Teacher's Wraparound Edition

World History

THE HUMAN EXPERIENCE

THE MODERN ERA

NATIONAL
GEOGRAPHIC
SOCIETY

Mounir A. Farah
Andrea Berens Karls

 **Glencoe**
McGraw-Hill

New York, New York   Columbus, Ohio   Woodland Hills, California   Peoria, Illinois

About the Authors

The **National Geographic Society**, founded in 1888 for the increase and diffusion of geographic knowledge, is the world's largest nonprofit scientific and educational organization. The Society has used sophisticated communication technologies and rich historical and archival resources to convey knowledge to a worldwide membership. The Educational Media Division has developed innovative educational programs— ranging from traditional print materials to multi-media programs including CD-ROMs, videodiscs, and software.

Mounir A. Farah, Ph.D. is a research historian and Associate Director of the Middle East Studies Program at the University of Arkansas, Fayetteville. Dr. Farah taught history and social science at New York University and Western Connecticut State University. He was a consultant to the Ministry of Education in Jordan and served as Coordinator of Social Studies in the Monroe, Connecticut public schools. Named Outstanding History Scholar-Teacher in New England and recipient of the Connecticut Council for the Social Studies Annual Award, Dr. Farah is a past president of the Connecticut Council for the Social Studies and of the Middle East Outreach Council.

Andrea Berens Karls is an educator and coauthor of Glencoe's *Global Insights*. Educated at Wellesley College and Harvard University, she has taught at both the elementary and secondary levels. Ms. Karls was formerly Program Associate at Global Perspectives in Education, Inc. She is a member of the National Council for the Social Studies and the American Historical Association.

About the Cover

In addition to painting the human figure, the fifteenth-century Italian artist Leonardo da Vinci recorded ideas about engineering that were well ahead of his time. Among Leonardo's many scientific drawings is this sketch of an experimental flying machine.

Leonardo's dream of human travel by air was finally fulfilled in the twentieth century. Today space engineers have developed space shuttles, such as the Discovery. Reusable for many missions, space shuttles blast off like rockets and land like airplanes.

Note: The Internet sites used in this textbook are not under the control of Glencoe/McGraw-Hill, and therefore Glencoe makes no representation concerning the content of the sites and their links.

Glencoe/McGraw-Hill

A Division of The McGraw-Hill Companies

Design and Production: DECODE, Inc.
Cover photograph: U.S. space shuttle *Discovery*, NASA; Leonardo da Vinci's sketch of a flying machine, Biblioteca Ambrosiana, Milan, Italy/Art Resource, NY

Send all inquiries to:
Glencoe/McGraw-Hill, 936 Eastwind Drive, Westerville, Ohio 43081

ISBN 0-02-800937-7 (Student Edition) ISBN 0-02-663951-3 (Teacher's Wraparound Edition)
Printed in the United States of America.

1 2 3 4 5 6 7 8 9 10 071/043 03 02 01 00 99 98

Academic Consultants

Teacher Reviewers

Table of Contents

*inter*NET CONNECTION

Visit the Glencoe Social Studies Web site at **glencoe.com/sec/socialstudies/** for unit-based activities you and your students can explore for this and other Glencoe Social Studies textbooks. There you will also find online versions of our *Current Events Update* and many more exciting resources!

Now Available

Online Resources from Glencoe Social Studies

Table of Contents

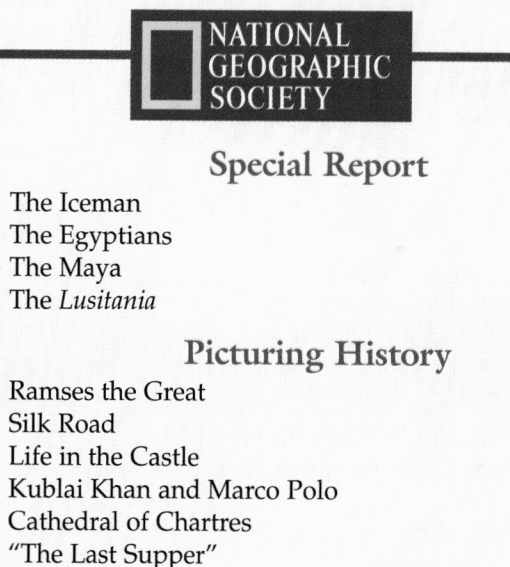

Multimedia Activity

Turning Points in World History

Surfing the "Net"

SKILLS

Social Studies Skills

Critical Thinking Skills

Study and Writing Skills

Technology Skills

Maps

Maps (continued)

Charts, Graphs, and Diagrams

Answering the Issue of Relevancy

Links to Today

Revolution … expansion … imperialism … How do you get your students to see that these concepts changed the world before *and during* their lifetimes? It's true that, unless your students see relevant reasons to study about the history of the world, they will not learn the lessons that history reveals. Your challenge every day is to generate high enthusiasm for learning by making strong connections between today's reality and the most telling stories and messages of the past.

Glencoe's *World History: The Human Experience in the Modern Era* is your primary tool for successful student motivation, second only to your masterful talents of instruction. It continually reminds students why the content *must* matter to them. Every unit opens with **Then & Now,** recognizing how history is directly embedded in our everyday lives. Each chapter and section opens with **The Storyteller,** personalizing the historical period by disclosing the thoughts and ideas of people from that time in their own words. Pivotal questions pointing to the era's **Historical Significance** open each chapter, and the Chapter Review imparts more relevancy in **Linking Past and Present.**

Then & Now

Historical Significance

The Storyteller

Living the History

You want your students to *experience* history, to comprehend another's situation from a different perspective, and to develop more active empathy with people from another time. You raise the level of authentic instruction by increasing the students' interactions with the content and with each other. Your students begin and end the study of each chapter in Glencoe's *World History: The Human Experience in the Modern Era* by writing in **Your History Journal,** where they explore real-world problems of another era, learning that no problem is totally objective and every point of view comes with a bias. **Footnotes to History** pique interest by revealing fascinating yet little-known facts about people, places, and events. And the classroom resource **History Simulations** take your students that much closer to actually being a part of history.

■ For Further Professional Reading

Adams, D., and M. Hamm. 1994. *New Designs for Teaching and Learning: Promoting Active Learning in Tomorrow's Schools.* San Francisco: Jossey-Bass Publishers.

Bower, B., J. Lobdell, and L. Swenson. 1994. *History Alive! Engaging All Learners in the Diverse Classroom.* New York: Addison-Wesley Publishing Company.

Newmann, F. M., and G. G. Wehlage. 1993. "Five Standards of Authentic Instruction." *Educational Leadership* 50(7): 8–12.

Other Program Resources

Rely on these additional resources to help students understand the relevancy of world history.

Teacher's Wraparound Edition
- Then & Now
- Linking Past and Present
- Global Gourmet
- You Don't Say…

Classroom Resources
- Historical Significance Chapter Activities
- Turning Points in World History Videodisc
- National Geographic Society CD-ROMs
- A&E Home Video®, THE HISTORY CHANNEL®, and Biography® videotapes
- World Music: Cultural Traditions

Linking Past and Present

Seeing the Big Picture

Learning for Understanding

Find Out ➤

Your students want to know what is most important among the millions of facts, key figures, significant events, and revealing interpretations in world history. You want them to know what it *all* means—recognizing the common themes from era to era and relating this information to today's hottest world headlines. Especially in this Information Age where data is at our fingertips, today's gauge of successful learning is not the quantity of information your students know but how well they understand. As coach and facilitator, your collaboration helps students become proficient in how to access information and derive meaning from it.

Who?What?Where?When?

Edith Cavell, an English nurse working in Belgium, was an Allied heroine of World War I. After the Germans occupied the country, she helped Belgian, French, and British soldiers escape. Arrested in 1915, she confessed and was sentenced to die by the firing squad. Her execution in October, though legally justified, aroused worldwide condemnation.

World History: The Human Experience in the Modern Era provides depth of understanding by consistently reinforcing historical trends, themes, and concepts. Beginning the unit with **A Global Chronology**, students see the relationships among important political, scientific, and social and cultural events. The text consistently puts events in perspective with time lines at the beginning of each chapter and section, too. Each unit ends with the **Unit Digest**, a synthesis of the important concepts discussed in each chapter.

1450   1500   **1550**   1600

1469 Lorenzo de' Medici rules Florence.

1508 Michelangelo begins painting the Sistine Chapel.

1517 Martin Luther promotes church reform.

Council **1563** of Trent ends.

The Spread of Ideas

Comprehending Concepts

You are convinced that knowing the "big picture" empowers students to learn more and to find new ways to learn. Investing them with the power of historians—to determine the essential questions, investigate for answers in a variety of sources, draw conclusions, and present their interpretations with vigor—builds critical thinkers, able researchers, and participating citizens. Through such work, students grasp the "big ideas" and understand how important they are in the study of history. Glencoe's *World History: The Human Experience in the Modern Era* opens each unit with **The Spread of Ideas**, which identifies an important concept in world history and explains how people from different parts of the world learned and reacted to these ideas during the epoch. Questions at the end of the feature help students in **Linking the Ideas**. The program communicates concepts by identifying **Chapter Themes** at the beginning of the chapter and reinforcing them in **Understanding Themes** in the Chapter Review. Students start each section of study with a **Find Out** question that channels their search for meaning.

Other Resources

Rely on these additional resources to help students see the "big picture."

Teacher's Wraparound Edition
- Section Theme Activity in Guided Practice
- Who?What?Where?When?

Classroom Resources
- Time Line Activities
- Chapter Themes: Graphic Organizers

■ For Further Professional Reading

Chuska, K. R. 1995. *Improving Classroom Questions: A Teacher's Guide to Increasing Student Motivation, Participation, and Higher-Level Thinking.* Bloomington, Ind.: Phi Delta Kappa Educational Foundation.

Thompson, L. J. 1995. *Habits of the Mind: Critical Thinking in the Classroom.* Lanham, Md.: University Press of America.

Williams, J. A. 1994. *Classroom in Conflict: Teaching Controversial Subjects in a Diverse Society.* Albany, N.Y.: State University of New York Press.

The Story of History

Telling the Story

Students' world views are only as broad as their life experiences. Once your students hear the powerful stories of the world's peoples, you know their views will broaden further. What's magical about the history of the world is that each story is brought to a personal level at which your students can ponder their ancestors' options. Through this personal identification, students imagine what it was like for people in that particular time and place—and learn from it. They are touched by the magic of the past through authentic voices, showcased in **The Storyteller** in Glencoe's *World History: The Human Experience in the Modern Era*, which dramatically open each new chapter study. Primary source quotations, integrated generously throughout the narrative, sustain the story's momentum. With so many stories to read and incredible people to learn about, students extend their world views and move toward acceptance of the many sides of the global story.

Other Program Resources

Rely on these additional resources to help students understand the world's many cultural perspectives.

Teacher's Wraparound Edition
- Cultural Diffusion
- Cultural Perspectives

Classroom Resources
- People in World History
- World Music: Cultural Traditions

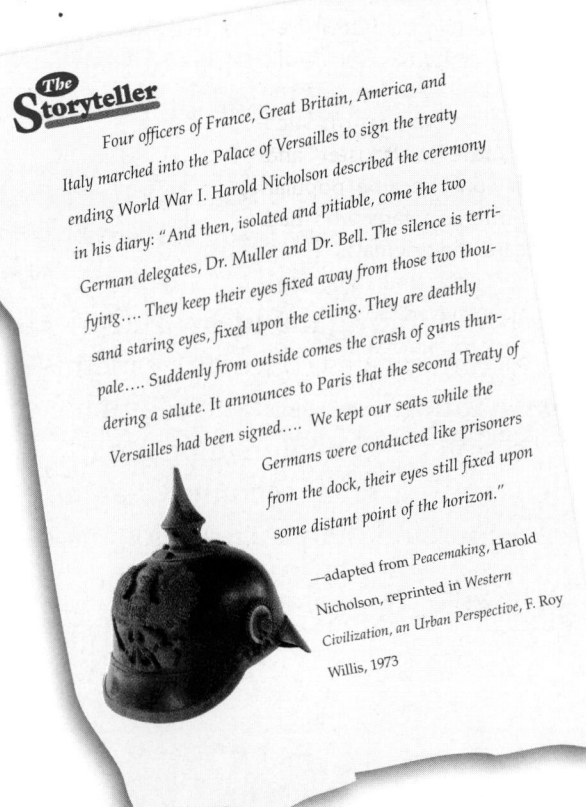

The Storyteller

Four officers of France, Great Britain, America, and Italy marched into the Palace of Versailles to sign the treaty ending World War I. Harold Nicholson described the ceremony in his diary: "And then, isolated and pitiable, come the two German delegates, Dr. Muller and Dr. Bell. The silence is terrifying.... They keep their eyes fixed away from those two thousand staring eyes, fixed upon the ceiling. They are deathly pale.... Suddenly from outside comes the crash of guns thundering a salute. It announces to Paris that the second Treaty of Versailles had been signed.... We kept our seats while the Germans were conducted like prisoners from the dock, their eyes still fixed upon some distant point of the horizon."

—adapted from *Peacemaking*, Harold Nicholson, reprinted in *Western Civilization, an Urban Perspective*, F. Roy Willis, 1973

Cultural Perspectives

Learning more about how world cultures of today and yesterday are interrelated is an important aspect of understanding the world's history. *World History: The Human Experience in the Modern Era* helps you make those intercultural connections. As our global community shrinks in size because of high-speed communication and transportation, it becomes increasingly important for students to see people different from themselves as interesting neighbors who have different ideas, customs, and languages, but who share many of the same values. In analyzing the progress and struggles of these groups over the course of human history—and witnessing the humanity throughout—students develop more positive attitudes toward others.

Cultural Diffusion

The Circle Is Unbroken The diffusion of African-influenced music continues. In the 1960s, British groups such as the Beatles, the Rolling Stones, and Led Zeppelin recorded blues and rhythm and blues classics written by Muddy Waters, Howlin' Wolf, and Willie Dixon, among others. The British versions of such songs as "Little Red Rooster" and "Seventh Son" became popular among American fans who had never heard the originals.

At the same time, blues and soul have traveled back across the Atlantic Ocean to influence Ali Farka Toure of Mali and other popular African musicians. Similarly, Caribbean musicians have incorporated elements of rap into merengue, from the Dominican Republic, and reggae, from Jamaica.

Cultural Perspectives

Navajo Code Talkers In 1943 the U.S. Marines recruited the Navajo to develop a military code that the Japanese could not break. Based on their oral language, the Navajo code talkers created the only unbreakable code in military history.

■ For Further Professional Reading

Brown, C. S. 1988. *Like It Was. A Complete Guide to Writing Oral History*. New York: Teachers and Writers Collaborative.

Davidman, L., and P. T. Davidman. 1994. *Teaching With a Multicultural Perspective: A Practical Guide*. New York: Longman.

Gay, G. 1994. *At the Essence of Learning: Multicultural Education*. West Lafayette, Ind.: Kappa Delta Pi.

Sherritt, C. 1990. *What Not To Do in the Name of Multiculturalism*. Contemporary Education 61(4): 215–16.

Visualizing History

Seeing is Believing

Your students were raised on cable TV and remote controls. It's plain and simple from students' perspectives—if they can't see it, they *don't* believe it. But bringing the people, places, and events of world history to your students is what Glencoe's *World History: The Human Experience in the Modern Era* does best. Interesting text and features are

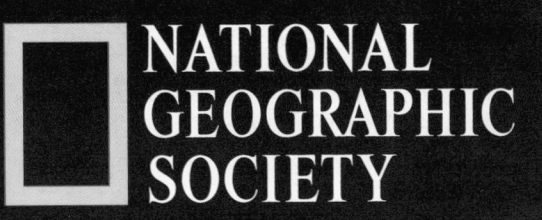

NATIONAL GEOGRAPHIC SOCIETY

accompanied by colorful illustrations, maps, charts, and photos. With the help of giants such as the National Geographic Society and ABCNews InterActive™, students witness the rich pageantry of the world's past through **STV Videodiscs**, **PictureShow CD-ROMs**, and **Turning Points in World History**. The *Picturing History* and *NGS Special Report* features in the student text are brought to you from the National Geographic Society.

Other Program Resources

Rely on these additional resources to help students visualize history.

Teacher's Wraparound Edition
- Visualizing History
- Images of the Times
- Making Connections Activities
- History & Art
- Curriculum Connection
- Connections: The Arts

Classroom Resources
- National Geographic Society Videodiscs
- NGS PictureShow CD-ROMs
- NGS Poster Sets and PicturePack Transparencies
- ABCNews InterActive™ Videodiscs
- Focus on World Art Prints
- A&E Home Video®, THE HISTORY CHANNEL®, and Biography® videotapes
- Chapter Transparencies
- World History and Art Transparencies

Images *of the* Times

Art as Experience

Nothing conveys the meaning of "god-king" more emphatically than examining the gold and precious stones on the stunning mask of Egyptian pharaoh Tutankhamen, one of the breathtaking posters in the **Focus on World Art Prints** collection. Prints displaying eighth-century Mayan civilization, medieval Europe, and nineteenth-century Africa, for example, bring students the color and artistry of times long ago. **Images of the Times**, a collection of art, sculpture, and other artifacts, also reveal the majesty of each period. Fine art appears continually throughout the text as illustrations and **History & Art**. Captions pose higher-order thinking questions that help students analyze what the art discloses about the people and the time in which they lived.

History & Art

Visualizing History

■ For Further Professional Reading

Epstein, T. L. 1994. "Sometimes a Shining Moment: High School Students' Representations of History Through the Arts." *Social Education* 58(3): 136–41.

Schubert, W., and G. Willis. 1991. *Understanding Curricula and Teaching Through the Arts*. Albany, N. Y.: State University of New York Press.

Geography in History

From the study of the emerging river valley civilizations in ancient times to the devastation of late twentieth-century natural disasters, the story of human history cannot be told without the influence of geographic features. Whether we talk about physical features—mountains blocking movement—or cultural features—dozens of ethnic groups and languages within a small region—geography has a significant impact on where and how people live.

Glencoe's *World History: The Human Experience in the Modern Era* understands that there is no time to teach geography separately from world history. By integrating important geographic information and the five geographic themes within the narrative and providing in-depth focus on geography in **Connections: Geography** features, this program helps students see the undeniable tie between geography and history. The extensive map program and accompanying **Map Study** questions help students improve their map-reading skills while recognizing the importance of location, place, region, movement, and human/environment interaction. The **Geography in History** questions in the Chapter Review reinforce themes and key concepts. The best in the field—the National Geographic Society—offers special multimedia resources that extend the student text—CD-ROMs, videodiscs, transparencies, posters, related references to *National Geographic*, and more!

Other Program Resources

Rely on these additional resources to help students understand the importance of geography in history.

Teacher's Wraparound Edition
- Geography Connection
- Map Study

Classroom Resources
- Geography and History Activities
- Student Desk Map
- Mapping History Activities
- Mapping History Overlay Transparencies

Occupation of Germany and Austria 1945

Germany and Austria were divided into zones. In 1955, Austria reunited as a neutral country.
Place What zone surrounded Berlin?

Integrating Literature and Writing into History

Concepts are better understood when information is presented in context rather than in unrelated bits and pieces. This means that integrating the important literature of particular eras within the study of history not only assists students in understanding the context of the people's lives but also reinforces verbal skills when completing writing assignments, such as the **Portfolio Project** at the beginning of each unit and **Your History Journal** at the start of each chapter.

Glencoe's *World History: The Human Experience in the Modern Era* provides an extensive excerpt from world literature for each unit in **Literature: Bridge to the Past**. This selection represents the time, the people, and the issues of the period, exposing students to literature of interdisciplinary consequence. Discussions and activities related to the selection assist the student in understanding its **Historical Connection** and **Contemporary Connection**. Information about the author and further examples of literature from the period extend student knowledge and understanding.

Other Program Resources

Rely on these additional resources to help students understand the importance of literature and writing in history.

Teacher's Wraparound Edition
- History and the Humanities
- About the Author
- Additional Literary Works of the Period

Classroom Resources
- World Literature Selections
- Source Readings

■ For Further Professional Reading

Danks, C. 1995. "Using Holocaust Short Stories and Poetry in the Social Studies Classroom." *Social Education* 59(6): 358–61.

Irvin, J. L., J. P. Lunstrum, C. Lynch-Brown, and M. F. Shepard. 1995. *Enhancing Social Studies Through Literary Strategies*. Washington, D.C.: National Council for the Social Studies.

Your History Journal

Portfolio Project

Addressing Multiple Learning Styles

With the advent of the 1980s and throughout the past 15 years, new discoveries about the inner workings and development of the brain and the nature of intelligence have replaced traditional beliefs that intelligence is entirely predetermined at birth. One of the most noted theories, advanced by Howard Gardner, is the theory of multiple intelligences, which contends that there are at least seven forms of intelligence that help us understand the world around us.

MULTIPLE LEARNING STYLES

Glencoe's *World History: The Human Experience in the Modern Era* provides you with a chapter activity for seven types of intelligences in each **Chapter Planning Guide**.

1 Verbal/Linguistic Learners

Students who exhibit this intelligence can argue, persuade, entertain, or instruct others effectively with words. They read regularly, can write clearly, and easily understand the written word. They retain facts readily, and love to play with the sounds of language.

Teachers can help develop this intelligence by using overhead projectors to convey information, providing audiocassettes for Chapter Digests, as well as assigning reading and writing. Writing a journal, like the **Your History Journal** in *World History: The Human Experience in the Modern Era*, will exercise linguistic intelligence.

2 Logical/Mathematical Learners

Students who exhibit this intelligence demonstrate the ability to reason, sequence, identify cause and effect, and create hypotheses. They see numerical patterns and can spot conceptual irregularities. They generally have a very rational outlook toward life, and love to develop "what if" scenarios.

Teachers can help develop this intelligence by discussing the pros and cons of important decisions made in world history and eliciting rationales for each side. To exercise this intelligence, students, for example, could sequence events in the **Time Line Activities** booklet.

3 Visual/Spatial Learners

Students who exhibit this intelligence think in terms of pictures and images. They are acutely aware of visual details and need to draw or sketch their ideas graphically. They easily see three-dimensional space and can transform content into images.

Teachers can help develop this intelligence by planning videodisc and CD-ROM presentations or by assigning readings in the *NATIONAL GEOGRAPHIC Magazine*, which depicts historical events with beautiful illustrations.

4 Auditory/Musical Learners

Students who exhibit this intelligence can produce rhythms and melodies. They sing in tune, keep time to music, and listen perceptively to different kinds of music. They can discern subtle differences in sounds and have "good ears."

Teachers can help develop this intelligence by incorporating more technology into lessons. Having students listen to the **Chapter Digests Audiocassettes** will exercise this intelligence. CD-ROMs also provide students with instant auditory directions and feedback.

5 Kinesthetic Learners

Students who exhibit this intelligence coordinate their body movements well, must move their bodies frequently, and can maneuver objects with skill. They have good tactile sensitivity, needing to touch things in order to learn about them, and can sense with their physical body.

Teachers can help develop this intelligence by asking students to perform basic tasks, such as constructing models, charts, or graphs that apply new knowledge. Students also practice new skills by using the **Student Self-Test and Review Software**.

6 Interpersonal Learners

Students who exhibit this intelligence understand and work well with other people. They demonstrate abilities to perceive others' moods, intentions, and desires. They can comfortably step into another's perspective of the world. Many class leaders have this intelligence.

Teachers can help develop this intelligence by integrating **History Simulations** and **Cooperative Learning Activities** into their plans. In such settings, students can seek help from another student or learn with a partner.

7 Intrapersonal Learners

Students who exhibit this intelligence can easily assess their own feelings, are very introspective, and enjoy meditation and soul-searching. They use their self-understanding to guide their lives and can be very goal-directed. They can be fiercely independent and highly self-disciplined. These students are likely to have opinions that set them apart from others and prefer to work alone. They take themselves very seriously yet have a realistic understanding of their strengths and weaknesses.

Teachers can help develop this intelligence by encouraging the use of a personal journal, asking for students' opinions on important issues, and encouraging the reading of autobiographies and biographies of important historical figures, such as those featured in **People in World History**. Analyzing the traits of figures who have been successful will help students analyze their own personal strengths.

8 Naturalist Learners

Students who exhibit this intelligence are able to observe, understand, and organize patterns in the natural environment. These skills of observing, collecting, and categorizing are also useful in the "human" environment to collect data and classify information.

Teachers can help develop this intelligence by integrating **Geography and History Activities, History Simulations,** and **Chapter Themes Graphic Organizers** into their plans.

What multiple intelligences mean to history teachers is that you must assign activities to students that accommodate their strongest intelligences but

frequently exercise their weakest intelligences. Although students may experience some difficulty by engaging in work from a different domain, they can strengthen the weaker intelligence over time. And by stretching their comfort zones, you help them strengthen their overall thinking and problem-solving abilities.

The resources available in *World History: The Human Experience in the Modern Era* guarantee that your classroom will be a multisensory environment, providing multiple paths for student learning.

Other Program Resources

Rely on these additional resources to help you provide for individual student needs.

Teacher's Wraparound Edition
- Multiple Learning Styles Chapter Activities
- Cooperative Learning Activities
- Key to Ability Levels
- Meeting Special Needs Activities

■ For Further Professional Reading

Armstrong, T. 1993. *Seven Kinds of Smart: Identifying and Developing Your Many Intelligences.* New York: Plume/Penguin Books Inc.

Csikszentmihalyi, M., K. Rathunde, and S. Whalen. 1993. *Talented Teenagers: The Roots of Success and Failure.* New York: Cambridge University Press.

Gardner, H. G. 1993. *Multiple Intelligences: The Theory in Practice.* New York: Basic Books, Inc.

Johnson, D. W., R. Johnson, E. J. Holubec, and P. Roy. 1984. *Circles of Learning: Cooperation in the Classroom.* Alexandria, Va.: Association for Supervision and Curriculum Development.

Kagan, S. 1990. *Cooperative Learning: Resources for Teachers.* San Juan Capistrano, Calif.: Resources for Teachers.

Implementing Block Scheduling

Advantages for Schools

For the schools themselves, the greatest advantage of block scheduling is a better use of resources. The schedule change does not require additional teachers or classrooms. It eliminates half of the time needed for class changes, which results in fewer discipline problems. Schools also report an increase in the overall quality of teacher instruction and student's time on task.

Advantages for Teachers

With block scheduling, teachers instruct fewer students each term, so students and teachers get to know each other better, and relationships improve. Teachers have time to provide additional one-on-one help and other resources for meeting the individual needs of students. Because block scheduling cuts in half the time needed for introducing and closing classes, teachers have more time to teach the key concepts of their discipline and become more focused themselves. Some schools report improved teacher morale, increased teacher effectiveness, and decreased burnout.

Block scheduling results in more frequent use of varied teaching approaches and more student-centered environments. Teachers venture away from discussion and lecture and use more productive models of teaching. Flexibility allows more opportunities for cooperative teaching strategies such as team teaching and interdisciplinary studies. Block scheduling also encourages activity-centered instruction; in Glencoe's *World History: The Human Experience in the Modern Era* Teacher's Wraparound Edition, such activities and research projects are specially coded for block schedules.

Advantages for Students

Student success rate is greater in a block scheduling format because students interact more with teachers and the content, learning more and retaining it longer. Students develop better problem-solving skills because they have more time to think.

In a block students study fewer subjects each term, making them better able to manage their workload.

Students experience fewer outside distractions and are better able to concentrate. They voice that there is more time to learn and more time to ask questions.

Students maximize use of the curriculum with a block schedule. They schedule required courses during the first term, and, if they do not pass the course, they can repeat it during the second term. Better students move ahead more quickly; block scheduling increases the number of students who take upper-level classes and earn advanced studies diplomas.

Utilizing Performance Assessment

Traditionally, in the social studies classroom, assessment has been at the end of study to measure how well students have learned the objectives of the unit of study. But today, in order to prepare students for future success in the adult world, more authentic forms of assessment, consisting of ongoing demonstrations of worthwhile, meaningful tasks, are in order.

Traditional Measures

Glencoe's *World History: The Human Experience in the Modern Era* provides you with both types of assessment. Traditional forms—**Chapter and Unit Tests**, **Section Quizzes**, and **Testmaker Software**—are available to evaluate knowledge of factual content and some forms of thinking skills.

Performance Measures

The alternative measures most often utilized by classroom teachers are projects, teacher observation, performance-based essays, and portfolios.

Tasks may be divided into three broad types: teacher-directed tasks, student-directed tasks, and collections over time. In **teacher-directed tasks**, students may be guided step-by-step through various phases of a task. For example, the teacher leads the class in brainstorming, but when students realize that they do not have enough information in order to be successful, the teacher serves as coach or facilitator.

Student-directed tasks are typically used at the end of a unit of study in the place of or in concert with traditional tests. The teacher explains clearly what is expected of the students in process and product and makes known the essential criteria.

Collections over time require longer periods to develop but are helpful in allowing the student to discover a broader application for what is learned than can be accomplished within a one-time task. The **Portfolio Project** assigned at the beginning of each unit in *World History: The Human Experience in the Modern Era* is an example.

Journals are often used as performance assessment because they contain samples of students' work collected over a period of time—often an entire grading period or even a semester. **Your History Journal**, assigned at the beginning of every chapter, provides students an opportunity not only to find information but also to make sense of it and put that information in context. The most common form of assessing authentic performance is by rubric, or by percent or points. You determine the components of the product, process, or task, and weight the completion of each according to its merits. A three-point rubric would show Score Point One as unacceptable performance and Score Point Three as completely successful. Each chapter's **Performance Assessment Activity**, suggested in *World History: The Human Experience in the Modern Era*, is accompanied with possible rubric features to help you plan your assessment strategies.

Other Resources

Rely on these additional resources to help students prepare portfolio items for assessment.

Teacher's Wraparound Edition
- Performance Assessment Activities
- Extra Credit Project

Classroom Resources
- Performance Assessment Strategies and Activities
- Student Self-Test and Review Software

Using Technology in the Classroom

Glencoe's software HOTLINE is 1-800-437-3715

Advances in technology continually debut, dramatically affecting all aspects of the social studies. Social studies instruction can include such advances, and Glencoe has developed many programs for successful integration of technology into your classroom.

Software

Student Self-Test and Review Software This highly motivational program allows students to check their comprehension by answering questions using the computer. If a student chooses a wrong answer, the computer explains why the choice is incorrect. The student may then try again. This process continues until the student chooses the correct answer. Chapter Summaries and a Glossary are also integrated in this software.

Testmaker Glencoe's Testmaker allows you to customize tests to fit your students' special needs. The software allows you to edit, reorder, and add questions as you desire and is available in Macintosh and DOS formats.

Vocabulary PuzzleMaker Because vocabulary development and comprehension is such an important part of social studies instruction, Glencoe has developed a special vocabulary program. The Vocabulary PuzzleMaker helps you create high-interest crossword puzzles and word searches.

The National Geographic Society has prize-winning resources. Fascinating audio and video clips exhibit history, languages, music, and cultural traditions of nations and civilizations.

Picture Atlas of the World

PictureShow CD-ROMs
- **Egypt and the Fertile Crescent**
- **India and China**
- **Greece and Rome**
- **The Middle Ages**
- **The Renaissance**
- **Age of Exploration**

Presentation Plus! CD-ROM is an exciting new presentation tool that enables you to present dynamic lessons for every unit, chapter, and section of *World History: The Human Experience in the Modern Era*. Presentation lessons include audio, graphics, links to videos, transparencies, content overviews, and much more. Use the provided lessons or customize for your classroom.

- **STV: World Geography**
- **STV: North America**
- **STV: Maya**

 The following videodiscs help students in their understanding of world history.

- **Turning Points in World History**
- **In the Holy Land**
- **Lessons of War**
- **Communism and the Cold War**

Videodiscs

If your school has a basic system consisting of a videodisc player and a television receiver, the videodiscs provide an effective and interesting tool for classroom presentations.

MindJogger Videoquiz The Mind-Jogger Videoquiz uses a game show format for review of key concepts. A bar code scanner allows you immediate access to specific chapters on the videodisc. The bar codes are placed on the Chapter Opener and Chapter Review pages of the Teacher's Wraparound Edition. The MindJogger Videoquiz is also available in a VHS format.

Surfing the History Net

You can join three history list servers:

- Send this message **Subscribe NCSS-L Your Name** to listproc2@bgu.edu to share information and ideas about K–12 social studies education, sponsored by the Instructional Technology Committee of the National Council for the Social Studies.
- Send **sub H-High-S Your Name Your School** to LISTSERV@msu.edu for inclusion in an ongoing discussion of curriculum, instructional strategies, and educational resources involved in teaching history.
- Send **Sub Histnews Your Name** to listserv@ukanvm. cc.ukans.edu for a newsletter for historians.

NOW AVAILABLE!
Visit the Glencoe Social Studies Web site at glencoe.com/sec/socialstudies/

The Internet

On the Internet if you know the name of the computer you want to contact, you look up its number, have your computer dial it, and talk to it. You can reach a specific person by using E-mail, being on a list server that sends information to its subscribers, or by subscribing to bulletin boards. The Internet, however, is used for much more than just receiving and sending messages.

World Wide Web

Getting information through the Internet became much easier with the development of the World Wide Web. You can scan the Web using "browsers"—programs such as Netscape and Mosaic. You can go directly to one of the million sources of information if you know an address called the Uniform Reference Locator (URL).

On-line Resources

Each Chapter Planning Guide in *World History: The Human Experience in the Modern Era* offers you easy-to-use Internet Connections. In addition to this unique feature, you may also wish to use the following Internet sites.

On-line resources for world history teachers are limitless. Sites are listed below with their URLs. When you type the address, you will reach the organization's "homepage," which tells you what is available at its site. Some are clearinghouses for other sources.

- **Armadillo from Rice University** http://chico.rice.edu/armadillo/about.html
- **CNN** http://www.cnn.com
- **ERIC Clearinghouses** http://ericir.syr.edu
- **American Geological Institute** http://jei.umd.edu/
- **Library of Congress** http://lcweb.loc.gov/homepage/lchp.html

- **Western European Studies (since 1945) Homepage** http://www.pitt.edu/~wwwes/
- **Yahoo** http://www.yahoo.com/

The following sites are particularly relevant to world history:

- **Interactive Communication Simulations, which is geared for students of global education** http://ics.soe.umich.edu/
- **EuroDocs for primary historical documents** http://library.byu.edu/~rdh/eurodocs/
- **Medieval Studies** http://sunsite.berkeley.edu/OMACL/
- **Program in International Educational Resources** http://www.yale.edu/pieris
- **Asian Institute of Technology, Bangkok, Thailand** http://www.ait.ac.th/

- **Resources on Japan** http://www.indiana.edu/~japan/odata.html
- **Resources on Africa** http://www.sas.upenn.edu/African_Studies/Home_Page/Country.html
- **Resources on Saudi Arabia** http://www.saudi.net/
- **Ultimate History** http://history.cc.ukans.edu/history/index.html

Newspapers from other countries summarize daily news:

German News in English http://www.mathematik.uni-ulm.de/germnews (in German) http://www.mathematik.uni-ulm.de/de-news/ (in English)

ANSA News Agency summaries (Italy) in English http://www.ansa.it/inglese2.html

The Times (London) http://www.the-times.co.uk/

Glencoe's unique Internet Connections are a continuing source of exploration. The sites listed here and elsewhere in the Teacher's Wraparound Edition are not under the control of Glencoe/McGraw-Hill and, therefore, Glencoe makes no representation concerning the content of the sites. We encourage teachers to preview these sites before students access them. Internet sites are sometimes under construction and may be incomplete and not always available. Sites may move or be removed.

Correlation to NCSS Ten Thematic Strands

In *Curriculum Standards for Social Studies: Expectations of Excellence,* the National Council for the Social Studies (NCSS) identified ten themes that serve as organizing strands for the social studies curriculum at every school level. These themes are interrelated and draw from all of the social science disciplines. Below is a correlation chart showing where the social studies themes are incorporated in *World History: The Human Experience in the Modern Era.*

Social Studies Theme	Incorporated Within *World History: The Human Experience in the Modern Era*			
I. Culture				
Human beings create, learn, and adapt culture. Human cultures are dynamic systems of beliefs, values, and traditions that exhibit both commonalities and differences. Understanding culture helps us understand ourselves and others.	Ch. 1 Ch. 2 Ch. 3 Ch. 4 Ch. 5 Ch. 6; S. 7	Ch. 7 Ch. 8; S. 1, 2, 3, 5 Ch. 9 Ch. 10; S. 1, 2, 4 Ch. 11; S. 2, 3, 4 Ch. 12; S. 1, 4	Ch. 13; S. 1, 3, 4 Ch. 14; S. 1, 3 Ch. 15; S. 3 Ch. 16; S. 1, 2 Ch. 17; S. 4 Ch. 18; S. 1, 4	Ch. 19; S. 2, 4 Ch. 20; S. 4 Ch. 21; S. 2, 5 Ch. 22; S. 2, 3 Ch. 23; S. 1 Ch. 24; S. 1, 4
II. Time, Continuity, and Change				
Human beings seek to understand their historic roots and to locate themselves in time. Such understanding involves knowing what things were like in the past and how things change and develop—allowing us to develop historic perspective and answer important questions about our current condition.	Ch. 1 Ch. 2 Ch. 3 Ch. 4 Ch. 5; S. 1 Ch. 6; S. 1, 3	Ch. 9 Ch. 10; S. 1, 3, 4 Ch. 11; S. 1, 3 Ch. 12 Ch. 13 Ch. 16; S. 1	Ch. 17; S. 1, 2, 4, 5 Ch. 18; S. 1 Ch. 19 Ch. 20; S. 3, 5 Ch. 21; S. 1	Ch. 22; S. 1 Ch. 23; S. 1 Ch. 24; S. 3 Ch. 25; S. 1 Ch. 26
III. People, Places, and Environment				
Technological advancements have insured that students are aware of the world beyond their personal locations. As students study content related to this theme, they create their spatial views and geographic perspectives of the world; social, cultural, economic, and civic demands mean that students will need such knowledge, skills, and understandings to make informed and critical decisions about the relationship between human beings and their environment.	Ch. 2 Ch. 3 Ch. 4 Ch. 10; S. 3	Ch. 12; S. 1, 2, 5 Ch. 13; S. 3 Ch. 15; S. 3, 5 Ch. 16; S. 1, 3	Ch. 21; S. 2 Ch. 22; S. 2 Ch. 23; S. 3	Ch. 24; S. 3 Ch. 25; S. 1 Ch. 26; S. 5
IV. Individual Development and Identity				
Personal identity is shaped by one's culture, by groups, and by institutional influences. Examination of various forms of human behavior enhances understanding of the relationships between social norms and emerging personal identities, the social processes which influence identity formation, and the ethical principles underlying individual action.	Ch. 1 Ch. 2 Ch. 3 Ch. 4 Ch. 5; S. 1, 4, 5	Ch. 6; S. 3 Ch. 9; S. 2, 3 Ch. 10; S. 1, 3, 4 Ch. 11; S. 2, 3 Ch. 12; S. 1, 3, 4	Ch. 13; S. 1, 3 Ch. 17; S. 1, 3, 4 Ch. 18; S. 1 Ch. 19 Ch. 20; S. 1, 3, 4	Ch. 21; S. 1 Ch. 23; S. 3 Ch. 24; S. 3 Ch. 25; S. 1 Ch. 26

Ch. = Chapter   S. = Section

V. Individuals, Groups, and Institutions

Institutions exert enormous influence over us. Institutions are organizational embodiments to further the core social values of those who comprise them. It is important for students to know how institutions are formed, what controls and influences them, how they control and influence individuals and culture, and how institutions can be maintained or changed.

Ch. 1	Ch. 7	Ch. 16	Ch. 22
Ch. 2	Ch. 8	Ch. 17; S. 4	Ch. 23
Ch. 3	Ch. 10	Ch. 18; S. 2, 3, 4	Ch. 24
Ch. 4	Ch. 11	Ch. 19	Ch. 25
Ch. 5; S. 4, 5	Ch. 12; S. 4	Ch. 20; S. 1, 3, 5	Ch. 26
Ch. 6; S. 2	Ch. 14	Ch. 21	

VI. Power, Authority, and Governance

Understanding of the historical development of structures of power, authority, and governance and their evolving functions in contemporary society is essential for the emergence of civic competence.

Ch. 1	Ch. 6; S. 2	Ch. 14	Ch. 19
Ch. 2	Ch. 7	Ch. 15	Ch. 21
Ch. 3	Ch. 8	Ch. 16; S. 2, 3, 4	Ch. 22
Ch. 4	Ch. 10	Ch. 17; S. 4	Ch. 23
Ch. 5; S. 1, 4, 5	Ch. 11	Ch. 18; S. 2, 3, 4	Ch. 24

VII. Production, Distribution, and Consumption

Decisions about exchange, trade, and economic policy and well-being are global in scope, and the role of government in policy making varies over time and from place to place. The systematic study of an interdependent world economy and the role of technology in economic decision making is essential.

Ch. 1	Ch. 7; S. 2, 3, 4	Ch. 14; S. 4, 5	Ch. 21
Ch. 2	Ch. 8; S. 1, 2, 3	Ch. 15; S. 3	Ch. 22; S. 1, 3
Ch. 3	Ch. 10; S. 1, 2, 3	Ch. 16; S. 1, 2	Ch. 23; S. 2, 3
Ch. 4	Ch. 11; S. 1, 2, 4	Ch. 17; S. 1, 4, 5	Ch. 24; S. 1, 2, 3
Ch. 5; S. 1, 2	Ch. 12; S. 1, 2, 4	Ch. 18	Ch. 25; S. 1, 2, 4
Ch. 6; S. 1, 3	Ch. 13; S. 1	Ch. 19; S. 4, 5	Ch. 26; S. 1, 2, 3, 5

VIII. Science, Technology, and Society

Technology is as old as the first crude tool invented by prehistoric humans, and modern life as we know it would be impossible without technology and the science which supports it. Today's technology forms the basis for some of our most difficult social choices.

Ch. 1	Ch. 6; S. 1	Ch. 13; S. 2, 3	Ch. 18; S. 4
Ch. 2	Ch. 8; S. 5	Ch. 14; S. 3	Ch. 19; S. 2, 4, 5
Ch. 3	Ch. 9; S. 1, 2	Ch. 15; S. 4	Ch. 20; S. 3, 4
Ch. 4	Ch. 11; S. 3	Ch. 16; S. 3	Ch. 21; S. 1, 2
Ch. 5; S. 1	Ch. 12; S. 1, 2, 3	Ch. 17; S. 1	Ch. 26; S. 5

IX. Global Connections

The realities of global interdependence require understanding of the increasingly important and diverse global connections among world societies before there can be analysis leading to the development of possible solutions to persisting and emerging global issues.

Ch. 1	Ch. 6; S. 2	Ch. 13; S. 4	Ch. 22; S. 6
Ch. 2	Ch. 7; S. 2, 3, 4	Ch. 14; S. 2	Ch. 24; S. 3
Ch. 4	Ch. 11; S. 4	Ch. 16; S. 1	Ch. 26; S. 5
Ch. 5; S. 2, 4			

X. Civic Ideals and Practices

All people have a stake in examining civic ideals and practices across time, in diverse societies, as well as in determining how to close the gap between present practices and the ideals upon which our democratic republic is based. An understanding of civic ideals and practices of citizenship is critical to full participation in society.

Ch. 2	Ch. 10	Ch. 16	Ch. 20; S. 1, 2, 5, 6
Ch. 3	Ch. 11; S. 1, 2, 4	Ch. 17	Ch. 21; S. 1, 2
Ch. 4	Ch. 13; S. 1, 2, 3, 5	Ch. 18; S. 1, 2, 3, 5	Ch. 22
Ch. 8	Ch. 14	Ch. 19; S. 2, 3, 4	Ch. 23
Ch. 9; S. 2, 3	Ch. 15; S. 2, 3, 4		

Scope and Sequence

Historical Themes

Students need to understand and be able to recognize the themes that appear throughout history. Students also need to develop the ability to apply these themes as they examine the effect of the past on the present and the future.

The central theme highlighted in each section appears in red. **Related themes are listed in black.**

Content Knowledge

Students need to have a knowledge of the disciplines that play an integral role in the social studies: history, literature, art and culture, science and technology, government and civics, geography, economics, and religion. Students also need to develop a keen understanding of how these subjects interact with one another.

Skills

These are the skills taught in the Chapter *Skills*. Each skill is reinforced in the *Skill Practice* found in the Chapter Reviews and in the **Skill Reinforcement Activities** booklet in the TCR.

Chapter	1	2	3	4	
Movement	Sections 1, 2	Sections 1, 2, 3, 4	Sections 1, 2, 3	Sections 1, 2, 3, 4	
Innovation	Sections 1, 2, 3	Sections 1, 2, 3, 4	Sections 1, 2, 3	Sections 1, 2, 3, 4	
Conflict/ Cooperation	Sections 1, 3	Sections 1, 2, 3, 4	Sections 2, 3	Sections 1, 2, 3, 4	
Revolution/ Reaction	Section 3	Sections 1, 2, 3, 4	Sections 1, 3	Sections 2, 3	
Change	Sections 1, 2, 3	Sections 1, 2, 3, 4	Sections 1, 2, 3, 4	Sections 1, 2, 3, 4	
Diversity/ Uniformity	Sections 2, 3	Sections 1, 2, 3, 4	Sections 1, 2, 3, 4	Sections 1, 2, 3, 4	
Cultural Diffusion	Sections 1, 2	Sections 1, 2, 3, 4, 5	Sections 1, 3, 4	Sections 1, 2, 3, 4	
Relation to Environment	Sections 1, 2, 3	Sections 1, 2, 3, 4, 5	Sections 1, 2, 3, 4	Sections 1, 2, 3, 4	
Regionalism/ Nationalism/ Internationalism	Section 3	Sections 1, 2, 3, 4, 5	Sections 1, 2, 3, 4	Sections 1, 2, 3, 4	
Literature, Art, and Culture	Sections 1, 2, 3	Sections 1, 2, 3, 4, 5	Sections 1, 2, 3, 4	Sections 1, 2, 3, 4	
Science and Technology	Sections 1, 2, 3	Sections 1, 2, 3, 4, 5	Sections 2, 3, 4	Sections 2, 3, 4	
Geography and Environment	Sections 1, 2, 3	Sections 1, 2, 3, 4, 5	Sections 1, 2, 3, 4	Sections 1, 2, 3, 4	
Economics	Sections 1, 2, 3	Sections 1, 2, 3, 4, 5	Sections 1, 2, 3, 4	Sections 1, 2, 3, 4	
Government/ Civics	Sections 1, 2, 3	Sections 1, 2, 3, 4, 5	Sections 1, 2, 3, 4	Sections 1, 2, 3, 4	
Religion	Sections 2, 3	Sections 1, 2, 3, 4, 5	Sections 1, 2, 3, 4	Sections 1, 2, 3, 4	
Skill Category	*Social Studies Skill*	*Critical Thinking Skill*	*Social Studies Skill*	*Social Studies Skill*	
Specific Skill	Finding Exact Location on a Map	Interpreting Point of View	Interpreting Demographic Data	Analyzing Historical Maps	

5	6	7	8	9	10	11
Sections 1, 2, 4, 5	Section 2	Section 1	Section 3	Section 3	Section 2	Sections 4, 5
Section 1	Section 1		Section 5	Sections 1, 2		
Sections 3, 4	Section 2	Section 1	Sections 1, 2, 3, 4, 5	Section 2	Sections 1, 3	Sections 2, 3, 4, 5
Section 5	Section 3	Sections 1, 3	Sections 4, 5	Section 3	Sections 2, 4	Sections 1, 3, 5
Sections 1, 5	Section 3	Sections 1, 4	Section 2	Section 1	Section 2	Sections 2, 3, 4
	Section 2		Sections 1, 3			
Sections 2, 4	Sections 1, 2	Sections 2, 3, 4				Section 4
	Sections 1, 2				Section 3	
			Sections 1, 2, 3		Section 3	Sections 4, 5
Sections 1, 2, 3		Section 2	Sections 2, 3	Section 3	Section 4	Sections 2, 3
Section 1	Section 1		Section 5	Sections 1, 2		Section 3
	Sections 1, 2		Sections 4, 5		Section 3	Sections 4, 5
Sections 1, 2	Sections 1, 3	Sections 2, 3, 4	Sections 1, 2, 3, 5		Sections 1, 2, 3	Sections 1, 2, 3, 4
Section 1	Section 2	Sections 1, 2, 3	Sections 1, 2, 3, 4, 5	Sections 2, 3	Sections 1, 2, 3, 4	Sections 1, 2, 3, 4
Section s 1, 2, 3, 4, 5	Section 3	Sections 1, 3	Sections 1, 2, 3, 5	Sections 1, 2, 3	Sections 1, 2	Sections 2, 3, 4
Critical Thinking Skill	*Technology Skill*	*Technology Skill*	*Study and Writing Skill*	*Technology Skill*	*Study and Writing Skill*	*Social Studies Skill*
Identifying Evidence	Using a Computerized Catalog	Using a Word Processor	Recognizing a Stereotype	Developing Multimedia Presentations	Outlining	Interpreting Graphs

Scope and Sequence

	Chapter	12	13	14	15
Historical Themes Students need to understand and be able to recognize the themes that appear throughout history. Students also need to develop the ability to apply these themes as they examine the effect of the past on the present and the future. **The central theme highlighted in each section appears in red. Related themes are listed in black.**	Movement	Sections 2, 3	Section 3	Section 2	
	Innovation	Sections 2, 3	Sections 2, 3, 4	Section 4	Section 3
	Conflict/ Cooperation	Section 4		Sections 2, 3, 4	Sections 1, 2, 4
	Revolution/ Reaction	Sections 2, 3		Section 3	Sections 4, 5
	Change	Sections 2, 3	Section 1	Sections 1, 4	Sections 3, 4
	Diversity/ Uniformity				Section 5
	Cultural Diffusion		Section 4	Section 2	
	Relation to Environment	Sections 1, 2, 5	Section 3		Sections 3, 5
	Regionalism/ Nationalism/ Internationalism			Section 5	Sections 1, 2
Content Knowledge Students need to have a knowledge of the disciplines that play an integral role in the social studies: history, literature, art and culture, science and technology, government and civics, geography, economics, and religion. Students also need to develop a keen understanding of how these subjects interact with one another.	Literature, Art, and Culture	Sections 1, 4	Sections 1, 3, 4		
	Science and Technology	Sections 1, 2. 3, 4	Sections 2, 3		Section 3
	Geography and Environment	Sections 1, 2, 5	Section 3	Sections 2, 4	Sections 3, 5
	Economics	Sections 1, 2, 4	Section 1	Sections 4, 5	Section 3
	Government/ Civics		Section 1	Sections 1, 2, 3, 5	Sections 1, 2, 3, 4, 5
	Religion			Sections 1, 3, 5	Section 3
Skills These are the skills taught in the Chapter *Skills*. Each skill is reinforced in the *Skill Practice* found in the Chapter Reviews and in the **Skill Reinforcement Activities** booklet in the TCR.	Skill Category	*Critical Thinking Skill*	*Technology Skill*	*Social Studies Skill*	*Study and Writing Skill*
	Specific Skill	Detecting Bias	Using E-Mail	Reading a Cartogram	Selecting and Using Research Sources

Scope and Sequence

16	17	18	19	20	21	22
Sections 1, 2			Section 4	Sections 1, 3		
Section 4	Section 3	Sections 1, 3	Section 4	Section 5	Section 3	
Sections 3, 4	Sections 1, 2, 3, 4, 5		Sections 1, 2, 3, 4	Sections 2, 3, 4	Sections 1, 2, 4	Sections 3, 4, 5
Section 3	Section 4		Section 3			Section 2
Section 2	Sections 4, 5	Section 2	Sections 2, 5		Sections 1, 2, 4	Section 1
	Section 5	Sections 3, 4		Section 3	Sections 2, 4	Section 5
Section 1						Section 6
Sections 1, 3					Section 2	Section 1
Sections 3, 4	Sections 1, 5	Section 1	Sections 1, 2, 5	Section 1	Sections 2, 3, 4	Sections 3, 4, 6
Sections 2, 3		Sections 1, 4	Section 4		Section 4	Section 2
Section 4	Section 3	Section 1	Section 4	Sections 2, 4, 5	Sections 3, 4	Sections 1, 2
Sections 1, 3	Sections 3, 5				Sections 1, 2	Section 1
Sections 1, 2	Sections 1, 4, 5	Sections 1, 2, 3, 4	Sections 4, 5		Sections 1, 2, 3, 4	Sections 1, 3
Sections 1, 2, 3, 4,	Sections 2, 3, 4	Sections 1, 2, 3, 4	Sections 1, 2, 3, 4, 5	Sections 1, 2, 5	Sections 2, 3, 4	Sections 1, 2, 5, 6
Section 1	Section 4		Section 2			Section 5
Technology Skill	*Social Studies Skill*	*Critical Thinking Skill*	*Critical Thinking Skill*	*Critical Thinking Skill*	*Social Studies Skill*	*Technology Skill*
Using the Internet	Interpreting Military Movements on Maps	Analyzing Political Cartoons	Identifying an Argument	Synthesizing Information	Understanding World Time Zones	Using a Spreadsheet

Scope and Sequence

Historical Themes

Students need to understand and be able to recognize the themes that appear throughout history. Students also need to develop the ability to apply these themes as they examine the effect of the past on the present and the future.

The central theme highlighted in each section appears in red. Related themes are listed in black.

Content Knowledge

Students need to have a knowledge of the disciplines that play an integral role in the social studies: history, literature, art and culture, science and technology, government and civics, geography, economics, and religion. Students also need to develop a keen understanding of how these subjects interact with one another.

Skills

These are the skills taught in the Chapter *Skills*. Each skill is reinforced in the *Skill Practice* found in the Chapter Reviews and in the **Skill Reinforcement Activities** booklet in the TCR.

Chapter	23	24	25	26
Movement		Section 2		Section 2
Innovation				Section 5
Conflict/ Cooperation	Sections 1, 2	Sections 1, 2, 3	Sections 1, 2, 3, 4	Sections 1, 3, 4
Revolution/ Reaction		Section 2	Sections 2, 3	Section 4
Change	Sections 1, 2, 3		Sections 2, 4	Sections 1, 2
Diversity/ Uniformity	Section 3			Sections 3, 5
Cultural Diffusion		Section 3		Section 5
Relation to Environment	Section 3	Sections 1, 2	Section 1	Section 5
Regionalism/ Nationalism/ Internationalism	Sections 1, 2, 3	Section 1	Sections 1, 2, 3, 4	Sections 1, 2, 3, 4, 5
Literature, Art, and Culture		Section 3		Sections 1, 4
Science and Technology				Section 5
Geography and Environment	Section 3	Sections 1, 2	Section 1	Section 5
Economics	Sections 2, 3	Sections 1, 2, 3	Sections 1, 2, 4	Sections 1, 2, 3, 5
Government/ Civics	Sections 1, 2	Sections 1, 2, 3	Sections 1, 2, 3, 4	Sections 1, 2, 3, 4
Religion		Sections 2, 3	Section 1	Section 4
Skill Category	*Study and Writing Skill*	*Study and Writing Skill*	*Technology Skill*	*Social Studies Skill*
Specific Skill	Writing a Research Report	Preparing a Bibliography	Developing a Database	Interpreting Statistics

Reference Atlas

Atlas Key

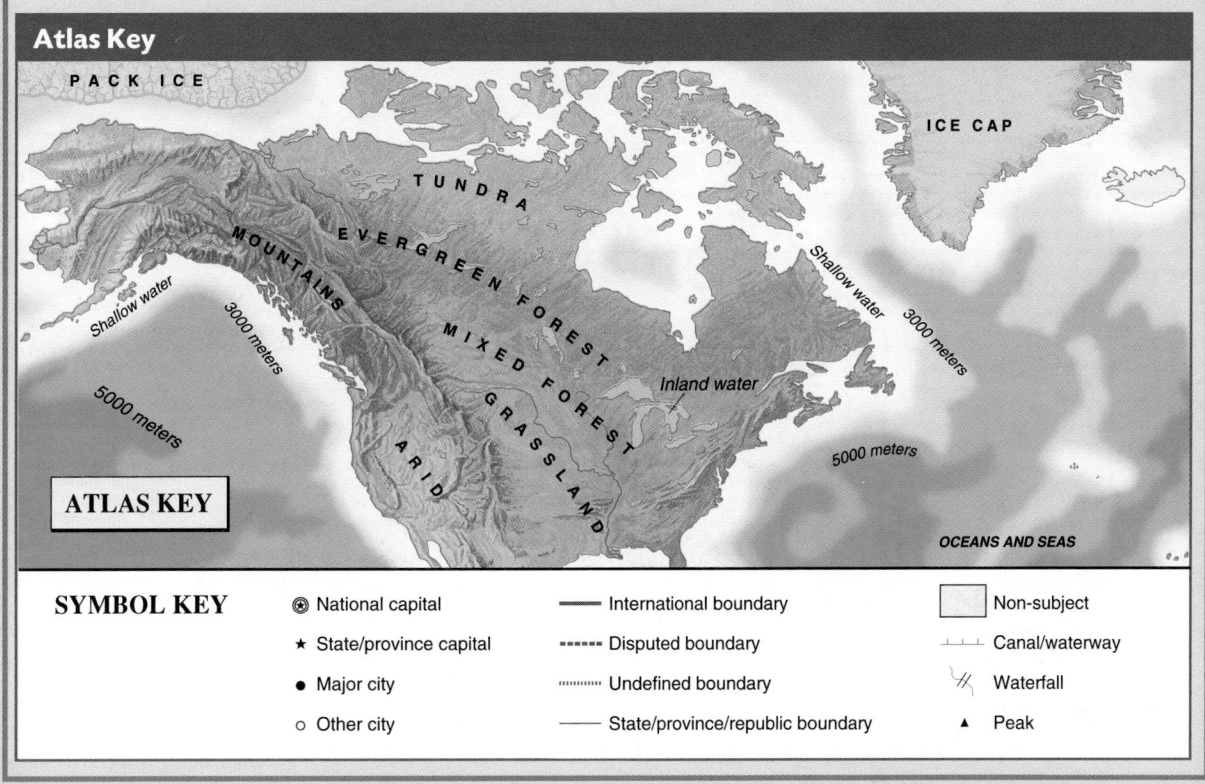

PACK ICE

ICE CAP

TUNDRA

EVERGREEN FOREST

MOUNTAINS

Shallow water

3000 meters

5000 meters

MIXED FOREST

Inland water

GRASSLAND

ARID

Shallow water

3000 meters

5000 meters

OCEANS AND SEAS

ATLAS KEY

SYMBOL KEY			
⊛ National capital	——— International boundary	▢ Non-subject
★ State/province capital	------ Disputed boundary	⊥⊥⊥ Canal/waterway
● Major city	.... Undefined boundary	⤨ Waterfall
○ Other city	——— State/province/republic boundary	▲ Peak

THE WORLD PHYSICAL/POLITICAL

- • World's most populous cities
- —— International boundary
- ----- Disputed boundary
- ········ Undefined boundary

0   1000   2000 Miles
0   1000   2000 Kilometers

Projection: Robinson

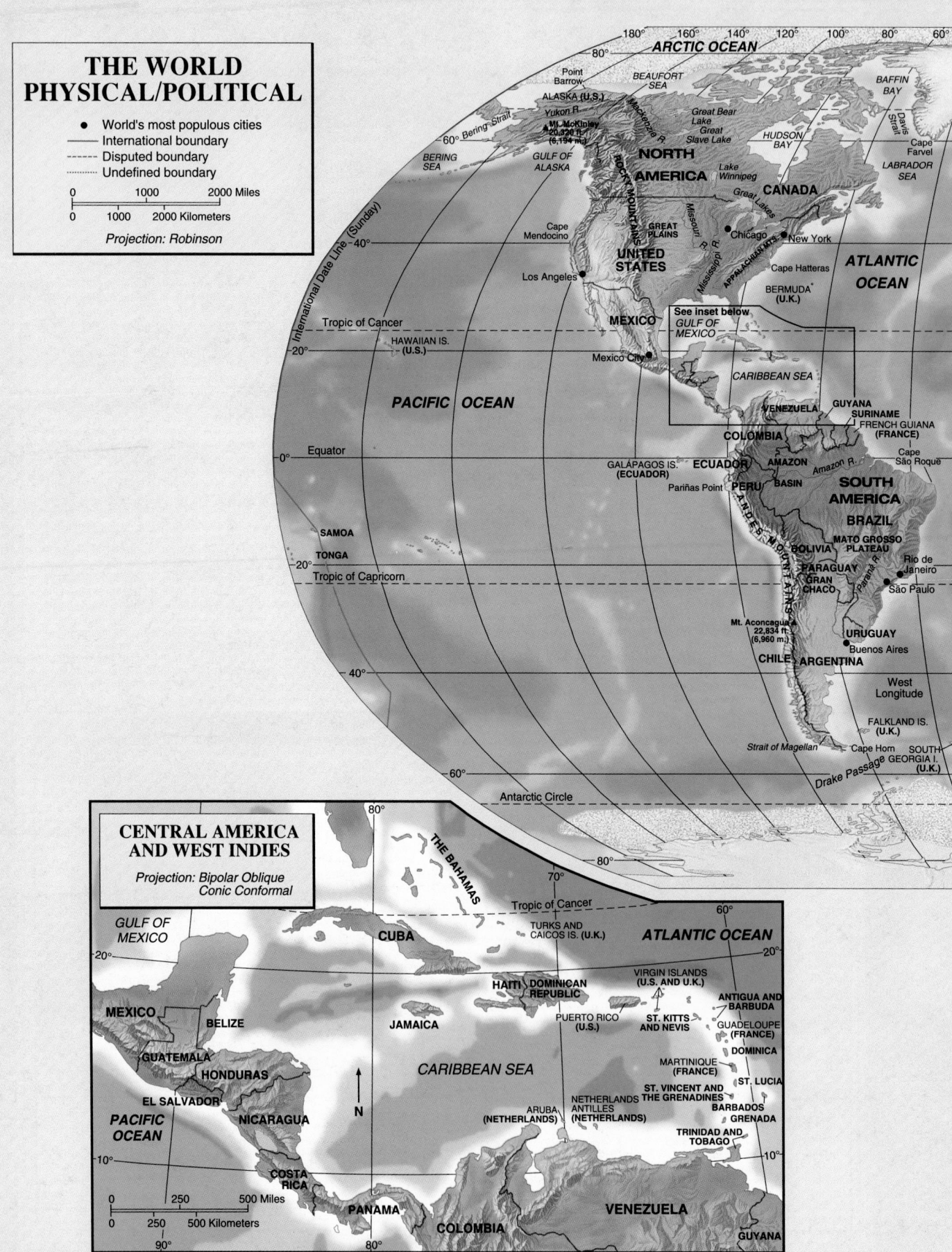

CENTRAL AMERICA AND WEST INDIES

Projection: Bipolar Oblique Conic Conformal

0   250   500 Miles
0   250   500 Kilometers

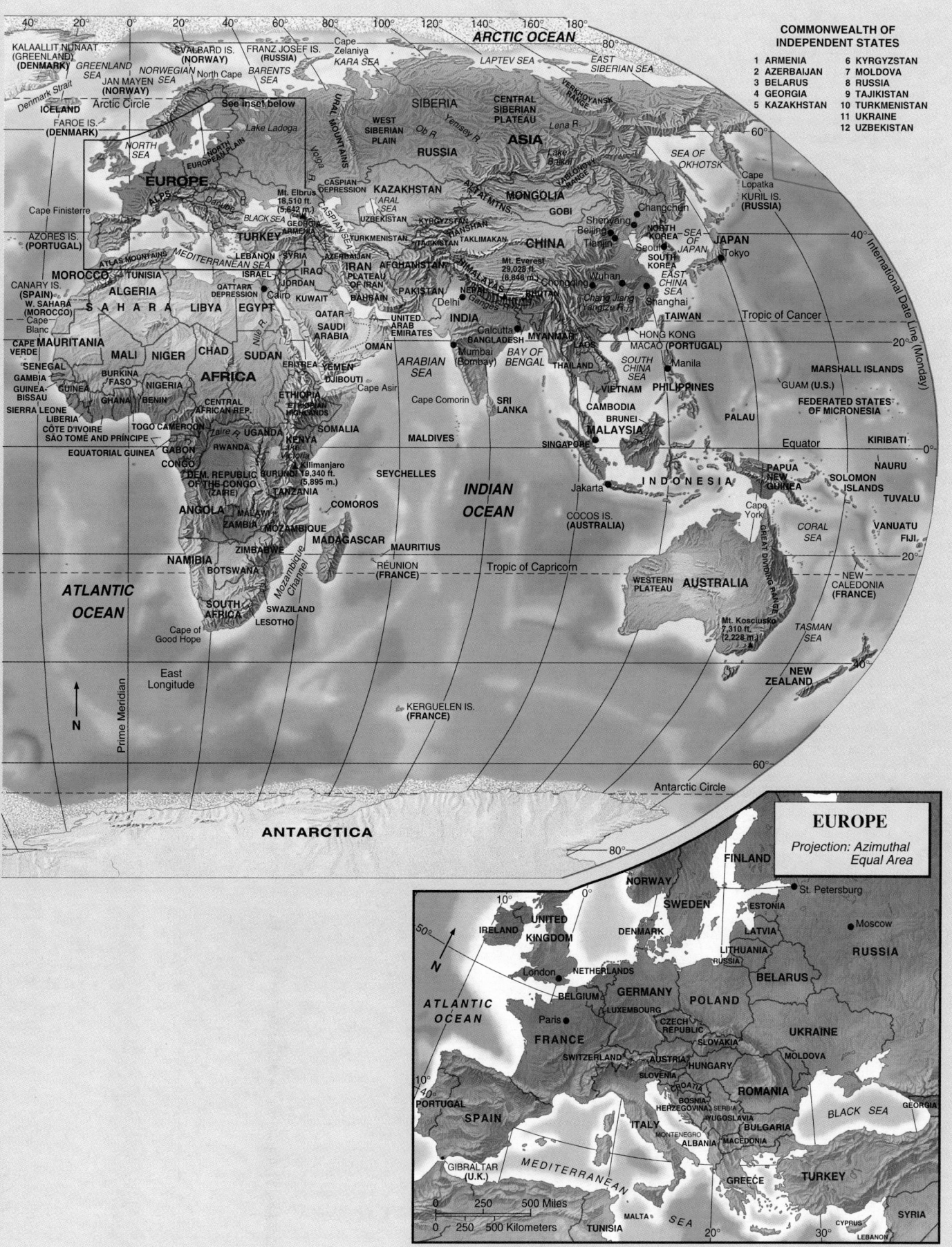

40° 20° 0° 20° 40° 60° 80° 100° 120° 140° 160° 180°

ARCTIC OCEAN

KALAALLIT NUNAAT
(GREENLAND)
(DENMARK)
*GREENLAND
SEA*
SVALBARD IS.
(NORWAY)
FRANZ JOSEF IS.
(RUSSIA)
Cape
Zelaniya
KARA SEA
LAPTEV SEA
*EAST
SIBERIAN
SEA*

Denmark Strait
*JAN MAYEN
(NORWAY)*
*NORWEGIAN
SEA*
North Cape
*BARENTS
SEA*

ICELAND
FAROE IS.
(DENMARK)
Arctic Circle
See Inset below
SIBERIA
**CENTRAL
SIBERIAN
PLATEAU**
*VERKHOYANSK
RANGE*

*NORTH
SEA*
EUROPE
Lake Ladoga
URAL MOUNTAINS
*WEST
SIBERIAN
PLAIN*
Yenisey R.
Ob R.
Lena R.
ASIA
Lake
Baikal
*SEA OF
OKHOTSK*

EUROPEAN PLAIN
ALPS
Danube
Volga R.
RUSSIA
KAZAKHSTAN
ALTAI MTNS.
MONGOLIA
GOBI
YABLONOVY RANGE
Cape
Lopatka
**KURIL IS.
(RUSSIA)**

Cape Finisterre
Mt. Elbrus
18,510 ft.
(5,642 m.)
*CASPIAN
DEPRESSION*
*ARAL
SEA*
TIANSHAN
Changchun
Shenyang
**NORTH
KOREA**
*SEA
OF
JAPAN*
JAPAN

AZORES IS.
(PORTUGAL)
BLACK SEA
GEORGIA
ARMENIA
CASPIAN SEA
TURKMENISTAN
KYRGYZSTAN
TAJIKISTAN
TAKLIMAKAN
Beijing
Tianjin
Seoul
**SOUTH
KOREA**
*EAST
CHINA
SEA*
Tokyo

TURKEY
LEBANON
SYRIA
AZERBAIJAN
UZBEKISTAN
HIMALAYAS
Mt. Everest
29,028 ft.
(8,848 m.)
CHINA
Chongqing
Wuhan
*Chang Jiang
Yangtze R.*
Shanghai
International Date Line (Monday)

MOROCCO TUNISIA
ISRAEL
IRAQ
JORDAN KUWAIT
BAHRAIN
IRAN
*PLATEAU
OF IRAN*
AFGHANISTAN
PAKISTAN
NEPAL
Ganges R.
BHUTAN
Delhi

ALGERIA
ATLAS MOUNTAINS
Cairo
EGYPT
QATAR
*QATTARA
DEPRESSION*
SAUDI
ARABIA
UNITED
ARAB
EMIRATES
OMAN
INDIA
BANGLADESH
Calcutta
Tropic of Cancer
MYANMAR
LAOS
HONG KONG
MACAO **(PORTUGAL)**
TAIWAN

CANARY IS.
(SPAIN)
W. SAHARA
(MOROCCO)
Cape
Blanc
S A H A R A
LIBYA
SUDAN
ERITREA
YEMEN
DJIBOUTI
Cape Asir
*ARABIAN
SEA*
Mumbai
(Bombay)
*BAY OF
BENGAL*
THAILAND
VIETNAM
PHILIPPINES
Manila
GUAM (U.S.)
MARSHALL ISLANDS

**CAPE
VERDE**
MAURITANIA
MALI NIGER CHAD
AFRICA
Niger R.
CENTRAL
AFRICAN REP.
ETHIOPIA
*ETHIOPIAN
HIGHLANDS*
Cape Comorin
SRI
LANKA
CAMBODIA
BRUNEI
MALAYSIA
PALAU
**FEDERATED STATES
OF MICRONESIA**

SENEGAL
GAMBIA
GUINEA-
BISSAU
BURKINA
FASO
NIGERIA
BENIN
UGANDA
SOMALIA
MALDIVES
*INDIAN
OCEAN*
SINGAPORE
Equator
KIRIBATI
0°

GUINEA
SIERRA LEONE
LIBERIA
GHANA
TOGO CAMEROON
CÔTE D'IVOIRE
SÃO TOMÉ AND PRÍNCIPE
EQUATORIAL GUINEA
GABON
CONGO
Zaire R.
RWANDA
*Lake
Victoria*
KENYA
SEYCHELLES
Jakarta
INDONESIA
**PAPUA
NEW
GUINEA**
SOLOMON
ISLANDS
NAURU
TUVALU

DEM. REPUBLIC
OF THE CONGO
(ZAIRE)
BURUNDI
*Kilimanjaro
19,340 ft.
(5,895 m.)*
TANZANIA
COMOROS
COCOS IS.
(AUSTRALIA)
Cape
York
*CORAL
SEA*
VANUATU
FIJI

ANGOLA
MALAWI
ZAMBIA
MOZAMBIQUE
MADAGASCAR
MAURITIUS
GREAT DIVIDING RANGE
NEW
CALEDONIA
(FRANCE)

*ATLANTIC
OCEAN*
NAMIBIA
ZIMBABWE
BOTSWANA
Mozambique Channel
RÉUNION
(FRANCE)
Tropic of Capricorn
WESTERN
PLATEAU
AUSTRALIA
20°

**SOUTH
AFRICA**
SWAZILAND
LESOTHO
Mt. Kosciusko
7,310 ft.
(2,228 m.)
*TASMAN
SEA*

Cape of
Good Hope
East
Longitude
40°

N

Prime Meridian
KERGUELEN IS.
(FRANCE)
**NEW
ZEALAND**

60°

Antarctic Circle

ANTARCTICA
80°

40° 20° 0° 20° 40° 60° 80° 60° 40° 20° 0° 20° 40°

EUROPE

*Projection: Azimuthal
Equal Area*

10° 0°

FINLAND
NORWAY
St. Petersburg
50°
IRELAND
**UNITED
KINGDOM**
SWEDEN
ESTONIA
Moscow
DENMARK
LATVIA
RUSSIA
London
NETHERLANDS
LITHUANIA
RUSSIA
BELARUS
*ATLANTIC
OCEAN*
BELGIUM
LUXEMBOURG
GERMANY
POLAND
Paris
FRANCE
CZECH
REPUBLIC
UKRAINE
SWITZERLAND
SLOVAKIA
AUSTRIA
HUNGARY
MOLDOVA
SLOVENIA
CROATIA
ROMANIA
10°
40°
PORTUGAL
BOSNIA
HERZEGOVINA
SERBIA
YUGOSLAVIA
BLACK SEA
GEORGIA
SPAIN
ITALY
MONTENEGRO
MACEDONIA
BULGARIA
ALBANIA
GIBRALTAR
(U.K.)
MEDITERRANEAN
GREECE
TURKEY
MALTA
SEA
CYPRUS
SYRIA
LEBANON
TUNISIA
20°
30°

0   250   500 Miles
0   250   500 Kilometers

N

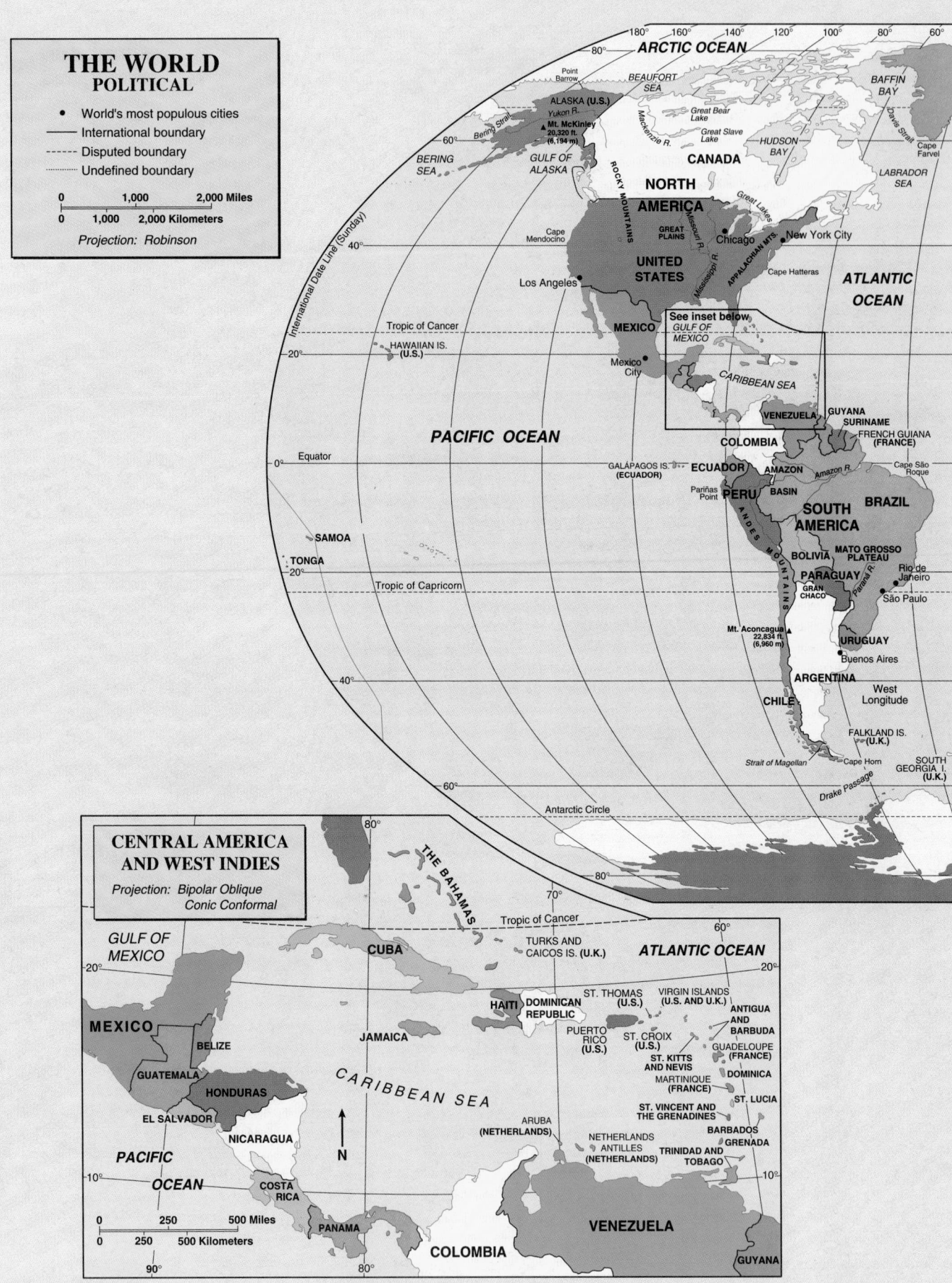

THE WORLD
POLITICAL

- • World's most populous cities
- —— International boundary
- --- Disputed boundary
- ···· Undefined boundary

| 0 | 1,000 | 2,000 Miles |
| 0 | 1,000 | 2,000 Kilometers |

Projection: Robinson

ARCTIC OCEAN

BEAUFORT SEA

BAFFIN BAY

Point Barrow

ALASKA (U.S.)

Yukon R.

Mt. McKinley
20,320 ft.
(6,194 m)

Great Bear Lake

Mackenzie R.

Great Slave Lake

Davis Strait

Cape Farvel

BERING SEA

Bering Strait

GULF OF ALASKA

ROCKY MOUNTAINS

CANADA

HUDSON BAY

LABRADOR SEA

NORTH AMERICA

Great Lakes

International Date Line (Sunday)

Cape Mendocino

GREAT PLAINS

Missouri R.

Chicago

New York City

UNITED STATES

Mississippi R.

APPALACHIAN MTS.

Cape Hatteras

ATLANTIC OCEAN

Los Angeles

Tropic of Cancer

See inset below

GULF OF MEXICO

MEXICO

HAWAIIAN IS. (U.S.)

Mexico City

CARIBBEAN SEA

PACIFIC OCEAN

VENEZUELA

GUYANA

SURINAME

FRENCH GUIANA (FRANCE)

COLOMBIA

Equator

GALÁPAGOS IS. (ECUADOR)

ECUADOR

AMAZON BASIN

Amazon R.

Cape São Roque

Pariñas Point

PERU

SOUTH AMERICA

BRAZIL

ANDES MOUNTAINS

SAMOA

MATO GROSSO PLATEAU

TONGA

BOLIVIA

Rio de Janeiro

Tropic of Capricorn

PARAGUAY

Paraná R.

São Paulo

GRAN CHACO

Mt. Aconcagua
22,834 ft.
(6,960 m)

URUGUAY

Buenos Aires

ARGENTINA

West Longitude

CHILE

FALKLAND IS. (U.K.)

Strait of Magellan

Cape Horn

SOUTH GEORGIA I. (U.K.)

Drake Passage

Antarctic Circle

CENTRAL AMERICA AND WEST INDIES

Projection: Bipolar Oblique Conic Conformal

THE BAHAMAS

Tropic of Cancer

GULF OF MEXICO

CUBA

TURKS AND CAICOS IS. (U.K.)

ATLANTIC OCEAN

MEXICO

HAITI

DOMINICAN REPUBLIC

ST. THOMAS (U.S.)

VIRGIN ISLANDS (U.S. AND U.K.)

ANTIGUA AND BARBUDA

BELIZE

JAMAICA

PUERTO RICO (U.S.)

ST. CROIX (U.S.)

GUADELOUPE (FRANCE)

GUATEMALA

ST. KITTS AND NEVIS

DOMINICA

CARIBBEAN SEA

MARTINIQUE (FRANCE)

ST. LUCIA

HONDURAS

ST. VINCENT AND THE GRENADINES

EL SALVADOR

N

ARUBA (NETHERLANDS)

BARBADOS

GRENADA

NICARAGUA

NETHERLANDS ANTILLES (NETHERLANDS)

TRINIDAD AND TOBAGO

PACIFIC OCEAN

| 0 | 250 | 500 Miles |
| 0 | 250 | 500 Kilometers |

COSTA RICA

PANAMA

VENEZUELA

COLOMBIA

GUYANA

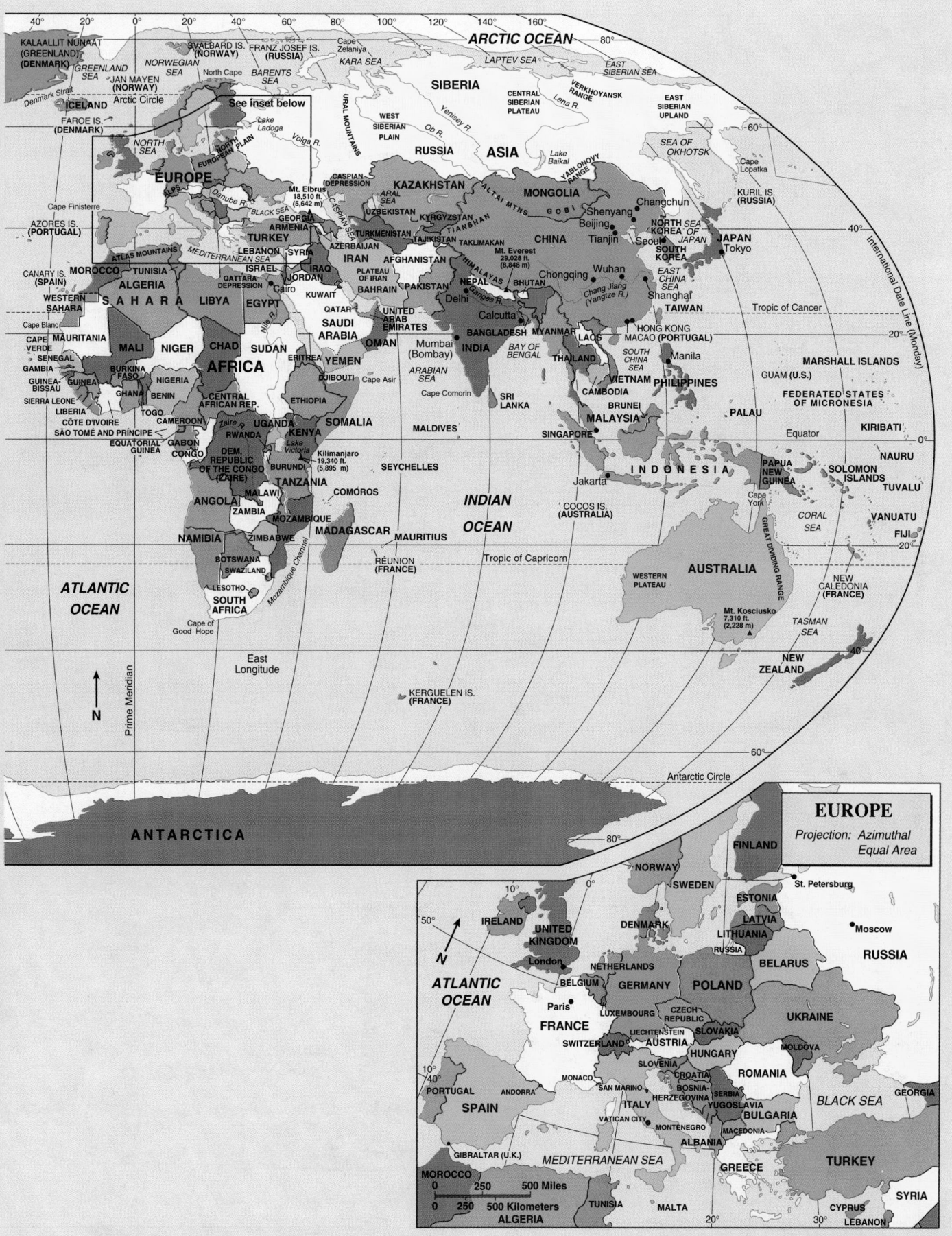

ARCTIC OCEAN

KALAALLIT NUNAAT (GREENLAND) (DENMARK)
GREENLAND SEA
JAN MAYEN (NORWAY)
SVALBARD IS. (NORWAY)
FRANZ JOSEF IS. (RUSSIA)
Cape Zelaniya
KARA SEA
LAPTEV SEA
EAST SIBERIAN SEA

NORWEGIAN SEA
BARENTS SEA
North Cape
SIBERIA
CENTRAL SIBERIAN PLATEAU
VERKHOYANSK RANGE
Lena R.
EAST SIBERIAN UPLAND

Denmark Strait
ICELAND
Arctic Circle
NORTH SEA
Lake Ladoga
WEST SIBERIAN PLAIN
Ob R.
Yenisey R.
RUSSIA
ASIA
Lake Baikal
SEA OF OKHOTSK
Cape Lopatka

FAROE IS. (DENMARK)
See inset below
Lake Onega
URAL MOUNTAINS
Volga R.
KAZAKHSTAN
ALTAI MTNS
MONGOLIA
Changchun
KURIL IS. (RUSSIA)

NORTH EUROPEAN PLAIN
EUROPE
Mt. Elbrus 18,510 ft. (5,642 m)
CASPIAN DEPRESSION
ARAL SEA
UZBEKISTAN
KYRGYZSTAN
TIANSHAN
GOBI
Shenyang
Beijing
NORTH KOREA
SEA OF JAPAN
JAPAN

ALPS
Danube R.
BLACK SEA
GEORGIA
ARMENIA
TURKEY
TURKMENISTAN
TAJIKISTAN
TAKLIMAKAN
CHINA
Tianjin
Seoul
SOUTH KOREA
Tokyo
Cape Finisterre

Cape Finisterre
AZORES IS. (PORTUGAL)
MEDITERRANEAN SEA
SYRIA
AZERBAIJAN
IRAN
AFGHANISTAN
Mt. Everest 29,028 ft. (8,848 m)
HIMALAYAS
Chongqing
Wuhan
EAST CHINA SEA
Shanghai

CANARY IS. (SPAIN)
ATLAS MOUNTAINS
MOROCCO
TUNISIA
LEBANON
ISRAEL
IRAQ
JORDAN
BAHRAIN
PAKISTAN
PLATEAU OF IRAN
NEPAL
Ganges R.
BHUTAN
Delhi
Chang Jiang (Yangtze R.)
TAIWAN

ALGERIA
QATTARA DEPRESSION
Cairo
KUWAIT
QATAR
Calcutta
Tropic of Cancer
HONG KONG
MACAO (PORTUGAL)

WESTERN SAHARA
S A H A R A
LIBYA
EGYPT
Nile R.
SAUDI ARABIA
UNITED ARAB EMIRATES
Mumbai (Bombay)
INDIA
BANGLADESH
MYANMAR
LAOS
SOUTH CHINA SEA
Manila
MARSHALL ISLANDS

Cape Blanc
CAPE VERDE
MAURITANIA
MALI
NIGER
CHAD
SUDAN
ERITREA
YEMEN
OMAN
ARABIAN SEA
BAY OF BENGAL
THAILAND
GUAM (U.S.)
FEDERATED STATES OF MICRONESIA

SENEGAL
GAMBIA
BURKINA FASO
NIGERIA
AFRICA
DJIBOUTI
Cape Asir
Cape Comorin
SRI LANKA
CAMBODIA
VIETNAM
PHILIPPINES
PALAU

GUINEA-BISSAU
GUINEA
GHANA
BENIN
CENTRAL AFRICAN REP.
ETHIOPIA
SOMALIA
MALDIVES
BRUNEI
MALAYSIA
KIRIBATI

SIERRA LEONE
LIBERIA
CÔTE D'IVOIRE
TOGO
CAMEROON
UGANDA
KENYA
SINGAPORE
Equator
NAURU

SÃO TOMÉ AND PRÍNCIPE
EQUATORIAL GUINEA
GABON
CONGO
DEM. REPUBLIC OF THE CONGO (ZAIRE)
RWANDA
BURUNDI
Lake Victoria
Kilimanjaro 19,340 ft. (5,895 m)
TANZANIA
SEYCHELLES
INDONESIA
Jakarta
PAPUA NEW GUINEA
SOLOMON ISLANDS
TUVALU

ANGOLA
MALAWI
ZAMBIA
MOZAMBIQUE
COMOROS
INDIAN OCEAN
Cape York
CORAL SEA
VANUATU
FIJI

NAMIBIA
ZIMBABWE
MADAGASCAR
MAURITIUS
RÉUNION (FRANCE)
Tropic of Capricorn
GREAT DIVIDING RANGE
NEW CALEDONIA (FRANCE)

BOTSWANA
SWAZILAND
Mozambique Channel
WESTERN PLATEAU
AUSTRALIA

ATLANTIC OCEAN
LESOTHO
SOUTH AFRICA
Cape of Good Hope
Mt. Kosciusko 7,310 ft. (2,228 m)
TASMAN SEA

East Longitude
NEW ZEALAND

Prime Meridian
N

KERGUELEN IS. (FRANCE)

Antarctic Circle

ANTARCTICA

International Date Line (Monday)

EUROPE
Projection: Azimuthal Equal Area

FINLAND
NORWAY
SWEDEN
ESTONIA
St. Petersburg
LATVIA
Moscow
IRELAND
UNITED KINGDOM
DENMARK
LITHUANIA
RUSSIA
London
NETHERLANDS
BELARUS
RUSSIA
ATLANTIC OCEAN
BELGIUM
GERMANY
POLAND
Paris
LUXEMBOURG
CZECH REPUBLIC
UKRAINE
FRANCE
LIECHTENSTEIN
SLOVAKIA
SWITZERLAND
AUSTRIA
MOLDOVA
SLOVENIA
HUNGARY
MONACO
CROATIA
ROMANIA
PORTUGAL
ANDORRA
SAN MARINO
BOSNIA-HERZEGOVINA
SERBIA
BLACK SEA
GEORGIA
SPAIN
ITALY
YUGOSLAVIA
BULGARIA
VATICAN CITY
Montenegro
MACEDONIA
GIBRALTAR (U.K.)
ALBANIA
MEDITERRANEAN SEA
GREECE
TURKEY
MOROCCO
0 250 500 Miles
0 250 500 Kilometers
TUNISIA
MALTA
CYPRUS
LEBANON
ALGERIA
SYRIA

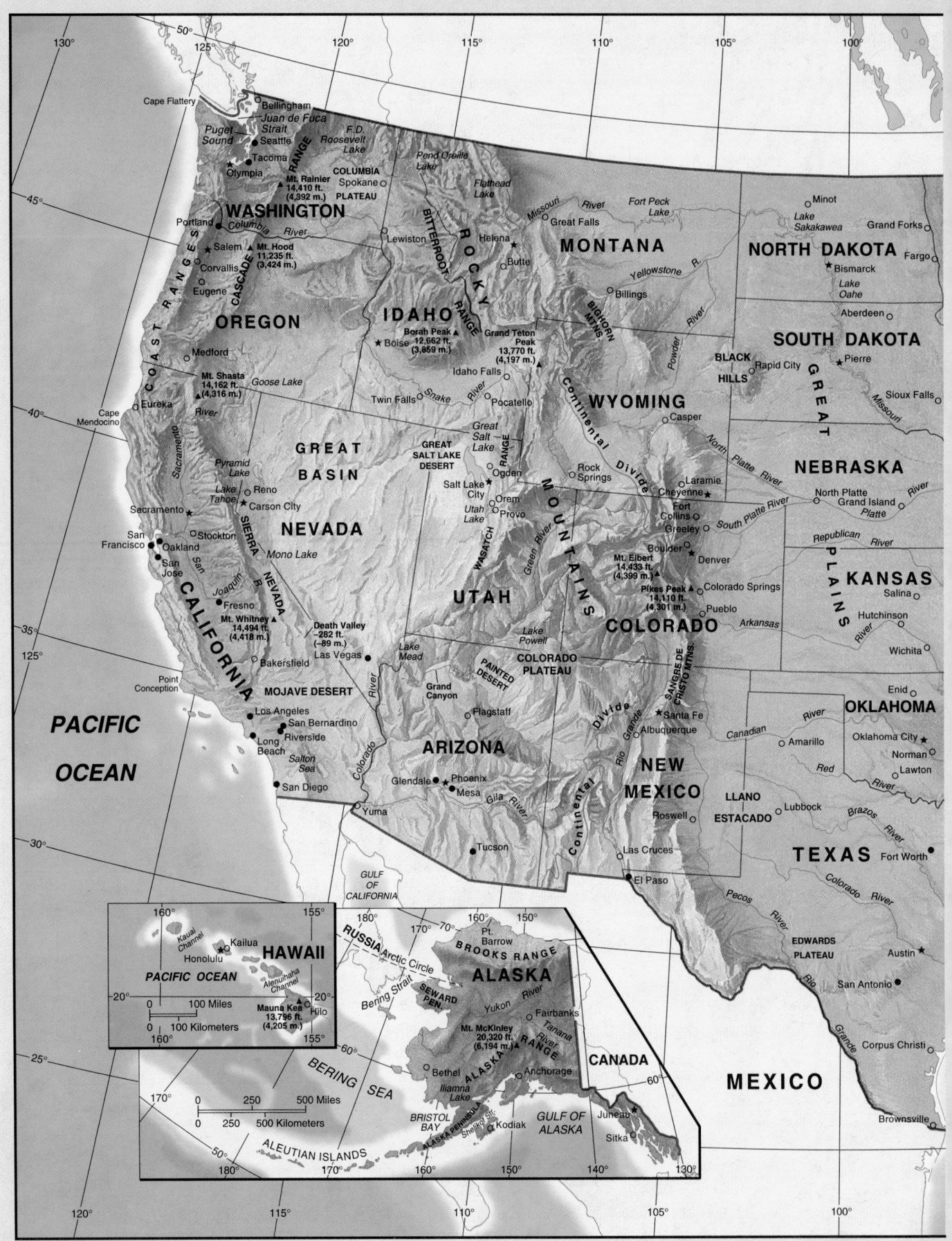

PACIFIC OCEAN

PACIFIC OCEAN

WASHINGTON
Cape Flattery
Bellingham
Juan de Fuca Strait
Puget Sound
Seattle
Tacoma
Olympia
Mt. Rainier 14,410 ft. (4,392 m.)
Portland
Salem
Mt. Hood 11,235 ft. (3,424 m.)
Corvallis
Eugene
F.D. Roosevelt Lake
COLUMBIA PLATEAU
Spokane
Pend Oreille Lake
Lewiston
Columbia River

OREGON
Medford
Mt. Shasta 14,162 ft. (4,316 m.)
Goose Lake

IDAHO
Boise
Borah Peak 12,662 ft. (3,859 m.)
Idaho Falls
Twin Falls
Snake River
Pocatello

BITTERROOT RANGE

MONTANA
Helena
Butte
Great Falls
Missouri River
Flathead Lake
Fort Peck Lake
Billings
Yellowstone R.
Powder River

WYOMING
Grand Teton Peak 13,770 ft. (4,197 m.)
Great Salt Lake
Casper
Rock Springs
Laramie
Cheyenne
BIGHORN MTNS.
Continental Divide

NORTH DAKOTA
Minot
Lake Sakakawea
Grand Forks
Bismarck
Fargo
Aberdeen

SOUTH DAKOTA
BLACK HILLS
Rapid City
Pierre
Sioux Falls
Missouri River
GREAT

NEBRASKA
North Platte
North Platte River
Grand Island
Platte
Republican River

COAST RANGES
Cape Mendocino
Eureka
Sacramento River

CALIFORNIA
Sacramento
Stockton
San Francisco
Oakland
San Jose
Fresno
San Joaquin River
Mt. Whitney 14,494 ft. (4,418 m.)
Bakersfield
Point Conception
Los Angeles
San Bernardino
Long Beach
Riverside
Salton Sea
San Diego

GREAT BASIN

NEVADA
Pyramid Lake
Lake Tahoe
Reno
Carson City
Mono Lake

SIERRA NEVADA

GREAT SALT LAKE DESERT
Great Salt Lake
Salt Lake City
Ogden
Orem
Provo
Utah Lake

WASATCH RANGE

UTAH
Lake Powell

COLORADO
Boulder
Denver
Fort Collins
Greeley
Colorado Springs
Mt. Elbert 14,433 ft. (4,399 m.)
Pikes Peak 14,110 ft. (4,301 m.)
Pueblo
Arkansas River
MOUNTAINS
SANGRE DE CRISTO MTNS.
Continental Divide

KANSAS
Salina
Hutchinson
Wichita
GREAT PLAINS

Death Valley -282 ft. (-89 m.)
Lake Mead
MOJAVE DESERT
Colorado River
Grand Canyon
PAINTED DESERT
COLORADO PLATEAU
Flagstaff

ARIZONA
Glendale
Phoenix
Mesa
Gila River
Yuma
Tucson

NEW MEXICO
Santa Fe
Albuquerque
Roswell
Las Cruces
El Paso
Rio Grande
Continental Divide
LLANO ESTACADO

OKLAHOMA
Amarillo
Oklahoma City
Norman
Lawton
Canadian River
Red River
Enid

TEXAS
Lubbock
Brazos River
Colorado River
Pecos River
Fort Worth
Austin
EDWARDS PLATEAU
San Antonio
Corpus Christi
Brownsville
Rio Grande

GULF OF CALIFORNIA

MEXICO

HAWAII
Kauai Channel
Kailua
Honolulu
PACIFIC OCEAN
Alenuihaha Channel
Mauna Kea 13,796 ft. (4,205 m.)
Hilo
0 100 Miles
0 100 Kilometers

ALASKA
RUSSIA
Arctic Circle
Pt. Barrow
BROOKS RANGE
SEWARD PEN.
Bering Strait
Yukon River
Tanana River
Fairbanks
Mt. McKinley 20,320 ft. (6,194 m.)
ALASKA RANGE
Bethel
Iliamna Lake
Anchorage
CANADA
Bristol Bay
ALASKA PENINSULA
Shelikof Str.
Kodiak
Juneau
Sitka
GULF OF ALASKA
BERING SEA
ALEUTIAN ISLANDS
0 250 500 Miles
0 250 500 Kilometers

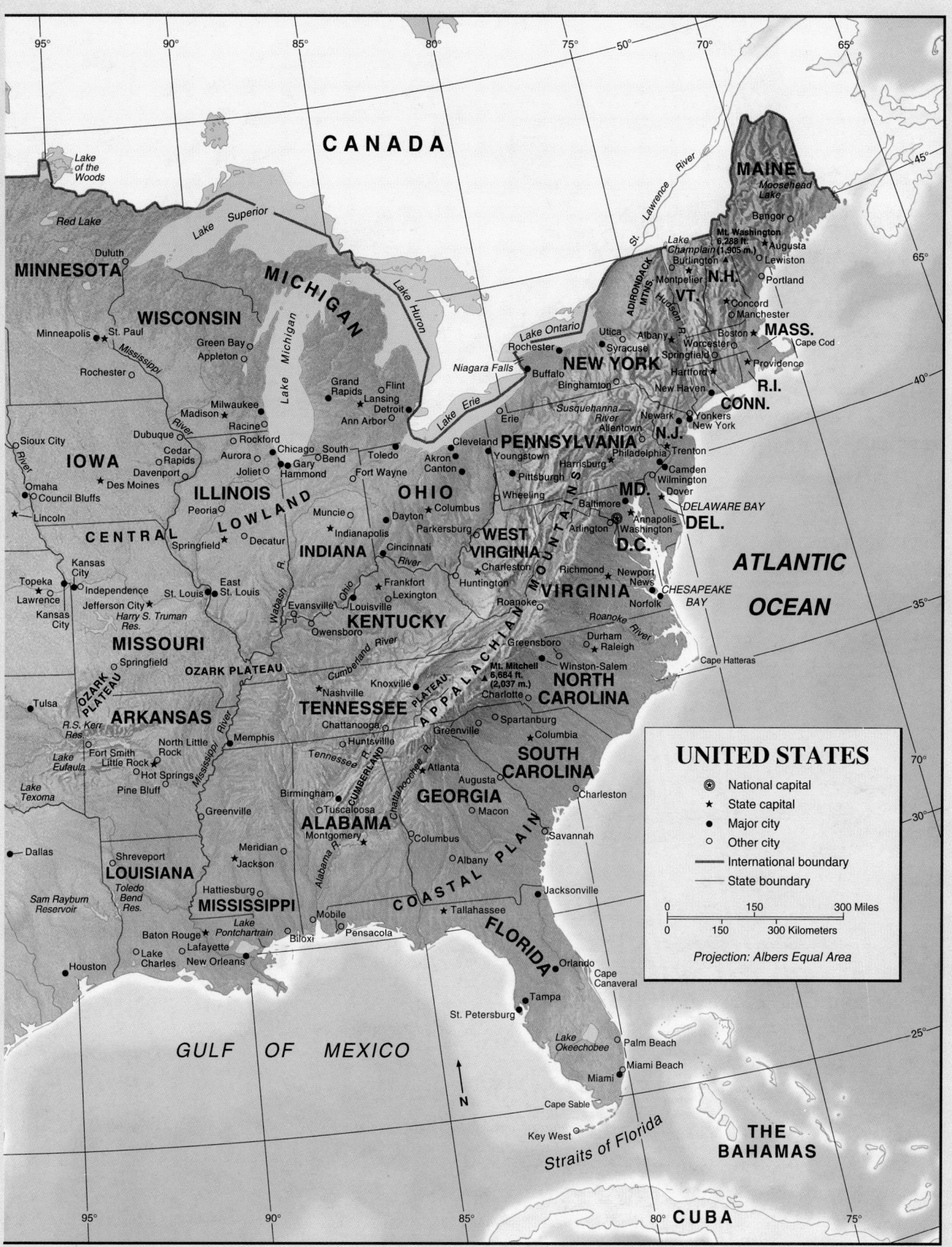

UNITED STATES

⊚ National capital
★ State capital
● Major city
○ Other city
━━━ International boundary
─── State boundary

0		150		300 Miles

0	150	300 Kilometers

Projection: Albers Equal Area

MEXICO, the CARIBBEAN, and CENTRAL AMERICA

✪ National capital

● Major city

—— International boundary

0   250   500 Miles

0   250   500 Kilometers

Projection: Azimuthal Equal Area

GULF OF CALIFORNIA

BAJA CALIFORNIA PENINSULA

Ciudad Juárez

Chihuahua

SIERRA MADRE OCCIDENTAL

MEXICAN PLATEAU

SIERRA MADRE ORIENTAL

Rio Grande

Monterrey

GULF OF MEXICO

Tropic of Cancer

San Pedro River

Tampico

León

Guadalajara

MEXICO

✪ Mexico City

Puebla

Veracruz

CAMPECHE BAY

Mérida

YUCATÁN PENINSULA

Balsas River

SIERRA MADRE DEL SUR

Belize City

Belmopan ✪

BELIZE

Dolores

GULF OF HONDURAS

GUATEMALA

El Progreso

Quezaltenango

Guatemala ✪

Tegucigalpa

Santa Ana

San Salvador ✪

EL SALVADOR

PACIFIC OCEAN

N

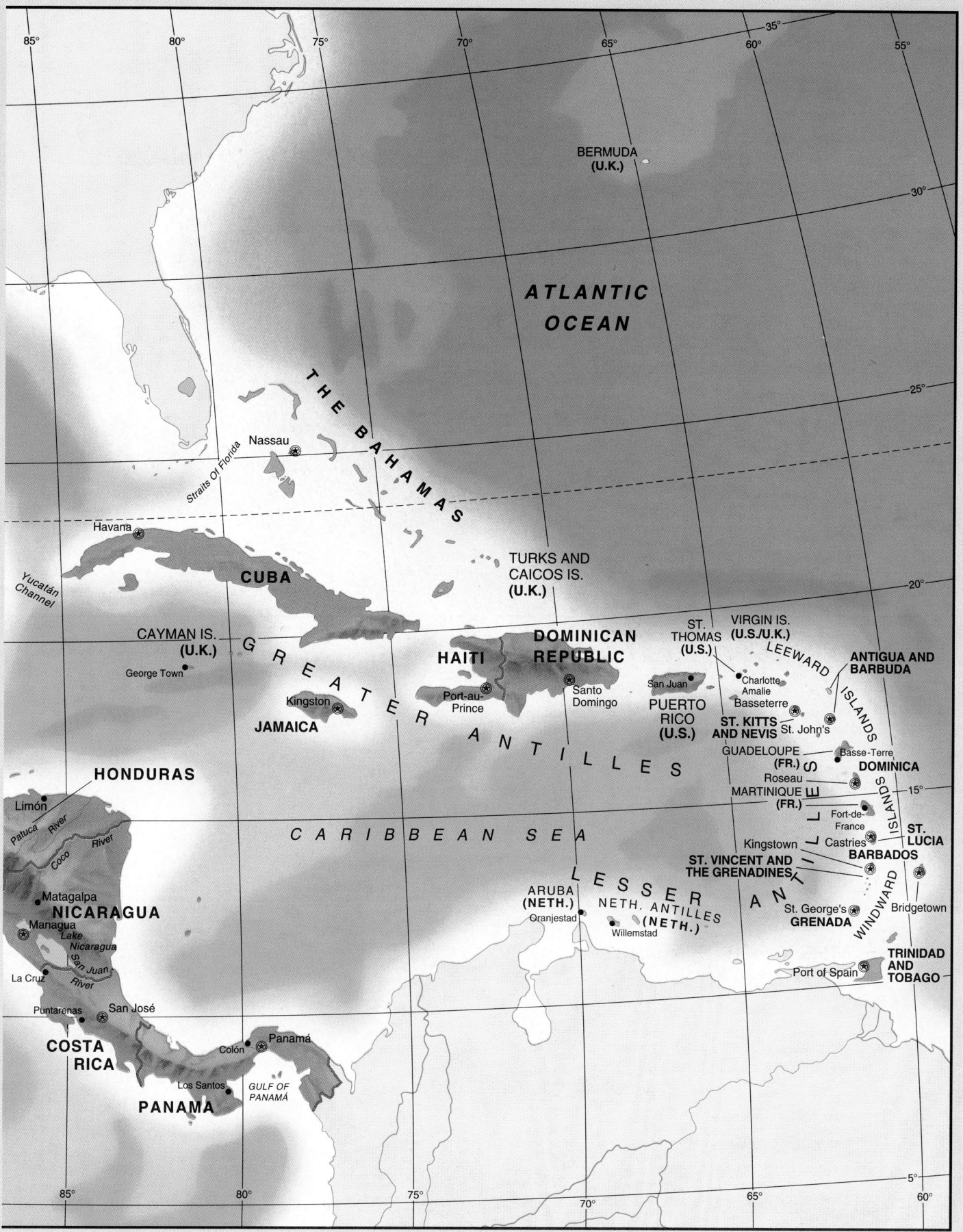

85° **80°** **75°** **70°** **65°** **35°** **60°** **55°**

30°

BERMUDA
(U.K.)

ATLANTIC
OCEAN

25°

T H E   B A H A M A S

Nassau

Straits Of Florida

Havana

Yucatán
Channel

CUBA

TURKS AND
CAICOS IS.
(U.K.)

20°

CAYMAN IS.
(U.K.)

George Town

Kingston

JAMAICA

G R E A T E R   A N T I L L E S

HAITI

Port-au-
Prince

**DOMINICAN
REPUBLIC**

Santo
Domingo

San Juan

ST.
THOMAS
(U.S.)

VIRGIN IS.
(U.S./U.K.)

Charlotte
Amalie

**PUERTO
RICO
(U.S.)**

Basseterre

**ST. KITTS
AND NEVIS**

L E E W A R D

St. John's

**ANTIGUA AND
BARBUDA**

I S L A N D S

HONDURAS

Limón

Patuca   River

Coco   River

River

Matagalpa

NICARAGUA

Managua

Lake
Nicaragua

San Juan

River

La Cruz

Puntarenas   San José

**COSTA
RICA**

Colón   Panamá

Los Santos

GULF OF
PANAMÁ

PANAMA

C A R I B B E A N   S E A

GUADELOUPE
(FR.)

Basse-Terre

DOMINICA

Roseau

MARTINIQUE
(FR.)

Fort-de-
France

Kingstown   Castries

**ST. VINCENT AND
THE GRENADINES**

BARBADOS

**ST.
LUCIA**

15°

W I N D W A R D

I S L A N D S

Bridgetown

ARUBA
(NETH.)

Oranjestad

NETH. ANTILLES
(NETH.)

Willemstad

L E S S E R   A N T I

St. George's

GRENADA

Port of Spain

**TRINIDAD
AND
TOBAGO**

5°

85° **80°** **75°** **70°** **65°** **60°**

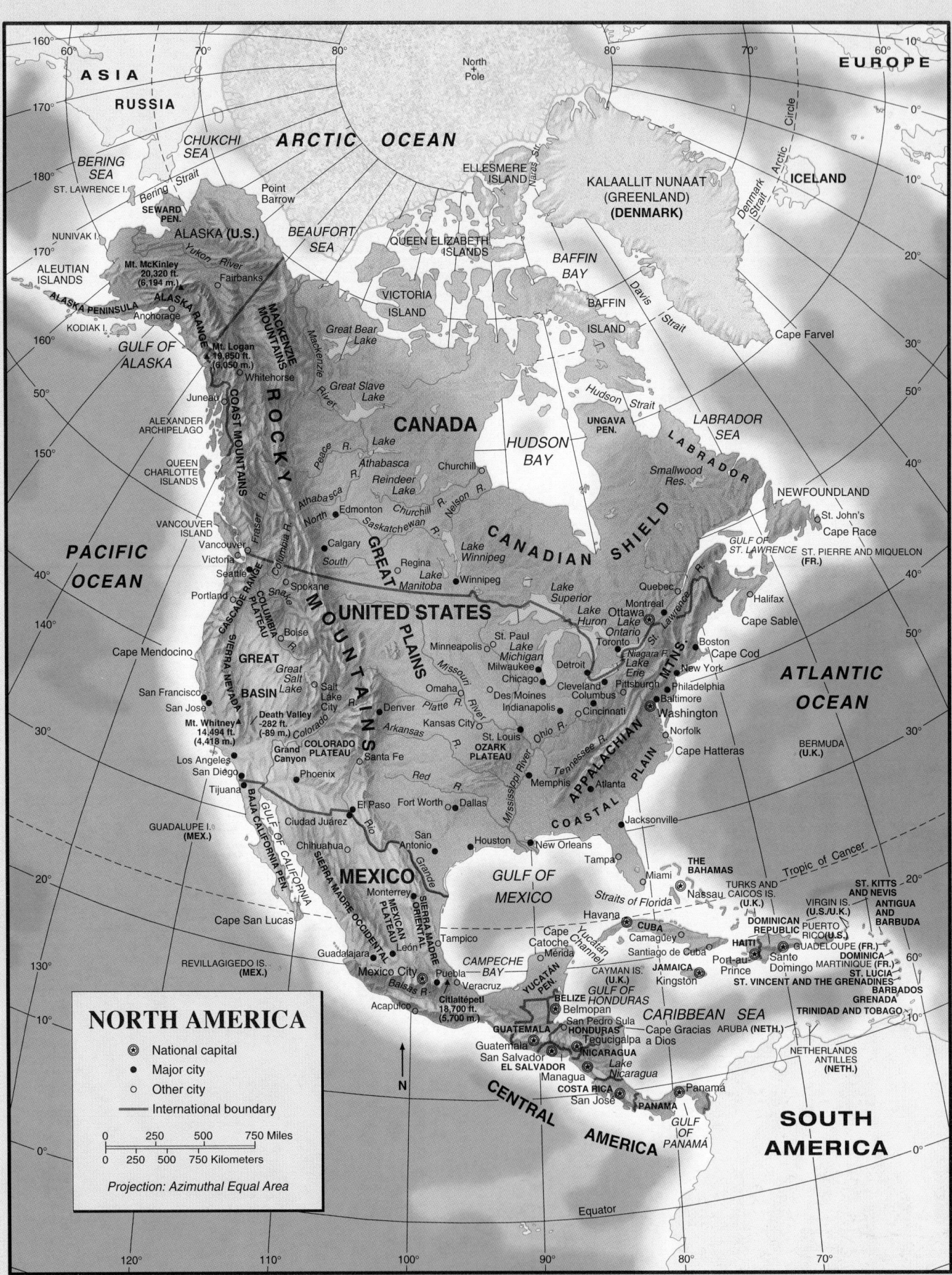

NORTH AMERICA

⊛ National capital
• Major city
○ Other city
— International boundary

| 0 | 250 | 500 | 750 Miles |
| 0 | 250 | 500 | 750 Kilometers |

Projection: Azimuthal Equal Area

NORTH AMERICA
CENTRAL AMERICA

CARIBBEAN SEA

GRENADA

MARGARITA I.

PARIA PEN.

TRINIDAD AND TOBAGO

Pt. Gallinas
GUAJIRA PEN.
Barranquilla
Cartagena
GULF OF DARIÉN
Maracay
Valencia
Caracas
Cumaná
Delta of the Orinoco
Maracaibo
Barquisimeto
VENEZUELA
Lake Maracaibo
MÉRIDA RANGE
Cúcuta
Bucaramanga
San Cristóbal
LLANOS
Orinoco River
Ciudad Guayana
Guri Res.
Ciudad Bolívar
GUYANA
Georgetown
Paramaribo
SURINAME
Van Blommestein Res.
Cayenne
FRENCH GUIANA (FR.)
GULF OF PANAMA
Medellín
Manizales
Cali
Bogotá
Tolima Peak 17,109 ft. (5,215 m.)
COLOMBIA
CORDILLERA OCCIDENTAL
CORDILLERA ORIENTAL
Magdalena R.
Meta R.
GUIANA
Angel Falls
PACARAIMA MOUNTAINS
GUIANA HIGHLAND
Essequibo R.
TUMUCUMAQUE MOUNTAINS
Cape San Francisco
Equator
Quito
Mt. Chimborazo 20,561 ft. (6,267 m.)
Ambato
Caquetá R.
Orinoco R.
Negro River
Branco R.
AMAZON
Delta of the Amazon
Cape Maguarinho
Equator
Portoviejo
Guayaquil
ECUADOR
Cuenca
Iquitos
Putumayo
Marañón River
BASIN
Manaus
Amazon River
Belém
São Luís
River
Fortaleza
Cape São Roque
Teresina
Natal
GULF OF GUAYAQUIL
Pariñas Point
PERU
Chiclayo
Trujillo
Chimbote
CORDILLERA ORIENTAL
Huascarán Peak 22,204 ft. (6,768 m.)
Ucayali River
Purus R.
Madeira River
Tapajós River
Xingu River
Tocantins River
Araguaia River
Tocantins R.
Parnaíba R.
SELVAS
BRAZIL
Rio Branco
Esperança Reservoir
Sobradinho Reservoir
PLATEAU OF BORBOREMA
Recife
Maceió
Aracaju
ANDES
Callao
Lima
Cuzco
Lake Titicaca
Ancohuma Peak 21,489 ft. (6,550 m.)
Mamoré R.
Guaporé R.
River
MATO GROSSO PLATEAU
São Francisco R.
BRAZILIAN HIGHLANDS
Salvador
TODOS OS SANTOS BAY
Point Carreta
PACIFIC OCEAN
La Paz
BOLIVIA
Cochabamba
Santa Cruz
Goiânia
Brasília
Arequipa
BOLIVIAN
Oruro
Sucre
Potosí
Lake Poopó
PLATEAU
Arica
Simão Res.
Júpia Res.
Tres Marias Reservoir
Belo Horizonte
Bandeira Peak 9,481 ft. (2,890 m.)
Antofagasta
ATACAMA DESERT
Salta
GRAN
CHACO
Pilcomayo R.
River
PARAGUAY
Campo Grande
Ilha Solteira Res.
Furnas Reservoir
Volta Redonda
Campinas
Juiz de Fora
Petrópolis
Nova Iguaçu
Niterói
Rio de Janeiro
Osasco
São Paulo
Santos
Santo André
Concepción
Tropic of Capricorn
Mt. Ojos del Salado 22,516 ft. (6,863 m.)
San Miguel de Tucumán
Resistencia
Santiago del Estero
Salado R.
Asunción
Paraguay River
Itaipu Res.
Paraná River
Iguaçu Falls
Curitiba
Tropic of Capricorn
SAN FÉLIX I. (CHILE)
SAN AMBROSIO I. (CHILE)
MOUNTAINS
Corrientes
Mt. Aconcagua 22,834 ft. (6,960 m.)
CÓRDOBA RANGE
Córdoba
Rosario
Mar Chiquita Lake
Santa Fe
Uruguay R.
Pôrto Alegre
Rivera
Lake dos Patos
Negro Res.
Lake Mirim
ATLANTIC OCEAN
JUAN FERNÁNDEZ IS. (CHILE)
Viña del Mar
Valparaíso
Santiago
Mendoza
ANDES
Paysandú
Montevideo
URUGUAY
Punta del Este
Buenos Aires
La Plata
RÍO DE LA PLATA
Cape San Antonio
CHILE
ARGENTINA
PAMPAS
Talcahuano
Concepción
Temuco
Salado River
Colorado River
Mar del Plata
Bahía Blanca
BLANCA BAY
Negro River
Rasa Point
VALDÉS DEPRESSION
GULF OF SAN MATÍAS
VALDÉS PEN.
PATAGONIA
Chubut R.
CHILOÉ ISLAND
CHONOS ARCHIPELAGO
Comodoro Rivadavia
GULF OF SAN JORGE
Cape Tres Puntas
Lake Buenos Aires
PEÑAS GULF
Lake San Martin
Lake Argentino
GRANDE BAY
Stanley
FALKLAND ISLANDS (U.K.)
QUEEN ADELAIDE ARCH.
Strait of Magellan
Punta Arenas
TIERRA DEL FUEGO
ESTADOS ISLAND
Cape Horn
SOUTH GEORGIA I. (U.K.)

N

SOUTH AMERICA

⊚ National capital
● Major city
○ Other city
━━ International boundary

0   250   500 Miles
0   250   500 Kilometers

Projection: Azimuthal Equal Area

EUROPE

- ◉ National capital
- ● Major city
- ○ Other city
- ▬▬ International boundary
- ▬ Republic boundary
- ⊥ Canal

```
0    100    200    300 Miles
0  100  200  300 Kilometers
```

Projection: Azimuthal Equal Area

ICELAND
Reykjavik

Arctic Circle

NORWEGIAN SEA

SCANDINAVIAN HIGHLANDS

FAROE IS. (DEN.)

Prime Meridian

Trondheim

SHETLAND IS. (U.K.)

NORWAY
Galdhøpiggen 8,097 ft. (2,468 m.)
Bergen
Oslo

SWEDEN
Uppsala
Lake Vänern
Stockholm
Lake Vättern

GULF OF BOTHNIA
ÅLAND I.

HIIUMAA I.
SAAREMAA I.
GOTLAND I.
ÖLAND I.

OUTER HEBRIDES IS.
Cape Wrath
ORKNEY ISLANDS

SCOTLAND
Glasgow
Edinburgh

NORTH SEA

Skagerrak

Kattegat
Göteborg

DENMARK
JUTLAND
Copenhagen
Odense
Malmö
BORNHOLM I.

BALTIC SEA

NORTHERN IRELAND (U.K.)
Belfast
ISLE OF MAN
IRISH SEA

PENNINE RANGE

UNITED KINGDOM

Dublin
IRELAND
Cork

Manchester
Liverpool
Leeds
Sheffield

ENGLAND
WALES
Cardiff
Birmingham
Bristol
London

Rostock
Szczecin
Gdańsk

RUSSIA

NORTH

POLAND
Poznań
Warsaw
Łódź

Cape Clear
St. George's Channel

Cape Finisterre

ATLANTIC OCEAN

English Channel
Strait of Dover

GUERNSEY I. (U.K.)
JERSEY I. (U.K.)

BRETON PEN.

Le Havre
Seine River
Paris
Marne R.

Nantes
Loire

Loire River

FRANCE

Hamburg
NETHERLANDS
Amsterdam
The Hague
Rotterdam
Antwerp
BELGIUM
Brussels
Liège
Bonn
LUXEMBOURG
Luxembourg

Mittelland Canal
Bremen
Essen
Dortmund
Cologne
Frankfurt

Elbe R.

Berlin
Magdeburg
Hannover

Marne-Rhine Canal
Rhine
Strasbourg

GERMANY
Leipzig
Dresden
Chemnitz

Oder R.

Wrocław

Prague
CZECH REPUBLIC
Brno

Katowice
Kraków
Ostrava

SLOVAKIA
Bratislava

Stuttgart
Danube River
Munich
Bodensee

Zürich
Bern
SWITZERLAND
Lausanne
Geneva
L. Geneva

LIECHTENSTEIN
Vaduz
Innsbruck

Linz
Salzburg
Vienna

AUSTRIA
Graz

Miskolc
Budapest

HUNGARY
L. Balaton
Pécs
Tisza R.

Cape Finisterre

BAY OF BISCAY

CANTABRIAN MTNS.
Bilbao

Porto

PYRENEES

Bordeaux
Garonne R.

Lyon
Mt. Blanc 15,771 ft. (4,807 m.)
Rhône R.

Mt. Rosa 12,203 ft. (4,634 m.)

ALPS

Turin
Milan
PO VALLEY
Po R.
Venice
Bologna

Ljubljana
SLOVENIA

Zagreb
CROATIA

DINARIC ALPS
Novi Sad
Sava R.
Belgrade

Toulouse
Midi Canal

CENTRAL MASSIF

Montpellier
Nice
Marseille
GULF OF LION

ANDORRA
Andorra la Vella

PORTUGAL
Lisbon
Setúbal
Tagus

Duero River
Valladolid

IBERIAN
Zaragoza
Madrid
Ebro River

Aneto Peak 11,168 ft. (3,404 m.)

PENINSULA

Barcelona

Guadiana River

SIERRA MORENA

SPAIN
Valencia

Seville

Granada
Málaga
Murcia

Strait of Gibraltar
GIBRALTAR (U.K.)

AFRICA

BALEARIC IS. (SP.)
Palma

CORSICA (FR.)

VATICAN CITY

SARDINIA (IT.)

Cagliari

TYRRHENIAN SEA

MONACO
Monaco

Florence

SAN MARINO
San Marino

APENNINES

Rome

ITALY

Naples

Bari

ADRIATIC SEA

Split

BOSNIA HERZEGOVINA
Sarajevo

MONTENEGRO

MACEDONIA

Tiranë
ALBANIA

G. OF TARANTO

Palermo
SICILY
Catania

PANTELLERIA (IT.)

MALTA
Valletta

IONIAN SEA
KEFALLINIA I.

MEDITERRANEAN

SEA

North Cape
30°   40°   70°   50°   60°   70°   80°

BARENTS SEA

Murmansk

KOLA PENINSULA

TIMAN RIDGE

Pechora R.

WHITE SEA

White Sea-Baltic Waterway

Arkhangel'sk

N. Dvina River   Vychegda River

Mt. Konzhakovskiy ▲
5,147 ft.
(1,569 m.)

FINLAND

Lake Onega

Kama R.

A S I A

Tampere
Lake Saimaa

Lake Ladoga

Sukhona River

Perm

U R A L   M O U N T A I N S

70°

Turku
Helsinki
Espoo

Volga-Baltic Waterway

Rybinsk Reservoir

Kama River

Ufa

50°

GULF OF FINLAND

St. Petersburg

Yaroslavl

Kazan

Ural River

Tallinn

ESTONIA

Chudskoye Lake

Nizhniy Novgorod

Kuybyshev Reservoir

GULF OF RIGA

LATVIA
Riga

Volga River

Volga-Baltic Waterway

Moscow

Samara

Orenburg

W. Dvina River

BALTIC PLAIN

EUROPEAN PLAIN

River

Oka

River

Tula

CENTRAL RUSSIAN UPLAND

VOLGA UPLAND

Volga River

LITHUANIA
Kaunas

Smolensk

RUSSIA

Vilnius

Minsk

Saratov

Volgograd Reservoir

Ural River

BELARUS

Don

Voronezh

River

KAZAKHSTAN

ARAL SEA

Pripet River

Desna R.

Kursk

Kiev

Kremenchug Reservoir

Kharkov

Lugansk

Volgograd

Volga River

DEPRESSION

Lvov

UKRAINE

Dniester R.

DNIEPER UPLAND

Dnepropetrovsk

Donetsk

Tsimlyansk Reservoir

Don River

CASPIAN

Astrakhan

40°

Krivoy Rog

Zaporozhye

Rostov

Delta of the Volga

CARPATHIAN MTNS.

MOLDOVA
Chisinau

Prut River

DNIEPER LOWLAND

Dnieper River

Kakhovka Res.

SEA OF AZOV

Krasnodar

Grozny

CASPIAN SEA

60°

Debrecen

Odessa

CRIMEA

Cluj-Napoca

ROMANIA
Timişoara   Braşov

Volga River

Mt. Elbrus
18,510 ft.
(5,642 m.)

C A U C A S U S   M T N S.

Bucharest

WALLACHIA PLAIN
Danube

River

Ruse

Constanţa

BLACK SEA

40°

SERBIA

Nis

BULGARIA
Sofia   Plovdiv

Burgas

Varna

Skopje

Musala Peak
9,536 ft.
(2,926 m.)

Salonika

PENINSULA   TURKEY

Bosporus

BALKAN

Larissa

Dardanelles
SEA OF MARMARA

AEGEAN SEA

A S I A

GREECE

Patras   Athens

Piraeus

PELOPONNESE PEN.

30°

RHODES

30°   40°   50°

CRETE (GR.)

Iráklion

60°
70°
80°
Arctic Circle
10°
0°
10°

EUROPE

ARCTIC OCEAN

FRANZ JOSEF ISLANDS

BARENTS SEA

Murmansk

KOLA PENINSULA

Cape Zelaniya

NOVAYA ZEMLYA

KARA SEA

Kara Strait

BALTIC SEA

GULF OF FINLAND

WHITE SEA

Baltic-White Sea Canal

Lake Ladoga

Arkhangel'sk

YAMAL PEN.

GYDAN PENINSULA

(RUSSIA)

St. Petersburg

Lake Onega

Volga-Baltic Waterway

VALDAI HILLS

N. Dvina R.

Vychegda R.

TIMAN RIDGE

Pechora River

Yenisey River

Urengoy

50°

20°

Minsk

BELARUS

Rybinsk Res.

Vologda

Sukhona R.

NORTHERN HILLS

Ob River

WEST SIBERIAN PLAIN

Lvov

DNIEPER UPLAND

Dnieper R.

Yaroslovl

Moscow

Ivanovo

Volga R.

Kamsk Res.

▲ Mt. Konzhakovskiy 5,147 ft. (1,569 m.)

URAL MOUNTAINS

Ob

Kiev

UKRAINE

DNIEPER LOWLAND

Tula

Ryazan'

Nizhniy Novgorod

Kazan

Izhevsk

Perm

R.

Vakh R.

MOLDOVA

Chisinau

Kharkov

Don River

Voronezh

Kuybyshev Res.

Ul'yanovsk

Kama R.

Yekaterinburg

Irtysh River

Odessa

Nikolayev

Krivoy Rog

Dnepropetrovsk

Penza

VOLGA UPLAND

Saratov

Tol'yatti

Samara

Ufa

Chelyabinsk

Tobol R.

River

30°

Zaporozh'ye

Donetsk

Lugansk

Tomsk

Mariupol

Rostov

SEA OF AZOV

Tsimlyansk Res.

Volgograd Reservoir

Volgograd

Ural R.

Orenburg

Ishim R.

Omsk

L. Chany

Novosibirsk

Kemerovo

BLACK SEA

Krasnodar

Volga R.

CASPIAN DEPRESSION

Astrakhan

KYRGYZ

TURGAY PLATEAU

Novosibirsk Res.

Novokuznetsk

40°

CAUCASUS MTNS

▲ Mt. Elbrus 18,510 ft. (5,642 m.)

STEPPE

Barnaul

GEORGIA

Tbilisi

KAZAKHSTAN

KAZAK UPLAND

Karaganda

▲ Mt. Belukha 14,783 ft. (4,506 m.)

ARMENIA

Yerevan

CASPIAN

Semipalatinsk

L. Zaysan

40°

AZERBAIJAN

AZERBAIJAN

Baku

SEA

USTYURT PLATEAU

ARAL SEA

Syr R.

BETPAK-DALA DESERT

Kzyl-Orda

Lake Balkhash

Ill R.

L. Alakol

PLAINS OF TURAN

KARA BOGAZ GOL GULF

TURKMENISTAN

UZBEKISTAN

Darya

ASIA

KARAKUM DESERT

Amu Darya

Ashkhabad

Samarkand

Tashkent

Bishkek

Almaty

L. Issyk-Kul

KYRGYZSTAN

30°

ALAY MOUNTAINS

Dushanbe

TAJIKISTAN

▲ Communism Pk. 24,590 ft. (7,495 m.)

50°
60°
70°
80°

A14   Reference Atlas

+ North Pole

ARCTIC
OCEAN

CHUKCHI
SEA

WRANGEL
ISLAND

Long Strait

BERING SEA

Bering Strait

CHUKOTSK
PEN.

Cape
Navarin

EAST SIBERIAN
SEA

Cherskiy

Anadyr R.

KOLYMA RANGE

KORYAK MTNS.

Cape Arkticheski

SEVERNAYA
ZEMLYA

NEW SIBERIAN
ISLANDS

Sannikov Strait

Laptev Strait

KOLYMA
PLAIN

Kolyma

Evensk

KARAGIN
ISLAND

KOMANDORSKIY
ISLANDS

Vil'kitskiy Strait

LAPTEV SEA

TAYMYR
PEN.

L. Taymyr

CHERSKIY RANGE

Indigirka

River

SHELIKHOV
GULF

SREDINNY RANGE

KAMCHATKA PENINSULA

▲ Mt. Klyuchevsk
15,584 ft.
(4,750 m.)

BYRRANGA
MTNS.

VERKHOYANSK RANGE

Verkhoyansk

River

Noril'sk

Koluy

Olenëk

Lena

Yakutsk

Magadan

Petropavlovsk-
Kamchatskiy

SEA OF OKHOTSK

Cape Lopatka

CENTRAL SIBERIAN

Markha R.

Vilyuy

River

SIBERIA

Tura

Tunguska

River

Vilyuysk
Reservoir

LENA PLATEAU

Cape Yelizavety

Lower

R.

R.

Aldan

SAKHALIN
ISLAND

KURIL ISLANDS

PLATEAU

ALDAN MTNS.

River

Terpeniya Point

RUSSIA

Yenisey River

Angara

Vitim

R.

STANOVOY RANGE

DZHUGDZHUR RA.

Uda R.

Tatar Strait

River

STANOVOY
UPLAND

Lena

Komsomol'sk

Amur

La Pérouse
Strait

Bratsk

Lake
Baikal

R.

Khabarovsk

Krasnoyarsk

Bratsk
Reservoir

YABLONOVY RANGE

R.

Chita

Ussuri River

SIKHOTE-ALIN RA.

Krasnoyarsk
Reservoir

Ulan-Ude

Shilka

L. Khanka

SAYAN
MOUNTAINS

Irkutsk

ASIA

Vladivostok

ALTAI MTNS.

SEA OF JAPAN

RUSSIA AND
THE EURASIAN REPUBLICS

⊛ National capital

● Major city

○ Other city

—— International boundary

| 0 | 250 | 500 Miles |
| 0 | 250 | 500 Kilometers |

Projection: Two-Point Equidistant

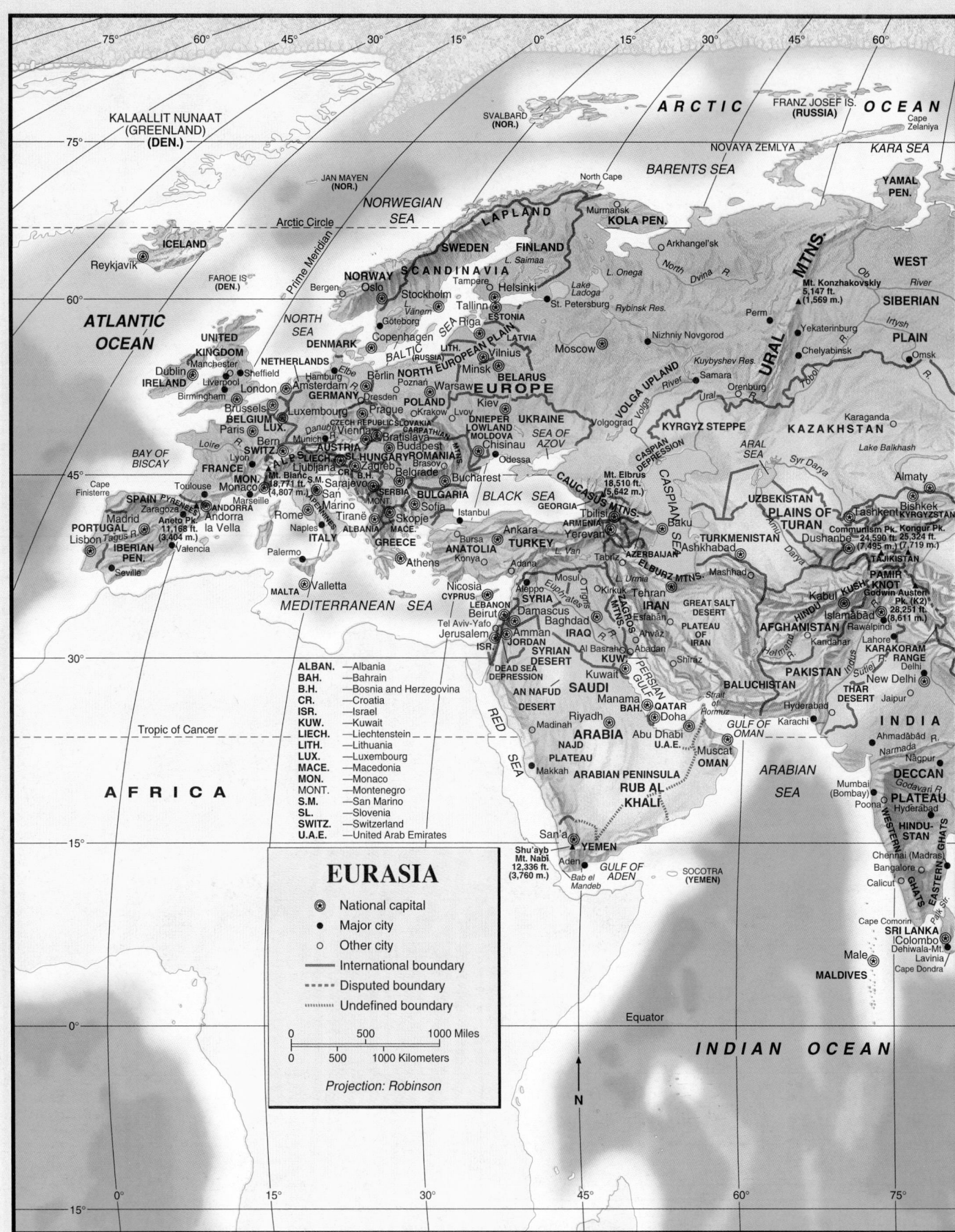

ARCTIC OCEAN

KALAALLIT NUNAAT
(GREENLAND)
(DEN.)

SVALBARD
(NOR.)

FRANZ JOSEF IS.
(RUSSIA)

Cape
Zelaniya

NOVAYA ZEMLYA

KARA SEA

BARENTS SEA

YAMAL
PEN.

JAN MAYEN
(NOR.)

North Cape

Arctic Circle

NORWEGIAN
SEA

LAPLAND

Murmansk

KOLA PEN.

Arkhangel'sk

WEST

ICELAND

SWEDEN

FINLAND

L. Onega

North
Dvina R.

Mt. Konzhakovskiy
5,147 ft.
(1,569 m.)

SIBERIAN

Reykjavík

NORWAY

Tampere

L. Saimaa

Lake
Ladoga

St. Petersburg

Rybinsk Res.

Perm

PLAIN

FAROE IS.
(DEN.)

Prime Meridian

Bergen

Oslo

Stockholm

Helsinki

Tallinn

ESTONIA

Nizhniy Novgorod

Yekaterinburg

Chelyabinsk

Ob

Irtysh R.

River

ATLANTIC
OCEAN

Göteborg

Riga

Moscow

Kuybyshev Res.

Omsk

UNITED
KINGDOM

DENMARK

Copenhagen

Vänern

BALTIC
SEA

LITH.
(RUSSIA)

LATVIA
Vilnius

Minsk

VOLGA UPLAND

Samara

Orenburg

URAL MTNS.

NETHERLANDS

Hamburg

Elbe

Berlin

Poznań

Warsaw

BELARUS

Kiev

Volgograd

Volga

Ural R.

Karaganda

KAZAKHSTAN

Dublin

Manchester

Sheffield

Liverpool

Amsterdam

GERMANY

Dresden

Prague

POLAND

Kraków

Lvov

UKRAINE

KYRGYZ STEPPE

Lake Balkhash

IRELAND

Birmingham

London

Brussels

Luxembourg

CZECH REPUBLIC
SLOVAKIA

DNIEPER
LOWLAND

MOLDOVA

CASPIAN
DEPRESSION

ARAL
SEA

BELGIUM

LUX.

Paris

Bern

Munich

Vienna

AUSTRIA

Bratislava

Budapest

HUNGARY

ROMANIA

Chisinau

Odessa

SEA OF
AZOV

Syr Darya

Almaty

SWITZ.

Danube

LIECH.

SL.

CR.

Brasov

Bucharest

BLACK SEA

Mt. Elbrus
18,510 ft.
(5,642 m.)

CASPIAN SEA

UZBEKISTAN

Tashkent

Bishkek

FRANCE

Loire R.

Lyon

Mt. Blanc
18,771 ft.
(4,807 m.)

Ljubljana

Zagreb

B.H.

Belgrade

SERBIA

GEORGIA

Tbilisi

Baku

PLAINS OF
TURAN

KYRGYZSTAN

BAY OF
BISCAY

Cape
Finisterre

Toulouse

Monaco

MON.

San
Marino

S.M.

Sarajevo

MONT.

BULGARIA

Sofia

CAUCASUS MTNS.

ARMENIA

Yerevan

AZERBAIJAN

TURKMENISTAN

Ashkhabad

Amu Darya

Dushanbe

Communism Pk.
24,590 ft.
(7,495 m.)

Kongur Pk.
25,324 ft.
(7,719 m.)

TAJIKISTAN

PAMIR
KNOT

SPAIN

Zaragoza

PYRENEES

ANDORRA

Andorra
la Vella

Marseille

Rome

MACE.

Skopje

Tiranë

Istanbul

Ankara

TURKEY

L. Van

Tabriz

Mashhad

KUSH KNOT

Godwin Austen
Pk. (K2)
28,251 ft.
(8,611 m.)

Madrid

Aneto Pk.
11,168 ft.
(3,404 m.)

Naples

ITALY

ALBANIA

GREECE

Bursa

Konya

Adana

Mosul

ELBURZ MTNS.

Tehran

GREAT SALT
DESERT

Kabul

Islamabad

HINDU

KARAKORAM
RANGE

PORTUGAL

Lisbon

Tagus R.

Valencia

Palermo

Athens

Nicosia

CYPRUS

Aleppo

Mosul

Kirkuk

Euphrates

Urmia

ZAGROS
MTNS.

Esfahan

PLATEAU
OF
IRAN

AFGHANISTAN

Rawalpindi

Kandahar

Lahore

Indus R.

Sutlej R.

New Delhi

Delhi

IBERIAN
PEN.

Seville

MALTA

Valletta

MEDITERRANEAN SEA

LEBANON

Beirut

SYRIA

Damascus

Baghdad

Tigris R.

IRAN

Ahvaz

Shiraz

Helmand R.

BALUCHISTAN

PAKISTAN

Hyderabad

Jaipur

THAR
DESERT

INDIA

Tel Aviv-Yafo

Jerusalem

ISR.

Amman

JORDAN

IRAQ

Al Basrah

Abadan

Karachi

Ahmadābād

Narmada R.

Nagpur

ALBAN. —Albania
BAH. —Bahrain
B.H. —Bosnia and Herzegovina
CR. —Croatia
ISR. —Israel
KUW. —Kuwait
LIECH. —Liechtenstein
LITH. —Lithuania
LUX. —Luxembourg
MACE. —Macedonia
MON. —Monaco
MONT. —Montenegro
S.M. —San Marino
SL. —Slovenia
SWITZ. —Switzerland
U.A.E. —United Arab Emirates

Tropic of Cancer

DEAD SEA
DEPRESSION

SYRIAN
DESERT

AN NAFUD
DESERT

KUW.

Kuwait

PERSIAN
GULF

Strait
of
Hormuz

Mumbai
(Bombay)

DECCAN
PLATEAU

Godavari R.

Poona

Hyderabad

AFRICA

Madinah

SAUDI

Riyadh

Manama

BAH.

QATAR

Doha

U.A.E.

Abu Dhabi

Muscat

OMAN

GULF
OF
OMAN

ARABIAN
SEA

WESTERN GHATS

HINDU-
STAN

RED
SEA

ARABIA

NAJD
PLATEAU

Makkah

ARABIAN PENINSULA

RUB AL
KHALI

Chennai (Madras)

Bangalore

Calicut

EASTERN GHATS

GHATS

San'a

Shu'ayb
Mt. Nabi
12,336 ft.
(3,760 m.)

Aden

YEMEN

GULF OF
ADEN

SOCOTRA
(YEMEN)

Cape Comorin

SRI LANKA

Colombo

Dehiwala-Mt.
Lavinia

Bab el
Mandeb

Male

MALDIVES

Cape Dondra

EURASIA

◎ National capital
● Major city
○ Other city
—— International boundary
---- Disputed boundary
····· Undefined boundary

0   500   1000 Miles
0   500   1000 Kilometers

Projection: Robinson

Equator

INDIAN OCEAN

N

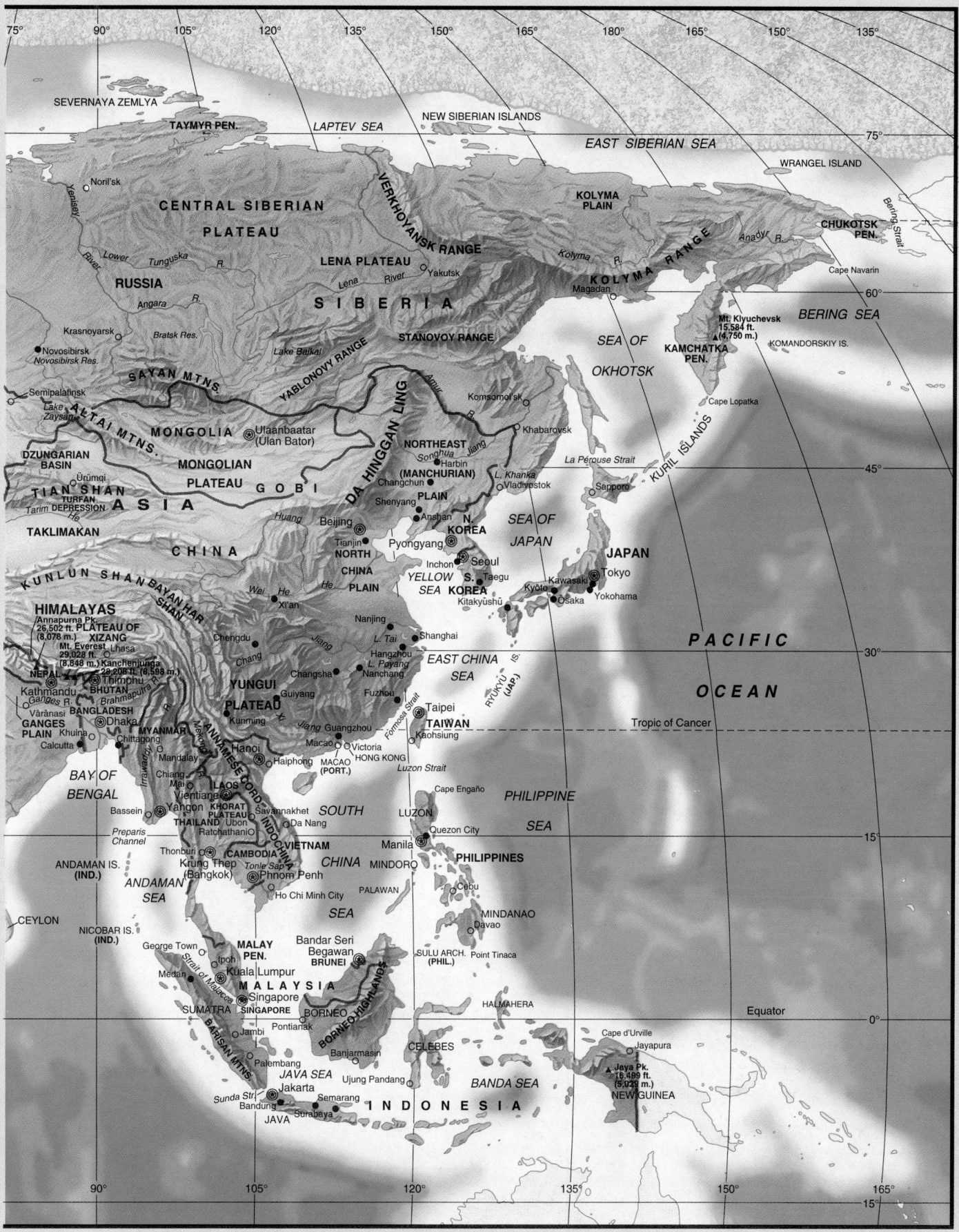

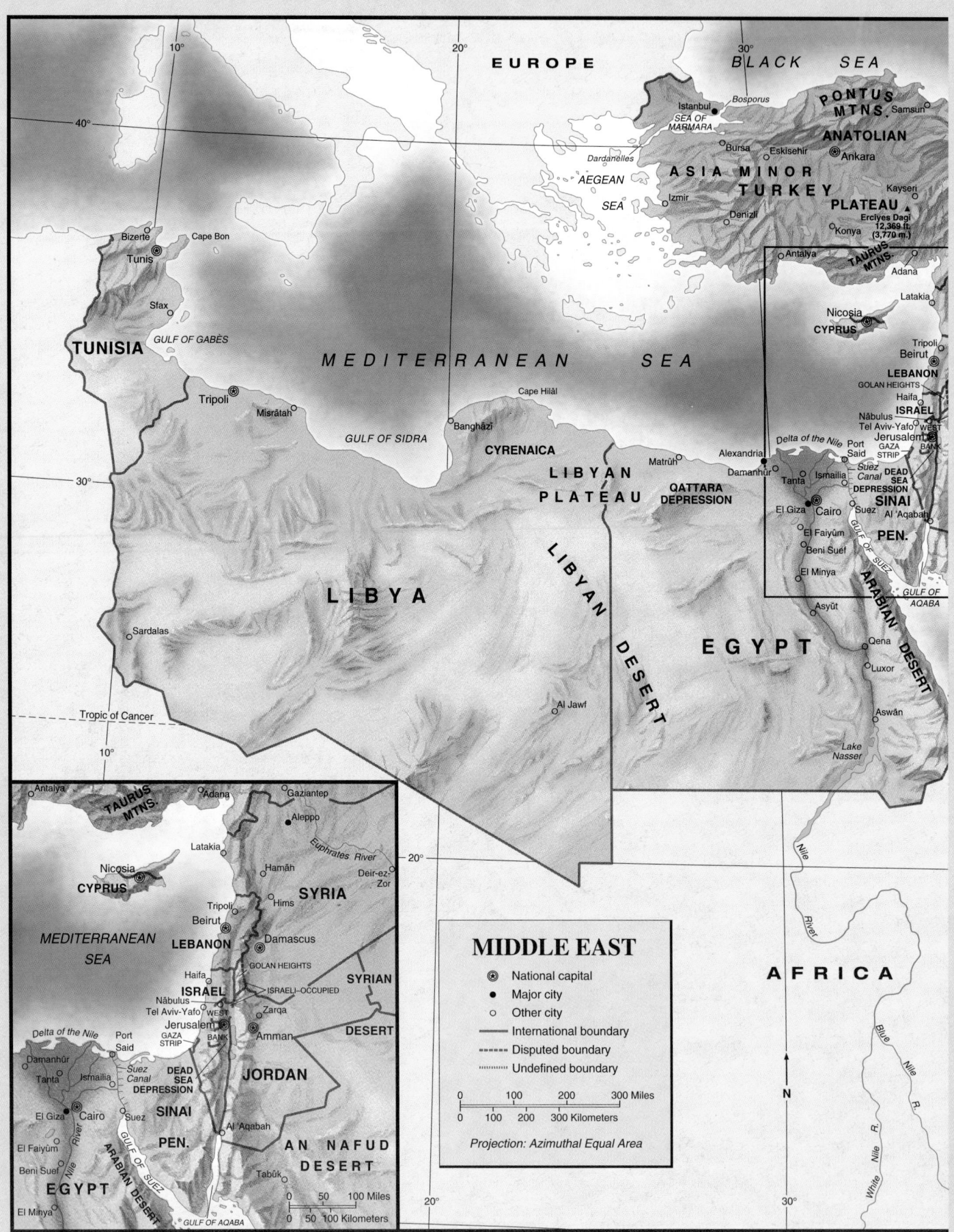

EUROPE

BLACK SEA

PONTUS MTNS.
Samsun

Istanbul
SEA OF MARMARA
Bosporus

ANATOLIAN

Dardanelles

AEGEAN SEA

Bursa Eskişehir ✪ Ankara
Izmir

ASIA MINOR
TURKEY

Denizli

Kayseri

PLATEAU
Erciyes Daği
12,369 ft.
(3,770 m.)
Konya

Antalya ▲

Adana

TAURUS MTNS.

Latakia

Nicosia ✪
CYPRUS

Tripoli
Beirut

Bizerte
Cape Bon

Tunis ✪

LEBANON

GOLAN HEIGHTS

Sfax

GULF OF GABÈS

TUNISIA

Haifa
Nâbulus
Tel Aviv-Yafo ✪ **WEST**
ISRAEL
Jerusalem ✪ BANK
GAZA
STRIP

Tripoli ✪
Misrātah

Cape Hilâl

MEDITERRANEAN SEA

Banghāzī

CYRENAICA

Matrûh

Alexandria •
Damanhûr
Tanta
Ismailia

Delta of the Nile Port Said

Suez Canal

DEAD SEA DEPRESSION

SINAI PEN.

Al 'Aqabah

GULF OF SUEZ

LIBYAN PLATEAU

QATTARA DEPRESSION

El Giza • Cairo
Suez

GULF OF SIDRA

LIBYA

LIBYAN DESERT

El Faiyûm
Beni Suef

El Minya

EGYPT

ARABIAN DESERT

GULF OF AQABA

Sardalas •

Asyût

Qena

Luxor

Tropic of Cancer

Al Jawf •

Aswân

Lake Nasser

Antalya •
TAURUS MTNS.
Adana •
Gaziantep

Aleppo •

Latakia

Nicosia ✪
CYPRUS

Hamâh
Hims

Euphrates River

Deir-ez-Zor

Tripoli •
Beirut ✪

SYRIA

MEDITERRANEAN SEA

LEBANON
Damascus ✪

GOLAN HEIGHTS

Haifa
Nâbulus
Tel Aviv-Yafo **WEST**
ISRAEL
Jerusalem ✪ BANK
GAZA
STRIP

ISRAELI-OCCUPIED

Zarqa •

SYRIAN

DESERT

Delta of the Nile Port Said

Damanhûr
Tanta
Ismailia

Suez Canal

DEAD SEA DEPRESSION

Amman ✪

JORDAN

Nile River

El Giza • Cairo
Suez

SINAI PEN.

Al 'Aqabah

AN NAFUD DESERT

El Faiyûm
Beni Suef

ARABIAN DESERT

GULF OF SUEZ

Tabûk •

EGYPT

El Minya

✪ *GULF OF AQABA*

MIDDLE EAST

- ✪ National capital
- • Major city
- ○ Other city
- —— International boundary
- ----- Disputed boundary
- ········ Undefined boundary

| 0 | 100 | 200 | 300 Miles |
| 0 | 100 | 200 | 300 Kilometers |

Projection: Azimuthal Equal Area

AFRICA

Nile River

Blue Nile

N

White Nile

Nile R.

0   50   100 Miles
0   50   100 Kilometers

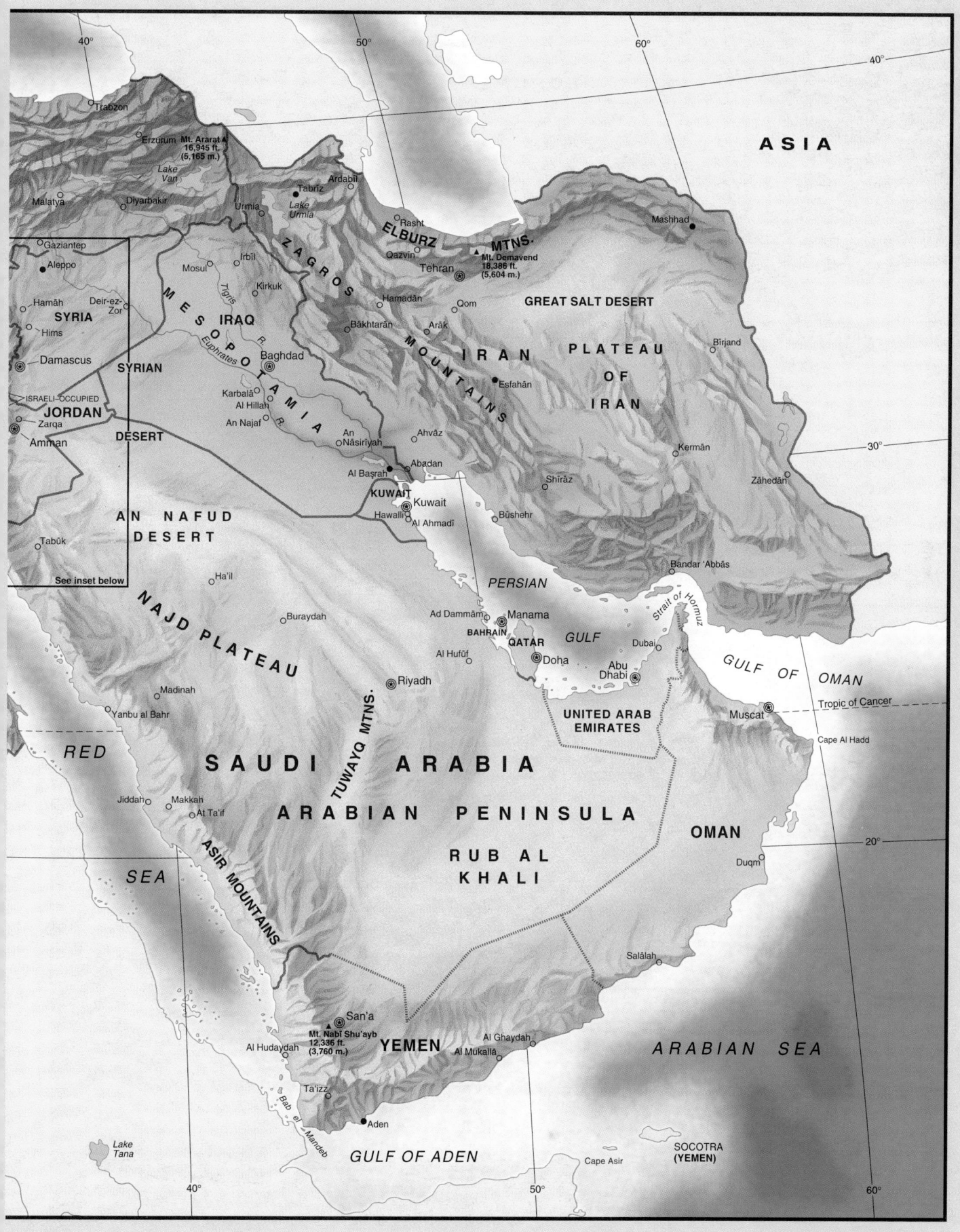

ASIA

Trabzon
Erzurum Mt. Ararat
16,945 ft.
(5,165 m.)
Lake
Van
Malatya   Diyarbakir
Ardabil   Mashhad
Tabriz
Urmia   Lake
Urmia
Rasht
ELBURZ
Gaziantep   Mosul   Irbil   Qazvin   MTNS.
Aleppo   Tehran   Mt. Demavend
Kirkuk   18,386 ft.
Hamāh   Deir-ez-   (5,604 m.)
Zor   SYRIA   Hamadān   GREAT SALT DESERT
Hims   Bākhtarān   Qom
Damascus   Baghdad   Arāk   Birjand
IRAQ   Esfahān   PLATEAU
SYRIAN   OF
ISRAELI-OCCUPIED   Karbalā   Ahvāz   IRAN
JORDAN   Al Hillah
Zarqa   An Najaf   Kermān
DESERT   An Nāsirīyah
Amman   Zāhedān
Abadan   Shīrāz
Al Basrah
Tabūk   KUWAIT   Būshehr
AN   NAFUD   Kuwait   Bandar 'Abbās
DESERT   Hawalli   Al Ahmadī
Ha'il
See inset below   PERSIAN
NAJD   PLATEAU   Buraydah   Ad Dammām   Manama   Strait of Hormuz
GULF
BAHRAIN   Dubai
Al Hufūf   QATAR   GULF OF OMAN
Madinah   Doha
Riyadh   Abu
Yanbu al Bahr   Dhabi
UNITED ARAB   Muscat   Tropic of Cancer
RED   EMIRATES
SAUDI   ARABIA   Cape Al Hadd
Jiddah   Makkah
SEA   At Ta'if   ARABIAN   PENINSULA   OMAN
ASIR   MOUNTAINS   RUB   AL
KHALI   Duqm
TUWAYQ MTNS.

Salālah
San'a
Mt. Nabī Shu'ayb   Al Ghaydah
12,336 ft.   Al Mukallā   ARABIAN   SEA
Al Hudaydah   (3,760 m.)   YEMEN
Ta'izz
Aden   SOCOTRA
(YEMEN)
Lake
Tana   GULF OF ADEN   Cape Asir

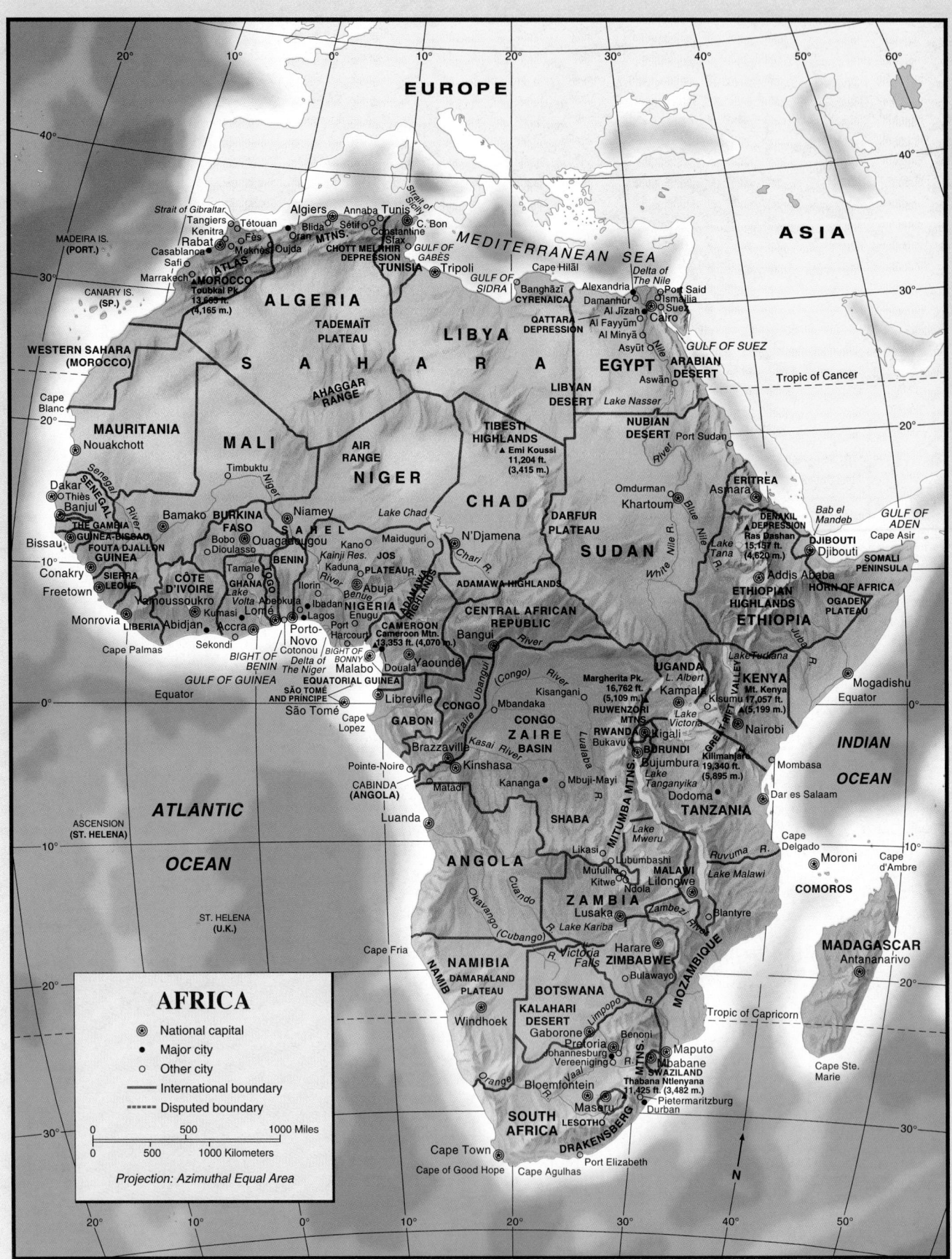

AFRICA

◎ National capital
● Major city
○ Other city
— International boundary
┅┅ Disputed boundary

| 0 | 500 | 1000 Miles |
| 0 | 500 | 1000 Kilometers |

Projection: Azimuthal Equal Area

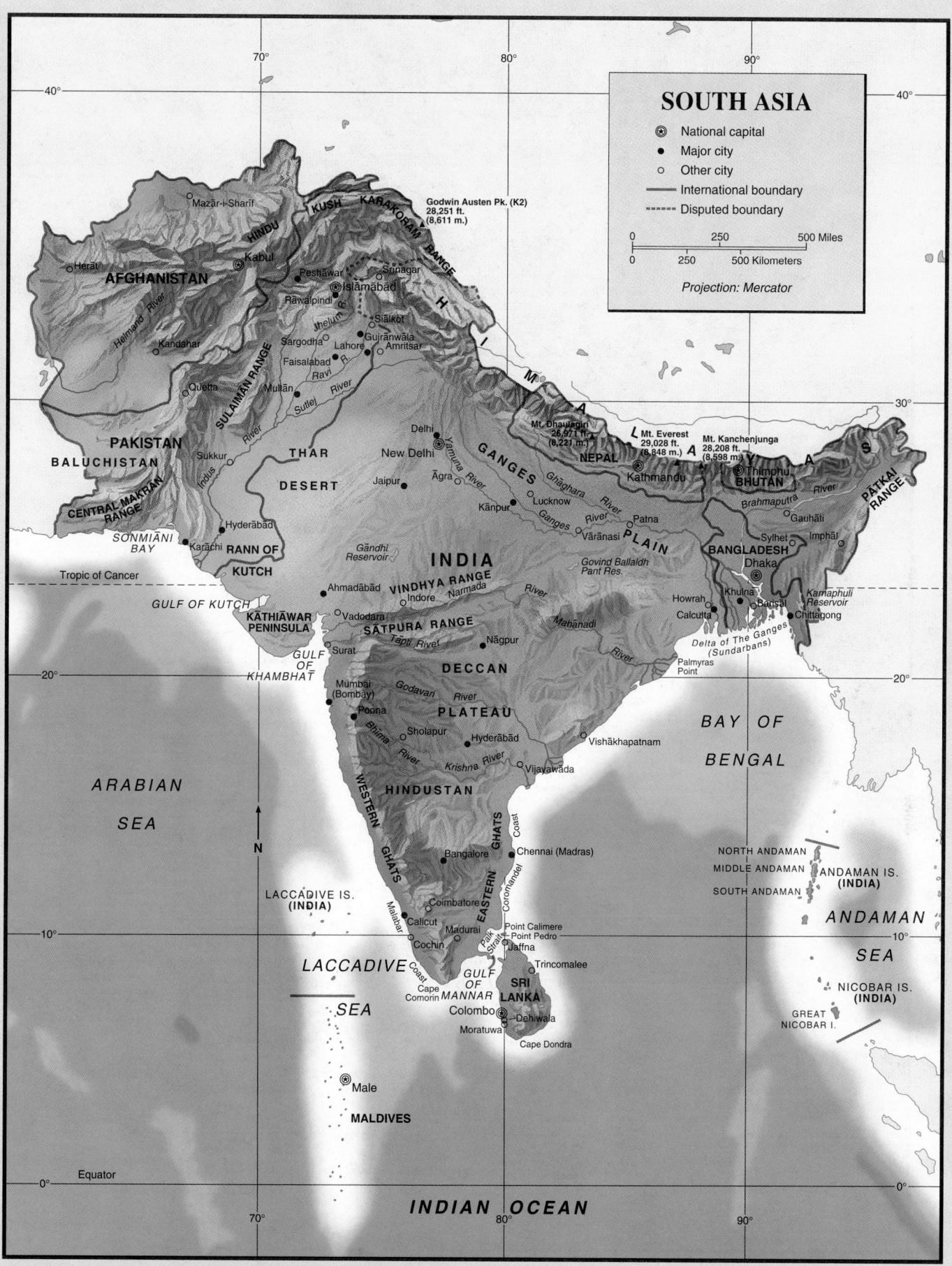

SOUTH ASIA

⊛ National capital
● Major city
○ Other city
— International boundary
---- Disputed boundary

0   250   500 Miles

0   250   500 Kilometers

Projection: Mercator

40°

70°

Mazār-i-Sharīf

HINDU KUSH

KARAKORAM RANGE

Godwin Austen Pk. (K2)
28,251 ft.
(8,611 m.)

Herāt

Kabul

AFGHANISTAN

Peshāwar

Srīnagar

Islāmābād

Rāwalpindi

Jhelum

Siālkot

Sargodha

Gujrānwāla

Lahore

Amritsar

Faisalabad

Ravi

R.

Kandahar

Mūltān

Sutlej

River

Quetta

SULAIMĀN RANGE

H I M A L A Y A S

30°

Mt. Dhaulāgiri
26,971 ft.
(8,221 m.)

Mt. Everest
29,028 ft.
(8,848 m.)

Mt. Kanchenjunga
28,208 ft.
(8,598 m.)

PĀTKAI RANGE

PAKISTAN

BALUCHISTAN

Sukkur

THAR

Delhi

New Delhi

Yamuna River

GANGES

NEPAL

Kathmandu

Thimphu

BHUTAN

River

Brahmaputra

Gauhāti

CENTRAL MAKRĀN RANGE

Indus

Jaipur

Āgra

Ghāghara

River

Imphāl

River

DESERT

Kānpur

Lucknow

Ganges

River

Patna

Sylhet

Sonmiāni
Bay

Karāchi

Hyderābād

RANN OF KUTCH

Gāndhī
Reservoir

INDIA

Vārānasi

PLAIN

BANGLADESH

Dhaka

Tropic of Cancer

GULF OF KUTCH

VINDHYA RANGE

Ahmadābād

Indore

Narmada

River

Govind Ballaldh
Pant Res.

Howrah

Khulna

Barisal

Karnaphuli
Reservoir

Vadodara

SĀTPURA RANGE

River

Calcutta

Chittagong

KĀTHIĀWAR PENINSULA

Surat

Tāpti River

Nāgpur

Mahānadi

Delta of The Ganges
(Sundarbans)

GULF OF KHAMBHĀT

20°

DECCAN

River

Palmyras
Point

B A Y   O F

20°

Mumbai
(Bombay)

Godavari

River

PLATEAU

B E N G A L

A R A B I A N

Poona

Bhima

Sholapur

Hyderābād

Vishākhapatnam

S E A

River

Krishna River

Vijayawada

HINDUSTAN

WESTERN GHATS

Bangalore

Chennai (Madras)

NORTH ANDAMAN

MIDDLE ANDAMAN

SOUTH ANDAMAN

ANDAMAN IS.
(INDIA)

EASTERN GHATS

Coromandel

Coast

LACCADIVE IS.
(INDIA)

Coimbatore

ANDAMAN

Calicut

Madurai

Point Calimere
Point Pedro

10°

Malabar

Cochin

Jaffna

SEA

Palk Strait

Trincomalee

10°

LACCADIVE

Coast

GULF OF MANNAR

SRI LANKA

NICOBAR IS.
(INDIA)

Cape Comorin

S E A

Colombo

Dehiwala

GREAT
NICOBAR I.

Moratuwa

Cape Dondra

⊛ Male

MALDIVES

Equator

0°

0°

Equator

INDIAN OCEAN

70°

80°

90°

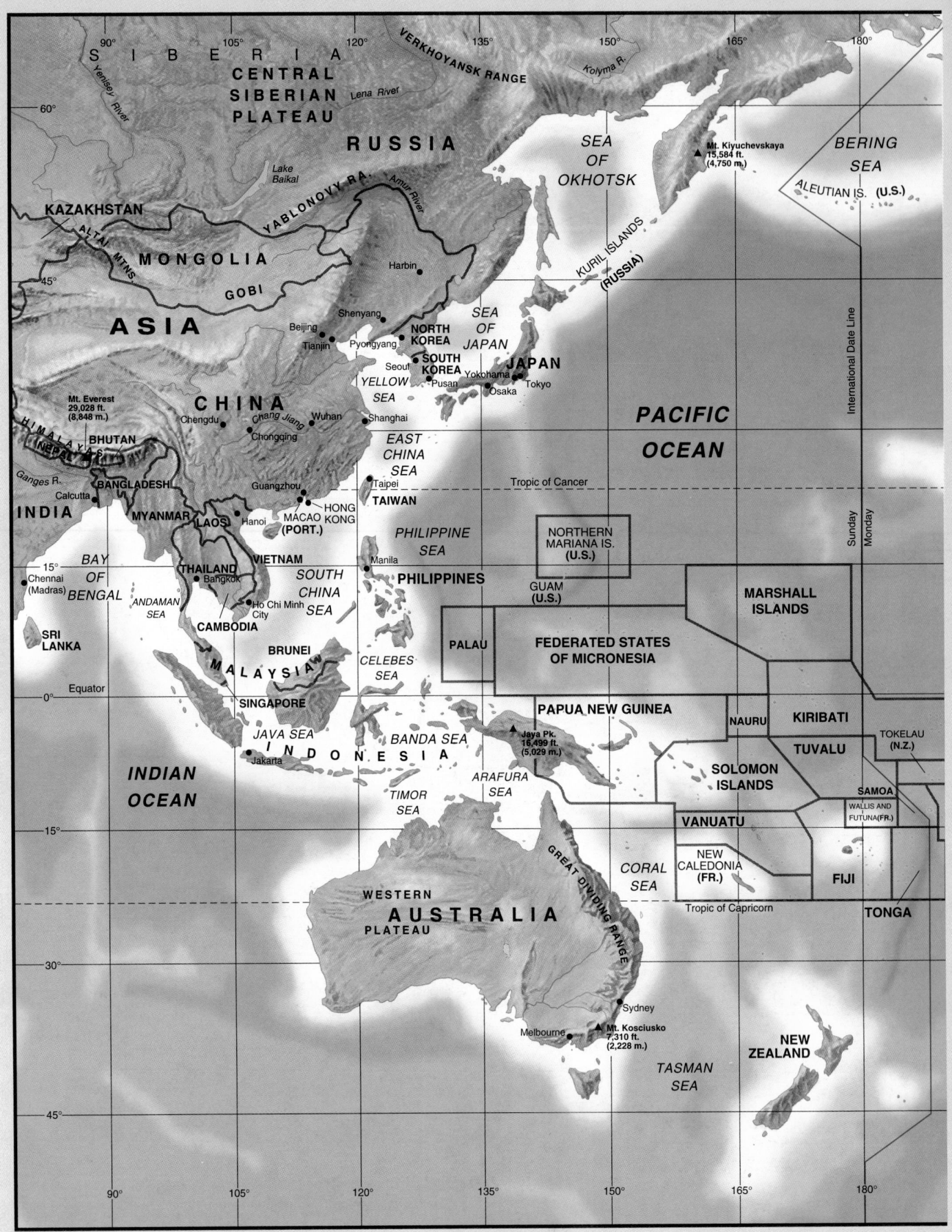

SIBERIA

CENTRAL
SIBERIAN
PLATEAU

Yenisey River

Lena River

VERKHOYANSK RANGE

Kolyma R.

RUSSIA

SEA
OF
OKHOTSK

Mt. Kiyuchevskaya
15,584 ft.
(4,750 m.)

BERING
SEA

ALEUTIAN IS. (U.S.)

Lake
Baikal

Amur River

KAZAKHSTAN

ALTAI
MTNS

YABLONOVY RA.

MONGOLIA

GOBI

KURIL ISLANDS
(RUSSIA)

ASIA

Harbin

Shenyang

Beijing

Tianjin

Pyongyang

NORTH
KOREA

SOUTH
KOREA

Seoul

JAPAN

SEA
OF
JAPAN

International Date Line

CHINA

Mt. Everest
29,028 ft.
(8,848 m.)

HIMALAYAS

BHUTAN

NEPAL

Ganges R.

BANGLADESH

Calcutta

INDIA

MYANMAR

Chengdu

Chang Jiang

Chongqing

Wuhan

Shanghai

YELLOW
SEA

Pusan

Yokohama

Osaka

Tokyo

Guangzhou

MACAO
(PORT.)

HONG
KONG

EAST
CHINA
SEA

Taipei

TAIWAN

PACIFIC

OCEAN

Tropic of Cancer

Sunday

Monday

LAOS

Hanoi

VIETNAM

THAILAND

Bangkok

BAY
OF
BENGAL

Chennai
(Madras)

ANDAMAN
SEA

Ho Chi Minh
City

CAMBODIA

SOUTH
CHINA
SEA

PHILIPPINE
SEA

Manila

PHILIPPINES

NORTHERN
MARIANA IS.
(U.S.)

MARSHALL
ISLANDS

SRI
LANKA

Equator

MALAYSIA

SINGAPORE

BRUNEI

CELEBES
SEA

GUAM
(U.S.)

PALAU

FEDERATED STATES
OF MICRONESIA

JAVA SEA

INDONESIA

Jakarta

BANDA SEA

Jaya Pk.
16,499 ft.
(5,029 m.)

PAPUA NEW GUINEA

NAURU

KIRIBATI

TOKELAU
(N.Z.)

INDIAN

OCEAN

TIMOR
SEA

ARAFURA
SEA

TUVALU

SOLOMON
ISLANDS

SAMOA

WALLIS AND
FUTUNA(FR.)

VANUATU

NEW
CALEDONIA
(FR.)

CORAL
SEA

FIJI

Tropic of Capricorn

TONGA

WESTERN
PLATEAU

AUSTRALIA

GREAT DIVIDING RANGE

Sydney

Melbourne

Mt. Kosciusko
7,310 ft.
(2,228 m.)

NEW
ZEALAND

TASMAN
SEA

90°   105°   120°   135°   150°   165°   180°

A22   Reference Atlas

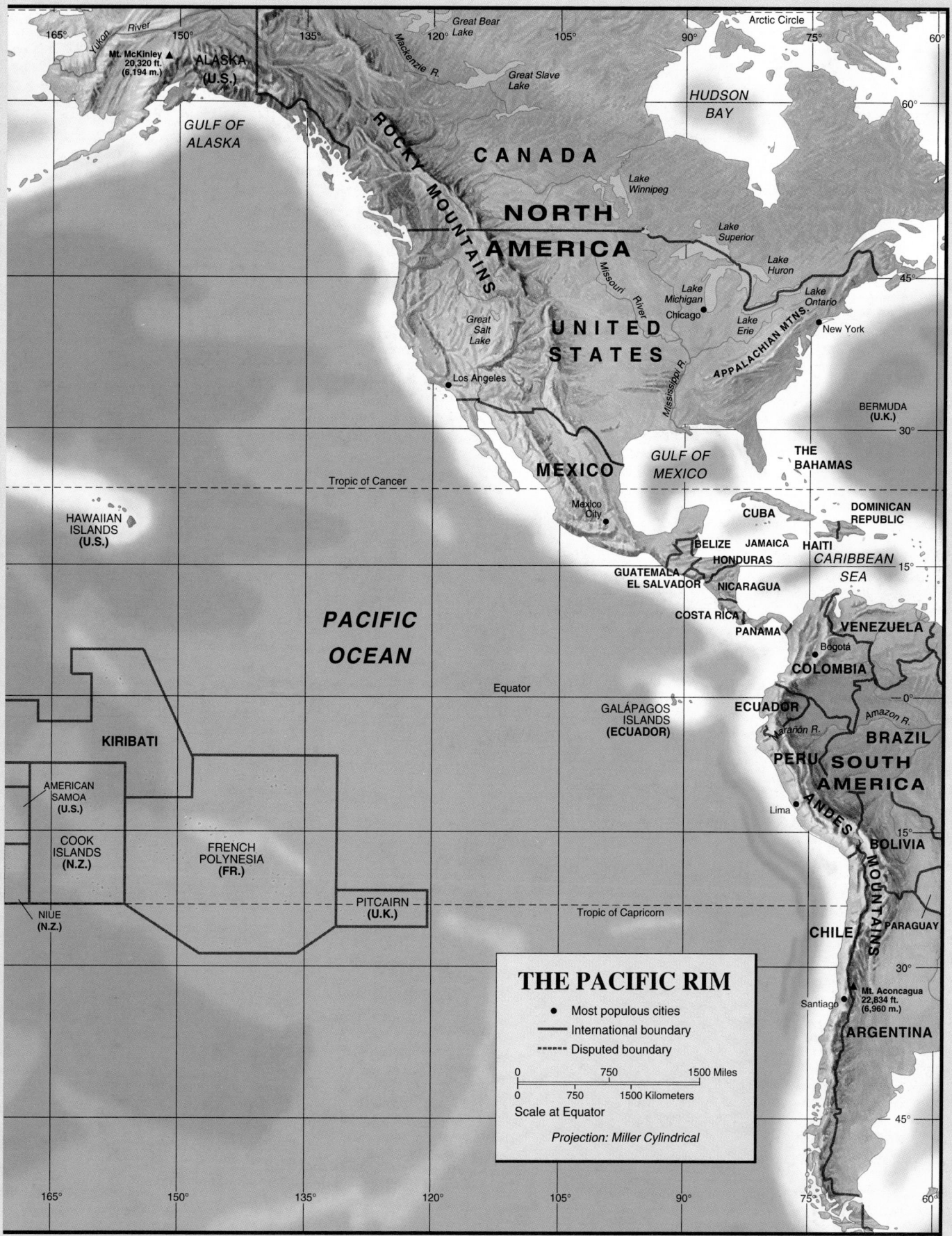

165°   150°   135°   120°   105°   90°   Arctic Circle   75°   60°

Yukon River   ▲ Mt. McKinley 20,320 ft. (6,194 m.)   ALASKA (U.S.)   *Mackenzie R.*   *Great Bear Lake*   *Great Slave Lake*   HUDSON BAY   60°

GULF OF ALASKA   ROCKY MOUNTAINS   CANADA   *Lake Winnipeg*   *Lake Superior*   *Lake Huron*   45°

NORTH AMERICA   *Missouri River*   *Lake Michigan*   • Chicago   *Lake Ontario*   *Lake Erie*   • New York   APPALACHIAN MTNS.

UNITED STATES   Great Salt Lake   • Los Angeles   *Mississippi R.*   BERMUDA (U.K.)   30°

Tropic of Cancer   MEXICO   GULF OF MEXICO   THE BAHAMAS

HAWAIIAN ISLANDS (U.S.)   Mexico City •   CUBA   DOMINICAN REPUBLIC   HAITI   CARIBBEAN SEA   15°

PACIFIC OCEAN   BELIZE   JAMAICA   HONDURAS   GUATEMALA   EL SALVADOR   NICARAGUA   COSTA RICA   PANAMA   VENEZUELA   Bogotá •   COLOMBIA

Equator   GALÁPAGOS ISLANDS (ECUADOR)   ECUADOR   *Marañón R.*   *Amazon R.*   0°

KIRIBATI   *Marañón R.*   BRAZIL   PERU   SOUTH AMERICA

AMERICAN SAMOA (U.S.)   Lima •   ANDES   15°

COOK ISLANDS (N.Z.)   FRENCH POLYNESIA (FR.)   BOLIVIA   MOUNTAINS

NIUE (N.Z.)   PITCAIRN (U.K.)   Tropic of Capricorn   CHILE   PARAGUAY

▲ Mt. Aconcagua 22,834 ft. (6,960 m.)   30°

THE PACIFIC RIM

- • Most populous cities
- —— International boundary
- ----- Disputed boundary

Santiago •   ARGENTINA

0   750   1500 Miles
0   750   1500 Kilometers
Scale at Equator

Projection: Miller Cylindrical   45°

165°   150°   135°   120°   105°   90°   75°   60°

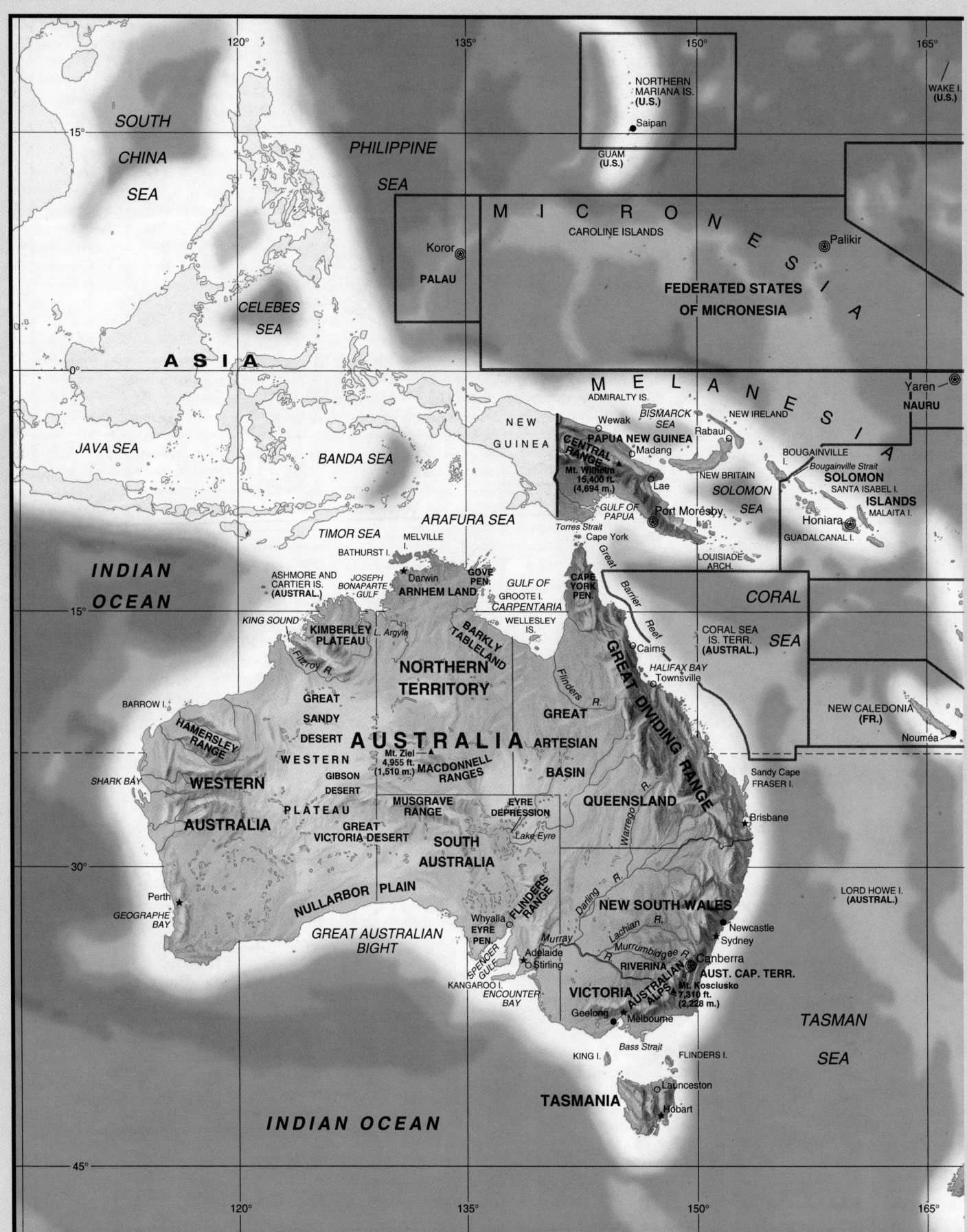

SOUTH

CHINA

SEA

PHILIPPINE

SEA

NORTHERN
MARIANA IS.
(U.S.)

• Saipan

GUAM
(U.S.)

WAKE I.
(U.S.)

M I C R O N E S I A

CAROLINE ISLANDS

Koror ⊛

PALAU

⊛ Palikir

FEDERATED STATES
OF MICRONESIA

ASIA

JAVA SEA

BANDA SEA

CELEBES
SEA

NEW
GUINEA

M E L A N E S I A

ADMIRALTY IS.

BISMARCK
SEA

Wewak •

PAPUA NEW GUINEA
CENTRAL
RANGE

Mt. Wilhelm
15,400 ft.
(4,694 m.)

• Madang

Lae ○

GULF OF
PAPUA

Port Morésby ⊛

NEW IRELAND

Rabaul ○

NEW BRITAIN

SOLOMON
SEA

Yaren ⊛

NAURU

BOUGAINVILLE
I.

Bougainville Strait

SOLOMON

SANTA ISABEL I.

ISLANDS
MALAITA I.

Honiara ○

GUADALCANAL I.

LOUISIADE
ARCH.

TIMOR SEA

ARAFURA SEA

Torres Strait
Cape York

INDIAN

OCEAN

MELVILLE
I.

BATHURST I.

ASHMORE AND
CARTIER IS.
(AUSTRAL.)

JOSEPH
BONAPARTE
GULF

Darwin ★

ARNHEM LAND

GOVE
PEN.

GROOTE I.

GULF OF
CARPENTARIA

WELLESLEY
IS.

CAPE
YORK
PEN.

Great
Barrier
Reef

Cairns ○

HALIFAX BAY

Townsville •

CORAL

CORAL SEA
IS. TERR.
(AUSTRAL.)

SEA

NEW CALEDONIA
(FR.)

Nouméa •

KING SOUND

KIMBERLEY
PLATEAU

Fitzroy R.

L. Argyle

BARKLY
TABLELAND

Flinders

NORTHERN

TERRITORY

GREAT

DIVIDING

RANGE

BARROW I.

HAMERSLEY
RANGE

GREAT

SANDY

DESERT

WESTERN

AUSTRALIA

Mt. Ziel ▲
4,955 ft.
(1,510 m.)

MACDONNELL
RANGES

GREAT

ARTESIAN

BASIN

QUEENSLAND

Warrego R.

R.

Sandy Cape
FRASER I.

Brisbane ★

LORD HOWE I.
(AUSTRAL.)

SHARK BAY

GIBSON
DESERT

WESTERN

PLATEAU

AUSTRALIA

MUSGRAVE
RANGE

GREAT
VICTORIA DESERT

EYRE
DEPRESSION

Lake Eyre

SOUTH

AUSTRALIA

Perth ★

GEOGRAPHE
BAY

NULLARBOR PLAIN

GREAT AUSTRALIAN

BIGHT

Whyalla ○

EYRE
PEN.

FLINDERS
RANGE

SPENCER
GULF

KANGAROO I.

ENCOUNTER
BAY

Adelaide ★
Stirling ○

Darling R.

Murray

NEW SOUTH WALES

Lachlan R.

Murrumbidgee R.

RIVERINA

VICTORIA

AUSTRALIAN
ALPS

Newcastle •
Sydney ★

Canberra ⊛
AUST. CAP. TERR.

Mt. Kosciusko
7,310 ft.
(2,228 m.)

TASMAN

SEA

Geelong ○
Melbourne ★

KING I.

Bass Strait

FLINDERS I.

AUSTRALIA

INDIAN OCEAN

TASMANIA

Launceston ○

Hobart ★

120° 135° 150° 165°

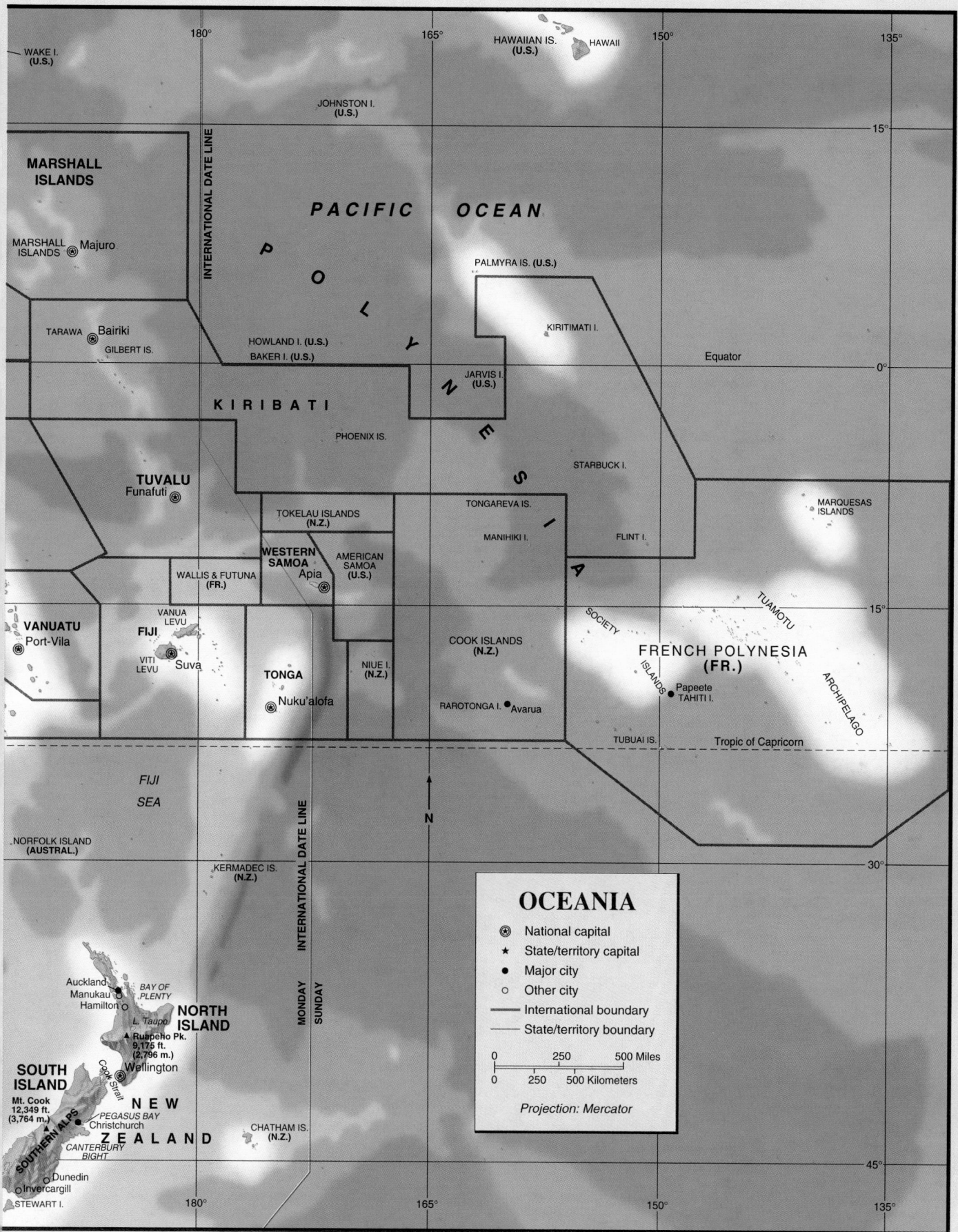

WAKE I. (U.S.)

180°

JOHNSTON I. (U.S.)

165°

HAWAIIAN IS. (U.S.)

HAWAII

150°

15°

135°

MARSHALL ISLANDS

PACIFIC OCEAN

MARSHALL ISLANDS ⊛ Majuro

P O L Y N E S I A

PALMYRA IS. (U.S.)

KIRITIMATI I.

TARAWA ⊛ Bairiki
GILBERT IS.

HOWLAND I. (U.S.)
BAKER I. (U.S.)

Equator

0°

KIRIBATI

JARVIS I. (U.S.)

PHOENIX IS.

STARBUCK I.

TUVALU
Funafuti ⊛

TOKELAU ISLANDS (N.Z.)

TONGAREVA IS.

MANIHIKI I.

FLINT I.

MARQUESAS ISLANDS

WESTERN SAMOA
Apia ⊛

AMERICAN SAMOA (U.S.)

VANUATU
● Port-Vila

WALLIS & FUTUNA (FR.)

VANUA LEVU

FIJI

VITI LEVU   Suva

SOCIETY

ISLANDS

TUAMOTU

15°

FRENCH POLYNESIA (FR.)

Papeete ●
TAHITI I.

ARCHIPELAGO

COOK ISLANDS (N.Z.)

NIUE I. (N.Z.)

TONGA
● Nuku'alofa

RAROTONGA I. ● Avarua

TUBUAI IS.

Tropic of Capricorn

FIJI SEA

INTERNATIONAL DATE LINE

N

NORFOLK ISLAND (AUSTRAL.)

KERMADEC IS. (N.Z.)

30°

INTERNATIONAL DATE LINE

MONDAY   SUNDAY

Auckland
Manukau ○
Hamilton ○

BAY OF PLENTY

L. Taupo
▲ Ruapehu Pk.
9,175 ft. (2,796 m.)

NORTH ISLAND

Wellington

SOUTH ISLAND

Mt. Cook
12,349 ft. (3,764 m.)

Cook Strait

N E W

PEGASUS BAY

● Christchurch

SOUTHERN ALPS

CANTERBURY BIGHT

Z E A L A N D

CHATHAM IS. (N.Z.)

○ Dunedin
○ Invercargill

STEWART I.

45°

180°

165°

150°

135°

OCEANIA

⊛ National capital
★ State/territory capital
● Major city
○ Other city
— International boundary
— State/territory boundary

0   250   500 Miles

0   250   500 Kilometers

Projection: Mercator

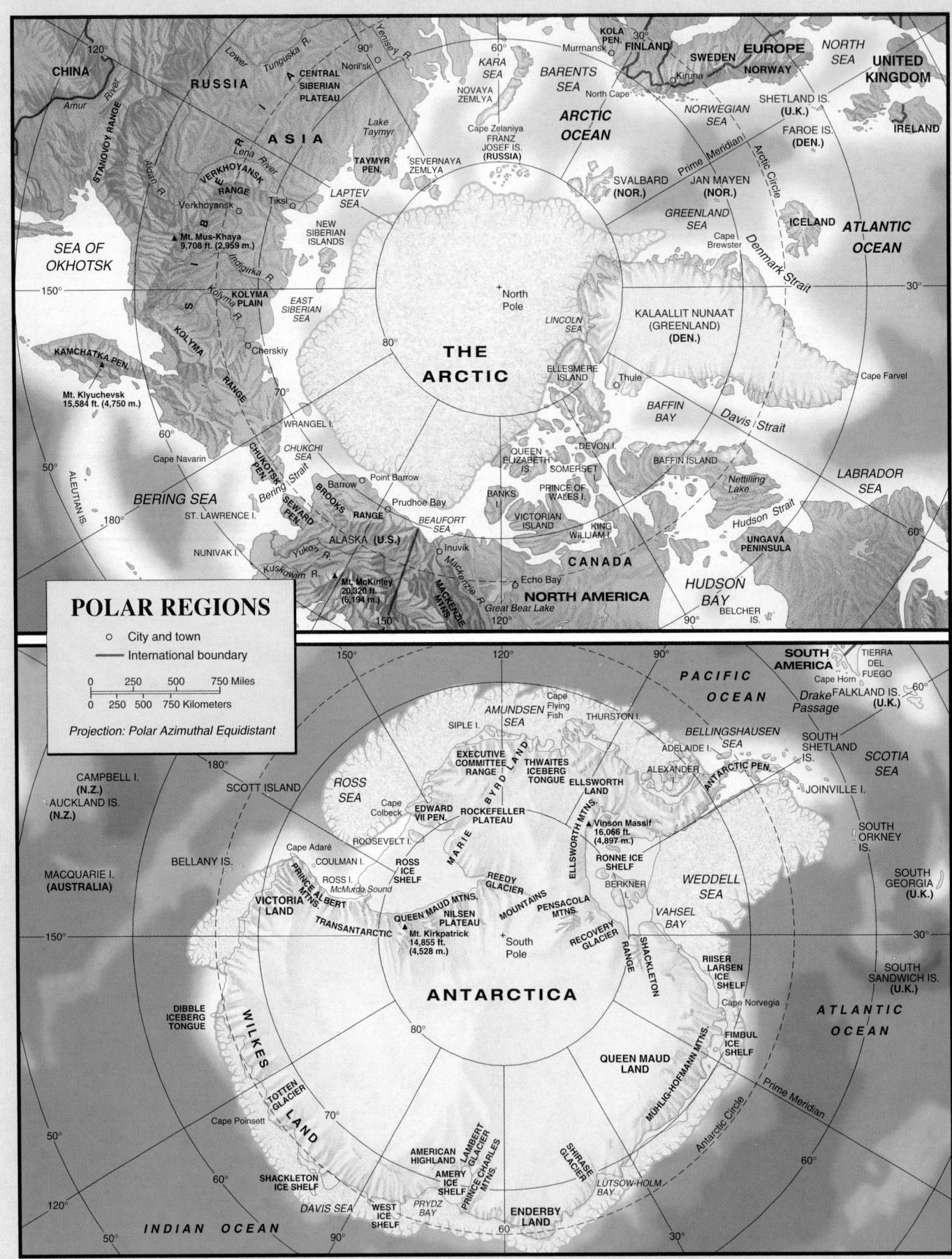

POLAR REGIONS

○ City and town
— International boundary

| 0 | 250 | 500 | 750 Miles |
| 0 | 250 | 500 | 750 Kilometers |

Projection: Polar Azimuthal Equidistant

THE ARCTIC

CHINA
RUSSIA
CENTRAL SIBERIAN PLATEAU
ASIA
STANOVOY RANGE
Amur
Lower
Tunguska R.
Yenisey R.
Noril'sk
Lena River
VERKHOYANSK RANGE
Verkhoyansk
Tiksi
Aldan R.
Indigirka R.
Mt. Mus-Khaya 9,708 ft. (2,959 m.)
SEA OF OKHOTSK
KOLYMA PLAIN
Kolyma R.
EAST SIBERIAN SEA
KOLYMA RANGE
Cherskiy
KAMCHATKA PEN.
Mt. Klyuchevsk 15,584 ft. (4,750 m.)
WRANGEL I.
CHUKOTSK PEN.
CHUKCHI SEA
Cape Navarin
BERING SEA
ALEUTIAN IS.
ST. LAWRENCE I.
SEWARD PEN.
Bering Strait
Barrow
Point Barrow
BROOKS RANGE
Prudhoe Bay
BEAUFORT SEA
NUNIVAK I.
Yukon R.
Kuskokwim R.
ALASKA (U.S.)
Mt. McKinley 20,320 ft. (6,194 m.)
MACKENZIE MTNS.
Inuvik
Mackenzie R.
Echo Bay
Great Bear Lake
NORTH AMERICA
CANADA
KARA SEA
NOVAYA ZEMLYA
Cape Zelaniya
FRANZ JOSEF IS. (RUSSIA)
TAYMYR PEN.
SEVERNAYA ZEMLYA
Lake Taymyr
LAPTEV SEA
NEW SIBERIAN ISLANDS
BARENTS SEA
Murmansk
KOLA PEN.
FINLAND
SWEDEN
NORWAY
EUROPE
Kiruna
North Cape
ARCTIC OCEAN
SVALBARD (NOR.)
JAN MAYEN (NOR.)
NORWEGIAN SEA
Prime Meridian
Arctic Circle
SHETLAND IS. (U.K.)
FAROE IS. (DEN.)
NORTH SEA
UNITED KINGDOM
IRELAND
ATLANTIC OCEAN
GREENLAND SEA
Cape Brewster
ICELAND
Denmark Strait
North Pole
80°
LINCOLN SEA
THE ARCTIC
KALAALLIT NUNAAT (GREENLAND) (DEN.)
Cape Farvel
ELLESMERE ISLAND
Thule
BAFFIN BAY
Davis Strait
70°
QUEEN ELIZABETH IS.
DEVON I.
SOMERSET I.
PRINCE OF WALES I.
BAFFIN ISLAND
Nettiling Lake
LABRADOR SEA
BANKS I.
VICTORIAN ISLAND
KING WILLIAM I.
Hudson Strait
UNGAVA PENINSULA
BELCHER IS.
HUDSON BAY
60°
90°

ANTARCTICA

PACIFIC OCEAN
SOUTH AMERICA
Cape Horn
TIERRA DEL FUEGO
Drake Passage
FALKLAND IS. (U.K.)
AMUNDSEN SEA
Cape Flying Fish
SIPLE I.
THURSTON I.
BELLINGSHAUSEN SEA
SOUTH SHETLAND IS.
SCOTIA SEA
EXECUTIVE COMMITTEE RANGE
BYRD LAND
THWAITES ICEBERG TONGUE
ELLSWORTH LAND
Adelaide I.
ALEXANDER I.
ANTARCTIC PEN.
JOINVILLE I.
ROSS SEA
Cape Colbeck
EDWARD VII PEN.
ROCKEFELLER PLATEAU
ELLSWORTH MTNS.
Vinson Massif 16,066 ft. (4,897 m.)
RONNE ICE SHELF
SOUTH ORKNEY IS.
SCOTT ISLAND
ROOSEVELT I.
MARIE
BERKNER I.
WEDDELL SEA
SOUTH GEORGIA (U.K.)
BELLANY IS.
Cape Adaré
COULMAN I.
ROSS I.
McMurdo Sound
ROSS ICE SHELF
REEDY GLACIER
PENSACOLA MTNS.
VAHSEL BAY
CAMPBELL I. (N.Z.)
AUCKLAND IS. (N.Z.)
PRINCE ALBERT MTNS.
VICTORIA LAND
QUEEN MAUD MTNS.
NILSEN PLATEAU
Mt. Kirkpatrick 14,855 ft. (4,528 m.)
Mountains
RECOVERY GLACIER
SHACKLETON RANGE
RIISER-LARSEN ICE SHELF
SOUTH SANDWICH IS. (U.K.)
MACQUARIE I. (AUSTRALIA)
TRANSANTARCTIC
South Pole
80°
ANTARCTICA
Cape Norvegia
ATLANTIC OCEAN
WILKES LAND
DIBBLE ICEBERG TONGUE
QUEEN MAUD LAND
MÜHLIG-HOFMANN MTNS.
FIMBUL ICE SHELF
TOTTEN GLACIER
Cape Poinsett
AMERICAN HIGHLAND
LAMBERT GLACIER
PRINCE CHARLES MTNS.
AMERY ICE SHELF
SHIRASE GLACIER
SHACKLETON ICE SHELF
DAVIS SEA
WEST ICE SHELF
PRYDZ BAY
ENDERBY LAND
LÜTSOW-HOLM BAY
Antarctic Circle
Prime Meridian
INDIAN OCEAN

Historical Atlas AND *World Data Bank*

Early Civilizations 3500 B.C –1700s B.C.

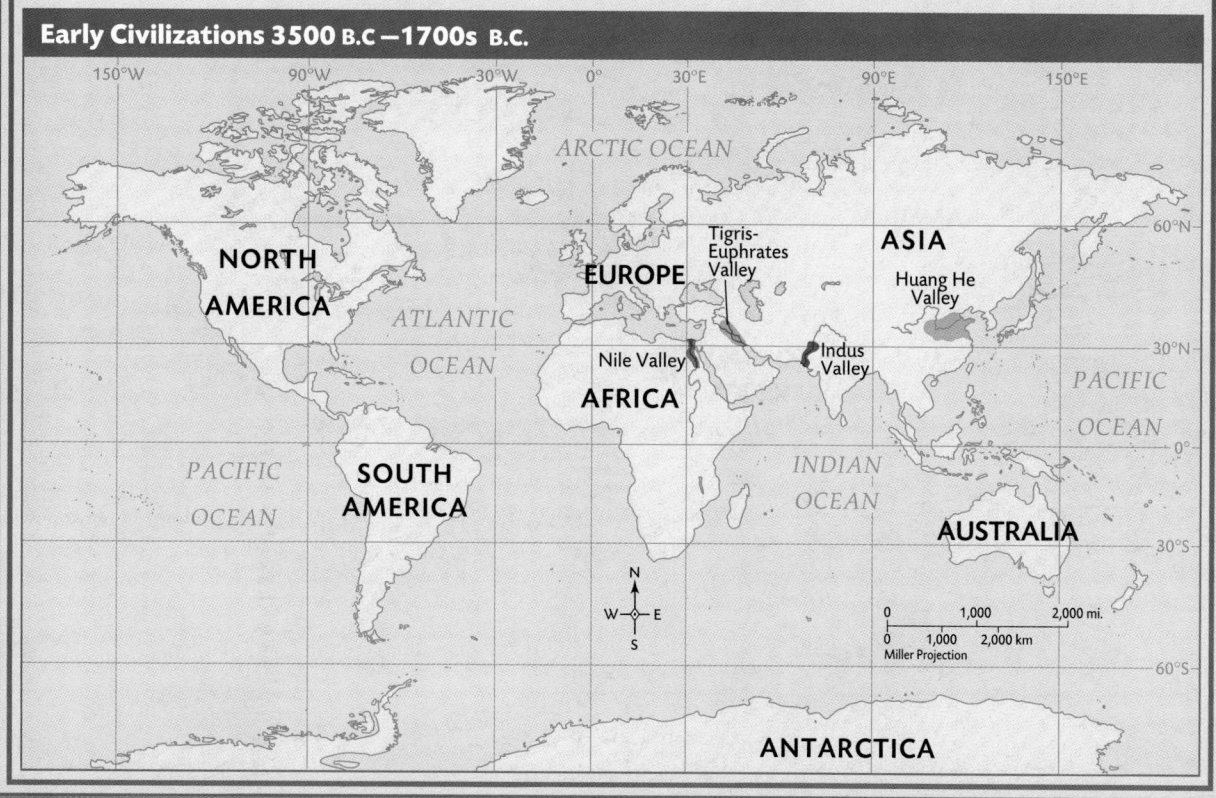

Ancient Empires A.D. 1—A.D. 500

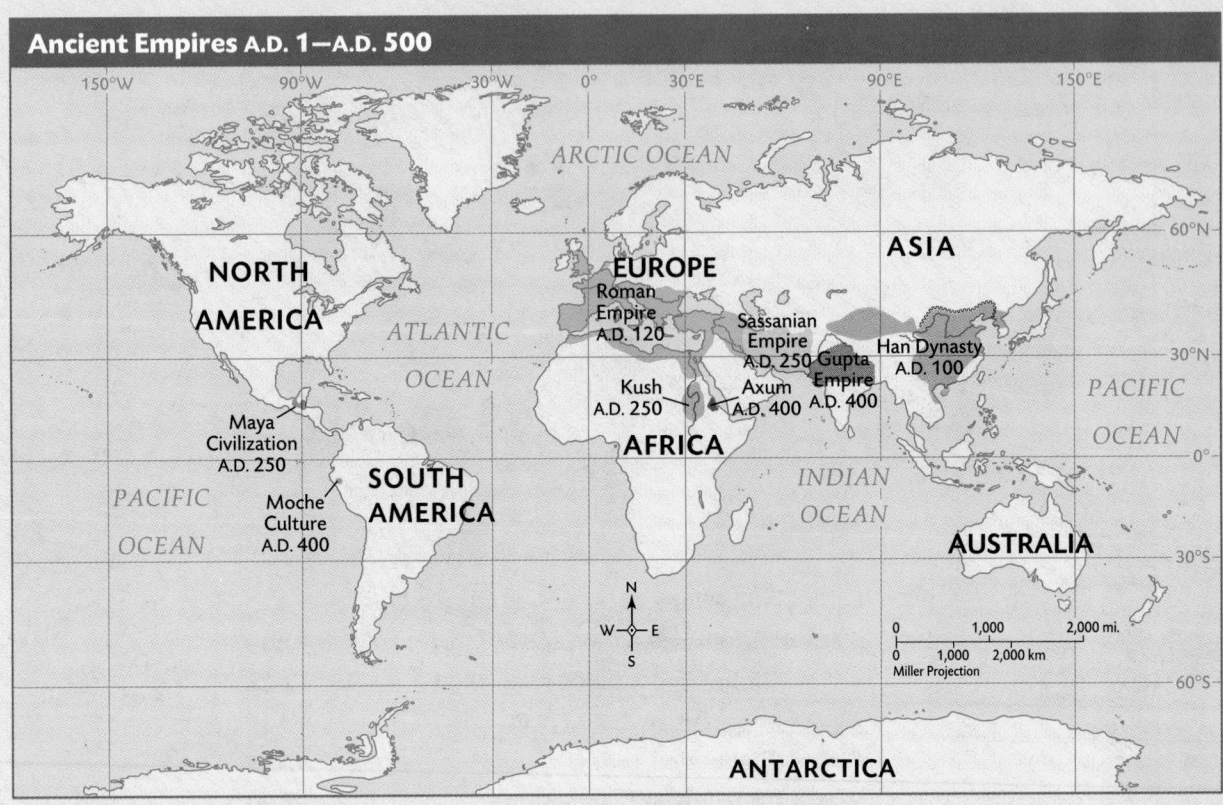

ARCTIC OCEAN

NORTH AMERICA

EUROPE

ASIA

ATLANTIC OCEAN

Roman Empire A.D. 120

Sassanian Empire A.D. 250

Han Dynasty A.D. 100

Gupta Empire A.D. 400

Kush A.D. 250

Axum A.D. 400

AFRICA

PACIFIC OCEAN

Maya Civilization A.D. 250

PACIFIC OCEAN

Moche Culture A.D. 400

SOUTH AMERICA

INDIAN OCEAN

AUSTRALIA

N
W—E
S

0   1,000   2,000 mi.
0 1,000 2,000 km
Miller Projection

ANTARCTICA

A New Global Age A.D. 800—A.D. 1500

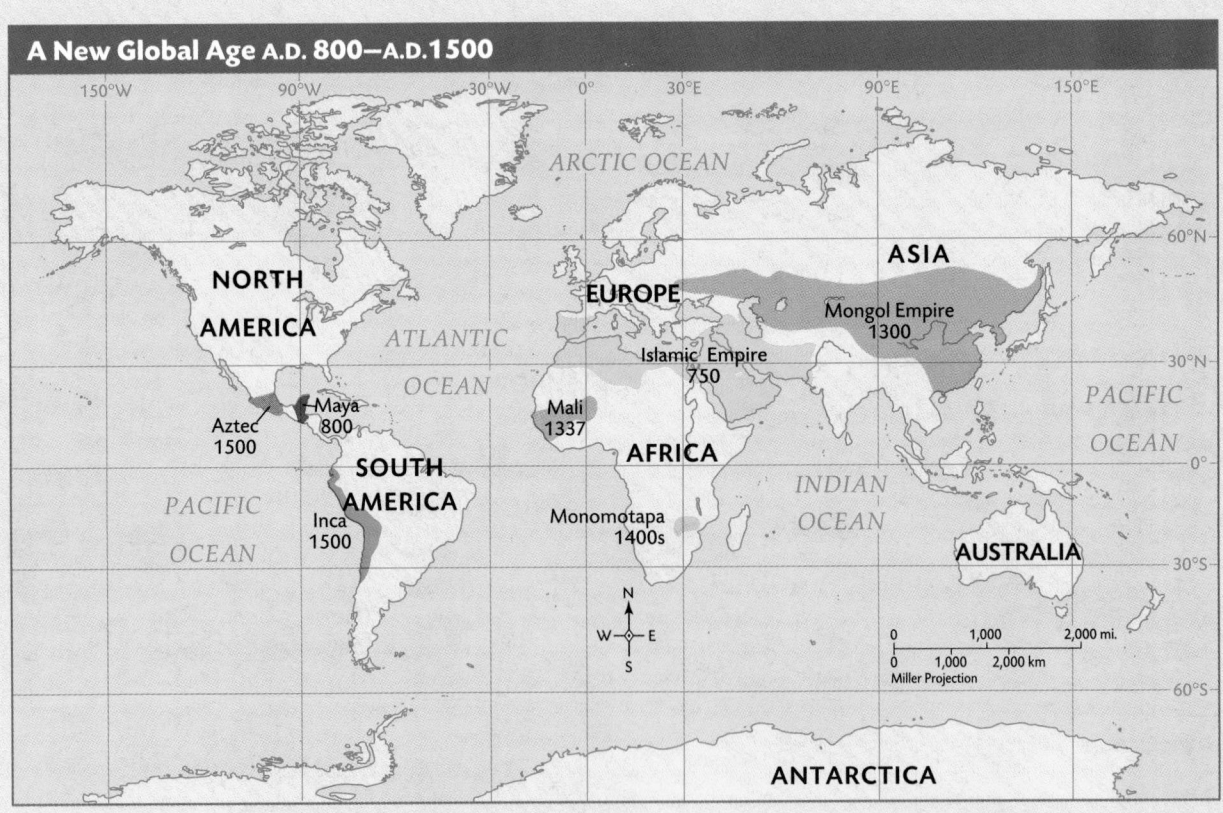

ARCTIC OCEAN

NORTH AMERICA

EUROPE

ASIA

ATLANTIC OCEAN

Mongol Empire 1300

Islamic Empire 750

Aztec 1500

Maya 800

Mali 1337

AFRICA

PACIFIC OCEAN

SOUTH AMERICA

INDIAN OCEAN

PACIFIC OCEAN

Inca 1500

Monomotapa 1400s

AUSTRALIA

N
W—E
S

0   1,000   2,000 mi.
0 1,000 2,000 km
Miller Projection

ANTARCTICA

Age of Imperialism 1870–1914

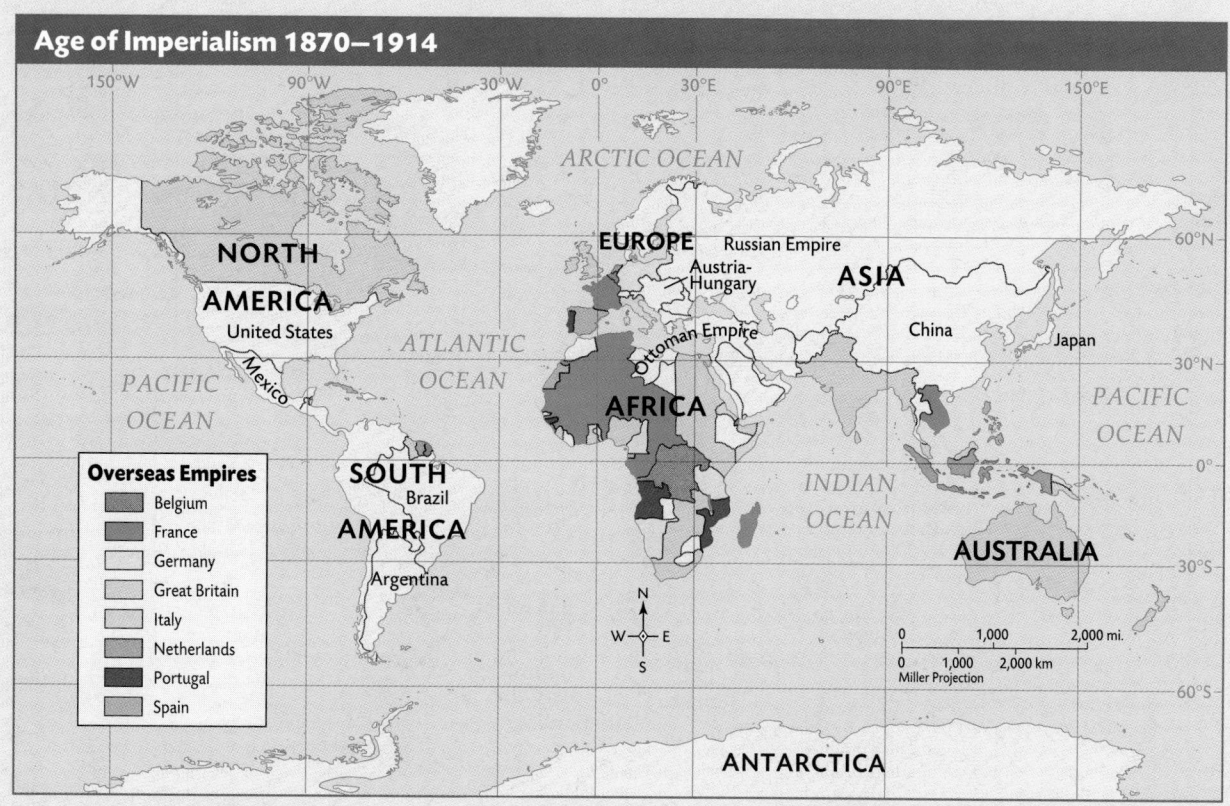

Overseas Empires
- Belgium
- France
- Germany
- Great Britain
- Italy
- Netherlands
- Portugal
- Spain

ARCTIC OCEAN

NORTH AMERICA

United States

Mexico

PACIFIC OCEAN

ATLANTIC OCEAN

SOUTH AMERICA

Brazil

Argentina

EUROPE

Russian Empire

Austria-Hungary

Ottoman Empire

AFRICA

ASIA

China

Japan

PACIFIC OCEAN

INDIAN OCEAN

AUSTRALIA

ANTARCTICA

N W E S

0 1,000 2,000 mi.
0 1,000 2,000 km
Miller Projection

Global Civilization Today

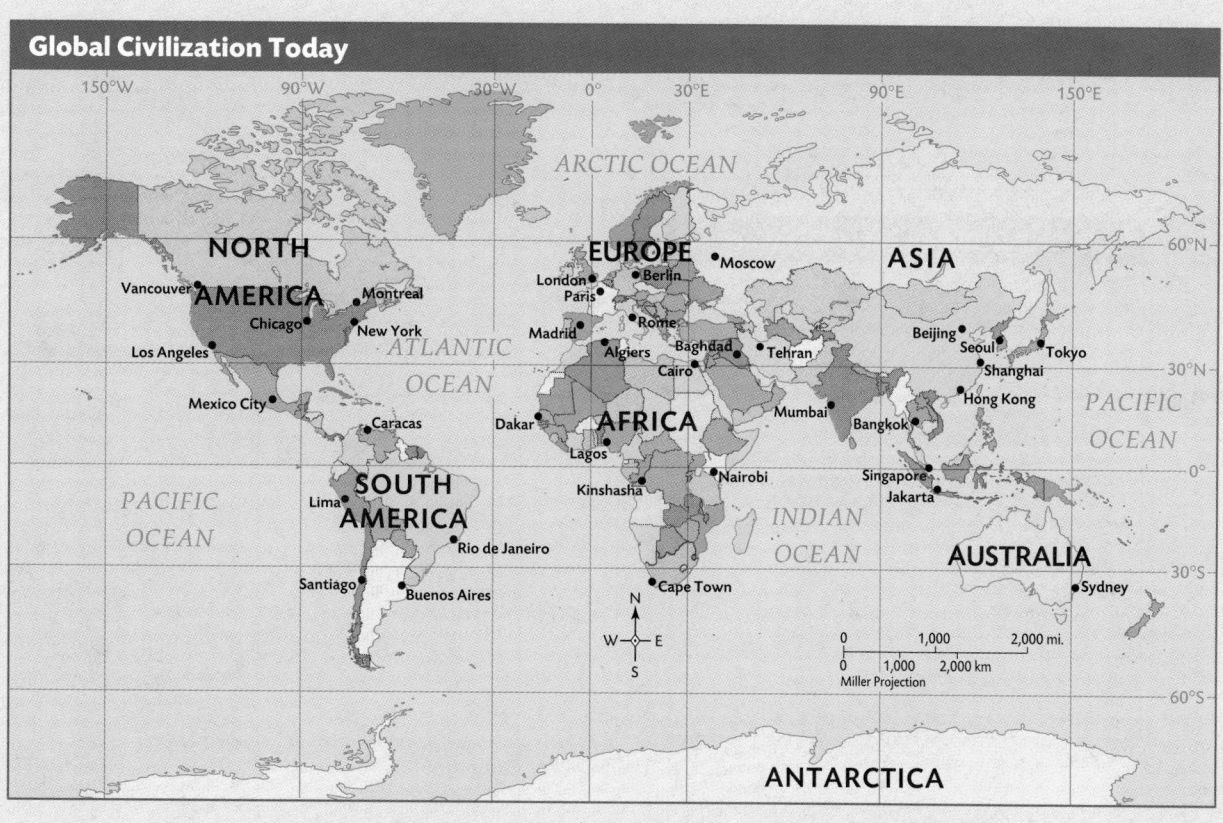

ARCTIC OCEAN

NORTH AMERICA

Vancouver
Montreal
Chicago
New York
Los Angeles
Mexico City
Caracas

SOUTH AMERICA
Lima
Santiago
Buenos Aires
Rio de Janeiro

ATLANTIC OCEAN

PACIFIC OCEAN

EUROPE
London
Paris
Berlin
Moscow
Madrid
Rome
Algiers
Baghdad
Cairo
Tehran

AFRICA
Dakar
Lagos
Kinshasha
Nairobi
Cape Town

ASIA
Beijing
Seoul
Tokyo
Shanghai
Hong Kong
Mumbai
Bangkok
Singapore
Jakarta

PACIFIC OCEAN

INDIAN OCEAN

AUSTRALIA
Sydney

ANTARCTICA

N W E S

0 1,000 2,000 mi.
0 1,000 2,000 km
Miller Projection

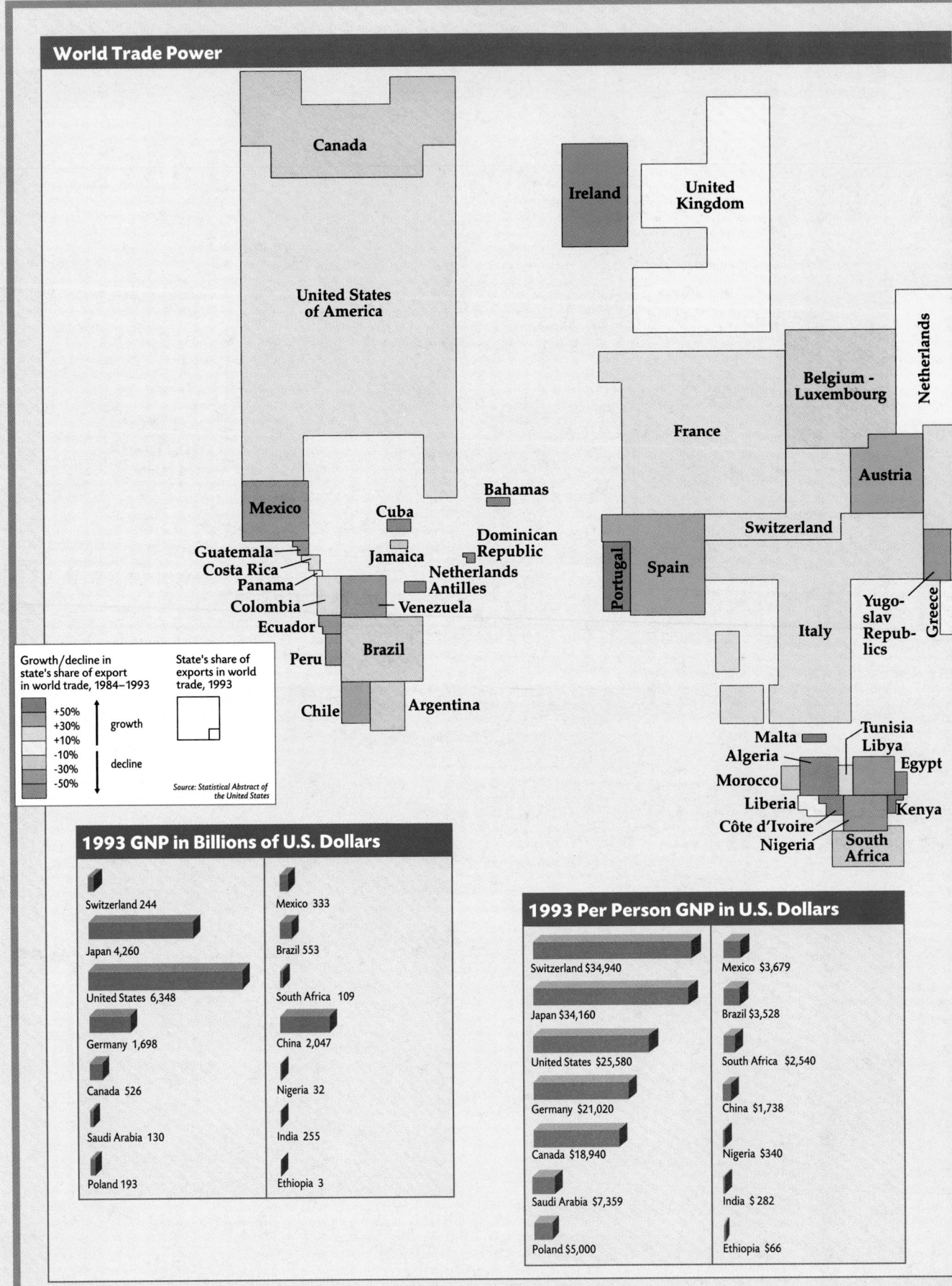

Canada

United States
of America

Ireland

United
Kingdom

Netherlands

Belgium -
Luxembourg

France

Austria

Switzerland

Portugal

Spain

Bahamas

Mexico

Cuba

Dominican
Republic

Jamaica

Guatemala
Costa Rica
Panama
Colombia
Ecuador

Netherlands
Antilles

Venezuela

Peru

Brazil

Italy

Yugo-
slav
Repub-
lics

Greece

Chile

Argentina

Malta

Tunisia
Libya

Algeria

Egypt

Morocco

Liberia

Côte d'Ivoire

Kenya

Nigeria

South
Africa

Growth/decline in state's share of export in world trade, 1984–1993

+50%
+30%   growth
+10%
-10%
-30%   decline
-50%

State's share of exports in world trade, 1993

Source: Statistical Abstract of the United States

1993 GNP in Billions of U.S. Dollars

Switzerland 244

Japan 4,260

United States 6,348

Germany 1,698

Canada 526

Saudi Arabia 130

Poland 193

Mexico 333

Brazil 553

South Africa 109

China 2,047

Nigeria 32

India 255

Ethiopia 3

1993 Per Person GNP in U.S. Dollars

Switzerland $34,940

Japan $34,160

United States $25,580

Germany $21,020

Canada $18,940

Saudi Arabia $7,359

Poland $5,000

Mexico $3,679

Brazil $3,528

South Africa $2,540

China $1,738

Nigeria $340

India $ 282

Ethiopia $66

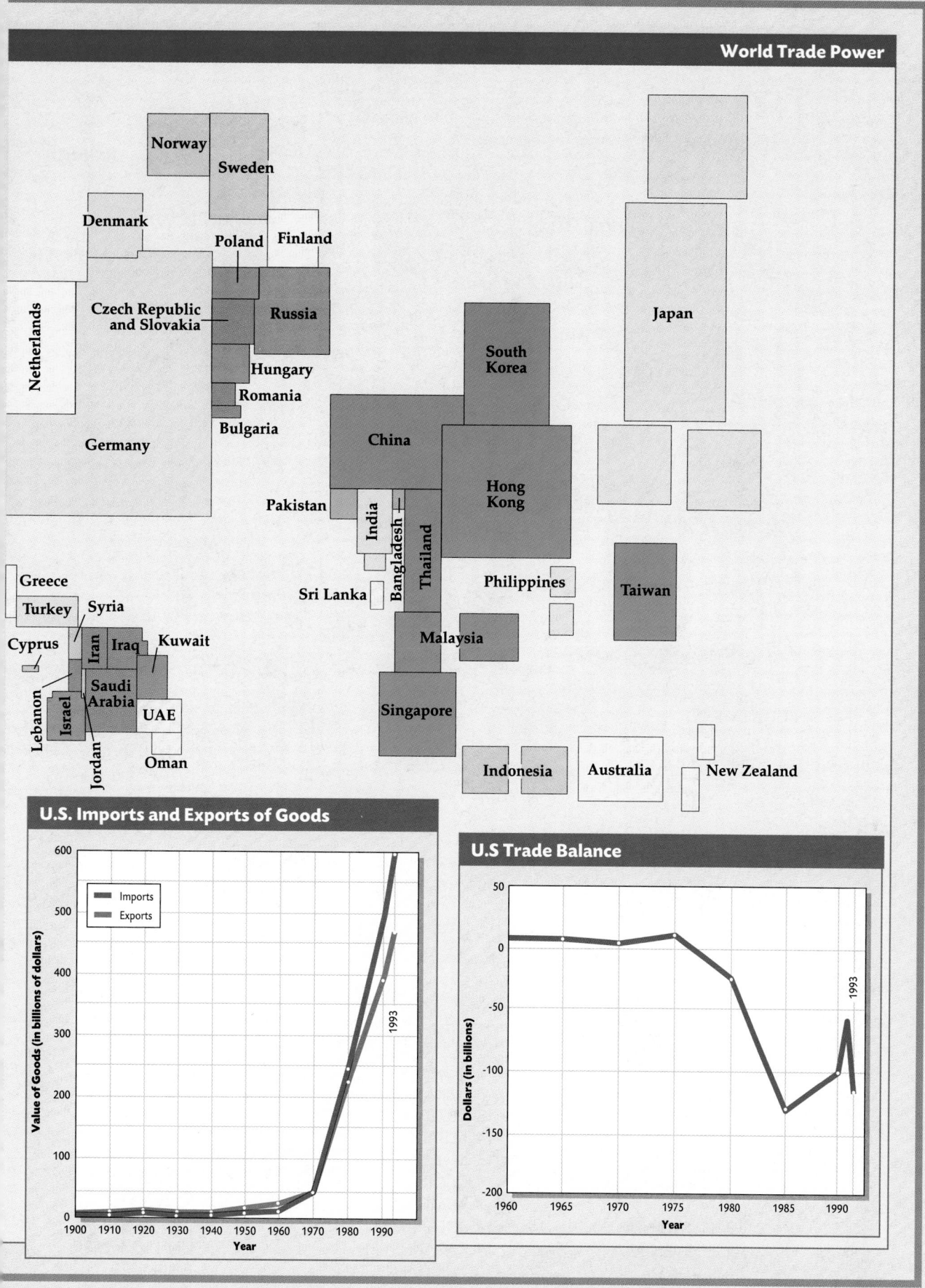

Norway

Sweden

Denmark

Poland   Finland

Czech Republic
and Slovakia   Russia

Netherlands

Hungary

Romania

Germany   Bulgaria

Japan

South
Korea

China

Hong
Kong

Pakistan

India

Bangladesh

Thailand

Greece

Turkey   Syria

Sri Lanka   Philippines

Taiwan

Cyprus   Iran   Iraq   Kuwait

Lebanon   Saudi
Arabia

Israel   UAE   Malaysia

Jordan   Oman

Singapore

Indonesia   Australia   New Zealand

U.S. Imports and Exports of Goods

Value of Goods (in billions of dollars)

- Imports
- Exports

1993

600
500
400
300
200
100

1900 1910 1920 1930 1940 1950 1960 1970 1980 1990

Year

U.S Trade Balance

Dollars (in billions)

50

0

-50

-100

-150

-200

1993

1960   1965   1970   1975   1980   1985   1990

Year

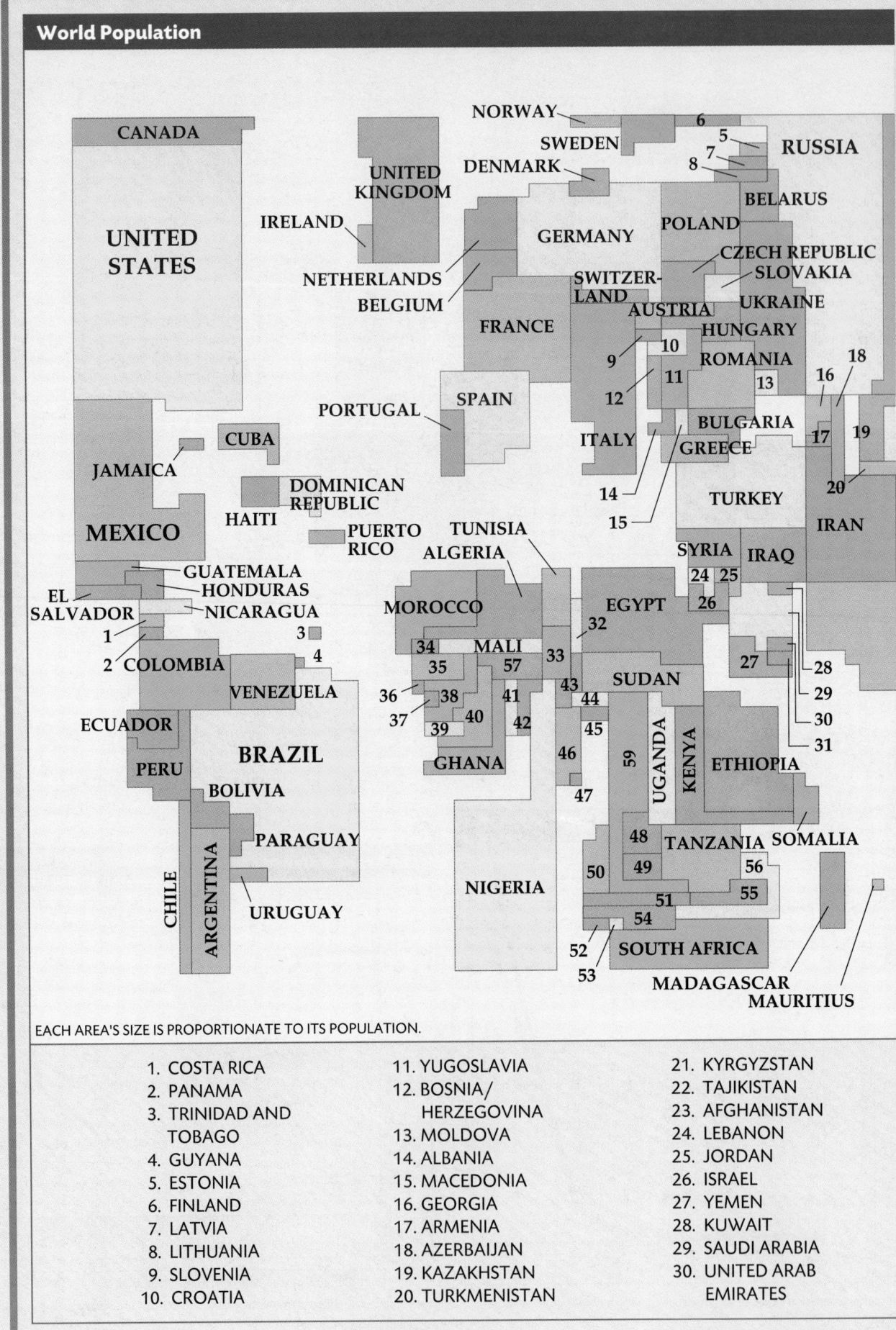

EACH AREA'S SIZE IS PROPORTIONATE TO ITS POPULATION.

1. COSTA RICA	11. YUGOSLAVIA	21. KYRGYZSTAN
2. PANAMA	12. BOSNIA/	22. TAJIKISTAN
3. TRINIDAD AND	HERZEGOVINA	23. AFGHANISTAN
TOBAGO	13. MOLDOVA	24. LEBANON
4. GUYANA	14. ALBANIA	25. JORDAN
5. ESTONIA	15. MACEDONIA	26. ISRAEL
6. FINLAND	16. GEORGIA	27. YEMEN
7. LATVIA	17. ARMENIA	28. KUWAIT
8. LITHUANIA	18. AZERBAIJAN	29. SAUDI ARABIA
9. SLOVENIA	19. KAZAKHSTAN	30. UNITED ARAB
10. CROATIA	20. TURKMENISTAN	EMIRATES

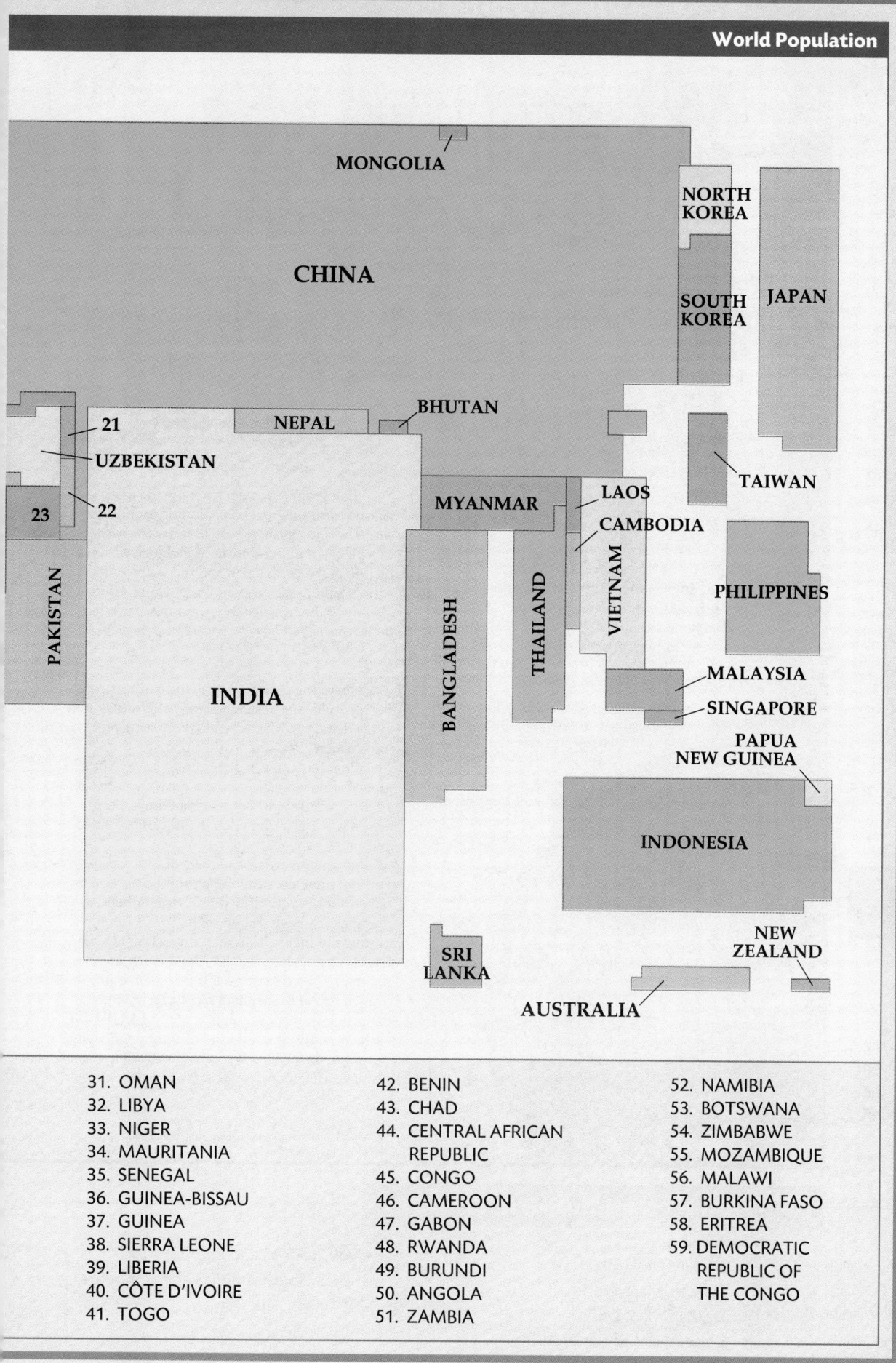

MONGOLIA

NORTH
KOREA

CHINA

SOUTH
KOREA

JAPAN

21

UZBEKISTAN

23

22

BHUTAN

NEPAL

TAIWAN

LAOS

MYANMAR

CAMBODIA

PAKISTAN

BANGLADESH

THAILAND

VIETNAM

PHILIPPINES

INDIA

MALAYSIA

SINGAPORE

PAPUA
NEW GUINEA

INDONESIA

NEW
ZEALAND

SRI
LANKA

AUSTRALIA

31. OMAN	42. BENIN	52. NAMIBIA
32. LIBYA	43. CHAD	53. BOTSWANA
33. NIGER	44. CENTRAL AFRICAN	54. ZIMBABWE
34. MAURITANIA	REPUBLIC	55. MOZAMBIQUE
35. SENEGAL	45. CONGO	56. MALAWI
36. GUINEA-BISSAU	46. CAMEROON	57. BURKINA FASO
37. GUINEA	47. GABON	58. ERITREA
38. SIERRA LEONE	48. RWANDA	59. DEMOCRATIC
39. LIBERIA	49. BURUNDI	REPUBLIC OF
40. CÔTE D'IVOIRE	50. ANGOLA	THE CONGO
41. TOGO	51. ZAMBIA	

Handbook Objectives

1. **Understand** the purpose and uses of globes and map projections.
2. **Identify** most commonly used geographic terms.
3. **Analyze** geographic factors that have shaped the course of historic events.

Vocabulary Pre-check

Survey the students' knowledge of geographic terms. Create three columns on the chalkboard with the following headings: *landforms*, *map elements*, and *bodies of water*.

List one term that fits each column, such as "canyon," "meridian," and "bay." Ask students to volunteer as many other terms for each column as they can.

Have students turn to page 4 and read the geographic dictionary. Then have them close their books and continue suggesting terms for each column on the chalkboard.

TEACH

NATIONAL
GEOGRAPHIC
SOCIETY

CD-ROM

PICTURE ATLAS OF THE WORLD

You and your students can see the challenges and solutions involved in making maps by viewing the Mapping Our World animation "Round Earth on Flat Paper."

GEOGRAPHY HANDBOOK

What Is Geography?

The story of humanity begins with **geography**—the study of the earth in all of its variety. Geography concerns the earth's land, water, and plant and animal life. It also tells you about the people who live on the earth, the places they have created, and how these places differ. The earth is a planet of diverse groups of people. A study of geography can help you see why the people of the earth are so diverse.

The Five Themes of Geography

The study of geography can be organized around five themes: **location**, **place**, **human/environment interaction**, **movement**, and **region**. Geographers use these five themes to study and classify all parts of the earth and its variety of human activity.

Geography and World History

World geography is especially important to the study of world history. Historians use geography to explain connections between the past and the present. They study how places

Behaim's Globe

looked in the past, how places and patterns of human activity have changed over time, and how geographic forces have influenced these changes.

GLOBES AND MAPS

Globes

Photographs from space show the earth in its true form—a great ball spinning around the sun. The only accurate way to draw the earth is as a globe, or a round form. A globe gives a true picture of the earth's size and the shape of the earth's landmasses and bodies of water. Globes also show the true distances and true directions between places.

Maps

A map is a flat drawing of the earth's surface. People use maps to locate places, plot routes, and judge distances. Maps can also display useful information about the world's peoples.

What advantages does a map have over a globe? Unlike a globe, a map allows you to see all areas of the world at the same time. Maps also show much more detail and can be folded and more easily carried.

Maps, however, have their drawbacks. As you can imagine, drawing a round object on a flat surface is very difficult. Cartographers, or mapmakers, have drawn many **projections**, or kinds of maps. Each map projection is a different way of showing the round earth on a flat map. This is because it is impossible to draw a round planet on a flat surface without distorting or misrepresenting some parts of the earth. As a result, each kind of map projection has some distortion. Typical distortions involve distance, direction, shape, and/or area.

GEOGRAPHY HANDBOOK RESOURCES

Reproducible Masters
- Glencoe Social Studies Outline Map Resource Book
- Building Skills in Geography Workbook

Transparencies
- NGS PicturePack Transparencies: Physical Geography of the World

Multimedia
- Student Desk Map
- Zip!Zap!Map! World
- Zip!Zap!Map! USA
- Picture Atlas of the World
- STV: World Geography:
  - Vol. 1: Asia and Australia
  - Vol. 2: Africa and Europe
  - Vol. 3: South America and Antarctica
- STV: North America

The Hemispheres

To determine location, distance, and direction on a map or globe, geographers have developed a network of imaginary lines that crisscross the earth. One of these lines, the **Equator**, circles the earth midway between the **North Pole** and the **South Pole**. It divides the earth into "half spheres," or **hemispheres**. The Northern Hemisphere includes all of the land and water between the Equator and the North Pole. The Southern Hemisphere includes all of the land and water between the Equator and the South Pole.

Another imaginary line running from north to south divides the earth into half spheres in the other direction. This line is called the **Prime Meridian**. Every place east of the Prime Meridian is in the Eastern Hemisphere. Every place west of the Prime Meridian is in the Western Hemisphere.

Latitude and Longitude

The Equator and the Prime Meridian are the starting points for two sets of lines used to find any location. The two sets measure distances north or south of the Equator, and east and west of the Prime Meridian.

One set of lines called **parallels** circle the earth and show **latitude**, which is distance measured in degrees (°) north and south of the Equator at 0° latitude. The letter *N* or *S* following the degree symbol tells you if the location is north or south of the Equator. The North Pole is at 90° North (*N*) latitude, and the South Pole is at 90° South (*S*) latitude.

Two important parallels in between the poles are the **Tropic of Cancer** at 23 1/2°N latitude and the **Tropic of Capricorn** at 23 1/2°S latitude. You can also find the **Arctic Circle** at 66 1/2°N latitude and the **Antarctic Circle** at 66 1/2°S latitude.

The second set of lines called **meridians** run north to south from the North Pole to the South Pole. These lines signify **longitude**, which is distance measured in degrees east (*E*) or west (*W*) of the Prime Meridian at 0° longitude. On the opposite side of the earth is the International Date Line, at about the 180° meridian.

The Grid System

Lines of latitude and longitude cross one another in the form of a **grid system**. You can use the grid system to find where places are exactly located on a map or globe. Each place on Earth has an address on the grid. This grid address is the place's **coordinates**—its degrees of latitude and longitude. For example, the coordinates of the city of San Francisco are 38°N latitude and 122°W longitude. This means that San Francisco lies about 38 degrees (°) north of the Equator and 122 degrees (°) west of the Prime Meridian. Where those two lines cross is called the **absolute location** of the city.

Map Symbols

Maps can direct you down the street, across the country, or around the world. There are as many different kinds of maps as there are uses for them. Being

Hemispheres

NORTHERN HEMISPHERE
North Pole
NORTH AMERICA
Equator
SOUTH AMERICA
South Pole
SOUTHERN HEMISPHERE

WESTERN HEMISPHERE   EASTERN HEMISPHERE
North Pole
NORTH AMERICA
EUROPE
AFRICA
Prime Meridian
SOUTH AMERICA
South Pole
ANTARCTICA

NORTHERN HEMISPHERE
North Pole
AFRICA
ASIA
Equator
AUSTRALIA
ANTARCTICA
South Pole
SOUTHERN HEMISPHERE

EASTERN HEMISPHERE   WESTERN HEMISPHERE
North Pole
ASIA
NORTH AMERICA
180°
PACIFIC OCEAN
AUSTRALIA
ANTARCTICA   South Pole

Geography Handbook **1**

NATIONAL GEOGRAPHIC SOCIETY

CD-ROM

PICTURE ATLAS OF THE WORLD

Have students view the Mapping Our World animation "Where in the World," which introduces the concepts of latitude and longitude.

Skills Practice

Reading a Diagram Have students look at the illustrations on this page. What hemisphere contains most of the landmass of the earth? *(the Northern Hemisphere)* What continents are entirely in the Western Hemisphere? *(North America and South America)* What line divides the earth into the Northern and Southern Hemispheres? *(Equator)* What line divides the earth into the Eastern and Western Hemispheres? *(Prime Meridian)*

Cultural Perspectives

Universal Language The grid system provides a kind of universal language. Citizens of all countries, no matter how different their cultures, speak the same language of latitude and longitude.

COOPERATIVE LEARNING ACTIVITY

Game Have students prepare a game called "My Grid Address." Students should write out grid address question cards, with each card containing one multiple-choice question regarding the grid address of a well-known location—a city, lake, mountain, and so on. A sample question format is "My grid address is 36° north latitude and 140° east longitude. What city am I? a. Madrid b. Tokyo c. New York d. Cairo." After students have completed at least 30-40 cards, organize them into teams and play "My Grid Address." Allow five points for each correct answer. **L1**

Types of Maps Explain that general purpose maps may include both physical and political information. Students should always carefully read the map title and key to determine the purpose of the map. Because of changes that occur in history, political maps should always identify the time period that they represent. If a political map does not identify a date, we usually assume that it is a current map.

Map Study

Have students look at the LANDSAT map and the San Francisco Bay Area map. Both maps are of the same general area.

Map Skills Practice

Reading a Map What is the value of the LANDSAT map? *(Changes to the earth's environment can be tracked by comparing LANDSAT maps over a period of time.)*

Have students each write a paragraph detailing the information about San Francisco that can be learned from the San Francisco Bay Area map. Have students read a detail from their paragraphs that they believe no other student recorded.

able to read a map begins with learning about its parts.

The **map key** explains the symbols used on the map. On a map of the world, for example, dots mark cities and towns. On a road map, various kinds of lines stand for paved roads, dirt roads, and interstate highways. A pine tree symbol may represent a state park, while an airplane is often the symbol for an airport.

An important first step in reading any map is to find the direction marker. A map has a symbol that tells you where the **cardinal directions**—north, south, east, and west—are positioned. Sometimes all of these directions are shown with a **compass rose**.

A measuring line, often called a **scale bar**, helps you find distance on the map. The map's **scale** tells you what distance on the earth is represented by the measurement on the scale bar. For example, 1 inch on a map may represent 100 miles on the earth. Knowing the scale allows you to visualize how large an area is, as well as to measure distances. Map scales are usually given in both miles and kilometers, a metric measurement of distance.

TYPES OF MAPS

Maps of many different kinds are used in this text to help you see the connection between world geography and the history of humanity.

General Purpose Maps

Maps that show a wide range of general information about an area are called **general purpose maps**. Two of the most common general purpose maps are physical maps and political maps. **Physical maps** show natural features, such as rivers and mountains. **Political maps** show places that people have created, such as cities or the boundaries of countries and states.

Special Purpose Maps

Special purpose maps show information on specific topics, such as climate, land use, or vegetation. Human activities, such as exploration routes, territorial expansion, or battle sites, also appear on special purpose maps. Colors and map key symbols are especially important on this type of map.

LANDSAT Maps

LANDSAT maps are made from photographs taken by camera-carrying LANDSAT satellites in space. The cameras record millions of energy waves invisible to the human eye. Computers then change this information into pictures of the earth's surface. With LANDSAT images, scientists can study whole mountain ranges, oceans, and geographic regions. Changes to the earth's environment can also be tracked using the satellite information.

LANDSAT map of
San Francisco Bay area

San Francisco

San Francisco
(38°N, 122°W)

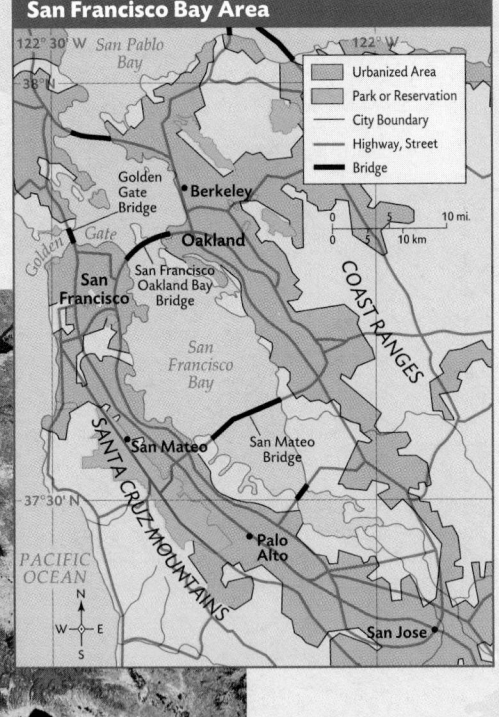

San Francisco Bay Area

122° 30' W — San Pablo Bay
38° N

- Urbanized Area
- Park or Reservation
- City Boundary
- Highway, Street
- Bridge

122° W

Golden Gate Bridge
Berkeley
Golden Gate
Oakland
San Francisco
San Francisco Oakland Bay Bridge
San Francisco Bay
COAST RANGES
SANTA CRUZ MOUNTAINS
San Mateo
San Mateo Bridge
37° 30' N
PACIFIC OCEAN
Palo Alto
San Jose

0 — 5 — 10 mi.
0 — 5 — 10 km

MORE ABOUT...

Cartography British sea captain James Cook was the greatest explorer and cartographer of the eighteenth century. In three voyages, undertaken between 1769 and 1779, Cook surveyed and charted huge areas of the Pacific Ocean. He also verified the existence of the continent of Antarctica and provided a wealth of information about the south Atlantic, south Indian, and Arctic Oceans. Using the latest scientific developments, Cook created incredibly accurate charts of his journeys. These charts revolutionized cartographic knowledge and practices.

CONTINENTS

Geographers divide most of the earth's land surface into seven large landmasses called **continents**. The continents are North America, South America, Europe, Africa, Asia, Australia, and Antarctica. Asia is the largest continent in size, and Australia is the smallest.

LANDFORMS

Landforms cover about 30 percent of the surface of the earth. **Landforms**, or the natural features of the earth's surface, include **mountains**, **hills**, **plateaus**, and **plains**. Geographers describe each landform by its **elevation**, or height above sea level, and by its **relief**, or changes in height.

Mountains

Mountains are the highest of the world's landforms. They rise from about 2,000 feet (610 m) to more than 20,000 feet (6,100 m) above sea level. One of the peaks in the Himalaya mountain ranges of central Asia is Mount Everest, the world's highest mountain. It towers 29,028 feet (8,848 m) above sea level. Other mountains, such as the Appalachians in eastern North America, are not as high. Mountains generally have high relief.

Hills, Plateaus, and Plains

Hills are lower than mountains and generally rise from about 500 to 2,000 feet (152 to 610 m) above sea level. They generally have moderate relief.

Plateaus are raised areas of flat or almost flat land. Most plateaus have low relief and vary in elevation from about 300 to 3,000 feet (91 to 914 m) above sea level. The world's largest plateau area is the Tibetan Plateau in central Asia. It covers about 715,000 square miles (1,852,000 sq. km) and has an average altitude of 16,000 feet (4,877 m) above sea level.

Plains are large areas of flat or gently rolling land that generally rise less than 1,000 feet (305 m) above sea level and have low relief. The world's largest plain is the North European Plain, which stretches for more than 1,000 miles (1,609 km) from the western coast of France to the Ural Mountains in Russia.

BODIES OF WATER

About 70 percent of the earth's surface is covered with water. Geographers identify bodies of water by their shapes and sizes. The major types include oceans, seas, bays, gulfs, lakes, and rivers.

Oceans and Seas

The largest bodies of water in the world are the four saltwater **oceans**—the Pacific, the Atlantic, the Indian, and the Arctic. The Pacific Ocean is the largest ocean, covering about 64 million square miles (165,760,000 sq. km)—more than all the land areas of the earth combined.

Seas are smaller bodies of salt water that are usually in part surrounded by land. The world's largest sea is East Asia's South China Sea, with an area of 1,148,500 square miles (2,975,000 sq. km).

Bays and Gulfs

Still smaller bodies of salt water are gulfs and bays. **Bays** are extensions of a sea usually smaller than a **gulf.** The largest bay in the world measured by shoreline is Hudson Bay, Canada, with a shoreline of 7,623 miles (12,265 km) and an area of 476,000 square miles (1,233,000 sq. km). Measured by area, the Bay of Bengal, in the Indian Ocean and bordering South Asia and part of Southeast Asia, is larger at 839,000 square miles (2,173,000 sq. km).

Lakes and Rivers

Other water features of the earth include lakes and rivers. A **lake** is a body of water completely surrounded by land. The world's largest freshwater lake is Lake Superior, one of the five Great Lakes between the United States and Canada. It has an area of 31,820 square miles (82,414 sq. km). The world's largest inland body of water, however, is the Caspian Sea, often considered a saltwater lake. Lying between Europe and Asia and east of the Caucasus Mountains, the Caspian Sea has a total area of 143,550 square miles (371,795 sq. km).

A **river** is a waterway flowing through land and emptying into another body of water. The world's longest river is the Nile River in Africa, which flows into the Mediterranean Sea from the highlands of East Africa. The Nile's length is about 4,160 miles (6,690 km).

Geography Handbook **3**

CURRICULUM CONNECTION

SCIENCE

It tastes really salty, but ocean water averages only about 3.5 percent salt. Of this, nearly 3 percent is sodium chloride (regular salt). The rest contains almost every chemical element on earth.

Landforms Mountains have fascinated people throughout history. They have provided refuge and asylum for those in danger; they have served as a buffer between warring states; they have challenged people for the sheer thrill of climbing them. How many mountain ranges or peaks can you name? Allow students a few minutes to list on the chalkboard several of the world's best known mountains. What historic event can you associate with any of the mountains on our list? *(Accept all legitimate answers such as Hannibal crossing the Alps, American settlers crossing the Rocky Mountains, the Inca building a refuge at Machu Picchu.)*

Cultural Perspectives

Terminology To promote communication, geographers the world over use the same terminology. The terms they use come from many different languages. For example, *tsunami* is a Japanese word meaning "overflowing wave," and *fjord* is a Norwegian word meaning "long, narrow bay."

TEACHER NOTES

_____
_____
_____
_____
_____

GEOGRAPHY HANDBOOK

you don't say...

The word *longitude* comes from the Latin word for "length," and *latitude* comes from the Latin word "breadth."

Who? What? Where? When?

There is a point on Earth with **"no" latitude and "no" longitude**. The absolute location where the Prime Meridian and the Equator intersect, off the African coast in the Atlantic Ocean, is 0° N-S, 0° E-W.

CURRICULUM CONNECTION

COMPUTER LITERACY

Computers have revolutionized cartography. They reduce distortions and calculate changes at incredible speeds. They gather, process, and store data about contour reliefs, ethnicities, economics, waterways, and much more. They even produce animated "flow maps," such as those that show storm movement.

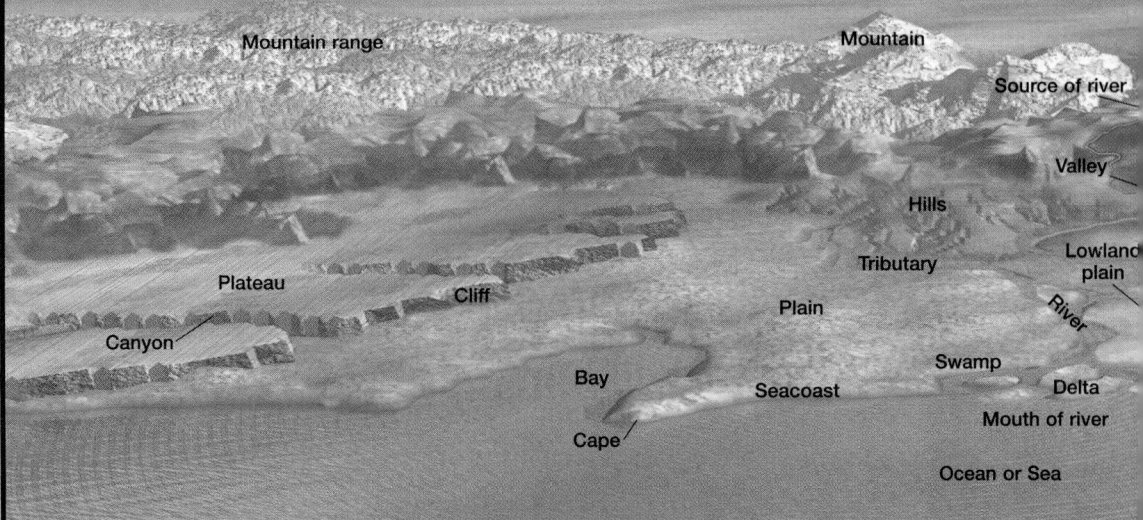

Mountain range — Mountain — Source of river — Valley — Hills — Lowland plain — Tributary — Plateau — Cliff — Plain — River — Canyon — Swamp — Delta — Bay — Seacoast — Mouth of river — Cape — Ocean or Sea

GEOGRAPHIC DICTIONARY

As you read about the world's geography and history, you will discover most of the terms listed and explained below. Many of the terms are pictured in the diagram above. Others you learned earlier in this Geography Handbook.

absolute location–exact location of a place on the earth described by global coordinates

basin–area of land drained by a given river and its branches; area of land surrounded by lands of higher elevations

bay–part of a large body of water that extends into a shoreline

canyon–deep and narrow valley with steep walls

cape–point of land surrounded by a body of water

channel–deep, narrow body of water that connects two larger bodies of water; deep part of a river or other waterway

cliff–steep, high wall of rock, earth, or ice

continent–one of the seven large landmasses on the earth

cultural feature–characteristic that humans have created in a place, such as language, religion, and history

delta–land built up from soil carried downstream by a river and deposited at its mouth

divide–stretch of high land that separates river basins

downstream–direction in which a river or stream flows from its source to its mouth

elevation–height of land above sea level

Equator–imaginary line that runs around the earth halfway between the North and South Poles; used as the starting point to measure degrees of north and south latitude

glacier–large, thick body of slowly moving ice, found in mountains and polar regions

globe–sphere-shaped model of the earth

gulf–part of a large body of water that extends into a shoreline, larger than a bay

harbor–a sheltered place along a shoreline where ships can anchor safely

highland–elevated land area with sloping sides such as a hill, mountain, or plateau, smaller than a mountain

island–land area, smaller than a continent, completely surrounded by water

isthmus–narrow stretch of land connecting two larger land areas

lake–a sizable inland body of water

latitude–distance north or south of the Equator, measured in degrees

longitude–distance east or west of the Prime Meridian, measured in degrees

lowland–land, usually level, at a low elevation

map–drawing of all or part of the earth shown on a flat surface

meridian–one of many lines on the global grid

MORE ABOUT...

Geographers work for the federal government in the Defense Mapping Agency, United States Geologic Survey, Central Intelligence Agency, Army Corps of Engineers, National Science Foundation, Smithsonian Institution, and Office of the Geographer in the Department of State.

State environmental and transportation agencies hire geographers as analysts, planners, and cartographers. In the private sector, geographers work as professors, researchers, and cartographers for high-tech computer mapmakers. Businesses as varied as fast-food chains and ski resorts consult geographers about optimal locations for new restaurants and effects of pollution on the slopes.

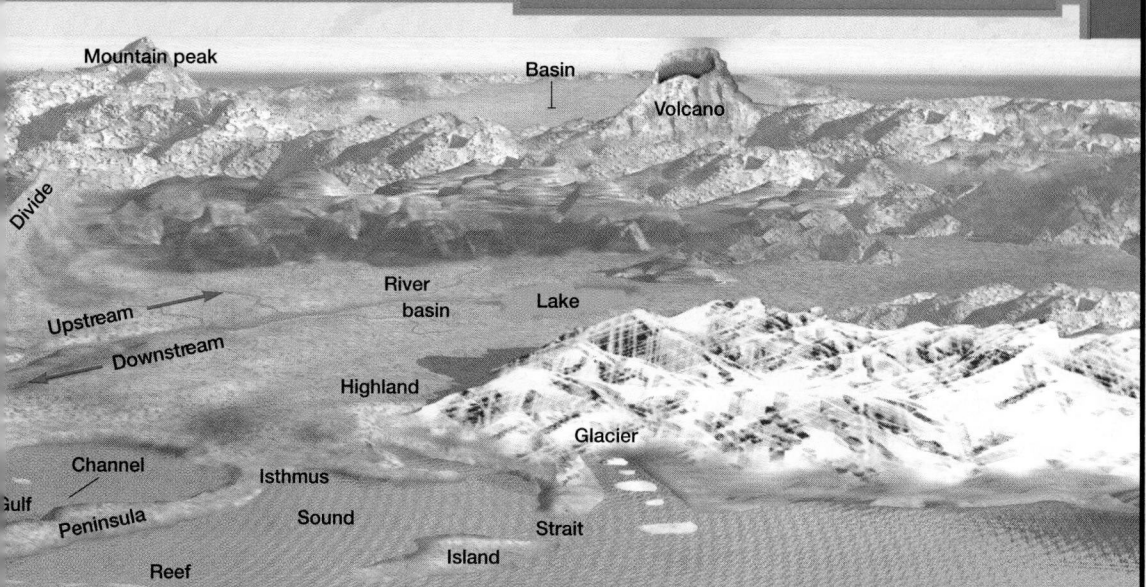

Mountain peak
Basin
Volcano
Divide
River basin
Lake
Upstream
Downstream
Highland
Glacier
Channel
Isthmus
Gulf
Peninsula
Sound
Strait
Reef
Island

Who?What?Where?When?

Flemish mathematician, geographer, and cartographer **Gerardus Mercator** created his well-known projection in 1568. This projection exaggerates areas as they increase in distance from the Equator, and has been favored by sailors for more than 400 years.

running from the North Pole to the South Pole, used to measure degrees of longitude

mesa–area of raised land with steep sides; smaller than a plateau

mountain–land with steep sides that rises sharply from surrounding land; larger and more rugged than a hill

mountain peak–pointed top of a mountain

mountain range–a series of connected mountains

mouth–(of a river) place where a stream or river flows into a larger body of water

ocean–one of the four major bodies of salt water that surrounds a continent

ocean current–stream of either cold or warm water that moves in a definite direction through an ocean

parallel–one of many lines on the global grid that circle the earth north or south of the Equator; used to measure degrees of latitude

peninsula–body of land almost surrounded by water

physical feature–characteristic of a place occurring naturally, such as a landform, body of water, climate pattern, or resource

plain–area of level land, usually at a low elevation

plateau–area of flat or rolling land at a high elevation

Prime Meridian–line of the global grid running from the North Pole to the South Pole at Greenwich, England; used as the starting point for measuring degrees of east and west longitude

relative location–position of a place on the earth in relation to other places

relief–changes in elevation, either few or many, that occur over a given area of land

river–large stream of water that runs through the land

sea–large body of water completely or partly surrounded by land

seacoast–land lying next to a sea or ocean

sea level–average level of an ocean's surface

sound–body of water between a shoreline and one or more islands off the coast

source–(of a river) place where a river or stream begins, often in high lands

strait–narrow stretch of water joining two larger bodies of water

tributary–small river or stream that flows into a large river or stream; a branch of the river

upstream–direction opposite the flow of a river; toward the source of a river or stream

valley–area of low land between hills or mountains

volcano–mountain created as liquid rock or ash are thrown up from inside the earth

 ### CURRICULUM CONNECTION

CIVICS

Geographic knowledge and perspectives help people be responsible citizens, especially when making decisions that affect their community, region, country, and world.

Who?What?Where?When?

One of the most violent **volcanic eruptions** in history occurred in 1883 on the island of Krakatau in Indonesia. The volcano collapsed from a height of 2,640 feet (692 meters) to 1,000 feet (300 meters) below sea level. Its collapse triggered a tidal wave that killed 36,000 people in nearby Java and Sumatra.

MORE ABOUT...

Geographic Information Systems (GIS) is a computer hardware and software system that can store, display, analyze, and map information. Geographers, urban planners, engineers, and utility companies use these systems. GIS are vital to planning because they enable us to combine data and look at layers of information at the same time. One GIS, for example, may begin with a digitized base map. A retailer wishing to make an informed decision about where to build a store may combine data such as population distribution, traffic movement, land availability, and real estate prices. Using the GIS, the retailer can see and analyze all this information at the same time.

Linking Past and Present

Climate The early Greeks established a classification of climate based only on what they knew of differences between where they lived and lands to the north and south of Greece. They called their own climate *temperate* because it posed few problems of shelter and clothing. They believed that the area south of the Mediterranean became increasingly hotter, so they called these lands *torrid*. Stories told by travelers from the north and the cold winter winds that came from that direction led the Greeks to call that area *frigid*.

Map Study

Map Skills Practice

Reading a Map What are four classifications that may be used to describe climate today? *(tropical, mid-latitude, high latitude, and dry)* What projection is this map? *(Robinson)*

Who?What?**Where?**When?

Climatologists agree that the **United States** has the most varied climate on Earth. With its tornadoes, hurricanes, thunderstorms, and blizzards, the climate of the United States also is one of the most violent and unpredictable.

CLIMATE

Climate is the usual pattern of weather events that occurs in an area over a long period of time. Climate is determined by distance from the Equator, by location near large bodies of water, and sometimes by positions near mountain ranges

The world's climates can be organized into four major regions: **tropical**, **mid-latitude**, **high latitude**, and **dry**. Some of these regions are determined by their latitude; others are based on the vegetation that grows in them.

Tropical Climates

Tropical climates get their name from the tropics, the areas along the Equator. Temperatures in the tropics change little from season to season. The warm tropical climate region can be separated into two types: tropical rain forest and tropical savanna.

The tropical rain forest climate region is wet in most months, with up to 100 inches (254 cm) of rain a year. In these areas, rain and heat produce lush vegetation and **rain forests**, dense forests that are home to millions of kinds of plant and animal life. The Amazon River basin in South America is the world's largest rain forest area.

The tropical **savanna** climate has two seasons—one wet and one dry. Savannas, or grasslands with few trees, occur in this region. Among the leading tropical savanna climate areas are southern India and eastern Africa.

Mid-Latitude Climates

Mid-latitude, or moderate, climates are found in the middle latitudes of the Northern and Southern Hemispheres. Most of the world's people live in this climate region. The mid-latitude region has a greater variety of climates than other regions. This variety results from the mix of air masses—warm air coming from the tropics and cool air coming from the polar regions. In most places, temperatures change with the seasons.

High Latitude Climates

High latitude, or polar, climate regions lie in the high latitudes of each hemisphere. Climates are cold everywhere in the high latitude regions, some more severe than others.

High latitude climate regions also include highland or mountainous regions even in lower

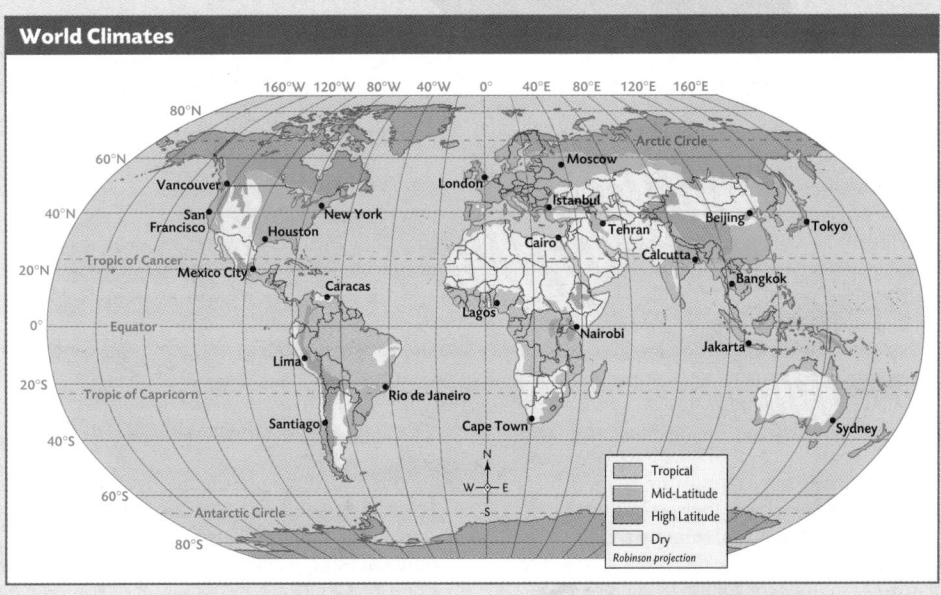

World Climates

COOPERATIVE LEARNING ACTIVITY

Survival Strategy Organize students into four or more groups. Assign each group a climate type. Encourage group members to imagine that they will be stranded for one year in a remote area that has their assigned climate type. Have groups plan a survival strategy to live in that climate. Each group should identify at least the following: (1) the type of shelter they need and will be able to make or obtain; (2) the type of clothing they need and will be able to make; and (3) the way they will obtain food and water. Have each group present their survival plan to the class, and have the class challenge each plan with situations or conditions likely to arise in the climate region.

L2

World Land Use and Resources

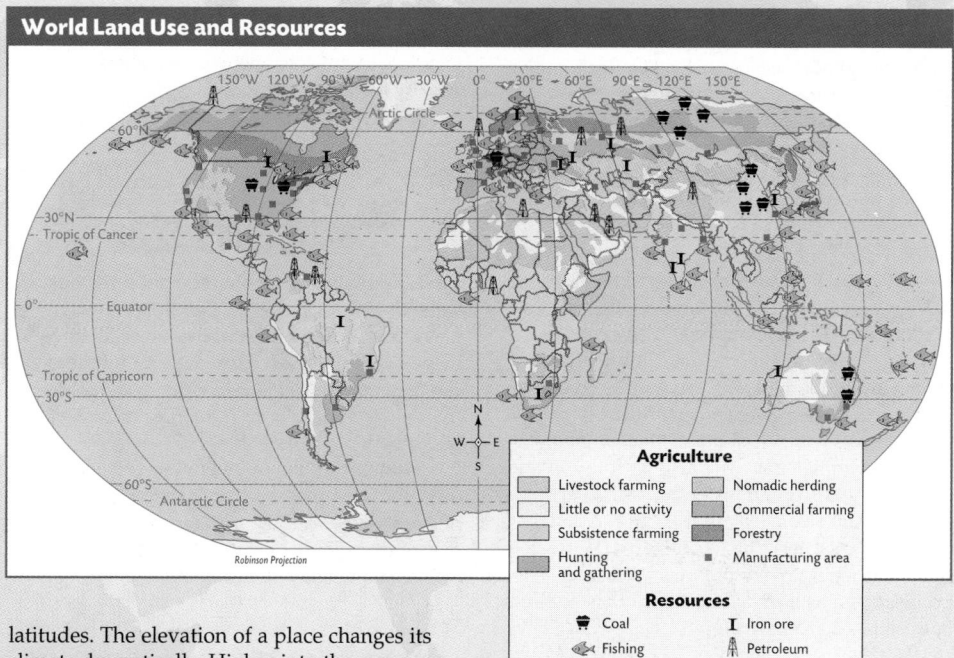

Agriculture

Livestock farming	Nomadic herding
Little or no activity	Commercial farming
Subsistence farming	Forestry
Hunting and gathering	■ Manufacturing area

Resources

🜨 Coal	I Iron ore
🐟 Fishing	⚒ Petroleum

Robinson Projection

latitudes. The elevation of a place changes its climate dramatically. Higher into the mountains, the air becomes thinner. It cannot hold the heat from the sun, so the temperature drops. Even in the tropics, snow covers the peaks of high mountains.

Dry Climates

Dry climate refers to dry or partially dry areas that receive little or no rainfall. Temperatures can be extremely hot during the day and cold at night. Dry climates can also have severely cold winters.

Nearly an eighth of the world's land surface is dry, with a rainfall of less than 10 inches (25 cm) per year. The Sahara in North Africa is the largest desert in the world. The area covered by the Sahara—3,579,000 square miles (9,270,000 sq. km)—is about the size of the United States.

NATURAL RESOURCES

Natural resources refer to anything from the natural environment that people use to meet their needs. Natural resources include fertile soil, clean water, minerals, trees, and energy sources. Human skills and labor are also valuable natural resources.

Renewable Resources

Some natural resources can be replaced as they are used up. These renewable resources can be replaced naturally or grown fairly quickly. Forests, grasslands, plant and animal life, and rich soil all can be renewable resources if people manage them carefully. A lumber company concerned about future growth can replant as many trees as it cuts. Fishing and whaling fleets can limit the number of fish and whales they catch in certain parts of the ocean.

Nonrenewable Resources

Metals and other minerals found in the earth's crust are nonrenewable resources. They cannot be replaced because they were formed over millions of years by geologic forces within the earth.

One important group of nonrenewable resources is fossil fuels—coals, oil, and natural gas. Industries and people depend on these fuels for energy and as raw materials for plastics and other goods. We also use up large amounts of other metals and minerals, such as iron, aluminum, and phosphates. Some of these can be reused, but they cannot be replaced.

Geography Handbook   7

Geography Handbook

Environmental Challenges Efforts to preserve a healthy environment date back hundreds of years. In A.D. 1253 the English Parliament placed bans on burning coal. The increasing use of fossil fuels, expanding populations, and the use of chemicals, however, present new challenges. Discuss the challenges presented on this page. Ask students to talk about how they view the future. Will people be able to preserve a healthy environment?

Who? What? Where? When?

Europe has few areas that have not been affected by human interaction. In recent years Europeans have taken steps to control pollution, despite the high costs. In some areas progress is slow. The estimated cost of cleaning up air pollution in eastern Europe ranges from $200 to $500 billion.

Geography's Impact on World History

Use the examples given for each unit as a launch pad for a general overview of world history.

Unit 1 Explain that most early civilizations developed near water. The Egyptians used the Nile, and many civilizations developed around the Mediterranean and near rivers in China. What are the essential needs that rivers and seas provided to early peoples? *(water for daily use, irrigation, transportation, fishing)*

Waves of Aryans from Europe swept into the Indus River valley around 1500 B.C. From there they spread into northern India. Why were river valleys good routes for early peoples to move from one location to another? *(Before roads,*

ENVIRONMENTAL CHALLENGES

When people use natural resources to make a living, they affect the environment. The unmanaged use of resources is a threat to the environment. Many human activities can cause pollution—putting impure or poisonous substances into the land, water, and air.

Land and Water

Only about 11 percent of the earth's surface has land good enough for farming. Chemicals that farmers use may improve their crops, but some also may damage the land. Pesticides, or chemicals that kill insects, can pollute rivers and groundwater, or water that fills tiny cracks in the rock layers below the earth's surface.

Other human activities also pollute soil and water. Oil spills from tanker ships threaten ocean coastal areas. Illegal dumping of dangerous waste products causes problems. Untreated sewage reaching rivers pollutes lakes and groundwater as well. Salt water can also pollute both soil and groundwater.

Air

Industries and vehicles that burn fossil fuels are the main sources of air pollution. Throughout the world, fumes from cars and other vehicles pollute the air. The chemicals in air pollution can seriously damage people's health.

These chemicals combined with precipitation may fall as acid rain, or rain carrying large amounts of sulfuric acid. Acid rain eats away the surfaces of buildings, kills fish, and can destroy entire forests.

Energy

All of the world nations need safe, dependable sources of energy. Fossil fuels are most often used to generate electricity, heat buildings, run machinery, and power vehicles. Fossil fuels, however, are nonrenewable resources. In addition, they contribute to air pollution. So today

---

many countries are trying to discover new ways of using renewable energy sources. Two of these ways are hydroelectric power, the energy generated by falling water, and solar energy, or energy produced by the heat of the sun.

GEOGRAPHY'S IMPACT ON WORLD HISTORY

Geographic factors have shaped the outcome of historical events. Landforms, waterways, climate, and natural resources all have helped or hindered human activities. In many cases, people have learned either to adapt to their environment or to transform it to meet their needs.

Throughout the units of your text, you will discover how geography has shaped the course of events in world history. Here are some examples of the role that geographic factors have played in the story of humanity.

Unit 1 The World Before Modern Times

Rivers contributed to the rise of many of the world's early civilizations. By 3000 B.C. the Sumerians of the Middle East had set up 12 prosperous city-states in the Tigris-Euphrates River valley. The Fertile Crescent, as the area is often called because of its relatively rich topsoil and its curved shape, was able to support city-state populations ranging from 20,000 to 250,000 people.

Landforms and waterways also affected the political relationships of the world's ancient peoples. For example, the rugged landscape of Greece divided the ancient Greeks into separate city-states instead of uniting them into a single nation. Furthermore, closeness to the sea caused the Greek city-states to expand their trade, culture, and sense of civic pride to other parts of the Mediterranean world.

From about A.D. 400 to A.D. 1500, regional civilizations developed at the crossroads of trade between different areas of the world. The city of Makkah (Mecca), in the Middle East's Arabian Peninsula, was a crossroads for caravans from North Africa, Palestine, and the Persian Gulf. The religion of Islam established a firm base in Makkah, from which it spread to other areas of the Middle East, North Africa, South Asia, and Southeast Asia.

---

rivers and the lowlands near rivers were the easiest routes to travel.)

Large oceans helped to separate people into regional civilizations. The Atlantic, the Indian, and the Pacific Oceans kept civilizations in the Americas, Asia, and Africa from much contact with each other. What people were most isolated from the rest of the world until the A.D. 1500s? *(the people in the Americas; some contact took place between Asia and Africa, Europe and Asia, and Europe and Africa in this period.)*

Unit 2 The modern world emerged largely as a result of cultural exchange among people who had once been separated

Unit 2 Emergence of the Modern World

The desire to control or to obtain scarce natural resources has encouraged trade and stimulated contact among the world's peoples. At the dawn of the modern era, Asians and Europeans came into contact with one another partly because Europeans wanted Asia's spices and silks.

When the Asiatic people known as the Mongols could no longer guarantee safe passage for traders on overland routes, Europeans were forced to consider new water routes to Asia. This opened a new global age that brought the peoples of Europe, Asia, Africa, and the Americas into closer contact with each other.

Unit 3 Age of Revolution

Climate often affects the way a country behaves toward its neighbors. For example, many of Russia's harbors stay frozen during much of the year. In the past, Russia has often gone to war with other countries to capture land for warm water ports.

Climate was also one reason why the Russians were able to stop the invasions of French ruler Napoleon Bonaparte in 1812 and the German dictator Adolf Hitler in 1941. The Russians were used to the bitter cold and snow of their country's winter, whereas the invaders were not.

Unit 4 Industry and Nationalism

Exploiting natural resources, such as coal and iron, was an important factor in the growth of the Industrial Revolution. During this time, power-driven machinery in factories replaced work done in homes. Modern industry started in Great Britain, which had large amounts of coal and iron ore for making steel. Throughout Europe and North America, the rise of factories that turned raw materials into finished goods prompted people eager for employment to move from rural areas to urban centers.

Also, the availability of land and the discovery of minerals in the Americas, Australia, and South Africa caused hundreds of thousands of Europeans to move to these areas in hope of improving their lives. These mass migrations were possible because of improvements in industrial technology and transportation that enabled people to overcome geographic barriers.

Unit 5 World in Conflict

Environmental disasters during the first part of the 1900s affected national economies in various parts of the world. For example, during the 1930s, winds blew away so much of the soil in the Great Plains of central North America that the area became known as the Dust Bowl. Ruined by the drought, many farmers packed up their belongings and headed west. It took many years of normal rainfall and improved farming techniques to transform the Great Plains from a Dust Bowl into productive land once again.

Unit 6 The Contemporary World

The world's peoples have become more aware of the growing scarcity of nonrenewable resources. Oil takes millions of years to form, and the earth's supply is limited. Industrialized countries like the United States consume far more oil than they produce and must import large amounts. Many experts believe that the world's fossil fuels will be used up if steps are not taken to limit their consumption and to find alternative sources of energy.

> ## Geography and History Journal
>
> *You are about to journey to the past to learn about the people and events that have shaped the world you live in today. Throughout your course of study, keep a record of the events discussed above and any other events in world history that have been affected by geography. When you come to the last unit, you may also want to explore how geography impacts current events or issues: For example, how has geography influenced peacekeeping missions in Bosnia and other parts of the world, or what would happen to Canada geographically if the province of Quebec were to separate and form an independent nation? On a world map locate the places where these historical events have occurred, and identify the units of study in your text in which they are discussed.*

the seemingly inexhaustible resources of the North American continent affect people's attitude toward these resources? *(Resources were exploited without much concern for their replacement or for the environment.)*

Unit 5 World War I grew out of national rivalries and the effects of imperialism. Imperialism was, in part, a quest for resources. What is a better way than conquest for a nation to obtain resources? *(Trade has been an effective means for Japan and many other nations.)*

Unit 6 As the world's population grows and more nations develop industrially, the demand for resources will increase. How can the world ensure adequate resources and avoid conflict over them? *(Science can research the use of alternative fuels; recycling can extend the use of resources; nations should consider the long-term costs and negative effects of war and explore the benefits of cooperation.)*

Using Your Geography and History Journal

An interesting and purposeful *Geography and History Journal* may be formatted using two columns in a notebook. For each chapter the student could list one or more events that were affected by specific geography listed in the first column. In the second column, the student could write a sentence explaining how geography helped shape history.

from each other. In what ways are cultural contacts increasing today? *(increased trade, travel, and telecommunications)*

Unit 3 Ideals of the American Revolution and the French Revolution affected people in other lands. Within a few years revolution spread through Latin America. Why did ideals of these revolutions spread so quickly? *(People had overcome the barriers that had separated civilizations—oceans and communications.)*

Unit 4 Available land and abundant natural resources helped to attract millions of people to the United States. How did

To help illustrate the link between history and geography, geographers have identified five themes that can be used to examine the role that geography plays.

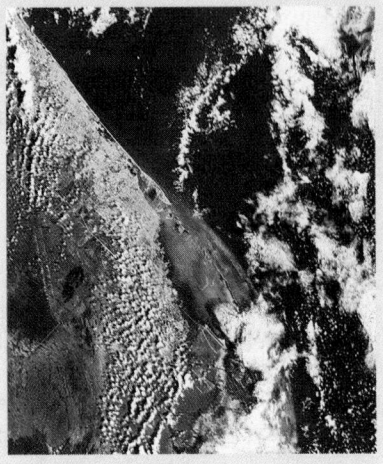

Modern mapmaking uses photography as a tool. A LANDSAT satellite provided data for this image of Miami, Florida.

1 **Location** serves as a starting point by asking, "Where is it?" To be more specific, there are two types of location. **Absolute location** refers to the exact location on the earth's surface as measured by latitude (lines north and south of the Equator) and longitude (lines east and west of the Prime Meridian). Every location on the earth can be found in this way.

Relative location is less precise. It helps you orient yourself to a location that is relative to something else. Relative location has been important historically as people decided where to build their cities and establish their civilizations.

This village in Tunisia, North Africa, is at the northern edge of the Sahara. Stone and mud brick buildings give the village and its surroundings a sense of place.

2 The idea of **Place** includes more than just where something is located. It includes those features and characteristics that give an area its own identity or personality. These can be *physical* characteristics—such as landforms, weather, plants, and animals—or *human* characteristics—language, religion, architecture, music, politics, and way of life.

3 **Human/Environment Interaction** focuses on how people respond to and alter their environment. To live comfortably or even to survive in many parts of the world, people must make changes in the environment or adapt to conditions they cannot change, or both.

How people choose to change their environment depends on their attitude toward the natural setting and on the technology they have available to change it.

Fishing is a major industry in Denmark, a small European nation nearly surrounded by water.

4 The **Movement** of people and things between places means that events in other places can have an impact on you personally. Transportation routes, communication systems, and trade connections link people and places throughout the world. Products, ideas, and information are sent around the globe, either slowly by ship or almost instantaneously by electronics.

The movement of people is particularly important because they can spread ideas and cultural characteristics from one place to another. Sometimes those ideas or characteristics are accepted in the new location, and the culture is changed by that linkage.

On the southern coast of China is Hong Kong, one of Asia's busiest ports.

Street signs and buildings in a historical area of Montreal reveal the French character of the Canadian province of Quebec.

5 A **Region** is an area that is unified by some feature or a mixture of features. It is used to generalize about parts of the earth's surface in either physical or human terms. A neighborhood is an example of a small region, while a cultural region that shares a common language would be a larger region. Other regions could be economic, where a particular economic activity is dominant, or political, where the same type of political system is followed.

Geography's Impact on History

While studying the history of the world, you will be learning about the people and events that have shaped the past and provide the framework for the future. As you read *World History: The Human Experience*, pay special attention to the ways in which geography has influenced history and fashioned the world in which you live.

Themes IN WORLD HISTORY

Relation to Environment
The ancient Egyptians develop a civilization in northeastern Africa's Nile River Valley.

Bust of infant sun god

Uniformity
Early Chinese dynasties establish and maintain a strong central government in East Asia.

Terra-cotta warriors—Qin dynasty

Change
Early modern Europe enjoys a cultural awakening based on ancient Greek and Roman ideas as well as on Christianity and Judaism.

Renaissance musicians

The Gas Factory

Cultural Diffusion
The Industrial Revolution begins in Great Britain and gradually spreads to other parts of the world.

Innovation
New technology transforms many aspects of life in the modern world.

Space shuttle lift-off

*W*orld history is a record of the adventures of humankind—both the famous and the ordinary—throughout thousands of years. By studying world history—by gazing across time—you can understand the past and recognize its contribution to the present and the future. World history tells of significant people and events. It also encompasses broad historical themes that happen again and again, providing meaning for events in the past and showing how they affect contemporary life.

World History: The Human Experience introduces 9 key historical themes. Each chapter highlights and develops several of these themes that demonstrate the interconnectedness of ideas and events. These events help organize your study of world history and make connections across time.

Cooperation/Conflict focuses on how people relate to each other throughout history—sometimes in cooperation, working together to accomplish a common goal, at other times in conflict, struggling against one another.

Revolution/Reaction deals with revolution, or the sudden overthrow of long-established ideas and organizations, contrasted with reaction, or the efforts to oppose new ideas and preserve traditional ways.

Change includes political, social, religious, cultural, and economic transformations that influence human activities throughout the centuries.

Diversity/Uniformity focuses on the diversity or variety of world peoples and customs, contrasted with the desire for uniformity or commonality in some societies.

Regionalism/Nationalism deals with a sense of loyalty and belonging, expressed in ties to a region, to a nation, or to the world as a whole—to the global community.

Innovation includes cultural, scientific, and technical breakthroughs that increase knowledge and impact the way people live and think.

Cultural Diffusion focuses on the spread of cultural expressions through a variety of means across nations, regions, and the world.

Movement involves the movement of people throughout history, including patterns of migration, exploration, and colonization as well as imperialism—people in one place on the globe exercising control over people in another place.

Relation to Environment emphasizes human-environment interchange—how people are affected by their environment and, in turn, how they affect that same environment.

Horn player, Benin

The World Before Modern Times

0:00 OUT OF TIME?

If time does not permit teaching each chapter in Unit 1, you may use the Unit Digest beginning on page 171, in conjunction with the Unit Digest Transparencies and Chapter Digest Audiocassettes with activities and tests.

Introducing the Unit

Unit 1 traces how ancient and medieval civilizations developed in Africa, the Middle East, Asia, and America. It then highlights each regional civilization's achievements, contacts, and influences on one another.

Unit Objectives

After reading Unit 1, students will be able to:

1. explain why the development of agriculture led to the growth of cities.
2. describe the society, government, religion, and culture found in each regional civilization.
3. trace interactions among regional civilizations through the spread of trade, ideas, and beliefs.
4. discuss the continuing development of regional civilizations separate from one another.

History *and the* Humanities

📖 Focus on World Art Prints
   6–9, 11–15, 17
🖌 World History and Art
   Transparencies 1, 3–19

Then & Now Scholars sometimes divide history into "pre-modern" and "modern" periods. "Pre-modern" refers to the time before the A.D. 1500s, when civilizations began to develop and advance in different parts of the world. Some of these civilizations were cut off from other regions, but trade and migrations gradually brought many of them into contact with each other. As ideas and products spread across continents, regional civilizations created prosperous centers of trade and produced highly developed social structures and governments. Some contact between civilizations caused conflict that lasted for decades or centuries. The positive contributions of these encounters, however, influenced the development of the "modern" period–the era of dynamic global changes that began during the A.D. 1500s and continues to the present.

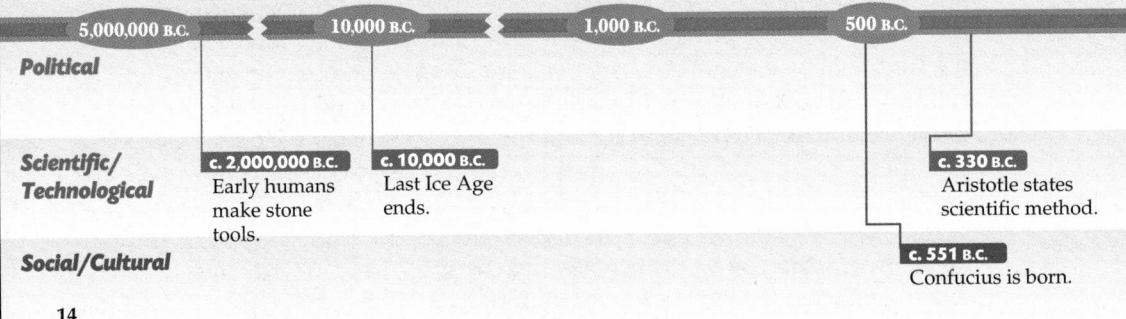

A Global Chronology

	5,000,000 B.C.	10,000 B.C.	1,000 B.C.	500 B.C.
Political				
Scientific/ Technological	**c. 2,000,000 B.C.** Early humans make stone tools.	**c. 10,000 B.C.** Last Ice Age ends.		**c. 330 B.C.** Aristotle states scientific method.
Social/Cultural				**c. 551 B.C.** Confucius is born.

14

Then & Now **Classical Legacy** The influence of ancient civilizations, particularly the classical civilizations of Greece and Rome, is visible in many aspects of modern American society. Examples include the use of Latin mottoes such as *E pluribus unum* inscribed on our currency; the neoclassical architecture of many public buildings, especially in Washington, D.C., and in state capitals; and even our form of government, which adopted the concepts of the senate and veto from the Roman Republic.

Have students brainstorm a list of things today that reflect the influence of ancient civilizations, prompting them from the examples above as necessary. Ask students why they think classical civilizations, especially Rome, have influenced the United States. Why was neoclassical

Mayan clay figurine of a man and a woman wrapped in a blanket, c. A.D. 700–1000. Campeche, Mexico

ABCNEWS INTERACTIVE™

VIDEODISC
Turning Points in World History

Side One,
Chapter 3

Title: *The Rise of Cities*
Subject: The inventions of the Sumerians in Mesopotamia enabled people to live together in communities for the first time.
Ask: What practice did the Sumerians create when they attempted to keep records of trading transactions? *(They created writing with symbols, which led to the creation of the alphabet.)*

History & Art
The Maya produced remarkably detailed sculptures and relief carvings using only stone tools.

Portfolio Project

Americans today share the benefits of foods, inventions, discoveries, and ideas from other people and places on the planet. Often we do not think about the civilizations past or present that contributed these things. Create a map on which you show some products or ideas that originated in each of the following areas: Africa, the Middle East, Asia, Europe, or the Americas.

Portfolio Project

You may wish to have students work in groups to create their maps. Have them skim the chapters of this unit to find products, inventions, and ideas from different regions.

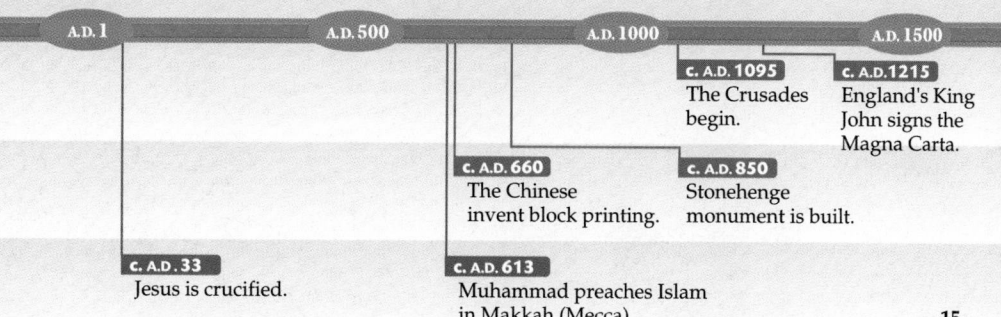

A.D. 1	A.D. 500	A.D. 1000	A.D. 1500

c. A.D. 1095
The Crusades begin.

c. A.D. 1215
England's King John signs the Magna Carta.

c. A.D. 660
The Chinese invent block printing.

c. A.D. 850
Stonehenge monument is built.

c. A.D. 33
Jesus is crucified.

c. A.D. 613
Muhammad preaches Islam in Makkah (Mecca).

15

architecture a popular style for public buildings? *(reflects power and solemnity, recalls the golden age of the Roman Republic)* Why was Latin often used for inscriptions and mottoes? *(Latin was the language of the learned for many centuries.)* Why do certain features of the federal and state governments stem from Roman institutions? *(Classical republican ideas influenced the Founders of the United States.)*

TEACH

Introduction

This feature focuses on a revolutionary breakthrough in human history—the invention of agriculture. Before they learned to farm, our ancestors spent nearly all their time hunting and gathering food. Because farming is much more efficient than hunting, it created food surpluses that allowed people to live in larger, permanent communities and to dedicate themselves to activities besides mere survival.

Who?What?Where?When?

Women and Agriculture
Many archaeologists believe that women invented the practice of agriculture. In hunter-gatherer societies, women collected fruit, nuts, and seeds. As they did so, women probably noticed that plants sprouted where seeds fell. Women probably invented the hoes they used to tend early farms. Only after the invention of the plow did men take over the job of raising crops.

Background Notes

Linking Past and Present

Farmers As farming methods have improved, fewer people are needed to produce the food we eat. In the nineteenth century, most Americans lived and worked on farms. Today less than 10 percent of Americans are farmers. In developing countries, farming is still the primary occupation of most people. In China, India, and Nigeria, for example, more than half the people are farmers.

Farming and Civilization

*B*etween 8,000 and 10,000 years ago, a quiet revolution took place. In scattered pockets of the Middle East, Asia, Africa, and the Americas, people learned to cultivate food-producing plants for the first time. As knowledge of farming gradually spread, it dramatically changed human culture. Farming encouraged the growth of permanent communities, which in turn became the seedbeds for the world's first civilizations.

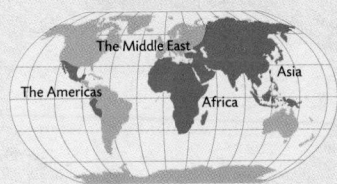

The Middle East
Breadbasket of the Ancient World

Greek grain storage jar

Today only sparse vegetation covers the foothills of Iran's Zagros Mountains. Erosion and overgrazing by sheep and goats have taken their toll. Around 8000 B.C., however, wild wheat known as emmer covered the hills. Experts believe it was here that the world's first farmers may have watched seeds fall to earth and sprout. This observation led these ancient wanderers to plant seeds.

Over time, knowledge of farming spread in a broad arc of fertile land that curved from the Persian Gulf to the Mediterranean Sea. Farmers gradually added other foods to their diets—barley, chickpeas, lentils, figs, apricots, pistachios, walnuts, and more. A hunger for these foods kept people in one place. Hunting and gathering lifestyles changed as people began to develop new ideas and skills. Slowly—very slowly—farming settlements grew into cities. Known by names such as Ur, Babylon, and Jericho, these cities were the centers of Earth's oldest civilizations.

Foothills of the Zagros Mountains

16

COOPERATIVE LEARNING ACTIVITY

Research Organize the class into groups of four or five students. Have each group select an agricultural product, such as corn, wheat, rice, soybeans, apples, bananas, or potatoes. Using encyclopedias and other reference works, as well as outline maps of the world, each group should identify the regions of the world that produce the product they selected. After students have completed the unit, lead a discussion about the importance of agriculture in the development of civilization. Have students discuss which farm products are most important today in their region, and then rank the products they investigated. **L1**

The Americas
Mexico and Peru: Farming and Diversity

For much of world history, distance separated the Americas from the rest of the world. But the independent invention of farming in the areas of present-day Mexico and Peru created cities as sophisticated as those in other regions. The crops that spurred their growth, however, differed from crops elsewhere. Few of the wild grains found on other continents grew in the Americas. The first farmers in the Americas used the seeds of other plants, especially squash and beans. They also developed two high-yield foods unknown to the rest of the world—potatoes and maize (corn). When distant civilizations made contact, ideas about agriculture accompanied the wide distribution of foods that early peoples had developed and cultivated.

Corn Dance by Frank Reed Whiteside

Asia and Africa
Expansion of Earth's Gardens

The farming revolution did not happen just once. It occurred several times in widely separated regions. More than 6,000 years ago, farmers along the upper Huang He in present-day northern China started planting millet. About 5,000 years ago, farmers near the mouth of the Chang Jiang in southern China learned to grow rice. At roughly the same time, farmers along the Nile River in the northern part of Africa harvested their first crops of wheat and barley.

Like the gardens of the Middle East, the gardens of China and northern Africa grew more diverse. By 3000 B.C., farmers cultivated soybeans, bananas, and sugarcane. Supported by the harvests, people had more time to think and dream. Soon they created things that were used by the civilizations of the Middle East—calendars, systems of writing, forms of art, and government.

Wood relief of farming activities, Yoruba peoples

LINKING THE IDEAS

1. How do experts think farming probably began?
2. Why is farming considered one of the most important inventions of human history?

Critical Thinking

3. **Cause and Effect** What is the connection between farming and the rise of ancient civilizations?

Geography

Place Ask students to look at the small map on page 16. Ask them to locate the early American civilizations that developed farming. *(Modern-day Mexico and Peru)* Have them identify other continents and regions where early societies learned to farm. *(Middle East, China, Africa)* What crops were grown in each region? *(Americas: squash, beans, corn, potatoes; Middle East: wild wheat, barley, chickpeas, lentils; China: rice; Africa: wheat, barley, soybeans, bananas, sugarcane)* Then have students use larger, specialized world maps, such as relief and rainfall maps, to describe conditions in these areas that may have contributed to the development of agriculture.

*C*ultural *D*iffusion

The Columbian Exchange After 1492 Europe and the Americas exchanged plants, animals, and microbes. The potato, a tuber of the Americas, became a staple food in Ireland and other parts of Europe. The potato, like corn, yields far more food per acre than does wheat. The growth of Europe's population after A.D. 1500 is partly due to the introduction of nutritious, hardy crops of the Americas—such as the potato, corn, and manioc (also called cassava or tapioca).

ANSWERS TO LINKING THE IDEAS

1. In the Middle East, people watched seeds sprout, then tried planting seeds themselves.
2. Farming produced food surpluses that allowed larger, permanent communities to develop, which became the world's first civilizations.
3. Early civilizations grew in areas that had pioneered farming and were well suited to agriculture because increasing numbers of people were freed to devote their time and energy to other pursuits.

A complete, 1-page lesson plan is provided for each section in the *Reproducible Lesson Plans* booklet.

The Rise of Civilizations

CHAPTER RESOURCES

	Reproducible Resources	Multimedia Resources
Chapter Opener	Chapter Themes: Graphic Organizer 1 Historical Significance Chapter Activity 1	MindJogger Videoquiz
Chapter Enrichment	Vocabulary Activity 1* Time Line Activity 1 Mapping History Activity 1 History Simulation 1 Geography and History Activity 1 Source Reading 1 Enrichment Activity 1 Critical Thinking Activity 1 Skill Reinforcement Activity 1 Building Skills in Geography Workbook, Unit 1, Lessons 3, 4, 5 Performance Assessment Activity 1	Ancient Civilizations Poster Set: *Ancient Egypt* World History and Art Transparencies 1, 2, 4 NGS PicturePack Transparency Sets: *Ancient Egypt, The Fertile Crescent, Ancient China, Ancient India* Vocabulary PuzzleMaker Software NGS PictureShow CD-ROMs: *Egypt and the Fertile Crescent, India and China, Middle and South America* Turning Points in World History: *The Rise of Cities, The Code of Hammurabi*
Chapter Review/Reteaching	Reteaching Activity 1 Skill Reinforcement Activity 1 Spanish Chapter Summary 1	Chapter 1 Digest Audiocassette, Activity, Test* Vocabulary PuzzleMaker Software Student Self-Test and Review Software MindJogger Videoquiz
Chapter Evaluation/Testing	Performance Assessment Activity 1 Chapter 1 Test, Forms A and B	Testmaker

* Also available in Spanish

0:00 OUT OF TIME? Assign the Chapter 1 summary in the Unit 1 Digest on pages 171–173, and the Chapter 1 Audiocassettes.

Block Schedule

Block scheduling differs from traditional class scheduling in the amount of time allotted to each period. The extended time frame provided by block scheduling affords you the opportunity to implement a greater number of research-oriented and activity-intense projects to motivate and involve your students. Activities that are particularly suited to use within the block scheduling framework are identified throughout this chapter by the following designation.

KEY TO ABILITY LEVELS

Teaching strategies have been coded for varying learning styles and abilities.

L1 BASIC activities for all students
L2 AVERAGE activities for average to above-average students
L3 CHALLENGING activities for above-average students
LEP LIMITED ENGLISH PROFICIENCY activities

Use Glencoe's *Presentation Plus!* multimedia teacher tool to easily present dynamic lessons that visually excite your students. Using Microsoft PowerPoint® you can customize the presentations to create your own personalized lessons.

SECTION RESOURCES

Daily Objectives	Reproducible Resources	Multimedia Resources
Section 1 **Human Beginnings** Specify the kinds of economic, political, and social changes that resulted from the rise of cities.	Reproducible Lesson Plan 1-1 Guided Reading Activity 1-1* Time Line Activity 1 Section Quiz 1-1*	Section Focus Transparency 1-1 World History and Art Transparency 1, *Woman's Head* Vocabulary PuzzleMaker Software Student Self-Test and Review Software Testmaker Turning Points in World History: *The Rise of Cities*
Section 2 **Civilizations in Africa and the Middle East** Explain how trading peoples influenced the development of Africa and the Middle East.	Reproducible Lesson Plan 1-2 Vocabulary Activity 1* Guided Reading Activity 1-2* History Simulation 1 Section Quiz 1-2*	Ancient Egypt Section Focus Transparency 1-2 Ancient Egypt; The Fertile Crescent World History and Art Transparency 2, *Tutankhamen's Throne;* Transparency 4, *Standard of Ur: Peace* Student Self-Test and Review Software Testmaker Turning Points in World History: *The Code of Hammurabi* Egypt and the Fertile Crescent
Section 3 **Civilizations in Asia and the Americas** Describe how Asians and Native Americans made use of their environments.	Reproducible Lesson Plan 1-3 Guided Reading Activity 1-3* Reteaching Activity 1 Enrichment Activity 1 Section Quiz 1-3* Performance Assessment Activity 1 Spanish Chapter Summary 1	Section Focus Transparency 1-3 Ancient India; Ancient China Vocabulary PuzzleMaker Software Student Self-Test and Review Software Testmaker India and China; Middle and South America

* Also available in Spanish

Chapter Activities

✔ Performance Assessment Activity

Planning a Documentary Have students take the roles of producers who must plan a documentary on early people. Have pairs of students prepare proposals for three thirty-minute segments, including where and when filming will take place, who will narrate, what types of people will be interviewed, what information will be presented, and the manner in which it will be presented (interview, graph, photo, and so on). Students may present proposals either in written or oral form, and should keep in mind that their audience will be potential financial backers for the project.

Possible Rubric Features
Content information, concept attainment, decision-making skills, quality and clarity of product

• *For an additional activity, refer to Activity 1 in the* Performance Assessment Strategies and Activities *booklet.*

ACTIVITY

From the Classroom of...

Nancy Sue Romerdahl, EdD.
Everett High School
Everett, WA

An Archaeological "Dig"
Materials: Pen and paper, and a woman's purse, with most contents (except personal items) remaining.
Procedure: Ask students to brainstorm how people and particularly history book authors come to "know" what they know.

Explain that this simulation is designed to show how historians and archaeologists use artifacts to make observations and then inferences from those observations. The "dig" is a woman's purse. Have the class list and describe items in the purse. Next, see how many inferences students can make about the purse and its owner. For example, if the purse contains contact lens solution, they might infer that the owner wears contacts; however, she might also be holding the solution for a relative. The class would discuss which is the stronger possibility. Then, if there is also an optometrist appointment card with her name on it this, added to the lens solution "find," becomes stronger evidence that she wears contacts.

After all the items are cataloged, and all reasonable inferences listed, have students write a probable description of the woman.

Following this activity, help students understand how archaeologists generate knowledge about people who left no written record.

MULTIPLE LEARNING STYLES

Verbal/Linguistic
Have students read outside sources about the origin and development of writing. Ask one or more students to report orally on the information obtained.

Auditory/Musical
Have students identify and bring to class one or more musical selections that they think would provide suitable background music for a visit to a cave in which prehistoric paintings have been found.

Kinesthetic
Have students mime the movements of a Neanderthal hunter or gatherer or both. Ask students to explain how they decided what movements would be appropriate.

Interpersonal
Have students form a panel to discuss this question: *As a small group of cave dwellers who have just begun to grow a few crops for food, how shall we divide up the work necessary to keep us alive?*

Additional Resources

NATIONAL GEOGRAPHIC SOCIETY

Teacher's Corner

INDEX TO NATIONAL GEOGRAPHIC MAGAZINE

The following articles may be used for research relating to this chapter:

- "The Most Ancient Americans," by Rick Gore, October 1997.
- "The Dawn of Humans," by Rick Gore, September 1997.
- "New Light on the Olmec," by George E. Stuart, November 1993.
- "Iraq, Crucible of Civilization," by Merle Severy, May 1991.
- "Kingdom of Kush," by Timothy Kendall, November 1990.

NATIONAL GEOGRAPHIC SOCIETY PRODUCTS AVAILABLE FROM GLENCOE

To order the following products for use with this chapter, contact your local Glencoe sales representative, or call Glencoe at 1-800-368-7344:

- *Egypt and the Fertile Crescent, India and China, Middle and South America (CD-ROMs)*
- *Ancient Egypt, The Fertile Crescent, Ancient India, Ancient China, Middle America (Transparencies)*
- *Ancient Egypt, The Fertile Crescent (Poster Sets)*

ADDITIONAL NATIONAL GEOGRAPHIC SOCIETY PRODUCTS

To order the following products for use with this chapter, call National Geographic Society at 1-800-368-2728:

- *Mysteries of Mankind (Video)*
- *PictureShow: Ancient Civilizations Library (CD-ROMs)*

BIBLIOGRAPHY

Literature About the Period
Auel, Jean M. *The Clan of the Cave Bear.* New York: Bantam, 1984 (paperback). A Cro-Magnon girl is adopted by a Neanderthal tribe.

Readings for the Student
Temple, Robert. *The Genius of China: 3,000 Years of Science, Discovery, and Invention.* New York: Simon and Schuster, 1989. Includes such inventions as the wheelbarrow, the stirrup, and the umbrella.

Readings for the Teacher
Coe, Michael, Dean Snow and Elizabeth Benson. *Atlas of Ancient America.* New York: Facts on File, 1986. The history of ancient America presented in maps, text, and pictures.

LOCAL OBJECTIVES

_____
_____
_____
_____
_____
_____
_____
_____
_____
_____
_____
_____
_____
_____
_____
_____
_____
_____
_____
_____
_____
_____
_____

interNET CONNECTION

Anthropology resources on the World Wide Web
AnthroLink:
http://www.buckley.pvt.k12.ca.us/AnthroLink/

Chapter Themes are listed by section on this chapter opening page of the Student Edition. A corresponding theme-based activity is available under "TEACH," and a theme-based question is asked in the Section and Chapter Reviews.

The Storyteller

Historical Setting Although Khufu was responsible for the largest monument ever built, surprisingly little is known about him, except for the length of his reign. He ruled for 23 years, around 2500 B.C. Much can be said about the extraordinary dimensions of his pyramid, however. It was originally 481 feet (147 meters) high. At its base, which covers about 13 acres (5.3 hectares), it is almost perfectly square, 755 feet (230 meters) to a side. The more than 2 million blocks of limestone in the pyramid average more than 2.5 short tons (2.3 metric tons) each. Most of them came from nearby quarries.

Historical Significance

Answers: *Early civilizations developed with the rise of cities. The cities grew because advances in agriculture—including irrigation—allowed specialization of labor, which in turn led to advances in technology.*

Early civilizations developed the basic elements of government, law, religion, economy, and social organization upon which our own global civilization rests.

5,000,000–500 B.C.

The Rise of Civilizations

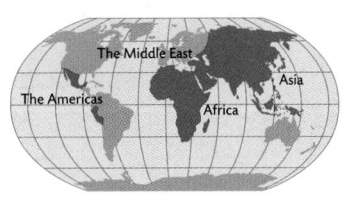

The Middle East
Asia
The Americas
Africa

Chapter Themes

▶ **Change** The earliest civilizations begin when farming settlements evolve into the first cities. *Section 1*
▶ **Cultural Diffusion** Armies, merchants, and religious thinkers spread new ideas and practices throughout Africa and the Middle East. *Section 2*
▶ **Relation to Environment** Peoples in Asia and the Americas adapt to a variety of environments. *Section 3*

The Storyteller

Under the blazing sun, a gigantic stone structure began to take shape on the desert sands of Egypt in northeastern Africa. A hundred thousand men toiled together, building a burial pyramid for Khufu, a king of Egypt about 2500 B.C. Gangs of laborers dragged huge blocks of limestone up winding ramps of dirt and brick to pile layer upon layer of stone. Farmers during the rest of the year, these laborers were compelled to work for the three or four months during which the annual flooding of the Nile River made farming impossible. It would take 20 years of their forced labor and more than 2 million blocks of stone before the Egyptians completed the massive pyramid. Today, the 5,000-year old Great Pyramid stands as a breathtaking reminder of the glories of one of the great civilizations that arose during the world's early history.

Historical Significance

What developments led to the rise of the world's first civilizations? How did these early civilizations lay the foundations for the global civilization that we know today?

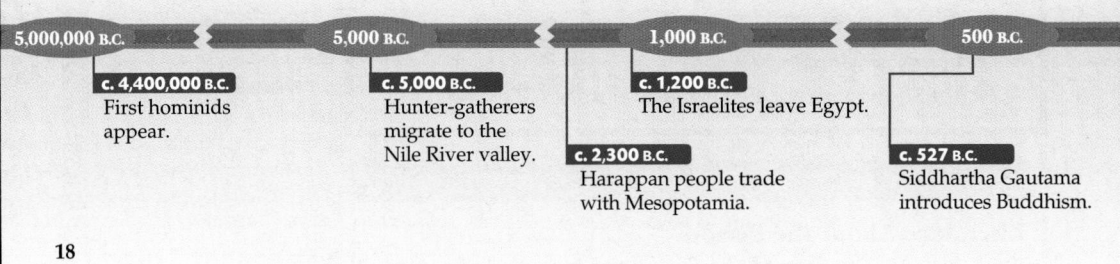

5,000,000 B.C.		5,000 B.C.	1,000 B.C.	500 B.C.

c. 4,400,000 B.C. First hominids appear.

c. 5,000 B.C. Hunter-gatherers migrate to the Nile River valley.

c. 1,200 B.C. The Israelites leave Egypt.

c. 2,300 B.C. Harappan people trade with Mesopotamia.

c. 527 B.C. Siddhartha Gautama introduces Buddhism.

18

Location Have students brainstorm a list of conditions that would have made it as easy as possible for early people to survive. *(Answers may include: warm climate all year long, plentiful water supply, abundant vegetation and wildlife.)* Next, have students use the Atlas of their text to locate areas of the world where these conditions exist. *(Answers may include: parts of South America, Africa, and South Asia.)* Finally, have students locate Ethiopia, northern Tanzania, and Kenya, where the remains of early people were actually found.

History & Art Fowling scene from a tomb at Thebes along the Nile River, Egypt.

History & Art Scenes depicting the sport of fowling are common in Egyptian tomb paintings. Here, a noble prepares to hurl a throwing stick at a flock of geese. Notice one woman holding the man's leg. What do you think this pose was intended to illustrate? *(personal attachment to the man; more than just a fowling scene, this is also a family scene)*

✔ **Performance Assessment**

Refer to the activity on page 18C of the Planning Guide.

📁 For an additional activity, refer to Activity 1 in the *Performance Assessment Strategies and Activities* booklet.

Your History Journal

Using a recent edition of an almanac, make a chart of the world's major religions, including the number of people who today are adherents of each religion.

Using Your History Journal

Students' charts should include the four religions with the greatest number of adherents worldwide. They are:
Christianity (1,955,229,000),
Islam (1,126,325,000),
Hinduism (793,075,000), and
Buddhism (325,275,000).

Chapter 1 *Rise of Civilizations* **19**

GLENCOE TECHNOLOGY

💿 **VIDEODISC**
Use MindJogger to preview chapter content.

MindJogger Videoquiz

‖‖‖‖‖‖‖‖‖ Chapter 1
Disc 1 Side A

 Also available in VHS.

✚ EXTRA CREDIT PROJECT

Essay Ask students why it is important to have an understanding of past events and their significance. Write on the chalkboard the following quotation from Cicero, a Roman statesman and orator: "To be ignorant of what happened before you were born is to be ever a child."

Have students write an essay in which they explain the meaning of Cicero's words. In the paper, have them explore the meaning and importance of history, discussing its relevance in today's world.

5,000,000 B.C.   200,000 B.C.   20,000 B.C.   A.D. 1

c. 4,400,000 B.C.
Earliest known human
ancestor lives in East Africa.

c. 200,000 B.C.
Homo sapiens
appear.

c. 8,000 B.C.
Agriculture begins.

SECTION THEME

▶ **Change** The earliest civilizations begin with the evolution of farming settlements into the first cities.

Find Out

Answer: *The earliest humans developed improved tools and discovered how to work metal. They domesticated both plants and animals. They began to live and work together in larger groups.*

FOCUS

Section Objective

Specify the kinds of economic, political, and social changes that resulted from the rise of cities.

BELLRINGER
Motivational Activity

Before taking roll at the beginning of the class period, project Section Focus Transparency 1-1 and have students answer the activity questions. Discuss students' responses.

This activity is also available as a blackline master.

Vocabulary Pre-check

Use the Vocabulary Puzzle-Maker to create a puzzle that reinforces the vocabulary terms in this section. **L1**

Section 1

Human Beginnings

Setting the Scene

▶ **Terms to Define**
prehistory, hominid, culture, technology, civilization, cultural diffusion

▶ **People to Meet**
the Neanderthals, the Cro-Magnons

▶ **Places to Locate**
East Africa, Jericho, Çatal Hüyük, Nile, Tigris, Euphrates, Indus, and Huang Rivers

Find Out What were the achievements of the earliest humans?

The Storyteller

The first sign of animal domestication we have discovered, at some of the earliest human settlements, is not of something that pulled a plow, or was eaten; it is evidence of the dog. This creature, which willingly chooses a human as the leader of its life-long pack, was humankind's first friend, it seems, as well as its best. Certain species began to thrive under human care; and humans rearranged their lives to care for the animals that now came to depend on them.

—adapted from *Women's Work: The First 20,000 Years*, Elizabeth Wayland Barber, 1994

Paleolithic scraper

---

istory tells the story of humankind. Because historians mostly use written records to gather information about the past, history is said to begin with the invention of writing about 5,500 years ago. But the story of humankind really begins in the time *before* people developed writing—the period called prehistory.

Using the best available evidence, scientists have traced the existence of the first humanlike creatures back to about 4.4 million years ago in **East Africa**. Human beings and the humanlike creatures that preceded them together belong to a group of beings named hominids (HAH•muh•nuhds).

According to one of the generally accepted theories, the first prehuman hominids stood about 3.5 to 5.0 feet (1.1 to 1.6 m) tall and walked on two legs. Known as *Australopithecus* (aw•STRAY•loh•PIH•thuh•kuhs), or "southern ape," they had small brains, flat noses, and large teeth. *Australopithecus* were most likely nomads–moving constantly in search of food. They may have used grass stems, twigs, sticks, or bones to dig roots.

Human Origins

Scientists use the Latin word *Homo*, which means "human," to name these hominids and all later human beings as well. Anthropologists today are still not certain whether a direct relationship connected *Australopithecus* and human beings or exactly when hominids became truly human. Scientists divided *Homo*–the genus of humans–into three species that differ somewhat in body structures and arose at different times in prehistory. The earliest of the three was *Homo habilis*, or "person with ability," who lived until about 1.5 million years ago. After *Homo habilis* lived the second type of early human–*Homo erectus*, or "person who walks upright"–who was, in turn, followed

---

SECTION RESOURCES

Reproducible Masters
- Reproducible Lesson Plan 1-1
- Guided Reading Activity 1-1
- Time Line Activity 1
- Section Quiz 1-1

Transparencies
- Section Focus Transparency 1-1
- World History and Art Transparency 1, *Woman's Head*

Multimedia
- Vocabulary PuzzleMaker Software
- Student Self-Test and Review Software
- Testmaker
- Turning Points in World History

between 100,000 and 200,000 years ago by *Homo sapiens*, or "person who thinks." All people living today belong to the species *Homo sapiens*.

The Ice Ages

Climactic changes played an important part in the development of early humankind. Between 2 million and 10,000 years ago, Earth experienced long periods of cold climate, known as the Ice Ages. During the Ice Ages, massive glaciers spread out from the Poles, scarring the landforms over which they crept. As the sheets of ice formed, the level of the oceans dropped more than 300 feet (90 m). As a result, some areas now separated by water were connected then by land bridges. Only the middle areas of the earth remained warm enough to support human and animal life.

Early human beings responded to the environmental changes of the Ice Ages in several ways. Some migrated to warmer places. Others developed ways to keep warm, such as clothing and fire. Those who could not adapt died from starvation or exposure.

Human Culture

In coping with their environment, prehistoric people developed the first types of human culture, or the way of life of a group of people. Culture includes the knowledge a people have, the language they speak, the ways in which they eat and dress, their religious beliefs, and their achievements in art and music.

One of the earliest aspects of culture that people developed was the use of tools. At first prehistoric people made crude tools of stone, which enabled them to skin small animals and cut pieces of meat. Improving their technology—the skills and useful knowledge available to them for collecting material and making the objects necessary for survival—early people later created specialized tools, such as food choppers, skin scrapers, and spear points.

The use of stone tools by early people led historians to apply the name Stone Age to the period before writing became established. Scholars divided the Stone Age into three shorter periods, depending on differences in toolmaking techniques. The earliest period, the Paleolithic (PAY•lee•uh•LIH•thihk), or Old Stone Age, began about 2.5 million years ago with the first toolmaking by *Homo habilis* and lasted until about 12,000 B.C. The Mesolithic (MEH•zuh•LIH•thihk) period, or Middle Stone Age, is usually dated from 12,000 B.C. to about 8000 B.C. The Neolithic (NEE•uh•LIH•thihk) period, or New Stone Age, lasted from about 8000 B.C. to 5000 B.C.

Mary Leakey, a noted paleoanthropologist, follows a trail of hominid footprints fossilized in volcanic ash. *What are hominids?*

Hunter-Gatherers

From their investigations of Paleolithic remains, scientists have gathered more information about *Homo erectus* than about earlier hominids. *Homo erectus* first appeared in Africa and lived from about 1.8 million to about 30,000 years ago. Their living areas covered a variety of environments from woodlands and grasslands in Africa to forests and plains in Europe and Asia.

Homo erectus at first were mostly food gatherers. Scientists believe the females gathered fruits, nuts, and seeds, while males searched for meat. Later the males hunted small animals with spears and clubs.

Migrations

Scientists disagree on when prehistoric people left Africa and moved to other parts of the world. They do know, however, that *Homo erectus* migrated from their native Africa to Asia and Europe. Skeletal remains found in Southeast Asia have led scientists to conclude that *Homo erectus* reached that region about 1.6 to 1.8 million years ago. *Homo erectus* was clearly well established in China by 460,000 years ago, and the earliest skeletal traces in Europe may also date back around 400,000 years.

Chapter 1 *Rise of Civilizations* **21**

TEACH

Guided Practice

THEME Change

Have students list some of the changes that evolved in early civilizations. Discuss the results of these changes. (*Irrigation made food surpluses possible; metalworking provided tools and weapons; ships promoted long-distance trading.*) L1

Visualizing History

Burial in volcanic ash is just one of a number of ways in which fossils are formed. Other conditions that led to the formation of fossils include quick burial in moist sediment, freezing (in cold areas), and engulfment in asphalt pits.

Answer to Caption: *All human beings as well as the humanlike creatures that preceded them are part of this group.*

Linking Past and Present

Global warming is a topic of concern today. Some scientists predict gradual increases in world temperatures. Unlike the natural forming and melting of glaciers in prehistory, global warming stems from human activities, such as burning fossil fuels. The result is heat trapped in the atmosphere.

COOPERATIVE LEARNING ACTIVITY

Bulletin Board Organize the class into three groups to prepare a bulletin board display showing the development of hominids from *Australopithecus* to *Homo habilis* to *Homo erectus*. Each group's contributions should include an illustration from a reliable source such as the *World Book Encyclopedia*, *Scientific American*, or *National Geographic*. Displays should also include an indication of the dates of the hominid category and a brief paragraph describing each type. Have students describe individual contributions and cite their sources before posting the bulletin board display. L1

Religion Have students discuss why the evidence of food, tools, and weapons at burial sites suggests to scientists a prehistoric belief in the afterlife. *(Answers might include the point that, since the articles would no longer be useful in the person's life, they must have been meant for an afterlife.)* **L2**

Critical Thinking Have students discuss how people's attitudes toward their environment might have changed as they began to raise crops and domesticate animals. *(One conclusion that students might draw is that hunter-gatherers live in nature, but farmers set out to control nature.)* **L3**

 World History and Art Transparency 1, *Woman's Head*

 **POINT**

The Neolithic Revolution
How did the Neolithic Revolution change the way people lived?
The practice of farming and the domestication of animals enabled people to have a steady food supply and to settle in villages as they no longer had to travel to hunt and gather food.

Language

By 50,000 B.C., *Homo erectus* may have been talking to each other instead of just making sounds to indicate emotions and directions. Language was one of humanity's greatest achievements. It enabled individuals to work with one another, to exchange ideas, and to pass beliefs and practices on to their offspring.

Appearance of *Homo Sapiens*

Evidence of early *Homo sapiens*, the modern human species, dates back about 200,000 years. When *Homo sapiens* appeared, cultural changes took place with greater frequency and sophistication.

The Neanderthals

The first *Homo sapiens* were probably **the Neanderthals** (nee•AN•duhr•TAWLZ), named after Germany's Neander Valley, where their remains were first discovered in the A.D. 1850s. Fossil evidence indicates that Neanderthal people originated in Africa and began spreading into Europe and Asia about 100,000 years ago.

Neanderthals stood about 5.5 feet (1.7 meters) tall and had stocky bodies. Like their predecessors, Neanderthals were nomadic hunter-gatherers who traveled in small groups. Their tool-making ability, however, was more sophisticated than that of *Homo erectus*. The Neanderthals were also more advanced culturally. They cared for their sick and aged, and they may have been the first to practice medicine.

Homo Sapiens Sapiens

Most scientists believe that modern humans, or *Homo sapiens sapiens*, originated in Africa about 50,000 years ago. Within 20,000 years, this new group had migrated to almost every continent in the world, including Australia, North America, and South America. Many scientists believe that as

 **Footnotes to History**

The First Razors
Archaeologists have unearthed evidence that prehistoric men were shaving as early as 18,000 B.C. Some Cro-Magnon cave paintings portray beardless men, and early Cro-Magnon grave sites contain sharpened shells that were the first razors. Later, people hammered razors out of bronze, and eventually, out of iron.

Homo sapiens sapiens appeared in various places, they may have come into contact with Neanderthals and even *Homo erectus*. With the extinction of the Neanderthals and *Homo erectus*, *Homo sapiens sapiens* became the only hominids left on Earth.

The Cro-Magnons

The earliest *Homo sapiens sapiens* in Europe are called **Cro-Magnons**, after the rock shelter in France where their remains were first found in the A.D. 1860s. Since then, Cro-Magnon remains have been found in other parts of the world.

Taller but less robust than the Neanderthals, Cro-Magnons made further advances in tool-making. With the invention of the stone ax, Cro-Magnons could chop down trees and shape them into canoes. Their development of the spear-thrower and the bow and arrow enabled them to hunt several animals at once and larger animals, too, such as wooly mammoths and bison.

As better hunting methods developed, groups of Cro-Magnons established permanent settlements and developed a more sophisticated culture. They created cave paintings like those found at Lascaux (la•SKOH) and Vallon-Pont-d'Arc (vah•YOHN•pohn•DAHRK), both in France, as well as those at numerous other cave sites in Spain and Africa. These hunting scenes may have been drawn to teach young hunters how to recognize prey or to pass on spiritual powers that would help the hunters.

 **POINT**

The Neolithic Revolution

During the Neolithic period and immediately after, humanity made one of its greatest cultural advances. New environments had developed with the end of the last Ice Age, and forests and grasslands appeared in many areas. Over some 5,000 years, people shifted from gathering and hunting food to producing food. This development, called the Neolithic Revolution, led to tremendous changes in the way people worked and lived.

The Neolithic Revolution took place slowly and began at different times in different parts of the world. Archaeologists have found evidence of agriculture in the Middle East dating as far back as 8000 B.C. In contrast, China and the Americas did not have agriculture until between 5000 B.C. and 4000 B.C.

Learning Style: Logical/Mathematical 4.4 million years—the approximate age of *Australopithecus*—may be hard for students to comprehend. Have them think of a grandmother-mother-daughter relationship. Three generations = 100 years. Add the word *great* to each previous generation—great-grandmother, great-great-grandmother, and so on. Have students calculate how many times *great* would have to be added to the word *grandmother* to name the ancestor that lived 1,000 years ago. *(27; the word* great *is not added for the first three generations)* Then have them figure how many times *great* would be used for a woman who lived 4.4 million years ago. *(132,000 less 3)* **L3**

The crops raised by Neolithic people varied from place to place, depending on the varieties of wild plants and on the crops best adapted to the region's climate. Early farmers used the sickle to cut grains, and domesticated, or tamed for human purposes, animals such as cattle, pigs, and sheep. Neolithic people also produced sun-hardened clay pottery for carrying and storing food and water.

Farming in many ways made life easier. It brought a steady food supply and enabled people to stay longer in one place. Farmers, however, had to work harder and longer than earlier hunters and gatherers.

The First Villages

Now that food could be produced, many more people survived. Scientists estimate that by 4000 B.C. the world population had risen to 90 million. Once they had agriculture, people could also settle permanently in communities instead of wandering as nomads. Soon agricultural villages of about 200 inhabitants began to develop where soil was fertile and water abundant. Archaeologists date one of the earliest such villages–**Jericho**, in the modern Israeli-occupied West Bank–back to 8000 B.C. Another village, **Çatal Hüyük** (CHAH•tuhl hoo•YOOK), in present-day Turkey, dates from 7000 B.C. to 6300 B.C.

Technological Advances

Neolithic farmers eventually made their work easier and more productive by inventing the plow and by training oxen to pull it. They also learned how to fertilize their fields with ashes, fish, and manure.

The relatively steady food supply quickened the pace of technological advance. Neolithic villagers invented the loom and began weaving textiles of linen and wool. They invented the wheel and used it for transportation. They found a way to make clay bricks for construction. They also

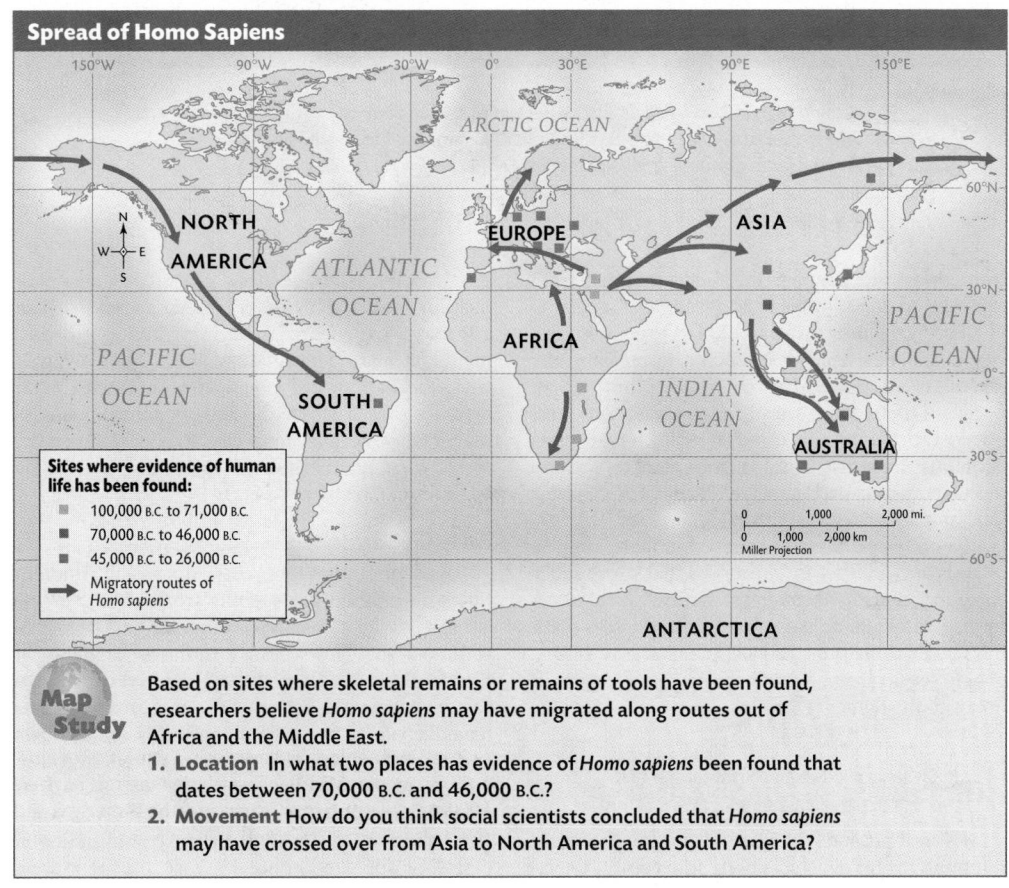

Spread of Homo Sapiens

Sites where evidence of human life has been found:
- 100,000 B.C. to 71,000 B.C.
- 70,000 B.C. to 46,000 B.C.
- 45,000 B.C. to 26,000 B.C.
- → Migratory routes of Homo sapiens

Map Study

Based on sites where skeletal remains or remains of tools have been found, researchers believe *Homo sapiens* may have migrated along routes out of Africa and the Middle East.

1. **Location** In what two places has evidence of *Homo sapiens* been found that dates between 70,000 B.C. and 46,000 B.C.?
2. **Movement** How do you think social scientists concluded that *Homo sapiens* may have crossed over from Asia to North America and South America?

Independent Practice

 Guided Reading Activity 1-1 **L1**

Time Line Activity 1

Environment Have students draw pictures of and report on some of the giant mammals that became extinct as the Ice Age ended. These could include the mammoth, giant beaver, and giant sloth. **L1 LEP**

Art Have students research and report on the cave paintings of French, Spanish, or African sites such as Vallon-Pont-d'Arc in France or the Altamira Cave in Spain. They might include illustrations in the report. **L2**

Map Study

Answers
1. *Asia and Australia*
2. *The two continents are so close at the Bering Strait that it is reasonable to assume they were once joined by a land bridge.*

MAKING CONNECTIONS ACTIVITY

Environment For many years people thought the remains of a vast river system lay hidden under the Sahara. When scientists studied the radar scan of the Sahara by the space shuttle *Columbia* in 1981, they saw a network of waterways, floodplains, and broad river valleys throughout southern Egypt and northern Sudan. Prompted by these images, in 1982 an Egyptian-American team excavated along the banks of an ancient river. They found tools and other artifacts believed to have been used by *Homo erectus* who lived and hunted in the fertile Sahara 200,000 years ago. Have students research to find other areas in which the climate has changed markedly in the past 200,000 years. **L2**

Visualizing History Behind high baked-brick walls the people of the ancient city of Mohenjo-Daro, near the Indus River in Pakistan, used four-wheeled carts to carry grain to a large granary. *What was the value of surplus food to the development of a civilization?*

Visualizing History Mohenjo-Daro was a great urban center that flourished from about 2500 B.C. to about 1500 B.C. A city with a perimeter of 3 miles (5 km), its streets were laid out in rectangular patterns. Houses, many of them two stories high, lined the streets. Drainage systems led into these brick-lined streets. The city had hilltop fortresses for protection and baths, probably for sacred rites.

Answer to Caption: *The economy depended on it; with surplus food fewer people had to farm and more could perform other types of work.*

Daily Life Have students use the information in the text as a guide to building a model of a Neolithic village such as the one discovered at Çatal Hüyük. **L2 LEP**

ASSESS

Check for Understanding

Assign Section 1 Review as homework or as an in-class activity.

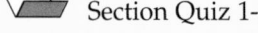 Use Student Self-Test and Review Software to review Section 1.

Evaluate

Section Quiz 1-1

 Use the Testmaker to create a customized quiz for Section 1.

Reteach

Have students review the roles of the following people in early cities: farmers, merchants, artisans, soldiers, rulers, priests.

learned how to hammer the metals copper, lead, and gold to make jewelry and weapons.

The agricultural way of life led to many other changes. People created calendars to measure the seasons and determine when to plant crops. Because their food supply depended on land ownership, people now cared about such matters as boundary lines and rules of inheritance. Warfare probably came into being as villages competed for land and water.

Neolithic people also believed in many deities, or gods and goddesses. The spirits that supposedly surrounded them throughout nature were transformed into humanlike gods and goddesses with the power to help or hurt people. Some Neolithic people set up shrines at which they offered gifts in honor of the deities.

Emergence of Civilization

Over thousands of years, some of the early farming villages evolved slowly into complex societies, known as civilizations. The people of a civilization lived in a highly organized society with an advanced knowledge of farming, trade, government, art, and science. The word *civilization* comes from the Latin word *civitas*, meaning "city," and most historians equate the rise of civilizations with that of cities. Because most city dwellers learned the art of writing, the rise of cities also marks the beginning of history.

Early Civilizations

As with agriculture, cities formed at different times in different parts of the world. Many of the earliest civilizations, however, had one thing in common: they rose from farming settlements in river valleys like that of the **Nile River** in northeastern Africa. The earliest cities that archaeologists have uncovered so far lie in the valley of the **Tigris** and **Euphrates** (yoo•FRAYT•eez) **Rivers** in southwest Asia and date back to about 3500 B.C. Cities arose in the **Indus River** valley in south Asia some 1,000 years later. The first urban communities in east Asia appeared about 1500 B.C. in the **Huang**

24 **Chapter 1** *Rise of Civilizations*

CRITICAL THINKING ACTIVITY

Supporting Generalizations Have students offer reasoned opinions as to which of the following they think was the most important advance in early civilizations—toolmaking, agriculture, or writing. Ask students to give an example of how early civilized people benefited from a particular development in toolmaking, agriculture, or writing. By the same token, ask students whether they consider technology, farming, or communication to be as important in modern human society. Have them give a modern-day example related to any one of these areas that they think makes their lives more "advanced" or "civilized." **L2**

(HWONG) **River** valley. By about 1000 B.C., cities were also flourishing in Europe and in the Americas, and by 750 B.C. in western Africa.

Early civilizations also shared several other basic features. With extra food, fewer men and women had to farm, and more could earn their living in other ways. People's labor became specialized, with different men and women doing different jobs. The civilization depended on advanced technology, such as metalworking skills. Each civilization always had some form of government to coordinate large-scale, cooperative efforts such as building irrigation systems. The people in each civilization also shared a system of beliefs.

Not all societies formed civilizations, however. Some people continued to live in small, agricultural villages, while others lived by hunting and gathering. Some nomadic people built a specialized culture that relied on moving herds of domesticated animals in search of good pasture.

Long-Distance Trade

Early civilizations learned to produce jewelry, weapons, and other goods from metals, such as copper, lead, and gold, or mixtures of metals, such as bronze. Harder than either copper or tin alone, bronze took a sharper cutting edge and was much easier to cast. The search for new sources of materials such as bronze led to the development of long-distance trade. Some long-distance trade moved overland by means of animal caravans. Other goods were transported by water. People floated down rivers on rafts. They made boats, propelling them in shallow water with poles and, in deeper water, with paddles and oars. After a time people learned how to harness the force of the wind, and rivers and seacoasts became filled with sailing ships.

Along with goods, ideas were actively shared. This exchange of goods and ideas when cultures come in contact is known as cultural diffusion. Although early civilizations developed many similar ideas independently, other ideas arose in a few areas and then spread throughout the world by cultural diffusion. When ancient peoples learned about the technology and ideas of different civilizations, the new knowledge stimulated them to improve their own skills and way of life.

The Rise of Cities

Early cities had from 5,000 to 30,000 residents. These cities faced new problems unknown in the Neolithic period. As their civilizations grew more complex, city dwellers developed ways to supervise agriculture and trade. First, they organized a group of government officials to oversee the collection, storage, and distribution of farming surpluses. These officials also directed the labor force needed for construction projects. Second, ancient cities hired professional soldiers to guard their territory.

Army leaders, government officials, and priests belonged to a ruling class often led by a king, although women also held positions of authority. Rulers often used religion to justify their powers. According to ancient beliefs, the land produced food only if the deities looked on the people with favor. One of the king's main tasks, therefore, was to assist priests in carrying out ceremonies to ensure an abundant harvest. The first kings were probably elected, but in time they inherited their positions.

Invention of Writing

Many historians believe that writing originated when priests kept records of wheat, livestock, and other items they received as offerings. At first the priests used marks and pictures, called pictograms, to represent products. Later, they used the

Enrich

Have students research cuneiform writing. Direct them to find out how different pictograms evolved into abstract symbols and how people of modern times learned to decode and read cuneiform inscriptions.

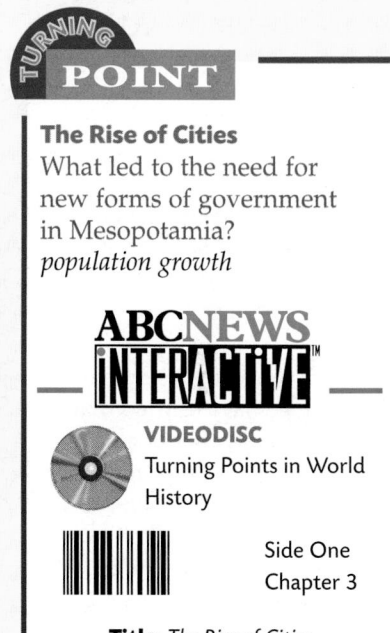

The Rise of Cities
What led to the need for new forms of government in Mesopotamia?
population growth

ABCNEWS INTERACTIVE™

VIDEODISC
Turning Points in World History

Side One
Chapter 3

Title: *The Rise of Cities*

CLOSE

Have students describe in their own words the migrations pictured on the map on page 23. Remind them to pay close attention to the symbols on the map that represent prehistoric time.

SECTION 1 REVIEW

Recall
1. **Define** prehistory, hominid, culture, technology, civilization, cultural diffusion.
2. **Identify** Paleolithic, Neolithic, Neanderthals, Cro-Magnons, Neolithic Revolution.

3. **Describe** briefly the basic features that characterized early civilizations.

Critical Thinking
4. **Evaluating Information** Does the use of agriculture by Neolithic peoples deserve to be

called a revolution? Give reasons to support your opinion.

Understanding Themes
5. **Change** How did technological changes in first civilizations improve toolmaking and the transportation of trade goods?

Chapter 1 *Rise of Civilizations* **25**

SECTION 1 REVIEW ANSWERS

1. All vocabulary words are defined in the Glossary.
2. Paleolithic, 21; Neolithic, 21; Neanderthals, 22; Cro-Magnons, 22; Neolithic Revolution, 22
3. Specialized labor; advanced technological skills; form of government; complex system of beliefs and values
4. Yes: agriculture led to huge and important changes in people's lives, such as living in villages.
5. **CHANGE** toolmaking: ability to make mixtures of metals such as bronze; transportation; advances in boatbuilding

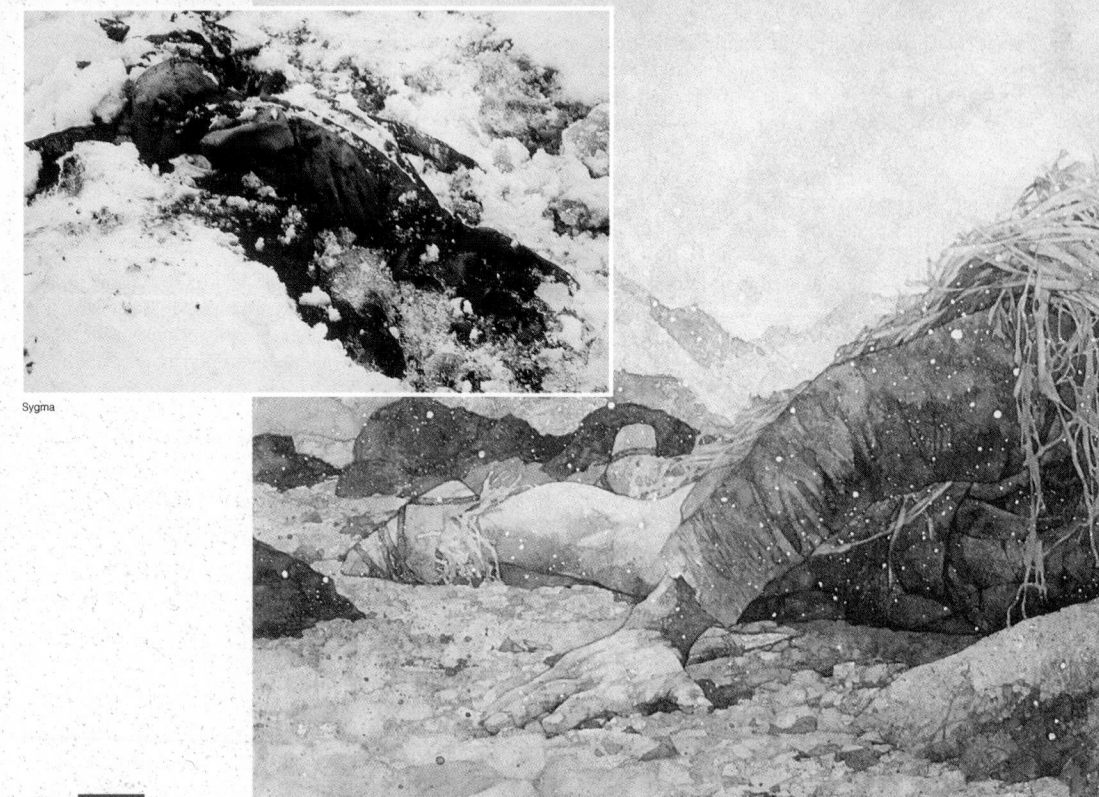

Sygma

Special Report Summary

In 1991 two German hikers discovered the body of a pre-historic man who had been frozen in a glacier in the Alps.

Scientists determined that the "Iceman" was at least 5,000 years old.

The Iceman lived during the Copper Age, which in Europe lasted from 4000 to 2200 B.C.

From the Iceman's posses-sions we have learned that he was a member of a com-munity which knew how to sew, make finely hewn tools of metal and flint, and use natural substances to combat illness.

TEACH

Points to Discuss

After students have read the selection, discuss the following: What two methods did scientists use to determine the Iceman's age? Which of the two is more exact? (estimating by style of ax, radiocarbon dating; the latter is more exact) What factors led the Ice-man and others of his time to

The Iceman

On September 19, 1991, Helmut and Erika Simon, a German couple hiking near the border between Austria and Italy, wandered slightly off the trail. Suddenly Erika Simon caught sight of a small head and pair of shoulders emerging from the ice. The Simons thought they had stumbled across a discarded doll. In fact, they had found the solitary prehistoric traveler now known around the world as the Iceman.

At first the Iceman was thought to be 4,000 years old—which would have made the discovery remarkable enough. Scientists later discovered that the Iceman was at least 5,000 years old! In comparison, Tutankh-amen, Egypt's boy-king, was born some 2,000 years later.

The Iceman is the oldest body ever retrieved from an Alpine gla-cier; the next-oldest was only 400 years old. At 10,530 feet (3,210 m),

◪ *Overcome by fatigue and cold, a mountaineer (above) lies down to die high in the Alps. Some 5,000 years later, the discovery of his well-preserved body, along with clothes and a copper ax, offers startling clues about how humans greeted the metal age in Europe.*

◪ *The Iceman (top) emerges from under a melting glacier.*

26   **Chapter 1**   *Rise of Civilizations*

TEACHER NOTES

_____
_____
_____
_____
_____

Sygma

climb high into the Alps? *(climatic warming made higher and higher altitudes good locations for hunting game or pasturing sheep; large veins of copper found there)* How did the discovery of copper change life for the prehistoric people who lived in the Alps? *(led to the development of trade routes, and of new, specialized occupations such as smelters and axmakers)* What evidence is there that the Iceman had a spiritual life? *(He had tattoo-like marks in places that no one could see, which suggests they were to confer supernatural power; he carried two pieces of fungi on a leather thong, an artifact which also might have been believed to confer power or protection, as it has no other more utilitarian purpose.)*

NGS Cartographic Division

the site where the Iceman lay is the highest elevation in Europe in which prehistoric human remains have been found. Not even traces of a campfire have ever been discovered at that height.

The body of the Iceman was preserved through sheer luck. Shortly after he died, the rocky hollow where he lay filled with snow. For thousands of years a glacier covered this pocket of snow, only a few yards over the Iceman's head. More commonly, a body caught in a glacier would be crushed and torn by the movement of the ice. Instead, the Iceman was naturally mummified.

In the four days following the discovery, many well-meaning hikers and officials tried to free the Iceman from the glacier. They took turns hacking and prodding around the body with ice axes and ski poles. Unfortunately, they damaged the Iceman and the artifacts found with him—in ways that 5,000 years of glaciation had not. One of the "rescuers" seized a stick to dig with, breaking it in the process; the stick turned out to be part of the hazelwood-and-larch frame of the Iceman's backpack, a type of ancient artifact never seen before. Workers also snapped off the top

▣ *The local coroner (above) and an assistant remove the corpse from his icy grave.*

▣ *The Iceman was found at an elevation of 10,530 feet (3,210 m) on the Austrian-Italian border. His tools and backpack frame were located near his body.*

Linking Past and Present

Archaeological Evidence Since the discovery of the Iceman, archaeologists have looked for other signs of prehistoric people in the high Alpine valleys where he died. They have found remains of campsites and flint tools from hunters who lived thousands of years before the Iceman. Many of these remains, as well as the Iceman's body, were found along a path which local shepherds still use.

Chapter 1 *Rise of Civilizations* **27**

FUN FACTS

- Although lung disease is often thought of as a symptom of modern life with its cigarette smoke and pollution, doctors found that the Iceman's lungs were as black as a smoker's. They attribute his condition to living in a shelter with an open fire.
- The development of metalworking

increased contact between peoples, as the early metalsmiths were traveling specialists. The Iceman had large amounts of copper in his hair, and may have been such a traveling coppersmith.

- Copper is the first metal prehistoric people put to utilitarian use. The oldest known

human-made metal is a copper pendant that dates from around 9500 B.C.

- Animals as well as humans have been preserved in ice. In Siberia, some 50 specimens of the long-extinct woolly mammoth have been found preserved in ice with their skin and flesh still intact.

 NATIONAL GEOGRAPHIC

CURRICULUM CONNECTION

MEDICINE

Doctors and scientists have used special instruments and techniques to study the Iceman's physical remains. Their studies have shown that he may have been in a weakened condition when he died, as he suffered from worms. X-rays of the Iceman's shinbones revealed that he endured several periods of illness or extreme hunger during the course of his life that arrested his growth.

you don't say...

Copper Age The Copper Age is also sometimes called the Chalcolithic Age, which means "Copper-Stone" Age. This name is fitting because in the early stages of this period, copper was used mainly for small precious objects, while many tools continued to be made of stone. Some of the Iceman's tools, for example his dagger, were made of flint, not metal.

end of the Iceman's six-foot-long bow. What remained of the Iceman's clothing was torn off, as were parts of his body, and an officer using a jackhammer left a gaping hole in the Iceman's hip. To be sure, none of the salvagers suspected how old the Iceman was.

Not until five days after the discovery did an archaeologist examine the Iceman's body. Basing his estimate on the style of the ax found with the body, the archaeologist guessed that the Iceman was 4,000 years old.

Once officials knew the Iceman's approximate age, a rigorous effort to stabilize his condition began. The mummy was placed in a freezer, where the temperature was kept at a constant 21°F (-6°C) and the humidity at 98 percent—conditions much the same as those of the ice in which he had lain. The Iceman was not removed from the freezer for more than 20 minutes at a time, and then only for the most important scientific research. Part of that research was carbon-dating the Iceman to verify how old he was. Further chemical analysis revealed that the blade of his ax was not bronze, but nearly pure copper. He was, in fact, unique: a mummy from the Copper Age, which lasted in central Europe roughly from 4000 B.C. to 2200 B.C. Two different laboratories concluded that he was 5,000 to 5,500 years old.

THE ICEMAN'S DOMAIN was the Alps, stretching from southeast France to the Swiss-German border, and from Austria to northern Italy. Five thousand years ago these mountains were a vast wilderness. In the Copper Age, hardy voyagers trekked these ranges, and the goods they traded traveled even farther. We know from his tools and clothes that the Iceman was one of these

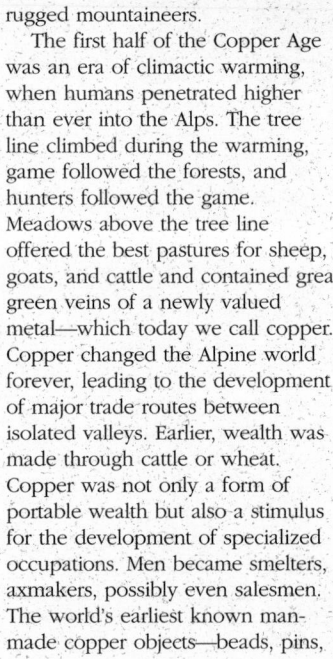

Iceman's artifacts photographed by Kenneth Garrett

rugged mountaineers.

The first half of the Copper Age was an era of climactic warming, when humans penetrated higher than ever into the Alps. The tree line climbed during the warming, game followed the forests, and hunters followed the game. Meadows above the tree line offered the best pastures for sheep, goats, and cattle and contained great green veins of a newly valued metal—which today we call copper. Copper changed the Alpine world forever, leading to the development of major trade routes between isolated valleys. Earlier, wealth was made through cattle or wheat. Copper was not only a form of portable wealth but also a stimulus for the development of specialized occupations. Men became smelters, axmakers, possibly even salesmen. The world's earliest known man-made copper objects—beads, pins,

A fragment of the Iceman's plaited-grass cape (above) was found next to his head.

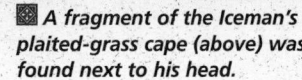 *This stone disk threaded with a leather thong (inset, top right) may have been worn to protect against evil.*

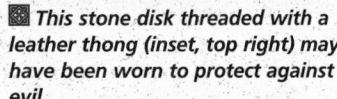 *The Iceman's copper ax is the oldest ever found in Europe with its bindings and handle intact (inset, bottom right).*

A fungus on a string may have been a first-aid kit (inset, above left).

and awls—were made about 8000 B.C. in Turkey and Iran. There is evidence of copper mining in the Balkans by 5000 B.C. From there the technology spread west, reaching the Alps a thousand years later.

TEACHER NOTES

_____
_____
_____
_____
_____
_____

his copper ax may tell us most. Its yew-wood handle ends in a gnarled joint, where a notch holds the blade. Dark birch gum held the blade firmly in position beneath a tightly wrapped thong of rawhide. It is a ribbed ax, rather than the more primitive flat ax that archaeologists would have expected to find.

Researchers who reconstructed what remained of the Iceman's clothing observed that his garment had been skillfully stitched together with sinew. Cruder repairs had been made, probably by the Iceman himself on his travels. This led researchers to believe that the Iceman had been part of a community, although he was used to fending for himself. Also, tiny pieces of a wheat that grew only at low altitudes, and bits of charcoal from a variety of trees found throughout the Alps were discovered with the Iceman, indicating that he may have come the South Tirol.

Included among the Iceman's possessions were a stick with a tip of antler used to sharpen flint blades; a deerskin quiver that contained 14 arrows; and an unfinished bow. His small flint dagger was similar to those found at other Copper Age sites, but no one had ever seen the kind of delicately woven sheath that held the dagger.

Central Europe's oldest known plow is more than a thousand years younger than the Iceman. Yet Copper Age artists cut images of plows on rocks. Rows of furrows have been found preserved at a major Copper Age religious complex excavated in northwest Italy, though experts believe plowing was ritualistic rather than agricultural.

The Iceman also had tattoo-like marks that might imply something about his spiritual life. Located on normally hidden places—his lower back, behind his knee, and on his ankle—the marks were not for

🔲 *The Iceman's head was reconstructed by John Gurche, an anthropologically trained artist. He first sculpted a replica of the skull by using computer images, X rays, and CT scans of the Iceman. Gurche then added clay to duplicate the Iceman's mummified face, complete with smashed nose and lip. Next, he added muscles and fatty tissue, nasal cartilage, and glass eyes. Finally he made a new model of the head with soft urethane, tinted to suggest wind-burned skin. He completed the replica of the Iceman's head by adding human hair.*

show. Perhaps they were meant to confer supernatural power or protection. So might the pair of fungi he carried, each pierced by a leather thong. Archaeologists have never seen anything like this artifact from that period. The fungi contain chemical substances now known to be antibiotic. If the Iceman used them to counteract illness, perhaps they also seemed magical to him.

We may never know what drew the Iceman to the mountain pass where he died. Perhaps he was a shepherd, a trader, or an outcast. But, in the late 20th century, it is our good fortune to have the opportunity to learn from this ambassador of the Copper Age.

Chapter 1 *Rise of Civilizations* **29**

The work of many researchers over the past 30 years tells us much about life during the Copper Age. Excavations have yielded bones that indicate that by around 5000 B.C. Alpine people had domesticated five animals: dogs, which were originally more important for food than companionship, cattle, sheep, goats, and pigs. Horses and chickens were still unknown in the Alps. Villagers grew wheat and barley and made linen clothes from flax. They had only recently discovered how to milk a cow and how to make cheese and butter. Their sheep may have been used for meat but not yet for wool. Many staple foods of today were still unknown, including potatoes, onions, and oats.

EVENTUALLY, THE ICEMAN'S possessions may tell us more than his body will. Of those possessions,

Cultural Perspectives

Human Development The era in which the Iceman lived, the Copper Age, represented the first stage of human development beyond the Stone Age. In addition to the discovery of metalworking techniques, people made numerous other advances. In some communities of the time, people wore clothes of woven fabric, extracted oil from plants, ate out of stone and wooden bowls, and lived in houses.

MORE ABOUT...

Metal How did early people learn how to make metal? Scientists speculate that the discovery was probably made using a pottery kiln, because ordinary cooking fires do not get hot enough. Copper oxides in powdered form were sometimes used as a glaze on pots. After firing such a pot, a potter may have discovered a small piece of copper in his kiln. If this happened more than once, he might eventually figure out that it was made when the heat interacted with the copper oxide.

| 3,000 B.C. | 2,000 B.C. | 1,000 B.C. | A.D. 1 |

c. 3,000 B.C.
Sumerians set up city-states in Mesopotamia.

c. 1,700 B.C.
Egypt's Queen Hatshepsut comes to power.

c. 1,200s B.C.
The Israelites first celebrate Passover.

c. 650 B.C.
The Assyrian Empire reaches its height.

SECTION THEME

▶ **Cultural Diffusion** Armies, merchants, and religious thinkers spread new ideas and practices throughout Africa and the Middle East.

Find Out

Answer: *Fertile river valleys enabled people to farm, trade promoted the spread of ideas and practices, and well-organized governments fostered cooperation.*

FOCUS

Section Objective

Explain how trading peoples influenced the development of Africa and the Middle East.

BELLRINGER
Motivational Activity

Before taking roll at the beginning of the class period, project Section Focus Transparency 1-2 and have students answer the activity questions. Discuss students' responses.

📁 This activity is also available as a blackline master.

Vocabulary Pre-check

📁 Use Vocabulary Activity 1 to introduce vocabulary terms.
L1 LEP

Section 2

Civilizations in Africa and the Middle East

Setting the Scene

▶ **Terms to Define**
dynasty, monarchy, bureaucracy, empire, polytheism, city-state, alphabet, monotheism, prophet

▶ **People to Meet**
Hatshepsut, Ramses II, Piankhi, Hammurabi, Moses, David, Darius I, Zoroaster

▶ **Places to Locate**
Thebes, Nubia, Kush, Fertile Crescent, Mesopotamia, Babylon, Jerusalem, Persepolis

Find Out
How did civilizations develop in Africa and the Middle East?

The Storyteller

King Hiram was pleased. Tyre, his capital city, was a bustling seaport. . . . Not only did the kings of Egypt and Babylon send ambassadors to Hiram's court, they also brought business to his land. Gold, copper, ivory, and linen from Egypt; precious stones from Babylon; silver from Asia Minor; and pottery from Crete enriched Tyre. In return, Tyre exchanged cedar, cut from the nearby mountains, and a vivid purple dye, harvested from murex shells found in the seas near the rocky coast. Hiram's people were Phoenicians, the people of the purple, the color—beautiful, costly, and rare.

—adapted from
The Bible as History,
Werner Keller,
translated by
William Neil, 1969

Phoenician ship

Cities and civilizations arose at different times in different parts of the world. The earliest civilizations are believed to have developed in Africa and the Middle East. One of the most important arose along the fertile banks of the Nile River in northeastern Africa.

The Nile Valley

As early as 5000 B.C., nomadic hunter-gatherers of northeastern Africa began to settle in an area of the Nile River valley later known as Egypt. They took up a farming life regulated by the river's seasonal rise and fall, growing cereal crops, such as wheat and barley. In time, their villages united into small kingdoms, each under the unrestricted rule of its king. About 3000 B.C., a leading king, Narmer, carried out conquests in the region and set up the first government that ruled all of Egypt. He governed the country from the capital city he had built known as Memphis.

Narmer's reign marked the beginning of the first Egyptian dynasty, or line of rulers from one family. From 3000 B.C. until 332 B.C., a series of 30 dynasties governed Egypt. Historians have organized the dynasties into three great periods: the Old Kingdom, the Middle Kingdom, and the New Kingdom.

The Egyptian Monarchy

During the Old Kingdom, which lasted from about 2700 B.C. to 2200 B.C., the Egyptians developed a strong national monarchy, or rule by a king or queen. They regarded their king as both a god and a political leader. The Egyptian ruler wielded absolute power, issuing commands regarded as the law of the land. Unable to carry out all official duties, the king delegated many tasks to a bureaucracy, a group of

---

SECTION RESOURCES

📁 **Reproducible Masters**
- Reproducible Lesson Plan 1-2
- Vocabulary Activity 1
- Guided Reading Activity 1-2
- History Simulation 1
- Section Quiz 1-2

📖 **Transparencies**
- Section Focus Transparency 1-2
- Ancient Egypt
- The Fertile Crescent
- World History and Art Transparency 2, *Tutankhamen's Throne;* and Transparency 4, *Standard of Ur: Peace*

Multimedia
- Ancient Egypt
- Student Self-Test and Review Software
- Testmaker
- Egypt and the Fertile Crescent
- Turning Points in World History

government officials, that carried out trade, collected taxes, and supervised the construction of dams, canals, and storehouses for grain.

The Egyptian Empire

During the Middle Kingdom, from about 2050 B.C. to 1800 B.C., Egyptian rulers governed the country from a new capital at **Thebes**. They supported irrigation projects that added thousands of acres to the land already under cultivation. The Theban rulers also launched military campaigns in the southern Nile River valley and sponsored trading expeditions to the Arabian Peninsula and East Africa.

After a period of foreign rule, the military leader, Ahmose, founded the first dynasty of the New Kingdom about 1600 B.C. Ahmose and his successors assumed the title pharaoh, an Egyptian word meaning "great house of the king." In the late 1400s B.C., a woman named **Hatshepsut** (hat•SHEHP•soot) became Egypt's pharaoh. She carried out an extensive building program, which included a great funeral temple and a tomb built into the hills of what is now called the Valley of the Kings.

Hatshepsut's stepson and successor Thutmose (thoot•MOH•suh) III carried out conquests in the Middle East and pushed the Egyptian frontier to the northern part of the Euphrates River. In a short time, Thutmose III had won an empire for Egypt, bringing many territories under one ruler. The Egyptian Empire grew rich from commerce and tribute from the conquered territories. The capital of Thebes, with its palaces, temples, and carved stone obelisks, reflected the wealth won by conquest. No longer isolated from other cultures, Egyptians benefited from cultural diffusion within their empire.

Decline and Recovery

About 1370 B.C., a pharaoh named Amenhotep (AH•muhn•HOH•TEHP) IV came to power. He broke with the Egyptian tradition of worshiping many deities. Amenhotep declared that Egyptians should worship only Aton, the sun-disk god, as the one supreme deity. Claiming to be Aton's equal, Amenhotep changed his royal name to Akhenaton (AHK•NAH•tuhn), which means "Spirit of Aton."

Akhenaton's reign had an unsettling effect on Egypt. Many of the common people and priests of the old religion opposed the religious reforms. At the same time, the army was unhappy about Egypt's loss of territories under Akhenaton's weak rule.

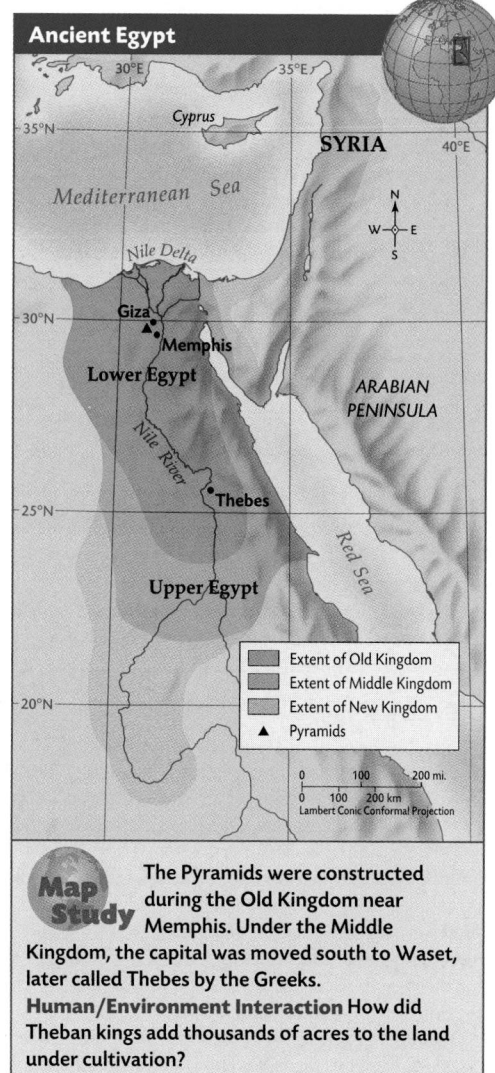

Ancient Egypt

Extent of Old Kingdom
Extent of Middle Kingdom
Extent of New Kingdom
▲ Pyramids

0   100   200 mi.
0   100   200 km
Lambert Conic Conformal Projection

Map Study The Pyramids were constructed during the Old Kingdom near Memphis. Under the Middle Kingdom, the capital was moved south to Waset, later called Thebes by the Greeks. **Human/Environment Interaction** How did Theban kings add thousands of acres to the land under cultivation?

After Akhenaton's death, the priests restored the old religion, and the army overthrew the dynasty and created a new one.

During the 1200s B.C., the pharaohs regained some of the territory and prestige that Egypt had lost during the previous century. One of these pharaohs, **Ramses II**, reigned for 67 years. He erected large statues of himself and built many temples and tombs. In A.D. 1995, archaeologists uncovered a vast underground tomb with at least 67 chambers that they believed to be the burial place of 50 of the 52 sons of Ramses II. The find,

Chapter 1 *Rise of Civilizations* **31**

TEACH

Guided Practice

THEME Cultural Diffusion

Ask students for a definition of the word *diffusion*. (*spreading or scattering widely*) Then ask if they know of other kinds of diffusion. (*scattering of light, spreading of different weather properties by air*) **L1**

Map Study

Answer

by supporting irrigation projects

Map Skills Practice

Reading a Map Why does the map suggest that ancient Egyptians made advances in transportation? (*parts of the New Kingdom are located across a large body of water, indicating ability to navigate and sail*)

Geography: Location Have students study the map of ancient Egypt on this page. Then ask them to use the Atlas in this text to find modern nations that fall within the boundaries of ancient Egypt during the New Kingdom. (*Egypt, Lebanon, Israel, Sudan, Cyprus, and part of Turkey*) **L1**

World History and Art Transparency 2, *Tutankhamen's Throne*; Transparency 4, *Standard of Ur: Peace*

COOPERATIVE LEARNING ACTIVITY

A Play Have the class write and perform a play about one of the people listed in the section. Organize the class into small groups. Have each group be responsible for a specific task in the project, such as researching the person chosen and the way of life during his or her time; writing the script, acting, making costumes, finding props, writing and designing programs; and designing sets (if needed). At each stage of the project, all students should be given an opportunity to react to the group task. Then have the students present the play to other classes. **L1**

Cultural Diffusion Have students locate Egypt on the map of the Middle East in the Atlas of this text. Discuss how Egypt's location at the crossroads between Africa and Asia provided opportunities for cultural diffusion. **L2**

Critical Thinking Remind students about the consensus that a writing system, a well-organized government, art and literature, and specialization of labor are the earmarks of civilization. Have students explain how ancient Egypt met these criteria. **L3**

Who?What?Where?When?

Nile Surroundings On the east bank of the Nile stood the commercial city of Thebes. On the west bank lay irrigated fields of black alluvium and green crops. At the edge of the fields rose a row of temples, each surrounded by a cluster of buildings. Several of these buildings were the homes of priests and scribes, but most were great storerooms holding the riches of the empire.

Religion Have students write an editorial explaining their position on this question: Did religion play a greater role in Egyptian society than it does in our society today? Tell students to respond according to their perception of the role of religion in today's society. **L3**

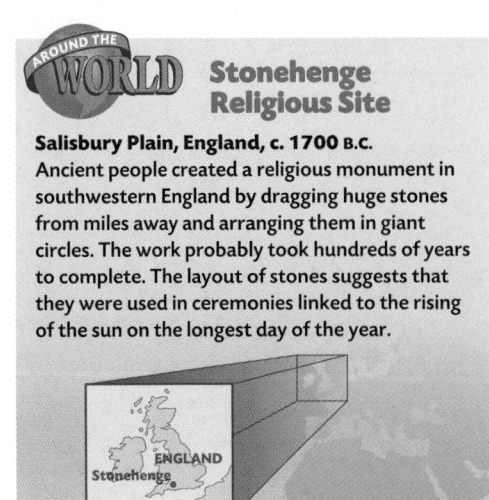

AROUND THE WORLD
Stonehenge Religious Site

Salisbury Plain, England, c. 1700 B.C. Ancient people created a religious monument in southwestern England by dragging huge stones from miles away and arranging them in giant circles. The work probably took hundreds of years to complete. The layout of stones suggests that they were used in ceremonies linked to the rising of the sun on the longest day of the year.

located near Ramses' own tomb, was hailed as one of the most historically significant discoveries in Egypt in the twentieth century.

Daily Life in Egypt

At the height of its glory, ancient Egypt was home to some 5 million persons, most of whom lived in the Nile Valley and in its fan-shaped delta near the Mediterranean Sea. Royalty, nobles, and priests formed the dominant class. They lived in large, elaborately decorated homes in the cities or on estates along the Nile River. The next influential social group–the middle class of artisans, scribes, merchants, and tax collectors–carried out Egypt's business activities. Middle-class homes–mostly in the cities–were comfortable but not elegant.

Most Egyptians belonged to the poor lower class. Many were farmers who paid rent to the king for the land on which they farmed. Farmers also worked on building projects, and some members of the lower class served the priests and the nobles. They lived in small villages of simple huts on or near the large estates along the Nile.

In the cities and in the upper class, the typical Egyptian family consisted of the husband, wife, and children. Outside the cities, especially among farmers and laborers, a family also included grandparents and other relatives.

The status of Egyptian women changed somewhat as the centuries passed. During the Old Kingdom, women were considered the property of their husbands and valued as producers of children. By the time of the empire, documents indicate

that women's legal rights had improved. Women could buy, own, and sell property in their own names, testify in court, and start divorce and other legal proceedings.

Egyptian Religion

Religion guided every aspect of Egyptian life. Egyptian religion was based on **polytheism**, or the worship of many deities. These included Amon-Ra, the sun god, and Osiris, the ruler of the realm of the dead. Because their religion stressed an afterlife, Egyptians devoted much time and wealth to preparing for survival in the next world. At first they believed that only kings and wealthy people could enjoy an afterlife. By the time of the New Kingdom, however, poor people could also hope for eternal life with Osiris's help.

The Egyptians believed that a king's soul continued to guide the kingdom after death. To honor their god-kings and to provide them with an eternal place of rest, the Egyptians of the Old Kingdom built lasting monuments–the Pyramids. Before entombing a dead king in his pyramid, Egyptian doctors first preserved the king's body from decay by a procedure called embalming. They wrapped the dried, shrunken body–called a mummy–with long strips of linen and placed it in an elaborate coffin.

Writing With Pictures

In their earliest writing system, called hieroglyphics, the Egyptians carved onto pieces of slate picture symbols, or hieroglyphs, to stand for objects, ideas, and sounds. For everyday business, however, the Egyptians used a cursive, or flowing, script known as hieratic, which simplified and connected the picture symbols.

Few people in ancient Egypt could read or write. Some Egyptians, though, did prepare at special schools for a career as a scribe in government or commerce. Scribes learned to write hieratic script on paper made from the papyrus reed.

Achievements in Science

Pyramids, temples, and other monuments bear witness to the architectural and artistic achievement of Egyptian artisans. These works, however, would not have been possible without advances in disciplines such as mathematics. The Egyptians developed a number system that enabled them to calculate area and volume, and they used principles of geometry to survey flooded land.

The Egyptians worked out an accurate 365-day calendar by basing their year not only on the movements of the moon but also on Sirius, the

MEETING SPECIAL NEEDS ACTIVITY

Language Delayed Ask several students who read English well to go through this section to find words related to the natural environment, such as *river, riverbank, delta, peninsula, plateau,* and so on. Working with partners who are language delayed, these students can help find pictures of the listed natural features in resource materials. Next, ask language-delayed students to prepare and present a simple natural-features map of their native country. Have students find similarities and differences between the geographic features of the student's country and those of Egypt. **L1 LEP**

© Louis Mazzatenta

Ramses the Great

TEACH

Not every well-preserved body from prehistoric times is a true mummy. Strictly speaking, a mummy is a dead body preserved by embalming. The technique of embalming seems to have been developed in Egypt about 2600 B.C. Bodies preserved from earlier times were the result of natural drying in the hot Egyptian sand. Mummification was costly, and at first only the wealthy could afford it. Still, mummified corpses of bulls, cats, and ibis have been found. Ask students why they think the Egyptians preserved these animals. (*The bull, cat, and ibis were sacred, associated with certain Egyptian gods.*)

T he mummy of Ramses the Great (above) lies in a display case on the second floor of the Egyptian Museum in Cairo. For many centuries before Ramses was brought to Cairo, the great pharaoh lay in his tomb near Luxor in a richly decorated coffin (left), embellished with symbols of Osiris, god f the afterlife. Ramses was nearly 90 when he died in 237 B.C. His mummy has remained intact for the last ,000 years.

Egyptians believed strongly in the afterlife and took great care to preserve the bodies of their pharaohs. Embalmers spent 70 days preparing the corpse of Ramses the Great. First they removed the internal organs and placed them in sacred jars. The heart was sealed in the body because Egyptians believed that it was the source of intellect as well as feeling and was needed in the afterlife. The brain, on the other hand, was thought to be useless and embalmers drew it out through the nose and threw it away. The body was then dried with salt, washed, coated with preserving resins, and wrapped in the hundreds of yards of linen. Recent medical tests show that Ramses suffered from arthritis, dental abscesses, gum disease, and poor circulation.

Chapter 1 *Rise of Civilizations* **33**

CURRICULUM CONNECTION

ARCHAEOLOGY

One of the impressive temple sites of Ramses II is Abu Simbel, located near the Nile River about 762 miles south of Cairo. In the 1960s the High Dam at Aswan would have flooded the site, but 51 countries contributed funds to move the temples block by block to higher ground farther inland.

**NATIONAL
GEOGRAPHIC
SOCIETY**

Use these materials to enrich student understanding of ancient Egyptian culture.

- **NGS PICTURESHOW CD-ROM**
  Egypt and the Fertile Crescent
- **NGS PICTUREPACK TRANSPARENCY SET**
  Ancient Egypt, The Fertile Crescent
- **ANCIENT CIVILIZATIONS POSTER SET**
  Ancient Egypt

History & Art Egyptian civilization obtained luxury items such as gold, ivory, and ebony as tribute from Nubia to the south.
Answer to Caption: *After 2000 B.C. the Nubian River civilization developed into the kingdom of Kush.*

History & Art Wall painting from the Metropolitan Museum of Art, New York City, New York. **Four late Bronze Age Nubian princes offer rings and gold to an Egyptian ruler.** *What happened to the Nubian River civilization after 2000 B.C.?*

bright Dog Star. Sirius rises annually in the sky just before the Nile's flood begins.

Egyptians also developed medical expertise recognized throughout the ancient world, having first learned about human anatomy in their practice of embalming. Egyptian doctors wrote directions on papyrus scrolls for using splints, bandages, and compresses when treating fractures, wounds, and diseases. Other ancient civilizations would later acquire much of their medical knowledge from the Egyptians.

Northeast African Kingdoms

In addition to Egypt, northeastern Africa was also the site of other civilizations. By 3000 B.C., a people called the Nubians had established a kingdom called **Nubia** in the southern part of the Nile River valley. The Nubian people, known for their military skills, maintained close contacts with Egypt. Some scholars believe that political ideas, such as monarchy, and various objects, like boats and eating utensils, reveal the early beginnings of close cultural links between Nubia and Egypt.

By 2000 B.C., the Nubian civilization had developed into the kingdom of **Kush**. The people of Kush used their Nile River location to develop trade. Their territory stood where trade caravans crossed the Nile, bringing gold, elephant tusks, and timber from the African interior. This strategic location brought wealth to the merchants and kings of Kush.

After a 500-year period of Egyptian rule, Kush became independent about 1000 B.C. In time Kush grew strong enough that a Kushite king **Piankhi** (pee•AHNK•hee) in 724 B.C. led a powerful army into Egypt and defeated the Egyptians. After this victory, Kushite kings ruled over both Egypt and Kush from their capital at Napata. The city boasted white sandstone temples, monuments, and pyramids fashioned in styles similar to those of the Egyptians.

In 671 B.C. the Assyrians, a people from the Middle East, invaded Egypt and forced the Kushites to return to their home territory. In spite of their defeat, the Kushites learned from the Assyrians the technology of making iron. They built a new capital at Meroë that became a major center for iron production. For about 150 years, the Kushite kingdom thrived. Then a new power—Axum, a kingdom located near the Red Sea—invaded Kush and ended its independence.

The Fertile Crescent

During the period of the early African civilizations, empires and kingdoms rose and fell in the Middle East's **Fertile Crescent**. This arc-shaped strip of fertile land stretched from the Mediterranean Sea to the Persian Gulf. About 3500 B.C., the Sumerians—a people from either central Asia or the Black Sea area—arrived in

34 Chapter 1 *Rise of Civilizations*

MAKING CONNECTIONS ACTIVITY

Technology In 1987 scientists from Egypt and the United States used advanced technology to view the remains of an ancient Egyptian boat that had been sealed inside a chamber for 4,600 years. To see inside without excavating and damaging the chamber, the scientists employed a special drill with technology invented for moon exploration. After drilling through the outer rock, they inserted a miniature video camera. Have students research other techniques used to handle and explore ancient Egyptian remains and report to the class on their findings. **L2**

Mesopotamia (MEH•suh•puh•TAY•mee•uh), the eastern part of the Fertile Crescent. They set up farming communities in the lower part of the Tigris-Euphrates River valley. Sumerian farmers built dams to control the unpredictable floodwaters and constructed canals to bring river water to irrigate their fields.

Sumerian City-States

By 3000 B.C. the Sumerians had formed 12 city-states in the Tigris-Euphrates valley. A typical Sumerian city-state consisted of the city itself and the surrounding land. Each was usually independent and governed by a king. A Sumerian king served both as political leader and as a high priest representing the city-state's deity. Although Sumerians honored many deities, each city-state claimed as its own one god or goddess to whom its citizens prayed and offered sacrifices.

Commerce and trade were important economic activities in the Sumerian city-states. Sumerian law regulated trading activities and outlined the roles of men and women. As the heads of households, men exercised great authority over their wives and children. Women did enjoy some legal rights, however. Like Egyptian women, they could buy and sell property and also operate their own businesses.

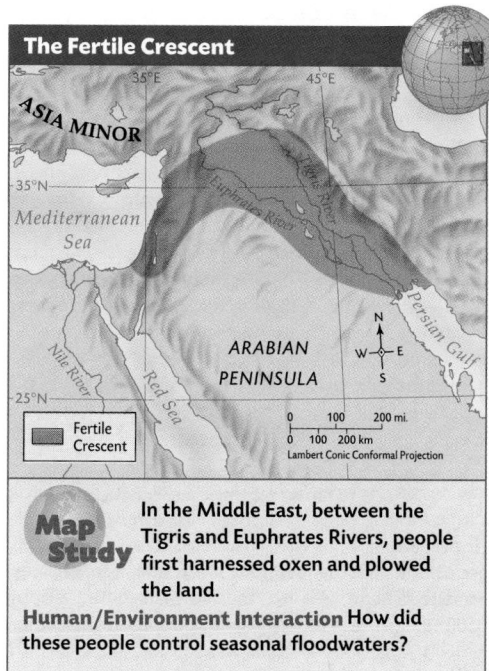

The Fertile Crescent

In the Middle East, between the Tigris and Euphrates Rivers, people first harnessed oxen and plowed the land.
Human/Environment Interaction How did these people control seasonal floodwaters?

To keep accounts and prepare documents, the Sumerians developed a system of writing known as cuneiform (kyoo•NEE•uh•FAWRM). This method began with pictograms and eventually evolved into a script that became–2,000 years later–a model for alphabetic systems of writing. Historians believe that the Sumerian writing system is the oldest in the world. They also credit the Sumerians with producing the world's oldest story–the tale of *Gilgamesh*. Written down before 1800 B.C., *Gilgamesh* tells the story of a godlike man who performs heroic deeds.

In addition, the Sumerians are known for numerous technological innovations. These include the wagon wheel to better transport people and goods, the arch to build sturdier buildings, the potter's wheel to shape containers, and the sundial to keep time. The Sumerians also developed a number system based on 60 and devised a 12-month calendar based on the cycles of the moon.

POINT

Hammurabi's Code

The Sumerian city-states eventually fell to foreign invaders in the 2000s B.C. The most powerful king in the Fertile Crescent at this time was Sargon I, ruler of the kingdom of Akkad (AH•KAHD) in northern Mesopotamia. Sargon's conquests united all of the city-states of Mesopotamia in one empire. After the decline of Sargon's empire, the Amorites, a Semitic people from western Syria, poured into Mesopotamia from the Mediterranean coastal land of Syria. The dynasty they founded at the city of **Babylon** later produced a ruler who would also dominate Mesopotamia: **Hammurabi**.

Hammurabi's greatest achievement was a collection of laws, developed in the 1700s B.C., that dealt with most aspects of daily life. Hammurabi's code clearly stated which actions were considered violations and assigned a specific punishment for each. The development of written law in Mesopotamia was a major advance toward justice and order. Before this achievement, people who had been offended often acted on their own and used violence against their opponents. Now, crimes against people or property became the concern of the whole community. Government assumed the responsibility of protecting citizens in return for their loyalty and service.

Chapter 1 *Rise of Civilizations* 35

Independent Practice

 Guided Reading Activity 1-2 **L1**

 History Simulation 1

Map Study

Answer
They built dams to control unpredictable floodwaters.

Map Skills Practice

Reading a Map Using the Atlas in this text, name a state or states in the United States that are approximately the same distance from the Equator as is the Fertile Crescent. (*Possible answers include: Georgia, Alabama, Mississippi, Texas, Arizona, New Mexico, southern California*)

POINT

Hammurabi's Law Code
How were punishments for crimes decided?
Punishments were to fit the crimes, like the biblical saying, "an eye for an eye."

VIDEODISC
Turning Points in World History

Side One
Chapter 4

Title: *The Code of Hammurabi*

CRITICAL THINKING ACTIVITY

Making Generalizations In learning about early history, students study many themes as they relate to early human beings—such as movement, innovation, and change. The same three themes apply to many civilizations. Have students write a paragraph on each theme as it relates to ancient Egypt. Ask volunteers to read their paragraphs in class. Then discuss the question: How do these three themes also apply to the history of the United States? **L2**

Critical Thinking Have students research Hammurabi's code of laws. Ask volunteers to present their findings in class. Students should understand that the code was an attempt to deal fairly with people in a political state made up of former independent states with different traditions. The code set up a social order based on individual rights. **L3**

Counting the Days

Our names for the days of the week also can be traced back to ancient times. The Babylonians named each of the seven days after a god who ruled one of the seven planets then visible. The Romans and the Anglo-Saxons simply substituted the names of their gods. The Babylonian god that ruled Jupiter, for example, was Marduk, who gave his name to the fifth day. The ancient Romans gave the name Jove to this day (in French, it is *jeudi*). The Anglo-Saxons in turn called it after their god Thor—*Thursday*.

ANSWERS

Our months are one or two days longer than the lunar month, and we add a day each leap year. Calendar reform—two calendars have been proposed: The Fixed Calendar (13 months with four weeks each month) and The World Calendar (12 months of 30 or 31 days). Students may point out practical difficulties of switching to a new calendar; or they may state that the reform proposals are designed to simplify the present calendar.

Trading Peoples

The civilizations of Mesopotamia and Egypt greatly influenced neighboring peoples in the Fertile Crescent–among them the Aramaeans (AR•uh•MEE•uhnz), the Phoenicians (fih•NEE•shuhnz) and the Lydians (LIH•dee•uhnz). In turn, these three trading peoples helped to spread their own cultures throughout the region and into much of the Mediterranean world. Traveling on sailing ships and by caravan, traders from the Fertile Crescent brought languages, customs, and ideas along with their trade goods.

About 1000 B.C. the Phoenicians developed a simplified alphabet—a series of written symbols that represent sounds–from earlier, more complicated systems that had been used in Mediterranean coastal areas of the Fertile Crescent. The Phoenician system later became the foundation of several alphabets, including Greek, which in turn became the basis of all Western alphabets.

The Lydians also made an important contribution to the Fertile Crescent's civilization: a money system using coins as mediums of exchange. Most traders in the region still relied on a system of barter for their transactions, exchanging their wares for other goods. The concept of money soon spread from the Lydians to other peoples of the region, whose rulers began to stamp their own coins.

The Israelites

Another people of the Fertile Crescent–the Israelites–adhered to monotheism, the belief in one all-powerful God whose commands were revealed by prophets, or holy messengers. The Israelites believed that God, whom they called Yahweh, determined right and wrong and expected people to deal justly with each other and to accept moral responsibility for their actions. The teachings of the Israelites exist today as the religion of Judaism. Judaism shares many beliefs with two other monotheistic religions that emerged in the Middle East—Christianity and Islam.

Counting the Days

How many days are there in a week? Different ancient peoples had more than one answer to this question. The Assyrians used a five-day week, while the Egyptians favored groupings of seven.

The modern week may trace its origins to the Jewish custom of observing a Sabbath day every seven days. Alternatively, our week may have originated in the Babylonian belief in the sacredness of the number seven–a belief probably linked either to the four seven-day phases of the moon or to the seven planets then visible in the heavens.

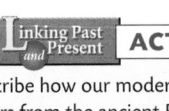

Ancient peoples often developed lunar calendars, based on the length of time it takes the moon to circle Earth, about 29 days. Of course, the lunar year of about 354 days did not correspond to the solar, or agricultural, year of 365 days. To solve this problem, Babylonian rulers added an extra month to certain years by royal decree.

Astronomers continued to try to adjust calendars to match the annual cycle of seasons. In 46 B.C. the Roman ruler Julius Caesar decreed that months should be longer than a lunar month. He also introduced January 1 as the first day of a new year. But not until A.D. 1582 were errors in the Julian calendar corrected by Pope Gregory XIII, who formalized a self-correcting system of leap years. The Gregorian calendar used today by most people in the Western world closely matches the solar year.

ACTIVITY

Describe how our modern calendar differs from the ancient Babylonian calendar. Then, research current proposals for calendar reform. Would you support any of the proposed changes? Why or why not?

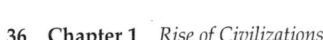

MORE ABOUT...

Deciphering the Rosetta Stone Jean-François Champollion, who deciphered the Rosetta stone, had a thorough knowledge of Coptic, the modern Egyptian language. He knew Greek as well, so he was able to read the entire text of the stone. The stone's inscription is a decree by Ptolemy V Epiphanes, king of Egypt from 203 to 181 B.C. The two forms of Egyptian writing on the stone are hieroglyphics and Demotic, the language of Egypt at the time the stone was inscribed. The black basalt stone–3 feet 9 inches (114 centimeters) high, 2 feet 4 1/2 inches (72 centimeters) thick–is on view at the British Museum in London.

Covenant and Exodus

The Bible traces Israelite origins to Abraham, a herder and trader who lived in Mesopotamia. Around 1900 B.C. Abraham and his household left Mesopotamia and settled in the coastal land of Canaan at the command of Yahweh. The Israelites believed that God made a covenant, or agreement, with Abraham at this time. "I will make of you a great nation" was God's promise to bless Abraham and his descendants if they would remain faithful.

Once in the land of Canaan, the descendants of Abraham shared the land with other related peoples, such as the Phoenicians and Philistines. After a severe drought brought a terrible famine to Canaan, the Israelites migrated to Egypt. There they lived peacefully for several generations, until the pharaohs began to enslave them. In the 1200s B.C., the Israelite leader **Moses** led his people out of Egypt in an exodus, or departure, into the Sinai Desert. Every year during the festival of Passover, Jews today retell the story of the Exodus from Egypt.

According to the Bible, during the long trek across the desert of the Sinai Peninsula, God renewed the covenant made with Abraham. Moses and the Israelites pledged to reject all gods other than the one true God and to obey God's laws, the most important of which would be called the Ten Commandments. The Ten Commandments, which later had a profound influence on the religious and moral outlook of the West, are recorded in the Biblical book of Exodus:

> 66 I the Lord am your God who brought you out of the land of Egypt, the house of bondage: You shall have no other gods beside Me.
> You shall not make for yourself a sculptured image. . . .
> You shall not swear falsely by the name of the Lord your God. . . .
> Remember the sabbath day and keep it holy. . . .

Visualizing History Scribes recopied the Torah carefully, comparing each letter and word to the original copy. *What important Jewish holy writings made up the Torah?*

> Honor your father and your mother, that you may long endure on the land that the Lord your God is giving you.
> You shall not murder.
> You shall not commit adultery.
> You shall not steal.
> You shall not bear false witness against your neighbor.
> You shall not covet . . . anything that is your neighbor's. 99
> —Exodus 20:2–14

In return for their loyalty, God promised the Israelites a safe return to the land of Canaan.

Settling the Land

Moses died before reaching Canaan, but his successor, Joshua, led the Israelites across the Jordan River into Canaan. For about 200 years, the Israelites fought the Philistines and the Canaanites who lived in the land. In 1012 B.C., **David**, a prominent military leader, became the Israelite king. He set up the capital at **Jerusalem**, organized a central government, and enlarged his kingdom's borders. During the reigns of David and his son Solomon, the Israelites enjoyed economic prosperity. Under Solomon's direction, a magnificent temple to God was built in Jerusalem.

Chapter 1 *Rise of Civilizations* **37**

Covenant and Exodus

Why do Jews today celebrate Passover?
to commemorate their departure from bondage in Egypt

Visualizing History To this day, after a scribe finishes copying the Torah onto parchment sheets, the sheets are sewn together with special thread made from animal muscles. The connected sheets are then attached to rollers.
Answer to Caption: *the first five books of the Bible: Genesis, Exodus, Leviticus, Numbers, and Deuteronomy*

Language Have students focus on the two Greek roots of the term for the early Israelites' major innovation: *monotheism*. After explaining that *monos* means "alone" or "single" and *theos* means "god," ask students for other words that incorporate either of the two roots. (*Answers may include* monogamy, monologue, monorail, *and* theocracy *and* theologian.) **L1**

Daily Life Ask students to find out some differences between the Hebrew alphabet and the English alphabet. (*The Hebrew alphabet is read from right to left and has essentially no vowels.*) **L2**

COOPERATIVE LEARNING ACTIVITY

Reading and Summarizing Organize the class into small groups. Give each group a copy of *Exodus*: Chapters 1–13. Have all groups read Chapters 3–4 and summarize the points made in the dialogue between God and Moses. Divide the remaining chapters among the groups. Ask each group to read its section and work together to summarize the arguments Moses used to convince Pharaoh to let the Hebrews leave Egypt. Regroup students so that each chapter has been read by someone in each new group. Tell students to learn from other group members about the chapters they did not read. Ask students to write a paragraph comparing the arguments in later chapters with the original dialogue between God and Moses. **L2**

Multicultural Have students read the following sections of the Hebrew Bible to see how the Israelites and the Hittites intermingled: Genesis 23, Genesis 26:34–35, II Samuel 11. Ask students to describe each interaction of the two peoples. **L2**

Geography: Movement Have students make travel plans for an ancient Greek who wants to visit one of the empires discussed in this section. Have them plot the route on an outline map, and then write a detailed description of it, including method of travel and a description of each site to be visited. **L2**

Geography: Environment In the Hanging Gardens, Nebuchadnezzar put plants that would remind his wife of her home in the mountains of Media (northwestern Iran). Have students make a catalog of plants that Nebuchadnezzar might have placed in the Hanging Gardens had his wife come from the students' own region. **L1 LEP**

ASSESS

Check for Understanding

Assign Section 2 Review as homework or as an in-class activity.

▣ Use Student Self-Test and Review Software to review Section 2.

Exile and Return

After Solomon's death in 922 B.C., the Israelite kingdom was divided into two parts: Israel in the north, and Judah in the south. In 722 B.C. the Assyrians of Mesopotamia conquered Israel, scattering its people throughout the Assyrian Empire. Then, in 586 B.C., another Mesopotamian people, the Chaldeans (kal•DEE•uhnz), gained control of Judah and destroyed the Temple in Jerusalem. They enslaved some of the city's residents and carried them off to exile in the Chaldean capital city of Babylon.

During this difficult period, a series of prophets arose among the Israelites, who were called Jews after the Babylonian exile. Some prophets, such as Jeremiah, condemned abuses in society and blamed the exile on the Jews' forgetting their duties to God and to one another. The prophets also helped the people of Judah retain their culture during the exile.

While in Babylon, the Jews no longer had a temple in which to worship God. Instead, small groups of Jews began to meet on the Sabbath, the holy day of rest, for prayer and discussion. The rise of local synagogues developed from these gatherings.

Many Jews continued to hope for a return to Jerusalem. Finally, in 539 B.C., the Persians, a people living east of the Fertile Crescent, conquered the Chaldeans. The Persian king allowed the Jewish exiles to return to Judah and to rebuild the Temple in Jerusalem. In the 400s B.C., Jewish holy writings were collected and organized into the Torah, made up of the first five books of the Bible: Genesis, Exodus, Leviticus, Numbers, and Deuteronomy. The Jewish Scriptures begin with the Torah and include the writings of the prophets.

Although a new Jewish community arose in Jerusalem, many Jews chose to remain in Babylon, and some migrated to other areas in the Middle East. Ever since this time, communities of Jews have existed outside their homeland in what has become known as the Diaspora, a Greek word meaning "scattered."

Middle Eastern Empires

The Phoenicians, Aramaens, Lydians, and Israelites gave the world their alphabets, languages, commercial practices, and religious beliefs. These peoples, however, lacked the military power of their neighbors, and the conquering armies of a series of warlike empires came to rule the Fertile Crescent.

The Hittites

About 2000 B.C., a warrior people known as the Hittites set up a well-organized kingdom in Asia Minor, the peninsula jutting eastward between the Mediterranean, Aegean, and Black Seas. The Hittites' fearsome army–the first in the Middle East to wield iron weapons extensively–pushed outward to conquer Syria to the south and part of Mesopotamia. The Hittite empire lasted until about 1200 B.C.

The Assyrians

The Hittites were followed by the Assyrians, a people living in northern Mesopotamia. By 650 B.C., the Assyrians had conquered an empire stretching from Asia Minor and the Persian Gulf into Egypt. Known as the most deadly fighting force in the Middle East, the Assyrian army fought with iron weapons and used battering rams against the walls of the cities they attacked. It treated conquered peoples cruelly, burning cities and torturing and killing thousands of captives.

Assyrian kings divided their vast empire into provinces. Officials sent from the central government collected taxes to support the army and to fund building projects. To improve communication, the Assyrians built a network of roads linking the provinces. In spite of the empire's strengths, rebellions by conquered peoples gradually weakened Assyrian rule.

The Chaldeans

In 612 B.C. a neighboring people, the Chaldeans, invaded and destroyed the Assyrian Empire. The Chaldeans were descended from people of Hammurabi's Babylonian Empire of the 1700s B.C. They reached the height of their power during the reign of one of their greatest rulers, King Nebuchadnezzar (NEH•byuh•kuhd•NEH•zuhr), from 605 B.C. to 562 B.C. Nebuchadnezzar rebuilt the Chaldean capital of Babylon into one of the largest, most beautiful cities of the ancient world. Babylon was especially known for its immense wall and its Hanging Gardens.

The Chaldeans were also noted for their interest in astrology. They recorded their observations of the stars and made maps that showed the position of the planets and the phases of the moon. Their studies laid the foundations for the science of astronomy.

The Persians

The Chaldeans were challenged by the Persians, who lived on a plateau between the Persian Gulf and the Caspian Sea, in the area of present-day Iran. In 539 B.C. under their king Cyrus II, the Persians seized

---

Babylon and then took control of the rest of the Chaldean Empire. In 525 B.C. Persian armies had conquered Egypt, bringing all of the Middle East under Persian rule. Unlike earlier empire-builders, the Persians were tolerant rulers who allowed conquered peoples to retain their own languages, religions, and laws.

During the late 400s B.C., the Persians waged war against the Greeks for control of Asia Minor. They tried to conquer Greece itself, but the campaign was a disaster and ended further Persian efforts toward western expansion.

The best organizer among the Persian kings was **Darius I**, who reigned from 522 B.C. to 486 B.C. Darius brought artisans from many of his conquered lands to build **Persepolis**, the most magnificent city in the empire. He assigned satraps, or governors, to rule the provinces of the empire. Inspectors called "Eyes and Ears of the King" made unannounced tours of the provinces and reported directly to the king on the activities of local officials. To advance trade throughout the empire and aid the movement of soldiers, Darius had Persian engineers improve and expand the network of roads first laid down by the Assyrians. The Royal Road, the most important thoroughfare in the empire, stretched more than 1,500 miles (2,400 km) from Persia to Asia Minor.

The Persians viewed their monarchy as a sacred institution. Persian kings commanded great

respect and were surrounded by pomp and pageantry. This style of kingship later shaped the development of monarchies in the Western world. Another influence of the Persians was religious in nature. About 570 B.C., **Zoroaster** (ZOHR•uh•WAS•tuhr), a Persian prophet, preached that the universe was divided by a struggle between a good supreme god, Ahura Mazda, and a lesser evil spiritual being, Ahriman. According to Zoroaster, all humans were caught up in this struggle and had to choose between good and evil. At the end of time, Ahura Mazda would triumph. Those on the side of good would be rewarded with eternal life; those who chose evil would be condemned after death to eternal darkness. Some scholars believe that Zoroaster's teachings about the afterlife may have influenced Judaism, Christianity, and Islam.

The Persian Empire

Persia, c. 640 B.C.
Extent of Persian Empire, c. 330 B.C.
→ Trade routes
— Royal Road

0   200   400 mi.
0 200 400 km
Mercator Projection

The Persians created four capital cities for their empire: Persepolis, Susa, Babylon, and Sardis.
Region How did the Persians win the loyalty of many different peoples in this vast empire?

SECTION 2 REVIEW

Recall
1. **Define** dynasty, monarchy, bureaucracy, empire, polytheism, city-state, alphabet, monotheism, prophet.
2. **Identify** Narmer, Hatshepsut, Thutmose III, Ramses II, Piankhi, *Gilgamesh*, Hammurabi, Moses,

David, Chaldeans, Hittites, Darius I, Zoroaster.
3. **Explain** the significance of Jerusalem to the Jews in exile in Babylon.

Critical Thinking
4. **Synthesizing Information** What reaction would you have

had to Akhenaton's reforms if you had been an Egyptian priest?

Understanding Themes
5. **Cultural Diffusion** Why was the Phoenician alphabet a significant development in the ancient Middle East?

Chapter 1 *Rise of Civilizations* 39

SECTION 2 REVIEW ANSWERS

1. All vocabulary words are defined in the Glossary.
2. Narmer, 30; Hatshepsut, 31; Thutmose III, 31; Ramses II, 31; Piankhi, 34; *Gilgamesh*, 35; Hammurabi, 35; Moses, 37; David, 37; Chaldeans, 38; Hittites, 38; Darius I, 39; Zoroaster, 39

3. The Jews longed to return to Jerusalem, the site of Solomon's temple.
4. Priests resented the loss of their power.
5. **CULTURAL DIFFUSION** It was more efficient for record keeping and correspondence and easier to learn than the previous systems.

Map Study

Answer
by respecting local customs

Map Skills Practice

Reading a Map What was the distance between Susa and Sardis along the Royal Road? *(about 1,400 miles or 2,253 kilometers)*

Evaluate

📁 Section Quiz 1-2

💻 Use the Testmaker to create a customized quiz for Section 2.

Linking Past and Present

Zoroastrians The Parsees of the Bombay area in India are modern Zoroastrians. Their ancestors traveled to India from Iran in the A.D. 700s to avoid Muslim persecution. The Parsees represent an important economic group in India. From about 1850 on, they proved successful in industries such as shipbuilding and the railways.

CLOSE

Ask students to reflect on the transitory nature of the empires built by the Hittites, Assyrians, Chaldeans, and Persians. What remains of the original empire in each case? (*Little remains of these empires; students might discuss ways in which each empire has indirectly affected later cultures.*)

NATIONAL GEOGRAPHIC *Special Report*

Special Report Summary

Discoveries at the Valley of the Kings in 1922 revealed the magnificence of ancient royalty in Egypt.

Discoveries made in 1988 and the early 1990s revealed details of lives of Egyptian commoners.

A bakery and skeletons reveal the diet and hard labor of the commoners.

Art, culture, and faith may have developed up from the average man and woman, rather than down from royalty.

TEACH

Points to Discuss

After students have read the feature, ask the following: **What archaeological remains indicate differences in life for royalty and for commoners?** *(Royal tombs and relics indicate great wealth; skeletons of workers reveal years of hard labor.)* **Why would people be willing to spend a life of toil and perhaps injury to build monumental tombs for their**

The Egyptians

The Valley of the Kings has seen more than its share of visitors. For thousands of years, travelers, warriors, and more recently, archaeologists have descended on this area on the outskirts of what is now Luxor to marvel at the magnificence of ancient Egypt. It was thought that most of

what there was to discover had been found after British explorer Howard Carter opened up the tomb of Tutankhamen in 1922.

Then in 1988, plans were made to build a parking lot over the site of Tomb 5, which had been discovered—and looted—years earlier. Wanting to make sure that the parking facility would not seal off anything important, Egyptologist Kent Weeks of the American University of

Cairo decided to make one last exploration of the tomb. To his surprise, beyond a few debris-choked rooms, he opened a door that led to the mostly unexcavated tomb of perhaps 50 of the sons of Ramses II, the powerful pharaoh who ruled Egypt from 1279 to 1212 B.C.

Though the tomb was emptied of valuables long ago, archaeologists consider Weeks's discovery a major find. Scientists and researchers hope

40 **Chapter 1** *Rise of Civilizations*

TEACHER NOTES

_____
_____
_____
_____
_____

pharaohs? *(Some scholars believe that the divine aspect of Egyptian society was expressed through the pharaoh, and building a tomb for the leader may have been an act of religious faith for the workers.)* **Why was the discovery of the bakery and the cemetery significant?** *(These finds were rich sources of information about the life of common Egyptians.)*

Cultural Perspectives

Burial Chambers Ancient Egyptians buried their kings in a secret chamber inside or beneath a pyramid. The pyramids protected and preserved the bodies, which the Egyptians believed was necessary for the soul to live forever. They filled the chamber with gold and other treasures as well as practical, everyday items. Egyptians believed that the king would need these things in the afterlife.

---

that artifacts found in the tomb will provide clues about Egyptian civilization during Egypt's last golden age.

For students of Judeo-Christian history, any information on Ramses' oldest son, Amen-hir-khopshef, would be a most important discovery. Ramses was in power when, in retribution for the enslavement of the Israelites, according to the Book of Exodus, the Lord "...smote all the firstborn in the land of Egypt, from the firstborn of Pharaoh that sat on his throne unto the firstborn of the captive that was in the dungeon."

The tomb and pyramids of

ancient Egypt hold many answers: These stone monuments have certainly established the immortality of the pharaohs. But what about the commoners, who vastly outnumbered the royalty? What of the men and women who gave their strength, sweat, and lives to create Egypt's lasting monuments? The widespread fame of the Sphinx and the Pyramids at Giza make it easy to forget that basic questions about Egyptian history have remained unanswered. Only recently have Egyptologists begun to fill in those gaps.

SEVERAL YEARS AGO, archaeologists began to excavate two sites—located about half a mile from the Sphinx—searching for signs of the

Offerings of food are carved in relief on an official's tomb (left).

Another pyramid nears completion about 2500 B.C. (above). Limestone facing blocks were quarried across the Nile and ferried to the work site. Teams then dragged the blocks to ramps made of rubble that were built around the pyramid during construction. Some experts believe that it took only 10,000 men—far below earlier estimates of up to 100,000—and 25 years to lay 5 million tons of rock. Half lion, half pharaoh, the Sphinx (in the foreground) is carved from an outcropping left unexcavated in a U-shaped quarry.

📖 Focus on World Art Print 7, Egyptian. *Mask of Tutankhamen*

📑 World History and Art Transparency 2, *Tutankhamen's Throne*

📑 Mapping History Overlay Transparency 2, *Ancient Egypt*

Chapter 1 *Rise of Civilizations* **41**

- The Pyramids are one of the Seven Wonders of the Ancient World.
- A broken section of the head of the Great Sphinx indicates that it may have been used as a target for gun practice at various times throughout history.

- The ancient Egyptians were among the first to use clocks and calendars, to produce books, and to devise formulas for finding the area and volume of geometric figures.
- One of the greatest treasures ever found

in ancient Egypt was the tomb of the boy-king Tutankhamen. When the tomb was opened in 1922, nearly 5,000 items from the fourteenth century B.C. came to light.

NATIONAL GEOGRAPHIC *Special Report*

Linking Past and Present

Tourism is an important economic activity in Egypt today. The warm, dry climate and magnificent relics from ancient times attract visitors from all over the world.

NATIONAL GEOGRAPHIC SOCIETY

Use these materials to enrich student understanding of ancient Egyptian culture.

- 💿 **NGS PICTURESHOW CD-ROM**
  Egypt and the Fertile Crescent
- **NGS PICTUREPACK TRANSPARENCY SET**
  Ancient Egypt
- **ANCIENT CIVILIZATIONS POSTER SET**
  Ancient Egypt

ordinary people who built the pyramids. Within months they uncovered the remains of many mud-brick buildings, including the oldest bakery yet discovered in Egypt.

This was a significant find. While the pyramids built Egypt by drawing its provinces together in a unified effort, it can be said that bread built the pyramids. For thousands of workers, a loaf of emmer-wheat bread—washed down with beer—was most likely the dietary staple.

At about the time the bakery was discovered, searchers also unearthed a cemetery of 600 graves of workers. Their skeletons revealed years of hard labor: Vertebrae were compressed and damaged from years of carrying heavy loads. Some skeletons were missing fingers and even limbs. A few of the tombs were adorned with mini-pyramids several feet high, made of mud brick. Nothing like these tiny pyramids had been found before. In the past, scholars believed that the pyramid form was invented as the shape for a royal tomb. However, Zahi Hawass, director general of the Giza Pyramids, thinks that the pyramid form actually may have arisen among the common people. He believes that the mini-pyramids evolved from sacred rectangular mounds found in tombs even older than the pharaohs' pyramids.

Life for most ancient Egyptians was hard. Society was built around a preoccupation with the pharaohs' immortality. But perhaps there were spiritual rewards for the common people in this devotion to their pharaohs. Some scholars think that ancient Egyptians believed not so much that the pharaoh was divine,

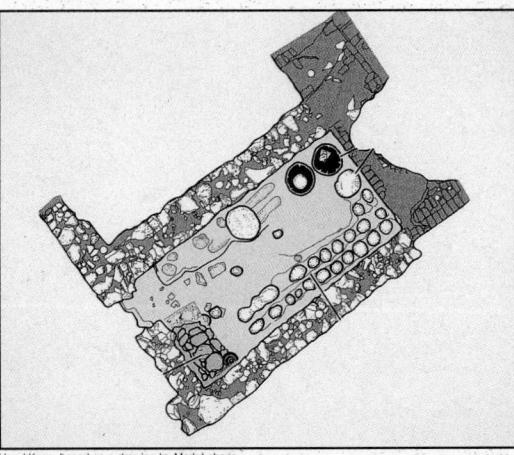

Hosul Kang, based on a drawing by Mark Lehner

Kenneth Garrett

🔲 *A drawing of an ancient bakery (top) was used to build this replica of an ancient Egyptian bakery near Saqqara, Egypt (bottom).*

but that through the pharaoh the divine nature of their society was expressed. Building a pyramid might have been an act of faith much as building a cathedral was in the Middle Ages.

Such recent discoveries about the life of the common people may lead to a new way of seeing ancient Egypt: not only as a brilliant civilization of the elite trickling down to the masses but also as a culture built

from the bottom up—a culture that stood on the daily toil of the workers and the beliefs of ordinary men and women.

Much of the emerging picture of daily life in ancient Egypt is one of arduous toil. The villages were crowded and dirty. Huts were made of thatch and mud brick. Men wore loincloths; women dressed in long sheaths with wide shoulder straps; and children went naked. On wooden sledges workers hauled the giant granite blocks that built the pyramids. Egypt created a vast agricultural empire, yet all the irrigation was done by hand. Farmers filled two heavy jars from the canals, then hung them from a yoke over their shoulders. Oxen dragging wooden plows tilled the fertile soil along the Nile, followed by lines of sowers who sang in cadence as they cast grains of emmer wheat from baskets.

There is much still to be learned and understood about daily life in ancient Egypt. The discovery of the bakery has provided insight into what sustained the masses; the bones in the commoners' graveyard tell us that life was not easy; the mini-pyramids illustrate that art, culture, and faith may have developed up from the average man and woman, rather than down from the royalty. For years Egyptologists have focused on the grandiose—and thereby disregarded most of Egyptian society. Eventually, however, our view of ancient Egyptian culture is broadening to encompass those responsible for creating it.

MORE ABOUT...

Recreation Although the ancient Egyptians were hard workers as farmers and pyramid builders, they also found time for leisure activities. Sailing on the Nile was a popular family pastime. Egyptians also enjoyed swimming and fishing on the Nile. Many Egyptians also liked to watch wrestling matches. The more adventurous hunted crocodiles, lions, hippopotamuses, and wild cattle with spears or bows and arrows. At home, Egyptians liked to play *senet*, a board game much like backgammon.

Kenneth Garrett

◼ *A potter was hired to make replicas of the old baking pots. A local worker (top left) heats the tops in a wood fire in preparation for baking.*

◼ *A kind of wheat known as emmer was supplied by a Californian who collects and grows ancient grains. The wet flour made from the emmer was left outside to collect free-floating native yeast spores and bacteria. (Store-bought yeast was not known to ancient Egyptians.) On baking day, the dough was placed into the pot bottoms and allowed to rise (bottom left). A hole for each pot was dug in the hot coals. The heated pot tops were then placed on the heated bottom halves and were placed in the coals to bake.*

◼ *Success! For perhaps the first time in more than 4,000 years, a loaf of emmer bread popped out of an Old Kingdom-style pot. Edward Wood (above), who has been baking ancient breads for 50 years, holds up a perfect loaf.*

Kenneth Garrett

Kenneth Garrett

Chapter 1 *Rise of Civilizations* **43**

CURRICULUM CONNECTION

MATHEMATICS
The Pyramid of Khufu contains more than 2 million stone blocks that average 2 1/2 short tons (2.3 metric tons) each. The pyramid was originally 481 feet (147 meters) high. Its base covers about 13 acres (5 hectares).

Global  Gourmet
Egypt Just as emmer-wheat bread was the staple in the pyramid builders diet, most villagers and poor city dwellers today eat a simple diet based on bread and *fool* (broad beans). For a typical evening meal, each person dips bread into a large communal bowl of vegetable stew.

Portfolio Project
Tell students that the study of ancient Egypt is called "Egyptology." Have students choose one of the following categories—architecture, woodworking, metalworking, or written records, and list five facts that they have learned about life in ancient Egypt.

TEACHER NOTES

SECTION THEME

▶ **Relation to Environment** Peoples in Asia and the Americas adapt to a variety of environments.

ind Out

Answer: *Asian and Native American civilizations developed agricultural techniques, religious beliefs, trading networks, governmental institutions, and an understanding of astronomy and mathematics.*

FOCUS

Section Objective

Describe how Asians and Native Americans made use of their environments.

BELLRINGER
Motivational Activity

Before taking roll at the beginning of the class period, project Section Focus Transparency 1-3 and have students answer the activity questions. Discuss students' responses.

📁 This activity is also available as a blackline master.

Vocabulary Pre-check
🖥 Use the Vocabulary Puzzle-Maker to create a puzzle that reinforces the vocabulary terms in this section. **L1**

---

c. 2500 B.C.
Settlements develop along the Indus River.

c. 1500 B.C.
Olmec civilization begins in Mexico.

c. 1028 B.C.
The Zhou establish a dynasty in China.

c. 527 B.C.
Siddhartha Gautama introduces Buddhism.

2500 B.C.   1500 B.C.   500 B.C.

Section 3

Civilizations in Asia and the Americas

Setting the Scene

▶ **Terms to Define**
varna, *dharma*, *jati*, reincarnation, karma, nirvana, yin and yang, slash-and-burn farming

▶ **People to Meet**
Siddhartha Gautama, Confucius (Kongfuzi), Laozi

▶ **Places to Locate**
Harappa, Mohenjo-Daro, Hindu Kush, Ganges Plain, Huang He valley, Mexico

ind Out   What were the major achievements of early civilizations in Asia and the Americas?

The Storyteller

Siddhartha stood still, as if a snake lay in his path. Suddenly the icy thought stole over him: he must begin his life completely afresh. "I am no longer what I was, . . I am no longer a hermit, no longer a priest, no longer a Brahmin. How can I return home? What would I do at home with my father? Study? Offer sacrifices? Practice meditation? All this is over for me now." He realized how alone he was. Now he was Siddhartha, the awakened. He must begin his life afresh. He began to walk quickly, no longer homewards, no longer looking back.

—from *Siddhartha*, Herman Hesse, translated by Hilda Rosner, 1957

About the same time as the rise of civilizations in Africa and the Middle East, civilizations also appeared in Asia and the Americas. These civilizations developed systems of government and belief, expanded their borders, and established networks of trade and commerce.

South Asia

East of Iran, the homeland of the Persians, lies the subcontinent of South Asia, a large triangular-shaped landmass that juts into the Indian Ocean. Today South Asia is made up of the nations of India, Pakistan, and Bangladesh.

Natural barriers separate the South Asian subcontinent from the rest of Asia. Water surrounds the landmass on the east and west. To the north rise two lofty mountain ranges–the Hindu Kush and the Himalayas. Plains sweep across the landscape to the south of the mountains. Across the plains flow three rivers–the Indus, Ganges (GAN•JEEZ), and Brahmaputra (BRAH•muh•POO•truh). Like the Nile Valley and the Tigris-Euphrates plains, these fertile river areas of South Asia have supported vast numbers of people over the ages.

The Indus River Valley

The first South Asian civilization arose in the Indus River valley about 2500 B.C. Archaeologists have uncovered the ruins of its two major cities: **Harappa** (huh•RA•puh), located in present-day Pakistan, and **Mohenjo-Daro** (moh•HEHN•joh DAHR•oh), situated near the Arabian Sea. The lack of written records, however, has made it difficult to learn as much about the Harappan civilization as is known about Egypt and Mesopotamia.

44 **Chapter 1** *Rise of Civilizations*

SECTION RESOURCES

📁 **Reproducible Masters**
• Reproducible Lesson Plan 1-3
• Guided Reading Activity 1-3
• Reteaching Activity 1
• Enrichment Activity 1
• Section Quiz 1-3
• Performance Assessment Activity 1
• Spanish Chapter Summary 1

🖥 **Transparencies**
• Section Focus Transparency 1-3
• Ancient India
• Ancient China

Multimedia
🖥 Vocabulary PuzzleMaker Software
🖥 Student Self-Test and Review Software
🖥 Testmaker
💿 India and China
💿 Middle and South America

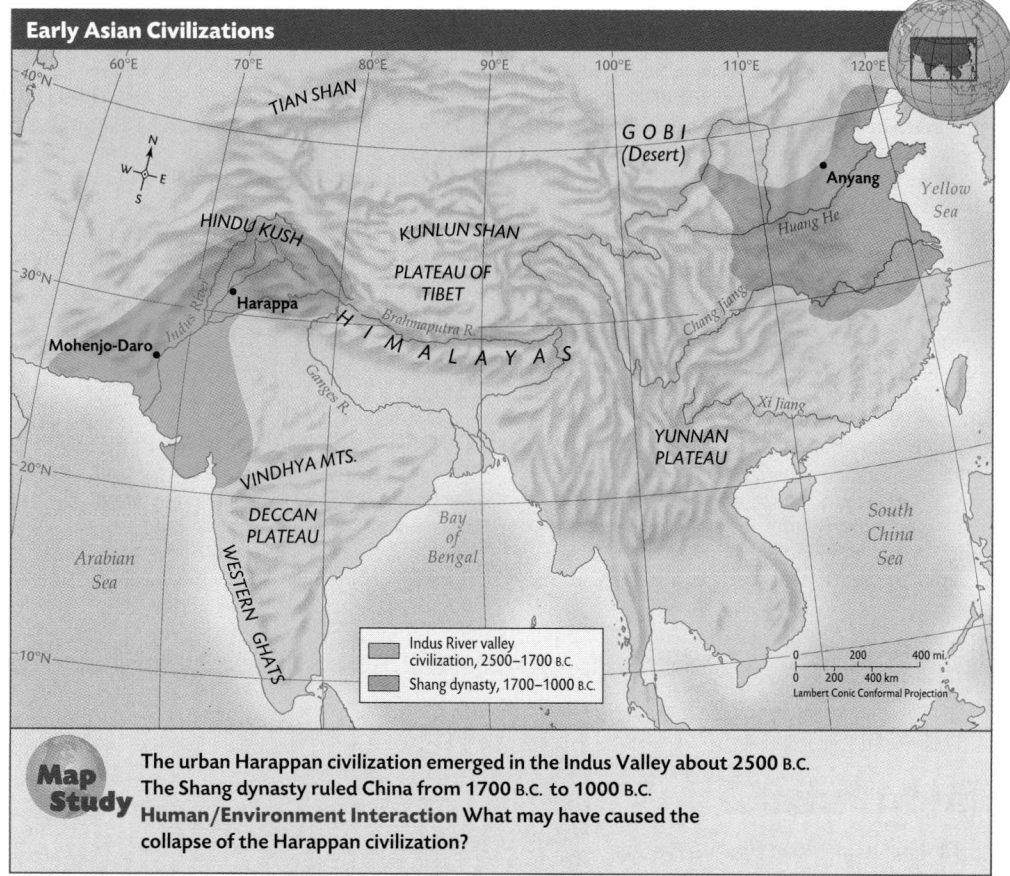

Early Asian Civilizations

Indus River valley civilization, 2500–1700 B.C.

Shang dynasty, 1700–1000 B.C.

0   200   400 mi.
0   200   400 km
Lambert Conic Conformal Projection

Map Study The urban Harappan civilization emerged in the Indus Valley about 2500 B.C. The Shang dynasty ruled China from 1700 B.C. to 1000 B.C. **Human/Environment Interaction** What may have caused the collapse of the Harappan civilization?

TEACH

Guided Practice

THEME **Relation to Environment** Using the map on page 163, ask students how the climatic conditions differed for the various North American cultures. (*Arctic and Far North: long winters with subzero temperatures; Northwest: mild winters and a cool, rainy climate much of the year; California Great Basin: warm, mild climate, with rivers making farming possible for most of year; Southwest: dry, desert climate, making farming more difficult; Great Plains: hot summers, very cold winters; Eastern Woodlands: temperate climate)* **L1**

Map Study

Answer
floods caused by climate changes, or violence—perhaps at the hands of invaders

Map Skills Practice

Reading a Map What features of physical geography, common to Egypt and Mesopotamia, were also vital to the Harappan and early Chinese civilizations? *(rivers)*

Geography: Movement Have students locate India on a map (in the text Atlas or other resource) and trace the route of conquering Aryans from central Asia to the northwestern part of the South Asian subcontinent (*modern Pakistan and northern India*). Also have them locate the area to which the Indus River valley people fled to escape Aryan capture *(southern part of Indian peninsula)*. **L1 LEP**

Based on archaeological evidence, historians do know that the Harappans had a sophisticated culture. Urban centers were well planned, and many city dwellers prospered from the production of clay pots, metallic vessels, jewelry, and cotton cloth. The discovery of Harrapan artifacts in Mesopotamia indicates that Indus Valley people traded with the people of Mesopotamia as early as 2300 B.C.

In spite of its prosperous economy, the Indus civilization had ended by 1500 B.C. Historians have many theories for what caused this collapse. Evidence of floods, for example, suggests possible climate changes. In the Mohenjo-Daro ruins are signs that some of its residents may have met a violent end, possibly at the hands of invaders.

Aryans

About 1500 B.C. waves of invaders from areas northwest of South Asia swept through passes in the **Hindu Kush** mountain range into the Indus River valley and the **Ganges Plain**. Known as Aryans, these warriors were distantly related to the Persians. They subdued the local inhabitants and developed a new civilization that eventually spread over much of South Asia. Aspects of this civilization endure today in the subcontinent, especially in the Republic of India.

The Aryans soon settled down into an agricultural way of life. In time they developed a complex social system consisting of four main social classes, or *varnas*. Each *varna* had its own dharma, or duties, and took pride in doing them well. Priests, or Brahmans, were the most honored *varna*. They were followed by the Kshatriyas (KSHA• tree•uhz), or warriors. Next in rank were merchants, artisans, and farmers, called Vaisyas (VYSH•yuhz); and unskilled laborers and servants, known as Sudras (SHOO•druhz).

By 500 B.C. the *varnas* had further divided into smaller groups known as *jati*. *Jati* were based on occupations and had their own rules for diet,

Chapter 1 *Rise of Civilizations* **45**

COOPERATIVE LEARNING ACTIVITY

Visual Presentations Organize the class into groups of five or six students. Have each group choose a topic from this list of suggestions: religion, architecture, city planning, farming, textiles, arts and crafts, commerce, and geography. Have groups research their topic as it pertains to Harappan civilization. They should then prepare visuals illustrating what they have learned about their topic. The items may be labeled, but the emphasis should be on a visual presentation. Each group should decide what task the members of the group will perform. Provide space for the groups to display their completed work. Discussion of the displays should include a time for questions and answers. **L2**

Daily Life Have students select one *varna*, or social group, to which they would want to belong (assuming they had a choice). Then have them tell or write a short explanation of why they chose the particular group. Students should mention the daily roles, rights, and duties of members of the category they have chosen. **L1 LEP**

NATIONAL GEOGRAPHIC SOCIETY

Use these materials to enrich student understanding of ancient India.

 NGS PICTUREPACK TRANSPARENCY SET
Ancient India

Who?What?Where?When?

Concepts of Time Western and Hindu beliefs differ profoundly. Consider the concept of time. Westerners see time as a steady, fixed progression. To Westerners, when a moment is gone, it is gone forever. Hindus see time as a revolving, endless circle. To Hindus, everything that happens today has happened before and will happen again.

marriage, and social customs. These groups lived in separate neighborhoods and did not mix socially with others. Outside the system of *varnas* and *jati* were the pariahs, or "untouchables." They did work that was considered unclean, such as skinning animals and tanning their hides for leather. The pariahs lived outside the villages and were shunned by most other people.

Epic Literature

The Aryans originally passed their traditions by word of mouth from generation to generation. Eventually they developed a written form of their spoken language, Sanskrit. Priests collected Aryan hymns and religious rituals into holy books known as Vedas (VAY•duhz). Also committed to writing were a number of epics, or long poems celebrating deities and legendary heroes.

One of these epics was the *Mahabharata* (muh•HAH•BAH•ruh•tuh). Considered the world's longest poem, it tells the story of a series of battles fought by two warrior families with the help of the gods. Included in the *Mahabharata* is the *Bhagavad Gita* (BAH•guh•VAHD GEE•tuh), or "Song of the Lord," one of the world's most important religious texts. It describes how the god Krishna appeared before the warrior Arjuna just before a battle, assured him that all souls survive death, and urged him to fulfill his duty as a warrior.

Another epic, the well-loved *Ramayana*, presents the moving tale of Rama and Sita (SEE•tuh). Rama was the ideal king; Sita, his faithful wife. Vividly describing the struggle between good and evil, the *Ramayana* tells how the demon Ravana captures Sita. When Rama finds that she is missing, he cries:

> ❝ Sita! Gentle Sita! If you have wanted to prove my love, if you are hiding from us, let the agony of my fear suffice. Come to me, my love, come to me!
> He stood there, both his arms held wide, as though half hoping she might run

Images *of the* Times

Hindu Beliefs

The three main gods of Hinduism are Brahma, Vishnu, and Siva. Brahma is creator of the world, Vishnu is preserver, and Siva is destroyer. These three are part of the same universal spirit.

Meeting to read holy writings such as the *Mahabharata* is a long-standing custom among Hindus in India.

46

Images *of the* Times   Hindu Beliefs

The Hindu religion is polytheistic, which means that followers worship many gods. Early Hindus worshiped gods that represented powers in nature—the sun and the rain, for example. In time, some Hindus began to believe that gods appear in various forms, and that these separate forms are part of one universal spirit called Brahman. These Hindus believed that Brahman consists of many divinities. The creation of religious art was itself regarded as an act of worship. Many Hindu shrines are literally covered with stone sculptures of nymphs, dwarfs, serpents, and demons. Sometimes these figures represent one of the principal gods, often Vishnu or Siva.

forward to his embrace. The country lay very still around him. Only the old tree shivered in every leafy spray and seemed to wring its hands for pity.

Slowly that gleam of hope faded, and his arms fell to his sides. 🙻

Rama at first doubts that Sita has been kidnapped. But he later realizes the truth, Sita is saved, and the couple is reunited. Like other Indian epics, the *Ramayana* ends happily, with good winning over evil.

Hinduism

As political and social organizations evolved, the Aryan religion, with its belief in many deities, slowly changed into Hinduism, the national religion of India. Hinduism was not founded on the teachings of one person, nor did it have one holy book. Instead it was based on different beliefs and practices, many of which had their roots in the Vedas and the Indian epics. Other ideas that became part of Hinduism came from religious thinkers who had grown discontented with the Aryan priests' complex external rituals. Between 800 B.C. and 400 B.C., their search for wisdom and truth was reflected in the religious writings known as the *Upanishads* (oo•PAH•nih•SHAHDZ).

The *Upanishads* view all of life as sacred. They state that all living things—gods, goddesses, humans, and animals—have souls that are part of one eternal spirit, sometimes called Brahman Nerguna. Because of this belief in the unity of life, many Hindus came to practice nonviolence toward living creatures, avoiding meat and not harming animals. The *Upanishads* teach that forms of self-denial such as fasting help people achieve union with the universal spirit. They encourage the practice of yoga, a discipline that combines physical and mental exercises designed to help one achieve a state of tranquillity.

Also presented in the *Upanishads* is the idea of reincarnation, or the rebirth of the soul. Hindus believe the soul passes through many lifetimes before it finally achieves union with the universal spirit. The *Upanishads* offer this picture of rebirth:

Much of India's fine art is related to its religions. Hindus built elaborate temples, such as this Mehsana Sun Temple (interior shown).

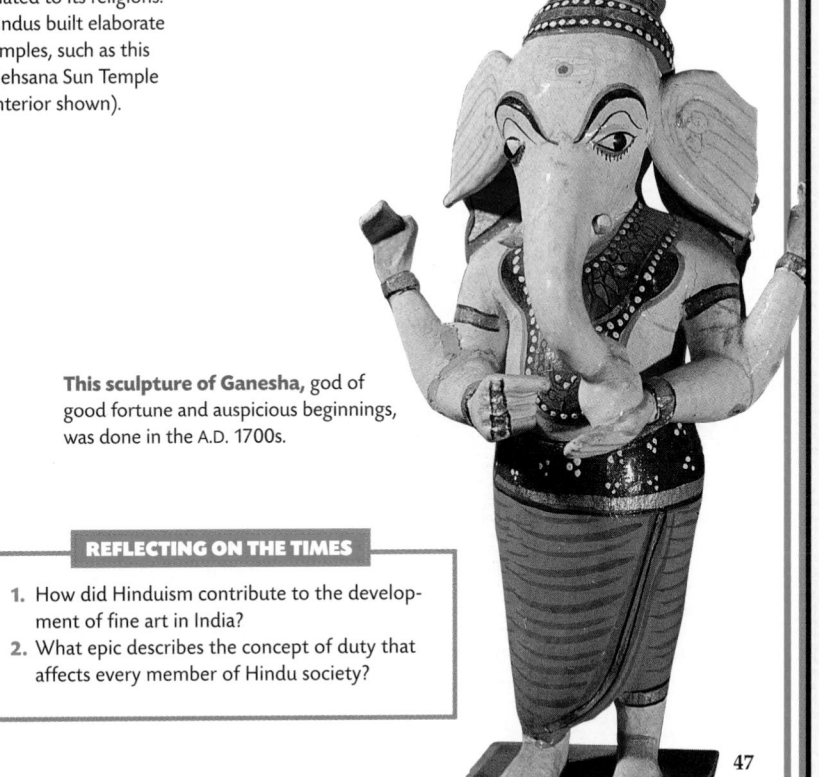

This sculpture of Ganesha, god of good fortune and auspicious beginnings, was done in the A.D. 1700s.

REFLECTING ON THE TIMES

1. How did Hinduism contribute to the development of fine art in India?
2. What epic describes the concept of duty that affects every member of Hindu society?

47

ANSWERS TO REFLECTING ON THE TIMES

1. The many gods and goddesses of Hinduism inspired much Indian art.
2. the *Mahabharata*

Visualizing History Oracle bones used to obtain advice about military campaigns were often inscribed with the question and answer and preserved as part of the king's records. *Why were such oracle bones stored by the rulers?*

Visualizing History Oracle-bone inscriptions were usually made on the shoulder blades of animals, mainly oxen, or else on turtle shells. The questions that were asked the priest concerned sacrifices, weather, war, hunting, travel, or luck. The form of the question had to yield a yes or no answer.
Answer to Caption: *to have a record of the king's question and the answer*

History & Art In two of his four hands, Siva holds symbols of his divine nature—the drum of creation and the flame of destruction. Apasmara, the dwarf beneath his foot, represents the illusions that Siva dispels. **Why do you think Siva is ringed by flames?** *(He is the god of destruction.)*
Answer to Caption: *Since all living things have souls, animals are sacred and cannot be killed.*

Rise of Buddhism
To what other parts of Asia and the world did Buddhism spread?
It spread to China, Japan, Korea, and the Middle East.

> As a caterpillar, having reached the end of a blade of grass, takes hold of another blade, then draws its body from the first, so the Self, having reached the end of his body, takes hold of another body, then draws itself from the first.

Hindus believed that the cycle of rebirth is determined by a principle called **karma.** According to this principle, how a person lives one life determines what form the person will take in the next life. To move toward the universal spirit, one must live a good life and fulfill one's dharma.

History & Art Siva, ringed by a circle of flames, dances on the back of the dwarf Apasmara. *Why do Hindus regard animals as sacred?*

48 **Chapter 1** *Rise of Civilizations*

Rise of Buddhism

During the 500s B.C., changes occurred in Indian religious life. Many devout Hindus became dissatisfied with external rituals and wanted a more spiritual faith. They left the towns and villages and looked for solitude in the hills and forests. Through meditation, many of these religious seekers developed new insights and became religious teachers. Their ideas and practices often led to the rise of new religions. The most influential of the new religions was Buddhism.

The Buddha
Siddhartha Gautama (sih•DAHR•tuh GOW•tuh•muh), the founder of Buddhism, began his life as a prince. Born around 566 B.C., Gautama was raised in luxury. As a young man, he continued to live a sheltered life, shielded from sickness and poverty. Tradition states that one day Gautama's charioteer drove him around his estates, and for the first time Gautama saw sickness, old age, and death. Shocked at these scenes of misery, Gautama decided to find out why people suffered and how suffering could be ended. At the age of 29, he left his wife and newborn son and wandered throughout India.

For seven years Gautama lived as a hermit, seeking the truth through fasting and self-denial. This did not lead him to the truth, however. One day, while meditating under a tree, Gautama gained a flash of insight that he felt gave him an answer to the problem of suffering. He began to share with others the meaning of his "enlightenment." Dressed in a yellow robe, he preached his message to people and

MEETING SPECIAL NEEDS ACTIVITY

Learning Style: Visual/Spatial Students who need additional guidance in following the chronology of the development of Hinduism and the emergence of Buddhism might prepare a list of events and dates from this chapter. (The list can also be written on the chalkboard.) Then have students place the events on a time line. Visual learners might benefit from drawing small pictures or symbols to illustrate events or people listed. Have students compare their time lines with the one on page 44. Students, working in pairs or small groups, may add important historical events from Chinese and early American history presented in this section. **L1**

began to gather followers. His closest friends began calling him the Buddha, or "Enlightened One."

Four Noble Truths

The Buddha developed a new religious philosophy. He outlined his main ideas in the Four Noble Truths. First, as he had discovered, all people suffer and know sorrow. Next, said Buddha, people suffer because their desires bind them to the cycle of rebirth. He told his followers:

> ❝ The thirst for existence leads from rebirth to rebirth; lust and pleasure follow. Power alone can satisfy lust. The thirst for power, the thirst for pleasure, the thirst for existence; there, O monks, is the origin of suffering. ❞

The third truth, said the Buddha, was that people could end their suffering by eliminating their desires. And according to the fourth truth, one could eliminate desire by following the Eightfold Path.

The Eightfold Path

The Buddha urged his disciples to do eight things: know the truth, resist evil, say nothing to hurt others, respect life, work for the good of others, free their minds of evil, control their thoughts, and practice meditation. By avoiding extremes and following the Eightfold Path, a person could attain nirvana, a state of freedom from the cycle of rebirth. In nirvana, a person would be in a state of oneness with the universe.

The Buddha rejected the varna system. He taught that a person's place in life depended on the person, not on the person's birth. He taught that anyone, regardless of caste, could attain enlightenment. He did not believe in the Hindu deities. He believed in reincarnation but taught that one could escape the cycle of suffering and reach nirvana by following the Eightfold Path.

Spread of Buddhism

After the Buddha's death, traveling Buddhist monks carried the new religion beyond India to other parts of Asia, especially to China, Japan, Korea, and Southeast Asia. As Buddhism spread, it contributed to a cultural flowering in architecture and the arts. Buddhist architects built stupas, or large stone mounds, over the bones of Buddhist holy people. Stupas were known for their elaborately carved stone railings and gateways. Paintings and statues of the Buddha, carved of polished stone or wood covered with gilt, adorned stupas and cave temples. Exquisite smaller statues were made from fine porcelain. Books about the Buddha's life and teachings were often beautifully illustrated.

Disagreements developed among the Buddha's followers, however, and two distinct branches of Buddhism eventually arose. One branch, known as Theravada, was the dominant form of Buddhism in South Asia and Southeast Asia. It remained fairly close in practice to the original teachings of the Buddha, regarding him as simply a teacher. The other branch of Buddhism, known as Mahayana, became established in China, Korea, and Japan. Mahayana encouraged the worship of the Buddha as a divine being and savior.

China

Even as the Harappans and later, the Aryans, were developing their cultures in South Asia, a major civilization emerged to the northeast in China. For many centuries rugged western mountains isolated the Chinese from the rest of the world and kept them focused on developing agriculture in eastern China's fertile river valleys and plains. The Chinese called their homeland *Zhong Guo* (JOONG GWAH), or "the Middle Kingdom." To them it was the center of the whole world and the one truly supreme civilization. The lack of outside contacts allowed the Chinese to develop one culture across many regions and a strong sense of national identity as well. As a result, China has the oldest continuous civilization in the world.

The Shang Dynasty

Very little is known about the origins of Chinese civilization. Archaeological finds dated to earlier than 5000 B.C. make it clear that eastern China's **Huang He valley**, like the river valleys of Egypt, the Fertile Crescent, and South Asia, invited settlement from very early times.

From the beginning of its recorded history until the early A.D. 1900s, China was ruled by dynasties.

NATIONAL GEOGRAPHIC SOCIETY

Use these materials to enrich student understanding of early China.

NGS PICTURESHOW CD-ROM
India and China

NGS PICTUREPACK TRANSPARENCY SET
Ancient China

CURRICULUM CONNECTION

LITERATURE
Hermann Hesse's novel *Siddhartha*, published in 1922, is a poetic expression of Indian philosophy. Hesse, a German, narrates how his young hero, the Brahman Siddhartha, after encountering the Buddha, sets off in search of self-fulfillment. His goal is to conquer suffering and fear, to attain serene contentment, and to see the unity in seeming contrasts—in short, to reach nirvana.

Critical Thinking Have students name the many technological advances of the Zhou dynasty. *(roads, horses, crossbow, improved writing system, iron plows, irrigation systems, flood control)* Have students suggest ways these advances could have led to population growth. **L2**

MAKING CONNECTIONS ACTIVITY

Environment Explain to students that like other early civilizations, India and China's economies were based on agriculture. Ask students to distinguish which features of the environment generally have the strongest impact on agriculture. *(water, physical terrain, climate, soil)* Have students identify those environmental features within the community or region where they live that would explain why agriculture is or is not an important segment of the local economy. If the local environment does not support agriculture, can the students see any connection between their local economy and local environmental factors? **L1**

Chinese Philosophies
How did Chinese philoso-
phies influence the society of
China?
*They provided ethical guidelines
for social and political life.*

Independent Practice

 Guided Reading Activity
1-3 **L1**

Geography: Place Have students
examine a physical map of China
and then write a brief explanation of why the ancient Chinese
thought of their country as the
"Middle Country" or the center
of the civilized world. (*China is
isolated by geographic barriers*) **L2**

A&E
HOME VIDEO.

*The following videotape
program is available from Glencoe:*

• **The Secret Burial Mounds
of Pre-Historic America**

To find classroom resources to
accompany this video, check the
following home page:
**A&E Television:
http://www.AandE.com**

In supporting a dynastic system, the Chinese believed that their rulers governed according to a principle known as the Mandate of Heaven. If rulers were just and effective, they received a mandate, or authority to rule, from heaven. If rulers did not govern properly, as indicated by poor crops or losses in battle, they lost the mandate to someone else who then started a new dynasty.

The first dynasty to be dated from written records in China is the Shang (SHAHNG), who ruled from about 1700 B.C. to 1000 B.C. Shang kings at first governed a small area in northern China. Later, their armies, equipped with bronze weapons and char-iots, conquered more distant territories and finally took over most of the Huang River valley.

Shang rulers were both political and religious leaders. As high priests, they had the authority to call upon the nature deities and the spirits of their ancestors. To do so, they had a priest scratch a ques-tion on an animal bone or tortoise shell. The priest then applied intense heat to the bone. The bone would crack, and the priest would interpret the pattern of cracks as the answer to the king's ques-tion. The bones were supposed to help the king to predict the future.

Under the Shang, the Chinese made a number of cultural achievements. Writers developed a script with many characters representing objects, ideas, or sounds and written in vertical columns. Artisans produced exquisite bronze objects, ivory and jade statues, silk, and pottery. Builders also constructed China's first cities.

The Zhou Dynasty

The Shang dynasty eventually weakened. About 1000 B.C., Wu, a ruler of a Shang territory in the northwest, marshaled his forces and marched on the capital. Wu killed the Shang king and estab-lished a new dynasty known as the Zhou (JOH).

Zhou rulers held sway over a vast realm. To control their holdings, Zhou kings set up an agri-cultural system in which local nobles owned the land and peasants worked it. By 700 B.C. political power was largely in the hands of the nobles. In the next centuries, the nobles fought small wars until, by the 200s B.C., several of their domains were locked in a struggle that ended Zhou rule.

Even though Zhou rulers lost their power, the Zhou are remembered for many technological advances. During the Zhou period, the Chinese built roads and expanded foreign trade. They obtained horses from western nomads, and formed a cavalry, or group of mounted warriors, along with horse-drawn chariots. The Zhou also added a deadly weapon: the crossbow. They further elaborated the

system of picture writing begun by the Shang, a system that is the ancestor of modern Chinese writing. Under the Zhou, iron plows were invented, irrigation systems were developed, and flood-control systems were begun. These and other advances led to population growth, and Zhou China became the world's most densely populated country.

Chinese Philosophies

In the latter half of the Zhou era, two major philosophies appeared in China that were to pro-foundly influence its culture. These philosophies—Confucianism and Daoism—neither dealt with the supernatural or with eternal life; both were focused instead on life in this world.

Confucianism

Confucianism developed from the teachings of **Kongfuzi** (KOONG•FUH•DZUH), a government official from Shandong Province. Known in the West as **Confucius,** he was born about 551 B.C. to a poor family. For over 12 years, Confucius traveled throughout northern China, seeking a position as an adviser to a ruler. He hoped that in such a posi-tion he could help end China's political and social disorder. Never able to get the post he wanted, Confucius finally found a way to spread his ideas by becoming a teacher.

Promoting order was Confucius's principal concern. He believed that everyone had a proper role in society. If each person would accept that role and perform his or her duties, social and political disorder would end. Confucius did not write books, but his followers collected his sayings and later published them in a collection called the *Analects.*

Individuals, Confucius taught, should live according to principles of ethics—good conduct and moral judgment. Ethics began with respect for family, especially elders, and reverence for the past and its traditions. Ethics should govern each person's behavior in these five primary relationships: ruler and subject, parent and child, husband and wife, old and young, friend and friend. Each person, Confucius believed, owed respect and obedience to those above him or her. Those above were expected to set a good example for those below.

Governments too had a duty: to set an example of right conduct. The ethical ruler had integrity, was

CRITICAL THINKING ACTIVITY

Making Comparisons Whereas the rulers of ancient China based their right to govern on the Mandate of Heaven, political rulers in today's democracies receive their right to govern based on the "Mandate of Voters." What does this mean? Have students look up the meaning of the word *mandate*. Ask students to explain how its meaning applies to ancient Chinese rulers and modern government officials. Can students see a connection between the Mandate of Heaven in China and the divine-right theory of monarchy which was at one time prevalent in Europe? **L3**

righteous, inspired loyalty, understood proper behavior, and appreciated culture. The Zhou government did not accept Confucius's teachings during his lifetime. Within a century after his death in 478 B.C., however, Confucian ethics were widely followed in China. Later scholars added their own ideas, and Confucius's teachings would serve as a basis for Chinese society and government until the A.D. 1900s.

Daoism

During the time of Confucius, a man called **Laozi** (LOW•DZUH), or "Old Master," taught ideas that in some ways seem the opposite of Confucianism. He rejected formal social structures and the idea that people must fill specific roles in society. Laozi's ideas were recorded in the *Dao De Jing*, one of the best-known of all Chinese classics.

Daoists believed that people should renounce worldly ambitions and turn to nature and the Dao–the eternal force that permeates everything in nature. By emphasizing harmony with nature, Daoists deeply influenced Chinese arts, particularly painting and poetry. Their concern for nature also led to studies of plants, animals, and minerals.

They followed examples from nature, as these lines suggest:

> " The highest good is like water.
>   Water gives life to the ten thousand things
>   and does not strive.
>   It flows in places men reject and so is like
>   the Dao.
>   In dwelling, be close to the land.
>   In meditation, go deep in the heart.
>   In dealing with others, be gentle and kind.
>   In speech, be true.
>   In ruling, be just. "

Daoist ideas were intertwined with the ancient Chinese concept of yin and yang, the two opposing forces believed to be present in all nature. Yin was cool, dark, female, and submissive, while yang was warm, light, male, and aggressive. Everything had both elements. For harmony the two elements had to be in balance. Human life and natural events, including the changing seasons, resulted from the interplay between yin and yang.

The concept of yin and yang helped the Chinese reconcile seeming opposites–like Dao simplicity and Confucian formality. In this way a person could be both a Confucianist and a Daoist. The concept of yin and yang later helped the Chinese to accept Buddhist ideas brought to China by monks and traders from India. ◆

The Americas

Human cultures and civilizations also emerged in the Americas. Recent archaeological finds indicate that humans were living in the Western Hemisphere as early as 40,000 years ago. Current theories claim that the first peoples in the Americas arrived in more than one migratory wave over a long period of time. Some groups may have migrated from Asia to North America over the then-exposed land bridge that today is the Bering Strait. Others may have traveled by boat along the Pacific coast from northern Asia to Alaska, then to South America.

Once in the Western Hemisphere, these early peoples dispersed throughout North America and South America. As they adapted to particular environments, they developed distinct ways of life. Some remained nomadic, while others settled and developed complex civilizations.

The Native Americans

The early Native Americans used the resources of their particular environment for basic needs of food, clothing, and shelter. If they lived near the ocean,

 History & Art Laozi on his buffalo. Guimet Museum, Paris, France. *How did the teaching of Laozi as recorded in the* Dao De Jing *influence Chinese arts and poetry?*

Chapter 1 *Rise of Civilizations* **51**

NATIONAL GEOGRAPHIC SOCIETY

Use these materials to enrich student understanding of early culture in the Americas.

💿 **NGS PICTURESHOW CD-ROM**
Middle and South America

ASSESS

Check for Understanding

Assign Section 3 Review as homework or as an in-class activity.

🖵 Use Student Self-Test and Review Software to review Section 3.

Evaluate

🗀 Section Quiz 1-3

🖵 Use the Testmaker to create a customized quiz for Section 3.

Reteach

Ask students to explain why Hinduism was not just a religion but a way of life for Indians. *(Religion was the basis for daily life, social groups, duties; religious texts explained life and culture; duty [dharma] was placed above all else; beliefs in self-denial and reincarnation influenced people's daily behavior.)*

History & Art Laozi was a scholar at the royal court of the Zhou dynasty. When he realized that the Zhou dynasty was in decline, he made a legendary voyage to the state of Qin. The guardian of the pass to the Qin state begged Laozi to write a book for him. The result was the *Dao De Jing*.
Answer to Caption: *Laozi's teachings influenced Chinese arts by emphasizing harmony with nature.*

Visualizing History The Olmec produced distinctive sculptures that are a combination of jaguars and human infants. Evidently the Olmec believed that in the distant past a union between a woman and a jaguar had produced a race of mythical creatures. *What is distinctive about the head of the statue? (It is cleft at the top; this is a typical feature of Olmec sculptures of mythical creatures.)*
Answer to Caption: *Jade carvings, figurines, and carved stone murals led them to make that inference.*

 Reteaching Activity 1

Enrich

Have students write a short essay supporting or rejecting the Hindu idea of ahimsa, the practice of nonviolence toward all living things.

 Enrichment Activity 1

CLOSE

Write on the chalkboard this statement from page 49: *China has the oldest continuous civilization in the world.* Have students explain what this statement means. Ask students to consider how isolation has affected China. *(Possible answer: It has built a strong national identity.)*

Visualizing History This jade ceremonial ax in the form of a feline monster is from the pre-Columbian Olmec culture. *Why do archaeologists believe that religion played an important role in Olmec life?*

people collected mussels and snails. Some groups fished in rivers and streams, while others hunted.

By about 5000 B.C., a group of hunter-gatherers in a highland area of present-day **Mexico** had discov-

ered that the seeds of maize, or corn, and other native plants could be planted and harvested, providing a reliable source of food. Farming eventually spread both north and south from Mexico, making possible permanently settled villages. In the present-day American Southwest, for example, the Hohokam about 300 B.C. adapted to their harsh desert environment by inventing techniques of irrigation to farm the land. They dug a canal to draw the waters of the Gila and Salt Rivers onto fields planted with maize, beans, and squash.

The Olmec

Between 1500 B.C. and 400 B.C., the Olmec civilization flourished in the swampy lowlands of eastern Mexico. Archaeologists have learned much about the Olmecs from their excavation of two major Olmec sites, San Lorenzo and La Venta. Evidence from these sites reveals that the Olmecs developed ceremonial centers, forms of hieroglyphic writing, and a calendar.

From jade carvings, figurines, and carved stone murals, archaeologists infer that religion played an important role in the lives of the Olmec. Many carvings show the Olmec god, a being with a human body and the catlike face of a jaguar, the large spotted wild cat that roamed the region. The Olmec believed the jaguar-god controlled their harvests.

Early Olmec farmers practiced what is known as slash-and-burn farming. To clear land, farmers cut down trees, let them dry, and then burned them. They planted maize among the fertile ashes. Since the soil became exhausted after a few years, farmers shifted fields and repeated the cycle on other lands.

Trade with other parts of Mexico and Central America was common. Olmec artifacts have been found throughout the region, and their ideas were echoed in later Native American civilizations.

SECTION 3 REVIEW

Recall
1. **Define** *varna, dharma, jati,* reincarnation, karma, nirvana, yin and yang, slash-and-burn farming.
2. **Identify** Harappa, the Aryans, *Upanishads,* Siddhartha Gautama, Four Noble Truths, Mandate of Heaven, Confucius, Laozi, the Hohokam, the Olmec.

3. **Use** the map on page 45 to list the major physical features of early civilizations in South Asia and China. Explain how these physical features affected the development of civilization in these areas.
Critical Thinking
4. **Making Comparisons** How would you compare Confucius

and Laozi in their ideas and ways of life? How did the philosophies of Confucianism and Daoism affect the development of Chinese civilization?
Understanding Themes
5. **Relation to Environment** How did early Native Americans depend on their environment and natural resources?

SECTION 3 REVIEW ANSWERS

1. All vocabulary words are defined in the Glossary.
2. Harappa, 44; the Aryans, 45; *Upanishads,* 47; Siddhartha Gautama, 48; Four Noble Truths, 49; Mandate of Heaven, 50; Confucius, 50; Laozi, 51; the Hohokam, 52; the Olmec, 52

3. Himalayas, Ganges River, Hindu Kush, Plateau of Tibet, Huang He, Chiang Jiang, Xi Jiang; fertile river valleys encouraged growth of civilizations; mountains isolated the Chinese and encouraged development of a common culture
4. Confucius favored a structured, orderly

society; Laozi looked to nature for the Dao, or way. Confucian ideas shaped China's government, while Daoism influenced the arts.
5. **RELATION TO ENVIRONMENT** They used the resources, such as shellfish, plants, and water.

Finding Exact Location on a Map

Your new friend invites you to her house. In giving directions, she says, "I live on Vine Street near the corner of Oak Avenue." She has pinpointed her exact location. We use a similar system to identify the exact location of any place on Earth.

Learning the Skill

Over many centuries, cartographers developed a grid system of imaginary lines–the lines of latitude and lines of longitude. Lines of latitude run east and west around the earth. Because they always remain the same distance from each other, they are also called parallels. The parallel lines of latitude measure distance north and south of the Equator, located at 0° latitude. Each line of latitude is one degree, or 69 miles (110 km), from the next. There are 90 latitude lines between the Equator and each Pole. For example, New York City lies 41° north of the Equator, or 41° N.

Lines of longitude, or meridians, run north and south from Pole to Pole. Unlike lines of latitude, lines of longitude are not always the same distance from each other. Lines of longitude are farthest apart at the Equator and intersect at each Pole. Longitude measures distance east and west of the Prime Meridian, located at 0° longitude. That line runs through Greenwich, England, in western Europe and through western Africa. Longitude lines increase east and west of the Prime Meridian to 180°. This meridian runs through the Pacific Ocean. New York City, for example, lies 74° west of the Prime Meridian, or 74° W.

With this system we can pinpoint the "grid address" of any place on Earth. On a map find the nearest line of latitude to the designated place. Then follow along this line until it crosses the nearest line of longitude. The point where the lines intersect is the grid address. For example New York City has this grid address: 41°N, 74°W.

Practicing the Skill

Use the map below to answer the following questions:
1. What is the approximate grid address of Babylon?
2. What city is located at approximately 30°N, 31°E?
3. What is the approximate grid address of Nineveh?
4. What is the approximate grid address of Tyre?

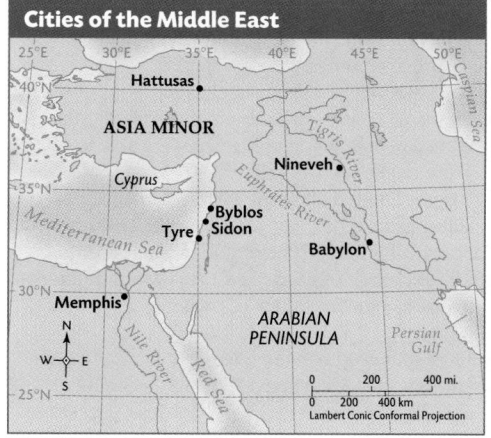

Cities of the Middle East

Applying the Skill

Create a travel itinerary for a tour of the ruins of ancient Egypt, Greece, or the Middle East. Choose at least 10 locations you would like to visit. Draw a map of the region, including grid lines. On the map, identify the approximate grid location of each place.

For More Practice

Turn to the Skill Practice in the Chapter Review on page 55 for more practice in finding exact location on a map

TEACH

Finding Exact Location on a Map
Have one or more students draw on the chalkboard a simplified map of the area around your school or a nearby residential or business district. (The school, or some other landmark, should be at the center, labeled "0.") With north at the top, the map should include 3 or 4 streets to the north, south, east, and west of the central point. These should be labeled with the street name and with a grid location: 1, 2, and 3 north; 1, 2, and 3 east; and so on. Then ask students to give grid locations for several street intersections, and vice versa.

Additional Practice

▱ Skill Reinforcement Activity 1

▱ Building Skills in Geography Workbook, Unit 1, Lessons 3, 4, 5

ANSWERS TO PRACTICING THE SKILL

1. 32°N, 44°E
2. Memphis
3. 36°N, 43°E
4. 33°N, 35°E

GLENCOE
TECHNOLOGY

VIDEODISC
Use MindJogger to review students' knowledge of the chapter.

MindJogger Videoquiz

Chapter 1
Disc 1 Side A

Also available in VHS.

Answers

Using Key Terms

1. f
2. l
3. c
4. b
5. e

Using Your History Journal

The 1998 *World Almanac* shows that 38,000 Buddhists live in Africa, 322 million in Asia, 1.5 million in Europe, 569,000 in Latin America, 920,000 in North America, and 200,000 in Oceania; of the world's Hindus, 2 million live in Africa, 787 million in Asia, 1.6 million in Europe, 760,000 in Latin America, 1.3 million in North America, and 323,000 in Oceania.

Reviewing Facts

1. Language enabled people to work together, exchange ideas, and pass on culture from generation to generation.
2. Empires politically unified diverse groups and stimulated the exchange of ideas, products, and peoples. They also promoted warfare on a larger scale than smaller political units.
3. the making and use of iron

Connections Across Time

Historical Significance Prehistoric people created the basics of human culture–for example, tools, language, and beliefs. In time, increased food supplies and a diverse labor force led to the rise of civilizations in various parts of the world. These civilizations built cities, created governments, developed writing systems, and devised laws. Their political ideas, social institutions, and cultural achievements were inherited by later peoples and became the foundation of the global civilization we know today.

Using Key Terms

Write the key term that completes each sentence. Then write a sentence for each term not chosen.

a. *varna*
b. civilizations
c. cultural diffusion
d. yin and yang
e. monotheism
f. slash-and-burn farming
g. technology
h. bureaucracy
i. hominids
j. alphabet
k. nirvana
l. empire

1. By using a technique known as _____, the Olmec people living in Mexico were able to grow crops, such as maize.
2. Sargon I united all of the Mesopotamian city-states in a single _____, which consisted of many different territories under one ruler.
3. The exchange of goods and ideas when different peoples come in contact is known as _____.
4. Over thousands of years, some of the early agricultural villages evolved into highly complex societies, known as _____.
5. The belief in one all-powerful god is known as _____.

Technology Activity

Using a Word Processor Search the Internet or your local library for information about the world's earliest civilizations. Using a word processor, create a chart comparing different civilizations. Include headings such as major contributions, cultural achievements, location, and time period. After comparing the contributions of the civilizations, write a paragraph explaining how these contributions have affected your life.

Using Your History Journal

Refer to a world almanac to determine how many Jews, how many Hindus, and how many Buddhists live in each region of the world today. Build a graph or create a world map that illustrates this information.

Reviewing Facts

1. Culture Explain why the development of language is one of humanity's greatest achievements.
2. Government Discuss how the rise of empires affected the peoples of the ancient Middle East.
3. Technology Discuss the kind of technology that was used by the people of Kush in northeastern Africa.
4. Culture Describe how the Israelites interpreted and applied the new idea of monotheism.
5. Culture State in your own words the Four Noble Truths of Buddhism.
6. Geography Discuss how China's location influenced the rise of its civilization.
7. History Name two principal sites where excavations have revealed an ancient Olmec culture.

Critical Thinking

1. Apply How did climactic changes affect the development of prehistoric peoples?
2. Analyze What actions taken by the Persian king Darius I made his rule so effective?
3. Compare How did the power of the Egyptian kings differ from those of the Shang kings? How were their powers the same?

---

4. One God determined right and wrong and expected people to deal fairly with one another and be morally responsible.
5. All people suffer; people suffer because desire binds them to the cycle of rebirth; eliminating desires will end suffering; and desire is eliminated by following the Eightfold Path.
6. Mountain barriers to the west largely isolated the early Chinese from other areas and enabled them to create the world's oldest continuous civilization on fertile eastern plains.
7. San Lorenzo and La Venta in Mexico

Critical Thinking

1. Colder climates led early humans to develop strategies for keeping warm; Ice Age land bridges led to migration into previously uninhabited areas.

Geography in History

1. **Movement** Refer to the map below. The Buddhist religion came to China from which area of the world?
2. **Location** What cities became major Buddhist sites in China?
3. **Region** What large geographic area shown on the map below was a major stronghold of Daoism?
4. **Region** What philosophical concept made it possible for much of China to incorporate the teachings of Confucius, Laozi, and the Buddha into a unified belief system?

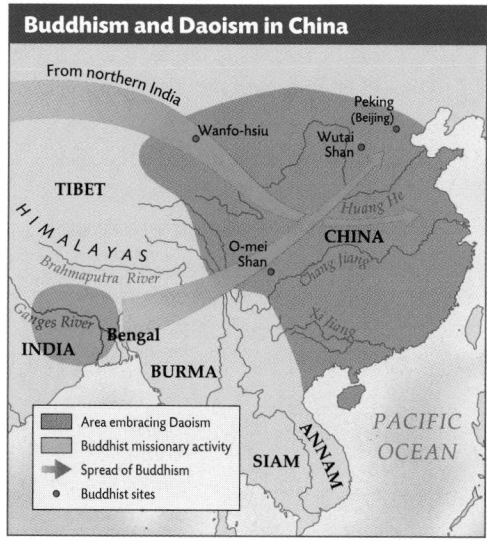

Buddhism and Daoism in China

Area embracing Daoism
Buddhist missionary activity
→ Spread of Buddhism
• Buddhist sites

Understanding Themes

1. **Change** How did city life differ from village life in the earliest civilizations?
2. **Cultural Diffusion** What technological and social advances in the twentieth century have made cultural diffusion easier and faster than in ancient times?
3. **Relation to Environment** How were the ancient Egyptians in northeast Africa and the Hohokam in the Americas similar in adapting to the environment? In what ways were they different?

Linking Past and Present

1. Hatshepsut was only one of the women who held prominent positions in ancient Egypt. What women have held high government positions in modern times?
2. What are some reasons for the decline of ancient civilizations? Would the same factors lead to the weakening of civilization today?
3. Early in the 1900s, India applied the Hindu principle of nonviolence to help win its independence from Great Britain. Do you think people can still use nonviolence effectively to win freedom?
4. Physical features isolated the Chinese from the rest of the world for centuries. What moves have the Chinese made recently to make greater contact with other cultures?

Skill Practice

Use the map "Greece and Persia" to answer the following questions.

1. What is the approximate location of Athens?
2. Which body of water lies entirely north of 40°N latitude?
3. What is the approximate location of Sparta?
4. What is the approximate location of Sardis?
5. What is the relative location of Sardis?
6. What Mediterranean island lies along the 35th parallel?

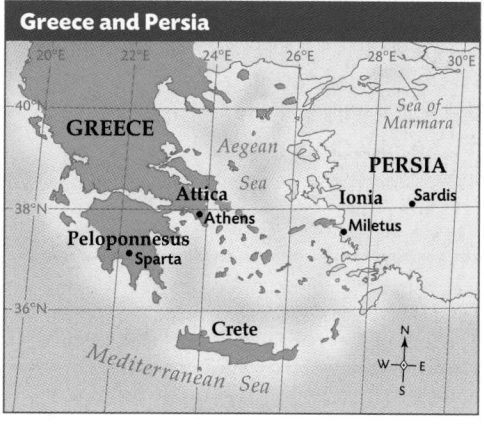

Greece and Persia

Chapter 1 *Rise of Civilizations* **55**

---

large-scale projects; labor more specialized in cities; long-distance trade and large ruling class developed in urban setting

2. **CULTURAL DIFFUSION** Answers may include computers and jet travel.
3. **RELATION TO ENVIRONMENT** Both peoples lived in dry climates but used irrigation water from rivers to grow crops. The Egyptians developed a powerful empire, bureaucracy, and army.

Linking Past and Present

1. Margaret Thatcher (Britain); Indira Gandhi (India); Golda Meir (Israel); Corazon Aquino (Philippines)
2. internal conflicts and invasion
3. Students should weigh consequences of violent action against those of nonviolence. They might mention nonviolence in the U.S. civil rights movement.
4. China now allows foreign firms to do business there, and Chinese citizens may study abroad. Curbs on freedom of movement remain for those within China.

Skill Practice

1. 38°N, 24°E
2. Sea of Marmara
3. 37°N, 22°E
4. 38°N, 29° E
5. east of Ionia, south of the Sea of Marmara, north of Miletus
6. Crete

---

2. divided Persian Empire into provinces; appointed military officials and tax inspectors from among conquered peoples; ordered surprise inspections of provinces; improved roads to encourage trade
3. Egyptian kings were regarded as gods, while Shang kings were not. Both were political and religious leaders, and both performed acts in order to benefit their people.

Geography in History

1. India
2. Wanfo-hsiu, Peking, Wutai Shan, O-mei Shan
3. from southeastern India
4. the yin-yang concept

Understanding Themes

1. **CHANGE** number of people larger in cities than in villages; cities promoted

Chapter Bonus Test Question

Ask students: Nonviolence has been espoused by many Hindus. How do you reconcile this fact with the fact that India has been involved in many armed struggles? *(not all Hindus believed in nonviolence)*

A complete, 1-page lesson plan is provided for each section in the *Reproducible Lesson Plans* booklet.

The Advance of Civilizations

CHAPTER RESOURCES

	Reproducible Resources	Multimedia Resources
Chapter Opener	Chapter Themes: Graphic Organizer 2 Historical Significance Chapter Activity 2	MindJogger Videoquiz

Chapter Enrichment	Vocabulary Activity 2*
	Time Line Activity 2
	Mapping History Activity 2
	History Simulation 2
	Geography and History Activity 2
	Source Reading 2
	People in World History Profiles 5–11
	World Art and Music Activity 2
	Enrichment Activity 2
	Critical Thinking Activity 2
	Skill Reinforcement Activity 2
	Performance Assessment Activity 2
		Focus on World Art Prints 8, 9, 11
		NGS Ancient Civilizations Poster Sets:
		  Ancient Greece, Ancient Rome
		World History and Art Transparencies
		  5, 6, 7, 8, 10
		NGS PicturePack Transparency Sets:
		  Ancient Greece, Ancient Rome,
		  Ancient India, Ancient China, Ancient
		  Central America, Ancient Africa
		Vocabulary PuzzleMaker Software
		NGS PictureShow CD-ROMs:
		  Greece and Rome, India and China,
		  The Americas
		Turning Points in World History:
		  Democracy in Greece
		STV: *Maya*

Chapter Review/Reteaching	Reteaching Activity 2 Skill Reinforcement Activity 2 Spanish Chapter Summary 2	Chapter 2 Digest Audiocassette, Activity, Test* Vocabulary PuzzleMaker Software Student Self-Test and Review Software MindJogger Videoquiz
Chapter Evaluation/Testing	Performance Assessment Activity 2 Chapter 2 Test, Forms A and B	Testmaker

* Also available in Spanish

0:00 OUT OF TIME? Assign the Chapter 2 summary in the Unit 1 Digest on pages 171–173, and the Chapter 2 Audiocassettes.

Block Schedule

Block scheduling differs from traditional class scheduling in the amount of time allotted to each period. The extended time frame provided by block scheduling affords you the opportunity to implement a greater number of research-oriented and activity-intense projects to motivate and involve your students. Activities that are particularly suited to use within the block scheduling framework are identified throughout this chapter by the following designation.

KEY TO ABILITY LEVELS

Teaching strategies have been coded for varying learning styles and abilities.

L1   **BASIC** activities for all students
L2   **AVERAGE** activities for average to above-average students
L3   **CHALLENGING** activities for above-average students
LEP   **LIMITED ENGLISH PROFICIENCY** activities

Use Glencoe's *Presentation Plus!* multimedia teacher tool to easily present dynamic lessons that visually excite your students. Using Microsoft PowerPoint® you can customize the presentations to create your own personalized lessons.

SECTION RESOURCES

Daily Objectives	Reproducible Resources	Multimedia Resources
Section 1 **Greece** Describe how the Greeks expressed their love of beauty and meaning.	Reproducible Lesson Plan 2-1 Guided Reading Activity 2-1* Section Quiz 2-1*	Ancient Greece Focus on World Art Print 8 Section Focus Transparency 2-1 Ancient Greece World History and Art Transparencies 5, 6 Vocabulary PuzzleMaker Software Student Self-Test and Review Software Testmaker *Democracy in Greece* Greece and Rome
Section 2 **Rome** Characterize life under the *Pax Romana* and the influence of early Christians on the later Roman Empire.	Reproducible Lesson Plan 2-2 Vocabulary Activity 2 Guided Reading Activity 2-2* Section Quiz 2-2*	Section Focus Transparency 2-2 Ancient Rome Student Self-Test and Review Software Testmaker Greece and Rome
Section 3 **Africa** Investigate what kinds of societies emerged in early Africa.	Reproducible Lesson Plan 2-3 Guided Reading Activity 2-3* Section Quiz 2-3*	Section Focus Transparency 2-3 Vocabulary PuzzleMaker Software Student Self-Test and Review Software Testmaker
Section 4 **Asia** Summarize the major advances the Indians and the Chinese made under strong central governments.	Reproducible Lesson Plan 2-4 Vocabulary Activity 2 Guided Reading Activity 2-4* Section Quiz 2-4*	Section Focus Transparency 2-4 Student Self-Test and Review Software Testmaker India and China World Music: Cultural Traditions 8
Section 5 **The Americas** Explain how trade encouraged the growth of city-states and kingdoms in the areas of present-day Mexico and Central America.	Reproducible Lesson Plan 2-5 Guided Reading Activity 2-5* Reteaching Activity 2 Enrichment Activity 2 Section Quiz 2-5* Performance Assessment Activity 2 Spanish Chapter Summary 2	Focus on World Art Print 11 Section Focus Transparency 2-5 Vocabulary PuzzleMaker Software Student Self-Test and Review Software Testmaker World Music: Cultural Traditions 2

* Also available in Spanish

Chapter Activities

 Performance Assessment Activity

An Ad Campaign Have students take the roles of ad executives for a museum exhibit about ancient Rome. They should create a series of ten magazine ads (or billboards) showcasing the most important aspects of what can be learned by visiting the exhibit. Ads/billboards may be described or actually drawn and should be placed in priority order for an audience of potential contributors who may decide to fund only a portion of the campaign. Students should write a reflection in which they explain and support their ranking.

Possible Rubric Features
Accuracy of content information, decision-making skills, quality of product, extent of support

• For an additional activity, refer to Activity 2 in the Performance Assessment Strategies and Activities booklet.

ACTIVITY

From the Classroom of...

**Lawrence J. Emsing
Arapahoe High School
Littleton, CO**

The Collapse of the Roman Empire
The purpose of this simulation activity is to get students to analyze and to understand the underlying causes for the eventual collapse of the Roman Empire in the West. Students will appreciate that multiple causation is a more historically satisfying explanation for complex events than single causation theories. This activity is designed to encourage: critical analysis of a major historical event, collaborative decision making within a small group, and advocacy skills.

Organize students into five groups, each representing a segment of the Roman population (wealthy landowners; urban poor in crowded Rome; rural poor in the provinces; the military; Christians, Jews, and other non-Roman religious sects). Groups will research and develop a plan for solving some of the many problems confronting the Empire. Each group will present its grievances and plans for addressing the grievances that will avert the fall as well as enhance their own position. The activity is designed to take 2–3 days depending on whether preparation time is included. After all groups have made their presentations, have students vote on which plan or plans for reform they would approve.

MULTIPLE LEARNING STYLES

Verbal/Linguistic
Have students write a detailed description of the Baths of Caracalla, one of the most elaborate of the Roman public baths.

Logical/Mathematical
Have students prepare a chart of Arabic numerals (1 through 15, then 20, 30, 40, 50, 60, 70, 80, 90, 100, 500, and 1,000), the corresponding Roman numerals, and the Latin names for the numerals. Have students research how Romans performed mathematical calculations using their numerals, and write a few simple examples.

Kinesthetic
Have students prepare a visual presentation of Roman architecture. They should present illustrations, diagrams, and pictures of some of the most important Roman structures from various periods, along with an explanation of each structure.

Intrapersonal
As students read Section 2, have them keep brief notes on each person mentioned. Then have them prepare a list of who they believe were the five most important Romans and briefly explain why they have chosen each person.

Additional Resources

NATIONAL GEOGRAPHIC SOCIETY

Teacher's Corner

INDEX TO NATIONAL GEOGRAPHIC MAGAZINE

The following articles may be used for research relating to this chapter:

- "The Royal Crypts of Copán," by George E. Stuart, December 1997.
- "The Roman Empire," by T. R. Reid, July 1997.
- "India," by Geoffery C. Ward, May 1997.
- "Genghis Khan," by Mike Edwards, December 1996.
- "Let the Games Begin," by Frank Deford, July 1996.

NATIONAL GEOGRAPHIC SOCIETY PRODUCTS AVAILABLE FROM GLENCOE

To order the following products for use with this chapter, contact your local Glencoe sales representative, or call Glencoe at 1-800-334-7344:

- *Greece and Rome, India and China, The Americas* (CD-ROMs)
- *Ancient Greece, Ancient Rome, Ancient Africa, Ancient India, Ancient China, Ancient Central America* (Transparencies)
- *Ancient Greece, Ancient Rome* (Poster Sets)
- *STV: Maya* (Videodisc)

ADDITIONAL NATIONAL GEOGRAPHIC SOCIETY PRODUCTS

To order the following products for use with this chapter, call National Geographic Society at 1-800-368-2728:

- *PictureShow: Ancient Civilizations Library* (CD-ROMs)
- *PicturePack: Geography of Africa* (Transparencies)
- *PictureShow: Geography of Asia* (CD-ROM)

BIBLIOGRAPHY

Literature About the Period
Davidson, Basil. *African Civilization Revisited.* Trenton: Africa World Press, 1991. Presents the story of Africa through a collection of historic chronicles and records.

Readings for the Student
Renault, Mary. *The Persian Boy.* New York: Bantam, 1988. The second of three novels about Alexander the Great.

Readings for the Teacher
Fairbank, John King. *China: A New History.* Cambridge: Harvard University Press, 1992. A survey of Chinese history from antiquity to the Tiananmen Square protests.

LOCAL OBJECTIVES

_____
_____
_____
_____
_____
_____
_____
_____
_____
_____
_____
_____
_____
_____
_____
_____
_____
_____
_____
_____
_____
_____

*inter*NET CONNECTION

Ancient Greek resources on the World Wide Web
The Ancient Greek World:
http://www.museum.upenn.edu/Greek_World/Intro.html

Chapter Themes are listed by section on this chapter opening page of the Student Edition. A corresponding theme-based activity is available under "TEACH," and a theme-based question is asked in the Section and Chapter Reviews.

Storyteller

Historical Setting Much of what we know about the life and teachings of Socrates comes to us from Socrates' most famous student, Plato. But Plato, according to some scholars, may have attributed ideas to Socrates that originated with Plato himself. Ask students why scholars might care whether the ideas should be attributed to Plato or Socrates. *(Scholars want to know how coherent and/or consistent their subject's ideas are and how they relate to the work of others; uncertain provenance makes this task harder.)*

Historical Significance

Answers: *Most of the societies were based on trade and commerce, although at different periods of their history, some emphasized military expansion.*

The achievements of these civilizations were varied but included political concepts such as democracy, engineering and building skills, and the development of scientific and mathematical principles.

Chapter
2

500 B.C.–A.D. 500
The Advance of Civilizations

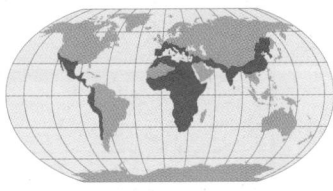

Chapter Themes

▶ **Innovation** The ancient Greeks develop a culture that becomes one of the foundations of Western civilization. *Section 1*

▶ **Cultural Diffusion** The Romans build an empire, spread Latin culture, and later, make Christianity the dominant religion in the West. *Section 2*

▶ **Movement** Migrations of Bantu-speaking peoples influence Africa's cultural development. *Section 3*

▶ **Uniformity** Indian and Chinese empires establish and maintain strong central governments. *Section 4*

▶ **Change** The Mesoamerican civilizations develop an understanding of astronomy and mathematics. *Section 5*

Storyteller

An outwardly unimpressive man, Socrates was nonetheless an intellectual giant in Greece during the late 400s B.C. One of his devoted followers described Socrates' day: "At early morning he was to be seen betaking himself to one of the promenades or wrestling grounds; at noon he would appear with the gathering crowds in the marketplace; and as day declined, wherever the largest throng might be encountered, there was he to be found, talking for the most part, while anyone who chose might stop and listen." Socrates was a supreme questioner who succeeded in getting people to analyze their own behavior. He was among a number of innovators living from 500 B.C. to A.D. 500 whose ideas and practices still shape our lives today.

Historical Significance

What kinds of societies developed in the world's advancing civilizations? Which of their achievements have had a lasting impact on the world's peoples?

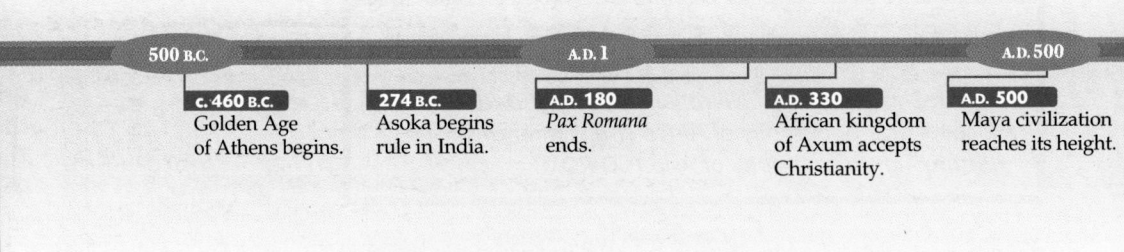

500 B.C.		A.D. 1		A.D. 500
c. 460 B.C. Golden Age of Athens begins.	274 B.C. Asoka begins rule in India.	A.D. 180 *Pax Romana* ends.	A.D. 330 African kingdom of Axum accepts Christianity.	A.D. 500 Maya civilization reaches its height.

56

GEOGRAPHY CONNECTION

Location Have students use the Atlas in their text to locate Europe, the Mediterranean Sea, Asia Minor, North Africa, and the Middle East—the regions controlled by the Roman Empire by A.D. 130. What problems might arise in governing such a vast area? *(delays in communications, need to provide defense against invaders and rebellions, tax collection)*

 Plato's School, a mosaic from the Hellenistic period. National Museum, Naples, Italy

Your History Journal

Advancing civilizations in both East and West achieved many "firsts" in the arts, politics, religion, and the sciences. Choose one contribution, invention, or discovery reported in this chapter, and write a short research report on its early history and its effect on your life.

Chapter 2   *The Advance of Civilizations*   **57**

History & Art   The School of Plato, in Athens, was commonly referred to as the Academy. It was located in a grove of trees said to have belonged to a man named Academus, a hero of the Trojan War. *Why do you think learning was important to the Greeks? (They believed people could develop themselves by thinking clearly.)*

✔ Performance Assessment

Refer to the activity on page 56C of the Planning Guide.

📁   For an additional activity, refer to Activity 2 in the *Performance Assessment Strategies and Activities* booklet.

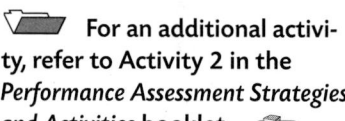

Using Your History Journal

Instruct students to include the approximate date of the innovation, the need that led to it, and the approximate date the innovation made its way beyond the country where it originated.

GLENCOE TECHNOLOGY

VIDEODISC
Use MindJogger to preview chapter content.

MindJogger Videoquiz

   Chapter 2
Disc 1 Side A

   Also available in VHS.

➕ EXTRA CREDIT PROJECT

Investigate Ask students to select one culture on the African continent to research and investigate further. Specifically, have them find out in what ways the culture's heritage has survived to the present. Have them present their findings to the class, using photographs or other visual aids to accompany their reports.

SECTION THEME

▶ **Innovation** The ancient Greeks develop a culture that becomes one of the foundations of Western civilization.

Find Out

Answer: *The ancient Greeks developed the Western version of drama, the Olympic Games, styles of architecture, scientific and mathematical principles, and the Western concept of democracy.*

FOCUS

Section Objective

Describe how the Greeks expressed their love of beauty and meaning.

BELLRINGER
Motivational Activity

Before taking roll at the beginning of the class period, project Section Focus Transparency 2-1 and have students answer the activity questions. Discuss students' responses.

This activity is also available as a blackline master.

Vocabulary Pre-check

Use the Vocabulary PuzzleMaker to create a puzzle that reinforces the vocabulary terms in this section. L1

1000 B.C. — 700 B.C. — 400 B.C. — 100 B.C.

- **c. 700s B.C.** Greeks found colonies in Mediterranean area.
- **c. 600 B.C.** Greeks perform the earliest plays.
- **c. 499 B.C.** Athenians and Persians fight the Battle of Marathon.
- **336 B.C.** Alexander becomes king of Macedonia.

Section 1

Greece

Setting the Scene

▶ **Terms to Define**
polis, tyrant, oligarchy, democracy, constitution, classical, tragedy, comedy

▶ **People to Meet**
Homer, Pericles, Socrates, Plato, Aristotle, Alexander the Great

▶ **Places to Locate**
Greece, Sparta, Athens, Marathon, Salamis, Olympia, Alexandria

Find Out What did the ancient Greeks achieve in politics, the arts, and the sciences?

The Storyteller

The Greek historian Herodotus reported that during the Persian Wars, some Greek deserters approached the Persian king Xerxes. Questioned about what the Greeks were about to do, they told him the truth: the Olympic Games were being held. They were going to watch the athletic competitions and chariot races. When asked what the prize was for such contests, they responded that the Olympic prize was an olive wreath. Upon hearing this, a Persian noble cried out in fear: "What kind of men are these? How can we be expected to fight against men who compete with each other for no material reward, but only for honor!"

The Parthenon on the Acropolis

—adapted from *The Histories,* Herodotus, translated by Aubrey de Selincourt

The ancient Greeks became the people who set their stamp on the Mediterranean region and who also contributed greatly to the way we live today. Every time you go to the theater or watch the Olympic Games on television, you enjoy an activity that has its roots in ancient Greece. Modern public buildings often reflect Greek architectural styles. Above all, the ancient Greeks helped develop the idea that all citizens should participate in the running of their government.

Ancient **Greece** included the southern part of Europe's Balkan Peninsula and a group of small, rocky islands, most of which dot the Aegean (ih•JEE•uhn) Sea near Asia Minor. Greece's low-lying, rugged mountains protected against invaders, but they also limited communication among the Greeks and prevented them from uniting under one government. Numerous harbors and closeness to the sea encouraged the Greeks to become traders, and they eventually founded colonies around the Mediterranean Sea.

Greek civilization had its origins in the Minoan and Mycenaean (MY•suh•NEE•uhn) civilizations that thrived in the area of the Aegean Sea between 3000 B.C. to 1000 B.C. From these early peoples, the Greeks derived their legends and heroes, which they commemorated in epic poetry. During the 700s B.C., a blind poet named **Homer** is believed to have composed the two most famous epics—the *Iliad* and the *Odyssey*. The Iliad tells of warrior heroes during the Trojan War, which probably took place about 1250 B.C. The *Odyssey* describes the adventures of the hero Odysseus as he returns home after the Trojan War.

Greek schools used the *Iliad* and the *Odyssey* to teach students values such as bravery, honor, dignity, and the love of beauty. In religion the Greeks worshiped gods and goddesses who were both humanlike and super powerful. They tried to be like the deities by doing everything to the best of their ability.

SECTION RESOURCES

Reproducible Masters
- Reproducible Lesson Plan 2-1
- Guided Reading Activity 2-1
- Section Quiz 2-1

Transparencies
- Section Focus Transparency 2-1
- Ancient Greece
- World History and Art Transparency 5, *Amphora from Vulci;* 6, *Nike of Samothrace*

Multimedia
- Ancient Greece
- Focus on World Art Print 8, *Laocoön*
- Vocabulary PuzzleMaker Software
- Student Self-Test and Review Software
- Testmaker
- Greece and Rome
- Turning Points in World History

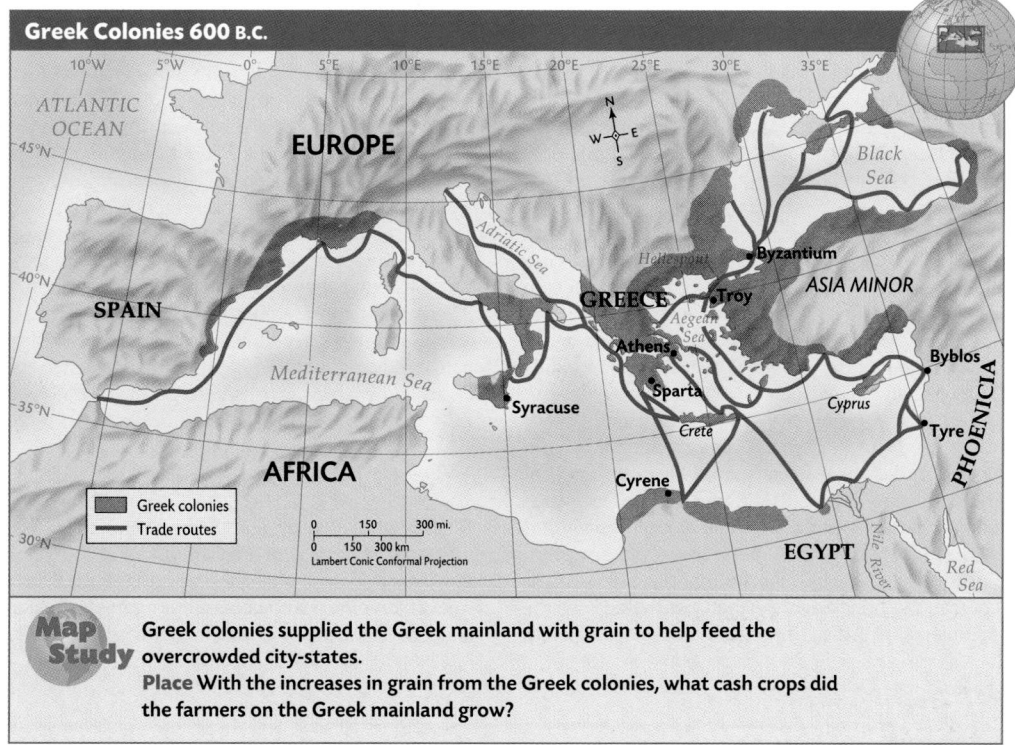

Greek Colonies 600 B.C.

ATLANTIC OCEAN

EUROPE

SPAIN

Mediterranean Sea

AFRICA

Adriatic Sea

GREECE

Athens

Sparta

Crete

Syracuse

Cyrene

Black Sea

Byzantium

Troy

Aegean Sea

ASIA MINOR

Cyprus

Byblos

Tyre

PHOENICIA

EGYPT

Nile River

Red Sea

■ Greek colonies
— Trade routes

0   150   300 mi.
0 150 300 km
Lambert Conic Conformal Projection

Map Study Greek colonies supplied the Greek mainland with grain to help feed the overcrowded city-states.
Place With the increases in grain from the Greek colonies, what cash crops did the farmers on the Greek mainland grow?

The Polis

By 700 B.C. the polis, or city-state, had emerged as the basic political unit of Greek civilization. A typical polis included a city and the surrounding villages and fields. Citizens—those who took part in polis government—had both rights and responsibilities. They could vote, hold public office, own property, and speak for themselves in court. In return the polis expected them to serve in government and to defend the polis in time of war.

Citizens, however, made up only a minority of the residents of a polis. In some cases, slaves and those who were foreign-born were excluded from citizenship, and before 500 B.C., so were men who did not own land. Greek women had no political or legal rights.

Colonies and Trade

By 700 B.C. heightened prosperity and increasing population had put a strain on Greece's limited food supplies. As a result, groups of people from each polis migrated to establish colonies in coastal areas around the Mediterranean and Black Seas.

Each overseas colony kept close ties with its metropolis, or "parent city." A colony supplied its metropolis with grain—wheat and barley. Farmers on the Greek mainland produced wine, olive oil, and other cash crops for export. Because vineyards and olive groves needed fewer workers than did grain fields, many farmers moved to the cities, where they learned crafts such as metalworking and pottery making. With more goods to sell, Greek merchants began trading throughout the Mediterranean region.

Toward Democracy

Economic growth changed Greek political life. Kings at first ruled Greek communities. By the 700s B.C., however, the kings had lost power to land-holding aristocrats, or nobles. Within 100 years merchants, artisans, and farmers challenged the power of the aristocrats.

Chapter 2 *The Advance of Civilizations* **59**

Chapter 2
Section 1

TEACH

Guided Practice

 **THEME** Innovation

Remind students that the word *innovation* means "something new." Ask them to recall innovations developed by earlier peoples. *(prehistoric: stone tools, agriculture, metalworking, boats; Egyptians: picture writing; Sumerians: cuneiform writing, wagon wheel, potter's wheel; early Chinese: picture writing, silk)* **L1**

Map Study

Answer
wine and olive oil

Map Skills Practice

Reading a Map How far from Greece were the most distant Greek colonies? *(around 1,200 miles [about 1,900 kilometers])*

 **POINT**

Toward Democracy
How did democracy develop in Athens?
Cleisthenes introduced a constitution that allowed all citizens to participate in the Assembly

 VIDEODISC
Turning Points in World History

Side One
Chapter 5

Title: *Democracy in Greece*

COOPERATIVE LEARNING ACTIVITY

Class Presentation Organize the class into small groups, and have each group find additional information about a Greek hero—either from the *Iliad* or the *Odyssey* or from myths. Each group should decide how best to present its information to the class and should assign tasks for the final presentation. Encourage students to be as inventive as possible. Some suggestions include: acting out a myth about a hero; recording information about the hero on audiotape; recording an oral/graphic presentation on videotape; delivering an oral/graphic presentation live; drawing and displaying posters that include a brief description of what is depicted. **L1**

City-States Have students research information about Greek city-states other than Athens and Sparta and report their findings to the class. Among the many that reward research are Argos, Corinth, Sicyon, Olympia, Delphi, Thebes, Miletus, and Ephesus. **L3**

NATIONAL GEOGRAPHIC SOCIETY

Use these materials to enrich student understanding of ancient Greek culture.

- **NGS PICTURESHOW CD-ROM**
  Greece and Rome
- **NGS PICTUREPACK TRANSPARENCY SET**
  Ancient Greece
- **ANCIENT CIVILIZATIONS POSTER SET**
  Ancient Greece

Linking Past and Present

Sailing the Aegean

Because Greek ships were small, they could carry very few provisions. As much as possible, ships hugged the coasts so that they could land frequently to take on food and water.

ANSWERS

Because Greek ships could sail easily only with the wind behind them; since the winds usually blew from north to south, sailing south was easy, but sailing north was difficult. Cargo today is transported by ships, trains, planes, and trucks.

As unrest among social groups increased, tyrannies arose in the city-states. A tyranny was created when one man, called a **tyrant**, seized power and ruled the polis single-handedly. Tyrants promoted trade, carried out many public works projects, and abolished debt slavery. The harshness of a few tyrants, however, gave *tyranny* its present meaning—rule by a cruel and unjust person.

Tyrants ruled various Greek city-states until about 500 B.C. From then until 336 B.C., most city-states became either oligarchies or democracies. In an **oligarchy** a few wealthy people hold power over the larger group of citizens. In a **democracy**, or government by the people, power lies in the hands of all the citizens.

The two major city-states of ancient Greece were **Sparta** and **Athens**. Although citizens of both Sparta and Athens participated in polis government, the two city-states differed greatly from each other. Sparta, located in the Peloponnesus (PEH•luh•puh•NEE•suhs) peninsula of southern Greece, was a warlike society that used its army to control its noncitizens. Athens, situated on the peninsula of Attica in central Greece, created a much freer society that was known for its artistic and intellectual achievements.

Like other Greek city-states, Athens excluded women and slaves from the political process. However, it did make a great contribution toward the development of the idea of democracy. In 507 B.C. the Athenian leader Cleisthenes introduced a **constitution**, or plan of government, which stated that all free men were citizens regardless of social class and could participate in the Assembly regardless of whether they owned land. In the Assembly, citizens were considered equal before the law and were guaranteed freedom of speech. This political change reduced much of the friction between social classes and enabled Athens to forge ahead.

War, Glory, and Decline

In 546 B.C. Persian armies conquered the Greek city-states of Ionia, in Asia Minor. About 50 years later, the Ionians, with the support of mainland Greeks, revolted unsuccessfully against Persian rule. The victorious Persian forces then set out to

---

CONNECTIONS

Geography

Sailing the Aegean

Because of their many natural harbors, the Greeks transported most goods by sea. Sea travel made good sense, given the rugged mountains of the Greek mainland. Besides, pack animals could carry only small loads short distances. Merchants found sea transport of bulky cargo—grain, timber, and even jugs of olive oil—to be practical and inexpensive.

Greek sailors could sail easily only when the wind was behind them. The prevailing northerly winds made the voyage from Athens to the Black Sea slow and difficult, but the return trip was quick and easy. Likewise, Greek ships could coast to Egypt, but they had to struggle to get home. Most ships managed only one round-trip per year.

Pottery jar showing a merchant ship

The typical Greek freighter was broad—about 25 feet (7.5 m) wide compared to a length of 80 feet (24 m). Rigged with a large square sail, this sturdy ship averaged only about 5 knots with the wind. Merchant ships usually sailed in fleets escorted by warships—galleys propelled by oarsmen.

Compare the ancient ships with today's diesel-driven giants. A container ship makes the round-trip between the United States and Europe in 21 days. It holds cargo in 1,000 containers—4 of which are the size of 1 Greek freighter. Some things have not changed, however. The Greek merchant fleet of today ranks among the largest in the world.

Linking Past and Present ACTIVITY

Explain why the ancient Greeks relied on the sea for the transport of goods. In what kinds of vessels did they sail? How has cargo transport changed since ancient times?

MEETING SPECIAL NEEDS ACTIVITY

Learning Style: Logical/Mathematical Many students have trouble understanding dates. This is especially true in the pre-Christian era (B.C.), when numbers grow smaller as the time advances—just the opposite of what happens in more recent history when dates are A.D.

Have students reproduce the time line on page 58 and then add the following events in the appropriate places: Persians conquer Ionia, Cleisthenes' constitution, battle of Salamis, end of the Peloponnesian War, death of Alexander the Great. **L2**

punish the mainland Greeks for helping the rebels.

The Persian Wars

In 490 B.C. Persian forces landed at the plain of **Marathon**, about 25 miles (40 km) north of Athens. The outnumbered, but well-disciplined, Greeks staged a surprise attack and defeated the Persians, who then withdrew to Asia Minor. Ten years later, the Persians returned to Greece. Preparing to challenge the Persians at sea, the Greeks first set up a delaying action on land. About 7,000 Greeks led by the Spartans stood firm against the Persians for three days at Thermopylae (thuhr•MAH•puh•lee), a mountain pass north of Athens. Even though these Greek soldiers suffered defeat, their heroic stand gave the Athenian-led

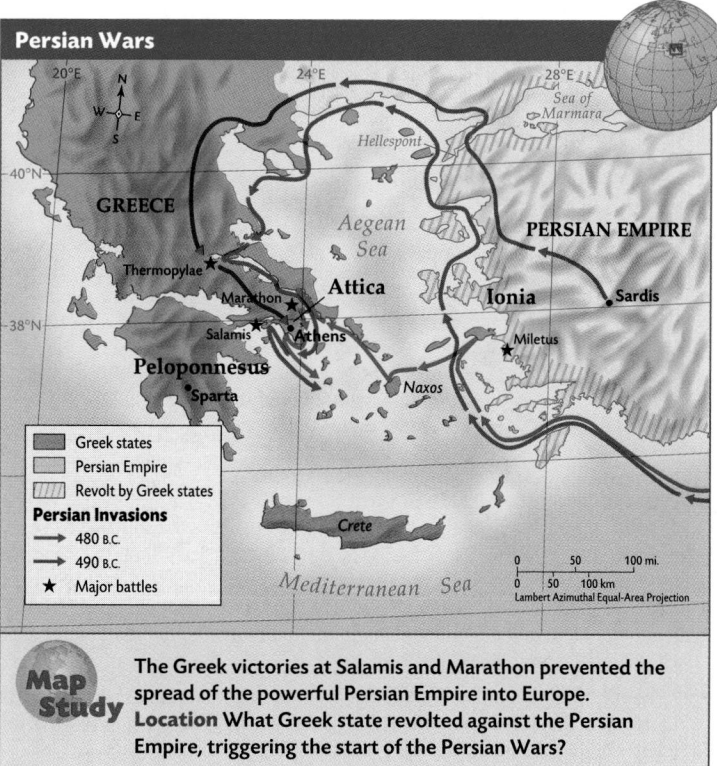

Persian Wars

Greek states
Persian Empire
Revolt by Greek states
Persian Invasions
→ 480 B.C.
→ 490 B.C.
★ Major battles

0   50   100 mi.
0   50   100 km
Lambert Azimuthal Equal-Area Projection

Map Study
The Greek victories at Salamis and Marathon prevented the spread of the powerful Persian Empire into Europe.
Location What Greek state revolted against the Persian Empire, triggering the start of the Persian Wars?

Greek navy the time it needed to draw the Persian fleet into a narrow body of water between Athens and the island of **Salamis**. Crowded together, the heavy Persian ships became easy targets for the faster and more maneuverable Greek ships. Although outnumbered, the Greek navy destroyed almost the entire Persian fleet.

With the end of the Persian threat at Salamis, the Greek city-states resumed their traditional quarrels. By this time Athens had emerged as the dominant Greek city-state. As Athenian economic and political power grew, several city-states joined Sparta in a war against Athens. Since Sparta was located in the Peloponnesus, historians have called this conflict the Peloponnesian War.

The Peloponnesian War lasted from about 431 B.C. to 404 B.C. At first it seemed as if Athens could hold out indefinitely, since Sparta had no navy. Sparta, however, eventually turned to the Persians for help in building a fleet. Then, in 430 B.C., a disastrous plague—probably typhus—struck Athens and wiped out more than a third of its population. The weakened Athenians faced a further blow when the Persian-financed Spartan navy destroyed their fleet.

After the Spartans laid siege to Athens itself, the Athenians finally surrendered in 404 B.C.

The Peloponnesian War brought setbacks to all of the Greek city-states, many of which declined in population and economic strength. Worst of all, the war's ferocity had undermined Greek confidence in their ability to rule themselves. When new invaders, the Macedonians, threatened Greece in the 350s B.C., the city-states were unable to resist.

Greek Civilization

During the mid-400s B.C., Greek civilization reached its cultural peak, particularly in the city-state of Athens. The ancient Greeks excelled in architecture, sculpture, painting, philosophy, and drama. They created works characterized by beautiful simplicity and graceful balance, an artistic style now called **classical**. Many cultural traditions of Western civilization—the civilization of Europe and those parts of the world influenced by Europeans—began in ancient Greece.

Chapter 2 *The Advance of Civilizations* **61**

Linking Past and Present

The Peloponnesian War demanded great sacrifice from Athens. It has been estimated that almost a third of its population was mobilized. By contrast, World War I mobilized 10 percent of the populations of the countries involved.

Global Gourmet

Greece Olives were a staple of the Greek diet because olive trees grow well in dry, rocky soil. Olive oil was so important to the Greek economy that when the Spartans attacked Athens, their first move was to destroy the olive groves surrounding the city in order to weaken the Athenian economy.

MAKING CONNECTIONS ACTIVITY

Sports The first modern marathon—named after the battle that led to the famous run of Pheidippides—was held at the Olympic Games in Athens in 1896. The length of the marathon varied until it was officially set in 1908 at 26 miles, 385 yards (42.19 kilometers). Have students research and report on famous marathons of today, such as those of Boston and New York City. Their reports should include the history of the event, the time and place in which it is staged, the average number of runners, the names of important recent winners, and the time it took these people to run the race. **L2**

Visualizing History

Many Romans shared the Greek ideal of perfecting the human body.
Answer to Caption: *by crowning them with wreaths of olive leaves and by holding parades in their honor*

you don't say...

"Orchestra" is a Greek word from the verb "to dance" and was first used to describe the space between the stage and the audience where the chorus performed. In modern times, the term designates both the area in front of the stage and the group of musicians that plays there.

Philosophy Draw a rectangle on the chalkboard and label it *philosophy*. Have volunteers draw and label within it smaller rectangles to represent other disciplines founded on philosophy. *(history, political science, biology)* Use this graphic organizer to brainstorm with students some fundamental questions in each of these disciplines; questions which a philosopher might address. *(Examples are: Can people uncover the truth about the past? What form of government best serves justice? What qualities define "life"?)* **L2 LEP**

 Focus on World Art Print 8, *Laocoön*

World History and Art Transparency 5, *Amphora from Vulci;* 6, *Nike of Samothrace*

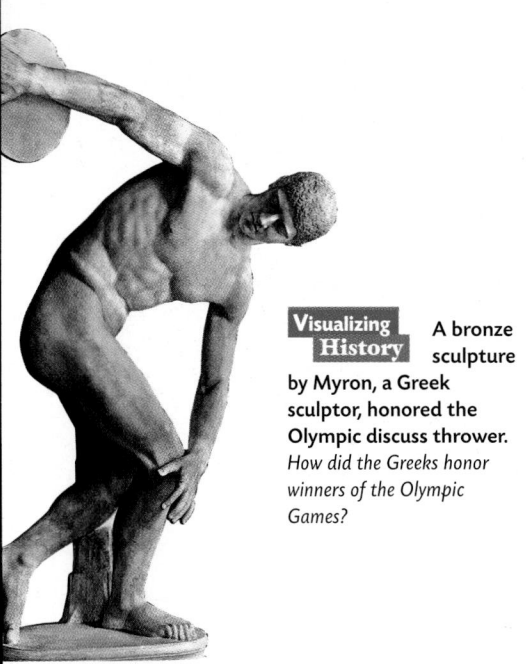

Visualizing History

A bronze sculpture by Myron, a Greek sculptor, honored the Olympic discus thrower. *How did the Greeks honor winners of the Olympic Games?*

The Visual Arts

After the Persian Wars, the Athenian general **Pericles** rebuilt Athens and made it the most beautiful city in Greece. The most famous structure built under Pericles, the Parthenon (the temple of the goddess Athena), still stands. Its graceful proportions perfectly balance width, length, and height.

In both painting and sculpture, the Greeks—because they emphasized the individual—excelled at portraying the human form. Today we can still see examples of their work in paintings on Greek vases and in statues of idealized human figures. Greek sculptors, such as Myron and Phidias (FIH•dee•uhs), focused on powerful deities and heroes; later, sculptors, such as Praxiteles (prak•SIH•tuhl•EEZ) carved ordinary people too.

Greek Drama

The Greeks were the first people to write and perform plays, which they presented twice a year at festivals to honor Dionysus, the god of wine and fertility. The earliest Greek plays were tragedies, dramatic works in which the lead characters struggle against fate only to be doomed—after much suffering—to an unhappy, or tragic, ending. Aeschylus (EHS•kuh•luhs), the first of the great writers of tragedies in the 400s B.C., wrote the *Oresteia*, a set of three plays dealing with the themes of guilt, revenge, punishment, and forgiveness. Another great tragedian, Sophocles (SAH•fuh•KLEEZ),

in his play *Oedipus Rex*, looks at human suffering, courage, and compassion. The last of the three great Greek tragedians—Euripides (yu•RIH•puh•DEEZ)—focuses on human responsibility and the horrors of war in the drama *The Trojan Women.*

Eventually the Greeks also wrote comedies, plays with humorous themes and happy endings. Aristophanes (ar•uh•STAH•fuh•NEEZ), the most famous writer of comedies, created imaginative social satire. In his works, such as *The Clouds*, he made witty comments about issues of his day and about leading figures—such as Euripides.

The Olympic Games

Believing that healthy bodies made the best use of nature's gifts, the ancient Greeks stressed athletics. Every four years they held a series of athletic contests for the glory of the chief god Zeus. Because these contests were held at the city of **Olympia**, they were called the Olympic Games.

Athletes came from all over the Greek-speaking world to compete in the Olympics. Only male athletes, however, were allowed to take part, and women were not permitted even as spectators. Games that honored the goddess Hera were held at a different location than Olympia and gave Greek women an opportunity to participate in running races.

The Greeks regarded Olympic winners as heroes. They crowned the victors with wreaths of olive leaves and held parades in their honor. Some city-states even excused outstanding athletes from paying taxes.

Philosophers

Greek philosophers, or thinkers, believed in the power of reason to explain all things. In their works, they laid the foundations for such disciplines as history, political science, biology, and logic, or the science of reasoning.

Socrates (SAH•kruh•TEEZ), the first major Greek philosopher, developed a teaching technique known as the Socratic method, in which students learned to clarify their thinking and to defend their ideas. One of Socrates' students, **Plato**, went on to devise an all-embracing philosophy that located the source of "truth" in ideas and not in information from the senses. Another philosopher, **Aristotle** (AR•uh•STAH•tuhl), influenced later thinkers with his work on logic and science. He was the first person to observe facts, classify them according to their similarities and their differences, and finally develop generalizations from his data. Although some of his specific beliefs were incorrect, Aristotle's method of inquiry would dominate European scientific thinking for centuries.

62   Chapter 2   *The Advance of Civilizations*

CRITICAL THINKING ACTIVITY

Determining Cause and Effect Ask students to comment on why historians consider the decline of Athens after the Peloponnesian War to be such a setback. Have students speculate on what could have occurred if Athens had won the war against Sparta and had continued to be prominent as before. Do students think other factors besides the outcome of the Peloponnesian War may have significantly contributed to Athens' decline? Ask students if they can think of parallel examples from recent history where the effects of warfare have weakened a nation's progress or influence. **L3**

Historians

The Greeks also used their intellectual skills in writing history. Until the 400s B.C., the Greeks had considered legends as history. Herodotus (hih•RAH•duh•tus), the first Greek historian, began to separate fact from legend by asking questions, recording answers, and checking the reliability of his sources. Another historian, Thucydides, (thoo•SIH•duh•DEEZ) is regarded as the first scientific historian because he carefully examined historical information and refused to accept supernatural explanations for events.

Scientists

The ancient Greeks passed on a great scientific heritage. They believed that the world is ruled by natural laws and that human beings can discover these laws by using reason. During the 500s B.C., the scientist Pythagoras (puh•THA•guh•ruhs) tried to explain everything in mathematical terms. He explored the nature of numbers, especially whole numbers and their ratios. Students of geometry still learn the Pythagorean theorem about the relationship of sides of a right-angled triangle.

Greek scientists also contributed to the field of medicine. Called "the father of medicine," the physician Hippocrates (hih•PAH•kruh•TEEZ) believed that diseases had natural, not supernatural, causes and that the body could heal itself. He strongly advocated proper health care, a sound diet, and plenty of rest. According to tradition, Hippocrates drafted a code for ethical medical conduct that has guided the practice of medicine for more than 2,000 years. Many doctors today recite the Hippocratic oath when they receive their medical degree.

Alexander's Empire

In the early 400s B.C., the Persians under Darius I, and then under his son Xerxes, had tried to conquer the Greek city-states but failed. Some 150 years later the Macedonians, a people who lived north of Greece in the Balkan Peninsula, made a similar attempt—and succeeded.

In 359 B.C. Philip II became king of Macedonia. As king, Philip determined to do three things: create a strong standing army, unify the quarreling Greek city-states under Macedonian rule, and destroy the Persian Empire.

Philip increased his army's fighting power by organizing his infantry into Greek-style phalanxes. Each phalanx consisted of 16 rows of lance-bearing foot soldiers closely arrayed with their shields forming a solid wall.

Visualizing History Greek physicians observed the many symptoms of disease and concluded that illnesses are not caused by evil spirits, but have natural causes. *What three prescriptions for health did Hippocrates suggest?*

The Greek city-states, weakened by the Peloponnesian War, would not cooperate with each other in resisting Philip. By 338 B.C. the Macedonian ruler controlled almost all of Greece.

Philip then prepared to lead the Greeks and Macedonians in a war against Persia. But in 336 B.C., he was murdered. His son Alexander, later known as **Alexander the Great**, became king.

Alexander the Great

Alexander was only 20 when he became the ruler of Macedonia and Greece. A commander in the Macedonian army since he was 16, Alexander was highly respected by his soldiers for his courage and military skill. He was also very well educated, for his father had him tutored by Aristotle for four years.

In 334 B.C. Alexander led his soldiers into Asia against the Persians. The first major encounter with the Persians took place at the Granicus River in western Asia Minor. Alexander's forces won, and he sent 300 suits of armor to Athens as an offering to the goddess Athena. Alexander then marched along the coast of Asia Minor, freeing the Ionian city-states from Persian rule.

The second battle between the Greeks and Persians took place in 333 B.C. at Issus, Syria. Once again, Alexander's superb tactics resulted in victory, forcing the Persian king Darius III to flee.

Chapter 2 *The Advance of Civilizations* **63**

Visualizing History The medical school founded by Hippocrates published the world's first work on epidemics, as well as a treatise on epilepsy.
Answer to Caption: *proper hygiene, a sound diet, and plenty of rest*

Independent Practice

Guided Reading Activity 2-1 **L1**

Biography Have students write a one- or two-page biography about any person discussed in this section. Students should research their subject to find information beyond that presented in the text. **L2**

Diversity Have students identify the diverse cultures that were part of Alexander's empire. (*Greek, Egyptian, Persian*) Then ask them to research what steps Alexander took to unify these cultures. (*by example, intermarriage, founding cities*) Have them explain which step they think was most effective. **L2 LEP**

Alexander's Inspiration Alexander the Great, like many ancient Greeks, spent much of his time either reading or listening to stories about heroic Greek exploits. According to Plutarch, a first century Greek biographer, one of Alexander's favorite stories was Homer's *Iliad*. Alexander had a copy of the epic poem that Aristotle had edited.

Alexander took it with him everywhere he traveled, keeping it with his dagger and his pillow at night. According to Plutarch, as Alexander set off to lead his troops into Asia, he first went straight to the ruins of Troy as a kind of pilgrimage. There he made a sacrifice to the goddess Athena and honored the burial spot of the hero Achilles.

you don't say...

"Barbarians" is a word that goes back to the Greeks, who applied the term to all non-Greeks. It was not a pejorative term, but simply a way of approximating a foreign language, which to the Greeks sounded like "bar-bar-bar."

Cultural Perspectives

Greek Influence The Romans borrowed heavily from Greek culture, especially after their conquest of Greece in 146 B.C. The poet Virgil, author of the *Aeneid*—the national epic of Rome—read and was inspired by Homer's works. Roman architects and sculptors imitated Greek styles. The Roman poet Horace put it this way: "Greece, taken captive, captured her savage conqueror."

ASSESS

Check for Understanding

Assign Section 1 Review as homework or as an in-class activity.

◙ Use Student Self-Test and Review Software to review Section 1.

Evaluate

🗁 Section Quiz 2-1

◙ Use the Testmaker to create a customized quiz for Section 1.

Instead of pursuing Darius, Alexander and his forces then moved south and conquered Phoenicia and Egypt. Discontented under Persian rule, the Egyptians welcomed Alexander and declared him pharaoh. In Egypt Alexander established a new city and named it **Alexandria** after himself.

In 331 B.C. Alexander again turned his attention eastward. He invaded Mesopotamia and smashed Darius's main army near the Tigris River. He went on to capture the city of Persepolis and declare himself ruler of the Persian Empire. Even this success was not enough for the young conqueror. In 327 B.C. Alexander led his soldiers into India, where they reached the Indus River valley. Alexander hoped to go farther yet, but his Macedonian veterans refused. Alexander therefore reluctantly turned around and went to Babylon, which he had made the capital of his empire. But the hardships of the journey had undermined his health, and he fell ill with a fever, probably malaria. In 323 B.C. Alexander the Great died at the age of 33.

Alexander's Goals

In assessing Alexander's achievements, it can be seen that when Alexander first set out with his army, his goal was to punish Persia for its invasion of Greece 150 years earlier. But as more and more territory came under his control, Alexander's views changed. His new vision was to create an empire that would unite Europe and Asia and combine the best of Greek and Persian cultures.

Alexander tried to promote his goal by example. He wore Persian dress and imitated the court life of Persian kings. He married a daughter of Darius III and encouraged some of his soldiers to marry Persian women. He enrolled Persians in his army. He also founded about 70 cities that served both as military outposts and centers for spreading the Greek language and culture throughout his empire.

A Divided Domain

Following Alexander's death, three of his generals—Ptolemy (TAH•luh•mee), Seleucus (suh•LOO•kuhs), and Antigonus (an•TIH•guh•nuhs)—eventually divided his vast empire into separate territories. Ptolemy and his descendants ruled Egypt, Libya, and part of Syria. The most famous Ptolemaic ruler was Cleopatra VII, who lost her kingdom to the Romans in 31 B.C.

Seleucus and his descendants—the Seleucids (suh•LOO•suds) at first controlled the rest of Syria, as well as Mesopotamia, Iran, and Afghanistan. After a while, however, they were forced to give up their eastern territory and withdraw to Syria. In 167 B.C. the Seleucids tried to put down a revolt of Jewish guerrillas led by Judah Maccabees. The kingdom of Judah, however, retained its independence.

The domain of Antigonus and his heirs consisted at first of Macedonia and Greece. But the Greek city-states soon declared their independence and once again began fighting with each other.

Hellenistic Culture

The political unity of Alexander's empire disappeared with his death, but the Greek language and culture continued to spread and flourish in the lands he had conquered. There, Hellenic ways of life mixed with elements of Middle Eastern culture to form a new culture, called Hellenism.

Hellenistic culture was concentrated in cities. The largest and wealthiest of these was Alexandria in Egypt. Alexandria was a major intellectual center that drew thinkers, writers, artists, and scientists from all over the Hellenistic world. In Alexandria and other Hellenistic cities, people focused on making a living rather than loyalty to a city or region. Women, especially in the upper classes, enjoyed more freedoms than they did in Hellenic times. Many learned to read and write, and they entered such occupations as real estate, banking, and government.

Alexander the Great

MEETING SPECIAL NEEDS ACTIVITY

Learning Style: Visual/Spatial Many students have problems understanding distances. Have students, in pairs or small groups, "translate" some of the distances of Alexander's time into comparable distances in the United States today. For instance, the extent of Alexander's conquests in Asia, from the Aegean coast to the Indus Valley, is approximately 2,800 miles (4,505 kilometers)—about the same as the east-west distance across the United States. If possible, have students present their findings to the class using a wall map of the United States. **L1**

Hellenistic Thinkers and Artists

During the Hellenistic period, the Greeks continued their interest in philosophy. Earlier Greek thinkers had focused on the world and the community in their pursuit of knowledge. Hellenistic philosophers, however, took a different approach. They gave more attention to the concerns of individuals. For example, Hellenistic thinkers focused on personal behavior, especially the question of how to achieve peace of mind. Three systems of thought attracted most Hellenistic thinkers: Cynicism, Epicureanism (EH•pih•kyu• REE •uh•NIH•zuhm), and Stoicism.

The best known Cynic was Diogenes (dy•AH• juh•NEEZ). He asserted that people would be happy if they gave up luxuries and lived simply, in accord with nature. The scholar Epicurus started the philosophy of Epicureanism, arguing that people should avoid both joy and pain by accepting the world as it is and living simply and quietly. The philosopher Zeno founded another viewpoint—Stoicism. The Stoics believed that natural laws governed human behavior. Therefore, people could gain happiness by ignoring their emotions, and instead following their reason. In this way, they were able to accept life's difficulties. Stoicism later affected both Roman and early Christian thinkers.

During the Hellenistic era, artists departed from the traditional Greek practice of showing idealized individuals and instead focused on people caught in the grip of powerful emotions. Hellenistic playwrights usually wrote comedies rather than tragedies. Menander, the most renowned Hellenistic playwright, specialized in comedies about everyday life.

Hellenistic scientists performed many experiments and formed new theories. For example, Euclid of Alexandria, collected and organized all information about geometry. Archimedes (AHR•kuh•MEE•deez) of Syracuse discovered the principle of buoyancy, and Eratosthenes (EHR•uh•TAHS•thuh•NEEZ) estimated the earth's circumference to within one percent of the correct figure.

Map Study

Alexander's Empire 336–323 B.C.

Alexander the Great united the Greeks and conquered an area stretching from Egypt to India.
1. **Movement** After freeing the Ionian city-states, in which direction did Alexander and his forces travel?
2. **Location** What key cities in the Persian Empire did Alexander conquer?

SECTION 1 REVIEW

Recall
1. **Define** polis, tyrant, oligarchy, democracy, constitution, classical, tragedy, comedy.
2. **Identify** Minoans, Homer, the *Iliad* and the *Odyssey*, Salamis, the Peloponnesian War, Pericles, Aeschylus, Socrates, Plato, Aristotle, Thucydides, Alexander the Great.
3. **Describe** how worship of Greek deities influenced architecture, art, and athletics.

Critical Thinking
4. **Analyzing Information** How did increased trade in the Mediterranean world affect political life in the Greek city-states?

Understanding Themes
5. **Innovation** How did Socrates and Hippocrates each contribute to the intellectual life of ancient Greece?

Chapter 2 Section 1

Map Study

Answers
1. *south and east*
2. *Babylon, Persepolis, and Susa*

Map Skills Practice

Reading a Map What major bodies of water bordered Alexander's empire? (*the Mediterranean, Black, Caspian, and Arabian Seas and the Persian Gulf*)

Reteach

Have students review the major innovations in thought discussed in this section.

Enrich

Have students compare the ancient Greek treatment of Olympic athletes with the treatment of professional athletes in the United States.

CLOSE

Write this quotation from the English poet Shelley on the board: "We are all Greeks." Have students discuss what they think the statement means in light of this section.

SECTION 1 REVIEW ANSWERS

1. All vocabulary words are defined in the Glossary.
2. Minoans, 58; Homer, 58; the *Iliad* and the *Odyssey*, 58; Salamis, 61; the Peloponnesian War, 61; Pericles, 62; Aeschylus, 62; Socrates, 62; Plato, 62; Aristotle, 62; Thucydides, 63; Alexander the Great, 63
3. Greek temples were built to venerate the deities. Greek artifacts often pictured the gods and goddesses, with many sculptures representing them. Greek plays honored Dionysus, while the Olympic Games honored Zeus.
4. Trade led to an increase in the number and wealth of nonlandowning merchants and artisans, who demanded a voice in the government and also wanted the government to encourage industry and promote trade.
5. **INNOVATION** Socrates: developed his Socratic method, forcing students to think clearly; Hippocrates: taught that diseases had natural causes and based his work on observation, thereby furthering the scientific method.

Block Schedule

Team Teaching This excerpt from *Antigone* may be presented in a team-teaching context, in conjunction with English or Language Arts.

Antigone

Historical Connection

Sophocles wrote during the Golden Age of Athens, an era in which Greek writers, philosophers, architects, and historians produced works that shaped all subsequent Western civilization. This excerpt from the play *Antigone* shows how thinkers of the time dealt with such basic issues as ethics and justice.

Background Information

Setting During the Golden Age of Athens, writers often set their works in the distant past. *Antigone* takes place in the city of Thebes in a mythological period long before Sophocles lived.

Characters Antigone: daughter of the deceased king of Thebes, niece of Creon, sister of Ismene, Polyneices, and Eteocles; Ismene: sister of Antigone; Creon: brother of the deceased king of Thebes.

Plot The main conflict is between Antigone, who wants to give her brother Polyneices an honorable burial, and Creon, her uncle, who argues that Polyneices was a traitor who does not deserve a burial. Antigone violates Creon's order and buries her brother. Antigone and Creon then debate the morality of her action.

from
Antigone
by Sophocles

*T*he Greek playwright Sophocles (about 496–406 B.C.) wrote about the conflict between conscience and authority in his play Antigone. *After Antigone's two brothers died battling each other for the throne of Thebes, her uncle, Creon, became king. Creon allowed one brother, Eteocles, an honorable burial. He declared, however, that the other brother, Polyneices, was a traitor whose body should be left for the "birds and scavenging dogs." Anyone attempting to bury Polyneices, he warned, would be stoned to death. Antigone's sister, Ismene, obeys Creon. Antigone, however, out of respect for her brother, buries him.*

Creon [*slowly, dangerously*]. And you, Antigone, You with your head hanging—do you confess this thing?

Antigone. I do. I deny nothing.

Creon [*to* SENTRY].   You may go. [*Exit* SENTRY] [*To* ANTIGONE] Tell me, tell me briefly: Had you heard my proclamation touching this matter?

Antigone. It was public. Could I help hearing it?

Creon. And yet you dared defy the law.

Antigone.   I dared. It was not God's proclamation. That final justice That rules the world below makes no such laws. Your edict, King, was strong, But all your strength is weakness itself against The immortal unrecorded laws of God. They are not merely now: they were, and shall be, Operative forever, beyond man utterly.

I knew I must die, even without your decree: I am only mortal. And if I must die Now, before it is my time to die, Surely this is no hardship: can anyone Living, as I live, with evil all about me, Think death less than a friend? This death of mine Is of no importance; but if I had left my brother Lying in death unburied, I should have suffered. Now I do not.
            You smile at me. Ah Creon.

ABOUT THE AUTHOR

Sophocles was born into a well-to-do family in ancient Greece. Many of his plays focused on one strong-willed individual who challenged authority, tradition, or the gods and goddesses. For example, Antigone defies the authority of the state to defend the honor of her brother. Although Sophocles wrote more than 100 plays, only 7 are known to exist today. Many of the lost plays won awards in the annual writing competition held in ancient Greece. In addition to writing, Sophocles served as a government administrator and a general in the Athenian army.

Think me a fool, if you like; but it may well be
That a fool convicts me of folly. . . .
Creon, what more do you want than my death?

Creon.   Nothing.
That gives me everything.

Antigone.   Then I beg you: kill me.
This talking is a great weariness: your words
Are distasteful to me, and I am sure that mine
Seem so to you. And yet they should not seem so:
I should have praise and honor for what I have done.
All these men here would praise me
Were their lips not frozen shut with fear of you.
[*Bitterly*] Ah the good fortune of kings,
Licensed to say and do whatever they please!

Creon. You are alone here in that opinion.

Antigone. No, they are with me. But they keep their tongues
in leash.

Creon. Maybe. But you are guilty,
and they are not.

Antigone. There is no guilt in reverence for the dead.

Creon. But Eteocles—was he not
your brother too?

Antigone. My brother too.

Creon.   And you insult
his memory?

Antigone [*softly*]. The dead man
would not say that I insult it.

Creon. He would: for you honor a
traitor as much as him.

Antigone. His own brother, traitor
or not, and equal in blood.

Creon. He made war on his country.
Eteocles defended it.

Antigone. Nevertheless, there are
honors due all the dead.

History & Art Actors preparing for a performance
(detail), the House of the Tragic Poet,
Pompeii. National Museum, Naples, Italy
What is the theme of Antigone?

OTHER WORKS OF SOPHOCLES

Jebb, Richard Claverhouse, trans. ***The
Complete Plays of Sophocles.*** New York:
Bantam, 1982.
Knox, M. W., trans. ***Oedipus the King.*** New
York: Pocket Books, 1972.

Watling, E. F., trans. ***Electra and Other Plays.***
New York: Penguin Books, 1954.
Williams, C. K., and Gregory W. Dickerson,
trans. ***Women of Trachus.*** New York: Oxford
University Press, 1978.

Literary Element Alliteration
occurs when words in a phrase
begin with a similar sound. The
first line by Creon uses alliteration, as in "head hanging." Later,
Antigone uses the phrase "a fool
convicts me of folly."

FOCUS

Before students read the excerpt,
list on the chalkboard people
who students feel have authority
over them, such as parents, teachers, and so on. Ask students to
describe hypothetical cases in
which they might choose to disobey a person having authority.
Help them see the difference
between ignoring authority and
principled disobedience.

TEACH

Interpretation
Ask students if they agree with
Antigone's claim that "All these
men here would praise me/Were
their lips not shut with fear of
you." Point out that ordinary
people may support a heroic
individual against a repressive
government. At other times, people see such an individual as a
threat to order and stability.

History & Art Pompeii was a
provincial Roman city buried in ash
and lava when the volcano Vesuvius
erupted in August of A.D. 79, killing
all its residents but preserving much
of the art and architecture.
Answer to Caption: *an individual
can stand up to authority, but at a price*

Bridge to the Past
Literature

Clarification

The choragos is the leader of the chorus, who serves as a narrator to smooth the flow of the story and adds commentary from the author.

Evaluation

Discuss the role of women in Greek society as portrayed in this excerpt. Students might consider how the play would differ if Antigone had been male instead of female. *(She would have taken the throne instead of Creon.)*

History & Art

Roman art was strongly influenced by Hellenic styles. Wealthy Romans not only had artists copy Greek originals but also sometimes brought artists from Greece to decorate their homes. **Answer to Caption:** *Students may say that since Ismene feared to act, mere words cannot redeem her.*

Linking Past and Present

Greek Dramas *Antigone* and other tragedies by Sophocles, such as *Oedipus the King*, *Oedipus at Colonus*, and *Electra*, are often staged today by college theater groups and by local repertory companies. Some students may wish to attend a performance in your area.

World Literature Selection 2

ASSESS

Assign **Responding to Literature** questions.

History & Art Wall painting of a Greek woman with flowers. National Museum, Naples, Italy
The Greeks admired beauty and virtue. *Does Ismene regain virtue by confessing a share in the crime?*

Creon. But not the same for the wicked as for the just.

Antigone. Ah Creon, Creon.
Which of us can say what the gods hold wicked?

Creon. An enemy is an enemy, even dead.

Antigone. It is my nature to join in love, not hate.

Creon [*finally losing patience*]. Go join them, then;
if you must have your love,
Find it in hell!

Choragos [*leader of a group of 15 citizens*]. But see, Ismene comes:
[*Enter Ismene, guarded.*] Those tears are sisterly, the cloud
That shadows her eyes rains down gentle sorrow.

Creon. You too, Ismene,

ADDITIONAL LITERARY WORKS OF THE PERIOD

Book of Songs. A collection of 300 poems from China dating to 1000 B.C.
Homer. *Iliad and Odyssey.* Ancient Greek epic poems that have greatly influenced Western literature.

Laozi. *The Classic of the Way and the Virtue.* Writings of the founder of Daoism, who lived in China in the 500s B.C.
Samhitas. Sacred Hindu hymns written in Sanskrit in India and compiled about 1000 B.C.

Snake in my ordered house, sucking my blood
Stealthily—and all the time I never knew
That these two sisters were aiming at my throne!

                                Ismene,
Do you confess your share in this crime, or deny it?
Answer me.

Ismene. Yes, if she will let me say so. I am guilty.

Antigone [*coldly*]. No, Ismene. You have no right to say so.
You would not help me, and I will not have you help me.

Ismene. But now I know what you meant; and I am here
To join you, to take my share of punishment.

Antigone. The dead man and the gods who rule the dead
Know whose act this was. Words are not friends.

Ismene. Do you refuse me, Antigone? I want to die with
you:
I too have a duty that I must discharge to the dead.

Antigone. You shall not lessen my death by sharing it.

Ismene. What do I care for life when you are dead?

Antigone. Ask Creon. You're always hanging on his opinions.

Ismene. You are laughing at me. Why, Antigone?

Antigone. It's a joyless laughter, Ismene.

Ismene.   But can I do nothing?

Antigone. Yes. Save yourself. I shall not envy you.
There are those who will praise you; I shall have honor, too.

Ismene. But we are equally guilty!

Antigone.   No more, Ismene.
You are alive, but I belong to death.

RESPONDING TO LITERATURE

1. Explain what Antigone means when she says to Creon, "But all your strength is weakness itself against the immortal unrecorded laws of God."
2. Quote a passage that demonstrates Antigone's bravery.
3. Explain whether you would like to live in a society in which individuals followed only their consciences.
4. **Making Inferences** Predict whether Creon actually would have Antigone stoned to death.

CLOSE

Ask students to put themselves in the positions of Antigone and Creon, and have them describe what moral dilemmas each faced. (*As ruler, Creon may feel he cannot back down from sentencing Antigone to death, but as her uncle, he may be reluctant to carry out the punishment. Antigone does not wish to die, but she feels it is dishonorable to leave her brother unburied.*)

Contemporary Connection

One underlying theme of *Antigone* is loyalty to family. Discuss the idea with students, asking if they feel they have a duty to be loyal to their families. Ask students to consider how far loyalty to family should go.

Portfolio Project

Have students draw on their own experience to write a short essay, agreeing or disagreeing with this statement: *There is no value more important than loyalty to family.*

ANSWERS TO RESPONDING TO LITERATURE

1. Antigone believes that her duty to obey the laws of the gods and goddesses is more important than obeying the laws of the state.
2. Her first line, "I do. I deny nothing," condemns her to die and so shows her courage.
3. Students may recognize that a society in which each person followed his or her conscience would be anarchic; on the other hand, they may sympathize with the right of individuals to determine what is right and wrong.
4. Some students may feel Creon's posture implies that he will have Antigone executed; others may feel that entering into a discussion with her means he might reconsider her punishment. At the end of the play, Creon banishes Antigone to a cave, where she commits suicide.

509 B.C.	264 B.C.	c. A.D. 30	A.D. 312
Rome becomes a republic.	Punic Wars begin.	Jesus preaches in Galilee.	Constantine begins rule.

SECTION THEME

▶ **Cultural Diffusion** The Romans build an empire, spread Latin culture, and later, make Christianity the dominant religion in the West.

ind Out

Answer: *through military expansion and the growth of a powerful government to meet the needs of its vast territories*

FOCUS

Section Objective

Characterize life under the *Pax Romana* and the influence of early Christians on the later Roman Empire.

BELLRINGER
Motivational Activity

Before taking roll at the beginning of the class period, project Section Focus Transparency 2-2 and have students answer the activity questions. Discuss students' responses.

This activity is also available as a blackline master.

Vocabulary Pre-check

Use Vocabulary Activity 2 to introduce vocabulary terms.
L1 LEP

Section 2

Rome and Early Christianity

Setting the Scene

▶ **Terms to Define**
republic, patrician, plebeian, tribune, aqueduct, messiah, disciple, pope

▶ **People to Meet**
Hannibal, Julius Caesar, Augustus, Nero, Marcus Aurelius, Virgil, Jesus, Paul, Constantine, Augustine

▶ **Places to Locate**
Italy, Rome, Carthage, Gaul, Judea

ind Out How did Rome change from a small republic into a vast empire?

Storyteller

The visitor was amazed. Aelius Aristides, an intelligent, educated, and well-travelled man, had never seen anything to rival Rome. And it was not just the city—it was everything that Rome represented: military might, sensible government, a healthy economy, and an elegant lifestyle. Who could help but admire an empire that commanded vast territories and diverse peoples, a military that

Augustus Caesar

conquered both armed forces and selfish ambition, a government where officials ruled not through arbitrary power but by law.

—adapted from *Oration on the Pax Romana,* Aelius Aristides, reprinted in *Sources of the Western Tradition,* Marvin Perry, 1991

To the west of Greece lies **Italy**, a narrow, boot-shaped peninsula that extends from Europe toward Africa, dividing the Mediterranean almost in half. Archaeological evidence suggests that people lived in Italy as early as 5000 B.C. During the next 4000 years, Italy's mild, moist climate and rich soil attracted waves of immigrants, who set up farms on the plains lying between the peninsula's mountains and foothills.

The most mysterious of these early peoples were the Etruscans, who lived in north central Italy. No one knows definitely where the Etruscans originally came from; and although the Etruscans wrote in an alphabet borrowed from the Greeks, modern scholars have been able to decipher only a few words. However, the Etruscans left behind burial chambers filled with expressive art and sculpture and other artifacts. Many tomb paintings show sports, religious ceremonies, banquets, and other scenes of daily life.

The Roman Republic

By the 600s B.C., the Etruscans had extended their rule over many peoples of the Italian Peninsula. Chief among these were the Latins, whose center was the city of **Rome**. In 509 B.C. the people of Rome finally drove out their Etruscan kings and set up a **republic**, a form of government in which the people elect their leaders.

Under the republic, Roman society consisted of **patricians**, a wealthy aristocratic class, and **plebeians** (plih•BEE•uhns), who made up most of Rome's inhabitants. The plebeians included wealthy, nonaristocratic townspeople and landowners, merchants, shopkeepers, farmers of small land holdings, and laborers. As citizens, both plebeians and patricians had the right to vote and

SECTION RESOURCES

Reproducible Masters
• Reproducible Lesson Plan 2-2
• Vocabulary Activity 2
• Guided Reading Activity 2-2
• Section Quiz 2-2

Transparencies
• Section Focus Transparency 2-2
• Ancient Rome

Multimedia
Student Self-Test and Review Software
Testmaker
Greece and Rome

were required to pay taxes and serve in the military. Plebeians, however, could not hold public office as patricians could.

Plebeians Against Patricians

The plebeians resented their lack of power. In 494 B.C. to obtain a greater voice in the government, they went on strike—refusing to serve in the army and threatening to set up their own republic. The patricians, frightened at the loss of their military and work forces, agreed to meet some of the plebeians' demands. The patricians in particular recognized the plebeians' chosen representatives, the tribunes, granting them power to veto any government decision.

The plebeians then pressed for more changes. Roman laws were unwritten, and only the patricians knew what the laws said. In 451 B.C. the plebeians finally got the patricians to engrave the laws on 12 bronze tablets for all to see. These Twelve Tables became the basis for all future Roman law.

Daily Life

During the republic, the Romans borrowed extensively from Greek culture. For example, they honored Greek deities, giving them Roman names. Roman life remained distinctly Roman, however. Families privately worshiped their ancestral spirits and turned to soothsayers, or priests who claimed to foretell the future.

The family was the basic unit of Roman society. In Roman families, the father, as the absolute head of the household, conducted religious ceremonies, controlled property, and supervised the education of his sons. Roman wives had few legal rights, but they had more freedom than Greek women. They hosted parties, shopped, and in some cases, acquired their own property and businesses. Roman children learned the values of thrift, discipline, self-sacrifice, and devotion to the family and the republic. Long after the Roman Republic ended, nostalgic reformers saw these as traditional Roman values.

From Republic to Empire

From about 500 B.C. to 300 B.C., Rome faced threats from its neighbors in Italy. To protect their republic, the Romans either conquered these opponents or forced them to ally with Rome. In this way the Romans subdued one rival after another, until, by 264 B.C., Rome ruled the entire peninsula.

Rome's success in war was due to its strong army. Roman generals organized their troops into legions, or divisions of 3000 to 6000 men. Known as

Visualizing History Roman legionaries, shown in a colorful mosaic, were well trained. *How did Roman soldiers help unite the Italian Peninsula?*

legionaries, these well-trained soldiers were stationed throughout Italy to defend strategic heights and river crossings. To link individual military settlements, the legions forged a chain of roads up and down the Italian Peninsula. As war yielded gradually to peace, some of these roads became major trade routes.

Roman Expansion

Between 264 B.C. and 146 B.C., Rome fought three conflicts known as the Punic Wars against the North African city-state of **Carthage**. The goal of both sides was to control the western Mediterranean. In the second Punic War, the Carthaginian general, **Hannibal**, marched his army from Spain to Italy, making a heroic crossing of the Alps on the way. Hannibal defeated the Roman forces sent against him, but the Romans rallied, forcing Hannibal to rush to Carthage's defense. The Roman general Publius Scipio (POO•blee•uhs SIH•pee•OH), finally defeated Hannibal's army at Zama, near Carthage in 202 B.C.

Rome's victory over Carthage was finally completed in 146 B.C., when Roman forces destroyed

Chapter 2 *The Advance of Civilizations* **71**

Guided Practice

THEME **Cultural Diffusion**
Have students cite specific examples of cultural diffusion mentioned in this section. *(diffusion of Roman law throughout the empire; Roman adaptation of Egyptian astronomy and Greek literature)* Discuss how Roman roads encouraged the diffusion of Roman culture throughout the empire, and ask what technologies in our world are important factors in cultural diffusion. *(satellite transmission of television signals; computer technology; ease and speed of world travel)* **L1**

Visualizing History The basic unit of the Roman legion was the maniple, which consisted of 120 men in 12 files and 10 ranks. The expression "rank and file," referring to common people, derives from this method of organizing Roman soldiers.
Answer to Caption: *To link their military settlements, Roman soldiers built a chain of roads that later became major trade routes.*

Change Ask students to give two examples of conflict leading to change in ancient Rome. *(overthrow of Etruscan rule, struggle between patricians and plebeians over who ruled the republic)* **L1**

COOPERATIVE LEARNING ACTIVITY

Wall Diagram The Romans borrowed extensively from other cultures, adapting Etruscan ritual duels, Etruscan and Greek deities, Greek styles of architecture and sculpture, and Greek medicine and science. Provide students with a wall-sized sheet of paper on which to show a composite of what Romans borrowed. Assign students to small groups. Have each group research one major topic and complete one portion of the wall diagram. Each group should divide tasks among its members: doing research, obtaining pictures or drawing illustrations, writing captions, explaining the group's work to the class. **L1**

Government The Roman Republic was founded to govern a city-state but floundered when Rome governed a vast empire. Have students list political changes that resulted from the growth of Roman territory. *(corrupt government officials, overtaxation, revolts)* **L2**

Use these materials to enrich student understanding of ancient Rome.

 NGS PICTUREPACK TRANSPARENCY SET Ancient Rome

Literature Have students work as individuals or in small groups to read and present to the class portions of Shakespeare's *Julius Caesar*. Suggest the following scenes: Caesar's assassination (III, i, 1–95); Marc Antony's address to the plebeians (III, ii); or the farewell of Brutus and Cassius (V, i, 70–125). **L2**

---

the city. Meanwhile, Roman forces to the east captured other territories. As a result of these conquests, Rome emerged as the undisputed master of the Mediterranean from Spain to Asia Minor.

The Republic in Crisis

Rome's military expansion flooded the Roman Republic with vast wealth, but it also led to the Republic's decline. Conquered peoples rebelled when corrupt Roman officials overtaxed them and grew wealthy at their expense. Putting down these revolts cost Rome troops and money, and the conquered lands soon began to strain Rome's resources.

Military expansion also disrupted Roman society. In both the conquered territories and Italy, wealthy Romans acquired large estates and used enslaved people to work the land. They forced small farmers out of business and bought up their lands. Landless farmers then streamed into Rome, only to discover that many jobs there were already being done by enslaved people. Angry and without hope, the new class of urban poor voted for any leader who promised a better way of life.

Reformers and Generals

Many Romans feared that the growth of landed estates and the spread of corruption threatened the Republic. Two wealthy brothers, Tiberius Gracchus and Gaius Gracchus, tried to reform Rome's political system. As tribunes, they introduced laws to limit the size of estates and to provide food and land to the poor. Patrician leaders, however, blocked these reforms, and both brothers were killed by their political enemies.

Roman generals also tried to promote—or block—reforms. In 107 B.C. General Gaius Marius gave poor people jobs in the army. With obedient soldiers supporting him, Marius forced the passage

Footnotes to History

A Roman Dinner Party In ancient Rome, dinner guests of wealthy Romans would recline on couches while slaves served them delicacies. Main course dishes might include boiled stingray garnished with hot raisins; boiled crane with turnips; roast hare in white sauce; leg of boar; wood pigeon baked in a pie; or roast flamingo cooked with dates, onions, honey, and wine.

---

of laws favoring the common people. In 88 B.C. Marius's dispute with another general, Lucius Cornelius Sulla, sparked a civil war. Sulla won and appointed himself dictator, or absolute ruler. He sided with the patricians against the common people and turned against reforms.

During the 50s B.C., still another general, **Julius Caesar**, decisively influenced Roman politics. Caesar's military triumphs in neighboring **Gaul** boosted his fortunes. By 45 B.C. he had overcome his political rivals and had taken over the Roman government as dictator for life. Under Caesar's leadership, the government gave jobs to the unemployed, public land to the poor, and citizenship to many conquered peoples. Caesar's most lasting reform was the Julian calendar, used in western Europe until early modern times.

Some Romans believed that Caesar was a wise ruler who had brought order and peace back to Rome. Others, however, considered him a tyrant who meant to end the republic and make himself king. To prevent this, on March 15, 44 B.C., a group of officials assassinated Caesar.

The Roman Empire

After a period of civil war, Caesar's grandnephew, Octavian, became undisputed ruler of Rome in 32 B.C. Five years later, Octavian gave himself the title **Augustus**, or "Majestic One." In doing so, he became Rome's first emperor and laid the foundation for a new state called the Roman Empire.

The Emperors

In the 40 years of his reign—from 27 B.C. to A.D. 14—Augustus introduced many reforms. He attacked government corruption, imported food for Rome's poor, and constructed magnificent buildings throughout the empire. Augustus's reign saw the beginning of the *Pax Romana*, or Roman Peace, which lasted about 200 years. The only major disturbances during those years occurred when new emperors came to power. For, although Augustus chose his own successor carefully, he failed to devise any law for the selection of later emperors.

Some of Augustus's successors were talented rulers; others proved to be inept. One of the worst emperors, **Nero**, suspected others of plotting against him and executed family members as well as political rivals. One of the best, **Marcus Aurelius** (aw•REE•lee•uhs), was both a skilled administrator and a noted philosopher.

Learning Style: Visual/Spatial Encourage students who are visual learners to find pictures of sites in today's Rome that date back to ancient times. Ask them to make copies of the pictures or to draw renditions of them, arrange them in a book with captions to identify them, and provide information about when and why they were built. Have them share their completed books with the rest of the class. Suggested sites include the Colosseum, the Arch of Constantine, the Arch of Titus, the Pantheon, the Baths of Caracalla. **L1 LEP**

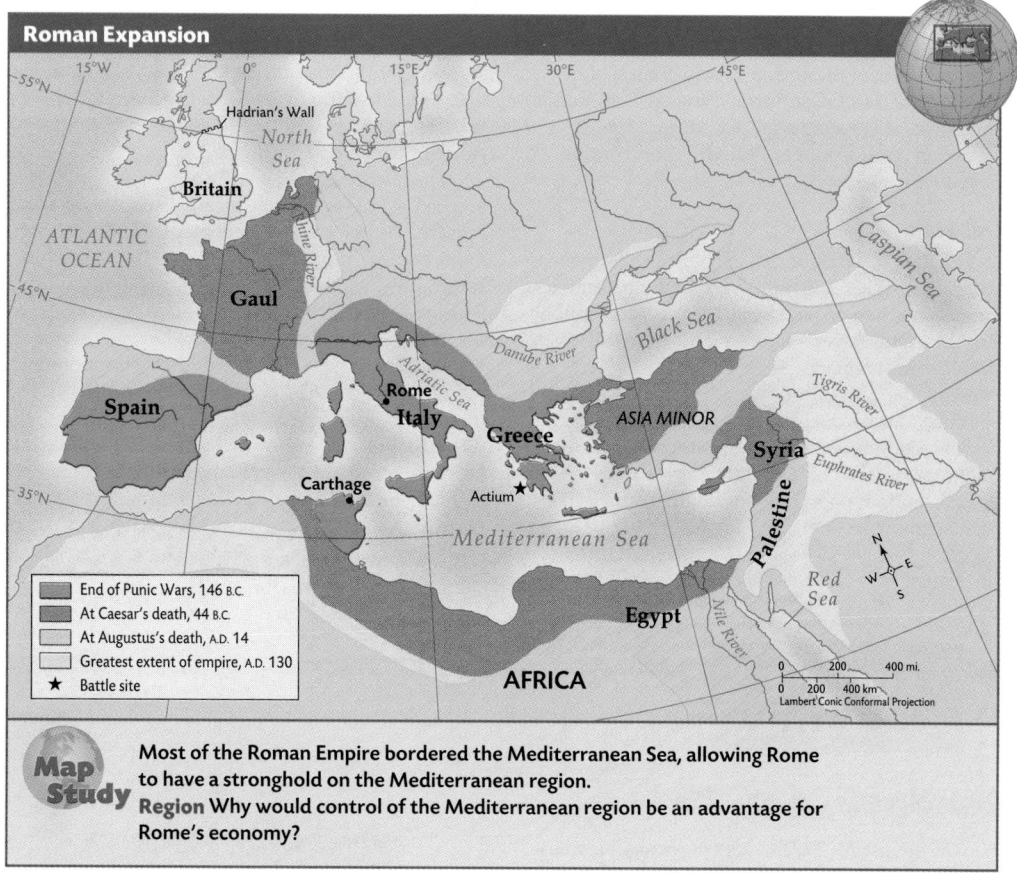

Roman Expansion

North Sea
Hadrian's Wall
Britain
ATLANTIC OCEAN
Gaul
Spain
Rome
Italy
Carthage
Actium ★
Mediterranean Sea
Greece
Adriatic Sea
Danube River
Black Sea
ASIA MINOR
Caspian Sea
Tigris River
Syria
Euphrates River
Palestine
Red Sea
Egypt
Nile River
AFRICA

Legend:
- End of Punic Wars, 146 B.C.
- At Caesar's death, 44 B.C.
- At Augustus's death, A.D. 14
- Greatest extent of empire, A.D. 130
- ★ Battle site

0   200   400 mi.
0   200   400 km
Lambert Conic Conformal Projection

Map Study Most of the Roman Empire bordered the Mediterranean Sea, allowing Rome to have a stronghold on the Mediterranean region.
Region Why would control of the Mediterranean region be an advantage for Rome's economy?

Law and Order

Under its emperors, Rome developed a legal system to unify the empire. Roman law stressed the authority of the state over the individual. It also accorded people definite legal rights, one of which was that an accused person should be considered innocent until proven guilty. Later Roman law formed the basis for the legal systems of many Western nations and of the Christian Church.

In addition to law, Roman emperors relied on the professional army to maintain order. As conditions became more peaceful, Roman legions were supplemented by troops recruited from the empire's many peoples. Even with forces combined, the emperor could count on having only about 300,000 troops, which was not enough to defend a border with a length of about 4,000 miles (6,440 km). Therefore, by A.D. 160, invasions by peoples outside the empire had become a continuing problem.

Trade, Engineering, and Science

During the *Pax Romana*, the Roman Empire enjoyed economic prosperity. Artisans in Italy made pottery, woven cloth, blown glass, and jewelry for sale throughout the empire. Outlying areas, such as Britain, Gaul, and Spain, sent to Italy minerals such as tin, iron, and lead. Thanks to Greek traders, silk cloth and spices reached Rome from India, China, and East Africa.

With increasing economic wealth, the Romans developed their talents in engineering and the sciences. Using a new building material—concrete, the Romans erected many impressive buildings, such as the temple of the Pantheon in Rome. They also built a 50,000-mile (80,000-km) network of roads that linked various parts of the empire and contributed to its unity. Roman engineering skills were especially demonstrated in the building of aqueducts, or artificial channels for carrying water.

Chapter 2 *The Advance of Civilizations* **73**

MAKING CONNECTIONS ACTIVITIES

The Calendar Romans helped shape the modern calendar. Have students do research and write a report summarizing Roman contributions to the calendar, including the names of the months and the division of the year into 12 months. Suggest that they also describe the shortcomings leading to calendar reform in the late 1500s. **L1**

Public Speaking The Romans helped define rules of rhetoric, or the art of using words persuasively, for oratory—the art of eloquent speaking. Have students research the life of Cicero, focusing on his contributions to these arts and describing some of his most famous orations. Encourage students to rehearse and deliver parts of his best-known orations. **L2**

Throughout the empire, scientists compiled information gathered from other cultures. The medical ideas of the ancient world compiled by the Greek physician Galen formed the basis of Roman medicine. Likewise, the observations of the Egyptian philosopher Ptolemy contributed to Roman astronomy.

Daily Life

Economic prosperity brought changes in Roman lifestyles. The family gradually became less significant than it had been during the republic. Romans had fewer children and were likely to divorce and remarry several times. Fathers lost some of the absolute power they had during the republic, and wives gained some legal rights. Society became less stable. Patricians might go bankrupt, lesser nobles might take a place in the Senate, and a poor person might even make a fortune in business.

Within each class, a consistent pattern of life formed. The wealthy often held public office, owned large farms outside the cities, ran factories, or directed trading firms. They lived comfortably in luxurious homes with marble walls, mosaic floors, running water, and baths.

The prosperity of the *Pax Romana* sometimes reached people of average means—shopkeepers and artisans. Although fewer people became very rich, more became moderately well-off. The majority in Rome, however, were still poor. Most Romans lived in flimsy wooden apartment buildings of six or seven stories that readily collapsed or caught fire.

Despite these trying conditions, the poor did not rebel against the government, because it offered them both free bread and free entertainment. By A.D. 160 Romans were celebrating 130 holidays a year. On some days teams of charioteers competed in races in the Circus Maximus, an arena seating more than 150,000. On other holidays, crowds could

Images *of the* Times

Pompeii, A.D. 79

On August 23–25, A.D. 79, the volcano Vesuvius erupted in southern Italy. The city of Pompeii was buried in a single day.

A detail from the Villa of the Mysteries shows that life for many in Pompeii offered many comforts and pleasures.

74

Images *of the* Times
Pompeii, A.D. 79

After the eruption of Vesuvius, Pompeii was buried under 19 to 23 feet (6 to 7 meters) of ash and debris. Herculaneum was covered by mud-lava to a depth of about 65 feet (20 meters).
An architect in the 1500s who was building a channel for drinking water discovered the ruins at Pompeii. Excavations of Herculaneum and Pompeii were begun in the 1700s and have continued, with interruptions, until the present. The earliest diggers were primarily treasure seekers, but in the mid-1800s archaeologists began to document their findings with care. Archaeologists have unearthed statue-covered public buildings, homes, shops, and luxurious villas.

watch gladiators fight each other or battle wild animals in stadiums like the Colosseum.

Language and Literature

Latin, Rome's official language, had a vocabulary far smaller than that of Greek or modern English; thus, many words expressed several meanings. Nevertheless, Latin remained the *lingua franca*, or common language, of Europe as late as the A.D. 1500s. Latin also forms the basis of the so-called Romance languages—Italian, French, Spanish, Portuguese, and Romanian—and supplies the roots for more than half of English words.

During the reign of Augustus, Latin literature entered a golden age. Cicero published his own beautifully written speeches. Ovid wrote love poetry and the *Metamorphoses*, a collection of verses based on Greek mythology. Horace, a poet, wrote about the shortness of life and the rewards of companionship. Horace's friend **Virgil** wrote the *Aeneid*, an epic poem comparable to those of Homer.

Rise of Christianity

The Romans worshiped many gods and goddesses. Beginning with Augustus, the government also expected people to honor the emperor as Rome's chief priest. Nevertheless, the empire's people were still allowed to worship freely, and a variety of religions flourished.

One of these religions was Judaism, whose homeland, Judah, became the Roman province of **Judea** in A.D. 6. Opposing Roman rule, some Jews clung to the ancient Jewish hope that a **messiah**, or savior, would bring deliverance. Others, believing that God would intervene on their behalf, rebelled against Rome. After two unsuccessful Jewish uprisings—one from A.D. 66 to A.D. 70, and the other in A.D. 132—the Romans renamed Judea *Palestine* and forced the Jews to leave Jerusalem and live in other

Rise of Christianity
What impact did Christianity have on the course of world history?
Christianity became the dominant religion of the West and profoundly influenced all areas of Western life and culture.

Independent Practice

Guided Reading Activity 2-2 **L1**

Geography: Place Have students trace a map of Italy. Ask them to research in an encyclopedia or other library reference books the Appian Way and other Roman roads and draw these on their maps. Have students include the names of towns or cities connected by the Appian Way. **L2 LEP**

CURRICULUM CONNECTION

LITERATURE
The story of the Trojan horse is only touched upon in Homer; in its fullest version, it is found in the *Aeneid*, the Latin epic poem by Virgil. The hero, Aeneas, supposedly founded Rome after having fought in the Trojan War.

Citizens of Pompeii were almost instantly overwhelmed by volcanic ash and fire. A plaster cast of victims serves as a stern reminder of Vesuvius's power.

REFLECTING ON THE TIMES

1. Why were so many artifacts from Pompeii so well preserved?
2. What do Roman wall paintings in Pompeii reveal about the lifestyles of upper-class Romans?

75

ANSWERS TO REFLECTING ON THE TIMES

1. The remains at Pompeii were preserved intact when the volcanic ash covering them hardened.
2. Many Romans became prosperous during the *Pax Romana,* and the government offered free entertainment to all.

Innovation Have students review
the meaning of innovation and
the way in which Christianity
grew out of Judaism. Ask students to explain how Christianity
could be considered an innovation. *(Although like Judaism it was
monotheistic and stressed ethical
behavior, it was an innovation in
teaching that Jesus was the Messiah
and that the kingdom of God was
close at hand.)* **L1 LEP**

Linking Past and Present

The Vandals so thoroughly
looted and destroyed Rome that
today we call someone who will-
fully destroys valuable objects a
vandal and deliberate destruction
of property *vandalism.*

ASSESS

Check for Understanding

Assign Section 2 Review as homework or as an in-class activity.

🔲 Use Student Self-Test and
Review Software to review
Section 2.

Visualizing History The walls of Roman catacombs host many depictions of
Christian art such as the Eucharistic Banquet version of
the Last Supper. *Why did the early Christians form churches?*

parts of the Mediterranean and the Middle East. In
their scattered communities, the Jews continued to
study the Torah. Between A.D. 200 and A.D. 500,
Jewish scholars assembled their various interpretations of the Torah into a book known as the Talmud.
To this day the Talmud remains an important book
of Jewish law.

Jesus

Meanwhile, a new monotheistic religion called
Christianity began to be practiced by some of the
Jews in the eastern Mediterranean. At first, both the
Romans and the earliest Christians thought of the
new religion as a sect, or group, within Judaism. As
Christians won over non-Jewish followers,
however, the faith diverged from its Jewish roots
and became a separate religion.

Christianity's origins can be traced to developments in Judea a few decades before the Jewish
revolts. About A.D. 26 to A.D. 30, a young Jew named
Jesus traveled through the region, preaching that
God's rule was close at hand. Jesus urged people to
turn away from their sins and practice deeds of kindness. He said that God was loving and forgiving
toward all who repented, no matter what evil they
had done or how lowly they were.

Jesus' **disciples**, or followers, believed that he
was the messiah; other Jews, believing that the
messiah had yet to come, disputed this claim. The
growing controversy over Jesus troubled local
Roman officials. They believed that anyone who
aroused such strong public feelings could endanger
Roman rule. In about A.D. 30, the Roman governor
arrested Jesus as a political rebel and ordered that
he be crucified—hung from a cross until dead. This
was a typical Roman way of punishing criminals.

The Spread of Christianity

After Jesus' death, his disciples proclaimed that
he had risen from the dead and had appeared to
them. They pointed to this as evidence that Jesus
was the messiah. His followers began preaching
that Jesus was the Son of God and the way of salvation. Small groups in the cities of the eastern
Mediterranean world accepted this message. Jews
and non-Jews who accepted Jesus and his teachings
became known as Christians—*Christos* was Greek
for "messiah." They formed churches—communities for worship, fellowship, and instruction.

Meanwhile, Christian missionaries spread
Christianity throughout the Roman world. One of
the most active was **Paul**, who traveled widely and
wrote on behalf of the new religion. Paul's letters to
various churches were later combined with the
Gospels, or stories about Jesus, and the writings of
other early Christian leaders. Together, these works
form the New Testament of the Bible.

Persecution and Triumph

Christians refused to honor the emperor as a
god and rejected military service. As a result, many
Romans accused the Christians of treason.
Although Roman officials did not hunt out the
Christians, they did kill those whom they believed
to be troublemakers. Such persecution lasted from
about the A.D. 60s to the early A.D. 300s.

About A.D. 312, however, a series of events
began that gradually transformed the position of
Christianity in the empire. In that year, according to
legend, the Roman general **Constantine** claimed to
experience a vision of a flaming cross before
leading his army into battle. When Constantine's
army won, the general credited both the vision and

CRITICAL THINKING ACTIVITY

Distinguishing Relevant Information Most early peoples did not hesitate to borrow from
other culture groups. For example, the Etruscans borrowed the Greeks' alphabet and even some of
their gods. Later, the Romans, after they established a far-flung empire, borrowed many features
from the peoples they conquered. Early Christians borrowed ideas from Judaism. Ask students to
offer some examples of features that American culture has borrowed from other cultures.
*(Examples: words from Latin, French, Greek, or Spanish; foods from Italy, China, or Mexico; holiday tradi-
tions such as the Christmas tree from Germany)* **L2**

the victory to the Christian God. Named emperor of Rome in A.D. 312, **Constantine** proclaimed equal rights for all religions, including Christianity. Later, in A.D. 392, the emperor Theodosius (THEE•uh•-DOH•shuhs) made Christianity the official religion of the Roman Empire.

The Early Church

From about A.D. 100 to A.D. 500, various Christian thinkers known as the Church Fathers wrote books explaining Christianity. Among these scholars was **Augustine**, a church official born in North Africa in A.D. 354. Augustine is believed to have written one of the world's first great auto-biographies. In his work, *Confessions,* Augustine describes how he was converted to Christianity:

❝ I heard from a neighboring house a voice, as of a boy or girl, I know not, chanting, and oft repeating, 'Take up and read; Take up and read.' . . . So . . . I arose, interpreting it to be no other than a command from God, to open the book [the Bible], and read the first chapter I should find. **❞**

—Augustine, *Confessions,* c. A.D. 398

By Augustine's time the Church was led by priests at the local level and bishops at the regional level. During the A.D. 400s, the bishop of Rome began to claim authority over the other bishops. Addressed by the Greek or Latin word *papa,* his name today is rendered *pope* in the English language. Latin-speaking Christians in the West regarded the **pope** as head of all of the churches. Greek-speaking Christians in the East, however, would not accept the authority of the pope over their churches. In time, the Latin churches as a group became known as the Roman Catholic Church. The Greek churches as a group became known as the Eastern Orthodox Church.

 **WORLD** **Sassanids Establish an Empire**

Persia, A.D. 200s
Ardashir I, king of Persis, defeated the Parthian army in a decisive victory, then entered the capital of Ctesiphon in triumph. There he was crowned King of Kings and established the Sassanid Empire, which lasted until A.D. 651. Ardashir founded or rebuilt many cities and made Zoroastrianism the state religion. A rock carving at Naqshi-Rustam shows Ardashir taking the symbol of royalty from the supreme Zoroastrian god.

Sassanid Empire

Roman Decline

During the A.D. 200s, Rome's power weakened as army legions struggled for control and Germanic groups invaded from the east. Political turmoil in turn led to economic disruption. From the late A.D. 300s, three successive emperors—Diocletian, Constantine, and Theodosius—tried to halt the empire's decline. They set up strict economic controls and sought new sources of revenue. Finally, to improve efficiency, the empire was split into eastern and western parts after Theodosius's death in A.D. 395. These reforms preserved the eastern empire but only delayed the downfall of the western part until the late A.D. 400s. By that time, Germanic groups—Ostrogoths, Vandals, Franks, Angles, and Saxons—had won control of much Roman territory. In doing so, however, they accepted the Latin language, Roman laws, and Christianity.

SECTION 2 REVIEW

Recall
1. **Define** republic, patrician, plebeian, tribune, aqueduct, messiah, disciple, pope.
2. **Identify** the Etruscans, the Twelve Tables, Hannibal, Julius Caesar, Augustus, *Pax Romana,* Nero, Marcus Aurelius, Virgil, the Talmud, Jesus, Paul,

Constantine, Augustine.
3. **Use** the map on page 73 to identify Roman expansion. When did the empire reach its greatest extent?

Critical Thinking
4. **Synthesizing Information** Which do you think had a greater impact on the fall of

the Roman Empire, internal difficulties or outside invaders? Why?

Understanding Themes
5. **Cultural Diffusion** List some of the advantages and disad-vantages to a non-Roman region of adopting Roman culture.

Evaluate

📁 Section Quiz 2-2

💿 Use the Testmaker to create a customized quiz for Section 2.

Reteach

Have students work in small groups to prepare time lines of events covered in this section. Then have groups present their time lines to the class, explaining the importance of each event.

Enrich

Have students interview a local Christian minister or priest or a Jewish rabbi about the Jewish roots of Christianity. Encourage students to tape-record the inter-view and to prepare a list of questions in advance. (Sample questions: What beliefs do Judaism and Christianity share? What are the significant differ-ences?) Have students report orally on their interviews.

CLOSE

Have students summarize the factors that led to the fall of Rome and discuss their relative importance. For example, did invasions have a greater impact than economic problems?

SECTION 2 REVIEW ANSWERS

1. All vocabulary words are defined in the Glossary.
2. the Etruscans, 70; the Twelve Tables, 71; Hannibal, 71; Julius Caesar, 72; Augus-tus, 72; *Pax Romana,* 72; Nero, 72; Mar-cus Aurelius, 72; Virgil, 75; the Talmud,

76; Jesus, 76; Paul, 76; Constantine, 76; Augustine, 77
3. in A.D. 130
4. Answers will vary. Internal difficulties weakened the government and made maintaining armies difficult. Outside

invaders brought disorder and isolated regions.
5. **CULTURAL DIFFUSION**
advantages: education and comforts to wealthy provincials; disadvantages: loss of local laws, customs, and languages

c. 500 B.C.
The Nok people
begin metal production.

c. 250 B.C.
Merchants from Egypt, Rome,
Persia, and India trade with Axum.

A.D. 330
Christianity becomes
Axum's official religion.

SECTION THEME

▶ **Movement** Migrations of Bantu-speaking peoples influence Africa's cultural development.

ind Out

Answer: *trading societies and close-knit agricultural communities with a wide variety of religious customs and traditions*

FOCUS

Section Objective

Investigate what kinds of societies emerged in early Africa.

BELLRINGER
Motivational Activity

Before taking roll at the beginning of the class period, project Section Focus Transparency 2-3 and have students answer the activity questions. Discuss students' responses.

🗁 This activity is also available as a blackline master.

Vocabulary Pre-check

🗁 Use the Vocabulary PuzzleMaker to create a puzzle that reinforces vocabulary terms in this section. **L1**

Section 3

Africa

Setting the Scene

▶ **Terms to Define**
oral tradition, savanna, matrilineal, age set

▶ **People to Meet**
Ezana

▶ **Places to Locate**
Axum, Adulis, Niger and Benue River valleys

 What kinds of societies emerged in early East Africa and early West Africa?

The Storyteller

African oral tradition contained stories full of wisdom, to be enjoyed by all. For example, where did death come from? A myth from Madagascar gave this answer. One day God asked the first couple what kind of death they wanted, one like that of the moon, or that of the banana? The couple was puzzled. God explained: the banana creates young plants to take its place, but the moon itself comes back to life every month. After consideration, the couple prayed for children, because without children they would be lonely, would have to do all the work, and would have no one to provide for. Since that time, human life is short on this earth.

—freely adapted from *The Humanistic Tradition*, Gloria K. Fiero, 1992

Mount Kilimanjaro

efore modern times, many African civilizations communicated knowledge about their past through oral traditions—legends and history passed by word of mouth from one generation to another. From these traditions and from archaeological finds, historians have discovered that early African peoples developed technologies and trade based on regional natural resources. Civilizations rose and declined and were influenced by the movement of people and by the way in which natural resources were developed.

Regions of Africa

The African continent can be divided into several large regions—North Africa, East Africa, West Africa, Central Africa, and Southern Africa. North Africa, bordering the Mediterranean Sea, has mild temperatures and frequent rainfall along its coastline. South of this thin, green coastal belt is a vast expanse of sand: the Sahara, the world's largest desert.

Inland areas of Africa's other regions feature a great central plateau covered by savannas, or treeless grasslands. However, there are also variations in landscape from region to region. In East Africa, the land beyond the eastern edge of the plateau becomes hilly or mountainous. In West Africa, the plateau descends to a narrow coastal plain that has a relatively unbroken coastline. Large areas of Central Africa near the Equator are covered by a lush tropical rain forest so thick that sunlight cannot penetrate to the forest floor. In Southern Africa, the landscape turns into a desert and cool, fertile highlands.

All of Africa's regions provide rich resources for their peoples. Civilizations developed where rainfall was plentiful, near lakes, or along rivers. As you learned in Chapter 1, the Egyptians and the Nubians developed the first African civilizations

SECTION RESOURCES

🗁 **Reproducible Masters**
• Reproducible Lesson Plan 2-3
• Guided Reading Activity 2-3
• Section Quiz 2-3

Transparencies
• Section Focus Transparency 2-3

Multimedia
🔲 Vocabulary PuzzleMaker Software
🔲 Student Self-Test and Review Software
🔲 Testmaker

along the Nile River in the eastern corner of North Africa. In this chapter you will study later civilizations that developed in other parts of the continent.

Axum

While the Nubian-based, Kushite kingdom thrived in the southern Nile River valley, a new power, **Axum**, arose to the south in the area of present-day Ethiopia near the Red Sea. The Axumites grew so strong that between A.D. 320 and A.D. 350, their armies invaded Kush and ended Kushite control of northeastern Africa.

A Trading Power

Because of its location along the Red Sea, Axum also emerged as a trading power. During the 200s B.C., merchants from Egypt, Greece, Rome, Arabia, Persia, and India sent ships laden with cotton cloth, brass, copper, and olive oil to Axum's main seaport at **Adulis**. Traders exchanged their goods for cargoes of ivory that the people of Axum hauled from Africa's interior.

The Coming of Christianity

Through trade Axum absorbed many elements of Roman culture, including a new religion: Christianity. A remarkable event led to the conversion of Axum's King **Ezana** to Christianity. Shipwrecked off the coast of Axum, two Christians from Syria were picked up and brought to King Ezana's court, where they lived for several years. The young men convinced Ezana that he should become a Christian. About A.D. 330 the king made Christianity the official religion in Axum. During this time, Christianity also became dominant in Kush and Egypt.

Axum's Accomplishments

In addition to borrowing from outside civilizations, the Axumites also accomplished much on their own. Their kings minted gold coins and built stone monuments 60 feet (18 m) tall. Axumite

Visualizing History **Church of St. Mary of Zion.** According to tradition, this church contains the original tablets of Moses, brought by King Menelik I to Axum. Menelik, the legendary founder of Axum's monarchy, was reputed to be the son of the Israelite king Solomon and the Arabian queen of Sheba. *How did Christianity come to Axum about A.D. 330?*

Chapter 2 *The Advance of Civilizations* **79**

TEACH

Guided Practice

THEME Movement

Ask students what the main reason for the Bantu migrations was. *(population increase, leading to a shortage of arable land)* Discuss with students how this reason for moving compares with other reasons. Point out that an inability to provide for themselves and their families, whether due to natural disaster, climate changes, or lack of local resources, is a common reason people migrate.

Visualizing History The kingdom of Axum was located in the northern part of modern Ethiopia. Emperor Haile Selassie was a member of Ethiopia's Amhara dynasty. Generations of this proud people are bound together by their Christian faith and traditional ways of life.
Answer to Caption: *When King Ezana of Axum converted to Christianity during the A.D. 300s, it became a state religion.*

COOPERATIVE LEARNING ACTIVITY

Archaeology Organize the class into groups of three to four students. Have each group select one culture covered in this section—Kush, Axum, Nok, or Bantu—for further study. Each group should work together to write a journal of an imaginary archaeological expedition that has uncovered artifacts from the selected culture. Each member of the group should participate in collecting and recording the information, drawing pictures of the artifacts, and drawing the location of the finds on maps of the site. **L2**

Map Study

Map Skills Practice

Reading a Map Where was Meroë located in relation to Thebes? With respect to Axum? *(south of Thebes; west of Axum)*

TURNING POINT

Bantu Migrations
How did the Bantu migrations affect the cultural development of early Africa?
They spread Bantu language to other parts of Africa. Later, the Bantu-speaking peoples became the dominant group in Africa south of the Sahara.

Independent Practice

Guided Reading Activity 2-3 **L1**

Geography: Movement Have students imagine that they are West African farmers who moved during the Bantu migrations to the grassland plateau around Lake Chad. Have them write a story about their experiences. Ask them what might have affected them the most—meeting new cultures or adapting to a new environment. **L3**

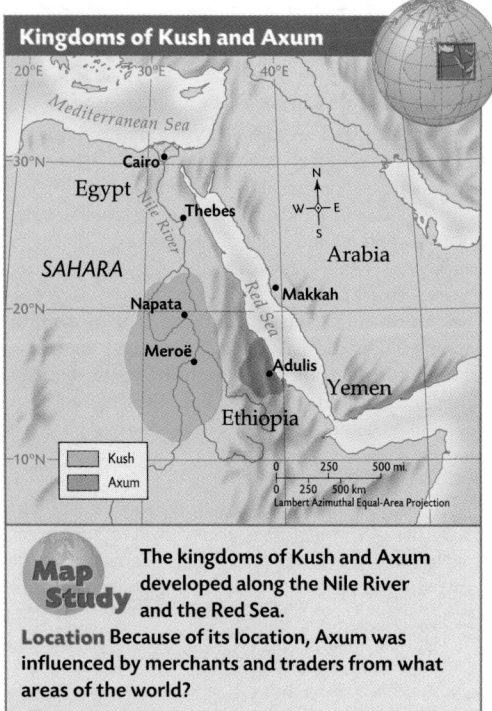

Kingdoms of Kush and Axum

Map Study

The kingdoms of Kush and Axum developed along the Nile River and the Red Sea.

Location Because of its location, Axum was influenced by merchants and traders from what areas of the world?

scholars developed a writing system for Ge'ez (jee • EHZ), the ancient language of Axum. They also knew Greek, the language of eastern Christianity, as well as Arabic dialects from the Arabian Peninsula that lay across the Red Sea from Axum. Axumite farmers learned to farm on terraces, or raised levels of land. Artisans made iron utensils for religious celebrations as well as for everyday use at home.

Axum began its decline when Arab merchants and soldiers from the Arabian Peninsula raided Axum's ports in the A.D. 600s. As a result, Axum lost much of its coastal territory and trade. Because the invading Arabs followed the new religion of Islam, many of the Axumites retreated inland to maintain their culture and to continue their practice of Christianity. Confined to the remote interior of East Africa, the rulers of Axum set up a Christian kingdom that became known as Ethiopia.

Nubia

While Axum prospered and declined, a number of small kingdoms emerged in the Nile Valley region of Nubia. These kingdoms prospered

from agriculture and trade. Nubia's major trading partner, Egypt, had accepted Christianity, and Christian missionaries from Egypt converted the Nubians to their religion during the A.D. 500s. Nubian Christianity remained a powerful influence in northeastern Africa for centuries. In the A.D. 1400s, the Nubian kingdoms finally collapsed as a result of invasion by Arab and Turkish followers of Islam.

TURNING POINT

The Bantu Migrations

Between 700 B.C. and 200 B.C., during Axum's rise to power, a West African civilization called the Nok had already established itself in the fertile **Niger and Benue River valleys**. In the 1940s archaeologists working in present-day, central Nigeria found terra-cotta, or baked clay, figurines that provided evidence of the Nok culture. Working in the Nok sites and other areas of West Africa, archaeologists also unearthed iron hoes and ax-heads. This latter discovery provided evidence that metal production had enabled African cultures south of the Sahara to farm their land more effectively.

As West African farmers used their iron tools to produce more food, the population increased. In time, arable land became scarce, causing widespread food shortages. Small groups of Africans began to migrate from West Africa to less populated areas. Other groups followed. Over about a thousand years, a great migration took place.

Historians call this mass movement the Bantu migrations because descendants of the people who migrated into central, eastern, and southern parts of the continent share elements of a language group known as Bantu.

The Bantu migrations did not follow a single pattern. Some villagers followed the Niger or other rivers, settling in one spot to farm for a few years and moving on as the soil became less fertile. Other groups penetrated the rain forests and grew crops along the riverbanks. Still others moved to the highland savannas of East Africa and raised cattle. Groups that settled on the eastern coastal plain grew new crops, such as bananas and yams, that had been brought to East Africa by traders from Southeast Asia.

As people pushed into new areas, they met other African groups that joined the migrants and adopted their ways of life. In time Bantu-speaking peoples became the dominant group in all parts of the continent apart from North Africa.

MEETING SPECIAL NEEDS ACTIVITY

Study Strategy Have students review the section and make note of natural resources or trade goods and locations where they can be found. Have students make a chart listing the name of the natural resource, its location(s), and the people who made use of the resource. They may use graphic symbols to represent the resources. **L1**

Africa South of the Sahara

Africans who spoke Bantu languages became divided into hundreds of ethnic groups, each with its own religious beliefs and cultural traditions. Ethnic groups living around A.D. 1000 formed close-knit communities where most families were organized into large households that included descendants of one set of grandparents.

Many villages were matrilineal societies in which villagers traced their descent through mothers rather than through fathers. However, when a young woman married, she became a member of her husband's family. To compensate the bride's family for the loss of a member, the husband's family gave the bride's family gifts of iron tools, goats, or cloth.

Even before marriage, specific jobs were assigned to groups of males and females of a similar age, called age sets. Boys younger than 10 or 12 herded cattle; girls of the same age helped their mothers plant as well as tend and harvest crops. At about 12 years old, boys and girls took part in ceremonies initiating them into adulthood. A boy remained with his age set throughout his life. After marriage, a young woman joined an age set in her husband's village.

Religious Beliefs

To most Africans, marriage customs and all other social laws and traditions were made by a single supreme god who created and ruled an orderly universe. The god rewarded those who followed social rules with abundant harvests and the birth of healthy children, and punished those who violated tradition with crop failures or illness.

Beneath the supreme god were many lesser deities who influenced the daily affairs of men and women. These deities were present in natural phenomena such as storms, mountains, and trees. Many Africans also believed that spirits of dead ancestors lived among the people of the village and guided their destiny.

The religious beliefs and family loyalties of most Africans maintained stability and support within villages. Most communities expected their members to obey the social rules they believed to have come from the supreme god.

Although African communities relied heavily on religious and family traditions to maintain a stable social structure, outside influences through trade and learning still managed to affect them. North Africans absorbed influences from the Arab world, whereas people in other regions of Africa adapted to Persian, Indian, and later, European influences. From these outsiders, African communities adopted many new customs, ideas, and languages.

The Arts

Various arts developed in early Africa. African sculpture included figures, masks, decorated boxes, and objects for ceremonial and everyday use. Most of these items were made of wood, bronze, ivory, or baked clay. The carving of masks and the performing of dances while wearing them symbolized the link between the living and dead. Those wearing the masks and performing the dances called upon ancestral spirits to provide guidance to the community.

Music rich in rhythm was interwoven with the fabric of everyday African life. It ranged from music performed at royal courts to village group singing that often provided the motivation and rhythm for various tasks, such as digging trenches or pounding grain. African musicians used a variety of drums as well as harps, flutes, pipes, horns, and xylophones.

Early African communities excelled in oral literature passed down from one generation to another. Often used in religious ceremonies and recited to music, oral literature included myths, legends, histories, stories, fables, poems, riddles, proverbs, and songs. It not only recorded the past but also taught traditions and values.

SECTION 3 REVIEW

Recall
1. **Define** oral tradition, savanna, matrilineal, age set.
2. **Identify** Axum, Ezana, Nubia, the Nok, Bantu.
3. **Locate** the map on page 80 that shows the east African kingdoms of Kush and Axum.

Why was Adulis an important city to the Axumites?

Critical Thinking
4. **Applying Information** Explain how trade with Egypt, the Mediterranean world, the Middle East, and South Asia influenced the

economy of Axum.

Understanding Themes
5. **Movement** How do the Bantu migrations in early Africa contrast with the Aryan migrations that took place in early South Asia?

ASSESS

Check for Understanding

Assign Section 3 Review as homework or as an in-class activity.

 Use Student Self-Test and Review Software to review Section 3.

Evaluate

Section Quiz 2-3

Use the Testmaker to create a customized quiz for Section 3.

Reteach

Distribute outline maps of Africa. Have students indicate the name, dates, and approximate location of the following: the kingdoms of Kush and Axum, Nok culture, and the Bantu-speaking peoples. Students may use the text or historical atlases.

Enrich

Have students read traditional African folktales. Have them work in groups of three or four to prepare an oral reading or dramatization of a tale they have read.

CLOSE

Have students create posters illustrating what they have learned about early African civilizations and ways of life. Display them on a bulletin board.

SECTION 3 REVIEW ANSWERS

1. All vocabulary words are defined in the Glossary.
2. Axum, 79; Ezana, 79; Nubia, 80; the Nok, 80; Bantu, 80
3. Adulis was a seaport for trade in the Red Sea area.
4. Mediterranean trade brought many resources and manufactured goods to Axum and stimulated the local production of ivory.
5. **MOVEMENT** Both migrations took place over long periods. The Bantu

migrations were peaceful, whereas the Aryan ones were the result of conquest. Both the Aryan and Bantu language families and customs blended with those of local peoples.

TEACH

Interpreting Point of View

Distribute copies of two reviews of the same movie, one favorable, one critical. After students have read both, ask them what the reviews reveal about the two critics' different perspectives, or points of view. Then have students read the skill and complete the practice questions.

Additional Practice

Skill Reinforcement Activity 7

Critical Thinking
SKILLS

Interpreting Point of View

Suppose you are interested in seeing a new science fiction movie, but you are hearing mixed reviews from your friends. Opinions range from "terrific" to "boring." People often have different opinions about the same people, events, or issues because they look at them from different points of view.

Learning the Skill

A point of view is a set of beliefs and values that affects a person's opinion. Many factors affect an individual's point of view, including age, sex, racial or ethnic background, economic class, and religion. In order to determine the accuracy of a description or the objectivity of an argument, first you must identify the speaker's point of view.

To interpret point of view in written material, read the material to identify the general subject. Then gather background information on that author that might reveal his or her point of view. Identify aspects of the topic that the author chooses to emphasize or exclude. Look for emotionally charged words such as *cruel, vicious, heartrending, drastic.* Also notice metaphors and analogies that imply an opinion such as, "If this budget can work, then pigs can fly."

If you are uncertain of an author's point of view, read a selection on the same topic by another author with a different background. By comparing works on the same subject, both points of view may become clear. This may not always be an easy task.

Practicing the Skill

Read the following excerpt from Ross E. Dunn's book *The Adventures of Ibn Battuta* and then answer these questions.

1. What is the general subject of the excerpt?
2. What do you know about Ibn Battuta that might reveal his point of view?
3. What emotionally charged words and phrases indicate his point of view?
4. Which aspects of Islamic leadership are praised and which are not?

" Sulayman came close to matching his brother's [Mansa Musa's] reputation for Islamic leadership and piety. Moreover, he ruled Mali in prosperity and peace. He was the sort of king from whom Ibn Battuta had come to expect an honorable and large-hearted reception. . . . Later, when Ibn Battuta had returned to his house, one of the scholars called to tell him that the sultan [Sulayman] had sent along the requisite welcoming gift.

'I got up, thinking that it would be robes of honor and money, but behold! It was three loaves of bread and a piece of beef fried in *gharti* [shea butter] and a gourd containing yoghurt. When I saw it I laughed, and was long astonished at their feeble intellect and their respect for mean things.' "

According to Dunn, Ibn Battuta found Sulayman to be "a miserly king from whom no great donation is to be expected," while Mansa Musa had been "generous and virtuous."

Applying the Skill

In a newspaper, find an editorial, column, or a letter to the editor that expresses a point of view that conflicts with your own. Write a brief paragraph analyzing the author's point of view and compare it to your point of view. Explain why you agree or disagree with the viewpoint of the author.

The Columbus Dispatch
An Independent Newspaper Serving Ohio Since July 1, 1871
JOHN F. WOLFE, Publisher, President and CEO
MICHAEL F. CURTIN, Editor
EDITORIALS
Ballot issue
Workers' comp to steal thunder from schools

For More Practice

Turn to the Skill Practice in the Chapter Review on page 97 for more practice in interpreting point of view.

ANSWERS TO PRACTICING THE SKILL

1. a comparison of the Islamic rulers Mansa Musa and his brother Sulayman
2. Ibn Battuta had received generous gifts from Sulayman's brother, Mansa Musa, so Battuta had expected the same kinds of gifts from Sulayman.
3. *honorable, largehearted, but behold!, I laughed and was long astonished, feeble intellect, respect for mean things*
4. Aspects praised: Ruled in prosperity and peace. Aspects not praised: Sulayman is said to have a feeble intellect and is called a miserly king.

400 B.C.		A.D. 1		A.D. 400

321 B.C.
Chandragupta Maurya founds dynasty.

c. 100 B.C.
Chinese invent paper.

c. A.D. 400
Buddhism becomes a popular religion in China.

Section 4

Asia

Setting the Scene

▶ **Terms to Define**
   "Arabic numerals," civil service, mandarin, acupuncture

▶ **People to Meet**
   Chandragupta Maurya, Asoka, Chandragupta I, Chandragupta II, Qin Shihuangdi, Liu Bang, Wudi

▶ **Places to Locate**
   Magadha, Great Wall of China, Silk Road

 **ind Out** What advances did the empires and dynasties make in India and China from 500 B.C. to A.D. 500?

The Storyteller

It troubled King Asoka that criminals continued their wrongdoing within his empire. Therefore he was proud of his latest merciful decree, carved on stone monuments: "Thus speaks the Beloved of the Gods . . . . This is my instruction from now on: Men who are imprisoned or sentenced to death are to be given three days respite. Thus their relations [relatives] may plead for their lives, or, if there is no one to plead for them, they may make their donations or undertake a fast for a better rebirth in the next life. For it is my wish that they should gain the next world."

—from Asoka and the Decline of the Mauryas, Romila Thapar, 1961

Lion-headed capital atop a Rock Edict pillar of Asoka

From 500 B.C. to A.D. 500, the peoples of India and China fashioned ideas that would result in unique civilizations. Meanwhile, their rulers established powerful empires and developed contacts with other parts of the world.

Indian Empires

Despite high mountain barriers in the north, India has never been completely cut off from other lands. The Aryans marched through mountain passes to invade the Indus River valley; later, others followed. In the 500s B.C., Persian ruler Darius I conquered lands in the Indus River valley. Alexander the Great invaded the same area in 327 B.C., and Indian merchants carried on a busy trade with the Roman Empire. In all that time, however, no Indian king or foreign conqueror had ever succeeded in uniting the separate kingdoms into one Indian nation.

At the time of Darius's invasion, one Indian kingdom, **Magadha**, was expanding in the north. King Bimbisara, who ruled Magadha from 542 B.C. to 495 B.C., added to the territory by conquest and marriage. Although Magadha declined after Bimbisara's death, it was to become the center of India's first empire.

The Mauryan Empire

At the time of Alexander's invasion, Magadha was only one of many small warring states in northern India. Then, in 321 B.C., **Chandragupta Maurya** (CHUHN•druh•GUP tuh MAH•oor•yuh), a military officer, proclaimed himself ruler of the northern Indian state. During his reign, Chandragupta Maurya founded a Mauryan kingdom that spread out from Magadha to embrace most of northern and central India.

Chapter 2 *The Advance of Civilizations* **83**

SECTION THEME

▶ **Uniformity** Indian and Chinese empires establish and maintain strong central governments.

F ind Out

Answer: *The Indians developed an efficient postal system, free hospitals, fine roads as well as art, literature, mathematics, and science. The Chinese made a variety of technological advances, strengthened central government, and created a civil service.*

FOCUS

Section Objective

Summarize the major advances the Indians and Chinese made under strong central governments.

BELLRINGER
Motivational Activity

 Before taking roll at the beginning of the class period, project Section Focus Transparency 2-4 and have students answer the activity questions. Discuss students' responses.

📁 This activity is also available as a blackline master.

Vocabulary Pre-check

📁 Use Vocabulary Activity 2 to introduce vocabulary terms.
L1 LEP

SECTION RESOURCES

📁 **Reproducible Masters**
• Reproducible Lesson Plan 2-4
• Vocabulary Activity 2
• Guided Reading Activity 2-4
• Section Quiz 2-4

Transparencies
• Section Focus Transparency 2-4

Multimedia
• Student Self-Test and Review Software
• Testmaker
• India and China
• World Music: Cultural Traditions, Lesson 8

TEACH

Guided Practice

THEME Uniformity

Have students assemble a list of the main features of the Qin empire. *(central government, standardized system of weights and measures, uniform coinage and law code, built roads and canals, began building Great Wall)* Help students to see how these features contributed to uniformity in China. **L1**

Map Study

Answers

1. *through the Khyber Pass in the Hindu Kush mountain range; from Central Asia*
2. *Ganges River*

Map Skills Practice

Reading a Map What areas of India that the Mauryas had controlled did the Guptas fail to conquer? *(Indus Valley and the Deccan Plateau)*

India's Golden Age

Why was the period of Indian empires considered a golden age?

Indian scientists, mathematicians, and artists made contributions that strengthened Hindu culture. Their scientific and mathematical achievements spread to the West and other parts of the world; for example, "Arabic" numerals and the concept of zero.

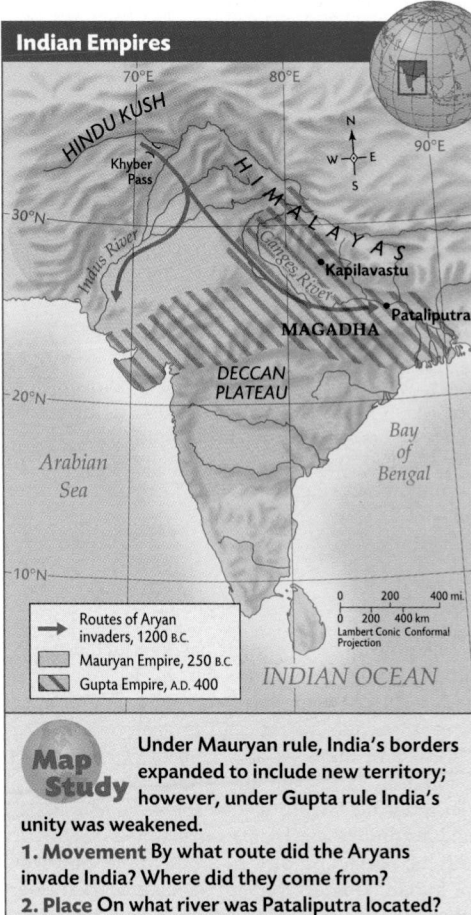

Indian Empires

Map Study

Under Mauryan rule, India's borders expanded to include new territory; however, under Gupta rule India's unity was weakened.

1. Movement By what route did the Aryans invade India? Where did they come from?
2. Place On what river was Pataliputra located?

Chandragupta Maurya was a skilled administrator whose achievements included the development of an efficient postal system. He kept control of his empire by maintaining a strong army and by using an extensive spy network.

Chandragupta's grandson, **Asoka** (uh•SHOH•kuh), who began his reign in 274 B.C., built an empire that covered two-thirds of the subcontinent. However, the horrors of war eventually turned Asoka to Buddhism, and he decided to become a ruler of peace and justice. During his reign, missionaries spread Buddhism throughout India and other parts of Asia.

Asoka issued laws stressing concern for other human beings. To make sure these laws became widely known, Asoka had them carved on rocks and on tall, stone pillars throughout the vast

empire. Asoka also improved the system of roads and provided free hospitals.

The Mauryan Empire declined after Asoka's death in 232 B.C. because his successors were not as enlightened as he was. They levied heavy taxes on the goods sold by merchants and seized large portions of the crops grown by peasants. Such harsh policies caused the people to turn against the Mauryas. When the last Mauryan ruler was murdered in 184 B.C., northern India again split into many small, warring kingdoms.

The Gupta Empire

About 500 years passed before much of India was again united. Then, in A.D. 310, **Chandragupta I** began to build an empire. He was not related to Chandragupta Maurya, but like that earlier ruler, he made Magadha the base of his kingdom.

Chandragupta I introduced the Gupta dynasty, which ruled northern India for more than 200 years. The Guptas governed a much smaller empire than the Mauryas, but they did manage to build a strong state, however, and did work to maintain unquestioned authority. They trained soldiers and used spies and political assassins. In short, they did whatever they felt had to be done to maintain power.

The Gupta Empire reached its height under **Chandragupta II**, who ruled from A.D. 375 to A.D. 415. By easing tax burdens, Chandragupta II gave people more freedom. Daily life, however, did not improve for women. During Aryan times, women had a say about whom they would marry. By the Gupta period, parents were choosing mates for their children, and child marriages were common. Women and mothers were highly respected, but they had little power or independence.

India's Golden Age

Under the Guptas, India enjoyed a golden age in the arts and sciences. The Gupta rulers encouraged learning based on the ideas found in the *Upanishads*. They made Hinduism the religion of the empire. Hindu temples were built—elaborate structures with brightly painted sculptures depicting tales in the *Mahabharata* and the *Ramayana*.

Gupta Learning

Learning flourished under the Guptas. The court welcomed poets, playwrights, philosophers, and scientists. Much of the writing was concentrated on

84 Chapter 2 *The Advance of Civilizations*

COOPERATIVE LEARNING ACTIVITY

Debate Have students form two groups, one to support Asoka and his followers, who opposed war, and the other to defend the Gupta rulers and warriors, who wanted to conquer more land. Be sure the groups are balanced in research and communications skills. Have each group break into smaller teams to discuss such issues as politics, law, religion, and economics. Then have students rejoin the larger groups to discuss findings. Key ideas should be written down and presented to the class in oral arguments by one or two spokespersons. Following the debate, discuss the major points made by both sides. Take a poll to see if the debate changed students' minds about the rulers and the peace-versus-war issue. **L1**

religion, but folktales were also popular. A collection of tales called the *Panchatantra* presented moral lessons through animals who acted like humans. Many of these stories eventually spread to the Middle East and West, where they were retold by other authors. Drama was also important during Gupta times. Kalidasa, the most famous playwright, wrote *Shakuntala*, a play about romantic love between a king and a forest maiden.

Mathematics

Gupta mathematicians contributed significantly to mathematics as it is today, making major advances in developing the principles of algebra. They also explained the concept of infinity and invented the concept of zero. The symbols they devised for the numbers one through nine were adopted by traders from the Middle East and so came to be called "Arabic numerals" in the West.

Gupta astronomers used these mathematical discoveries to advance their understanding of the universe. They realized that the earth is round, and they had some knowledge of gravity. In medicine, Gupta doctors set bones, performed operations, and invented hundreds of medical instruments.

International Trade

Many countries benefited from Gupta achievements, as both ideas and products traveled along land and sea routes that connected India to the rest of the world. Indian exporters traded such items as gems, spices, cotton, teak, and ebony for horses from Arabia and central Asia, silk from China, and gold from Rome.

End of the Golden Age

After Chandragupta II's death in A.D. 415, the Gupta Empire began to fail. As the government weakened, the Guptas faced invasions along India's northwestern border. By A.D. 600, the Gupta Empire had dissolved into a collection of small states.

However, much of the culture that was uniquely Indian survived. Many aspects of India's life today grew out of the social structures, the religions, and the arts and sciences of the Maurya and Gupta periods.

China

While the Mauryas ruled India, the Qin (CHIN) dynasty set up the first powerful central government in China. Westerners would later call the nation *China* after the Qin, whose first ruler added the title Shihuangdi (SHUR•HWONG•DEE), or First Emperor, to his name.

A tireless ruler, **Qin Shihaungdi** set out to create a government directly under his control. He reorganized the empire into military districts, appointing officials to govern them. This system prevented local lords from becoming strong enough to challenge the power of the central government.

The First Emperor made other changes to further centralize his control. He devised a system of weights and measures to replace the various systems used in different regions. He standardized coins, instituted a uniform writing system, and set up a law code throughout China. To stifle opposition, he cracked down on local nobles and burned the books of writers who opposed his policies.

Qin had grandiose plans for his empire, and he used forced labor to accomplish them. Gangs of Chinese peasants dug canals and built roads. To Qin, one building project seemed especially urgent—shoring up China's defenses to the north. Earlier rulers had built walls to prevent attacks by nomadic invaders. Qin ordered those walls connected. Over several years some 300,000 peasants toiled—and thousands died—before the work was done. Eventually the wall stretched more than 4,000 miles (6,436 km). Rebuilt by later rulers, the **Great Wall of China** stands today as a monument to Qin's ambition and to the peasants who carried out the emperor's will.

Han Rulers

In 207 B.C. **Liu Bang** (LYOH BONG), a military official, overthrew the Qin government and soon declared himself the emperor of a new dynasty, the Han. Under the Han, China enjoyed a 400-year period of prosperity and stability, later referred to as the *Pax Sinica* (PAHKS SIH•nuh•kuh), the Chinese Peace. The *Pax Sinica* coincided with the *Pax Romana* in the West.

The Han dynasty reached its peak during the reign of **Wudi** (WOO•DEE), who ruled from 141 B.C. to 87 B.C. An ambitious ruler, Wudi conquered lands to the north, including Korea and Manchuria, south into Southeast Asia, and west as far as northern India.

Wudi reformed government by laying the foundation of a civil service, a system that in theory allowed anyone with ability to attain public office. In practice, Wudi's system favored the wealthy, for education was expensive, and usually only the wealthy could afford to obtain enough education to pass the exams. As a result of Wudi's reforms, a new class of well-educated civil servants, called mandarins, controlled the government, and they would continue to do so until the early 1900s.

Politics Discuss with students the "positive" (*public projects, art, learning*) and the "negative" (*wars, repression*) historical developments that occurred during the Mauryan and Gupta Empires. **L2**

CURRICULUM CONNECTION

EDUCATION

Learning in the Gupta Empire was furthered by several fine universities in northern India. One of them, the university at Nalanda, with eight colleges and three libraries, attracted students from all over Asia.

NATIONAL GEOGRAPHIC SOCIETY

Use these materials to enrich student understanding of ancient India.

🌐 **NGS PICTURESHOW CD-ROM**
India and China

Social Class Work with students to organize a chart showing the social classes in ancient China. List the classes in order of hierarchy. Next to each class, list its characteristics. **L2**

MEETING SPECIAL NEEDS ACTIVITY

Learning Style: Visual/Spatial Have students trace a map of the area from East Asia to western Europe as far as Rome. Have them draw in and label on the map the physical features of the area, the primary cities of the dynasties covered in this section, and the Silk Road between China and Rome. **L1**

TEACH

Tell students that for more than 2,000 years, the Silk Road and its extensions westward into Roman territory made up the world's longest road. The travel distance along the length of the road and its western extensions totaled 8,000 miles (12,800 km). Ask students in which direction the silk traveled. *(westward)* Point out to students that among the ideas China received via the road were Christianity and Buddhism.

CURRICULUM CONNECTION

ENGINEERING

Part of the Silk Road is currently in use as a paved highway linking Pakistan and Sinkiang Uihgur Autonomous Region, China. The ancient trade route was the inspiration for a United Nations' plan for a trans-Asian highway.

Thomas J. Abercrombie

Silk Road

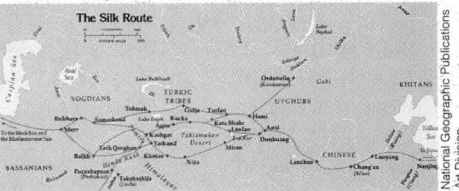

National Geographic Publications Art Division

A caravan of men and mules walk a trail that once formed part of the old Silk Road, a network of paths cutting across Asia from the Pacific coast of China to the Mediterranean Sea. The route, first traveled many years before the Christian era, was the passageway not only for Chinese silk but for a great range of products including jade and fruit, ideas and paintings. Today it is still possible to see how poles and rocks created the actual highway over which goods moved throughout many centuries—before ships, trains, buses, and airplanes replaced mules and packs.

You can trace the length of the trip on the accompanying map. A trader setting forth from the Chinese city of Nanjing would soon leave Chinese territory and enter a world of Muslim ethnic groups and treacherous terrain. The trail loops south and north of the scorching Takla Makan Desert and rises high through mountain passes across the Pamir Mountains. The whole trip was far too long for a single caravan to undertake. Instead, Chinese or Persian merchants dealt with central Asian middlemen from lands such as Afghanistan and Turkestan. ⊕

86 Chapter 2 *The Advance of Civilizations*

After Wudi's reign, Han power declined until the dynasty eventually fell in A.D. 220. However, Han achievements in government, technology, science, and the arts were lasting.

Family Life

Confucian values governed all aspects of life in Han China. The family was supreme in Chinese society. It was the focus of life, bound together strongly by mutual love, loyalty, and dependence. Family members, however, did not relate to each other as equals. The oldest male in the home, usually the father, was dominant. Every family member knew his or her place and understood its duties, and each was careful not to bring dishonor on the family by failing in these duties. Moreover, the duty to family members did not stop at death; all were expected to pay respect to departed ancestors.

Under the Confucian system, women were subordinate to men. Some women, however, were able to gain respect in Chinese homes. With marriage and motherhood, they became revered. Other opportunities for women, such as education, were limited. In spite of Confucianism's predominance, women fared better under the Han than they would in later centuries. They could inherit property, and they could remarry after a husband's death.

Society and Economy

Chinese society consisted of landowners, peasants, and merchants. Landowning families were wealthy and lived in tile-roofed mansions with courtyards and gardens. They filled their rooms with fine furniture and adorned them with silk wall hangings and carpets. Wealthy families feasted on a rich variety of foods.

Probably 90 percent of the Chinese people were peasants. The wealth that supported the lifestyles of the rich was gained from the hard labor of the peasants who cultivated the land.

The peasants raised livestock and toiled long hours in the grain fields. They faced constant threats from floods and from famine. As rent for the land, peasants turned over part of their produce to the landowner. The government required them to pay taxes and to work one month each year on public works projects such as road building. In times of conflict, peasants were drafted into the army as soldiers.

At the bottom of Chinese society were merchants—a group that included shopkeepers, traders, service workers, and even bankers. In spite of the great wealth that many merchants accumulated, Chinese society generally held them in contempt. Confucianism taught that the pursuit of profit was an unworthy pastime for the "superior" individual.

Literature

Although the Qin burned thousands of books, many survived in royal libraries and secret private collections. Particularly prized was a collection of books called the Five Classics, some of which were written before Confucius. All candidates for the civil service were required to master them. No better example is recorded of the Chinese reverence for history.

The oldest of the Five Classics, the *Book of Songs*, preserves some of the earliest Chinese poems, written between 1000 B.C. and 600 B.C. The poems deal with political themes, ritual, and romance. Many seem contemporary, with their everyday topics and simple, concrete imagery—this one, for example:

> ❝Near the East Gate
> Young women go
> Like so many clouds all day.
> Like drifting clouds
> A thought of them
> Soon blows away.
>
> There. White robe
> and a blue scarf—
> she makes my day.
>
> Near the Great Tower and Wall
> Go slender girls
> Like reeds by river's edge:
> Like bending reeds
>
> A thought of them
> Soon passes by. ❞

The *Book of Documents* records political speeches and documents from early in the Zhou dynasty, including the earliest statement of the Mandate of Heaven. The *Book of Changes* presents a complex system for foretelling the future and choosing a course of action. In *Spring and Autumn Annuals* Confucius reported major events that occurred in the state of Lu between 722 B.C. and 481 B.C.

The Five Classics were thought to carry solutions to most problems. Officials studied them closely to find support for their positions, such as the conduct of political leaders. Accounts of solar eclipses, meteor showers, and droughts were used to show what terrifying events and disasters could befall poor political leaders.

Chapter 2 *The Advance of Civilizations* **87**

 World Music: Cultural Traditions, Lesson 8

NATIONAL GEOGRAPHIC SOCIETY

Use these materials to enrich student understanding of Chinese culture.

 **NGS PICTURESHOW CD-ROM**
India and China

Independent Practice

Guided Reading Activity 2-4 **L1**

ASSESS

Check for Understanding

Assign Section 4 Review as homework or as an in-class activity.

 Use Student Self-Test and Review Software to review Section 4.

Evaluate

Section Quiz 2-4

Use the Testmaker to create a customized quiz for Section 4.

Reteach

Ask students to name the important people from this section and several contributions from each of the major empires.

Enrich

Have students discuss some of the reasons that "golden ages" end, using the Mauryan and Gupta Empires as examples.

Chapter 2 *The Advance of Civilizations* **87**

Visualizing History

Visualizing History According to legend, in about 2700 B.C. Chinese emperor Huangdi ordered his wife to find out what was killing his mulberry trees. Finding white worms eating and spinning shiny cocoons on the leaves, she accidentally dropped a cocoon into hot water. When she removed a thin thread unwinding from the cocoon, she discovered silk.
Answer to Caption: *the Silk Road*

POINT

Chinese Science and Technology
What were specific achievements of Chinese science and technology?
astronomical calculations (solar year), medical treatments (acupuncture), paper, gunpowder, wheelbarrow

CLOSE

Ask students to imagine that they live in China in A.D. 200. Have them decide which family role (father, mother, eldest son, youngest son, daughter, daughter-in-law) they would like best and least, and why.

Visualizing History Women prepare newly woven silk. Han weavers created beautiful damasks of many colors. *How did Chinese arts and inventions spread to other civilizations?*

The Han Chinese encouraged literary pursuits and made literature available to everyone. An especially valuable work produced during the Han dynasty period was the *Historical Record*. Written by Sima Qian during the reign of Wudi, it is the first true history of China.

POINT

Chinese Science and Technology

Besides literature, China also made major contributions in science and technology. By the 300s B.C., Chinese astronomers had calculated the length of the solar year as 365 1/4 days. They gazed through bronze tubes equipped with a device that divided the sky into measured segments, allowing them to make accurate measurements. They kept valuable records of solar and lunar eclipses and comet sightings.

Medicine

Chinese physicians recognized nutrition as vital and realized that some diseases resulted from vitamin deficiencies. Although they did not identify vitamins as such, the Chinese discovered and prescribed foods that would correct some problems. They also understood that many herbs had medicinal value.
Chinese doctors treated ailments and relieved pain with acupuncture, a technique in which the skin is pierced with thin needles at vital points. They believed acupuncture restored the balance between yin and yang in a person's body.

Inventions

Many inventions in ancient China were especially vital to Chinese life and economy. Made by the Chinese since prehistoric times, silk was in great demand as a trade item; its worth was attested to by the name of one of history's greatest trade routes—the **Silk Road**. Caravans carried the precious cargo as far as Rome.

Paper was probably invented by 100 B.C., although it was officially credited to an inventor from about 200 years later. Other inventions included mining and construction. Miners, using iron drill bits driven by workers on seesaw-like levers, drilled boreholes to obtain salt from the earth. Another invention was the wheelbarrow, which was first used on building sites around 100 B.C.

These are only a few examples from a list of Chinese "firsts," which also includes the first printed books, the earliest technologies for casting bronze and iron, the suspension bridge, the compass, the wheelbarrow, and gunpowder. Such achievements caused China to remain far ahead of Europe in science and technology until the A.D. 1300s.

SECTION 4 REVIEW

Recall
1. **Define** "Arabic numerals," civil service, mandarin, acupuncture.
2. **Identify** Chandragupta Maurya, Asoka, Chandragupta I, Chandragupta II, *Panchatantra*, Qin Shihuangdi, Liu Bang, Wudi, the Five Classics.

3. **Locate** the map of the Indian subcontinent on page 84, and find the Mauryan Empire and the Gupta Empire. Compare and contrast the geographical sizes, territorial boundaries, and physical features of these Indian empires.

Critical Thinking
4. **Making Comparisons** Compare a typical Han Chinese family with families you consider typical of America today.
Understanding Themes
5. **Uniformity** How did Qin Shihuangdi unify China?

SECTION 4 REVIEW ANSWERS

1. All vocabulary words are defined in the Glossary.
2. Chandragupta Maurya, 83; Asoka, 84; Chandragupta I, 84; Chandragupta II, 84; *Panchatantra,* 85; Qin Shihuangdi, 85; Liu Bang, 85; Wudi, 85; the Five Classics, 87

3. The Mauryan Empire covered more territory than the Gupta; unlike the Mauryas, the Guptas never controlled the Indus River valley.
4. Answers will vary. Students may refer to the strict Han family hierarchy with the

father at the top, obedience and respect due to those above, and limited opportunities for women.
5. **UNIFORMITY** standardized coins; uniform legal system, weights and measures

c. A.D. 100
The Teotihuacános dominate central Mexico.

c. A.D. 300
Mayan civilization reaches its peak.

c. A.D. 800
Mayan civilization begins to decline.

A.D. 1   A.D. 400   A.D. 800

Chapter 2
Section 5

Section 5

The Americas

Setting the Scene

▶ **Terms to Define**
  obsidian

▶ **People to Meet**
  the Maya, the Teotihuacános, the Toltec

▶ **Places to Locate**
  Monte Albán, Yucatán Peninsula, Teotihuacán, Tula

ind Out ▶ How did trade encourage the growth of city-states and kingdoms in the areas of present-day Mexico and Central America?

The Storyteller

How did the world begin? According to Mayan myth, "All was in suspense, all calm, in silence; all motionless, still, and the sky was empty. . . . There was neither man, nor animal, birds, fishes, crabs, trees, stones, caves, ravines, grasses, nor forests; there was only the sky. . . . There was nothing standing; only the calm water, the placid sea, alone and tranquil. Nothing existed. There was only silence in the darkness, in the night. Only the Creator[s] were there. By nature they were great thinkers. They decided: when day dawned for the first time, the human being must appear. Thus they spoke. 'Let there be light, let there be dawn in the sky and on the earth.'"

—adapted from *Sources of World History,* edited by Mark A. Kishlansky, 1995

Chichén Itzá temple figure

B etween 500 B.C. and A.D. 500, a series of Native American civilizations emerged in the areas of present-day Mexico and Central America. Amid volcanic mountains, cool valleys, dense rain forests, and dry, forested plains, early farmers developed methods that produced plentiful harvests and supported large populations. Maize was their basic crop.

Ruins of ancient cities reveal an astonishing way of life. Ideas from earlier civilizations were adopted and modified by later ones. Although each culture had unique features, they shared common elements. Archaeologist have labeled them together as Mesoamerican civilizations. The prefix *meso-* means "middle" and refers to the fact that these people lived in the middle land area that joins North America and South America. Descendants of the early Mesoamericans continue to live in this region and maintain many of their early traditions.

The Zapotec

As you learned in Chapter 1, the Olmecs were the earliest people to develop a civilization in Mexico. After the Olmec, the Zapotec people (ZAH•puh•TEHK), began a civilization about 500 B.C. The Zapotec built their capital city, **Monte Albán,** on a mountain in the valley of Oaxaca (wah•HAH•kah) in southern Mexico. They flattened the mountaintop to create a large plaza, around which they designed a temple area. They also carved the slopes of the mountain into terraces for agriculture and housing.

The Zapotec produced the earliest written texts in Mexico and Central America. They carved on stone slabs records of their conquests, religious rituals, and contacts with other peoples. After the Zapotec empire collapsed about A.D. 750, the Zapotec people abandoned Monte Albán. They set up several smaller kingdoms, but these territories were later conquered by other Native American groups.

Chapter 2 *The Advance of Civilizations* **89**

Chapter 2
Section 5

SECTION THEME

▶ **Change** The Mesoamerican civilizations develop an understanding of astronomy and mathematics.

ind Out ▶

Answer: *City-states and kingdoms grew up around trading centers.*

FOCUS

Section Objective

Explain how trade encouraged the growth of city-states and kingdoms in the areas of present-day Mexico and Central America.

BELLRINGER
Motivational Activity

Before taking roll at the beginning of the class period, project Section Focus Transparency 2-5 and have students answer the activity questions. Discuss students' responses.

📁 This activity is also available as a blackline master.

Vocabulary Pre-check

📁 Use the Vocabulary PuzzleMaker to create a puzzle that reinforces the vocabulary terms in this section. **L1**

SECTION RESOURCES

📁 **Reproducible Masters**
• Reproducible Lesson Plan 2-5
• Guided Reading Activity 2-5
• Reteaching Activity 2
• Enrichment Activity 2
• Section Quiz 2-5
• Performance Assessment Activity 2
• Spanish Chapter Summary 2

📖 **Transparencies**
• Section Focus Transparency 2-5

Multimedia
📱 Focus on World Art Print 11
💿 Vocabulary PuzzleMaker Software
💿 Student Self-Test and Review Software
💿 Testmaker
🎵 World Music: Cultural Traditions, Lesson 2

TEACH

Guided Practice

THEME Change

Ask students to make a written list of the innovations of the Maya, the Teotihuacános, and the Toltec. Ask volunteers to read their lists and have the class point out any omissions. **L1**

Visualizing History

The Aztec borrowed the rain god Tlaloc from the Teotihuacános. At the center of the Aztec capital was a temple where victims were sacrificed to Tlaloc. **Answer to Caption:** *the Mexican Plateau*

Economics Mayan farmers produced large surplus crops of maize that they brought to market to trade for other goods made by craftspeople. Ask students to explain what made Mayan trade successful. *(The Maya had trade routes throughout Mexico and Central America; merchants traveled by road, river, and sea.)* **L1**

📖 Focus on World Art Print 11, Mayan. *Presentation of Captives to a Maya Ruler*

🎵 World Music: Cultural Traditions, Lesson 2

Independent Practice

📁 Guided Reading Activity 2-5 **L1**

Daily Life Have students read the article on Teotihuacán in the December 1995 *NATIONAL GEOGRAPHIC*. Ask them to summarize some of the recent discoveries about that city. **L2**

Visualizing History The Teotihuacáno rain god Tlaloc is shown in an *incensario* (container for burning incense) from A.D. 400–700. *Where was the Teotihuacáno civilization located?*

The Maya

As early as 900 B.C., another Native American group, **the Maya**, began to settle the **Yucatán Peninsula** of present-day Mexico. Influenced by the Olmec, the Maya built cities consisting of temple-pyramids, houses, terraces, and courts. Mayan ruins can now be found throughout the region in diverse terrains: highlands, lowlands, and coastal plains. The Maya adapted to their various environments, developing different farming practices, languages, and governments.

Mayan civilization reached its peak between A.D. 300 and A.D. 900. Instead of uniting into one empire, the Maya were divided into a patchwork of city-states linked by a common culture, political ties, and trade. Royalty, priests, and nobles made up the ruling class in each Mayan city-state. Under them were farmers, merchants, and artisans. Laborers and enslaved people made up the lowest social group.

Religion

Religion was at the center of Mayan life. The Maya believed in two levels of existence. One level was the daily physical life they lived. The second level was the Otherworld, a spiritual world peopled with gods, the souls of ancestors, and other supernatural creatures. The two levels were closely intertwined. Actions on each level could influence the other. Mayan myths explained the workings of this world and the Otherworld.

Mayan kings were spiritual leaders as well as political leaders. They were responsible for their people's understanding of the Otherworld and for their behaving in ways that would keep the gods pleased. Rulers performed rituals and ceremonies to satisfy the gods. In their great cities, the Maya constructed plazas, temples, and huge pyramids— symbolically sacred mountains—where thousands of people could gather for special ceremonies and festivals.

Images on Mayan temples, sacred objects, and pottery provide clues about Mayan beliefs and practices. The rain god, Chac, appears frequently. Images depict other gods in the form of trees, jaguars, birds, monkeys, serpents, reptiles, fish, and shells. Monsters combine parts of several creatures.

Blood symbols also appear. Human sacrifices and bloodletting rituals were part of Mayan practice. These ceremonies were considered important to appease the gods and to maintain and renew life.

Some festivals also included a ceremonial ball game, called *pok-a-tok*. For this game, the Maya invented the use of solid rubber balls about the size of basketballs. Players wearing protective padding batted the balls back and forth across a walled court. These games recalled games played by mythical Mayan heroes.

Sciences

Like the ancient Greeks, the Maya believed that the movements of the sun, moon, and planets were journeys of gods across the sky. Since the gods controlled nature—including harvests—charting the movements of the celestial bodies was essential.

To do this charting, Mayan priests became excellent mathematicians and astronomers. Mayans built on the earlier work of the Olmec. Mayans developed a system of mathematics using the base 20. They used three symbols to represent numbers. A dot stood for the number one; a bar was five; and a shell figure symbolized zero. Rather than expressing place value with the highest place to the left, the Maya expressed their numbers vertically with the largest place at the top. The Maya also developed accurate calendars, a 260-day sacred calendar and another 360-day calendar. The calendars were used to predict eclipses, schedule religious ceremonies, and determine times to plant and harvest.

COOPERATIVE LEARNING ACTIVITY

Chart Organize the class into five groups, corresponding to the five subheadings in the section covering the Maya. Distribute a large sheet of poster board to each group. The groups should use the poster board to display information about their subheading that is not found in the text. Each group should select a coordinator responsible for assigning specific tasks to every group member. When each group has filled in its piece of poster board with additional information, mount the display so that it forms a comprehensive chart presenting information on Mayan culture. One member of each group should present its findings to the rest of the class. **L2** 📦

Economy

The Mayan economy was based on agriculture and trade. In addition to maize, farmers grew beans, squash, pumpkins, chili peppers, and tomatoes. Slash-and-burn farming continued in some areas. Elsewhere the Maya produced larger harvests by intensively farming raised plots surrounded by canals.

Perhaps as often as every five days, farmers brought surplus crops to the open-air markets of the major cities. Maize and other produce were traded for cotton cloth, jade ornaments, pottery, fish, deer meat, and salt.

Mayan merchants participated in long-distance trade throughout Mexico and Central America. Traders transported their cargoes by canoes on rivers and coastal waterways. Overland, goods were carried on human backs, for large-wheeled vehicles and beasts of burden to haul them were unknown.

Writings

The Maya were one of the first Native American peoples to develop a writing system. They wrote in accordion-folded books made of flattened bark covered with a thin layer of plaster. Four of these books have survived. They also carved inscriptions in clay, and on jade, bone, shells, and large stone monuments. Only within the past 25 years have linguists made major breakthroughs in translating Mayan writing. Linguists discovered that some inscriptions are phonetic syllables, while others represent full words. The Maya recorded the genealogy of their kings and royal families, mythology, history, ritual practices, and trade.

Collapse

By A.D. 900 the Maya in the lowlands showed signs of collapse. They stopped building, abandoned many of their cities, and moved elsewhere. Why this happened is unclear. There is evidence of increasing conflict and warfare among Mayan royal and nonroyal families. Non-Mayan outsiders were also attacking. Agricultural breakdown, perhaps caused by warfare or by erosion and over-farming, may have produced rising malnutrition, sickness, and death rates.

Other Mesoamericans

In a high, fertile valley 30 miles (48 km) northeast of present-day Mexico City, **the Teotihuacános** (TAY•oh•TEE•wuh•KAHN•ohs) flourished for about 750 years. By A.D. 100, they dominated the centrally located Mexican Plateau. At its height their main city, **Teotihuacán**, had an estimated 120,000 to 200,000 inhabitants.

Teotihuacán was laid out on a grid. The most important buildings were built along the north-south axis. Excavations of the ruins have revealed 600 pyramids, 2,000 apartment compounds, 500 workshop areas, and a huge marketplace. A valuable source of obsidian was near Teotihuacán. Obsidian, a volcanic glass, was used for sharp-edged tools, arrowheads, and other objects. It was easily traded, because Teotihuacán lay on the trade routes east to the Gulf of Mexico and to the south.

Teotihuacán declined about A.D. 750. Historians still are uncertain about the reasons for its decline. Drought may have been the cause, or invasion by **the Toltec**, a people from the north.

The Toltec people were the next group to control central Mexico. With a powerful army, they conquered land as far south as the Yucatán Peninsula. The Toltec capital of **Tula** was the center of a powerful mining and trading empire. Their gods, Quetzalcoatl (ket•suhl•KWAH•tuhl), the "plumed serpent" god of the air, and Tezcatlipoca (tehz•KAHT•lee•POH•kuh), the god of war, would be adopted by the Aztec, a later Mesoamerican group. When invaders destroyed Tula in A.D. 1170, the Toltecs' empire collapsed.

SECTION 5 REVIEW

Recall
1. **Define** obsidian.
2. **Identify** the Zapotec, Monte Albán, the Maya, the Teotihuacános, the Toltec, Quetzalcoatl.
3. **Use** the map on 165 to locate the area settled by the Maya. What large city did the Maya establish? On what landform was it located?

Critical Thinking
4. **Synthesizing Information** What common cultural features linked the Mesoamerican civilizations?

Understanding Themes
5. **Change** What variety of factors might have contributed to the collapse of the Mayan civilization?

SECTION 5 REVIEW ANSWERS

1. All vocabulary words are defined in the Glossary.
2. the Zapotec, 89; Monte Albán, 89; the Maya, 90; the Teotihuacános, 91; the Toltec, 91; Quetzalcoatl, 91
3. Chichén Itzá, Yucatán Peninsula
4. maize as basic food; markets for trade; importance of religion; complex cultures
5. **CHANGE** increased conflict and warfare among Mayan families; outside attacks; decline of agriculture caused by warfare, erosion, or over-farming; rising sicknesses

---

ASSESS

Check for Understanding
Assign Section 5 Review as homework or as an in-class activity.

 Use Student Self-Test and Review Software to review Section 5.

Evaluate
 Section Quiz 2-5

 Use the Testmaker to create a customized quiz for Section 5.

Reteach
Write on the board the following sentence from page 89: *Although each culture had unique features, they shared common elements.* Ask students to identify first the unique features of each of the cultures covered in the section and then the elements common to all of them.

 Reteaching Activity 2

Enrich
Have students write a short report comparing Mayan hieroglyphics and pyramids with those of ancient Egypt.

 Enrichment Activity 2

CLOSE

Ask students how a culture is reflected in its art and architecture. Have them describe the types of art and architecture characteristic of the Mesoamerican civilizations.

Special Report Summary

In 1989 archaeologists went to Guatemala to learn why the great Mayan civilization vanished more than 1,000 years ago.

↓

Interpreting artifacts and hieroglyphs, they found that the rulers of the city of Dos Pilas had won control of other cities in the region.

↓

In A.D. 761 the subject kingdoms attacked Dos Pilas. The people of Dos Pilas tore down palaces to build defensive walls, but they were overrun.

↓

Scholars believe that the warfare among rival Mayan kings reduced farming, disrupted trade, and killed young people, contributing to the decline of Mayan civilization.

TEACH

Points to Discuss

After students have read the feature, ask: Why did a team of archaeologists go to Guatemala in 1989? *(to learn why the golden age of the Maya ended in the ninth century A.D.)* What did archaeologists use to learn more about the Maya? *(potsherds, bones, monuments, spearheads, trash, fortifications, and a hieroglyphic stairway)* How did the archaeological finds change our view of Mayan society? *(not a series of peaceful kingdoms with ceremonial centers, but wracked by battle and human sacrifice)*

The Maya

Some 2,000 years ago, the lowland Mayan civilization of what is now Central America flourished. A society dating to 1200 B.C., the Maya developed the most complex writing system in the Americas, built majestic temple-pyramids and palaces, and mastered astronomy and mathematics. Then suddenly, in the A.D. 800s, the record of life in the region fell silent: The people stopped erecting monuments, carving hieroglyphic texts, and making pottery. Their cities lay in ruins, their fields and villages were abandoned to the jungle, and the great civilization of the Maya vanished.

What happened to end the golden age of the Maya more than a thousand years ago? To answer that question, in 1989 an international team of archaeologist, sponsored in part by the National Geographic Society and Vanderbilt University, went to the Petexbatún rain forest of northern Guatemala. Amid the ruins of the ancient city of Dos Pilas, the team set to work on one of archaeology's greatest mysteries.

92   Chapter 2   *The Advance of Civilizations*

TEACHER NOTES

_____
_____
_____
_____
_____

Enrico Ferorelli

History *and the* Humanities

Focus on World Art Print 11, Mayan. *Presentation of Captives to a Maya Ruler*

Cultural Perspectives

Mayan Innovations The Maya learned to make a durable cement using burnt lime, which they used for temples and other structures. The pyramids at Tikal rise to 230 feet. Mayan priests also made exact calculations of dates; they estimated the beginning of history to have been August 10, 3113 B.C.

NATIONAL GEOGRAPHIC SOCIETY

VIDEODISC
STV: Maya

Side 2
Frames 15839–38987
Title: *End of Classic Period*
Subject: Evidence of warfare and violence in Mayan society
Ask: What evidence found in 1990 proved that the Maya were violent? *(hieroglyphic text that told of battles)*

After setting up a fully functioning camp complete with a computer lab and drafting workstations, scientists began their task. They studied thousands of potsherds, scores of monuments, bone fragments, spearheads, trash heaps, and miles of fortifications of Dos Pilas—built by renegades from the great Mayan center of Tikal—and nearby cities.

One spectacular find that told the fate of the Maya was a hieroglyphic stairway. Five limestone steps, about 20 feet wide, each with two rows of glyphs carved on the risers, climb to the base of the royal palace near the main plaza at Dos Pilas. Experts at deciphering glyphs were on hand to translate each glyph as it was uncovered. The story on the steps gives an account of the battles of the first ruler of the Petexbatún (referred to as Ruler 1) against his brother at Tikal, some 65 miles northeast of Dos Pilas.

One of the epigraphists summed up the inscription: "It begins by talking about the 60th birthday of

A Mayan warrior-king is portrayed on a stela carved in A.D. 731. Discoveries at Dos Pilas have led to new theories on the collapse of the Mayan civilization along the border of Guatemala and Mexico.

A stairway of five long steps (top) came to light during excavations at the Dos Pilas site.

Chapter 2 *The Advance of Civilizations* 93

FUN FACTS

- At the height of Mayan civilization, the city of Tikal and its environs may have had as many as 60,000 residents.
- The Maya used corbel vaulting in their buildings, a complex technique that supports arches and domes.
- The Maya constructed buildings and carved sculptures without the use of metal tools.
- Mayan farmers experimented with the domestication of many varieties of corn, beans, and other food crops.
- Mayan temples were often built in alignment with astronomical phenomena.

NATIONAL
GEOGRAPHIC *Special Report*

Linking Past and Present

Mayan Ruins Until the mid-1800s most Mayan ruins lay hidden and unknown in the jungles of Mexico and Central America. When the sites were discovered, priceless sculptures were often looted and sold. Today, Mayan ruins are protected by the governments of Mexico, Guatemala, and Belize.

▨ *As Vanderbilt graduate student Stacy Symonds excavated a defensive wall, she discovered the hieroglyphic stairway beneath it. Here she records information about the glyphs.*

Ruler 1, that he danced a ritual dance. As you read down the steps, the glyphs give a historical sequence to his reign. We think Ruler 1 left Tikal and started a splinter kingdom at Dos Pilas. There's an emblem glyph——which is like a political title —for Tikal, and both brothers claimed it. Ruler 1 was defeated, but then there was another war. This time Dos Pilas won."

Although the glyphs told archaeologist about the origin of a dynasty, what was even more intriguing was a stone wall built on top of the stairs during the kingdom's fall. Less than a hundred years after memorializing their founder, the people of Dos Pilas threw a wall up over his monument in what must have been a desperate attempt to

protect themselves. Why did the people of Dos Pilas build defensive walls, which are rarely found at Mayan sites?

The second and third rulers of Dos Pilas changed traditional warfare when they set forth on campaigns of expansion. Digging a 30-foot shaft into the burial temple of Ruler 2, archaeologist discovered hieroglyphs on fine pottery that offered more clues. These glyphs suggest that Ruler 2, who reigned from A.D. 698 to A.D. 726, expanded the influence of Dos Pilas and gained control of other cities through marriage and political alliances.

Ruler 3 went on to wed a royal lady from the city of Cancuén and to dominate the entire region. He traveled to the cities of Tamarindito, Aguateca, Seibal, and others to perform ceremonies and quell unrest. After Ruler 3 died in A.D. 741, Ruler 4 took control, living mostly at Aguateca—by then a twin capital— which rests on a limestone bluff high above Lake Petexbatún.

In A.D. 761 something went wrong. According to hieroglyphs, the kings of the Petexbatún had overextended their domain. There had been hints of trouble for more than a decade: Ruler 4 had spent much of his 20-year reign racing from one end of the realm to the other, performing bloodletting rituals, leading battles, and contracting alliances. He used every technique to sustain the kingdom, but to no avail.

Then the city of Tamarindito threw off the yoke of Dos Pilas. Hieroglyphs at Tamarindito tell us that its warriors attacked the capital and killed Ruler 4.

About that time the citizens of Dos Pilas made a valiant last stand. In desperation they ripped stones from temples and monuments, including the tomb of Ruler 2 and the hieroglyphic stairway. They tore

down much of the royal palace to build two walls around the central palaces and temples.

The surviving nobles deserted their citizens and fled to Aguateca, proclaiming themselves the new rulers of the kingdom. They chose Aguateca as its final capital because of its defensive location. The people of Aguateca held out for about 50 years, but disappeared in the early A.D. 800s

✀

IN A SPAN of only a few hundred years the kingdom rose, expanded, and collapsed as a succession of kings moved from limited conflict to widespread warfare. Scholars have argued that the Mayan civilization simply outgrew its environment, exhausting the soil and creating environmental and economic stress. But another possibility is that intensive warfare forced the Maya, at least in the Petexbatún area, to move close to fortresses such as Aguateca, where they would have soon run out of fertile land. Perhaps farmers were limited to fortified areas near cities that could provide protection, forcing them to forsake traditional agricultural practices that had sustained them for hundreds of years. The wars must have disrupted trade, upset population distribution, destroyed crops, and killed young farmer-warriors, exacting a huge price.

Scholars have added greatly to our view of Mayan society. Once regarded as a network of ceremonial centers ruled by peaceful priest-kings, Mayan civilization is no longer seen that way. Battle and human sacrifice were aspects of life. Perhaps siege warfare was ultimately too costly for the Maya. For years to come, scientists will study the ruins in the Petexbatún rain forest researching changes that may have contributed to the collapse of the lowland Mayan civilization.

MORE ABOUT...

Mayan Women The archaeologist Tatiana Proskouriakoff (1909–1985) was a leading expert on Mayan civilization. Proskouriakoff pioneered research on the role of women in Mayan society by analyzing female figures in Mayan sculpture. She argued that Mayan women were often the founders of dynasties and suggested that descent among the Maya may have been matrilineal.

**Before
A.D. 761**

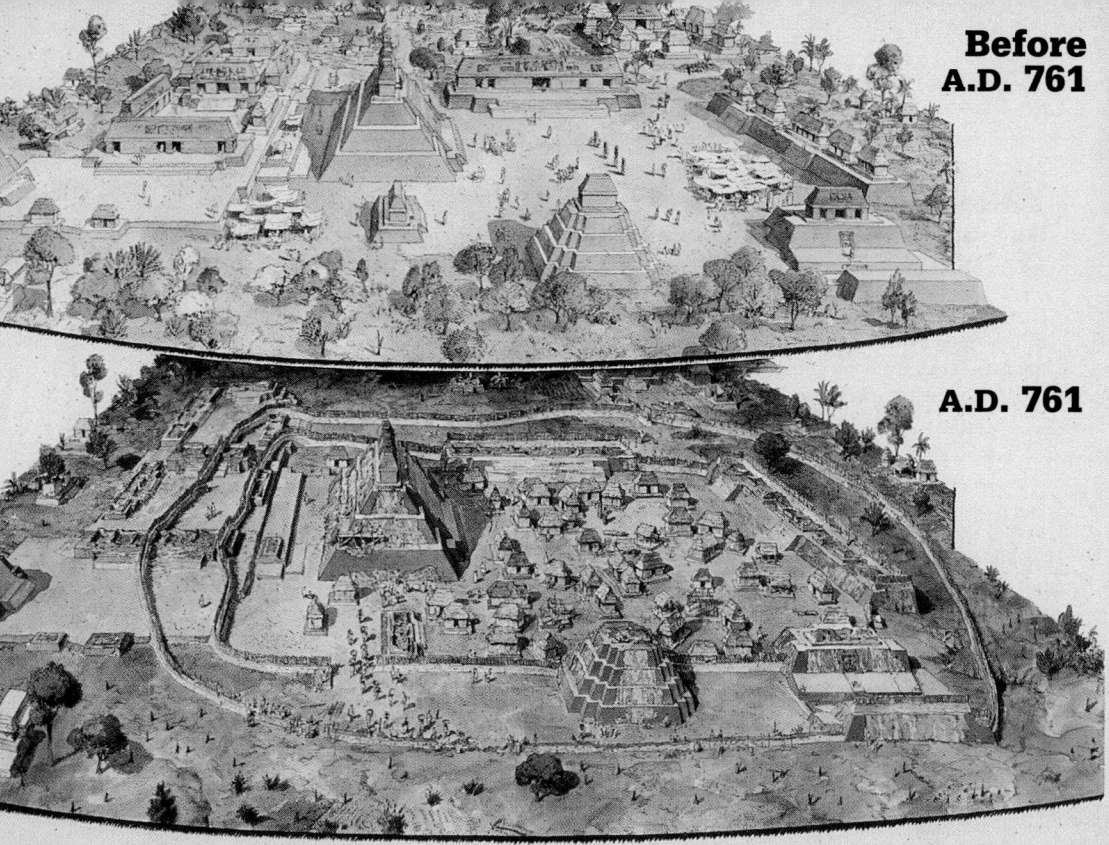

A.D. 761

Enrico Ferorelli

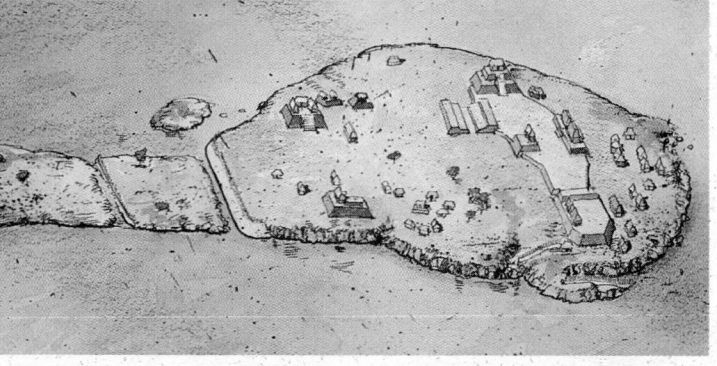

Enrico Ferorelli

CURRICULUM CONNECTION

LITERATURE

In the A.D. 1500s, Mayan myths were written down in an epic called *Popol Vuh*. The epic describes the universe before the creation of the earth: "There is not yet one person, one animal, bird, fish, crab, tree, rock, hollow, canyon, meadow, forest. Only the sky alone is there; the face of the earth is not clear. Only the sea alone is pooled under all the sky; there is nothing whatever gathered together. It is at rest; not a single thing stirs."

Global Gourmet

Central America Corn and beans remain essential ingredients in the diet of the people of southern Mexico, Guatemala, and Belize. Corn is ground and pounded flat to make tortillas, the pancake-shaped bread popular throughout the region.

Portfolio Project

Remind students of the importance of religion to the Maya. Then ask them to write a brief essay discussing how the people of Dos Pilas probably felt when they tore down temples and palaces to build defensive walls.

In proper Mayan style Dos Pilas's ceremonial precinct (above, top) featured palaces for rulers and temples to the gods. But an apparent golden age came to an abrupt end in A.D. 761 (above, bottom). After the killing of Ruler 4, warfare consumed the region. Residents tore down facades of temples and palaces to raise two walls. A cleared area between the walls likely served as a killing alley. Seeking refuge, farmers moved into the plaza and erected huts. Soon the city was abandoned.

A peninsula became an island (left, top and bottom) as defenders of the Lake Petexbatún port dug three moats across the neck of land. At the tip of the island, a walled wharf protected a canoe landing. Perhaps the enemy proved too strong or conditions too harsh, for the outpost was abandoned.

Chapter 2   *The Advance of Civilizations*   **95**

TEACHER NOTES

_____

_____

_____

_____

_____

Chapter 2 Review

GLENCOE TECHNOLOGY

VIDEODISC
Use MindJogger to review students' knowledge of the chapter.

MindJogger Videoquiz

Chapter 2
Disc 1 Side A

  Also available in VHS.

Answers

Using Key Terms

1. k
2. j
3. a
4. b
5. f

Using Your History Journal

Suggest to students that they use reference books to amplify their knowledge of domestic and foreign policies of the civilizations described.

Reviewing Facts

1. pride in being Greek; love of life; desire for excellence; determination to meet fate with dignity
2. Rome ceased to be a republic and became an empire.
3. Achievements include: made advances in principles of algebra; explained concept of infinity and invented concept of zero; devised symbols for numbers 1 to 9.
4. Main groups: landowners, peasants, merchants
5. Located in central Nigeria, the Nok produced terra-cotta figurines and iron tools.
6. astronomy, mathematics

96 Chapter 2 *The Advance of Civilizations*

Connections Across Time

Historical Significance From about 500 B.C. to A.D. 500, major civilizations in different parts of the world produced achievements in a variety of fields that still influence people today. Political leaders introduced stable forms of government, uniform codes of law, and opportunities for economic and cultural development. Various religions instilled spiritual ideals and produced great achievements in the arts. Philosophic and scientific thinkers established systems of thought and institutions of learning. Finally, merchants created trading networks that encouraged the exchange of ideas and practices.

Using Key Terms

Write the key term that completes each sentence. Then write a sentence for each term not chosen.

a. polis
b. civil service
c. classical
d. pope
e. tragedies
f. aqueducts
g. obsidian
h. plebeians
i. democracy
j. messiah
k. oral tradition
l. acupuncture
m. savanna

1. Early African peoples communicated their culture through _____ —legends and history passed by word of mouth.
2. Many Jews hoped for a ____, or savior, to deliver them from Roman rule.
3. The ____, the basic political unit of ancient Greece, included a city and the surrounding villages and fields.
4. Chinese students took examinations for positions in the ___, a system that allowed anyone with abilities to attain public office.

Technology Activity

Building a Database Search the Internet or your local library for additional information about the Olympic Games. Build a database by collecting information about recent Olympic Game results of both summer and winter sporting events. Include headings such as the name of the event, when it first became an event, if participated in by both sexes, and the number of medals each country obtained.

96 Chapter 2 *The Advance of Civilizations*

Using Your History Journal

Imagine that you are either a young Roman legionary stationed in a remote part of the Roman Empire or a Chinese student preparing to take a civil service examination. Write a letter describing the accomplishments of your civilization to a person who lives in another civilization.

5. Throughout the Roman Empire, Roman engineers built _____, or artificial channels for carrying water from one area to another.

Reviewing Facts

1. **Culture** State the values of Greek civilization that were found in the literary works the *Iliad* and the *Odyssey*.
2. **Government** Describe how Rome's political system changed when Augustus Caesar came to power.
3. **Science** List some of the achievements of Indian mathematicians during the Gupta Empire.
4. **Culture** Identify three main social groups that made up Chinese society during the Han era.
5. **Culture** Identify the Nok people, their location, and their major cultural achievements.
6. **Science** Explain the scientific fields in which the Maya excelled.

Critical Thinking

1. **Apply** How did Sparta's values affect its educational system?

Critical Thinking

1. Sparta's military values instilled respect for the military and prepared citizens for warfare.
2. Through trade, commerce, and expanded contacts in the cities, Greek and Middle Eastern cultures blended to form Hellenistic culture.
3. During the republic family life was stable, and people held similar values.
4. Fierce wars might have continued to characterize the Indian empires; it would have encompassed more territory but had less cultural advancement.
5. The country might be less productive if merchants were held in low esteem.
6. They encountered new environments and objects, which needed new words, and they adopted words from the languages of the people they met.

2. **Synthesize** How did Alexander the Great's founding of cities throughout his empire help create a new culture?

3. **Analyze** What evidence suggests that Roman society was more stable during the time of republic than it had been during the time of the empire?

4. **Synthesize** What might have happened if Asoka had not been horrified while viewing carnage after a fierce battle?

5. **Synthesize** Think about how merchants were viewed in Han society and why. How might the United States be different if we felt that way about merchants?

6. **Evaluate** Language changed as people moved into various regions of Africa. Why do you think this happened?

Understanding Themes

1. **Innovation** What might contemporary theater be like if a playwright such as Aristophanes had not lived?

2. **Cultural Diffusion** How might Roman roads have helped to foster cultural diffusion?

3. **Movement** How did migration and population movements affect the development of early Africa?

4. **Uniformity** What steps did Asoka take to bring unity to his empire?

5. **Change** How did trade affect the development of Mesoamerican civilizations?

Skill Practice

Read the following African proverbs carefully. Then answer the questions for each proverb.

- Familiarity breeds contempt; distance breeds respect.
- When you follow in the path of your father, you learn to walk like him.

1. What is the general subject of each proverb?
2. Describe the point of view expressed in each proverb.
3. Do you agree with the point of view? Make sure you are able to support your answer with specific reasons.

Linking Past and Present

1. The Olympic Games were revived in 1896. In what ways do today's Olympic Games resemble those of ancient Greece? In what ways do they differ?

2. Ideas of Greek civilization have affected much of American culture. Choose one area such as medicine, philosophy, politics, art, or sport. Reread information about that area in the chapter. Then list as many examples of influences on American culture as you can.

3. Ancient China and India produced a variety of products that were exchanged for goods from other parts of the world. What ideas and products from these lands have become popular in the West in recent years? What factors account for their popularity?

Geography in History

1. **Location** Refer to the map below. Which area (east or west) was more heavily influenced by Christianity by A.D. 200?

2. **Movement** How did Constantine encourage the spread of the Christian religion in the Roman Empire?

3. **Place** According to the map below, which city in western Europe had the largest concentration of Christians by A.D. 200?

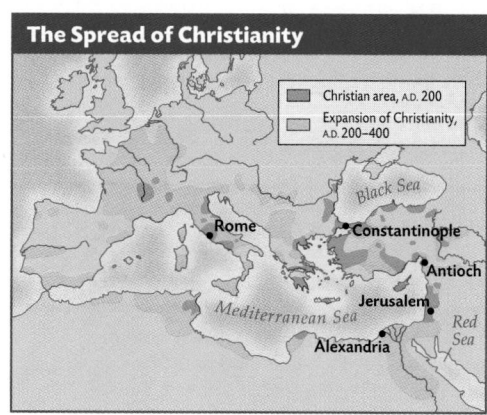

The Spread of Christianity

Christian area, A.D. 200
Expansion of Christianity, A.D. 200–400

Rome · Constantinople · Antioch · Jerusalem · Alexandria
Black Sea · Mediterranean Sea · Red Sea

Chapter 2 The Advance of Civilizations **97**

---

1. The modern Olympics include summer and winter games alternating every two years; many of the events today are the same as those of ancient times. Today's Olympics feature athletes from all over the world, not just Greeks; women can watch and participate; many additional events have been added.

2. Answers will vary.

3. clothing and other consumer goods; they might mention the spread of Indian and Chinese religious ideas among Westerners; growing interest might stem from the larger role these countries are playing in world affairs

Geography in History

1. east

2. credited military victories to the Christian God; gave Christians freedom of worship; resolved differences among Christian leaders; ordered churches constructed

3. Rome

? Chapter Bonus Test Question

Ask students: "Beware of Greeks bearing gifts" is a common expression. What event in Greek history or legend does it refer to, and what does it mean? Give an example of a situation in which someone today might use this expression. *(The event is the Trojan War; the "gift" a wooden horse given to the Trojans that secretly contained Spartan soldiers. People should be wary of gifts coming from unlikely givers.*

Understanding Themes

1. **INNOVATION** Perhaps the only type of play would be tragedy.

2. **CULTURAL DIFFUSION** Ease of travel between Rome and the provinces facilitated trade and other contacts.

3. **MOVEMENT** They brought Bantu cultures to most of Africa south of the Sahara.

4. **UNIFORMITY** He issued laws stressing concern for other human beings; provided free health care; built new roads.

5. **CHANGE** Trade among the parts of Mesoamerica led to the spread of ideas and objects.

Skill Practice

Answers should allow more time for essay questions than for short answer questions and should include time for reviewing answers.

A complete, 1-page lesson plan is provided for each section in the *Reproducible Lesson Plans* booklet.

Regional Civilizations

CHAPTER RESOURCES

	Reproducible Resources	Multimedia Resources
Chapter Opener	Chapter Themes: Graphic Organizer 3 Historical Significance Chapter Activity 3	MindJogger Videoquiz

Chapter Enrichment	Vocabulary Activity 3*
	Time Line Activity 3
	Mapping History Activity 3
	History Simulation 3
	Geography and History Activity 3
	Source Reading 3
	People in World History Profiles
	   17, 18, 19, 21, 22, 26
	World Art and Music Activity 3
	Enrichment Activity 3
	Critical Thinking Activity 3
	Performance Assessment Activity 3
		NGS Poster Set: *The Middle Ages*
		Focus on World Art Prints 13, 14
		World History and Art Transparencies
		   12, 13, 14, 15, 17
		NGS PicturePack Transparency Set:
		   The Middle Ages
		Vocabulary PuzzleMaker Software
		World Music: Cultural Traditions,
		   Lessons 4, 5, 8, 9
		NGS PictureShow CD-ROM:
		   The Middle Ages
		Turning Points in World History:
		   Jerusalem: City of Three Faiths
		STV: World Geography, Vol. 1, *Asia*

Chapter Review/Reteaching	Reteaching Activity 3 Skill Reinforcement Activity 3 Spanish Chapter Summary 3	Chapter 3 Digest Audiocassette, Activity, Test* Vocabulary PuzzleMaker Software Student Self-Test and Review Software MindJogger Videoquiz
Chapter Evaluation/Testing	Performance Assessment Activity 3 Chapter 3 Test, Forms A and B	Testmaker

* Also available in Spanish

0:00 OUT OF TIME? Assign the Chapter 3 summary in the Unit 1 Digest on pages 170–173, and the Chapter 3 Audiocassettes.

Block Schedule

Block scheduling differs from traditional class scheduling in the amount of time allotted to each period. The extended time frame provided by block scheduling affords you the opportunity to implement a greater number of research-oriented and activity-intense projects to motivate and involve your students. Activities particularly suited for use within the block scheduling framework are identified throughout this chapter by the following designation.

KEY TO ABILITY LEVELS

Teaching strategies have been coded for varying learning styles and abilities.

L1 BASIC activities for all students
L2 AVERAGE activities for average to above-average students
L3 CHALLENGING activities for above-average students
LEP LIMITED ENGLISH PROFICIENCY activities

Use Glencoe's *Presentation Plus!* multimedia teacher tool to easily present dynamic lessons that visually excite your students. Using Microsoft PowerPoint® you can customize the presentations to create your own personalized lessons.

SECTION RESOURCES

Daily Objectives	Reproducible Resources	Multimedia Resources
Section 1 **Eastern Christian Lands** Investigate the role of Christianity in Byzantine, Armenian, Georgian, and Slavic societies.	Reproducible Lesson Plan 3-1 Guided Reading Activity 3-1* Time Line Activity 3 People in World History Profiles 17, 18 Source Reading 3 Section Quiz 3-1*	Section Focus Transparency 3-1 World History and Art Transparency 12 Vocabulary PuzzleMaker Software Student Self-Test and Review Software Testmaker
Section 2 **Islamic Civilization** Explain how the Islamic state expanded and spread to other parts of the world.	Reproducible Lesson Plan 3-2 Vocabulary Activity 3* Guided Reading Activity 3-2* People in World History Profile 19 Geography and History Activity 3 History Simulation 3 Mapping History Activity 3 Section Quiz 3-2*	Section Focus Transparency 3-2 World History and Art Transparency 14 Student Self-Test and Review Software Testmaker Turning Points in World History: *Jerusalem: City of Three Faiths*
Section 3 **Early Medieval Europe** Name the achievements of medieval European monarchs.	Reproducible Lesson Plan 3-3 Guided Reading Activity 3-3* People in World History 21, 22 Section Quiz 3-3*	Focus on World Art Print 14 NGS Poster Set: *The Middle Ages* Section Focus Transparency 3-3 World History and Art Transparency 15 NGS PicturePack Transparency Set: *The Middle Ages* Vocabulary PuzzleMaker Software Student Self-Test and Review Software Testmaker NGS PictureShow CD-ROM: *The Middle Ages*
Section 4 **Asia's Pacific Rim** Explain how Koreans, Japanese, and Southeast Asians were influenced by the cultures of China and India.	Reproducible Lesson Plan 3-4 Vocabulary Activity 3* Guided Reading Activity 3-4* Reteaching Activity 3 Enrichment Activity 3 Section Quiz 3-4* Performance Assessment Activity 3 Spanish Chapter Summary 3	Section Focus Transparency 3-4 World History and Art Transparency 17 Student Self-Test and Review Testmaker World Music: Cultural Traditions, Lessons 8, 9 Picture Atlas of the World

* Also available in Spanish

Chapter Activities

✔ *Performance Assessment Activity*

Writing a Historical Fiction Narrative Have students take the role of authors to develop a historical fiction story set in medieval Europe. Students should combine accounts of actual leaders with those of fictitious characters. You may wish to have on hand a dictionary of old English terms from which students can draw words to make their narratives more authentic. Have students share their narratives with the class.

Possible Rubric Features

Accuracy and extent of content information, concept attainment, elaboration and detail, clarity and organization

• *For an additional activity, refer to Activity 3 in the* Performance Assessment Strategies and Activities *booklet.*

ACTIVITY

From the Classroom of...

Amy Chevalier
Sun Prairie High School
Sun Prairie, WI

Be a Medieval

Have students identify with an individual from medieval Europe by assuming a role and communicating a message to another party.

Have students choose the character whose identity they will assume, the type of communication they wish to use, their audience, and the subject matter of the message they will convey. They may choose from the following list, or use ideas of their own.

Characters: a ruler (Clovis, Pepin, Charlemagne), a noble (a mayor of the palace, a knight, a lord or a lady), a member of the clergy (Pope Gregory, an abbot, monk, cardinal, or friar), a Viking, a serf

Communication: letter, poem, speech, decree, sermon, editorial, song

Audience: a family member (for example, a cousin in Constantinople), a church congregation, peasants on the manor, the king, the pope

Subject of Message: Viking raids, feudal battles, living conditions on the manor, change in taxation, new laws for the manor, heresy in the Church, life in the castle

Students may also choose to authenticate their document when they present it. For example, they may choose to write it in an old-style script.

MULTIPLE LEARNING STYLES

Verbal/Linguistic
As students study the people of the Middle Ages, read portraits from Chaucer's Prologue to *The Canterbury Tales* aloud to them. Discuss the details provided by Chaucer on the following characters in relation to information provided in the text: the Knight, the Wife of Bath, the Squire, the Monk, the Friar, the Parson, and the Prioress.

Visual/Spatial
Have the class work together to create a mural in the fashion of the Bayeux Tapestry. Have them include portraits of people from the chapter, including details of their dress and objects that symbolize their station in life. For instance, students might depict a knight in full armor with a shield showing his coat of arms.

Kinesthetic
Have students research a key medieval ceremony, such as homage or the admission of a squire to knighthood. Then have them stage a reenactment, with a narrator explaining the steps in the ceremony.

Interpersonal
Have students work in groups to create advertisements for some of the many technological improvements that date from the Middle Ages. Have one or two students in each group research, one student draw or create other visuals, and another student write the text for the ad. Students should work together to divide and coordinate the various tasks. Some possible subjects for the ads are trousers, barrels, skis, the horse collar, horseshoes, and the water mill. Display the ads in the classroom as you cover Chapter 3.

Additional Resources

NATIONAL GEOGRAPHIC SOCIETY

Teacher's Corner

INDEX TO NATIONAL GEOGRAPHIC MAGAZINE

The following articles may be used for research relating to this chapter:

- "Searching for the Scythians," by Mike Edwards, September 1996.
- "The Three Faces of Jerusalem," by Alan Mairson, April 1996.
- "The Basques," by Thomas J. Abercrombie, November 1995.
- "The Hanseatic League: Europe's First Common Market," by Edward Von Der Porten, October 1994.

NATIONAL GEOGRAPHIC SOCIETY PRODUCTS AVAILABLE FROM GLENCOE

To order the following products for use with this chapter, contact your local Glencoe sales representative, or call Glencoe at 1-800-334-7344:

- *The Middle Ages (CD-ROM)*
- *The Middle Ages (Transparencies)*
- *The Middle Ages (Poster Set)*

ADDITIONAL NATIONAL GEOGRAPHIC SOCIETY PRODUCTS

To order the following products for use with this chapter, call National Geographic Society at 1-800-368-2728:

- *STV World Geography, Vol. 1, Asia (Videodisc)*

BIBLIOGRAPHY

Literature About the Period
Murasaki, Shikibu. *The Tale of Genji.* New York: Knopf, 1992. Novel considered to be one of Japan's greatest works of fiction.
Readings for the Student
Guerber, H. A., ed. *Middle Ages.* New York: Avenel Books, 1985. Covers Charlemagne, Arthur and his knights, and other tales of the Middle Ages.
Readings for the Teacher
Esposito, John L. *Islam: The Straight Path.* Expanded ed. New York: Oxford University Press, 1991. Clear, up-to-date survey of Islam.

LOCAL OBJECTIVES

interNET CONNECTION
Islamic resources on the World Wide Web
Understanding Islam:
http://darkwing.uoregon.edu/ ~kbatarfi/islam.html

Introducing
Chapter 3

CHAPTER THEMES

Chapter Themes are listed by section on this chapter opening page of the Student Edition. A corresponding theme-based activity is available under "TEACH," and a theme-based question is asked in the Section and Chapter Reviews.

The Storyteller

Historical Setting For more than 2,000 years, the Chinese used competitive exams as a way of selecting government workers. The civil service exam such as the one described here was the last in a series of tests a Chinese student had to pass in order to be offered a government post. First the student took a local exam. If he passed it, he took a provincial exam. The final step was an empirewide exam, given every three years. Applicants were tested on their knowledge of Chinese poetry and the writings of Confucius. Of the hundreds of thousands of men who took these exams, only a few hundred passed.

Historical Significance

Answer: *They developed and passed on systems of religion, law, and government as well as alphabets and literary and artistic skills to neighboring peoples.*

Chapter
3
A.D. 500–A.D. 1300
Regional Civilizations

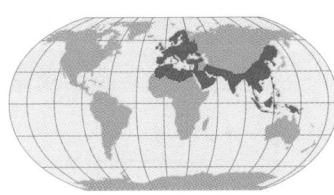

Chapter Themes

▶ **Innovation** Eastern Christian lands develop distinctive religious beliefs and art forms. *Section 1*
▶ **Movement** Armies and merchants spread Islam throughout the Middle East, North Africa, and into Spain and Asia. *Section 2*
▶ **Conflict** Western European kings, feudal lords, and popes struggle for political dominance. *Section 3*
▶ **Cultural Diffusion** The civilizations of India and China influence neighboring peoples in Asia. *Section 4*

The Storyteller

In China in the year A.D. 1200, a lone student sat behind a desk in a room furnished only with a lamp, some paper, a writing brush, and an inkstone. He labored over a grueling government exam designed to test his knowledge of Confucian texts. He worried because examiners could fail a person for even a single misquotation. If he passed, he would be one of the Song emperor's officials. If he failed, he would have to hawk cheap goods in the streets.

Civil service examinations helped ancient China maintain a consistent government no matter which dynasty was in power. Between A.D. 500 and A.D. 1300, China was among a number of civilizations in various parts of the world that developed stable governments and societies. The accomplishments of these regional civilizations had a lasting effect on world history.

Historical Significance

How did regional civilizations in Europe and Asia influence each other and the rest of the world?

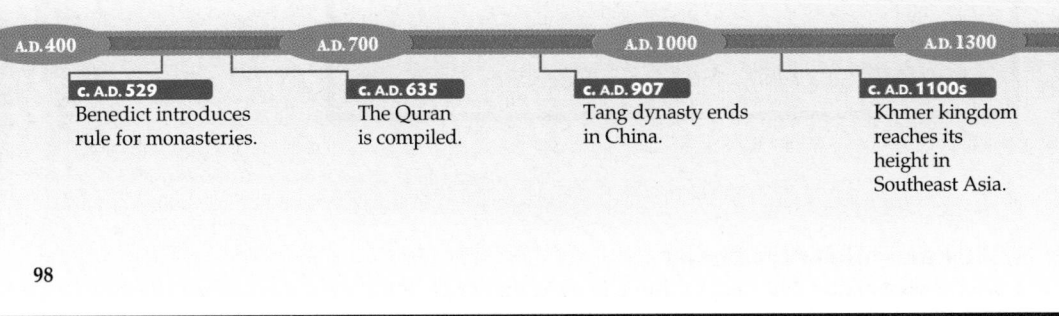

A.D. 400	A.D. 700	A.D. 1000	A.D. 1300
c. A.D. 529 Benedict introduces rule for monasteries.	**c. A.D. 635** The Quran is compiled.	**c. A.D. 907** Tang dynasty ends in China.	**c. A.D. 1100s** Khmer kingdom reaches its height in Southeast Asia.

98

GEOGRAPHY CONNECTION

Location Have students locate a number of Arab nations on a map, including Iran, Saudi Arabia, and Egypt. Explain that, contrary to what many people believe, these countries are not home to the majority of the world's Muslims. The majority of the world's 1 billion Muslims are not Arab but rather Asian and African. Have students locate Indonesia, Bangladesh, Pakistan, India, central Asia, and Nigeria. Where are the world's largest Muslim communities found? *(in these regions)* Point out that there are also large Muslim communities in France and England, in Bosnia, and in the United States.

Visualizing
History A partial view of the summer palace constructed under
Emperor Ch'ien Lung. Bibliothèque Nationale, Paris, France

Visualizing History

Members of the Chinese imperial family lived in elaborate palace complexes. Secluded and sheltered from the outside world, most of them knew little about the lives of their subjects.

Performance Assessment

Refer to the activity on page 98C of the Planning Guide.

 For an additional activity, refer to Activity 3 in the *Performance Assessment Strategies and Activities* booklet.

Using Your History Journal

Suggest that students look for details of everyday life among Slavs, Arabs, and Europeans in the three excerpts from the literature of these regional civilizations.

Your History Journal

From A.D. 500 to A.D. 1300, the literature of the world's regional civilizations reflected a variety of themes. Read an excerpt from the Slavic Primary Chronicle, *the Islamic* A Thousand and One Nights, *and the western European the* Song of Roland. *Take notes about life in each particular civilization at the time.*

GLENCOE TECHNOLOGY

VIDEODISC
Use MindJogger to preview chapter content.

MindJogger Videoquiz

Chapter 3
Disc 1 Side A

 Also available in VHS.

Chapter 3 *Regional Civilizations* 99

✚ EXTRA CREDIT PROJECT

Martial Arts Asian civilizations developed several different systems of martial arts. Have students research one or more of these: tai chi chuan (Chinese), tae kwon do (Korean), or karate (Japanese). They should find out where, how, and when the discipline originated and what role it plays in society today. If possible, have students demonstrate or show pictures of some of the basic principles and movements of the system they choose.

A.D. 400

A.D. 800

A.D. 1200

A.D. 527
Justinian becomes eastern Roman emperor.

A.D. 787
Church council at Nicaea approves use of icons.

A.D. 980
Vladimir becomes Grand Prince of Kiev.

A.D. 1054
Eastern and Western churches split.

SECTION THEME

▶ **Innovation** Eastern Christian lands develop distinctive religious beliefs and art forms.

Find Out

Answer: *Christianity provided the peoples of the Byzantine Empire, Armenia, and Georgia with a sense of national identity and unity and served as the basis for innovations in the arts and architecture.*

FOCUS

Section Objective

Investigate the role of Christianity in the Byzantine Empire and its neighbors.

BELLRINGER
Motivational Activity

Before taking roll at the beginning of the class period, project Section Focus Transparency 3-1 and have students answer the activity questions. Discuss students' responses.

This activity is also available as a blackline master.

Vocabulary Pre-check

Use the Vocabulary Puzzle-Maker to create a puzzle that reinforces the vocabulary terms in this section. **L1 LEP**

Section 1

Eastern Christian Lands

Setting the Scene

▶ **Terms to Define**
schism, theology, icon, mosaic, monastery, principality

▶ **People to Meet**
Constantine, Justinian, Theodora, Cyril, Methodius, Tiridates III, Tamara, Vladimir

▶ **Places to Locate**
Byzantine Empire, Constantinople, Armenia, Georgia, Dnieper River, Kiev, Moscow

Find Out
What role did Christianity play in the development of the Byzantine Empire and its neighbors?

The Storyteller

Byzantium [Constantinople] was in flames. A mob was screaming insults at Emperor Justinian and Empress Theodora. The emperor swiftly ordered the imperial treasury loaded onto ships to prepare for escape. Half crazed and without hope, Justinian held a final council of a few loyal friends; Theodora was present. After the military generals expressed their

fears, Theodora suddenly rose and broke the silence. "I do not choose to flee," she said. "Never shall I see the day when I am not saluted as the empress. . . . You have the money, the ships are ready, the sea is open. As for me, I shall stay." Hearing her, the others took heart. That day, Theodora saved Justinian's throne.

—adapted from *Theodora, Empress of Byzantium,* Charles Diehl, 1972

Theodora, detail of mosaic

After the Roman Empire's division in A.D. 395, the eastern half became known as the **Byzantine Empire.** At its height in the A.D. 500s, the Byzantine Empire included most of the Balkan Peninsula, Asia Minor, Syria, and Egypt. By A.D. 1000 Byzantine civilization had influenced neighboring peoples, such as the Armenians, the Georgians, and the Slavs.

Byzantine Foundations

The Byzantine Empire traced its origins to the time of the Roman emperor **Constantine**. In A.D. 330 Constantine built the city of **Constantinople,** later the Byzantine capital, at a strategic place where Europe and Asia meet. Located on a peninsula, Constantinople overlooked the Bosporus, the narrow strait between the Sea of Marmara and the Black Sea. A second strait, the Dardanelles, connects the Sea of Marmara and the Aegean Sea, which leads to the Mediterranean. The straits made Constantinople a crossroads for trade between Europe and Asia, and the location of the city on a peninsula offered natural protection from attack. As a result Constantinople became a major economic, political, and cultural center of the Roman Empire.

A Cultural Blend

After Rome's fall the Byzantine Empire inherited Roman traditions, and the city of Constantinople became known as the New Rome. Byzantine civilization, however, was more than a continuation of the old Roman Empire. Many Byzantines were Greek, spoke the Greek language, and practiced a distinct form of the Christian faith known as Eastern Christianity, or Eastern Orthodoxy. However, the empire's population consisted of many peoples, including Egyptians, Syrians, Arabs, Armenians, Jews, Persians, Slavs, and Turks. These varied peoples and cultures gave the Byzantine Empire an

---

SECTION RESOURCES

Reproducible Masters
- Reproducible Lesson Plan 3-1
- Guided Reading Activity 3-1
- People in World History Profiles 17, 18
- Time Line Activity 3
- Source Reading 3
- Section Quiz 3-1

Transparencies
- Section Focus Transparency 3-1
- World History and Art Transparency 12, *Theodora and Attendants*

Multimedia
- Vocabulary PuzzleMaker Software
- Student Self-Test and Review Software
- Testmaker

international character. Between A.D. 500 and A.D. 1200, Byzantine civilization developed into one of the most advanced in the world, and its people had a higher standard of living than the people of western Europe.

Justinian's Rule

From A.D. 527 to A.D. 565, the early Byzantine Empire was ruled by one of its greatest emperors: **Justinian.** Justinian's enthusiasm for knowledge and hard work began when he was a young court official during the reign of his uncle, Emperor Justin I. Later as emperor, Justinian aimed to restore the unity of the Roman Empire. Between A.D. 533 and A.D. 555, Byzantine forces reconquered Italy, North Africa, and Roman lands in Spain that had fallen to Germanic invaders. The successful reconquest, however, exhausted Byzantine resources, and funds were low for defending the empire's eastern borders from Persian attacks. Within a generation of Justinian's death, the Byzantine Empire lost many of its outlying territories.

Justinian, however, had many lasting accomplishments to his credit. Under his direction, a commission of scholars codified, or classified, the empire's Roman laws that had accumulated without organization or classification. The commission's work was recorded in a massive collection of books—the *Corpus of Civil Law,* or the Justinian Code—that preserved Rome's legal heritage and later became the basis for most European legal systems.

Also under Justinian, Byzantine art and architecture thrived and received their distinct character. The emperor ordered the construction of new roads, fortresses, and churches. His most famous project was the church of Hagia Sophia, "Holy Wisdom," in Constantinople. The largest and most beautiful church in the empire, Hagia Sophia still stands today as one of the world's great architectural landmarks.

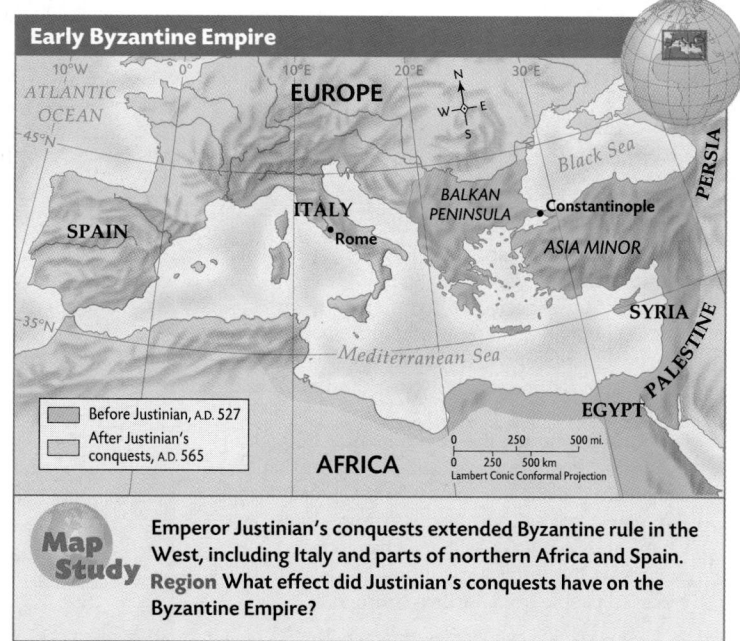

Early Byzantine Empire

Before Justinian, A.D. 527
After Justinian's conquests, A.D. 565

0   250   500 mi.
0 250 500 km
Lambert Conic Conformal Projection

Map Study Emperor Justinian's conquests extended Byzantine rule in the West, including Italy and parts of northern Africa and Spain. **Region** What effect did Justinian's conquests have on the Byzantine Empire?

Church and State

Strong ties linked Byzantine emperors and the Eastern Church. Regarded as God's representatives on Earth, emperors tried to unify the Byzantine Empire under one Christian faith, a practice that sometimes led to the persecution of Jews and non-Greek Christians. They also frequently played a major role in church affairs by appointing church officials, defining styles of worship, and using the Church's wealth for government purposes. Emperors strengthened their authority by intervening in disputes over church beliefs. In doing so, they often came into conflict with the Western Church. Since the A.D. 400s, the pope in Rome had claimed supreme leadership of all Christians; the Eastern Church opposed this claim. By A.D. 1054 this dispute over religious authority—as well as various doctrinal, political, and geographical differences—had led to a schism (SIH•zuhm), or separation, of the Church into the Roman Catholic Church in the West and the Eastern Orthodox Church in the East.

Byzantine Civilization

From A.D. 500 to A.D. 800, when western Europe was in decline, the Byzantine Empire was a brilliant center of civilization. Its scholars preserved ancient Greek and Roman works and helped

Chapter 3 *Regional Civilizations* **101**

TEACH

Guided Practice

THEME Innovation

Introduce students to a Byzantine architectural innovation: the large central church dome. Explain that although domes were not a new architectural feature, Byzantine domes were used in a new geometrical setting—flanked by smaller domes—and were higher and wider than any previous domes. If possible, bring to class pictures of ancient Roman domed buildings for students to compare. **L1 LEP**

Justinian's Rule

How did Justinian's reign contribute to world civilization? *The Justinian Code became the basis for most European legal systems, and Byzantine art and architecture flourished under Justinian's rule.*

Answer
Justinian's conquests were very expensive. The empire had little money left to protect its eastern borders.

Map Skills Practice

Reading a Map By how much did the Byzantine Empire grow after Justinian became emperor? *(Justinian's conquests nearly doubled the size of his empire.)*

COOPERATIVE LEARNING ACTIVITY

Geography Organize a travel agency in which teams of students provide information to people traveling to Constantinople during Justinian's rule. One team can plan important stops on a tour of the city; another can provide information on climate and food; while a third can prepare travel posters. The team that plans the stops should prepare a map showing the route the tour will take. Each team should research the various points of interest (such as the Hagia Sophia and the Hippodrome). On completion of the project, display the map, posters, travel brochures, and itineraries. **L1**

Visualizing History
The Russian language and other Slavic languages are closely related. The Cyrillic alphabet, which is based largely on the Greek alphabet and originally had 43 letters, eventually became the basis for the culture of the entire Slavic world.
Answer to Caption: *A modified form of the Cyrillic alphabet, containing 33 letters, is used by the Russians, Ukrainians, Bulgarians, and Serbs today.*

Who?What?Where?When?

Justinian's wife, **Theodora**, had remarkable intellectual gifts and an indomitable will. She actively helped Justinian shape his policies. Theodora also built hospitals for the poor and homes for destitute women.

Art Have students draw an icon. They should choose a subject from an illustration in the text or another source and copy it in the Byzantine manner. Students should try to use the same colors as those used by Byzantine artists. Ask students to observe the motionless aspect of the faces. **L2 LEP**

Politics Encourage students to consider the factors that led to the fall of the Byzantine Empire. Using library research, have them create a time line tracing the decline of the empire after the reign of Justinian. **L2**

World History and Art Transparency 12, *Theodora and Attendants*

---

spread classical knowledge to the western world. The Byzantines also excelled in explaining Christian theology, or religious teachings. They created new art forms and brought the religion of the Eastern Orthodox Church to eastern Europe.

Byzantine Life

Byzantine society was divided into social groups organized according to levels of rank. The family was the center of social life. Byzantine women were expected to live partly in seclusion, although they had gained some rights through the efforts of Justinian's wife, **Theodora**.

Most Byzantines made a living through farming, herding, or working as laborers. Farmers paid heavy taxes that supported the government. Although the Byzantine economy was based on agriculture, commerce thrived in cities such as Constantinople. For gems, spices, and textiles from South Asia, China, and Southeast Asia, merchants traded everything from Byzantine agricultural goods and furs to enslaved people from northern Europe.

Art

Byzantine art primarily focused on religious subjects. Icons, or religious portraits, were the most popular art form. Icons of Jesus, his mother Mary, and the saints were displayed on the walls of churches, homes, and shrines. The Byzantines also excelled in the art of mosaic, or pictures made of many tiny pieces of colored glass or flat stone set in plaster. Byzantine emperor Constantine VII, historian, painter, and author, described one mosaic:

> **"** As you move, the figures seem to move, too. You could swear that their eyes are turning and shining and that their garments are rustling . . . the Byzantine mosaicist has succeeded in creating the illusion that his jig-saw puzzle has come to life. **"**

Religious scholars of the Byzantine Empire created another art form, the illuminated manuscript. These were books decorated with elaborate designs, beautiful lettering, and miniature paintings. Illuminated manuscripts and other Byzantine art forms influenced the art of other civilizations in Europe and the Middle East.

Spread of Christianity

The Byzantines were influential in the development and spread of Christianity. Near the end of the A.D. 300s, devout Christians throughout the Byzantine Empire formed religious communities

---

Visualizing History St. Jacob holding script in the Cyrillic alphabet, a modified form of the Greek alphabet. *What peoples use the Cyrillic alphabet today?*

called monasteries. In the monasteries, men called monks sought to develop a spiritual way of life apart from the distractions and cares of the world. Christian women who did the same were called nuns and lived in quarters of their own that were known as convents.

Monasteries and convents soon played an important role in Byzantine life. They helped the poor and ran hospitals and schools for needy children. They also spread Byzantine arts and learning. Monasteries sent missionaries to neighboring peoples to convert them to the Christian faith.

Among the most successful missionaries were the brothers **Cyril** and **Methodius**. About A.D. 863 Cyril devised an alphabet for the Slavic languages. Known today as the Cyrillic (sih•RIHL•ihk) alphabet in honor of its inventor, this script is still used by Russians, Ukrainians, Bulgarians, and Serbs. When Cyril and Methodius presented the

---

MEETING SPECIAL NEEDS ACTIVITY

Language Delayed Encourage students who have difficulty defining terms to search through the text for new words and jot them down on index cards. Assign partners to work together to define the terms on the backs of the cards. Have students use the words in another context to ensure understanding. The entire class can use the set of cards for review at the end of the chapter and before the unit test. **L1 LEP**

Slavs with Cyrillic translations of the Bible and church ceremonies, they won many converts to Eastern Orthodox Christianity.

Decline and Fall

From its founding, the Byzantine Empire suffered frequent attacks by invading armies. Among them were Germanic Lombards, Slavs, Avars, Bulgars, Persians, and Arabs. In A.D. 1071 a group of invaders—the Seljuk (SEHL•JOOK) Turks, a central Asian people who practiced the religion of Islam—defeated the Byzantines at the town of Manzikert. As the Seljuks advanced, the Byzantine emperor sought aid from the Western Church. Western European expeditions sent by the pope, however, were more interested in taking Palestine, the homeland of Christianity, from Islamic control than in helping the Byzantines. In A.D. 1204 western European soldiers, attracted by Byzantine wealth, even attacked Constantinople and temporarily imposed their rule on the city and its surrounding area.

By the late A.D. 1300s, the years of fighting had severely weakened the Byzantines, reducing their territory to only Constantinople and part of Greece. In A.D. 1453 new Islamic invaders from central Asia, the Ottoman Turks, finally captured Constantinople and ended the Byzantine Empire. Despite the empire's fall, the Byzantine heritage lived on in the civilizations developed by neighboring peoples in eastern Europe.

Armenia and Georgia

During the time of the Byzantine Empire, Christian civilizations arose in the kingdoms of **Armenia** and **Georgia**. Both Armenia and Georgia lay south of the Caucasus Mountains between the Black and Caspian Seas. Although the Caucasus made travel by land difficult, plains and valleys between the mountains allowed missionaries, traders, and invaders to pass between Europe and Asia.

In the early A.D. 300s, Armenia and Georgia came under the influence of Christianity. The Armenian king **Tiridates** (TEER•eh•DAH•teez) **III** and most of his people accepted the new faith, and Armenia became the first officially Christian country in the world. According to tradition, through the efforts of a Christian woman named Nino, the Georgians accepted Christianity shortly thereafter.

Between A.D. 300 and A.D. 1200, Armenia and Georgia were prosperous kingdoms. In A.D. 451, the warrior Vartan Mamikonian (VAHR•tahn mah•mih•KOH•nee•uhn) defeated Persian forces and secured Armenia's freedom. In the late A.D.

1100s and early A.D. 1200s, the Georgians made great advances in the arts and sciences under Queen **Tamara** (tah•MAH•rah).

By the end of this period, however, both Armenia and Georgia had become a battleground among the Persians, the Byzantines, and various Islamic groups that rivaled each other for control of the Caucasus region. Centuries later, in the early A.D. 1800s, the two kingdoms became part of the Russian Empire to the north.

The Slavs

During the Byzantine era, the Slavs were among the largest groups of eastern Europe. Slavic communities north of the Black Sea traded with the Byzantine Empire and northern Europe. They controlled the middle part of a major trade route that ran north across the Black Sea, up the **Dnieper River**, then overland to the Baltic Sea. From Slavic trading posts along the Dnieper emerged a civilization that eventually developed into today's nations of Ukraine, Belarus, and Russia.

Kievan Rus

The *Primary Chronicle,* a collection of early Slavic history and legends, states that Viking warriors from Scandinavia to the north helped lay

Visualizing History This ancient monastery stands as a symbol of the influence of Byzantine **Christianity.** *What primary role did monasteries have in Byzantine society?*

Chapter 3 *Regional Civilizations* **103**

Visualizing History  Monasteries played a key role in the revival of Russian civilization, much as they did in medieval Europe. Early Russian monasteries were often built near cities, and many monks took part in local political, economic, or military activities outside the monastery. **Answer to Caption:** *Monasteries helped the poor and ran hospitals and schools for needy children. They also spread Christianity as well as Byzantine arts and learning.*

CURRICULUM CONNECTION

LITERATURE

Georgia enjoyed a golden age during the reign of Queen Tamara. Her court welcomed artists and poets, including Shota Rustaveli, whose epic poem, *The Knight in the Tiger Skin*, was dedicated to the queen. Set in Arabia, the poem tells a tale of courtly love, emphasizing courage, loyalty, and patriotism. It has been translated into French, Russian, Japanese, and other languages.

Independent Practice

📁 Guided Reading Activity 3-1 **L1**

📁 People in World History Profiles 17, 18

MAKING CONNECTIONS ACTIVITY

Daily Life Have students bring in works of folk art, literature, and music and examples of foods from the Balkan Peninsula and Slavic areas. Some might prepare recipes from Turkey, Armenia, and Russia. Other students can locate collections of folktales and perform a dramatic reading. Still others might play recordings of typical folk music of the region. Possibly someone from the community can share a traditional costume or perform a folk dance. **L1**

Chapter 3
Section 1

Map Study

Answer

Traders would have traveled north-west from Kiev to Sweden.

Map Skills Practice

Reading a Map How would Kiev's location have been favorable to Byzantine trade? *(Kiev was centrally located along the Dnieper River between Sweden and Constantinople.)*

ASSESS

Check for Understanding

Assign Section 1 Review as home-work or as an in-class activity.

 Use Student Self-Test and Review Software to review Section 1.

Evaluate

📁 Section Quiz 3-1

💻 Use the Testmaker to create a customized quiz for Section 1.

Reteach

Ask students to explain the sig-nificance of waterways and mobility in early Russia.

Enrich

Have students research the life of the Empress Theodora. Direct them to focus especially on what she did to improve the lives of women in the empire.

CLOSE

Help the class summarize the sec-tion by asking them to list three important contributions of Byzan-tine civilization.

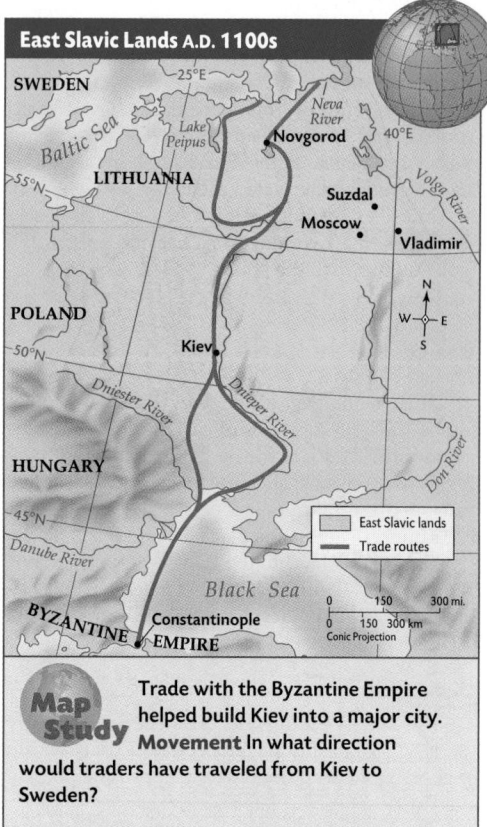

East Slavic Lands A.D. 1100s

Map Study

Trade with the Byzantine Empire helped build Kiev into a major city. **Movement** In what direction would traders have traveled from Kiev to Sweden?

In A.D. 989 contacts with the Byzantine Empire had led Prince **Vladimir** of Kiev to abandon the tradi-tional Slavic worship of nature deities and to adopt Eastern Orthodox Christianity. Vladimir's aim was to unify Kievan Rus and make it a more powerful civilization. After Vladimir's conversion, princes, warriors, and then the common people gradually accepted the new religion.

The acceptance of Eastern Orthodoxy brought Byzantine culture to Kievan Rus. The Byzantines introduced the Slavs to colorful rituals, elaborate church architecture, the spirituality of the monas-teries, and the making of icons. The people of Kievan Rus also learned to write their language in the Cyrillic alphabet. Basing its civilization on Byzantine traditions, Rus enjoyed a golden age during the A.D. 1000s and A.D. 1100s. Kiev became a glittering city of churches and palaces whose culture outshone that of any in western Europe at the time.

Rise of Moscow

In A.D. 1240 the Mongols, a warrior group from central Asia, invaded Kievan Rus and completely destroyed Kiev. The Mongols taxed the Slavs and demanded their allegiance but allowed the Slavs to keep their religion and their local governments. After Kiev's fall, political power in Kievan Rus shifted from Kiev in the south to various towns in the northeast. One of these northern settlements, **Moscow**, became a prosperous town because of its location near vital land and water routes.

Moscow advanced its position among the Slavic lands by cooperating with the Mongols. Using war and diplomacy, the princes of Moscow expanded their territory and formed the principality of Muscovy. Moscow's importance further grew in A.D. 1325 when the metropolitan, or leader of the Orthodox Church in the Eastern Slavic lands, moved there. In A.D. 1380, Muscovite forces finally defeated the Mongols at the Battle of Kulikovo. Within two hundred years, Moscow's rulers would lay the foun-dation of the powerful Slavic empire of Russia.

---

the foundations of Slavic government. About A.D. 880, the Viking prince Oleg conquered **Kiev**, a fortress-village on the Dnieper River. Control of Kiev enabled Oleg to dominate the river trade route. By A.D. 900 Kiev had become the major city of a region of Slavic territories known as Kievan Rus.

At its height during the A.D. 1000s and A.D. 1100s, Kievan Rus was a collection of city-states and principalities, or territories ruled by princes. Each region enjoyed local self-government; however, they all paid special respect to the Grand Prince of Kiev.

SECTION 1 REVIEW

Recall
1. **Define** schism, theology, icon, mosaic, monastery, principality.
2. **Identify** Constantine, Justinian, Theodora, Cyril, Methodius, Manzikert, Tiridates III, Tamara, Vladimir.

3. **Explain** why the Bosporus and the Dardanelles are considered strategic waterways.

Critical Thinking
4. **Analyzing Information** How were Byzantine emperors and the Eastern Church linked?

Understanding Themes
5. **Innovation** How did Chris-tianity affect culture in the Byzantine Empire, Georgia, Armenia, and Kievan Rus? What was the role of art and religion in these lands?

104 Chapter 3 *Regional Civilizations*

SECTION 1 REVIEW ANSWERS

1. All vocabulary words are defined in the Glossary.
2. Constantine, 100; Justinian, 101; Theodora, 102; Cyril, 102; Methodius, 102; Manzikert, 103; Tiridates III, 103; Tamara, 103; Vladimir, 104
3. They link the Mediterranean and Black

Seas, and they provide access to trade.
4. Byzantine emperors appointed church officials, set the style of worship, and intervened in church disputes.
5. **INNOVATION** It stimulated and inspired cultural creativity; they helped give them a sense of identity and unity.

A.D. 570
Muhammad is born.

A.D. 661
Umayyads establish
Islamic empire.

A.D. 830
Baghdad reaches its height
as a major center of learning.

Section 2

Islamic Civilization

Setting the Scene

▶ **Terms to Define**
  hajj, caliph, mosque, bazaar, calligraphy

▶ **People to Meet**
  Muhammad, Mu'awiyah, Harun al-Rashid, al-Razi, Omar Khayyám, Moses Maimonides, Ibn-Khaldun

▶ **Places to Locate**
  Arabian Peninsula, Makkah, Madinah, Damascus, Baghdad

 **ind Out** How did the Islamic state expand, and what were the achievements of Islamic civilization?

The Storyteller

From the far reaches of the Mediterranean to the Indus River valley, the faithful approached the holy city. Despite different nationalities, customs, and languages, all had the same objective—to worship together at the holiest shrine of Islam, the Kaaba in Makkah. One such traveler was Mansa Musa, king of Mali in western Africa. After consulting with his seers, Musa had prepared carefully for the long journey he and his attendants would take. He was determined to go, not only for his own religious fulfillment, but also to recruit teachers and leaders, so that his land could learn more of the Prophet's teachings.

—adapted from *The Chronicle of Seeker*, Mahmud Kati, reprinted in *The Human Record*, Alfred J. Andrea and James H. Overfield, 1990

Pilgrimage to Makkah

etween the Red Sea and the Persian Gulf lies the **Arabian Peninsula**, a large wedge of land consisting mostly of arid plains and deserts. The Arabian Peninsula is the home of the Arabs, distant relations to the Israelites, Phoenicians, and Chaldeans. In ancient times, the Arabs were nomadic herders who lived in tribes, each made up of related families. By the A.D. 500s, however, many tribes had settled around oases, or fertile areas near springs and water holes, to pursue either farming or trade.

Eventually groups of Arab merchants founded prosperous market towns. The most important of these towns was **Makkah** (Mecca), a crossroads of commerce about 50 miles (80 km) inland from the Red Sea. People from all over the peninsula traveled to Makkah to trade animal products for weapons, dates, grain, spices, jewels, silk, and perfumes. Arabs also visited Makkah to worship at the peninsula's holiest shrine, the Kaaba, which contained statues of the many Arab deities. The business the pilgrims brought to Makkah made its merchants wealthy.

Revelation

By A.D. 600 business ties had gradually replaced tribal ties in the Arab trading towns, and the old tribal rules were no longer adequate. At the same time, the Byzantine and Persian Empires were threatening to take over Arab lands. The Arabs had a common language, but they lacked a sense of unity and had no central government to face these challenges.

Meanwhile, many Arabs, dissatisfied with their traditional religion, searched for a new faith. This spiritual ferment contributed to the emergence of the monotheistic religion known as Islam, which means "submission to the will of Allah (God)." This faith would bring the Arabs into closer contact with other civilizations and change Arab history.

Chapter 3 *Regional Civilizations* **105**

▶ **Movement** Armies and merchants spread Islam through the Middle East and North Africa, and into Spain and Asia.

 **ind Out**

Answer: *It expanded through the conquests of the early caliphs; Islamic civilization made many advances in the arts and sciences. These advances spread to other parts of the world through trade and intellectual contacts.*

FOCUS

Section Objective

Explain how the Islamic state expanded and affected a variety of cultures.

BELLRINGER
Motivational Activity

Before taking roll at the beginning of the class period, project Section Focus Transparency 3-2 and have students answer the activity questions. Discuss students' responses.
This activity is also available as a blackline master.

Vocabulary Pre-check

Use Vocabulary Activity 3 to introduce vocabulary terms.
L1 LEP

SECTION RESOURCES

📁 **Reproducible Masters**
• Reproducible Lesson Plan 3-2
• Vocabulary Activity 3
• Guided Reading Activity 3-2
• People in World History Profile 19
• Geography and History Activity 3
• History Simulation 3

• Mapping History Activity 3
• Section Quiz 3-2

📁 **Transparencies**
• Section Focus Transparency 3-2
• World History and Art Transparency 14, *Court of the Lions, The Alhambra*

Multimedia
🖥 Student Self-Test and Review Software
🖥 Testmaker
🌀 Turning Points in World History

TEACH

Guided Practice

THEME Movement

Ask students to what regions Islam spread under "the Rightly Guided Caliphs." *(Palestine, Syria, Iraq, Persia, Egypt, bringing the Persian Empire under Muslim control and reducing the Byzantine Empire)* Under the Umayyads? *(eastward to the borders of India and China, westward across North Africa and into Spain)* Ask why the Arabs were able to conquer such a vast, diverse area. *(religious duty to spread Islam to other peoples; promise of paradise for those who died in jihad; weakened condition of defeated empires)* **L1**

Visualizing History

Arabic is the religious language of all Muslims. Although classical Arabic—the form of the language found in the Quran—is uniform throughout the Arab world, colloquial Arabic includes several different dialects.
Answer to Caption: *The Quran is the set of Islamic holy scriptures.*

POINT

The Islamic Community
In what way was the creation of the Islamic community a turning point in history? *It politically unified the Arabs and enabled them to spread Islam to other parts of the Middle East and the world.*

Visualizing History Because the Quran was written in Arabic, Muslims of many cultures adopted Arabic as a universal language. *Why is the Quran important to Islam?*

Muhammad

The prophet of Islam, **Muhammad**, was born in Makkah around A.D. 570. According to Islamic tradition, Muhammad about A.D. 610 experienced visions in which he heard a voice calling him to be the apostle of the one true deity—Allah, the Arabic word for God. Muhammad then preached to the people of Makkah that there was only one God whom people everywhere must worship and obey. He also told the Makkans to live their lives in preparation for the day of judgment, when God would punish evildoers and reward the just.

Muhammad won converts among his family and Makkah's poor. Most Makkans, however, rejected Muhammad's message. Wealthy merchants and religious leaders especially feared that monotheistic worship would end the profitable pilgrimages to Makkah. They began to persecute Muhammad and the Muslims, or the followers of Islam.

Makkan threats against his life finally forced Muhammad to seek help in Yathrib, a small town north of Makkah. The departure of Muhammad and his followers to Yathrib is known in Muslim history as the *Hijrah* (HIH•jruh), or emigration. The year in which the *Hijrah* took place, A.D. 622, marks the beginning of the Islamic era and is the first year of the Muslim calendar.

POINT

The Islamic Community
Yathrib accepted Muhammad as God's prophet and its ruler. As the center of Islam, Yathrib became known as Madinat al-Nabi, "the city of the prophet," or **Madinah** (muh•DEE•nuh). While in Madinah, Muhammad laid the foundation of an Islamic state. In the Madinah Compact of A.D. 624, he decreed that all Muslims were to place loyalty to the Islamic community above loyalty to their tribe. As a result of the Compact, all areas of life were placed under the divine law given to Muhammad and recorded in the Quran (kuh•RAHN), the holy scriptures of Islam. Muhammad also extended protection to Jews and Christians who accepted Islam's political authority.

Eventually the Makkans invaded Yathrib, forcing the Muslims to retaliate in self-defense. In the resulting battles, the Muslims defeated Makkan forces. The Makkans—and later, other Arab groups throughout the Arabian Peninsula—accepted Islam and became part of the Islamic state.

While Madinah remained Islam's political capital, Makkah became its spiritual capital. The Muslims destroyed the idols in the Kaaba and turned the shrine into a place of worship for Muslim pilgrims. Once in a lifetime, every Muslim was expected to participate in the hajj, or annual pilgrimage, to Makkah.

After a brief illness, Muhammad died at Madinah in A.D. 632. He left behind two major achievements. The first achievement was the formation of a religious community based on carefully preserved sacred writings. The second was the example of his life as an interpretive guide for Muslims to follow.

Spread of Islam

After Muhammad's death, a group of prominent Muslims chose a leader, whom they called *khalifah* (kuh•LEE•fuh) or **caliph** (KAY•luhf), meaning "successor." The first four caliphs followed Muhammad's example, kept in close touch with the people, and asked the advice of other Muslim leaders. For these reasons, Muslims have called them the Rightly Guided Caliphs.

Conquests

The Rightly Guided Caliphs sought to protect and spread Islam. Their military forces carried

---

COOPERATIVE LEARNING ACTIVITY

Oral Report Organize the class into three groups. Have each group research one of the three main holy places in Jerusalem—the Western Wall, the Church of the Holy Sepulchre, or the Dome of the Rock. Each group should present an oral report that traces the site's history and explains its importance to Jews, Christians, or Muslims. Suggest that students include drawings or photographs and a diagram of the city showing the site's location. After the presentations, ask why it is significant that these sites are all in the same city. Students should not only understand that the Middle East was the birthplace of three major world religions, but also consider the sensitive political question of who should control Jerusalem today. **L2**

Islam beyond the Arabian Peninsula. In addition to religious motives, the Arabs were eager to acquire the agricultural wealth of the neighboring Byzantine and Persian Empires to meet the needs of their growing population.

By A.D. 661 Arab armies had substantially reduced Byzantine territory and had brought the Persian Empire completely under Muslim control. In the next century Muslim warriors carried Islam east to the borders of India and China. In the west they swept across North Africa and into Spain, the southernmost area of Christian western Europe. Muslim forces advanced halfway into France before the Christian Franks stopped them at the Battle of Tours in A.D. 732. This battle halted the spread of Islam into western Europe.

Muslim Divisions

While Muslim armies were achieving military success, rival groups fought for control of the caliphate, or the office of the caliph. In A.D. 661 Ali, the fourth caliph and a son-in-law of Muhammad, was fatally stabbed by a disillusioned follower. **Mu'awiyah** (moo•UH•wee•uh), one of Ali's most powerful rivals, became the first caliph of the powerful Umayyad (oo•MY•uhd) dynasty.

Followers of Ali, known as the Shiite (SHEE• EYET), never accepted Mu'awiyah's rule. When Ali died in A.D. 680, they claimed the caliphate for Ali's son, Husayn (hoo•SAYN). Umayyad troops, however, killed Husayn and a group of his followers in a battle at Karbala in present-day Iraq.

The murders of Ali and Husayn led to a permanent schism in the Islamic world. The majority of Muslims, known as the Sunni (SU•NEE), or "followers of the way," follow the teachings of Muhammad, the tradition followed by the Rightly Guided Caliphs. In Sunni Islam, the caliph may be any devout Muslim who is accepted by the people.

The Shiite, the smaller group of Muslims, live mostly in present-day Iraq and Iran. They believe that the caliphate should be held only by descendants of Muhammad through his daughter Fatimah and her husband Ali.

The Umayyads

The Umayyad dynasty, which was founded by Mu'awiyah, ruled from A.D. 661 to A.D. 750. Umayyad rulers stressed the political, rather than the religious, aspect of their office. To unite the lands conquered by the Arabs, the Umayyads moved the capital from Madinah to **Damascus**,

ABCNEWS INTERACTIVE™

VIDEODISC
Turning Points in World History

Side One
Chapter 6

Title: *Jerusalem: City of Three Faiths*
Subject: Discussion of the importance of the Holy City to three faiths
Ask: Why is Jerusalem important to Muslims? *(because Muhammad ascended from Jerusalem to heaven)*

Geography: Movement Have students draw or trace a map of the Arabian Peninsula. Have them locate and label Madinah, Makkah, the Red Sea, the Arabian Sea, and the Persian Gulf. Ask students to look at the map on this page. Why was the Arabian Peninsula a good starting point for the spread of Islam? *(near overland trade routes and Red Sea and Persian Gulf water routes)* **L2**

Map Study

Answer
The Muslim defeat at the Battle of Tours prevented the spread of Islam into France.

Map Skills Practice

Reading a Map Which caliphs added most of the territory in Europe and North Africa? *(Umayyads)* Which added most of the territory in Asia and North Africa? *(the Rightly Guided Caliphs)*

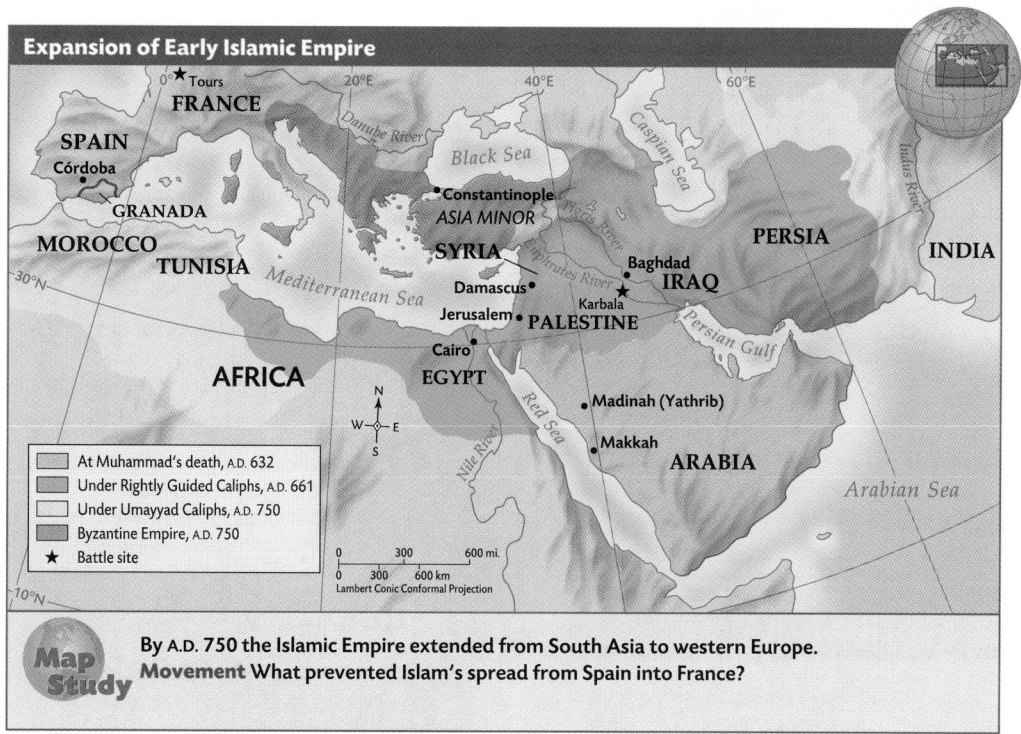

Expansion of Early Islamic Empire

At Muhammad's death, A.D. 632
Under Rightly Guided Caliphs, A.D. 661
Under Umayyad Caliphs, A.D. 750
Byzantine Empire, A.D. 750
★ Battle site

0   300   600 mi.
0   300   600 km
Lambert Conic Conformal Projection

Map Study By A.D. 750 the Islamic Empire extended from South Asia to western Europe. **Movement** What prevented Islam's spread from Spain into France?

Chapter 3 *Regional Civilizations* **107**

MEETING SPECIAL NEEDS ACTIVITY

Learning Style: Verbal/Linguistic Ask students to imagine that they are followers of Muhammad in Madinah during his lifetime. Have them write letters to Muhammad praising him for the improved status of women under Islam. Letters should mention specific improvements, such as abolishing the killing of female infants. Proofread each student's letter individually, pointing out mistakes in grammar, fuzzy passages, and unclear statements. Give specific suggestions as to how to improve these weaknesses. **L2**

Critical Thinking Have students list reasons for the rise of the Abbasids. Have them single out the reason they consider most important and defend it in a written paragraph or in a class discussion. (*Choices might include Shiite opposition to the Umayyads, or non-Arab Muslims' dissatisfaction with Umayyad policies.*) **L2**

Economics Have students discuss how they think the spread of Islam enriched the Islamic state. They may discuss such topics as new tax monies, trading opportunities, natural resources, and skills of conquered peoples. Explain that the Arabs also absorbed the traditions of the conquered peoples and synthesized them into a unique culture. **L3**

World History and Art Transparency 14, *Court of the Lions, The Alhambra*

Syria, which was more centrally located in the expanding state. They also made Arabic the official language, built roads, and established postal routes. One of the strengths of Umayyad rule was a civil service made up of well-trained bureaucrats who had served as officials in the Byzantine and Persian Empires.

Umayyad rule also improved conditions for many, particularly Jews and non-Greek Christians, who had suffered under Byzantine rule. They had to pay a special tax, but they were tolerated because they believed in one God. The great Arab commander Khalid ibn al-Walid, who had led the conquest of Syria and Persia, described Muslim policy:

> In the name of Allah, the compassionate, the merciful, this is what Khalid ibn al-Walid would grant to the inhabitants of Damascus. . . . He promises to give them security for their lives, property, and churches. Their city wall shall not be demolished, neither shall any Muslim be

quartered in their houses. Thereunto we give to them the pact of Allah and the protection of His Prophet, the Caliphs and the believers. So long as they pay the tax, nothing but good shall befall them. "

The Abbasids

Despite this enlightened outlook, Umayyad rule caused dissatisfaction among non-Arab Muslims. They paid higher taxes, received lower wages in the army and government, and were discriminated against socially. In A.D. 747 various anti-Umayyad groups joined forces, and in three years of fighting, overwhelmed the Umayyads. The new caliph, Abu'l-'Abbas, established the Abbasid (uh•BA•suhd) dynasty and had a new city, **Baghdad**, built on the banks of the Tigris River. Baghdad lay at the crossroads of the trade routes that stretched from the Mediterranean Sea to East Asia.

The Abbasid Empire reached its height under Caliph **Harun al-Rashid** (ha•ROON ahl•rah•SHEED), who ruled from A.D. 786 to A.D. 809.

Images of the Times

Islamic Art and Architecture

Inspired by their faith, artists and architects of Islam created unequaled geometric designs, floral patterns, and calligraphy.

Carpets and other textiles were turned into fine art pieces by the skilled hands of Islamic weavers.

Ornate bookbinding reflected the importance of the book in Islamic civilization.

108

Images of the Times — Islamic Art and Architecture

Although the Quran neither prohibits nor allows the representation of living things, by the middle of the eighth century such a prohibition became a standard element of Islamic thought. In spite of this prohibition, Islamic artists produced elaborate arabesques and developed a stylistic form of calligraphy.

The Alhambra (in Arabic, "the red," probably from the color of the outer wall's bricks) was built in Granada, Spain, mainly between A.D. 1238 and A.D. 1358. The Alhambra has six courts, of which the Court of the Myrtles is the most famous. It leads into the huge Hall of Ambassadors.

During this time, the Abbasids developed a sophisticated, urban civilization based on the diversity of the empire's peoples. Harun and his successors lived in splendor apart from their subjects, but they worked to ensure equality among all Muslims, Arab and non-Arab. They set up a new ruling group that included Muslims of many nationalities.

The Abbasids ruled the Islamic state from A.D. 750 to A.D. 1258; during this time, however, many of lands won earlier by the Umayyads broke free from Baghdad. In central Asia, Persian Muslims set up the Samanid dynasty and transformed cities, such as Bukhara, Samarkand, and Tashkent, into major commercial, religious, and educational centers. Meanwhile, one of the last Umayyad princes fled to Spain and set up an independent Umayyad state there. Also, the Fatimids, an Egyptian dynasty, gained control over areas in North Africa and the Middle East. By the A.D. 1000s, the Abbasids ruled little more than the area around Baghdad.

Islamic Life

Although the Islamic state had a diverse population, Islam and the Arabic language provided a sense of unity. The widespread use of Arabic, the language of the Quran, enabled government officials, thinkers, and scientists from different lands to communicate with one another.

Family Life

Early Islam stressed the equality of all believers before God; however, as in the case of Christian and Jewish communities of the time, Islamic communities gave men and women distinct roles and rights. The Quran told male Muslims that "men are responsible for women." A woman's social position was therefore defined by her relationship as wife, mother, daughter, or sister to the male members of her family. Islam did, however, improve the position of women. It forbade the tribal custom of killing female infants and also limited polygamy (puh•LIH•guh•mee),

Court of the Myrtles, Alhambra, Granada, Spain, remains as a striking example of intricate Islamic architectural design.

Social Life Have students write paragraphs defending or rebutting the following statement: "Outside the home, Islamic society was a man's world." Use students' paragraphs as a springboard for a class discussion of gender roles in Muslim society. **L2**

Independent Practice

Guided Reading Activity 3-2 **L1**

People in World History Profile 19

Time Line Ask students to chart the chronology of the Islamic state. Have them find the year of as many significant events as possible and arrange the events in chronological order on their charts. Provide these dates to get students started:

ca. 570 birth of Muhammad

632 death of Muhammad; succession of Abu Bakr as first caliph

1258 Mongols capture Baghdad, ending Abbasid caliphate **L1**

REFLECTING ON THE TIMES

1. What details characterize the interior walls of the Court of the Myrtles?
2. Why do you think the decorative arts flourished in the Islamic world during this period?

109

ANSWERS TO REFLECTING ON THE TIMES

1. geometric designs, calligraphy, floral patterns
2. The Islamic state was prosperous; as it expanded into new territories, it synthesized local traditions into Islamic forms.

Social Life Ask students to research the status of women in the Islamic state and in another culture such as that of Native Americans. Have students write a paper that compares the status and the relative freedom and independence of women in both cultures. Display the papers or have several students read their papers aloud in class. **L2**

you don't say...

Originally, **"bazaar"** referred to the public market districts of Persian towns. The word spread from Persia to Arabia and other parts of the Islamic state, including Turkey, North Africa, and India. In current English usage it may mean a store offering many types of goods for sale, a sale of contributed articles to benefit a cause, or a Middle Eastern marketplace.

Puzzle Have students make a crossword puzzle by using Islamic words from this section. The puzzle may include proper nouns, common nouns, adjectives, and verbs. Students should construct a grid for their puzzle and write short clues for the words. Have students solve each other's puzzles. **L2**

or the practice that allowed a man to have more than one wife. Also, a woman had complete control over her own property.

Cities and Trade

Although most Arabs lived in rural or desert places, the leadership of the Islamic state came from the cities. Many cities, such as Damascus, in Syria, developed as trading centers even before the rise of Islam. Others, such as Kufa, in Iraq, developed from military towns set up during the conquests.

The main religious, government, and business buildings were at the center of the city. Dominating the skyline were graceful mosques, or Muslim places of worship, and their slender minarets, or towers from which people were called to prayer five times daily. Mosques usually included schools, shelters for travelers, and a prayer hall, where worshipers gathered on Friday.

Another important area in the typical Muslim city was the bazaar, or marketplace. Muslim merchants dominated trade throughout the Middle East and North Africa until the A.D. 1400s. Caravans traveled overland from Baghdad to China. Muslim traders crossed the Indian Ocean gathering cargoes of Indian rubies, Chinese silk, and Southeast Asian spices. Gold, ivory, and enslaved people were brought from Africa. From the Islamic world came spices, textiles, glass, and carpets.

The destination of these goods was the city bazaars. In major cities the bazaars consisted of mazes of shops and stalls, often enclosed to shut out the glare of the sun. Buyers at the major bazaars included Europeans who purchased Asian goods and then shipped them across the Mediterranean Sea to Italy and other parts of Europe.

Rural Areas

Because of the dry climate and the scarcity of water, growing food was difficult in most of the Islamic territory. Farmers, however, worked efficiently. They increased yields by irrigating their fields, rotating crops, and fertilizing the land. Most productive land was held by large landowners who received grants from the government. They had large estates and employed farmers from nearby villages. Muslim farms produced wheat, rice, beans, melons, cucumbers, mint, apricots, and figs.

Islamic Science and Art

The use of Arabic encouraged cultural diffusion throughout the Islamic world. Between the A.D. 800s and the A.D. 1300s, Islamic scientists, thinkers,

and artists made important contributions in many areas of the sciences and the arts. In mathematics, astronomy, chemistry, and medicine, Muslim scholars based their work on two main intellectual traditions. The first, and most important, was that of Greece. The second was that of India, which came to the Arabs by way of Persia.

Mathematics

As you read in Chapter 2, Gupta mathematicians in India devised the numerals we know as Arabic numerals and the concept of zero. Muslim mathematicians adopted these numerals and used them in a place-value system. In this system, today used worldwide, a number's value is determined by the position of its digits. The place-value system made possible great achievements in mathematics.

Muslim mathematicians invented algebra and expressed equations to define curves and lines. Their work in geometry led to the development of trigonometry, which was used to calculate the distance to a star and the speed of a falling object. Mathematicians were also interested in practical applications, such as devising pumps and fountains and applying their skills to building and surveying.

Astronomy and Geography

Muslim astronomers made observations of the skies and produced physical and mathematical models of the universe. They improved on a Greek device called the astrolabe, with which they determined the positions of stars, the movements of planets, and the time. The astrolabe made navigation easier and safer.

Using the astrolabe, Muslim geographers measured the size and circumference of the earth with accuracy unmatched until the 1900s. From such studies, geographers concluded that the earth was round, although most continued to accept the Greek theory that heavenly bodies revolve around the earth. By the A.D. 1100s, Muslim geographers had determined the basic outlines of Asia, Europe, and North Africa and had produced the first accurate maps of the Eastern Hemisphere.

Chemistry and Medicine

Muslims developed the equipment and methods that are still used in modern chemistry. The renowned chemist and physician **al-Razi** (ahl•RAH•zee), who lived from A.D. 865 to A.D. 925, classified chemical substances as animal, mineral, or vegetable, a classification system that remains in use today.

Islamic physicians also made breakthroughs in medicine. Al-Razi compiled a medical encyclopedia describing the origins and symptoms of diseases. In

MAKING CONNECTIONS ACTIVITIES

The Arts Muslims reproduced their sacred text, the Quran, in beautiful handwritten script. Other cultures have done likewise. Have students work together to create a bulletin-board display showing examples of how Christian, Jewish, and Islamic sacred scriptures have been written by scribes over the ages.

L2

Religion Have students research the Muslim celebration that occurs on the last day of Ramadan. Have them write short reports in which they compare customs for that holiday with those for Christmas or Hanukkah. **L2**

the A.D. 900s, the doctor Ibn Sina (IH•buhn SEE•nuh) produced the *Canon of Medicine,* a volume that offered diagnosis and treatment for many illnesses. Another physician, Ibn al-Haytham, founded the science of optics, or the study of light and its effect on sight. As a result of these and other achievements, Muslim medicine was centuries ahead of the medicine practiced in the West.

Art and Literature

Islamic artistic creativity reached its fullest development in architecture, particularly in the building and decorating of mosques. Muslim theologians, opposed to idol worship, discouraged artists from making images or pictures of living creatures. Instead, artists used the beautiful script of written Arabic in an art form known as calligraphy (kuh•LIH•gruh•fee), or the art of elegant handwriting, to decorate public walls with passages from the Quran. Often calligraphy was accompanied by geometric designs entwined with plants, leaves, flowers, and stars.

Until the A.D. 600s, Arabic literature consisted mostly of poetry passed orally from one generation to the next. After the rise of Islam, religion had much influence in the creation of Arabic literature. The Quran, the first and greatest work in Arabic prose, was familiar to every Muslim, and its style influenced Islamic writing.

During the Abbasid period, Islamic literature blossomed as a result of contact with Greek thought, Hindu legends, and Persian court epics. One of the best known works of this time is the *Rubaiyat* by **Omar Khayyám** (OH•MAHR KY•YAHM), a Persian mathematician and poet. You may also have heard some of the stories found in *A Thousand and One Nights,* also known as *The Arabian*

History & Art Turkish miniature depicting angels, from the *Ajac, ib Mahlukat* by Sururi, A.D. 1500s. British Museum, London, England *What cultural influences shaped the development of Islamic arts?*

Nights—stories such as "Sinbad the Sailor," "Aladdin and His Lamp," and "Ali Baba and the Forty Thieves." Originating in the Middle East, India, and other lands, the tales reflect the multinational character of the Islamic state.

Philosophy and History

Muslim philosophers tried to reconcile the teachings of the Quran with Greek philosophy. They believed that religious truths could be analyzed and defended using logic. Many of their works were translated into Latin and later brought a

Who?What?Where?When?

Kufic script is the earliest Islamic style of calligraphy used to transcribe the Quran. The script's name comes from the Iraqi city of Kufa, where it may have originated. Kufa was a center of Arab culture and learning from the eighth to the tenth centuries. From about the twelfth century, Kufic script was not generally used except as a decorative border around later scripts.

ASSESS

Check for Understanding

Assign Section 2 Review as homework or as an in-class activity.

🖥 Use Student Self-Test and Review Software to review Section 2.

History & Art According to Islamic myth, God created angels from light before creating Adam from clay. With the exception of Iblis (Satan), all the angels obeyed God's order to bow down to Adam. Upon dying, a person is questioned by two angels. The archangel Israfil will blow a trumpet to awaken the dead for the day of resurrection.
Answer to Caption: *the Quran and contact with Greek thought, Hindu legends, and Persian court epics*

CRITICAL THINKING ACTIVITY

Making Comparisons/Drawing Conclusions The Muslims made important contributions in many fields of human knowledge and endeavor: mathematics, astronomy, geography, chemistry, medicine, philosophy. Have students decide in which area they think Muslim contributions were the most significant. Have them write one-page papers defending their choice. Their arguments should include comparisons with Islamic achievements in other fields. **L2**

Visualizing
History
In A.D. 642 the
Arabs conquered Isfahan, which is
about 210 miles (340 kilometers)
south of Tehran. The founder of the
Seljuk dynasty made Isfahan its capital. Although Isfahan declined after
the fall of the Seljuks in about A.D.
1200, the city's fortunes began to
rise in A.D. 1598, when Shah Abbas I
the Great transformed it into one of
the most magnificent cities of the
seventeenth century. Today the city
is a major textile center.
Answer to Caption: *The early
historical events of Islam are traced
in chronicles.*

Evaluate

 Section Quiz 3-2

Use the Testmaker to create a
customized quiz for Section 2.

Reteach

Ask students to write five sentences that describe specific
Islamic achievements in areas
such as mathematics, astronomy,
and medicine. Have students
read their sentences in class and
correct any misstatements.

Enrich

Have students find out more
about the four Rightly Guided
Caliphs and write a two-page
report about them.

CLOSE

Have students make a chart that
compares the major features of
Islamic civilization with those of
another civilization they have
studied, such as Egyptian, Greek,
Roman, or Byzantine.

Visualizing History A modern Islamic mosque in Isfahan, Iran, one of the most
magnificent cities in the early Muslim world. *What kind of
writings traced the early historical events of Islam?*

new understanding of philosophy to western
Europe. Ibn-Rushd, a judge in Córdoba, was the
most noted Islamic thinker, and Christian scholars
in western Europe later used his commentaries on
Aristotle.

Moses Maimonides (my•MAH•nuh•
DEEZ), a Spanish Jew born in A.D. 1135, was a noted
philosopher who lived in Egypt. Like several
Muslim scholars, Maimonides attempted to reconcile religious faith and reason. One of
his major contributions, *Guide to the Perplexed*,
was written in Arabic and later translated into
Hebrew and Latin. After his death in A.D. 1204,
Maimonides was recognized as one of the world's
great philosophers.

Because their religion was based on historical
events, Islamic scholars were interested in writing
history. At first they wrote chronicles, or accounts
in which events are arranged in the order in which
they occurred. Later, historians began to organize
their accounts around events in the lives of rulers
and others. The first Muslim historian to examine
history scientifically was a North African diplomat
named **Ibn-Khaldun** (IH•buhn-KAL•DOON). He
looked for laws and cause-and-effect relationships
to explain historical events. Ibn-Khaldun believed
that history was a process shaped by geography
and economics as well as by moral and spiritual
forces. Ibn-Khaldun's work later influenced
European historical writing.

SECTION 2 REVIEW

Recall
1. **Define** hajj, caliph, mosque,
bazaar, calligraphy.
2. **Identify** Muhammad, Quran,
Mu'awiyah, the Shiite, the
Sunni, Harun al-Rashid, al-Razi,
Omar Khayyám, Moses
Maimonides, Ibn-Khaldun.

3. **Explain** What made life
possible in the harsh environment of the Arabian Peninsula?
Critical Thinking
4. **Analyzing Information** In
what ways was Islam a unique
religion? In what ways was it
similar to other religions that

were also founded in the Middle
East Judaism and Christianity?
Understanding Themes
5. **Movement** How did expansion affect the ethnic diversity
of the Islamic state? How did
expansion affect the state's
stability?

112 **Chapter 3** *Regional Civilizations*

SECTION 2 REVIEW ANSWERS

1. All vocabulary words are defined in the
Glossary.
2. Muhammad, 106; Quran, 106; Mu'awiyah,
107; the Shiite, 107; the Sunni, 107;
Harun al-Rashid, 108; al-Razi, 110; Omar
Khayyám, 111; Moses Maimonides, 112;

Ibn-Khaldun, 112
3. oases, tribal ties, cooperation
4. Answers may refer to pre-Islamic idol worship or to Christian reverence for icons.
5. **MOVEMENT** Expansion increased
diversity but led to instability.

A.D. 496
Frankish King Clovis accepts Catholicism.

C. A.D. 900
Feudalism takes hold in Northern France.

C. A.D. 1000
Peasants begin to use three-field system to farm.

A.D. 1215
England's King John signs Magna Carta.

Section 3

Early Medieval Europe

Setting the Scene

▶ **Terms to Define**
feudalism, chivalry, manorialism, serf, sacrament, lay investiture, heresy, friar, common law

▶ **People to Meet**
Clovis, Charlemagne, Benedict, Gregory VII, Innocent III, Francis of Assisi, Alfred the Great, William the Conqueror, Philip Augustus, Otto the Great

▶ **Places to Locate**
Frankish Empire, France, Germany, Italy, Scandinavia, England

Find Out How were loyalties maintained in a divided and often violent Europe?

The Storyteller

Alcuin, a Benedictine monk, arose to begin his day. The day's work in a monastery depended on sunlight hours, for candles were expensive and no one in medieval times had access to cheap artificial light. Because it was winter, Alcuin had to get up at 2:30 A.M., and go to bed at 6:30 P.M. after sunset.

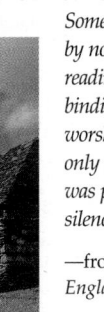

Sometimes he was already tired by noon! His workday included reading, choir practice, bookbinding, sewing, gardening, and worship services—which were the only times during the day that he was permitted to break his vow of silence and speak.

—from *Monastic Life in Medieval England*, J.C. Dickinson, 1962

Irish monastery

By A.D. 500, Germanic invasions had all but destroyed the western Roman Empire. Trade declined, cities fell into decay, and law and order vanished. For most people, life did not extend beyond the tiny villages where they were born, lived, and died.

Western Europe was so backward because of this decline that the early part of this period was once called "the Dark Ages." Scholars later combined the Latin terms *medium* (middle) and *aevum* (age) to form the term *medieval*, recognizing that this period was an era of transition between ancient and modern times. Out of the violent medieval period, or the Middle Ages, a dynamic new European civilization arose. It combined elements of classical and Germanic cultures with Christian beliefs.

The Frankish Empire

During the A.D. 400s, the Franks, who settled in what is now France and western Germany, emerged as the strongest Germanic group. Their early rulers, known as Merovingian (MEHR•uh•VIHN•jee•uhn) kings for the ruler Merowig, held power until the early A.D. 700s.

Merovingian Rulers

In A.D. 481 a brutal and wily warrior named **Clovis** became king of the Franks. Fifteen years later, Clovis became the first Germanic ruler to accept Catholicism. Clovis's military victories and his religious conversion gave his throne stability.

By A.D. 700 the Frankish kingdom had declined. Political power gradually passed from kings to government officials known as mayors of the palace. In A.D. 714 Charles Martel, or "Charles

Chapter 3 *Regional Civilizations* **113**

Chapter 3 Section 3

SECTION THEME

▶ **Conflict** European kings, feudal lords, and popes struggle for political dominance.

Find Out

Answer: *They were maintained through the Church, feudal ties, and the manorial system.*

FOCUS

Section Objective
Name the achievements of medieval European monarchs.

BELLRINGER
Motivational Activity

Before taking roll at the beginning of the class period, project Section Focus Transparency 3-3 and have students answer the activity questions. Discuss students' responses.

This activity is also available as a blackline master.

Vocabulary Pre-check
Use the Vocabulary Puzzle-Maker to create a puzzle that reinforces the vocabulary terms in this section. **L1**

SECTION RESOURCES

Reproducible Masters
- Reproducible Lesson Plan 3-3
- Guided Reading Activity 3-3
- People in World History Profiles 21, 22
- Section Quiz 3-3

Transparencies
- Section Focus Transparency 3-3
- World History and Art Transparency 15, *Cover of the Lindau Gospels*
- The Middle Ages

Multimedia
- The Middle Ages
- Focus on World Art Print 14
- Vocabulary PuzzleMaker Software
- Student Self-Test and Review Software
- Testmaker
- The Middle Ages

TEACH

Guided Practice

THEME Conflict

Discuss the word *conflict* as it applies to England in this section. What specific conflicts are mentioned in the text? (*military conflicts between the Anglo-Saxons and the Danes and between the English and the Normans; political conflicts between the monarchy and the nobility*) **L1 LEP**

Map Study

Answer

France, Belgium, the Netherlands, most of Germany and Austria, northern Italy

Map Skills Practice

Reading a Map How far from north to south did the Frankish Empire stretch at its greatest extent? (*about 1,000 miles [1,600 kilometers]*)

Charlemagne's Realm

Why was the formation of Charlemagne's realm a significant milestone?

It was the first time most western Europeans were under one government since the time of the Roman Empire; although it did not outlast him, Charlemagne's empire became a model for later efforts toward European unity.

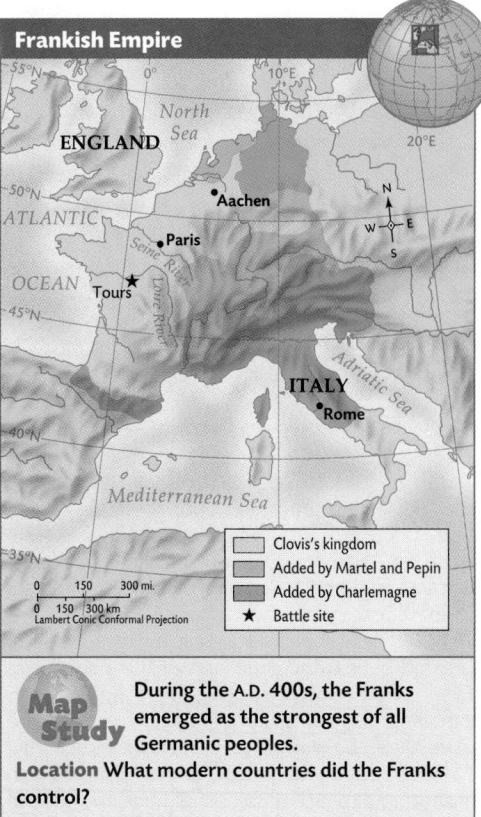

Frankish Empire

- ENGLAND
- North Sea
- ATLANTIC OCEAN
- Aachen
- Paris
- Seine River
- Tours ★
- Loire River
- Rhine River
- ITALY
- Rome
- Adriatic Sea
- Mediterranean Sea

	Clovis's kingdom
	Added by Martel and Pepin
	Added by Charlemagne
★	Battle site

0 150 300 mi.
0 150 300 km
Lambert Conic Conformal Projection

Map Study During the A.D. 400s, the Franks emerged as the strongest of all Germanic peoples.
Location What modern countries did the Franks control?

---

the Hammer" became mayor of the palace. When Muslim forces threatened Europe in A.D. 732, Charles led the successful defense of Tours, in France. This victory won him great prestige and ensured that Christianity would remain the dominant religion of Europe.

Charlemagne's Realm

In the A.D. 750s, Martel's son, Pepin the Short, became king of the Franks and strengthened Frankish ties to the pope in Rome. Pepin's son, **Charlemagne,** or Charles the Great, became the Frankish king in A.D. 771. Charlemagne was one of Europe's great monarchs. During his reign Charlemagne nearly doubled the borders of his kingdom to include Germany, France, northern Spain, and most of Italy. His enlarged domain

became known as the **Frankish Empire**. For the first time since the fall of Rome, most western Europeans were ruled by one government.

Because few western Europeans could read and write, Charlemagne encouraged the formation of schools in churches and monasteries. He gathered scholars from all over Europe to teach in his palace school. These scholars helped preserve classical learning by making accurate Latin copies of ancient religious manuscripts and Roman classics. When knowledge spread from Charlemagne's court to other areas of Europe, western Europeans became united by a common set of ideas.

A Christian Empire

One of the ideas that united western Europeans was the creation of a Christian Roman Empire. In A.D. 800 Charlemagne came to Rome to defend Pope Leo III against the Roman nobles. To show his gratitude, Leo crowned Charlemagne the new Roman emperor. As protector of the Church and ruler of much of western Europe, Charlemagne wanted the title, but he had misgivings about receiving it from the pope. By crowning a monarch, the pope seemed to be saying that church officials were superior to rulers.

In spite of his concern, Charlemagne accepted his duties as emperor and worked to strengthen the empire. Because the central bureaucracy was small, he relied on local officials to assist him. These officials solved local problems, stopped feuds, protected the weak, and raised armies for the emperor. Each year royal messengers went on inspections after which they informed Charlemagne about the performance of the local administrators. The emperor also traveled throughout the empire observing the work of his officials firsthand.

More than anything else, Charlemagne's forceful personality held his empire together. His death in A.D. 814 left a void that his successors could not fill. In A.D. 843 Charlemagne's three feuding grandsons agreed in the Treaty of Verdun to divide the Frankish Empire. Charles the Bald took the western part, an area that covered most of present-day **France**. Louis the German acquired the eastern portion, which today is **Germany**. Lothair, who became the Holy Roman emperor, took a strip of land in the middle of the empire stretching from the North Sea southward to **Italy**.

Invasions

While internal feuding weakened the Frankish domains, invasions by Muslims, Slavs, Magyars, and Vikings nearly destroyed them. The most threatening attacks came from the Vikings, raiders from

---

COOPERATIVE LEARNING ACTIVITY

Role Play Have the class create a historical account of a medieval village under Viking attack. Some students should take on the roles of Vikings, keeping a record of their voyage, their intentions, and their strategies for attack. Other students may assume the roles of clergy members, keeping the village's official records. Still others may represent the villagers, recording the raid with drawings of the encounter. Encourage students to research and to include vivid details in their projects. Conclude the activity with a class presentation. **L1 LEP**

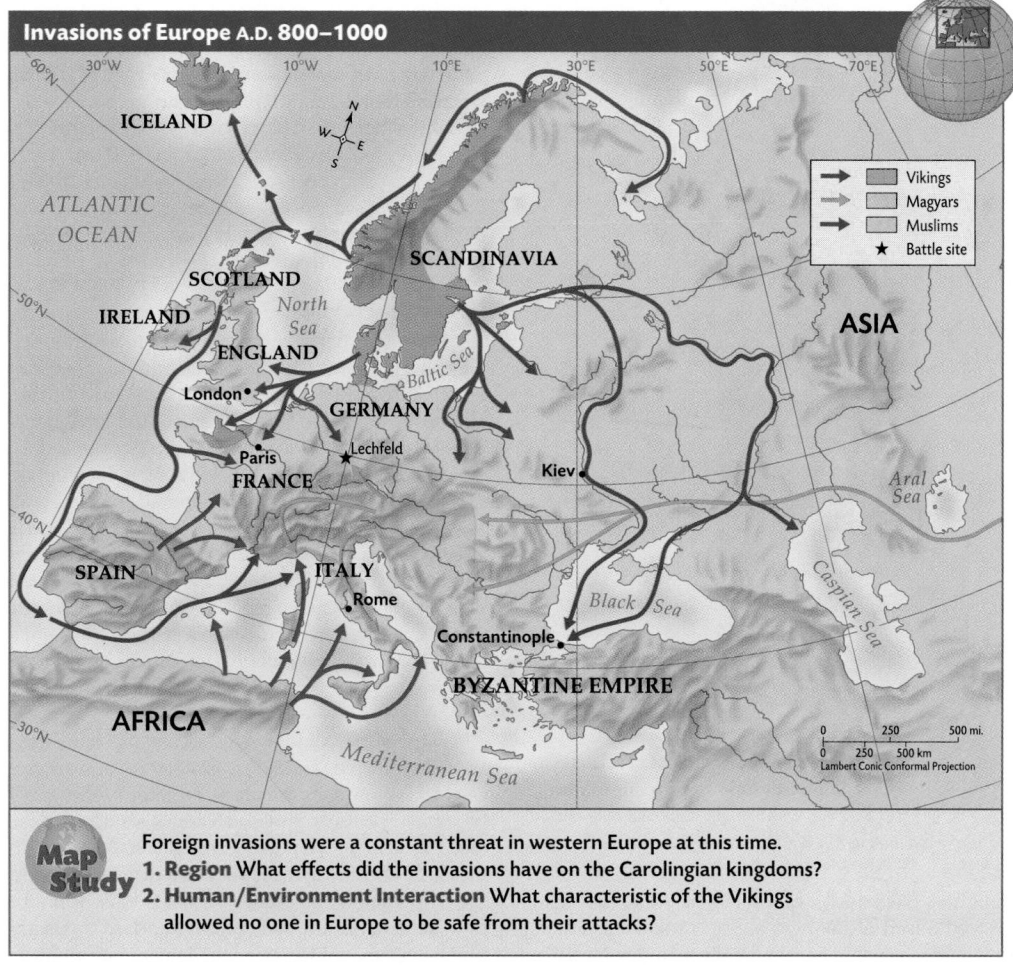

Invasions of Europe A.D. 800–1000

ICELAND

ATLANTIC OCEAN

SCOTLAND
IRELAND
ENGLAND
London
Paris
FRANCE
SPAIN

SCANDINAVIA
North Sea
Baltic Sea
GERMANY
Lechfeld
ITALY
Rome

ASIA
Kiev
Aral Sea
Black Sea
Caspian Sea
Constantinople
BYZANTINE EMPIRE

AFRICA
Mediterranean Sea

→ Vikings
→ Magyars
→ Muslims
★ Battle site

0 250 500 mi.
0 250 500 km
Lambert Conic Conformal Projection

Foreign invasions were a constant threat in western Europe at this time.
1. **Region** What effects did the invasions have on the Carolingian kingdoms?
2. **Human/Environment Interaction** What characteristic of the Vikings allowed no one in Europe to be safe from their attacks?

Scandinavia to the north. Skilled in sailing and trading, the Vikings moved along the Atlantic and Mediterranean coasts of Europe. They temporarily held England and northwestern France and also settled in present-day Ukraine and Russia. By A.D. 1000 some Viking groups had settled the North Atlantic islands of Greenland and Iceland, and even reached North America.

Feudalism

The people of western Europe suffered at the hands of the Vikings and other invaders. These raids isolated communities and severely weakened the authority of monarchs. Trade diminished, and many areas faced economic collapse. With the decline of central government, a new political system known as feudalism took hold in northern France around A.D. 900 and spread through the rest of western Europe by the A.D. mid-1000s.

Feudal Relationships

Feudalism was a highly localized form of government that stressed ties of mutual aid between kings and nobles. Kings turned to lords, or nobles, and granted them fiefs, or estates with peasants. Lords receiving the fiefs were given many governmental powers as well as the right to pass on these lands and responsibilities to their heirs. In return, nobles used income from their fiefs to provide mounted warriors called knights, horses, and battle equipment for the royal army.

In theory, feudal relationships were like a pyramid. The king was at the top. In the middle were various ranks of lords. At the bottom were

Chapter 3 *Regional Civilizations* **115**

MEETING SPECIAL NEEDS ACTIVITY

Learning Style: Verbal/Linguistic Some students may have difficulty differentiating between feudalism, a political system, and manorialism, an economic system. Have students write on the chalkboard the headings *Political* and *Economic*. Then introduce various activities, and ask students to place them in the appropriate column. Activities might include voting, shopping, baby-sitting, eating at a restaurant, depositing a check, and writing a letter to the editor of the local paper. **L1**

Visualizing History A suit of armor made of steel, brass, and leather belonging to an English knight, Master Jacobe. *What knightly code became the basis of good manners in Western society?*

knights. Each lord was a vassal—a noble who served a lord of the next higher rank. In practice, however, a noble might be both a lord and a vassal, since a noble could pledge his allegiance to more than one lord. Conflicts of loyalty often arose if one of a vassal's lords went to war with another.

Because of the lack of a strong central government, warfare occurred frequently in feudal society. As a result, every noble built a castle, or fortified manor house, for defense against enemies. To prepare for combat and develop their military skills, knights participated in mock battles called tournaments. As time passed, medieval society took steps to limit the brutality caused by war. For example, the behavior of knights was governed by a code of chivalry. This code called for knights to be brave in battle, fight fairly, keep promises, defend Christianity, and treat women of noble birth in a courteous manner. Chivalry eventually became the basis for the development of good manners in Western society.

During the Middle Ages, French epics known as *chansons de geste,* or "songs of high deeds," celebrated the courage of feudal warriors. The *Song of Roland,* written around A.D. 1100, gives an account of the chivalrous defense of Christianity by Charlemagne's soldiers. In southern France in the A.D. 1100s and A.D. 1200s, traveling poet-musicians known as troubadours composed poems and songs about love and the feats of knights. They helped define the ideal knight celebrated in the code of chivalry.

Life of the Nobility

Within his fief, a lord had almost total authority. He collected rents from peasants and administered justice in disputes between his vassals. Any outside attempt to seize the land or control the inhabitants of his fief met with violent resistance.

In contrast to a lord, a lady, or noblewoman, had few, if any, rights. A noblewoman could be wed as early as her twelfth birthday to a man her father selected. Her primary duties lay in bringing up children and taking care of the household. Some women, however, shared the supervision of the estate with the lord and took over their husband's duties while the men were away at war.

Peasant Life

During the Middle Ages, economic life across Europe centered around a system of agricultural production called manorialism. In return for a lord's protection, peasants provided various services for the lord. Chief among the peasants' obligations were to farm the lord's land and to make various payments of goods.

The manors, or estates, of lords varied in size from several hundred to several hundred thousand acres. Each manor included the lord's manor house, pastures for livestock, fields for crops, forest areas, and a village where the peasants lived. Most of the peasants were serfs, people who were bound to the

Footnotes to History **Identifying a Knight** To identify themselves, knights had individual designs painted on their shields and tunics. Each particular design became known as the knight's coat of arms. In noble families, coats of arms were passed down from one generation to the next. The flags of some modern countries are based on the system of designs that were developed by the knights.

1–Moat; 2–Drawbridge; 3–Guardroom; 4–Latrine; 5–Armory; 6–Soldiers' quarters; 7–Kitchen garden; 8–Storerooms and servants' quarters; 9–Kitchen; 10–Great hall; 11–Chapel; 12–Lord and lady's quarters; 13–Inner ward

Harry Bliss

Life in the Castle

The medieval castle was both fortress and home. The first castles, raised in the A.D. 900s, were square towers encircled by wooden ramparts. By the A.D. 1100s, castles had become mighty stone fortresses. From the towers and walls archers took aim and soldiers dumped boiling liquids on attackers. The castle was surrounded by a moat—a body of water encircling the castle—that could be crossed when a drawbridge was let down.

Inside it was crowded, smelly, dirty, and damp. The animals ate and slept with the people, and the smell of animal and human waste was everywhere. The occupants of the castle had to contend with cold earthen or stone floors, drafty halls, smoky rooms, and windows without glass that let in cold and heat along with light. Not even the lord and lady had their own private room. Grand but never comfortable, the castle's main purpose was military security.

TEACH

Tell students that the center of castle activity was the great hall, which changed greatly during the castle-building period. Though initially drafty, smoky, and dark, it gradually became more comfortable with tapestries on the walls and balconies for musicians. Ask students which part of the castle they think was the most important. (*Answers will vary. Without walls and a moat, a castle could be stormed. But without a well, livestock, and gardens, the inhabitants would starve during a siege.*)

CURRICULUM CONNECTION

LITERATURE
One of Europe's best-preserved castles is the Castle of Chillon, built in Switzerland on an island in Lake Geneva. A famous poem by Lord Byron, published in 1816, tells the story of "The Prisoner of Chillon," who was imprisoned in the castle for so long that he lost his desire for freedom.

Cultural Perspectives

Castles Medieval castles had their origins in the early Byzantine Empire. Byzantine general Belisarius constructed square forts with tall corner towers during his North African campaigns. Muslim conquerors of North Africa copied the idea and built similar structures in Spain. Castles spread from there to France during the tenth century, where they were first used as private fortresses.

Uniformity The goal of the medieval Church was to unify western Europe in accordance with the teachings and beliefs of Christianity. Does the Catholic Church play the same role today in the Western world? (No, because it is not the only Christian church, and there are other non-Christian religions as well.) What factors tend to create uniformity in the United States today? (Answers will vary but might include: the English language, our government under the Constitution, and the mass media.) **L2**

World History and Art Transparency 15, *Cover of the Lindau Gospels*

Global Gourmet

Southern Europe The knot-shaped pretzels that we enjoy today were the creation of medieval monks, given as rewards to children for memorizing their prayers. (The Latin word *pretiola* means "small reward.") The shape represented the folded arms of children at prayer.

Visualizing History An illustration from the *Trés Riches Heures du Duc de Berry* shows peasants at work outside a castle. *Why did feudal lords need castles?*

manor and could not leave it without permission. But the serfs were not slaves—they could not be "sold" apart from the land on which they lived.

Warfare and invasions made trade almost impossible, so the manor had to produce nearly everything its residents needed. The manorial system normally produced only enough food to support the peasants and the lord's household. However, farmers developed new ways to boost productivity and to ease the threat of famine. For example, a new, heavier type of plow improved methods of planting and reduced the amount of time spent in the fields. Also, instead of dividing plots of land into two fields, one of which lay fallow, or unsown, each year, farmers in the A.D. 1000s began using a three-field system. One field might be planted with winter wheat, a second with spring wheat and vegetables, and a third left

fallow. The next year, different crops were planted in the fallow field. One of the two remaining fields was planted, and the other one was left fallow until the next year. This system produced more crops than the old system and helped to preserve the soil.

Poverty and hardship characterized peasant life, and few serfs lived beyond the age of 40. Famine, disease, and war were constant dangers. A monk of Canterbury described an English serf's account of his day:

66 I work very hard. I go out at dawn, driving the oxen to the field, and I yoke them to the plough; however hard the winter I dare not stay home for fear of my master; but, having yoked the oxen and made the ploughshare and coulter fast to the plough, every day I have to plough a whole acre or more. 99
—from Aelfric, *Colloquy*, A.D. 1005

Serfs like this man lived in tiny, one-room houses with dirt floors, no chimney, and one or two crude pieces of furniture—perhaps a table and stools. People slept huddled together for warmth. Coarse bread, a few vegetables from their gardens, and grain for porridge made up their usual diet. Meat was a rarity.

In spite of hardships, peasants were able to relax on Sundays and holy days. They enjoyed dancing, singing, and such sports as wrestling and archery. In addition, there were other amusements, such as religious plays, pageants, and shows by minstrels, or singers.

The Church

During the Middle Ages, the Catholic Church was the dominant spiritual influence in western Europe. For most people, the Church was the center of their lives. Only a small number of Europeans—mainly Jews and Muslims—did not recognize the Church's authority.

In its teachings, the Catholic Church stressed that all people were sinners and dependent on God's grace, or favor, for salvation. The only way to receive grace was by taking part in the sacraments, or church rituals. The most important sacrament was the eucharist, or holy communion, which commemorated Jesus' death on the cross.

Medieval people generally had a limited understanding of church rituals. Worship was conducted in Latin, a language few people understood. Moreover, few worshippers could read or write. What the

118 Chapter 3 *Regional Civilizations*

India, A.D. 760
Emperor Krishna of the Rashtrakuta dynasty ordered construction of the Kailasa Temple at Ellora. The temple, completed in A.D. 760, was cut from a single outcropping of rock. It was 165 feet (50 m) long and 96 feet (29 m) high. Kailasa was dedicated to the Hindu god Siva. Its elaborate carvings featured Hindu gods and mythological figures in various poses.

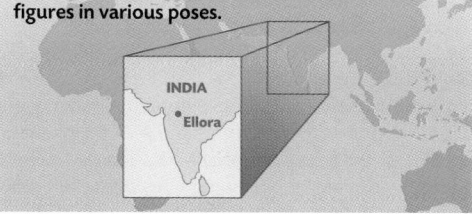

average person learned about the Christian faith came from the statues, paintings, and later the stained glass windows that adorned medieval churches.

Church Leaders

Although the Church's primary mission was spiritual, the decline of Rome in the A.D. 400s led the Church to assume many political and social tasks. During this time the bishop of Rome, now called the pope, became the strongest political leader in western Europe. He also continued to claim spiritual authority over all Christians.

The pope and the bishops and priests under him formed what is called the secular clergy because they lived in *saeculo*, a Latin phrase that means "in the world." Other clergy, known as regular clergy, lived by a *regula*, or rule. Regular clergy included monks and nuns who lived apart from society. These Christians played an important role in strengthening the medieval Church.

Monks and Missionaries

In A.D. 529 a Roman official named **Benedict** founded a monastery at Monte Cassino in Italy. His monastery became a model for monks in other communities. Benedict drew up a list of rules that provided for manual work, meditation, and prayer. According to the Benedictine Rule, the life of monks was one of poverty, chastity, and obedience to the directives of an abbot, or monastery head.

Women took part in monastic life by living in a convent under the direction of an abbess. Known as nuns, they lived simply and alternated prayer with activities such as spinning, weaving, and sewing.

They also taught needlework and the medicinal use of herbs to the daughters of the nobility.

Although monks and nuns lived apart from society, they played a crucial role in medieval life. Since few people could read or write, the regular clergy preserved ancient religious works and the classical writings. Scribes copied books by hand; creating illuminated manuscripts decorated with rich colors and detailed pictures.

Monasteries and convents also provided schools for young people, hospitals for the sick, food for the needy, and guest houses for weary travelers. They taught peasants carpentry and weaving and made improvements in agriculture that they passed on to others. Some monks and nuns became missionaries.

Pope Gregory I was so impressed with the Benedictine Rule that he adopted it to spread Christianity in Europe. In A.D. 597 he sent monks to England, where they converted the Germanic Anglo-Saxons to Catholicism. From England, missionaries carried Christianity to northern Germany. During the A.D. 600s, monasteries in Ireland sent missionaries throughout western Europe. By the A.D. mid-1000s, most western Europeans had become Catholics.

Visualizing History A young boy, having obtained the office of bishop, carries sacred church relics. *How did Pope Gregory try to stop the selection of church officials by secular rulers?*

Chapter 3 *Regional Civilizations* **119**

 **NATIONAL GEOGRAPHIC SOCIETY**

Use these materials to enrich student understanding of the culture of the Middle Ages.

- **NGS PICTURESHOW CD-ROM**
  The Middle Ages
- **NGS PICTUREPACK TRANSPARENCY SET**
  The Middle Ages

Independent Practice

📁 Guided Reading Activity 3-3 **L1**

Religion Have students speculate on what the various attractions of monastic life might have been. *(Answers may include: opportunity to better serve and worship God; desire to study or to develop the particular skills used in monasteries and convents; for women, a chance to escape a life of childbearing and child rearing.)* Discuss which of these were spiritual in nature and which were worldly. **L3**

Visualizing History Bones and other remains of saints were honored and place in elaborately decorated receptacles called reliquaries. **Answer to Caption:** *He criticized the practice of lay investiture.*

MORE ABOUT...

Church Influence Nobles gave little thought to hurting or killing peasants, serfs, and villagers, burning their crops and barns, or killing their livestock. The Church tried to stop feudal violence and bloodshed. Late in the A.D. 900s, a movement within the Church called the Peace of God tried to protect certain persons or places from violence. For example, no feudal warfare could take place on church property. Knights were forbidden to attack people on their way to church. In A.D. 1017 the Church tried to put a further ban on fighting under the Truce of God. Under this restriction, fighting was forbidden from Wednesday evening until Monday morning, on holidays, and during the religious seasons of Christmas and Lent.

The Arts Have students create posters in the style of medieval stained glass to tell a story about people or events they have studied in this section. Possible subjects include Francis of Assisi, missionary efforts in Europe, a church ritual, or the Albigensian crusade. **L2 LEP**

Biography Have students select one of the popes discussed in this section—Gregory I, Gregory VII, or Innocent III. Have them research his life, write a brief summary of his major accomplishments, and share their findings with the class. **L3**

📁 People in World History Profiles 21, 22

Linking Past and Present

Electing a Pope The pope today is still elected by a gathering of cardinals, called a "conclave." They meet no later than the twentieth day after the death of a pope and vote by secret ballot until they can achieve a two-thirds majority on a given candidate.

The Church's Power

During the Middle Ages, the Catholic Church helped to govern western Europe. This political role boosted the Church's wealth and power. Church officials received donations of land and money from rich nobles who wanted to perform acts of piety. As a result, local lords began to control many church offices and lands, contrary to church tradition. They often appointed relatives as bishops or abbots, instead of awarding those offices to the most qualified people. Furthermore, as religious leaders and monasteries grew wealthier, many church officials became increasingly careless about carrying out their religious duties.

Church Reform

By the A.D. 900s, many devout Christians were calling for reform. The reform movement began in the monasteries and soon spread throughout much of western Europe. Many reformers wanted a spiritually renewed Church to be the final authority in Western society. In A.D. 1059 a church council declared that political leaders could no longer choose the pope. Instead, the pope would be elected by a gathering of cardinals—high church officials in Rome ranking directly below the pope. In addition, the reformers insisted that the pope, not secular rulers such as lords and kings, should be the one to appoint bishops and other officials to church offices.

In A.D. 1073 a reform-minded monk named Hildebrand became Pope **Gregory VII**. Gregory believed that the pope should have complete jurisdiction over all church officials. He especially criticized the practice of lay investiture, in which secular rulers gave the symbols of office, such as a ring and a staff, to the bishops they had appointed.

Innocent III, one of the most powerful popes, also tried to reform the Catholic Church. In A.D. 1215 he called a church council that laid down strict rules for the clergy and took action to stop the spread of heresy, or the denial of church teachings. In the Middle Ages, heresy was regarded as seriously as the crime of treason is viewed today.

Other reformers of the Church during the early A.D. 1200s were friars, or wandering preachers. At a time when church leaders were criticized for their love of wealth and power, the friars lived simply and depended on gifts of food and shelter to survive. They followed monastic rules but did not isolate themselves from the rest of the Christian community. Instead, they lived in towns and preached Christianity to the people.

The best-known friars were the Franciscans and the Dominicans. The Franciscans, founded about A.D. 1210 by **Francis of Assisi**, became known for their cheerful trust in God and their respect for nature as a divine gift. The Dominicans, set up by a Spanish priest named Dominic in A.D. 1215, were well-educated preachers who could reply to the arguments of heretics. Because they were well-known and liked, both groups of friars kept many people loyal to the teachings of the Catholic Church.

The Inquisition

Church officials at first relied on persuasion to convert heretics, or those who challenged church teachings. When that failed, they used force. To seek out and punish people suspected of heresy, the Church set up a court in A.D. 1232 known as the Inquisition. Those brought before the court were urged to confess their heresies and seek forgiveness. Often, however, Inquisition officials accused people without sufficient proof; sometimes they even used torture to obtain confessions. Those who did not repent faced punishments ranging from imprisonment to loss of property and even execution.

The Inquisition, church councils, and the friars were all indications of the Church's power during the Middle Ages. By the A.D. 1000s, however, that influence was increasingly being challenged by secular rulers.

Rise of Monarchies

After Charlemagne's reign in the late A.D. 700s, European monarchs were often rulers in name only. Their lands and power were gradually lost to nobles, and the feudal system emerged to maintain law and order. However, beginning in the A.D. 1000s and A.D. 1100s, many European monarchs began to build strong states.

England

In the A.D. 400s, Germanic Angles, Saxons, and Jutes invaded the island of Britain, conquered the native Celts (KEHLTZ), and eventually set up several kingdoms. About four hundred years later, they were joined by Danes, or Danish Vikings from Scandinavia. In the late A.D. 800s, King Alfred of Wessex, known as **Alfred the Great**, defeated the Danes and united the Anglo-Saxon domains into one kingdom that became known as "Angleland," or **England**.

The Anglo-Saxon kings who followed Alfred were weak rulers. When the last of their number died in A.D. 1066, three rivals claimed the throne. One of these claimants was William, Duke of Normandy, who ruled a strong feudal territory in

COOPERATIVE LEARNING ACTIVITY

Role Play Organize the class into three groups. One group will represent missionaries who have been ordered by Pope Gregory I to convert the people of England and should describe their thoughts and goals as they prepare to leave continental Europe. The second group will represent monks and nuns who teach the young and help the sick and needy, and should explain how their work benefits others. The third group will represent the regular clergy who copy books by hand in order to preserve ancient learning, and should portray the life of a scribe. The members of each group should explain why their work is important, what their goals are, and how their work reflects their Christian beliefs. **L2**

Europe A.D. 1160

KINGDOM OF NORWAY
KINGDOM OF SWEDEN
KINGDOM OF SCOTLAND
IRELAND
WALES
North Sea
KINGDOM OF DENMARK
Baltic Sea
PRUSSIA
KIEVAN RUS
KINGDOM OF ENGLAND
London
Saxony
Aachen
Rhine River
HOLY ROMAN EMPIRE
KINGDOM OF POLAND
ATLANTIC OCEAN
Normandy
Paris
KINGDOM OF FRANCE
KINGDOM OF NAVARRE
Lechfeld
VENETIAN TERRITORIES
Venice
KINGDOM OF HUNGARY
KINGDOM OF LEÓN
Aquitaine
Genoa
Danube River
Black Sea
PORTUGAL
KINGDOM OF ARAGON
KINGDOM OF CASTILE
Corsica
Rome
BYZANTINE EMPIRE
Córdoba
Sardinia
KINGDOM OF SICILY
MUSLIM TERRITORY
Mediterranean Sea

0   150   300 mi.
0   150   300 km
Lambert Conic Conformal Projection

Map Study

In the A.D. 1100s Europe was divided into many separate kingdoms that eventually became nations.
1. **Region** According to the map, what kingdom controlled the most amount of land?
2. **Region** What kingdoms posed the greatest threat to the Holy Roman Empire?

northwestern France. William gathered a force of soldiers and invaded England in A.D. 1066. At the Battle of Hastings, he defeated his major rival for the throne, won the English crown, and earned the name **William the Conqueror**.

To keep the loyalty of his Norman vassals, William gave them the lands of Anglo-Saxon nobles. He also set up a Great Council of royal officials, bishops, and nobles to advise him. In the A.D. 1100s, William's successors, Henry I, and later, Henry II, further strengthened the English monarchy by developing a system of royal courts. In place of the old feudal rules, which differed from lord to lord, Henry II established a common law throughout the kingdom. Soon a system of trial by jury was developed to determine the guilt or innocence of those accused of crimes.

Henry II's son, John, was an ineffectual ruler whose unpopularity increased when he increased taxes and punished his enemies without trial. Alarmed at the loss of their feudal rights, a group of nobles in A.D. 1215 forced John to sign the Magna Carta, or Great Charter. Placing clear limits on royal power, the charter prevented the king from collecting taxes without the consent of the Great Council. It also guaranteed freemen, or non-serfs, the right of trial by jury. Designed to protect feudal rights, the Magna Carta over time guaranteed the rights of all English people.

A major step toward representative government occurred in A.D. 1295 when Edward I called into session the Model Parliament. This assembly of representatives from the clergy, the nobility, and the townspeople soon advised the king on matters of

Chapter 3 *Regional Civilizations* **121**

Map Study

Answers
1. *Holy Roman Empire*
2. *Kingdom of Poland, Kingdom of Hungary*

Map Skills Practice

Reading a Map What three kingdoms were located in what is now Spain? (*Aragon, Castile, and Navarre*)

 Focus on World Art Print 14, French. *William Exhorts His Troops*, from the Bayeux Tapestry

---

Cultural Perspectives

Language For years after the Norman Conquest, two languages were spoken in England—Norman French by the upper classes and Anglo-Saxon English by the lower classes. This double heritage is preserved in the English language today. The words for animals in the field (in the Middle Ages, tended by the lower classes) are Anglo-Saxon: *ox, pig,* and *sheep.* The words for cooked meat (served to the upper classes) are French: *beef, pork,* and *mutton.*

 **CURRICULUM CONNECTION**

GOVERNMENT
Unlike the United States, the United Kingdom has no single written constitution. Instead, it is governed according to a series of laws and charters. The oldest of them is the Magna Carta.

MEETING SPECIAL NEEDS ACTIVITY

Study Strategy Have students make a list of each of the major figures discussed in this section. In a second column, they should write the name of the person or group with which the first figure was in conflict. Then students should make a check mark next to the victor. For instance, Alfred the Great (checked) would be paired with Danes; William of Normandy (checked) with Anglo-Saxons; and so on. **L1**

ASSESS

Check for Understanding

Assign Section 3 Review as homework or as an in-class activity.

 Use Student Self-Test and Review Software to review Section 3.

Evaluate

📁 Section Quiz 3-3

💿 Use the Testmaker to create a customized quiz for Section 3.

Reteach

Have students review the major theme of this section, conflict, as it applies to England, France, and the Holy Roman Empire.

Enrich

Have students research the life of St. Francis of Assisi or St. Dominic and present their findings to the class.

CLOSE

Have students summarize the main advantages and disadvantages of the manorial system.

---

government. By A.D. 1400 Parliament had divided into two chambers: the House of Lords, made up of nobles and clergy, and the House of Commons, consisting of knights and townspeople.

France

After Charlemagne's death in A.D. 814, the Frankish lands disintegrated into separate feudal territories. In A.D. 987 a noble named Hugh Capet seized the French throne from the weak Frankish king. Capet controlled only the area around the city of Paris in northern France. However, by the A.D. 1100s, the king of the Capetian (kuh•PEE•shuhn) dynasty had strengthened the power of the French monarchy and brought French feudal lords under royal control.

Philip II, known as **Philip Augustus**, was one of the most effective French monarchs. During his long reign from A.D. 1180 to A.D. 1223, Philip doubled the area of his domain through marriage and conquests. By appointing loyal officials and forming a semipermanent royal army, he further weakened the power of the feudal nobles.

Philip's grandson, Louis IX, banned private warfare, made royal courts dominant over feudal courts, and decreed that only the king had the right to mint coins. A very religious man, Louis was admired for his chivalry and high moral character. His advice to his son reveals these characteristics:

❝ [Have] a tender pitiful heart for the poor ... [and] hold yourself steadfast and loyal toward your subjects and your vassals, without turning either to the right or to the left, but always straight, whatever may happen. And if a poor man have a quarrel with a rich man, sustain the poor rather than the rich, until the truth is made clear, and when you know the truth, do justice to them. ❞

Louis IX's grandson, Philip IV, increased France's territory and trade by defeating both England and Flanders in war. To pay for the wars, he raised taxes and taxed new groups, such as the clergy. Although the pope opposed taxing the clergy, he could not force Philip to back down. Before he died in A.D. 1314, Philip summoned the Estates-General, an assembly of nobles, clergy, and townspeople. He wanted to use the assembly to raise taxes nationally rather than locally. The Estates-General, however, never became as powerful as Parliament in England. French kings kept a firm hand on government affairs.

The Holy Roman Empire

While the monarchs of England and France were building strong central governments, the rulers of Germany set out to create a powerful Christian empire in the heartland of Europe. In A.D. 955, Germany's Otto I, or **Otto the Great**, defeated the Magyars at the Battle of Lechfeld. He then set his sights on Italy. In A.D. 962 Pope John XII sought Otto's help against Roman nobles who opposed the pope. In return for the German king's help, the pope crowned Otto Emperor of the Romans.

Otto and his successors claimed the right to intervene in the election of popes, and Otto himself appointed and deposed several popes. As the Church's power increased, popes claimed the right to anoint and depose kings. These two conflicting claims led to centuries of dispute between the Holy Roman emperors and the Roman Catholic popes. This ongoing rivalry weakened the throne of the Holy Roman emperor.

Powerful German lords also prevented the Holy Roman emperors from building a strong, unified state. Their challenges to the emperor caused civil wars that divided Germany. Conflicts with neighboring Poland, Bohemia, and Hungary also weakened the emperor's power.

SECTION 3 REVIEW

Recall
1. **Define** feudalism, chivalry, manorialism, serf, sacrament, lay investiture, heresy, friar, common law.
2. **Identify** Clovis, Charlemagne, the Vikings, Benedict, Gregory VII, Innocent III, Francis of Assisi, Alfred the Great, William the Conqueror,

Magna Carta, Philip Augustus, Otto the Great.
3. **Explain** how the Catholic Church provided the link between the ancient world and the medieval world.

Critical Thinking
4. **Making Comparisons** Contrast the reign of Charlemagne with those of his

Frankish successors. Why do you think Charlemagne was successful in enlarging and maintaining his empire?

Understanding Themes
5. **Conflict** Why did conflicts develop between popes and European monarchs? Could their disputes have been resolved peacefully? Explain.

SECTION 3 REVIEW ANSWERS

1. All vocabulary words are defined in the Glossary.
2. Clovis, 113; Charlemagne, 114; the Vikings, 114; Benedict, 119; Gregory VII, 120; Innocent III, 120; Francis of Assisi, 120; Alfred the Great, 120; William the Conqueror, 121; Magna Carta, 121; Philip Augustus, 122; Otto the Great, 122

3. It preserved much of the learning of the classical world.
4. Charlemagne had a more forceful personality than his successors. His empire owed its success to the emperor's personality, to his wise use of local officials and royal messengers, and to his first-hand contact with all areas of his realm.

5. **CONFLICT** Conflicts developed over whether ecclesiastical or secular leaders had supreme authority, especially in the appointment of religious officials. Answers will vary as to whether conflicts could have been resolved peacefully.

c. A.D. 649
Empress Wu begins to rule the Chinese empire.

A.D. 938
The Vietnamese defeat the Chinese in the Battle of Bach Dang River.

c. A.D. 1100s
Zen Buddhism reaches Japan from China.

Section 4

Asia's Pacific Rim

Setting the Scene

▶ **Terms to Define**
meritocracy, shamanism, clan, shogun, samurai, daimyo, animism

▶ **People to Meet**
Tai Cong, Empress Wu, Duo Fu, Li Bo, Sejong, Prince Shotoku, Yoritomo Minamoto, the Khmer, Ngo Quyen, Ramkhamhaeng

▶ **Places to Locate**
Changan, Heian Kyo (Kyoto), Angkor Wat, Pagan, Sukhothai, Srivijaya Empire

ind Out What Chinese achievements influenced the growth of civilizations in Korea, Japan, and Southeast Asia?

The Storyteller

Thoughtfully, Gui Xi considered the civil service examination. He was to select a single line of poetry and, using his finest calligraphy, write it on a silk scroll. Then he must create a painting linked to the chosen text, filling the scroll. To pass this vital test a man needed to be able to read, drawing conclusions and inferences. He also needed to demonstrate proficiency in the brush arts, a discipline requiring many years to master. Gui Xi recollected the steps essential to writing and painting. One must first find the spirit, rhythm, and thought, then one could seek to control the scenery, brush, and ink. For good work to result, mental and physical aspects must balance.

—adapted from *Record of Brush Methods: Essay on Landscape Painting,* Ching Hao, reprinted in *Varieties of Visual Experience,* 1991

Chinese calligraphy

From the A.D. 500s to the A.D. 1300s, prosperous civilizations developed along the rim of Asia bordering the Pacific Ocean. China, the most powerful empire in the region, reached the peak of its cultural development during this period. At the same time, China's neighbors—Korea, Japan, and the kingdoms of Southeast Asia—combined Chinese ways with their own and other foreign traditions to create distinct civilizations.

China

After a long period of disorder, a new dynasty known as the Sui reunited China about A.D. 589. Sui rulers increased the power of the central government, modeling their rule on the traditions of the Han dynasty. They rebuilt the former Han capital at **Changan** (CHONG•ON), repaired the Great Wall, and constructed a system of roads and canals to unite northern and southern China. However, to accomplish these projects, the Sui used crews of forced laborers. As the harshness of Sui rule increased, peasant rebellions occurred throughout China.

The Tang Dynasty

In A.D. 618 a rebellious noble named Li Yuan (LEE YOO•AHN) overthrew the Sui and established the Tang (TONG) dynasty, which lasted until A.D. 907. Under the Tang, the Chinese expanded their borders to include new territories in central Asia, Korea, and Southeast Asia.

The military genius behind Tang expansion was the emperor **Tai Cong** (TIE TSOONG). Not only was Tai Cong a warrior, but he was also a shrewd administrator. By restoring a strong central government in China, he maintained control of his enormous empire while continuing to expand it.

To obtain a position in the Tang government, candidates had to pass civil service examinations.

SECTION THEME

▶ **Cultural Diffusion** The civilizations of India and China influence neighboring peoples in Asia.

ind Out

Answer: *The Koreans, Japanese, and Southeast Asians (especially the Vietnamese) adopted many elements of Chinese culture, including forms of writing, religion, art, medicine, astronomy, philosophy, and government practices.*

FOCUS

Section Objective

Explain how Koreans, Japanese, and Southeast Asians were influenced by the cultures of China and India.

BELLRINGER
Motivational Activity

Before taking roll at the beginning of the class period, project Section Focus Transparency 3-4 and have students answer the activity questions. Discuss students' responses.

This activity is also available as a blackline master.

Vocabulary Pre-check

Use Vocabulary Activity 3 to introduce vocabulary terms.
L1 LEP

Reproducible Masters
• Reproducible Lesson Plan 3-4
• Vocabulary Activity 3
• Guided Reading Activity 3-4
• Reteaching Activity 3
• Enrichment Activity 3
• Section Quiz 3-4

• Performance Assessment Activity 3
• Spanish Chapter Summary 3

Transparencies
• Section Focus Transparency 3-4
• World History and Art Transparency 17, *Angkor Wat*

Multimedia
📀 Student Self-Test and Review Software
📀 Testmaker
📀 World Music: Cultural Traditions, Lessons 8, 9
📀 Picture Atlas of the World

TEACH

Guided Practice

THEME Cultural Diffusion

Using a wall map if possible, point out the major origins of cultural influence (*India, China*), the region affected (*the countries of Southeast Asia*), and the water routes by which cultural elements traveled (*Bay of Bengal, South China Sea, Mekong River*). **L1 LEP**

Uniformity List on the chalkboard some of the factors that made for a uniform Chinese culture: a strong centralized government, good transportation between the different parts of the country, availability of written literature. Ask students who restored strong central government in China (*Tai Cong*), who improved transportation (*Tang rulers*), and what invention made it easier to make literature available to people in China (*block printing*). **L1**

History & Art Tang porcelain and other crafts were widely admired. In many Asian languages, the word for "Chinese" became a synonym for "superior."
Answer to Caption: *roads and waterways*

Under Tang rule, these tests measured the degree to which candidates had mastered Confucian principles. Because almost any male could take these examinations, the Chinese government claimed that it was a meritocracy—a system in which people are chosen and promoted for their talents and performance. But in practice it did not meet this ideal. Few young men from poor families could afford to pay tutors to help them prepare for the exams. Most could not spare the time away from their labor to study on their own.

Prosperity and Trade

Under the Tang, China had a prosperous economy. **Empress Wu**, one of the influential members of her dynasty, opened up new areas for farming and encouraged trade. Other Tang rulers also carried agricultural reforms and enforced the peace that enabled farmers to till the land. In the Chang Jiang (Yangtze River) region, farmers were able to experiment with new strains of rice and better methods for growing them—both of which led to greater crop yields. With more food available, the Chinese population increased as well.

Political stability and agricultural prosperity enabled China to increase its contacts with the outside world. New and improved roads helped government officials to perform their duties. They also enabled merchants to increase trade with people from Japan, India, and the Middle East.

Chinese luxury goods, such as silk and pottery, passed through central Asia along the Silk Road. Beginning in central China, traders' camel caravans traveled north to the Great Wall and then headed west, crossing into central Asia just north of the Tibetan plateau. Some traveled as far west as Syria. These caravans brought Chinese goods and ideas to other cultures and returned with foreign products and new ideas as well. The Buddhist, Christian, and Islamic religions came to China by way of the Silk Road. During the Tang dynasty, Buddhism especially became very popular in China.

As trade increased the wealth of the empire, the Tang capital at Changan grew into the largest city in the world. Dazzling tales attracted merchants and scholars from countries throughout Asia to this city of 2 million people. Visitors to Changan spoke of wide, tree-shaded avenues and two vast market squares where merchants sold goods from Asia and the Middle East.

Tang Arts

The Tang period brought many achievements in learning and the arts. Scholars compiled encyclopedias, dictionaries, and official histories of China. Chinese Buddhist monks developed the technique

History & Art *Four Travelers on Horseback*, porcelain figures from the Tang dynasty
Chinese potters discovered how to make porcelain in the A.D. 800s by firing pieces at very high temperatures. *What constructions helped merchants trade fine Chinese wares with other countries?*

COOPERATIVE LEARNING ACTIVITY

Technology Organize the class into four groups. Ask each group to choose one of the technological advances of the Tang and Song dynasties: porcelain, block printing, the compass, or gunpowder. Have each group research its topic to learn more about when and how the invention came about, how it was used, and how knowledge of it spread. If possible, each group should find illustrations of its subject. Then have the groups present their findings to the class. **L2**

of block printing—carving the text of a page into a block of wood, then reproducing the page by inking the wood and pressing a piece of paper onto it. Also, during the Tang period, Chinese artisans made a fine translucent pottery that became a prized commodity known in the West as "china."

The Tang period was a great age of poetry. Two of China's greatest poets, **Duo Fu** (DWA FOO) and **Li Bo** (LEE BWAW), aimed to create mood and atmosphere in their works. Many of their poems reveal the Chinese love of nature.

Tang Decline

For a time the cultural splendor of Tang China masked its military weakness. However, the Tang ruler's vulnerability to attack was revealed in A.D. 751, when Turkish armies in central Asia successfully revolted against China. They cut off China's trade routes to the Middle East, and they put an end to the exchange of goods and ideas along the Silk Road. Border wars and internal unrest in famine-stricken provinces plagued the Tang from the late A.D. 700s on. In A.D. 907, this turmoil finally caused the fall of the dynasty.

The Song Dynasty

From A.D. 907 to A.D. 960, China was ruled by a series of military dynasties. Then a military general named Zhao Kuangyin (JOW KWONG•YIN) seized the throne and established the Song (SOONG) dynasty.

To strengthen their hold on China, Song rulers introduced an official state philosophy that combined Confucian values with elements of Buddhism and Daoism. They also firmly supported the civil service system that the Tang had restored. Scholarly civil servants who passed the tests eventually formed a wealthy elite group, called mandarins by Westerners.

During the Song dynasty, China's population increased along with trade and commerce. Although poverty persisted among the lower classes, the upper and middle classes enjoyed one of the highest standards of living in the world at that time.

Song rulers encouraged prosperity by pursuing peaceful policies. Instead of raising large armies, they supported public works projects, including the digging of irrigation ditches and canals. They expanded sea trade with foreign lands, such as India and Southeast Asia. The introduction of new crops from Southeast Asia, such as tea and a faster-growing rice plant, further boosted China's farming economy. With farming, trade, and commerce all thriving, urban centers prospered.

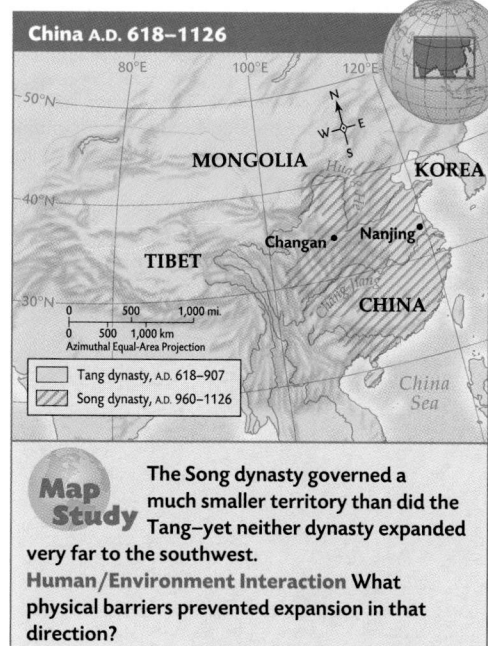
China A.D. 618–1126

Tang dynasty, A.D. 618–907
Song dynasty, A.D. 960–1126

Map Study The Song dynasty governed a much smaller territory than did the Tang—yet neither dynasty expanded very far to the southwest. **Human/Environment Interaction** What physical barriers prevented expansion in that direction?

Song Arts and Sciences

Song achievements in the arts and sciences were many. The cuisine which people recognize today as distinctively Chinese originated during the Song dynasty. Experts regard Song porcelain as the best ever made. Landscape painting reached its peak during Song rule.

Song inventors perfected the compass, a tool that enabled Chinese sailors to navigate on journeys far offshore. They also produced gunpowder, first used in fireworks and later in military weapons. Bamboo-tube rocket launchers charged with gunpowder made the Song army a powerful fighting force.

China's enemies, however, were eventually able to obtain the secrets of Song military technology. Thus, using the Song Empire's own technology against it, the Mongols were able to completely capture northern China in A.D. 1234 and bring about the fall of the Song dynasty in southern China in A.D. 1279.

Korea

Korea forms a peninsula on the east coast of Asia, extending southward toward the East China Sea. Historically Korea has acted as a bridge between its two powerful neighbors, China and Japan. Beginning in the 100s B.C., the Koreans

Chapter 3 *Regional Civilizations* 125

Map Study

Answer
the mountain ranges of eastern Tibet

Map Skills Practice

Reading a Map At their greatest extent, how far did the domains of the Tang dynasty stretch from east to west? *(about 3,000 miles [4,825 kilometers])*

Cultural Diffusion Ask students how religions—Buddhism, Christianity, Islam—might come to China "by way of the Silk Road."*(Answers will vary but might include via missionaries, by books, and by traders who practiced these religions.)* **L3**

World Music: Cultural Traditions, Lesson 8

NATIONAL GEOGRAPHIC SOCIETY

CD-ROM
PICTURE ATLAS OF THE WORLD

You and your students can see the Grand Canal, the Great Wall, and the Silk Road by clicking China's "Photos" button.

Global Gourmet

China Chopsticks, the eating implements used by Asians, originated in China as early as the Shang dynasty. Most Asian food is served in bite-sized pieces making it easier to handle with the slender sticks. The Chinese word for chopsticks, *kuai-zi*, is a pun on the word *kuai*, which means both "quick" and "piece."

MEETING SPECIAL NEEDS ACTIVITY

Attention Deficiency Chinese food is very popular in the United States. Students who have trouble focusing their attention should enjoy learning more about some of their favorite dishes. They might use cookbooks or other library resources. (These students might be helped in their research by other students with longer attention spans.) If possible, a Chinese meal could be prepared for the class and presented along with informative commentary. **L2 LEP**

Literature Encourage students to find a poem by Duo Fu or Li Bo or another poet of the Tang or Song dynasty. Ask them to copy their selection so that it can be displayed on a bulletin board. **L1 LEP**

**Visualizing
History** When the kingdom of Silla dominated Korea, absolute monarchy flourished. Although the rulers granted land to aristocrats, the land reverted to the central government when the nobles died.
Answer to Caption: *all of Korea*

Technology Review the principles behind the Chinese system of writing. (*Hundreds of characters were needed to represent objects, ideas, and sounds.*) Why would an innovation like the Korean system of hangul be an improvement? (*Because it was alphabetic, requiring only 24 symbols. This made it much easier for the average person to learn.*) **L2**

adopted elements of Chinese culture and blended them with their own rich traditions.

Early History

Historians believe the first Koreans were immigrants from northern Asia. These settlers lived in villages, grew rice, and made tools and other implements of bronze. They practiced shamanism, a belief that good and evil spirits inhabit both living and nonliving things. Shamans, or priests, interceded between the spirit world and humans.

**Visualizing
History** Shown here is the world's oldest astronomical observatory in Asia. It was built at Silla, Korea, from 365 stones. *How much territory did the kingdom of Silla hold by A.D. 668?*

126   Chapter 3   *Regional Civilizations*

About 109 B.C. Korea came under Chinese rule. But after the fall of the Han dynasty, Koreans regained control of their peninsula and, by A.D. 313, eventually formed three kingdoms—Silla, Paekche (pah•EHK•chee), and Koguryo. During the Three Kingdoms period, from 57 B.C. to A.D. 668, the Koreans adopted many elements of Chinese culture, including Confucianism, Buddhism, calligraphy, and ideas about government. They also used Chinese knowledge of arts and sciences to make their own unique civilization. In A.D. 668 the kingdom of Silla finally conquered all of Korea, ushering in a period of peace, prosperity, and creativity.

The Yi Dynasty

In A.D. 1392 a dynasty called the Yi came to power in Korea. The Yi called their kingdom Choson and built Hanyang—today the city of Seoul—as their capital. They opened schools to teach Chinese classics to civil service candidates and made a form of Confucianism the state doctrine. Under one of the greatest Yi rulers, King **Sejong**, scholars devised *hangul,* an alphabet that uses 14 consonants and 10 vowels to represent Korean sounds.

Although the Japanese tried to capture Korea in A.D. 1592, the Yi dynasty managed to successfully rebuff the Japanese invaders, mainly because of an invention created by Korean Admiral Yi-Sun-shin. The admiral's ironclad warships, or "turtle ships," devastated the Japanese fleet. Although the Koreans won the war, they did not escape unscathed. In the years that followed, Koreans increasingly avoided contact with the outside world and eventually isolated themselves so thoroughly that Korea became known as the "Hermit Kingdom."

Japan

Just 110 miles (177 km) east of Korea lies the Japanese archipelago, or chain of islands. As the map on page 130 shows, Japan consists of four large islands—Honshu, Shikoku, Kyushu, and Hokkaido—and many smaller ones.

Island Geography

Because of this island geography, the Japanese formed their civilization mostly in isolation from mainland Asian civilizations, except for China. Although the Japanese borrowed from Chinese civilization, their customs and traditions were different from those of most other Asian peoples.

MAKING CONNECTIONS ACTIVITIES

Religion Have students research the Japanese tea ceremony, focusing especially on the symbolism of the ritual. Encourage students to do a demonstration of a tea ceremony for the rest of the class. **L2**

The Arts Have students research ikebana, the Japanese art of flower arranging. On the basis of the information they find, have students create an arrangement that conforms to the principle of ikebana. Most libraries have books on the subject. **L3**

Visualizing History Mount Fuji and Lake Ashi at Hakone, Japan. *How did the physical beauty of the land affect Japanese art?*

Visualizing History The graceful shape of Mount Fuji has made this volcanic mountain famous all over the world. The temples and shrines on its slopes—and even in its craters—draw hundreds of thousands of climbers every year. **Answer to Caption:** *It inspired Japanese painters and poets with deep reverence for nature.*

The geography of these islands influenced the formation of Japanese culture in other ways as well. Because much of the land is mountainous—less than 20 percent of it is suitable for farming—the Japanese learned to get most of their food from the sea. They also learned to rely on the sea for protection from invaders—being a natural barrier to invasion from the mainland—and yet to regard it as a route of transport between the islands. The physical beauty of the land inspired deep reverence for nature in works by many Japanese painters and poets. However, nature has often brought trying times to Japan. The Japanese islands have suffered much from volcanic eruptions, earthquakes, floods, and typhoons.

Early Japan

Japan was first settled about 10,000 years ago, but little is known about its earliest inhabitants. During the 200s B.C. and 100s B.C., invaders from the Asian mainland entered Japan. They introduced agriculture and the use of bronze and iron to the peoples already living there.

In early Japan, separate clans, or groups based on family ties, ruled their own regions. Clan members practiced a religious belief called Shinto, or "the way of the gods." People in each clan honored a common ancestor as their special *kami*, or spirit. Followers of Shinto believed that *kami* also dwelled within people, animals, and even nonliving

objects such as rocks and streams. To honor this *kami*—and the *kami* of their ancestors—they held numerous festivals and rituals. Often these ceremonies were conducted by the chief of the clan, who acted as both military leader and priest.

By about A.D. 400, the Yamato, a militarily strong clan based in central Japan, extended its rule over most of the country. Although other clans continued to rule their own lands, they owed their loyalty to the Yamato chief. In effect, he became the emperor of Japan.

Initially the emperor had a great deal of political power. By the A.D. 500s, however, the emperor had become more of a ceremonial figure who carried out religious rituals. The real power was held by aristocratic families.

China's Influence on Japan

From A.D. 400 to A.D. 700, the Japanese developed close ties to Korea and China. During this period the Chinese Empire had one of the most advanced civilizations in the world. The Japanese were impressed with Chinese achievements and began to model their society on Chinese principles and methods. For example, the Japanese adopted

Cultural Perspectives

The Ainu Because of Japan's geographic isolation, the country today has very few minorities. There is, however, one group that may have descended from the very first inhabitants of Japan. They are called Ainu, and most of them live on the northernmost main island, Hokkaido. Although most of the 15,000 Ainu have intermarried with other Japanese, a few still live in isolated villages, where they follow their traditional way of life.

Religion Many Japanese practice Shinto along with Buddhism. Have students write a report on Shinto, describing the beliefs and practices of this religion. **L2**

China's Influence on Japan
What influence did China have on the development of Japanese culture?
The Chinese profoundly influenced Japanese culture, bringing their writing system, forms of government and society, and Buddhist religion to Japan.

CRITICAL THINKING ACTIVITY

Making Comparisons Although Korea and Japan have many things in common, there are also profound differences between them. Have students compare and contrast the two countries, perhaps using a double-column format with side headings such as: *mythological origins; major historical periods to about A.D. 1400; cultural borrowings from China;* and *native cultural contributions.* **L3**

History & Art Lady Murasaki's novel depicts Prince Genji and his courtiers as refined members of the nobility. To succeed at court, an aristocrat had to be skilled as a musician, poet, and calligrapher, and be wise in the ways of elegant courtship.
Answer to Caption: *Lady Shikibu Murasaki*

Politics Have students research Taika reforms. Ask them to use library resources to describe some of the reforms and draw conclusions about their effects. **L3**

Linking Past and Present

Nara Temples During the Nara period in Japan, hundreds of temples were built at the capital city of Nara. Today, 1,300 years later, many of these temples still stand. Their beauty and historic interest draw some 10 million visitors a year.

Who?What?Where?When?

Early Japanese Writings The earliest known Japanese books are the *Kojiki* (Records of Ancient Matters), completed in A.D. 712, and the *Nihon shoki* (Chronicles of Japan), completed in A.D. 720. The two works combine actual events with myths that trace the imperial family to the foundations of the world. Their purpose was to give the court—then under Chinese influence—a history that could compete with that of the Chinese.

History & Art *The Lady Fujitsubo Watching Prince Genji Departing in the Moonlight* by A. Hiroshige and U. Toyokuni, A.D. 1853. *What author may have written the world's first novel,* The Tale of Genji?

the Chinese characters for writing to create their own writing system. They also accepted Buddhism, which was brought to Japan by Chinese and Korean missionaries.

About A.D. 587 **Prince Shotoku**, the most powerful official at the emperor's court, gave his support to Buddhism. He ordered the construction of Buddhist monasteries and temples and sent officials and students to China to study. When Shotoku heard about the Chinese Confucian ideas of government, he wrote a constitution for Japan in which he set forth general principles that explained how government officials should act.

In A.D. 646 government officials instituted the Taika, or "Great Change" reforms. These reforms attempted to establish a strong central government patterned after that of China. Although these reforms were somewhat effective at increasing the central government's control over the clans, most clan leaders refused to give up their land. Even after the Taika reforms, Japan remained much divided under the control of regional clan leaders.

Greater government centralization did not take place until A.D. 710, when Japan built its first permanent capital at Nara. A smaller version of China's Changan, Nara had an imperial palace, broad streets, large public squares, rows of Chinese-style homes, and Buddhist temples. During the Nara period, the Japanese produced their first written literature, mainly poetry and histories of early Japan.

The Heian Period

In A.D. 794 the Japanese established a new capital, **Heian Kyo**, "the City of Peace and Tranquillity," later called **Kyoto**. For more than 1,000 years, this city remained the capital of Japan.

During the Heian period, central government in Japan was largely in the hands of aristocratic families such as the Fujiwara. Because they had little political power, the emperor and his court had time to support the arts.

Life at the Heian court was known for its elegance, good manners, and love of natural beauty. Court officials and their wives wrote stories, travel diaries, and essays. They composed poems for special occasions and exchanged them in letters. Calligraphy was as important as the poem itself, for a person's handwriting was taken to be an indication of his or her character. People were even said to fall in love upon seeing each other's handwriting.

During the Heian period, women of the court produced Japan's first great prose literature. Lady Shikibu Murasaki wrote *The Tale of Genji*, which some believe to be the world's first novel. Filled with poems about the beauty of nature, the novel chronicles the life and loves of a fictional prince named Genji.

The Way of the Warrior

In A.D. 1156 the rule of the Fujiwara family came to a end. A dispute soon developed between

MORE ABOUT...

Lady Murasaki The author of *The Tale of Genji* was born about A.D. 978 and died around A.D. 1014. Her real name is unknown; the name by which she is called is that of the heroine of her novel. After the death of her husband, Fujiwara Nobutaka, Lady Murasaki served at court. It was during this time that she wrote *The Tale of Genji*. It has been recognized as a masterpiece ever since. In the thirteenth century, a 54-volume commentary appeared; more recently, a Japanese publisher issued a 1,200-page *Tale of Genji Encyclopedia.*

two powerful court families: the Taira and the Minamoto. The families fought a decisive battle in A.D. 1185 in which the Taira were defeated. To the head of the Minamoto family, the emperor then gave the title shogun, or great general, and **Yoritomo Minamoto** became the real political and military power. While the emperor remained with his court in the capital of Kyoto carrying on ritual tasks, Yoritomo and his soldiers ran a shogunate, or military government, from Kamakura near present-day Tokyo.

The shogunate proved to be quite strong. During the A.D. 1200s, Mongol warriors from China tried twice to invade Japan but did not succeed. On the second occasion, when a typhoon destroyed the Mongol fleet, the Japanese thought of the storm as the kamikaze, or "divine wind," and took it to be confirmation that their islands were indeed sacred.

In A.D. 1336 the Ashikaga family gained control of the shogunate. But the family failed to get control of regional warriors. Japan soon broke into individual warring states, leaving the shogun and the emperor as mere figureheads.

The powerful landowner-warriors in the countryside were called samurai. The most powerful samurai became daimyo (DY•mee•OH), or lords.

Like the medieval knights of feudal Europe who pledged their loyalty to lords, samurai pledged their loyalty and military service to their daimyo. Poor rice farmers paid high taxes for the right to farm a daimyo's lands. In return, that daimyo provided the farmers with protection.

The samurai fought on horseback with bows, arrows, and steel swords. They dressed in loose-fitting armor. The samurai followed a strict code of honor called Bushido, meaning "the way of the warrior." Bushido stressed bravery, self-discipline, and loyalty. It demanded that the samurai endure suffering and defend his honor at all costs. If a samurai was dishonored or defeated, he was expected to commit suicide.

Growth of a Merchant Class

Despite the political turmoil during its feudal period, Japan developed economically at this time. Workshops on daimyo estates produced arms, armor, and iron tools. Each region began to specialize in goods such as pottery, paper, textiles, and lacquerware. Trade increased between regions.

The increasing trade led to the growth of towns around the castles of the daimyos. Japanese merchants began to trade with Chinese and Korean

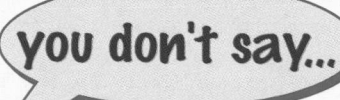

"Tycoon" is an English word that now applies mainly to business leaders. It comes to us from China by way of Japan. The Chinese term for "great prince," *ta kuin*, was adapted by the Japanese as *taikun* and used to describe the shogun.

Linking Past and Present

The *kamikaze*, or "divine wind" that saved Japan from Mongol defeat in A.D. 1281, never lost its importance for the Japanese. During World War II, Allied planes bombed Japan from aircraft carriers. Suicide pilots, their planes loaded with explosives, dived into the aircraft carriers in an effort to stave off defeat. Admired at home and feared by the Allies, they were known as kamikaze pilots.

CONNECTIONS The Arts

Samurai Arts

Kiyomatsu, a samurai hero

In the A.D. 1100s, the rise of military rule in Japan brought in a new style of art. Supported by daimyo and samurai, artists created paintings highlighting the skill and bravery of soldiers. These works show warriors in richly patterned clothing, riding magnificent horses and wielding long swords. The expressions of the rider and his horse often convey wild—but controlled—emotions.

Today in Japan the samurai artistic tradition is most prominent in movies and television. Many popular Japanese films are samurai tales set in feudal times and filled with action and adventure. Akira Kurosawa, one of the world's renowned directors, has made a number of samurai movies. His film *The Hidden Fortress*—about a brave general who leads an endangered princess to safety—helped inspire American director George Lucas to create the epic film *Star Wars*.

Linking Past and Present ACTIVITY

Study a painting with a samurai theme. What values are expressed in the painting? You might want to view the films *The Hidden Fortress* and *Star Wars*. In what ways do you think these films reflect samurai values? In what ways do you think they do not?

Samurai Arts

The samurai's loyalty to his overlord was absolute. Nothing was to come before it—not duties to wife, parents, or children. Although the samurai and the European feudal knight had this tradition of loyalty to one's lord in common, the two were quite different in other ways. The samurai did not go to battle to defend a lady or for religious motives, as his European counterpart often did.

ANSWER

Students might suggest values, such as bravery, heroism, or the strength of the human spirit against adversity. They may note that these same values are expressed in the films.

Chapter 3 *Regional Civilizations* **129**

COOPERATIVE LEARNING ACTIVITY

Panel Presentation Organize the class into groups of four or five. Each group is to become a panel of experts on a Japanese topic. Subjects may include ikebana (flower arranging); the tea ceremony; Kabuki theater; architecture; the samurai; and various customs relating to food, clothing, manners, or holidays. Choose a leader for each group. Each member of each group should prepare a five-minute presentation on one aspect of the team's subject. **L2**

Government Ask students to summarize the changes in Japan's form of government from Yamato times to the fourteenth century. *(clan rule: with Taika reforms, stronger central government; Nara: greater centralization; Heian: power struggles and rise of shogunate)* **L3**

Independent Practice

📁 Guided Reading Activity 3-4 **L1**

Music Have students find recordings of Korean or Japanese music to share with the class. Samples could include koto (a harplike instrument) or samisen (a three-stringed banjo) music, or a recording of folk songs. **L2 LEP**

Map Study

Answer
fertile soil, a warm climate, and abundant rain

Map Study Practice

Reading a Map Why do you think Southeast Asia was never united under a single ruler or political system? *(It would be difficult to subdue, much less hold together, a region that includes so many peninsulas and islands scattered over a wide region.)*

Religion Encourage students to find out more about animism, the beliefs and practices associated with it, and the areas where it has flourished. Have them compile their findings in a brief written report. **L3**

---

merchants. The Japanese exported raw materials such as lumber, pearls, and gold, as well as finished goods, such as swords and painted fans. The Japanese imported items such as medicines, books, and pictures.

Religion and the Arts

By the 1200s Buddhism had spread from the nobles to the common people. The opening words of *The Tale of the Heike* describe the Buddhist sentiments that were prevalent in Japan during its feudal period:

❝ In the sound of the bell of the Gion Temple echoes the impermanence of all things. The pale hue of the flowers of the teak tree show the truth that they who prosper must fall. The proud do not last long, but vanish like a spring-night's dream. And the mighty ones too will perish in the end, like dust before the wind. ❞

In the late A.D. 1100s, a new form of Buddhism called Zen reached Japan from China. The followers of Zen rejected book learning and logical thought, embracing instead bodily discipline and meditation. They believed that by meditation a student could free his mind and arrive at enlightenment. Zen won widespread support among the samurai because it taught them to improve their battle skills by freeing the mind from distractions to better concentrate on the object or target.

Zen perfected art forms and rituals such as ikebana, or flower arranging, meditation gardens, and the tea ceremony. Ikebana grew out of the religious custom of placing flowers before images of Buddha. The Zen practice of meditation gave rise to meditation gardens, which consisted of carefully placed rocks surrounded by neatly raked sand. Meditation sparked the tea ceremony, an elegant, studied ritual for serving tea. One tea master said the ceremony was intended to "cleanse the senses. . . so that the mind itself is cleansed from defilements." These and other arts and rituals derived from Buddhism remain popular in Japan today.

Southeast Asia

While culturally diverse societies flourished in China, Korea, and Japan from about A.D. 500 until A.D. 1300, Southeast Asia emerged as a center of civilizations. Lying south of China and east of India, Southeast Asia developed early as a crossroads of trade. During the A.D. 100s, an exchange of goods and ideas began between India and Southeast Asia. This exchange led Southeast Asians to adopt many elements of Indian culture. For instance, at that time, traveling Indian traders and scholars introduced to Southeast Asia the Sanskrit language and the religions of Hinduism and Buddhism. Indian literature, law codes, political ideas, and arts also deeply affected the cultures of the region.

Southeast Asians nevertheless retained many of their own traditions. They continued to perform the art of shadow puppetry, to make intricately patterned cloth called batik, and to play their own unique instruments and music—all achievements that Southeast Asians originated without Indian influence. They also held to **animism**, the idea that spirits inhabit living and nonliving things.

Map: Western Pacific Rim A.D. 700

Map labels: 100°E, 120°E, 140°E, 50°N, 30°N, 10°N, 0°
Hokkaido, Honshu, Silla, JAPAN, Nara, Shikoku, KOREA, Kyushu, CHINA, INDIA, PACIFIC OCEAN, Red River, INDOCHINA PENINSULA, (PHILIPPINES), Strait of Malacca, MALAY PENINSULA, SUMATRA, (INDONESIA), INDIAN OCEAN, Borobudur, JAVA
0 300 600 mi. / 0 300 600 km
Azimuthal Equal-Area Projection

Map Study Much of Southeast Asia (shown in purple on the map) lies in the tropics. **Region** What conditions in this region have made farming an important part of the economy?

The Khmer

In A.D. 802 **the Khmer** (kuh•MEHR) people of the mainland Southeast Asian country of Cambodia established a great Hindu-Buddhist empire with its capital at Angkor. The Khmer Empire reached its peak during the A.D. 1100s, when it conquered much of the land that now includes Laos, Thailand, and Vietnam.

The empire's wealth came primarily from its rice production. With income from bountiful harvests, Khmer rulers supported mammoth construction projects. Adapting Indian building techniques to create their own distinctive architecture, the Khmer built hundreds of temples that glorified Hindu and Buddhist religious figures. The most elaborate of these buildings was **Angkor Wat**, a temple complex covering nearly a square mile.

The Khmer king poured so much of the empire's wealth into building projects that he severely weakened the kingdom. This excess, along with rebellions against Khmer rule and infighting among members of the royal family, further crippled the empire. In A.D. 1431 the Thai, a neighboring Southeast Asian people, captured the capital city of Angkor, bringing an end to Khmer rule.

Vietnam

East of Cambodia and south of China lies the area of present-day Vietnam. Because of Vietnam's proximity to China, the Vietnamese accepted Confucianism, Daoism, and Buddhism as well as Chinese forms of writing and government. They retained many of their own traditions, however. While accepting Chinese religions, the Vietnamese continued their practice of animism. The Vietnamese also wrote and spoke their own Vietnamese language, though in writing it they used Chinese characters.

China controlled Vietnam almost continuously from about 200 B.C. to A.D. 939, but the Vietnamese fought hard to retain—and then to regain—their independence. In A.D. 39 two Vietnamese sisters, Trung Trak and Trung Nhi, clad in armor and riding atop elephants, led a successful revolt against the Chinese. For two years Vietnam was independent of China, but then the Chinese returned in greater numbers and defeated the Vietnamese.

During the confusion after the overthrow of the Tang dynasty, the Vietnamese took advantage of China's disunity to revolt again. The Chinese sent a fleet of warships to Vietnam to try to subdue the rebels. In A.D. 938, however, under the leadership of **Ngo Quyen** (noo chu•YEHN), the Vietnamese defeated the warships in the Battle of the Bach Dang River.

After the Song dynasty gained control of China, the Song emperor threatened the Vietnamese with invasion. To keep peace with China, the Vietnamese agreed to send tribute in the form of gifts to the Chinese emperor. In return, China agreed not to invade Vietnam.

Myanmar

The easternmost area of mainland Southeast Asia today includes the country of Myanmar (Burma). The first peoples to extensively settle most of present-day Myanmar were the Mons and the Tibeto-Burmans. Although they developed their own traditions, the Mons and the Tibeto-Burmans accepted Buddhism and other aspects of Indian culture from visiting South Asian sailors and traders.

During the 500s B.C., the Tibeto-Burmans became the dominant group and pushed the Mons southward. In A.D. 849 they set up a capital city called **Pagan** (pah•GAHN), which eventually became a center of Buddhist learning and culture. Skilled architects transformed Pagan from a small settlement into a city of elaborate Buddhist temples and monasteries.

During the A.D. 1200s, Mongol armies captured Pagan and ended its glory. Although Burman culture was preserved, a united kingdom did not arise again in Myanmar until the A.D. 1500s.

The Thai

More than four out of every five people who live in the Southeast Asian country of Thailand today belong to the ethnic group called Thais. They are descendants of people who began migrating south from China about A.D. 700. About A.D. 1238 the Thais established their first kingdom at **Sukhothai** (SOO•kah•TY) in the north-central part of the country.

The Sukhothai kingdom lasted only about 100 years, but it was known for its wise leaders. The kingdom's greatest monarch, King **Ramkhamhaeng** (rahm•KAHM•hong) ruled from A.D. 1275 to A.D. 1317. He made Sukhothai into a center of learning and the arts. During Ramkhamhaeng's reign, the Thai developed an alphabet and writing system based on the Khmer script. Artisans from China taught the making of porcelain, and Buddhist monks from South Asia won most of the Thai people to Buddhism. Beautiful Buddhist temples, with many levels of roofs, rose gracefully above the skyline of Sukhothai.

In A.D. 1350 a prince named Ramathibodi (rah•MAH•thee•BOH•dee) overthrew the last Sukhothai ruler and founded a new Thai kingdom known as Ayutthaya (ah•YOO•thy•yuh). He set up

Chapter 3 *Regional Civilizations* **131**

Architecture After the decline of the Khmer kingdom, the capital city of Angkor fell into ruins and was covered with rain forest growth. Have students research the rediscovery and rebuilding of Angkor, beginning in the late A.D. 1800s. **L2**

World History and Art Transparency 17, *Angkor Wat*

World Music: Cultural Traditions, Lesson 9

Who?What?Where?When?

Tran Hung Dao One of the greatest of all Vietnamese heroes is Tran Hung Dao, a military leader who defeated the Mongol forces of Kublai Khan. His biggest victory was a naval engagement in A.D. 1288. Kublai Khan's fleet was ripped apart by iron-tipped spears that Hung Dao had planted upright under water.

ASSESS

Check for Understanding

Assign Section 4 Review as homework or as an in-class activity.

Use Student Self-Test and Review Software to review Section 4.

Evaluate

 Section Quiz 3-4

Use the Testmaker to create a customized quiz for Section 4.

TEACHER NOTES

Reteach

Have students identify the
countries of Southeast Asia and
summarize the major cultural
elements they adopted from India
(*Hinduism, Buddhism, Sanskrit*)
and China (*Confucianism, written
language*).

 Reteaching Activity 3

Enrich

Have students do the necessary
research to create a travel
brochure for a Southeast Asian
country they would like to visit.

 Enrichment Activity 3

CLOSE

Have students summarize the
areas of Southeast Asian culture
in which the people retained their
own traditions. (*shadow puppetry,
batik, music, animism, architectural
styles, Vietnamese language*)

---

his capital south of Sukhothai
and up the Chao Phraya (chow
PRY•uh) River from where
Bangkok, the present Thai
capital, is today.

The Ayutthaya kingdom
lasted for about 400 years, with a
succession of 33 kings. At its
height, it held control over large
areas of Southeast Asia, including parts of Myanmar and
the Malay Peninsula. Like Sukhothai, Ayutthaya was an important center of Buddhist learning
and culture. Economically prosperous, Ayutthaya carried on
trade in teakwood, salt, spices,
and hides with China and neighboring Asian kingdoms.

Seafaring Kingdoms

Many kingdoms in early
Southeast Asia developed
around strategic ports. The Indonesian islands
became a crossroads in the expanding international
trade that stretched from the Arabian Peninsula to
China. Merchants of many lands—Arabs, Chinese,
Indians, and Persians—traded such products as
porcelain, textiles, and silk for Southeast Asian
spices and valuable woods. Beginning in the A.D.
400s, Buddhism and Hinduism became major religious influences in maritime Southeast Asia.

The **Srivijaya** (SHRIH•vih•JAY•uh) **Empire**
arose on the islands of Java and Sumatra in present-day Indonesia. Lasting from about A.D. 600 to A.D.
1100, the Srivijaya Empire was one of the region's
most powerful seafaring powers. It controlled shipping along the Strait of Malacca that separates
Sumatra from the Malay Peninsula. By the end of the
1100s, Srivijaya was reduced to a small kingdom and

Visualizing
History Wat Mahathat, an ancient Buddhist
temple now restored, is in Sukhothai
Historic Park, which was opened to the public in
1980. *What was accomplished in Sukhothai's golden age?*

the Majapahit (mah•jah•PAH•heet) kingdom began
to dominate the Indonesian islands.

During the early A.D. 1200s, Muslim traders
from the Arabian Peninsula and India brought Islam
to the peoples of the Malay Peninsula and Indonesia.
The first major center of Islam in Southeast Asia was
Melaka, a port kingdom on the southwestern coast
of the Malay Peninsula. From Melaka, Islam spread
throughout the Indonesian islands. By the A.D. 1500s
a number of Muslim trading kingdoms were
competing for control of the islands.

SECTION 4 REVIEW

Recall
1. **Define** meritocracy,
shamanism, clan, shogun,
samurai, daimyo, animism.
2. **Identify** Tai Cong, Empress
Wu, Duo Fu, Li Bo, Sejong,
Prince Shotoku, Yoritomo
Minamoto, Ngo Quyen,
Sukhothai, Ramkhamhaeng,
Srivijaya.

3. **Locate** the city of Changan in
central China on the map on
page 125. How was Changan
restored years after the Han
dynasty collapsed?
Critical Thinking
4. **Evaluating Information**
Which would you prefer to
follow, the ideals of the Heian
court or the samurai code of

Bushido? Why? What effects
might each have had on the
people of Japan?
Understanding Themes
5. **Cultural Diffusion** What
were some of the ways in which
the cultures of China, India,
and the Arabian Peninsula
influenced the peoples of
Southeast Asia?

SECTION 4 REVIEW ANSWERS

1. All vocabulary words are defined in the
Glossary.
2. Tai Cong, 123; Empress Wu, 124; Du Fo,
125; Li Bo, 125; Sejong, 126; Prince
Shotoku, 128; Yoritomo Minamoto, 129;
Ngo Quyen, 131; Sukhothai, 131;
Ramkhamhaeng, 131; Srivijaya, 132
3. It was rebuilt as a public works project.

4. Answers will vary. Heian: stress on beauty;
Bushido: stress on self-discipline. Both the
court and the military placed heavy taxes on
the common people.
5. **CULTURAL DIFFUSION** China:
Confucianism, Daoism, writing, governmental system; India: Hinduism, Buddhism,
building techniques, law, political ideas

Interpreting Demographic Data

Demographic data are statistics about a population, or a group of people. Demographic data can tell us a great deal about where and how people live.

Learning the Skill

Demographers measure populations in different ways. Sometimes they count the number of people living in a country or region. By comparing these numbers, we can determine which countries have more people than others.

Suppose, however, that country A and country B each has five million people, but country A has five times more land area than country B. Country B would be more crowded, or more densely populated, than country A. Population density measures the number of people living within a certain area. Demographers also measure the population distribution, or the pattern of settlement within a country. For example, in Egypt most people live in the fertile Nile River valley, and few people live in the desert.

Demographic data also describe population growth. Zero population growth occurs when births equal deaths. If births exceed deaths, the population is shrinking. Population growth is expressed as a percentage rate. Demographers use growth rates to predict the future size of a population. A population pyramid is a graph showing the age distribution of a population.

If the pyramid is wider at the bottom than at the top, the population is growing. If a pyramid is smaller at the bottom, the population is shrinking.

Practicing the Skill

The graphs on this page show demographic data for seven countries in the modern Islamic world. Use the graphs to answer these questions.

1. What kind of demographic data appears in each graph?
2. Which three countries have the largest total populations?
3. Which two countries are growing fastest?
4. How is population size related to growth rates in the graphs of these countries?

Applying the Skill

At the library, find demographic data about your city or county, and illustrate it in a table, graph, or map. You could show population increase or decrease, population distribution, population growth rates, or age distribution. Write a short paragraph interpreting your data.

For More Practice

Turn to the Skill Practice in the Chapter Review on page 135 for more practice in interpreting demographic data.

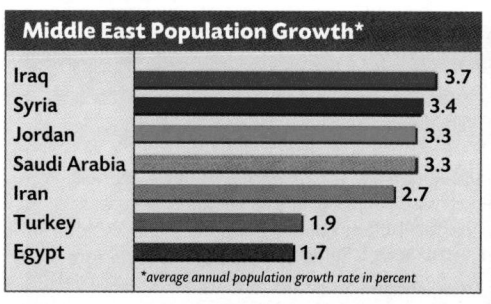

Selected Middle East Populations, 1996*

Iran	66,094
Egypt	63,575
Turkey	62,484
Iraq	21,422
Saudi Arabia	19,409
Syria	15,608
Jordan	4,212

(in thousands)

Source: Information Please Almanac, 1997.

Middle East Population Growth*

Iraq	3.7
Syria	3.4
Jordan	3.3
Saudi Arabia	3.3
Iran	2.7
Turkey	1.9
Egypt	1.7

average annual population growth rate in percent

TEACH

Interpreting Demographic Data
Before the class reads the skill, ask students if they know the meaning of the word *demography*. *(the science of the statistics of populations)* Ask them what other words they can think of that share one of the two roots of the word *demography*. *(for example, democracy, geography, biography)* Then ask them what conclusions they might reach from the following information:

1. The number of students entering twelfth grade in the imaginary country of Utopia has been on the decline since 1990.
2. The number of students entering kindergarten in Utopia has been on the rise since 1995. *(They will probably conclude that after a decline in the birthrate for a number of years, Utopia is witnessing a rise in the birthrate.)* Now have students read the skill and complete the practice questions.

Additional Practice

◤ Skill Reinforcement Activity 11

◤ Building Skills in Geography Workbook, Unit 2, Lesson 4

ANSWERS TO PRACTICING THE SKILL

1. The graph on the left presents a simple count of the number of people in each country. The graph on the right compares the rate of population growth in the same countries.
2. Iran, Turkey, Egypt
3. Iraq, Syria
4. The four countries with the smallest populations are experiencing the highest rates of growth. The three countries with the largest populations are experiencing a lesser percentage rate of growth.

GLENCOE
TECHNOLOGY

VIDEODISC
Use MindJogger to review students' knowledge of the chapter.

MindJogger Videoquiz

Chapter 3
Disc 1 Side A

Also available in VHS.

Answers

Using Key Terms
1. i
2. a
3. g
4. j
5. k

Using Your History Journal

Students should consider how military, intellectual, economic, or religious motives shaped the characters of the peoples whose values these works describe.

Reviewing Facts

1. preserved the legal heritage of Rome; served as the basis for later European legal systems
2. Answers may include advances in astronomy, geography, medicine, chemistry, mathematics, literature, decorative arts, architecture.
3. Church hierarchy, the Church's feudal ties, fighting heresy
4. son of the founder of the Tang dynasty; expanded empire and restored strong central government
5. the samurai code of honor; stressed bravery, self-discipline, loyalty

Connections Across Time

Historical Significance Contacts among the world's regional civilizations of Asia led to an exchange of ideas and practices. The Byzantines spread Orthodox Christianity and classical learning to neighboring peoples in Europe. The people of the Islamic Empire spread Islam, preserved much ancient knowledge, and made advances in the arts and sciences. Western Europeans passed on Catholic Christianity and forms of government and learning. In east Asia, China transmitted elements of its civilization to Japan, Korea, and Southeast Asia.

Today, because of numerous technological advances, cultural diffusion occurs on a global scale and affects many peoples. Thus, Westerners learn a great deal from the peoples of Asia, and Asians, likewise, benefit from their encounters with Westerners.

Using Key Terms

Write the key term that completes each sentence. Then write a sentence for each term not chosen.

a. mosaic
b. feudalism
c. clans
d. meritocracy
e. samurai
f. monasteries
g. shogun
h. shamanism
i. mosque
j. serfs
k. calligraphy
l. caliph

1. At noon on Fridays, many Muslims pray together in a _____.
2. Artists in the Byzantine Empire excelled in the art of _____, or pictures made of tiny pieces of glass or stone set in plaster.
3. In A.D. 1185 the Japanese emperor gave the title _____, or great general, to Yoritomo Minamoto.
4. Peasants in medieval Europe were often ___, people who were bound to the lord's manor.
5. Islamic artists used the beautiful script of Arabic in _____, or the art of elegant handwriting.

Technology Activity

Using the Internet Locate a Web site dealing with the history of the Cyrillic alphabet. Focus your search by using phrases such as *Cyrillic alphabet* and *Slavic languages*. Create a bulletin board showing examples of Cyrillic words with their English translations. When possible, include illustrations.

Using Your History Journal

*From your notes on the **Primary Chronicle**, **A Thousand and One Nights**, and the **Song of Roland**, write a short description of the manners, customs, and values of the civilizations and peoples described in the work.*

Reviewing Facts

1. **Citizenship** Explain the significance of the Justinian Code to later generations.
2. **Culture/Science** List some achievements of Islamic civilization in science and the arts.
3. **Culture** List the factors that helped maintain religious uniformity in medieval Europe.
4. **Government** Identify Tai Cong and name his important political achievements.
5. **Culture** Explain the code of Bushido and its impact on the Japanese.

Critical Thinking

1. **Analyze** How was the title of New Rome both suitable and unsuitable for Constantinople?
2. **Contrast** How did the rule of the Abbasids differ from the early Islamic community?
3. **Synthesize** Use a diagram to explain the relationships among medieval nobles, knights, and peasants.
4. **Evaluate** In what ways did Chinese innovations change the cultures of Korea and Japan?

Critical Thinking

1. Constantinople adopted some of its Roman heritage, but it also developed its own culture and was influenced by the Middle East.
2. Early Islamic state was mostly Arab; under the Abbasids, the population was larger and very diverse, and people had more leisure for cultural pursuits.
3. It should outline feudalism and manorialism.
4. They altered almost every aspect of society: religion, philosophy, ideas about government, science, and the arts.

Geography in History

1. to Labrador (Canada) and possibly Vinland (Newfoundland)
2. They were looking for riches, adventure, and land.
3. Their homeland bordered the northern Atlantic.

Geography in History

1. **Place** Refer to the map below. Where did Leif Eriksson's journey lead him?
2. **Movement** What reasons did Vikings have for leaving Scandinavia and venturing out into the Atlantic?
3. **Human/Environment Interaction** Why did the Vikings sail across the far northern part of the Atlantic rather than through the warmer waters to the south?
4. **Location** After leaving Scandinavia, which landmasses did the Vikings explore?
5. **Place** What two islands in the North Atlantic Ocean were settled by Vikings? What three areas explored by the Vikings are today part of Canada.

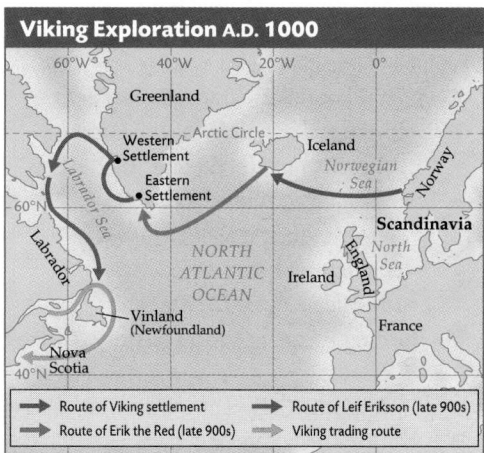

Viking Exploration A.D. 1000

Route of Viking settlement
Route of Erik the Red (late 900s)
Route of Leif Eriksson (late 900s)
Viking trading route

Understanding Themes

1. **Innovation** Using Byzantine civilization as an example, explain how one civilization's ideas can be adapted to other societies.
2. **Movement** How was the Umayyad's decision to move the Islamic capital from Madinah to Damascus a result of Islamic expansion?
3. **Conflict** How did the conflict between England's King John and the nobles eventually have positive results for all English people?
4. **Cultural Diffusion** What are some of the similarities between Southeast Asian cultures and Chinese culture?

Linking Past and Present

1. Explain the historical reasons why Russia has a continuing interest in eastern Europe.
2. What words in the English language have their origins in the Arabic language?
3. How have Japan's have samurai values helped it to become a world leader in industry today?

Skill Practice

Study the population pyramid below and then answer these questions.

1. What is the general shape of the graph?
2. What percentage of the female population is between 0 and 19 years old?
3. Are there equal numbers of males and females in this population? How can you tell?
4. What conclusion can you draw about the growth rate in this population? On what data do you base this conclusion?

Age Distribution in Jordan

Age	% of Pop'n	Male	Female	% of Pop'n	Age
70+	0.8%			0.8%	70+
60-69	1.2%			1.1%	60-69
50-59	2.4%			2.2%	50-59
40-49	3.8%			3.4%	40-49
30-39	4.5%			4.2%	30-39
20-29	8.1%			7.3%	20-29
10-19	13.9%			12.4%	10-19
0-9	17.6%			16.3%	0-9

640   320   0   320   640

Total Population: 4,212,000
Total Male Population: 2,161,000
Total Female Population: 2,051,000
Life Expectancy (Male): 71 years
Life Expectancy (Female): 74 years

Sources: Broderbund Software, Inc., CIA World Factbook 1996.

Linking Past and Present

1. Both the Russians and many of the peoples in eastern Europe share a common past as Slavic peoples.
2. Answers may include *bazaar*, *algebra*, and *sherbert*.
3. Heian values, emphasizing taste and beauty, are reflected in the simple, elegant design of Japanese buildings, goods, and rituals. Bushido, stressing self-discipline and loyalty, may underlie the Japanese work ethic.

Skill Practice

1. bottom-heavy pyramid
2. 28.7 percent
3. No, the male bars of the pyramid are longer—signifying more males in the population.
4. The population growth rate is high; the population pyramid is much wider at the bottom than at the top.

Chapter Bonus Test Question

Ask students: Medieval society operated under a system of mutual obligations. What kinds of mutual obligations exist in our own society today? (*An example might be government: citizens pay taxes and in return are provided such services as defense.*)

---

4. Iceland, Greenland, North America
5. Iceland and Greenland; Labrador, Newfoundland, and Nova Scotia.

Understanding Themes

1. **INNOVATION** The Byzantine Church used architectural ideas from Eastern sources; Byzantine culture was modified when its civilization mingled with other sources.

2. **MOVEMENT** As the Islamic state expanded, its central location changed.

3. **CONFLICT** It resulted in the Magna Carta, which limited the power of the monarch.

4. **CULTURAL DIFFUSION** Confucian principles and use of civil service exams; systems of writing; arts, such as porcelain

A complete, 1-page lesson plan is provided for each section in the *Reproducible Lesson Plans* booklet.

Toward a New World

CHAPTER RESOURCES

	Reproducible Resources	Multimedia Resources
Chapter Opener	Chapter Themes: Graphic Organizer 4 Historical Significance Chapter Activity 4	MindJogger Videoquiz
Chapter Enrichment	Vocabulary Activity 4* Time Line Activity 4 Mapping History Activity 4 History Simulation 4 Geography and History Activity 4 Source Reading 4 People in World History Profiles 24, 25, 27, 28 World Art and Music Activity 4 Enrichment Activity 4 Critical Thinking Activity 4 Skill Reinforcement Activity 4 Performance Assessment Activity 4	NGS Poster Set: *The Middle Ages* Focus on World Art Prints 15, 17 World History and Art Transparencies 8, 10, 16, 18 NGS PicturePack Transparency Sets: Physical Geography of the World, *Africa South of the Sahara, The Middle Ages, Ancient Central America, Ancient South America* NGS PictureShow CD-ROMs: *The Middle Ages, The Americas* Turning Points in World History: *The Crusades* STV: World Geography, Vol. 1, *Asia* World Music: Cultural Traditions, Lessons 1, 2, 8, 9
Chapter Review/Reteaching	Reteaching Activity 4 Skill Reinforcement Activity 4 Spanish Chapter Summary 4	Chapter 4 Digest Audiocassette, Activity, Test* Vocabulary PuzzleMaker Software Student Self-Test and Review Software MindJogger Videoquiz
Chapter Evaluation/Testing	Performance Assessment Activity 4 Chapter 4 Test, Forms A and B	Testmaker

* *Also available in Spanish*

0:00 OUT OF TIME? Assign the Chapter 4 summary in the Unit 1 Digest on pages 171–173, and the Chapter 4 Audiocassettes.

Block Schedule

Block scheduling differs from traditional class scheduling in the amount of time allotted to each period. The extended time frame provided by block scheduling affords you the opportunity to implement a greater number of research-oriented and activity-intense projects to motivate and involve your students. Activities that are particularly suited to use within the block scheduling framework are identified throughout this chapter by the following designation.

KEY TO ABILITY LEVELS

Teaching strategies have been coded for varying learning styles and abilities.

L1 BASIC activities for all students
L2 AVERAGE activities for average to above-average students
L3 CHALLENGING activities for above-average students
LEP LIMITED ENGLISH PROFICIENCY activities

Use Glencoe's *Presentation Plus!* multimedia teacher tool to easily present dynamic lessons that visually excite your students. Using Microsoft PowerPoint® you can customize the presentations to create your own personalized lessons.

SECTION RESOURCES

Daily Objectives	Reproducible Resources	Multimedia Resources
Section 1 **Asian Empires** Describe how the Mongols acquired the world's largest land empire.	Reproducible Lesson Plan 4-1 Vocabulary Activity 4* Guided Reading Activity 4-1* Section Quiz 4-1*	Section Focus Transparency 4-1 World History and Art Transparency 10, *Buddha* Student Self-Test and Review Software Testmaker STV: World Geography, *Asia*
Section 2 **A New Europe** Explain how the growth of towns affected the society of medieval Europe.	Reproducible Lesson Plan 4-2 Guided Reading Activity 4-2* Section Quiz 4-2*	NGS Poster Set: *The Middle Ages* Focus on World Art Print 15, *Saint George and the Dragon*; 17, *Saint Jerome in His Study* Section Focus Transparency 4-2 NGS PicturePack Transparency Set: *The Middle Ages* World History and Art Transparency 16, *May* Vocabulary PuzzleMaker Software Student Self-Test and Review Software Testmaker Turning Points in World History: *The Crusades* NGS PictureShow CD-ROM: *The Middle Ages*
Section 3 **African Kingdoms and City-States** Describe how trade was carried out in West Africa.	Reproducible Lesson Plan 4-3 Vocabulary Activity 4* Guided Reading Activity 4-3* Section Quiz 4-3*	Section Focus Transparency 4-3 World History and Art Transparency 8, *Gold Pendant Mask* Student Self-Test and Review Software Testmaker
Section 4 **The Americas** List the factors that led to the rise and decline of the Aztec and Inca Empires.	Reproducible Lesson Plan 4-4 Guided Reading Activity 4-4* Reteaching Activity 4 Enrichment Activity 4 Section Quiz 4-4* Performance Assessment Activity 4 Spanish Chapter Summary 4	Section Focus Transparency 4-4 NGS PicturePack Transparencies: *Physical Geography of the World* World History and Art Transparency 18, *Mola Stitchery* Vocabulary PuzzleMaker Software Student Self-Test and Review Software Testmaker World Music: Cultural Traditions, Lesson 1

* Also available in Spanish

Chapter Activities

✔ Performance Assessment Activity

Starting a Modern-Day Crusade Have students expand their concept of *crusade* by researching modern-day crusades such as the women's movement, the March of Dimes crusade against polio, and so forth. After students have developed various perspectives on crusades, have them choose an issue for which they would "crusade." Students should take the roles of social activists and develop a plan for their crusade, including major events, strategies, people they would involve, and so on.

Students should also complete a reflection in which they compare their crusade to that of medieval times.

Possible Rubric Features
Accuracy of content information, research skills, organization of plan, decision-making skills

• *For an additional activity, refer to Activity 4 in the* Performance Assessment Strategies and Activities *booklet.*

ACTIVITY

From the Classroom of...

Hank Poehling
Central High School
La Crosse, Wisconsin

Compare and Contrast
The purpose of this project is to acquaint students with the historical impact of the Black Death on medieval European society. In comparing the Black Death to AIDS, students will understand the relevance of history as they also examine a contemporary problem. In addition, they receive beneficial AIDS education.

Have students produce a project comparing and contrasting the Black Death (bubonic plague) with AIDS, working either individually or in groups of up to four. The type of project can be left up to each individual or group—a display, a video newscast, a reenactment, a news-style magazine. Tell students that the following areas must be addressed in the project:
- causes of both diseases
- symptoms of both diseases
- how both are spread
- any known or possible cures for both
- the effects of each disease on the individual
- the effects of each disease on society

Allow about two weeks for the projects. On the due date, have all groups and individuals make a formal presentation of their projects to the class.

MULTIPLE LEARNING STYLES

Verbal/Linguistic
Have students prepare a talk show program about dissent within the Church during the High Middle Ages. The guests to be interviewed might include a corrupt clergyman, Pope Clement V, John Wycliffe, and Jan Hus. Students should research the lives of these figures. Then some students may act the parts of each of these figures, based on the research, and others may serve as panel members and the host of the show. Both host and panel members should research sufficiently to enable them to prepare a set of questions in advance of the show.

Visual/Spatial
Have the class work together to create a mural in the fashion of the tapestries that were popular as wall hangings during the Middle Ages. First have them research the art of tapestry and the tapestries of the Middle Ages. Then they can design a tapestry or set of tapestries, depicting some motif or event from this chapter. Students may choose such themes as the Crusades, a medieval fair, a battle of the Hundred Years' War, or some other theme. Display the completed tapestry designs in class.

Auditory/Musical
Have students present a short musical based on portraits from the General Prologue to Chaucer's *The Canterbury Tales*. Students may choose to write their lyrics either to music typical of the Middle Ages or to contemporary music.

Intrapersonal
Have students write essays in which they state whether they would have supported or opposed Wycliffe or Hus during the late Middle Ages. Ask them to explain the reasons for their stand.

Additional Resources

NATIONAL GEOGRAPHIC SOCIETY

Teacher's Corner

INDEX TO NATIONAL GEOGRAPHIC MAGAZINE

The following articles may be used for research relating to this chapter:

- "Genghis Khan," by Mike Edwards, December 1996.
- "African Gold," by Carol Beckwith and Angela Fisher, October 1996.
- "Mural Masterpieces of Ancient Cacaxtla," by George E. Stuart, September 1992.

NATIONAL GEOGRAPHIC SOCIETY PRODUCTS AVAILABLE FROM GLENCOE

To order the following products for use with this chapter, contact your local Glencoe sales representative, or call Glencoe at 1-800-334-7344:

- *The Middle Ages, Native Americans 1, Native Americans 2, The Americas (CD-ROMs)*
- *The Middle Ages, Ancient Central America, Ancient South America, Native Americans 1, Native Americans 2 (Transparencies)*
- *The Middle Ages (Poster Set)*

ADDITIONAL NATIONAL GEOGRAPHIC SOCIETY PRODUCTS

To order the following products for use with this chapter, call National Geographic Society at 1-800-368-2728:

- *PicturePack: Geography of Africa (Transparencies)*

BIBLIOGRAPHY

Literature About the Period
Bierhorst, John, ed. *The Hungry Woman: Myths and Legends of the Aztecs.* New York: William Morrow, 1984. More than two dozen Aztec tales.

Readings for the Student
McKissack, Patricia and Frederick. *The Royal Kingdoms of Ghana, Mali, and Songhay.* New York: Henry Holt, 1994. Examines the civilizations of West Africa.

Readings for the Teacher
Armstrong, Karen. *Holy War: The Crusades and Their Impact on Today's World.* New York: Doubleday, 1991. Analyzes the effects of the Crusades on current relations among Christians, Jews, and Muslims.

LOCAL OBJECTIVES

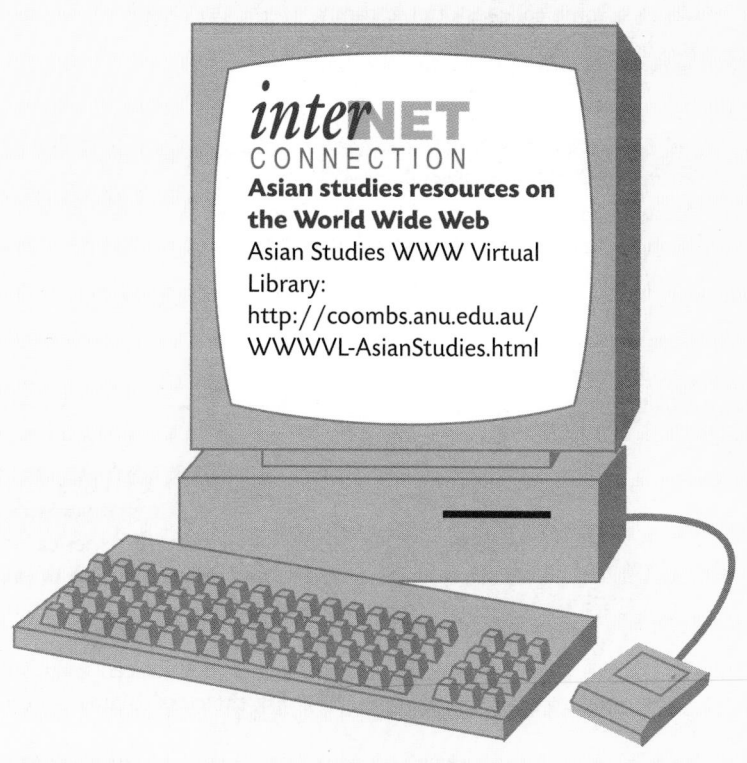

*inter*NET CONNECTION

Asian studies resources on the World Wide Web
Asian Studies WWW Virtual Library:
http://coombs.anu.edu.au/WWWVL-AsianStudies.html

CHAPTER THEMES

Chapter Themes are listed by section on this chapter opening page of the Student Edition. A corresponding theme-based activity is available under "TEACH," and a theme-based question is asked in the Section and Chapter Reviews.

The Storyteller

Historical Setting In medieval Latin, the word *universitas* meant "corporation," and the earliest universities were corporations of students and masters. These corporations received charters from popes and emperors but were entitled to govern themselves as long as they stayed away from heretical or atheistic teachings. Along with this freedom came financial independence, which meant that teachers had not only to charge fees but also to please those they taught in order to attract enough students to guarantee themselves a living. As the letter from the student to his father shows, students also had financial worries. Some colleges offered room and board to the poorest students.

Historical Significance

Answers: *Developing trade networks among different regions of the world; rise of a middle class of merchants and bureaucrats; emerging technology in areas such as shipping and land transport; expansion of government activities.*

Chapter
4
A.D. 1000–A.D. 1500
Toward a New World

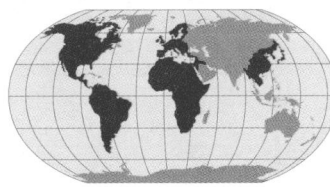

Chapter Themes

▶ **Movement** The Mongols of central Asia conquer China and parts of Europe. *Section 1*
▶ **Innovation** Advances in commerce, learning, and the arts change medieval Europe. *Section 2*
▶ **Cultural Diffusion** Africa's trade with Europe and Asia affects African cultures. *Section 3*
▶ **Change** The Aztec and the Inca establish powerful empires in Mexico and Central America. *Section 4*

The Storyteller

"Well-beloved father," wrote a medieval student, "I have not a penny, nor can I get any save through you, for all things at the University are so dear: nor can I study in my [law books], for they are all tattered. Moreover, I owe ten crowns in dues to the [university administrator], and can find no man to lend them to me.

"Well-beloved father, to ease my debts . . . at the baker's, with the doctor . . . and to pay . . . the laundress and the barber, I send you word of greetings and of money."

This letter from a European student of the A.D. 1200s sounds very much like something a modern student might write. At that time, however, the university was something new. It was part of a number of changes that were transforming life in Europe and other parts of the world during the period from A.D. 1000 to A.D. 1500. These changes prepared the way for the coming of the modern world.

Historical Significance

What features of modern civilization had their beginnings during the period from A.D. 1000 to A.D. 1500?

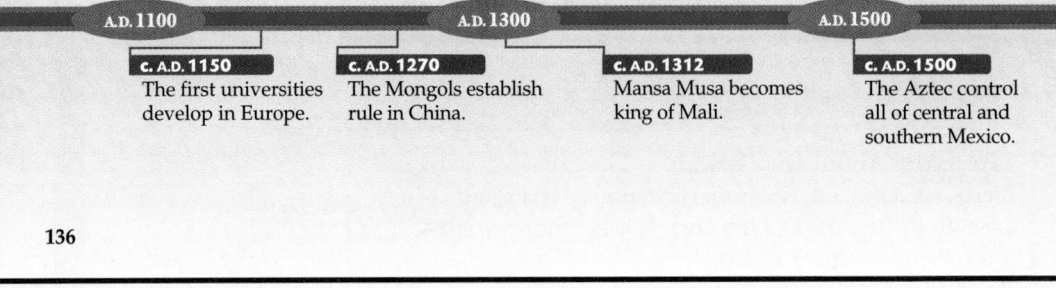

A.D. 1100	A.D. 1300	A.D. 1500
c. A.D. 1150 The first universities develop in Europe.	c. A.D. 1270 The Mongols establish rule in China.	c. A.D. 1312 Mansa Musa becomes king of Mali.	c. A.D. 1500 The Aztec control all of central and southern Mexico.

136

GEOGRAPHY CONNECTION

Location Have students find North America and South America on a map and draw an outline of each continent on tracing paper. Have them look at the map on page 163, find and draw a heavy line around the corresponding area on their traced map, and label it *North American Cultures*. Next ask the class to draw a heavy line around Mexico, Guatemala, Belize, Honduras, and El Salvador. Tell them that about half of Mexico, all of Guatemala and Belize, and parts of Honduras and El Salvador are included in Mesoamerica, where a variety of civilizations flourished. Have them label this area *Mesoamerican Cultures*. Finally, have them draw a heavy line around Ecuador, Peru, and Bolivia and label this area *Inca Empire*.

History
& Art *The Church Militant and Triumphant,* a fresco from the A.D. 1300s by Andrea
de Bonaiuto. The Spanish Chapel in Santa Maria Novella, Florence, Italy

---

Your History Journal

Copy or obtain a blank map of the world. As you read the chapter, place 10 to 20 key events on your map in the regions where they occurred. Include the dates of the these events.

✚ EXTRA CREDIT PROJECT

Research Report The Crusades are of interest from a military as well as a religious perspective. Ask students to prepare a report that compares and contrasts the organization, tactics, and effectiveness of the Crusader and Muslim armies. Suggested resources: R. C. Finucane, *Soldiers of the Faith: Crusaders and Moslems at War;* J. Godfrey, *1204: The Unholy Crusade;* H. E. Mayer, *The Crusades;* and J. Riley-Smith, *The Crusades: A Short History.*

History & Art
The church of Santa Maria Novella was founded by the Dominicans, who were named after a Spanish priest. But in Latin the words *Domini Canes* mean the "dogs of God." Why did de Bonaiuto include dogs in his fresco? *(The Dominicans served God in hunting out heresy like hounds served hunters by tracking prey.)*

✔ *Performance* Assessment

Refer to the activity on page 136C of the Planning Guide.

📁 **For an additional activity, refer to Activity 4 in the** *Performance Assessment Strategies and Activities* **booklet.**

Using Your History Journal

Students may want to use different colors to represent different types of events, such as red for military engagements, blue for political matters (the founding of cities and/or dynasties), and so on.

GLENCOE TECHNOLOGY

VIDEODISC
Use MindJogger to preview chapter content.

MindJogger Videoquiz

‖‖‖‖‖‖‖‖‖‖   Chapter 4
              Disc 1 Side A

 Also available in VHS.

A.D. 1200	A.D. 1300	A.D. 1400

c. A.D. 1206
Genghis Khan becomes
ruler of all Mongol tribes.

c. A.D. 1260
Kublai Khan becomes
emperor of China.

A.D. 1398
Timur Lenk (Tamerlane)
sacks Samarkand in
central Asia.

SECTION THEME

▶ **Movement** The Mongols of
central Asia conquer China and
parts of Europe.

Find Out ▶

Answer: *At the time, their armies
formed the most skilled fighting force in
the world. They employed terror and
Chinese techniques of siege warfare.*

FOCUS

Section Objective

Describe how the Mongols
acquired the world's largest land
empire.

BELLRINGER
Motivational Activity

Before taking roll at the
beginning of the class
period, project Section
Focus Transparency 4-1
and have students answer
the activity questions. Discuss
students' responses.
☞ This activity is also available as a blackline master.

Vocabulary Pre-check

☞ Use Vocabulary Activity 4
to introduce vocabulary terms.
L1 LEP

Section 1

Asian Empires

Setting the Scene

▶ **Terms to Define**
steppe, khan

▶ **People to Meet**
Genghis Khan, Kublai Khan, Marco Polo, Timur
Lenk (Tamerlane)

▶ **Places to Locate**
Mongolia

Find Out ▶ How did the Mongols acquire the
world's largest land empire?

The Storyteller

*The caravan halted for the night. Chaghatai, the
leader, before retiring posted a sign and fastened bells
around the animals' necks. Maffeo, a young foreigner,
wondered at these precautions. Chaghatai explained
that strange things may happen in the Desert of Lop.
"When a man is riding by night through this desert
and something happens to make him . . . lose touch
with his companions . . . he hears spirits talking. . . .
Often these voices make him stray from the path. . . .
For this reason bands of travellers make a point of
keeping very close together. . . . And round the necks
of all their beasts they fasten little
bells, so that by listening to the
sound they may prevent them from
straying from the path."*

—from *The Travels of Marco Polo,*
Marco Polo, translated by
Ronald Latham, 1958

Chinese porcelain figure

138 Chapter 4 *Toward a New World*

From the A.D. 1000s to the A.D. 1400s,
invaders from the steppe—or wide,
grassy plains of central Asia—
conquered territories in eastern Asia, the Middle
East, and eastern Europe. Originally nomads, the
invaders settled in many of the conquered areas.
They adapted to the local cultures, advanced trade,
and encouraged the exchange of goods and ideas.

The Steppe Peoples

At the beginning of the A.D. 1000s, large
numbers of nomadic groups roamed the steppe of
central Asia. Loosely organized into clans based on
family ties, they depended on the grazing of
animals for their livelihood. To protect their
pastures and provide for a growing population,
they organized under powerful chiefs. The chiefs
formed cavalry units of warriors armed with bows
and arrows. These nomadic peoples became a military threat to surrounding territories. They carried
out a series of invasions that transformed the
cultures of eastern Asia, the Middle East, and
eastern Europe.

The Seljuk Turks

The first people of the steppe to engage in
conquest were the Turks. Around A.D. 800 weak
Abbasid rulers centered in Baghdad hired Turkish
warriors to fight in their armies. As a result, the
Turks became powerful and soon controlled the
Abbasid government. Later, about A.D. 1000, a
group of Muslim Turks called the Seljuk Turks
moved from central Asia into the Middle East.
There they formed settlements and restored the
Sunni caliphate. The Seljuks also gained control of
the main trade routes between eastern Asia, the
Middle East, and Europe. They benefited from this
trade and used their wealth to build an empire.

SECTION RESOURCES

☞ **Reproducible Masters**
• Reproducible Lesson Plan 4-1
• Vocabulary Activity 4
• Guided Reading Activity 4-1
• Section Quiz 4-1

📽 **Transparencies**
• Section Focus Transparency 4-1
• World History and Art Transparency 10,
  Buddha

Multimedia
🖥 Student Self-Test and Review Software
💾 Testmaker
📀 STV: World Geography, *Asia*

Visualizing History Some people in Mongolia still live in yurts, circular domed tents of skins or felt stretched over a lattice frame. *Why did ancient Mongols choose this kind of housing?*

Seljuk warriors also invaded the highlands and plains of Asia Minor. There they defeated the Byzantines at the Battle of Manzikert in A.D. 1071. About 20 years later, the Seljuks also conquered Palestine, arousing great concern in western Europe about the safety of Christian pilgrims and holy places in the area.

Though the Seljuks were skilled warriors, they were unable to develop a well-organized government to rule their territories. Seljuk rulers lacked strong traditions of government administration and had difficulties holding the empire together. Local officials ignored the central government and acted like independent rulers. They began to fight each other for control of land. Weakened by internal upheavals, the Seljuks became prey to new nomadic invaders from central Asia.

The Mongols

During the late A.D. 1100s, the Mongols became the dominant nomadic group in central Asia. Their homeland was **Mongolia**, a region of forests and steppe northwest of China. In this wild and isolated area, they wandered from pasture to pasture with their herds of sheep, horses, and yaks, or long-haired oxen. Because of their nomadic life, the Mongols lived in movable tents called yurts. Their principal foods were meat and mare's milk. In a few fertile areas, Mongol farmers established small communities. There women raised grains while men herded animals.

Genghis Khan

Like other nomads, the Mongols at first were divided into clans. They were expert fighters on horseback, using bow and arrow. About A.D. 1206 a Mongol leader named Temujin (teh•MOO•juhn) organized the scattered clans under one government. He brought together Mongol laws in a new code known as the *yasa*. Under Temujin's guidance, an assembly of tribal chiefs met for the first time to plan military campaigns and to appoint future leaders.

Temujin's greatest achievement was in military affairs. He organized the Mongol armies into disciplined cavalry units. These units were then placed under the command of officers chosen for their abilities and not for their family ties. These changes made the Mongols the most skilled fighting force in the world at that time. As a result of his efforts, Temujin was recognized as khan, or absolute ruler. Now called **Genghis Khan** (JEHN•guhs KAHN), or "universal ruler," he set out to create a large empire.

Mongol Conquests

The Mongol armies under Genghis Khan first conquered the other steppe peoples, most of whom were Turks. These victories brought tribute money to the Mongol state as well as new recruits for the

Chapter 4 *Toward a New World* **139**

TEACH

Guided Practice

THEME Movement

Explain that the steppes are a region of dry, treeless plains covered with grass. They are very hot in summer and bitter cold in winter. **Why would this kind of topography encourage the movement of peoples?** (*The harsh environment could not long support a large population; people would have to move to find new sources of food for themselves and their animals.*) **L1**

Visualizing History Some modern yurts have stoves and wooden floors and are even equipped with electricity. **Answer to Caption:** *because the Mongols were nomads and yurts are easily moved*

Daily Life The horse was basic to the culture of the Mongols. Have one or more students research (a) the kind of horses the Mongols rode, and (b) what made the Mongols such good riders. **L2**

Mongol Conquests
Why were the Mongol conquests so successful?
The Mongols were skilled horse riders who gained tribute and recruits from conquered peoples. From the Chinese, they adopted techniques of siege warfare. This combination enabled the Mongols to have the largest land empire in history.

COOPERATIVE LEARNING ACTIVITY

TV Interview Organize the class into five teams, and assign each a Mongol leader: Genghis Khan, Ogadai, Batu, Helagu, Timur Lenk. One member of each team should play the role of announcer, one should act as interviewer, and one should be the guest. Team members should research the man to be interviewed and write questions and answers for the interview. Allow time for team members to share what they have learned and to plan the interview. Then have each team present its interview to the class. **L2**

Map Study

Answer

by bringing peace

Map Skills Practice

Reading a Map What Mongol settlement is today the capital of China? *(Cambaluc [Beijing])*

NATIONAL GEOGRAPHIC SOCIETY

VIDEODISC

STV: World Geography, Volume 1

Side One, Frames 13631–17712

Title: *Asia*

Subject: Interior and North Asia

Ask: What is the winter climate of the taiga like? *(Winters are long, very cold, and days are short.)*

Cultural Perspectives

Burial Secrets No one knows where Genghis Khan is buried. According to Mongol tradition, a ruler's grave was hidden and kept secret. The ground was trampled, trees were planted on it, and those who actually buried the ruler were executed.

World History and Art Transparency 10, *Buddha*

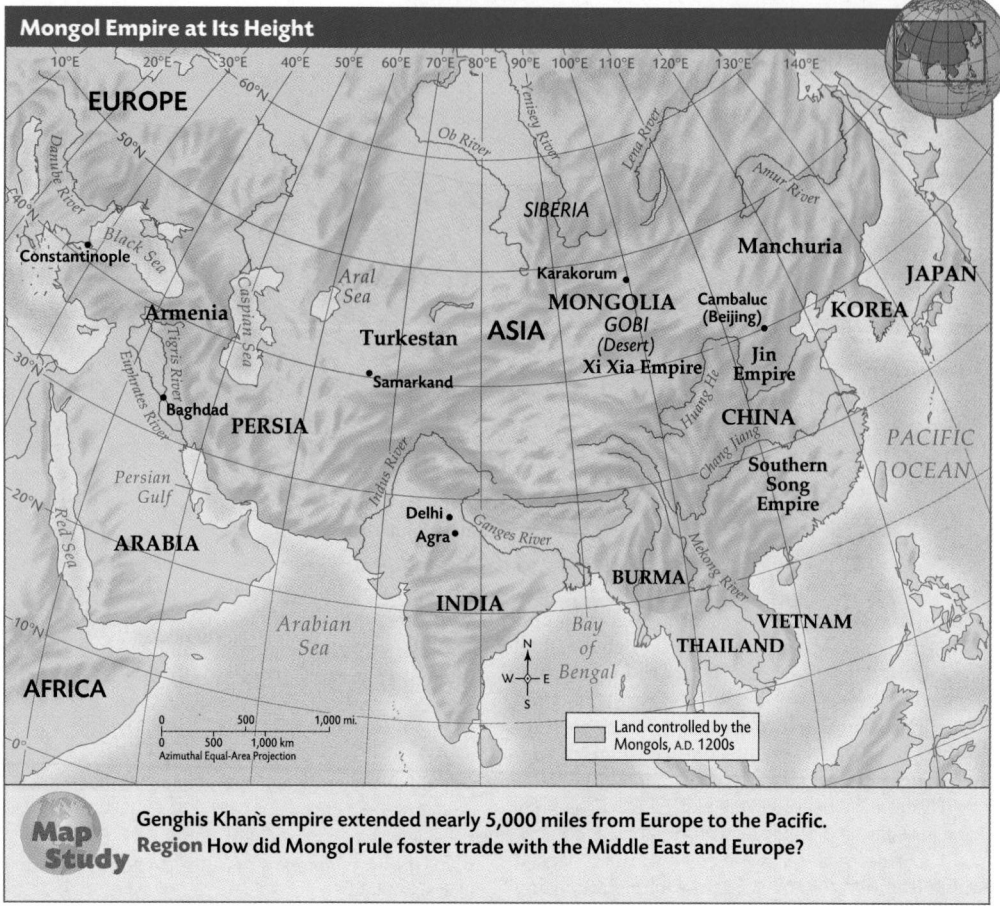

Mongol Empire at Its Height

Genghis Khan's empire extended nearly 5,000 miles from Europe to the Pacific.
Region How did Mongol rule foster trade with the Middle East and Europe?

Land controlled by the Mongols, A.D. 1200s

Mongol armies. By A.D. 1211 the Mongols were strong enough to attack major civilizations. In that year, 100,000 Mongol horsemen invaded China. While fighting the Chinese, the Mongols learned Chinese techniques of siege warfare. Using gunpowder, storming ladders, and battering rams, they won significant victories against their opponents. In spite of Genghis Khan's death in A.D. 1227, the Mongols continued their advance. By A.D. 1270 all of China was in their hands, and a Mongol dynasty ruled the country.

Under Ogadai (OH•guh•DY) Khan, the other Mongol forces moved westward. During the A.D. 1230s and A.D. 1240s, a Mongol army led by the commander Batu (bah•TOO) conquered Russian territories and then crossed the Carpathian Mountains into eastern and central Europe. Upon hearing of Ogadai's death, Batu's army returned to

Russia. There they awaited the selection of a new khan. Meanwhile, Ogadai's widow ruled the Mongols.

During the same period, another group of Mongols invaded the Middle East. Using terror to subdue the region, the Mongols destroyed cities and killed large numbers of people. In A.D. 1258 the commander Helagu (heh•lah•GOO) captured and ransacked Baghdad, the old Abbasid capital, and enslaved its inhabitants. The destruction of Baghdad represented a major setback to Islamic civilization. However, the Mongol advance was finally halted by the Mamluks, a Muslim military group that ruled Egypt.

The Mongol Empire

The Mongols created the largest land empire in history. Their territories extended from China to the

---

MEETING SPECIAL NEEDS ACTIVITY

Language Delayed To help make studying easier for students with limited English proficiency, ask other students to record this chapter on tape for home study. Have several students divide the chapter, with each student recording a few paragraphs. Ask students who use the tapes to summarize orally the main ideas of each section. These same students could prepare questions about the chapter and quiz their classmates. **L1 LEP**

frontiers of western Europe. Many of the great trade routes between Europe and Asia passed through Mongol lands. During the A.D. 1200s, Mongol rule brought peace to the region. This advanced the growth of trade and encouraged closer cultural contacts between East and West.

The Mongols respected the highly advanced culture of conquered groups and learned from them. In China, Mongol rulers gradually adopted Chinese ideas and practices. In Persia and central Asia, Mongol settlers converted to Islam and intermarried with the local Turkish population. Turkish became the principal language of the region. The Mongols of Russia, however, kept their traditional customs and lived apart from the Slavs. They settled in the empty steppe region north of the Caspian Sea. From there, they controlled the Slavic principalities located in the northern forests.

The unity of the Mongol Empire did not last long. All Mongols gave allegiance to the khan in Mongolia. However, local rulers became increasingly independent. By the end of the A.D. 1200s, Mongol territories in Russia, central Asia, Persia, and China had developed into separate and independent domains.

The Yuan Dynasty

During the A.D. 1200s, the Mongols invaded China and established the Yuan (YOO•AHN), or Mongol, dynasty. They became the first conquerors to rule most of the country.

Kublai Khan

The first great Mongol emperor of China was **Kublai Khan** (KOO•BLUH KAHN). A grandson of Genghis Khan, Kublai ruled from A.D. 1260 to A.D. 1294. Kublai Khan extended Mongol rule beyond China's borders. He conquered Korea in the north and part of Southeast Asia. He made two attempts to invade Japan, using Chinese and Korean ships. Both efforts failed because the Mongols were not skilled in naval warfare.

Although Kublai complied with some Chinese traditions to better control the Chinese, he tried to maintain Mongol culture. Government documents were written first in Mongolian and then translated into Chinese. Furthermore, the highest positions in the emperor's court were given to Mongols or foreigners.

The most famous of these foreigners appointed to government posts may have been a Venetian named **Marco Polo**. According to Polo, he arrived in China in A.D. 1271 and stayed 17 years, traveling through Mongol territory on the Khan's missions. After Polo returned to Italy, his tales of the splendor of Chinese civilization astounded Europeans.

Mongol Government and Society

Like traditional Chinese rulers, the Mongol emperors of China were regarded as absolute rulers. In addition to heading the bureaucracy, the emperors provided government funds for schools and temples. They gave charitable aid to the elderly and sick. Public granaries were maintained to provide food in time of famine. China's Mongol rulers also built canals, roads, and irrigation systems. A notable achievement of the Mongol emperors was the construction of a permanent capital at Cambaluc. With its palaces and parks, Cambaluc was one of the world's most beautiful cities. At its center was the emperor's palace. It was a large building with many courtyards and halls. The grounds of the palace had lakes, hills, orchards, and grassy plains grazed by animals.

Under Mongol rule, Chinese civilization broke with past traditions and developed new styles in the arts. The most important changes occurred in literature. Because many Chinese were not admitted to government service, scholars turned to creative writing. They developed Chinese drama, in which lively action was combined with realistic portrayals of human characters. Many plays were written in the language of the common people rather than the language of scholars. Chinese theater had little scenery and furnishings. The actors, all of whom were male, wore elaborate costumes and sang rather than spoke their lines. An orchestra placed on stage provided background music.

Mongol rulers made Buddhism the state religion. However, they permitted the practice of Confucianism and Daoism. They also allowed the introduction of Christianity and Islam into China. These two religions, however, won only a comparatively small number of Chinese converts.

Mongol Peace and Decline

Travelers, such as Marco Polo who arrived in China in A.D. 1271 and stayed for 17 years, were able to journey throughout China because the Mongols enforced a relatively stable order. Merchants could safely travel the roads built by the Mongols. Mongol rule thus fostered trade and connections with Europe.

Through contact with the Middle East, Russia, and Europe, the Chinese obtained enslaved people as well as products such as glass, hides, clothes, silver, cotton, and carpets. In return, Europeans

Independent Practice

Guided Reading Activity 4-1 **L1**

ASSESS

Check for Understanding

Assign Section 1 Review as homework or as an in-class activity.

Use Student Self-Test and Review Software to review Section 1.

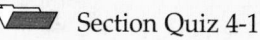

Who?What?Where?When?

The city of **Pagan**, in what is now Myanmar, controlled a large area along the Irrawaddy River. Among the visitors to this kingdom was Marco Polo, who was impressed by its magnificent monasteries and temples.

Evaluate

Section Quiz 4-1

Use the Testmaker to create a customized quiz for Section 1.

MAKING CONNECTIONS ACTIVITY

Guerrilla Warfare Kublai Khan's first major expedition into Vietnam failed in the 1200s. The Mongols' cavalry could not proceed in the rain forests of Vietnam. They then reorganized the cavalry into an army, thinking they were unbeatable. The Vietnamese, however, periodically unleashed guerrilla raids and ultimately defeated the Mongols.

During the Vietnam War in the 1960s and 1970s, U.S. troops faced many of the same problems that the Mongols had 700 years earlier. Ask students to look up information on the Vietnam War and name some of the similarities. *(unfamiliar climate, hit-and-run attacks, difficulty in finding the Vietcong forces, overconfidence in American military)* **L2**

TEACH

Tell students that, after Marco Polo's return, he was captured and imprisoned by the Genoese, archrivals of the Venetians. There he dictated his book, known in English as the *Travels of Marco Polo*, to a fellow prisoner. It was instantly popular and soon known all over Europe (even though this was before the days of printing). **Why, do you think, were Europeans of Polo's time eager to read his book?** *(Answers will vary but should include the fact that East Asia was practically unknown to Europe at the time.)*

CURRICULUM CONNECTION

LITERATURE

One of the most famous poems of the English Romantic period is "Kubla Khan," by Samuel Taylor Coleridge. Published in 1816, it portrays Kublai Khan's court as a place of fantastic beauty.

The Bodleian Library, Oxford, Ms. Bodl. 264, fol.219ᵇ

Kublai Khan and Marco Polo

This medieval English manuscript shows the Chinese emperor Kublai Khan presenting golden tablets to Marco Polo and his family to ensure their safe passage back to the West. In A.D. 1297 Marco Polo wrote an account of a trip he claimed to have made to China, and his book eventually became popular with the small literate class in Europe. The painter who embellished this manuscript had never met Marco Polo nor had he ever seen a picture of an Asian. Maybe that's why the emperor looks European rather than Asian.

The Mongol rulers of China put the country in closer touch with the Middle East and Europe. The Mongolian khans were outsiders who distrusted, and were distrusted by, their Chinese subjects. The khans turned to outsiders to help them rule, especially after Kublai Khan moved the Chinese capital to Beijing. The Polos (Marco Polo's father and uncle accompanied him to China) were but three of hundreds of European and Muslim merchants and artisans who moved in and out of China. But Marco Polo became famous, both in his time and in ours, because he wrote a book about his adventures. The Polos may have brought Chinese noodles back to Europe, and other European and Muslim travelers brought Chinese inventions such as gunpowder and the compass back to the West. This transfer of technology had a major impact on the history of Europe. ⊕

142 Chapter 4 *Toward a New World*

benefited from the increased trade with China as they obtained exotic products such as silk, porcelain, and tea.

After Kublai Khan died in A.D. 1294, a series of weak successors took over the throne. The Chinese, still resentful of foreign rule, began to stage rebellions against these rulers. Finally, in A.D. 1368, a young Buddhist monk named Zhu Yuanzhang (JOO YOO•AHN•JAHNG) led an army against the capital and overthrew the Yuan dynasty.

Timur Lenk

About the same time as the overthrow of the Mongol dynasty in China, another powerful nomadic force emerged from central Asia. In the A.D. 1390s, a Turkish-Mongol chief named **Timur Lenk** (in English, **Tamerlane**) rose to power in the region. As a youth, Timur was known for his athletic abilities, especially in horse riding. He began his rise as leader of a small nomadic tribe and extended his rule through numerous wars with neighboring tribes.

A devout Muslim, Timur hoped to spread Islam to new areas of Asia. His religious zeal also made him oppose Muslims who differed with his understanding of Islam. Claiming descent from Genghis Khan, Timur united the Turkish-Mongols and extended their rule over much of the Middle East. In A.D. 1398 Timur's armies also invaded the Indian subcontinent and defeated the forces of the ruling Delhi sultan at the Battle of Panipat.

Although Timur was ruthless, the people under his rule created important centers of civilization in central Asia. The most influential city in the region was Samarkand which Timur established at the capital of his empire. A wealthy trading and craft center, it became known for its beautifully decorated mosques and tombs. Many of these architectural monuments contained colorful turquoise, gold, and marble mosaics. Samarkand also became a center of scholarship and science. Astronomers

there set up an observatory and drew up astronomical tables that were later used by European scientists during the 1600s.

In A.D. 1402 Timur and his armies swept into Asia Minor, defeating another Turkish group—the Ottomans—at Ankara. Timur's effort to gain territory and establish his dominance in Asia Minor never succeeded. In A.D. 1405 Timur died of fever and was buried in Samarkand. The huge empire soon collapsed. The Ottomans were able to regain their lost lands and began the building of a state that eventually spread throughout the Middle East.

Visualizing History The name Timur Lenk means "Timur the Lame." This Mongol leader was wounded by an arrow when he was a young man. **Answer to Caption:** *Samarkand*

Reteach

Have students summarize the main conquests of the Mongols.

Enrich

Have students research and report on present-day Mongolia, especially its people's way of life.

Linking Past and Present

Mogul Rule In the 1500s, a descendant of both Genghis Khan and Timur Lenk led a Mongol conquest of India. His people, who ruled India for 200 years, were called Moguls, from the Persian word for Mongol. A Mogul ruler named Shah Jahan built the Taj Mahal, one of the most beautiful buildings in the world.

CLOSE

Ask students to summarize the positive and negative consequences of Mongol rule.

SECTION 1 REVIEW

Recall
1. **Define** steppe, khan.
2. **Identify** the Seljuk Turks, the Mongols, Genghis Khan, Kublai Khan, Marco Polo, Timur Lenk (Tamerlane).
3. **Explain** why the empire

founded by the Seljuk Turks declined so quickly.

Critical Thinking
4. **Synthesizing Information** What factors led the steppe peoples to expand their territories and to create empires?

Understanding Themes
5. **Movement** How did the conquests of Mongol warriors contribute to the spread of culture and ideas throughout much of Asia and parts of Europe?

SECTION 1 REVIEW ANSWERS

1. All vocabulary words are defined in the Glossary.
2. Seljuk Turks, 138; Mongols, 139; Genghis Khan, 139; Kublai Khan, 141; Marco Polo, 141; Timur Lenk, 143
3. The Seljuk Turks failed to develop an efficient means of governing, especially at the

local level, which was essential to holding their empire together.
4. The steppe could not support an expanding population.
5. **MOVEMENT** By creating a large, peaceful empire, the Mongols encouraged the spread of culture.

A.D. 1100   A.D. 1300   A.D. 1500

c. A.D. 1150
French architects begin
to build in Gothic style.

A.D. 1204
Crusaders sack
Constantinople.

A.D. 1348
Black Death spreads
throughout Europe.

A.D. 1469
Ferdinand of Aragon and
Isabella of Castile marry.

Section 2

A New Europe

Setting the Scene

▶ **Terms to Define**
the Crusades, charter, money economy, guilds, scholasticism, vernacular, czar

▶ **People to Meet**
Pope Urban II, Joan of Arc, Henry VII, Ferdinand of Aragon, Isabella of Castile, Ivan III, John Wycliffe

▶ **Places to Locate**
Venice, Flanders, Castile, Aragon

 **ind Out**   How did the growth of trade, towns, and monarchies affect the society of medieval Europe?

Storyteller

   Geoffrey de Renneville was footsore, thirsty, and covered with dust. He had joined the Crusade as an adventure. The Crusaders had traveled for weeks and were beset by flies, raids by bandits, disease, poor food, and limited drink. The cavalcade stopped and the weary men dropped into an uneasy slumber. Suddenly, they were startled awake by the cry "Help for the Holy Sepulchre!" One by one the knights took up the cry. Shouting with the others, Geoffrey was reminded of the Crusade's purpose.

   —adapted from *The Dream and the Tomb*, Robert Payne, 1984

Leaving for the Crusades

uropean life in the early Middle Ages was characterized by decentralized government, warfare, cultural isolation, and wretched living conditions. Trade was sparse, and agricultural production—the mainstay of the economy—was inefficient.

   By A.D. 1100, however, conditions in Europe had begun to improve. Some European monarchs succeeded in building strong central governments. Better farming methods led to larger crop yields and a growth in population. Towns and trade began to reappear. The Church held a powerful sway over the emotions and energies of the people. Changes in religion, society, politics, and economics made the High Middle Ages—the period between A.D. 1050 and A.D. 1270—a springboard for a new and brilliant civilization in western Europe.

TURNING POINT

The Crusades

   The transformation of medieval society began with a holy war over Jerusalem, a sacred city to Jews, Muslims, and Christians alike. During the High Middle Ages, European Christians undertook a series of military expeditions—nine in all—to recover the Holy Land from the Muslims. These expeditions were called the Crusades, from the Latin word *crux*, meaning "cross." Those who fought were called Crusaders because they vowed to "take up the cross."

First Crusade
   In the A.D. 600s, Arab Muslims had conquered Jerusalem and the entire region of Palestine. The new Arab rulers generally allowed Christian pilgrims to travel to Jerusalem without interference. During the A.D. 1200s, however, the Seljuk Turks from central Asia took control of Jerusalem.

Their conquest left Palestine in chaos, and the hazards of pilgrimage increased. The Seljuks also threatened the Byzantine Empire, especially Constantinople. As a result of this threat, the Byzantine emperor wrote to the pope in A.D. 1095 requesting military assistance from the West.

In the autumn of A.D. 1095, **Pope Urban II** attended a council of church leaders at Clermont, France. At this gathering he called for a Crusade. In a stirring sermon, the pope urged Europe's Christians to cease fighting among themselves and to recapture Palestine from the Seljuks. He promised that those who joined the crusade would enjoy both spiritual and material rewards.

The crowd enthusiastically responded with cries of *"Deus vult!"* (God wills it!). Knights and peasants alike vowed to join the expedition to Palestine. For knights, the Crusade was a welcome chance to employ their fighting skills. For peasants, the Crusade meant at least a temporary release from feudal bonds. Adventure and the possibility of wealth were other reasons to join the Crusade.

During the First Crusade, which began in A.D. 1096, three armies of Crusader knights and volunteers traveled separately from western Europe to the eastern Mediterranean. On the way, many of them killed Jews and sometimes massacred entire Jewish communities. These killings reflected the heightened hatred of non-Christians that came with the First Crusade and marked the onset of a long period of Christian persecution of the Jews.

Led by French nobles, the three Crusader armies finally met in Constantinople in A.D. 1097. From there, they made their way to Jerusalem, enduring the hardships of desert travel as well as quarrels among their leaders. In June A.D. 1099, the Crusaders finally reached the holy city. After a siege of almost two months, Jerusalem fell. Crusaders swarmed into the city and killed most of its Muslim and Jewish inhabitants.

Soon after the conquest, the religious zeal of the Crusaders cooled, and many knights returned home. Those who stayed set up feudal states in Palestine.

Second Crusade

Less than 50 years after the First Crusade, the Seljuks conquered part of the Crusader states in Palestine. Pope Eugenius IV called for a Second Crusade to regain the territory. Eloquent sermons by the monk Bernard of Clairvaux (KLAR•VOH) persuaded King Louis VII of France and Holy Roman Emperor Conrad III to lead armies to Palestine. The Second Crusade, which lasted from A.D. 1147 to A.D. 1149, was unsuccessful. Louis VII

 **Pope Urban II arrives at the Council of Clermont.** *What did the pope ask the people to do?*

and Conrad III quarreled constantly and were ineffective militarily. They were easily defeated by the Seljuks.

Third Crusade

A diplomatic and forceful leader named Saladin (SA•luh•DEEN) united the Muslim forces and then captured Jerusalem in A.D. 1187. The people of western Europe were stunned and horrified. Holy Roman Emperor Frederick Barbarossa of Germany, King Philip Augustus of France, and King Richard I of England assembled warriors for the Third Crusade. This "Crusade of Kings" lasted from A.D. 1189 to A.D. 1192 and was no more successful than the Second Crusade. The German and French forces returned home, and Richard continued the struggle alone.

Although his army defeated the Muslims in several battles, Richard could not win a decisive victory over Saladin's well-trained and dedicated forces. After three years of fighting, Richard signed a truce with Saladin. The Muslims refused to turn over Jerusalem but allowed Christian pilgrims entry to the city.

Chapter 4   *Toward a New World*   **145**

TEACH

Guided Practice

THEME Innovation

Have students give some examples of innovations that developed during the High Middle Ages. *(heavier plows and collar harnesses, trade fairs, money economy, universities)* **L1 LEP**

 When he was born to noble parents about A.D. 1035 in the Champagne region of France, the baby who would become pope some 53 years later was named Odo. **Answer to Caption:** *to recapture Palestine from the Seljuks*

TURNING POINT

The Crusades
How did the Crusades encourage Europeans to increase trade?
Increased knowledge of Asia's civilizations increased the demand for imported goods.

VIDEODISC
Turning Points in World History

Side One
Chapter 7

Title: *The Crusades*

COOPERATIVE LEARNING ACTIVITY

Drawing Maps Have students work in small groups to research and prepare maps of the various routes used by the Crusaders to reach the Middle East. (For example, early Crusaders from France and Germany sailed from Italy to Greece or crossed Europe to Constantinople, then marched across present-day Turkey. Later Crusaders sailed from the Mediterranean coast to ports in Palestine.) Assign each student a task, such as tracing the area from western Europe to the Middle East, drawing in topographic features, drawing the routes used by the Crusaders, or illustrating maps with pictures pertaining to the Crusaders or dangers they encountered. Display and discuss the completed maps in class. **L2**

Map Study

Answer
about 1,875 miles (3,017 km)

Map Skills Practice

Reading a Map About how far did Crusaders on the First Crusade travel before reaching Jerusalem? *(about 2,000 miles [3,218 km])*

Literature Have students read Sir Walter Scott's *Ivanhoe*, whose main character is a Crusader. Ask them to report to the class on the Christian-Jewish interactions depicted in the novel. **L3**

Focus on World Art Print 15, *Saint George and the Dragon*; 17, *Saint Jerome in His Study*

World History and Art Transparency 16, *May*

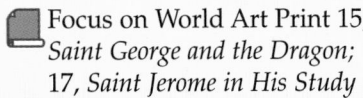

The following videotape program is available from Glencoe:
- **Richard the Lionheart**

NATIONAL GEOGRAPHIC SOCIETY

Use these materials to enrich student understanding of the Middle Ages.

📖 **NGS POSTER SET**
The Middle Ages

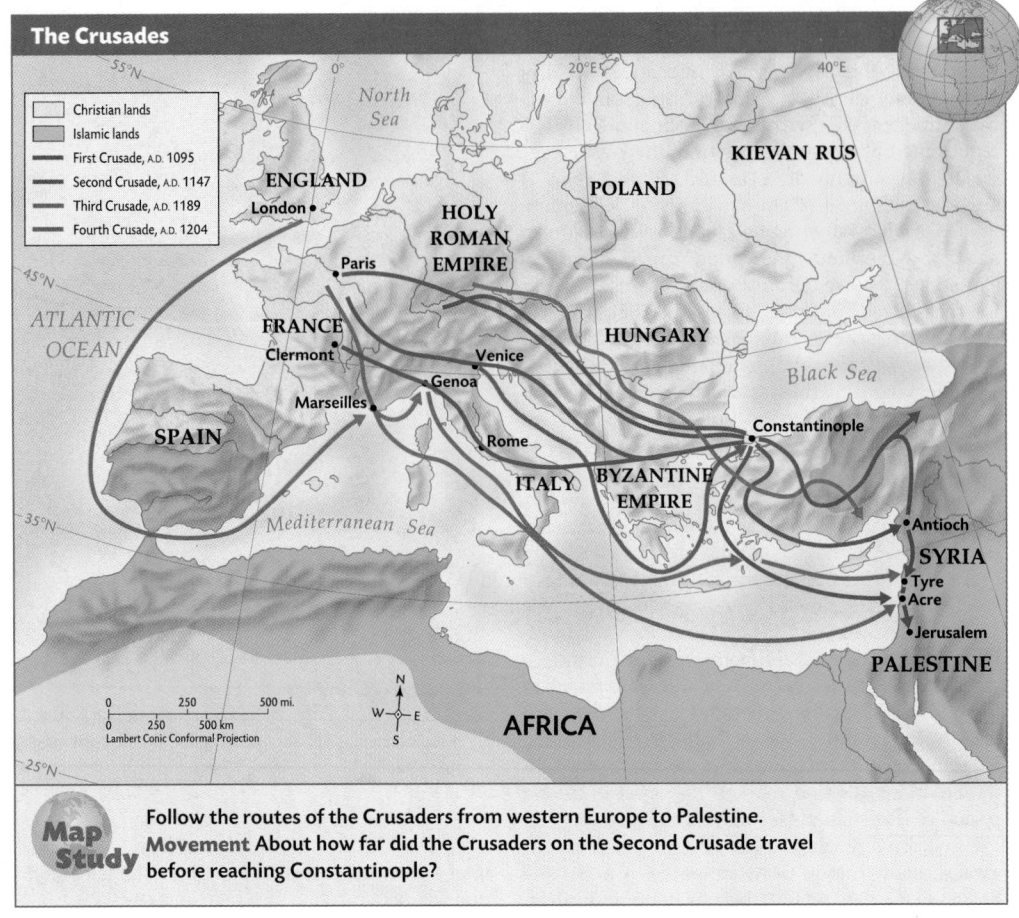

The Crusades

Legend:
- Christian lands
- Islamic lands
- First Crusade, A.D. 1095
- Second Crusade, A.D. 1147
- Third Crusade, A.D. 1189
- Fourth Crusade, A.D. 1204

Map labels: North Sea, KIEVAN RUS, POLAND, ENGLAND, London, HOLY ROMAN EMPIRE, Paris, ATLANTIC OCEAN, FRANCE, Clermont, HUNGARY, Venice, Genoa, Black Sea, Marseilles, SPAIN, Rome, Constantinople, ITALY, BYZANTINE EMPIRE, Mediterranean Sea, Antioch, SYRIA, Tyre, Acre, Jerusalem, PALESTINE, AFRICA

Scale: 0 250 500 mi. / 0 250 500 km
Lambert Conic Conformal Projection

Map Study Follow the routes of the Crusaders from western Europe to Palestine. **Movement** About how far did the Crusaders on the Second Crusade travel before reaching Constantinople?

Effects of the Crusades

Other Crusades followed in the A.D. 1200s, but none succeeded in winning permanent Christian control of Palestine. In fact the Muslims slowly conquered all the remaining Christian territories. Nonetheless, the Crusades had a major impact on the development of western Europe. In Europe the Crusades helped break down feudalism and increase the authority of kings. Kings levied taxes and raised large armies of fighting forces. Some nobles died in battle without leaving heirs, and their lands passed to kings. To raise money for weapons and supplies, many lesser nobles sold their estates or allowed their serfs to become free farmers on the land or artisans in the towns.

Contact between the Crusaders and the more advanced Byzantine and Muslim civilizations broadened European views of the world. In addition, European cities—especially Venice and Genoa in Italy—became more prosperous and powerful due to increased trading in the Mediterranean. Contact with the East spurred a new demand for luxury goods: spices, sugar, melons, tapestries, silk, and other items previously hard to come by.

Finally, the Crusades improved European technology. From the Muslims, the Crusaders learned how to build better ships and make more accurate maps. They began to use the magnetic compass to tell direction. The Crusaders also learned new military skills, especially in siege techniques. Weaponry significantly improved as well.

The Crusades had less impact on the Muslims. Crusader states were relatively weak in an area divided among powerful Muslim rivals. The arrival of the Crusaders, however, helped unite the Muslims against a common enemy.

MEETING SPECIAL NEEDS ACTIVITY

Learning Style: Visual/Spatial To reinforce the ideas presented in this section, have students who are visual learners draw a series of illustrations depicting important events and people. Illustrations could include Pope Urban II delivering his call for the First Crusade, a series of drawings depicting the journeys of Crusaders to the Holy Land, or a portrait of King Richard I of England. Ask the artists to work with other students to create text that explains their drawings. Display the completed drawings and accompanying text in the classroom. **L1 LEP**

European Revival

The Crusades advanced the transformation of western Europe from a backward, often violent, society to a civilization that exhibited some early features of modern Western civilization. Towns grew, trade expanded, and learning and the arts thrived.

Agricultural Advances

During the A.D. 1000s, Europe's agricultural production increased. Using the three-field system, a heavier plow that cut through difficult soil, and fast-moving horses instead of slower oxen, farmers were able to produce more food and to cultivate new lands. Nobles and freeholders—peasants not bound to the land—moved to new areas, clearing forests, draining swamps, and building villages. In one of the largest migrations of the time, Germans moved to eastern Europe, doubling the territory they controlled.

Growth of Towns

As the land began to feed more people, the population naturally increased. During the A.D. 1000s and A.D. 1100s, the number of towns in western Europe grew tremendously. Many towns developed beside well-traveled roads or near waterways. For protection, townspeople built walls around their communities. Inside the walls most buildings were of wood and had thatch roofs, making fire a constant hazard.

Medieval towns had almost no sanitation facilities, causing the rapid spread of diseases such as diphtheria, typhoid, influenza, and malaria. In crowded towns such diseases often turned into epidemics and took many lives. The worst of these epidemics ravaged Europe between A.D. 1348 and A.D. 1350, killing one-third of the population and earning the name the Black Death.

The Middle Class

The medieval town, or *burg,* created the name for a new class of people. In Germany they were called *burghers;* in France, the *bourgeoisie* (BURZH•WAH•ZEE); and in England, *burgesses.* The name originally referred to anyone living in a town. Gradually it came to mean a middle class of merchants, bankers, and artisans who made money rather than relying on the land for a living.

Conflict gradually developed between the middle class and the traditional feudal classes. City dwellers resented owing taxes and services to lords. They wanted to run their own affairs and have their own laws. In the A.D. 1000s, Italian towns used the power they gained from trade and commerce to form independent city-states. In other areas of Europe, kings and nobles granted townspeople charters, documents that gave them the right to control their own affairs. At the same time, many towns remained a part of a kingdom or feudal territory.

Trade and Money

The growth of towns caused a rapid expansion of trade. Important land and water routes connected western Europe with the Mediterranean, eastern Europe, and Scandinavia. Italian towns such as **Venice** controlled the Mediterranean trade after A.D. 1200, bringing silks and spices from Asia to Europe. The town of **Flanders**, a region that includes present-day northern France and southern Belgium, became the center of trade on Europe's northern coast. Towns along the Baltic coast formed the Hanseatic League, which carried out trade between eastern Europe and the North Atlantic. The textiles produced by many European towns were traded at Middle Eastern markets for porcelain, velvet, silk, and silver.

In medieval Europe, merchants at first used the barter system, exchanging one good for another. When this method proved to be impractical, they developed a money economy, based on the use of money as a common medium of exchange.

The rise of a money economy had far-reaching consequences for the growth of Europe. Initially, it led to the growth of banking. Since traders came from many countries, they carried different currencies with different values. Moneychangers—often Jews or Italians—determined the value of the various currencies and exchanged one currency for another. They also developed procedures for transferring funds from one place to another, received deposits, and arranged loans, thus becoming the first bankers in Europe.

As the money economy grew, it put the feudal classes in an economic squeeze. Kings, clergy, and nobles became dependent on money from banks to pay their expenses. To pay off their loans, they had to raise taxes, sell their lands, or demand money in place of traditional feudal services. As serfs became able to buy their freedom, the feudal system declined.

Guilds

During the A.D. 1100s, European merchants and artisans organized themselves into business associations called guilds. The primary function of the merchant guild was to maintain a monopoly of the local market for its members. To accomplish this end, merchant guilds severely restricted trading by foreigners in their city and enforced uniform pricing. Craft guilds, by contrast, regulated the work of artisans and established strict rules

Economics Have students explain the consequences of the rise of a money economy. Ask how it affected banking. *(led to the growth of banking)* How did a money economy affect the feudal system? *(It weakened feudalism by forcing lords to become dependent on money for expenses and by enabling serfs to buy their freedom.)* **L2**

Critical Thinking Have students discuss the benefits of the guild system. How did guilds help not only guild members but also society at large? *(ensured high quality)* What were some disadvantages? *(Students may answer that guilds could fix prices at an unfair level or that discouraging competition also discouraged growth of business.)* **L3**

> ### *Cultural Perspectives*
> **Early Universities** Although modern universities had their origins in medieval Europe, Arabs had founded universities nearly 200 years earlier. The Fatimids founded Cairo's al-Azhar University in A.D. 970. It remains the world's chief center of Islamic and Arabic learning.

MAKING CONNECTIONS ACTIVITY

Movement Have students use a map to locate the city of Jerusalem (in the present country of Israel), as well as England, France, Germany, and Italy. Have students discuss some of the difficulties that physical geography presented to medieval armies traveling from Europe to Jerusalem. *(crossing the Alps, crossing the mountains of the Macedonian peninsula, traveling through the Syrian and Palestinian deserts, the dangers of open sea voyages on the Mediterranean)*

you don't say...

Burg The term *burg* originally meant a fortified town or castle. As part of town names, it appeared in the German *-burg*, the French *-bourg*, and the English *-borough* and *-bury*. Today in Europe one can find Hamburg, Strasbourg, Edinburgh, and Canterbury; in the United States there is Pittsburgh, Harrisburg, Jonesboro, and Salisbury.

The Plague

In addition to the physical effects, the psychological effects of the Black Death were also significant. Many people, searching for answers to the scourge, turned to mysticism and superstitious practices. They often found little spiritual guidance among the clergy, who fell ill and died at the same alarming rate as the general population. As the number of educated priests declined, religious orders began to recruit less qualified individuals, which lowered the overall intellectual level of the Church.

ANSWERS

Students may discuss the advances in medicine during modern times that have helped control the spread of diseases and have lessened their economic impact. When people exposed to an infection in one part of the world travel to another part, they can infect people with whom they come into contact.

---

concerning prices, wages, and employment. Although both merchant and craft guilds prohibited competition, they set standards of quality to protect the public from shoddy goods.

Craft guilds were controlled by masters, or artisans who owned their own shops and tools. Trainees known as apprentices worked for a master without pay for a certain length of time. An apprentice then became a journeyman and received pay. When a journeyman became skilled at his craft, he submitted a special sample of his work—a masterpiece—to the guild for approval. If the sample was approved, the journeyman became a master and could set up his own shop.

Aside from business activities, guilds provided benefits such as medical care and unemployment relief for their members. Guilds also organized social and religious life by sponsoring banquets, holy day processions, and outdoor plays.

Universities

During the Early Middle Ages, most people were illiterate. Education was controlled by the clergy, and students attended monastery and cathedral schools to prepare for work as church officials. As towns grew, the need for educated officials and lawyers stimulated a new interest in learning. Around A.D. 1150 students and teachers began meeting away from monastery and cathedral schools. They formed organizations that became known as universities.

The university at first was not so much a place as it was a group of scholars organized like a guild for the purpose of learning. In most classes a teacher read the text and discussed it, while students took notes on slates or committed as much information as possible to memory. To qualify as a teacher, students had to pass an examination leading to a degree, or certificate of completion.

By the end of the A.D. 1200s, universities had spread throughout Europe. Most southern European universities were modeled after the law school at Bologna (buh•LOH•nyuh), Italy, and specialized in law and medicine. Universities in northern Europe, on the other hand, specialized in liberal arts and theology. These were generally modeled after the University of Paris.

CONNECTIONS

Geography

The Plague

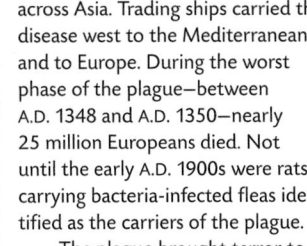

The Black Death

The Black Death—known today as the bubonic plague—was the worst medieval epidemic. It began in China and spread across Asia. Trading ships carried the disease west to the Mediterranean and to Europe. During the worst phase of the plague—between A.D. 1348 and A.D. 1350—nearly 25 million Europeans died. Not until the early A.D. 1900s were rats carrying bacteria-infected fleas identified as the carriers of the plague.

The plague brought terror to many medieval Europeans, who saw it as God's punishment. As deaths increased, production declined, and prices and wages rose. To cut costs, many landowners switched from farming to sheep raising (which required less labor) and drove villagers off the land. Merchants in towns laid off workers and demanded laws to limit wages. These setbacks, as well as the fear of plague, sparked peasant and worker uprisings. It would take at least a century for western Europe to recover.

Today, plague occasionally occurs in developing areas of Asia, Africa, and South America. Knowledge of disease prevention and the development of vaccines, however, have largely isolated plague outbreaks and reduced their devastating impact on societies.

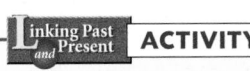
ACTIVITY

Examine the effects of disease on medieval and modern societies. How is the spread of disease related to human movement?

CRITICAL THINKING ACTIVITY

Making Inferences The general climate in Palestine where the Crusaders fought was similar to that of the western United States and Mexico—a combination of semi-desert and Mediterranean climates. Average temperature in Palestine was between 60° and 70°F (16°–21°C), similar to temperatures throughout the southern United States. Considering that most Crusaders came from countries in northern Europe, ask students to surmise what effects the climate and temperature in Palestine would have had on them. How do students think the climate and temperature would have affected the Muslim forces?. **L1**

New Learning

At medieval universities, scholars studied classical writings, especially the works of Aristotle. Many church leaders opposed the study of Aristotle, fearing that his ideas threatened Christian teachings. In contrast, some scholars thought the new knowledge could be used to support Christian ideas. They applied Aristotle's philosophy to theological questions and developed a system of thought called scholasticism. In seeking to reconcile classical philosophy with the Church's teachings, the supporters of scholasticism believed that all knowledge could be integrated into a coherent whole.

In the A.D. 1200s, the most important scholastic thinker was Thomas Aquinas (uh•KWY•nuhs), a brilliant theologian and philosopher who taught philosophy in Paris and Naples. In his work *Summa Theologica* (a summary of religious thought), Aquinas claimed that reason was a gift from God that could provide answers to basic philosophical questions. The Catholic Church later accepted and promoted Aquinas's way of teaching and thinking.

Medieval Literature

The renewed interest in learning promoted advances in literature and the arts. Most medieval literature was written in the vernacular, or language of everyday speech, of the writer. Instead of using Latin as a common language, people spoke the language of their own country—English, German, French, Italian, or Spanish. These vernacular languages helped give each kingdom of Europe a separate identity. Use of vernacular languages in writing made literature accessible to more people.

Some outstanding works of literature were written in the vernacular in the A.D. 1300s. Dante Alighieri (DAHN•tay A•luh•GYEHR•ee) wrote the *Divine Comedy*, an epic poem in Italian. Written over a period of several years, the poem discusses medieval ideas of life after death by describing an imaginary journey from hell to heaven.

In England a government official named Geoffrey Chaucer began *The Canterbury Tales* in A.D. 1386 and continued the series of tales, probably right up to his death in A.D. 1400. The narrative poems brilliantly describe a group of pilgrims, representing people of various classes and occupations, who tell stories to amuse one another on their way to a shrine at Canterbury, England.

Medieval Art

Early medieval churches were built in a style called Romanesque, which combined features of Roman and Byzantine structures. Romanesque churches had thick walls, columns set close together, heavy curved arches, and small windows. About A.D. 1150 French architects began to build in a new style called Gothic. They replaced Romanesque heavy walls and low arches with flying buttresses. These stone beams, extending out from the wall, took the building's weight off the walls. This allowed the walls to be thinner, with space for stained-glass windows. The ceiling inside was supported by pointed arches made of narrow stone ribs reaching out from tall pillars. These supports allowed architects to build higher ceilings and more open interiors.

Medieval painters turned their attention to a smaller art form, the illuminated manuscript. Adorned with brilliantly colored illustrations and often highlighted with gold leaf, these works were miniature masterpieces whose beauty has endured to the present day.

Strengthening of Monarchy

During the High Middle Ages, political power steadily shifted from feudal nobles to kings or queens. Gradually the influence of the clergy and nobles diminished as educated common people and laymen became advisers to monarchs. Despite the strengthening of monarchy and central government, feudal disputes continued to spark conflict throughout Europe.

The Hundred Years' War

Between A.D. 1337 and A.D. 1453, the kings of France and England fought the Hundred Years' War—actually a series of wars—for control of French territory. Another cause of the conflict was the desire of English monarchs to obtain the French throne.

Despite being poorer and less populated than France, England won the early battles of the Hundred Years' War, which were fought on French soil. English unity at home and superior military tactics contributed to this success. With the use of two new weapons—the Welsh longbow and a portable firearm that was a forerunner of the cannon—English archers and foot soldiers won the war's greatest victories in the Battle of Crécy (kray•SEE) in A.D. 1346 and the Battle of Agincourt (A•juhn•KORT) in A.D. 1415.

By A.D. 1429 when French fortunes had reached their lowest, a young peasant woman named **Joan of Arc** helped bring about a dramatic reversal. Joan led a French army and ended the

---

Literature Have students read the General Prologue to Chaucer's *The Canterbury Tales* and write a character sketch of three different pilgrims. Select several students to read their character sketches aloud. **L3**

NATIONAL GEOGRAPHIC SOCIETY

Use these materials to enrich student understanding of the Middle Ages.

- **NGS PICTURESHOW CD-ROM**
  The Middle Ages
- **NGS PICTUREPACK TRANSPARENCY SET**
  The Middle Ages

Global Gourmet

France The first important French cookbook was written during the Middle Ages. Taillevent, the chef of King Charles VI, wrote *Le Viander* around 1375. Although Taillevent is the name of one of the finest restaurants in modern Paris, the recipes in Taillevent's cookbook aim not at bringing out the flavor of food but rather at disguising it, since the lack of refrigeration often led to spoilage.

MORE ABOUT...

Chaucer Geoffrey Chaucer apparently was a native Londoner, born about 1342. He attended the universities at Cambridge and Oxford, traveled in northern Europe, then studied law. He served three English kings as a court official, public servant, and diplomat. At the same time he carried on a second career as a poet, philosopher, and translator. Upon his death, Chaucer was buried in Westminster Abbey, a rare honor for a commoner. The Canterbury Tales were written in the London dialect of the Middle English vernacular. The popularity of Chaucer's poems is thought to have been a great influence in making this dialect the basis for modern English.

History & Art *La Pucelle* is French for "the Maid." **How is Joan dressed?** *(in men's clothes)* Among the charges of blasphemy brought against Joan in her trial was her wearing of men's clothes.
Answer to Caption: *Her courage rallied the French around the king and drove the English out of France.*

Critical Thinking Have students recap the developments they have learned about in Section 2 that led to the decline of feudalism. Then have them explain how the Hundred Years' War further hastened its decline. *(revival of trade and growth of towns; new ways of fighting led to need for standing armies rather than feudal soldiers)* **L3**

Independent Practice

Guided Reading Activity 4-2 **L1**

Biography The French estates of Eleanor of Aquitaine were a source of dispute during the Hundred Years' War. An extraordinary woman in her own right, Eleanor was more than the wife and mother of French and English kings. Have students research the life of Eleanor of Aquitaine and write a brief summary of their findings. **L2**

History & Art *"La Pucelle!" Jeanne d' Arc Leads Her Army* by Franck Craig, 1907. Musée d' Orsay, Paris, France *What did the "Maid of Orleans" accomplish for the French?*

English siege of the town of Orleans (AWR•lay•AHN). Betrayed by rivals of the French king, Charles VII, Joan later became a prisoner of the English, who burned her to death. Inspired by Joan's courage, the French rallied around Charles VII and drove the English out of France. When the war ended in A.D. 1453, the port of Calais was the only French territory still in English hands.

The Hundred Years' War had a noticeable impact on European affairs. The conflict contributed to national unity in both France and England. It also hastened the decline of feudalism. The use of the longbow and firearms made feudal methods of fighting based on castles and mounted knights obsolete. Monarchs replaced feudal soldiers with national armies made up of hired soldiers. Maintaining these armies, however, was expensive. Monarchs turned to townspeople and the lower nobility for new sources of revenue. These groups willingly paid taxes and made loans to monarchs in return for security and good government.

France

By the end of the Hundred Years' War, the French monarchy had gained much power and prestige. Wartime emergencies allowed kings to collect national taxes, maintain permanent armies, and assert royal authority.

Louis XI, son of Charles VII, set out to unite France by taking back lands held by French nobles that had once been part of the royal territory. Louis especially wanted Burgundy, one of the most prosperous regions of Europe. However, its ruler, Charles the Bold, wanted Burgundy to be an independent state.

Louis was a shrewd diplomat. Rather than fight Charles openly, he encouraged quarrels between Burgundy and the neighboring Swiss. After Charles was killed in a battle with the Swiss in A.D. 1477, Burgundy was divided into two parts: the northern half, Flanders, went to Charles's daughter Mary; the remainder became part of France.

Through a series of reforms, Louis strengthened the bureaucracy of government, kept the nobles under royal control, and promoted trade and agriculture. By the end of his reign, France was strong and unified, and its monarch ruled with increased power.

England

After the Hundred Years' War, England became mired in a civil war as nobles struggled for control of the English throne. This 30-year conflict, known as the Wars of the Roses (because of the symbols of the two rival royal families), began in A.D. 1455. The royal house of Lancaster bore the red rose; its rival, the house of York, a white rose.

150 **Chapter 4** *Toward a New World*

COOPERATIVE LEARNING ACTIVITY

Readers' Theater Have groups of students prepare and present readings from the play *Saint Joan* by George Bernard Shaw, choosing suitable passages for presentation, assigning and reading the roles, preparing and presenting a synopsis of the play, and explaining the scenes.

Advanced students may prefer to present readings from Shakespeare's *Henry V*, Act IV, Scenes iii–viii, which dramatize the Battle of Agincourt from the English point of view. Much of the dialogue in this scene is in French; students taking French classes might especially enjoy the challenge. Make sure they use an edition with adequate footnotes, such as the Arden Shakespeare, and that they do not overlook the humor in Scene iv. **L3**

Adam Woolfitt

Cathedral of Chartres

The cathedral stands out against a lowering sky. The old town of Chartres, France, crowds the foreground, where artisans, merchants, bakers, and stonemasons once lived, clustered near the great church. At the center of the photograph, the rose window provides a perfect example of medieval stained glass. The two towers, one ornate, the other plain, were finished in different periods. They pierce the sky—giving form to the faith and spirit of Europe's Middle Ages.

The cathedral reflects the technology of the High Middle Ages. Built before A.D. 1300, Chartres Cathedral, located about 50 miles southwest of Paris, is one of many works of Gothic architecture expressing both the fervor of the medieval era and the revival of the European economy, beginning around A.D. 1000. The growth of towns such as Chartres was a result of such changes. The combination of new building techniques, financial resources, and professional skills enabled the construction of the great cathedrals of Europe. ⊕

Chapter 4 *Toward a New World* **151**

TEACH

Tell students that the rose window (also called a wheel window) was a richly decorated circular window. Toward the mid-1100s the rose window began to be used widely in Gothic churches. Ask students to explain why stained glass art is not static. (*As sunlight changes in intensity, direction, and color during the day, the effect of the stained glass changes.*) Ask students which windows of Chartres Cathedral are the first to come fully to life. (*the east windows, because the sun rises in the east*)

CURRICULUM CONNECTION

RELIGION
Numerous street names in today's Chartres, such as *Rue aux Juifs*, recall the presence of an important medieval Jewish community there. The city's Saint-Hilaire Hospital probably originated as a synagogue.

The Arts When Ferdinand and Isabella captured the Moorish province of Granada, they gained some remarkable examples of Moorish art and architecture, such as the Alhambra. Have students research and report on the art and architecture of Moorish Spain. Have them give an oral summary, bringing pictures to share with the class. **L2**

Linking Past and Present

Religion Not until 1990 did Spain officially overturn the 1492 order calling for the expulsion or conversion of the Jews. The 1990 accord places not only Judaism but also Protestantism on par with Roman Catholicism in Spain.

ASSESS

Check for Understanding

Assign Section 2 Review as homework or as an in-class activity.

⊙ Use Student Self-Test and Review Software to review Section 2.

Political Cartoon Have students draw a political cartoon about an event or issue in this section, such as the Babylonian Captivity, the Great Schism, or the behavior of corrupted clergy. Display the cartoons in class. **L3**

During the Wars of the Roses, Edward, duke of York, overthrew the weak Lancaster dynasty and became King Edward IV. As king, Edward worked to strengthen royal government and to promote trade. Edward's death in A.D. 1483 brought uncertainty to England. The heirs to the throne were the late king's two young sons. Edward's brother Richard, however, proclaimed himself King Richard III and locked his young nephews in the Tower of London, where they were probably murdered. Richard finally fell to the forces of Henry Tudor, a Lancaster noble, on Bosworth Field in A.D. 1485.

Henry became King **Henry VII**, the first Tudor king. Henry steadily eliminated rival claimants to the throne, avoided expensive foreign wars, and gradually reasserted royal power over the lords and nobles. As a result, the English monarchy emerged from the Wars of the Roses strengthened and with few challengers. The Tudor dynasty ruled England for more than 100 years until A.D. 1603.

Spain

During the late A.D. 1400s, Spain emerged from a period of turmoil and warfare to become an important European power. Even before Pope Urban called for the Crusades, the Christian kingdoms of northern Spain were engaged in the *Reconquista* (RAY•kohn•KEES•tuh), or reconquest, of the lands the Muslims had taken in the A.D. 700s. By A.D. 1250 the Iberian Peninsula consisted of three Christian kingdoms: Portugal in the west, **Castile** in the center, and **Aragon** on the Mediterranean coast. Only Granada in the south remained in the hands of the Moors, or Spanish Muslims.

In A.D. 1469 **Ferdinand of Aragon** and **Isabella of Castile** were married. The two kingdoms maintained separate governments, however, and assemblies known as *cortes* (KOR•tays) limited royal power. Jewish and Muslim communities in Castile and Aragon had their own laws and elected their own officials.

The two monarchs, however, strengthened the powers of the Crown in Castile. In A.D. 1492 their armies forced the surrender of the last Moorish stronghold at Granada. Shortly afterward, Ferdinand and Isabella ended the traditional policy of toleration for minority groups. They believed that all Spaniards had to be Catholic if Spain was to become one nation. Spanish Jews and Muslims were given the choice to convert to Catholicism or leave Spain. The persecution and departure of many Jews and Muslims, known for their banking, business, and intellectual skills, weakened Spain's

economy and culture. The two monarchs set up the Spanish Inquisition, a court that enforced Catholic teachings. The fear caused by the Spanish Inquisition further strengthened the power and authority of the Spanish monarchs.

Russia

While royal power expanded in western Europe, the principality of Muscovy in eastern Europe laid the foundation of the Slavic empire of Russia. In the late A.D. 1300s, after years of cooperation with its Mongol rulers, Muscovy began to assert its independence and drive out the Mongols. In A.D. 1480 during the rule of **Ivan III**, Muscovy finally refused to pay taxes to the Mongols. With this step, Muscovy's long submission to the Asian rulers was over.

Free of Mongol controls, Ivan III brought many of the eastern Slavic territories under Muscovy's rule. The lands Ivan ruled, now known as Russia, were a hundred times as large as the original Muscovite state. As a result of these conquests, he became known as Ivan the Great. Other factors also strengthened Ivan's rule. After Constantinople fell to the Ottoman Turks in A.D. 1453, Muscovy stood alone as the center of the Eastern Orthodox world. In A.D. 1472 Ivan III took the title czar, or caesar, the title used by the Roman and Byzantine emperors. The Russian Orthodox Church identified its interests with those of the Russian ruler. Church leaders stressed the importance of obedience to the czar and the government.

Russia's religious leaders and political rulers also encouraged the development of a unique national style of icon painting and building construction. Ivan III had western European and Russian architects rebuild the Moscow Kremlin, or fortress. In spite of Western influences on its construction, the Kremlin became known for the typically Russian splendor of its beautiful onion-domed churches and ornately decorated palaces. Today the Kremlin in Moscow is still a center of government, religion, and culture for Russia.

The Troubled Church

During the upheavals of the Late Middle Ages—caused by warfare, the plague, and religious controversy—many people in western Europe turned to the Catholic Church for comfort and reassurance. In spite of this increase in religious devotion, the temporal authority of the Church was weakening due to the influence of strong monarchs and national governments. A growing middle class

152 **Chapter 4** *Toward a New World*

MEETING SPECIAL NEEDS ACTIVITY

Learning Style: Visual/Spatial Organize the class into small groups of three to five students. Each group should include one student who draws well. Have each group choose a topic related to medieval life and draw several designs for stained glass treatment. Each group should then select a single design to prepare for presentation using poster board and colored tissue paper. After the design has been sketched in pencil on the poster board, students should work together to cut out the design and glue the tissue paper to the back of the poster. Have each group present its finished project to the class. **L1 LEP**

of educated townspeople and a general questioning of the Church's teachings also contributed to this decline.

Exile and Division

From A.D. 1315 to A.D. 1377, popes settled in Avignon, France, to escape the civil wars that were disrupting Italy. This long period of exile at Avignon came to be known as the Babylonian Captivity, after the period of the exile of the Jews in Babylon in the 500s B.C. With the pope in France, people feared that the papacy had come under the control of French monarchs. Others disliked the concern the Avignon popes showed for increasing church taxes and making church administration more efficient. They believed the popes had become corrupted by worldly power and were neglecting their spiritual duties.

Finally, in A.D. 1377, Pope Gregory XI left Avignon and returned to Rome. After his death a year later, the Church faced the dilemma of being led by two and later, even three popes. In A.D. 1414, a church council at Constance in Germany finally forced the resignation of all three popes and elected Pope Martin V, ending this controversy known as the Great Schism. The long period of disunity, however, had seriously weakened the spiritual and political authority of the Church.

Church Reform

Church authorities also abused their power by charging fees for services and selling church positions. The Church's growing wealth angered many devout Europeans who called for reform during the late 1300s and early 1400s.

In England, the scholar **John Wycliffe** criticized the Church's teachings as well as its wealth and corruption. He claimed that the Bible, not the pope, was the sole source of religious truth. Wycliffe began to translate the Bible from Latin into English so that people could read it for themselves.

In central Europe, the Czech preacher Jan Hus called for change based on biblical principles. Hus

Visualizing History Italian bankers, from *Treatise on the Seven Vices: Avarice*. The Church viewed lending with the intent to charge interest as evil. *What problems did the Church face during the late Middle Ages?*

was burned at the stake as a heretic. His heroic death, however, led many people to regard him as a martyr. Church and political leaders condemned both Hus and Wycliffe, but ideas of religious reform continued to spread throughout Europe and erode the church's authority.

SECTION 2 REVIEW

Recall
1. **Define** the Crusades, charter, money economy, guilds, scholasticism, vernacular, czar.
2. **Identify** Pope Urban II, Joan of Arc, Henry VII, Ferdinand of Aragon, Isabella of Castile, Ivan III, John Wycliffe.

3. **Explain** the effects of the Babylonian Captivity and the Great Schism on the late medieval Church.

Critical Thinking
4. **Applying Information** Select one European monarchy, and discuss the ways that it changed

during the course of the Middle Ages.

Understanding Themes
5. **Innovation** Choose one of the following, and trace its effect on medieval society: three-field system, money economy, guilds.

Chapter 4 *Toward a New World* 153

SECTION 3 REVIEW ANSWERS

1. All vocabulary words are defined in the Glossary.
2. Pope Urban II, 145; Joan of Arc, 149; Henry VII, 152; Ferdinand of Aragon, 152; Isabella of Castile, 152; Ivan III, 152; John Wycliffe, 153
3. They seriously undermined the pope's authority, aroused resentment against papal

power, and led to calls for reform within the Church.
4. Answers should describe that country's monarchy and its effects on social, political and economic life.
5. **INNOVATION** Answers should reflect the chosen topic's significance.

Evaluate

Section Quiz 4-2

Use the Testmaker to create a customized quiz for Section 2.

Reteach

Have students work in small groups to list the important features of each Crusade discussed in this section. Have the groups compare and discuss their lists.

Enrich

The son of the English king Edward III was known as the Black Prince because he wore black armor. Have students research the Black Prince and his role in the Hundred Years' War. Ask them to summarize his career in a brief written report.

CLOSE

Summarize the ways the monarchy was strengthened during the period covered in this section and the causes for this change. Have students debate the advantages and disadvantages of a strong monarchy.

A.D. 700
c. A.D. 900
Arab and Persian merchants
trade in East Africa.

A.D. 1100
c. A.D. 1275
Mali conquers
surrounding territory.

A.D. 1500
A.D. 1493
Askia Muhammad
begins rule in Songhai.

Section 3

African Kingdoms and City-States

Setting the Scene

▶ **Terms to Define**
ghana, monopoly, multicultural

▶ **People to Meet**
Sundiata Keita, Mansa Musa, Ibn Battuta, Askia Muhammad

▶ **Places to Locate**
Ghana, Mali, Timbuktu, Songhai, Kilwa

**ind Out** How did African territories develop as a result of inland and overseas trade?

Storyteller

The poets of Mali preserved the history of their people. Hear one speak: "I teach kings the history of their ancestors so that the lives of the ancients might serve them as an example, for the world is old, but the future springs from the past. My word is pure and free of all untruth. . . .Listen to my word, you who want to know, by my mouth, you will learn the history of Mali. By my mouth you will get to know the story of the ancestor of great Mali, the story of him who . . . surpassed even Alexander the Great. . . . Whoever knows the history of a country can read its future."

Horn player, Benin

—from *Sundiata: An Epic of Old Mali* in *The Humanistic Tradition*, Gloria K. Fiero, 1992

While monarchies flourished in medieval Europe, a series of prosperous kingdoms and city-states emerged in Africa. Their rise was aided by the knowledge of iron-smelting. This technology spread from the northeastern African kingdom of Kush to other parts of the continent.

In West Africa between A.D. 300 and A.D. 1500, Africans mined gold and other mineral resources. An active trade developed between them and various Islamic peoples outside the region. Through their trade contacts with the followers of Islam, African cultures gradually adopted Islamic cultural elements such as language and religion.

Kingdom of Ghana

The first of the West African trading kingdoms was **Ghana** (GAH•nuh). According to legend Ghana was founded about A.D. 200. Around A.D. 350, the people of Ghana learned how to smelt iron. With iron swords and lances, Ghanaian warriors expanded the boundaries of their country. They also gained control over West Africa's major trade routes.

**POINT**

The Gold-Salt Trade

Ghana became one of the richest trading civilizations in Africa due to its location midway between Saharan salt mines and tropical gold mines. There was two-way traffic by caravan between cities in North Africa and Ghana. Muslim traders from North Africa sent caravans loaded with cloth, metalware, swords, and salt across the

western Sahara to northern settlements in Ghana. Large caravans from Ghana traveled north to Morocco, bringing kola nuts and farming produce. Ghanaian gold was traded for Saharan salt brought by Muslim traders.

Salt was an important trade item for the people of Ghana. They needed salt to preserve and flavor their foods. Using plentiful supplies of gold as a medium of exchange, Ghanaian merchants traded the precious metal for salt and other goods from Morocco and Spain.

Masudi, a Muslim traveler, writing about A.D. 950, described how trade was conducted:

❝ The merchants . . . place their wares and cloth on the ground and then depart, and so the people of [Ghana] come bearing gold which they leave beside the merchandise and then depart. The owners of the merchandise then return, and if they are satisfied with what they have found, they take it. If not, they go away again, and the people of [Ghana] return and add to the price until the bargain is concluded. ❞

A Wealthy Empire

Between A.D. 300 and A.D. 1200, the kings of Ghana controlled a trading empire that stretched more than 100,000 square miles (259,000 sq. km). Because the ghana, or king, ruled such a vast region, the land became known by the name of its ruler—Ghana. Ghanaian kings prospered from the taxes they imposed on goods that entered or left their kingdom. One emperor—Kinissai—owned a thousand horses. An Arab chronicler states that each horse "slept only on a carpet, with silken rope for a halter." Another wealthy ruler, according to an Arab traveler, tied his horse to an enormous gold nugget weighing thirty pounds (14 kg).

The Coming of Islam

Ghana reached the height of its economic and political power as a trading kingdom in the A.D. 800s and A.D. 900s. The salt and gold trade moving through Ghana brought Islamic ideas and customs to the kingdom. Muslims held court positions, and many Ghanaians converted to Islam.

The religion of Islam had an enormous impact on Ghana. It strengthened the mutually profitable partnership between the Ghanaians and traders from Islamic centers in North Africa and the Middle East. The new faith also provided administrative, legal, and commercial practices that suited the needs of the growing Ghanaian empire. The

blending of Islamic learning and local African customs advanced the empire's cultural and political development.

Ghana's Decline

At the end of the A.D. 1000s, an attack on the Ghanaian trade centers by the Almoravids, a Muslim group from North Africa, led to the eventual decline of Ghana. Groups of Ghanaians broke away to form Islamic communities that developed into many small independent states.

Kingdom of Mali

Mali, one of the small states to break away from Ghana, became a powerful kingdom that eventually ruled much of West Africa. The word *Mali* means "where the king resides" and is an appropriate name for a kingdom that gained much of its power and influence from its kings. **Sundiata Keita**, one of Mali's early kings, defeated his leading rival in A.D. 1235 and began to conquer surrounding territories. By the late A.D. 1200s, Mali's territory included the old kingdom of Ghana.

Sundiata Keita

Sundiata Keita carried out policies to strengthen his new empire. He organized a permanent army and divided the kingdom into provinces, each headed by a general. The generals kept the peace and saw that there was enough food for the people. To strengthen ties with different groups in the kingdom, Sundiata moved his capital from place to place.

Sundiata also worked to bring economic prosperity to Mali. He sought to improve agricultural production, and he restored the trans-Saharan trade routes that had been interrupted by the Almoravid attacks. He ordered soldiers to clear large expanses of savanna and burn the grass that had been cleared to provide fertilizer for crops of peanuts, rice, sorghum, yams, beans, onions, and grains. With the benefit of adequate rainfall, agriculture flourished

 **Footnotes to History**

Golden Monarchs
Ghana's rulers became very wealthy from the taxes they imposed on the gold and salt trade. They wore elaborate gold headdresses and adorned themselves with jewelry. One ruler's dogs even wore collars and bells made of silver and gold.

THEME Cultural Diffusion
Develop a working definition of the term *cultural diffusion* by asking students to think of ways they have changed as a result of contact with other persons or groups. *(the transfer of religion, customs, traditions, arts, and language from one people to another)* How did trade contacts with Arabs affect the development of African cultures? *(The Arabs brought with them the religion of Islam, written language, and other elements of Islamic culture that were adopted by West Africans.)* **L1 LEP**

TURNING POINT

The Gold-Salt Trade
How did Ghana expand West Africa's geographic contacts? *Ghana, a kingdom located in West Africa, traded its gold for much-needed salt and other products that came from North Africa and Spain.*

Who?What?Where?When?

The Silent Trade The trade exchange described by Masudi is also known as "the silent trade." It has been described by other writers, including Herodotus, as the method often used by peoples who have no common language.

COOPERATIVE LEARNING ACTIVITY

Simulation Game Have students role-play the interactions between the various groups that made up the East African trading community: coastal traders; traders from inland kingdoms; and merchants and traders from Muslim lands, India, and China. Organize the class into groups of three or four for this activity.

Create game cards to represent trade articles such as ivory, gold, copper, iron tools, carvings, cotton, silk, glass beads, and porcelain. Allow time for small groups to meet to discuss and plan strategies for their trading activities. Discuss the impact of this trade on the economies of the various African empires and city-states. **L1**

CURRICULUM CONNECTION

GEOGRAPHY

Mali is within three climatic zones: the Sudanic of the south with temperatures of 75° to 86°F; the Sahel with temperatures of 73° to 97°F; and the Saharan area with temperatures ranging from 117°F in the daytime to 39°F at night.

Economics List the products the West Africans exchanged for Arab goods. (*gold, kola nuts, and farm produce*) Ask what Arab goods they chiefly traded for. (*cloth, metalware, swords, salt*) Challenge students to name items people use today that come from Africa. (*gold, diamonds for jewelry, agricultural products such as cocoa and coffee, petroleum, and carvings*) Discuss ways early and modern African trading patterns are similar. (*Africans still trade precious metals and agricultural products for items they need.*) **L3**

World History and Art Transparency 8, *Gold Pendant Mask*

Who?What?Where?When?

Timbuktu was an important site for the gold-salt trade in the A.D. 1300s. Today it is the administrative center of Mali. Small salt caravans are still evident, but no gold trade exists. The city has air service, but it is more accessible by camel or boat.

in Mali. With larger tracts of land under cultivation, farmers produced surplus crops that the government then collected as taxes.

Sundiata Keita used colorful ceremonies to impress the people with his power. When he appeared in public, trumpeters announced his arrival. He sat on an ebony throne under an arch made from large elephant tusks. He never spoke directly to people. Instead, requests were answered by servants standing at the foot of the stairs leading to the throne.

Mansa Musa

Mali's greatest king was **Mansa Musa**, who ruled from A.D. 1312 to A.D. 1332. By opening trade routes and protecting trade caravans with a powerful standing army, Musa maintained the economic prosperity begun by Sundiata. He also introduced Islamic culture to Mali.

A Muslim himself, Musa enhanced the prestige and power of Mali through a famous pilgrimage to Makkah in A.D. 1324. It took more than 14 months to cover the 3,000 miles (4,800 km). Arab writers report that Musa traveled in grand style. He took with him 12,000 servants, each dressed in silk or brocade and carrying bars of gold. Musa gave away many of these gold bars to poor people he met along the way. As a result of this trip, news of Mansa Musa and Mali's wealth reached as far as Europe. In fact, so much gold was given away on Mansa Musa's journey that the world price of gold fell.

At Makkah, Musa persuaded a Spanish architect to return with him to Mali. There the skilled architect built great mosques and other fine buildings, including a palace for Musa in the capital of **Timbuktu** (TIHM•BUHK•TOO). Timbuktu became an important center of Muslim art and learning mainly through the efforts of Mansa Musa, who encouraged Muslim scholars to teach at his court.

As a result of Islamic influence, written contracts and the use of credit became standard practices in the commerce and trade of Mali. Literacy also became

Images of the Times

Africa's Religious Heritage

Religion played a central role in the development of African cultures. Islam became the dominant religion in the north.

The Great Mosque at Timbuktu Founded around A.D. 1100, the city of Timbuktu became a major center of trade and site of an important Islamic school.

Altar of the Hand, Benin Beginning in the A.D. 1200s, the kingdom of Benin emerged as a wealthy trading state. The *oba*, or king, became the political, economic, and spiritual leader of the people.

156

Images of the Times
Africa's Religious Heritage

Africa's indigenous religious beliefs were not universal but ethnic in scope. Thus, each ethnic group had its own name for the supreme being, its own account of the creation and the origin of death, and its own magic, initiation rites, and rituals. Nearly all Africans, however, believed in a supreme being that was the origin of all things and presided over a realm of lesser beings and a host of animate and inanimate forces. These religious beliefs and practices permeated every phase of life on the African continent.

important. At first, only important merchants and government officials could read. In time, however, Islam contributed to the advancement of learning among the population as a whole.

Ibn Battuta

Shortly after the death of Mansa Musa in A.D. 1337, the kingdom of Mali became the destination for one of the great explorations of the premodern world. Almost two centuries before Columbus set off for the Americas, an Arab traveler and author named **Ibn Battuta** began his travels in A.D. 1325 to the far corners of the Islamic world—from North Africa to China and back. He returned home three decades later as one of history's great travelers and travel writers. Battuta's journeys totaled 75,000 miles (121,000 km). Ibn Battuta's final journey brought him to Mali and its fabled city of Timbuktu.

Mali's Decline

During the A.D. 1330s, Mali came under attack by Berbers, a people living in the Saharan expanses to the north. They raided the empire's territory and captured the city of Timbuktu. From the south, warriors from the rain forest region also attacked Mali's frontiers. Inside the kingdom, people living in the **Songhai** region of the Niger River valley had long resented losing control over their political destiny and rebelled against the empire. By the middle of the A.D. 1500s, Mali had split into several independent states.

Kingdom of Songhai

The rebellious Songhai, who were skilled traders, farmers, and fishers, were led by strong leaders. During the late A.D. 1400s, their ruler, Sunni Ali, fought many territorial wars and managed to conquer the cities of Timbuktu and Djenné, expanding his empire to include most of the West African savanna. These conquests enabled Songhai to become the largest of the three West African trading kingdoms.

Terra-cotta heads, c. early 1600s, commemorate the deceased members of the royal family among the Akan peoples of southern Ghana.

REFLECTING ON THE TIMES

1. How did religion influence the arts and other aspects of culture in Africa?
2. In what way did Africans honor royalty?

157

Religion Tell students that the main religion of the Republic of Mali is still Islam. Today 90 percent of the people are of that faith. What might have attracted a traveler like Battuta to Timbuktu? (*It was on an important caravan route and was a center of Islamic culture.*)

The following videotape program is available from Glencoe:

• **The Last Elephants of Timbuktu**

To find classroom resources to accompany this video, check the following home page:

A&E Television: http://www.AandE.com

Linking Past and Present

Timbuktu At the time of the kingdom of Mali, Timbuktu became a major center for trade, learning, and scholarship. Merchants, religious leaders, and scholars mingled in this Muslim city. After it was attacked by Moroccan invaders in 1593, Timbuktu was never again a leading city. Today Timbuktu is a small provincial town; however, hints of its former glory are visible in its mosques and monuments.

ANSWERS TO REFLECTING ON THE TIMES

1. Africans made artifacts with religious themes and built places of worship. Islam especially promoted the growth of education.
2. African rulers were portrayed on artifacts; other members of royalty were also commemorated in the arts: for example, the Akan made terra-cotta heads of deceased members of their royal family.

Map Study

Answer

the Sahara and attacks by the Almoravids

Map Skills Practice

Reading a Map Have students determine how far it is across the Sahara from Timbuktu north to Morocco. *(about 1,000 miles [1,700 km])* Discuss how long such a journey might have taken when traveling on foot or by camel.

Independent Practice

📁 Guided Reading Activity 4-3 **L1**

Biography Have students use library resources to find interesting details and insights about early African leaders such as Sundiata Keita, Mansa Musa, Sunni Ali, or Askia Muhammad. Students may prepare oral or written reports on their findings.

you don't say...

Swahili is a Bantu language originally spoken on the east coast of Africa. The word comes from an Arabic word meaning "coast." It is the only Bantu language with a written literature. The name "Uhura," a character from the original Star Trek series, comes from the Swahili word *uhuru,* meaning "freedom."

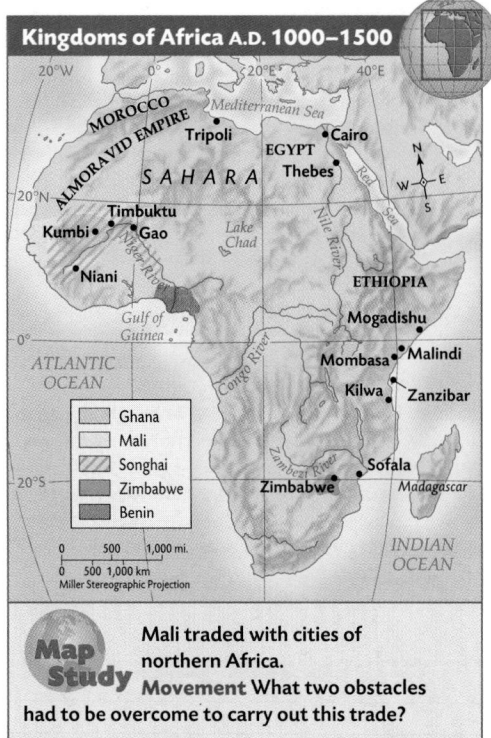

Kingdoms of Africa A.D. 1000–1500

- Ghana
- Mali
- Songhai
- Zimbabwe
- Benin

0   500   1,000 mi.
0   500 1,000 km
Miller Stereographic Projection

Map Study Mali traded with cities of northern Africa.
Movement What two obstacles had to be overcome to carry out this trade?

Sunni Ali

Although Songhai had defeated the armies of Mali in battle, Sunni Ali adopted many of the administrative and legal practices that had been developed by Mansa Musa. Governing Songhai from the city of Gao, Ali maintained a huge army equipped with armor, camels, and horses. He also had a large navy that patrolled the Niger River. Sunni Ali was a Muslim ruler, but when he died, rule fell to his son, a non-Muslim. The Muslim population of Songhai overthrew Ali's son and brought a Muslim ruler to the throne.

Askia Muhammad

Under the new ruler, **Askia Muhammad**, the Songhai Empire reached the height of its glory. Askia Muhammad extended the empire even more and culture flourished, especially in Timbuktu. Askia welcomed teachers, doctors, poets, students, and religious leaders from Asia and Europe.

Ruling from A.D. 1493 to A.D. 1528, Askia Muhammad divided Songhai into five huge provinces, each with a governor, a tax collector, a court of judges, and a trade inspector—very much like the government structure of China in the A.D. 1400s. Everyone used the same weights and

measures and followed the same legal system. Only members of the ruling Songhai could become political leaders or join the cavalry. Other groups had special tasks, such as caring for the army's horses or serving at the royal court. Most enslaved people, often prisoners of war, worked as farmers.

Devoted to Islam, Muhammad introduced laws based on the teachings of the holy book of Islam, the Quran. Lesser crimes were sometimes overlooked, but those who committed major crimes such as robbery or idolatry received harsh punishments. Askia Muhammad appointed Muslim judges to uphold Islamic laws.

Songhai's Decline

Despite its power, Songhai lasted only about 100 years. In A.D. 1528 Askia Muhammad was overthrown by his son. A series of struggles for the throne followed, leading to a weakened central government. Around A.D. 1589 the rulers of Morocco sent an army across the Sahara to attack Songhai. Moroccan soldiers, armed with guns and cannons, easily defeated the Songhai forces fighting with only swords, spears, and bows and arrows. By A.D. 1600 the Songhai Empire had ended.

East Africa

While empires rose and fell in West Africa, trade spurred the development of prosperous communities along the coast of East Africa. As in West Africa, trade contacts with the Muslim world enabled East African coastal areas to adopt the religion of Islam and Islamic cultural practices.

Coastal City-States

As early as 500 B.C., coastal areas of East Africa were trading with the Arabian Peninsula and South Asia. East Africans used monsoon winds to sail across the 2,500-mile (4,023-km) stretch of Indian Ocean that separates Africa from India. By the A.D. 900s, Arab and Persian merchants had settled on the East African coast and controlled the trade there. From these foreign merchants, local Africans quickly learned about seafaring and the practices of long-distance trade. They founded their own settlements along the East African coast and in northern Madagascar.

By A.D. 1200 small East African trading settlements had become thriving city-states taxing the goods that passed through their ports. Traders from the interior of Africa brought ivory, gold, iron, and rhinoceros horn to the east coast to trade for Indian cotton and silk and Chinese porcelain.

MEETING SPECIAL NEEDS ACTIVITY

Study Strategy Students who have difficulty remembering the names of many different places may be helped by seeing that some place-names in history are still in use today. Refer students to the map of Africa shown on this page. Direct students to write down the place-names shown on the map and in the map key. Then have them turn to a modern map of Africa, such as shown on page A20 in the Reference Atlas of the textbook. Have them note and record those place-names that appear on both maps. Ask them why they think some names are no longer on the map. It might be helpful to remind students that some place-names in earlier United States history are no longer found on a map. **L1**

The port of **Kilwa** had a virtual *monopoly*, or sole control or ownership, of the gold trade with the interior of Africa. Its rulers collected heavy taxes from traders of other countries. The people of Kilwa used their wealth to extend their power over neighboring city-states. They also used it to dress in fine cotton and silk and to fill their four-story houses with vases and hangings from India and China.

Malindi and Mombasa, both ports farther north on the coast, were also important centers, as was Sofala, a port in what is present-day Mozambique. The iron mined in the surroundings of these three city-states was widely used in the Arabian Peninsula and South Asia.

The island of Zanzibar was also an important center of trade. Sailors from the islands of Southeast Asia as well as India and China came to Zanzibar in search of ivory and gold, which was brought to Zanzibar ports from the coastal city-states of East Africa.

Blending of Cultures

By the A.D. 1300s, the city-states of East Africa had reached the height of their prosperity. They had become truly *multicultural* centers—populated by a variety of cultural groups. Within each city-state, Islamic and African cultures blended. For the most part, Arab and Persian merchants ruled the trading states. They converted many Africans to Islam.

Arab merchants married local women who had converted to Islam. Families having members with African and Islamic cultural backgrounds began speaking Swahili, a Bantu language that included Arabic and Persian words. The people of the East African coastal city-states also developed an Arabic form of writing that enabled them to write about their history.

East African rulers were either Arab governors or African chieftains. They used coral from Indian Ocean reefs to build magnificent mosques, palaces, and forts. For example, the palace of Kilwa's ruler had more than 100 rooms, an octagonal bathing pool, and separate sections for residential and business purposes.

Central and Southern Africa

The growth of trading kingdoms and city-states in East Africa was matched by the rise of powerful states in the interior regions of Central and Southern Africa. The Bantu-speaking inland kingdoms mined rich deposits of copper and gold. During the A.D. 900s, inland mining companies in Central and Southern Africa traded minerals and ivory with the East African coastal city-states. There Muslim traders brought carpets from Arab lands, glass beads, cotton, silk, and Chinese porcelain from India and Southeast Asia to exchange for the products of Africa's interior.

Great Zimbabwe

One of the best-known inland trading kingdoms was Karanga, which arose in present-day Zimbabwe. The Bantu-speaking people of Karanga originated in West Africa. About A.D. 100 a population explosion, or a large and sudden growth in population, took place. Since the land could not support the increased number of people, many West Africans began to leave their homeland to look for new homes.

By A.D. 700 some of the Bantu-speaking migrants had settled on a high plateau between the Zambezi and Limpopo Rivers of south central Africa. Their descendants, known as the Shona, eventually formed the kingdom of Karanga in this region.

The Shona were essentially cattle raisers. The need to defend their large herds and grazing lands led to the growth of a centralized state under a royal dynasty. During the A.D. 1300s, the kings of Karanga acquired new wealth from the export of gold that was mined from rich deposits within their territory. About this time, they ordered the building of nearly 300 stone-walled fortresses throughout the kingdom. The largest fortress was called the Great Zimbabwe—meaning "stone house"—and served as the political and religious center of the kingdom.

The oval stone wall of the Zimbabwe enclosure was 30 feet (9.15 m) high and was made from 900,000 stones fitted together without mortar. Within the wall was a maze of interior walls and hidden passages that protected the circular house of the Zimbabwe chief. Near the house, archaeologists have uncovered a platform with several upright stones that may have been the place where the chief held court.

Territorial Divisions

For nearly five centuries, Karanga and the other Bantu states grew wealthy from their control of the chief routes between the gold mines and the sea. However, during the A.D. 1500s, Bantu states in Southern Africa struggled in civil wars that brought disorder to the kingdoms and disrupted trade. The Karanga territories were split between two rival forces. The northern territory was called Monomotapa. The southern territory was taken over by the Changamire dynasty.

Chapter 4   *Toward a New World*   **159**

Innovation Ask students to identify some aspects of the East African or Bantu cultures that represented an innovation. **L1**

ASSESS

Check for Understanding

Assign Section 3 Review as homework or as an in-class activity.

 Use Student Self-Test and Review Software to review Section 3.

Evaluate

Section Quiz 4-3

 Use the Testmaker to create a customized quiz for Section 3.

Reteach

Hold a class discussion in which students compare the bartering practices of the Ghanaian and Arab traders with their own experiences buying and selling.

Enrich

Have students research to learn more about the archaeological excavation of the Great Zimbabwe or similar stone building sites at Khami, Natetali, and Mapungubwe. Encourage students to create visual representations.

MAKING CONNECTIONS ACTIVITY

Location   Ask students to locate the following physical features on a wall map or in the Atlas in their texts: the Nile, Niger, Senegal, Zambezi, and Limpopo Rivers; the Red Sea; the Sahara; the Sahel; and the Great Rift Valley. **Why didn't Africa's rivers provide easy routes into and out of the interior?** *(Many contain rapids and great waterfalls.)* Lead students to notice how few natural harbors are found on the African continent. Discuss the significance of this lack of harbors. *(The lack of protected harbors and navigable rivers would tend to isolate cultures and make land transport the major access route into the interior of the continent.)* **L2**

Visualizing History The Great Zimbabwe is located in what was once the British colony of Rhodesia. When Rhodesia became independent, it took Zimbabwe as its new name.
Answer to Caption: *political and religious center; fortress*

CLOSE

Have students create a chart that compares the achievements of the early African cultures with another civilization that they have studied. Headings should include *Religion, Agriculture, Architecture, Literature, Trade Networks,* and *Science and Technology.*

Visualizing History This view shows the circular stone ruins of the Great Zimbabwe with an exterior wall more than 800 feet in circumference. *What functions did this "stone house" serve?*

The Changamire Empire became stronger than the Monomotapa Empire. Changamire rulers took over Great Zimbabwe and built the fortress's largest structures. At the same time, European explorers arrived along the East African coast. Eager to control the sources of gold, ivory, and copper, the Europeans threatened the survival of the African civilizations in the continent's interior. While trading contacts with the Europeans were at first encouraged, Changamire rulers blocked European efforts to expand inland. They succeeded in limiting European control to coastal areas until the Changamire Empire's fall in the early 1800s.

The Southern Tip of Africa

By A.D. 1500 the southernmost part of Africa, the region that is the present-day Republic of South Africa, had become the homeland of many different peoples. In the western part of this area lived two ethnic groups—the Khoikhoi and the San. The Khoikhoi raised cattle and sheep, while the San lived by hunting wild game. Meanwhile, Bantu-speaking peoples populated the eastern part. They had entered the region from the north about A.D. 300. Ruled by chiefs, these Bantu-speaking peoples grew grain, raised livestock, and made iron tools and weapons.

SECTION 3 REVIEW

Recall
1. **Define** ghana, monopoly, multicultural.
2. **Identify** Sundiata Keita, Mansa Musa, Timbuktu, Ibn Battuta, Askia Muhammad, Kilwa, Great Zimbabwe.
3. **Locate** Timbuktu on the map on page 158. How did Timbuktu become an important center of Islamic culture during the A.D. 1300s?

Critical Thinking
4. **Analyzing Information** Why was trade vital to the kingdoms of West African?

Understanding Themes
5. **Cultural Diffusion** What new aspect of cultural life developed in the city-states of East Africa as a result of contacts among traders in Africa, East Asia, South Asia, and the Middle East?

---

160 **Chapter 4** *Toward a New World*

SECTION 3 REVIEW ANSWERS

1. All vocabulary words are defined in the Glossary.
2. Sundiata Keita, 155; Mansa Musa, 156; Timbuktu, 156; Ibn Battuta, 157; Askia Muhammad, 158; Kilwa, 159; Great Zimbabwe, 159
3. Mansa Musa encouraged Islamic scholars to teach in his capital and hired a skilled architect to build great mosques.
4. They needed salt to preserve their food and could obtain it only through trade.
5. **CULTURAL DIFFUSION** the Swahili language, a Bantu language with a written form

A.D. 1325
The Aztec found their capital, Tenochtitlán.

C. A.D. 1400
Eastern Woodland peoples form the Iroquois League.

C. A.D. 1438
The Inca emperor Pachacuti comes to power.

Section 4

The Americas

Setting the Scene

▶ **Terms to Define**
potlatch, confederation, hierarchy

▶ **People to Meet**
the Kwakiutl, the Pueblo, the Apache, the Navajo, the Plains peoples, the Mound Builders, the Aztec, the Inca, the Moche, Pachacuti

▶ **Places to Locate**
Great Plains, Cahokia, Tenochtitlán, Cuzco

ind Out What factors led to the rise and decline of civilizations and empires in the Americas?

The Storyteller

A Navajo tale describes the origin of the twelve months of the year: First Man and First Woman built a hogan in which to live. Turquoise Boy and White Shell Girl came from the underworld to live with them. "It is not unwise that we plan for the time to come, how we shall live," said First Man. First Woman and First Man whispered together during many nights. They planned that there should be a sun, and day and night. Whenever Coyote, called First Angry, came to make trouble and asked them what they were doing, they told him: "Nothing whatsoever." He said, "So I see," and went away. After he had gone, they planned the twelve months of the year.

—adapted from *The Portable North American Indian Reader,* edited by Frederick W. Turner III, 1974

Navajo rug

From about A.D. 1000 to A.D. 1500, the population of the Americas increased as food supplies improved. By the time Europeans arrived in the Western Hemisphere around A.D. 1500, about 30 million to 100 million Native Americans belonging to more than 2,000 different groups were inhabiting the two continents of North America and South America. About 15 to 20 million of these early inhabitants lived in the present-day United States and parts of Canada.

North Americans

Much of what we know about the early people of North America north of Mexico comes from the work of archaeologists. Archaeological digs have uncovered homes, burial mounds, pottery, baskets, stone tools, and the bones of people and animals in the Arctic and Northwest, California and the Great Basin, the Southwest, the Great Plains, and the Eastern Woodlands. By studying these artifacts, archaeologists have discovered that there were distinct regional differences. People who settled in a particular region developed a common culture. Gradually the arts and crafts and religious customs of each region grew to be distinct from those of other regions, a pattern historians call cultural differentiation. In each region, culture reflected the local geography and natural resources.

The Arctic and Northwest

The early people of the Arctic lived in the cold northern regions of present-day Canada and Alaska. The severe climate of this region prohibited farming. Thus, small bands of extended families moved about, hunting and fishing. Many Arctic people lived in small villages of pit houses, covered with dome-shaped roofs of whalebone and driftwood. Villagers hunted whales, sea lions, seals, and water birds. They ate the meat and used the skins to make warm, protective clothing.

SECTION THEME

▶ **Change** The Aztec and the Inca establish powerful empires in Mexico and South America.

ind Out

Answer: *Skill in war and governance led to the rise of empires; internal disruption and outside invasions led to their decline.*

FOCUS

Section Objective
List the factors that led to the rise and decline of the Aztec and Inca Empires.

BELLRINGER
Motivational Activity

Before taking roll at the beginning of the class period, project Section Focus Transparency 4-4 and have students answer the activity questions. Discuss students' responses.
This activity is also available as a blackline master.

Vocabulary Pre-check
Use the Vocabulary PuzzleMaker to create a puzzle that reinforces the vocabulary terms in this section. **L1**

SECTION RESOURCES

Reproducible Masters
- Reproducible Lesson Plan 4-4
- Guided Reading Activity 4-4
- Reteaching Activity 4
- Enrichment Activity 4
- Section Quiz 4-4
- Performance Assessment Activity 4
- Spanish Chapter Summary 4

Transparencies
- Section Focus Transparency 4-4
- Physical Geography of the World
- World History and Art Transparency 18, *Mola Stitchery*

Multimedia
- Vocabulary PuzzleMaker Software
- Student Self-Test and Review Software
- Testmaker
- World Music: Cultural Traditions, Lesson 1

TEACH

Guided Practice

THEME Change

Ask students to list the changes instituted by the Aztec and the Inca that enabled them to flourish. *(centralized government, productive farming techniques)* **L1**

Visualizing History

 Have students design their own totem to either reflect their family history or to show what is important to them. **Answer to Caption:** *in the Iroquois League*

NATIONAL GEOGRAPHIC SOCIETY

TRANSPARENCIES

PHYSICAL GEOGRAPHY OF THE WORLD

Display the following to enrich student understanding of Native American environments.

2. Sonoran Desert, U.S.
3. Rocky Mountains, Canada
4. Grand Canyon, U.S.
6. Mississippi River, U.S.
8. Baffin Island, Canada
9. Appalachian Mountains, U.S.

Visualizing History In the Northwest a totem represented a bond of unity and was the symbol and protector of the group. *How were Native Americans in the Northeast organized?*

In contrast to the cold and snow of the Arctic, the thickly forested seacoast of the Pacific Northwest had a milder climate. Rainfall was plentiful, and mild winters and warm ocean currents kept rivers and bays free of ice. Like the people of the Arctic, those who settled along the Pacific Coast—**the Kwakiutl**, for example—hunted whales, fish, and other sea animals as their main source of food. Forests of the Northwest provided additional sources of food—small forest animals and acorns. The people of the Northwest also used other resources from the surrounding forests and rivers. With stone and copper woodworking tools they split cedar, fir, and redwood trees into planks to make houses and large canoes. They also developed ways to harvest salmon with fiber nets, stone-tipped spears, and elaborate wooden traps called weirs.

Society among the Kwakiutl and other Northwest peoples was organized into lineages, each of which claimed to be descended from a mythical ancestor. A lineage group lived together in a single, large house and owned the right to use or display special designs, songs, ceremonies, or prized possessions, such as patterned sheets of copper. A lineage maintained exclusive use of its own fishing area and berry-picking grounds. The wealth of each lineage was displayed and given away as gifts at festive gatherings called potlatches. At a potlatch a chief might give away canoes, blankets, and other goods. In turn, guests might bring the chief deerskins and food.

To obtain items they could not make themselves, some people of the Northwest developed trading networks with people living farther south. Traders paddled redwood canoes along the coast, stopping at villages along the shore to exchange goods. Trade networks stretched from southern Alaska to northern California.

California—Great Basin

Native Americans living along the California coast enjoyed a warm climate and an abundance of food resources. Many communities lived on diets of abalone and mussels. Near San Francisco Bay, archaeologists have found evidence of this diet in heaps of discarded shells that date from 2000 B.C. In addition to shellfish, the first Californians fished for sea bass, hunted seals, and gathered berries and nuts. Having such abundant resources made food gathering easier for the people living in this region.

Like other Native Americans, they developed elaborate religious ceremonies designed to worship nature spirits that inhabited all of the natural world, but especially those spirits related to animals or plants used for food. The Chumash, who lived in the area of present-day southern California, would gather together at harvest festivals to celebrate the goodness of the earth. Villagers participated in dances and games.

Compared with those living along the coast, people living farther inland scratched their living from a harsh desert and mountain environment. Great Basin people moved about in small bands, living in windbreak shelters and eating seeds, grasshoppers, and small animals.

Southwest

In the Southwest, Native American peoples adapted to their harsh environment by improving techniques of irrigation to farm the land. Between A.D. 1000 and A.D. 1300, a group of Southwest people known as **the Pueblo** developed a culture in present-day northern Arizona and New Mexico. The Pueblo grew maize in fields terraced like a series of stair steps to check the erosion of topsoil caused by heavy late summer rains. They employed a style of building that used adobe, a sun-dried brick easy to produce under desert conditions. The Pueblo often built their villages under ledges on the sides of cliffs to shade residents from the desert sun and to make the villages easier to defend.

Religious leaders governed Pueblo villages. They led religious ceremonies to ensure the harmony between humans and the spiritual world. The Pueblo believed that if harmony existed, the

---

COOPERATIVE LEARNING ACTIVITY

Bulletin Board Organize the class into five groups, corresponding to the five different regions inhabited by native North Americans. Ask each group to select one of the peoples identified in the text as living in "their" region. Have them research and prepare a bulletin-board display on that people, highlighting aspects of daily life and customs. Among the topics students should consider are layout of villages and buildings, the development of crafts, food-gathering techniques, and religious ceremonies. Each group member should have a specific role to play in preparing the display. **L1 LEP**

spirits would provide rain for crops and small game for food.

Another important Southwest group known as **the Apache** lived in areas that were unsuitable for farming. They hunted wild birds and rabbits and gathered plants. Sometimes they raided Pueblo fields; other times they traded meat and animal hides with Pueblo villagers for maize and other food supplies. A neighboring people, **the Navajo**, did manage to raise a breed of sheep that could live on the sparse desert vegetation.

Great Plains

In contrast to the sparse rocky and desert environment of the Southwest, vast expanses of grassland covered the **Great Plains**, stretching from the Rocky Mountains to the Mississippi River. This environment provided a different challenge for the early people who inhabited the region. Native Americans adapting to life on the plains needed a reliable source of food. Farming in the region was difficult, as the thick plains sod was hard to plow. Moreover, maize needs more water than is naturally available on most parts of the Great Plains.

Although some farming was done along streams, most of **the Plains people** depended on one abundant resource—the great herds of bison, or buffalo, that roamed the plains. From earliest times, the Kiowa, Crow, Blackfoot, and other people of the plains followed the herds from one grazing ground to another. They used every part of the bison for their food, clothing, shelter, and tools.

Eastern Woodlands

Unlike the Plains people who depended on the bison, Native Americans of the woodlands east of the Mississippi River hunted a large variety of animals. Deer, turkeys, geese, and squirrels were common in eastern forests. Like the Plains people, Woodland people made use of every part of the animals they killed. They ate deer meat, wore deer-

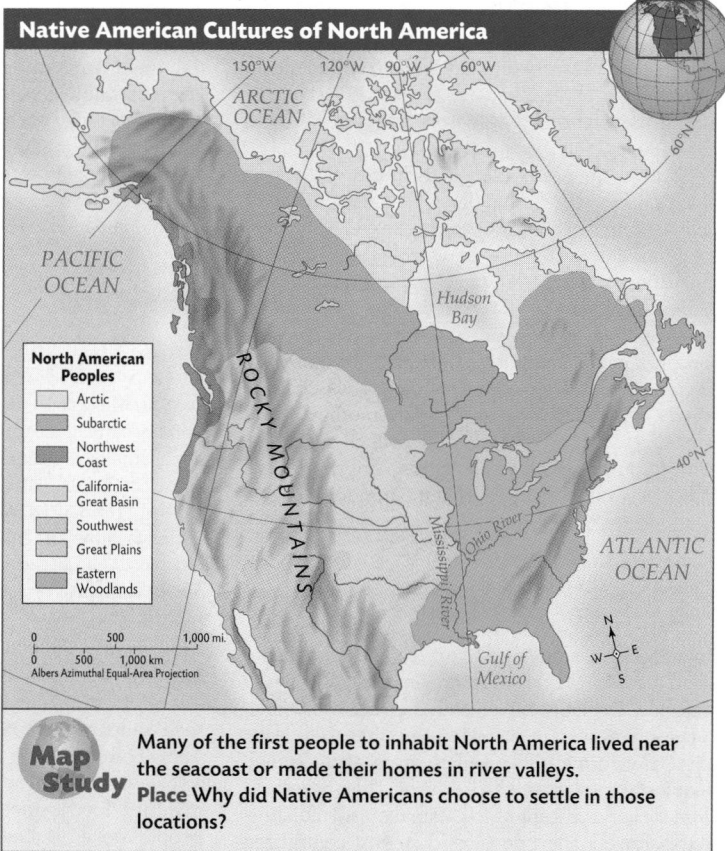

Native American Cultures of North America

North American Peoples
- Arctic
- Subarctic
- Northwest Coast
- California–Great Basin
- Southwest
- Great Plains
- Eastern Woodlands

0   500   1,000 mi.
0   500   1,000 km
Albers Azimuthal Equal-Area Projection

Map Study Many of the first people to inhabit North America lived near the seacoast or made their homes in river valleys. **Place** Why did Native Americans choose to settle in those locations?

skin clothing, and made tools out of animal bones and antlers. Since summers were warm, rainfall abundant, and soil fertile throughout most of the Eastern Woodlands, the people of this region lived in farming villages and grew crops such as corn, squash, beans, and tobacco.

In the Ohio and Mississippi River valleys, groups of Native Americans known as **the Mound Builders** erected large earthen mounds. Archaeologists today believe that the mounds were used as ceremonial structures or as tombs for leaders. A number of mounds were made in the shape of animals.

From about A.D. 700 to A.D. 1700, productive farming in the Mississippi River valley led to the rise of towns and cities. Each town had a ceremonial center of earthen platforms and was probably governed by a high-ranking group of individuals, perhaps warriors. One of the largest urban centers was **Cahokia** (keh•HOH•kee•eh), on the east bank of the Mississippi in present-day Illinois. A huge temple mound dominated the city. Around the

Chapter 4 *Toward a New World* **163**

Map Study

Answer
Rivers and coastal areas provided a supply of fish that people used for food. River valleys and coastlands also provided good land for farming. People living in these areas could use boats for travel and trade.

Map Skills Practice

Reading a Map What two natural boundaries marked the region of the Great Plains people? (*Rocky Mountains, Mississippi River*)

♪ World Music: Cultural Traditions, Lesson 1

you don't say...

"**Mississippi**," the name of the principal river of the United States, comes from an Algonquian word meaning "big river."

MEETING SPECIAL NEEDS ACTIVITY

Learning Style: Visual/Spatial Help students distinguish among the cultures described in this section by asking them to draw pictures representing each one. Guide students through the text to make sure they select appropriate images for each culture, such as a whalebone for people of the Arctic, a totem pole for people in the Northwest, a buffalo for the Plains people, and a pyramid for the Aztec. Students may also use outside sources. **L1 LEP**

HOME VIDEO.

The following videotape program is available from Glencoe:

- **The Secret Burial Mounds of Pre-Historic America**

To find classroom resources to accompany this video, check the following home page:

A&E Television: http://www.AandE.com

Independent Practice

Guided Reading Activity 4-4 **L1**

Literature Have students find one or two examples of Native American poetry and stories in the library and share a reading of one with the class. Ask them to explain its purpose in the culture, such as its use in religious ceremonies or celebrations. **L2**

Geography: Location Have students locate both the Aztec and Inca Empires, as well as the Mayan civilization studied in Chapter 2, on a map of Mexico and Central America. Discuss with students why so many civilizations arose in the same area. **L2**

World History and Art Transparency 18, *Mola Stitchery*

World Music: Cultural Traditions, Lesson 2

---

temple stretched clusters of workshops, houses, farms, and other mounds used for religious ceremonies. The largest Native American city built north of Mexico, Cahokia housed about 10,000 people during its height of power from about A.D. 900 to A.D. 1100.

Native Americans living in the northeastern part of the present-day United States had a high level of political organization compared with the peoples of the plains and the Southwest. During the A.D. 1500s, the Cayuga, Mohawk, Oneida, Onondaga, and Seneca formed the League of the Iroquois—a confederation, or loose union of tribes or territories. A council of representatives from each group met to discuss and resolve disputes, but every clan had an elderly female known as a "clan mother," who named and deposed chiefs and council members. When Europeans invaded Native American land, they met strong resistance from the Iroquois League.

Native American Empires

From the A.D. 1300s to the A.D. 1500s, two powerful civilizations—**the Aztec** and **the Inca**—ruled areas of Mexico, Central America, and South America. Both the Aztec and the Inca were latecomers to power. In scarcely more than 200 years, they transformed themselves from little-known peoples to masters of vast empires. They borrowed from earlier civilizations to create their own distinctive cultures. They developed highly centralized

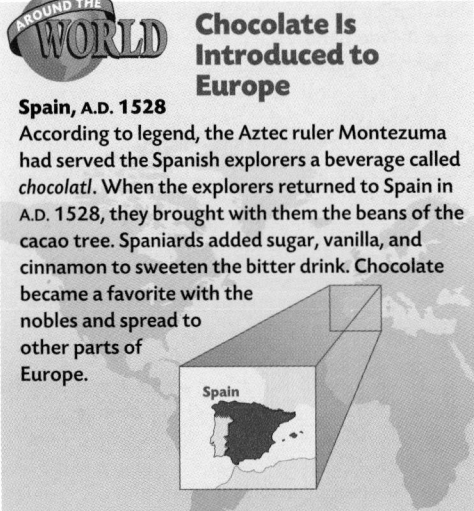

Chocolate Is Introduced to Europe

Spain, A.D. 1528
According to legend, the Aztec ruler Montezuma had served the Spanish explorers a beverage called *chocolatl*. When the explorers returned to Spain in A.D. 1528, they brought with them the beans of the cacao tree. Spaniards added sugar, vanilla, and cinnamon to sweeten the bitter drink. Chocolate became a favorite with the nobles and spread to other parts of Europe.

Spain

---

governments and became productive farmers, master builders, artisans, and weavers. Although they held quite different religious beliefs, religion was important to both peoples and motivated their expansion. Both sophisticated civilizations came to sudden ends in the early A.D. 1500s, when they were overwhelmed and destroyed by Spanish invaders from Europe.

The Aztec

The early Aztec were semi-nomadic hunters and warriors who migrated from the north into central Mexico in the A.D. 1200s. They founded what became the capital of their empire in A.D. 1325 on a small, uninhabited island near the western shore of Lake Texcoco. The Aztec named their capital **Tenochtitlán** (tay•NAWCH•teet•LAHN). Today it is the site of Mexico City.

Tenochtitlán

The Aztec turned Tenochtitlán into an agricultural center and marketplace. Since land for farming was scarce on the island, they built *chinampas*, or artificial islands, by piling mud from the bottom of the lake onto rafts secured by stakes. These became floating gardens where farmers grew a variety of crops, including corn and beans. With a plentiful food supply, the population grew and people moved outside the city to the mainland. A network of canals, bridges, and causeways was built to connect the mainland with the capital city.

At the center of Tenochtitlán, the Aztec built impressive white stone pyramids, temples, plazas, palaces, arsenals, and ball courts. The location of main temples and the layout of main streets was partly based on astronomical principles.

A huge market was located in another part of the city. Goods arrived by canoes on Tenochtitlán's many canals or by bearers carrying loads in backpacks. Maize, chili peppers, cotton textiles, rubber, obsidian, copper, jewelry, jaguar skins, and live eagles could be found there. Cacao beans, enjoyed by the wealthy for making chocolate, were used as currency in the market.

Building an Empire

Strengthened by early alliances with neighboring city states, the Aztec then conquered more distant rivals. By A.D. 1500 their empire stretched from north-central Mexico to the border of Guatemala, and from the Atlantic Ocean to the Pacific Ocean. Conquered peoples had to pay

---

MAKING CONNECTIONS ACTIVITY

Political Influences Many historians think that American settlers were influenced in their development of a new government by the confederations they observed among the Native Americans on the east coast. In a confederation, each Native American group continued to manage its internal affairs, but all the groups banded together to fight outside enemies. The League of the Iroquois served as a model for the Albany Plan of Union in the A.D. 1750s and the Articles of Confederation in the A.D. 1780s. Have students look up information about the Albany Plan and the Articles and note the similarities between them and the Iroquois confederation. **L3**

heavy tribute in the form of food, clothing, raw materials, and prisoners for sacrifice.

As the Aztec Empire expanded, Tenochtitlán prospered. Estimates of the city's population by A.D. 1500 range from 120,000 to 200,000. Goods and tribute came to the city from all parts of the empire.

Government and Society

The Aztec civilization was organized as a hierarchy—divided into levels of authority—each level more powerful than the level below it. At the top was the emperor. His power came from his control of the army and was reinforced by religious beliefs.

Emperors were aided by a chief priest who was to communicate with the gods and relay their wishes back to the emperor. A council of noble princes and three honored classes of warriors managed the day-to-day affairs of the empire.

The Aztec social order had four classes: nobility, commoners, serfs, and slaves. Land could be owned by noble families and commoners. Commoners included priests, merchants, artisans, and farmers. Serfs were farm workers tied to noble lands. The lowest class included criminals and debtors, as well as female and children prisoners of war. Male prisoners of war were sacrificed to the Aztec gods.

Religion

Religion was the driving force behind the Aztec emphasis on war and sacrifice. Borrowing religious beliefs from the Maya and the Toltecs, the Aztec believed that live human sacrifices were necessary to keep the gods pleased and to ensure abundant harvests. Records show that as many as 20,000 prisoners were sacrificed at the dedication of a great temple-pyramid.

Much Aztec art reflected religious and military themes. The walls of temple-pyramids were decorated with scenes of gods or battles. Poets and writers glorified Aztec gods and the legendary history of the Aztec people. One poem ends with the proud question, "Who could conquer Tenochtitlán?" The empire proved to be more fragile than the poet dreamed. Tenochtitlán faced rebellions from its outlying territories that weakened the empire. In A.D. 1521 these groups joined Spanish explorers in invading and destroying Aztec villages and cities.

The Inca

In South America, along the Pacific coast and in the Andes Mountains, other civilizations developed independently of Mesoamerica. In the late A.D.

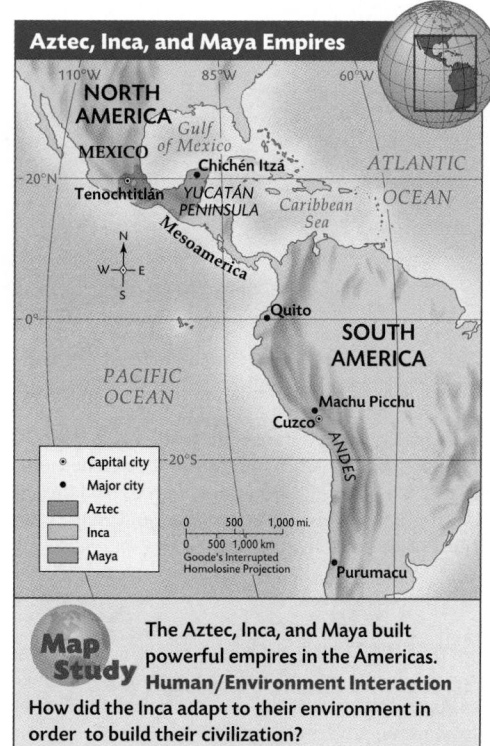

Aztec, Inca, and Maya Empires

- ⊙ Capital city
- • Major city
- Aztec
- Inca
- Maya

0   500   1,000 mi.
0 500 1,000 km
Goode's Interrupted
Homolosine Projection

Map Study

The Aztec, Inca, and Maya built powerful empires in the Americas. **Human/Environment Interaction** How did the Inca adapt to their environment in order to build their civilization?

1980s, archaeological finds revealed that complex societies first emerged in South America between 3000 B.C. and 2100 B.C., 2,000 years earlier than previously thought and 1,000 years earlier than in Mesoamerica.

One of the early peoples was **the Moche**, who flourished on the north coast of present-day Peru between A.D. 100 and A.D. 600. In A.D. 1987 the discovery of a noble's pyramid tomb proved that the Moche had a social order based on ranks, skilled artisans who produced ornaments of gold, silver, and copper, and religious beliefs that included a sacrifice ceremony.

Rise of the Inca

The Inca began as one of many small tribes competing for scarce fertile land in the highland valleys of the Andes. Around A.D. 1200 the Inca settled in **Cuzco** (KOOS•koh), which became their capital. They raided other tribes and slowly established a powerful empire.

The decisive period of Inca expansion began in A.D. 1438, when **Pachacuti**, the ninth Inca ruler, came to power. He and his son, Topa Inca Yupanqui, have been compared to Philip and Alexander the Great of Macedonia. By persuasion,

Chapter 4 *Toward a New World* **165**

Chapter 4 *Toward a New World* **165**

Map Study

Answer
They adjusted to high altitudes.

Map Skills Practice

Reading a Map Where was Machu Picchu located? *(in the Andes Mountains of central Peru, about 50 miles [80 kilometers] northwest of Cuzco)*

Science, Technology, and Society
Encourage students to make a tabletop model or drawing of Aztec *chinampas*. Pair students with limited English proficiency with native English-speaking classmates to help with research using an encyclopedia or other resources. After research and completion of the model or drawing, have students summarize the importance of *chinampas* to Aztec society. **L2 LEP**

ASSESS

Check for Understanding

Assign Section 4 Review as homework or as an in-class activity.

🖳 Use Student Self-Test and Review Software to review Section 4.

Evaluate

📁 Section Quiz 4-4

🖳 Use the Testmaker to create a customized quiz for Section 4.

CRITICAL THINKING ACTIVITY

Making Comparisons Ask students to compare features of government, society, the economy, religion, and culture among the peoples living in Mesoamerica and in Europe between A.D. 1000 and A.D. 1500. In what ways did the two regions resemble each other? *(centralized governments, the importance of religion, distinct social classes)* How did they differ? *(the practice of human sacrifice)* Encourage students to debate which features of Mesoamerican life may have been more advanced than those found in Europe at the same time. **L2**

Visualizing History Have students research the kinds of buildings uncovered by modern archaeologists in Machu Picchu.
Answer to Caption: *They built a network of roads.*

Reteach

Have students make a chart on the chalkboard summarizing the religion, economy, and government of the Aztec and Inca.

 Reteaching Activity 4

Enrich

Have students research the plants Native Americans used for medicinal purposes. Recommend that they use a variety of library resources: encyclopedias, nature magazines, and nonfiction works.

 Enrichment Activity 4

CLOSE

Conduct a class discussion on how geographic location affects culture. Ask students to give examples from the text and their outside reading. Have them focus on customs, housing styles, clothing, or food preparation that depended on specific resources.

---

threats, and force, they extended Inca boundaries far to the north and south.

The Inca Empire eventually included all of present-day Peru, much of Chile, and parts of Ecuador, Bolivia, and Argentina. It stretched more than 2,500 miles (4,020 km) through coastal deserts, dry highlands, fertile river valleys, and rain forests. Most of the Inca lived in the Andes highlands and adjusted to high altitudes. Cuzco was 11,600 feet (3,535 m) above sea level.

Government and Society

Pachacuti created a strong central government to control the vast realm. He permitted local rulers to continue governing conquered territories as long as they were loyal. He introduced a system of tribute collections, military posts, and local work regulations to closely bind outlying lands to the central government. To unify the diverse people of the empire, the Inca established an imperial language—Quechua (KEH•chuh•wuh).

The Inca emperor and his officials closely regulated the lives of the common people. As a divine ruler, the emperor owned all land and carefully regulated the growing and distribution of foods, such as potatoes and quinoa (KEEN•WAH), a protein-rich grain. Each year, to prevent uprisings, government officials redistributed land among the farmers within a province. Farmers and other commoners had to earn the right to own luxury

goods by doing extra work for the government—which included repairing bridges, constructing public buildings, cultivating lands owned by religious leaders, and serving in the army. Under the emperor's direction, Inca officials supervised work crews in the building of a network of roads and woven fiber suspension bridges that linked the various parts of the empire.

As a divine ruler, the Inca emperor was believed to have contact with the deities. Like the Aztec, the Inca believed in many deities, including a creator god and a sun god, whom they worshiped in a variety of religious ceremonies. Food and animals were typical sacrificial offerings, but human sacrifices were also made for special events. In A.D. 1995 archaeologists working in the ice fields of the Peruvian Andes discovered the frozen, carefully preserved body of a teenage Inca woman. The food fragments and ceramic shards in the woman's coffin seemed to indicate that she was a sacrificial victim offered by Inca priests to appease the gods.

Inca Decline

The obedient, well-disciplined Inca would prove to be no match for the Spanish conquerors who arrived in South America in A.D. 1533. In spite of fierce resistance, the Inca Empire declined and eventually disappeared. Aspects of Inca culture, however, have survived among the Inca descendants living today in western South America.

SECTION 4 REVIEW

Recall
1. **Define** potlatch, confederation, hierarchy.
2. **Identify** the Kwakiutl, the Pueblo, the Apache, the Navajo, the Plains peoples, the Mound Builders, the Aztec, the Inca, the Moche, Pachacuti.

3. **Use** the maps in the Atlas to describe the physical geography of Mexico and western South America. How did geography affect the civilizations there?

Critical Thinking
4. **Analyzing Information** Compare the structure of the

Iroquois League with that of the government of the United States.

Understanding Themes
5. **Change** Contrast the methods used by the Aztec and the Inca to expand and administer their empires.

SECTION 4 REVIEW ANSWERS

1. All vocabulary words are defined in the Glossary.
2. the Kwakiutl, 162; the Pueblo, 162; the Apache, 163; the Navajo, 163; the Plains people, 163; the Mound Builders, 163; the Aztec, 164; the Inca, 164; Moche, 165; Pachacuti, 165

3. Mexico: diverse terrains, mountain chains, and volcanoes led to innovative farming practices; western South America: coastal deserts, dry highlands, fertile river valleys, and rain forests led to struggle for fertile land and need to adjust to high altitudes.

4. Each group in the Iroquois League sent representatives to a council; each state in the United States sends elected representatives to Congress.
5. **CHANGE** Aztec: heavy tribute imposed on conquered peoples; Inca: resettled rebellious peoples

Analyzing Historical Maps

When you walk through your town, you may see changes in progress. Perhaps a new restaurant has opened, or an old factory has been torn down. Change also takes place on a larger scale across nations and continents. Historical maps illustrate political, social, and cultural change over time.

Learning the Skill

To analyze a historical map, first read the title to identify its theme. Then identify the chronology of events on the map. Many historical maps show changes in political boundaries over time. For example, the map below of the Frankish Empire uses colors to show land acquisitions under three different rulers. On the other map, however, colors represent areas controlled by different rulers at the same time. Read the map key, labels, and captions to determine what time periods and changes appear on the map.

To compare historical maps of the same region in different time periods, first identify the geographic location and time period of each map. Then look for similarities and differences. Which features have remained the same and which have changed? What groups control the area in each map? Has the country or empire grown larger or smaller over time? Have other features changed?

After analyzing the information on historical maps, try to draw conclusions about the causes and effects of these changes.

Practicing the Skill

The two maps on this page show the same region in different time periods. Study both maps and answer these questions.
1. What is the time period of each map?
2. How did the Frankish Empire change from A.D. 500 to A.D. 800?
3. Did France grow larger or smaller between A.D. 800 and A.D. 1400?
4. What other changes appear on these maps?

Applying the Skill

Compare a map of Europe today with a map of Europe in A.D. 1985 or earlier. Identify at least five changes that have occurred since the early A.D. 1980s.

For More Practice

Turn to the Skill Practice in the Chapter Review on page 169 for more practice in analyzing historical maps.

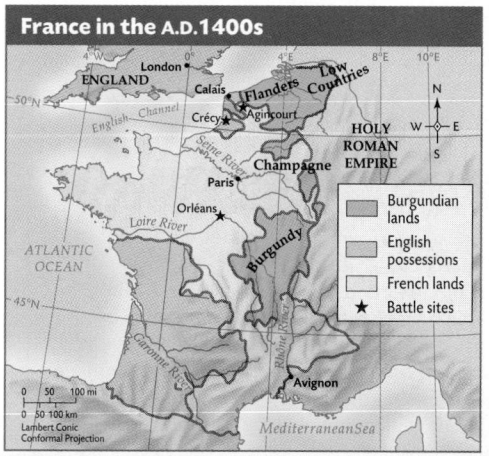

Frankish Empire A.D. 481–814

Clovis's kingdom
Added by Martel and Pepin
Added by Charlemagne
★ Battle site

France in the A.D. 1400s

Burgundian lands
English possessions
French lands
★ Battle sites

TEACH

Analyzing Historical Maps Before students read the skill, ask them whether they think of maps as static or changing and to justify their answers. Then ask them to name some other kinds of maps with which they are familiar. *(Students might mention weather maps, topographic maps, astronomical maps.)* Ask them to indicate what kinds of changes those maps can illustrate. *(Weather maps clearly show changing weather patterns; changes in topographic maps of the same region over time might show the formation of a new island from vulcanism; changes in astronomical maps of the same region over time might show the appearance of a comet.)* When students are sufficiently familiar with the idea that maps of different kinds can serve as records of change, have them read the skill and complete the practice questions.

Additional Practice

🗀 Skill Reinforcement Activity 13

🗀 Building Skills in Geography Workbook, Unit 1, Lesson 13

ANSWERS TO PRACTICING THE SKILL

1. The map on the left shows the Frankish Empire from A.D. 481 to A.D. 814; the map on the right shows France in the A.D. 1400s.
2. It spread east and south to include parts of present-day Spain, Italy, Switzerland, and the Benelux countries.
3. smaller
4. Answers may include that France was divided up among various rulers, and its boundaries changed over time.

Chapter 4 Review

GLENCOE
TECHNOLOGY

VIDEODISC
Use MindJogger to review students' knowledge of the chapter.

MindJogger Videoquiz

Chapter 4
Disc 1 Side A

  Also available in VHS.

Answers

Using Key Terms
1. c
2. i
3. l
4. k
5. a

Using Your History Journal
Students might want to consider using various colors to represent different types of events.

Reviewing Facts
1. It brought peace and security and fostered trade with Europe.
2. Increased trade led to the development of a money economy and a system of banking. Towns grew in size and population. The growth of trade and urban life undermined feudalism.
3. People from the middle class served as advisers to monarchs; the middle class gained freedom from feudal duties in return for financial support of monarchs.
4. Timbuktu
5. It was an island city.

Critical Thinking
1. Answers will vary, but the Mongols' major asset—military

Connections Across Time

Historical Significance The period from A.D. 1000 to A.D. 1500 was one of growth in many areas of the world. In Asia, Africa, and the Americas, powerful empires fostered economic expansion, trade, and cultural advances. In medieval Europe, the growth of trade, towns, and centralized governments set the stage for Europe's later global expansion.

During this period trade networks gradually brought Africa, Europe, the Middle East, South Asia, and East Asia into contact with each other and encouraged the exchange of ideas and practices. Such contact between cultures caused conflict that lasted for decades, even centuries; yet at other times, ideas and ideals were peacefully adopted.

Using Key Terms

Write the key term that completes each sentence. Then write a sentence for each term not chosen.

a. money economy
b. charter
c. scholasticism
d. vernacular
e. multicultural
f. potlatches
g. czar
h. ghana
i. monopoly
j. hierarchy
k. guilds
l. confederation

1. Scholars in medieval Europe developed a system of thought known as _____ that sought to reconcile Christian faith and human reason.
2. Among Native Americans of the Pacific Northwest, the wealth of each lineage group was given away at _____.
3. During the A.D. 1100s, European merchants and artisans organized themselves into business associations called _____.
4. Aztec society was based on a _____, which consisted of the emperor, nobles, commoners, serfs, and slaves.
5. The rise of a _____ in western Europe led to the growth of banking.

Technology Activity

Using the Internet Access the Internet to locate a Web site about the Inca Empire. Use a search engine to help focus your search by using phrases such as *inca empire, mesoamerican civilizations*, or *native amerians*. Create a bulletin board using the information found, and incorporate illustrations of Inca culture and artifacts.

Using Your History Journal

Choose one region from your map of the world. Draw that region on a separate sheet of paper. From the section of Chapter 4 that provides information on your chosen region, list 5 to 10 important facts or events beside your map.

Reviewing Facts

1. **Explain** how Mongol rule benefited China.
2. **Discuss** new business methods that developed in western Europe during the A.D. 1300s and A.D. 1400s. How did they change society?
3. **Explain** why townspeople supported the rise of strong monarchies in western Europe.
4. **Name** the city that became a major center of trade and Islamic art and learning in Mali.
5. **State** what was unique about the location and geography of the Aztec city of Tenochtitlán.

Critical Thinking

1. **Synthesize** Do you think the strengths of Mongol society would benefit a nation today? Why or why not?
2. **Evaluate** How would Europe be different today if there had been no Crusades?
3. **Making Comparisons** Compare the causes for the decline of each of the three West African kingdoms.
4. **Synthesize** What were some daily activities of the Eastern Woodlands peoples?
5. **Analyze** How did the rise and decline of the Aztec and Inca Empires differ?

---

strength—is still regarded as necessary for a strong nation.
2. lack of cultural diffusion and hostility between Christians and Muslims
3. Ghana: Islamic peoples from North Africa attacked Ghanaian trade centers, which led to the empire's decline; Mali: attacked from north and south and faced internal rebellion; Songhai: the central government weakened and Morocco attacked with superior weapons.
4. hunting, farming
5. Aztec demanded tribute of conquered peoples; Inca resettled rebellious peoples; Aztec decline hastened by alliance of conquered peoples, whom they had mistreated, with Spanish; fall of Inca to Spanish eased by obedient national character.

Skill Practice

Study the map "Spread of the Black Death" and answer the questions below.

1. What is the topic and time period of this map?
2. What does color represent?
3. When and where did the Black Death begin?
4. In which direction did the Black Death spread? How does the map show this?
5. What factor do you think caused this pattern of the epidemic?

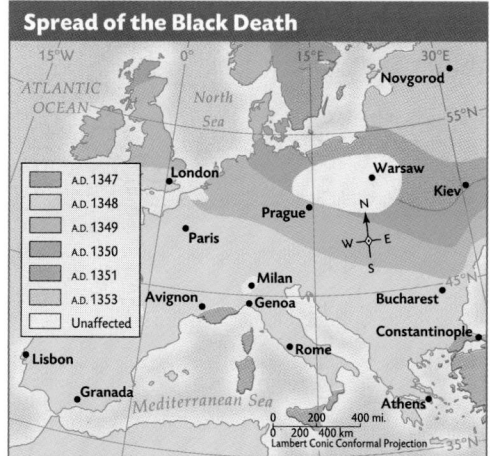

Spread of the Black Death

Legend:
- A.D. 1347
- A.D. 1348
- A.D. 1349
- A.D. 1350
- A.D. 1351
- A.D. 1353
- Unaffected

Cities: Novgorod, Warsaw, Kiev, London, Prague, Paris, Milan, Avignon, Genoa, Bucharest, Constantinople, Rome, Lisbon, Granada, Athens

0 200 400 mi.
0 200 400 km
Lambert Conic Conformal Projection

Understanding Themes

1. **Movement** The Mongols conquered a vast inland empire spanning parts of Europe and Asia, but ruled it relatively briefly. Provide a hypothesis that might explain this situation.
2. **Innovation** Choose one medieval innovation and describe its influence on medieval Europe. Do the same for a modern innovation and modern society.
3. **Cultural Diffusion** How did trade affect cultural diffusion in West Africa? From what areas did the West African kingdoms receive new ideas and practices?
4. **Change** How did the arrival of the Spaniards in the Americas affect the development of Aztec and Inca civilizations?

Linking Past and Present

1. The Crusades were a series of "holy wars" conducted by Christians against Muslims. Can you find examples of holy wars in modern times?
2. Gold helped make Ghana a powerful empire. Name another natural resource that has benefited African countries today.
3. What impact do Native American traditions have on life in the Americas today? In what ways has modern civilization been affected by the early Native Americans?

Geography in History

1. **Movement** Refer to the map below. In the A.D. 1500s and A.D. 1600s, Native American civilizations declined as the whole region came under the rule of powerful European nation-states. The triangular trade linked four continents between A.D. 1600 and A.D. 1760. How, do you think, did trade change population in the Americas, especially in the Caribbean islands?
2. **Cultural Diffusion** What positive and negative changes, do you think, might have resulted from the cultural contacts of peoples from four different continents?

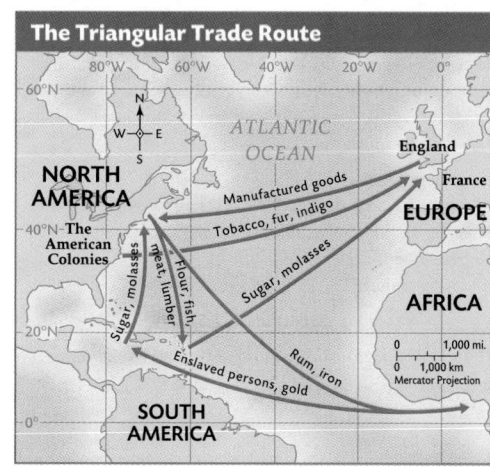

The Triangular Trade Route

NORTH AMERICA — The American Colonies

ATLANTIC OCEAN

England, France, EUROPE, AFRICA, SOUTH AMERICA

Manufactured goods
Tobacco, fur, indigo
Sugar, molasses
Sugar, molasses
Flour, fish, meat, lumber
Rum, iron
Enslaved persons, gold

0 1,000 mi.
0 1,000 km
Mercator Projection

3. **CULTURAL DIFFUSION** Trade brought the culture of the Islamic world to West Africa.
4. **CHANGE** Both civilizations were destroyed.

Linking Past and Present

1. Conflict between Islamic groups and the West; some Arab groups and Israel; Protestant and Catholic groups in Northern Ireland; Hindu and Muslim groups in South Asia
2. Answers may include diamonds and other gems as well as oil and copper.
3. Native American traditions have left their impact on language, recreation (for example, lacrosse, use of hammocks, canoeing), and diet. Respect for the environment, similar to the Native Americans, has become a concern of modern society.

Geography in History

1. Many enslaved Africans were imported; Europeans settled there.
2. positive: exchange of products, resources, ideas; negative: enslavement of local populations

Chapter Bonus Test Question

Ask students: What similarities do you see between the rise of urban civilization in the Americas and the rise of early urban civilizations in the Near East? *(Answers may include: location in areas that are warm year-round; the building of huge structures such as pyramids; development of astronomy and calendars.)*

Skill Practice

1. spread of the Black Death in the A.D. 1300s
2. where plague spread to at different times
3. China in A.D. 1347
4. north and west; colors correspond to dates, showing northern and westward movement
5. As ships sailed from Asia to the Mediterranean, the plague spread from China to ports in southern Europe and beyond.

Understanding Themes

1. **MOVEMENT** Answers will vary; a possible hypothesis might be that they were skilled fighters but not good administrators, and so could not hold their domains together.
2. **INNOVATION** Answers will vary; possible answer is computer technology today has strengthened interdependence among nations.

ABCNEWS iNTERACTIVE™

VIDEODISC
Turning Points in World History

Side One
Chapter 7

Title: *The Crusades*

If you do not have access to a videodisc player, **Turning Points in World History** is also available in VHS.

Internet Sites

The following are possible sites for completing the "Net" activities:

Native Web:
http://www.maxwell.syr.edu/nativeweb/index.html

The Azteca Web Page:
http://www.azteca.net/aztec

Not on the "Net"...

If students have limited or no access to the Internet, have them complete "The Aztecs" activity by using resources in the school or public library to find information on the Aztecs. Encourage students to use the following subjects to help them locate sources in the library's computerized or traditional card catalog: government, religion, innovations, contributions.

Students may use the information they locate to help them create their fact sheet.

 **ABCNEWS iNTERACTIVE™**

Turning Points in World History

The Crusades

Setting up the Video

Work with a group of your classmates to view "The Crusades" on the videodisc *Turning Points in World History*. The Crusades left lasting effects on the economic and political development of western Europe. Improvements abounded in the areas of new knowledge, trade, and technology. This program introduces the Crusades and the changes that occurred in European culture, art, and architecture.

Hands-On Activity

Create an oral history by interviewing a person about his or her experiences during a modern-day "crusade" (such as the civil rights or women's rights movements) that has left a lasting effect on our society. Create questions to ask this individual during a recorded interview. Share the results of your interview with the class.

Side One, Chapter 7

View the video by scanning the bar code or by entering the chapter number on your keypad and pressing Search. (Also available in VHS format.)

Surfing the "Net"

The Aztecs

The Aztecs held a vast empire until the early A.D. 1500s, when they were ultimately defeated by Spanish invaders from Europe. Their civilization was very advanced in areas such as building, agriculture, and the creation of a highly centralized government. To learn more about the Aztecs, access the Internet.

Getting There
1. Go to a search engine. Type in the phrase *aztec culture*.
2. After typing in the phrase, enter words such as those below to focus your search:
   - *government*
   - *religion*
   - *innovations*
   - *contributions*

3. The search engine should provide you with a number of links to follow. Links are "pointers" to different sites on the Internet and commonly appear as blue underlined words.

What to Do When You Are There
Click on the links to navigate through the pages of information and gather your findings. Create a fact sheet of information about all aspects of Aztec culture. Include information such as type of government, agriculture, religion, and innovations. Include an accompanying map showing the Aztec Empire sphere of influence.

INTERNET ADDRESS BOOK

Use this space to record frequently used addresses.

_____

_____

_____

_____

_____

Unit 1 | Digest

From about 3500 B.C. to about A.D. 1500, civilizations developed independently in different parts of the world. For hundreds of years, they had little contact with one another. However, as time passed, these civilizations spread, and their peoples began to exchange ideas and practices.

Chapter 1
The Rise of Civilizations

Humans have probably lived on Earth about 2 million years, but the story of world history begins only about 5,500 years ago with the invention of writing. Other significant changes were the rise of farming and village life. In time, some farming villages became cities that served as centers of civilizations, or highly organized societies. The earliest civilizations arose in river valleys in Africa and Asia, where fertile soil and an available water supply made agriculture productive.

Africa and the Middle East

Along Africa's Nile River, the Egyptians founded a civilization about 3100 B.C. Egyptian monarchs built royal tombs, temples, and palaces as well as an empire that fostered long-distance trade and the exchange of ideas.

In Mesopotamia, the land between the Tigris and Euphrates Rivers, the Sumerians and other peoples set up city-states and empires. Their achievements included the wheel, one of history's first law codes, and cuneiform, perhaps the world's oldest writing system.

For several hundred years after 1200 B.C., various other Middle Eastern peoples left their mark on world history. Phoenician traders created an alphabet on which Western alphabets were modeled. The Israelites, later called Jews, practiced monotheism—the belief in one all-powerful god—that formed the basis of Judaism, Christianity, and Islam. The Hittites, Assyrians, Chaldeans, and Persians set up empires that advanced trade and cultural exchanges.

Asia

In South Asia's Indus River valley, the Harrappans built well-planned cities. By 1000 B.C.

Aryan invaders had conquered northern India. India's languages, social structure, and Hindu religion emerged from Aryan roots. During 500s B.C., Siddartha Gautama, known to his followers as the Buddha, or Enlightened One, laid the foundation of Buddhism, one of the world's major religions.

Meanwhile, the people of China built their first cities and established a form of government based on dynasties, or ruling families. Under the Zhou dynasty, two major philosophies—Confucianism and Daoism—emerged. Based on the teachings of Kongfuzi, or Confucius, Confucianism stressed moral standards and social duties. Daoism, derived from the thinker Laozi, stressed harmony with nature.

The Americas

Archaeologists believe that people were living in the Americas as early as 40,000 years ago. By about 5000 B.C., hunter-gatherers in present-day Mexico learned to cultivate maize and other native plants. This discovery spread from Mexico to other parts of the Americas. Between 1500 B.C. and 400 B.C., the Olmec emerged as the first of a series of American civilizations.

SURVEYING CHAPTER 1

1. **Relating to the Enviornment** Why did early civilizations arise in river valleys?
2. **Relating Ideas** What major world religions emerged in early civilizations?

Chapter 2
The Advance of Civilizations

From about 500 B.C. to A.D. 500, civilizations made further advances in various parts of the world. Each had unique traits, but they all had common features—a stable political system, one or more major religions, and an interest in the arts and sciences.

Greece

The seafaring Greeks founded colonies around the Mediterranean Sea. Each Greek polis, or city-state, especially Athens, encouraged its citizens to

---

The Unit Digest offers a chapter-by-chapter summary that can be used for any of the following teaching purposes:
- *Preview* one chapter or an entire unit,
- *Review* some or all of the chapters,
- *Condense* when specific chapters or units have not been taught, or
- *Reteach* chapters that students have studied in the unit.

PREVIEW

Use the Unit 1 Digest Transparencies to preview the highlights of the unit.

REVIEW

Cultural Diffusion Have students brainstorm examples of ways that cultural diffusion took place during the period covered in Unit 1. Discuss the examples and decide which three were the most important. (*Answers may include: Migrating peoples spread their culture; trading peoples exchanged ideas as well as goods; empire builders brought large territories under the control of one ruler.*) **L2**

Use Student Self-Test and Review Software to review any chapters that students have studied in Unit 1.

CLASSROOM RESOURCES FOR UNIT 1 DIGEST

Preview
- Unit 1 Digest Transparencies

Review
- Time Line Activities 1, 2, 3, 4
- Student Self-Test and Review Software, Chapters 1, 2, 3, 4
- MindJogger Videoquiz, Chapters 1, 2, 3, 4

Condense
- Chapter Digests Audiocassettes, Chapters 1, 2, 3, 4

Reteach
- Reteaching Activities 1, 2, 3, 4
- Chapter Digests Audiocassettes, Chapters 1, 2, 3, 4

Religion Ask students to identify the religions that arose during the time period of Unit 1 that are still practiced today. Have students tell where each religion originated and where it first spread. *(Christianity: began among Jewish disciples of Jesus in Judea, spread through Roman Empire. Hinduism: evolved in India from early Aryan beliefs. Buddhism: the Buddha lived in India; Buddhism spread to China and Southeast Asia.)* **L1**

History Ask students to consider how the decline of a civilization can affect what we know about world history. Ask them to consider efforts by new civilizations to preserve the traditions and knowledge of fallen empires. *(Students should recognize that if a civilization leaves few artifacts, we will know little about it; by preserving useful elements of earlier cultures, newer civilizations preserve our knowledge of the past.)* **L2**

CONDENSE

🎧 Use Chapter Digest Audiocassettes to introduce chapters that students have not studied in Unit 1. Spanish Chapter Digest Audiocassettes are also available.

Discuss Have students read the **Unit Digest** and discuss the **Surveying the Unit** questions. **L1**

RETEACH

Time Line Have students summarize Unit 1 by creating a time line that shows at least 10 key events and developments from 3500 B.C. to A.D. 1500.

---

participate in government, thereby introducing the Western concept of democracy. By the 400s B.C., Greek victories over the Persian Empire had ushered in a golden age of culture. During this time the Greeks laid the foundations of Western philosophy, science, mathematics and the arts. By 330 B.C. Alexander the Great had conquered an empire stretching from Greece and Egypt to India. Under his rule Greek culture spread eastward and mixed with Middle Eastern ideas to form the Hellenistic civilization.

Rome

Rome used its army to build an empire that ruled the Mediterranean world. The Romans developed a system of laws and built roads, aqueducts, and public buildings. Meanwhile, Christianity, based on the life and teachings of Jesus or Nazareth, spread from the Middle East throughout the Roman world. Christianity became the official religion of the empire in A.D. 392.

Africa

In northeast Africa, trading civilizations such as Kush and Axum imported new ideas and religions along with goods. Meanwhile, the Bantu migrations spread culture to other parts of Africa. Family traditions rooted in religious beliefs governed life in African villages.

Asia

Powerful empires developed in Asia. Two ruling groups—the Mauryas and later the Guptas—founded empires in India. Under the Guptas, mathematicians developed "Arabic numerals" and the concept of zero. The Qin and Han dynasties of China expanded China's borders, increasing contacts with the outside world. Under the Han emperor Wudi, the Chinese adopted a civil service in which officials were appointed on the basis of examinations. The Chinese of this period made contributions in science and technology, such as the first printed book, paper, gunpowder, and acupuncture.

The Americas

From about 500 B.C. to A.D. 500, the Maya ruled present-day Mexico and Central America. They developed a complex writing system, built temple-pyramids, and mastered mathematics and astronomy. Later, the Toltec set up a mining and trading empire in central Mexico.

SURVEYING CHAPTER 2

1. **Relating Ideas** How did the Greeks and the Romans influence Western civilization?
2. **Making Comparisons** How do ancient India and ancient America compare in their achievements?

Chapter 3
Regional Civilizations

From A.D. 500 to A.D. 1300, regional civilizations established bases of power in various parts of the world. Expanded trade routes spread ideas and practices from one people to another.

The Byzantines

After A.D 395 Byzantine civilization developed in the eastern Roman Empire from the blending of the classical heritage, Christian faith, and Middle Eastern influences. Constantinople, the capital, was a major crossroads of trade and culture. Among Byzantine achievements were the Justinian Code—the revision of Roman law that later became a model for the legal systems of western Europe—and the spread of Christianity to the Slavs of eastern Europe.

Islamic Civilization

The preaching of Muhammad in the early A.D. 600s led to the rise of the monotheistic religion of Islam in the Arabian Peninsula. A powerful Islamic empire later developed in the Middle East and North Africa under the Umayyad and Abbasid dynasties. Islamic scholars made advances in mathematics, astronomy, geometry, and medicine. Islamic sciences and arts influenced western Europe.

Early Medieval Europe

After Rome's decline in the A.D. 400s, Christianity, the classical heritage, and Germanic culture created a new civilization in Europe. Feudalism—a system joining ties of loyalty among nobles to land ownership and military service—aimed to provide security in an age of conflict. Monarchs were generally weak, but the kings of England and France worked to strengthen central government in their lands. The Catholic Church meanwhile deeply affected western Europeans. Communities known as monasteries preserved writings, set up schools, and spread Christianity.

CHAPTER 1
1. Fertile soil and an available water supply made agriculture productive.
2. Judaism, Hinduism, Buddhism, Confucianism, Daoism

CHAPTER 2
1. Greeks: democracy, drama, philosophy, science/arts; Romans: system of laws; methods of building

2. Both had achievements in mathematics.

CHAPTER 3
1. Korea, Japan and parts of Southeast Asia
2. impact of Islamic art, architecture, and literature

CHAPTER 4
1. Benefits: Civilizations were enriched by cultural diffusion, and the interchange of ideas about technology and government advanced the

---

Unit 1 Digest

Answer to Caption: *fewer than 50 years*

Outline Map Have students use an outline map of the world to locate and give approximate dates for the following: Byzantine Empire, Islamic state, Frankish Empire, Tang dynasty, kingdoms of Kush and Mali, and Aztec and Inca Empires. **L1**

 Reteaching Activities 1, 2, 3, 4

Chapter Digests Audiocassettes, Chapters 1, 2, 3, 4

Asia's Pacific Rim

From about A.D. 500 to A.D. 1300, civilizations developed along Asia's Pacific Rim. China's influence extended to parts of Southeast Asia, and to Korea and Japan. Isolated from mainland Asia, the Japanese developed a feudal system in which landowning nobles used warriors known as samurai to fight for them.

SURVEYING CHAPTER 3

1. **Relating Ideas** What areas of Asia were influenced by the spread of Chinese culture?
2. **Analyzing Trends** How did the rise of Islam affect western Europe?

Chapter 4
Toward a New World

From A.D. 1000 to A.D. 1500, civilizations came into closer contact with each other through trade and conquests. Yet they remained largely independent of one another, with their histories continuing to develop along separate lines.

From A.D. 1000 to A.D. 1400, peoples from central Asia, such as Mongols, conquered vast areas in Europe and Asia. In China a series of dynasties—the Tang, Song, and Yuan—created stable government, expanded Chinese frontiers, promoted trade with the West, and encouraged the arts, science, and technology. During Yuan times Europeans became increasingly interested in China as a result of the reports of travelers and traders.

Beginning in the late A.D. 1000s, Christian western Europeans began the Crusades to end Muslim rule of Palestine. The Crusades did not regain "the Holy Land," but they did open western Europe to new ways of life and stimulated trade with the East. Meanwhile, Europe's economy and culture revived with the growth of trade, towns, banking, and universities. All of these developments brought about the decline of feudalism. By the A.D. 1300s, monarchy was the major political institution in Europe.

From about A.D. 1000 to A.D. 1500, trading kingdoms emerged in Africa. The rulers of Ghana traded gold for salt brought by Islamic traders. Mali later became a rich trading empire under its ruler, Mansa Musa. Songhai developed an Islamic legal system. Trade also brought prosperity and Islamic culture to East African coastal states.

By the early A.D. 1400s, various Native American groups flourished in the Americas. The Aztecs of central Mexico waged war on neighboring peoples and built an empire centered in the magnificent capital, Tenochtitlán. Along the western coast of South Africa, the Inca conquered an empire ruled by a strong central government and linked by a vast network of roads.

SURVEYING CHAPTER 4

1. **Defending a Point of View** Do you think cultural diffusion benefits or hinders the growth of a civilization? Explain.
2. **Making Comparisons** How did governments in different parts of the world develop in response to challenges?

GLENCOE TECHNOLOGY

VIDEODISC
Use MindJogger to review any chapter in Unit 1.

MindJogger Videoquiz

 Chapter 1 Disc 1 Side A

 Chapter 2 Disc 1 Side A

 Chapter 3 Disc 1 Side A

Chapter 4 Disc 1 Side A

 Also available in VHS.

ANSWERS TO SURVEYING THE UNIT

development of all civilization. Hinderance: Cultural diffusion was often accompanied by conflict, with one group dominating another.
2. Answers will vary. Examples: Governments in the ancient Middle East developed in response to the challenge of using river waters for agriculture; the Chinese created a civil service to provide order and effective control of the economy; Rome changed from a republic to an empire as conquests brought diverse lands and peoples under its rule; African empires emerged from the gold trade; medieval European Feudalism developed in response to foreign invasions and the collapse of central government.

Introducing the Unit

Unit 2 focuses on how the Renaissance, the Reformation, and the age of exploration dramatically changed Europe and much of the rest of the world. The unit also explores the way Asian civilizations enriched their own cultures by adapting elements of Western culture.

Unit Objectives

After reading Unit 2, students will be able to:

1. explain how the Renaissance emphasized individualism and how the Protestant Reformation established new forms of Christianity.
2. understand how Europeans explored and colonized the Americas, Asia, and Africa.
3. trace the growing power of monarchs and the rise of strong nation-states in Europe from the 1500s to the 1700s.
4. examine the powerful Ottoman, Persian, Mogul, Chinese, and Japanese Empires and understand the cultural achievements of Asia.

Portfolio Project

Students may work in groups to gather information. Students can learn about early banks on pages 222–223. This activity may be a method of authentic assessment.

Unit **2** 1400–1800

Emergence of the Modern World

Chapter 5
Renaissance and Reformation

Chapter 6
Expanding Horizons

Chapter 7
Empires of Asia

Chapter 8
Royal Power and Conflict

Then **& Now**

The Renaissance and Reformation changed European culture and created powerful political alliances. Europeans set out on uncharted seas to explore the world as powerful European monarchs competed for trade, influence, and territory. While the peoples of the Americas struggled against European invaders, civilizations in Asia reached pinnacles of cultural achievement.

Every time you use paper money or write a check, you are trusting in a system based on banking that originated during this period. As European trade and commerce increased, merchants turned to bankers for the capital to finance their ventures. Wealthy banking families even made loans to European monarchs. By the 1600s government-chartered banks began to replace family-owned banks. These banks issued banknotes and checks that made trading in heavy coins obsolete.

A Global Chronology

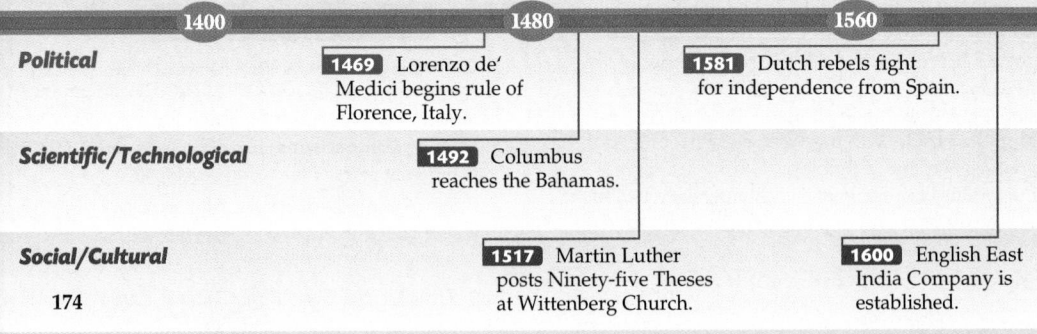

	1400	1480	1560
Political		**1469** Lorenzo de' Medici begins rule of Florence, Italy.	**1581** Dutch rebels fight for independence from Spain.
Scientific/Technological		**1492** Columbus reaches the Bahamas.	
Social/Cultural		**1517** Martin Luther posts Ninety-five Theses at Wittenberg Church.	**1600** English East India Company is established.

174

Then **& Now**

Power In this unit students will learn about the emergence of powerful and wealthy nation-states in Europe and the creation of European colonies in the Americas, Africa, and Asia. Explain that Spain, Portugal, France, Britain, and Holland were the leading commercial and naval powers of the Renaissance and Reformation.

Ask students to make a list of the most powerful nations in the world today, using wealth and

Title: *Age of Exploration*
Subject: Western Europeans
seek new routes to Asia.
Ask: In what ways was the age
of exploration a turning point?
(Europeans gained territory; indige-nous peoples were mistreated, killed, or died from disease; new crops introduced to Europe.)

History & Art

Galileo Galilei was
an Italian astronomer, physicist, and
mathematician who embodied the
Renaissance humanists' ideal of
thinking independently. He was
tried and convicted of heresy for
maintaining that the earth revolved
around the sun, rather than vice
versa.

History *and the* Humanities

  Focus on World Art Prints
- 16 *Portrait of a Noblewoman*
- 20 *The Attributes of Painting*

World History and Art
Transparencies
- 20 *Mona Lisa*
- 22 *View of Toledo*
- 24 *Taj Mahal*
- 25 *Shah Jahan and One of His
Sons Riding in Escort*

  World Music: Cultural
Traditions, Lessons 2, 3, 7

Portfolio Project

Banks originated as places
to store money. They then made
loans to merchants and others
who needed capital. Today
banks perform a variety of
financial services. Do you know
what services your local bank
offers? Visit two local banks and
pick up several advertising
brochures. Compare such things
as interest rates, the cost of hav-ing a checking account, and the
types of loans available. Create
a table that shows the different
services of early banks and
modern banks.

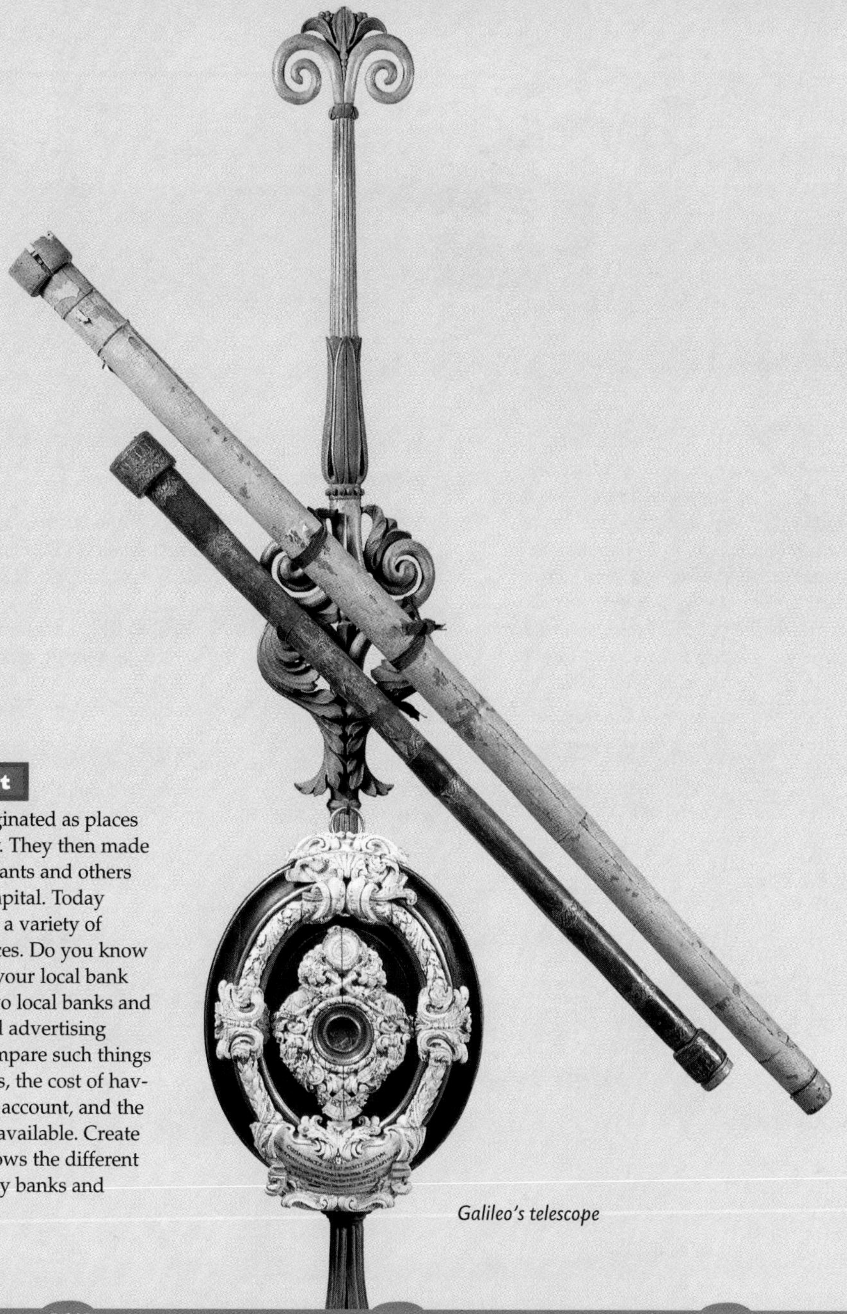

Galileo's telescope

1640   **1720**   **1800**

1642 English Civil War begins.

1763 Peace of
Paris ends Seven
Years' War.

1795 Russia, Prussia, and
Austria divide Poland among
themselves.

1717 Lady Mary Wortley
Montagu introduces inoculation
against smallpox.

1608 First checks are used to
replace cash in the Netherlands.

1764 Mozart writes his
first symphony at age 8.

175

---

military power as their criteria. **Are any countries on both lists? Which?** *(Britain and France)* **Why
are some nations wealthy and powerful?** *(They possess abundant natural resources, an industrial and
technological base, and an educated population.)* **What causes nations to lose their position as world
leaders?** *(loss of economic predominance, limited resources and population, competition of newly industrialized nations)*

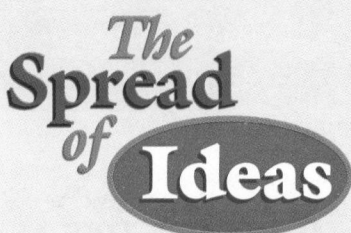

The Spread of Ideas

TEACH

Introduction

This feature focuses on the spread of musical forms from Africa to the Americas as an unintended consequence of the Atlantic slave trade. In North America and the Caribbean, the distinctive African musical forms evolved into spirituals, blues, ragtime, jazz, rock and roll, rap, reggae, calypso, and salsa, among other styles.

Background Notes

Linking Past and Present

Several elements of African music have profoundly influenced modern popular forms, particularly rhythmic polyphony, a more complex and compelling rhythmic style than those of European origin. The minor third, a regular feature of West African music, also became an essential element of blues and rock and roll.

Geography

Movement After reaching North America, African-influenced music was at first found mainly in the Deep South. Early blues masters such as Robert Johnson and Blind Lemon Jefferson came from the Mississippi Basin, and New Orleans and Memphis emerged as centers of the new style. During the Great Depression, millions of African Americans moved north, and the blues traveled with them to St. Louis, Kansas City, Chicago, and New York.

The Spread of Ideas

Music

*I*n the 1400s and 1500s, European ships edged into uncharted waters. These voyages set the stage for one of the greatest cultural exchanges in history, as people from Europe, Africa, and the Americas came face-to-face for the first time. One of the products of this exchange was the birth of "America music," a collection of styles deeply rooted in West Africa.

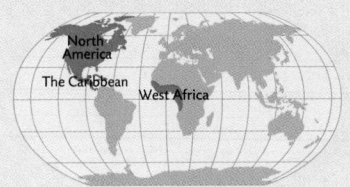

West Africa
Traditional Rhythms

"We are almost a nation of dancers, musicians, and poets," recalled a West African named Olaudah Equiano. "Every great event ... is celebrated ... with songs and music suited to the occasion."

Equiano's words highlighted the importance of music to everyday life among the varied peoples of West Africa. Here musicians won fame for the skill with which they played complicated rhythms on drums, flutes, whistles, and stringed instruments. People added the sounds of their voices to a rhythm known as a call-and-response pattern. A leader would sing out a short piece of music, and people would sing it back to the beat of a drum.

African-style drum

COOPERATIVE LEARNING ACTIVITY

Map Have students use a large outline map of the world to show the diffusion of musical forms from Africa to the Americas, Europe, and back to Africa. Have them label musical centers such as West Africa and New Orleans. Suggest that they use thumbtacks and colored thread to show the paths that music has traveled. Display the finished map in the classroom.

Also encourage students to bring in examples of older forms of music, such as ragtime, blues, jazz, and rhythm and blues, and try to identify similarities and differences in their musical styles.

L1 LEP

North America
New Musical Forms

The musical heritage of West Africa traveled to the Americas aboard European slave ships. To endure the pains of slavery, West Africans kept alive musical patterns that reminded them of their ancestral homelands. Because most West Africans came as laborers, work songs took root first. The rhythmic patterns of these songs set the pace for repetitious tasks. West African laborers added field hollers—long calls by a worker in which other workers answered back. Outside the fields, enslaved Africans cried out for freedom in religious folk songs known as spirituals.

Over hundreds of years, these musical forms came together to create new styles. The blues grew out of the field songs and spirituals of slavery. Ragtime echoed the complicated rhythms of West African music. On these foundations grew yet other styles—jazz, rock 'n' roll, and rap.

Chicago 1955 by
Ben Shahn

Steel drums of the Caribbean

The Caribbean
Afro-Caribbean Beats

The sounds of West Africa could be heard wherever large enslaved African populations lived in the Americas. On islands in the Caribbean, the beat of bongos, the conga, the tambour, and other West African drums became the soul of Afro-Caribbean music. Added to the drums were European instruments such as the Spanish guitar and a variety of Native American instruments such as the marimba (xylophone), maraca, and wooden rhythm sticks called claves. Out of this blend of influences emerged a range of styles as diverse as the Caribbean islands themselves—reggae, calypso, salsa, and more.

LINKING THE IDEAS

1. What are some of the features of West African music?
2. How did West African music influence musical styles in North America and the Caribbean?

Critical Thinking

3. **Evaluating Information** Which styles of music that you listen to at least once a week are influenced by West African musical patterns?

Unit 2   *Emergence of the Modern World*   **177**

The Spread of Ideas

Who?What?Where?When?

W. C. Handy was a pioneer of jazz and blues. The son of a minister, Handy became a musician over his father's protests. As a young man, he played the cornet in minstrel shows, later forming his own band. In 1912 he published "Memphis Blues," originally composed for a political campaign, and one of the first popular blues songs.

Cultural Diffusion

The Circle Is Unbroken The diffusion of African-influenced music continues. In the 1960s, British groups such as the Beatles, the Rolling Stones, and Led Zeppelin recorded blues and rhythm and blues classics written by Muddy Waters, Howlin' Wolf, and Willie Dixon, among others. The British versions of such songs as "Little Red Rooster" and "Seventh Son" became popular among American fans who had never heard the originals.

At the same time, blues and soul have traveled back across the Atlantic Ocean to influence Ali Farka Toure of Mali and other popular African musicians. Similarly, Caribbean musicians have incorporated elements of rap into merengue, from the Dominican Republic, and reggae, from Jamaica.

ANSWERS TO LINKING THE IDEAS

1. complicated rhythms and call-and-response patterns
2. Musical forms such as work songs, field hollers, and spirituals evolved into modern forms of music such as jazz, rock and roll, rap, salsa, reggae, and calypso.
3. Answers should explain the West African connection.

A complete, 1-page lesson plan is provided for each section in the *Reproducible Lesson Plans* booklet.

Renaissance and Reformation

CHAPTER RESOURCES

	Reproducible Resources	Multimedia Resources
Chapter Opener	Chapter Themes: Graphic Organizer 5 Historical Significance Chapter Activity 5	MindJogger Videoquiz
Chapter Enrichment	Vocabulary Activity 5* Time Line Activity 5 Mapping History Activity 5 History Simulation 5 Geography and History Activity 5 Source Reading 5 People in World History Profiles 29, 30 World Literature Selection 4 World Art and Music Activity 5 Enrichment Activity 5 Critical Thinking Activity 5 Skill Reinforcement Activity 5 Performance Assessment Activity 5	Focus on World Art Print 16, *Portrait of a Noblewoman* NGS Poster Set: *The Renaissance* World History and Art Transparency 20, *Mona Lisa*; 21, *Herzogenburg Monastery* Chapter Transparency 5 NGS PicturePack Transparency Set: *The Renaissance* Vocabulary PuzzleMaker Software NGS PictureShow CD-ROM: *The Renaissance* World Music: Cultural Traditions, Lesson 3 Turning Points in World History
Chapter Review/Reteaching	Reteaching Activity 5 Skill Reinforcement Activity 5 Spanish Chapter Summary 5	Chapter 5 Digest Audiocassette, Activity, Test* Vocabulary PuzzleMaker Software Student Self-Test and Review Software MindJogger Videoquiz
Chapter Evaluation/Testing	Performance Assessment Activity 5 Chapter 5 Test, Forms A and B	Testmaker

* Also available in Spanish

0:00 OUT OF TIME? Assign the Chapter 5 summary in the Unit 2 Digest on pages 283–285, and the Chapter 5 Audiocassettes.

Block Schedule

Block scheduling differs from traditional class scheduling in the amount of time allotted to each period. The extended time frame provided by block scheduling affords you the opportunity to implement a greater number of research-oriented and activity-intense projects to motivate and involve your students. Activities that are particularly suited to use within the block scheduling framework are identified throughout this chapter by the following designation.

KEY TO ABILITY LEVELS

Teaching strategies have been coded for varying learning styles and abilities.

L1 **BASIC** activities for all students
L2 **AVERAGE** activities for average to above-average students
L3 **CHALLENGING** activities for above-average students
LEP **LIMITED ENGLISH PROFICIENCY** activities

Use Glencoe's *Presentation Plus!* multimedia teacher tool to easily present dynamic lessons that visually excite your students. Using Microsoft PowerPoint® you can customize the presentations to create your own personalized lessons.

SECTION RESOURCES

Daily Objectives	Reproducible Resources	Multimedia Resources
Section 1 **The Italian Renaissance** Identify the factors that inspired the Renaissance.	Reproducible Lesson Plan 5-1 Vocabulary Activity 5* Guided Reading Activity 5-1* People in World History Profile 30 Geography and History Activity 5 Time Line Activity 5 History Simulation 5 Section Quiz 5-1*	NGS Poster Set: *The Renaissance* Section Focus Transparency 5-1 Chapter Transparency 5 World History and Art Transparency 20, *Mona Lisa* NGS PicturePack Transparency Set: *The Renaissance* Student Self-Test and Review Software NGS PictureShow CD-ROM: *The Renaissance*
Section 2 **The Northern Renaissance** Explain how the Renaissance reached northern Europe.	Reproducible Lesson Plan 5-2 Vocabulary Activity 5* Guided Reading Activity 5-2* Section Quiz 5-2*	Focus on World Art Print 18, Pieter Brueghel. *The Wedding Dance* Section Focus Transparency 5-2 Student Self-Test and Review Software Testmaker
Section 3 **The Protestant Reformation** Discuss how Luther's religious reforms led to Protestantism, a new branch of Christianity.	Reproducible Lesson Plan 5-3 Vocabulary Activity 5* Guided Reading Activity 5-3* People in World History Profile 29 Section Quiz 5-3*	Section Focus Transparency 5-3 Student Self-Test and Review Software Testmaker Turning Points in World History: *The Reformation*
Section 4 **The Spread of Protestantism** Identify the different forms of Protestantism that emerged in Europe as the Reformation spread.	Reproducible Lesson Plan 5-4 Vocabulary Activity 5* Guided Reading Activity 5-4* Section Quiz 5-4*	Section Focus Transparency 5-4 Student Self-Test and Review Software Testmaker
Section 5 **The Catholic Reformation** Describe how the Catholic Church tried to halt the spread of Protestantism.	Reproducible Lesson Plan 5-5 Guided Reading Activity 5-5* Reteaching Activity 5 Enrichment Activity 5 Section Quiz 5-5* Performance Assessment Activity 5 Spanish Chapter Summary 5	Focus on World Art Print 5 Section Focus Transparency 5-5 World History and Art Transparency 21, *Herzogenburg Monastery* Vocabulary PuzzleMaker Software Student Self-Test and Review Software Testmaker

* Also available in Spanish

Chapter Activities

 Performance Assessment Activity

Renaissance and Reformation Have students take the roles of merchants, artisans, and other citizens of Italy and Germany during this era. Pair students and have them write a series of letters to each other in which they give details of the events happening at the time and express their feelings and attitudes regarding the developments and reforms. Each student should write at least five letters that are detailed, persuasive in tone and style, and responsive to the previous letter received.

Possible Rubric Features

Accuracy of content, persuasiveness, concept attainment, appropriateness of inferences and predictions, clarity of organization

• *For an additional activity, refer to Activity 5 in the* Performance Assessment Strategies and Activities *booklet.*

ACTIVITY

From the Classroom of...

Carla Eileen Heckstall Franklin K. Lane High School Brooklyn, NY

Renaissance Art and Modern Art

Organize the class into two groups. Have one group review pictures of artwork from the Renaissance. (You may use pictures from the text.) Have the other group review pictures of modern art, preferably from the 1990s. (Use pictures from art magazines or museum or gallery catalogs.)

Ask both groups to select two or three pictures and try to identify values the artists were trying to depict. Have students compare the list of values from the Renaissance art with the list from the modern art.

MULTIPLE LEARNING STYLES

Verbal/Linguistic
Have students research and then debate the following statement: Without the Renaissance, the Reformation could never have taken place.

Logical/Mathematical
Have students create a time line of major events that occurred during the Renaissance and Reformation.

Visual/Spatial
Have students design a bulletin-board display that identifies famous Renaissance paintings, sculptures, and buildings.

Auditory/Musical
Have students collect and present examples of court, church, and popular music that were common in Europe during the Renaissance and Reformation.

Kinesthetic
Have students research and reenact the meeting with Luther at the Diet of Worms in 1521. Remind them to clearly present and defend the points of view of the Catholic Church and of Martin Luther.

Additional Resources

NATIONAL GEOGRAPHIC SOCIETY

Teacher's Corner

INDEX TO
NATIONAL GEOGRAPHIC MAGAZINE

The following articles may be used for research relating to this chapter:

- "Venice," by Erla Zwingle, February 1995.
- "Out of the Darkness: Michelangelo's Last Judgment," by Meg Nottingham Walsh, May 1994.
- "A Renaissance for Michelangelo," by David Jeffrey, December 1989.
- "Restoration Reveals the Last Supper," by Carlo Bertelli, November 1983.
- "Carrara Marble: Touchstone of Eternity," by Cathy Newman, July 1982.

NATIONAL GEOGRAPHIC SOCIETY PRODUCTS AVAILABLE FROM GLENCOE

To order the following products for use with this chapter, contact your local Glencoe sales representative, or call Glencoe at 1-800-334-7344:

- *PictureShow: The Renaissance (CD-ROM)*
- *The Renaissance (Transparencies, Poster Set)*

ADDITIONAL NATIONAL GEOGRAPHIC SOCIETY PRODUCTS

To order the following products for use with this chapter, call National Geographic Society at 1-800-368-2728:

- *Nations of the World Series, "East Germany." (Video)*

BIBLIOGRAPHY

Literature of the Period
Castiglione, Baldassare. *The Book of the Courtier.* Translated by George Bull. New York: Penguin, 1976. Contemporary handbook of courtly etiquette.
Readings for the Student
Rabb, Theodore K. *Renaissance Lives: Portraits of an Age.* New York: Pantheon, 1993. The Renaissance through the lives of fifteen Renaissance men and women.
Readings for the Teacher
Lucas, Henry. *The Renaissance and the Reformation.* New York: Harper, 1960. Historical survey of the Renaissance, Reformation, and the Catholic Reformation.

LOCAL OBJECTIVES

Reformation resources on the World Wide Web
The Catholic Encyclopedia:
The Reformation:
http://www.csn.net/advent/cathen/12700b.htm

Chapter Themes are listed by section on this chapter opening page of the Student Edition. A corresponding theme-based activity is available under "TEACH," and a theme-based question is asked in the Section and Chapter Reviews.

The Storyteller

Historical Setting The House of Este, which ruled Ferrara from the 1200s through the 1500s, was one of the most influential families in Italian politics. Ercole I, father of Isabella d'Este, used marriage as a means of consolidating his political and military position. He himself had married the daughter of the king of Naples. Not only did he arrange Isabella's marriage to the Marquis of Mantua, Francesco Gonzaga, but his two other daughters married the rulers of Bologna and Milan.

Historical Significance

Answers: *During the Renaissance, interest in the art, literature, and values of classical Greece and Rome caused Europeans to place greater emphasis on life here and now and on the worth of each individual, as well as to view themselves as part of a world larger than their town or village.*

During the Reformation, many northern Europeans left the Catholic Church and joined new Protestant religions. In some countries, the king became head of the new church. In other countries, the church controlled the government. Protestant religions with small numbers of followers were often persecuted. Their members sought religious freedom and separation of church and state.

Chapter
5
1400–1600
Renaissance and Reformation

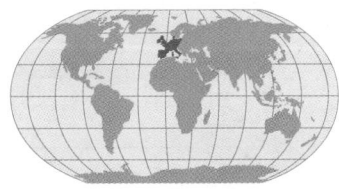

Chapter Themes

▶ **Innovation** The Renaissance leads to an artistic and intellectual awakening in Europe. *Section 1*
▶ **Cultural Diffusion** Renaissance ideas and artistic styles spread from Italy to northern Europe. *Section 2*
▶ **Conflict** Martin Luther's protests against the Catholic Church result in Protestantism. *Section 3*
▶ **Cultural Diffusion** Protestant religious groups spread reform through northern Europe. *Section 4*
▶ **Reaction** The Catholic Church enacts its own reform, the Catholic Reformation. *Section 5*

The Storyteller

Isabella d'Este, married in 1490 at the age of 16 to the Marquis of Mantua, played a vital role in ruling the Italian city-state of Mantua. A brilliant and well-educated young woman who loved Latin literature, Isabella gathered a fashionable assemblage of artists and statesmen in her sparkling court. In a room decorated with ornately carved woodwork and paintings that illustrated Greek myths, Isabella entertained her guests to her own lute recitals and poetry readings. Isabella was one of the many Italians of her time who rediscovered and repopularized Greek and Roman classics, educating their contemporaries to the glories of their classical past after a thousand years of neglect. The word Renaissance, *coming from the French word meaning "rebirth," was coined to refer to this rebirth of interest in classical ideas and culture.*

Historical Significance

What happened during the Renaissance that changed Europeans' outlook on the world? How did the Reformation shape the religious and political life of Europe?

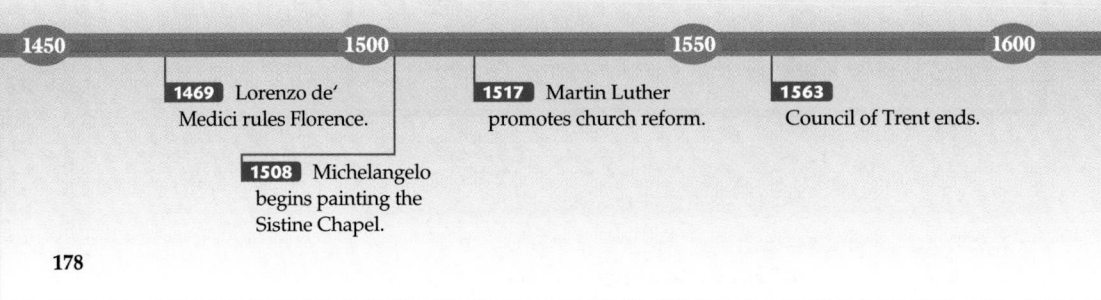

1450	1500	1550	1600

1469 Lorenzo de' Medici rules Florence.

1508 Michelangelo begins painting the Sistine Chapel.

1517 Martin Luther promotes church reform.

1563 Council of Trent ends.

178

Location Have students locate Italy, France, the Low Countries (present-day Belgium, Luxembourg, and the Netherlands), Germany, England, and Switzerland on a physical map of Europe in the Atlas of this book. What main geographic barrier separates Italy from these other countries? *(mountains: the Alps)* How could this barrier have affected the spread of new ideas? *(The mountains would have made overland travel difficult.)* **L1**

 History & Art   Detail of *The Court* by Andrea Mantegna.
Palazzo Ducale, Mantua, Italy

 History & Art   Tell students that Andrea Mantegna served as painter to the Gonzaga court at Mantua from 1460 until his death in 1506. Besides executing large frescoes for the palace, Mantegna painted smaller works for Isabella d'Este's study. How does the artist show Gonzaga's importance in this fresco? (*He is seated in an armchair, surrounded by family and servants, and is being consulted about some kind of business.*)

✔ Performance Assessment

Refer to the activity on page 178C of the Planning Guide.

📁 **For an additional activity, refer to Activity 5 in the *Performance Assessment Strategies and Activities* booklet.**

Your History Journal

Choose a Renaissance sculptor, architect, or painter mentioned in this chapter. Research and write a short report on the work and influence of this person.

Using Your History Journal

Have students use their journals to take notes, organize their ideas, and write a rough draft of the report.

GLENCOE TECHNOLOGY

 VIDEODISC
Use MindJogger to preview chapter content.

MindJogger Videoquiz

   Chapter 5
Disc 1 Side A

    Also available in VHS.

➕ EXTRA CREDIT PROJECT

Research First-person accounts and other information about the Renaissance and Reformation are available in many books. Have students research and report to the class on a person, event, or artwork from this historical period that is not detailed in the chapter. Suggest that students use vivid quotations from the first-person accounts and use descriptive language in their own explanations.

1400   1450   1500

1436 Filippo Brunelleschi   **c. 1490** Florence enjoys   **c. 1500** Rome becomes a major
completes dome for Florence   economic prosperity.   center of Renaissance culture.
Cathedral.

▶ **Innovation** The Renaissance leads to an artistic and intellectual awakening in Europe.

Find Out

Answer: *the discovery of Greek and Roman works, rise of humanism, opening of new schools, and the rise of a wealthy middle class in cities*

FOCUS

Section Objective

Identify the factors that inspired the Renaissance.

BELLRINGER
Motivational Activity

Before taking roll at the beginning of the class period, project Section Focus Transparency 5-1 and have students answer the activity questions. Discuss students' responses.
    This activity is also available as a blackline master.

Vocabulary Pre-check

    Use Vocabulary Activity 5 to introduce vocabulary terms. **L1 LEP**

Section 1

The Italian Renaissance

Setting the Scene

▶ **Terms to Define**
   humanism, secular, individualism, sonnet, doge

▶ **People to Meet**
   Niccolò Machiavelli, Lorenzo de' Medici, Michelangelo Buonarroti, Leonardo da Vinci

▶ **Places to Locate**
   Florence, Rome, Venice

 What factors inspired the Renaissance?

The Storyteller

Michelangelo finished the Sistine Chapel in September 1512. Pope Julius came to see the completed work. One man had covered ten thousand square feet with the greatest wall painting in Italy. Michelangelo wrote to his father, "I have finished the chapel which I have been painting. The Pope is very satisfied…. Your Michelangelo, sculptor, in Rome." The artist, tired and in poor health, went home to Florence, hoping for rest and relaxation.

—adapted from *Michelangelo The Man*, Donald Lord Finlayson, 1935

Ancestors of Christ, detail from the Sistine Chapel

The Renaissance—the period from about 1350 until 1600 during which western Europeans experienced a profound cultural awakening—was in many ways a continuation of the Middle Ages, but it also signaled the beginning of modern times. The Renaissance caused educated Europeans to develop new attitudes about themselves and the world around them.

The Renaissance began first in the city-states of Italy. Unlike other areas of Europe, Italy had largely avoided the economic crisis of the late Middle Ages. Italian towns remained important centers of Mediterranean trade and boosted their production of textiles and luxury goods.

More than other Europeans, Italians were attached to classical traditions. The ruins of ancient Roman buildings, arches, and amphitheaters constantly reminded them of their heritage. Moreover, through trade Italian towns remained in close contact with the Byzantine Empire, where scholars preserved the learning of ancient Greece.

Humanism

Through renewed contact with the classics, Italian scholars improved their understanding of Greek and Latin, studied old manuscripts, and copied the classical writing style. This interest in classical learning, however, was more than just a fascination with ancient times. It led to a new intellectual movement known as humanism that focused on secular, or worldly, themes rather than on the religious ideas that had concerned medieval thinkers. Humanists—the scholars who promoted humanism—accepted classical beliefs and wanted to use them to renew their own society. Among the most important beliefs was individualism, an emphasis on the dignity and worth of the individual person.

SECTION RESOURCES

    Reproducible Masters
- Reproducible Lesson Plan 5-1
- Vocabulary Activity 5
- Guided Reading Activity 5-1
- People in World History Profile 30
- Geography and History Activity 5
- Time Line Activity 5

- History Simulation 5
- Section Quiz 5-1

Transparencies
- Section Focus Transparency 5-1
- Chapter Transparency 5
- World History and Art Transparency 20
- The Renaissance

Multimedia
- The Renaissance
- Student Self-Test and Review Software
- Testmaker
- The Renaissance

Another was the idea of human improvement, that people should develop their talents through many activities: politics, sports, and the arts.

Education and Literature

Humanists believed that education could help people improve themselves. They opened schools that taught the *studia humanitas*, or humanities—Greek, Latin, history and philosophy, the subjects taught in ancient times. These schools became so popular that humanists began to replace the clergy as teachers of the sons of the wealthy.

Humanism also inspired new forms of literature written in the vernacular and focusing on personal feelings. During the 1300s, Francesco Petrarca, or Petrarch (PEE•TRAHRK), wrote sonnets, or short poems, that expressed his love for Laura, a woman who had died during the Black Death. His friend, Giovanni Boccaccio, in the work *Decameron*, described young people who tell stories to divert their attention from the plague's horrors.

As the Renaissance developed, writers also focused on the topics of individual ambition and success. During the 1500s, Benvenuto Cellini, a goldsmith and sculptor, glorified his achievements in one of the first modern autobiographies. In a popular manual, *The Book of the Courtier*, Baldassare Castiglione (bahl•dahs•SAHR•ray kahs•steel•YOHN•ay) gave advice to men and women on the Renaissance ideal of good behavior. Men were to be skilled in many activities; women were to be graceful, attractive, and courteous. The diplomat **Niccolò Machiavelli** (mak•ee•uh•VEHL•ee) wrote *The Prince*, a book that realistically analyzed the politics of Renaissance Italy. Rulers, Machiavelli said, should be ready to use force and deceit to hold power. Critics charged that *The Prince* justified immoral behavior in politics, but Machiavelli's book appealed to power-hungry Renaissance rulers. It also influenced the thought and actions of later political leaders.

Scholarship

Humanist scholars influenced more than just literature. With their independent thinking, they began to challenge long-accepted traditions, assumptions, and institutions. As they made all sorts of unsettling discoveries, it further validated their desire to challenge and question nearly everything—even long-standing church traditions. For example, in an exciting piece of Renaissance detective work, the scholar Lorenzo Valla determined that a document that supposedly provided the legal basis for the pope's supremacy over kings was actually a forgery.

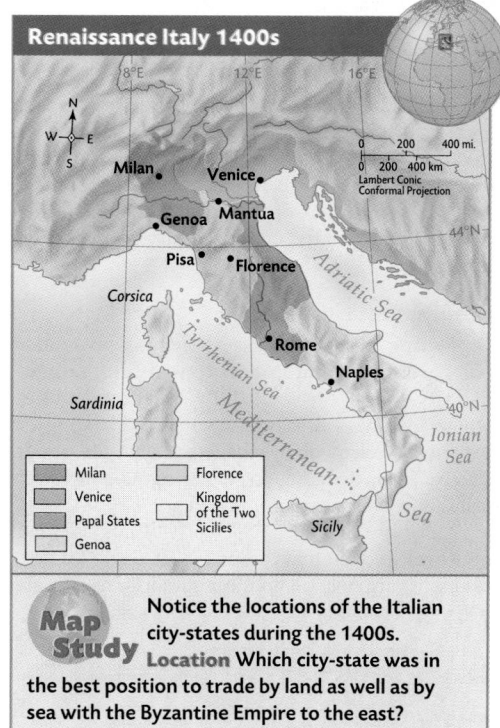

Renaissance Italy 1400s

Milan • Venice • Genoa • Mantua • Pisa • Florence • Rome • Naples

Corsica • Sardinia • Sicily

Adriatic Sea • *Tyrrhenian Sea* • *Mediterranean Sea* • *Ionian Sea*

Milan
Venice
Papal States
Genoa
Florence
Kingdom of the Two Sicilies

Map Study Notice the locations of the Italian city-states during the 1400s. **Location** Which city-state was in the best position to trade by land as well as by sea with the Byzantine Empire to the east?

Through their teaching and writing, humanists reawakened the educated public to classical values. They also encouraged a ferment of new ideas that eventually spread from Italy throughout Europe and reshaped European civilization.

City Life

Town life was stronger in Italy than in other parts of Europe. As a result, Italians could easily discard feudalism and other medieval institutions that had their origins in the rural north. Italy did not become unified as did France and England. Wealthy and successful, most Italian communes, or communities, resisted the efforts of emperors, kings, and nobles to control them. They became independent city-states, each of which included a walled urban center and the surrounding countryside.

Social Groups

The Italian city-states fashioned a new social order in which wealth and ability mattered more than aristocratic titles and ownership of land. Wealthy merchants and bankers replaced the

Chapter 5 *Renaissance and Reformation* **181**

TEACH

Guided Practice

THEME Innovation

Ask students to volunteer examples from this section of innovations in literature and art that resulted from the influence of humanism. *(new forms of writing, such as sonnets and autobiography; literature in the common language instead of Latin; more lifelike art; classical as well as religious themes in painting and sculpture)* Write their suggestions on the chalkboard. **L1**

Map Study

Answer
Venice

Map Skills Practice

Reading a Map In which part of Italy were most of its great Renaissance cities located? *(north)*

NATIONAL GEOGRAPHIC SOCIETY

Use these materials to enrich student understanding of the Renaissance.

- **NGS PICTURESHOW CD-ROM** The Renaissance
- **NGS PICTUREPACK TRANSPARENCY SET** The Renaissance
- **NGS POSTER SET** The Renaissance

COOPERATIVE LEARNING ACTIVITY

Oral Reports Have students compare the Renaissance in Milan, Mantua, and Genoa. Organize students into three teams, each studying one city. Have each team split into subgroups to research a topic such as government, economy, patrons of the arts, women, painting, sculpture, or architecture in their city. When research is complete, have subgroups report their findings to the whole team. Then have each team prepare an overall summary of its research. Ask each team to select a member to present orally to the class the team's overall summary of its Renaissance city. **L2**

Geography: Movement Have students review a map of the Byzantine Empire to explain how Italy's trade routes helped maintain the influence of earlier cultures. *(Routes across the Adriatic, Ionian, and Mediterranean Seas led to Greece and Turkey as well as to other countries of the Byzantine Empire.)* **L1**

HOME VIDEO

The following videotape is available from Glencoe:

• **The Miraculous Canals of Venice**

To find classroom resources to accompany this video, check the following home page:

A&E Television: http://www.AandE.com/

 Chapter Transparency 16

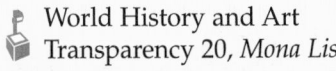 World History and Art Transparency 20, *Mona Lisa*

 History Simulation 16

Who?What?Where?When?

Machiavelli's *The Prince* was roundly denounced by the Medici family, even though it had been dedicated to Lorenzo de' Medici. To express his political views to a wider audience, Machiavelli turned to writing plays. His comedy *Mandragola* is considered one of Italy's best Renaissance plays.

---

landed nobility as the most powerful social and political group—the upper class. Shopkeepers and artisans ranked below the wealthy merchants, forming a moderately prosperous middle class that employed large numbers of poor workers. Most of these workers—who were the majority of town dwellers—came to urban areas from the countryside. At the bottom of the social order were the peasants who worked on the country estates of the upper class.

Government

During the Renaissance, Italy was not under one government, but instead consisted of individual city-states, each ruled by wealthy families whose fortunes came from commercial trading or banking. Workers often rebelled against the upper classes. Their demands for equal rights and lower taxes, however, were suppressed.

During the 1400s, social conflicts created upheaval so often that certain city-states felt it necessary to turn over all political authority to a single powerful leader to restore peace. These powerful political leaders were called signori (seen•YOHR•ee). Some signori ruled as dictators, using violence to maintain control. Others successfully ensured popular loyalty by improving city services, supporting the arts, and providing festivals and parades for the lower classes.

While dealing with internal unrest, city-states also fought with each other in territorial disputes. But the prosperous merchants and bankers, unlike the nobility they had supplanted, did not want to fight in these battles. Since military service would interfere with conducting business and trade, the signori chose to replace citizen-soldiers with hired soldiers known as condottieri (KAHN•duh•TYEHR•ee).

Hiring condottieri made wars very costly. To avoid this expense, signori began to seek territorial gain through negotiated agreements. To carry out this policy, they assembled the first modern diplomatic services. Permanent ambassadors were appointed to represent their city-states at foreign

Images of the Times

Art of the Italian Renaissance

The Italian Renaissance produced a host of great Italian artists and sculptors. Among the most notable of these were Michelangelo, Raphael, and Leonardo da Vinci.

Michelangelo created *David*, a gigantic marble sculpture, while at home in Florence between 1501 and 1504. A painter, architect, sculptor, and poet, he has had an unparalleled influence on Western art.

182

Images of the Times

Art of the Italian Renaissance

Leonardo da Vinci's *Mona Lisa* has fascinated art lovers and the general public for centuries. To this day, art critics and historians still do not know for sure who the woman in the painting is or why she is smiling. Some say that a wealthy Florentine merchant named Giocondo commissioned Leonardo to paint a portrait of his third wife. This painting became the famous *La Gioconda*, also known as *Mona Lisa*. Toward the end of his life, Leonardo sold the painting to Francis I, the king of France, who hung it in the Louvre in Paris where it can still be seen today.

courts. The city-states also worked out an agreement among all the city-states that no one city-state would be allowed enough power to threaten the others. During the 1500s other European states adopted similar agreements with one another and also began to practice diplomacy.

Although the Italian city-states had much in common, each developed its own characteristic life. Three cities in particular played leading roles in the Renaissance: **Florence**, **Rome**, and **Venice**.

Florence

Originally a republic, Florence in the 1400s came under the control of a prominent banking family known as the Medici (MEH•duh•chee). Medici rulers helped to foster the spirit of humanism among the city-state's scholars and artists. With this spirit alive throughout the city, Florence became the birthplace of the Italian Renaissance.

Cosimo de' Medici gained control of Florence in 1434. He worked to end worker uprisings by introducing an income tax that placed a heavier burden on wealthier citizens. He used the tax revenues to make city improvements, such as sewers and paved streets, that benefited everyone. Cosimo also worked to establish peaceful relations between the city and its neighbors.

Cosimo's grandson **Lorenzo de' Medici** ruled Florence from 1469 to 1492, and he continued policies like those of his grandfather. He used his wealth to support artists, philosophers, and writers and to sponsor public festivals. As a result of the city's prosperity and fame, Lorenzo was known as "the Magnificent."

During the 1490s Florence's economic prosperity, based mostly on the banking and textile industries, began to decline with increasing competition from English and Flemish cloth makers. Tired of the Medici rule, discontented citizens rallied in support of a Dominican friar named Girolamo Savonarola (SA•vuh•nuh•ROH•luh). In fiery sermons before hundreds of people, Savonarola attacked the Medici for promoting ideas that he claimed were causing the downfall of Florence:

Leonardo da Vinci painted the *Mona Lisa* during a period of intensive study in Florence in 1503. His talent was also expressed in sculpture, architecture, and engineering.

Raphael painted the *School of Athens* for Pope Julius II. When Raphael died in Rome on his 37th birthday, the whole city mourned. His funeral mass was celebrated at the Vatican.

REFLECTING ON THE TIMES

1. What Renaissance values are reflected in the paintings and sculpture shown in this feature?
2. Why are there many similarities in style and subject matter among works of the Italian Renaissance?

183

ANSWERS TO REFLECTING ON THE TIMES

1. lifelike, strong individuals; accurate and natural portrayal of the human form; balance and harmony of subject details
2. The Italian Renaissance artists were all influenced by humanism; because they studied and worked in the same cities, they were in contact with and came to influence one another.

Independent Practice

Guided Reading Activity 5-1 **L1**

Daily Life Have students use outside sources to research one of the following types of Renaissance persons: wealthy banker or merchant, shopkeeper, artisan, manual worker, or peasant. Ask students to write a diary entry for a typical day in their person's life. **L2**

Biography

The following videotapes are available from Glencoe:

- **Michaelangelo: Artist and Man**
- **Leonardo da Vinci: Renaissance Master**

you don't say...

Penknife During the 1400s, penknives were just that—knives for trimming quill pens, whose points quickly became dull. After metal pen points were invented, "*penknife*" came to mean any small blade that could be carried in a pocket.

Linking Past and Present

Tunics, mid-thigh-length garments worn over tights, were fashionable attire for many young Renaissance men. Today, many women favor a similar style of clothing—a long, loose sweater or shirt worn over pants.

History & Art Brunelleschi, a Florentine goldsmith, began his artistic career in 1401 by entering the contest to design the doors of Florence's baptistry. When Ghiberti's design was chosen, Brunelleschi turned to architecture. What characteristics of Renaissance art are shown in his sculpture? *(emotions shown, people and animals look lifelike)* **Answer to Caption:** *designing a dome for the Cathedral of Florence*

Critical Thinking Have students research Savonarola's impact on life in Florence. Then have them write a letter to the editor of a Florence newspaper either in support of or in opposition to Savonarola. Encourage students whose letters express opposite points of view to compare them. **L3**

📁 People in World History Profile 30

📁 Geography and History Activity 5

📁 Time Line Activity 5

Cultural Perspectives

Renaissance **palazzi** took their name from the Latin word *palatium*, which meant the area in Rome where the emperors built their homes. The English word *palace*, which also comes from *palatium*, refers to homes of royalty. In Italian, however, *palazzo* simply means a large urban home.

History & Art Brunelleschi's sculpture of the sacrifice of Isaac was a contest entry for the east doors of the Baptistry in Florence. *Brunelleschi lost but is remembered for what architectural feat?*

> ❝ In the mansions of the great prelates and great lords there is no concern save for poetry and the oratorical art. Go … and see; [you] shall find them all with books of the humanities in their hands.… Arise and come to deliver [your] Church from the hands of the devils! ❞

So many people were won over by Savonarola that the Medici family was forced to turn over the rule of Florence to his supporters. On Savonarola's advice, the city's new leaders imposed strict regulations on public behavior. Gambling, swearing, and horse racing were banned. Savonarola urged his listeners to repent of their "worldly" ways. He had crowds make bonfires to burn books, paintings, fancy clothes, and musical instruments.

Savonarola soon aroused a great deal of opposition to his preaching. His criticism of church officials angered the pope. Many people in Florence disliked his strict ways. In 1498 Savonarola was hanged for heresy, and the Medici family returned to power. By this time, however, Florence's greatness had passed.

Rome

During the 1500s Rome emerged as a leading Renaissance city. In Rome, the pope and the cardinals living in the Vatican made up the wealthiest and most powerful class.

Eager to increase their prestige, Renaissance popes rebuilt the ancient city. Architects constructed large churches and palaces, and artists created magnificent paintings and sculptures to decorate these buildings. Scholars came from all over Europe to study manuscripts and books in the Vatican Library.

Renaissance popes often placed political goals ahead of religious duties. In ruling Rome and its surroundings, they sent ambassadors to other lands, collected taxes, and fought wars. The most politically minded pope was Alexander VI. Elected pope in 1492, Alexander had bribed the College of Cardinals to vote for him. Once in office, he used the wealth of the Church to support his family, the Borgias. He especially encouraged his son Cesare, who raised an army and conquered much of central Italy.

After Alexander's death in 1503, his successors, Julius II and later Leo X, promoted artistic projects to beautify Rome. Their most notable effort was the rebuilding of St. Peter's Basilica, the largest church in the Christian world.

Venice

Another Renaissance center was Venice, the port city on the Adriatic Sea. Venice's economic power, enjoyed since the Crusades, was fading because of changing trade routes and Muslim invasions in the east. However, the city's role as a link between Asia and western Europe still drew traders from all over the world. Venetian shipyards also turned out huge galleys, and Venetian workshops produced high quality glass.

One benefit of Venice's prosperity was political stability. Venice's republican government was headed by an elected **doge**, (DOHJ), or leader. The doge officially ran the city, but the wealthiest merchants meeting in committee as the Council of Ten held the real power. This council passed laws, elected the doge, and even had to be consulted should the doge's son want to marry.

Influenced by Byzantine as well as western European culture, Venice was known for its artistic achievements. Painters, such as Titian, Tintoretto, and Giorgione, used brilliant oil colors to portray rural landscapes and classical and religious themes. Venetian architects, such as Sansovino and Palladio, erected buildings in the classical style.

184 Chapter 5 *Renaissance and Reformation*

MEETING SPECIAL NEEDS ACTIVITY

Learning Style: Visual/Spatial Encourage students who are strong visual learners to draw pictures of some activities representative of the Italian Renaissance. Drawings might include humanist scholars teaching the new learning, Cosimo de' Medici ending a peasant uprising, Savonarola preaching to the people of Florence, a papal banquet, or a meeting of the doge of Venice and the Council of Ten. Have students display their drawings in the classroom. Number each drawing (1, 2, 3, and so on). Then have each class member view the display and identify what activity is illustrated by each drawing. **L1 LEP** 📦

Renaissance Arts

What were the unique characteristics of Renaissance art? The humanists' emphasis on cultivating individual talent inspired Italian artists to express their own values, emotions, and attitudes. No longer content with creating symbolic representations of their subjects, artists made their subjects as lifelike and captivating as possible. Although much of the art was still devoted to religious subjects, it had more secular, or worldly, overtones. Interest in ancient Greece and Rome moved artists to include classical mythology as well as biblical themes in their works.

To make their creations lifelike and captivating, artists experimented with new techniques. For example, they learned to create a sense of perspective, which gave their paintings depth. They studied anatomy so they could portray human figures more accurately and naturally. Artists also learned to depict subtleties of gesture and expression to convey human emotions. Much of their work consisted of frescoes, or paintings done on damp plaster.

The public in Renaissance Italy appreciated works of art and hailed great artists as geniuses. Nobles and townspeople used art to decorate homes as well as churches. They lavishly rewarded artists and gave them a prominent place in society.

Architecture

During the Middle Ages, cathedral architects had pointed soaring arches and spires heavenward for the glory of God. During the Renaissance, however, Italian architects returned to the classical style. On churches, palaces, and villas they substituted domes and columns from classical Greek and Roman architecture for the medieval arches and spires. They sought both comfort and beauty in their buildings, adorning them with tapestries, paintings, statues, finely made furniture, and glass windows. Unlike the anonymous architects of the Middle Ages, Renaissance architects took credit for their fine buildings.

The most famous Italian Renaissance architect was Filippo Brunelleschi (BROO•nuhl•EHS•kee), best known for the dome he designed and completed in 1436 for the Cathedral of Florence. Until Brunelleschi submitted his design, no one had been able to come up with a way to construct a dome large or strong enough to cover the cathedral without the dome collapsing from its own weight. Brunelleschi's design—based on his own study of the domes, columns, and arches of ancient Rome—was considered to be the greatest engineering feat of the time.

Sculpture

Renaissance sculpture reflected a return to classical ideals. The free-standing statues of nude figures sculpted in bronze or marble during the Renaissance resembled ancient Greek and Roman sculptures of nude figures much more than they did medieval sculptures. Human figures in medieval sculptures had usually been portrayed in a stiff, stylized manner.

Some of the best-known Renaissance sculptors—Donatello, Michelangelo, and Ghiberti (gee•BEHR•tee)—came from Florence. There the Medicis opened a school for sculptors. Donatello was the first sculptor since ancient times to cast a large, free-standing nude statue. Although the sculptor **Michelangelo Buonarroti** later went to Rome to sculpt works for the pope, he learned his craft in Florence. Forentine sculptor Lorenzo Ghiberti took 21 years to create 10 biblical scenes on bronze doors for Florence's cathedral baptistry.

Painting

Italian Renaissance painters departed from the flat, symbolic style of medieval painting to begin a more realistic style. This change first appeared in the early 1300s when the Florentine artist-sculptor-architect Giotto (jee•AH•toh) effectively captured human emotions in a series of frescoes portraying the life of Francis of Assisi. In the 1400s Florentine

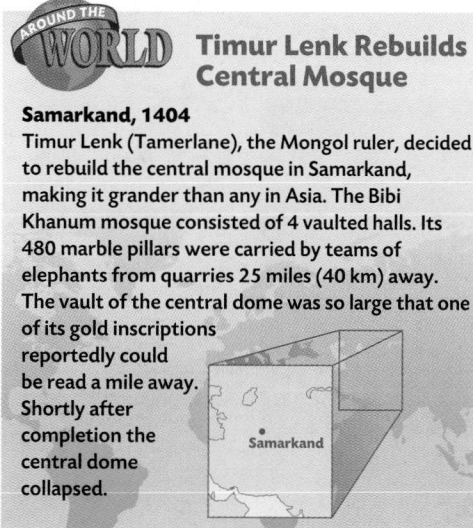

Timur Lenk Rebuilds Central Mosque

Samarkand, 1404

Timur Lenk (Tamerlane), the Mongol ruler, decided to rebuild the central mosque in Samarkand, making it grander than any in Asia. The Bibi Khanum mosque consisted of 4 vaulted halls. Its 480 marble pillars were carried by teams of elephants from quarries 25 miles (40 km) away. The vault of the central dome was so large that one of its gold inscriptions reportedly could be read a mile away. Shortly after completion the central dome collapsed.

Renaissance Arts
What changes did Renaissance artists bring to the arts of Europe?
They broke with medieval symbolism and brought a new realism to the arts, experimenting with new techniques, such as perspective; much Renaissance art was still devoted to religious topics, but Renaissance artists also turned to classical mythology.

 **CURRICULUM CONNECTION**

THE ARTS
Renaissance artists used perspective to create a three-dimensional effect in their two-dimensional works. Objects in such paintings achieve depth and distance because the artist draws the viewer's eye to an invisible vanishing point.

ASSESS

Check for Understanding
Assign Section 1 Review as homework or as an in-class activity.

🔲 Use Student Self-Test and Review Software to review Section 1.

MAKING CONNECTIONS ACTIVITY

Sports The Renaissance revived the Greek concept that an ideal person participated in a variety of activities, including sports. Have students research and report to the class on one of the following popular Renaissance games or sports: javelin hurling, tennis, chess, archery, fencing, boxing, falconry, hunting, and gambling. Tell students to explain how these sports or games are alike or different from the same activities today. Ask students to bring props for their reports and, if possible, to give a brief demonstration of the skills needed for their game or sport. **L2**

TEACH

Tell students that to show life and activity, Leonardo chose to illustrate the moment when Jesus says that one of his disciples will betray him. The disciples are caught as they ask, "Is it I?" Encourage students to compare this painting with religious paintings of the Middle Ages and to note the differences in style and subject matter.

More About...

The Last Supper A friend of Leonardo's suggested that he leave the face of Jesus incomplete so viewers would not compare Jesus to the disciples.

CURRICULUM CONNECTION

TECHNOLOGY

Because Leonardo believed that an artist's most important work was thinking and planning rather than the actual painting or brush strokes, he didn't use the standard fresco technique of painting on wet plaster, which required quick, certain strokes. Instead, he painted *The Last Supper* on dry plaster with tempera. That is why the painting soon started to deteriorate. ⊕

"The Last Supper"

Victor R. Boswell, Jr.

"One of you shall betray me," said Jesus, sitting amid the disciples gathered around in a flurry of worry, gossip, and fear. Between 1495 and 1497 Leonardo da Vinci painted *The Last Supper* on the walls of a monastery in Milan, Italy. Unstable paint and centuries of wear slowly destroyed the mural. In 1977 restoration of the painting began, as shown in the detail (above) depicting the apostles Matthew, Thaddeus, and Simon. The larger view of the master-piece (left) shows visitors clustered around while restorers continue their work.

Da Vinci was one of the most famous painters of the Italian Renaissance. During the Renaissance the peoples of Europe began to see themselves as Europeans rather than as members of the kingdom of Christendom whose single passport was belief. The Renaissance was a period of upheaval and change in religion, politics, and economy. The arts flourished. Writers began using the language of their own nations instead of Latin. Painters, architects, and sculptors experimented with new techniques. Expressing his belief in the newfound power of paintings, da Vinci boasted that the painter could "even induce men to fall in love with a picture that does not portray any living woman." Indeed, people throughout the ages have fallen in love with *The Last Supper*. ⊕

186 Chapter 5 *Renaissance and Reformation*

artist Masaccio (muh•ZAH•chee•oh) employed lighting and perspective in his paintings to give depth to the human body and to set off his figures from the background. He thus created an even greater sense of realism than Giotto had.

One of the greatest Renaissance artists was **Leonardo da Vinci** (VIHN•chee). A citizen of Florence, he did much of his work in Milan and Rome. Da Vinci is best known for the *Mona Lisa*, a portrait of a strangely smiling young woman of Florence, and *The Last Supper*, a wall painting of Jesus' last meal with his disciples. In both works, da Vinci skillfully portrayed the subjects' personalities, thoughts, and feelings. He also made designs in notebooks on astronomy, mathematics, and anatomy. These drawings often pictured parachutes, flying machines, and other mechanical inventions far ahead of his time.

Another outstanding Renaissance artist—Michelangelo Buonarroti—began his career as a sculptor in Florence. There he did a famous marble statue of David, after the heroic biblical king. Later in Rome he sculpted *La Pietà* (PEE•ay•TAH), which shows the dead Jesus in the arms of his mother, Mary. Most of Michelangelo's sculptures were awesome in size and suggested controlled but intense emotions.

In 1508 Pope Julius II hired Michelangelo to work at the Vatican, painting the ceiling of the Sistine Chapel with scenes from the Bible. All of Michelangelo's painted figures resembled sculptures. They had well-formed muscular bodies that expressed vitality and power. Michelangelo ended his career by designing the dome of the new St. Peter's Basilica.

Like Michelangelo, the artist Raphael Santi worked at the Vatican. He completed a series of paintings on classical and religious themes for the pope's apartment. Raphael is most noted for his paintings of Mary, the mother of Jesus. These works were done in bright colors and reflected the Renaissance ideals of grace, harmony, and beauty.

History & Art *La Pietà* by Michelangelo Buonarroti. St. Peter's Basilica, The Vatican, Rome, Italy
What is the subject of La Pieta?

Women and the Arts

Although Renaissance women had few roles independent of men, some of them did contribute to the arts. These women were either daughters of artists who trained in their fathers' workshops or children of noblemen, who were expected to have literary, musical, and artistic skills. Among the most celebrated female artists were the portrait painters Lavinia Fontana and Sofonisba Anguissola (soh•foh•NIHZ•bah ahn•gwee•SOH•lah). An Italian noblewoman, Anguissola became a painter at the Spanish royal court of King Philip II.

Chapter 5 *Renaissance and Reformation* **187**

History & Art Tell students that Michelangelo executed *La Pietà* in Rome for a French cardinal. The idea for showing the dead Jesus across his mother's lap came from German art, but Michelangelo rendered his work in classic Greek form. From what material is *La Pietà* made? (*marble*)
Answer to Caption: *the crucified Jesus in the arms of his mother Mary*

Evaluate

Section Quiz 5-1

Use the Testmaker to create a customized quiz for Section 1.

Reteach

Have students review the characteristics of humanism and give examples of how humanism was expressed by major Renaissance artists and writers.

Enrich

Have students write an essay in which they explain who they think was the most important person of the Italian Renaissance.

CLOSE

Write on the chalkboard: *Important Innovations of the Renaissance.* Ask volunteers to write what they think were the most important innovations in literature, education, art, architecture, and government during this period.

SECTION 1 REVIEW

Recall
1. **Define** humanism, secular, individualism, sonnet, doge.
2. **Identify** Niccolò Machiavelli, Lorenzo de' Medici, Savonarola, Michelangelo Buonarroti, Leonardo da Vinci.
3. **Discuss** the meaning of the term "Renaissance." To what does it refer? What were its major characteristics?

Critical Thinking
4. **Making Comparisons** How does the role of female artists today compare with that of female artists in Renaissance times?

Understanding Themes
5. **Innovation** Identify one masterpiece in Renaissance literature or the arts. Explain how it reflects Renaissance ideals. Also state what subject is represented.

SECTION 1 REVIEW ANSWERS

1. All vocabulary words are defined in the Glossary.
2. Niccolò Machiavelli, 181; Lorenzo de' Medici, 183; Savonarola, 183; Michelangelo Buonarroti, 185; Leonardo da Vinci, 187
3. It means "rebirth", referring to the cultural awakening in Italy and the rest of Europe from 1300s to 1500s; creative period in the arts; a focus on worldly rather than religious values; regard for individual worth and human achievement.
4. Answers will vary but should mention that Renaissance female artists had more limited opportunities. Generally, they had artist-fathers who trained them or were noblewomen.
5. **INNOVATION** Answers will vary but should focus on the Renaissance depiction of lifelike realistic figures from the Bible, classical mythology, or daily life.

188   Chapter 5   Renaissance and Reformation

SECTION THEME

▶ **Cultural Diffusion** Renaissance ideas and artistic styles spread from Italy to northern Europe.

ind Out

Answer: *Wars, trade, and the printing press helped bring Renaissance ideas from Italy to northern Europe.*

FOCUS

Section Objective

Explain how the Renaissance reached northern Europe.

BELLRINGER
Motivational Activity

Before taking roll at the beginning of the class period, project Section Focus Transparency 5-2 and have students answer the activity questions. Discuss students' responses.

☞ This activity is also available as a blackline master.

Vocabulary Pre-check

☞ Use Vocabulary Activity 5 to introduce vocabulary terms.
L1 LEP

1400	1450	1500	1550

c. 1456 Johannes Gutenberg uses movable metal type in printing.

1494 Francis I of France invades Italy.

1509 Desiderius Erasmus writes *The Praise of Folly*.

Section 2

The Northern Renaissance

Setting the Scene

▶ **Terms to Define**
châteaux

▶ **People to Meet**
Johannes Gutenberg, François Rabelais, Desiderius Erasmus, Pieter Brueghel, Thomas More, William Shakespeare

▶ **Places to Locate**
the Low Countries

 **ind Out** How did the Renaissance reach northern Europe?

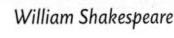 **Storyteller**

When Shakespeare's play Hamlet *opened in London, about 2,000 people crowded in to see the performance. Admission was one penny. Down in front of the stage, where it was standing room only, the crowd could be noisy. One writer complained: "Such heaving, and shoving, such pushing and shouldering—especially by the women! Such care for their clothes, that no one step on their dress;.... Such smiling and winking.... Never mind the stage—it is a comedy to watch them!"*

—freely adapted from *Shakespeare: Of an Age For All Time*, The Yale University Festival Lectures, edited by Charles Tyler Prouty, 1954

William Shakespeare

uring the late 1400s, Renaissance art and humanist ideas—characterized by a revival of interest in classical antiquity—began to filter northward from Italy to France, England, the Netherlands, and other European countries. War, trade, travel, and a newly invented method of printing helped to promote this cultural diffusion. The people of the Northern Renaissance adapted ideas of the Italian Renaissance to their own individual tastes, values, and needs.

Spreading Ideas

War, as usual, helped spread ideas by furthering contact between people of different cultures. After France invaded Italy in 1494, French kings and their warrior-nobles became fascinated by Italian Renaissance art and fashions. In 1517 King Francis I brought Leonardo da Vinci to his court in France, thus helping to promote the entry of Renaissance ideas into northern Europe. Other European monarchs also developed an enthusiasm for the Renaissance. Kings and queens so eagerly supported scholars and artists that the number of humanists in the north grew rapidly along with the popularity of humanist ideas.

At the same time, Italian traders living in the north set an example for northern European merchants, who began to appreciate wealth, beauty, personal improvement, and other Renaissance values. These northern merchants—having only recently become successful enough to afford lifestyles based upon such values—began to spend their wealth on education, fine houses, and material goods. Some northern Europeans began to travel to Italy to study with Italian masters. Thus began the emergence of a newly educated middle class.

188   Chapter 5 *Renaissance and Reformation*

SECTION RESOURCES

 **Reproducible Masters**
• Reproducible Lesson Plan 5-2
• Vocabulary Activity 5
• Guided Reading Activity 5-2
• Section Quiz 5-2

Transparencies
• Section Focus Transparency 5-2

Multimedia
💻 Focus on World Art Print 18
💿 Student Self-Test and Review Software
💿 Testmaker

This spread of knowledge among the middle class was aided by the invention of the printing press. By the 1400s, German engravers had developed movable type, in which the type was set into adjustable molds, inked, and then pressed onto a sheet of paper. In 1456 **Johannes Gutenberg** printed a complete edition of the Bible using movable metal type. As a result of this invention, books were published more quickly and less expensively. Production of humanist texts could now begin to match the new-found desire for such works.

Although Italian Renaissance ideas became quite popular in the north, they were not merely transplanted there. Rather, northern scholars interpreted them according to their own individual ways of thinking. Furthermore, the people of each northern culture adapted these ideas to suit their own needs and traditions.

The French Renaissance

The French Renaissance had a character all its own. French architects blended medieval Gothic towers and windows with the classical arches used by Italian architects to create châteaux (sha•TOHZ), or castles, for Francis I and his nobles. These large country estates were erected primarily in the Loire River valley. The château of Chambord is a fine example.

Many French Renaissance writers borrowed extensively from the new literary forms of the Italian Renaissance. Inspired by Petrarch's sonnets, Pierre Ronsard (rohn•SAHR) wrote his own sonnets with common humanist themes such as love, the passing of youth, and the poet's immortality. Michel de Montaigne (mahn•TAYN) may have based his informal and direct style on Italian literary models. He cultivated the literary form called the personal essay, a short prose composition written to express clearly the personal view of a writer on a subject. In his essay "Of the Disadvantages of Greatness," Montaigne analyzed the authority of royalty:

> 66 The most difficult occupation in the world, in my opinion, is to play the part of a king worthily. I excuse more of their faults than people commonly do, in consideration of the dreadful weight of their burden, which dazes me. It is difficult for a power so immoderate to observe moderation.... 99

Physician-monk **François Rabelais** (RA•buh •LAY), France's most popular Renaissance author, wrote comic tales, satires, and parodies on a broad spectrum of contemporary life. He rejected the

Erasmus by Quentin Metsys. The "Prince of the Humanists" joined a love for the classics with respect for Christian values. *What reforms did Christian humanists promote?*

Middle Ages' focus on the afterlife and believed that people should enjoy life to the fullest. Exceptionally knowledgeable and gifted as a writer, he also wrote on such subjects as law, medicine, politics, theology, botany, and navigation.

Northern Europe

The Italian Renaissance was enthusiastically accepted by the wealthy towns of Germany and **the Low Countries** (present-day Belgium, Luxembourg, and the Netherlands). Universities and schools promoted humanist learning, and printers produced a large quantity of books. Latin was still the main scholarly language, but writers increased their use of German and Dutch.

Christian Humanism

Unlike in Italy, the Renaissance in northern Europe had a more religious tone. Groups of scholars, known as Christian humanists, wanted reforms in Catholicism that would eliminate abuses and restore the simple piety of the early Church. They believed that humanist learning and Bible study were the best ways to promote these goals.

The most famous Christian humanist, **Desiderius Erasmus** (dehz•ih•DEER•ee•uhs ih•RAZ•muhs), inspired his colleagues to study

TEACH

Guided Practice

THEME Cultural Diffusion

Ask students how ideas were transported during the time of the Northern Renaissance. *(war, as when France invaded Italy; traveling merchants; new, more affordable printed books)* **L1**

Visualizing History With the help of the printing press, Erasmus became a best-selling author.
Answer to Caption: *They wanted to eliminate abuses in the Catholic Church and restore piety through humanist learning and Bible study.*

Literature Have students identify the contributions of Ronsard, Montaigne, Erasmus, Thomas More, and Shakespeare. **L2**

Focus on World Art Print 18, Pieter Brueghel. *The Wedding Dance*

Who? What? Where? When?

The Book of Manners by Giovanni della Casa stated, "Anyone whose legs are too thin, or exceptionally fat, ... should not wear vivid or parti-colored hose, in order not to attract attention to his defects."

Independent Practice

Guided Reading Activity 5-2 **L1**

Government Have students research to compare the views of Montaigne and Machiavelli on how a ruler should exercise authority. **L3**

COOPERATIVE LEARNING ACTIVITY

Analyzing Art Assign students to small groups to study the works of one of the following Northern Renaissance artists: Pieter Brueghel the Elder, Jan van Eyck, Albrecht Dürer, Lucas Cranach the Elder, or Hans Holbein the Younger. Tell students to use art history books to analyze their artist's works. Suggest that they record evidence of daily activities, occupations, social classes, entertainment, clothing, hairstyles, and housing shown in these works. Remind groups that each member should be responsible for a task, such as organizing research, recording the group's discussion, making photocopies, or presenting the group's analysis to the class. Tell students to include pictures of artworks in their reports to the class. **L2**

History & Art Brueghel, disguised as a peasant, attended village fairs and recorded dances and children's games in his sketchbook.
Answer to Caption: *realistic portraits, religious themes, landscapes, and scenes of daily life*

ASSESS

Check for Understanding

Assign Section 2 Review as homework or as an in-class activity.

▣ Use Student Self-Test and Review Software to review Section 2.

Evaluate

▱ Section Quiz 5-2

▣ Use the Testmaker to create a customized quiz for Section 2.

Reteach

Have students create a list on the chalkboard of specific accomplishments and innovations of the Northern Renaissance that show the influence of ideas from Italy.

Enrich

Have students write a report using outside sources on criticisms of Renaissance society by Thomas More, Rabelais, or Montaigne.

CLOSE

Lead students in a brief discussion that summarizes major characteristics of Northern Renaissance literature, painting, and architecture.

 Peasant's Dance by Pieter Brueghel the Elder. **The painting emphasizes the enjoyments of common people.** *What four subjects did northern European realistic artists paint?*

Greek and Hebrew so that they could understand older versions of the Bible written in these languages. Erasmus also used biting humor to make people take a more critical view of society. He specifically attacked the wealth of Renaissance popes. In his noted work, *In Praise of Folly*, he describes these popes, claiming that they were so corrupt they no longer practiced Christianity:

❝ Scarce any kind of men live more [devoted to pleasure] or with less trouble.... To work miracles is ... not in fashion now; to instruct the people, troublesome; to interpret the Scripture, [too bookish]; to pray, a sign one has little else to do ... and lastly, to die, uncouth; and to be stretched on a cross, infamous. ❞

Northern European Painters

Artists in northern Europe developed a style of painting that relied more on medieval than classical models. In the early 1400s, a group of Flemish painters, led by the brothers Jan and Hubert van Eyck (EYEK), painted scenes from the Bible and daily life in sharp, realistic detail. They developed the technique of painting in oils. Oils provided artists with richer colors and allowed them to make changes on the painted canvas. Painting in oils soon spread to Italy. Meanwhile, Italian Renaissance art reached northern Europe. Artists such as Albrecht Dürer and **Pieter Brueghel** (BROY•guhl) combined Italian technique with the artistic traditions of their homelands. They painted realistic portraits, religious themes, landscapes, and scenes of daily life.

The English Renaissance

Renaissance ideas did not spread to England until 1485, when the Wars of the Roses—bloody conflicts over who was the rightful heir to the throne—ended. Ultimately, the Tudor family defeated the York family, bringing the Tudor king Henry VII to power. Henry invited Italian Renaissance scholars to England, where they taught humanist ideas and encouraged the study of classical texts.

English humanists expressed deep interest in social issues. **Thomas More**, a statesman and a friend of Erasmus, wrote a book that criticized the society of his day by comparing it with an ideal society in which all citizens are equal and prosperous. The book, written in Latin, was called *Utopia*.

The English Renaissance was especially known for drama. The best-known English playwrights were **William Shakespeare** and Christopher Marlowe. They drew ideas for their works from medieval legends, classical mythology, and the histories of England, Denmark, and ancient Rome. Shakespeare dealt with universal human qualities such as jealousy, ambition, love, and despair so effectively that his plays are still relevant to audiences today.

SECTION 2 REVIEW

Recall
1. **Define** châteaux.
2. **Identify** Johannes Gutenberg, Michel de Montaigne, François Rabelais, Desiderius Erasmus, Jan and Hubert van Eyck, Pieter Brueghel, Thomas More, William Shakespeare.

3. **Describe** some elements of Italian Renaissance architecture used by French architects. How did they transform French architecture?

Critical Thinking
4. **Applying Information** Choose one writer or artist

from the Northern Renaissance and explain how the works of this writer or artist reflected Renaissance ideas.
Understanding Themes
5. **Cultural Diffusion** How did Italian Renaissance ideas spread to northern Europe?

190 **Chapter 5** *Renaissance and Reformation*

SECTION 2 REVIEW ANSWERS

1. All vocabulary words are defined in the Glossary.
2. Johannes Gutenberg, 189; Michel de Montaigne, 189; François Rabelais, 189; Desiderius Erasmus, 189; Jan and Hubert van Eyck, 190; Pieter Brueghel, 190; Thomas More, 190; William Shakespeare, 190
3. French architects used classical columns

from the Italian Renaissance but blended them with medieval Gothic towers and windows in their châteaux.
4. Answers should incorporate humanistic themes of the Renaissance.
5. **CULTURAL DIFFUSION** through war, travels, and books

1517 Martin Luther preaches against indulgences.

1520 The Church condemns Luther's works.

c. 1550 Lutheranism spreads through northern Europe.

Section 3

The Protestant Reformation

Setting the Scene

▶ **Terms to Define**
justification by faith, indulgences, vocation

▶ **People to Meet**
Martin Luther, Pope Leo X

▶ **Places to Locate**
Wittenberg, Worms

Find Out How did Luther's religious reforms lead to Protestantism, a new branch of Christianity?

The Storyteller

In later years, Martin Luther remembered the fateful day he entered the monastery: "Afterwards I regretted my vow, and many of my friends tried to persuade me not to enter the monastery. I, however, was determined to go through with it.... I invited certain of my best men friends to a farewell party.... In tears they led me away; and my father was very angry ... yet I persisted in my determination. It never occurred to me to leave the monastery." Luther's break with the Church was an even bigger decision than the one to enter monastic life.

—adapted from *Luther and His Times*, E.G. Schweibert, 1950

Martin Luther

The Renaissance values of humanism and secularism stimulated widespread criticism of the Catholic Church's extravagance. By about 1500, educated Europeans began calling for a reformation—a change in the Church's ways of teaching and practicing Christianity. In Germany the movement for church reform eventually led to a split in the Church that produced a new form of Christianity known as Protestantism. The series of events that gave birth to Protestantism is known as the Protestant Reformation.

Martin Luther

The Protestant Reformation was begun by a German monk named **Martin Luther**, born in 1483, the son of middle-class townspeople. His father wanted him to become a lawyer, but Luther was interested in religion. In 1505 he was nearly struck by lightning in a thunderstorm. Terrified that the storm was God's way of punishing him, the law student knelt and prayed to Saint Anne. In return for protection, he promised to become a monk. Shortly thereafter, Luther entered a monastery.

As a young monk, Luther struggled to ensure his soul's salvation. He would confess his sins for hours at a time. Yet still he worried that God might not find him acceptable.

Then he read Saint Paul's Epistle to the Romans: "He who through faith is righteous shall live"—and Luther's worries dissolved. He interpreted this to mean that a person could be made just, or good, simply by faith in God's mercy and love. Luther's idea became known as justification by faith. Luther later stated that because of this discovery he felt as if he "had been born again and had entered Paradise through wide open gates."

Chapter 5 *Renaissance and Reformation* **191**

SECTION THEME

▶ **Conflict** Martin Luther's protests against the Catholic Church result in Protestantism.

Find Out

Answer: *When the Catholic Church banned Luther's works and excommunicated him, and the Diet of Worms declared him a heretic, Luther formed a new religion.*

FOCUS

Section Objective

Discuss how Luther's religious reforms led to Protestantism, a new branch of Christianity.

BELLRINGER
Motivational Activity

Before taking roll at the beginning of the class period, project Section Focus Transparency 5-3 and have students answer the activity questions. Discuss students' responses.

This activity is also available as a blackline master.

Vocabulary Pre-check

Use Vocabulary Activity 5 to introduce vocabulary terms.
L1 LEP

SECTION RESOURCES

Reproducible Masters
- Reproducible Lesson Plan 5-3
- Vocabulary Activity 5
- Guided Reading Activity 5-3
- People in World History Profile 29
- Section Quiz 5-3

Transparencies
- Section Focus Transparency 5-3

Multimedia
- Student Self-Test and Review Software
- Testmaker
- Turning Points in World History: *The Reformation*

TEACH

Guided Practice

THEME Conflict

Important historical events often occur when ideas come into conflict. Ask students to describe conflicting ideas that led to the development of Lutheranism. **L1**

POINT

Luther's Protest

How did Luther's protest affect European religious life? *His protest led to the rise of Protestantism. In challenging the pope's authority, Luther also contributed to ending the religious unity of western Europe.*

VIDEODISC
Turning Points in World History

Side One
Chapter 8

Title: *The Reformation*
Ask: Who was Martin Luther? *(a professor and priest who founded Lutheranism)*

Independent Practice

 Guided Reading Activity 5-3 **L1**

Linking Past and Present

ANSWER
Books were printed at less cost and were able to circulate, aiding in the spread of ideas. The printing press got Luther's books quickly into readers' hands—spreading Protestantism; imprints from computer files, the development of the Internet and E-mail

POINT

Luther's Protest

Luther's ideas gradually matured and eventually brought him into conflict with the Church. At this time **Pope Leo X** was trying to raise money to rebuild St. Peter's Basilica in Rome. To this end, the pope sold church positions to his friends and also authorized sales of indulgences.

Indulgences were certificates issued by the Church that were said to reduce or even cancel punishment for a person's sins—as long as one also truly repented. People purchased indulgences believing that the document would assure them admission to heaven. John Tetzel, the Church's agent for selling indulgences in northern Germany, even went so far as to promise peasants that indulgences would relieve them of guilt for *future* sins. He also encouraged people to buy indulgences for the salvation of their dead relatives. Tetzel's sale of indulgences inspired a popular jingle: "Once you hear the money's ring, the soul from purgatory is free to spring." (According to church teaching, purgatory is a place in the afterlife where people are made fit for heaven.)

Luther, a professor and priest in the town of **Wittenberg**, preached against the sale of indulgences. He also lectured against other church practices he believed were corrupt. Then, on October 31, 1517, Luther nailed on the door of the Wittenberg Church a placard with 95 theses, or statements, criticizing indulgences and other church policies.

Breaking With Rome

Printed copies of the Ninety-five Theses spread quickly all over Germany. Sales of indulgences declined sharply. Encouraged by this reaction, Luther published hundreds of essays advocating justification by faith and attacking church abuses.

Pope Leo X responded to the decline in indulgence sales by sending envoys to Germany to persuade Luther to withdraw his criticisms. But Luther refused. In 1520 the pope formally condemned Luther and banned his works. In 1521 Pope Leo X excommunicated Luther from the Church.

CONNECTIONS

Science and Technology

Printing

Before the 1400s books had to be copied by hand—a time-consuming method. Consequently, books were rare, owned and read only by scholars and the wealthy. Gutenberg's invention of movable type changed all that: books could be produced faster at lower cost; more people were able to buy books and expand their knowledge; and traditional ideas were questioned. German printers quickly adopted Gutenberg's invention and set up similar printing presses in other European countries.

Martin Luther was one of the first authors to benefit from the new technology. Since his books could be reproduced inexpensively and in large quantities, they could be easily obtained throughout Europe shortly after Luther completed them. Thus, Luther was able to spread his ideas and gain widespread support before the Catholic Church could respond.

In the past few decades, more advances have been made in printing than in all the years since Gutenberg. Today high-speed machines and computer technology together have revolutionized the printing industry. Images are now transferred onto paper directly from computer files. The development of copy machines and laser printers has also made smaller printing jobs easier.

Gutenberg's press

Linking Past and Present **ACTIVITY**

Describe how Gutenberg's printing press transformed European society during the 1400s and 1500s. How did Luther benefit from Gutenberg's invention? Explain how computer technology and other innovations have transformed printing and other means of communication today.

192 Chapter 5 *Renaissance and Reformation*

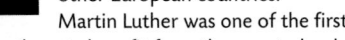
COOPERATIVE LEARNING ACTIVITY

Role Play Organize the class into five groups and have each group create a short television interview spot in which students interview either Tetzel on the sale of indulgences, Luther on his Ninety-five Theses, Pope Leo X on excommunicating Luther, Prince Frederick of Saxony on hiding Luther, or Luther on the teachings of Lutheranism. Encourage students to conduct research at the library. Have each group select a member to act as an interviewer and another member to be interviewed. All group members should prepare questions for the interview. After all interviews have been presented, have the class summarize the events that led to the Reformation. **L2**

History & Art *Luther Preaching to the Faithful*, (artist unknown). National Museum, Copenhagen, Denmark *What was Luther's view of vocations?* **(below) Indulgence box—an item that Luther opposed.**

Tell students that the painting illustrates many of Luther's beliefs: the importance of the sermon in services, having believers physically closer to the minister, baptism and the Lord's Supper as the only sacraments, simplified interior of churches.
Answer to Caption: *All occupations were vocations through which people could serve God and their neighbors.*

Shortly after Luther's excommunication, a diet, or council, of German princes met in **Worms**, Germany, to try to bring Luther back into the Church. They decided that Luther should take back his criticisms of the papacy. Meanwhile, Luther traveled to Worms as crowds of cheering people lined the road. Luther strode into the assembly hall and, when asked to take back his teachings, gave this reply: "I am bound by the Sacred Scriptures I have cited … and my conscience is captive to the Word of God. I cannot and will not recant [take back] anything.… God help me." Luther, condemned as a heretic and outlaw, was rushed out of Worms and hidden at a castle in Wartburg by a friend, Prince Frederick of Saxony.

While in hiding, Luther translated the New Testament into German. Earlier German translations of the Bible were so rare and costly that few people had them. With Luther's more affordable translation, most people could now read the Bible.

Lutheranism

After Worms, Luther laid the foundation of the first Protestant faith: Lutheranism. While Catholicism stressed faith and good works in salvation and the importance of church teaching as a spiritual guide, Lutheranism emphasized salvation by faith alone and the Bible's role as the only source of religious truth. Lutheran services centered on biblical preaching rather than ritual and were held in the language of the people instead of Latin. In this way people could understand and participate in the services. Luther and his followers also held that the Church was not a hierarchy of clergy, but a community of believers. All useful occupations, not just the priesthood, were vocations, or callings, in which people could serve God and neighbor.

Lutheranism brought a new religious message to Germany, but it also stirred social unrest among peasants wanting to end serfdom. When a major peasant revolt erupted in 1525, Luther, fearing social chaos, backed the princes against the peasants. The princes cruelly put down the uprising, killing thousands of people. Lutheranism became a more conservative movement as a result; however, it had already sown the seeds of more radical Protestant movements that would transform Europe's religious landscape.

ASSESS

Check for Understanding
Assign Section 3 Review as homework or as an in-class activity.

Use Student Self-Test and Review Software to review Section 3.

Evaluate
Section Quiz 5-3

Use the Testmaker to create a customized quiz for Section 3.

Reteach
Ask students to explain the relevance of justification by faith and the sale of indulgences to Luther's break from the Catholic Church.

Enrich
Have students imagine that they are living in Germany in the 1500s. Ask them to assert a Catholic or Lutheran point of view in a letter to the editor about the implications of Luther's reforms on the Catholic Church in Germany.

CLOSE

Have students list reasons that Lutheranism attracted many followers across Germany.

SECTION 3 REVIEW		
Recall 1. **Define** justification by faith, indulgences, vocation. 2. **Identify** Protestant Reformation, Martin Luther, Pope Leo X. 3. **Discuss** the religious changes	brought by Luther's protest against the Catholic Church. **Critical Thinking** 4. **Synthesizing Information** If you wanted to protest against something today, what medium would you use to communicate	your cause? Why? **Understanding Themes** 5. **Conflict** Why did the pope ask Luther to recant his beliefs and then excommunicate him when Luther would not do so?

SECTION 3 REVIEW ANSWERS	
1. All vocabulary words are defined in the Glossary. 2. Protestant Reformation, 191; Martin Luther, 191; Pope Leo X, 192 3. stress on faith and the Bible alone for salvation; biblical preaching; services in the vernacular; and stress on the holiness of all useful vocations	4. Possible answers might include television and newspapers, but students should give reasons for their choice of medium. 5. **CONFLICT** Possible answer: The pope exercised his authority as head of the Catholic Church in an attempt to stop criticism of a church practice.

1509 John Calvin is born.

1525 Huldrych Zwingli establishes theocracy in Zurich.

1536 John Calvin publishes *The Institutes of the Christian Religion.*

1558 Queen Elizabeth I establishes Anglicanism in England.

SECTION THEME

▶ **Cultural Diffusion** Protestant religious groups spread reform throughout northern Europe.

⌐ind Out ▶

Answer: *Zwinglism, Calvinism, Anabaptism, Anglicanism, and Puritanism*

FOCUS

Section Objective

Identify the different forms of Protestantism that emerged in Europe as the Reformation spread.

BELLRINGER
Motivational Activity

Before taking roll at the beginning of the class period, project Section Focus Transparency 5-4 and have students answer the activity questions. Discuss students' responses.

◻ This activity is also available as a blackline master.

Vocabulary Pre-check

◻ Use Vocabulary Activity 5 to introduce vocabulary terms.
L1 LEP

Section 4

The Spread of Protestantism

Setting the Scene

▶ **Terms to Define**
theocracy, predestination

▶ **People to Meet**
Huldrych Zwingli, John Calvin, the Anabaptists, Henry VIII, Catherine of Aragon, Anne Boleyn, Mary, Elizabeth I

▶ **Places to Locate**
Zurich, Geneva

⌐ind Out ▶ What different forms of Protestantism emerged in Europe as the Reformation spread?

The Storyteller

Mary Queen of Scots was a prisoner for seventeen long years. What was she to do, as she and her keeper's wife sat together all that time? She could sew. Over the years, she and her attendant ladies embroidered seas of fabric: tablecloths, cushions, and hangings, every piece scattered with coats of arms and emblems, every piece sprinkled with gold and silver spangles to catch the light. Some became gifts; but occasionally her presents were rudely refused. Her own son, King James VI, returned a vest his mother had embroidered for him because she had addressed it to "The Prince of Scotland."

—adapted from *Mary Queen of Scots*, Roy Strong and Julia Trevelyan Oman, 1972

Mary Queen of Scots

Although the Protestant Reformation spread throughout Europe in the 1500s, divisions began to appear within the movement soon after it had started. Not only did the Protestant reformers not believe in the same methods; they did not even agree on the same goals.

Swiss Reformers

After the rise of Lutheranism in Germany, many preachers and merchants in neighboring Switzerland separated from Rome and set up churches known as Reformed. **Huldrych Zwingli**, a Swiss priest who lived from 1484 to 1531, led the Protestant movement in Switzerland. Like Luther, Zwingli stressed salvation by faith alone and denounced many Catholic beliefs and practices, such as purgatory and the sale of indulgences. Unlike Luther, though, Zwingli wanted to break completely from Catholic tradition. He wanted to establish a theocracy, or church-run state, in the Swiss city of **Zurich**. By 1525 Zwingli had achieved this goal. But in 1531 war broke out over Protestant missionary activity in the Catholic areas of Switzerland. Zwingli and his force of followers were defeated by an army of Catholics.

In the mid-1500s **John Calvin**, another reformer, established the most powerful and influential Reformed group in the Swiss city of **Geneva**. Here Calvin set up a theocracy similar to Zwingli's rule in Zurich.

Born in 1509, Calvin grew up in Catholic France at the start of the Reformation. He received an education in theology, law, and humanism that prompted him to study the Bible very carefully and to formulate his own Protestant theology. In 1536 Calvin published his theology in *The Institutes of the Christian Religion*, soon one of the most

SECTION RESOURCES

◻ **Reproducible Masters**
• Reproducible Lesson Plan 5-4
• Vocabulary Activity 5
• Guided Reading Activity 5-4
• Section Quiz 5-4

🕯 **Transparencies**
• Section Focus Transparency 5-4

Multimedia
◻ Student Self-Test and Review Software
◻ Testmaker

popular books of its day, influencing religious reformers in Europe and later in North America.

The cornerstone of Calvin's theology was the belief that God possessed all-encompassing power and knowledge. Calvin contended that God alone directed everything that has happened in the past, that happens in the present, and that will happen in the future. Thus, he argued, God determines the fate of every person—a doctrine he called predestination.

To advance his views, Calvin tried to turn the city of Geneva into a model religious community. He began this project in 1541 by establishing the Consistory, a church council of 12 elders that was given the power to control almost every aspect of people's daily lives. All citizens were required to attend Reformed church services several times each week. The Consistory inspected homes annually to make sure that no one was disobeying the laws that forbade fighting, swearing, drunkenness, gambling, card playing, and dancing. It dispensed harsh punishments to people who disobeyed any of these laws. This strict atmosphere earned Geneva the title "City of God" and attracted reformers from all parts of Europe.

Visitors to Geneva helped to spread Calvinism, or John Calvin's teaching, throughout Europe. Because the Calvinist church was led by local councils of ministers and elected church members, it was easy to establish in most countries. Furthermore, the somewhat democratic structure of this organization gave its participants a stake in its welfare and inspired their intense loyalty.

The people of the Netherlands and Scotland became some of Calvin's most ardent supporters. John Knox, a leader of the Reformation in Scotland, and other reformers used Calvin's teachings to encourage moral people to overthrow "ungodly" rulers. They preached, as Calvin had, "We must obey princes and others who are in authority, but only insofar as they do not deny to God, the supreme King, Father, and Lord, what is due Him." Calvinism thus became a dynamic social force in western Europe in the 1500s and contributed to the rise of revolutionary movements later in the 1600s and 1700s.

Radical Reformers

Several new Protestant groups in western Europe, called the Anabaptists, initiated the practice of baptizing, or admitting into their groups, only adult members. They based this practice on the belief that only people who could make a free and informed choice to become Christians should be allowed to do so. Catholic and established Protestant churches, in contrast, baptized infants, making them church members.

Many Anabaptists denied the authority of local governments to direct their lives. They refused to hold office, bear arms, or swear oaths, and many lived separate from a society they saw as sinful. Consequently, they were often persecuted by government officials, forcing many Anabaptists to wander from country to country seeking refuge.

Although most Anabaptists were peaceful, others were fanatical in their beliefs. These zealots brought about the downfall of the rest. When in 1534 radical Anabaptists seized power in the German city of Münster and proceeded to burn books, seize private property, and practice polygamy, Lutherans and Catholics united to crush them. Together they killed the Anabaptist leaders and persecuted any surviving Anabaptist believers.

As a result, many Anabaptist groups left Europe for North America during the 1600s. In the Americas, the Anabaptists promoted two ideas that would become crucial in forming the United States of America: religious liberty and separation of church and state. Today, Protestant groups such as the Baptists, Mennonites, and Amish all trace their ancestry to the Anabaptists.

England's Church

Reformation ideas filtered into England during the 1500s. A serious quarrel between King Henry VIII and the pope, however, brought these ideas to the forefront.

The quarrel arose over succession to the throne. Although Henry's wife Catherine of Aragon had borne six children, only one child, Mary, survived. Henry wanted to leave a male heir to the throne so that England might not be plunged into another civil war like the Wars of the Roses. Believing that Catherine was too old to have more children, the king decided to marry Anne Boleyn. In 1527 Henry

Footnotes to History

King Henry VIII
Henry VIII was a typical Renaissance ruler who tried to excel in many areas. He enjoyed tennis, jousting, music, and discussions about religion and the sciences. He wrote a book of theology and composed several pieces of music, one of which may have been the song "Greensleeves."

TEACH

Guided Practice
THEME Cultural Diffusion
Using a wall map, have students trace the spread of Protestantism from Germany to other European countries. **L1 LEP**

Politics Have students make a chart in which they show the country, leader, relation to government, and basic beliefs of Zwinglism, Calvinism, the Anabaptists, and Anglicanism. (*Example: Zwinglism—Zurich, Swirtzerland; Huldrych Zwingli; theocracy; salvation by faith alone.*) **L2**

Biography

The following videotapes are available from Glencoe:
- **Henry VIII**
- **Elizabeth I: The Virgin Queen**

Independent Practice
Guided Reading Activity 5-4 **L1**

ASSESS

Check for Understanding
Assign Section 4 Review as homework or as an in-class activity.

Use Student Self-Test and Review Software to review Section 4.

COOPERATIVE LEARNING ACTIVITY

Panel Discussion Organize the class into five groups to prepare and present a panel discussion of Reformation movements in one of the following countries: Switzerland, Scotland, the Netherlands, England, or Germany (Anabaptists). Using outside sources, each group member should focus on a specific topic, such as leadership, religious beliefs, relationship to government, or important political events. Have each group appoint a member to serve as moderator or timekeeper. After each group member presents his or her topic, have the moderator summarize the panel's main points. After all panels have made their presentations, encourage the class to compare and contrast these Reformation movements. **L2**

History & Art

Henry VIII was an absolute monarch. By placing his allies in positions of power in Parliament, he totally controlled England. **Answer to Caption:** *to show that breaking from the Catholic Church was the will of the English people, not merely a whim of his own*

Evaluate

Section Quiz 5-4

Use the Testmaker to create a customized quiz for Section 4.

Reteach

On the chalkboard, draw a time line from 1500 to 1600. On the time line, have volunteers mark important events from this section.

Enrich

Have students research the more recent history of one of the Protestant groups mentioned in this section. Have them prepare brief reports that include size of the sect today and where most members live, current beliefs and practices, and how the latter have evolved since the group's founding.

CLOSE

Ask students to compare the reasons that England became Protestant with the reasons Switzerland adopted Protestantism. Have students note major points.

History & Art *Henry VIII*, a portrait by Hans Holbein, shows the king's splendid royal attire, reflecting his authority. *Why did Henry seek Parliament's support in breaking with the Catholic Church?*

asked the pope to agree to a divorce between himself and Catherine. But Catherine's nephew was the powerful Holy Roman Emperor Charles V, upon whom the pope depended for protection. Charles wanted Catherine to remain as queen of England in order to influence the country's policies in favor of his own interests. The pope refused Henry's request.

Henry would not be thwarted. With Parliament's support, he had a series of laws passed that separated the English Church from the pope. The most important law, the Act of Supremacy passed in 1534, made Henry head of the English Church instead of the pope. Despite this break with Rome, Henry was not a Protestant reformer. The new Church of England kept Catholic doctrines and forms of worship. Devout Catholics, however, opposed the king's rule of the Church. The most noted Catholic, the humanist scholar Thomas More, was beheaded for treason in 1535. Henry took other measures against supporters of the old religion. Between 1536 and 1540, he closed monasteries and convents, seized their land, and shared the gains with nobles and other high officials. In this way, the king filled his treasury and ensured influential support for his religious policies.

Henry also worked to strengthen the succession to the throne. He had the Church of England end his marriage to Catherine and then wed Anne Boleyn. Anne bore him a daughter, Elizabeth. In the years that followed, Henry married four more times but had only one son, Edward. When Henry died in 1542, 10-year-old Edward succeeded him to the throne. The young king was dominated by devout Protestant officials who introduced Protestant doctrines into the Church of England.

When Edward VI died in his teens, his Catholic half-sister **Mary** became queen. Mary tried to restore Catholicism in England and ended up burning hundreds of Protestants at the stake. This persecution earned her the nickname of "Bloody Mary" and only served to strengthen her people's support for Protestantism.

After Mary's death in 1558, her Protestant half-sister, **Elizabeth I**, became queen. To unite her people, Elizabeth followed a moderate course in religion. She made the English Church Protestant with some Catholic features. Anglicanism, as this blend of Protestant belief and Catholic practice was called, pleased most English people. However, radical Protestants known as Puritans wanted to "purify" the English Church of Catholic rituals. Although at first small in numbers, the Puritans gradually became influential both in the Church of England and the English Parliament.

SECTION 4 REVIEW

Recall
1. **Define** theocracy, predestination.
2. **Identify** Huldrych Zwingli, John Calvin, the Anabaptists, Henry VIII, Catherine of Aragon, Anne Boleyn, Edward VI, Mary, Elizabeth I.

3. **Explain** why divisions appeared among the different reformers within the Protestant movement.

Critical Thinking
4. **Making Comparisons** How did the Calvinists and Anabaptists differ in their attitudes toward the government church members participating in government activities?

Understanding Themes
5. **Cultural Diffusion** Why did the Catholic Church want to stop the spread of Protestant ideas?

196 Chapter 5 *Renaissance and Reformation*

SECTION 4 REVIEW ANSWERS

1. All vocabulary words are defined in the Glossary.
2. Huldrych Zwingli, 194; John Calvin, 194; the Anabaptists, 195; Henry VIII, 195; Catherine of Aragon, 195; Anne Boleyn, 195; Edward VI, 196; Mary, 196; Elizabeth I, 196
3. The reformers had different goals and ideas about how to reform the Church.
4. The Anabaptists denied the authority of government in their lives and did not take part in government activities; the Calvinists set up a church-run state that had control over people's daily lives.
5. **CULTURAL DIFFUSION** Possible answer: The Catholic Church was losing members, money, and power, as well as influence over European governments.

Critical Thinking SKILLS

Identifying Evidence

In a geography trivia game, you picked the following question: What is the longest river in the world? The game card says it is the Amazon River, but you think it is the Nile River. Your friends insist that you are wrong. How can you prove you are right?

You must identify evidence that will establish your claim. In the example above, you could consult an atlas, almanac, or encyclopedia to find the lengths of both rivers. In fact, you are correct! The Nile River is 4,160 miles long, while the Amazon is 4,000 miles long.

Learning the Skill

There are four basic kinds of evidence: 1) oral accounts (eyewitness testimony); 2) written documents (diaries, letters, books, articles); 3) objects (artifacts); and 4) visual items (photographs, videotapes, paintings). These kinds of evidence fall into one of two categories—primary evidence and secondary evidence.

Primary evidence is produced by participants or eyewitnesses to events. Eyewitness accounts or photographs of a fire are examples of primary evidence. Secondary evidence is produced later, by those who have not experienced the events directly. Textbooks and encyclopedias are examples of secondary evidence.

To identify evidence that proves a claim, first clearly define the claim. Search available information to find the kind of evidence that can prove or disprove the claim. Compare the pieces of evidence to see if they agree. Also, rate the objectivity of your evidence. In the example above, the sources you consulted— atlas, almanac, or encyclopedia—are all reliable sources of information.

However, if you are using primary sources such as letters, diaries, and news accounts, carefully assess which evidence is most reliable.

Practicing the Skill

Read the claim below. Then read each piece of evidence that follows. Decide which pieces of evidence prove the claim to be true and explain why.

Claim: *Humanism's emphasis on the value of the individual led to artistic flowering in the Renaissance.*

1. In Renaissance Italy humanist scholars opened schools to promote the study of history, philosophy, Latin, and Greek.
2. Renaissance artists used painting and sculpture to convey human emotions and values.
3. In Rome, the pope and cardinals made up the wealthiest and most powerful class of people.
4. In England, William Shakespeare wrote plays that dealt with universal human qualities such as jealousy, ambition, love, and despair.
5. The invention of the printing press spread knowledge of humanism throughout the newly emerging middle class.

Applying the Skill

Think about this claim: The humanist values of the Renaissance still dominate modern American culture. Find at least five pieces of evidence from newspapers, magazines, and other sources to prove or disprove this claim.

For More Practice

Turn to the Skill Practice in the Chapter Review on page 207 for more practice in identifying evidence.

1525   1550   1575

1536 Pope Paul III calls for reforms.   **1540** Ignatius of Loyola founds Society of Jesus.   **1563** Council of Trent ends.

Find Out

Answer: *The Catholic Church began its own reformation, eliminating abuses, clarifying theology, and sending out missionaries to reclaim Catholic lands.*

FOCUS

Section Objective
Describe how the Catholic Church tried to halt the spread of Protestantism.

BELLRINGER
Motivational Activity

Before taking roll at the beginning of the class period, project Section Focus Transparency 5-5 and have students answer the activity questions. Discuss students' responses.
📁 This activity is also available as a blackline master.

Vocabulary Pre-check
🔲 Use the Vocabulary PuzzleMaker to create a puzzle that reinforces the vocabulary terms in this section. **L1**

Section 5

The Catholic Reformation

Setting the Scene
▶ **Terms to Define**
  seminary, baroque

▶ **People to Meet**
  Pope Paul III, the Jesuits, Ignatius of Loyola

▶ **Places to Locate**
  Trent

 **Find Out** How did the Catholic Church try to halt the spread of Protestantism?

The Storyteller

The Inquisition sometimes used "ordeals" to determine guilt or innocence, confident that God would give victory to an innocent person and punish the guilty. In the "Trial of the Cross," both parties, accuser and accused, stood before a cross with arms outstretched. The first to drop his arms was judged guilty. In the "Trial by Hot Water," the accused lifted a stone from the bottom of a boiling cauldron. If, after three days, his wound had healed, he was innocent. In the "Trial by Cold Water," the accused was tied up and lowered into water. If he sank, he was innocent. If he floated, he was guilty.

—from The Medieval Inquisition, Albert Clement Shannon, 1983

Trial of Books *(detail)*

Most of the people in Spain, France, Italy, Portugal, Hungary, Poland, and southern Germany remained Catholic during the Protestant Reformation. Nevertheless, Catholicism's power was threatened by Protestantism's increasing popularity in northern Europe. To counter the Protestant challenge, Catholics decided to enact reforms. The Catholic Church had had a history of periodic reform since the Middle Ages. Thus, in the movement that came to be known as the Counter-Reformation, or Catholic Reformation, the Church eliminated many abuses, clarified its theology, and reestablished the pope's authority over church members.

TURNING POINT

Reaffirming Catholicism

During the 1530s and 1540s, **Pope Paul III** set out to reform the Church and stem the Protestant advance. To establish the goals of the Catholic Reformation, he called a council of bishops at **Trent**, Italy, in 1545.

The Council of Trent
The Council of Trent, which met in several sessions until 1563, reaffirmed Catholic teachings that had been challenged by the Protestants. Salvation, it declared, comes through faith and good works, and church tradition is equal to the Bible as a source of religious truth. The Latin Vulgate translation of the Bible was made the only acceptable version of scripture.

The Council also put an end to many church abuses. It forbade the selling of indulgences. Clergy were ordered to follow strict rules of behavior. The

---

SECTION RESOURCES

📁 **Reproducible Masters**
• Reproducible Lesson Plan 5-5
• Guided Reading Activity 5-5
• Reteaching Activity 5
• Enrichment Activity 5
• Section Quiz 5-5
• Performance Assessment Activity 5
• Spanish Chapter Summary 5

🔲 **Transparencies**
• Section Focus Transparency 5-5
• World History and Art Transparency 21

Multimedia
📘 Focus on World Art Print 16
🔲 Vocabulary PuzzleMaker Software
🔲 Student Self-Test and Review Software
🔲 Testmaker

The Council of Trent by Titian. **Held off and on for about 20 years, this church council reaffirmed Catholic doctrine and introduced reforms.** *What Bible was made the only acceptable version?*

Council decided that each diocese had to establish a seminary, or theological school, to ensure a better-educated clergy.

The Inquisition

To deal with the Protestant threat, Pope Paul also strengthened the Inquisition. As you read in Chapter 3, the Inquisition was a church court set up to stamp out heresy. In addition to carrying out its traditional functions, the Inquisition in the 1500s introduced censorship to curtail humanist and Protestant thinking. In 1543 it published the Index of Forbidden Box, a list of works considered too immoral or irreligious for Catholics to read.

The Arts

The Church also used the arts to further the Catholic Reformation. The Council of Trent maintained the Church's elaborate art and ritual, and it declared that the Mass should be said only in Latin.

Church art and Latin ritual were to serve as sources of inspiration for educated and less educated Catholics alike. Many artists were influenced by the intensely emotional devotion of the Catholic Reformation. One of these was the Greek painter Domenikos Theotokopoulos, known in Spain as El Greco, or "The Greek." Residing in Spain, El Greco painted the saints in distorted figures that showed strong religious feelings.

As the Catholic Reformation spread through Europe, it helped spark a new style of art and architecture called baroque (buh•ROHK). The Renaissance arts had shown restraint, simplicity, and order, but the baroque arts stressed emotion, complexity, and exaggeration for dramatic effect. In painting, Peter Paul Rubens of Flanders was a master of the baroque style. He painted large altarpieces of emotional religious scenes as well as mythological subjects. Another master was the Spaniard Diego Velázquez, who painted portraits at the Spanish royal court. Among the most famous

Chapter 5 *Renaissance and Reformation* **199**

Map Study

Answer

Religious wars broke out.

Map Skills Practice

Reading a Map Which Protestant religion was a significant minority in largely Catholic France? *(Calvinism)*

Independent Practice

Guided Reading Activity 5-5 **L1**

Foreign Affairs Have students choose an area where the Jesuits sent missionaries, such as China, Japan, or North America, and research the Jesuits' activities and accomplishments there. Let students share this information with the class. **L2**

Diplomacy Have students write a brief report on the safe-conducts issued to Protestants who addressed the Council of Trent. **L3**

Cultural Perspectives

No More Latin In the 1960s the Catholic Church convened the Second Vatican Council (the First Vatican Council had met in 1869 and 1870). One result was the decision to say Mass in the vernacular language of each country rather than in Latin.

ASSESS

Check for Understanding

Assign Section 5 Review as homework or as an in-class activity.

Use Student Self-Test and Review Software to review Section 5.

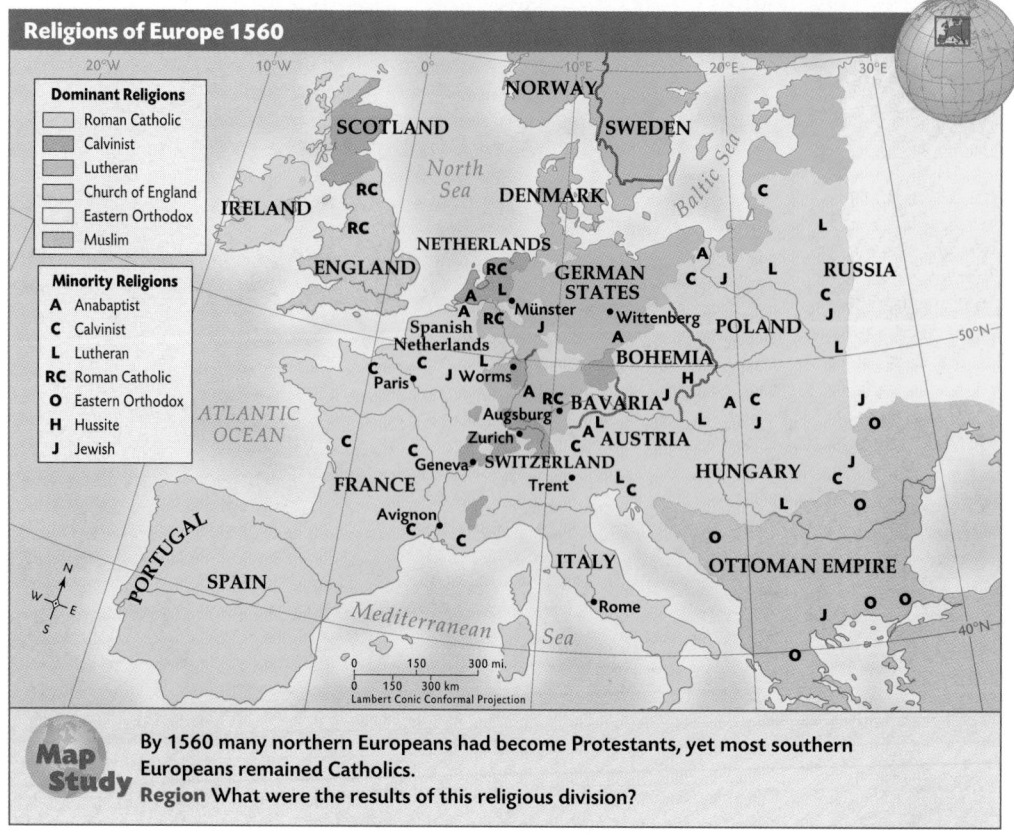

Religions of Europe 1560

Dominant Religions
- Roman Catholic
- Calvinist
- Lutheran
- Church of England
- Eastern Orthodox
- Muslim

Minority Religions
- **A** Anabaptist
- **C** Calvinist
- **L** Lutheran
- **RC** Roman Catholic
- **O** Eastern Orthodox
- **H** Hussite
- **J** Jewish

0   150   300 mi.
0   150   300 km
Lambert Conic Conformal Projection

Map Study By 1560 many northern Europeans had become Protestants, yet most southern Europeans remained Catholics.
Region What were the results of this religious division?

---

baroque architects was the Italian artist Gian Lorenzo Bernini. His best known work is the public square of St. Peter's Basilica in Rome, which is enclosed by two great semicircles of columns.

Spreading Catholicism

The Church also set out to win converts and to strengthen the spiritual life of Catholics. Many religious orders and individuals in the Church became involved in these efforts.

Ignatius of Loyola

In 1540 the pope recognized a new religious order, the Society of Jesus, or **Jesuits**. Founded by **Ignatius of Loyola**, the Jesuits worked to spread Catholicism and combat heresy.

Ignatius was a Spanish noble whose military career had ended abruptly when he was wounded in battle. During a long recovery, he found comfort in the lives of the saints and vowed to serve God.

The outcome of his vow was the founding of the Jesuits, who followed a strict spiritual discipline and pledged absolute obedience to the pope.

The Jesuits wore the black robes of monks, lived simple lives, but did not withdraw from the world. They preached to the people, helped the poor, and set up schools. They also served as advisers in royal courts and founded universities. Jesuit centers of learning taught not only theology but also physics, astronomy, mathematics, archaeology, and other subjects.

As missionaries, the Jesuits helped strengthen Catholicism in southern Germany, Bohemia, Poland, and Hungary. They also carried their message to the Americas, Africa, and Asia. The Jesuit priest Matteo Ricci, for example, traveled to China and preached Christianity at the court of the Ming emperor. To make his message relevant to Chinese needs, Ricci learned to speak Chinese and dressed in Chinese clothing. Although he had little success in spreading his religious beliefs, Ricci shared with Chinese scholars his knowledge of European arts and sciences.

200 Chapter 5 *Renaissance and Reformation*

Study Strategy Have students divide Section 5 into three parts according to the following headings: *Reforms in the Catholic Church, Missionary Activity of the Catholic Church, Results of the Reformation.* Then have students find similar headings in the text and write at least three outcomes under each heading. *(For example: Missionary Activity—Jesuit order formed; Jesuits retained church members in southern Germany, Bohemia, Hungary, and Poland; Jesuits establish universities throughout Europe.)* Tell students that *Reforms in the Catholic Church* corresponds with "Redefining Catholicism" in the text. **L2**

Teresa of Avila

Another supporter of Catholic renewal was the Spanish nun Teresa of Avila. Born to a noble family in 1515, Teresa entered a Carmelite convent. Daily life there, however, was not strict enough for the deeply religious Teresa, so she set up her order of Carmelite nuns. With the pope's approval, Teresa later opened many new convents throughout Spain. Made a saint after her death, Teresa became known for her spiritual writings that rank among the devotional classics of Christianity.

A Divided Europe

While Catholicism carried out reforms, the Catholic Holy Roman Emperor Charles V tried, but failed, to stem the spread of Protestantism in his domains. Finally, in 1555, Charles and the German princes signed the Peace of Augsburg, which allowed each prince—whether Catholic or Lutheran—to choose the religion of his subjects.

This treaty set the stage for the division of Europe into a Protestant north and a Catholic south, a division that remains to this day. Northern Germany and Scandinavia were Lutheran as a result of the efforts of monarchs and princes. Areas of southern Germany, Switzerland, the Netherlands, and Scotland—with their economic wealth based in towns—held to Calvinism. England set up its own Anglican Church, a blend of Protestantism and Catholicism under royal control.

There were many reasons why Europeans in large numbers supported Protestantism. One reason was undoubtedly religious conviction. However, nonreligious factors were also involved. German princes often favored Protestantism in order to increase their power. They made Protestantism the official religion of their territories, placing it under their control. They also seized lands and wealth owned by the Catholic Church. Townspeople also rallied to the new faith, which supported their business practices. Above all, northern Europeans saw Protestantism as a way to

 Visualizing History Jesuit missionaries in Japan are depicted by a Japanese painter. *Who founded the Society of Jesus?*

defy an Italian-controlled Catholic Church that drew so much money from their homelands.

During the 1500s and early 1600s, religious wars engulfed Europe, bringing widespread killing and destruction. In France, a struggle for the monarchy heightened bitter fighting between French Protestants, or Huguenots, and the Catholic majority. Both sides carried out terrible atrocities. The most infamous event was the Saint Bartholomew's Day Massacre. On that day—August 24, 1572—violence erupted that led to the killing of 3,000 Huguenots.

Religious bigotry also brought hard times to European Jews caught in the middle of the Christian feuding. One exception to this pattern of intolerance was the Netherlands, which took in Jews driven out of other areas of Europe.

SECTION 5 REVIEW

Recall
1. **Define** seminary, baroque.
2. **Identify** Pope Paul III, the Jesuits, Ignatius of Loyola.
3. **List** the educational opportunities provided by the Jesuits.

Critical Thinking
4. **Analyzing Information** List any three of the reforms proposed by the Council of Trent. Beside each, give the Protestant viewpoint to which it responded.

Understanding Themes
5. **Reaction** Evaluate the actions the Church took to halt the spread of Protestantism and their effects. Which were successful, and which were not?

Visualizing History In 1549 the Jesuits began their mission to Japan under the Spanish priest Francis Xavier. He learned Japanese and recommended that other missionaries follow local customs and use the native language.
Answer to Caption: *Ignatius of Loyola*

Evaluate
 Section Quiz 5-5

▣ Use the Testmaker to create a customized quiz for Section 5.

Reteach
Have students summarize the Catholic Church's activities to halt the Protestant Reformation.

 Reteaching Activity 5

Enrich
Have students do research on the Inquisition, the methods it employed, and how and why it eventually ended.

📁 Enrichment Activity 5

CLOSE

Have students make a wall chart summarizing the work of the Inquisition and the Council of Trent.

SECTION 5 REVIEW ANSWERS

1. All vocabulary words are defined in the Glossary.
2. Pope Paul III, 198; the Jesuits, 200; Ignatius of Loyola, 200
3. physics, astronomy, mathematics, archaeology, linguistics, biology, chemistry, and genetics, as well as Roman

Catholic theology and philosophy
4. Sample answer: Council of Trent—salvation achieved through faith and works; Protestant viewpoint—salvation achieved by faith alone
5. **REACTION** Sample answer: Catholic missionary activities were

successful because they retained many church members; the Inquisition was unsuccessful because it aroused fears in Protestant countries of what might happen if Catholicism were restored.

Literature

Team Teaching This excerpt from *The Prince* may be presented in a team-teaching context, in conjunction with English or Language Arts.

The Prince

Historical Connection

Machiavelli's advice on how to rule a kingdom helps us to understand the way people in any age compete for power. He emphasizes how rulers really act, not how they should behave, a reflection of the focus on human behavior that began in Europe in the 1400s.

Background Information

Setting Machiavelli lived in a time of political instability in Italy. Tyranny, war, and corruption were common. Machiavelli believed that an effective ruler had to impose peace so that the country could progress.

Literary Elements Tone is the outlook of the writer toward his or her material. Machiavelli tries to achieve an objective tone. For example, when he describes "men in general" as "ungrateful, fickle, and deceitful," he neither condemns nor praises them for these traits.

Machiavelli's theme, the central idea in *The Prince*, is that the end justifies the means. The point of his handbook is to help a ruler stay in power at whatever cost.

Literature

from

The Prince

by Niccolò Machiavelli

ike many other Renaissance thinkers, Niccolò Machiavelli (1469–1527) analyzed human actions rather than spiritual issues. Unlike many of his contemporaries, however, he focused on the selfish side of human nature more than on humanity's potential for progress. Machiavelli observed how successful politicians won and secured power. He sent his thoughts to an Italian prince, hoping to win a position as an adviser. His ruthlessly honest look at how politicians act both confirms and challenges the views we have toward our leaders.

t is the custom of those who are anxious to find favor in the eyes of a prince to present him with such things as they value most highly or in which they see him take delight. Hence offerings are made of horses, arms, golden cloth, precious stones and such ornaments, worthy of the greatness of the Prince. Since therefore I am desirous of presenting myself to Your Magnificence with some token of my eagerness to serve you, I have been able to find nothing in what I possess which I hold more dear or in greater esteem than the knowledge of the actions of great men which has come to me through a long experience of present-day affairs and continual study of ancient times. And having pondered long and diligently on this knowledge and tested it well, I have reduced it to a little volume which I now send to Your Magnificence. Though I consider this work unworthy of your presence, nonetheless I have much hope that your kindness may find it acceptable, if it be considered that I could offer you no better gift than to give you occasion to learn in a very short space of time all that I have come to have knowledge and understanding of over many years and through many hardships and dangers. I have not adorned the work nor inflated it with lengthy clauses nor pompous or magnificent words, nor added any other refinement or extrinsic ornament wherewith many are wont to advertise or embellish their work, for it has been my wish either that no honor should be given it or that simply the truth of the material

ABOUT THE AUTHOR

Machiavelli was born into a poor family in Florence, Italy. For many years he served the ruler of Florence as an ambassador and military adviser. In 1512 Lorenzo de' Medici seized power in Florence and dismissed Machiavelli, who later settled in the countryside where he wrote *The Prince*. Machiavelli dedicated the book to Lorenzo de' Medici in the hope the ruler would forgive him and allow him back into the government.

In *The Prince*, Machiavelli says what many rulers believed but would never have dared declare in public. For centuries *Machiavelli* has been synonymous with amoral cunning.

and the gravity of the subject should make it acceptable....

As for the exercise of the mind, the prince should read the histories of all peoples and ponder on the actions of the wise men therein recorded, note how they governed themselves in time of war, examine the reasons for their victories or defeats in order to imitate the former and avoid the latter, and above all conduct himself in accordance with the example of some great man of the past....

We now have left to consider what should be the manners and attitudes of a prince toward his subjects and his friends. As I know that many have written on this subject I feel that I may be held presumptuous in what I have to say, if in my comments I do not follow the lines laid down by others. Since, however, it has been my intention to write something which may be of

use to the understanding reader, it has seemed wiser to me to follow the real truth of the matter rather than what we imagine it to be. For imagination has created many principalities and republics that have never been seen or known to have any real existence, for how we live is so different from how we ought to live that he who studies what ought to be done rather than what is done will learn the way to his downfall rather than to his preservation. A man striving in every way to be good will meet his ruin among the great number who are not good. Hence it is necessary for a prince, if he wishes to remain in power, to learn how not to be good and to use his knowledge or refrain from using it as he may need....

Here the question arises; whether it is better to be loved than feared or feared than loved. The answer is that it would be desirable to be both

Visualizing History Machiavelli advised Lorenzo de' Medici, who became the ruler of Florence in 1513, to be as cunning as his grandfather, Lorenzo the Magnificent, shown here. *Why did Machiavelli believe it is better to be feared than loved?*

FOCUS

Have students brainstorm a list of words that can be applied to politicians today. After they have come up with five or more words, ask them whether the connotations of each word are positive or negative.

Visualizing History The Medici were a leading family of Florence. Originally physicians—the family name means "doctors" in Italian—they later founded one of Italy's most important banking houses. **Answer to Caption:** *It is safer to be feared, if one must choose.*

TEACH

Evaluation

Point out that Machiavelli believed rulers could learn lessons from history. Ask students whether they agree with this idea. They may feel that although historical examples are often referred to in contemporary debates, history rarely teaches clear-cut lessons.

Comparison

Ask students to compare their view of human nature with that of Machiavelli. Challenge them to come up with examples that support their views. If they share Machiavelli's pessimism, they might use crime statistics to support the claim that people need to be strictly controlled. If they disagree with Machiavelli, they might point to the amount of charitable work people do.

OTHER WORKS OF OR ABOUT MACHIAVELLI

Bondanella, Peter, and Mark Musa, trans. *The Portable Machiavelli.* New York: Viking, 1979.

Detmold, Christian, trans. *Discourse on the First Ten Books of Livy.* New York: Modern Library, 1940.

History of Florence and the Affairs of Italy. Washington, DC: M. W. Dunne, 1901.

Hale, J.R., ed. and trans. *The Literary Works of Machiavelli.* New York: Oxford University Press, 1961.

Visualizing History

Cesare Borgia became famous throughout Italy as a brilliant but ruthless military tactician. When Machiavelli held Borgia up as a model ruler, many Italians were appalled.
Answer to Caption: *when it is not to his advantage or when his reasons for giving his word are no longer valid*

Interpretation

Discuss with students the implications of Machiavelli's ideas for a democracy. Some students may argue that if people are deceitful, a democracy is bound to fail. Others may argue that because people are deceitful, a democracy is the best way to check the power of individuals.

 World Literature Selection 2

Linking Past and Present

Ethics Machiavelli pioneered the idea that rulers should be held to a looser moral standard because, to stay in power, they had to ignore ethics. Are politicians today held to a looser or stricter moral standard than ordinary citizens?

ASSESS

Assign **Responding to Literature** questions.

CAES·BORGIA·VALENTINV

Visualizing History This portrait of Cesare Borgia embodies the pride and confidence of the prince about whom Machiavelli wrote his political commentary. Borgia, the son of the controversial Pope Alexander VI, used his position as duke of Romagna to enhance papal political power. *When should a leader not keep his word, according to Machiavelli?*

but, since that is difficult, it is much safer to be feared than to be loved, if one must choose. For on men in general this observation may be made: they are ungrateful, fickle, and deceitful, eager to avoid dangers, and avid for gain, and while you are useful to them they are all with you, offering you their blood, their property, their lives, and their sons so long as danger is remote, as we noted above, but when it approaches they turn on you. Any prince, trusting only in their words and having no other preparations made, will fall to his ruin, for friendships that are bought at a price and not by greatness and nobility of soul are paid for indeed, but they are not owned and cannot be called upon in time of need. Men have less hesitation in offending a man who is loved than one who is feared, for love is held by a bond of

obligation which, as men are wicked, is broken whenever personal advantage suggests it, but fear is accompanied by the dread of punishment which never relaxes....

Hence a wise leader cannot and should not keep his word when keeping it is not to his advantage or when the reasons that made him give it are no longer valid. If men were good, this would not be a good precept, but since they are wicked and will not keep faith with you, you are not bound to keep faith with them....

So a prince need not have all the aforementioned good qualities, but it is most essential that he appear to have them. Indeed, I should go so far as to say that having them and always practicing them is harmful, while seeming to have them is useful. It is good to appear clement [merciful], trustworthy, humane, religious, and

---

ADDITIONAL LITERARY WORKS OF AND ABOUT THE PERIOD

Cao Xueqin. *Dream of the Red Chamber.* New York: Pantheon, 1958. Story of the problems faced by a well-to-do Chinese family in the 1700s.

Shakespeare, William. *Hamlet. Riverside Shakespeare.* Boston: Houghton Mifflin, 1974. Tragedy written in 1603 about a Danish prince and his Machiavellian uncle.

honest, and also to be so, but always with the mind so disposed that, when the occasion arises not to be so, you can become the opposite. It must be understood that a prince and particularly a new prince cannot practice all the virtues for which men are accounted good, for the necessity of preserving the state often compels him to take actions which are opposed to loyalty, charity, humanity, and religion. Hence he must have a spirit ready to adapt itself as the varying winds of fortune command him. As I have said, so far as he is able, a prince should stick to the path of good but, if the necessity arises, he should know how to follow evil.

A prince must take great care that no word ever passes his lips that is not full of the above mentioned five good qualities, and he must seem to all who see and hear him a model of piety, loyalty, integrity, humanity, and religion. Nothing is more necessary than to seem to possess this last quality, for men in general judge more by the eye than the hand; as all can see but few can feel. Everyone sees what you seem to be, few experience what you really are and these few do not dare to set themselves up against the opinion of the majority supported by the majesty of the state. In the actions of all men and especially princes, where there is no court of appeal, the end is all that counts. Let a prince then concern himself with the acquisition or the maintenance of a state; the means employed will always be considered honorable and praised by all, for the mass of mankind is always swayed by the appearances and by the outcome of an enterprise....

I am not ignorant of the fact that many have

The Pier and the Ducal Palace (detail) by Luca Carlevaris. *According to the principles of Machiavelli, why should a ruler carefully maintain the exterior of the palace?*

held and hold the opinion that the things of this world are so ordered by fortune and God that the prudence of mankind may effect little change in them, indeed is of no avail at all. On this basis it could be argued that there is no point in making any effort, but we should rather abandon ourselves to destiny. This opinion has been the more widely held in our day on account of the great variations in things that we have seen and are still witnessing and which are entirely beyond human conjecture. Sometimes indeed, thinking on such matters, I am minded to share that opinion myself. Nevertheless I believe, if we are to keep our free will, that it may be true that fortune controls half of our actions indeed but allows us the direction of the other half, or almost half....

CLOSE

Organize the class into small groups. Ask each group to prepare a rebuttal to Machiavelli's ideas. They could address his views of human nature, his analysis of politics, or the long-term effectiveness of his political tactics.

Contemporary Connection

Machiavelli says that a successful ruler must always appear good but can seldom afford to actually *be* good. Have students discuss the idea of appearances versus reality. Then have them write a short essay in which they analyze a person whose appearance belied his or her real nature.

RESPONDING TO LITERATURE

1. Describe in your own words Machiavelli's view of human nature.
2. Write a brief essay giving an example that explains whether today's politicians follow Machiavelli's advice.
3. Propose an alternative principle to Machiavelli's

view that "where there is no court of appeal, the end is all that counts."
4. **Making Judgments** Do you think individuals should follow Machiavelli's advice in dealing with their family, friends, and classmates? Why or why not?

Portfolio Project

Have students write an essay in which they discuss the qualities *they* believe a good political leader should have. Encourage them to support their assertions with examples from history and current events.

ANSWERS TO RESPONDING TO LITERATURE

1. Student answers should recognize that the view is largely pessimistic.
2. Essays should indicate that students understand Machiavelli's belief that politicians' lying is justified.
3. One alternative is the belief that immoral actions cannot lead to a moral end.

4. Answers will vary. Some students may realize that Machiavelli believed standards governing personal relationships differed from those he recommends to princes. Students should give supporting reasons for their views.

Chapter 5 Review

Answers

Using Key Terms

1. a   4. g
2. b   5. i
3. j

Using Your History Journal

Suggest that students research one of the following: Mennonites, Puritans, Huguenots, or Quakers.

Reviewing Facts

1. They were governed by wealthy families; social classes included nobles and bankers; middle class of shopkeepers and artisans; peasants and workers.
2. Renaissance art and architecture were based on classical styles and were more realistic and life-like, and more individualistic and worldly.
3. They brought about greater religious diversity in Europe, aided in reviving religious faith, and ushered in a period of religious warfare.
4. Henry wished to divorce Catherine of Aragon, and the pope denied permission.
5. Ignatius of Loyola founded the Jesuits, an order devoted to strengthening Catholicism and halting the spread of Protestantism; also promoted mission-

---

Connections Across Time

Historical Significance During the Renaissance, Europeans focused less on religion and the afterlife and more on individual achievement and on worldly concerns. Like the ancient Greeks and Romans whom they admired, Europe's educated classes stressed human achievement and supported the arts.—especially architecture, painting, and sculpture.

With a renewed interest in learning, Europeans began to question age-old traditions and called for church reforms. When changes did not take place, some Europeans broke away from Catholicism and formed Protestant churches. Protestantism—emphasizing individual salvation and the worthiness of ordinary occupations—profoundly influenced the lands and cultures of northern Europe.

Using Key Terms

Write the key term that completes each sentence. Then write a sentence for each term not chosen.

a. baroque   h. theocracy
b. humanism   i. doge
c. seminary   j. sonnet
d. vocations   k. châteaux
e. indulgences   l. secular
f. predestination   m. individualism
g. justification by faith

1. The Catholic Reformation made use of a new style of art known as _____.
2. _____, or the Renaissance interest in the ancient classical writings, sparked an interest in human creativity and fulfillment.
3. A _____ was a Renaissance form of writing that dealt with the theme of love.
4. _____ is the belief that a person could be made good simply by faith in God's mercy and love.
5. The Italian city of Venice had a republican style of government headed by an elected official called a _____.

Technology Activity

Using a Computerized Card Catalog Make use of a library's computerized card catalog to choose a Renaissance artist to research. Find information about the person's life and achievements. Using your research, create an oral history about that person by role-playing him or her. Have the class ask you questions about your life and your contributions to the Renaissance. Your responses should reflect your researched information.

Using Your History Journal

One effect of the Reformation was the migration of thousands of people to colonial America. Research and write a brief history of one religious group's migration. Create a map that shows the origin and destination(s) of that group.

Reviewing Facts

1. **Government/Culture** Explain how the city-states of Renaissance Italy were governed. What social classes were present in the typical city-state?
2. **Culture** Describe how the art and architecture of the Renaissance differed from the art and architecture of the Middle Ages.
3. **History** Discuss why the Protestant and Catholic Reformations were important turning points in the history of Europe.
4. **Culture** Explain why Henry VIII separated from the Catholic Church and created the Church of England.
5. **Culture** State how Ignatius of Loyola and Teresa of Avila helped to reform Catholicism.

Critical Thinking

1. **Apply** Why did the Medici rulers use tax revenues to fund public works projects that benefited all the citizens of Florence?
2. **Analyze** What were the causes of the Protestant Reformation? Could the Reformation have occurred without a reformer such as Luther?

---

ary work and education; Teresa of Avila encouraged religious devotion and founding of convents.

Critical Thinking

1. to win the loyalty of Florence's lower classes; to make improvements such as sewers and paved streets
2. dissatisfaction with church corruption; humanist questioning of church teaching; rise

of princes and middle classes who resented church wealth and controls
3. They led to the religious division of Europe into Protestant and Catholic areas; students might note that religious differences play a smaller role in Europe's largely secular political life today.
4. figures and horses are lifelike and set off from the background; subject matter drawn from everyday life

3. **Evaluate** How did the religious reformations of the 1500s affect Europe? How might Europe's religious heritage affect efforts toward unity today?

4. **Analyze** Apollonio Giovanni, an Italian artist, painted the entry of a group of cavaliers into a town in the 1300s, shown below. In what ways does this painting show how Renaissance artists broke away from traditional forms?

Understanding Themes

1. **Innovation** Why did the Renaissance begin in Italy? How did the movement change European thought and culture?

2. **Cultural Diffusion** How did the people of northern Europe adapt Italian Renaissance ideas to their society?

3. **Conflict** Could the conflict between Luther and the pope have been resolved if either had reacted differently? Explain.

4. **Cultural Diffusion** What factors helped Protestant ideas to spread so rapidly?

5. **Reaction** In what ways could the Catholic Reformation be called the Counter-Reformation?

Skill Practice

Use the information in Chapter 5 to find evidence for each claim below. Then decide which claim you support.

1. Martin Luther was a sincere believer who only wanted to reform the Catholic Church.

2. Martin Luther was a rebel intent on splitting the Catholic Church.

Linking Past and Present

1. Do you think ancient Greek and Roman culture influences artists, architects, and writers as much today as it did during the Renaissance? Why or why not?

2. What ideas of the Protestant Reformation do you think affect the United States today?

Geography in History

1. **Location** What is the approximate location of the first Spanish bishopric in South America?

2. **Region** In what geographic region were most Spanish missions established during the 1500s?

3. **Human/Environment Interaction** Large areas of South America were unreached by missionaries in the first 200 years of Spanish, Portuguese, and French mission activity. What geographic feature contributed to this?

4. **Place** What river did Jesuit missionaries use as a means of gaining access to the interior of South America?

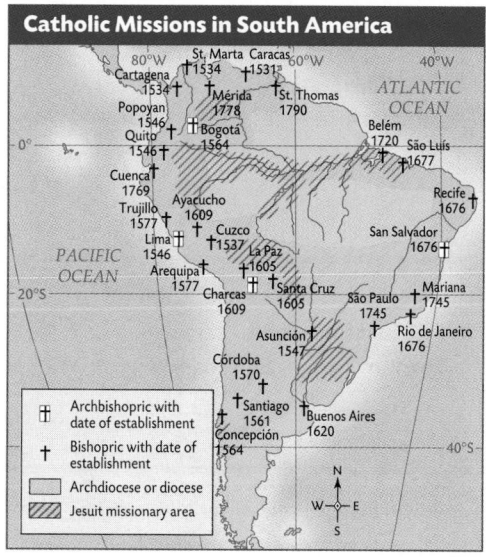

Catholic Missions in South America

oppression, and rulers eager to seize church property

5.  **REACTION** The Catholic Reformation was a response or reaction that countered the Protestant Reformation.

Skill Practice

Evidence for (1) may include the fact that Luther had had sincere struggles of conscience as a monk, had eventually become a priest, and had not proposed leaving the Church until after Worms; (2) may include the fact that Luther proclaimed his Ninety-five Theses in a challenging manner and made them as widely known as possible.

Linking Past and Present

1. Yes: Western art is founded on classical styles developed by the Greeks and Romans. No: artists are exploring diverse non-Western influences and rejecting established rules in favor of individual expression.

2. Answers might mention separation of church and state and the value of diversity and toleration, both of which came from the radical wing of the Protestant Reformation.

Geography in History

1. 66°W, 10°N
2. the northern and western coastal regions
3. tropical rain forests
4. Amazon

? Chapter Bonus Test Question

Ask students: Why was the time ripe for the Protestant Reformation? *(Answers may include: Italian humanism brought an emphasis on secular ideas, and Christian humanism in northern Europe focused on criticizing abuses in the Church and returning to the Church's piety.)*

Understanding Themes

1.  **INNOVATION** Town life was stronger in Italy, enabling Italians to easily discard feudal ways and accept new ideas. Also, the classical tradition was stronger in Italy, once the center of the Roman Empire. The Renaissance led to a focus on classical learning and the values of individualism and human achievement; society also became more secular in tone, although religious values were also held.

2. **CULTURAL DIFFUSION** Many added a religious emphasis to the classical ideals of the Italian Renaissance.

3. **CONFLICT** Possible answer: Luther sought to reform the Church not break from it, and he might not have broken away had the pope responded thoughtfully to him.

4. **CULTURAL DIFFUSION** printing press, vernacular translations of the Bible, peasants wanting freedom from church

A complete, 1-page lesson plan is
provided for each section in the
Reproducible Lesson Plans booklet.

Expanding Horizons

CHAPTER RESOURCES

Chapter Opener	**Reproducible Resources** Chapter Themes: Graphic Organizer 6 Historical Significance Chapter Activity 6	**Multimedia Resources** MindJogger Videoquiz
Chapter Enrichment	Vocabulary Activity 6* Time Line Activity 6 Mapping History Activity 6 History Simulation 6 Geography and History Activity 6 Source Reading 6 People in World History Profiles 31, 32 World Art and Music Activity 6 Enrichment Activity 6 Critical Thinking Activity 6 Skill Reinforcement Activity 6 Building Skills in Geography Workbook, Unit 1, Lesson 11 Performance Assessment Activity 6	Focus on World Art Print 1, Jan Vermeer. *The Artist and His Model as Klio* World History and Art Transparencies 22, 23 Mapping History Overlay Transparency 11, *Triangular Trade Routes*; 12, *17th Century Latin American Viceroyalties* Chapter Transparency 6 NGS PicturePack Transparency Set: *The Age of Exploration, 1 & 2* Vocabulary PuzzleMaker Software NGS PictureShow CD-ROM: *The Age of Exploration, 1 & 2* Turning Points in World History
Chapter Review/Reteaching	Reteaching Activity 6 Skill Reinforcement Activity 6 Spanish Chapter Summary 6	Chapter 6 Digest Audiocassette, Activity, Test* Vocabulary PuzzleMaker Software Student Self-Test and Review Software MindJogger Videoquiz
Chapter Evaluation/Testing	Performance Assessment Activity 6 Chapter 6 Test, Forms A and B	Testmaker

* Also available in Spanish

0:00 OUT OF TIME?   Assign the Chapter 6 summary in the Unit 2 Digest on pages 283–285, and the Chapter 6 Audiocassettes.

Block Schedule

Block scheduling differs from traditional class scheduling in the amount of time allotted to each period. The extended time frame provided by block scheduling affords you the opportunity to implement a greater number of research-oriented and activity-intense projects to motivate and involve your students. Activities that are particularly suited to use within the block scheduling framework are identified throughout this chapter by the following designation.

KEY TO ABILITY LEVELS

Teaching strategies have been coded for varying learning styles and abilities.

L1 **BASIC** activities for all students
L2 **AVERAGE** activities for average to above-average students
L3 **CHALLENGING** activities for above-average students
LEP **LIMITED ENGLISH PROFICIENCY** activities

Use Glencoe's *Presentation Plus!* multimedia teacher tool to easily present dynamic lessons that visually excite your students. Using Microsoft PowerPoint® you can customize the presentations to create your own personalized lessons.

SECTION RESOURCES

Daily Objectives	Reproducible Resources	Multimedia Resources
Section 1 **Early Explorations** Explain why Europeans risked dangerous ocean voyages to discover sea routes to other parts of the world.	Reproducible Lesson Plan 6-1 Vocabulary Activity 6* Guided Reading Activity 6-1* History Simulation 6 Time Line Activity 6 Source Reading 6 Section Quiz 6-1*	Section Focus Transparency 6-1 Chapter Transparency 6 Student Self-Test and Review Software Testmaker Turning Points in World History: *Age of Exploration*
Section 2 **Overseas Empires** Describe how Europeans exploited the lands and the peoples they found in Africa, Asia, and the Americas.	Reproducible Lesson Plan 6-2 Vocabulary Activity 6* Guided Reading Activity 6-2* People in World History Profiles 31, 32 Mapping History Activity 6 Geography and History Activity 6 Section Quiz 6-2*	Section Focus Transparency 6-2 Mapping History Overlay Transparency 11, *Triangular Trade Routes*; 12, *6th Century Latin American Viceroyalties* NGS PicturePack Transparency Set: *The Age of Exploration, 1 & 2* Student Self-Test and Review Software Testmaker NGS PictureShow CD-ROM: *The Age of Exploration, 1 & 2* Turning Points in World History: *Age of Exploration*
Section 3 **Changing Ways of Life** Analyze how increased trade and colonial expansion set the stage for a global economy.	Reproducible Lesson Plan 6-3 Guided Reading Activity 6-3* Reteaching Activity 6 Enrichment Activity 6 Section Quiz 6-3* Performance Assessment Activity 6 Spanish Chapter Summary 6	Focus on World Art Print 1, Jan Vermeer. *The Artist and His Model as Klio* Section Focus Transparency 6-3 World History and Art Transparency 22, *View of Toledo*; 23, *Mission San Xavier del Bac* Vocabulary PuzzleMaker Software Student Self-Test and Review Software Testmaker

* Also available in Spanish

Chapter Activities

✔ *Performance Assessment Activity*

A Court Case After students have studied the causes for and results of the era of exploration and mercantilism, have them demonstrate their understanding by taking the roles of modern-day government officials in one of the countries explored by Spain, England, and so on. Students who represent countries of the same empire should form groups to brainstorm ideas and plan a course of action intended to file suit in court and claim damages from the exploring country for lasting harm done to the explored country. Ideas may be presented in the form of a speech to a jury or testimony of experts in a role play, or letters laying out a plan of action.

Possible Rubric Features
Accuracy of content information, concept attainment, collaborative planning, argumentation, clarity of presentation (letter), and impact on audience

• *For an additional activity, refer to Activity 6 in the* Performance Assessment Strategies and Activities *booklet.*

ACTIVITY
From the Classroom of...

Scott Shephard
Watertown Senior High
School
Watertown, SD

Why We Explore
Encourage students to think about the general reasons humans explore. This activity also encourages students to compare the motives of explorers from the age of exploration with those of explorers from other eras of investigation.

On the board, write the headings *Motives, Risks,* and *Significant Gains.* Ask students what they know about Christopher Columbus and fill in the chart with facts about his explorations.

Next, give students a list of famous explorers such as Neil Armstrong, Lewis and Clark, Yuri Gagarin, Marco Polo, and Edmund Hillary. Have students use classroom resources to find out about these people, then add facts about them to the chart on the board.

As a follow-up to this activity, ask students to draw some generalizations about the following: Why do we explore? Do the risks of exploration ever outweigh the gains? Was Columbus's voyage riskier than the *Apollo 11* moon mission? As a final evaluation, you might ask students to write an essay that compares and contrasts Columbus with another explorer they choose in the areas of motives, risks, and gains.

MULTIPLE LEARNING STYLES

Verbal/Linguistic
During the age of exploration, many Europeans believed in terrible sea monsters and odd beings that inhabited unknown lands. Have students research and report on some of these legends.

Logical/Mathematical
Have students create a time line of all the voyages of exploration and all the colonial activities described in this chapter.

Visual/Spatial
Have students research Columbus's life and create a mural that summarizes its highlights.

Auditory/Musical
Many old folk songs, such as "Upon Sir Francis Drake's Return," relate stories about the sea. Have students locate such folk songs and report on them. Students may refer to the *Oxford Book of Sea Songs*, edited by Roy Palmer (New York: Oxford University Press, 1986) or obtain recordings of some of the songs from the public library and play them for the class.

Additional Resources

NATIONAL GEOGRAPHIC SOCIETY

Teacher's Corner

INDEX TO NATIONAL GEOGRAPHIC MAGAZINE

The following articles may be used for research relating to this chapter:

- "La Salle's Last Voyage," by Lisa Moore LaRoe, May 1997.
- "San Diego: An Account of Adventure, Deceit, and Intrigue," by Franck Goddio, July 1994.
- "African Slave Trade: The Cruelest Commerce," by Colin Palmer, September 1992.
- "Portugal's Sea Road to the East," by Merle Severy, November 1992.
- "La Isabela: Europe's First Foothold in the New World," by Kathleen A. Deagan, January 1992.
- "Pizarro: Conqueror of the Inca," by John Hemming, February 1992.
- "Track of the Manila Galleons," by Eugene Lyon, September 1990.

NATIONAL GEOGRAPHIC SOCIETY PRODUCTS AVAILABLE FROM GLENCOE

To order the following products for use with this chapter, contact your local Glencoe sales representative, or call Glencoe at 1-800-334-7344:

- *PictureShow: The Age of Exploration, 1 & 2 (CD-ROM)*
- *Age of Exploration (Transparencies)*

BIBLIOGRAPHY

Literature of the Period
Las Casas, Bartolomé de. *A Short Account of the Destruction of the Indies.* Translated and edited by Nigel Griffin. New York: Penguin, 1992. A Dominican missionary's critical account, written in 1552, of the Europeans' brutal treatment of the Native Americans.

Readings for the Student
Yue, Charlotte and David. *Christopher Columbus: How He Did It.* Boston: Houghton Mifflin, 1992. Describes the technology and knowledge on which Columbus's voyages were based.

Readings for the Teacher
The Times Atlas of World Exploration: 3,000 Years of Exploring, Explorers, and Mapmaking. Edited by Felipe Fernandez-Armesto. New York: Harper Collins, 1991. A comprehensive survey.

LOCAL OBJECTIVES

_____
_____
_____
_____
_____
_____
_____
_____
_____
_____
_____
_____
_____
_____
_____
_____
_____
_____
_____
_____
_____
_____
_____
_____

interNET
CONNECTION
Early exploration resources on the World Wide Web
Discoverers Web Home page:
http://www.win.tue.nc/cs/fm/engels/discovery/index.html

CHAPTER THEMES

Chapter Themes are listed by section on this chapter opening page of the Student Edition. A corresponding theme-based activity is available under "TEACH," and a theme-based question is asked in the Section and Chapter Reviews.

The Storyteller

Historical Setting At first Columbus failed to persuade the monarchs of Portugal, England, and France to finance his plan of finding a sea route to Asia by sailing west across the Atlantic Ocean. The deeply religious Catholic queen, Isabella of Spain, was impressed by Columbus's stated intention to use the proceeds of his expedition to seize Jerusalem from the Muslims and to rebuild the Temple of the Jews there. At the queen's insistence, a commission of experts evaluated Columbus's plan but rejected it. Only after Spain's conquest of Granada (January 1492) was Isabella persuaded (April 1492) by royal treasurer Luis de Santangel to seize the opportunity offered by Columbus's plan.

Historical Significance

Answer: *The age of exploration brought the people of Europe, Asia, the Americas, and Africa south of the Sahara into direct contact for the first time and led to a transfer of ideas and products. However, the European process of colonization took a great toll in human life and often had a negative impact on cultures that were conquered.*

Chapter
6   1400–1750

Expanding Horizons

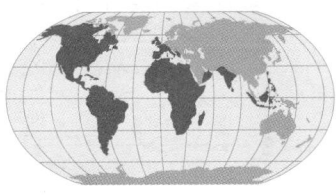

Chapter Themes

▶ **Innovation** European sailors borrow technological and navigational ideas from Asia. *Section 1*

▶ **Movement** European nations establish colonies in the lands they explore in Asia, Africa, and the Americas. *Section 2*

▶ **Change** The wealth of overseas colonies sparks the Commercial Revolution in Europe. *Section 3*

The Storyteller

On the night of October 11, 1492, Christopher Columbus scanned the horizon, praying that landfall was near. "About 10 o'clock at night, while standing on the sterncastle, I thought I saw a light to the west. It looked like a little wax candle bobbing up and down. It had the same appearance as a light or torch belonging to fishermen or travellers…."

The light flickered out, though, and the ship sailed on. The moon rose, but no land appeared. Two hours later, the boom of a cannon roared across the water. A sailor aboard the Pinta, *the fastest of the expedition's three ships, had sighted land. For Spain and other nations of Europe, the land that appeared in the darkness was part of a far greater treasure. As a result of Columbus's voyage, contacts increased among Europeans, Native Americans, Africans, and Asians.*

Historical Significance

How were Europe, Asia, Africa, and the Americas changed as the result of cross-cultural contacts from the 1400s to the 1700s?

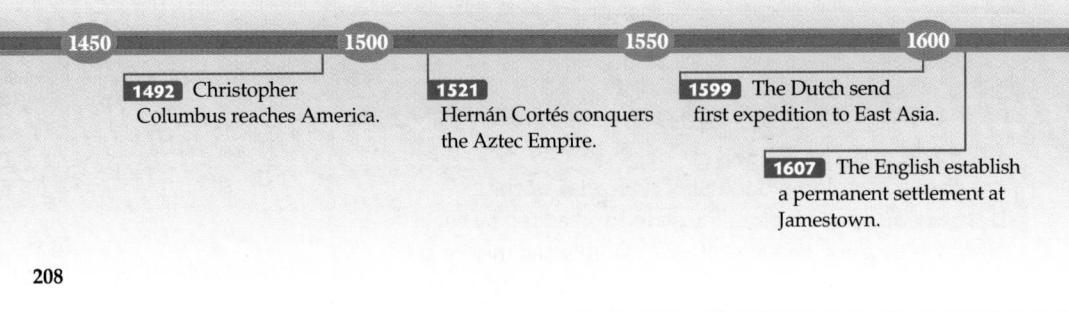

1450   **1500**   **1550**   **1600**

1492 Christopher Columbus reaches America.

1521 Hernán Cortés conquers the Aztec Empire.

1599 The Dutch send first expedition to East Asia.

1607 The English establish a permanent settlement at Jamestown.

208

GEOGRAPHY CONNECTION

Location Using a world map or globe, have students locate Portugal, Spain, the Netherlands, England, France, North and South America, the islands of the Caribbean, Africa, the East Indies (now Indonesia), India, and the Philippines. Into what three major oceans are the great waters of the world divided? *(Pacific, Atlantic, Indian)* Which ocean is the largest and which the smallest? *(The Pacific is the largest and the Indian the smallest.)* Have students note the distances from Europe to India, the islands of Indonesia, and the coast of the Americas. **L1**

Although Dutch artists painted pictures with nautical subjects throughout the seventeenth century, English painters began to respond artistically to their country's nautical activity only at the beginning of the eighteenth century. English artists such as Samuel Scott put on canvas faithful depictions of actual scenes in English seaports.

Visualizing History This busy English port of the 1700s reveals England's position as one of Europe's major seafaring nations.

 Performance Assessment

Refer to the activity on page 208C of the Planning Guide.

 For an additional activity, refer to Activity 6 in the *Performance Assessment Strategies and Activities* booklet.

Your History Journal

Imagine crossing the Atlantic, the Pacific, or the Indian Ocean in the early 1600s. Compared to today, ships were small, and the journey was neither safe nor pleasant. Write a diary of a few days on such a voyage.

Using Your History Journal

Suggest that students consider such basic aspects of daily life aboard ship as diet, sleeping conditions, and sanitary facilities.

GLENCOE TECHNOLOGY

 VIDEODISC
Use MindJogger to preview chapter content.

MindJogger Videoquiz

 Chapter 6
Disc 1 Side A

 Also available in VHS.

Chapter 6 *Expanding Horizons* **209**

➕ EXTRA CREDIT PROJECT

Issues in History Historians are still debating whether the early explorers should be viewed primarily as heroes or as exploiters. Have students research this question and report to the class not only on the contributions to knowledge that resulted from the voyages of exploration but also on their negative impact on Native American cultures. Suggested resources: H. Faber, *The Discoverers of America*; M. E. Jones, ed., *Christopher Columbus and His Legacy*; S. E. Morison, *The Great Explorers: The European Discovery of America*; and R. Wright, *Stolen Continents: The Americas Through Indian Eyes Since 1492.*

1432 Prince Henry the Navigator's explorers reach the Azores.

1488 Bartholomeu Dias of Portugal sails to the tip of Africa.

1519 Magellan expedition sets sail from Seville, Spain.

SECTION THEME

▶ **Innovation** European sailors borrow technological and navigational ideas from Asia.

Answer: *Their hopes for profit and for spreading Christianity made the risks seem worthwhile.*

FOCUS

Section Objective

Explain why Europeans risked dangerous ocean voyages to discover sea routes to other parts of the world.

BELLRINGER
Motivational Activity

Before taking roll at the beginning of the class period, project Section Focus Transparency 6-1 and have students answer the activity questions. Discuss students' responses. This activity is also available as a blackline master.

Vocabulary Pre-check

Use Vocabulary Activity 6 to introduce vocabulary terms.
L1 LEP

Section 1

Early Explorations

Setting the Scene

▶ **Terms to Define**
cartographer, line of demarcation, circumnavigation

▶ **People to Meet**
Prince Henry the Navigator, Bartholomeu Dias, Vasco da Gama, Christopher Columbus, Ferdinand Magellan

▶ **Places to Locate**
Cape of Good Hope, Strait of Magellan

Find Out Why did Europeans risk dangerous ocean voyages to discover sea routes to other parts of the world?

The Storyteller

Wealth was on everyone's mind when they thought about the New World. Ferdinand and Isabella wrote, "We have commanded [Columbus] to return ... because thereby our Lord God is served, His Holy Faith extended and our own realms increased." The King and Queen offered financial incentives for accompanying Columbus: "Whatever persons wish to ... dwell in ... Hispaniola ... shall pay no tax whatsoever and shall have for their own ... the houses which they build and the lands which they work...." As a final enticement, Columbus insisted, "The Indians are the wealth of Hispaniola—for they perform all labor of men and beasts."

Spanish treasure

—adapted from *Ferdinand and Isabella*, Felipe Fernández-Armesto, 1975

---

n the 1400s European explorers tested uncharted oceans in search of a better trade route to Asia. They left their homelands filled with a desire for gold, glory, and for spreading Christianity. In just over 250 years, their ventures had destroyed and built empires at a great cost in human life. Their efforts, however, linked people of different cultures and ended forever the isolation of the world's major civilizations.

Age of Exploration

Europe in the 1300s had depended on spices from Asia. Such spices as pepper, cinnamon, and nutmeg were in great demand. Used chiefly to flavor and preserve meat, spices were also used for perfumes, cosmetics, and medicine.

The spice trade was controlled by Arab and Venetian merchants. Chinese and Indian traders sold spices to Arab merchants, who then shipped the cargoes overland to Europe and reaped huge profits in the sale of the spices to the Venetians. Europeans, eager to amass quick fortunes through direct trade with Asians, began to look for quicker routes eastward. Because the Mongols by the mid-1300s could no longer guarantee safe passage for traders on overland routes, Europeans were forced to consider the sea as a possible route to Asia.

Several motivations led Europeans into an era of exploration. Not only did merchants seek a profitable trade with Asia, but also church leaders sought to halt the expansion of Islam and to spread Christian teachings. Learning and imagination also played a part. Renaissance thinkers had expanded the European world view to include new possibilities for exploration and discovery.

Overseas voyages would end Europe's isolation and set it on the path of worldwide expansion.

SECTION RESOURCES

Reproducible Masters
- Reproducible Lesson Plan 6-1
- Vocabulary Activity 6
- Guided Reading Activity 6-1
- History Simulation 6
- Time Line Activity 6
- Source Reading 6
- Section Quiz 6-1

Transparencies
- Section Focus Transparency 6-1
- Chapter Transparency 6

Multimedia
- Student Self-Test and Review Software
- Testmaker
- Turning Points in World History: *Age of Exploration*

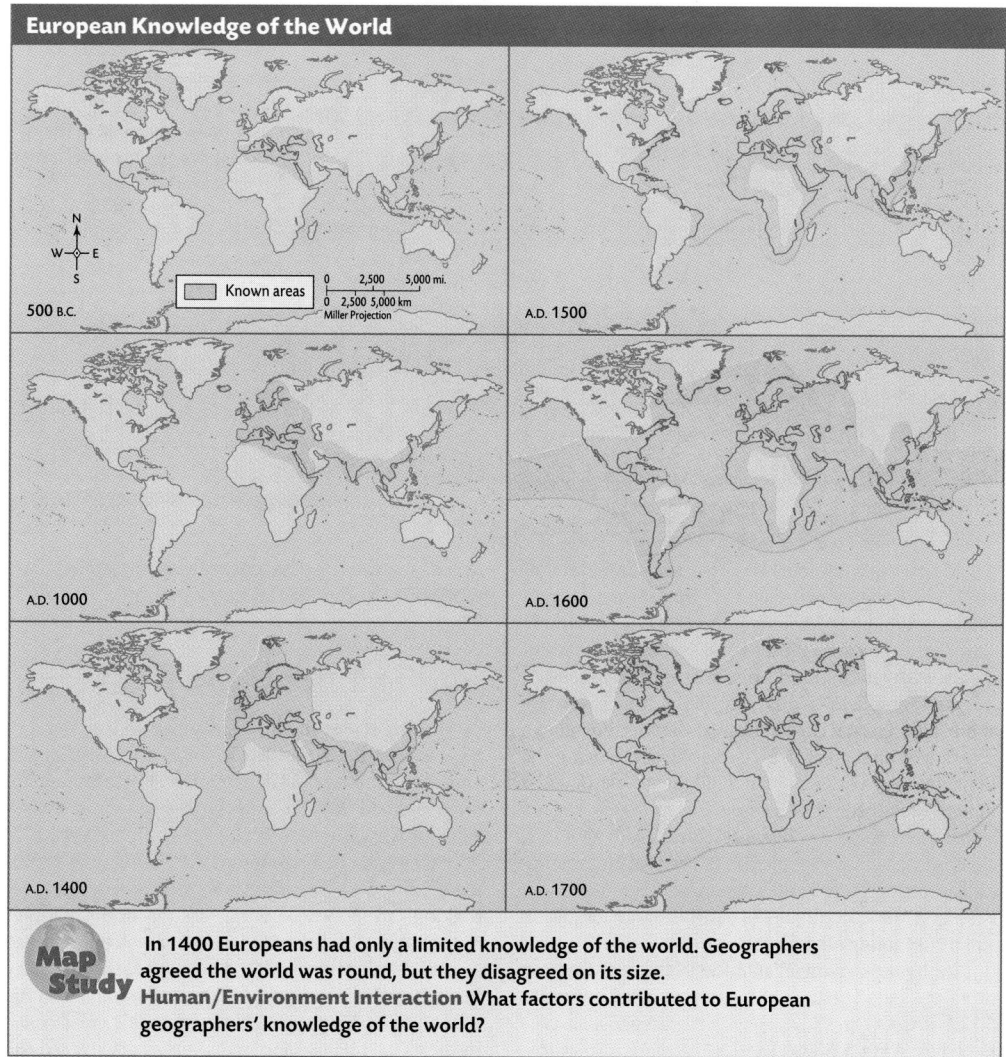

European Knowledge of the World

Known areas

0   2,500   5,000 mi.
0 2,500 5,000 km
Miller Projection

500 B.C.

A.D. 1500

A.D. 1000

A.D. 1600

A.D. 1400

A.D. 1700

Map Study In 1400 Europeans had only a limited knowledge of the world. Geographers agreed the world was round, but they disagreed on its size. **Human/Environment Interaction** What factors contributed to European geographers' knowledge of the world?

They would also prepare the way for the rise of the world's first global age.

Technology of Exploration

Open-water ocean sailing—necessary to find a water route to Asia—required sailors trained in navigation, accurate maps, and oceangoing ships. For exploration to succeed, ships had to be able both to leave the coastal waters and sight of land and to return home. Ancient navigators stayed close to the coast, using landmarks to determine their position. Later, sailors who traveled beyond sight of land used the positions of stars and the sun

to determine in which direction they were traveling. Hourglasses told them how long they had traveled. Keeping track of speed, direction, and time theoretically enabled a captain to tell where the ship was. However, these calculations were very inaccurate.

The compass, of Chinese origin, enabled sailors to determine geographical direction. By 1100, sailors used the astrolabe—perfected by the Arabs—to determine the altitude of the sun or other heavenly bodies. But in practice, standing on the deck of a heaving ship, few ship captains had the skill and patience that the astrolabe required.

Chapter 6 *Expanding Horizons* **211**

TEACH

Guided Practice

THEME Innovation

Have students discuss the design innovations of the caravel that contributed to successful voyages by the Portuguese and Spanish. (*lateen sails, multiple masts, rudder at stern*) **L1**

Map Study

Answer
inventions such as the compass and the astrolabe, and the reappearance of Ptolemy's maps in Europe

POINT

Age of Exploration
What impact did European voyages of exploration have on the course of world history?
They ended Europe's long isolation and set it on the paths of global expansion and greater contact among different regions of the world. In the course of this expansion, indigenous peoples were greatly affected.

VIDEODISC
Turning Points in World History

Side One
Chapter 9

Title: *Age of Exploration*

COOPERATIVE LEARNING ACTIVITY

Cultural Life Early Spanish and Portuguese explorers encountered many different cultures in the Americas (including Arawak, Carib, Maya, Aztec, Inca). Organize the class into small groups and have each group research and report on one of the indigenous American cultures. Remind students that each group member is responsible for contributing to the overall effort. Each student should be assigned one of the following areas to research: geographic location and method of subsistence, arts and crafts, religious beliefs, customs, and the effect of European contact on the culture. One or more students may illustrate the report. **L2**

Chapter 6
Section 1

The American artist J.L.G. Ferris painted *The Eve of Discovery*, showing a caravel as it may have appeared in the 1400s. *Why was the caravel a good ship for sailing up rivers?*

An astrolabe

Visualizing History

A true caravel had four masts, one with square sails, the other three with lateen sails. The *Niña* and the *Pinta*, two of Columbus's three ships for the historic 1492 voyage, were caravels. Astrolabes were in use as early as the sixth century but came into wide use by Europeans and Muslims from the early Middle Ages.
Answer to Caption: *Its rudder made it maneuverable, and it drew little water, allowing it to travel in shallow waters.*

Literature Have students read an excerpt from one of Columbus's journals. Discuss what the excerpt reveals about Columbus and his times. **L2**

 History Simulation 6

 Chapter Transparency 6

Independent Practice

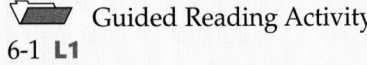 Guided Reading Activity 6-1 **L1**

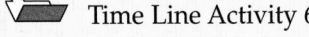 Time Line Activity 6

 Source Reading Activity 6

Global Gourmet

Americas Florida's citrus industry can be traced back to Columbus's second voyage to the Americas in 1493. The citrus seeds the navigator brought to the West Indies took root there and eventually made their way to Mexico and Florida.

Maps were another problem for early navigators. Most maps were wildly inaccurate, drawn from scattered impressions of travelers and traders. Cartographers, or mapmakers, filled their parchments with lands found only in rumor or legend.

Cartographers' skills gradually improved. By about 1300, coastal charts showed the Mediterranean coastline with a great degree of accuracy. During the Renaissance, works by the Hellenistic astronomer Ptolemy reappeared in Europe. His maps, improved over the centuries by Byzantine and Arab scholars, gave Europeans a new picture of the world. Ptolemy also introduced the grid system of map references based on the coordinates of latitude and longitude still in use today all over the world.

Innovations were also made in the construction of ships. Late in the 1400s, shipwrights began to outfit ships with triangle-shaped lateen sails perfected by Arab traders. These sails made it possible for ships to sail against the wind, not simply with it. Shipwrights also abandoned using a single mast with one large sail. Multiple masts, with several smaller sails hoisted one above the other, made ships travel much faster. In addition, moving the rudder from the ship's side to the stern made ships more maneuverable.

In the 1400s a European ship called a caravel incorporated all these improvements. The caravel was up to 65 feet (20 m) in length with the capability of carrying about 130 tons (118 metric tons) of cargo. Because a caravel drew little water, it allowed explorers to venture up shallow inlets and to beach the ship to make repairs. A Venetian mariner called the caravels "the best ships that sailed the seas." The caravels also carried new types of weapons—rifles and cannons.

Portugal Leads the Way

Portugal was the first European country to venture out on the Atlantic Ocean in search of spices and gold. Between 1420 and 1580, Portuguese captains pushed farther and farther down the west coast of Africa in search of a sea route to Asia.

Although **Prince Henry the Navigator**, son of King John I of Portugal, was not a sailor—never making an ocean voyage—he brought together mapmakers, mathematicians, and astronomers to study navigation. He also sponsored many Portuguese exploratory voyages westward into the Atlantic and southward down Africa's west coast. In the early 1400s Henry's explorers discovered the Azores, the Madeira Islands, and the Cape Verde Islands. These discoveries were the foundation of what in the 1500s became the Portuguese Empire.

In August 1487 **Bartholomeu Dias** left Portugal, intent upon finding the southern tip of Africa. In 1488 his expedition discovered the southern tip of Africa, which was later named the **Cape of Good Hope**. Dias's voyage proved that ships could reach East Asia by sailing around Africa.

In 1497 four ships led by **Vasco da Gama** sailed from Portugal for India. The expedition rounded the Cape of Good Hope, made stops at trading centers along the east coast of Africa, and landed at Calicut on the southwest coast of India in 10 months. There da Gama found Hindus and

212 **Chapter 6** *Expanding Horizons*

Learning Style: Visual/Spatial Have students work in pairs or small groups to summarize in pictures on poster board the achievements of Portugal and Spain described in this section. Try to pair competent illustrators with verbally proficient students. Tell students to discuss how the pictures should best convey the information. After the picture or pictures have been sketched and colored in, the groups should write labels summarizing the information the pictures convey. After the posters are completed, display them in the classroom. **L1 LEP**

Richard Schlecht

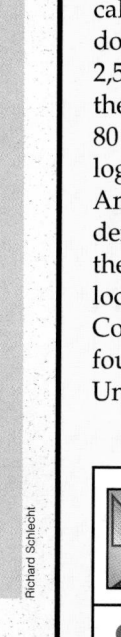

"Little Girl"

The *Niña*—"Little Girl"—was Christopher Columbus's favorite ship, a small, fast, seaworthy vessel about 67 feet long. Descriptions of the *Niña* discovered in a Spanish document from the period have enabled historians to draw pictures of what the craft actually looked like. In this drawing the lines in red show the *Niña's* sails and riggings. The document also revealed that the *Niña* had four masts, not two or three, as previously believed. Columbus's beloved "Little Girl," the most technically advanced craft of her day, probably made three of his four voyages to the Americas.

The Europe of 1500 was on the brink of the modern era. Monarchs Isabella and Ferdinand of Spain could command Columbus and other explorers, who combined knowledge of sophisticated naval technologies with bravery and determination. In quick succession Columbus (1492), Vasco da Gama (1498), and Magellan (1519–21), among others, linked Europe with the rest of the world. The sea-sheltered Americas were invaded. The slave trade expanded and brought much of Africa into the shadow of the Americas. The Muslim peoples of Africa and Asia lost their central position as guardians of trade between Europe, Asia, and Africa. Within a few centuries, the whole world came within European explorers' reach. ⊕

Chapter 6 *Expanding Horizons* **213**

TEACH

Tell students that the fifteenth-century document describing the *Niña* is only one of many so-called Columbus documents. The documents include more than 2,500 notes Columbus wrote in the margins of his books, about 80 letters and notes, copies of the log from his first trip to the Americas, and his will. Ask students where they think most of the books and manuscripts are located. *(Spain)* Tell them that Columbus documents are also found in Italy, France, and the United States.

CURRICULUM CONNECTION

GEOGRAPHY

Columbus's seafaring interest may have been shaped by the geography of his birthplace, the seaport Republic of Genoa, in today's Italy. Lacking much fertile land and surrounded by powerful rival cities like Milan and Florence, many inhabitants of Genoa looked to the Mediterranean Sea in search of their fortunes.

Calico, a cotton cloth that began to be used after 1495, is a shortened version of "Calicut cloth." The first place to export calico was the Indian city Calicut.

Biography

The following videotape program is available from Glencoe.

- **Christopher Columbus: Explorer of the New World**

ASSESS

Check for Understanding

Assign Section 1 Review as homework or as an in-class activity.

⦿ Use Student Self-Test and Review Software to review Section 1.

History & Art
After being dismissed in 1487 by advisers to Ferdinand and Isabella, Columbus did not allow the rejection to cause him to abandon his plan.
Answer to Caption: *He made three voyages after the initial voyage.*

Muslims trading fine silk, porcelain, and spices that made the glass beads and trinkets of the Portuguese appear shoddy.

Da Gama tried to persuade the ruler of Calicut and Muslim merchants in India to trade with the Portuguese. He had little success and returned home. In Portugal, however, da Gama was regarded as a national hero. He had pioneered a water route to India, and he had provided a glimpse of the riches that could come from direct trade with the East.

Spain's Quest for Riches

In the late 1400s Spain ended a long period of internal turmoil and wars against the Moors. Under King Ferdinand and Queen Isabella, Spain entered the race for Asian riches by backing the expeditions of an Italian navigator named **Christopher Columbus**.

Columbus Crosses the Atlantic

In 1492 Christopher Columbus approached Queen Isabella with an intriguing plan—to reach India by sailing west across the Atlantic. For years

History & Art *Columbus Before the Queen* by Peter Rothermel, 1842. National Museum of American Art, Washington, D.C. **Seven years of persistent pleading earned Spain's support.** *How many voyages did Columbus make seeking proof that he had discovered a new route to India?*

214 Chapter 6 *Expanding Horizons*

Columbus had tried unsuccessfully to persuade other European rulers to finance his voyage. With Queen Isabella his persistence paid off.

In August 1492 Columbus sailed from Spain with three small ships. He calculated the distance to India to be 700 leagues, about 2,200 nautical miles; he knew that the actual distance might be greater. To calm the crews' fears, he showed them a log that understated the distance they had sailed from home.

The days out of sight of land wore on and on, however, and the terrified sailors begged Columbus to turn back. After a false sighting of land, the crews began to talk of mutiny. Columbus reluctantly agreed to turn back if they did not reach land within three days.

After midnight on the second day, the expedition sighted land. In the morning Columbus and his men went ashore, becoming the first Europeans to set foot on one of the islands of the Bahamas. Columbus wrote of the inhabitants:

❝ The islanders came to the ships' boats, swimming and bringing us parrots and balls of cotton thread … which they exchanged for … glass beads and hawk bells … they took and gave of what they had very willingly, but it seemed to me that they were poor in every way. They bore no weapons, nor were they acquainted with them, because when I showed them swords they seized them by the edge and so cut themselves from ignorance. ❞

Believing he was off the coast of India, Columbus called the islanders "Indians." Columbus spent the next three months exploring the islands Hispaniola (present-day Haiti and the Dominican Republic) and Cuba in search of gold. Although he found enough gold to raise Spanish hopes, he saw no evidence of the great civilizations of Asia.

When Columbus returned to Spain, Ferdinand and Isabella gave him the title "Admiral of the Ocean Sea, Viceroy and Governor of the Islands he hath discovered in the Indies." Before he died in 1506, Columbus made three more voyages to the Caribbean islands and South America seeking proof that he had discovered a new route to Asia. He died certain that he had.

Even without sure proof, it was difficult for anyone to dispute Columbus's claim. Maps of the time did not show any landmass between Europe and Asia. It was not until 1507 that another Italian explorer, Amerigo Vespucci (veh•SPOO•chee), suggested that Columbus had discovered a "New World." In honor of Vespucci, the name *America* began to appear on maps that included the newly discovered lands.

MAKING CONNECTIONS ACTIVITIES

Technology Have students research and write a brief illustrated report on developments in ship design and construction from antiquity through the age of exploration. Make sure they include mention of Henry the Navigator's role in encouraging the building of new types of ships. **L2**

Cartography Ask students to research and write a brief report on the history of cartography from antiquity (beginning with Babylonian maps on clay tablets) through the age of exploration. Encourage them to focus on how the discoveries of explorers such as Columbus and Magellan transformed the world maps of those days. **L2**

Dividing the World

Both Spain and Portugal wanted to protect their claims in the Americas and turned to the pope for help. In 1493 the pope drew a line of demarcation, an imaginary line running down the middle of the Atlantic from the North Pole to the South Pole. Spain was to have control of all lands to the west of the line, while Portugal was to have control of all lands to the east of the line.

The Portuguese, however, feared that their line was so far to the east that Spain might take over their Asian trade. As a result, in 1494 Spain and Portugal signed the Treaty of Tordesillas (TAWR•duh•SEE•yuhs), an agreement to move the line of demarcation farther west. The treaty divided the entire unexplored world between just two powers, Spain and Portugal.

Voyage of Magellan

In 1519 an expedition led by **Ferdinand Magellan**, a Portuguese soldier of fortune, set sail from Seville under the Spanish flag to find a western route to Asia. The five ships and 260-man crew sailed across the Atlantic and made their way along the eastern coast of South America, searching every bay and inlet for this route.

Along the coast of Argentina, crews of three of the ships attempted a mutiny because Magellan had decided to halt the expedition until spring. Magellan executed the captain who had instigated the mutiny, regained control of the fleet, and resumed the expedition. Finally, near the southern tip of South America, the ships reached a narrow water passageway now called the **Strait of Magellan**. The ships threaded their way through the maze of rocky islands in the 350-mile- (504-km-) long strait. Strong currents and unpredictable gales separated one ship from the others, and its crew forced its return to Spain. Another was shipwrecked.

Magellan's ship and the two other remaining ships finally passed through the strait into the South Sea, which had been discovered and named six years earlier by Vasco Núñez de Balboa. Because the water was so calm, Magellan renamed it the Pacific Ocean. The fleet then sailed nearly four months before reaching land. Water and food ran out, and some sailors died. One of the crew wrote in his journal, "We ate biscuit, which was no longer biscuit, but powder of biscuits swarming with worms, for they had eaten the good."

At last the ships reached the present-day Philippines. Caught in a skirmish between a local chief and his enemy, Magellan was killed. The surviving crew escaped and sailed for Spain.

In 1522, after three years at sea, the last ship with its 18 survivors arrived at Seville, completing the first circumnavigation, or circling of the globe. The spices they brought back barely covered the cost of the voyage, but the expedition had a value far beyond money. It proved that the world was round and much larger than anyone had believed, that the oceans of the world were connected, and that the lands discovered by Columbus were not part of Asia.

 Discovery of Magellan Strait (artist unknown). **By this point in Magellan's voyage, one ship foundered on the rocks and another turned back.** *What did the journey prove?*

Chapter 6 Section 1

History & Art Until the opening of the Panama Canal (1914) shortened the water route from the Atlantic to the Pacific, the Strait of Magellan remained an important sailing-ship route.

Answer to Caption: *that the world was round and larger than previously believed, that the oceans were connected, and that the lands Columbus discovered were not part of Asia*

Evaluate

Section Quiz 6-1

Use the Testmaker to create a customized quiz for Section 1.

Reteach

Organize the class into two groups. Ask both groups to prepare a quiz based on the information discussed in this section. Then have the members of each group take the other group's quiz.

Enrich

Have students use library resources to research the expeditions of Amerigo Vespucci or Vasco Nuñez de Balboa. Then have them prepare a script about the explorer's expedition.

CLOSE

Write these headings on the chalkboard: *Country Financing Voyage, Explorer, Discovery, Date, Result.* Ask volunteers to provide the information for each heading.

SECTION 1 REVIEW

Recall
1. **Define** cartographer, line of demarcation, circumnavigation.
2. **Identify** Prince Henry the Navigator, Bartholomeu Dias, Vasco da Gama, Christopher Columbus, Ferdinand Magellan.

3. **Explain** why Portugal and Spain wanted to find a sea route to Asia.

Critical Thinking
4. **Synthesizing Information** Using the text as a resource, write a journal entry describing your experiences as a sailor on an expedition of Dias, Columbus, Magellan, or da Gama.

Understanding Themes
5. **Innovation** What sciences and new technologies led to voyages of exploration?

SECTION 1 REVIEW ANSWERS

1. All vocabulary words are defined in the Glossary.
2. Henry, 212; Dias, 212; da Gama, 212; Columbus, 214; Magellan; 215
3. quest for riches, desire to spread Christianity

4. Students should include details of the expedition they select.
5. **INNOVATION** sciences: cartography, math, astronomy; technologies: compass, astrolabe, caravels

1500 Pedro Alvares Cabral claims Brazil for Portugal.

1532 Francisco Pizarro of Spain invades the Inca Empire.

1608 France's Samuel de Champlain founds Quebec.

1640 English planters introduce sugarcane in the West Indies.

SECTION THEME

▶ **Movement** European nations establish colonies in the lands they explore in Asia, Africa, and the Americas.

Find Out

Answer: *They enslaved the peoples and imposed their religion on them and commandeered the lands' valuable resources.*

FOCUS

Section Objective

Describe how Europeans exploited the lands and the peoples they found in Africa, Asia, and the Americas.

BELLRINGER
Motivational Activity

Before taking roll at the beginning of the class period, project Section Focus Transparency 6-2 and have students answer the activity questions. Discuss students' responses.

This activity is also available as a blackline master.

Vocabulary Pre-check

Use Vocabulary Activity 6 to introduce vocabulary terms.
L1 LEP

Section 2

Overseas Empires

Setting the Scene

▶ **Terms to Define**
conquistador, triangular trade, the Middle Passage

▶ **People to Meet**
Pedro Alvares Cabral, Hernán Cortés, Montezuma II, Francisco Pizarro, Atahualpa, Henry Hudson, Jacques Cartier, Samuel de Champlain, John Cabot

▶ **Places to Locate**
Brazil, Peru, West Indies, Quebec, Jamestown

Find Out
How did the Europeans exploit the lands and the peoples they found in Africa, Asia, and the Americas?

The Storyteller

Native Americans digging gold

John Sparke, who traveled with English admiral John Hawkins, wrote an account of the inhabitants of the Florida coast in 1589: "They have for apothecary [medicine] herbs, trees, roots, and gum, myrrh, and frankincense, with many others, whereof I know not the names.... Gold and silver they want [lack] not, for when the Frenchmen came, they offered it for little or nothing. They received for a hatchet two pounds of gold. The soldiers, being greedy, took it from them, giving them nothing for it. When the Floridians perceived that, they stopped wearing their gold ornaments, for fear that they would be taken away."

—from *The Hawkins Voyages,* edited by Clements R. Markham, reprinted in *The Annals of America,* 1968

216   **Chapter 6**   *Expanding Horizons*

The Treaty of Tordesillas claimed to divide the world between Spain and Portugal. Only Spain and Portugal, however, recognized the treaty. The Netherlands, France, and England soon joined them in a race to exploit wealth from the lands beyond Europe.

Portugal and Spain

Portugal's main interest lay in Africa and Asia, and in trade rather than colonization. When the Portuguese became the first Europeans to reach the Indian Ocean, they found themselves in waters already thoroughly explored by seafarers from Asian lands. Eager to seize control of the spice trade, the Portuguese reacted quickly to Vasco da Gama's voyage to India. In 1500, less than six months after da Gama's return, 13 ships were dispatched to Calicut. Led by **Pedro Alvares Cabral**, the Portuguese won a bloody trade war with Muslim merchants and defeated a large Arab fleet to establish Portuguese control of the Indian Ocean.

The Portuguese then built naval bases along the Indian Ocean—along the Persian Gulf and in Southeast Asia. They soon controlled shipping in the Indian Ocean. Next, they expanded eastward toward the Moluccas, or the Spice Islands. From the Spice Islands, the Portuguese established trading ports in China and Japan.

Portugal also colonized the area of present-day **Brazil**. Cabral claimed this territory as he swung west across the Atlantic to India in 1500. Because this area of South America juts east of the line of demarcation, it became Portuguese. The rest of South America had been claimed by Spain.

Settlers in Brazil grew income-producing crops such as sugarcane, tobacco, coffee, and cotton. Because the local population did not supply enough labor, enslaved people were brought from Africa. By the late 1500s, Brazil was one of Portugal's most important colonies.

SECTION RESOURCES

Reproducible Masters
- Reproducible Lesson Plan 6-2
- Vocabulary Activity 6
- Guided Reading Activity 6-2
- People in World History Profiles 31, 32
- Mapping History Activity 6
- Geography and History Activity 6
- Section Quiz 6-2

Transparencies
- Section Focus Transparency 6-2
- Mapping History Overlay Transparencies 11, 12
- The Age of Exploration, 1 & 2

Multimedia
- Student Self-Test and Review Software
- Testmaker
- The Age of Exploration, 1 & 2
- Turning Points in World History: *Age of Exploration*

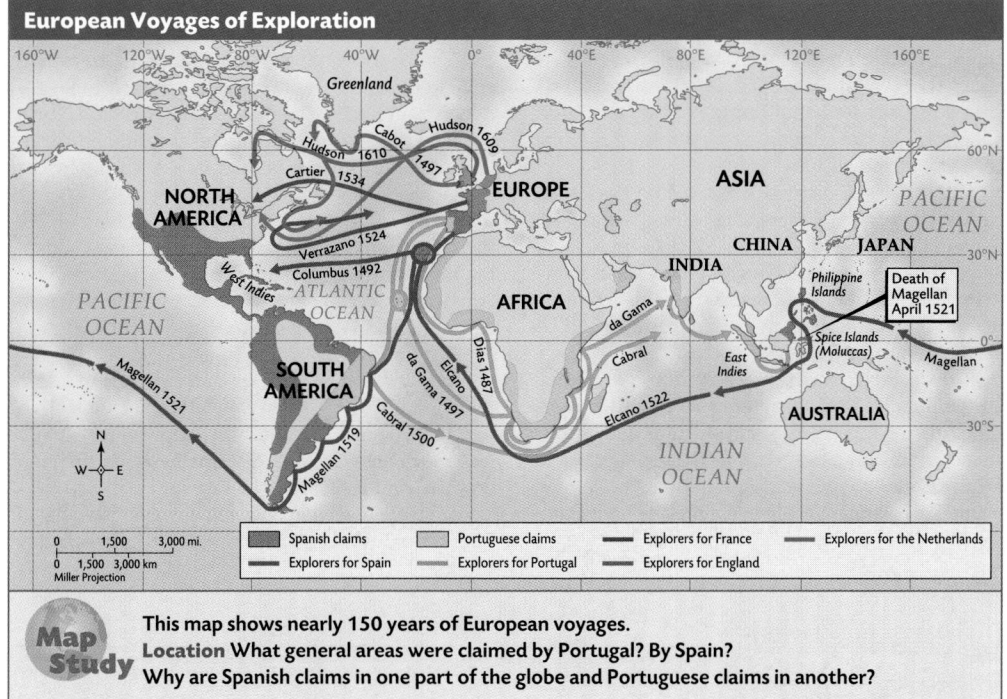

European Voyages of Exploration

Spanish claims | Portuguese claims | Explorers for France | Explorers for the Netherlands
Explorers for Spain | Explorers for Portugal | Explorers for England

Map Study

This map shows nearly 150 years of European voyages.
Location What general areas were claimed by Portugal? By Spain?
Why are Spanish claims in one part of the globe and Portuguese claims in another?

TEACH

Guided Practice

THEME Movement

Have students discuss the movement of goods and people described in this section. Ask them to name some examples of colonies and trading settlements. (*Portugal: Brazil; Spain: West Indies and the Americas; the Netherlands: Indonesia and Africa*) Have students give examples of some of the goods exported from these areas. (*Brazil: sugarcane, tobacco, coffee, cotton; West Indies and the Americas: animal hides, sugar, tobacco; Indonesia: sugar, spices, coffee, tea*) **L1**

Map Study

Answer

Portugal's claims are primarily in Africa, India, Southeast Asia, and the tip of Brazil; Spain's claims are in the Americas and the Philippines; the Line of Demarcation set by the Treaty of Tordesillas divided the world between Spain and Portugal.

Map Skills Practice

Reading a map How did the destinations change over time? (*After Columbus crossed the Atlantic, explorers searched for a western, rather than an eastern, route to the East Indies.*)

 People in World History Profiles 31, 32

 Mapping History Overlay Transparency 11, *Triangular Trade Routes*; 12, *17th Century Latin American Viceroyalties*

Spain

Spanish conquistadors, or conquerors, came to the Americas "to serve God and his Majesty, to give light to those who were in darkness and to grow rich as all men desire to do."

One conquistador, **Hernán Cortés**, landed in Mexico in 1519 with about 600 men, 16 horses, and a few cannons. Guided by Malinche (mah•LIHN •chay), a Native American woman who learned Spanish, Cortés allied with local enemies of the Aztecs and journeyed inland to Tenochtitlán. Meanwhile, in the Aztec capital, messengers told the Aztec ruler **Montezuma II** that the approaching soldiers were "supernatural creatures riding on hornless deer, preceded by wild animals on leashes, dressed in iron." Thinking that Cortés might be the long-awaited god-king Quetzalcoatl returning from the east, Montezuma offered gifts of gold.

Tenochtitlán's riches were beyond anything the Spaniards had ever seen. Soon fighting broke out. With the advantage of horses and guns, the Spanish force ultimately slaughtered thousands of Aztec people. Within three years, Aztec resistance had ended and Cortés ruled Mexico.

In 1532 another conquistador, **Francisco Pizarro**, invaded the Inca Empire in present-day

Peru. The Spaniards' arrival followed a conflict in which the Incan ruler **Atahualpa** (AH•tuh•WAHL •puh) won the throne from a brother. Aided by Native American allies, Pizarro captured Atahualpa and had thousands of Inca massacred. Although a ransom was paid for Atahualpa's release, the Spaniards killed him anyway. Inca resistance continued, but Spanish forces eventually conquered vast stretches of Inca territory in South America.

Building an Empire

By the 1600s, Spain's empire in the Americas included much of North America and South America as well as islands in the **West Indies**. Keeping close watch over their empire, Spanish monarchs named viceroys, or royal representatives, to rule local provinces with the advice of councils of Spanish settlers.

Spain had two goals for its American empire—to acquire its wealth and to convert Native Americans to Christianity. Farmers set up plantations, or large estates, for the growing of sugarcane; landowners drew gold and silver from mines. At the same time priests founded missions—settlements where many Native Americans lived, worked, and adopted European ways.

Chapter 6 *Expanding Horizons* **217**

COOPERATIVE LEARNING ACTIVITY

Research Organize the class into four research groups and ask each group to become experts on one period in the life of Rembrandt. One group might focus on the artist's early years (1606–1625), another the Leiden years (1625–1631), a third his Amsterdam years (1632–1640), and a fourth his last years (1640–1669). Each group member should have a specific assignment, with some students focusing on specific paintings, etchings, or drawings of each period. After individual students compile their research notes, each group should meet to plan a presentation format—panel discussion, poster presentation, or short dramatic sketch. Each group should make its presentation to the entire class. **L2**

NATIONAL GEOGRAPHIC SOCIETY

Use these materials to enrich student understanding of the age of exploration.

- **NGS PICTURESHOW CD-ROM**
  The Age of Exploration, 1 & 2

- **NGS PICTUREPACK TRANSPARENCY SET**
  The Age of Exploration, 1 & 2

Independent Practice

📁 Guided Reading Activity 6-2 **L1**

📁 Mapping History Activity 6

📁 Geography and History Activity 6

Religion Explain to the class that Spain and France were predominantly Roman Catholic countries. The English and Dutch were primarily Protestant. Ask students how much importance each nation placed on converting the native populations it encountered to Christianity. *(Jesuit missionaries from France and Spain were the most dedicated to conversion.)* **L2**

Biography

The following videotape is available from Glencoe:

- **Ponce de León: The First Conquistador**

Under the encomienda system, Spanish monarchs granted landowners the right to use Native American labor. Native Americans, however, were enslaved and mistreated. Disease also took its toll. Exposed to diseases from Europe for the first time, millions of Native Americans died during the first 50 years of Spanish rule.

A few priests, such as Bartolomé de Las Casas, tried to protect the Native Americans. The Spanish government responded with laws meant to end abuses, but the laws were never enforced. In many cases, Native Americans resisted Spanish rule on their own by preserving their local cultures and by staging periodic revolts.

The decline in the Native American population led the Spaniards to bring over enslaved workers from Africa. As sugarcane production and profits soared, more and more Africans arrived to work in the fields and in various trades. In time, the coming together of African, Native American, and European peoples in Spain's American colonies gave rise to a new culture.

Colonies of the Netherlands

The Netherlands was also interested in expansion. In the late 1500s the Dutch won their independence from Spain. This small country on the North Sea had few natural resources and limited farmland. A large Dutch middle class saw commerce as the key to survival.

The period of the 1600s was the golden age of the Netherlands. Dutch ships were efficient, carrying more cargo and smaller crews than other ships. Amsterdam became the world's largest commercial city, and the Dutch enjoyed the world's highest standard of living.

The first Dutch expedition to East Asia returned in 1599. Three years later the Dutch chartered the Dutch East India Company to expand trade and ensure close relations between the government and enterprises in Asia.

In 1619 the company set up headquarters at Batavia on the island of Java in present-day Indonesia. Soon the Dutch controlled island trade

---

Images of the Times

The Dutch Republic

With no monarchy or aristocracy, the tastes and ideals of society as reflected in Dutch art were determined largely by the middle class.

The Flower Vendor and the Vegetable Vendor by Arnout de Muysor focuses on two important themes in Dutch painting of this period—middle-class life and trade.

The World Upside-down by Jan Steen, the son of a brewer, is representative of his earthy, humorous scenes of ordinary people.

218

Images of the Times   The Dutch Republic

The formal name of the Dutch Republic was the United Provinces of the Netherlands. Formed in 1579, the republic experienced a golden age during the seventeenth century, when it was not only the center of a world colonial empire but also a center of international finance and culture. The comic perspective of Jan Steen (1626–1679) makes him unique among leading seventeenth-century Dutch painters. Gabriel Metsu (1629–1667) began painting religious subjects but found the life of the marketplace better suited to his personality. Rembrandt (1606–1669) movingly conveyed the human aspect of all his subjects, whether drawn from the Bible, history, mythology, or everyday life.

in sugar, spices, coffee, and tea. Using Batavia as a base, the Dutch pushed the Portuguese and English out of Asian outposts. After taking Malacca from the Portuguese in 1641, the Netherlands controlled all trade with the Spice Islands. The Dutch also used force against local Muslim rulers to win lands and ports in the region.

At the same time, the Dutch set out for North America. An English navigator, **Henry Hudson**, claimed land for the Dutch along the Atlantic coast of North America, and in 1621 the government chartered the Dutch West India Company to establish colonies in the Americas. The company founded New Amsterdam on Manhattan Island at the mouth of the Hudson River. This settlement was soon a center for European and colonial trade.

The Dutch established a colony in Africa as well. In 1652 Dutch farmers known as Boers settled at the Cape of Good Hope to provide fresh food and water for sailing ships. By the 1700s, however, Dutch power was declining, and England had emerged as Europe's leading maritime nation.

French and English Colonies

The French and the English played only a small part in the early voyages of exploration. Religious conflicts and civil wars kept their interests focused at home. During the 1500s, however, France and England searched for overseas trading colonies.

Thwarted by the Portuguese and later the Dutch control of Asian markets, England and France turned toward North America and the Caribbean. In general, the French companies sought quick profits from trade rather than the long-term investment of farming. For the English, colonies could provide the raw materials—lumber, fish, sugarcane, rice, and wheat—they would otherwise have to purchase from other countries.

France

In 1524 the French hired an Italian captain, Giovanni da Verrazano, to find a Northwest Passage through America to Asia. Da Verrazano explored the North American coast from North

Geography: Movement Have students work in pairs to locate information, including maps, about the explorations of Cartier, Champlain, Marquette, and Joliet. Ask them to draw maps showing each explorer's routes and claims in North America. **L3**

Linking Past and Present

Wall Street, the major financial center of the United States, gets its name from a wall built by the colonists of New Amsterdam in 1653. The wall, meant to protect the colonists from enemy attacks, fell down within a few years. When the colonists built a road in its place, it became known as Wall Street.

ABCNEWS INTERACTIVE™

 VIDEODISC
Turning Points in World History

Side One
Chapter 9

Title: *Age of Exploration*
Subject: As western Europeans sought new routes to Asia, they found lands unknown to them; Europeans seeking wealth and power conquered these lands.
Ask: In what ways was the age of exploration a turning point in history? *(Indigenous peoples were mistreated, killed, or died from disease; new crops were brought to Europe, and other crops were introduced to the Americas.)*

Rembrandt van Rijn, the celebrated Dutch painter, earned fame with his portraits of himself and of his family. Although he died poor and forgotten, his paintings were of more spiritual depth than those of his contemporaries.

REFLECTING ON THE TIMES

1. How does Dutch art compare with art from a nation like France that had a monarch and nobility?
2. Why did Rembrandt's work receive greater acclaim after he died?

219

ANSWERS TO REFLECTING ON THE TIMES

1. Dutch art focuses on middle-class, not aristocratic, concerns.
2. People later responded to the spiritual depth of his portraits and paintings.

ASSESS

Check for Understanding

Assign Section 2 Review as homework or as an in-class activity.

 Use Student Self-Test and Review Software to review Section 2.

Evaluate

Section Quiz 6-2

 Use the Testmaker to create a customized quiz for Section 2.

The following videotape program is available from Glencoe:
- **Pocahontas: Her True Story**

Carolina to Maine without success. Ten years later the French navigator **Jacques Cartier** continued the search and sailed up the St. Lawrence River to the site of the present-day city of Montreal. He claimed much of eastern Canada for France.

In 1608 **Samuel de Champlain,** a French mapmaker, founded **Quebec,** the first permanent French settlement in the Americas. In 1673 missionaries Jacques Marquette and Louis Joliet explored the Mississippi Valley. Later, Robert Cavelier, known as Sieur de La Salle, claimed the entire inland region surrounding the Mississippi River for France.

Like the Spanish, the French sent Jesuit missionaries to convert Native Americans to Christianity. French explorers traded the Native Americans blankets, guns, and wine for animal skins. Trapping, fishing, and lumbering were also profitable.

Some French settlers went to the West Indies, where they claimed the islands of St. Kitts, Martinique, and Guadeloupe. The French brought enslaved Africans to work on sugar and tobacco plantations on the islands. Although most of their interests were in North America, the French also established trading posts in India.

England

England also showed an interest in overseas trade. In 1497 the Italian-born navigator **John Cabot** explored the coast of present-day Newfoundland. During the 1500s, English sea captains, such as Francis Drake, raided Spanish ships for gold and silver. English overseas expansion, however, did not begin until the founding of the English East India Company in 1600. This trading enterprise set up posts in India and Southeast Asia.

During the 1600s, the English also founded settlements in the Americas. On West Indian islands, such as Jamaica, they introduced sugarcane, worked by enslaved African labor. **Jamestown,** the earliest English settlement in North America was founded in 1607 in present-day Virginia. In 1620 devout Protestants, calling themselves Pilgrims, sought religious freedom by establishing Plymouth in present-day Massachusetts. Before landing, the Pilgrims set down rules for governing Plymouth in the Mayflower Compact:

> **❝** We, whose names are underwritten… having undertaken for the glory of God, and advancement of the Christian faith…a voyage to plant [a] colony…do…enact, constitute, and frame …just and equal Laws…as shall be

thought most [appropriate] and convenient for the general good of the colony. **❞**

In the 1600s and 1700s, English settlements arose and thrived along the eastern coast of North America. In northern areas, family-operated farms emerged, while in southern areas, plantation farming based on African enslaved labor was established. Although English monarchs supervised these settlements by sending out governors, the English in North America enjoyed a large degree of self-government in their representative assemblies modeled on the English Parliament.

English settlement, however, pushed out the earlier inhabitants, the Native Americans. Concerned about land, the English had little desire to Christianize Native Americans, although they adopted Native American farming methods and foods, such as corn and beans. On the other side, Native Americans fought back to save their lands, but disease and food shortages had reduced their numbers. As the settlers expanded inland, they also came into conflict with the Dutch and the French. By 1765, after a series of wars, the English had emerged as the leading European power in much of North America.

Slave Trade

In the 1600s European territories in the Americas based their economies on agricultural products that required intensive labor. Enslaved Africans planted and harvested sugar, tobacco, and coffee crops. They also worked silver mines.

The Triangular Trade

The slave trade was part of what was called the triangular trade. Ships sailed the legs of a triangle formed by Europe, Africa, and the Americas. Typically, European ships left their home ports carrying manufactured goods—knives, swords, guns, cloth, and rum. In West Africa the ship captains traded their goods with local rulers for enslaved people, most of whom were war captives. During the second leg of the journey, the ships brought enslaved Africans across the Atlantic to various Caribbean islands or to mainland areas in North America and South America. The enslaved Africans were sold, and the money was used to buy sugar, molasses, cotton, and tobacco. Finally, the ships returned to Europe to sell the goods purchased in America.

The Middle Passage

An enslaved person's journey from the west coast of Africa to the lands of the Americas was a ghastly ordeal called the Middle Passage. This middle leg of the triangular trade originated from ports along a 3,000-mile (4,800-km) stretch on the west coast of Africa. Captured by other Africans, enslaved Africans were sold to European slave traders along the coast for transport to American plantations.

Because large cargoes brought large profits, the slave traders packed the captives as tightly as possible. Below deck, each African occupied a space only 4 or 5 feet (122 cm to 153 cm) long and 2 or 3 feet (60 cm to 92 cm) high. Chained together, they could neither stand nor lie at full length. In the darkness and stifling heat, many Africans suffocated or died of disease.

Estimates of the number of enslaved Africans brought to America range from 10 to 24 million. One in five who began the trip did not survive it. Because of the enormous value of their "cargo," however, slave traders made some effort to keep the enslaved people alive. Psychological torment may have been worse than physical conditions. Some Africans committed suicide by jumping overboard. Others simply lost the will to live and refused to eat. Enslaved people on hunger strikes were fed forcibly.

An Enslaved Person's Life

Africans who survived the long Middle Passage faced another terror when they arrived in American ports: the slave auction. Examined and prodded by plantation owners, most Africans were sold to work as laborers—clearing land, hoeing, planting, weeding, and harvesting. The work was hard, the hours long, and life expectancy short. Because many

Visualizing History A deck plan shows tightly packed ranks of enslaved people on a ship bound from Africa to the Americas. *What did enslaved people experience on the Middle Passage?*

Europeans believed that Africans were physically suited to hard labor, especially in hot, humid climates, the enslaved people were viewed as nothing more than a unit of labor to exploit for profit.

Resistance

In addition to its inhumanity, the slave trade wrenched untold numbers of young, productive Africans from their homelands. This population loss at least temporarily weakened many African societies. As a result, many Africans tried to resist the slave trade. One of them was Affonso I, ruler of Kongo in central Africa. As a Christian, Affonso favored contact with Europeans but spoke out against the trade in human lives. The slave trading network, however, was too powerful for Affonso and other African opponents to end it.

Enslaved people also acted to obtain freedom. Despite heavy odds, a few escaped their masters and got far enough away to set up their own free communities. The ultimate weapon, however, was mass rebellion. In many areas of the Americas, enslaved people outnumbered free populations, who constantly feared uprisings. The most successful uprising occurred in the French-ruled West Indian island of Saint Domingue. There, a prolonged rebellion in the 1790s led to the creation of the republic of Haiti in 1804. By the early 1800s, humanitarian concerns and fear of uprisings both had fueled an anti-slavery movement that saw slavery as an evil bringing only violence, oppression, and suffering.

SECTION 2 REVIEW

Recall
1. **Define** conquistador, triangular trade, the Middle Passage.
2. **Identify** Pedro Alvares Cabral, Hernán Cortés, Montezuma II, Francisco Pizarro, Atahualpa, Henry Hudson, Jacques Cartier, Samuel de Champlain, Jacques Marquette, Louis Joliet, John Cabot.
3. **State** the goals that Spain had for its American empire.

Critical Thinking
4. **Making Comparisons** How did treatment of Native Americans differ in the colonies of Spain, France, and England?

Understanding Themes
5. **Movement** What motivated Europeans to move from their countries to the Americas?

Chapter 6 *Expanding Horizons* **221**

SECTION 2 REVIEW ANSWERS

1. All vocabulary words are defined in the Glossary.
2. Cabral, 216; Cortés, 217; Montezuma II, 217; Pizarro, 217; Atahualpa, 217; Hudson, 219; Cartier, 220; Champlain, 220; Marquette and Joliet, 220; Cabot, 220
3. "to serve God and his Majesty, to give light to those who were in darkness and to grow rich as all men desire to do"
4. Spain converted, enslaved, and abused Native Americans; France traded with and converted them.
5. **MOVEMENT** They sought national prestige, wealth, religious freedom, and religious converts.

1400   1500   1600

c. 1400s Increased trade leads to advanced banking methods.

c. 1500s The nation replaces the city and the village as Europe's primary economic unit.

c. 1600 Europe's population reaches 100 million.

SECTION THEME

▶ **Change** The wealth of overseas colonies sparks the Commercial Revolution in Europe.

Find Out

Answer: *They linked the nations of the world economically.*

FOCUS

Section Objective

Analyze how increased trade and colonial expansion set the stage for a global economy.

**BELLRINGER
Motivational Activity**

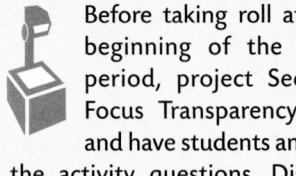

Before taking roll at the beginning of the class period, project Section Focus Transparency 6-3 and have students answer the activity questions. Discuss students' responses.

This activity is also available as a blackline master.

Vocabulary Pre-check

Use the Vocabulary Puzzle-Maker to create a puzzle that reinforces the vocabulary terms in this section. **L1**

Section 3

Changing Ways of Life

Setting the Scene

▶ **Terms to Define**
joint-stock company, entrepreneur, mercantilism, bullion, balance of trade

▶ **Places to Locate**
Florence, Augsburg

Find Out
How did increased trade and colonial expansion set the stage for a global economy?

The Storyteller

The English and French considered piracy against Spain practically a religious crusade. Pirates sometimes held Holy Communion before starting a raid on a Spanish ship! The strangest pirate fleet of all, based in England, attacked Spaniards passing anywhere near, and openly sold their stolen cargo in the market. Even their Spanish prisoners were publicly auctioned for prices set by the ransom money each one might bring. Public opinion finally forced Elizabeth I to put a stop to all this: She declared the pirates public outlaws—"Rascals of the Sea."

—adapted from *The Pirate Picture*, Rayner Thrower, 1980

Pirate ship

The age of exploration brought far-reaching changes to global cultures. Overseas trade and the conquest of empires expanded Europe's economy. This search for wealth led to the rise of modern capitalism, an economic system in which money is invested in business to make profits.

TURNING POINT

The Commercial Revolution

By the 1600s the nation had replaced the city and village as the basic economic unit in Europe. Nations competed for markets and trade goods. New business methods were instituted for investing money, speeding the flow of wealth, and reducing risks in commercial ventures. These changes, which came to be known as the Commercial Revolution, formed the roots of modern financial and business life.

New Business Methods

Launching an overseas trading venture was a major undertaking. The financial backer of the voyage had to raise money for supplies and to hire a crew. Often several years passed before a fleet finished trading overseas and returned home. Only then could the initial investment be recovered. Governments and rich merchants alone had enough money to back such trading voyages, and even they needed financial assistance.

At first merchants turned to bankers for the money to finance their ventures. Families like the Medici of **Florence**, Italy and the Fuggers of **Augsburg**, Germany loaned money as part of their operations. By the 1500s these families were so wealthy that they accepted deposits, made loans, and transferred funds over long distances. Both banking families had branches in several European cities and also made loans to European monarchs.

Visualizing History This European port scene by Jan Griffier the Elder shows the mix of cultures that resulted from the increased trade between Europeans and the rest of the world. *How did merchants protect themselves against losses?*

By the 1600s, however, these banking families were beginning to be replaced by government-chartered banks. The banks accepted deposits of money and charged interest on loans. Before long the banks began to provide other services. They issued banknotes and checks, making large payments in heavy coins a thing of the past. They acted as money changers, exchanging currencies from other countries. The banks even provided official exchange rates for foreign currency.

Individual merchants who wanted to invest in exploration often raised money by combining their resources in joint-stock companies, organizations that sold stock, or shares, in the venture, enabling large and small investors to share the profits and risks of a trading voyage. If a loss occurred, investors would lose only the amount they had invested in shares. This sharing of risk provided a stable way of raising funds for voyages.

A few joint-stock companies became rich and powerful through government support. For example, the Dutch government gave the Dutch East India Company a monopoly in trade with Africa and the East Indies. It also gave the company the power to make war, to seize foreign ships, to coin money, and to establish colonies and forts. In return

the government received customs duties, or taxes on imported goods, from the company's trade.

Increase in Money

As gold and silver flowed into Europe from abroad, the supply of coined money increased. This, in turn, led to inflation, or a dramatic rise in prices. Money, however, became more widely available for large enterprises, and ideas changed about the nature and goals of business. Gradually, a sys-

Footnotes to History

Spanish Doubloons and Pieces of Eight

During the 1500s, Spanish ships called galleons sailed the seas loaded with gold doubloons and silver pieces of eight. Minted from the plunder of Central and South American mines, the coins were a favorite target for pirates of other nations. Today, marine archaeologists have explored a number of sunken galleons and recovered hundreds of doubloons and pieces of eight—still worth a fortune.

COOPERATIVE LEARNING ACTIVITY

Research Organize the class into three groups and assign to each group one of the following European banking families: the Medici, the Fuggers, the Rothschilds. Have each group prepare an oral report on the family. Have students include in their report brief biographical sketches of prominent members of the family, aspects of their daily life, what became of the family with time. Each group should decide how best to present to the class the results of its research. Possibilities include a dramatic skit, poster presentation, or panel discussion. **L2**

TEACH

Guided Practice

THEME Change

Discuss how entrepreneurs could change the social structure of a nation that previously had a stable social hierarchy. Ask students what happens when common people can accumulate wealth that had previously been available only to nobility. *(Common people become empowered by wealth; they demand more rights from government.)* **L1**

Visualizing History In the early 1600s, the Dutch Republic modified the port city of Amsterdam to make it more suitable as a base for expanding sea power. Other nations, anxious to emulate the Netherlands' success as a commercial empire, imitated Dutch techniques of planning port cities.

Answer to Caption: *They combined resources in joint-stock companies, enabling them to share profits and risks.*

The Commercial Revolution
How did the Commercial Revolution transform Europe's economy?
The nation replaced the city and village as Europe's basic economic unit; new business institutions, such as joint-stock companies, opened opportunities for investment and increased the flow of wealth. The roots of modern business methods can be traced to the Commercial Revolution.

Focus on World Art Print 1, Jan Vermeer. *The Artist and His Model as Klio*

 World History and Art Transparency 22, *View of Toledo*; 23, *Mission San Xavier del Bac*

Independent Practice

 Guided Reading Activity 6-3 **L1**

The Commercial Revolution

The founder of England's Royal Exchange was merchant and financier Sir Thomas Gresham (1518/19–1579). He had the Royal Exchange built in London in order to provide a convenient place for merchants and traders to conduct business. The Royal Exchange was first called the "Bourse," from the French word for purse. Queen Elizabeth issued a royal proclamation in 1571 that changed its name. Today the London International Financial Futures Exchange stands on the site of the original Royal Exchange.

ANSWER

Joint-stock companies shared risks and costs among several investors. Both joint-stock companies and corporations raise money through sale of stock to a number of investors; joint-stock companies were involved in overseas trading ventures and were forerunners of today's corporations, which are large-scale organizations involved in a number of business activities.

tem based on the belief that the goal of business was to make profits took shape. Individuals known as **entrepreneurs** combined money, ideas, raw materials, and labor to make goods and profits. Profits were then used to expand the business and develop new ventures.

An entrepreneur in the cloth industry, for example, would buy wool and employ spinners to make the wool into yarn. Weavers and dyers would also be hired to turn the yarn into cloth. The entrepreneur would then sell the cloth on the open market for a price that brought a profit. Of course, entrepreneurs took risks when they put up capital for businesses. They could lose their investment if prices fell or workers could not produce goods at a specified time or for a specific market.

In the 1600s the greatest increase in trade took place in the countries bordering the Atlantic Ocean—Portugal, Spain, England, and the Netherlands—in large part because they had the largest colonial empires. Italian cities such as Venice and Genoa, formerly the leading trade centers in Europe, found themselves cut out of overseas trade as trade routes and fortunes gradually moved westward toward the Atlantic Ocean and the Americas.

Mercantilism

A new theory of national economic policy called **mercantilism** also appeared. This theory held that a state's power depended on its wealth. Accordingly, the goal of every nation was to become as wealthy as possible.

Europeans believed that the measure of a nation's wealth was the amount of **bullion**, or gold and silver it owned. One Venetian summed up the general feeling about bullion: "[It is] the sinews of all government, it gives it its pulse, its movement, its mind, soul, and it is its essence and its very life. It overcomes all impossibilities, for it is the master … without it all is weak and without movement."

Under mercantilism, nations could gain wealth by mining gold and silver at home or overseas. Thus, Spain sent conquistadors to the Americas to seize the silver and gold mines of the Aztec and Inca Empires. Governments could also gain wealth through trade. Nations sought to create a favorable **balance of trade** by exporting more goods than they imported. The gold and silver received for exports would exceed that paid for imports. This greater wealth meant greater national power and influence in the world.

CONNECTIONS
Economics
The Commercial Revolution

Queen Elizabeth opens the Royal Exchange

Europe's economic prosperity during the 1500s and 1600s made European merchants eager to increase their fortunes. Overseas trade, however, was costly and dangerous. Individual merchants found it impossible to take the entire burden on themselves. If a voyage failed, the merchant would lose everything.

This uncertainty led to the rise of joint-stock companies, which shared expenses, risks, and profits by selling stock to many investors. Joint-stock companies became so popular that stock exchanges, where investors could buy and sell stock, developed in western Europe.

Setting up a joint-stock company involved getting a charter from the monarch, who controlled merchant trade. Charters became important in the founding of settlements and trading ventures in the Americas. Also, with their emphasis on shared risk and gain, joint-stock companies were the forerunners of modern corporations. Today, the Hudson's Bay Company, chartered in 1670 to operate the fur trade in Canada, exists as a large retail corporation with many business interests.

Linking Past and Present ACTIVITY

Explain why joint-stock companies were popular among merchants. Compare and contrast the joint-stock company of the 1600s with the modern corporation.

MEETING SPECIAL NEEDS ACTIVITY

Learning Style: Visual/Spatial Work with students who learn best by producing or decoding graphic information to prepare a balance-of-trade chart of a hypothetical nation's imports and exports. For example, under the heading *Imports*, students might list raw materials and goods. Put a hypothetical dollar value next to each entry. Under the heading *Exports*, they should list items and give a hypothetical dollar value for each item. Have students explain why a nation must have a balance of trade. Ask what happens if more money is spent for imported goods than is received for exported goods. *(The nation goes into debt.)* Ask students how this applies to nations today. **L2**

Coffeehouses, such as this one depicted in London in 1668, were places to converse about the news of the day—fires, feasts, riots, weddings, plays, and scandals. *Besides coffee, what other foods and drinks were introduced to Europe in this period?*

To increase national wealth, governments often aided businesses producing export goods. They sold monopolies, or the right to operate free of local competition, to producers in certain key industries. They also set tariffs, or taxes on imported goods, to protect local industries from foreign competitors.

Colonies, or overseas territories ruled by a parent country, were highly valued in the mercantilist system. They were both the sources of raw materials as well as vital markets for finished goods provided by the parent country. The primary reason for having colonies was to help make the parent country self-sufficient.

European Daily Life

The Commercial Revolution had a noticeable impact on European society. Merchants prospered most from the expansion of trade and empire. They began to surpass the nobility in both wealth and power. Hereditary nobles had to rely on rents from their lands for wealth, but rents did not rise as fast as prices.

The newly rich entrepreneurs set trends in lifestyles. Coffeehouses became their favorite gathering places where business and gossip were exchanged. A Spaniard described a coffeehouse in Amsterdam in 1688:

❝ [They] are of great usefulness in winter, with their welcoming stoves and tempting pastimes; some offer books to read, others gaming-tables and all have people ready to converse with one; one man drinks chocolate, another coffee, one milk, another tea

and practically all of them smoke tobacco …In this way they can keep warm, be refreshed and entertained for little expense, listening to the news. ❞

Joseph de la Vega, *The Wheels of Commerce*, 1817

In the countryside, however, peasants lived as meagerly as they ever had. The French writer Jean de La Bruyère (LAH•broo•YEHR) remarked that European peasants worked like animals, lived in hovels, and survived on a diet of water, black bread, and roots.

A Global Exchange

During the Commercial Revolution, Europe's population grew rapidly. In 1450 Europe had about 55 million people; by 1650, Europeans numbered about 100 million. They also had become more mobile. Towns expanded outside their walls as more and more people left rural areas to be closer to centers of trade.

Europe's growing population demanded more goods and services. This demand was met by Europe's increasing contacts with the rest of the world. As Europe's trade expanded, it contributed to a worldwide exchange of people, goods, technologies, ideas, and even diseases that had profound consequences for the entire globe.

Known as the Columbian Exchange, after Christopher Columbus, the transfer of products from continent to continent brought changes in

Chapter 6 *Expanding Horizons* **225**

Until the middle of the nineteenth century, when daily newspapers and home mail delivery became the norm, London coffeehouses served as informal mail depots and suppliers of newspapers. **Answer to Caption:** *corn, potatoes, chocolate, and tea*

A Global Exchange
How did increased global trade after the 1400s affect the world's people?
A worldwide exchange of people, goods, technologies, ideas, and even diseases brought changes in ways of life throughout the world. New foods and crops helped increase population in Asia, Africa, Europe, and the Americas. European influences, however, often had a disruptive impact on cultures outside of Europe.

ASSESS

Check for Understanding
Assign Section 3 Review as homework or as an in-class activity.

🖵 Use Student Self-Test and Review Software to review Section 3.

Evaluate

🗁 Section Quiz 6-3

🖵 Use the Testmaker to create a customized quiz for Section 3.

MAKING CONNECTIONS ACTIVITIES

Cultural Life Have students research and prepare short reports comparing and contrasting the role of the coffeehouse in the cultural life of London with that of the café in Paris and Vienna. Students who wish to bring their reports up to date may also include speculations on why coffeehouses have become so popular in American cities today. **L2**

Religion Missionary work continues around the world today. Ask students to research and prepare short oral reports describing the nature of contemporary missionary activity. Encourage them to focus not only on Christian missionaries but also on efforts by eastern religions, Lubavitcher Hasidic Jews, and Muslims to attract converts. **L2**

History & Art   Man-o'-war is another name for a warship. The Portuguese and Spanish and then the French were probably first to cross the ocean with warships outfitted with cannons.
Answer to Caption: *economic pressure, wars, and religious persecution*

Reteach

Have students work in small groups to list and discuss the most significant changes brought about by overseas empires and the Commercial Revolution.

   Reteaching Activity 6

Enrich

Have students research and write short reports on the life of Sir Thomas Gresham, founder of the Royal Exchange.

   Enrichment Activity 6

CLOSE

Have students prepare a television talk show about the impact of overseas empires on Europe and on the indigenous peoples. Appoint one student as host and several students as experts. The rest of the class should act as audience. The host should direct a series of questions at the experts and encourage audience participation.

History & Art   *Man-o'-War Firing a Salute* by Jan Porcellis. **Building an empire called for military strength in this period of intense European rivalry.** *What caused many Europeans to venture to America?*

ways of life throughout the world. Europeans brought wheat, grapes, and livestock to the Americas. From Native Americans, Europeans acquired food items such as corn, potatoes, tomatoes, beans, and chocolate, which they brought back to Europe. Easy-to-grow food crops, such as the potato, fed Europe's growing population. Some foods, such as corn, also spread to Asia and Africa, boosting population growth there. From Asia and Africa, Europeans brought to Europe and the Americas tropical products—bananas, coffee, tea, and sugarcane—and luxury goods, such as ivory, perfumes, silk, and gems.

New global trading links increased the movement of people and cultures from continent to continent. Europeans, seeking wealth or fleeing economic distress and religious persecution, moved to the Americas and other parts of the world. They exchanged food, ideas, and practices with the peoples living in these areas. European influences profoundly affected local cultures. European traders spread European languages, and European missionaries taught Christianity and European values. Wealthy Europeans, in turn, developed an interest in the arts, styles, and foods of Asia, especially Chinese porcelain, Indian textiles, and Southeast Asian spices. At the same time, the drastic decline of the Native American populations and the forcible removal of Africans to the Americas revealed that European expansion often had a disruptive effect on cultures in other parts of the world.

SECTION 3 REVIEW

Recall
1. **Define** joint-stock company, entrepreneur, mercantilism, bullion, balance of trade.
2. **Identify** capitalism and discuss the changes of the Commercial Revolution that led to its rise.
3. **Discuss** the changes brought by European expansion to other parts of the globe.

Critical Thinking
4. **Synthesizing Information** Imagine that you are an entrepreneur of the 1700s. Invent a way for making profits by using your capital and talents.

Appraise the potential risks and profits in your venture.

Understanding Themes
5. **Change** Decide which class of European society benefited most from the Commercial Revolution. Why?

SECTION 3 REVIEW ANSWERS

1. All vocabulary words are defined in the Glossary.
2. It is an economic system in which money is invested in business to make a profit; new business methods, rising prices and available money to invest, and government encouragement of wealth through mercantilist system

3. It led to an exchange of goods and ideas throughout the world; people moved from continent to continent, voluntarily or forcibly, European influences increased.
4. Students' answers should reflect a historically accurate assessment of potential risks and gains.

5. **CHANGE** merchants and bankers; as handlers of financial transactions, they would make sure they received a share of profit. Working classes would benefit least. Workers would be hired at low pay to ensure owner profits.

Using a Computerized Card Catalog

By now you probably have been assigned several research reports. Skill in using a computerized card catalog will help you find the information you need to complete your assignment.

Learning the Skill

Go to the card-catalog computer in your school or local library. What information do you need? Type in the name of an author or performer (for tapes, cassettes, and CDs); the title of a book, videotape, audiocassette, or CD; or a subject heading. You will access the on-line, or computerized card catalog that lists all the library's resources for that topic. The computer will list on screen the title's author, or the information you requested.

The "card" that appears on screen will provide other information as well, including the year the work was published, who published it, what media type it is, and the language in which it is written or recorded. Use this information to determine if the material meets your needs. Then check to see if the item is available. In addition, find the classification (biography, travel, and so on) and call number under which it is shelved.

Practicing the Skill

This chapter discusses explorers. The following steps will help you use the computerized card catalog to find additional information on the subject "explorers":

1. Type "s/explorers."
2. From the list of subjects that appears on the screen, determine which might apply to European explorers from the 1400s to the 1700s.
3. Follow the instructions on the computer screen to display all the titles under each subject you selected. For example, the

instructions might be to type the line number next to the subject and press RETURN.
4. Determine which of the books, videos, audiocassettes, and CDs now on the screen you want to learn more about.
5. What do the instructions on the screen tell you to do to find more details?
6. What do the instructions on the screen tell you to do if you want to find out how many copies of the title the library owns and if and where a copy is available?

Applying the Skill

Use the computerized card catalog in your school or local library to identify four resources—books, videotapes, CDs, or audiocassettes—you can use to write two reports. Write one report on French explorer Jacques Cartier, and the other report on technological advances in exploration from 1400 to 1700.

For More Practice

Turn to the Skill Practice in the Chapter Review on page 229 for more practice in using a computerized card catalog.

TEACH

Using a Computerized Card Catalog This skill introduces the use of the computer in finding library materials. After students have read **Learning the Skill,** have them use the library computer to follow the instructions in **Practicing the Skill** and in **Applying the Skill.** If the school library does not have a computerized card catalog, make arrangements with the public library to work with students. You might arrange a class field trip to the library for that purpose.

Point out to students the advantage of a computerized card catalog—the ability of the computer to narrow the student's search for information. If the student does not know or remember the name of a specific book or author, the subject heading can guide the student in the right direction.

Additional Practice

Skill Reinforcement Activity 6

ANSWERS TO PRACTICING THE SKILL

Answers will vary depending on the computer program in use and the resources available in the library system.

GLENCOE TECHNOLOGY

VIDEODISC
Use MindJogger to review students' knowledge of the chapter.

MindJogger Videoquiz

Chapter 6
Disc 1 Side A

 Also available in VHS.

Answers

Using Key Terms

1. g   **4.** e
2. a   **5.** h
3. b

Using Your History Journal

Advise students to find specific data for their journal entries by reviewing the material about these cultures in Chapter 4.

Reviewing Facts

1. Causes: European interest in a more direct trade route to Asia; improved navigational technology; European investment overseas; Effects: European overseas empires; exchange of ideas, products, and peoples among several continents; better food supplies and rising populations; Negative Consequences: enslavement of Africans and the spread of diseases that ravaged Native Americans

2. triangular sails, multiple masts, a stern-operated rudder, and a shallow draft that enabled it to sail faster, sail against the wind, maneuver better, and go into inlets and to the beach for repairs

3. They had limited land for agriculture and few natural resources. A large middle class had developed

Connections Across Time

Historical Significance The period from the 1400s to the 1700s is often called the first global age. During this time, the peoples of Europe, Asia, Africa, and the Americas came into direct contact. Through exploration, the size and dimensions of the world and its oceans became known. Europeans established overseas empires, bringing prosperity to their homelands. However, the European process of establishing colonies often left a negative impact on the cultures that Europeans encountered. In the long run, the meeting of civilizations throughout the world laid the foundation of the global community that we know today, with its exchange of ideas and practices among different peoples.

Using Key Terms

Write the key term that completes each sentence. Then write a sentence for each term not chosen.

a. cartographers
b. circumnavigation
c. conquistadors
d. entrepreneurs
e. joint-stock companies
f. line of demarcation
g. Middle Passage
h. mercantilism
i. balance of trade
j. bullion
k. triangular trade

1. An enslaved person's journey from Africa to the Americas was known as the _____.
2. As a result of discoveries made by early European explorers, _____ were able to draw maps with greater accuracy.
3. In 1522 Ferdinand Magellan's crew arrived at Seville, Spain, completing the first _____, or circling of the globe.
4. _____, or organizations that sold stock in ventures, enabled large and small investors to share the risks and profits of a trading voyage.
5. The theory of _____ held that a nation's power rested on its accumulated wealth.

Technology Activity

Using a Spreadsheet Search the Internet or your local library for additional information about early European explorers and their achievements. Organize your information by creating a spreadsheet. Include headings such as name, regions of exploration, types of technology used, and contributions. Provide a map of the world labeling oceans, continents and the routes that European explorers took in discovering the world.

Using Your History Journal

Exploration brought people from Europe into contact with the cultures of Asia, Africa, and the Americas for the first time in this period. Imagine and describe such a meeting. Remember that these people did not, when meeting, understand each other's language or culture.

Reviewing Facts

1. **History** Identify the causes and effects of European expansion in the 1500s.
2. **Technology** Describe the improvements that shipbuilders incorporated in the caravel.
3. **Economics** Explain why the Dutch turned to commerce instead of agriculture in the late 1500s.
4. **Government** Identify the Mayflower Compact and discuss politics in England's colonies.
5. **Citizenship** Describe what the Middle Passage was like for enslaved Africans.
6. **History** Explain in what ways the French and the English differed in their aims for their colonies.
7. **Economics** State how a joint-stock company enabled small investors to profit from a major voyage.

Critical Thinking

1. **Apply** Why did Columbus's plan to reach Asia by a western route appeal to Spain?
2. **Analyze** Were the English and the Spanish justified in colonizing the Americas? Why or why not?

---

and was ready for commercial expansion.

4. Agreement signed by Pilgrims in 1620 that set down principles for governing their settlement; English colonists developed English political system by establishing their own representative assemblies apart from Parliament.

5. a terrifying psychological and physical ordeal for the captives

6. The French were interested in trade; the English sought raw materials.

7. It reduced the risk of individual investors.

Critical Thinking

1. Spain sought quicker routes to Asia's wealth.
2. Students should support their position.
3. Possible answers: The colonies would have been less successful economically. Fewer Europeans would have gone there.
4. European explorers ventured overseas; exchange of goods, ideas, and peoples; Euro-

3. **Evaluate** How would the colonies have been different if Europeans had not used slave labor?
4. **Synthesize** Why is the era from the 1400s to the 1700s called the Age of Exploration? What are its major features? What was its impact?
5. **Evaluate** How did the influx of wealth from the colonies help bring about the Commercial Revolution in Europe?
6. **Analyze** What were the results of Ferdinand Magellan's circumnavigation?
7. **Apply** Why were the Dutch eager to establish overseas colonies?

Geography in History

1. **Place** What European city was the first to have potatoes for consumption?
2. **Movement** Why were potatoes introduced into Sweden and Finland so much later than they were in other nations?
3. **Human/Environment Interaction** How would new crops such as the potato affect agriculture?

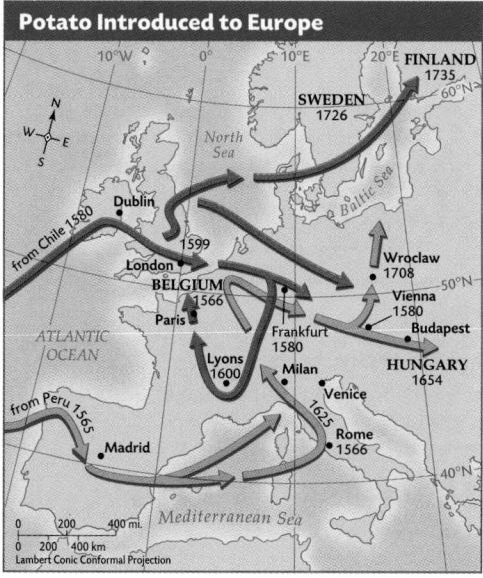

Potato Introduced to Europe

Understanding Themes

1. **Innovation** How did Chinese and Arab discoveries aid European voyages of exploration?

2. **Movement** How did the Columbian Exchange affect changes in world populations?
3. **Change** How did the Commercial Revolution encourage more European voyages of exploration and colonization?

Linking Past and Present

1. History books used to say that Columbus "discovered" America. What did they mean, and why do we no longer see his voyage in this way?
2. Making profits motivated early entrepreneurs. Is this still the goal of entrepreneurs today?
3. Compare and contrast modern space explorations with European voyages of exploration. Consider the technologies used, the ways explorations were funded, and the impact of these ventures on human knowledge.

Skill Practice

Use the card catalog computer in your school library to find out more about Spain's empire from the 1500s to the 1700s.

1. Type "s/Spain."
2. From the list of subjects that appears on screen determine which might apply to Spain's empire from the 1500s to the 1700s.
3. Follow the instructions on the computer screen to display all the titles under each subject you selected. Which book on the screen do you want to learn more about?
4. Who is the author and publisher of the book and in what year was the book published?
5. What is the call number of the book?
6. Is the book available?
7. Go back to the screen that displays all the titles under the subject you selected. Are there any videotapes, audiocassettes, or CDs listed? If so, which resource do you want to learn more about? What is the call number? Is the resource available?

Chinese compass, the astrolabe perfected by Arabs, and lateen sails used by Muslims.
2. **MOVEMENT** Africans brought to the Americas, Native American populations reduced.
3. **CHANGE** It made it easier to finance such voyages and for more people to profit from them.

Linking Past and Present

1. Before his voyages, Europeans were unaware of the Americas. Today we have a world perspective rather than a Eurocentric one.
2. Some students may agree, or may argue that entrepreneurs today, regulated by laws and conscience, may base their decisions on factors besides profit.
3. Technology—the development of shipping and navigation in early modern times and that of rockets, shuttles, and on-site planetary exploration craft today; funding—the role of government and private ventures then and now; human knowledge—enlarging mental horizons about dimensions of earth and understanding of solar system.

Skill Practice
Answers will vary depending on the resources available.

Chapter Bonus Test Question

Ask students: How would the world today be different if the age of exploration had never occurred? *(only local or possibly regional economies; there would be no interracial problems; Native Americans would constitute entire population of North and South America; products and ideas would not have spread; geographical knowledge limited.)*

pean overseas empires established, often with negative effects on local cultures.
5. Entrepreneurs needed expanded banking services for business outside Europe.
6. Magellan's voyage proved the world was round and larger than previously believed, that the oceans were connected, and that Columbus had not reached Asia.
7. The Dutch middle class saw trade as a means of survival.

Geography in History
1. Madrid
2. Potatoes came from the west to England and Spain. Sweden and Finland were more isolated from trade with the rest of Europe.
3. They added to, and sometimes replaced, crops that were being grown.

Understanding Themes
1. **INNOVATION** Europeans used the

A complete, 1-page lesson plan is provided for each section in the *Reproducible Lesson Plans* booklet.

Empires of Asia

CHAPTER RESOURCES

	Reproducible Resources	Multimedia Resources
Chapter Opener	Chapter Themes: Graphic Organizer 7 Historical Significance Chapter Activity 7	MindJogger Videoquiz
Chapter Enrichment	Vocabulary Activity 7* Time Line Activity 7 Mapping History Activity 7 History Simulation 7 Geography and History Activity 7 Source Reading 7 People in World History Profiles 33, 34 World Art and Music Activity 7 Enrichment Activity 7 Critical Thinking Activity 7 Skill Reinforcement Activity 7 Performance Assessment Activity 7	Focus on World Art Print 10, Kitagawa Utamaro. *Reflected Beauty* World History and Art Transparency 24, *Taj Mahal*; 25, *Shah Jahan and One of His Sons Riding in Escort* Chapter Transparency 7 Vocabulary PuzzleMaker Software Picture Atlas of the World World Music: Cultural Traditions, Lessons 7, 8, 9
Chapter Review/Reteaching	Reteaching Activity 7 Skill Reinforcement Activity 7 Spanish Chapter Summary 7	Chapter 7 Digest Audiocassette, Activity, Test* Vocabulary PuzzleMaker Software Student Self-Test and Review Software MindJogger Videoquiz
Chapter Evaluation/Testing	Performance Assessment Activity 7 Chapter 7 Test, Forms A and B	Testmaker

* Also available in Spanish

0:00 OUT OF TIME? Assign the Chapter 7 summary in the Unit 2 Digest on pages 283–285, and the Chapter 7 Audiocassettes.

Block Schedule

Block scheduling differs from traditional class scheduling in the amount of time allotted to each period. The extended time frame provided by block scheduling affords you the opportunity to implement a greater number of research-oriented and activity-intense projects to motivate and involve your students. Activities that are particularly suited to use within the block scheduling framework are identified throughout this chapter by the following designation.

KEY TO ABILITY LEVELS

Teaching strategies have been coded for varying learning styles and abilities.

L1 BASIC activities for all students
L2 AVERAGE activities for average to above-average students
L3 CHALLENGING activities for above-average students
LEP LIMITED ENGLISH PROFICIENCY activities

Use Glencoe's *Presentation Plus!* multimedia teacher tool to easily present dynamic lessons that visually excite your students. Using Microsoft PowerPoint® you can customize the presentations to create your own personalized lessons.

SECTION RESOURCES

Daily Objectives	Reproducible Resources	Multimedia Resources
Section 1 **Muslim Empires** Describe how Muslim rulers controlled and governed much of the Middle East, North Africa, and India between the 1500s and 1800s.	Reproducible Lesson Plan 7-1 Vocabulary Activity 7* Guided Reading Activity 7-1* Time Line Activity 7 History Simulation 7 People in World History Profile 33 Section Quiz 7-1*	Section Focus Transparency 7-1 Chapter Transparency 7 World History and Art Transparency 24, *Taj Mahal*; 25, *Shah Jahan and One of His Sons Riding in Escort* Student Self-Test and Review Software Testmaker World Music: Cultural Traditions, Lesson 7
Section 2 **Chinese Dynasties** Analyze why China flourished and then declined during the Ming and Qing dynasties.	Reproducible Lesson Plan 7-2 Vocabulary Activity 7* Guided Reading Activity 7-2* Section Quiz 7-2*	Section Focus Transparency 7-2 Student Self-Test and Review Software Testmaker World Music: Cultural Traditions, Lesson 8 Picture Atlas of the World
Section 3 **The Japanese Empire** Explain why Japan was more adaptable to changes than China before the 1800s.	Reproducible Lesson Plan 7-3 Vocabulary Activity 7* Guided Reading Activity 7-3* Geography and History Activity 7 People in World History Profile 34 Section Quiz 7-3*	Focus on World Art Print 10, Kitagawa Utamaro. *Reflected Beauty* Section Focus Transparency 7-3 Student Self-Test and Review Software Testmaker World Music: Cultural Traditions, Lesson 8
Section 4 **Southeast Asia** Explain how the Thai kingdom was able to keep its independence while other parts of Southeast Asia gradually came under European control.	Reproducible Lesson Plan 7-4 Guided Reading Activity 7-4* Reteaching Activity 7 Enrichment Activity 7 Section Quiz 7-4* Performance Assessment Activity 7 Spanish Chapter Summary 7	Section Focus Transparency 7-4 Vocabulary PuzzleMaker Software Student Self-Test and Review Software Testmaker World Music: Cultural Traditions, Lesson 9

* Also available in Spanish

Chapter Activities

 Performance Assessment Activity

Creating a Television Series Have students take the roles of producers who want to find the perfect location for a historical television series for a network. Students should work alone or in pairs to study the empires of Asia and develop proposals for the investors for the site they think people of today would find most interesting. The proposals should include descriptions of the setting, possible historical characters, possible problems for episode story lines, and the type of series that would be created. Students might present their proposals orally with visuals or in writing.

Possible Rubric Features
Accuracy of content information, concept attainment, decision-making process skills, creative thinking, clarity and organization of presentation or proposal

• *For an additional activity, refer to Activity 18 in the* Performance Assessment Strategies and Activities *booklet.*

ACTIVITY

From the Classroom of...

**Jon Kilgore
Moline High School
Moline, IL**

The Quest for Japan
Prepare a list of review questions about Chapter 7. Then divide an outline map of Japan into 10 or 12 sections. Assign each a value between 1 and 5 (representing a number of questions). Organize the class into five groups or families and assign each group one of the sections on the map as its family's home. The families are competing to take over the rest of Japan. Let each group in turn decide which section it wants to "enter." In order to gain that territory, the group must answer correctly the designated number of questions for the section. If a group chooses to enter an occupied section, it must compete with the group already there. The groups take turns answering questions until one answers incorrectly and loses. When all sections have been taken, the "family" with the most territory wins.

MULTIPLE LEARNING STYLES

Verbal/Linguistic
Have students debate the following proposition: Western influence on the countries of East Asia in the early modern period was more helpful than harmful.

Visual/Spatial
Select books on Indian and Persian art from the library and bring them to class. Have each student choose a different miniature painting and write a short description of it.

Kinesthetic
Have students prepare a large map of East and Southeast Asia, indicating on it some of the most important points of contact between Europeans and Asians, such as Macao, the Philippines, and Java. (They might use different colored tacks, pushpins, or labels to represent the various European countries.)

Additional Resources

NATIONAL GEOGRAPHIC SOCIETY

Teacher's Corner

INDEX TO NATIONAL GEOGRAPHIC MAGAZINE

The following articles may be used for research relating to this chapter:

- "Sumo," by T. R. Reid, July 1997.
- "China's Gold Coast," by Mike Edwards, March 1997.
- "The New Saigon," April 1995.
- "Ibn Battuta: Prince of Travelers," by Thomas J. Abercrombie, December 1991.
- "The World of Süleyman the Magnificent," by Merle Severy, November 1987.
- "When the Moguls Ruled India," by Mike Edwards, April 1985.

NATIONAL GEOGRAPHIC SOCIETY PRODUCTS AVAILABLE FROM GLENCOE

To order the following products for use with this chapter, contact your local Glencoe sales representative, or call Glencoe at 1-800-334-7344:

- *STV: World Geography (Videodisc)*
- *Picture Atlas of the World (CD-ROM)*

LOCAL OBJECTIVES

_____
_____
_____
_____
_____
_____
_____
_____
_____
_____
_____
_____
_____
_____
_____
_____
_____
_____
_____
_____
_____
_____

BIBLIOGRAPHY

Literature of the Period
Tsao Hsueh-Chin. *The Dream of the Red Chamber.*
Westport, CT: Greenwood Press, 1975. Written in the eighteenth century, this is considered to be China's greatest novel.
Readings for the Student
Ebrey, Patricia B., ed. *Chinese Civilization: A Sourcebook, 2nd rev. ed.* New York: Free Press, 1993.
Readings for the Teacher
Clayre, Alasdair. *The Heart of the Dragon.*
Boston: Houghton Mifflin, 1985. A look at China today, with reference to its history.
Savory, R.M., ed. *Introduction to Islamic Civilization.* New York: Cambridge University Press, 1976. Essays about Islam.

*inter*NET CONNECTION
Thailand resources on the World Wide Web
Thailand: The big picture 1997:
http://www.nectec.or.th/index.html

Chapter Themes are listed by section on this chapter opening page of the Student Edition. A corresponding theme-based activity is available under "TEACH," and a theme-based question is asked in the Section and Chapter Reviews.

The Storyteller

Historical Setting Suleiman had begun his campaign against Europe in 1521, soon after coming to power. (It was an Ottoman tradition for a new ruler to celebrate with a military campaign.) Although Suleiman was successful in his attacks on Hungary, well-organized resistance, coupled with supply difficulties and bad weather, contributed to his defeat in Vienna.

Historical Significance

Answers: *One kind—represented by the Ottoman, Persian, and Mogul Empires—was founded by Muslim steppe peoples. New dynasties in China were characterized by a strong central government, while in Japan the ruling shoguns had lost much power to the daimyos. A new type of empire, the European colonial empire, began to transform Southeast Asia, although the Thai emperors managed to preserve their people's independence.*

Asian response to European arrivals ranged from cordial (Philippines) to suspicious (China) to hostile (Japan).

Chapter
7
1350–1850
Empires of Asia

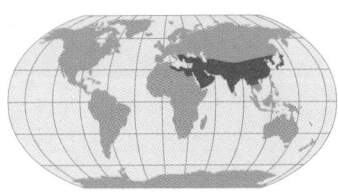

Chapter Themes

▶ **Movement** Muslim rulers govern empires that cover vast regions of Asia, North Africa, and Europe. *Section 1*
▶ **Cultural Diffusion** China is directly challenged by its contacts with western European cultures. *Section 2*
▶ **Reaction** Japan enforces isolationist policy to keep out Western influences. *Section 3*
▶ **Change** Southeast Asian lands face the growth of European trade and commerce in their region. *Section 4*

The Storyteller

Within the city walls of Vienna, Austria, people quaked as thundering cannonballs signaled the beginning of the Turkish siege of the city on September 27, 1529. Occupying the surrounding hills were 100,000 Turkish soldiers led by their skilled commander Suleiman.

By mid-October, Turkish troops twice had broken through part of Vienna's walls, but failed to capture the city as the Austrians and their allies rushed to plug the breaches. This clash between European and Asian armies was one of many encounters between different civilizations during the early modern period.

Historical Significance

What kinds of empires arose in Asia during the early modern period? How did they respond to the arrival of Europeans in their areas?

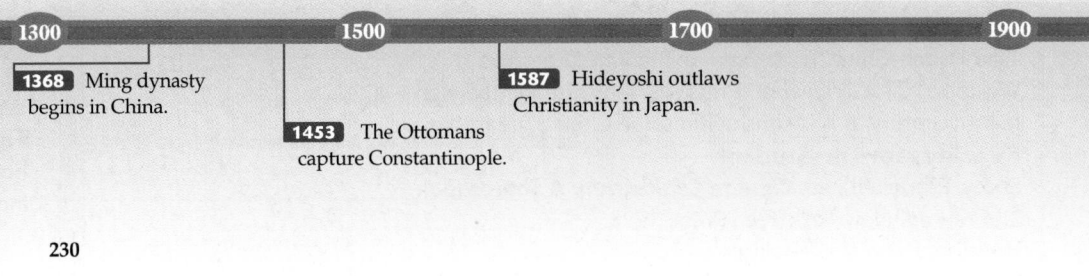

1300	1500	1700	1900

1368 Ming dynasty begins in China.

1453 The Ottomans capture Constantinople.

1587 Hideyoshi outlaws Christianity in Japan.

230

Region Use a wall map or one of the maps in the Atlas to review with students the distinguishing geographic features of the major regions discussed in this chapter: eastern Europe, western Asia, North Africa, South Asia, East Asia, and Southeast Asia. How might geography make it easier to govern Japan than the Ottoman Empire? *(Japan covers a relatively small area, whereas the Ottoman Empire stretched thousands of miles from the western Mediterranean to the Gulf of Aden.)* **L2**

Voyage of the Emperor Qianlong (detail of a scroll), Qing dynasty.
Musée Guimet, Paris, France

History & Art This painting dates from the 1700s, when China was ruled by the Manchus, a non-Chinese people from Manchuria. Their empire—the largest in Chinese history—included Nepal, Outer Mongolia, Taiwan, and parts of Southeast Asia. *What other rulers of China governed large empires?* *(the Han, around 200 B.C.–A.D. 200; and the Mongols, in the 1200s)*

Performance Assessment

Refer to the activity on page 230C of the Planning Guide.

For an additional activity, refer to Activity 7 in the *Performance Assessment Strategies and Activities* booklet.

Your History Journal

Research one of the following topics, make notes, and write an outline for a short paper: the Imam Mosque of Isfahan, the Taj Mahal, the Forbidden City, and the Imperial Palace of Tokyo.

Using Your History Journal

Headings might include *When* and *Where Built*, *Description* and *Culture/Values Reflected* for each of the places.

GLENCOE TECHNOLOGY

VIDEODISC
Use MindJogger to preview chapter content.

MindJogger Videoquiz

Chapter 7
Disc 1 Side B

  Also available in VHS.

Chapter 7 *Empires of Asia* 231

✚ EXTRA CREDIT PROJECT

Bulletin Board Have students create a bulletin-board display on one of the great centers of Asian civilization during the period discussed in this chapter, such as Istanbul, Isfahan, Delhi, Beijing, or Kyoto. Their displays should include, if possible, a plan of the city, summaries describing its economic and political importance, pictures of notable buildings and other features, and details on the daily life of its people. The displays should also include a few pictures showing what the city is like today. **L2**

SECTION THEME

▶ **Movement** Muslim rulers govern empires that cover vast regions of Asia, North Africa, and Europe.

ind Out

Answer: *They had absolute power and were aided by the common faith of Islam, large bureaucracies, and powerful military forces.*

FOCUS

Section Objective

Describe how Muslim rulers controlled and governed much of the Middle East, North Africa, and India between the 1500s and 1800s.

BELLRINGER
Motivational Activity

Before taking roll at the beginning of the class period, project Section Focus Transparency 7-1 and have students answer the activity questions. Discuss students' responses.
▭ This activity is also available as a blackline master.

Vocabulary Pre-check

▭ Use Vocabulary Activity 7 to introduce vocabulary terms.
L1 LEP

1500   1700   1900

1526 Babur founds the Mogul dynasty in India.

c. 1740 Nader Shah expands the empire of Safavid Persia.

1856 The Hatt-I Humayun decree sets out reforms for the Ottoman Empire.

Section 1

Muslim Empires

Setting the Scene

▶ **Terms to Define**
sultan, grand vizier, janissary, *millet*

▶ **People to Meet**
Suleiman I, Shah Abbas, Babur, Akbar

▶ **Places to Locate**
Istanbul, Isfahan, Delhi

ind Out How did Muslim rulers control and govern much of the Middle East, North Africa, and India between the 1500s and 1800s?

The Storyteller

On the day that Jahangir was crowned emperor of the Moghuls [Moguls], favorable omens abounded. His coronation was a scene of splendor, illuminated by nearly three thousand wax lights in branches of gold and silver. By his command, the imperial crown was brought to him. On each of the twelve points of this crown was a single diamond.... At the point in the center was a single

pearl ... and on different parts of the same were set two hundred rubies. The Emirs of his empire, waiting for Jahangir's commands, were covered from head to foot in gold and jewels.

—adapted from *Memoirs of the Emperor Jahangir Written by Himself*, translated by David Price, reprinted in *The Human Record*, Alfred J. Andrea and James H. Overfield, 1990

Mogul warriors

232 **Chapter 7** *Empires of Asia*

Between the 1400s and the 1800s, three Muslim empires—the Ottoman Empire, the Persian Empire, and the Mogul Empire—conquered and controlled much of eastern Europe, central Asia, and India respectively. Strong leaders used powerful armies to amass territory that gave them economic control over major trade routes. As these empires spread into new areas, the religion and culture of Islam also expanded.

The Ottoman Empire

During the late 1200s, Turkish clans—calling themselves Ottoman Turks after their first leader, Osman—settled part of Asia Minor and began conquests to build an empire. They conquered much of Byzantine territory, making Constantinople their capital in 1453. Extending their Muslim empire even farther, by the 1500s the Ottomans controlled the Balkan Peninsula and parts of eastern Europe. By the end of their rule in the early 1900s, they had acquired much of the Middle East, North Africa, and the Caucasus region between the Black and Caspian Seas.

The Ottoman Empire maintained a strong navy in the Mediterranean to protect the lucrative trade they controlled there. Alarmed by the threat to their trade and to Christianity, Europeans under Philip II of Spain fought and defeated the Ottoman fleet at the Battle of Lepanto in 1571. But the Ottomans rebuilt their navy and remained a significant seapower until the 1700s.

Suleiman I

Suleiman I was one of the early Ottoman rulers who strengthened Muslim forces prior to the Battle of Lepanto. He was a multitalented man—a heroic military commander, a skillful administrator, and a patron of the arts. Ruling from 1520 to 1566, Suleiman received the name "The Lawgiver" for his work in organizing Ottoman laws.

SECTION RESOURCES

▭ **Reproducible Masters**
- Reproducible Lesson Plan 7-1
- Vocabulary Activity 7
- Guided Reading Activity 7-1
- Time Line Activity 7
- History Simulation 7
- People in World History Profile 33
- Section Quiz 7-1

Transparencies
- Section Focus Transparency 7-1
- Chapter Transparency 7
- World History and Art Transparencies 24, 25

Multimedia
- Student Self-Test and Review Software
- Testmaker
- World Music: Cultural Traditions, Lesson 7

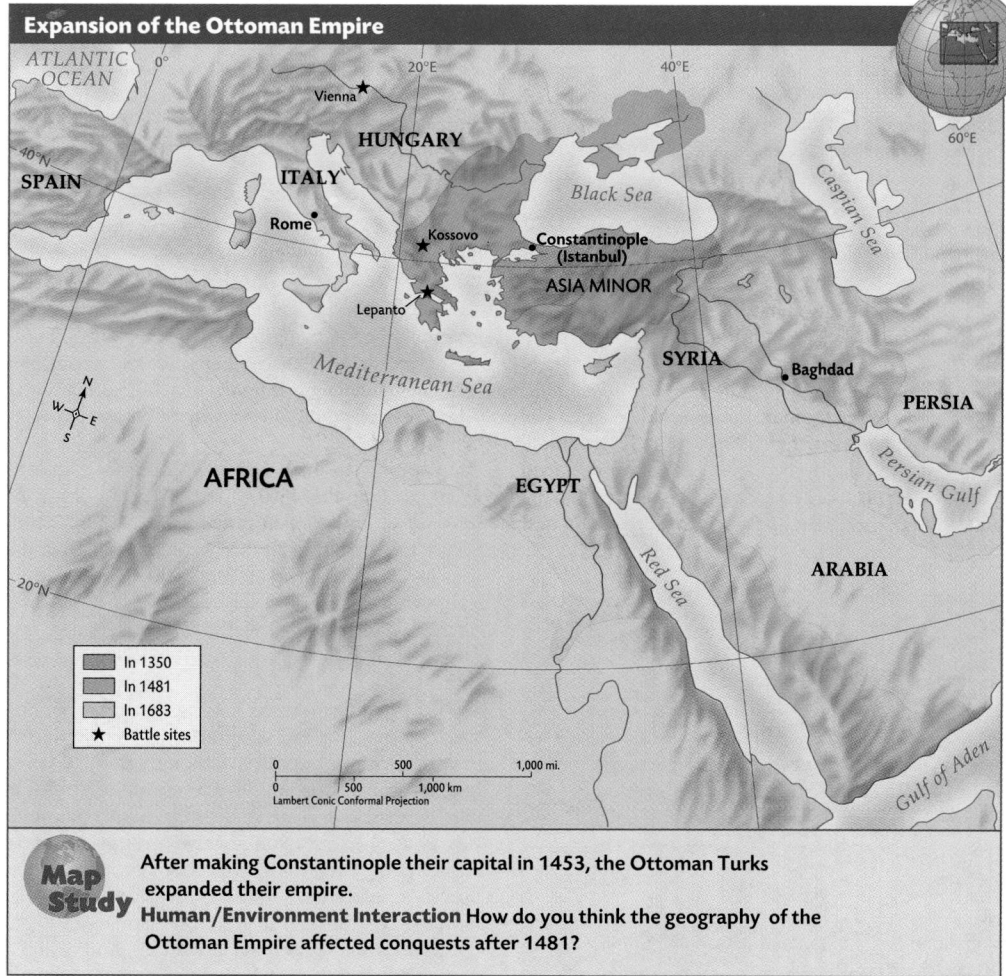

Expansion of the Ottoman Empire

ATLANTIC OCEAN
SPAIN
HUNGARY
Vienna ★
ITALY
Rome •
Kossovo ★
Lepanto ★
Constantinople (Istanbul)
ASIA MINOR
Black Sea
Caspian Sea
Mediterranean Sea
SYRIA
Baghdad •
PERSIA
AFRICA
EGYPT
Persian Gulf
Red Sea
ARABIA
Gulf of Aden

Legend:
- In 1350
- In 1481
- In 1683
- ★ Battle sites

0   500   1,000 mi.
0 500 1,000 km
Lambert Conic Conformal Projection

Map Study After making Constantinople their capital in 1453, the Ottoman Turks expanded their empire.
Human/Environment Interaction How do you think the geography of the Ottoman Empire affected conquests after 1481?

Suleiman acted as both the sultan, or political ruler, and the caliph, or religious leader; he enjoyed absolute authority. To rule effectively, however, Suleiman needed support from his personal advisers, the bureaucracy, a group of religious advisers known as the Ulema, and a well-trained army. A grand vizier, or prime minister, headed the bureaucracy that enforced the sultan's decisions throughout the empire. The Ulema made rulings on questions of Islamic law, and the army held much control within the empire by conquering and controlling new territories.

The Ottomans recruited officers from among the conquered peoples of their empire. An elite corps of officers called janissaries came from the Balkans, where Christian families were required by the Ottomans to turn over young boys to the govern-

ment. Converted to Islam, the boys received rigorous training that made them a loyal fighting force.

Ottoman Law

Because the empire was so large, Ottoman Muslims ruled diverse peoples, including Arabs, Greeks, Albanians, Slavs, Armenians, and Jews. The population was divided into several classes: a ruling class made up of the sultan's family and high government officials; the nobility, which administered agricultural estates; and the largest class, the peasants who worked on those estates.

To accommodate these diverse populations, the government made special laws affecting those who did not practice Islam, the empire's official religion. Non-Muslims were allowed to practice their faith. Ottoman law also permitted the empire's diverse

Chapter 7 *Empires of Asia* **233**

TEACH

Guided Practice

THEME Movement

Ask students why Muslim peoples like the Ottomans, Persians, and Moguls might have wanted to expand their territory. *(to gain control of trade routes; to spread their religion; to protect the lands they already governed)* **L1**

Map Study

Answer

Much of Asia Minor is mountainous. Ottoman invaders had to be familiar with mountain passes and inaccessible areas before they attacked their enemies.

Map Skills Practice

Reading a Map **Which modern countries, wholly or in part, were ruled by the Ottoman Empire at its greatest extent?** *(Turkey, Bulgaria, Romania, Greece, Hungary, Egypt, Libya, Tunisia, Algeria, Saudi Arabia, Yemen, Syria, Jordan, Israel, Iraq)*

Religion Have students review the main tenets of Islam, with emphasis on the Five Pillars (Chapter 3). **What is the main difference between Shiite and Sunni Muslims?** *(Shiites believe that only a descendant of Muhammad possesses true spiritual [and political] power; Sunnis believe that any devout Muslim can hold this authority.)* **L2**

History Simulation 7

World History and Art Transparency 24, *Taj Mahal*; 25, *Shah Jahan and One of His Sons Riding in Escort*

COOPERATIVE LEARNING ACTIVITY

Quiz Game Organize the class into three groups representing the Ottomans, Safavids, and Moguls. Have each team prepare questions about its empire. Encourage students to ask about the arts, foods, religious beliefs, and social codes of the cultures they represent. Each group should select one person to record the questions on note cards, with the answers on the back. Each team should choose ten questions and present these to the rest of the class as a quiz game. **L1**

Compare Ask students to compare the treatment of subject peoples by the Ottomans, Safavids, and Moguls. (*Ottomans: Non-Muslims could practice their own religion and run their own communities if they paid a tax; Safavids: forced everyone to adopt Shiite Islam; Moguls: Akbar encouraged religious tolerance, but later Moguls persecuted Hindus.*) **L3**

🎵 World Music: Cultural Traditions, Lesson 7

Who?What?Where?When?

The Janissaries By 1826 this military force had grown so large—135,000 strong—and so powerful that the sultan was forced to massacre all its members.

Independent Practice

 Guided Reading Activity 7-1 **L1**

📁 Time Line Activity 7

📁 People in World History Profile 33

Visualizing History

Although Suleiman was credited with many achievements, the governmental reforms of his reign were due largely to his vizier, Ibrahim Pasha, a man of Greek origin.
Answer to Caption: *They could practice their own religion and manage their own affairs if they paid a tax.*

religious groups to run affairs in their own *millets*, or communities, and choose their own leaders to present their views to the Ottoman government.

The Ottoman Islamic civilization borrowed many elements from the Byzantine, Persian, and Arab cultures they had absorbed. Mosques, bridges, and aqueducts reflected this blend of styles. The Christian city of Constantinople was transformed into a Muslim one and renamed **Istanbul**. Ottoman architects renovated Hagia Sophia into a mosque and then planned new mosques and palaces that added to Istanbul's beauty. Ottoman painters produced detailed miniatures and illuminated manuscripts.

Decline of the Ottomans

By 1600 the Ottoman Empire had reached the peak of its power; thereafter it slowly declined. Even at its height, however, the empire faced enemies on its borders. Conquests ended as the Ottomans tried to fight both Persians and

Visualizing History **Portrait of Suleiman, "The Lawgiver," from the late 1600s.** *What provision did the Ottoman law make for peoples of diverse religions?*

Europeans. In 1683 Polish King John III Sobieski led European forces in ending an Ottoman siege of Vienna. This European victory dealt a decisive blow to the Ottoman Empire. When Ottoman military conquests ceased, massive poverty and civil discontent afflicted Ottoman lands.

Reform

By the 1700s, the Ottoman Empire had fallen behind Europe in trade and military technology. Russia and other European nations began taking Ottoman territory, and local rulers in North Africa gradually broke away from Ottoman control. In the 1800s uprisings in the Balkans led to freedom for the Greeks, Serbs, Bulgarians, and Romanians. Unsuccessful revolts in Armenia and Arabia were brutally crushed.

Wanting to halt Ottoman decline, Ottoman rulers during the 1800s used European ideas to reform and unify the empire. In 1856 Sultan Abdul-Mejid I issued the Hatt-I-Hamayun, a sweeping reform decree that created a national citizenship, reduced the authority of religious leaders, and opened government service to all peoples.

Reaction

Powerful resistance to change grew among the religious leaders, who had lost civil authority in their own communities. Although many Muslim, Jewish, and Christian leaders protested reform, merchants and artisans in the individual communities welcomed it. Non-Turkish groups, such as Armenians, Bulgarians, Macedonians, and Serbs, however, had little interest in any reform that would save the empire. They began to think of themselves as separate nationalities and wanted nation-states of their own.

After Abdul-Mejid's death in 1861, the reform movement lacked the strong leadership needed to guarantee its success. To gain public support, reformers known as the Young Ottomans overthrew the weak sultan Abdul-Aziz and replaced him with Abdul-Hamid II.

At first the new sultan went along with the reformers. In 1876 he proclaimed a new constitution. He affirmed the unity of the empire and promised individual liberties for his subjects. In 1877 the first Ottoman parliament met in Istanbul. But later that same year Abdul-Hamid II decided to resist reform. He suddenly dissolved the parliament and ended constitutional rule. The sultan believed that moving the Ottoman government toward liberalism would lead to ruin. To further protect the empire from change, he drove many of the Young Ottomans into exile. Then he imposed absolute rule.

MEETING SPECIAL NEEDS ACTIVITY

Study Strategy Have students work alone or in small groups to develop topic sentences for this section—first, for the section as a whole; second, for each of the three peoples discussed; and third, for each paragraph of the section. After they have developed their sentences, each one should be read aloud and discussed briefly. **L1**

Safavid Persia

To the east of the Ottoman Empire lay Persia, a land that had once been part of the Islamic Empire, but which had broken away because of religious differences. In the 1500s Shiite Muslims, bitter enemies of the Ottoman Turks, conquered the land of present-day Iran. The Shiite leader, Ismail (ihs•MAH•EEL), conquered and unified the numerous people living there, declaring himself to be the founder of the Safavid (sah•FAH•weed) dynasty.

Safavid rulers required all of their Persian subjects to accept the Shiite form of Islam. Belief in the Shia branch of Islam distinguished people living in Persia from neighboring Sunni Muslim peoples—the Arabs and Turks.

Shah Abbas

The Safavid leader **Shah Abbas** came to the throne in 1587. His army regained some western territory lost to the Ottomans in previous years. Then the shah sought allies against the Ottomans even among such Christian states as England. The English used their alliance with Persia to seize the strategic Persian Gulf port of Hormuz in 1622, gaining control of the Persian silk and East Indian spice trade.

With his empire secure against the Ottoman forces, Shah Abbas set up his court in **Isfahan**, which became one of the most magnificent cities in the entire Muslim world. Towering above the city was the blue dome of the Imam Mosque, which was covered with lacy white decorations. Near the mosque, Abbas had a three-story palace built for his personal use. He also ordered beautiful streets and parks constructed throughout the city.

During the reign of Abbas, Persian spread as the language of culture, diplomacy, and trade in most of the Muslim world. Later the language spread to India. Urdu, spoken in Pakistan today, is partly based on Persian.

Nader Shah

After the death of Shah Abbas in 1629, inept Safavid rulers weakened the empire, bringing on its decline. In 1736, after the Safavid decline, Nader Shah came to power. He expanded the Persian Empire to its greatest height since Darius. But after his assassination in 1747, territory was lost and the country was divided.

In the late 1700s another Turkic group, the Qajar dynasty, seized the Persian throne and established a new dynasty in Tehran. The Qajars ruled Persia until 1925.

The Imam Mosque in Isfahan (in present-day Iran) was built by Shah Abbas during the early 1600s. *What cultural impact did Safavid Persia have on the Muslim world?*

The Mogul Empire

Even before the Ottomans and the Safavids built their empires, Islamic invaders from central Asia had conquered much of northern India by the 1100s. The invaders set up a sultanate, or Muslim kingdom, in **Delhi** in 1206. Once order was restored, northern India prospered economically and culturally. Traditional Hindu culture survived the invasions and blended with Islamic civilization.

Timur Lenk in India

By the late 1300s the Muslim Mongol ruler, Timur Lenk (Tamerlane), had conquered much of central Asia and made Samarkand the capital of his empire. Although a devout Muslim, Timur Lenk was also a ruthless leader. His forces sacked the city of Delhi in 1398, killing thousands and leaving the city in rubble. After Timur Lenk's death, his Islamic

Visualizing History Under Shah Abbas, Isfahan included 162 mosques, 48 schools, 1,802 commercial buildings, and 283 baths, according to one account. **Answer to Caption:** *The Persian language spread through much of the Muslim world.*

Biography Have students write an article on Suleiman the Magnificent, Shah Abbas, Babur, or Akbar. Have them assume that they interviewed the ruler in order to write the article in a question-and-answer format. They should include information about the man's interests, religious beliefs, and political goals. **L2**

News Report Have students write a news report on the Battle of Lepanto or the Battle of Panipat. Remind them that news reports tell who, what, where, when, and why. **L3**

Global Gourmet

Middle East A favorite food for barbecues is shish kebab, meat and vegetables grilled on a skewer. The English term comes from Armenia, whose people adapted it from the Turkish words *sis* ("skewer") and *kebabi* ("roast mutton").

Chapter 7 *Empires of Asia* **235**

MAKING CONNECTIONS ACTIVITIES

Architecture One of Istanbul's most famous buildings, the Christian church of Hagia Sophia, has undergone several changes in its long history. Have students research these changes, ending with a description of the building today. **L2**

Religion Although Sikhs have never been as numerous as Hindus or Muslims in India, their religious group has played an important role in the country. Have students research the basic tenets of Sikhism and summarize the role Sikhs have played in Indian politics, especially in recent years. **L2**

TEACH

Tell students that the name of this tomb comes from the title of Shah Jahan's favorite wife, Mumtazi Mahal, which means "Chosen of the Palace." (Her actual name was Arjumand Banu.) For his own resting place, the emperor planned to build a replica of the Taj Mahal in black marble across the Jumna River from his wife's tomb. He lost his throne, however, before he could do so. Ask students for their responses to Tagore's description of the Taj Mahal.

Who?What?Where?When?

Shah Jahan was a conqueror as well as a builder, extending Mogul rule over areas of central India. But his reign ended unhappily, with his four sons struggling for the throne. His son Aurangzeb declared himself emperor in 1658 and confined his father to a fort for the last six years of his life.

Taj Mahal

The beauty of the Taj Mahal has awed visitors for centuries. A pear-shaped dome crowns the square central building, complete with a reflecting pool. The marble surface glitters with semiprecious stones: jade from China; turquoise from Tibet; lapis lazuli from Afghanistan; chrysolite from Egypt; and mother-of-pearl from the Indian Ocean. Inside all this wealth and beauty lies Mumtazi Mahal, wife of the Mogul emperor of India, Shah Jahan, who ruled from 1628 to 1658. He fell in love with Mumtazi at 16 and adored his queen throughout her life. In 1629, shortly after Shah Jahan's reign began, Mumtazi died in childbirth, after giving birth to their 14th child. Her death left him in black despair, and in his grief he decided to build the world's greatest tomb.

Or so goes the legend. Contemporary scholars argue that Shah Jahan built the Taj Mahal not only as a resting place for his well-loved wife—and later for himself—but also as a symbol of his power and wealth. The Moguls were Muslims—outsiders and conquerors who ruled India in an absolute monarchy. Their administration left India weak and, by the 1800s, vulnerable to British conquest. In their art and architecture they gave India a more lasting legacy. "The Taj Mahal," wrote Indian poet Rabindranath Tagore, is "like a solitary tear suspended on the cheek of time." ⊕

empire disintegrated; yet northern India would face other Muslim invasions.

Akbar the Great

In the early 1500s **Babur**, who was a descendant of Timur Lenk, led another attack on northern India. Using artillery and with cavalry riding elephants and horses, Babur conquered Delhi at the Battle of Panipat in 1526. Then he set up the Mogul dynasty, the Persian name for Mongol, which lasted three centuries in India. Unlike Timur Lenk, the Moguls encouraged orderly government, and they expanded the arts.

Babur's grandson, **Akbar**, was a benevolent ruler who brought peace and order to northern India. Recognizing that most of the people he ruled were Hindus, Akbar encouraged religious tolerance to end quarrels between Hindus and Muslims. Whereas Muslims believed in one God, Hindus worshiped many deities. Hindus and Muslims differed about sacred foods, social organization, and religious customs. To reduce tension among his people, Akbar repealed a tax on Hindus.

Extremely curious about all religions, Akbar invited religious scholars of other faiths to his court to learn about other religions. He concluded that all religions revealed the same divine truth, whatever their external practices were. He tried to set up a new religion that he called Divine Faith. The new religion included features of many of the world's religions such as Islam, Hinduism, and Christianity.

Mogul Civilization

Under Akbar's rule music, painting, and literature flourished in Mogul India. Mogul rulers made their lavish courts centers of art and learning. Although Akbar could not read, he understood the value of education and set up a large library, employing more than 100 court painters to illustrate the elegantly bound books.

Another Mogul ruler, Shah Jahan, created one of the world's most beautiful buildings—the Taj

 Akbar Hunting Tigers Near Gwalior by Husain Haqqash, c. 1580, from the *Akbar-Nama*. Victoria and Albert Museum, London, England *How did Akbar encourage religious tolerance?*

Mahal at Agra—a magnificent example of Muslim architecture. Muslim architects introduced the arch and dome to India, and in trading contacts with China, Muslim merchants brought gunpowder, paper, and Chinese porcelain to Mogul India.

Mogul Decline

During the late 1600s, Mogul rulers, such as Shah Aurangzeb, abandoned religious toleration. They persecuted India's Hindu majority as well as the Sikhs, followers of Sikhism (SEE•KIH•zuhm), a new religion founded by the teacher Nanak in the 1500s. Sikhism holds to a belief in one God and teaches that good deeds and meditation bring release from the cycle of reincarnation. Today there are about 14 million Sikhs, most of whom live in the northern Indian state of Punjab. During the late 1600s, both Sikhs and Hindus rebelled against the Moguls and helped weaken Mogul authority. As Mogul central government declined, local rulers became more independent.

SECTION I REVIEW

Recall
1. **Define** sultan, grand vizier, janissary, *millet*.
2. **Identify** Suleiman I, Hatt-I Humayun, Shah Abbas, Babur, Akbar.
3. **Use** the map on page 233 to compare the Ottoman Empire's boundaries in 1481 to those in 1683. How did the growth of the Ottoman Empire lead to decline?

Critical Thinking
4. **Making Comparisons** How did Shah Abbas's patronage of the arts compare to that of a contemporary European monarch?

Understanding Themes
5. **Movement** How do you think the movement of Muslims into northern India affected the people already living there?

History & Art Akbar's interest in religion led him to invite Jesuit missionaries to his court, but they failed to convert him to Christianity. **Answer to Caption:** *by repealing a tax on Hindus*

ASSESS

Check for Understanding

Assign Section 1 Review as homework or as an in-class activity.

Use Student Self-Test and Review Software to review Section 1.

Evaluate

Section Quiz 7-1

Use the Testmaker to create a customized quiz for Section 1.

Reteach

Have students review which territories were ruled by each of these peoples at their height: Ottomans, Safavids, Moguls.

Enrich

Have students research a famous landmark in Istanbul, Isfahan, or Delhi and write a description of it.

CLOSE

Ask: Would you have preferred to live under Suleiman, Shah Abbas, or Akbar? Why?

SECTION I REVIEW ANSWERS

1. All vocabulary words are defined in the Glossary.
2. Suleiman I, 232; Hatt-I-Humayun, 234; Shah Abbas, 235; Babur, 237; Akbar, 237
3. It led to border warfare; when military conquests stopped, poverty and discontent spread.
4. Many contemporary rulers also encourage civic improvements and construction of beautiful buildings.
5. **MOVEMENT** It led to conflicts with the people living there, who were Hindu; eventually it led to the development of a new religion, Sikhism, an attempt to unite Islam and Hinduism.

1405 China begins first seagoing expedition.

1644 The Manchus establish the Qing dynasty.

1800 China's population reaches 350 million.

Find Out

Answer: *In each dynasty, strong governments were followed by weak and corrupt ones.*

FOCUS

Section Objective

Analyze why China flourished and then declined during the Ming and Qing dynasties.

Vocabulary Pre-check

Use Vocabulary Activity 7 to introduce vocabulary terms.
L1 LEP

Chinese Dynasties

Setting the Scene

▶ **Terms to Define**
junk, queue, labor-intensive farming

▶ **People to Meet**
Hong Wu, Yong Le, Zheng He

▶ **Places to Locate**
Beijing, the Forbidden City

 **Find Out**   Why did China flourish and then decline during the Ming and Qing dynasties?

The Storyteller

The examination process for civil servants was riddled with corruption. "There are too many men who claim to be pure scholars and yet are stupid and arrogant," K'ang-hsi [Kangxi] fumed. Incompetent examiners were set on memorization instead of independent thinking. Candidate lists were manipulated to favor specific provinces.

Some candidates even hired people to take the exams for them. As an active ruler K'ang-hsi was determined to have officials who were able and efficient. He addressed the problems by holding the exams under armed supervision and reading the exam papers himself.

—adapted from *Emperor of China: Self-Portrait of K'ang-hsi*, translated by Johnathan D. Spence, reprinted in *The Human Record*, Alfred J. Andrea and James H. Overfield, 1990

Han civil service exam

In 1368, after the Yuan dynasty fell, a new era of reform began. The Ming and the Qing dynasties built strong central governments that implemented agricultural and public works projects. As food production and trade increased, so did China's population. At the same time, China looked to earlier achievements to invigorate its culture. After years of prosperity, Chinese emperors isolated themselves from their people and the outside, resulting in government corruption, rebellions, and decline.

The Ming Dynasty

After 89 years of Mongol rule, a military officer named Zhu Yuanzhang (JOO YOO•AHN•JAHNG) led a rebellion that overthrew the Yuan dynasty. Born into a poor peasant family, Zhu had been a Buddhist monk before entering the army. In 1368 he became emperor, taking the name **Hong Wu** and establishing his capital at Nanjing. For the first time in more than 1,000 years, the Son of Heaven was of peasant origin. Hong Wu gave the name *Ming* ("brilliant") to his dynasty, which would rule China for nearly 300 years.

Peace and Stability

The Ming dynasty brought peace and stability to China. Hong Wu and the early Ming rulers imposed new law codes, reorganized the tax system, and reformed local government.

The new law codes were harsher than those of previous Chinese dynasties. Scholars, traditionally exempt from corporal punishment, had to endure public whippings if they displeased the emperor and his officials. Formerly, the saying was that "a gentleman could be ordered to die but should never be humiliated."

Visualizing History The Forbidden City in the heart of the city of Beijing contains hundreds of buildings. Many of these buildings housed the emperors of China and their imperial court from 1421 to 1911. *How did the Ming Emperor Yong Le contribute to Chinese scholarship?*

Chinese persons replaced Mongols in all civil service posts, and Confucianism again became the empire's official doctrine. The Ming dynasty restored the old examination system, making the tests even stricter than in earlier dynasties.

Strong rulers at the beginning of the dynasty enforced peace throughout the land. With peace and additional revenues from a reformed tax system, economic prosperity came to China. But northern China had been devastated by nomadic invaders. To encourage farmers to move there, the government offered free land, tools, seeds, and farm animals. Farmers reclaimed and restored much of the land in the north, and the policy helped secure the northern frontier from invaders.

With more land under cultivation, farmers could sell their surplus produce at local markets. Government workers repaired and maintained the canal system that connected local markets. Increased agricultural productivity also freed workers for nonfarming tasks. Artisans in larger numbers expanded the production of silk, textiles, tea, and porcelain to meet the demands of growing urban populations. Thus, trade within China

increased, enriching merchants in cities such as Shanghai and Guangzhou (GWONG•JOH).

As city merchants and artisans grew wealthier, they demanded more popular entertainments and learning. The third Ming emperor, **Yong Le**, ordered 2,000 scholars to compile a treasury of Chinese histories and literature. This massive library included neo-Confucian writings from the Song dynasty and also many Buddhist scriptures.

Ming writers preferred the novel to other forms of fiction. Their works were based largely on tales told over the centuries by storytellers. One of the most popular novels, *The Romance of the Three Kingdoms*, describes military rivalries at the end of the Han era.

Chinese Exploration

The early Ming emperors spent government money on a navy that could sail to foreign ports and collect tribute for the emperor. The ships,

Chapter 7 *Empires of Asia* **239**

COOPERATIVE LEARNING ACTIVITY

Chart Organize students into two teams, one to focus on the Ming dynasty, the other on the Qing. Each team should make a chart organizing the text information about its dynasty. Among the topics to be included are *Leaders, Religion, Trade Policies, Economics, European Contacts,* and *Cause of Decline.* Each team member should be responsible for one topic. The team members should jointly decide on the chart's format and organization. After completion, the charts should be displayed for the entire class. **L1**

Guided Practice

THEME Cultural Diffusion

Ask: How did China's culture spread beyond its boundaries during the Ming and Qing dynasties? (*by seagoing expeditions and trade*) How did foreign influences enter China during the Ming dynasty? (*via Portuguese traders and Jesuit missionaries*) **L1**

Visualizing History The Forbidden City was so called because no one but a member of the imperial household could enter it. Its numerous buildings were erected in only five years but required a million workers to construct.

Answer to Caption: *He had scholars compile a treasury of Chinese history and literature.*

History Review with the class the three dynasties that preceded the Ming: the Tang (618–907), the Song (960–1279), and the Yuan of the Mongols (1260–1368). Ask them to name a well-known ruler from each one. (*Tang: Tai Cong, Empress Wu; Song: Zhao Kuangyin; Yuan: Kublai Khan*) **L2**

Chinese Exploration

What was the long-term outcome of Chinese voyages of exploration?

Although the Chinese established trading links with Southeast Asia, Africa, and the Middle East, Ming emperors saw no great benefit from the voyages and halted them. China retreated into isolation at a time when Europe was expanding its global outreach.

Government Remind students that the Manchus formed a small minority in China. Ask how these non-Chinese exerted their control. *(by adopting some Chinese traditions, such as Confucian ideals; by favoring Manchus as officers and soldiers; by reserving top government jobs for Manchus and having Manchu supervisors for lesser employees)* **L3**

 World Music: Cultural Traditions, Lesson 8

NATIONAL GEOGRAPHIC SOCIETY

CD-ROM
PICTURE ATLAS OF THE WORLD

View traditional ceremonies that open games in Urumqi, a Muslim city deep in Central Asia, by clicking China's "Video" button.

Linking Past and Present

Chinese New Year Although China today uses the Gregorian calendar, its traditional New Year is still celebrated in both China and Chinese communities living outside China. Occurring on the second new moon after the winter solstice, it falls between January 21 and February 19. A time of clearing out the old, Chinese New Year has traditionally been an occasion for thorough housecleaning, paying debts, and giving charity to the poor.

---

known as **junks**, usually traveled along the coastline, but they could also venture into open water.

From 1405 to 1433, emperors sent out seven seagoing expeditions. Their purpose was "glorifying Chinese arms in the remote regions and showing off the wealth and power of the [Middle] Kingdom." The leader of the voyages was a Chinese Muslim named **Zheng He** (JUNG HUH).

Zheng He took his first fleet to the nations of Southeast Asia. In later voyages he reached India, sailed up the Persian Gulf to Arabia, and even visited eastern Africa. Everywhere he went, he demanded that the people submit to the emperor's authority. If they refused, he applied force; rulers who accepted were rewarded with gold or silk.

Zheng He brought back trade goods and tribute from many lands. From Africa he returned home with animals for the emperor's zoo. As a result of Zheng He's voyages, Chinese merchants settled in Southeast Asia and India and spread Chinese culture.

Later Ming emperors, however, did not follow through: ocean voyages were costly, and in the early 1400s China concentrated its funds on military forces to combat threats from nomadic tribes to the north. The emperor's officials saw no great benefit in exploring expeditions and halted them. The government discouraged trade with foreign countries partly because Confucian philosophy regarded trade as the lowest of occupations. The emperor even forbade construction of seagoing vessels.

Inside the Forbidden City

To help defend the northern border, Yong Le shifted his capital from Nanjing to Cambaluc, renaming it **Beijing** (BAY•JING), which means "northern capital." He ordered the city completely rebuilt, modeled after the great Tang capital of Changan. For 16 years, from 1404 to 1420, workers labored on its construction. On the Chinese New Year's Day in 1421, the government moved to Beijing.

A visitor entering Beijing walked through the great gate in the 30-foot-(9-meter-) high southern wall. Government workers passed through the Gate of Heavenly Peace to the offices of the Imperial City.

Images *of the* Times

Chinese Life

Under the stable, centralized rule of the Ming and Qing dynasties, crafts, industry, and agriculture flourished.

Breeding the silkworm required patience, but the reward was income from trade.

The Gate of Supreme Harmony at Beijing's Forbidden City is guarded well by a centuries-old lion.

Images *of the* Times
Chinese Life

China generally prospered in the early modern period. One development that helped the economy during the Qing dynasty was the growth of private banks. For the first time in Chinese history, merchants and traders were able to secure loans, transfer funds from one part of the empire to another, and use banknotes—along with coins—as payment.

Farther north, across a moat and through the Meridian Gate, stood **the Forbidden City**, where the emperor and his family lived. The Forbidden City had two main sections: one for the emperor's personal use and another for state occasions. The main courtyard outside the gate held 90,000 people. The emperor sometimes appeared before guests here, but ordinary people stayed out or faced a penalty of death.

The residential section of the Forbidden City consisted of many palaces with thousands of rooms. Pavilions and gardens gave comfort to the imperial family, who spent their days in fabulous splendor. Later Ming emperors devoted much of their time to pleasure. In the last 30 years of one emperor's reign, he met with his closest officials only five times.

Corrupt officials, eager to enrich themselves, took over the country. As law and order collapsed, Manchu invaders from Manchuria attacked the northern frontier settlements. Revenues for military spending were limited by the expenses of the lavish court. The Manchus managed to conquer a weakened China.

The Qing Dynasty

In 1644 the Manchus set up a new dynasty, called the Qing (CHING), or "pure." For only the second time in history, foreigners controlled all of China. The Manchus slowly extended their empire to the north and west, taking in Manchuria, Mongolia, Xinjiang (SHIN•JEE•ONG), and Tibet. The offshore island of Taiwan became part of the empire in 1683. For almost 300 years the Qing dynasty ruled over the largest Chinese empire that ever existed.

Adapting Chinese Culture

The Manchus had already accepted Confucian values before invading China. Their leaders understood that these precepts benefited the ruling class. Ruling over an empire in which Chinese outnumbered Manchus by at least 30 to 1, the Manchu rulers controlled their empire by making every effort to adopt many of the native Chinese customs and traditions.

A **Ming porcelain bowl** painted in underglaze displays the familiar blue willow pattern.

Iron workers decorate this Chinese vase preserved in the Golestan Palace, Tehran, Iran.

REFLECTING ON THE TIMES

1. What artistic creation was done under the emperor's patronage?
2. How do these objects and scenes reflect life under the Ming and Qing dynasties?

241

Independent Practice

Guided Reading Activity 7-1 **L1**

Daily Life Have students prepare advertisements to encourage farmers during the Ming dynasty to move to northern China. In their ads, students should mention some of these government benefits: free land, tools, seeds, and farm animals. **L2**

Politics Have students brainstorm a list of topics related to the Taiping Rebellion. Examples are: Western reactions, the leader of the rebellion, the government's response to the rebellion. Ask each student to research one topic, taking notes on index cards. Have students make oral reports to the class and turn their cards in to you after the presentation. **L3**

Cultural Perspectives

Foot-binding The Manchus tried unsuccessfully to outlaw an ancient custom of foot-binding of girls. The Chinese not only admired small feet but also believed in restricting women's freedom. Long strips of cloth were used to turn the toes under and keep the feet three or four inches long. For centuries, only women who did heavy work could escape this painful procedure, for normal feet made a woman unfit for marriage. The practice did not die out until the 1900s.

ANSWERS TO REFLECTING ON THE TIMES

1. porcelain
2. China enjoyed stable government under emperors who patronized artists and architects. The Chinese also enjoyed economic prosperity based on trade and the production of practical and luxury items.

Chapter 7
Section 2

 **inking Past and Present**

Feeding China

Providing for China's growing population was made easier by an innovation introduced by the Manchus—the use of storehouses in each province. By storing reserves of grain, these granaries helped avert famine in years when crops were poor.

ANSWER

In the past, farmers terraced the land and received new food products; and the government sponsored irrigation systems and canals. Today, government has encouraged the profit motive among farmers; dams, bridges, and other public works have been constructed. Answers may include: use of power-driven machinery to cultivate more land; extensive cultivation, however, can lead to soil erosion, and chemicals in fertilizers run off into vital water supplies and contaminate them.

Who?What?Where?When?

Matteo Ricci—known to the Chinese as Li Ma-tou—was the most famous Jesuit missionary to China. He and his fellow Jesuits impressed the Chinese not only with their knowledge of Chinese but also with their tolerance for Chinese customs. For example, they allowed their congregations to discharge fireworks during Mass, in accordance with Chinese religious practice.

CONNECTIONS Economics

Feeding China

During the Ming and Qing eras, China expanded its agricultural production. Rapid population growth, particularly in eastern China, made it necessary for farmers to grow more food. Terracing—the steplike areas that farmers dug out of hillsides—helped them make full use of their lands. To help farmers water their crops and transport them to market, the government continued building canal and irrigation systems.

Chinese irrigation

Meanwhile, new crops from the Americas arrived in China on Chinese ships that traveled regularly to Southeast Asia. During the 1500s, Spanish ships brought sweet potatoes, maize, and peanuts as well as silver and gold from the Americas to the Philippines. There Chinese merchants exchanged silk or porcelain for the precious metals and exotic foods. All these factors helped make China's population the largest in the world.

Today, China is still the world's most populous country, despite government efforts to limit population growth. Farm production also has significantly risen because of better opportunities for farmers to make profits on the open market. Electricity reaches many villages, and a few rural households now operate small factories and businesses. Dam construction, bridge building, and other public works have transformed rural China, while new products have come to China through increased trade with other parts of the world.

inking Past and Present ACTIVITY

Discuss past and present ways used by the Chinese to expand food production. In doing so, how have they changed their environment? How have modern farming practices affected the environment in various parts of the world?

Manchus kept control by naming Manchus to the officer corps and by ensuring that most of the soldiers were Manchus. To control the Chinese civil service, Manchus reserved the top jobs in the government hierarchy for their people. Even Chinese officials in lower positions had a Manchu supervisor monitoring their work. Critical military and government positions thus remained loyal to the Manchu leadership.

In 1645 the Manchu emperor ordered all Chinese men to shave their heads leaving a single queue, or braid, at the back of their heads—or be executed. Among the people this order was known as "Keep your hair and lose your head" or "Lose your hair and keep your head." The upper classes had to adopt the Manchu tight, high-collared jacket and abandon their customary loose robes. But in spite of the many-layered controls, the Manchu rulers took on more elements of Chinese culture.

The Qing were fortunate in having able emperors in the first years of their rule. Emperor Kangxi, who ruled from 1661 to 1722, reduced taxes and undertook public works projects, such as flood control. Kangxi, himself a poet, also sponsored Chinese art. Other emperors secured new territory, extending the Qing Empire.

Daily Life

The Manchus made few changes in China's economy. The government-sponsored work projects and internal peace contributed to economic prosperity in the 1700s. Agricultural improvements increased food production, whereupon China's population exploded, from about 150 million in 1600 to 350 million in 1800. China was the most populous country in the world.

More than three-fourths of the Chinese people lived in rural areas. In the south where Chinese farmers worked as tenants, each family farmed its plot and paid rent to a landlord. In the north, more families owned their land. But because a family divided its land among its sons, over the generations the average peasant's share of land shrank.

As population increased, every inch of land had to be made productive. Although the Chinese had invented such simple machines as the wheelbarrow and paddle-wheel pumps, farmers depended on human labor for most farm tasks. In hill country, farm workers dug flat terraces into the hillsides where rice and other crops could be grown. Workers carried pails of water to fill the rice paddies. This labor-intensive farming, in which work

---

MEETING SPECIAL NEEDS ACTIVITY

Language Delayed To encourage active participation by students for whom English is a second language, organize the class into two groups. Have one represent a Chinese family in Beijing during the Ming dynasty, the other a Turkish family in Istanbul during the same period. Each group should prepare an itinerary for a visiting student from the other country. Tasks should include gathering information about the places on the itinerary and role-playing an interaction between the hosts and the visitor. Each student should participate by explaining at least one aspect of the culture or describing one historic place to the guest. **L1 LEP**

is performed by human effort, contrasts with agriculture in which the hard work is done by animals or machinery.

Subsistence farming was not a year-round occupation during the Qing dynasty. Many farmers grew cash crops such as cotton, rather than just their own food. A writer in the 1700s described the life of farm families in one district:

> 66 The country folk only live off their fields for the three winter months.... During the spring months, they ... spin or weave, eating by exchanging their cloth for rice.... The autumn is somewhat rainy, and the noise of the looms' shuttles is once again to be heard everywhere in the villages.... Thus, even if there is a bad harvest ... our country people are not in distress so long as the other counties have a crop of cotton [for them to weave]. 99

Silk production provided extra income for farm families. They grew mulberry trees, whose leaves provided food for silkworms. From the leaves women and girls plucked the cocoons and carefully unwound them. Then the silk was ready for those who spun it into thread and others who wove it into silk cloth.

Internal trade flourished during the Qing period. There was a lively exchange of goods within and between the various regions of China. Great merchant families made fortunes trading rice, silk, fish, timber, cloth, and luxury goods. The growth of trade prompted specialization. Some regions were famous for textiles; others for cotton, porcelain, tea, or silk. At Jingdezhen, the emperor's porcelain factory employed thousands of workers. Artists painted delicate patterns or scenes on vases, bowls, and plates. Others made chemical glazes that formed a hard, shiny surface on the pottery after it was fired in a hot kiln.

Contacts With Europeans

European demand for Chinese goods such as silk and porcelain was high, attracting European ships to China's coast. The first Europeans arrived in China during the Ming dynasty. In 1514 Portuguese caravels landed near Guangzhou. The Chinese called Portuguese sailors ocean devils, and local officials refused to deal with them. Nonetheless, by 1557 the Portuguese had built a trading base at Macao.

Jesuit missionaries followed the Portuguese traders with the dream of converting China's huge population to Christianity. Although most Chinese officials were not interested in Christianity, the Jesuits' scientific knowledge impressed them. In 1611 the emperor placed a Jesuit astronomer in charge of the Imperial Calendar, and in years to come Jesuits gained other government positions. They also converted some court officials to Christianity. By the 1700s, however, Qing rulers worried that Jesuits were too involved in government affairs and forced the missionaries to leave. The Jesuits had failed to make China a Christian nation.

Qing Decline

During the 1700s corruption and internal rebellions forced the Qing dynasty into a slow decline. As the population grew, the government raised taxes to support public services. High-ranking officials, however, kept much of the revenue. Peasant rebellions followed.

By 1850 the Qing faced the Taiping Rebellion. The leader of this revolt came in contact with Christian missionaries and developed his version of Christianity. He organized many Chinese into a political movement to replace the Qing dynasty with a "Heavenly Kingdom of Great Peace." Lasting 14 years, the rebellion left much of southern China destroyed and the central government weakened. Thus undermined, the Qing faced new threats from foreign imperialistic powers.

SECTION 2 REVIEW

Recall
1. **Define** junk, queue, labor-intensive farming.
2. **Identify** Hong Wu, Yong Le, Zheng He, the Forbidden City, the Manchus.
3. **Use** the world map on pages A4 and A5 in the Atlas to determine the distance Chinese

explorers traveled to reach the east coast of Africa. How does this record compare to Prince Henry's expeditions?

Critical Thinking
4. **Evaluating Information** How did the achievements of the Ming and Qing dynasties differ? Did the Qing build on the

successes of the Ming, or did they create a completely new civilization?

Understanding Themes
5. **Cultural Diffusion** What might have happened if the Chinese had continued moving westward? Would China have colonized as Europeans did?

ASSESS

Check for Understanding
Assign Section 2 Review as homework or as an in-class activity.

Use Student Self-Test and Review Software to review Section 2.

Evaluate
Section Quiz 7-2

Use the Testmaker to create a customized quiz for Section 2.

Reteach
Have students summarize the similarities between the Ming and Qing dynasties. (*Agricultural development was encouraged, internal trade thrived, the arts flourished, foreigners were met with suspicion, rulers accepted Confucian values.*)

Enrich
Have students research the way silk was produced in the 1500s and 1600s in China. Have them prepare diagrams and oral reports on the process.

CLOSE

Have students summarize relations between China and the rest of the world during the Ming and Qing dynasties.

SECTION 2 REVIEW ANSWERS

1. All vocabulary words are defined in the Glossary.
2. Hong Wu, 238; Yong Le, 239; Zheng He, 240; the Forbidden City, 240; the Manchus, 241
3. Chinese explorers traveled about 5,000 miles (8,000 kilometers) to the east coast of Africa. This was much farther

than Prince Henry traveled; his longest expedition was about 2,000 miles (3,200 kilometers), along Africa's west coast.
4. The Ming were known for their overseas voyages, the Qing for conquests that made the Chinese Empire the largest that ever existed. The Qing built on Ming successes.

5. **CULTURAL DIFFUSION** Answers will vary. The Chinese would probably have met stiff resistance from the Ottomans, among others. It is unlikely that they would have set up colonies since they were interested mainly in internal development and protecting their borders.

1600 Tokugawa Ieyasu wins the Battle of Sekigahara.

1636 Act of Seclusion forbids Japanese to leave the country.

c. 1700s Japanese cities grow in size and population.

SECTION THEME

▶ **Reaction** Japan enforces isolationist policy to keep out Western influences.

ꟷind Out

Answer: *This was a period of turmoil for Japan, so people were more open to new social, economic, and religious ideas and practices. By contrast, the 1500s to the 1700s were years of stability in China.*

FOCUS

Section Objective

Explain why Japan was more adaptable to changes than China before the 1800s.

BELLRINGER
Motivational Activity

Before taking roll at the beginning of the class period, project Section Focus Transparency 7-3 and have students answer the activity questions. Discuss students' responses.

▭ This activity is also available as a blackline master.

Vocabulary Pre-check

▭ Use Vocabulary Activity 7 to introduce vocabulary terms.
L1 LEP

Section 3

The Japanese Empire

Setting the Scene

▶ **Terms to Define**
sankin-kotai, metsuke, geisha, haiku

▶ **People to Meet**
Oda Nobunaga, Toyotomi Hideyoshi, Tokugawa Ieyasu, Francis Xavier, Matsuo Basho

▶ **Places to Locate**
Edo, Nagasaki

ꟷind Out
Why was Japan more adaptable to changes than China before the 1800s?

The Storyteller

Yamaga Soko bowed deeply. The shogun, Tokugawa Ieyasu, would determine if Yamaga was prepared to assume a samurai's responsibilities. "In peacetime, we should not be oblivious to the danger of war. Should we not then prepare ourselves for it?" asked Tokugawa. Yamaga understood that many considered the use of arms evil. "Beyond these military duties, we have other functions. We are examples for all society, leading simple and frugal lives," Yamaga responded. Not only would the samurai excel at death; they should also cultivate all aspects of life. Tokugawa spoke again, "A samurai's life calls for constant discipline. Are you, Yamaga Soko, prepared to devote yourself to this?"

—adapted from *Sources of Japanese Tradition,* reprinted in *The Human Record,* Alfred J. Andrea and James H. Overfield, 1990

Samurai in combat

While China enjoyed stability in the 1400s and 1500s, Japan experienced a period of turmoil. The shogun was a mere figurehead, and the emperor performed only religious functions. Daimyos, who controlled their own lands, waged war against their neighbors as feudal lords had done in Europe in the 1400s. "The strongest eat and the weak become the meat" was a Japanese expression of the time. Warriors showed no chivalry or loyalty. This time of local wars left Japan with a political system known as the Tokugawa shogunate that combined a central government with a system of feudalism.

Tokugawa Shogunate

Oda Nobunaga (oh•DAH noh•boo•NAH •gah) was the first military leader to begin uniting the warring daimyos. He announced his ambition on his personal seal: "to bring the nation under one sword." After winning control of a large part of central Japan, Nobunaga led his army against the capital city of Kyoto in 1568. Five years later, amid the chaos caused by the weak Ashikaga (ah•shee•KAH •gah) family, Nobunaga deposed the Ashikaga shogun. Meanwhile, his forces had moved against Buddhist military strongholds around Kyoto. After a 10-year siege, he won and so became the most powerful man in the country. In 1582, however, a treacherous soldier murdered him.

Toyotomi Hideyoshi

Power then shifted to Nobunaga's best general, **Toyotomi Hideyoshi** (toh•yoh•TOH•mee HEE•day •YOH•shee), who rose from a peasant family to his high position in the military. By 1590 Hideyoshi had forced Japan's daimyos to pledge their loyalty to him. Acting as a military dictator, Hideyoshi furthered his goal of unity by disarming the peasants to prevent them from becoming warriors. In 1588 he ordered the "great sword hunt," demanding that

---

SECTION RESOURCES

▭ **Reproducible Masters**
- Reproducible Lesson Plan 7-3
- Vocabulary Activity 7
- Guided Reading Activity 7-3
- Geography and History Activity 7
- People in World History Profile 34
- Section Quiz 7-3

Transparencies
- Section Focus Transparency 7-3

Multimedia
- Focus on World Art Print 10
- Student Self-Test and Review Software
- Testmaker
- World Music: Cultural Traditions, Lesson 8

all peasants turn in their weapons. To stabilize the daimyo realms he controlled, he imposed laws that prevented warriors from leaving their daimyo's service to become merchants or farmers. The laws also prevented farmers and merchants from becoming warriors.

Hideyoshi, planning to expand Japan's power abroad, invaded Korea as a step toward conquering China. The invasion had another purpose—to rid the country of warriors who could start rebellions at home. However, as you learned in Chapter 14, Admiral Yi's Korean turtle ships thwarted Hideyoshi's conquest.

Tokugawa Ieyasu

After Hideyoshi's death in 1598, a third leader, **Tokugawa Ieyasu** (toh•kuh•GAH•wah ee•YAH•soo), completed the work of unification. At the Battle of Sekigahara (seh•kee•gah•HAR•ah) in 1600, Ieyasu defeated the last of his opponents. Three years later, Ieyasu asked the emperor to make him shogun. The Tokugawa family retained the shogunate for 250 years.

Tokugawa Rule

Ieyasu established his government headquarters at the fishing village of **Edo**, present-day Tokyo. There he built a stone fortress protected by high walls and moats. Today, the fortress is the Imperial Palace, but during the Tokugawa shogunate, the Japanese emperor continued to live in Kyoto. Although the emperor remained the official leader of Japan, the shogun exercised the real power.

After taking control, Ieyasu reassigned the daimyos' lands. He divided the daimyos into three groups: Tokugawa relatives, longtime supporters of the Tokugawa family, and those who came to the Tokugawa side only after the Battle of Sekigahara. He issued the most productive lands near Edo to the Tokugawa relatives. The others—potential enemies—received less desirable lands in outlying areas of Japan.

To ensure daimyo loyalty, Ieyasu set up a system called *sankin-kotai*, or attendance by turn. Each daimyo had to travel to Edo every other year, bringing tribute and remaining in the shogun's service for a full year. Thus, half the daimyos were directly under the shogun's control at any one time. Even when the daimyos returned to their estates, they had to leave their families at Edo as hostages.

The daimyos spent much of their income traveling to and from Edo and maintaining several households. They also had to get the shogun's permission to marry and to repair or build their castles. *Sankin-kotai* kept them weak, obedient to the

shogun, and less able to rebel against the government. Much like Louis XIV of France, the shogun turned his aristocracy into courtiers who were carefully watched and controlled.

Political System

The Tokugawa family and a select group of daimyos controlled the government. Together they made up the Council of Elders, the leading administrative body. Assisting the Council, as the "eyes and ears" of the state, was a group of officials known as the *metsuke*. The *metsuke* toured the country and reported on possible uprisings or plots against the shogun. A genuine bureaucracy began to develop, working on the principles of joint decision making and promotion based on talent and success.

Social Classes

Before 1600 there had been some social mobility between classes in Japan. Hideyoshi and Ieyasu

Visualizing History As a member of a professional class of women, a geisha might serve a samurai in song or dance, by playing a musical instrument, or engaging in stimulating conversation. *What were the symbols of authority permitted only to a samurai?*

Chapter 7 *Empires of Asia* **245**

Independent Practice

📁 Guided Reading Activity 7-3 **L1**

📁 Geography and History Activity 7

📁 People in World History Profile 34

Art Have students use library resources to prepare a report on one of these Japanese artists: Hiroshige, Hokusai, or Utamaro. In their reports to the class, have them tell something about the artist, the style of art for which he was known, and the subject matter of his work. Encourage students to show examples of the artist's work. **L2**

Linking Past and Present

Kurosawa Feudal Japan has been brought to life in the movies of today. In dramatizing the past, few have excelled more than the great Japanese film director, Akira Kurosawa. His *Seven Samurai* tells the story of poor villagers who hire samurai to fight off bandits. Kurosawa's film was the basis for a popular American Western, *The Magnificent Seven*.

Visualizing History

In the early 1700s, Edo's population of more than 1,000,000 made it the largest city in the world.
Answer to Caption: *samurai, farmers, artisans, and merchants*

---

had both risen to the top from lowly backgrounds. To maintain social stability and limit future rivals, they introduced measures that froze the Japanese social structure.

Under Tokugawa rule, the Japanese were divided into four social classes. At the top were the samurai, including the daimyos, who held all political power. They alone could wear symbols of authority: a sword and a distinctive topknot in their hair. The farmers, as major food producers, were the second-highest class. They were followed by artisans who made goods. Merchants were at the bottom of society, because they only exchanged goods and thus were not productive.

No one could change his social class or perform tasks that belonged to another class. One samurai recalled that his father took him out of school because he was taught arithmetic—a subject fit only for merchants. A character in a popular puppet play, written by the author Chikamatsu, described the proper order of society:

> A samurai's child is reared by samurai parents and becomes a samurai himself because they teach him the warrior's code. A merchant's child is reared by merchant parents and becomes a merchant because they teach him the way of commerce. A samurai seeks a fair name in disregard for profit, but a merchant, with no thought to his reputation, gathers profit and amasses a fortune. This is the way of life proper to each. This strict social order helped maintain peace and stability throughout Japan. "

Visualizing History In Tokugawa Japan, cities became leading centers of Japanese culture. Artisans began to produce goods for a growing urban market. *What social classes made up Tokugawa Japan?*

Tokugawa Ethics

Tokugawa ethics placed loyalty to the shogun above the family. Duty and honor became the central values. Individuals had to develop strict inner discipline to live up to the requirements of their assigned place in life. These values gradually spread from the samurai through all social classes in Japan.

Over the course of time, Tokugawa rules for personal conduct evolved into complex rituals and etiquette. Minute details came to have heavy symbolic meaning. They became a way to maintain conformity and control. This was important for a society that had a large population and only a small area of productive land.

Contacts With the West

The peace and order of the Tokugawa shogunate were interrupted when the first Europeans—the Portuguese—arrived in Japan in 1543. Although the Japanese looked upon Europeans as barbarians, the warrior society saw that European weapons meant power. They purchased muskets and cannon to defeat their opponents.

Roman Catholic missionaries soon followed the Portuguese merchants. **Francis Xavier**, the earliest of the Jesuit priests who came to Japan, admired the Japanese people. To convert them, the Jesuits adopted their customs. Jesuit missionaries learned the subtleties of conversing in polite Japanese and set up a tea room in their houses so that they could receive their visitors properly.

After Xavier won the support of some local daimyos, Christianity spread rapidly. Oda Nobunaga himself lent support to the Christians, for during this time he was moving against the Buddhist monasteries that were serving as military strongholds. Jesuits trained Japanese priests to create a strong Japanese Christian church. By 1614 the Jesuits had converted 300,000 Japanese.

Many Japanese welcomed the first contact with Westerners, whose customs and styles became widespread in Japanese society. Even for Japanese who had not converted to Christianity, Christian symbols became fashionable. A missionary described non-Christian daimyos who would wear "rosaries of driftwood on their breasts, hang a

---

Visualizing History Merchants from the West arrive in Japan accompanied by Jesuit missionaries. *How did Christian missionary activity end under Tokugawa rule?*

Visualizing History One reason Christianity grew quickly in Japan was that when a daimyo adopted the faith, all the people subordinate to him did so, too.
Answer to Caption: *The shoguns outlawed Christianity, crucified some priests, and killed converts or forced them to emigrate.*

Compare Ask students to compare the Tokugawa period with the Renaissance in Europe. Have them include how the Japanese turned toward pleasure and away from the spirituality of Buddhism. This project can be in the form of a chart or a written report. **L3**

crucifix from their shoulder or waist … they think it good and effective in bringing success in daily life."

Hideyoshi began to suspect that Christian influence could be harmful to Japan. He had heard of Spanish missionaries in the Philippines who had helped establish Spain's control over the islands. In 1587 Hideyoshi outlawed Christianity. Although some priests were crucified, Hideyoshi generally did not enforce his ban on the religion.

Tokugawa Ieyasu and his successors also feared that Christianity threatened their power and so continued to persecute Christians, killing them or forcing them to leave Japan. When Japanese Christians in the port city of **Nagasaki** defied authorities and refused to disband, the government attacked their community in 1637 and finally wiped them out in 1638.

Japan's Policy of Isolation

The Tokugawa rulers, deciding that contact with outsiders posed too many dangers, laid down edicts. Their seclusion policy lasted 200 years. The Act of Seclusion of 1636 forbade any Japanese to leave the country and added, "All Japanese residing abroad shall be put to death when they return home." The government banned construction of ships large enough for ocean voyages.

Japan barred all Europeans except the Dutch. Unlike the Spanish and the Portuguese, the Dutch were interested only in trade, not conquest or religious conversion of the Japanese. For this reason, after 1641 the Tokugawa government confined the Dutch to a tiny island in Nagasaki harbor where they and a few Chinese carried on a tightly regulated trade. Through the Dutch traders, a trickle of information about the West continued to flow into Japan.

Despite Japan's geographic isolation and the Tokugawa policy of isolation, Japan's society and economy continued to change internally. During the early Tokugawa period, agriculture brought wealth to daimyos and samurai, who profited from the rice produced on their lands. Merchants, in turn, grew wealthy by lending money to daimyos and samurai.

Footnotes to History

Karate
Karate is unarmed combat in which a person uses primarily the hands or feet to strike a blow at an opponent. This martial art began on the island of Okinawa near Japan. During the 1600s, Okinawa's Japanese conquerors forbade the local people to own weapons. In response, many Okinawans learned to turn their hands and feet into fighting instruments.

POINT

Japan's Policy of Isolation
How did Tokugawa policies affect Japan and the rest of the world?
Japan was largely isolated from economic and cultural contacts with the West; however, its society and economy developed internally. Agriculture flourished, and cities grew in size and population.

Chapter 7 *Empires of Asia* **247**

MAKING CONNECTIONS ACTIVITIES

Daily Life The Japanese inn, or *ryokan*, preserves many features of Japanese life as they have been for centuries. Have students research the subject and present their findings to the class. Travel guides to Japan would be a good source of information. **L2**

Art Have students research classical Japanese theater, including Noh and Kabuki. Have them use their findings to make a presentation to the class. Encourage students to use visual aids—pictures, photos, and if possible video footage—in their presentations. **L1 LEP**

CURRICULUM CONNECTION

THE ARTS

Japanese prints *(ukiyo-e)* influenced many European artists in the 1800s. Among the painters who admired and imitated their flat, decorative style were Vincent van Gogh, Henri de Toulouse-Lautrec, and Édouard Manet.

ASSESS

Check for Understanding

Assign Section 3 Review as homework or as an in-class activity.

 Use Student Self-Test and Review Software to review Section 3.

Evaluate

Section Quiz 7-3

Reteach

Have students make charts for the Tokugawa era (1600–1868). Under headings such as *Government, Society,* and *Foreign Relations,* have them summarize the main events of this period.

Enrich

Have students read the classic *A Book of Five Rings* and prepare a brief book report, including biographical material about the author, Miyamoto Musachi.

CLOSE

Discuss Japan's location and how it furthered a policy of isolation. Ask students what would be different in our society if Japan had remained isolated. *(Answers may include that we would lack many innovative electronics products.)*

First Public Opera House Opens

Venice, Italy, 1637
The Teatro San Cassiano—the world's first public opera house—opened in Venice in 1637. Early baroque operas consisted of recitatives, or informational parts, sung by soloists accompanied by one or two instruments. The arias, or solos expressing a character's feelings, allowed opera singers to show off their vocal skills. By the late 1600s, operas were being written and performed in England, France, and Germany. Italian opera, however, remained the accepted style.

As the daimyos became a debtor class, the merchant class became more powerful.

The system of *sankin-kotai* also helped merchants to prosper and trade to increase, because merchants provided the goods and services that the daimyos needed on their twice-yearly trips to Edo. To smooth the daimyos' journey, the government built roads, which also made it easier for traders to take their goods to distant regions. Rest stations along the roads often grew into trading or administrative towns of considerable size.

At the same time, the demands for increased taxes led the daimyos to increase agricultural yields. As agriculture became more efficient, farming required fewer people. Unemployed farm workers moved to prosperous towns and cities, seeking work as artisans. In urban centers such as Edo, Kyoto, and Osaka, social order began to break down and class distinctions became less rigid.

Social life in the cities converged on bathhouses, restaurants, and theaters. Japanese merchants and samurai could relax in the company of geishas, women who were professional entertainers. Geishas were trained in the arts of singing, dancing, and conversation. Urban amusement centers also provided employment for playwrights, artists, and poets. At this time a new form of theater known as Kabuki developed. Kabuki became popular for its portrayal of historical events and emotion-filled domestic scenes. Another form of drama that arose during this period was the elaborate Japanese puppet theater called Bunraku, in which three-man teams manipulated each puppet as a backstage chorus sang a story.

A popular form of art called ukiyo-e developed from the demand for prints of famous actors and their plays. At first, ukiyo-e prints were black-and-white, but soon ornate, brightly colored prints appeared in street stalls. Printed on delicate rice paper, they are highly prized collectors' items today.

A new form of poetry called haiku (HY•koo) also became popular among city people. In only 17 syllables, the haiku was to express a thought that would surprise the reader. **Matsuo Basho**, one of the great haiku masters, wrote this haiku:

> 66 In my new clothing
> I feel so different
> I must
> Look like someone else. 99

As cities grew in size and population during the 1700s and 1800s, the ban on foreign contacts was gradually relaxed. Some Japanese began to study Western medicine in books that the Dutch brought to Nagasaki. Their interest in the so-called Dutch learning spread to Western science and technology. However, it would not be until the other Europeans arrived in the 1800s that Japan would begin to absorb other Western ideas.

SECTION 3 REVIEW

Recall
1. **Define** *sankin-kotai, metsuke,* geisha, haiku.
2. **Identify** Oda Nobunaga, Toyotomi Hideyoshi, Tokugawa Ieyasu, Francis Xavier, Matsuo Basho.
3. **Describe** how the *sankin-kotai* system affected the daimyos.

How did shoguns benefit from the system? How was the emperor affected?
Critical Thinking
4. **Synthesizing Information** Imagine that you lived in Japan during the Tokugawa shogunate. Which social class would you have wanted to

belong to? Explain.
Understanding Themes
5. **Reaction** Explain why Japan reacted to Western ideas by adopting a policy of isolation. How did this reaction affect Japan's development over the next few centuries?

SECTION 3 REVIEW ANSWERS

1. All vocabulary words are defined in the Glossary.
2. Oda Nobunaga, 244; Toyotomi Hideyoshi, 244; Tokugawa Ieyasu, 245; Francis Xavier, 246; Matsuo Basho, 248
3. It weakened the daimyos while strengthening the shoguns. The emperor, having little power to begin with, was probably not

much affected.
4. Answers should reflect an understanding of social classes.
5. **REACTION** The Tokugawa rulers believed Western religious ideas were harmful; it prevented the Japanese from acquiring much knowledge of Western ideas and technology until the 1800s.

Using a Word Processor

There are several ways to create a professional looking printed document. You may use a word processor or a computer word processing software program. A word processor is a keyboard-operated terminal with a video display.

Learning the Skill

When you open most word processors, you are initially presented with a blank document. To create a new document, simply begin typing. Use the following tips to help you format the document to make it look the way you want:

1. Text fonts, or size and style of type, can be chosen. To choose font or size and style of type, click **Font** on your Standard toolbar.
2. Text can be made to appear **bold**, *italicized*, or underlined. To do this, first highlight the text (drag the cursor, or pointer, over the text with the left mouse button depressed). Then choose the modification mentioned above (the way you do this depends on the word processor you are using).
3. Press **Tab** to indent a paragraph. Press **Enter** to start a new paragraph.
4. To insert new text in a line, move the cursor to the point where you want the line to go and type. The word processing program moves the existing text to the right to make room for the new text.
5. When you finish typing, click the **Spell Check** button on the Standard toolbar to check the spelling of your document.

Practicing the Skill

This chapter focuses on the empires of Asia from 1350 through 1850. Create a newspaper article about an important event during one of these empires. Be sure to include a headline in your article. To use a word processor to create this document, complete the following steps.
1. Choose a font and the text size from the stan-

dard toolbar. Use a different text and size for your headline than you use for the rest of the text.
2. Type two or three paragraphs of copy about the event you chose for your article. As you type, make modifications to the text, such as bold, italics, or underlining.
3. Press **Tab** to indent a paragraph. Press **Enter** to start a new paragraph.
4. Insert new text in a line.
5. Use **Spell check** to check the spelling of your document.

Applying the Skill

Using a word processor, create an official-looking document that explains the Ottoman Laws described on pages 233–234 of this textbook.

For More Practice

Turn to the Skill Practice in the Chapter Review on page 255 for more practice in using a word processor.

ANSWERS TO PRACTICING THE SKILL

Answers will vary depending on the event chosen to write about. Check for accurate use of word processing functions, such as fonts, paragraph indents, spelling, and so on.

TEACH

Using a Word Processor If possible, schedule computer lab time so students can get practice in using a word processor. As students follow the instructions in **Learning the Skill,** point out that word processing programs automatically "wrap" the text to the next line when the text reaches the right margin. Tell them to make sure that they do not press **Enter** at the end of each line of text, unless they are starting a new paragraph.

Help students find the toolbar on the screen of their computer. Have them practice word processing techniques using the functions shown on the toolbar. For example, have them practice moving text around on a page. Have students move several lines of text. Say to students, "Highlight the text you wish to remove and then click the Cut button (or scissors icon) on the toolbar. Next, position your cursor (insertion point) in the location that you want to move the cut text and click the Paste button (or jar of paste icon). The cut text appears at your cursor. If you accidentally drag or paste text to the wrong place, click the Undo or Edit button on the toolbar."

To learn other word processing methods, have students read their word processor user's manual or click the Help button on their toolbar.

Skill Reinforcement Activity 7

SECTION THEME

▶ **Change** Southeast Asian lands face the growth of European trade and commerce in their region.

Find Out

Answer: *Thai rulers encouraged competition among foreign nations so that no single one could gain control.*

FOCUS

Section Objective

Explain how the Thai kingdom was able to keep its independence while other parts of Southeast Asia gradually came under European control.

BELLRINGER
Motivational Activity

Before taking roll at the beginning of the class period, project Section Focus Transparency 7-4 and have students answer the activity questions. Discuss students' responses.

This activity is also available as a blackline master.

Vocabulary Pre-check

Use the Vocabulary PuzzleMaker to create a puzzle that reinforces the vocabulary terms in this section. **L1**

1500	1700	1900

1511 Portuguese seize port of Melaka on the Malay Peninsula.

1565 Spaniards found a colony in the Philippines.

1767 Troops from Burma seize Ayutthaya.

1868 Chulalongkorn becomes king of Siam.

Section 4

Southeast Asia

Setting the Scene

▶ **Terms to Define**
colony, *datus*, animism

▶ **People to Meet**
Trailok, Phraya Chakkri, Mongkut, Chulalongkorn

▶ **Places to Locate**
Manila, Java, Indochina, Bangkok

Find Out How was the Thai kingdom able to keep its independence while other parts of Southeast Asia gradually came under European control?

The Storyteller

The century-old Bayon Temple of Angkor swarmed with workers. Huge stone faces with faint, haunting smiles gazed in all directions. A European merchant stepped closer to examine the temple and nearly collided with a monk. When asked about the faces, the monk replied, "This old Hindu shrine will become a Buddhist temple. Jayavarman, our king, has adopted the Buddhist religion and wishes to introduce its teaching throughout our land. Sculptors have been commissioned to create new images on the temple. Most important is the image of boddhisattva, a compassionate being who looks everywhere for souls to save."

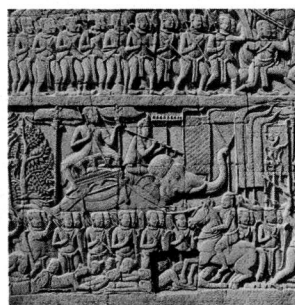

—freely adapted from *World History*, Volume 1, William Duiker and Jackson Spielvogel, 1994

Relief from Bayon Temple of Angkor

By the mid-1400s, Southeast Asia was carrying on extensive trade with other regions. This was partly because of its location on the water route between India and China. In addition, Southeast Asia produced valuable spices and woods that people in other parts of the world wanted to buy.

European Influences

In the early 1500s the first European explorers reached Southeast Asia in search of new trade routes and products. With the coming of the Europeans, Southeast Asian kingdoms faced a growing challenge to their independence and traditional ways of life.

The Portuguese Spice Trade

Coming from India, the Portuguese were the first Europeans to reach Southeast Asia in the early 1500s. They set out to control the region's lucrative spice trade which, for many years, had been controlled by Muslim traders. In 1511 Portuguese soldiers captured the most important of the Muslim ports—Melaka, on the west side of the Malay Peninsula.

During the next 25 years, the Portuguese built a number of new trading posts in Southeast Asia. They patrolled the seas near the islands of present-day Indonesia to keep out the ships of other countries. The Portuguese also tried to spread Catholicism in maritime Southeast Asia. They had little success, however, because most Southeast Asian islanders resented Portuguese disregard for their traditional cultures.

Spanish Rule in the Philippines

The Spaniards were eager to find their own route to the spices of Southeast Asia. In 1519 Ferdinand Magellan, exploring for Spain, reached Southeast Asia by sailing westward around the

---

SECTION RESOURCES

Reproducible Masters
• Reproducible Lesson Plan 7-4
• Guided Reading Activity 7-4
• Reteaching Activity 7
• Enrichment Activity 7
• Section Quiz 7-4
• Performance Assessment Activity 7
• Spanish Chapter Summary 7

Transparencies
• Section Focus Transparency 7-4

Multimedia
• Vocabulary PuzzleMaker Software
• Student Self-Test and Review Software
• Testmaker
• World Music: Cultural Traditions, Lesson 9

Visualizing History During the 1600s, the Netherlands reached its height as a seafaring power. Dutch merchant ships sailed the seas from the Caribbean region to the East Indies (Indonesia). *How did the Dutch win control of the Indonesian island of Java?*

TEACH

Guided Practice

THEME Change

Ask students to list the foreigners who brought change to Southeast Asia beginning in the 1500s. *(Portuguese, Spanish, English, Dutch, French)* **What goal did they all have in common?** *(trade)* **L1 LEP**

Geography Using a wall map or a map in the Atlas of this book, review with the class the geographical features of the Southeast Asian regions of special concern in this chapter: the Malay Peninsula, Indonesia, the Philippines, Indochina, Siam (Thailand), and Burma (Myanmar). **L2**

Visualizing History During the golden age of the Netherlands—the 1600s—this small country was among the most powerful and influential nations on the earth.
Answer to Caption: *using force to get the English to leave; gaining concessions from local rulers in exchange for their help*

Economics Discuss with students the advantages and disadvantages to a parent country of having colonies. *(advantages: control over subject peoples, assured source of raw materials, assured market for goods from the home country; disadvantages: need for supervision by parent country, drain on parent country's resources)* **L3**

World Music: Cultural Traditions, Lesson 9

southern tip of South America. Magellan and his crew landed in the Philippines, becoming the first Europeans to visit these islands.

In 1565 the Spanish founded a colony, or overseas territory ruled by a parent country, in the Philippines. Although the Spanish did not find spices in the Philippines, they did find fertile land and an excellent location for trade. Spanish soldiers and officials established a fortified settlement at **Manila** on the island of Luzon. Manila's magnificent harbor made the Philippines a valuable link in Spain's trade with Asia and the Americas.

The Spaniards gradually expanded their control to other parts of the islands. They persuaded many of the *datus*, or local rulers, to pledge loyalty to Spain in return for keeping their regional powers. Under Spanish rule, most of the people of the Philippines—largely of Malay and Chinese descent—accepted many Spanish customs as well as the Roman Catholic faith. Spanish Roman

Catholic clergy established missions, learned the local languages, taught the people European agricultural methods, and introduced new crops—such as maize (corn) and cocoa—from the Americas. Spain's control of the Philippines would last well into the late 1800s.

Dutch Traders in Indonesia

By the end of the 1500s, English and Dutch traders were also wanting a share in the Southeast Asian spice trade. After breaking Portuguese control of the trade, they began to fight each other. During the 1620s, the Dutch finally succeeded in forcing the English to leave the islands that now make up present-day Indonesia. A further step toward Dutch control of the islands came in 1677 when the ruler of Mataram, a kingdom on the island of **Java**, asked the Dutch to help him defeat a rebel uprising. In return for their assistance, the Dutch received important trading rights and

Chapter 7 *Empires of Asia* **251**

COOPERATIVE LEARNING ACTIVITY

Debate Organize the class into two groups representing advisers to a Southeast Asian ruler. Europeans, who have been trading with their country, now want to establish a colony there. One group should argue in favor of the colony while the other group opposes it. Each participant should contribute specific reasons in support of their group's stand. **L2**

Independent Practice

📁 Guided Reading Activity 7-4 **L1**

Daily Life Have students, as Spanish settlers living in the Philippines in the 1600s, write to friends in Spain urging them to emigrate and explaining why life as a colonist offers a good future. **L2**

Government Have students research the present-day Chakkri ruler of Thailand. In brief reports, have them summarize his role and compare it with that of the founder of the dynasty, Phraya Chakkri. **L3**

Linking Past and Present

The King and I In the 1860s King Mongkut employed a Welsh governess, Anna Leonowens, to tutor his children. Her story was told in a popular book of the 1940s, *Anna and the King of Siam*. The book in turn served as the basis for the musical *The King and I*, two movies, and a television serial.

Visualizing History

In a single year, King Trailok had 500 statues of the Buddha cast, hoping to prevent a repetition of the great famine that had devastated his country the year before.
Answer to Caption: *Hinduism and animism*

Javanese lands. Through similar agreements and by force, the Dutch had gained control of most of the other Indonesian islands by the late 1700s.

The French in Vietnam

The French were latecomers in the European pursuit of trade and colonies in Southeast Asia. Beginning in the 1600s, French traders based in India carried out only limited trade with the Vietnamese and other peoples in the Southeast Asian region of **Indochina**. Because of the weakness of this trade link, the Vietnamese and their Indochinese neighbors were able to keep the French from taking control of their area. Roman Catholic missionaries from France, however, converted many Vietnamese to Christianity.

By the early 1800s most of Indochina was ruled by local emperors who came from the region of Annam in present-day Vietnam. At this time, Indochina was predominantly Chinese in culture. Devoted to Confucian ideas, the Annamese emperors persecuted their Christian subjects and tried to keep Indochina closed to Europeans. Angered at the policies of the Annamese court, the French in 1858 returned to Southeast Asia in force. Their stated purpose was to protect local Christians from persecution. However, they also wanted Indochina's rubber, coal, and rice. In the 1860s the French began to colonize the region.

The Thai Kingdom

While European influence grew throughout Southeast Asia, the independent kingdom of Ayutthaya (ah•YU•tuh•yuh) continued to flourish in the area that is present-day Thailand. Under a series of powerful kings, the Thai people of Ayutthaya developed a rich culture based on Buddhism, Hinduism, and animism, the idea

Visualizing History This bronze bas–relief of the Buddha reveals the important role that Buddhism has played in unifying the Thai people and in supporting their rulers. *What other religious influences shaped the development of Thai culture?*

---

that both living and nonliving things have spirits or souls.

Trailok's Rule

One of the most powerful Ayutthaya monarchs was King **Trailok**, who ruled from 1448 to 1488. Trailok set up a strong central government with separate civil and military branches directly responsible to him. He also brought local leaders to Ayutthaya and put them in charge of new governmental offices. These officials were required to live in the capital where the king could easily oversee their work.

Trailok set up a rigid class system based on loyalty to the Thai monarchy. All male Thai were given the use of varying amounts of land according to their rank. Nobles and merchants were given as much as 4,000 acres (1,620 ha), while enslaved people, artisans, and other subjects with little status received 10 acres (4 ha) or less. Women were not included in this distribution of land.

Expansion

While the Ayutthaya kingdom set its internal affairs in order, Thai soldiers fought battles with neighboring peoples, such as the Khmer, Burmans, and Malays. Through conquests, the Ayutthaya kingdom grew to almost the size of present-day Thailand. In 1431 Thai soldiers from Ayutthaya captured Angkor Wat and destroyed it. They also overcame the Malays in the south as well as smaller Thai kingdoms in the north.

During the mid-1500s a border dispute led to war between the Ayutthaya kingdom and Burma (Myanmar). Soldiers from Burma briefly captured the city of Ayutthaya in 1569, but the Thai king Naresuan defeated Burma's ruler in the Battle of Nong Sarai in 1593.

European Contacts

The 1500s also saw the beginning of European contacts with Ayutthaya. The Portuguese and later the Dutch and the English sent delegations to the kingdom to encourage trade. For much of the 1600s, Thai rulers allowed Europeans the right to carry out trade in their territory. In 1612

MEETING SPECIAL NEEDS ACTIVITY

Learning Style: Kinesthetic Some students may need help understanding the nature of trade in Southeast Asia in early modern times. Organize the class into small groups and assign each one a Southeast Asian trade item, such as cloves, cinnamon, cassia, nutmeg, ebony, or rosewood. Have each group find an example of its item to bring to class. Also, have each group research its item, finding out where in the region it is from and how it was used by Europeans. **L1**

British traders took a letter from King James I to the Thai monarch. They reported back that the city of Ayutthaya, with its palaces and Buddhist temples, was as large and awesome as London.

The Thai, however, became concerned that Europeans wanted to colonize as well as trade. In 1688 a Thai group that opposed European influences took over the kingdom. The new rulers expelled most of the Europeans except for a few Dutch and Portuguese traders. The kingdom closed its ports to the West until 1826.

The Bangkok Era

Free of European influence, Thai rulers hoped for a period of calm. Burma, however, wanted to resume the conflict with Ayutthaya that it had lost in the late 1500s. In 1767 an army from Burma defeated the Thai and sacked and burned the city of Ayutthaya. The Thai, however, soon rallied after the disaster. Phraya Taksin (PRY•uh tahk•SEEN), a Thai general, led his troops against Burma's army and drove it out of the region.

After proclaiming himself king, Taksin forced rival Thai groups to accept his rule. He reigned until 1782, when rebel leaders overthrew him. The rebels called on General **Phraya Chakkri** (PRY•uh SHAH•kree) to be the new Thai monarch. Chakkri founded the royal dynasty that still rules Thailand today. Chakkri built a new capital called **Bangkok** on the Chao Phraya River. Under Chakkri's rule, the reborn Thai kingdom became known as Siam.

Reforming Monarchs

By the mid-1800s Europeans were pressuring Thai rulers to widen trade opportunities in Siam. King **Mongkut** recognized the threat that Western colonial nations posed to the independence of his kingdom. He moved quickly to protect Siam by setting foreign nations against one another through competition.

Mongkut achieved this goal by allowing many Western nations to have commercial opportunities

Visualizing History King Mongkut ruled Siam from 1851 to 1868. He increased the powers of the monarchy while supporting social reforms to improve the conditions of his subjects. *How did Mongkut work to preserve Siam's independence?*

in the kingdom. The Thai king welcomed what he judged to be the positive influences of Western commerce on his country. He encouraged his people to study science and European languages with the Christian missionaries who had accompanied European traders to the kingdom.

After Mongkut's death in 1868, his son **Chulalongkorn** (choo•lah•LAHNG•kohrn) came to the throne. Like Mongkut, Chulalongkorn worked to modernize Siam while protecting the kingdom from European controls. He ended slavery, founded schools, encouraged his people to study abroad, and built railways and roads.

SECTION 4 REVIEW

Recall
1. **Define** colony, *datus*, animism.
2. **Identify** Melaka, Manila, Trailok, Phraya Chakkri, Bangkok, Mongkut, Chulalongkorn.
3. **Locate** Southeast Asia on the map on page 130, and explain

why it attracted European explorers, traders, and missionaries during the 1500s and 1600s.

Critical Thinking
4. **Making Comparisons** How do you think the Spanish conquest of the Philippine Islands differed from the

Portuguese conquest of the Indonesian islands?

Understanding Themes
5. **Change** How did the Thai kings Mongkut and Chulalongkorn respond to the growth of Western influence in their region?

Chapter 7 *Empires of Asia* **253**

SECTION 4 REVIEW ANSWERS

1. All vocabulary words are defined in the Glossary.
2. Melaka, 250; Manila, 251; Trailok, 252; Phraya Chakkri, 253; Bangkok, 253; Mongkut, 253; Chulalongkorn, 253
3. It was strategically located between India and China, and it had desirable natural resources.

4. The Spanish established colonies, not just trading posts. Also, they had more success in spreading Christianity.
5. **CHANGE** Both welcomed some Western education and innovations but also protected Siam from foreign control.

Visualizing History Mongkut spent 25 years as a monk before he became king. He also studied Latin, English, mathematics, and astronomy.
Answer to Caption: *By giving commercial opportunities to many different nations, he set them against one another and thus reduced their power.*

ASSESS

Check for Understanding

Assign Section 4 Review as homework or as an in-class activity.

 Use Student Self-Test and Review Software to review Section 4.

Evaluate

 Section Quiz 7-4

 Use the Testmaker to create a customized quiz for Section 4.

Reteach

Have students review the role of European traders in Southeast Asia.

 Reteaching Activity 7

Enrich

Have students research and report on the death of Magellan in the Philippine Islands.

 Enrichment Activity 7

CLOSE

Have students summarize how Southeast Asia in the late 1800s differed from what it had been in the early 1500s.

Chapter 7 Review

GLENCOE
TECHNOLOGY

VIDEODISC
Use MindJogger to review students' knowledge of the chapter.

MindJogger Videoquiz

Chapter 7
Disc 1 Side B

  Also available in VHS.

Answers

Using Key Terms

1. h   4. c
2. g   5. k
3. d

Using Your History Journal

Remind students that they should back up any generalizations they make with specific details about the place they write about.

Reviewing Facts

1. Ottoman, Safavid (Persian), Mogul
2. The Ottomans were Sunni Muslims; the Persians were Shiites and bitter enemies of the Ottomans.
3. The Moguls were Muslims, unlike their Hindu subjects. Rulers like Akbar were tolerant, but later Moguls persecuted Hindus.
4. to display China's wealth and power and to obtain trade and tribute
5. staffed army with Manchus; reserved top government jobs for Manchus; had Manchus monitor Chinese officials; enforced Manchu hair and clothing styles
6. Geishas were female professional entertainers who were trained in

254 Chapter 7 *Empires of Asia*

Connections Across Time

Historical Significance From 1350 to 1850 many social and political changes came to Asia. Islam continued to expand and reached South Asia as a result of the Mogul invasions. Despite efforts at toleration, conflicts developed between Muslims and Hindus that still divide South Asia today.

During the early modern period, China turned inward instead of meeting the challenge of the West. Japan and Siam at first took the same route; however, they eventually introduced reforms that preserved their freedom. In Japan's case, reforms also enabled it to compete successfully with Western countries.

Using Key Terms

Write the key term that completes each sentence. Then write a sentence for each term not chosen.

a. geisha
b. grand vizier
c. haiku
d. janissaries
e. *sankin-kotai*
f. colony
g. labor-intensive farming
h. sultan
i. queue
j. *datus*
k. *millets*

1. The Ottoman leader Suleiman I acted as both the _____, or political ruler, and the caliph, or religious leader.
2. During the Manchu dynasty, the Chinese practiced _____ in which workers dug flat terraces into hillsides to grow rice.
3. Ottoman sultans maintained a special corps of soldiers known as _____ who were noted as a fierce and loyal fighting force.
4. Japanese writers developed _____, a form of poetry made up of 17 syllables, that became popular among city people.
5. Ottoman law allowed religious groups to run affairs in their own _____, or communities.

Technology Activity

Using a Computerized Card Catalog Use a computerized card catalog to locate sources about traditional Japanese customs that are practiced in Japan today. Write an essay discussing how political power, leadership, and loyalty in traditional Japan compare to how these characteristics are viewed in modern democracies. Share your opinions with the rest of the class.

254 Chapter 7 *Empires of Asia*

Using Your History Journal

From your notes and outline write a three-page paper on one of the four sites listed on page 231. Discuss what that place reveals about the civilization that built it.

Reviewing Facts

1. **History** Name the three great Muslim empires in eastern Europe, central Asia, and India.
2. **Culture** Define the relationship between Sunni Muslims and Shiite Muslims living in the Ottoman Empire and the Persian Empire.
3. **Culture** Explain how the Moguls' religion brought them into conflict with the majority of India's people. Describe how Mogul rulers reacted.
4. **History** Explain the purpose of the voyages of Zheng He.
5. **History** List the steps taken by the Manchus to maintain their control over China.
6. **Culture** Describe the role of geishas in Japan.
7. **Culture** Discuss the effects of the shogunate's policies on Japan's Christian population.

Critical Thinking

1. **Apply** How did religious differences cause strife between Muslim empires?
2. **Evaluate** Would you consider Suleiman I a successful ruler? Why was he called "The Lawgiver" by the Ottomans?
3. **Analyze** How did Akbar's religious tolerance in India differ from that of the Manchus in China?

---

the arts of singing, dancing, and conversation. They worked in expanding urban areas to entertain merchants and samurai.
7. Fearing the spread of Christian and Western influences, shoguns persecuted Christians, killing them or forcing them to leave Japan.

Critical Thinking

1. The Safavids, as Shiite Muslims, were bitterly opposed to the Ottomans, who were Sunnis.

2. yes; because of his work in organizing Ottoman laws
3. Akbar invited representatives of all faiths to his court because he was curious about different religions. The Manchus allowed Christian missionaries into China but were only interested in their scientific knowledge.
4. Answers should reflect knowledge of the various governments.
5. The Moguls (who were Muslims) conquered

4. **Evaluate** Which government described in this chapter was most successful in meeting its people's needs? Why?

5. **Evaluate** How did the movement of Islamic peoples affect northern India? What impact did Islam have on religion in this part of India?

6. **Analyze** What factors led to China's growth in both land and population during the Qing dynasty? How did government policies contribute to this growth?

7. **Evaluate** Was the Ming dynasty's policy of isolationism beneficial to China? Explain.

8. **Analyze** How did new urban centers in Japan influence growth in the arts and entertainment?

Geography in History

1. **Region** Refer to the map below that shows the political divisions of Japan about 1560. For more than a century, feudal lords fought for control of territory. How many Daimyo clans ruled in Japan during this period?

2. **Location** What is the relative location of the Takeda domains?

3. **Human/ Environment Interaction** What geographic conditions helped make it possible for Japan to enforce a policy of isolation from the rest of the world in the 1600s?

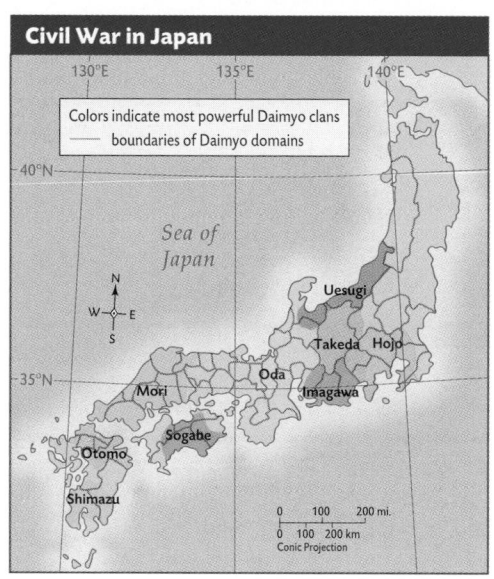

Civil War in Japan

Colors indicate most powerful Daimyo clans
— boundaries of Daimyo domains

Sea of Japan

Uesugi
Takeda Hojo
Oda
Mori Imagawa
Sogabe
Otomo
Shimazu

0   100   200 mi.
0 100 200 km
Conic Projection

Understanding Themes

1. **Movement** What areas of Asia came under the rule of the Muslim empires?

2. **Cultural Diffusion** How did Christianity spread to China? To Japan?

3. **Reaction** What good and bad effects resulted from Japan's policy of isolation?

4. **Change** What development was crucial in advancing Dutch control of the islands of Indonesia?

Linking Past and Present

1. Do you think it is possible for today's nations to follow a policy of isolation like Japan's in the early modern period? Have any tried to?

2. From the 1300s to the 1800s powerful Asian rulers took drastic measures to implement changes that they supported. Is a powerful ruler or a strong central government necessary today for technological advancement and economic prosperity? Give reasons to support your position.

Skill Practice

Using a word processor or a computer word processing software program, create a one-page professional-looking document using the subject of Japan's isolationist policy—The Act of Seclusion of 1636. For example, you might wish to create a letter written by the Tokugawa rulers to European rulers or create a handbill that was given out to European traders to warn them about the isolation policy. Be sure to complete the following steps while creating your document:

1. use more than one font and text size
2. use bold, italics, and underlining
3. include paragraph indents
4. run spell check
5. try other word processing techniques that help create a professional-looking document

Chapter 7 *Empires of Asia* **255**

2.  **CULTURAL DIFFUSION** via Jesuit missionaries; by European Roman Catholic missionaries

3. **REACTION** Good: internal trade thrived and merchants became wealthy; roads were built; towns grew. Bad: Japan did not absorb many Western ideas until the 1800s.

4. **CHANGE** The ruler of Mataram asked for Dutch help in putting down rebels.

Linking Past and Present

1. Isolation is harder today because of modern communications; Albania, Cambodia, and North Korea.

2. Answers will vary.

Skill Practice

Answers will vary but content should include: Contact with outsiders posed too many dangers; Japanese were forbidden to leave Japan; the government banned construction of ships large enough for ocean voyages; Europeans, except Dutch, were barred from the country; Dutch were confined to a tiny island in Nagasaki harbor.

Chapter Bonus Test Question

Ask students: In your view, what is the most important difference between the Muslim empires of western and South Asia and the older cultures of East Asia? (*In the former, Islam was a driving force, while in the latter, people maintained other religious traditions. The western and South Asian empires, at least in the beginning, resulted from expansive, outward thrusts; in East Asia, civilizations turned inward.*)

northern India, initiating a continuing conflict between Hinduism and Islam.

6. Manchus made conquests in the north and west; its population increased because of peace and improvements in agriculture.

7. yes; the Ming had the funds to fight off nomadic tribes because they had stopped putting money into ocean voyages

8. As cities grew and class divisions weakened, there was a larger market for entertainment.

Geography in History

1. nine

2. south of Uesugi territory, north of Imagawa lands, west of Hojo domains

3. It is an island nation.

Understanding Themes

1. **MOVEMENT** western Asia and South Asia

A complete, 1-page lesson plan is provided for each section in the *Reproducible Lesson Plans* booklet.

Royal Power and Conflict

CHAPTER RESOURCES

	Reproducible Resources	Multimedia Resources
Chapter Opener	Chapter Themes: Graphic Organizer 8 Historical Significance Chapter Activity 8	MindJogger Videoquiz
Chapter Enrichment	Vocabulary Activity 8* Time Line Activity 8 Mapping History Activity 8 History Simulation 8 Geography and History Activity 8 Source Reading 8 People in World History Profiles 35, 36 World Art and Music Activity 8 Enrichment Activity 8 Critical Thinking Activity 8 Skill Reinforcement Activity 8 Performance Assessment Activity 8	Focus on World Art Print 19, Jan Steen. *The Dancing Couple*; 20, Jean-Baptiste Simeon Chardin. *The Attributes of Painting* World History and Art Transparency 26, *The French Ambassadors*; 22, *View of Toledo* Chapter Transparency 8 Vocabulary PuzzleMaker Software Picture Atlas of the World World Music: Cultural Traditions, Lesson 3
Chapter Review/Reteaching	Reteaching Activity 8 Skill Reinforcement Activity 8 Spanish Chapter Summary 8	Chapter 8 Digest Audiocassette, Activity, Test* Vocabulary PuzzleMaker Software Student Self-Test and Review Software MindJogger Videoquiz
Chapter Evaluation/Testing	Performance Assessment Activity 8 Chapter 8 Test, Forms A and B	Testmaker

* Also available in Spanish

0:00 OUT OF TIME? Assign the Chapter 8 summary in the Unit 2 Digest on pages 283–285, and the Chapter 8 Audiocassettes.

Block Schedule

Block scheduling differs from traditional class scheduling in the amount of time allotted to each period. The extended time frame provided by block scheduling affords you the opportunity to implement a greater number of research-oriented and activity-intense projects to motivate and involve your students. Activities that are particularly suited to use within the block scheduling framework are identified throughout this chapter by the following designation.

KEY TO ABILITY LEVELS

Teaching strategies have been coded for varying learning styles and abilities.

L1 BASIC activities for all students
L2 AVERAGE activities for average to above-average students
L3 CHALLENGING activities for above-average students
LEP LIMITED ENGLISH PROFICIENCY activities

Use Glencoe's *Presentation Plus!* multimedia teacher tool to easily present dynamic lessons that visually excite your students. Using Microsoft PowerPoint® you can customize the presentations to create your own personalized lessons.

SECTION RESOURCES

Daily Objectives	Reproducible Resources	Multimedia Resources
Section 1 **Spain** Explain why Philip II and other Spanish monarchs had difficulty ruling the Spanish Empire.	Reproducible Lesson Plan 8-1 Vocabulary Activity 8* Guided Reading Activity 8-1* Time Line Activity 8 Geography and History Activity 8 Section Quiz 8-1*	Section Focus Transparency 8-1 Chapter Transparency 8 Student Self-Test and Review Software Testmaker
Section 2 **England** Recognize how Tudor monarchs influenced English and European affairs.	Reproducible Lesson Plan 8-2 Vocabulary Activity 8* Guided Reading Activity 8-2* Section Quiz 8-2*	Section Focus Transparency 8-2 World History and Art Transparency 22, *View of Toledo* Student Self-Test and Review Software Testmaker World Music: Cultural Traditions, Lesson 3
Section 3 **France** Describe the kind of monarchy that developed in France under the Bourbon monarchs.	Reproducible Lesson Plan 8-3 Vocabulary Activity 8* Guided Reading Activity 8-3* Section Quiz 8-3*	Focus on World Art Print 20, Jean-Baptiste Simeon Chardin. *The Attributes of Painting* Section Focus Transparency 8-3 World History and Art Transparency 26, *The French Ambassadors* Student Self-Test and Review Software Testmaker
Section 4 **The German States** Examine how the Thirty Years' War differed from prior European wars.	Reproducible Lesson Plan 8-4 Vocabulary Activity 8* Guided Reading Activity 8-4* Section Quiz 8-4*	Focus on World Art Print 8, Jan Steen. *The Dancing Couple* Section Focus Transparency 8-4 Student Self-Test and Review Software Testmaker
Section 5 **Russia** Understand how the power of Russian czars differed from that of other European monarchs.	Reproducible Lesson Plan 8-5 Guided Reading Activity 8-5* History Simulation 8 Reteaching Activity 8 Enrichment Activity 8 Section Quiz 8-5* Performance Assessment Activity 8 Spanish Chapter Summary 8	Section Focus Transparency 8-5 Vocabulary PuzzleMaker Software Student Self-Test and Review Software Testmaker Picture Atlas of the World

* Also available in Spanish

Chapter Activities

Performance Assessment Activity

A Resume for a Political Candidate After students have studied the leaders in this chapter, have them think about their qualities and actions and then consider what they believe is required of our government leaders today. Each student should create a resume for a candidate for current office based on what they know of the real leaders presented in the chapter, choosing the qualities and actions that best support their vision for modern times. The task may be extended by having students make visual representations of their ideal candidates. Students should include a reflection that defines their vision of those qualities needed in a candidate today and why they chose specific qualities.

Possible Rubric Features
Accuracy of content information, appropriateness of choices for vision communicated, organization and format of resume, argumentation and level of support for qualities and actions chosen

• *For an additional activity, refer to Activity 8 in the* Performance Assessment Strategies and Activities *booklet.*

ACTIVITY

From the Classroom of...

Allan Solomonson
West High School
Wausau, WI

Power of Monarchs
Help students understand how monarchs consolidated their power and how they ensured that their monarchies would survive into the next generation.

Write the following words on an overhead transparency, the chalkboard, or a worksheet: *prestige, privilege, organization, personality, diplomacy, opulence, conflict.* Give each student a half sheet of paper or a large note card. Have them select the word that most accurately describes a monarch of their choosing. Using the paper or note card, students should write a short essay explaining why that word is most appropriate. This can be done in class or as a homework assignment.

Use the ideas of the students as a springboard for a discussion on the power of monarchs of this era. For example, ask students to consider what legacy these monarchs left that enabled the monarchy or the nation to survive.

MULTIPLE LEARNING STYLES

Verbal/Linguistic
Have students discuss and evaluate the positive and negative aspects of Louis XIV's reign.

Logical/Mathematical
Have students use the maps in this chapter to compute and compare the approximate areas of the Spanish Hapsburgs, Austrian Hapsburgs, Holy Roman Empire, Dutch Netherlands, and Brandenburg-Prussia at their largest.

Visual/Spatial
Have students create a mural that depicts major events in the reigns of Elizabeth I, Philip II, Louis XIV, and Peter the Great.

Kinesthetic
Have students draw a large outline map of Europe and hang it on the bulletin board. Using tacks and labels, identify the Hapsburg territories.

Additional Resources

NATIONAL GEOGRAPHIC SOCIETY

Teacher's Corner

INDEX TO NATIONAL GEOGRAPHIC MAGAZINE

The following articles may be used for research relating to this chapter:

- "The Tale of the *San Diego*," by Frank Goddio, July 1994.
- "The Living Tower of London," by William R. Newcott, October 1993.
- "St. Petersburg: Capital of the Tsars," by Steve Raymer, December 1993.
- "Inside the Kremlin," by Jon Thompson, January 1990.
- "Shakespeare Lives at the Folger," by Merle Severy, February 1987.
- "Legacy from the Deep: Henry VIII's Lost Warship," by Margaret Rule, May 1983.

NATIONAL GEOGRAPHIC SOCIETY PRODUCTS AVAILABLE FROM GLENCOE

To order the following products for use with this chapter, contact your local Glencoe sales representative, or call Glencoe at 1-800-334-7344:

- *Picture Atlas of the World (CD-ROM)*

LOCAL OBJECTIVES

_____
_____
_____
_____
_____
_____
_____
_____
_____
_____
_____
_____
_____
_____
_____
_____
_____
_____
_____
_____
_____
_____

BIBLIOGRAPHY

Literature of the Period
Shakespeare, William. *The Riverside Shakespeare.* Boston: Houghton Mifflin, 1974. Authoritative collection of Shakespeare's complete works, including historical background.
Readings for the Student
Dumas, Alexandre. *The Three Musketeers.*
Translated by Jacques Le Clercq. New York: Random House, 1950. Exaggerated tale of swashbucklers in France during the reign of Louis XIII.
Readings for the Teacher
Fraser, Antonia. *The Weaker Vessel.* New York: Knopf, 1984. An exploration of women's roles in seventeenth-century England.

inter**NET** CONNECTION

Early modern Europe resources on the World Wide Web
Early Modern Europe:
http://www.wilpaterson.edu/hmss/history/study/ws2/set1b.htm

CHAPTER THEMES

Chapter Themes are listed by section on this chapter opening page of the Student Edition. A corresponding theme-based activity is available under "TEACH," and a theme-based question is asked in the Section and Chapter Reviews.

The Storyteller

Historical Setting The opening text reveals one view of the social life of the upper class during the reign of Louis XIV. An evening at Versailles generally began at 6:00 P.M. and could last until 8:00 A.M. the next morning. During that time, activities might include eating two suppers, attending a comedy and a ballet, and dancing at a ball.

It is not surprising that Louis's sister-in-law went hunting—Louis kept 1,000 hounds at Versailles for that sport. France's poor, on the other hand, spent their days working on the estates of the rich, plowing fields, or working in cities at any job that would assure them food to eat and a roof over their heads.

Historical Significance

Answers: *Monarchs tried to strengthen the power of the throne, build up the national economy, and increase military strength. In Spain and France, monarchs also tried to promote a national culture.*

French expansion led to wars with Spain, the Netherlands, and Austria. Russian expansion led to wars with Poland, Sweden, and the Ottoman Empire.

Chapter
8

1500–1750

Royal Power and Conflict

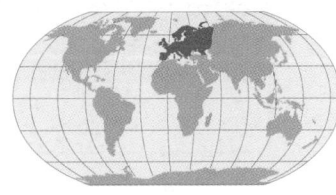

Chapter Themes

▶ **Conflict** Spanish and English monarchs engage in a dynastic struggle. *Section 1*
▶ **Change** Tudor monarchs bring stability and prosperity to England. *Section 2*
▶ **Uniformity** France's Louis XIV strengthens absolute monarchy in France and limits rights of religious dissenters. *Section 3*
▶ **Conflict** Dynastic and religious conflicts divide the German states. *Section 4*
▶ **Innovation** Peter the Great attempts to modernize Russian society. *Section 5*

The Storyteller

"We hunted all morning, got back around 3 o'clock in the afternoon, changed, went up to gamble until 7 o'clock, then to the play, which never ended before 10:30, then on to the ball until 3 o'clock in the morning.... So you see how much time I had for writing."

Princess Elizabeth-Charlotte, sister-in-law of France's King Louis XIV, described court life at the Palace of Versailles in a letter to a friend as an endless round of social activities. A man of tremendous energy and drive, Louis routinely devoted eight or nine hours daily to matters of state, regularly rode and hunted, ate with great enthusiasm, and expected courtiers, or members of his court, to do the same as well.

Historical Significance

How did monarchs build strong nation-states in early modern Europe? How did their efforts in national expansion contribute to Europe's legacy of territorial disputes and wars?

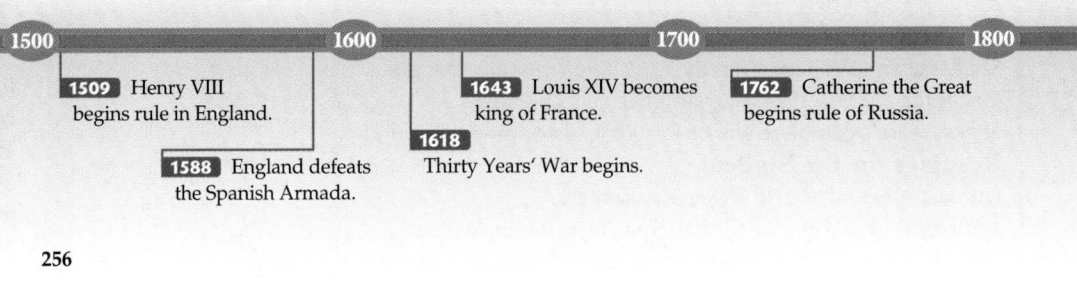

| 1500 | 1600 | 1700 | 1800 |

1509 Henry VIII begins rule in England.

1588 England defeats the Spanish Armada.

1643 Louis XIV becomes king of France.

1618 Thirty Years' War begins.

1762 Catherine the Great begins rule of Russia.

256

GEOGRAPHY CONNECTION

Location Use the Atlas to review with students the locations of England, Spain, Prussia, the Netherlands, Russia, Austria, and France. What is unique about England's geographical situation? *(England is an island.)* In what way is Russia different from other European countries? *(Russia covers a vast amount of land.)*

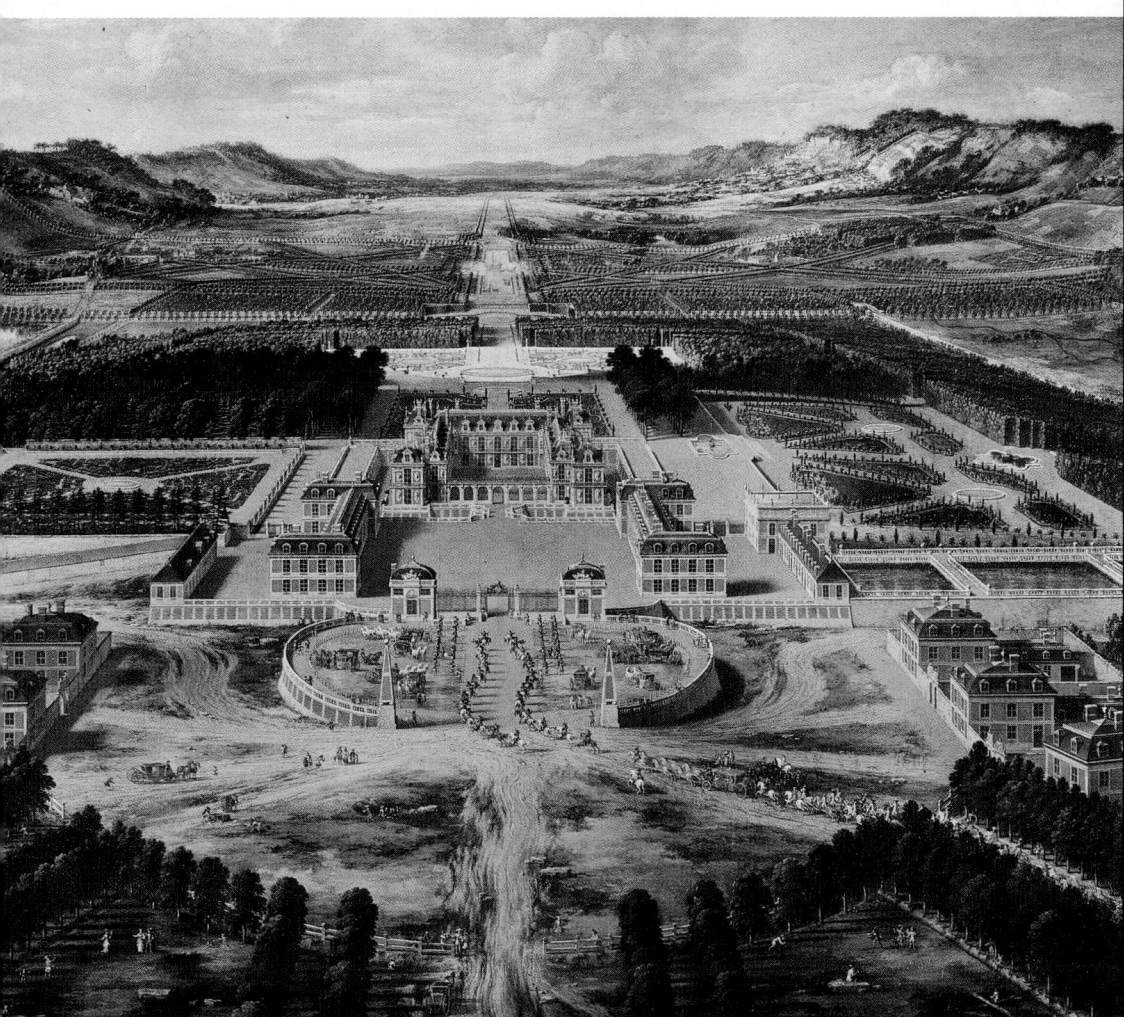

Visualizing History Versailles was so expensive to build that Louis XIV destroyed some of the bills to avoid criticism from his ministers. On several occasions during his reign, it was the scene of elaborate and enormously expensive festivals that lasted for as long as a week.

✓ Performance Assessment

Refer to the activity on page 256C of the Planning Guide.

For an additional activity, refer to Activity 8 in the *Performance Assessment Strategies and Activities* booklet.

Using Your History Journal

After students have finished their time lines, have them research the topic they find the most important or most interesting.

GLENCOE TECHNOLOGY

 VIDEODISC
Use MindJogger to preview chapter content.

MindJogger Videoquiz
 Chapter 8
Disc 1 Side B

 Also available in VHS.

Visualizing History The vast palace and grounds of Versailles lie outside of Paris, France. Versailles was home to France's monarchs and the royal court during the late 1600s and most of the 1700s.

Your History Journal

Choose a country from this chapter. As you read the section, create a time line of important events between 1500 and 1750. Include the reigning monarchs, expansions of territory, laws, and conflicts.

Chapter 8 *Royal Power and Conflict* **257**

➕ EXTRA CREDIT PROJECT

Essay Many great writers wrote during the period covered here. These include Corneille, Racine, and Molière (France); Shakespeare (England); Cervantes (Spain); and Goethe (Prussia). Have students read excerpts from the works of two of these writers and write an essay comparing and contrasting their style and themes. Students may also draw conclusions, if warranted, about how any differences or similarities in the writers' styles reflect differences or similarities in the political, economic, and social life of the writers' homelands. **L3**

SECTION THEME

▶ **Conflict** Spanish and English monarchs engage in a dynastic struggle.

ind Out

Answer: *There was no uniform system of government; Philip faced opposition from Protestants, and costly wars damaged the economy.*

FOCUS

Section Objective

Explain why Philip II and other Spanish monarchs had difficulty ruling the Spanish Empire.

BELLRINGER
Motivational Activity

Before taking roll at the beginning of the class period, project Section Focus Transparency 8-1 and have students answer the activity questions. Discuss students' responses.

📁 This activity is also available as a blackline master.

Vocabulary Pre-check

📁 Use Vocabulary Activity 8 to introduce vocabulary terms.
L1 LEP

1500 ——— **1550** ——— **1600** ——— **1650**

| **1556** Philip II becomes king of Spain. | **1588** The English defeat the Spanish Armada. | **c. 1590s** Aragon revolts against Castilian control. | **1647** Plague kills thousands of Spaniards. |

Section **1**
....

Spain

Setting the Scene

▶ **Terms to Define**
absolutism, divine right, armada, inflation

▶ **People to Meet**
Philip II, the Marranos, the Moriscos, Charles II

▶ **Places to Locate**
Madrid

ind Out ▶ Why did Philip II and other Spanish monarchs have difficulty ruling the Spanish Empire?

The Storyteller

The Duke of Alva's son, ten-year-old Alejandro, was ecstatic. He had been appointed as a page to King Philip—an excellent beginning to a career with the Spanish court. Alejandro would learn to fence and to perform feats of horsemanship, as well as the rudiments of reading and writing. In five or six years, when he completed his education, Alejandro would become a member of His Majesty's court and would be expected to serve at arms. That position was the fulfillment of most young men's desires. If he proved himself truly outstanding, he might become one of Philip's personal attendants, a position usually reserved for the sons of princes.

Philip II

—from *Charles V and Philip His Son*, Marino Cavalli, reprinted in *The Portable Renaissance Reader*, Mary Martin McLaughlin, 1977

258 Chapter 8 *Royal Power and Conflict*

In the 1500s and 1600s, European monarchs sought to create powerful kingdoms in which they could command the complete loyalty of all their subjects. This form of government, known as **absolutism**, placed absolute, or unlimited, power in the monarch and his or her advisers. The strength of absolutism rested on **divine right**—the political idea that monarchs receive their power directly from God and are responsible to God alone for their actions. An absolute monarchy, it was reasoned, would unify diverse peoples and bring greater efficiency and control.

During the age of absolutism, the Hapsburgs remained Europe's most powerful royal family. But their lands were too scattered for any one person to rule effectively. To remedy this problem, Charles V retired in 1556 and divided the empire, leaving the Hapsburg lands in central Europe to his brother, Ferdinand, who became Holy Roman emperor. He gave Spain, the Netherlands, southern Italy, and Spain's overseas empire to his son, **Philip II**.

Philip II

Philip II, who ruled from 1556 to 1598, was the most powerful monarch in Spanish history. A devout Catholic, Philip saw himself as the leading defender of the faith. His efforts to end Protestantism in his domains made him the enemy of all Protestants. Son of the Holy Roman Emperor Charles V and Isabella of Portugal, Philip worked to increase the Hapsburg family's power throughout Europe. This effort led Philip to involve Spain in a number of costly European wars.

Known as the Prudent King, Philip II was cautious, hardworking, and suspicious of others. He built a granite palace called El Escorial, which served as royal court, art gallery, monastery, and tomb for Spanish royalty. There Philip spent most of his time at his desk, carefully reading and

---

SECTION RESOURCES

📁 **Reproducible Masters**
• Reproducible Lesson Plan 8-1
• Vocabulary Activity 8
• Guided Reading Activity 8-1
• Time Line Activity 8
• Geography and History Activity 8
• Section Quiz 8-1

Transparencies
• Section Focus Transparency 8-1
• Chapter Transparency 8

Multimedia
• Student Self-Test and Review Software
• Testmaker

responding to hundreds of documents from all over the empire. Bureaucrats advised him and handled routine matters, but he made all decisions and signed all papers that he received.

Unrest

Philip II faced many difficulties in ruling Spain. The Spanish kingdoms had united when Ferdinand of Aragon married Isabella of Castile in 1469. A uniform system of government for the entire country, however, had not been set up. Separate laws and local authorities remained in place, but the ways of Castile eventually came to dominate Spanish life. In the 1500s Castile had more territory, people, and wealth than any other part of Spain.

Philip II made Castile the center of Spain and the empire. **Madrid**, located in Castile, became the capital. The Castilian, or literary, form of Spanish was spoken at the royal court. Most of Philip's advisers came from Castile. Trade from the overseas empire was controlled by the Castilian city of Seville, and Castilian merchants benefited most from trade. Leaders in Aragon and other Spanish provinces resented the dominance of Castile, and in the 1590s Aragon revolted. The revolt was put down, but discontent continued into the 1600s.

Religious Policy

Philip had to deal with a number of troubling religious issues in his European domains. He was concerned about the loyalty of large religious minorities in Spain. These minorities included Protestants, **the Marranos** (Jews who had converted to Christianity), and **the Moriscos** (Muslims who had become Christians). Philip supported the Inquisition's efforts to uproot the heresies believed to exist among these groups. He personally attended several *autos da fé,* the elaborate public rituals of sentencing usually followed by executions. The Inquisition was so thorough that Protestantism never took hold in Spain. Its actions, however, led to a revolt by the Moriscos in 1569. The revolt was brutally crushed, and finally in 1609 the Moriscos were expelled from the country.

In 1567, when Philip had sought to impose Catholicism on the Netherlands, Dutch Protestants rebelled against his rule. This conflict proved to be long, bloody, and complex. The Dutch declared their independence in 1581, but the fighting continued. England gave support to the Dutch and to the English "sea dogs" who raided Spanish ships in their ports. Meanwhile, Philip extended his crusading zeal into the eastern Mediterranean, where in 1571 he defeated the Ottoman Turks in a naval battle at Lepanto off the coast of Greece.

The Spanish Armada entered the English Channel in late July, 1588. *What advantages did the English fleet have over the Spanish Armada?*

Spanish Armada

Catholic Spain faced a growing challenge from Protestant England. Philip at first had supported Elizabeth I as England's queen against the pope's wishes. When Elizabeth aided the Dutch, Philip decided to act against her.

In 1586 Philip laid plans to invade England. In May 1588 a force of 130 ships and 33,000 men, known as the Spanish Armada, sailed for the English coast. (An armada is a fleet of warships organized to carry out a mission.) Two months later, the Armada entered the English Channel in crescent formation. The English had faster, more maneuverable ships and longer-range cannons than did the Spaniards. Yet they were unable at first to block the Spanish formation. English fire ships, however, were able to separate the Spanish vessels. Running out of shot and short of water, the Spanish fleet retreated to the stormy North Sea. After circling the northern tip of Great Britain, a number of Spanish ships later sank near the rocky coasts of Scotland and Ireland.

The defeat of the Armada not only ended Philip's plan to invade England, it also marked the beginning of Spain's decline as a sea power. During the next two centuries, the Dutch Netherlands, England, and France would gradually reduce Spanish might in Europe and around the world.

TEACH

Guided Practice

THEME Conflict

Ask students to identify the conflict that underlay Philip's struggles both at home and abroad. *(the conflict between Philip's Roman Catholic faith and Protestantism)* **L1**

Visualizing History The Spanish ships varied in size and condition. There were transport ships, freighters, dispatch boats, and small cruisers. Still, they made up the greatest sea force Europe had ever seen. **Answer to Caption:** *The English had faster ships and better cannons.*

Spanish Armada
Why was the failure of the Spanish Armada a significant event in European affairs? *It marked the beginning of Spain's decline as a great sea power and the rise of England to a prominent position in European affairs.*

Chapter Transparency 8

Independent Practice

Guided Reading Activity 8-1 **L1**

Time Line Activity 8

Geography and History Activity 8

COOPERATIVE LEARNING ACTIVITY

Research Organize students into three groups. Have each group research and write a report about one of the Spanish minorities during Philip II's reign—Protestants, Marranos, or Moriscos. Reports should include information about the daily life, professions, reasons for conversion or defiance in the face of danger, persecution during the Spanish Inquisition, and decisions people made to flee Spain or to stay in spite of persecutions. Ask the groups to draw some connections between treatment of minorities and the eventual decline of Spain. Students should delegate tasks of finding information, organizing ideas, making outlines and note cards, and writing the drafts. **L2**

Answer
primarily Spain, southern Italy, Sicily, Sardinia, the Netherlands

ASSESS

Check for Understanding

Assign Section 1 Review as homework or as an in-class activity.

 Use Student Self-Test and Review Software to review Section 1.

Evaluate

📁 Section Quiz 8-1

🖥 Use the Testmaker to create a customized quiz for Section 1.

Reteach

Ask volunteers to give oral summaries of important events during the rule of Philip II and during the decline of the Hapsburg rulers after his death.

Enrich

Have students make a time line reflecting the events of the section. Ask them to chart positive events above the line and negative events below it.

CLOSE

Write *Strengths* and *Weaknesses* on the chalkboard and ask students to list items under each heading for the Spanish Hapsburgs they have studied.

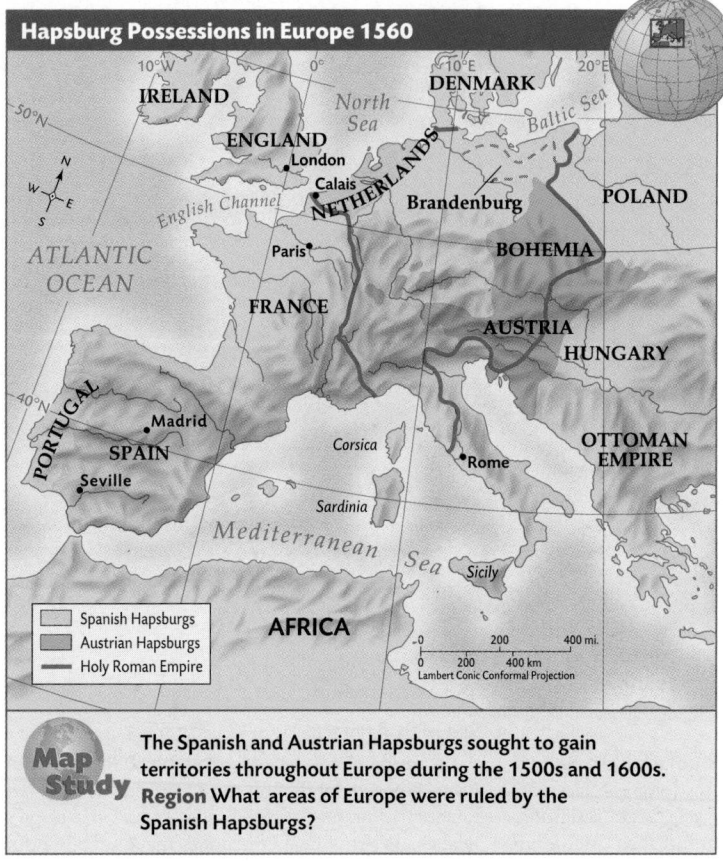

Hapsburg Possessions in Europe 1560

Map Study

The Spanish and Austrian Hapsburgs sought to gain territories throughout Europe during the 1500s and 1600s. **Region** What areas of Europe were ruled by the Spanish Hapsburgs?

Last of the Spanish Hapsburgs

The period from 1550 to 1650 is called Spain's cultural *siglo de oro*, or "golden century." Midway through this era, the Spanish author Miguel de Cervantes (suhr•VAN•teez) wrote *Don Quixote*, a novel about a landowner who imagines himself a knight called to perform heroic deeds. In making fun of medieval romances of chivalry, *Don Quixote*

presented a new kind of hero who did not conform to commonly accepted beliefs and practices.

Cervantes's novel also symbolized the steady decline of Spain as a European power. Despite Spain's resource-rich overseas empire, costly wars drained the national treasury, forcing the government to borrow money from foreign bankers. This, along with the flow of gold and silver from the Americas, led to inflation, an abnormal increase in currency resulting in sharp price rises. In addition, Spain's industry and agriculture declined. The government excessively taxed and weakened the industrious middle class. It also expelled the Muslims and Jews, many of whom were skilled artisans and merchants.

Philip II's successors lacked his political skills and turned the government over to corrupt and incompetent nobles. Spain became involved in a series of European wars, and overtaxed citizens in various parts of the empire rebelled. **Charles II**, who became king in 1665, was the last of the Spanish Hapsburgs. No one expected him to rule long, since he was physically and mentally weak. Although Charles later married, he did not have any children. With no heirs to the throne of Spain, European monarchs plotted to control the succession to the Spanish throne.

SECTION I REVIEW

Recall
1. **Define** absolutism, divine right, armada, inflation.
2. **Identify** Philip II, El Escorial, the Marranos, the Moriscos, Spanish Armada, Charles II.
3. **Use** the map of the Hapsburg domains above to locate Spain, Portugal, and the Netherlands. Why was the Netherlands opposed to Hapsburg rule?

Critical Thinking
4. **Analyzing Information** Why did Philip II send the Spanish Armada against England? What was the outcome of this effort?

Understanding Themes
5. **Conflict** What were the reasons for internal unrest in the Spanish Empire under Philip II's rule? How did Philip respond?

260 **Chapter 8** *Royal Power and Conflict*

SECTION I REVIEW ANSWERS

1. All vocabulary words are defined in the Glossary.
2. Philip II, 258; El Escorial, 258; Marranos, 259; Moriscos, 259; Spanish Armada, 259; Charles II, 260
3. The Protestant Dutch resented Philip's attempt to reimpose Catholicism on them.
4. Philip was angered by England's support of Protestants in the Netherlands; Spanish Armada was defeated.
5. **CONFLICT** resentment by other provinces of Castile's dominance, religious persecutions, declining economy; by crushing any revolts

1547 Henry VIII dies.

1558 Elizabeth I becomes queen of England.

1597 Poor Law makes local areas responsible for care of the unemployed.

Section 2
England

Setting the Scene

▶ **Terms to Define**
  gentry, yeomen, balance of power

▶ **People to Meet**
  Henry VII, Henry VIII, Elizabeth I, William Shakespeare

▶ **Places to Locate**
  Scotland, Ireland

ᚱind Out How did Tudor monarchs influence English and European affairs?

Storyteller

On this day, Elizabeth would be crowned Queen of England. London was arrayed with pavilions and bright banners, and the city's fountains offered wine, not the usual brackish water. Alison Crisp eagerly awaited the royal procession to Westminster Abbey. Although only six years of age, she would present a costly gift to Elizabeth from the Orphans Home board of directors. When the procession neared, the queen commanded her coachmen to stop. Alison flawlessly presented the gift. As the queen prepared to move on, Alison surprised her with another gift, a bouquet of flowers she had picked. With Elizabeth's acceptance of the child's humble offering, the rapport between the queen and her people strengthened.

—from *Description of Elizabeth I's Coronation Procession in 1559,* John Hayward, in *The Past Speaks,* L.B. Smith and J.R. Smith, 1993

Elizabeth I

ngland, like Spain, developed a strong monarchy. Its Tudor dynasty, which ruled from 1485 to 1603, brought unity to the country after a long period of decline and disorder. Tudor monarchs were hardworking, able, and popular. They greatly expanded the power and authority of the Crown. They were not, however, as absolute in their rule as other European monarchs. Instead, institutions such as Parliament and the courts of law set bounds to the authority that Tudor monarchs could exercise.

Early Tudors

Henry VII, the first Tudor monarch, became king in 1485 after the Wars of the Roses. He used shrewd maneuvering to disarm his rivals and to increase the prestige of his family. Most of Henry's close advisers came from the gentry and merchant classes. Titles were given to these officials, who formed a new aristocracy dependent on the king.

Henry VII helped rebuild England's commercial prosperity. He encouraged the expansion of foreign trade, especially the export of finished woolens to the Netherlands, Germany, and Venice. He promoted the improved collection of taxes as well as careful government spending. In foreign policy Henry avoided war, using diplomacy and the arrangement of suitable royal marriages to strengthen England's interests abroad.

Henry VIII

The second Tudor to rule was **Henry VIII**, son of Henry VII and the most powerful of all Tudor monarchs. Unlike his father, Henry VIII fought wars on the European continent and began to make England a great naval power. His personal life, however, would have a lasting effect on English history. In his pursuit of a male heir, Henry married six times. He worked with Parliament to obtain his personal goals and to break with the Catholic

Chapter 8 *Royal Power and Conflict* **261**

▶ **Change** Tudor monarchs bring stability and prosperity to England.

ᚱind Out

Answer: *They rebuilt commercial prosperity, expanded the power of the Crown, increased foreign trade, established a balance of power in Europe, and made Scotland and Ireland allies of England.*

FOCUS

Section Objective

Recognize how Tudor monarchs influenced English and European affairs.

BELLRINGER
Motivational Activity

Before taking roll at the beginning of the class period, project Section Focus Transparency 8-2 and have students answer the activity questions. Discuss students' responses.

🗁 This activity is also available as a blackline master.

Vocabulary Pre-check

🗁 Use Vocabulary Activity 8 to introduce vocabulary terms.
L1 LEP

SECTION RESOURCES

🗁 **Reproducible Masters**
• Reproducible Lesson Plan 8-2
• Vocabulary Activity 8
• Guided Reading Activity 8-2
• Section Quiz 8-2

Transparencies
• Section Focus Transparency 8-2
• World History and Art Transparency 22

Multimedia
🔲 Student Self-Test and Review Software
🔲 Testmaker
💿 World Music: Cultural Traditions, Lesson 3

TEACH

Guided Practice

THEME Change

Tudor monarchs used their strong personalities and diplomatic skills to bring about change in England. Write *Henry VII*, *Henry VIII*, and *Elizabeth I* on the chalkboard. Ask students to name some of the changes each of these monarchs brought and list them on the chalkboard. (*Sample answers: Henry VII, expanded foreign trade; Henry VIII, established Anglican Church; Elizabeth I, ushered in one of England's greatest cultural periods.*) **L1 LEP**

Government Tudor rule differed from the absolute rule of Philip II. Both dynasties had successes and failures. Ask students to take a position on whether the Spanish Hapsburgs or the English Tudors were more successful in ruling their kingdoms and why. Students should consider the personal traits and public actions of monarchs. Ask volunteers to judge the positions and point out those with well-supported arguments. **L2**

Biography

The following videotape programs are available from Glencoe:

- **Elizabeth I: The Virgin Queen**
- **Henry VIII**

Church. As a result of this cooperation, the House of Commons increased its power during Henry VIII's reign. Henry, however, furthered support for his policies by seizing monastery lands and selling them to wealthy landowners.

Edward VI and Mary I

After Henry VIII's death in 1547, England entered a brief period of turmoil. Edward VI, Henry's son and successor, was only 9 years old when he became king. He died in 1553 after a short reign. Protestant nobles then plotted to prevent Edward's Catholic half-sister, Mary, from becoming queen. The English people, however, supported Mary's claim to the Tudor throne.

Mary's Catholic policies soon offended the English. Despite strong opposition, Mary married Philip II of Spain in 1554. The next year, she restored Catholicism and had about 300 Protestants burned at the stake for heresy. At Philip's urging, Mary involved England in a war with France. As a result, England lost the port of Calais, its final foothold on the European continent. Many English people feared that England would be controlled by Spain. Before this fear could be realized, Mary died childless, and the throne then passed to her Protestant half-sister, Elizabeth.

Elizabeth I

Elizabeth I became queen in 1558, when she was 25 years old. She was shrewd, highly educated, and had a forceful personality. With a sharp tongue she asserted her iron will, causing sparks to fly in exchanges with Parliament. Elizabeth, however, used her authority for the common good of her people. On frequent journeys throughout the kingdom Elizabeth earned the loyalty and confidence of her subjects. During her travels, Elizabeth stayed at the homes of nobles who entertained her with banquets, parades, and dances.

Elizabeth's reign was one of England's great cultural periods. Poets and writers praised

Images of the Times

Tudor England

Under Tudor monarchs, England enjoyed a period of stability and relative prosperity.

Mary I married Philip II of Spain in 1554, against the wishes of her Protestant subjects. This coat of arms represents the marital union of the two monarchs.

262

Images of the Times — Tudor England

What was life like for the people? Houses of plaster and brick with thatched roofs now had glass windows, but people still needed candles or torches for light at night. Floors had no carpets, but tapestries were hung on walls. Furniture was strong and cut of walnut or oak to last for centuries. People of all classes had a garden by the house. Elizabethan England was an age of fashion. Men wore hats of many shapes and colors outside the home and in church. They wore their hair long and grew beards. Women often wore wigs, used cosmetics, wore jewelry, and had pierced ears. Both men and women wore pleated collars, called ruffs, made of fabric, pasteboard, and wire.

Elizabeth in their works. The theater flourished under playwrights such as **William Shakespeare**. During Elizabeth's reign, English was transformed into a language of beauty, grace, vigor, and clarity.

Marriage

People fully expected that Elizabeth would marry and that her husband would rule. The common attitude of the time was that only men were fit to rule and that government matters were beyond a woman's ability. Elizabeth, however, was slow in seeking a husband. She had learned from the lesson of her sister Mary: to marry a foreign prince would endanger England. At the same time, marrying an Englishman would cause jealousies among the English nobility. In the end, Elizabeth refused to give up her powers as monarch for the sake of marriage. To one of her suitors she stormed, "God's death! My lord, I will have but one mistress [England] and no master." Elizabeth's refusal to marry caused a great deal of speculation as to who would succeed her.

Court and Government

In matters of government, Elizabeth was assisted by a council of nobles. With her approval they drafted proclamations, handled foreign relations, and supervised such matters as the administration of justice and the regulation of prices and wages. These advisers were assisted by small staffs of professional but poorly paid bureaucrats.

Although Parliament did not have the power to initiate legislation, it could plead, urge, advise, and withhold approval. These powers gave Parliament some influence, especially when it was asked to consider tax laws.

The task of enforcing the queen's law was performed by unpaid respected community members known as justices of the peace. Most justices belonged to the rural landowning classes. They knew both the law and local conditions. They maintained peace, collected taxes, and kept the government informed of local problems. Their voluntary participation in support of the government was a key to its success.

The Court of Elizabeth I was known for its love of fashions and style. Noble men and women who served the queen wore elegant clothes and enjoyed music and the arts.

The Globe Theater in London was the site where many of William Shakespeare's plays—tragedies, comedies, and histories—were performed.

REFLECTING ON THE TIMES

1. Why is Elizabeth's reign considered one of England's great cultural eras?
2. Why was Mary I an unpopular ruler?

263

ANSWERS TO REFLECTING ON THE TIMES

1. It was a time when the English language, theater, art, and music all thrived.
2. People feared her Catholic policies and a loss of power because of her marriage to Philip of Spain.

World History and Art Transparency 22, *View of Toledo*

World Music: Cultural Traditions, Lesson 3

Independent Practice
Guided Reading Activity 8-2 **L1**

Time Line Assign pairs of students to make a biographical time line of Tudor royalty. Using encyclopedias or biographical dictionaries, have them write brief descriptions of each Tudor ruler and place it next to the appropriate birth date on the time line. **L2 LEP**

Women in History Women were very influential during the Tudor reign. Have students research and report on one of the following: a wife of Henry VIII; Mary I; Elizabeth I; Mary, Queen of Scots; Margaret Pole; or Lady Jane Grey. **L3**

Linking Past and Present

Shakespeare's plays are as popular today as they were in Elizabethan England. Through the centuries, directors have adapted productions of the plays to fit contemporary situations. In some cases they have changed everything except the basic plot line. *Romeo and Juliet*, a story of ill-fated lovers in Verona, Italy, was transformed into *West Side Story*, a 1950s musical about lovers caught in the conflict between rival New York City gangs. Changes in time period and culture do not change the universal theme of the original play.

ASSESS

Check for Understanding

Assign Section 2 Review as homework or as an in-class activity.

🖥 Use Student Self-Test and Review Software to review Section 2.

you don't say...

"To take the chair," or to preside, is an expression that came from Tudor times. A chair with a back was a luxury then; most people sat on stools or benches. The chair, then, was reserved for the master or mistress of the house or the honored guest.

History & Art Elizabeth Tudor was an extraordinary individual who had had little security, hope, or love in her life. With the freedom of the throne, however, she was able to do as she chose. She chose to appeal to her subjects and earn their love. **Answer to Caption:** *England developed a balance of power with European nations.*

CURRICULUM CONNECTION

ASTRONOMY

In his twenties, Edmund Halley published a paper on planetary orbits, financed Newton's first edition of *Principia*, and predicted that in 75 years there would be a reappearance of a comet that appeared in 1682. When the comet returned, it was named Halley's comet.

Social and Economic Policy

Elizabeth believed in the importance of social rank. During the late 1500s, English society was led by the queen and her court. Next were prominent nobles from the great landed families and a middle group of **gentry**, or lesser nobles, merchants, lawyers, and clergy. This group provided the source of Tudor strength and stability. The lowest social rank was comprised of **yeomen**, or farmers with small landholdings, and laborers.

Government laws and policies closely regulated the lives of the common people. The Statute of Apprentices of 1563 declared work to be a social and moral duty. It required people to live and work where they were born, controlled the movement of labor, fixed wages, and regulated apprenticeships. The Poor Laws of 1597 and 1601 made local areas responsible for their own homeless and unemployed. These laws included means to raise money for charity and to provide work for vagabonds.

Elizabeth inherited a monarchy that was badly in debt. Royal revenues, which came from rents of royal land, fines in court cases, and duties on imports, barely covered annual expenses. The queen, however, spent lavishly on court ceremonies to show the power and dignity of the monarchy. In other matters, she showed the greatest financial restraint, leading many to call her a "pinchpenny."

To raise funds without relying on Parliament, Elizabeth sold off royal lands, offices, licenses, monopolies, and the right to collect customs. These measures helped but could not solve the problem. England faced the costs of war and mounting inflation. Elizabeth was therefore forced to turn to Parliament for funds. When she ended her reign, England remained badly in debt.

Foreign Policy

By Elizabeth's time, England had lost all of its possessions on the European continent. France was too powerful for England to defeat in order to regain territories. Although England could not completely withdraw from continental affairs, it developed a foreign policy suitable for a small island nation with limited resources.

For security, the English relied on the English Channel to protect their island from European invaders. Building and maintaining a strong navy was therefore important in defending the nation. For that reason, Elizabeth continued the efforts begun by her Tudor predecessors to build such a navy.

History & Art *Elizabeth I* by George Glower, 1596. National Portrait Gallery, London, England **A woman of keen intellect, Elizabeth I was gifted in music, languages, and the arts. In addition, she was an excellent public speaker.** *What foreign policy strategy did England develop under Elizabeth I's reign?*

COOPERATIVE LEARNING ACTIVITY

Research Have students research Shakespeare, the Elizabethan theater, and London in the middle and late 1500s. Organize the class into several groups and ask each group to choose different tasks: write a biography of Shakespeare; make a model of the Globe or Black Friars theater; give an oral report or write a fictional diary entry describing London in the 1500s—its theater audience and its actors; stage a specific scene from a play (such as *Henry VIII*) to be discussed and performed; make drawings of costumes used on Shakespeare's stage. The class could combine their efforts in creating a Shakespeare Festival, including appropriate musical and dramatic recordings and samples of foods from the 1500s. **L2** 📦

Spain and France posed the greatest naval threats to England. The attack of the Spanish Armada made England realize the dangers of an alliance between Spain and France. England might be able to defeat one power, but certainly not both. As a result, the English relied on diplomacy as well as sea power to protect their interests.

During Elizabeth's reign, England worked to balance the power of European nations. In international affairs, balance of power refers to the system in which each nation helps to keep peace and order by maintaining power that is equal to, or in balance with, rival nations. One nation cannot overpower another. If one nation becomes more powerful than the other, a third nation can reestablish the balance by supporting the second nation.

Under Elizabeth's rule, England operated as the third balancing nation. In the early part of Elizabeth's reign, England and Spain feared the power of the French. England cooperated with Spain in order to keep France out of the Netherlands. Later, when the Netherlands revolted against Philip II, the English supported the rebels and allied with the weaker power against the stronger one.

Scotland was largely Catholic and hostile toward England during the 1550s. Although part of **Ireland** was under English rule, the rest of the country resisted English armies. To protect English interests, Elizabeth sought to solidify her ties with Scotland and Ireland so they could not be used as bases for Spanish and French attacks on England.

In the 1560s, with Elizabeth's help, Scotland became Protestant and an ally of England. Mary Stuart, later known as Mary, Queen of Scots, was Elizabeth's cousin. She was forced to abdicate her position as queen of Scotland in 1567. She later fled to England, where her presence caused controversy. Mary was a Catholic and heir to the English throne. Many English Protestants feared she would try to replace Elizabeth. In 1586 Mary was accused of plotting with English and foreign Catholics against Elizabeth. Public fears of a Catholic monarchy were strong. In 1587 Elizabeth finally agreed to Mary's

Visualizing History Sir Francis Drake was one of England's most famous explorers and military leaders. After sailing around the world, Drake was knighted in 1581 by Queen Elizabeth I. His naval warfare later helped make England a major sea power. *What European nation was England's primary enemy during the time of Elizabeth I and Francis Drake?*

execution, although she was hesitant to sentence to death another monarch.

In the 1590s, England carried out military campaigns in Ireland to conquer the Irish. With Scotland and Ireland allied with England, a period of temporary peace came to the British Isles.

Elizabeth died in 1603 at the age of 69. With her death came the end of the Tudor dynasty. King James VI of Scotland, the Protestant son of Mary, Queen of Scots, became the new monarch of England. As James I, he founded the Stuart dynasty and united Scotland and England under a common ruler.

SECTION 2 REVIEW

Recall
1. **Define** gentry, yeomen, balance of power.
2. **Identify** Henry VII, Henry VIII, Edward VI, Mary I, Elizabeth I, William Shakespeare, Poor Laws, James I.

3. **Explain** England's foreign policy under Elizabeth I.

Critical Thinking
4. **Evaluating Information** Contrast the effect on English history of Henry's many marriages with the effect of

Elizabeth I's refusal to marry.

Understanding Themes
5. **Change** How did the rule of the Tudor monarchs, especially the rule of Elizabeth I, affect the development of England?

Visualizing History Prospects of future Armada attacks on England and the subsequent financial burdens of war led Elizabeth to encourage Drake and his sea captains to attack foreign vessels carrying treasure from the Americas and claim the booty.
Answer to Caption: *Spain*

Evaluate

 Section Quiz 8-2

 Use the Testmaker to create a customized quiz for Section 2.

Reteach

Ask students to list the political tactics used by Tudor rulers. *(use of Parliament to grant favors, foreign policy based on diplomacy, a balance of power)*

Enrich

Have students assume the role of someone who might have lived between 1485 and 1603. Ask them to choose under which ruler—Henry VIII, Edward VI, Mary I, or Elizabeth I—they would like to have lived and why.

CLOSE

Hold a discussion on how religion affected the policies of the Tudors and whether this influence strengthened or weakened England.

SECTION 2 REVIEW ANSWERS

1. All vocabulary words are defined in the Glossary.
2. Henry VII, 261; Henry VIII, 261; Edward VI, 262; Mary I, 262; Elizabeth I, 262; William Shakespeare, 263; Poor Laws, 264; James I, 265

3. It was a policy of cooperation with Spain to balance the power of France and keep the French out of the Netherlands.
4. Henry's marriages caused a split with the Catholic Church; Elizabeth's refusal to marry prevented foreign claims to the

English throne.
5. **CHANGE** Elizabeth strengthened the monarch's ties with Parliament, subdued religious dissent, encouraged cultural development, and established a balance of power among European nations.

SECTION THEME

▶ **Uniformity** France's Louis XIV strengthens absolute monarchy in France and limits rights of religious dissenters.

Find Out

Answer: *Bourbon kings developed an absolute monarchy in France.*

FOCUS

Section Objective

Describe the kind of monarchy that developed in France under the Bourbon monarchs.

BELLRINGER
Motivational Activity

Before taking roll at the beginning of the class period, project Section Focus Transparency 8-3 and have students answer the activity questions. Discuss students' responses.

📁 This activity is also available as a blackline master.

Vocabulary Pre-check

📁 Use Vocabulary Activity 8 to introduce vocabulary terms.
L1 LEP

1550   1600   1650   1700

1598 Henry IV issues the Edict of Nantes.   **1648** Fronde uprising grips Paris.   **1661** Louis XIV takes sole charge of the government.   **1701** War of the Spanish Succession begins.

Section 3

France

Setting the Scene

▶ **Terms to Define**
intendant

▶ **People to Meet**
Henry IV, Cardinal Richelieu, Louis XIV

▶ **Places to Locate**
Versailles

Find Out
What kind of monarchy developed in France under the Bourbon monarchs?

The Storyteller

A flourish of trumpets sounded. The crowd of courtiers bowed as King Louis entered the Grand Salon at Versailles, accompanied by his attendants. The Duke of Saint-Simon, one of many noblemen whose power Louis was systematically eclipsing, was nonetheless required to be present. He observed that the king "liked splendor, magnificence, and profusion in everything: you pleased him if you shone through the brilliancy of your houses, clothes, tables, equipages." Because everyone tried to emulate the king, a taste for extravagance and luxury was spreading through all classes of society.

—adapted from *The Memoires of the Duke of Saint-Simon*, reprinted in *Aspects of Western Civilization, Volume II,* Perry M. Rogers, 1988

Louis XIV's lavish court life

After a period of religious conflict, peace was restored to most of France when Henry of Navarre became King **Henry IV** in 1589. He founded the Bourbon dynasty, which ruled France with some interruptions until the early 1800s. During most of that time, Bourbon kings maintained an absolute monarchy that was imitated by monarchs throughout Europe.

Henry IV

Henry IV was a Protestant, but he converted to Catholicism to quiet his Catholic opponents. Believing that people's religious beliefs need not interfere with their loyalty to the government, Henry issued the Edict of Nantes in 1598 to reassure the Huguenots, the name given to France's Protestants. The edict allowed Protestant worship to continue in areas where the Protestants were a majority, but barred Protestant worship in Paris and other Catholic strongholds. The edict granted Huguenots the same civil rights as Catholics.

These actions ended religious strife and enabled France to rebuild itself. With the help of his minister of finance, Henry restored the Crown's treasury, repaired roads and bridges, and supported trade and industry. He also tried to restore discipline in the army and bring order to the government bureaucracy. All of these royal policies were put into effect without the approval of the Estates-General and thus laid the foundation for the absolute rule of later Bourbon monarchs.

Cardinal Richelieu

When Henry IV was assassinated in 1610, his 9-year-old son, Louis XIII, became king. Louis's mother, Marie de Medici, was regent for the next 7 years. In 1617 Louis gained the throne by force and exiled his mother from court. A few years later, he

---

SECTION RESOURCES

📁 **Reproducible Masters**
- Reproducible Lesson Plan 8-3
- Vocabulary Activity 8
- Guided Reading Activity 8-3
- Section Quiz 8-3

Transparencies
- Section Focus Transparency 8-3
- World History and Art Transparency 26

Multimedia
- Focus on World Art Print 20, Jean-Baptiste Simeon Chardin. *The Attributes of Painting*
- Student Self-Test and Review Software
- Testmaker

gave power to one of her advisers, **Cardinal Richelieu**.

Gradually Louis gave complete control of the government to the cardinal, who set out to build an absolute monarchy in France. To realize this goal, Richelieu had to reduce the power of the nobles and the Huguenots.

When Louis XIII came to the throne, the nobility was in control of the provinces. Nobles collected taxes, administered justice, appointed local officials, and even made alliances with foreign governments. To end the nobles' power, Richelieu destroyed their fortified castles and stripped them of their local administrative functions. The nobility retained social prestige, while authority in local government affairs was given to special agents of the Crown known as intendants. Non-nobles, Richelieu believed, would not assert themselves and challenge the king's authority.

Richelieu also sought to take away the military and territorial rights given to the Huguenots by the Edict of Nantes. The Huguenots were seen as a threat to the French state. In 1625 radical Huguenots revolted against Louis XIII. After the defeat of Protestant forces at the seaport of La Rochelle in 1628, Richelieu took away the Huguenots' right to independent fortified towns. The Huguenots were, however, allowed to keep their religious freedom.

Having weakened the monarchy's internal enemies, Richelieu sought to make France the supreme power in Europe. He strengthened the French army and took steps to build up the economy. In order to strengthen national unity, he supported French culture. Under Richelieu's direction, France's leading writers in 1635 organized the French Academy. The Academy received a royal charter to establish "fixed rules for the language … and render the French language not only elegant but also capable of treating all arts and sciences." In the following century, French became the preferred language of European diplomacy and culture.

Louis XIV

Louis XIV is recognized as the most powerful Bourbon monarch. He became king in 1643 at the age of 5. At first, France was ruled by his two regents—his mother, Anne of Austria, and Cardinal Mazarin, Richelieu's successor. When Mazarin died in 1661, Louis announced that he would run his own government. He was then 23 years old.

The 72-year reign of Louis XIV was the longest in European history. It set the style for European

Cardinal Richelieu strengthened France's economy by promoting the manufacture of luxury goods. He also gave charters to commercial companies for overseas trade. *How did Richelieu encourage the growth of French culture?*

monarchies during the 1600s and 1700s. During his own lifetime, Louis was known as the Sun King, around whom the royalty and nobility of Europe revolved. He set up a lavish court and surrounded himself with pomp and pageantry. Louis's monarchy had power as well as style. Although Louis relied on a bureaucracy, he was the source of all political authority in France. In one of his audiences, he is said to have boasted, *"L'état, c'est moi!"* ("I am the state!").

Absolute Rule

Louis emphasized a strong monarchy because of his fear of disorder without it. As a child, he had lived through the Fronde, a series of uprisings by nobles and peasants that occurred between 1648 and 1653. During the Fronde, royal troops lost control of Paris and mobs rioted in the streets. The young Louis and his regents were called to give an account of their actions before the *Parlement*, or supreme court of law, in Paris. The Fronde was crushed, but Louis never forgot this attempt to limit royal power. As king, he intended never to let it happen again.

Louis XIV's feelings about absolute monarchy were later supported by Jacques Bossuet (ZHAHK baw•SWAY), the leading church official of France during the 1600s. Bossuet's defense of the divine

COOPERATIVE LEARNING ACTIVITY

Research Organize the class into groups of four or five students. Assign a report on the life and actions of Henry Navarre (Henry IV), who converted to Catholicism and issued the Edict of Nantes to restore religious peace to France. Each group should decide on a thesis for their report. Individual students could research Henry's personal and political life, Huguenot beliefs, the St. Bartholomew's Day Massacre, consequences of the Edict of Nantes, or other information that would support the group's thesis. Each member should submit research notes to the person who will write the draft of the report. After group approval and editing, a member should copy the report in final form. **L2**

TEACH

Guided Practice

THEME Uniformity

The efforts of Cardinal Richelieu and Louis XIV brought uniformity of language, government, and religion to France. Discuss the importance of this uniformity and ask which institutions were unified. (*a predominant religion, common language, uniform currency, laws, taxes, culture, customs*) **L1**

Visualizing History Richelieu was devoted to his pursuit of power for France. He taxed the peasantry and used the taxes to build up the military in order to destroy the power of the Hapsburgs in Europe.
Answer to Caption: *He directed the establishment of the French Academy, which helped standardize and refine the French language.*

Science, Technology, and Society
Display pictures of the interior and exterior of Versailles from history, art, or architecture books. Ask students to comment on Versailles as a " perfect symbol" for Louis XIV and his court. Contrast Versailles with descriptions of French peasant life. **L1 LEP**

Politics Have students discuss the effects of Cardinal Richelieu's policies on France during the reign of Louis XIII. (*brought stability to government by ending powers of nobility, took away political power of Huguenots, built a strong army, strengthened economy, improved and standardized French language*) **L3**

origins of monarchy became one of the most famous justifications of absolute rule. He wrote:

> 66 What grandeur that a single man should embody so much! ... Behold this holy power, paternal and absolute, contained in a single head: you see the image of God in the king, and you have the idea of royal majesty. 99

According to Bossuet, subjects had no right to revolt even if the king was unjust. Kings need account to no one except God, but they should act with humility and restraint because "God's judgment is heaviest for those who command."

Court Life

After the Fronde, Louis made plans to live outside of Paris. He moved his court and government to a new palace that he built at **Versailles**. The Palace of Versailles was a large, splendid structure. No expense was spared, for Versailles was to demonstrate the wealth, power, and glory of France.

The palace had elegant royal apartments, sweeping staircases, mirrored halls, priceless tapestries, and lavish formal salons and dining rooms. There were offices for government bureaucrats as well as tiny, cramped rooms where officials lived. As many as 10,000 people lived at Versailles. Outside the palace were acres of formal gardens, filled with marble sculptures and fountains.

In this setting Louis felt secure from the danger of Parisian mobs. Here he had the nobility attend his court so that he could control them. Instead of using the nobles in government service, Louis had them wait on him in a round of daily court rituals. The nobility depended on the king's favor for pensions, court posts, and protection from creditors.

In exchange for ending the nobles' power, Louis freed them from taxation. To nobles and nonnobles alike, he sold many offices with salaries. The sale of offices provided needed royal income but became a long-term drain on the treasury.

Government Policies

Louis continued the efforts of Henry IV and Richelieu to strengthen the power of the monarch and the state. He followed the tradition of Richelieu and chose his top advisers not from the nobility, but from middle-class families. Sons often succeeded their fathers in government service.

Although Louis was an absolute monarch, he was not able simply to change the traditions of his country's feudal past. Legal systems varied throughout France. Private tolls and customs were levied on

goods moving from one province to another. Weights and measures were not uniform. There were separate authorities and districts for financial, judicial, religious, and administrative affairs.

If Louis had tried to change these practices, it would have disrupted the kingdom and endangered his throne. Instead, the king kept the traditional ways, but added to them new administrative offices and practices. Two key people aided Louis XIV in his efforts—Jean-Baptiste Colbert (kohl •BEHR) and François Michel Le Tellier, the Marquis de Louvois (loov•WAH). As economic and financial minister, Colbert followed mercantilist policies to promote trade and industry. Louvois served as minister of war and helped make France's army the strongest in Europe.

Taxation

While reforming some aspects of government practice, Louis failed to adjust the complicated and unjust tax system. The poor carried most of the tax burden, while nobles, clergy, and government officials were exempt from many payments. Independent tax collectors often made large profits from their work, but they were allowed to continue this practice since the money they provided was needed to support the army.

The unreformed tax system heightened the economic differences between the regions of France. Since any visible improvement in one's farm or household might lead to higher tax payments, there was little desire to improve one's output. The tax system encouraged people to move from heavily taxed regions to regions with lower taxes. As a result, heavily taxed regions became poorer.

Religious Policy

Louis regarded the Huguenots as a threat to his absolute monarchy. Many Huguenots were military leaders and prosperous merchants. They often controlled local commerce. In spite of their high social standing, the Huguenots faced mounting persecution from Louis's government. The king wanted the Huguenots to accept Catholicism. He believed that, in this way, they would prove their loyalty to the throne. In 1685 the Edict of Nantes was repealed. Huguenots could no longer practice their religion, and their children had to become Catholics.

The result of the king's policy was the emigration of about 200,000 Huguenots to such places as the Netherlands, England, and England's American colonies. Many of these talented people contributed to the economic growth and prosperity of the lands where they settled.

Expansion

Louis XIV pursued a bold and active foreign policy. His goal was to expand the glory and power of France. Other European rulers were fearful of Louis's desire for expansion, and as a result, allied in opposition to France.

At the end of Louis XIV's reign, Europe was concerned about the succession to the Spanish throne. It was expected that Charles II of Spain would die without an heir. Both France and Austria had claims to the throne. The rest of Europe was alarmed that the balance of power would be disrupted if France inherited Spain's vast empire. Prior to Spanish king Charles II's death, the European powers worked out a plan to divide the Spanish Empire. The will of Charles II upset this plan by stating that the entire empire should remain intact and pass to Louis XIV's grandson, Philip of Anjou. Louis XIV accepted the provisions of the will. When Charles II died in 1700, Philip of Anjou became King Philip V of Spain. As a result, Europe was plunged into a conflict known as the War of the Spanish Succession.

Conflict

The War of the Spanish Succession lasted from 1701 to 1713. During the conflict England, the Dutch Netherlands, and Austria led a Grand Alliance of European nations against France and Spain.

Peace was finally restored with the Treaty of Utrecht in 1713. England and the Dutch Netherlands recognized Philip V as king of Spain, on the condition that France and Spain never be united under one crown. England gained trade advantages with the Spanish colonial empire. France, however, was forced to surrender the North American provinces of Nova Scotia and Newfoundland to England. The War of the Spanish Succession drained the French treasury, brought increased poverty, and created opposition to Louis's rule.

Louis XIV's Legacy

France enjoyed one of its most brilliant cultural periods under Louis XIV. Builders and artisans designed and decorated palaces and churches. Artists and playwrights portrayed the daily life of the king's court, the nobility, and the lower classes. Louis's building projects and his wars, however, had left the country near financial ruin. The ways in which Louis weakened the French nobility also had their costs. The nobles lost their ability to govern, but not the desire for power. The peasants and the middle class resented the privileges and wealth of the nobles. After Louis XIV's death in 1715, the nobility sought to expand its power under Louis's great-grandson, Louis XV. Conflicts between the nobles and the middle and lower classes would bring France to the brink of revolution.

SECTION 3 REVIEW

Recall
1. **Define** intendant.
2. **Identify** Henry IV, Edict of Nantes, Cardinal Richelieu, Louis XIV, Treaty of Utrecht.
3. **Explain** how Henry IV tried to

bring religious peace to France.
Critical Thinking
4. **Evaluating Information** What do you think were the successes and failures of Louis XIV's reign?

Understanding Themes
5. **Uniformity** What were Cardinal Richelieu's political goals? How did Richelieu reduce the power of the nobility? Of the Huguenots?

SECTION 3 REVIEW ANSWERS

1. All vocabulary words are defined in the Glossary.
2. Henry IV, 266; Edict of Nantes, 266; Cardinal Richelieu, 266; Louis XIV, 267; Treaty of Utrecht, 269
3. issued the Edict of Nantes
4. Louis XIV elevated French culture and brought every aspect of French life under

his control; he antagonized nobility, Huguenots, and the poor, setting the stage for future conflict.
5. **UNIFORMITY** Richelieu sought to build a strong monarchy; he stripped the nobility of their administrative powers and repealed the Edict of Nantes.

ASSESS

Check for Understanding

Assign Section 3 Review as homework or as an in-class activity.

▣ Use Student Self-Test and Review Software to review Section 3.

Linking Past and Present

Molière was a great writer of comic theater during Louis XIV's reign. One of his plays, *L' Ecole des Femmes* or *School for Wives*, is considered the first great comedy of French theater and is still frequently performed. It is said that France loves Molière as England loves Shakespeare.

Reteach

Have students create a biographical outline, chronologically listing the major figures of this section and including examples of how each person helped or hindered France.

Enrich

Have students research the decorative arts of this period in France and make a short oral report, including visuals.

CLOSE

Have students explain how the reign of Louis XIV built on policies begun during the time of Louis XIII, giving specific examples.

ind Out

Answer: *All major European powers except England became involved.*

FOCUS

Section Objective

Examine how the Thirty Years' War differed from prior European wars.

BELLRINGER
Motivational Activity

Before taking roll at the beginning of the class period, project Section Focus Transparency 8-4 and have students answer the activity questions. Discuss students' responses.

This activity is also available as a blackline master.

Vocabulary Pre-check

Use Vocabulary Activity 8 to introduce vocabulary terms.
L1 LEP

1600   **1700**   **1800**

1618 Czechs revolt against Hapsburg rule.

1648 Treaty of Westphalia ends Thirty Years' War.

1740 Maria Theresa becomes empress of Austria.

1763 Seven Years' War ends.

Section 4

The German States

Setting the Scene

▶ **Terms to Define**
pragmatic sanction

▶ **People to Meet**
Maria Theresa, Frederick II

▶ **Places to Locate**
Austria, Prussia

ind Out   How was the Thirty Years' War different from prior European wars?

$\mathcal{S}$*toryteller*

Thomas Taylor traveled slowly and cautiously from Dresden to Prague. He was overwhelmed by a harshness he had never witnessed in his native England. Life all around him was insecure and uncomfortable. Violent outlaws roamed the highways, torture was part of the judicial process, executions were horrible, famine and disease were evident in every town. Taylor detoured around public refuse heaps, swarming with rats and carrion crows. He dodged the bodies of executed criminals dangling from the gallows. Taylor had heard rumors of war. If the rumors were true, he judged it would be long, brutal and terrible.

—freely adapted from *The Thirty Years' War*, C.V. Wedgwood, 1961

The Thirty Years' War

While the Bourbons were building the strongest monarchy in Europe, the Hapsburgs of Austria were trying to set up their own absolute monarchy in central and eastern Europe. Their efforts renewed tensions between Europe's Catholics and Protestants. This eventually led to yet another conflict—the Thirty Years' War. Though most of the fighting took place in Germany, all the major European powers except England became involved.

The Thirty Years' War

Conflicts between Catholics and Protestants had continued in Germany after the Peace of Augsburg in 1555. These disputes were complicated by the spread of Calvinism, a religion that had not been recognized by the peace settlement. Furthermore, the Protestant princes of Germany resisted the rule of Catholic Hapsburg monarchs.

In 1618 the Thirty Years' War began in Bohemia, where Ferdinand of Styria had become king a year earlier. Ferdinand was also the Hapsburg heir to the throne of the Holy Roman Empire. An enemy of Protestantism who wanted to strengthen Hapsburg authority, Ferdinand began his rule by curtailing the freedom of Bohemian Protestants, most of whom were Czechs. In 1618 the Czechs rebelled and took over Prague. Soon the rebellion developed into a full-scale civil war—Ferdinand and the Catholic princes against the German Protestant princes. Philip III of Spain, a Hapsburg, sent aid to Ferdinand.

The Czech revolt was crushed by 1620 and, over the next 10 years, the Czechs were forcefully reconverted to Catholicism. Instead of ending, however, the war continued. Protestant Denmark now fought against the Hapsburgs, hoping to gain German territory. The Danes were soon defeated and forced to withdraw. Then Sweden entered the war to defend the Protestant cause. By this time the

---

war had been going on for 12 years, and religious issues were taking second place to political ones. In 1635, under Cardinal Richelieu, Roman Catholic France took up arms against the Roman Catholic Hapsburgs to keep them from becoming too powerful.

For 13 more years the war dragged on—rival armies plundering the German countryside and destroying entire towns. Historians estimate that Germany lost about one-third of its people.

When the conflict finally ended in 1648, the outcome was the further weakening of Germany and the rise of France as Europe's leading power. The Peace of Westphalia ending the war recognized Calvinism among the official religions and divided the Holy Roman Empire into more than 300 separate states. The Hapsburgs still ruled Austria and Bohemia, but their control of the other German states was in name only, thus ending their hope of establishing an absolute monarchy over all of Germany.

Austria

After the Thirty Years' War, the Austrian Hapsburgs concentrated on building a strong monarchy in **Austria**, Hungary, and Bohemia. Austria was still the most powerful of the German states. In 1683 the Austrians, with the aid of the Poles, lifted an Ottoman siege of Vienna. By 1718, Austrian armies had regained territory in the Balkan Peninsula from the Ottomans. As a result of the War of the Spanish Succession, the Austrians received the Spanish Netherlands and acquired lands in Italy.

In 1740, 23-year-old **Maria Theresa** inherited the throne of Austria from her father, Holy Roman

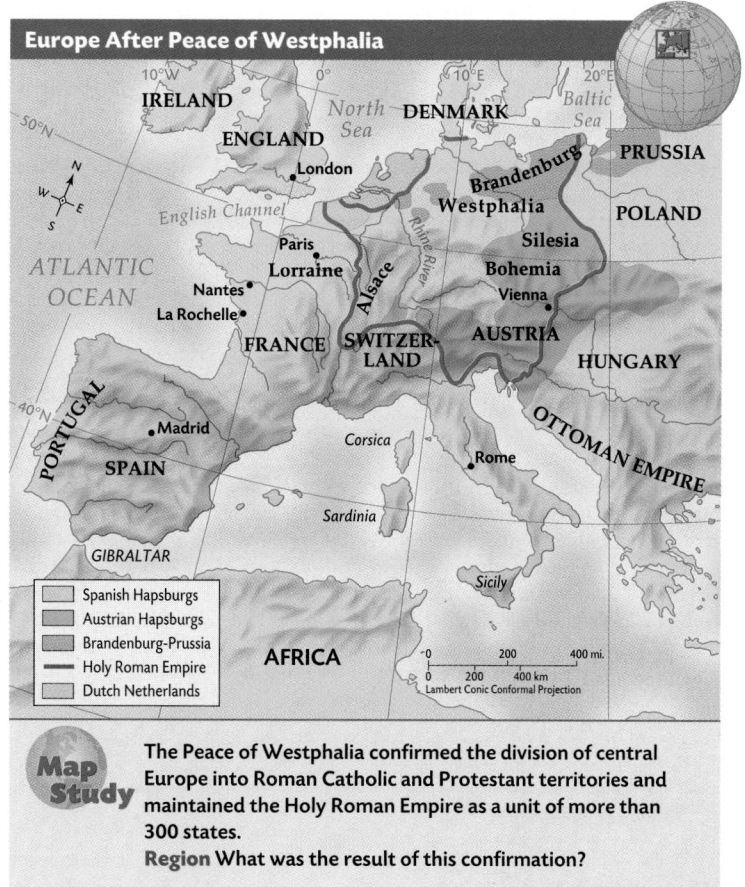

Europe After Peace of Westphalia

- Spanish Hapsburgs
- Austrian Hapsburgs
- Brandenburg-Prussia
- Holy Roman Empire
- Dutch Netherlands

Map Study

The Peace of Westphalia confirmed the division of central Europe into Roman Catholic and Protestant territories and maintained the Holy Roman Empire as a unit of more than 300 states.
Region What was the result of this confirmation?

Emperor Charles VI. According to law and custom, women were not permitted to rule Austria. In 1718 Charles had convinced the monarchs of Europe to accept a pragmatic sanction, or royal decree having the force of law, by which Europe's rulers promised not to divide the Hapsburg lands and to accept

Footnotes to History

Tulip Mania
During the Thirty Years' War, western Europeans fell in love with tulips. Dutch traders brought tulip bulbs into Europe from Ottoman Turkey beginning in the 1500s, and gardeners in the Netherlands and other parts of Europe took a liking to the blossoms. This led to a public craze for tulips that reached a peak in the 1630s.

Chapter 8   *Royal Power and Conflict*   **271**

TEACH

Guided Practice

THEME Conflict
In discussing the conflicts involved in the Thirty Years' War, ask students to recall religious conflicts that were a part of earlier periods. (*Romans and early Christians; Hindus and Muslims in India; Christians and Muslims in the Holy Land*) **L1**

Map Study

Answer
France became the leading power.

Map Skills Practice

Reading a Map What are the major cities in the Hapsburg territories? (*Madrid, Vienna*)

Geography Have students compare the map of the Hapsburg holdings in Section 1 on page 260 to the map in this section. Ask them to identify the changes that took place between the time represented by the earlier map and the time represented by this one. (*Holy Roman Empire is smaller; Hapsburg holdings smaller; Brandenburg-Prussia is new; Switzerland and Dutch Netherlands are now independent states; France is larger.*) **L2**

Focus on World Art Print 19, Jan Steen. *The Dancing Couple*

Who?What?Where?When?

Maria Theresa of Austria not only ruled the foreign affairs of the Holy Roman Empire but also raised 16 children. One of her daughters, Marie Antoinette, became queen of France.

Chapter 8 Section 4

Independent Practice

 Guided Reading Activity 8-4 **L1**

Political Cartoon Have students assume the role of a political cartoonist during the Austrian Succession or the Seven Years' War. Have them depict a major event in a cartoon for the *Prussian Press.* Subjects might include the fight over Silesia or alliances formed by different countries. **L2 LEP**

ASSESS

Check for Understanding

Assign Section 4 Review as homework or as an in-class activity.

🖲 Use Student Self-Test and Review Software to review Section 4.

The Sounds of Bach

In the Germany of Bach's time, music was taught in schools, and most people could play an instrument. The chief instrument was the organ, but string and keyboard (clavier) instruments were gaining in popularity. Bach favored the organ and composed 143 chorale preludes for it. Of these, 45 were compiled in a "little organ book" for his oldest son and other students.

ANSWERS

Bach's music was lively and complex in style. His work was largely neglected. Today, he is regarded as an esteemed musician and has had an impact on popular music ranging from Walt Disney classics to rock music.

---

female succession to the Austrian throne.

Maria Theresa had not received any training in political matters, yet she proved to be a clever and resourceful leader. Overcoming the opposition of the nobility and most of her ministers, Maria Theresa greatly strengthened the Austrian central government. She reorganized the bureaucracy, improved tax collection, and furthered the building of roads. Understanding that the unity of her empire depended on a strong economy, Maria Theresa ended trade barriers between Austria and Bohemia and encouraged exports. She also used government funds to boost the production of textiles and glass.

Prussia

Maria Theresa faced a number of enemies in Europe. One of these was France, the traditional rival of the Hapsburgs. In the 1700s a new European rival rose to prominence in northeastern Germany. Brandenburg-Prussia was ruled by the Hohenzollern family, which had governed the territory of Brandenburg since the 1400s. During the Thirty Years' War, they gained control of **Prussia** and other widely scattered lands in Germany.

Great Elector

One of the greatest of the Hohenzollern monarchs was Frederick William. He held the title "Great Elector." After the Thirty Years' War, Frederick William increased the strength of Brandenburg-Prussia by creating a permanent standing army. To meet the cost of his army, he proposed raising taxes. The Junkers, or nobles, opposed this plan. Frederick William then worked out a compromise with them. He permitted only Junkers to be landowners, freed them from taxes, and gave them full power over the peasants. In return, the Junkers agreed that Frederick William could tax townspeople and peasants. These two groups were too weak to organize and oppose this increased burden. In 1663 the Junkers further strengthened their ties to the Hohenzollerns. They pledged allegiance to Frederick William. As a result of this alliance with the Junkers, Frederick William was able to become an absolute ruler.

Frederick William was succeeded by his son Frederick I. Frederick aided the Austrian Hapsburgs against Louis XIV in the War of the Spanish Succession. As a reward, Frederick was given the title of king. He was, however, a weak ruler who did little to strengthen his country.

CONNECTIONS

The Arts

The Sounds of Bach

Johann Sebastian Bach

Born in Eisenach, Germany, in 1685, Johann Sebastian Bach was one of the world's most talented composers. He wrote music for the Lutheran Church, wealthy nobles, and other musicians. Bach's work reflects the baroque style of music, which reached its height during the early 1700s. Baroque music was characterized by lively, complex dramatic compositions that appealed to the listener's mind and emotions.

Bach is especially known for two types of baroque music—counterpoint and fugue. In counterpoint, two or more melodies are combined. In the fugue, several instruments or voices play together, each playing the same melodies but with variations.

For about 50 years after Bach's death in 1750, his work was neglected. Today Bach is esteemed as a brilliant musician, and his influence has touched even modern popular music and film. Walt Disney had Mickey Mouse conducting Bach's *Toccata and Fugue in D Minor* in the 1940 movie classic *Fantasia.* Bach's style is at least hinted at in the rock song *A Whiter Shade of Pale* and in rock musician Jethro Tull's jazz-like arrangement of the *Bourrée* from the *E Minor Lute Suite.*

 **ACTIVITY**

Explain why Johann Sebastian Bach's work is called "baroque." How was he regarded after his death? How is he regarded today? What impact has Bach had on modern music?

272 **Chapter 8** *Royal Power and Conflict*

MEETING SPECIAL NEEDS ACTIVITY

Learning Style: Visual/Spatial Help students who learn better visually to understand the conflicts involved between European powers during the Thirty Years' War or the War of the Austrian Succession by guiding them to make diagrams illustrating the actions and reactions, causes and effects, or problems and solutions of that time. For example, students might list problems or causes in one column, effects in another column, then draw arrows between the causes and effects. **L2 LEP**

Frederick William I

Frederick William I, who ruled from 1713 to 1740, was a powerful leader. He centralized the Prussian government, uniting all functions into one bureaucracy under his direct control. He supported production and trade and brought more revenue into the government treasury. Known as the Royal Drill Sargeant, Frederick William devoted his life to the Prussian army and made it the most efficient fighting force in Europe. Royal agents recruited men from rural areas of Germany. Frederick William I especially delighted in recruiting tall soldiers. He formed a special "regiment of giants" that he drilled himself.

Frederick II

In 1740 **Frederick II**, Frederick William I's son, became king of Prussia. As a boy, Frederick preferred music and art to horseback riding and military drills. However, when he became king, Frederick adopted his father's military ways and set out to expand Prussian territory. Frederick the Great, as he became known, rejected Austria's pragmatic sanction and seized the Austrian province of Silesia.

Frederick's attack on Silesia began a conflict called the War of the Austrian Succession. Prussia's forces were stronger than those of Austria. In spite of Austria's disadvantage, the Austrian empress, Maria Theresa, decided to send her forces into battle. Spain and France backed Prussia, while Great Britain (formed in 1707 as the result of a union between England and Scotland) and the Dutch Netherlands supported Austria.

After seven years of fighting, in 1748 the European powers signed the Treaty of Aix-la-Chapelle, which officially recognized Prussia's rise as an important nation. Frederick was allowed to keep Silesia; Maria Theresa was able to hold the rest of her domain: Austria, Hungary, and Bohemia.

The Austrian ruler, however, was not satisfied with the treaty and was determined to recover Silesia. To this end, Maria Theresa changed her alliance from Great Britain to France. She also gained the support of Russia since Prussia's Frederick II was

an archenemy of Empress Elizabeth of Russia. These alliances set the stage for further conflict.

The Seven Years' War—from 1756 to 1763—was a worldwide conflict in which Great Britain and France competed for overseas territory, and Prussia opposed Austria, Russia, France, and other nations. The war between Austria and Prussia erupted in 1756. After victories in Saxony—a German state and an ally of Austria—and after a later victory over the Austrians in Silesia, Frederick II signed a peace agreement that enabled him to retain most of Silesia.

The struggle between Great Britain and France in North America was known as the French and Indian War. The British and French also fought in India. At the Treaty of Paris in 1763, France gave up most of French Canada and its lands east of the Mississippi River to Great Britain. Great Britain also replaced France as the leading power in India. As a result of the Seven Years' War, Great Britain emerged as the strongest colonial empire and Prussia retained the province of Silesia.

The War of Jenkins' Ear

Caribbean Sea, 1739
The War of Jenkins' Ear was part of a series of conflicts among European nations in the 1700s. In the waters off Florida, an English smuggler named Robert Jenkins lost his ear in a fight with Spaniards in 1731. Jenkins' appearance in Parliament in 1738 further incited public opinion against Spain. The result was war, declared in June 1739, over possession of Georgia and commercial rivalry at sea. Within a year, the War of Jenkins' Ear had become part of the more serious War of Austrian Succession.

Caribbean Sea

| SECTION 4 REVIEW |

Recall
1. **Define** pragmatic sanction.
2. **Identify** Ferdinand of Styria, Peace of Westphalia, Maria Theresa, Frederick II, Silesia.
3. **State** what primary factor

caused the Thirty Years' War. What were the war's results?

Critical Thinking
4. **Analyzing Information** How did Maria Theresa strengthen the central government in Austria

and in her other domains?

Understanding Themes
5. **Conflict** How did the many conflicts among the German states affect the balance of power?

Who?What?Where?When?

Sans Souci Frederick II planned and had built a one-story summer palace, Sans Souci. French for "without cares," Sans Souci was the king's favorite retreat. It was famous for its midnight suppers, at which Frederick surrounded himself with educated men.

Evaluate

Section Quiz 8-4

Use the Testmaker to create a customized quiz for Section 4.

Reteach

Have students work in small groups to write summaries of conflicts discussed in this section.

Enrich

Have students voice their opinions about the shifting of alliances in order to achieve political goals. Were these the decisions of a wise monarch or signs of disloyalty and ingratitude? (*Answers will vary. Students should mention the balance of power theory.*)

CLOSE

Ask students to offer opinions about the justification of war and bloodshed that raged throughout Europe before and during the Thirty Years' War. Ask how they might have reacted if they had lived in the 1600s.

| SECTION 4 REVIEW ANSWERS |

1. All vocabulary words are defined in the Glossary.
2. Ferdinand of Styria, 270; Peace of Westphalia, 271; Maria Theresa, 271; Frederick II, 273; Silesia, 273
3. Ferdinand of Styria's attempts to end Protestantism and strengthen Hapsburg

rule by curtailing Bohemian Protestants' freedom; ensuing Czech revolt; other Protestant countries became involved
4. Government took responsibilities for services such as public health, prisons, and roads; ended trade barriers; used government funds to encourage

production of textiles and glass to build the economy.
5. **CONFLICT** weakened German states and allowed France to become dominant

1533 Ivan IV (the Terrible) begins rule.

1689 Peter I (the Great) becomes czar.

1721 Russia secures areas of Baltic coastline.

1796 Catherine II (the Great) dies.

SECTION THEME

▶ **Innovation** Peter the Great attempts to modernize Russian society.

ind Out

Answer: *Russian czars were all-powerful and able to crush the nobility, the Church, and the towns.*

FOCUS

Section Objective

Understand how the power of Russian czars differed from that of other European monarchs.

BELLRINGER
Motivational Activity

Before taking roll at the beginning of the class period, project Section Focus Transparency 8-5 and have students answer the activity questions. Discuss students' responses.

📂 This activity is also available as a blackline master.

Vocabulary Pre-check

🖥 Use the Vocabulary PuzzleMaker to create a puzzle that reinforces the vocabulary terms in this section. **L1**

Section 5

Russia

Setting the Scene

▶ **Terms to Define**
boyar, *dvorianie*, serf

▶ **People to Meet**
Ivan IV, Peter I, Catherine II

▶ **Places to Locate**
Poland, Siberia, St. Petersburg

 How did the power of Russian czars differ from that of other European monarchs?

The Storyteller

When first posted, no one could believe the decree. Czar Peter had ordered all children from the nobility and clerical classes [clergy] to study mathematics and geometry. Those who refused were forbidden to marry until they mastered the material. Such commands seemed absurd and many scoffed at the czar's ability to enforce his demands. However, teachers arrived in each district and local taxes were increased for support. Priests likewise received notification and no priest dared solemnize a marriage without proper certification. Father Konstantin looked sadly at the couple before him and explained, "You do not have the proper certification. I cannot marry you."

—adapted from *Decree on Compulsory Education of the Russian Nobility*, reprinted in *The Human Record, Volume 2*, Alfred J. Andrea and James H. Overfield, 1990

Russian Orthodox Bishop

Between 1500 and 1800, Russia made tremendous territorial gains and became a major European power. Slavs elsewhere lost ground and were taken over by other powers.

In southeastern Europe, the Ottoman Turks ruled most of the Balkan Peninsula and the Serbs, Bosnians, and Macedonians who lived there. Under the Ottomans, some of these Slavs converted to Islam, while the rest remained Eastern Orthodox. Hungary ruled the Croats (KROH•ATZ), and Austria controlled the Slovenes (SLOH•VEENZ). Both these Slavic peoples remained Roman Catholic and oriented to western Europe.

In central Europe, Austria ruled the Slovaks and Czechs. Neighboring **Poland** had been an important European power from the late 1300s. Polish monarchs created one of the larger states of Europe, but by the 1600s Poland had gradually weakened. Ukrainian subjects rebelled against Polish rule in the mid-1600s and allied with Russia. By 1764 almost all of Ukraine was under Russian control. In the late 1700s Prussia, Austria, and Russia divided Poland among themselves. The Belarus region and its people, the Belarussians, passed from Polish to Russian control at this time.

Rise of Russia

From the 1200s to the early 1700s, Russia was isolated from western European developments, such as the Crusades, the Renaissance, and the Reformation. Russia developed its own civilization based on the values of the Eastern Orthodox Church and the Byzantine Empire. The Russian monarchy became all-powerful and easily crushed its opponents. The nobility, the established church, and the towns—all of whom had posed repeated opposition to royal power elsewhere in Europe—never posed the same challenge in Russia.

274 Chapter 8 *Royal Power and Conflict*

SECTION RESOURCES

📂 **Reproducible Masters**
- Reproducible Lesson Plan 8-5
- Guided Reading Activity 8-5
- History Simulation 8
- Reteaching Activity 8
- Enrichment Activity 8
- Section Quiz 8-5

- Performance Assessment Activity 8
- Spanish Chapter Summary 8

🎞 **Transparencies**
- Section Focus Transparency 8-5

Multimedia
- 🖥 Vocabulary PuzzleMaker Software
- 🖥 Student Self-Test and Review Software
- 🖥 Testmaker
- 💿 Picture Atlas of the World

Ivan IV

The most powerful of the early czars was **Ivan IV**, who ruled from 1533 to 1584. Known as Ivan "the Terrible" or "the Awesome," he was at once learned, religious, and cruel. Ivan became czar at the age of three. While growing up, he was caught between rival groups of nobles who sought to rule the country. He witnessed much cruelty and was never able to rid himself of his early memories. As an adult, Ivan saw treason everywhere and arrested, exiled, or executed many of his closest advisers. In a fit of rage, he even killed his own son.

Ivan took many steps against the **boyars** (boh•YAHRZ), or nobles, to reduce their potential threat to his throne. He seized their scattered lands and placed them under his direct control. The former owners were uprooted and dispersed. On the seized land, which made up about one-half of the country, Ivan placed his own loyal people. They became a secret police force, the *oprichniki*, (aw•PREECH•nee•kee) and terrorized the rest of the country.

Ivan IV also increased Russia's trade with western Europe and worked to expand his borders. Despite Russia's vast size, it had few seaports free of ice throughout the year. Gaining more access to the sea for trade and security became a major goal of Russian rulers. During the late 1500s, Ivan conquered Mongol lands east and south of Moscow but waged unsuccessful war against Poland, Lithuania, and Sweden for territory near the Baltic Sea.

The Time of Troubles

After Ivan's death in 1584, Russia drifted toward chaos. During the "Time of Troubles," from 1598 to 1613, noble feuds over the throne, peasant revolts, and foreign invasions plagued the country. Finally in 1613, an assembly of clergy, nobles, and townsmen named 17-year-old Michael Romanov as czar. Michael began the Romanov dynasty that ruled Russia until 1917.

During the 1500s and 1600s, Russian society experienced many changes. Boyars became more closely tied to the czar's service, townspeople lost what little influence they had on government, and peasants were bound to the land as a virtually enslaved workforce. To escape, many peasants moved to borderlands south of Moscow. In Ukraine, some formed self-governing villages of warrior pioneers and their families and became known as Cossacks. Peasants, traders, and adventurers also moved into **Siberia**, the vast stretch of land east of European Russia.

Visualizing History Peter the Great, a man of restless energy and sometimes hasty decisions, attempted many reforms. *What reforms did he introduce to make Russia more like western European nations?*

Peter the Great

In 1689 **Peter I**, known as Peter the Great, came to the throne. He was a towering figure, nearly 7 feet (2 m) tall. Peter had boundless energy and volcanic emotions. During his reign, he sought to bring Russia into the mainstream of European civilization.

Encounter With the West

As a young man, Peter enjoyed practical subjects, such as mechanics, geography, and military strategy. He sought out tutors among the foreign community in Moscow to learn the basic skills of navigation and shipbuilding. He discovered that Russian knowledge of the outside world was quite limited. Most Russians were illiterate peasants; only a few nobles were well educated.

After becoming czar, Peter took an 18-month study tour of England and the Netherlands. He visited shipyards, factories, mills, and laboratories. He learned carpentry and developed enough skill in surgery and dentistry to want to practice on others.

Chapter 8 *Royal Power and Conflict* **275**

TEACH

Guided Practice

THEME Innovation

Discuss and list on the chalkboard the changes that occurred in Russia between the time of Ivan the Terrible and Catherine the Great. Ask what advances were made in political control, the arts, science, and technology. *(Sample answers: nobility given land in exchange for government service; printing press introduced into Russia; new capital built; army and navy modernized)* **L1 LEP**

Visualizing History Because Peter had such stores of energy, he found relaxation difficult. Although hunting was a favorite sport of many monarchs, Peter refused to hunt; however, he sailed whenever he could. He also enjoyed playing chess and carried a folding leather chessboard with him so he could play with anyone at any time.

Answer to Caption: *required court members to wear Western-style clothes; included women in social gatherings; invited foreign experts to train Russians in sciences, naval warfare, shipbuilding, and foreign languages; increased the power of the central government*

Comparing Catherine the Great has been compared by historians to England's Elizabeth in her ability to rule and in the significance of her reign. Have students prepare a chart comparing the two rulers and their accomplishments. **L2**

 History Simulation 8

COOPERATIVE LEARNING ACTIVITY

Research Have students work in small groups to research and report on the daily life of women in Russia during the time of Peter the Great and Catherine the Great, as well as women in Russia today. Scholarly works on Russian feminism of the past and the present are available in local libraries. Have groups plan how to delegate the work—some students may research, and others may write the reports. Topics to consider might be family responsibilities, intellectual interests, types of work, and political concerns of the women. Copies of photographs from the resources will help the groups describe the life of women then and now. **L2**

TEACH

Explain to the class that the building of a city on the marshes of the Neva River was a major project. Peter hired hundreds of foreign architects and thousands of Russian workers to create a city described as the "Venice of the North." **What feature unique to a city like Venice would be useful for a city built on a broad river and marshes?** *(a network of canals)* Tell students that St. Petersburg became the country's main industrial center and one of the world's most brilliant cultural centers.

Who? What? Where? When?

St. Petersburg arrived late as a major city in the world. In the American colonies, New York was already 75 years old, Boston was 73, and Philadelphia was 60. St. Petersburg was the capital of the Russian Empire for 200 years.

NATIONAL
GEOGRAPHIC
SOCIETY

CD-ROM

PICTURE ATLAS OF THE WORLD

You and your students can see a skyline view of St. Petersburg and the Winter Palace (now the Hermitage Museum) by clicking Russia's "Photos" button.

Peter's Great City

Where he first set foot on the Baltic coast, legend has it, Peter the Great proclaimed: "Here there shall be a town." On May 16, 1703, Russian workers laid the foundations for a fortress on the Baltic coast. The city of St. Petersburg soon spread out, and in 1712 Peter made it the new capital of Russia. A traveler in his youth, he was determined that his new capital would imitate the imposing European cities he had visited. St. Petersburg did not remain the capital of Russia, but the new city offered Peter the Great a chance to consolidate the power of the Russian central government and to drag Russia into the modern world. Many changes were inaugurated: He

G.D. Talbot

forbade men to wear beards or to dress in the traditional long robes called caftans. He simplified the Cyrillic alphabet. He was relentless. At times he even resorted to terror. But he transformed Russia and made his new city on the Baltic Sea a window to the West.

Today Peter's legacy is everywhere: in the shipyards, the research centers, and the architecture of ornate palaces such as the Winter Palace (center), completed during the reign of Catherine the Great in 1762. "I have a whole labyrinth of rooms ... and all of them are filled with luxuries," she wrote of the Winter Palace and the adjoining Hermitage, where Pavilion Hall (top) fills one small corner. ●

276 Chapter 8 *Royal Power and Conflict*

When he returned home, Peter forced the Russian nobility to adopt the ways of western Europe. He ordered members of the court to wear western European clothing. Men entering Moscow were forced to shave their beards or pay a fine. Women, who had always been excluded from social gatherings, were ordered to attend parties.

Peter sent Russians abroad to study shipbuilding, naval warfare, mathematics, and foreign languages. He invited foreign experts to train Russians. His greatest effort to open Russia to Europe was the building of a new capital, which he named **St. Petersburg**. Located at the mouth of the Neva River near the Baltic Sea, St. Petersburg became Russia's "window to the West."

Foreign Policy

Peter's goal was to make Russia a European power. He expanded Russia's borders in the south, east, and northwest. In 1689 Russia forced China to accept Russian control of Siberia. In the early 1700s, the Danish navigator Vitus Bering claimed for Russia what became known as the Bering Strait between Siberia and Alaska. Russian settlements eventually started in Alaska and even California.

During much of Peter's reign, Russia fought Poland, Sweden, or the Ottoman Empire. Russian failures to win warm-water ports on either the Baltic or Black Seas convinced Peter to modernize the military. His reforms paid off in 1721, when Russia defeated Sweden and won control of the eastern end of the Baltic region.

Government Administration

Peter made sweeping changes in the Russian government. Borrowing ideas from France, he introduced a central bureaucracy and placed local governments under its control. Peter brought the Eastern Orthodox Church under his direct authority. In place of a single independent church leader, Peter created the Holy Synod, a council of bishops responsible to the government.

Peter also created a new class of nobles called *dvorianie* (DVOH•ree•YAH•nee•YUH), who, in return for government service, were allowed to own hereditary, landed estates. A noble's duty to the czar started at age 15 and continued until death.

Peter used privileges and force to make the established nobility accept government service. Nobles were given full control over the serfs, or peasant laborers who worked the estates and were bound to the land. While freedom for peasants had gradually increased in western Europe, the opposite was true in Russia.

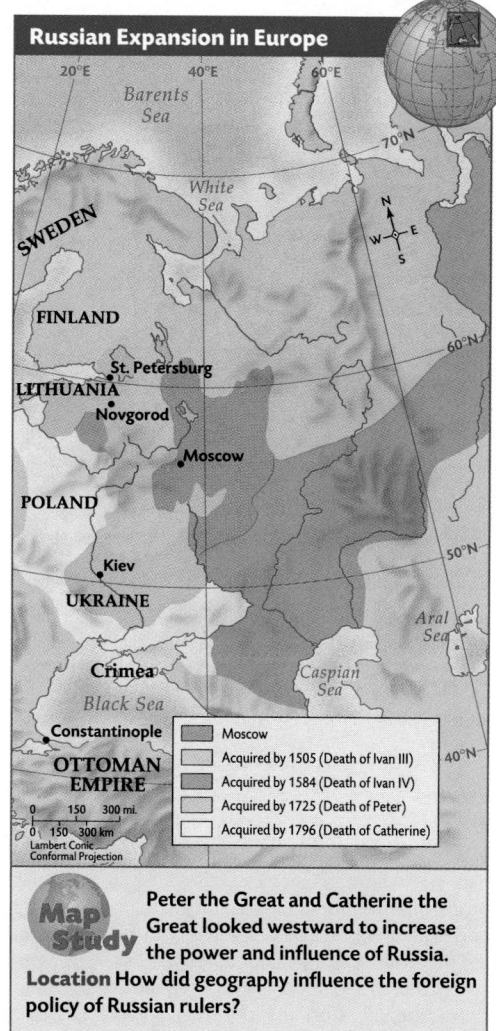

Russian Expansion in Europe

	Moscow
	Acquired by 1505 (Death of Ivan III)
	Acquired by 1584 (Death of Ivan IV)
	Acquired by 1725 (Death of Peter)
	Acquired by 1796 (Death of Catherine)

0   150   300 mi.
0   150   300 km
Lambert Conic
Conformal Projection

Map Study Peter the Great and Catherine the Great looked westward to increase the power and influence of Russia. **Location** How did geography influence the foreign policy of Russian rulers?

Finally, Peter changed the tax laws to increase government income and efficiency. Under the plan, nobles paid no taxes. As in France, the tax burden fell on the poorest classes.

Economic Changes

To stimulate economic growth, Peter brought agriculture and craft production under strict government control. He gave incentives to increase production in favored areas such as mining and metalworking. New production centers were provided with land, money, and workers. Most of the workers were tied to their trades as the serfs were to the land.

Chapter 8 *Royal Power and Conflict* **277**

Independent Practice

 Guided Reading Activity 8-5 **L1**

Map Study

Answer

Russia was a vast northern country whose population centers were far from ports that were ice-free throughout the year; Russian rulers wanted to expand to acquire coastal areas with warm water outlets.

Map Skills Practice

Reading a Map The acquisition of Crimea gave Russia access to what important body of water? (*Black Sea*)

The following videotape program is available from Glencoe:

• **Secrets of the Romanovs**

To find classroom resources to accompany this video, check the following home page:

A&E Television:
http://www.AandE.com/

Linking Past and Present

City Renamed Peter the Great had the new city named St. Petersburg after himself. Later it was renamed Leningrad after the Communist revolutionary leader Vladimir Lenin. Today the city has been re-renamed and is again called St. Petersburg.

MEETING SPECIAL NEEDS ACTIVITY

Mixed Learners To help students who learn better by discussing a topic and also to help those who have limited use of the language, have students work in groups of three. Each student should select part of the section to study, outline, and then "teach" to the other members of the group. Suggest that they each write a short quiz for the others to take at the end of the teaching session. **L1 LEP**

History & Art In the midst of her political and military career, Catherine wrote plays, poems, fairy tales, and memoirs. She encouraged literature and the arts, and architecture flourished under her reign. The famous Hermitage, which became her art gallery, was built as an addition to the Winter Palace. **Answer to Caption:** *a peasant rebellion*

ASSESS

Check for Understanding

Assign Section 5 Review as homework or as an in-class activity.

 Use Student Self-Test and Review Software to review Section 5.

Evaluate

Section Quiz 8-5

Reteach

Have students work in small groups to summarize the achievements and the acts of oppression of each major ruler in Section 5. Guide a class discussion based on their summaries.

Reteaching Activity 8

Enrich

Have students debate the following: Catherine the Great was not great.

Enrichment Activity 8

CLOSE

Ask students which Russian monarch they would rather serve and in what capacity. *(Answers should reflect the ability and morality of the monarch.)*

History & Art *Portrait of Catherine the Great* by Alexandre Roslin. Musée des Beaux Arts, La Rochelle, France *What changed Catherine's mind about the equality of all people?*

Effects

Peter's reforms strengthened Russia's role in foreign affairs. In his own country, however, Peter had only limited success. His domestic policies broke the traditional Eastern Orthodox culture that had united nobles and peasants. With Peter's reign, a dangerous split developed between the few who accepted European ways and the many who clung to traditional values. An observer noted: "The tsar pulls uphill alone with the strength of ten, but millions push downhill." Many of Peter's reforms were incomplete and hasty. Yet his measures brought Russia into the mainstream of western European civilization.

Catherine the Great

After Peter's death in 1725, Russia was ruled by a series of weak or ordinary monarchs. The next notable ruler was **Catherine II**. In 1762, Catherine seized the throne from her weak husband, Peter III, and ruled as empress of Russia until 1796. Although born a German princess, Catherine easily adopted Russian ways and earned the respect of her people.

As monarch, Catherine was greatly influenced by leading western European thinkers. She studied their works and corresponded with a number of them. For a time, she believed that all people were born equal and that it was "contrary to the Christian faith and to justice to make slaves of them."

Early in her reign, Catherine considered freeing the serfs. A peasant rebellion that threatened her rule, however, made Catherine change her mind. To ensure the continued support of the nobles, she released them from the government service required by Peter I. Catherine also allowed the nobles to treat their serfs as they pleased. During Catherine's reign, more peasants were forced into serfdom than ever before, and their conditions worsened. The common people of Russia had fewer rights than those in any other part of Europe. When groups of them revolted, Catherine brutally crushed the uprisings.

A successful foreign policy earned her the name Catherine the Great. She significantly expanded Russia's borders to the south and achieved the goal of securing a warm-water port on the Black Sea. In making this gain, Russian armies defeated the Ottoman Turks. In the west, Catherine acquired territory from Poland. Prussia and Austria took the rest of Poland, which then ceased to exist until 1919.

Catherine was the last of the great absolute monarchs of the 1700s. By the time of her death in 1796, new ideas of liberty and equality had spread throughout western Europe. These new ideas directly challenged and questioned the age-old institution of monarchy.

SECTION 5 REVIEW

Recall
1. **Define** boyar, *dvorianie*, serf.
2. **Identify** Ivan IV, the Romanovs, Peter I, Catherine II.
3. **Locate** the cities of Moscow and St. Petersburg on the map on page 277. Why did Czar Peter the Great move the Russian capital from Moscow to St. Petersburg?

Critical Thinking
4. **Synthesizing Information** How did the reigns of Peter the Great and Catherine the Great affect the Russian nobility and the common people?

Understanding Themes
5. **Innovation** How did Peter the Great try to make Russia accept western European ideas and practices?

SECTION 5 REVIEW ANSWERS

1. All vocabulary words are defined in the Glossary.
2. Ivan IV, 275; the Romanovs, 275; Peter I, 275; Catherine II, 278
3. to open Russia to Europe
4. Peter used privileges and force to make the nobility accept government service; bound serfs to the land and granted nobles full control over them; Catherine released the nobles from government service; under her the lot of the common people worsened.
5. **INNOVATION** He brought foreign experts to teach the European ways and sent Russians abroad.

Critical Thinking SKILLS

Recognizing a Stereotype

Emanuella asks her friend Ashley if she would date a football player. Ashley says, "No way. Football players are all muscle and no brains." Ashley has expressed a stereotype—an oversimplified description of a group. Because stereotypes may be both inaccurate and harmful, we must learn to recognize them in speaking, writing, and thinking.

Learning the Skill

A stereotype can describe any group—a gender, race, religion, country, region, city, neighborhood, school, or profession. Stereotypes blur or ignore the characteristics of individuals within the group. In the example above, Ashley may reject the friendship of a very considerate and intelligent person just because he plays football. While this is a negative stereotype, other stereotypes may have positive or neutral connotations. "Blondes have more fun," for example, is a positive stereotype. Negative stereotypes, however, are the least accurate and most harmful.

Stereotypes can influence not only our attitude about a group's members, but also can affect our behavior toward them. History is full of examples of oppression and persecution directed at particular groups of people. Negative stereotypes usually accompany and support these destructive acts.

Because stereotypes are so common, it is easy to ignore or accept them. Instead, learn how to recognize and evaluate them. Certain words, phrases, and thoughts signal the presence of stereotypes. In any kind of material, written or oral, first notice characteristics attributed to a particular group. Look for exaggerations, often indicated by words such as *all*, *none*, *every*, *always*, and *never*. Identify strong negative adjectives such as *lazy*, *sneaky*, *cruel*, and *corrupt*. Note a consistently positive or negative tone to the description.

Once you recognize a stereotype, then evaluate its accuracy. Think about whether the stereotype puts a positive or negative slant on the information concerning a specific group. Ask yourself: Does this stereotype agree or disagree with what I know about individual members of this group?

Practicing the Skill

Each statement below contains a stereotype held by people from the 1500s to the 1700s. Identify the stereotype in each statement. Identify any words or phrases that helped you recognize the stereotype, and tell whether it has a negative, positive, or neutral connotation.

1. England is an isle fouled by heretics and barbarians. (*Spain, 1554*)
2. It is against the law, human and divine, that a woman should reign and have empire above men. (*England, 1560*)
3. The Italians are so jovial and addicted to music that nearly every countryman plays on the guitar, and will commonly go into the field with a fiddle. (*England, 1600*)
4. Do not put such unlimited power into the hands of husbands. Remember all men would be tyrants if they could. [We ladies] will not hold ourselves bound by any laws in which we have no voice, or representation. (*United States, 1776*)

Applying the Skill

Identify three stereotypes about groups within your community. For each stereotype, write a paragraph evaluating its accuracy by recalling your own experiences with individual members of the group.

For More Practice

Turn to the Skill Practice in the Chapter Review on page 281 for more practice in recognizing a stereotype.

Critical Thinking SKILLS

TEACH

Recognizing a Stereotype Most students will understand and be aware of the problem of negative stereotypes. Suggest that they take time to consider positive stereotypes and the actual harm that can come from them, too. Ask students to brainstorm positive stereotype examples from television programs, movies, and magazine advertisements. For example, they might discuss the positive body images portrayed in the media, such as the scent ads, hairstyles, and fashions that are supposed to make life wonderful. Ask students to discuss the impact of these advertisements on young people and the problems they cause for self-esteem in the teenage population.

Additional Practice

Skill Reinforcement Activity 8

ANSWERS TO PRACTICING THE SKILL

1. English people were opposed to Catholicism; words *fouled*, *heretics*, and *barbarians* are used for their negative connotations; a negative stereotype
2. only men should be rulers of countries; words "against the law" very absolute; a negative stereotype
3. Italians are happy and musical; *every* shows exaggeration; a positive stereotype
4. husbands, men in general, are not to be trusted with power; negative word *tyrants* and use of *all*; a negative stereotype

GLENCOE
TECHNOLOGY

VIDEODISC
Use MindJogger to review students' knowledge of the chapter.

MindJogger Videoquiz

Chapter 8
Disc 1 Side B

 Also available in VHS.

Answers

Using Key Terms
1. f   4. e
2. j   5. b
3. h

Using Your History Journal

Students should give supporting facts to explain the reason for their opinion.

Reviewing Facts

1. Hapsburgs, Spain and Austria; Tudors, England; Bourbons, France; Romanovs, Russia; Hohenzollern, Brandenburg-Prussia

2. European monarchs were at their pinnacle of power, emphasizing divine right—monarchs worked to unify their nations and build strong central government bureaucracies; they emphasized their power and wealth by building palaces and staging magnificent ceremonies.

3. by cooperating with Parliament and selling monastery lands to wealthy landowners

4. It ended a long period of religious warfare in France between Catholics and Protestants; granted Protestants equal rights with Catholics; and moved toward acceptance of religious toleration.

5. He built St. Petersburg and made

Connections Across Time

Historical Significance One of the results of the Age of Monarchy was the emergence of strong national states in Europe. Absolute monarchs centralized their governments and established powerful military forces to protect and to expand their countries' natural borders.

Monarchs plunged Europe into wars over territorial, religious, and economic issues. By forcefully asserting their power, monarchs created the national boundaries that would form the basis of modern Europe. Later wars would modify the boundaries but not change them completely. Today, monarchs reign but do not rule in several European democracies.

Using Key Terms

Write the key term that completes each sentence. Then write a sentence for each term not chosen.

a. absolutism   g. armada
b. balance of power   h. inflation
c. intendants   i. yeomen
d. serfs   j. pragmatic sanction
e. divine right   k. *dvorianie*
f. boyars

1. Ivan IV of Russia took steps against the _____ to reduce their potential threat to his throne.
2. In 1718 the Holy Roman emperor Charles VI convinced Europe's monarchs to accept a _____ in which they promised to accept Maria Theresa as the future Hapsburg monarch.
3. During Spain's decline as a European power, its economy suffered from _____, an abnormal increase in currency resulting in sharp price increases.
4. During the 1600s and the 1700s, European monarchs claimed to rule by _____, the theory that monarchs derive their power from God.
5. During Elizabeth I's reign, England worked for a _____ on the Continent to prevent one European power from becoming too strong.

Technology Activity

Building a Database Search the Internet or your library for additional information about European monarchies since the early 1500s. Build a database collecting biographical information about European monarchies from the 1500s to present day. Include information such as name of monarchy, country, date of coronation, achievements, and names of heirs.

Using Your History Journal

Choose an event from the country time line you created. Write a short opinion paper on why you believe that this was the most significant development, person, or decision in that nation during the period 1500 to 1750.

Reviewing Facts

1. **History** List at least four European royal families and their countries during the period from about 1500 to about 1800.
2. **History** Identify major characteristics of Europe's age of absolutism.
3. **Government** Explain how England's Henry VIII strengthened support for his policies.
4. **Citizenship** State why Henry IV's issuing of the Edict of Nantes was a significant event.
5. **History** Identify the changes that Peter the Great brought to Russia.

Critical Thinking

1. **Analyze** How were the Hapsburg and Tudor monarchies of the 1500s similar? How were they different? Which one do you think was more successful?
2. **Synthesize** Imagine you are a soldier during the Thirty Years' War. Describe how you joined the army and what conditions were like during the war. What hopes do you have for the future?
3. **Evaluate** Consider the leadership style of Maria Theresa of Austria, who had no training in political matters. Can a person today be a successful political leader with no prior training or experience?

---

it the capital; expanded Russia's borders; built a navy and factories; introduced newspapers and books and western European styles and customs.

Critical Thinking

1. Similarities: both strong monarchies, sought to increase wealth, faced internal unrest. Differences: Hapsburg Empire vaster; Hapsburgs Protestant and Tudors Catholic; Hapsburgs a

larger family with many branches.

2. I joined the army because it was the only way to escape hanging. Conditions during the war were terrible. I was hungry most of the time and often wounded; most of my friends died. I have little hope for the future because my home has been destroyed and the land ruined.

3. Students may conclude that political leaders need training in diplomacy and negotiation.

4. **Evaluate** Which of the monarchs described in this chapter do you most admire? Which one do you least admire? Explain your reasons.

5. **Evaluate** What does the portrait of Frederick the Great below reveal about the values and characteristics of the Prussian monarchy?

Understanding Themes

1. **Conflict** How did Spain's rivalry with England develop during the period from about 1500 to about 1750?

2. **Change** How did Tudor monarchs bring stability to England?

3. **Uniformity** How did Louis XIV try to strengthen French loyalty to his monarchy?

4. **Conflict** What dynastic and religious issues divided the German states?

5. **Innovation** Why did Peter the Great want to make innovations in government and society?

Skill Practice

The following lines from William Shakespeare's plays include stereotypes that were common in 16th-century England. Identify each stereotype and any words or phrases that helped you recognize it.

1. "Frailty, thy name is woman!"
2. "These Moors are changeable in their moods."
3. "This Hebrew will turn Christian; he grows kind."
4. "Today the French … all in gold, like heathen gods, shone down the English."

Linking Past and Present

1. European monarchs in the 1600s and 1700s resolved their territorial disputes and ambitions through war. How do present-day leaders resolve disputes? Explore the similarities and the differences between contemporary world leaders and monarchs in early modern Europe.

2. European monarchs in the 1600s and 1700s were powerful leaders who claimed to rule by divine right. What is the position of monarchs in Europe today? How is power exercised in modern European governments?

Geography in History

1. **Location** Refer to the map below. Along what body of water did Pomerania lie? What was the population loss over much of its area?

2. **Place** Of Bohemia, Saxony, and Silesia, which area had suffered the least population loss?

3. **Region** In general, what parts of the Holy Roman Empire retained the most population? Why do you think this was so?

Population Loss 1618–1648

Up to 15%   33–66%
15–33%   Over 66%   — Boundary of Holy Roman Empire

Bourbons fought Hapsburgs for power; Hohenzollerns of Prussia fought Austrian Hapsburgs.

5. **INNOVATION** He wanted to make Russia more like western Europe.

Skill Practice

1. all women are weak; woman used to mean "all women"; negative

2. Moors (Africans) are moody people; "these Moors" means "all Moors"; negative

3. Jews are not kind—kindness is a Christian trait; negative

4. the French looked splendid; *all in gold* and *gods* show exaggeration; positive

Linking Past and Present

1. Today leaders try to resolve disputes through negotiations and diplomacy, but sometimes conflicts still result in war.

2. Most European monarchs today are mainly figureheads with power exercised by a prime minister and national legislature.

Geography in History

1. Baltic Sea; over 66 percent
2. Saxony
3. western parts, Brunswick, and Saxony; there were more rebellions and wars in the other territories, depleting the population

Chapter Bonus Test Question

Ask students: If you could spend an evening with one of the rulers you have met in this chapter, who would it be and what would you do? (*Answers should reflect knowledge of the ruler's life and accomplishments.*)

4. Students should give supporting facts to explain why they admire or do not admire a particular monarch.

5. reflects a dignified, serious, and strong leader

Understanding Themes

1. **CONFLICT** England supported the Dutch fight for independence against Spain and raided Spanish ships; Philip invaded England with Armada to rid himself of Elizabeth's interference; that defeat led to Spain's decline.

2. **CHANGE** They unified the country, expanded foreign trade, and built a strong navy.

3. **UNIFORMITY** kept nation's traditional ways, chose top advisers from middle classes, repealed Edict of Nantes

4. **CONFLICT** Catholic Hapsburgs fought Protestant German princes; Catholic

VIDEODISC
Turning Points in World History

Side One
Chapter 9

Title: *Age of Exploration*

If you do not have access to a videodisc player, **Turning Points in World History** is also available in VHS.

Internet Site

The following is a possible site for completing the "Net" activity:

The Atocha Home Page:
http://www.ocf.berkeley.edu/~mars/

Not on the "Net"...

If students have limited or no access to the Internet, have them complete the "Sunken Treasures" activity by using resources in the school or public library to find information on sunken treasures. Encourage students to use the following subjects to help them locate sources in the library's computerized or traditional card catalog: sunken treasure, spanish history, florida keys.

Students may use the information they locate to help them create their chart and map.

ABCNEWS INTERACTIVE™ Turning Points in World History

Age of Exploration

Setting up the Video

Work with a group of your classmates to view "Age of Exploration" on the videodisc *Turning Points in World History*. The voyages of the age of exploration opened new doors for European explorers to gain new contacts for trade, expansion, and innovation that profoundly changed European culture. This program highlights the history of European exploration and speculates about future trends for modern explorers.

Side One, Chapter 9

View the video by scanning the bar code or by entering the chapter number on your keypad and pressing Search. (Also available in VHS format.)

Hands-On Activity

Research information about current discoveries that are taking place in space explorations. Using a word processor, write a minireport about the latest findings. Share your results with the rest of the class.

Surfing the "Net"

Sunken Treasures

During the 1500s, Spanish galleons were constantly searching for treasure to take back to Spain. Typically, the loot included precious stones, gold doubloons, and silver pieces of eight. Many treasure-laden vessels were sunk due to bad weather or pirates trying to steal the fortune in the midst of a battle. To find out more about recent discoveries of sunken treasures, access the Internet.

Getting There

Follow these steps to gather information about sunken treasure.
1. Go to a search engine. Type in the phrase *sunken treasure*.
2. After typing in the phrase, enter words such as the following to focus your search:
   - *spanish history*   - *florida keys*   - *location*
3. The search engine should provide you with a number of links to follow. Links are "pointers" to different sites on the Internet and commonly appear as blue underlined words.

What to Do When You Are There

Click on the links to navigate through the pages of information and gather your findings. Using a word processor, create a chart to organize your information. Include headings such as location of a sunken galleon, date of sinking, date of discovery, and treasure recovered from the galleon. Include a map labeling the location of discovered sunken ships.

INTERNET ADDRESS BOOK

Use this space to record frequently used addresses.

_____
_____
_____
_____
_____

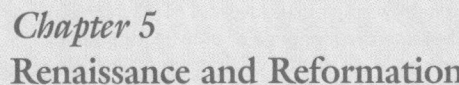

Unit 2 Digest

F rom 1400 to the mid 1700s, rulers in various parts of the world increased the power and prestige of their territories. In Europe two major movements—the Renaissance and the Reformation—encouraged Europeans to gain new knowledge, explore lands overseas, acquire new resources, and spread Christianity.

Religion, politics, and economic needs also spurred new developments in Asia. There, Muslim empires ruled over vast areas between the Mediterranean Sea and South Asia. Other parts of Asia—China, Japan, and Southeast Asia—developed their traditional cultures while facing growing challenges from European explorations. A new age dawned in which the world's different civilizations for the first time came into close contact with each other.

History & Art *The Marriage of Giovanni Arnolfini and Giovanna Cenami* by Jan van Eyck, 1434. National Gallery, London, England *What values were popular throughout Renaissance Europe?*

Chapter 5
Renaissance and Reformation

In the 1300s scholars in Italy revived the ancient Greek ideal of individual achievement. Their interest in the classics sparked a new era of European thought and art known as the Renaissance. For the first time since the fall of Rome, European artists and writers emphasized the value of human activities and feelings in their works. This represented a departure from the medieval concern with religion and spiritual values. During the Italian Renaissance, highly talented people—such as Michelangelo Buonarroti and Leonardo da Vinci—also created works of art that have been admired throughout the centuries for their technical skill and beauty.

From Italy the Renaissance spread to northern Europe, where it became more religious in its emphasis. Scholars such as Erasmus and Thomas More called for simpler forms of worship and other church reforms. Johannes Gutenberg's use of movable type in printing made an increasing number of books at cheaper prices available to more people. As a result, Renaissance ideas spread rapidly and challenged traditional religious and cultural beliefs.

Protests against church abuses soon led to a split in Western Christianity. Reformers such as

Martin Luther and John Calvin criticized the pope's authority and many Catholic teachings and practices. Their two major ideas—that the Bible, rather than church tradition, was the source of authority and that salvation was by faith alone—won support throughout northern Europe and led to a new form of Christianity known as Protestantism. In England, the monarch replaced the pope as head of the Church in England. Later the English Church became Protestant with Catholic features.

To counter Protestantism, the Roman Catholic Church began its own reform movement to correct church abuses and to more clearly define its teachings. As part of this effort, the pope sent the Jesuits, a new religious order, as missionaries to Protestant areas in Europe and non-Christian areas in Asia.

Chapter 6
Expanding Horizons

During the 1400s, Muslims and Italians controlled the rich overland spice trade from Asia. Wanting to share in this wealth, European countries bordering the Atlantic Ocean sought a direct sea route to the spice-producing islands of Southeast Asia. Advances in navigation by Chinese and Muslim inventors made their oceangoing voyages possible. By the 1500s, Portugal had discovered a

Unit 2 *Emergence of the Modern World* **283**

Unit 2 Digest

The Unit Digest offers a chapter-by-chapter summary that can be used for any of the following:
- *Preview* one chapter or an entire unit,
- *Review* some or all of the chapters,
- *Condense* when specific chapters or units have not been taught, or
- *Reteach* chapters that students have studied in the unit.

PREVIEW

Use the Unit 2 Digest Transparencies to preview the highlights of the unit.

History & Art

Answer to Caption: *human activities and feelings*

REVIEW

Critical Thinking From the illustrations in this unit, have students choose one example of Western painting or architecture and one example of Eastern art or architecture. Then have students write a short essay comparing the styles of the two works and suggesting what each work reveals about the society that created it. **L3**

Use the Student Self-Test and Review Software to review any chapters that students have studied in Unit 2.

CLASSROOM RESOURCES FOR UNIT 2 DIGEST

Preview
- Unit 2 Digest Transparencies

Review
- Time Line Activities 5, 6, 7, 8
- Student Self-Test Software, Chapters 5, 6, 7, 8
- MindJogger Videoquiz, Chapters 5, 6, 7, 8

Condense
- Chapter Digests Audiocassettes, Chapters 5, 6, 7, 8

Reteach
- Reteaching Activities 5, 6, 7, 8
- Chapter Digests Audiocassettes, Chapters 5, 6, 7, 8
- Turning Points in World History

CONDENSE

 Use Chapter Digests
Audiocassettes to introduce chapters that students have not studied in Unit 2. Spanish Chapter
Digests Audiocassettes are also
available.

Discuss Have students read the
Unit Digest and discuss the
Surveying the Unit questions.

GLENCOE
TECHNOLOGY

VIDEODISC
Use the MindJogger to
review any chapter in Unit 2.

MindJogger Videoquiz

Chapter 5
Disc 1 Side A

Chapter 6
Disc 1 Side A

Chapter 7
Disc 1 Side B

Chapter 8
Disc 1 Side B

Also available in VHS.

route to South Asia around the southern tip of
Africa. Its traders followed the route and founded
trading centers in India and Southeast Asia.

Portugal's rival, Spain, joined in the effort to
reach Asia. By 1522, Columbus, Magellan, and
other explorers under Spain's flag had reached the
Americas or had circled the globe. The Spaniards
later set up a large overseas empire that included
Mexico, Central America, most of South America,
and the Philippines.

France, England, and the Netherlands led the
search for shorter routes to Asia, and they eventually
surpassed Spain in overseas exploration. The Dutch
acquired Portugal's spice trade in Southeast Asia.
France traded with Native Americans in North
America's interior lands. England set up colonies or
trading posts in the Americas and South Asia.

European overseas expansion brought riches to
European countries. However, the same expansion
often had both a positive and negative impact on
the cultures that Europeans encountered.
Europeans brought new skills, beliefs, and goods to
overseas areas. Peoples in Asia, Africa, and the
Americas, however, saw their traditional cultures
undermined by European expansion, and millions
died of mistreatment or diseases brought by
Europeans. Portugal, Spain, and England relied on
enslaved people from Africa to work their plantations and mines in the Americas.

The slave trade became part of the larger trading network that was beginning to link Europe,
Asia, Africa, and America. Gold and silver from the
Americas to Europe increased trade between
Europe and Asia, where demand for the precious
metals was high. European manufactured goods
flowed around the world, while agricultural products, such as corn, chocolate, yams, potatoes, coffee,
and tea, came to Europe from Asia, Africa, and the
Americas. All of these exchanges, both positive and
negative, contributed to the rise of the global community that we know today.

Chapter 7
Empires of Asia

From the late 1400s to the 1700s, three Muslim
empires—the Ottoman, the Safavid Persian, and
the Mogul—ruled parts of Asia, Europe, and Africa.
The Ottomans controlled the Middle East and
much of North Africa and Europe's Balkan
Peninsula. Suleiman I, who ruled from 1520 to 1566,
strengthened government administration, but later
military defeats at Lepanto (1571) and Vienna

**During the 1500s and 1600s,
European explorers, traders, and
missionaries traveled the seas to Africa, the Americas, and Asia.** *What earlier developments in European
finance and business encouraged voyages of exploration?*

(1683) halted the Ottoman advance into Europe. To
the east, the Safavid dynasty ruled Persia, or present-day Iran. Under Safavid leadership, Persia
enjoyed a flowering of culture, and the Persian language became the language of culture, diplomacy,
and trade in most of the Muslim world. Muslims
from central Asia conquered northern India and set
up the Mogul dynasty. Akbar, a Muslim ruler of the
1500s, fostered religious tolerance among Muslims
and Hindus. Mogul rulers encouraged the arts—
music, painting, and literature.

In China the Ming dynasty, which ruled from
1368 to 1644, encouraged the development of agriculture and sponsored overseas explorations that
sailed as far as Africa and Arabia. Although the
expeditions brought back rich tribute, the Chinese
did not continue their voyages of discovery. In 1644
Manchu invaders conquered China and set up the
Qing dynasty. Internal peace and government-
sponsored improvements brought prosperity and
increased population. During the 1700s, government corruption and internal revolts weakened the
dynasty. Meanwhile, the Chinese faced new threats
from European explorations in their part of the
world.

In the 1500s Japan's warrior classes came under
the rule of a military leader known as a shogun.
During this period, Portuguese traders reached
Japan, and European Catholic missionaries made
many converts among the Japanese. Fearing this
foreign influence, Japan's military leaders closed
Japan's borders to all except a few Dutch traders.

Visualizing History The Ottoman ruler Selim I, who was crowned in 1512, fought wars of expansion against the neighboring Persians and Egyptians. *What areas eventually made up the territory of the Ottoman Empire?*

From the 1400s to the 1800s, large areas of Southeast Asia came under European influence. The Thai kingdom (Siam) was the only Southeast Asian area to remain free of European control. Thai kings built a strong central government and employed reforms that preserved their country's independence.

Chapter 8
Royal Power and Conflict

During the 1500s and 1600s, European monarchs strengthened their thrones and created powerful central governments. Their efforts paved the way for the rise of modern nation-states in Europe.

In Spain, Philip II sought national unity by using the Spanish Inquisition to force Protestants, Jews, and Muslims to accept Catholicism. His religious policy sparked revolts, especially among the Protestant Dutch in the Spanish-ruled Netherlands.

Protestant England supported the Dutch and challenged Spanish sea power. After the defeat of the Spanish Armada by the English in 1588, Spain began to lose much of its power. During the 1600s, the Spanish monarchy and economy declined, although Spain still held on to its overseas empire.

English Tudor monarchs, such as Henry VIII and Elizabeth I, brought England peace and stability. They increased royal power while allowing Parliament and other non-royal institutions to flourish. As the English economy prospered, the first steps were taken toward building an overseas empire based on trade.

Elsewhere in Europe, wars of religion between Protestants and Catholics shaped political boundaries and brought much hardship to Europe's people. When the Hapsburg monarchs of Austria tried to advance Catholicism and curtail Protestant liberties, war erupted among central Europe's Protestant and Catholic rulers. Other European nations, including Catholic France and Protestant Sweden, entered this conflict known as the Thirty Years' War. The Peace of Westphalia finally ended the war in 1648. By this time, the concerns of Europe's rulers had shifted from enforcing religious uniformity to extending their own political powers.

From 1600 to 1789, European monarchs wielded great power. They believed in the theory of absolute monarchy, which held that kings and queens ruled as representatives of God and were responsible to God alone, not to parliaments or citizens. In France, monarchs such as Louis XVI created a strong royal government that became the model for other European royal houses. Louis also sought to expand French territory in a series of wars that cost France thousands of lives and much wealth. During the 1700s, major wars between France and Great Britain (formed by a union in 1707 between England and Scotland) spread overseas to Europe's colonies. By the 1760s, France had lost much of its overseas empire to Great Britain.

Meanwhile, Russia, once largely isolated from European affairs, began to take on an international role under the rule of Peter the Great. Peter rebuilt the Russian state, enhanced its military power, and increased contacts with western Europe. His reforms, however, created a large gap between the Europeanized upper classes and the traditionally Russian lower classes.

SURVEYING UNIT 2

1. **Chapter 5** How did the use of movable type in printing affect developments in Europe during the 1500s?
2. **Chapter 6** What effect did European expansion have on Europeans? On peoples living in Asia, Africa, and the Americas?
3. **Chapter 7** Would the world be different if China had continued its voyages of exploration? Explain.
4. **Chapter 8** How did Ottoman, Mogul, or Ming rulers in Asia compare with monarchs in Europe during the period from the 1500s to the 1700s?

Unit 2 *Emergence of the Modern World* **285**

ANSWERS TO SURVEYING THE UNIT

CHAPTER 7 Answers will vary, but students should recognize that if China had continued its voyages of exploration, European expansion and influences in various parts of the world might have been checked or limited by Asian ones.

CHAPTER 8 European and Asian rulers faced similar problems—how to keep the peace among diverse peoples and how to bring more wealth to their empires. Their tactics were also similar: as absolute monarchs, they created centralized states with large bureaucracies.

Unit 2 Digest

Visualizing History

Answer to Caption: *Middle East, North Africa, the Balkans*

RETEACH

Review Chart Have students prepare a chart with columns headed *Europe, Asia, Africa,* and *The Americas.* Then have them brainstorm a list of the effects that the Renaissance and the age of exploration had in each region.

 Reteaching Activities 5, 6, 7, 8

 Chapter Digests Audiocassettes, Chapters 5, 6, 7, 8

ABCNEWS INTERACTIVE™

VIDEODISC
Turning Points in World History

Side One, Chapter 8
Title: *The Reformation*
Ask: Why did Martin Luther begin questioning Church practices? *(He was disturbed by abuses in the Catholic Church.)*

Side One, Chapter 9
Title: *Age of Exploration*
Ask: Why is the age of exploration considered a turning point? *(Europeans came into contact with lands and people unknown to them, irrevocably changing both cultures forever.)*

Unit 2 *Emergence of the Modern World* **285**

Introducing the Unit

Unit 3 focuses on the revolutionary changes that transformed early modern Europe, including the Scientific Revolution and political revolutions in England, the United States, and France. The ideas of liberalism, nationalism, and democracy are also explored.

Unit Objectives

After reading Unit 3, students will be able to:
1. explain how the Scientific Revolution changed the way people looked at their world and how the Enlightenment advanced new social and political ideas.
2. compare the causes and results of the English and American Revolutions.
3. understand the different phases of the French Revolution and trace the ways in which that revolution and the Napoleonic period transformed Europe.

Portfolio Project

Student reports should include the major inventions and developments in the technologies they study. This activity may be an appropriate method of authentic assessment.

Unit **3** 1500–1830

Age of Revolution

Chapter 9
Scientific Revolution

Chapter 10
English and American Revolutions

Chapter 11
The French Revolution

Then & Now *The discoveries and writings of the Age of Revolution ignited a fuse of knowledge that exploded in a scientific revolution so complete and far-reaching that the years from 1500 to 1830 are often called "the beginning of the modern age."*

Every time you have your temperature taken with a mercury thermometer, receive medication through a fine-needled syringe, let a doctor listen to your heartbeat through a stethoscope, or have your tooth drilled by a dentist, you are seeing instruments invented during the Age of Revolution. When you study a cell through a microscope or a star through a telescope, you are using equipment developed to fill the needs of sixteenth- and seventeenth-century scientists for precise, accurate scientific instruments. Even the simple multiplication symbol × was proposed during this age of scientific revolution.

A Global Chronology

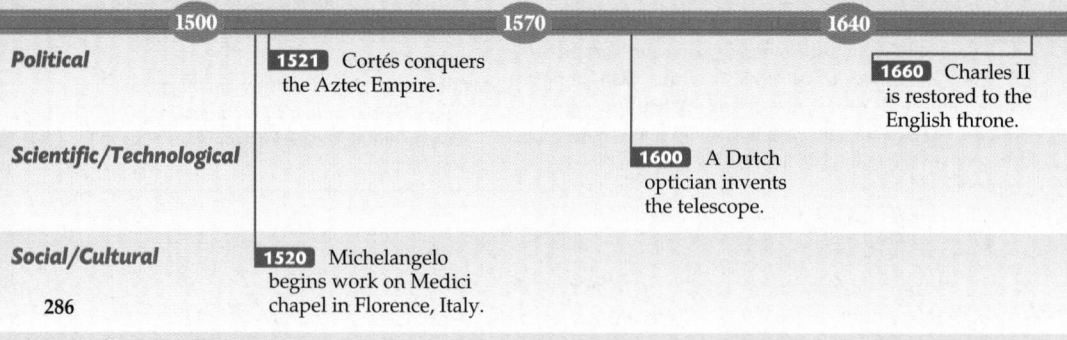

	1500	1570	1640
Political	**1521** Cortés conquers the Aztec Empire.		**1660** Charles II is restored to the English throne.
Scientific/Technological		**1600** A Dutch optician invents the telescope.	
Social/Cultural	**1520** Michelangelo begins work on Medici chapel in Florence, Italy.		

286

Then & Now **Science and Society** In this unit students will learn how breakthroughs in science and philosophy—the Scientific Revolution and the Enlightenment—eventually had repercussions on the political and social systems of Europe, North America, and elsewhere.

Have students think about the ways that science and technology influence the way we think and live today. How have scientific breakthroughs by NASA and the space shuttle program influenced our lives? *(Many breakthroughs in telecommunications, air travel, and computer science are*

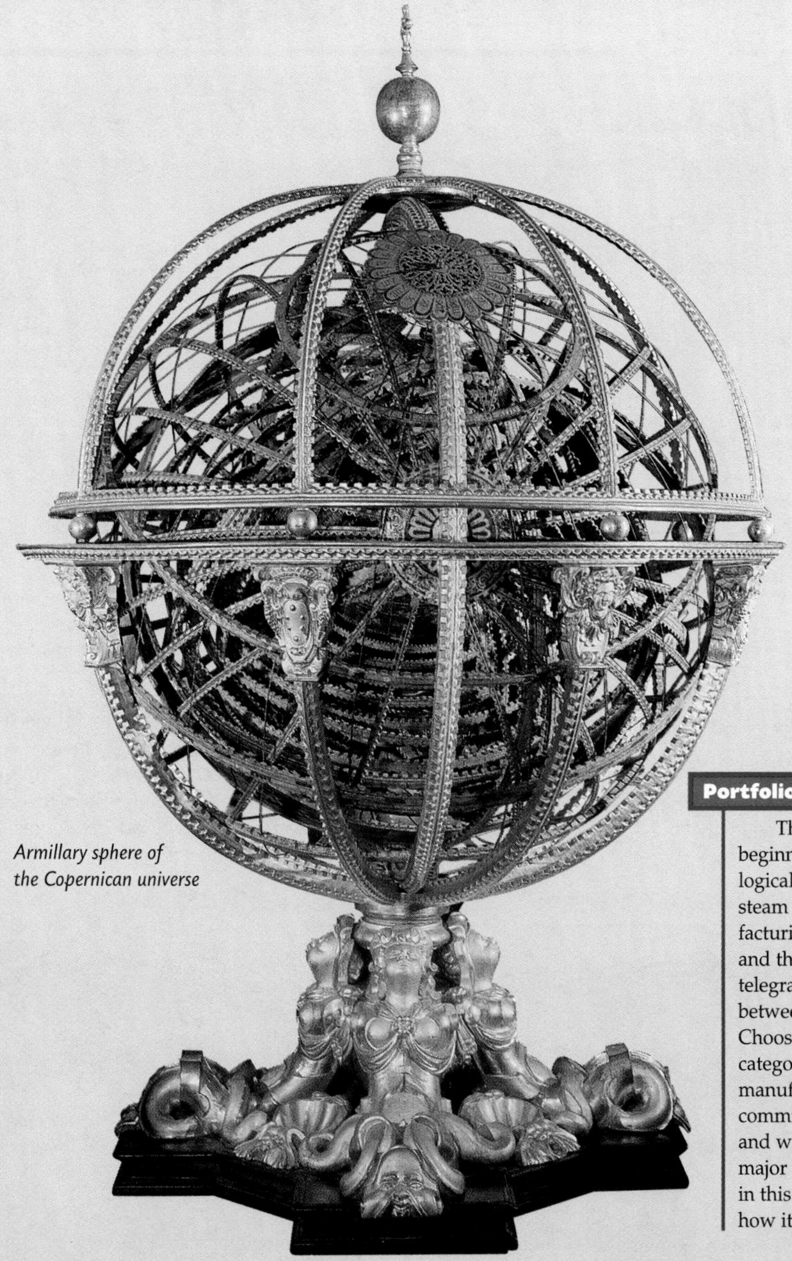

Armillary sphere of
the Copernican universe

Portfolio Project

This unit marks the beginning of great technological achievements. The steam engine, textile manufacturing, the electric battery, and the semaphore (visual telegraph) were all developed between 1750 and 1800. Choose one of the following categories—engines, textile manufacturing, electricity, or communications. Research and write a report on the major historical developments in this technology, including how it affects your life today.

History *and the* Humanities

World History and Art Transparencies
- 27 *The Letter*
- 28 *Blue Boy*
- 29 *Napoleon Crossing the Alps*

ABCNEWS INTERACTIVE™

 VIDEODISC
Turning Points in World History

 Side One, Chapter 11

Title: *French Revolution*
Subject: French Revolution
Ask: What great changes in the way people thought about political rights and freedoms took place in this period? *(The idea of the divine right of monarchs to rule gave way to individual rights and rule by popular consent.)*

1710

1789 The French Revolution begins.

1687 Isaac Newton states the theory of gravity.

1799 Rosetta stone found in Egypt makes deciphering hieroglyphics possible.

1740 Frederick the Great introduces freedom of the press and of worship in Prussia.

1780

1850

1832 The British Parliament passes the Reform Bill.

1804 Ludwig van Beethoven composes his Third Symphony, the *Eroica*.   287

History & Art

The Polish astronomer Copernicus (1473–1543) discredited the ancient idea that the earth was at the center of the solar system and that the sun moved around it. "I began to consider the mobility of the Earth," Copernicus wrote, "even though the idea seemed absurd."

---

civilian applications of space program technology.) **In what ways have computers and the information superhighway created new possibilities for political activity?** *(Through the Internet and E-mail, individuals from around the world can communicate cheaply and instantly about issues that concern them.)* **How does our knowledge about the transmission of diseases affect our behavior?** *(We take precautions like washing our hands before eating, getting vaccinations, avoiding contact with blood and other body fluids.)*

The Spread of Ideas

TEACH

Introduction

This feature focuses on the movement of revolutionary ideas between Europe and the Americas. The challenge of early scientists such as Galileo to established authority led to the questioning of long-held ideas about government, religion, and society, as well as science. In the United States, France, and Haiti, revolutionaries tried to put new ideas about government into practice.

Background Notes

Linking Past and Present

Ideas of the 1700s continue to reverberate in this century. When Ho Chi Minh declared Vietnam's independence from France in 1945, his speech began: "All men are created equal. The Creator has given us certain inviolable Rights; the right to Life, the right to be Free, and the right to achieve Happiness. These immortal words are taken from the Declaration of Independence of the United States of America in 1776."

The Spread of Ideas

Revolution

In the 1600s and 1700s, revolution bounced back and forth across the Atlantic. The pattern started with the arrival of the first English colonists in North America. They carried with them ideals born of the English Revolution. They believed that governments existed to protect the rights and freedoms of citizens.

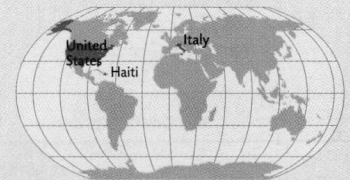

The United States
Revolutionary Ideas

In 1776 the colonists fought a revolution, making clear the principles of freedom and rights in the Declaration of Independence:

> We hold these truths to be self-evident, that all men are created equal, that they are endowed by their Creator with certain unalienable rights, that among these are life, liberty, and the pursuit of happiness.

These ideas bounced back across the Atlantic to influence the French Revolution. French rebels in 1789 fought in defense of *Liberté, Egalité, Fraternité* (Liberty, Equality, Fraternity). In drafting their declaration of freedom, French revolutionaries repeated the principles of the American Declaration of Independence: "Men are born and remain free and equal in rights."

Signing of the Declaration of Independence

288 Unit 3 *Age of Revolution*

COOPERATIVE LEARNING ACTIVITY

Wall Map and Display Have students work together to create a wall map and display that shows the origins of the ideas behind the American, French, and Haitian Revolutions. Organize the class into three groups, letting each group take one of the revolutions. Have members research their revolution, generating a list of philosophers, events, and other specific influences. For each item on the list, students should be sure to name the country of origin. When the lists have been completed, have students organize them by country in a format suitable for display. Have them mount the lists to the sides of a wall map, then use thumbtacks and colored yarn to show how various ideas traveled. **L2**

Italy
The Age of Revolution

The spread of ideas—specifically, revolutionary ideas—forms the subject of Unit 3. The spark that sent the spirit of revolution flashing across Europe and the Americas began in the minds of sixteenth-century European scientists. These thinkers challenged established ideas defended by the Roman Catholic Church. Church officials tried to stop the spread of new scientific ideas. But once unleashed, the ideas respected neither authority nor geographic boundary. Defiance of one authority, in this case, the Church, soon led people to question other authorities as well. The result was the intellectual and political upheavals that historians call the Age of Revolution.

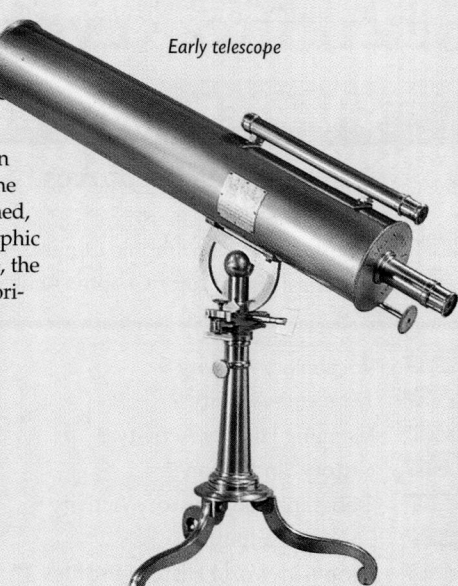

Early telescope

Haiti
Exporting Revolution

In 1791 the ideals of the American and French Revolutions traveled across the Caribbean and the Atlantic to the French-held island colony of Saint Domingue. Inspired by talk of freedom, enslaved Africans took up arms. Led by Toussaint-Louverture, they shook off French rule. In 1804 Saint Domingue, present-day Haiti, became the second nation in the Americas to achieve independence from colonial rule. "We have asserted our rights," declared the revolutionaries. "We swear never to yield them to any power on earth."

Toussaint-Louverture

Geography

Movement Americans living in France before the French Revolution actively promoted the principles of the new republic across the Atlantic. "Everyone here is trying their hands at forming declarations of rights," wrote Thomas Jefferson, whose advice was often sought by Lafayette and other moderate revolutionaries. Ask students to name other ways ideas of revolution may have traveled between the different locations of revolution shown on the map on page 288. (*Answers may include trade, newspapers, scholars exchanging books.*)

Cultural Diffusion

Containing Antislavery The success of the Haitian Revolution terrified American slaveholders, who feared that the overthrow of slavery in Haiti would inspire their own enslaved people to rebel. In the southern United States, tighter restrictions were placed on both enslaved and free African Americans. In 1802 Jefferson's postmaster general advised a senator from Georgia against letting enslaved people deliver the mail: "After the scenes which St. Domingo has exhibited to the world, we cannot be too cautious in attempting to prevent similar evils.... Everything which tends to increase their knowledge of natural rights ... or that affords them an opportunity ... of establishing a chain and line of intelligence, must increase your hazard."

LINKING THE IDEAS

1. What was the role of government according to the American colonists?
2. What ideals did the Americans and the French share?

Critical Thinking

3. **Cause and Effect** Why do you think revolutionary ideas respect neither authority nor geographic boundaries?

Unit 3 *Age of Revolution* **289**

ANSWERS TO LINKING THE IDEAS

1. to protect the rights and freedoms of citizens
2. belief in freedom and equal rights
3. Answers will vary. Students may feel that revolutionary ideas spread quickly when traditional authority has lost touch with the times. The desire for freedom and opportunity motivates people in all times and places.

A complete, 1-page lesson plan is provided for each section in the *Reproducible Lesson Plans* booklet.

Scientific Revolution

CHAPTER RESOURCES

	Reproducible Resources	Multimedia Resources
Chapter Opener	Chapter Themes: Graphic Organizer 9 Historical Significance Chapter Activity 9	MindJogger Videoquiz

Chapter Enrichment	Vocabulary Activity 9*
	Time Line Activity 9
	Mapping History Activity 9
	History Simulation 9
	Geography and History Activity 9
	Source Reading 9
	People in World History Profiles 37, 38
	World Art and Music Activity 9
	Enrichment Activity 9
	Critical Thinking Activity 9
	Skill Reinforcement Activity 9
	Performance Assessment Activity 9
		World History and Art
		  Transparency 27, *The Letter*
		
		Chapter Transparency 9
		Vocabulary PuzzleMaker Software
		Picture Atlas of the World
		Turning Points in World History:
		  The Scientific Revolution

Chapter Review/Reteaching	Reteaching Activity 9
	Skill Reinforcement Activity 9
	Spanish Chapter Summary 9
		Chapter 9 Digest Audiocassette,
		  Activity, Test*
		Vocabulary PuzzleMaker Software
		Student Self-Test and Review
		  Software
		MindJogger Videoquiz

Chapter Evaluation/Testing	Performance Assessment Activity 9 Chapter 9 Test, Forms A and B	Testmaker

* Also available in Spanish

0:00 OUT OF TIME? Assign the Chapter 9 summary in the Unit 3 Digest on pages 367–369, and the Chapter 9 Audiocassettes.

Block Schedule

    Block scheduling differs from traditional class scheduling in the amount of time allotted to each period. The extended time frame provided by block scheduling affords you the opportunity to implement a greater number of research-oriented and activity-intense projects to motivate and involve your students. Activities that are particularly suited to use within the block scheduling framework are identified throughout this chapter by the following designation.

KEY TO ABILITY LEVELS

Teaching strategies have been coded for varying learning styles and abilities.
- **L1 BASIC** activities for all students
- **L2 AVERAGE** activities for average to above-average students
- **L3 CHALLENGING** activities for above-average students
- **LEP LIMITED ENGLISH PROFICIENCY** activities

Use Glencoe's *Presentation Plus!* multimedia teacher tool to easily present dynamic lessons that visually excite your students. Using Microsoft PowerPoint® you can customize the presentations to create your own personalized lessons.

SECTION RESOURCES

Daily Objectives	Reproducible Resources	Multimedia Resources
Section 1 New Scientific Ideas Discuss how scientific thought changed during the 1600s.	Reproducible Lesson Plan 9-1 Guided Reading Activity 9-1* Time Line Activity 9 People in World History Profile 37 Geography and History Activity 9 Section Quiz 9-1*	Section Focus Transparency 9-1 Chapter Transparency 9 Vocabulary PuzzleMaker Software Student Self-Test and Review Software Testmaker Turning Points in World History: *The Scientific Revolution*
Section 2 Impact of Science Analyze the effects that changes in scientific thought had on thinking in other fields.	Reproducible Lesson Plan 9-2 Vocabulary Activity 9* Guided Reading Activity 9-2* History Simulation 9 Section Quiz 9-2*	Section Focus Transparency 9-2 Student Self-Test and Review Software Testmaker Turning Points in World History: *The Scientific Revolution*
Section 3 Triumph of Reason Identify the factors that helped Enlightenment ideas spread throughout Europe.	Reproducible Lesson Plan 9-3 Guided Reading Activity 9-3* People in World History Profile 38 Reteaching Activity 9 Enrichment Activity 9 Section Quiz 9-3* Performance Assessment Activity 9 Spanish Chapter Summary 9	Section Focus Transparency 9-3 World History and Art Transparency 27, *The Letter* Vocabulary PuzzleMaker Software Student Self-Test and Review Software Testmaker Turning Points in World History: *The Scientific Revolution*

* Also available in Spanish

Chapter Activities

✔ Performance Assessment Activity

A Last Will and Testament Have students think about the developments that occurred during the Scientific Revolution and list them in order of importance, giving a rationale for their choices. Students should then match each of the items on their list to a current-day group, individual, or country that would be a logical recipient of the invention or development if left to them in a will by the inventor or initiator. Students should then write a collective last will and testament for all of the people highlighted in the chapter. Wills should include a rationale with each beneficiary listed.

Possible Rubric Features
Accuracy of content information, argumentation and level of support, organization and clarity, research skills, ability to make logical connections

• *For an additional activity, refer to Activity 9 in the* Performance Assessment Strategies and Activities *booklet.*

ACTIVITY

From the Classroom of...

Ross Bennett Brown
Franklin K. Lane High School
Brooklyn, NY

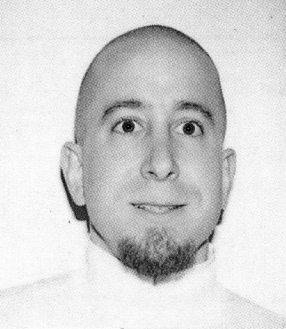

The Scientific Method in Action

Have students employ the scientific method in order to solve a problem. One problem that works well involves a simple chemistry exercise. You will need some filter paper cut into 4-inch strips, paper clips, cups with about 1 inch of water in them, and green felt-tipped pens. Begin by drawing a dot about 1 inch from the end of a strip of filter paper. Ask students what will happen when the dot makes contact with water. This is their *hypothesis*. Most will suggest smearing. Pierce the other end of the filter paper with a paper clip and use the clip to suspend the paper in the cup so that the end with the dot is just touching the water, but the dot remains above the water. This is the *experiment*. The water is drawn up the filter paper, and when it reaches the dot, the green separates into blue and yellow. We could not know this without the process of hypothesis followed by the careful observation of events during the experiment.

Since the result is almost always different from students' hypotheses, it is likely to stimulate in the class the same sort of excitement that seventeenth-century scientists might have felt conducting their own experiments.

MULTIPLE LEARNING STYLES

Verbal/Linguistic
Ask each student to select a discovery or invention of the 1600s and then write a promotional flyer or commercial promoting it. Have students present their commercials to the class.

Visual/Spatial
Have students draw political cartoons illustrating one of the controversies associated with the Enlightenment. Incorporate all the cartoons into a book.

Auditory/Musical
Have students listen to a recording of Leonard Bernstein's musical version of Voltaire's *Candide*. Ask them to write a sentence describing the connection between the lyrics of at least five songs and Enlightenment ideas.

Kinesthetic
Have students prepare models of the universe according to Aristotle and according to Copernicus. Have them use diagrams in astronomy textbooks or other reference books as a guide.

Additional Resources

NATIONAL GEOGRAPHIC SOCIETY

Teacher's Corner

INDEX TO NATIONAL GEOGRAPHIC MAGAZINE

The following articles may be used for research relating to this chapter:

- "The Hubble Telescope," by William R. Newcott, April 1997.
- "Sir Joseph Banks," by T. H. Watkins, November 1996.
- "Information Revolution," by Joel L. Swerdlow, October 1995.
- "Humboldt's Way," by Loren McIntyre, September 1985.

NATIONAL GEOGRAPHIC SOCIETY PRODUCTS AVAILABLE FROM GLENCOE

To order the following products for use with this chapter, contact your local Glencoe sales representative, or call Glencoe at 1-800-334-7344:

- *Picture Atlas of the World (CD-ROM)*

LOCAL OBJECTIVES

BIBLIOGRAPHY

Literature of the Period
Voltaire. *Candide and Other Stories.* Translated by Roger Pearson. New York: Oxford University Press, 1990. Voltaire's most popular philosophical novel and other stories.
Readings for the Student
Boorstin, Daniel. *The Discoverers: A History of Man's Search to Know His World and Himself.* New York: Random House, 1983. Contains much fascinating and readable information on Copernicus, Kepler, Galileo, Newton, and others.
Readings for the Teacher
Cohen, I. Bernard. *Science and the Founding Fathers: Science in the Political Thought of Thomas Jefferson, Benjamin Franklin, John Adams and James Madison.* New York: Norton, 1995. Explains how the Founders incorporated scientific reasoning into the Constitution.

*inter*NET
CONNECTION
Age of Enlightenment resources on the World Wide Web
Age of Enlightenment:
http://history.evansville.net./enlighte.html

CHAPTER THEMES

Chapter Themes are listed by section on this chapter opening page of the Student Edition. A corresponding theme-based activity is available under "TEACH," and a theme-based question is asked in the Section and Chapter Reviews.

The Storyteller

Historical Setting Despite the fact that Leeuwenhoek never attended a university, he became one of the world's greatest scientific pioneers. Though England and Holland were trade rivals and enemies in several wars, Leeuwenhoek shared his scientific ideas with the Royal Society of London, one of the oldest scientific societies in Europe. In October 1678, in his eighteenth letter to the Royal Society, Leeuwenhoek described "these little animals" revealed by his microscope in a drop of water. Today scientists know they are not animals at all but rather bacteria. Leeuwenhoek also discovered red blood cells when he turned his microscope on a drop of human blood.

Historical Significance

Answers: *By introducing a philosophy of knowledge based on observation, experiment, and reason, the Scientific Revolution challenged faith and traditional ideas in many areas.*

New scientific discoveries and new applications continue to challenge accepted ideas and introduce new ways of life.

Chapter 9

1600–1830

Scientific Revolution

Chapter Themes

▶ **Innovation** European interest in science leads to discoveries and ideas based on reason. *Section 1*
▶ **Conflict** Changing views based on science and reason conflict with traditional beliefs. *Section 2*
▶ **Reaction** Reason and order are applied to many human endeavors. *Section 3*

The Storyteller

Antonie van Leeuwenhoek, a Dutch cloth merchant in the late 1600s, found that his unusual hobby unlocked the door to an unknown world. By carefully grinding very small lenses out of clear glass, van Leeuwenhoek discovered that he could make things look much bigger than they appeared to the naked eye.

Soon the Dutch merchant turned his lenses to everything he could find—from the cloth he had just bought to the scales of his own skin. His most remarkable find was tiny microorganisms, which he described as "wretched beasties" with "incredibly thin feet" swimming through a tiny universe.

New technology such as van Leeuwenhoek's microscope and scientific study in general captured the imagination of many European people in the 1600s. A scientific revolution would lead to a new era in Western thought.

Historical Significance

How did the scientific revolution of the 1600s and 1700s transform European society? What impact has the growth of science had on the world today?

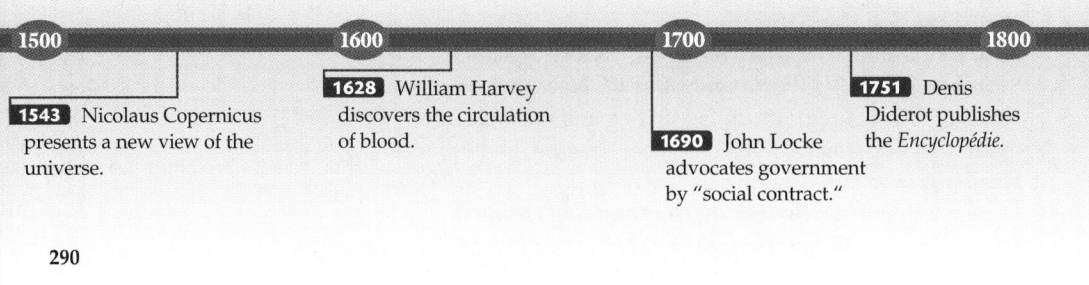

1500	1600	1700	1800

1543 Nicolaus Copernicus presents a new view of the universe.

1628 William Harvey discovers the circulation of blood.

1690 John Locke advocates government by "social contract."

1751 Denis Diderot publishes the *Encyclopédie*.

290

GEOGRAPHY CONNECTION

Movement Point out that scientific ideas traveled quickly and frequently between France, the Netherlands, and England. Have students locate these countries on a map. What route did ideas have to take between the two countries on the European continent and England? *(They had to cross the English Channel.)* How far across is the English Channel at its narrowest? *(about 20 miles [34 kilometers])* How did people cross the Channel at the time of the Scientific Revolution? *(by boat)* What options are available to people crossing the Channel today? *(boat, train, ferry, airplane, Chunnel)* **L1**

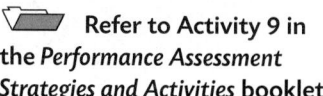

History & Art Around 1662 a group of French scientists began to hold periodic private meetings in Paris. In 1666 the Royal Academy of Sciences was established to formalize those meetings. Construction of the observatory began the following year. Today the academy's building in Paris is headquarters of the International Time Bureau, which sets standard time for the world's observatories.

✔️ **Performance Assessment**

Refer to the activity on page 290C of the Planning Guide.

📁 Refer to Activity 9 in the *Performance Assessment Strategies and Activities* booklet.

History & Art *The Establishment of the Academy of Science and the Foundation of the Observatory by Louis XIV by Henri Testelin. Musée National du Chateau de Versailles, Versailles, France*

Using Your History Journal

Encourage students to include direct quotations from the scientists whose discoveries or inventions they choose. A good resource is Daniel J. Boorstin, *The Discoverers* (New York: Random House, 1983).

Your History Journal

Research a scientific discovery or invention from the 1600s. Write the story of the discovery or invention as it might have appeared in a publication at the time.

GLENCOE
TECHNOLOGY

VIDEODISC
Use MindJogger to preview chapter content.

MindJogger Videoquiz

Chapter 9
Disc 1 Side B

Also available in VHS.

Chapter 9   *Scientific Revolution*   **291**

1600   1700   1800

1632 Galileo Galilei   1687 Isaac Newton   1774 Joseph Priestley
stands trial for his ideas.   publishes the *Principia*.   discovers oxygen.

SECTION THEME

▶ **Innovation** European interest in science leads to discoveries and ideas based on reason.

ind Out

Answer: *Observation, experiment, and reason began to replace mysticism and ancient writings as the basis for scientific thought.*

FOCUS

Section Objective

Discuss how scientific thought changed during the 1600s.

BELLRINGER
Motivational Activity

Before taking roll at the beginning of the class period, project Section Focus Transparency 9-1 and have students answer the activity questions. Discuss students' responses. This activity is also available as a blackline master.

Vocabulary Pre-check

🔲 Use the Vocabulary PuzzleMaker to create a puzzle that reinforces vocabulary terms in this section. **L1**

Section 1

New Scientific Ideas

Setting the Scene

▶ **Terms to Define**
hypothesis, ellipses, scientific method, calculus, alchemist

▶ **People to Meet**
Nicolaus Copernicus, Johannes Kepler, Galileo Galilei, Francis Bacon, René Descartes, Isaac Newton, Andreas Vesalius, William Harvey, Robert Hooke, Robert Boyle, Joseph Priestley, Antoine and Marie Lavoisier

▶ **Places to Locate**
Poland

 **ind Out** How did scientific thought change during the 1600s?

Storyteller

Christina, Grand Duchess of Tuscany, was intrigued. She had asked the renowned Galileo to describe his studies to her. "Nature," he explained in his letter, "never transgresses the laws imposed upon her, or cares whether her reasons and methods of operation are understandable to men." But Christina knew that others might find Galileo's opinions dangerous, for he also claimed that one could learn truth from these studies as much as from religion. "I do not feel obliged to believe that the same God who has endowed us with senses, reason, and intellect has intended us to forgo their use."

—adapted from *Letter to Christina of Tuscany,* reprinted in *Western Civilization: Sources, Images, and Interpretations,* Dennis Sherman, 1995

Galileo Galilei

Magic, mysticism, and ancient writings ruled scientific thought in Europe throughout the Middle Ages. Scholars based their ideas on theories proposed almost a thousand years before by ancient Greek thinkers such as Aristotle, Ptolemy, and Galen. During the Middle Ages, most Europeans believed that the earth was flat, and they accepted the Catholic Church's view that the earth was the center of the universe. According to church doctrine, God created the universe to serve people. Therefore, the Church reasoned, the people's home—the earth—must be at the center of the universe.

In the 1600s, however, such ideas would topple as a scientific revolution spread throughout Europe. New technology, combined with innovative approaches to seeking knowledge, led to a breakthrough in Western thought. At the forefront of this scientific revolution was a Polish astronomer named **Nicolaus Copernicus.**

A Scientific Revolution

Copernicus started his scientific career at the University of Kraków in **Poland** in 1492—the same year in which Christopher Columbus reached the Americas. Like Columbus, Copernicus began his questioning in a time when few people dared to question age-old beliefs and superstitions.

As Copernicus delved into his studies, he became convinced that ideas commonly accepted about the universe were wrong. Copernicus believed that the earth was round and that it rotated on its axis as it revolved around the sun. The sun stayed still at the center of the universe.

Copernicus realized, however, that his ideas were revolutionary and even dangerous. Disputing or even questioning traditional views about the universe could mean persecution, excommunication, or even imprisonment. To avoid this risk, Copernicus worked in privacy, without publishing

---

SECTION RESOURCES

📁 Reproducible Masters
- Reproducible Lesson Plan 9-1
- Guided Reading Activity 9-1
- Time Line Activity 9
- People in World History Profile 37
- Geography and History Activity 9
- Section Quiz 9-1

📱 Transparencies
- Section Focus Transparency 9-1
- Chapter Transparency 9

Multimedia
- 🔲 Vocabulary PuzzleMaker Software
- 🔲 Student Self-Test and Review Software
- 🔲 Testmaker
- 🔲 Turning Points in World History:
  The Scientific Revolution

Visualizing History In 1633, the Inquisition in Rome found Galileo guilty of heresy and sentenced him to life imprisonment. Recanting many of his views, Galileo was allowed to serve his sentence at home. *Why was Galileo charged with heresy?*

his ideas. The Polish scientist spent more than 30 years writing his treatise. Friends who realized the significance of Copernicus's ideas helped publish his work just before his death.

New Theories About the Universe

Other scientists took Copernicus's ideas and ventured even further into a scientific understanding of the universe. Copernicus had based his hypotheses, or theories that attempt to explain a set of facts, on study and observations. He could not provide proof, however, because the necessary mathematics was not available to him at the time. In the late 1500s, the Danish astronomer Tycho Brahe (TEE•koh BRAH•uh) set up an observatory to study heavenly bodies and accumulated much data on planetary movements. After Brahe's death, the German astronomer and mathematician **Johannes Kepler** used Brahe's data with the goal of providing mathematical proof for Copernicus's hypotheses.

Using mathematical formulas, Kepler did show that the planets revolve around the sun. His findings, however, also refuted some of Copernicus's views. For example, Kepler proved that the planets move in oval paths called ellipses—not in circles as Copernicus had believed. He also found that planets do not always travel at the same speed, but

move faster as they approach the sun and slower as they move away from it.

Challenging the Church

Kepler challenged the teachings of many academic and religious leaders. Because Kepler was a Protestant, however, he did not have to fear the Catholic Church. His Catholic contemporary, the Italian mathematician **Galileo Galilei**, did face considerable opposition from church leaders.

In 1609 Galileo built his own telescope and observed the night skies. His discovery of moons circling a planet convinced him that the Copernican theory about the earth revolving around the sun was correct. Because these moons revolved around Jupiter, Galileo reasoned, not all heavenly bodies revolved around the earth. It was possible that some planets did move around the sun.

In 1632 Galileo published his ideas. Soon afterward, the Catholic Church banned the book. The Church would not tolerate Galileo's spreading of ideas that contradicted its own position. An outraged Pope Urban VIII demanded that Galileo come to Rome and stand trial.

Urban's threats of torture and possible death forced Galileo to recant many of his statements and publicly state that he had gone too far in some of his writing:

Chapter 9 *Scientific Revolution* 293

Readers' Theater and Discussion Organize the class into four groups. Have the members of three groups prepare five scenes each from Bertolt Brecht's *Life of Galileo* to read dramatically to the class. Have the members of the fourth group make an intensive study of the facts of Galileo's life. After the three groups have completed their classroom reading of the entire play, have members of the fourth group run a panel discussion comparing Brecht's dramatic treatment of characters and events with their actual historical models. **L3**

TEACH

Guided Practice

THEME Innovation

New interest in science led to discoveries and philosophies based on reason. Guide students to a definition of reason. *(the power of acquiring intellectual knowledge based on facts or premises)* Ask students to give an example from this section of an innovator who used reason to advance an idea. *(Possible answer: Galileo reasoned that, as moons circle Jupiter, so planets circle the sun.)* **L1**

Visualizing History Galileo's *Dialogue Concerning the Two Chief World Systems—Ptolemaic and Copernican*, published in 1632, had been approved by the censors. But after the Jesuits claimed that it could do more damage to Catholicism "than Luther and Calvin put together," the pope had Galileo prosecuted for ignoring a warning the Church had made 16 years earlier, prohibiting him from "teaching or discussing Copernicanism in any way."
Answer to Caption: *He published ideas that contradicted the Church's earth-centered view of the universe.*

Chapter Transparency 9

Biography

The following videotape program is available from Glencoe:

• **Sir Isaac Newton: The Gravity of Genius**

Newton's Universe
Why was Newton's thinking important in the scientific revolution?

Newton's work suggested that precise mathematical formulas could be used to describe an orderly universe. This idea greatly influenced the thinking of his own age and all later scientific thought.

VIDEODISC
Turning Points in World History

Side One
Chapter 10

Title: *The Scientific Revolution*
Ask: What changes took place in European society in the seventeenth century that led to the Scientific Revolution? *(People began to challenge traditional thinking and began to see the world differently.)*

Independent Practice

📁 Guided Reading Activity 9-1 **L1**

📁 Time Line Activity 9

📁 People in World History Profile 37

📁 Geography and History Activity 9

❝ I, Galileo Galilei, … swear that with honest heart and in good faith I curse … the said heresies and errors as to the movement of the earth around the sun and all other heresies and ideas opposed to the Holy Church; and I swear that I will never assert or say anything either orally or in writing, that could put me under such suspicion. ❞

Galileo continued his work after the trial. As he experimented with the motion of objects on the earth, he helped to establish the universal laws of physics. Among these discoveries was the law of inertia, which specifies that an object remains at rest or in straight-line motion unless acted upon by an external force. Other investigations into the workings of the pendulum helped to advance its application as a time controller in clocks.

New Ways of Thinking

As European scientists revolutionized the world of astronomy, philosophers such as **Francis Bacon** and **René Descartes** incorporated scientific thought into philosophy. Bacon, an English philosopher, claimed that ideas based solely on tradition or unproven facts should be discarded completely.

To Bacon, truth resulted only from a thorough investigation of evidence. He helped develop what is known today as the scientific method. The scientific method is made up of several steps. The scientist begins with careful observations of facts or things. Then the scientist tries to find a hypothesis to explain the observations. By experimenting, the scientist then tests the hypothesis under all possible conditions and in every possible way to see whether it is true. Finally, if careful and repeated experiments show that the hypothesis does prove true under all conditions, it is considered a scientific law. In other words, a scientific truth is not assumed—it is deduced from observations and a series of thorough experiments.

Like Bacon, French philosopher and mathematician René Descartes believed that truth must be reached through reason. The inventor of analytic geometry, Descartes saw mathematics as the perfect model for clear and certain knowledge. In 1637 he published *Discourse on Method* to explain his philosophy. In the book, Descartes began his search for knowledge by doubting everything except his own existence. He believed he had found one unshakable and self-evident truth in the statement "I think, therefore I am."

Newton's Universe

In 1642, after Bacon and Descartes had transformed European thinking, one of the most influential figures in modern science was born in England. His name was **Isaac Newton**. Newton used the scientific method as he studied science and mathematics. He once commented, "Asking the correct question is half the problem. Once the question is formulated there remains to be found only proof.… "

At Cambridge University, Newton was a below-average student with few friends. He almost left school without realizing his mathematical genius. But one of his teachers recognized his ability and began tutoring him. With this help Newton quickly became an eager and successful student. He explored the most complicated mathematics of his day, reading the writings of Copernicus and Galileo.

In 1665 an outbreak of the plague closed the university and forced Newton to return to his family's farm. There, he began his ground-breaking studies in mathematics and physics. The legend of Newton's apple originated during these years. It was claimed that while sitting in his garden one day, Newton watched an apple fall to the ground. The apple's fall led him to the idea of gravity.

Nearly 20 years later, in 1687, Newton published his theories about gravity and other scientific concepts in his book *Mathematical Principles of Natural Philosophy*, often called *Principia*. Newton offered in the *Principia* a new understanding of the universe, explaining and expanding the work of Copernicus, Galileo, and Kepler.

The book stated Newton's theory of universal gravitation, explaining why the planets move as they do. According to this theory, the force of gravity not only prevents objects from flying off the

Footnotes to History

The Circus Identified by Newton, centripetal force pulls an object traveling in a circular path toward the center of the circle. In 1768 the English performer Philip Astley relied on centripetal force to perform stunts on horseback while the horse ran in a circle at full gallop. He took his horse show to Paris in 1774, beginning the first circus. *Circus* is the Latin word for "circle."

MEETING SPECIAL NEEDS ACTIVITY

Attention Deficiency To help students with attention problems organize and remember information about the people in this section, have them list these people's names. Tell students that remembering information is often easier if it is classified in some way. They can classify the names on their lists by scientific field. Organize students into small groups or pairs to identify the scientists' fields and then quiz each other; for example, "Who was Boyle?" "Boyle was a chemist." After students know these facts, have pairs add another fact about each person, then quiz each other again. For example, "Who was Boyle?" "Boyle was a chemist who is often called the founder of modern chemistry." **L1**

CONNECTIONS
Science and Technology

Bubbling Waters

Have you ever sipped a fizzy soft drink to settle an upset stomach? People have long believed that bubbling waters contain healing properties. For centuries royalty and wealthy Europeans sought the health benefits of the mineral-rich, bubbling springs scattered throughout Europe.

Scientists in Europe and the United States attempted to reproduce these effervescent waters. In 1775 the French chemist Antoine Lavoisier identified the gaseous compound as carbon dioxide. In 1782 the English chemist Thomas Henry described how to make artificial carbonated waters commercially. Factories and bottling

Soft drink advertisement

plants soon began operating in London, Paris, Dublin, and Geneva.

"Soft drinks" were originally sold in drugstores in the United States as syrupy tonics used for medicinal purposes. In the early 1800s it became popular to combine these tonics with carbonated water. Bottled colas appeared on the market in the late 1800s.

Today mineral waters and carbonated beverages are popular throughout the world. People like the tangy, sparkling taste provided by carbonation, which also prevents spoilage.

Linking Past and Present ACTIVITY

Determine whether or not carbonated soda has a positive or negative effect on your health. Can you think of any inventions or technologies that have been produced by the soft-drink industry?

revolving earth, but it also holds the entire solar system together by keeping the sun and the planets in proper orbits. To prove his theory, Newton developed calculus, a system of mathematics that calculates changing forces or quantities.

Newton's work greatly influenced the thinking of his own age and all later scientific thought. It suggested that precise mathematical formulas could be used to describe an orderly universe.

Studying the Natural World

As astronomy, philosophy, and mathematics advanced at an incredible pace, so too did the sciences of anatomy and chemistry. Like astronomy and physics, anatomy had been based on ancient works. Most knowledge of anatomy had come from the work of Galen, an ancient Greek.

Because Roman law forbade the dissection of human corpses, Galen formulated his theories of human anatomy by dissecting dogs and apes. Galen did make many anatomical discoveries, such as the existence of blood within the arteries, but he also held many mistaken views. Galen believed, for example, that the liver digested food and processed it into blood. A thousand years would pass before anyone began to question his findings.

Investigating the Human Body

French lawmakers in the 1500s also considered dissecting human bodies illegal. This limitation, however, did not stop a young medical student from making great advances in anatomy. Self-assured and outspoken, **Andreas Vesalius** made it clear to his professors that because Galen's views were based on dissected apes and dogs, his beliefs about human anatomy could not be accepted as truth. By dissecting human bodies, Vesalius made ground-breaking discoveries in anatomy. In 1543 he published his work in *On the Structure of the Human Body*.

Almost 100 years later, English physician **William Harvey** made a discovery that also disproved many of Galen's hypotheses. From his direct observations of humans, Harvey concluded that blood circulates throughout the body, pumped by the heart and returning through the veins. His findings astounded a medical world that had based its beliefs about circulation on Galen.

As Vesalius and Harvey explained the workings of the human body, English scientist **Robert Hooke** made a more fundamental biological discovery—the cell. Using the newly invented microscope, Hooke recognized cells in vegetable tissue. He called them "cells" because they reminded him of the cells in a honeycomb.

Chapter 9 *Scientific Revolution* **295**

MAKING CONNECTIONS ACTIVITIES

Mathematics/Science Have students who are talented in math or physics do a demonstration for the rest of the class explaining one of Newton's laws of physics or the basic principle of calculus. Encourage students to use objects or chalkboard diagrams. **L3**

Social Life Antoine and Marie Lavoisier are only one pair of married scientific collaborators. Have students research and write short reports about the fruitful collaborative efforts of other scientist couples, such as Marie and Pierre Curie, Irène and Frédéric Joliot-Curie, or Carolyn and Eugene Shoemaker. **L2**

ASSESS

Check for Understanding

Assign Section 1 Review as homework or as an in-class activity.

○ Use Student Self-Test and Review Software to review Section 1.

Evaluate

Section Quiz 9-1

○ Use the Testmaker to create a customized quiz for Section 1.

Reteach

Have students independently review the section and create a time line that lists important discoveries and persons. Discuss and create a class time line.

Enrich

Have students choose an innovator from the section, then choose a pivotal day in that innovator's life and write a journal entry in that person's voice for that day. A suggestion is Galileo's journal on a day during his heresy trial.

CLOSE

Write the words *before* and *after* on the chalkboard. Have students take turns choosing a person mentioned in this section and describing an accepted theory before and after this person's work. For example, having chosen Vesalius, a student would describe anatomy before and after Vesalius.

Franklin Experiments With Electricity

Philadelphia, Pennsylvania, 1752
American scientist and inventor Benjamin Franklin performed an experiment to prove his theory that lightning is electricity. During a thunderstorm, Franklin flew a homemade kite with a wire attached to it. A bolt of lightning struck the wire and traveled down the wet kite string to a key fastened at the end, where it caused an electric spark. Franklin reported the results in his pamphlet *Experiments and Observations in Electricity*.

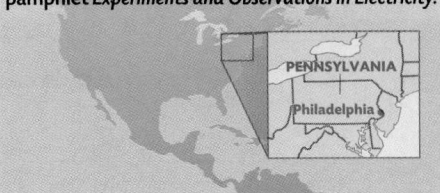

Experimenting With Chemistry

European scientists working in the field of chemistry joined their peers in astronomy, mathematics, and medicine in challenging traditional ideas. By careful scientific experimentation, **Robert Boyle** was primarily responsible for taking chemistry from its mystical and unscientific origins and establishing it as a pure science.

When Boyle was born into an Irish noble family in 1627, the chemistry of the day was alchemy. People who practiced alchemy, called alchemists, spent much of their time trying to transform base metals, such as lead and copper, into precious metals, such as silver and gold. They also held to the age-old belief that all matter was made up of four elements: earth, fire, water, and air.

Boyle criticized alchemists and attacked the theory of the four elements in his book *The Skeptical Chymist*, published in 1661. Boyle proved that air could not be a basic element because it was a mixture of several gases. He also defined an element as a material that cannot be broken down into simpler parts by chemical means.

A century later, in 1774, an English chemist and clergyman named **Joseph Priestley** conducted further experiments into the properties of air and discovered the existence of oxygen. His study of the properties of carbon dioxide resulted in his invention of carbonated drinks. Toward the end of his career, Priestley wrote, "Every year of the last twenty or thirty has been of more importance to science … than any ten in the preceding century."

In France, **Antoine Lavoisier** contributed still more to knowledge about oxygen. Lavoisier conducted scientific experiments that probed the nature of air and discovered that materials do not throw off a substance called phlogiston when burned, as commonly believed, but rather they consume oxygen. Lavoisier discovered the nature of combustion, which results from the chemical union of a flammable material with oxygen.

Marie Lavoisier contributed significantly to her husband's work. She learned English and Latin so that she could translate scientific essays and books for him. She also read numerous articles and condensed them so that he could be informed on many scientific subjects. Madame Lavoisier also made illustrations for her husband's writing.

Perhaps more significant than any single discovery in the 1700s was the application of the scientific view to an understanding of the world. Influenced by the discoveries in science, European philosophers in the 1700s began to apply the scientific method to all human ideas and practices. Most people, caught up in the daily struggle for survival, at first took little notice. In the years to come, however, science would profoundly alter humanity's view of the world.

SECTION 1 REVIEW

Recall
1. **Define** hypothesis, ellipses, scientific method, calculus, alchemist.
2. **Identify** Nicolaus Copernicus, Johannes Kepler, Galileo Galilei, Francis Bacon, René Descartes, Isaac Newton, Andreas Vesalius, William Harvey, Robert Hooke, Robert Boyle, Joseph Priestley, Antoine and Marie Lavoisier.
3. **List** three scientific discoveries that were made during the period from 1500 to 1800.

Critical Thinking
4. **Analyzing Information** What was the scientific revolution? How did it change the way Europeans viewed the universe and the workings of the human body?

Understanding Themes
5. **Innovation** How did Robert Boyle revolutionize chemistry by applying the scientific method?

SECTION 1 REVIEW ANSWERS

1. The words are defined in the Glossary.
2. Copernicus, 292; Kepler, 293; Galileo, 293; Bacon, 294; Descartes, 294; Newton, 294; Vesalius, 295; Harvey, 295; Hooke, 295; Boyle, 296; Priestley, 296; Lavoisiers, 296
3. sun-centered solar system; universal gravitation; blood circulation; the cell; oxygen

4. It was the use of reason, mathematics, and technology to understand the physical universe; they relied less on traditional authority, religion, and magic and turned to experimentation, individual experience, and the scientific method to understand the world around them.

5. **INNOVATION** Boyle used the scientific method to disprove the old theory of the four elements and define the true nature of an element, thereby establishing chemistry as a pure science.

1651 Thomas Hobbes publishes *Leviathan*.

1662 Charles II establishes the Royal Society of London.

1700s Deism becomes popular in Europe and America.

Section 2

Impact of Science

Setting the Scene

▶ **Terms to Define**
natural law, natural rights, pacifism, deism

▶ **People to Meet**
Thomas Hobbes, John Locke, Thomas Jefferson, Hugo Grotius, William Penn

▶ **Places to Locate**
Pennsylvania

 What effects did changes in scientific thought have on thinking in other fields?

The Storyteller

Donald MacAdam bent forward to hear better. The lecturer was about to read from a new poem from the pen of Nicolas Boileau-Despreaux.

*"What-e'er you write of Pleasant or Sublime,
Always let sense accompany your Rhyme:
Falsely they seem each other to oppose;
Rhyme must be made with Reason's Laws to close:
And when to conquer her you bend your force,
The Mind will Triumph in the Noble Course."*

Donald wondered, how would poetry survive if it must always be so rational?

—adapted from The Reasonableness of Poetry, reprinted in From Absolutism to Revolution, edited by Herbert H. Rowen, 1964

European salon conversation

s scientists made revolutionary discoveries about people, nature, and the universe, popular interest in science spread throughout Europe. Using new technology such as the microscope, scientists and amateurs alike looked with wonder at the world inside a drop of pond water. Others tinkered and prodded in their home laboratories, studying gases and other substances. At social gatherings across Europe, people discussed the latest findings with lively interest.

Monarchs helped the new sciences by supporting scientific academies, observatories, and museums. In England Charles II established the Royal Society of London in 1662. The group included Isaac Newton and Robert Boyle among its members. In 1666 Louis XIV of France supported the founding of the French Academy of Science. These societies provided financial support to scientists and published scientific books and journals.

Exploring Political Ideas

The advances in science led philosophers and other thinkers to believe that if systematic laws governed the workings of nature and the universe, it followed that political, economic, and social relationships could also be understood through reasoned analysis. Scientific thought and method profoundly influenced political theory. Political philosophers believed in the idea of natural law, or a universal moral law that, like physical laws, could be understood by applying reason.

Two English philosophers, **Thomas Hobbes** and **John Locke**, grappled with their ideas of natural law and government during the 1600s, as England struggled with the political tensions of a civil war. The country was torn between people who wanted the king to have absolute power and those who thought the people have the right to govern themselves.

Chapter 9 *Scientific Revolution* **297**

SECTION THEME

▶ **Conflict** Changing views based on science and reason conflict with traditional beliefs.

Answer: *Thinkers began to use reasoned analysis to scrutinize political theory, legal practice, and religious beliefs.*

FOCUS

Section Objective

Analyze the effects that changes in scientific thought had on thinking in other fields.

BELLRINGER
Motivational Activity

Before taking roll at the beginning of the class period, project Section Focus Transparency 9-2 and have students answer the activity questions. Discuss students' responses.

This activity is also available as a blackline master.

Vocabulary Pre-check

Use Vocabulary Activity 9 to introduce vocabulary terms. **L1 LEP**

SECTION RESOURCES

Reproducible Masters
- Reproducible Lesson Plan 9-2
- Vocabulary Activity 9
- Guided Reading Activity 9-2
- History Simulation 9
- Section Quiz 9-2

Transparencies
- Section Focus Transparency 9-2

Multimedia
- Student Self-Test and Review Software
- Testmaker
- Turning Points in World History: *The Scientific Revolution*

TEACH

Guided Practice

THEME Conflict

Ask students how they would react if they encountered ideas that conflicted with their beliefs; for example, if someone argued that we descend from extraterrestrials. Have students list conflicts of ideas in this section. **L1**

History Simulation 9

Picturing History ➡️

Tell students that many historians of science challenge claims that Galileo was the first to disprove Aristotle's notions about the relationship between the speed of falling bodies and their weight. Medieval philosophers had pointed out Aristotle's mistake more than 1,000 years before Galileo, and other scientists in the 1500s had also challenged Aristotle's claim. Nonetheless, it is universally agreed that Galileo did make careful experiments of vertically falling objects by rolling balls down inclined planes. Scientists today study falling bodies by using equipment unavailable to Galileo: strobe lights and video cameras.

VIDEODISC
Turning Points in World History

Side One
Chapter 10

Title: *The Scientific Revolution*
Ask: What scientist perfected the telescope? *(Galileo)*

Tower Physics

In a modern re-creation (left) of Galileo's famous experiment from the Leaning Tower of Pisa, two lighted plastic balls, one heavier than the other, plummet to the ground at once—a result the scientific community of Galileo's day refused to acknowledge. In 1591 Italian scientist Galileo Galilei (right) wanted to test the Aristotelian theory of motion—the idea that when two bodies of unequal weight are dropped simultaneously, the heavier object will hit the ground first. So he dropped a ten-pound weight and a one-pound weight from the top of the bell tower.

Galileo's experiment demonstrated that objects of different weights fell at the same rate—hit the ground at the same time—if one allowed for the impact of air resistance. Galileo proved Greek philosopher Aristotle's theory of motion wrong. In investigating the science of the motion of bodies, Galileo was part of the scientific revolution, a reformulation of ideas that overturned those held by medieval thinkers and the Catholic Church. Scientists began carefully testing old theories of how the material world worked; they used careful measurements, exact observations, and precise experiments. The conflict between these new ideas and the power of the older theories forced the new scientists to develop techniques to prove their claims. Today we call this the scientific method—and admire men like Galileo, who sought to understand motion by dropping things from the tallest building in Pisa. ⊕

298 Chapter 9 *Scientific Revolution*

MORE ABOUT...

Science and Motion In July 1971, *Apollo 15* astronaut David Scott performed Galileo's demonstration on the moon, where there is no air. He dropped a hammer and a feather at the same time to show conclusively that in the absence of air resistance, a heavy object will hit the ground at the same time as a lighter one.

Hobbes Explores Government

Thomas Hobbes used the idea of natural law to argue that absolute monarchy was the best form of government. He believed that violence and disorder came naturally to human beings and that without an absolute government, chaos would occur. In his book *Leviathan*, published in 1651, Hobbes wrote about a state in which people lived without government. The book showed how "nasty, brutish, and short" life in such a world would be.

Hobbes believed that people should form a social contract, an agreement to give up their freedom and live obediently under a ruler. In this way, they would be governed by a monarch who would protect them and keep their world peaceful and orderly. According to Hobbes, people generally do not have the right to rebel against their government, no matter how unjust it might be.

Locke Offers a Different View

Another English philosopher, John Locke, also based his theories on the idea of natural law. He came to a different conclusion, however. Like Hobbes, Locke held that government was based on a social contract and that it was necessary to establish order. Unlike Hobbes, he believed that people in a state of nature are reasonable and moral, and that they have natural rights, or rights belonging to all humans from birth. These included the right to life, liberty, and property.

In *Two Treatises of Government*, Locke stated that people created government to protect natural rights. A government functioned best when its powers were limited and it was acceptable to all citizens. However, if a government failed in its basic duty of protecting natural rights, people had the right to overthrow the government.

Locke's writings were widely read throughout Europe and the Americas. Ironically, many of the ideas that the American colonists later used to justify their independence from Britain came from Locke and other British thinkers. For example, **Thomas Jefferson** based much of the Declaration of Independence on Locke's ideas about the social contract and the right of people to overthrow an unjust government.

Reason Influences Law

As Europeans searched for new principles that would meet the standards of reason, great changes were made in the practice of law. Incorporating scientific or reasoned thought in applying the law helped to end unjust trials. Lawmakers placed less value on hearsay and on confessions made under torture in determining the guilt or innocence of suspected criminals.

In the 1600s several people made the first attempts to create a body of international law. A Dutch jurist named **Hugo Grotius** called for an international code based on natural law. He believed that one body of rules could reduce the dealings of governments to a system of reason and order.

In the American colonies, **William Penn**, founder of the Quaker colony of **Pennsylvania**, believed in pacifism, or opposition to war or violence as a means of settling disputes. Penn advocated an assembly of nations committed to world peace.

Examining Religion

Many Europeans also applied reason to religious beliefs. Members of the upper and middle classes increasingly turned away from traditional religious views, and Europe became a more secular society. In the 1700s a new religious philosophy called deism swept through Europe and America. Although believing in God, Deists often denounced organized religion, declaring that it exploited people's ignorance and superstitions. Deism was intended to construct a simpler and more natural religion based on reason and natural law. Its followers asserted the rightness of humanity's place in an orderly universe.

SECTION 2 REVIEW

Recall
1. **Define** natural law, natural rights, pacifism, deism.
2. **Identify** Thomas Hobbes, John Locke, Thomas Jefferson, Hugo Grotius, William Penn.

3. **Explain** Locke's social contract theory. What was its impact?

Critical Thinking
4. **Making Comparisons** Contrast Hobbes's views with Locke's views.

Understanding Themes
5. **Conflict** What was the purpose of the new religious philosophy known as deism, and how did deism conflict with traditional religion?

SECTION 2 REVIEW ANSWERS

1. The words are defined in the Glossary.
2. Hobbes, 297; Locke, 297; Jefferson, 299; Grotius, 299; Penn, 299
3. Government was based on a contract, which could be broken if rights were not upheld; it was later used to justify revolutions, such as the American revolution.

4. Hobbes argued that people need absolute governments to prevent chaos. Locke argued that people may overthrow any government that denies them their natural rights.
5. **CONFLICT** Deism was based on reason and natural law. Deists claimed organized religion exploited people.

Independent Practice
Guided Reading Activity 9-2 **L1**

ASSESS

Check for Understanding
Assign Section 2 Review as homework or as an in-class activity.

Use Student Self-Test and Review Software to review Section 2.

Evaluate
Section Quiz 9-2

Use the Testmaker to create a customized quiz for Section 2.

Reteach
Review with students the concept of natural law, the political philosophies of the time, and the political changes that took place.

Enrich
Remind students that ideas covered in this section still affect today's world. Have students make a list of contemporary thinkers, ideas, and technologies they think will still affect the world 300 years from now.

CLOSE

Help students create a flowchart showing how the scientific method affected other areas of thought, such as politics, law, and religion. Incorporate material from Section 1 and leave room for additions from Section 3.

c. 1736 John Wesley promotes religious revival in Great Britain.

1748 Baron de Montesquieu publishes *The Spirit of Laws.*

1780s Joseph II of Austria introduces Enlightenment reforms.

SECTION THEME

▶ **Reaction** Reason and order are applied to many human endeavors.

▶ind Out ▶

Answer: *Enlightenment ideas were spread through the writings of philosophers and other Enlightenment thinkers and through discussions in salons.*

FOCUS

Section Objective

Identify the factors that helped Enlightenment ideas spread throughout Europe.

BELLRINGER
Motivational Activity

Before taking roll at the beginning of the class period, project Section Focus Transparency 9-3 and have students answer the activity questions. Discuss students' responses.

📁 This activity is also available as a blackline master.

Vocabulary Pre-check

🔘 Use the Vocabulary PuzzleMaker to create a puzzle that reinforces the vocabulary terms in this section. **L1**

Section 3

Triumph of Reason

Setting the Scene

▶ **Terms to Define**
philosophe, salon, enlightened despot, classicism, metaphysics, romanticism

▶ **People to Meet**
Madame de Pompadour, Denis Diderot, Baron de Montesquieu, Voltaire, Jean-Jacques Rousseau, Immanuel Kant, John Wesley

▶ **Places to Locate**
Paris

▶ind Out ▶ What factors helped Enlightenment ideas to spread throughout Europe?

The Storyteller

The notorious criminal Jean Chatel had just been executed. Moments before his death, the priests announced that the murderer had confessed all his sins and received absolution. Therefore, he had died in a state of grace and his soul would eventually reach Paradise. The proclamation greatly disturbed Joseph Leveque and his friends. They had just read Voltaire's comments about universal toleration. How could good and bad be defined in such absolute terms? They asked themselves and each other, would the Creator condemn Confucius and Socrates to limitless torment, while blessing a villain simply because he died according to a prescribed formula?

Voltaire

—adapted from *Treatise on Toleration*, Voltaire, reprinted in *The Human Record*, Alfred J. Andrea and James H. Overfield, 1990

Compared to their ancestors, who lived in a world that seemed to be run by inexplicable forces and filled with magic, Europe's new thinkers believed that their scientific approach helped illuminate and clarify both the natural world and the study of human behavior. As a result, the period in Europe from the late 1600s through the 1700s came to be called the Age of Enlightenment.

Men and women of the Enlightenment studied the world as though they were looking at it for the first time. No longer held back by tradition, they defined the world in their own way, using science as their base. Natural scientists analyzed and classified thousands of animals, insects, and plants. Geologists drew maps of the earth's surface. Astronomers continued to make discoveries about the universe.

Largely due to reading Newton's *Principia*, Enlightenment thinkers perceived the universe as a machine governed by fixed laws. They saw God as the master mechanic of the universe—the builder of a machine who provided laws and then allowed it to run on its own, according to these orderly principles. They also believed in progress, or the idea that the world and its people could be improved.

Such radically new perceptions and ideas started a philosophical revolution. Jean Le Rond d'Alembert, a French mathematician, claimed that the new method of thinking and the enthusiasm that accompanied it had "brought about a lively fermentation of minds, spreading through nature in all directions like a river which has burst at its dams."

Spreading Ideas

The thinkers of the Enlightenment who spread these exciting new ideas came to be called philosophes (FEE•luh•ZAWFS), the French word for "philosopher." Most philosophes passionately believed in Locke's political philosophy and

---

SECTION RESOURCES

📁 **Reproducible Masters**
- Reproducible Lesson Plan 9-3
- Guided Reading Activity 9-3
- People in World History Profile 38
- Reteaching Activity 9
- Enrichment Activity 9
- Section Quiz 9-3

- Performance Assessment Activity 9
- Spanish Chapter Summary 9

📄 **Transparencies**
- Section Focus Transparency 9-3
- World History and Art Transparency 27

Multimedia
- 🔘 Vocabulary PuzzleMaker Software
- 🔘 Student Self-Test and Review Software
- 🔘 Testmaker
- 🔘 Turning Points in World History: *The Scientific Revolution*

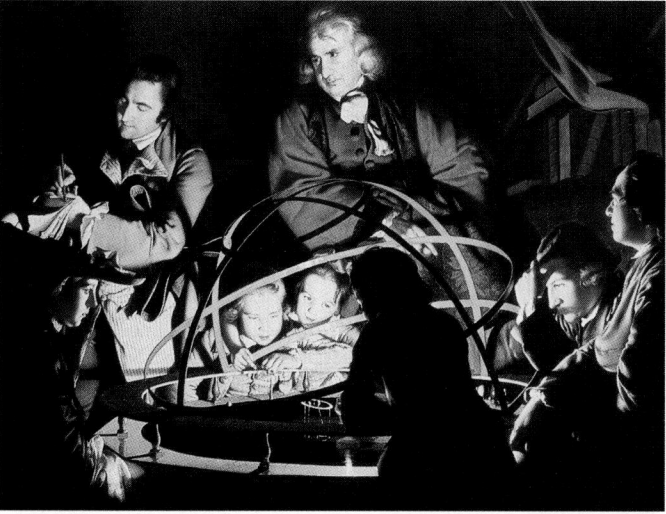

Newton's scientific theories. Most disapproved of superstition and religious opposition to new scientific endeavors. They believed in both freedom of speech and the individual's right to liberty. Many philosophes were talented writers whose essays and books helped to spread and popularize ideas and beliefs of the Enlightenment.

Activity in Paris

France was the most active center of ideas. In **Paris** especially, the new intellectuals delighted in gatherings called salons held in the homes of wealthy patrons. In a salon, writers, artists, and educated people of the growing middle class mingled with men and women of the nobility. Besides discussing the philosophies of the day, salon guests prized the art of conversation and often engaged in contests to see who had the sharpest wit.

Wealthy and influential women ran many of the popular salons. **Madame de Pompadour** was perhaps the most celebrated. A mistress to Louis XV, Pompadour's intelligence and courtly charm won the admiration of many philosophes.

A remarkable achievement compiled by some of the most prominent philosophes of the Enlightenment was the *Encyclopédie*. First published in 1751, these 28 volumes covered everything then known about the sciences, technology, and history in more than 3,000 pages crammed with illustrations.

The *Encyclopédie* was initially conceived to be simply a French translation of a two-volume English encyclopedia, but its editor, **Denis Diderot** (dee•DROH), had a work of much greater scope in mind. Diderot devoted much of his life to this project. Among other things, the *Encyclopédie* criticized the Church and government and praised religious tolerance.

The Catholic Church banned the *Encyclopédie*. When Diderot discovered that the printer, frightened by the controversial material in the volumes, had omitted passages that might offend the Church's leaders, he became enraged and screamed at the printer:

> ❝ You have massacred … the work of twenty good men who have devoted to you their time, their vigils, their talents, from a love of truth and justice, with the simple hope of seeing their ideas given to the public…. ❞

For their writings, Diderot and several others went to prison. Still, the *Encyclopédie* was widely read and its ideas spread all through Europe.

Montesquieu

A contributor to the *Encyclopédie* and one of the most learned of the philosophes in political matters was Charles-Louis de Secondat, the **Baron de Montesquieu** (MAHN•tuhs•KYOO). His master work, *The Spirit of Laws*, appeared in two volumes in 1748.

After studying various existing governments, Montesquieu wrote about his admiration for the English government and promoted the idea of separating governmental powers. Montesquieu believed that power should be equally divided among the branches of government: the legislative

TEACH

Guided Practice

THEME Reaction

Have students describe some of the different ways specific people reacted to Enlightenment ideas. Suggest that they consider the reactions of Madame de Pompadour, Diderot, Voltaire, Frederick II, Rousseau, and John Wesley. **L1**

Visualizing History The orrery gets its name from Charles Boyle, fourth earl of Orrery, who probably had the device invented by George Graham. **Answer to Caption:** *Newton*

Global Issues Ask students to restate Voltaire's words: "I disapprove of what you say, but I will defend to the death your right to say it." Then have them identify countries in which Voltaire's approach to free speech could and could not be practiced today. **L2**

Point of View To help students better understand opposition to the ideas of the Enlightenment, have them summarize the nature of the objections of Jean-Jacques Rousseau, Immanuel Kant, Count von Zinzendorf, and John Wesley. **L3**

World History and Art Transparency 27, *The Letter*

COOPERATIVE LEARNING ACTIVITY

Role Play Organize the class into two groups to plan a gathering in a salon. Have each student in one group select a favorite individual from this chapter. Have students in the other group choose roles as members of the middle class or the nobility. Students should research the individuals, the lifestyles of the different social classes, and the salons. They should then plan the setting and select a topic for the gathering. Remind students that salons were places where middle-class writers, artists, and educated people could mingle with the nobility. To stimulate conversation, you may wish to visit the salon in the guise of a noble person. **L2**

ABCNEWS INTERACTIVE™

VIDEODISC
Turning Points in World History

Side One, Chapter 10

Title: *The Scientific Revolution*
Ask: What is your interpretation of this statement, "If there is one evil in the world today for which there is no excuse, it is the evil of stupidity"? *(Students may suggest that the statement seems to say that there is no excuse for lacking knowledge, because everyone has the ability and opportunity to expand their knowledge.)*

Independent Practice

📁 Guided Reading Activity 9-3 **L1**

📁 People in World History Profile 38

Critical Thinking Ask students to write a short paper stating whether they agree or disagree with Rousseau that human beings are naturally good. Ask them to give examples supporting their opinions. **L2**

Linking Past and Present

Encyclopedias—from the Greek words for "general education"—continue to be published along the lines of the French *Encyclopédie*. Although encyclopedias vary in length, format, and content, all aim at presenting up-to-date knowledge in a conveniently accessible form.

---

branch, which made the laws; the executive branch, which enforced them; and the judicial branch, which interpreted the laws and judged when they were violated.

Montesquieu strongly believed in the rights of individuals. His work powerfully influenced the writing of the constitutions in many countries, including the United States.

Voltaire

Perhaps the most celebrated of the philosophes was François-Marie Arouet, known to the world by his pen name, **Voltaire**. A French author and Deist, Voltaire wrote poetry, plays, essays, and books in a style that was entertaining and often satirical. *Candide*, his most celebrated satire, challenged the notion that everything that happens is for the best in "the best of all possible worlds."

In his youth, Voltaire twice served time in the Bastille, the notorious prison in Paris. His satirical works that mocked the Church and the royal court of France earned him one prison term; he received the other term when he was accused of insulting a nobleman. After his second offense, Voltaire was given a choice between further imprisonment and exile from France. He chose the latter. When Voltaire moved to England, he felt unfettered in an atmosphere of political and religious freedom.

During the three years he spent in England, Voltaire wrote books promoting Bacon's philosophy and Newton's science. Voltaire deeply admired the English ideal of religious liberty and its relative freedom of the press. Voltaire is credited with the famous statement in defense of free speech, "I disapprove of what you say, but I will defend to the death your right to say it."

Women and the Enlightenment

Enlightenment ideas about equality and freedom spread throughout Europe, but they were not

Images *of the* Times

Salon Society

During the Enlightenment, Europe's high society gathered in the salons of wealthy patrons to discuss the ideas and events of the day.

Upper-class society of the 1700s enjoyed card games as well as intellectual discussions.

Images *of the* Times   Salon Society

The salon of Marie-Thérèse Rodet Geoffrin (1699–1777), held in the Hôtel de Rambouillet from 1749 to 1777, drew artists and writers from France and beyond. Although she was the daughter of a valet and lacked a formal education, her native intelligence and her marriage to a rich manufacturer enabled her to be an excellent hostess. Madame Geoffrin underwrote the *Encyclopédie* project.

When Jeanne-Antoinette Poisson (1721–1764) became King Louis XV's mistress in 1745, he made her marchioness of Pompadour. A patron of the arts, Madame de Pompadour also introduced the pompadour hairstyle, in which the hair is raised up over the forehead in a roll.

applied to women. Although some upper- and middle-class women hosted salons, women generally did not participate in public life on an equal basis with men. Their rights were limited to the home and family. By the mid-1700s, a small but vocal number of women began to affirm women's equality with men. In *A Vindication of the Rights of Women*, the British author Mary Wollstonecraft favored equal education for women and men so that both sexes could contribute equally to society.

Some Leaders Initiate Reform

The Enlightenment attracted the support of European monarchs eager to bring political and social change to their countries. These leaders became enlightened despots, or rulers who sought to govern by Enlightenment principles while maintaining their royal powers.

Prussia's Frederick II, the most famous of the enlightened despots, ruled as an absolute monarch.

Yet he believed that as king, he was the "first servant of the state," dedicated to the welfare of his realm. Frederick's reforms included abolishing the use of torture except for treason and murder, establishing elementary schools, and promoting industry and agriculture. Frederick corresponded with Voltaire, and it was the French philosophe who first honored Frederick with the title "the Great." In one letter Frederick wrote to Voltaire:

66 My chief occupation is to fight the ignorances and the prejudices in this country.… I must enlighten my people, cultivate their manners and morals, and make them as happy as human beings can be; as happy as the means at my disposal permit me to make them. 99

Catherine II of Russia also exchanged letters with Voltaire and other philosophes. She made reforms in law and government but was inclined to praise Enlightenment values more than practice

Literature Have students read English translations of Molière's *Les Précieuses Ridicules* (1659) or *Les Femmes Savantes* (1672). Have them write a short report for class presentation in which they describe how Molière satirizes the pretensions of middle-class women *(les précieuses)* and male participants in salon society. **L3**

Who?What?Where?When?

Marie de Vichy-Chamrond, marchioness of Deffand (1697–1780), was the hostess of another important French salon. Her salon attracted not only writers and socialites but also scientists.

In her mid-fifties, after losing her sight, Madame du Deffand engaged the younger Julie de Lespinasse (1732–1776) to assist her in entertaining. Jealous of Mademoiselle de Lespinasse's popularity with her guests, the older woman dismissed her in 1764. However, that action brought about the end of her salon when many of her former patrons chose to follow the fired cohostess.

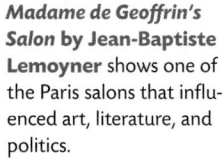

Parisian aristocratic women often posed for their portraits dressed as classical mythological figures.

Madame de Geoffrin's Salon by Jean-Baptiste Lemoyner shows one of the Paris salons that influenced art, literature, and politics.

REFLECTING ON THE TIMES

1. How did salon gatherings in Europe during the 1700s reflect Enlightenment ideals?
2. What role do you think women played in the salon society of the 1700s?

303

Who?What?Where?When?

Rococo During the period of salons, the French decorative arts were characterized by fanciful and intricate decoration in a style that became known as rococo. Furniture, porcelain, clocks, chandeliers, and draperies all were testaments to the middle-class worship of beauty.

ANSWERS TO REFLECTING ON THE TIMES

1. At salons individuals exercised their right to speak freely and to disagree with their rulers, both ideals of the philosophes.
2. Women both hosted salons and participated in salon debates. The salons not only broadened the social views of its female participants but also expanded their role in society.

Visualizing
History The Grand-
Théâtre, Bordeaux, was the largest
theater in France before the French
Revolution. Although Victor Louis
(1731–1800) was disliked by many
because of his bad temper and con-
ceited nature, his work was admired.
Best known for his construction of
theaters, Louis also planned the gardens of the Palais Royal.
Answer to Caption: *The classical
style often used simple geometric forms
and drew on subjects from classical
mythology.*

Who?What?Where?When?

Moses Mendelssohn (1729–
1786) was an important Jewish
figure during the Enlightenment.
Son of a poor scribe, the brilliant
Mendelssohn taught himself
both philosophy and foreign languages by reading the works of
John Locke and other Enlightenment figures. Mendelssohn
became a renowned philosopher
and literary figure. His life
demonstrated that religion could
coexist with the Enlightenment's
emphasis on reason.

Cultural Perspectives

Hasidism was founded by followers of Israel Baal Shem Tov, a
Jewish mystic and miracle worker. Although Hasidism was dealt
a devastating blow by the murder of millions of European Jews
in the Holocaust, it is a growing
movement today, with flourishing centers in New York and
Israel and active outreach activities around the world.

Visualizing
History The Grand Théâtre was built by the French architect Victor
Louis in the mid-1700s. Located in the French city of Bordeaux,
this magnificent theater reflects the dominant classical style of the time. *What
were two major characteristics of the classical style?*

them. For example, Catherine spoke out against serfdom but forced more peasants into serfdom than ever before. When groups of serfs revolted, she brutally crushed the uprisings.

The most far-reaching measures of enlightened despotism occurred in Austria. As a Catholic, Empress Maria Theresa disagreed with the secularism of the Enlightenment. However, she introduced humanitarian reforms, including setting up elementary schools and freeing all serfs who worked on her estates. Her son, Joseph II, carried reforms even further. He abolished serfdom completely, made land taxes equal for peasants and nobles, and named middle-class officials instead of nobles to government posts. He gave freedom to the press and took property from the Catholic Church, using the money to support hospitals. The Austrian monarch also granted religious freedom to the empire's Protestants and Jews.

Most of Joseph's reforms failed, however. His abrupt changes antagonized too many people. Rebellion by the nobles forced him to repeal many reforms. Joseph's brother and successor, Leopold II, revoked most of Joseph's remaining laws.

Throughout Europe, nobles and church leaders, afraid of losing too much political power to the common people, frustrated many reform efforts made by enlightened despots. In addition, many monarchs backed away from Enlightenment ideals when they realized that their own positions would be threatened by giving too much power to their subjects. In doing so, they struck down many of the political reforms that might have prevented the violent revolutions that were to come.

Classical Movements

The worlds of art, music, and literature also shared in the Enlightenment beliefs. Writers, artists, and architects strove to achieve the ideals of Greek and Roman classicism, which to them represented ultimate order and reason. Using classical titles and imitating classical themes and styles, artists of the Enlightenment attempted to capture the refined and simplified spirit of the ancients.

Architects built palaces, opera houses, and museums based on the architecture of ancient Rome. They used simple forms, such as squares and circles, rather than the elaborate swirls of the baroque style.

Sculptors and painters also emulated the ideals and forms of antiquity. Whereas artists following the baroque style tended to appeal to their viewers with elegant, swirling forms, these artists sought a return to a calm, rational style of art that would

MEETING SPECIAL NEEDS ACTIVITY

Learning Style: Auditory/Musical Listening to authentic musical pieces will help students with a sensitivity to harmony, melody, rhythm, and tone better understand the different musical styles of the age of Enlightenment. Play some works from the baroque period (1600–1750) by Bach or Handel, and then some from the classical period (1750–1820) by Haydn or Mozart. Ask students to describe some of the ways the two styles differ. *(Answers may include: the use of repetition in baroque music, and the balance and contrast among movements of a classical work.)* **L2**

appeal to the mind through the logic and geometry of its forms.

Sculptors such as Antonio Canova created works based on subjects from classical mythology. Jean-Antoine Houdon carved sculptures of contemporary figures, such as Voltaire, in poses that recall portraits of ancient philosophers.

In painting, Jacques-Louis David (dah•VEED) also drew from classical subjects and forms. *The Oath of the Horatii*—showing Roman soldiers vowing to fight for Rome—and other David works reveal a balance and simplicity that results in monumental images. David used uncomplicated primary colors—reds, yellows, and blues—to create powerful contrasts and accent the clarity of his forms.

Writers worked to achieve the classical ideal while maintaining their devotion to the concept of reason. Often, imitation of a classical model resulted in an ornate and affected style that was focused more on form than on content. French dramatists Molière, Jean Racine, and Pierre Corneille as well as English poets John Dryden, Alexander Pope, and John Milton mastered the classical tradition.

Musical composers of the Enlightenment also stressed classical elements such as balance, contrast, and refined expression of emotion. At the same time, they witnessed a great evolution in music. Music made the transition from merely supporting religious services and dance and opera companies, to being an "art" in its own right. For the first time, people began going to concerts for the pleasure of listening to the music itself.

The piano, evolving in the 1700s, allowed musicians to produce much greater ranges of loudness and softness. The violin was perfected at the same time, changing the sound of music. As composers grouped similar instruments, they laid the foundations for chamber music and the modern orchestra. Germany's Johann Sebastian Bach, Great Britain's German-born George Frideric Handel, and Austria's Joseph Haydn and Wolfgang Amadeus Mozart were among the musicians of this era.

Enlightenment Opponents

Not everyone agreed with the ideas of the Enlightenment. Some saw the structured and ordered view of the universe as overly rational and devoid of emotion and feeling. English poet William Blake exclaimed, "God is not a mathematical diagram!"

Jean-Jacques Rousseau

During the 1700s the French philosopher **Jean-Jacques Rousseau** criticized what he saw as his era's excessive reliance on reason and claimed that people should rely more on instinct and emotion. Born in Geneva, Switzerland, to French Huguenot parents, Rousseau became a leading thinker and writer of his day. He believed that human beings were naturally good but that civilization and institutions were corrupting. He urged people to throw off civilization and return to nature, as far as that was possible. In 1760 he published *La Nouvelle Héloise*, a novel that described the beauties of nature and the pleasures of simple country life. The book influenced people from every level of society. Even the queen of France, Marie Antoinette, had a cottage built for herself at Versailles, where she enjoyed pretending to be a milkmaid.

A second book, *Émile* (1762), used the novel form to emphasize the importance of education in the development of human personality. In *Émile*, Rousseau called for a type of education that would preserve what he believed was a child's natural goodness.

In 1762 Rousseau also published his most famous work, *The Social Contract*. It began, "Man is born free, and everywhere he is in chains." According to Rousseau, sovereignty, or the right to rule, rested in the people. Therefore, the people had the right to remove the "chains" of an oppressive society and to create a government devoted to the common good. The basis of government, Rousseau held, is a social contract through which people give

Visualizing History The Austrian composer Wolfgang Amadeus Mozart died before the age of 36, but he still left the world more than 600 musical works. *Who were three other noted classical musicians?*

Who?What?Where?When?

Alexander Pope (1688–1744), the English poet, reflected the tenets of the Scientific Revolution in his *An Essay on Man*, in which he described nature as "A mighty maze! but not without plan."

ASSESS

Check for Understanding

Assign Section 3 Review as homework or as an in-class activity.

 Use Student Self-Test and Review Software to review Section 3.

Visualizing History
A child prodigy, Mozart (1756–1791) began composing music at age five, and at age six he played for the Austrian empress. Among his most popular pieces are the serenade *A Little Night Music* (1787) and the operas *The Marriage of Figaro* (1786) and *Don Giovanni* (1787).
Answer to Caption: *Bach, Handel, and Haydn*

Evaluate
Section Quiz 9-3

 Use the Testmaker to create a customized quiz for Section 3.

MAKING CONNECTIONS ACTIVITIES

Religion Hasidism is only one example of a religious movement grounded in mysticism. Have students prepare short oral reports on mysticism in other religions and periods. **L2**

Religion Expressions of religious tolerance proliferated during the Enlightenment. Have students prepare short oral reports on the views on religious tolerance of two or more of these figures: Gotthold Ephraim Lessing, John Locke, William Penn, Voltaire. **L2**

The Arts Not only classicism but also other artistic styles flourished during the Enlightenment. Have students prepare illustrated reports on the baroque style of the 1600s and 1700s or on the rococo style that flourished from about 1700 to 1780. **L1 LEP**

Visualizing History The
Methodists got their name from
critics who disparaged their belief in
methodical study and devotion.
Wesley (1703–1791) briefly served
as a missionary in the North American colony of Georgia. In 1784 he
declared that Methodist societies
were completely independent of the
Church of England.
Answer to Caption: *the value of
personal religious experience*

Reteach

Write on the chalkboard all the
terms to define and names of
people to meet in this section.
Call on different students to identify each term or name.

 Reteaching Activity 9

Enrich

During the Enlightenment, with
more people reading than ever
before, the novel came into its
own. Have students read all or
part of an English or French
novel from this period (for example, Richardson's *Clarissa*, Field-
ing's *Tom Jones*, Prévost's *Manon
Lescaut*) and report to the class on
how it compares with more modern novels.

 Enrichment Activity 9

CLOSE

Have students write their reactions to the Enlightenment. Ask
them to imagine how they might
have felt in the 1700s when faced
with these new ideas. Collect the
papers and then read their ideas
aloud. Using the students' ideas
as a guide, review the ways people of the time reacted to the
ideas of the Enlightenment.

Visualizing History John Wesley, a clergyman of the
Church of England, founded the
Protestant movement known as Methodism. His out-
door preaching drew large crowds. *What value did
Methodism stress?*

up their individual rights to the "general will," the
will of the majority. Those opposing the "general
will," however, must accept it or "be forced to be
free." By opposing injustice and supporting government by the people, *The Social Contract* has
shaped democratic thought from the 1700s to the
present. However, dictators have used its ideas
about the "general will" to justify their policies.

Immanuel Kant

Another critic of the Enlightenment was
the German thinker **Immanuel Kant**. He believed
that reason could not answer the problems of
metaphysics—the branch of philosophy that deals
with spiritual issues such as the existence of God. In
his work *Critique of Pure Reason* (1781), Kant asserted that reality consisted of separate physical and
spiritual worlds and that the methods for knowing

varied greatly in these two realms. In the physical
world, knowledge came through the senses and
reason; in the spiritual world, it was acquired
through faith and intuition. Thus, ideas and feelings about religion, morality, and beauty were true
even though reason and science could not explain
them.

Religious Movements

Not only philosophers, but ordinary men and
women found something lacking in the
Enlightenment's emphasis on reason. Many rejected deism, the religion of reason, and searched for a
religion that was more emotionally satisfying.

In Germany, Count von Zinzendorf established
the Moravian Brethren, which emphasized the
emotional and mystical side of Christianity. In
England, a movement called Methodism, led by
John Wesley, also stressed the value of personal
religious experience. Methodism was a reaction to
the cold formality of the Church of England.

The need for a religion with more feeling also
led to a Catholic revival in France. In eastern Europe, Hasidism, which promoted mysticism and
religious zeal—as opposed to an emphasis on external ritual—spread among Jews. All of these religious movements rejected reason in favor of an
enthusiastic faith.

As people questioned the philosophies of the
Enlightenment, classicism in the arts gave way to
romanticism, which was a cultural movement that
celebrated emotion and the individual. These developments marked the ending of the Age of
Enlightenment. Tired of the privileged ruling classes and inspired by new ideas such as the writings of
Rousseau, the lower classes began to demand more
rights. The sun set on the tranquil world of the
Enlightenment as history moved on to a period of
tumult and revolution.

SECTION 3 REVIEW

Recall
1. **Define** philosophe, salon,
   enlightened despot, classicism,
   metaphysics, romanticism.
2. **Identify** the Enlightenment,
   Madame de Pompadour,
   Denis Diderot, Baron de
   Montesquieu, Voltaire,

   Jean-Jacques Rousseau,
   Immanuel Kant, John Wesley.
3. **Describe** some of the main
   ideas of the Enlightenment
   thinkers.

Critical Thinking
4. **Making Comparisons** How
   do John Locke's ideas about

   government compare with
   those of Jean-Jacques
   Rousseau?

Understanding Themes
5. **Reaction** In what ways did
   Europeans of the 1700s react
   to Enlightenment ideas and
   values?

---

306 **Chapter 9** *Scientific Revolution*

SECTION 3 REVIEW ANSWERS

1. All vocabulary words are defined in the
   Glossary.
2. Enlightenment, 300; Mme. de Pompadour,
   301; Diderot, 301; Montesquieu, 301;
   Voltaire, 302; Rousseau, 305; Kant, 306;
   Wesley, 306
3. belief in reason, natural law, classical
   themes and ideals
4. Both believed in a social contract and that

   people had a right to overthrow an unjust
   government; Locke stressed the natural
   rights of the individual that government
   had to protect, while Rousseau emphasized
   individual acceptance of the will of the
   majority.
5. **REACTION** Some rejected reason
   in favor of more emotional movements in
   philosophy, religion, and art.

Developing Multimedia Presentations

You have been assigned a research report to present to your class. You want to really hold the attention of your classmates. How can you do this? One way is to use a variety of media.

Learning the Skill

At its most basic, a multimedia presentation involves using several types of media. To discuss the Age of Enlightenment, for example, you might show photographs or slides of the art, play and listen to recordings of the music or literature, or present a video of a play written during this time period.

You can also develop a multimedia presentation on a computer. Multimedia as it relates to computer technology is the combination of text, video, audio, and animation in an interactive program.

In order to create multimedia productions or presentations on a computer, you need to have certain tools. These may include traditional computer graphic tools and draw programs, animation programs that make still images move, and authoring systems that tie everything together. Your computer manual will tell you which tools your computer can support.

Practicing the Skill

This chapter focuses on the Age of Revolution from 1500 to 1830. Ask yourself questions such as the following to develop a multimedia presentation on the politics of that era:

- Which forms of media do I want to include? Video? Sound? Animation? Photographs? Graphics? Other?
- Which of these media forms does my computer support?
- What kind of software programs or systems do I need? A paint program? A draw program? An animation program? A program to create interactive, or two-way, communication? An authoring system that will allow me to change images, sound, and motion?
- Is there a "do-it-all " program I can use to develop the kind of presentation I want?

Applying the Skill

Keeping in mind the four guidelines given above, write a plan describing a multimedia presentation you would like to develop. Indicate what tools you will need and what steps you must take to make the presentation an exciting reality.

For More Practice

Turn to the Skill Practice in the Chapter Review on page 309 for more practice in developing multimedia presentations.

ANSWERS TO PRACTICING THE SKILL

Answers will vary, depending on students' imaginations, the aspects of the topic they want to present, and the hardware and software available. Make sure that students have checked their computers' capabilities and the available software. You might give students the option of working in groups.

Technology
SKILLS

TEACH

Developing Multimedia Presentations This skill helps students develop the ability to create multimedia presentations. Point out that this ability will do more than make for interesting classes. It might also prove helpful to them as they enter the workplace. Encourage students to look at this skill as an adventure. Have students brainstorm a list of possible forms of media that could be used in a multimedia presentation. Even suggestions that seem quite unusual may yield interesting possibilities.

Discuss the technologies pictured in the photograph. Also demonstrate some of the media appliances that are available to students in your school or local library. For example, you might play recordings of music from the Age of Enlightenment while you present a slide show of artwork from the same time period. You might ask staff members in the technology/media department of your school to help with the demonstration. Ask a guest speaker to discuss and demonstrate the development of multimedia presentations on a computer to your students. If possible, try to schedule computer lab time so that students can sample software and begin to build their own presentations

Additional Practice

Skill Reinforcement Activity 9

Chapter 9 Review

Answers

Using Key Terms
1. f   4. b
2. e   5. j
3. g

Using Your History Journal

Encourage students to include personal as well as scientific details, just as a TV interviewer would ask questions about the scientist's or inventor's private life as well as his or her professional achievements.

Reviewing Facts

1. Copernicus: sun-centered solar system; Galileo: observations with telescope support Copernican model; Kepler: planets move around sun in ellipses; Newton: gravity holds solar system together

2. sun is at the center of the solar system and that the planets move around the sun; living matter composed of cells and that blood circulates through body; truth of physical universe known through scientific method; use of reason to make laws just and workable

3. Answers will vary. Possible answer: Historians began to use the scientific method, posing and testing hypotheses about the past.

308 Chapter 9 *Scientific Revolution*

Connections Across Time

Historical Significance The scientific revolution and the Enlightenment marked a turning point in the history of human thought. Scientists and thinkers constructed a new understanding of knowledge that stressed observation, experimentation, and reasoning rather than reliance on faith and tradition. Thinkers analyzed the existing political systems and focused on the rights of individuals. Their views challenged the concept of absolute monarchy and paved the way for the rise of democracy.

The Age of Enlightenment continues to shape our lives. The United States Constitution incorporates many Enlightenment beliefs, and scientists employ approaches in research today that are based on the scientific method.

Using Key Terms

Write the key term that completes each sentence. Then write a sentence for each term not chosen.

a. philosophes   g. pacifism
b. classicism   h. enlightened despots
c. salons   i. scientific method
d. hypotheses   j. deism
e. natural law   k. metaphysics
f. romanticism   l. natural rights

1. _____, with its emphasis on emotion and the individual, opposed the values of the Enlightenment.
2. Political philosophers of the Enlightenment believed in the idea of _____, or a universal moral law that, like physical laws, could be understood by applying reason.
3. William Penn believed in _____ and favored the creation of an assembly of nations committed to world peace.
4. Enlightenment writers, artists, and architects strove to achieve the ideals of _____, which to them represented ultimate order and reason.
5. The philosophy of _____ favored a simpler religion based on reason.

Technology Activity

Using a Word Processor **Search** the Internet or a library for information about the achievements of European scientists during the scientific revolution. Use a word processor to organize your research into a chart. Include headings such as name of the scientist, country, year of discovery, and achievements. Write a paragraph explaining which discovery you believe had the greatest impact on modern civilization.

Using Your History Journal

Rewrite the story of a scientific discovery or invention from the 1600s as a television news story. Include an interview with the inventor or discoverer.

Reviewing Facts

1. **Science** Explain how Copernicus, Galileo, Kepler, and Newton each added something new to an understanding of the solar system.
2. **Culture** Describe the ways in which European thinking about the universe, philosophy, and law changed during the Enlightenment.
3. **History** Explain how the study of history was influenced by the Enlightenment.
4. **Government** State the political idea advocated by Montesquieu that can be found in the United States Constitution.
5. **Culture** Identify two philosophers in the 1700s who disagreed with Enlightenment ideas. What were their views?

Critical Thinking

1. **Apply** How did classical art reflect the values of the Enlightenment? Give examples to support your answer.
2. **Synthesize** Why do you suppose a belief in witches and ghosts largely became a thing of the past in Europe after the period of the Enlightenment?
3. **Evaluate** Were the 1700s an era of optimism or pessimism? Explain.

---

4. the separation of powers, rights of individuals
5. Rousseau thought that people should rely more on instinct and emotion than on reason, that people are naturally good, and that they have the right to rise up against a government. Kant believed reason could not explain problems of metaphysics, asserted that human feelings about religion, beauty, and morality are real even though not explainable by reason.

Critical Thinking

1. It emphasized form and order. Examples will vary; students may refer to classical architects' preference for squares and circles rather than elaborate swirls, or to David's concern for simplicity of form.
2. People began to rely on observation, reason, and the scientific method instead of superstition.
3. Some may argue that it was an optimistic age

4. **Synthesize** Do scientific laws apply to human society in the way that they apply to the physical universe? Why or why not?
5. **Analyze** Why were the enlightened despots unable to carry out thorough reforms?
6. **Evaluate** Has science fulfilled the promise of progress that it seemed to hold in the 1700s? Why or why not? Give examples.

Geography in History

1. **Region** Refer to the map below. What conclusion can you draw about European interest in science and learning during the period of the 1500s and 1600s?
2. **Place** In what two nations were organizations founded for people interested in sharing scientific information?
3. **Movement** How do you think scientific ideas and theories spread from one nation of Europe into other nations?

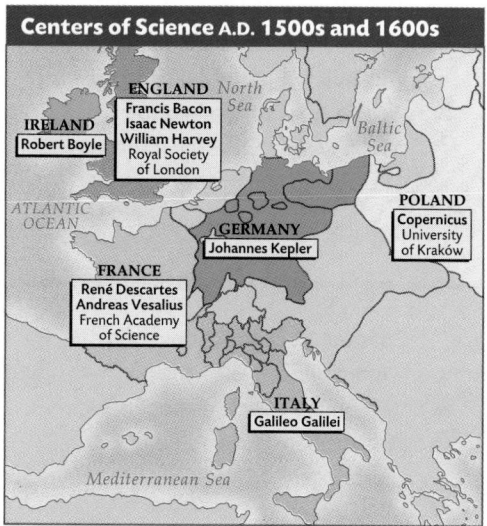

Understanding Themes

1. **Innovation** How did the scientific revolution change the ways in which Europeans investigated the natural world?

2. **Conflict** Catholic Bishop Bossuet said that the skepticism of the philosophes was an "unending error, a risk-all boldness, a deliberate dizziness, in a word, a pride that cannot accept its proper cure, which is legitimate authority." Explain the bishop's view in your own words. What does he mean by "legitimate authority"?
3. **Reaction** What religious movements formed as a reaction to the ideas of the Enlightenment thinkers? Why?

1. William Penn envisioned an assembly of nations working for world peace. What modern organization reflects Penn's idea?
2. Classical movements in music, art, and literature reflected the spirit of the Enlightenment. Does popular music, art, and literature reflect how people feel about society today? Why or why not? Give examples.
3. Do you agree or disagree with Jean-Jacques Rousseau's view that people are naturally good but that civilization and institutions make them evil? Give examples from modern life to support your viewpoint.

Skill Practice

Study the list of topics below. Choose one of the topics and explain how you would use at least three types of media in a presentation to best teach the topic to a class.

1. Michelangelo's work
2. The causes of the French Revolution
3. The American Revolution
4. The Scientific Revolution of the 1600s and 1700s
5. The Salon Society of the 1700s
6. Religious movements of the 1700s

Chapter 9 Review

Understanding Themes

1. **INNOVATION** relied on observation, reason, and the scientific method instead of tradition
2. **CONFLICT** The philosophes should give up their questioning and accept the views of the Church, the "legitimate authority."
3. **REACTION** Methodism, the Moravian Brethren, and Hasidism formed. Each emphasized personal faith as opposed to emphasis on reason.

1. the United Nations
2. Students should support claims.
3. Students should support claims.

Skill Practice
Answers will vary, depending on students' imaginations, the aspects of the topic they want to present, and the hardware and software available. Make sure that students have checked their computers' capabilities and the available software. You might give students the option of working in groups.

? Chapter Bonus Test Question

In 1611 English poet John Donne wrote that "new philosophy calls all in doubt." Similarly, in our times, many people are troubled by the destabilizing effects of new scientific methods. **Ask students:** What are three areas of scientific research today that some people find unsettling? *(Answers will vary but may include: manipulation of human reproduction, tinkering with genetic information.)*

because people looked favorably on new ideas and believed reason could provide the answers to many of life's problems.
4. Answers will vary. Some may argue that human emotions and actions vary too much to be predictable by law.
5. Many nobles felt threatened by the powers monarchs were giving common people, and so they frustrated reform efforts.
6. Answers will vary. Some may argue that scientific breakthroughs have enhanced the quality of life, others that new technologies have threatened environmental viability.

Geography in History
1. People all over Europe were interested in science.
2. England, France
3. Writers and traveling scholars and scientists spread ideas.

A complete, 1-page lesson plan is provided for each section in the Reproducible Lesson Plans booklet.

English and American Revolutions

CHAPTER RESOURCES

	Reproducible Resources	**Multimedia Resources**
Chapter Opener	Chapter Themes: Graphic Organizer 10 Historical Significance Chapter Activity 10	MindJogger Videoquiz

Chapter Enrichment	Vocabulary Activity 10*
	Time Line Activity 10
	Mapping History Activity 10
	History Simulation 10
	Geography and History Activity 10
	Source Reading 10
	People in World History Profiles 39, 40
	World Art and Music Activity 10
	Enrichment Activity 10
	Critical Thinking Activity 10
	Skill Reinforcement Activity 10
	Writer's Guidebook, Lesson 11
	Performance Assessment Activity 10
		World History and Art
		   Transparency 28, *Blue Boy*
		Mapping History Overlay
		   Transparency 13, *European Claims*
		   in North America
		
		Chapter Transparency 10
		Vocabulary PuzzleMaker Software
		Picture Atlas of the World
		World Music: Cultural Traditions,
		   Lesson 1

Chapter Review/Reteaching	Reteaching Activity 10
	Skill Reinforcement Activity 10
	Spanish Chapter Summary 10
		Chapter 10 Digest Audiocassette,
		   Activity, Test*
		Vocabulary PuzzleMaker Software
		Student Self-Test and Review
		   Software
		MindJogger Videoquiz

Chapter Evaluation/Testing	Performance Assessment Activity 10 Chapter 10 Test, Forms A and B	Testmaker

* Also available in Spanish

0:00 OUT OF TIME? Assign the Chapter 10 summary in the Unit 3 Digest on pages 367–369, and the Chapter 10 Audiocassettes.

Block Schedule

   Block scheduling differs from traditional class scheduling in the amount of time allotted to each period. The extended time frame provided by block scheduling affords you the opportunity to implement a greater number of research-oriented and activity-intense projects to motivate and involve your students. Activities that are particularly suited to use within the block scheduling framework are identified throughout this chapter by the following designation.

KEY TO ABILITY LEVELS

Teaching strategies have been coded for varying learning styles and abilities.

L1 **BASIC** activities for all students
L2 **AVERAGE** activities for average to above-average students
L3 **CHALLENGING** activities for above-average students
LEP **LIMITED ENGLISH PROFICIENCY** activities

Use Glencoe's *Presentation Plus!* multimedia teacher tool to easily present dynamic lessons that visually excite your students. Using Microsoft PowerPoint® you can customize the presentations to create your own personalized lessons.

SECTION RESOURCES

Daily Objectives	Reproducible Resources	Multimedia Resources
Section 1 **Civil War** Identify factors that led to civil war in England.	Reproducible Lesson Plan 10-1 Vocabulary Activity 10* Guided Reading Activity 10-1* Time Line Activity 10 History Simulation 10 People in World History Profile 40 Section Quiz 10-1*	Section Focus Transparency 10-1 Chapter Transparency 10 Student Self-Test and Review Software Testmaker
Section 2 **A King Returns to the Throne** Describe how England established a constitutional monarchy.	Reproducible Lesson Plan 10-2 Vocabulary Activity 10* Guided Reading Activity 10-2* Section Quiz 10-2*	Section Focus Transparency 10-2 World History and Art Transparency 28, *Blue Boy* Student Self-Test and Review Software Testmaker
Section 3 **Road to Revolt** Identify factors that led to disagreement and eventual conflict between the British and the American colonies.	Reproducible Lesson Plan 10-3 Vocabulary Activity 10* Guided Reading Activity 10-3* Geography and History Activity 10 Section Quiz 10-3*	Section Focus Transparency 10-3 Student Self-Test and Review Software Testmaker World Music: Cultural Traditions, Lesson 1
Section 4 **A War for Independence** Describe the kind of government Americans established after the American Revolution.	Reproducible Lesson Plan 10-4 Guided Reading Activity 10-4* People in World History Profile 39 Reteaching Activity 10 Enrichment Activity 10 Section Quiz 10-4* Performance Assessment Activity 10 Spanish Chapter Summary 10	Section Focus Transparency 10-4 Mapping History Overlay Transparency 13, *European Claims in North America* Vocabulary PuzzleMaker Software Student Self-Test and Review Software Testmaker

* Also available in Spanish

Chapter Activities

 **Performance Assessment Activity**

A Time Capsule Have students suppose that they have found a time capsule from the era of the English and American Revolutions. Have them list and make visuals of artifacts they might find inside evoking revolutionary attitudes and events. Have them design a container and make a list with visuals of items they would select for a current-day time capsule representing a revolutionary activity of our time. Students should write a reflection explaining their choices for both capsules.

Possible Rubric Features

Concept attainment, accuracy of content information, decision-making process skills, analytical thinking, research skills, ability to make logical connections, organization and clarity of product

• *For an additional activity, refer to Activity 10 in the* Performance Assessment Strategies and Activities *booklet.*

ACTIVITY

From the Classroom of...

Mike Nitzel
Moline High School
Moline, IL

The Revolutionary Times
Organize the class into two groups—one group to write and assemble an American Revolution newspaper, the other group to write and assemble an English Revolution newspaper. Each newspaper should have three sections: Causes of the Revolution; Events of the Revolution; Effects of the Revolution.

Each student should write an article dealing with one of the three topics listed above. Articles should be typed in columns, with titles and by-lines, as in a real newspaper. Each student should also create an advertisement or political cartoon reflective of the period. Let each group put their newspaper together. Students may need to cut and paste and use a copy machine to give their newspapers a professional look. Make a copy of both newspapers for each student and have the class discuss how the American and English Revolutions were similar, how they were different, and how each advanced the ideas of limited government and/or democracy.

MULTIPLE LEARNING STYLES

Verbal/Linguistic
Have students write news reports about the American Revolution as if they were assigned to do a feature on George Washington, the Second Continental Congress, or a town that had been the site of a battle.

Logical/Mathematical
Have students make a time line that shows steps in the English kings' loss of power and Parliament's increase in power. Ask students to display the time line on a bulletin board.

Visual/Spatial
Have students develop pictorial histories of the Glorious Revolution that illustrate the major events before, during, and after this revolution. Remind students to include captions that explain the events. Encourage students to display completed projects in the classroom.

Auditory/Musical
Have students listen to the Chapter 21 Digest Audiocassette, stopping at two-minute intervals to write summary sentences.

Kinesthetic
Have students research life in England under Cromwell. Then ask them to dramatize their research, showing the effects of Puritan rule on daily life.

Additional Resources

 **NATIONAL GEOGRAPHIC SOCIETY** | **Teacher's Corner**

INDEX TO NATIONAL GEOGRAPHIC MAGAZINE

The following articles may be used for research relating to this chapter:

- "Two Revolutions," by Charles McCarry, July 1989.
- "Yorktown Shipwreck," by John D. Broadwater, June 1988.
- "James Madison, Architect of the Constitution," by Alice J. Hall, September 1987.

NATIONAL GEOGRAPHIC SOCIETY PRODUCTS AVAILABLE FROM GLENCOE

To order the following products for use with this chapter, contact your local Glencoe sales representative, or call Glencoe at 1-800-334-7344:

- *GTV: The American People (Videodiscs)*
- *GTV: A Geographic Perspective on American History (Videodiscs)*

ADDITIONAL NATIONAL GEOGRAPHIC SOCIETY PRODUCTS

To order the following products for use with this chapter, call National Geographic Society at 1-800-368-2728:

- *PictureShow: Story of America Library, 1 (CD-ROM)*

LOCAL OBJECTIVES

_____

BIBLIOGRAPHY

Literature of the Period
Defoe, Daniel. *Robinson Crusoe.* New York: Oxford University Press, 1981. The adventures of a man stranded on an island who survives through ingenuity and hard work.
Readings for the Student
Meltzer, Milton. *The American Revolutionaries: A History in Their Own Words, 1750–1800.* New York: Crowell, 1987. Ordinary Americans as well as leaders tell their stories through letters, diaries, and pamphlets.
Readings for the Teacher
Draper, Theodore. *A Struggle for Power: The American Revolution.* New York: Times Books, 1996. A thoroughly researched and penetrating analysis of the struggles that led to the American Revolution.

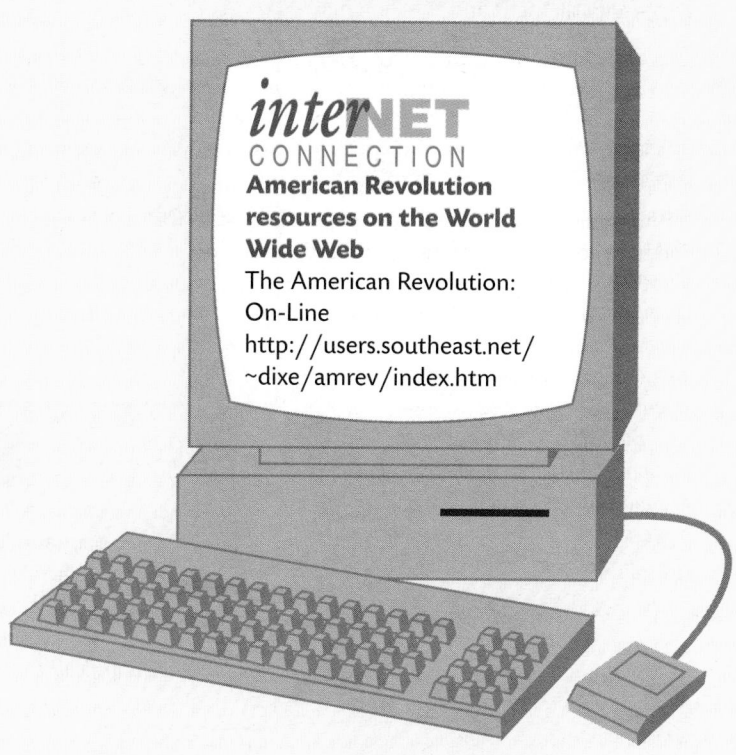

interNET CONNECTION
American Revolution resources on the World Wide Web
The American Revolution: On-Line
http://users.southeast.net/~dixe/amrev/index.htm

CHAPTER THEMES

Chapter Themes are listed by section on this chapter opening page of the Student Edition. A corresponding theme-based activity is available under "TEACH," and a theme-based question is asked in the Section and Chapter Reviews.

Storyteller

Historical Setting The death of Charles I in 1649 marked the beginning of a new era in the relationship between the English people and their rulers. Never before had an English monarch been tried and executed by the people. In the past, English monarchs had been murdered or killed in battle, but a monarch's divine right to rule had never been challenged. The idea of the divine right of kings was gradually replaced by the idea of the social contract—that governments are created by an agreement between rulers and their people. In 1776, Great Britain's thirteen colonies declared their independence because Parliament and the king had broken the social contract.

Historical Significance

Answers: *The English Revolution limited the power of the monarchy and increased the power of Parliament and the rights of the people. The American Revolution ended both the power of the king and of Parliament over the thirteen colonies.*

Both the English and American Revolutions led to the development of constitutional government that specified the powers of the government and protected the rights of the governed.

English and American Revolutions

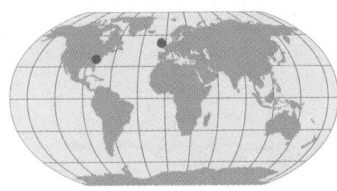

Chapter Themes

▶ **Conflict** Disputes over the monarchy plunge England into civil war. *Section 1*
▶ **Change** The English Parliament limits the monarchy's powers. *Section 2*
▶ **Conflict** The American colonies resist British control. *Section 3*
▶ **Revolution** The American colonies revolt against Great Britain and form the United States of America. *Section 4*

Storyteller

In 1649 a crowd gathered around a public platform near Whitehall Palace in London. There they watched Charles I, the king of England, prepare to die. The king made a short speech, prayed silently, and then knelt with his head on the block.

With just one blow, the executioner severed the king's head from his body. At that moment, the crowd uttered "such a [groan] by the thousands then present as I never heard before and desire I may never hear again," said a seventeen-year-old boy present at the execution.

By the late 1600s, England would undergo two revolutions limiting the power of the monarch. A new political age was dawning in England and throughout the world.

Historical Significance

How did the English and American Revolutions change government and society in the English-speaking world? What impact did the two revolutions have on the development of democracy?

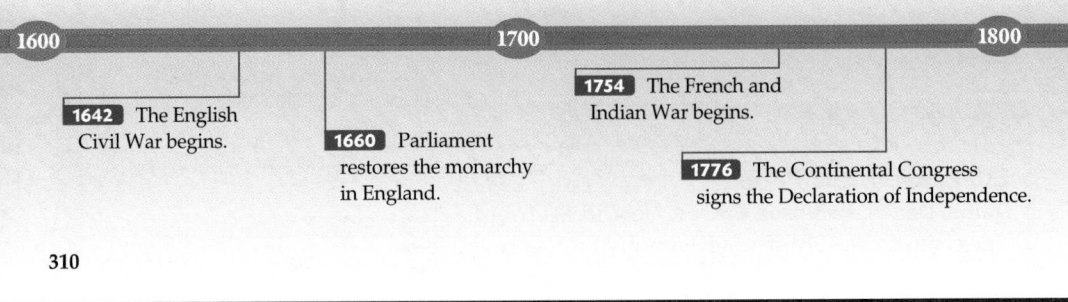

1600	1700	1800

1642 The English Civil War begins.

1660 Parliament restores the monarchy in England.

1754 The French and Indian War begins.

1776 The Continental Congress signs the Declaration of Independence.

310

GEOGRAPHY CONNECTION

Location On a map in the Atlas of their textbook, have students locate England, Scotland, and Ireland in the United Kingdom, and the United States and Canada in North America. **Why was England able to exercise control over Scotland and Ireland?** *(Both countries were close in distance to England.)* **Why did England have difficulty conducting war against the thirteen colonies?** *(The long distance across the ocean made it difficult to ship supplies and to issue orders.)* **L1**

History
& Art
After Naseby, 1645 by Edgar Bundy, c. 1850. John Noott Galleries,
Worcester, England

History & Art

Cromwell's defeat of Charles I at Naseby was important both militarily and politically. Charles lost his infantry, artillery, and most of his cavalry. Most important, he left behind letters that showed his plan to bring Irish troops into England and to repeal laws against Catholics. *How do you think Parliament felt about Charles when they found out about these letters?* (*Parliament probably thought there was no way they could negotiate with Charles; they would have to defeat him.*)

Performance Assessment

Refer to the activity on page 310C of the Planning Guide.

For an additional activity, refer to Activity 10 in the *Performance Assessment Strategies and Activities* booklet.

Using Your History Journal

Encourage students, where possible, to give the origins of the ideas in their list.

Your History Journal

In this chapter English and American people make major changes to their governments. What should be the basic ideas upon which government is built? List the ideas you believe to be basic.

GLENCOE TECHNOLOGY

VIDEODISC
Use MindJogger to preview chapter content.

MindJogger Videoquiz

Chapter 10
Disc 1 Side B

 Also available in VHS.

✚ EXTRA CREDIT PROJECT

Battle Map Have students research one of the battles from the English Civil War or the American Revolution. Then ask students to draw a map of this battle, showing nearby towns, physical features, the line of approach of the opposing armies, and important points in the battle. Remind students to provide a key to the map and to write a caption that explains the importance of the battle to the war. **L2 LEP**

1600		1620		1640		1660

1603 Queen Elizabeth I dies.

1625 Charles I becomes king of England.

1640 The Long Parliament meets in London.

1653 Oliver Cromwell is named Lord Protector.

SECTION THEME

▶ **Conflict** Disputes over the monarchy plunge England into civil war.

**ind Out**

Answer: *Parliament wanted to limit the monarch's powers, ensure that monarchs would not reestablish the Catholic Church, have more control over taxation and other government policies, and protect individual rights of the people. The religious dispute between Puritans in Parliament and the Church of England was another factor that led to civil war.*

FOCUS

Section Objective

Identify factors that led to civil war in England.

BELLRINGER
Motivational Activity

Before taking roll at the beginning of the class period, project Section Focus Transparency 10-1 and have students answer the activity questions. Discuss students' responses.

This activity is also available as a blackline master.

Vocabulary Pre-check

Use Vocabulary Activity 10 to introduce vocabulary terms.
L1 LEP

Section 1

Civil War

Setting the Scene

▶ **Terms to Define**
divine right, martial law, royalist, commonwealth

▶ **People to Meet**
James I, the Puritans, Charles I, the Cavaliers, the Roundheads, Oliver Cromwell

▶ **Places to Locate**
Scotland, Ireland

ind Out What factors led to the outbreak of civil war in England?

The Storyteller

"I say you are no Parliament; I will put an end to your sitting; call them in, call them in." Oliver Cromwell brought in two lines of men armed with muskets, adjourned the session, and locked the doors. That afternoon he intruded upon the Council of State and tried the same. But the chairman, Bradshaw, who had faced worse from King Charles, faced Cromwell. "Sir, we have heard what you did in the morning, and before many hours all England will hear it; but sir, you are mistaken to think that the Parliament is dissolved; for no power under heaven can dissolve them but themselves; therefore take you notice of that."

Oliver Cromwell

—from *Oliver Cromwell*, John Morley, M.P., 1901

lizabeth I, daughter of Henry VIII and Anne Boleyn, ruled England from 1558 to 1603. She was a strong monarch, but she did not have absolute power. Elizabeth took into consideration the views of Parliament, which grew more politically involved during her reign.

An able leader, Queen Elizabeth recognized the importance of the goodwill of the people—and of Parliament. She once said, "Though God has raised me high, yet this I account the glory of the crown, that I have reigned with your loves." For its part, Parliament was willing to defer to the popular queen. After Elizabeth died in 1603, Parliament, especially the House of Commons, was determined to increase its control over national policy. This move by Parliament resulted in a conflict with the Crown that tore the nation apart.

Opposition to the Crown

Because Elizabeth died childless, **James I**, the son of Elizabeth's cousin, Mary, Queen of Scots, became king in 1603. James, a member of the Stuart family, was the king of **Scotland** when he assumed the English throne.

King and Parliament

Soon after James became king of England, problems arose with the English Parliament. James professed his belief in divine right—that monarchs derive their power directly from God and that such power is absolute. He lectured the Parliament:

❝ Kings are not only God's lieutenants upon earth and sit upon God's throne, but even by God himself they are called Gods.... I will not be content that my power be disputed on. ❞

Such statements aroused the resentment among the members of Parliament.

SECTION RESOURCES

Reproducible Masters
- Reproducible Lesson Plan 10-1
- Vocabulary Activity 10
- Guided Reading Activity 10-1
- Time Line Activity 10
- History Simulation 10
- People in World History Profile 40
- Section Quiz 10-1

Transparencies
- Section Focus Transparency 10-1
- Chapter Transparency 10

Multimedia
- Student Self-Test and Review Software
- Testmaker

James I's greatest political weakness was his constant need to ask Parliament for money. He spent huge sums of money on the government as well as on himself and his advisers. After one of James's parties, a member of Parliament remarked that James had "given away more plate [money] than Queen Elizabeth did in her whole reign." When Parliament refused to vote him enough funds, James resorted to other means of raising money, such as selling titles of nobility.

Parliament also criticized the king's foreign policy. James's decision to end a war with Spain created outrage in Parliament. The war repayments that were part of the peace treaty put England deep into debt. Opposition to James's policies grew even stronger when James tried to arrange the marriage of his son, Charles, to a Spanish Catholic princess. Fearing the return of Catholics to power, the people celebrated when James's marriage plans for his son failed.

Religion and the Monarchy

England's unsettled religious issues only added to the tension between Parliament and the Crown. In the 1600s most English people belonged to the Church of England, but they had differences of opinion about the doctrine and rituals of the Church. One powerful group of dissenters, or opponents, within the Church was **the Puritans.** They wanted the Church to be "purified" of remaining Catholic rituals and symbols. Many Puritans in Parliament called for these reforms.

James I, as head of both church and government in England, thought that anyone who criticized the Church of England was not a loyal subject. When James had become king, the Puritans presented him with a petition asking for reforms to be made in the Church of England. Not only did James reject the suggested changes, he warned the Puritans that if they did not conform to the Church of England, he would "harry [force] them out of the land." When the king refused to support the Puritan cause, the Puritans turned against him. Because of James's policies, many Puritans left England and settled in North America.

Despite his controversial ways, James I made a lasting and important contribution to the religion and literature of the English-speaking world. In 1604 he had a group of scholars prepare a new translation of the Bible from Greek and Hebrew into English. The new version appeared in 1611 and became known as the "King James" Bible. Written in the eloquent prose and poetry of Shakespeare's time, it became the best-known English version of the Bible.

Portrait of Charles I Hunting by Anthony Van Dyck, c. 1636. The Louvre, Paris, France *Why were the English Parliament and people unhappy with Charles by 1628?*

Charles Inherits the Throne

When James I died in 1625, his son Charles became king. **Charles I** inherited the country's religious conflicts and political divisions. Like his father, Charles opposed the Puritans and believed in the divine right of kings. Adding to the tension, Charles eventually married a Catholic woman—Henrietta Maria, sister of France's King Louis XIII.

Early in his reign, Charles asked Parliament for money to fight a war against Spain and France. When it gave him only a fraction of the sum he had requested, the king dissolved Parliament immediately and tried to raise money without its consent. Charles then forced landowners to give "loans" to the government. When they refused, he put them in jail. People were outraged by the king's behavior.

People were also angered by Charles's demand to billet, or board and lodge, his troops in private homes. The king also placed some areas under martial law, or temporary military rule with limitations on individual rights. Thus, discontent ran high when Charles again called Parliament into session in 1628.

Chapter 10 *English and American Revolutions* **313**

TEACH

Guided Practice

THEME Conflict

Tell students that the English Civil War was the result of the deep conflict between Parliament and James I and later Charles I. Help students identify the source of the conflict. (*James and Charles believed in the divine right of kings; Parliament wanted more control over government policy, raising money, and reforms in the Church of England.*) **L1**

History & Art Van Dyck was a Flemish artist who specialized in portraits of Flemish, Italian, Spanish, and English nobles. In 1632 King Charles I made Anton Van Dyck his court painter and knighted him Sir Anthony Van Dyck.

Answer to Caption: *Charles I had dissolved Parliament, tried to raise money without Parliament's consent, forced landowners to lend him money and put them in jail if they refused, forced people to lodge soldiers in their homes, and placed some areas of England under martial law.*

Politics Have students make a two-column chart that lists Parliament's grievances against James I and Charles I. **L2**

 Chapter Transparency 10

 History Simulation 10

Who?What?Where?When?

English Catholics In spite of England's anti-Catholic laws, about one-fourth of the population was Catholic in 1634.

COOPERATIVE LEARNING ACTIVITY

Role Play Organize students into three groups to stage the trial of Charles I: the prosecution, the defense, and witnesses for the prosecution and for the defense. Have students choose a classmate to play Charles and another to play Cromwell. Have students from the appropriate group research arguments for the prosecution, arguments for the defense, and background on witnesses. Have each group select a few representatives to work with the other groups' representatives to prepare dialogue for the role play. Encourage students to ad lib as well. If possible, videotape the students' presentation. **L2**

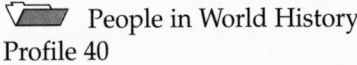
History & Art The Pilgrims were a dissenting sect that separated from the Church of England and left England on the *Mayflower* to start a new life in New England. In the Mayflower Compact, Pilgrim leaders agreed to form a government for the good of their colony. **How did this differ from government in England?** *(The king claimed to rule by divine right, and ordinary people had no role in government.)*

Answer to Caption: *Leaders of the Church of England persecuted Puritans and Pilgrims.*

Economics Have students discuss how collecting taxes became a point of conflict between Charles I and Parliament. *(When Parliament refused to give King Charles the money he asked for to fight France and Spain, the king tried to raise money without Parliament's consent. In exchange for approval of additional taxes, Parliament forced the king to sign the Petition of Right forbidding him from again collecting taxes without parliamentary consent.)* **L3**

Independent Practice

Guided Reading Activity 10-1 **L1**

Time Line Activity 10

People in World History Profile 40

Political Cartoon Have students draw a political cartoon about the English Civil War, perhaps lampooning Charles I or Cromwell, expressing ideas of Roundheads or Cavaliers, or depicting the tragedy of civil war. **L2 LEP**

History & Art *Pilgrims Signing the Mayflower Compact* by Percy Moran, c. 1900. The Pilgrim Hall Museum, Plymouth, Massachusetts *Why did groups like the Pilgrims and the Puritans leave England?*

By this time England was at war with both France and Spain. Parliament, however, was now ready to press changes on the king. In return for its approval of additional taxes to support the war, Parliament forced Charles to sign the Petition of Right. The Petition severely limited Charles's power in four ways. First, the king was forbidden to collect taxes or force loans without Parliament's consent. Second, the king could not imprison anyone without just cause. Third, troops could not be housed in a private home against the will of the owner. Fourth, the king could not declare martial law unless the country was at war.

Charles's desire to maintain his power, however, was not checked by the Petition of Right. Nearly a year after Parliament had authorized funds in return for his signature on the document, Charles dissolved Parliament and vowed never to call it again. For the next 11 years, Charles ruled without the advice or consent of the Parliament. He continued to collect taxes and imprison opponents—ignoring the Petition of Right he had signed.

At the same time, Charles deepened the religious divisions within England. He named William Laud to be Archbishop of Canterbury, the leading official of the Church of England. Laud and Charles persecuted the Puritans. They denied Puritans the right to preach or to publish. They burned Puritan

writings, and punished outspoken Puritans with public whippings.

As a result, thousands of Puritans sought religious freedom in the English colonies in America. Their exodus from England from 1630 through 1643 is known as the Great Migration. Most Puritans, however, remained in their homeland, determined to fight Charles and others who opposed them.

Charles and Archbishop Laud then turned their attention to Scotland. In an effort to establish the Church of England in Scotland, the king and the archbishop tried to force the Calvinist Church of Scotland to accept the Church of England's prayer book. The Scots rejected the new prayer book and formed a National Covenant, or agreement, in which they pledged to preserve their religious freedom. Outraged by the king's actions, they were prepared to go to war to do so.

Beginnings of the Civil War

By 1640 the Scots had invaded England. In dire need of money, Charles was forced to recall a Parliament that he had ignored for 11 years. The members of Parliament, however, refused to discuss anything without first voicing their complaints about Charles's handling of religious and political issues. As a result, Charles dissolved this Parliament, known as the Short Parliament, after only 3 weeks.

Charles became so desperate for money that he had no choice but to summon Parliament once again. By this time members of Parliament were seething with anger and demanded to voice their complaints to the king. Controlled by Puritans, this session of Parliament, called the Long Parliament, would meet for almost 20 years.

The Long Parliament was determined to decrease Charles's power. The members abolished the special courts used to imprison Charles's opponents and passed a law requiring Parliament to be called every 3 years. They ended all forms of illegal taxation and jailed and later executed the hated Archbishop Laud.

While Parliament convened, trouble erupted in **Ireland**. Relations between England and Ireland had been strained since the 1100s. The Irish people remained Roman Catholic and refused to accept the Church of England. What angered the Irish most was the continuing English practice of seizing land from Irish owners and giving it to English and Scots settlers. In 1641 the Irish rebelled. Faced with rebellion in both Scotland and Ireland, Charles was at the mercy of the Puritan-controlled Parliament.

MEETING SPECIAL NEEDS ACTIVITY

Learning Style: Visual/Spatial Collect several portraits of Charles I and Oliver Cromwell for students to analyze. Ask students to list the appearance, characteristics, qualities, and interests of each man as shown in their portraits. Let students discuss similarities and differences that they notice between the two men. Finally, ask students how their differences led to the conflict of the English Civil War. **L1 LEP**

As the Puritans grew stronger, a *royalist*, or pro-monarchy, group formed in Parliament. It was made up of people who supported the king and opposed Puritan control of the Church of England. As time went on, debates between Puritans and royalists became more heated.

Despite resistance by the royalists, Parliament in June 1642 sent Charles "Nineteen Propositions" that made Parliament the supreme power in England. Charles, however, refused to agree to its demands. With a dramatic personal appearance, Charles led troops into the House of Commons and attempted to arrest five of its leaders. The five were hidden and protected from capture. The king's use of force meant there could be no compromise. Both Charles and Parliament prepared for war.

The English Civil War

Charles gathered an army that included nobles and landowners in the north and west of the country. They were called **the Cavaliers** because many belonged to the king's cavalry, or armed horsemen. Supporters of Parliament and Puritans drew their strength from the south and east of England. They were called **the Roundheads** because many of them had close-cropped hair.

Parliament organized its military forces under the leadership of **Oliver Cromwell**. Cromwell was a very religious man and a brilliant military commander. His rigorous training and firm discipline of the parliamentary forces led to several decisive victories. After nearly four years of conflict, the royalist armies surrendered in May 1646. Parliament had won complete control of the English government. The Puritans removed their remaining opponents from Parliament, leaving behind what was known as the Rump Parliament.

After a failed attempt to escape from his enemies, Charles surrendered in 1647. The army then tried, sentenced, and executed the king in 1649. It was a shocking moment for many English people, no matter how they felt about Charles.

A New Government

After the execution, the Rump Parliament ended the monarchy and set up a republic known as a *commonwealth*, a state ruled by elected representatives. From the outset, the new government faced much opposition. It relied on Cromwell's army to crush royalist uprisings in Scotland and Ireland. Severe measures were placed on Ireland's Catholic majority, many of whom were killed or lost lands to Protestant landlords. In England, Cromwell and his officers later suppressed the Levellers, a group wanting the vote for all men.

Overseas, the republic's mercantilist policies advanced English trade. The Navigation Act (1651) required that imports be brought to England in English ships or in ships of the country producing the goods. This law angered the Dutch, who had grown rich from carrying goods to England on their ships. A strengthened English navy, however, met the Dutch threat. During the 1650s, English military victories over the Dutch and later the Spanish heightened England's position as a European power.

At home, Cromwell dismissed the ineffectual Rump Parliament and placed England under military rule, with himself as Lord Protector. Cromwell's government granted religious freedom to all non-Anglican Protestants, but enforced Puritan rules requiring people to attend church and to avoid drinking, swearing, and gambling. When Cromwell died in 1658, his son Richard was unable to maintain the government. Most English people were tired of military rule and unhappy with Puritan restrictions. In 1660 a newly elected Parliament restored the monarchy under Charles I's son, Charles II. Representative government and individual rights would survive, however. No English monarch would ever be able to claim absolute power again.

SECTION 1 REVIEW

Recall
1. **Define** divine right, martial law, royalist, commonwealth.
2. **Identify** James I, the Puritans, Charles I, Petition of Right, William Laud, the Cavaliers, the Roundheads, Oliver Cromwell.
3. **Discuss** how the Puritans shaped English religion and politics in the 1600s.

Critical Thinking
4. **Analyzing Information** How did Elizabeth I and the Stuart monarchs James I and Charles I differ in getting what they wanted from Parliament?

Whose methods were more effective? Why?

Understanding Themes
5. **Conflict** What problems did Parliament face before the English Civil War? After the war? Did Parliament achieve its political goals?

Chapter 10 *English and American Revolutions* **315**

SECTION 1 REVIEW ANSWERS

1. All vocabulary words are defined in the Glossary.
2. James I, 312; the Puritans, 313; Charles I, 313; Petition of Right, 314; William Laud, 314; the Cavaliers, 315; the Roundheads, 315; Oliver Cromwell, 315
3. The Puritans aimed to rid the Church of England of Catholic rituals; they opposed absolute monarchy and advanced cause of representative parliamentary government.
4. Elizabeth worked with Parliament; the Stuarts insisted on their divine right as kings. Elizabeth's methods were more successful; Parliament usually did what she wanted whereas the Stuarts brought England into a civil war.
5. **CONFLICT** Answers will vary. Possible answer: No. Before the English Civil War, Parliament faced problems with an overbearing monarchy. After the war, it had to contend with Cromwell's autocratic rule.

ASSESS

Check for Understanding
Assign Section 1 Review as homework or as an in-class activity.

Use Student Self-Test and Review Software to review Section 1.

Evaluate
Section Quiz 10-1

Use the Testmaker to create a customized quiz for Section 1.

Reteach
Organize students into groups of six. Give each group six slips of paper with one of these roles on each slip: *James I, Charles I, Oliver Cromwell, a Puritan, a Cavalier,* and *Archbishop Laud.* Let students play charades with the roles on these slips of paper.

Enrich
Have students write a report comparing the structure of government under Charles I with government under Cromwell as Lord Protector.

CLOSE

Have students create a flowchart that traces events in England from 1603 to 1658.

1650   1700   1750

1688	The Glorious Revolution brings William III and Mary II to the English throne.
1707	The Act of Union unites England and Scotland.
1714	George I becomes king of Great Britain.

Section 2

A King Returns to the Throne

Setting the Scene

▶ **Terms to Define**
constitutional monarchy, habeas corpus, cabinet, prime minister

▶ **People to Meet**
Charles II, the Whigs, the Tories, William III, Mary II, George I, Sir Robert Walpole

▶ **Places to Locate**
London

 How did England establish a constitutional monarchy?

𝒮toryteller

"What pillars and arches to be pulled down! What new ones to be erected! What scaffold and engines to lay the foundation of an endless and incalculable future expenditure." The authorities in charge of restoring St. Paul's Cathedral believed Christopher Wren's designs went too far and would cost too much. Just when it seemed as though the great architect would have to change his plans, disaster changed everything. In the Great Fire of London, buildings were demolished overnight. At St. Paul's Cathedral, heated stones

flew like grenades and lead ran in rivers down the streets. Wren would design a new cathedral.

—adapted from *The Architecture of Wren*, Kerry Downes, 1982

Christopher Wren

As the son of Charles I, **Charles II** had faced danger throughout the English Civil War and Cromwell's rule. He risked death on the battlefield as he joined the royalist forces in their fight and in their defeat. He saw his father imprisoned and put to death. He narrowly escaped his own capture and execution by disguising himself as a servant and fleeing to the European continent.

In Europe, Charles wandered from country to country. While some European rulers received him as royalty, others threatened him with arrest as a fugitive. In his own country, the Puritans kept a close watch on Charles. Since he was the direct heir to the English throne, Charles posed a threat to their political power. By the time Parliament had restored the monarchy, Charles had learned a good deal about pleasing people he needed for support and safety. Charles willingly accepted a change from the absolute power of his ancestors.

The Merry Monarch

When Charles II returned to **London**, on May 29, 1660, the English people celebrated wildly. They felt released from a violent, unstable period followed by harsh Puritan rule. A court member described the happiness of the English people as they rejoiced in a lavish parade marking the king's return:

❝ A triumph of above 20,000 horse and foot soldiers, brandishing their swords and shouting with inexpressible joy; the ways strewed with flowers, the bells ringing, the streets hung with tapestry, fountains running with wine…. I stood and beheld it, and blessed God. ❞

This period, in which the House of Stuart was returned to the throne, is called the Restoration. In contrast to the severe and religious rule of Cromwell, Charles II was known as the Merry Monarch. He loved parties, games, and witty conversation. He supported the arts, science, and entertainment. People once again danced and enjoyed sports and theater. Charles married a Portuguese princess; and though they had no children, he fathered illegitimate children by his mistresses.

Dealing With Religious Questions

Outwardly, Charles was a member of the Church of England; secretly, however, he favored Catholicism. Although hoping for religious toleration, the king recognized that the settlement of England's religious divisions rested on Parliament. During the 1660s, the largely royalist Cavalier Parliament passed the Clarendon Code, a series of laws that made the Church of England once again the state religion. Only Church of England members could attend the universities, serve in Parliament, or hold religious services. Hundreds of Puritan clergy were driven from their churches.

During this time of troubles for the Puritans, the Puritan writer John Milton wrote *Paradise Lost* (1667), generally considered to be the greatest epic poem in the English language. *Paradise Lost* retells the biblical story of creation, the devil's revolt against God, and the fall of Adam and Eve.

Limiting Royal Power

In addition to its anti-Puritan policies, Parliament kept limits on royal power. All laws that Charles I had accepted, such as the Petition of Right, were still in effect. The Restoration thus gave England a constitutional monarchy, a form of government in which the monarch's powers are limited by a constitution. Rather than being a single document, however, England's constitution was made up of many documents—such as the Magna Carta and the Petition of Right—plus other laws and customs. Although Charles II disagreed with some of the reforms he never fought Parliament forcefully. Charles was determined to avoid his father's fate.

The French ambassador to England was astonished at the mood of the country. In France, the king had absolute power. The ambassador commented

The Arts

Rebuilding London

In 1666 a major fire destroyed much of London. Over the next decades, it was rebuilt as a beautiful capital. One of the men chosen to work on the commission rebuilding the city was Christopher Wren, a noted mathematician and astronomer at Oxford University. He is best known, however, as the architect of St. Paul's Cathedral, a London landmark begun in 1675.

The new St. Paul's Cathedral was the first major church built for Anglican worship, and Wren designed it to be an impressive, monumental structure. He used classical and baroque styles to produce a cathedral that combined orderliness with dramatic visual effects. Wren also designed other architecturally attractive churches for the city.

During World War II, the area around

St. Paul's Cathedral

St. Paul's Cathedral was heavily bombed by the German air force. St. Paul's was spared extensive damage, but other Wren churches were among the many buildings destroyed. Since then, heavily bombed areas, including some of these churches, have been rebuilt.

Today, skyscrapers rather than churches dominate the landscape of central London. As the city has built upward, it has also spread outward. A number of new towns have arisen in outlying areas, separated from central London by a greenbelt, a wide band of open country.

Linking Past and Present — ACTIVITY

Discuss how Christopher Wren contributed to the architecture of London in the 1600s. How has the city's appearance changed since World War II? In what ways is London like, or unlike, other modern cities?

Chapter 10 *English and American Revolutions* 317

COOPERATIVE LEARNING ACTIVITY

Documentary Assign the class the task of producing a documentary television show about the London fire of 1666. Have students choose a producer to coordinate the class project. Then organize the class into teams. Have teams research, write, and present "hard news" about the fire, such as its origin, how far it spread, number of casualties, buildings destroyed, or plans for rebuilding. Ask other teams to prepare on-the-scene features about the fire, such as interviews with local residents, firefighters, or government officials. If possible, videotape the presentation for the basis of a class discussion later. **L2**

TEACH

Guided Practice

THEME Change

On the chalkboard, write the following column headings: *Monarchy's Power, Parliament's Power, Religious Problems*. Then write these row headings: *Charles II, James II, William and Mary, Anne, George I, George II*. Help students complete the chart to show how England's government changed between 1660 and 1760. **L1 LEP**

Critical Thinking Lead a discussion about why the English reestablished the monarchy yet limited the ruler's power through a constitutional monarchy. **L2**

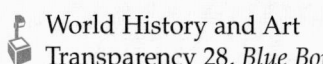 World History and Art Transparency 28, *Blue Boy*

Linking Past and Present

Rebuilding London

London builders and craftsmen took more than 30 years to complete St. Paul's Cathedral. The dome, its most famous feature, has an inner dome and a much taller outer dome. Light enters the cathedral through an opening in the middle of the inner dome.

ANSWERS

Christopher Wren built St. Paul's Cathedral and many other Anglican churches in London, combining baroque and classical styles. After World War II bombings, many areas of London were rebuilt; skyscrapers came to dominate churches; answers will vary, but should mention that like other modern cities, London has expanded upward and outward.

Cultural Perspectives

Church of England Today in England, the Church of England is also known as the Anglican Church. In the United States, followers of the beliefs of the Church of England belong to the Episcopal Church. The Anglican Church is still the official church in the United Kingdom.

Independent Practice

📂 Guided Reading Activity 10-2 **L1**

Government Have students research to prepare a chart that compares rights in the English Bill of Rights with those in the United States Bill of Rights. Ask students to indicate on their charts the rights common to both countries' bills of rights. **L2**

CURRICULUM CONNECTION

EDUCATION

The College of William and Mary, founded in 1693 in Williamsburg, Virginia, was named for England's king and queen. It is the second oldest institution of higher learning in the United States. Harvard University is the oldest.

you don't say...

Tory comes from an Irish word for "robber" or "royalist outlaw." During the fight for the Exclusion Bill, Tory became an unflattering term for people who supported the monarchy and the Church of England.

 **Religious Revolution in the Colonies**

Maryland, 1689
The colony of Maryland had been founded as a refuge for Roman Catholics, with religious freedom for all people. Maryland Protestants resented having Roman Catholic Charles Calvert as the colony's owner. In 1689 Protestants took over Maryland and passed anti-Catholic legislation. The laws required children of mixed marriages to be raised as Protestants and imposed fines for sending children to Catholic schools abroad.

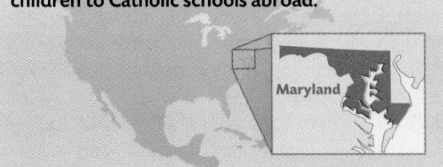

Maryland

on the changes in England in a letter to the French king, Louis XIV:

> ❝ This government has a monarchical appearance because there is a King, but at bottom it is far from being a monarchy.... The members of Parliament are ... allowed to speak their mind freely.... ❞

While the English celebrated the end of Puritan rule, they were struck by two disasters. In 1665 the plague returned to London for the last time, killing as many as 100,000 people. Later, a terrible raging fire destroyed much of London. Some people falsely blamed Catholics for setting the fire as part of a plan to gain control of the country.

Establishing Political Parties

Opposition to Catholicism helped to spark the growth of England's first political parties. The parties grew out of a debate over who would succeed Charles as the king of England. Because Charles had no legitimate children, James II, Charles's brother, was next in line to be king. James, who was a practicing Catholic, ignited the fears of a revival of Catholic power in England.

In 1679 Parliament tried to pass the Exclusion Bill, which would have kept James from becoming king. During this conflict, those members of Parliament who wanted to exclude James from the throne were known as **the Whigs.** Those who defended the hereditary monarchy were referred to as **the Tories.**

In a compromise, the Tories agreed to defeat the Exclusion Bill by accepting another bill supported by the Whigs. The Whig-proposed bill established the principle of habeas corpus as law. According to habeas corpus, a person could not be held in prison by the king (or anyone else) without just cause or without a trial. It was another step that increased individual rights and reduced those of the Crown.

A Bloodless Revolt

When Charles II died in 1685, his Catholic brother, James II, became king, effectively ending the peaceful relations between Parliament and the Crown. James wanted absolute power and claimed he had the right to suspend the law. Ignoring Parliament's religious laws, James appointed Catholics to government and university positions. He also allowed people of all Christian faiths to worship freely.

The Glorious Revolution

These actions alarmed many of the members of Parliament, but they tried to be patient. They were waiting for James to die and for the English throne to pass to his Protestant daughter Mary, who was married to William of Orange, the ruler of the Netherlands.

In 1688, however, a royal birth prompted Parliament to take action. James's second wife bore a son, who would be raised a Catholic. He would inherit the throne, rather than the Protestant Mary. Both Whig and Tory leaders united against James and invited Mary's husband William to invade England and take over the Crown. James fled to France when he realized he had little support in England. **William III** and **Mary II** gained the English throne without battles or bloodshed. This peaceful transfer of power was so welcome and so different from previous struggles that the English called it the Glorious Revolution.

New Limits on Royal Power

At previous coronations, English kings and queens had sworn to observe the laws and customs established by their royal ancestors. In 1689, however, William and Mary swore an oath that they would govern the people of England "according to the statutes in Parliament agreed upon, and the laws and customs of the same."

In that same year, Parliament further strengthened its power by passing the Bill of Rights. According to the Bill of Rights, the king could not

Learning Style: Verbal/Linguistic Have students imagine they have been selected by Parliament to write a letter either to Charles II asking him to return as king or to William and Mary inviting them to be monarchs. Remind students to include the conditions under which the monarchs will rule. Suggest that students research styles for writing letters in the 1600s. Encourage students to share their completed letters with the class. **L2**

raise taxes or maintain an army without the consent of Parliament and could not suspend laws. Further, it declared that Parliament should be held often and that there should be freedom of debate in sessions of Parliament.

The Bill of Rights also guaranteed certain individual rights. It guaranteed the right to a trial by jury, outlawed cruel and unusual punishment for a crime, and limited the amount of bail money that could be required for a person to be temporarily released while awaiting trial. Citizens were given the right to appeal to the monarch and to speak freely in Parliament.

In 1689 the exiled James II landed in Ireland and led Irish Catholics in a revolt to recapture the Crown. Although the uprising failed a year later, English Protestants controlling Irish affairs began to exclude the Catholic majority in Ireland from government and business. This action only deepened the hatred Irish Catholics had for English policies.

Anti-Catholic feelings throughout the country also led the English Parliament in London to pass more legislation limiting the Crown's power. In the Act of Settlement (1701), Parliament excluded any Catholic from inheriting the English throne.

Parliament and the Crown

The Bill of Rights and the Act of Settlement made it clear that Parliament had won the long battle with the Crown. England was still a monarchy, but a king or queen could not rule without Parliament's consent.

England was not yet a true democracy, however. Although members of the House of Commons were elected, only male property owners—250,000 people out of 6 million, or 4 percent of the population—had the right to vote. Members of the House of Commons were not paid, so only the wealthy could afford to run for office. Parliament was controlled by people of property—nobles, gentry, wealthy merchants, and clergy.

Succession and Union

The power of Parliament further increased when Mary's sister Anne succeeded William in 1702. (Mary had died in 1694.) At the same time, Parliament had to establish a new order of succession to the throne. Since Anne had no living children to succeed her, she would be succeeded by the children of Sophia, a Protestant granddaughter of James I. Sophia was married to the German elector, or ruler, of Hanover. In short, the English throne

would pass to the heirs or heiresses from the German House of Hanover.

Yet there still remained a danger that the Scots might prefer a Stuart monarch to a member of the House of Hanover. Parliament also feared that the Scots would form an alliance with France against England. After negotiations with the Scots, who were militarily and economically weak, the two governments signed the Act of Union in 1707. It united the two countries into a new nation called Great Britain. Both the English and the Scots would now be "British." Although the Scots gave up their own parliament, they were given representation in the English Parliament. Scotland also retained its own Calvinist religion, and its own laws, courts, and educational system as well.

Visualizing History In 1688 Parliament presented the Crown of England to William and Mary. *Why did Parliament decide to give the Crown to the royal couple?*

Linking Past and Present

William III At the Battle of the Boyne in Ireland on July 12, 1690, William III defeated the army of James II. He also ended the political power of Irish Roman Catholics. In 1695 Protestants in what is now Northern Ireland formed the Orange Society, named for William III who was also William of Orange.

Visualizing History Sixteen years before the Glorious Revolution, William had gained control of the Netherlands through another revolution. Although by right of birth the office of stadtholder should have been his (his father held it), it had fallen into the hands of Jan de Witt. A revolution in 1672 made William stadtholder.
Answer to Caption: *Parliament wanted England to have Protestant rulers instead of Catholic.*

ASSESS

Check for Understanding

Assign Section 2 Review as homework or as an in-class activity.

▣ Use Student Self-Test and Review Software to review Section 2.

MAKING CONNECTIONS ACTIVITY

The Arts After the long winter of Puritan rule, the arts blossomed in England during the Restoration period. Have students choose an area of the arts, such as architecture, drama, furniture design, music, or painting, and prepare an oral report about it in England from 1660 to 1760. Tell students to describe important people and works, how the works reflected the times, and whether these people and works have any impact on the arts today. Suggest that students illustrate their reports. Then display the illustrations on a classroom bulletin board. **L2**

Chapter 10
Section 2

Visualizing History Robert Walpole wears a powdered wig in this portrait. This fashion spread from France to England in the late 1600s. Men with short hair did not want to be mistaken for Roundheads. **Answer to Caption:** *prime minister*

Evaluate

Section Quiz 10-2

Use the Testmaker to create a customized quiz for Section 2.

Reteach

Have students discuss the evolution of England's constitutional monarchy from 1660 to 1760.

Enrich

Have students write a research report on one of England's literary figures of this period, such as Alexander Pope, Jonathan Swift, Daniel Defoe, Richard Steele, or Joseph Addison.

CLOSE

Ask students to create a time line that includes important events and people discussed in Section 2. Have students write a brief explanation next to each event or person.

Visualizing History Sir Robert Walpole became a close friend of King George II and Queen Caroline. He directed policy as the leading cabinet official. *What title did the main cabinet official earn?*

Political Parties and the Cabinet

During Anne's reign (1702-1714), Parliament's political powers continued to increase. Anne was unskilled in British politics and sought guidance from a cabinet, a small group of advisers selected from the House of Commons. Because a cabinet made up of both Whigs and Tories often quarreled, it became the custom to choose cabinet members only from the party holding a majority of the seats in Parliament.

Anne died in 1714, and Sophia's son **George I** took the throne according to the Act of Settlement. George had been raised in Germany, and did not speak English very well.

George I relied on the cabinet even more than Anne had. Eventually, **Sir Robert Walpole**, the leader of the Whigs, gained control of the cabinet. Although he spoke no German, Walpole advised the king. Walpole's position as head of the cabinet was later called prime minister, the chief executive of a parliamentary government. Walpole remained prime minister when a new king, George II, took the throne in 1727. With the king's encouragement, Walpole gradually took over many political responsibilities: managing finances, appointing government officials, and requesting the passage of laws. He helped avoid wars and allowed the North American colonies to grow without interference from the British government.

In 1760 George III, grandson of George II, became king at the age of 22. George III greatly expanded the British Empire through victory in a war against France. Great Britain gained Canada and all of France's territory east of the Mississippi River. The cost of waging the war—and the ways in which George III and his ministers tried to deal with that cost—would eventually lead to rebellion in Great Britain's American colonies.

SECTION 2 REVIEW

Recall
1. **Define** constitutional monarchy, habeas corpus, cabinet, prime minister.
2. **Identify** Charles II, the Restoration, the Whigs, the Tories, William III, Mary II, Bill of Rights, George I, Sir Robert Walpole.

3. **Explain** why Charles II was called the Merry Monarch. How was his reign different from that of his father, Charles I?

Critical Thinking
4. **Analyzing Information** How did the royal power of William and Mary compare with that of Charles II? How had

Parliament's powers expanded by the time William and Mary came to the throne?

Understanding Themes
5. **Change** Briefly describe how England evolved into a constitutional monarchy. What rights did individual citizens gain as a result of this change?

---

320 **Chapter 10** *English and American Revolutions*

SECTION 2 REVIEW ANSWERS

1. All vocabulary words are defined in the Glossary.
2. Charles II, 316; the Restoration, 317; the Whigs, 318; the Tories, 318; William III, 318; Mary II, 318; Bill of Rights, 318; George I, 320; Sir Robert Walpole, 320
3. Charles II loved social life, the arts, and entertainment. Charles II accepted limited power; Charles I insisted on the divine right of kings.
4. Charles II accepted the Petition of Right and agreed not to be involved in church affairs; William and Mary agreed to rule only with Parliament's consent.
5. **CHANGE** Parliament gradually took greater control as it forced monarchs to give up much of their power. Individuals gained the right to a fair trial, freedom from cruel and unusual punishment, and the right to speak freely in Parliament.

1725 ———————————— 1750 ———————————— 1775

c. 1730 Colonial assemblies win the right to limit royal governors' salaries.

1754 The French and Indian War begins.

1763 British proclamation bans colonial settlement west of the Appalachians.

1774 First Continental Congress meets in Philadelphia.

Section 3

Road to Revolt

Setting the Scene

▶ **Terms to Define**
duty, direct tax, boycott

▶ **People to Meet**
George Grenville, George III, John Adams, Patrick Henry, George Washington, Samuel Adams

▶ **Places to Locate**
New York City, Boston, Philadelphia

 What factors led to disagreement and eventual conflict between the British and the American colonies?

The Storyteller

Boston's newspapers announced that a ship bearing tea would arrive soon. All over town, this handbill appeared: "Friends! Brethren! Country–men! That worst of plagues, the detested tea, shipped for this port by the East India Company, is now arrived in this harbor; the hour of destruction or manly opposition to the machinations [schemes] of tyranny stares you in the face; every friend … is now called upon … to make a united and successful resistance. Boston, November 29, 1773."

—adapted from *Tea Leaves, Being a Collection of Letters and Documents Relating to the Shipment of Tea to the American Colonies …, 1970*

Boston Tea Party

While Great Britain struggled through civil war and a changing government, its colonies in America changed as well. By the mid-1700s, 13 colonies thrived on the eastern coast of North America. As more people migrated to North America to escape religious persecution or to gain a new start in life, the population of the colonies grew to more than 1.5 million by 1763.

Since most of the colonists were British, they shared a common language and political background. Although many radical political ideas—ideas about republicanism, universal suffrage, liberty, and equality—had died out in Great Britain, many political radicals had fled to the colonies. Here the old ideas stayed alive. In the colonies, there was no aristocracy. The hardships of life on the frontier and the easy availability of land tended to blur class divisions. Each American colony had a representative assembly, much like Parliament in Great Britain, and the colonists were used to governing themselves.

The British Empire in America

Except for regulating trade, the British government generally left the colonies alone. In the British mercantilist view, the American colonies were valuable to Great Britain only to the extent that they benefited British trade. The role of the colonies was to produce goods—mostly raw materials—that could not be produced in Great Britain, and to provide markets for British manufactured goods.

By the early 1700s, the colonies pulsated with economic activity. In the South, plantations produced tobacco, rice, and indigo with the labor of thousands of enslaved Africans. Settlers in the rich farming land of the Middle Colonies grew enough food to feed their families and trade throughout the year. New England colonists turned to the sea because of their poor soil and harsh climate. In 1673

Chapter 10 *English and American Revolutions* **321**

SECTION RESOURCES

Reproducible Masters
- Reproducible Lesson Plan 10-3
- Vocabulary Activity 10
- Guided Reading Activity 10-3
- Geography and History Activity 10
- Section Quiz 10-3

Transparencies
- Section Focus Transparency 10-3

Multimedia
- Student Self-Test and Review Software
- Testmaker
- World Music: Cultural Traditions, Lesson 1

Guided Practice

THEME Conflict

Have students recall acts of Parliament that caused conflicts in the colonies. (*Stamp Act, Declaratory Act, Intolerable Acts, Quebec Act, tax on tea*) Encourage students to discuss why the colonists disliked these acts. (*Colonists were not represented in Parliament.*) **L1 LEP**

Cause and Effect Help students make a flowchart on the chalkboard that shows the sequence of cause and effect from the Stamp Act to the First Continental Congress. (*For example: the Stamp Act caused colonists to call the Stamp Act Congress, whose actions in turn caused Parliament to repeal the Stamp Act.*) **L3**

Biography

The following videotape programs are available from Glencoe:

- **King George III: Mad or Maligned?**
- **Patrick Henry: Voice of Liberty**

Who?What?Where?When?

Colony Names The colonies of Maryland, Virginia, North and South Carolina, and Georgia were named after the following English rulers: Henrietta Maria, wife of Charles I; Elizabeth I, who was known as the Virgin Queen; Charles I and Charles II; and George II.

---

a sea captain described busy Boston Harbor, reporting that "ships arrive dayly from Spain, France, Holland & Canarys bringing all sorts of wine, linens, silks, and fruits, which they transport to all the other plantations...."

To protect this profitable trade with its colonies, Parliament passed a series of Navigation Acts in the 1600s. According to these laws, the colonists were required to export certain products only to Great Britain or to other British colonies. In addition, all goods going to the colonies had to first pass through Great Britain, where a **duty**, or tax, had to be paid before shipment to the colonies. Finally, all goods going to or coming from the colonies were to be carried by ships built in British or colonial ports.

The colonists did not suffer as much as one might imagine from the effects these laws had on trade. Actually, the Navigation Acts had some benefits. Some colonies were able to develop a strong shipping industry, and some businesses grew prosperous in the absence of foreign competition. Moreover, the British government was never able to adequately enforce these laws. Smuggling goods in and out of ports along the coast became a major part of colonial trade.

Colonial Political Power

As people in the colonies grew more settled and economically secure, they also became more involved in their government. Most of the colonies were managed by a governor appointed by the king. The royal governor then appointed judges and other officials, but each colony also had an elected assembly. Voting in the colonies was restricted to men who owned property or paid taxes, as it was in Great Britain. In the colonies, however, it was much easier to acquire land. A much greater percentage of the population therefore could vote for their government.

The assemblies often struggled with the royal governors for power in the same way that Parliament and the Crown struggled in Great

---

Images of the Times

Colonial America

The colonies became prosperous and began to drift away from Great Britain. When the British Parliament tried to take control, Americans revolted.

A New England dame school fulfilled the Massachusetts General Court's requirement for public school financed by taxes.

A creche doll with a wooden face and glass inset eyes looked much like an adult. Colonists treated their children as miniature adults.

322

Images of the Times   Colonial America

Teaching children how to read so they could understand the Bible on their own was the main purpose of early New England schools. The *New England Primer*, the principal textbook, taught children their ABC's starting with "Adam" and ending with "Zaccheus." Prayers were also part of the *New England Primer*. Both boys and girls went to dame schools. When it came time to learn how to write, however, the boys advanced to grammar schools, whereas education ended for most girls.

Britain. These power struggles were often over money. In the early 1700s assemblies won the right to limit the salaries of governors and judges. If a governor would not do as colonists desired, the assembly would reduce or withhold his salary for the next year. In 1731 the New Hampshire assembly refused to pay the governor's salary for five years.

The assemblies also held fast to their right to approve any taxes requested by the Crown or governors. This issue would become a central point of conflict between the colonies and Great Britain. Just as the British Parliament had fought hard for its right to approve or refuse any taxes, so too would the American colonists.

Tightening Colonial Controls

A bitter rivalry between Great Britain and France for territory in North America would eventually lead the British government to interfere more actively in the colonial economy. A dispute over French and British land claims in North America as well as rights to the rich North American fur trade led France and Great Britain to war in 1754. The conflict, called the French and Indian War, brought French troops and French Canadian colonists against British forces and the American colonists. Some Native Americans fought on behalf of the British, while others supported the French.

After six years of war, the British-led forces finally defeated the French in 1760. Three years later, a treaty was signed in Paris. Under the treaty's terms, Great Britain acquired nearly all of France's possessions in North America, including Canada and lands in the area that lay west of the Appalachian Mountains.

Great Britain's empire had grown both in size and in power, but at a considerable cost. The war strained the British economy, and defending the huge new lands they had gained would cost the British even more.

George Grenville, whom **George III** appointed First Lord of the Treasury in 1763, took the first

"**The Wise Men of Gotham,**" a political cartoon, appeared in a colonial paper in 1776. It shows the British killing the American goose that laid the golden egg (trade) for the British.

The Stamp Act required stamps such as this on all legal documents. Colonists protested vigorously.

A Half Penny Sheet

REFLECTING ON THE TIMES

1. Why did colonial legislatures instead of Parliament exercise authority in matters such as education?
2. Why did colonists object to Parliament's authority in the Stamp Act?
3. What attitude toward British policies is reflected in the cartoon "The Wise Men of Gotham"?

323

📁 Geography and History Activity 10

🎵 World Music: Cultural Traditions, Lesson 1

Independent Practice

📁 Guided Reading Activity 10-3 **L1**

Economics Have students write paragraphs explaining why Great Britain wanted to control colonial imports and exports. *(to protect colonial trade from competition with other countries)* **L2**

Foreign Affairs Have students use outside resources to write an essay on why the French believed they had a right to the land in the Ohio Valley during the French and Indian War. **L3**

Who?What?Where?When?

Paris has served as the site for the signing of several peace treaties. In addition to the treaty that ended the French and Indian War, the treaties that ended both the American Revolution and United States involvement in the Vietnam War were signed there. The treaty that ended World War I was signed at Versailles, a few miles from Paris.

Global  Gourmet

America Native Americans invented succotash, a stew made of corn, lima beans, and meat from bears or wild birds. Colonists soon learned how to make this one-dish meal.

Visualizing
History Crispus
Attucks, an African American, was
one of the five colonists killed during the Boston Massacre.
Answer to Caption: *Parliament
repealed most taxes except for the tax
on tea.*

Who?What?Where?When?

John Peter Zenger In the early
1700s, colonial newspapers did
not criticize government officials. When John Peter Zenger's
New York Weekly Journal printed
letters against New York's governor, Zenger was arrested. When
Zenger's lawyer produced evidence proving the truth of the
criticisms, a jury acquitted Zenger. Zenger's acquittal is usually
viewed as the first American case
to uphold freedom of the press.

ASSESS

Check for Understanding

Assign Section 3 Review as homework or as an in-class activity.

🖲 Use Student Self-Test and
Review Software to review
Section 3.

Evaluate

📁 Section Quiz 10-3

🖲 Use the Testmaker to create a
customized quiz for Section 3.

Visualizing
History Bitter feelings erupted
in bloodshed on March
5, 1770, in Boston, when British soldiers
fired into a crowd and killed five people.
This incident became known to the
colonists as the Boston Massacre. *What
happened as a result of the unrest in Boston?*

steps to solve these problems. Grenville issued a
proclamation that said the colonists could not, for
the time being, settle in the lands west of the
Appalachians. This move, he hoped, would avoid
wars with Native Americans until Great Britain had
the area under control and could gradually open
the land to settlers. The colonists, however, were
eager to build new settlements in the west, and they
were outraged by this attempt to stop them.

Grenville also believed that colonists should
help pay the costs of their own defense. He began
raising money by enforcing the Navigation Acts
with the British navy. British warships hunted
down smugglers, who were then tried in British
military courts rather than in colonial courts.
Another new law allowed British troops to be
housed in colonists' homes.

It was the Stamp Act, however, that most infuriated the colonists. Passed in 1765, the Stamp Act
was different from previous tax measures because it
was a direct tax—a tax paid directly to the government rather than being included in the price of
goods. It required that all printed materials, from
newspapers and shipping documents to playing
cards, bear a stamp to show that a tax had been
paid to Great Britain. Colonial lawyers, tavern
owners, merchants, and printers were most affected by the Stamp Act.

Colonial Protests

Colonists reacted to these measures quickly.
They protested with a boycott—a refusal to buy
British goods. They attacked stamp agents and
burned stamps in the streets. In 1765 nine colonies
sent 28 representatives to a Stamp Act Congress in

New York City. The Congress resolved that
Parliament could not tax the colonies because the
colonies did not have representatives in Parliament.
They rallied under the cry "No taxation without
representation!" and insisted that only their own
colonial assemblies had the right to tax them. The
British Parliament repealed the Stamp Act in 1766.
The struggle for control of the colonies, however,
had begun in earnest. **John Adams**, a colonial
leader from Massachusetts, wrote in his diary:

“ The people have become more attentive to
their liberties, … and more determined to
defend them.… Our presses have groaned,
our pulpits have thundered, our legislatures
have resolved, our towns have voted; the
crown officers have everywhere trembled,
and all their little tools and creatures been
afraid to speak and ashamed to be seen. ”

Unrest in Boston

The British Parliament reasserted its right to
pass laws governing the colonies in the Declaratory
Act of 1766. The next year Great Britain placed new
taxes on glass, lead, paper, and tea coming into the
colonies. Royal agents trying to enforce these laws
pleaded for British soldiers to protect them from
the angry colonists.

In 1770 the first clash between the Americans
and British troops took place. Two regiments of
British troops had been sent to **Boston** to support the
governor. One evening a squad of soldiers was
harassed by a Boston crowd throwing snowballs and
rotten eggs. Gunfire erupted, and five people died in
what became known as the Boston Massacre.

Because of the unrest in Boston, Parliament
repealed most of the taxes but kept the tax on tea.

COOPERATIVE LEARNING ACTIVITY

Posters Organize the class into small groups to research and make posters about colonial scientists, doctors, and inventors, such as John Lining, John Winthrop, Benjamin Franklin, James Logan,
Benjamin Banneker, Samuel Higby, Thomas Cadwalader, David Rittenhouse, or others that students choose. Ask students to include written information and illustrations about these people's
lives, discoveries, and inventions on their posters. When each group has decided on a subject, the
tasks of research, writing, and illustration should be divided up among group members. Have students display completed posters around the classroom. Allow time for students to examine the
posters and write one interesting fact that they learned from each poster. **L2** 📋

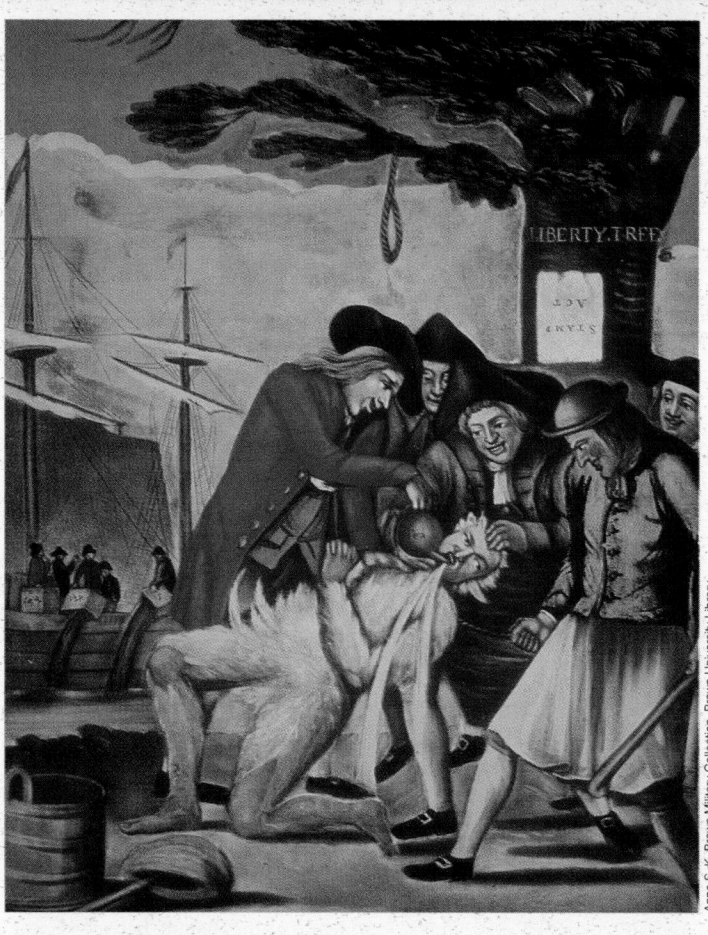

Anne S. K. Brown Military Collection, Brown University Library

Tarred and Feathered

This 1774 British cartoon depicting the tarring and feathering of a British customs officer made a simple point: The American rebels were not men of goodwill simply petitioning for parliamentary representation. The American upstarts, the cartoon implied, were revolutionaries determined to upset the prevailing order in both the Americas and Europe.

In January 1774 a mob took a customs officer named John Malcolm, tarred and feathered him, and then beat him with clubs and ropes until he agreed to speak against His Majesty's government. Even then the mob did not let him go but led him half-naked through the snow for four hours. By then the skin hung off his back in strips and his body was frozen solid—or so the British governor of Massachusetts wrote in his report to the British secretary of state. The men of Massachusetts thus earned a reputation for violence and disorder. The cartoon of Malcolm's ordeal made good anticolonial propaganda in Great Britain, and the idea of hot tar on human flesh still sears our imaginations with the violence of the Revolutionary period. ⊕

Chapter 10 *English and American Revolutions* **325**

TEACH

Tell students that the Boston Tea Party took place on December 16, 1773, and that this British cartoon is a response to that event. Have students carefully examine the cartoon. **What activity is going on in the background?** *(the Boston Tea Party)* **What other colonial protest is referred to in the cartoon?** *(protest against the Stamp Act)* **What do you think the noose hanging from the tree might have symbolized?** *(that the cause of liberty might require that people die)*

Linking Past and Present

Propaganda in the form of cartoons and stories is still used to make an enemy look like a monster and to rally citizens behind a cause. During the Persian Gulf War, stories and cartoons showed Saddam Hussein as a baby killer. Iraqi troops were supposed to have killed Kuwaiti babies by taking them out of incubators and removing the incubators to Iraq. The stories were later found to be incorrect.

Linking Past and Present

Patriots and Minutemen Colonists who favored American independence were called Patriots. New England's minutemen were volunteer soldiers who could be assembled quickly. Today *Minuteman* and *Patriot* continue to be used by the United States military as names for modern missile systems. Patriot missiles helped defeat Iraq in the Persian Gulf War in 1991.

Visualizing History

During the American Revolution, the states and local militias adopted their own flags. The rattlesnake with the warning "Don't Tread on Me" appeared on several of these flags.
Answer to Caption: *At the Congress, leaders from the different colonies met face to face for the first time and were united for a common cause.*

Reteach

Have students make a chart about events that led to the American Revolution. Help them fill in information under the following headings: *Event, Date, What Happened, Outcome of Event.*

Enrich

Have students read a book—fiction or nonfiction—related to events of this section, write a report, and deliver their report orally to the class.

CLOSE

Ask students to imagine they are attending a protest meeting at the Old South Meetinghouse. Assign one or two students to give brief speeches about the "tyranny" of the British, addressing some specific issue, such as the Boston Massacre. Have other students, acting as participants at the meeting, stand up and "speak their minds" about the issues.

Rattlesnake Flag 1776

Visualizing History
The Rattlesnake Flag with 13 alternating red and white stripes warns: "Don't Tread on Me." *What was the significance of the thirteen colonies sending delegates to the First Continental Congress?*

In an effort to keep the British East India Company from going bankrupt, a special law was passed that allowed it to sell tea in the colonies without paying tax. Because their tea could be sold more cheaply, it hurt the business of colonial tea merchants. The Boston colonists decided to retaliate. Disguised as Native Americans, the colonists dumped wooden chests of British tea into Boston Harbor.

The British quickly punished the Massachusetts colonists for the Boston Tea Party by passing what the colonists called the Intolerable Acts. These laws closed Boston Harbor until the tea had been paid for and required colonists to feed and house British soldiers in their homes. The acts also greatly reduced the colonists' right of self-government. Town meetings, for example, could not be held more than once a year without special permission from the royal governor. Parliament also passed the Quebec Act, placing Canada and territories north of the Ohio River under a separate government, thus closing the area to colonists.

The First Continental Congress

The latest repressive measures of the British convinced the thirteen colonies to form a union of resistance. On September 5, 1774, 56 colonial delegates met at **Philadelphia** at the First Continental Congress. The Congress marked an important event in colonial affairs in which leaders from different colonies met face to face. Usually, most colonies considered their differences with Great Britain individually. Now they were united as a group. **Patrick Henry**, a leading statesman from Virginia, commented: "There are no differences between Virginians, Pennsylvanians, New Yorkers, and New Englanders. I am not a Virginian but an American." **George Washington** of Virginia and **Samuel Adams** of Massachusetts were among the leading members of the Congress.

The Congress, which met for more than 7 weeks, resolved that the "English colonists … are entitled to a free and exclusive power of legislation in their several provincial legislatures." In other words, only the colonial assemblies should have the right to make laws in the colonies. Although the Congress recognized Parliament's right to regulate trade, the Congress agreed that the colonies would not import goods from Great Britain after December 1774. After September 1775, they resolved not to send colonial goods to Great Britain.

Many colonists, however, were determined to take more radical steps to end British rule. In every colony a volunteer army was organized and weapons collected. In New England, minutemen (so named because they could be ready for battle on a minute's notice) drilled on village greens, while the town officials stored ammunition, weapons, and food. In the Southern Colonies, planters recruited soldiers at their own expense. It began to appear that the dispute between Great Britain and the colonies would be settled only by force.

SECTION 3 REVIEW

Recall
1. **Define** duty, direct tax, boycott.
2. **Identify** Navigation Acts, French and Indian War, George Grenville, George III, Stamp Act, John Adams, First Continental Congress, Patrick Henry, George Washington, Samuel Adams.
3. **Explain** why relations between Great Britain and the colonies worsened after the French and Indian War.

Critical Thinking
4. **Evaluating Information** Do you think that the British monarch and his ministers were right in expecting the colonists to shoulder the burden of defending the American colonies? What other approaches might Grenville have taken?

Understanding Themes
5. **Conflict** Compare and contrast Parliament's struggles for power with the king with the American colonists' later struggle for control of their own affairs. What were the key issues for Parliament? For the colonists?

SECTION 3 REVIEW ANSWERS

1. All vocabulary words are defined in the Glossary.
2. Navigation Acts, 322; French and Indian War, 322; George Grenville, 323; George III, 323; Stamp Act, 324; John Adams, 324; First Continental Congress, 326; Patrick Henry, 326; George Washington, 326; Samuel Adams, 326
3. The British government began to interfere in colonial affairs and to tax the colonies in order to pay for the war.
4. Answers may include that colonists should have paid something for the French and Indian War, but Grenville should have consulted colonial legislatures about acceptable ways to raise money.
5. **CONFLICT** Both struggles were for more control over the taxing power and for protection of rights. The difference was that Parliament fought to limit the power of the king and change the government, whereas the colonists wanted more representation within the established British government.

Study and Writing SKILLS

Outlining

To sketch a scene, first you would draw the rough shape, or outline, of the picture. Then you would fill in this rough shape with details. Outlining written material is a similar process. You begin with the rough shape of the material and gradually fill in the details.

Learning the Skill

Outlining has two important functions. When studying written material, it helps you identify main ideas and group together related facts. In writing, it helps you put information in a logical order.

There are two kinds of outlines–formal and informal. An informal outline is similar to taking notes. You write only words and phrases needed to remember ideas. Under the main ideas, jot down related but less important details. This kind of outline is useful for reviewing material before a test.

A formal outline has a standard format. In a formal outline, label main heads with Roman numerals, subheads with capital letters, and details with Arabic numerals. Each level would have at least two entries and should be indented from the level above. All entries use the same grammatical form. If one entry is a complete sentence, all other entries at that level must also be complete sentences.

When outlining written material, first read the material to identify the main ideas. In textbooks, section heads provide clues to main topics. Then identify the subheads. Place details supporting or explaining subheads under the appropriate head.

Practicing the Skill

Study the outline below of Chapter 10, Section 1 and then answer these questions.
1. Is this an example of a formal or an informal outline?
2. What are the three main headings?

3. How do subheads under the heading "Commonwealth" relate to this main idea?
4. Give two examples of grammatical consistency in this outline.

    I. Monarchy
      A. James I
        1. Believed in the divine right of kings
        2. Fought with Parliament over money and religion
      B. Charles I
        1. Continued to believe in divine right
        2. Tried to rule without Parliament
        3. Lost the Civil War and was beheaded
    II. Commonwealth
      A. England ruled by Parliament
      B. Army led by Cromwell
   III. Military dictatorship
      A. Headed by Oliver Cromwell
      B. Enforced Puritan rules

Applying the Skill

Write a formal outline for Section 2 of this chapter.

For More Practice

Turn to the Skill Practice in the Chapter Review on page 333 for more practice in outlining.

Oliver Cromwell

Study and Writing SKILLS

TEACH

Outlining On the chalkboard, write the following main headings for an informal outline about activities of a typical school day: *Morning, Afternoon, Evening.* Have students add indented subheads and further indented supporting details under each main head. For example: *At home* and *At school* could be subheads under *Morning. Get up, Get dressed*, and *Eat breakfast* could be details under *At home.* Be sure students have at least two subheads under each head and at least two details under each subhead. Students should maintain grammatical consistency within each level of the outline. Convert students' outline to a formal outline by placing Roman numerals, capital letters, and Arabic numerals in the appropriate places. Then have students read the skill and complete the practice questions.

Additional Practice

📁 Skill Reinforcement Activity 10

📁 Writer's Guidebook, Lesson 11

ANSWERS TO PRACTICING THE SKILL

1. formal outline
2. Monarchy, Commonwealth, Military dictatorship
3. The subheads describe affairs in England during the Commonwealth.
4. The main headings are nouns and the numbered subheads are verb phrases.

1775 British and American forces exchange fire at Lexington and Concord.

1781 British General Cornwallis surrenders at Yorktown.

1783 Great Britain recognizes American independence.

1787 Delegates in Philadelphia write the United States Constitution.

SECTION THEME

▶ **Revolution** The American colonies revolt against Great Britain and form the United States of America.

ind Out ▶

Answer: *At first, the Americans had a weak confederacy, but then they wrote a constitution that set up a federal system with a strong central government.*

FOCUS

Section Objective

Describe the kind of government Americans established after the American Revolution.

BELLRINGER
Motivational Activity

Before taking roll at the beginning of the class period, project Section Focus Transparency 10-4 and have students answer the activity questions. Discuss students' responses.

📁 This activity is also available as a blackline master.

Vocabulary Pre-check

💿 Use the Vocabulary Puzzle-Maker to create a puzzle that reinforces the vocabulary terms in this section. **L1**

Section 4

A War for Independence

Setting the Scene

▶ **Terms to Define**
revolution, confederation, federal system

▶ **People to Meet**
Paul Revere, George Washington, Thomas Paine, Thomas Jefferson

▶ **Places to Locate**
Yorktown

ind Out What kind of government did the Americans establish after the American Revolution?

The Storyteller

Mercy Warren lived through the American Revolution and wrote about its horrors. "The roads [were] filled with frighted women and children; some in carts with their tattered furniture, others on foot fleeing into the woods. But what added greatly to the horrors of the scene, was our passing through the bloody field at Monotong, which was strewed with mangled bodies. We met one affectionate father with a cart, looking for his murdered son.... " She concluded one of her letters, "Be it known unto Britain, even American daughters are politicians and patriots, and will aid the good work with their female efforts."

Powder horn

—adapted from *The Women of the American Revolution*, Elizabeth F. Ellet, 1850

ostilities between the American colonists and the British broke out near Boston in 1775. People there were outraged by the British government. Their seaport was still closed because of the Boston Tea Party, causing many Bostonians to lose their jobs. As British troops filled the city, rumors accusing the "redcoats" of robberies and murders swept through shops, inns, and other meeting places.

Sensing the tension in the city, the British Parliament ordered the governor of Massachusetts, General Thomas Gage, to seize the colonists' military supplies. Before dawn on April 19, 1775, Gage sent a troop of 700 British soldiers to destroy weapons collected in the town of Concord, about 18 miles (29 km) from Boston.

Colonists **Paul Revere** and William Dawes learned of the British plan and rode to warn the colonial minutemen. As the British marched into Lexington on their way to Concord, they found about 70 farmers and villagers blocking their path. When the colonists refused to put down their guns, a shot was fired, though no one knows which side fired first. In the skirmish, British soldiers killed 8 colonists; later at Concord, the "redcoats" held off a sharp attack by more minutemen.

As the British troops marched back toward Boston, colonists fired at them from behind buildings, trees, and stone walls. The next day, almost 300 British soldiers and nearly 100 colonists lay dead. The British were humiliated. No one expected the colonists to be any match for the professional British soldiers.

Moving Toward Separation

News of the colonial attack on the British troops spread throughout the American colonies.

328 **Chapter 10** *English and American Revolutions*

SECTION RESOURCES

📁 **Reproducible Masters**
• Reproducible Lesson Plan 10-4
• Guided Reading Activity 10-4
• People in World History Profile 39
• Reteaching Activity 10
• Enrichment Activity 10
• Section Quiz 10-4

• Performance Assessment Activity 10
• Spanish Chapter Summary 10

📁 **Transparencies**
• Section Focus Transparency 10-4
• Mapping History Overlay Transparency 13

Multimedia
💿 Vocabulary PuzzleMaker Software
💿 Student Self-Test and Review Software
💿 Testmaker

 History & Art *Signing of the Declaration of Independence* by John Trumbull, c. 1825. The Yale University Art Gallery, New Haven, Connecticut **To the British, those who signed the Declaration of Independence committed an act of treason.** *How did the document justify revolution?*

TEACH

Guided Practice

THEME Revolution

Help students arrive at a definition of revolution as used in this section. *(violent overthrow of the government)* Have them explain how the American Revolution fits their definition. **L1 LEP**

When the Second Continental Congress gathered in Philadelphia one month after the battles at Lexington and Concord, it immediately organized an army and named **George Washington** as military commander.

Many colonists, however, still resisted the idea of declaring war on Great Britain. The Congress tried one last time to arrange a peaceful compromise with Parliament and the king. They sent a proposal, called the Olive Branch Petition, to King George III. When the British government refused the petition, chances of a peaceful settlement between Great Britain and the American colonies grew dimmer. To more and more colonists, independence seemed the only answer.

A Call to Part

The most stirring arguments in favor of independence came from the pen of colonist **Thomas Paine**. Paine, who recently had come to the American colonies from Great Britain, wrote a pamphlet called *Common Sense* in January 1776. In it he called upon the colonists to break away from Great Britain. Paine promoted independence for economic, social, and moral reasons:

❝ Every thing that is right begs for separation from [Great] Britain. The Americans who have been killed seem to say, 'TIS TIME TO PART. England and America are located a great distance apart. That is itself strong and natural proof that God never expected one to rule over the other. ❞
—Thomas Paine, *Common Sense*, 1776

Common Sense circulated widely and helped to convince thousands of American colonists that it was "time to part." The delegates to the Congress sensed the changing mood in the colonies and assigned five of their best thinkers and writers to prepare a declaration of independence that would clearly state their resolve.

The Declaration of Independence

Thomas Jefferson, a young Virginian, was the principal author of the colonists' declaration of independence. The document set forth the colonists' reasons for separation from Great Britain. Jefferson, like many other colonial leaders, knew and valued the works of John Locke and other Enlightenment thinkers. He incorporated many of their ideas into the Declaration of Independence.

The Declaration stated that individuals have certain basic rights that cannot be taken away by any government. Focusing on John Locke's concept of the "social contract," the Declaration announced that governments are created by an agreement, or contract, between the rulers and those ruled. If a ruler loses the support of the people by taking away basic rights, the people have a right to change the government through rebellion. The beginning of the Declaration reads:

❝ We hold these truths to be self-evident, that all men are created equal, that they are endowed by their Creator with certain unalienable Rights, that among these are Life, Liberty, and the pursuit of Happiness. That to secure these rights, Governments are instituted among Men, deriving their just powers from the consent of the governed; that whenever any Form of Government becomes destructive of those ends, it is the Right of the People to alter or to abolish it.... ❞

The Declaration continued with a long list of the ways in which Great Britain and George III had

History & Art Trumbull served as George Washington's aide-de-camp during the war and did not start this painting until 1789. To portray Jefferson correctly, Trumbull made sketches of him in France where Jefferson served as United States ambassador.
Answer to Caption: *It said revolution was justified if a ruler took away basic rights of the people, which King George III had.*

Comparison Have students list the advantages and the disadvantages of the Americans and the British during the American Revolution. **L2**

Mapping History Overlay Transparency 13, *European Claims in North America*

Biography

The following videotape programs are available from Glencoe:

• **Paul Revere: The Midnight Rider**

• **Thomas Jefferson: Philosopher of Freedom**

Chapter 10 *English and American Revolutions* **329**

COOPERATIVE LEARNING ACTIVITY

Dramatization Organize the class into two groups and have each group prepare a play dramatizing the debate about and writing of either the Declaration of Independence or the Constitution. Be sure that each student has a task, such as researching Enlightenment ideas that influenced the documents, investigating background information on the main participants who wrote and debated the documents, writing dialogue that includes a discussion of the Enlightenment ideas, or acting in the drama. After each dramatization has been presented, allow the audience to ask questions. **L2**

Independent Practice

 Guided Reading Activity 10-4 **L1**

📂 People in World History Profile 39

Daily Life Have students research the daily routine of American or British soldiers during the American Revolution. Ask them to draw pictures or to write a first-person narrative describing a soldier's experiences. **L2 LEP**

TURNING POINT

United States Government
Why was the formation of the United States government an important event in world history?
Formed in an age of monarchy, the United States was a republic with a written constitution. The Constitution of the United States was an example of a social contract based on popular sovereignty, separation of powers among government branches, and guarantees for protecting citizen's rights. The American republic became a model for people everywhere seeking freedom.

ASSESS

Check for Understanding

Assign Section 4 Review as homework or as an in-class activity.

🖥 Use Student Self-Test and Review Software to review Section 4.

Evaluate

 Section Quiz 10-4

🖥 Use the Testmaker to create a customized quiz for Section 4.

---

abused their power and concludes that "these United Colonies are and of Right ought to be Free and Independent States."

On July 4, 1776, the Congress adopted the Declaration of Independence. A few days later, George Washington had the Declaration read to his troops to inspire them and give them hope as war loomed ahead. Cheers went up from the ranks when the reading was done. That night some of the troops joined a crowd of townspeople who pulled down a statue of George III.

The War for Independence

The Declaration of Independence made a reconciliation with the British impossible. The only course open to the colonists was revolution, the violent overthrow of a government. For the revolutionary leaders, now seen as traitors to the British king, failure would mean death. As Benjamin Franklin said, "Yes, we must, indeed, all hang together, or, most assuredly, we shall all hang separately."

The War of Independence was long and bitter. The Americans did not have an army that could face the British in the open field, but they did have a skillful general in Washington. They also had military help from the French, who wanted to revenge the losses of the Seven Years' War. France, however, did not enter the conflict until American victory seemed certain.

The British had the disadvantage of trying to fight a long-distance war. Also, they had to conquer the whole country to win. The Americans had only to hold out until the British admitted defeat.

The turning point came in October 1777 with a British defeat at Saratoga, New York. The

---

Footnotes to History

"Yankee Doodle" The song "Yankee Doodle" was first sung by the British to mock the American colonists:

"Yankee Doodle came to town,
Riding on a pony;
He stuck a feather in his cap
And called it macaroni."

"Macaroni" was a term used for British men who thought they dressed in style but actually looked ridiculous. The colonists loved the tune and added verses of their own to make it a song of defiance.

American victory persuaded France to come in on the American side. Spain followed in 1779. Faced with a naval war against France and Spain, Great Britain became less interested in defeating its rebellious colonies. In October 1781 the Americans forced the British army to surrender at **Yorktown**, Virginia.

TURNING POINT

United States Government

In 1783 Great Britain recognized American independence. At first, the United States was a confederation, or a loose union of independent states, under the Articles of Confederation. Its central government, however, was too weak to deal effectively with national problems. In 1787 the nation's leaders meeting in Philadelphia wrote the Constitution of the United States, a strong, but flexible, framework for a new national government.

The Constitution

The Constitution set up a federal system, in which political authority was divided between the national government and state governments. It also provided for a separation of powers among the national government's executive, legislative, and judicial branches, an idea that came directly from Montesquieu's *The Spirit of Laws*. A system of checks and balances enabled each branch to limit the power of the other branches.

Under the Constitution, the United States was a republic with an elected president instead of a hereditary monarch. Elections held in 1789 made George Washington the first President of the United States. Yet, at the time, only white males who met certain property qualifications could vote in elections. Among the groups excluded were women, African Americans, and Native Americans. Not until this century would the right to vote—and other civil rights—be extended to all adult Americans.

In 1789, however, the United States was closer to democratic rule than any other country in the world. That same year, a Bill of Rights was added to the Constitution in the form of ten amendments. It affirmed the principle that people had basic liberties that government must protect. These liberties included freedom of religion, speech, and the press, as well as the right to private property and to trial by jury. As in the case of the vote, not all Americans at first had equal protection under the law but would later be included.

MEETING SPECIAL NEEDS ACTIVITY

Study Strategy Have students outline this section using the following Roman numeral heads: *I. The move toward separation, II. The War of Independence, III. The new government.* Help students correctly place the following subheads in the outline: *Olive Branch Petition, Common Sense, Declaration of Independence, American advantages and disadvantages, British advantages and disadvantages, Articles of Confederation, Constitution.* Then have students find at least two details to place under each subhead. **L1**

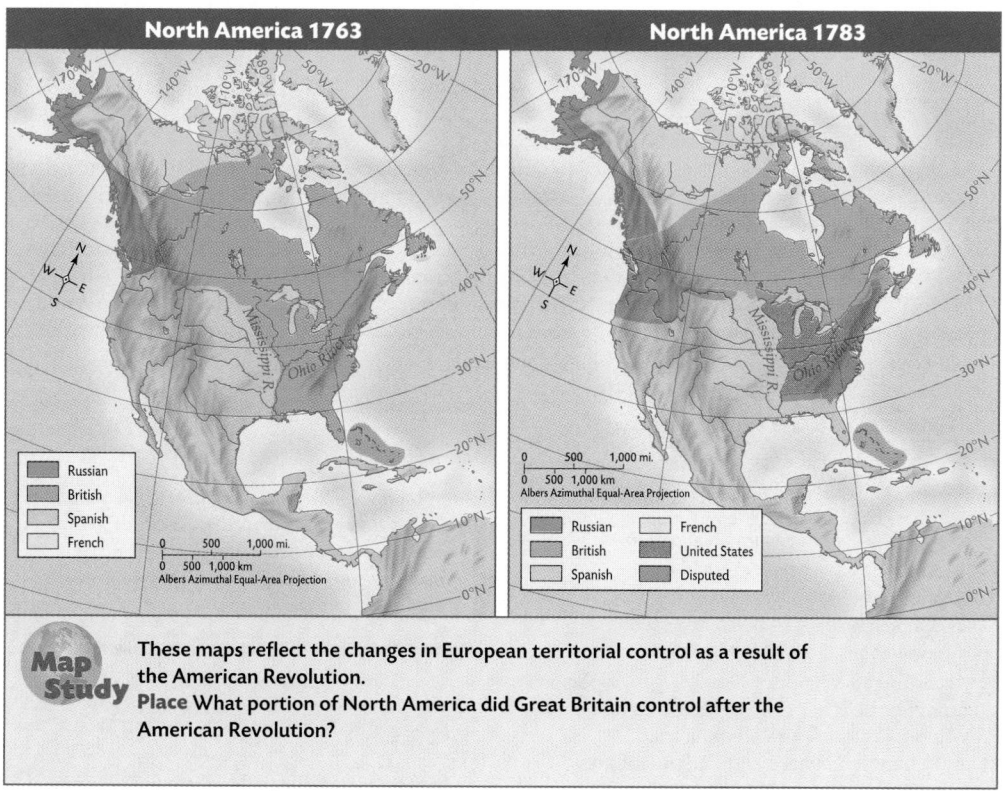

North America 1763

Russian
British
Spanish
French

0   500   1,000 mi.
0 500 1,000 km
Albers Azimuthal Equal-Area Projection

North America 1783

Russian   French
British   United States
Spanish   Disputed

0   500   1,000 mi.
0 500 1,000 km
Albers Azimuthal Equal-Area Projection

Map Study
These maps reflect the changes in European territorial control as a result of the American Revolution.
Place What portion of North America did Great Britain control after the American Revolution?

Map Study

Answer
most of Canada and islands in the Caribbean Sea

Map Skills Practice

Reading a Map What other country had large holdings in North America in 1783? *(Spain)*

Reteach

Have students make a list of the most significant people and events discussed in this section. Then have students compare their lists and discuss the significance of each person and event.

 Reteaching Activity 10

Enrich

Have students research how Locke's ideas (social contract) and Montesquieu's ideas (separation of powers) became part of American political theory.

Enrichment Activity 10

CLOSE

Have students write a brief summary of the events covered in this section. Then have them write what they think is the significance of the events and how those events affect their lives today. Discuss.

The Republic's Significance

The creation of the American republic proved that Enlightenment values could work in practice. Based on the ideas of Locke, Montesquieu, and Rousseau, the Constitution of the United States was an example of a social contract based on the sovereignty of the people, with separation of powers among government branches and guarantees for protecting natural rights. Since their writing, the Constitution and the Declaration of Independence both have inspired peoples throughout the world seeking freedom from oppression. In the 1700s and 1800s, many Europeans and Latin Americans appealed to these American documents of liberty in ending absolute monarchy and creating new forms of government. In the 1900s people in many lands throughout the world did the same in their struggles against empires and dictators.

SECTION 4 REVIEW

Recall
1. **Define** revolution, confederation, federal system.
2. **Identify** Paul Revere, George Washington, Thomas Paine, Thomas Jefferson, the Declaration of Independence.
3. **Explain** the basic message of the Declaration of Independence. Why did the American colonists believe the Declaration was necessary?

Critical Thinking
4. **Evaluating Information** Do you think that if Great Britain had treated the colonists differently, they would have been content to remain under British rule? Support your answer.

Understanding Themes
5. **Revolution** Compare the Americans' attempts to organize a new form of government with those of the English after executing King Charles I. Did both governments ensure representation and individual rights?

Chapter 10 *English and American Revolutions* 331

SECTION 4 REVIEW ANSWERS

1. All vocabulary words are defined in the Glossary.
2. Paul Revere, 328; George Washington, 329; Thomas Paine, 329; Thomas Jefferson, 329; Declaration of Independence, 329
3. Individuals have basic rights that government cannot take away. Because the king had taken basic rights from the colonists, they had the right to rebel; they couldn't tolerate the British government any longer.
4. Answers may vary. Possible answer: If the British government had compromised, the Americans would not have revolted.
5. **REVOLUTION** After the English Civil War, Cromwell suspended Parliament, became a military dictator, and placed the people under strict laws. After the American Revolution, Congress wrote a new Constitution to which they added the Bill of Rights to protect individual liberties.

Chapter 10 Review

GLENCOE TECHNOLOGY

VIDEODISC
Use MindJogger to review students' knowledge of the chapter.

MindJogger Videoquiz

Chapter 10
Disc 1 Side B

 Also available in VHS.

Answers

Using Key Terms

1. a   **4.** i
2. b   **5.** e
3. l

Using Your History Journal

Suggest that students examine bylaws or constitutions from several school or community organizations as models for their key ideas.

Reviewing Facts

1. royal powers were limited and certain individual rights were guaranteed
2. Harsh Puritan rule made the English people eager to restore the monarchy.
3. Both parties united against James II and invited William and Mary of Orange to rule England according to laws of Parliament.
4. Causes: Quarrels over religion, taxes, and royal power between Stuart monarchs and Parliament; Effects: temporary creation of republic; long-term limits on royal power and emergence of parliamentary supremacy; England became a constitutional monarchy with royal powers limited and Parliament supreme
5. Causes: rift between England and colonies over taxation, representation, and trade; Effects: U. S.

Connections Across Time

Historical Significance The English and American Revolutions helped to establish the rights of citizens within a representative government. In England, and later Great Britain, the monarchy steadily lost power, Parliament became supreme, and legal documents guaranteed certain individual rights.

In the United States, the colonists established a republic with a written constitution, separation of powers, and an elected president. The Bill of Rights spelled out the rights of individual citizens that government could not violate. The American Revolution would become a source of inspiration to people seeking freedom throughout the world.

Using Key Terms

Write the key term that completes each sentence. Then write a sentence for each term not chosen.

  a. habeas corpus   g. constitutional monarchy
  b. divine right   h. federal system
  c. duty   i. royalists
  d. prime minister   j. direct tax
  e. commonwealth   k. confederation
  f. revolution   l. martial law

1. According to the principle of _____, a person cannot be held in prison by the government without just cause or without a trial.
2. A rift between James I and Parliament grew deeper when the king publicly professed his belief in _____.
3. During times of _____, military authorities are given temporary rule and individual rights are limited.
4. In the English Civil War, supporters of the monarchy were known as _____.
5. When the monarchy was abolished in 1649, England became a _____, a state governed by elected representatives.

Technology Activity

Using the Internet Access the Internet to locate a Web site about the history of the English Civil War. Use a search engine to help focus your search by using words such as *charles I*, *oliver cromwell* or *english civil war*. Based on your research, write a position paper addressing whether you agree that monarchs should have divine right, or whether parliament should have more control over government policy, raising money, and reforms in the Church of England.

Using Your History Journal

From your list of key ideas that should be the basis of government, write a short constitution or structure for governing a small group—a club, voluntary organization, or a community.

Reviewing Facts

1. Government/Citizenship State the changes brought by the English Bill of Rights.
2. Government Discuss how the military rule of Oliver Cromwell helped set the stage for the Restoration in 1660.
3. Government Describe the Glorious Revolution.
4. History Identify the causes and effects of the English Civil War. How did it change England? How did it later affect America?
5. History State the causes and effects of the American Revolution. What was its impact?

Critical Thinking

1. Apply What political ideas transformed England and America during the 1600s and 1700s? Are these ideas relevant today? Explain.
2. Contrast How has American voting changed since the 1700s? What factors do you think have brought about this change?
3. Evaluate How were the ideas of separation of powers and checks and balances applied to the government of the United States? Why were these ideas adopted by the framers of the Constitution? How do they affect you today?

---

became an independent republic and model for others struggling for freedom

Critical Thinking

1. social contract theory, government by the people, separation of powers, constitutional government; these ideas are at the heart of modern democratic government
2. The vote was limited to white males with certain property qualifications; today the franchise has been extended to include all adult Americans. Changes have come about through the belief in equality for all citizens.
3. The federal government was divided into legislative, executive, and judicial branches. Checks and balances allowed each branch to limit the powers of the other branches.
4. John Locke's ideas about the social contract was the basis of the Declaration of Independence.

4. Synthesize How did the Enlightenment influence the American Revolution?

Geography in History

1. Region Refer to the map below. One of Great Britain's major challenges in the American Revolution was to control rebellion over a wide area. How far is it from the Battle of Saratoga to the Battle of Camden, South Carolina?

2. Movement Why did most British troop movement from one location to another occur by sea?

3. Region The dates and stars identify major Revolutionary battles. How do these battles indicate a shift in the region of the most significant battles from the earliest to the latest period?

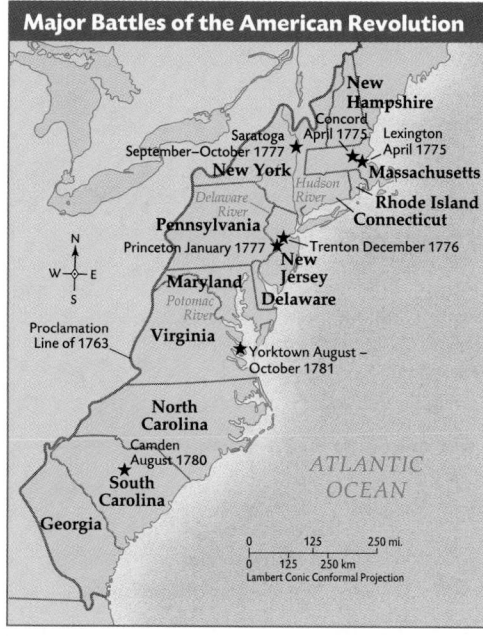

Major Battles of the American Revolution

ATLANTIC OCEAN

New Hampshire · Concord April 1775 · Lexington April 1775 · Saratoga September–October 1777 · New York · Massachusetts · Hudson River · Delaware River · Rhode Island · Connecticut · Pennsylvania · Princeton January 1777 · New Jersey · Trenton December 1776 · Maryland · Potomac River · Delaware · Proclamation Line of 1763 · Virginia · Yorktown August–October 1781 · North Carolina · Camden August 1780 · South Carolina · Georgia

N W E S

0 125 250 mi.
0 125 250 km
Lambert Conic Conformal Projection

Understanding Themes

1. Conflict What factors caused the conflict between Parliament and the Stuart monarchs?

2. Change Why do you think the English restored the monarchy after the Commonwealth? What changes came to the monarchy after 1660?

---

3. Conflict How did the British punish Massachusetts colonists after the Boston Tea Party?

4. Revolution Why did the American Revolution lead to a stable republic in the colonies, while the English Civil War did not do so in England?

Linking Past and Present

1. Some of the Revolutionary quarrels concerned taxes. In what ways does the United States today struggle with the issue of fair taxation?

2. After 1945, many peoples won their freedom from Great Britain. Compare their struggles with that of Americans in the 1700s.

3. The United States and Great Britain today are both democracies. How are their governments similar? How are they different? To what extent do they base their political principles on the events of the 1600s and 1700s?

Skill Practice

Complete the following formal outline for Section 3, "Road to Revolt."

I. Great Britain's American Empire
  A. Economic relationship between Great Britain and colonies
  B. _____
    1. Some colonial products exported only to Great Britain
    2. _____
    3. No foreign-made ships in colonies
II. _____
  A. Structure of colonial governments
    1. _____
    2. Elected assemblies
  B. Early power struggles
    1. Limited salaries of officials
    2. _____
III. Tightening British Control
  A. Effects of French and Indian War
    1. _____
    2. _____
  B. Stamp Acts
IV. _____
  A. Boston Massacre
  B. _____
  C. First Continental Congress

---

the Americans worked together to form a stable government. After the English Civil War, Cromwell ruled as a dictator.

Linking Past and Present

1. Congress makes some changes in the tax laws in response to various groups' calls for fairness.

2. Some places in the British Empire (Canada), achieved independence gradually and without revolution, while other places (India and Kenya), engaged in some kind of struggle.

3. Both have representative governments. Britain has a constitutional monarchy; the U.S. is headed by a president. Both are influenced by Enlightenment ideas.

Skill Practice

I.B. Navigation Acts
I.B.2. All goods going to colonies first pass through Great Britain
II. Colonial Political Power
II.A.1. Governors appointed by king
II.B.2. Had right to approve taxes requested by the Crown or governors
III.A.1. Land west of the Appalachians closed to colonists
III.A.2. Navigation Acts enforced
IV. Events Leading to War
IV.B. Intolerable Acts

? Chapter Bonus Test Question

Ask students: Why did England reestablish the monarchy after the Civil War while the Americans set up a constitutional government after their revolution? *(Between the English Civil War and the American Revolution, the Enlightenment occurred that brought forth Locke's and Montesquieu's ideas about government.)*

Geography in History

1. about 700 miles [about 1,126 kilometers]
2. It was easier and faster to move by sea.
3. They show that the war started in the northern colonies and moved south.

Understanding Themes

1. **CONFLICT** The Stuart monarchs believed in the divine right of kings, and Parliament thought the monarch's powers

---

should be limited by law. Parliament and the Stuarts also had conflicts over religion.

2. **CHANGE** They were tired of conflicts in Parliament and of harsh Puritan rule; it became a constitutional monarchy.

3. **CONFLICT** passed the Intolerable Acts, required colonists to quarter British soldiers, reduced self-government, and closed land north of Ohio River

4. **REVOLUTION** After the Revolution,

A complete, 1-page lesson plan is provided for each section in the *Reproducible Lesson Plans* booklet.

The French Revolution

CHAPTER RESOURCES

	Reproducible Resources	Multimedia Resources
Chapter Opener	Chapter Themes: Graphic Organizer 11 Historical Significance Chapter Activity 11	MindJogger Videoquiz
Chapter Enrichment	Vocabulary Activity 11* Time Line Activity 11 Mapping History Activity 11 History Simulation 11 Geography and History Activity 11 Source Reading 11 People in World History Profiles 41, 42 World Literature Selection 5 World Art and Music Activity 11 Enrichment Activity 11 Critical Thinking Activity 11 Skill Reinforcement Activity 11 Building Skills in Geography Workbook, Unit 2, Lesson 8 Performance Assessment Activity 11	World History and Art Transparency 29, *Napoleon Crossing the Alps* Mapping History Overlay Transparency 14, *France and Europe* Chapter Transparency 11 Vocabulary PuzzleMaker Software Turning Points in World History: *French Revolution*
Chapter Review/Reteaching	Reteaching Activity 11 Skill Reinforcement Activity 11 Spanish Chapter Summary 11	Chapter 11 Digest Audiocassette, Activity, Test* Vocabulary PuzzleMaker Software Student Self-Test and Review Software MindJogger Videoquiz
Chapter Evaluation/Testing	Performance Assessment Activity 11 Chapter 11 Test, Forms A and B	Testmaker

* *Also available in Spanish*

0:00 OUT OF TIME? Assign the Chapter 11 summary in the Unit 3 Digest on pages 367–369, and the Chapter 11 Audiocassettes.

Block Schedule

Block scheduling differs from traditional class scheduling in the amount of time allotted to each period. The extended time frame provided by block scheduling affords you the opportunity to implement a greater number of research-oriented and activity-intense projects to motivate and involve your students. Activities that are particularly suited to use within the block scheduling framework are identified throughout this chapter by the following designation.

KEY TO ABILITY LEVELS

Teaching strategies have been coded for varying learning styles and abilities.

L1 **BASIC** activities for all students
L2 **AVERAGE** activities for average to above-average students
L3 **CHALLENGING** activities for above-average students
LEP **LIMITED ENGLISH PROFICIENCY** activities

Use Glencoe's *Presentation Plus!* multimedia teacher tool to easily present dynamic lessons that visually excite your students. Using Microsoft PowerPoint® you can customize the presentations to create your own personalized lessons.

SECTION RESOURCES

Daily Objectives	Reproducible Resources	Multimedia Resources
Section 1 **The Old Order** Explain how France's class structure contributed to the French Revolution.	Reproducible Lesson Plan 11-1 Vocabulary Activity 11* Guided Reading Activity 11-1* Time Line Activity 11 People in World History Profile 41 Section Quiz 11-1*	Section Focus Transparency 11-1 Chapter Transparency 11 Student Self-Test and Review Software Testmaker Turning Points in World History: *French Revolution*
Section 2 **Constitutional Government** List the political reforms the National Assembly adopted for France.	Reproducible Lesson Plan 11-2 Vocabulary Activity 11* Guided Reading Activity 11-2* Source Reading 11 Section Quiz 11-2*	Section Focus Transparency 11-2 Student Self-Test and Review Software Testmaker Turning Points in World History: *French Revolution*
Section 3 **Dawn of a New Era** Explain why the French Revolution led to war between France and its neighbors.	Reproducible Lesson Plan 11-3 Vocabulary Activity 11* Guided Reading Activity 11-3* History Simulation 11 People in World History Profile 42 Section Quiz 11-3*	Section Focus Transparency 11-3 Student Self-Test and Review Software Testmaker Turning Points in World History: *French Revolution*
Section 4 **Napoleon's Empire** Relate how Napoleon built and then lost an empire.	Reproducible Lesson Plan 11-4 Vocabulary Activity 11* Guided Reading Activity 11-4* Geography and History Activity 11 World Art and Music Activity 11 Section Quiz 11-4*	Section Focus Transparency 11-4 World History and Art Transparency 29, *Napoleon Crossing the Alps* Mapping History Overlay Transparency 14, *France and Europe* Student Self-Test and Review Software Testmaker
Section 5 **Peace in Europe** Evaluate the success of the plans of the reactionaries to thwart the spread of liberalism in Europe.	Reproducible Lesson Plan 11-5 Guided Reading Activity 11-5* Reteaching Activity 11 Enrichment Activity 11 Section Quiz 11-5* Performance Assessment Activity 11 Spanish Chapter Summary 11	Section Focus Transparency 11-5 Mapping History Overlay Transparency 14, *France and Europe* Vocabulary PuzzleMaker Software Student Self-Test and Review Software Testmaker

* Also available in Spanish

Chapter Activities

✔ Performance Assessment Activity

A Concerned Citizen Speaks to the Government This chapter provides an example of how isolated incidents of conflict can spread. Ask students to think of analogous situations today (for example, gangs, crime families, political factions). Have each student assume the role of a citizen who is concerned about one of these situations and would like to bring its seriousness to the attention of the city council, state legislature, or United Nations. In their speeches, students should refer to the French Revolution for historical perspective, making connections with details in their modern-day examples. Have students deliver their speeches to collaborative groups of eight, with the listeners assuming the roles of members of the body being addressed.

Possible Rubric Features

Concept attainment, research skills, ability to make connections, clarity and impact of speech, accuracy of content information, appropriateness of speech to audience

• *For an additional activity, refer to Activity 11 in the* Performance Assessment Strategies and Activities *booklet.*

ACTIVITY

From the Classroom of...

**Susan E. Szachowicz
Brockton High School
Brockton, MA**

The Congress of Vienna Convenes

Organize the class into five groups, representing Austria, Great Britain, Russia, Prussia, and France, and direct each group to select one spokesperson to be Metternich, Castlereagh, Alexander I, Frederick William III, and Talleyrand. Provide each group with an overview of the Congress and its purpose; information specific to their country, which includes their delegate's role at the Congress and their country's goals, vital interests, and demands, and an outline map of Europe at the height of Napoleon's power. Each group should now develop their lists of demands and redraw the map of Europe as they would like to see it. Then convene the Congress by having the representative from each group offer their proposals and maps to the entire class. Questioning and negotiating should proceed until a plan acceptable to all is developed. Finally, the class plan should be compared to the actual decision made at the Congress of Vienna and similarities and differences noted.

MULTIPLE LEARNING STYLES

Verbal/Linguistic
Have students research and then debate the following question: Was Napoleon's legacy positive or negative?

Logical/Mathematical
Have students create a time line of major events that occurred during the French Revolution.

Visual/Spatial
Students may create a comic book that chronicles the life of a French peasant family living outside Paris at the time of the French Revolution. Each section should focus on a particular event that occurred in Paris between 1789 and 1815.

Kinesthetic
Have students draw a large outline map of Europe and hang it on the bulletin board. Using thumbtacks and labels, identify locations of major events during the French Revolution.

Additional Resources

NATIONAL GEOGRAPHIC SOCIETY

Teacher's Corner

INDEX TO NATIONAL GEOGRAPHIC MAGAZINE

The following articles may be used for research relating to this chapter:

- *France: Bicentennial of the Great Revolution, Special Issue,* July 1989.
- "Two Revolutions," by Charles McCarry, July 1989.
- "Napoleon," by John J. Putman, February 1982.

NATIONAL GEOGRAPHIC SOCIETY PRODUCTS AVAILABLE FROM GLENCOE

To order the following products for use with this chapter, contact your local Glencoe sales representative, or call Glencoe at 1-800-334-7344:

- *Picture Atlas of the World (CD-ROM)*

ADDITIONAL NATIONAL GEOGRAPHIC SOCIETY PRODUCTS

To order the following products for use with this chapter, call National Geographic Society at 1-800-368-2728:

- *Democratic Government Series, "France." (Video)*

BIBLIOGRAPHY

Literature of the Period
Dickens, Charles. *A Tale of Two Cities.* New York: Dutton, 1970. A romantic novel that takes place during the French Revolution.
Readings for the Student
Forester, C. S. *Mr. Midshipman Hornblower.* Boston: Little, Brown, 1940. The first of eleven sea stories set in the era of the Napoleonic Wars.
Readings for the Teacher
Evenson, Norma. *Paris: A Century of Change, 1878–1978.* New Haven: Yale University Press, 1979. Historical and social changes in France as reflected in the city of Paris, from its rebuilding under Napoleon III.

LOCAL OBJECTIVES

_____
_____
_____
_____
_____
_____
_____
_____
_____
_____
_____
_____
_____
_____
_____
_____
_____
_____
_____
_____
_____
_____
_____

interNET CONNECTION
French Revolution resources on the World Wide Web
The French Revolution:
http://www.powerup.com.au/~rdale/rev.htm

CHAPTER THEMES

Chapter Themes are listed by section on this chapter opening page of the Student Edition. A corresponding theme-based activity is available under "TEACH," and a theme-based question is asked in the Section and Chapter Reviews.

The Storyteller

Historical Setting Marie-Victoire Monnard was one of 15 children in her family. She was also one of thousands of young women who sewed hats and dresses in workshops throughout Paris. Like many of them, she lived in a dormitory for seamstresses.

Monnard is writing during a phase of the French Revolution called the Reign of Terror. From September 1793 to July 1794, revolutionaries declared a policy of terror against anyone who publicly disagreed with their policies. In time, hundreds of thousands of suspects filled French jails, and revolutionary courts handed down more than 17,000 death sentences.

Historical Significance

Answers: *Waves of violence and bloodshed swept across France during the revolution. In time, people became desensitized to the cruelties.*

The French Revolution destroyed the entire structure of royal absolutism and ended the social order based on aristocratic privilege. It set the stage for democratic movements around the world during the next century.

Chapter
11
1700–1830
The French Revolution

Chapter Themes

▶ **Revolution** The French overthrow their absolute monarchy. *Section 1*
▶ **Change** The National Assembly establishes a constitutional government. *Section 2*
▶ **Conflict** The new French Republic faces enemies at home and abroad. *Section 3*
▶ **Movement** Napoleon becomes France's emperor and conquers much of Europe. *Section 4*
▶ **Reaction** European leaders try to reestablish the old order. *Section 5*

The Storyteller

In 1792 the violence of the French Revolution filled the streets of Paris, where a young seamstress named Marie-Victoire Monnard lived and worked. Walking back to her workshop one afternoon, Marie-Victoire saw six large carts coming toward her. The 13-year-old girl later wrote in her diary, "The carts were full of men and women who had just been slaughtered … legs and arms and heads nodded and dangled on either side of the carts."

The next year she wrote again about the carts, "People just went on working in the shops when they passed by, often not even bothering to raise their heads to watch or to turn their backs to avoid the grisly sight."

Historical Significance

What happened during the French Revolution that allowed people to become accustomed to the bloodied bodies? How did the French Revolution alter society in Europe? What lasting effects did it have on the rest of the world?

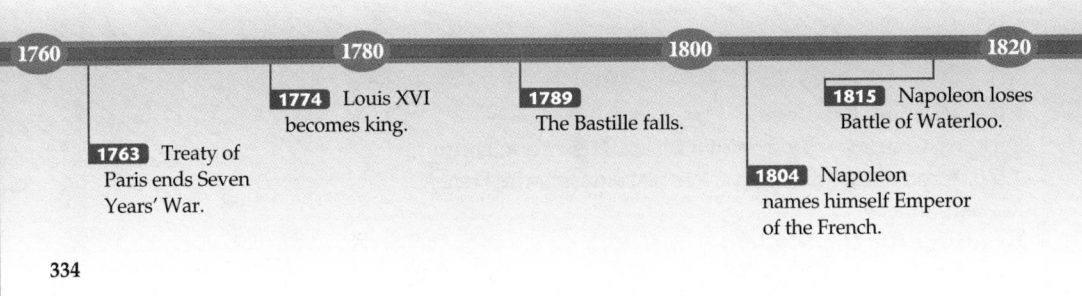

1760	1780	1800	1820

1763 Treaty of Paris ends Seven Years' War.

1774 Louis XVI becomes king.

1789 The Bastille falls.

1804 Napoleon names himself Emperor of the French.

1815 Napoleon loses Battle of Waterloo.

334

GEOGRAPHY CONNECTION

Location Have students locate France, England, Spain, the Netherlands, and their capitals on a map in the Atlas of their textbook. What is the distance from Paris to each of these capitals? Have students compare these distances to those between Washington, D.C., and Cleveland, Ohio; and New York City and Dallas, Texas. How did geography affect relations among these nations in Europe? *(Because the nations were so close together, anything that one nation did affected its neighbors. National rivalries were intense.)* **L2**

History & Art *Assault on the Bastille,* (artist unknown)
Musée National du Chateau de Versailles, Versailles, France

History & Art On July 14, 1789, an angry mob stormed the Bastille, a Paris prison. Bastille Day is a national holiday in France, much like July 4th in the United States, because the revolt that followed overthrew the French monarchy. What evidence of violence does the painting contain? *(The mob has weapons, there are bodies on the ground, and there is smoke in the air.)*

Performance Assessment

Refer to the activity on page 334C of the Planning Guide.

For an additional activity, refer to Activity 11 in the *Performance Assessment Strategies and Activities* booklet.

Your History Journal

Imagine living through the tumultuous events of the French Revolution. Choose a point of view represented by one of the following: a Catholic bishop, a landed aristocrat, a wealthy merchant, a poor artisan, or a peasant. From your chosen viewpoint, describe your reactions to three major events of the times as you read the chapter.

Using Your History Journal

Journal entries may be in diary form. Have students keep a diary of their reactions to various events of the French Revolution.

GLENCOE **TECHNOLOGY**

VIDEODISC
Use MindJogger to preview chapter content.

MindJogger Videoquiz

Chapter 11
Disc 2 Side A

Also available in VHS.

Chapter 11   *The French Revolution*   **335**

✚ EXTRA CREDIT PROJECT

Report Interesting events and first-person accounts of the French Revolution are available in many books. Have students research and report to the class on an event of the French Revolution that is not detailed in the chapter. Suggest that students use vivid quotations from the first-person accounts. **L1**

1774 Louis XVI becomes king of France.

1786 Banks refuse to lend money to the government.

1789 Great Fear breaks out.

SECTION THEME

▶ **Revolution** The French overthrow their absolute monarchy.

ind Out

Answer: *The great inequalities led to resentment among the people.*

FOCUS

Section Objective

Explain how France's class structure contributed to the French Revolution.

BELLRINGER
Motivational Activity

Before taking roll at the beginning of the class period, project Section Focus Transparency 11-1 and have students answer the activity questions. Discuss students' responses.

📁 This activity is also available as a blackline master.

Vocabulary Pre-check

📁 Use Vocabulary Activity 11 to introduce vocabulary terms.
L1 LEP

Section 1

The Old Order

Setting the Scene

▶ **Terms to Define**
  estate, tithe, bourgeoisie

▶ **People to Meet**
  Louis XVI, Marie Antoinette

▶ **Places to Locate**
  Versailles, Paris, the Bastille

ind Out
Why was France's class system a cause of the French Revolution?

𝒮toryteller

Fear tightened young Claudette Leroux's throat as she waited for the questioning. She could not deny that she was smuggling salt. She could only explain that the gabelle—the tax on salt—made the cost ten times what it should be. French peasants simply could not afford the Farmers General's prices. She wondered who gave these corrupt officials the power to store, inspect, tax, register, and force people to buy their salt. Did anyone understand the peasants' plight?

—adapted from *Citizens: A Chronicle of the French Revolution*, Simon Schama, 1989

Peasant woman's burden

At its height, the absolute monarchy in France controlled the richest and possibly the most powerful state in Europe. The French aristocracy set European trends in literature, clothing, art, and ideas for change. Yet the majority of the people did not share the wealth or privileges of the aristocracy. Working men and women who had few rights yearned for a better way of life. The success of the American Revolution fueled their desire for change.

French Society Divided

The source of the unhappiness lay within France's class system, which fostered great inequalities among the French people. All French people belonged to one of three estates, or orders of society. The estates determined a person's legal rights and status. The Catholic clergy formed the First Estate. The nobility formed the Second Estate. Everyone else, 97 percent of the French people, made up the Third Estate.

Members of the Third Estate deeply resented the privileges that members of the First and Second Estates enjoyed. For example, neither the First Estate nor the Second Estate was required to pay taxes. The nobility received high positions in the Church, in the government, and in the army, and they could also hunt and carry swords. Third Estate members enjoyed none of these social and political privileges. No matter how successful and well-educated Third Estate members became, they were always excluded from the First and Second Estates—simply because of the families into which they were born.

The First Estate
The First Estate consisted of Roman Catholic clergy and made up about 1 percent of the population. The First Estate comprised two groups: the higher clergy and the lower clergy.

336   **Chapter 11**   *The French Revolution*

SECTION RESOURCES

📁 **Reproducible Masters**
- Reproducible Lesson Plan 11-1
- Vocabulary Activity 11
- Guided Reading Activity 11-1
- Time Line Activity 11
- People in World History Profile 41
- Section Quiz 11-1

📑 **Transparencies**
- Section Focus Transparency 11-1
- Chapter Transparency 11

Multimedia
- Student Self-Test and Review Software
- Testmaker
- Turning Points in World History: *French Revolution*

The City and Port of Tolone (Toulon) by Joseph Vernet. The Louvre, Paris, France **The bourgeoisie in French cities enjoyed wealth and leisure, but few political rights.** *Where had they learned about freedom and social justice?*

Bishops and abbots, noblemen by birth, made up the higher clergy. These powerful men controlled between 5 and 10 percent of the land in France and enjoyed many privileges. At their disposal were the revenues from their land as well as a tithe, or a 10 percent tax on income, from each church member. Although this money was used to support schools, aid poor people, and maintain church property, it also paid for the grand lifestyles the higher clergy enjoyed, often at the expense of their religious duties.

The lower clergy, made up of parish priests, came from poorer backgrounds and were socially more a part of the Third Estate. Many lower clergy members who carried out religious duties, ran schools, and cared for the poor resented the luxurious lifestyles of the higher clergy.

The Second Estate

The nobility, the Second Estate, formed about 2 percent of the population and owned about 25 percent of the land in France. Like the upper clergy, the members of the Second Estate enjoyed many privileges and lived in great style.

The nobility held high posts in the government and the military. Some resided in the palace at **Versailles**. Others lived in lavish homes on inherited land, some of which they rented to peasants to farm. The Second Estate's main income came from the feudal dues they collected from the peasants who lived on and worked their land.

The Third Estate

The Third Estate made up the largest social group in France during the late 1700s. Peasants and artisans, as well as members of the bourgeoisie (BURZH•WAH•ZEE), or middle class, belonged to the Third Estate. Yet they had very few political rights or privileges.

The doctors, lawyers, merchants, and business managers of the bourgeoisie generally lived in the towns and cities. Educated and well-to-do, they had read Enlightenment works and believed in freedom and social justice.

Other members of the Third Estate, such as thousands of poor artisans and their families, also lived in the cities. Artisans worked for low wages and in poor working conditions. Many lived in the slums of **Paris**.

The peasants, the Third Estate's largest group, lived in rural areas. Although they owned 40 percent of the land, they were very poor because of the payments they had to make to the other estates. These payments included a tithe to the clergy; feudal dues and fines to the nobles; and a land tax to the king. Although members of the Third Estate worked hard, they had no effective voice in the government.

Growing Unrest

Unhappy with this unfair social structure, the people of the Third Estate began to call for change. An Englishman traveling in France saw this growing unrest reflected in a conversation he had with a peasant woman:

> ❝ Walking up a long hill … I was joined by a poor woman who complained of the times, and that it was a sad country; … she said her husband had but a morsel of land, one cow, and a poor little horse, yet they had [42 lbs.] of wheat and three chickens to pay as rent to one [lord], and [4 lbs.] of oats, one chicken and 1s. [shilling] to pay to another, besides very heavy tailles and other taxes. ❞
>
> —Arthur Young, from *Travels*, 1789

Chapter 11 *The French Revolution* **337**

TEACH

Guided Practice

THEME Revolution

Ask students to brainstorm definitions of the term *revolution*. When are people justified in choosing revolution as a solution to political problems? **L1**

History & Art Toulon, on the southeast coast of France, is the principal site of modern-day France's Mediterranean fleet. **Answer to Caption:** *They had read Enlightenment works.*

VIDEODISC
Turning Points in World History

Side One
Chapter 11

Title: *French Revolution*
Ask: Why was 1789 considered "the best of times" for some and "the worst of times" for others in France? *(It was the best of times for the clergy and nobility because they had power and privileges while paying no taxes. It was the worst of times for peasants who went hungry and paid high taxes.)*

Religion Ask students to define the phrase "separation of church and state." *(Religions do not have a formal say in government decisions, and the government has no control over religions.)* Then discuss the relationship between church and state in France and its results. **L3**

COOPERATIVE LEARNING ACTIVITY

Debate Explain that the French government faced heavy debt in 1789. To pay the debt, the king wanted to increase taxes. The clergy and nobility had been exempt from taxation. Would they accept some of the burden now? Organize students into three groups, representing the First, Second, and Third Estates. Each group should prepare a statement and choose a person to present its position on taxation. Allow time for discussion, then vote on each proposal for tax apportionment. Each estate receives one vote. Members of each estate must arrive at a consensus before voting. **L3**

Chapter Transparency 11

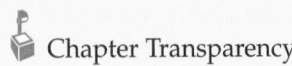

The following videotape program is available from Glencoe:

- **Marie Antoinette: Tragic Queen**

Independent Practice

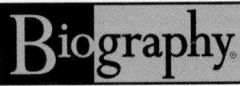 Guided Reading Activity 11-1 **L1**

Time Line Activity 11

People in World History Profile 41

Who?What?Where?When?

French aid to the American Revolution represented a large portion of the French government's debt in 1788. Between 1776 and 1781, France lent the American government almost 19 million livres, or about $6 million.

Linking Past and Present

Tricolor The French revolutionaries established the red, white, and blue flag, called the tricolor, that France continues to use today.

ASSESS

Check for Understanding
Assign Section 1 Review as homework or as an in-class activity.

Use Student Self-Test and Review Software to review Section 1.

As a growing population put increasing demands on resources, and the cost of living in France increased, the peasants' anger rose. Nobles also charged the peasants higher fees for the use of such equipment as mills and wine presses.

At the same time, artisans in the cities faced higher prices while their wages stayed the same. Members of the bourgeoisie also wanted change. Although they were prosperous, they wanted more political power. Nobles, too, were unhappy. They resented the king's absolute power and wanted to increase their political influence in the government.

A growing financial crisis in government only added to the country's problems. The 1700s had begun with debts from the wars waged by Louis XIV. The extravagant court of Louis XV had further enlarged this debt.

In 1774 Louis XV's 19-year-old grandson followed his grandfather to the throne as **Louis XVI**. His wife, **Marie Antoinette**, was a year younger. In spite of his inexperience, the young king recognized the growing financial crisis. Supporting the American Revolution had only increased his debt. After initiating government cost-cutting measures, Louis decided that he had no choice but to begin taxing the nobility and the clergy. Both groups, however, refused to be taxed.

By 1786 banks began to refuse to lend money to the ailing government. The economy suffered a further blow when crop failures caused bread shortages in 1788 and 1789. When the privileged classes refused to aid the government, Louis made a bold choice. He summoned the Estates-General to meet in May 1789 in Versailles. Only in this way could he get additional taxes.

Calling the Estates Together

The Estates-General, which had not met since 1614, was made up of delegates representing each estate. The king hoped that the gathering would agree to new taxes on the First and Second Estates. The nobles, however, intended to use the Estates-General to protect their privileges, weaken royal power, and gain control of the government. Because each estate in the Estates-General had a single vote, the nobles hoped that the First and Second Estates together could easily dominate the Third Estate.

Members of the Third Estate refused this plan. Claiming that they had more right to represent the nation than either the clergy or the nobles, Third Estate delegates called for a joint meeting of the three estates, with each delegate voting as an individual. The Third Estate was as large as the other

---

two combined, and many reform-minded nobles and clergymen supported their views. A mass meeting would give the Third Estate a majority vote. A clergy member who supported the Third Estate, the Abbé Sieyès (see•AY•YEHS), wrote:

❝ Therefore, what is the Third Estate? Everything; but an everything shackled and oppressed. What would it be without the privileged order? Everything, but an everything free and flourishing. Nothing can succeed without it, everything would be infinitely better without the others. ❞

The king, however, insisted that the estates meet separately. Refusing the king's demands, the representatives of the Third Estate, most of whom were members of the bourgeoisie, were eventually locked out of the Estates-General. They named themselves the National Assembly and gathered at a nearby indoor tennis court with deputies from the other estates who supported their cause. Here the representatives took an oath, known as the Tennis Court Oath, promising not to disband until they had written a constitution for France.

The king recognized the danger of letting the Third Estate alone draw up a constitution. He ordered the first two estates to join the Third Estate in the National Assembly. Fearing trouble, he also called for troops to concentrate in areas around Paris.

A Call to Revolt

In the National Assembly, delegates loudly voiced their unhappiness with the rigid French social order and the government. While the upper clergy and nobility fought to keep their privileges, some members of the Third Estate called for complete social equality. The spirit of rebellion against the government also spread throughout Paris. Debates raged on streets and in cafes. Some members of the Third Estate even physically attacked people who would not support their cause.

The king only added to the anxiety by gathering more troops at his palace in Versailles. Fearing that he planned to dissolve the National Assembly and halt reforms, the citizens reacted. They focused their action on a Paris prison called **the Bastille** (ba•STEEL).

The Fall of the Bastille
To many French people, the Bastille symbolized the injustices of the monarchy. On July 14, 1789, a huge mob surrounded the Bastille in an attempt to

---

MEETING SPECIAL NEEDS ACTIVITY

Learning Style: Visual/Spatial Encourage students who are strong visual learners to draw pictures of some of the early events of the French Revolution. Drawings might include women protesting the lack of bread, the Tennis Court Oath, the storming of the Bastille, and peasants seizing landlords' property. Then have a group of students arrange the drawings in chronological order along a time line on a bulletin board. **L1 LEP**

History & Art *The Oath of the Tennis Court,* detail from a painting by L.C.A. Couder **The National Assembly, locked out of the meeting hall for three days, resumed their meeting at an indoor tennis court.** *What caused members to fear that the National Assembly would be dissolved by force?*

steal weapons needed to defend the National Assembly. Tensions grew as the angry crowd tried to force its way into the fortress.

Hoping to calm the crowd, the prison commander finally lowered a drawbridge. The mob, however, angrily pressed forward into the main courtyard. Armed with axes, they freed the 7 prisoners held in the Bastille. The soldiers opened fire, and 98 rioters were killed. The prison commander and several soldiers were also killed as the rioters took over the prison. This outbreak led to the formation of a revolutionary government in Paris.

Violence in the Countryside

The storming of the Bastille released a wave of violence throughout France called the Great Fear. When rumors spread wildly that nobles had hired robbers to kill peasants and seize their property, the peasants armed themselves. No robbers came, but fear fanned the peasants' anxiety into violence. Swearing never again to pay feudal dues, they drove some landlords off their property. Peasants broke into manor houses, robbed granaries, and destroyed feudal records. The first wave of the French Revolution had struck.

SECTION 1 REVIEW

Recall
1. **Define** estate, tithe, bourgeoisie.
2. **Identify** Louis XVI, Marie Antoinette, National Assembly, Tennis Court Oath.
3. **Use** a chart to describe France's class system under the rule of

King Louis XVI. What conflicts set the nobility against the members of the Third Estate?

Critical Thinking
4. **Analyzing Information** July 14, Bastille Day, is celebrated in France like an independence

day. Why is it an important national event?

Understanding Themes
5. **Revolution** When did events in France become a revolution? Give specific evidence to support your reasoning.

Chapter 11 *The French Revolution* 339

1789 National Assembly adopts Declaration of the Rights of Man and of the Citizen.

1791 New French constitution is presented to the people.

1792 France declares war on Austria.

SECTION THEME

▶ **Change** The National Assembly establishes a constitutional government.

ind Out

Answer: *Reforms included abolition of feudal dues and tithes; taxing of nobles; the opening of government, army, and church offices to all male citizens; the protection of basic civil rights; the confiscation of church lands and government assumption of some church expenses; requirement that parishes elect their own priests; limitation of royal powers; and the establishment of a national legislature whose members would be elected by the people.*

FOCUS

Section Objective

List the political reforms the National Assembly adopted for France.

BELLRINGER
Motivational Activity

Before taking roll at the beginning of the class period, project Section Focus Transparency 11-2 and have students answer the activity questions.
📁 This activity is also available as a blackline master.

Vocabulary Pre-check

📁 Use Vocabulary Activity 11 to introduce terms. **L1 LEP**

Section 2

Constitutional Government

Setting the Scene

▶ **Terms to Define**
unicameral legislature, émigré

▶ **People to Meet**
Pope Pius VI

ind Out What political reforms did the National Assembly adopt for France?

The Storyteller

Sharp differences of political opinion disrupted the Paris opera. At a performance of Iphigenia *the chorus sang "Let us honor our Queen." Royalists applauded, but the opposing party booed. Lainez, an actor who remarked that "every good Frenchman should love the king and queen," was thrown a laurel wreath. Two days later, the revolutionaries would not let Lainez act until he had trampled that wreath underfoot.*

—adapted from *Blood Sisters, The French Revolution in Women's Memory*, Marilyn Yalom, 1993

French social groups

s violence swept the countryside, the National Assembly worked to form a new government. This task was complicated by power struggles among royalists, moderates, and radicals. Most royalists still favored absolute monarchy, but a growing number of moderates wanted the king to share power with a new legislature. Their leader was the Marquis de Lafayette, who had aided the colonists in the American Revolution. A radical group, the Paris Commune, won control of Paris's city government and pushed for an end to the monarchy.

End of the Old Order

Peasant unrest and urban violence finally forced the National Assembly to make reforms. On August 4, 1789, the nobles in that body voted to end their privileges. In a session lasting until 2 A.M., deputies wept and cheered as the last remains of feudalism in France were destroyed. The nobles gave up feudal dues as well as their exemption from taxation. They also agreed that all male citizens could hold government, army, or church office.

The Declaration of Rights

With the old order abolished, the deputies turned to ensuring the equality of all citizens before the law. Inspired by the American Declaration of Independence and Constitution, as well as the English Bill of Rights, the National Assembly composed the Declaration of the Rights of Man and of the Citizen in late August 1789. It is in the French Constitution today.

The Declaration of Rights, which incorporated the ideas of Enlightenment writers Locke, Montesquieu, and Rousseau, stated that all people are equal before the law. It also guaranteed freedom

---

SECTION RESOURCES

📁 **Reproducible Masters**
• Reproducible Lesson Plan 11-2
• Vocabulary Activity 11
• Guided Reading Activity 11-2
• Source Reading 11
• Section Quiz 11-2

Transparencies
• Section Focus Transparency 11-2

Multimedia
🔘 Student Self-Test and Review Software
🔘 Testmaker
🔘 Turning Points in World History:
French Revolution

of speech, press, and religion, and protected against arbitrary arrest and punishment.

The Declaration, however, did not grant equal rights to women. When the journalist Olympe de Gouges and other women called for equality, revolutionary leaders rejected their demands. Women did, however, benefit from reforms that made divorce easier and allowed them to inherit property.

March to Versailles

The king refused to accept the new reforms and the Declaration of Rights. This rejection raised the fears of the citizens of Paris that he would take action against the National Assembly. The people wanted Louis to move to Paris from his countryside palace in the town of Versailles to show his support for the Assembly.

In October 1789 thousands of women demanding bread marched in the rain to the king's palace in Versailles. Wielding sticks and pitchforks, the angry mob surrounded the palace, shouting for the king and queen. As the cries grew louder and armed guards were not able to hold back the surging crowd, the king declared at last, "My friends, I will go to Paris with my wife and children."

That afternoon, women waving banners and loaves of bread on bayonets surrounded the king's carriage as it drove from Versailles to Paris. In Paris, fervent anti-royalists watched the king, Marie Antoinette, and their two children. A few days later the National Assembly moved to Paris.

A New France

With the king and the National Assembly settled in Paris, government affairs began to move forward again. The delegates could turn their attention to political reforms.

Political Reforms

One problem faced by the National Assembly was government financing. With the backing of a liberal bishop, Maurice de Talleyrand, the Assembly in 1790 voted to take and sell church lands to pay off the huge government debt. To weaken the power of the Catholic Church, it also passed the Civil Constitution of the Clergy, a measure that placed the French Church under government control and turned the clergy into elected, salaried officials. The Civil Constitution created a deep rift between the Church and the Revolution. **Pope Pius VI** condemned the legislation, and many clergy refused to accept it. Other opponents of the Civil Constitution were many conservative peasants in the provinces.

The Constitution of 1791

In 1791 the National Assembly presented a new constitution to the people. The constitution kept the monarchy but limited royal powers. It set up a uni-cameral legislature, or one-house assembly, whose members were to be chosen by voters. Although equal rights were declared for all, the suffrage, or

Visualizing History *Louis XVI Arrested at Varennes* (engraving) After an attempted escape in June 1791, the royal family was watched closely in Paris. *Why did revolutionary leaders declare war on Austria?*

TEACH

Guided Practice

THEME Change
Have students create a chart listing changes brought about by the National Assembly in the right-hand column and the corresponding state of affairs before the revolution in the left-hand column. **L1**

Critical Thinking Write the following sentence on the chalkboard: *I am king, and I have the God-given right to rule France. Signed, Louis XVI.* Discuss how this belief influenced events in France. **L2**

VIDEODISC
Turning Points in World History

   Side One
Chapter 11

Title: *French Revolution*
Ask: What American document inspired the "Rights of Man"? *(the Declaration of Independence)*

Visualizing History Louis XVI and his family planned to cross the border into the Austrian Netherlands, northeast of France, and put down the revolution with help from Austrian troops stationed there. Marie Antoinette was from Austria.
Answer to Caption: *They feared Austria would try to reinstate Louis XVI as an absolute monarch.*

COOPERATIVE LEARNING ACTIVITY

Newspaper Have the class work together to plan the front page of *The Revolutionary Times*, a newspaper chronicling the events of the French Revolution through Louis XVI's failed flight to Varennes. After students have read Section 2, organize them into groups and have each group list the stories and visuals they would put on the front page. Students may get ideas for visuals from illustrations in Chapter 11. Groups can decide which event gets the top headline and where the other lead articles and visuals should go. Then, as a class, have groups decide on final placement of stories and visuals. **L2**

AROUND THE WORLD
Revolution in Saint Domingue

August 12, 1791
The French National Assembly, supporting human rights, decided to give the vote to enslaved Africans and people of mixed race in the French colony of Saint Domingue (Haiti). When the planters on the island refused to comply, a major controversy broke out. Enslaved Africans rose in revolt against the plantation owners. Nearly 100,000 of the colony's half million enslaved people participated in the rebellion.

Saint Domingue

the right to vote, was limited to only males who paid a minimum tax.

To the moderates, the Constitution of 1791 had achieved their goals. It guaranteed basic rights and created a limited monarchy largely controlled by the wealthy middle class and freed from the power of the Church and the nobles. However, many French people were not happy with the Constitution. For some, the reforms had gone too far; for others, not far enough. Delegates in the newly elected Legislative Assembly were seated according to their political beliefs: the reactionary royalists on the right; the moderates in the center; and the radicals, who wanted a republic, on the left. Today political scientists use the terms *right, center,* and *left* to describe similar political positions.

As political groups became more divided, France entered one of the most tumultuous periods in its history. Disagreements led to unrest and violence throughout the country. Many upper-class people feared the breakdown of law and order.

Decline of the Monarchy

Living in Paris, Louis XVI and Marie Antoinette were aware of the unrest. In June 1791 they decided to flee to Austria, where the queen's brother was emperor. Disguised as ordinary people, the royal family left Paris in a carriage late at night.

A bystander recognized the king at a road stop in Varennes, a town east of Paris. Soldiers immediately arrested the royal family, returning them to Paris. A virtual prisoner, Louis reluctantly accepted the limited monarchy established by the National Assembly. The limited monarchy, though, had little chance of success, for the people distrusted the king and were leaning toward a republic.

As news of the revolt against the French monarchy spread to neighboring countries, monarchs in the German states and the Austrian Empire began to worry about the stability of their own governments. French émigrés (EH•mih•GRAY), nobles who had fled France, hoped to restore Louis XVI to full power. The émigrés tried to convince the leaders of these governments that their own rule would be threatened unless they smashed the revolution before it spread.

Meanwhile French revolutionary leaders, fearing that Austria would try to reinstate Louis, declared war on Austria in 1792. Austria was soon supported by other monarchies, including Prussia and Sardinia.

War threw France into total upheaval. In August 1792, Paris crowds attacked the king's palace and killed many royal guards. Seeking protection, the king and his family fled to the Legislative Assembly. There they were given no safety; instead the radicals voted for their imprisonment. A month later, Paris mobs carried out the "September massacres," killing imprisoned nobles and priests accused of political crimes. Meanwhile, the radicals, backed by Paris crowds, took over the Assembly and called for a National Convention to create a new constitution. They also extended the vote to all males, whether or not they owned property.

SECTION 2 REVIEW

Recall
1. **Define** unicameral legislature, émigré.
2. **Identify** the Declaration of the Rights of Man and of the Citizen, Civil Constitution of

the Clergy, Pope Pius VI.
3. **Discuss** the Legislative Assembly's impact on modern politics.

Critical Thinking
4. **Analyzing Information** Contrast the views of French

moderates and radicals. What type of government did each want?

Understanding Themes
5. **Change** How did the Civil Constitution of the Clergy affect church-government relations?

1793 King Louis XVI is beheaded on the guillotine.

1795 The Directory comes to power in France.

1799 Napoleon helps to overthrow the Directory.

Section 3

Dawn of a New Era

Setting the Scene

▶ **Terms to Define**
conscription, coup d'état

▶ **People to Meet**
Jacobins, Girondists, Napoleon Bonaparte

▶ **Places to Locate**
Prussia, Valmy

 Why did the French Revolution lead to war between France and its neighbors?

The Storyteller

Paul Lemieux was both excited and anxious. At age 16 he had just received a notice that he would be one of the 3,000 young citizens to attend the new School of Mars. The Committee of Public Safety created the new school for learning and public military instruction. He read the Committee's report, "Loyalty to your own families must end when the great family calls you. The Republic leaves to parents the guidance of your first years, but as soon as your intelligence devel-

A sans-culotte

ops, it loudly proclaims the right it has over you. You are born for the Republic and not to be the pride of family despotism or its victims...." Paul wondered how this choice would affect his life.

—from *The Era of the French Revolution, 1789-1799,* Leo Gershoy, 1957

n September 1792 the French revolutionary leaders faced the result of their declaration of war on Austria and **Prussia**. Prussian troops had taken the major French fort of Verdun, and the road to Paris was now open for them. As fear gripped the country, Georges-Jacques Danton, a revolutionary orator, exclaimed: "All are burning with a desire to fight! We need boldness ... and France will be saved."

In response to Danton's words, thousands of volunteers came forward to defend the revolution. A week later, thoughts of defeat vanished when the French army won an astonishing victory at **Valmy**, less than 100 miles (161 km) from Paris. The French commander later wrote in his diary:

❝ Our soldiers were badly clothed, they had no straw to sleep on, no blankets, they sometimes went two days without bread. I never once saw them complain.... The tiredness and hardship they have suffered have been rewarded. The enemy has [yielded] to the season, misery, and illness. Its formidable army is in flight, its numbers halved.... ❞

—Commander Dumouriez, 1792

The victory at Valmy boosted the spirits of the revolutionaries. French forces had halted the powerful armies of Europe's monarchs and had saved the revolution for the time being.

TURNING POINT

The French Republic

As cannons thundered at Valmy, the National Convention met in Paris to create a new government for France. Shouts of "Long live the Nation!" echoed through the chamber as the delegates ended the monarchy and made France a republic.

Chapter 11 *The French Revolution* **343**

SECTION THEME

▶ **Conflict** The new French Republic faces enemies at home and abroad.

ind Out

Answer: *When Europe's monarchies threatened the revolution, French leaders formed an army to spread "liberty, equality, and fraternity" all over Europe.*

FOCUS

Section Objective
Explain why the French Revolution led to war between France and its neighbors.

BELLRINGER
Motivational Activity

 Project Section Focus Transparency 11-3 and have students answer the questions.
Available as a blackline master

Vocabulary Pre-check
Use Vocabulary Activity 11 to introduce vocabulary terms.
L1 LEP

TURNING POINT

The French Republic
What were the achievements of the first French Republic? *France received its first democratic constitution and introduced the metric system.*

SECTION RESOURCES

Reproducible Masters
• Reproducible Lesson Plan 11-3
• Vocabulary Activity 11
• Guided Reading Activity 11-3
• History Simulation 11
• People in World History Profile 42
• Section Quiz 11-3

Transparencies
• Section Focus Transparency 11-3

Multimedia
• Student Self-Test and Review Software
• Testmaker
• Turning Points in World History: *French Revolution*

Guided Practice

THEME Conflict

Have students imagine that the classroom is the National Convention. Tell students at the back that they are sitting on high benches. Which groups do you represent? What are the views of these groups? (sans-culottes and Jacobins; radical) Tell students at the front that they are Girondists and those in the middle that they are the Plain. Have these two groups explain their views. Then ask students from the front and back to try to persuade the middle to support their points of view on the revolution. **L2**

Literature Write the following quote from the opening of Charles Dickens's *A Tale of Two Cities* on the chalkboard: "It was the best of times, it was the worst of times …" Discuss how this quote applies to the French Revolution. **L2**

History & Art The Trianon and its gardens, a royal retreat on the grounds at Versailles complete with a theater, lake, river, and village, became a symbol of the excesses of Marie Antoinette. Why did the French people resent the queen's lifestyle? (She continued her luxurious life while ordinary citizens did not have enough to eat.)

Answer to Caption: *They began dressing more simply—men wearing long, plain trousers and women wearing long, straight dresses.*

The National Convention met from 1792 to 1795. Its members—who were all male and mostly lawyers, doctors, and other middle-class professionals—passed into law a number of democratic reforms. The Convention wrote France's first democratic constitution. The constitution placed political power in a single national legislature based on universal male suffrage, meaning that every man could vote, whether or not he owned property. Convention members also replaced the monarchy's confusing system of weights and measures with the metric system still used throughout the world today.

The National Convention also adopted a new calendar, naming September 22, 1792—the date of the republic's creation—as the first day of the Year I of Liberty. The year was divided into months with such names as *Nivôse* ("the snowy month"), *Germinal* ("seed time"), and *Thermidor* ("the warm month"). Although this calendar did not last, it and the other democratic reforms expressed the French people's hope that the republic would be the dawn of a new era of freedom.

Death of a King

Before it could enter the republican era, the Convention had to deal with the legacy of the past. Its first task was to decide Louis XVI's fate. In November 1792 a large iron box holding Louis's secret correspondence with foreign monarchs was found in the royal palace. Although the letters provided little evidence against Louis, the radicals successfully used them to discredit the royal family.

In December 1792 Louis was tried before the Convention and convicted of having "conspired against the liberty of the nation." In January 1793 he was beheaded on the guillotine—a killing machine the revolutionaries had adopted as a humane means of execution. As he faced execution, the king reportedly said:

> I forgive my enemies; I trust that my death will be for the happiness of my people, but I grieve for France and I fear that she may suffer the anger of the Lord. **"**

History & Art *Marie Antoinette in the Park of Trianon* by Antoine Vestier **Because of her extravagance, the people referred to the queen as "Madame Deficit."** *How did Parisians show their feelings about elaborate clothes?*

Parisian crowds joyously celebrated the king's death. For them, it meant that there was no turning back; the republic would remain.

Toward the Future

In the days that followed, republican enthusiasm swept the country. Parisians were the most fervent. The *sans-culottes*—Paris's shopkeepers, artisans, and workers—saw themselves as heroes and heroines and demanded respect from the upper classes.

Soon even wealthy Parisians addressed each other as "citizen" or "citizeness" rather than "mister" or "madame." They rejected elaborate clothes and powdered wigs in favor of simple styles. Men wore long trousers instead of knee-length breeches (hence the name *sans-culottes*, meaning "without breeches"); women wore long dresses in the style of ancient Rome.

While the nation celebrated the republic, debate over the revolution's future erupted in the Convention. There, supporters of the *sans-culottes* and extreme radicals called the **Jacobins** (JA•kuh•buhns) formed the Mountain, so called because its members sat on high benches at the rear of the hall. Under leaders such as Maximilien Robespierre, Georges-Jacques Danton, and Jean-Paul Marat, the Mountain saw itself as the defender of the revolution and as the voice of the people.

Across the aisle was a group of moderates known as **Girondists** (juh•RAHN•dihsts), because many of them came from the Gironde, a region in southwestern France. The Girondists felt that the revolution had gone far enough and wanted to

Role Play Organize the class into three or four groups and have each group create a television interview program in which ordinary citizens during the French Revolution talk about the times in which they live. Have each group select a television host and individuals to act as guests. The guests could be a shopkeeper, a Jacobin, a Girondist, a *sans-culottes*, a farm woman, a soldier in the French army, and a housewife. The host and students acting as the audience should prepare questions through which the guests reveal important historical developments and how these events affected them. **L2**

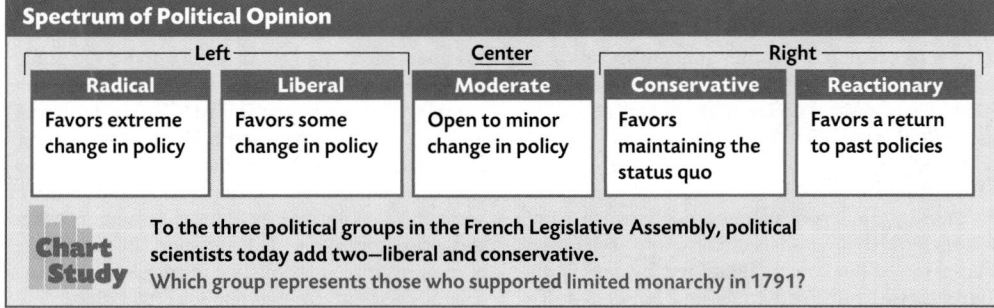

Spectrum of Political Opinion

Left		Center	Right	
Radical	Liberal	Moderate	Conservative	Reactionary
Favors extreme change in policy	Favors some change in policy	Open to minor change in policy	Favors maintaining the status quo	Favors a return to past policies

Chart Study To the three political groups in the French Legislative Assembly, political scientists today add two—liberal and conservative. Which group represents those who supported limited monarchy in 1791?

protect the wealthy middle class from radical attacks. They organized support to resist the growing strength of the Mountain in Paris.

Seated between these two rivals on the main floor was a group called the Plain. It was made up of undecided deputies who were a majority of the Convention. As the influence of the *sans-culottes* increased during 1793, members of the Plain came to support the Mountain. Together, they helped make the revolution more radical, more open to extreme and violent change.

Spreading the Revolution

Meanwhile, Europe's monarchs viewed events in France with horror. After Louis's execution, they feared democratic revolutions could spread from France and endanger their thrones and their lives. In January 1793 the monarchs of Great Britain, the Netherlands, Spain, and Sardinia joined those of Austria and Prussia in an alliance against the revolutionary government of France.

French Expansion

At the same time, France's leaders were determined to overthrow royalty everywhere. Early in 1793 Danton declared that "the kings in alliance try to frighten us, [but] we hurl at their feet, as a gage of battle, the French king's head." He then called upon French forces to expand France's territories to their natural frontiers: the Alps, the Pyrenees, the Rhine River, and the Mediterranean Sea.

In response to this call, an army made up of volunteers poured outward from France, eager to seize the natural frontiers and to bring "liberty, equality, and fraternity" to Europe's peoples. Although poorly trained, the French forces often caught the enemy off guard and won many battles. The enemy's professional soldiers, however, soon inflicted on the French a string of defeats. In despair, the French commander in chief abandoned his troops and surrendered.

As French forces retreated, the National Convention took steps to repel the foreign invasion. It formed the Committee of Public Safety to direct the entire war effort. In the summer of 1793 the Committee adopted conscription, or the draft, calling up all men between the ages of 18 and 45 for military service. It also called upon the skills and resources of all civilians, both men and women. The Committee turned the conflict into what has been called the world's first "people's war."

The Revolution in Crisis

While waging war, France's revolutionaries had to struggle with problems at home. A fierce civil war raged in western France as royalist peasants revolted against the revolutionaries. They were angered by the drafting of their sons to fight a war they opposed. Mobs in French cities rioted to protest rising food prices and food shortages.

Meanwhile, the government itself was embroiled in a political crisis. The Girondists accused the Jacobins of seeking the favor of the mob. The Jacobins responded by charging that the Girondists were secretly royalists. The Jacobins in the Mountain won control of the Convention and arrested Girondist delegates.

In retaliation Girondist supporters rebelled against the Jacobins in the Convention. During the uprising Charlotte Corday, a loyal Girondist supporter, killed the Jacobin leader Marat and was sent to the guillotine.

 **Footnotes to History**

The Wax Museum A young Swiss woman living in Paris immortalized the revolution's leaders by making wax models of them. She escaped to London, where she opened a museum—Madame Tussaud's Exhibition—that is open today.

Chapter 11 *The French Revolution* 345

Chapter 11 Section 3

Chart Study

Answer *Conservative*

Practice

Reading a Chart Which group held the most political power in France by the summer of 1792? *(the radicals)*

Critical Thinking Ask students to name some of the tactics of the Reign of Terror. *(suspension of rights, neighborhood watch committees)* Then ask them if they can think of any other historical periods when such tactics were used. *(Answers may include Hitler's Germany; Salem, Massachusetts, during the witch trials.)* **L3**

 VIDEODISC Turning Points in World History

 Side One Chapter 11

Title: *French Revolution*
Ask: What was the motto for the French Revolution? *("Liberty, Equality, and Fraternity")*

MEETING SPECIAL NEEDS ACTIVITY

Study Strategy Have students work in small groups to outline important events in the French Revolution—from September 1792 to October 1799—covered in Section 3. Information in the outline should include dates, people, and places for each event as well as the significance of the event to the revolution as a whole. Let groups share their outlines. **L2**

Independent Practice

📁 Guided Reading Activity
11-3 **L1**

📁 People in World History
Profile 42

Time Line Have students create a
time line of events in Section 3.
Ask students to write a paragraph describing each event and
its significance. **L1**

Biography Have students choose
a person from the French
Revolution and write a short
biography of him or her. Tell students to include information
from Section 3 as well as from
other sources. **L2 LEP**

Global Gourmet

Paris Bread was the mainstay in
the diet of the average Parisian in
1789. A typical French worker ate
a four-pound loaf a day.
Supplying bread for the city's
more than 600,000 inhabitants
was a major production. It is not
surprising that it was often a
problem as well. Bread shortages
played a significant role in the
onset of the French Revolution.

you don't say...

Jacobin was originally used to
refer to priests of the Dominican
order whose first religious house in
Paris was on the Rue St. Jacques.
When the radical group made up of
Robespierre, Marat, and others met
in a former Dominican religious
house, the French radicals became
known as Jacobins. Today the word is
used to refer to people with radical
views.

The Reign of Terror

Overwhelmed by enemies at home and abroad,
the Jacobins set out to crush all opposition within
France. This effort, known as the Reign of Terror,
lasted from July 1793 to July 1794.

Crushing Opposition

During the Terror, neighborhood watch committees hunted down suspected traitors and turned
them over to the courts. Pressured by mobs, the
courts carried out swift trials and handed down
harsh sentences. Innocent people often suffered—
many of them sentenced because of false statements
made by hostile neighbors. Among the victims of
the Terror was Marie Antoinette, Louis XVI's wife.
Royalty and aristocrats, however, were only a few of
those killed. Historians estimate that about 85
percent of the 40,000 people who died were
probably commoners—merchants, laborers, and
peasants. The Committee of Public Safety ruled
France, and Robespierre ruled the committee.

Republic of Virtue

Meanwhile, the Jacobin-controlled Committee
of Public Safety went about setting up the "Republic
of Virtue." By this the Jacobins meant a democratic
republic made up of good citizens. Toward this end,
the Committee opened new schools and promoted
the idea of universal elementary education. In economic matters, it issued pamphlets to teach farmers
agricultural skills and introduced temporary wage
and price controls to halt inflation. In the area of
human rights, it abolished slavery in France's
colonies and encouraged religious toleration.

Radical revolutionaries, however, bitterly
opposed Catholicism because of its traditional links
with monarchy and its claim to be the sole
source of religious truth. They closed churches or
turned them into "temples of reason." Fearing a
further loss of support for the revolution among
believers, the Committee opposed these actions.
Robespierre himself sponsored the worship of a
Supreme Being in an effort to unite Catholics,
deists, and nonbelievers.

Images of the Times

Revolutionary Life

*Although the causes of the French Revolution
had existed for years, the events of 1789
sparked the beginning of the revolution.*

After a failed harvest caused
bread prices to increase, about
6,000 Parisian women marched
on Versailles.

Tri-color badge

346

Images of the Times

Revolutionary Life

The *bonnet rouge* or red liberty cap became a symbol of loyalty to the revolution. The cap came from
the head wrap used by enfranchised formerly enslaved Romans. At first, the caps were held high on
poles during meetings and ceremonies. Then the Jacobins started wearing them to their meetings.
Soon they became the obligatory headgear of all French patriots. Citizens were forced to wear them
under pain of beating or death. The king even wore one after the invasion of the Tuileries Palace.

End of the Terror

By the spring of 1794, the French had taken the offensive in the war. With the republic out of danger, Danton and his supporters called for an end to the Terror. Robespierre, however, accused them of treason and had them sent to the guillotine. Fearing for their own safety, other leaders then turned against Robespierre and had him executed. The day after the execution, a Paris newspaper expressed the relief that everyone felt: "We are all throwing ourselves into each other's arms."

After Robespierre's death, the Jacobins lost power and the Terror came to an end. A reaction against Jacobin ideas began, and the wealthier middle class took control of the Convention. Fashions changed as people rebelled against the "Republic of Virtue." Once again, people wore knee breeches, luxurious dresses, and wigs. Price controls were relaxed, and prices rose sharply, causing hardship for the poor. Riots broke out, but the leaderless lower classes were easily put down by the army. By mid-1794, many people even favored a restoration of the monarchy.

The Directory

After Robespierre's fall the Convention briefly carried on as France's government. In 1795 it wrote a new constitution. Universal male suffrage was ended; only citizens who owned property could vote. This constitution, in effect, brought the government under the control of the wealthy middle class. The constitution also set up an executive council of five men called directors. The Directory, as the council was called, ruled with a two-house legislature.

Once in power the Directory faced many enemies. Despite the Terror, enough royalists remained to threaten a takeover. Even more alarming was the growing discontent of the radical *sans-culottes*, angered by food shortages and rising prices. During its rule from 1795 to 1799, the Directory used the army to put down uprisings by both groups.

Meanwhile, the Directory made little effort to resolve a growing gap between the rich and the poor people of France. It was having its own problems: the revolutionary government was on the

Symbols of the revolution carried the message of liberty, equality, and fraternity—or death.

UNITE·INDIVISIBILITE
DE·LA·REPUBLIQUE
LIBERTE·EGALITE
FRATERNITE·OULA·MORT

REFLECTING ON THE TIMES

1. Why would these images cause European monarchs to react in horror?
2. How might peasants in neighboring European countries react?

347

ANSWERS TO REFLECTING ON THE TIMES

1. Seeing citizens rising up in arms against another monarch and willing to die to gain liberty, equality, and fraternity might cause them to worry that these views could spread to their own countries.
2. They might think that they too could rise up against their monarchs.

Cultural Perspectives

Revolutionary Titles Just as the French revolutionaries addressed every person as "Citizen" rather than by titles such as "Sir" or "Madam," the Communists during the Russian Revolution addressed one another as *"Tovarishch"* (meaning "Comrade"). In both cases, the attempt was to show equality of people within a cause. "Comrade" later came to mean a member of the Communist party, not just a citizen of the country.

Who?What?Where?When?

The revolutionary calendar helped secularize revolutionary France by not including Sundays and church feast days. The new calendar contained 12 months, each with 30 days broken into 3 weeks made up of 10 days each. The remaining 5 days of the year were feast days dedicated to the *sans-culottes*. France reverted to the Gregorian calendar on January 1, 1806.

ASSESS

Check for Understanding

Assign Section 3 Review as homework or as an in-class activity.

 Use Student Self-Test and Review Software to review Section 3.

Evaluate

Section Quiz 11-3

Use the Testmaker to create a customized quiz for Section 3.

TEACH

Tell students that the inventor of the guillotine, Dr. Joseph Ignace Guillotin, was a member of the Constituent Assembly and was regarded as a kindly man. Up until the revolution, the punishment of decapitation was viewed as a privilege reserved for nobles. Dr. Guillotin proposed that it be the punishment for anyone accused of a capital crime, regardless of class. He developed his machine to make the process as quick and painless as possible. Point out that people's concepts of "cruel and unusual punishments" have changed over the years. Ask students what they feel constitutes cruel and unusual punishment today.

Linking Past and Present

Guillotine Dr. Guillotin's invention was not the first such machine. Similar decapitating machines had been used in Germany and Italy; in Yorkshire, England; and in Scotland. The guillotine continued to be used in France until 1981, when the French abolished capital punishment.

CURRICULUM CONNECTION

TECHNOLOGY

The Legislative Assembly assigned the guillotine project to a committee that hired a German mechanic to build the machine. To make sure that the new beheading machine worked properly, experiments were conducted on dead bodies at a Paris hospital.

James L. Stanfield

Guillotine

This dreaded machine, pictured here in eerie stillness, embodies the violence and upheaval of the French Revolution. Yet this device used to chop off heads represents not only the terror of the revolution but also its reforms. The guillotine was adopted as a more humane form of capital punishment, a civilized advance over hanging or the executioner's ax. The swift, sharp blade was, according to its French inventor, Dr. Joseph-Ignace Guillotin, "a cool breath on the back of the neck."

A saga of social and political upheaval, the French Revolution transformed the people of France from subjects of an absolute monarch to citizens of a nation. The revolution marked the beginning of the modern age in Europe. "It roused passions," said 19th-century French writer Alexis de Tocqueville, that "revolutions had never before excited." In France people still argue over its importance and meaning. ⊕

brink of bankruptcy, and the directors were beset by financial and moral scandals in their personal lives. As the Directory appeared more and more inept, French people of all classes looked to the power of the army to save France from ruin.

Napoleon Takes Over

As the Directory faced growing unpopularity at home, the French army won victories in the continuing war with the European monarchies. One of the many able French military leaders who attracted public attention was a young general named **Napoleon Bonaparte**.

Napoleon's Early Fame

During the French Revolution, Napoleon's great military skills won him quick promotion to the rank of general. In 1795, at age 26, he crushed an uprising against the Directory. Napoleon placed his artillery so that he cleared the streets of Paris "with a whiff of grapeshot."

A year later Napoleon married Josephine de Beauharnais, a leader of Paris society. Using Josephine's connections, he won command of the French army that was fighting the Austrians in Italy. Upon arriving, Napoleon improved the soldiers' conditions and mustered their support.

Rapidly moving and massing French forces at weak points on the enemy's line, Napoleon defeated the Austrians. He forced them to sign a peace treaty giving France control over most of northern Italy. Napoleon, France's leading general, was now ready to influence events at home.

Napoleon's Bold Move

In 1799 Napoleon seized his opportunity. For more than a year, he had been fighting the British in Egypt, hoping to cut off Britain's trade with the Middle East and India. Napoleon won victories on land against Egyptian forces. However, the British

History & Art *Napoleon Crossing the Great St. Bernard* by Jacques-Louis David. Chateau de Malmaison, Ruiel-Malmaison, France **Known for his classical style, David was the leading artist of the French Revolution.** *How does David portray Napoleon?*

navy under Admiral Horatio Nelson destroyed the French fleet that was located at a harbor east of Alexandria. French forces were left stranded among the Pyramids. Hearing of the troubled political situation back home, Napoleon abandoned his army in Egypt and returned to France.

Napoleon landed unannounced on the French Mediterranean coast in October 1799. When he entered Paris, he was greeted by cheering crowds. Quickly, Napoleon joined leaders in a coup d'état, or a quick seizure of power, against the Directory.

SECTION 3 REVIEW

Recall
1. **Define** conscription, coup d'état.
2. **Identify** Jacobins, Girondists, Reign of Terror, Napoleon Bonaparte.
3. **Locate** France's "natural frontiers" according to Danton. Why do you think Danton

called for France's expansion to its "natural frontiers"?
Critical Thinking
4. **Applying Knowledge** Select a revolutionary leader such as Robespierre and show how he or she succeeded—or failed—in carrying out the ideals of "lib-

erty, equality, and fraternity."
Understanding Themes
5. **Conflict** What conditions led to the Reign of Terror? Why did the French revolutionaries use such violent and drastic measures to advance their cause?

SECTION 3 REVIEW ANSWERS

1. All the vocabulary words are defined in the Glossary.
2. Jacobins, 344; Girondists, 344; Reign of Terror, 346; Napoleon Bonaparte, 349
3. the Alps, the Pyrenees, the Rhine River, and the Mediterranean Sea; to increase French lands and to spread revolutionary

ideals
4. Answers will vary. Possible answer: Leaders such as Robespierre failed in carrying out the revolutionary ideals because they persecuted many innocent people.
5. **CONFLICT** The Reign of Terror was the outgrowth of the

revolutionaries' fears that the revolution would be overthrown. Because they were desperate and the government was in such a chaotic state, the revolutionaries resorted to violence to maintain their power.

SECTION THEME

▶ **Movement** Napoleon becomes France's emperor and conquers much of Europe.

ind Out

Answer: *He built his empire through military leadership and diplomatic alliances. The empire fell apart when his allies saw him as a threat.*

FOCUS

Section Objective

Relate how Napoleon built and then lost an empire.

BELLRINGER
Motivational Activity

Before taking roll at the beginning of the class period, project Section Focus Transparency 11-4 and have students answer the activity questions. Discuss students' responses.
This activity is also available as a blackline master.

Vocabulary Pre-check

Use Vocabulary Activity 11 to introduce vocabulary terms.
L1 LEP

1800   1810   1820

1802 France signs Treaty of Amiens with Great Britain.

1804 Napoleon names himself Emperor of the French.

1812 Napoleon invades Russia.

1815 Duke of Wellington wins Battle of Waterloo.

Section 4

Napoleon's Empire

Setting the Scene

▶ **Terms to Define**
dictatorship, plebiscite, nationalism

▶ **People to Meet**
Duke of Wellington, Alexander I, Louis XVIII

▶ **Places to Locate**
Trafalgar, Moscow, Waterloo

ind Out   How did Napoleon build and then lose an empire?

 **Storyteller**

Carl von Clausewitz, a military theoretician, analyzed the French disaster in Russia: "[Napoleon] had hoped from that centre [Moscow], to influence by opinion [St.]Petersburg and the whole of Russia.… He reached Moscow with 90,000 men, he should have reached it with 200,000. This would have been possible if he had handled his army with more care and forbearance. But these were qualities unknown to him.… It is, moreover, to be considered as a great neglect … to have made so little preparation as he did for retreat."

—translated from *Campaign of 1812 in Russia,* Carl von Clausewitz, 1835

Napoleon Bonaparte

In 1804 Napoleon named himself Emperor of the French. At the brilliant coronation ceremony in Paris, the people witnessed an astonishing act. Napoleon took the crown from the pope's hands and placed it on his own head. Napoleon's action spoke loudly of his intention to be a strong ruler. How had the French government been transformed from a democracy to an empire in five short years?

The Consulate

After his successful overthrow of the Directory in 1799, Napoleon had proclaimed a new constitution, which theoretically established a republic. The constitution actually set up a dictatorship, a government headed by an absolute ruler. The executive branch was a committee of three members, called consuls, who took their title from ancient Rome. Napoleon, however, became First Consul and quickly concentrated power in his own hands.

Restoring Order

Napoleon wanted to bring order to the country. One of his first goals was to restructure the government. Although he tried to keep many of the revolutionary reforms, Napoleon replaced elected local officials with men he appointed himself. He also placed education under the control of the national government, creating technical schools, universities, and secondary schools. The secondary schools, called lycées (lee•SAY), were designed to provide well-educated, patriotic government workers. Although students who attended the lycées came mostly from wealthy families, some poorer students received scholarships. In this way the French schools were a step toward a public school system open to all children.

Napoleon also changed the country's financial system. He created the Bank of France and required that every citizen pay taxes. The collected taxes

---

History & Art
The Consecration of Emperor Napoleon I and the Coronation of the Empress Josephine (detail) by Jacques-Louis David. The Louvre, Paris, France
In imitation of Pepin and Charlemagne, Napoleon seized the crown from Pope Pius VII and placed it on his own head in 1804. A virtual dictator, Napoleon had the support of most people in France. *How had Napoleon earlier made peace with the Catholic Church?*

were deposited in the bank and used by the government to make loans to businesses. These changes gradually brought inflation and high prices under control.

Napoleon's many supporters welcomed his strong government and the peace and order it brought. In 1802 Napoleon named himself Consul for life. This move was overwhelmingly approved by a plebiscite, or popular vote.

The Napoleonic Code

Many historians say that Napoleon made his greatest impact on French law. Old feudal and royal laws were often contradictory and confusing. To make French law clear and consistent, Napoleon had a new law code written. Commonly known as the Napoleonic Code, it was based on Enlightenment ideas, such as the equality of all citizens before the law, religious toleration, and advancement based on merit. However, the Code placed the state above the individual. For example, it limited freedom of speech and press by allowing the censorship of books, plays, and pamphlets. Women also lost many of the rights they had gained during the revolution. Male heads of households were given extensive authority over wives and minor children.

The Church

Napoleon also made peace with the Catholic Church. Realizing that French Catholics had objected to the Civil Constitution of the Clergy, he negotiated an agreement called the Concordat of 1801 with Pope Pius VII. In this agreement Napoleon acknowledged that Catholicism was the religion of the majority of French people but affirmed religious toleration for all. Napoleon did, however, retain the right to name all bishops, who had to swear allegiance to the state. The pope agreed to accept the loss of church lands; in return the state agreed to pay salaries to the Catholic clergy.

Building an Empire

Although Napoleon proved that he was an able administrator, he was more interested in building

Chapter 11 *The French Revolution* **351**

TEACH

Guided Practice

THEME Movement
Using the map in their book as a guide, have students identify on a wall map key places in Napoleon's movement through Europe. *(march across the Alps into Italy and Austria, site of Battle of Trafalgar, march into Russia)* **L1 LEP**

History & Art Napoleon's coronation took place in Paris in the cathedral of Notre Dame. **Why do you think Napoleon chose to be crowned emperor in a church?** *(to show that as emperor he had some control over the Church)*
Answer to Caption: *Napoleon and Pope Pius VII had agreed to the Concordat of 1801.*

Critical Thinking If ever a man has been considered great, it is Napoleon. Historians have traditionally referred to him, like Alexander more than 2,000 years earlier, as Napoleon "the Great." Have students summarize the strengths and accomplishments that earned Napoleon this appellation. Discuss whether, in their opinion, Napoleon was greater than other leaders they have read about. **L3**

World History and Art Transparency 29, *Napoleon Crossing the Alps*

Mapping History Overlay Transparency 14, *France and Europe*

COOPERATIVE LEARNING ACTIVITY

Report Organize the class into groups to research changes Napoleon brought to France and whether these changes are still in effect. Assign each group one of the following topics: restructuring of government, educational system, financial system, legal system (Napoleonic Code), and Concordat of 1801. Have each group present an oral report to the class. Encourage groups to use charts, graphs, and pictures to illustrate their reports. After groups have given their reports, encourage a class discussion about Napoleon's impact on France. **L2**

Independent Practice

📁 Guided Reading Activity 11-4 **L1**

📁 Geography and History Activity 11

📁 World Art and Music Activity 11

Diary Have students write a diary entry or draw an illustration from the viewpoint of a French soldier involved in the march toward Moscow or in the retreat from Russia. **L2 LEP**

Judgment Have students label two columns *Positive* and *Negative* on a sheet of paper. Ask students to list Napoleon's actions, placing them under the appropriate heading. Some actions may be viewed as both positive and negative. (*example: replaced turmoil of revolution with orderly government—positive; put himself at head of a dictatorship —negative*) **L3**

Who?What?Where?When?

Metric System During the revolution French scientists developed the metric system. Before that, France had no uniform system of weights and measures. In 1801 the government made the metric system France's only system of weights and measures. Since then, the metric system has spread to most countries in the world.

---

an empire. Soon after becoming First Consul, Napoleon commanded the French forces that defeated both Italy and Austria. He also persuaded Russia to withdraw from the war. Though Napoleon was not able to defeat the British navy, the British were ready for peace because their commerce had suffered during the war. The two powers signed the Treaty of Amiens in March 1802.

Over the next few years Napoleon combined his talents as a masterful military leader and brilliant diplomat to build an empire. In 1804 he named himself Emperor of the French and soon set his armies on the road to conquest.

The Battle of Trafalgar

Despite his successes on the continent of Europe, Great Britain remained Napoleon's most tenacious enemy. By 1805 Napoleon felt he was ready to invade Great Britain from the English Channel; his fleet never made it that far, however. In October 1805 at the Battle of **Trafalgar**, off the southern coast of Spain, the British admiral Lord Nelson soundly defeated the French navy, removing once and for all the possibility of a French invasion of Great Britain.

Economic Blockades

After Trafalgar, Napoleon decided to use economic warfare against the British. He believed he could defeat Great Britain by destroying its economic lifeline—trade. In a plan called the Continental System, Napoleon ordered all European nations he had conquered to stop trade with the British. In another decree he forbade British imports entry to the European ports that he controlled. Napoleon also required Russia and Prussia to go along with the blockade of British goods.

Meanwhile, Great Britain responded to the trade blockade with a counterthreat: Any ship on its way to a European port had to stop first at a British port. Napoleon responded that he would seize any ship that did so.

This conflict put the United States and other neutral nations in a difficult position. The United States relied heavily on its trade with both Great Britain and France. If the United States ignored the British threat, American ships would be seized by the British navy. If the United States obeyed the British, the French navy would seize its ships. This conflict on the seas was one of the causes that eventually led to the War of 1812 between the United States and Great Britain.

Despite the blockades, the aggressive British navy did maintain control of the seas, and Napoleon's Continental System failed. French trade

suffered, and the French economy worsened. Yet Napoleon's empire kept growing as he continued to win battles on land.

Napoleonic Europe

By 1812 Napoleon controlled most of Europe. France's boundaries now extended to the Russian border. Through successful French military conquests, Napoleon became king of Italy, his brother Joseph became king of Naples and later Spain, and his other brother, Louis, became king of Holland. Napoleon then abolished the Holy Roman Empire and created the Confederation of the Rhine, a loose organization of the German states. This move led Prussia to declare war on France, but the French easily crushed the weak Prussian army.

The people who lived in the countries under Napoleon's rule resented paying taxes to France and sending soldiers to serve in Napoleon's armies. This resentment ignited in the conquered people a feeling of **nationalism**, the yearning for self-rule and restoration of their customs and traditions. Nationalism helped stir revolts against French rule throughout Europe.

The first signs of trouble appeared in Spain, where Spanish forces carried out guerrilla warfare, or hit-and-run attacks, on French forces. In 1812, aided by British troops under the command of Arthur Wellesley (later named **Duke of Wellington**), the Spaniards overthrew their French occupiers. They reinstated their old king under a system of limited monarchy. Prussia also joined in the revolt against Napoleon, as nationalist leaders rebuilt its army and amassed political support in the hope of ridding themselves of French rule.

Downfall of the Empire

When Russia joined the movement against Napoleon, it signaled the end of the empire. Czar **Alexander I** of Russia viewed Napoleon's control of Europe as a threat to Russia. Additionally, Napoleon's Continental System had hurt the Russian economy. In 1811 Alexander withdrew from the Continental System and resumed trade with Great Britain.

The Invasion of Russia

Alexander's withdrawal outraged Napoleon, leading him to invade Russia. Napoleon assembled a massive army of 600,000 soldiers from countries

---

MEETING SPECIAL NEEDS ACTIVITY

Learning Style: Auditory/Musical Tell students that the composer Beethoven had greatly admired Napoleon, seeing the general as the embodiment of the spirit of the French Revolution. Beethoven originally dedicated his Third Symphony to Napoleon. He retracted the dedication when Napoleon proclaimed himself emperor, renaming the work "Heroic Symphony to celebrate the memory of a great man." It has become known as the *Eroica*. Have students who are strong auditory/musical learners listen to the Third Symphony. Have them select segments that they feel especially express the spirit of Napoleonic or revolutionary France and play these for the rest of the class. **L2 LEP**

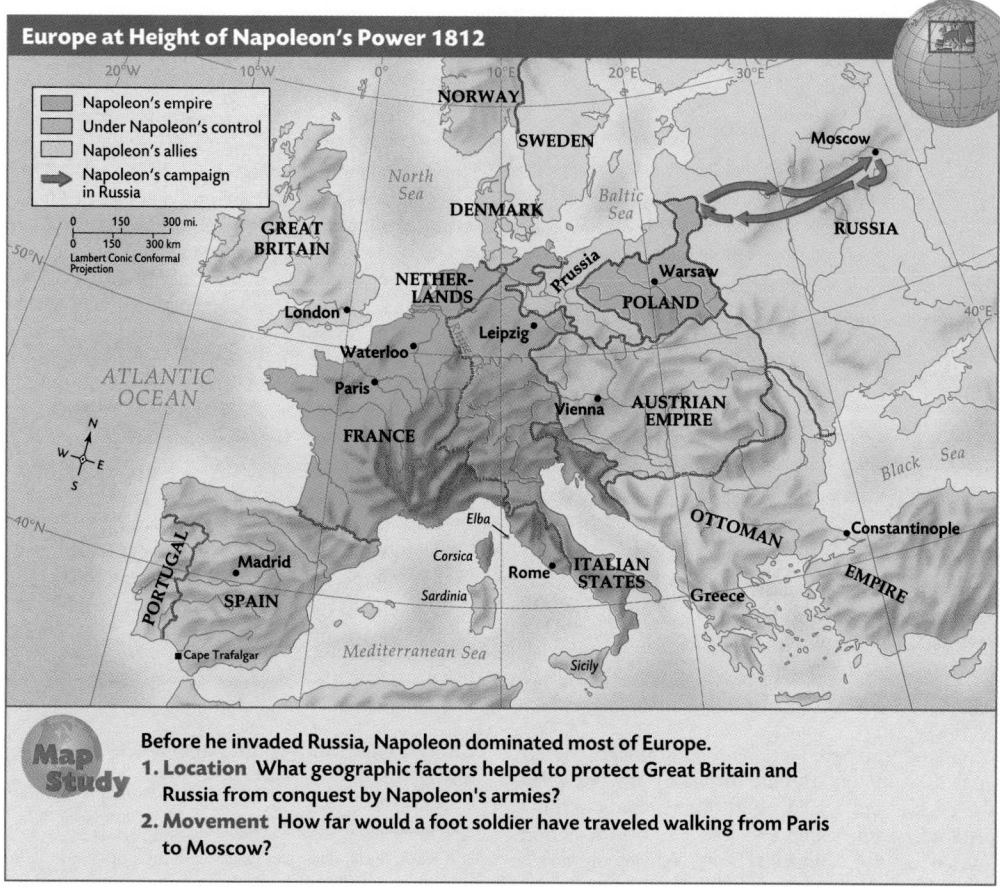

Europe at Height of Napoleon's Power 1812

Napoleon's empire
Under Napoleon's control
Napoleon's allies
Napoleon's campaign in Russia

0   150   300 mi.
0   150   300 km
Lambert Conic Conformal Projection

NORWAY
SWEDEN
Moscow
North Sea
DENMARK
Baltic Sea
RUSSIA
GREAT BRITAIN
NETHER-LANDS
Prussia
Warsaw
POLAND
London
Leipzig
Waterloo
Paris
Vienna
AUSTRIAN EMPIRE
FRANCE
ATLANTIC OCEAN
Black Sea
Elba
Corsica
Rome
ITALIAN STATES
OTTOMAN
Constantinople
EMPIRE
Madrid
SPAIN
Sardinia
Greece
PORTUGAL
Cape Trafalgar
Mediterranean Sea
Sicily

Map Study

Before he invaded Russia, Napoleon dominated most of Europe.
1. **Location** What geographic factors helped to protect Great Britain and Russia from conquest by Napoleon's armies?
2. **Movement** How far would a foot soldier have traveled walking from Paris to Moscow?

throughout Europe. The long French march toward **Moscow** began in May 1812. The Russians, however, refused to yield to Napoleon's threat. They retreated to central Russia, adopting a "scorched-earth policy" in which they burned everything as they went. On September 14, one of Napoleon's men finally saw the city of Moscow from a nearby hill. But the day after the French entered Moscow, a giant fire, probably started by Russian patriots, destroyed most of the city.

Shortly afterward the harsh Russian winter began to set in, and the French army could not remain in Russia without shelter. Despite the difficult conditions, Napoleon delayed before ordering a retreat. When the French troops finally did withdraw, the Russians relentlessly attacked them. Amid the extreme conditions the retreat became a rout. Of the 600,000 soldiers who entered Russia, about 400,000 died of battle wounds, starvation, and exposure.

Defeat

The Russian blow to Napoleon's power ruined him. From all directions his enemies—Russians, Prussians, Spaniards, English, Austrians, Italians—sent armies against Napoleon's forces. Russia and Prussia announced a War of Liberation. Joined by Austria, they defeated Napoleon at Leipzig in Saxony, part of present-day Germany, in October 1813.

By March 1814 the allies were in Paris, forcing Napoleon to surrender and abdicate as emperor. The victors restored the French throne to **Louis XVIII**, a member of the Bourbon family and the brother of Louis XVI. Napoleon was exiled to Elba, an island off the coast of Italy. The boundaries of France were reduced to those of 1792.

Still determined to rule, Napoleon returned to France on March 1, 1815, and easily won widespread popular support. The troops of the restored Bourbon king, Louis XVIII, deserted to their former

Chapter 11 *The French Revolution* **353**

Map Study

Answers
1. *Great Britain: the English Channel; Russia: harsh winters*
2. *about 1,700 miles (2,700 kilometers)*

Map Skills Practice

Reading a Map What countries were Napoleon's allies? (*Norway, Denmark, Prussia, Austrian Empire*)

Linking Past and Present

Napoleonic Code France exported the Napoleonic Code to its empire in Europe and its colonies in North America. Today Louisiana, once part of France's lands in America, is the only state with laws still based on the Napoleonic Code.

ASSESS

Check for Understanding

Assign Section 4 Review as homework or as an in-class activity.

⊙ Use Student Self-Test and Review Software to review Section 4.

Evaluate

🗀 Section Quiz 11-4

⊙ Use the Testmaker to create a customized quiz for Section 4.

MAKING CONNECTIONS ACTIVITY

Daily Life During the years of the French Empire, clothing and furniture were made in what became known as the Empire style. Have students prepare an oral report about this style, using reference materials in a local library on the history of fashion and furniture. Encourage them to find out how this style became popular, if it spread to other countries, if it influenced other styles, and if it remained popular in later years. Ask students to make sketches or use pictures showing the Empire style in their reports. **L1 LEP**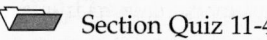

Music of Revolutions

Claude-Joseph Rouget de Lisle's marching song received the title "The Marseillaise" four months after he wrote it. Troops from Marseilles sang it as they stormed the Tuileries on August 10, 1792.

ANSWER

It appeals to people's emotions, music unites them in a common cause; answers may include high school and college "fight songs" or songs such as "We Are the World."

Reteach

Have students summarize Napoleon's greatest accomplishments and greatest defeats. *(for example, accomplishments: legal and educational reforms; defeats: defeat at Trafalgar, retreat from Russia)*

Enrich

Have students discuss what Napoleon could have done differently to make his return from Elba a success.

CLOSE

Let students discuss what they consider the most important changes in Europe caused by Napoleon's rule in France.

Music of Revolutions

Rouget de Lisle Singing "The Marseillaise" at Dietrich's *by Isidore Pils*

The French Revolution found its voice in a rousing military march written in 1792 by Joseph Rouget de Lisle, a young captain in the army engineers. The march, later known as "The Marseillaise," rallied French citizens by sounding the call to battle:

To arms, citizens!
Form your battalions,
Let us march, let us march!

"The Marseillaise" became the French national anthem in 1795. Because of its revolutionary character, it was banned under the reigns of Napoleon, Louis XVIII, and Napoleon III. It once again became the national anthem in 1879.

The best-known and most enduring song of the American Revolution was "Yankee Doodle." The British had originally used the term "yankee" as an insult. Singing "Yankee Doodle" as they marched, the British showed scorn for the American soldiers. The American colonists, however, turned the insult into a battle cry for freedom.

Revolutionary and protest groups today use music to gain public support. For example, since the 1960s, "We Shall Overcome" has been a unifying force in movements for freedom throughout the world.

Linking Past and Present ACTIVITY

Examine ways in which revolutionary music can be used to motivate people. Can you think of cases today where music is used to unite people around a cause?

---

commander when Napoleon announced, "Your general, summoned to the throne by the prayer of the people and raised upon your shields, is now restored to you; come and join him." In a period known as the Hundred Days, Napoleon again reigned as emperor. To avoid war he announced that France wanted no more territory.

The European governments, however, feared that Napoleon might regain his former strength. Determined to stop him, the armies of Prussia, Great Britain, and the Netherlands advanced toward France under the command of the Duke of Wellington. Napoleon met them at **Waterloo** in the Austrian Netherlands in June 1815; the French troops were decisively defeated. Napoleon was then placed under house arrest on the island of Saint Helena in the South Atlantic. He died there in 1821.

Napoleon's Legacy

Napoleon did not allow true representative government. He did, however, secure the revolution in France and spread throughout Europe ideas such as equality before the law, religious toleration, and advancement by merit rather than by birth. Napoleon's rule also set uniform standards of government, reformed tax systems, promoted education, and improved agriculture and industry. After the collapse of Napoleon's empire, many Europeans still wanted to keep these benefits from the French Revolution. They especially did not forget their taste of freedom from absolute monarchy.

SECTION 4 REVIEW

Recall
1. **Define** dictatorship, plebiscite, nationalism.
2. **Identify** the Napoleonic Code, the Continental System, Duke of Wellington, Alexander I, Louis XVIII, Waterloo.

3. **Discuss** the changes brought by the Napoleonic Code.
Critical Thinking
4. **Making Comparisons** Compare Napoleon's rule after the French Revolution to Cromwell's rule after the

English Civil War.
Understanding Themes
5. **Movement** How did the principles of the French Revolution spread throughout Europe and contribute to the rise of nationalism?

SECTION 4 REVIEW ANSWERS

1. All vocabulary words are defined in the Glossary.
2. Napoleonic Code, 351; Continental System, 352; Duke of Wellington, 352; Alexander I, 352; Louis XVIII, 353; Waterloo, 354
3. It made French law clear and consistent, basing it on Enlightenment ideas such as the equality of all citizens before the law. However, it placed the state above the individual and limited rights of women and children.
4. Both were stern military leaders who restored order to countries after a period of political chaos.
5. **MOVEMENT** While emperor, Napoleon helped spread the principles of the French Revolution; however, he also aroused resentment in the peoples he conquered by making them pay taxes to France and provide soldiers for his armies. This resentment, coupled with the inspiration of the new ideals of liberty, led to the development of nationalism.

Interpreting Graphs

When you divide a pizza among four people, it is easy to estimate where the circle should be sliced. A circle graph is similar to a round pizza. Circle graphs are useful for showing percentages, such as 25 percent of a pizza. A line or bar graph, however, can be used to show changes over a period of time.

Most graphs also use words to identify or label information. These steps will help you interpret graphs.

- Read the title.
- Read the captions and text.
- Determine the relationships among all sections of the graph.

Learning the Skill

The circle on the right is like a clock. It visually compares the time periods from the following information about revolution and empire in France between 1789 and 1815.

1. **Estates-General and National Assembly**
   May 1789–September 1791
   Limited constitutional monarchy
2. **Legislative Assembly**
   October 1791–September 1792
   New constitution; delegates seated according to political beliefs
3. **National Convention**
   September 1792–October 1795
   King executed; Reign of Terror
4. **Directory**
   October 1795–November 1799
   New constitution with bicameral legislature, five executive directors; Napoleon seizes control
5. **Consulate**
   December 1799–May 1804
   New constitution sets up three consuls; Napoleon rules
6. **Empire**
   May 1804–June 1815
   Napoleon I, emperor until overthrown

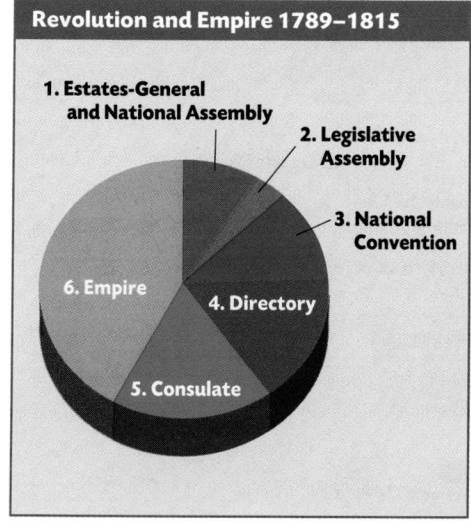

Revolution and Empire 1789–1815

1. Estates-General and National Assembly
2. Legislative Assembly
3. National Convention
4. Directory
5. Consulate
6. Empire

Practicing the Skill

Study the graph and answer the following questions.
1. What was the longest of the six periods of the French Revolution?
2. What was the shortest of the six periods?
3. About what percentage of the total time did Napoleon rule France (during the Consulate and Empire)?
4. About what percentage of the time did the Directory rule?

Applying the Skill

Draw a circle graph showing the major divisions of your day.

For More Practice

Turn to the Skill Practice in the Chapter Review on page 365 for more practice in interpreting graphs.

TEACH

Interpreting Graphs Conduct a class survey by counting the number of students who travel to school on foot, by bicycle, on a school bus, by public transportation, or by car. (Have students choose the method they use the most often.) Note the results on the chalkboard and call on volunteers to convert these numbers into percentages. Next, draw a circle on the chalkboard and explain that it represents the whole class, or 100 percent. Divide the circle into sections to represent the percentages of the subgroups. Have students note how the circle illustrates the relationship of the parts to the whole. Then have students read the skill and complete the practice questions.

Additional Practice

📁 Skill Reinforcement Activity 11

📁 Building Skills in Geography Workbook, Unit 2, Lesson 8

ANSWERS TO PRACTICING THE SKILL

1. Empire
2. Legislative Assembly
3. about 66 percent
4. about 15 percent

356 Chapter 11 The French Revolution

1810   1815   1820   1825

1814 Congress of Vienna meets.

1819 Carlsbad Decrees impose censorship in Prussia.

1821 Greek nationalists revolt against Turkish rule.

SECTION THEME

▶ **Reaction** European leaders try to reestablish the old order.

Find Out

Answer: *They were fairly successful, restoring absolute monarchies throughout Europe. However, liberals and nationalists did continue to demonstrate and fight for reforms in several countries.*

FOCUS

Section Objective

Evaluate the success of the plans of the reactionaries to thwart the spread of liberalism in Europe.

BELLRINGER
Motivational Activity

Before taking roll at the beginning of the class period, project Section Focus Transparency 11-5 and have students answer the activity questions. Discuss students' responses.

▱ This activity is also available as a blackline master.

Vocabulary Pre-check

▣ Use the Vocabulary PuzzleMaker to create a puzzle that reinforces the vocabulary terms in this section. **L1**

Section 5

Peace in Europe

Setting the Scene

▶ **Terms to Define**
buffer state, reactionary, liberalism

▶ **People to Meet**
Prince Klemens von Metternich

▶ **Places to Locate**
Vienna

 How successful were the plans of the reactionaries to thwart the spread of liberalism in Europe?

The Storyteller

Vienna, native city of Haydn, home of Brahms, and host to Europe's greatest musicians, was known for its opera and its pageantry. The medieval streets of the old city, dominated by the tall Gothic tower of St. Stephen's Cathedral, were once occupied by Napoleon's troops. Now Vienna would host the victorious assembled aristocracies. The czar of Russia, the kings of Prussia, Denmark, Bavaria, and Saxony, and the nobility dined at forty lavish tables in the Hofburg. Colorful military parades, fireworks, balls in the Grand Hall, and Beethoven's concerts all served to disguise the serious discussions that would establish Europe's "balance of power."

The Old University in Vienna

—adapted from *Western Civilization, an Urban Perspective,* F. Roy Willis, 1973

Walking along the streets of **Vienna**, Austria, in the autumn of 1814 were the kings, princes, and diplomats who had gathered for a peace conference known as the Congress of Vienna. With Napoleon in exile, the delegates had come to Vienna to restore order and stability in Europe after nearly 25 years of war.

The Congress met from September 1814 to June 1815. Nearly every European nation sent delegates, but the Congress's main work was done by Austria's **Prince Klemens von Metternich** of Austria, Russia's Czar Alexander I, and Great Britain's Lord Robert Castlereagh (KAS•uhl•ray). Prince Maurice de Talleyrand, once a bishop, represented defeated France.

The Congress of Vienna

Austria's chief minister, Prince Klemens von Metternich, served as host to the Congress and presided over it. Metternich believed that in order to establish European stability, Europe should be restored to the way it was before the French Revolution. To achieve his goal, Metternich maintained that settlements reached at Vienna would be guided by three principles: compensation, legitimacy, and balance of power. Compensation meant that all countries should be repaid for the expenses they incurred while fighting the French. By legitimacy, Metternich meant restoring to power the royal families who had ruled before Napoleon. Finally, balance of power meant that no country should ever again dominate continental Europe.

Redrawing the Map

As the victors of the war claimed their rewards, they redrew the map of Europe. France was forced to give up its recently gained territory and to pay a large indemnity, or compensation, to other countries for war damages. Although Great Britain did not gain land in continental Europe, it took from France most of its remaining islands in the West

---

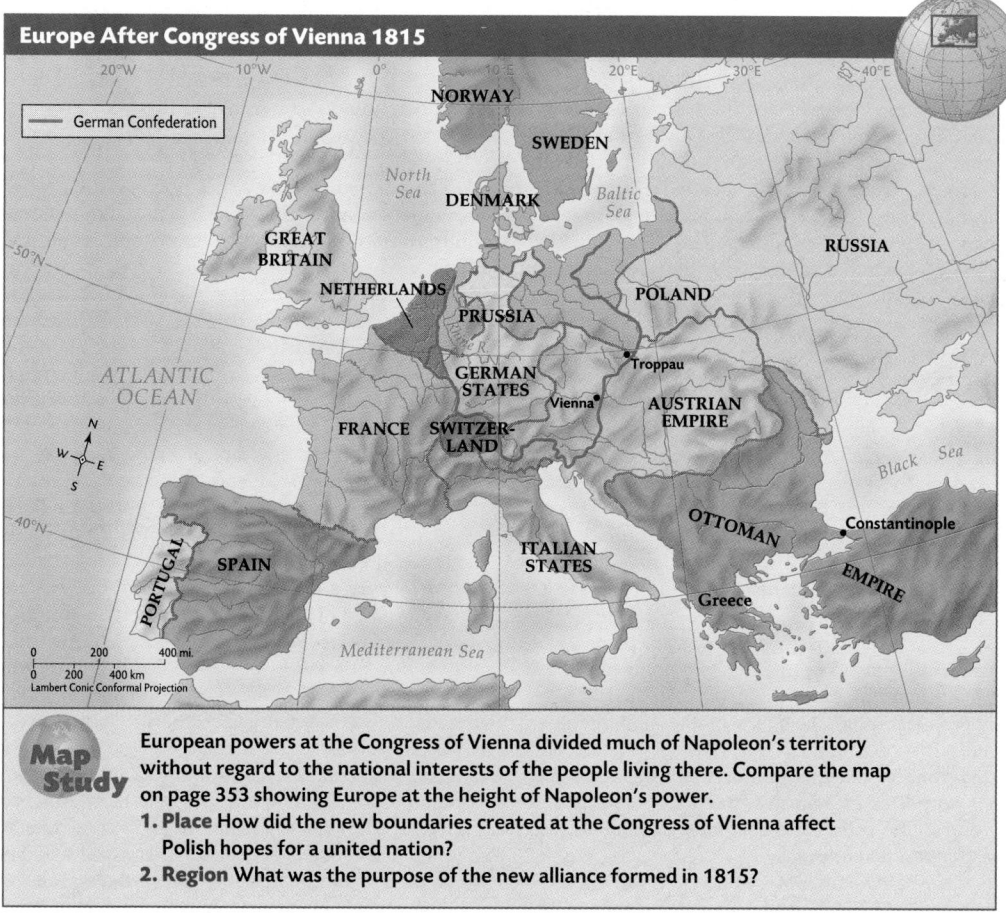

Europe After Congress of Vienna 1815

— German Confederation

NORWAY
SWEDEN
North Sea
DENMARK
Baltic Sea
GREAT BRITAIN
RUSSIA
NETHERLANDS
POLAND
PRUSSIA
ATLANTIC OCEAN
GERMAN STATES
Troppau
Vienna
FRANCE
SWITZERLAND
AUSTRIAN EMPIRE
Black Sea
OTTOMAN
Constantinople
ITALIAN STATES
EMPIRE
PORTUGAL
SPAIN
Greece
Mediterranean Sea

0   200   400 mi.
0   200   400 km
Lambert Conic Conformal Projection

Map Study

European powers at the Congress of Vienna divided much of Napoleon's territory without regard to the national interests of the people living there. Compare the map on page 353 showing Europe at the height of Napoleon's power.

1. **Place** How did the new boundaries created at the Congress of Vienna affect Polish hopes for a united nation?
2. **Region** What was the purpose of the new alliance formed in 1815?

Indies. Austria gained the Italian provinces of Lombardy and Venetia as well as territory on the eastern coast of the Adriatic Sea.

At the conference Prussia and Russia also made it known that they wanted to expand their borders by seizing formerly French-held lands. Yet Great Britain and Austria feared that increased Prussian and Russian influence in central Europe would lead to an imbalance of power on the continent. To put pressure on Prussia and Russia, Great Britain and Austria made an agreement with France. The agreement bound the three powers—Great Britain, Austria, and France—to resist any further Prussian or Russian territorial expansion in Europe by armed force if it was necessary.

In the end a compromise was reached. Prussia received extensive territories along the Rhine River and almost half the kingdom of Saxony for its compensation. Russia received most of the Polish

territory formerly held by Prussia and Austria. This increased the Polish territory held by Russia. A new kingdom of Poland was then formed under the czar.

Restoring the Monarchies

Once the territorial compensation was settled, delegates at the Congress of Vienna turned to stabilizing European governments. Believing that divine-right monarchy was necessary for proper order, the delegates made settlements based on legitimate claims to the throne and restored the absolute monarchs who ruled Europe before Napoleon. The Congress reestablished royal dynasties in France, Spain, Portugal, Naples, Sardinia, and Sicily. In France the Congress officially recognized the Bourbon heir Louis XVIII as the legitimate, or legal, ruler.

To safeguard other ruling dynasties, the Congress placed further controls on France. It

Chapter 11 *The French Revolution* **357**

TEACH

Guided Practice

THEME Reaction

Have students describe reactionary measures taken by the Congress of Vienna to restore Europe to pre-French Revolution status. *(restored absolute monarchies, formed an alliance to keep liberalism and nationalism in check)* **L1**

Map Study

Answers

1. *Poland's hopes were crushed; Polish lands were divided among Russia, Prussia, and Austria.*
2. *to prevent democratic revolutions in Europe*

Map Skills Practice

Reading a Map Compare this map with the map on page 353. Which European states gained French land in 1815? *(the Netherlands, Prussia, German States, and Italian States)*

Geography: Movement Using the map showing Europe after the Congress of Vienna in 1815, have students describe how the map of Europe was redrawn. *(Prussia received territories along the Rhine, almost half of Saxony; Russia received Polish territory formerly held by Prussia and Austria, increased Polish territory held by Russia.)* **L3**

Mapping History Overlay Transparency 14, *France and Europe*

COOPERATIVE LEARNING ACTIVITY

Report Organize the class into three groups. Have one group create a large map of Europe after the Congress of Vienna, using the map in their book as a guide. Have the second group make a wall chart listing countries that participated in the Congress of Vienna, the major leaders who represented each country, and the terms of the Quadruple Alliance. Have the third group make a wall chart listing countries and leaders who reacted against the Congress of Vienna's work and the results of their reactions. Remind students to use library resources when needed. Have groups display their work on a "Congress of Vienna" bulletin-board display. **L2**

Independent Practice

 Guided Reading Activity
11-5 **L1**

Foreign Affairs Have students
create a chart with three columns
titled *Holy Alliance, Quadruple
Alliance,* and *Concert of Europe.* In
each column, have students write
short statements describing the
alliance. *(for example: Holy
Alliance: by order of Czar Alexander
I, called for Christian rulers in
Europe to cooperate as a union of
monarchs)* **L1**

Essay Have students write a
short essay explaining what the
Carlsbad Decrees were and why
they were instituted. **L3**

Linking Past and Present

Carlsbad Decrees The repressive measures of the 1819
Carlsbad Decrees ended student
protests for reform. Students in
the 1980s and 1990s also used
protests as a way to achieve
change. Student protests in
China were brutally put down;
but in South Africa and Eastern
Europe, protests and pressure
from other countries helped
bring about change.

Visualizing History
Parties, balls,
and pageantry reminded delegates
of what life had been like before the
revolution.
Answer to Caption: *to establish
peace and stability in Europe*

ASSESS

Check for Understanding

Assign Section 5 Review as homework or as an in-class activity.

---

reduced French borders to those of 1790 and established buffer states, or neutral territories, around
French territory. To the north of France, the
Austrian Netherlands and the Dutch Netherlands
became one country under the Dutch ruler. Thirty-
nine independent German states formed the
German Confederation, headed by Austria.
Switzerland regained its neutrality and independence as a federal league of states. The Italian kingdom of Piedmont united with the Mediterranean
island of Sardinia.

Forces Changing Europe

The diplomats responsible for most of the
agreements made at the Congress of Vienna were
reactionaries, people who opposed change and
wanted to return things to the way they had been in
earlier times. They strongly felt that Europe could
maintain peace only by returning to the tradition of
strong absolute monarchies in effect before the
French Revolution.

The reactionaries hoped that their plans would
thwart the spread of liberalism, a political philosophy influencing European peoples in the 1800s. The
liberals accepted the ideas of the Enlightenment
and the democratic reforms of the French
Revolution. Believing in individual freedom, liberals supported ideas such as freedom of speech, freedom of the press, and religious freedom—which
had led to revolution.

The reactionaries also hoped to crush the rise of
nationalism throughout Europe. When they redrew
national boundaries, the delegates reflected the
wishes of the rulers rather than those of the people
they governed. The new boundaries thwarted the
nationalistic hopes of many European groups. For

example, the boundaries crushed the Polish people's hopes for a united nation of their own.
Instead, their land was parceled out among their
neighbors: Austria, Prussia, and Russia.

Alliances

The diplomats knew that nationalistic desires
for independence, democratic rule, and national
unity could well lead to revolution, and revolution
threatened everything they believed in. To prevent
democratic revolutions, they agreed to form new
alliances. Great Britain, Austria, Prussia, and Russia
joined in the Quadruple Alliance to maintain the
settlements of Vienna. The four powers concluded
the alliance in November 1815. France was admitted three years later, when the members of the
alliance met for the first time at Aix-la-Chapelle.

According to the alliance agreement, representatives of the great powers were to meet periodically to discuss the security of Europe. Their goals
included preservation of territorial boundaries set
at the Congress of Vienna, exclusion of Napoleon
Bonaparte and his heirs from French rule, and prevention of any revolutionary movements from taking hold in Europe.

With the goals of securing international order
based on "Justice, Christian Charity, and Peace,"
Czar Alexander I of Russia created the Holy
Alliance. Issued in the name of the czar, the Prussian
king, and the Austrian emperor, the Holy Alliance
called for Christian rulers in Europe to cooperate as
a union of monarchs. Metternich dismissed the idea
as "a loud-sounding nothing." Nevertheless, all the
invited rulers joined the Holy Alliance except Pope
Pius VII and the British government. The pope had
said that "from time immemorial the papacy had
been in possession of Christian truth and needed no
new interpretation of it." The British government

Visualizing History The serious
work of the
Congress of Vienna was nearly
overshadowed by lavish
entertainment—plays, musicals, and balls. *What did
Metternich want to achieve by a
balance of power?*

358

Reading Comprehension The principles that guided Metternich at the Congress of Vienna were
compensation, legitimacy, and balance of power. Help students find these terms in Section 5. Ask
them to explain what Metternich meant by these principles and how he carried them out. Then
have students work in pairs to write three original sentences, each using one of these terms. Let
students share their sentences. **L1**

excused itself on the grounds that, without approval by Parliament, such an alliance would violate the British constitution.

The Concert of Europe

The two alliances encouraged European nations to work together to preserve the peace. The members decided to have regular meetings to settle international problems. These meetings became known as the Concert of Europe. This system helped to avoid major European conflicts by resolving local problems peaceably.

For nearly 30 years, Metternich used the system set up by the Congress of Vienna to achieve his own political goals: to oppose liberalism and nationalism and to defend absolute monarchies in Europe. His system of beliefs came to be known as the Metternich system.

Metternich's political goals and the Concert of Europe did not go unchallenged, however. In Germany university students demonstrated for liberal reforms and national unity. Alarmed by this revolutionary activity, Metternich persuaded King Frederick William III of Prussia to pass a series of repressive measures in 1819. These so-called Carlsbad Decrees imposed strict censorship on all publications and suppressed freedom of speech. Metternich, with the support of the Prussian king, managed to end student agitation in Germany, but new challenges to the status quo arose in other areas.

Liberal reformers in Spain, for example, forced their monarch to agree to constitutional government in 1820. Metternich pressured members of the Quadruple Alliance to intervene in European countries and their territories to prevent the spread of liberalism. Great Britain, with a tradition of liberalism in government, opposed the action and broke from the alliance. Metternich's system did prevail, however, as French troops restored the Spanish king to full power. But the spirit of revolt did not die, for

 Visualizing History Metternich pushed for the creation of the Quadruple Alliance. *What was the alliance's major role?*

Spanish colonies in Latin America successfully revolted against Spanish control during the 1820s.

The Greeks also fought for their independence in 1821 when Greek nationalists revolted against Turkish rule. Metternich intervened by attempting to stop other countries from aiding the rebellion. The British and the French provided assistance to the Greek nationalists despite Metternich's threats. Greece finally won independence from the Ottoman Empire in 1829.

The stable political system Metternich envisioned throughout Europe would soon be under attack. The nationalistic spirit fostered by the French Revolution would not die in Europe.

SECTION 5 REVIEW

Recall
1. **Define** buffer state, reactionary, liberalism.
2. **Identify** the Congress of Vienna, Prince Klemens von Metternich, Quadruple Alliance.
3. **List** the three guiding principles Metternich used at the Congress of Vienna.

Critical Thinking
4. **Making Comparisons** Compare and contrast the political philosophies of a liberal and a reactionary in the 1800s.

Understanding Themes
5. **Reaction** Why were the countries at the Congress of Vienna mostly represented by reactionaries? What effect did their views and policies have on the spread of liberalism and nationalism throughout Europe?

Chapter 11 *The French Revolution* **359**

Chapter 11
Section 5

 Visualizing History Metternich dominated European politics for 30 years after the Congress of Vienna. **Answer to Caption:** *maintaining the settlements made in Vienna*

Use Student Self-Test and Review Software to review Section 5.

Evaluate
Section Quiz 11-5

Use the Testmaker to create a customized quiz for Section 5.

Reteach
Have students summarize how the alliances formed after 1814 contributed to peace in Europe.

 Reteaching Activity 11

Enrich
Have students research the effect of Great Britain withdrawing from the Quadruple Alliance.

Enrichment Activity 11

CLOSE

Ask students to make a wall chart summarizing the work of the Congress of Vienna and the Concert of Europe.

SECTION 5 REVIEW ANSWERS

1. All vocabulary words are defined in the Glossary.
2. Congress of Vienna, 356; Prince Klemens von Metternich, 356; Quadruple Alliance, 358
3. compensation, legitimacy, balance of power
4. Liberals accepted the ideas of the Enlightenment and the French Revolution. Reactionaries wanted to reestablish absolute monarchies.
5. **REACTION** Monarchies in the various countries had returned to power. Reactionaries redrew boundaries to reflect the wishes of the rulers rather than the people they governed, thus igniting nationalistic revolts throughout Europe.

Block Schedule

Team Teaching This excerpt from *Les Misérables* may be presented in a team-teaching context, in conjunction with English or Language Arts.

Les Misérables

Historical Connection

This excerpt from Hugo's novel portrays the social conflicts that wracked France in the 1820s. The bitter argument between the young man and his grandfather reflects the division between monarchists and supporters of the French Republic that persisted long after Napoleon's death.

Background Information

Setting The scene takes place in 1827. Napoleon died in 1821, and the French monarchy has been restored. The spirit of republicanism, here represented by the memory of Marius's father, continues to influence the younger generation.

Characters Monsieur Gillenormand: grandfather of Marius, a bourgeois supporter of the monarchy; Marius: an 18-year-old who is beginning to develop political consciousness.

Plot Marius's grandfather and aunt search his belongings and find a note stating that Napoleon had made Marius's father a baron. When Marius arrives, the grandfather ridicules all republicans as bandits; Marius in turn insults the French monarchy. The scene ends with Gillenormand ordering Marius from his home.

360 Chapter 11 *The French Revolution*

from
Les Misérables
by Victor Hugo

A s we have seen, literature can be a bridge to the past, transporting us to a world that may seem strange or obscure at first, but that has much in common with our own. Across the gap between then and now we can see faces that we recognize, situations that are familiar, hopes that we share. The selection that follows was written by one of France's most celebrated writers, Victor Hugo. Hugo lived from 1802 to 1885, a time of dramatic and violent change for France. In this scene, Monsieur Gillenormand snoops through the belongings of his grandson, Marius. Assisting the grandfather is Marius's aunt. Marius's father has recently died.

M . Gillenormand, who had risen early like all the elderly who are in good health, had heard [Marius] come in, and hurried as fast as he could with his old legs, to climb to the top of the stairs where Marius's room was, to give him a kiss, question him while embracing him, and find out something about where he had come from.

But the youth had taken less time to go down than the old man to go up, and when Grandfather Gillenormand went into the garret room, Marius was no longer there.

The bed had not been disturbed, and on it were trustingly laid the coat and the black ribbon.

"I like that better," said M. Gillenormand.

And a moment later he entered the drawing room [room for receiving guests] where Mlle. Gillenormand the elder was already seated, embroidering her carriage wheels.

The entrance was triumphant.

In one hand M. Gillenormand held the coat and in the other the neck ribbon, and cried out, "Victory! We are about to penetrate the mystery! We shall know the end of the mystery, unravel the wanton ways of our rascal! Here we are right to the core of the romance. I have the portrait!"

In fact, a black shagreen box, rather like a medallion, was fastened to the ribbon.

The old man took this box and looked at it for some time without opening it, with that air of desire, delight, and anger, with which a poor,

360 Chapter 11 *The French Revolution*

BOUT THE AUTHOR

Victor Hugo expressed in his writing his concern for the poor, his belief in democracy, and his desire for social reform. In the mid-1840s, he won election to the French Chamber of Peers, where he advocated public funding of education and the broadening of the voting franchise. After the republican government of France was overthrown, he left the country to live in Belgium and Great Britain. In the middle of his almost twenty-year exile, he published *Les Misérables*. In 1870 he returned to France. By then, he was a successful and well-known writer. When Hugo died, huge throngs of Parisians marched in his funeral procession.

hungry devil sees an excellent dinner pass right under his nose, when it is not for him.

"For it is clearly a portrait. I know all about these things. They are worn tenderly against the heart. What fools they are! Some abominable floozy, probably enough to bring on the shudders! Young people have such bad taste nowadays!"

"Let's see, father," said the old maid.

The box opened by pressing a spring. They found nothing in it but a piece of paper carefully folded.

"More and more predictable," said M. Gillenormand, bursting with laughter. "I know what that is. A love letter!"

"Ah! Then let's read it!" said the aunt.

And she put on her spectacles. They unfolded the paper and read this:

"*For my Son.*—The emperor made me a baron on the battlefield of Waterloo. Since the Restoration contests this title I have bought with my blood, my son will take it and bear it. I need not say that he will be worthy of it."

The feelings of the father and daughter are beyond description. They felt chilled as by the breath of a death's head [skull]. They did not exchange a word. M. Gillenormand, however, said in a low voice, and as if talking to himself, "It is the handwriting of that bandit."

The aunt examined the paper, turned it over every which way, then put it back in the box.

At that very moment, a little rectangular package wrapped in blue paper fell out of the coat pocket. Mademoiselle Gillenormand picked it up and unwrapped the blue paper. It was Marius's hundred

[calling] cards. She passed one of them to M. Gillenormand, who read: *Baron Marius Pontmercy.*

The old man rang. Nicolette [the chambermaid] came. M. Gillenormand took the ribbon, the box, and the coat, threw them all on the floor in the middle of the drawing room, and said:

"Take those things away."

A full hour passed in complete silence. The old man and the old maid sat with their backs turned to one another, and were probably each individually thinking over the same things. At the end of that hour, Aunt Gillenormand said, "Pretty!"

A few minutes later, Marius appeared. He was just coming home. Even before crossing the

Visualizing History A French salon displays the wealth of the bourgeoisie. With the end of the revolution, the return of social class distinctions accompanied the restoration of the monarchy. *Why was Monsieur Gillenormand angry about Marius's calling cards?*

Literary Elements Repetition is the use of a word or phrase over and over to achieve some effect. In his tirade against the republicans, the grandfather repeats "I don't know" and "all," revealing that he has strong opinions but little knowledge.

Irony is the use of a word in a way that conveys the opposite of its usual meaning. When Marius's aunt says, "Pretty!" she means that the situation has become unpleasant and uncomfortable.

FOCUS

Point out to students that Gillenormand and Marius still harbor passionate feelings more than a decade after Napoleon's defeat. **By showing that the conflict between monarchists and republicans had not disappeared, what is Hugo saying about the issues at stake in the French Revolution?** (*that they were crucial, life-or-death matters*) **Are there issues or events that arouse such strong emotion today?** (*Answers will vary.*)

Visualizing History The literal meaning of the French word *salon* is "room" or "chamber." Later it came to refer to gatherings of intellectuals.

Answer to Caption: *He probably felt that only the king, not a usurper like Napoleon, had the right to make Marius's father a baron.*

OTHER WORKS BY VICTOR HUGO

Cobb, Walter J., trans. *The Hunchback of Notre Dame.* New York: New American Library, 1965.

The Works of Victor Hugo. New York: W.J. Black, 1928.

TEACH

Literary Analysis

Ask students to consider Monsieur Gillenormand's statement that a bourgeois like himself cannot live under the same roof with a baron. **Why is it ironic that Marius would have a higher social position than his grandfather?** *(because Marius and his father are supposedly republicans, not aristocrats)*

Visualizing History

In 1848 a wave of rebellions and near-revolutions challenged the old regimes of Europe. In France, the failed popular movement paved the way for the rise of Napoleon III, the nephew of Napoleon Bonaparte, who ruled as emperor from 1852 to 1870. **Answer to Caption:** *Gillenormand seems coldhearted.*

Evaluation

To describe the rage that Marius feels when his father is insulted, Hugo compares him to a priest and to a fakir. Discuss with students why Hugo compared Marius to religious figures. Many supporters of the revolution were not religious; Hugo may be implying that their politics had become a religion.

Literary Analysis

Discuss how Hugo builds tension in the final scene in the excerpt. By describing how the grandfather walks across the room, Hugo draws the scene out and involves the reader in the conflict.

World Literature Selection 5

Visualizing History A republican club meets in Paris in 1848. Victor Hugo's concern for the common people underlies much of his writing. Social commentary and support for democratic movements mark his works in the 1850s and 1860s. *How does the character of Monsieur Gillenormand portray aristocracy?*

threshold of the drawing room, he saw his grandfather holding one of his cards in his hand; the old man, on seeing him, exclaimed with his crushing air of sneering bourgeois superiority, "Well! Well! Well! Well! Well! So you are a baron now. My compliments. What does this mean?"

Marius blushed slightly, and answered, "It means I am my father's son."

M. Gillenormand stopped laughing, and said harshly, "Your father; I am your father."

"My father," resumed Marius with downcast eyes and stern manner, "was a humble and heroic man, who served the Republic and France gloriously, who was great in the greatest history that men have ever made, who lived a quarter of a century in the camps, under fire by day, and by night in the snow, in the mud, and the rain, who captured colors [flags], who was twenty times wounded, who died forgotten and abandoned, and who had but one fault; that was to have too dearly loved two ingrates [ungrateful persons], his country and me."

This was more than M. Gillenormand could bear. At the word, "Republic," he rose, or rather, sprang to his feet. Every one of the words

ADDITIONAL LITERARY WORKS OF THE PERIOD

Brontë, Charlotte. *Jane Eyre.* New York: Modern Library, 1993. Story of bright, self-possessed young woman of humble origins who falls in love with a troubled, wealthy Englishman.

Dickens, Charles. *Oliver Twist.* New York: Penguin, 1966. Novel about a poor English boy struggling to survive in the slums of London.

Stowe, Harriet Beecher. *Uncle Tom's Cabin.* New York: Penguin, 1981. Antislavery novel that helped turned Northerners against the institution of slavery.

Swift, Jonathan. *Gulliver's Travels.* New York: Oxford, 1977. Biting satire about English society and the human race in general.

Marius had just spoken, produced on the old royalist's face the effect of a blast from a bellows on a burning coal. From dark he had turned red, from red to purple, and from purple to flaming.

"Marius!" he exclaimed, "abominable child! I don't know what your father was! I don't want to know! I know nothing about him and I don't know him! But what I do know is that there was never anything but miserable wretches among them! That they were all beggars, assassins, thieves, rabble in their red bonnets! I say all of them! I say all of them! I don't know anybody! I say all of them! Do you hear, Marius? Look here, you are as much a baron as my slipper! They were all bandits, those who served Robespierre! All brigands who served Bu-o-na-parté! All traitors who betrayed, betrayed, betrayed! Their legitimate king! All cowards who ran from the Prussians and English at Waterloo! That's what I know. If your father is among them I don't know him, I'm sorry, so much the worse. Your humble servant, sir!"

In turn, it was Marius who now became the coal, and M. Gillenormand the bellows. Marius shuddered in every limb, he had no idea what to do, his head was burning. He was the priest who sees all his wafers thrown to the winds, the fakir [member of a Muslim religious order] seeing a passerby spit on his idol. He could not allow such things to be said before him. But what could he do? His father had just been trodden underfoot and stamped on in his presence, but by whom? By his grandfather. How could he avenge the one without outraging the other? It

was impossible for him to insult his grandfather, and it was equally impossible for him not to avenge his father. On one hand a sacred tomb, on the other a white head. For a few moments he felt dizzy and staggering with all this whirlwind in his head; then he raised his eyes, looked straight at his grandfather, and cried in a thundering voice: "Down with the Bourbons, and that great hog Louis XVIII!"

Louis XVIII had been dead for four years; but that made no difference to him.

Scarlet as he was, the old man suddenly turned whiter than his hair. He turned toward a bust of the Duc de Berry that stood on the mantel and bowed to it profoundly with a sort of peculiar majesty. Then he walked twice, slowly and in silence, from the fireplace to the window and from the window to the fireplace, covering the whole length of the room and making the parquet creak as if an image of stone were walking over it. The second time, he bent toward his daughter, who was enduring the shock with the stupor of an aged sheep, and said to her with a smile that was almost calm, "A baron like Monsieur and a bourgeois like myself cannot remain under the same roof."

And all at once straightening up, pallid, trembling, terrible, his forehead swelling with the fearful radiance of anger, he stretched his arm towards Marius and cried out, "Be off!"

Marius left the house.

The next day, M. Gillenormand said to his daughter, "You will send sixty pistoles [old gold coins] every six months to that blood drinker, and never speak of him to me again."

RESPONDING TO LITERATURE

1. What political conflict of the period does the heated clash between Marius and his grandfather represent?
2. What sort of person is Monsieur Gillenormand?
3. If Marius's father had not been a hero at the Battle of Waterloo, do you think Marius still would have become a revolutionary? Explain your answer.
4. **Supporting an Opinion** Was the era of the French Revolution and Napoleon "the greatest history that men have ever made," as Marius claims? Support your answer with evidence.

ANSWERS TO RESPONDING TO LITERATURE

1. Marius was a republican, a supporter of political reform, while his grandfather was a conservative royalist.
2. Answers might include that he is nosy, brash, unprincipled, and insulting, but that he does plan to send money to his grandson after throwing him out.
3. Students may feel that because of his temperament, Marius would be a republican whether or not his father had fought with Napoleon.
4. Answers will vary; students may say that the fact that the revolution dramatically changed not only French but also European history makes this claim justified.

Literature

Linking Past and Present

Les Misérables was made into one of the most popular musical plays of the 1990s. Students may be interested in listening to the soundtrack of the play.

ASSESS

Assign **Responding to Literature** questions.

CLOSE

After students have read the excerpt, ask them to discuss the high-handed treatment that Marius receives from his grandfather. Are conflicts between older and younger people common today? What issues lead to disagreements between them? (*Answers will vary.*)

Contemporary Connection

The musical *Les Misérables* has been playing on Broadway for more than 10 years. *Les Misérables* has also been made into five movies, including a 1935 version starring Charles Laughton and Fredric March. The universal appeal of its themes has extended for more than 100 years. The themes of Hugo's popular story—conflicting political loyalties and generation gaps—are as applicable today as when the book was published.

Portfolio Project

Write a script for a brief dialogue between a member of the older generation and yourself. The subject could be a political or social issue.

GLENCOE
TECHNOLOGY

VIDEODISC
Use MindJogger to review students' knowledge of the chapter.

MindJogger Videoquiz

Chapter 11
Disc 2 Side A

  Also available in VHS.

Answers

Using Key Terms
1. j   4. k
2. i   5. l
3. c

Using Your History Journal

Students should consider how the lives of the characters they chose and how France changed as a result of Napoleon's reign.

Reviewing Facts

1. Causes: inequality of the estates; influence of Enlightenment and American Revolution; cost of living increases; government financial crisis; Effects: creation of constitutional government and Declaration of Rights; fall of the monarchy; establishment of republic; Reign of Terror; European wars; rise of Napoleon; spread of nationalism throughout Europe
2. to destroy the monarchy
3. abolition of feudal dues and tithes, taxation of nobles, Declaration of Rights of Man and of the Citizen
4. Women were involved in street protests and demanded equal rights; peasants revolting in countryside to end feudal remnants; workers and artisans in

Connections Across Time

Historical Significance The French Revolution's ideals of "liberty, equality, and fraternity" continue to inspire people around the world. In parts of Africa, China, the Middle East, and Latin America, people of diverse backgrounds struggle for political freedom.

Many of these struggles have been ignited by feelings of nationalism, as people yearn for self-rule and the return of their traditions. As Napoleon learned in the collapse of his empire, even the strictest military control cannot suppress the power of nationalism.

Using Key Terms

Write the key term that completes each sentence. Then write a sentence for each term not chosen.

a. bourgeoisie
b. buffer states
c. conscription
d. coup d'état
e. émigrés
f. estate
g. dictatorship
h. liberalism
i. nationalism
j. plebiscite
k. reactionaries
l. tithe
m. unicameral legislature

1. Napoleon Bonaparte's move to become Consul for life was supported by a _____ , or popular vote.
2. Intense feelings of _____ caused people to fight for self-rule and a return to their traditional customs.
3. French revolutionaries resorted to _____ , or drafting civilians, in their fight against European powers.
4. _____ wanted to return absolute monarchs to Europe after the collapse of Napoleon's empire in 1814.
5. Before the revolution the Catholic Church in France was supported by a _____ , or a 10 percent tax on income.

Technology Activity

Developing a Multimedia Presentation Use a computerized card catalog or the Internet to find information about the French Revolution and the American Revolution. Using images from the Internet, create a short multimedia presentation comparing the two revolutions. Include a plan describing the type of multimedia presentation you would like to develop and the steps you will take to ensure its success.

Using Your History Journal

Napoleon's army lost 400,000 soldiers in the retreat from Russia. Many more died in other battles. Were the reforms of the French Revolution worth its cost? Answer this question from the viewpoint of the character you chose at the beginning of the chapter in an opinion article for a French newspaper to be published upon the death of Napoleon in 1821.

Reviewing Facts

1. **History** Identify the causes and effects of the French Revolution.
2. **History** Explain why Louis XVI was executed.
3. **Government** List three accomplishments of the French National Assembly.
4. **Citizenship** Describe the role of women, peasants, and urban workers in the French Revolution.
5. **History** Describe the Concert of Europe.

Critical Thinking

1. **Apply** Why was the creation of a French republic a significant turning point in history?
2. **Apply** What Enlightenment ideas affected the French Revolution?
3. **Synthesize** What circumstances, if any, justify a violent revolution? What other means could be used to change an unfair or tyrannical system of government?
4. **Evaluate** In your opinion, did Napoleon's thirst for power help or hurt France? Europe?

towns favored republican government and pushed the revolution toward greater equality and social changes.
5. meetings of members of the Quadruple Alliance and the Holy Alliance to keep peace in Europe

Critical Thinking

1. France was the first large European state that overthrew a monarchy and established a democratic republic. It became a model for democratic government elsewhere.
2. rule by the people expressed in extension of voting rights, equality of all citizens before the law, written constitutions and declarations of citizens' rights, and representative government with elected officials
3. Possible answer: suppression of basic rights; work within the system or use of nonviolent protest

Geography in History

1. **Location** Refer to the map below. What is the global address of Paris?
2. **Place** What role did agriculture play in starting the French Revolution?
3. **Movement** Why did Napoleon want to prevent British ships from trading at various European ports?

Western Europe 1789

Understanding Themes

1. **Revolution** What similarities and differences do you see between the American and the French Revolutions?
2. **Change** What specific rights did the Declaration of Rights apply to French citizens? How did the Declaration and other revolutionary events affect the position of French women?
3. **Conflict** How did violence and fear among the French people contribute to Napoleon's seizure of power?
4. **Movement** How did the desire to expand his European empire help to bring about the downfall of Napoleon?
5. **Reaction** How did the Congress of Vienna

show itself to be a strong reaction to revolutionary ideals?

Linking Past and Present

1. Napoleon tried to use military force to unite Europe under his rule. What attempts have been made in this century to forcibly bring Europe or large areas of Europe under one form of government?
2. Unity remains a goal of many Europeans. What recent efforts are peacefully uniting the countries of Europe?

Skill Practice

The diagram below shows the growth of the French army in the early years of the French Revolution. The graph is divided into sizes relative to the additions made to the army between 1791 and 1793. Study the diagram and answer the following questions.

1. How large was the French army in the summer of 1792?
2. How many troops were added to France's army in 1793?
3. What was the total number of French troops called into service during this period?
4. If this information were on a bar graph, the horizontal axis (line) would list the dates. The vertical axis would have labels in units of 100,000 each. What would each bar represent?

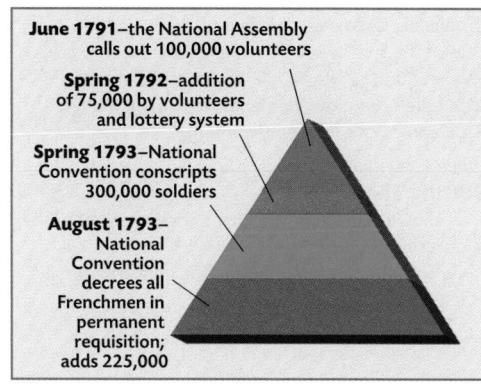

June 1791–the National Assembly calls out 100,000 volunteers

Spring 1792–addition of 75,000 by volunteers and lottery system

Spring 1793–National Convention conscripts 300,000 soldiers

August 1793– National Convention decrees all Frenchmen in permanent requisition; adds 225,000

Chapter 11 The French Revolution **365**

before the law; freedom of speech, press, religion; freedom from arbitrary arrest and punishment; the Declaration of Rights did not grant women equality with men. Women did benefit from reforms that made divorce easier and allowed them to inherit property. The Napoleonic Code later removed some of these rights.

3. **CONFLICT** Napoleon was able to use his popularity and success as a military leader to seize political power.
4. **MOVEMENT** It led to many wars and finally to military defeat.
5. **REACTION** Its actions restored monarchies and built alliances to prevent democratic revolutions.

Linking Past and Present

Answers might mention Hitler's conquest of Europe during World War II and the USSR's control of Eastern Europe after World War II; union of East and West Germany and the European Community.

Skill Practice
1. 175,000 soldiers
2. 300,000 soldiers
3. 700,000 soldiers
4. number of soldiers

? Chapter Bonus Test Question

Ask students: Why was the time ripe for revolution in France in 1789? (*widespread knowledge of Enlightenment ideas; example of the successful American Revolution; high national debt plus several poor harvests; seeming indifference of king, queen, and nobles for plight of peasants and workers*)

---

4. Possible answer: Napoleon's thirst for power led to France's downfall; French conquests antagonized other Europeans but in doing so stimulated the rise of nationalism among them.

Geography in History
1. about 48°N, about 2°E
2. Poor wheat harvests that made peasants' financial conditions worse and caused bread shortages in cities fueled the discontent.

3. Napoleon wanted to destroy the lifeline of the British economy, which was trade.

Understanding Themes
1. **REVOLUTION** Similarities: People fought for political representation and rights. Differences: Americans did not go through a period of terror or try to spread the revolution to other countries.
2. **CHANGE** All people were equal

VIDEODISC
Turning Points in World History

Side One
Chapter 10

Title: *The Scientific Revolution*

 If you do not have access to a videodisc player, **Turning Points in World History** is also available in VHS.

Internet Site

The following is a possible site for completing the "Net" activities:

The Napoleon Series
http://www.ping.be/napoleon.series/index.html

Not on the "Net"...

If students have limited or no access to the Internet, have them complete the "Napoleonic Code" activity by using resources in the school or public library to find information on the Napoleonic Code. Encourage students to use the following subjects to help them locate sources in the library's computerized or traditional card catalog: Napoleonic Code, principles, government, law.

Students may use the information they locate to help them create their chart.

ABCNEWS INTERACTIVE™ Turning Points in World History

The Scientific Revolution

Setting up the Video

Work with a group of your classmates to view "The Scientific Revolution" on the videodisc *Turning Points in World History*. The scientific revolution played a large role in shaping the world as we know it today. The seventeenth century changed dramatically from a reliance on faith and mysticism to include scientific thinking that led to many new inventions. This program examines the scientific revolution and its effects on civilization.

Hands-On Activity

Collect the following items for an invention you will create: two plastic spoons, one rubber band, two paper clips, a sheet of paper measuring 8x11, and a roll of scotch tape. Use all of the items to invent a gadget for practical use. Demonstrate your invention to the class.

 Side One, Chapter 10

View the video by scanning the bar code or by entering the chapter number on your keypad and pressing Search. (Also available in VHS format.)

Surfing the "Net"

Napoleonic Code

One of Napoleon's greatest gifts to France was his contribution to French civil law. In the Napoleonic Code, he changed old feudal laws to laws that were consistent and included some revolutionary reforms. The Napoleonic Code was a compromise between the ideas of the French Revolution and older ideas. It gave new freedoms to the people, for example, but maintained the system of inheritance. To learn about the Napoleonic Code look on the Internet.

Getting There

Follow these steps to gather information about the Napoleonic Code.
1. Go to a search engine. Type in the phrase *napoleonic code*.

2. After typing in the phrase, enter words such as the following to focus your search:
   • *principles*   • *government*   • *law*
3. The search engine should provide you with a number of links to follow. Links are "pointers" to different sites on the Internet and commonly appear as blue underlined words.

What to Do When You Are There

Click on the links to navigate through the pages of information and gather your findings. Using a word processor, create a chart comparing the American Bill of Rights to the Napoleonic Code. Share your findings with the class.

INTERNET ADDRESS BOOK

Use this space to record frequently used addresses.

_____
_____
_____
_____
_____

From about 1600 to the early 1800s, people in the Western world lived through a time of revolution, or swift and far-reaching change. During this period, Western thinkers laid the foundation of modern science and developed new ideas about society and politics. The two most important ideas were democracy—the right of the people to take an active part in government—and nationalism—the right of people who share a common culture to have their own nation. In some areas, people influenced by the new ideas rebelled against monarchs in the hope of creating better and more democratic societies.

Chapter 9
Scientific Revolution

During the 1500s and 1600s, European thinkers began relying on their own reasoning rather than automatically accepting traditional beliefs. In their investigation of nature, they gradually developed the scientific method, a way of finding scientific truth through observation and experimentation. They also developed new instruments, such as the telescope and microscope, to help them in their work. Over time, each discovery or invention led to others, creating an explosion of knowledge known as the scientific revolution.

The advance of science transformed the European understanding of the natural world. The work of scientists such as Galileo and Isaac Newton enabled Europeans to view the universe as a huge, orderly machine that worked according to definite laws that could be stated mathematically. Many European thinkers also came to believe that people could also use reason to discover the natural laws governing human behavior. They claimed that once these laws were known, people could use the laws to improve their society. English philosophers Thomas Hobbes and John Locke applied scientific reasoning to the study of government. Locke's basic conclusions—that government's authority rested on popular consent, and that the people had a right to overthrow an unjust government—were later important in the development of democracy in Europe and North America.

During the 1700s Europeans boasted they had entered an Age of Enlightenment, when the light of reason would free all people from the darkness of ignorance and superstition. They looked to France as the leading center of Enlightenment thought. Through the printed word and at public gatherings, French thinkers called philosophes claimed that science and reason could be used to promote progress in all areas of human life.

Visualizing History The Copernican model of the universe placed the sun at the center. Ptolemy's second-century model had the sun and the planets revolving around Earth. *The work of what two scientists enabled Europeans to view the universe as a huge, orderly machine?*

Unit 3   *Age of Revolution*   **367**

The Unit Digest offers a chapter-by-chapter summary that can be used for any of the following:
- **Preview** one chapter or an entire unit,
- **Review** some or all of the chapters,
- **Condense** when specific chapters or units have not been taught, or
- **Reteach** chapters that students have studied in the unit.

PREVIEW

Use the Unit 3 Digest Transparencies to preview the highlights of the unit.

Visualizing History

Answer to Caption: *Galileo and Newton*

REVIEW

Use the Student Self-Test and Review Software to review any chapters that students have studied in Unit 3.

Dialogue Organize the class into groups. Have each group pick one intellectual, political, or social change of the time covered in the unit and write a dialogue between a supporter and an opponent of the change. Then have volunteers present the dialogue to the class. Use the dialogues as springboards for discussion. *(examples: for and against the Copernican view of the universe, American independence, or the execution of Louis XVI)* **L2**

CONDENSE

Chapter 10
English and American Revolutions

While Europe experienced a revolution in science and ideas, its monarchs faced growing opposition to royal authority. The first successful challenge to the power of monarchy came in England. There, during the 1640s, a violent civil war between supporters of the Crown and the supporters of Parliament ended with the monarchy's defeat. A republic under the leading parliamentary general Oliver Cromwell brought reforms and efficient government, but most English people grew to resent its Puritan rules. In 1660 the monarchy was restored, with the king and Parliament sharing power in an uneasy relationship.

In 1685 James II, a Roman Catholic, angered the English with his desire to restore Catholicism and a strong monarchy. In 1688 Protestant nobles in Parliament invited Mary, James's Protestant daughter, and William of Orange, her husband and the ruler of the Netherlands, to take the throne. In return, William and Mary agreed to a Bill of Rights that assured the English people basic civil liberties and made the monarch subject to Parliament. During the next 100 years, England developed into a constitutional monarchy, in which the monarch's authority was limited and Parliament became the major political institution.

During the mid-1700s, Great Britain (formed by a union of England and Scotland in 1707) tried to tighten its control over its recently acquired overseas empire, especially in North America. Already enjoying a large measure of self-government, the North American colonies opposed Parliament's efforts to enforce trade laws and impose taxes on them. They began to press for even more freedom from the home country.

During the 1700s, relations between Great Britain and the North American colonies steadily worsened. The arrival of British troops in North America to put down colonial protests signaled the beginning of the American Revolution. In 1776, 13 of the colonies declared their freedom from British rule and became a new nation—the United States of America. Five years later, the American victory at

Visualizing **History** Mocking British Rule, *Horse Throwing His Master* represented American colonists in revolt against the British monarchy. *How did colonial economic interests help to ignite the American Revolution?*

Yorktown ended the war, and in 1783 the British officially recognized the independence of their former colonies. Following the Revolutionary War, the 13 newly independent states in 1788 ratified the Constitution of the United States. This document established the framework for a federal republic and later provided a Bill of Rights that protected personal liberties. From the 1700s to the present century, the democratic ideals of the American Revolution have inspired colonial peoples struggling to escape from the hold of empires.

History **& Art** *The Spirit of '76 by* Archibald Willard. Abbot Hall, Marblehead, Massachusetts **Revolution was romanticized in the art of the 1800s.** *Why did the American colonies rebel?*

ANSWERS TO SURVEYING THE UNIT

CHAPTER 9 Scientific discoveries convinced European political thinkers that rational laws governed human behavior just as they did the natural world. They believed that people could use the laws to improve society.

CHAPTER 10 The Enlightenment ideas that government must serve the people and protect basic rights were reflected in the American Revolution, in which the colonists claimed their rights had been violated by Great Britain and that they therefore were entitled to form a new government that would protect their rights.

History & Art *Battle at Eylau* **by Antoine Jean Gros** **Severe November weather froze the French troops as they retreated from Moscow.** *What two factors brought about the downfall of Napoleon's empire?*

Chapter 11
The French Revolution

The American Revolution influenced the French people, who became increasingly critical of their monarchy. Under the rule of King Louis XVI, France's nobles and clergy enjoyed power and privileges, while the majority of people paid most taxes and had little say in the government. In 1789, social injustice, economic distress, and Enlightenment ideas combined to spark the French Revolution.

The early period of the Revolution saw the creation of a constitutional monarchy with a representative form of government. Delegates in the new National Assembly ended class privileges and guaranteed rights for all citizens. The king's refusal to accept the Revolution and the threat of foreign invasion, however, led to the monarchy's overthrow and the formation of a democratic republic. The revolutionaries then raised a large army to push back the foreign invaders and carried out a Reign of Terror at home to crush opposition to the Revolution.

Instability eventually brought the general Napoleon Bonaparte to power in 1799. Although

Napoleon professed revolutionary ideals, he made himself emperor. With a powerful army, he brought much of Europe under French control. By 1814, the combined might of France's enemies and the growth of anti-French nationalism in conquered lands led to Napoleon's defeat. European leaders at the Congress of Vienna sought to limit French power and restore monarchies in Europe. Democracy and nationalism, however, emerged as powerful forces in the 1800s.

SURVEYING UNIT 3

1. **Chapter 9** Why did European political thinkers during the Enlightenment stress the importance of natural laws?
2. **Chapter 10** How was Enlightenment thought reflected in the political events and the political changes that took place in North America during the 1700s?
3. **Chapter 11** Compare the political revolutions in England, North America, and France. Which revolution was the most conservative? Which was the most radical? Explain your answers.

Unit 3 *Age of Revolution* 369

Unit 3 Digest

History & Art

Answer to Caption: *the combined military might of France's enemies and the growth of anti-French nationalism in conquered lands*

RETEACH

Flowchart Have students create a flowchart that summarizes the major events of each revolution in the unit.

Reteaching Activities 9, 10, 11

Chapter Digests Audio-cassettes, Chapters 9, 10, 11

 VIDEODISC
Turning Points in World History

 Side One
Chapter 11

Title: *French Revolution*
Ask: Why did the French revolutionaries storm the Bastille prison? *(The Bastille represented royal authority and the injustice of the government.)*

ANSWERS TO SURVEYING THE UNIT

CHAPTER 11 Answers will vary. The English Revolution may be seen as the most conservative because it kept the monarchy while advancing civil liberties; the American Revolution overthrew the monarchy and established a republic, but its political changes were not accompanied by sweeping social changes; the French Revolution may be viewed as the most radical because of the widespread social upheavals that accompanied the fall of monarchy and the birth of the French republic.

Introducing the Unit

Unit 4 focuses on the Industrial Revolution and the rapid political, social, and cultural changes that transformed the world in the 1700s and 1800s.

Unit Objectives

After reading Unit 4, students will be able to:

1. understand the technological innovations and new economic developments of the Industrial Revolution.
2. trace new political, economic, and scientific ideas and the growth of popular culture.
3. describe the revolutionary and reform movements that reshaped politics of Europe and the Americas in the 1800s.
4. explain how nationalists unified Italy and Germany and challenged autocracy in Russia and Austria-Hungary.
5. discuss the effects of European and United States imperialism in Asia, Africa, and Latin America.

Portfolio Project

Students can find information on the Internet, in world almanacs and general encyclopedias, as well as in books such as *The Encyclopedia of American Facts and Dates*. This activity may be an appropriate method of authentic assessment.

Unit **4** 1750–1914

Industry and Nationalism

Then & Now

For centuries wealthy landowners in Europe controlled a static agricultural economy. Peasant families farmed strips of land, and small industries and trades met local needs. Then, in England in the late 1700s, innovations in farming made agriculture a profitable business. An agricultural revolution helped start a revolution in industry, beginning in textiles. The factory system expanded the power and wealth of the middle class. While scientific and medical advances improved life for many, in much of Europe the poor remained powerless.

How long would it take you to walk to school? The railroad began the revolution in transportation. When a German engineer redesigned the internal combustion engine to run on gasoline, the automobile took center stage. Within a few decades the automobile would transform society in every industrial country.

A Global Chronology

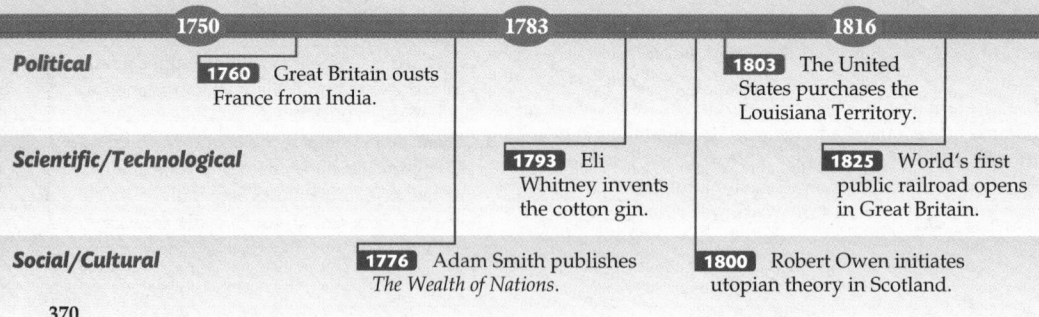

	1750	1783	1816
Political	**1760** Great Britain ousts France from India.		**1803** The United States purchases the Louisiana Territory.
Scientific/Technological		**1793** Eli Whitney invents the cotton gin.	**1825** World's first public railroad opens in Great Britain.
Social/Cultural		**1776** Adam Smith publishes *The Wealth of Nations*.	**1800** Robert Owen initiates utopian theory in Scotland.

370

Then & Now

Nationalism In this unit students will learn about the rise of nationalism in Europe, including nationalist movements in the Balkans (pages 473–474). Ask students to discuss regions of the world where nationalism has led to violence in recent years. Why is nationalism such a powerful feeling throughout the world? (*Answers will vary. Some students may feel that nationalism or patriotism is a natural feeling.*) In what ways has nationalism been a positive force in recent history? (*It led to dramatic restructuring*

Steam locomotive and wood car

Portfolio Project

Graphs can show the dramatic changes caused by the Industrial Revolution. Create several graphs that illustrate these changes from the early 1800s to the 1900s. Subjects of your graphs for any industrializing nation or group of nations may include: population growth; spread of railroads; and production of goods such as cotton, steel, coal, and oil. Libraries and the Internet have good historical references for these statistics. After completing the graphs, write a list of questions that can be answered from the data shown in each graph.

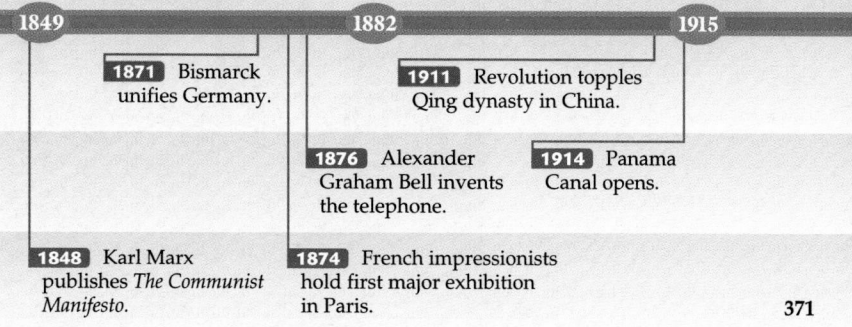

1849   1882   1915

1871 Bismarck unifies Germany.

1911 Revolution topples Qing dynasty in China.

1876 Alexander Graham Bell invents the telephone.

1914 Panama Canal opens.

1848 Karl Marx publishes *The Communist Manifesto.*

1874 French impressionists hold first major exhibition in Paris.

371

ABCNEWS
INTERACTIVE™

 VIDEODISC
Turning Points in World History

Side Two, Chapter 3
Title: *The Industrial Revolution*
Ask: How was the development of the railroad instrumental in the new industrial economy? *(The railroad transported goods being made in the factories.)*

---

of the Soviet Union and the Communist regimes of Eastern Europe.) Where has nationalism led to violence in recent years? *(former Soviet Union, former Yugoslavia, Rwanda, Liberia)* Why has nationalism sometimes led to violence? *(Answers will vary. Students may mention that political boundaries often do not correspond to distribution of ethnic groups.)* Do you think that every distinct ethnic group should form its own nation? Why or why not? *(Answers will vary. Students may realize that the idea would lead to the splitting up of nearly all nations that now exist.)*

Visualizing History

A network of rail lines spread across Europe and North America after 1820. Railroads opened up vast new markets and spurred the growth of large factories.

The Spread of Ideas

TEACH

Introduction

This feature focuses on the spread of the Industrial Revolution from its beginnings in Great Britain to the United States and Japan.

Background Notes

Linking Past and Present

Today, industrial technology moves quickly from one country to another. For example, computer software, microelectronics, and industrial chemicals, once produced almost entirely in Europe, Japan, and the United States, are now exported from Brazil, India, Korea, and Taiwan. The reduction in trade barriers under GATT (General Agreement on Tariffs and Trade) has made the movement of technology even easier.

Geography

Movement The Industrial Revolution caused unprecedented movement among people as farmers in many lands left their farms to work in factories, often in far-off places. Skilled European workers came to the United States in the early 1800s to work in cotton mills like the one Slater built in Pawtucket. In the 1820s one observer noted that a mix of workers from different parts of Britain made problems for one mill owner: "I cannot conceive a more uncomfortable situation than … to be surrounded by a mixture of Irish, Yorkshire, and west of England workmen. Whatever advice he might receive from the one party would be condemned by the others…."

The Spread of Ideas

Industrialization

*T*he rise of industry changed the world forever. So dramatic were the changes that historians have labeled the period the Industrial Revolution. Although the revolution began in Britain, it respected neither time nor place. The revolution traveled beyond Britain to touch every nation on earth.

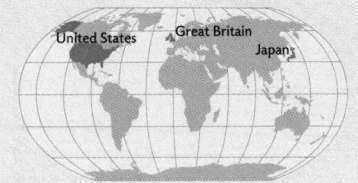

Great Britain
Workshop of the World

The birth of industry needed certain preconditions: the science, incentive, and money capital to build machines; a labor force to run them; raw materials and markets to make the system profitable; and efficient farms to feed a new group of workers. At the start of the 1700s, Great Britain possessed all these conditions. Here industrialism first took root.

As with the development of agriculture, no one person can be credited with the invention of industry. Instead, it grew from the innovations of individuals who developed machines to do work formerly done by humans and animals. One inventor built on the ideas of another. In 1705, for example, Thomas Newcomen devised a crude steam engine to pump water out of coal mines. In 1769 James Watt improved upon Newcomen's work and built a more efficient steam engine. Other inventors adapted Watt's engine to run cloth-making machines. Business owners soon brought machines and workers together in a single place called a factory.

By the 1800s, industry had catapulted Great Britain into a position of world leadership. "[Britain has] triumphantly established herself as the workshop of the world," boasted one leader. It was impossible to monopolize this idea. Workshops began to hum in America.

James Watt

Watt's steam engine

COOPERATIVE LEARNING ACTIVITY

Reports Have students brainstorm a list of important technologies today (prompt them if necessary to consider semiconductors, satellites, fiber optics, biotechnology, software, and high-resolution television). Then organize the class into groups and have each group research and prepare an oral report on one technology. Reports should indicate, if possible, where the technology was first developed and where it is produced today. Then have students from each group present their report to the class. Encourage students to include visuals in their reports. **L2**

The Spread of Ideas

The United States
The Revolution Spreads

Great Britain tried to keep the secrets of industry locked up. It forbade the export of industrial machines. It also barred the people who built and operated the machines from leaving the country. In 1787, however, a young factory supervisor named Samuel Slater found a way to escape. He disguised himself as a farmhand and boarded a ship for New York.

Working entirely from memory, Slater built a mill in Pawtucket, Rhode Island. On December 20, 1790, the mill turned out the first machine-made cotton yarn produced in America.

Within two years, Slater had sales offices in Salem, New York City, Baltimore, and Philadelphia. As Slater's mills turned out cotton, the United States began churning out its own brilliant industrial inventors. They produced more than just machines. They came up with new industrial principles such as Eli Whitney's use of standardized parts and Henry Ford's use of the assembly line. Together these two ideas gave the world mass production—a concept that would revolutionize people's lives around the globe.

Matthew Perry's steamboat in Tokyo Bay

Samuel Slater's mill

Japan
The Search for Markets

In 1853, the Industrial Revolution traveled to Japan in the form of a fleet of United States steamships sent to open the island to trade. "What we had taken as a fire at sea," recalled one Japanese observer, "was really smoke coming out of their smokestacks."

The military power produced by United States industry shook the Japanese. Recalled the same observer, "What a joke, the steaming teapot fixed by America—Just four cups [ships], and we cannot sleep at night."

The Japanese temporarily gave in to American demands. But they also vowed that they too would possess industry. By the start of the 1900s, Japan had joined other industrial nations in the search for markets. By 1914 Japan's merchant fleet was the sixth largest in the world and their foreign trade had increased one hundred-fold in value in fifty years.

LINKING THE IDEAS

1. How was the idea for a cotton mill brought from Great Britain to the United States?
2. What feature of the American fleet most impressed the Japanese in 1853?

Critical Thinking

3. **Drawing Conclusions** Why did the British want to control the spread of an idea that made production of goods easier?

Unit 4 *Industry and Nationalism* 373

Cultural Diffusion

Military-Industrial Complex The Japanese understood that a nation could not have a strong military without industrializing. After Britain defeated China in the Opium War of the 1830s, one Japanese commented: "Why did an upright and righteous great country like China lose to an insolent, unjust, and contemptible country like England? It is because [the rulers of China] prided themselves on their superiority, regarded the outside world with contempt, and paid no heed to the progress of machinery in foreign countries."

ANSWERS TO LINKING THE IDEAS

1. Samuel Slater memorized the mill design and left England by pretending to be a farmer.
2. their steam engines
3. Britain wanted to maintain a monopoly over industrial production.

A complete, 1-page lesson plan is provided for each section in the *Reproducible Lesson Plans* booklet.

Age of Industry

CHAPTER RESOURCES

	Reproducible Resources	Multimedia Resources
Chapter Opener	Chapter Themes: Graphic Organizer 12 Historical Significance Chapter Activity 12	MindJogger Videoquiz
Chapter Enrichment	Vocabulary Activity 12* Time Line Activity 12 Mapping History Activity 12 History Simulation 12 Geography and History Activity 12 Source Reading 12 People in World History Profiles 43, 44 World Art and Music Activity 12 Enrichment Activity 12 Critical Thinking Activity 12 Skill Reinforcement Activity 12 Performance Assessment Activity 12	World History and Art Transparency 30, *Le Moulin de la Galette* Chapter Transparency 12 Vocabulary PuzzleMaker Software Turning Points in World History: *The Industrial Revolution*
Chapter Review/Reteaching	Reteaching Activity 12 Skill Reinforcement Activity 12 Spanish Chapter Summary 12	Chapter 12 Digest Audiocassette, Activity, Test* Vocabulary PuzzleMaker Software Student Self-Test and Review Software MindJogger Videoquiz
Chapter Evaluation/Testing	Performance Assessment Activity 12 Chapter 12 Test, Forms A and B	Testmaker

* Also available in Spanish

0:00 OUT OF TIME? Assign the Chapter 12 summary in the Unit 4 Digest on pages 505–507, and the Chapter 12 Audiocassettes.

Block Schedule

Block scheduling differs from traditional class scheduling in the amount of time allotted to each period. The extended time frame provided by block scheduling affords you the opportunity to implement a greater number of research-oriented and activity-intense projects to motivate and involve your students. Activities that are particularly suited to use within the block scheduling framework are identified throughout this chapter by the following designation.

KEY TO ABILITY LEVELS

Teaching strategies have been coded for varying learning styles and abilities.

L1 **BASIC** activities for all students
L2 **AVERAGE** activities for average to above-average students
L3 **CHALLENGING** activities for above-average students
LEP **LIMITED ENGLISH PROFICIENCY** activities

Use Glencoe's *Presentation Plus!* multimedia teacher tool to easily present dynamic lessons that visually excite your students. Using Microsoft PowerPoint® you can customize the presentations to create your own personalized lessons.

SECTION RESOURCES

Daily Objectives	Reproducible Resources	Multimedia Resources
Section 1 **Living From the Land** Describe what daily life was like before the rise of modern industry.	Reproducible Lesson Plan 12-1 Vocabulary Activity 12* Guided Reading Activity 12-1* Time Line Activity 12 Section Quiz 12-1*	Section Focus Transparency 12-1 Chapter Transparency 12 Student Self-Test and Review Software Testmaker Turning Points in World History: *The Industrial Revolution*
Section 2 **The Beginnings of Change** Explain why the Industrial Revolution began in Great Britain.	Reproducible Lesson Plan 12-2 Vocabulary Activity 12* Guided Reading Activity 12-2* Geography and History Activity 12 Section Quiz 12-2*	Section Focus Transparency 12-2 Student Self-Test and Review Software Testmaker Turning Points in World History: *The Industrial Revolution*
Section 3 **The Growth of Industry** Analyze how new technology advanced the growth of industry.	Reproducible Lesson Plan 12-3 Guided Reading Activity 12-3* People in World History Profiles 43, 44 History Simulation 12 Section Quiz 12-3*	Section Focus Transparency 12-3 Vocabulary PuzzleMaker Software Student Self-Test and Review Software Testmaker Turning Points in World History: *The Industrial Revolution*
Section 4 **A New Society** Describe how the Industrial Revolution affected people's lives.	Reproducible Lesson Plan 12-4 Vocabulary Activity 12* Guided Reading Activity 12-4* Reteaching Activity 12 Enrichment Activity 12 Section Quiz 12-4* Performance Assessment Activity 12 Spanish Chapter Summary 12	Section Focus Transparency 12-4 World History and Art Transparency 30, *Le Moulin de la Galette* Student Self-Test and Review Software Testmaker Turning Points in World History: *The Industrial Revolution*

* Also available in Spanish

Chapter Activities

Performance Assessment Activity

Students as Inventors Have students assume the roles of modern-day inventors who have identified a clear need for a new product. Ask them to draw up plans for an invention to fill the need, determine an area of the world in which to manufacture it, and suggest possible ways to finance the project. Students will then create a proposal including a diagram and map of manufacturing and distribution. Included in the proposal should be the likely impact of the manufacturing in the area under consideration. As an alternative, you might suggest the type of invention needed, have several groups come up with proposals, then debate the relative merits of their proposals for location and investment.

Possible Rubric Features

Accuracy of research; thoroughness in meeting criteria for labor force, capital, natural resources, and need; organization and clarity of presentation and visuals

• *For an additional activity, refer to Activity 12 in the* Performance Assessment Strategies and Activities *booklet.*

ACTIVITY

From the Classroom of...

**Edward Thomas
Elmont Memorial High School
Elmont, NY**

Analyzing Effects of Industrialization

Ask students what products or inventions have been important during the 1990s. Have students discuss the ways each product or invention has affected their lives and society as a whole, both positively and negatively. Then have students list products and inventions from the Age of Industry, along with their effects in both rural and urban regions. Use these lists as a springboard for a general discussion of the changes in lifestyle brought about by industrialization. Be sure students mention the movement of many people from rural to urban areas. Ask students if any of the problems brought about by industrialization are still present in society.

MULTIPLE LEARNING STYLES

Verbal/Linguistic
Have students read Charles Dickens's *Hard Times* and write a book report analyzing how the novel presents relations between industrialists and workers. Have them consider these questions: Who are the heroes? Who are the villains? How does Dickens's portrayal compare with this chapter's discussion of the situation?

Logical/Mathematical
Have students select one or more stocks and follow their progress on the stock market for several days or weeks. If possible, they should research the companies they select and learn something about their development.

Visual/Spatial
Have students construct a graph showing the growth of Europe's population from 1600 to 1900.

Kinesthetic
Have students select an invention of the period and prepare a model or detailed diagram showing how it works.

Additional Resources

NATIONAL GEOGRAPHIC SOCIETY

Teacher's Corner

INDEX TO NATIONAL GEOGRAPHIC MAGAZINE

The following articles may be used for research relating to this chapter:

- "Robot Revolution," by Curt Suplee, July 1997.
- "Information Revolution" by Joel L. Swerdlow, October 1995.
- "George Washington's Patowmack Canal," by Wilbur E. Garrett, June 1987.

ADDITIONAL NATIONAL GEOGRAPHIC SOCIETY PRODUCTS

To order the following products for use with this chapter, call National Geographic Society at 1-800-368-2728:

- *Wired World (Video)*
- *Inventors and Inventions (Video)*
- *Technology's Price (Video)*

BIBLIOGRAPHY

Literature of the Period
Trollope, Anthony. *The Way We Live Now.* London: Trollope Society, 1992. Witty dissection of English society in the Industrial Age.
Zola, Émile. *Germinal.* New York: Vintage Books, 1994. Outspoken attack on harsh conditions in French coal mines.
Readings for the Student
Dickens, Charles. *Oliver Twist.* New York: Dodd, Mead, 1984. An orphan's adventures in seamy, industrial London.
Readings for the Teacher
Avery, Gillian. *The Echoing Green: Memories of Victorian Youth.* New York: Viking, 1974. Diaries and memoirs re-create life in the 1800s.

LOCAL OBJECTIVES

*inter*NET CONNECTION
Industrial Revolution resources on the World Wide Web
Age of Industry:
http://history.evansville.net/industry.html

CHAPTER THEMES

Chapter Themes are listed by section on this chapter opening page of the Student Edition. A corresponding theme-based activity is available under "TEACH," and a theme-based question is asked in the Section and Chapter Reviews.

The Storyteller

Historical Setting Children had worked for centuries before the onset of the Industrial Revolution. They had worked on their families' farms and had been apprenticed at a variety of skilled crafts. But with the advent of the industrial age, working children's lives were little better than those of enslaved peoples. They worked in factories and in mines. They toiled long hours in the cold and the dark, handling dangerous machinery for very low wages.

Historical Significance

Answers: *Many nations developed urban industrial economies. New inventions led to the growth of factories, and these in turn led to the growth of manufacturing cities. The middle class expanded in size and wealth. Harsh conditions for working people led to the development of labor unions.*

Today industrialized nations have advanced technology and high standards of living; nonindustrialized nations try to gain these benefits by industrializing.

Chapter
12
1700–1914

Age of Industry

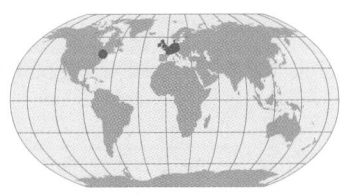

Chapter Themes

▶ **Relation to Environment** Before the Industrial Revolution of the 1700s and 1800s, most Europeans live in isolated rural villages and depend on the land. *Section 1*
▶ **Innovation** A series of inventions and new procedures in agriculture and industry transform economies in Europe and North America. *Section 2*
▶ **Change** Throughout the Western world, new urban centers based on industry develop along with the rise of new social classes. *Section 3*
▶ **Conflict** Workers in Europe and North America organize to gain better wages and improved working conditions. *Section 4*

The Storyteller

Change swept through Europe and North America as new coal mines and iron works began to dominate rural landscapes. Susan Pitchforth, an 11-year-old British girl, was just one of the millions of men, women, and children who left farming villages to find work in these growing industries.

Like countless others, Susan suffered difficult and dangerous industrial working conditions. When the British Parliament investigated horrible conditions in coal mines, young Susan told them her story:

"I have worked at this pit going on two years … I walk a mile and a half to my work, both in winter and summer. I run 24 [loads] a day; I cannot come up till I have done them all."

Historical Significance

What changes took place in Europe and North America during the Industrial Revolution? How does the Industrial Revolution affect life throughout the world today?

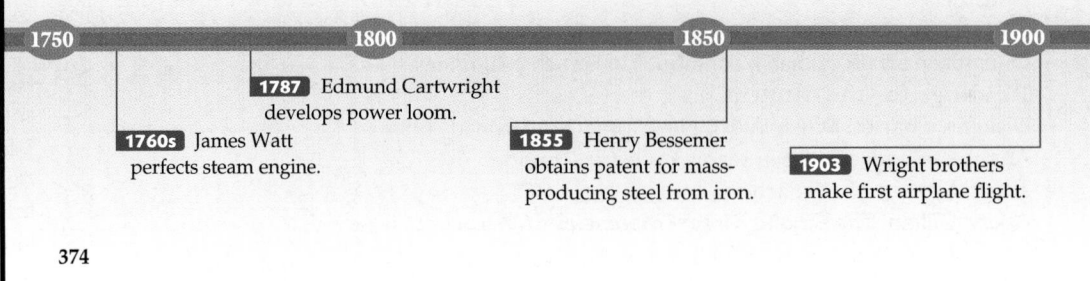

1750 — 1800 — 1850 — 1900

1787 Edmund Cartwright develops power loom.

1760s James Watt perfects steam engine.

1855 Henry Bessemer obtains patent for mass-producing steel from iron.

1903 Wright brothers make first airplane flight.

374

GEOGRAPHY CONNECTION

Location Have students locate Great Britain (England, Scotland, Wales) in the Atlas in their textbook or on a wall map. What geographic features do you see? *(Britain is an island nation; there are many harbors and rivers.)* How might these features help stimulate industry? *(Isolation from continental Europe would protect Britain from invasion and warfare; harbors and rivers aid transportation.)* **L1**

 Coalbrookdale by Night by Philip de Loutherberg.
Science Museum, London, England

History & Art
 Tell students that Coalbrookdale was an important center of English industrialization. It was here, in the early 1700s, that entrepreneur Abraham Darby first used coke—a coal product—to smelt iron. Previously, manufacturers had used charcoal, a wood product, with the result that England's forests were being depleted.

✔ Performance Assessment

Refer to the activity on page 374C of the Planning Guide.

📁 For an additional activity, refer to Activity 12 in the *Performance Assessment Strategies and Activities* booklet.

Using Your History Journal

Students may use different colors for different industries, such as textiles, iron and steel, and transportation and communication.

Your History Journal

Build a time line of inventions of the Industrial Revolution beginning with John Kay's improved loom and ending with the first airplane.

GLENCOE
TECHNOLOGY

VIDEODISC
Use MindJogger to preview chapter content.

MindJogger Videoquiz

 Chapter 12
Disc 2 Side A

 Also available in VHS.

➕ EXTRA CREDIT PROJECT

Biography Have students investigate one of the men who helped bring about the agricultural revolution: Robert Bakewell, Charles Townshend, or Jethro Tull in England, or John Deere in the United States. Students should report, orally or in writing, on what the man contributed and the difference his contribution made to agricultural production. **L2**

c. 1700s Domestic system is widespread in European towns and villages.

c. 1750 About 75 percent of Europeans live in rural areas.

SECTION THEME

▶ **Relation to Environment**
Before the Industrial Revolution of the 1700s and 1800s, most Europeans live in isolated rural villages and depend on the land.

Find Out

Answer: *Most people lived in small villages and depended mainly on agriculture to make a living. They worked hard, lived always under the threat of disease, seldom ventured far from their village, and expected to die fairly young.*

FOCUS

Section Objective

Describe what daily life was like before the rise of modern industry.

BELLRINGER
Motivational Activity

Before taking roll at the beginning of the class period, project Section Focus Transparency 12-1 and have students answer the activity questions. Discuss students' responses.
This activity is also available as a blackline master.

Vocabulary Pre-check

Use Vocabulary Activity 12 to introduce vocabulary terms.
L1 LEP

Section 1

Living From the Land

Setting the Scene

▶ **Terms to Define**
domestic system

▶ **People to Meet**
Charles Dickens

▶ **Places to Locate**
London

Find Out What was daily life like before the rise of modern industry?

The Storyteller

Landlords increased their income by removing common farmers from their rented fields. An anonymous poem passed judgment on the enclosure of Thornborough landlords in 1798:

Ye Thornbro' youths bewail with me;
Ye shepherds lay your pipes aside,
    No longer tune the merry
       glee,
    For we are rob'd of all
       our pride.
    The time alas will soon
       approach,
    When we must all our
       pasture yield;
    The wealthy on our
       rights encroach
    And will enclose our
       common field.

Haymaking in rural England

—adapted from *English Parliamentary Enclosure,* Michael Turner, 1980

During the 1700s and 1800s, a series of innovations in agriculture and industry led to profound economic and social change throughout Europe and the United States. Urban industrial economies emerged in these areas and eventually spread around the world. This transformation, which became known as the Industrial Revolution, began when power-driven machinery in factories replaced work done in homes—altering the way people had lived and worked for hundreds of years.

Cloth making provides a dramatic example of the far-reaching effects of the Industrial Revolution. In the 1700s a home weaver worked many hours to produce a yard of cloth. A century later, a worker operating machines in a textile mill could make 50 times more cloth.

As adventurous businesspeople brought machines and workers together in factories, industries produced mass quantities of goods. Millions of people in search of new opportunities to make a living left rural villages to find factory work in growing towns and cities. A new era of mechanization had arrived.

A Harsh Way of Life

Before the dawn of the Industrial Revolution in the 1700s, people lived in much the same way their ancestors had lived for hundreds of years. Nature's seasons and religious traditions measured time, and social change was rare. Relying almost solely on farming to make a living, people planted and harvested fields, hoped for good weather, and lived always under the threat of disease.

Families, both rich and poor, remained relatively small because of a very high infant death rate. One baby in three died in his or her first year of life,

---

SECTION RESOURCES

Reproducible Masters
- Reproducible Lesson Plan 12-1
- Vocabulary Activity 12
- Guided Reading Activity 12-1
- Time Line Activity 12
- Section Quiz 12-1

Transparencies
- Section Focus Transparency 12-1
- Chapter Transparency 12

Multimedia
- Student Self-Test and Review Software
- Testmaker
- Turning Points in World History: *The Industrial Revolution*

and only one in two people reached age 21. Life expectancy hovered around age 40. People expected life to be short and harsh. As one mother in the 1770s said after her baby's death, "One cannot grieve after her much, and I have just now other things to think of."

Only 25 percent of Europeans lived in towns or cities in the 1700s. **London** was the largest city in Europe in 1750 with about 700,000 people. Yet it too had a rural character. The famous British novelist **Charles Dickens** described the sights of a London morning in the early 1800s:

> 66 By degrees, other shops began to be unclosed, and a few scattered people were met with. Then, came straggling groups of labourers going to their work; then men and women with fish baskets on their heads; donkey carts laden with vegetables; chaise carts filled with live-stock or whole carcasses of meat, milk women with pails; an unbroken concourse of people.... 99
> —Charles Dickens, *Oliver Twist*, 1837

Most people in preindustrial times lived in small country villages consisting of a few hundred people. Many never ventured beyond the village borders. When braver people traveled to other cities and towns, their tales delighted their less worldly neighbors.

Village Life

Virtually all rural villagers were farmers. Wealthy landowners controlled the majority of the village land, renting most of it to small farming families. Families owned or rented small strips of land in several areas of the village. This practice ensured both fair land distribution and economic protection should disaster strike any one field. Farmers worked the land cooperatively, jointly deciding what crops to grow and when to plant and harvest.

In most of the villages, private and public lands were not separated or fenced off. The public lands, called the village commons, consisted of woodlands, pastures, and less fertile land near the village. For centuries, farmers could gather wood and

History & Art   *Harvest Scene* by George Vicat Cole. Christie's, London, England   *What were the village commons?*

graze their livestock on the commons. Poorer farmers even used these public lands for raising crops.

Village economies were limited largely to the local area because transporting goods to other areas was difficult and unprofitable. Rain turned the few roads into muddy rivers. For this reason, villages had to be nearly self-sufficient. People grew enough food for their families and perhaps a small amount to sell to nearby towns. They made their own homes, clothes, and tools from products raised in the fields or gathered from the land.

The richest rural landowners lived on sprawling country estates with a huge main house, cottages, several barns, and extensive fields. Landowners and their families lived lavishly. Servants ran the households and catered to the families' needs.

People who rented land from the landowners lived quite differently. Most lived in small, smoky, poorly lighted cottages with dirt floors. Since the poorest farming families often did not have barns, they sometimes shared their cramped living quarters with farm animals.

All daily activities revolved around farming, an occupation dominated by tradition. Farmers used the same simple methods and tools their ancestors had used and relied on nature to provide good growing seasons. Nature, however, was never predictable, and harvests ranged from plentiful to disastrously small.

Everyone in the farming family worked hard. From morning to night, husband, wife, and children worked together. Boys helped their fathers in

---

COOPERATIVE LEARNING ACTIVITY

Demonstration Organize the class into groups and assign each one a crop commonly grown in preindustrial Europe: wheat, rye, barley, and so on. Each group should then research to find out how the crop was planted, cultivated, harvested, and processed in the days before machinery. Groups should present their findings in the form of a demonstration and a report, including information on the agricultural tools used. **L3**

TEACH

Guided Practice

THEME Relation to Environment
Ask students to identify some positive features—perhaps things they lack in their own lives—of life in a preindustrial farm village. (*Answers will vary but might include a feeling of community, little crime, and a sense of accomplishment that comes with self-reliance.*) **L1**

History & Art   Before the Industrial Revolution, Britain produced almost all its own foodstuffs except for sugar.
Answer to Caption: *land that all villagers could use*

Daily Life Have half the class take the role of magazine reporter and the other half that of a village inhabitant—landowner, farmer, and so on. Reporters should interview villagers about what it is like to live in the village. **L2**

 VIDEODISC
Turning Points in World History

Side Two, Chapter 3
Title: *The Industrial Revolution*
Ask: What kinds of power did inventors use to run new machines? (*water, steel, coal*)

Chapter Transparency 12

Independent Practice

 Guided Reading Activity 12-1 **L1**

 Time Line Activity 12

Technology Have students make a flowchart showing the steps involved in creating a woolen garment under the domestic system. **L2**

ASSESS

Check for Understanding

Assign Section 1 Review as homework or as an in-class activity.

▣ Use Student Self-Test and Review Software to review Section 1.

Evaluate

📁 Section Quiz 12-1

▣ Use the Testmaker to create a customized quiz for Section 1.

Reteach

Organize students into small groups. Each group should list the key characteristics of preindustrial farming, preindustrial mining, and the early wool industry. As the groups share their lists, write major points on the board.

Enrich

Have students draw cartoons showing the best and worst features of rural life in the preindustrial age.

CLOSE

Remind students that people often use the phrase "the good old days" out of nostalgia for the past. Have them write an essay explaining whether the preindustrial era could be considered good.

the fields or at the workbench. Girls helped their mothers with chores such as milking cows and household duties such as churning butter and preparing meals.

Early Industries

In addition to farming, many people worked in small industries or in coal mines. These industries met local needs for goods such as coal, glass, iron, and clothing and employed a small number of workers. Since many workers were also farm workers, work schedules were coordinated with the agricultural cycle.

During harvest time nail makers, glassblowers, ironworkers, and miners helped farmers with the crops; likewise, in the winter farmworkers worked in the mines and in the workshops. This close relationship between farming and industry provided a steadier income to workers than either farming or industry alone.

Making Wool

In Great Britain, the woolen industry had for centuries been second only to farming in the numbers of people it employed and in the volume of trade it created. In the 1700s the demand for wool grew so great that merchants hired workers to produce woolens in their own homes. This system of labor, called the domestic system, spread to other industries such as leather working and lace making and was a widespread method used throughout Europe in the 1700s.

The domestic system depended on a network of workers. In the case of wool, a merchant first bought the raw fiber and divided it among several families. Women and children usually cleaned, sorted, and spun the fiber into thread or yarn. Men usually did the actual weaving. Then the merchant collected the yarn, paid the spinner a fee, and took the yarn to a weaver. The material next went to a fuller, who shaped and cleaned the material, and at last to the dyer for coloring. Finally, the merchant took the finished products to market and sold them for the highest possible price.

The domestic system had many benefits. Workers set their own hours and could tend to duties at home during work breaks. Women cared for children, tended vegetable gardens, and cooked meals while they earned money at home. Men carried on farming tasks, such as plowing and planting fields. Children also helped their parents. In one British region, children attended special schools to learn the art of lace making. With this skill they contributed to the family income. The domestic system provided work and income during hard times, saving many families from starvation. Its simple rural domestic practices later became the basis on which the technology and skills of the Industrial Revolution were built.

Mining Coal

The domestic system also had its place in coal mining. Coal fields often lay under farmland. The people who worked the mines often became farm laborers during the harvest, and farm horses pulled coal wagons from the pits. In some coal fields, women and children even hauled baskets of coal from the pits. One observer described these loaded baskets, saying it was "frequently more than one man could do to lift the burden."

With the money earned from mining or farmwork, country people might buy in nearby towns the few things they could not manufacture for themselves. Craftspeople sold handmade guns, furniture, and clothing in their small shops. Some craftspeople sent their goods to foreign markets in exchange for imported goods and traded the rest for food from nearby farmers and products from other local craftspeople.

Yet changes to this way of life were on the horizon. The development of new machinery and sources of power would soon upset the domestic system, transforming forever the way people lived and worked.

SECTION 1 REVIEW

Recall
1. **Define** the domestic system.
2. **Identify** the Industrial Revolution, Charles Dickens.
3. **Describe** the advantage of coordinating the work schedules in small industries with farming cycles.

Critical Thinking
4. **Predicting Trends** During the Industrial Revolution, many traditions were abandoned. How could abandoning tradition help the small farming villages?

How might it hurt them?

Understanding Themes
5. **Relation to the Environment** Where did most people live during preindustrial times? What was their most important occupation?

SECTION 1 REVIEW ANSWERS

1. All vocabulary words are defined in the Glossary.
2. Industrial Revolution, 376; Charles Dickens, 377
3. Laborers could earn a steadier income because they could work in industry part-time and farm part-time.
4. It might help them by increasing production and raising the standard of living; it might harm them by weakening community ties.
5. **RELATION TO ENVIRONMENT**
   in rural villages; farming

c. 1700s British landowners extend enclosures and displace farmers.

1787 Edmund Cartwright develops power loom.

1807 Robert Fulton designs first practical steamboat.

Section 2

The Beginnings of Change

Setting the Scene

▶ **Terms to Define**
enclosure movement, capital, entrepreneur, factory system

▶ **People to Meet**
James Hargreaves, Richard Arkwright, Edmund Cartwright, Eli Whitney, James Watt, Henry Bessemer, Robert Fulton

 **ind Out** Why did the Industrial Revolution begin in Great Britain?

The **Storyteller**

About 210,000 men built the first railroads in Britain. They called themselves "navvies." Mostly the men worked in silence. The only British navvies whose singing was noticed were the Welsh, whose songs were mainly hymns. Most other songs that navvies sang while they worked have disappeared. One tune, however, heard on the railway in 1859 gives some insight into the navvies' lives:

> *…I'm a navvy on the line.*
> *I get me five-and-twenty bob a week,*
> *Besides me overtime.*
> *Roast Beef and boiled beef*
> *An' puddin' made of eggs….*

—adapted from *The Victorian Railway*, Jack Simmons, 1991

Early train

For hundreds of years, British farmers had planted crops and kept livestock on unfenced private and public lands. Village society depended on this age-old system of farming and grazing. By the late 1700s, however, wealthy British landowners would end this open-field system, which had been slowly giving way to private ownership since the 1100s.

The landowners felt that larger farms with enclosed fields would increase farming efficiency and productivity. Parliament supported this enclosure movement, passing laws that allowed landowners to take over and fence off private and common lands. In the 1700s the enclosure movement transformed rural Great Britain. Many small farmers dependent on village lands were forced to move to towns and cities to find work. At the same time, landowners practiced new, more efficient farming methods.

To raise crop yields, landowners mixed different kinds of soils and used new crop rotation systems. One landowner, Lord Charles Townshend, urged the growing of turnips to enrich exhausted soil. Another reformer, Robert Bakewell, bred stronger horses for farm work and fatter sheep and cattle for meat. The inventor Jethro Tull developed a seed drill that enabled farmers to plant seeds in orderly rows instead of scattering them over the fields. As innovation and competition replaced traditional methods, agriculture underwent a revolution that improved the quality, quantity, and profitability of farm goods.

Great Britain Leads the Way

This agricultural revolution helped Great Britain to lead the Industrial Revolution. Successful farming businesses provided landowners with money to invest in growing industries. Many

Chapter 12 *Age of Industry* **379**

▶ **Innovation** A series of inventions and new procedures in agriculture and industry transform economies in Europe and North America.

 **ind Out**

Answer: *because of its supply of capital, its rich natural resources, and its growing population; also, the agricultural revolution provided landowners with money to invest in industry and led farmworkers to leave their homes and look for work in industry*

FOCUS

Section Objective
Explain why the Industrial Revolution began in Great Britain.

BELLRINGER
Motivational Activity

Before taking roll at the beginning of the class period, project Section Focus Transparency 12-2 and have students answer the activity questions. Discuss students' responses.
This activity is also available as a blackline master.

Vocabulary Pre-check
Use Vocabulary Activity 12 to introduce vocabulary terms.
L1 LEP

SECTION RESOURCES

📁 **Reproducible Masters**
• Reproducible Lesson Plan 12-2
• Vocabulary Activity 12
• Guided Reading Activity 12-2
• Geography and History Activity 12
• Section Quiz 12-2

📽 **Transparencies**
• Section Focus Transparency 12-2

Multimedia
🖥 Student Self-Test and Review Software
🖥 Testmaker
🎞 Turning Points in World History:
  The Industrial Revolution

TEACH

Guided Practice

THEME Innovation

Ask students why they think textiles were in the forefront of technological innovation. (*A British textile industry already existed but could not meet the increasing demand for cloth.*) **L1**

Visualizing History

One indication of the enormous growth of the textile industry was the increase in cotton imports: in the 1760s Britain imported 4 million pounds (1,816 kilograms) of cotton yearly; by the 1830s it was importing 300 million pounds (13,620,000 kilograms).
Answer to Caption: *by passing laws that helped business*

Economics Ask students why the British had surplus capital to invest in the late 1700s. (*Landowners benefited from new large-scale farming; they and others also profited from overseas commerce, including the slave trade.*) **L2**

Time Line Have students construct a time line of important eighteenth-century developments in the textile industry. **L2**

Visualizing History The task of beating cotton by hand was replaced by a beating and lapping machine in the 1700s. *How did Parliament encourage investment in industry?*

displaced farmers became industrial workers. These factors added to the key elements for industrial success that Great Britain already possessed—capital, natural resources, and labor supply.

Money and Industry

Capital, or money to invest in labor, machines, and raw materials, is essential for the growth of industry. Many British people became very wealthy during the 1700s. Landowners and other members of the aristocracy profited not only from new large-scale farming but also from overseas commerce and the slave trade, as you learned in Chapter 6. At the same time, an emerging middle class of British merchants and shopkeepers had grown more prosperous from trade.

Industry provided the aristocracy and the middle class with new opportunities to invest their money. By investing in growing industries, they stood a good chance of making a profit. Parliament encouraged investment by passing laws that helped the growing businesses.

Natural Resources

Great Britain's wealth also included its rich supply of natural resources. The country had fine harbors and a large network of rivers that flowed year-round. Water provided power for developing industries and transported raw materials and finished goods.

Great Britain also had huge supplies of iron and coal, the principal raw materials of the Industrial Revolution. Iron and the steel made from it proved to be the ideal materials for building industrial machinery. An abundance of coal also helped to fuel industry.

Large Labor Supply

Perhaps the country's greatest natural resource was its growing population of workers. Improvements in farming led to an increased availability of food. Better, more nutritious food allowed people to enjoy longer, healthier lives. In just one century, England's population nearly doubled, growing from about 5 million in 1700 to about 9 million in 1800.

The changes in farming also helped to increase the supply of industrial workers. With the introduction of machinery such as the steel plow, farms needed fewer workers. Former farmworkers left their homes to find jobs in more populated and industrialized areas.

Ambitious British people in the middle and upper classes organized and managed the country's growing industries. These risk-taking entrepreneurs (AHN•truh•pruh•NUHRS), or businesspeople, set up industries by bringing together capital, labor, and new industrial inventions.

By the mid-1700s, the British domestic system was ready for change. The textile industry led the way.

Growing Textile Industries

In the 1700s people in Great Britain and overseas were eager to buy cool, colorful cotton cloth. Since the domestic system could not meet the demand, cotton merchants looked for new ways to expand production. A series of technological advances would revolutionize cloth production.

Advances in Machinery

One of the first innovations in cloth making occurred at the dawn of the Industrial Revolution. Weaving cloth was difficult and time-consuming work. Weavers had to push a shuttle back and forth across a loom by hand. Then they had to beat the

---

woof—the threads that run crosswise—down tightly against the previous row. The width of the fabric was limited by the distance a weaver could "throw" the shuttle.

In 1733 British clock maker John Kay improved the loom with his "flying shuttle." Instead of pushing the shuttle by hand, the weaver simply pulled sharply on a cord, and the shuttle "flew" across the loom. Wider fabrics could be woven at a faster pace.

Using the flying shuttle, weavers could produce two to three times more material; thus they needed more yarn than ever from the spinners. To answer this need, **James Hargreaves**, a weaver-carpenter, in the 1760s invented a more efficient spinning machine that he called the spinning jenny. Early models of the spinning jenny enabled one person to spin 6 to 7 threads at a time; later refinements increased this number to 80 threads.

While the spinning jenny revolutionized spinning in the home, another invention revolutionized spinning in factories and industrial settings. In 1768 **Richard Arkwright**, a struggling barber with a great interest in machines, developed the water frame, a huge spinning machine that ran continually on waterpower.

By 1779 spinner Samuel Crompton combined the best features of the spinning jenny and the water frame into a new machine called the "spinning mule." It produced strong thread that could be woven into high-quality muslin cloth. Until this time, such fine cloth had to be imported from Asia.

Producing More Cloth

The new spinning machines produced more yarn or thread than there were weavers to use it. In 1787 **Edmund Cartwright**, a British poet and minister, answered this shortage of weavers with the development of a power loom. Running on horse, water, or steam power, the mechanical loom made it possible for weavers to keep up with the amount of yarn produced.

These new inventions created a growing need for raw cotton. Yet raw cotton was expensive because cleaning the seeds out of it was a slow and tedious job. In 1793 **Eli Whitney**, an American inventor, developed a machine that cleaned cotton 50 times more quickly than a person could. The cotton gin helped the booming British textile industry to overcome its last major hurdle on its journey toward full mechanization.

ABCNEWS INTERACTIVE™

VIDEODISC
Turning Points in World History

Side Two, Chapter 3
Title: *The Industrial Revolution*
Ask: How did the Industrial Revolution change population settlement patterns? *(People moved to the cities where they could work in factories.)*

Independent Practice

📁 Guided Reading Activity 12-2 **L1**

📁 Geography and History Activity 12

Telecast Ask students to imagine that they are TV journalists. Instruct them to present a class "telecast" discussing a technological development in Britain. **L2**

Linking Past and Present

An Industrial City

Cities grew at an incredible pace as Britain industrialized. In 1801, Manchester was the only city aside from London whose population exceeded 100,000. In only 20 years, it was joined by Glasgow, Edinburgh, Liverpool, and Birmingham.

ANSWERS

It was close to coal fields, at the junction of three rivers, and on a canal that connected to the sea; yes, in purely material terms; no, if quality of life is considered; answers will vary

---

CONNECTIONS
Geography

An Industrial City

The growth of industrial cities depended on geographic factors such as the availability of raw materials and accessible routes. The city of Manchester in northern England has had many geographic advantages. It lies close to coal fields and the Irwell and Mersey rivers. A canal connects the city to the Irish Sea, making Manchester an inland port.

Despite being a wool trade center, Manchester retained a rural atmosphere in the 1700s. Merchants lived in city townhouses, and people enjoyed sailing on the Irwell River. During the 1800s, Manchester grew into a textile-manufacturing city with world markets. Mills and warehouses replaced private homes in many areas, and

Manchester, England

the Irwell became so polluted it was described as "a flood of liquid manure." Some Britons at the time saw Manchester's transformation as evidence of the evils of industrialization. Others, however, saw the change as a symbol of progress.

During the first half of the 1900s, Manchester's production of textiles declined steadily. The growth of other businesses, however, helped the city and its surrounding communities to retain their economic importance in the British economy. Today, Manchester is England's third largest urban area, after London and Birmingham, and is still a major center of trade and finance.

Linking Past and Present ACTIVITY

Discuss how Manchester became an industrial city. Do you think that what happened to Manchester can be called "progress"? How do cities today compare/contrast with cities of the 1800s?

Chapter 12 *Age of Industry* **381**

Visualizing
History Because the cotton gin made cotton growing more profitable, it stimulated U.S. production of the crop and thus entrenched slavery in the South.
Answer to Caption: *It removed the seeds from the cotton.*

POINT

The Factory System
How did the factory system transform production?
It brought workers and machines together under the control of managers to produce goods in greater quantity and with more efficiency.

ASSESS

Check for Understanding

Assign Section 2 Review as homework or as an in-class activity.

Use Student Self-Test and Review Software to review Section 2.

Evaluate

 Section Quiz 12-2

Use the Testmaker to create a customized quiz for Section 2.

Reteach

Have students review the three main reasons Britain led the way in industrialization.

Enrich

Have students debate which innovation discussed in this section they think was most important.

CLOSE

Ask students why they think the Industrial Revolution is sometimes called the Machine Age.

Visualizing
History Eli Whitney's original cotton gin was a simple device that one person could turn by hand. *What task did the cotton gin perform?*

POINT

The Factory System

Since the new textile machinery was too large and costly for most workers to use in their homes, industrialists gradually moved cloth production out of workers' cottages and into the large buildings they built near major waterways. This marked the beginning of the **factory system**, an organized method of production that brought workers and machines together under the control of managers. The waterways powered the machines and provided transportation for raw materials and finished cloth.

As the factory system spread, manufacturers required more power than horses and water could provide. Steam power answered these growing needs. In the 1760s a Scottish mathematician named

James Watt designed an efficient steam engine. Watt's steam engine helped to set the Industrial Revolution in full motion. Factories that had once closed down when the river froze or flowed too low could now run continuously on steam power. The steam engine also enabled industrialists to build factories far from waterways.

Industrial Developments

The use of factory machinery increased demand for iron and steel. In response, the iron industry developed new technologies. In the mid-1800s William Kelly, an American ironworker, and **Henry Bessemer**, a British engineer, developed methods to inexpensively produce steel from iron. Steel answered industry's need for a sturdy, workable metal.

At the same time, people worked to advance transportation systems throughout Europe and the United States. Improvements to the slow, often impassable roadways began when private companies began building and paving roads. Two Scottish engineers, Thomas Telford and John McAdam, further advanced road making with better drainage systems and the use of layers of crushed rock.

Water transportation also improved. In 1761 British workers dug one of the first modern canals to link coal fields with the industrial city of Manchester. Soon, a canal building craze began both in Europe and the United States.

A combination of steam power and steel would soon revolutionize both land and water transportation. In 1801 British engineer Richard Trevithick first brought steam-powered travel to land. He devised a steam-powered carriage that ran on wheels, and three years later, a steam locomotive that ran on rails. Later, in 1807 **Robert Fulton**, an American inventor, designed the first practical steamboat. Railroads and steamboats laid the foundations for a global economy and opened up new forms of investment.

SECTION 2 REVIEW

Recall
1. **Define** enclosure movement, capital, entrepreneur, factory system.
2. **Identify** James Hargreaves, Richard Arkwright, Edmund Cartwright, Eli Whitney, James Watt, Henry Bessemer, Robert Fulton.

3. **List** the factors that favored the early growth of industry in Great Britain.
Critical Thinking
4. **Synthesizing Information** Write a diary entry describing the thoughts of a British farmer who has lost land because of the enclosure movement.

Understanding Themes
5. **Innovation** Is an Industrial Revolution still happening today? If so, name some of today's revolutionary inventions or technological developments. How have these inventions and technological developments changed modern life?

SECTION 2 REVIEW ANSWERS

1. All vocabulary words are defined in the Glossary.
2. James Hargreaves, 381; Richard Arkwright, 381; Edmund Cartwright, 381; Eli Whitney, 381; James Watt, 382; Henry Bessemer, 382; Robert Fulton, 382
3. surplus capital, ample natural resources, and a growing population of workers

4. Entries might express nostalgia about the "good old days," sadness about leaving the old home, or anger at the landlord.
5. **INNOVATION** Developments include electronic communication, medical breakthroughs, and high-speed transportation. Results include global interdependence and longer life span.

1839 Germany builds its first major railway.

c. 1870 The United States becomes an industrial equal of Great Britain and Germany.

1895 Guglielmo Marconi develops wireless telegraph.

Section 3

The Growth of Industry

Setting the Scene

▶ **Terms to Define**
industrial capitalism, interchangeable parts, division of labor, partnership, corporation, depression

▶ **People to Meet**
Eli Whitney, Frederick Taylor, Henry Ford, Samuel Morse, Guglielmo Marconi, Alexander Graham Bell, Thomas Edison, Rudolf Diesel, Wilbur and Orville Wright

 **ind Out** How did new technology advance the growth of industry?

The Storyteller

The people on the street in Paris waited impatiently for word from inside the store. "It works!" cried a spectator suddenly. Someone held up a hand. "Not so much noise. The people in Brantford [Canada] are talking ... and singing. It can be heard as plain as day." Now everyone wanted a turn at the receiver. Finally, at eleven o'clock the crowd went home. Mr. Bell's telephone was a success.

—adapted from *The Chord of Steel, The Story of the Invention of the Telephone*, Thomas B. Costain, 1960

Alexander Graham Bell's telephone

In 1789 a tall, ruddy young British worker boarded a ship bound for New York, listing his occupation in the ship's record as farmer. Although he looked like the farmer he claimed to be, Samuel Slater was actually a smuggler. Slater was stealing a valuable British commodity—industrial know-how. The 21-year-old spinner headed for the United States with the knowledge of how to build an industrial spinning wheel. When he arrived two months later, Slater introduced spinning technology to the United States.

By keeping spinning and other technologies secret, Great Britain had become the most productive country in the world. To maintain its position, Parliament passed laws restricting the flow of machines and skilled workers to other countries. Until 1824 the law that Samuel Slater had ignored prohibited craftspeople from moving to other countries. Another law made it illegal to export machinery. Nonetheless, by the late 1820s many mechanics and technicians had left Great Britain, carrying industrial knowledge with them.

Spread of Industry

As British workers left the country, Great Britain gave up trying to guard its industrial monopoly. Wealthy British industrialists saw that they could make money by spreading the Industrial Revolution to other countries.

In the mid-1800s, financiers funded railroad construction in India, Latin America, and North America. In Europe, British industrialists set up factories, supplying capital, equipment, and technical staff. The industrialists earned Great Britain the nickname "the workshop of the world." In other lands, however, large-scale manufacturing based on the factory system did not really take hold

---

▶ **Change** Throughout the Western world, new urban centers based on industry develop along with the rise of new social classes.

 **ind Out**

Answer: *It speeded up communications and transportation and, in electricity, furnished a new source of power.*

FOCUS

Section Objective

Analyze how new technology advanced the growth of industry.

BELLRINGER
Motivational Activity

Before taking roll at the beginning of the class period, project Section Focus Transparency 12-3 and have students answer the activity questions. Discuss students' responses.

This activity is also available as a blackline master.

Vocabulary Pre-check

▣ Use the Vocabulary PuzzleMaker to create a puzzle that reinforces the vocabulary terms in this section. **L1**

TEACH

Guided Practice

THEME Change

Write the headings *Topic* and *Changes* on the chalkboard. Under *Topic*, list *Communications, Energy, Production Methods,* and *Business Organization*. Have a volunteer complete the chart as you elicit information from the class. **L1**

VIDEODISC
Turning Points in World History

Side Two, Chapter 3
Title: *The Industrial Revolution*
Ask: What happened to housing as a result of the mass movement of people to cities? *(Housing became hard to find, resulting in the outgrowth of slums.)*

POINT

Growth of Big Business
What factors enabled big business to achieve economic growth?
use of machines, development of mass production and division of labor, and formation of new types of business organization

History & Art Although Germany and France lagged behind Britain in the Industrial Revolution, they soon made rapid progress.
Answer to Caption: *Great Britain, Germany, and the United States*

---

until 1870 or later. The major exceptions were France, Germany, and the United States.

Because the French government encouraged industrialization, France developed a large pool of outstanding scientists. In spite of this, France's industrialization was slow-paced. The Napoleonic Wars had strained the economy and depleted the workforce. For a long time the French economy depended more on farming and small businesses than on new industries. Yet with the growth of mining and railway construction, railway lines radiated in every direction from Paris by 1870.

Germany's efforts to industrialize proved more successful. Before 1830 Germans brought in some machinery from Britain and set up a few factories. In 1839 they used British capital to build the country's first major railway. In the following decade, strong coal, iron, and textile industries emerged. Even before the German states united in 1871, government funding had helped industry to grow.

At the same time, industrialization increased in the United States, especially in the Northeast. British capital and machinery, combined with American mechanical skills, promoted new indus-try. In time, shoe and textile factories flourished in New England. Coal mines and ironworks expanded in Pennsylvania. By 1870 the United States ranked with Great Britain and Germany as one of the world's three most industrialized countries.

POINT
Growth of Big Business

A major factor in spurring industrial growth was capitalism, the economic system in which individuals and private firms, not the government, own the means of production—including land, machinery, and the workplace. In a capitalist system, individuals decide how they can make a profit and determine business practices accordingly.

Industrialists practiced industrial capitalism, which involved continually expanding factories or investing in new businesses. After investing in a factory, industrial capitalists used profits to hire more workers and buy additional raw materials and new machines.

History & Art *Beirmeister and Wain Steel Forge* by P. S. Kroyer. Statens Museum, Copenhagen, Denmark **Industrialization spread throughout Europe.** *What were the three most industrialized nations in 1870?*

COOPERATIVE LEARNING ACTIVITY

Report Organize the class into groups. Have each group study innovations in transportation during the Industrial Revolution: railroads, steamships, and automobiles. Assign each team member a specific topic, such as method of operation, economic impact, and most common uses. After completing their research, team members should share information. Each team should then combine individual reports into a summary. One member of each team should present the group's summary. **L2**

Mass Production

Looking to increase their profits, manufacturers invested in machines to replace more costly human labor. Fast-working, precise machines enabled industrialists to mass-produce, or to produce huge quantities of identical goods.

In the early 1800s **Eli Whitney**, inventor of the cotton gin, contributed the concept of interchangeable parts that increased factory production. Whitney's system involved machine-made parts that were exactly alike and easily assembled or exchanged. In the past, handmade parts were not uniform—each differed from the next to some degree.

By the 1890s industrial efficiency had become a science. **Frederick Taylor** encouraged manufacturers to divide tasks into detailed and specific segments of a step-by-step procedure.

Using Taylor's plan, industrialists devised a division of labor in their factories. Each worker performed a specialized task on a product as it moved by on a conveyor belt. The worker then returned the product to the belt where it continued down the line to the next worker. Because products were assembled in a moving line, this method was called the assembly line.

American automobile manufacturer **Henry Ford** used assembly-line methods in 1913 to mass-produce his Model T automobiles. Ford described the assembly line this way:

❝ The man who places a part does not fasten it. The man who puts in a bolt does not put in a nut; the man who puts on the nut does not tighten it. Every piece of work in the shop moves; it may move on hooks, on overhead chains…. No workman has anything to do with moving or lifting anything. Save ten steps a day for each of the 12,000 employees, and you will have saved fifty miles of wasted motion and misspent energy. **❞**

—Henry Ford, *Ford*, 1913

As Ford produced greater quantities of his cars, the cost of producing each car fell, allowing him to drop the price. Millions of people could then buy what earlier only a few could afford.

Organizing Business

As production increased, industrial leaders developed various ways to manage the growing business world and to ensure a continual flow of capital for business expansion. In addition to individual and family businesses, many people formed partnerships. A partnership is a business organization involving two or more entrepreneurs who can raise more capital and take on more business than if each had gone into business alone. Partners share management responsibility and debt liability.

Corporations take the idea of partnership many steps further. Corporations are business organizations owned by stockholders who buy shares in a company. Stockholders vote on major decisions concerning the corporations. Each vote carries weight according to the number of shares owned. Shares decrease or increase in value depending on the profits earned by the company. In the late 1800s, as industries grew larger, corporations became one of the best ways to manage new businesses.

Business Cycles

As market needs grew more complex, individual businesses concentrated on producing a particular kind of product. This increase in specialization made growing industries dependent on each other. When one industry did well, other related industries also flourished. A great demand for cars, for example, led to expansion in the petroleum industry. Likewise, bad conditions in one industry often spread rapidly to other related industries.

The economic fate of an entire country came to rest on business cycles, or alternating periods of business expansion and decline. Business cycles follow a certain sequence, beginning with expansion. In this "boom" phase, buying, selling, production, and employment rates are high. When expansion ends, a "bust" period of decreased business activity follows. The lowest point in the business cycle is a depression, which is characterized by bank failures and widespread unemployment. As industry increasingly dominated the economy, more people suffered during "bust" periods.

Science and Industry

Amateur inventors relying heavily on trial and error produced most industrial advances at the beginning of the Industrial Revolution. By the late 1800s, manufacturers began to apply more scientific findings to their businesses.

Communications

Science played an important role in the development of communications. In the 1830s **Samuel Morse**, an American inventor, assembled a working model of the telegraph. Using a system of dots and dashes, the telegraph carried information at high speeds. Soon telegraph lines linked most European and North American cities.

📁 History Simulation 12

Bio**graphy**®

The following videotape programs are available from Glencoe:

- **Henry Ford: Tin Lizzy Tycoon**
- **J. Pierpont Morgan: Emperor of Wall Street**
- **Wilbur & Orville Wright: Dreams of Flying**

Independent Practice

📁 Guided Reading Activity 12-3 **L1**

📁 People in World History Profiles 43, 44

Who?What?Where?When?

The corporation had its roots in the joint-stock companies that were formed during the Commercial Revolution of the 1600s. Most joint-stock companies were simple trading companies, however. A corporation, like a person, can own property, buy and sell goods, and bring lawsuits. Its stockholders have limited liability. This means that, if the corporation fails, no stockholder is liable for more than his or her original investment.

Business Have students research and report on a contemporary stock exchange, such as the New York Stock Exchange. Students' reports should summarize how the exchange is organized and how it works. **L3**

TEACH

Remind students that the chief metal for centuries was iron. But cast iron, though hard, was brittle, and wrought iron was malleable but soft. People knew that steel was better—hard but not brittle—but it was expensive to make. Only with the Bessemer process, developed in the mid-nineteenth century, did inexpensive steel become widely available. Ask students if they think Benton's mural is a realistic portrayal of steel manufacturing. *(Answers will vary. Some may say it represents a romantic view of a mill.)*

CURRICULUM CONNECTION

MATHEMATICS

As industrialization spread, a common system of weights and measures became necessary. Most countries of the world adopted the metric system, first developed in France in the 1790s. Its basic measurement, the meter, equals one ten-millionth of the distance along a meridian from the Equator to one of the Poles.

Detail from "Steel," mural by Thomas Hart Benton, The New School for Social Research, NY

Steel

Coal, iron, and steel; railroads, steamships, and airplanes; factories, skyscrapers, and steel forges: This was the new world of the age of industry depicted by artist Thomas Hart Benton in this mural painted in 1930. This section, called "Steel," was taken from a drawing Benton had sketched of a Maryland steel plant. The workers in the mural are skilled and strong, the kind of American citizens who will make the American democracy, originally designed for an agricultural world, thrive in the industrial environment.

The Industrial Revolution began in Great Britain in the late 1700s. By applying steam power to iron machinery the British profoundly transformed how things were made. These new industries began to change how people worked, where they lived, how they ate, and what they needed to know in order to survive. After 1870 the United States and Germany began to take the lead in industrialization, and steel became the most important metal used in industry. In this mural Benton welded a new industrial image to an older republican ideal. ⊕

Other advances in communications included the development of the radio. Although British physicist James Clerk Maxwell in 1864 promoted the idea that electromagnetic waves travel through space at the speed of light, it took 30 years to apply this idea to technology. Italian inventor **Guglielmo Marconi** devised the wireless telegraph in 1895. This machine was later modified into the radio.

Development of the telephone in 1876 is credited to **Alexander Graham Bell**, a Scottish-born American teacher of the deaf. Tiny electrical wires carrying sound allowed people to speak to each other over long distances.

Electricity

By the early 1900s, scientists had devised ways to harness electrical power. As a result, electricity replaced coal as the major source of industrial fuel. In 1831 Michael Faraday, a British chemist and physicist, had discovered that moving a magnet through a coil in a copper wire would produce an electric current. Over 40 years later, in the 1870s, an electric motor was based on this principle.

An American inventor made great strides in the development of electricity. In 1877 **Thomas Edison** invented the phonograph, which reproduced sound. Two years later, he made electric lighting cheap and accessible by inventing incandescent lightbulbs.

Energy and Engines

The Industrial Revolution surged forward with advances in engines. In the late 1880s Gottlieb Daimler, a German engineer, redesigned the internal-combustion engine to run on gasoline. The small portable engine produced enough power to propel vehicles and boats. Another German engineer, **Rudolf Diesel**, developed an oil-burning internal-combustion engine that could run industrial plants, ocean liners, and locomotives. These inventions ushered in the age of the motor car.

 **World's Highest Railroad Is Built**

Peru, 1870
Henry Meiggs, an American engineer, began building Peru's Central Railway in 1870. Meiggs died before his ambitious project was completed, but the Central Railway remains one of the world's great engineering marvels. The standard-gauge railroad begins at sea level, near Lima, and climbs through the Andes to Huancayo. At its highest point, the Central Railway reaches an altitude of nearly 16,000 feet (5,000 m), higher than the tallest peak in the Alps.

Gasoline engines carried aviation technology to new levels of achievement. In the 1890s Germany's Ferdinand von Zeppelin streamlined the dirigible, a 40-year-old balloonlike invention that could carry passengers. Meanwhile, other scientists experimented with flying heavier aircraft. The American inventors **Wilbur and Orville Wright** achieved success in 1903 with the first flight of a motorized airplane. Although the first flight covered a distance of only 120 feet (37 m), the brothers flew their wooden airplane a distance of 100 miles (161 km) only 5 years later.

The new airplanes and other vehicles needed a steady supply of fuel for power and rubber for tires and other parts. As a result, the petroleum and rubber industries skyrocketed. Innovations in transportation, communications, and electricity changed life at an amazing rate. The world sped forward into an era of ever-increasing mechanization.

SECTION 3 REVIEW

Recall
1. **Define** industrial capitalism, interchangeable parts, division of labor, partnership, corporation, depression.
2. **Identify** Eli Whitney, Frederick Taylor, Henry Ford, Samuel Morse, James Clerk Maxwell, Guglielmo Marconi, Alexander Graham Bell, Michael Faraday, Thomas Edison, Rudolf Diesel, Wilbur and Orville Wright.
3. **List** factors that aided the growth of industrial capitalism.

Critical Thinking
4. **Synthesizing Information** Imagine you are a teenager living in the early 1900s. Choose one invention mentioned in this section and describe how it has changed your life.

Understanding Themes
5. **Change** What effects do you think that industrial advancements, such as mass production and the assembly line, have had on workers' lives?

ASSESS

Check for Understanding

Assign Section 3 Review as homework or as an in-class activity.

▪ Use Student Self-Test and Review Software to review Section 3.

Who?What?Where?When?

Guglielmo Marconi, inventor of the wireless telegraph, was inspired to experiment with science after reading a biography of Benjamin Franklin.

Evaluate

▱ Section Quiz 12-3

▪ Use the Testmaker to create a customized quiz for Section 3.

Reteach

Have students review the growth of big business, as described in this section.

Enrich

Ask students to investigate how internal-combustion engines are used today and give brief oral reports on their findings.

CLOSE

Have students show how capital was necessary to develop innovations summarized in this section.

SECTION 3 REVIEW ANSWERS

1. All vocabulary words are defined in the Glossary.
2. Eli Whitney, 385; Frederick Taylor, 385; Henry Ford, 385; Samuel Morse, 385; James Clerk Maxwell, 387; Guglielmo Marconi, 387; Alexander Graham Bell, 387; Michael Faraday, 387; Thomas Edison, 387; Rudolf Diesel, 387; Wilbur and Orville Wright, 387
3. investment in machines; use of interchangeable parts; specialized labor; use of the assembly line; new methods of business organization
4. Answers should reflect a knowledge of inventions in this section.
5. **CHANGE** Students may say that in many cases, industrial advancements have led to boredom and dissatisfaction; however, by lowering product costs, they have enabled more workers to buy more products.

c. 1800 Combination Acts passed by British Parliament ban labor unions.

1845 Massachusetts mill workers petition state for better working conditions.

1870 British Parliament legalizes labor's right to strike.

c. 1900 Labor union membership grows steadily in Europe and North America.

SECTION THEME

▶ **Conflict** Workers in Europe and North America organize to gain better wages and improved working conditions.

Find Out

Answer: *As the middle class expanded, separate spheres developed for men and women. People worked in factories more than on farms. Wages were low, and often the whole family worked. Conditions and pay were so poor that workers formed unions to fight more effectively against factory owners.*

FOCUS

Section Objective

Describe how the Industrial Revolution affected people's lives.

BELLRINGER
Motivational Activity

Before taking roll at the beginning of the class period, project Section Focus Transparency 12-4 and have students answer the activity questions. Discuss students' responses.

📁 This activity is also available as a blackline master.

Vocabulary Pre-check

📁 Use Vocabulary Activity 12 to introduce vocabulary terms.

L1 LEP

Section 4

A New Society

Setting the Scene

▶ **Terms to Define**
labor union, collective bargaining

▶ **Places to Locate**
Massachusetts

Find Out
How did the Industrial Revolution affect people's lives?

The Storyteller

Factory inspectors interviewed a little boy who worked carrying coal early in the Industrial Revolution:

> I don't know how old I am; father is dead; mother is dead also. I began to work when I was about 9. I first worked for a man who used to hit me with the belt or with tools and fling coals at me. I left him and went to see if I could get another job. I used to sleep in the old pits that had no more coal in them; I laid upon the shale all night. I used to eat whatever I could get; I ate for a long time the candles that I found in the pits. I work now for a man who serves me well; he pays me with food and drink.

—freely adapted from *Hard Times, Human Documents of the Industrial Revolution*, E. Royston Pike, 1966

Child at work

efore the Industrial Age, a person's position in life was determined at birth, and most people had little chance of rising beyond that level. Few managed to rise above their inherited place in the rigid European society.

As the Industrial Revolution progressed throughout the 1700s and 1800s, however, new opportunities made the existing social structure more flexible. Many people, such as inventor Richard Arkwright, used their talents and the opportunities presented by the Industrial Age to rise from humble beginnings to material success.

The youngest of 13 children of poor parents, Arkwright trained to become a barber. Yet machines, not his barbershop, occupied his time and energy. Spurred by the developments in the textile industry, Arkwright developed the huge water-frame spinning wheel that was powered by water and spun continuously. Arkwright persuaded investors to join him in establishing textile mills throughout Great Britain.

Soon Arkwright's mills employed more than 5,000 people. He amassed a great fortune, became active in politics, and was eventually knighted by Great Britain's King George III.

The Rise of the Middle Class

Although few businesspeople in Europe and America prospered as Arkwright had, industrialization did expand the size, power, and wealth of the middle class. Once made up of a small number of bankers, lawyers, doctors, and merchants, the middle class now also included successful owners of factories, mines, and railroads. Professional workers such as clerks, managers, and teachers added to the growing numbers.

Many wealthy manufacturers and other members of the middle class strongly believed in education as the key to business success. Politically

---

SECTION RESOURCES

📁 **Reproducible Masters**
- Reproducible Lesson Plan 12-4
- Vocabulary Activity 12
- Guided Reading Activity 12-4
- Reteaching Activity 12
- Enrichment Activity 12
- Section Quiz 12-4

- Performance Assessment Activity 12
- Spanish Chapter Summary 12

📀 **Transparencies**
- Section Focus Transparency 12-4
- World History and Art Transparency 30, *Le Moulin de la Galette*

Multimedia
- 💿 Student Self-Test and Review Software
- 💿 Testmaker
- 💿 Turning Points in World History: *The Industrial Revolution*

active, they became involved in many reform efforts, including education, health care, prison improvements, and sanitation.

Middle-Class Lifestyles

As European and American middle-class men rose in society and assumed the role of sole provider for families, family life began to change. By the end of the late 1800s, stereotypes emerged from the middle class that created and reinforced the idea that men and women occupied different roles based on differences in their characters. Men centered their energy on the workplace, while women concentrated their efforts on maintaining the home and bringing up children.

As soon as the family could afford it, a middle-class woman would hire domestic help. The number of her servants increased with her wealth. In 1870 an English guidebook listed the sequence in which women hired new help. First she "hires a washerwoman occasionally, then a charwoman, then a cook and housemaid, a nurse or two, a governess, a lady's maid, a housekeeper…." Servants, usually women, did the more difficult and unpleasant household chores, such as carrying loads of wood and coal, washing laundry, and cleaning house.

As middle-class women freed themselves from more tedious labor, they devoted their time to other occupations, such as educating their children, hand-sewing and embroidering, and planning meals. Magazines for women proliferated at this time, instructing housewives in everything from cooking and housekeeping to geography and natural science.

A typical day for one American middle-class woman in the early 1800s began at 6:00 A.M. and lasted until after 10:00 P.M. After waking up the family, the woman fed her infant son and then sat down to breakfast with her family. She read the Bible to her other three children, prayed with the servants, and then ordered the meals for the day. During the day she wrote letters, took one child to the park, and supervised the older daughters in feeding the younger children and folding up the laundry. The woman's schedule continued after nightfall. "After tea," she wrote, "read to [the children] till bedtime…."

Middle-class parents sent their boys to school

Visualizing History During the late 1800s, the middle classes in North America and Great Britain stressed the importance of leisure activities shared by the entire family. *How did middle-class male and female roles differ?*

to receive training for employment or preparation for higher education. Sons often inherited their fathers' positions or worked in the family business. Most daughters were expected to learn to cook, sew, and attend to all the workings of the household so that they would be well prepared for marriage.

Lives of the Working Class

As the middle class in Europe and America grew, so too did the working class in even greater numbers. The members of this class enjoyed few of the new luxuries that the upper and middle classes could now afford. Most people in the working classes had once labored on rural farms and now made up the majority of workers in new industries. Workers depended solely on the money they earned to buy what they needed. Unlike in earlier days, they did not grow or make what their families needed.

Footnotes to History

Shampoo
In the early 1900s, 25-year-old Joseph Breck tried in vain to find a cure for premature baldness. His efforts, however, led to a full line of hair care products that replaced the harsh soaps used at that time. Breck's businesses soon led the United States in shampoo production.

Chapter 12 *Age of Industry* 389

Chapter 12 *Age of Industry* 389

TEACH

Guided Practice

THEME Conflict
Discuss the conflicts between industrialists and workers. Why did conflict arise between mill owners and the workers in their factories? *(Industrialists wanted to maximize profits by keeping wages low and hours long; laborers wanted to improve their quality of life by doing the opposite.)* **L1**

Visualizing History Along with music, middle-class families enjoyed reading aloud, playing card games such as whist, and acting out charades.
Answer to Caption: *Men focused on the workplace, while women concentrated on the home.*

Daily Life Ask students to compare the roles of men and women in the middle class with those of working-class men and women. *(Middle-class men and women had very different roles, the men involved in the world of work and the women caring for the children and the house. Among the working classes, both men and women worked long hours.)* **L2**

Biography

The following videotape program is available from Glencoe:
- **The Astors: High Society**

COOPERATIVE LEARNING ACTIVITY

Debate Organize the class into two groups, one representing workers and the other representing factory owners. Workers should present the grievances they have against management (poor working conditions, low pay, dangerous conditions, and so on). Management should counter with the benefits factory owners have conferred on society (wages, lower costs for products, and so on). Each team member should speak when the debate is held. **L2**

World History and Art Transparency 30, *Le Moulin de la Galette*

Economics Have students assume the role of entrepreneur, imagining that they are starting their own business. They should choose a form of business organization—individual ownership, partnership, or corporation—and explain why it is best for their particular enterprise. **L3**

VIDEODISC
Turning Points in World History

Side Two, Chapter 3
Title: *The Industrial Revolution*
Ask: What were working conditions like for children? *(Children worked long hours for low pay in terrible conditions.)* How did workers express their opposition to poor work conditions? *(They formed unions and lobbied for government regulation to protect workers.)*

Independent Practice

Guided Reading Activity 12-4 **L1**

Music Have students prepare an oral report on a labor song such as "Sixteen Tons." (Several such songs can be found in the *Folksinger's Wordbook*.) Students should present the lyrics of the songs and summarize the background of the specific events and people mentioned. **L2**

At the Mercy of Machinery

When British and American industrialists first established mill towns such as Lowell, Manchester, Sheffield, and Fall River, work conditions were tolerable. As industrial competition increased, however, work became harder and increasingly more dangerous. Managers assigned workers more machines to operate and insisted that workers perform their tasks as fast as possible throughout the day.

Under the system of division of labor, workers did the same tasks over and over again, and did not have the satisfaction of seeing the completed work. The combination of monotonous work and heavy, noisy, repetitive machinery made the slightest interruption in the work potentially dangerous. Many workers—often children—lost fingers and limbs, and even their lives, to factory machinery.

Time ruled the lives of the industry workers down to the second. On the farms, workers' days had followed the sun and the weather. Now rigid schedules clocked by ringing bells commanded their every minute. One woman who worked in a Lowell, **Massachusetts**, textile mill wrote about her frustration in 1841:

> ❝ I am going home, where I shall not be obliged to rise so early in the morning, nor be dragged about by the factory bell, nor confined in a close noisy room from morning to night. I shall not stay here.... Up before day, at the clang of the bell—and out of the mill by the clang of the bell—into the mill, and at work in obedience to that ding-dong of a bell—just as though we were so many living machines. ❞
> —anonymous worker, *The Lowell Offering*

In the textile mills, workers spent 10 to 14 hours a day in unventilated rooms filled with lint and dust. Diseases such as pneumonia and tuberculosis spread throughout the factories, killing many workers. In coal mines, workers faced the danger of working with heavy machinery and of breathing in coal dust in the mines.

Images *of the* Times

The Industrial Age

Industrialization brought new products and leisure activities to many people. It also produced terrible working conditions that gave rise to labor unions.

A badge of an early labor union represents the cooperative efforts of workers to seek fair wages and a more humane workplace.

390

Images *of the* Times

The Industrial Age

The courtyard shown here was ringed by tiny houses. In complexes like this, a house usually had just two rooms, one per family. The only light and air came through the courtyard, for other houses backed up to the ones shown. There was no running water. A common tap and a single toilet in the courtyard served all the families that lived there. In American cities such as New York, old houses were subdivided into tiny, dark apartments. Several families often lived in a single room. In New York's Lower East Side, 290,000 people lived in one square mile. Yet rents were 25 to 30 percent higher than in middle-class neighborhoods uptown.

For these long hours at dangerous work, employees earned little to support themselves and their families. Factory owners kept workers' wages low so that their businesses could make profits. Women often made half the wages as men for the same job. Children were paid even less.

Workers' Lives

To earn enough money, whole families worked in the factories and mines, including small children as young as 6 years old. Children often worked 12-hour shifts, sometimes longer and through the night, with only a short break to eat a small meal.

Working-class children did not usually go to school, spending most of the day working instead. Many became crippled or ill from working under unhealthful and dangerous conditions. In 1843 an observer wrote that a child worker in the brick-fields "works from 6 in the morning till 8 or 9 at night … Finds her legs swell sometimes … and [suffers] pains and aches between the shoulders, and her hands swell."

For many women, the industries offered new opportunities for independence. For centuries, women's choices were limited almost entirely either to marriage or to life in a convent. Now they could earn a living. Textile mills in New England, for example, provided young single women an opportunity to make money while making new friends. These "mill girls" lived together in mill boardinghouses where they often gathered in study groups devoted to reading and discussing literature.

Yet for the majority of working-class women and their families, life consisted of a difficult working life and an uncomfortable home life. Workers often lived in crowded, cold apartments in poorly constructed tenement housing near factories. Sometimes whole families lived in one or two rooms.

Because the mill owners often owned the workers' housing, they controlled the rent and decided when and whether to improve living conditions. New urban problems complicated life. Human and industrial waste contaminated water supplies and spread diseases such as cholera and typhoid. In the

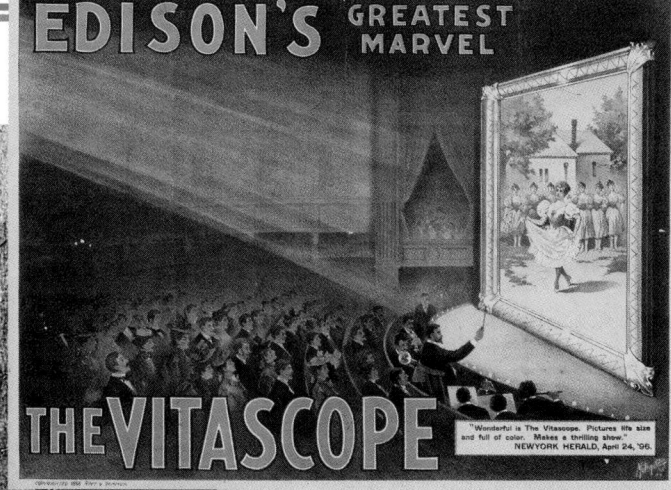

Edison's Vitascope, an early type of motion picture projector, fascinated large audiences.

Children of the working class were often underfed and without schooling. Many in this London tenement lived with discouraged parents. Others worked alongside adults.

REFLECTING ON THE TIMES

1. Why did labor unions organize in the industrial period?
2. How did the Industrial Revolution tend to divide people into separate classes?

391

ANSWERS TO REFLECTING ON THE TIMES

1. because workers on their own could not effectively stand up to the powerful mill owners
2. It enabled the middle class to get richer but made workers' lives poorer and harsher; also, the wealth of the middle class was gained by exploiting laborers.

Daily Life Have students research and report on men's and women's clothing during some period of the Industrial Revolution. Their reports should answer such questions as: Did social classes dress differently, and if so, how? Ask students what conclusions they can draw about the period by studying its clothing. **L3**

Who?What?Where?When?

Luddites, who were named after a (probably legendary) worker named Ned Ludd, organized an early protest against industrialization. In the early 1800s, these English laborers smashed textile machines that were putting them out of work. Some of the Luddites were hanged, and others were transported to Australia.

Cultural Perspectives

Women's Rights Middle-class married women during the industrial age benefited from domestic help, but they had few legal rights. In England, for example, a woman forfeited to her husband not only her property but also her right to control it. A man could will his wife's property to someone without her consent.

ASSESS

Check for Understanding

Assign Section 4 Review as homework or as an in-class activity.

◼ Use Student Self-Test and Review Software to review Section 4.

Workers Unite
How did industrial workers
unite to deal with labor and
social issues that affected
their lives?
*They formed workers associations
and labor unions to demand
better pay and working conditions
either through strikes or collective
bargaining.*

The I.W.W.
(Industrial Workers of the World)
was a militant American labor organization of the early 1900s.
Answer to Caption: *Among other
things, they circulated blacklists.*

Evaluate

 Section Quiz 12-4

Use the Testmaker to create a
customized quiz for Section 4.

Reteach

Have students form two groups.
Have one group present a skit
showing typical middle-class life;
have the other group present a
skit showing working-class life
during the time.

 Reteaching Activity 12

Enrich

Have students draw a cartoon
expressing a factory worker's dissatisfaction.

 Enrichment Activity 12

CLOSE

Have students summarize the
social changes that accompanied
the Industrial Revolution.

THE **I.W.W.** is COMING!

JOIN THE ONE BIG UNION

Visualizing History Through posters, early labor unions
called for unity, realizing that the
individual worker was powerless. *How did factory
owners try to prevent unionization?*

late 1800s, Holyoke, a Massachusetts mill town, had
the highest infant mortality rate in the United States.

Workers Unite

Although governments in western Europe
began to recognize the workers' complaints and initiate reforms, workers still labored under harsh conditions. Only through forming organized labor
groups were workers able to begin to improve their
working conditions in the late 1800s and early 1900s.

Workers knew that they could not fight successfully as individuals against the factory owners.
They had to join together into groups to make their
problems heard. In Great Britain, many workers
joined to form worker associations, which were
groups dedicated to representing the interests of
workers in a specific industry. The associations
hoped to improve the wages and working conditions of their members. Eventually these worker
associations developed into labor unions both in
Europe and in the United States in the 1800s.

Union Tactics

Workers in labor unions protested in many
ways. They organized strikes, in which every worker refused to work. Other times, in sit-down strikes,
workers stopped working but refused to leave their
work area.

Despite these efforts, unions faced great opposition. Manufacturers complained that the shorter
hours and higher wages would add to production
costs, increase the price of goods, and hurt business. To discourage workers from joining unions,
factory owners added the names of suspected
union members to a blacklist to prevent them from
getting jobs throughout the industry. The British
Parliament even banned unions in the Combination
Acts of 1799 and 1800.

Yet British workers kept their cause alive. They
finally won their cause in the 1820s when
Parliament agreed that workers could meet to discuss working hours and wages. In the following
years, skilled British workers formed unions based
on a specific trade or craft. Because they had valuable skills, these trade union members were able to
bargain with employers. When union leaders and
an employer meet together to discuss problems and
reach an agreement, they practice collective bargaining. The British unions' power increased in the
1870s after Parliament legalized strikes.

Following the skilled trade unions' success,
unskilled workers formed unions in the late 1880s. By
the beginning of the 1900s, union membership grew
steadily in Europe and the United States.

SECTION 4 REVIEW

Recall
1. **Define** labor unions, collective
   bargaining.
2. **Identify** Combination Acts.
3. **Discuss** what effect the separation of home and work had on

middle-class and working-class
people in America and Europe.
Critical Thinking
4. **Analyzing Information** Why
   were industrialists often able to
   subject workers to poor work-

ing conditions?
Understanding Themes
5. **Conflict** What were some of
   the problems that factory workers faced? Why did they form
   labor unions to solve them?

SECTION 4 REVIEW ANSWERS

1. All vocabulary words are defined in the
   Glossary.
2. Combination Acts, 392
3. effect on middle class: created separate
   spheres for men and women; effects on
   working class: both men and women subject to harsh factory conditions much of the
   day, had impoverished home lives

4. because factory workers were unskilled
   and many others would be willing to take
   their place
5. **CONFLICT** Factory workers
   faced long hours, low pay, and difficult
   and often dangerous working conditions.
   They formed unions to gain strength in
   numbers.

Critical Thinking SKILLS

Detecting Bias

Suppose you see a billboard showing two happy customers shaking hands with "Honest Harry," the owner of a used-car sales business. The ad says, " Visit Honest Harry for the best deal on wheels." That evening you see a television program that investigates used-car sales businesses. The report says that many of these businesses cheat their customers.

Each message expresses a strong bias. A bias is an inclination or prejudice that inhibits impartiality. Most people have preconceived feelings, opinions, and attitudes that affect their judgment on many topics. For this reason, ideas that profess to be facts may turn out to be opinions. Detecting bias enables us to evaluate the accuracy of information.

Learning the Skill

In detecting bias, first identify the writer's or speaker's purpose. For example, the billboard ad is a marketing tool for selling cars. We would expect that it has a strong bias. The television report may also have a bias, because bad news attracts more viewers.

Another clue to identify bias is emotionally charged language such as *exploit*, *terrorize*, and *cheat*. Also look for visual images that provoke an emotional response. For example, in the television report an interview with a person who bought a "lemon" automobile may elicit a strong response.

Look for overgeneralizations such as *unique*, *honest*, and *everybody*. Notice italics, underlining, and punctuation that highlights particular ideas. Watch for opinions stated as facts without substantiating evidence. Finally, examine the material to determine whether it presents equal coverage of differing views.

Practicing the Skill

Industrialization produced widespread changes in society and widespread disagreement on its effects. While many people hailed the abundance of manufactured goods, others criticized its impact on working people. Karl Marx and Friedrich Engels presented their viewpoint on industrialization in the *Communist Manifesto* in 1848. Read the following excerpt and then answer these questions.

1. What is the purpose of this manifesto?
2. What are three examples of emotionally charged language?
3. According to Marx and Engels, which is more inhumane—the exploitation by feudal lords or by the bourgeoisie? Why?
4. What bias about industrialization is expressed in this excerpt?

    “ The bourgeoisie *[the class of factory owners and employers]* … has put an end to all feudal, patriarchal, idyllic relations. It has pitilessly torn asunder the motley feudal ties that bound man to his "natural superiors," and has left remaining no other nexus *[link]* between man and man than naked self-interest, than callous "cash payment." It has drowned the most heavenly of ecstasies of religious fervor, of chivalrous enthusiasm … in the icy water of egotistical calculation.… In one word, for exploitation, veiled by religious and political illusions, it has substituted naked, shameless, direct, brutal exploitation. ”

Applying the Skill

Find written material about a topic of interest in your community. Possible sources include editorials, letters to the editor, and pamphlets from political candidates and interest groups. Write a short report analyzing the material for evidence of bias.

For More Practice

Turn to the Skill Practice in the Chapter Review on page 395 for more practice in detecting bias.

Critical Thinking SKILLS

TEACH

Detecting Bias Point out that everyone is biased. Without using reason, people rely on gut emotional reactions, favoring some things—a sports team, a political party—and disapproving of others—a nationality, a breed of dog. Have students list, anonymously, two biases of theirs, either positive or negative. After collecting these, read some of them aloud for class discussion. Which are positive and which negative? How might they be helpful or harmful?

Additional Practice

Skill Reinforcement Activity 12

ANSWERS TO PRACTICING THE SKILL

1. to arouse negative feelings about capitalists and capitalism
2. Emotionally charged language includes: *idyllic, pitilessly, naked, callous, heavenly, ecstasies, chivalrous, egotistical, shameless, brutal.*
3. exploitation by the bourgeoisie; at least feudal relations were accompanied by religious faith and chivalry
4. It is a totally negative force. It has destroyed all ties between people except for the "naked self-interest" expressed through a cash nexus.

VIDEODISC

Use MindJogger to review students' knowledge of the chapter.

MindJogger Videoquiz

Chapter 12
Disc 2 Side A

Also available in VHS.

Answers

Using Key Terms

1. l
2. d
3. f
4. c
5. k

Using Your History Journal

Of special interest to students would be the telephone, electricity, and the automobile.

Reviewing Facts

1. the widespread change from human labor to machines; Causes: agricultural revolution providing more food for more people; availability of capital for investment; development of factory system based on steam power; Effects: more and cheaper goods, new social classes, growth of cities, short-term suffering for workers, but long term improvement in standards of living

2. It provided a source of power that enabled factories to be built in more locations.

3. Women and children worked long hours in unhealthy and dangerous conditions in factories.

4. (Industry) James Watt, the steam engine; (Transportation) Robert Fulton, first practical steamboat; (Communication) Alexander Graham Bell, telephone

5. Great Britain lost its industrial monopoly as its ideas and prod-

---

Historical Significance The Industrial Revolution has led to seemingly limitless possibilities. Many of the cities created by the early factories have grown and prospered. International business today is carried on with the aid of computer technology.

The Industrial Age has carried with it many social problems as well as a depletion of natural resources. Today, people face the challenge of combining economic development with preservation of the environment.

Using Key Terms

Write the key term that completes each sentence. Then write a sentence for each term not chosen.

a. factory system
b. partnership
c. division of labor
d. corporation
e. enclosure movement
f. collective bargaining
g. industrial capitalism
h. entrepreneurs
i. labor unions
j. domestic system
k. capital
l. depression

1. The lowest point in the business cycle is a _____, which is characterized by bank failures and widespread unemployment.
2. A _____ is a business organization owned by stockholders who buy shares in the company and vote on major decisions concerning the future of the business.
3. When union leaders and an employer meet together to discuss problems and reach an agreement, they practice _____.
4. Under a _____, workers perform a particular task on a product as it is moved by on a conveyor belt.
5. Money invested in labor, machines, and raw materials is known as _____.

Technology Activity

Using E-mail Locate an E-mail address for your chamber of commerce. Compose a letter requesting information about various industries in your area. Create an illustrated pamphlet of information about area industries. Include advancement of technology within these industries, and their impact on the community. Provide a circle graph illustrating the percentage of people employed by specific industries within your community.

Using Your History Journal

From your time line of inventions choose one invention that you believe affects your life every day. How would people live today without this invention? Write a paragraph describing life without it.

Reviewing Facts

1. **Technology/Society** Identify the Industrial Revolution, and list its causes and effects.
2. **Technology** Explain the role of steam engine in the development of the factory system.
3. **Technology/Society** Discuss the impact of industrialization on working-class women and children.
4. **Science** Identify three inventors in industry, transportation, and communication, and list their individual contributions.
5. **Technology/Society** Track the spread of industry. How did industrialization differ from country to country?

Critical Thinking

1. **Apply** How did the Industrial Revolution affect Great Britain's social structure?
2. **Analyze** In what ways did the life of a farm laborer differ from the life of a factory worker?
3. **Synthesize** Great Britain had an early lead in industrialization. Which factor was the most critical in this development? Why?
4. **Evaluate** What do you see as the positive and negative effects of the Industrial Revolution?

---

ucts spread abroad; France's industrial development proceeded slowly, allowing farming and small businesses to remain dominant in its economy; with government aid, industry forged ahead in Germany; the United States developed its industry in the Northeast, using British capital and local mechanical skills; Japan developed into an industrial power by 1914.

Critical Thinking

1. It increased social mobility and enlarged both the middle class and the working class.
2. Farm laborers worked in accordance with the seasons and the days, not a fixed time schedule; they also had greater autonomy.
3. capital, natural resources, or a growing labor force
4. positive—growth of cities, higher standard of living; negative—exploitation of labor, degra-

5. Evaluate How can consumer demand influence technological development?

Geography in History

1. **Region** Refer to the map below. Why did England have an advantage in developing heavy industry?
2. **Place** What industrial center is closest to several iron ore and coal fields?
3. **Movement** Railways in northern Scotland and Ireland were not built for transporting iron and coal. How can you tell this from the map? What may have been transported on these railways?

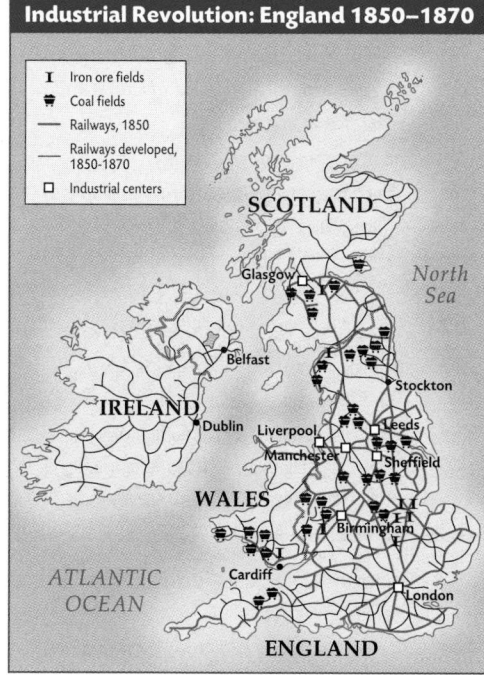

Industrial Revolution: England 1850–1870

- **I** Iron ore fields
- Coal fields
- — Railways, 1850
- Railways developed, 1850-1870
- □ Industrial centers

SCOTLAND

Glasgow

North Sea

Belfast

Stockton

IRELAND

Dublin Liverpool Leeds

Manchester Sheffield

WALES

Birmingham

ATLANTIC OCEAN

Cardiff

London

ENGLAND

Understanding Themes

1. **Relation to Environment** How were industry and farming related during the period before the Industrial Revolution?

2. Innovation It is often said that "necessity is the mother of invention." Using one invention in this chapter, illustrate this statement.

3. Change Do you think that progress is a necessary result of change? Give examples.

4. Conflict How have differences between employers and workers produced positive effects for workers in the modern world?

Linking Past and Present

1. What effects do you see from the Industrial Revolution in your everyday life?
2. What changes and challenges has industry presented society in recent years?
3. The Industrial Revolution replaced many handcrafted items with mass-produced ones. What things that we use today are made mostly by hand?

Skill Practice

Read the following excerpt from "The Gospel of Wealth," an 1889 essay by Andrew Carnegie. Then answer the questions that follow.

❝ The contrast between the palace of the millionaire and the cottage of the laborer with us today measures the changes which had come with civilization. The change, however, is not to be deplored, but welcomed as highly beneficial. It is well, nay, essential for the progress of the race that the houses of some should be homes for all that is highest and best in literature and the arts, and for all the refinements of civilization, rather than that none should be so. Much better this great irregularity than universal squalor. ❞

1. Does the term *cottage* coincide with the description of how workers lived that is found on page 391?
2. How does Carnegie's use of this term indicate bias?
3. How does Carnegie justify large differences in lifestyle between rich and poor?
4. How does Carnegie describe the condition of most of humanity, except the wealthy?

Chapter 12 *Age of Industry* **395**

3. **CHANGE** Possible answer: No, the factory system, for example, brought with it exploitation of workers, child labor, and slums.

4. **CONFLICT** In industrialized nations, unions and government regulation have helped workers achieve good wages, benefits, and decent working conditions.

Linking Past and Present

1. rapid transportation, instant communication, and a huge range of inexpensive mass-produced items
2. the need to adapt to electronic technology, to protect the environment, to lessen the gap between industrialized and nonindustrialized nations
3. some items of clothing and furnishings (e.g., hand-knit sweaters), works of art (e.g., paintings), some musical instruments (e.g., violins, pianos)

Skill Practice

1. Answers will vary.
2. He infers that all laborers live in cottages or squalor.
3. as a progress of civilization
4. universal squalor

Chapter Bonus Test Question

Ask students: In "exporting" the Industrial Revolution to nonindustrialized nations, what do you think would be the single most important element of the nineteenth-century revolution described in this chapter to introduce? *(Technological innovations might include steel manufacturing, electric power, good roads, labor unions)*

dation of environment

5. If enough people want an innovative good or service, individuals or businesses will try to develop it.

Geography in History

1. England had plenty of iron ore and coal.
2. Birmingham
3. Neither of these areas has iron or coal fields. The railways may have carried agricultural

products to industrial areas and industrial goods to Ireland and Scotland.

Understanding Themes

1. **RELATION TO ENVIRONMENT** Often, families were engaged in both: part-time farming and part-time industry through the domestic system.
2. **INNOVATION** The textile industry offers many good examples.

A complete, 1-page lesson plan is provided for each section in the *Reproducible Lesson Plans* booklet.

Cultural Revolution

CHAPTER RESOURCES

	Reproducible Resources	Multimedia Resources
Chapter Opener	Chapter Themes: Graphic Organizer 13 Historical Significance Chapter Activity 13	MindJogger Videoquiz
Chapter Enrichment	Vocabulary Activity 13* Time Line Activity 13 Mapping History Activity 13 History Simulation 13 Geography and History Activity 13 Source Reading 13 People in World History Profiles 38, 45, 46 World Literature Selection 6 World Art and Music Activity 13 Enrichment Activity 13 Critical Thinking Activity 13 Skill Reinforcement Activity 13 Performance Assessment Activity 13	Focus on World Art Prints 2, 5, 22 World History and Art Transparency 31, *In the Garden*; 32, *Sunday Afternoon on the Island of La Grande Jatte*; 34, *Starry Night* Mapping History Overlay Transparency 16, *Global Ancestry of Americans* Chapter Transparency 13 Vocabulary PuzzleMaker Software Turning Points in World History: *The Industrial Revolution* Communism and the Cold War: • *Perspectives on Capitalism* • *Perspectives on Communism*
Chapter Review/Reteaching	Reteaching Activity 13 Skill Reinforcement Activity 13 Spanish Chapter Summary 13	Chapter 13 Digest Audiocassette, Activity, Test* Vocabulary PuzzleMaker Software Student Self-Test and Review Software MindJogger Videoquiz
Chapter Evaluation/Testing	Performance Assessment Activity 13 Chapter 13 Test, Forms A and B	Testmaker

* Also available in Spanish

0:00 OUT OF TIME? Assign the Chapter 13 summary in the Unit 4 Digest on pages 505–507, and the Chapter 13 Audiocassettes.

Block Schedule

Block scheduling differs from traditional class scheduling in the amount of time allotted to each period. The extended time frame provided by block scheduling affords you the opportunity to implement a greater number of research-oriented and activity-intense projects to motivate and involve your students. Activities that are particularly suited to use within the block scheduling framework are identified throughout this chapter by the following designation.

KEY TO ABILITY LEVELS

Teaching strategies have been coded for varying learning styles and abilities.

L1 **BASIC** activities for all students
L2 **AVERAGE** activities for average to above-average students
L3 **CHALLENGING** activities for above-average students
LEP **LIMITED ENGLISH PROFICIENCY** activities

Use Glencoe's *Presentation Plus!* multimedia teacher tool to easily present dynamic lessons that visually excite your students. Using Microsoft PowerPoint® you can customize the presentations to create your own personalized lessons.

SECTION RESOURCES

Daily Objectives	Reproducible Resources	Multimedia Resources

Section 1
New Ideas
Explain why Karl Marx advocated doing away with the capitalist system.
	Reproducible Lesson Plan 13-1
	Guided Reading Activity 13-1*
	People in World History Profile 38
	Time Line Activity 13
	Section Quiz 13-1*
		Section Focus Transparency 13-1
		
		Chapter Transparency 13
		Vocabulary PuzzleMaker Software
		Student Self-Test and Review Software
		Testmaker
		Communism and the Cold War:
		  • *Perspectives on Communism*
		  • *Perspectives on Capitalism*

Section 2 **The New Science** List advances made in science between 1750 and 1914 that have improved life today.	Reproducible Lesson Plan 13-2 Guided Reading Activity 13-2* People in World History Profiles 45, 46 Section Quiz 13-2*	Section Focus Transparency 13-2 Vocabulary PuzzleMaker Software Student Self-Test and Review Software Testmaker
Section 3 **Popular Culture** Analyze why the population grew dramatically in Europe and North America during the 1800s.	Reproducible Lesson Plan 13-3 Vocabulary Activity 13* Guided Reading Activity 13-3* Geography and History Activity 13 Section Quiz 13-3*	Section Focus Transparency 13-3 Mapping History Overlay Transparency 16, *Global Ancestry of Americans* Student Self-Test and Review Software Testmaker Turning Points in World History: *The Industrial Revolution*
Section 4 **Revolution in the Arts** Describe how writers and artists in Europe and North America reflected changes in society between 1750 and 1914.	Reproducible Lesson Plan 13-4 Guided Reading Activity 13-4* History Simulation 13 Reteaching Activity 13 Enrichment Activity 13 Section Quiz 13-4* Performance Assessment Activity 13 Spanish Chapter Summary 13	Focus on World Art Print 2, Franz Marc. *Stables*; 5, Paul Klee. *Palace, Partially Destroyed*; 22, Vincent van Gogh. *Hospital at Saint-Rémy* Section Focus Transparency 13-4 World History and Art Transparency 31, *In the Garden*; 32, *Sunday Afternoon on the Island of La Grande Jatte*; 34, *Starry Night* Vocabulary PuzzleMaker Software Student Self-Test and Review Software Testmaker

* Also available in Spanish

Chapter Activities

✓ *Performance Assessment Activity*

Reform Inquiry and Projection Reforms covered in this chapter took place in government, working conditions, medicine, education, art, and urban life. Have students research reform efforts today in the same areas in order to complete a compare-and-contrast matrix. After students have drawn conclusions about the continuity and change in these areas, ask them to predict the reform movements that might occur after another 50 to 100 years. As a concluding activity, students can create a collage, mural, chart, or multimedia slide show including symbols and illustrations of the past, present, and future reform movements.

Possible Rubric Features
Accuracy of content information; accuracy, relevance, and degree of research; plausibility of predictions; originality, impact, and clarity of visuals

• *For an additional activity, refer to Activity 13 in the* Performance Assessment Strategies and Activities *booklet.*

ACTIVITY

From the Classroom of...

Charles Dixon
High School Redirection
Brooklyn, NY

Rise of Socialism Round Robin

Have students read from "A Better Society" to the end of Section 1 in the text (pages 399–401) and outline the ideas of the different reformers. Ask students to head a sheet of paper *During the 1800s socialism began to ...* , then write an end to the sentence, using information from their outlines.

Have students exchange papers six times (each time with someone new). After each exchange have students add a sentence to the paper they have just received. On the last exchange instruct students to write concluding sentences. Have several students read their completed paragraphs and use these as a springboard for discussion.

MULTIPLE LEARNING STYLES

Logical/Mathematical
Have students create a time line that tracks the major social, cultural, and scientific developments of the period. Students should include details from the text and from class discussions and activities.

Visual/Spatial
Have students produce an art journal filled with their own drawings and paintings done in the different artistic styles presented in this chapter.

Auditory/Musical
Have students listen to Schiller's "Ode to Joy," sung as part of Beethoven's Ninth Symphony. Ask them to write new words of their own that seem appropriate to the music.

Kinesthetic
Have students plan and attend a field trip to a nearby museum whose collection includes works by the artists discussed in this chapter. If possible, arrange to be led through the collection by a docent.

Additional Resources

Teacher's Corner

INDEX TO
NATIONAL GEOGRAPHIC MAGAZINE

The following articles may be used for research relating to this chapter:

- "Vincent van Gogh," by Joel L. Swerdlow, October 1997.
- "Sir Joseph Banks," by T. H. Watkins, November 1996.
- "Viruses," by Peter Jaret, July 1994.
- "Paris: La Belle Epoque," by Eugen Weber, July 1989.
- "The World of Tolstoy," by Peter T. White, June 1986.

ADDITIONAL NATIONAL GEOGRAPHIC
SOCIETY PRODUCTS

To order the following products for use with this chapter, call National Geographic Society at 1-800-368-2728:

- *Capitalism, Socialism, Communism Series,* "Communism," "Socialism," "Capitalism." (Videos)

BIBLIOGRAPHY

Literature of the Period
Dreiser, Theodore. *Sister Carrie.* Edited by Donald Pizer. New York: Norton, 1970. Includes backgrounds, sources, and criticism in addition to an authoritative text of the naturalist novel.
Readings for the Student
Briggs, Asa. *A Social History of England: From the Ice Age to the Channel Tunnel.* London: Weidenfeld and Nicolson, 1994. Offers the human side of change, drawing on artistic, economic, and political developments.
Readings for the Teacher
Heilbroner, Robert L. *The Worldly Philosophers.* New York: Simon and Schuster, 1980. Discusses Smith, Ricardo, Malthus, Marx, and the utopian Socialists.

LOCAL OBJECTIVES

*inter***NET**
CONNECTION
Art history resources on the World Wide Web
ArtSource:
http://www.uky.edu/
Artsource/artsourcehome.html

CHAPTER THEMES

Chapter Themes are listed by section on this chapter opening page of the Student Edition. A corresponding theme-based activity is available under "TEACH," and a theme-based question is asked in the Section and Chapter Reviews.

The Storyteller

Historical Setting Dreiser (1871–1945) wrote this description of Chicago in his first novel, *Sister Carrie.* Dreiser is considered a member of the literary movement of naturalism, which began in the mid-1800s in France. According to Dreiser and other naturalists, social, economic, and biological forces control human actions and destinies. Dreiser lived and worked in Chicago for several years. He wrote about the city in his autobiographies, journalistic articles, and novels. Although Dreiser believed that cities were the source of power and wealth, he also believed that most city-dwellers were fated to lives of poverty and degradation.

Historical Significance

Answers: *Economic reformers developed theories of socialism and Marxism as alternatives to capitalism; scientists began to understand the nature of living matter and of the atom, and they made advances in medicine.*

Improved nutrition, sanitation, and medical practices resulted in healthier, longer-lived populations. People became more mobile, and many moved to cities. There, leisure-time activities spread, but many people still lived in poverty and in dismal conditions.

Artists reacted to the changes in society through movements such as romanticism, realism, symbolism, and impressionism.

Chapter
13
1750–1914
Cultural Revolution

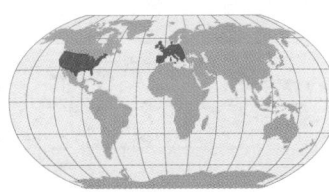

Chapter Themes

▶ **Change** Political and economic philosophies attempt to make sense of a changing industrial world. *Section 1*

▶ **Innovation** Scientific discoveries lead to improved health and revolutionary views about the natural world and human society. *Section 2*

▶ **Movement** People move from rural to urban areas and from continent to continent in search of better lives. *Section 3*

▶ **Innovation** Artists and writers in the Western world reflect the changes in urban industrial society. *Section 4*

The Storyteller

A new world was in the making. Factories boomed. Cities grew. By the late 1800s, steamships and trains allowed people to move in search of better lives. American novelist Theodore Dreiser described the excitement that drew people to Chicago:

"Its many and growing commercial opportunities gave it widespread fame, which made of it a giant magnet, drawing to itself, from all quarters, the hopeful and the hopeless…. It was a city of over 500,000 with the ambition, the daring, the activity of a metropolis of a million."

The Industrial Revolution also brought challenges to Europeans and North Americans. Cities became overcrowded, and the gap between rich and poor widened. People struggled to make sense of an increasingly complex society.

Historical Significance

What changes occurred in the economics, the sciences, and the arts of the West between 1750 and 1914? How did these changes alter people's values and daily lives?

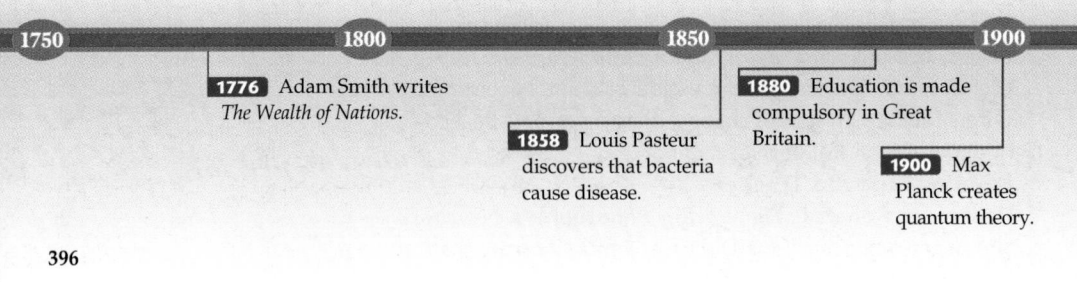

1750	1800	1850	1900

1776 Adam Smith writes *The Wealth of Nations.*

1858 Louis Pasteur discovers that bacteria cause disease.

1880 Education is made compulsory in Great Britain.

1900 Max Planck creates quantum theory.

396

GEOGRAPHY CONNECTION

Location Have students locate Chicago on a map. What two great North American waterways does the Chicago River lie between? *(It empties into Lake Michigan, and its arms nearly reach the drainage basin of the Mississippi River.)* Explain to students that several factors helped transform Chicago into the interior land and water hub of the expanding United States: The opening of the Erie Canal in 1825 connected the Atlantic Ocean and the Great Lakes; the completion of the Illinois and Michigan Canal in 1848 linked the Great Lakes and Mississippi River systems; and the railroad system in 1856 turned the city into the nation's chief rail center.

 History & Art Boulevard Des Capuchines and Théâtre de Vaudeville, 1889, by Jean Beraud. Musée Carnavalet, Paris, France

✔ **Performance Assessment**

Refer to the activity on page 396C of the Planning Guide.

📁 For an additional activity, refer to Activity 13 in the *Performance Assessment Strategies and Activities* booklet.

Your History Journal

This chapter introduces thinkers and reformers who wanted to create a better society. Write an essay suggesting ways to improve the society in which we live today.

Using Your History Journal

Suggest that students research the goals of some reformers active in the United States today, such as Ralph Nader or Amory Lovins.

Chapter 13 *Cultural Revolution* 397

GLENCOE **TECHNOLOGY**

VIDEODISC
Use MindJogger to preview chapter content.

MindJogger Videoquiz
Chapter 13
Disc 2 Side A

▶ Also available in VHS.

✚ **EXTRA CREDIT PROJECT**

Socialist Reformers Have students research and report to the class on the life and work of one of the early French utopian Socialist reformers, such as Count Claude Henri de Saint-Simon (1760–1825) or Charles Fourier (1772–1837). Suggested resources: A. J. Booth, *Saint-Simon and Saint-Simonism*; F. E. Manuel, *The Prophets of Paris*; A. Gray, *The Socialist Tradition*.

▶ **Change** Political and economic philosophies attempt to make sense of a changing industrial world.

Find Out

Answer: *He believed it exploited workers.*

FOCUS
Section Objective

Explain why Karl Marx advocated doing away with the capitalist system.

BELLRINGER
Motivational Activity

Project Section Focus Transparency 13-1 and have students answer the activity questions.
Also available as a blackline master

Vocabulary Pre-check

Use the Vocabulary PuzzleMaker to create a puzzle that reinforces the vocabulary terms in this section. **L1**

TURNING POINT

Capitalist Ideas
What did early industrial capitalists believe about the role of government in the economy? *They believed in laissez-faire and worked to end the restrictions of the mercantilist system.*

1800		1850		1900
1837 David Ricardo writes about the "iron law of wages."		**1847** British Parliament passes the Ten Hours Act.		**1867** Karl Marx publishes *Das Kapital*.

Section 1
New Ideas

Setting the Scene

▶ **Terms to Define**
laissez-faire, utilitarianism, socialism, proletariat, bourgeoisie, communism

▶ **People to Meet**
Adam Smith, David Ricardo, Jeremy Bentham, John Stuart Mill, Robert Owen, Karl Marx, Friedrich Engels

 **Find Out** Why did Karl Marx advocate doing away with the capitalist system?

The Storyteller

Karl Marx, the chief architect of communism, was always and everywhere a student. At an early age his withdrawal from all university activities except the intellectual brought stern advice from his father:

"My clever and gifted son Karl passes wretched and sleepless nights, wearying body and mind with cheerless study…. But what he builds today he destroys again tomorrow…. At last the body begins to ail and the mind gets confused, whilst ordinary folk … attain their goal if not better at least more comfortably than those who condemn youthful pleasures and undermine their health…."

—from *The Life and Teaching of Karl Marx*, M. Beer, 1921

Karl Marx

398 Chapter 13 *Cultural Revolution*

English essayist William Hazlitt, writing in the early 1800s, described Europe in the critical years after the French Revolution:

❝ There was a mighty ferment in the heads of statesmen and poets, kings and people. According to the prevailing notions, all was to be natural and new. Nothing that was established was to be tolerated…. The world was to be turned topsy-turvy. ❞

The Western world did appear to be turning upside down, as society underwent a transformation. In little more than 100 years, the Industrial Revolution converted Europe from a farming economy centered in the country to an industrial economy based in urban areas.

Industry in the short term brought great wealth to a few and imposed hardships on the many. In the long run, however, it provided material benefits to all people. Still, the gap between "haves" and "have nots" remained to create unrest in many societies.

Capitalist Ideas

During the Industrial Revolution, European thinkers for the first time studied and explained how capitalism worked. Rejecting mercantilism with its government controls, many supported laissez-faire (LEH•SAY•FAHR), a policy allowing business to operate without government interference. Laissez-faire, from a French term meaning "let them alone," was developed in France during the 1700s by the Physiocrats. These thinkers valued land as the primary source of national wealth. They held that fewer taxes and regulations would enable farmers to grow more produce. In the early 1800s, the middle-class owners of railroads, factories, and

---

Reproducible Masters
• Reproducible Lesson Plan 13-1
• Guided Reading Activity 13-1
• People in World History Profile 38
• Time Line Activity 13
• Section Quiz 13-1

Transparencies
• Section Focus Transparency 13-1
• Chapter Transparency 13

Multimedia
Vocabulary PuzzleMaker Software
Student Self-Test and Review Software
Testmaker
Communism and the Cold War:
• *Perspectives on Capitalism*
• *Perspectives on Communism*

mines began supporting laissez-faire. They believed that freedom from government controls would mean a growing economy with material progress for all people.

Adam Smith

Industrial leaders relied on the ideas of **Adam Smith**, a Scottish economist who set down the workings of a laissez-faire economy. In *The Wealth of Nations* (1776), Smith stated that an economy works best when the natural forces of supply and demand operate without government interference. In such a free market, individual sellers and buyers act on self-interest. Smith did not think this was necessarily bad, believing that a natural order in the universe made all individual striving for self-interest add up to the common good. Businesses compete to produce goods as inexpensively as possible, and consumers buy the best goods at the lowest prices. Efficient producers make more profit, hire more workers, and continue to expand, to everyone's benefit.

As the Industrial Revolution gathered momentum and spread throughout the world, Smith's ideas profoundly influenced economic thought and practice. By the 1850s, Great Britain, the world's leading industrial power, had adopted free trade and other laissez-faire policies.

Malthus and Ricardo

Not all thinkers, however, held Smith's optimism about the future. Thomas Malthus, an Anglican clergyman, wrote in *An Essay on the Principle of Population* (1798) that poverty, famine, and misery were unavoidable because population was increasing faster than the food supply. Influenced by Malthus, the British economist **David Ricardo** stated in his "iron law of wages" that rapid population growth would lead only to fierce competition for jobs, lower wages, and higher unemployment. Continual poverty was all that was in store for the working class. As strong believers in laissez-faire, both Malthus and Ricardo opposed government aid to the poor. Instead, they believed that the poor could help themselves by working hard, saving their earnings, and having fewer children.

Because of these gloomy theories, people in the 1800s called economics "the dismal science." However, the forecasts of Malthus and Ricardo were not fulfilled. Population continued to rise, but as a result of the agricultural revolution, the food supply grew even faster. By the 1900s, higher living standards and lower birth rates prevailed in many

Grim-faced young coal mine workers in Kingston, Pennsylvania, pose for the camera. *How would photographs such as this support criticism of laissez-faire economics?*

Western countries such as Great Britain, the United States, and Germany. Yet, industrialization benefited some more than others and fueled demands for reforms that would create a more just society.

A Better Society

During the 1800s, reformers set out to improve the lives of the disadvantaged, especially enslaved people and the urban poor. At the same time, a new generation of thinkers questioned laissez-faire and urged government to work for a better society.

Evangelicals and Reform

During the late 1700s and early 1800s, a series of religious awakenings swept through the Protestant churches. The outcome of these revivals was Evangelicalism, a movement that joined personal faith with social improvement. Some Evangelicals supported strict laissez-faire; others, however, believed that government needed to involve itself in the lives of the disadvantaged. One of the most noted participants in the Evangelical cause was William Wilberforce, a member of Parliament. Opposed to slavery, Wilberforce had Parliament pass a bill in 1807 that ended the British slave trade. Later, in 1833—the year of Wilberforce's death—Parliament abolished slavery throughout the British Empire.

Chapter 13 *Cultural Revolution* **399**

TEACH

Guided Practice

THEME Change

Have students brainstorm things they would change about present-day society if they could create their own utopian community. At the end of the brainstorming session, have students vote on the changes they would make. **L1**

Visualizing History Not until 1916 did the U.S. Congress pass the first federal child labor law. Among other provisions, that law set the minimum age for work in mines at 16. **Answer to Caption:** *It depicts the dismal life of children exploited by the system.*

ABCNEWS INTERACTIVE™

 VIDEODISC Communism and the Cold War

Side One, Chapter 7
Frames 13483–14256
Title: *Perspectives on Capitalism*
Ask: What is the underlying idea behind capitalism? *(individual initiative)*

Side One, Chapter 8
Frames 14264–14893
Title: *Perspectives on Communism*
Ask: In communism, what was "the ideal society"? *(one in which everyone is happy, no competition)*

COOPERATIVE LEARNING ACTIVITY

Newsletters Organize the class into several groups. Have each group prepare the front page of a newsletter advocating an economic policy presented in this section, such as laissez-faire or socialist economics. Each group should choose a name for its newsletter that suggests its point of view (for example, *Voice of the People* for a socialist perspective) and select a time period between 1750 and 1914. The groups should research economic issues of that time, which might include unionization, worker strikes, or labor reform. After selecting topics for a number of front-page stories, group members should write the articles or illustrate them. Completed front pages can be displayed in class. **L3**

Visualizing History Posters became a popular means of conveying simple messages in the 1860s after the invention of color lithography allowed for inexpensive and easy production.
Answer to Caption: *public control of the means of production and equal distribution of wealth*

Economics Explain that proponents of laissez-faire economics still believe in a minimum of governmental interference in the economy. They argue that if businesses are allowed to operate freely, competition will keep prices low and quality high. Ask the class to discuss the implications of this policy and ways it might affect today's society. **L3**

 Chapter Transparency 13

Independent Practice

📁 Guided Reading Activity 13-1 **L1**

📁 People in World History Profile 38

📁 Time Line Activity 13

Visualizing History Many socialist groups used posters and cartoons to win support for the overthrow of Europe's monarchies as well as the capitalist system. *What were two other goals of the socialist movement?*

Another Evangelical leader, Lord Shaftesbury, promoted laws to limit working hours for women and children. Aiding Shaftesbury's efforts were parliamentary commissions investigating factories and mines. Commission reports detailing miserable working conditions raised a public outcry. Parliament responded with the first factory laws of the industrial era. Passed during the 1830s and 1840s, these measures regulated child employment in factories, prohibited women and children from working in underground mines, and established a 10-hour day in textile factories for children under 18 and women.

Utilitarian Reformers

Many secular social reformers also believed that laissez-faire policies should be changed to allow for some government involvement in economic and social affairs. British philosopher **Jeremy Bentham** promoted utilitarianism, the idea that society should work for "the greatest happiness for the greatest number" of citizens. To Bentham, laws should be judged by their usefulness, whether they advanced human happiness and reduced human misery. To this end, Bentham called for a better code of law, education for all, a public health service, and improved prisons.

Bentham's follower, **John Stuart Mill**, challenged strict views of laissez-faire economics, calling on government to distribute national wealth more justly by taxing income. However, he also held a firm belief in individual freedom. In works such as *On Liberty*

(1859), Mill stated that freedom of thought and discussion promoted social progress and supported extending the vote to all adults. A believer in full democracy, Mill advocated equal rights for women.

TURNING POINT

Rise of Socialism

Not everyone in Europe agreed with the capitalist way of thinking in the early 1800s. Some people believed that ending the misery of workers required eliminating capitalism completely. They advocated socialism—the belief that the means of production—capital, land, raw materials, and factories—should be owned and controlled by society, either directly or through the government. In this way, wealth could be distributed equally among all citizens.

Early Socialism

Some early advocates of socialism planned and built communities where everyone was supposed to share equally in the benefits of the industrial age. Among the first to establish such a community was **Robert Owen**, a wealthy Welsh manufacturer. Owen believed that competition caused society's problems. Thus, he reasoned that if cooperation replaced competition, life would improve.

In 1800 Owen set out to prove his point in New Lanark, a dreary Scottish mill town. In time he reconstructed it into a model industrial community. Although he did not turn the textile mill completely over to the workers, he greatly improved their living and working conditions. In 1825 Owen stopped managing New Lanark and bought New Harmony, Indiana, where he tried to set up a cooperative community. New Harmony, however, did not meet with the same success as New Lanark. Feuding among Owen and the residents led Owen to return to Great Britain.

Marx and Engels

German philosopher **Karl Marx** dismissed the ideas of the early socialists as impractical and set out to provide a scientific basis for socialism. The son of a prosperous German lawyer, Marx received a doctorate in history and philosophy. When his radical views got him into trouble with the Prussian government, he fled to Paris. There in 1844 he met **Friedrich Engels**. Engels was on his way home from one of his father's factories in Manchester, England. Horrified by what he saw there, Engels wrote a classic book called *The Condition of the Working Class in England*.

Marx later settled in London, and he and Engels became lifelong friends and collaborators. Engels, a successful businessman, supported Marx, who devoted his life to writing about economics.

Marx's Theories

Marx based his ideas in part on the teachings of the German philosopher G.W.F. Hegel. Hegel taught that changing ideas were the major force in history. As ideas clashed, new ideas emerged. This produced new changes, conflicts, and ideas.

Like Hegel, Marx believed that history advanced through conflict. In Marx's view, however, economics was the major force for change. Production was at the base of every social order. Laws, social systems, customs, religion, and art all developed in accord with a society's economic base.

The most important aspect of the economic base was the division of society into classes. The class that controlled production became the ruling class. The only way to make the ruling class give up control was through revolution. Therefore, conflict between classes was inevitable. Marx stated "class struggle," was what pushed history forward.

Marx argued that Europe had moved through four stages of economic life—primitive, slave, feudal, and capitalist. During the primitive stage, people produced only what they needed to live. There was no exploitation, or unfair use of a person for one's own advantage. Once tools were developed, however, and people could produce a surplus, they became exploitable. From then on, history was a class struggle. It was the "haves" against the "have–nots."

Marx believed that capitalism was only a temporary phase. As the makers of goods, the proletariat, or the working class, was the true productive class. An economic crisis in one of the advanced industrial countries would give the proletariat the chance to seize control from the bourgeoisie (BURZH•WAH•ZEE), or middle class. The proletariat would then build a society in which the people owned everything. Without private property, classes would vanish, and the government would wither away. In this last stage, known as communism, the governing principle would be "from each according to his ability, to each according to his need."

Marx and Engels published their views in *The Communist Manifesto* in 1848. In it they appealed to the world's workers:

> **❝** Let the ruling classes tremble at a Communist revolution. The proletarians have nothing to lose but their chains. They have a world to win. Working men of all countries, unite! **❞**

In 1867 Marx developed his ideas further in the work *Das Kapital*.

The Socialist Legacy

History did not proceed by Marx's plan. When Marx was writing, workers' poverty contrasted sharply with industrialists' wealth. By 1900 conditions had changed in western Europe. Workers could buy more with their wages than they could 50 years earlier. Rather than overthrow their governments, workers gained the right to vote and used it to correct the worst social ills. They also remained loyal to their individual nations rather than ally with workers in other countries to promote revolution.

In time, democratic socialism developed in western Europe. Democratic Socialists urged public control of some means of production, but they respected individual values and favored democratic means to implement Socialist policies.

In the early 1900s, however, revolution swept Russia, a largely agricultural society. There a small group of Marxist revolutionaries had developed a radical form of socialism that became known as "communism." Rising to power in the revolution, the Russian communists imposed their beliefs on the country and shunned democratic values.

| **SECTION I REVIEW** |

Recall
1. **Define** laissez-faire, utilitarianism, socialism, proletariat, bourgeoisie, communism.
2. **Identify** Adam Smith, David Ricardo, Jeremy Bentham, John Stuart Mill, Robert Owen, Karl Marx,

Friedrich Engels.
3. **Explain** why, according to Adam Smith, a laissez-faire policy would promote economic progress and social harmony.

Critical Thinking
4. **Making Comparisons** How are the viewpoints of the Evangelicals and the Utilitarians

similar? How are they different?
Understanding Themes
5. **Change** Why did industrialization make people think about the causes and cures of poverty? Can poverty be totally eliminated? Which thinkers of the period would agree with your views?

| **SECTION I REVIEW ANSWERS** |

1. All vocabulary words are defined in the Glossary.
2. Smith, 399; Ricardo, 399; Bentham, 400; Mill, 400; Owen, 400; Marx, 400; Engels, 400
3. Without governmental interference, businesses compete to produce goods as inexpensively as possible, and consumers buy the best goods at the lowest prices. Efficient producers make more profit, hire more workers, and continue to expand, to everyone's benefit.
4. They both wanted to reform society and eliminate injustices; the Evangelicals were motivated by religion—the Utilitarians were secular and sought to change society on the basis of the principle of usefulness, whether a practice advanced human happiness or reduced human misery.
5. **CHANGE** Industrialization created societies of haves and have-nots. Students should support their answers with explanations.

ASSESS

Check for Understanding

Assign Section 1 Review as homework or as an in-class activity.

🖱 Use Student Self-Test and Review Software to review Section 1.

Evaluate

📁 Section Quiz 13-1

🖱 Use the Testmaker to create a customized quiz for Section 1.

Reteach

Organize students into small groups. Each group should make lists of the advantages and disadvantages of a socialist and a capitalist society.

Enrich

Have students investigate public reactions to reformers such as Robert Owen and Karl Marx. **Did public support for their ideas grow stronger or weaker during the 1800s?** Have students report to the class.

CLOSE

Tell students to imagine that they are living in 1880 and that a large factory opened in their town a year ago. Have students write a diary entry describing the changes in the town brought about by the factory.

402 Chapter 13 *Cultural Revolution*

SECTION THEME

▶ **Innovation** Scientific discoveries lead to improved health and revolutionary views about the natural world and human society.

ind Out

Answer: *The discovery of bacteria; the introduction of vaccines; the introduction of anesthesia; the development of genetics, psychology, and atomic theory have all led to improved lives for people today.*

FOCUS

Section Objective

List advances made in science between 1750 and 1914 that have improved life today.

BELLRINGER
Motivational Activity

Before taking roll at the beginning of the class period, project Section Focus Transparency 13-2 and have students answer the activity questions. Discuss students' responses.

📁 This activity is also available as a blackline master.

Vocabulary Pre-check

🔲 Use the Vocabulary PuzzleMaker to create a puzzle that reinforces the vocabulary terms in this section. **L1**

1750	1800	1850	1900

1796 Edward Jenner invents smallpox vaccine.

1803 John Dalton develops atomic theory.

1859 Charles Darwin publishes *On the Origin of Species.*

1898 Marie Sklodowska Curie and Pierre Curie discover radium.

Section 2

The New Science

Setting the Scene

▶ **Terms to Define**
   cell theory, evolution, genetics, atomic theory, sociology, psychology

▶ **People to Meet**
   Charles Darwin, Gregor Mendel, Edward Jenner, Louis Pasteur, John Dalton, Marie Sklodowska Curie, Pierre Curie, Ivan Pavlov, Sigmund Freud

ind Out What advances made in science between 1750 and 1914 have improved life today?

The Storyteller

Family in London slum

Dr. Hugh Barrett's hands shook with anger as he met with the industrial board of directors. They had requested his presence because many workers were falling ill and dying, costing them loss of labor. They hoped that modern medicine could offer a cure. Dr. Barrett tried to explain. "Cholera and typhoid will continue to rage as long as elementary hygiene is impossible. The congested, unsanitary housing—all your workers can afford on the wages you give them—is a breeding ground for disease." His persuasive words fell on deaf ears. What good is it, he wondered, to explain how disease is transmitted, if his recommendations were not to be followed?

—freely adapted from *History of Private Life, Volume 4, From the French Revolution to the Great War,* edited by Michelle Perrot, 1987

During the 1800s and early 1900s, scientific discoveries were beginning to unravel some intriguing mysteries. Not only did discoveries help our understanding of life and the universe, they also led to medical advances, longer life spans, and cures for deadly diseases.

New Look at Living Things

In the 1600s scientists had observed under a microscope the cells that make up living things, but they did not understand what they saw. It was not until 1838 that German botanist Mathias Schleiden and biologist Theodor Schwann formulated the cell theory: All living things are made up of tiny units of matter called cells. They also discovered that all cells divide and multiply, causing organisms to grow and mature.

The Diversity of Life

Cell theory could not explain why the world has so many kinds of plants and animals. In the 1800s scientists proposed the theory that all plants and animals descended from a common ancestor by evolution over millions of years. During that time, they said, plants and animals had evolved from simple to complex forms.

In France, the scientist Jean-Baptiste de Lamarck observed similarities between fossils and living organisms. He found that an animal's parts—its legs, for example—might grow larger or smaller depending on how much it used them. He suggested that living things adapt to their environment and then pass the changes on to the next generation. Lamarck's theory, though later disproved, influenced **Charles Darwin**, a British naturalist who would build his own theory of evolution.

In December 1831 Charles Darwin set off on a world voyage on HMS *Beagle*, a British naval ship. While traveling he became curious about the great

---

SECTION RESOURCES

📁 **Reproducible Masters**
• Reproducible Lesson Plan 13-2
• Guided Reading Activity 13-2
• People in World History Profiles 45, 46
• Section Quiz 13-2

🔲 **Transparencies**
• Section Focus Transparency 13-2

Multimedia
🔲 Vocabulary PuzzleMaker Software
🔲 Student Self-Test and Review Software
🔲 Testmaker

variety of plants and animals. He also wondered why some kinds had become extinct while others lived on.

Influenced by the theories of Malthus, Darwin developed a theory of evolution based on natural selection. In his book *On the Origin of Species*, Darwin stated that most animal groups increase faster than the food supply and are constantly struggling for survival. The plants and animals that survive are better adapted to their environment, so that they alone live on, producing offspring having the same characteristics. In another book, *The Descent of Man*, Darwin traced human evolution from animal species. Darwin's writings created controversy because many religious leaders believed that his views contradicted the biblical account of creation and ignored divine purpose in the universe.

Development of Genetics

In the 1860s **Gregor Mendel** wondered how plants and animals pass characteristics from one generation to another. Mendel, an Austrian monk, experimented with pea plants. He concluded that characteristics are passed from one generation to the next by tiny particles. The particles were later called genes, and Mendel's work became the basis for genetics, the science of heredity.

Medical Advances

Through most of history, diseases have killed more people than famines, natural disasters, and wars. In the 1800s knowledge of living organisms brought medical advances that would give people longer, healthier lives.

Fighting Disease

Smallpox, which killed millions of people over the centuries, was one of the most dreaded diseases. In 1796 **Edward Jenner**, an English doctor, noticed that dairy workers who had contracted cowpox, a mild disease, never caught smallpox. Jenner hypothesized that he could prevent smallpox by injecting people with cowpox. To prove his theory, Jenner injected a boy with cowpox serum and later with smallpox serum. As Jenner expected, the boy contracted cowpox but not smallpox. Jenner had given the world's first vaccination.

About 50 years later, **Louis Pasteur**, a French chemist, learned why Jenner's vaccination worked. In the 1850s Pasteur discovered bacteria, or germs, and proved that they cause infectious diseases. He also discovered that bacteria do not appear spontaneously, but instead reproduce like other living

---

CONNECTIONS
Science *and* Technology

Triumph Over an Ancient Enemy

When a wine maker asked his friend French scientist Louis Pasteur to find out why some wines turned sour as they fermented, science and medicine vaulted into a new era. Pasteur discovered that the wines would not sour if they were heated to a specific temperature and bottled without contact with the air.

With his microscope, Pasteur saw that tiny microbes were destroyed in this heating, later called pasteurization. He had proved that the germs that caused contamination came from an outside source. Pasteur worked to show that bacteria were carried in the air, on hands or clothes, and in other ways. He developed

Louis Pasteur

the theory that bacteria can cause disease, and he argued that bacteria could be killed only by heat or other means.

Pasteur applied his knowledge of bacteria to fighting diseases. In the 1880s he developed a successful vaccine against rabies. That same decade, the Pasteur Institute was founded in Paris, with Pasteur as director. Today, as one of the world's leading research centers, the Institute has been involved in medical breakthroughs to control many deadly diseases. In 1983 Institute researchers were the first to isolate the AIDS virus.

 **ACTIVITY**

Discuss how Pasteur developed the germ theory of disease and changed people's thinking about illness. How does his work influence the world today?

Chapter 13 *Cultural Revolution* 403

TEACH

Guided Practice

THEME Innovation

Guide students in a discussion about innovations in today's society caused by modern scientific breakthroughs. **L1 LEP**

Triumph Over an Ancient Enemy

Although as a child Pasteur (1822–1895) seemed interested only in drawing, he went on to become a major contributor to science and industry. In 1854, as dean of the science faculty at the University of Lille, he not only offered evening classes for the workers of that industrial city but also exposed his day students to the factories. In 1857 he became director of scientific studies at France's most prestigious university, the École Normale Supérieure, but after a decade he devoted himself to research. He helped the French economy by finding the bacteria threatening the silk industry. His groundbreaking work in the prevention of rabies led to the opening of the Pasteur Institute in Paris, which he headed until his death.

ANSWER
While investigating why some wines turned sour, Pasteur learned that germs that cause contamination come from an outside source. Once people knew that bacteria can cause disease, they could take protective measures. Pasteur's lasting legacy is the Pasteur Institute.

Guided Reading Activity 13-2 **L1**

 People in World History Profiles 43, 44

Geography: Movement Have students research Darwin's voyage. (Refer to his book *Journal of Researches into the Geology and Natural History of the Various Countries Visited by H.M.S. Beagle.*) Have them locate on a world map the stops Darwin made and report his conclusions. **L2**

ASSESS

Check for Understanding

Assign Section 2 Review as homework or as an in-class activity.

⊙ Use Student Self-Test and Review Software to review Section 2.

Evaluate

 Section Quiz 13-2

⊙ Use the Testmaker to create a customized quiz for Section 2.

Reteach

Assign students to work in small groups to create a chart summarizing key information in this section. Have students include these column heads in their charts: *Scientist, Development, Date, Uses.*

Enrich

Have students research a scientist mentioned in the section.

CLOSE

Have students imagine that they are journalists in 1899. Ask them to write an article summarizing the major scientific developments of the past century.

---

things. Pasteur knew then that they could be killed and that many diseases could be prevented.

New Approaches to Surgery

Surgery benefited from advances in chemistry. Until the mid-1800s, surgeons could operate only when their patients were forcibly held down. The experience was gruesome and often fatal. In the 1840s a Boston dentist demonstrated surgery using ether. When ether was administered, patients slept through their operations, feeling no pain. Sir James Simpson, a professor at the University of Edinburgh, investigated the use of another sleep-producing chemical, chloroform. Using the anesthetics ether and chloroform led to painless surgery.

Still, many people died after surgery because of infection introduced during the procedure. Joseph Lister, an English surgeon, searched for a way to destroy bacteria and make surgery safe. He found that carbolic acid could be used to sterilize medical instruments. Lister's use of an antiseptic moved surgery into a new era.

Breakthroughs in Physics

The explosion of ideas also advanced the physical sciences. Expanding the ideas of Galileo and Newton, scientists created our modern ideas about atomic energy. Atomic theory is the idea that all matter is made up of tiny particles called atoms.

John Dalton, an English chemist, provided proof of this theory. He discovered that elements are composed of atoms, and that all atoms of an element are identical and unlike the atoms of any other element. Dalton then determined chemical formulas showing which atoms make up specific elements.

Until the 1890s scientists believed that atoms were solid and indivisible; then in 1895 German physicist Wilhelm K. Roentgen discovered X rays, or high-energy electromagnetic waves that could penetrate solid matter. Later scientists showed that X rays are made up of particles of electricity called electrons, which are part of every atom.

These beginnings led scientists to frame modern physics. In 1898 the physicists **Marie Sklodowska** (skluh•DAWF•skuh) **Curie** and **Pierre Curie** discovered the highly radioactive element of radium and proved that it emits energy. In 1900 German physicist Max Planck theorized that energy is not continuous, but is released in separate units called quanta. Planck's quantum theory eventually helped Albert Einstein develop his theory of relativity, leading us to the nuclear age.

Social Sciences

Meanwhile, other scientists used the scientific method to study human behavior. This led to the development of two new social sciences—sociology, the study of human behavior in groups, and psychology, the science of human behavior in individuals. The French thinker Auguste Comte (KOHNT) was one of the founders of sociology. Comte believed that society, like nature, operated by certain laws. He stated that once these laws were discovered, people could apply scientific methods to the study of human social groups.

In the 1890s **Ivan Pavlov**, a Russian researcher, experimented with animals to see what effects outside stimuli had on their behavior. His findings suggested that human actions were unconscious reactions to stimuli and could be changed by training. Another researcher who held that an unconscious part of the mind governs human behavior was the Austrian physician **Sigmund Freud** (FROYD). Freud's theories led to psychoanalysis, a method of treatment to discover people's motives.

SECTION 2 REVIEW

Recall
1. **Define** cell theory, evolution, genetics, atomic theory, sociology, psychology.
2. **Identify** Charles Darwin, Gregor Mendel, Edward Jenner, Louis Pasteur, John Dalton, Marie Sklodowska Curie, Pierre Curie,

Ivan Pavlov, Sigmund Freud.
3. **Describe** Charles Darwin's theory of natural selection and how it changed thinking about the development of life.

Critical Thinking
4. **Applying Information** Explain in writing how a scientist discussed in Section 2

helped to change the ideas of the day.
Understanding Themes
5. **Innovation** How are the scientific understandings of the 1800s and early 1900s being expanded today? What impact are scientific discoveries having on your life?

SECTION 2 REVIEW ANSWERS

1. All vocabulary words are defined in the Glossary.
2. Darwin, 402; Mendel, 403; Jenner, 403; Pasteur, 403; Dalton, 404; Marie and Pierre Curie, 404; Pavlov, 404; Freud, 404
3. Natural selection, the idea that those species that are best adapted to their environment survive, challenged religious ideas

about the divine origins of life.
4. Answers will vary. Students should use specific details to support their answers.
5. **INNOVATION** Answers will vary. Students should use specific details to support their answers.

1837 Mary Lyon opens the first women's college in the United States.

1858 Frederick Law Olmsted designs New York City's Central Park.

c. 1890s Many Russian Jews flee persecution and settle in the United States.

Section 3

Popular Culture

Setting the Scene

▶ **Terms to Define**
emigration, immigration, urbanization

▶ **People to Meet**
Frederick Law Olmsted, Mary Lyon

▶ **Places to Locate**
London, New York City, Paris

ind Out ▶ Why did population grow dramatically in Europe and North America during the 1800s?

The Storyteller

A book titled Host and Guest *described dining for wealthy Europeans in the late 1800s:* "The first course consists of soups and fish, followed by boiled poultry, ham or tongue, roasts, stew, etc.; with vegetables ... curries, hashes, cutlets, patties, etc. For the second course, roasted poultry or game at the top and bottom, with dressed vegetables, omelets, macaroni, jellies, creams, salads, preserved fruit, and all sorts of sweet things and pastry are employed.... The third course consists of game, confectionary, the more delicate vegetables dressed in the French way...." Dessert, of course, followed.

—adapted from *Manners and Morals in the Age of Optimism, 1848-1914,* James Laver, 1966

Dining scene in Victorian England

As the 1900s began, the new science and technology were making a difference throughout Europe and North America. Most people could now expect a longer and healthier life. The rate of infant mortality dropped in the late 1800s, and life expectancy climbed. In 1850 the average person lived about 40 years; by 1900 most people could expect to live beyond 50.

Thus, as industrialization grew, so did world population. At the beginning of the Industrial Revolution, 140 million people lived in Europe. By 1850, about 100 years later, Europe's population had soared to 266 million. In Europe and the United States, the first industrialized areas, the rate of population growth was highest.

Improved Living Conditions

The medical advances of the 1800s were partly responsible for this dramatic growth in population. So too was the availability of more and better food. Before 1740 many people died of starvation and of diseases caused by vitamin deficiency such as rickets. At that time a person's entire daily diet might have consisted of three pounds of bread.

In the 1800s, however, bread ceased to be the staple it had been for centuries. With new machinery and scientific methods, farmers could produce many kinds of foods. Potatoes, nutritious and easy to grow, became popular. Methods for preserving foods, including canning and eventually refrigeration, enabled people to take advantage of the greater variety of food that was available.

One observer of working-class life in London during the late 1890s wrote: "A good deal of bread is eaten and tea is drunk especially by the women and children, but ... bacon, eggs and fish appear regularly in the budgets. A piece of meat cooked on Sundays serves also for dinner on Monday and Tuesday." Some Europeans imported corn from the

Chapter 13 *Cultural Revolution* **405**

SECTION THEME

▶ **Movement** People move from rural to urban areas and from continent to continent in search of better lives.

**ind Out** ▶

Answer: *Scientific developments led to a decline in infant mortality and a rise in life expectancy. The availability of more and better food also helped people to live longer.*

FOCUS

Section Objective

Analyze why the population grew dramatically in Europe and North America during the 1800s.

BELLRINGER
Motivational Activity

Before taking roll at the beginning of the class period, project Section Focus Transparency 13-3 and have students answer the activity questions. Discuss students' responses.

▱ This activity is also available as a blackline master.

Vocabulary Pre-check

▱ Use Vocabulary Activity 13 to introduce vocabulary terms.
L1 LEP

TEACH

Guided Practice

THEME Movement

Guide students in discussing the positive and negative aspects of population movement. *(positive: new opportunities; negative: new-comers often face discrimination)* Ask students for examples from other periods and from personal experiences. **L1**

Critical Thinking Organize the class into groups such as the working poor, industrialists, and government officials. Have students role-play a public meeting on urban health and housing during the 1800s. Encourage students to discuss health issues such as housing and clean air. **L3**

VIDEODISC
Turning Points in World History
Side Two
Chapter 3

Title: *The Industrial Revolution*
Ask: What was the "price" of the Industrial Revolution? *(Some negative effects include pollution, overcrowding in cities, exploitation of workers.)*

 Mapping History Overlay Transparency 16, *Global Ancestry of Americans*

United States and fruit and frozen meat from Australia and New Zealand.

Seeking a Better Life

As the population grew, people became more mobile. Railroads revolutionized not only the food people ate, but also the way they lived. In 1860 London's Victoria Station opened, making it easier for Londoners to leave their crowded city. Steamships carried people to other countries and continents in search of a better life. Between 1870 and 1900, more than 25 million people left Europe for the United States; others moved to South America, South Africa, and Australia.

For a number of reasons, some Europeans chose emigration, leaving their homelands to settle elsewhere. Some looked for higher-paying jobs and better working conditions. Others sought to escape discrimination and persecution by oppressive governments. Still others hoped to escape famine.

Advertisements of steamship companies, along with low fares, lured many immigrants to the United States. Industries looking for cheap labor offered additional encouragement. Some American industrialists sent recruiters whose task was to urge people to leave Europe and obtain permanent jobs and homes in the United States.

Twelve-year-old Mary Antin joined thousands of Russian Jews fleeing persecution in 1894. Many years earlier Mary's father had decided on immigration, or coming to settle permanently in a foreign land. His new homeland was the United States. Mary, her mother, and her brothers and sisters endured a harrowing journey across Europe and the Atlantic Ocean to join him in Boston, Massachusetts. Mary wrote of her experiences: "And so suffering, fearing, brooding, and rejoicing, we crept nearer and nearer to the coveted shore until on a glorious May morning ... our eyes beheld the Promised Land and my father received us in his arms."

Most people left their homelands knowing that they would never see their parents or their birthplace again. The ocean voyage often proved a frightening experience. One youngster

Images of the Times

Leisure Time

An urban environment offered many people new opportunities for leisure activities.

A Bicycle was a fashionable new means of getting around, for those who could afford it.

Perth Station, Going South by George Earl captures the happy confusion of a London holiday.

406

Images of the Times   Leisure Time

Bicycles were exhibited as early as 1818, but the first to become popular was the 1861 machine produced by a French father-and-son team. The bicycle soon gave rise to such leisure-time activities as bicycle touring and bicycle racing.

Railway travel had become very popular in England by the 1840s. British writer Sydney Smith said in an 1842 letter to *The Morning Leader*, "Railway travelling is a delightful improvement of human life."

Iced desserts originated in Asia, but the ice-cream soda was first served in 1874 in Philadelphia, and the ice-cream cone had its debut at the St. Louis World's Fair in 1904.

remembered "the howling darkness, the white rims of the mountain-high waves speeding like maddened dragons toward the tumbling ship."

When the immigrants reached their new homes, many learned that their troubles had only begun. Now they had to find housing and jobs in strange surroundings where they did not know the culture or the language. Some people took advantage of the European immigrants, who seemed to them strange "foreigners."

From Country to City

During the 1800s and early 1900s, many people moved within their own country. Cities around the world were absorbing newcomers who were moving from rural villages to find new opportunities. As farms grew larger and more mechanized, they needed fewer workers. The growing industries in or near the cities offered new and challenging ways to make a living.

Although the new city dwellers faced no language barriers, some of their problems were similar to those of the European immigrants. Their old life was gone, with its known boundaries, familiar people, and established routines. Although work was plentiful, living quarters in the cities were often cramped, and neighbors might be less friendly than people they had known. British poet Lord Byron summed up the feelings of many newcomers to the city:

> ❝ I live not in myself, but I become a
> Portion of that around me: and to me
> High mountains are a feeling, but the hum
> Of human cities torture. ❞

Growth of Cities

The movement of people into the cities resulted in the urbanization, or the spread of city life, of the industrialized countries. A country is urbanized when more people live in cities than in rural areas. Great Britain is a prime example. In 1800 **London**

Ice cream delighted these children and their mother at the St. Louis World's Fair in 1904.

REFLECTING ON THE TIMES

1. What do these scenes reveal about the economic status of the people depicted?
2. Why are no poor people shown in these three images?

407

ANSWERS TO REFLECTING ON THE TIMES

1. All the people are sufficiently wealthy to be able to take time off from work and to pay for excursions and treats.
2. The poor had no disposable income to pay for leisure-time activities or treats.

ℬiography

The following videotape programs are available from Glencoe:

- **The Rockefellers**
- **The Pulitzers**
- **P. T. Barnum: American Dreamer**

Independent Practice

📁 Guided Reading Activity 13-3 **L1**

📁 Geography and History Activity 13

Brochure Ask students to investigate one of the cultural institutions founded during this period, such as the Louvre or the Albert Hall. Have students create a brochure for the institution, describing its most interesting features and encouraging people to visit it. **L1**

Environmental Issues Have students do further research into the environmental conditions in the large cities of the period, such as London. Have them write letters to the editor as urban dwellers protesting the conditions they see around them. **L2**

Who?What?Where?When?

Pogroms, or government-sponsored attacks against Jews, led two million East European Jews to seek refuge in the United States between 1881 and the outbreak of World War I. This massive migration accounted for 85 percent of the movement between Europe and America during that period.

Linking Past and Present

Urbanization According to current estimates, about half the world's population will live in urban areas by the year 2000, a sharp contrast with 1800, when less than 3 percent lived in cities of 20,000 or more.

Who?What?Where?When?

Settlement houses, or institutions to improve urban neighborhood living conditions, were founded in the 1880s. The most famous United States settlement house was Hull House in Chicago, founded in 1889 by Jane Addams and Ellen Gates Starr. Although Hull House no longer stands, the Hull House Association still operates about 25 Chicago community centers.

Who?What?Where?When?

Jacob Riis (1849–1914) was a Danish immigrant whose *How the Other Half Lives* (1890), a photojournalistic exposé of the terrible conditions of the urban poor, resulted in improved conditions.

ASSESS

Check for Understanding

Assign Section 3 Review as homework or as an in-class activity.

🖲 Use Student Self-Test and Review Software to review Section 3.

---

was its only city with a population of more than 100,000. By 1851 Britain had 9 such cities. In the same year, and for the first time, slightly more than half of the British people lived in cities. By 1914 that figure had reached 80 percent.

Urbanization was taking place elsewhere as well. In 1914, 60 percent of the Germans, 50 percent of the Americans, and 45 percent of the French were city dwellers.

As people moved to cities, they began to marry earlier. Children could increase a family's income by working in factories. As a result, people had more children, adding to the population.

The cities' growth soon outpaced their ability to provide needed housing and sanitation. Few cities had building codes that mandated adequate housing. Houses were built close together in long rows, one against another. The workers crowded together in damp, cold, unsanitary rooms, with fire a constant danger.

The factories added to the unpleasant city environment. Here is a report on the working conditions of British miners in 1843: "Sheffield is one of the dirtiest and most smoky towns I ever saw. The town is also very hilly, and the smoke ascends the streets, instead of leaving them…. One cannot be long in the town without experiencing the necessary inhalation of soot."

City Services

City governments in Europe and the United States began to look for solutions to the overwhelming troubles. They saw that one of the most pressing problems was sanitation. An observer in the British city of Leeds reported, "The ashes, garbage, and filth of all kinds are thrown from the doors and windows of the houses upon the surface of the streets and courts." Ditches and open sewers carried waste from public toilets. Polluted water encouraged epidemics of cholera and other diseases, especially in the crowded slums.

In the late 1800s, the germ theory and the newly invented iron pipe spurred city leaders to clean up their cities. They installed closed sewer lines and improved garbage collection. Police and fire protection created safer cities.

As city planning progressed, a number of city governments set aside areas as parks. In **New York City**, landscape architect **Frederick Law Olmsted** saw the need for "a simple, broad, open space of clean greensward [grassy turf]" enclosed by a large enough green space to "completely shut out the city." With the architect and landscape designer Calvert Vaux, Olmsted designed Central Park in 1858.

Leisure Time

Leisure time activities expanded for the middle classes and for the working classes. Men and women took more outings and enjoyed more cultural activities. Newspapers helped to make people interested in places and events outside of their own neighborhoods and communities.

In the 1700s the fine arts were available only to the wealthy upper classes. Concerts were performed in palaces and grand homes, or they were performed in churches. Wealthy aristocrats, prosperous merchants, and religious leaders commissioned cultural events and artworks, such as concerts and paintings, to commemorate special events or to honor special people.

In the 1800s, however, fine art and music became available to middle- and working-class people in the city. City governments in Europe and North America built concert halls and opera houses, such as London's vast Royal Albert Hall, erected in 1871. Cities sponsored the opening of art museums, such as the great Louvre (LOOV) Museum in **Paris**.

When people were not visiting libraries and museums, they went to amusement parks, which provided shows, rides, games, and food. Sports such as soccer and rugby began to be organized between cities and around the nation. Many people also enjoyed archery, lawn tennis, and cricket.

New Interest in Education

In the early 1800s, when governments began to support public schools, their reasons were political. For example, the Prussian government established public schools to train its people in citizenship and in devotion to the monarchy and the army. In the

Footnotes to History

Moving to the Suburbs During the late 1800s, suburbs, or small communities next to large cities, grew in Europe and the United States along with the development of streetcar lines and railroads. Middle-class people could afford to live in less urban areas and ride the trolley or train to their jobs in the city. In the United States, suburban growth greatly increased in the 1950s as more and more families were able to buy one or two automobiles.

COOPERATIVE LEARNING ACTIVITY

Interview Assign students to work in pairs to investigate a social issue discussed in this section. Students should take the roles of an interviewer and an interviewee, write a script for an interview, and perform it for the class. Possible interview "pairs" include a journalist and an immigrant discussing the experience of traveling to a new country, a public official and an urban newcomer discussing the difficulty of adjusting to crowded city living and working conditions, or a journalist and Mary Lyon discussing the benefits of education for women. **L2** 📦

United States, government support for public schools grew out of a desire to foster national unity after the Revolutionary War.

By the late 1800s, as people grew more and more interested in improving their lives, they became more actively involved in promoting education. Both in Europe and the United States, they supported education that was funded by the government and available to everyone. Believing education would improve their children's chances for a better life, they voted for increased educational opportunities. Schools and colleges were also established to provide better training for teachers.

The new kind of society—urbanized and industrialized—also benefited from the cause of public education. Industrialists needed employees who could read and write. Advanced technologies based on science depended on workers who had scientific training. Many people came to see that an ever more complex society would demand a well-educated populace. People were needed who could participate intelligently in public affairs.

Education for Women

Education for women was a hotly debated topic in the 1800s. Some felt that women's roles as wives and homemakers did not require education. Others believed women should be given the same educational opportunities as men. Girls were included in the laws providing education to all. Still, they could usually attend only elementary schools. Access to secondary education was limited only to the wealthy few.

Determined to offer higher education to women, some people began to open secondary schools and colleges especially for them. In 1837 American educator **Mary Lyon** opened the first women's college, the Mount Holyoke Female Seminary, which later became Mount Holyoke College in Massachusetts. In 1874 the London School of Medicine was opened, and after two years of bitter debate, the British Parliament finally allowed women to be registered as doctors.

History & Art *Piccadilly Circus, 1912* by Charles Ginner. Tate Gallery, London, England **The circular street of Piccadilly Circus was built near the shopping district of London.** *By 1914, what percent of the British lived in cities?*

Results of Education

The advances in education created a growing demand for accessible reading materials. Magazines and books became popular. Libraries with large collections opened as early as the 1840s in major cities such as Paris and London. Lending libraries loaned books for small fees.

Mass-circulation newspapers were first printed at this time, and by 1860, more than 3,000 newspapers were published in the United States. Newspaper publishers benefited from the combination of rapid communication provided by the telegraph, cheaper printing methods, and improved distribution by railroad and steamship.

History & Art Tell students that in England, a *circus* is an open circle, square, or plaza where several streets converge. Six busy streets meet at Piccadilly Circus, which, together with Trafalgar Square, is one of two huge intersections in London's West End.
Answer to Caption: *80 percent*

Evaluate

Section Quiz 13-3

Use the Testmaker to create a customized quiz for Section 3.

Reteach

Have students meet in small groups of five or six to discuss the review questions. Circulate to monitor progress.

Enrich

Have students research the popular culture of their town or city during the 1800s and report on topics such as entertainment, economic growth, and population shifts.

CLOSE

Tell students to imagine they are immigrants living in a large city in the late 1800s. Have them write a letter to friends at home describing their new homeland.

SECTION 3 REVIEW

Recall
1. **Define** emigration, immigration, urbanization.
2. **Identify** Frederick Law Olmsted, Mary Lyon.
3. **List** three improvements in city life that were made in the 1800s and the early 1900s.

Critical Thinking
4. **Making Comparisons** How do attitudes about women's education today differ from attitudes in the late 1800s? Explain reasons for the differences.

Understanding Themes
5. **Movement** Why did many people in Europe and North America move in the late 1800s and early 1900s? Do the same reasons apply today?

SECTION 3 REVIEW ANSWERS

1. All vocabulary words are defined in the Glossary.
2. Olmsted, 408; Lyon, 409
3. sewer lines, improved garbage collection, police and fire protection, development of parks
4. Most people today believe that all opportunities available to men should also be available to women; to enable women to take advantage of these opportunities on equal terms, they need an equivalent education. Many people in the 1800s felt a woman's role as wife and homemaker did not require an education. Reasons for the differences will vary but may include that seeing women perform successfully in such formerly all-male roles as doctors, lawyers, and engineers has changed people's thinking.
5. **MOVEMENT** Answers should include the search for better jobs and working conditions and the need to escape from discrimination, famine, and persecution. Similar reasons apply today.

TEACH

Using E-Mail As electronic communication becomes an ever-increasing part of our daily lives, students almost inevitably will find that they must know how to send and receive E-mail. You might begin discussion of this feature by taking a class survey to find out if anyone frequently corresponds in this fashion. Also discuss the advantages of sending E-mail rather than phoning or sending messages through the post office. *(faster and cheaper)*

In discussing components of an E-mail system, mention that it is possible to attach documents and other kinds of files to E-mail messages. For example, a student can send an essay to a friend without typing it again as part of a message itself.

Demonstrate sending a message and opening and printing a received message. Then demonstrate how to send a message with an attached file and opening and printing a received message with an attached file. If possible, schedule time in the computer lab so that students can send E-mail on their own.

Additional Practice

Skill Reinforcement
Activity 13

Using E-Mail

Sharing information, thoughts, and feelings with others is communication. *Telecommunication* refers to communicating at a distance through the use of a telephone, video, or computer. How can you communicate using your computer?

Learning the Skill

In order to use your computer to telecommunicate, you must add two parts to it. The first part is a piece of hardware called a *modem*. A modem is a device that enables computers to communicate with each other through telephone lines.

The second part is *communications software* which lets your computer prepare and send information to the modem. It also lets your computer receive and understand the information it receives from the modem.

Electronic mail, or *E-mail*, for short, is one way of sending and receiving messages electronically. Anyone who is part of an E-mail network can send and receive private messages.

Before you can send or receive E-mail, you must obtain an E-mail address. This address identifies the location of your electronic "mailbox"—the place where you receive your E-mail. To send an E-mail message to another person you must include that person's E-mail address, just as you might address an envelope. There is no central listing of E-mail addresses. The best way to find out an address is to ask the person for their address.

Many corporations are using E-mail communications, which makes some environmentalists happier. More electronic communication means less use of paper and more saved trees.

Practicing the Skill

To send a message to a friend on an E-mail network, complete the following steps.

1. Select the "message" function from your communications software.
2. Type in the E-mail address.
3. Type in your message. Proofread it for errors.
4. Select the "send" function.

The E-mail system places the message in the receiver's "mailbox." He or she can read the message at any time—and then send you a reply.

Applying the Skill

Many scientific discoveries took place in the mid-1700s to the early 1900s. Use E-mail to contact a librarian. Ask for recommendations of young adult books related to scientific discoveries from 1750–1914.

For More Practice

Turn to the Skill Practice in the Chapter Review on page 421 for more practice in using E-mail.

ANSWERS TO PRACTICING THE SKILL

If possible, have students who are familiar with E-mail help you guide novices through the process of sending a message. Because of computer availability, you may find it more practical to have groups of students work together on the activity.

1750 ———— **1800** ———— **1850** ———— **1900**

c. 1780 Romanticism becomes a leading cultural movement.

1854 Charles Dickens writes *Hard Times.*

c. 1873 Impressionist movement begins in France.

c. 1890 Symbolist movement reacts against industrial civilization.

Section 4

Revolution in the Arts

Setting the Scene

▶ **Terms to Define**
  romanticism, realism, symbolism, impressionism, Postimpressionism

▶ **People to Meet**
  Peter Tchaikovsky, Johann Wolfgang von Goethe, George Sand, Honoré de Balzac, Charles Dickens, Leo Tolstoy, Claude Monet, Vincent van Gogh

▶ **Places to Locate**
  Paris

Find Out How did writers and artists in Europe and North America reflect changes in society between 1750 and 1914?

The Storyteller

Gustave frowned as he read his mother's letter. "I am tired of seeing your talent receive no recognition. You must acknowledge what people want. You need to cater to the popular taste ... paint imaginary scenes of Roman or medieval heroes. Then your paintings might win prizes or be purchased by influential collectors." Gustave Courbet would not follow the crowd or popular tastes, just because others were doing it. He would paint images of his own time.

—freely adapted from *Realism*, Linda Nochlin, 1971

Landscape
by Gustave Courbet

uropean and American artists in the 1800s mirrored society's mixed feelings about the rapid disappearance of the old order and the uncertainty of the new. A growing middle class created a larger audience for music, literature, and poetry. Formerly, artists had depended on patronage by the wealthy. Now, although some artists sought support in the new industrial society, others rebelled against middle-class values and shunned patronage of any kind, preferring to work independently. Those who rebelled would dominate the arts in the late 1700s and early 1800s.

The Romantic Movement

By the late 1700s, artists had begun to react to the Enlightenment's emphasis on order and reason. The French philosopher Jean-Jacques Rousseau taught that people were naturally good and needed only to be free. In rejecting society's formal structures and rules, Rousseau anticipated romanticism, a movement in which artists would emphasize human emotion and imagination over reason.

Romantic artists tried to free themselves from the rigid forms and structures of neoclassical art. Rejecting the mechanization and ugliness of industrialized society, many turned to nature, glorifying its awesome power and quiet beauty.

Many romantic artists looked to the past, admiring the mythical heroes of old. They felt compassion for the weak and oppressed, and they celebrated the lives of "simple peasants." The struggle for personal freedom and heroic rebellion against society's established rules are frequent themes in their works. The French poet Charles Baudelaire described the movement: "Romanticism is precisely situated neither in choice of subject nor in exact truth, but in a way of feeling."

Chapter 13 *Cultural Revolution* **411**

SECTION THEME

▶ **Innovation** Artists and writers in the Western world reflect the changes in urban industrial society.

Find Out

Answer: *Reaction to emphasis on reason led to emotion-filled works of romantics; by the mid-1800s artists rejected romanticism as sentimental and embraced realism. Symbolist writers and painters sought to escape ugly realities by creating images evoked by symbols.*

FOCUS

Section Objective
Describe how writers and artists in Europe and North America reflected changes in society between 1750 and 1914.

BELLRINGER
Motivational Activity

Before taking roll, project Section Focus Transparency 13-4 and have students answer the activity questions.

This activity is also available as a blackline master.

Vocabulary Pre-check
Use the Vocabulary PuzzleMaker to create a puzzle that reinforces the vocabulary terms in this section. **L1**

SECTION RESOURCES

Reproducible Masters
• Reproducible Lesson Plan 13-4
• Guided Reading Activity 13-4
• History Simulation 13
• Reteaching Activity 13
• Enrichment Activity 13
• Section Quiz 13-4

• Performance Assessment Activity 13
• Spanish Chapter Summary 13

Transparencies
• Section Focus Transparency 13-4
• World History and Art Transparencies 31, 32, 34

Multimedia
• Focus on World Art Prints 2, 5, 22
• Vocabulary PuzzleMaker Software
• Student Self-Test and Review Software
• Testmaker

TEACH

Guided Practice

THEME Innovation

Ask students to scan the section and provide examples of innovations in art. *(They may point out any of the movements discussed or specific examples within them, such as the emphasis on emotion and imagination by the romantics.)* Ask students to cite examples of innovations in art, music, or literature that they have noticed in their lifetimes. **L1**

History *and the* Humanities

 Focus on World Art Prints
- 2 Franz Marc. *Stables*
- 5 Paul Klee. *Palace, Partially Destroyed*
- 22 Vincent van Gogh. *Hospital at Saint-Rémy*

 World History and Art Transparencies
- 31 *In the Garden*
- 32 *Sunday Afternoon on the Island of La Grande Jatte*
- 34 *Starry Night*

History Simulation 13

 **History & Art** Tell students that a fjord is a long, narrow arm of the sea bordered by steep cliffs.
Answer to Caption: *It is dramatic and celebrates nature and freedom of the human spirit.*

Romantic Music

The composers of the Enlightenment had emphasized form and order, but romantic composers departed from traditional forms and styles. They often fused music with imaginative literature, creating operas—dramas set to music—and *lieder* (LEED•uhr)—art songs, or poems set to music.

Romantic music was meant to stir the emotions—whether in large works, such as symphonies by German composer Ludwig van Beethoven (BAY•TOH•vuhn) or Russian composer **Peter Tchaikovsky** (chy•KAWF•skee), or in smaller, more intimate works, such as piano pieces by Poland's Frédéric Chopin (SHOH•PAN) or the *lieder* of Austria's Franz Schubert. Melodies from folk music added emotional power to romantic music, as in works by Czech composer Antonín Dvořák (DVAWR•ZHANK), whose *Symphony From the New World* echoes American spirituals.

Romantic Literature

Like romantic composers, romantic writers created emotion-filled, imaginative works. Early leaders of the romantic movement in literature

History & Art *Girl With Goats by a Fiord* by Hans Dahl. Christie's, London, England **This painting exemplifies romantic ideals.** *What characteristics of romanticism does the painting show?*

412 Chapter 13 *Cultural Revolution*

include German writers Friedrich von Schiller and **Johann Wolfgang von Goethe** (GUHR•tuh). Schiller glorified freedom fighters, such as the legendary hero William Tell. His drama with that title is about the medieval Swiss struggle for freedom. Goethe is best known for *Faust*, a drama about human striving and the need for redemption.

France produced some of the most popular romantic writers. Alexandre Dumas's novel *The Three Musketeers* recounts the exploits of three dashing adventurers in the 1600s. Aurore Dupin, better known as **George Sand**, made peasants and workers heroes in her fiction. The novels of Victor Hugo, the foremost French romanticist, include *The Hunchback of Notre Dame* and *Les Misérables*, tales portraying human suffering with compassion and power.

Romanticism also influenced Great Britain. Scots writer Sir Walter Scott won a huge following with his historical novels *Ivanhoe*, *Quentin Durward*, and *The Talisman*. Another Scot, Robert Burns, showed deep feeling for nature and romantic love in his poetry. English poet and painter William Blake attacked the growing results of industrialization in *Songs of Innocence* and *Songs of Experience*. Similar themes fill the works of English poets Samuel Taylor Coleridge, William Wordsworth, John Keats, Percy Bysshe Shelley, and Lord Byron.

Romantic Painting

Painters, like writers, reflected romantic ideals. Turning from the order, clarity, and balance of the neoclassical style, painters began to portray exotic, powerful subjects in a dramatic and colorful way. For example, the painting *Liberty Leading the People*, by Eugène Delacroix (DEH•luh•KWAH), shows the figure of Liberty as a brave woman carrying a flag and leading patriots through the streets of **Paris**. Like many other romantic works, the painting was meant to stir the emotions, not appeal to the intellect.

The Turn Toward Realism

In the mid-1800s, some artists began to reject the sentimentality of romanticism. They sought to portray life in a realistic manner. In France, painter Gustave Courbet (kur•BAY) expressed the idea behind this style, known as realism: "Painting … does not consist of anything but the presentation of real and concrete things." Realist painters and writers wished to portray life as it was, not to escape from it.

Courbet's own large, somber canvases called attention to the less fortunate members of society and their difficult circumstances. *Burial at Ornans*

COOPERATIVE LEARNING ACTIVITY

Art Magazine Have students work together to produce a magazine displaying their literary and artistic accomplishments. Contributions must be in the style of one of the artistic movements of the period described in this section and may include paintings, drawings, poetry, songs, and so on. Some students should be responsible for assembling and organizing the materials by movement. Others may do interviews of the contributors or write articles evaluating the works. **L2 LEP**

National Gallery of Art

French Impressionists

Purest of the impressionists, Claude Monet captured the essence of light and air. A stiff breeze swirls through *Woman With a Parasol—Madame Monet and Her Son*, painted between 1875 and 1878. "His pictures always were too draughty for me!" commented fellow impressionist Edgar Degas. "If it had been any worse, I should have had to turn up my coat collar." Unlike Monet and other French impressionists who insisted on painting from life, Degas was the master of the fleeting moment. He relied on quick sketches and his memory of posture, light, and color, and painted later at his studio.

One of Monet's paintings entitled *Impression—Sunrise*, exhibited in a Paris art show gave impressionism its name. An art critic reviewing the show ridiculed the painting and invented the term "impressionism." French impressionists such as Monet, Degas, and others rebelled against the strict traditions and rules of the art world of the late 1800s to capture the natural appearances of objects. Using dabs and strokes of primary colors, they tried to give the impression of actual reflected light. They often painted outdoors, trying to capture natural light, shadow, and color on canvas. ⊕

Chapter 13 *Cultural Revolution* **413**

TEACH

The impressionist style is said to have had its origins at a French riverside café called La Grenouil-lière, where Monet and Renoir began meeting in 1869. Until that time, both men had employed an ordinary naturalist style in their work. But upon gazing out at the sun sparkling on the rippling river waters, they felt that a new technique was needed to capture that delightful play of light. From then on Monet began to work at finding ways of rendering an *impression* of the many different effects of light. "Light is the principal person in the picture," he once said. **What characteristics of impressionist painting can you see in "Woman With a Parasol"?** *(Students may point to the pattern of separate brushstrokes, the brilliant color, the feathery lightness.)*

CURRICULUM CONNECTION

POLITICS

Many artists of the time took sides in the Dreyfus affair, a military-political scandal that polarized French society during the last half of the 1890s. Monet and Pissarro were among the artists believing that the charge of treason against Captain Alfred Dreyfus, the only Jew on the General Staff of the French army, was unfounded (as in fact it proved to be). Cézanne, Rodin, Renoir, and Degas believed in Dreyfus's guilt.

Independent Practice

 Guided Reading Activity 13-4 **L1**

Biography Have students research the life of one of the artists of the period and write a brief biography. Tell students to include information on education, training, major works, and public acceptance. **L1**

Biography

The following videotape program is available from Glencoe:

- **The Hunchback of Notre Dame**

The Arts Have students assemble copies of paintings from the period covered in this section and report to the class on the techniques and subject matter of the different artists. Instruct them to identify the movement each work represents and to point out characteristics of the movement. **L3**

ASSESS

Check for Understanding

Assign Section 4 Review as homework or as an in-class activity.

🖳 Use Student Self-Test and Review Software to review Section 4.

Evaluate

 Section Quiz 13-4

🖳 Use the Testmaker to create a customized quiz for Section 4.

 **Futabatei Publishes** *The Drifting Clouds*

Japan, 1889
Beginning in the 1880s, Western ideas began to influence Japanese writing. A group of Japanese authors, who had been educated in Western languages, broke from traditional forms of literature. These writers believed that Japan's technological development should be accompanied by the development of modern European-style literary works. In 1889 Futabatei Shimei produced a novel titled *The Drifting Clouds* which helped establish the novel as a respected form of Japanese literature.

portrayed peasants from his hometown standing around the grave of a loved one. By the end of the 1850s, other French artists had joined Courbet in painting realistically. Among the most notable were Honoré Daumier (doh•MYAY) and Jean-François Millet (mee•YAY).

Realism in Literature

Realism also flourished in literature. French writer **Honoré de Balzac** grouped about 90 of his novels and short stories of French life in the 1800s into a collection he called *The Human Comedy*. Many described frankly the greed and stupidity that Balzac saw in the growing middle class. Gustave Flaubert (floh•BEHR), another French writer, portrayed the conflict between dreary realities and romantic dreams in *Madame Bovary*, the story of a young woman married to a dull provincial doctor.

The English novelist, Mary Ann Evans wrote under the pen name George Eliot. Her novels portrayed the rigidity and senselessness of the British social order. **Charles Dickens**, the foremost English realistic writer, spoke out on behalf of the poor. Dickens focused on the deplorable conditions in the prisons, hospitals, and poorhouses of London. In his novel *Hard Times*, he attacked the materialism of Coketown, a fictional city.

Russian writers came to be known for their penetrating novels about the human spirit. The novels of Russian writer **Leo Tolstoy** also reflected his compassion for the peasants and gave his analysis of social customs. *War and Peace* is a family novel in which Tolstoy takes five families through the

---

stages of life. It is also a historical novel about Napoleon's invasion of Russia in 1812.

The works of American novelist Theodore Dreiser belong to a pessimistic style of realism called naturalism, in which writers tried to apply scientific methods to imaginative writing. In Dreiser's novel *An American Tragedy*, a young man is executed for killing his pregnant girlfriend. To Dreiser, the man is a victim whose tragedy results from circumstances over which he has no control.

Symbolism

Some writers became disgusted with what they viewed as the ugly and brutal realities of European industrial civilization. To escape, they created a world of shadowy images evoked by symbols. This movement, called **symbolism**, began in France and was led by the poet Stéphane Mallarmé (MA•LAHR•MAY), who believed that "to name an object is to destroy three-quarters of the enjoyment of a poem, which is made up of the pleasure of guessing little by little." He and his followers, Paul Verlaine (vehr•LAYN) and Arthur Rimbaud (ram•BOH), gave impressions by suggestion rather than by direct statement.

Symbolism spread to the other arts and to other countries. The symbolists focused on the exotic, using imagery to suggest the world of the spirit. Intellectuals applauded this effort, but the average person found symbolism difficult to understand.

New Trends in Painting

Intense competition and rigid, traditional standards characterized the artistic world in the 1800s. An artist's works had to be considered "correct" and the subject matter "proper" by judges at London's Royal Academy of Art or Paris's École des Beaux-Arts (School of Fine Arts). Acceptance by those schools and a place in their yearly exhibitions were crucial to a beginning artist's success.

In 1863 the École turned down more than 3,000 of the 5,000 works that were submitted for its approval—the highest proportion of rejections that anyone could remember. Napoleon III, the French emperor at the time, decided to hold an exhibit to let the public see the paintings that had been rejected by the École. Those paintings delighted many people and gave the painters renewed hope that their works would win recognition.

Impressionism

During the 1870s, a group of French artists developed a style called **impressionism**. The

---

Learning Style: Logical/Mathematical Have students with good computer skills access information from the World Wide Web on the artistic movements described in this section. Ask them to print out the information they find and distribute it to the class. Then they can explain to the class how they located the information and point out ways it enhances the coverage available in the text. **L2**

impressionist painters abandoned many of the rules on which earlier painters had based their art—rules about proper subject matter and traditional techniques of line, perspective, and studio lighting. Fascinated by color and light, the impressionists sought to capture the momentary impression a subject made on their senses. They moved out of the studio and into the real world, choosing to work outdoors, in theaters, and in cafes.

Pierre-Auguste Renoir (REHN•WAHR) painted idealized portraits of women and children and outdoor scenes. **Claude Monet** (moh•NAY), one of the most famous impressionists, painted series of paintings on the same subject to show variations in light and color during various times of the day and seasons of the year.

Postimpressionism

In the late 1880s some artists turned away from impressionism. Known as Postimpressionists, they formed their styles independently to express in different ways the chaos and complexity around them. One of their leaders was Paul Cézanne (say•ZAN). Earlier, he had identified with romanticism and impressionism. By the 1880s he had laid the foundation for Postimpressionism when he declared, "I do not want to reproduce nature, I want to re-create it."

Georges Seurat (suh•RAH), another Postimpressionist, applied science to his paintings. He developed a method called pointillism, placing small dabs of color close together to produce a three-dimensional effect. His painting *A Sunday Afternoon on the Island of La Grande Jatte* consists of thousands of different-colored dots.

Paul Gauguin (goh•GAN) moved to the Pacific island of Tahiti, where he painted *Where do we come from? What are we? Where are we going?* It was an attempt to find universal truths in the symbols of a nonindustrial culture.

The son of a Dutch minister, **Vincent van Gogh** (van GOH) led an unhappy life. After failing at the ministry, he turned to painting. Within two years,

 The Swing by Pierre-Auguste Renoir, 1876. Musée d'Orsay, Paris, France *What did France's impressionist painters, such as Renoir and Monet, seek to capture in their works?*

he produced most of the paintings for which he is known, using brilliant colors and distorted forms to make intense statements.

Henri de Toulouse-Lautrec (tu•LOOZ loh•TREHK) used Paris nightlife as a major subject. He painted with vivid detail, using bright colors to catch the reality of lives he portrayed. His use of line and color in posters of Paris's Moulin Rouge nightclub attracted worldwide attention.

SECTION 4 REVIEW

Recall
1. **Define** romanticism, realism, symbolism, impressionism, Postimpressionism.
2. **Identify** Peter Tchaikovsky, Johann Wolfgang von Goethe, George Sand, Honoré de Balzac, Charles Dickens, Leo Tolstoy, Claude Monet, Vincent van Gogh.
3. **Explain** what factors led to the rise of realism.

Critical Thinking
4. **Analyzing Information** How might the painting *Liberty Leading the People* have influenced French attitudes about revolution?

Understanding Themes
5. **Innovation** How was nature significant in romantic art?

History & Art Tell students that the Musée d'Orsay is situated in the former Gare d'Orsay, a railroad station in Paris. After being remodeled, the building was reopened in 1986 as a museum specializing in the different schools of French art of the middle to late 1800s.
Answer to Caption: *They sought to capture the momentary impression a subject made on their senses.*

Reteach

Ask each student to write three questions on the section's content. Then have students meet in groups and exchange questions.

Reteaching Activity 13

Enrich

Have students who are musically inclined research trends in post-romantic music of the late 1800s and early 1900s. Have them summarize their findings in brief reports to the class that include taped excerpts of compositions.

Enrichment Activity 13

CLOSE

Have students write a brief paragraph explaining which artistic movement described in this section they find most visually pleasing and which they like least.

SECTION 4 REVIEW ANSWERS

1. All vocabulary words are defined in the Glossary.
2. Tchaikovsky, 412; Goethe, 412; Sand, 412; Balzac, 414; Dickens, 414; Tolstoy, 414; Monet, 415; van Gogh, 415
3. Students might mention reactions to romantic sentimentality, to the Industrial Revolution, or to the Scientific Revolution.
4. Answers will vary. Possible answer: The patriotic emotions it stirred might have encouraged people to revolt against a government that seemed unresponsive to the people's needs.
5. **INNOVATION** Answers will vary but might include the idea that nature's awesome power and quiet beauty inspired artists who rejected industrialized society's mechanization and ugliness.

Block Schedule

Team Teaching This excerpt from *The Beggar* may be presented in a team-teaching context, in conjunction with English or Language Arts.

The Beggar

Historical Connection

Industrialization increased the number of poor city dwellers. Societies had to decide how to treat those unable to support themselves.

Background Information

Setting The story is set in a Russian city in the late 1800s. During this period many Russians moved to the city to find work and escape the poverty and tedium of rural life.

Characters Lushkoff: a poor alcoholic who survives by begging; Skvortsoff: a wealthy lawyer who prides himself on his compassion for the needy; Olga: Skvortsoff's cook who often supervises Lushkoff

Plot Skvortsoff, though angered by Lushkoff's lies, hires him to cut wood and do other chores. Eventually Lushkoff is able to find a better job as a notary. Years later the two men meet again at the theater, where Skvortsoff takes credit for teaching Lushkoff the value of work. The former beggar confesses that he never chopped any wood; Olga did it all.

Bridge to the Past

Literature

from

The Beggar
by Anton Chekhov

Anton Chekhov, who died in 1904 at age 44, wrote several plays and short stories that became classics of Russian literature. The issue he confronts in the following excerpt—how to help those in need—remains a vital issue today. A wealthy lawyer, Skvortsoff, is angered by the lies a beggar tells to win sympathy and money from passersby. Skvortsoff complains to the beggar that "you could always find work if you only wanted to, but you're lazy and spoiled and drunken!"

"By God, you judge harshly!" cried the beggar with a bitter laugh. "Where can I find manual labor? It's too late for me to be a clerk because in trade one has to begin as a boy; no one would ever take me for a porter because they couldn't order me about; no factory would have me because for that one has to know a trade, and I know none."

"Nonsense! You always find some excuse! How would you like to chop wood for me?"

"I wouldn't refuse to do that, but in these days even skilled wood-cutters find themselves sitting without bread."

"Huh! You loafers all talk that way. As soon as an offer is made you, you refuse it. Will you come and chop wood for me?"

"Yes, sir; I will."

"Very well; we'll soon find out. Splendid—we'll see—"

Skvortsoff hastened along, rubbing his hands, not without a feeling of malice, and called his cook out of the kitchen.

"Here, Olga," he said, "take this gentleman into the wood-shed and let him chop wood."

The tatterdemalion [clothed in ragged garments] scarecrow shrugged his shoulders, as if in perplexity, and went irresolutely after the cook. It was obvious from his gait that he had not consented to go and chop wood because he was hungry and wanted work, but simply from pride and shame, because he had been trapped by his own words. It was obvious, too, that his strength had been undermined by vodka and

---

BOUT THE AUTHOR

Anton Chekhov grew up in Taganrog, a city on the Black Sea. His father, a recently freed serf, struggled to make a living as a grocer. From this childhood poverty, Chekhov developed a sympathy for the poor and working classes. He worked as a medical doctor among the poor during his adult life. His real interest, however, was writing. As a young man, Chekhov began writing short humorous tales to add to his income. As he grew older, he wrote plays and more serious short stories. He occasionally wrote nonfiction, including an account of convicts on Russia's Sakhalin Island. Often ill, Chekhov died of tuberculosis in 1904.

that he was unhealthy and did not feel the slightest inclination for toil.

Skvortsoff hurried into the dining room. From its windows one could see the wood-shed and everything that went on in the yard. Standing at the window, Skvortsoff saw the cook and the beggar come out into the yard by the back door and make their way across the dirty snow to the shed. Olga glared wrathfully at her companion, shoved him aside with her elbow, unlocked the shed, and angrily banged the door.

"We probably interrupted the woman over her coffee," thought Skvortsoff. "What an ill-tempered creature!"

Next he saw the pseudo-teacher, pseudo-student seat himself on a log and become lost in thought with his red cheeks resting on his fists. The woman flung down an ax at his feet, spat

angrily, and, judging from the expression of her lips, began to scold him. The beggar irresolutely pulled a billet [log] of wood toward him, set it up between his feet, and tapped it feebly with the ax. The billet wavered and fell down. The beggar again pulled it to him, blew on his freezing hands, and tapped it with his ax cautiously, as if afraid of hitting his overshoe or of cutting off his finger. The stick of wood again fell to the ground.

Skvortsoff's anger had vanished and he now began to feel a little sorry and ashamed of himself for having set a spoiled, drunken, perchance sick man to work at menial labor in the cold.

"Well, never mind," he thought, going into his study from the dining room. "I did it for his own good."

An hour later Olga came in and announced

History & Art *Religious Procession in the Province of Kursk* by Ilya Repin. Tretyakov Gallery, Moscow, Russia **Ilya Repin painted realistic scenes of everyday Russian life.** *How does Chekhov portray Russian life in his story "The Beggar"?*

Bridge to the Past
Literature

Literary Element Irony is the contrast between what is anticipated and what actually occurs. The unexpected twist at the end of the story—that Lushkoff did little work for Skvortsoff—makes the lawyer's comments about the value of hard work ironic.

FOCUS

Ask students how they respond when they see someone asking for money. Discuss how they feel toward the individual and whether they think about why the person might have to beg.

History & Art In the late 1800s when Chekhov wrote, Russia was still a vast, overwhelmingly agrarian society. There was a sharp contrast between the urban lifestyle of city dwellers in Moscow and St. Petersburg and the way that poor, deeply religious former serfs lived in the countryside.
Answer to Caption: *Students may feel Russia was marked by strong class differences but that members of different classes still had regular contact and that there was some social mobility.*

Chapter 13 *Cultural Revolution* **417**

OTHER WORKS BY ANTON CHEKHOV

Frayn, Michael, trans. *Chekhov: Plays.* Methueun UK: Heinemann, 1988.
Garnett, Constance, trans. *The Duel and Other Stories.* New York: Echo Press, 1984.

Garnett, Constance, trans. *The Steppe.* Gloucester: Sutton, 1987.
Mamet, David, ed. *Uncle Vanya.* New York: Grove Press, 1988.

Chapter 13 *Cultural Revolution* **417**

TEACH

Literary Analysis

Students may recall being told by English teachers to avoid the passive voice, a sentence structure in which the writer does not make clear who carried out an action. However, Chekhov, or the translator of this story, used the passive voice to good effect. When Olga enters, she "announced that the wood had been chopped." The construction avoids stating who actually chopped the wood, which the reader does not learn until the end of the story.

History & Art

In the late 1800s Russian women had few rights. A wife had no legal rights except through her husband; a widow was entitled to inherit only one-seventh of her husband's real estate.
Answer to Caption: *Unknown to Skvortsoff, Olga, his cook, played the key role in reforming Lushkoff.*

Interpretation

Point out to students that Skvortsoff obviously considers himself a good judge of character. Yet he misunderstands both his cook, whom he calls "ill-tempered" but who is actually very kind, and Lushkoff, who he believes was reformed by hard work but was actually changed by the cook's sympathy. Ask students what Chekhov might have been saying about how well upper-class Russians understood the poor. (*They did not understand the poor well at all.*)

 World Literature Selection 6

History & Art *Female Farmers* by Kazimir Malevich. Russian State Museum, St. Petersburg, Russia **Malevich used modern painting techniques to portray the life of peasant women in rural Russia.** *What role does Olga play in Chekhov's story?*

that the wood had all been chopped.

"Good! Give him half a ruble [the Russian unit of currency]," said Skvortsoff. "If he wants to he can come back and cut wood on the first day of each month. We can always find work for him."

On the first day of the month the waif made his appearance and again earned half a ruble, although he could barely stand on his legs. From that day on he often appeared in the yard and every time work was found for him. Now he would shovel snow, now put the wood-shed in order, now beat the dust out of rugs and mattresses. Every time he received from twenty to forty kopecks [one kopeck equals one-hundredth of a ruble], and once, even a pair of old trousers were sent out to him.

When Skvortsoff moved into another house he hired him to help in the packing and hauling of the furniture. This time the waif was sober, gloomy, and silent. He hardly touched the furniture, and walked behind the wagons hanging his head, not even making a pretense of appearing busy. He only shivered in the cold and became embarrassed when the carters jeered at him for his idleness, his feebleness, and his tattered, fancy overcoat. After the moving was over Skvortsoff sent for him.

"Well, I see that my words have taken effect," he said, handing him a ruble. "Here's for your pains. I see you are sober and have no objection to work. What is your name?"

"Lushkoff."

"Well, Lushkoff, I can now offer you some

ADDITIONAL LITERARY WORKS OF THE PERIOD

Futabatei, Shimei. *Ukigumo.* Novel about Japanese modernization.
Hernandez, José. *Martin Fierro.* Epic poem about an Argentinian gaucho.

London, Jack. *Call of the Wild.* Tale of a dog that returns to the wilderness.
Wharton, Edith. *Ethan Frome.* Tragic novel set in rural New England.

other, cleaner employment. Can you write?"

"I can."

"Then take this letter to a friend of mine tomorrow and you will be given some copying to do. Work hard, don't drink, and remember what I have said to you. Good-bye!"

Pleased at having put a man on the right path, Skvortsoff tapped Lushkoff kindly on the shoulder and even gave him his hand at parting. Lushkoff took the letter, and from that day forth came no more to the yard for work.

Two years went by. Then one evening, as Skvortsoff was standing at the ticket window of a theater paying for his seat, he noticed a little man beside him with a coat collar of curly fur and a worn sealskin cap. This little individual timidly asked the ticket seller for a seat in the gallery and paid for it in copper coins.

"Lushkoff, is that you?" cried Skvortsoff, recognizing in the little man his former wood-chopper. "How are you? What are you doing? How is everything with you?"

"All right. I am a notary [a clerk who certifies legal documents] now and get thirty-five rubles a month."

"Thank Heaven! That's fine! I am delighted for your sake. I am very, very glad, Lushkoff. You see, you are my godson, in a sense. I gave you a push along the right path, you know. Do you remember what a roasting I gave you, eh? I nearly had you sinking into the ground at my feet that day. Thank you, old man, for not forgetting my words."

"Thank you, too," said Lushkoff. "If I hadn't come to you then I might still have been calling

myself a teacher or a student to this day. Yes, by flying to your protection I dragged myself out of a pit."

"I am very glad, indeed."

"Thank you for your kind words and deeds. You talked splendidly to me then. I am very grateful to you and to your cook. God bless that good and noble woman! You spoke finely then, and I shall be indebted to you to my dying day; but, strictly speaking, it was your cook, Olga, who saved me."

"How is that?"

"Like this. When I used to come to your house to chop wood she used to begin: 'Oh, you sot [drunkard], you! Oh, you miserable creature! There's nothing for you but ruin.' And then she would sit down opposite me and grow sad, look into my face and weep. 'Oh you unlucky man! There is no pleasure for you in this world and there will be none in the world to come. You drunkard! You will burn in hell. Oh, you unhappy one!' And so she would carry on, you know, in that strain. I can't tell you how much misery she suffered, how many tears she shed for my sake. But the chief thing was—she used to chop the wood for me. Do you know, sir, that I did not chop one single stick of wood for you? She did it all. Why this saved me, why I changed, why I stopped drinking at the sight of her I cannot explain. I only know that, owing to her words and noble deeds a change took place in my heart; she set me right and I shall never forget it. However, it is time to go now; there goes the bell."

Lushkoff bowed and departed to the gallery.

RESPONDING TO LITERATURE

1. Explain how the beggar Lushkoff's character and behavior change between the beginning of Chekhov's story and the conclusion of the story.
2. Contrast Skvortsoff's plan for helping Lushkoff improve his life and what actually helped Lushkoff.
3. What advice do you think Chekhov would give to people today who want to help the poor?
4. **Predicting an Outcome** What might have happened if Skvortsoff had found out immediately that Olga was chopping the wood for Lushkoff?

ANSWERS TO RESPONDING TO LITERATURE

1. Lushkoff stops drinking and begging and takes a respectable job as a notary.
2. Skvortsoff thought he would help Lushkoff by giving him work. Instead, Olga helped him by showing real concern.
3. Students may feel Chekhov was saying that people should help the poor out of genuine compassion, not a sense of superiority.
4. He probably would have stopped hiring Lushkoff. He probably would have scolded Olga.

Literature

ASSESS

Assign **Responding to Literature** questions.

CLOSE

After students have read the excerpt, point out to them that Chekhov came from a very humble background. Ask them to discuss whether Chekhov was sympathetic to Lushkoff when he was a beggar. Does Chekhov seem to blame society in general or Lushkoff himself for Lushkoff's poverty? (*Since Lushkoff reforms through his own efforts, Chekhov seems to point to individual responsibility for poverty in this story.*)

Contemporary Connection

The Cherry Orchard and other Chekhov plays are often presented by regional theater companies. Students may also be interested in watching the film *Uncle Vanya on 42nd Street*, a play within a play that deals with a production of the famous drama by Chekhov, directed by Louis Malle.

Portfolio Project

Have students interested in issues of unemployment, poverty, and substance abuse choose and research a specific topic in one of these areas and write a brief essay.

Chapter 13 Review

GLENCOE TECHNOLOGY

VIDEODISC
Use MindJogger to review students' knowledge of the chapter.

MindJogger Videoquiz

Chapter 13
Disc 2 Side A

  Also available in VHS.

Answers

Using Key Terms

1. f   4. l
2. g   5. c
3. i

Using Your History Journal

Encourage students to comment on the universality and timelessness of Chekhov's subject.

Reviewing Facts

1. They preferred not to have the government restrict their ability to make money.
2. Smith's analysis of capitalism stressed the importance of a free market in advancing economic growth and social progress; his ideas shaped people's understanding of capitalist economies worldwide; Marx believed he had discovered a scientific socialism and stressed the importance of class warfare as the "engine of history." His views influenced revolutionaries.
3. Marie and Pierre Curie discovered radium; Max Planck theorized that energy is released in units known as quanta; Albert Einstein developed his theory of relativity. They laid the foundations of modern physics and the nuclear age.

CHAPTER 13 REVIEW

Connections Across Time

Historical Significance The Industrial Revolution created new businesses and social classes. Living standards improved although a wide gap separated rich and poor.

Today Communist ideas have been discredited and capitalism is the world's dominant economic system. Since the 1930s, democratic societies have combined capitalism with social welfare

policies. The role of government in social affairs, however, currently provokes much debate, and there are calls for greater personal responsibility and less government involvement.

Using Key Terms

Write the key term that completes each sentence. Then write a sentence for each term not chosen.

a. atomic theory   g. socialism
b. evolution   h. sociology
c. laissez-faire   i. genetics
d. immigration   j. emigration
e. impressionism   k. urbanization
f. realism   l. psychology

1. In the mid-1800s artists and writers in Europe and North America developed a style called _____ that often called attention to the less fortunate members of society.
2. Supporters of _____ believe that society, directly or through the government, should own the means of production.
3. The research of Gregor Mendel laid the foundation for the development of _____, the science of heredity.
4. Freud's theory that human actions grew out of subconscious motives led to the development of the science of _____.
5. Supporters of _____ believed that people should be able to buy and sell, hire and fire, free from government interference.

Technology Activity

Using the Internet Search the Internet for a Web site that provides additional information about the history of Marxism. Use a search engine to help focus your search by using words such as *karl marx, history,* and *socialism.* Write a research report based on your findings. Explain Marx's stages toward true communism, and provide examples of governments that were influenced by Karl Marx's ideas.

420   Chapter 13   *Cultural Revolution*

Using Your History Journal

After reading the literature selection from "The Beggar" by Anton Chekhov, write a review of the piece. Do you agree or disagree with Chekhov's assumptions about the poor? Why?

Reviewing Facts

1. **Economics** Explain why business leaders during the 1800s promoted laissez-faire economics.
2. **Economics** Discuss the impact of the ideas of Adam Smith and Karl Marx on world history.
3. **Science** List the contributions of Marie Curie and other physicists and state their impact.
4. **Economics** Identify the factors that led to the rise and spread of socialism in the 1800s.
5. **Culture** Describe one work by each of these writers: Hugo, Tolstoy, Dreiser.

Critical Thinking

1. **Apply** What are three examples of the romantics' emphasis on emotion?
2. **Analyze** How did Charles Darwin's theories answer his question about the great variety of living things?
3. **Synthesize** A frame of reference is a set of ideas that determines how something will be understood. Explain how the Industrial Revolution would be viewed from a capitalistic frame of reference and a Marxist frame of reference.
4. **Evaluate** Write a letter to the editor of an 1800s newspaper, expressing your views on secondary-school education for women.

4. the belief that capitalism could not remedy social ills and that equal distribution of wealth was needed; when capitalism brought some social improvements, many socialist movements discarded revolution and favored democratic means to introduce socialist reforms
5. Hugo's *Les Misérables*: romantic novel portraying human suffering with compassion; Tolstoy's *War and Peace*: realistic historical novel about Napoleon's 1812 invasion of

Russia; Dreiser's *An American Tragedy*: naturalistic novel about a young man executed for killing his pregnant girlfriend

Critical Thinking

1. Answers may include examples from painting, literature, or music.
2. Natural selection explained that only those species best adapted to their environment survive.

420 Chapter 13 *Cultural Revolution*

5. Analyze The painting *Dinner at Haddo House* shows the lifestyle of the wealthy. How did this show of wealth further separate social classes?

Understanding Themes

1. **Change** According to Karl Marx, what steps would societies follow in moving toward the goal of communism?
2. **Innovation** Describe one innovation of the 1800s and early 1900s in each of these sciences: biology, physics, psychology. How did each innovation affect people's lives?
3. **Movement** How did improved methods of transportation affect the movement of people and products?
4. **Innovation** Select a cultural movement such as romanticism, realism, symbolism, impressionism, or Postimpressionism, and explain how the movement reflected the way people felt about changes in the 1800s.

Linking Past and Present

Explain why modern Russia has turned to capitalism from the radical Socialism born during the Industrial Revolution.

Skill Practice

Using your communications software, type a message to another student naming your favorite writer or artist from one of the following artistic movements. Explain why this artist is your favorite.

- Romanticism
- Realism
- Symbolism
- Impressionism
- Postimpressionism

Geography in History

1. **Place** Refer to the map "Population Growth in the United Kingdom." What were the major industrial cities of the United Kingdom by 1900?
2. **Place** How much did the population per square mile in the London and Bristol areas grow during this period?

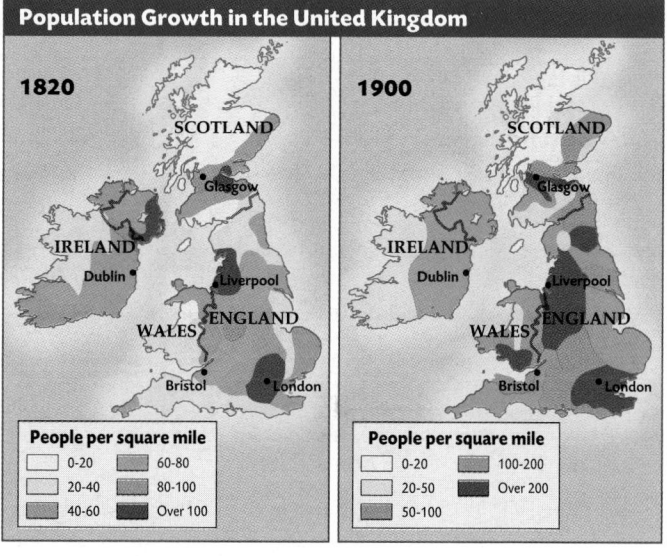

Population Growth in the United Kingdom

1820 / 1900

SCOTLAND — Glasgow — IRELAND — Dublin — Liverpool — WALES — ENGLAND — Bristol — London

People per square mile
0-20, 20-40, 40-60, 60-80, 80-100, Over 100 (1820)
0-20, 20-50, 50-100, 100-200, Over 200 (1900)

Chapter 13 *Cultural Revolution* 421

methods in medicine; theory of the unconscious led to psychoanalysis

3. **MOVEMENT** People became more mobile. Railroads enabled people to eat food grown elsewhere and encouraged travel.
4. **INNOVATION** Answers should reflect an understanding of cultural movements.

Linking Past and Present

Answers should mention the strengths of the free market in promoting economic growth and material prosperity, while communism with its controls failed to provide incentives for work and the goods and services that people wanted.

Skill Practice

Messages will vary depending on the writer or artist chosen by the students. Make sure the students have used the steps for sending E-mail as described on page 634.

Geography in History

1. London, Bristol, Liverpool, Glasgow, Dublin
2. London: from over 100 people per square mile to over 200 per square mile; Bristol: increased no more than 20 people per square mile

❓ Chapter Bonus Test Question

Ask: How would you respond to the romantic poet Keats's famous statement, "Beauty is truth, truth beauty,—that is all/Ye know on earth, and all ye need to know"? (*Keats's statement reflects the romantics' rejection of the increasing mechanization of industrialized society.*)

3. Answers should mention the capitalist's faith in the self-regulating marketplace to provide benefits for all with minimal government involvement and the Marxist belief in the importance of class conflict, the revolutionary overthrow of capitalism by the workers, and the creation of a classless society.
4. Answers may focus on the equality of men and women.
5. It emphasized the great gap between rich and poor.

Understanding Themes

1. **CHANGE** primitive, slave, feudal, and capitalist—before the proletariat seized control, creating a society without private property, class distinctions, or government
2. **INNOVATION** discovery of bacteria led to new approaches in disease prevention; discovery of X rays led to new diagnostic

A complete, 1-page lesson plan is provided for each section in the *Reproducible Lesson Plans* booklet.

Democracy and Reform

CHAPTER RESOURCES

	Reproducible Resources	Multimedia Resources
Chapter Opener	Chapter Themes: Graphic Organizer 14 Historical Significance Chapter Activity 14	MindJogger Videoquiz
Chapter Enrichment	Vocabulary Activity 14* Time Line Activity 14 Mapping History Activity 14 History Simulation 14 Geography and History Activity 14 Source Reading 14 People in World History Profiles 47, 48 World Art and Music Activity 14 Enrichment Activity 14 Critical Thinking Activity 14 Skill Reinforcement Activity 14 Performance Assessment Activity 14	World History and Art Transparency 33, *The Banjo Lesson* Mapping History Overlay Transparency 16, *Global Ancestry of Americans* Chapter Transparency 14 Vocabulary PuzzleMaker Software World Music: Cultural Traditions, Lessons 1, 2, 3, 10 Lessons of War: *Why Soldiers Fight*
Chapter Review/Reteaching	Reteaching Activity 14 Skill Reinforcement Activity 14 Spanish Chapter Summary 14	Chapter 14 Digest Audiocassette, Activity, Test* Vocabulary PuzzleMaker Software Student Self-Test and Review Software MindJogger Videoquiz
Chapter Evaluation/Testing	Performance Assessment Activity 14 Chapter 14 Test, Forms A and B	Testmaker

* Also available in Spanish

0:00 OUT OF TIME? Assign the Chapter 14 summary in the Unit 4 Digest on pages 505–507, and the Chapter 14 Audiocassettes.

Block Schedule

Block scheduling differs from traditional class scheduling in the amount of time allotted to each period. The extended time frame provided by block scheduling affords you the opportunity to implement a greater number of research-oriented and activity-intense projects to motivate and involve your students. Activities that are particularly suited to use within the block scheduling framework are identified throughout this chapter by the following designation.

KEY TO ABILITY LEVELS

Teaching strategies have been coded for varying learning styles and abilities.

L1 **BASIC** activities for all students
L2 **AVERAGE** activities for average to above-average students
L3 **CHALLENGING** activities for above-average students
LEP **LIMITED ENGLISH PROFICIENCY** activities

Use Glencoe's *Presentation Plus!* multimedia teacher tool to easily present dynamic lessons that visually excite your students. Using Microsoft PowerPoint® you can customize the presentations to create your own personalized lessons.

SECTION RESOURCES

Daily Objectives	Reproducible Resources	Multimedia Resources
Section 1 **Reform in Great Britain** Describe how political change came to Great Britain during the 1800s.	Reproducible Lesson Plan 14-1 Vocabulary Activity 14* Guided Reading Activity 14-1* Time Line Activity 14 History Simulation 14 Section Quiz 14-1*	Section Focus Transparency 14-1 Chapter Transparency 14 Student Self-Test and Review Software Testmaker World Music: Cultural Traditions, Lesson 3
Section 2 **The Dominions** Relate how new societies emerged in Canada, Australia, and New Zealand.	Reproducible Lesson Plan 14-2 Vocabulary Activity 14* Guided Reading Activity 14-2* Geography and History Activity 14 Section Quiz 14-2*	Section Focus Transparency 14-2 Student Self-Test and Review Software Testmaker World Music: Cultural Traditions, Lesson 10
Section 3 **Political Struggles in France** Identify the changes in government that France underwent during the 1800s.	Reproducible Lesson Plan 14-3 Vocabulary Activity 14* Guided Reading Activity 14-3* Section Quiz 14-3*	Section Focus Transparency 14-3 Student Self-Test and Review Software Testmaker
Section 4 **Expansion of the United States** Explain how the United States changed during the 1800s.	Reproducible Lesson Plan 14-4 Vocabulary Activity 14* Guided Reading Activity 14-4* People in World History Profile 47 Section Quiz 14-4*	Section Focus Transparency 14-4 World History and Art Transparency 33, *The Banjo Lesson* Mapping History Overlay Transparency 16, *Global Ancestry of Americans* Student Self-Test and Review Software World Music: Cultural Traditions, Lesson 1 Lessons of War: *Why Soldiers Fight*
Section 5 **Latin American Independence** Relate how the countries of Latin America won independence.	Reproducible Lesson Plan 14-5 Guided Reading Activity 14-5* People in World History Profile 48 Reteaching Activity 14 Enrichment Activity 14 Section Quiz 14-5* Performance Assessment Activity 14 Spanish Chapter Summary 14	Section Focus Transparency 14-5 Vocabulary PuzzleMaker Software Student Self-Test and Review Software Testmaker World Music: Cultural Traditions, Lesson 2

* *Also available in Spanish*

Chapter Activities

Performance Assessment Activity

An Import/Export Company Organize students into groups that will assume the roles of owners of an import/export company. First, each group will review the expansions and reforms of the era and predict how various parts of the world would be different today if none of these had occurred—including differences today in government, foreign affairs, trade, language, travel and tourism, and economics. Each group will then create five scenarios of how they would acquire merchandise for their companies from different parts of the world studied in this chapter. Each scenario should reflect the long-term effects of one of the expansions or reforms.

Possible Rubric Features
Accuracy of content information; collaborative skills; logical predicting; plausibility of scenarios; and thoroughness in including criteria related to government, trade, language, foreign affairs, economics, and tourism

• *For an additional activity, refer to Activity 14 in the* Performance Assessment Strategies and Activities *booklet.*

ACTIVITY

From the Classroom of...

**Chuck Kloes
Beverly Hills High
School
Beverly Hills, CA**

The Irish Question: A Solution Satisfactory to Whom?
Prepare "point of view" sheets for both sides of the Irish question—Sheet A listing four to five arguments in support of granting home rule to all of Ireland, and Sheet B listing four to five arguments in support of maintaining English control over Northern Ireland. Organize the class into A and B groups to debate the question and pass out the sheets. Give the groups 15 minutes to study the sheets, collect data, and prepare their presentations. Have each group select two students to be spokespersons, with you acting as moderator. After the debate, hold a class discussion about what students learned from the exercise.

MULTIPLE LEARNING STYLES

Verbal/Linguistic
Tell students to imagine going on a tour of Europe and North and South America during the 1800s. Have them keep a journal of their travels and record their impressions of culture, environment, society, and special events.

Logical/Mathematical
Have students create a time line that tracks the major political, social, and cultural struggles of the period. Ask students to include details from the text as well as class presentations.

Visual/Spatial
Have students make a large wall map of the Oregon, Santa Fe, and California Trails. Have them mark key physical geographic features and main stopping places.

Auditory/Musical
Ask students to research and report on the music of this period in Europe, the British dominions, the United States, or Latin America. They might select a sample from each area or concentrate on just one location. They may present their findings to the class.

Additional Resources

NATIONAL GEOGRAPHIC SOCIETY — Teacher's Corner

INDEX TO NATIONAL GEOGRAPHIC MAGAZINE

The following articles may be used for research relating to this chapter:

- "El Libertador: Simón Bolívar," by Bryan Hodgson, March 1994.
- "The Itch to Move West: Life and Death on the Oregon Trail," by Boyd Gibbons, August 1986.
- "The Travail of Ireland," by Joseph Judge, April 1981.

NATIONAL GEOGRAPHIC SOCIETY PRODUCTS AVAILABLE FROM GLENCOE

To order the following products for use with this chapter, contact your local Glencoe sales representative, or call Glencoe at 1-800-334-7344:

- *GTV: The American People (Videodiscs)*
- *GTV: A Geographic Perspective on American History (Videodiscs)*

ADDITIONAL NATIONAL GEOGRAPHIC SOCIETY PRODUCTS

To order the following products for use with this chapter, call National Geographic Society at 1-800-368-2728:

- *Nations of the World Series, "Australia." (Video)*
- *Heritage of the Black West (Video)*

LOCAL OBJECTIVES

_____
_____
_____
_____
_____
_____
_____
_____
_____
_____
_____
_____
_____
_____
_____
_____
_____
_____
_____
_____
_____
_____

interNET CONNECTION
British resources on the World Wide Web
The Victorian Web:
http://www.stg.brown.edu/projects/hypertext/landow/victorian/victov.html

BIBLIOGRAPHY

Literature of the Period
Eliot, George. *The Mill on the Floss.* New York: Bantam, 1987. Novel explores family relationships while taking a critical look at British middle-class values.

Readings for the Student
Davis, William C., ed. *Touched by Fire: A Photographic Portrait of the Civil War*. Boston: Little, Brown, 1985. Portrays the tragedy of the American Civil War.

Readings for the Teacher
Hoppen, K. Theodore. *Ireland Since 1800: Conflict and Conformity.* White Plains, NY: Longman, 1989. This survey of Irish history examines the social, economic, and political aspects of recent Irish history.

Chapter Themes are listed by section on this chapter opening page of the Student Edition. A corresponding theme-based activity is available under "TEACH," and a theme-based question is asked in the Section and Chapter Reviews.

The Storyteller

Historical Setting Richard Cobden, an English political leader and economist, became a great supporter of the democratic movement and of laws to protect the interests of the middle class. Cobden worked for peace and argued against the British foreign policy of intervention to maintain the balance of power. He was a strong advocate of free trade and played a key role in the fight to repeal the Corn Law.

Historical Significance

Answers: *Ideals of individual liberty and self-government spread among the middle and working classes who demanded the vote and social reforms; Latin Americans broke with Spain and set up independent republics; however, democracy was often elusive.*

Chapter
14
1800–1914
Democracy and Reform

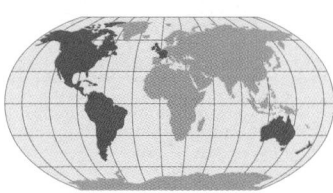

Chapter Themes

▶ **Change** Great Britain carries out democratic reforms. *Section 1*
▶ **Movement** Immigrants from Great Britain and other countries settle Canada, Australia, and New Zealand. *Section 2*
▶ **Revolution** France undergoes political upheaval during the 1800s. *Section 3*
▶ **Change** The United States extends its borders and develops its economy. *Section 4*
▶ **Nationalism** Latin American nations achieve self-government. *Section 5*

The Storyteller

British politician Richard Cobden stood before the House of Commons in 1845. In a loud voice, he demanded that the middle and working classes be given more representation in a government that unfairly favored the landed aristocracy. Cobden declared:

"I say without being revolutionary ... that the sooner the power of this country is transferred from the landed ruling class, which has so misused it, and is placed absolutely ... in the hands of the intelligent middle and industrious classes, the better for the condition and destinies of this country."

While Cobden worked for change within the British political system, people in Europe and Latin America faced fiercer and often bloody struggles for democratic reform. By the end of the 1800s, democracy had triumphed in many parts of the world.

Historical Significance

Why did democratic reform movements develop and flourish in Europe and other parts of the world? How did independence change the lives of people in Latin America?

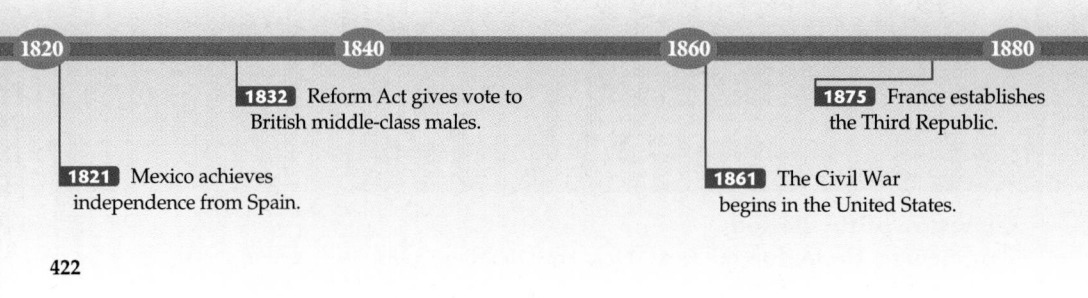

1820	1840	1860	1880

1832 Reform Act gives vote to British middle-class males.

1875 France establishes the Third Republic.

1821 Mexico achieves independence from Spain.

1861 The Civil War begins in the United States.

422

GEOGRAPHY CONNECTION

Location Using a world map, have students use a scale of miles to estimate distance between Great Britain and Australia *(approximately 8,000 miles [13,000 km])* and the distance between Spain and Ecuador *(approximately 6,000 miles [10,000 km])*. Ask students what effect these distances might have on the relationship between the country and the colony. *(It might have made it difficult for the countries to govern their distant colonies efficiently or knowledgeably; it might have increased the colonies' desire for independence.)*

History & Art: *Celebration of the Concorde of May 21, 1848* by Jean Jacques Champin. Musée de la Ville de Paris, Musée Carnavalet, Paris, France

Your History Journal

On an outline map of the world, draw and label all the territories once held by Great Britain and the dates when they became self-governing, or independent.

Chapter 14 *Democracy and Reform* **423**

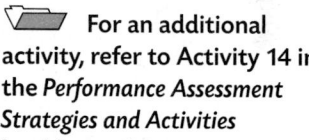

Introducing Chapter 14

History & Art The work to build the Place de la Concorde began in 1755. Almost a hundred years later, during the reign of Louis-Philippe, it was completed with the addition of the Egyptian obelisk. The Place de la Concorde has been the arena for many historic events including guillotine executions in the 1790s.

✔ **Performance Assessment**

Refer to the activity on page 422C of the Planning Guide.

📁 For an additional activity, refer to Activity 14 in the *Performance Assessment Strategies and Activities* booklet.

Using Your History Journal

Suggest that students use colored pencils or pens to color code the territories on their maps. They should label neatly with black pen.

GLENCOE TECHNOLOGY

 VIDEODISC
Use MindJogger to preview chapter content.

MindJogger Videoquiz

Chapter 14
Disc 2 Side A

 Also available in VHS.

➕ **EXTRA CREDIT PROJECT**

Research To further their understanding of the period covered in this chapter, have students investigate one of the following topics: the potato famine of 1845–1847, schools and education on the frontier, the California gold rush, the Dreyfus affair, or the penal colonies of Australia. Ask students to prepare an outline first, then write the report and present it to the class. **L2**

424   Chapter 14   Democracy and Reform

SECTION THEME

▶ **Change** Great Britain carries out democratic reforms.

Find Out ▶

Answer: *Electoral reform, the reorganization of political parties, and the dynamic leadership of prime ministers Gladstone and Disraeli brought peaceful change in government in Britain during the 1800s.*

FOCUS

Section Objective

Describe how political change came to Great Britain during the 1800s.

BELLRINGER
Motivational Activity

Before taking roll at the beginning of the class period, project Section Focus Transparency 14-1 and have students answer the activity questions. Discuss students' responses.

This activity is also available as a blackline master.

Vocabulary Pre-check

Use Vocabulary Activity 14 to introduce vocabulary terms.
L1 LEP

1825	1850	1875	1900

1837 Victoria becomes queen of Great Britain.

1867 Reform Act extends vote to all male homeowners and renters.

1886 Gladstone introduces Irish home rule legislation.

1900 Trade unionists and Socialists begin to form the Labour party.

Section 1

Reform in Great Britain

Setting the Scene

▶ **Terms to Define**
apportion, disenfranchised, suffragette, home rule

▶ **People to Meet**
the Chartists, Queen Victoria, William Gladstone, Benjamin Disraeli, the Fabians, Emmeline Pankhurst, Charles Stewart Parnell

▶ **Places to Locate**
Ireland

Find Out ▶ How did political change come to Great Britain during the 1800s?

The Storyteller

When women first lobbied for voting rights, some critics feared that if they won the vote, men would become women's servants. Political cartoons and works of art appeared that showed sour-faced men caring for babies and wringing out dirty laundry, while women happily rode around in carriages or talked excitedly around the ballot box. Other opponents claimed that if women won the vote, they would spend all their time at the polls. One poster nicknamed a woman who ran for office "Susan Sharp-Tongue, the Celebrated Man Tamer."

—adapted from *On To Victory, Propaganda Plays of the Woman Suffrage Movement*, edited by Bettina Friedl, 1987

Woman suffrage rally

political change in Great Britain took place gradually and peacefully. The British government moved toward greater democracy through evolution rather than revolution. By the 1800s Great Britain was a limited constitutional monarchy. The monarch's authority consisted only of the rights to encourage, to warn, and to be consulted by those who really governed Great Britain. Actual executive power belonged to the Cabinet led by the prime minister, while Parliament maintained legislative control.

Although all British people in theory were represented in the House of Commons, the British government was not a true democracy in the early 1800s. Political power remained with the landed aristocracy, while the middle and working classes had no voting rights.

Electoral Reforms

In the early 1800s some rural districts were well represented in the House of Commons, while growing industrial areas had little representation. Factory workers, farm laborers, and the middle class began to demand that they receive a greater political voice. The liberal minority party, the Whigs, continually introduced bills to give voting rights to more people and to **apportion**, or divide and share, electoral districts more fairly. The Whigs' efforts were repeatedly defeated by the Tory party, which opposed such bills.

When the Whigs came to political power in 1830, however, their demands could no longer be ignored. In 1832 the Whigs forced the king to announce that he would create as many new lords as necessary to give the reform bill a majority in the House of Lords. To avoid this action, the lords gave in and passed the bill.

424   **Chapter 14**   *Democracy and Reform*

The Reform Act of 1832

The Reform Act of 1832 lowered the property qualifications for voting and gave more middle-class males the right to vote. The proportion of voters increased from 1 in 100 to 1 in 32 men. The act also took representation rights away from areas that had declined in population. With 143 seats freed in the House of Commons, the heavily populated cities finally increased their representation. One observer recalled the moments after the passing of the reform bill:

> ❝ We shook hands and clapped each other on the back, and went out laughing, crying … into the lobby. And no sooner were the outer doors opened than another shout answered that within the House. All the passages … were thronged by people who had waited till four in the morning to know the issue [outcome]. ❞

Reform Movements

While the Reform Act gave middle-class men the right to vote, it only frustrated the industrial and farm workers, who remained disenfranchised, or deprived of the right to vote. These disenfranchised citizens banded together to demand further reforms. In a document called *A People's Charter*, **the Chartists**, an important reform group of the working class, proposed political changes. The Chartists' demands included voting rights for all adult men, no property qualifications for voting, a secret ballot, salaries for members of Parliament so that the middle and lower classes could take seats, and equal electoral districts.

The Chartists submitted two petitions to Parliament, one with more than a million signatures and the other with more than 3 million. Parliament rejected both petitions. After the defeat, the Chartists had little success and their movement faded by the 1850s. Parliament did, however, eventually pass many of their reforms.

Another reform movement, the Anti-Corn Law League, was supported by the middle class. The aim of the League was to repeal the Corn Law, which since 1815 had severely limited and taxed the importation of foreign grain. Wealthy landowners benefited from the law, as it ensured them a profitable hold on the grain market. Middle-class industrialists fought the Corn Law because it forced them to pay higher wages to workers to enable them to buy bread.

The League—the first major political pressure group in Great Britain—captured public attention with lectures, pamphlets, books, and meetings.

Visualizing History In this British cartoon, Prime Minister Benjamin Disraeli presents the crown of India to Queen Victoria. *What other noted prime minister served during Victoria's reign?*

When an Irish crop failure forced Great Britain to import much grain, Parliament responded to the pressure and repealed the Corn Law.

Political Parties

One result of electoral reform was more elaborate organization of political parties. Before 1800 both parties—the Tories and the Whigs—represented wealthy landowners. They had no formal organization. They were actually loose groups of politicians with common interests. As more middle-class men gained voting rights, the old parties reorganized to win support from the new voters. After 1832 the Tory and Whig parties began to change into the modern Conservative and Liberal parties.

Support for the Conservative party came largely from the aristocracy and members of the old Tory party. The industrial and commercial classes and members of the old Whig party supported the Liberal party. Both parties eventually competed for middle-class and working-class votes.

Political Leadership

This era of political reform took place during the reign of **Queen Victoria**. She came to the throne in 1837 at age 18 and reigned for 64 years. Two brilliant prime ministers—**William Gladstone** and **Benjamin Disraeli**—served during Victoria's reign. Both men offered dynamic leadership for the

---

COOPERATIVE LEARNING ACTIVITY

Role Play Have students form groups to role-play a visit to Ireland by members of the British Parliament. Tell students to imagine that they are living in the mid-1800s and that some members of Parliament are visiting Ireland to hear the people's views on home rule. Select one group of five or six students to be observers. Have remaining students represent: members of Parliament who oppose or favor home rule, Irish Catholics, and a group of Irish Protestants. Have students who have assumed roles debate the issue of home rule. At the conclusion of the debate, have the observers comment on the effectiveness of each faction's arguments. **L2**

TEACH

Guided Practice

THEME Change

Work with students to create a chart on the chalkboard listing the changes caused by the Reform Act of 1832. **L1 LEP**

Visualizing History The rise of British political cartoons came with the movement toward greater democracy. These caricatures became a popular way to communicate political messages and influence voters. In this cartoon the artist is commenting on the well-known fact that Queen Victoria was very fond of Disraeli and had offered him a peerage.
Answer to Caption: *William Gladstone*

Diagram Have students list events that influenced the democratic reform movement in Great Britain during the 1800s. *(Whigs coming to power in 1830, formation of the Chartists)* Help students make a diagram showing the cause-and-effect relationships between these events and specific reforms. **L2**

Debate Have students take the following roles: industrial workers, middle-class landowners, and members of the House of Lords. Lead an impromptu debate on the Reform Act of 1832. **L3**

 History Simulation 14

Chapter Transparency 14

World Music: Cultural Traditions, Lesson 3

Chapter 14
Section 1

Independent Practice

 Guided Reading Activity 14-1 **L1**

 Time Line Activity 14

Geography: Location Using the Atlas in their textbook, have students locate Ireland and write a brief paragraph about the conflict between the Irish and the British, focusing especially on the locations of the places involved. **L1 LEP**

Women Ask students to investigate the Women's Social Political Union or the lives of Emmeline, Christabel, and Sylvia Pankhurst and report on the women's rights movements. Ask them to describe the strategies used to gain public attention and support and then tell whether they agree with the strategies. **L2**

Critical Thinking Have students recall the cultural, economic, and political history of Great Britain and how it may have contributed to a male, landowner-dominated political system. Ask them to list specific changes that may have brought about the reevaluation of this political system in the 1800s. *(the Industrial Revolution)* **L3**

Linking Past and Present

Protests To publicize their cause, British suffragists went to extraordinary lengths, including arson, bombing of monuments, window smashing, and hunger strikes. These tactics were also used by Vietnam War protesters in the 1960s.

---

emerging Liberal and Conservative parties. Through their efforts Great Britain continued toward full democracy.

William Gladstone

William Gladstone of the Liberal party served 4 times as prime minister between 1868 and 1894. His first term, from 1868 to 1874, became known as the Great Ministry because of his many social reforms. Deeply religious, Gladstone always sought to apply morality to politics.

Gladstone directed reforms in such areas as government administration, education, and elections. A civil service reform of 1870 made appointments to most civil service positions dependent on competitive examinations. The Education Act of 1870 divided the country into school districts, which were maintained by local control. With the Ballot Act of 1872, Gladstone satisfied the old Chartist demand for the secret ballot. He also changed election districts. The Redistribution Act of 1885 divided Britain into electoral districts almost equal in population.

Benjamin Disraeli

Benjamin Disraeli of the Conservative party first gained fame in Great Britain as a novelist and later as a politician. He served two terms as prime minister—his first term briefly in 1868 and his second term from 1874 to 1880.

Disraeli believed that the Conservative party could save aristocratic traditions while cautiously adopting democratic reforms. He realized that blocking change would be damaging to the Conservative party, which began to base its primary support among the upper middle class.

In 1867 Disraeli had introduced a Conservative-backed reform bill. By lowering property qualifications for voters, the Reform Bill of 1867 extended the vote to all male homeowners and most men who rented property. The bill increased the electorate by about 1 million men, adding to it many working-class voters.

Growth of Democracy

The British government changed in the last quarter of the 1800s. As steps were taken toward democracy, the working class, women, and Irish Catholics began to influence political life.

Rise of Labor

Political reforms inspired many groups to fight for increased rights. Labor unions had been steadily growing and gaining political strength since the mid-1700s. By the time of Gladstone's Great Ministry, unions had become a way of life among the working classes. Laborers from nearly every trade organized into unions, which achieved great gains by staging strikes and demonstrations.

At the same time that labor unions were growing stronger, socialism was also gaining followers. In 1884 a group of middle-class intellectuals formed the Fabian Society, an organization whose aim was to peacefully and gradually prepare the way for a Socialist government. Through education, its members promoted social justice such as improved conditions and fair wages for workers. Unlike labor unions, **the Fabians** favored parliamentary action over strikes and demonstrations.

In 1900 trade unionists and Socialists laid the foundation for a new political party—the Labour party—to speak for the working class. Labour party supporters backed the reform-minded Liberal government elected in 1906. Together the Liberal and Labour members of Parliament promoted government reform to improve workers' lives. Between 1906 and 1914, new legislation provided the working classes with old-age pensions, a minimum wage, unemployment assistance, and health and unemployment insurance.

A Constitutional Crisis

To finance these measures, the Liberal government called for higher taxes in the budget of 1909. The largely Conservative House of Lords vehemently opposed the proposed taxation, because it directly threatened the wealth of the aristocracy.

The contest ended in victory for the House of Commons when the 1911 Parliament Act narrowed the powers of the House of Lords by removing money bills from their control. This action symbolized the aristocracy's political decline.

Women Demand Greater Rights

Women also sought to benefit from Great Britain's move toward more representative democracy. British women, mostly from the middle class, spoke out for political and social equality in the mid-1800s. In the 1850s women's rights activists fought to win property rights for married women. Their efforts led to the passage of the Married Women's Property Acts of 1870 and 1882, which gave women increased legal control over a family's earnings and property.

Achieving women's voting rights came more slowly. Although women had gained the right to vote in local elections in 1869, they still could not vote on a national level. In 1903 **Emmeline**

426 Chapter 14 *Democracy and Reform*

MEETING SPECIAL NEEDS ACTIVITY

Mixed Learners Because of the large amount of information conveyed in this chapter, allow students with learning disabilities to work in study groups. Help them to graphically organize the material by using time lines, charts, and diagrams to show relationships and to serve as study aids. Encourage students who need challenges to explore the section topics in detail. Direct them to key events that had major repercussions or that typify other similar situations. Have students look for cause-and-effect relationships. Establish a forum by which students can share their research with the class in a meaningful way, such as by a panel discussion. **L2**

Pankhurst and her two daughters, Christabel and Sylvia, founded the Women's Social and Political Union (WSPU). They led a voting rights campaign on behalf of all British women and became known as suffragettes. The WSPU attracted attention to its cause through street demonstrations and hunger strikes. The violence cost the movement much support. Nevertheless, the movement grew. In 1918 Parliament finally granted women over 30—along with all men—the right to vote. Ten years later, it gave the vote to all women over 21.

Ireland

Like others in the British Isles, Irish Catholics sought greater participation in the government. Their ultimate goal, however, was to govern themselves. For centuries, English and Scots Protestants who had settled in **Ireland** enjoyed almost total political and economic control of the island. This privileged minority owned large amounts of land. They rented it at high prices to Irish Catholic peasants, who were prohibited from purchasing land. Most Irish people lived in poverty. Ireland was predominantly Catholic, and a law requiring Catholics to pay taxes to the Anglican Church of Ireland only intensified anti-British feeling.

In 1801 Parliament had passed the Act of Union, joining Ireland and Great Britain. This union entitled Ireland to representation in Parliament, but it was not until 1829 that Catholics in the British Isles won the right to vote and hold office. Although these acts increased their rights, most Irish people still demanded to rule themselves.

Irish hatred of British rule heightened when a disastrous potato famine known as the "Great Hunger" hit the country in the 1840s. Because peasants were forced to export the grain they grew in order to pay their high rents, they came to rely on the potato as their main source of food. In 1845 a deadly fungus destroyed much of the potato crop,

 Visualizing History Irish activists seeking home rule riot in Belfast in 1872. *What minority group controlled most of the land in Ireland for centuries?*

and the British government sent inadequate aid to Ireland during the famine. In four years, at least one million Irish died of starvation and disease. Millions more emigrated to the United States, Canada, and Australia.

Various groups fought for Irish rights. **Charles Stewart Parnell**—Irish-born member of a Protestant family—led Irish nationalists who sought to have the question of home rule, or self-government, heard in Parliament. Liberal Prime Minister Gladstone tried to pass legislation granting Irish home rule. His action split the Liberal party, and the measure was defeated. In 1914 Parliament finally passed a home rule bill, but it never went into effect. Irish Protestants threatened to fight British troops if Parliament enforced it.

| SECTION 1 REVIEW |

Recall
1. **Define** apportion, disenfranchised, suffragette, home rule.
2. **Identify** the Chartists, Anti-Corn Law League, Queen Victoria, William Gladstone, Benjamin Disraeli, the Fabians,

Emmeline Pankhurst, Charles Stewart Parnell.
3. **List** three democratic reforms that occurred in Great Britain during the 1800s.
Critical Thinking
4. **Synthesizing Information** Imagine that you are an Irish

Catholic farmworker living in Ireland in the 1800s. Express your feelings and attitudes about the British government.
Understanding Themes
5. **Change** What might have happened if Parliament had opposed democratic reform?

SECTION 1 REVIEW ANSWERS

1. All vocabulary words are defined in the Glossary.
2. Chartists, 425; Anti-Corn Law League, 425; Queen Victoria, 425; William Gladstone, 425; Benjamin Disraeli, 425; the Fabians, 426; Emmeline Pankhurst, 427; Charles Stewart Parnell, 427
3. Reform Act of 1832, civil service reform of

1870, Ballot Act of 1872
4. Answers will vary but should include a sense of anger and frustration.
5. **CHANGE** Answers will vary. Possible answer: British lower classes might have staged a revolution against the wealthy ruling classes.

Chapter 14
Section 1

ASSESS

Check for Understanding
Assign Section 1 Review as homework or as an in-class activity.

Use Student Self-Test and Review Software to review Section 1.

Visualizing History The population of the city of Belfast in 1872 was largely Protestant with much opposition to home rule.
Answer to Caption: *English and Scots Protestants*

Evaluate
Section Quiz 14-1

Use the Testmaker to create a customized quiz for Section 1.

Reteach
Have students review the material and write one sentence that summarizes the key idea under each heading in the section.

Enrich
Have students imagine that they are journalists working for a political magazine in the 1830s. Have them write an article on the growth of democracy in Great Britain, focusing on the people who have recently been given the vote and those who are still struggling to obtain it.

CLOSE

Have students write six newspaper headlines that report the main ideas discussed in this section.

1850   1875   1900   1925

1840 Treaty of Waitangi guarantees Maori rights in New Zealand.

1867 British North America Act forms the Dominion of Canada.

1885 Canadian Pacific Railway links eastern and western parts of Canada.

1901 Australia becomes a dominion in the British Empire.

SECTION THEME

▶ **Movement** Immigrants from Great Britain and other countries settle Canada, Australia, and New Zealand.

Find Out

Answer: *Settlers in Canada, Australia, and New Zealand sought self-government, developed the natural resources, and enlarged the areas of British settlement.*

FOCUS

Section Objective

Relate how new societies emerged in Canada, Australia, and New Zealand.

BELLRINGER
Motivational Activity

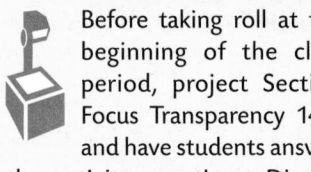

Before taking roll at the beginning of the class period, project Section Focus Transparency 14-2 and have students answer the activity questions. Discuss students' responses.

This activity is also available as a blackline master.

Vocabulary Pre-check

Use Vocabulary Activity 14 to introduce vocabulary terms.
L1 LEP

Section 2

The Dominions

Setting the Scene

▶ **Terms to Define**
dominion

▶ **People to Meet**
the Loyalists, Lord Durham, John A. Macdonald, the Aborigines, the Maori

▶ **Places to Locate**
Canada, Australia, New Zealand

 How did new societies emerge in Canada, Australia, and New Zealand?

The Storyteller

On the long sea voyage to Australia, first-class passengers could go anywhere on board; other passengers, traveling more cheaply, were more restricted. Seamen were most restricted of all, and after three months on board, got their revenge for staying below-deck in curious ways.

Sometimes the crew would protest their rights by tossing a pig or sheep down among the cabins at night, to invade the passengers' space and keep them awake. One emigrant wrote in her diary: "From every quarter of the cabin you could hear the 'Ma, Ma' during the greater part of the night."

—adapted from *Sailing to Australia*, Andrew Hassam, 1994

Immigrant mother and children

As Great Britain moved toward greater democracy, the British Empire reached its height. With its colonies making up one-fourth of the world's land and people, Great Britain became the richest and most powerful country in the world. Political changes also took place in the empire, especially in territories largely inhabited by British settlers. Colonies such as **Canada**, **Australia**, and **New Zealand** sought self-government.

Canada

By the mid-1800s, Canada consisted of a number of British colonies dependent on the British government. The colonial population was ethnically divided. One part was French, another immigrant British, and a third part descendants of **the Loyalists**—Americans loyal to Great Britain during the American Revolution. Most Britons and Loyalists lived in Nova Scotia, New Brunswick, and near the Great Lakes. The French were concentrated in the Saint Lawrence River valley.

In 1763, as a prize for their victory in the French and Indian War, the British gained control of Quebec, which included most of French Canada. From that time, the French in Quebec firmly resisted British colonial rule. The predominantly Catholic French population were irritated by the influx of British immigrants, English-speaking and Protestant, that began about 1760.

To solve the growing English and French problem, the British government passed the Constitutional Act of 1791. This law divided Quebec into two colonies: Lower Canada and Upper Canada. Lower Canada remained French-speaking, but Upper Canada became English. Each colony had an assembly whose laws were subject to veto by a governor appointed by the British government. This arrangement worked until political differences brought rebellion in each colony.

428 Chapter 14 *Democracy and Reform*

SECTION RESOURCES

📁 Reproducible Masters
- Reproducible Lesson Plan 14-2
- Vocabulary Activity 14
- Guided Reading Activity 14-2
- Geography and History Activity 14
- Section Quiz 14-2

Transparencies
- Section Focus Transparency 14-2

Multimedia
- Student Self-Test and Review Software
- Testmaker
- World Music: Cultural Traditions, Lesson 10

Visualizing History Quebec City, founded in 1608, is Canada's oldest city. Located on the St. Lawrence River, Quebec City was a major lumber and ship-building center during the 1800s. *What three groups contributed to the founding of Canada?*

TEACH

Guided Practice

THEME Movement

Ask students to recall other periods or places where two cultures clashed as a result of colonization. *(the Spanish and the Aztec; British colonists and Native Americans)* Point out that culture clashes occurred in the British dominions. Ask students to predict how these clashes might affect the indigenous peoples in the Dominions. *(Colonization usually results in negative effects on native peoples.)* **L2**

Visualizing History

It was in the mid-1820s that unemployment in Britain and Ireland spurred a great migration to Canada. Many of the people who came were fairly wealthy and educated.
Answer to Caption: *French-speaking settlers, American Loyalists and their descendants, and British settlers*

🎵 World Music: Cultural Traditions, Lesson 10

THE HISTORY CHANNEL.

The following videotape program is available from Glencoe:

• **Transcontinental Railroads**

To find classroom resources to accompany this video, check the following home page:
The History Channel: http://www.historychannel. com

By the late 1830s the French began to feel threatened by the growing English-speaking minority. Meanwhile, the British-Loyalist community was divided by disagreements between the conservative upper-class leadership and a group of liberal reformers who wanted a share in government. In 1837 unrest triggered rebellions in both colonies.

Canadian Self-Government

Uprisings in both Upper Canada and Lower Canada convinced the British that they had a serious problem in North America. In 1838 the British Parliament ordered **Lord Durham** to Canada to investigate. In a report to Parliament, Durham urged granting virtual self-government to Canada. Durham insisted that the real authority should be an elected assembly, not a British-appointed governor-general or the British government in London. With acceptance of the Durham report by the British Parliament, self-government developed in Canada. This pattern was later adopted by other territories of the British Empire.

In 1867 the British Parliament passed the British North America Act. This law established Canada as a dominion, or a self-governing territory owing allegiance to the British king or queen. The British North America Act joined Upper Canada (Ontario), Lower Canada (Quebec), Nova Scotia, and New Brunswick in a confederation called the Dominion of Canada. This act became the basis of the modern nation of Canada. In that same year, Canadian voters elected their first parliament. The first Canadian prime minister was **John A. Macdonald**, a Scottish-born lawyer.

Expanding Canadian Territory

At first the Dominion of Canada consisted of four provinces in the southeast, extending from the Great Lakes to the Atlantic Ocean. Then, in 1869 the dominion acquired the Northwest Territory, which extended west across vast prairies and forestlands and north to the Arctic wilderness. Most of this area was populated by Native Americans and European and American fur traders. Following sporadic violence between traders and Native Americans, the Canadian government set up and sent westward a special law-keeping force known as the Northwest Mounted Police. The police largely won the respect and loyalty of the Native Americans before the arrival of large numbers of Canadian settlers.

Canada further expanded its territory during the late 1800s. From the eastern part of the Northwest Territory, the province of Manitoba was formed in 1870. In 1871 British Columbia, a separate British colony on the Pacific coast, became a province. In 1873 tiny Prince Edward Island near the Atlantic Ocean joined Canada. To link the eastern provinces with the western provinces, the Canadian Pacific Railway was completed in 1885. This made possible the development of the Canadian prairies. In 1905 the prairie provinces of Saskatchewan and Alberta were added to the dominion.

Australia and New Zealand

On the other side of the world—in the south and southwest Pacific—the British colonies of Australia and New Zealand also sought self-government.

Chapter 14 *Democracy and Reform* **429**

COOPERATIVE LEARNING ACTIVITY

Documentary Have students work in groups to develop a television documentary on the settlement of Australia or New Zealand. In each group (one for Australia and one for New Zealand) have students take on the roles of writers, researchers, on-location reporters, British settlers, native groups, and British government officials. Other students in each group may produce maps and other graphic materials. Have students research information as necessary and then write and produce the documentary. If possible, record the performance on videotape. **L2** 📦

Independent Practice

 Guided Reading Activity
14-2 **L1**

 Geography and History
Activity 14

Multicultural Have students
imagine themselves as settlers in
one of the Dominions. Ask them
to write letters describing their
lives to friends in Great Britain.
Suggest that students describe
their work, their relationship
with native people and other settlers, their remoteness from
England, and the rigors of living
on a frontier. **L2**

ASSESS

Check for Understanding

Assign Section 2 Review as homework or as an in-class activity.

■ Use Student Self-Test and
Review Software to review
Section 2.

Evaluate

 Section Quiz 14-2

■ Use the Testmaker to create a
customized quiz for Section 2.

Reteach

Have students create a time line
documenting the development of
the British dominions.

Enrich

Have students research the work-
ing of modern government in
Canada, Australia, or New
Zealand.

CLOSE

Ask students to write an essay
summarizing changes in the
Dominions during the 1800s.

Footnotes to History

Australian Language
Australian English has its
own unique words: some
come from the Aboriginal languages; others from
the experiences of European settlers in the outback—the dry, open Australian interior. "Waltzing
Matilda," Australia's best-known song, captures
the flavor of Australian speech in this region:
> "Once a jolly swagman [hobo] camped by a
> billabong [waterhole]
> Under the shade of a coolibah tree,
> And he sang as he watched and waited till
> his billy [milkpail] boiled
> Who'll come a-waltzing Matilda [tramp the
> roads carrying a blanket roll] with me?"

Australia

Initially, Great Britain established Australia as a
prisoners' colony to relieve overcrowded British jails.
By 1860, after a gold rush lured new immigrants, the
population reached 1 million, and the practice of
transporting prisoners to Australia was abolished.

In settling the land, Europeans came into contact with **the Aborigines**, the original people of
Australia. Many early European settlers treated the
Aborigines badly, occupied their land, and killed
many of them. Large numbers of Aborigines died
from diseases introduced by the Europeans.

The increase in European settlement called for
a better administration of colonial Australia. By the
late 1800s Australia was made up of six British
colonies—New South Wales, Victoria, Queensland,
Tasmania, Western Australia, and South Australia.
In 1901 Parliament made Australia a dominion that
included the colonies plus a region known as the
Northern Territory.

New Zealand

The first Europeans to settle in New Zealand
were from James Cook's expedition in 1770.
Hunters from Great Britain and the United States
set up whaling stations during the 1790s. New
Zealand also attracted timber traders.

Foreigners brought many problems to the original inhabitants, known as **the Maori**. Firearms, for
example, increased warfare among the Maori tribes.
Foreigners also brought diseases to which the Maori
had no immunity, causing an almost 50 percent
reduction in the Maori population in 20 years.

In an effort to provide law for the Maori and
the settlers, British naval officers and Maori chiefs
concluded the Treaty of Waitangi in 1840. The treaty
protected Maori rights, including property rights,
while the Maori gave the British sovereignty over
New Zealand. In 1840 the first permanent British
settlements were founded at Wellington and
Wanganui. Their economies were based on wool
exports to British markets.

As with Australia, New Zealand's British population was small until the discovery of gold. The
gold discovery also brought conflict between the
newcomers and the Maori.

Prospectors unsuccessful in finding gold in
New Zealand remained to farm. To gain more land,
they violated those Maori land rights guaranteed
by the treaty with the British. During the Maori
Wars in the mid-1800s, the New Zealand government sided with the newcomers and seized some
Maori land for public use.

New Zealand received a constitution from Great
Britain in 1852 and became a largely self-governing
colony. In the 1890s, the New Zealand government
carried out an extensive program of social reforms,
such as pensions for the elderly and protection of
workers' rights. At this time Great Britain itself had
not yet introduced many of these reforms. In 1907
New Zealand finally became a dominion within the
British Empire.

SECTION 2 REVIEW

Recall
1. **Define** dominion.
2. **Identify** the Loyalists, Lord
   Durham, John A. Macdonald,
   British North America Act,
   Northwest Mounted Police,
   the Aborigines, the Maori,
   Treaty of Waitangi.
3. **State** the terms of the Treaty
   of Waitangi. Were its terms
   carried out?

Critical Thinking
4. **Evaluating Information** The
   Canadians at first wanted to
   call their confederation "the
   Kingdom of Canada." The
   British government, however,
   suggested the term *dominion*
   because they felt *kingdom*
   would be offensive to the
   United States. Why might
   Americans find *kingdom* an
   offensive title?

Understanding Themes
5. **Movement** What was the
   original purpose for British
   settlement of Australia?

---

430 Chapter 14 *Democracy and Reform*

SECTION 2 REVIEW ANSWERS

1. All vocabulary words are defined in the
   Glossary.
2. Loyalists, 428; Durham, 429; Macdonald,
   429; British North America Act, 429;
   Mounted Police, 429; Aborigines, 430;
   Maori, 430; Waitangi, 430
3. The treaty protected Maori rights, including
   property rights, and gave the ownership of

New Zealand to the British. The terms were
violated; British settlers later took Maori
lands with the backing of the government.
4. Americans had fought to be independent
   from the "kingdom" of Great Britain and
   favored republican governments.
5. **MOVEMENT** Australia was a prisoners' colony.

1830 Revolution overthrows Bourbon dynasty.

1848 Voters elect Louis-Napoleon president.

1870 Revolutionaries establish Commune of Paris.

1890s The Dreyfus affair divides French society.

Section 3

Political Struggles in France

Setting the Scene

▶ **Terms to Define**
ultraroyalist, coup d'état, plebiscite

▶ **People to Meet**
Charles X, Louis Philippe, Louis-Napoleon, General Georges Boulanger, Alfred Dreyfus

▶ **Places to Locate**
Paris

 What changes in government did France undergo during the 1800s?

The Storyteller

Louis-Napoleon Bonaparte (Emperor Napoleon III) had grand ideas for the government of France—including a grand role for himself. Of course, he would not revive the excesses of royalty that France had groaned under before. Still, Frenchmen could not help but notice that his plans for the new constitution of France included the following ideas: "The executive power vests in the Emperor alone. The Emperor is the supreme head of the state; he commands the national forces both on land and sea; declares war, makes treaties of peace, of alliance, and of commerce...."

—adapted from *The Political and Historical Works of Louis Napoleon Bonaparte*, Volume 1, 1852

Louis-Napoleon Bonaparte

The Congress of Vienna sought to reduce France's might and restore traditional monarchs to their thrones. Although the European balance of power was restored, Congress delegates found their plans for monarchy frustrated as liberal and nationalist ideas spread among the peoples of Europe. The clash between old and new ideologies, or systems of thought and belief, sparked revolutions throughout Europe from the 1820s to the 1840s.

 **POINT**

Revolt in France

Because of its revolutionary traditions, France was the center point of these upheavals. In 1815 the Congress of Vienna restored the Bourbon monarchy under Louis XVIII. Many French republicans accepted Louis because he was willing to rule as a constitutional monarch.

After Louis's death in 1824, his brother and successor **Charles X** set out to restore absolute monarchy—with help from the ultraroyalists—nobles favoring a return to the old order. When Charles tried to repay nobles for lands lost during the revolution, liberals in the legislative assembly opposed him. The king then dissolved the assembly and held new elections; but voters only elected more liberals to reject Charles's policies. Finally the king issued the July Ordinances, measures designed to dissolve the assembly, end press freedom, and restrict voting rights.

On July 27, 1830, angry Parisian workers and students rose up against the king. By July 29, after *Les Trois Glorieuses* (three glorious days) they forced

SECTION THEME

▶ **Revolution** France undergoes political upheaval during the 1800s.

ind Out

Answer: *France went from a monarchy to the Second Empire, to the Commune, and finally to a republic.*

FOCUS

Section Objective

Identify the changes in government that France underwent during the 1800s.

BELLRINGER
Motivational Activity

Before taking roll, project Section Focus Transparency 14-3 and have students answer the activity questions.

This activity is also available as a blackline master.

Vocabulary Pre-check

Use Vocabulary Activity 14 to introduce vocabulary terms.
L1 LEP

TEACH

Guided Practice

THEME Revolution

Based on their knowledge of the French Revolution, guide students in a discussion about how the events described in this section can be called a continuation of the original French Revolution of 1789. *(French people revolted against monarchy installed after Napoleon's downfall.)* **L1 LEP**

POINT

Revolt in France
Why were political developments in France during the early 1800s influential in other areas of Europe?
France became a model of democratic political action. Upheavals there against monarchical government sparked similar uprisings against royal authority in other parts of Europe.

Visualizing History The 1848 uprising lasted three days. Louis Philippe had called the National Guard to keep order, but they sided with the rioters, and the municipal police force was too small to control the citizens. The mobs took over. This was considered a fairly bloodless revolution as revolutions go.
Answer to Caption: *It was replaced by an empire headed by Louis-Napoleon Bonaparte.*

Chart Guide students in making a chart to organize the succession of French governments presented in this section. Use the following heads: *French Leader, Form of Government, Cause of Downfall.* **L2**

Visualizing History The Revolution of 1848 that began in France triggered revolts throughout Europe. *What happened to the Second Republic within four years of its constitution?*

Charles X to give up his right as monarch and abdicate the throne. The fallen king fled to Great Britain.

The "Citizen-King"

After the chaos had subsided, revolutionary leaders set up a new constitutional monarchy that did not have close ties to the old aristocracy. **Louis Philippe**, a cousin of Charles, accepted the throne. Because he dressed and behaved like a middle-class person, Louis Philippe became known as the "Citizen-King" and won the support of the growing middle class.

From 1830 to 1848, however, many French people became discontented with Louis Philippe's government. At heart, the "Citizen-King" favored the wealthy, and many working-class citizens began to demand political reforms, especially voting rights.

Louis Philippe refused their demands. When they appealed to Prime Minister François Guizot (gee•ZOH), he too refused. Frustrated, leaders organized political banquets, where they called for an extended vote and Guizot's resignation.

The Revolution of 1848

In 1848 Guizot canceled a banquet, fearing a demonstration. This order, however, came too late. On February 22, crowds flooded the streets, singing "The Marseillaise" and shouting protests against Guizot. Louis Philippe called in troops, but the soldiers sympathized with the rebels and joined them. Over the next days, at least 52 civilians were killed or wounded. The disturbances forced Louis Philippe to abdicate and flee to Great Britain. The Revolution of 1848 ended with the rebels proclaiming France a republic.

432 **Chapter 14** *Democracy and Reform*

Inspired by events in France, revolutionaries in other European countries also fought for greater political rights. Political discontent in Austria, Italy, and Prussia was particularly significant. In these areas, however, the political status quo was more or less maintained despite the uprisings.

The Second Empire

When the political turmoil in France had finally subsided, the revolutionary leaders proclaimed the Second Republic of France and set out to create a new constitution. The French constitution featured many democratic reforms, including a legislative branch called the National Assembly, the election of a president, and an extension of voting rights to all adult men. Nine million men eagerly set off to the polls to elect a new National Assembly in the spring of 1848. Only briefly, however, would the French enjoy the freedoms brought by the Second Republic.

The Rise of Louis-Napoleon

In presidential elections held in December 1848, French voters gave **Louis-Napoleon** Bonaparte, the nephew of Napoleon Bonaparte, an overwhelming victory. Louis-Napoleon's popularity came more from his name than from his political skills. The name "Napoleon" reminded the French people of the greatness their nation had once enjoyed under Napoleon I.

Although Louis-Napoleon presented himself as a democratic reformer, the president hoped to use his popularity to make himself an emperor. To guarantee victory, Louis-Napoleon worked to win

COOPERATIVE LEARNING ACTIVITY

News Broadcast Organize students into broadcast teams to provide coverage of the revolutions in France. Each team should divide up responsibility to research and prepare stories that provide a rounded picture of events in one of the revolutions. Each team member should have a role as a news anchor, on-the-scene reporter, or subject of an interview. Have teams report on events, reactions of royalists, republicans, leaders, and the person-in-the-street. Remind students to base their reports on actual events and actual people when possible. Have them write scripts and present their broadcasts to the class. You may want to videotape the presentations. **L2**

the support of powerful groups in France—the army, the Church, the middle class, and the peasants. For example, in 1849 he won the confidence of French Catholics by ordering French troops to help the pope suppress an attempt by Italian nationalists to set up a republic in Rome. He also gave the Church more control over French education.

This support for the Catholics, however, created an uproar in **Paris**. Demonstrators opposing support for the pope filled the streets. Alarmed by the mob action, the National Assembly restricted people's rights in order to keep law and order. They also revoked voting rights for about a third of the voters.

Louis-Napoleon used this uproar to his advantage by convincing the French people that the republic was a failure. Deciding to take control of the French government, Louis-Napoleon directed a coup d'état, or a quick seizure of power, on December 2, 1851. He dissolved the National Assembly and arrested many of his opponents. With shrewd planning, he won popular support by reestablishing voting rights for all French men.

Louis-Napoleon then called for a plebiscite, or national vote, asking the people to give him the power to create a new French constitution. The people enthusiastically gave him their support. Now Louis-Napoleon had complete legislative and executive control, and the people appeared happy with the order and stability he provided. In a second plebiscite, a large percentage of the people approved the transformation of the French republic into a hereditary empire. In 1852 Louis-Napoleon became Napoleon III, Emperor of France.

Although Napoleon III restricted the press and limited civil liberties, he had a successful economic program. During the 1850s French industrial growth doubled and foreign trade tripled. France built new railroads and roads, including Paris's famous wide boulevards.

The Crimean War

In 1854 Napoleon III led France into the Crimean War. The war pitted France and Great Britain against Russia and arose from the interests that all three countries had in the Ottoman Empire. The immediate cause of the conflict was a dispute between France and Russia over which of them had the right to protect Christians in the empire or those visiting the Holy Land. In this dispute the Ottoman emperor sided with France.

Angered by the decision, Russia's Czar Nicholas I in July 1853 seized Ottoman territory in the Balkans. This Russian invasion upset both Great Britain and France, who wanted to protect their trade and financial interests in the Middle East. After the

Ottoman Empire declared war on Russia in October 1853, Great Britain, France, and the tiny Italian kingdom of Sardinia eventually joined the conflict.

In the fall of 1854, French and British armies invaded the Russian-ruled Crimean Peninsula on the north shore of the Black Sea. At first, little fighting occurred as the armies battled cold, violent storms, and disease. By war's end, disease would cause more deaths on both sides than war injuries. Among British forces, however, a nurse, Florence Nightingale, improved hospital care and saved many lives. In the fall of 1855, French and British forces finally defeated the Russians, who lacked supplies, reinforcements, and railroads. The 1856 Treaty of Paris ending the war made Russia return some of the Ottoman territory it had seized and banned warships and forts around the Black Sea.

End of the Empire

In 1870 conflict with Prussia ended Napoleon III's empire. Alarmed by Prussia's growing power, Napoleon made his most costly error in judgment: he declared war on the Prussians on July 19, 1870.

Few French or foreign observers anticipated the quick and relatively easy defeat of France in the Franco-Prussian War. The French armies were slow to mobilize, and German forces crossed into France with little armed resistance. The Prussians defeated the French in just over six weeks. On September 2, after winning a decisive victory at Sedan, the Prussians took Napoleon III as prisoner.

History & Art *The Siege of Paris* by Ernest Meissonier. The Louvre, Paris, France *What impact did the Franco-Prussian conflict of 1870–1871 have on France and the government of Napoleon III?*

Independent Practice

📁 Guided Reading Activity 14-3 **L1**

Daily Life Have students work in small groups and take the roles of ordinary French people in the late 1800s. Have them role-play casual conversations in which they reveal the average person's thoughts about the political events of the day. **L2**

Critical Thinking Ask students to list factors that contributed to the revolutions described in this section. **L3**

History & Art Two million Parisians were cut off from all contact with the outside world during the siege. The Prussians formed a continuous front of about 52 miles with 150,000 men and 700 guns. How might the four-month siege have affected people's daily lives? *(They would have been cut off from food and fuel supplies and suffered severe hardships.)*
Answer to Caption: *France was easily defeated by Prussia, and the government of Napoleon III collapsed.*

Who?What?Where?When?

Florence Nightingale became a nurse at a time when it was not considered a noble profession, and in 1854 led a group of British nurses to the Crimean War. Her efforts at the battle zone transformed the appalling conditions and won her worldwide fame. In 1864 she helped inspire the organization of the International Red Cross.

MEETING SPECIAL NEEDS ACTIVITY

Study Strategy To help students learn the information in this section, suggest that they outline it. They should list each major head and any subheads, leaving space under these heads to write the key figures, dates, and events as they read about them. They should look up words they do not understand and write the definitions to reinforce remembering them. They might continue this strategy with other chapters. **L1**

CURRICULUM CONNECTION

LITERATURE

The author of *Les Misérables*, Victor Hugo, was banished to the Channel Island of Guernsey for opposing Louis-Napoleon. His famous novel portrays nineteenth-century problems and events of France during the post-Napoleonic period.

The Development of Photography

Tell students that in 1839 in France, photographs were displayed for the first time. By the 1850s, photographers were heading west in the United States and recording the frontier. They carried bulky cameras and used glass plates for negatives instead of small rolls of film as are used today. The photographer's covered wagon served as a darkroom.

ANSWER

Photography provided them with exact images of people and events. Answers will vary. Possible answer: Photography has a major influence on people's lives given the importance of television.

When the news of the emperor's capture reached Paris on September 4, crowds filled the streets and forced the collapse of the Second Empire. The people of Paris endured a Prussian siege for four months before a truce was signed.

Making Peace With Prussia

The French people elected a new National Assembly, dominated by royalists, to make peace with Prussia. The Assembly surrendered the provinces of Alsace and Lorraine and agreed to pay 5 billion francs—the equivalent of 1 billion dollars—to Prussia. Prussian forces further humiliated France by staging a victory march through Paris. The people of Paris, strong republicans who wanted a renewal of the war with Prussia instead of peace, were angered by the peace terms. They sank into despair after their loss.

In March the National Assembly set about restoring order in France, particularly in Paris. The provisional government inspired an angry outcry when it demanded that Parisians pay the rents and the debts that had been suspended during the siege. At the same time, the Assembly stopped payments to the National Guard, which many Parisian workers had joined during the Prussian siege. These drastic measures led to unrest and to an uprising in Paris.

The Commune of Paris

During the revolt, the workers established a Socialist government known as the Commune of Paris. The leaders of the Commune refused to recognize the National Assembly and called for the conversion of France into a decentralized federation of independent cities. The Commune declared war on the propertied classes and the Church. It advocated an end to government support for religion, the adoption of a new revolutionary calendar, and the introduction of a 10-hour workday.

In a bitter civil war, the National Assembly took the offensive and reasserted its control over Paris. Armies pushed past the Commune's barricades throughout the strife-ridden city. In defiance, the supporters of the Commune burned public buildings, including the Tuileries Palace and the City Hall. During the "Bloody Week" in May 1871, the Assembly's powerful military forces arrested nearly 40,000 people and killed more than 20,000. The horror of rebellion set back the political and social advances made by workers and caused distrust between France's middle and working classes.

CONNECTIONS

Science and Technology

The Development of Photography

Early Camera

For centuries scientists tried to record lasting images, but it was not until 1826 that the world's first camera was made. Its inventor, the Frenchman Joseph Niépce, produced a blurry image of a farmyard by coating a metal plate with a light-sensitive chemical. In 1837 Louis Daguerre perfected Niépce's methods and fixed an image on silver-coated copper. Daguerreotypes, as these images were called, produced detailed pictures.

Photography progressed rapidly throughout the 1800s. Some photographers took portraits of wealthy families. Others risked their lives photographing the horrors of war. Gradually scientific and technical discoveries made cameras more efficient and easier to operate. In 1888 George Eastman developed the small, lightweight, and relatively inexpensive box camera. Mass-produced, the box camera put photography into the hands of millions.

Today, a picture can be taken simply by aiming the camera and pressing a button. In sophistication, cameras range from simple fixed-focus models to ones that have many lenses and built-in features.

 **ACTIVITY**

Discuss how photography helped people record their lives in the 1800s. In what ways does photography affect events today? Consider the power of the media.

MAKING CONNECTIONS ACTIVITIES

Science and Technology Have students investigate the photographic process. Have them present their findings to the class in the form of a detailed diagram that shows the stages of the printing process. **L2**

Photography Students can research the lives and the work of pioneers in photography. Examples include Mathew Brady and his photographs during the Civil War, George Eastman and the development of the Eastman-Kodak company, or Julia Cameron, a British pioneer of portrait photography. Have students present their findings to the class. **L2**

The Third Republic

After the fall of the Commune, the dispirited French again tried to rebuild their government. This proved to be a difficult task, as royalists and republicans alike fought bitterly over the form the government should take.

Finally, in 1875 a new constitution made France once again a republic. The Third Republic's constitution provided for a two-house legislature. The two houses elected a president, who served for four years and who had little real power. Every official act required the full support of both houses of the legislature to be signed into law. A cabinet of ministers was responsible for government policy, and the post of premier was created to handle all executive business.

Threats to the Republic

Although France had finally established itself as a republic, the new government was particularly vulnerable to attack. One of its greatest threats came from **General Georges Boulanger** (BOO •lahn•ZHAY), who was a popular war hero. Boulanger urged the French people to seek revenge against Prussia. He launched a campaign to demand the election of a new legislature in 1888.

Boulanger won great support from royalists and others who opposed the republic. In 1889 his supporters urged him to overthrow the Third Republic with a coup d'état. When the government ordered him arrested for treason, Boulanger fled the country to Belgium. Without the direction of its popular leader, the Boulanger movement collapsed.

A second threat to the republic in the early 1890s centered around the construction of a canal through Panama. The canal would provide France with a waterway connecting the Atlantic and Pacific Oceans.

When the Panama Company collapsed and the Panama project failed, thousands of French stockholders lost all of the money they had invested. Charges of dishonesty and poor managerial practices erupted. The scandal spread to the highest government offices, as members of both houses were accused of accepting bribes to get more funding for the troubled project. The Panama scandal partly benefited France's growing Socialist movement. In 1893 nearly 50 Socialists won seats in the national legislature.

The Dreyfus Affair

The 1890s saw the Third Republic's greatest crisis—the Dreyfus affair. In 1894 **Alfred Dreyfus**, a French army officer, was convicted by a military court of selling military secrets to the Germans and sentenced to a life term on Devil's Island, a prison colony off the coast of French Guiana in South America. The French army was, at the time, influenced by anti-Semitic views, and its suspicion had fallen on Dreyfus, who was Jewish.

Dreyfus, however, protested his innocence and it soon became known that another officer was the real traitor and that the official evidence used in Dreyfus's trial had been forged. In an article, "*J'accuse* (I Accuse)", the novelist Émile Zola took a strong stand in support of Dreyfus. In 1899 a new trial was ordered, but the military court, unable to admit error, found Dreyfus guilty once again. This time, Dreyfus won a presidential pardon, and a civilian court later declared him innocent.

While it lasted, the Dreyfus affair deeply divided France. Republicans, Socialists, and anti-Catholics united to defend Dreyfus and to discredit the military. Wanting to uphold the army's honor, royalists, nationalists, and many Catholics joined anti-Semites—those hostile to Jews—in regarding Dreyfus as guilty.

Despite its divisiveness, the Dreyfus affair proved that republican government was able to survive in France. The immediate effect of the affair was to bring to power radical republicans and Socialists, who carried out changes such as the separation of church and state in 1905.

SECTION 3 REVIEW

Recall

1. **Define** ultraroyalist, coup d'état, plebiscite.
2. **Identify** Charles X, Louis Philippe, Louis-Napoleon, Commune of Paris, General Georges Boulanger, Alfred Dreyfus.

3. **Explain** how the French government changed under the rule of Louis-Napoleon.

Critical Thinking

4. **Analyzing Information** Why was the government of the Third Republic especially vulnerable to political opposition?

Understanding Themes

5. **Revolution** Trace France's political history during the 1800s. What factors sparked revolutions in 1830 and 1848? What impact did these revolutions have on the rest of Europe?

Chapter 14 Democracy and Reform **435**

ASSESS

Check for Understanding

Assign Section 3 Review as homework or as an in-class activity.

 Use Student Self-Test and Review Software to review Section 3.

Evaluate

Section Quiz 14-3

Reteach

Have students review the section and create an outline of events.

Enrich

Ask students to write a short story about France during the nineteenth century. They should use historical events as the backdrop for their stories.

CLOSE

Have students draw a series of political cartoons reflecting the changes in French government from the Revolution of 1830 to the creation of the Third Republic in 1875.

SECTION 3 REVIEW ANSWERS

1. All vocabulary words are defined in the Glossary.
2. Charles X, 431; Louis Philippe, 432; Louis-Napoleon, 432; Commune of Paris, 434; General Georges Boulanger, 435; Alfred Dreyfus, 435
3. It became an empire under an autocratic emperor.
4. It was young and unstable.
5. **REVOLUTION** France went from a constitutional monarchy to a republic to an empire to a republic. The revolutions were sparked by popular discontent with monarchies that limited democratic expression. The revolutions in France stirred similar uprisings in other parts of the continent.

ind Out

Answer: *The United States grew in size, wealth, and power during the 1800s and went through a civil war that resulted from sectional conflicts.*

FOCUS

Section Objective

Explain how the United States changed during the 1800s.

**BELLRINGER
Motivational Activity**

Before taking roll at the beginning of the class period, project Section Focus Transparency 14-4 and have students answer the activity questions. Discuss students' responses.
⎙ This activity is also available as a blackline master.

Vocabulary Pre-check

⎙ Use Vocabulary Activity 14 to introduce vocabulary terms.
L1 LEP

1800   1850   1900

1803 The United States gains the Louisiana Purchase.

1846 War begins between the United States and Mexico.

1865 The Civil War ends.

c. 1890s Immigrants arrive in the United States from eastern and southern Europe.

Section 4
....

Expansion of the United States

Setting the Scene

▶ **Terms to Define**
sectionalism, secede, ratify

▶ **People to Meet**
Thomas Jefferson, Abraham Lincoln, Susan B. Anthony, Woodrow Wilson

▶ **Places to Locate**
Louisiana Purchase, Gadsden Purchase

 **ind Out**   How did the United States change during the 1800s?

The Storyteller

During the Civil War when Confederate casualties returned in large numbers from the front, buildings quickly became makeshift hospitals. Miss Sally Tomkins was one of the most tireless workers among the many brave women who served in the overcrowded places of mercy. As a "soldier without a gun," she received a commission in the Confederate Army as well as a commendation—the only such commission ever issued to a woman, and a unique "first" for any American army. In a note to the War Department, she said: "I accepted the commission … but would not allow my name to be placed on the payroll of the army."

—adapted from *A Pictorial History of the Confederacy*, Lamont Buchanan, 1951

Civil War nurse and patient

While many political upheavals shook Europe during the 1800s, the United States grew in size, wealth, and power. The vast area of forests and plains west of the original colonies lured American settlers by the thousands, and no European powers with colonial interests blocked their westward drive. The conflicts between European countries during the early years of the nation had created opportunities for the United States to acquire more territory.

The Young Nation Grows

The United States gained its biggest territorial prize as a result of Napoleon I's desire to conquer his most hated enemy, Great Britain. In 1803 Napoleon was preparing to go to war against Great Britain and needed money to finance it. Desperate for money, Napoleon offered to sell the French-owned Louisiana territory to the United States. With a quick stroke of the pen and a payment of $15 million, President **Thomas Jefferson** acquired the **Louisiana Purchase**—all the land between the Mississippi River and the Rocky Mountains. The area eventually formed 13 states.

The United States also gained land as a result of Spain's internal conflicts. Weakened by political and financial problems, Spain ceded, or gave up, Florida in 1819.

Later acquisitions of new land from other nations proved to be not so easy or peaceful. In 1845 the Republic of Texas was annexed to the United States. By 1846 this territorial gain resulted in a conflict between the United States and Mexico that escalated into war. The United States defeated the Mexicans in 1848, and in the resulting treaty Mexico gave up a vast area that later formed all of California, Utah, and Nevada and parts of

---

Denver Public Library, Western History Department

Pioneers

You can see the fatigue in the faces of these pioneers, moving West in Conestoga wagons. Prairie stretched behind them, mountains ahead—and an unbearable distance to go. From the settlement of Jamestown in 1607 to the settlement of the West two centuries later, Americans explored, moved, and endured unspeakable hardships. Their journeys stretched their endurance, as they battled hunger, Native Americans, and the difficulties of the terrain itself. The West was dry: Wood shrank; wheels fell off wagons; and the hooves of oxen split. "Dust is two or three inches in depth and as fine as flour," one pioneer wrote. "We cannot see the wagons

next to us...." Settled into new homes, the pioneers' hardships did not end. Families lived through winters so harsh that cows, sheathed in ice, had to be brought inside. Summers brought plagues of grasshoppers and prairie fires. And always there was isolation and loneliness.

By 1860 the United States stretched from the Atlantic to the Pacific. But expansion brought problems for the nation as well as benefits. The territory won in the Mexican-American War (1846–1848) shifted the issue of slavery into the political mainstream with such force that it took the Civil War to resolve the conflict between North and South. ⊕

Chapter 14 *Democracy and Reform* **437**

TEACH

Tell students that the first wagon trains to go West set out in 1841 from one of a number of towns in Missouri along the Missouri River called "jumping-off places." They headed toward Oregon or California. Supplies were fresh, animals were healthy, the Kansas prairie was flat, and this beginning part of the trip was the easiest. Hardships and fatigue came later on the trails. How do you think this pioneer life affected the lives of children? *(Answers will vary but may include that children grew up faster because they faced so many dangers and hardships at a young age and because they had to shoulder adult responsibilities for the good of their families.)*

Who? What? Where? When?

Willa Cather was a journalist and novelist who wrote many stories about the plains of Nebraska. At the age of nine, she had to move with her parents from Virginia to the West. She portrays the psychological trauma of that move in *My Ántonia*.

Guided Practice

 **Change**

Discuss with students the changes that occurred in the United States as it expanded rapidly. Emphasize the impact of rapid expansion and westward migration on daily life. Help them to visualize heading West without knowing much about your destination. **L1**

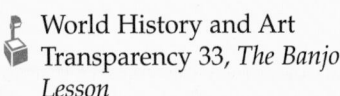

Rise of the United States
How did the United States increase its political power during the 1800s?
It expanded democratic rights, used its resources to build an economy based on agriculture and industry, and overcame divisions, although by means of a bloody civil war.

Geography: Movement Have students recall how the colonists slowly expanded their settlements along the east coast. Have students describe the stages in westward expansion. Point out that between 1607 and 1890, the idea of expansion was part of the American consciousness. Ask students what people mean today when they think of expansion. **L3**

World Music: Cultural Traditions, Lesson 1

World History and Art Transparency 33, *The Banjo Lesson*

Mapping History Overlay Transparency 16, *Global Ancestry of Americans*

Colorado, Arizona, Wyoming, and New Mexico. This large acquisition of territory added a sizable Hispanic population to the United States.

Farther north, the United States argued with Great Britain over the exact borders of the Oregon Country. In a treaty with Great Britain, the United States gained this vast region. Oregon, Washington, and Idaho, as well as parts of Wyoming and Montana, were later created from this territory.

By the mid-1800s, only one step remained in the country's move across the continent. In 1853 James Gadsden, the American ambassador to Mexico, gave Mexico $10 million for 45,000 square miles (116,550 sq. km) of land in southern New Mexico and Arizona, south of the Rio Grande.

With the **Gadsden Purchase**, the United States finally stretched from "sea to shining sea." This westward expansion brought new opportunities to settlers, who forged communities and built states in the new lands. The expansion also brought suffering—loss of land, culture, and often life—to Native Americans who had inhabited lands in the West for centuries.

Rise of the United States

As Americans moved westward, democratic rights in the United States expanded. When the nation was first founded, the right to vote and hold public office was generally restricted to white male property owners.

The people of the West sought to extend these voting rights. All of the new states adopted constitutions that granted the right to vote to all men. These new states gradually gained power in Congress, and, over time, their liberal policies influenced the country. By 1856 every state had granted all white men the vote.

An Expanding Economy

Many factors contributed to the rapid growth of the American economy. The Industrial Revolution, which began in Great Britain, spread to

Images *of the* Times

The Civil War

There had always been economic and cultural differences between the North and the South. In 1861 these differences led to the American Civil War, or the War Between the States.

Antislavery feeling in the North was stimulated by Harriet Beecher Stowe's *Uncle Tom's Cabin*, a novel portraying slavery at its worst. The book sold 300,000 copies in 1852, its first year of publication.

Union naval forces took New Orleans in May 1862. In the Civil War, both North and South suffered heavy losses, but the North's industrial strength gave it an advantage over the agricultural South.

438

Images *of the* Times   The Civil War

Harriet Beecher Stowe wrote most of *Uncle Tom's Cabin* in Brunswick, Maine; she had spent exactly one weekend in a slave state. Stowe said that the powerful death scene of Uncle Tom came to her in a vision while she was in church.

Although slavery was the primary moral issue dividing the North and the South, the abolition of slavery was not the main reason that hundreds of thousands of men joined the Northern army in the early days of the war. Most of them did not agree with the abolitionists; they viewed their own efforts as a struggle to preserve the Union.

the United States. Busy commercial regions filled with factories and heavily populated cities characterized the North. Irish, German, and Scandinavian immigrants joined the Northern workforce, settling in cities and farmlands. Northern workers received pay for their labor, as well as the right to leave their jobs for better ones. This system of work was called free labor.

In contrast, the South became the chief producer of raw cotton for the booming British textile industry. The South's economy remained primarily agricultural and depended on the labor of enslaved African Americans. Most white Southerners, even those who held no enslaved people, believed in slave labor. As the United States expanded, it was clear that the different economic interests of the two regions would cause conflict.

A Nation Divided

The differences in their economies led the two regions, the North and the South, to take widely different positions on many political and economic issues. The result was sectionalism, the devotion to the political and economic interest of a region or a section of the country. The most divisive issue, however, was slave labor. The South wanted to expand slavery into the territories gained during the Mexican War. The North wanted these new western areas to remain territories employing free labor.

By 1860 the United States consisted of 18 free states and 15 slave states. In the presidential election of 1860, proslavery and antislavery forces vied for power. When **Abraham Lincoln** won the presidency, the South feared he would abolish slavery.

To protest the election, South Carolina decided to secede, or withdraw, from the Union. Other Southern states followed suit. By February 8, 1861, seven states had joined to form their own nation, the Confederate States of America. In Washington, D.C., Congress worked on a compromise, but to no avail. When Lincoln was sworn in as President in March, he declared that "no state, upon its own mere motion, can lawfully get out of the Union." By April the divided nation was at war. The Civil

Union and Confederate caps reveal the war's colors: blue for the North (shown right), and gray for the South (shown left). More Americans died in the Civil War than in any other conflict in American history.

REFLECTING ON THE TIMES

1. What major issue helped spark conflict between the North and the South?
2. Why was the Civil War unique in American history?

439

Biography

The following videotape programs are available from Glencoe:

- **Lewis & Clark**
- **Crazy Horse**
- **Frederick Douglass**
- **Susan B. Anthony: Rebel for a Cause**

Independent Practice

Guided Reading Activity 14-4 **L1**

People in World History Profile 47

Critical Thinking Organize students into small groups to consider whether a state should have the right to withdraw from the United States. Have each group take one side of the issue and gather information. Then each group should choose a member to participate in a class debate on the issue. **L3**

Linking Past and Present

States' Rights Today United States government officials continue to disagree about whether certain issues, such as school integration, should be controlled by the federal or by the state government.

ANSWERS TO REFLECTING ON THE TIMES

1. slavery
2. It was a war fought on American soil.

Map Study

Answer

France, Spain, Britain, Russia

Map Skills Practice

Reading a Map Which acquisitions allowed the United States to stretch from "sea to shining sea"? *(Oregon Country, 1846; Mexican Cession, 1848; Gadsden Purchase, 1853)*

VIDEODISC
Lessons of War

Side One, Chapter 4
Frames 8662–11204
Title: *Why Soldiers Fight*
Subject: Discussion and images of what motivates soldiers to fight
Ask: What motivates people to volunteer in the armed services? *(Most volunteer because they feel a sense of patriotic duty and loyalty to their country.)*

ASSESS

Check for Understanding

Assign Section 4 Review as homework or as an in-class activity.

 Use Student Self-Test and Review Software to review Section 4.

Evaluate

Section Quiz 14-4

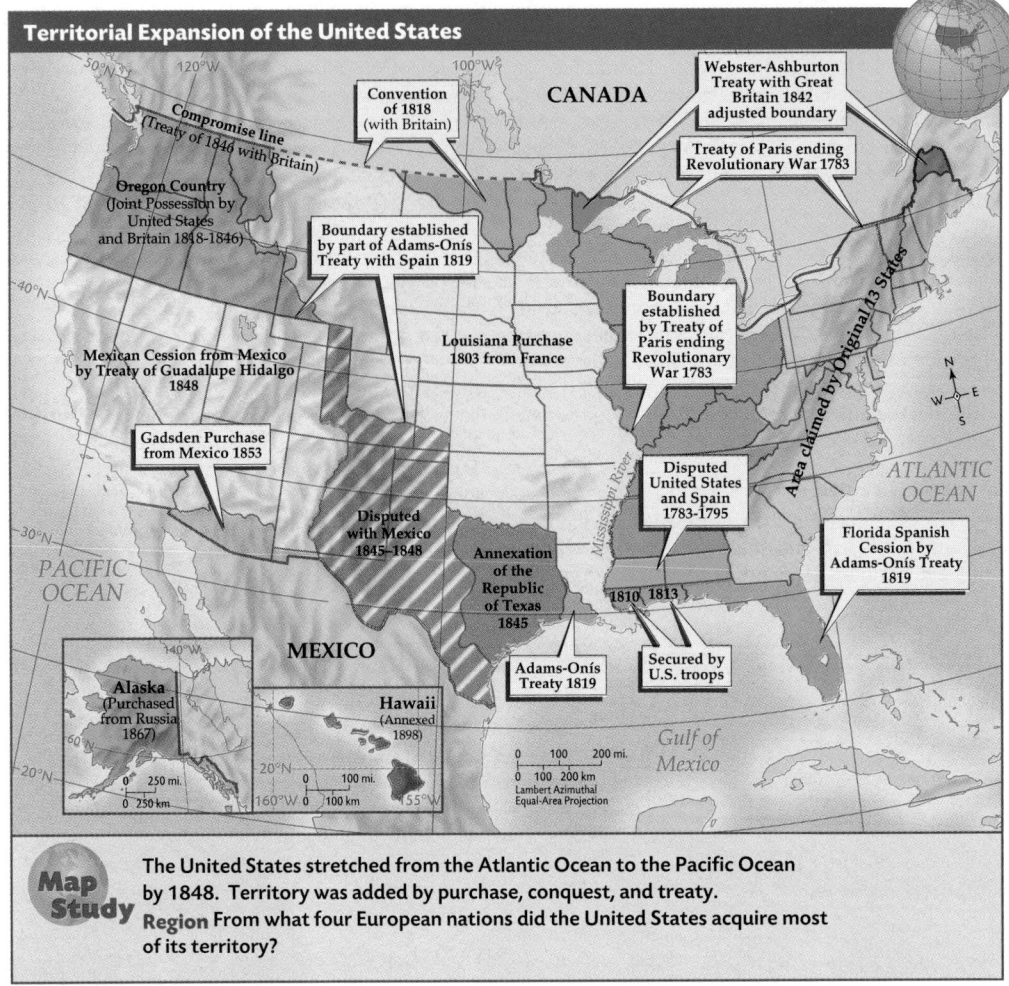

Territorial Expansion of the United States

Map Study

The United States stretched from the Atlantic Ocean to the Pacific Ocean by 1848. Territory was added by purchase, conquest, and treaty.
Region From what four European nations did the United States acquire most of its territory?

War, pitting North against South and lasting from 1861 to 1865, was one of the bloodiest struggles of the 1800s.

Although the North had 22 million people and the South only 9 million, of which nearly a third were enslaved, Southern forces won many early victories under skilled military leaders such as Robert E. Lee. Later, however, the North threw the full weight of its massive resources against the South.

After four years of war that claimed the lives of more than 600,000 Americans, the Northern forces defeated the Confederate forces. After the war, Congress passed three amendments to the Constitution of the United States. These amendments abolished slavery and gave formerly enslaved African Americans citizenship and equal protection under the law, as well as the right to vote. The nation set about to rebuild itself.

A New Society

After the Civil War, the growth of industries and cities in the United States continued with new vigor. Across the country textile mills, lumberyards, mines, and factories increased their output. In 1900 oil fields provided about 130 times more oil than they had in 1860, ironworks 10 times more iron, and steelworks almost 60 times more steel. The "captains of industry" who developed and invested in these thriving industries amassed great fortunes and gained widespread admiration.

COOPERATIVE LEARNING ACTIVITY

Discussion Groups Organize the class into groups to discuss the ways American life might be different if the Civil War had not been fought and the country had remained divided into two separate nations. Have each group focus on a different topic, such as economy, international relations, labor, government, or culture. One person from each group should take notes on the discussion and report the group's ideas to the class. Encourage students from the other groups to ask questions after each presentation. **L1**

Immigration

As industry grew, so did the nation's population. Between 1870 and 1900, the number of Americans doubled from approximately 38 million to 76 million. Immigrants contributed significantly to this growth. Before the Civil War, most immigrants had come from northern Europe, mainly the British Isles, Germany, and Scandinavia. The Irish potato famine of the 1840s brought nearly 1 million Irish people to the United States. The failed German revolution of 1848 had prompted many disappointed liberals and intellectuals to leave their homeland.

After the Civil War, immigration from northern Europe decreased, while immigration from southern and eastern Europe increased. By 1900, immigrants from Italy, Russia, and Austria-Hungary made up more than three-fourths of the United States's foreign-born population. After landing at Ellis Island in New York, most of these immigrants headed for urban areas to work.

Along the West coast by the late 1800s, communities of Asian immigrants thrived. Chinese immigrants first came to California in the late 1840s to find gold and stayed to work in the mines and build railroads. By 1900, immigrants from Japan had also arrived in the country. Anti-Asian feelings, however, led to legal limits or bans on further Asian immigration. Also, Asian Americans faced widespread discrimination, much of which lasted well into the 1900s.

Women's Rights

As women gained economic opportunities, they also demanded political equality. A women's rights movement had flourished in the 1850s under leaders such as Lucretia Mott and Sojourner Truth. During the late 1800s, women known as suffragists fought hard for women's right to vote. Forming organizations such as the National Woman Suffrage Association (NWSA), suffragists such as Elizabeth Cady Stanton and **Susan B. Anthony** wrote books,

Visualizing History During the late 1800s and early 1900s, suffragists pushed for an amendment to the Constitution granting women the right to vote. *By 1918, in which of the states could women vote?*

testified before state legislatures, and spoke at public meetings to urge votes for women.

Slowly women achieved the right to vote at the state level, beginning with Wyoming, Colorado, and Utah. By 1918 women had gained full suffrage in many Western states, Michigan, Illinois and New York. Finally, because of women's contribution in World War I, it became impossible for politicians to ignore women's demands. In September 1918 President **Woodrow Wilson** asked Congress to pass a constitutional amendment guaranteeing the vote to all United States citizens 21 years of age and older regardless of their sex. In 1920 Congress decided to **ratify**, or approve, the Nineteenth Amendment.

SECTION 4 REVIEW

Recall
1. **Define** sectionalism, secede, ratify.
2. **Identify** Thomas Jefferson, Louisiana Purchase, Abraham Lincoln, the Civil War, Susan B. Anthony, Woodrow Wilson.
3. **Explain** how the United States acquired territory to achieve its present-day continental borders.

Critical Thinking
4. **Analyzing Information** How did the Industrial Revolution in the North contribute to the outbreak of the Civil War?

Understanding Themes
5. **Change** Describe the changes to the economy of the United States in the late 1800s. What caused these changes?

Chapter 14 *Democracy and Reform* 441

Chapter 14
Section 4

SECTION 4 REVIEW ANSWERS

1. All vocabulary words are defined in the Glossary.
2. Thomas Jefferson, 436; Louisiana Purchase, 436; Abraham Lincoln, 439; the Civil War, 440; Susan B. Anthony, 441; Woodrow Wilson, 441
3. Louisiana Purchase; annexation of Texas; territory gained through Mexican-American War; Oregon Country; Gadsden Purchase
4. It caused the North to build factories and rely on free labor. Cotton farming boomed in the South to meet demands from British textile industry. The South relied on slave labor. These economic differences led to the Civil War.
5. **CHANGE** The economy boomed in the late 1800s; it was caused by the increase in production that began during the Civil War.

1804 Haiti proclaims its independence.

1819 Simón Bolívar defeats Spaniards at the Battle of Boyacá.

1825 Portugal recognizes Brazil's independence.

SECTION THEME

▶ **Nationalism** Latin American nations achieve self-government.

ind Out

Answer: *Revolts and uprisings and, in the case of Brazil, a constitutional convention brought independence to Latin American countries.*

FOCUS

Section Objective

Relate how the countries of Latin America won independence.

BELLRINGER
Motivational Activity

Before taking roll at the beginning of the class period, project Section Focus Transparency 14-5 and have students answer the activity questions. Discuss students' responses.

⬛ This activity is also available as a blackline master.

Vocabulary Pre-check

◉ Use the Vocabulary PuzzleMaker to create a puzzle that reinforces the vocabulary terms in this section. **L1**

Section 5

Latin American Independence

Setting the Scene

▶ **Terms to Define**
peninsulares, creoles, mestizos

▶ **People to Meet**
François Toussaint-Louverture, Miguel Hidalgo, Simón Bolívar, José de San Martín, Pedro I

▶ **Places to Locate**
Haiti, Mexico, Central America, Venezuela, Argentina, Chile, Peru, Brazil

 **ind Out** How did the countries of Latin America win independence?

The Storyteller

Simón Bolívar sent a joyous letter to a fellow general on January 8, 1822, displaying his belief in a unified America. He wrote, "America's greatest day has not yet dawned. We have indeed driven out our oppressors, smashed the tablets of their

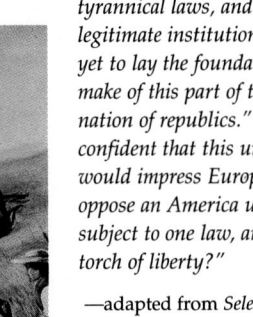

tyrannical laws, and established legitimate institutions; but we have yet to lay the foundation ... that will make of this part of the world a nation of republics." Bolívar was confident that this unified America would impress Europe: "Who shall oppose an America united in heart, subject to one law, and guided by the torch of liberty?"

—adapted from *Selected Writings of Bolívar,* compiled by Vicente Lecuna and edited by Harold A. Bierck, Jr., 1951

Simón Bolívar

For 300 years Spain and Portugal held colonies in the Americas without facing serious threats to their rule. In the early 1800s, however, the situation changed. Inspired by the American and French Revolutions, Latin Americans sought an end to colonial rule and joined independence movements.

Ruling the Colonies

Like other European nations, Spain and Portugal regarded their Latin American colonies with a mercantilist view—the idea that colonies existed chiefly to increase the home countries' wealth. Mexico, Peru, and Brazil contained large deposits of gold and silver as well as forests that yielded valuable exotic woods such as mahogany and ebony.

Farming provided another major source of colonial income. Spanish and Portuguese monarchs granted huge tracts of fertile land to explorers and nobles for the growing of cash crops, such as corn, sugar, and cocoa. The landowners then forced the Native Americans to work the farms. When they died from forced labor and diseases that the Europeans had introduced to the Americas, the Spanish and the Portuguese imported large numbers of enslaved Africans.

The Catholic Church also played a critical role in the colonial economies, strengthening Spanish and Portuguese rule in Latin America. Both the Spaniards and the Portuguese brought the Catholic religion with them to the Americas. Priests and monks converted the Native Americans who worked on the farms to Catholicism and taught them loyalty to the Crown.

The colonial governments and the clergy worked very closely together. Clergymen held high

---

SECTION RESOURCES

⬛ **Reproducible Masters**
• Reproducible Lesson Plan 14-5
• Guided Reading Activity 14-5
• People in World History Profile 48
• Reteaching Activity 14
• Enrichment Activity 14
• Section Quiz 14-5

• Performance Assessment Activity 14
• Spanish Chapter Summary 14

♪ **Transparencies**
• Section Focus Transparency 14-5

Multimedia
◉ Vocabulary PuzzleMaker Software
◉ Student Self-Test and Review Software
◉ Testmaker
♪ World Music: Cultural Traditions, Lesson 2

government offices. The government, in turn, supported the Church. By 1800 the Catholic Church controlled almost half the wealth of Latin America.

Over the years, colonists became increasingly unhappy with colonial rule. They resented the trade restrictions and high taxes Spain and Portugal imposed upon them. Most of all, they resented the rigid colonial social structure.

A Rigid Social Order

Social classes based on privilege divided colonial Latin America. Colonial leaders, called *peninsulares*, were born in Spain or Portugal and stood at the top level of the social order. Appointed by the Spanish and Portuguese governments, the *peninsulares* held all important military and political positions. Below them were the colonial-born white aristocrats, called creoles. Although they controlled most of the land and business in the colonies, the creoles were regarded as second-class citizens by the *peninsulares*. The creoles envied the privileged leadership positions that were held exclusively by the *peninsulares*.

At the bottom of the colonial social pyramid were the majority of Latin Americans. Some were Native Americans. Others were of African or African and European ancestry. The largest of this group, however, were mestizos (meh•STEE•zohz), Latin Americans of mixed Native American and European ancestry. Spurned by the ruling white classes, these Latin Americans faced social and racial barriers in colonial society. They worked as servants for *peninsulares* and creoles, and as unskilled laborers and carpenters. Some worked as plantation overseers and farmhands.

Growing Discontent

In the 1800s Latin Americans began to challenge the rigid social order and its controls with revolts throughout Latin America. The creoles played the largest leadership roles in these conflicts. Wealthy and well educated, many were well versed in the liberal political philosophies of the Enlightenment, but their colonial birth prevented them from holding the highest government positions. The creoles were eager to take control of Latin American affairs.

Uprising in Haiti

Although the Spanish and Portuguese colonies were ripe for revolt, the first successful uprising in the Latin American colonies took place in the French colony of **Haiti** (Saint Domingue), on the island of

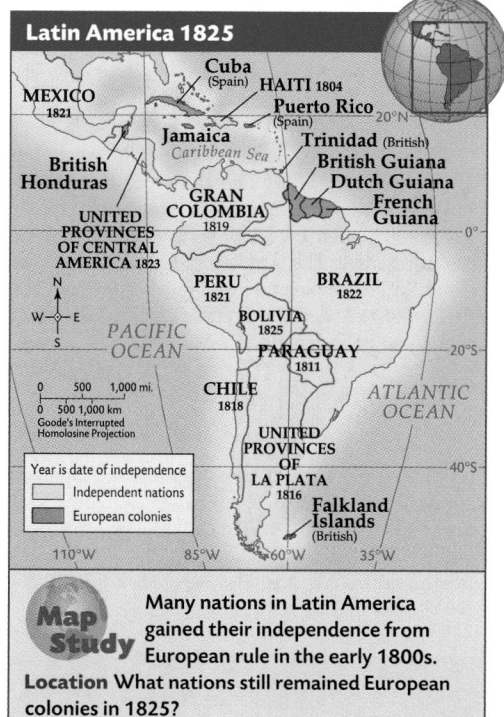

Latin America 1825

Cuba (Spain)
HAITI 1804
Puerto Rico (Spain)
MEXICO 1821
Jamaica
Caribbean Sea
British Honduras
Trinidad (British)
British Guiana
Dutch Guiana
French Guiana
GRAN COLOMBIA 1819
UNITED PROVINCES OF CENTRAL AMERICA 1823
PERU 1821
BRAZIL 1822
BOLIVIA 1825
PACIFIC OCEAN
PARAGUAY 1811
CHILE 1818
ATLANTIC OCEAN
UNITED PROVINCES OF LA PLATA 1816
Falkland Islands (British)

0   500   1,000 mi.
0 500 1,000 km
Goode's Interrupted Homolosine Projection

Year is date of independence
Independent nations
European colonies

Map Study

Many nations in Latin America gained their independence from European rule in the early 1800s. **Location** What nations still remained European colonies in 1825?

Hispaniola in the Caribbean Sea. Huge plantations of sugar, cotton, and coffee spread across the mountains and valleys of the lush tropical land. France and many other countries depended on the tiny colony for their supply of sugar and coffee.

The plantations were owned by French planters and worked by the colony's enslaved African population. More than 500,000 of the 560,000 people living in Haiti in the late 1700s were enslaved or had been. The few French planters who controlled the French colony often went to severe and brutal extremes to control the African majority.

Unrest erupted in the early 1790s when enslaved Africans led by a formerly enslaved man named **François Toussaint-Louverture** (TOO•SAN LOO•vuhr•TYUR) revolted, setting fire to plantation homes and fields of sugarcane. One observer described the horrifying scene:

❝ Picture to yourself the whole horizon a wall of fire, from which continually rose thick vortices [whirling columns] of smoke, whose huge black volumes could be likened only to those frightful storm-clouds ... for nearly three weeks we could

TEACH

Guided Practice

THEME Nationalism

Review with students the definition of *nationalism*. (*the feeling that people of the same culture should have their own nation*) Ask students how nationalism can lead to revolution. (*People revolt against foreign governments in an effort to rule themselves.*) Have students cite examples of present-day or historic nationalistic struggles. (*Answers may include: Palestinian Arabs; Bosnians in former Yugoslavia.*) **L1**

Map Study

Answer

Cuba, British Honduras, Trinidad, British Guiana, Dutch Guiana, French Guiana, Falkland Islands, Puerto Rico

Map Skills Practice

Reading a Map What is the only Latin American country that is completely landlocked? (*Paraguay*)

Multicultural Discuss the rigid social order in South American colonies. Ask students to compare this with the Estate system that existed before the French Revolution of 1789. (*Both were rigid social orders that a person was born into; the small number of people in the top classes created discontent.*) **L3**

🎵 World Music: Cultural Traditions, Lesson 2

COOPERATIVE LEARNING ACTIVITY

Creating a Constitution Organize students into teams: priests, *peninsulares*, mestizos, and Creoles. Tell students that their colony has just achieved independence from Spain and they now have the opportunity to form a new government. Have students research the social and economic interests and goals of their groups. Next have the groups discuss their concerns and draw up a platform stating their positions and their goals for the new government. Then have the teams meet in a constitutional convention to create the laws for their new government. Allow students to debate their needs and draw up a constitution. Emphasize the importance of negotiation and compromise throughout the activity. **L2** 📦

Independent Practice

📁 Guided Reading Activity 14-5 **L1**

📁 People in World History Profile 48

Geography: Location Have students imagine that they are on a journey through Latin America. Tell them to keep a journal in which they record their impressions of the geography. Ask them to draw conclusions about the difficulties early Latin Americans may have had in communicating and transporting goods. **L1**

Broadcast Have students investigate the revolution in Haiti. Then have students form news teams to report key events throughout the period. Students may write news stories or produce a news broadcast. **L2**

Linking Past and Present

Mexican Independence On September 16, 1810, Father Hidalgo rang the bells in his small church in the village of Dolores and shouted the *Grito de Dolores* (Cry of Dolores) in which he demanded independence. To this day, the president of Mexico rings a bell in Mexico City each September 16 and repeats the *Grito de Dolores*.

---

barely distinguish between day and night, for so long as the rebels found anything to feed the flames, they never ceased to burn.... 🙶

In 1802 Napoleon sent forces to take control of the colony. Captured by French officers, Toussaint-Louverture was imprisoned in France, where he died in 1803. Then a wave of yellow fever aided the revolutionaries. The epidemic swept across the colony, killing thousands of French soldiers. The rebel army defeated the French, and in 1804 Haiti proclaimed its independence.

Mexico Struggles for Freedom

One of the earliest uprisings against Spanish rule occurred in **Mexico**, which at that time was part of New Spain. In 1810 a Catholic priest named **Miguel Hidalgo** led the fight against the Spanish government in Mexico. Hidalgo cared deeply for

History & Art *Father Miguel Hidalgo,* a fresco by José Clemente Orozco, 1937. Governor's Mansion, Guadalajara, Mexico *What two groups made up the rebel force that Hidalgo led against the Spanish army?*

the poverty-stricken Native Americans and mestizos in his parish of Dolores. In addition to political freedom, he also wanted to end slavery and to improve living conditions for Mexico's poor. To Hidalgo, revolt was the only way to bring change to Mexico.

On September 16, 1810, Hidalgo gave a stirring address that became known as "el Grito de Dolores" —the cry of Dolores. In the speech, he called on Mexicans to fight for "Independence and Liberty." Hidalgo then led Native Americans and mestizos on a freedom march to Mexico City that eventually turned into an armed movement. In spite of early advances, Hidalgo and his forces faced mounting opposition from the Spaniards and their Mexican creole allies. In 1811 the well-trained Spanish army finally overwhelmed the rebels, and Hidalgo was captured and executed.

Another priest, José María Morelos, took charge of the revolution after Hidalgo died. Morelos captured a large portion of southern Mexico. In 1813 he called a conference that declared Mexico's independence from Spain. Morelos's forces fought the Spaniards but were defeated in 1815. Like Hidalgo, Morelos was executed.

Despite many battles, Mexico did not gain full independence until 1821. That year, a liberal revolt in Spain threatened to overthrow the monarchy and establish a constitution. This reform frightened wealthy Mexican creoles, who feared such a change might infringe on their own privileges. To make sure this did not happen, they declared independence from Spain in 1821.

Ironically, their leader was Agustín de Iturbide (EE•TUR•BEE•thay), the army officer who had crushed Morelos's movement. Iturbide made himself emperor in 1822, but opposition to his oppressive rule developed. The Mexican people soon deposed Iturbide and declared their country a republic in 1823.

When Mexico became a republic, the Central American provinces in New Spain declared their independence. In Guatemala, representatives established the United Provinces of **Central America**. In the 1830s leaders divided the region into the countries of Costa Rica, El Salvador, Guatemala, Honduras, and Nicaragua.

Spanish South America

Creoles in the Spanish colonies of South America gained an opportunity for independence in 1808 when Napoleon seized control of the Spanish government. The refusal of the Spanish

---

MEETING SPECIAL NEEDS ACTIVITY

Study Strategy Reading comprehension is often greatly aided by presentation of background information or "schema." The schema is developed from the reader's current knowledge and then extended with new information from text, lecture, pictures, and media. Have students with comprehension problems research the meeting between San Martín and Bolívar in Guayaquil in July 1822, or the meeting between O'Higgins and San Martín in Chile in 1818. Have students take the roles of these leaders and reproduce a probable conversation from each point of view. **L2**

American colonists to acknowledge Napoleon's government resulted in revolts throughout the empire. In addition, Spain's fight against France, together with the colonies' isolation from their home country, left the Spanish weak and vulnerable to attack. Three outstanding leaders—Simón Bolívar, José de San Martín, and Bernardo O'Higgins—led South American colonies in their fight against Spanish rule.

Simón Bolívar, a creole from **Venezuela**, led many colonies to independence. Bolívar believed in equality and saw liberty as "the only object worth a man's life." Bolívar had witnessed the reforms of the French Revolution. Called "the Liberator," Bolívar devoted his life to freedom for Latin Americans.

In 1810 Bolívar started a revolt against the Spaniards in Caracas. After nearly 9 years of fighting, Bolívar crushed Spain's power in northern South America at the Battle of Boyacá in 1819. During the next 20 years, Bolívar and his forces won freedom for the present-day countries of Venezuela, Colombia, Panama, Bolivia, and Ecuador.

While Bolívar fought in Venezuela, another revolutionary leader, **José de San Martín** of **Argentina**, led Latin American armies over the Andes Mountains and into **Chile**. In Chile, San Martín joined Bernardo O'Higgins. Together, their forces successfully achieved independence for Chile in 1818. San Martín then set off to free **Peru** in 1820. Within a year he captured Lima and declared Peru independent.

In July 1822 San Martín and Bolívar met in the Ecuadorian port of Guayaquil (GWY•uh•KEEL) to discuss the future of Latin America. Though they shared a common goal, they could not agree on strategy and policy. San Martín finally decided to withdraw from the revolt and allowed Bolívar to take command. By 1826 Bolívar and his armies had liberated all of South America.

Brazil Gains Independence

Brazil achieved its independence without the bloodshed that accompanied the liberation of Spanish America. In 1808 Napoleon's French army had invaded Portugal, causing the Portuguese royal family to flee to Brazil.

King João transferred his monarchy to Brazil, declaring Rio de Janeiro capital of the Portuguese Empire. João immediately introduced governmental reforms in Brazil. He reinstated more favorable trade laws by opening Brazil's ports to the world. João also worked to make the agriculture and

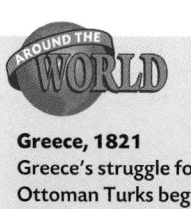

Greeks Fight for Independence

Greece, 1821
Greece's struggle for independence from the Ottoman Turks began in 1821 when Greek fighters gained control of the Peloponnesus and many islands in the Aegean Sea. But in 1825, a combined army of Turks and Egyptians regained these regions. France, Great Britain, and Russia came to Greece's aid in 1827 and defeated the Turkish-Egyptian fleet in the Battle of Navarino. By 1829 both the Turks and the Egyptians left Greece, and Greece became independent that year.

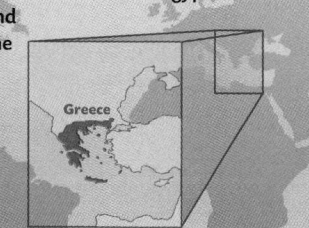

mining industries more profitable. Soon both industry and commerce were flourishing.

The liberal ruler brought Brazilians increasing opportunities by funding public education, including military academies, an art school, and medical schools. With these reforms Brazil moved quickly toward independence, and in 1815 João made Brazil a self-governing kingdom within the Portuguese Empire.

King João came to love the semitropical land of mountains and endless forests; he chose to remain there after Napoleon was defeated in 1815. In 1820, however, liberals took over the Portuguese government. Determined to save his throne, he returned to Portugal. He left Brazil in the hands of his 23-year-old son, Dom Pedro.

The new Portuguese government fought to make Brazil a colonial possession again. Leaders ended free trade and many of the other advantages Brazil had enjoyed under João's monarchy. They also demanded that Dom Pedro abandon his rule and immediately return to Portugal. Supported by his father, Dom Pedro declared that he would remain in Brazil. Dom Pedro defied Portuguese leaders by calling a constitutional convention and answered their angry response with a cry of "Independence or death!"

In September 1822 Brazil won full independence from Portugal. Three months later Dom Pedro was

Cultural Perspectives
Other Revolts The spirit of revolt also swept through China during the 1800s. The Taiping Rebellion (1850–1864) tore the country apart when a group combining Christian and ancient Chinese beliefs attempted to create a perfect society with an equal division of land among the people. In 1899–1900, a Chinese group led the Boxer Rebellion in which they tried to protect their traditions against Western influences.

Who?What?Where?When?
Brazil is the fifth-largest country in the world. It encompasses an area greater than that of the 48 contiguous states of the United States.

ASSESS

Check for Understanding
Assign Section 5 Review as homework or as an in-class activity.

Use Student Self-Test and Review Software to review Section 5.

MAKING CONNECTIONS ACTIVITY

Religion The Roman Catholic Church was extremely powerful in Latin America in the nineteenth century. Have students investigate the role of the Church in Latin America today and answer the question: How has the role of the Church changed in Latin America during the past 150 years? Students should research the Church's role in the social affairs of the people, in economics, and in political affairs. After doing the research, students should present the information in a panel presentation. **L2**

Evaluate

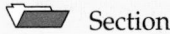 Section Quiz 14-5

🖥 Use the Testmaker to create a customized quiz for Section 5.

Reteach

Ask students to imagine they have to write a history of the Latin American independence movement. Ask them to create an outline of the topics and key information they would include in their book.

 Reteaching Activity 14

Enrich

Remind students that the main reason European powers wanted colonies was for their raw materials. Ask students to report on how the economies of selected Latin American countries have changed since the days of colonialism.

 Enrichment Activity 14

CLOSE

Have students make lists of general causes for revolutions based on revolutions they have studied thus far. Have them write a brief explanation of how the Latin American revolutions were similar to and different from others they have studied.

---

crowned Emperor **Pedro I** of Brazil. With Pedro ruling the empire under a constitution, Brazil became the only independent country in South America to freely choose a constitutional monarchy as its form of government.

Meanwhile, João maintained his support of his beloved Brazil by refusing to allow the Portuguese government to send new military forces to fight the rebels. Great Britain also pressured Portugal to end its battle. In 1825 Portugal finally recognized Brazil's independence.

Challenges to Growth

By the mid-1820s most Latin American countries had won their independence. Their next task was to achieve national unity and a stable government. These goals, however, were difficult to reach. Simón Bolívar, who had dreamed of uniting all of northern South America into one large and powerful state, became so disappointed and disillusioned that he wrote, "Those who have toiled for liberty in South America have plowed the sea."

Common Problems

In trying to build stable and prosperous nations, Latin Americans faced a number of challenges. One obstacle was the geography of Central and South America. High mountains and thick jungles made transportation and communication difficult, hindering trade and economic growth. Vast areas of fertile land remained undeveloped. Population centers, separated by physical barriers, became rivals instead of allies.

Other problems were part of Latin America's colonial heritage. Spanish and Portuguese rule had given the Latin Americans little practice in governing themselves. Instead, they were used to authoritarian government, which was not responsible to the people and demanded obedience from them.

In the colonial system, political power was in the hands of the executive branch of government.

The judicial branch was weak and limited, and the legislative branch was practically nonexistent. Latin Americans had strong, well-educated leaders, but they had no experience in the legislative process. Simón Bolívar complained that the colonial system had kept his people in a state of "permanent childhood" with regard to knowledge of running a government. "If we could have at least managed our domestic affairs and our internal administration, we could have acquainted ourselves with the process and machinery of government," he wrote.

Independence did not bring about much change in social conditions in Latin America. Catholicism remained the official religion, and Church and government continued to be closely tied. The new countries also continued to maintain a separation between upper and lower classes. The dominant group was now the creoles instead of the *peninsulares*. Creoles owned the best land and controlled business and government. Their privileged position was resented, especially by the mestizos.

Continuing Political Conflicts

Soon after independence, political conflicts increased. Liberals called for separation of Church and state, the breakup of large estates, higher taxes on land, public social services, and civilian control of the government. Most of the liberals were mestizos, intellectuals, or merchants who wanted free trade. Opposed to this group were the creoles, most of whom were rich landowners, church leaders, and military officers. These conservatives favored strong central government and a powerful Church and army.

The decades that followed the wars for independence saw an ongoing struggle for economic strength and social justice. Although many South American governments were republics in appearance, many actually were military dictatorships. Today, there still remains in many Latin American countries a vast gap between the ruling rich and the underprivileged poor.

SECTION 5 REVIEW

Recall
1. **Define** *peninsulares*, creoles, mestizos.
2. **Identify** François Toussaint-Louverture, Miguel Hidalgo, Simón Bolívar, José de San Martín, Pedro I.

3. **Explain** why creoles were strong supporters of independence movements in Latin America.

Critical Thinking
4. **Making Comparisons** How did the independence movement in Mexico differ from that in Brazil?

Understanding Themes
5. **Nationalism** Did independence bring social advances in Latin American countries? Why or why not?

SECTION 5 REVIEW ANSWERS

1. All vocabulary words are defined in the Glossary.
2. François Toussaint-Louverture, 443; Miguel Hidalgo, 444; Simón Bolívar, 445; José de San Martín, 445; Pedro I, 445
3. They were educated in the political philosophies of the Enlightenment and frustrated by the rigid social order imposed by the ruling Spaniards and Portuguese.
4. The independence movement in Mexico was violent; in Brazil, the king granted independence without violence.

5. **NATIONALISM** Answers will vary. Possible answer: No, there was still separation between upper and lower classes; creoles assumed the positions formally held by the *peninsulares* and ignored the needs of the mestizos.

Reading a Cartogram

O n most maps, land areas are drawn in proportion to the actual surface areas on the earth. On some maps, however, a small country may appear much larger than usual, and a large country may look much smaller. Even the shapes of the countries may look different. If maps are supposed to outline the earth's features, why are these maps so distorted?

Learning the Skill

Maps that distort country size and shape are called **cartograms**. In a cartogram, country size reflects some value *other* than a land area, such as population or gross national product. For example, on a conventional map Canada appears much larger than India. In a cartogram showing world population, however, India would appear larger than Canada because it has a much larger population. The cartogram is a tool for making visual comparisons. At a glance, you can see how each country or region compares with another in a particular value.

To use a cartogram, first read the title and key to identify what value the cartogram illustrates. Then examine the cartogram to see which countries or regions appear. Find the largest and smallest countries. Compare the cartogram with a conventional land-area map to determine the degree of distortion of particular countries. Finally, draw conclusions about the topic.

Practicing the Skill

Study the cartogram shown at the top right and answer these questions.
1. What is the subject of the cartogram?
2. Which country appears largest on the cartogram? Which appears smallest?
3. Compare the cartogram to the map of Europe found in the Atlas. Which countries are most distorted in size compared to a land-area map?

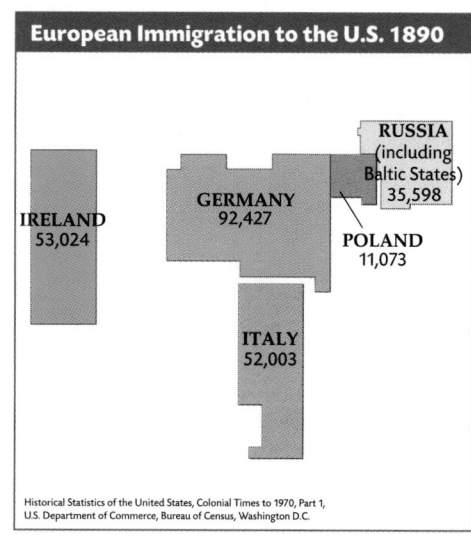

European Immigration to the U.S. 1890

RUSSIA (including Baltic States) 35,598

GERMANY 92,427

IRELAND 53,024

POLAND 11,073

ITALY 52,003

Historical Statistics of the United States, Colonial Times to 1970, Part 1, U.S. Department of Commerce, Bureau of Census, Washington D.C.

4. What accounts for these distortions?

Applying the Skill

At the library, find statistics that compare some value for different states or countries. For example, you might compare the number of farms in each state, or annual oil consumption of countries in North America. Be creative in your choice of value.

Convert these statistics into a simple cartogram. Determine the relative size of each country or state according to the chosen value. If the United States consumes five times more oil than does Mexico, then the United States should appear five times larger.

For More Practice

Turn to the Skill Practice in the Chapter Review on page 449 for more practice in reading a cartogram.

TEACH

Reading a Cartogram Suggest that students imagine they are members of a city school board charged with the responsibility of planning where the city needs new schools. The standard city map shows the various residential areas and the borders of school districts. Ask students to consider how a cartogram would help them. Suggest that if it showed at a glance the relative numbers of school-age children in each district, this would help them to judge the capacity needs. Ask students to brainstorm other situations where a cartogram would be helpful.

Additional Practice

Skill Reinforcement Activity 14

ANSWERS TO PRACTICING THE SKILL

1. European immigration to the United States in 1890
2. Germany; Poland
3. Ireland and Russia
4. the number of immigrants these nations sent to the United States relative to their size

Chapter 14 Review

Answers

Using Key Terms
1. c   4. k
2. l   5. b
3. j

Using Your History Journal
Have students refer to the maps they made of Britain's territories and choose one to write about. Be sure they supply details and sources.

Reviewing Facts
1. most British middle-class men; British working-class men, women
2. Middle-class French people felt that Louis Philippe favored the rich; they overthrew his government.
3. Napoleon felt that Prussia was gaining too much power; the Prussians defeated the French, and Napoleon's empire collapsed.
4. Louisiana Purchase; Mexican Cession; Oregon Country; Gadsden Purchase
5. Toussaint-Louverture, Hidalgo, Bolívar, San Martín, O'Higgins

Critical Thinking
1. Alike: Both had a monarchy that people wanted to change. Differ-

Connections Across Time

Historical Significance The 1800s saw the growth of democracy and nationalism in Europe and the Americas. In Great Britain, the British dominions, and the United States, democracy came peacefully. In France and Latin America, violent upheavals led to democracy or independence.

Although some revolts of the 1800s were unsuccessful, they planted the seeds of self-government in some Central and Eastern European countries. Today, many of the nations of the world are democracies with guarantees of protection for citizens' rights.

Using Key Terms

Write the key term that completes each sentence. Then write a sentence for each term not chosen.

a. creoles
b. disenfranchised
c. dominion
d. home rule
e. seceded
f. ratify
g. *peninsulares*
h. sectionalism
i. ultraroyalists
j. suffragettes
k. plebiscite
l. mestizos

1. A self-governing country other than Great Britain that recognizes the British monarch as its head of state is called a _____.
2. _____ are Latin Americans of mixed Native American and European ancestry.
3. Women in Great Britain who led a voting rights campaign for women became known as _____.
4. In 1851 Louis-Napoleon called for a _____, or national vote, asking the French people to give him support to create a new constitution.
5. While the Reform Act of 1832 gave middle-class men the right to vote, agricultural laborers, factory workers, and women remained _____.

Technology Activity

Using a Computerized Card Catalog Use the computerized card catalog in your school or local library to locate sources about Latin American countries. Research current information about a country from that region. Organize your research into a fact sheet. Include headings such as history, culture, religion, demographics, economics, and government. Provide a map of your country illustrating features such as mountain ranges, bodies of water, natural resources, and major cities.

Reviewing Facts

1. **Citizenship** List the groups in Great Britain that gained the right to vote under the Reform Act of 1832. What groups were still excluded from voting?
2. **Government** Explain why many French people came to oppose the constitutional monarchy of Louis Philippe. How did this opposition affect Louis Philippe's rule?
3. **History** Explain why France went to war in 1870. What was the result of the conflict?
4. **Geography** Identify three land acquisitions that significantly expanded the territorial borders of the United States in the 1800s.
5. **Government** Name three leaders who helped win freedom for Latin American countries.

Critical Thinking

1. **Apply** Compare the movement toward democratic reform in Great Britain with similar movements in France under Louis Philippe. How were they alike? How did they differ?
2. **Synthesize** How did expansion and the Civil War affect the growth of democracy and civil rights in the United States?

---

ent: The British democratic movements were peaceful; the French movement was violent.
2. Settlers moving west set up state governments and pressed for extension of voting rights, and their liberal policies soon influenced the country; the Civil War ended slavery and ushered in constitutional guarantees of civil rights for African Americans.
3. With European nations involved in conflict, the United States was able to expand its territory with few prohibitions. European countries were willing to sell North American land to raise money for their wars at home.

Geography in History
1. Great Britain
2. United States
3. the potato famine
4. Possible answers: the revolts in Europe; economic instability; colonization of territory.

3. Evaluate How did conflict in Europe in the 1800s contribute to the development of the United States?

Geography in History

1. Movement Refer to the map below. Which European nation lost the most emigrants in this period?

2. Movement To which nation did most Europeans migrate during this period?

3. Human/Environment Interaction What caused many Irish people to migrate to the United States in the 1840s?

4. Region What circumstances in Europe caused millions of people to migrate during this period?

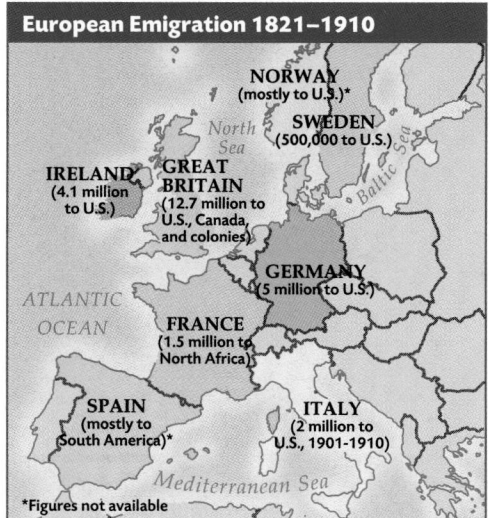

European Emigration 1821–1910

Understanding Themes

1. Change From your reading, would you say that the method of gradual reform was the best way that the British could have taken to change their government and society in the 1800s?

2. Movement How did British settlement of the dominions affect the original inhabitants?

3. Revolution Why do you think revolutions are often followed by governments led by dictators?

4. Change How did immigration affect the economic growth of the United States?

5. Nationalism How did the American Revolution affect Latin America in the early 1800s?

1. British and American women fought to win the right to vote. What rights do women seek today? Are their methods today similar to or different from past methods?
2. After slavery was abolished in the United States, African Americans and other groups still had to struggle for equality. What educational and employment opportunities do some Americans seek today?
3. The Irish were granted home rule in 1914, but it never went into effect. How does this relate to the politics in Ireland today?

Skill Practice

Study the cartogram below and then answer these questions.

1. What is the subject of the cartogram?
2. Which country appears largest on the cartogram? Which appears smallest?
3. Compare the cartogram to a world map or globe. Which countries are most distorted in size compared to a land-area map?
4. What accounts for these distortions?

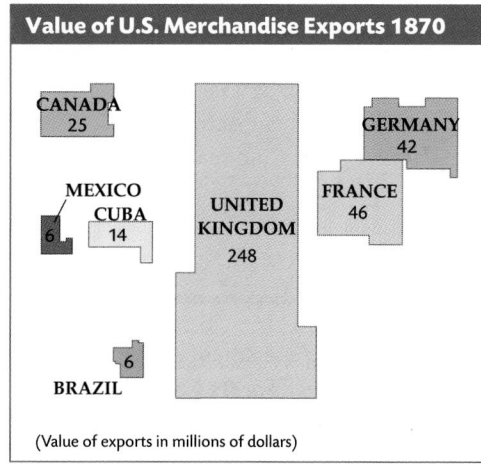

Value of U.S. Merchandise Exports 1870

(Value of exports in millions of dollars)

Chapter 14 *Democracy and Reform* **449**

cans to end colonial rule and join independence movements in their territories.

1. Possible answer: Women still seek equal pay for equal work and an end to sex discrimination. Methods used today by the women's movement are less dramatic and violent.
2. Possible answer: African Americans continue to seek legislation to fight discrimination.
3. The Irish Catholics in Northern Ireland continue to resent British rule and use terrorist tactics to protest.

Skill Practice

1. value of United States merchandise exports in 1870
2. United Kingdom; Mexico or Brazil
3. Canada, the United Kingdom, Brazil
4. the value of these countries' United States merchandise exports relative to their size

Chapter Bonus Test Question

Ask students: What political, social, economic, or other conditions make it easiest for a country to achieve democratic government with civil rights for all citizens? What conditions make it most difficult? *(Answers may include that some history of self-government or of limitations on the power of the monarch make it easiest; traditions of absolute rule and a rigid social class structure make it most difficult.)*

Understanding Themes

1. CHANGE Possible answer: It seems that Great Britain's way of achieving democracy was the smoothest, most stable, and longest lasting.

2. MOVEMENT It brought them deadly diseases, took away their land, and led to conflicts that killed many native peoples.

3. REVOLUTION Possible answer: The people have been used to being ruled by an autocratic government and may not know how to go about ruling themselves. It may be difficult for opposing factions to agree on the best way of establishing the new government.

4. CHANGE Immigrants provided the workforce for the expanding United States industries.

5. NATIONALISM The example of the American Revolution inspired Latin Ameri-

A complete, 1-page lesson plan is provided for each section in the *Reproducible Lesson Plans* booklet.

Reaction and Nationalism

CHAPTER RESOURCES

	Reproducible Resources	Multimedia Resources
Chapter Opener	Chapter Themes: Graphic Organizer 15 Historical Significance Chapter Activity 15	MindJogger Videoquiz
Chapter Enrichment	Vocabulary Activity 15* Time Line Activity 15 Mapping History Activity 15 History Simulation 15 Geography and History Activity 15 Source Reading 15 People in World History Profiles 49, 50 World Art and Music Activity 15 Enrichment Activity 15 Critical Thinking Activity 15 Skill Reinforcement Activity 15 Writer's Guidebook, Lesson 9 Performance Assessment Activity 15	Mapping History Overlay Transparency 17, *Revolutionary Centers in Europe 1820–1848* Chapter Transparency 15 Vocabulary PuzzleMaker Software Turning Points in World History: *The Russian Revolution*
Chapter Review/Reteaching	Reteaching Activity 15 Skill Reinforcement Activity 15 Spanish Chapter Summary 15	Chapter 15 Digest Audiocassette, Activity, Test* Vocabulary PuzzleMaker Software Student Self-Test and Review Software MindJogger Videoquiz
Chapter Evaluation/Testing	Performance Assessment Activity 15 Chapter 15 Test, Forms A and B	Testmaker

* Also available in Spanish

0:00 OUT OF TIME? Assign the Chapter 15 summary in the Unit 4 Digest on pages 505–507, and the Chapter 15 Audiocassettes.

Block Schedule

Block scheduling differs from traditional class scheduling in the amount of time allotted to each period. The extended time frame provided by block scheduling affords you the opportunity to implement a greater number of research-oriented and activity-intense projects to motivate and involve your students. Activities that are particularly suited to use within the block scheduling framework are identified throughout this chapter by the following designation.

KEY TO ABILITY LEVELS

Teaching strategies have been coded for varying learning styles and abilities.

L1 BASIC activities for all students
L2 AVERAGE activities for average to above-average students
L3 CHALLENGING activities for above-average students
LEP LIMITED ENGLISH PROFICIENCY activities

Use Glencoe's *Presentation Plus!* multimedia teacher tool to easily present dynamic lessons that visually excite your students. Using Microsoft PowerPoint® you can customize the presentations to create your own personalized lessons.

SECTION RESOURCES

Daily Objectives	Reproducible Resources	Multimedia Resources
Section 1 **The Unification of Italy** Explain how nationalism led to a united Italy in the 1860s.	Reproducible Lesson Plan 15-1 Vocabulary Activity 15* Guided Reading Activity 15-1* History Simulation 15 Time Line Activity 15 Section Quiz 15-1*	Section Focus Transparency 15-1 Chapter Transparency 15 Student Self-Test and Review Software Testmaker
Section 2 **The Unification of Germany** Identify the methods Bismarck used to unite the German states.	Reproducible Lesson Plan 15-2 Vocabulary Activity 15* Guided Reading Activity 15-2* Section Quiz 15-2*	Section Focus Transparency 15-2 Student Self-Test and Review Software Testmaker
Section 3 **Bismarck's Realm** Analyze how Bismarck's policies affected the German Empire.	Reproducible Lesson Plan 15-3 Vocabulary Activity 15* Guided Reading Activity 15-3* Section Quiz 15-3*	Section Focus Transparency 15-3 Student Self-Test and Review Software Testmaker
Section 4 **Empire of the Czars** Explain why revolutionary movements developed in Russia.	Reproducible Lesson Plan 15-4 Guided Reading Activity 15-4* Geography and History Activity 15 Section Quiz 15-4*	Section Focus Transparency 15-4 Vocabulary PuzzleMaker Software Student Self-Test and Review Software Testmaker Turning Points in World History: *The Russian Revolution*
Section 5 **Austria-Hungary's Decline** Describe how the growth of nationalistic feelings affected the empire of Austria-Hungary.	Reproducible Lesson Plan 15-5 Vocabulary Activity 15* Guided Reading Activity 15-5* Reteaching Activity 15 Enrichment Activity 15 Section Quiz 15-5* Performance Assessment Activity 15 Spanish Chapter Summary 15	Section Focus Transparency 15-5 Mapping History Overlay Transparency 17, *Revolutionary Centers in Europe 1820–1848* Student Self-Test and Review Software Testmaker

* Also available in Spanish

Chapter Activities

 Performance Assessment Activity

A Portfolio of Examples The concepts featured in this chapter include sectionalism, nationalism, and empire. Ask students to make connections with their own lives by creating a portfolio of contemporary examples of these concepts. For each example, have students discuss the positive and negative roles played by diversity and unity in the situation. Students may include examples from politics, business, city, and the family. As a concluding activity, have students write a reflection in their portfolios in which they explain how diversity and unity affect their lives.

Possible Rubric Features

Concept attainment for concepts and themes studied, organization and classification of portfolio, analytical skills, clarity and detail of reflection

• *For an additional activity, refer to Activity 15 in the* Performance Assessment Strategies and Activities *booklet.*

ACTIVITY

From the Classroom of...

**Kimberly C. Felder
Frederick Douglass
Academy
New York, NY**

Nationalism Then and Now

Organize students into four groups: Germany, Italy, Russia, and Austria-Hungary. Have each group use the text to review the nationalistic struggle in its country, or provide groups with fact sheets. Then have each group write a letter to the editor of a newspaper in their country, arguing a nationalistic position.

Distribute magazine and newspaper articles about current nationalistic struggles (try to include letters to the editor). Have the entire class compare the late twentieth-century struggles with the nationalistic movements of the nineteenth century.

MULTIPLE LEARNING STYLES

Verbal/Linguistic

Have students write an essay comparing the effects of war on the governments of Italy, Germany, Russia, Austria-Hungary, and the Ottoman Empire during the last half of the 1800s. Ask students to consider how war strengthened or weakened the existing governments and what political changes war brought about.

Logical/Mathematical

Have students make a time line that shows the main events in the spread of nationalism through Italy, Germany, Russia, Austria-Hungary, and the Ottoman Empire.

Visual/Spatial

Have students create a picture gallery of the many personalities mentioned in the chapter. Have them accompany each copy of a portrait with a thumbnail sketch that provides the person's nationality and principal accomplishments.

Auditory/Musical

Have students develop a musical collage of works by Richard Wagner, Giuseppe Verdi, and Modest Mussorgsky that show the spirit of nationalism.

Kinesthetic

Have students create a board game that uses Bismarck's domestic and foreign strategies to bring about a unified Germany.

Additional Resources

NATIONAL GEOGRAPHIC SOCIETY
Teacher's Corner

INDEX TO NATIONAL GEOGRAPHIC MAGAZINE

The following articles may be used for research relating to this chapter:

- "Reinventing Berlin," by Peter Ross Range, December 1996.
- "Crimea: Pearl of a Fallen Empire," by Peter T. White, September 1994.
- "The Morning After: German Revisited," by William S. Ellis, September 1991.
- "Berlin's Ode to Joy," by Priit J. Vesiland, April 1990.
- "St. Petersburg: Capital of the Tsars," by Steve Raymer, December 1993.

ADDITIONAL NATIONAL GEOGRAPHIC SOCIETY PRODUCTS

To order the following products for use with this chapter, call National Geographic Society at 1-800-368-2728:

- *The Democratic Government Series: German (Video)*
- *Russia's Last Tsar (Video)*
- *Voices of Leningrad (Video)*

LOCAL OBJECTIVES

_____
_____
_____
_____
_____
_____
_____
_____
_____
_____
_____
_____
_____
_____
_____
_____
_____
_____
_____
_____
_____
_____
_____

BIBLIOGRAPHY

Literature of the Period
Dostoyevsky, Fyodor. *The Possessed.* Translated by Constance Garnett. New York: Modern Library, 1963. A Russian novel about nineteenth-century revolutionaries.

Readings for the Student
Snyder, L. L. *A Comparative History of Nationalism.* New York: Holt, 1976. An introduction to the different varieties of nationalism.

Readings for the Teacher
Knapton, Ernest John, and Thomas Kingston Derry. *Europe: 1815–1914.* New York: Scribners, 1965. Comprehensive history of Europe that includes cultural, social, and economic trends as well as political, diplomatic, and military themes.

interNET CONNECTION

Russian Revolution resources on the World Wide Web
The Russian Revolution:
http://www.barnsdle.demon.co.uk/russ/rusrev.html

Chapter Themes are listed by section on this chapter opening page of the Student Edition. A corresponding theme-based activity is available under "TEACH," and a theme-based question is asked in the Section and Chapter Reviews.

The Storyteller

Historical Setting Giuseppe Mazzini, born in Genoa in 1805, founded Young Italy, a secret society whose goal was the unification of Italy. Mazzini spent most of his life in exile under a sentence of death. While in Switzerland, he and exiles from Poland and Germany founded Young Europe. Their vision was a Europe of many free nations coming together through an elected assembly that would regulate matters of common interest. Mazzini helped form other nationalist groups across Europe, such as Young Switzerland, Young Germany, Young Poland, Young Spain, and Young Russia.

Historical Significance

Answers: *French nationalism under Napoleon brought parts of Europe into the French Empire. When the Congress of Vienna broke up the French Empire and divided much of Europe among Prussia, Russia, and Austria, it set the stage for nationalist movements among groups in lands controlled by those nations.*

Nationalist feelings in the Balkans led to World War I and to the recent war in Bosnia; Hitler's nationalistic program to unite the German people and create a German Empire led to World War II; nationalist feelings in Africa and Asia led to the breakup of the British and French Empires.

Chapter
15
1815–1914
Reaction and Nationalism

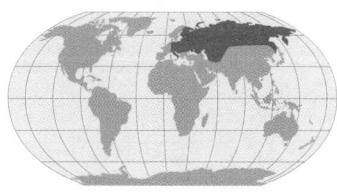

Chapter Themes

▶ **Nationalism** The rise of nationalism contributes to the unification of Italy. *Section 1*
▶ **Conflict** Bismarck uses war and diplomacy to bring unity to Germany. *Section 2*
▶ **Change** Bismarck's German Empire allows for economic growth but limits political freedoms. *Section 3*
▶ **Reaction** Russian czars oppose the forces of liberalism and nationalism in the Russian Empire. *Section 4*
▶ **Diversity** The large empire of Austria-Hungary contains many different nationalities seeking self-rule. *Section 5*

The Storyteller

One Sunday in 1821, 16-year-old Giuseppe Mazzini walked along a street in Genoa, Italy. Suddenly a tall, black-bearded stranger approached him. With a piercing look, the stranger held out his hand for money and said, "for the refugees of Italy." Everyone knew that the refugees were those who had recently rebelled against the Austrians to win independence for Italy.

Forty years later, Mazzini—now a leader of the Italian nationalist movement—wrote of this incident: "That day was the first in which … [I realized that] … we Italians could and therefore ought to struggle for the liberty of our country." During the early 1800s feelings of nationalism similar to Mazzini's began to stir all across Europe.

Historical Significance

How has the force of nationalism repeatedly changed the map of Europe? What impact has nationalism had on European and world developments in the twentieth century?

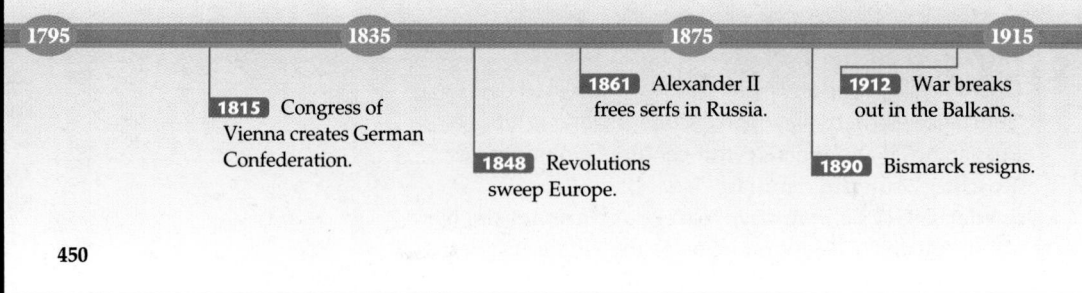

1795	1835	1875	1915

1815 Congress of Vienna creates German Confederation.

1848 Revolutions sweep Europe.

1861 Alexander II frees serfs in Russia.

1912 War breaks out in the Balkans.

1890 Bismarck resigns.

450

Location On a historical map of Europe of about 1860, have students locate the independent Italian states and German states, the Russian Empire, Austria, Hungary, and the Ottoman Empire. Why would Austria-Hungary and Russia be interested in land in the Ottoman Empire? *(The Ottoman Empire bordered both Austria-Hungary and Russia.)* Then have students compare the historical map with a present-day map of Europe. What area in present-day Italy remains part of the Papal States? *(Vatican City)*

History & Art In 1860 Giuseppe Garibaldi had conquered the Kingdom of the Two Sicilies in southern Italy, while Victor Emmanuel II had brought most of northern Italy into his kingdom. When the two men met at the bridge of Teano, Garibaldi surrendered his conquests to Victor Emmanuel and hailed him as king of Italy.

History & Art _Meeting at Teano_ by Cesare Maccari. Palazzo Pubblico, Siena, Italy
A desire to unite Italy brought together Sardinia's King Victor Emmanuel II (left) and the revolutionary leader Giuseppe Garibaldi (right).

Your History Journal

Write a report on a subtopic from "Powder Keg in the Balkans" in Section 5 of this chapter. Suggested titles: Decline of the Ottoman Empire, The Crimean War, Russo-Turkish War, The Congress of Berlin, Russian Objectives in the Balkans, British Objectives in the Balkans.

Chapter 15   _Reaction and Nationalism_   **451**

Performance Assessment

Refer to the activity on page 450C of the Planning Guide.

 For an additional activity, refer to Activity 15 in the _Performance Assessment Strategies and Activities_ booklet.

Using Your History Journal

Have students research one of the suggested report topics by using outside sources. Suggest that they take notes for their report in their journals.

GLENCOE TECHNOLOGY

VIDEODISC
Use MindJogger to preview chapter content.

MindJogger Videoquiz

Chapter 15
Disc 2 Side B

 Also available in VHS.

✚ **EXTRA CREDIT PROJECT**

Oral Report Have students use outside sources to do in-depth research on one of the people mentioned in this chapter or on a person or group not mentioned in the chapter that was involved in a European nationalist movement during the 1800s. Suggest that they cover the background, education, social position, political ideas, and political actions of the person or group. Ask them to analyze the success or failure of their person or group.

1820   **1860**   **1900**

1831 Giuseppe Mazzini founds Young Italy.

1861 Italians establish a united kingdom.

1871 Victor Emmanuel II moves the capital from Florence to Rome.

Section 1

The Unification of Italy

Find Out

Answer: *The desire for a politically united Italy caused the Italians to over- throw Austrian rule and look to the king of Sardinia as a unifying force. After fighting started, people in many regions of Italy overthrew their rulers and united with the Kingdom of Sardinia to become the nation of Italy.*

FOCUS

Section Objective

Explain how nationalism led to a united Italy in the 1860s.

BELLRINGER
Motivational Activity

Before taking roll at the beginning of the class period, project Section Focus Transparency 15-1 and have students answer the activity questions. Discuss students' responses.
🗁 This activity is also avail- able as a blackline master.

Vocabulary Pre-check

🗁 Use Vocabulary Activity 15 to introduce vocabulary terms.
L1 LEP

Setting the Scene

▶ **Terms to Define**
nationalism, nation-state, guerrilla warfare

▶ **People to Meet**
Giuseppe Mazzini, Charles Albert, Victor Emmanuel II, Count Camillo di Cavour, Giuseppe Garibaldi

▶ **Places to Locate**
Florence, Genoa, Sicily, Sardinia, Rome

 **Find Out** How did nationalism lead to a unit- ed Italy in the 1860s?

The Storyteller

As the crowd shouted "Viva Verdi!", Giuseppe Verdi smiled. He understood the phrase's double meaning. Although the throng appreciated his operas, they were actually demon- strating for a unified Italy. The Risorgimento, those wishing for a unified Italy, adopted Verdi's music as a rally-cry supporting Victor Emmanuel, the king of Sardinia. When people cheered "Viva Verdi," the occupying Austrians thought they were praising the musician. But the words meant Viva Vittorio Emanuele, Re D'Italia—*long live Victor Emmanuel, king of Italy.*

—adapted from *A History of Western Music,* Donald J. Grout and Claude V. Palisca, 1988

The Musician Giuseppe Verdi *by Boldini*

452 Chapter 15 *Reaction and Nationalism*

From about the 1100s to the 1800s, central Europe was made up of numerous king- doms, principalities, and free cities. Stimulated by the desire for economic growth, by the success of the American Revolution, and by the experience of the Napoleonic Wars, a small but dedicated group of Italians and Germans worked to unify these territories into nations in the 1800s. The desire for national independence that inspired them, known as nationalism, became one of the most powerful forces at work in Europe during the 1800s.

In 1815 the modern nation of Italy did not yet exist. At that time the Italian Peninsula was divided into a number of independent states, many of which had foreign rulers. A French Bourbon monarch ruled the Kingdom of the Two Sicilies, while Austria controlled Lombardy and Venetia and the pope controlled the Papal States.

In addition to political divisions, cultural and economic differences divided the regions of the Italian Peninsula. Not only did people speak differ- ent dialects of the Italian language, but trade barri- ers and poor transportation discouraged the flow of goods and people. To move goods the 200 miles (322 km) from **Florence** to Milan often took 8 weeks.

While cultural and economic divisions contin- ued into the 1900s, a growing unification move- ment eventually swept aside the political divisions on the Italian Peninsula. By the 1860s, Italy had become a single country.

Early Attempts

The name given to the movement for Italian unity was *Risorgimento* (ree•ZAWR•jih•MEHN •toh), meaning the "resurgence" or "revival."

Giuseppe Mazzini was its most effective speaker. A native of **Genoa** and a bold and active leader in the fight for Italian independence, Mazzini founded in 1831 a secret society called Young Italy. The goal of this society was to transform Italy into an independent sovereign nation. According to Mazzini, the nation-state, a political organization consisting of one nationality rather than several nationalities, was very important. Through it, people in one unified country with common ideals could best contribute their efforts to the well-being of all its citizens.

In January 1848, Mazzini-inspired nationalists led a republican revolution in **Sicily**. Some weeks later, news of larger revolutions in France and Austria sparked uprisings throughout the Italian Peninsula. When fighting began against Austrian forces in Lombardy and Venetia, King **Charles Albert** of the Kingdom of **Sardinia** joined the war to expel the foreigners. Nationalists pressured the rulers of Naples, Tuscany, and the Papal States to send troops against the Austrians.

By April 1848 the united Italian forces had almost succeeded in driving the Austrians from the peninsula. Then, saying that he opposed a war with another Catholic country, Pope Pius IX suddenly withdrew his troops. Naples followed suit. Their withdrawal enabled Austria to defeat the army of Charles Albert and reestablish its control over Lombardy and Venetia.

The pope's decision infuriated Italian nationalists. In November 1848 angry mobs forced the pope to flee the city. Nationalists proclaimed **Rome** a republic and summoned Mazzini to the capital to head the government. The expulsion of the pope, however, aroused the Catholic governments of Naples, Spain, and France. As a result, Louis-Napoleon sent a French army to Rome. His troops occupied the city and restored the pope to power.

The events of 1848 caused many Italians to lose faith in Mazzini's revolutionary methods. They became more conservative and turned to Charles Albert, who had earned their respect with his brave stand against the Austrians. Nationalists now looked to Sardinia to lead the struggle for Italian unification.

Count Cavour's Diplomacy

In 1849 **Victor Emmanuel II**, Charles Albert's son, became king of Sardinia. During the next few years Victor Emmanuel II toiled to keep popular support for the unity movement alive. He was greatly helped in his efforts by a shrewd and determined adviser named **Count Camillo di Cavour**.

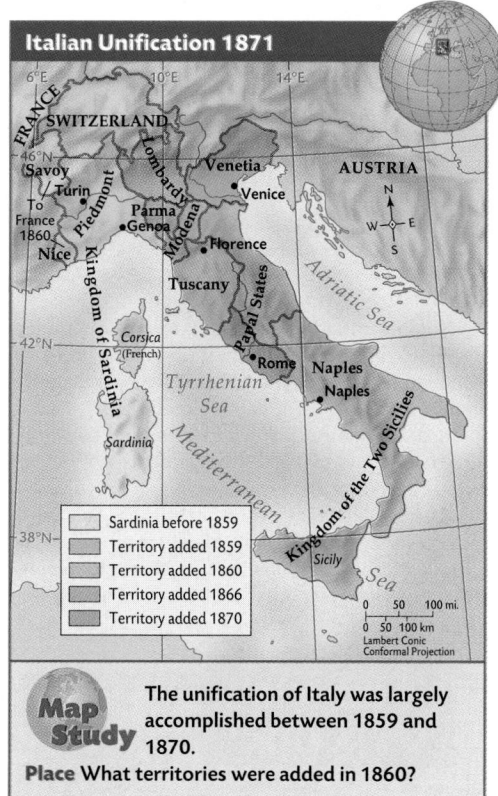

Italian Unification 1871

Sardinia before 1859
Territory added 1859
Territory added 1860
Territory added 1866
Territory added 1870

0   50   100 mi.

0   50   100 km
Lambert Conic
Conformal Projection

Map Study The unification of Italy was largely accomplished between 1859 and 1870.

Place What territories were added in 1860?

Physically, Cavour was not impressive, as this description by a contemporary illustrates:

> ❝ The squat … pot-bellied form; the small, stumpy legs; the short, round arms, with the hands stuck constantly in the trousers' pockets … and the sharp grey eyes, covered by the goggle spectacles … The dress itself seemed a part and property of the man. ❞

Cavour's looks were deceptive, however. Hidden behind the rumpled clothes and strange appearance was a bold, intelligent man of great personal charm. By the time of the Crimean War in 1854, Cavour dominated Sardinia's council of ministers. His major goals were the promotion of rapid industrial growth, the reduction of the Catholic Church's influence, and the advancement of Sardinia's national interests in foreign affairs.

The defeat of Sardinia in 1848 convinced Cavour that the kingdom needed the aid of a foreign power to expel Austria and achieve Italian

Chapter 15 *Reaction and Nationalism* **453**

TEACH

Guided Practice

THEME Nationalism

Help students define *nationalism*. Discuss how nationalism can unify people in a country or can lead to war and to discrimination against minority groups. Conclude by asking students to give examples of nationalism at work in the world today. **L1**

Map Study

Answer
Parma, Modena, Tuscany, part of the Papal States, and the Kingdom of the Two Sicilies

Map Skills Practice

Reading a Map When did Venetia become part of Italy? *(1866)*

Geography: Place Refer students to the map on this page. Have students identify the changing political loyalties of the major islands west of Italy. Which ones became part of a unified Italy? *(Sardinia and Sicily)* Which one did not? *(Corsica)* Let students discuss the importance of political loyalties of islands. *(important for trade and military strategy)* **L2**

Critical Thinking Have students discuss whether Cavour's problems with Garibaldi were justified. *(No; Garibaldi surrendered his conquests to Victor Emmanuel II.)* **L2**

 Chapter Transparency 15

 History Simulation 15

COOPERATIVE LEARNING ACTIVITY

Time Line Organize students into three groups to construct a chronology showing the unification of Italy. Have one group gather information on key people, writing short descriptions of their roles. Have the second group prepare short written descriptions about key events and their dates. Have the third group design and draw the time line, incorporating information from the other two groups. Have this group post the time line on a classroom bulletin board or wall. Encourage the class to use the time line as a reference. **L1**

Independent Practice

📁 Guided Reading Activity 15-1 **L1**

📁 Time Line Activity 15

Chart Have students create a chart with the following column headings: *Mazzini, Count Cavour, Victor Emmanuel II, Garibaldi.* Include the following topics for rows: *Goals and Ideals, Events and Dates, Impact on Unification.* Suggest students use outside sources to complete the chart. **L2 LEP**

Biography Have students research the life of Pope Pius IX and write a short biography. Suggest that students include the following topics in their biographies: Pius IX's early reforms, his views on and role in Italian unification, his removal from Rome, the doctrine of papal infallibility. **L3**

you don't say...

Carbonari means "charcoal burners" in Italian. It was the name of one of the first Italian secret societies for the overthrow of foreign governments in Italy. Although charcoal is black, it gives off a bright glow when burning. This was associated with the light of freedom and liberty.

unity. To win such aid, Cavour decided to support France and Britain in the Crimean War. One historian later called this action "one of the most brilliant strokes of statecraft in the nineteenth century."

By sending an army to the Crimea in 1854, Sardinia established a claim to equality with the other warring nations. Participating in the war also won Sardinia admittance to the Congress of Paris, which settled treaty matters after the war.

War With Austria

Not long after the Crimean War, in the summer of 1858, Cavour met secretly with Napoleon III at Plombiéres-les-Bains in France. There Napoleon III promised to aid Sardinia in expelling Austria if Sardinia found itself at war. In return, Sardinia agreed that it would give the provinces of Savoy and Nice to France in the event of an Italian-French victory over Austria. Cavour next forced Austria to declare war against Sardinia. He did this by encouraging nationalist groups in Lombardy to revolt. When Austria demanded that Sardinia withdraw

its support of the rebels, Sardinia refused. Austria declared war in April 1859. As he had promised, Napoleon III led a force of 120,000 French soldiers to aid Sardinia.

The combined forces of France and Sardinia defeated the Austrians at Magenta and Solferino in June 1859. Austria was on the run. The French suffered heavy losses, however, and Napoleon III feared the loss of public support at home if the fighting in Italy continued.

Without consulting Cavour, Napoleon III withdrew from the fighting in July and signed a treaty with Emperor Francis Joseph of Austria. By the terms of the treaty, Austria gave Lombardy to Sardinia but retained control of Venetia. When Cavour read these terms, he became furious. He insisted that Victor Emmanuel II continue to fight. Believing that victory was impossible without France, the king refused.

The fighting, however, did not stop. People in Tuscany, Parma, Modena, and the papal province of Romagna overthrew their rulers in late 1859 and

Images of the Times

Uniting Italy

Before 1860 Italy was made up of many separate states. After 1860 it became a united kingdom but remained culturally and economically divided. The deepest division was between northern and southern parts of the country.

Southern Italy remained a leading rural and agricultural area. Traditional customs were strong, and artisans excelled in various crafts.

454

Images of the Times
Uniting Italy

"We have made Italy, now we have to make Italians," remarked Massimo d'Azeglio, a former prime minister of the Piedmont, after 1860. This task was especially hard to accomplish in southern Italy, where few local people had actively taken part in the fight for unification. Many of the peasants who lived in this region had to scratch out a living working as laborers or as tenants on large estates. Poverty and unemployment were common throughout the south, and the new government lacked revenue for relief, job programs, and education. Because of lack of work, many southern Italians migrated to North Africa and the Americas. From there, they sent money home to their families.

early 1860. Their new governments demanded the right to unite with Sardinia. To gain Napoleon III's consent for this unification, Cavour gave Savoy and Nice to France. In April 1860 Victor Emmanuel II accepted the territories into his kingdom.

Garibaldi Seizes the South

Southern Italy remained isolated from the revolutionary fever sweeping the rest of the peninsula, but at the death of Ferdinand II, ruler of the Kingdom of the Two Sicilies, Italian nationalists prepared for a revolution. Their leader was a charismatic military commander and adventurer named **Giuseppe Garibaldi**.

As a young man, Garibaldi had joined Young Italy. Forced into exile after taking part in the 1830 uprisings, he went to South America, where he fought in several revolutionary wars. As a result of this experience, Garibaldi became an expert in guerrilla warfare, a method of warfare using hit-and-run tactics. Garibaldi returned to Italy in 1848 and took part in Mazzini's short-lived Roman Republic. When the Roman Republic fell in 1849, Garibaldi again fled his homeland, this time to the United States.

Sensing that the people of the Kingdom of the Two Sicilies were ready to revolt, Garibaldi returned to Italy in 1860. After collecting a thousand volunteers in Genoa, he set out for Sicily. When his troops faltered in the midst of the first battle of the Sicilian campaign, Garibaldi rallied them to victory. In a few weeks, he gained total control of the island.

He then crossed to the mainland and advanced toward Naples. The army of the Kingdom of the Two Sicilies proved no match for the guerrilla tactics of Garibaldi's Red Shirts, so called because of the color of their uniforms. Naples fell, and the king of the Two Sicilies fled.

Garibaldi's successes in the south made Cavour nervous. He worried about his fellow countryman's political ambitions. To prevent Garibaldi

Who?What?Where?When?

Giuseppe Garibaldi Between 1850 and 1860, Garibaldi lived on Staten Island in New York City. He made a meager living working in a friend's candle factory.

Linking Past and Present

Guerrilla warfare, such as that which Garibaldi's Red Shirts were known for, has been used since biblical times. During the American Revolution, Francis Marion, the "Swamp Fox," led guerrilla groups against the British in South Carolina. More recently, guerrilla warfare proved effective during the Vietnam War.

ASSESS

Check for Understanding

Assign Section 1 Review as homework or as an in-class activity.

Use Student Self-Test and Review Software to review Section 1.

Northern Italy became a highly urbanized and industrialized region. The city of Milan was known both for its economic prosperity and its festive outdoor celebrations.

Tuscany, a region in north-central Italy, was known for its picturesque villages and vineyards as well as the cultural city of Florence.

REFLECTING ON THE TIMES

1. How was Italy organized politically before 1860?
2. What economic and social differences distinguished northern Italy from southern Italy?

455

ANSWERS TO REFLECTING ON THE TIMES

1. Italy was divided into several independent states.
2. Northern Italy became highly industrialized and urbanized; southern Italy remained a rural, agricultural area.

Chapter 15
Section 1

Visualizing History After gaining control of Sicily in 1860, Giuseppe Garibaldi and his forces left the island for the Italian mainland. *What type of warfare did Garibaldi carry out on behalf of Italian national unity?*

from further victories, Cavour sent an army into the Papal States. On September 18 the forces of Sardinia defeated the papal army at Castelfidaro. The victory kept Cavour in control of the campaign for national unity.

When voters in southern Italy supported union with Sardinia in October 1860, Garibaldi surrendered his conquests to Victor Emmanuel II. By February 1861 the whole peninsula, with the exception of Rome and Venetia, was united under one government. Victor Emmanuel II was now king of the newly created constitutional monarchy of Italy.

Building a New Nation

Three months after the unification of Italy, Count Cavour died. His last words were "Italy is made. All is safe." Despite Cavour's optimism, many difficult problems faced the new nation. For example, national unification had not erased the profound cultural and economic divisions that separated the south and north of Italy. The south was poor and agricultural, while the north had begun to industrialize. The gap in the standards of living between the two regions fueled discontent and hampered unification efforts.

In the name of national unity, Sardinia often tried to force its laws and customs onto the other Italian states. This tactic only fanned resentment. Former rulers also encouraged discontent. When some of these rulers tried to regain their thrones, bloody civil wars erupted.

Gradually the Italian government developed a unified military force and a national educational system. It built railroads, linking not only the south with the north but also Italy with the rest of Europe. While these developments were important steps in the process of unification, cultural and economic barriers remained.

Another problem concerned the location of the nation's capital. Most Italians thought that **Rome** should be the capital of the new nation. During the 1860s, however, the pope still ruled the city. In addition, the Austrians continued to control Venetia.

Italy again sought foreign help to solve a political problem. In 1866 Italy allied itself with Prussia in a war against Austria. In return, Prussia promised to give Venetia to Italy. Although Austria defeated Italian forces in the conflict, the Prussian victory was so overwhelming that Prussia gave Venetia to Italy anyway.

Foreign intervention also played a role in helping Italy win Rome. When war broke out between France and Prussia in 1870, Napoleon III withdrew French troops that had been protecting the pope. Italian troops then entered Rome and conquered the pope's territory. In 1871 Victor Emmanuel II moved the national capital from Florence to Rome. The political unification of Italy was finally complete.

SECTION 1 REVIEW

Recall
1. **Define** nationalism, nation-state, guerrilla warfare.
2. **Identify** Giuseppe Mazzini, Charles Albert, Victor Emmanuel II, Count Camillo di Cavour, Giuseppe Garibaldi.

3. **List** three problems Italy faced after unification.
Critical Thinking
4. **Applying Information** Select a leader in the movement for Italian unification and show how that leader furthered the

aims of the movement.
Understanding Themes
5. **Nationalism** Explain how the papacy and the Catholic Church responded to the rise of nationalism in the Italian Peninsula.

1820   1840   1860   1880

1834 German states create the *Zollverein*.

1866 Prussia and Austria fight Seven Weeks' War.

1871 William I becomes emperor of a united Germany.

Section 2

The Unification of Germany

Setting the Scene

▶ **Terms to Define**
realpolitik, kaiser, chancellor

▶ **People to Meet**
William I, Otto von Bismarck

▶ **Places to Locate**
Frankfurt, Austria, Prussia, Schleswig, Holstein

 **Find Out** What methods did Bismarck use to unite the German states?

The Storyteller

Klaus von Erlach was impressed by Otto von Bismarck's message, although many of Klaus's fellow aristocrats disliked the Iron Chancellor, considering him a traitor to his class. Who other than a great leader, Klaus wondered, would be able to defend a change of political opinion? As Bismarck stated, "The man who does not learn also fails to progress and cannot keep abreast of his time. People are falling behind when they remain rooted in the position they occupied two years ago." If Germany was to progress, the old systems would have to adapt.

—adapted from "Professorial Politics," Otto von Bismarck, reprinted in *Sources of World History*, Mark A. Kishlansky, 1995

Otto von Bismarck

Germany was the last of the great European powers to achieve complete political unity. In 1815, 39 independent German states stretched north and south from the Baltic Sea to the Alps, and east and west from the Rhine River to the Russian Empire. Political rivals Austria and Prussia were the most powerful of these German states.

While Great Britain and France were developing as strong industrial nations, Germany remained divided and economically disadvantaged. The Reformation and the Thirty Years' War contributed to Germany's social and political divisions. Antagonisms between Protestant and Catholic states ran deep. By 1871, however, the German states—excluding Austria and Switzerland—had united into a single nation.

Steps Toward Unity

The Congress of Vienna had created the German Confederation in 1815 as a buffer against possible future French expansion. This first major step toward German unity established closer economic ties between the German states and helped pave the way for greater political union.

The German Confederation loosely tied together the numerous German states with a diet, or assembly, sitting at **Frankfurt**. **Austria** dominated the confederation. Its position as head of the diet eventually brought it into conflict with **Prussia**. Neither Austria nor the smaller German states wanted to see a united Germany. Austria feared the economic competition, while the smaller states feared domination by Prussia.

The largest of the German states, Prussia had a well-organized government and a strong economy. Political power in Prussia lay in the hands of

Chapter 15 *Reaction and Nationalism* **457**

SECTION THEME

▶ **Conflict** Bismarck uses war and diplomacy to bring unity to Germany.

Find Out

Answer: *war and diplomacy*

FOCUS

Section Objective
Identify the methods Bismarck used to unite the German states.

BELLRINGER
Motivational Activity

Before taking roll at the beginning of the class period, project Section Focus Transparency 15-2 and have students answer the activity questions. Discuss students' responses.
This activity is also available as a blackline master.

Vocabulary Pre-check
Use Vocabulary Activity 15 to introduce vocabulary terms.
L1 LEP

SECTION RESOURCES

Reproducible Masters
• Reproducible Lesson Plan 15-2
• Vocabulary Activity 15
• Guided Reading Activity 15-2
• Section Quiz 15-2

Transparencies
• Section Focus Transparency 15-2

Multimedia
• Student Self-Test and Review Software
• Testmaker

Chapter 15 *Reaction and Nationalism* **457**

TEACH

Guided Practice

THEME Conflict

Have students make a chart on the chalkboard that shows the participants, purpose, and outcomes of the war against Denmark, the Seven Weeks' War, and the Franco-Prussian War. **L1 LEP**

Map Study

Answers

1. *Prussia*
2. *a well-organized government and a strong economy*

Map Skills Practice

Reading a Map **For what practical reason would Prussia want a united Germany?** *(to unite the two parts of Prussia)*

Economics Lead a discussion about economic issues involved in unification. Have students include the *Zollverein* and Bismarck's budget for the army. **L2**

Government Hold an informal class debate on the advantages and disadvantages of Bismarck's policy of realpolitik. Conclude the debate by having students discuss whether realpolitik is a force in political policy today. Encourage students to give examples of realpolitik from current events. **L3**

---

influential aristocratic landowners called Junkers (YUN•kuhrs), but members of the rising business class demanded a share of political power. To reduce trade barriers, German states in 1834 formed a *Zollverein*, or economic union. This step toward unity strengthened the influence of Prussia, while weakening that of Austria, in German affairs.

In 1848, as revolutions swept Europe, power in the German states shifted to the liberals. From all parts of Germany, delegates met in the Frankfurt Assembly to unite the country under a liberal constitution. Internal feuding, however, weakened this effort, allowing the conservatives to regain control. In 1849 the Prussian military forced the Assembly's closure and later put down street revolts. Many liberal and radical Germans fled abroad, especially to the United States. During the 1850s, in Germany as in other parts of Europe, conservatives in many cases came to control nationalist causes.

Rise of Bismarck

German conservatives looked to Prussia for help in uniting Germany. In 1861 **William I** became king of Prussia. Opposed to liberal ideas, William believed in a strong military and took steps to expand the Prussian army. Liberal German nationalists, however, saw no use for a strong military except to control the Prussian people. They wanted the king to adopt democratic policies to gain support from the other German states. As a result, liberal deputies in the Prussian assembly overwhelmingly defeated new taxes to support a larger army.

Frustrated by the defeat, the king appointed as his new prime minister a man who shared his views on army reconstruction. That man was **Otto von Bismarck**. A Junker himself, Bismarck had served in the Prussian assembly and as ambassador to Russia and France. He shared the king's view that Prussia needed a strong government and army to achieve German unity. A brilliant negotiator, Bismarck embraced the policy of **realpolitik**, the right of the nation-state to pursue its own advantage by any means, including war and the repudiation of treaties.

In September 1862 Bismarck defied the finance committee of the Prussian assembly. He declared that the great issues of the times would not be decided "by speeches and majority decisions … but by blood and iron." When the lower house again refused to approve the new army budget, Bismarck pushed the program through by simply collecting the necessary taxes without authorization.

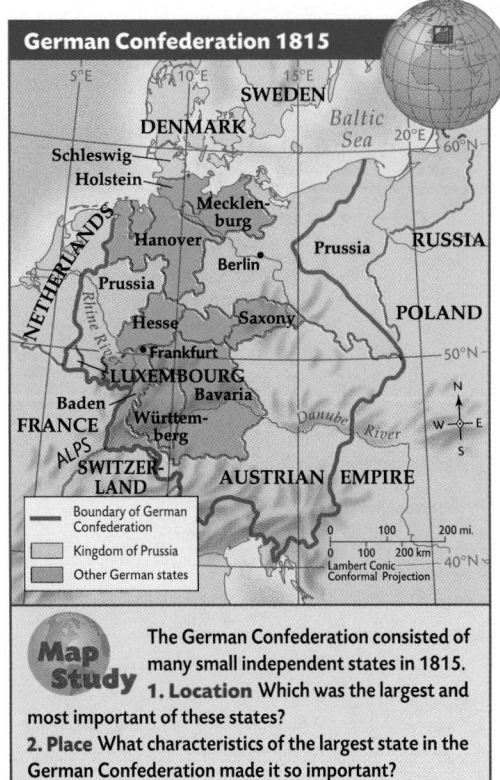

German Confederation 1815

Map Study

The German Confederation consisted of many small independent states in 1815.
1. **Location** Which was the largest and most important of these states?
2. **Place** What characteristics of the largest state in the German Confederation made it so important?

Three Wars

Bismarck once said, "Show me an objective worthy of war and I will go along with you." As prime minister, he found several worthy objectives. His initial goal was to raise money for army expansion. Then he wanted Prussia to use its military and economic power to reduce Austrian influence among the German states. Finally, he planned to arrange the unification of all German states except Austria and Switzerland under Prussian domination. To accomplish these objectives, Bismarck went to war three times.

War Against Denmark

By inheritance, the king of Denmark ruled the territories of **Schleswig** and **Holstein**. Schleswig's population was part German and part Danish; Holstein's population was entirely German. When King Christian IX proclaimed Schleswig a Danish province in 1863, Germans in both territories appealed to the larger German states for support.

COOPERATIVE LEARNING ACTIVITY

Role Play Organize the class into six groups to role-play the diplomatic stands taken by Germany and its rivals in the war with Denmark, the Seven Weeks' War, and the Franco-Prussian War. Have three groups research Germany's position in each war and the other three groups each research Denmark's, Austria's, and France's positions. Suggest that students gather data about their assigned country's goals and relations with their opposing country. Then have each pair of rival groups present their dramatizations in the order in which they occurred: the war with Denmark, the Seven Weeks' War, and the Franco-Prussian War. **L2**

To prevent Danish annexation of Schleswig, Bismarck persuaded Austria to join Prussia in declaring war against Denmark in 1864. Prussia and Austria soon won this war and forced Denmark out of the disputed provinces. By mutual agreement, Prussia took control of Schleswig, and Austria took over the administration of Holstein. This arrangement strained the relationship between these rival powers.

The war accomplished two of Bismarck's objectives. First, it made Europe aware of Prussia's military might and influence. Second, the tension resulting from the war settlement gave Bismarck the excuse he wanted for going to war with Austria.

Seven Weeks' War

One month before the invasion of Schleswig, Bismarck wrote to his envoy in Paris:

❝ You do not trust Austria. Neither do I. But I consider it the correct policy at present to have Austria with us. Whether the moment of parting will come, and on whose initiative, we shall see.... I am not in the least afraid of war, on the contrary ... you may very soon be able to convince yourself that war also is included in my program. ❞

Bismarck prepared for war by stripping Austria of possible allies. He gained Russia's goodwill by offering the czar aid against Polish rebels in 1863. He offered France possible "compensations" for its neutrality in case of an Austro-Prussian war. He also forged an alliance with Italy by supporting its claim to Venetia in return for military support against Austria.

Bismarck gained public support for his actions when Austria sided with the duke of Augustenburg, who claimed title to Schleswig and Holstein. To prevent an alliance between Austria and the duke, Bismarck ordered Prussian troops into Austrian-occupied Holstein. When Austria then asked the German Confederation to take military action against Prussia for this invasion, Bismarck responded by declaring war against Austria.

The war between Austria and Prussia began on June 15, 1866, and ended in a Prussian victory just seven weeks later. For Bismarck, the conflict had been a limited war with limited objectives. Its purpose was to separate Austria from Germany and

CONNECTIONS Geography

A Divided Land

Germany's geography has made it a country of distinct regions. Throughout German history, rivers have drawn people in different directions. The north-flowing Rhine, Weser, and Oder Rivers have linked the peoples of these river valleys to the northern plains. In southern Germany, the Danube River has oriented people of that region to the southeast.

Mountains and highland areas—especially the Alps and the Central Highlands—have isolated populations

A divided Berlin

and strengthened local dialects and traditions.

In the past, political and religious conflict heightened divisions; Swabians considered Westphalians as foreigners, and Bavarians regarded Prussians as archrivals. This regionalism led Germans to resist political unity until the late 1800s. In the 1900s, the German defeat in World War II and the rivalry between the United States and the Soviet Union caused Germany's division into eastern and western parts. With communism's fall, Germany finally reunited in 1990.

Linking Past and Present ACTIVITY

Discuss the geographical and historical factors contributing to German regionalism. What has been the relationship between regionalism and national unity in the United States?

Linking Past and Present

German Unification Bismarck used three wars to unify Germany, but another German-caused war—World War II—left Germany divided for 45 years. In 1990 West Germany and East Germany were reunited as one country.

Independent Practice

📁 Guided Reading Activity 15-2 **L1**

Comic Strip Have students draw an action comic strip of the major events that led to German unification. Suggest that they include the German Confederation, *Zollverein*, rise of Bismarck, the three wars, William I, the Ems telegram, and the government of the empire. **L2**

— **Linking Past and Present** —

A Divided Land

Germany is made up of three major geographic areas: the northern Lowlands, the Central Highlands, and the southern mountains. These physical divisions hindered political unification of the German states.

ANSWER

Geographic factors: mountains, highlands, and flow of major rivers; historical: political and religious strife. Because of its large size and varied geography, regionalism has also existed in the United States; regional differences between North and South led to the Civil War; since the late 1800s, a growing economy and common beliefs in liberty and democracy, however, have united the country while respecting regional differences.

MEETING SPECIAL NEEDS ACTIVITY

Study Strategy Organize students into four groups, with the most students in group three. Assign each group one of the four main headings in the section. Ask each group to prepare an outline of its part of the section. Remind students to include important dates and explanations of why certain people, places, and events were important to German unification. Make photocopies of each group's outline to distribute to students in all the groups. **L2**

Answer

to unite the eastern and western parts of Prussia

Map Skills Practice

Reading a Map To which central European country did a united Germany pose the biggest threat? *(Austria-Hungary)*

CURRICULUM CONNECTION

MILITARY HISTORY

In 1841 Johann Nikolas Dreyse designed the Prussian needle gun. Using this breech-loading rifle, the Prussian army defeated the Austrian army at the Battle of Sadowa in 1866 during the Seven Weeks' War. Lying down on the ground, Prussian soldiers outfired the standing Austrians who used muzzle-loading rifles.

Cultural Perspectives

German Dialects The German language has many dialects. When Germany was first united, speakers of Low German dialects had trouble understanding Swabians in southern Germany. Eastern Rhinelanders could not easily communicate with southwestern Saxons. In addition, minority groups spoke French, Lithuanian, Polish, and Danish.

ASSESS

Check for Understanding

Assign Section 2 Review as homework or as an in-class activity.

end the chance for a united Germany under Austrian control. In the end, Bismarck did not want to destroy Austria with a harsh peace settlement. He knew that he would probably need an alliance with Austria in the future.

The treaty ending the war was negotiated in the city of Prague. The settlement dissolved the German Confederation and gave Holstein to Prussia and Venetia to Italy. The treaty also called for "a new organization of Germany without the participation of Austria."

This "new organization" became the North German Confederation in 1867. It embraced all the German states north of the Main (MYN) River. The Confederation's constitution gave each state the right to manage its domestic affairs, but put foreign policy and national defense in the hands of Prussia. Legislative authority was vested in a federal council composed of representatives from the various governments and a diet, or assembly, elected by universal male suffrage.

The establishment of a strong confederation by Prussia made Bismarck a hero among German nationalists. Bismarck's work of uniting Germany, however, was not finished.

The Franco-Prussian War

The southern German states, which were largely Catholic, remained outside the new German confederation. Most of them feared Protestant Prussia's military strength and its control of Germany. The kingdoms of Bavaria and Württenberg (WUHR•tehm•BUHRG), in particular, steadfastly opposed German unification under Prussian rule. They would accept German unification only if Prussia gave up some of its authority in a united government. Prussia would not agree to this, however.

France posed the most serious obstacle to a united Germany. Napoleon III would not accept German unification unless France received some territory—its compensation for not joining Austria in the Seven Weeks' War. To resolve the situation, Bismarck again chose war.

Some historians believe that Bismarck was responsible for the Franco-Prussian War. In his memoirs, Bismarck had written that "a Franco-German [Prussian] war must take place before the construction of a united Germany could be realized." If Napoleon III had not wanted war as much as Bismarck, however, the war may never have taken place. Bismarck knew that he could not invade France without public support. Instead, he had to lure France into war, taking advantage of Napoleon III's weakness in foreign policy and of the French public's current anti-Prussian feeling.

460 Chapter 15 *Reaction and Nationalism*

German Unification 1871

Prussia before 1866
Territory added 1867
Territory added 1871

Map Study Bismarck succeeded in unifying Germany in just 15 years. **Location** Why do you think it was important to Prussia to add northern Germany to its territory?

Bismarck's chance came in 1870 in connection with the Hohenzollern candidacy for the Spanish throne.

A revolution in 1868 had deposed Queen Isabella of Spain. The Spanish government offered the throne to Prince Leopold of Hohenzollern, a Catholic cousin of William I of Prussia. Fearing a Spanish-German alliance against France, Napoleon III protested the offer. William brushed aside this protest, but Leopold later voluntarily declined the throne.

In July 1870, France demanded a promise from William that a Hohenzollern would never sit on the Spanish throne. William, who was vacationing at the German resort of Ems, refused. In a telegram to Bismarck, he described the details of his meeting with the French ambassador. To make it appear that William had deliberately insulted the French envoy, Bismarck altered the Ems telegram and released it to the press. Newspaper coverage of the supposed insult enraged the French, leading Napoleon to declare war on Prussia.

The fighting began on July 19, 1870. More anti-French than anti-Prussian, the southern German states allied with Prussia. With highly efficient military forces, the Prussians easily defeated the French.

MAKING CONNECTIONS ACTIVITY

Music and Literature Have students research and write brief reports on one of the following German composers or writers: Richard Wagner, Johannes Brahms, Gustav Mahler, Anton Bruckner, Friedrich Nietzsche, Gustav Freytag, Leopold von Ranke, or Heinrich von Treitschke. Ask students to include the major works and main ideas of the person chosen and to discuss the person's views about the unification of Germany. **L2**

History & Art
Otto von Bismarck by Franz von Lenbach, Art History Museum, Vienna, Austria **Otto von Bismarck poses in military uniform with a Prussian helmet. He came from the Junker class of Prussia and supported a strong monarchy.** *What does Bismarck's style of dress reveal about the German Empire formed in 1871?*

 History & Art Fashionable parties in the German Empire were not complete without officers splendidly attired in imperial uniforms. Bismarck even wore his uniform in the parliament.
Answer to Caption: *It shows that the German Empire was founded on militaristic, authoritarian values.*

◎ Use Student Self-Test and Review Software to review Section 2.

Evaluate
📁 Section Quiz 15-2

◎ Use the Testmaker to create a customized quiz for Section 2.

Reteach

Have students orally summarize material under each of the section's major headings.

Enrich

Have students write a brief essay on why the Junkers felt that Bismarck had betrayed his class by giving the industrial, business class a share in political power.

CLOSE

Have students discuss whether Germany could have been unified without war.

Bismarck then gained support from all the German states for the unification of Germany under Prussia.

Formation of an Empire

On January 18, 1871, William I assumed the title of kaiser, or emperor, of a united Germany. He ruled over a domain that stretched from the Baltic sea in the north to the Alps in the south. Bismarck became the German chancellor, or chief minister.

The new empire united 25 German states into one federal union. Although each state had its own ruler, and some had their own armies and diplomatic staffs, the kaiser headed the national government. He had authority to make appointments, command the military in time of war, and determine foreign policy. Prussian Junkers now shared power with wealthy industrialists. Unification did not make Germany a model democratic state.

William's son, Crown Prince Frederick of Prussia, was a liberal and a supporter of reform. He deplored the means Bismarck used to bring about the unification of Germany. In his diary, he wrote of his despair: "We are no longer looked upon as the innocent victims of wrong, but rather as arrogant victors." While he foresaw many of the consequences of Bismarck's policies, Frederick did nothing to change them.

SECTION 2 REVIEW

Recall
1. **Define** realpolitik, kaiser, chancellor.
2. **Identify** William I, Otto von Bismarck.
3. **Locate** Schleswig and Holstein on the map on page 460. Why do you think the Danish king claimed Schleswig and not Holstein as a Danish province?

Critical Thinking
4. **Synthesizing Information** Imagine that you are a member of the Prussian assembly opposed to Bismarck's policy for German unification. What alternative policy would you have suggested to William I?

Understanding Themes
5. **Conflict** Compare Bismarck's methods for achieving the unification of Germany with Cavour's methods for bringing about the unification of Italy.

SECTION 2 REVIEW ANSWERS

1. All vocabulary words are defined in the Glossary.
2. William I, 458; Otto von Bismarck, 458
3. Schleswig is directly south of Denmark and part of the same peninsula. Holstein is more a part of the mainland.
4. Answers will vary but may include that offering people greater participation in government rather than threats of force might have gained their support for unification.
5. **CONFLICT** Both Cavour and Bismarck planned the unification of their respective countries; both used military means to achieve their objective; both used foreign help to achieve unification—although Bismarck relied more on his own Prussian army than on foreign troops.

1870		1885		1900		1915

1872 Bismarck expels Jesuits from Germany.

1883 German government provides health insurance to workers.

1888 William II becomes emperor of Germany.

1913 Germany's standing army numbers more than 800,000 soldiers.

Section 3

Bismarck's Realm

Setting the Scene

▶ **Terms to Define**
papal infallibility, militarism

▶ **People to Meet**
Pope Pius IX, Ferdinand Lassalle, William II

Find Out How did Bismarck's policies affect the German Empire?

The Storyteller

Erich Klein's Uncle Karl enjoyed talking politics and was eager to explain the German political system to his American nephew. "Germany consists of twenty-six different states that were once independent but now are united. Each state has its own governmental officials and hereditary princes, but they are all subject to Kaiser [William] I." Erich remarked, "This government sounds similar to the United States." Uncle Karl agreed, but mentioned an important difference: "The Kaiser was not elected. He was acclaimed by the various princes who were willing to concede their power so that aristocracy by birth would remain within the German government."

Kaiser William I

—adapted from *Im Vaterland [In the Fatherland]*, Paul V. Bacon, 1910

Victory on the battlefield brought about Germany's political unity, but the Germans were not united as a people. Religious, economic, social, and political divisions remained. German leaders now had to encourage a sense of common purpose in the population.

Bismarck became the key figure in early German nation building. With the support of Kaiser William I, Bismarck took charge of policy in the German Empire. Over the years, he faced several direct challenges to the German nation-state and his own political authority.

Bismarck and the Church

One of the first challenges Bismarck faced was with the Catholic Church in the so-called Kulturkampf (kul•TUR•KAHMF), or cultural struggle, between Church and state. After German unification, Catholics in Germany organized the Center party to represent their interests in opposition to the predominantly Protestant Prussians.

Bismarck viewed Catholicism as an antinationalist force and consequently supported the Protestants in political affairs. In part, he was annoyed at the popularity of the Center party. He was also worried about an 1870 proclamation by Catholic bishops in Rome declaring papal infallibility—the doctrine that the pope, when speaking on matters of faith and morals, is infallible, or free from error.

Since the Jesuits, in Bismarck's eyes, were papal agents working to destroy the German Empire, the chancellor launched his campaign against the Church by expelling the Jesuits from Germany in 1872. One year later, the German legislature began passing a series of laws aimed at destroying Catholic influence in Germany. These so-called May Laws deprived Catholic bishops of much of their authority and even required that weddings be performed by secular officials. In response,

462   Chapter 15   *Reaction and Nationalism*

SECTION THEME

▶ **Change** Bismarck's German Empire allows for economic growth but limits political freedoms.

Find Out

Answer: *Bismarck's policies left Germany militarily and economically strong but prevented the development of a parliamentary democracy. Also, the working class was disgruntled about poor working and living conditions.*

FOCUS

Section Objective

Analyze how Bismarck's policies affected the German Empire.

BELLRINGER
Motivational Activity

Before taking roll at the beginning of the class period, project Section Focus Transparency 15-3 and have students answer the activity questions. Discuss students' responses.

This activity is also available as a blackline master.

Vocabulary Pre-check

Use Vocabulary Activity 15 to introduce vocabulary terms.
L1 LEP

SECTION RESOURCES

Reproducible Masters
• Reproducible Lesson Plan 15-3
• Vocabulary Activity 15
• Guided Reading Activity 15-3
• Section Quiz 15-3

Transparencies
• Section Focus Transparency 15-3

Multimedia
 Student Self-Test and Review Software
 Testmaker

Pope Pius IX declared the laws invalid and broke diplomatic ties with Germany.

Bismarck soon realized that he was fighting a losing battle. Instead of weakening the Center party, Bismarck's repressive measures strengthened it. In the legislative elections of 1877, the Center party gained even more seats. Even the Junker-controlled Conservative party began to oppose Bismarck's policies. Knowing that he needed the support of the Center party to defeat a serious challenge from the Socialists, Bismarck sought to make peace with the Catholics.

When Pope Pius IX died in 1878, his successor, Leo XIII, made an effort to heal the rift with Germany. Eventually, the German legislature repealed most laws directed against Catholics. By 1881 the Kulturkampf was over.

Germany's Industrial Growth

Prior to unification, Germany was not a great industrial nation. Primarily agricultural, the German states lagged far behind Great Britain in the production of textiles, coal, iron, and steel. Knowing that Germany's position as a major political and military power depended on a strong economy, German political and business leaders worked to expand the nation's industry. By the mid-1800s, advances in many areas began to transform Germany's economy. The establishment of the *Zollverein* had already encouraged economic growth and spurred efforts to improve transportation. After unification, investment capital from Great Britain, France, and Belgium helped to modernize industrial production and establish a mechanized factory system.

The development of deep-pit coal mining in the provinces along the Rhine and the opening of new coal mines in the Saar made available large reserves of cheap fuel for the new plants. Cities grew rapidly. Many young men and women streamed in from the villages to work in the new factories. As a result, at the end of the 1800s, Germany finally became a major industrial power.

The economic changes sweeping Germany conferred on at least some of its people the highest standard of living in Europe. The middle class and the business leaders benefited enormously from the rapid industrialization of the country. Every improvement in factory machinery, however, resulted in lower wages and higher unemployment for many German workers. They lived in crowded, filthy tenements and toiled long hours under dangerous working conditions.

Visualizing History Pope Leo XIII took a more conciliatory approach to new forms of secular government than did earlier popes. *What effect did Leo's papacy have on church relations with Bismarck's Germany?*

Workers and Socialism

Poor wages, long workdays, and job uncertainty made German workers receptive to a more hopeful vision of the future. They looked forward to a democratic social order in which they would no longer be exploited. To help bring about this new order in Germany, **Ferdinand Lassalle**, a writer and labor leader, founded the Universal German Workingmen's Association in 1863. Although he called himself a Socialist and a disciple of Karl Marx, Lassalle did not preach revolution. Whereas Marx called for the workers of the world to revolt against capitalism, Lassalle advocated mass political action to change the system.

Lassalle was a national celebrity who knew Bismarck and lectured him on the workers' plight. He did not live long enough, however, to finish the fight, for he was killed in a duel in 1864. The party he founded grew slowly until it merged with the Social Democratic party in 1875 and became a major political force.

Chapter 15 *Reaction and Nationalism* **463**

TEACH

Guided Practice

THEME Change

Have students make two lists, one showing economic changes in the German Empire under Bismarck, the other showing social changes. **L1 LEP**

Visualizing History Although Pope Leo XIII worked to reconcile with Germany, he continued to support the papacy's conservative political views, remaining opposed to freedom of speech, freedom of conscience, freedom of worship, and separation of church and state. **Answer to Caption:** *Pope Leo XIII worked to heal the rift between the papacy and Germany. German laws against Catholics were repealed and Kulturkampf ended by 1881.*

Religion Have students discuss the goals and outcome of Bismarck's Kulturkampf with the Catholic Church. **L2**

Cause and Effect Have students identify the causes and effects of the rise of socialism in the German Empire. **L3**

Independent Practice

Guided Reading Activity 15-3 **L1**

ASSESS

Check for Understanding

Assign Section 3 Review as homework or as an in-class activity.

Use Student Self-Test and Review Software to review Section 3.

TEACH

Tell students that to get Ludwig II to join the German Empire, Bismarck promised Bavaria its own post office and a separate peacetime army. Bismarck also had Ludwig send William I a letter inviting him to be emperor of Germany. Ludwig received the equivalent of $45,000 a year in exchange for the letter. What do you think he spent the money on? (*castles*) Within a week of being declared insane and losing his throne in 1886, Ludwig was found drowned in a lake near Neuschwanstein.

Linking Past and Present

Neuschwanstein Today nearly 1 million people tour Neuschwanstein each year. Many more people see a model of Ludwig's famous castle at the Disney theme parks. Cinderella's castle, the heart of Fantasyland, was patterned after Neuschwanstein.

Richmond Crawford, Jr.

Mad Ludwig's Castle

Ludwig II, King of Bavaria, ruled the independent German kingdom of Bavaria until 1871 and built for himself the storybook Neuschwanstein castle. He came to the throne unprepared to rule but enthusiastic about indulging his two passions: opera and palaces. Ludwig's castles were based on his romantic vision of the past. In each new mansion, rooms were decorated to look like scenes from the famous operas of nineteenth-century composer Richard Wagner. Ludwig's dreamy castles glorified and enshrined a bygone Germany. Ludwig's ministers, who had to find t cash to pay for his follies, finally had him declar insane and removed from power. Today his castle one of Germany's leading tourist attractions.

While Ludwig dreamed and listened to roman operas, Count Otto von Bismarck set about uniti the German Confederation and creating a mode German nation through military strength. "The gre questions of the age," Bismarck once remarked, "a not settled by speeches and majority votes ... but iron and blood." ⊕

464 **Chapter 15** *Reaction and Nationalism*

Bismarck and the Socialists

Despite his association with Lassalle, Bismarck believed that any Socialist party was out to change the government and that it therefore posed a serious threat to the German Empire. To destroy the Socialist movement in Germany, he set out to crush its organization. In 1878 the German legislature passed an anti-Socialist bill introduced by Bismarck. Although the bill did not outlaw the party itself, it banned all Socialist meetings and publications.

Bismarck's efforts to suppress the Socialists met with only temporary success. Consequently, Bismarck changed his tactics. He tried to show the workers that the government, and not the Socialists, had their true interests at heart. He directed the passage of several bills that gave workers some measure of comfort and security. In 1883, for example, the Sickness Insurance Law gave limited compensation to those who missed work because of illness. In 1889 the Old Age Insurance Law protected industrial workers in retirement.

Bismarck's reform efforts, however, did not go far enough to end the popularity of the Socialists. In 1890 the Social Democratic party won 35 seats in the legislature. With strong Socialist backing, the legislature refused to renew Bismarck's anti-Socialist law.

The Fall of Bismarck

In 1888 Kaiser William I died at the age of 91. Crown Prince Frederick, his liberal-minded son, succeeded him. Frederick III, however, died about 100 days after his coronation. **William II**, his son, succeeded him as emperor in 1888.

Only 29 years old at the time of his coronation, William II was a man of great energy and strong conservative opinions. Like his grandfather, William I, he favored militarism, or support for a powerful military prepared for war. His belief in the absolute authority of the emperor immediately

Visualizing History After steering the German ship of state for thirty years, Bismarck resigned in 1890. This cartoon was published upon Bismarck's departure from office. *What is the cartoon saying about Bismarck's relationship with Kaiser William II?*

brought him into conflict with Bismarck. Bismarck wanted the kaiser to leave political affairs to him.

Under William I, Bismarck often got his way by threatening to resign. When Bismarck offered his resignation in 1890, the kaiser accepted it. Much to Bismarck's surprise, William II "sent the veteran pilot over the side," as a popular cartoon of the time illustrated Bismarck's dismissal.

Bismarck's policies had left Germany strong, but they frustrated the German people. His strict rule prevented the development of a parliamentary democracy. With Bismarck gone, William II was free to pursue his own policies. During his reign Germany became one of the world's major industrial and military powers.

SECTION 3 REVIEW

Recall
1. **Define** papal infallibility, militarism.
2. **Identify** Kulturkampf, Pope Pius IX, Ferdinand Lassalle, William II.
3. **List** the economic and

technological advances that contributed to the growth of industry in Germany.

Critical Thinking
4. **Evaluating Information** Predict what might have happened if Frederick III had not died so

soon after becoming kaiser.

Understanding Themes
5. **Change** What tactics did Bismarck use in his attempt to block challenges from Catholicism and the Socialist movement?

Chapter 15 Section 3

Visualizing History Tell students that after William II accepted Bismarck's resignation, William made Bismarck a duke, offered him a gift of cash, and sent Bismarck a portrait. Bismarck accepted the title and portrait but refused the money.
Answer to Caption: *Bismarck, the dignified elder statesman, is being dismissed by the young, upstart kaiser.*

Evaluate

Section Quiz 15-3

Use the Testmaker to create a customized quiz for Section 3.

Reteach

Have students make a chart that shows how Bismarck influenced political, economic, social, and religious developments in the German Empire.

Enrich

Have students write a brief essay on Bismarck's Kulturkampf, which includes their views of separation of church and state.

CLOSE

Have students discuss struggles Bismarck had with the legislature during his years as chancellor. (*Kulturkampf alienated many legislators; legislature refused to renew anti-Socialist laws introduced by Bismarck.*)

SECTION 3 REVIEW ANSWERS

1. All vocabulary words are defined in the Glossary.
2. Kulturkampf, 462; Pope Pius IX, 463; Ferdinand Lassalle, 463; William II, 465
3. the earlier establishment of the *Zollverein*; influx of investment capital from Britain, France, and Belgium; establishment of a modern factory system; the

development of deep-pit coal mining along the Rhine; opening of new coal mines in the Saar; growth of cities
4. Answers may vary but should include that since Frederick was liberal-minded, he might have promoted liberal reforms.
5. **CHANGE** Bismarck expelled the Jesuits and deprived bishops of their

authority, encouraged passage of anti-Catholic and anti-Socialist laws, and directed passage of laws that gave workers some measure of comfort and security as a way to blunt the Socialist challenge.

SECTION THEME

▶ **Reaction** Russian czars oppose the forces of liberalism and nationalism in the Russian Empire.

F̄ind Out ▶

Answer: *Few Russians were satisfied with the czars' halfway reforms. Students and intellectuals with strong ideals but little practical political experience espoused revolutionary and violent measures.*

FOCUS

Section Objective

Explain why revolutionary movements developed in Russia.

BELLRINGER
Motivational Activity

Before taking roll at the beginning of the class period, project Section Focus Transparency 15-4 and have students answer the activity questions. Discuss students' responses.

▭ This activity is also available as a blackline master.

Vocabulary Pre-check

▣ Use the Vocabulary PuzzleMaker to create a puzzle that reinforces the vocabulary terms in this section. **L1**

1815   1845   1875   1905

| 1825 The Decembrist uprising fails. | 1855 Nicholas I dies. | c. 1870 Populist movement reaches out to peasants. | 1905 Nicholas II issues the October Manifesto. |

Section 4

Empire of the Czars

Setting the Scene

▶ **Terms to Define**
autocracy, emancipation, zemstvo, anarchy, nihilist, Russification, pogrom, soviet, duma

▶ **People to Meet**
Alexander I, Nicholas I, Alexander II, Nicholas II, Empress Alexandra, Mensheviks, Bolsheviks, Lenin

▶ **Places to Locate**
Poland, St. Petersburg

F̄ind Out  Why did revolutionary movements develop in Russia?

The Storyteller

Prince Peter Kropotkin, a student in the Corps of Pages for the sons of the aristocracy, went to the opera with his friends the evening after Czar Alexander proclaimed an end to serfdom. The students planned to sing the hymn

"God Save the Czar," and expected that everyone would join them. When they arrived they found the band of the opera was already playing the hymn, which was drowned immediately in enthusiastic cheers from all parts of the hall. This night, Prince Kropotkin thought, was undoubtedly the czar's finest hour.

—adapted from *A Source Book for Russian History from Early Times to 1917*, reprinted in *Sources of World History*, Mark A. Kishlansky, 1995

Czar Alexander II

In the early 1800s the Russian Empire stretched from Europe to the Pacific Ocean. More than 60 nationalities, speaking over 100 different languages, populated this vast territory. Although Slavs, including Russians, comprised nearly two-thirds of the population, many other European, Middle Eastern, and Asiatic peoples lived within the empire.

The agricultural economy of the Russian Empire was more oppressive but not much more effective than it had been during the Middle Ages. Serfdom, long in decline in western Europe, still bound the peasants living and working in rural areas. As a result of this entrenched agricultural system, Russia's level of industrialization remained lower than that of western Europe.

As an autocracy, a government in which one person rules with unlimited authority, the political structure of the Russian Empire had also remained much as it was in the days of Peter the Great. The forces of reform, already at work in western Europe in the early 1800s, soon threatened this traditional economic and political order of the Russian Empire.

Autocracy on the Defensive

Alexander I, who ruled from 1801 to 1825, dreamed of improving Russia's system of government and even granted a constitution to Russian-ruled **Poland** for a brief period of time. Convinced by the Napoleonic Wars that he was the savior of Europe, Alexander soon lost his desire to improve social, political, and economic conditions within his country.

The Russian officers who fought in the Napoleonic Wars were impressed by the reforms they saw in western Europe. Many of these officers joined secret societies to discuss the need in their country for economic reform, for a constitutional government, and for freeing the serfs. In December

---

SECTION RESOURCES

▭ **Reproducible Masters**
• Reproducible Lesson Plan 15-4
• Guided Reading Activity 15-4
• Geography and History Activity 15
• Section Quiz 15-4

Transparencies
• Section Focus Transparency 15-4

Multimedia
▣ Vocabulary PuzzleMaker Software
▣ Student Self-Test and Review Software
▣ Testmaker
◉ Turning Points in World History: *The Russian Revolution*

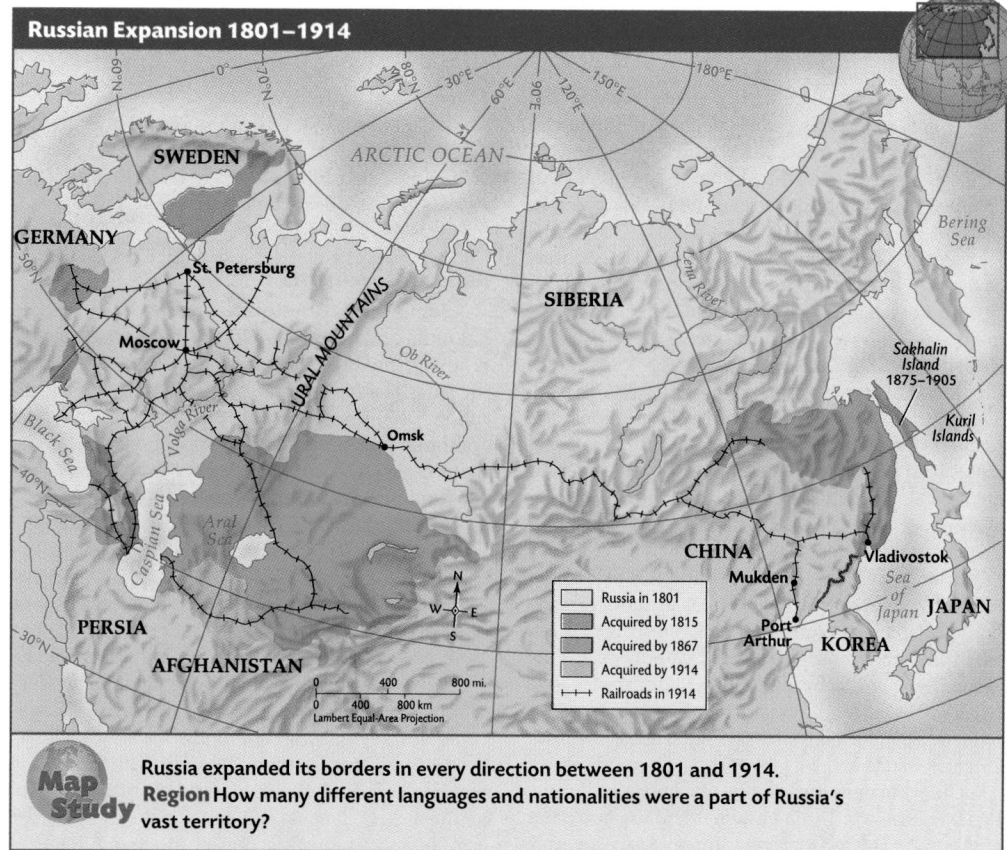

Russian Expansion 1801–1914

SWEDEN
ARCTIC OCEAN
GERMANY
St. Petersburg
Moscow
SIBERIA
Ob River
Lena River
URAL MOUNTAINS
Volga River
Omsk
Black Sea
Aral Sea
Caspian Sea
Sakhalin Island 1875–1905
Kuril Islands
Bering Sea
CHINA
Mukden
Port Arthur
Vladivostok
Sea of Japan
JAPAN
KOREA
PERSIA
AFGHANISTAN

	Russia in 1801
	Acquired by 1815
	Acquired by 1867
	Acquired by 1914
++	Railroads in 1914

0   400   800 mi.
0   400   800 km
Lambert Equal-Area Projection

Map Study Russia expanded its borders in every direction between 1801 and 1914. **Region** How many different languages and nationalities were a part of Russia's vast territory?

1825, some of these officers took advantage of the uncertainty about the transfer of power after Alexander I's death and staged a military revolt.

Although the government quickly crushed the so-called Decembrist Revolt, the uprising had two very different effects. Its leaders were seen as martyrs and inspired later generations of revolutionaries. In the short term, however, the uprising hardened the determination of Alexander I's successor, **Nicholas I**, to strengthen the autocracy and suppress all opposition.

Under Nicholas I, the secret police had unlimited power to arrest and imprison people without trial and to censor the press. Despite Nicholas I's efforts to resist change, demands for reform persisted during the 1830s and 1840s. Russian losses in the Crimean War underscored the fact that the Russian Empire was in serious trouble. Nicholas, however, was too ill to begin any reforms. Following Nicholas I's death in 1855, his son **Alexander II** undertook the task of saving the autocracy and preventing a revolution.

Alexander II and Reforms

Russia's humiliating defeat in the Crimean War revealed the extent to which the nation lagged behind the other European powers militarily and economically. One major reason for Russia's backwardness was its system of serf labor. To progress, Russia needed to industrialize, but to industrialize, the factories needed a steady source of cheap labor. Only the serfs could provide this labor force, but they were not free to leave the land.

On March 3, 1861, Alexander II decreed the emancipation, or freeing, of the serfs. Although the serfs attained legal freedom, they received no land individually. Their village communities, called mirs, were granted varying amounts of the landlords' holdings, for which they had to undertake a 50-year mortgage. Peasants could not leave the mirs without paying their share, so they were still bound to the worst land and had an additional tax to pay. The landlords kept the best land and

Chapter 15 *Reaction and Nationalism* **467**

Chapter 15 *Reaction and Nationalism* **467**

TEACH

Guided Practice

THEME Reaction

Help students recall the definition of *reaction* as it applies to government and politics. (*a maintenance of or return to a former political or social order*) Have students discuss how this definition fits the Russian czars. (*The czars suppressed all opposition.*) **L1 LEP**

Map Study

Answer
People of 60 nationalities speaking 100 different languages lived in the Russian Empire.

Map Skills Practice

Reading a Map What does the heavy concentration of railroads in the western part of the empire indicate? (*That part of Russia was the most heavily populated, the most urban, and the most industrial.*)

Critical Thinking Have students compare the methods of Russia's anarchists, nihilists, Mensheviks, and Bolsheviks. Ask what goal all four groups had in common. (*ending the autocracy*) **L3**

The following videotape programs are available from Glencoe:

• **The Fabulous World of Faberge**

• **Nicholas & Alexandra**

To find classroom resources to accompany these videos, check the following home page:

**A&E Television:
http://www.AandE.com/**

COOPERATIVE LEARNING ACTIVITY

Panel Discussion Organize the class into five groups and have each group research the following groups of Russian society: the aristocracy, the landowners, the intellectuals, the urban workers, and the peasants. Have each group assemble a composite portrait of its class. Suggest that students include in their portraits the major characteristics, occupations, interests, and problems of the class. Have each group assign one of those topics to one or more group members to present in a panel discussion. After each group has presented its panel, encourage students to predict possible outcomes of these class differences for Russia. **L2**

VIDEODISC
Turning Points in World History

Side Two
Chapter 5

Title: *The Russian Revolution*
Ask: Why was the Russian Revolution a turning point in history? *(A Communist government was established.)*

Independent Practice

📁 Guided Reading Activity 15-4 **L1**

📁 Geography and History Activity 15

Who?What?Where?When?

Fabergé Eggs In the 1880s, Alexander III appointed Peter Carl Fabergé jeweler to the imperial court. Each Easter, Fabergé's workshop designed a special Easter egg for the czar to present to the czarina. These eggs, made of jewels and precious metals, opened to reveal a surprise, such as a miniature peacock or basket of flowers.

Global Gourmet

Russia Beef stroganoff, made of thinly sliced beef, onions, sour cream, and seasonings served with egg noodles, is a popular dish in Europe and the United States. It was created for Count Paul Stroganov, a liberal adviser of Alexander I.

---

received compensation from the government for their losses.

Many peasants gave up farming rather than return to bondage. Landless peasants moved from the farms to the cities, adding to the growing numbers of unskilled urban workers. Their discontent revealed itself in occasional minor uprisings and produced new stirrings of revolutionary activity in the Russian Empire.

Because the emancipation decree took control of the provinces away from the landowners, it also created the need for a new system of local government. An 1864 law created this new system. Locally elected assemblies called zemstvos took charge of provincial matters such as schools and health care. Three groups could vote in zemstvo elections: the nobility, the wealthy townspeople, and the peasants. The vote was weighted, however, so that noblemen and rich taxpayers dominated the local assemblies.

Czar Alexander II became known as the Czar Liberator for freeing the serfs and for his many reforms. In addition to those already mentioned, he limited the use and authority of the secret police, eased restrictions on the press, modernized the judicial system, and expanded the educational system. Alexander also reorganized the Russian army, reducing the period of active military service from 25 years to 6 years.

Unfortunately, the reforms of Alexander II satisfied few Russians. The landowners had lost both land and power. The peasantry had made few economic gains. Conservatives feared weakening of the autocracy, while reformers pushed for even greater changes. Designed to stem discontent, the reforms failed to halt the growth of revolutionary movements.

Footnotes to History

A Sickly Prince
In 1904 Czar Nicholas II and Empress Alexandra finally had a son—an heir to the throne— after four girls. Tragically, Alexis suffered from hemophilia, an inherited disease preventing the normal clotting of blood. To ease her son's agonies, Alexandra relied on a mystic healer named Grigori Rasputin (ra•SPYOO•tuhn). Rasputin's apparent success in helping Alexis gave him great political influence over the czar. This in turn increased Nicholas's isolation from his people and the forces of change sweeping his empire.

Terror and Reaction

Among the most vocal critics of the Russian government during Alexander II's reign were intellectuals and students from the upper and middle classes. Although these reformers had strong ideals, they had little practical political experience and almost no direct contact with the Russian people, especially the peasants.

Radical Movements

Some radical reformers, such as Michael Bakunin, advocated anarchy, or the absence of government, and called for the complete destruction of the state, the family, law, property, and other institutions. Nihilists (from the Latin *nihil*, meaning "nothing") also rejected all traditions, believing that Russia would have to destroy the czarist autocracy and build a completely new society.

Beginning in the early 1870s, many reformers became active in a new movement known as populism. The populists believed that the peasants would eventually lead a revolution, overthrow the czar, and establish a socialist society. To further their cause, groups of students and intellectuals went to the villages to prepare the peasants for revolution. The peasants, however, often grew suspicious of the young revolutionaries and sometimes even turned them over to the police. Frustrated by their lack of success, many populists turned to violent tactics.

The most radical faction of the revolutionaries plotted the assassinations of key officials in order to frighten the government into making radical reforms. Beginning in 1866, revolutionaries made several attempts to assassinate Alexander II. Although Alexander insisted that these radicals be crushed, he eventually responded to popular pressure by drafting a plan to establish a national assembly. Before the plan could be enacted, however, a young revolutionary killed the czar with a bomb in 1881.

Alexander III

Alexander III, who succeeded his father, vowed to maintain the old order and crush revolutionaries. He warned that he would not tolerate a constitution and reduced the powers of the zemstvos. Reversing his father's reforms, he abolished autonomy in the schools, restored censorship of the press, and extended the powers of the secret police.

To protect the autocracy, Alexander III used a resurgence of nationalism to promote a policy of Russification. Designed as an attempt to unite the empire's many peoples, Russification instead

---

MEETING SPECIAL NEEDS ACTIVITY

Learning Style: Visual/Spatial Have students who are visual learners research outside sources and then draw a picture depicting one of the following people in czarist Russia: a member of the imperial family, a wealthy landowner, a revolutionary intellectual, an urban worker, or a peasant. Suggest that students characterize the position of the person through clothing, hairstyle, facial expression, surroundings, and tools or equipment. Set aside space on a bulletin board for completed drawings. **L1 LEP**

Visualizing History In August 1905 the czar proposed to give peasants but not urban workers the right to vote for duma representatives. In response, urban workers and students led a general strike for 10 days in October that has often been described as the most effective strike in history. *Why was this a successful strike? (The czar issued the October Manifesto making Russia a constitutional monarchy.)*
Answer to Caption: *It vowed to maintain the old order and cracked down on revolutionary opposition, extending the powers of the secret police.*

Visualizing History **Moscow workers, students, and intellectuals fought czarist troops during the 1905 Revolution.** *How did the czarist government under Alexander III and Nicholas II deal with its opponents?*

became an official policy of intolerance and persecution of non-Russian peoples. Anyone who questioned the czar's authority, who spoke a language other than Russian, or who followed a religion other than Eastern Orthodoxy risked prosecution.

Russification singled out the Jews in particular for persecution. Government decrees deprived Jews of the right to own land and forced them to live in a certain area of the empire called the Pale. The government also encouraged bloody pogroms, or organized massacres of a minority group, in Jewish communities.

POINT

The Revolution of 1905

After Alexander III's death in 1894, many Russians were disappointed when his son **Nicholas II** stated he would also rule as an autocrat. The new czar, however, lacked the strong will to make absolute rule effective. He was easily influenced by those around him, particularly his wife, **Empress Alexandra**, who wanted their son to inherit an autocracy.

During the reign of Nicholas II, a revolutionary mood swept over Russia. Peasants grew increasingly dissatisfied; national minorities called for an end to persecution; and middle-class reformers pushed for a constitutional monarchy. At the same time, the emancipation of the serfs and rapid industrialization had resulted in a marked increase in the size of the urban working class. Russian factories at the turn of the century lacked proper lighting, ventilation, and sanitation. Workers toiled long hours for little pay and lived in terrible, overcrowded housing. Not surprisingly, then, urban workers joined the ranks of the dissatisfied.

Russian Marxists

By the early 1900s several revolutionary groups in Russia followed the teachings of Karl Marx. Their members believed that the working class, not the peasants, would lead the revolution. The **Mensheviks** believed that Russia needed to develop into an industrial state with a sizable working class before a socialist revolution could occur. The more radical **Bolsheviks**, led by Vladimir Ilyich Ulyanov—commonly known as **Lenin**—believed that a small party of professional revolutionaries

Chapter 15 Reaction and Nationalism **469**

POINT

The Revolution of 1905
How did the Revolution of 1905 affect Russian government under the czars?
It nearly overthrew the monarchy, forcing the autocratic czar to grant concessions to liberals and revolutionaries, especially the creation of a legislature.

Linking Past and Present

Secret police have been known since Greek and Roman times. In 1825 the Russian czar established the first modern version of the secret police, giving them the power not only to arrest but also to try and to punish anyone who opposed the czar's power. From 1954 to 1991, the KGB was the Soviet Union's secret police, questioning and trying suspects and sending those with questionable loyalty to forced labor camps, psychiatric hospitals, and prisons. With the USSR's collapse, the KGB was disbanded.

ASSESS

Check for Understanding

Assign Section 4 Review as homework or as an in-class activity.

 Use Student Self-Test and Review Software to review Section 4.

Evaluate

Section Quiz 15-4

 Use the Testmaker to create a customized quiz for Section 4.

Reteach

Have students make an outline of Section 4 showing czarist reforms and reactions. Tell students to use the names of the five czars discussed in this section as the main headings for their outlines.

Enrich

Have students do further research and then write an essay about the events and outcome of the Revolution of 1905.

CLOSE

Have students draw evidence from Section 4 to support the following statement: Czarist reforms were incomplete, aroused opposition, and were always followed by reactionary measures.

---

could use force to bring about a socialist society in the near future.

Upheavals

War between Russia and Japan in 1904 over control of Manchuria furthered the Socialists' cause. Russian land forces suffered major setbacks, and a Russian fleet attempting to deliver supplies lost many ships in a Japanese attack. With the mediation of the United States, the war-exhausted empires finally concluded a peace agreement in 1905.

Russia's humiliating military performance heightened already mounting opposition to the czar's government by urban workers, middle-class thinkers, and peasants. The war had strained the Russian economy, raising food prices while keeping wages low.

Spontaneous strikes began to break out in many cities throughout the empire. On Sunday, January 22, 1905, about 200,000 workers marched in a peaceful procession to the czar's palace in **St. Petersburg** to present a petition for reform. Palace soldiers opened fire on the crowd, killing hundreds of workers. Bloody Sunday, as the demonstration was called, sparked riots and strikes in most industrial centers and set off a wave of political protests.

Middle-class organizations drew up programs for political reform. The zemstvos issued lists of demands. In the spring of 1905, the first soviets, or workers' councils, formed to voice workers' grievances. From all reformist and revolutionary groups came the cry for the establishment of a representative government elected by universal suffrage.

In October 1905, angry workers seized control of the major cities in a general strike. As disorder and violence in the cities and rural areas continued, Nicholas II announced a law providing for the election of a national **duma**, or legislature. The czar, however, proposed that the Duma serve as an advisory council rather than a genuine legislative body. Instead of appeasing the Russian people, the measure set off more nationwide strikes.

Slavery Is on Its Way Out

Washington, D.C., 1863
During the American Civil War, President Abraham Lincoln issued the Emancipation Proclamation that eventually led to the end of slavery in the United States. This historic document declared freedom for all enslaved people in the Confederacy—the states that were in rebellion against the Union. The Emancipation Proclamation strengthened the Union's war effort and made the war a fight against slavery. It also weakened the Confederacy by discouraging France and England from entering the war.

The events of October forced Nicholas to yield reluctantly to the demands of his people. The czar issued the October Manifesto, granting civil rights to citizens and allowing the Duma to make laws. In theory, Russia had become a constitutional monarchy; however, in practice, Nicholas continued to keep his powers. Stern measures to restore order, including pogroms against the Jews and the arrest of peasant and labor leaders, remained in place. When the Duma tried to act independently of the czar, Nicholas quickly dissolved it.

Nicholas II's ability to silence opposition was only temporary. Russia's many serious troubles had not been resolved. On the eve of World War I, growing numbers of peasants, workers, national minorities, and middle-class reformers supported an immediate end to the autocracy. Their demands and the stress of war would soon bring revolution to Russia.

SECTION 4 REVIEW

Recall
1. **Define** autocracy, emancipation, zemstvo, anarchy, nihilist, Russification, pogrom, soviet, duma.
2. **Identify** Alexander I, Nicholas I, Alexander II, Nicholas II, Empress Alexandra, Mensheviks,

Bolsheviks, Lenin.
3. **Name** the two major Russian revolutionary groups that followed the teachings of Karl Marx, and explain the differences between the two.

Critical Thinking
4. **Applying Information** Select

one of the Russian czars and tell how his policies affected the Russian Empire.

Understanding Themes
5. **Reaction** Why was effective reform difficult to achieve in Russia during the reign of Nicholas II?

SECTION 4 REVIEW ANSWERS

1. All vocabulary words are defined in the Glossary.
2. Alexander I, 466; Nicholas I, 467; Alexander II, 467; Nicholas II, 469; Empress Alexandra, 469; Mensheviks, 469; Bolsheviks, 469; Lenin, 469
3. Mensheviks and Bolsheviks: The Mensheviks believed that a revolution would

take place when Russia was industrialized and had a large working class. The Bolsheviks believed that a small revolutionary party using force could bring about a socialist society.
4. Answers may vary but should include both the reforms and reactionary measures.

5. **REACTION** Answers may vary but should include that Nicholas II gave in to reforms only when he was forced to but remained determined to maintain his power and the autocracy of the czars.

Section 5

Austria-Hungary's Decline

Setting the Scene

▶ **Terms to Define**
  dual monarchy, jingoism

▶ **People to Meet**
  Francis Joseph, Francis Deak

▶ **Places to Locate**
  Austria, Vienna, Hungary, Bohemia, Moravia, Serbia, Bulgaria, Romania, Montenegro, Bosnia and Herzegovina

 **ind Out** How did the growth of nationalistic feelings affect the empire of Austria-Hungary?

⒮toryteller

Josef Heismann knew that the army was edgy. Once a powerful force, Austria was now regarded as second-rate. Inflammatory newspaper articles called for Austria to annex Bosnia, Serbia, and other Slav republics. Josef read an army newspaper article calling for an immediate invasion: "On us depends the future of our Empire. If we return victorious, we shall not only have conquered a foreign land: we shall have won back Austrian self-respect, given new life to the Imperial idea and vanquished … the enemy in our midst."

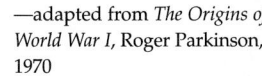

—adapted from *The Origins of World War I*, Roger Parkinson, 1970

Austrian soldiers of the 1860s

In the early 1800s, in addition to Russia and the Ottoman Empire, there was a third dominant power in eastern Europe: **Austria**. The Austrian Empire at this time contained more than 11 different national groups, including the Germans of Austria and the Magyars of Hungary.

Like Russia, Austria lacked national and geographical unity. Also as in Russia, life in Austria remained almost feudal at the beginning of the 1800s. A powerful landed nobility controlled a large peasant population and resisted any change in the old agricultural system. Through strict censorship and the arrest and intimidation of protesters, the government sought to stem the forces of nationalism and revolution sweeping through Europe.

The Revolution of 1848

As you learned in Chapter 11, the principal political figure in Austria during the early 1800s was Prince Klemens von Metternich, who held the office of minister of foreign affairs from 1809 to 1848. Metternich believed that democratic and nationalist movements would destroy the Austrian Empire and threaten peace in Europe. As a result, Metternich worked to crush all revolutionary activity, both within and outside the empire.

Despite Metternich's conservative policies, however, the revolutionary movement that had begun in France in 1848 spread to Austria the same year. Throughout the empire, nationalist groups demanded freedom of speech and press, peasant relief from feudal dues, and a representative government. The Austrian Empire seemed on the verge of collapse.

The tide of revolutionary activity was to turn once more, however. Infighting among nationalist groups and within radical factions with different

Chapter 15 *Reaction and Nationalism* **471**

TEACH

Guided Practice

THEME Diversity

Have students list the national groups that were part of Austria-Hungary by 1914. **L1 LEP**

Geography: Regions Have students use the map on page 473 to name the areas that bordered the Austro-Hungarian Empire. (*Germany, Russia, Romania, Serbia, Montenegro, Italy, Switzerland*) Have students discuss how cultural ties between these neighbors and ethnic groups within Austria-Hungary could threaten the coherence of the empire. **L2**

Analyzing Information Have students explain how the Congress of Berlin and the Treaty of Bucharest set the stage for further conflict in the Balkans. **L3**

Mapping History Overlay Transparency 17, *Revolutionary Centers in Europe 1820–1848*

Visualizing History 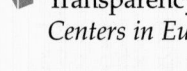 Although Francis Joseph was both an emperor and a king, he has been described as being at heart "a simple soul with Spartan tastes." Francis Joseph was usually painted wearing the white jacket and red trousers of the Austrian army.

Answer to Caption: *the transformation of Austria-Hungary into a dual monarchy, with Hungary as an independent kingdom on an equal level with Austria*

---

political ideas enabled conservative forces to strike back. In **Vienna**, for example, conflict between middle-class moderates who wanted to reform the political system and radical workers who wanted to overthrow it weakened the revolutionary movement. By October 1848, the government once more occupied the capital. When Emperor Francis Ferdinand resigned his throne, his nephew, **Francis Joseph**, became emperor at the age of 18.

Francis Joseph moved quickly to restore the conservative order. He dissolved the revolutionary assembly and rejected the new constitution. Although threatened, the old regime had managed to withstand revolutionary change by playing one nationalist faction against another.

Throughout his 68-year reign, Francis Joseph struggled to maintain a unified empire. Neither repressive measures nor reforms, however, helped ease the nationalist tensions that threatened Austria. At the same time, a series of foreign crises further weakened the empire. In 1859 Austria was forced to give up the Italian province of Lombardy. Then in 1866, during the Seven Weeks' War with Prussia, Austria lost its influence over its German states as well.

The Dual Monarchy

Francis Joseph's efforts to strengthen his authority were most effectively challenged by the

Magyars of **Hungary**. In 1848 Hungarian nationalists led by Louis Kossuth declared Hungary an independent republic, but this achievement was short-lived. With Russian help, Austrian forces defeated the Hungarian nationalists, and Hungary was restored to the Austrian Empire. After Austria's defeat in the Seven Weeks' War (1866), however, Francis Joseph realized that his empire's stability depended on better relations with the Hungarians. He met with Hungarian leader **Francis Deak** to see if a compromise could be worked out.

After months of negotiations, Austria and Hungary finally reached an agreement in 1867. The *Ausgleich* (OWS•glyk), or Compromise, restored Hungary's independence and divided the Austrian Empire into a dual monarchy: the empire of Austria and the kingdom of Hungary. Francis Joseph remained ruler of both areas. He kept his title as emperor of Austria, and the Hungarians crowned him king of Hungary.

In addition to sharing a monarch, the two states had common ministries of foreign affairs, war, and finance. A system of committees handled other matters of mutual concern. In internal affairs, however, Austria and Hungary were completely independent of each other. Each had its own constitution, prime minister, and parliament.

While Austria and Hungary were independent politically, they were dependent on each other economically. Industrialized Austria supplied manufactured goods for the peoples of the dual

Visualizing History Francis Joseph ruled the Austrian Empire for 68 years. When he came to the throne in 1848, Europe was in the midst of revolutions. When he died in 1916, Europe was in the midst of World War I. *What change did Francis Joseph agree to in 1867 in order to save his empire?*

472 **Chapter 15** *Reaction and Nationalism*

COOPERATIVE LEARNING ACTIVITY

Fact File Organize the class into groups of two or three students to research and prepare fact files on the following ethnic groups in the Austro-Hungarian Empire: Germans, Magyars, Italians, Romanians, Czechs, Serbs, Croatians, Slovaks, Poles, Slovenes, and Ukrainians. Have each group gather information on the culture, language, religion, traditions, national dress, and political goals of one ethnic group. Tell students to organize this information on no more than two sheets of paper. Choose a few students to compile each group's information into a "Fact File on Ethnic Groups in Austria-Hungary." Make the Fact File available to the class as a source of information. **L1**

monarchy. Agricultural Hungary supplied food products. Their cooperation, however, was not without conflict. Disputes inevitably developed between Austria and Hungary over foreign trade, tariffs, and currency.

During the mid-1800s, Austrian industrial growth had been slow. After the creation of the dual monarchy, however, the empire's production of coal, iron, steel, and manufactured goods grew rapidly. The territories of **Bohemia** and **Moravia** became the empire's leading industrial centers, producing machine tools, textiles, armaments, shoes, and chemicals. The concentration of industry in Bohemia and Moravia caused a more rapid urbanization in those areas.

The dual monarchy was satisfactory to both the Austrian-Germans, who maintained power in Austria, and the Magyars, who controlled Hungary. Other nationalities remained discontented. Three-fifths of the population of Austria-Hungary were Slavs—Poles, Czechs, Slovaks, Serbs, and Bosnians— who had no voice in the government. Many Slavic nationalist groups dreamed of breaking free from the Austro-Hungarian Empire and forming a large Slav kingdom. Their discontent became a threat to the empire's unity.

Powder Keg in the Balkans

By the mid-1800s, the Ottoman Empire had declined to a weakened and diminished state. In 1829 Greece won its independence. By 1850 the Ottomans had lost the provinces of Moldavia and Wallachia to Russia and Algeria to France. In addition, Egypt, Arabia, and several Balkan territories had gained their autonomy.

Foreign powers watched the decline of the Ottoman Empire closely. Austria hoped to expand into the Balkan region. France sought to protect persecuted Catholics within the empire. Great Britain feared disruption of its Mediterranean trade. The primary objective of these foreign powers, though, was to prevent Russian expansion into the region. "We have a sick man on our hands," declared Czar Nicholas I, referring to Turkey, and Russia stood ready to contribute to its final collapse.

During the Crimean War, from 1854 to 1856, France, Great Britain, and Sardinia helped defend the Ottoman Empire against Russia's advances. Although the Ottoman allies defeated Russia in this war, the empire continued to lose power and territory. In 1875 nationalists in the Balkan states of **Serbia**, **Bulgaria**, and **Romania** rose up in revolt, demanding immediate independence from Turkey. The Turks brutally suppressed these revolts with widespread massacres.

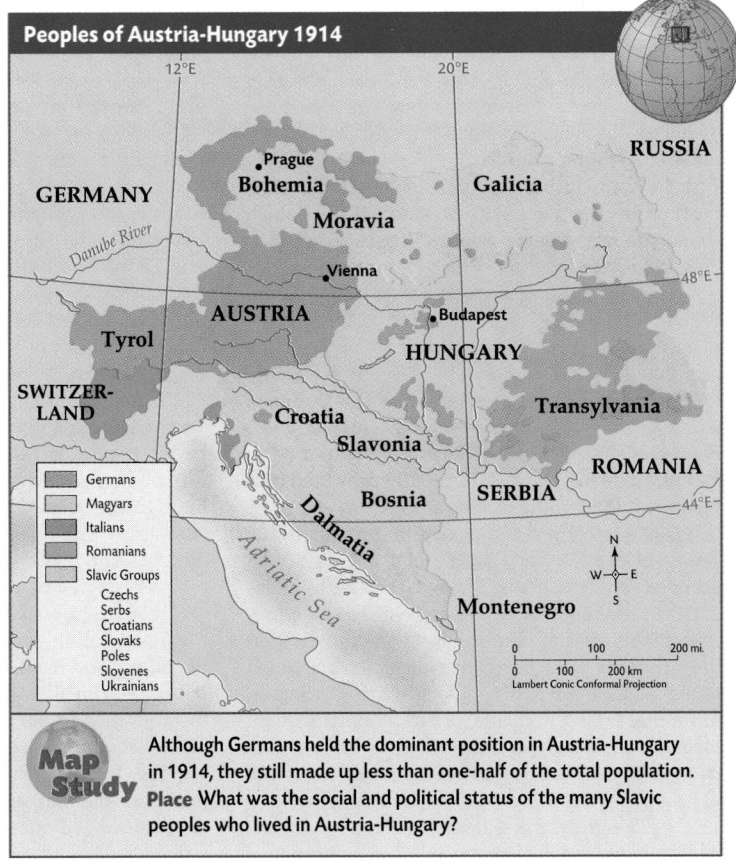

Peoples of Austria-Hungary 1914

Germans
Magyars
Italians
Romanians
Slavic Groups
  Czechs
  Serbs
  Croatians
  Slovaks
  Poles
  Slovenes
  Ukrainians

Map Study Although Germans held the dominant position in Austria-Hungary in 1914, they still made up less than one-half of the total population. **Place** What was the social and political status of the many Slavic peoples who lived in Austria-Hungary?

Map Study

Answer
They had no voice in their government.

Map Skills Practice

Reading a Map Which nationality group lived throughout Austria-Hungary? (*the Germans*)

Independent Practice

⬦ Guided Reading Activity 15-5 **L1**

Multicultural Have students research and write a brief history on one of the following ethnic groups from early times through the present: Magyars, Romanians, Serbs, Croatians, Bosnians, Poles, Lithuanians, Slovaks, Bohemians, Moravians, or Slovenes. **L2**

Global 🍲 Gourmet

Hungary Hungary's first people, the Magyars, were nomads. As such they needed food that traveled well without spoiling. *Gulyás*, cubes of seasoned, cooked, dried meat added to hot water and any local vegetables, became an instant soup or stew. Today the ingredients in *gulyás*, or goulash, are fresh.

ASSESS

Check for Understanding
Assign Section 5 Review as homework or as an in-class activity.

⬦ Use Student Self-Test and Review Software to review Section 5.

MEETING SPECIAL NEEDS ACTIVITY

Learning Style: Visual/Spatial To help students better visualize the location of ethnic groups in the Austro-Hungarian and Ottoman Empires, have them work in pairs using a historical atlas to draw a map of these areas. Ask students to label the map with the ethnic groups. Then have students compare their maps with a map of present-day Europe. Help students identify the countries in which these ethnic groups now live. **L2 LEP**

Evaluate

 Section Quiz 15-5

Use the Testmaker to create a customized quiz for Section 5.

Reteach

Have students make a time line from 1848 to 1913 of major events covered in Section 5.

 Reteaching Activity 15

Enrich

Have students redraw the map on page 473 to show how they would have divided Austria-Hungary into independent countries based on nationality.

 Enrichment Activity 15

CLOSE

Have students discuss why the Balkans were called "the powder keg of Europe."

The Congress of Berlin

In 1877 Russia went to war on behalf of the Slavic people in the Balkan Peninsula. Publicly embracing the Slavic nationalist movement because it suited the government's imperial ambitions, Russia used the conflict known as the Russo-Turkish War to justify its expansion into Balkan territory. The Treaty of San Stefano (1878), which ended the war, created a large Russian-controlled Bulgarian state.

As news of Russian victories reached Great Britain, the public cried out for war. A popular slogan in Great Britain at the time captured the heightened public sentiment: "We don't want to fight, but by jingo, if we do, we've got the men, we've got the ships, we've got the money, too." From this slogan came the term jingoism, used to describe extreme patriotism, usually provoked by a perceived foreign threat.

The great European powers protested the Treaty of San Stefano. In the end a congress of European leaders met in Berlin, Germany, to revise it. At the meeting, which began in June 1878, representatives of the European powers divided Bulgaria into three parts, one of which remained under Ottoman rule. Neighboring Serbia, **Montenegro**, and Romania, on the other hand, won their complete independence. Britain gained control of Cyprus, and Austria-Hungary won the Balkan provinces of **Bosnia and Herzegovina**.

The Congress of Berlin satisfied few. Russia lost its war gains, and the Ottoman Empire lost much of its European territory. In addition, the congress dealt with the Balkan states inequitably, granting independence for some, but not all, of the people of any given nationality.

Balkan Conflict

By 1912 the Balkan states had joined forces and moved to free members of their respective nationalities from Ottoman rule. Encouraged by Italy's easy victory over the Turks in North Africa, the Balkan League—consisting of Bulgaria, Greece, Montenegro, and Serbia—declared war on Turkey in 1912. As a result of the war, the Ottomans lost all of their European territory with the exception of Istanbul and a small surrounding area.

Unity among members of the Balkan League was short-lived. No sooner had the Balkan states won the war than they began to fight among themselves over the lands they had gained. Before the war, Serbia and Bulgaria had secretly arranged for land distribution in case of victory. After the war, Bulgaria refused to go along with the plan. The Bulgarians did not want to give up territory won directly in battle.

To keep their land, the Bulgarians in June 1913 attacked Greek and Serb forces in the disputed area. In this second Balkan War, Montenegro and Greece sided with Serbia against Bulgaria. Romania joined the fighting when it saw the opportunity to win land from Bulgaria. The Balkan conflict brought new hope to the Ottomans. Seeing the chance to recover its own lost European territory, the Ottoman Empire attacked Bulgaria.

The fighting ended in 1913 with the Treaty of Bucharest, and the disputed land was redistributed. Bulgaria, which lost the war, surrendered much of the land it had won from the Ottomans in the previous Balkan conflict.

The Treaty of Bucharest did not bring lasting peace to the Balkans. Serbia's increased power encouraged nationalism among Slavs and threatened Austria-Hungary. Russia, in supporting the pan-Slavic movement, sought to extend its own influence in the Balkans. The French, British, and German governments tried to preserve the existing balance of power to prevent either Austria-Hungary or Russia from gaining greater influence in the area. It is not difficult to see why writers of the time called the Balkans "the powder keg of Europe." It seemed inevitable that events in the Balkans would sooner or later explode into a major European war.

SECTION 5 REVIEW

Recall
1. **Define** dual monarchy, jingoism.
2. **Identify** Francis Joseph, Francis Deak, the Congress of Berlin.
3. **List** two ways in which Austria and Hungary were dependent upon each other in the dual

monarchy. List two ways they were independent of each other.

Critical Thinking
4. **Analyzing Information** How did Austria-Hungary and Russia differ from the Balkan countries in their reasons for

intervening in the Ottoman Empire's problems?

Understanding Themes
5. **Diversity** Explain how ethnic diversity contributed to the decline of Austria-Hungary. Could this decline have been avoided? Why or why not?

SECTION 5 REVIEW ANSWERS

1. All vocabulary words are defined in the Glossary.
2. Francis Joseph, 472; Francis Deak, 472; Congress of Berlin, 474
3. Austria and Hungary were dependent on each other in matters of foreign affairs and finance; they were independent in internal affairs, and each had its own constitution, prime minister, and parliament.
4. The Balkan countries wanted to win independence from the Ottoman Empire. Austria-Hungary and Russia wanted to expand their control into the Balkans.
5. **DIVERSITY** Answers will vary but should include that the many ethnic groups in the empire had more allegiance to their own group than to the empire. Because nationalism was spreading across Europe, the Austrian Empire's decline probably could not have been avoided.

Selecting and Using Research Sources

You have to write a report, so you head off to the library. There you are surrounded by bookshelves filled with books. Where do you begin?

Learning the Skill

Libraries contain many kinds of research sources. Understanding the content and purpose of each type will help you find relevant information more efficiently. Here are brief descriptions of important sources:

Reference Books Reference books include encyclopedias, biographical dictionaries, atlases, and almanacs.

An encyclopedia is a set of books with short articles on many subjects arranged alphabetically. General encyclopedias present a wide range of topics, while specialized encyclopedias have articles on a theme—i.e., an encyclopedia of music.

A biographical dictionary provides brief biographies listed alphabetically by last names. Each biography gives data such as the person's place and date of birth, occupation, and achievements.

An atlas is a collection of maps and charts for locating geographical features and places. An atlas can be general or thematic. An atlas contains an alphabetical index of place names that directs you to the map(s) where that place appears.

An almanac is an annually updated reference that provides current statistics together with historical information on a wide range of subjects.

Card Catalog The library's catalog, on computer or cards, lists every book in the library. Search for books by author, title, or subject. Each listing gives the book's call number and location. Computer catalogs also show whether the book is currently available.

Many libraries have joined networks. A library network usually has a single computer catalog listing all the books in the network. A patron can borrow any book in the system. Find out whether your library is part of a network.

Periodical Guides A periodical guide is a set of books listing topics covered in magazine and newspaper articles.

Computer Databases Computer databases provide collections of information organized for rapid search and retrieval.

If you have trouble finding the needed information, ask the librarian for help.

Practicing the Skill

Suppose you are going to Germany and want to learn more about the country before you go. Read the research questions below. Then decide which of the following sources you would use to answer each question and why.

a. encyclopedia
b. atlas
c. historical atlas
d. almanac
e. biographical dictionary
f. catalog entry: Germany—travel
g. catalog entry: Germany—modern history
h. periodical guide

1. Where is each city on the trip itinerary located?
2. What are the places of interest in each city?
3. What have been the major events in German history since 1800?
4. What political issues face Germany today?

Applying the Skill

Use research resources from your school or local library to research the following topic:

What medical treatment was given to Czarevitch Alexis, son of Nicholas II and Alexandra? How has medical care of hemophiliacs improved since 1910? List your sources.

For More Practice

Turn to the Skill Practice in the Chapter Review on page 477 for more practice in selecting and using research sources.

Selecting and Using Research Sources Make arrangements with the director of the school's resource center to have the class use the center to review various kinds of research sources: general and specialized encyclopedias, atlases, dictionaries, almanacs, periodical guides, the card catalog, and computerized databases such as Infotrak. Organize the class into several groups. Have each group familiarize itself with one of the above kinds of sources. Have each group describe to the class how to use the source and the kinds of information that can be found in that source. Then have students read the skill and complete the practice questions.

Additional Practice

📁 Skill Reinforcement Activity 15

📁 Writer's Guidebook, Lesson 9

ANSWERS TO PRACTICING THE SKILL

1. atlas; provides collection of maps
2. catalog entry: Germany—travel; entry deals with travel in Germany
3. encyclopedia; provides information on many subjects; catalog entry: Germany—modern history
4. periodical guide; lists article topics covered in current magazines and newspapers

Chapter 15 Review

GLENCOE
TECHNOLOGY

VIDEODISC
Use MindJogger to review students' knowledge of the chapter.

MindJogger Videoquiz

Chapter 15
Disc 2 Side B

 Also available in VHS.

Answers

Using Key Terms
1. a **4.** h
2. g **5.** j
3. f

Using Your History Journal

Suggest that students use the encyclopedia to gain an understanding of the history of the conflict in Bosnia.

Reviewing Facts
1. After the events of 1848, Italian nationalists lost faith in Mazzini and turned to the king of Sardinia, respected for his brave stand against the Austrians, to lead the struggle for unification.
2. Mazzini, Cavour, Victor Emmanuel II, Garibaldi
3. The *Zollverein* was an economic union that established a uniform tariff among the German states. Because Prussia formed the *Zollverein* and was the largest of the German states, Prussia was able to outmaneuver Austria.
4. economic, social, religious, political, and cultural divisions
5. Landowners lost land and power; peasants made few gains; conservatives feared autocracy was weakened; reformers wanted

Connections Across Time

Historical Significance The forces of nationalism changed the map of Europe dramatically in the 1800s. In the 1860s, the independent states on the Italian Peninsula united into the nation of Italy. Nationalism, however, weakened the Austrian Empire, where

About 10 years later, a loose confederation of states in the heart of Europe became the modern nation of Germany.

Nationalism, however, weakened the Austrian Empire, where various ethnic groups wanted independence. Nationalist tensions increased throughout Europe during the late 1800s and early 1900s. They pushed European nations closer to an all-out war.

Using Key Terms

Write the key term that completes each sentence. Then write a sentence for each term not chosen.

a. anarchy
b. duma
c. jingoism
d. nationalism
e. Russification
f. autocracy
g. dual monarchy
h. nihilists
i. kaiser
j. pogroms
k. emancipation
l. zemstvo

1. In the 1800s some radical reformers in Russia called for _____, the complete destruction of the government, the family, law, property, and other institutions.
2. In 1867 Austria and Hungary reached an agreement to transform the Austrian Empire into a _____, consisting of two separate but interrelated kingdoms.
3. During the 1800s the Russian Empire was an _____, a government in which one person rules with unlimited authority.
4. Among Russian revolutionaries, the _____ rejected all traditions, believing that Russia would have to completely build a new society.
5. The Russian government encouraged bloody _____, or organized massacres, in Jewish communities of the Russian Empire.

Technology Activity

Using a Word Processor **Search** the Internet or your local library for sources about the history of Russian czars. Using a word processor or software, create a genealogy chart of the Romanov dynasty. Include a short report explaining why the empire of the czars ended and how it impacted Russian culture.

Using Your History Journal

Read two or three recent news magazine reports on Bosnia and Herzegovina. Write an essay about how to achieve lasting peace in the Balkans.

Reviewing Facts

1. **Government** Explain how Sardinia gained control of the Italian struggle for unification.
2. **Government** Identify the leaders of Italy's unification movement.
3. **Economics** Describe the *Zollverein*. How did it help Prussia lead the German Confederation?
4. **Government** List the challenges that faced the new German state.
5. **Government** Explain why the reforms of Alexander II satisfied few Russians.
6. **History** State the effects of the 1905 Revolution on Russian government and society.

Critical Thinking

1. **Apply** How did foreign powers help Italians achieve independence?
2. **Contrast** How did the problems that Italy faced after unification differ from the problems that Germany faced?
3. **Synthesize** Why do you think Austria agreed to the compromise with Hungary that established the dual monarchy?
4. **Evaluate** What do you think might have happened if Russia's Czar Nicholas II had given the Duma full legislative power?

greater reforms.
6. The 1905 Revolution shook the autocracy to its foundations. Strikes forced the czar to grant a national legislature and civil rights; however, after the uprisings were suppressed, he tried to return to autocratic rule.

Critical Thinking
1. Britain and France recognized Italy's sovereignty because Italy supported them in the

Crimean War; France agreed to help the Italians expel Austria from the peninsula; Prussia agreed to give Italy Venetia for Italy's help in defeating Austria in the Seven Weeks' War.
2. Germany faced divisions based on religion and dialects; Italy was threatened by former rulers of the Italian states and Austria still controlled some Italian land.
3. After losing the Seven Weeks' War, Austria

Geography in History

1. **Place** Refer to the map below. In what two areas was most of the fighting during the Russo-Japanese War?
2. **Movement** Across what two bodies of water were Japanese troops transported to the war zone?
3. **Movement** What railway helped in moving Japanese forces north?
4. **Region** What effect did Russia's setback in this region have on the czar's government?

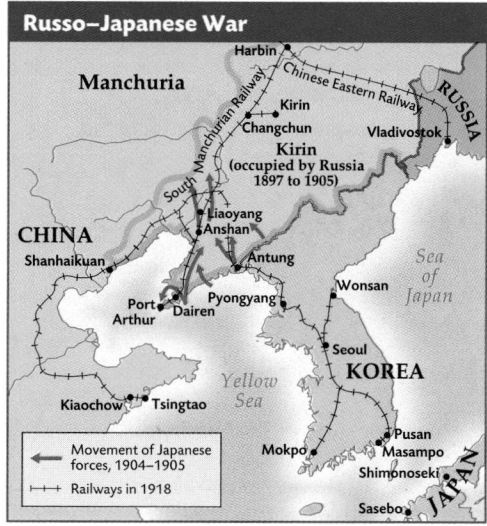

Russo–Japanese War

Understanding Themes

1. **Nationalism** How did the rise of nationalism spur the unification movement in Italy?
2. **Conflict** How did Bismarck promote his goal of German unification?
3. **Change** What changes came to Germany's economy after unification?
4. **Reaction** How did the policies of Alexander III affect the Jews and other non-Russian groups within the Russian Empire?
5. **Diversity** How did the great diversity of nationalities in the Austrian Empire lead to the establishment of the dual monarchy in the mid-1800s?

Linking Past and Present

1. Bismarck had the difficult task of forging a strong, united German nation. What problems did he face? What problems have confronted German leaders since the early 1990s in reuniting Germany today after nearly 50 years of division into Communist and democratic areas?
2. Alexander III carried out a policy of Russification that led to intolerance and persecution of non-Russian groups in the Russian Empire. Are similar policies carried out today in Russia and the other countries of the former Soviet Union? Explain your answer.

Skill Practice

For each research question below, decide which of these sources would provide relevant information.

a. encyclopedia
b. atlas
c. historical atlas
d. almanac
e. biographical dictionary
f. catalog entry: European history 19th century
g. catalog entry: nationalism
h. periodical guide

1. How have the borders of the countries discussed in Chapter 15 changed since World War I?
2. What are the latest population statistics for Germany, Italy, Austria, Hungary, and Russia?
3. What were Otto von Bismarck's greatest accomplishments?
4. What nationalist struggles have occurred in Europe in the last decade?

strong and prosperous industrial economy.
4.  **REACTION** Alexander III tried to force Russian language and ways on the non-Russian peoples; he exerted strong pressure on the Jews who were singled out for persecution. The government forced Jews to live in the Pale and encouraged bloody massacres of Jewish communities.
5. **DIVERSITY** The nationalist movements of the empire's many ethnic groups had left Austria in a weakened position. When the Magyars in Hungary asked for greater independence, Francis Joseph agreed to the dual monarchy.

Linking Past and Present

1. Bismarck faced problems with the Catholic Church and Socialists. Since 1990, Germany has faced economic differences between former East and West Germans and has had to protect foreign minority workers.
2. yes; Russia's move against the Chechen independence movement

Skill Practice
1. c   3. e
2. d   4. g, h

Chapter Bonus Test Question

Ask students: How did the goals of nationalism differ between the people in Italy and Germany and the people in the Austrian, Russian, and Ottoman Empires? *(Nationalism in Italy and Germany sought to unite the separate states in each of those countries, but nationalism in the Austrian, Russian, and Ottoman Empires sought independence for their various ethnic groups.)*

was in a weakened bargaining position.
4. Russia might have evolved into a constitutional monarchy.

Geography in History
1. along the coast of the Yellow Sea; along the South Manchurian Railway
2. Sea of Japan, Yellow Sea
3. South Manchurian Railway
4. It weakened the government.

Understanding Themes
1. **NATIONALISM** caused the Italian people to move toward independence from foreign countries and to unite the Italian states into one country
2. **CONFLICT** He carried out a policy of realpolitik, using a combination of war and diplomacy to advance the interests of the Prussian state.
3. **CHANGE** Germany developed a

A complete, 1-page lesson plan is provided for each section in the *Reproducible Lesson Plans* booklet.

The Age of Imperialism

CHAPTER RESOURCES

	Reproducible Resources	Multimedia Resources
Chapter Opener	Chapter Themes: Graphic Organizer 16 Historical Significance Chapter Activity 16	MindJogger Videoquiz
Chapter Enrichment	Vocabulary Activity 16* Time Line Activity 16 Mapping History Activity 16 History Simulation 16 Geography and History Activity 16 Source Reading 16 People in World History Profiles 51, 52 World Art and Music Activity 16 Enrichment Activity 16 Critical Thinking Activity 16 Skill Reinforcement Activity 16 Performance Assessment Activity 16	World History and Art Transparency 35, *Ono Waterfall* Chapter Transparency 16 Vocabulary PuzzleMaker Software

Chapter Review/Reteaching	Reteaching Activity 16
	Skill Reinforcement Activity 16
	Spanish Chapter Summary 16
		Chapter 16 Digest Audiocassette,
		   Activity, Test*
		Vocabulary PuzzleMaker Software
		Student Self-Test and Review
		   Software
		MindJogger Videoquiz

Chapter Evaluation/Testing	Performance Assessment Activity 16 Chapter 16 Test, Forms A and B	Testmaker

* Also available in Spanish

0:00 OUT OF TIME? Assign the Chapter 16 summary in the Unit 4 Digest on pages 505–507, and the Chapter 16 Audiocassettes.

Block Schedule

Block scheduling differs from traditional class scheduling in the amount of time allotted to each period. The extended time frame provided by block scheduling affords you the opportunity to implement a greater number of research-oriented and activity-intense projects to motivate and involve your students. Activities that are particularly suited to use within the block scheduling framework are identified throughout this chapter by the following designation.

KEY TO ABILITY LEVELS

Teaching strategies have been coded for varying learning styles and abilities.

L1 **BASIC** activities for all students
L2 **AVERAGE** activities for average to above-average students
L3 **CHALLENGING** activities for above-average students
LEP **LIMITED ENGLISH PROFICIENCY** activities

Use Glencoe's *Presentation Plus!* multimedia teacher tool to easily present dynamic lessons that visually excite your students. Using Microsoft PowerPoint® you can customize the presentations to create your own personalized lessons.

SECTION RESOURCES

Daily Objectives	Reproducible Resources	Multimedia Resources
Section 1 **Pressures for Expansion** Identify the political, economic, and social causes of imperialism.	Reproducible Lesson Plan 16-1 Vocabulary Activity 16* Guided Reading Activity 16-1* Time Line Activity 16 Section Quiz 16-1*	Section Focus Transparency 16-1 Chapter Transparency 16 Student Self-Test and Review Software Testmaker
Section 2 **The Partition of Africa** List the effects imperialism had on the continent of Africa.	Reproducible Lesson Plan 16-2 Vocabulary Activity 16* Guided Reading Activity 16-2* People in World History Profile 52 History Simulation 16 Section Quiz 16-2*	Section Focus Transparency 16-2 Student Self-Test and Review Software Testmaker
Section 3 **The Division of Asia** Describe how the countries of Asia responded to imperialism.	Reproducible Lesson Plan 16-3 Guided Reading Activity 16-3* Geography and History Activity 16 People in World History Profile 51 Section Quiz 16-3*	Section Focus Transparency 16-3 World History and Art Transparency 35, *Ono Waterfall* Vocabulary PuzzleMaker Software Student Self-Test and Review Software Testmaker
Section 4 **Imperialism in the Americas** Explain how Latin Americans responded to the growth of American influence in their region.	Reproducible Lesson Plan 16-4 Vocabulary Activity 16* Guided Reading Activity 16-4* Reteaching Activity 16 Enrichment Activity 16 Section Quiz 16-4* Performance Assessment Activity 16 Spanish Chapter Summary 16	Section Focus Transparency 16-4 Student Self-Test and Review Software Testmaker

* Also available in Spanish

Chapter Activities

Performance Assessment Activity

Conducting a Draft Assign students to cooperative groups, with each group representing a world power of the era discussed in the chapter. The whole class should brainstorm a list of all of the areas of the world that once were under the control of these powers. Then give each group approximately 30 minutes to organize a strategy for drafting countries or areas from this list for their empires. On the second day, the actual draft will occur. It should be patterned after the NFL or NBA drafts, where each group has a limited amount of time to make a choice, at which time the country is removed from the list. Groups of world powers may work out trades among themselves as well, following any agreed-upon rules of the drafting system. As a final product, the groups should submit a record sheet of each of their transactions and drafts with a rationale for each.

Possible Rubric Features

Accuracy of content information, decision-making skills, collaborative skills, concept attainment for imperialism and empires, organization of plan

• *For an additional activity, refer to Activity 16 in the* Performance Assessment Strategies and Activities *booklet.*

ACTIVITY

From the Classroom of...

**Scott L. Miles—
Teacher of the Year,
Wisconsin Council for
the Social Studies
Wausau West High
School Wausau, WI**

Establishing Colonies in Africa

Assign small groups a European nation and give them a list of goals for the country's colonial activities in Africa. (For example, Portugal: secure African coastal areas to help develop secure trade routes with Asia.)

Spread out a large piece of paper on the classroom floor and draw a large outline map of Africa. Provide each nation (small group) with a length of yarn based on their relative strength. Some suggested lengths are: Portugal (9 ft.), England (26 ft.), France (22 ft.), Germany (12 ft.), Spain (6 ft.), and Italy (6 ft.). You may wish to use a separate color for each nation. Then ask students to place the yarn on the map to mark off territory in such a way as to meet their country's objectives.

Compare the map with an actual colonial map of the continent. How accurate was your country in fulfilling its objectives? How do colonial boundaries (maps) compare with current national boundaries? What problems would this cause for African nations?

MULTIPLE LEARNING STYLES

Verbal/Linguistic

Have students assume the role of a newspaper editor during the 1800s. Have them prepare editorials entitled either "The Case for Imperialism" or "The Case Against Imperialism." Their editorials should include examples that support their opinion.

Logical/Mathematical

Have students create a circle graph showing how much of Africa was controlled by the various colonial powers during the Age of Imperialism. Have them obtain rough area figures by comparing colonial boundaries with those of modern nations and then consulting an almanac or encyclopedia. Areas can be converted to percentages of the total area of the continent.

Visual/Spatial

Have students trace the continents of Europe, Asia, Africa, and the Americas, including the Pacific islands. Have them label countries discussed in the chapter and create a key using different colors to indicate the European power that ruled each country. Then have students color their maps accordingly, creating a map for the Age of Imperialism.

Auditory/Musical

Have students prepare a short musical skit about one of the events described in this chapter, such as the Sepoy Rebellion or U.S. involvement in Mexico from 1914 until 1917.

Additional Resources

NATIONAL GEOGRAPHIC SOCIETY

Teacher's Corner

INDEX TO NATIONAL GEOGRAPHIC MAGAZINE

The following articles may be used for research relating to this chapter:

- "Malaysia," by T.R. Reid, August 1997.
- "French Polynesia," by Peter Benchley, June 1997.
- "India," by Geoffrey C. Ward, May 1997.
- "Hong Kong," by Mike Edwards, March 1997.
- "Burma, the Richest of Poor Countries," by Joel L. Swerdlow, July 1995.
- "Hagi: Where Japan's Revolution Began," by N. Taylor Gregg, June 1984.

NATIONAL GEOGRAPHIC SOCIETY PRODUCTS AVAILABLE FROM GLENCOE

To order the following products for use with this chapter, contact your local Glencoe sales representative, or call Glencoe at 1-800-334-7344:

- *PicturePack: Physical Geography of the World (Transparencies)*

LOCAL OBJECTIVES

_____
_____
_____
_____
_____
_____
_____
_____
_____
_____
_____
_____
_____
_____
_____
_____
_____
_____
_____
_____
_____
_____
_____
_____

BIBLIOGRAPHY

Literature of the Period
Forster, E. M. *A Passage to India.* New York: Harcourt Brace, 1989. A novel about life in India under British rule.

Readings for the Student
Conrad, Joseph. *Heart of Darkness.* New York: Norton, 1987. Conrad's grim 1902 story of one man's journey up the Congo River, accompanied by backgrounds, sources, and critical essays.

Readings for the Teacher
Said, Edward W. *Culture and Imperialism.* New York: Knopf, 1993. A literary critic's interpretation of the relationship between imperialism and literature.

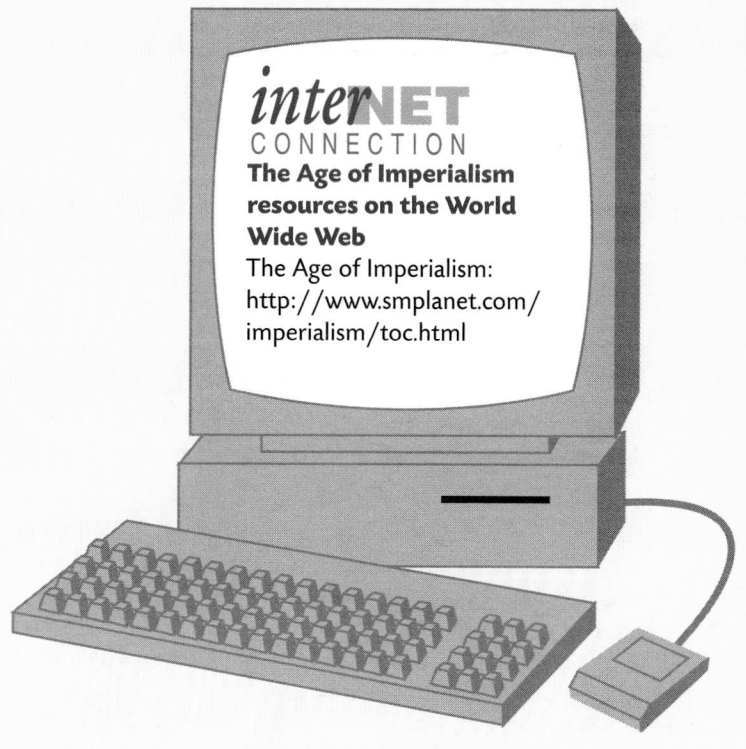

inter**NET**
CONNECTION
The Age of Imperialism resources on the World Wide Web
The Age of Imperialism: http://www.smplanet.com/imperialism/toc.html

CHAPTER THEMES

Chapter Themes are listed by section on this chapter opening page of the Student Edition. A corresponding theme-based activity is available under "TEACH," and a theme-based question is asked in the Section and Chapter Reviews.

The Storyteller

Historical Setting The incident that led to the Sepoy Rebellion reveals how Great Britain, like many of the imperialist powers in the 1800s, imposed its own culture and values on its colonized peoples. Imperialists were often contemptuous of the sacred beliefs and rituals of the people in their colonies, often to the point of wiping out other cultures in the name of progress. Where colonized peoples tried to resist imperialist pressures to discard traditional ways of life, tension—and sometimes fighting—occurred. In many cases, such as the Sepoy Rebellion, simple ignorance or thoughtlessness about local customs and beliefs created hostile feelings between imperialists and colonial peoples.

Historical Significance

Answers: *Colonized people in those regions were introduced to Western traditions and technologies for the first time—sometimes against their will. Often, they were also led to reject native customs and beliefs. Imperialists exploited laborers in colonial areas and sometimes split up families and villages.*

Western rule inspired the rise of nationalist movements that ultimately brought independence.

Chapter
16
1800–1914
The Age of Imperialism

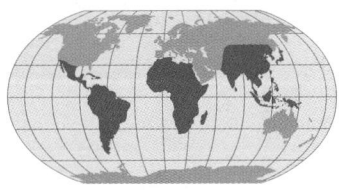

Chapter Themes

▶ **Movement** Political, economic, and social factors lead to a new period of expansion known as the Age of Imperialism. *Section 1*
▶ **Change** European powers divide most of Africa into colonies, and Africans resist European intervention and colonialism. *Section 2*
▶ **Reaction** India and China come under European control or influence, while Japan adopts reforms to meet the Western challenge. *Section 3*
▶ **Nationalism** Nationalism intensifies in Latin America as United States involvement in the region increases. *Section 4*

The Storyteller

No one knows how the rumor started, but it spread quickly. The bullets for the new rifles, the story went, were greased with the fat of cows and pigs. The sepoys, Indian soldiers in the British army, were outraged. Because Hindus regarded the cow as sacred and Muslims could not touch pork, using these bullets would violate the beliefs of both groups. As a result, the sepoys started a rebellion in May 1857 that soon engulfed much of India.

The Indian Revolt of 1857 was not an isolated incident. As European powers acquired new territories in the 1800s, conflicts between colonial rulers and colonial peoples developed. By the early 1900s European nations ruled large parts of Asia and Africa, while the United States was expanding its interests in Latin America.

Historical Significance

How did the spread of empires affect peoples in Asia, Africa, and Latin America? How did colonial peoples respond to Western rule?

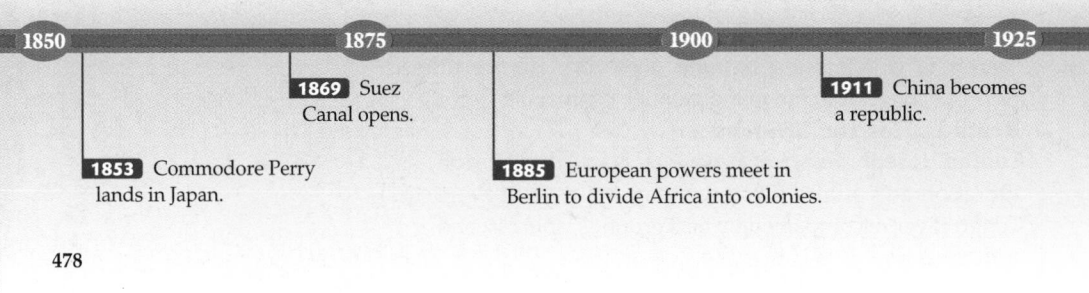

| 1850 | | 1875 | | 1900 | | 1925 |

1869 Suez Canal opens.

1911 China becomes a republic.

1853 Commodore Perry lands in Japan.

1885 European powers meet in Berlin to divide Africa into colonies.

478

GEOGRAPHY CONNECTION

Location Have students locate on a world map some of the regions in which the British acquired possessions during the Age of Imperialism, including South Africa, India, and the Pacific islands. Then have them locate the British dominions they studied in Chapter 25, including Canada, Australia, and New Zealand. What was required to rule such a large and far-flung empire? *(Answers may include: a large navy and merchant fleet, a sizable army, many adventurous and loyal citizens.)* **L1**

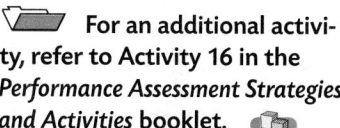

Visualizing History An Indian prince hosts a British officer at a nautch (a form of entertainment by professional dancers).

Your History Journal

Draw or copy the map "Imperialism in Africa 1914" on page 486 of this chapter. Then, using the map of modern Africa in the Atlas as a guide, write in the new national names and draw in present boundaries.

Chapter 16 *The Age of Imperialism* **479**

c. 1800 Age of Imperialism begins.

c. 1840s French citizens settle in Algeria.

1899 British author Rudyard Kipling writes the poem "The White Man's Burden."

SECTION THEME

▶ **Movement** Political, economic, and social factors lead to a new period of expansion known as the Age of Imperialism.

ind Out

Answer: *competition for international power and prestige, desire for new markets and sources of raw materials, religious fervor, and feelings of racial and cultural superiority*

FOCUS

Section Objective

Identify the political, economic, and social causes of imperialism.

BELLRINGER
Motivational Activity

Before taking roll at the beginning of the class period, project Section Focus Transparency 16-1 and have students answer the activity questions. Discuss students' responses.
This activity is also available as a blackline master.

Vocabulary Pre-check

Use Vocabulary Activity 16 to introduce vocabulary terms.
L1 LEP

Section 1

Pressures for Expansion

Setting the Scene

▶ **Terms to Define**
imperialism, colony, protectorate, sphere of influence

▶ **People to Meet**
Cecil Rhodes, Rudyard Kipling

▶ **Places to Locate**
Algeria, Australia, New Zealand, Rhodesia (Zimbabwe)

ind Out What were the political, economic, and social causes of imperialism?

The Storyteller

In India, British schools taught English and required students to adopt Christianity. The wife of a British official described attending a graduation ceremony in the year 1886. "The proceedings began with a hymn. The children sang pretty well, though in a harsh voice…. Then a boy stood up, put his hands together, and repeated the Lord's Prayer. Others followed him, and then Mr.

Summers [the teacher] read a chapter from the Old Testament about Adam and Eve…. We could just tell he was speaking of the various nations—English, Parsee, [Muslim], Hindu, all came from Adam and Eve, we were all one family here."

—adapted from *An Indian Journal*, Nora Scott, 1994

Indians and British

The term imperialism is a Latin word from the days of the Roman Empire. Imperialism means one country's domination of the political, economic, and social life of another country. About 2,000 years ago, imperial Rome controlled most of the Mediterranean world. By the end of the 1800s, a handful of European countries, together with the United States, controlled nearly the entire world. Not surprisingly, the era between 1800 and 1914 has come to be known as the Age of Imperialism.

The imperialism of the 1800s resulted from three key factors. First, nationalism prompted rival European nations to build empires in their competitive quests for power. Second, the Industrial Revolution created a tremendous demand for raw materials and expanded markets, which prompted industrialized nations to seek new territories. Finally, both religious fervor and feelings of racial and cultural superiority inspired Europeans to impose their cultures on distant lands.

Political Rivalries

In the mid-1800s European countries saw themselves as actors on the world stage, and each country wanted to play a starring role. If Great Britain started a small colony in distant Asia or Africa, France had to start one too—and so did Belgium, Germany, Italy, Holland, Spain, Portugal, and Russia.

Once begun, the quest for colonies became a continuing enterprise that seemed to have no limits. Slow and difficult communication between remote territories and European capitals often enabled colonial governors and generals to take matters into their own hands. If a colony's borders did not provide military security, for instance, military officials

---

SECTION RESOURCES

Reproducible Masters
- Reproducible Lesson Plan 16-1
- Vocabulary Activity 16
- Guided Reading Activity 16-1
- Time Line Activity 16
- Section Quiz 16-1

Transparencies
- Section Focus Transparency 16-1
- Chapter Transparency 16

Multimedia
- Student Self-Test and Review Software
- Testmaker

Visualizing History In this cartoon Bismarck (representing Germany), John Bull (representing Great Britain), and Uncle Sam (representing the United States) decide the fate of Samoa. *What phrase described Great Britain's vast overseas holdings?*

based in the colony used their armies to expand the colony's borders. This strategy worked well enough until colonial governments started claiming the same territories. Then new conflicts arose, and European troops found themselves facing off on remote battlefields in Africa and Asia.

Desire for New Markets

The Industrial Revolution of the 1800s knew no borders. Factories in Europe and the United States consumed tons of raw materials and churned out thousands of manufactured goods. The owners and operators of these factories searched constantly for new sources of raw materials and new markets for their products. They hoped to find both in foreign lands.

Rubber, copper, and gold came from Africa, cotton and jute from India, and tin from Southeast Asia. These raw materials spurred the growth of European and American industries and financial markets, but they represented only the tip of the iceberg. Bananas, oranges, melons, and other exotic fruits made their way to European markets. People in Paris, London, and Berlin drank colonial tea, coffee, and cocoa with their meals and washed themselves with soap made from African palm oil.

The colonies also provided new markets for the finished products of the Industrial Revolution. Tools, weapons, and clothing flowed out of the factories and back to the colonies whose raw materials had made them possible.

Seeking New Opportunities

Imperialism involved more than just guns, battles, raw materials, and manufactured goods. Colonies needed people who were loyal to the imperialist country. Great Britain, France, and Germany needed British, French, and German citizens to run their newly acquired territories and keep them productive.

Throughout the 1800s European leaders urged their citizens to move to far-off colonies. Many of them responded. In the 1840s, for example, thousands of French citizens sailed across the Mediterranean Sea to **Algeria**, where they started farms and estates on lands seized from local Algerian farmers.

The British, meanwhile, emigrated to the far corners of the globe, hoping to find opportunities not available at home. Many rushed to **Australia** and **New Zealand** in the 1850s in search of gold. As the British government continued to acquire vast tracts of land in Africa, Asia, and the Pacific, the phrase "the sun never sets on the British Empire" became a popular way of describing Great Britain's vast holdings.

Strong-minded individuals saw emigration as a chance to strike it rich or make a name for themselves. Perhaps the most spectacular success story of the era belonged to **Cecil Rhodes**, a British adventurer who made a fortune from gold and diamond mining in southern Africa. Rhodes went on to found a colony that bore his name: **Rhodesia** (now **Zimbabwe**).

Chapter 16 *The Age of Imperialism* 481

TEACH

Guided Practice

THEME Movement

Have students begin a discussion of the concept of movement during the Age of Imperialism by first considering their own personal travels. Ask them how traveling to new places has changed their views of the world, of other people, and of themselves. **L1**

Visualizing History John Bull, who first appeared as a literary character in 1712, later became the caricaturist's symbol for England. He was usually portrayed as a solid and jovial figure. The original Uncle Sam is said to have been Samuel Wilson, a businessman from Troy, New York, who supplied beef to the army during the War of 1812. **Why are the three men not looking at one another?** *(The cartoonist seems to imply that each country stubbornly resisted the others' arguments.)*
Answer to Caption: *"The sun never sets on the British Empire."*

Economics Discuss the close connection between the Industrial Revolution in Europe and America and the rise of imperialism. Review the effects of industrialization discussed in Chapter 23. Include the idea that the colonies that provided raw materials also became new markets for mass-produced goods. **L3**

Chapter Transparency 16

Independent Practice

Guided Reading Activity 16-1 **L1**

Time Line Activity 16

COOPERATIVE LEARNING ACTIVITY

Oral Reports Organize students into groups of three or four. Assign each group a topic that has something to do with daily life in India under the British (for example, Indian ceremonies, Indian religious life, the role of Indian women, transportation, agriculture, tiger hunts). Have each group member take on a specific task, such as library work, note taking, or presenting. Have the spokesperson for each group present a 10-minute report. Then open the topic for class discussion.

L2

Essay Have students write an essay summarizing the causes and effects of imperialism. The essays should include an intro-duction; a paragraph each for political, economic, and social causes and effects; and a conclu-sion. **L1**

ASSESS

Check for Understanding

Assign Section 1 Review as home-work or as an in-class activity.

 Use Student Self-Test and Review Software to review Sec-tion 1.

Evaluate

🗂 Section Quiz 16-1

🖥 Use the Testmaker to create a customized quiz for Section 1.

Reteach

Have students create an outline for Section 1 using the main headings and subheadings as a guide. Go over the outlines in class, creating a group outline on the chalkboard so that students can check their understanding of major ideas.

Enrich

Assign each student a person or event to research (for example, Cecil Rhodes or Perry's opening of Japan). Have them summarize their research in a three-minute class presentation.

CLOSE

Ask students how their own views on imperialism have changed after reading Section 1. *Is it possible that imperialism led to progress? How? Why? For whom?*

"Civilizing" Mission

Some emigrants had motives that went beyond mere personal glory and profit. Religious and humanitarian impulses inspired many individuals to leave their secure lives at home and head for the distant colonies. The desire to spread Western tech-nology, religion, customs and traditions also fueled colonial expansion.

During the Age of Imperialism, growing num-bers of Catholic and Protestant missionaries decid-ed to bring the Christian message to the most remote corners of Africa and Asia. Over the decades they set up hundreds of Christian missions and preached to thousands of Africans and Asians throughout these two continents. Like many other Europeans and Americans of this period, these mis-sionaries believed that Christianity and Western civilization together could benefit and transform the world.

The missionaries were not military conquerors, but they did try to change people's beliefs and prac-tices. They believed that, in order to become "civi-lized," the people of Africa and Asia would have to reject their old religions and convert to Christianity. To achieve this goal, missionaries built churches and taught Christian doctrine. Missionaries often set up schools and hospitals as well.

Other Europeans also believed that Western civilization was superior to the civilizations of colo-nial peoples. As a result, some colonial officials tried to impose Western customs and traditions on the people they conquered. These officials insisted that their colonial subjects learn European lan-guages, and they encouraged Western lifestyles as well. They also discouraged colonial peoples from practicing traditional customs and rituals.

Some Europeans seized on the theory of social Darwinism as proof of their cultural superiority. This theory adapted Darwin's ideas about the evo-lution of animals—particularly his notion of "the survival of the fittest"—to explain differences among human beings. Social Darwinists believed that white Europeans were the "fittest" people in the world and that Western nations had a duty to spread Western ideas and traditions to "backward" peoples living overseas.

In 1899 the British writer **Rudyard Kipling** cap-tured the essence of the imperialist attitude in his famous poem "The White Man's Burden." Kipling addressed the poem to the United States, which at this time had just begun to acquire and govern colonies of its own:

> ❝ Take up the White Man's burden—
> Send forth the best ye breed—
> Go bind your sons to exile
> To serve your captives' need;
> To wait in heavy harness
> On fluttered folk and wild—
> Your new-caught, sullen peoples,
> Half-devil and half-child. ❞

Forms of Imperialism

Imperial nations gained new lands through treaties, purchases, and military conquest. Once in power, they used several forms of territorial con-trol. The first of these, a colony, was a territory that an imperial power ruled directly through colonial officials. A protectorate had its own government, but its policies were guided by a foreign power. A sphere of influence was a region of a country in which the imperial power had exclusive invest-ment or trading rights.

Within these general forms of control, each imperial nation exercised its power differently. For example, the French used their colonial officials not only to govern but to spread French culture and to make territories overseas extensions of France. The British, by contrast, focused strictly on administra-tion and were less inclined to convert colonial peo-ples to British ways. In many cases, the British allowed local rulers to govern territories as their representatives.

SECTION 1 REVIEW

Recall
1. **Define** imperialism, colony, protectorate, sphere of influence.
2. **Identify** Cecil Rhodes, Rudyard Kipling.

3. **List** five raw materials that imperial powers took from their colonies. What did they send to these colonies?

Critical Thinking
4. **Evaluate** What does the Kipling poem reveal about his attitude toward Africans and Asians?

Understanding Themes
5. **Movement** Explain why the period from 1800 to 1914 is the Age of Imperialism.

SECTION 1 REVIEW ANSWERS

1. All vocabulary words are defined in the Glossary.
2. Rhodes, 481; Kipling, 482
3. Raw materials included rubber, copper, cot-ton, jute, tin, gold, bananas and other exot-ic fruits, coffee, tea, cocoa, and palm oil. The colonies were sent manufactured goods such as tools, weapons, and clothing.
4. The colonists were childlike, in need of dis-cipline and instruction.
5. **MOVEMENT** During this period, European powers extended their control over people and territories overseas to acquire new markets, to spread European values, and to provide security in the face of increasing power rivalries.

c. 1870 David Livingstone explores Africa.

1896 The Ethiopians defeat the Italians in the battle of Adowa.

1904 The French win special rights in Morocco.

1910 The British form the Union of South Africa.

Section 2

The Partition of Africa

Setting the Scene

▶ **Terms to Define**
partition

▶ **People to Meet**
David Livingstone, Abd al-Qadir, Muhammad Ali, Samory Touré, Menelik II, the Afrikaners, Shaka

▶ **Places to Locate**
Morocco, Egypt, the Sudan, Liberia, Ethiopia, Union of South Africa

 What effects did imperialism have on the continent of Africa?

The Storyteller

An eyewitness to the opening ceremonies for the Suez Canal reported: "Fireworks in front of the Viceroy's Palace. Open house everywhere.... Luxurious dinners, vintage wines, exquisite fish, partridges, wild duck. Seven or eight thousand people sitting down to dinner in the middle of the desert. It was like something out of the Arabian Nights.... *At last I got back to my houseboat....*

Opening of Suez Canal

All through the night I could hear the noise of the fair—the sound of music, the banging of fireworks, and the shouting of happy revelers."

—adapted from *World Ditch, The Making of the Suez Canal,* John Marlowe, 1964

Until the 1800s Europeans knew little of Africa beyond its northern, western, and southern coasts. Then, in the mid-1800s, a few brave explorers began to venture into the African interior. The most famous of these was Scottish doctor and missionary **David Livingstone**, who first went to Africa in 1840. For the next 30 years, Livingstone explored wide tracts of central and eastern Africa, setting up Christian missions and sending back to Great Britain detailed reports of his discoveries, such as Victoria Falls.

When Europeans temporarily lost touch with Livingstone late in the 1860s, the *New York Herald* hired a British journalist and explorer named Henry M. Stanley to track him down. Their famous meeting in 1871 is best remembered for Stanley's understated greeting, "Dr. Livingstone, I presume?" With help from European financial backers, Stanley went on to lead several major expeditions through central Africa himself.

The publicity surrounding the explorations of Livingstone and Stanley generated new interest in Africa throughout Europe. This interest swelled when subsequent explorers sent back excited reports about the continent's abundance of resources. Reports such as these helped set off a mad European scramble for Africa between 1880 and 1914. One European country after another laid claim to parts of Africa. In 1885, 14 nations met in Berlin, Germany, and agreed to partition, or divide, the prize King Leopold II of Belgium called "this magnificent African cake." By 1914 European nations controlled 90 percent of the continent.

North Africa

 The world's largest desert—the Sahara—stretches across North Africa from the Atlantic

Chapter 16 *The Age of Imperialism* **483**

SECTION THEME

▶ **Change** European powers divide most of Africa into colonies, and Africans resist European intervention and colonialism.

Find Out

Answer: *By 1914 European nations controlled 90 percent of Africa, whose native populations and resources they exploited. In some places families and even whole villages were split up. Africans were taught to reject their own customs and beliefs in favor of European ways.*

FOCUS

Section Objective

List the effects imperialism had on the continent of Africa.

BELLRINGER
Motivational Activity

Before taking roll at the beginning of the class period, project Section Focus Transparency 16-2 and have students answer the activity questions. Discuss students' responses.
This activity is also available as a blackline master.

Vocabulary Pre-check

Use Vocabulary Activity 16 to introduce vocabulary terms.
L1 LEP

SECTION RESOURCES

📁 **Reproducible Masters**
- Reproducible Lesson Plan 16-2
- Vocabulary Activity 16
- Guided Reading Activity 16-2
- People in World History Profile 52
- History Simulation 16
- Section Quiz 16-2

📽 **Transparencies**
- Section Focus Transparency 16-2

Multimedia
- Student Self-Test and Review Software
- Testmaker

Visualizing History British explorer Sir Henry Morton Stanley finds missionary David Livingstone in Africa. *What ended Britain's imperialist dispute with France over the Sudan?*

TEACH

Guided Practice

THEME Change

Discuss the changes brought to Africa as a result of imperialist expansion and conflict. Focus on changes involving local inhabitants, land, and culture. Ask students to explain which changes they perceive as good and which they view as bad. *(Students may point to new products and the establishment of better transportation and trade routes as good; they may point to the inhuman treatment of Africans by people such as Leopold II and the land devastation caused by wars as bad.)* **L1**

Visualizing History

The historic meeting between Livingstone and Stanley took place in Ujiji, in Central Africa, on November 10, 1871.
Answer to Caption: *British recognition of French control of Morocco*

Critical Thinking Ask students to speculate on Italy's reasons for "settling" Libya. **Why was controlling Libya better than having no imperialist claim at all?** *(Possible answer: It gave Italy a foot in the door to further expansion in Africa—to Ethiopia, for example.)* **L3**

 History Simulation 16

Independent Practice

Guided Reading Activity 16-2 **L1**

People in World History Profile 52

Ocean to the Red Sea. Most of the people in North Africa live on a thin strip of land located north of the Sahara along the Mediterranean coast. Here the land is fertile and the climate mild. In the early 1800s Muslim Arabs under the authority of the Ottoman ruler in Istanbul governed the large territories west of Egypt, which at that time were called Tripoli, Tunis, and Algiers. Today Tripoli, Tunis, and Algiers are the independent North African countries of Libya, Tunisia, and Algeria.

The French in North Africa

In 1830 King Charles X of France ordered an invasion of Algiers with the aim of colonizing that country. French troops encountered stiff resistance from the Algerians, whose leader was **Abd al-Qadir** (AB•duhl KAH•duhr). About 10 years passed before 100,000 French soldiers finally subdued the determined Algerians. After conquering Algiers, the French seized neighboring Tunis in 1881 and secured special rights in **Morocco** in 1904. About 1 million French people settled in North Africa during these years of struggle.

Britain and Egypt

During the early 1800s, Ottoman **Egypt** was virtually independent under its governor, **Muhammad Ali**. Muhammad Ali's armies conquered neighboring lands, making Egypt a power in the eastern Mediterranean. To modernize Egypt, Ali reformed tax and land systems, encouraged industry, and supported irrigation projects to boost cotton production. Under Ali's successors, however, Egypt's debts rose along with European influence.

In 1859 a French entrepreneur, Ferdinand de Lesseps, set up a company to build the Suez Canal. Joining the Mediterranean and Red Seas, this waterway became a vital shortcut between Europe and Asia and was especially valued by the British as an important link to India. In 1875 Great Britain gained effective control of the canal when Egypt sold its canal shares to the British to pay off its debts. During the next few years, British influence increased over Egypt. In 1882 British forces put down a revolt led by nationalist leader Ahmed Arabi, and Egypt became a British protectorate.

Meanwhile, in **the Sudan**, south of Egypt, a Muslim revival stirred nationalist feelings. Since the 1880s, the Sudanese, under their leader the Mahdi, had challenged British expansion. In 1898, however, British forces, using Maxim machine guns, defeated the more simply armed Sudanese army at the Battle of Omdurman. Soon after the battle, the British also confronted a French force at Fashoda, bringing Great Britain and France to the brink of war. In the end, the French withdrew their army and their claim to the Sudan when the British recognized French control of Morocco.

Italy Seizes Libya

Libya lies between Egypt on the east and Algeria and Tunisia on the west. Known as Tripoli in the 1800s, the country had almost no economic value, but it was coveted by Italy, the nearest European nation. Entering the imperialist race late, Italy was eager to establish an African empire. After seeking guarantees of neutrality from other European nations, Italy in 1911 declared war on the Ottoman Empire, which ruled Tripoli. Italy easily

484 Chapter 16 *The Age of Imperialism*

COOPERATIVE LEARNING ACTIVITY

News Report Have students prepare an in-depth news report on the Boer War in the style of a prime-time television news program. Organize students into four groups—those who will gather information about the war and the issues surrounding it, those who will prepare written copy for the telecast, those who will represent the Afrikaners and the British in interviews, and those who will serve as reporters and anchors for the show. If possible, videotape the show for presentation to other classes. **L2**

defeated the Ottoman Turks and took Tripoli as a colony, renaming it Libya. Libya was the last country in North Africa to be conquered by European nations.

West, Central, and East Africa

West, Central, and East Africa have varied landscapes: mountains, plains, deserts, and rain forests. During the 1800s, these regions consisted of many territories, each with its own history and traditions. Europeans, however, exploited the Africans' lack of political unity and swallowed up most of these lands in the late 1800s.

West Africa

In the 1500s and 1600s Europeans traded along the coasts of Africa. From West African coastal trading posts, they carried out the transatlantic slave trade that provided labor for plantations and mines in the Americas. West African states traded salt, gold, and iron wares with the Europeans, but some local rulers also supplied prisoners of war to the slave trade.

During the early 1800s, many Western nations declared an end to the slave trade and abolished slavery. Slave trading, however, continued as Arab and African traders sent people from Central and East Africa to perform slave labor in the Middle East and Asia. Meanwhile, West African states, weakened by the population losses of the slave trade, traded natural products, such as palm oil, ivory, rubber, cotton, and cacao beans, for European manufactured goods.

To control this trade and to expand their coastal holdings, European nations began to push inland in the 1870s. Before this time, Europeans had avoided inland Africa because of the difficult terrain and deadly diseases, such as malaria. In the late 1800s, the discovery of the natural ingredient, quinine, to fight malaria and the use of steamships for river transportation made European exploration of inland Africa easier. By 1900, European powers, especially Great Britain and France, had acquired vast new territories in West Africa.

European expansion, however, did not go unchallenged. In the 1890s West African rulers, such as **Samory Touré** (sah•MOHR•ree too•RAY) and Behanzin, led armies against the French. In the Gold Coast, the Ashanti queen Yaa Asantewaa rallied her people against British expansion. All of these efforts were defeated by well-armed European forces. By 1900, **Liberia** was the only remaining independent state in West Africa. Established in 1822 by free African Americans, Liberia became a republic in 1847. Its ties to the United States made it off limits to European expansion.

Central and East Africa

In 1877 the explorer Henry M. Stanley reached the mouth of the Congo River. He later described the river as a "grand highway of commerce to … Central Africa." As a result of Stanley's exploration, Belgium's King Leopold II claimed the Congo region as his own private plantation. He enslaved the Congolese people and had them cut down forests for rubber trees and kill elephant herds for ivory tusks. In pursuing his ambitions, Leopold stripped the Congo of many people and resources.

Leopold's brutal control of the Congo lasted about 20 years, despite the world's outrage. In 1908 he finally agreed to give his plantation to the Belgian government in return for a large loan. Thus, in that year, the Congo region owned by Leopold became the Belgian Congo.

Visualizing History This wood carving of a man reading a book is a Yoruba artist's depiction of a Swedish missionary. *Besides establishing missions, what were other European objectives in Africa?*

Role Play Ask students to assume the persona of Henry Stanley, David Livingstone, or Cecil Rhodes and write letters describing the details of everyday life and their discoveries. **L2**

Multicultural The imperialists, with their desire to colonize and control Africa, often clashed with the diverse indigenous groups. Have students research some of the original inhabitants of Africa and their relations with the imperialists and report to the class on their findings. This exercise may be done in small groups. **L3**

Literature Have students read Joseph Conrad's *Heart of Darkness* as background for studying imperialism in the Congo. Have them prepare written reports. Some may wish to work together to prepare a class presentation on different aspects of imperialism as presented in Conrad's story. **L3**

Visualizing History Southwestern Nigeria is home to the Yoruba peoples. Yoruba sculptures of humans are distinctive for their bulging eyes and flat lips.
Answer to Caption: *to exploit the continent's resources for their own purposes, to control trade to their own advantage, and to enhance their national prestige by increasing their overseas possessions*

MEETING SPECIAL NEEDS ACTIVITY

Learning Disability For the benefit of students with learning problems, organize the entire class into five groups, making sure that each group has a similar mix of students of different abilities. Assign each group one area of Africa covered in the section: North Africa (including Egypt and Libya), West Africa, Central Africa, East Africa, and southern Africa. Have the students in each group use the material in the chapter and an encyclopedia to prepare a brief oral report on the history of their region. Then ask one person in each group to present its oral report to the other groups. **L1**

Linking Past and Present

Apartheid, the South African policy of segregation, has taken on a more general meaning. The word is sometimes used to refer to any practice anywhere that separates people by race, social class, gender, and so on.

Chapter 16
Section 2

Who?What?Where?When?

South Africa's Orange Free State and **Transvaal** provinces both get their names from rivers. The Orange River forms part of the Orange Free State's southern boundary, and the Vaal River forms part of the Transvaal's southern boundary. Transvaal means "across the Vaal." Afrikaners first crossed both rivers in the early 1800s.

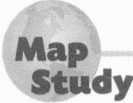

you don't say...

Trek, an arduous journey, comes from the Afrikaans word meaning "to draw a vehicle or to migrate." In South Africa a trek is also a stage of a journey, between two stopping places.

Map Study

Answer

It shortened the distance between Europe and Asia; it was a vital link between the British and their Indian empire.

Map Skills Practice

Reading a Map Which two European imperialist powers controlled the most territory in Africa in 1914? *(France, Great Britain)*

While the Belgians were claiming the Congo Basin, the British, the Germans, and the Italians were doing the same in East Africa. The only country in East Africa to remain independent during this period was **Ethiopia**, located in a remote region known as the Horn of Africa. Beginning in the 1880s, Italy tried to conquer this country, but the Italians underestimated the determination of their opponent, Ethiopia's Emperor **Menelik II**. As emperor, Menelik had conquered many small kingdoms and reunified the Ethiopian Empire.

When the Italians attacked Ethiopia in 1896, Menelik's well-trained forces crushed the invaders at the battle of Adowa. His victory was so devastating

Imperialism in Africa 1914

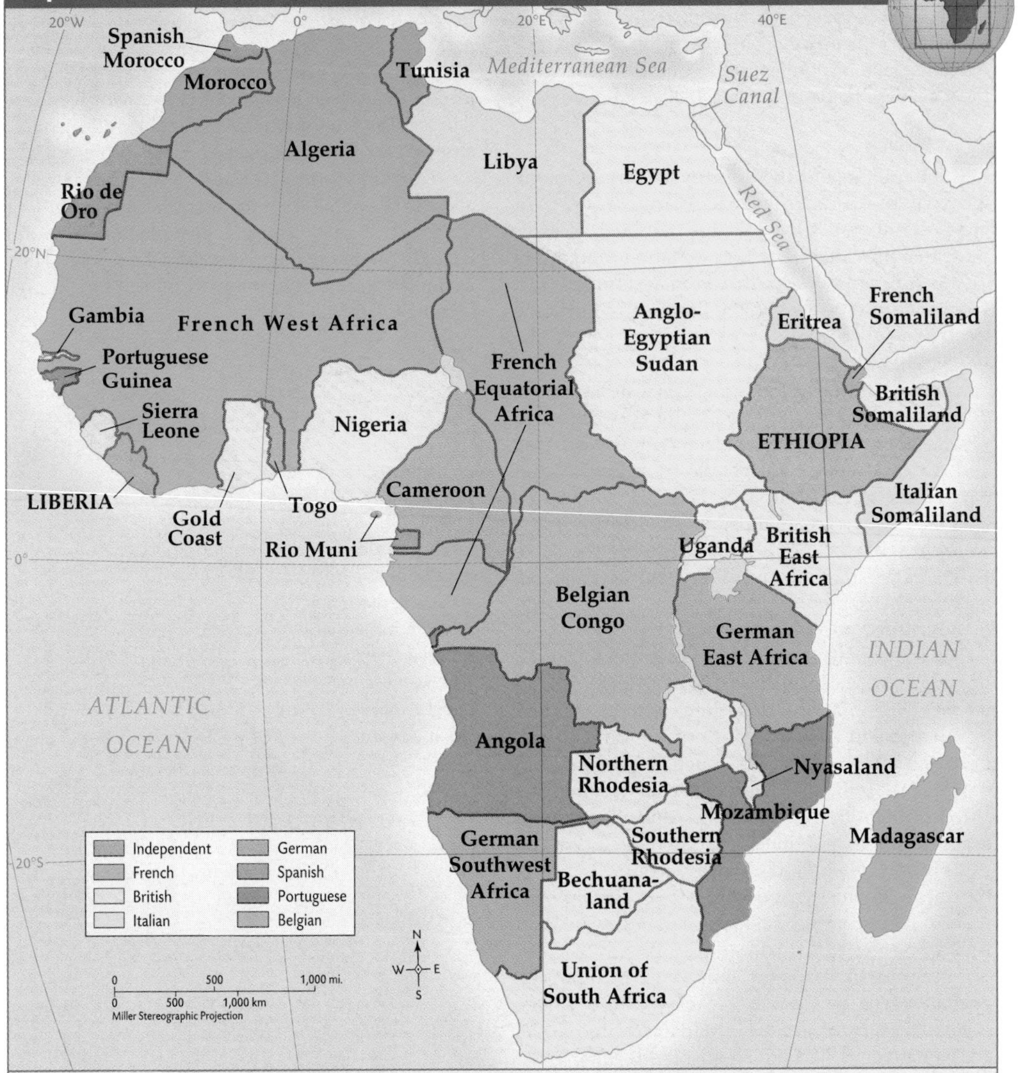

20°W
0°
20°E
40°E
20°N
0°
20°S
Spanish Morocco
Morocco
Tunisia
Mediterranean Sea
Suez Canal
Algeria
Libya
Egypt
Red Sea
Rio de Oro
Gambia
French West Africa
Portuguese Guinea
Sierra Leone
LIBERIA
Gold Coast
Togo
Nigeria
Rio Muni
Cameroon
French Equatorial Africa
Anglo-Egyptian Sudan
Eritrea
French Somaliland
British Somaliland
ETHIOPIA
Italian Somaliland
Uganda
British East Africa
Belgian Congo
German East Africa
INDIAN OCEAN
ATLANTIC OCEAN
Angola
Northern Rhodesia
Nyasaland
Mozambique
Madagascar
German Southwest Africa
Southern Rhodesia
Bechuana-land
Union of South Africa
Independent
French
British
Italian
German
Spanish
Portuguese
Belgian
N
S
E
W
0 500 1,000 mi.
0 500 1,000 km
Miller Stereographic Projection

Map Study By 1914 only two independent countries remained in all of Africa.
Movement How did the Suez Canal affect global trading patterns?

MAKING CONNECTIONS ACTIVITY

The Arts Have some students watch the video *Out of Africa* (1985), which takes place around the time of World War I, when discontented European settlers moved in waves to East Africa. Ask students to summarize what the film shows about the effects of imperialism on both Africans and Europeans of the time. Have other students watch movies set in South Africa, such as *Sarafina!* (1992), *A World Apart* (1988), *Overindulgence* (1987), and the more recent *Cry, the Beloved Country* (1996). Ask them to write brief reviews of the movies, focusing on the long-lasting effects of imperialism on the country's inhabitants. Use students' reactions to the various movies as a springboard for a general discussion of the effects of imperialism in Africa. **L2**

Visualizing History King Menelik is shown here with his chiefs. *How did Ethiopia's emperor prevent Italy and other nations from establishing imperialist control of Ethiopia?*

that no Europeans dared invade his country again during his lifetime. Ethiopia and Liberia were the only two African nations to escape European domination completely during the Age of Imperialism.

Southern Africa

Dutch settlers came to southern Africa in 1652 and established the port of Cape Town. For the next 150 years, **the Afrikaners**, as these settlers came to be called, conquered the lands around the port. The lands they eventually acquired became known as Cape Colony.

Before construction of the Suez Canal, the quickest sea route to Asia from Europe was around the Cape of Good Hope at the southern tip of Africa. Sensing the strategic value of Cape Colony, the British seized it during the Napoleonic Wars in the early 1800s. The Afrikaners resented British rule, particularly laws that forbade the enslaving of black Africans. The white Afrikaners believed that they were superior to black Africans and that God had ordained slavery.

In the 1830s about 10,000 Afrikaners, whom the British called *Boers* (the Dutch word for "farmers"), decided to leave Cape Colony rather than live under British rule. In a move known as the Great Trek, the Afrikaners migrated northeast into the interior. Here they established two independent republics, the Transvaal and the Orange Free State. The constitution of the Transvaal stated, "There shall be no equality in State or Church between white and black."

The Afrikaners fought constantly with their neighbors. First they battled the powerful Zulu nation for control of the land. Under their king **Shaka**, the Zulu in the early 1800s had conquered a large empire in southern Africa. The Zulu and Boers were unable to win a decisive victory. Finally, in 1879, the British became involved in battles with the Zulu. Under their king, Cetywayo, the Zulu at first defeated British forces. With guns and greater numbers, however, the British eventually destroyed the Zulu Empire.

Conflict also developed between the British and the Boers. During the 1880s, British settlers moved into the Boer-ruled Transvaal in search of gold and diamonds. Eager to acquire this mineral wealth for Great Britain, Cecil Rhodes—now prime minister of Cape Colony—and some other British leaders wanted all of South Africa to come under British rule. They began pressuring the Boers to grant civil rights to the British settlers in the Transvaal. Growing hostility between the British and the Boers finally erupted in 1899 into the Anglo-Boer War, which the British won three years later.

In 1910 Great Britain united the Transvaal, the Orange Free State, Cape Colony, and Natal into the **Union of South Africa**. The constitution of this British dominion made it nearly impossible for nonwhites to win the right to vote. As one black African writer of the time said, "The Union is to be a Union of two races, namely the British and the Afrikaners—the African is to be excluded."

Racial equality became a dominant issue in South African affairs after the formation of the Union. Several nonwhite South African groups tried to advance their civil rights against the white minority government. Mohandas K. Gandhi, a lawyer from India, worked for equality for Indians in South Africa. He urged the Indians to disobey laws that discriminated against them. Gandhi's efforts brought some additional rights for the Indian community.

South Africa's black majority also was stirred into action against racial injustices. In 1912 black South Africans founded the South African Native

Chapter 16 *The Age of Imperialism* **487**

CRITICAL THINKING ACTIVITY

Recognizing Ideologies On the chalkboard write these statements quoted on page 487: "There shall be no equality in State or Church between white and black" and "The Union is to be a Union of two races, namely the British and the Afrikaners—the African is to be excluded." Without glossing over American racial problems, ask students to suggest some aspects of American national ideology that enabled more rapid advances in the civil rights movement in this country than in South Africa. (*Students may point to the assertion in the Declaration of Independence "that all Men are created equal, that they are endowed by their Creator with certain unalienable Rights...."*) **L3**

Geography

Coastal Trading Centers

Dakar, Senegal

"The king of the white people wishes to find out a way by which we may bring our own merchandise to you and sell everything at a much cheaper rate," said British explorer Mungo Park to a West African king in 1805. Park was interested in the possibilities of trade on the Niger River.

Like the other great rivers of Africa—the Congo, the Nile, and the Zambezi—the Niger flows to the sea. To the European traders of the 1800s, few places were more important than the mouth of a river. These were the only places where the large trading ships could unload European manufactured goods in exchange for African raw materials.

At the mouth of the Niger in the late 1800s, trade centered on palm oil. The British used the oil for making soap. Barrels of the precious oil were floated down the Niger and collected at depots, or ports, with names like Calabar and Port Harcourt.

Today these ports are growing cities that draw people from all parts of Nigeria. Port Harcourt now has a population of 400,000 inhabitants, while Calabar has about 160,000. Both ports still provide oil to the world, but today it is crude oil, the lifeblood of the world's industries and transportation.

Linking Past and Present — ACTIVITY

Explain why Mungo Park was interested in Africa. Why did the mouths of African rivers become centers of trade with Europeans? Describe African port cities today.

Linking Past and Present

Coastal Trading Centers

Scottish-born Mungo Park (1771–1806) was trained as a surgeon and began his explorations in 1792 as medical officer of a ship bound for trade in the East Indies. Park survived many adventures, which he recounted in the popular book *Travels in the Interior Districts of Africa* (1797). He died by drowning in 1806, when his second expedition to the Niger was attacked.

ANSWERS

He was interested in establishing the Niger River as a trading route for the British. They were places where European trading ships could unload manufactured goods in exchange for raw materials transported from the African interior; growing cities with increasing population and ports that supply crude oil to world industrial centers.

CLOSE

Many countries vied for Africa during the Age of Imperialism. Have students summarize five or six main reasons for the scramble for Africa.

National Congress (SANNC). The SANNC's goal was to work for black rights in South Africa. In 1923 the SANNC shortened its name to the African National Congress (ANC).

Effects of Imperialism

Imperialism had profound effects on Africa. These effects varied from colony to colony, but they centered mainly on economic and social life. The imperialists profited from the colonies by digging mines, starting plantations, and building factories and ports. They hired Africans at low wages and imposed taxes that had to be paid in cash. Men were often housed in dormitories away from their families and subjected to brutal discipline.

Schools set up by Europeans taught Africans that European ways were best. In some cases, African traditions declined, although most Africans held on to their cultures while accepting some European ways. For example, many Africans came to accept some form of Christianity.

By the early 1900s, a western-educated elite had emerged in many European colonies in Africa. These Africans condemned imperialism as contrary to western ideals of liberty and equality. They founded nationalist groups to push for self-rule. By the end of the twentieth century, Africa's peoples had won their political independence from European rule.

SECTION 2 REVIEW

Recall
1. **Define** partition.
2. **Identify** David Livingstone, Abd al-Qadir, Muhammad Ali, Samory Touré, Menelik II, the Afrikaners, Shaka.
3. **Locate** the countries of North Africa on the map on page 486. What geographical feature separates these countries from the rest of Africa?

Critical Thinking
4. **Analyzing Information** How did European rule affect civil rights in South Africa? What steps did Africans and Asians take to bring about change?

Understanding Themes
5. **Change** What were the main causes and effects of the European partition of Africa?

SECTION 2 REVIEW ANSWERS

1. All vocabulary words are defined in the Glossary.
2. Livingstone, 483; al-Qadir, 484; Muhammad Ali, 484; Touré, 485; Menelik, 486; Afrikaners, 487; Shaka, 487
3. the Sahara
4. The Afrikaners imposed slavery on Africans; the British abolished slavery but Africans did not have full rights with whites; Asians practiced disobedience against discriminatory laws while Africans formed the South African Native National Congress, later African National Congress, to work for black rights.
5. **CHANGE** It resulted from European rivalries and interest in Africa's resources and potential markets. The imperialists hired Africans at low wages, laid waste their land, and destroyed traditional ways of life.

Section 3

The Division of Asia

Setting the Scene

▶ **Terms to Define**
sepoy, viceroy, sphere of influence, culture system, westernization

▶ **People to Meet**
Ci Xi, Sun Yat-sen, Matthew C. Perry, Mutsuhito, Diponegoro, Emilio Aguinaldo

▶ **Places to Locate**
Beijing, the East Indies, the Philippines, Indochina

 How did the countries of Asia respond to imperialism?

The Storyteller

"Until the year 1924 I was the only foreigner privileged to witness and to participate in the great ceremonies…." So wrote Reginald Johnston, Professor of Chinese at the University of London, and witness to the end of an empire in the "Palace of Cloudless Heaven" within the Forbidden City. "It was not without difficulty that even the emperor was able to … invite a few 'ocean-men' to witness the New Year ceremonial which took place on February 5, 1924. It turned out to be the last occasion on which the ceremony was performed.

China's Forbidden City

Before another year had passed, the life of the Manchu court had come to an end."

—adapted from *Twilight in the Forbidden City,* Reginald F. Johnston, 1934

In his book *Description of the World,* written in 1298, Italian explorer Marco Polo relates the many stories he heard about Zipangu, an East Asian island with a supposedly inexhaustible supply of gold. Polo never did visit Zipangu, now called Japan, but his description of its imagined treasures, and of the Asian riches he did see, inspired generations of Europeans. They looked eastward to Asia, dreaming of wealth.

The British in India

European trade with Asia opened up in the 1500s as sea routes replaced difficult overland routes. British involvement in India dates back to this period, when English traders first sailed along India's coast. In 1600 some of these traders formed the East India Company, which later became one of the richest and most powerful trading companies the world had ever known.

After its founding, the East India Company built trading posts and forts in strategic locations throughout India. The French East India Company did the same and challenged the British for control of the India trade. In 1757 Robert Clive, a British East India Company agent, used an army of British and Indian troops to defeat the French at the Battle of Plassey. During the next hundred years, the British expanded their territory in India through wars and commercial activity.

The Sepoy Rebellion

As a result of steady expansion, the East India Company came to control most of India by 1857. Their power was tested that year, however, when the sepoys, or Indian soldiers, rebelled against their British commanders. Long before the greased bullet rumor discussed at this chapter's beginning triggered the Indian Revolt of 1857, sepoy resentment had been growing over British attempts to impose Christianity and European customs on them.

Chapter 16 *The Age of Imperialism* **489**

SECTION THEME

▶ **Reaction** India and China come under European control or influence, while Japan adopts reforms to meet the Western challenge.

Find Out

Answer: *In India and China, nationalist movements developed; Japan industrialized and became a major world power.*

FOCUS

Section Objective

Describe how the countries of Asia responded to imperialism.

BELLRINGER
Motivational Activity

Before taking roll at the beginning of the class period, project Section Focus Transparency 16-3 and have students answer the activity questions. Discuss students' responses.
This activity is also available as a blackline master.

Vocabulary Pre-check

🖵 Use the Vocabulary PuzzleMaker to create a puzzle that reinforces the vocabulary terms in this section. **L1**

SECTION RESOURCES

📁 **Reproducible Masters**
• Reproducible Lesson Plan 16-3
• Guided Reading Activity 16-3
• Geography and History Activity 16
• People in World History Profile 51
• Section Quiz 16-3

📊 **Transparencies**
• Section Focus Transparency 16-3
• World History and Art Transparency 35, *Ono Waterfall*

Multimedia
🖵 Vocabulary PuzzleMaker Software
🖵 Student Self-Test and Review Software
🖵 Testmaker

TEACH

Guided Practice

THEME Reaction

Write the words *China* and *Japan* on the chalkboard. Lead students in a comparison and contrast of Chinese and Japanese reactions to Western influence. Summarize student comments on the appropriate place on the chalkboard. (*China: People rebelled, first in the Opium War, then in the Boxer Rebellion, but foreign influence increased; Japan: New leaders worked to make Japan a great power capable of competing with modern, industrialized Western nations.*) **L1**

Map Study

Answer
Kashmir, the Rajput States, Hyderabad, Mysore

Map Skills Practice

Reading a Map In which period did Great Britain seize the largest amount of territory in India? *(1805–1856)*

Economics Discuss the importance of the Chinese opium trade to the merchants in imperialist countries. What were the effects of smuggling opium into China besides the exchange of merchandise? *(war between Britain and China)* What effects do you think this trade had on the Chinese people? *(The use of opium led to illness and less productive lives.)* **L2**

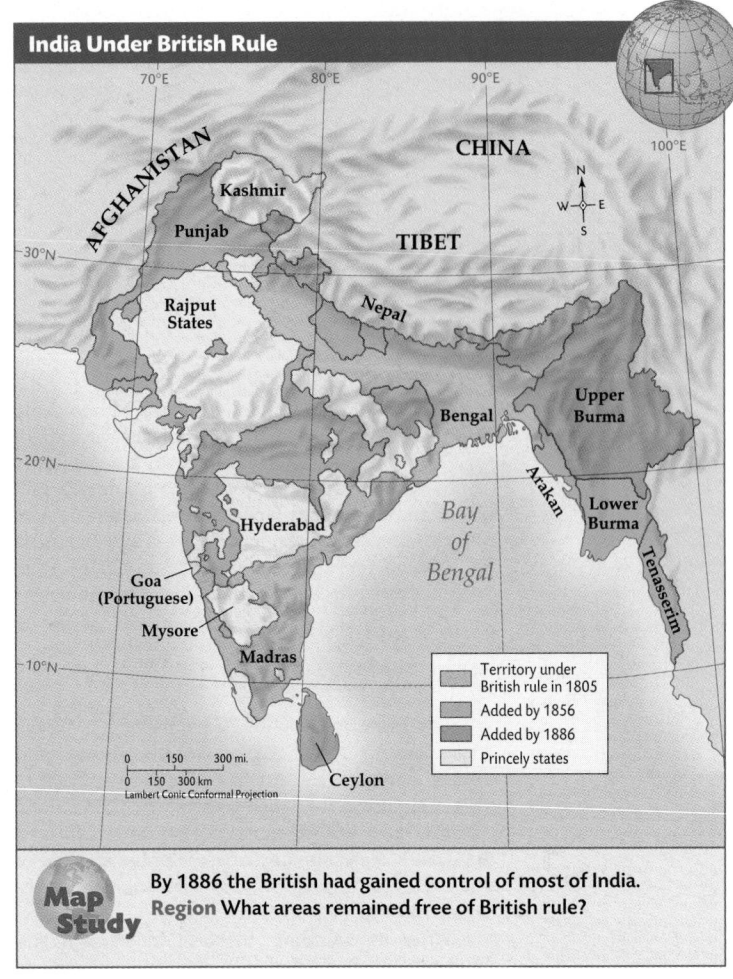

India Under British Rule

Territory under British rule in 1805
Added by 1856
Added by 1886
Princely states

0   150   300 mi.
0   150 300 km
Lambert Conic Conformal Projection

Map Study By 1886 the British had gained control of most of India. **Region** What areas remained free of British rule?

The sepoy rebellion spread across northern and central India, in some places resulting in the massacre of British men, women, and children. Within a year, British forces put down the uprising. In revenge for the massacres, they killed thousands of unarmed Indians. The revolt left bitterness on both sides and forced the British to tighten their control of India. In 1858 Parliament ended the East India Company and sent a **viceroy** to rule as the monarch's representative. Treaties secured the loyalty of the remaining independent Indian states.

Indian Nationalism

The British government tried to quell further unrest in India by spending vast amounts of money on India's economic development. It built paved roads and an extensive railway system; it installed telegraph lines and dug irrigation canals; and it established schools and universities.

At the same time, British colonial officials discriminated against Indians and forced them to change their ancient ways, often with tragic results. Indian farmers, for example, were told to grow cotton instead of wheat, because British textile mills needed cotton. The lack of wheat then led to severe food shortages that killed millions of Indians during the 1800s.

Outraged by the food shortages and other problems, many Indians wanted to move toward self-rule. In 1885 a group of Indian business and professional leaders formed the Indian National Congress. Accepting western ideas such as democracy and equality, the Congress at first used peaceful protest to urge the British to grant more power to Indians. Later, as the Congress party, it led the long struggle for complete independence.

China Faces the West

While the British increased their hold on India, they and other Europeans developed trade with China. During the 1500s, Chinese civilization had been highly advanced, and the Chinese at that time had little interest in European products. There was only limited trade between China and Europe during the next 300 years. During this period, while technological changes transformed Europe, China's political, economic, and military position weakened under the Qing dynasty. Qing emperors ruled China from 1644 to 1912.

The Unequal Treaties

In the early 1800s, British merchants found a way to break China's trade barriers and earn huge

---

COOPERATIVE LEARNING ACTIVITY

Debate Have students prepare a debate between the British officials who ruled India and the Indian National Congress. Have students on one team portray members of the British government and defend their rule in India by citing the progress they have brought to the country. Have students on the other team portray the Indians who dispute this assertion and cite the problems they face as a result of British rule. Have each group member contribute by gathering data, forming arguments, or suggesting practice questions. **L3**

profits. In exchange for Chinese tea, silk, and porcelain—and to avoid paying cash—the merchants smuggled a drug called opium, which they obtained from India and Turkey, into China. In 1839 Chinese troops tried to stop the smuggling. When the British resisted, war broke out. The British used gunboats to bombard Chinese ports and easily defeated the Chinese, who lacked modern weapons.

British victory in the Opium War in 1842 led to the Treaty of Nanking, the first of many "unequal treaties" that forced China to yield many of its rights to Western powers. The Nanking treaty granted the British payment for war losses as well as the island of Hong Kong. British citizens in China also gained extraterritoriality, the right to live under their own laws and courts. Over the next 60 years, the "unequal treaties" increased foreign influence in China and weakened the Qing dynasty. Civil wars, such as the Taiping Rebellion (1850-1864), also eroded the dynasty's control.

By the 1890s, European powers as well as Japan claimed large sections of China as spheres of influence—areas where they had exclusive trading rights. Coming late to the imperialist scramble, the United States did not claim a sphere of influence. Instead, it tried to open China to the trade of all nations through the Open Door Policy. Deadlocked by their own rivalries, the other powers reluctantly agreed to this policy in 1899.

Chinese Responses

To modernize China, some reformers during the late 1800s began a "self-strengthening" movement. This program involved importing both Western technology and educational methods. They also worked to improve agriculture, strengthen the armed forces, and end the European practice of extraterritoriality.

Lack of government support stalled these efforts. Chinese weakness was only further exposed in an 1894 war against a modernizing Japan that ended in China's defeat and loss of territory. From China, Japan gained the island of Taiwan and the Liaodong Peninsula as well as trading benefits in Chinese territory. The Japanese also ended China's influence in Korea.

After this setback, reformers regained influence with the support of the young emperor Guang Xu (gwawng SHYOO). They launched the Hundred Days of Reform to modernize the government and encourage new industries. However, conservatives led by the emperor's mother, **Ci Xi** (TSUH•SEE), returned to power, arrested the emperor, and halted the reforms.

By the late 1890s, anti-foreign feelings in China had led to the formation of secret societies dedicated to removing diplomats, entrepreneurs, missionaries, and other foreigners from the country. One group, the Righteous and Harmonious Fists, practiced a Chinese form of boxing, and Westerners named its members Boxers. In 1900 the Boxers carried out attacks against foreigners and Chinese Christians, besieging foreign communities in **Beijing**, the Chinese capital. In response, the Western powers and Japan sent a multinational force that ended the uprising. The empress, who had supported the Boxers, reversed her policy.

The Revolution of 1911

After the Boxer Uprising, Ci Xi struggled to hold on to power. She agreed to allow foreign troops to remain in China and gave in to some of her people's demands for change. For example, she established schools and reorganized the government. But it was too little, too late. Many Chinese believed that a modern republic should replace the Qing dynasty. In their view, the only way to achieve this goal was through revolution.

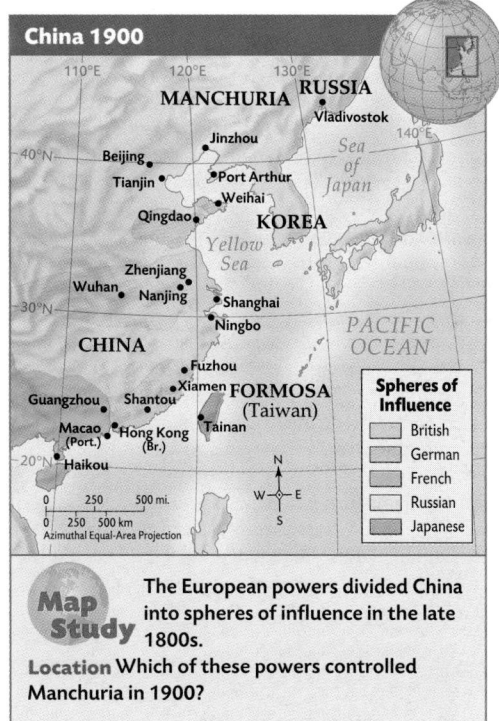

China 1900

110°E · 120°E · 130°E

MANCHURIA RUSSIA
Vladivostok
Jinzhou
140°E
40°N Beijing
Tianjin · Port Arthur
Weihai
Qingdao · KOREA
Yellow
Sea
Zhenjiang
Wuhan · Nanjing
30°N · Shanghai
· Ningbo PACIFIC OCEAN
CHINA
· Fuzhou
·Xiamen FORMOSA
Guangzhou Shantou (Taiwan)
Macao · Hong Kong Tainan
(Port.) (Br.)
20°N Haikou

Spheres of Influence
- British
- German
- French
- Russian
- Japanese

0 · 250 · 500 mi.
0 · 250 · 500 km
Azimuthal Equal-Area Projection

N W–E S

Map Study The European powers divided China into spheres of influence in the late 1800s.

Location Which of these powers controlled Manchuria in 1900?

Map Study

Answer
Russia controlled Manchuria in 1900.

Map Skills Practice

Reading a Map Which non-European nation had a sphere of influence in China? (*Japan*)

Critical Thinking Have students analyze and discuss the reasons the British dissolved the East India Company. What were their main concerns? (*fear of rebellion and of conflict with local inhabitants*) What seems to have concerned them least about the Sepoy Rebellion? (*the feelings and sacred beliefs of the sepoys*) **L3**

World History and Art Transparency 35, *Ono Waterfall*

Who?What?Where?When?

Surendranath Banerjea The history of the brilliant Indian Surendranath Banerjea (1848–1946) sheds light both on imperialist oppression and on the rise of colonial nationalism. Although Banerjea scored higher on the Indian Civil Service exam than most British test takers, every effort was made to prevent him from having a successful career. After giving up on British justice, Banerjea founded a nationalist political organization. His political persistence combined with the pronunciation of his first name led to his nickname, "Surrender Not."

MEETING SPECIAL NEEDS ACTIVITY

Learning Style: Visual/Spatial Ask students who learn best by producing and decoding graphic information to depict events such as the Sepoy Rebellion or the Dutch presence in Southeast Asia in drawings, graphs, or political cartoons. Encourage them to share their work with the class as a way of reinforcing the section's main ideas. **L2**

Independent Practice

 Guided Reading Activity 16-3 **L1**

 Geography and History Activity 16

 People in World History Profile 51

TURNING POINT

Modernization of Japan
How did Meiji leaders transform Japan during the late 1800s?
They created a parliamentary form of government, industrialized the economy, and built up the military, making Japan a world power by the early 1900s.

Interview Have students research Matthew Perry's dealings with the Japanese and prepare a television interview with questions and answers for Perry and the Japanese shoguns who signed treaties with him. Have students prepare and present a "Special News Report" for U.S. citizens eager to know the outcome of Perry's dealings with the Japanese. Some students can take the role of reporters and others can represent Perry, members of his crew, and the Japanese. **L2**

Who?What?Where?When?

Shogun James Clavell's novel *Shogun*, and the 10-hour television miniseries based on it, tell the story of Blackthorne, an English sailor shipwrecked among the feudal Japanese.

The revolutionaries wanted China to regain its former power and influence. One of them, a doctor named **Sun Yat-sen**, wrote in the early 1900s: "Today we are the poorest and weakest nation in the world and occupy the lowest position in international affairs. Other men are the carving knife and serving dish; we are the fish and the meat."

In 1905 Sun and other revolutionaries formed the United League (later known as the *Guomindang*, or Nationalist party). Their goal was to modernize China on the basis of the "Three Principles of the People": nationalism (freedom from foreign control), democracy (representative government), and livelihood (economic well-being for all Chinese). The revolutionary cause was strengthened in 1908 when Ci Xi died, and two-year-old Prince Pu Yi became emperor. Three years later, revolution swept China as peasants, workers, soldiers, and court officials turned against the weak dynasty. Sun Yat-sen hurried home from a fund-raising tour of the United States. In January 1912, he became the first president of the new Chinese republic.

TURNING POINT
Modernization of Japan

Japan's dealings with the European powers began in much the same way as China's, but they ended differently. European traders first came to the island country in the 1500s. Like the Chinese, the Japanese were uninterested in European products, and they cut off almost all trade with Europe in the early 1600s. At the time a military commander called a shogun ruled Japan. Although the country also had an emperor, he had no real power.

Japan did not trade again with the outside world until 1853, when four American warships commanded by Commodore **Matthew C. Perry** sailed into the bay at Edo (present-day Tokyo). Perry wanted Japan to begin trading with the United States. The shogun, knowing what had happened to China in the recent Opium War, decided early in 1854 to sign a treaty with Perry.

Images *of the* Times

The British Empire

From the late 1700s to the early 1900s, Great Britain ruled the world's largest overseas empire. British territories were found in every continent.

British naval forces demonstrated British power in countries that were not directly under Queen Victoria's crown. Here a British ship attacks Chinese warships off the coast of China.

492

Images *of the* Times The British Empire

The period of British rule in India is often called the Raj, from the Sanskrit word for "rule" or "king." It comes from the same root as *raja*, an Indian prince, yet during the Raj, the princes' powers were limited by the British. India was considered "the jewel in the crown," that is, Great Britain's prize possession.

The canopied elephant saddle is called a howdah. The Australian outback is called the bush.

The Meiji Leaders

In the first five years after Perry's arrival, the shogun signed trade treaties with Britain, France, Holland, Russia, and the United States. Since the treaties favored the imperialist powers, the Japanese people called them unequal treaties, just as the Chinese had. Unhappiness with the treaties led to the overthrow of the shogun in 1868. A group of samurai gave its allegiance to the new emperor, **Mutsuhito**, but kept the real power to themselves. Because Mutsuhito was known as the Meiji (MAY•jee), or "Enlightened" emperor, Japan's new rulers were called the Meiji leaders.

The Meiji leaders tried to make Japan a great power capable of competing with Western nations. Adopting the slogan "Rich country, strong military" they brought the forms of parliamentary government to Japan, strengthened the military, and worked to transform the nation into an industrial society. The Meiji leaders established a system of universal education designed to produce loyal, skilled citizens who would work for Japan's mod-ernization. In this way, the Japanese hoped to create a new ruling class based on talent rather than birth.

Industrialization

In the 1870s Japan began to industrialize in an effort to strengthen its economy. The Japanese did this with little outside assistance. They were reluctant to borrow money from the West, fearing foreign takeovers if loans could not be repaid. In any case, most Western banks were not interested in making loans to Japan, because they considered the country a poor financial risk.

The Japanese government laid the groundwork for industrial expansion. It revised the tax structure to raise money for investment. It also developed a modern currency system and supported the building of postal and telegraph networks, railroads, and port facilities.

Beginning in the late 1880s, Japan's economy grew rapidly. A growing population provided a continuing supply of cheap labor. The combination of new technological methods and cheap labor

Literature Have students choose a work by Rudyard Kipling, such as *Plain Tales from the Hills*, *Kim*, *Soldiers Three and Other Stories*, *The Man Who Would Be King*, or a collection of his poems. Have them write a report on the work, concentrating on Kipling's literary uses of Indian culture, people, and geography. **L3**

Cultural Perspectives

Madama Butterfly Puccini's popular opera *Madama Butterfly*, which was first performed in 1904, dramatizes some of the consequences of Japan's relationship with the West. It is the tragic story of the love affair between a young Japanese girl and Lieutenant Pinkerton, an officer in the United States Navy. The opera provided the model for the modern musical *Miss Saigon*, though set in a different location and historical period.

Global Gourmet

India Chutney, whose name comes from the Hindi word *chatni*, is a relish that originated in east India. Chutney, which has remained popular in Great Britain since the Age of Imperialism, usually combines mangoes or other fruits with onions, raisins, sugar, and spices. Indian curry is typically served with one or more chutneys.

India was the most important British possession. This painting shows a British military officer traveling by elephant through northern India with his cavalry and foot soldiers.

Australia drew many British settlers, who made their homes in the harsh outback, or semi-dry interior, as well as in coastal areas.

REFLECTING ON THE TIMES

1. What types of people were found throughout Great Britain's empire?
2. In the 1800s, people often said that "the sun never sets on the British Empire." What do you think this phrase meant?

493

ANSWERS TO REFLECTING ON THE TIMES

1. Europeans: military officials, adventurers, missionaries, ordinary settlers; indigenous peoples: laborers, minor officials, soldiers
2. Britain's imperial holdings covered such a vast portion of the globe that, when it was nighttime in one part of the holding (Canada and the Caribbean), it was daytime in another part (India and Australia).

Who?What?Where?When?

The Philippines Spanish explorers who colonized the Philippines in the 1500s named the island country after King Philip II of Spain (1527–1598).

Global Gourmet

The Philippines Typical of Filipino food are two items made of fermented seafood: *bagoong* is a fish paste, and *patis* is a flavoring sauce. Both have a sour-salty taste.

ASSESS

Check for Understanding

Assign Section 3 Review as homework or as an in-class activity.

 Use Student Self-Test and Review Software to review Section 3.

Evaluate

Section Quiz 16-3

Use the Testmaker to create a customized quiz for Section 3.

Reteach

Create a group outline of the section on the board. Have students contribute oral summaries of each part for a class discussion.

---

allowed Japan to produce low-priced goods. Wars at the turn of the century further stimulated Japan's economy and helped it enter new world markets. By 1914 Japan had become one of the world's leading industrial nations.

Japan as a World Power

By the 1890s the Meiji leaders had taken great strides toward creating a modern nation. Japan had acquired an efficient government, a vigorous economy, and a strong military. Needing more natural resources, the Japanese government began to establish its own overseas empire. The first prize it attempted to take was Korea.

When the people of Korea revolted against their Chinese rulers in 1894, Japan decided to intervene. Japanese troops easily defeated the Chinese army in the Sino-Japanese War. Although Korea officially became independent, Japan gained partial control of its trade. Over the next few years, thousands of Japanese settled in Korea.

Korea also figured in Japan's next war. The Russian Empire had interests in Korea as well, and its interests began to clash with Japan's. Even more important was neighboring Manchuria, where the Russians kept troops and had a naval base at Port Arthur. In 1904 the Japanese navy launched a surprise attack on Port Arthur. Few people expected Japan to win the Russo-Japanese War, but the Japanese piled up victory after victory. The conflict ended in 1905, when Russia signed a treaty granting the country of Japan control over Korea and other nearby areas.

Japan's victory over Russia inspired non-Western nationalist leaders throughout the world. It proved that the European empires could be defeated if one had the will and determination. On the other hand, Japan had now become an imperialist country itself. It annexed Korea as a colony in 1910 and continued to expand its empire for the next 35 years.

Footnotes to History

A Teenage Emperor Mutsuhito was only 15 when he became Japan's emperor in 1867. During his 44-year reign, he often led the way in adopting Western customs. He cut his traditional topknot, a tuft of hair on the top of the head, and wore European-style clothes. While previous emperors lived apart from the people, Mutsuhito rode around Tokyo in an open carriage and toured the countryside.

Southeast Asia

Southeast Asia consists of two distinct geographic areas. Island Southeast Asia is made of two archipelagos, or groups of islands: **the East Indies** and **the Philippines**. To the north and west lies mainland Southeast Asia. It includes all of the territories that occupy the Indochinese and Malay Peninsulas.

The growth of imperialism in these areas followed a familiar pattern. Beginning in the 1500s, imperialist powers came, saw, and conquered. Over the next 400 years Portugal, Spain, the Netherlands, Great Britain, France, and the United States all set up colonies in that region. They ranged in size from the huge Dutch East Indies that included thousands of islands to the tiny British settlements on the island of Singapore.

The Islands of Southeast Asia

For centuries, the island region of Southeast Asia had attracted foreign traders and colonizers. At the beginning of the 1800s, the Dutch controlled most of the East Indies and Spain controlled the Philippines.

The Dutch East Indies, present-day Indonesia, had many natural resources, including rich soil. Farmers grew coffee, pepper, cinnamon, sugar, indigo, and tea; miners dug for tin and copper; loggers cut down ebony, teak, and other hardwood trees. The Dutch government used a method of forced labor called the culture system to gather all these raw materials. The Dutch also discouraged westernization, or the spread of European civilization. The enormous profits the Dutch received from the East Indies made the colony the envy of the imperialist powers.

Diponegoro, a native prince from the East Indian island of Java, started a revolt against the Dutch in 1825. Although it lasted 10 years, this revolt eventually ended in failure, and the Dutch encountered little real opposition for the next 80 years. One of the Dutch governors put it this way: "We have ruled here for 300 years with the whip and the club and we shall still be doing it in another 300 years." In the early 1900s, the Dutch won control of the entire archipelago, extending their rule into northern Sumatra and the Celebes. But within a generation, nationalist forces would bring the Dutch East Indian empire to its knees.

The Spanish rule of the Philippines resembled the Dutch rule of the Dutch East Indies. Native Filipinos worked for very low wages, if any, on tobacco and sugar plantations owned by wealthy Spaniard landowners. During the 1800s the

---

MAKING CONNECTIONS ACTIVITIES

Daily Life Ask students to research and then write short reports on the similarities and differences among the cuisines of China, Japan, India, and Southeast Asia. **L1**

Science, Technology, and Society Have students research the improvements made by the Japanese under the Meiji leaders. Have students pay particular attention to modern Japanese business philosophy and its influence on American corporations. **L2**

Visualizing
History This view of Whampoa Reach in China (about 1860) shows an English barque and an American ship. *How did Western trade and commerce affect Southeast Asia?*

Visualizing
History In 1844 China and France signed the Treaty of Whampoa, which expanded French rights within that port.
Answer to Caption: *Colonial landowners and trading companies changed traditional ways of life and damaged the landscape.*

Filipinos' resentment grew until it finally exploded into revolution in 1896.

When the United States declared war on Spain in 1898, the American government promised to free the Philippines in return for the rebels' help against the Spanish. After winning the Spanish American War, the United States broke its promise and ruled the Philippines as a colony. The Filipinos led by **Emilio Aguinaldo** (ah•gee•NAHL•doh) then arose against American rule, but United States troops defeated them two years later.

Mainland Southeast Asia

The mainland region of Southeast Asia consisted of several large territories in the early 1800s, including Burma (present-day Myanmar) and Malaya in the west, Vietnam in the east, and Siam (Thailand), Cambodia, and Laos in the middle. All through the 1800s, Great Britain and France struggled for domination of the area—more for military gain—than for economic reasons.

The British swept into Burma from India in the 1820s. Over the next 60 years, they took full control of Burma and neighboring Malaya. Meanwhile, the French were slowly conquering **Indochina**, the region that includes present-day Vietnam, Cambodia, and Laos. They, too, established complete control in the 1880s.

Squeezed between the two growing blocks of British and French territory lay the kingdom of Siam. In 1893 the French invaded Siam, sending forces into Bangkok, the capital city. Great Britain and France avoided armed conflict, however, when they agreed to define their spheres of influence in Southeast Asia. As a result of the agreement, Siam remained independent.

European rivalries for control of resources brought much disturbance to mainland Southeast Asia. Western influences changed traditional ways of life. Colonial landowners and trading companies forced local farmers and workers to grow cash crops, mine coal, and cut teak trees.

Enrich

Have students prepare comic strips depicting a specific event in this section, such as the Sepoy Rebellion, the Boxer Rebellion, or the colonization of the Dutch East Indies. After students present their work in class, display the comic strips until completing Chapter 16.

CLOSE

Have students hold a class discussion on the topic "Positive and Negative Outcomes of Imperialism in Asia." Have them decide whether imperialism was a constructive or destructive force in the late 1800s and early 1900s.

SECTION 3 REVIEW

Recall
1. **Define** sepoy, viceroy, sphere of influence, culture system, westernization.
2. **Identify** Ci Xi, Sun Yat-sen, Matthew C. Perry, Mutsuhito, Diponegoro, Emilio Aguinaldo.

3. **Explain** why the British government dissolved the East India Company.
Critical Thinking
4. **Synthesizing Information** How did European imperialism differ in India, China, and

Southeast Asia?
Understanding Themes
5. **Reaction** How did the Japanese succeed in avoiding extensive Western interference in its affairs, while China could not?

SECTION 3 REVIEW ANSWERS

1. All vocabulary words are defined in the Glossary.
2. Ci Xi, 491; Sun Yat-sen, 492; Perry, 492; Mutsuhito, 493; Diponegoro, 494; Emilio Aguinaldo, 495
3. because of the Sepoy Rebellion
4. In India, Britain ruled closely and developed Western institutions. In China, various

European powers held spheres of influence. In Southeast Asia, a number of European powers ruled colonies in a variety of ways; make sure students use specific facts.
5. **REACTION** Japan industrialized and created a strong military, becoming a power in its own right.

TEACH

Using the Internet The Internet is a powerful research tool. It can provide students with more recent information than would appear in books or magazines. The Internet offers access to a world of resources that may not be available in students' school or local libraries. The Internet also gives students an interactive way to learn.

Discuss the need for an Internet provider. Students probably have heard of such providers as America OnLine and Prodigy. Use the yellow pages to mention a few local Internet services as well. If possible, ask a representative from a local provider to speak to the class about Internet. Discuss various World Wide Web browsers. If you have access to the Internet at school, demonstrate and supervise its use.

As you talk about URLs— Web page addresses—point out that although they all start with http://, that prefix is not always followed by *www*. Also mention some of the domain designations that may end a URL—*.com* for a commercial organization, and *.gov* for a government organization.

Additional Practice

Skill Reinforcement
Activity 16

Technology
SKILLS

Using the Internet

Have you heard the expression, "surfing the Net?" This means you can search through the Internet to find information on many subjects. You won't get wet, but you sure can learn a lot and have fun!

Learning the Skill

The Internet is a global computer network that offers many features, including the latest news and weather, stored information, E-mail, and on-line shopping. Before you can connect to the Internet and use the services it offers, however, you must have three things: a computer, a modem, and a service provider. A service provider is a company that, for a fee, gives you entry to the Internet.

Once you are connected, the easiest and fastest way to access sites and information is to use a "Web browser," a program that lets you view and explore information on the World Wide Web. The Web consists of many documents called "Web pages," each of which has its own address, or Uniform Resource Locator (URL). Many URLs start with the keystrokes *http://*

Practicing the Skill

This chapter focuses on the Age of Imperialism, when the Panama Canal and the Suez Canal were completed. Surf the Internet to learn about the history of these canals.

1. Log on the Internet and access one of the World Wide Web search tools, such as Yahoo at website http://www.yahoo.com *or* Lycos at http://www.lycos.com *or* WebCrawler at http://www.webcrawler.com
2. Search by category or by name. If you search by category in Yahoo, for example, click on *Social* Science. To search by name, type in *Panama Canal and Suez Canal*.

3. Scroll the list of Web pages that appears when the search is complete. Select a page to bring up and read or print it. Repeat the process until you have enough information you can use to develop a short report on the two major canals completed during the Age of Imperialism.

Applying the Skill

Go through the steps just described to search the Internet for information on the Sepoy Rebellion in India. Based on the information, write an article for your school newspaper or magazine about your topic.

For More Practice

Turn to the Skill Practice in the Chapter Review on page 503 for more practice in using the Internet.

ANSWERS TO PRACTICING THE SKILL

Some report details about the Panama and Suez canals will vary and will arise from varying information. You might have groups of students use different search tools and later discuss the helpfulness of each one.

1823 The United States proclaims the Monroe Doctrine.

1898 The United States declares war on Spain.

1914 The Panama Canal opens.

Section 4

Imperialism in the Americas

Setting the Scene

▶ **Terms to Define**
arbitration

▶ **People to Meet**
James Monroe, José Martí, William McKinley, Theodore Roosevelt, Benito Juárez, Porfirio Díaz, Emiliano Zapata, Francisco "Pancho" Villa, Venustiano Carranza, Woodrow Wilson

▶ **Places to Locate**
Cuba, Puerto Rico, the Virgin Islands, Isthmus of Panama, Mexico

Find Out How did Latin Americans respond to the growth of American influence in their region?

The Storyteller

Frederic Remington was one of the first "foreign correspondents"—a journalist in Cuba during the Spanish-American War. He wrote: "At night I lay up beside the road outside of Siboney, and cooked my supper by a soldier fire, and lay down under a mango-tree on my raincoat, with

my haversack for a pillow. I could hear the shuffling of the marching troops, and see by the light of the fire near the road the ... sweaty men."

—adapted from *Frederic Remington and the Spanish-American War*, Douglas Allen, 1971

Teddy Roosevelt and the Rough Riders

On the floor of the Senate in 1898, United States Senator Albert J. Beveridge delivered a stirring speech on America's growing role as a world power:

66 Fate has written our policy for us; the trade of the world must and shall be ours. We will establish trading-posts throughout the world as distributing-points for American products.... Great colonies governing themselves, flying our flag and trading with us, will grow about our posts of trade. 99

Senator Beveridge's grand ambition capped a half-century of growing American influence in world affairs. The imperialist powers of Europe had already laid claim to much of the world. Now that the United States had grown considerably in size, wealth, and power, it was determined to use the Monroe Doctrine to block the spread of European imperialism in neighboring Latin America, an area that includes Mexico, the Caribbean islands, Central America, and South America. In doing so, the United States was also promoting its own brand of imperialism that involved the penetration of new economic markets and the acquisition of overseas territories.

TURNING POINT

The Monroe Doctrine

Even before the independence of all the Latin American countries was well established, Spain had sought the support of other European powers in reconquering its former colonies. Both the United States and Great Britain opposed Spain's

Chapter 16 *The Age of Imperialism* **497**

SECTION THEME

▶ **Nationalism** Nationalism intensifies in Latin America as United States involvement in the region increases.

Find Out

Answer: *They rebelled against American rule.*

FOCUS

Section Objective

Explain how Latin Americans responded to the growth of American influence in their region.

BELLRINGER
Motivational Activity

Before taking roll at the beginning of the class period, project Section Focus Transparency 16-4 and have students answer the activity questions. Discuss students' responses.
 This activity is also available as a blackline master.

Vocabulary Pre-check

 Use Vocabulary Activity 16 to introduce vocabulary terms.
L1 LEP

SECTION RESOURCES

 Reproducible Masters
• Reproducible Lesson Plan 16-4
• Vocabulary Activity 16
• Guided Reading Activity 16-4
• Reteaching Activity 16
• Enrichment Activity 16
• Section Quiz 16-4
• Performance Assessment Activity 16

• Spanish Chapter Summary 16

 Transparencies
• Section Focus Transparency 16-4

Multimedia
 Student Self-Test and Review Software
 Testmaker

TEACH

Guided Practice

THEME Nationalism

Ask students to write a definition of *nationalism*. Discuss students' ideas about nationalism and refer to nationalist leaders discussed in the section (Martí, Juárez, Díaz, Carranza, "Pancho" Villa, Zapata). Then ask students to name some locations where nationalist movements have arisen recently. *(former Yugoslav republics, republics of the former Soviet Union, the West Bank and Gaza Strip under Israeli control, Basque separatists in Spain)* **What do nationalist movements hope to gain or preserve?** *(cultural and political independence)* **L1**

Visualizing History

 A U.S. military government controlled Cuba from 1898 to 1902. In 1903 Cuba signed a treaty granting the United States a permanent lease on Guantánamo Bay, where it built a large naval base. From 1906 to 1909, American forces occupied Cuba again.
Answer to Caption: *Cuba's sugar and tobacco plantations were important to Spain's economy.*

TURNING POINT

The Monroe Doctrine

Why was the Monroe Doctrine an important statement of American foreign policy? *It warned against further European influence in the Western Hemisphere and was later used to justify American involvement in the region.*

Visualizing History
United States Marines hoist the American flag in Cuba. *What was Spain's economic interest in Cuba?*

plan. The United States did not want a strong European power so close to its borders. Great Britain had developed good trade relations with the Latin Americans and did not feel that its commercial interests would be served by the return of Spanish control to the Americas.

Great Britain suggested to the United States that a joint warning be issued to the various European powers. However, President **James Monroe** and Secretary of State John Quincy Adams decided to act alone. In 1823 Monroe warned the European powers not to interfere in the countries of the Western Hemisphere. The Monroe Doctrine, as it was later called, contained two major points:

❝1. The American continents, by the free and independent condition which they have assured and maintain, are hence forth not to be considered as subjects for future colonization by any European powers.

2. We should consider any attempt on their part to extend their system to any portion of this hemisphere as dangerous to our peace and safety. **❞**

At the time the Monroe Doctrine was declared, it was not clear what the United States would do if European powers tried to conquer any part of Latin America. The support of the British Royal Navy, however, ensured that the infant states of Latin America would remain free to determine their own political destinies.

As the United States grew in strength during the late 1800s and early 1900s, it began to make its power felt in Latin America. In 1895, when Great Britain was in conflict with Venezuela over the boundaries of British Guiana, the United States urged that the dispute be submitted to arbitration, or settlement by a third party that is agreeable to both sides. Appealing to the Monroe Doctrine, the United States Department of State issued a strong warning to the British to pressure them into accepting arbitration. Aware of the power of the United States and involved with problems in its empire, Great Britain agreed to a peaceful settlement. ▬

The Spanish-American War

Soon after the Guiana border dispute was settled, the United States turned its attention to **Cuba**. Cuba and the neighboring island of **Puerto Rico** were still Spanish colonies in the late 1800s. Cuba was particularly important to Spain, which reaped huge profits from the island's many sugar and tobacco plantations.

In 1895 **José Martí**, a writer and political activist, led Cubans in a revolution against Spanish rule. Cuba's Spanish leaders embarked on a bloody attack on the rebel forces. Martí was killed in a battle against the Spaniards, and Spanish troops rounded up thousands of Cubans and sent them to prison camps where conditions were brutal. Disease and starvation soon claimed more than 400,000 Cuban lives.

Remember the *Maine*!

The struggle of the Cubans for freedom attracted much sympathy in the United States. American newspapers printed vivid stories describing the cruelty and killings in Cuba. Soon, prominent American politicians began clamoring for war with Spain. Businesspeople who had invested in Cuba also joined in. Finally, in January 1898, President **William McKinley** ordered the battleship *Maine* to Havana, the capital of Cuba, to demonstrate growing American interest in Cuban affairs. A few weeks later, an explosion ripped through the *Maine* while it was still anchored in Havana harbor, sinking the ship and killing 260 American sailors.

The cry "Remember the *Maine*!" swept across the United States. American newspapers left little doubt that Spain was responsible for the disaster. In April 1898, under pressure from all sides, McKinley asked Congress to declare war on Spain. The Spanish-American War lasted four months and ended with a victory for the United States.

COOPERATIVE LEARNING ACTIVITY

Research Organize students into several small groups. Have each group research U.S. relations with the Philippines during one of these time periods: immediately after the Spanish-American War (the period discussed in this section), during World War I, during World War II, during the cold war, and at the present time. Have each group divide the tasks of gathering data, preparing summaries of the material, providing a time line to accompany the summaries, and exhibiting the material in a class presentation. **L2**

Bettmann

George F. Mobley

Panama Canal

The Panama Canal was a testament to the skill of American engineers. The enormous lock gates (under construction, left) were made of steel plates attached to a skeleton of steel girders. (Note the size of the men working around these gates.) Each gate weighed 700 tons (784 short tons) but was hollow and could float. Because they were buoyant, the gates exerted less stress on their hinges as the gates were opened and closed. Without the significant advances made in technology during the 1800s, this canal could not have been built.

Without President Theodore Roosevelt (center) the

Harvard College Library

Panama Canal would not have been built. During his presidency he decided that the United States would build a canal across the Isthmus of Panama—and he made it happen. Roosevelt wanted to boost American power and to compete more effectively with the imperial powers of Europe and Japan. The Panama Canal helped accomplish this goal by strengthening the military posture of the United States. The canal eliminated 7,800 miles (12,550 km) from the sea voyage between New York and San Francisco. It cost $380 million and tens of thousands of lives, and took ten years to complete. ⊕

Chapter 16 *The Age of Imperialism* **499**

TEACH

Tell students that there were several reasons for Lesseps's failure to build a Panama Canal. The French not only did not have the necessary tools for implementing such a huge task of digging but also lacked the medical knowledge needed to control the epidemics of tropical disease that decimated the laborers. In addition, dishonest political backers of Lesseps siphoned off cash from the company, which went bankrupt in 1889.

 **CURRICULUM CONNECTION**

MEDICINE

Beginning in 1904, Colonel William C. Gorgas, the U.S. physician who had wiped out yellow fever in Havana, Cuba, after the Spanish-American War, began an effort to eliminate malaria, yellow fever, and bubonic plague from the Isthmus of Panama. By destroying the mosquitoes that carry the first two diseases and the rats that carry the third, Gorgas dramatically lowered the death toll.

Linking Past and Present

Teddy Bears The stuffed bears that generations of children have cherished are named for President Theodore Roosevelt. After a cartoonist depicted him with a bear cub, toymakers began to produce the stuffed animals that are still called teddy bears.

Independent Practice

 Guided Reading Activity 16-4 **L1**

Cartoon Have students draw political cartoons depicting a major event from the section and present them to the class. **L2**

Foreign Policy Have students research and write short reports on public reaction to a more recent attempt by the United States to shape political events in Latin America by supporting the Nicaraguan *contras*. Ask students to consider how attitudes toward American intervention have changed over the century. **L3**

ASSESS

Check for Understanding

Assign Section 4 Review as homework or as an in-class activity.

🖳 Use Student Self-Test and Review Software to review Section 4.

Evaluate

 Section Quiz 16-4

🖳 Use the Testmaker to create a customized quiz for Section 4.

Reteach

Ask students to explain the importance of the Monroe Doctrine and the Roosevelt Corollary to U.S. imperialism. Have them provide examples of the influence each had on the events covered in Section 4.

🖳 Reteaching Activity 16

American Territorial Gains

During the late 1800s, the United States made many significant territorial gains. In 1867 it purchased Alaska from Russia, and in 1898 annexed Hawaii, shortly after American entrepreneurs on the islands had overthrown the Hawaiian queen Liliuokalani (lee•lee•oo•oh•kah•LAH•nee). As a result of the Spanish-American War, the United States gained from Spain territories in the Pacific Ocean (the Philippines and Guam) and in the Caribbean Sea (Puerto Rico). Although independent, Cuba was under American protection. In 1917 the United States purchased **the Virgin Islands** (St. Thomas, St. John, and St. Croix) from Denmark.

The Panama Canal

Victory in the Spanish-American War made the United States a world power. It became important for the United States to be able to move its fleet quickly between the Pacific and Atlantic Oceans. What was needed was a canal across the **Isthmus of Panama**, a narrow neck of land that linked Central America and South America.

For centuries, Europeans and Americans had dreamed of building a canal across Central America. In the 1880s the Frenchman Ferdinand de Lesseps, who had built the Suez Canal, tried—and failed—to build a canal in Panama. Thirteen years after the bankruptcy of de Lesseps's company, United States President **Theodore Roosevelt** received the backing of Congress to acquire the Panama canal rights and property.

In 1902 Panama was part of Colombia. Roosevelt tried to negotiate a treaty with Colombia that year that would give the United States land to build the canal in Panama. When Colombia refused to sign the treaty, Roosevelt and the American public were outraged.

Roosevelt soon developed a plan, however. With his approval, American agents encouraged the people of Panama to revolt against the government of Colombia. They did so on the night of November 3, 1903, with the help of the United States Navy, which prevented Colombian troops from landing. The rebellion was over by the next day, and the new Republic of Panama quickly signed a treaty granting the United States the land to build the Panama Canal.

Construction of the canal began in 1904 and took 10 years to complete. More than 40,000 workers cut through hills, built dams, and drained swamps until the two mighty oceans were connected. Many of the workers, however, died of malaria

and yellow fever. This problem eventually was solved by implementing a sanitation program to control disease-carrying mosquitoes. When the first ship finally steamed through the canal in August 1914, the canal was hailed as one of the world's great engineering feats.

Possession of the Panama Canal gave the United States even more of a stake in Latin America. Thus, the United States continued to exert its power in the region throughout the early 1900s. In 1904 President Theodore Roosevelt extended the Monroe Doctrine in what became known as the Roosevelt Corollary. Under this addition, the United States would actively intervene to force Latin American countries to honor their foreign debts. During the next two decades, United States forces intervened in such countries as the Dominican Republic, Haiti, and Nicaragua. The United States hoped its interventions would provide stability and prepare the way for democracy. Most Latin Americans, however, viewed American actions as moves to turn their countries into "colonies" of the United States and to protect foreign businesses that were exploiting their resources.

Mexico

During the 1800s and early 1900s, the United States became deeply involved in the affairs of its southern neighbor, **Mexico**. During the 1830s, opposition to the dictatorial rule of General Antonio López de Santa Anna grew in the Mexican state of Texas, where many Americans had settled. In 1835 the Americans and some Mexicans in Texas revolted and the next year set up an independent republic. Ignoring Mexican opposition, Texas in 1845 joined the American republic as a state, and conflict soon developed between Mexico and the United States. Despite the bravery of its soldiers, Mexico lost the Mexican War. In the Treaty of Guadalupe Hidalgo (1848), nearly half of Mexico's territory went to the United States.

Reform and Conflict

After the Mexican War, Mexico entered an era of change known as La Reforma. In 1855 Mexican voters chose **Benito Juárez**, a lawyer of Native American background, as president. Juárez reduced the power of the military, separated church and state, and improved the lot of impoverished farmers. In 1863, when Mexico could not pay its foreign debts, French troops occupied Mexico City. Juárez fled the capital to organize a guerrilla movement in the countryside. In 1864 Mexican conservatives, supported by the French, named Austrian Archduke

MEETING SPECIAL NEEDS ACTIVITY

Language Delayed Some students who speak English as a second language may come from families with personal experiences in countries fighting against outside intervention. Ask these students to interview a parent or an acquaintance with such experience. Have them write the interviews in their native language. Then work with them individually as they translate their interviews into English. Read some of the translated interviews to the class as a basis for class discussion. **L1 LEP**

Maximilian emperor of Mexico. In 1867 the French, under American pressure, withdrew their troops from Mexico, and Juárez returned to power after his forces had ousted and executed Maximilian.

Four years after Juárez's death in 1872, General **Porfirio Díaz** seized power. To ensure "Order and Progress," Díaz strengthened the army and limited individual freedoms. Under Díaz's harsh rule, however, Mexico made economic advances, building railroads, developing industries, expanding farmlands, and opening new mines. Unfortunately, for the Mexican people, most profits went to foreign investors and wealthy landowners. While the rich prospered, most Mexicans remained poor farmers, working on large estates for low wages.

The Mexican Revolution

Discontent with Díaz eventually led to revolution. From 1910 to 1920, Mexico was engulfed by the first major social upheaval in modern Latin America. During this time, armies of farmers, workers, ranchers, and even *soldaderas*, or women soldiers, fought the authorities and each other across Mexico. The unrest also sparked a wave of Mexican immigration to the United States.

The revolution began when Francisco Madero, a liberal reformer, and his supporters overthrew Díaz in 1910. Once in power, Madero was murdered by one of his generals, Victoriano Huerta. A year later, Huerta himself was toppled from power by Mexican revolts and American intervention.

No strong leader emerged to take Huerta's place. Instead, three revolutionary leaders—**Emiliano Zapata**, **Francisco "Pancho" Villa**, and **Venustiano Carranza**—competed for power. Using the battle cry, *"Tierra y Libertad!"* (Land and Liberty!), Zapata and his followers fought for the rights of impoverished farmers. Like Zapata, Villa proposed radical reforms. The more conservative

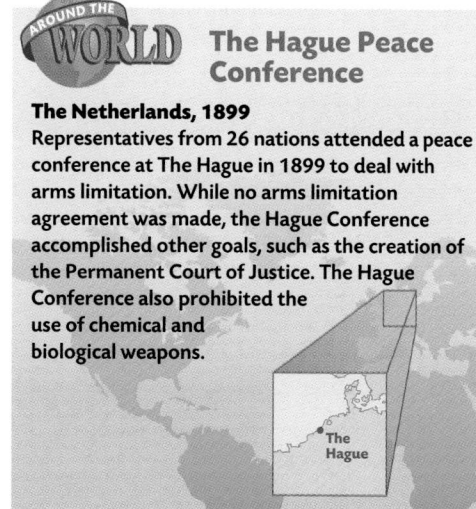

The Hague Peace Conference

The Netherlands, 1899
Representatives from 26 nations attended a peace conference at The Hague in 1899 to deal with arms limitation. While no arms limitation agreement was made, the Hague Conference accomplished other goals, such as the creation of the Permanent Court of Justice. The Hague Conference also prohibited the use of chemical and biological weapons.

The Hague

Carranza, however, was able to become president in 1915 with American support. In retaliation, Villa crossed the border into New Mexico and killed 18 Americans. United States President **Woodrow Wilson** then sent American troops into Mexico to capture Villa. American entry into World War I in 1917 led to the withdrawal of these troops.

That same year, Carranza reluctantly introduced a liberal constitution but was slow in carrying out reforms. Force was often used against Carranza's opponents. For example, in 1919 a pro-Carranza military officer murdered Zapata, who had protested Carranza's disregard of land reform. A year later, Carranza himself was killed during a revolt that brought General Álvaro Obregón to power. As the revolutionary violence began to subside in the early 1920s, relations between Mexico and the United States were less tense. The memory of American intervention, however, lingered in the minds of Mexicans for years to come.

SECTION 4 REVIEW

Recall
1. **Define** arbitration.
2. **Identify** James Monroe, Monroe Doctrine, José Martí, William McKinley, Theodore Roosevelt, Benito Juárez, Porfirio Díaz, Emiliano Zapata, Francisco "Pancho" Villa, Venustiano Carranza, Woodrow Wilson.
3. **Explain** the impact of the Monroe Doctrine and the Roosevelt Corollary.

Critical Thinking
4. **Analyzing Information** Why do you think the United States government was so concerned about maintaining its influence in Latin America during the late 1800s and early 1900s?

Understanding Themes
5. **Nationalism** What factors led to the Mexican Revolution that began in 1910?

SECTION 4 REVIEW ANSWERS

1. All vocabulary words are defined in the Glossary.
2. Monroe, 498; Monroe Doctrine, 498; Martí, 498; McKinley, 498; Roosevelt, 500; Juárez, 501; Díaz, 501; Zapata, 501; "Pancho" Villa, 501; Carranza, 501; Wilson, 501
3. to keep out European powers and to justify U.S. intervention in Latin America
4. It wanted to establish itself as a contender in the imperialist competition.
5. **NATIONALISM** pent-up grievances after years of dictatorship under Díaz; demands for social justice for mestizos and Native Americans

POINT

The Mexican Revolution
Why was the Mexican revolution a major development in Latin American history?
It was the first major social upheaval in modern Latin America, resulting in reforms to benefit peasants and workers.

Enrich

Arrange for students to see a video of *Viva Zapata!*, the 1952 film chronicling the life of the Mexican revolutionary leader. Ask students to imagine they are newspaper or television movie critics and to write a review of the film for submission or for class presentation.

Enrichment Activity 16

CLOSE

Have students divide a sheet of paper into three columns. In one column have them summarize their reactions to imperialism as if they were supporters of Woodrow Wilson in 1914–1916. In the second column have them summarize their reactions to imperialism as if they were supporters of "Pancho" Villa in 1914–1916. In the third column have them summarize their reactions to imperialism in their own voices.

Chapter 16 Review

GLENCOE
TECHNOLOGY

VIDEODISC
Use MindJogger to review students' knowledge of the chapter.

MindJogger Videoquiz

Chapter 16
Disc 2 Side B

 Also available in VHS.

Answers

Using Key Terms
1. a   4. i
2. f   5. c
3. e

Using Your History Journal

Suggest that students update the history of and make predictions for the same nation they chose to highlight when they began the chapter.

Reviewing Facts
1. through treaties, purchases, and conquest; French: spread their culture overseas; British: allowed local rulers to represent them
2. Suez (Asia/Africa): joined Mediterranean and Red Seas and facilitated trade between Europe and Asia; Panama (Central America): linked Caribbean Sea and Pacific Ocean; helped U.S. Navy to guard the nation's two coasts.
3. Missionaries spread Christianity and set up schools and hospitals; they also spread European ways.
4. Asians: China did not readily adapt Western ways, but western-educated elite later established a republic; Japan modernized and became an imperial power; Africa: resisted colonization; western-educated elite formed nationalist movements; Latin America: although independent, resisted

502 Chapter 16 *The Age of Imperialism*

CHAPTER 16 REVIEW

Connections Across Time

Historical Significance The Age of Imperialism brought much of the globe under Western control. An unparalleled exchange of ideas and products resulted. European ways, however, often disrupted many cultures.

By the mid-1900s, after two world wars and many smaller conflicts, Europe saw its world leadership pass to the United States. Meanwhile, nationalist movements in Africa, Asia, and Latin America challenged the West's control of global events.

Using Key Terms

Write the key term that completes each sentence. Then write a sentence for each term not chosen.

a. sepoys   f. imperialism
b. protectorate   g. spheres of influence
c. partition   h. viceroy
d. arbitration   i. culture system
e. westernization j. colony

1. Before revolting in 1857, _____ had resented British attempts to impose Christianity and European customs on them.
2. _____ means one country's control of the political, economic, and social life of another country.
3. The acquisition of colonies by Europeans led to _____, or the spread of European civilization to other parts of the world.
4. In the East Indies, the Dutch used a method of forced labor called the _____ to gather raw materials and harvest crops.
5. In 1885, 14 nations met in Berlin, Germany, and agreed to _____ the continent of Africa among themselves.

Technology Activity

Using the Internet Search the Internet for a Web site that provides a map of the world around 1900 that includes political boundaries and a distance scale. Color code all countries that the British Empire controlled. Describe the relative location of the countries that were part of the British Empire in terms of the approximate distance from each country to Great Britain. Use the distance scale on the map. Then organize your findings in a chart. In addition, find out which countries remain under British control today.

502 Chapter 16 *The Age of Imperialism*

Using Your History Journal

Choose one nation in Africa and research its history from the colonial era to the present. Write a short paper about your chosen country's independence and its prospects for the future.

Reviewing Facts

1. **History** Explain how imperial nations acquired and ruled overseas lands. In what ways did the British and the French differ in ruling their empires?
2. **Geography** Identify the locations and state the significance of the Suez and Panama Canals.
3. **Culture** Describe the role of religion in the spread of Western values during the 1800s.
4. **History** Identify how Asians, Africans, and Latin Americans reacted to Western imperialism after the mid-1800s.

Critical Thinking

1. **Apply** How did science, industry, and technology aid the growth of imperialism?
2. **Evaluate** Why was Japan able to establish itself as an imperial and military power?
3. **Synthesize** How did imperialism affect peoples in Africa, Asia, and Latin America? What impact did imperialism have on the peoples of Europe and North America?
4. **Analyze** Contrast the ways in which the Age of Imperialism contributed to the growth of unity in the world with the ways in which it contributed to disunity.

American intervention and sought social justice; Mexican Revolution

Critical Thinking
1. New mass-produced weapons of war enabled Europeans to defeat non-European peoples that had simpler technologies. Japan, however, modernized and became an imperial power.
2. It modernized its government and schools, and built industry and a strong military.

3. Africans and Asians faced cultural challenges from European rule; however, they often used western values to condemn imperialism. Latin Americans opposed United States intervention; Europeans and North Americans believed their ways were superior.
4. It promoted unity by bringing people from around the world into closer contact; it promoted disunity by sparking wars and other conflicts.

502 Chapter 16 *The Age of Imperialism*

Geography in History

1. **Place** Refer to the map below. What two large bodies of water does the Panama Canal connect?
2. **Human/Environment Interaction** Why do you think engineers chose this particular location in which to build the canal?
3. **Location** Why is the Pacific Ocean located on the southeast side of this map?
4. **Region** What geographic features of this region made building the canal difficult?

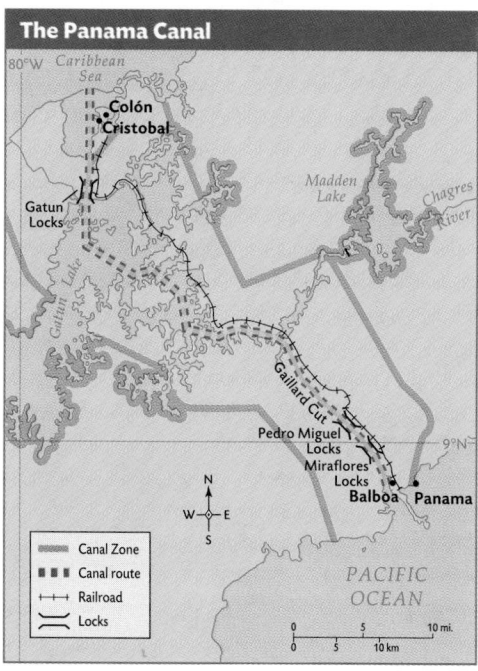

The Panama Canal

Legend:
— Canal Zone
▪▪▪ Canal route
┼─┼ Railroad
═ Locks

0   5   10 mi.
0   5   10 km

Understanding Themes

1. **Movement** What factors stimulated outward expansion by the European powers in the Age of Imperialism?
2. **Change** How did Africans react to the changes brought by the spread of imperialism in Africa?
3. **Reaction** In what two ways did Indian nationalists respond to British rule in India?

4. **Nationalism** Trace the events of the Mexican Revolution. Why was the Revolution an important development in modern Latin America?

Linking Past and Present

1. Historical context refers to the setting in which an event occurs. Throughout the 1900s the United States continued to intervene in Latin America. Investigate three recent interventions, and explain how the historical context surrounding American interventions has changed from 1900 to the present.
2. Have attitudes about imperialism changed from the 1800s to the present time? Explain. What factors do you think account for any changes?
3. Does imperialism exist in some form today? What factors do you think account for any changes? If imperialism exists today, does it differ from the imperialism of the 1800s?
4. Examine the role of the South African Native Congress (SANNC) in South Africa after its founding in 1912. As the African National Congress (ANC) after 1923, how did the organization's involvement change under independent white-dominated South African governments from the 1920s to the early 1990s? How does the ANC influence developments in South Africa today?

Skill Practice

Using the steps described on page 496 search the Internet for informaiton about one of the following topics from the Age of Imperialism. Write an article for the school newspaper or magazine based on the information you retrieved about your topic.

- writings of Rudyard Kipling
- establishment of Liberia
- African Imperialism 1914
- Cecil Rhodes
- Russo-Japanese War
- Spanish-American War

the Indian National Congress to fight for Indian independence.
4.  **NATIONALISM** The Revolution started as a revolt against dictatorship; soon it became a social upheaval; leaders sought varying kinds of social justice, especially land reforms. The Revolution was the first social upheaval in modern Latin America.

Linking Past and Present

1. After 1945 the cold war affected U.S. involvements in Latin America. About 1900 the U.S. focused on intervention by traditional European powers. During the entire period U.S. concerns included regional stability, democracy, and protection of U.S. interests.
2. Students should support their opinions.
3. A typical response: imperialism still exists in an economic sense, because many politically free but economically weak nations rely on other nations for aid.
4. SANNC was founded to work for black rights. As the ANC, it continued this goal after the introduction of apartheid. By the 1960s, ANC militancy rose as government crackdowns grew harsh; today the ANC is the largest political party in South Africa.

Skill Practice
Articles will vary depending on the chosen topic and the information found on the Internet.

❓ Chapter Bonus Test Question

Ask students: How did the motives behind the age of exploration differ from those behind the Age of Imperialism? *(less pressure to find sources of raw materials and new markets for products during the age of exploration)*

Geography in History
1. Atlantic and Pacific Oceans
2. The distance across the continent is shortest there.
3. because the isthmus bends where the Panama Canal was dug, putting the Pacific Ocean south and east of the Atlantic
4. its jungles, hills, and swamps

Understanding Themes
1. **MOVEMENT** national rivalries, the desire for raw materials and markets, search for new opportunities, a "civilizing" mission
2. **CHANGE** Leaders such as Samory Touré and Shaka fought Europeans; some Africans accepted European rule with allowances for limited self-government.
3. **REACTION** Indians revolted during the Sepoy Rebellion, and they later formed

ABCNEWS INTERACTIVE™

VIDEODISC
Turning Points in World History

Side Two
Chapter 1

Title: *The Industrial Revolution*

If you do not have access to a videodisc player, **Turning Points in World History** is also available in VHS.

Internet Sites

The following are possible sites for completing the "Net" activities:

The Age of Imperialism:
http://www.smplanet.com/imperialism/toc.html

City Net
http://www.city.net

Not on the "Net"...

If students have limited or no access to the Internet, have them complete the "Imperialism" activity by using resources in the school or public library to find information on imperialism in Latin America. Encourage students to use the following subjects to help them locate sources in the library's computerized or traditional card catalog: history, colonialism, imperialism, independence.

Students may use the information they locate to help them create their news reports.

 **Turning Points in World History**

The Industrial Revolution

Setting up the Video

Work with a group of your classmates to view "The Industrial Revolution" on the videodisc *Turning Points in World History*. The Industrial Revolution started in the late 1700s and changed the way people lived. The introduction of modern machines and the building of factories brought both technical advancement and its own set of problems. This program examines the social issues of the Industrial Revolution and where we are today within our own technological revolution.

Side Two, Chapter 3

Hands-On Activity

Using multimedia tools, create a presentation about present technology innovations and how these advancements are changing people's lives. Be sure to include some innovations that affect how most people live their daily lives.

View the video by scanning the bar code or by entering the chapter number on your keypad and pressing Search. (Also available in VHS format.)

Surfing the "Net"

Imperialism

During the Age of Imperialism, world powers lay claim to different parts of the world. Spheres of influence included the region of Latin America. Access the Internet to find out about the effects of imperialism on Latin American countries.

Getting There

Follow these steps to gather more information about the history of various Latin American countries.
1. Find a search engine. Type in the name of a *Latin American country*.
2. After typing in the name of a Latin American country, enter words such as these to focus your search:

- *history*
- *colonialism*
- *imperialism*
- *independence*

3. The search engine should provide you with a number of links to follow. Links are "pointers" to different sites on the Internet and commonly appear as blue underlined words.

What to Do When You Are There

Click on the links to navigate through the pages of information and gather your findings. Create a news report researching the specific country's history of colonialism, and how the country attained its independence. Videotape all news reports and show to other classes.

INTERNET ADDRESS BOOK

Use this space to record frequently used addresses.

_____

_____

_____

_____

Unit 4 Digest

From the late 1700s to the early 1900s, the primarily rural, agricultural economies of Europe and North America developed into industrial economies based on cities, factories, and manufactured goods. This sweeping transformation became known as the Industrial Revolution, and its effects would eventually impact the rest of the world.

During the 1800s, the rise of industry in the Western world—Europe and North America—inspired people living in these areas to push for social and political reforms. At the same time, Western nations, seeking new markets and resources, expanded overseas trade and strengthened their control of foreign areas. The peoples of Asia, Africa, and Latin America faced enormous challenges as their cultures were threatened by forceful Western takeovers.

 *The Gas Factory at Courcelles* by Ernest Jean Delahae. Musée du Petit Palais, Paris, France *How did increasing industrialization affect the social order?*

Chapter 12
Age of Industry

The Industrial Revolution began in Great Britain during the late 1700s. Wealthy British landowners at this time took over more agricultural land and used new farming methods to increase crop yields. With more food available, people were able to live healthier, longer lives. As these changes spread throughout Great Britain and the rest of Europe, the population increased dramatically.

Meanwhile, farmers displaced by rural changes moved to the cities to find work. This growing urban population, combined with skilled inventors who provided new technology and business people who had money and organizational skills, helped to ignite the Industrial Revolution. The availability of natural resources—coal, iron, and water power—led to the use of power-driven machinery in factories. This new kind of manufacturing replaced the handwork done in the home.

From Great Britain, industrialization spread to the rest of Europe and to North America, creating a new social order in the Western world. A growing middle class of prosperous factory owners and managers began to exert political power, while an even larger working class pressed for reforms to end poor working conditions and improve their lives.

Chapter 13
Cultural Revolution

Western Europeans and North Americans sought solutions to the social divisions arising in the new industrial society. Some thinkers, such as the British philosopher Adam Smith, held that capitalism, or private ownership of industry, benefited society as a whole and should operate without government controls. Others, including British philosophers Jeremy Bentham and John Stuart Mill, accepted capitalism, but held that it needed some government regulation to ensure a just society for all classes. Still others, such as the German thinker Karl Marx, believed that capitalism promoted sharp inequalities and that it would be replaced by socialism, a system in which the workers by themselves or through government would control industry for the public good.

The Age of Industry also saw many exciting advances in science, from new ideas about human origins to new methods for fighting diseases. In addition, improved means of transportation enabled people to leave their native lands to seek new opportunities in other parts of the world. Increased interest in education led to the spread of literacy as public schools and libraries were established

Unit 4 *Industry and Nationalism* 505

The Unit Digest offers a chapter-by-chapter summary that can be used for any of the following:
- *Preview* one chapter or an entire unit,
- *Review* some or all of the chapters,
- *Condense* when specific chapters or units have not been taught, or
- *Reteach* chapters that students have studied in the unit.

PREVIEW

Use the Unit 4 Digest Transparencies to preview the highlights of the unit.

History & Art
Answer to Caption: *The middle class grew, but life for factory workers worsened.*

REVIEW

Use the Student Self-Test and Review Software to review any chapters that students have studied in Unit 4.

History Lead students in a discussion of the power of nationalism to prompt political change. Have the class agree on a definition of nationalism. *(the desire of people sharing a common culture to have their own nation-state)* Then have students write two or three paragraphs about the role nationalism played in European political events during the 1800s. **L2**

CLASSROOM RESOURCES FOR UNIT 6 DIGEST

Preview
- Unit 4 Digest Transparencies

Review
- Time Line Activities 12, 13, 14, 15, 16
- Student Self-Test and Review Software, Chapters 12, 13, 14, 15, 16
- MindJogger Videoquiz, Chapters 12, 13, 14, 15, 16

Condense
- Chapter Digests Audiocassettes, Chapters 12, 13, 14, 15, 16

Reteach
- Reteaching Activities 12, 13, 14, 15, 16
- Chapter Digests Audiocassettes, Chapters 12, 13, 14, 15, 16
- Turning Points in World History

CONDENSE

 Use Chapter Digests Audio-cassettes to introduce chapters that students have not studied in Unit 4. Spanish Chapter Digests Audiocassettes are also available.

Discuss Have students read the **Unit Digest** and discuss the **Surveying the Unit** questions.
L1

GLENCOE TECHNOLOGY

VIDEODISC
Use MindJogger to review any chapter in Unit 4.

MindJogger Videoquiz

 Chapter 12
Disc 2 Side A

 Chapter 13
Disc 2 Side A

 Chapter 14
Disc 2 Side A

 Chapter 15
Disc 2 Side B

 Chapter 16
Disc 2 Side B

Also available in VHS.

---

throughout Europe and North America. Instead of following one approach, artists and writers responded to the industrial age in a variety of ways.

Chapter 14
Democracy and Reform

Economic and social changes inspired new political movements in Europe and the Americas during the 1800s. In some countries, political change was gradual and relatively peaceful; in other countries, it was sudden and often violent.

Great Britain was the world's strongest economic and political power during most of the 1800s. The British government moved slowly toward democracy as political parties came to control Parliament and more people gained voting rights. Social reforms somewhat improved the lives of workers, women, and other groups traditionally outside of the political system. Overseas colonies such as Canada, Australia, and New Zealand won increasing self-rule within the British Empire.

France's political development was more violent and uncertain than that of Britain, with the French government changing in form several times—from empire to monarchy to republic to empire to republic—during the course of the 1800s. France developed industrially during this period, but agriculture still remained an important part of its economy. The most enduring achievements of France's Third Republic, created in 1875, were its safeguards of civil liberties and educational reforms.

The United States was the world's most advanced democracy during the 1800s. Although Native Americans, African Americans, women, and other groups often faced rejection, discrimination, or second-class status, an increasing number of Americans were able to participate in the political process and fulfill their dreams of a better life. The country also steadily expanded westward toward the Pacific Ocean. A growing debate over slavery, however, led to territorial division and a bloody civil war in the early 1860s during the administration of President Abraham Lincoln. After the Civil War, the United States, once more united, became increasingly industrialized, attracted large numbers of immigrants, and emerged as a world power.

In Latin America, the Enlightenment and the American and French Revolutions influenced the growth of independence movements. During the late 1700s and early 1800s, Latin Americans, under the leadership of Touissant L'Ouverture, Simón Bolívar, José de San Martín, and others, won their freedom from Spanish, Portuguese, or French rule. The newly independent Latin American countries, however, lacked experience in self-rule, and military dictators frequently came to power during the 1800s. National unity was often hindered by a huge social gap that divided wealthy landowners from impoverished farmers.

Chapter 15
Reaction and Nationalism

Nationalism, or the desire of people sharing the same culture to have their own nation, became one of the most powerful forces in Europe during the 1800s. In some cases, people struggled to unify small, individual states into one nation. In others people fought to break free from large empires.

In Italy, Austrian rule, territorial divisions, and the pope's opposition had long hindered the growth of a united nation. During the 1800s, leaders such as Giuseppe Garibaldi and Count Camilo di Cavour rallied Italian and international support to expel Austria, end the pope's political power, and join individual territories into a united Italy. In 1861 Italy became a constitutional monarchy, but national unity was hindered by differences between its industrial north and its agricultural south.

A similar quest for unity took place in Germany, which was divided into numerous independent territories. There, Otto von Bismarck, the prime minister of the largest territory, Prussia, used diplomacy and the Prussian army to create a German Empire by 1871. While in office, Bismarck discouraged the growth of democracy, although he enacted social reforms for German workers. Conflict between Bismarck and the kaiser, or emperor, William II, led to Bismarck's resignation in 1890. By this time, Germany had become a prosperous industrial nation with claims to world power.

To the east, the Russian Empire generally resisted nationalism and democracy. Czar Alexander II, however, recognized that some changes were necessary if the empire was to survive. In the 1860s he freed the serfs and reformed aspects of the empire's government. Radicals wanting a revolution assassinated Alexander II in 1881, and political repression returned under his successors, Alexander III and Nicholas II. Meanwhile, the advance of industry in the empire created a small, urban working class that became a major political force after 1900. Strikes

506 Unit 4 *Industry and Nationalism*

ANSWERS TO SURVEYING THE UNIT

CHAPTER 12 A growing urban working class, skilled inventors who provided new technology, businesspeople with money and organizational skills, and the availability of natural resources contributed to the Industrial Revolution in Great Britain.

CHAPTER 13 Smith believed that an unregulated capitalism would bring prosperity to all; Marx believed that capitalism produced sharp inequalities and that it would be replaced by socialism, a system in which the workers by themselves or through government controlled industry for the public good.

and protests after the Russian Empire's setbacks in a war with Japan forced limited political reforms from the czar.

The Austrian Empire also tried to resist political change, but faced growing demands for independence and reform from its diverse nationalities. In 1867, after Austria's defeat in a war with Prussia, Austrian Emperor Francis Joseph agreed to give Hungary equal standing with Austria in the empire. Meanwhile, the Slavic peoples of the empire continued to push for greater political rights.

Chapter 16
The Age of Imperialism

Between 1800 and 1914, various Western nations carried out policies of imperialism, in which they sought to control the political, economic, and social life of countries in Asia, Africa, and Latin America. Three key factors led to the rise of imperialism: competition among Western countries for more territory, their demand for raw materials and new markets, and feelings of cultural and racial superiority that influenced Western peoples to impose their cultures on distant lands.

Beginning in the 1870s, European nations expanded their control over Africa, dividing the continent among themselves and exploiting its rich variety of natural resources. In spite of African resistance, only two African nations—Ethiopia and Liberia—had managed to escape European control by 1914.

 Visualizing History The Boxers in China launched a series of attacks against foreigners in 1900. *What were "spheres of influence"?*

In India, an uprising in 1857 brought direct British control over Indian affairs. To prevent further unrest, the British took steps to develop India economically, but many Indians failed to benefit from the growth of railroads and industries. In 1885 nationalists formed the Indian National Congress, beginning a long struggle for independence.

Also, during the 1800s, European powers intervened in China. Using military power or the threat of it, they claimed large areas of China as spheres of influence—areas where they had exclusive trading rights. When the Chinese fought back in the Boxer Uprising of 1900, the Europeans quickly crushed the revolt. In 1912 Chinese revolutionaries overthrew the weakened Qing dynasty and set up a republic.

The United States in 1853 forced the Japanese to open their doors to trade, sending shock waves through Japanese society. The Meiji leaders who came to power in Japan during the 1860s decided to make Japan a great power capable of competing with the West. They reformed Japan's government and began to industrialize the nation. By 1914 Japan had emerged as a modern industrial nation.

During the era of imperialism, the United States used the Monroe Doctrine to oppose European involvement in Latin America. At the same time, the United States government and American businesses were becoming increasingly involved in Latin American affairs. In the early 1900s, American military forces often intervened in Latin American countries when either government policies or social unrest threatened American interests. This involvement heightened tensions between the United States and Latin America. Anti-American feelings were often a factor in the upsurge of nationalism that swept through the region during this period. The Mexican Revolution, which lasted from 1910 to about 1920, was the first major social upheaval in modern Latin America.

SURVEYING UNIT 4

1. **Chapter 12** What factors led to the Industrial Revolution in Great Britain?
2. **Chapter 13** How did Adam Smith and Karl Marx differ in their view about economics and society?
3. **Chapter 14** How did Great Britain differ from France in the advance toward democracy?
4. **Chapter 15** What effect did nationalism have on Italy? On the Austrian Empire?
5. **Chapter 16** Why did imperialism become a significant force in world affairs during the 1800s?

Visualizing History

Answer to Caption: *Spheres of influence were areas of China where European powers had exclusive trading rights.*

RETEACH

Review Chart Have students create a review chart that summarizes the goals of colonizing nations and the resistances made by those colonized.

 Reteaching Activities 12, 13, 14, 15, 16

Chapter Digests Audio-cassettes, Chapters 12, 13, 14, 15, 16

ABCNEWS INTERACTIVE™

 **VIDEODISC**
Turning Points in World History

Side Two
Chapter 3

Title: *The Industrial Revolution*
Ask: What kind of revolution are we experiencing today? *(a technological revolution)*

ANSWERS TO SURVEYING THE UNIT

CHAPTER 14 Great Britain moved slowly toward democracy by giving more people voting rights and enacting social reforms, while France experienced many changes in its form of government until a republican democracy was established in 1875.

CHAPTER 15 Nationalism helped unite the territories of the Italian Peninsula into a single nation; it caused divisions within the Austrian Empire by arousing the desire for self-rule among the empire's many nationalities.

CHAPTER 16 rivalry among European nations for more territory; their demand for raw materials and new markets; and ideas of superiority that influenced Europeans to impose their cultures on distant lands

Introducing the Unit

Unit 5 focuses on the political movements and global conflicts that gripped the world between 1914 and 1945, including the rise of fascism and communism in Europe, the growth of national-ism in the developing world, and World War I and World War II.

Unit Objectives

After reading Unit 5, students will be able to:

1. discuss the causes, events, and results of World War I.
2. trace the growth of fascist and Communist dictatorships in Italy, Germany, and the Soviet Union.
3. explain the upsurge of nation-alism in Asia, Africa, and Latin America from 1919 to 1939.
4. discuss the causes of World War II and the major political realignments that followed the war.

Portfolio Project

For their radio news reports, have students choose events from the time lines on pages 508–509, 512, 544, 570, and 600. Tell them that their reports should begin with a catchy opener and be brief and live-ly. This activity may be an appropri-ate method of authentic assessment.

Unit **5**

1914–1945

World in Conflict

Chapter 17
World War I

Chapter 18
Between Two Fires

Chapter 19
Nationalism in Asia, Africa, and Latin America

Chapter 20
World War II

Then & Now

Nationalism and imperialism had dire conse-quences for Europe and the world. When national pride and the scramble for overseas territories dictated foreign rela-tions among industrial states, conflict was inevitable. Two world wars resulted. Never before in the history of civilization had the world endured devastation on such a massive scale.

When you climb aboard a jetliner, you may reflect on the tech-nology of air travel developed in this period. After World War II, many people hoped that the refined instruments of war could be turned to peaceful purposes. The power of the atom could be used to produce energy rather than bombs. Airplanes, developed in World War I and refined in World War II, could become a major means of transportation.

A Global Chronology

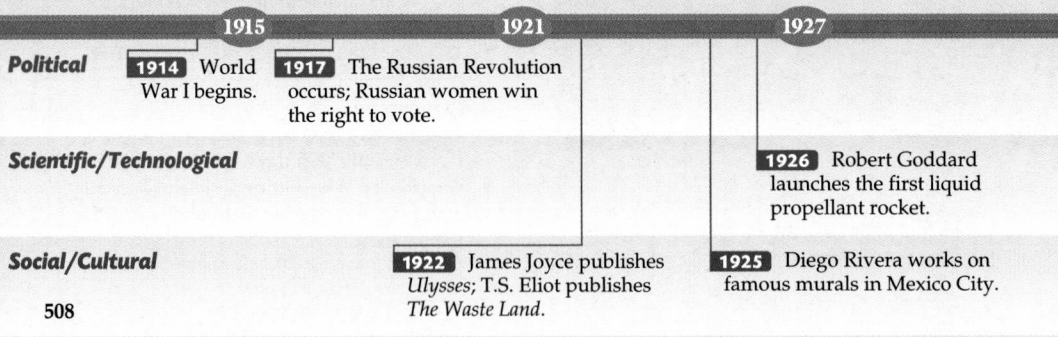

	1915	1921	1927
Political	**1914** World War I begins.	**1917** The Russian Revolution occurs; Russian women win the right to vote.	
Scientific/Technological			**1926** Robert Goddard launches the first liquid propellant rocket.
Social/Cultural		**1922** James Joyce publishes *Ulysses*; T.S. Eliot publishes *The Waste Land*.	**1925** Diego Rivera works on famous murals in Mexico City.

508

Then & Now

Why War? In this unit, students will learn how democracy and peace broke down twice in Europe during the first half of the twentieth century, leading to the bloodiest conflicts in world history.

Ask students to think about the causes of war in general, particularly more recent conflicts involving the United States such as the Vietnam War and the Persian Gulf War. What are the main reasons that nations go to war? *(Answers will vary. Students may feel that*

A 1938 Zenith console radio

Portfolio Project

In the 1930s and 1940s radio reported dramatic news to anxious listeners. At first radio news was simply news-paper-style writing that was read on the air. Soon radio news developed a style of its own. Listen to a few radio news stories. How do they lead in? How much detail is given? How long is the typi-cal report? From the dramatic developments of 1930–1945, compose several radio news reports and read them as an announcer on audiotape.

History and the Humanities

 World History and Art Transparencies
- 36 *Three Musicians*
- 37 *I Want You for the U.S. Army*
- 38 *Migrant Mother*
- 39 *Bird in Space*
- 40 *Zapatistas*
- 41 *Turkestan Oriental Rug*
- 42 *The Red Stairway*

 World Music: Cultural Traditions, Lessons 1, 2, 6, 9

ABCNEWS INTERACTIVE™

 VIDEODISC
Turning Points in World History

Side Two
Chapter 4

Title: *Assassination Ignites World War I*
Ask: Why did the assassination of the archduke plunge Europe into war? *(A web of European alliances caused most major nations to declare war.)*

Visualizing History

The first com-mercial radio station began to broadcast in the United States in 1920; only two years later more than 500 stations were broadcasting throughout the country. With radio, human society entered the modern era of instant communications, including special reports and live, on-the-scene broadcasting.

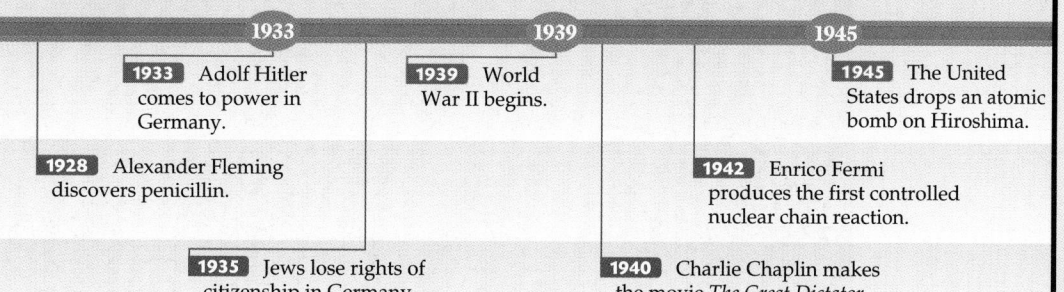

1933 Adolf Hitler comes to power in Germany.

1928 Alexander Fleming discovers penicillin.

1935 Jews lose rights of citizenship in Germany.

1939 World War II begins.

1940 Charlie Chaplin makes the movie *The Great Dictator*.

1945 The United States drops an atomic bomb on Hiroshima.

1942 Enrico Fermi produces the first controlled nuclear chain reaction.

509

conflicting ideologies or interests between two nations, or aggressive actions by one nation, are the main causes of war.) Are democratic governments more or less likely to go to war than dictatorships? Why? (Some students may feel that democracies are less likely to resort to war; others may point out that Britain and the United States, the world's oldest democracies, have fought many wars.) Is war ever justi-fied as a way of achieving foreign policy goals? (Answers will vary; some students may feel that at times war cannot be avoided or is the lesser of two evils; others may respond that war is never justified.)

The Spread of Ideas

TEACH

Introduction

This feature focuses on efforts by the international community to achieve collective security, first through the League of Nations, established after World War I, and later through the United Nations, set up in the aftermath of World War II.

Background Notes

Linking Past and Present

As students will read on pages 538–540, American President Woodrow Wilson was the prime mover of the League of Nations; the failure of the Senate to approve American participation was a blow to Wilson and the League. In contrast, today the United States is a leading funder and supporter of the United Nations, even though there is often heated debate in Congress about American participation in UN peacekeeping missions.

Geography

Movement Since 1989, troops from around the world have participated in UN observer and peacekeeping missions in Latin America, Africa, and Europe. Among the most important have been observer groups to monitor elections in Nicaragua, Haiti, and South Africa and peacekeeping missions in the former Yugoslavia, the republic of Georgia, and Somalia. Ask students what problems the growing number of UN missions in recent years may have created. (*The UN has been burdened with ballooning costs and funding shortages.*)

The Spread of Ideas

International Peacekeeping

The 1900s taught people the meaning of world war. No previous century in history had ever seen conflicts that literally spanned the globe. In addition to numerous regional conflicts, the 20th century witnessed two world wars. As the scope of war grew, so did the commitment to collective security—the principle in which a group of nations join together to promote peace.

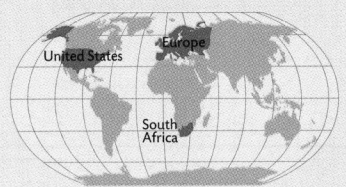

Europe
The League of Nations

As early as 1828, an American named William Ladd sought to establish a Congress of Nations to settle international disputes and avoid war. Nearly a century later, at the end of World War I, the victorious nations set up a "general association of nations" called the League of Nations.

By 1920 42 nations had sent delegates to the League's headquarters in Geneva, Switzerland. Another 21 nations eventually joined, but conspicuously absent was the United States. Opponents in the United States Senate had argued that membership in the League went against George Washington's advice against "entangling alliances."

When the League failed to halt warlike acts in the 1930s, these same opponents pointed to the failure of collective security. The League was a peacekeeper without a sword—it possessed neither a standing army nor members willing to stop nations that used war as a method of diplomacy.

UN distribution center in the Gaza Strip

510 Unit 5

COOPERATIVE LEARNING ACTIVITY

Role Play Have students brainstorm a list of international conflicts today. Then organize students into small groups. Assign each group a conflict from the list. Have them role-play an attempt by the United Nations to resolve the situation. In each group, have some students represent the two parties in conflict and others represent UN mediators. Have students discuss the sources of the conflict, then draw up and if possible agree to a peace treaty. Each group can describe its dilemma to the class and explain whether—and why—they could or could not resolve it. **L3**

Rwandan child at a refugee camp

The United States
The United Nations

Non-membership in the League did not protect the United States from the horrors of war. The Japanese air attack on Pearl Harbor, Hawaii, ended the notion that the United States could isolate itself from the rest of the world.

As World War II drew to a close, the United States hosted a meeting in San Francisco to create a new global peacekeeping organization. Here delegates from 50 nations hammered out the Charter of the United Nations. The document's Preamble sets forth a formula for international peace:

We the peoples of the United Nations, determined to save succeeding generations from the scourge of war, which twice in our lifetime has brought untold sorrow to mankind and to reaffirm faith in fundamental human rights ... and to promote social progress and to better standards of life and to promote our strength to maintain international peace and security, and to ensure ... that armed force shall not be used, save in the common interest ... have resolved to combine our efforts to accomplish these aims.

In the years following, the United Nations (UN) attempted to eliminate the root causes of war. In 1946 it founded the UN Educational, Scientific, and Cultural Organization (UNESCO) and the UN Children's Fund (UNICEF). These agencies promoted global education and the well-being of children. Two years later, in 1948, United States delegate Eleanor Roosevelt convinced the UN to adopt The Universal Declaration of Human Rights. This committed the UN to the elimination of oppression wherever it existed.

South Africa
The Power of World Opinion

Like the League of Nations, the UN could be only as strong as its members were prepared to make it. The development of atomic weapons, however, was a powerful incentive for members to cooperate. By 1995, the UN had taken part in 35 peacekeeping missions—some successful, some failures. It also had provided protection for more than 30 million refugees.

The UN's ability to use world opinion to promote justice was perhaps best tested in South Africa. In 1977 the UN urged nations to use an arms embargo and economic sanctions against South Africa until apartheid was lifted. In 1994 South Africa held its first all-race elections. Many believed this was a major triumph for collective international action.

UN troops in Beirut, Lebanon

LINKING THE IDEAS

1. What factors made it difficult for the League of Nations to promote world peace?
2. What methods has the United Nations used to encourage peace?

Critical Thinking

3. **Forming Opinions** The United Nations Declaration of Human Rights sees injustice in one part of the world as a threat to peace in all parts of the world. Do you agree? Why or why not?

Unit 5 *World in Conflict* **511**

Cultural Diffusion

International Cooperation and Popular Music Since the 1970s the spirit of international cooperation has influenced the world of rock music. In the early 1970s, a number of rock musicians, including George Harrison and Bob Dylan, held a concert to raise money for famine victims in the newly created nation of Bangladesh (formerly part of Pakistan). In the 1980s Bob Geldof of the Boomtown Rats organized Band Aid, featuring many recording artists such as Sting and Phil Collins, to raise money for famine relief in Ethiopia.

ANSWERS TO LINKING THE IDEAS

1. It had no army, and its members were not willing to use force to stop aggression.
2. The UN has tried to eliminate the causes of war through UNESCO and UNICEF and has used peacekeeping missions, arms embargoes, and economic sanctions to promote peace.
3. Answers will vary. Some students may feel that injustice creates instability that can lead to war.

A complete, 1-page lesson plan is provided for each section in the *Reproducible Lesson Plans* booklet.

World War I

CHAPTER RESOURCES

	Reproducible Resources	Multimedia Resources
Chapter Opener	Chapter Themes: Graphic Organizer 17 Historical Significance Chapter Activity 17	MindJogger Videoquiz
Chapter Enrichment	Vocabulary Activity 17* Time Line Activity 17 Mapping History Activity 17 History Simulation 17 Geography and History Activity 17 Source Reading 17 People in World History Profiles 53, 54 World Art and Music Activity 17 Enrichment Activity 17 Critical Thinking Activity 17 Skill Reinforcement Activity 17 Performance Assessment Activity 17	World History and Art Transparency 36, *Three Musicians*; 37, *I Want You for the U. S. Army* Mapping History Overlay Transparency 18, *World War I* Chapter Transparency 17 Vocabulary PuzzleMaker Software Turning Points in World History: *Assassination Ignites World War I* Lessons of War: *How Wars Begin—World War I* Communism and the Cold War: *Perspectives on Communism*
Chapter Review/Reteaching	Reteaching Activity 17 Skill Reinforcement Activity 17 Spanish Chapter Summary 17	Chapter 17 Digest Audiocassette, Activity, Test* Vocabulary PuzzleMaker Software Student Self-Test and Review Software MindJogger Videoquiz
Chapter Evaluation/Testing	Performance Assessment Activity 17 Chapter 17 Test, Forms A and B	Testmaker

* Also available in Spanish

0:00 OUT OF TIME? Assign the Chapter 17 summary in the Unit 5 Digest on pages 631–633, and the Chapter 17 Audiocassettes.

Block Schedule

Block scheduling differs from traditional class scheduling in the amount of time allotted to each period. The extended time frame provided by block scheduling affords you the opportunity to implement a greater number of research-oriented and activity-intense projects to motivate and involve your students. Activities that are particularly suited to use within the block scheduling framework are identified throughout this chapter by the following designation.

KEY TO ABILITY LEVELS

Teaching strategies have been coded for varying learning styles and abilities.

L1 **BASIC** activities for all students
L2 **AVERAGE** activities for average to above-average students
L3 **CHALLENGING** activities for above-average students
LEP **LIMITED ENGLISH PROFICIENCY** activities

Use Glencoe's *Presentation Plus!* multimedia teacher tool to easily present dynamic lessons that visually excite your students. Using Microsoft PowerPoint® you can customize the presentations to create your own personalized lessons.

SECTION RESOURCES

Daily Objectives	Reproducible Resources	Multimedia Resources
Section 1 **The Seeds of War** Identify the underlying causes of World War I.	Reproducible Lesson Plan 17-1 Vocabulary Activity 17* Guided Reading Activity 17-1* Time Line Activity 17 Section Quiz 17-1*	Section Focus Transparency 17-1 Chapter Transparency 17 Student Self-Test and Review Software
Section 2 **The Spark** Describe the series of events that provided the spark that ignited World War I.	Reproducible Lesson Plan 17-2 Vocabulary Activity 17* Guided Reading Activity 17-2* Section Quiz 17-2*	Section Focus Transparency 17-2 Student Self-Test and Review Software Turning Points in World History: *Assassination Ignites World War I*
Section 3 **The War** Specify where and how World War I was fought.	Reproducible Lesson Plan 17-3 Guided Reading Activity 17-3* History Simulation 17 Geography and History Activity 17 Section Quiz 17-3*	Section Focus Transparency 17-3 Mapping History Overlay Transparency 18, *World War I* World History and Art Transparency 36, *Three Musicians*; 37, *I Want You for the U. S. Army* Vocabulary PuzzleMaker Software Student Self-Test and Review Software Lessons of War: *How Wars Begin–World War I*
Section 4 **The Russian Revolution** Summarize the events that led to the Russian Revolution.	Reproducible Lesson Plan 17-4 Vocabulary Activity 17* Guided Reading Activity 17-4* Section Quiz 17-4*	Section Focus Transparency 17-4 Student Self-Test and Review Software Communism and the Cold War: *Perspectives on Communism*
Section 5 **Peace at Last** Explain why the Treaty of Versailles was ultimately unsuccessful.	Reproducible Lesson Plan 17-5 Guided Reading Activity 17-5* Reteaching Activity 17 Enrichment Activity 17 Section Quiz 17-5* Performance Assessment Activity 17 Spanish Chapter Summary 17	Section Focus Transparency 17-5 Vocabulary PuzzleMaker Software Student Self-Test and Review Software Testmaker

* Also available in Spanish

Chapter Activities

✔ Performance Assessment Activity

A Chain of Events Have students assume the role of scriptwriters for a television episode about a time traveler. Each student will think of one event of the World War I era to change, then predict the chain of events that would have flowed from the changed event and describe how the war would have been different because of it. Then have students write a brief summary of the chain of events, choose real actors to play the parts of the significant individuals, decide on how the time traveler will be able to make the proposed change, and choose locations for the scenes (either real or with designed sets). Students will then present their ideas to a group whose members play the roles of producers.

Possible Rubric Features
Accuracy of content information, logical predictions, appropriateness of sets and locales for events, clarity of presentation, originality, and summarization skills

• *For an additional activity, refer to Activity 17 in the* Performance Assessment Strategies and Activities *booklet.*

ACTIVITY

From the Classroom of...

Kathleen M. Slane
Rockville High School
Vernon, CT

World War I Propaganda Posters

Show the class a number of World War I propaganda posters, designed by members of both the Allied Powers and the Central Powers. Explain to students that they will design propaganda posters for either the Allied forces or the Central forces. Number slips of paper with a 1 or 2, representing the Allied or Central forces. Place the slips of paper in a container and have each student (or group of students) pick one to determine the alliance system for which they will create a poster.

Students may create posters that demonstrate the following: (1) support for the Red Cross, (2) women's roles in wartime, (3) financial support through the purchase of war bonds, (4) fear of the opposing forces, (5) savagery of the opposing forces, (6) patriotism for their country and loyalty to the cause.

Display the completed posters in the classroom. Have students study each poster and answer the following questions: Which country or alliance system designed this propaganda poster? How do you know? What was the important message of the poster? Can you think of examples of propaganda that present-day countries utilize?

MULTIPLE LEARNING STYLES

Verbal/Linguistic
Have students select poems from the World War I era and read them aloud in class as a basis for discussion.

Logical/Mathematical
Have students debate the following proposition: War unites the people of a country as nothing else can.

Auditory/Musical
Have students listen to a tape or CD of World War I songs. On the basis of these, ask what generalizations they can make about the armies and/or civilians of the time.

Kinesthetic
Have students use models or diagrams to explain to the rest of the class the workings of one of the new pieces of military technology used in World War I. They might choose machine guns, tanks, submarines, or fighter planes.

Additional Resources

NATIONAL GEOGRAPHIC SOCIETY

Teacher's Corner

INDEX TO NATIONAL GEOGRAPHIC MAGAZINE

The following articles may be used for research relating to this chapter:

- "Riddle of the Lusitania," by Robert D. Ballard, April 1994.
- "The Bolshevik Revolution: Experiment That Failed," by Dusko Doder, October 1992.

NATIONAL GEOGRAPHIC SOCIETY PRODUCTS AVAILABLE FROM GLENCOE

To order the following products for use with this chapter, contact your local Glencoe sales representative, or call Glencoe at 1-800-334-7344:

- *GTV: The American People (Videodiscs)*
- *GTV: A Geographic Perspective on American History (Videodiscs)*

ADDITIONAL NATIONAL GEOGRAPHIC SOCIETY PRODUCTS

To order the following products for use with this chapter, call National Geographic Society at 1-800-368-2728:

- *1914–1918: World War I (Video)*
- *1917: Revolution in Russia (Video)*
- *The Rise and Fall of the Soviet Union (Video)*
- *Last Voyage of the Lusitania (Video)*

LOCAL OBJECTIVES

_____
_____
_____
_____
_____
_____
_____
_____
_____
_____
_____
_____
_____
_____
_____
_____
_____
_____
_____
_____
_____
_____
_____
_____

*inter*NET CONNECTION

World War I resources on the World Wide Web
World War I: Trenches on the Web
http://www.worldwar1.com

BIBLIOGRAPHY

Literature of the Period
Hemingway, Ernest. *A Farewell to Arms.* New York: Macmillan, 1988. A romantic novel by a writer who served as an ambulance driver during the war.
Remarque, Erich Maria. *All Quiet on the Western Front.* New York: Fawcett, 1987. A novel about the destruction of a generation of young German soldiers in World War I.
Readings for the Student
Taylor, A.J.P. *The First World War: An Illustrated History.* New York: Perigee, 1980. Includes many photographs and an informative commentary.
Readings for the Teacher
Tuchman, Barbara W. *The Guns of August.* New York: Bantam, 1980. A vivid account of the crucial first six weeks of World War I.

CHAPTER THEMES

Chapter Themes are listed by section on this chapter opening page of the Student Edition. A corresponding theme-based activity is available under "TEACH," and a theme-based question is asked in the Section and Chapter Reviews.

 The Storyteller

Historical Setting Erich Maria Remarque, author of *All Quiet on the Western Front*, was 18 when he was drafted into the German army. He saw action on the Western Front, where he was wounded.

The novel's hero, Paul Baumer, volunteers enthusiastically for the army but is soon disillusioned by the carnage. "How senseless is everything," he says, "when such things are possible.... A hospital alone shows what war is." Baumer is killed on the Western Front, on a day that is otherwise "all quiet."

Historical Significance

Answers: *It differed in scope (fought on several continents), scale (heavy casualties), and the destructiveness of the weapons used, including poison gas and machine guns.*

The war ended several empires and created many small countries. Among its legacies were the decimation of a generation of young men, widespread impoverishment, and lasting resentments and animosities.

Chapter
17 1914–1920
World War I

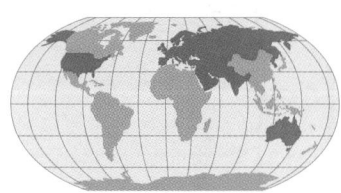

Chapter Themes

▶ **Cooperation** European powers form a series of alliances before World War I. *Section 1*
▶ **Conflict** Tensions between the two European alliances erupt into a European-wide conflict. *Section 2*
▶ **Conflict** The European war is transformed into a war that engulfs much of the world; the global conflict directly affects many civilians as well as soldiers. *Section 3*
▶ **Revolution** Revolution in Russia overthrows the czar and brings Lenin and the Bolsheviks to power. *Section 4*
▶ **Internationalism** The Treaty of Versailles provides for the creation of a League of Nations to mediate international disputes. *Section 5*

The Storyteller

To survive days of bombardment on the Western Front during World War I, men crouched down in deep ditches. During these times there was nothing to do but wait and watch. Finally, they would receive orders to attack:

"Suddenly the nearer explosions cease. The shelling continues but it has lifted and falls behind us, our trench is free. We seize the hand-grenades, pitch them out in front of the dug-out and jump after them. The bombardment has stopped and a heavy barrage now falls behind us. The attack has come."

In this passage from All Quiet on the Western Front, *Erich Maria Remarque captures the chaos and horror of what is now called World War I. When this war broke out in the summer of 1914, most Europeans thought it would be over by Christmas. Instead, it lasted four long years and changed Europe and the world forever.*

Historical Significance

In what ways was World War I different from previous wars? How did it affect the countries and peoples involved? What impact did it have on the future course of the 1900s?

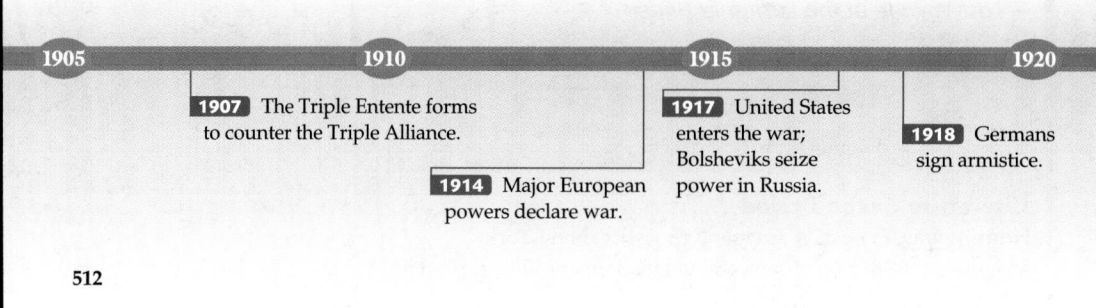

1905	1910	1915	1920

1907 The Triple Entente forms to counter the Triple Alliance.

1914 Major European powers declare war.

1917 United States enters the war; Bolsheviks seize power in Russia.

1918 Germans sign armistice.

512

GEOGRAPHY CONNECTION

Location On a wall map, have students locate the countries that became the Central Powers: Germany, Austria-Hungary, the Ottoman Empire, and Bulgaria. Then have them locate the countries that became the (European) Allies: Britain, France, Russia, Belgium, Serbia, Montenegro, and later, Romania, Greece, Portugal, and Italy. **L1 LEP**

History & Art *American Troops Arriving in Paris July 14, 1918* by J. F. Foucher. West Point Museum, West Point, New York

✔ *Performance Assessment*

Refer to the activity on page 512C of the Planning Guide.

📁 **For an additional activity, refer to Activity 17 in the *Performance Assessment Strategies and Activities* booklet.**

Using Your History Journal

The main participants were Ypres: Germans and British; *Lusitania*: Germans, British, Americans; Verdun: Germans, French.

Your History Journal

Write a letter home as a first-person account of one of the following events: Poison gas at Ypres, the Sinking of the Lusitania, the Battle of Verdun.

GLENCOE
TECHNOLOGY

VIDEODISC
Use MindJogger to preview chapter content.

MindJogger Videoquiz

Chapter 17
Disc 2 Side B

 Also available in VHS.

Chapter 17 *World War I* **513**

✚ EXTRA CREDIT PROJECT

Deadly Influenza In the last months of the war, the world was struck by a pandemic of influenza that killed more people than the war itself. Have students research and report on the pandemic: where and when it began; how the disease manifested itself; and the total number of casualties.

SECTION THEME

▶ **Cooperation** European powers form a series of alliances before World War I.

Find Out

Answer: *The main causes were competition for resources and territories, nationalism, and militarism.*

FOCUS

Section Objective

Identify the underlying causes of World War I.

BELLRINGER
Motivational Activity

Before taking roll at the beginning of the class period, project Section Focus Transparency 17-1 and have students answer the activity questions. Discuss students' responses.
This activity is also available as a blackline master.

Vocabulary Pre-check

Use Vocabulary Activity 17 to introduce vocabulary terms.
L1 LEP

1880		1890		1900		1910

1882 Italy joins Germany and Austria-Hungary to form the Triple Alliance.

1894 France and Russia become allies to counter the Triple Alliance.

c. 1900 Germany has the most powerful weapons and the best army in Europe.

1905 France and Germany come close to war over Morocco

Section 1
....
The Seeds of War

Setting the Scene

▶ **Terms to Define**
militarism, conscription, alliance system, *entente*

▶ **People to Meet**
Otto von Bismarck

▶ **Places to Locate**
Morocco, Alsace-Lorraine, Bosnia-Herzegovina

Find Out What were the underlying causes of World War I?

The Storyteller

Herbert Marlow, foreign editor for a large United States newspaper, was amazed. His correspondents in Paris, Vienna, and Berlin had all wired similar reports concerning European nationalism and attitudes favoring war. Roland Doregelès wrote, "No more poor or rich ... there were only Frenchmen." Stefan Zweig in Vienna

observed, "As never before, thousands and hundreds of thousands felt what they should have felt in peacetime, that they belonged together." Marlow reread Philipp Scheidermann's dispatch from Berlin, resolving to use it as his headline. Scheidermann had noted Germans proclaiming "It is the hour we yearned for."

German military parade

—adapted from articles reprinted in *Sources of the Western Tradition*, edited by Marvin Perry, 1991

In the summer of 1914, an assassination took place in the Austro-Hungarian province of Bosnia in the Balkans. Although some people mourned, there was no broad sense of outrage or alarm. There had been other assassinations in the recent past with no major consequences.

Within weeks, it became apparent that this assassination was different. By August, the major European powers were at war with each other. The war was to last from 1914 to 1918; it led to the development of new weapons that changed warfare forever. By the time it was over, the war had involved most nations of the world and was the largest that the world had ever seen.

It was known as the Great War, the "war to end all wars." The name by which it was called was not important. The changes it brought about were. The way of life that had existed before the war was destroyed. Empires were swept away, and governments toppled. European dominance of the world was shaken. The war marked the close of a long era of international peace.

European Rivalries

Since the mid-1800s, rivalries had been building up and intensifying among some of the countries of Europe. As Western nations industrialized, each sought the most favorable conditions for economic growth. This led to intense competition. As industrialization spread, the competition grew keener. One by one, Great Britain, France, Germany, Austria-Hungary, Russia, and Italy sought to acquire new markets and to establish and expand global empires.

Great Britain wanted to maintain the lifelines of its empire and keep open the sea-lanes it needed for trade. It also wanted to make sure no other nation became strong enough to attack it. France was intent on adding mineral-rich **Morocco** to its gains.

SECTION RESOURCES

Reproducible Masters
- Reproducible Lesson Plan 17-1
- Vocabulary Activity 17
- Guided Reading Activity 17-1
- Time Line Activity 17
- Section Quiz 17-1

Transparencies
- Section Focus Transparency 17-1
- Chapter Transparency 17

Multimedia
- Student Self-Test and Review Software
- Testmaker

Race to the South Pole

Antarctica, 1911
Two European explorers–Roald Amundsen of Norway and Robert Scott of Great Britain–became engaged in a dramatic race to reach the South Pole. Amundsen and his companions began crossing the Ross Ice Shelf on October 19, 1911. They traveled on skis and used dogsleds to carry their supplies. They arrived at the South Pole on December 14. Scott and his party reached the Pole in January to find a Norwegian flag and a message from Amundsen. Then tragically, Scott and all his companions died on the return trip.

Germany hoped to gain economic control of the declining Ottoman Empire. Austria-Hungary set out to gain territorial access through the Balkans to the Aegean Sea. Russia aspired to take control of the Bosporus and the Dardanelles near the Black Sea and to extend the influence it already had over Manchuria in East Asia.

Competition turned to hostility as one power crossed another in its efforts to accomplish its goals. In 1898, for example, Great Britain and France confronted one another over rival claims in Egypt and the Sudan. The following year, Germany started to build the Berlin-Baghdad railway, which created resentment among both the British and the Russians. The British feared that the railroad would interfere with their interests in India and reduce traffic through the Suez Canal. The Russians thought the railroad interfered in their traditional areas of interest. In 1905, 1908, and 1911, Germany and France came close to war over control of Morocco.

Nationalism

Contributing to the tension was a growing spirit of nationalism. Nationalism had unified Germany and was rapidly becoming popular in France. There, French nationalists sought revenge against Germany for depriving France of the border provinces of **Alsace-Lorraine** in the 1870–1871 Franco-Prussian War.

The French novelist Victor Hugo urged France to "have but one thought: to reconstitute her forces, gather her energy, nourish her sacred anger.... Then one day she will be irresistible. Then she will take back Alsace-Lorraine." This put the Germans on their guard. They were well aware that the issue of Alsace-Lorraine was not settled permanently.

Slavic Nationalism

In Austria-Hungary, nationalism was creating the most violent tensions in Europe. The empire's Slavs were attracted to Pan-Slavism, the idea that the Slavs had a historic mission to develop their culture and unite into an empire. Slavic nationalists in neighboring Serbia supported the Slavs of Austria-Hungary. They wanted their own country to be the center of a South Slav, or Yugoslav, nation. This new Slavic state would be formed out of Slavic territories in Austria-Hungary.

Austria-Hungary was alarmed by Serbian activities in the Balkans. It feared that the idea of a Yugoslav state would attract restless Slavic groups in Austria-Hungary. Such a development would harm the security of the empire and lead to its eventual breakup.

In 1908 Austria-Hungary annexed the Slavic territories of **Bosnia-Herzegovina**, once the provinces of the Ottoman Empire. Angered at the Austro-Hungarian move, Serbia called on Russia, its traditional protector, for help. Russia, however, was still weak from the Russo-Japanese War and was not ready to fight again. In addition, Russia had made a secret deal with the Austro-Hungarians. The Russians had agreed to let Austria-Hungary have Bosnia-Herzegovina in exchange for the right for Russian warships to go through the Dardanelles. So, Russia persuaded the Serbs to restrain themselves. Then, Russia discovered that Austria-Hungary had made its move before Russia could get its part of the deal. As a result, the Russians were bitter.

Balkan Wars

The first Balkan war in 1912 further inflamed the Serbs. One of Serbia's war aims had been to acquire Albania, a small territory along the coast of the Adriatic Sea, an arm of the Mediterranean Sea. This would give Serbia the water outlet it desired. When, after winning the war, Serbia did not get Albania, Serb resentment grew even stronger.

In 1913 a second Balkan war broke out. Albania was made independent, frustrating once again Serbian ambitions. In this war, as in the last one, the Russians had not been able to support Serbia. This upset the Serbs and humiliated the Russians. Austria-Hungary, meanwhile, became increasingly worried about its future role in European affairs.

Chapter 17 *World War I* **515**

Chapter 17 Section 1

TEACH

Guided Practice

THEME Cooperation
Ask students to suggest different reasons why nations cooperate. *(Possible answers: for protection against mutual enemies, to help poorer nations, to increase trade and wealth, to manage common natural resources wisely.)* Ask which of these reasons are most likely to lead to war. *(protection against mutual enemies)* **L1**

Militarism Have students name the main components of militarism in the period before World War I. *(winning allies, increasing military spending, stockpiling arms, conscription, universal military training)* Ask which of these elements can be found in societies today. *(Answers will vary, but students may mention high levels of military spending.)* **L2**

Time Line Have students create a time line of the alliance systems formed between 1872 and 1907. Ask a volunteer to record the time line on the chalkboard. **L2**

Chapter Transparency 17

Who?What?Where?When?

Slavs, modern descendants of an ancient people, are related mainly by their similar languages. Slavs include the Russians, Ukrainians, Poles, Czechs, Slovaks, Bulgarians, Croatians, Slovenes, Serbs, and Macedonians.

COOPERATIVE LEARNING ACTIVITY

Roundtable Organize the class into small groups. Each group should represent one of the major nations that eventually became the Central Powers and the Allies. Have each "nation" list its grievances and fears vis-à-vis the others. Then have them reevaluate their lists in light of one factor changing—for example, if Germany agreed to return Alsace-Lorraine to France. Discuss how small incidents can lead to major shifts in alignments. **L3**

Chapter 17 *World War I* **515**

Independent Practice

 Guided Reading Activity 17-1 **L1**

 Time Line Activity 17

Competition Have students explain briefly why each of the following caused tension among the European powers: Berlin-Baghdad railway; Morocco; Alsace-Lorraine; Dardanelles. **L2**

ASSESS

Check for Understanding

Assign Section 1 Review as homework or as an in-class activity.

 Use Student Self-Test and Review Software to review Section 1.

Evaluate

 Section Quiz 17-1

 Use the Testmaker to create a customized quiz for Section 1.

Reteach

Have students summarize the chief factors that constituted the "seeds" of war.

Enrich

Have students list the alliances the United States maintains today.

CLOSE

Have students point out on a map the main areas of tension in Europe, the Middle East, and Africa in 1914. For each area, have students indicate whether the tensions were due principally to nationalistic feelings or imperialist rivalries.

Militarism

As tensions began to rise, so did militarism, the glorification of war and the military. The European powers assessed each other's military strength. They compared military training programs and levels of spending. They also looked at levels of industrialization and tried to estimate how fast a nation could ready its troops for battle.

Diplomats maneuvered to win new allies. Military leaders argued for increased military spending and more arms. After 1870, all the powers except Great Britain adopted conscription, the compulsory call-up of civilians for military service, and universal military training. They were sure that their national security depended almost entirely on the technology, skill, and readiness of their military forces.

Each nation's actions caused a reaction in the other nations. For example, when Germany decided in 1898 to expand its navy, Great Britain felt threatened. The Germans argued that they needed a larger navy to protect colonial and merchant shipping and "for the general purpose of greatness." Great Britain claimed that as an island nation that depended on trade for many vital supplies, it had to be able to control the seas. To do this, said the British, they had to maintain a navy as large as the combined fleet of their two nearest rivals.

Alliances

Along with militarism came a hardening of the alliance systems, or the defense agreements among nations. In 1873 **Otto von Bismarck** created the Three Emperors' League, which united Germany, Austria-Hungary, and Russia. His purpose was to isolate France by attaching all of its possible friends to Germany. The Emperors' League, however, did not last very long because of Austrian-Russian rivalry in the Balkans. Bismarck then created a new and stronger alliance with Austria-Hungary.

In 1882 Italy joined the Austrian-German alliance, and it became known as the Triple Alliance. Italy joined because it wanted allies against France. The Italians were angry with the French for occupying Tunis, or present-day Tunisia, in North Africa. They also were afraid that the French might send an army to defend the pope, with whom they were having a dispute. The three powers of the Triple Alliance agreed that if any one member became involved in a war with two or more enemies, the others would provide support.

In 1890 another alliance began to evolve as Russia and France developed friendlier relations. In 1894 Russia and France signed a military alliance in which they agreed to come to each other's aid in case of an attack by either Germany or Austria-Hungary, or by both powers. This was followed in 1904 by the Entente Cordiale between France and Great Britain. The term *entente* refers to a friendly understanding between two nations that, at the same time, lacks the binding commitments of a full-fledged alliance. Three years later, Great Britain and Russia settled their conflicting ambitions in the Middle East and central Asia.

All of these agreements developed into the Triple Entente, a loose alliance between France, Russia, and Great Britain. Russia, an autocratic monarchy, and France, a democratic republic, were willing to ally out of a common fear of Germany and Austria-Hungary. Great Britain, a democratic monarchy, was willing to join because it was alarmed by Germany's naval-building program. It felt hard pressed to protect its empire on its own.

Thus, by 1907, the great powers of Europe had aligned themselves in two opposing combinations. On one side stood the Triple Alliance. On the other stood the Triple Entente. Instead of making their members more secure, however, these alliances threatened the peace of the continent. Given the conditions of the Triple Alliance and the Triple Entente, a minor conflict between rival nations had the potential to involve all major European powers in war.

SECTION 1 REVIEW

Recall
1. **Define** militarism, conscription, alliance system, *entente*.
2. **Identify** Otto von Bismarck, Triple Alliance, Triple Entente.
3. **Locate** Germany on the map on page 518. Why was Germany at a disadvantage in fighting an all-European war?

Critical Thinking
4. **Evaluating Information** What were the factors that led to alliances before the outbreak of World War I?

Understanding Themes
5. **Cooperation** Given the conditions that existed in Europe before 1914, could the nations of that continent have avoided a major war? If so, how?

SECTION 1 REVIEW ANSWERS

1. All vocabulary words are defined in the Glossary.
2. Otto von Bismarck, 516; Triple Alliance, 516; Triple Entente, 516
3. Its central location meant that it had to fight on two fronts.
4. fear of military threats from rival powers; nationalistic rivalries; imperialistic rivalries
5. **COOPERATION** Answers will vary. Possible answer: They probably could have avoided a major war if some differences had been negotiated.

JUNE, 1914   JULY, 1914   AUGUST, 1914

JUNE 28, 1914 Slav nationalist assassinates Austria's Archduke Francis Ferdinand.

JULY 28, 1914 Austria-Hungary declares war on Serbia.

AUGUST 1, 1914 Germany declares war on Russia.

AUGUST 4, 1914 Great Britain declares war on Germany.

Chapter 17
Section 2

Section 2

The Spark

Setting the Scene

▶ **Terms to Define**
ultimatum, mobilization

▶ **People to Meet**
Francis Ferdinand, Gavrilo Princip, William II, Nicholas II

▶ **Places to Locate**
Sarajevo, Serbia

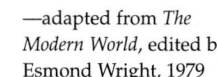 What series of events provided the spark that ignited World War I?

The Storyteller

Nearly one month after Archduke Francis Ferdinand was assassinated at the Bosnian capital of Sarajevo, some European leaders suspected that the crisis would pass. Newspaper headlines carried other stories. Cabinet minister Lloyd George of Britain told the House of Commons: "I cannot help thinking that civilization which is able to deal with disputes among individuals and small communities ... should be able to extend its operations to the larger sphere of disputes among states." Before he finished his address, Austria had delivered an ultimatum to Serbia. World War I was about to begin.

Assassination at Sarajevo

—adapted from *The Modern World*, edited by Esmond Wright, 1979

---

ntil 1914, a false optimism prevailed in Europe. Although military buildups continued, most Europeans did not really think there would be a major war. Almost a century of relative peace had followed the Congress of Vienna. The absence of a major war for so long a period had lulled many Europeans into believing that such a war would not ever happen again.

Major social reforms and important scientific advances during the 1800s reinforced the belief that the world was improving steadily and that people had outgrown the need for war to solve their problems. Most countries were enjoying economic prosperity. A war would destroy what had been built up over the years. Despite this optimism, war did come, triggered by the assassination in the Balkans. That event set in motion the diplomatic moves that ended in war.

Trouble in the Balkans

On June 28, 1914, Archduke **Francis Ferdinand**, nephew and heir to Austro-Hungarian Emperor Francis Joseph, paid a visit to **Sarajevo** (SAR•uh•YAY•voh), the capital of Bosnia-Herzegovina. Francis Ferdinand planned, upon becoming emperor, to give the Slavs of Bosnia-Herzegovina and other parts of the empire a voice in the government equal to that of the Austrians and Hungarians. This political action might have defused the movement for a separate Slavic state.

Before the archduke and his wife, Sophie, began their ride through the streets of Sarajevo in an open car, seven young assassins had already taken their places along the route. All were members of a secret nationalist group based in **Serbia** known as the Black Hand, or Union of Death. Although the archduke and Sophie survived the first assassin's attempt, their luck did not hold.

Chapter 17 *World War I* **517**

SECTION THEME

▶ **Conflict** Tensions between the two European alliances erupt into a European-wide conflict.

Answer: *the assassination of Archduke Francis Ferdinand, declarations of war, mobilizations by Austria-Hungary, Russia, Germany, France, and Britain*

FOCUS

Section Objective
Describe the series of events that provided the spark that ignited World War I.

BELLRINGER
Motivational Activity

Project Section Focus Transparency 17-2 and have students answer the questions.
This activity is also available as a blackline master.

Vocabulary Pre-check
Use Vocabulary Activity 17 to introduce vocabulary terms.
L1 LEP

POINT

Trouble in the Balkans
What was the significance of the assassination of Austrian Archduke Ferdinand?
It triggered World War I by bringing the two rival European alliances into conflict.

SECTION RESOURCES

Reproducible Masters
• Reproducible Lesson Plan 17-2
• Vocabulary Activity 17
• Guided Reading Activity 17-2
• Section Quiz 17-2

Transparencies
• Section Focus Transparency 17-2

Multimedia
• Student Self-Test and Review Software
• Testmaker
• Turning Points in World History: *Assassination Ignites World War I*

TEACH

Guided Practice

THEME Conflict

Have students study the map on page 518, then create a list of all the possible sources of conflict between the major powers in Europe at this time. Discuss how one of these sources of conflict might have led to World War I if Archduke Ferdinand had not been assassinated. **L1**

Map Study

Answer

Triple Entente countries, they surrounded the Triple Alliance countries and had better access to the sea

Map Skills Practice

Reading a Map What geographic advantages did the Central Powers have over the Allied Powers? *(They had better access to western Asia; also, because they were centrally located, they could move troops quickly from one theater of war to another.)*

VIDEODISC
Turning Points in World History

Side Two
Chapter 4

Title: *Assassination Ignites World War I*

Ask: Why did the assassination of the archduke plunge Europe into war? *(A web of European alliances caused most major nations to declare war.)*

Europe in 1915

Central Powers
Allied Powers
Neutral nations

World War I split Europe into two armed camps.
Location Which side do you think had the better strategic location: the Triple Alliance or the Triple Entente countries?

When the couple's car took a wrong turn, 19-year-old **Gavrilo Princip** (gah•VREE•loh PREEN•seep) fired his gun, fatally wounding them both.

German Support

Although the assassination had not occurred in Serbia, Austro-Hungarian leaders held the Serbians responsible. They were encouraged in this line of thinking by their German allies and by Count Leopold Berchtold, the Austro-Hungarian foreign minister. On July 5, Berchtold sent an envoy to Berlin to talk to the German emperor, **William II**. William assured the envoy that Germany would give its full support to any actions Austria-Hungary might take against Serbia. The next day, the German chancellor officially repeated this promise to the Austro-Hungarian government. In effect, Germany gave Austria-Hungary permission to do with Serbia as it pleased.

Declaration of War

On July 23, Austria-Hungary gave Serbia an ultimatum, a set of final conditions that must be accepted to avoid severe consequences. The ultimatum demanded that Serbia allow Austro-Hungarian officials into the country to suppress all subversive movements there and to lead an investigation into the archduke's murder. Austria-Hungary gave Serbia 48 hours to agree to these terms or face war. Berchtold knew, however, that the ultimatum "would be wholly impossible for the Serbs to accept."

Although the ultimatum outraged Serbian leaders, they knew that their nation was not ready for war with Austria-Hungary. Therefore, on July 25, they responded in a conciliatory manner. They rejected, however, the demand that Austro-Hungarian officials take part in the investigation and trial of those involved in the assassination.

COOPERATIVE LEARNING ACTIVITY

Dramatization Organize students into small groups and have them stage a series of radio or television newscasts devoted to the outbreak of World War I. Each group should select a critical date from June 28 to August 4. They should incorporate researched information with the text material. Have groups include comments by participants, descriptions of citizen responses, and speculation as to what will happen next. **L3**

The Serbian answer did not satisfy Austria-Hungary. Consequently, on July 28, 1914, exactly one month after the assassination of Archduke Ferdinand, Austria-Hungary declared war on Serbia. Both countries immediately issued general orders for mobilization, the gathering and transport of military troops and fighting equipment in preparation for war. News of these mobilizations spread quickly across the European continent.

A European War

Many Europeans still believed war could be avoided. The major European powers pushed each other to the brink of war, believing that the other side would back down at the last minute. They were tragically mistaken.

Russia was the first to act once Austria-Hungary declared war. Knowing it had lost face often in the past, the Russian government had to support Serbia now or risk the bitter hatred of all the Slavs in the Balkan region. Although the czar was convinced that Germany would fight, he had also been assured through diplomatic channels that France would support Russia.

Consequently, on July 30, Czar **Nicholas II** ordered a general mobilization of his armed forces against both Austria-Hungary and Germany. Austria-Hungary mobilized against Russia the following day. Once Russia's intentions were clear, France and Great Britain showed their hands.

On July 31, Germany issued Russia an ultimatum to cancel its mobilization order or face war. On the same day, Germany also delivered an ultimatum to France. France had 18 hours to decide whether or not it would remain neutral if Germany went to war with Russia. France's answer was to give its support to Russia. When Czar Nicholas did not even reply to Germany's ultimatum, Germany declared war on Russia on August 1. Two days later, Germany declared war on France as well.

The British, meanwhile, were divided on the question of going to war. They still hoped to avoid conflict through negotiations. They did not make it clear whether or not they would support France and Russia. Germany hoped that Great Britain would stay neutral.

The same day that Germany declared war on Russia, however, the German army marched into Luxembourg. The Germans then demanded passage across Belgium, claiming that France intended to invade that country at any moment. Belgium was a neutral country whose borders and neutrality had been guaranteed in an 1839 treaty signed by Great Britain, Russia, France, and Germany.

The Belgians refused the Germans entry into their territory and appealed to Great Britain for help. When the Germans went ahead and invaded Belgium on August 3, Britain protested and sent an ultimatum to the German government that demanded withdrawal of German forces from Belgium. The German chancellor responded by calling the 1839 treaty "a scrap of paper." This left the British little choice. On August 4, Britain declared war on Germany.

The outbreak of war in August 1914 was generally greeted with confidence and rejoicing by the peoples of Europe. In an outburst of patriotic enthusiasm, crowds gathered in the streets, squares, and railway stations of European cities to cheer on the military forces of their respective nations. As the conflict unfolded, most Europeans believed in the war as a matter of defending their country's honor or upholding "right against might."

Few people, however, imagined how long or how devastating a war between the powers of Europe could be. Designed to protect nations against their enemies, the European alliance systems instead dragged a whole continent into war. What began as a local dispute between Austria-Hungary and Serbia eventually became a global conflict that had no clear, limited objective.

SECTION 2 REVIEW

Recall
1. **Define** ultimatum, mobilization.
2. **Identify** Francis Ferdinand, Gavrilo Princip, William II, Nicholas II.
3. **Locate** Serbia on the map on page 518. How did Serbia's location affect its relations with Austria-Hungary?

Critical Thinking
4. **Evaluating Information** Historians have long argued over which European nation was most responsible for the start of World War I. Using examples to support your statements, explain which country you think was most responsible for the war.

Understanding Themes
5. **Conflict** Why do you think World War I came as a surprise to many Europeans?

Chapter 17   *World War I*   519

SECTION 2 REVIEW ANSWERS

1. The words are defined in the Glossary.
2. Francis Ferdinand, 517; Gavrilo Princip, 518; William II, 518; Nicholas II, 519
3. Overshadowed by its neighbor, Serbia was either dependent on Austria-Hungary for protection or vulnerable to attack.
4. Answers will vary. Possibilities: Austria-Hungary, because of its rigid ultimatum; Germany, because of the tacit permission it gave Austria-Hungary.
5. **CONFLICT** The period preceding it was one of optimism. Europeans were proud of their material progress. Also, there had been no major wars since the time of Napoleon.

Time Line Have students create a time line on the chalkboard listing events from the assassination of Francis Ferdinand (June 28) to Britain's declaration of war against Germany (August 4). **L2**

Independent Practice

📁 Guided Reading Activity 17-2 **L1**

Biography Have students research Gavrilo Princip and write a short biographical sketch of him, including what happened to him after the assassination of Archduke Francis Ferdinand. **L2**

ASSESS

Check for Understanding

Assign Section 2 Review as homework or as an in-class activity.

🔘 Use Student Self-Test and Review Software to review Section 2.

Evaluate

📁 Section Quiz 17-2

🔘 Use the Testmaker to create a customized quiz for Section 2.

Reteach

Have students recount in their own words the causes of World War I.

Enrich

Have students write an essay on how World War I might have been avoided.

CLOSE

Have students discuss why the Balkans have been called "the powder keg of Europe."

| 1914 | 1915 | 1916 | 1917 |

1914 French and German armies collide in the Battle of the Marne.

1915 German submarine sinks British passenger liner *Lusitania*.

1916 Allies withdraw forces from the Gallipoli Peninsula.

1917 American newspapers publish the Zimmermann telegram.

SECTION THEME

▶ **Conflict** The European war is transformed into a war that engulfs much of the world; the global conflict directly affects many civilians as well as soldiers.

Find Out

Answer: *the Western and Eastern Fronts in Europe, in western Asia, and at sea; infantry attacks, trench warfare, naval battles, blockades, tanks, airplanes, and submarines*

FOCUS

Section Objective

Specify where and how World War I was fought.

BELLRINGER
Motivational Activity

Before taking roll at the beginning of the class period, project Section Focus Transparency 17-3 and have students answer the activity questions. Discuss students' responses.

☐ This activity is also available as a blackline master.

Vocabulary Pre-check

☐ Use the Vocabulary PuzzleMaker to create a puzzle that reinforces the vocabulary terms in this section. **L1**

Section 3

The War

Setting the Scene

▶ **Terms to Define**
belligerent, propaganda, war of attrition, trench, contraband

▶ **People to Meet**
Alfred von Schlieffen, Helmuth von Moltke, Joseph Jacques Joffre, Henri-Philippe Pétain, Winston Churchill, Woodrow Wilson

▶ **Places to Locate**
Paris, Tannenberg, Verdun, Gallipoli

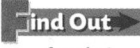  **F**ind Out Where and how was World War I fought?

The Storyteller

François was only 8 years old when war's realities entered his small French village. Gendarmes delivered the official notice of death on the field of honor to the towns, villages, and farms. A hush fell when the names were read. Then the word spread. "Gustave was killed, the little clerk who had looked so handsome in his cavalryman's uniform. Alcide, Jules, Léon, Maurice, Rèmi, Raoul—all killed." In horror, François watched his neighbors' grief. Childhood playmates, cousins, the only sons of families, and brothers all perished in battle. "They remained on their battlefields in the great military cemeteries, neat and orderly, hidden forever."

French soldiers in the trenches

—adapted from "World War I: A Frenchman's Recollections," reprinted in *The Global Experience*, vol. 2, 1987

By August 1914 the major powers of Europe had lined up against each other. Germany and Austria-Hungary, joined by the Ottoman Empire and Bulgaria, became known as the Central Powers. Great Britain, France, Russia, Serbia, Belgium, and, later, Japan and Montenegro, became known as the Allied Powers, or Allies. Claiming that Austria-Hungary and Germany had acted aggressively rather than defensively, Italy remained neutral.

In spite of their military buildups, none of the European powers was fully prepared for what lay ahead. For example, cavalry and horse-drawn vehicles still played an important role in each nation's army—traditions that were quickly discarded. Nations from both sides also seriously underestimated the length of the war. No country had stockpiled enough war materials or ammunition to last more than six months. The widespread feeling among Europeans was that the war would be over by Christmas.

The Schlieffen Plan

Germany's invasion of Belgium on August 3 had been part of the Schlieffen Plan, a war strategy that German General **Alfred von Schlieffen** (SHLEE•fuhn) drew up in 1905. Germany's main problem was that it had enemies in both the east and the west. Schlieffen assumed, however, that Russia would be slow to mobilize. As a result, Schlieffen believed that the Germans could reach Paris and defeat the French in six weeks and then move on to the Eastern Front and fight against Russian forces.

Schlieffen's plan ran into problems from the beginning. First, German Commander **Helmuth von Moltke** led his troops through an area of Belgium that proved to be heavily fortified. Second, Moltke encountered far stronger resistance than anyone had expected; the German advance was

520 Chapter 17 *World War I*

SECTION RESOURCES

📁 Reproducible Masters
• Reproducible Lesson Plan 17-3
• Guided Reading Activity 17-3
• History Simulation 17
• Geography and History Activity 17
• Section Quiz 17-3

📊 Transparencies
• Section Focus Transparency 17-3
• Mapping History Overlay Transparency 18, *World War I*
• World History and Art Transparencies 36, 37

Multimedia
☐ Vocabulary PuzzleMaker Software
☐ Student Self-Test and Review Software
☐ Testmaker
◉ Lessons of War:
How Wars Begin—World War I

delayed until August 20. Third, the Russian army mobilized far more quickly than Schlieffen had estimated, necessitating the movement of two German divisions to the Eastern Front.

The Germans were held up further when they met British forces in the north of France. British troops eventually had to retreat, but they fought expertly and inflicted heavy losses on the Germans. At the same time, the French attacked another wing of the German army in Alsace-Lorraine. The French offensive eventually collapsed but not before delaying the German advance yet again.

The Battle of the Marne

France struggled to recover after the defeat at Alsace-Lorraine. The French chief of command, General **Joseph Jacques Joffre**, pulled back his troops to protect **Paris**. While many Parisians fled the city, General Joseph Simon Gallieni strengthened the army in Paris to the point that it was able to launch a counterattack. To speed troops into position, the French army requisitioned several hundred Parisian taxis.

On September 5 the French and German armies collided in northeastern France in the Battle of the Marne. After four days of shelling, the French finally pushed the Germans back a distance of about 50 miles (80 km) from Paris. The attack saved Paris from the Germans and boosted French morale. Although German forces continued to hold much of France's heavily industrialized areas, the German retreat from the Battle of the Marne signified the abandonment of the Schlieffen Plan. It also made it clear that neither side was capable of defeating the other quickly or easily.

A Russian Disaster

Russia, meanwhile, kept its word to the French and sent troops into battle even before its military was fully mobilized. The speed with which the Russians moved surprised Germany and Austria-Hungary. By August 13 the Russians had invaded East Prussia from the south and from the east. This attack diverted German troops from the attack against the French and British during the first critical weeks of the war.

Russia's success did not last long. At the end of August, Russian and German troops met at **Tannenberg** in present-day Poland. There the Russians suffered a disastrous defeat from which they never fully recovered. At Tannenberg, the Germans were able to encircle and destroy the Russian army. They killed more than 30,000 Russian soldiers and took 92,000 prisoners. German casualties numbered only about 13,000.

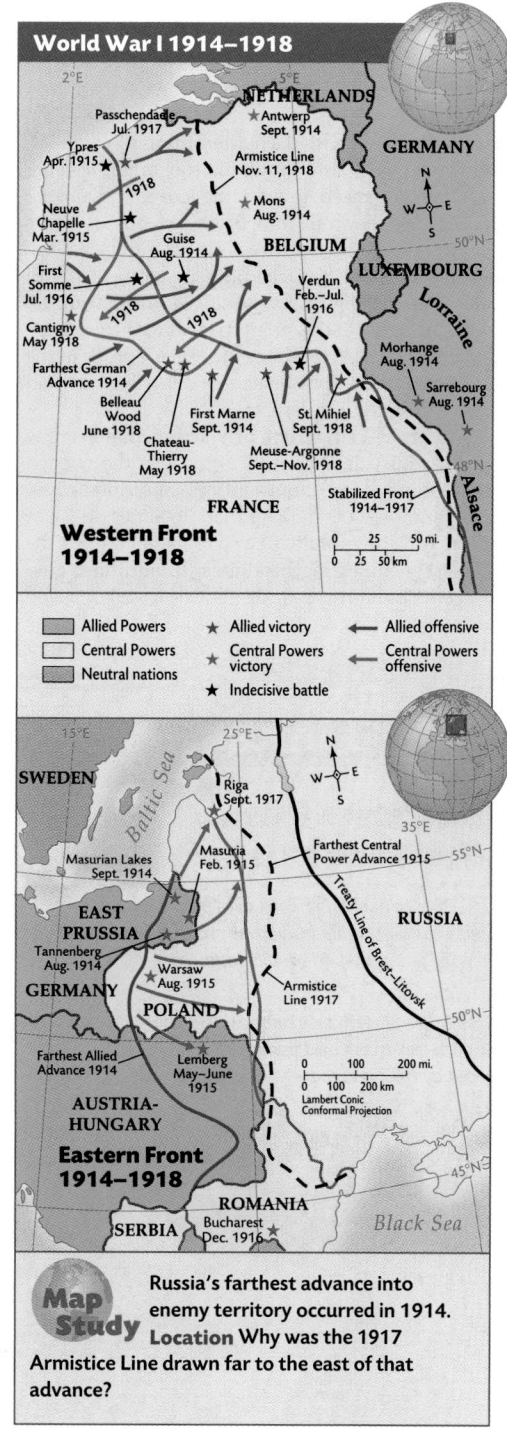

World War I 1914–1918

Western Front 1914–1918

Allied Powers · ★ Allied victory · ← Allied offensive
Central Powers · ★ Central Powers victory · ← Central Powers offensive
Neutral nations · ★ Indecisive battle

Eastern Front 1914–1918

Map Study Russia's farthest advance into enemy territory occurred in 1914. **Location** Why was the 1917 Armistice Line drawn far to the east of that advance?

TEACH

Guided Practice

THEME Conflict

Have students write several reasons trench warfare was so deadly. Discuss these reasons as a class. Focus especially on how trench warfare resulted in a state of deadlock. (*Machine guns made successful offenses almost impossible; neither side had a way to break through the other's lines.*) **L1**

Military History Have students explain the significance of the Battle of the Marne. (*It signified the end of the Schlieffen Plan and also showed that the war would not end quickly.*) **L2 LEP**

Geography: Location Ask students why they think the Germans attacked the Allies through Belgium rather than more directly across Alsace and Lorraine. (*France probably expected a German attack from the east and so fortified its eastern boundary more heavily than its northern border with Belgium. Also, Alsace and Lorraine, once French, might have been more hostile to the Germans than Belgium was.*) **L3 LEP**

Map Study

Answer
By 1917 the Central Powers had pushed the front that far to the east.

Map Skills Practice

Reading a Map What aspects of fighting on the Western Front did not characterize the Eastern Front? (*indecisive battles, a stabilized front*)

COOPERATIVE LEARNING ACTIVITY

Report Have students research and present an oral report on the first six weeks of World War I. Assign each of five groups one of the following: the invasion of Belgium, the German sweep through France toward Paris, the retreat of the Allies, Russian mobilization and early victories ending at Tannenberg, and the Battle of the Marne. Individual students should gather information on a specific topic within his or her group. Then ask each group to present its report to create a composite picture. **L2**

History Simulation 17

 World History and Art Transparency 36, *Three Musicians*; 37, *I Want You for the U.S. Army*

Mapping History Overlay Transparency 18, *World War I*

ABCNEWS INTERACTIVE™

VIDEODISC
Lessons of War

Side One, Chapter 5
Frames 11214–15727
Title: *How Wars Begin—World War I*
Subject: Exploration of the reasons behind war, specifically World War I
Ask: What did Germany wish to accomplish in World War I? *(Germany wanted to become a world power.)* What did Austria-Hungary want to acquire? Who helped them to accomplish this? *(Austria-Hungary wanted to acquire Serbian territory and asked Germany for help.)*

Biography

The following videotape program is available from Glencoe:

- **Red Baron: Master of the Air**

Years of Deadlock

After the Battle of the Marne, the Germans and the Allies began a series of battles known as "the race to the sea," with each attempting to reach the North Sea first and outflank the other. As the Germans advanced toward the ports of Dunkirk and Calais, they ran into British troops at Ypres (EEPR), a town in southwestern Belgium. The battle that followed brought high casualties to both sides. Despite the heavy sacrifices, there were no breakthroughs. At this point the war in the west settled into a stable front from the Swiss border to the North Sea coast. By November 1914 the war had already reached a stalemate.

All of the belligerent, or warring, nations now had to adjust their plans. To produce the needed ships, guns, food, ammunition, and medicines, large numbers of civilians had to enter the war effort. To raise morale, newspapers gave even the smallest victories big headlines. In addition, governments used propaganda—ideas or rumors used to harm an opposing cause—to portray the enemy as beastly and inhuman. Making peace with such an enemy seemed unthinkable.

Trench Warfare

By early 1915 the war on the Western Front had turned into a deadly war of attrition, in which each side tried to wear down the other side by constant attacks. To protect themselves, soldiers on both

Footnotes to History

Holiday Cheer
On Christmas Day, 1914, fighting stopped, and British and German soldiers met in "no-man's-land" to chat, play soccer, and pose for photographs! Officers, however, quickly ended these goodwill meetings, and the soldiers returned to their positions to take up firing at one another again.

Images of the Times

Industry Generates War Materials

More than any previous war, World War I demanded large-scale industrial production of military and transportation equipment.

This German officer's helmet and the English gas mask and pack were produced by their respective war industries.

522

Images of the Times
Industry Generates War Materials

The Allies faced problems in supplying their troops because they had expected the war to be short and mobile. But when soldiers dug in on the Western Front, they needed much larger quantities of war materials, especially ammunition, than had been foreseen. Not only were supplies short, but hundreds of the skilled male workers needed to produce more shells had volunteered for or been drafted into the army. For many of the warring nations, women workers provided vital help in war industries.

sides dug trenches, or ditches. Eventually, two parallel trenches stretched for about 500 miles (805 km) in an unbroken line from Switzerland to the North Sea. Land mines and barbed wire protected the area in front of each trench. The desolate area that separated the two sides, which could vary from a half a mile to a few yards, was known as "no-man's-land."

Soldiers lived in the trenches for weeks at a time, fighting boredom and terror. They endured cold, mud, rats, and disease. To attack, the soldiers charged "over the top" of their own trenches and ran across "no man's land" to the enemy's trenches. As attackers struggled through the barbed wire, their opponents mowed them down with heavy artillery and machine guns.

Throughout 1915, battle followed battle, and casualties mounted. At the battle of Ypres, the Germans introduced a new weapon—poison gas. From cylinders in their trenches, they released yellow-green chlorine gas. The wind carried the gas into French trenches, causing blindness, choking, vomiting, torn lungs, and death. Wilfred

Owen, an English poet and soldier, described the horrors of poison gas in his poem "Dulce et Decorum Est" (1916):

“ Gas! Gas! Quick, boys!—An ecstasy of
   fumbling,
Fitting the clumsy helmets just in time;
But someone still was yelling out and
   stumbling
And flound'ring like a man in fire or lime …
Dim, through the misty panes and thick
   green light,
As under a green sea, I saw him drowning. ”

Verdun and the Somme

The year 1916 opened with the war on the Western Front still stalemated. Although Italy had denounced the Central Powers six months earlier and entered the war on the side of the Allies, it had gained little ground after four battles against the Austro-Hungarians. Then in February 1916, the Germans made a move. They staged a surprise

Who?What?Where?When?

"Dulce et Decorum Est" The title of Wilfred Owen's poem is the first phrase of a line from the Latin poet Horace, "Dulce et decorum est pro patria mori," meaning "It is sweet and honorable to die for one's country." Owen's use is ironic—fitting for a man who himself was killed on the battlefield.

Independent Practice

📁 Guided Reading Activity 17-3 **L1**

📁 Geography and History Activity 17

Science, Technology, and Society Have students research and report on the use of poison gas in World War I—the different types used, when and where employed, effects, and effectiveness. **L2**

Who?What?Where?When?

Edith Cavell, an English nurse working in Belgium, was an Allied heroine of World War I. After the Germans occupied the country, she helped Belgian, French, and British soldiers escape. Arrested in 1915, she confessed and was sentenced to die by the firing squad. Her execution in October, though legally justified, aroused worldwide condemnation.

Propaganda Have students research and report on the propaganda issued by both sides during World War I. If possible, they should bring examples, such as posters, to class. **L2**

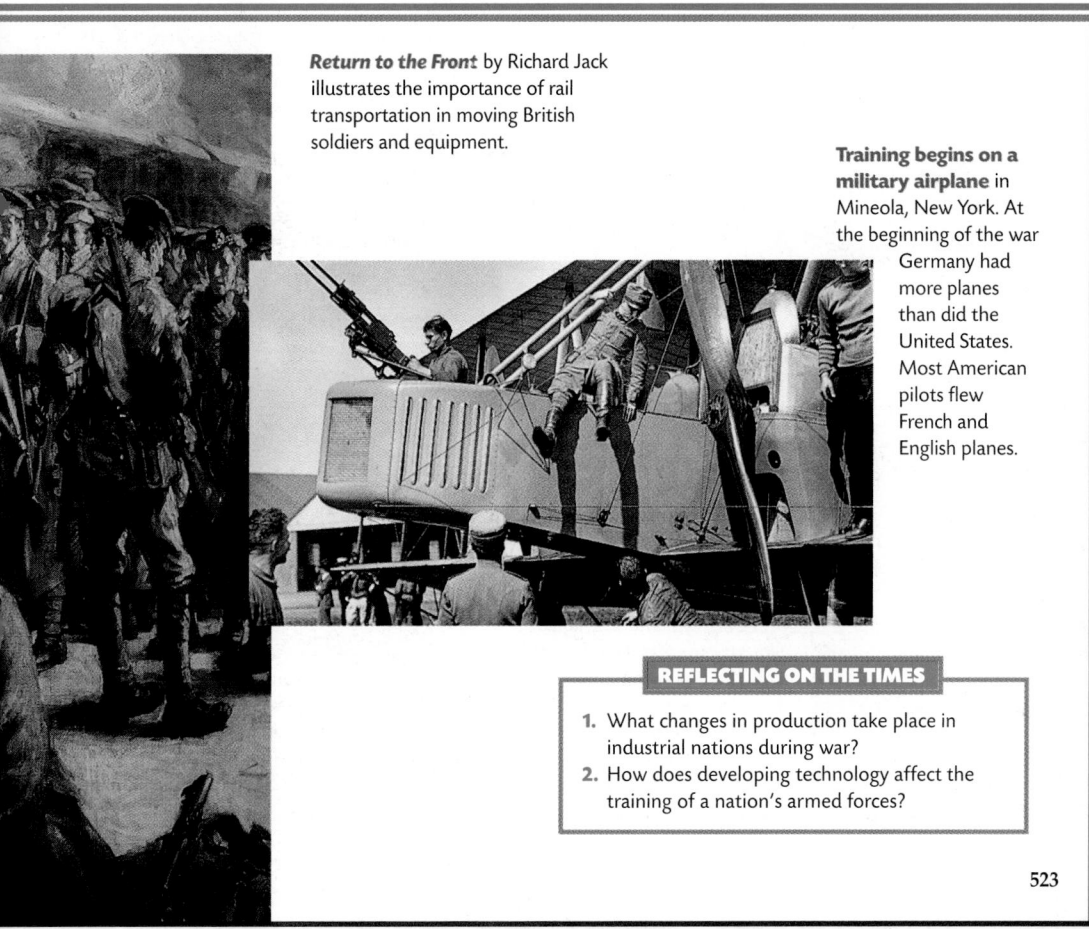

Return to the Front by Richard Jack illustrates the importance of rail transportation in moving British soldiers and equipment.

Training begins on a military airplane in Mineola, New York. At the beginning of the war Germany had more planes than did the United States. Most American pilots flew French and English planes.

REFLECTING ON THE TIMES

1. What changes in production take place in industrial nations during war?
2. How does developing technology affect the training of a nation's armed forces?

523

ANSWERS TO REFLECTING ON THE TIMES

1. They must switch from making peacetime goods to meeting wartime needs. They have to do so quickly, since lives are at stake.
2. Troops must be trained in the use of new and unfamiliar technologies; specialization is often the result, with specific personnel trained to use specific equipment.

Literature Have students read the entire Owen poem, "Dulce et Decorum Est,"and comment on its meaning. In particular, ask them to speculate what effect Owen hoped to achieve through his choice of title. **L3**

you don't say...

Blimp The German dirigibles known as zeppelins, which were used to drop bombs on London, had their counterpart in British balloons known as blimps. The English word comes from the original designation—*B* for balloon and *limp* indicating that the gas bag was not rigid, having no metal framework.

Linking Past and Present

Flaming Coffins

Because World War I aircraft were so vulnerable, the men who flew them were widely admired. Pilots who shot down five enemy planes were known as "aces." Among the best-known aces of the war were Georges Guynemer of France, Manfred von Richthofen of Germany, "Mick" Mannock of England, and Eddie Rickenbacker of the United States.

ANSWERS

They were flimsily built and had no brakes. There was no radio communication, either. Modern planes are safer, faster, and more maneuverable, with jet engines, thinner and flatter wings, and heat-resistant materials.

---

attack against French forces at **Verdun**, a massive fortress in northeastern France on the Meuse River. The French, under General **Henri-Philippe Pétain** (PAY•TAN), rallied to the cry "They shall not pass." After six months, the French still held firm, and the Germans finally abandoned the attack. The Battle of Verdun was one of the bloodiest of the war. Before the struggle ended, both sides had suffered more than a half-million casualties.

Later that year, the British, aided by a small French force, launched a similar offensive against the Germans in the Somme River valley in northern France. The Battle of the Somme turned out to be as terrible and inconclusive as the one at Verdun, costing the Germans about 500,000 men, the British 400,000, and the French 200,000. Although the British introduced another new weapon during this battle—an armored vehicle called the tank—it made little difference to the outcome of the struggle. Tanks were still too clumsy and slow to be an effective weapon, and the generals on both sides did not yet understand how best to use them.

The Eastern Front

The Eastern Front in Russia was less entrenched than the Western Front in France; the war there was far more mobile, involving constant changes in battlefield positions. Neither side, however, was able to achieve a complete victory.

In 1915 Germany and Austria-Hungary made determined efforts to remove Russia from the war. As the least industrialized of the European powers, Russia did not have the resources and skills to fight a modern conflict. By year's end, the Russians had been forced to give up territory greater than the whole of France. In addition to suffering a staggering number of casualties, they had lost ammunition and guns equal to the amount they had possessed when the war began. The Allies, however, had promised Russia control of Constantinople and the Dardanelles if their side won the war.

Inspired by this agreement, the Russians went to work rebuilding their army. In March 1916 they launched an offensive against the Germans but made little headway. A few months later, however, they fared much better against Austria-Hungary. In addition to capturing many cities, they took several hundred thousand prisoners. They paid a heavy toll in the process, however, losing more than a million men and most of their supplies.

Although morale in the Russian army suffered greatly as a result of the 1916 offenses, their efforts

---

CONNECTIONS
Science and Technology

Flaming Coffins

Airplanes added a new dimension to fighting in World War I. For the first time, combat took place not only on land and at sea but also in the air. Crude but operational, these noisy, pitching, and bucking machines were not built with the pilot's safety foremost in mind. The typical plane was made of thin wood reinforced by steel wire. Its body and wings were covered by cloth coated with a highly flammable liquid. The pilot sat on a seat directly over the fuel tank. Fire was such a constant danger that airplanes were often referred to as "flaming coffins."

Battle between German and British planes

Brakes did not exist on World War I-era planes. On takeoff, the crew had to hold the plane back while the pilot revved the engine. On landing, the pilot had to turn the engine off and on to slow the approach. Once the pilot was airborne, contact with the ground was possible only if an unwieldy Morse code transmitter was on board.

Today, military aircraft are safer, faster, and more maneuverable. For example, the development of jet engines has enabled planes to fly much faster than before. Other recent innovations increasing the speed and range of planes include the development of thinner and flatter wings and the use of more effective heat-resistant materials.

Linking Past and Present **ACTIVITY**

In what sense were World War I airplanes "crude" vehicles? Compare World War I-era military aircraft with that of today.

MEETING SPECIAL NEEDS ACTIVITY

Mixed Learners Encourage students needing extra reinforcement to summarize the material under each subhead in this section in a manner of their own choosing. Some students may elect to prepare oral summaries. Students may be divided into small groups. Each group would assign a subsection to pairs of students who would prepare the summaries.

Visual learners might draw a series of cartoons depicting such subjects as the battles, the weapons used, or trench warfare. Gifted students may use outside resources to enhance their summaries. This activity may be done in groups or individually. **L2 LEP**

Visualizing
History These heavy guns were not enough to overcome the resistance of the Turks at Gallipoli. *What were Churchill's three main goals in attacking Turkey?*

helped the Allies on the Western Front. The Germans had to transfer several divisions from the west to the east, hampering the effectiveness of their attack at Verdun.

Gallipoli Campaign

As the war dragged on and casualties soared, each side tried to find ways to turn the war in its favor. In Great Britain, First Lord of the Admiralty **Winston Churchill**—head of the British navy—asked, "Are there not other alternatives than sending our armies to chew barbed wire in Flanders?" Churchill favored opening an offensive on the Dardanelles strait, which Turkey controlled. This strait was the only practical means of supplying Russia and of strengthening Serbia. From there, the Allies could take Constantinople and possibly put the Ottoman Empire out of the war. This offensive, Churchill believed, might also lead to the collapse of Austria-Hungary.

Churchill's idea had merit. The Allies' initial offensive in early 1915 nearly succeeded, but a lack of coordination, planning, and reinforcements gave

the Turks time to rearm. When the Allies followed up in April with a land attack on the peninsula of **Gallipoli** (guh•LIH•puh•lee), the Turks drove them back. On January 9, 1916, the Allies finally gave up the effort and withdrew the last of their troops from the area.

On the Seas

The British, meanwhile, had been using their naval superiority to dominate the seas. They were determined to keep the Germans from invading Great Britain and to keep war materials from reaching the Central Powers by sea. The Germans were just as determined to disrupt Allied shipping. Both Great Britain and Germany depended heavily on the seas for their food and war materials. Without those goods, neither country could continue the war.

Great Britain blockaded all ports under German control at the start of the war. The blockade was so effective that Germany had to receive most of its supplies through the neutral countries of Holland, Denmark, Sweden, and Norway. The

Chapter 17 *World War I* **525**

TEACH

Tell students that the main line of trenches on the Western Front was established by November 1914. It ran almost 500 miles from the North Sea to Switzerland. One reason it became relatively fixed as soon as it did was that both sides were too exhausted and too short of war materials to launch major offensives in the fall; over the winter, troops had an opportunity to dig in and make their positions more defensible. Ask students why both sides were in such bad shape after only four months of war. *(They expected a short war and had not stockpiled enough arms and ammunition.)*

Linking Past and Present

Gallipoli One of the most effective movies ever made about World War I is *Gallipoli* (1981). It tells the story of two Australian soldiers who take part in the unsuccessful Allied attack on the Turkish peninsula.

Hulton Picture Company

In the Trenches

In the Dardanelles Campaign of 1915 these soldiers of the British Empire fought to capture Gallipoli. Held by the Ottoman Empire, Gallipoli was a strategic location for supplying Russia and the Eastern Front of the war. These troops have hastily dug a trench on their way up a hillside. There they could make use of periscopes and wait for their officers to decide whether they should go "over the top." Three of the men in this photo are Australian. The heavy losses sustained by Australian troops in the Gallipoli Campaign fostered a new sense of Australian identity.

It was on the Western Front, however, in France and Belgium, that trench warfare was most gruesome. In ditches and tunnels called trenches the armies of the Allies and the Central Powers settled into a war of position. The units of horse cavalry that had pranced proudly into war were replaced by foot soldiers hunkered into trenches, facing the enemy across a no-man's-land of barbed wire. Stuck in mud and water, soldiers lived alongside lice and rats amid the smell of dead horses and dead men. It was a war, British poet Wilfred Owen wrote, "obscene as cancer" and "bitter as ... vile." ⊕

Germans protested that the blockade violated international law and called it "the hunger blockade." Ignoring these protests, the British also stopped ships they suspected of carrying contraband, or prohibited goods. They escorted these ships into port and seized their cargoes.

Submarine Warfare

To wear down British sea power, the Germans introduced submarine warfare. At first, German submarines, or U-boats, struck only warships. In 1915 they also began to strike civilian and commercial ships, many of which were carrying supplies to the Allies. In May 1915 a German U-boat torpedoed the British passenger liner *Lusitania*. About 1,200 people, including 128 Americans, were killed. The Germans justified the attack, arguing the *Lusitania* carried weapons.

By March 1916, German U-boats had sunk other British and French ships. This led President **Woodrow Wilson** to issue an ultimatum to the Germans. He threatened to sever diplomatic relations if Germany did not agree to stop attacking passenger and freight vessels. The Germans responded by ending unrestricted submarine warfare for a while.

In May 1916, the only major battle between the British and German fleets took place off the coast of Denmark. Both sides claimed victory, but the Battle of Jutland as it was called still left the British in control of the seas and the Germans bound by the British blockade.

United States Enters War

One of the most important events of 1917 was the decision of the United States to enter the war. Until this point, American public opinion was divided about the conflict in Europe. For example, many Irish Americans were staunchly anti-British, and many German Americans sided with the Central Powers. Many other Americans, mostly of English, Scottish, and Scots Irish descent, favored the Allies. The majority of Americans, however, agreed with President Woodrow Wilson that the war was strictly a European conflict. While incidents such as the sinking of the *Lusitania* in 1915 angered them, Americans were not ready to take an active part in the war.

Meanwhile, in Europe, the Germans did not want the Americans to enter the war. At the same time, they were determined to break the British blockade and end British control of the seas. They believed that the way to do this was by resuming a policy of unrestricted submarine warfare. As a result, Germany announced that beginning February 1, 1917, it would sink any merchant ships heading to British or western European ports. President Wilson responded by breaking off diplomatic relations with Germany.

Tensions between the two countries grew worse in March 1917 when American newspapers printed the Zimmermann telegram, a message from the German foreign minister, Arthur Zimmermann, to his ambassador in Mexico. Zimmermann promised that, in return for Mexican support, Germany would help Mexico to regain New Mexico, Texas, and Arizona. The British had passed on the Zimmermann telegram to the American government, and the message's publication heightened anti-German attitudes in the United States.

After the German sinking of four American merchant ships, President Wilson on April 2, 1917, asked Congress for a declaration of war and called upon Americans to help "make the world safe for democracy." American financial aid and military intervention would tip the scales in favor of an eventual Allied victory.

SECTION 3 REVIEW

Recall
1. **Define** belligerent, propaganda, war of attrition, trench, contraband.
2. **Identify** Alfred von Schlieffen, Helmuth von Moltke, Joseph Jacques Joffre, Henri-Philippe Pétain, Winston Churchill, Woodrow Wilson.

3. **Locate** Gallipoli and the Dardanelles on the map on page 518. Why was an Allied military campaign carried out there?

Critical Thinking
4. **Synthesizing Information** Create your own strategy for avoiding a stalemate in trench warfare. Determine the main

factors working against a breakthrough in this type of warfare.

Understanding Themes
5. **Conflict** Explain how World War I was a new kind of war. Consider objectives, strategy, and technology in the course of your explanation.

Chapter 17 *World War I* 527

United States Enters War
How did American entry into World War I affect the conflict? *It added military and economic strength to the Allies at a time when they were being exhausted by the fighting.*

Use the Testmaker to create a customized quiz for Section 3.

Reteach

Discuss the following topics with students: the major events on the Western Front, on the Eastern Front, and at sea; technological advances used, and their effects; events prior to and following the entrance of the United States into the war.

Enrich

Have students read Mark Helprin's *A Soldier of the Great War* for a vivid account of an Italian soldier's experiences. Have them select several passages and present an oral reading in class.

CLOSE

Have students summarize the situations of the Allies and the Central Powers in the spring of 1917. *(The prospect of victory was slim for both sides at this point.)*

SECTION 3 REVIEW ANSWERS

1. All vocabulary words are defined in the Glossary.
2. Alfred von Schlieffen, 520; Helmuth von Moltke, 520; Joseph Jacques Joffre, 521; Henri Pétain, 524; Winston Churchill, 525; Woodrow Wilson, 527
3. An Allied offensive through the Gallipoli Peninsula and the Dardanelles was the

only means of supplying Russia and of strengthening Serbia.
4. Answers will vary but should show an understanding of trench warfare.
5. **CONFLICT** Old strategies did not take into account the contingencies of war and surprise moves by the enemy. In World War I, strategists had

to react to many new situations as they arose; new technology—machine guns, land mines, submarines, tanks, airplanes—made it possible to kill people in unprecedented numbers.

Special Report Summary

In 1915 a German submarine sank the British luxury liner *Lusitania*, killing more than 1,000 people and helping draw the United States into World War I.

To clear up questions about the sinking, scientists used a robot vehicle to examine the wreck on the ocean floor.

Although the ship was carrying arms, the team found that the weapons had not exploded when a torpedo struck the *Lusitania*. This disproved a once-popular theory of why the ship sank so fast.

The team hypothesized that the powerful secondary explosion that caused the ship to sink in only 18 minutes was probably caused by the ignition of coal dust in a storage compartment.

Bettmann

The Lusitania

Passengers boarding the British liner R.M.S. *Lusitania* in New York on May 1, 1915, for the voyage to Liverpool, England, knew of Germany's threat to sink ships bound for the British Isles. England and Germany had been fighting for nine months. Still, few passengers imagined that a civilized nation would attack an unarmed passenger steamer without warning.

Built eight years earlier, the *Lusitania* was described as a "floating palace." German authorities, however, saw her as a threat. They accused the British government of using the *Lusitania* to carry ammunition and other war materials across the Atlantic.

With her four towering funnels, the liner looked invincible as she left New York on her last voyage. Six days later, at 2:10 p.m. on May 7, 1915, Walther Schwieger, the 30-year-old commander of the German submarine U 20, fired a single torpedo at the *Lusitania* from a range of about 750 yards.

Captain William Turner of the *Lusitania* saw the torpedo's wake from the navigation bridge just before impact. It sounded like a "million-ton hammer hitting a steam boiler a hundred feet high," one passenger said. A second, more powerful explosion followed, sending a geyser of water, coal, and debris high above the deck.

Listing to starboard, the liner began to sink rapidly at the bow, sending passengers tumbling down her slanted decks. Lifeboats on the port side were hanging too far inboard to be readily launched, while those on the starboard side

528 **Chapter 17** *World War I*

TEACHER NOTES

_____
_____
_____
_____
_____

EVENING EDITION—7:30 O'CLOCK—LATEST

LUSITANIA SUNK

Not Known How Many Passengers Saved

TORPEDOED BY GERMANS, REMAINED AFLOAT 12 HOURS

Titanic Historical Society Inc.

TEACH

Points to Discuss

After students have read the feature, ask the following: **Why did the sinking of the *Lusitania* anger many Americans?** *(because sinking the unarmed passenger vessel killed more than 1,000 civilians, including 123 Americans)* **What questions were raised about the sinking?** *(Was the ship warned about German submarines? Why did one torpedo sink it so fast? Was it armed, as Germany claimed? What caused a second explosion?)* **What did researchers learn by examining the wreck with a robot vehicle?** *(They found that weapons carried by the* Lusitania *had not exploded, and they hypothesized that the second explosion was caused by the ignition of coal dust.)*

were too far out to be easily boarded. Several overfilled lifeboats spilled occupants into the sea. The great liner disappeared under the waves in only 18 minutes, leaving behind a jumble of swimmers, corpses, deck chairs, and wreckage. Looking back upon the scene from his submarine, even German commander Schwieger was shocked. He later called it the most horrible sight he had ever seen.

News of the disaster raced across the Atlantic. Of 1,959 people aboard, only 764 were saved. The dead included 94 children and infants.

Questions were immediately raised. Did the British Admiralty

give the *Lusitania* adequate warning? How could one torpedo have sunk her? Why did she go down so fast? Was there any truth to the German claim that the *Lusitania* had been armed?

From the moment the *Lusitania* sank, she was surrounded by controversy. Americans were outraged by the attack, which claimed the lives of 128 U.S. citizens. Newspapers called the attack "deliberate murder" and a "foul deed," and former President Theodore Roosevelt demanded revenge against Germany. The attack on the *Lusitania* is often credited with drawing the United States into

🔲 **The Lusitania *arrives in New York on her maiden voyage in 1907 (opposite page).***

🔲 **In the two days prior to the attack on the Lusitania, the German submarine U 20 had sunk three ships off Ireland's southern coast. Yet the captain of the Lusitania, who had received warnings by wireless from the British Admiralty, took only limited precautions as he approached the area. Headlines in Boston and New York report the terrible news of the sinking of the Lusitania on May 7, 1915 (above).***

Chapter 17 *World War I* **529**

- Woodrow Wilson's secretary of state, William Jennings Bryan, resigned rather than sign a strongly worded protest Wilson sent to Germany after the *Lusitania*'s sinking.
- The name of the ship came from the ancient Roman province of Lusitania, which made up the region that is now Portugal and western Spain.
- The cargo of arms and ammunition that the *Lusitania* was carrying weighed about 173 tons.
- The British admiralty had recommended that the *Lusitania* follow a zigzag course, changing direction every few minutes, to avoid torpedo attacks.

Linking Past and Present

Shipwrecks In recent years a number of wrecked ships have been raised from the ocean bottom by scientists and entrepreneurs. The salvage operations have generated controversy about the ownership of the materials recovered, which can be worth millions of dollars.

Among the better-known cases are the Padre Island wrecks in Texas and the case of *Nuestra Señora de la Atocha* in Florida.

CURRICULUM CONNECTION

SCIENCE AND TECHNOLOGY

The first submarine to be used in combat was built by an American, David Bushnell, in 1776, and was used during the Revolutionary War. It was made of wood and moved by means of a hand-turned propeller. (The craft was used in an unsuccessful attempt to blow up a British warship in New York harbor.) By the late 1800s, an American engineer named Simon Lake had made considerable advances in submarine technology, including the use of horizontal rudders for diving and water ballast for submergence. However, the U.S. Navy was slow to see the merits of Lake's work. It wasn't until several European governments had made use of Lake's ideas in the early 1900s that he was hired by the United States.

World War I. President Woodrow Wilson—though he had vowed to hold Germany responsible for its submarine attacks—knew that the American people were not ready to go to war. It was almost two more years before the United States joined the conflict in Europe.

A British judge laid full blame on the German submarine commander, while the German government claimed that the British had deliberately made her a military target. Tragically, inquiries following the sinking of the *Lusitania* revealed that Captain Turner had received warnings by wireless from the British Admiralty, but took only limited precautions as he approached the area where U 20 was waiting.

Rumors of diamonds, gold, and valuables locked away in *Lusitania's* safes have prompted salvage attempts over the years. To date, no treasure has ever been reported.

Perhaps the biggest puzzle has been the hardest to solve: Why did the liner sink so fast? Newspapers speculated that the torpedo had struck ammunition in a cargo hold, causing the strong secondary explosion. Divers later reported a huge hole in the port side of the bow, opposite where munitions would have been stored.

HOPING TO SETTLE the issue, a team from the Woods Hole Oceanographic Institution, sponsored by the National Geographic Society, sent their robot vehicle Jason down to photograph the damage. Fitted with cameras and powerful lights, the robot sent video images of the wreck by fiber-optic cable to a control room on the surface ship, *Northern Horizon*. A pilot maneuvered Jason with a joystick, while an engineer relayed instructions to the robot's computers. Other team members watched for recognizable

objects on the monitors. In addition to using Jason to make a visual survey of the *Lusitania*, the team of researchers and scientists also used sonar to create a computerized, three-dimensional diagram of how the wreck looks today.

From this data, it was discovered that the *Lusitania's* hull had been flattened—in part by the force of gravity—to half its original width. When Jason's cameras swept across the hold, looking for the hole reported by divers shortly after the sinking, there was none to be found. Indeed, no evidence was found that would indicate that the torpedo had detonated an explosion in a cargo hold, undermining one theory of why the liner sank.

Questions about her cargo have haunted the *Lusitania* since the day she went down. Was she carrying illegal munitions as the Germans have always claimed? In fact, she was. The manifest for her last voyage included wartime essentials such as motorcycle parts, metals, cotton goods, and food, as well as 4,200 cases of rifle ammunition, 1,250 cases of shrapnel (not explosive), and 18 boxes of percussion fuses. The investigation conducted by the Woods Hole team and Jason suggested that these munitions did not cause the secondary blast that sent the *Lusitania* to the bottom. So what did?

One likely possibility was a coal-dust explosion. The German torpedo struck the liner's starboard side about ten feet below the waterline, rupturing one of the long coal bunkers that stretched along both sides. If that bunker, mostly empty by the end of the voyage, contained explosive coal dust, the torpedo might have ignited it. That would explain all the coal found scattered on the seafloor near the wreck.

The *Lusitania's* giant funnels have long since turned to rust, an eerie

Brown Brothers

UPI/Bettmann

marine growth covers her hull, and her superstructure is ghostly wreckage. Yet the horror and fascination surrounding the sinking of the great liner live on. With today's high-technology tools, researchers and scientists at Woods Hole and the National Geographic Society have provided another look—and some new answers—to explain the chain of events that ended with the *Lusitania* at the bottom of the sea.

German U-Boat Attacks After the sinking of the *Lusitania*, German submarines continued to torpedo merchant vessels without warning. In March 1910, fearing the United States would enter the war, Germany stopped the attacks. With the war stalemated, however, Germany resumed unrestricted submarine attacks in February 1917, sinking four American ships in just two months. Wilson cited German violations of "freedom of the seas" as a reason for entering the war in April 1917.

ENLIST

Bowman Gray Collection, University of North Carolina, Chapel Hill

Jonathan Blair

Jonathan Blair

◩ Captain William Turner of the Lusitania, (opposite page, top); Walther Schwieger, commander of the German submarine U 20 (opposite page, bottom).

◩ Homer, a small robot, (left) explores a hole in the stern of the Lusitania that was cut by a salvage crew to recover silverware and other items.

◩ *A provocative poster (left) depicted drowning innocents and urged Americans to enlist in the armed forces. For the women pictured above, the image was all too real. Alice Drury (above left) was a young nanny for an American couple on the Lusitania. She and another nanny were caring for the couple's children: Audrey, Stuart, Amy, and Susan. Alice was about to give Audrey a bottle when the torpedo hit. Alice wrapped Audrey in a shawl, grabbed Stuart, and headed for the lifeboats. A crewman loaded Stuart, but when Alice tried to board, the sailor told her it was full. Without a life jacket and with Audrey around her neck, Alice jumped into the water. A woman in the lifeboat grabbed her hair and pulled her aboard. Audrey's parents were rescued too, but Amy, Susan, and the other nanny were lost. Alice and Audrey Lawson Johnston (above right) have remained close ever since.*

you don't say...

"There is such a thing as a man being too proud to fight," President Wilson explained on May 10. Although Wilson had sent several stern diplomatic notes to Germany following the *Lusitania*'s sinking, he had stopped short of delivering an ultimatum that would lead to war. Most Americans were horrified by the attack, but they supported Wilson's measured response.

─── **Portfolio Project** ───

Have students discuss the effect of the *Lusitania*'s sinking on U.S. public opinion. Organize the class into two groups and have each write a short newspaper editorial either for or against going to war with Germany as a result of the attack on the *Lusitania*.

Chapter 17 *World War I* 531

TEACHER NOTES

_____
_____
_____
_____
_____

1916   1918   1920

1917 Czar Nicholas II abdicates.

1918 Bolshevik Russia and Germany sign Treaty of Brest-Litovsk.

1919 Reds and Whites fight civil war.

Section 4

The Russian Revolution

Setting the Scene

▶ **Terms to Define**
provisional government, communism

▶ **People to Meet**
Nicholas II, Grigori Rasputin, Alexander Kerensky, Vladimir Ilyich Lenin, Leon Trotsky

▶ **Places to Locate**
Petrograd, Siberia, Poland, Ukraine

 **ind Out** What events led to the Russian Revolution?

The Storyteller

Thousands filled the hall, waiting for Trotsky's speech. The crowd was tense, waiting. When Trotsky appeared, they applauded, but briefly, so as to hear that much sooner what he would say. Trotsky spoke of current conditions, and then continued. "The Soviet government will give everything the country contains to the poor and the men in the trenches. You, bourgeois, have two fur caps!—give one of them to the soldier, who's freezing in the trenches." The crowd surrounding Trotsky was aroused almost to ecstasy. This, actually, was already an insurrection. A transformation had begun.

Leon Trotsky

—adapted from *The Russian Revolution*, N. N. Sukharov, translated by Joel Carmichael, 1917

World War I proved to be the breaking point for czarist rule in Russia. By 1917, morale in the Russian army had reached bottom. As many as one-fourth of the Russian soldiers, having no weapons of their own, had to pick up the guns of dead soldiers. Inadequate transport made grave food shortages even worse. Almost all of the country's resources went to supply the army, making the human and financial costs of war increasingly unbearable.

A nurse at the Russian front in 1917 described the situation that helped bring about the collapse of the autocracy and the establishment of a Communist state:

❝ Discontent among the masses in Russia is daily becoming more marked. Disparaging statements concerning the Government are being voiced…. "Bring the men home!" "Conclude peace!" "Finish this interminable war once and for all!" Cries such as these penetrate to the cold and hungry soldiers in their bleak earthworks, and begin to echo among them. Now that food has grown scarce in Petrograd (St. Petersburg) and Moscow, disorder takes the shape of riots and insurrections. We are told that mobs of the lower classes parade the streets shouting 'Peace and Bread!' ❞

Fall of the Czar

Events leading to the fall of the czar began to accelerate in the last half of 1916. Czar **Nicholas II** and his wife, Alexandra, had already become unpopular because of the czar's political incompetence and the couple's reliance on the mystic healer **Grigori Rasputin** (ra•SPYOO•tuhn). Wanting to

---

SECTION THEME

▶ **Revolution** Revolution in Russia overthrows the czar and brings Lenin and the Bolsheviks to power.

ind Out

Answer: *Russia's participation in World War I, with its hardships for both soldiers and civilians; the unpopularity of Czar Nicholas II*

FOCUS

Section Objective

Summarize the events that led to the Russian Revolution.

BELLRINGER
Motivational Activity

Before taking roll at the beginning of the class period, project Section Focus Transparency 17-4 and have students answer the activity questions. Discuss students' responses.

📁 This activity is also available as a blackline master.

Vocabulary Pre-check

📁 Use Vocabulary Activity 17 to introduce vocabulary terms.
L1 LEP

SECTION RESOURCES

📁 **Reproducible Masters**
• Reproducible Lesson Plan 17-4
• Vocabulary Activity 17
• Guided Reading Activity 17-4
• Section Quiz 17-4

📝 **Transparencies**
• Section Focus Transparency 17-4

Multimedia
🖥 Student Self-Test and Review Software
🖥 Testmaker
💿 Communism and the Cold War: *Perspectives on Communism*

save the monarchy, two relatives of the czar assisted in killing Rasputin in December 1916.

Rasputin's death did not solve the monarchy's problems. Public anger against the government mounted as a result of food and fuel shortages, and strikes erupted across the country. On March 8, 1917, and for the next few days, hundreds of thousands of men and women gathered in the streets of **Petrograd** (the Russian name given to St. Petersburg). Demanding food and an end to the war, the crowds shouted, "Down with the czar!" On March 11 and 12, the troops the government ordered to put down the riots refused to fire on the crowds. Many soldiers joined the protesters.

When the czar ordered his generals at the front to crush the rebellion, they told him that any troops they might send to the capital would also join the rioters. With the country sinking into chaos, the czar finally abdicated on March 15, ending the 300-year-old Romanov dynasty. The March revolution was a spontaneous uprising of working people and soldiers. It caused the loss of relatively few lives and took place, surprisingly, without the leadership of its revolutionary intellectuals, most of whom were living in exile abroad.

The Provisional Government

After Czar Nicholas II's abdication, political authority in Russia passed into the hands of a temporary central government known as the provisional government. This new regime called for elections later in the year to choose a constituent, or constitutional, assembly. The constituent assembly would then establish a permanent government.

The provisional government, which consisted of middle-class Duma representatives, soon had a rival for power—the Petrograd Soviet of Workers' and Soldiers' Deputies. Members of the Petrograd Soviet were workers and peasants belonging to different socialist groups. The majority were either Mensheviks or Social Revolutionaries, the political heirs of the Populists. A smaller, more radical group was the Bolsheviks.

One man who moved easily between the provisional government and the Petrograd Soviet was **Alexander Kerensky** (keh•REHN•skee). A moderate socialist, Kerensky served first as the provisional government's minister of justice and then as its prime minister. He also belonged to the executive committee of the Petrograd Soviet.

The Petrograd Soviet became a model for the founding of other soviets throughout Russia.

Together, the soviets called for an immediate peace, the transfer of land to the peasants, and the control of factories by workers. As the Russian economy continued to collapse under the war effort, this three-point program gained great popularity among the Russian masses.

In spite of the suffering and anger of the Russian people, however, the provisional government did not withdraw from the war. Desertion, worsening transportation problems, and a drop in already low armament production plagued the Russian army. Preoccupied with war policy, the provisional government could not carry out the social reforms proposed by the soviets. As a result, the government lost much of its popular support, a factor that contributed to its eventual downfall.

Lenin

As the provisional government struggled to maintain order, a variety of revolutionary groups vied to fill the power vacuum. Since their split into two factions in 1903, the Mensheviks and the Bolsheviks had competed for control of Russia's revolutionary movement. By 1917 the Mensheviks far outnumbered the Bolsheviks. Because they believed that a socialist revolution would be the work of the masses, however, the Mensheviks did not make concrete plans to seize control of the Russian government.

The more radical Bolsheviks, on the other hand, believed that a socialist society could be introduced immediately by force. They claimed that a small group of dedicated revolutionaries could carry out the revolution with the help of a relatively small working class and the peasants. They also believed that Russia's revolution would spread worldwide. Their leader, **Vladimir Ilyich Lenin**, urged them to make plans to topple the provisional government from power.

Born in 1870, Lenin came from a middle-class provincial background. When Lenin was in high school, his older brother, Alexander, became involved in a plot to assassinate Czar Alexander III, the father of Nicholas II. The attempt failed, however, and the government hanged Lenin's brother and four fellow conspirators in 1887. Alexander's death made a powerful impression on Lenin, who dedicated his life to promoting a revolution.

In 1895 the Russian government arrested Lenin for his activities and exiled him to **Siberia**. After his release, he went to Germany, Great Britain, and Switzerland, where he wrote revolutionary articles and kept a close eye on the political situation in

TEACH

Guided Practice

THEME Revolution

Have students review the earlier Russian Revolution, that of 1905. How was the situation different in 1917? *(widespread dissatisfaction caused by Russian participation in World War I)* **L1**

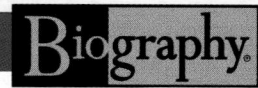

The following videotape program is available from Glencoe:

- **Rasputin: The Mad Monk**

Independent Practice

Guided Reading Activity 17-4 **L1**

CURRICULUM CONNECTION

SCIENCE

After the execution of Czar Nicholas II and his family, their bodies were disfigured by acid and thrown into unmarked graves. Not until the 1990s were systematic efforts made to locate and identify the Romanovs. When some likely remains were found, they were subjected to DNA analysis. Prince Philip, husband of Britain's Queen Elizabeth II, also was tested. DNA from his blood matched DNA from a bone fragment, proving that one of the bodies was that of Philip's relative, Czarina Alexandra.

VIDEODISC
Communism and the Cold
War

Side One, Chapter 8
Frames 14264–14893
Title: *Perspectives on Communism*
Subject: Discussion of the ideals
of communism
Ask: What did the Soviet Union
feel it could teach the world? *(It
felt the world needed to be taught to
work collectively.)*

Literature Have students
research and report on one of the
following: Maksim Gorky, a
champion of the revolutionary
movement in Russia; Alexander
Blok, who wrote "The Twelve," a
poem about the revolution; or
Vladimir Mayakovsky, who popularized the revolution. **L3**

The Bolshevik Revolution
What change did the
Bolshevik Revolution bring
to Russia and the rest of the
world?
*It established the world's first
Communist state in Russia and
promoted the spread of communism elsewhere.*

Russia. After hearing the news of the March 1917
revolution, he wanted to return to Russia as soon as
possible. Since Germany wanted Russia out of the
war and knew that Lenin would promote a withdrawal, it provided him with a special "sealed"
train that allowed no one to enter or exit during the
trip. Lenin's goal upon his arrival in Russia was to
organize the Bolsheviks and seize power from the
provisional government.

Lenin realized that the provisional government
could not maintain the support of the soldiers,
peasants, and workers. His slogan, "Peace, Land,
and Bread," promised the Russian people that
Russia would withdraw from the war, that the
peasants would be given land, and that everyone
would have enough to eat. Another point in Lenin's
program was that the soviets should become the
nation's only government. This goal was summed
up in the slogan "All power to the soviets!"

The Bolshevik Revolution

During the summer of 1917, a number of demonstrations against the provisional government broke
out across Russia. Blaming these demonstrations on
the Bolsheviks and calling Lenin a German agent, the
government issued arrest warrants for all Bolshevik
leaders, forcing Lenin into hiding. By late August,
however, the Bolsheviks started to show new
strength in local elections, and by mid-September
they had gained control of the Petrograd Soviet.

Two months later, in November 1917, the
Bolsheviks staged a coup d'etat in Petrograd, overthrowing the provisional government in the name
of the soviets. Bolshevik soldiers, workers, and
sailors took over the main post office, the telephone
system, electrical generating plants, and train stations. When the Bolsheviks turned the guns of the
battleship *Aurora* against the Winter Palace, the former home of the czar, the ministers of the provisional government quickly surrendered. As a
result, the revolution was relatively bloodless.

In spite of the Bolshevik coup, the election for
the constituent assembly still took place in late
November. Of those elected, 420 seats went to the
Social Revolutionaries and only 225 to the
Bolsheviks. When the assembly met in Petrograd in
January 1918, however, the Bolsheviks dissolved it
after only one day.

Claiming absolute power, the Bolsheviks laid
the foundation of a socialist state—ending private
ownership of property, distributing land among the

peasants, and giving workers control of factories
and mines. The Bolsheviks began calling themselves Communists and their political viewpoint,
based on the ideas of Marx and Lenin, communism.
The Communists and their supporters in other countries created an international movement to spread
their revolution throughout the world.

Civil War

In addition to building a socialist state, Lenin
also sought peace with Germany. At a heavy price,
Russia in March 1918 signed the Treaty of Brest-
Litovsk, losing much western territory and a third
of the population. Meanwhile, the Bolsheviks faced
challenges from within the former empire.
Powerful nationalist movements set up independent governments in Estonia, Latvia, Lithuania,
Poland, **Ukraine**, and the Caucasus lands of
Armenia, Georgia, and Azerbaijan. Although in
theory allowing these countries to break away from
Russia, the Communists in practice used force to
gain control in Ukraine and the Caucasus.

Reds and Whites

During the early months of 1918, Russia also
slipped into a devastating civil war between the
Communists and their political opponents. In this
conflict, the Communists were called Reds, because
they favored the red flag of revolution. Their opponents—royalists, liberal democrats, and moderate
socialists—became known as the Whites.

Lenin's government was determined not to
yield power. Under the Communist leader, **Leon
Trotsky**, the Red Army was organized to defend the
Communist state. Trotsky restored discipline to
military ranks, using force and education to foster
loyalty to communism.

The Whites promised to defeat the Reds quickly and get Russia back into World War I against the
Central Powers. As a result, they received soldiers
and military aid from the Allies and the United
States. The foreign intervention did little to help the
Whites, but it stirred Russian nationalist support
for the Communists and increased Communist distrust of the West.

For three grim years, the fighting raged across
the vast landscape. Both sides burned villages and
killed civilians. When the Whites captured an area,
they killed all suspected Communists. The Reds
did the same to "counter-revolutionaries," or those
believed to be opposed to communism. In the
meantime, workers and peasants were starving and
the nation's economy was crumbling.

MEETING SPECIAL NEEDS ACTIVITY

Study Strategy Students may have trouble following the events in the chaotic period of the
Russian Revolution. Have them construct a chart with dates (from 1916 to 1922) along the side and
these headings across the top: *Leader(s) of Government; Political/Social Events.* **L3**

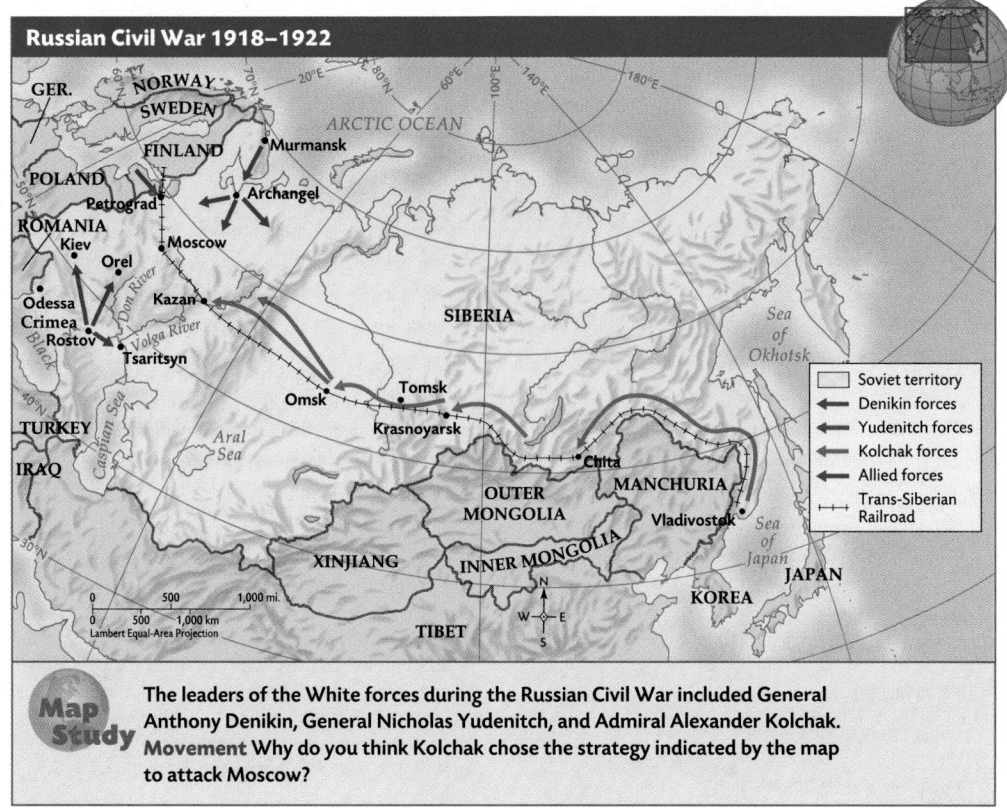

Russian Civil War 1918–1922

☐	Soviet territory
←	Denikin forces
←	Yudenitch forces
←	Kolchak forces
←	Allied forces
⊢⊢⊢	Trans-Siberian Railroad

Map Study

The leaders of the White forces during the Russian Civil War included General Anthony Denikin, General Nicholas Yudenitch, and Admiral Alexander Kolchak. **Movement** Why do you think Kolchak chose the strategy indicated by the map to attack Moscow?

The Terror

During the upheaval, the Communists further tightened their hold on Russia. They imposed a policy called "war communism"—taking direct control of industry and forcing peasants to send food to the starving cities. Lenin also used terror as a weapon against his opponents. In 1918 Communist soldiers killed the imprisoned czar and his family. A secret police force, the Cheka, arrested anyone considered an "enemy of the revolution." In keeping with communism's anti-religious viewpoint, Lenin placed severe restrictions on the Russian Orthodox Church.

Many Socialists who had backed Lenin's revolution now withdrew their support and fled Russia. At the same time, the Whites suffered from a lack of unity among their royalist, liberal, and moderate socialist supporters. Outnumbered, disorganized, and poorly equipped, the White armies finally admitted defeat. By 1921 Lenin had extended Communist control throughout the war-ravaged country.

SECTION 4 REVIEW

Recall
1. **Define** provisional government, communism.
2. **Identify** Nicholas II, Grigori Rasputin, Alexander Kerensky, Vladimir Ilyich Lenin, Leon Trotsky.
3. **Discuss** the main differences that separated the Mensheviks and the Bolsheviks.

Critical Thinking
4. **Evaluating Information** Do you think Lenin was justified in closing down the democratically elected constituent assembly in January 1918? Why or why not?

Understanding Themes
5. **Revolution** Why was the Russian Revolution a significant turning point in world history? What impact did it have on Russian and global affairs?

SECTION 4 REVIEW ANSWERS

1. The words are defined in the Glossary.
2. Nicholas II, 532; Rasputin, 532; Kerensky, 533; Lenin, 533; Trotsky, 534
3. Mensheviks: revolution should be the work of the masses; Bolsheviks: revolution could occur by force by a small group of revolutionaries plus workers and peasants
4. Answers should show understanding of Bolsheviks' political beliefs.
5. **REVOLUTION** It led to the collapse of one of the world's most powerful monarchies and the foundation of the world's first socialist state. Communism became the ideological basis of the Soviet Union, which sought to export revolution and/or expand its territory. This contributed to the cold war rivalry with the United States after World War II.

Map Study

Answer
He hoped that if he could seize control of the Trans-Siberian Railroad, he could control an important supply line and transport his troops to the main theater of action.

Map Skills Practice

Reading a Map From what regions did Denikin and Yudenitch attack? (*Denikin: from the Crimea, south of Moscow; Yudenitch: from the Baltic region, in the north*)

ASSESS

Check for Understanding

Assign Section 4 Review as homework or as an in-class activity.

⊞ Use Student Self-Test and Review Software to review Section 4.

Evaluate

🗀 Section Quiz 17-4

⊞ Use the Testmaker to create a customized quiz for Section 4.

Reteach

Have students review the goals of the Bolsheviks and discuss why they appealed to the Russian people.

Enrich

Have the class watch the film *Dr. Zhivago* and discuss its message and impact.

CLOSE

Have students summarize the effects of World War I on the Russian Revolution.

1917
1917 United States declaration of war raises Allied morale.

1918
1918 President Woodrow Wilson presents Fourteen Points.

1919
1919 Allies sign Treaty of Versailles.

Section 5

Peace at Last

ind Out

Answer: *because it left Germany weakened, humiliated, and resentful*

FOCUS

Section Objective

Explain why the Treaty of Versailles was ultimately unsuccessful.

BELLRINGER
Motivational Activity

Before taking roll at the beginning of the class period, project Section Focus Transparency 17-5 and have students answer the activity questions. Discuss students' responses.

This activity is also available as a blackline master.

Vocabulary Pre-check

Use the Vocabulary PuzzleMaker to create a puzzle that reinforces the vocabulary terms in this section. **L1**

Setting the Scene

▶ **Terms to Define**
convoy, armistice, reparation, mandate, cordon sanitaire

▶ **People to Meet**
T.E. Lawrence, Ferdinand Foch, Woodrow Wilson, Georges Clemenceau, David Lloyd George, Vittorio Orlando

▶ **Places to Locate**
Fiume

 **ind Out** Why was the Treaty of Versailles ultimately unsuccessful?

The Storyteller

Four officers of France, Great Britain, America, and Italy marched into the Palace of Versailles to sign the treaty ending World War I. Harold Nicholson described the ceremony in his diary: "And then, isolated and pitiable, come the two German delegates, Dr. Muller and Dr. Bell. The silence is terrifying…. They keep their eyes fixed away from those two thousand staring eyes, fixed upon the ceiling. They are deathly pale…. Suddenly from outside comes the crash of guns thundering a salute. It announces to Paris that the second Treaty of Versailles had been signed….

We kept our seats while the Germans were conducted like prisoners from the dock, their eyes still fixed upon some distant point of the horizon."

—adapted from *Peacemaking*, Harold Nicholson, reprinted in *Western Civilization, an Urban Perspective*, F. Roy Willis, 1973

German officer's helmet

536 Chapter 17 *World War I*

Russia's withdrawal from the war was offset by the entry of the United States into the conflict. American intervention boosted Allied morale and gave the Allies much needed resources, both industrial and human. It took time for the Americans to build and train an army, but the American navy was of immediate help. United States Admiral William S. Sims introduced the idea of the convoy to guard Allied ships from German U-boats. Under the successful convoy system, merchant ships crossed the Atlantic in clusters surrounded by warships for protection. At the same time, improvements in mines and underwater explosives—as well as the use of the airplane for air surveying and bombing—changed the way the war was being fought.

Turning the Tide

Until American forces arrived, the fighting along the trench lines in the Western Front continued without lasting gains for either side. In April 1917 a French offensive stalled, leading to losses so great that French forces mutinied. The British, in order to keep the Germans from taking advantage of French weakness, launched an offensive into Flanders, a coastal region of northern France and eastern Belgium. Heavy rains, however, made the clay soil of Flanders an impassable expanse of mud. In November, the fighting finally came to an end at Passchendaele (PAH•shehn•dayl). Casualties were so enormous that both the British and the Germans were reaching the end of their reserves.

Total War

By 1917, the pressures of war had brought notable changes to the societies of fighting countries. The demands of a large-scale mechanized war required the efficient use of human and natural resources. Governments therefore carried out the principle of total war, directing all people and resources to the

---

war effort. Greatly increasing their powers, governments on both sides recruited, drafted, trained, and supplied large armies. They raised taxes and borrowed vast sums of money. They also placed controls on capitalist economies, setting prices and wages, rationing goods, and banning strikes. Even in democratic countries, censorship of the press and other media was imposed in an effort to control public opinion and to keep morale high.

Women also played an important role in the war effort. As millions of men went to the battlefields, many women took their places in factories making weapons and supplies. Other women became military nurses or joined special branches of the armed forces. War work proved the abilities of women in areas once limited to men. Although women had to leave many jobs after the war, their contributions had boosted their self-confidence and in the long term aided the ongoing struggle for women's rights. By war's end, many countries were ready to grant the vote to women.

Global War

World War I reached beyond Europe to other parts of the world. European imperialist nations obtained badly needed resources from their empires. They also turned to recruits from their overseas possessions to fight on the Western Front. Meanwhile, in parts of Asia and Africa, Allied forces, including those of Japan, won victories that enabled them to take control of German colonies.

For their services, colonial Asians and Africans expected citizenship or independence at war's end; however, they were often disappointed when European empires were not only preserved but often extended at their expense. In the Middle East, the Arabs, seeking freedom from Ottoman rule, backed the Allied cause. While the war on the Western Front was deadlocked, they helped the British advance in the Middle East and finally conquer the Ottoman Turks. For example, Arab guerilla fighters, led by **T.E. Lawrence**, a young British officer, harassed the Ottoman Turks and gave the British information about important Turkish military positions. Unknown to the Arabs, however, the British and the French had in the 1916 Sykes-Picot Agreement already determined to divide the defeated Ottoman Empire among themselves.

End of Fighting

In July 1918 an Allied breakthrough on the Western Front finally came. Under the unified command of French General **Ferdinand Foch** (FAWSH), Allied forces stopped a huge German offensive that had moved them back to within 40 miles (60 km) of

Visualizing History More than 2 million American soldiers made up of 42 infantry divisions served in France before the war ended in 1918. *How did the arrival of American troops affect the war's outcome?*

Paris. Aided by the arrival of American forces, the Allies then launched a counterattack that pushed the exhausted Germans back to the border of Germany. In September, German generals told Kaiser Wilhelm II that the war could not be won.

The collapse of other Central Powers followed. The Ottoman Turks asked for peace after an Allied drive through the Balkans, and the Austro-Hungarians surrendered following their defeat by the Italians at Vittorio Veneto in northern Italy. The Austro-Hungarian military collapse led to the revolt of the empire's many nationalities and the end of the Hapsburg monarchy.

Although the German army stood firm, morale in Germany gave way. On November 9, 1918, the kaiser abdicated, and a German republic was proclaimed. On November 11, the Germans signed an armistice, or agreement to end the fighting.

Effects of the War

The war shattered Europe's aristocratic order and increased political and social instability. Boundaries had to be redrawn in various parts of the world. Human misery also had become commonplace. Nearly 9 million soldiers were dead, and another 21 million of them were wounded.

Chapter 17 *World War I* **537**

TEACH

Guided Practice

THEME Internationalism
Ask students to define *internationalism. (having to do with two or more nations)* Then have them list the goals of the United States, Britain, and France in drafting a peace settlement after World War I. **L1 LEP**

Visualizing History U.S. soldiers, known as the American Expeditionary Force, were commanded by General John J. Pershing. This was the first American army ever sent to Europe.
Answer to Caption: *They helped bolster Allied morale and provided much needed human and industrial resources.*

Geography: Location Have students look at the map on page 540 and locate the new European nations created after the war. *(Finland, Estonia, Latvia, Lithuania, Poland, Czechoslovakia, Austria, Hungary, Yugoslavia)* **L2 LEP**

Linking Past and Present

Lafayette After the first U.S. troops landed in France, an American officer announced: "Lafayette, we are here." He was referring to the services rendered to the colonists during the American Revolution by a French aristocrat, the Marquis de Lafayette, who served as a valuable aide to George Washington.

COOPERATIVE LEARNING ACTIVITY

Presentation Organize the class into three groups to research and report on World War I in the Middle East. One group should research the life of T. E. Lawrence. The second group should research Britain's role on the Middle Eastern front, including its broken promise of Arab independence. The third group should research the goals and participation of the Arab peoples involved. All three groups should then meet to share their data in a presentation to the rest of the class. **L3**

Graph Study

Answers
Russia; the United States; Russia was the least industrialized of the great powers and was ill-equipped to fight a mechanized war; the United States entered the war later and its troops had a powerful industrial economy behind them.

Practice

Reading a Chart Which side had the heavier casualties, the Allies or the Central Powers? *(the Allies)*

Independent Practice

 Guided Reading Activity 17-5 **L1**

Time Line Ask students to create a time line of events that led to Allied victory. They should begin with May 1917 (the first convoy) and end with the armistice in November 1918. **L2 LEP**

Biography.

The following videotape program is available from Glencoe:

• **Woodrow Wilson: Reluctant Warrior**

Linking Past and Present

November 11, 1918—the day World War I ended—is a time when members of the armed services are honored in many of the former Allied countries. It is called Veterans Day in the United States, Remembrance Day in Canada, and Armistice Day in Britain.

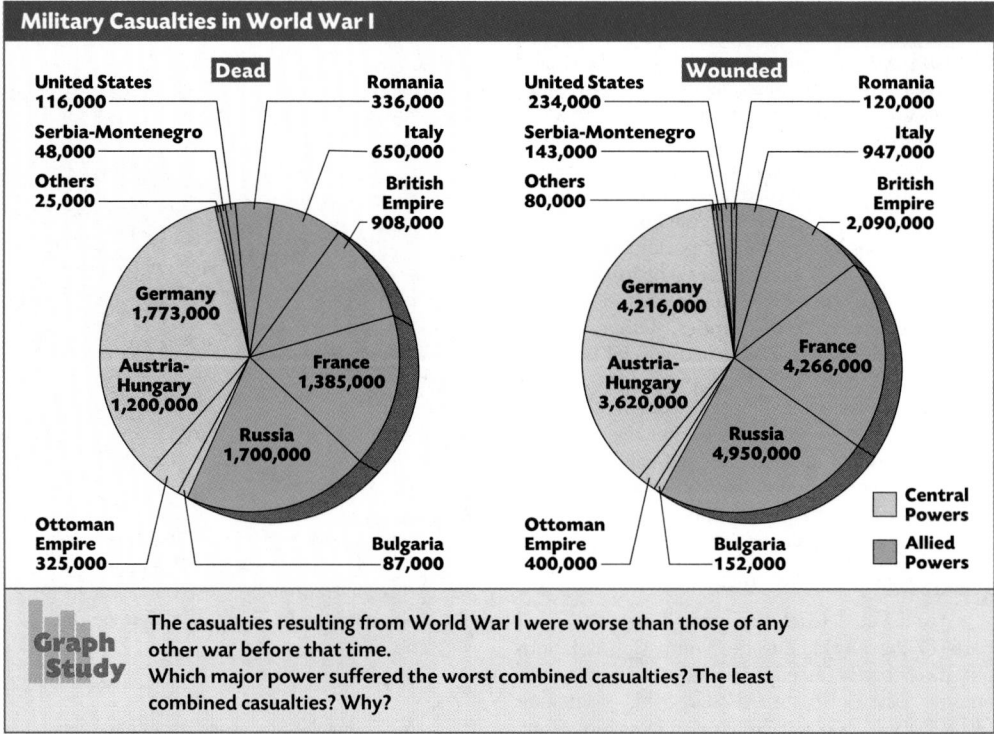

Military Casualties in World War I

Dead

United States 116,000
Romania 336,000
Serbia-Montenegro 48,000
Italy 650,000
Others 25,000
British Empire 908,000
Germany 1,773,000
France 1,385,000
Austria-Hungary 1,200,000
Russia 1,700,000
Ottoman Empire 325,000
Bulgaria 87,000

Wounded

United States 234,000
Romania 120,000
Serbia-Montenegro 143,000
Italy 947,000
Others 80,000
British Empire 2,090,000
Germany 4,216,000
France 4,266,000
Austria-Hungary 3,620,000
Russia 4,950,000
Ottoman Empire 400,000
Bulgaria 152,000

Central Powers
Allied Powers

Graph Study The casualties resulting from World War I were worse than those of any other war before that time.
Which major power suffered the worst combined casualties? The least combined casualties? Why?

In addition, about 13 million civilians were dead of disease and starvation. Mass deaths or killings on a grand scale, such as those of the Armenians under the rule of the Ottoman Turks in 1915, added to the list of horrors.

Angry at Armenian support for the Allies and fearful of Armenian nationalism, the Turkish government decided to use the war as an excuse to end the long history of animosity between Turks and Armenians. The Turkish army first removed all Armenian soldiers from its ranks and deported them to labor camps. Then they rounded up Armenian civilians, roped them together, and drove them into the desert to starve. In other cases they destroyed whole Armenian villages and shot the inhabitants. Some historians have estimated that more than 1 million Armenians lost their lives in this slaughter.

Restoring the Peace

The hopes of many Europeans and North Americans focused on United States President **Woodrow Wilson**. Even before the war ended,

Wilson had put forth his Fourteen Points, a peace plan whose terms included international recognition of freedom of the seas and of trade, limitations on arms, and an end to all secret alliances. Wilson's plan also called for just settlements of colonial claims, the right of self-rule for all nations, and the establishment of a "general assembly of nations" to settle future problems peacefully. It was these points that Germany thought would be the basis of peace negotiations.

For the most part, everyone seemed to agree that Wilson's points should be the guiding framework for the peace settlement. There were only two major reservations—one was Great Britain's. Control of the seas had been a major British war aim vital to British interests. Great Britain depended on foreign trade for its survival and still ruled a vast overseas empire. The British, therefore, objected to the idea of open seas. The other reservation was held by France. Wilson had stated that there should be "no annexations, no contributions, and no punitive damages" as a result of the war. France believed that some statement demanding reparations, or payments for damages, should be included in any peace settlement.

MEETING SPECIAL NEEDS ACTIVITY

Learning Style: Visual/Spatial Have students compare the map of Europe in 1919 on page 540 with the map of Europe in 1915 on page 518. Ask them to make a list of all the ways Europe changed as a result of World War I. **L1 LEP**

The Paris Peace Conference

In January 1919, delegates from 27 nations gathered in Paris to work out 5 separate peace treaties known as the Peace of Paris. The Allies did not invite representatives from the defeated Central Powers or Russia. In a break with tradition, heads of state attended the conference. President Wilson represented the United States; Prime Minister **Georges Clemenceau** (KLEH•muhn•SOH), France; Prime Minister **David Lloyd George**, Britain; and Prime Minister **Vittorio Orlando**, Italy. Most of the decisions were made by these "Big Four."

It soon became clear that there was a large gap between the idealistic goals of Wilson and the nationalistic goals of the French, British, and Italian leaders. Lloyd George and Clemenceau wanted to make Germany pay for the war. Wilson's chief aim was to win support for his idea of an international assembly of nations. The League of Nations, as Wilson called it, became a bargaining point. Again and again, Wilson gave in on other issues to ensure the acceptance of the League of Nations.

The Treaty of Versailles

The Treaty of Versailles, the most important treaty of the Peace of Paris, spelled out the details of the Allied settlement with Germany. Lloyd George and Clemenceau prevailed in their goal to punish Germany. Militarily, the treaty reduced the German army and banned conscription and the manufacture of major war weapons.

The treaty reduced Germany in size as well. Germany had to return Alsace-Lorraine, seized in the Franco-Prussian War of 1870, to France. For a period of 15 years, France would also control the coal-rich Saar Basin, while Allied forces together would occupy the Rhineland region of Germany.

In the east, Germany had to renounce the Treaty of Brest-Litovsk. The Allies also reestablished an independent Poland out of lands held by Germany, Austria-Hungary, and Russia. So that it had access to the Baltic Sea, Poland received the Polish Corridor, a strip of land separating East Prussia from the rest of Germany.

The Treaty of Versailles stripped Germany of all of its overseas colonies as well. The Allies received all of Germany's overseas possessions as mandates, territories administered by other countries. Great Britain and France divided Germany's African colonies, Australia and New Zealand split the German Pacific islands south of the Equator, and Japan took the German Pacific islands north of the Equator.

Although these terms were harsh, France and Great Britain were still not satisfied. The Allies also demanded that Germany accept blame for causing the war and that it pay reparations for Allied war costs and damages.

The Allies signed the treaty at the Palace of Versailles on June 28, 1919. Only four of Wilson's Fourteen Points and nine supplementary principles emerged intact in the treaty. The most important of these was the Covenant of the League of Nations.

Other Settlements

The Allied Powers signed separate peace agreements with Austria, Bulgaria, Hungary, and Turkey. In them, the greatest attention was given to territorial matters. The Allies recognized the breakup of Austria-Hungary. Austria was left a small, economically weak country. Italy received from Austria German-speaking areas near the Brenner Pass in the Alps. Italy also wanted the port of **Fiume** on the Adriatic, but Wilson refused to agree.

New nations emerged in eastern Europe from the ashes of the old German, Russian, and Austro-Hungarian empires. These included Finland, Estonia, Latvia, Lithuania, Poland, Czechoslovakia, and Yugoslavia. The Allies, particularly France, regarded these countries as a cordon sanitaire (kawr•DOHN sah•nee•TEHR), or quarantine line, that would serve as a buffer against any potential threat from Russia or Germany. In creating Yugoslavia, the Serbs achieved their goal of forming a nation of South Slavic peoples. Hungary lost territory to Yugoslavia, Czechoslovakia, and Romania, while Bulgaria lost land to Yugoslavia, Greece, and Romania.

In the Middle East, the Allies divided what was left of the Ottoman Empire. The Arabs did not receive the independence that Great Britain had promised them. Instead, Palestine, Transjordan, and Iraq became British mandates. At the same time, Lebanon and Syria became French mandates.

Bitter Fruits

A general disillusionment set in after World War I. Slogans such as "the war to end all wars" and "to make the world safe for democracy" rang hollow after years of slaughter. In addition to killing millions of people, the war destroyed the homes and lives of millions more. Many people suddenly found themselves to be minorities within newly formed nations. Others who believed they would become the citizens of independent nations found their hopes dashed by the settlements. Those whose lands were defeated were embittered by the loss of territory and prestige.

Cultural Perspectives

Anti-German feeling reached near-hysteria in many of the Allied countries during World War I. In the United States, German-language instruction was dropped from schools. In Britain, King George V changed his family name from Wetlin to Windsor, and the Battenberg family changed theirs to Mountbatten.

CURRICULUM CONNECTION

SCIENCE

Vitamins had been isolated before World War I. Only with the war, when medical examinations of draftees revealed widespread malnourishment, did people realize how important they were. Of 2.5 million British draftees examined in 1917–1918, 41 percent were in poor health, mainly because of inadequate nutrition.

ASSESS

Check for Understanding

Assign Section 5 Review as homework or as an in-class activity.

🔲 Use Student Self-Test and Review Software to review Section 5.

MAKING CONNECTIONS ACTIVITY

Literature For writers who took part in World War I, the war was an unforgettable experience. Have students research and write brief biographies of writers who wrote fiction or memoirs about their experiences. Possible subjects include Robert Graves, Siegfried Sassoon, e. e. cummings, John Dos Passos, and Ernest Hemingway. Encourage students to read an actual work by their subject as well. **L2**

Map Study

Answer

Russia

Map Skills Practice

Reading a Map What European countries created after World War I no longer exist today? *(Czechoslovakia, Yugoslavia)*

Evaluate

 Section Quiz 17-5

Use the Testmaker to create a customized quiz for Section 5.

Reteach

Have students list the major participants at the Paris Peace Conference and summarize the aims of each.

 Reteaching Activity 17

Enrich

Have students research and write an essay on the history and activities of the present-day United Nations as an outgrowth of the earlier League of Nations. Ask students to compare the UN and the League in terms of their effectiveness.

 Enrichment Activity 17

CLOSE

Have a roundtable discussion about the ways the Treaty of Versailles prepared the way for World War II. Include the provisions of the treaty and the role that U.S. isolationism played in the aftermath.

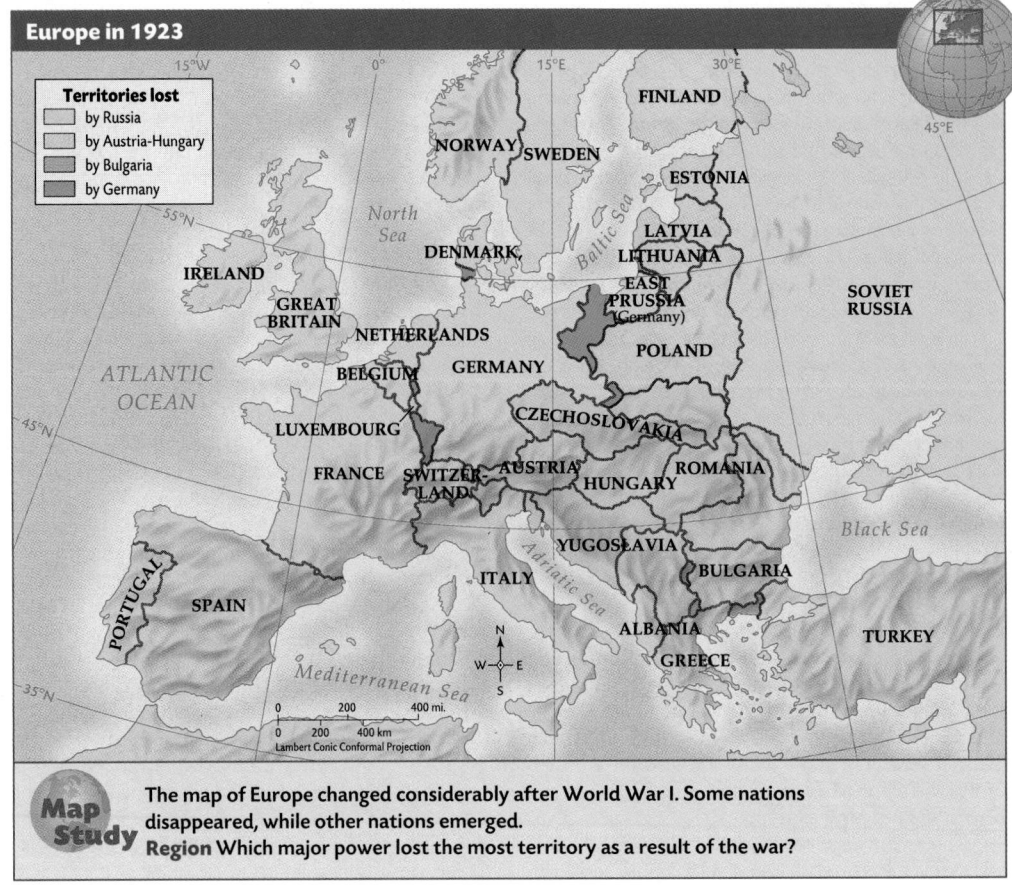

Europe in 1923

Territories lost
- by Russia
- by Austria-Hungary
- by Bulgaria
- by Germany

Map Study The map of Europe changed considerably after World War I. Some nations disappeared, while other nations emerged.
Region Which major power lost the most territory as a result of the war?

The Germans felt an especially deep sense of resentment about their loss in World War I. Because they had fought mostly on foreign territory and used resources from other countries to supplement their own, German economic strength remained largely intact. The harsh provisions of the Treaty of Versailles, however, left Germany weakened and humiliated as well as deprived of great-power status. This made reconciliation with the Allies very difficult. The Germans' festering resentment burst forth upon the world with an even greater violence two decades later in the form of Nazism.

SECTION 5 REVIEW

Recall
1. **Define** convoy, armistice, reparation, mandate, cordon sanitaire.
2. **Identify** Woodrow Wilson, Ferdinand Foch, T. E. Lawrence, the Fourteen Points, Georges Clemenceau, David Lloyd George, Vittorio Orlando.

3. **Discuss** the effect of Ottoman Turkish policies on the Armenian population.

Critical Thinking
4. **Analyzing Information** How do you think a German citizen in 1919 would have felt about the provisions of the Treaty of Versailles?

Understanding Themes
5. **Internationalism** Explain some of the problems created by the Treaty of Versailles. How did this treaty lay the foundation for another international conflict? How could it have been written to prevent this?

SECTION 5 REVIEW ANSWERS

1. The words are defined in the Glossary.
2. T. E. Lawrence, 537; Foch, 537; Wilson, 538; the Fourteen Points, 538; Clemenceau, 539; George, 539; Orlando, 539
3. Angry at Ottoman support for the Allies and fearful of Armenian nationalism, the Ottomans rounded up Armenians and drove them into the desert. They destroyed Armenian villages and shot the inhabitants. More than 1 million Armenians died in this slaughter.
4. angry, humiliated, vengeful
5. **INTERNATIONALISM** Because of its harsh terms, it caused bitter resentment; if punishments had been lessened, or if Germany had been present at the peace conference, future conflict might have been avoided.

Interpreting Military Movements on Maps

Although wars begin over many different issues, they all end up as fights to control territory. Because wars are basically fought over land, maps are particularly good tools for seeing the "big picture" of a war.

Learning the Skill

The map key is essential in interpreting military maps. The key explains what the map's colors and symbols represent. Use the following steps to study the key:

- Determine what color scheme appears on the map. Usually, colors represent different sides in the conflict.
- Identify all symbols. These may include symbols for battle sites, victories, types of military units and equipment, fortifications, and so on.
- Study the arrows, which show the direction of military movements. Because these movements occur over periods of time, some maps give dates showing when and where the troops advanced and retreated.

Once you have carefully studied the key and the map, try to follow the progress of the battle or campaign that is shown. Notice where each side began, in which direction it moved, where the two sides met and fought, and which side claimed victory.

Practicing the Skill

The map on this page shows the Middle East front during World War I. Study the map and then answer the following questions.

1. On which side did Arabia and Egypt fight?
2. Which side won the crucial battle of the Dardanelles?
3. Describe the movement of the Central Powers offensive.
4. When did the Allied Powers win the most battles in the Middle East?

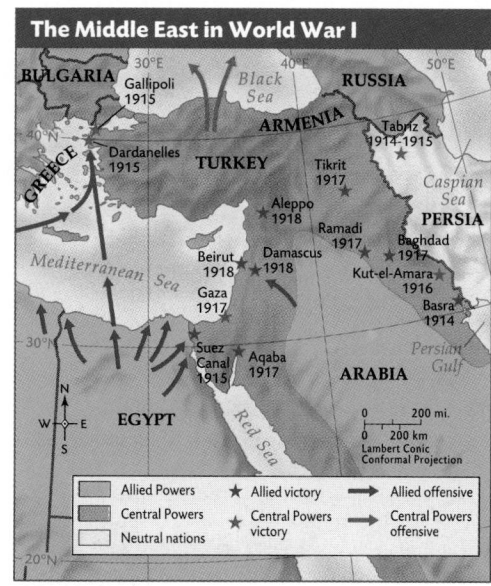

The Middle East in World War I

▢ Allied Powers	★ Allied victory	→ Allied offensive
▢ Central Powers	★ Central Powers victory	→ Central Powers offensive
▢ Neutral nations		

Applying the Skill

Choose one of the maps (showing the Western Front and the Eastern Front of World War I) on page 521. Study your map selection carefully. Then write a paragraph answering the following questions.

1. Where did most of the fighting occur?
2. Which side made the most significant advance in 1914?
3. How did each side progress on this front as the war continued?
4. Did either side win a decisive victory on this front?

For More Practice

Turn to the Skill Practice in the Chapter Review on page 543 for more practice in interpreting military movements on maps.

TEACH

Interpreting Military Movements on Maps Ask students to make their own military maps of an engagement in an imaginary war. They should use two different colors to represent the opposing sides; different symbols or colors for the victories of each side; and arrows to show the direction of troop movements. The students should label land and water areas and a few important towns or cities. The map should also include a key explaining what the various colors and symbols represent.

Additional Practice

▱ Skill Reinforcement Activity 17

ANSWERS TO PRACTICING THE SKILL

1. on the Allied side
2. the Central Powers
3. from the Ottoman Empire north across the Black Sea toward Russia
4. 1917

GLENCOE
TECHNOLOGY

VIDEODISC
Use MindJogger to review students' knowledge of the chapter.

MindJogger Videoquiz

Chapter 17
Disc 2 Side B

Also available in VHS.

Answers

Using Key Terms
1. i   4. k
2. d   5. f
3. b

Using Your History Journal

Remind students to write their letters at the appropriate time.

Reviewing Facts
1. 1914: assassination of Archduke Ferdinand and beginning of World War I; 1917: United States entry into World War I, the Russian Revolution; 1918: Armistice ending World War I
2. It abandoned the Schlieffen Plan.
3. about 30 million soldiers were killed or wounded; about 13 million civilians
4. Peace: Russian withdrawal from the war; Land: land to the peasants; Bread: enough food for everyone. "All power to the soviets" meant that these local organizations would govern Russia.
5. freedom of the seas; freedom of trade; arms limitations; an end to secret alliances; just settlement of colonial claims; self-rule for all nations; "general assembly of nations"
6. Large numbers of women entered

542 **Chapter 17** *World War I*

Connections Across Time

Historical Significance World War I brought weapons of mass destruction. The resulting slaughter on the battlefields destroyed the image of war as a heroic undertaking.

Many people also became disillusioned about the war's aftermath. World War I swept away the old order in Europe and redrew the map of the continent. It caused widespread economic suffering and ended in a controversial peace settlement that sowed the seeds for another, even more destructive, war. After World War I, Europe's global power began to ebb.

Using Key Terms

Write the key term that completes each sentence. Then write a sentence for each term not chosen.

a. armistice	g. trenches
b. contraband	h. alliance system
c. convoy	i. provisional government
d. entente	j. reparations
e. propaganda	k. communism
f. mobilization	l. ultimatum

1. After Czar Nicholas's abdication, political authority in Russia passed into the hands of a _____.
2. In 1904, Great Britain and France signed an _____ that settled key colonial disputes.
3. The British stopped ships on the high seas that they suspected carried _____, or prohibited goods.
4. The Bolsheviks founded an international revolutionary movement based on _____, the political viewpoint stemming from the ideas of Marx and Lenin.
5. Warring countries issued general orders for _____, the gathering and transport of military troops and fighting equipment.

Technology Activity

Using E-mail Use your local library or access the Internet to locate an E-mail address for an organization that deals with World War I. Compose a letter requesting information about World War I submarine warfare. Using your response, create a bulletin board of the history of the American submarine during the Great War. Provide pictures and captions showing different types of submarines.

542 **Chapter 17** *World War I*

Using Your History Journal

Take the role of a parent and answer the letter you wrote as a first-person account of the war. Include words of encouragement and try to explain the significance of the war effort.

Reviewing Facts

1. **History** State the significance of the following dates: 1914, 1917, and 1918.
2. **History** Explain how Germany's war strategy changed after the Battle of the Marne.
3. **History** State how many soldiers were killed or wounded in World War I. How many civilians died of disease or starvation?
4. **Culture** Explain the social changes promised by the Bolshevik slogans.
5. **History** List five of the Fourteen Points that United States President Woodrow Wilson presented at the Paris peace conference in 1919.
6. **Culture** State the role and contributions of women during World War I. What was their standing in society after the war?

Critical Thinking

1. **Evaluate** How did Lenin's beliefs and goals differ from those of Wilson? Which leader has had the greater impact on world history?
2. **Apply** How did sea power have a major effect on the outcome of World War I?
3. **Analyze** How were technological advances in weaponry most responsible for the military stalemate during much of World War I?

the labor force; others became nurses or served in armed forces; their post-war contributions led to obtaining the vote.

Critical Thinking
1. Lenin's stress on revolution and dictatorial government v. Wilson's affirmation of democratic values, self-determination, and free institutions.
2. The British maintained an extremely effective blockade of Germany. Germany's submarine warfare did extensive damage but also brought the United States into the war.
3. Machine guns, heavy artillery, and trenches made it hard for either side to mount a decisive offensive attack on the other.

Understanding Themes
1. **COOPERATION** because they were all afraid of Germany

Understanding Themes

1. **Cooperation** Why do you think Great Britain, France, and Russia put aside their differences to form the Triple Entente?
2. **Conflict** Name a war goal for each of these countries: Serbia, Austria-Hungary, Russia, and France. Discuss a situation today where a conflict over national goals might lead to war.
3. **Conflict** What were the causes of World War I? What key events affected its outcome? How did World War I affect global affairs?
4. **Revolution** Name the main causes of the Russian Revolution of 1917. How did the Russian Revolution differ from the American Revolution in its causes and global impact?
5. **Internationalism** Do you think the peace settlement after World War I promoted the success of the League of Nations? Explain.

Skill Practice

Study the map "Russian Civil War 1918–1922" and answer the questions that follow.

1. From which direction did the Allied forces invade Russia?

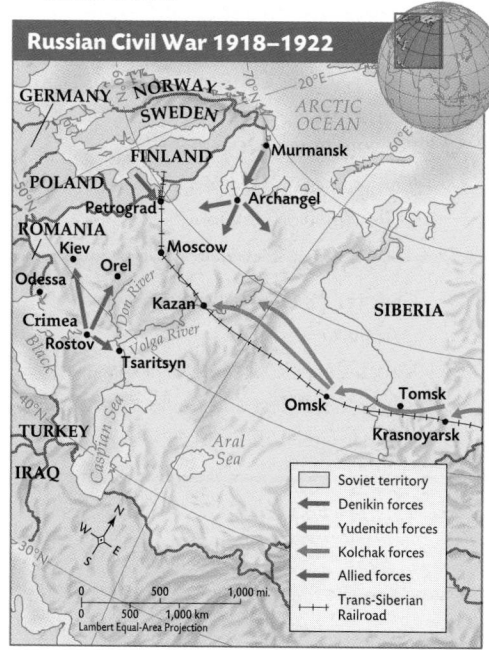

Russian Civil War 1918–1922

2. Where did Denikin's forces begin and in what direction did they move?
3. Why do you think Kolchak chose his route to Moscow?
4. Which military group advanced on Russian territory from Poland?

Geography in History

1. **Place** Refer to the map below. What five European nations had built up the largest standing armies during World War I?
2. **Location** How do you think Germany's location affected its military strategy?
3. **Movement** When war broke out, which side had the more challenging task of moving troops and materials, the Allies or the Central Powers? Why?

Mobilized Forces During World War I

Linking Past and Present

1. How do conflicts in the Balkans before World War I compare with those in the region today?
2. The ideal of self-determination was not granted to European colonies after World War I. Where do struggles for self-determination continue today? How are they faring?

Skill Practice

1. from the northwest
2. Denikin's forces began in the Crimea and moved north.
3. He hoped to seize control of the Trans-Siberian Railroad, which would give him control of an important supply line into Russia and enable him to use the railroad to transport his troops.
4. Yudenitch forces

Geography in History

1. Germany, Russia, Great Britain, France, Austria-Hungary
2. It had to worry about two fronts of fighting.
3. the Allies, because their territories were split in two by the Central Powers

Linking Past and Present

1. Students should stress ethnic and national rivalries as the cause of conflicts.
2. Chechens in the Russian Federation; Basques in Spain; Quebec; Kurds in the Middle East; Tamils in Sri Lanka; Kashmiris in South Asia; and Tibetans in China.

? Chapter Bonus Test Question

Ask students: One clause of the Versailles Treaty put all the blame for causing World War I on Germany. Do you think this was just? *(Yes: War might have been avoided if Germany had not given Austria-Hungary permission to do with Serbia as it pleased. No: The intransigence of Austria-Hungary was also to blame, and without the terrorism of Serbian nationalists, the war might not have broken out at all.)*

2. **CONFLICT** Serbia: to be the center of a new South Slav nation; Austria-Hungary: to gain territory through the Balkans to the Aegean Sea and to contain Slavic nationals; Russia: an Adriatic port; France: return of Alsace-Lorraine; possibilities include the former Yugoslavia and the former Soviet Union.
3. **CONFLICT** Militarism, rivalries among alliances, imperialist expansion; it led to a Communist dictatorship based on force;
the American Revolution, caused by political and economic differences, led to a democratic republic
4. **REVOLUTION** Shortages of food and fuel, dissatisfaction with the monarchy, war casualties. Answers might mention a common element of dissatisfaction with the regime in power.
5. **INTERNATIONALISM** No, it created bad feeling.

A complete, 1-page lesson plan is provided for each section in the *Reproducible Lesson Plans* booklet.

Between Two Fires

CHAPTER RESOURCES

	Reproducible Resources	Multimedia Resources
Chapter Opener	Chapter Themes: Graphic Organizer 18 Historical Significance Chapter Activity 18	MindJogger Videoquiz
Chapter Enrichment	Vocabulary Activity 18* Time Line Activity 18 Mapping History Activity 18 History Simulation 18 Geography and History Activity 18 Source Reading 18 People in World History Profiles 55, 56 World Art and Music Activity 18 Enrichment Activity 18 Critical Thinking Activity 18 Skill Reinforcement Activity 18 Writer's Guidebook, Lesson 10 Performance Assessment Activity 18	Focus on World Art Print 3, Thomas Hart Benton. *The Wreck of the Ole '97*; 4, Sargent Johnson. *Forever Free*; 23, René Magritte. *The Human Condition 1* World History and Art Transparency 38, *Migrant Mother*; 39, *Bird in Space*; 43, *The Persistence of Memory* Chapter Transparency 18 Vocabulary PuzzleMaker Software World Music: Cultural Traditions, Lesson 1 Lessons of War: *The Enemy* Communism and the Cold War: *Growing Up Communist*
Chapter Review/Reteaching	Reteaching Activity 18 Skill Reinforcement Activity 18 Spanish Chapter Summary 18	Chapter 18 Digest Audiocassette, Activity, Test* Vocabulary PuzzleMaker Software Student Self-Test and Review Software MindJogger Videoquiz
Chapter Evaluation/Testing	Performance Assessment Activity 18 Chapter 18 Test, Forms A and B	Testmaker

* Also available in Spanish

0:00 OUT OF TIME? Assign the Chapter 18 summary in the Unit 5 Digest on pages 631–633, and the Chapter 18 Audiocassettes.

Block Schedule

Block scheduling differs from traditional class scheduling in the amount of time allotted to each period. The extended time frame provided by block scheduling affords you the opportunity to implement a greater number of research-oriented and activity-intense projects to motivate and involve your students. Activities that are particularly suited to use within the block scheduling framework are identified throughout this chapter by the following designation.

KEY TO ABILITY LEVELS

Teaching strategies have been coded for varying learning styles and abilities.

L1 **BASIC** activities for all students
L2 **AVERAGE** activities for average to above-average students
L3 **CHALLENGING** activities for above-average students
LEP **LIMITED ENGLISH PROFICIENCY** activities

Use Glencoe's *Presentation Plus!* multimedia teacher tool to easily present dynamic lessons that visually excite your students. Using Microsoft PowerPoint® you can customize the presentations to create your own personalized lessons.

SECTION RESOURCES

Daily Objectives	Reproducible Resources	Multimedia Resources
Section 1 **The Postwar World** Describe the trends that dominated the arts and popular culture from 1919 to 1939.	Reproducible Lesson Plan 18-1 Vocabulary Activity 18* Guided Reading Activity 18-1* Time Line Activity 18 Chapter Themes: Graphic Organizer 18 Section Quiz 18-1*	Focus on World Art Print 3, Thomas Hart Benton. *The Wreck of the Ole '97*; 4, Sargent Johnson. *Forever Free*; 23, René Magritte. *The Human Condition 1* Section Focus Transparency 18-1 Chapter Transparency 18 World History and Art Transparency 39, *Bird in Space*; 43, *The Persistence of Memory* Student Self-Test and Review Software Testmaker World Music: Cultural Traditions, Lesson 1
Section 2 **The Western Democracies** Explain why democratic government survived in the United States, Great Britain, and France during the post-World War I era.	Reproducible Lesson Plan 18-2 Vocabulary Activity 18* Guided Reading Activity 18-2* Section Quiz 18-2*	Section Focus Transparency 18-2 World History and Art Transparency 38, *Migrant Mother* Student Self-Test and Review Software Testmaker
Section 3 **Fascist Dictatorships** Identify the factors that led to the rise of Fascist dictatorships in Italy and Germany after World War I.	Reproducible Lesson Plan 18-3 Guided Reading Activity 18-3* History Simulation 18 Geography and History Activity 18 Section Quiz 18-3*	Section Focus Transparency 18-3 Vocabulary PuzzleMaker Software Student Self-Test and Review Software Testmaker Lessons of War: *The Enemy*
Section 4 **The Soviet Union** Examine how Joseph Stalin's rule transformed the Soviet Union.	Reproducible Lesson Plan 18-4 Guided Reading Activity 18-4* Reteaching Activity 18 Enrichment Activity 18 Section Quiz 18-4* Performance Assessment Activity 18 Spanish Chapter Summary 18	Section Focus Transparency 18-4 Vocabulary Puzzlemaker Software Student Self-Test and Review Software Testmaker Communism and the Cold War: *Growing Up Communist*

* Also available in Spanish

Chapter Activities

✓ Performance Assessment Activity

Newsreel Explain that in the 1920s and 1930s (before television), movie theaters showed newsreels along with the feature film. Newsreels included narration and footage of what was happening nationally and around the world, and they often included propaganda. Have small groups of students choose an important event and write newsreel scripts, including headlines and visuals. Then groups can combine their scripts into a 10- or 15-minute production. One student from each group may narrate its segment.

Possible Rubric Features

Accuracy of content information, concept attainment, originality and creativity of product, clarity, organization of ideas, and collaborative skills

• For an additional activity, refer to Activity 18 in the Performance Assessment Strategies and Activities booklet.

ACTIVITY

From the Classroom of...

**Loretta Smithson
Elsinore High School
Lake Elsinore, CA**

Experiencing the Holocaust

Organize the class into small groups to research the roots and results of anti-Semitism. Assign each group a different area to research: (1) a history of the Hebrew people, including the Diaspora (A.D. 70); (2) a history of Jewish expulsion from European countries (e.g., Spain, 1493); (3) excerpts of writings or speeches by famous people (e.g., Martin Luther); (4) excerpts from books or stories of the Holocaust (e.g., *The Blue Tattoo*); (5) reasons given by Nazis for their treatment of European Jews; and (6) world reactions to Nazi treatment of the Jews.

Provide students with the condensed materials they need for their categories, and encourage them to prepare their information in interesting ways for group presentations, such as charts, maps, diagrams, slides.

After group presentations, let students share their analyses of the materials provided, then conduct a class discussion on the meaning of genocide and its implications for world events today (in Bosnia, for example).

MULTIPLE LEARNING STYLES

Verbal/Linguistic
Have students create a front page for a newspaper of the postwar period. Allow students to divide the work for the page: research and writing, editing, laying out the copy, printing, and distributing to the class.

Visual/Spatial
For a mock international TV news special, have students imagine they are news reporters on assignments in one of the following countries: Great Britain, France, Germany, Italy, or the Soviet Union. They are to cover an event in postwar Europe, or a special feature on daily life in their country.

Auditory/Musical
Suggest that students collect music from the 1920s and present a sampling as a concert for the class. They should include both popular and classical selections. Part of the project should include a program for the audience that lists the composers, songwriters, and musicians along with brief biographical sketches, and the names of the works.

Kinesthetic
Ask students to research the currency of each of the countries mentioned in the chapter. Have students collect samples, either real or photocopied, of the currencies. Remind students that some of the nations may have had a change in currency during the postwar period. Have students create a display for the class.

Additional Resources

NATIONAL GEOGRAPHIC SOCIETY

Teacher's Corner

INDEX TO NATIONAL GEOGRAPHIC MAGAZINE

The following articles may be used for research relating to this chapter:

- "Our Man in China," by Mike Edwards, January 1997.
- "U.S.S. Macon: Lost and Found," by J. Gordon Vaeth, January 1992.

NATIONAL GEOGRAPHIC SOCIETY PRODUCTS AVAILABLE FROM GLENCOE

To order the following products for use with this chapter, contact your local Glencoe sales representative, or call Glencoe at 1-800-334-7344:

- *GTV: The American People (Videodiscs)*
- *GTV: A Geographic Perspective on American History (Videodiscs)*

ADDITIONAL NATIONAL GEOGRAPHIC SOCIETY PRODUCTS

To order the following products for use with this chapter, call National Geographic Society at 1-800-368-2728:

- *1929–1941: The Great Depression (Video)*
- *The Superliners: Twilight of an Era (Video)*
- *Secrets of the Titanic (Video)*

LOCAL OBJECTIVES

_____
_____
_____
_____
_____
_____
_____
_____
_____
_____
_____
_____
_____
_____
_____
_____
_____
_____
_____
_____
_____
_____
_____

BIBLIOGRAPHY

Literature of the Period
Hemingway, Ernest. *The Sun Also Rises.* New York: Scribner, 1926. A novel about English and American expatriates in France and Spain after World War I.

Readings for the Student
Laqueur, Walter. *Stalin: The Glasnost Revelations.* Scribner, 1990. A review of a new body of evidence about Stalin and modern-day Russia.

Readings for the Teacher
Garraty, John. *The Great Depression.* San Diego: Harcourt, 1986. Focuses on the Great Depression from a global perspective.

interNET CONNECTION

Joseph Stalin resources on the World Wide Web
The Stalin Archive:
http://acs2.bu.edu:8001/~sbern/stalin.htm

Chapter Themes are listed by section on this chapter opening page of the Student Edition. A corresponding theme-based activity is available under "TEACH," and a theme-based question is asked in the Section and Chapter Reviews.

 **S**toryteller

Historical Setting Hitler was a master speechmaker. His personal architect, Albert Speer, recalled in his memoirs that when he first heard Hitler speak, he was immediately charmed by his style. He had expected a fanatic man dressed in uniform. Instead Hitler appeared in a blue suit and seemed almost shy. He had a gift for adjusting to his audience. Hitler spoke with hypnotic persuasiveness that cast a mood that transformed his listeners.

Historical Significance

Answers: *Economic depressions, unemployment, and social unrest led to the rise of dictatorships in postwar Europe.*

Democratic governments had to become involved in social reforms, adapt to changing technology, and (except for the United States) deal with major debts and rebuild damaged territory.

Chapter
18
1919–1939
Between
Two Fires

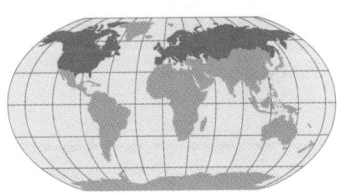

Storyteller

From early evening until long past midnight, Nazi stormtroopers and youth groups marched in disciplined columns through Berlin. For many of the young people in that torchlight parade in the 1930s, their marching was only a beginning. They looked forward to a bright future, playing important roles in creating a new Germany out of the confusion and trouble that surrounded them. To them, Hitler seemed like a deliverer who would restore Germany's greatness.

Years later, a number of them looked back on that night, appalled at how little they really knew about the Nazis. But the economic and political chaos caused by World War I and the Great Depression led many Europeans to support powerful dictators during the 1920s and 1930s.

Chapter Themes

▶ **Innovation** The period after World War I brings revolutionary changes in science, the arts, and popular culture. *Section 1*
▶ **Change** The Great Depression forces governments in Europe and North America to increase their involvement in social and economic affairs. *Section 2*
▶ **Uniformity** Fascist governments in Italy and Germany limit individual liberties and stress loyalty to the state. *Section 3*
▶ **Uniformity** Communist leaders in the Soviet Union impose state control on society and crush opposition. *Section 4*

Historical Significance

What factors led to the rise of dictatorships in Europe after World War I? How were democratic nations affected by the social and economic crises that came after the end of World War I?

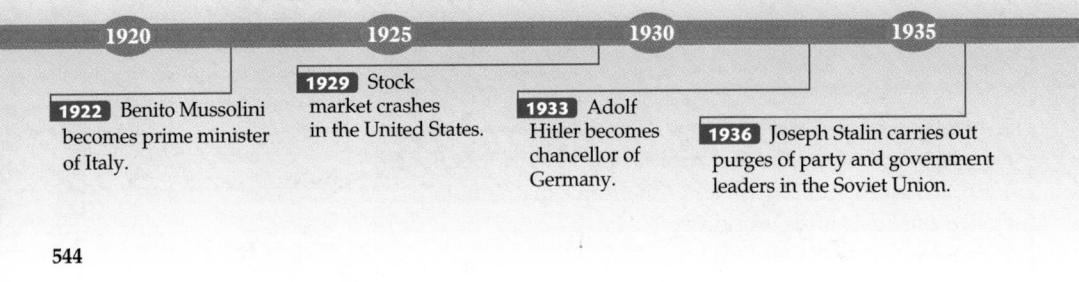

1920	1925	1930	1935

1922 Benito Mussolini becomes prime minister of Italy.

1929 Stock market crashes in the United States.

1933 Adolf Hitler becomes chancellor of Germany.

1936 Joseph Stalin carries out purges of party and government leaders in the Soviet Union.

544

GEOGRAPHY CONNECTION

Location To help students realize where events of this chapter took place, have them find the United States, Great Britain, France, Germany, the Commonwealth of Independent States, and Italy on a world map. **What geographic factor made it possible for the United States to escape economic problems and get on with life immediately after World War I?** *(Its distance from battle sites kept it from being physically damaged and allowed people to isolate themselves from Europe's problems.)*

Automat, Edward Hopper, 1927. Des Moines Art Center Permanent Collection, Des Moines, Iowa

Your History Journal

Interview an older person about his or her feelings and perceptions in the period between 1930 and 1941. Use the chapter to formulate questions about events. Take notes during the interview, or write down your impressions soon afterward.

History & Art Edward Hopper (1882–1967) was an American artist known for his realistic paintings of loneliness and boredom. He depicted characters in all-night restaurants or in lonely settings such as this automat. The world he revealed was stark and impersonal. What detail in this picture tells you that the setting is not a modern fast-food restaurant? *(radiator)*

✔ *Performance Assessment*

Refer to the activity on page 544C of the Planning Guide.

📁 For an additional activity, refer to Activity 18 in the *Performance Assessment Strategies and Activities* booklet.

Using Your History Journal

Students might find it helpful to tape-record the interview. This will allow them to capture all of the details and get accurate quotes.

GLENCOE TECHNOLOGY

VIDEODISC
Use MindJogger to preview chapter content.

MindJogger Videoquiz

Chapter 18
Disc 2 Side B

 Also available in VHS.

➕ EXTRA CREDIT PROJECT

The Commonwealth Students might research the history of Canada or Australia during the postwar years. They should find out about the relationship with Great Britain, the economies, social issues, Canadians' relationship with France, and developments in literature, the arts, and sciences in those countries. Have students prepare reports to share with the whole class.

546 Chapter 18 *Between Two Fires*

SECTION THEME

▶ **Innovation** The period after World War I brings revolutionary changes in science, the arts, and popular culture.

Find Out

Answer: *Breaking with tradition and experimenting with new styles dominated the arts and popular culture of the 1920s and 1930s.*

FOCUS

Section Objective

Describe the trends that dominated the arts and popular culture from 1919 to 1939.

BELLRINGER
Motivational Activity

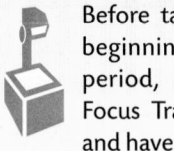

Before taking roll at the beginning of the class period, project Section Focus Transparency 18-1 and have students answer the activity questions. Discuss students' responses.

☞ This activity is also available as a blackline master.

Vocabulary Pre-check

☞ Use Vocabulary Activity 18 to introduce vocabulary terms.
L1 LEP

1920   1930   1940

1920 United States women win the vote.

1926 Ernest Hemingway writes *The Sun Also Rises.*

1935 Dance bands reach height of popularity.

Section 1

The Postwar World

Setting the Scene

▶ **Terms to Define**
cubism, surrealism, jazz, choreographer

▶ **People to Meet**
Albert Einstein, Sigmund Freud, T.S. Eliot, Pablo Picasso, Sergey Prokofiev, Walter Gropius

▶ **Places to Locate**
Hollywood

Find Out What trends dominated the arts and popular culture from 1919 to 1939?

The Storyteller

There was trouble in Hollywood. One of Tinseltown's biggest names, with a bigger screen following than 90 percent of the stars, according to columnist Louella Parsons, had "fallen afoul of the censors in a big way." Censor boards throughout the nation were receiving vigorous complaints about the "devilish, naughty" behavior of this national celebrity. Terry Ramsaye wrote in the Motion Picture Herald, "It's the old, old story. If nobody knows you, you can do anything, and if everybody knows you, you can't do anything—except what everyone approves." The star was Mickey Mouse.

—adapted from *Of Mice and Magic*, Leonard Maltin, 1987

Hollywood landmark

"ARMISTICE SIGNED, END OF THE WAR!" proclaimed *The New York Times* headline on November 11, 1918. In the United States and Europe, people exploded in a frenzy of celebration. The critic and author Malcolm Cowley wrote later of the feeling of euphoria that marked the end of the war: "We danced in the streets, embraced old women and pretty girls, swore blood brotherhood with soldiers in little bars...." But the excitement did not last. "On the next day," continued Cowley, "...we didn't know what to do."

World War I marked the great divide between the old and the new. The war changed the way many people looked at the world, and the disillusionment it caused led artists and intellectuals on a restless search for something new. The postwar period was a time for breaking with tradition and experimenting with new styles in politics and culture.

Changing Patterns of Life

Warren Harding was elected President of the United States in 1920, promising a "return to normalcy." But there was no going back to the past. The war had changed the world too much for that to be possible. Instead, people in both North America and Europe began to experiment with new customs and ways of life.

New Trends in Culture and Style

In the postwar era, women gained a new level of independence. With the ratification of the Nineteenth Amendment in 1920, women in the United States won the right to vote at last. Women also won the vote in most other Western countries following the war.

Many women now demanded other freedoms as well. Throwing off the inhibitions of the prewar era, some women in the United States and western

---

SECTION RESOURCES

☞ **Reproducible Masters**
- Reproducible Lesson Plan 18-1
- Vocabulary Activity 18
- Guided Reading Activity 18-1
- Time Line Activity 18
- Chapter Themes: Graphic Organizer 18
- Section Quiz 18-1

Transparencies
- Section Focus Transparency 18-1
- Chapter Transparency 18
- World History and Art Transparencies 39, 43

Multimedia
- Focus on World Art Prints 3, 4, 23
- Student Self-Test and Review Software
- Testmaker
- World Music: Cultural Traditions, Lesson 1

Europe began to use rouge and lipstick openly. Their skirts rose from a few inches above the ankle to an inch above the knee. They cropped their hair to a shingle bob and aimed for a carefree, little-boy look. Thus attired, the "flapper" created a revolution in manners and morals.

In the postwar era, not only the flapper but people in general disdained the familiar and the commonplace. They wanted heroes who were larger than life. Babe Ruth, the "Sultan of Swat," was the king of baseball. Tennis champions Big Bill Tilden and Helen Wills Moody became national heroes. When Gertrude Ederle swam the English Channel and Charles Lindbergh flew nonstop from Long Island to Paris, the public saluted them with tumultuous ticker-tape parades on Broadway.

Amid all the hoopla, bankers and business leaders were having a heyday. The war had opened new prospects for economic development. President Calvin Coolidge neatly summed up the nation's focus in the 1920s when he said, "The business of America is business."

The Impact of Technology

New forms of technology altered people's lifestyles and brought people closer together in the 1920s. The decade following World War I witnessed a revolution in transportation and communication throughout the world.

The automobile had perhaps the greatest impact on European and American society. A network of highways began to crisscross Europe and the United States. People could now move easily from place to place, and move they did. The United States, in particular, became an increasingly mobile society. Americans traveled farther afield on vacations and moved from rural areas to cities.

Radio also brought about dramatic changes. By exposing millions of people to the same news and entertainment shows, radio helped to produce a more homogeneous, or uniform, culture. Through its advertisements, radio also stimulated the public's desire for consumer goods. Advertisers learned the art of motivation, and ads now played on people's insecurities and self-doubts. "Why had he changed so in his attentions?" queried a forlorn-looking woman in an ad for a leading mouthwash.

Many products of the new technology eased the burden of the homemaker. With the advent of packaged foods, refrigerators, vacuum cleaners, and electric irons, people had more leisure time. Instead of working at home, they could take a drive, listen to the radio, or go out dancing. Millions spent their idle moments with another new product of technology: the movies.

A Revolution in Ideas

New inventions had an enormous impact on people's daily lives in the postwar period. At the same time, exciting new ideas in physics and psychology transformed the way people looked at themselves and the world.

Physics

In 1905 German physicist **Albert Einstein** introduced his theories of relativity, shattering Newton's view of the universe as a machine that operated by universal laws. According to Einstein, there are no absolutes in measuring time and space. Time and space instead depend on the relative motion of bodies in space. For example, the speed of two trains appears differently to bystanders on the station platform than it does to passengers on the trains.

Einstein also held that the speed of light is constant, and that all matter has energy. If matter could be broken down and changed into energy, the amount of energy would be enormous. Einstein's formula $E=MC^2$ was finally supported in 1945 when scientists tested the first atomic bomb in New Mexico.

Although too difficult for the average person to understand, Einstein's views had an impact beyond physics. To many people, his views seemed to reinforce the idea that there were no absolutes in any field of knowledge or in moral values.

Psychology

The Austrian physician **Sigmund Freud** (FROYD) revolutionized people's ideas about how the human mind works. After observing many patients, Freud concluded that the unconscious mind plays a major role in shaping behavior. The unconscious, he said, is full of memories of events from early childhood. If the memories are especially painful, people sometimes suppress them. Such suppression may lead to a variety of mental disorders.

When Freud first introduced his theories in the late 1800s, many people ridiculed or attacked them. By the 1920s, however, his ideas about human

Footnotes to History

Fads
The 1920s was a time when many fads swept the United States. These ranged from crossword puzzles, to stunts, such as sitting on the top of flagpoles for days at a time, to parlor games, such as mah-jongg, a Chinese version of rummy played with tiles.

Chapter 18 *Between Two Fires* **547**

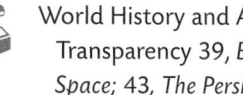
Chapter 18 *Between Two Fires* **547**

Independent Practice

📁 Guided Reading Activity
18-1 **L1**

📁 Time Line Activity 18

📁 Chapter Themes: Graphic
Organizer 18

History & Art Picasso did not complete Stein's face during the actual sitting. When he did finish it, he painted the face from memory in a sculptural, masklike style. This was indicative of the move Picasso would soon make into cubism. **Answer to Caption:** *Artists and writers broke with long-established traditions and experimented with new styles, media, and subject matter.*

Biography

The following videotape programs are available from Glencoe:

• **Amelia Earhart: Queen of the Air**

• **Admiral Richard Byrd**

you don't say...

Cubism, as a name, had its origin in a comment by art critic Louis Vauxhouses. Vauxhouses described Georges Braque's works as reducing things to "geometrical schemas, to cubes." Although there were no cubes in cubist painting, the name stuck.

History & Art *Gertrude Stein* by Pablo Picasso, 1906. The Metropolitan Museum of Art, New York, New York **The Spanish painter Pablo Picasso and the American writer Gertrude Stein were two of the major cultural figures of the 1920s and 1930s.** *What were two major characteristics of the arts during the period between the world wars?*

psychology had become more accepted and influential. Freud's theories eventually led to new approaches in the treatment of mental illness, in child rearing, and in education.

Upheaval in the Arts

The break between old and new following World War I was perhaps most sharply defined in the arts. In painting, music, literature, and dance, artists abandoned long-accepted traditions. The avant-garde experimented with new styles, media, and subject matter. Often the public greeted their pioneering efforts with cries of shock and protest.

Literature

Many of the period's writers had been disillusioned by World War I and its aftermath. The war had destroyed their belief in the traditional values of middle-class society. In expressing that disillusionment, they broke new literary ground.

In his poems *The Waste Land* and "The Hollow Men," for example, American-born poet **T.S. Eliot** used a patchwork style that juxtaposed different literary, religious, and historical references to convey a sense of despair about life. German novelist Thomas Mann, Czech novelist Franz Kafka, and British novelist Virginia Woolf also experimented

with new literary techniques. Both in terms of their style and content, all of these writers represented a sharp break with the literature of the past.

While they echoed Eliot's sense of disenchantment, American writers such as Ernest Hemingway and F. Scott Fitzgerald developed markedly different literary styles. For instance, in his 1926 novel *The Sun Also Rises*, Hemingway used a lean, straightforward style to tell the tale of Americans and Britons who roamed France and Spain, living for the moment while trying to find meaning in their lives. In contrast, Fitzgerald used a more elaborate poetic style in his 1925 novel *The Great Gatsby* to explore the atmosphere and excesses of the Roaring Twenties.

Several years earlier, in 1922, Irish novelist James Joyce had published *Ulysses*, an in-depth account of a day in the lives of three ordinary people in Dublin. *Ulysses* was a landmark in the development of the modern novel. Influenced by Freud's theories, Joyce developed a style known as "stream of consciousness" in which he presented the inner thoughts—rather than just the external actions—of his characters. Joyce's psychological emphasis and his earthy language caused a storm of protest, which led to a number of court battles over the publication of his novel.

In the late 1920s and the 1930s, many writers became interested in important social issues of the

548 Chapter 18 *Between Two Fires*

day. Langston Hughes, Claude McKay, and Zora Neale Hurston, who belonged to an African American literary movement known as the Harlem Renaissance, explored the African American experience in America. In *The Grapes of Wrath*, John Steinbeck described the plight of Oklahoma farmers who, in the midst of a severe drought, abandoned their farms and moved to California. John Dos Passos's *U.S.A.* trilogy was a broader social criticism of conditions in American society during the postwar period.

Painting

The postwar world also saw a revolution in the visual arts. Artists no longer tried to be realistic in their works. Instead they developed radical new styles and redefined the nature of painting. In 1907, the Spanish painter **Pablo Picasso** created an uproar in the art world when he painted *Les Demoiselles d'Avignon*. The painting was the earliest example of cubism, an abstract art form that uses intersecting geometric shapes. Cubist painters transform their subjects by flattening them, cutting them up, rearranging different portions of them, and altering shapes and colors to fit their own vision. As Picasso explained: "Art is a lie that makes us realize the truth."

Another development was Dada, an art form that aimed to shock middle-class viewers. Dada stressed absurdity and the role of the unpredictable in life. For example, the paintings and poems of Dada consisted of meaningless and random arrangements of objects and words. Dada's reliance on the imagination led to surrealism, an art form that used dreamlike images and unnatural combinations of objects. Influenced by Freud, surrealist painters tried to find a new reality by exploring the unconscious mind. The Spanish painter Salvador Dali created such realistically impossible images as limp watches set in bleak landscapes.

In the tradition of Steinbeck and Dos Passos, other artists used their talents to attack social problems. In their paintings and photographs, social realists such as Ben Shahn, Peter Blume, and Dorothea Lange showed the human suffering caused by the Depression of the 1930s. Although not a realist, Pablo Picasso protested the horrors of Spain's civil war in his symbolic painting *Guernica*.

Music and Dance

Composers also broke new ground after the war. Several eastern European composers transformed the classical form. **Sergey Prokofiev**

(sehr•GAY pruh•KAWF•yuhf), a Russian, composed driving and dissonant music that lacked the familiar harmonies of traditional forms. Critics dubbed him the "age of steel composer." Prokofiev, however, later composed more pleasant sounding symphonies and operas.

Arnold Schoenberg (SHUHN•BUHRG), a self-taught Austrian composer, made radical changes in music theory. Instead of harmonies based on the traditional eight-note scale, he proposed new musical arrangements based on 12 equally valued notes. In his groundbreaking composition, *Pierrot Lunaire* (1912), Schoenberg used harsh, dissonant music to express what he regarded as the decay of Western civilization. His composition outraged conservative audiences.

Meanwhile, in the United States, musicians were creating their own distinctive sound. The 1920s was "the golden age of jazz." What some have called the only art form to originate in the United States, jazz is a mixture of American folk songs, West African rhythms, harmonies from European classical music, and work songs from the days of slavery. Trumpet player Louis Armstrong, blues singer Bessie Smith, and pianist Jelly Roll Morton popularized the new music which soon spread throughout the world.

The postwar era also saw a transformation in the art of dance. Performing barefoot in a loose tunic, the American dancer Isadora Duncan changed people's ideas about dance. Another American, Martha Graham, expanded on Duncan's style and turned modern dance into a striking new art form.

Visualizing History Pablo Picasso's mural painting *Guernica* expresses the horror of the bombing of the town of Guernica during the civil war that devastated Spain in the 1930s. *What changes developed in the visual arts after World War I?*

Chapter 18 *Between Two Fires* **549**

Chapter 18
Section 1

ASSESS

Check for Understanding

Assign Section 1 Review as homework or as an in-class activity.

🖳 Use Student Self-Test and Review Software to review Section 1.

Evaluate

🗂 Section Quiz 18-1

🖳 Use the Testmaker to create a customized quiz for Section 1.

Reteach

Have students independently review the section and list important dates, discoveries, movements, and people on a time line. Some students may wish to do additional research to fill in gaps. Discuss the time lines in class and combine them to make a class time line.

Visualizing History Picasso, in addition to creating lasting works of art, also expanded our definition of what art could be. His art was very influential among artists during his own lifetime and remains so among artists today.
Answer to Caption: *Artists turned from realism to abstraction, showing basic artistic forms and probing the subconscious rather than portraying everyday scenes. They also commented on social problems in their works.*

MAKING CONNECTIONS ACTIVITY

The Arts Motion pictures became a major industry in the 1920s. One of the earliest silent film stars was British comedian Charlie Chaplin. Sound was added to films in the late 1920s. Have students research the movie industry and the technological advances it made during the postwar decade. Have students work in pairs to write a report on their findings and then design a poster advertising a movie of the era. This was the time of *Dracula* with Bela Lugosi, Greta Garbo in *Mata Hari*, Jeanette MacDonald and Nelson Eddy in *Rose Marie*, and Fred Astaire and Ginger Rogers in *Top Hat*. Suggest that students bring to class a video of one of the old films; groups of students could plan a small film festival. **L2** 📼

TEACH

Point out that the people in the status symbol cars wearing fancy dresses and tuxedos were the wealthy set. Entertainment for millions of others often centered around a more modest piece of technology—the radio. By 1925 the listening audience was put at 50 million, and radio advertising was making an incredible impact. *What radio shows or stars have you heard about from that era? (some shows: "Fibber McGee and Molly," "Baby Snooks," "Flash Gordon," "Little Orphan Annie," "Inner Sanctum"; stars: Jack Benny, Burns and Allen, Edgar Bergen and Charlie McCarthy, Kate Smith)*

you don't say...

Clarence Darrow also defended Nathan Leopold and Richard Loeb, two university students accused of murdering a classmate, in 1924. Darrow did not believe in capital punishment, even though the men admitted to the murder. Darrow introduced psychiatrists and neurologists to the courtroom battle and opened a new era in murder trials by entering the first "temporary insanity" plea.

Flying High

Racing down a dark road, the young men and women in this photograph enjoy a new freedom. Cars were important throughout the industrialized world of Europe and North America, and the American auto industry led the global market. The automobile brought mobility to many Americans during the years following World War I. It was all part of a new lifestyle called the Roaring Twenties.

Behind the gaiety and frivolity, however, the 1920s was a decade in which a new urban style of living came into conflict with an older rural way of life. In the United States this conflict was played out again and again: Politician and orator William Jennings Bryan battled lawyer Clarence Darrow in the famous Scopes trial over whether or not public schools should teach Darwinian science. Farms failed and farmers lost their land, while the sounds of the new prosperity played on radios in their living rooms. The new city slickers were jazz age flappers, like the ones here, racing along unpaved roads in a fancy new Stutz Bearcat. ◉

Sergey Diaghilev (dee•AH•guh•LEHF), the Russian impresario, or sponsor, developed modern ballet, which blended modern dance with classical ballet. When Russian composer Igor Stravinsky wrote *The Rite of Spring* (1913) for Diaghilev and his company of dancers, the Ballets Russes, it was a turning point for ballet. The leaping dance steps that ballet star Vaslav Nijinsky (VAHT•slahv nuh •ZHIHN•skee) performed to Stravinsky's music created a sensation. George Balanchine, who had been a choreographer, or dance arranger, with the Ballets Russes, expanded on Diaghilev's work after moving from the Soviet Union to the United States.

Architecture

The 1920s and 1930s saw striking new designs in buildings and furnishings. **Walter Gropius** founded the Bauhaus (BOW•HOWS) school of design in Weimar (VY•MAHR), Germany. He and his followers created a simple, unornamented style of design. Linking beauty to practicality, Gropius pioneered geometric concrete and glass structures in both Germany and the United States.

In the United States, Frank Lloyd Wright blended his structures with their natural surroundings. Because of their low horizontal form, his houses seem to grow out of the ground. Instead of creating boxlike rooms, Wright reduced the number of walls so that one room flowed into another.

Popular Culture

While the revolutionary developments taking place in art and music may not have had an immediate effect on the lives of ordinary people, films and big bands did. In the postwar era, **Hollywood** productions dominated the movie screens of the world. The movies reflected the new morality of the "Jazz Age" and the doctrine of living for the moment. During the 1930s the public flocked to movie theaters, where for 10 cents they could escape the harsh realities of hard economic times.

In the early part of the century, the creative use of the camera elevated the motion picture to an art form. In *The Last Laugh*, a silent film directed by German filmmaker F.W. Murnau, the camera work is so expressive that the story is told entirely without subtitles. British actor and director Charlie Chaplin also broke new ground in his films while delighting millions of moviegoers with his humor.

But in 1927 motion pictures found their voice. *The Jazz Singer*, starring American actor Al Jolson, changed motion pictures overnight and signaled the beginning of the end of the era of silent films. During the early 1930s American musicals, gangster movies, and horror movies were popular. However, some filmmakers tried to educate as well as entertain their audiences. *I Am a Fugitive From a Chain Gang* (1932) was a forceful indictment of the Southern penal system, while *Mr. Smith Goes to Washington* (1939) showed the effects of political corruption.

The public also sought escape from their troubles on the ballroom floor. In the 1930s and 1940s, dance bands reached their greatest popularity. Tommy Dorsey, Count Basie, Benny Goodman, Duke Ellington, Artie Shaw, and their swing bands performed in ballrooms and hotels all across America. Swing was the new word for music played with a happy, relaxed jazz beat. But if swing was not everyone's cup of tea, there were alternatives. The bands of Guy Lombardo and Sammy Kaye played traditional waltzes and fox-trots.

Obviously, the social upheavals and economic hardships that World War I created did not dampen the creative spirit following the war. During this era artists introduced new styles in every major art form. They took little interest in politics and reform. Many cried out against conformity and retreated into individualism. At times it seemed as if they were transforming the world with their radical new visions of life. But the euphoria did not last. The stock market crash that took place on Wall Street in late October 1929 signaled for the United States and much of the world an economic depression that had devastating and deadly consequences.

Chapter 18
Section 1

Cultural Perspectives

Jazz, created by African American musicians in the United States, incorporated many sources. It grew out of spiritual music, old ballads, children's jingles, minstrel music, and the rag-time piano music of the early 1920s. In New Orleans it was common for bands in funeral processions to play hymns on the way to the funeral and then break out in joyful jazz tunes afterward. Singing and dancing crowds would tag along after the band. Today jazz is a popular form of music throughout the world.

Enrich

Have students choose one of the literary works or paintings mentioned in the section, read or study it, and report on it to the class.

CLOSE

Discuss with students how World War I changed the way people viewed the world. Review the artistic and scientific advances and cultural movements of the time. Help students conclude that the postwar world had adopted a style of "living for the moment."

SECTION 1 REVIEW

Recall
1. **Define** cubism, surrealism, jazz, choreographer.
2. **Identify** Albert Einstein, Sigmund Freud, T.S. Eliot, Pablo Picasso, Sergey Prokofiev, Walter Gropius.
3. **Explain** how women shaped

many of the changes that came to Western societies after World War I.

Critical Thinking
4. **Analyzing Information** The era after World War I was a time for breaking with tradition. How could abandoning

traditions help a society? How might it harm a society?

Understanding Themes
5. **Innovation** What impact did technological advances in transportation and communication have on American culture in the 1920s?

SECTION 1 REVIEW ANSWERS

1. All vocabulary words are defined in the Glossary.
2. Albert Einstein, 547; Sigmund Freud, 547; T. S. Eliot, 548; Pablo Picasso, 549; Sergey Prokofiev, 549; Walter Gropius, 551
3. Women won the right to vote and influ-

enced elections; they became more independent and were involved in changes affecting fashion and behavior patterns.
4. Answers will vary. Possible answer: New creative spirit can spur inventions and improvements; however, some traditions are still valuable and should not be

abandoned.
5. **INNOVATION** They made society more homogeneous, brought people together more easily, and made life easier so there was more leisure time.

Chapter 18
Section 2

SECTION THEME

▶ **Change** The Great Depression forces governments in Europe and North America to increase their involvement in social and economic affairs.

Find Out

Answer: *because the governments in these nations intervened in new ways in social and economic affairs, taking steps to improve life for people suffering in the Great Depression*

FOCUS

Section Objective

Explain why democratic government survived in the United States, Great Britain, and France during the post-World War I era.

BELLRINGER
Motivational Activity

Before taking roll at the beginning of the class period, project Section Focus Transparency 18-2 and have students answer the activity questions. Discuss students' responses.

This activity is also available as a blackline master.

Vocabulary Pre-check

Use Vocabulary Activity 18 to introduce vocabulary terms. **L1 LEP**

1920	1925	1930	1935

1926 The General Strike paralyzes Great Britain.

1933 Franklin D. Roosevelt introduces the New Deal.

1936 French voters elect a Socialist government.

Section 2

The Western Democracies

Setting the Scene

▶ **Terms to Define**
disarmament, general strike, coalition

▶ **People to Meet**
Franklin D. Roosevelt, Ramsay MacDonald, Eamon De Valera, Léon Blum

▶ **Places to Locate**
Washington, D.C., Irish Free State

Find Out Why did democratic government survive in the United States, Great Britain, and France during the post-World War I era?

The Storyteller

Throughout 1932 the lines had grown. They formed at banks, as investors tried to withdraw their savings before the bank collapsed. They formed at factory gates and employment offices. Men lost their jobs, lost their homes. They swallowed their pride and formed another line—for relief. If there was none to be found, another line waited. As one eyewitness reported, "We saw a crowd of some 50 men fighting over a barrel of garbage which had been set outside the back door of a restaurant."

—adapted from *Since Yesterday*, Frederick Lewis Allen, 1939

Depression-era food line

Peace brought neither stability nor lasting prosperity to the Western democracies, which paid a heavy price for their victory in World War I. Although the United States suffered comparatively minor financial losses, huge war debts threatened the economic and political stability of Great Britain and France. The West did enjoy a brief period of prosperity in the 1920s, but a global economic depression soon followed. This depression further weakened the Western democracies in the 1930s, making it difficult for them to counter the rising totalitarian threat in Italy and Germany.

The United States

The United States emerged from World War I in better shape than its allies. No battles were fought on American soil, and because of its late entry into the conflict, America suffered far fewer casualties than the other nations. Moreover, unlike the economies of many European countries, the American economy remained strong until 1929.

Cutting Foreign Ties

President Woodrow Wilson wanted the United States to assume a greater role in world affairs following the war. Americans, however, were weary of war and of the foreign entanglements that had dragged the nation into war. They wanted to return to a life of isolation, free from international problems.

An idealistic man, Wilson had seized on the notion of a League of Nations as the cornerstone of a lasting peace. But the newly elected Republican majorities in Congress had no wish to accommodate the Democratic President. When Congress failed to ratify the Treaty of Versailles in 1919, it also rejected American membership in the League. The absence of the United States significantly weakened the

SECTION RESOURCES

Reproducible Masters
- Reproducible Lesson Plan 18-2
- Vocabulary Activity 18
- Guided Reading Activity 18-2
- Section Quiz 18-2

Transparencies
- Section Focus Transparency 18-2
- World History and Art Transparency 38, *Migrant Mother*

Multimedia
- Student Self-Test and Review Software
- Testmaker

League's effectiveness as a strong international peacekeeping organization.

Meanwhile, many Americans feared the effects of communism on the United States. In 1919 and 1920 this "red scare" led to the expulsion of suspected foreign-born radicals. Some native-born Americans also opposed immigration from southern and eastern Europe. In response, Congress enacted limits to immigration from Europe. Earlier laws had already excluded or limited Asian immigration

From Boom to Depression

Unlike Europe, the United States emerged from the war with a dynamic industrial economy. It was now a nation lending, instead of borrowing, money. American industries produced a major share of the world's manufactured goods, and many industrial workers earned higher wages. As a result of this prosperity, more Americans were willing to take risks. Some bought expensive goods on credit. Others entered the stock market, buying stocks on margin, that is, they paid only part of the cost and borrowed the rest from brokers.

Despite the soaring "bull market," the economy had underlying weaknesses. Most farmers faced hardships because of falling farm prices. Also, in certain industries, workers did not see their wages rise as fast as the production of goods. As a result, many people held back from buying goods that factories were rapidly turning out. This combination of slow demand and overproduction paved the way for an economic crisis.

In late October 1929, concern about the economy led brokers to call in loans. When investors were unable to pay, a financial panic began. Stock prices tumbled, wiping out the fortunes of many investors. This stock market crash sparked the Great Depression of the 1930s. In the three years after the crash, prices fell and many businesses and banks closed. Sales dropped off, forcing a production slump. Salaries and wages also fell, and many workers lost their jobs. By 1933 more than 13 million American workers were unemployed—nearly one-fourth of the nation's workforce.

Many Americans believed that direct relief for the needy was the responsibility of the individual, the family, and the local community. Government-funded relief, they held, would destroy American self-reliance and lead to socialism. However, in these desperate times, not everyone agreed.

Geography

The Dust Bowl

American farmers in the 1930s suffered greatly from the Great Depression, but their hardships also came from a devastating drought that afflicted the central United States from 1933 to 1937. As the Great Plains became powder-dry, winds lifted vital topsoil in clouds of dust that turned day into night. Dust storms had swept over the area before, but never on such a large and destructive scale.

The roots of this disaster lay well in the past. Ranchers' cattle overgrazed an area that experienced scant rainfall. The ranchers were followed by farmers, who planted wheat. These early settlers plowed land that should never have been cultivated, and they farmed

Dust Bowl scene

it badly. They did not use contour plowing to check erosion, rotate their crops, or plant trees as windbreaks to hold the soil.

Ruined by drought, about 200,000 farm families headed West, especially to California. They found little relief in their new home—only low-paying jobs and the resentments of local residents opposed to their coming. It took many years of normal rainfall and improved farming methods to transform the Great Plains into productive land again. In addition to agriculture, the region today prospers from petroleum and coal mining.

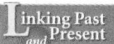

Linking Past and Present **ACTIVITY**

Describe the factors that created the Dust Bowl. What did many Dust Bowl farmers do in the 1930s? How has the region developed since that time?

Chapter 18 *Between Two Fires* **553**

TEACH

Guided Practice

THEME Change

Discuss how the aftermath of the war changed the economies in France, Great Britain, and the United States. Ask students to comment on the drastic change in the United States when the stock market crashed. **L1**

From Boom to Depression
How did the Great Depression affect people's ideas about the role of government in society? *With large numbers of workers unemployed and on relief, people during the Great Depression began to expect government to take a greater role in finding solutions to social and economic problems.*

Linking Past and Present

The Dust Bowl

Lead students in a discussion of how the weather and other natural phenomena affect business, the economy, and daily life. Ask them to consider how heavy rains and flooding, unexpected snow and freezing, and hurricanes affect farmers and orchard growers.

ANSWERS

overgrazing of land, drought, poor farming methods; they headed west to find work in California; normal rainfall and improved farming methods restored productivity and petroleum and coal mining also became important to the region's economy

Chapter 18
Section 2

World History and Art Transparency 38, *Migrant Mother*

Independent Practice

Guided Reading Activity 18-2 **L1**

Visualizing History A general strike is labor's strongest weapon, and when it occurs society can be thrown into upheaval. Winston Churchill had prepared for such a strike in 1926. Police were mobilized, troops dispatched, and thousands of upper- and middle-class volunteers drove trucks, taxis, and locomotives. It was an emergency, but one with little violence.
Answer to Caption: *The war had reduced Great Britain's standing in world markets; its privileged standing in foreign trade was upset by challenges from new competitors; it became a debtor nation.*

Broadcast Have students write the script for a 1930s radio news broadcast. They may use facts from the text or conduct additional research. The broadcast should also include weather or sports or some other feature related to the country of origin of the broadcast. **L2 LEP**

Linking Past and Present

"Happy Days Are Here Again," the popular jingle that Franklin D. Roosevelt used as his 1932 campaign song, is still played today at the Democratic party's national conventions.

Visualizing History During the 1920s and 1930s, economic downturns led to labor unrest in many western democracies. British workers especially carried out strikes for better wages. *What was Great Britain's economic standing after World War I?*

The New Deal

In 1932 voters elected a new President, former New York governor **Franklin D. Roosevelt.** Roosevelt had campaigned on the promise of "a new deal" for the American people. He believed that the federal government had to aid the stricken economy and provide relief for the unemployed.

In the first 100 days of his administration, in the spring and early summer of 1933, Roosevelt sent a number of bills to Congress that quickly became laws. These measures regulated the banks and stock market and established production guidelines for industry and agriculture. To put people back to work, the government established public works projects to build roads, dams, bridges, homes, and parks. Later New Deal legislation provided for social security and unemployment insurance. Although Roosevelt's New Deal policies were not entirely successful in ending the Depression, they did much to restore the confidence of the nation.

Foreign Affairs

The American government was concerned with more than just domestic affairs during the 1920s and 1930s. Despite its rejection of the League of

Nations and binding alliances, the United States did take steps to prevent a future world war. In 1922 it played host in **Washington, D.C.,** to an international conference on disarmament, the reduction of military weapons. At this conference, the United States signed a treaty with Japan and Great Britain limiting the number of naval warships each could stockpile. The leading powers at the conference also agreed to seek peaceful rather than military solutions to disagreements.

In 1928 the United States and France signed the Kellogg-Briand Pact, which denounced war as a means of settling disputes. Eventually, nearly all the nations of the world signed this agreement. Unfortunately, it was nothing more than a statement of intentions and had no powers of enforcement.

Great Britain

Although World War I increased the United States's economic and political influence, it cost Great Britain its position as a leading economic power in the world. Before the war British banks lent money to nations all over the globe. But the war

554 Chapter 18 *Between Two Fires*

MEETING SPECIAL NEEDS ACTIVITY

Physical Disability For students who have chronic illnesses and are absent from classes fairly often, it is helpful to provide materials that can be used at home or in the hospital. If there are special oral class presentations, tape them for home use. Assign a special book report or research project to make up for missed class lectures. When a cooperative learning activity has a task that can be done at home, assign it to the student who must be absent often. **L2**

was costly, and Great Britain was forced to borrow heavily from the United States. As a result, Great Britain became a debtor instead of a creditor nation.

The war also cost Great Britain its privileged position in world trade. American and Japanese companies captured many British overseas markets during the war. In addition, Great Britain's factories were old and the equipment outdated. Countries like the United States and Japan, which had industrialized later, had newer factories and more modern equipment. Consequently, they could produce goods at a lower cost. Many factories in Great Britain closed or cut back production after the war. By 1921 more than 2 million workers had lost their jobs.

The General Strike

Great Britain's economic woes reached a crisis point in 1926. Coal miners were engaged in a bitter strike for higher wages that year. For months the coal companies had refused to give in to their demands. In an effort to end the stalemate, the coal miners convinced many other trade union workers to join in a general strike, a strike involving all or a large number of a nation's workers. On May 4 all transport workers, dockers, public utility employees, and workers in the building trades and heavy industry walked off their jobs. The government declared a state of emergency and called out the troops to run essential services.

In the end, the General Strike was a failure. By December 1926 the coal strike had also collapsed. In 1927 Parliament passed the Trade Disputes Act, which made general strikes illegal.

Rise of the Labour Party

Despite the failure of the General Strike, British workers gained political strength during the 1920s. During this decade the Labour party became the second leading party in the country after the Conservatives. In 1924 and again in 1929, Labour governments were elected to office. Each time, King George V named Scottish Labour leader **Ramsay MacDonald** prime minister. Because the Labour party supported Socialist policies, its rise to power alarmed the Conservatives and their wealthy supporters. However, once in power, MacDonald and other Labour leaders tempered many of their radical demands.

The Dominions and Ireland

During the 1920s and 1930s, Great Britain still held on to most of its empire. However, dominions, such as Canada and Australia, became completely independent states. In 1931 Parliament passed the Statute of Westminister, which established the

 **Visualizing History** Irish nationalist leader Michael Collins, speaking here to crowds in the Irish capital of Dublin, negotiated a 1921 treaty with the British. *What changes did the treaty bring to Ireland?*

Commonwealth of Nations, a voluntary association linking Great Britain and its former colonies on an equal basis.

One of Great Britain's major problems was its relationship with Ireland. Unwilling to wait for home rule, militant Irish nationalists on Easter 1916 had revolted against the British. The brutal crushing of the Easter Uprising by British forces increased Irish support for full independence. In 1921 moderate leaders in Ireland and Great Britain signed a compromise agreement. The Catholic southern part of Ireland became a dominion known as the **Irish Free State**. The largely Protestant northern counties remained joined to Great Britain as Northern Ireland.

Wanting full independence for all of Ireland, Irish radicals, led by **Eamon De Valera**, revolted against the Irish Free State. The Irish government suppressed this uprising, but Irish elections in 1932 brought De Valera to power. Five years later, the country's name was changed to Eire, and a president replaced the British monarch as head of state.

France

World War I had an even more devastating effect on France than on Great Britain. In the four years of fighting, the combatants had destroyed thousands of square miles of farmland and forests and reduced villages and cities to rubble. French casualties were enormous. Half of the males

Visualizing History Michael Collins was a courageous and a very popular Irish leader. He was successful in raising funds for the Irish war for independence and organized an intelligence service for the Irish Republican Army. As commander of the Free State army, Collins took strong actions to end fighting but was killed in an ambush in County Cork in 1922.

Answer to Caption: *It divided the island of Ireland into two parts: the southern part became known as the Irish Free State, a dominion separate from Great Britain; the northern counties remained part of Great Britain and were known as Northern Ireland.*

CURRICULUM CONNECTION

LITERATURE

In the postwar world of Great Britain, A. A. Milne offered a protected and imaginary world for children in *Winnie-the-Pooh* and *The House at Pooh Corner*. Two other well-known children's stories of the time were Margery Williams Bianco's *The Velveteen Rabbit* and Hugh Lofting's *The Story of Doctor Doolittle.*

MAKING CONNECTIONS ACTIVITIES

Literature Have students read John Steinbeck's novel *The Grapes of Wrath* about farmers making the journey from the Dust Bowl area to California. Have them report to the class on how Steinbeck portrayed the life these people led. **L2**

The Arts Movies were an extremely popular form of entertainment for Americans in the 1930s. Suggest that students view a video of one or two hit films from the era, such as *It Happened One Night* or *Footlight Parade*. Discuss as a class what sorts of movies appealed to people during the time of the Depression. **L1 LEP**

Biography

The following videotape programs are available from Glencoe:

- **FDR: The Years of Crisis**
- **Eleanor Roosevelt: A Restless Spirit**

ASSESS

Check for Understanding

Assign Section 2 Review as homework or as an in-class activity.

▣ Use Student Self-Test and Review Software to review Section 2.

Evaluate

◻ Section Quiz 18-2

▣ Use the Testmaker to create a customized quiz for Section 2.

Reteach

Write the headings *Causes* and *Effects* on the chalkboard and create a class chart to help students review the causes and effects of World War I.

Enrich

Have students use the chart from **Reteach** to write a short report on what they think were the most important effects of World War I on the Western democracies.

CLOSE

Lead a discussion about why democracy survived in the United States, Great Britain, and France after World War I despite serious economic and political problems.

 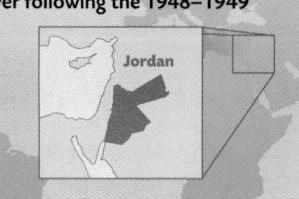

Jordan Gains Independence

Jordan, 1921
After World War I, lands east and west of the Jordan River were administered by Great Britain. In 1921 the territory east of the Jordan gained partial self-government. This land—then called Transjordan—won full independence in 1946 as a monarchy under King Abdullah. The country was renamed Jordan after it annexed the West Bank of the Jordan River following the 1948–1949 Arab-Israeli war.

between the ages of 18 and 32 were killed in the fighting.

Troubled Years

Like Great Britain, France faced severe economic problems after the war. High unemployment and soaring inflation caused terrible hardships. The French government was nearly bankrupt, and its war debts were staggering. As a result of these financial problems, France's factories, railways, and canals could not be quickly rebuilt.

The political picture was as bleak as the economic one. Many political parties competed for votes. Since each party received seats in the national legislature according to its percentage of the vote, no party ever won a majority of seats. In order to form a government, several parties had to band together into a coalition, or alliance of factions, but the coalition governments often fell apart soon after they were formed.

Extremist groups on both the left and the right also threatened the political stability of the nation. Communists and Socialists struggled for power against Fascists, extreme nationalists favoring a strong government, and outbreaks of violence were common.

The Popular Front

In 1934 the political crisis reached a head. Fascist groups rioted in Paris, killing several people. Fearing a Fascist takeover, the Communists appealed to leaders of the Socialist party for "a broad Popular Front to combat fascism and for work, liberty, and peace."

The new coalition won enough votes in a 1936 election to form a government. **Léon Blum**, the Socialist leader, became prime minister. The Popular Front was in power for about a year, but in that short time it passed many new laws that benefited workers and farmers.

Foreign Policy

Exhausted and drained by World War I, France wanted, above all else, to prevent another war. Consequently, the French government supported the League of Nations in the postwar years and worked to create a series of alliances to contain Germany. But it also sought friendly ties with Germany's new democratic Weimar Republic. In 1925 France signed the Locarno Treaties with Germany, Italy, Belgium, and Great Britain that appeared to ensure a lasting peace.

As added insurance against a future German invasion, France built a series of fortifications that were 200 miles (320 km) long called the Maginot (MA•zhuh•NOH) Line. This stretch of concrete bunkers and trenches extended along France's border with Germany. French military leaders boasted that the Maginot Line could never be crossed. What they failed to consider was that past German invasions had come through Belgium, whose border with France remained virtually undefended.

SECTION 2 REVIEW

Recall
1. **Define** disarmament, general strike, coalition.
2. **Identify** Franklin D. Roosevelt, Ramsay MacDonald, Commonwealth of Nations, Eamon De Valera, Léon Blum.
3. **Explain** how World War I affected the economies of the United States, Great Britain, and France.

Critical Thinking
4. **Evaluating Information** Why do you think the democracies of the United States, Great Britain, and France survived despite postwar political, economic, and social problems?

Understanding Themes
5. **Change** How did President Franklin D. Roosevelt's New Deal change the role the federal government played in American society after 1933?

SECTION 2 REVIEW ANSWERS

1. All vocabulary words are defined in the Glossary.
2. Roosevelt, 554; MacDonald, 555; Commonwealth of Nations, 555; De Valera, 555; Blum, 556
3. It had a devastating effect on the economies of Great Britain and France; the United States emerged with a strong economy.
4. Answers will vary. Students may conclude that democracy was more firmly established in these countries or that the governments of these nations took bold new steps to meet citizens' needs.
5. **CHANGE** The federal government became more actively involved in domestic affairs.

Section 3

Fascist Dictatorships

Setting the Scene

▶ **Terms to Define**
totalitarianism, fascism, corporate state, syndicate, *Kristallnacht*, concentration camp

▶ **People to Meet**
Benito Mussolini, Adolf Hitler

▶ **Places to Locate**
Weimar

 **ind Out** What factors led to the rise of Fascist dictatorships in Italy and Germany?

The Storyteller

Alice Hamilton was dismayed. Twenty-five years earlier, she had spent a year in Frankfurt as a student. She now returned to visit the city only to find the lovely Römer Platz draped with Nazi flags. The city's children and young people also had changed. Formerly they played games; now they marched in regular ranks. Where tuneful songs had been sung in public houses, militant music blared forth. Mrs. Hamilton understood why this transformation had taken place. Hitler was inspiring Germany's impoverished, hopeless youth to believe they were the elect of the earth.

—adapted from "The Youth Who Are Hitler's Strength," *New York Times Magazine*, October 8, 1933. Alice Hamilton. Reprinted in *Sources of the Western Tradition*, Marvin Perry, 1991

Nazi poster

fter World War I, political, economic, and social strife engulfed many Western nations. Long-established democracies remained strong in the United States and Great Britain, but in Italy, Germany, and Russia, a new form of dictatorship known as totalitarianism emerged. Totalitarian governments aimed at total control over every aspect of citizens' lives. Under totalitarianism, the individual was viewed as a servant of the state and was allowed few personal freedoms. Books, radio, films, the arts, and the schools were used to promote the government's political philosophy.

Totalitarianism grew out of World War I. To fight a total war, democratic and autocratic governments alike had temporarily assumed sweeping powers. After the war, totalitarian dictatorships extended such powers further, using their vast authority to remodel entire societies and conquer other lands. In seeking these goals, totalitarian governments came into conflict with each other and with the Western democracies. Their actions set the stage for the beginning of another world war.

Rise of Fascism in Italy

After World War I, a general mood of dissatisfaction gripped the people of Italy. Italian nationalists were outraged that the Paris peace treaties had not given Italy huge portions of territory from the Central Powers. Returning veterans found no work, workers went on strike or took over factories, and peasants seized land. Reeling from an economic downturn, the government was unable to relieve the mounting discontent.

These chaotic conditions favored the rise of **Benito Mussolini** (MOO•suh•LEE•nee). Born in 1883, Mussolini came from a working-class family. As a young journalist, he was active in Socialist politics; but during the war, he switched loyalties and became an ardent nationalist.

Chapter 18 *Between Two Fires* 557

SECTION THEME

▶ **Uniformity** Fascist governments in Italy and Germany limit individual liberties and stress loyalty to the state.

 **ind Out**

Answer: *Economic problems, social chaos, and unemployment led to the rise of dictatorships in Italy and Germany.*

FOCUS

Section Objective

Identify the factors that led to the rise of Fascist dictatorships in Italy and Germany after World War I.

BELLRINGER
Motivational Activity

Before taking roll at the beginning of the class period, project Section Focus Transparency 18-3 and have students answer the activity questions. Discuss students' responses.
📁 This activity is also available as a blackline master.

Vocabulary Pre-check

🔲 Use the Vocabulary PuzzleMaker to create a puzzle that reinforces the vocabulary terms in this section. **L1**

SECTION RESOURCES

📁 **Reproducible Masters**
• Reproducible Lesson Plan 18-3
• Guided Reading Activity 18-3
• History Simulation 18
• Geography and History Activity 18
• Section Quiz 18-3

🔖 **Transparencies**
• Section Focus Transparency 18-3

Multimedia
🔲 Vocabulary PuzzleMaker Software
🔲 Student Self-Test and Review Software
🔲 Testmaker
🔲 Lessons of War:
   The Enemy

TEACH

Guided Practice

THEME Uniformity

Ask students if they would like to live in a uniform society. Have them give examples from Fascist Italy and Nazi Germany to illustrate the effects of imposed uniformity. List these examples on the chalkboard as they are given. **L1**

Visualizing History Point out what effect Mussolini's military attire and disciplined stance would have on the people. When *Il Duce* was in power there were no purges, but he was able to intimidate people with the threat of terror.

Answer to Caption: *Mussolini promised "something to everyone," then used street violence and political pressure to destroy his opponents and get himself named prime minister.*

Recognizing Ideologies Write two headings on the chalkboard: *What the People Wanted* and *What Mussolini Had to Offer*. Encourage students to fill in the chart during class discussion. Ask students to make a similar chart for Adolf Hitler. **L2**

Biography

The following videotape program is available from Glencoe:

- **Mussolini: Italy's Nightmare**

Visualizing History Italian dictator Benito Mussolini salutes soldiers at a military parade. He dreamed of making Italy a great nation and reviving the Roman Empire. *How did Mussolini come to power in Italy?*

Mussolini formed a new political party in 1919 called the *Fasci di Combattimento*, or Fascist party. Fascism (FA•SHIH•zuhm) is a political philosophy that advocates the glorification of the state, a single-party system with a strong ruler, and an aggressive form of nationalism. Like communism, fascism gave the state absolute authority. But fascism defended private property, although with some government regulation, and the class structure. According to its principles, the nation's cause was to be advanced at all cost even by war.

Mussolini's Road to Power

Conditions in Italy continued to deteriorate in the months following the war. The value of the lira

declined steadily, the price of bread rose, and a shortage of coal hampered industrial production. To express their dissatisfaction, workers staged a series of strikes that paralyzed the country. In September 1920, workers in Lombardy and Piedmont took over the factories. Mussolini showed his support for the strikers in a speech at Trieste:

> **❝** I demand that the factories increase their production. If this is guaranteed to me by the workers in place of the industrialists, I shall declare without hesitation that the former have the right to substitute themselves … [for] the latter. **❞**

The unrest spread to rural Italy. Peasants seized land from wealthy landowners, and tenant farmers refused to pay their rents. The situation was so chaotic that the middle and upper classes feared a Communist revolution. Ever the politician, Mussolini offered "a little something to everyone." To appease the landowners, he vowed to end the unrest and protect private property. To woo the workers, he promised full employment and workers' benefits. He pleased nationalists by pledging to restore Italy to its former greatness.

By 1922 the Fascists were ready to use force in a bid for power. The Blackshirts, as Mussolini's followers were called, did not rely on verbal assaults alone to achieve their goals. They physically attacked political opponents in the streets and drove elected officials from office.

Believing that fascism was a useful way of controlling the Socialists and workers, the democratic government did nothing to stop the Blackshirts. As a result, Mussolini grew even bolder. In October 1922 the Fascists staged a march on Rome. Mussolini waited in Milan to see how the government would react. Believing that the Fascists were planning to seize power, the cabinet asked King Victor Emmanuel III to declare martial law. The king refused, and the cabinet resigned. Instead of calling for new elections, the monarch named Mussolini prime minister.

Mussolini's Dictatorship

Mussolini quickly put an end to democratic rule in Italy. In a 1924 election, Blackshirts used their now familiar brutal tactics to make sure that Italians voted for Fascist candidates. As a result, Fascists won a majority of seats in the Italian parliament. The Fascist-controlled parliament gave Mussolini sweeping new powers. After this election Mussolini began calling himself *Il Duce* (eel DOO•chay), "The Leader."

COOPERATIVE LEARNING ACTIVITY

Debate Organize the class into two groups to debate this statement: Mussolini's rule was good for Italy. Have the members of each group agree on assignments within the group as they prepare for the debate. Inform them that they will need to conduct research to support their positions. Remind students that to hold a good debate, statements must be based on fact, not opinion. Be sure to allow both sides time to make rebuttal arguments. Explain to students the bases on which you determine the winning team (thoroughness of research, clarity and force of arguments, presentation, and so forth). **L3**

To consolidate his power, Mussolini reorganized the Italian government and established a corporate state. Under the corporate state, Mussolini hoped to bring workers and employers together and consequently to end the political quarreling that he associated with a democratic, multiparty system. To this end, he banned non-Fascist parties and ordered that syndicates, or corporations of workers and employers, be formed in each industry. Each syndicate sent representatives to a legislature in Rome that set policies on wages, production, and distribution. In theory, the corporate state was a new form of democracy; in practice, it was a political tool expressly designed for strengthening Mussolini's power.

Many Italians bitterly opposed fascism. They mourned the loss of democracy and individual freedoms. The Fascists arrested, assaulted, and murdered any who dared speak out against the abuses. "The masses must obey," thundered Mussolini. "They cannot afford to waste time searching for truth."

A majority of Italians, however, supported Mussolini. They believed he had done Italy a great service by preventing a Communist revolution and had brought order to the nation. After all, they said, he "made the trains run on time."

By building up Italy's armed forces, Mussolini did solve the unemployment problem. Even more important, he rekindled the feelings of patriotism and nationalism that had lain dormant in the Italian people. He made it clear to Italians that it was in their destiny to recapture all the greatness that had made the glory of ancient Rome. He would use all the economic and human resources available to make Italy a great power again.

The Weimar Republic

While Mussolini was establishing fascism in Italy, the Allies were preoccupied with ensuring that Germany would never again threaten peace. As a result, the Treaty of Versailles limited the size of Germany's armed forces and required the Germans to form a democratic government. While many Germans believed that democracy had become inevitable after the breakdown of the monarchy, few really believed in it.

In early 1919 Germans went to the polls and elected delegates to a national assembly. Meeting in **Weimar**, the assembly drafted a constitution for Germany establishing a democratic republic. The republic, which lasted from 1919 to 1933, was called the Weimar Republic.

Soon after the Weimar Republic became a reality, political instability and violence threatened to overwhelm it. In 1920 nationalist army officers tried to overthrow the government in a coup d'état. Like many other Germans, they claimed that Weimar leaders had betrayed the nation by accepting the Treaty of Versailles. Although the revolt was suppressed, the government failed to overcome widespread opposition to its policies.

Reparations

More than just political problems threatened Germany. Great Britain and France promised their citizens that the German government would pay reparations for the full cost of the war. The Allies set this cost at $35 billion. Already beset by serious economic problems, the German government in 1922

Visualizing History The blockade of Germany in World War I and postwar reparations on Germany brought hardships to many German citizens. These women in Berlin are searching in a garbage pile for food. *What form of government did Germany have between 1919 and 1933?*

Chapter 18 *Between Two Fires* **559**

VIDEODISC
Lessons of War

Side Two, Chapter 11
Frames 40065–44679
Title: *The Enemy*
Subject: A discussion of the process of "demonization," which causes people to see their enemies not as human beings
Ask: Why is it important for governments to "dehumanize" the enemy? *(When the enemy is dehumanized, soldiers and others are justified in their killing of the "monsters.")*

Daily Life Ask students to list some freedoms that we take for granted that would be suppressed under Fascist rule. Have a student read the United States Bill of Rights to stimulate a follow-up discussion. **L3**

History Simulation 18

Visualizing History German citizens struggled to survive in a time of increasing inflation. People in the United States were also finding food hard to get and spent hours waiting in breadlines or at soup kitchens.
Answer to Caption: *a democratic republic*

MEETING SPECIAL NEEDS ACTIVITY

Reading Comprehension Suggest that students who have difficulty reading the text take notes as they read. Have them list the headings and write any important ideas, events, and people under the headings. They should also write words they are unsure of and look them up in a dictionary as they study. By the end of the chapter, students will have completed a guide for studying. **L1**

Rise of Nazism
How did the rise of Nazism affect Germany and the world?
It ended democracy and established a totalitarian state in Germany; it persecuted opponents and sought to destroy the Jews; its expansionist program set the stage for World War II.

Independent Practice

📁 Guided Reading Activity 18-3 **L1**

📁 Geography and History Activity 18

Biography Have students list the steps in Hitler's rise to power. They may begin with his forming the Brownshirts and conclude with his taking the title of *Der Führer.* **L1 LEP**

Critical Thinking Have students write short essays comparing and contrasting the ways Hitler and Mussolini rose to power. Instruct students to include the conditions that favored each ruler's coming to power. **L2**

Economics Ask students to research the topic of inflation. Have them find or calculate what the inflation rate of the German mark was in 1923, then compare that figure to the current inflation rates in Germany and the United States. **L3**

Global 🌍 Gourmet

Italy is known for its traditional pasta dishes but it also has some foods that reflect German influence. Northeastern Italy has such dishes as sauerbraten, wurst, and strudel (marinated meat, sausage, and a pastry).

announced that it could not under present circumstances meet its obligations.

France, however, insisted that Germany pay its debt. To ensure this result, French troops marched into Germany's industrial Ruhr Valley in 1923 and took control of the coal mines and steel mills. Angered at the French invasion, German workers went on strike while their government paid them. With income from Ruhr industries going to France, Germany had lost an important asset.

Inflation

To meet expenses, the German government printed more and more paper money. As a result, inflation soared. Before the war, 4 marks equaled 1 American dollar. By late 1923, it took 4 trillion marks to equal 1 dollar. Inflation wiped out the savings of many middle-class Germans.

In the mid-1920s, Germany finally saw some relief ahead from its troubles. The French reached a compromise with the Germans that eased payments, and they left the Ruhr. Freed of debt and strengthened by American loans, Germany entered a five-year period of relative prosperity. But the seeds of discontent had already been sown.

Rise of Nazism

Among the political parties challenging the Weimar Republic was the National Socialist Workers' party, or Nazi party. One of its first recruits was World War I veteran **Adolf Hitler**. Born in Austria in 1889, Hitler failed in his efforts to become a successful artist. After the war, he settled in Munich and joined the Nazi party.

Hitler soon formed the Brownshirts, a private army of young veterans and street thugs. During the inflationary crisis of 1923, Hitler made an attempt to seize power. With armed Brownshirts outside, Hitler jumped on a table in a Munich beer hall and announced, "The revolution has begun!"

Images *of the* Times

Life in Nazi Germany

During the 1930s, Hitler's National Socialist party ruled Germany with an iron hand. Many Germans accepted the Nazi dictatorship, believing that it would solve the country's problems. Other Germans, however, suffered under Hitler's rule.

Adolf Hitler at a Nazi rally accepts flowers from a German child. German children were taught in schools to honor Hitler as Germany's savior.

German young people joined Nazi youth groups where they participated in parades and athletics and learned Nazi ideas.

560

Images *of the* Times — Life in Nazi Germany

When the Nazis took power in 1933, terror against the Jews escalated. November 9, 1938—*Kristallnacht* (named "The Night of Broken Glass" because of the shattered glass strewn all over German cities)—marked the beginning of the Nazis' open persecution of the Jews. Almost 8,000 Jewish businesses were destroyed, homes were broken into and looted, and 177 synagogues were gutted. Main streets everywhere were littered with glass. This night of terror was the start of massive arrests and transportation of Jews to concentration camps.

When the police intervened and arrested Hitler, however, the revolt quickly collapsed.

While in prison, Hitler wrote his autobiography, *Mein Kampf* (My Struggle). In Hitler's view, the Germans were not responsible for losing the war. He blamed the Jews and the Communists for the German defeat. He also declared that the Germans were a "master race" whose destiny was to rule the world. Hitler saw himself as the leader who would unite all German-speaking people into a new empire that would dominate other groups.

After his release from prison, Hitler resumed his activities. When the Great Depression struck in 1929, he appealed to German workers and industrialists alike with his promise to end unemployment and restore Germany's military might. In the early 1930s, the Nazis won a large number of seats in the multiparty Reichstag, or legislative lower house. With the government paralyzed by divisions, conservative politicians decided to back Hitler and use him for their own ends. In 1933 Hitler became chancellor. Through entirely legal means, the Nazis had come to power.

Hitler in Power

Hitler's goal all along was the creation of a totalitarian state. Because the Nazis were still a minority in the Reichstag, however, he planned to hold a new election. But a week before it was to be held, the Reichstag building mysteriously caught fire and burned to the ground. Hoping to reduce Communist support among the workers, Hitler blamed the Communists for the fire. In the election, the Brownshirts forced German voters to back the Nazis. When the Nazi-dominated Reichstag met after the election, it voted Hitler emergency powers to deal with the "Communist threat."

Hitler used his new powers to crush his opponents and consolidate his rule. All political parties, except the Nazi party were banned, and constitutional guarantees of freedom of speech, assembly, press and religion were ended. The Nazi government took over the labor unions and regulated production and wages. It also tried to control the Christian churches and silence clergy who opposed Nazi policies.

The Jews of Germany were persecuted by the Nazis. Nazi groups often terrorized Jewish people and vandalized Jewish-owned businesses.

REFLECTING ON THE TIMES

1. How were Germany's young people influenced by the Nazis?
2. How did Nazi rule affect Germany's Jews?

561

Chapter 18
Section 3

ASSESS

Check for Understanding

Assign Section 3 Review as homework or as an in-class activity.

Use Student Self-Test and Review Software to review Section 3.

Evaluate

Section Quiz 18-3

Reteach

Review with students the differences in postwar life in the United States, Great Britain, France, Italy, and Germany. Discuss the reasons democracy continued in the United States, France, and Great Britain, but not in Italy and Germany.

Enrich

Show students a documentary film of Nazi rallies in the 1930s such as the Nazi propaganda film *Triumph of the Will* or the American propaganda film *Nazi Strike.* Discuss the feelings they have after seeing and hearing Hitler speak.

Who?What?Where?When?

The Sound of Music, the Rodgers and Hammerstein musical, depicts the Nazi takeover of Austria.

ANSWERS TO REFLECTING ON THE TIMES

1. Young people were taught Nazi ideas at school and in youth groups.
2. Hitler's rule led to the persecution of Germany's Jews.

After becoming dictator of Germany in 1933, Adolf Hitler often held large rallies to inspire the loyalty of Germans. Hitler also adopted the slogan *Ein Volk, Ein Reich, Ein Führer* (One People, One Empire, One Leader). *What ambitions did Adolf Hitler have for Germany?*

Linking Past and Present

Anne Frank was a Jewish girl who kept a diary during the two years she spent hiding with her family in an attic in Amsterdam. She was arrested in 1944 and sent to the Nazi death camp at Bergen-Belsen, where she died at the age of 15. Her account, *The Diary of a Young Girl*, was published in 1952. More than thirty years later, in 1987, Miep Gies, the woman who hid the Frank family, wrote her own story, *Anne Frank Remembered*, about life under Nazi occupation and what she remembers of Anne Frank.

Visualizing
History Point out the Hitler salute in the photo and explain that this "Heil Hitler" salute became a famous gesture associated with Hitler.
Answer to Caption: *Hitler wanted to expand German territory and make it into a mighty world power.*

CLOSE

Hold a class discussion to help students outline what led to the rise of Fascist dictatorships in Italy and Germany. For each country, have students create a flowchart of the events on the chalkboard. Encourage students to copy the flowchart and use it for reference.

Attacks on the Jews

Hitler directed his most bitter attacks against the Jews. In 1935 the Nuremberg Laws stripped Jews of their citizenship and their right to hold public office. The laws barred Jewish students from schools and destroyed Jewish businesses. In the *Kristallnacht* of November 9 and 10, 1938, members of the Nazi party attacked Jews on the streets and vandalized Jewish businesses, homes, and synagogues. Hitler's secret police, the Gestapo, arrested Jews and other opponents of the government by the thousands. Many of these opponents were shot. Others were sent to concentration camps, large prison camps where political prisoners or refugees were confined.

Hitler was suspicious of even his closest supporters. He particularly feared radical members among the Brownshirts and set out to weaken their ranks. On June 30, 1934, the "Night of Long Knives," Hitler had hundreds of Brownshirts and their leaders shot.

The Third Reich

Assured of absolute power, Hitler took the title of *der Führer* (duhr FYUR•uhr), "the Leader." He called his government the Third Reich (RYK), or Third Empire, and boasted it would last 1,000 years. To reach this end, he set about restoring Germany's military might. He ignored the provisions of the Versailles Treaty, which limited the size of the German army, and ordered German factories to begin turning out guns, ammunition, airplanes, tanks, and other weapons. He made no secret of his ambitions to expand Germany's territory: "Today, Germany; tomorrow, the world!"

Hitler also brought all intellectual and artistic activity in Germany under his control and imposed his own ideas on the arts. To glorify Nazism, he made plans to rebuild Berlin in the style of monumental classical architecture. He discouraged the artistic experimentation that had flourished during the 1920s. As a result, many of Germany's most talented artists and scientists—among whom were Walter Gropius, Arnold Schoenberg, Sigmund Freud, and Albert Einstein—fled the country.

Hitler actively used the press, radio, and movies to flood Germany with propaganda praising the Nazi cause. In its propaganda, the government stressed the importance of a strong military and devotion to the nation and its leader. Hitler also set up organizations for young people between the ages of 6 and 18. These organizations aimed to mold German youth to accept Nazi ideas.

SECTION 3 REVIEW

Recall
1. **Define** totalitarianism, fascism, corporate state, syndicate, *Kristallnacht*, concentration camp.
2. **Identify** Benito Mussolini, Weimar, Adolf Hitler.

3. **Explain** how Italians differed regarding Mussolini.
Critical Thinking
4. **Analyzing Information** Why did fascism appeal to many Italians and Germans in the

decade following World War I?
Understanding Themes
5. **Uniformity** Analyze the type of government Germany had under the Nazis. What were its goals?

SECTION 3 REVIEW ANSWERS

1. All vocabulary words are defined in the Glossary.
2. Benito Mussolini, 557; Weimar, 559; Adolf Hitler, 560
3. Most Italians believed that Mussolini had saved Italy from communism and had brought order to the nation; others mourned the loss of democracy and individual freedoms.
4. because the economic and social chaos created by war and depression made both Italy and Germany ripe for Fascist-style revolution
5. **UNIFORMITY** Germany was a totalitarian state under the Nazi party led by Adolf Hitler. All other political parties were banned; constitutional freedoms were ended; controls were placed on all aspects of society; goals were to make Germany militarily strong, end the depression in Germany, and eliminate Jews/various opponents from Germany.

Critical Thinking SKILLS

Analyzing Political Cartoons

Do you enjoy reading the comics section in the newspaper? Most people enjoy reading comic strips. Cartoons, however, also appear on the editorial page. These are opinions on political issues. Political cartoons are good sources of historical information because they reflect opinions on current affairs.

Learning the Skill

A political cartoonist relies mostly on images to communicate a message. Using caricature and symbols, political cartoons help readers see relationships and draw conclusions about events. A caricature exaggerates a detail in a drawing such as a subject's features. Cartoonists use caricature to create a positive or negative impression of a subject. For example, if a cartoon shows one figure three times larger than another, it implies that one figure is more powerful than the other.

A symbol is an image or object that represents something else. For example, a cartoonist may use a crown to represent monarchy. Symbols often represent nations or political parties. The bald eagle and Uncle Sam are common symbols for the United States. A bear often stands for Russia. A dragon might be used to stand for China.

To analyze a political cartoon, first identify the topic and principal characters. Read labels and messages. Note relationships between the figures and symbols. Review your knowledge of the cartoon's topic to determine the cartoonist's viewpoint and message.

Practicing the Skill

The political cartoon on this page, published in 1938, makes a statement about the dictatorships that developed in Europe after World War I and the reaction of the Western democracies toward the newly formed dictatorships. Study the cartoon and then answer these questions.

1. What do the figures represent?
2. Why is the standing figure so large?
3. What is the standing figure holding and what is it attached to?
4. What is the message of the cartoon?

Applying the Skill

Choose a current issue on which you hold a strong opinion. It can be a school, local, national, or international issue. Draw a political cartoon expressing your opinion on this issue. Show it to a friend to find out if the message is clear. If not, revise the cartoon to clarify its point.

For More Practice

Turn to the Skill Practice in the Chapter Review on page 569 for more practice in analyzing a political cartoon.

WOULD YOU OBLIGE ME WITH A MATCH PLEASE ?

Chapter 18   *Between Two Fires*   **563**

Critical Thinking SKILLS

TEACH

Analyzing Political Cartoons
Bring some political cartoons to class, such as the ones that appear on the editorial page of many newspapers. Before having the class read the skill, distribute copies of the cartoons. *What is each cartoon's message and how did you figure it out?* After a short class discussion, ask students to read the skill and complete the practice questions.

Ask students to look for political cartoons in newspapers and magazines and bring them to class. Have students apply what they learned about analyzing political cartoons to explain the cartoons to the class.

Additional Practice

📁 Skill Reinforcement Activity 18

ANSWERS TO PRACTICING THE SKILL

1. The seated figure represents Western democracies. The standing figure represents the dictatorships.
2. The standing figure is large because it implies that dictatorships are becoming more powerful than democracies.
3. The standing figure is holding a rope that is attached to a bomb.
4. The dictatorships are setting the stage for the beginning of another world war with Western democracies.

Chapter 18   *Between Two Fires*   **563**

ind Out

Answer: *Stalin's rule created a climate of repression and terror, purged the nation of those who opposed him, and put all artistic and cultural activities under the Communist party's control.*

FOCUS

Section Objective

Examine how Joseph Stalin's rule transformed the Soviet Union.

**BELLRINGER
Motivational Activity**

Before taking roll at the beginning of the class period, project Section Focus Transparency 18-4 and have students answer the activity questions. Discuss students' responses.

   This activity is also available as a blackline master.

Vocabulary Pre-check

 Use the Vocabulary PuzzleMaker to create a puzzle that reinforces the vocabulary terms in this section. **L1**

| 1920 | | 1930 | | 1940 |

1921 Lenin announces New Economic Policy.   **1928** Stalin promotes collective farms.   **1932** "Terror famine" sweeps Ukraine.

Section 4

The Soviet Union

Setting the Scene

▶ **Terms to Define**
   nationalization, dictatorship of the proletariat, collectivization, kulak, purge, Socialist realism

▶ **People to Meet**
   Vladimir Ilyich Ulyanov (Lenin), Leon Trotsky, Joseph Stalin, Maksim Gorky

▶ **Places to Locate**
   Georgia, Ukraine

ind Out   How did Joseph Stalin's rule transform the Soviet Union?

ℭ**toryteller**

It was 35 degrees below zero when the team set out for work at Magnitogorsk. They would weld fittings to the blast furnaces 100 feet off the ground. It was hazardous work, for ice coated every surface. Three hours into the day a rigger fell off the scaffolding. Badly injured, he was carried to the first-aid station. His shaken companions talked of the need to improve the scaffolding. The foreman, however, blamed the workers. "You ploughboys don't know how to be careful. You don't pay as much attention as you should. People will fall, but we are building blast furnaces all the same, aren't we?"

Soviet construction project, 1930s

—adapted from *Behind the Urals: An American Worker in Russia's City of Steel*, John Scott, reprinted in *The Global Experience*, Volume 2, 1987

y 1921 Russia had endured the horrors of world war, revolution, and civil war. In the course of seven years of conflict, 27 million people had perished. Most had died on the battlefields and in countless guerrilla engagements, but millions had died of disease and starvation as well. In addition, the nation's transport system was in ruins, the peasants were in open revolt, and the economy was plunging toward collapse. At the Tenth Party Congress, Red Army director Leon Trotsky proclaimed: "We have destroyed the country in order to defeat the Whites."

Lenin in Power

In their struggle for survival during the civil war, **Vladimir Ilyich Ulyanov** (ool•YAH•nuhf), also known as **Lenin**, and the Bolsheviks had introduced an economic policy called war communism in 1918. Under war communism, the government carried out a policy of nationalization, in which it brought under state control all major industries. Applying the principle that those who would eat must work, the government required everyone between the ages of 16 and 50 to hold a job. It also erected a huge bureaucratic administration that wielded tremendous power but was extremely inefficient.

In 1921 Lenin tried to bring order out of the chaos that both war and government policy had caused. He announced a plan called the New Economic Policy, or NEP. Major industries such as steel, railroads, and large-scale manufacturing remained under government control. But in an attempt to stimulate the economy, Lenin allowed some private businesses to operate. In a startling departure from Marxist theory, NEP permitted small manufacturers and farmers to own their own businesses and to sell what they produced for a profit.

In 1922 the Communists changed the official name of the country from Russia to the Union of

---

Soviet Socialist Republics (USSR), or the Soviet Union. During this time, Lenin and other Communist leaders also completed a new constitution. This constitution stated that the USSR was a Socialist state, meaning that the government controlled the means of production.

In theory this state, called the dictatorship of the proletariat, was controlled by workers. But in practice the leadership of the Communist party controlled the workers. It was, as German Communist party member Rosa Luxemburg observed: "… a dictatorship, to be sure, not the dictatorship of the proletariat, however, but only the dictatorship of a handful of politicians." The classless society envisioned by Marx was, in the Soviet Union, a pyramid, with the party boss at the top and the peasants at the bottom.

The non-Russian nationalities in the USSR did not fare much better than the peasants. Because Lenin did not want to break up the old Russian Empire into independent states, he gave each major nationality its own republic with its own bureaucracy. In reality, however, the central government in Moscow still made the important decisions for these republics. In spite of the government's talk about equality for all nationalities, the Russians remained the dominant group in the Soviet Union and largely determined its policies.

Trotsky and Stalin

In 1922 Lenin suffered two strokes that left him permanently disabled. He died two years later at the age of 54.

The struggle to succeed Lenin began during his final illness. The two main contenders for the position were **Leon Trotsky** and **Joseph Stalin**. Next to Lenin, Trotsky had been the most important person in the Communist party. He had played a key role in the Bolshevik Revolution and had built the Red Army into a powerful fighting force. Trotsky came from a middle-class background and was a scholar who contributed many new ideas to the Marxist movement. He was also a speaker of great power and eloquence.

Born in **Georgia**, a territory south of Russia, Stalin was the son of artisans. A seminary student in his youth, Stalin was punished for reading books about revolution and social conditions, including novels such as Les Misérables. Stalin later renounced Russian Orthodoxy and became a Marxist revolutionary. Unlike Trotsky, Stalin was a skilled administrator. In 1922 he rose to the post of general secretary of the Communist party.

Visualizing History Lenin's New Economic Policy (NEP) helped put the Soviet Union's economy back on its feet in the early 1920s. In what way did NEP depart from Marxist theory?

Trotsky and Stalin held fundamentally different views about the path the Soviet Union should follow. Like Lenin, Trotsky believed in the theory of a "permanent revolution." He believed that only when the Russian Revolution had touched off uprisings all over the world could Socialists build an ideal society in the Soviet Union. Stalin, in contrast, declared it possible and necessary to "build socialism in a single country." By this he meant that the Soviet Union should concentrate on growing strong first, before it tried to spread revolution around the world.

Trotsky was better known than Stalin, both at home and in the Comintern (Communist International), an organization of Communist parties from all over the world. Moreover, Trotsky had been closer to Lenin. Nevertheless, Stalin managed to outmaneuver Trotsky politically. As general secretary, Stalin had the authority to appoint and remove officials. He gradually gained control of the party bureaucracy. As soon as he was securely in power, Stalin exiled Trotsky to Siberia and then expelled him from the Soviet Union. Trotsky eventually settled in Mexico City, where he continued to write about communism and the Soviet Union. An assassin acting on Stalin's orders murdered Trotsky in 1940.

Chapter 18 *Between Two Fires* **565**

TEACH

Guided Practice

THEME Uniformity

Ask students to imagine the United States government taking total control of all industrial and agricultural production. Have students tell ways such control would change daily life. (*Average citizens could not own businesses; the government would control the supply of food and industrial products.*) Ask students how they would react to such a government. **L1**

Visualizing History Lenin's New Economic Policy was a radical change that opened the way for a modified form of capitalism. Whereas selling for profit had once been a crime against the state, it was now officially encouraged. However, along with Lenin's strategy to get the economy moving came a new tightening of discipline.
Answer to Caption: *It allowed small manufacturers and farmers to own businesses and sell their products for a profit.*

Literature Lead a discussion on Socialist realism, or the literary and artistic style that became obligatory under Stalin's rule. Ask what the aim of art was under Socialist realism. Discuss how this style stifled artistic expression. **L3**

Independent Practice

Guided Reading Activity 18-4 **L1**

VIDEODISC
Communism and the Cold War

Side One, Chapter 9
Frames 14929–17326
Title: *Growing Up Communist*
Ask: What did the leaders of the Soviet Union feel they could teach the world? *(to work collectively)*

Answer
This land gave Russia greater access to the Black Sea and created a larger buffer between Germany and Russia.

Stalin's Dictatorship
What were the major features of Stalin's dictatorship?
One of the world's most brutal governments, Stalin's dictatorship employed terror through the secret police, purged Old Bolshevik leaders and secured mastery of the Communist party, and sought control of the arts.

ASSESS

Check for Understanding
Assign Section 4 Review as homework or as an in-class activity.

▣ Use Student Self-Test and Review Software to review Section 4.

Russia 1914–1922

[MAP]

Map Study
Russia gave up a vast amount of territory in the 1918 Treaty of Brest-Litovsk.
Region Why was the land Russia regained by 1922 particularly valuable to the nation?

Five-Year Plans

Fearing war with the West, Stalin wanted to rapidly transform the Soviet Union into an industrial power. In 1928 he declared an end to NEP and announced the first of his Five-Year Plans, a program that set economic goals for a five-year period. The plan brought all industrial and agricultural production under government control. It also provided for housing, health care, and other services.

While promising a better future, Stalin demanded sacrifices from the Soviet people. The first Five-Year Plan concentrated on building heavy industry. Consumer goods were produced in small amounts and were of inferior quality.

Responsibility for administering the plan lay in the hands of bureaucrats in Moscow. Theirs was a difficult task requiring tight control and careful planning. Not surprisingly, they made plenty of mistakes. For example, one Soviet enterprise

---

purchased its nail supply from a nail factory many miles away, while a nail factory across the street was shipping its goods a similar distance. Despite the mistakes, the first Five-Year Plan was a success in spurring industrial growth.

Collective Farms

In agriculture, Stalin's plan called for collectivization, a system of farming in which the government owned the land and used peasants to farm it. Stalin believed that collective farms would be more efficient. They would not only produce food for the Soviet people but produce it for export as well. By increasing agricultural exports, Stalin hoped to pay for Soviet industrialization without borrowing from the capitalist West.

Stalin also planned to use collectivization to intimidate the Soviet Union's peasant majority, most of whom were fiercely anti-Communist. Kulaks, or the most prosperous peasants, especially opposed collectivization. They had prospered under NEP and did not want to give up their land, livestock, and machinery. Fighting broke out in the countryside when the government tried to impose its plans. Thousands of peasants and their families were killed or arrested and sent to labor camps in Siberia. Stalin also took measures to crush anti-Communist resistance in **Ukraine**. By seizing the region's grain during the terrible winter of 1932, Stalin promoted a "terror famine," causing the deaths of millions of Ukrainian peasants.

Results

The first Five-Year Plan transformed the Soviet Union into an industrial power, but the human cost of the plan was enormous. Industrial workers received low wages, or none at all, and food was often limited in quantity. Millions of people died because of rural unrest, and collective farms were often unable to provide enough grain to feed the nation's population.

Stalin's Dictatorship

Stalin ruled the Soviet Union from the mid-1920s until his death in 1953. During this period he established one of the most brutal dictatorships the world has ever seen. Stalin demanded complete obedience from the people he ruled and got it through an effective use of terror. He granted the secret police immense power, which they used to scrutinize every aspect of the nation's social and

---

Study Strategy To visually clarify the information in this section, have students create a chart that summarizes the changes brought about by Lenin and Stalin in the Soviet Union. Headings for one axis of the chart might include *Major Industries, Small Businesses, Agriculture, Non-Russian Nationalities, Communist Party, The Arts, Comintern.* Headings for the other axis would be *Stalin, Lenin.*
L2

political life. Agents of the secret police encouraged workers to spy on each other and children to spy on their parents. Those accused of disloyalty were either shot or sent to labor camps in Siberia. The secret police and their activities helped to create a climate of fear in Soviet society.

Purges

In the 1930s Stalin began a methodical attack upon his potential enemies. Even members of the Communist party did not escape the reach of Stalin and his secret police. In 1934 an unknown assailant, probably acting on Stalin's orders, assassinated a high party official. Stalin used the event to rid himself of opponents and strengthen his hold on the party. He had millions of Communist party members expelled from the party, arrested and put in labor camps, or shot.

Stalin then turned against the Old Bolsheviks. These officials had been associates of Lenin and Stalin in the early days of the movement. Because some of them had sided with Trotsky, Stalin moved in 1936 to purge, or remove, them from any position where they could threaten his leadership. He had them arrested and put on trial. In open court in Moscow, with foreign reporters looking on, they pleaded guilty to false charges of treason, murder, and other crimes. Although these prisoners showed no signs of mistreatment, many Western experts have since concluded that the secret police used psychological torture to break their wills.

The Arts

Stalin also set out to put all artistic and cultural activities under the Communist party's control. In

Visualizing History The Soviet government used posters to glorify Soviet achievements and to urge people to carry out the goals of the Communist party. *How did Stalin strengthen his hold on the Soviet Union and the Communist party?*

1934 he put **Maksim Gorky**, one of the Soviet Union's leading writers, in charge of all Soviet culture. Gorky promoted a new literary style that soon became obligatory in the arts: Socialist realism. Writers and artists created a "new reality" by glorifying Soviet heroes and achievements, while denouncing the rumors about forced labor and terror. Artists who violated these dictates faced exile or imprisonment in labor camps.

Stalin's restrictions had a chilling effect on Soviet artists. Although talented writers and artists struggled to survive, most official artistic works were predictable and uninspiring.

The Comintern

In 1919 Lenin had established the Communist International, or Comintern. The goal of the Comintern was to encourage Communist parties in other countries to overthrow their governments by legal or illegal means and to establish Soviet-style regimes. While Stalin at first gave low priority to Comintern affairs, he later took more seriously the relations of the Soviet Union to the Communist parties in other countries. Stalin eventually decided to dissolve the Comintern in 1943, to win the favor and approval of the Western Allies during World War II.

---

spread propaganda by bombarding the Soviets with his portraits—they were hung in schoolrooms and every public building. **Answer to Caption:** *He used terror tactics to demand obedience. He expelled millions of Communists from the party. All Soviet citizens accused of disloyalty were arrested and either placed in labor camps or shot.*

Evaluate

📁 Section Quiz 18-4

💻 Use the Testmaker to create a customized quiz for Section 4.

Reteach

Review with students the economic and cultural changes that took place under Lenin and Stalin. Discuss these items from the points of view of the leaders and the general public.

📁 Reteaching Activity 18

Enrich

Books and music can bring the period to life. Suggest that students read *And Quiet Flows the Don* by Mikhail Sholokov or listen to the music of Rimsky-Korsakov or Shostakovich.

📁 Enrichment Activity 18

CLOSE

Have students discuss what post-war life was like for the average citizen in the Soviet Union. Have students compare this picture to postwar life in Italy, Germany, and the Western democracies.

SECTION 4 REVIEW

Recall
1. **Define** nationalization, dictatorship of the proletariat, collectivization, kulak, purge, Socialist realism.
2. **Identify** Vladimir Ilyich Ulyanov (Lenin), Leon Trotsky, Joseph Stalin, Georgia, Ukraine, Maksim Gorky.
3. **Describe** how the communists governed the Soviet Union.

Critical Thinking
4. **Analyzing Information** How did Stalin transform the Soviet Union? What effects did Stalin's policies have on the Soviet

people? Are these effects still felt today? Explain.

Understanding Themes
5. **Uniformity** Predict what might have happened if Trotsky—and not Stalin—had succeeded Lenin.

SECTION 4 REVIEW ANSWERS

1. All vocabulary words are defined in the Glossary.
2. Lenin, 564; Trotsky, 565; Stalin, 565; Georgia, 565; Ukraine, 566; Gorky, 567
3. It was a totalitarian state under the Communist party. The government was highly centralized in Moscow and controlled industry and agricultural production.
4. He brought all major industries and agriculture under strict government control; many peoples died or suffered hardships from harsh government policies; society is freer but more disorganized.
5. **UNIFORMITY** Answers will vary. Students may conclude that Trotsky's regime may have been less repressive.

Chapter 18 Review

Answers

Using Key Terms
1. i
2. b
3. d
4. k
5. c

Using Your History Journal
Be sure students have used some quotes from the interviews.

Reviewing Facts
1. automobiles, radios, vacuum cleaners, packaged foods, refrigerators, movies, and electric irons
2. T. S. Eliot, new style of writing; Pablo Picasso, introduced cubism; Salvador Dali, surrealist paintings; Arnold Schoenberg, brought 12-note scale to music.
3. Americans were weary of war and international problems.
4. nationalist outrage about peace treaties and land; strikes; peasant seizure of lands; economic downturn; political paralysis; high unemployment, especially among veterans; influence of Mussolini
5. war debts, inflation, unemployment, political instability, Hitler fostered belief in supremacy of Germans
6. Mussolini formed the Fascists, gave the state absolute authority; Hitler joined the new Nazi party and crushed Communist

568 Chapter 18 *Between Two Fires*

Connections Across Time

Historical Significance After World War I, scientists and artists in the West broke with old traditions and sought a "new reality." Meanwhile, economic and political instability posed challenges to democratic societies, which took emergency steps to save their economies. In lands where democracy was weak, such as Italy and Germany, social and economic upheaval led to the rise of Fascist governments. At the same time, a brutal Communist dictatorship emerged in the Soviet Union. Tensions between totalitarian and democratic nations paved the way for a new global conflict.

Using Key Terms

Write the key term that completes each sentence. Then write a sentence for each term not chosen.

a. cubism
b. coalition
c. surrealism
d. fascism
e. purge
f. kulaks
g. concentration camps
h. disarmament
i. corporate state
j. nationalization
k. *Kristallnacht*
l. general strike

1. Under the _____, Mussolini hoped to bring workers and employers together.
2. Because there were numerous political parties, the formation of a government in France required a _____ of several parties.
3. _____ is a political philosophy that glorifies the state, supports a single-party system under a strong leader, and promotes an aggressive form of nationalism.
4. In the _____, members of the Nazi party attacked Jews on the streets and vandalized Jewish businesses, homes, and synagogues.
5. The art form of _____ used dreamlike images and unnatural combinations of objects.

Technology Activity

Developing a Multimedia Presentation Search the Internet or your local library for sources on World War I. Based on your research, create a multimedia presentation about the economic effects of World War I on Western countries. Use images from the Internet in your presentation. Include a plan describing the type of presentation you would like to develop and the steps you will take to ensure a successful presentation.

568 Chapter 18 *Between Two Fires*

Using Your History Journal

Use your notes from the interview of a person who lived through the period between the wars. Write an account of how events affected ordinary people's lives.

Reviewing Facts

1. **Technology** List the technological advances in the 1920s and 1930s that impacted people.
2. **Culture** Identify three artists who produced changes in literature, art, music, or architecture. Describe the contributions each made.
3. **History** Explain why the United States retreated into isolationism after World War I.
4. **Culture** Explain the rise of fascism in Italy.
5. **Culture** Discuss how Hitler rose to power.
6. **Government** Explain how Hitler and Mussolini strengthened their political power.
7. **Economics** Identify Lenin's NEP.
8. **Government** Describe how Stalin defeated Trotsky.

Critical Thinking

1. **Apply** Why was World War I a watershed event in the twentieth century?
2. **Apply** How did Einstein's theories affect twentieth-century science and culture?
3. **Analyze** Compare totalitarianism and democracy. Why did totalitarian governments rise to power after World War I?
4. **Analyze** How does the term "Night of Terror" describe *Kristallnacht*?

---

opponents until he gained control.
7. put major industries under government control but permitted small manufacturers and farmers to own businesses
8. Stalin was a more skilled administrator and used his post to gain control politically.

Critical Thinking
1. It radically changed the way people looked at the world.

2. Einstein's theories laid the foundation of modern physics with his understanding of relativity and atomic theory; made possible the development of uses for atomic energy.
3. Totalitarianism sees individual as a servant of the state, while democracy sees government as the servant of individuals. Totalitarian governments arose in countries that had many social and economic problems and weak democratic traditions. The conditions of war

5. Synthesize To aid Germany's economic recovery after World War I, how might the Allies have structured the peace settlements?

6. Compare How does fascism differ from communism? How do both differ from capitalism?

7. Analyze Salvador Dali was influenced by Sigmund Freud. How is Freud's influence evident in *The Persistence of Memory* (1931)?

The Persistence of Memory, *Salvador Dali.*
Museum of Modern Art, New York, New York

Understanding Themes

1. **Innovation** How did new movements in literature and the arts reflect changes after World War I?

2. **Change** How was Roosevelt's New Deal similar to Stalin's Five-Year Plan? How was it different?

3. **Uniformity** Why did the Nazis try to control labor unions and the Christian churches? Why did they mistreat Germany's Jewish population?

4. **Uniformity** How did Lenin try to unify all non-Russian republics under one government?

During the 1920s and 1930s the automobile, motion pictures, and the radio transformed the way Americans lived. What technological advances shape our lives today? Are they negative or positive? Explain.

Skill Practice

Study the cartoon and answer the questions.

1. Who is the figure in the cartoon?
2. What country does the flag represent?
3. What is the message of the cartoon?

Geography in History

1. **Place** In which countries did Fascist governments come to power during the 1930s?

2. **Region** In what region of Europe were 10 of the 11 democracies in the 1930s?

Politics of Europe 1930s

Democratic
Fascist
Conservative, repressive

FINLAND
NORWAY
SWEDEN
ESTONIA
LATVIA
LITHUANIA
North Sea
IRELAND
DENMARK
GREAT BRITAIN
NETHER-LANDS
GERMANY
POLAND
BELGIUM
CZECHO-SLOVAKIA
LUXEMBOURG
AUSTRIA
ROMANIA
SWITZER-LAND
HUNGARY
FRANCE
YUGOSLAVIA
ATLANTIC OCEAN
BULGARIA
ITALY
PORTUGAL
SPAIN
ALBANIA
GREECE
Mediterranean Sea

0 200 400 mi.
0 200 400 km
Lambert Conic Conformal Projection

Understanding Themes

1. **INNOVATION** reflected disillusionment and search for new ideas and ways of portraying the world

2. **CHANGE** Both plans brought enormous changes in the two countries and increased the governments' involvement in social and economic affairs. The New Deal did not demand great sacrifices from the people.

3. **UNIFORMITY** The Nazis wanted to create a totalitarian state and silence these groups; because they blamed the Jews for German defeat in World War I and saw the Jews as inferior.

4. **UNIFORMITY** gave each nationality its own republic but had Moscow make the important decisions

the computer, lasers, microwaves, and televisions; answers will vary

Skill Practice

1. Communists
2. United States
3. Americans did not want Communists in the United States.

Geography in History

1. Germany, Italy
2. northwestern Europe

Chapter Bonus Test Question

Ask students: Given the state in which Germany, Italy, and Russia found themselves after World War I, could they have achieved economic health and national self-respect by any means other than totalitarianism? Explain your answer.

had increased government powers (temporarily) even in democracies.

4. It describes the terrorizing and assault on Jews and their property by the Nazis.

5. Possible answer: The Allies should have imposed milder terms on Germany and reduced its war debt payments.

6. Fascism defended private property and class structure and made the nation supreme. Communism, in theory, did away with private property and class division and worked for a workers' revolution. Fascism and communism both emphasize the role of the state in all areas of life, especially in the economy. Capitalism, although limited by some regulations, allows a free market of private owners who make their own economic decisions.

7. Answers should mention that the bizarre images reflect Dali's attempt to explore the unconscious mind.

A complete, 1-page lesson plan is provided for each section in the *Reproducible Lesson Plans* booklet.

Nationalism in Asia, Africa, and Latin America

CHAPTER RESOURCES

	Reproducible Resources	Multimedia Resources
Chapter Opener	Chapter Themes: Graphic Organizer 19 Historical Significance Chapter Activity 19	MindJogger Videoquiz

Chapter Enrichment	Vocabulary Activity 19*
	Time Line Activity 19
	Mapping History Activity 19
	History Simulation 19
	Geography and History Activity 19
	Source Reading 19
	People in World History Profiles 57, 58
	World Literature Selection 7
	World Art and Music Activity 19
	Enrichment Activity 19
	Critical Thinking Activity 19
	Skill Reinforcement Activity 19
	Performance Assessment Activity 19
		World History and Art
		  Transparency 40, *Zapatistas*; 41,
		  Turkestan Oriental Rugs
		
		Chapter Transparency 19
		Vocabulary PuzzleMaker Software
		In the Holy Land: *Arab violence*
		  1919–1921
		Lessons of War:
		  Philosophy of Nonviolence

Chapter Review/Reteaching	Reteaching Activity 19
	Skill Reinforcement Activity 19
	Spanish Chapter Summary 19
		Chapter 19 Digest Audiocassette,
		  Activity, Test*
		Vocabulary PuzzleMaker Software
		Student Self-Test and Review
		  Software
		MindJogger Videoquiz

Chapter Evaluation/Testing	Performance Assessment Activity 19 Chapter 19 Test, Forms A and B	Testmaker

* Also available in Spanish

0:00 OUT OF TIME? Assign the Chapter 19 summary in the Unit 5 Digest on pages 631–633, and the Chapter 19 Audiocassettes.

Block Schedule

Block scheduling differs from traditional class scheduling in the amount of time allotted to each period. The extended time frame provided by block scheduling affords you the opportunity to implement a greater number of research-oriented and activity-intense projects to motivate and involve your students. Activities that are particularly suited to use within the block scheduling framework are identified throughout this chapter by the following designation.

KEY TO ABILITY LEVELS

Teaching strategies have been coded for varying learning styles and abilities.

L1 **BASIC** activities for all students
L2 **AVERAGE** activities for average to above-average students
L3 **CHALLENGING** activities for above-average students
LEP **LIMITED ENGLISH PROFICIENCY** activities

Use Glencoe's *Presentation Plus!* multimedia teacher tool to easily present dynamic lessons that visually excite your students. Using Microsoft PowerPoint® you can customize the presentations to create your own personalized lessons.

SECTION RESOURCES

Daily Objectives	Reproducible Resources	Multimedia Resources
Section 1 **New Forces in the Middle East and Africa** Identify how the forces of nationalism affected events in the Middle East and Africa after World War I.	Reproducible Lesson Plan 19-1 Vocabulary Activity 19* Guided Reading Activity 19-1* People in World History Profile 58 Section Quiz 19-1*	Section Focus Transparency 19-1 Chapter Transparency 19 Student Self-Test and Review Software Testmaker In the Holy Land: *Arab violence 1919–1921*
Section 2 **India's Struggle for Independence** State the methods Gandhi used in India's struggle for independence from British rule.	Reproducible Lesson Plan 19-2 Vocabulary Activity 19* Guided Reading Activity 19-2* Section Quiz 19-2*	Section Focus Transparency 19-2 Student Self-Test and Review Software Testmaker Lessons of War: *Philosophy of Nonviolence*
Section 3 **China's Drive for Modernization** Explain the factors that divided and the factors that united nationalist forces in China.	Reproducible Lesson Plan 19-3 Vocabulary Activity 19* Guided Reading Activity 19-3* Time Line Activity 19 Section Quiz 19-3*	Section Focus Transparency 19-3 Student Self-Test and Review Software Testmaker
Section 4 **Militarism in Japan** Describe how militarism shaped the development of Japan after World War I.	Reproducible Lesson Plan 19-4 Vocabulary Activity 19* Guided Reading Activity 19-4* History Simulation 19 Mapping History Activity 19 Section Quiz 19-4*	Section Focus Transparency 19-4 Student Self-Test and Review Software Testmaker
Section 5 **Nationalism in Latin America** Analyze why nationalism in Latin America brought conflict with the United States.	Reproducible Lesson Plan 19-5 Vocabulary Activity 19* Guided Reading Activity 19-5* World Art and Music Activity 19 People in World History Profile 57 Reteaching Activity 19 Enrichment Activity 19 Section Quiz 19-5* Performance Assessment Activity 19 Spanish Chapter Summary 19	Section Focus Transparency 19-5 World History and Art Transparency 40, *Zapatistas* Student Self-Test and Review Software Testmaker

* Also available in Spanish

Chapter Activities

✔ Performance Assessment Activity

Point/Counterpoint For the concepts of pacifism and militarism, organize students into groups of four to role-play a point/counterpoint segment on public television. Each group will research a current problem that has led to violence or that threatens to erupt in violence in Asia, Africa, the Middle East, or Latin America. After groups have gathered information from newspapers or magazines, have two students from each group present the pacifist response to solving the problem and two students present the militarist perspective. During the role play, students should refer to principles or historical examples to justify their positions.

Possible Rubric Features
Concept attainment, accuracy of content information, clarity of oral presentation, effect on audience, collaborative skills, persuasion and argumentation skills

• *For an additional activity, refer to Activity 19 in the* Performance Assessment Strategies and Activities *booklet.*

ACTIVITY

From the Classroom of...

**James Kim
Polytechnic
Preparatory Country
Day School
Brooklyn, NY**

China's Drive for Modernization
Have students create either a Nationalist (Guomindang) or Communist newspaper. Once they have read the chapter, have each student select a topic for an article. After researching their topics at the library, students should write rough drafts, then use peer editing to edit the drafts and prepare final versions of their articles. Have students type the articles, select a name for their paper, and lay out the copy. The newspaper can be photocopied or printed for distribution and display.

MULTIPLE LEARNING STYLES

Verbal/Linguistic
Have students select one of the countries discussed in this chapter and imagine that they live in that country during the time period under study. Ask them to write a letter to the editor of a newspaper in which they express their opinions about an incident described in the chapter.

Visual/Spatial
Give students an outline map of the world. As they read the chapter, have them fill in the names of the countries, continents, and regions they are studying. At the end of the chapter, put an enlarged version of the outline map on the bulletin board. Organize the class into two teams and hold a geography bee. Have teams take turns trying to identify places mentioned in the chapter. The team that correctly identifies the most places wins.

Auditory/Musical
Have students write and present a short class musical based on the rise of nationalism in one of the countries described in this chapter.

Kinesthetic
Have students choreograph and perform a dance that displays through movement the struggle for independence in one of the countries described in this chapter.

Additional Resources

NATIONAL GEOGRAPHIC SOCIETY

Teacher's Corner

INDEX TO NATIONAL GEOGRAPHIC MAGAZINE

The following articles may be used for research relating to this chapter:

- "The Promise of Pakistan," by John McCarry, October 1997.
- "India," by Geoffrey C. Ward, May 1997.
- "African Gold," by Carole Beckwith and Angela Fisher, October 1996.
- "Eritrea Wins the Peace," by Charles E. Cobb, Jr., June 1996.
- "Simon Bolivar," by Bryan Hodgson, March 1994.
- "Who Are the Palestinians?" by Tad Szulc, June 1992.

BIBLIOGRAPHY

Literature of the Period
Malraux, André. *Man's Fate.* Translated by Haakon M. Chevalier. New York: Random, 1990. First published in 1933, this French novel is based on the struggle between the Communist Reds and Chiang Kai-shek's Blues in the Shanghai insurrection of 1927.

Readings for the Student
Paz, Octavio. *The Labyrinth of Solitude: The Other Mexico, Return to the Labyrinth of Solitude, Mexico and the U.S.A., The Philanthropic Ogre.* Translated by Lysander Kemp, Vara Milos, and Rachel Phillips Belash. New York: Grove Press, 1985. Perceptive studies of Mexican character and culture by the acclaimed poet.

Readings for the Teacher
Rose, Norman. *Chaim Weizmann: A Biography.* New York: Viking, 1986. Life of the Zionist leader whose work in England led to the Balfour Declaration.

LOCAL OBJECTIVES

_____
_____
_____
_____
_____
_____
_____
_____
_____
_____
_____
_____
_____
_____
_____
_____
_____
_____
_____
_____
_____

interNET CONNECTION

Indian independence resources on the World Wide Web
Free India: Celebrating 50 years of India's Freedom:
http://www.freeindia.org/

CHAPTER THEMES

Chapter Themes are listed by section on this chapter opening page of the Student Edition. A corresponding theme-based activity is available under "TEACH," and a theme-based question is asked in the Section and Chapter Reviews.

The Storyteller

Historical Setting U.S. Marines had occupied Nicaragua since 1912. In 1927 the United States backed Emiliano Chamorro, who had seized power from the elected president. Sandino (1893–1934) refused to accept the U.S.-imposed regime and led several hundred followers to the mountains of northern Nicaragua. His ability to evade capture by U.S. forces and the Nicaraguan National Guard not only turned Sandino into a popular hero but also encouraged anti-American sentiment throughout the hemisphere. After the Marines withdrew in 1933, Sandino attended a peace conference with the head of the National Guard, Anastasio Somoza, who abducted and murdered the guerrilla leader. In 1962 the Sandinista National Liberation Front was formed with the goal of overthrowing the Somoza family dictatorship. The Sandinistas overthrew Somoza in July 1979 and governed Nicaragua until 1990.

Historical Significance

Answer: *World War I shattered the old order in Europe while the Versailles peace conference raised hopes for self-determination in many colonies, leading to the growth of nationalist and independence movements between 1919 and 1939.*

Nationalism in Asia, Africa, and Latin America

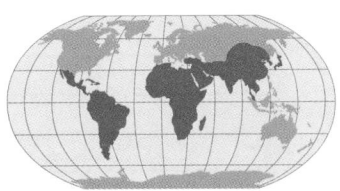

Chapter Themes

▶ **Nationalism** Hope for a new world after World War I leads to the rise of nationalism in the Middle East and Africa. *Section 1*
▶ **Change** Gandhi calls for nonviolence in India's struggle for independence from British rule. *Section 2*
▶ **Conflict** Nationalists, Communists, and the Japanese compete for control of China. *Section 3*
▶ **Conflict** Japan's militarism and expansionism place it on a collision course with the West. *Section 4*
▶ **Change** Nationalist forces in Latin America oppose increased American intervention in the region. *Section 5*

The Storyteller

"I swear before country and history that my sword will defend our nation's dignity, that it will be a sword for the oppressed. I accept the invitation to fight…. The last of my soldiers, the soldiers of freedom for Nicaragua, may die; but before that, more than a battalion of your blond invaders will have bitten the dust of my wild mountains."

With these fighting words, General Augusto César Sandino challenged the United States Marines in 1927. Sandino was trying to drive out the "blond invaders" who had occupied Nicaragua for 15 years. In the years following World War I, nationalist leaders such as Sandino struggled to end foreign control and win independence for their countries around the globe.

Historical Significance

What factors led to the growth of nationalist and independence movements in Asia, Africa, and Latin America between 1919 and 1939?

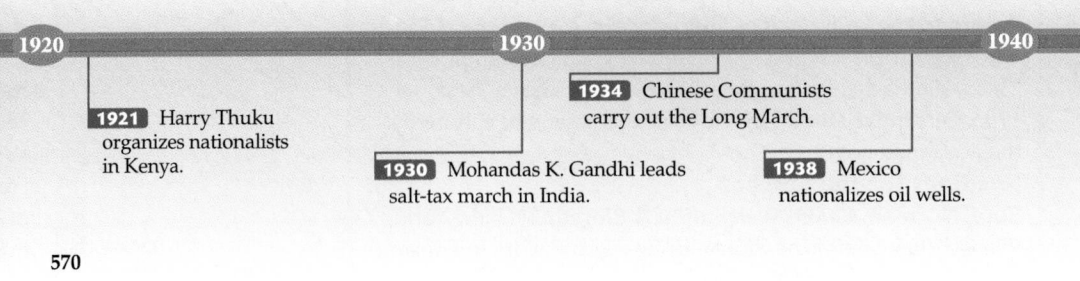

1920

1921 Harry Thuku organizes nationalists in Kenya.

1930

1930 Mohandas K. Gandhi leads salt-tax march in India.

1934 Chinese Communists carry out the Long March.

1940

1938 Mexico nationalizes oil wells.

570

GEOGRAPHY CONNECTION

Location Have students use a globe to locate the Middle East, Africa, India, China, Japan, and Central America. In which hemisphere does each region or country lie? *(Central America is in the Western Hemisphere; all the other locations are in the Eastern Hemisphere.)*

History & Art *The Destruction of the Old Order* by José Clemente Orozco. National Preparatory School, Mexico City, Mexico

Your History Journal

Choose a major event that occurred after 1930 in one of the nations featured in this chapter. Write a short radio news report describing the event for broadcast in the United States.

History & Art Orozco is considered the most important modern muralist to work in fresco, the technique of applying watercolors to a moist plaster surface. While he did not fight in the Mexican Revolution, his political cartoons rallied support for General Venustiano Carranza. Orozco lived in the U.S. on several occasions, and in 1932–1934 he painted a series of frescoes at Dartmouth College in Hanover, New Hampshire.

✔ Performance Assessment

Refer to the activity on page 570C of the Planning Guide.

 Refer to Activity 19 in the *Performance Assessment Strategies and Activities* booklet.

Using Your History Journal

If possible, have students listen to Edward R. Murrow's radio broadcasts on the recording, *I Can Hear It Now, 1919–1949: 30 Years of Audible History.*

GLENCOE TECHNOLOGY

VIDEODISC
Use MindJogger to preview chapter content.

MindJogger Videoquiz

Chapter 19
Disc 3 Side A

 Also available in VHS.

✚ EXTRA CREDIT PROJECT

Oral Report Ask students to research the events leading to the Balfour Declaration, the importance of that document in the establishment of Israel, and Britain's short-lived commitment to it. Have students summarize their findings in a brief oral report. Suggested resources: R. Sanders, *The High Walls of Jerusalem: A History of the Balfour Declaration and the Birth of the British Mandate for Palestine;* W. Laqueur, *A History of Zionism.*

1917

1917 The British issue the Balfour Declaration.

1927

1929 Nigerian women oppose British tax.

1937

1936 Egypt becomes independent.

SECTION THEME

▶ **Nationalism** Hope for a new world after World War I leads to the rise of nationalism in the Middle East and Africa.

ind Out

Answer: *Nationalist movements caused economic, political, and cultural ferment in Turkey, Iran, Palestine, Egypt, Kenya, and Nigeria.*

FOCUS

Section Objective

Identify how the forces of nationalism affected events in the Middle East and Africa after World War I.

BELLRINGER
Motivational Activity

Before taking roll at the beginning of the class period, project Section Focus Transparency 19-1 and have students answer the activity questions. Discuss students' responses.

📁 This activity is also available as a blackline master.

Vocabulary Pre-check

📁 Use Vocabulary Activity 19 to introduce vocabulary terms.

L1 LEP

Section 1

New Forces in the Middle East and Africa

Setting the Scene

▶ **Terms to Define**
self-determination, fez, shah

▶ **People to Meet**
Kemal Atatürk, Reza Shah Pahlavi, Theodor Herzl, Saad Zaghlul, Harry Thuku, Jomo Kenyatta, Nnamdi Azikiwe

▶ **Places to Locate**
Turkey, Iran, Palestine, Egypt, Kenya, Nigeria

 **ind Out** How did the forces of nationalism affect events in the Middle East and Africa after World War I?

ᵀʰᵉ Storyteller

Fawaz Khourey listened as a delegate at the Arab Students Congress in Paris read the committee report. "I am an Arab. I believe Arabs constitute one nation. This nation's sacred right is to be sovereign in her own affairs. Her ardent nationalism drives her to liberate our homeland, uniting all parts, and finding political, economic, and social institutions more sound and more compatible than existing ones."

—adapted from *Arab Nationalism: An Anthology,* edited by Sylvia G. Haim, reprinted in *Documents in World History,* Volume 2, 1988

Paris mosque

t the end of World War I, European powers continued to control most of the Middle East and Africa. Many colonies had assisted the Allies during the war, hoping to gain their independence as a reward. President Woodrow Wilson of the United States raised their hopes in 1918 by endorsing the concept of self-determination: the right of national groups to set up independent nations.

But instead of relaxing their grip, the European powers tightened it. Nationalists prepared to fight for independence and organized political demonstrations. They were eager to establish modern countries where their own cultures could flourish.

Turkey

For nearly 500 years, Turkish emperors called sultans ruled the vast Ottoman Empire, which at one time included parts of eastern Europe, the Middle East, and North Africa. During the 1800s, however, large sections of this empire broke away or were conquered. When World War I began, the Ottomans joined forces with Germany, hoping to save their remaining lands.

War With Greece

The Allied victory in World War I dashed Ottoman hopes. The Ottoman sultan, or ruler, lost all of his lands except the area of present-day **Turkey.** In 1919 the Greeks invaded Turkey in an attempt to complete the destruction of the Ottoman Empire. Turkish general Mustafa Kemal, however, rallied forces to his country's defense. Kemal led a political group known as the Young Turks who wanted reforms to modernize Turkey. Turkish armies under Kemal counterattacked and defeated the Greeks in 1922.

SECTION RESOURCES

📁 **Reproducible Masters**
- Reproducible Lesson Plan 19-1
- Vocabulary Activity 19
- Guided Reading Activity 19-1
- People in World History Profile 58
- Section Quiz 19-1

🕯 **Transparencies**
- Section Focus Transparency 19-1
- Chapter Transparency 19

Multimedia
- 💿 Student Self-Test and Review Software
- 💿 Testmaker
- 💿 In the Holy Land: *Arab violence 1919–1921*

The Turkish victory led to dramatic changes. The sultan gave up his throne, and the Turks formed a new country, the Republic of Turkey. Kemal became its first president. The new government moved the capital from Istanbul to Ankara, a city near the center of the country. Believing that Turkey needed to industrialize in order to assert its role in world affairs, Kemal's government established industries and planned their growth. Tariffs on imports were raised to protect the new industries from foreign competition and to reduce dependence on foreign countries.

Kemal's Reforms

Kemal carried out a number of radical reforms in Turkish society. As a result of Kemal's policies, Turkey adopted a Western way of life. The Turks began using the Western calendar, the Latin alphabet, and the metric system. Kemal ordered men to stop wearing the fez, a traditional hat, and he tried to rid the country of the custom of veiling among women. He also urged Turks to use Western-style last names. To Westernize the government, he reformed the legal code and separated government and religion.

Some of Kemal's changes were designed to promote national pride among the Turks. For example, he urged Turks to "purify" their language by ridding it of all words that had Persian or Arabic origins. He also changed his own name to **Kemal Atatürk** (keh•MAHL AT•uh•TUHRK), which means "father of the Turks."

In defense of his reforms, Kemal said: "We have suffered much. This is because we have failed to understand the world. Our thoughts and our mentality will become civilized from head to toe." Kemal ruled Turkey with an iron fist until his death in 1938. His policies were not always popular, but he changed Turkey from an ancient empire into a modern nation.

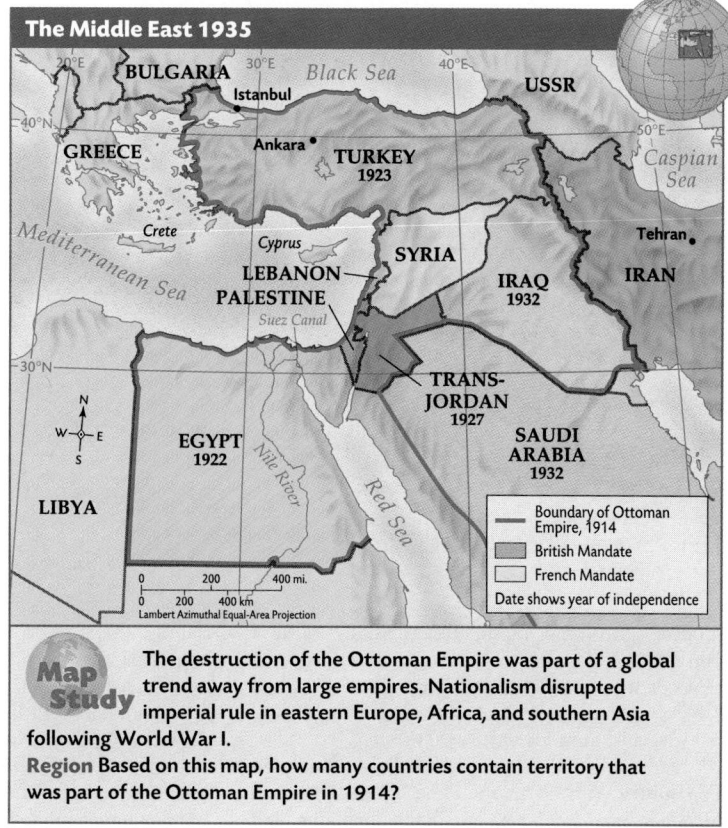

The Middle East 1935

Boundary of Ottoman Empire, 1914
British Mandate
French Mandate
Date shows year of independence

Map Study

The destruction of the Ottoman Empire was part of a global trend away from large empires. Nationalism disrupted imperial rule in eastern Europe, Africa, and southern Asia following World War I.

Region Based on this map, how many countries contain territory that was part of the Ottoman Empire in 1914?

Iran

Located between Turkey and Pakistan, **Iran** is a land of mountains, deserts, and oil. At the end of World War I this land, known by its historic name of Persia, was ruled by a shah, or king. However, Great Britain and the Soviet Union each had controlling interests in Persia's oil fields.

In 1921 nationalist forces led by Reza Khan, an army officer, wanted to cut back the foreign influence on their government and economy. The nationalists overthrew the shah and set up a new government. Like Atatürk, Reza Khan built schools, roads, and hospitals, and he allowed women more freedom. Improved communications helped unite the diverse groups in the country. Although adopting many Western ways, he tried to reduce Western political influence in Persia.

Reza wanted to change the Persian monarchy into a republic. However, traditional Muslim leaders opposed this change, so Reza ruled as a dictator. Later, in 1925, he declared himself shah and

Chapter 19 *Nationalism in Asia, Africa, and Latin America* **573**

TEACH

Guided Practice

THEME Nationalism

Write on the chalkboard Sandino's statement quoted on page 570: "I swear before country and history that my sword will defend our nation's dignity, that it will be a sword for the oppressed." Although the statement was made by a Nicaraguan general, it may have been echoed by nationalist leaders in other areas of the world. Have students explain how Sandino's statement might have rallied the support of Nicaraguans. **L1**

People in World History Profile 58

Map Study

Answer
eight countries

Map Skills Practice

Reading a Map Which region did Britain control through a mandate? *(Palestine)*

Geography: Location Have students study the map on this page. What body of water lies west of Palestine? *(Mediterranean Sea)* What country now exists in the area that was a British mandate? *(Israel)* What nations bordered Syria in 1935? *(Turkey, Iraq, Transjordan, Palestine, Lebanon)* **L2**

Chapter Transparency 19

Independent Practice

Guided Reading Activity 19-1 **L1**

COOPERATIVE LEARNING ACTIVITY

Posters Organize the class into two groups and assign one group Turkey and the other Iran. Have each group list the ways its country modernized and adopted certain elements of Western countries following World War I. Then ask the groups to research the subsequent history of each country, including the reaction against westernization in Iran. Have students create posters illustrating daily life in Turkey and Iran today. Encourage students to use photographs from magazines or newspapers to illustrate their posters. When the posters are completed, have students discuss how life in secular Turkey differs from life in Iran's Islamic republic. **L3**

Visualizing History Although he served in a series of governments that collaborated with the British, Zaghlul (1857–1927) became a nationalist when he realized that Britain had no intention of granting independence to Egypt.
Answer to Caption: *Kemal Atatürk of Turkey and Reza Shah Pahlavi of Iran*

Linking Past and Present

Iran In 1979 a revolutionary movement led by Muslim religious leader Ayatollah Ruholla Khomeini overthrew Reza Shah's son, Mohammad Reza Pahlavi, and declared Iran an Islamic republic. Although Khomeini died in 1989, Iran continues to follow his anti-Western orientation and commitment to Muslim fundamentalism.

VIDEODISC
In the Holy Land

Side One, Chapter 15
Frame: 20841
Title: *Arab violence 1919–1921*
Subject: Jewish and Palestinian perspectives of anti-Jewish rioting and violence
Ask: As a result of the Balfour Declaration, Jewish immigration to Israel increased. What was the effect of this on the Arabs? *(They felt threatened because others were claiming their homeland. This resulted in riots, strikes, and violence.)*

---

adopted the new name **Reza Shah Pahlavi** (rih•ZAH SHAH PAL•uh•vee). Pahlavi was the name of the ancient Persian language. Reza Shah Pahlavi earned money from Persia's oil fields and factories and from his vast royal estates.

During the 1930s, Reza Shah Pahlavi aligned his country with Germany. He admired Hitler, in part because he believed that Germans and Persians shared a common ancestry in the ancient Aryan, or Indo-European, peoples. In 1935 he changed the country's name from Persia to Iran, a variation of the word *Aryan*. In 1941, when Great Britain and the Soviet Union were at war with Germany, British and Soviet forces deposed Reza Shah Pahlavi and replaced him with his son, Mohammad Reza Pahlavi. The new ruler permitted British and Soviet troops to remain in Iran.

Palestine

While Iran was trying to free itself from European control, another Middle Eastern region was just coming under British domination. After World War I, the newly formed League of Nations gave Great Britain a mandate over **Palestine**. This region had been part of the Ottoman Empire. Britain was eager to benefit from control of Palestine's strategic location at the eastern end of the Mediterranean Sea.

In Palestine, the nationalism of two groups—Jews and Arabs—came into conflict. The Jews claimed the land on the basis of their biblical heritage and the continuing presence of Jews in the area since ancient times. Arabs pointed out that their ancestors had lived there for many centuries also. During this period, Palestine's small number of Jews and large number of Arabs lived together peacefully most of the time.

Beginning in the late 1800s, the number of Jews in Palestine began increasing. European Jews, facing harsh anti-Jewish pogroms in Russia and stirred by a growing sense of nationalism, believed they should reestablish a Jewish national homeland in Palestine. This movement, known as Zionism, became an organized political force in the late 1890s under the leadership of **Theodor Herzl**, a prominent Austrian Jewish writer and journalist. By World War I, about 500,000 Arabs and 85,000 Jews lived in Palestine.

During World War I, the British government promised independence to the Arabs in return for their help against the Ottoman Turks and also promised a homeland to the Jews. The Balfour Declaration—a letter from British Foreign Secretary Arthur Balfour in 1917 to the English Zionist Federation—promised Great Britain's help in establishing "a national home for the Jewish people" in Palestine. Great Britain's pledge of support, however, was on the condition that the civil and religious rights of other communities be protected. In September 1923, the British mandate officially came into force in Palestine in spite of Great Britain's conflicting promises to the area's Jewish and Arab communities.

MEETING SPECIAL NEEDS ACTIVITY

Learning Disability To check the progress of students with learning problems, ask them to identify the country described in each of the following statements:
1. In 1922 the British granted this country limited independence. *(Egypt)*
2. It was originally known as Persia. *(Iran)*
3. Greece invaded this country in 1919. *(Turkey)*
4. Reza Khan became its leader and eventually declared himself shah. *(Iran)*
5. Mustafa Kemal introduced radical reforms here. *(Turkey)* **L1**

Under the British mandate, tensions heightened between Arabs and Jews. As the persecution of Jews in Nazi Germany increased, so did Jewish immigration to Palestine. As more Jews moved into a region long inhabited by Arabs, the two groups clashed. Riots broke out, resulting in hundreds of casualties. When Great Britain tried to limit Jewish immigration, Zionists responded in anger. By the end of the 1930s, Great Britain's ambiguous promises had angered both Jews and Arabs, and the conflict in Palestine was worsening.

Egypt

Palestine's neighbor **Egypt** also confronted troubles after World War I. Under British occupation since 1882, Egypt was beginning to feel the power of nationalism. **Saad Zaghlul** (zag•LOOL) led the nationalist forces in Egypt demanding independence. The British tried to weaken the nationalist cause by arresting Zaghlul, but their action only sparked riots and violence. Finally, in 1922, Great Britain granted Egypt limited independence. However, the British kept control of the Suez Canal.

Tensions continued over the next decade between Egypt and Great Britain. But when Italy invaded Ethiopia in 1935, the British decided they needed Egypt's help to prevent further Italian aggression. As a result, the British government granted Egypt its complete independence in 1936 and helped it become a member of the League of Nations the following year. Great Britain also withdrew all British troops from Egypt, except for those in the Suez Canal zone.

Kenya

South of Egypt, in central East Africa, lay another part of Great Britain's empire: **Kenya**. During World War I, about 45,000 Kenyans died while helping the British fight the Germans in East Africa. The survivors returned home after the war with dreams of independence and a new life. However, instead of granting Kenya its independence, the British allowed European settlers to seize the land of many Kenyans in order to start large coffee plantations and other agricultural operations. The settlers hired Kenyans at low wages and made them work under harsh conditions. Resentment of British rule in Kenya gave rise to a

Imperialist Boundaries

During the late 1800s, European powers carved up Africa without respect to the continent's historic ethnic boundaries. Colonial boundary lines split groups of people and joined them to other groups with different religious beliefs, customs, and languages. This often led to unwanted rivalries and hostilities. Nowhere was this problem more evident than in Nigeria.

Nigeria is home to more than 250 separate ethnic groups. The three largest are the Hausa, the Yoruba, and the Ibo. In the days before colonial rule, each group controlled its own territory. When the British united the region in 1914, Hausa,

Nigerian nationalist Nnamdi Azikiwe

Yoruba, and Ibo peoples were part of the same country for the first time. They eyed each other with suspicion.

After independence arrived in 1960, the struggle for unity continued in Nigeria. However, hostilities flared into warfare in 1967. Eastern Nigeria seceded and established the independent state of Biafra. The Nigerian government eventually won the war and reclaimed Biafra, but the country remains haunted by the prophetic words that nationalist leader Obafemi Awolowo spoke in 1947: "Nigeria is not a nation. It is a mere geographical expression."

ACTIVITY

Explain the statement: "Nigeria is not a nation. It is a mere geographical expression." Why have Nigerians been reluctant to unite?

Chapter 19 *Nationalism in Asia, Africa, and Latin America* **575**

Imperialist Boundaries

Awolowo (1909–1987) himself was a leader of the Yoruba people. He studied law in London, where he wrote *Path to Nigerian Freedom* (1947), a call for his homeland's independence. Upon his return to Nigeria, he founded the Action Group, a Yoruba political party. After Nigeria attained independence in 1960, Awolowo turned to socialism and spent some years in prison.

ANSWERS

Nigeria's nationhood is based on place, not on a common culture. Ethnic groups formerly in control of their own territories were reluctant to live as one people.

ASSESS

Check for Understanding

Assign Section 1 Review as homework or as an in-class activity.

▣ Use Student Self-Test and Review Software to review Section 1.

MAKING CONNECTIONS ACTIVITIES

The Arts Have students watch videos of *Lawrence of Arabia*, the 1962 screen biography of T. E. Lawrence, the British leader of the Arab revolt against the Ottoman Empire, and *Exodus*, the 1960 film about the last days of the British mandate in Palestine and the clash of Arab and Zionist nationalists there after the birth of Israel.

Have students write brief reports in which they evaluate the complex British role in the region as depicted in the two films. **L2**

Politics Have students research and write brief reports comparing the lives and political goals of Theodor Herzl, founder of political Zionism, and Yasir Arafat, leader of the Palestine Liberation Organization. **L2**

Evaluate

 Section Quiz 19-1

Use the Testmaker to create a customized quiz for Section 1.

Reteach

Have students explain why the experience of World War I promoted the concept of self-determination among colonial peoples of Africa and the Middle East. (*Many hoped to receive their independence in exchange for fighting with the Allies.*)

Enrich

Ask students to imagine that they are one of the nationalist leaders described in this section. Have them write a short speech directed at a European audience, demanding independence for their homeland.

CLOSE

Write the following on the chalkboard: *No matter how small or weak, every nation has the right to decide its own form of government and to manage its own affairs.* Ask students to discuss whether they agree with this statement in principle and if they think it is practical in real life.

protest movement in 1921 led by **Harry Thuku** (THOO•koo). The protesters complained about high colonial taxes and strict British labor laws. Colonial officials promptly arrested Thuku, and in the riot that followed, British troops killed about 25 Kenyans. The British government then exiled Thuku from Kenya.

In Thuku's absence, **Jomo Kenyatta** took over the growing nationalist movement. Instead of fighting the British in Kenya for independence, Kenyatta took his struggle to the center of British power in London. By meeting with government officials in the 1920s and 1930s, he succeeded in making progress—but at a very slow pace. He later recalled his frustrations:

> 66 By driving [the African] off his ancestral lands, the Europeans have robbed him of the material foundations of his culture, and reduced him to a state of serfdom incompatible with human happiness.... It is not in his nature to accept serfdom forever. He realizes that he must fight unceasingly for his own complete emancipation; for without this he is doomed to remain the prey of rival imperialisms. 99
> —Jomo Kenyatta, *Facing Mount Kenya*, 1938

In spite of Kenyatta's efforts for independence, when World War II began in 1939, Kenya remained firmly in British hands.

Nigeria

Across the continent from Kenya, on the west coast of Africa, lies **Nigeria**. The British controlled this region of Africa as well, and they made large fortunes from Nigeria's rubber, oil, and tin. As in Kenya, the British imposed heavy taxes on men and strict labor laws.

In 1929 Nigerian women learned that they too

Visualizing History Jomo Kenyatta wrote a book, *Facing Mount Kenya*, that explained how British rule had disrupted his country's culture. *How did Kenyatta try to obtain Kenya's independence?*

would be taxed. When a group of unarmed women protested by attacking British goods and property, police fired on them, killing 50.

The violent ending of the women's uprising drove many Nigerians to adopt nonviolent methods in their struggle for independence. One of these Nigerian nationalists was **Nnamdi Azikiwe** (eh•nahm•dee ah•zee•KEE•WEE), who started the newspaper *The West African Pilot* in 1937. He wrote many articles in favor of independence, not only for Nigeria but for all of Africa. "Africa needs a pilot," he wrote once. "Those who follow the true pilot, believing they are on the right track, will find their way to their destination."

SECTION I REVIEW

Recall
1. **Define** self-determination, fez, shah.
2. **Identify** Kemal Atatürk, Reza Shah Pahlavi, Theodor Herzl, Saad Zaghlul, the Balfour Declaration, Harry Thuku, Jomo Kenyatta, Nnamdi Azikiwe.

3. **State** the goal of the reforms introduced by Kemal Atatürk.

Critical Thinking
4. **Evaluating Information** The British in Kenya said they were "exercising a trust on behalf of the African population." What does that phrase imply about

Great Britain's attitude toward Africans?

Understanding Themes
5. **Nationalism** What were the reasons for the rise of nationalism in the Middle East and Africa at the end of World War I?

SECTION I REVIEW ANSWERS

1. All vocabulary words are defined in the Glossary.
2. Atatürk, 573; Reza Shah, 574; Balfour Declaration, 574; Zaghlul, 575; Thuku, 576; Kenyatta, 576; Azikiwe, 576
3. He wanted to westernize Turkey.
4. The British thought they knew what was best for Africans.

5. **NATIONALISM** Colonial peoples wanted to establish modern nations where their own cultures could flourish.

1919 The Amritsar Massacre heightens anti-British feeling in India.

1930 Mohandas K. Gandhi leads protest against British rule.

1935 The British Parliament passes the Government of India Act.

Chapter 19 Section 2

Section 2

India's Struggle for Independence

Setting the Scene

▶ **Terms to Define**
pacifist, civil disobedience, satyagraha

▶ **People to Meet**
Mohandas K. Gandhi, Mohammed Ali Jinnah, Jawaharlal Nehru

▶ **Places to Locate**
India, Amritsar, Ahmadabad

 **ind Out** What methods did Gandhi use in India's struggle for independence from British rule?

The Storyteller

Riswati and Kamala, once friendly neighbors in Bombay, had not spoken to each other for months—since relations between Muslims and Hindus had deteriorated. The British could use the problem as an excuse for delaying Indian independence. The two women had argued over which group, Muslims or Hindus, was more to blame. Kamala recalled the example of Mohandas Gandhi and resolved to visit Riswati and renew their friendship. Perhaps she could quote Gandhi saying, "It does not matter to me that we see things from different angles of vision." Kamala caught sight of Riswati at the market. Quickly she crossed the square toward her old friend.

—adapted from *Communal Unity*, M.K. Gandhi, reprinted in *World Civilizations*, Volume 2, 1994

Mohandas Gandhi

When World War I began, the most important territory in the British Empire was **India**. As in the Middle East and Africa, nationalism was spreading in India. Some Indians wanted independence. Many were willing to remain in the British Empire but demanded home rule. Two of the largest nationalist organizations were the Indian National Congress and the Muslim League.

During World War I, Indian nationalists supported Great Britain and its allies. More than a million Indian soldiers fought on the battlefields of the Middle East and Africa. Indian wheat fed the Allied troops, and Indian cotton kept them clothed. In return for this aid, Great Britain promised in 1917 to support eventual self-rule for India.

The Amritsar Massacre

Independence did not come easily to India. After the war, the Indian National Congress staged demonstrations to protest British rule. The nationalist movement, however, was divided by religion. The Hindu majority and the Muslim minority did not trust each other. The British authorities in India encouraged that distrust.

A second difficulty was British opposition. Many Britons were unwilling to see their empire's power reduced and staunchly opposed freeing India. In 1919 Great Britain imposed on India harsh laws intended to stifle opposition to British rule. British officials could arrest nationalists without cause and jail them without trial.

British repression reached an extreme in the Punjabi city of **Amritsar** in April 1919. The British had outlawed all large gatherings and declared that they would respond to any violation with force. When 10,000 unarmed Indians assembled in a

---

SECTION THEME

▶ **Change** Gandhi calls for non-violence in India's struggle for independence from British rule.

ind Out

Answer: *Gandhi used nonviolent methods such as protest marches and boycotts of British goods.*

FOCUS

Section Objective

State the methods Gandhi used in India's struggle for independence from British rule.

BELLRINGER
Motivational Activity

Before taking roll at the beginning of the class period, project Section Focus Transparency 19-2 and have students answer the activity questions. Discuss students' responses.
This activity is also available as a blackline master.

Vocabulary Pre-check

Use Vocabulary Activity 19 to introduce vocabulary terms.
L1 LEP

SECTION RESOURCES

Reproducible Masters
- Reproducible Lesson Plan 19-2
- Vocabulary Activity 19
- Guided Reading Activity 19-2
- Section Quiz 19-2

Transparencies
- Section Focus Transparency 19-2

Multimedia
- Student Self-Test and Review Software
- Testmaker
- Lessons of War: *Philosophy of Nonviolence*

TEACH

Guided Practice

THEME Change

Discuss the purpose of the boycott led by Gandhi. Ask students to explain why this tactic might be more effective at achieving change than a demonstration. *How did the boycott attack the underlying logic of imperialism? (The empire was supposed to benefit England economically.)* **L1**

Visualizing History The Indian National Congress, founded in 1885, led the movement for independence, and was also India's ruling party from 1947 to 1977.

Answer to Caption: *South Africa*

Gandhi's Campaign

How did Gandhi's campaign affect India's relationship with Great Britain?

His use of nonviolence weakened British authority and helped lead to India's independence.

VIDEODISC
Lessons of War

Side Two, Chapter 6
Frames 12636–20751
Title: *Philosophy of Nonviolence*
Ask: Identify two people in history who exemplified nonviolent protest. *(Mohandas Gandhi and Martin Luther King, Jr.)*

Visualizing History During the 1920s and 1930s, Gandhi was India's leading nationalist. He worked to promote unity between Hindus and Muslims in the Indian National Congress party. *Where did Gandhi first use nonviolent methods to protest injustices?*

walled garden in Amritsar for a political meeting, the local commander decided that the British needed to demonstrate their authority. Without warning, British troops blocked the only entrance to the garden and began firing into the trapped crowd. When the firing ceased, nearly 400 people, including many children, lay dead. Another 1,200 people were wounded. Criticized for his action, the British commander declared:

> ❝ I fired and continued to fire until the crowd dispersed, and I consider this is the least amount of firing which would produce the necessary moral effect.... If more troops had been at hand, the casualties would have been greater. ❞

Gandhi and the West Mohandas K. Gandhi has had a profound influence on people in the West. He served as a model for Martin Luther King, Jr. King led the African American civil rights struggle until his assassination in 1968. Like Gandhi, King protested injustice with nonviolent boycotts and marches.

Indians across the country were shocked by the brutal massacre and the general's justification of it. In large numbers, they came together in meeting after meeting, more determined than ever to drive the British out of their land. However, they needed a strong leader to spearhead their struggle.

Gandhi's Campaign

In the months following the Amritsar Massacre, **Mohandas K. Gandhi** became the leading Indian nationalist. Born in India of middle-class parents in 1869, Gandhi had been educated in England. He later practiced law in South Africa, where he and other Indians experienced mistreatment because of their dark skin.

Until 1914 Gandhi lived in South Africa and led protests against racial discrimination. He was a pacifist, a person opposed to using war and other violence to settle disputes. In keeping with his beliefs, Gandhi used protest methods based on civil disobedience, or the refusal to obey laws that are considered unjust.

When Gandhi returned to India, he began working with the Indian National Congress and led a nonviolent movement for self-government and for greater tolerance among the country's many social and religious groups. Gandhi urged Indians to reject much of Western civilization for its use of brute force, its worship of money, and its prejudicial attitudes toward non-Western peoples. Gandhi's understanding of India's problems made him popular throughout the country. The Indian people called Gandhi *Mahatma*, meaning "great soul."

Gandhi's doctrine of moral nonviolent protest won him international attention. He believed that one could force an evil person or government to change by challenging it directly, but without violence. Gandhi used the term satyagraha (suh•TYAH•gruh•huh), which means "truth force," to describe the nonviolent protests he led after the Amritsar Massacre. One effective form of protest was the boycott, in which Indians refused to buy British cloth and other manufactured goods. As a step toward independence, Gandhi urged Indians to begin spinning their own cloth.

Gandhi practiced what he preached by spinning cloth for a half hour every day. He made the spinning wheel the symbol of the National Congress, and he wore nothing but simple homespun clothes for the rest of his life.

COOPERATIVE LEARNING ACTIVITY

Debate Organize the class into two groups to debate the following statement: "Gandhi's nonviolent philosophy made India's independence movement less effective than it would have been, had force been used." Each group should research the issue and organize its argument before the debate takes place, dividing the work into research, organization of information, and presentation of information, and assigning these tasks to subgroups. You might want to have students conduct this debate before another class and let the members of that class vote on the more persuasive argument. **L2**

Gandhi's courage inspired millions of Indians to join in protests. In 1922, however, the British arrested Gandhi, and he disappeared from active protest for the rest of the decade. Undaunted, the Indian National Congress continued to protest, but it achieved very little success until Gandhi's return in 1930.

Toward Independence

Gandhi planned his next major protest around salt. In India's hot climate, the millions of people who worked in fields and factories needed salt to replace what they lost daily in sweat. The British controlled the salt mines and the ocean salt fields. They taxed every grain of salt they sold and jailed Indians who gathered salt on their own.

In 1930 Gandhi protested the salt tax. First he led thousands of his followers on a 200-mile (322-km) march from **Ahmadabad** to the sea, where they made salt from sea water. One month later, Gandhi openly defied British authority by wading into the sea and picking up a lump of salt. The British did not dare arrest him, but they did arrest thousands who followed his example. To quell the mounting protests, they arrested him a month later, but the protests only increased. Webb Miller, a British journalist, described one such protest, in which a group of Indians marched on a heavily guarded salt mine: "Although every one knew that within a few minutes he would be beaten down, perhaps killed, I could detect no signs of wavering or fear.... There was no fight, no struggle; the marchers simply walked forward until struck down."

This pattern continued throughout the 1930s. As Indians protested, the British responded with guns and clubs. Their violence could not stop the millions of people motivated by nationalism.

Limited Self-Rule

Under pressure from the nationalist movement, the British began to give Indians more political power. In 1935 the British Parliament passed the Government of India Act, which created a constitution for India. This measure gave provincial legislatures control over the making of law in the provinces. Areas such as agriculture, education, public health, and public works came under the control of the provincial governments. The British government retained control of national lawmaking, finance, defense, and foreign affairs.

The majority of Indian nationalists rejected the act, wanting complete independence. However, the Indian National Congress, at the insistence of Gandhi, finally accepted it as the first step toward self-rule. The Indian historian K.M. Panikkar states that with the Government of India Act, "British authority in India was in full retreat, in the administrative field no less than in the political and economic fields." Nevertheless, independence was not yet won.

Hindu-Muslim Relations

Even as India moved toward independence in the 1930s, conflicts among Indians increased. For every Muslim, India had three Hindus. As independence approached, the Muslims began worrying about their future treatment by the Hindus, and many joined the Muslim League.

In 1937 the Indian National Congress, controlled by Hindus, won election majorities in 7 out of 11 provinces. Muslims came to power in the others. This heightened bitter feelings. The Muslim League, headed by **Mohammed Ali Jinnah**, split with the Congress party. It demanded a separate Muslim nation for the millions of Muslims in India. The Hindus, led by **Jawaharlal Nehru**, a follower of Gandhi, wanted a united India.

Although a Hindu, Gandhi was concerned about the deepening rift between Hindus and Muslims. His pleas for toleration were largely ignored by both groups. As 1939 ended, India continued its long struggle for freedom. But now the nationalist movement had split in two, and not even Gandhi could put it together again.

SECTION 2 REVIEW

Recall
1. **Define** pacifist, civil disobedience, satyagraha.
2. **Identify** Mohandas K. Gandhi, Mohammed Ali Jinnah, Jawaharlal Nehru.
3. **List** the three countries in which Gandhi spent most of his life. Locate these countries on the Atlas map on pages A-5 and A-6.

Critical Thinking
4. **Synthesizing Information** What could Hindus have done to keep Muslims united with them against the British?

Understanding Themes
5. **Change** What nonviolent methods did Mohandas K. Gandhi use to bring about change?

SECTION 2 REVIEW ANSWERS

1. All vocabulary words are defined in the Glossary.
2. Gandhi, 578; Jinnah, 579; Nehru, 579
3. Gandhi was born in India, educated in Great Britain, and worked in South Africa before returning to India.
4. Answers will vary but may include the guarantee of a voice for Muslims in political decisions or support of strong civil rights laws.
5. **CHANGE** He led marches and urged Indians to boycott British goods and to make their own cloth and salt.

Independent Practice

Guided Reading Activity 19-2 **L1**

Critical Thinking Have students discuss under what conditions, if any, it is proper to break the law. Ask them to consider whether someone who breaks an unjust law should accept punishment, and what moral point a person makes by intentionally breaking the law.

ASSESS

Check for Understanding

Assign Section 2 Review as homework or as an in-class activity.

Use Student Self-Test and Review Software to review Section 2.

Evaluate

Section Quiz 19-2

Use the Testmaker to create a customized quiz for Section 2.

Reteach

Have each student write one review question for each of the three major parts of this section. Ask students to exchange their questions with a classmate and answer each other's questions.

Enrich

Have students watch a video of the 1982 screen biography *Gandhi*. Ask them to write a brief review as if they were a critic.

CLOSE

Have students create two lists on the chalkboard, one of British actions to prevent Indian independence, and the other of measures taken by Indian nationalists to win self-rule.

SECTION THEME

▶ **Conflict** Nationalists, Communists, and the Japanese compete for control of China.

ind Out

Answer: *They were united in their wish to control the threat from Japan but divided by political conflicts.*

FOCUS

Section Objective

Explain the factors that divided and the factors that united nationalist forces in China.

BELLRINGER
Motivational Activity

Before taking roll at the beginning of the class period, project Section Focus Transparency 19-3 and have students answer the activity questions. Discuss students' responses.

This activity is also available as a blackline master.

Vocabulary Pre-check

Use Vocabulary Activity 19 to introduce vocabulary terms.
L1 LEP

Section 3

China's Drive for Modernization

Setting the Scene

▶ **Terms to Define**
warlord

▶ **People to Meet**
Sun Yat-sen, Yuan Shigai, Chiang Kai-shek, Mao Zedong

▶ **Places to Locate**
Nanjing, Guangzhou, Manchuria

ind Out
What divided nationalist forces in China, and what united them?

The Storyteller

Wai Zhou watched a small man addressing a group in the square. "China has become a colony of all the Powers," he proclaimed. This was nothing new, Wai Zhou thought, just another agitator seeking an audience. But the man continued, "Foreigners often refer to the Chinese nation as a bowl of loose sand. To revive nationalism we must expand our small group loyalty to a very large group. The people must learn to read and write. China must become a democracy. Those who till the soil should own it." The speaker outlined a plan for Chinese independence. Completely won over, Wai Zhou asked a bystander who the speaker was. "I heard him called Sun Yat-sen," the man replied.

—adapted from *Lectures on Nationalism*, Sun Yat-sen, reprinted in *Lives and Times*, James P. Holoka and Jiu-Hwa Lo Upshur, 1995

Sun Yat-sen

---

nlike India, China was never entirely controlled by a European country. However, despite its independence and population size, China did not have the military power to command respect. That they lacked the respect of Europeans was shown by the final terms of the Versailles peace conference that followed World War I. The Versailles Treaty had a provision granting Japan economic control of the Shandong (SHON•DOONG) Peninsula of northeastern China. This provision was a humiliating and surprising blow to the Chinese. During and after World War I, China was torn apart by internal divisions, and the foreign powers took advantage of China's weakness.

The Chinese Republic

As you read in Chapter 16, the Chinese revolutionary leader **Sun Yat-sen** formally declared China a republic in January 1912. Sun dreamed of a free, democratic society. However, just two months after taking office, he was ousted by a military strongman, **Yuan Shigai** (YOO•AHN SHUR•GIE). Yuan quickly turned the new republic into a dictatorship. Meanwhile, Sun organized and formed the nationalist Guomindang (KWOH•MIHN•DAHNG) party, tried and failed to overthrow Yuan, and then fled to Japan.

When Yuan died in 1916, China slipped into chaos. Local military leaders called warlords divided the vast country among themselves. An almost continual state of civil war followed.

Sun Yat-sen returned to China in 1917 and tried in vain to restore strong central government to China and rebuild the Guomindang party. Then in 1923, with aid from the Soviet Union and an ambitious young officer named **Chiang Kai-shek**

SECTION RESOURCES

Reproducible Masters
- Reproducible Lesson Plan 19-3
- Vocabulary Activity 19
- Guided Reading Activity 19-3
- Time Line Activity 19
- Section Quiz 19-3

Transparencies
- Section Focus Transparency 19-3

Multimedia
- Student Self-Test and Review Software
- Testmaker

Visualizing History Chiang Kai-shek was appointed commander of the National Revolutionary Army in 1926. By the end of 1928 the last major faction of warlords pledged obedience to the National Government. *What other party opposed the warlords?*

TEACH

Guided Practice

THEME Conflict

Have students discuss the difficulties faced by Sun Yat-sen in creating a new China. *(ousted by Yuan Shigai shortly after taking office; failed in his attempt to overthrow Yuan with his Guomindang party; failed to restore strong central government)* **L1**

Visualizing History To strengthen the moral fiber of the nation, Chiang (1887–1975) encouraged a movement to teach Confucian morals. **Answer to Caption:** *the Communists*

Independent Practice

🗁 Guided Reading Activity 19-3 **L1**

🗁 Time Line Activity 19

Politics Have students imagine that they are members of the Red Army trying to gain the support of peasants in the countryside. Have them write a short speech that deals with issues of concern to Chinese peasants. **L2**

Linking Past and Present

Taiwan After Mao won control of the Chinese mainland, Chiang headed the Nationalist government in exile on Taiwan from 1949 until his death in 1975. China continued to regard Taiwan as a renegade province. Although tensions between the two eased in the late 1980s, they intensified again in the 1990s.

(JEE•AHNG KY•SHEHK), the Guomindang army grew rapidly in strength. Sun Yatsen died in 1925. Three years later, Chiang led the army to victory over the warlords and established a government in the city of **Nanjing**.

Though undemocratic, government under the Guomindang promoted economic development by building schools, roads, and railways. However, the Guomindang did very little to raise the living standards of the peasants who comprised the vast majority of the population of China.

Rivalry With the Communists

Many peasants, along with intellectuals and urban workers, supported another party that opposed the warlords: the Communists. During Chiang's drive against the warlords, Communist soldiers provided him with crucial military support. But in 1927 the Communists attempted to take over the Guomindang party and failed. Chiang turned against the Communists and tried to wipe them out. In Shanghai, **Guangzhou**, and other cities, Guomindang soldiers killed tens of thousands of Communists.

As Chiang began his purge, tens of thousands of Communists fled to the mountains in the southern province of Jiangxi (jee•AHNG•SHEE). Here they gathered their strength and formed the Red Army, led by the son of a prosperous peasant family, **Mao Zedong** (MOW DZUH•DOONG). Mao

believed that the Communists could still triumph with the help of China's millions of peasants:

 In a very short time, in China's central, southern, and northern provinces, several hundred million peasants will rise like a mighty storm, like a hurricane, a force so swift and violent that no power, however great, will be able to hold it back. 🙰

—Mao Zedong, *Report on an Investigation,* 1926

Living conditions for China's peasants had changed little over the centuries. They worked small plots of land and turned over most of their crops to wealthy landlords. The Red Army gained popular support in rural areas of the country by overthrowing local landlords and distributing their land to the peasants. Before long, the Red Army included nearly 30,000 peasant troops.

The success of the Red Army worried Chiang. In the early 1930s he ordered a series of "extermination campaigns" in an attempt to destroy this rival army. Mao fought back, however, using his own strategies: "The enemy advances, we retreat; the enemy camps, we harass; the enemy tires, we attack; the enemy retreats, we pursue."

Mao's military plans worked at times, but by October 1934, the Guomindang had nearly surrounded the Communists with a million troops. Mao decided to retreat once again, leading about 100,000 followers out of Jiangxi Province in a desperate gamble for survival.

Chapter 19 *Nationalism in Asia, Africa, and Latin America* **581**

COOPERATIVE LEARNING ACTIVITY

Reports Organize the class into two groups to report on the influence of Chinese students on the politics of China. Each group member should have a specific task, such as researching, organizing, or summarizing. Have one group examine the political role Chinese students played in the early part of this century and the other group research the role Chinese students have played in politics in recent years, including the Tiananmen Square demonstrations of June 1989. **L2**

ASSESS

Check for Understanding

Assign Section 3 Review as homework or as an in-class activity.

🖭 Use Student Self-Test and Review Software to review Section 3.

Evaluate

📂 Section Quiz 19-3

🖭 Use the Testmaker to create a customized quiz for Section 3.

Reteach

Have students list statements on the chalkboard summarizing the main events in China's drive for unity and modernization.

Enrich

Have students watch a video of the 1987 film *The Last Emperor*. Have them write reports analyzing the way the film uses the story of Pu Yi as a mirror reflecting China's passage from feudalism through revolution toward a modern society.

CLOSE

Have students create a time line covering the key events in Chinese history from 1919 to 1939. Have them write summary statements describing the political situations in China in 1919 and 1939.

Visualizing History Mao Zedong led the Communist retreat known as the Long March. Some Communists survived the ordeal in spite of harsh weather and rugged terrain. *From what Chinese force were the Communists fleeing?*

The Long March

Mao's retreat from Jiangxi lasted for one year and covered about 6,000 miles (9,600 km). During that time the Red Army marched an average of 16 miles (26 km) a day, across rivers and mountains, and defeated 10 provincial armies—all the while

being chased by Guomindang military forces. The Chinese Communists called the arduous undertaking the Long March.

At times the line of marching Communist soldiers stretched out for nearly 50 miles (80 km). One of these soldiers later recalled the march:

“ If it was a black night and the enemy far away, we made torches from pine branches or frayed bamboo, and then it was truly beautiful. At the foot of a mountain, we could look up and see a long column of lights coiling like a fiery dragon up the mountainside. From the summit we could look in both directions and see miles of torches moving forward like a wave of fire. A rosy glow hung over the whole route of the march. ”

Conditions on the Long March were far from rosy, however. Thousands of soldiers froze or starved to death, and others died in battle. Of the original 100,000 troops, fewer than 8,000 remained at the end of the march in 1935.

Threat From Japan

While Chiang and Mao battled each other in 1931, the Japanese had conquered the large section of northeast China known as **Manchuria**. Now it appeared that Japan wanted even more land, and Chiang's advisers urged him to confront the Japanese. Mao offered assistance but was rejected by Chiang. Manchurian forces then kidnapped Chiang and held him prisoner until he finally agreed to end his war with the Communists.

However, unity between Chiang and Mao could not stop the Japanese invasion that came eight months later. By 1939 Japan controlled most of eastern China. Chiang withdrew to the interior of the country, where Mao was awaiting the proper moment to strike back. Before that moment arrived, the entire world was at war.

SECTION 3 REVIEW

Recall
1. **Define** warlord.
2. **Identify** Sun Yat-sen, Yuan Shigai, Chiang Kai-shek, Mao Zedong.
3. **List** the groups of Chinese who

supported the Communists most strongly.

Critical Thinking
4. **Analyzing Information** Why do you think Mao decided to undertake the Long March?

What other choices did he have?

Understanding Themes
5. **Conflict** What conflicts kept China in turmoil after World War I?

SECTION 3 REVIEW ANSWERS

1. All vocabulary words are defined in the Glossary.
2. Sun Yat-sen, 580; Yuan Shigai, 580; Chiang Kai-shek, 580; Mao Zedong, 581
3. The Communists attracted support from peasants, urban workers, and intellectuals.
4. Answers will vary. Possible answer: Mao

may have believed the Long March would build solidarity among members of the Red Army.

5. **CONFLICT** Fighting occurred among the warlords, between the Guomindang and the Communists, and against the Japanese.

1915   1925   1935

1915 Japan forces China to accept the Twenty-One Demands.

1925 Japanese parliament grants vote to all males.

1932 Army officers assassinate Japanese prime minister.

Chapter 19 Section 4

Section 4

Militarism in Japan

Setting the Scene

▶ **Terms to Define**
population explosion, heavy industry, *zaibatsu*

▶ **People to Meet**
Hirohito

▶ **Places to Locate**
Manchuria

 How did militarism shape Japan during the period after World War I?

The Storyteller

Japan's Total War Research Institute drafted a secret strategy for the Japanese government. Called the "Greater East Asia Co-Prosperity Sphere," the plan outlined the establishment of a "zone of peaceful living and common prosperity for the peoples of East Asia." Japan would be the stabilizing power. The influence of all other nations would be driven out. The "New Order of East Asia" was an idea that did not include independence based on national self-determination. Instead, Japan would establish a new morality whose basic principle would be the Imperial Way.

—adapted from *Sources of the Japanese Tradition,* edited by W.T. deBary, reprinted in *Sources of World Civilization,* Volume 2, 1994

Japanese cavalry in China

Like China, Japan, an independent country, had fought on the side of the Allies in World War I. During the conflict, the Japanese supplied weapons to their European partners, particularly to Russia. At the same time, they took advantage of the war to expand their economic and political influence in East Asia. In addition to ruling Korea and Taiwan, Japan pressed for an enlargement of its role in China. In 1915 Japanese diplomats forced the Chinese government to accept a list of terms known as the Twenty-One Demands. The Twenty-One Demands, in effect, made China a Japanese protectorate.

Japan and the West

When World War I ended, Japan received Germany's Pacific islands north of the Equator as mandates from the League of Nations. The Japanese also entered into a series of military and commercial agreements with the Western powers. A disarmament conference held in Washington, D.C., in 1922 led to a five-power agreement among Japan, Great Britain, the United States, Italy, and France that allowed Japan to become the world's third-largest naval power after Great Britain and the United States. Yet, in spite of this and other gains, the Japanese were bitter toward the West.

First, Japan felt that the West did not accept it as an equal. In 1919 the League of Nations, dominated by Western powers, refused to accept Japan's demand for a statement on racial equality in the League's charter. The Japanese regarded this rejection as a humiliation. In 1924 the United States banned further Japanese immigration to its shores. In response, the Japanese staged demonstrations and boycotted American goods.

The Japanese were angered further by the West's refusal to support Japanese policy in China. Japan wanted to tie China closer to itself; the West wanted to retain the Open Door policy. As a result

Chapter 19 *Nationalism in Asia, Africa, and Latin America* **583**

SECTION THEME

▶ **Conflict** Japan's militarism and expansionism place it on a collision course with the West.

 **ind Out**

Answer: *Militarism pervaded all aspects of Japanese life–from foreign policy to education.*

FOCUS

Section Objective

Describe how militarism shaped the development of Japan after World War I.

BELLRINGER Motivational Activity

Before taking roll at the beginning of the class period, project Section Focus Transparency 19-4 and have students answer the activity questions. Discuss students' responses.

This activity is also available as a blackline master.

Vocabulary Pre-check

Use Vocabulary Activity 19 to introduce vocabulary terms. **L1 LEP**

SECTION RESOURCES

Reproducible Masters
- Reproducible Lesson Plan 19-4
- Vocabulary Activity 19
- Guided Reading Activity 19-4
- History Simulation 19
- Mapping History Activity 19
- Section Quiz 19-4

Transparencies
- Section Focus Transparency 19-4

Multimedia
- Student Self-Test and Review Software
- Testmaker

TEACH

Guided Practice

THEME Conflict

To help students understand how population density encouraged Japanese expansionism, have them consider the relative areas of Japan (145,856 square miles [377,767 square km]) and California (158,706 square miles [411,049 square km]). By 1925 Japan's population was about 60 million; have students find out the current population of California. Ask students to discuss how Japan's growth led to aggressive policies. **L1**

Visualizing History

After Chiang Kai-shek's Nationalist government made Nanking (now Nanjing) the capital of a united China in 1928, the city thrived. When the city fell to the Japanese in 1937, between 40,000 and 300,000 civilians were killed. From then until Japan's defeat in World War II, Nanjing was ruled by puppet governments. **Answer to Caption:** *His advisers feared the emperor would be removed and that extremism would increase if he opposed militarism.*

Independent Practice

 Guided Reading Activity 19-4 **L1**

 History Simulation 19

 Mapping History Activity 19

Biography

The following videotape program is available from Glencoe:
- **Hirohito**

Visualizing History Young Japanese students celebrate the fall of Nanjing to Japanese forces in 1938. *Why was Emperor Hirohito unable to thwart the spread of militarism in Japan?*

of Western pressure, Japan had to abandon the Twenty-One Demands and recognize Western interests in China.

Social and Political Tensions

After World War I, Japan faced social and economic challenges at home. Of major concern was a population explosion, or dramatic increase in population. Japan's population had increased from nearly 35 million in 1872 to about 60 million in 1925. This rate of increase was a challenge because of the already high density of population on the Japanese islands.

Japan's Industrial Growth

Since emigration was cut off to such places as the United States, the Japanese looked for other ways to cope. They placed new emphasis on manufacturing and foreign trade. It was hoped that new factories and markets would provide employment for large numbers of people.

Government-controlled banks provided the needed capital to encourage the expansion of heavy industry, or the manufacture of machinery and equipment needed for factories and mines. Industries important to national defense, especially

steel and the railroads, were owned by the government, but most of the Japanese economy was in the hands of large privately owned businesses known together as the *zaibatsu* (zy•BAHT•soo).

During the 1920s and 1930s Japan's industry grew rapidly, and Japanese manufactured goods began to flood world markets. Increased manufacturing, however, stimulated the desire for raw materials. Since Japan had few mineral resources of its own, it was forced to look overseas for them.

Social and Political Changes

Meanwhile, Japan's working class increased in importance. Because of overpopulation in the countryside, land already scarce was continually subdivided among farmers. Rural economic woes enabled farm villages to provide the bulk of labor for the new urban industries. Along with male workers, many young women from rural areas found jobs in the factories.

Labor unions became more powerful and increased their membership to more than 300,000 members by the end of the 1920s. The growth of the urban, working-class population produced movements demanding social changes. Several efforts by intellectuals to organize Socialist groups, however, were speedily met with police repression.

During this period, the urban middle class expanded as well. Japanese cities became great metropolitan areas and centers of middle-class culture. The Tokyo-Yokohama area, devastated by a terrible earthquake in 1923, took on a new appearance as Western influences increasingly shaped the tempo of urban life. American music, dancing, and sports especially became popular, and rising standards of living and expectations produced the need for more and better higher education.

With the growth of the working and middle classes, steps were taken toward greater political democracy. In 1925 the Japanese parliament granted universal male suffrage; voters increased from 3 million to 14 million. Japanese women, however, did not receive the right to vote until 1947.

Political Weaknesses

In spite of these gains, democracy remained very limited in Japan. Political power was actually in the hands of nobles and urban industrialists. The emperor, **Hirohito**, was a constitutional monarch. However, he was a powerful symbol of traditional authority. Behind the emperor was an influential group of military leaders, who were opposed to democratic reforms.

The appeal of antidemocratic nationalist groups increased as the economy deteriorated in

---

COOPERATIVE LEARNING ACTIVITY

Roundtable Discussion Have students make a list of the social and economic problems that Japan faced after World War I. The list should include rapid population growth, need for raw materials, scarce farmland, limited democracy, and political repression. Organize the class into groups and have each group think of several possible solutions to one problem. Then hold a roundtable discussion in which representatives from each group try to work out peaceful solutions to Japan's challenges. **L2**

the 1930s. A worldwide fall in prices caused by the Great Depression devastated Japan's silk factories and other industries. Millions of workers lost their jobs and could not find new ones. Some began to starve, and children went begging in the streets. In November 1930 an assassin from a secret society shot Prime Minister Osachi Hamaguchi (oh•SAH •chee hah•mah•GOO•chee). Teetering on the brink of economic chaos, many impoverished farmers and workers in Japan looked to strong-minded military leaders such as Hashimoto Kingoro (hah•shee•MOH•toh keen•GOH•roh) for answers:

❝ We are like a great crowd of people packed into a small and narrow room, and there are only three doors through which we might escape, namely emigration, advance into world markets, and expansion of territory. The first door … has been barred to us by the anti-Japanese immigration policies of other countries. The second door … is being pushed shut by tariff barriers.... Japan should rush upon the last door [expansion of territory]. **❞**

—Hashimoto Kingoro, *Addresses to Young Men*

Militarism and Daily Life

During the 1930s, militarism began to influence all aspects of Japanese life—from foreign policy to education. Supporters of the military program opposed the spread of Western lifestyles in Japan and favored traditional Japanese ways. Military dress, including items such as the samurai swords, appealed to nationalist sentiments. Young children even carried out military drills in schools and participated in parades.

Military Expansion

In September 1931 the Japanese military demonstrated just how powerful it had become.

Without seeking approval from the government, army leaders decided to invade the northeastern region of China known as **Manchuria**. In short order, they launched an invasion. It was clear that the Japanese government could no longer control its own army. In five months the powerful Japanese army had conquered Manchuria.

The conquest of Manchuria was a clear sign of the plans of the military to dominate the Japanese government at home and expand Japanese influence abroad. The principal opposition to democratic government came from young military officers. Largely from rural backgrounds, they opposed the urban luxuries of the politicians and readily accepted extremist ideas.

By the early 1930s extremist groups in the military were ready to use violence to bend the government to their will. In 1932 army officers assassinated a prime minister who dared to oppose their views. Then, in 1936, another group of officers led an armed revolt against the government. Although the revolt collapsed, it did not halt the steady takeover of government policy making by the military. By early 1937 the army and the government had become one and the same.

Many democratically minded Japanese hoped that Emperor Hirohito would try to thwart the spread of militarism. As a crown prince, the emperor had traveled in the West and had a keen appreciation of Western ways. Palace advisers, however, feared that any strong stand by the emperor would only increase the extremism of the military leaders. Above all, they feared that the emperor would be removed from office and that the Japanese monarchy would be abolished.

As international criticism of Japan's expansion grew, many Japanese rallied to the support of their soldiers and the military leaders. With no powerful political opposition at home, Japan's military leaders looked forward to conquering all of Asia. Their dreams of a mighty Japanese empire—like the dreams of German and Italian rulers—brought the world to war.

SECTION 4 REVIEW

Recall
1. **Define** population explosion, heavy industry, *zaibatsu*.
2. **Identify** Hirohito.
3. **Locate** the Manchurian Plain on the map on pages A16 and A17 of the Atlas. Explain why

the location of this region made it valuable to the Japanese.

Critical Thinking
4. **Synthesizing Information** Imagine you are an unemployed worker in Japan in the 1930s. Would you support the

new military powers? Why or why not?

Understanding Themes
5. **Conflict** What steps did the military take to increase its hold on the Japanese government?

SECTION 4 REVIEW ANSWERS

1. All vocabulary words are defined in the Glossary.
2. Hirohito, 584
3. It was a nearby region and China was preoccupied with internal conflicts.
4. Answers will vary. Students might suggest that a strong military government might provide work through expanding war

industries.

5. **CONFLICT** invaded Manchuria without government approval in 1931, assassinated a prime minister who opposed it in 1932, rebelled against the government in 1936, and steadily took over government policy making

---

Linking Past and Present

Japan's Military The Japanese Constitution of 1947 not only abolished the country's army and navy but also pledged that Japan would abandon war as a political tool. The prohibition was observed so strictly that it was not until February 1996 that 45 Japanese soldiers—the first Japanese troops to participate in peacekeeping operations—joined UN forces in the Golan Heights.

ASSESS

Check for Understanding

Assign Section 4 Review as homework or as an in-class activity.

 Use Student Self-Test and Review Software to review Section 4.

Evaluate

Section Quiz 19-4

 Use the Testmaker to create a customized quiz for Section 4.

Reteach

Have students state how Japan's geography contributed to its problems during the late 1800s and early 1900s.

Enrich

Have students imagine that they are Japanese civilians opposed to militarism living in Tokyo during the 1930s. Have them write diary entries responding to key events during the decade.

CLOSE

Have students make two lists, one of the problems that Japan confronted in the 1920s and 1930s, and one of solutions pursued by Japanese militarists.

Critical Thinking SKILLS

TEACH

Identifying an Argument In preparation for this lesson, find two newspaper editorials or opinion pieces that make opposing arguments on the same issue. Before having the class read the skill, distribute copies of the pieces. After students have read the editorials, ask them to identify the argument and supporting reasons in each piece. Now have students read the skill and complete the practice questions.

Additional Practice

Skill Reinforcement Activity 19

Critical Thinking SKILLS

Identifying an Argument

Have you ever argued with someone about a political or social issue? In everyday conversation, the word *argument* refers to a conflict involving two or more opinions. However, in writing and in formal debate, an argument is the full presentation of a single opinion. It is important to learn how to identify a writer's or speaker's argument to fully understand and evaluate the position.

Learning the Skill

The main idea of an argument is its thesis, or the writer's basic position or viewpoint on the subject. In some arguments the thesis is stated explicitly. In others, you must read carefully to determine the writer's position.

The writer supports the thesis with reasons and supports the reasons with examples or facts. For instance, suppose your parents have said that it would be better if you did not have a car to drive until after your 18th birthday. They support their thesis with these reasons: 1) other forms of transportation are available; and 2) you will be a more mature and better driver by that age. They support the first reason with these facts: you live in a city with good public transportation; your best friend has a car and frequently drives you to school. They support the second reason with accident statistics of younger and older drivers.

Before accepting or rejecting an argument, evaluate its strengths and weaknesses. Determine the validity of each reason. How well is each reason supported by facts and examples? Does the author's bias invalidate the argument? In the above example, your parents may be biased; they may want to protect your safety and keep their car insurance rates low for another year. Despite this bias, however, they still may have a strong argument if the supporting facts are true.

Practicing the Skill

Read the quotation from Jomo Kenyatta

below, and review the discussion of Kenya in Section 1, pages 575–576. Then answer the following questions.
1. What is Kenyatta's thesis in this quotation?
2. What reasons does Kenyatta give to support this thesis?
3. What facts support Kenyatta's statement that Europeans have robbed Africans of their birthright?
4. What bias does Kenyatta show in his statement? Do the facts outweigh his bias? Why or why not?

66 By driving [the African] off his ancestral lands, the Europeans have robbed him of the material foundations of his culture, and reduced him to a state of serfdom incompatible with human happiness…. It is not in his nature to accept serfdom forever. He realizes that he must fight unceasingly for his own complete emancipation; for without this he is doomed to remain the prey of rival imperialisms. 99
—Jomo Kenyatta, *Facing Mount Kenya*, 1938

Applying the Skill

Find an article in a recent newspaper or magazine that states an argument about a political or historical issue. Identify the thesis of the argument and major reasons and evidence supporting it. Decide whether you accept or reject this argument and explain why.

For More Practice

Turn to the Skill Practice in the Chapter Review on page 599 for more practice in identifying an argument.

586 **Chapter 19** *Nationalism in Asia, Africa, and Latin America*

ANSWERS TO PRACTICING THE SKILL

1. Europeans have robbed Africans of the material foundations of their culture.
2. Europeans drove Africans from their lands, reducing them to serfdom. Unless Africans emancipate themselves, they will continue to be subject to outside powers.
3. Britain refused to grant independence to Kenya and violently suppressed protests; Europeans settled on African lands and employed Africans on plantations for very low wages.
4. Kenyatta reveals an anti-European bias with emotional words such as *robbed, serfdom, emancipation, prey*. Student evaluations may differ, but point out that, despite his bias, the facts support Kenyatta's thesis.

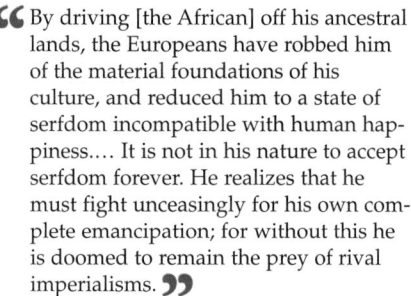

The timeline at top

1915 | **1925** | **1935**

1917 Mexico ratifies a new constitution.

1930 José F. Uriburu leads successful coup in Argentina.

1934 Lázaro Cárdenas becomes president of Mexico.

Chapter 19
Section 5

Section 5

Nationalism in Latin America

Setting the Scene

▶ **Terms to Define**
cooperatives, nationalization

▶ **People to Meet**
Lázaro Cárdenas, Juan Vicente Gómez, Hipólito Irigoyen, José F. Uriburu, Getúlio Vargas, Augusto César Sandino

▶ **Places to Locate**
Mexico, Venezuela, Argentina, Brazil, Nicaragua

 **ind Out** Why did nationalism in Latin America bring conflict with the United States?

The Storyteller

"Let us forget the marble of the Acropolis and the towers of the Gothic cathedrals. We are the sons of the hills and the forests. Stop thinking of Europe. Think of America!" The words of Ronald de Carvallo, a Brazilian nationalist, rang in Lucio Costa's ears. He resolved to break with traditional forms and create architecture appropriate for Brazil. He visualized a style integrating art and nature—murals, sculptures, and tiles with gardens and decorative painting.

—adapted from Latin America, A Concise Interpretive History, E. Bradford Burns, 1994

Palacio Do Ilamarati, Brasilia

After World War I, economic change and nationalism swept Latin America. Although the region's economy remained basically agricultural, the oil and mineral industries became increasingly important. Much of the investment that developed these resources was from the United States, Great Britain, France, Germany, and Italy. Anger at foreign influence led to growing nationalism among Latin Americans of all backgrounds. Rubén Darío, a noted Nicaraguan writer, had expressed the view of many Latin Americans:

❝ The United States is grand and powerful.
Whenever it trembles, a profound shudder runs down the enormous backbone of the Andes.
If it shouts, the sound is like the roar of a lion....
But our own America, which has had poets since the ancient times ...
and has lived, since the earliest moments of its life,
in light, in fire, in fragrance, and in love—
the America of Moctezuma and Atahualpa,
the aromatic America of Columbus,
Catholic America, Spanish America ...
our America lives. And dreams. And loves.
And it is the daughter of the Sun. Be careful.
Long live Spanish America! ❞
—Rubén Darío, "To Roosevelt," 1903

Economic Changes

In the 20 years following World War I, Latin Americans continued to grow coffee, bananas,

SECTION THEME

▶ **Change** Nationalist forces in Latin America oppose increased American intervention in the region.

 **ind Out**

Answer: *Nationalism in Latin America brought conflict with the United States because of increased American intervention.*

FOCUS

Section Objective

Analyze why nationalism in Latin America brought conflict with the United States.

BELLRINGER
Motivational Activity

Before taking roll at the beginning of the class period, project Section Focus Transparency 19-5 and have students answer the activity questions. Discuss students' responses.
This activity is also available as a blackline master.

Vocabulary Pre-check

Use Vocabulary Activity 19 to introduce vocabulary terms.
L1 LEP

Chapter 19 *Nationalism in Asia, Africa, and Latin America* **587**

SECTION RESOURCES

Reproducible Masters
- Reproducible Lesson Plan 19-5
- Vocabulary Activity 19
- Guided Reading Activity 19-5
- World Art and Music Activity 19
- People in World History Profile 57
- Reteaching Activity 19
- Enrichment Activity 19

- Section Quiz 19-5
- Performance Assessment Activity 19
- Spanish Chapter Summary 19

Transparencies
- Section Focus Transparency 19-5
- World History and Art Transparency 40, *Zapatistas*

Multimedia
- Student Self-Test and Review Software
- Testmaker

TEACH

Guided Practice

THEME Change

Write on the chalkboard the following line from Rubén Darío's poem quoted on page 587: *"Whenever it trembles, a profound shudder runs down the enormous backbone of the Andes."* Ask students to interpret the sentence. **How did economic changes in Latin America after World War I make the poem even more relevant?** *(Latin America became even more tied to global markets.)* **L1**

Global Issues Ask students to discuss the ways in which the United States was involved in Latin America following World War I. *(It kept a military presence in Nicaragua, Haiti, the Dominican Republic, Panama; it was involved in the economies of many countries through ownership of oil wells and other businesses.)* **L2**

Politics Have students explain what the United States promised to do under the Good Neighbor policy. *(not to interfere militarily in the affairs of other countries)* Initiate a discussion of why this was a change from the actions of the United States before this time. *(The United States had formerly kept a strong military presence in Latin America.)* **L3**

World Art and Music Activity 19

World History and Art Transparency 40, *Zapatistas*

wheat, corn, beans, sugarcane, and other crops in large amounts. However, industrial growth—particularly in the United States and western Europe—increased the demand for tin, copper, silver, oil, and other raw materials from Latin America. As mineral exports increased, Latin Americans had more cash with which to buy imports. More and more of the Latin American economy became tied to global markets.

When world prices for raw materials increased, Latin American economies improved. However, in the 1920s, prices for coffee, sugar, and other raw materials plunged. The price declines foretold the global economic depression that was soon to occur. Like much of the world, Latin America suffered high unemployment and low prices for its products in the decade of the Great Depression, 1929–1939.

Mexico's Oil Economy

Oil was one of the vital resources for growing industries, and **Mexico** was an important source of oil. Mexico entered the postwar era, still reeling from its own bloody and divisive revolution that had begun in 1910. However, a stable, one-party system was evolving that seemed able to maintain order and unity. Mexico's constitution, ratified in 1917, authorized the government to protect workers from exploitation and to require private property owners to act in the public interest.

Despite the constitution, reforms came slowly until 1934. In that year, **Lázaro Cárdenas** (KAHR•duhn•AHS) was elected to the presidency. Over the next six years, his government carried out other reforms in the spirit of the 1910 revolution. First, Cárdenas directed the redistribution of vast tracts of land to landless peasants. To increase agricultural production, the Mexican government also encouraged the formation of cooperatives, farm organizations operated by and for the peasants. By 1940 more than half of all Mexicans farmed land they could finally call their own.

Cárdenas's main goal, however, was to make Mexico economically independent of foreign countries. His government especially wanted to bring

Images of the Times

Mexican Murals

During the 1930s, Mexican artists painted colorful murals showing key themes and events in Mexico's history. Many of these murals still decorate outer and inner walls of government buildings, theaters, universities, and hospitals throughout the country.

Distribution of the Land by Diego Rivera. Court of Fiestas, Secretaria de Educacion Publica, Mexico City, Mexico

588

Images of the Times   Mexican Murals

Mexican murals won world renown after World War I, and controversy made Diego Rivera (1886–1957) the best-known Mexican muralist. A mural he was commissioned to paint for the Detroit Institute of Arts was attacked for being antireligious, and a fresco he did for New York's Rockefeller Center was ultimately destroyed because it included a portrait of the Bolshevik leader Lenin.

Siqueiros (1896–1974) also used his art to convey his radical political beliefs. Over the course of his lifetime, his Communist sympathies and work for labor unions landed him in jail and drove him into exile at different times.

the industrial economy under Mexican control. In 1937 Cárdenas supported an oil workers' strike. At the time, many Mexican workers had gone on strike against their British and American employers, demanding higher wages and better working conditions. Cárdenas urged the oil companies to meet their demands, but the companies refused. After a year of futile negotiations, Cárdenas carried out a policy of nationalization of foreign-owned oil wells on March 18, 1938, declaring them the property of the government. He explained his actions by reaching all the way back to a colonial law written by the Spanish king in 1783, which had been retained in the new constitution: "The Mines are the property of My Royal Crown, [including] all bitumens [minerals] and juices of the earth."

The British and American companies were furious, but the Mexican people were ecstatic. They celebrated March 18 as the day of their "Declaration of Economic Independence." Cárdenas, meanwhile, defused the crisis by offering to pay a fair price for the oil wells. With World War II looming on the horizon, Great Britain and the United States soon accepted this offer. They did not want an angry Mexico to sell its oil to Japan and Germany.

The nationalization of Mexico's oil fields signaled the arrival of economic nationalism in Latin America. For Mexico it was a clean break from the economic dependence of the past.

Changes in Venezuela

Another oil-rich country, **Venezuela**, followed a course unlike that of Mexico, but more like that of other Latin American countries that had a single source of wealth. Between 1908 and 1935, President **Juan Vicente Gómez** ruled Venezuela as a dictator. During this period, engineers discovered oil along Venezuela's Caribbean coast. By the late 1930s Venezuela was the third-largest oil-producing country in the world. However, British, Dutch, and American oil companies controlled the Venezuelan oil industry. Gómez, instead of nationalizing the oil companies, worked closely with them. He, his

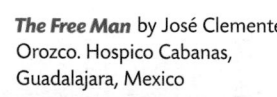

The Free Man by José Clemente Orozco. Hospico Cabanas, Guadalajara, Mexico

From Porfirio's Dictatorship to the Revolution (detail with Martyrs) by David Alfaro Siqueiros. Museo Nacional de Historia, Castillo de Chapultepec, Mexico City, Mexico

REFLECTING ON THE TIMES

1. What three leading Mexican artists painted murals during the 1930s?
2. Based on the murals, what do you think are some major themes in Mexican history?

589

Independent Practice

📁 Guided Reading Activity 19-5 **L1**

Economics Organize students into two groups. Have one group write a pamphlet in favor of the nationalization of foreign-owned oil wells in Mexico, and the other a pamphlet against nationalization. Tell students to support their arguments by forecasting the long-term effects of state ownership of the wells. **L2**

The Arts Have students research Latin American artists and writers whose work dealt with nationalist issues. Then ask students to deliver brief oral reports describing how the artists' political beliefs shaped their work. Suggest that they bring in reproductions of artwork if possible. **L3**

📁 People in World History Profile 57

you don't say...

Latin America The region consisting of Mexico, Central America, South America, and the islands of the Caribbean gets its name from the Latin language. When Europeans began to settle the area during the late 1400s, they brought their languages and customs with them. These languages—Spanish, Portuguese, and French—all derived from ancient Latin. They are the main languages of Latin America to this day.

ANSWERS TO REFLECTING ON THE TIMES

1. Diego Rivera, José Clemente Orozco, and David Alfaro Siqueiros
2. transforming Mexico into a more independent and equitable society, economically as well as politically

Visualizing History By the 1930s, Buenos Aires had become a city of wide avenues and public buildings. Its prosperity rested on the export of beef and other agricultural products. *How did the Great Depression affect Argentina's political life during the 1930s?*

political allies, and oil companies prospered, but most Venezuelans did not.

Gómez used the oil profits to strengthen his government. He paid off his country's huge national debt to European bankers and created a strong army. He also used some of the profits for his personal benefit.

After Gómez died in 1935, workers and students around the country rioted to protest the domination of their country by foreign oil companies and their Venezuelan partners. The army intervened to stop the protests and remained in charge of the country for the next several decades.

Democracy and the Military

Venezuela was one of many Latin American countries in which a small group of people prospered from the natural wealth found in the country. It was also typical in that the military intervened to put down protests that threatened business interests. Argentina and Brazil are two of the other countries in which democracy failed to take hold.

Argentina Becomes Fascist

In 1916 **Argentina** held its first open presidential election in which every male could vote. The winner, **Hipólito Irigoyen** (ee•PAW•lee•TOH IHR•ih•GOH•YEHN), obtained most of his support from urban workers and the middle class. They elected him because of his party's success in achieving electoral reforms. During his first administration, Irigoyen carried through social reforms that improved factory conditions, boosted workers' wages, and regulated working hours. He advocated other democratic reforms and efforts to help the poor. After serving six years as president, Irigoyen proudly claimed:

> We have held public office in obedience to the popular mandate and inspired by the duty to make reparation … for all the injustices, moral and political, collective and individual, that have long dishonored the country.

In 1928 Irigoyen was again elected president. His second term, however, aroused widespread opposition, and he did not complete his term in office. Although he was personally popular, his government had often been ineffective. He was slow to make decisions, so that official documents needing his attention piled up on his desk awaiting action. More important, corrupt aides stole money from the national treasury. In addition, few Argentinians believed any more in the democratic process by which Irigoyen had won office.

Angered by inefficiency and corruption and opposed to democracy, General **José F. Uriburu** led a successful coup against Irigoyen in 1930. With the coming of the Great Depression, Argentina was divided between Socialist and Fascist political

National Archives

Sending in the Marines

American marines in Nicaragua unload a cannon to help defend their military position. The United States has a history of military intervention in the Central American nation of Nicaragua. In the early years of the 1900s American interest in Nicaragua increased with the building of the Panama Canal, with growing pressure to defend the hemisphere against British and German threats, and with expanding United States involvement in Central American trade.

In 1912, U.S Marines landed in Nicaragua to ensure the payment of its debts and remained there for the next 13 years. In 1927, American forces again intervened to put down an uprising by nationalist leader Augusto César Sandino (left, center figure). Sandino fought American involvement in his country's domestic affairs—and failed. American forces remained in Nicaragua until 1933.

During the years between the two world wars the empires of Europe began to crumble. In the Western Hemisphere President Hoover pulled American troops out of Nicaragua, and President Franklin D. Roosevelt declared a Good Neighbor policy with Latin America. Nevertheless, imperialism endured until after World War II. ⊕

Chapter 19 *Nationalism in Asia, Africa, and Latin America* **591**

TEACH

Tell students that for many years before the United States began construction of the Panama Canal, Americans had hoped to build a canal across Nicaragua to link the Atlantic and Pacific Oceans. **What was the political group that controlled Nicaragua from 1979 until 1990 called, and why?** *(They were called Sandinistas in honor of Nicaragua's nationalist hero, Sandino.)*

CURRICULUM CONNECTION

THE ARTS
Nicaraguan poet and essayist Rubén Darío (1867–1916) was a founder of the literary movement called modernism. Many literary historians date the birth of modernism to the 1888 publication of *Azul*, Darío's first major work, and the movement's peak to the 1896 publication of his *Prosas profanas*.

ASSESS

Check for Understanding

Assign Section 5 Review as homework or as an in-class activity.

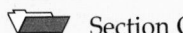 Use Student Self-Test and Review Software to review Section 5.

Evaluate

📁 Section Quiz 19-5

 Use the Testmaker to create a customized quiz for Section 5.

Reteach

Write this heading on the chalkboard: *Latin America and the Global Economy.* Have students list facts that show how the world market affected Latin America. *(Lists might include increased U.S. and European demand for raw materials from Latin America; sale of exports increased Latin American purchases of imports; U.S. investment in Latin America led to interventions to protect American interests.)*

AROUND THE WORLD

Major Oil Discovery

Saudi Arabia, 1938
In 1933 the government of Ibn Saud granted an American oil company the right to explore for oil in the newly united kingdom of Saudi Arabia. After a major oil deposit was discovered on the Arabian Peninsula, other oil companies joined to form the Arabian American Oil Company (Aramco) in 1944. After World War II, large-scale oil production brought immense wealth to Saudi Arabia and enabled Ibn Saud's government to build roads, schools, and hospitals throughout the country.

movements. To maintain social order, the army began to assume an important role in the Argentine government.

Uriburu, like Italy's Mussolini, believed in fascism. He cancelled elections and tried to abolish the congress. For the remainder of the 1930s, military men and their sympathizers ruled Argentina. They faked elections, suppressed their opponents, and consolidated their power. Democracy was dead in Argentina, destroyed by the military.

Brazil's Popular Dictator

Brazil, like Argentina, fell under an authoritarian government. In 1930 President **Getúlio Vargas** took power. Seven years later, Vargas proclaimed a new constitution that made him a virtual dictator. He strengthened the government by transferring powers from the cities and states to the national government. He won support from many Brazilians for his willingness to oppose the interests of large businesses. To gain working-class support, Vargas's administration increased wages, shortened working hours, and gave unions the right to organize. Vargas's supporters called him "father of the poor" for these efforts.

Vargas, with the support of the military, was able to keep Brazil united and stable until 1945. In that year, a democratic revolt threw him out of power. When Vargas refused to leave office, military leaders stepped in and forced Vargas out of office. Although the military did not actually rule in Brazil, their support was crucial in deciding who did.

Ties With the United States

During the 1920s and 1930s, the mineral wealth of Latin America attracted American businesses, which invested heavily in the region. To protect American economic interests, the United States intervened militarily in Central America and the Caribbean countries.

Increased American Intervention

In 1912 United States Marines had invaded **Nicaragua** when the country failed to pay its debts. American forces landed again during the 1920s to protect United States interests. Rebel forces led by General **Augusto César Sandino** resisted the Americans and tried to force a United States withdrawal. To help the American soldiers, the United States government trained a loyal Nicaraguan army called the National Guard. By the mid-1930s the National Guard was able to defeat the rebels. Its leader, Anastasio Somoza, seized power in 1936. From that time until 1979, the Somoza family ruled Nicaragua with American support.

During the early 1900s, American troops also occupied Haiti and the Dominican Republic as well as Nicaragua. This American military intervention, as well as the growth of American economic influence, was deeply resented by many Latin Americans. Latin American nationalists particularly opposed the Roosevelt Corollary. They stated that no country had the right to intervene in the affairs of another. They also claimed that, while the United States was exploiting their raw materials, Latin America was getting few economic benefits in return. Anti-Americanism was especially strong during the Great Depression. At this time, world market prices for raw materials fell sharply. This decline increased hardships among Latin Americans dependent on trade with North America and Europe.

Good Neighbor Policy

Aware of growing resentment, the United States tried to improve relations with its southern neighbors. Following his election in 1928, United States President Herbert Hoover went on a good-will tour of Latin America. He hoped to show that the United States regarded its Latin American neighbors as equals. At the same time, Secretary of State Joshua Reuben Clark began to restate the meaning of the Monroe Doctrine. In a memorandum issued in December 1928, Clark held that the Monroe Doctrine's warning that European powers could not interfere in Latin America did not mean that the United States had the right to interfere.

592   Chapter 19   *Nationalism in Asia, Africa, and Latin America*

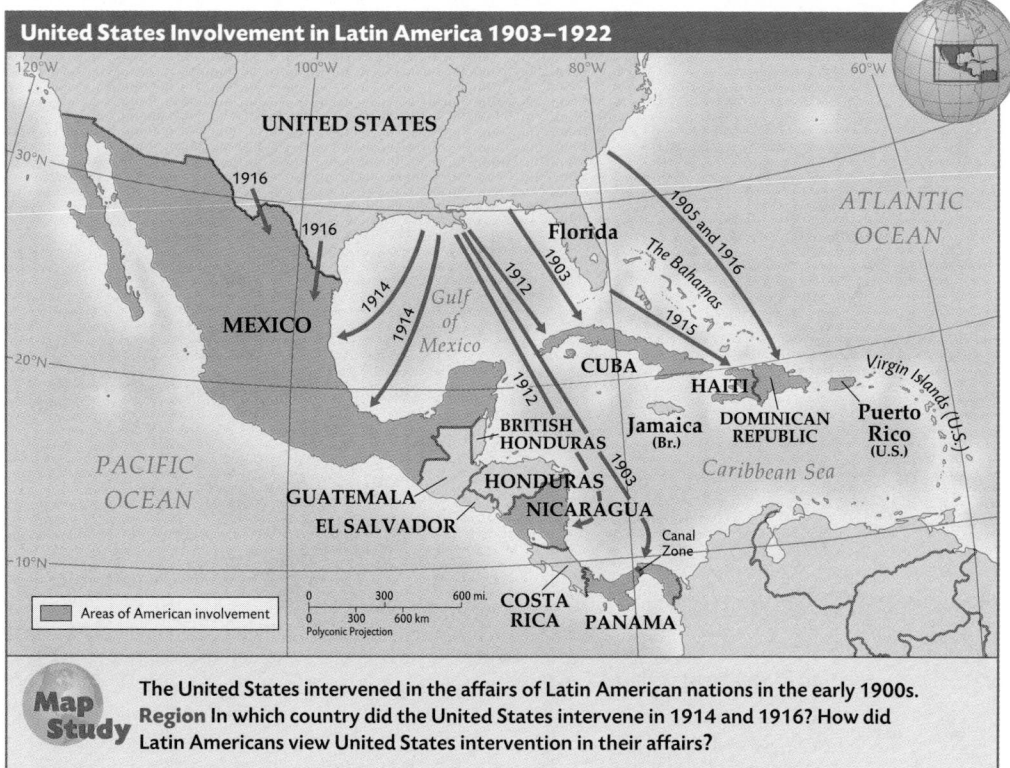

United States Involvement in Latin America 1903–1922

UNITED STATES

1916
1916

Florida
1903

The Bahamas

ATLANTIC OCEAN

1905 and 1916

1914
1914

Gulf of Mexico

MEXICO

1912

1912

CUBA

HAITI

1915

Virgin Islands (U.S.)

BRITISH HONDURAS

Jamaica (Br.)

DOMINICAN REPUBLIC

Puerto Rico (U.S.)

PACIFIC OCEAN

Caribbean Sea

GUATEMALA
EL SALVADOR

HONDURAS
NICARAGUA

1903

Canal Zone

COSTA RICA   PANAMA

Areas of American involvement

0   300   600 mi.
0 300 600 km
Polyconic Projection

Map Study The United States intervened in the affairs of Latin American nations in the early 1900s. **Region** In which country did the United States intervene in 1914 and 1916? How did Latin Americans view United States intervention in their affairs?

In 1933 President Franklin D. Roosevelt, Hoover's successor, announced the Good Neighbor policy toward Latin America. He declared, "I would dedicate this nation to the policy of the good neighbor—the neighbor who resolutely respects himself, and because he does so, respects the rights of others." The Good Neighbor policy renounced past United States military intervention in the region. To prove his good intentions, Roosevelt ended American restrictions on the sovereignty of

Cuba. He also ordered the withdrawal of American troops from Haiti and Nicaragua.

In 1933 the United States took another step toward improving its relationship with Latin America. Diplomats from the United States joined with their Latin American counterparts at the Pan American conference in Montevideo, Uruguay. After much discussion, all parties signed an agreement stating: "No state has the right to intervene in the internal or external affairs of another."

SECTION 5 REVIEW

Recall
1. **Define** cooperatives, nationalization.
2. **Identify** Lázaro Cárdenas, Juan Vicente Gómez, Hipólito Irigoyen, José F. Uriburu, Getúlio Vargas, Augusto César Sandino, the Good Neighbor policy.

3. **Describe** major political and economic trends in Latin America during the period between the world wars.

Critical Thinking
4. **Making Comparisons** How did Mexico and Venezuela differ in their response to European

and American control of their oil industries?

Understanding Themes
5. **Change** Does the United States have the right to intervene in the affairs of other countries? Explain, using recent examples.

Map Study

Answer
Mexico; Latin Americans resented U.S. interference in their national affairs.

Map Skills Practice

Reading a Map What nations border Costa Rica? (*Nicaragua and Panama*)

📁 Reteaching Activity 19

Enrich

Have students select one leader from this section and research his life. Have them write a brief essay about the leader that focuses on whether he was good or bad for his country.

📁 Enrichment Activity 19

CLOSE

Review with students the political and economic changes that were occurring in Latin America during the period after World War I. (*the revolution in Mexico, struggles for economic independence, conflicts over freedom from interference by the United States*)

SECTION 5 REVIEW ANSWERS

1. All vocabulary words are defined in the Glossary.
2. Cárdenas, 588; Gómez, 589; Irigoyen, 590; Uriburu, 590; Vargas, 592; Sandino, 592; the Good Neighbor policy, 593
3. Military rule, anti-American feeling, and industrialization

4. Mexico nationalized its oil industry; Venezuela worked closely with foreign oil companies.
5. **CHANGE** Answers will vary but might include discussions of U.S. intervention in Somalia, Haiti, or Bosnia.

Bridge to the Past
Literature

Block Schedule

Team Teaching This excerpt from *Gifts of Passage* may be presented in a team-teaching context, in conjunction with English or Language Arts.

Gifts of Passage

Historical Connection

British rule dramatically affected Indian society. In British schools, government offices, and elsewhere, the diverse peoples of India met and interacted with the British but not on terms of equality.

Background Information

Setting The incident takes place in the Indian city of Zorinabad about 1928. The British still ruled India, but the Indian independence movement was growing stronger.

Characters Santha: a five-year-old girl from whose point of view the story is told; Premila: Santha's eight-year-old sister; Headmistress: the Englishwoman who runs the Anglo-Indian school; Mother: the mother of Santha and Premila

Plot Santha and Premila start to attend an Anglo-Indian school, where the headmistress assigns them British names because she does not think she can pronounce Indian names. When Premila takes her first test, her teacher separates the Indian students because she thinks they will cheat. Premila, with Santha, leaves the school in anger.

from

Gifts of Passage

by Santha Rama Rau

Santha Rama Rau, born in Madras, India, in 1923, spent her childhood in India, England, and South Africa. In each place, she closely watched the way people from different backgrounds related with one another. Advances in transportation and communication have sharply increased the interactions of people from different cultures. Today these interactions shape the world more than ever before. In the following excerpt, Rau recalls her early experiences at a school for English and Indian children in India.

At the Anglo-Indian day school in Zorinabad to which my sister and I were sent when she was eight and I was five and a half, they changed our names. On the first day of school, a hot, windless morning of a north Indian September, we stood in the headmistress's study and she said, "Now you're the *new* girls. What are your names?"

My sister answered for us. "I am Premila, and she"—nodding in my direction—"is Santha."

The headmistress had been in India, I suppose, fifteen years or so, but she still smiled her helpless inability to cope with Indian names. Her rimless half-glasses glittered, and the precarious bun on the top of her head trembled as she shook her head. "Oh, my dears, those are much too hard for me. Suppose we give you pretty English names. Wouldn't that be more jolly? Let's see, now—Pamela for you, I think." She shrugged in a baffled way at my sister. "That's as close as I can get. And for *you*," she said to me, "how about Cynthia? Isn't that nice?"

My sister was always less intimidated than I was, and while she kept a stubborn silence, I said "Thank you," in a very tiny voice....

That first day at school is still, when I think of it, a remarkable one. At that age, if one's name is changed, one develops a curious form of dual personality. I remember having a certain detached and disbelieving concern in the actions of "Cynthia," but certainly no responsibility. ...

ABOUT THE AUTHOR

Santha Rama Rau is the daughter of an Indian government official. When she was young, India was still part of the British Empire. Many Indian leaders and administrators, including Rau's father, were strongly influenced by British culture. Her father, for example, was educated in England. Rau herself attended Wellesley College in Massachusetts. She has written a number of novels and nonfiction works, including essays about her childhood and her extensive travels, as well as a stage play based on the novel *A Passage to India*, by E. M. Forster.

Visualizing History During the years of British rule, the Indian subcontinent had a wealthy upper class of princes and their families. This upper-class Indian family of the 1940s practiced traditional ways but was also familiar with the customs of the British aristocracy. *What are the British teachers' attitudes toward ordinary Indians in the story by Santha Rama Rau?*

Accordingly, I followed the thin, erect back of the headmistress down the veranda [porch] to my classroom feeling, at most, a passing interest in what was going to happen to me in this strange, new atmosphere of School.…

I can't remember too much about the proceedings in class that day, except for the beginning. The teacher pointed to me and asked me to stand up. "Now, dear, tell the class your name."

I said nothing.

"Come along," she said, frowning slightly. "What's your name, dear?"

"I don't know," I said, finally.

The English children in the front of the class—there were about eight or ten of them—giggled and twisted around in their chairs to look at me. I sat down quickly and opened my eyes very wide, hoping in that way to dry them off. The little girl with the braids put out her hand and very lightly touched my arm. She still didn't smile.

Most of the morning I was rather bored. I looked briefly at the children's drawings pinned to the wall, and then concentrated on a lizard clinging to the ledge of the high, barred window behind the teacher's head. Occasionally it would shoot out its long yellow tongue for a fly, and then it would rest, with its eyes closed and its belly palpitating, as though it were swallowing several times quickly. The lessons were mostly concerned with reading and writing and simple numbers—things that my mother had already taught me—and I paid very little attention. The teacher wrote on the easel blackboard words like

Chapter 19 *Nationalism in Asia, Africa, and Latin America* **595**

OTHER WORKS BY SANTHA RAMA RAU

The Adventuress. New York: Harper, 1970.
East of Home. New York: Harper, 1950.
Home to India. New York: Harper, 1945.
My Russian Journey. New York: Harper, 1959.

Remember the House. New York: Harper, 1956.
This Is India. New York: Harper, 1954.
View to the Southeast. New York: Harper, 1957.

Visualizing History Many upper-class Indians strongly supported the movement for independence. Like the Latin American creoles who fought for independence from Spain in the early 1800s, members of this upper class had the most to gain from independence since they would become the ruling elite of the new nation.
Answer to Caption: *superficially friendly but condescending and mistrustful*

Literary Element Imagery consists of the words and phrases that a writer uses to evoke particular sights, sounds, smells, or other sensations for the reader. In this excerpt, for example, Rau helps readers picture the headmistress by describing her "rimless half-glasses" and "precarious bun."

FOCUS

As students read, ask them to think about the importance of name giving in the story. Santha and her sister are given British names, as is Santha's friend, Nalini. But other characters, such as the headmistress and the teachers, are not referred to by name at all. Discuss what Rau may have intended by not giving names to certain characters. Why might Rau have chosen to focus on names, and their significance, at this moment in Indian history? *(Names establish identity, and the struggle for an Indian identity was part of the independence movement.)*

TEACH

Literary Analysis

Rather than simply tell the reader that she was bored during her first day in school, Rau describes a lizard on the wall in vivid detail. The description of the lizard takes the reader's mind off the classwork, just as the actual lizard distracted Santha.

Comparison

Discuss the difference between Santha's view of games and that of the British children. The way the children played reflected their basic values about individual achievement and group cooperation. Discuss how games today may reflect the values of students in schools in the United States.

Clarification

Discuss how social-class relationships affect even school students. Rau, even as a five-year-old child, knew that friendship between Indian and British or Anglo-Indian children was "out of the question." Have students consider how Rau knew that social equality between British and Indian students was impossible.

 World Literature Selection 7

"bat" and "cat," which seemed babyish to me; only "apple" was new and incomprehensible.

When it was time for the lunch recess, I followed the girl with braids out onto the veranda. There the children from the other classes were assembled. I saw Premila at once and ran over to her, as she had charge of our lunchbox. The children were all opening packages and sitting down to eat sandwiches. Premila and I were the only ones who had Indian food—thin wheat cha-patties [a type of bread], some vegetable curry, and a bottle of buttermilk. Premila thrust half of it into my hand and whispered fiercely that I should go and sit with my class, because that was what the others seemed to be doing....

I had never really grasped the system of competitive games. At home, whenever we played tag or guessing games, I was always allowed to "win"—"because," Mother used to tell Premila, "she is the youngest, and we have to allow for that." I had often heard her say it, and it seemed quite reasonable to me, but the result was that I had no clear idea of what "winning" meant.

When we played twos-and-threes that afternoon at school, in accordance with my training, I let one of the small English boys catch me, but was naturally rather puzzled when the other children did not return the courtesy. I ran about for what seemed like hours without ever catching anyone, until it was time for school to close. Much later I learned that my attitude was called "not being a good sport," and I stopped allowing myself to be caught, but it was not for years that I really learned the spirit of the thing....

It was a week later, the day of Premila's first test, that our lives changed rather abruptly. I was sitting at the back of the class, in my usual inattentive way, only half listening to the teacher. I had started a rather guarded friendship with the girl with the braids, whose name turned out to be Nalini (Nancy, in school). The three other Indian children were already fast friends. Even at that age it was apparent to all of us that friendship with the English or Anglo-Indian children was out of the question. Occasionally, during the class, my new friend and I would draw pictures and show them to each other secretly.

The door opened sharply and Premila marched in. At first, the teacher smiled at her in a kindly and encouraging way and said, "Now, you're little Cynthia's sister?"

Premila didn't even look at her. She stood with her feet planted firmly apart and her shoulders rigid, and addressed herself directly to me. "Get up," she said. "We're going home."

I didn't know what happened, but I was aware that it was a crisis of some sort. I rose obediently and started to walk toward my sister.

"Bring your pencils and your notebook," she said.

I went back for them, and together we left the room. The teacher started to say something just as Premila closed the door, but we didn't wait to hear what it was.

In complete silence we left the school grounds and started to walk home. Then I asked Premila what the matter was. All she would say was "We're going home for good."...

When we got to our house the ayah [maid] was just taking a tray of lunch into Mother's room. She immediately started a long, worried questioning about what are you children doing back here at this hour of the day.

Mother looked very startled and very concerned, and asked Premila what had happened.

Premila said, "We had our test today, and she made me and the other Indians sit at the back of the room, with a desk between each one."

Mother said, "Why was that, darling?"

"She said it was because Indians cheat," Premila added. "So I don't think we should go back to that school."

Mother looked very distant, and was silent a long time. At last she said, "Of course not, darling." She sounded displeased.

We all shared the curry she was having for lunch, and afterward I was sent off to the beautifully familiar bedroom for my siesta. I could hear Mother and Premila talking through the open door.

Mother said, "Do you suppose she understood all that?"

ADDITIONAL LITERARY WORKS OF THE PERIOD

Mistral, Gabriela. *Feeling.* Poems for children by one of Chile's most famous writers.
Natsume, Sóseki. *The Three-Cornered World.* Story of a Japanese artist who visits a small village.
Tagore, Rabindranath. *Gitanjali.* Poetry about India, religion, and nationalism.

Visualizing History These Indian women are dressed in the sari, a garment of several yards of material draped so that one end forms a skirt and the other a shoulder or head covering. *How do you think the two Indian girls in the story dressed for their classes at the British school?*

Premila said, "I shouldn't think so. She's a baby."

Mother said, "Well, I hope it won't bother her."

Of course, they were both wrong. I understood it perfectly, and I remember it all very clearly. But I put it happily away, because it had all happened to a girl called Cynthia, and I never was really particularly interested in her.

RESPONDING TO LITERATURE

1. Why did Santha and her sister leave school?
2. Explain why Santha was unable to tell the class her name.
3. When the headmistress gives Santha and her sister new names, what can you determine the headmistress thought of Indian culture?
4. **Demonstrating Reasoned Judgment** Explain why Santha's mother would or would not keep her children home permanently from the Anglo-Indian school.

ANSWERS TO RESPONDING TO LITERATURE

1. because a British teacher assumed that Indian students cheated
2. Answers may vary but might suggest that Santha had not accepted her British name but realized her real name would not be accepted by the teacher.
3. The headmistress does not value Indian culture and feels it should be replaced by British customs.
4. Answers will vary. Students may say that the mother is forced to face the fact that to get a good, that is British, education, her daughters must confront British racism.

Visualizing History Clothing can make a powerful statement about identity. A woman's decision to wear a veil in secular Muslim nations like Egypt and Turkey, for example, is a way to identify with traditional Muslim values.
Answer to Caption: *Answers will vary but may include Western styles of dress, especially uniforms.*

ASSESS

Assign **Responding to Literature** questions.

CLOSE

After students have read the excerpt, ask them how they would react if they were Indian students in Premila's classroom. Discuss what other ways they might have found to protest their treatment by the British teachers.

Contemporary Connection

Students interested in learning more about India might wish to see the films of the great Indian director Satyajit Ray, including *The World of Apu* and *Pather panchali*.

Portfolio Project

Have students write an essay in which they tell what steps they think a teacher ought to take to overcome or prevent prejudice among the different ethnic groups represented in his or her classroom.

GLENCOE TECHNOLOGY

VIDEODISC
Use MindJogger to review students' knowledge of the chapter.

MindJogger Videoquiz

Chapter 19
Disc 3 Side A

 Also available in VHS.

Answers

Using Key Terms

1. a   4. c
2. i   5. d
3. b

Using Your History Journal

Suggest that students model their feature on those presented on all-news radio broadcasts.

Reviewing Facts

1. soldiers, wheat, and cotton; greater control over their government
2. Kemal Atatürk, Reza Shah, Chiang Kai-shek, Mao Zedong, and José Uriburu, among others
3. Gandhi's nonviolent protest effectively undermined British claims to rule India.
4. Atatürk separated government and religion and had Turks follow Western ways. Reza Shah built schools, roads, and hospitals.
5. Nigerian women held protests against British taxes.
6. Mexican President Cárdenas nationalized foreign oil wells.

Critical Thinking

1. The two forms work together. In

Connections Across Time

Historical Significance World War I shattered the old order in Europe and stirred nationalist feelings in lands under Western colonial rule. During the 1900s dozens of new nations in Asia, Africa, and the Americas either emerged from the ashes of old empires or asserted their independence from powerful neighbors. In addition, newly developing countries began to follow economic policies based on nationalism. Governments in these lands sometimes took over foreign-owned industries and limited foreign investment when national sovereignty seemed threatened.

Using Key Terms

Write the key term that completes each sentence. Then write a sentence for each term not chosen.

a. warlords
b. nationalization
c. pacifist
d. *zaibatsu*
e. cooperatives
f. heavy industry
g. shah
h. population explosion
i. self-determination
j. civil disobedience

1. After Yuan Shigai's death in 1916, local military leaders called _____ divided China among themselves.
2. United States President Woodrow Wilson raised the hopes of colonial peoples by endorsing the principle of _____.
3. In 1938 the Mexican government carried out a policy of _____ in which it took over the foreign-owned oil industries.
4. Mohandas K. Gandhi was a _____, a person opposed to using war and other means of violence to settle disputes.
5. The privately owned part of the Japanese economy in the 1920s and 1930s was largely in the hands of large companies known as _____.

Technology Activity

Using a Computerized Card Catalog Use a computerized card catalog to locate information about nationalism in Asia, Africa, and Latin America after World War I. Using your research, create a bulletin board focusing on the themes of "global nationalism." Include time lines for each region, showing significant events related to nationalism. List similarities and differences you see among the nationalist movements.

Using Your History Journal

Write a three-minute radio news feature about the setting and causes of the event you described in Your History Journal news report at the beginning of the chapter.

Reviewing Facts

1. **History** Name the contributions that India made to the war effort in World War I. What did Great Britain promise India in return?
2. **Government** Identify three leaders who would agree with the statement "Political power grows out of the barrel of a gun."
3. **History** Describe the influence of Gandhi on India's struggle for freedom.
4. **History** List the reforms introduced by Kemal Atatürk in Turkey and Reza Shah in Iran.
5. **Culture** Discuss the role of women in the nationalist movement in Nigeria after World War I.
6. **History** Identify the major event in 1938 that marked the arrival of economic nationalism in the countries of Latin America.

Critical Thinking

1. **Apply** How does political control relate to economic control? Give examples from Egypt or India.
2. **Apply** How did religious differences hamper the Indian independence movement? Give examples to support your opinion.

Egypt, Britain asserted political control in order to retain the Suez Canal. In India, Britain's political control maintained a profitable trade in cotton, wheat, and other raw materials.
2. Differences split the independence movement just as it was gaining power.
3. Nationalist movements had to grow stronger so that the cost of retaining colonial control outweighed the profits of imperialism.

4. Students might refer to murals on pages 588–589 and discuss such themes as revolution and social justice. These themes first appeared in Western art during the 1800s and have since become international.
5. Possible answer: While Egypt, India, and other countries either won or moved toward breaking free of the West's political control, countries such as Iran and Turkey adopted many elements of Western culture.

3. **Analyze** In 1939 most of Africa and much of Asia were European colonies. What conditions needed to change before self-determination could be achieved by all countries? Give examples to support your answer.

4. **Synthesize** Name a 1930s Mexican mural and state its theme. Could artists of other cultures and eras have also used this theme? Explain.

5. **Evaluate** Did the global influence of the West become more or less widespread in the two decades after World War I? Give examples to support your opinion.

Geography in History

1. **Location** Refer to the map below. What is the relative location of the Sea of Japan?

2. **Movement** Approximately how many miles would the Japanese military have had to transport troops across the Sea of Japan to invade Manchuria (Northeast Plain) in 1931?

3. **Region** Along what major rivers might the Japanese have traveled to gain access to central China? What obstacles would they have faced?

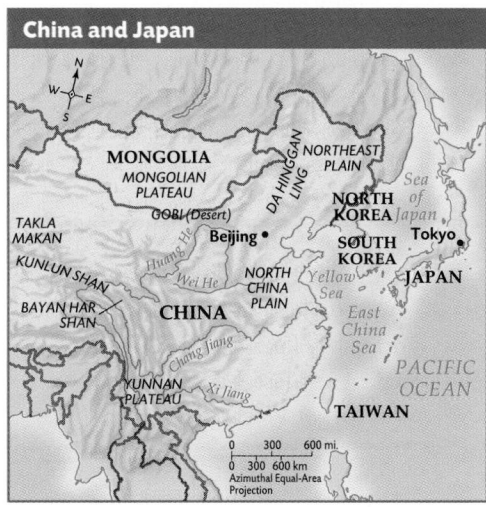

China and Japan

Understanding Themes

1. **Nationalism** In what countries of Africa and the Middle East did nationalism lead to self-

determination in the period 1919 to 1939?

2. **Change** How did the British respond to Gandhi's campaign for Indian independence?

3. **Conflict** Do you think Mao Zedong and Chiang Kai-shek were wise to put aside their differences and unite against Japan? Explain.

4. **Conflict** What were the main areas of disagreement that resulted in conflict between Japan and the West after World War I?

5. **Change** How did nationalism change Latin America following World War I?

Linking Past and Present

1. Review Gandhi's major criticisms of Western civilization. Were they accurate? Do they apply today?

2. Do you think nationalism is stronger or weaker throughout the world today than it was in the 1920s and 1930s? Give examples from current events that support your opinion.

Skill Practice

Read the quotation below by Hashimoto Kingoro and review the discussion of Japan in Section 4, pages 583–585. Then answer the questions below.

❝ We are like a great crowd of people packed into a small and narrow room, and there are only three doors through which we might escape, namely emigration, advance into world markets, and expansion of territory. The first door … has been barred to us by the anti-Japanese immigration policies of other countries. The second door … is being pushed shut by tariff barriers … Japan should rush upon the last door [expansion of territory]. ❞

—Hashimoto Kingoro, *Addresses to Young Men*

1. What is Kingoro's thesis in this argument?
2. What reasons does he give to support this thesis?
3. What evidence in Section 4 supports Kingoro's thesis?
4. Do you accept or reject Kingoro's argument? Explain your answer.

the West's insistence that Japan abandon the Twenty-One Demands and recognize Western interests in China.

5. **CHANGE** Mexico nationalized its oil fields, breaking with past economic dependence; Nicaraguans fought U.S. Marines; anti-Americanism spread throughout the region.

Linking Past and Present

1. the West's violence, materialism, and self-righteousness, compared with the spirituality of India; answers will vary.

2. Answers will vary. Students should support their answers.

Skill Practice

1. In order to support its large population, Japan must expand its territory.

2. Japan is overcrowded. The only solutions are emigration, capturing world markets, or expanding its territory. The first two options are closed by hostile foreign powers, leaving only the third.

3. Japan had a population explosion; the United States banned Japanese immigration in 1924; Western countries forced Japan to abandon the Twenty-One Demands on China.

4. Answers may vary.

❓ Chapter Bonus Test Question

Ask students: How does Mao's statement, "Political power grows out of the barrel of a gun," apply to the revolutions discussed in this chapter? *(Answers may include: Not all the revolutions were violent, but brute force played a key role in many of them.)*

Geography in History

1. It lies between Japan to the east and Korea and China to the west.

2. about 600 miles (965 km)

3. Huang He, Wei He, Chang Jiang, Xi Jiang; mountains

Understanding Themes

1. **NATIONALISM** Turkey, Iran, and Egypt

2. **CHANGE** They arrested Gandhi,

keeping him from active protest and weakening the Indian National Congress.

3. **CONFLICT** Even though the Chinese were unable to stop the invasion, they were more likely to prove effective as a united force.

4. **CONFLICT** Japan felt humiliated by the League of Nations' rejection of its demand for a statement on racial equality, by the U.S. ban on Japanese immigration, and by

A complete, 1-page lesson plan is provided for each section in the *Reproducible Lesson Plans* booklet.

World War II

CHAPTER RESOURCES

	Reproducible Resources	Multimedia Resources
Chapter Opener	Chapter Themes: Graphic Organizer 20 Historical Significance Chapter Activity 20	MindJogger Videoquiz
Chapter Enrichment	Vocabulary Activity 20* Time Line Activity 20 Mapping History Activity 20 History Simulation 20 Geography and History Activity 20 Source Reading 20 People in World History Profiles 59, 60 World Art and Music Activity 20 Enrichment Activity 20 Critical Thinking Activity 20 Skill Reinforcement Activity 20 Performance Assessment Activity 20	World History and Art Transparency 42, *The Red Stairway* Mapping History Overlay Transparencies 19, 20, 21 Chapter Transparency 20 Vocabulary PuzzleMaker Software Turning Points in World History: • *The Holocaust* • *Dropping the Atomic Bomb* Lessons of War: • *Can a Battle Change History?* • *Appeasement: Munich Pact* • *At the Front* • *Laws of War*
Chapter Review/Reteaching	Reteaching Activity 20 Skill Reinforcement Activity 20 Spanish Chapter Summary 20	Chapter 20 Digest Audiocassette, Activity, Test* Vocabulary PuzzleMaker Software Student Self-Test and Review Software MindJogger Videoquiz
Chapter Evaluation/Testing	Performance Assessment Activity 20 Chapter 20 Test, Forms A and B	Testmaker

* Also available in Spanish

0:00 OUT OF TIME?   Assign the Chapter 20 summary in the Unit 5 Digest on pages 631–633, and the Chapter 20 Audiocassettes.

Block Schedule

Block scheduling differs from traditional class scheduling in the amount of time allotted to each period. The extended time frame provided by block scheduling affords you the opportunity to implement a greater number of research-oriented and activity-intense projects to motivate and involve your students. Activities that are particularly suited to use within the block scheduling framework are identified throughout this chapter by the following designation.

KEY TO ABILITY LEVELS

Teaching strategies have been coded for varying learning styles and abilities.

L1 **BASIC** activities for all students
L2 **AVERAGE** activities for average to above-average students
L3 **CHALLENGING** activities for above-average students
LEP **LIMITED ENGLISH PROFICIENCY** activities

Use Glencoe's *Presentation Plus!* multimedia teacher tool to easily present dynamic lessons that visually excite your students. Using Microsoft PowerPoint® you can customize the presentations to create your own personalized lessons.

SECTION RESOURCES

Daily Objectives	Reproducible Resources	Multimedia Resources
Section 1 **The Path to War** Explain in what sense World War II was a product of World War I.	Reproducible Lesson Plan 20-1 Vocabulary Activity 20* Guided Reading Activity 20-1* Chapter Themes: Graphic Organizer 20 People in World History Profile 59 Time Line Activity 20 Section Quiz 20-1*	Section Focus Transparency 20-1 Chapter Transparency 20 Student Self-Test and Review Software Lessons of War: *Appeasement: Munich Pact*
Section 2 **War in Europe** Describe how Hitler took over most of Europe and how Great Britain and the United States responded to German expansion.	Reproducible Lesson Plan 20-2 Vocabulary Activity 20* Guided Reading Activity 20-2* People in World History Profile 60 Section Quiz 20-2*	Section Focus Transparency 20-2 Mapping History Overlay Transparency 19, *Europe in June, 1942* Student Self-Test and Review Software Lessons of War: *Laws of War*
Section 3 **A Global Conflict** Describe how the Soviet Union and the United States entered World War II.	Reproducible Lesson Plan 20-3 Vocabulary Activity 20* Guided Reading Activity 20-3* History Simulation 20 Section Quiz 20-3*	Section Focus Transparency 20-3 Student Self-Test and Review Software Lessons of War: *At the Front* Turning Points in World History: *The Holocaust*
Section 4 **Turning Points** Explain how the tide of war turned in favor of the Allies during 1942 and 1943.	Reproducible Lesson Plan 20-4 Vocabulary Activity 20* Guided Reading Activity 20-4* Geography and History Activity 20 Section Quiz 20-4*	Section Focus Transparency 20-4 Mapping History Overlay Transparency 20, *Southeast Asia Prior to World War II* Student Self-Test and Review Software Lessons of War: *Can a Battle Change History?*
Section 5 **Allied Victories** Understand how new technology affected the conduct and outcome of World War II.	Reproducible Lesson Plan 20-5 Guided Reading Activity 20-5* Reteaching Activity 20 Enrichment Activity 20 Section Quiz 20-5* Performance Assessment Activity 20 Spanish Chapter Summary 20	Section Focus Transparency 20-5 Mapping History Overlay Transparency 21, *Battle Sites in the Pacific* World History and Art Transparency 42, *The Red Stairway* Vocabulary PuzzleMaker Software Student Self-Test and Review Software Testmaker Turning Points in World History: *Dropping the Atomic Bomb*

* Also available in Spanish

Chapter Activities

✓ Performance Assessment Activity

World War III After studying the factors contributing to the two world wars, have students predict the likelihood of a third world war. Organize students into small groups to develop a scenario including real countries, leaders, and plausible issues they believe have the potential to trigger a third world war. Students then should write a treaty or suggest some other plan they think could avert the crisis. Have each group present its detailed scenario as well as its treaty or plan to the rest of the class. Then have the class discuss and vote on which scenario for World War III is the most plausible and which treaty or plan would be most effective in averting war.

Possible Rubric Features

Accuracy of information, plausibility of predictions, problem-solving skills, research skills

• *For an additional activity, refer to Activity 20 in the* Performance Assessment Strategies and Activities *booklet.*

ACTIVITY

From the Classroom of...

Jill M. Frimel and Gene A. Brunswick
Solon High School
Solon, OH

Atomic Bombs

Students will experience the complex decision-making process that led to the dropping of atomic bombs on Japan. Students will need to be familiar with the events of the Pacific theater of World War II, including Japanese resistance in Okinawa, kamikaze attacks on U.S. ships, and projections of massive casualties in a direct invasion of Japan.

Have partners discuss what they know about the decision to use atomic weapons against Japan. Then assign students one of the following roles: member of U.S. Congress today; member of U.S. Congress in 1945; U.S. civilian in 1945; Japanese civilian in 1945; U.S. military officer in 1945; U.S. soldier in 1945; and a human rights activist today. Have students present their different views to the class. Then have the class discuss Truman's decision and vote for or against the use of atomic bombs.

MULTIPLE LEARNING STYLES

Verbal/Linguistic
Have students interview family or community members who remember World War II. Suggest that students make a list of questions before conducting their interviews. Have students present oral reports to the class based on their interviews.

Logical/Mathematical
Have students make a time line that shows the main events of World War II. Suggest that they record European events on one side of the time line and Asian events on the other.

Visual/Spatial
Have students design a bulletin board that depicts the battles and destruction of World War II.

Auditory/Musical
Have students make a tape recording of the voices of World War II. Suggest that they locate recordings of Edward R. Murrow's reports on the war; wartime speeches by Roosevelt or Churchill; songs popular during the war; and any other recordings they can find. Remind them to record the voices in chronological order before they present their tapes to the class.

Kinesthetic
Have students construct a model that shows the strategies and outcome of one of the following events of World War II: D-Day landing, Battle of the Bulge, Battle of Guadalcanal, or the Battle of Stalingrad.

Additional Resources

NATIONAL GEOGRAPHIC SOCIETY

Teacher's Corner

INDEX TO NATIONAL GEOGRAPHIC MAGAZINE

The following articles may be used for research relating to this chapter:

- "Hiroshima," by Ted Gup, August 1995.
- "Blueprints for Victory," by John F. Shupe, May 1995.
- "The Wings of War," by Thomas B. Allen, March 1994.
- "Pearl Harbor: A Return to the Day of Infamy," by Thomas B. Allen, December 1991.
- "Remembering the Blitz," by Cameron Thomas, July 1991.
- "Ghosts of War in the South Pacific," by Peter Benchley, April 1988.

NATIONAL GEOGRAPHIC SOCIETY PRODUCTS AVAILABLE FROM GLENCOE

To order the following products for use with this chapter, contact your local Glencoe sales representative, or call Glencoe at 1-800-334-7344:

- *GTV: The American People (Videodisc)*
- *GTV: A Geographic Perspective on American History (Videodisc)*

ADDITIONAL NATIONAL GEOGRAPHIC SOCIETY PRODUCTS

To order the following products for use with this chapter, call National Geographic Society at 1-800-368-2728:

- *Lost Fleet of Guadalcanal (Video)*
- *Search for Battleship Bismarck (Video)*

BIBLIOGRAPHY

Literature of the Period
Frank, Anne. *The Diary of a Young Girl.* New York: Doubleday, 1972. First-person account of a young Jewish girl and her family who spent years hiding from the Nazis.
Readings for the Student
Ryan, Cornelius. *The Longest Day.* New York: Simon and Schuster, 1984. Detailed, exciting account of D-Day and the Normandy invasion.
Readings for the Teacher
Leckie, Robert. *Delivered from Evil: The Saga of World War II.* New York: Harper, 1987. A complete history of World War II told in the style of a novel.

LOCAL OBJECTIVES

interNET CONNECTION
World War II resources on the World Wide Web
World War II on the Web:
http://www.bunt.com/~mconrad/

Chapter Themes are listed by section on this chapter opening page of the Student Edition. A corresponding theme-based activity is available under "TEACH," and a theme-based question is asked in the Section and Chapter Reviews.

**The
Storyteller**

Historical Setting The invasion of Normandy launched by the Allies in June 1944 was not their first invasion of German-occupied France. In 1942 the Allies launched a raid on the seaport town of Dieppe. About two-thirds of the 6,000 soldiers who took part in this attack were killed, wounded, captured, or reported missing. However, the defeat at Dieppe did provide the Allies with valuable information that was used two years later when planning the D-Day invasion.

Historical Significance

Answers: *By the end of World War II, the balance of power had shifted away from Europe.*
The United States and the Soviet Union held the balance of power.

Chapter
20   1930–1945
World War II

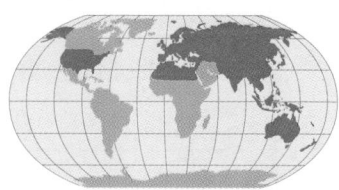

Chapter Themes

▶ **Movement** Japan, Italy, and Germany carry out expansionist policies. *Section 1*
▶ **Cooperation** The United States and Great Britain move slowly toward an alliance, while Germany and Italy make major territorial gains in Europe and the Mediterranean. *Section 2*
▶ **Conflict** Two separate and opposing alliances, the Allies and the Axis, wage a worldwide war. *Section 3*
▶ **Conflict** The Allies make major gains against the Axis Powers. *Section 4*
▶ **Innovation** New military technologies, such as the atomic bomb, affect the outcome of World War II. *Section 5*

**The
Storyteller**

On June 6, 1944, the Allies mounted an all-out attack against German forces in Normandy, France. Years later an American soldier named Elliott Johnson could still vividly recall the events of the day:

"I remember going up to the highest part of that ship and watching the panorama around me unfold. In my mind's eye, I see one of our ships take a direct hit and go up in a huge ball of flames. There were big geysers coming up where the shells were landing and there were bodies floating, face down, face up."

The invasion of Normandy was one of the key events of World War II. Although the war began in 1939, it had its roots in the peace treaties that settled World War I.

Historical Significance

How did World War II affect the world balance of power? What nations emerged from conflict as world powers?

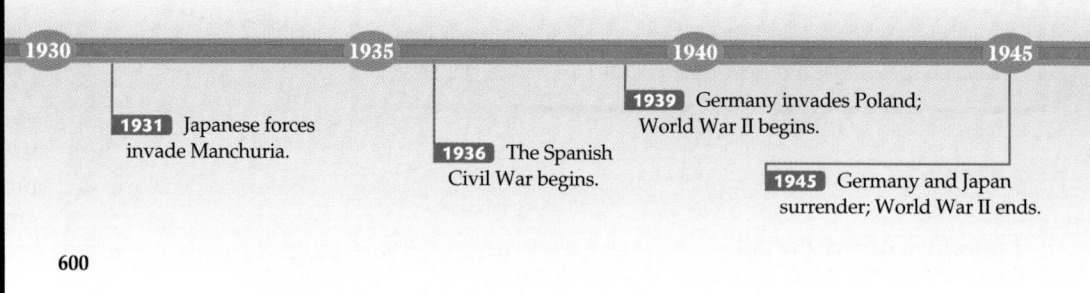

1930	1935	1940	1945

1931 Japanese forces invade Manchuria.

1936 The Spanish Civil War begins.

1939 Germany invades Poland; World War II begins.

1945 Germany and Japan surrender; World War II ends.

600

GEOGRAPHY CONNECTION

Location On a large wall map of the world or on the world map in the Atlas of their textbook, have students locate the following countries that took part in World War II: Germany, Italy, Japan, China, Poland, Finland, Norway, Denmark, France, Germany, the former Soviet Union (now the Commonwealth of Independent States), the United States, Egypt, Libya, and the Philippines. Why was this war called a world war? (*World War II involved countries in all parts of the world.*)

Visualizing History Allied forces led by the United States land in the Pacific island of Bougainville, the largest of the Solomon Islands.

Visualizing History The United States entered World War II on December 8, 1941, one day after Japan's surprise attack on the American naval and air base at Pearl Harbor in Hawaii. The victory at Bougainville was part of America's strategy of "island-hopping" to capture Japanese-held islands in the Pacific.

 Performance Assessment

Refer to the activity on page 600C of the Planning Guide.

Refer to Activity 20 in the *Performance Assessment Strategies and Activities* booklet.

Using Your History Journal

Tell students to note major events and turning points in World War II as they read the chapter. Then, from their notes, ask them to select the ten most significant events and tell why they were important to the outcome of the war.

Your History Journal

Create a two-column chart that shows the significance of ten key events in World War II. In column one list the event and date. In column two write a short statement of why the event was important to the outcome of the war.

 GLENCOE
TECHNOLOGY

VIDEODISC
Use MindJogger to preview chapter content.

MindJogger Videoquiz

Chapter 20
Disc 3 Side A

 Also available in VHS.

✚ EXTRA CREDIT PROJECT

Prisoners of War Have students use outside sources to do in-depth research on a prisoner-of-war camp run by the Germans, the Japanese, or the Allies. Have them write a report that includes information on general living conditions, work done by prisoners, chances for recreational activities, escape attempts, and compliance with international law on treatment of prisoners of war.

1930   1935   1940

1933 Japan withdraws from the League of Nations.   **1936** Germany occupies the Rhineland.   **1938** European powers meet at the Munich Conference.

SECTION THEME

▶ **Movement** Japan, Italy, and Germany carry out expansionist policies.

ind Out

Answer: *The peace treaties that ended World War I left Italy, Germany, and Japan dissatisfied, laying the groundwork for another world war.*

FOCUS

Section Objective

Explain in what sense World War II was a product of World War I.

BELLRINGER
Motivational Activity

Before taking roll at the beginning of the class period, project Section Focus Transparency 20-1 and have students answer the activity questions. Discuss students' responses.

▭ This activity is also available as a blackline master.

Vocabulary Pre-check

▭ Use Vocabulary Activity 20 to introduce vocabulary terms.
L1 LEP

Section 1

The Path to War

Setting the Scene

▶ **Terms to Define**
collective security, sanctions, appeasement

▶ **People to Meet**
Chiang Kai-shek, Benito Mussolini, Haile Selassie, Francisco Franco, Adolf Hitler, Joseph Stalin, Neville Chamberlain

▶ **Places to Locate**
Manchuria, Ethiopia, Spain, the Rhineland, Austria, Czechoslovakia

ind Out
In what sense was World War II a product of World War I?

The Storyteller

Joseph Stalin sent an invitation to formal negotiations to Adolf Hitler, the Nazi dictator. Hitler read the note and drummed both fists

Joseph Stalin

against the wall, exclaiming, "Now I have the world in my pocket." German Foreign Minister Joachim von Ribbentrop and Stalin arranged the division of Europe and agreed never to attack each other, then celebrated with an elaborate dinner. Each side toasted the other and told jokes the other side did not find funny. After dinner, in a final show of hospitality, Stalin drew the German foreign minister aside and told him that he personally could guarantee, on his word of honor, that the Soviet Union would not betray its partner.

—adapted from *Joseph Stalin: Man and Legend*, Ronald Hingley, 1974

In the 1930s the Western democracies watched uneasily as militaristic dictatorships came to power in Europe and Asia. Despite their fears, Britain, France, and the United States could not agree on what steps to take to ensure their collective security, or what was needed to defend their common interests against enemy attack. Much of the unrest in Europe and Asia can be traced to the peace settlements made at the end of World War I. Great Britain, France, and the United States were substantially satisfied with these settlements; however, Japan, Italy, and Germany were not.

Japan's Expansion in Asia

Japan was the first of the nondemocratic powers to reveal its territorial ambitions in the interwar period. With limited natural resources of its own, Japan depended heavily on foreign sources for raw materials and on foreign markets for finished goods. To acquire more of these materials and markets, Japan sought new territories for conquest.

The Japanese military used a bomb explosion on the South Manchurian Railway in September 1931 as an excuse to overrun **Manchuria**. The following year Japan established Manchuria as an independent state, renamed it Manchukuo, and set up former Chinese emperor Pu Yi as puppet ruler.

When China protested in the League of Nations about Japan's actions, the League ordered a commission under British statesman Lord Lytton to investigate the affair. Lytton's commission laid the blame squarely on Japan and ordered the Japanese government to return Manchuria to China. The League voted overwhelmingly in favor of this recommendation, to which Japan responded in March 1933 by withdrawing from the League. The Manchurian incident not only revealed that the League of Nations was powerless, but also boosted the expansionist ambitions of Italy and Germany.

SECTION RESOURCES

▭ **Reproducible Masters**
- Reproducible Lesson Plan 20-1
- Vocabulary Activity 20
- Guided Reading Activity 20-1
- Chapter Themes: Graphic Organizer 20
- People in World History Profile 59
- Time Line Activity 20
- Section Quiz 20-1

Transparencies
- Section Focus Transparency 20-1
- Chapter Transparency 20

Multimedia
- Student Self-Test and Review Software
- Testmaker
- Lessons of War:
  Appeasement: Munich Pact

In the early 1930s, the Japanese military wanted to acquire the rich oil reserves of the East Indies to supply its ships and airplanes. But to control the East Indies, Japan needed Chinese ports. Consequently, in the summer of 1937, Japanese forces invaded China and captured major eastern and southern cities. In the capital of Nanjing, they engaged in mass brutality, killing over 200,000 civilians. Meanwhile, the Nationalist government of **Chiang Kai-shek** retreated inland and later allied with the Western powers. From 1937 to 1945, the Nationalists, the Chinese Communists, and the Japanese fought each other for control of China.

Visualizing History Haile Selassie (center) appealed to the League of Nations for action against Italian aggression in Ethiopia. The League's failure to halt Axis expansion led to its own downfall. *Why were the League's sanctions against Italy ineffective?*

Italy's Conquest of Ethiopia

The relative ease with which Japan acquired Manchuria encouraged Italy to make a similar move. Italy's goal was to secure control of the ancient kingdom of **Ethiopia** in eastern Africa. In 1934 Italian and Ethiopian forces clashed in a disputed zone on the border of Ethiopia and Italian Somaliland. When the Italian dictator, **Benito Mussolini**, demanded an apology and reparations, the Ethiopians responded by asking the League of Nations to investigate the matter. The League decided that because each side viewed the area where the incident took place as its own territory, neither side was to blame.

The League's decision did not satisfy Mussolini, who thought an Ethiopian colony would enhance Italy's image as a world power. Consequently, in October 1935, Mussolini ordered the Italian army to invade Ethiopia. In a dramatic appearance at the League of Nations, Ethiopian Emperor **Haile Selassie** appealed for help. This time the League condemned the action and voted to impose economic sanctions, measures designed to stop trade and other economic contacts, against Italy. The League forbade its members to sell Italy arms and certain raw materials. But the sanctions did not include oil, coal, and iron, all vital to Italy's war efforts.

Once again the League's actions were ineffective. Mussolini completed his conquest of Ethiopia, and in May 1936 he formally annexed the African nation.

Spanish Civil War

A civil war in **Spain** further inflamed the international situation in the 1930s. After presiding over years of social and economic chaos, King Alfonso XIII abdicated in 1931, and Spain became a republic. The new republican government immediately began a program of social reforms. It ended the Catholic Church's role in educating Spanish youth and redistributed land from nobles to peasants.

As a result of these and other reforms, many right-wing groups in Spain opposed the republic and wished to restore the old order. In July 1936 right-wing army chiefs staged an uprising in Spanish Morocco that soon spread to Spain. For three years the conservative Spanish Nationalists, led by General **Francisco Franco**, and the left-wing Loyalists, or Spanish Republicans, battled for control of Spain.

Early in the fighting several foreign powers intervened in the Spanish war. The Soviets supported the Loyalists, while the Germans and Italians aided the Nationalists. Volunteers from Britain, France, the United States, and other countries around the world flocked to Spain to join the International Brigade and fight for the Republican cause against fascism. The governments of the Western democracies, however, refused to intervene because they feared a general European war.

Germany's dictator, **Adolf Hitler**, viewed German participation in the Spanish Civil War as a

Chapter 20 *World War II* **603**

TEACH

Guided Practice

THEME Movement

Ask several students to point out on a wall map the areas that Japan, Italy, and Germany invaded. (*Japan: Manchuria and China; Italy: Ethiopia; Germany: the Rhineland, Austria, Czechoslovakia*) **L1 LEP**

Visualizing History After Italy invaded Ethiopia, Haile Selassie lived in England for several years, helping plan the liberation of Ethiopia. When he returned to power, he wrote a new constitution that provided for universal suffrage. In 1974, with drought and starvation plaguing the country, Ethiopians deposed the aging ruler. A year later, Ethiopia's last emperor died.
Answer to Caption: *The sanctions did not include oil, coal, and iron—all of which helped Italy's war effort.*

Economics Have students discuss the economic reasons for Japan's expansionism. (*the need for raw materials, markets, and ports*) **L2**

 Chapter Transparency 20

Chapter Themes: Graphic Organizer 20

Independent Practice
Guided Reading Activity 20-1 **L1**

People in World History Profile 59

Time Line Activity 20

VIDEODISC
Lessons of War

Side Two, Chapter 3
Frames 3466–5635
Title: *Appeasement: Munich Pact*
Subject: British Prime Minister Neville Chamberlain's attempt to keep peace with Germany in 1938
Ask: What did Hitler demand at the Munich Conference? *(that the Sudetenland be given to Germany)*

Global Issues Have students imagine that they are newspaper editors in 1938. Ask them to list the events that have pushed the world toward another war. Then have them write an editorial titled "On the Brink of War" that offers suggestions on how to diffuse the powder keg. **L3**

THE HISTORY CHANNEL.

The following videotape program is available from Glencoe:

• **World War II: The War Chronicles** (Seven Video Set)

To find classroom resources to accompany this video, check the following home page:

The History Channel: http://www.historychannel.com

---

way to strengthen ties with Italy and to secure a vital supply of Spanish iron ore and magnesium. Hermann Goering, head of the Luftwaffe—or German air force—saw an opportunity "firstly, to prevent the further spread of Communism; secondly, to test my young Luftwaffe in this or that technical aspect." To accomplish these goals, Goering formed the Condor Legion, an all-German air and ground force. They used Spanish towns and cities as testing grounds for new weapons and military tactics, such as the combined use of fire and high-explosive bombs.

By the summer of 1936, the Nationalists had taken most of western Spain. When the Soviets stopped sending aid to the Loyalists in 1938, Franco launched his final offensive. In March 1939 Franco entered Madrid, the last of the Loyalist strongholds. The civil war had ended, but more than half a million Spaniards had died, and much of the country lay in ruins. Although Spain joined Italy and Germany as countries headed by fascist dictators, Franco did not ally himself with Italy and Germany.

Hitler on the Offensive

The same year the Spanish Civil War broke out, Hitler made his move in Germany. The German dictator was convinced that Germany needed more *lebensraum*, or living space, for its expanding population. In his book, *Mein Kampf (My Struggle)*, Hitler wrote:

> **"** Only an adequate large space on this earth assures a nation freedom of existence….We must hold unflinchingly to our aim … to secure for the German people the land and soil to which they are entitled…. **"**

Footnotes to History

Writers at War
The Spanish Civil War became a crusade for many writers. In *For Whom the Bell Tolls*, American writer Ernest Hemingway describes an idealistic American fighting the Fascist forces in Spain. The English novelist George Orwell, in *Homage to Catalonia*, presents his experiences on the Aragon front and his nearly fatal gunshot wound.

Occupying the Rhineland

Since 1919, the Versailles Treaty had forbidden German troops in **the Rhineland**, a German region between the Rhine and the French border. This ban was designed to provide security to France. Hitler gambled that if he violated the treaty, France and Great Britain would do nothing to stop him. In March 1936, therefore, Hitler sent troops into the Rhineland. France had the right to take military action, and Britain had the obligation to back France with its own armed forces. Neither country acted, however, because neither was willing to risk a war.

In October 1936, Hitler and Mussolini agreed to the Rome-Berlin Axis, an alliance that they hoped would be the "axis" around which world affairs would turn. Known thereafter as the Axis Powers, Italy and Germany later joined Japan in the Anti-Comintern Pact, an alliance against Soviet communism. Viewing the Pact as a threat to his country, the Soviet dictator **Joseph Stalin** urged the West to unite against the Axis. But the West, fearing war and distrusting Stalin, refused.

Seizing Austria

Hitler, meanwhile, grew bolder. For a long time he had dreamed of *Anschluss* (ANSH•luhs)—the joining of **Austria** to Germany. "German-Austria must return to the great mother country," he wrote. "One blood demands one Reich."

In 1934 Hitler had tried to take over Austria but backed down when Mussolini responded by mobilizing Italy's troops. In 1938, now that Germany and Italy were allies, Hitler tried again. He invited the Austrian chancellor to Berchtesgaden, his mountain retreat in the German Alps, and bullied him into appointing Nazis to key posts in Austria. The Austrian chancellor appealed to Britain and France for help, but once more the two major democracies in Europe did nothing. In March 1938 Hitler sent German troops into Austria and then proclaimed it part of Germany. He insisted that he was only promoting political stability in central Europe by uniting German-speaking peoples into one country. The Western democracies, however, refused to take military action.

Tension Builds in Europe

Austria was the first victim of Hitler's policy of expansion. **Czechoslovakia** was the next. In the late 1930s, Czechoslovakia was the only democratic nation in central Europe. It held a key strategic position in the region. Its standard of living was second only to that of

---

MEETING SPECIAL NEEDS ACTIVITY

Learning Style: Visual/Spatial Have students who are strong visual learners work together to review information in Section 1 and plan political cartoons based on these topics: Japan sets up puppet government in Manchuria; Italy takes Ethiopia; Condor Legion bombs Spain; League of Nations fails to stop aggression; Hitler grabs Austria. Display completed cartoons on the bulletin board and hold a class discussion on what the cartoons say about events of the 1930s. **L2**

Germany. Czechoslovakia also had a strong army and alliances with France and the Soviet Union.

The nation of Czechoslovakia was created by treaty at the end of World War I. In addition to Czechs and Slovaks, it had 1 million Hungarians, half a million Ruthenians, and more than 3 million Germans. During the 1930s these minorities began to demand more freedom than they had received under the terms of the treaties, creating serious problems for the Czechoslovak government. Hitler took advantage of Czechoslovakia's ethnic problems to destroy the country.

Sudeten Crisis

On September 12, 1938, Hitler demanded that the Germans of the Sudetenland, a heavily fortified region in northwestern Czechoslovakia, be given the right of self-determination. Czechoslovak leaders responded by proclaiming martial law. In an effort to avert an international crisis, British Prime Minister **Neville Chamberlain** suggested to Hitler that they meet to discuss the matter. France supported his request.

Chamberlain met with Hitler in Germany on September 15, 1938. There Hitler demanded that the Sudetenland be given to Germany. At a second meeting a week later, Chamberlain accepted Hitler's demands. He thought that a policy of appeasement, granting concessions to maintain peace, would stabilize Europe. As the British and their French allies searched for a peaceful solution, Hitler raised his demands. The Sudetenland, he stated, must be united with Germany.

The Munich Conference

On September 29, Chamberlain met with Hitler a third time in Munich, Germany. Also attending were French Premier Édouard Daladier and Italy's dictator Benito Mussolini. Czechoslovakia and the Soviet Union were not represented.

Mussolini offered a "compromise" that gave Germany control over the Sudetenland. In return, Hitler promised to respect Czechoslovakia's sovereignty. He also promised not to take any more European territory and to settle future disputes by peaceful negotiation. Still hoping to avoid war,

Visualizing History In May 1938 Adolf Hitler (left) visited Rome, Italy, to meet with his Italian ally Benito Mussolini (right). The visit was designed to demonstrate the unity of the Rome-Berlin Axis. *What role did Mussolini play in the Czech crisis later that year?*

Great Britain and France accepted the terms. On September 30, Czechoslovakia reluctantly accepted the Munich Agreement.

Chamberlain returned home to cheering crowds, proclaiming that he had ensured "peace in our time." He trusted Hitler and believed that the Nazis would cause no more trouble. Events soon proved him wrong. On March 15, 1939, Hitler sent his armies into Czechoslovakia and took control of the western part of the country. The eastern part, Slovakia, became a German puppet state. After the takeover the Western democracies could no longer maintain their illusions about Hitler's plans and began to prepare for war.

The Coming of War

More German demands followed the Munich agreement. In March 1939 Hitler turned his attention to eastern Europe. He forced Lithuania to give up the German-speaking city of Memel. Next the German dictator put pressure on Poland, threatening to take over the Baltic port of Danzig

Chapter 20 *World War II* **605**

Visualizing History Hitler and Mussolini first met in Venice in 1934, but little came of that first encounter. Mussolini remarked to an aide, "I don't like the look of him." Yet, two years later, the two men formed the Rome-Berlin Axis.
Answer to Caption: *Mussolini offered a compromise that gave the Sudetenland to Germany in return for Hitler's promise to respect Czechoslovakia's sovereignty, to take no more European territories, and to settle future disputes by peaceful negotiation.*

Linking Past and Present

Realpolitik, the idea that a state should pursue its own interests without regard for ethics or morality, was first used in the 1860s and 1870s when Bismarck united the German states into the German Empire. Hitler applied realpolitik ruthlessly in the 1930s as he conquered neighboring countries. Today the term is often employed to mean "power politics."

The Coming of War
How did Hitler's invasion of Poland change the course of European affairs?
His invasion ended the European democracies' policy of appeasement and started World War II in Europe.

MAKING CONNECTIONS ACTIVITY

Foreign Affairs Have students choose one of the following topics and write a brief report on it: Japan's attack on Nanjing, Haile Selassie and the League of Nations, Germany's advance into the Rhineland, the Nationalist victory in the Spanish Civil War, or the Munich Agreement. Tell students to use issues of popular magazines from the 1930s, such as *The Saturday Evening Post, Time,* and *Life* for their research. Have them include quotes and copies of pictures in their reports. **L2**

ASSESS

Check for Understanding

Assign Section 1 Review as homework or as an in-class activity.

 Use Student Self-Test and Review Software to review Section 1.

Evaluate

Section Quiz 20-1

Use the Testmaker to create a customized quiz for Section 1.

Reteach

Have students explain the connection of the following people to acts of aggression in the 1930s: Pu Yi, Benito Mussolini, Haile Selassie, Francisco Franco, Adolf Hitler, Joseph Stalin, and Neville Chamberlain.

Enrich

Have students write a paragraph explaining why Germany, Italy, and Japan eventually became allies.

CLOSE

Have students summarize how aggressive expansion, a weak League of Nations, appeasement, and secret treaties led to the outbreak of war in 1939.

---

and the Polish Corridor, a narrow strip of Polish land that separated the German region of East Prussia from the rest of Germany. Great Britain and France promised to help Poland defend its borders if it became necessary. The Polish government accepted the support of the Western democracies and firmly rejected Hitler's demands.

The West and the Soviets

To defend Poland, the democracies had to consider the Soviet Union, Poland's neighbor but also its traditional enemy. During the late 1930s, Stalin had urged the Western powers to do something about Hitler. He suspected that the Munich Agreement was an attempt by the British and the French to turn Hitler's attention away from the West and toward the Soviet Union. Chamberlain, on the other hand, did not trust Stalin. He suspected that the Soviet leader wanted to extend his influence in eastern Europe. This confusion as to whether the Fascists or the Communists were the greater enemy contributed to the coolness of the British and the French toward Stalin.

Despite Chamberlain's suspicions and his lack of faith in the fighting ability of the Soviet army, he asked the Soviets to join Britain and France in an alliance to contain Nazism. Stalin agreed on the condition that the Western powers acknowledge the Soviet right to occupy a broad zone stretching from Finland to Bulgaria. Chamberlain refused Stalin's request, deepening Stalin's suspicion that the West would like nothing better than to see Germany and the Soviet Union destroy each other.

Nazi-Soviet Talks

Stalin believed that Hitler's desire for "living space" would eventually lead the German dictator to move into the rich agricultural areas of eastern Europe. Because he doubted that the West would

come to his country's aid if Germany threatened it, Stalin began secret talks with the Germans. On August 23, 1939, the Soviet Union and Germany signed the Nazi-Soviet Nonaggression Pact.

According to the agreement, Germany and the Soviet Union pledged that they would never attack each other. Moreover, each would remain neutral if the other became involved in a war. Stalin and Hitler also secretly agreed to create spheres of influence in eastern Europe. Germany would occupy the western part of Poland, while the Soviet Union would govern the eastern part. They agreed to include Finland, part of Romania, and the Baltic republics of Estonia, Latvia, and Lithuania in the Soviet sphere of influence.

Neither Stalin nor Hitler had any illusions about their agreement. They were long-term enemies who, for their own purposes, needed a short-term arrangement. Stalin still believed that war with Germany was inevitable. But he thought that the pact would improve Soviet security. If nothing else, it would buy the Soviets time to prepare for war. Hitler saw the pact as a means of securing Germany's eastern border. If he did not have to worry about fighting the Soviets, he would be free to act as he wanted.

The pact shocked Western leaders, who realized that it destroyed the last barrier to war. The West had also lost a potential ally, and Hitler had won a pledge of neutrality that freed him to pursue his military objectives regarding Poland. Hitler remained convinced, however, that the West would do nothing if he moved against Poland. "The men of Munich," he said, "will not take the risk." With this thought in mind, Hitler sent his armies across the Polish frontier on September 1, 1939. However, he had finally misjudged what the Western leaders would do. Two days after Hitler's invasion of Poland, Great Britain and France declared war on Germany. World War II had begun.

SECTION 1 REVIEW

Recall
1. **Define** collective security, sanctions, appeasement.
2. **Identify** Chiang Kai-shek, Benito Mussolini, Haile Selassie, Francisco Franco, Adolf Hitler, Joseph Stalin, Neville Chamberlain.
3. **Locate** Czechoslovakia on the

map on page 608. What about this country's location gave it such strategic value in Hitler's eyes?

Critical Thinking
4. **Evaluating Information** What major factors do you think contributed to the outbreak of World War II?

Understanding Themes
5. **Movement** How was the response by the League of Nations to Japanese expansion in 1933 similar to the response by the Western democracies to German expansion in 1938? How was it different? Explain your response.

SECTION 1 REVIEW ANSWERS

1. All vocabulary words are defined in the Glossary.
2. Chiang Kai-shek, 603; Benito Mussolini, 603; Haile Selassie, 603; Francisco Franco, 603; Adolf Hitler, 603; Joseph Stalin, 604; Neville Chamberlain, 605
3. Czechoslovakia separated Germany from Austria, which had already been con-

quered by Germany.
4. dissatisfaction with World War I peace treaties; expansionist policies of Germany, Japan, and Italy; appeasement policies of the democracies; Stalin's pact with Hitler; lack of U.S. participation in world affairs; weaknesses of the League of Nations; social and economic disloca-

tion as a result of the Depression
5. **MOVEMENT** The response of both the League of Nations and the Western democracies was so weak and ineffective that it encouraged more aggression.

1939 The Soviet Union fights Finland.

1940 France surrenders to Germany; the Battle of Britain begins.

1941 Franklin D. Roosevelt and Winston Churchill issue the Atlantic Charter.

Section 2

War in Europe

Setting the Scene

▶ **Terms to Define**
blitzkrieg, blitz, cash-and-carry policy, lend-lease

▶ **People to Meet**
Winston Churchill, Charles de Gaulle, Franklin D. Roosevelt

▶ **Places to Locate**
Finland, Norway, London, Libya

 **ind Out** How did Hitler take over most of Europe, and what was the response of Great Britain and the United States to German expansion?

The Storyteller

Saturday night, August 24th, 1940, the first German bombs fell on London. That September, bombing became more frequent and deadly as waves of planes came over the city. For hours bombers would attack; then, to fight the fires, thousands of firefighters went into action. Many Londoners lost their homes. An observer reported that boats normally used by tourists on vacation became evacuation boats "chugging along the riverside … defying high explosive and incendiary bombs, walls of flame, and clouds of choking fumes.… With a few bundles of clothes the refugees climbed aboard and were taken by river to the safety zone or ferried across to the opposite bank."

German bombers

—adapted from *The Lost Treasures of London*, William Kent, 1947

On September 1, 1939, the German Luftwaffe roared toward its targets in Poland, spreading panic and confusion with its bombs. At the same time, armored tank divisions known as panzers swept across the Polish border. Next came the infantry, a million and a half strong, in motorized vehicles. This was blitzkrieg, or "lightning war," a new German strategy aimed at taking the enemy by surprise.

The blitzkrieg worked with speed and efficiency, devastating Poland in a few weeks. Great Britain and France could not move fast enough to send troops to Poland. The Soviet Union, meanwhile, quickly moved its forces to occupy the eastern half of that nation.

Stalin also forced the Baltic republics of Latvia, Lithuania, and Estonia to accept Soviet military bases. When he tried to do the same with **Finland**, war broke out. The Finns held out heroically until March before the Soviets forced them to surrender. As a result of their victory, the Soviets moved their frontier 70 miles (112 km) to the west, making the city of Leningrad less vulnerable to German attack.

Hitler Looks to the West

All through the winter and spring of 1939–1940, the western front was quiet. The Germans called this period the "sit-down war," or *Sitzkrieg*, while the West dubbed it the "phony war." Many hoped that an all-out war could still be avoided.

When Finland capitulated to the Soviets, however, the British took steps to ensure that the same fate would not befall **Norway**. In early April 1940, they mined Norwegian waters to block any ships trading with Germany. Hitler used the mining to support his claim that the Allies were about to invade Scandinavia. He delivered an ultimatum to Norway and Denmark, demanding that they accept the "protection of the Reich." The Danes accepted his demands; the Norwegians did not.

Chapter 20 *World War II* **607**

SECTION THEME

▶ **Cooperation** The United States and Great Britain move slowly toward an alliance, while Germany and Italy make major territorial gains in Europe and the Mediterranean.

 **ind Out**

Answer: *by a policy of blitzkrieg, "lightning war," which took the enemy by surprise; Britain declared war on Germany. The United States supplied Britain with food and weapons.*

FOCUS

Section Objective
Describe how Hitler took over most of Europe and how Great Britain and the United States responded to German expansion.

BELLRINGER
Motivational Activity

Before taking roll at the beginning of the class period, project Section Focus Transparency 20-2. This activity is also available as a blackline master.

Vocabulary Pre-check
Use Vocabulary Activity 20 to introduce vocabulary terms.
L1 LEP

SECTION RESOURCES

Reproducible Masters
- Reproducible Lesson Plan 20-2
- Vocabulary Activity 20
- Guided Reading Activity 20-2
- People in World History Profile 60
- Section Quiz 20-2

Transparencies
- Section Focus Transparency 20-2
- Mapping History Overlay Transparency 19, *Europe in June, 1942*

Multimedia
- Student Self-Test and Review Software
- Testmaker
- Lessons of War: *Laws of War*

TEACH

Guided Practice

THEME **Cooperation**

Have students find examples in Section 2 of countries cooperating, or working together for their common good. *(Britain mined Norwegian waters to keep German ships out, helped the French, and sent troops to Belgium; the United States supplied food and weapons to Britain; Hitler sent Rommel to help the Italians in Libya.)* **L1**

Map Study

Answer

Ireland, Portugal, Spain, Switzerland, Turkey, Sweden

Map Skills Practice

Reading a Map What countries did Germany invade in 1941? *(Yugoslavia, Lithuania, Latvia, Estonia, the Soviet Union)*

Military History Have students compare the fall of France with the Battle of Britain. **L2**

Politics Have students examine the reasons for the downfall of Neville Chamberlain and discuss why Great Britain's attitude toward Germany changed when Winston Churchill became prime minister. **L3**

Biography

The following videotape program is available from Glencoe:

- **The Complete Churchill**
  (Four Video Set)

Axis Expansion Into Europe 1935–1941

Legend:
- Allied nations
- Neutral nations
- Axis nations
- Occupied by Germany
- Occupied by Italy
- Vichy France and colonies
- → Axis offensive
- --- Siegfried Line
- --- Maginot Line

By the end of 1941, Germany had seized control of much of Europe.
Location Which European nations chose to remain neutral during the war?

The Invasion of Scandinavia

In the early morning hours of April 9, three small German transports steamed into the harbor of Copenhagen, the Danish capital. After meeting little resistance, the Germans took control of Denmark. That same morning, German forces also landed along the coast of Norway. British forces had been busy laying mines in Norwegian waters in an effort to cut off German shipment of iron ore from neighboring Sweden. Within hours, however, the Germans had seized Norway's major cities, including the capital of Oslo.

Although Germany now controlled Norway, the Norwegian invasion proved costly. Germany lost a large number of destroyers and cruisers. On the other hand, Hitler won the outlet to the Atlantic that he needed to ensure that the German navy would not be bottled up in the Baltic Sea like it had in World War I.

News of the fall of Norway and Denmark caused an uproar in the British House of Commons. The Labour and Liberal opposition strongly attacked Prime Minister Neville Chamberlain and his policies. Knowing that he had lost the confidence of his own Conservative party as well, Chamberlain stepped down. On May 10, 1940, King George VI summoned **Winston Churchill** to Buckingham Palace and asked him to form a new

608   Chapter 20   *World War II*

COOPERATIVE LEARNING ACTIVITY

Video Presentation Organize the class into three groups to create a 15-minute video documentary about Germany's early military offensives in World War II. Assign each group one of the following topics: the conquest of Poland, fall of France (include the Low Countries and Dunkirk), or the Battle of Britain. Suggest that students use pictures of events and people, sound effects, "interviews," speeches, and songs in their films. Each group should choose a narrator for its segment, and one student to act as a coordinator with the other groups. When the documentaries are completed, have students present them to other classes. **L3**

government. Churchill, one of the few politicians to warn of the Nazi danger in the 1930s, was now prime minister.

The Fall of France

On that same momentous date, the war began in earnest on the western front. Along the Maginot Line, the British and French watched and waited. The Maginot Line was impressive, but it had one major flaw. It had a 50-mile (80-km) gap in the Ardennes. Although the Germans had invaded through Belgium and the Ardennes during World War I, the French still believed that the forests, swamps, and hills of that region were a sufficient barrier. A French tank commander, **Charles de Gaulle**, pleaded for more tanks and planes, but the French command insisted that the Maginot Line was impenetrable.

Hitler, meanwhile, carried out a massive attack on the Low Countries—Luxembourg, the Netherlands, and Belgium. Before dawn on May 10, 1940, German troops parachuted into the Netherlands. It was the first large-scale airborne attack in the history of warfare and caught the Dutch by surprise. Five days after the start of the invasion, the Dutch capitulated.

On the same day that Germany invaded the Netherlands, Britain and France moved their best troops into Belgium. German panzers swept into the Ardennes and began to encircle them. Other panzer divisions drove through Luxembourg and raced toward France.

Dunkirk

Although the Belgian forces fought valiantly, they did not hold out as long as had been expected. The Germans were now rolling through undefended open country. They pushed westward toward the English Channel, trapping the Belgian, British, and French forces in the northwest corner of France. The only hope for the Allies was an evacuation by sea from the French port of Dunkirk. With German forces within sight of the coast, the rescue of 300,000 Allied soldiers seemed impossible. But for reasons never entirely understood, Hitler ordered his forces to halt.

The British Admiralty began a desperate rescue operation at Dunkirk on May 26. A ragtag armada of 850 vessels, ranging from destroyers and cruisers to trawlers, tugs, yachts, and fishing boats, left England and set sail for Dunkirk. Civilians operated many of the smaller boats. Over the next nine days, under fierce air and ground attack, this hastily assembled fleet rescued the Allied armies.

The evacuation of Dunkirk was a stunning

military achievement, but as Churchill said, "wars are not won by evacuations." Faced with an unprepared French army and a confused French government, the Germans continued their sweep into France and on June 14 entered Paris. A week later France signed an armistice with Germany.

Vichy and the Free French

By the terms of the armistice, the Germans occupied all of northern France and the Atlantic coastline to the Spanish border. In southern France, the Nazis set up a puppet government in the city of Vichy under French Marshal Henri Pétain. Pétain and other officials in the so-called Vichy government collaborated with the Germans. Many French citizens, on the other hand, continued to fight for freedom. In Britain, de Gaulle organized a Free French government, while in France many joined the French Resistance, an underground movement that opposed the German occupation.

Battle of Britain

All that stood between Hitler and German domination of western Europe was Winston Churchill and the determined British people. Hitler expected that Britain would seek peace with Germany, but he misjudged the resolve of the British. Alone and only partially prepared, Britain faced the mightiest military machine the world had ever seen.

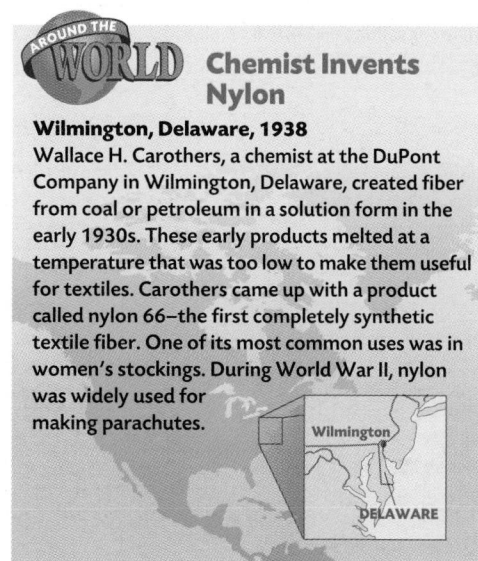

AROUND THE WORLD
Chemist Invents Nylon

Wilmington, Delaware, 1938
Wallace H. Carothers, a chemist at the DuPont Company in Wilmington, Delaware, created fiber from coal or petroleum in a solution form in the early 1930s. These early products melted at a temperature that was too low to make them useful for textiles. Carothers came up with a product called nylon 66–the first completely synthetic textile fiber. One of its most common uses was in women's stockings. During World War II, nylon was widely used for making parachutes.

Wilmington

DELAWARE

Mapping History Overlay Transparency 19, *Europe in June, 1942*

Who?What?Where?When?

Radar The invention of radar, an early-warning system against incoming aircraft, by physicist Robert Watson-Watts in 1935 helped the British defeat the German Luftwaffe in the Battle of Britain.

Independent Practice

📁 Guided Reading Activity 20-2 **L1**

📁 People in World History Profile 60

Art Have students research and write a brief report on the work of a World War II correspondent or photojournalist such as Edward R. Murrow, Alan Moorehead, Robert Capa, Margaret Bourke-White, Max Alpert, or Henri Cartier-Bresson. **L2**

Literature Have students research Winston Churchill's World War II speeches and write a brief report that explains how Churchill's oratory rallied the British people. Ask students to use quotations from Churchill in their reports. **L3**

Cultural Perspectives

Finland In the war between Finland and the Soviet Union (November 1939–March 1940), Finnish ski patrols in white camouflage maneuvered over Finland's snow-covered fields. They cut off Soviet supplies, isolated Soviet patrols, and stranded entire brigades. Eventually, 400,000 Soviet troops were massed against Finland's army of 33,000.

MEETING SPECIAL NEEDS ACTIVITY

Study Strategy To help students better understand terms used in Section 2, have them make a minidictionary for the following words: *blitzkrieg, sitzkrieg, capitulate, ultimatum, panzer, armada, Luftwaffe, neutrality, cash-and-carry policy,* and *lend-lease.* Tell them first to alphabetize the words, then find them in Section 2 and either determine their meaning from context or look them up in the dictionary or the Glossary of their textbook. Then have students write a good definition for each word and use each in a sentence. **L1**

VIDEODISC
Lessons of War

Side One, Chapter 12
Frames 46153–50167
Title: *Laws of War*
Subject: The rules that place limits on the types of weapons that can be used in war and against whom they can be used
Ask: What rule is supposed to protect civilians? *(Civilians should not be "injured or killed on purpose"; there should be no attacks on residential areas.)*

you don't say...

Quisling, a word that means "traitor," comes from the name of Vidkun Quisling, a Norwegian Nazi who helped the Germans take over Norway in 1940. During the war Quisling headed Norway's government under direction from Germany.

THE HISTORY CHANNEL.

The following videotape program is available from Glencoe:

• **Churchill & the Cabinet War Rooms**

To find classroom resources to accompany this video, check the following home page:

The History Channel: http://www.historychannel.com

On May 13, 1940, Churchill delivered his first speech before the House of Commons. He told the Commons that he had "nothing to offer but blood, toil, tears, and sweat." He ended the speech with these words:

“ You ask, what is our policy? I will say: it is to wage war, by sea, land, and air, with all our might and with all the strength that God can give us: to wage war against a monstrous tyranny, never surpassed in the dark, lamentable catalogue of human crime. That is our policy. You ask, what is our aim? I can answer in one word: Victory—victory at all costs, victory in spite of all terror, victory, however hard and long the road may be; for without victory, there is no survival. ”

Immediately after France fell, Hitler began making plans to invade Great Britain. Hitler and the German High Command soon realized that this invasion depended on winning air supremacy over the English Channel and destroying British airfields and vital industries. To accomplish this goal, the Luftwaffe began bombing the southern coast of Britain in early August 1940. The bombings damaged four aircraft factories and five Royal Air Force (RAF) airfields, but British fighter planes known as Hurricanes and Spitfires shot down 75 German planes. From then on, Hermann Goering, head of the German air force, focused his attacks on the RAF. From August 24 to September 6, Goering sent over 1,000 planes a day. The RAF lost 466 fighters and 103 pilots, but it inflicted even heavier losses on the Germans.

Seeking to do better, the Luftwaffe changed tactics once again, switching its attack to massive night bombings of **London**. For 57 consecutive nights, from September 7 to November 3, German bombers pounded London in its great blitz, or series of air raids. In one night alone, the Luftwaffe dropped 70,000 fire bombs on Britain's capital. The devastation was enormous, killing and injuring thousands of

Images *of the* Times

The Blitz

During World War II, German bombers rained destruction on London and strategic targets in an attempt to knock out Great Britain's defenses and force the British to surrender.

Many London school children were evacuated to safer parts of Great Britain and even overseas to escape the bombing.

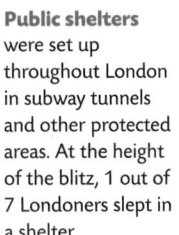

Public shelters were set up throughout London in subway tunnels and other protected areas. At the height of the blitz, 1 out of 7 Londoners slept in a shelter.

610

Images *of the* Times The Blitz

During the war, about two million children were evacuated to the countryside from London and other British cities. There, many of these city children played on grass and climbed trees for the first time. The government paid the children's hosts for their care. Some children lived in cottages, while others stayed at large country estates. Parents and children were reunited periodically when the government offered reduced train fares to the country. Knowing that their children were safe helped parents carry on with the war effort.

civilians, damaging light, power, and gas lines and destroying buildings, roads, and railways. But the bombings did not break the British people's morale.

The Luftwaffe never did gain air supremacy over Britain. While incurring heavy losses of its own, the RAF downed more than 1,700 German aircraft during the Battle of Britain, and in so doing, blocked Hitler's invasion. Churchill spoke for all Britons when he said of the RAF pilots: "Never in the field of human conflict was so much owed by so many to so few."

Anglo–American Cooperation

Throughout the early phase of the war, the United States expressed its determination to remain neutral. Even before the fighting began, the United States Congress had enacted laws designed to prevent American involvement in the war. The Neutrality Acts, passed in 1937, prohibited arms shipments, loans, and credit to belligerent nations. Congress later banned the export of armaments, "for the use of either of the opposing forces" in the Spanish Civil War.

President **Franklin D. Roosevelt**, however, became convinced that Germany's expansion endangered American security and that Britain and France could not stop Hitler without American aid. Throughout his campaign for the presidency in 1940, Roosevelt tried to rally national opinion. And as they listened to news reports of German aggression, Americans became more sympathetic to Britain's plight.

After Dunkirk, Churchill appealed to the United States for help. Roosevelt gave the British 50 old American naval destroyers in return for the right to maintain American bases in Newfoundland, Bermuda, and the British West Indies. He also convinced Congress that a cash-and-carry policy—a program in which Great Britain traded cash for desperately needed supplies—would allow the United States to supply the British without risking the loss

The Royal Air Force (RAF) won the Battle of Britain, the first battle ever fought to control the air. RAF pilots intercepted German planes with the help of ground radar stations that warned of the German planes' approach.

The bombing of London, which lasted nightly beginning in September 1940, caused much ruin, but failed to break the determined spirit of the British people.

REFLECTING ON THE TIMES

1. What did the Germans achieve by bombing London during World War II?
2. How did the British people respond to the German attacks?

611

Rommel had trained his troops for desert warfare on a sandy peninsula on the Baltic Sea. To prepare them for desert conditions, Rommel housed them in overheated barracks and held them to strict rations of food and water.
Answer to Caption: *to stop German troops that were sweeping through Yugoslavia and Greece*

Visualizing History In the spring of 1941, Erwin Rommel, "The Desert Fox" drove the British out of Libya into Egypt. *Why had Churchill diverted some troops from Africa to southeast Europe?*

Evaluate

◤ Section Quiz 20-2

▣ Use the Testmaker to create a customized quiz for Section 2.

Reteach

Have students write paragraphs that summarize the information under each main heading in Section 2.

Enrich

Have students write short essays about the resistance movement against the Nazis in occupied France.

CLOSE

Call on volunteers to trace the major events in World War II from September 1939 to April 1941 in chronological order on a map of Europe and North Africa. Ask other students to tell the significance of each event.

of American neutrality. Throughout 1940 this policy enabled the British to import American food and armaments. They paid cash and transported the goods in their own ships.

But the cost of the war drained the British treasury. Britain ordered 12,000 airplanes from the United States in 1940 but could not pay for them. On Roosevelt's urging, Congress approved a policy of lend-lease. It authorized the President to lend war equipment to any country whose defense he deemed vital to the national security of the United States.

On August 9, 1941, Churchill met with Roosevelt on a British battleship off the Newfoundland coast to discuss war aims. The leaders issued a joint declaration called the Atlantic Charter. It upheld freedom of trade and the right of people to choose their own government. But it also called for the "final destruction of Nazi tyranny."

Eastern Europe and Africa

While Hitler was conquering much of western Europe, Mussolini was dreaming of building a Mediterranean empire for his own country—Italy. On June 10, 1940, Mussolini declared war on France and Britain. Italy's armies in **Libya** were poised for an attack on the British forces guarding Egypt and the Sudan. Although vastly outnumbered, the British attacked the Italians on December 9. In the following weeks they scored victory after victory against the Italians stationed along Libya's north coast.

Churchill, however, halted this advance and diverted some of the troops to stop a German advance in southeast Europe that had already claimed Romania, Bulgaria, and Hungary. It was a fatal decision. German forces, sweeping through Yugoslavia and Greece in April 1941, forced the British into a second Dunkirk. Although most British troops escaped by sea, they left behind their tanks and 12,000 men. Meanwhile, Hitler sent Erwin Rommel, a brilliant general who had led the 7th Panzer Division in France, to take command of a tank force in Libya and rescue the Italians. By April 11, Rommel had pushed the British out of northern Libya, except for a small force at Tobruk.

SECTION 2 REVIEW

Recall
1. **Define** blitzkrieg, blitz, cash-and-carry policy, lend-lease.
2. **Identify** Winston Churchill, Charles de Gaulle, Franklin D. Roosevelt.
3. **Explain** why Neville

Chamberlain stepped down as British prime minister in 1940.
Critical Thinking
4. **Analyzing Information** What mistakes did French military leaders make that led to the fall of France?

Understanding Themes
5. **Cooperation** How did the United States government in the early 1940s move from a policy of isolationism to a policy of openly assisting the British in the war effort against the Nazis?

SECTION 2 REVIEW ANSWERS

1. All vocabulary words are defined in the Glossary.
2. Winston Churchill, 608; Charles de Gaulle, 609; Franklin D. Roosevelt, 611
3. The German conquest of Norway and Denmark showed that appeasement had

failed, and Chamberlain lost the support of all three political parties.
4. French military leaders assumed that the Maginot Line would stop an invasion even though Germany had invaded through Belgium in World War I.

5. **COOPERATION** Because Roosevelt believed that German aggression threatened American security, he convinced Congress to adopt the cash-and-carry and lend-lease policies.

Synthesizing Information

If you want to play the guitar, you must learn different skills: how to hold the instrument, play various chords, and read music. By putting together, or synthesizing, this information, you will learn to play the guitar.

Learning the Skill

When synthesizing information, we combine information obtained from separate sources. To write a research report, for example, you study the topic in several sources—encyclopedias, books, articles, and so on. Eventually, you synthesize this information and write the report.

Before synthesizing information, first analyze each source separately. Determine the value and reliability of each source. Then, look for connections and relationships among the different sources. Some information may conflict with your existing knowledge, or may present exceptions to the general rule.

Practicing the Skill

Study the passage and the map on this page. Then answer the following questions.
1. What is the main idea of the passage?
2. What information does the map add to your knowledge of this topic?
3. By synthesizing the two sources, what conclusion can you draw about the extent of the Nazis' "final solution."

“ I have received a report which is of the greatest importance.… It is stated in this report that very large numbers of … Jews first deported to Poland or directly sent to [Auschwitz-] Birkenau in the well-known cattle-trucks from Germany, France, Belgium, Holland, Greece, etc. have been killed in these establishments. The bodies have been burnt in specially constructed stoves and the ashes have been used as fertilizers. All those who died by starvation or ill-treatment in the various labour-camps nearby were also burned in these stoves. ”
—Letter from Richard Lichtheim of the Jewish Agency, June 19, 1944

Applying the Skill

Find two sources of information on the same topic and write a short report. In your report, answer these questions: What kinds of sources did you use—primary or secondary? What are the main ideas in these sources? How does each source add to your understanding of the topic? Do the sources support or contradict each other?

For More Practice

Turn to the Skill Practice in the Chapter Review on page 629 for more practice in synthesizing information.

Nazi Concentration and Death Camps

TEACH

Synthesizing Information Ask students to write detailed directions from your classroom to the principal's office, to the cafeteria, or to the gym. Have students exchange directions with a classmate. Then pass out copies of a school map. Have students compare the written directions with the map. How do the two sources differ? *(For example: The written directions are more personal; the map gives options of other routes.)* Does the information from each source lead to the same locations? *(yes)* Tell students that when they prepare material for reports, they must first synthesize, or combine, information from several sources. Then have students read the skill and complete the practice questions.

Additional Practice

Skill Reinforcement Activity 20

ANSWERS TO PRACTICING THE SKILL

1. It describes the systematic extermination of Jews in Nazi concentration camps.
2. The map shows the location of Auschwitz-Birkenau and other concentration camps and killing centers.
3. This was happening not only at Auschwitz but also at camps throughout occupied Europe.

JUNE 1941 German forces invade the Soviet Union.

JULY 1941 The Nazis order the mass killing of Europe's Jews.

NOV. 1941 German forces reach the outskirts of Moscow.

DEC. 1941 Japan stages surprise attack on Pearl Harbor; the United States enters World War II.

Section 3

A Global Conflict

Setting the Scene

▶ **Terms to Define**
scorched-earth policy, Holocaust, genocide

▶ **People to Meet**
Isoroku Yamamoto

▶ **Places to Locate**
Moscow, Kiev, Leningrad, Dachau, Warsaw, Auschwitz, Pearl Harbor

Find Out How did the Soviet Union and the United States enter World War II?

The Storyteller

In 1942 a young Jewish woman wrote: "Of course, it is our complete destruction they want! But let us bear it with grace.... And a camp needs a poet, one who experiences life there, even there

... and is able to sing about it.... At night, as I lay in the camp on my plank bed ... I was sometimes filled with an infinite tenderness, and lay awake for hours letting all the many, too many impressions of a much too long day wash over me, and I prayed, 'Let me be the thinking heart of these barracks.' And that is what I want to be again. The thinking heart of a whole concentration camp."

Surviving in a concentration camp

—from *An Interrupted Life, the Diaries of Etty Hillesum, 1941–1943,* translated by Arno Pomerans, 1983

𝒯n the spring of 1941, Great Britain stood alone against Nazi Germany, which now controlled almost all of western Europe. In Africa, the Nazi General Erwin Rommel had succeeded in pushing the British back and had taken control of most of Libya. In Asia, meanwhile, the Japanese held Manchuria and controlled much of China. By the end of 1941, the expansive war would grow even larger. Events since June drew two more major powers into the conflict: the Soviet Union and the United States.

Invasion of the Soviet Union

Having failed in his attempt to defeat Great Britain, Hitler now turned his attention to the Soviet Union. Only by conquering the vast Soviet steppe, Hitler reasoned, could the "living space" believed vital to Germany's future be gained. He also wanted the wheat of Ukraine and the oil reserves of the Caucasus region.

On June 22, 1941, Hitler launched Operation Barbarossa, a massive attack on the Soviet Union. Despite British warnings and the massing of German troops along the border, the invasion took Stalin by surprise. In the first few days of fighting, the Germans destroyed the greater part of the Soviet air force, disabled thousands of Soviet tanks, and captured half a million Soviet soldiers. As German divisions advanced deeper into Soviet territory, Stalin appealed to his people to resist the invasion and issued his famous scorched-earth policy. If the Germans forced Soviet forces to retreat, Stalin ordered, Soviet citizens should destroy everything that could be of use to the invaders.

By November 1941 German armies had pushed 600 miles (960 km) inside the Soviet Union to the outskirts of **Moscow**. In addition to controlling 40 percent of the Soviet population, the Germans had captured **Kiev** and begun the siege of **Leningrad**. Yet the Soviets refused to surrender. Young Soviet

614 Chapter 20 *World War II*

soldiers rallied to the cry, "Behind us is Moscow—there is no room left for retreat!" The Germans faced not only a steely Soviet resistance but another equally formidable foe—the Russian winter. A German soldier described the conditions:

❝ We had no gloves. We had no winter shoes. We had no equipment whatsoever to fight or withstand the cold…. We lost a considerable part of our equipment…. Due to the cold we lost a lot of people who got frost-bitten, and we had not even the necessary amount of ointments, or the most simple and primitive things to fight in…. Guns didn't fire anymore. Even our wireless equipment didn't work properly anymore because the batteries were frozen hard…. ❞

On December 2, 1941, German troops began an assault on Moscow, and in just one day they drew within sight of the city's center. It was as far as they ever got. When all seemed lost, the Soviets staged a counterattack and forced a German retreat.

The Nazi Order

Hitler wanted to conquer the Soviet Union as part of his plan to create a "New Order" in Europe. In the new world that Hitler envisioned, the Nazis would rule Europe and exploit its resources. In addition to enslaving the conquered peoples and forcing them to work for the German "master race," the Nazis would exterminate "undesirable elements" such as the Jews and the Slavs.

The Nazis began to implement Hitler's plan by plundering the occupied countries. They seized art treasures, raw materials, and factory equipment. At the same time, the Nazis drove millions into forced labor and concentration camps and massacred millions more. Between 1939 and 1944, about 7.5 million people were deported to Germany and put to work in factories, fields, and mines. Many people in the occupied countries, however, joined underground resistance movements to combat the Nazis.

The Holocaust

Beginning in 1941, Nazi leaders carried out a plan that aimed at the complete extermination of all Jews in Europe. During the next four years, the

Visualizing History The powerful German panzers were no match for the harsh Soviet winter of 1941. The intense cold froze lubricating oil and cracked engine blocks. *What other problems did the German invaders encounter during that winter?*

Nazis murdered more than 6 million Jews. This mass destruction of the Jewish people based on racial grounds has become known as the Holocaust. Another 6 million people, including the Slavs and Gypsies, also were killed by the Nazis.

Beginnings

In mid-1940, the Nazis began to persecute Jews in the lands they had conquered. They expelled Jews from jobs and schools and forced them to wear yellow badges showing the Star of David, an ancient Jewish symbol. Some Jews managed to flee Nazi-occupied Europe; others went into hiding; but many more failed to escape and were sent to concentration camps, such as **Dachau** (DAH•KOW) in southern Germany.

The largest number of Jews in Nazi-occupied Europe lived in areas of Poland and the Soviet Union. To control this sizable Jewish population, the Nazis at first forced the Jews into specially designated areas of towns and cities called ghettos. The largest ghetto was in **Warsaw**, where almost half a million Jews were kept.

Life in the ghettos was unbearable. Families had to crowd into unsanitary housing, and contagious diseases spread rapidly. The Nazis deliberately tried to starve residents by allowing only small amounts of food. As a result, tens of thousands died in the ghettos from hunger, disease, and the cold. Despite their suffering, many people courageously tried to live as normally as possible. For example, many young people carried out their education by attending secret classes organized and taught by adults.

TEACH

Guided Practice

THEME Conflict

Remind students that World War II began as a European conflict but expanded to become a global conflict by the end of 1941. Have students point out on a map of the world the areas involved in the war by December 8, 1941. **L1 LEP**

Visualizing History Have students review Napoleon's invasion of Russia in the winter of 1812. Remind students that geography often plays a vital role in war. *In what ways did Napoleon and Hitler make the same mistakes? (They underestimated the effects of the Russian winter and the resistance of the Russian people.)*
Answer to Caption: *They were without winter clothing and medical supplies.*

POINT

The Holocaust
Why was the Holocaust a major development in twentieth-century world affairs? *Hitler's murder of 6 million European Jews is an example of genocide. It reflected the extent to which totalitarian governments violated human rights in pursuing their ideological goals.*

 VIDEODISC
Turning Points in World History

 Side Two
Chapter 6

Title: *The Holocaust*

COOPERATIVE LEARNING ACTIVITY

Panel Discussion Assign small groups of students to research one of the following topics: *Kristallnacht*; the Warsaw ghetto; German use of slave labor; artworks and gold stolen by Germany from occupied countries. Have each group present a panel discussion based on their research. After all panels have been presented, have the class discuss how Hitler's "New Order" was carried out through these various activities. **L2**

Linking Past and Present

Genocide Since World War II, the German people have accepted collective responsibility for the campaign of genocide carried out by the Nazis. In 1996 Germany's head of state, President Roman Herzog, proclaimed January 27 a national day of commemoration for the victims of National Socialism. That day is the anniversary of the liberation of the Auschwitz concentration camp.

Political Policies Have students compare the goals and methods of Hitler's "New Order" with Japan's plans to create an "Asia for Asiatics." **L2**

Let Us Never Forget

Controversy surrounded some of the exhibits in the Holocaust Memorial Museum. Jews and non-Jews, concentration camp survivors, and others, all agreed on the need for a museum that accurately portrayed the horrors of the Holocaust. Such items as actual collections of the shoes, teeth, and hair taken from prisoners were, however, deeply disturbing to some visitors. A few compromises were made, but the museum stands as a truthful account of millions of people who will not be forgotten.

ANSWERS
They created artwork as an outlet for some of their pain; in books, artwork, movies, and memorials.

The Killing Squads

The German invasion of the Soviet Union in June 1941, proved to be a turning point in the Nazi mistreatment of the Jews. At that time, the Nazis turned from the forced emigration and imprisonment of Jews to the mass murder of them. Special units of Nazi soldiers known as the SS moving with the German army acted quickly to kill any Jews they could find in occupied Soviet territory. Captured Jews had to surrender their valuables and were forcibly marched to open areas on the outskirts of captured towns and cities. There they were shot, and their bodies dumped into mass graves. The killing squads murdered more than a million Jews and hundreds of thousands of other innocent people. At Babi Yar, near Kiev in Ukraine, about 35,000 Jews were murdered in two days of shooting.

The Final Solution

In January 1942, Nazi party and German government leaders secretly agreed to what they called "the final solution to the Jewish question in Europe." The "final solution" was the Nazi code word for the destruction of all European Jews. Never before had a modern state set out on a campaign of genocide, the deliberate, carefully planned killing of an entire people on the basis of race, politics, or culture.

Beginning in the summer of 1942, the Nazis arrested and rounded up Jews throughout occupied Europe by the hundreds of thousands. The Jews then were transported by train or trucks to death camps, such as **Auschwitz** (AUSH•VIHTS) in Poland, where most eventually died. Many of the people in the camps were murdered in poison gas chambers. Others died of starvation or were the victims of cruel experiments carried out by Nazi doctors.

Response and Resistance

The Nazis tried to keep the killings and death camps secret from the world. Even European Jews at first had been unaware of the fate in store for them. But once they became aware of Nazi intentions, Jews fought back in Warsaw and other European ghettos. However, Jewish resistance groups in the ghettos were outnumbered and lacked the arms to fight the Germans. In spite of their heroic efforts, Jewish resistors were easily defeated.

Some Jews who succeeded in escaping from the ghettos formed fighting units in densely forested areas of eastern Europe. Others joined regular

Let Us Never Forget

From 1941 to 1945, Jewish artists, musicians, and writers in the Theresienstadt concentration camp created moving artistic expressions of their Holocaust experiences. Since World War II, their works—and those of others—have stirred hearts and consciences of people everywhere about one of the most horrifying events of our century.

In his memoir called *Night* (1958), the Romanian-born writer Elie Wiesel (vee•ZEHL), a Holocaust survivor, described the horrors he witnessed in the Auschwitz and Buchenwald camps. Another writer, the Australian Thomas Keneally, in his 1982 novel

Concentration camp survivors

Schindler's List, tells a powerful true story about Oskar Schindler, a German manufacturer who saved his Jewish workers from the Holocaust. The American filmmaker Steven Spielberg later turned Keneally's novel into an Oscar Award-winning movie in 1993.

Another 1993 event relating to the Holocaust was the opening of the United States Holocaust Memorial Museum in Washington, D.C. Through exhibits, videos, and special lectures, the museum commemorates the millions of Jews and others murdered by the Nazis during World War II.

ACTIVITY

Explain how people in the Theresienstadt concentration camp tried to cope with their ordeal. How has the Holocaust been artistically commemorated since World War II?

CRITICAL THINKING ACTIVITY

Identifying Alternatives Remind students that Churchill and Roosevelt feared that Stalin would impose Communist governments on the countries liberated by the Soviets from German control. Have students research the events in East Germany, Poland, Hungary, Czechoslovakia, Romania, Bulgaria, and Yugoslavia from 1945 to 1950. Encourage them to discuss other ways the fate of Eastern Europe might have been handled at the Yalta Conference. **L3**

Visualizing History When the Nazis advanced throughout Europe in 1939 and 1940, they rounded up Jews—such as these residents of Warsaw, Poland—and forced them to work as slave laborers. Later, the Nazis killed or imprisoned millions of Jews. *How did the Allies react to the Nazi persecution and killing of Europe's Jews?*

Allied forces fighting the Nazis. One Jewish resistance fighter was Hannah Senesh, a Hungarian Jew who had emigrated to Palestine in 1939. Allied forces dropped her and other parachutists into German-controlled Hungary to organize resistance efforts. Before she could accomplish her mission, she was captured and executed.

A major factor hindering Jewish resistance both in the ghettos and the forests was the widespread lack of support for the Jews. Anti-Semitic Europeans in occupied areas helped the Nazis hunt down Jews, and pro-Nazi governments, such as those of France, Italy, and Hungary, sent tens of thousands of Jews to the death camps. Even banks in neutral Switzerland accepted and profited from the money and valuables stolen from Jews by the Nazis. Even as late as the 1990s, much of this wealth had yet to be returned to the families of the rightful owners.

Most people in occupied areas, however, did nothing, thinking that the plight of the Jews did not concern them or fearing punishment if they got involved. Despite dangers, a small number of courageous people did provide help to the Jews and other persecuted people. Denmark, alone among the occupied countries, actively resisted the Nazi regime's efforts to remove its Jewish citizens.

During the Holocaust, evidence reached the outside world about the Nazi mistreatment of Jews and other groups. However, little action was taken.

Allied governments believed that fighting the war and defeating the Nazis was the only way they could help those suffering from Nazi injustices. The full horror of the Holocaust was not realized until Allied forces had liberated the concentration camps and death camps in 1945.

Japanese Expansion

After seizing much of China in the 1930s, Japan shifted its attention to the European colonies in East and Southeast Asia and their stores of raw materials. Taking advantage of Hitler's offensive in Europe, the Japanese acquired many of these territories. The collapse of France and the Low Countries left French Indochina and the Dutch East Indies virtually defenseless. And when the Germans threatened to invade Great Britain, the British withdrew their fleet from Singapore, leaving that colony open to attack as well.

In July 1940 the Japanese government announced its plan to create a "new order in greater East Asia." Proclaiming "Asia for the Asiatics," Japan moved to establish the "Greater East Asia Co-prosperity Sphere," an appeal to Asians who wanted to rid their lands of European rule. First, it asked France for the right to build airfields and station troops in northern Indochina. After gaining this foothold, Japan invaded southern Indochina.

Chapter 20 *World War II* **617**

Visualizing History In October 1940 the Nazis forced all 400,000 of Warsaw's Jews to move into a walled, 1-square-mile (2.6-square-kilometer) area known as the Warsaw Ghetto. Warsaw's Jews resisted the Nazis, but more than 300,000 died in the ghetto or were deported to Nazi labor or death camps. On April 18, 1943, Nazi forces blew up the ghetto's synagogue, killing 14,000 people. The remaining 42,000 Jews were sent to labor camps.
Answer to Caption: *Rumors of Nazi atrocities had reached the Allies, but little action was taken on behalf of the Jews. Many governments did not believe the rumors and devoted their main attention to winning the war.*

History Simulation 20

Biography

The following videotape program is available from Glencoe:
• **FDR: The War Years**

Independent Practice
Guided Reading Activity 20-3 **L1**

NATIONAL GEOGRAPHIC PICTURING HISTORY

National Archives

TEACH

Tell students that on February 19, 1942, President Roosevelt signed Executive Order 9066, which authorized the War Department to move 112,000 Japanese American men, women, and children from the West Coast to crude internment camps farther inland. These Americans lost their constitutional rights, property, businesses, and homes. Despite this policy, Japanese Americans remained loyal to the United States. None was ever brought to trial for espionage or sabotage. **Why do you think Roosevelt signed this order?**

Linking Past and Present

Reparations Not until 1988 did the U.S. government acknowledge the wrong done to Japanese Americans during World War II. That year, President Ronald Reagan signed a bill that gave surviving internees a formal apology and reparations for their suffering during internment.

ABCNEWS INTERACTIVE™

VIDEODISC
Lessons of War

Side Two, Chapter 8
Frames 25814–28652
Title: *At the Front*
Subject: Contributions of minorities in World War II
Ask: How did the Japanese American 442nd Regimental Combat Team of World War II prove themselves during the war? *(This regiment was even more successful than the other units.)*

Japanese Americans

During World War II Japanese Americans were feared and hated by many other Americans, especially those living on the West Coast. In Oakland, California, the Japanese American owner of this small store—in an attempt to prevent its burning or looting—put up a sign asserting his loyalty: "I am an American." This very American scene emphasizes the cruelty of persecuting Japanese American businessmen. After the Japanese bombed Pearl Harbor, U.S. politicians spoke with fiery rhetoric, and newspapers ran hate stories that fanned the fear and antagonism against Japanese Americans.

This campaign of hate was a symptom of the brutality of the war in the Pacific. Both sides, Japanese and American, found it necessary to demonize the enemy so that their own soldiers could fight a long and hard war, and their own civilian populations could fully support their country's war effort, despite wartime shortages, extra-long working hours, or family members killed in the war. ⊕

MORE ABOUT...

Japanese American Soldiers The 442nd Regimental Combat Team, a Japanese American unit, helped the Allies win control of Italy. Altogether, almost 26,000 Japanese Americans fought for the United States during World War II.

The United States retaliated by placing an embargo, or ban, on the sale of scrap iron to Japan. In response, Japan signed the Tripartite Pact with Germany and Italy on September 27, 1940. Under this pact, the three powers affirmed the right of every nation to "receive the space to which it is entitled" and pledged to cooperate to reach that goal as well as to come to one another's aid if attacked.

Pearl Harbor

When the Japanese invaded southern Indochina on July 24, 1941, President Roosevelt demanded that they withdraw—not only from Indochina but also from China. To back up his demands, Congress placed an embargo on oil and froze all Japanese assets in the United States. Negotiations with the Japanese government continued during the summer and fall.

Japan decided to go to war with the United States because it believed the United States stood in the way of its plans for expansion in the East. To defeat American military forces, however, Japanese leaders knew they had to destroy the American Pacific fleet based at **Pearl Harbor** in Hawaii. Although most American and Japanese leaders believed that Pearl Harbor was safe from attack, Admiral **Isoroku Yamamoto**, the commander of the Japanese navy, did not agree. He convinced Japanese leaders that bombers taking off from aircraft carriers and equipped with newly designed torpedoes for use in shallow water could effect a successful surprise attack on Pearl Harbor. In November 1941 Yamamoto's plan was put into effect, and the Japanese fleet set sail for Hawaii.

Meanwhile, negotiations between the United States and Japan had broken down. By now Roosevelt knew that the Japanese were "poised for attack," but was convinced that Japan's move would be in Southeast Asia. As a precaution, United States military leaders sent all aircraft carriers and half the army's planes from Pearl Harbor.

On the morning of December 7, the Japanese attack squadron took off from their carrier decks and began the attack on Pearl Harbor. Within the first 25 minutes of the attack, they sank or damaged the battleships *Arizona, Utah, Oklahoma, West Virginia,* and *California*. The Japanese success was even greater than they had hoped. In all, they sank or disabled 19 American ships and destroyed 188 airplanes. They also killed more than 2,400 people and wounded 1,100. Fortunately for the United States, its aircraft carriers were at sea and escaped the attack. Calling December 7 "a date which will live in infamy," President Roosevelt, in an appearance before Congress the next day, asked for and received a declaration of war against Japan.

The Allies

The United States was now officially at war. On December 11, 1941, Germany and Italy honored their pledge to Japan in the Tripartite Pact by declaring war on the United States. Great Britain, backing the United States, declared war on Japan.

Although mistrust still lingered between the Western democracies and the Soviet Union, they put aside their differences in their resolve to defeat their common enemy. Meanwhile, the fighting in the Soviet Union remained fierce. Vast areas of the country were under German occupation. The Germans had completely surrounded Leningrad, trapping 3 million people. Within two years, nearly 1 million of its people died from cold, hunger, and starvation.

Stalin urged the Allies to open a "second front" in Europe as quickly as possible. Although President Roosevelt favored a second front, Winston Churchill was opposed to it. He knew that Great Britain would have to bear the brunt of any second-front operation. Consequently, the two Allied leaders postponed plans for an invasion of Europe. Instead, they laid plans for military campaigns in North Africa and the Mediterranean area.

SECTION 3 REVIEW

Recall

1. **Define** scorched-earth policy, Holocaust, genocide.
2. **Identify** Isoroku Yamamoto.
3. **Explain** Adolf Hitler's reasons for attacking the Soviet Union

in June 1941.

Critical Thinking

4. **Analyzing Information** How did the "New Order" that Germany's Adolf Hitler wanted to create in Europe affect differ-

ent groups of people living on that continent?

Understanding Themes

5. **Conflict** How did World War II turn into a large-scale global conflict?

Chapter 20   *World War II*   **619**

SECTION 3 REVIEW ANSWERS

1. All vocabulary words are defined in the Glossary.
2. Isoroku Yamamoto, 619
3. Hitler wanted "living space" for Germany as well as the Soviet Union's farmland and oil deposits.
4. Hitler's "New Order" exploited the

resources of the conquered countries and enslaved or exterminated the conquered people.

5. **CONFLICT** Germany invaded the Soviet Union and Japan attacked Pearl Harbor, causing the United States to enter the war.

Pearl Harbor
How did Pearl Harbor change the course of World War II?
The Japanese attack brought the United States, with its powerful military potential, into World War II.

ASSESS

Check for Understanding

Assign Section 3 Review as homework or as an in-class activity.

⊙ Use Student Self-Test and Review Software to review Section 3.

Evaluate

🗀 Section Quiz 20-3

⊙ Use the Testmaker to create a customized quiz for Section 3.

Reteach

Have students summarize the events that brought the Soviet Union and the United States into World War II.

Enrich

Have students research the raw materials Japan gained by invading French Indochina and the Dutch East Indies.

CLOSE

Have students discuss how the entry of the Soviet Union and the United States into the war changed the balance of forces between the Allies and the Axis.

1941	1942	1943

MAY 1941 British naval forces sink German battleship *Bismarck*.

October 1942 British halt German advance in North Africa at El Alamein, Egypt.

FEB. 1943 German forces at Stalingrad surrender to the Soviets.

Section 4

Turning Points

SECTION THEME

▶ **Conflict** The Allies make major gains against the Axis powers.

Find Out

Answer: *The Soviet victory at Stalingrad, the German surrender in North Africa, the Allied invasion of Italy, and the American victories in the Pacific turned the tide of the war.*

FOCUS

Section Objective

Explain how the tide of war turned in favor of the Allies during 1942 and 1943.

**BELLRINGER
Motivational Activity**

Before taking roll at the beginning of the class period, project Section Focus Transparency 20-4 and have students answer the activity questions. Discuss students' responses. ◤ This activity is also available as a blackline master.

Vocabulary Pre-check

◤ Use Vocabulary Activity 20 to introduce vocabulary terms.
L1 LEP

Setting the Scene

▶ **Terms to Define**
kamikaze

▶ **People to Meet**
Erwin Rommel, Bernard Montgomery, Dwight D. Eisenhower, Douglas MacArthur, Chester W. Nimitz

▶ **Places to Locate**
Stalingrad, Casablanca, Sicily, Guadalcanal

 **Find Out** How did the tide of war turn in favor of the Allies during 1942 and 1943?

ℭ*The* Storyteller

A kamikaze attack on an American aircraft carrier, the Hornet, *was recorded in photographs and by eyewitness accounts such as this one: "His [plane] already with flame blossoming on its underside, appeared high above the* Hornet's *starboard quarter. Perhaps dead or dying, [the pilot] did not release his bomb but kept coming directly at the carrier. He did not miss.... Ruptured fuel tanks sprayed the signal bridge with burning gasoline, while the wrecked airplane smashed into the flight deck...." The impact and burning fuel killed and maimed many men, and fires blazed for two hours.*

—adapted from *The First Team and the Guadalcanal Campaign*, John B. Lundstrom, 1994

Japanese kamikaze pilot

In the early months of 1942, the war was going badly for the Allies. By destroying much of the American fleet at Pearl Harbor, Japan had gained control of the Pacific Ocean and cleared the way for a seaborne invasion of American, British, and Dutch territories in that region. In December 1941 Japanese forces had captured the British colony of Hong Kong and invaded the Malay Peninsula. In the West, meanwhile, Rommel controlled a large area of North Africa, and German forces held the upper hand in the Soviet Union as well.

Despite these successes, the Axis powers would never again enjoy such a strong position. By the end of 1942, the tide of the war had begun to turn in favor of the Allies.

Sea and Air Battles

Even before the United States entered the war, it was shipping food and war supplies to Britain under the Lend-Lease Act. But German submarines, or U-boats, threatened this vital lifeline across the Atlantic. By the end of 1939, U-boats had already sunk 114 Allied and neutral ships. German air attacks also took their toll.

To make matters worse for the Allies, the new German battleship *Bismarck*, accompanied by the new cruiser *Prinz Eugen*, entered the fight in May 1941. With 11 Allied convoys either at sea or about to sail, the British hastily dispatched several ships to intercept the Nazis. On May 23 they sighted the two German ships in the Denmark Strait between Iceland and Greenland and opened fire. In the battle that followed, the *Bismarck* sank the British battle cruiser *Hood* and damaged a new British battleship before slipping away to safety.

Three days later, on May 26, a British patrol plane spotted the *Bismarck* about 600 miles (965 km) off the French coast. In the battle that followed, the *Bismarck* sustained at least eight

620 Chapter 20 *World War II*

SECTION RESOURCES

◤ **Reproducible Masters**
• Reproducible Lesson Plan 20-4
• Vocabulary Activity 20
• Guided Reading Activity 20-4
• Geography and History Activity 20
• Section Quiz 20-4

Transparencies
• Section Focus Transparency 20-4
• Mapping History Overlay Transparency 20, *Southeast Asia Prior to World War II*

Multimedia
▣ Student Self-Test and Review Software
▣ Testmaker
▣ Lessons of War: *Can a Battle Change History?*

torpedo hits before it finally sank. With this crucial victory, the British put an end to German efforts to win the Battle of the Atlantic with surface ships. Gradually, the Allies devised new methods for protecting their convoys against U-boats as well.

As they fought for control of the Atlantic, the Allies carried out an air offensive against Germany. These attacks were directed at factories, railroads, dockyards, and cities and towns. Their purpose was to destroy German war industries and weaken the will of the civilian population to continue the war.

Stalingrad

In July 1942 the military situation in the Soviet Union looked desperate. With the Soviet army in full retreat, the Germans were approaching **Stalingrad**, a major industrial center on the Volga River. In angry exchanges with Churchill, Stalin continued to press for a second front in the West to take some of the military pressure off his nation. But in August Churchill went to Moscow to tell Stalin that there would be no second front in 1942.

On August 22 the Germans attacked Stalingrad. Because it was named after Stalin, losing the city would have been a blow to Soviet morale. As determined to protect Stalingrad as Hitler was to take it, Stalin ordered that the city be held at all costs.

The Soviets launched a counterattack in September and encircled the German troops threatening the city. They cut off German supply lines. Although the Soviets and the frigid winter weather were closing in on the Germans, Hitler refused to allow his troops to retreat. By the time German officers finally surrendered in February 1943, the German army had lost the best of its troops. Many historians now view the Soviet victory at Stalingrad as the major turning point of World War II. By killing about 100,000 German soldiers, capturing 80,000 more, and seizing large quantities of German military equipment, the Soviet Union broke the back of the Nazi military machine.

War in the Desert

In January 1942 Allied forces in North Africa were struggling to regain ground lost to the Germans. They faced a formidable foe. **Erwin Rommel,** commander of the Afrika Korps, applied blitzkrieg tactics to warfare in the desert. His exploits earned him the nickname "the Desert Fox."

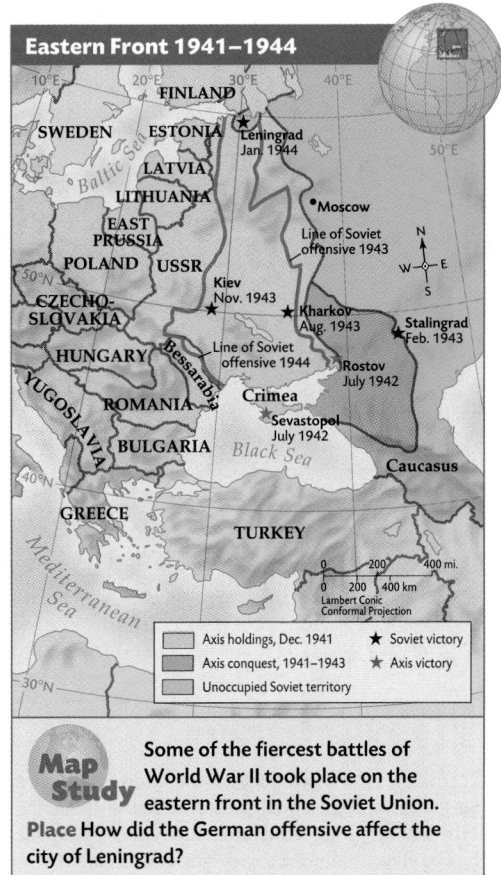

Eastern Front 1941–1944

Map Study Some of the fiercest battles of World War II took place on the eastern front in the Soviet Union. **Place** How did the German offensive affect the city of Leningrad?

In the spring of 1942, Rommel pushed the British two-thirds of the way back to the Egyptian frontier. He struck again at the end of May, but the British, under General **Bernard Montgomery**, stopped him two months later at El Alamein (EL A•luh•MAYN), a railway junction about 70 miles (112 km) from Alexandria. In October Montgomery launched a counterattack that forced the Germans back across the Egyptian-Libyan frontier and ended with the British capture of Tripoli, the capital of Libya, in January 1943.

As Montgomery was advancing westward, the Allies were landing troops in Morocco and Algeria as part of a planned offensive against Rommel. By advancing from the east and from the west, the Allies hoped to trap Rommel with their "pincers" strategy. But the Allied landings met with heavy resistance from the Vichy French, who governed French North Africa. To end the fighting, Allied commander **Dwight D. Eisenhower** struck a deal with Admiral François Darlan, a Vichy official. In

Chapter 20 *World War II* **621**

TEACH

Guided Practice

THEME Conflict

List the following events on the chalkboard: the sinking of the *Bismarck*; victory at Stalingrad; the battle of El Alamein in North Africa; the invasion of Sicily; the capture of Malaya, Singapore, Burma, Dutch East Indies, Guam, Wake Island, and the Philippines; Battles of the Coral Sea, Midway, and Guadalcanal. Have students identify the combatants and the victors of each event. **L1 LEP**

Map Study

Answer

It was surrounded by German forces who laid siege to the city. Within two years, about 1 million people died from cold, starvation, and disease.

POINT

Stalingrad
Why was Stalingrad a major turning point in World War II? *The Battle of Stalingrad put the Germans on the defensive on the Eastern Front and marked the beginning of the turning of the tide in favor of the Allies.*

Mapping History Overlay Transparency 20, *Southeast Asia Prior to World War II*

Independent Practice

Guided Reading Activity 20-4 **L1**

Geography and History Activity 20

COOPERATIVE LEARNING ACTIVITY

Biographies Organize the class into two groups. Have one group use outside sources to prepare a biography of Franklin Roosevelt, and the other group to do the same for Winston Churchill. Tell students to focus on how each man developed the qualities he needed to serve as a wartime leader. Students should examine factors such as education, military experience, personality traits, charisma, oratory skills, and ideals. Have both groups present their reports and then have them draw up a list of leadership qualities shared by FDR and Churchill. **L2**

Map Study

Answer

The Allies invaded Italy from Tunisia because it was the closest point to Italy.

Map Skills Practice

Reading a Map Where in North Africa did the Allies win victories in 1943? *(Tripoli, Kasserine Pass, Tunis, Bizerte)*

VIDEODISC
Lessons of War

Side One, Chapter 6
Title: *Can a Battle Change History?*
Subject: The Battle of Midway
Ask: Why was the Battle of Midway considered a turning point in World War II history? *(Stopping Japan at Midway changed the direction of the war.)*

Biography

The following videotape programs are available from Glencoe:

• **General Douglas MacArthur: Return of a Legend**

• **Dwight D. Eisenhower: Commander-in-Chief**

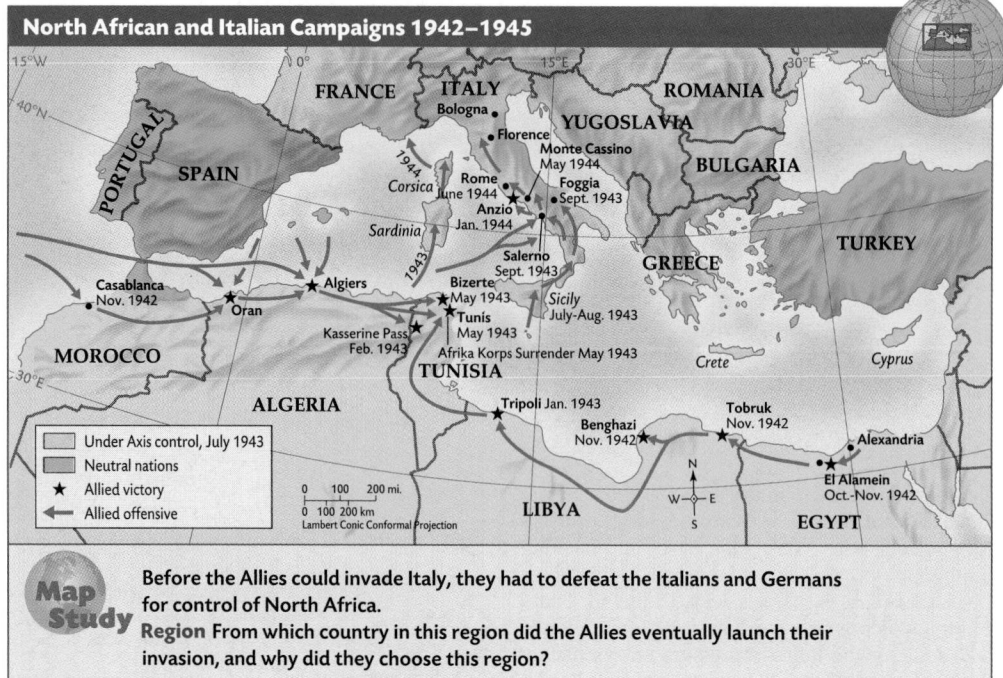

North African and Italian Campaigns 1942–1945

Map Study

Before the Allies could invade Italy, they had to defeat the Italians and Germans for control of North Africa.

Region From which country in this region did the Allies eventually launch their invasion, and why did they choose this region?

---

return for Allied support of his claim to French North Africa, Darlan ordered an end to the resistance. With the armistice concluded in November 1942, the Free French, under Charles de Gaulle, joined the Allies in Africa. Meanwhile, in a series of powerful attacks, the Allies began closing the pincers. When Rommel flew to Berlin to tell Hitler that the situation was hopeless, the Nazi dictator rejected his general's assessment and barred Rommel from returning to Africa. But Rommel was right. In May 1943, General von Arnim, the new commander of the German forces in Tunisia, surrendered. The Allies now controlled all of North Africa.

Invasion of Italy

In early 1943, the American and British chiefs of staff and political leaders met at **Casablanca** in Morocco to discuss their next move. Because they wanted to secure communications in the Mediterranean and intensify the pressure on Italy, they decided to invade **Sicily**, the large island near the southern tip of the Italian Peninsula.

Under the command of General Eisenhower, the Allies began a combined air and sea attack on **Sicily** in July 1943. The seaborne landings met little

resistance at first, but when the Allies approached Messina, on the extreme northeastern tip of the island, the Germans put up a stronger fight to cover their withdrawal across the Strait of Messina. In six days nearly 40,000 German and 70,000 Italian troops escaped to Italy.

The conquest of Sicily led quickly to Mussolini's downfall. On July 25, King Victor Emmanuel III, pressed into action by antiwar factions, fired Mussolini and had him arrested. The new prime minister, Marshal Pietro Badoglio, soon dissolved the Fascist party and on September 3 signed a secret act of surrender.

That same day, Allied forces crossed the Strait of Messina and landed in Calabria on the Italian mainland. The broadcast announcement of Badoglio's unconditional surrender caught the Germans by surprise, but they recovered in time to occupy Rome two days later, forcing the king and Badoglio to withdraw to the south. The Germans later rescued Mussolini and put him in control of northern Italy.

For the remaining months of 1943 and early months of 1944, the Allies fought their way up the Italian Peninsula. Allied troops could not penetrate the German defenses at Monte Cassino, a sixth-century monastery located on a mountaintop that dominated the road to Rome. In the end it took a

---

MEETING SPECIAL NEEDS ACTIVITY

Learning Style: Kinesthetic Have students who are kinesthetic learners create a "war map" showing one of the following conflicts of the war: the Soviet offensive, the war in the desert, the invasion of Italy, or the war in the Pacific. Tell students to re-create the area of conflict and then illustrate how the Allied forces took the offensive and achieved victory. Suggest that they use markers, flags, or pictures to illustrate the actions in the conflict. Display completed maps in the classroom and encourage students to explain their maps. **L2 LEP**

massive artillery bombardment and almost five months for the Allies to dislodge the Germans in May 1944. One month later, on June 4, Allied forces entered Rome.

Pacific War

While war raged in Europe, Japan took over much of Southeast Asia and the Pacific. At first welcomed as liberators, the Japanese soon were hated by local peoples for their killing of civilians and taking of property. Resistance groups arose to fight Japanese forces.

Meanwhile, the Allies were able to make some gains. In May 1942, in the Battle of the Coral Sea, the Allies claimed a victory. And in June, at the Battle of Midway, the Americans defeated the Japanese navy and ended Japanese naval superiority in the Pacific.

Japanese Empire 1910–1945

USSR
MONGOLIA
Manchukuo
KOREA   JAPAN
CHINA   Hiroshima
HONG KONG
BURMA   Okinawa
TAIWAN   Iwo Jima
FRENCH INDOCHINA   PHILIPPINES
THAILAND
MALAYSIA
DUTCH EAST INDIES
INDIAN OCEAN
Sakhalin
Kuril Island
Attu
Aleutian Islands
PACIFIC OCEAN
Midway Islands
Hawaiian Islands
Mariana Islands
Guam
Marshall Islands
Caroline Islands
Coral Sea
Solomon Islands
Gilbert Islands
AUSTRALIA

Area held by Japan in 1910
To 1931
To 1941
To 1942
Anglo-American advances, 1943–1945
Soviet advances, 1945
★ Allied victory

0   500   1,000 mi.
0   500 1,800 km
Mercator Projection

Map Study
Between 1931 and 1942, Japan took over large areas of East Asia, Southeast Asia, and the Pacific.
Region Why were the Japanese able to seize the European colonies in this region so easily in 1941 and 1942?

To follow up this victory, the Americans launched an attack against the Pacific island of **Guadalcanal** in early August. While troops under General **Douglas MacArthur** attacked the Japanese on land, naval forces under Admiral **Chester W. Nimitz** confronted them at sea. The six-month land, sea, and air battle for control of the island ended in victory for the Allies. Guadalcanal was the first in a series of island battles the Americans fought as they leapfrogged their way north to Japan. Their strategy was to capture some

islands and bypass others. Those bypassed would be cut off from supplies and made to "wither on the vine."

After Guadalcanal, the Americans paused to build up their Pacific forces. When the American advance resumed in November 1943, Japanese leaders called upon their soldiers to die for their homeland. Japanese pilots known as **kamikazes** volunteered for suicide missions, crashing their bomb-laden aircraft into Allied bases and ships. The Japanese were far from ready to surrender.

SECTION 4 REVIEW

Recall
1. **Define** kamikaze.
2. **Identify** Erwin Rommel, Bernard Montgomery, Dwight D. Eisenhower, Douglas MacArthur, Chester W. Nimitz.
3. **Locate** Stalingrad on the map

on page 619. Why was the Battle of Stalingrad a major turning point in World War II?
Critical Thinking
4. **Synthesizing Information** How did Hitler's decisions contribute to Germany's defeats in

both Stalingrad and North Africa?
Understanding Themes
5. **Conflict** Why did the Allies decide to "leapfrog" their way to Japan rather than launch a direct attack?

SECTION 4 REVIEW ANSWERS

1. The word is defined in the Glossary.
2. Erwin Rommel, 621; Bernard Montgomery, 621; Dwight D. Eisenhower, 621; Douglas MacArthur, 623; Chester W. Nimitz, 623
3. In the Battle of Stalingrad, the best of the German army was destroyed.
4. Hitler refused to allow the German forces

to withdraw from Stalingrad and refused to end the North African campaign even after it had become hopeless.
5. **CONFLICT** By capturing some islands and leapfrogging over others, the Allies hoped to cut off supplies to the bypassed islands, forcing them to surrender.

Map Study

Answer
The European powers were preoccupied with Hitler.

ASSESS

Check for Understanding
Assign Section 4 Review as homework or as an in-class activity.

🖲 Use Student Self-Test and Review Software to review Section 4.

Evaluate
📁 Section Quiz 20-4

🖲 Use the Testmaker to create a customized quiz for Section 4.

Reteach
Using a large wall map, have students show Allied progress in the Atlantic, Soviet Union, North Africa, Italy, and the Pacific in 1942–1943.

Enrich
Have students watch the film *North Star* (also called *Armored Attack*), made in 1943, which shows the German invasion of the Soviet Union. Have students write a short essay describing the attitude toward the Soviet Union reflected in the film.

CLOSE

Organize the class into two groups. Have each group make a list in chronological order of ten key events from this section. Combine the two lists into one top-ten list.

SECTION THEME

▶ **Innovation** New military technologies, such as the atomic bomb, affect the outcome of World War II.

ind Out

Answer: *The use of the atomic bomb, developed secretly by the United States, quickly ended the war.*

FOCUS

Section Objective

Understand how new technology affected the conduct and outcome of World War II.

BELLRINGER
Motivational Activity

Project Section Focus Transparency 20-5 and have students answer the activity questions.
This activity is also available as a blackline master.

Vocabulary Pre-check

◉ Use the Vocabulary PuzzleMaker to create a puzzle to reinforce vocabulary. **L1**

TURNING POINT

D-Day
How did D-Day affect the Allied cause in World War II?
It opened the Western front in the war, giving the Western Allies a beachhead against the Nazis on the European mainland.

JUNE 1944	DEC. 1944	JUNE 1945	DEC. 1945

JUNE 6, 1944 (D-Day) Allies land in Normandy.

DEC. 16, 1944 Battle of the Bulge begins.

MAY 8, 9, 1945 V-E (Victory in Europe) Day celebrated in Allied countries.

AUG. 6, 1945 The United States drops atomic bomb on Hiroshima, Japan.

Section 5

Allied Victories

Setting the Scene

▶ **Terms to Define**
D-Day, partisan

▶ **People to Meet**
George Patton, Harry S Truman, Clement Attlee

▶ **Places to Locate**
Rhine River, Berlin, Yalta, Potsdam, Hiroshima, Nagasaki

 **ind Out** How did new technology affect the conduct and outcome of World War II?

The Storyteller

An American woman, living in Russia, later recalled how hope for Allied rescue was everywhere in Russia during the spring of 1944:

"They knew it must come this summer, for the war was already in Europe.... On a day in early June the air was split by a radio announcement: 'Stand by for a special broadcast at 1:45.' We knew what it would be. Everybody knew. 'Today, June 6, 1944, early in the morning, General Eisenhower's forces began landing operations on the northern coast of France.'" The long-awaited second front was a reality. People laughed and slapped each other on the back.

—adapted from *Fifty Russian Winters, An American Woman's Life in the Soviet Union*, Margaret Wettlin, 1992

American troops land in Normandy

To fight the Axis, Allied democracies geared their economies for war production, rationed goods, and regulated prices and wages. The wartime emergency limited citizens' rights, but unemployment ended as factories turned out weapons and supplies. With men joining the military, women in large numbers entered industry and served in supporting roles in the armed forces. Outside of the democracies, women supported the Allied cause by fighting in the resistance forces of occupied Europe; in the Soviet Union, they saw combat as ground soldiers and pilots.

TURNING POINT

D-Day

At a 1943 conference in Tehran, Iran, Roosevelt and Churchill told Stalin about their plan to open a second front the following spring. Meanwhile, General Eisenhower assembled a force of 176,000 soldiers, 600 warships, and 10,000 aircraft in England for Operation Overlord, the invasion of France. On June 6, 1944, D-Day, or the day of attack, convoys carrying troops and equipment sailed across the English Channel to the French province of Normandy. British bombers attacked German coastal defenses, and Allied airborne troops parachuted into France to assist the invasion. As battleship guns pounded German positions, Allied soldiers moved from their landing craft onto the beaches, fighting their way forward amid German machine-gun fire.

Despite the battle's confusion and the heavy German resistance, the invasion was a success. From their Normandy foothold, the Allies launched an offensive against the Germans. By early August, American tank commander General **George Patton** and his forces were racing across northern France. At the same time, in Paris, French resistance fighters rose up against the occupying Germans.

SECTION RESOURCES

▶ **Reproducible Masters**
• Reproducible Lesson Plan 20-5
• Guided Reading Activity 20-5
• Reteaching Activity 20
• Enrichment Activity 20
• Section Quiz 20-5
• Performance Assessment Activity 20
• Spanish Chapter Summary 20

Transparencies
• Section Focus Transparency 20-5
• Mapping History Overlay Transparency 21, *Battle Sites in the Pacific*
• World History and Art Transparency 42, *The Red Stairway*

Multimedia
◉ Vocabulary PuzzleMaker Software
◉ Student Self-Test and Review Software
◉ Testmaker
◉ Turning Points in World History

Allied Offensive in Europe June 1944–May 1945

Legend:
→ Allied offensive
← German offensive
Land held by Allies, Sept. 1944
Land held by Allies, Jan. 1945
Land held by Allies, May 1945
Land held by Germans, May 1945

NORWAY
FINLAND
SWEDEN
ESTONIA
LATVIA
LITHUANIA
IRELAND
North Sea
Baltic Sea
GREAT BRITAIN
DENMARK
Antwerp Sept. 4
Bremen Apr. 26
Hamburg May 3
Rouen Aug. 30
Brussels Sept. 3
GERMANY
Berlin Apr. 22–May 2
D-Day June 6
Cologne Mar. 7
Torgau Apr. 25
POLAND
Brest Sept. 18
Battle of the Bulge Dec. 16–Jan. 16
Paris Aug. 25
Nuremberg Apr. 20
Metz Nov. 22
CZECHOSLOVAKIA
ATLANTIC OCEAN
Orléans Aug. 16
SWITZER-LAND
Munich Apr. 30
Vienna Apr. 13
Budapest Feb. 13
FRANCE
AUSTRIA
HUNGARY
ROMANIA
PORTUGAL
SPAIN
Corsica
ITALY
Adriatic Sea
YUGOSLAVIA
Black Sea
BULGARIA
ALBANIA
Spanish Morocco
Sardinia
Sicily
GREECE
TURKEY
Mediterranean Sea
Crete

0   150   300 mi.
0   150   300 km
Lambert Conic Conformal Projection

Map Study From D-Day in June 1944 to its surrender in May 1945, Germany was in full retreat on both the western and eastern fronts.
Location Where did the one German offensive occur during this period?

Pressured on all sides, German forces retreated, and on August 25, Allied troops, led by Free French forces, entered Paris.

Victory Over Germany

Months before D-Day, Soviet forces advanced steadily toward Germany from the east. By the summer of 1944, they had pushed the Germans out of Soviet territory and were moving into eastern Europe. Despite the Allied gains, Hitler was convinced that a surprise offensive in the west might still

reverse the Allied advance. In December 1944, the Germans cut through the center of the American forces, creating a bulge in the Allied line of troops. The Allies finally checked the German drive at Bastogne, Belgium, and in March 1945, stormed across the **Rhine River**, Germany's historic defense barrier. By this time, Germany's cities had undergone repeated Allied air attacks, which destroyed industrial centers and killed hundreds of thousands of people.

Meanwhile, from the east, the Soviets inflicted a savage revenge on the German population and fought their way into the city of **Berlin**. In late April, American and Soviet troops met on the Elbe

Chapter 20   *World War II*   **625**

COOPERATIVE LEARNING ACTIVITY

Mapmaking Organize the class into five groups. Each group will be responsible for mapping one of the following military campaigns from June 1944 to August 1945: Operation Overlord, the Battle of the Bulge, the Soviet advances, the Pacific Campaign, and the bombing of Japan. Instruct each group to create a map of their campaign using poster paper and markers. Suggest that they use maps from the text as well as from other sources as guides. Tell them to show the locations of battles, troop movements, flight patterns, and strategies. Have each group prepare a brief written summary that explains the campaign. When the maps are completed, ask each group to present its map and summary to the class. **L3 LEP**

TEACH

Guided Practice

THEME Innovation
Have students describe how strategies used in the D-Day invasion and in capturing Pacific islands helped the Allies, and how the atomic bomb quickly ended the war. **L1**

Map Study

Answer
the Battle of the Bulge

Cultural Perspectives
Navajo Code Talkers In 1943 the U.S. Marines recruited the Navajo to develop a military code that the Japanese could not break. Based on their oral language, the Navajo code talkers created the only unbreakable code in military history.

Mapping History Overlay Transparency 21, *Battle Sites in the Pacific*

World History and Art Transparency 42, *The Red Stairway*

CURRICULUM CONNECTION

TECHNOLOGY
After D-Day, PLUTO (Pipe-Line Under The Ocean), a pipeline under the English Channel, supplied 700 tons of gasoline a day for Allied trucks and tanks advancing across Europe.

Independent Practice

Guided Reading Activity 20-5 **L1**

Chapter 20 *World War II* **625**

VIDEODISC

Turning Points in World History

Side Two
Chapter 7

Title: *Dropping the Atomic Bomb*
Ask: What cities were bombed?
(Hiroshima and Nagasaki, Japan)

TURNING POINT

Victory Over Japan
How did the way in which the United States defeated Japan affect future world events? *For the first time, the atomic bomb was used in warfare, forcing Japan's surrender. It opened the atomic age, in which nuclear weapons played a role in global rivalry.*

ASSESS

Check for Understanding

Assign Section 5 Review as homework or as an in-class activity.

Use Student Self-Test and Review Software to review Section 5.

Visualizing History The Soviet army, aided by the Royal Air Force, fought for nine days to win control of Berlin. On April 30, 1945, Soviet tanks reached the Reichstag, the German parliament building, which they bombarded until afternoon. **Answer to Caption:** *The Western Allies crossed the Rhine and by April 11 reached the Elbe, where they later met Soviet armies coming from the east.*

River. On May 7, the Germans surrendered unconditionally, and the next day was proclaimed V-E (Victory in Europe) Day in the Allied democracies; May 9 was celebrated as V-E Day in the Soviet Union. With the German surrender, the war in Europe had finally ended. The end also came for the Fascist dictators. Italian partisans, or resistance fighters, had shot Mussolini, and Hitler had committed suicide in an underground chamber in Berlin.

Yalta and Potsdam

In February 1945, Roosevelt, Churchill, and Stalin had met at **Yalta**, a Black Sea resort in the Soviet Union, to discuss issues affecting the postwar world. The Allied leaders proposed that France and China join their countries in forming the United Nations, a permanent international organization to maintain peace after the war. They also agreed to divide Germany, as well as the city of Berlin, into four zones that Great Britain, France, the United States, and the Soviet Union would occupy.

Visualizing History Celebrating the Red Army's capture of Berlin, a group of Soviet troops unfurl the Soviet flag over the ruins of the German parliament building. *What advances were made by the Western Allies during the spring of 1945?*

Roosevelt and Churchill obtained from Stalin a promise to hold free elections in Soviet-occupied eastern Europe. In return, they gave Stalin the eastern part of Poland. Poland would receive German land in return for yielding its eastern territory.

To hasten the end of the Pacific conflict, the Western leaders sought and received Stalin's promise to declare war on Japan. In return, Stalin gained the Kuril Islands and the southern part of Sakhalin Island. These islands, located off the coast of Siberia in the northern Pacific Ocean, were ruled by Japan.

Six months later, the Allies met in **Potsdam** in Germany, but by this time some of the key participants had changed. After Franklin D. Roosevelt died in April, **Harry S Truman** succeeded him as President. Although Churchill was there at the opening, his Conservative party lost the general election, and **Clement Attlee** of the Labour party replaced him as prime minister halfway through the conference.

The atmosphere at Potsdam was also quite different from that at Yalta. The Allies made plans for the occupation of Germany and issued an ultimatum to Japan demanding unconditional surrender. However, more issues were raised than were settled. New tensions over the future of Europe were beginning to pull apart the wartime alliance.

TURNING POINT

Victory Over Japan

By end of 1944, an Allied victory over Japan seemed inevitable. American planes bombed Japanese cities, and General Douglas MacArthur regained the Philippines. In early 1945, the Americans defeated the Japanese in bloody battles on the Pacific islands of Iwo Jima and Okinawa, and the British completed the destruction of Japanese forces in Southeast Asia. Despite setbacks, Japan's military leaders, such as General Hideki Tojo, refused to surrender.

When Japan rejected an American ultimatum in July, President Truman decided to use a new secret weapon—the atomic bomb. His stated reason for using the bomb against Japan was to end the war swiftly and to avoid the enormous loss of life that would have resulted from an American invasion of the Japanese home islands. Concerned about growing Soviet-American rivalry, Truman also may have used the bomb to impress the Soviets with American military might.

On August 6, 1945, an American plane dropped an atomic bomb on **Hiroshima**, a munitions center. The blast leveled most of the city. When no response

---

MAKING CONNECTIONS ACTIVITY

Women's Roles The day-to-day activities of women in Allied, Axis, and occupied countries changed during the war. Have students research and write a report on how the war affected women's daily lives in the United States, Great Britain, France, Germany, Italy, the Soviet Union, or Poland. Suggest that students include in their reports changes in home life, work opportunities, and military roles as well as popular images of women's roles. **L1**

Visualizing History In February 1945, Allied leaders Winston Churchill, Franklin D. Roosevelt, and Joseph Stalin met at Yalta on the USSR's Crimean Peninsula. They discussed a number of issues related to the post-war Europe. *What major agreement was made at Yalta regarding the war against Japan?*

came from Japan, three days later the Americans dropped a second atomic bomb on the port city of **Nagasaki**. Altogether, about 200,000 Japanese died in both cities. In the following months, many more would die from the blasts' radioactivity.

On August 14, 1945, Japan finally surrendered. A few weeks later, on September 2 (proclaimed V-J—or Victory over Japan—Day by the Allies) Japanese officials signed the official surrender document on board the American battleship *Missouri* anchored in Tokyo Bay. World War II was over.

Effects of the War

More than 70 million people fought in World War II. The casualties were staggering. Altogether, some 55 million people perished because of the conflict. The Soviet Union lost 22 million people, Germany almost 8 million, Japan 2 million, and the United States almost 300,000. In addition, millions of people in Europe and Asia died in campaigns of genocide.

After the war the Allies began to address the wrongs committed by the Axis Powers. Between November 1945 and September 1946, trials held at Nuremburg, Germany, brought many Nazi leaders to justice for pursuing "aggressive war" and for "committing crimes against humanity." Similar war crimes trials were held in Japan and Italy.

In addition to the casualties, many areas of Europe and Asia lay in ruins. The use of deadly new weapons made World War II the most destructive war in history. Heavy aerial bombing and shifting battlelines left as many as 12 million people homeless. Food, medicine, and clothing, were in short supply. One Japanese student recalls life after the war:

> 66 When winter came we were really miserable. We had neither food nor clothing.... We were told to go to the countryside and find food wherever we could. There was nothing in Tokyo.. 99

For millions of people the suffering and hardships lasted long after the war's end.

SECTION 5 REVIEW

Recall
1. **Define** D-Day , partisan.
2. **Identify** George Patton, Harry S Truman, Clement Attlee.
3. **Explain** why Operation Overlord has been called "unmatched in history."

Critical Thinking
4. **Analyzing Information** War crimes trials after World War II held Axis leaders responsible for actions in wartime. Give examples of similar trials after recent conflicts. Why were these trials held?

Understanding Themes
5. **Innovation** World War II was even more costly in the destruction of human life and property than World War I. What factors made World War II the most destructive war in the history of the world?

Chapter 20 *World War II* **627**

Chapter 20 Review

GLENCOE
TECHNOLOGY

VIDEODISC
Use MindJogger to review students' knowledge of the chapter.

MindJogger Videoquiz

Chapter 20
Disc 3 Side A

Also available in VHS.

Answers

Using Key Terms
1. d
4. h
2. j
5. k
3. l

Using Your History Journal
Remind students to use examples to show how the event affected other developments in the war.

Reviewing Facts
1. It could only make recommendations and impose sanctions. Welcomed as liberators in some cases, the Japanese treated conquered peoples cruelly, killing civilians and seizing property.
2. Austria and Czechoslovakia
3. Causes: ineffective World War I peace treaties; dislocations caused by economic depression; expansionist policies of Fascist dictators; weakness of the League of Nations; United States isolationism; Effects: widespread loss of life, misery, homelessness; weakening of European powers and their empires; rise of the superpowers; development of nuclear weapons; the founding of the United Nations
4. The U.S. stood in the way of Japan's expansionist policy. Realizing that war with the U.S. was inevitable, Japan wanted to

628 Chapter 20 *World War II*

Connections Across Time

Historical Significance World War II dramatically shifted the world balance of power. Weakened by the conflict, European nations lost their empires and their dominance of world affairs. In their place emerged the United States and the Soviet Union—superpowers and rivals with nuclear arsenals capable of unleashing global mass destruction. Meanwhile, scores of newly independent nations arose from the ashes of the European empires and presented their own distinct outlooks on world affairs. One hopeful development in the postwar world was the United Nations, an international body dedicated to world peace. Another was the increased attention given to human rights as a result of the horrors of the Holocaust and Japanese atrocities in Asia.

Using Key Terms

Write the key term that completes each sentence. Then write a sentence for each term not chosen.

a. blitzkrieg
b. sanctions
c. lend-lease
d. appeasement
e. kamikazes
f. partisan
g. D-Day
h. scorched-earth policy
i. genocide
j. Holocaust
k. collective security
l. cash-and-carry policy

1. British Prime Minister Chamberlain pursued _____ with Nazi Germany in hopes of stabilizing Europe.
2. In the _____, the Nazis murdered almost 6 million Jews during the war.
3. The _____ allowed the United States to supply the British in return for payment without risking American neutrality.
4. Joseph Stalin tried to thwart the German invasion of his country by a _____.
5. During the 1930s, the Western democracies were unable to agree on what steps to take to ensure their _____.

Technology Activity

Using the Internet Search the Internet for a World War II Web site that includes memoirs or excerpts from Holocaust survivors. Copy or print a part of the memoirs that you find especially moving. Create a bulletin board about the Holocaust. Post the excerpts on the bulletin board under the heading "Voices of World War II." Include pictures of the Holocaust with captions underneath providing explanations.

628 Chapter 20 *World War II*

Using Your History Journal

Select one event from your chart about important events in World War II. Write a paragraph showing how the event affected other developments in the war.

Reviewing Facts

1. **Citizenship** Explain why the League of Nations could not stop Japan's expansion. How did Japan treat its conquered peoples?
2. **History** List the countries that Germany occupied before the outbreak of war.
3. **History** Identify the causes and effects of World War II.
4. **History** Explain Japan's attack on Pearl Harbor.
5. **Citizenship** Identify the Holocaust and discuss the different stages of its implementation.

Critical Thinking

1. **Apply** Why did the Western democracies let Hitler overrun much of Europe before trying to stop him?
2. **Analyze** What factors account for the response the world gave to the Holocaust?
3. **Synthesize** If the Japanese had not bombed Pearl Harbor, would the United States have entered the war? Explain your position.
4. **Evaluate** Was the United States justified in using the atomic bomb to end the war with Japan?

---

destroy its Pacific fleet.
5. It was the deliberately planned attempt by the Nazis to exterminate Europe's Jews; included in its sweep were other groups such as Slavs and Gypsies. At first the Nazis used forced emigration and imprisonment. Later, after the invasion of the Soviet Union, Nazi SS forces rounded up and shot large numbers of Jews. Finally, the Jews were sent to the death camps for extermination.

Critical Thinking
1. They thought that by appeasing Hitler they could maintain peace.
2. Within Nazi-occupied areas, anti-Semitic people helped the Nazis round up Jews; most people did nothing, fearing punishment or believing that it was none of their concern; Allied governments, aware of the death camps, did nothing, either, believing that carrying out the war was the only way

Understanding Themes

1. **Movement** What were Hitler's objectives in Europe? What were Japan's objectives in Asia?
2. **Cooperation** What assistance did the United States provide to Great Britain before American entry into the conflict?
3. **Conflict** Why did Stalin press the Allies to establish a second front in Europe?
4. **Conflict** Why did the Western Allies at Yalta agree to give Stalin the Kuril Islands and the southern part of Sakhalin Island?
5. **Innovation** What effect did new technology have on the war?

Geography in History

1. **Location** Refer to the map below. What were the relative locations of territories held in France by the Allies in September 1944?
2. **Region** What areas touching the Mediterranean Sea were in Allied control by September 1944?
3. **Movement** Beginning in June 1944, the Allied strategy was to pressure Germany on two fronts —East and West. How does the map show that the plan was a successful way to end the war?
4. **Location** Where did Soviet and American forces meet in April 1945?

The Allies Regain Europe

inking Past and Present

1. To avert war with Germany, the European democracies allowed Hitler to occupy Czechoslovakia. How did the United Nations react to Iraq's occupation of Kuwait in 1990? Do you think the United Nations made the correct decision? Explain.
2. In the 1940s, several publications called Churchill "Man of the Century." Do you think he still deserves the title? Explain.

Skill Practice

Reread the section of Chapter 20 that describes the bombing on Hiroshima, pages 626–627. Then read the passage on this page written six years later by a survivor. Use the two sources to answer the questions below.

“ I was eating breakfast … when there was bright light in front of my eyes and an indescribable orange light surged in.… It must have been ten or fifteen minutes later when I recovered consciousness.… but I could see nothing because the place was filled with white smoke.… I tried to stand up and fell again.… What on earth had happened? …

I looked over my shoulder and saw our house was a flattened wreck, and at the back waves of swirling flames were threatening to sweep down on us at any moment.… I suddenly heard my sister's voice calling, 'Someone help me! …' She was my own sister but the sight of her was horrifying. Her dark hair which reached her shoulders, that hair was now pure white. At the side of her mouth was a crescent-shaped gash through which her gums were pitifully exposed, and from which bright red blood flowed… When I saw this figure my sister had been transformed into, for a fleeting moment, I just couldn't think that it was her. I was afraid even to go near her. ”

—Eiko Matsunaga, 11th grade girl, 1951

1. What is the topic of the two sources?
2. What information does the textbook give about this topic?
3. How does the passage add to your understanding of this topic?

5. **INNOVATION** New technology extended the scope of the war and increased its devastation.

Geography in History
1. northwest and southeast France
2. southeastern France, Corsica, Sardinia, Italy, Sicily, North Africa
3. It shows that the Allies steadily gained territory on both the eastern and western fronts throughout late 1944 and late 1945.
4. in Germany

inking Past and Present

1. The UN sent a multinational force to the Middle East to expel Iraq from Kuwait. Answers will vary but should include that Iraqi aggression might have continued had the UN not responded as it did.
2. Answers might state that Churchill's firm stand in the Battle of Britain gave the British the courage to face the Nazis.

Skill Practice
1. the dropping of the atomic bomb on Hiroshima
2. The textbook explains why the bomb was dropped and gives facts about the time, place, extent of damage, and outcome.
3. Matsunaga tells what she saw, heard, and felt physically and emotionally. It makes the personal suffering very real.

Chapter Bonus Test Question

Ask students: How were the gains made by Stalin at Yalta similar to those made by Hitler at the Munich conference? *(Both men got what they wanted in exchange for promises they didn't keep: Hitler got the Sudetenland and then took over the rest of Czechoslovakia; Stalin got Poland but instead of holding elections made Poland a Communist state.)*

to help people suffering under Nazi injustice.
3. Yes; because the Atlantic Charter called for the destruction of Nazi tyranny.
4. Students should explain their opinions.

Understanding Themes
1. **MOVEMENT** Hitler wanted to control all of Europe, including the Soviet Union, to obtain "living space" for the "master race." Japan wanted to establish a "Greater East Asia Co-Prosperity Sphere."
2. **COOPERATION** The United States gave the British old destroyers, supplied food and weapons through the cash-and-carry policy, and lent war equipment through the lend-lease policy.
3. **CONFLICT** because the Soviet Union was fighting the Nazis alone
4. **CONFLICT** in exchange for Stalin's promise to enter the war against Japan

ABCNEWS INTERACTIVE™

VIDEODISC
Turning Points in World History

Side Two
Chapter 6

Title: *The Holocaust*

If you do not have access to a videodisc player, **Turning Points in World History** is also available in VHS.

Internet Sites

The following are possible sites for completing the "Net" activities:

The United Nations:
http://www.un.org/

Free India: Celebrating 50 Years of India's Freedom:
http://www.freeindia.org/

Not on the "Net"...

If students have limited or no access to the Internet, have them complete the "Mohandas K. Gandhi and India" activity by using resources in the school or public library to find information on Gandhi and India. Encourage students to use the following subjects to help them locate sources in the library's computerized or traditional card catalog: India, soulforce, independence.

Students may use the information they locate to help them design their banners.

ABCNEWS INTERACTIVE™ Turning Points in World History

The Holocaust

Setting up the Video

Work with a group of your classmates to view "The Holocaust" on the videodisc *Turning Points in World History*. The Holocaust was a horrific period in history when the Nazi regime was responsible for murders and crimes against 6 million Jews. This program examines the impact on those who experienced Nazi control during the 1930s and 1940s.

Hands-On Activity

Using the Holocaust theme, create a haiku. The Japanese haiku is one of the shortest types of lyric poetry. The haiku is made up of 17 syllables arranged in three lines. The first line has 5 syllables, the second 7, and the third 5.

Side Two, Chapter 6

View the video by scanning the bar code or by entering the chapter number on your keypad and pressing Search. (Also available in VHS format.)

Surfing the "Net"

Mohandas K. Gandhi and India

The early 1900s brought a great struggle for India concerning the issue of independence from Great Britain. Mohandas K. Gandhi provided leadership for independence by practicing active nonviolence. To learn more about Gandhi and the nonviolent movement, access the Internet.

Getting There

Follow these steps to gather information about Mohandas Gandhi.
1. Go to a search engine. Type in the phrase *mohandas gandhi.*
2. After typing in the phrase, enter words such as these to focus your search:
   • *india*   • *soulforce*   • *independence*

3. The search engine should provide you with a number of links to follow. Links are "pointers" to different sites on the Internet and commonly appear as blue underlined words.

What to Do When You Are There

Click on the links to navigate through the information and gather your findings. Organize into cooperative groups of three. Design large banners promoting peace and nonviolence for today's world. Share your banner with the other groups. Be sure to explain why you chose particular symbols, language, or colors for your banner.

INTERNET ADDRESS BOOK

Use this space to record frequently used addresses.

Unit 5 Digest

Two destructive wars engulfed the world in the first half of the 1900s. World War I brought about the collapse of European monarchies, triggered a Communist revolution in Russia, and left many countries in chaos. This turmoil, the bitterness created by the peace treaties ending the war, and a worldwide economic depression that started in 1929 led to the rise of dictatorships in Germany, Italy, and Japan.

During the 1930s, the world once again was set on a course toward war. When it arrived, World War II proved to be the most destructive in history. At its end, European dominance of world affairs had ended, with many new nations arising from the ashes of the overseas European empires. Above all, two superpowers—the United States and the Soviet Union—were extending their power and struggling for global influence.

Chapter 17
World War I

In the late 1800s and early 1900s, nationalism and imperialism led the nations of Europe to form two rival alliances: the Triple Alliance, made up of Germany, Austria-Hungary, and Italy, and the Triple Entente (later, the Allies), consisting of France, Great Britain, and Russia. Conflict between the two armed camps broke out following the assassination of the heir to the Austrian throne in June 1914. For four years, the belligerents fought on land, at sea, and in the air, using new weapons, such as machine guns, tanks, airplanes, and poison gas. In western Europe the war quickly settled into a stalemate along two parallel lines of trenches stretching from Switzerland to the North Sea. In eastern Europe and the Middle East, constant changes occurred in battlefield positions, but neither side was able to achieve a speedy total victory.

To try to cut off Germany's supply lines, Great Britain blockaded German ports. The Germans struck back with U-boats, or submarines. German sinking of American merchant ships eventually brought the neutral United States into the war on the side of the Allies. The United States gave the Allies much-needed human and material resources; and in November 1918, Germany finally surrendered.

The war brought sweeping changes. The Ottoman, Russian, and Austro-Hungarian empires collapsed, and new nations emerged from the breakup. The peace settlement at Versailles, France, made Germany responsible for the war and imposed a heavy financial penalty on its people. The war also increased human misery on a large scale, with millions of soldiers and civilians dead or wounded. Mass killings, such as those of the Armenians under Ottoman rule, added to the list of horrors. Finally, revolution in Russia led to the rise of communism as a force in world affairs.

Chapter 18
Between Two Fires

World War I destroyed the West's belief in progress and created feelings of disillusionment. In the postwar era, European and American artists and writers rejected the past and experimented with new styles and subject matter. Innovative forms of technology, such as the automobile and the radio, transformed people's lives and brought the world closer together.

The United States came out of the war in far better shape than its allies. The 1920s were boom years for the American economy, but the general prosperity hid the fact that farmers and workers were worse off than before the war. Finally, in 1929, wild speculation led to a stock market crash, and the nation fell into a major economic depression that had worldwide effects.

Although war and depression had a terrible effect on Great Britain and France, democracy managed to survive in these nations. Germany and Italy also faced setbacks, but these countries did not have strong democratic traditions. Amid political and economic chaos in Italy, Benito Mussolini in 1922 set up a Fascist dictatorship that stressed nationalism and military strength. In Germany Nazi party leader Adolf Hitler came to power in 1933 with a similar program that also included persecution of the Jews, whom he blamed for Germany's economic woes.

Dramatic changes were also occurring in the Soviet Union. After seizing power, Lenin and the Bolsheviks, renamed Communists, tried to quickly

The Unit Digest offers a chapter-by-chapter summary that can be used for any of the following:

- *Preview* one chapter or an entire unit,
- *Review* some or all of the chapters,
- *Condense* when specific chapters or units have not been taught, or
- *Reteach* chapters that students have studied in the unit.

PREVIEW

Use the Unit 5 Digest Transparencies to preview the highlights of the unit.

REVIEW

Cause and Effect Ask students to give examples of some of the indirect results of World War I and its aftermath that destabilized both Europe and the rest of the world. *(the Russian Revolution; the rise of dictators in Italy and Germany; the growth of nationalist movements in Asia, Africa, and Latin America)* Then discuss how World War I contributed to these developments and decide which were the most important in causing World War II. **L1**

CLASSROOM RESOURCES FOR UNIT 7 DIGEST

Preview
- Unit 5 Digest Transparencies

Review
- Time Line Activities 17, 18, 19, 20
- Student Self-Test and Review Software, Chapters 17, 18, 19, 20
- MindJogger Videoquiz, Chapters 17, 18, 19, 20

Condense
- Chapter Digests Audiocassettes, Chapters 17, 18, 19, 20

Reteach
- Reteaching Activities 17, 18, 19, 20
- Chapter Digests Audiocassettes, Chapters 17, 18, 19, 20
- Turning Points in World History

Unit 5
Digest

CONDENSE

⌒ Use Chapter Digests Audiocassettes to introduce chapters that students have not studied in Unit 5. Spanish Chapter Digests Audiocassettes are also available.

Discuss Have students read the **Unit Digest** and discuss the **Surveying the Unit** questions.
L1

Visualizing History

Answer to Caption: *Stalin put industry and agriculture under state control, and set up a brutal dictatorship.*

GLENCOE TECHNOLOGY

VIDEODISC
Use MindJogger to review any chapter in Unit 5.

MindJogger Videoquiz

 Chapter 17
Disc 2 Side B

 Chapter 18
Disc 2 Side B

 Chapter 19
Disc 3 Side A

 Chapter 20
Disc 3 Side A

 Also available in VHS.

▣ Use the Student Self-Test and Review Software to review any chapters that students have studied in Unit 5.

632 Unit 5 *World in Conflict*

Visualizing History Lenin guided the affairs of the Soviet state through civil war and economic collapse until his death in January 1924. *What changes did Lenin's successor, Joseph Stalin, bring to the Soviet Union?*

impose a new socialist order but faced widespread opposition. In 1921 Lenin strengthened Communist power by allowing limited capitalism. After Lenin's death in 1924, Joseph Stalin won a political power struggle with his rival, Leon Trotsky. Beginning in the late 1920s, Stalin brought all Soviet industry and agriculture under state control. He also removed suspected opponents from leadership positions, and promoted a famine that cost many lives in Ukraine, a stronghold of anti-Communist nationalism. Other Soviet citizens also suffered imprisonment, exile, and death under Stalin's grim rule.

Chapter 19
Nationalism in Asia, Africa, and Latin America

After World War I, the European powers retained control of their colonies. But in the years following the conflict, nationalist groups arose in Asia and Africa that challenged continued European rule in these areas.

Weakened by internal discord, the Ottoman Empire crumbled during the war. After halting a Greek invasion in 1922, the Turks removed their Ottoman ruler and formed the Republic of Turkey. Persians, too, asserted their independence and gave Persia a new name—Iran.

Although Great Britain granted Egypt independence in 1936, it controlled neighboring Palestine and continued to rule African colonies such as Kenya and Nigeria. Despite India's contribution to the British war effort, Great Britain refused to grant the Indians independence. Mohandas K. Gandhi and other Indian nationalists organized nonviolent protests against British rule, including strikes and a refusal to buy British goods.

In China, the nationalist Guomindang army led by Chiang Kai-shek gained power. During the late 1920s, Chiang turned on his Chinese Communist allies, many of whom fled to the mountainous inte-

632 Unit 5 *World in Conflict*

rior of China. When the Japanese invaded China in the 1930s, however, Chiang again joined with the Communists in an effort to repulse the invaders.

In Japan military leaders became a powerful force in the 1920s and 1930s. They believed that Japan could solve the problems of a growing population and limited resources by conquering new territories. By the late 1930s, the military had won complete control of the government and embarked on a collision course with the United States and Western powers.

Although most Latin American countries had won political independence before the 1920s, they remained economically dependent on the United States. They also faced American military intervention whenever internal unrest threatened American interests. In the early 1930s, United States President Franklin D. Roosevelt worked for good relations with Latin America. He proclaimed the Good Neighbor policy, in which the United States would refrain from intervention.

Chapter 20
World War II

The desire of Fascist dictatorships for more territory increasingly threatened world peace during the 1930s. The League of Nations, which had been formed after World War I to preserve peace, proved powerless to stop the drift toward war.

Adolf Hitler aimed to bring much of Europe under Nazi control. When the German leader threatened to invade Czechoslovakia in 1938, Great Britain and France negotiated the Munich Agreement that gave Hitler the part of Czechoslovakia that he demanded. This policy of appeasement—or compromise with the dictatorships—to avoid war only increased Hitler's expansionism. In early 1939, Hitler took over all of Czechoslovakia, and in September of that year secured the help of the Soviet Union in attacking Poland. The Nazi assault on Poland led Great Britain and France to declare war on Germany.

ANSWERS TO SURVEYING THE UNIT

Chapter 17 Nationalism and imperialism led to rivalries among European powers, which in turn led to the formation of competing alliances.

Chapter 18 The war and economic depression placed burdens on many nations; Italy and Germany, not having the strong democratic traditions of Great Britain and France, fell prey to

Fascist movements that promised to restore national greatness.

Chapter 19 Most of Latin America was politically independent, but economically dependent on the United States. Latin American nationalists opposed American military intervention in Latin American affairs. In other parts of the

632 Unit 5 *World in Conflict*

Visualizing History

After Pearl Harbor, San Francisco prepared for possible Japanese air attacks by sandbagging buildings. *Why was the Japanese attack on Pearl Harbor a significant event?*

In the spring of 1940, German forces took control of Norway and Denmark, and then invaded the Low Countries and France, pushing British and French forces to the English Channel. France surrendered in June, leaving the British to fight Hitler alone. In the summer and fall of 1940, Great Britain, under the leadership of Winston Churchill, fought and won a crucial victory over Germany in the air conflict known as the Battle of Britain. By 1941, however, Nazi Germany had conquered large areas of Europe, and in June of that year, launched a large-scale invasion of the Soviet Union.

Meanwhile, the United States remained neutral in the conflict, although it supplied the British with equipment to fight the war. To prevent the Americans from interfering with its expansionist thrust in East Asia and the Pacific, Japan attacked the United States fleet at Pearl Harbor, Hawaii. The Pearl Harbor attack brought the United States into the war on the side of the Allies—Great Britain, the Soviet Union, the Free French, and other anti-Fascist governments and nations.

Not until 1942 did the tide begin to turn in favor of the Allies. Americans defeated Japanese naval forces at the Battle of Midway in the Pacific Ocean. In 1943, Soviet forces threw back a German offensive at Stalingrad, and British and American forces pushed the Germans out of North Africa. From there, the Allies launched an invasion of Sicily and the Italian Peninsula.

In June 1944, Western Allied forces invaded Normandy in France and pushed toward Germany as Soviet troops advanced from the east. In April 1945 Western and Soviet allies met at the Elbe River, and the following month Germany surrendered. When Japan refused to surrender, the United States dropped its new secret weapon, the atomic bomb, on Hiroshima and Nagasaki in August. Days later Japan surrendered.

World War II was over, but much of Europe lay in ruins, and millions of people had died. The most shocking horror in a war filled with atrocities was the Holocaust, the killing of over 6 million Jews by the Nazis in a campaign of genocide, or the deliberate killing of a racial, political, or cultural group. Among the political changes brought by the war was the division of Europe into Communist and non-Communist areas.

SURVEYING UNIT 5

1. **Chapter 17** What general factors led to the outbreak of World War I?
2. **Chapter 18** What common problems did many nations face in the 1920s and 1930s? Why did democracy survive in Great Britain and France, while it collapsed in Italy and Germany?
3. **Chapter 19** How did nationalism in Latin America during the 1920s and 1930s differ from nationalism in Asia and Africa?
4. **Chapter 20** How were the causes of World Wars I and II different? How were they similar?

ANSWERS TO SURVEYING THE UNIT

world, nationalists were struggling for political freedom from Western colonial rule.

Chapter 20 Differences: World War I developed out of rivalries among European powers for territory, prestige, and security; World War II emerged from the territorial ambitions of Fascist dictatorships and the failure of the League of Nations and the democratic nations to respond seriously to the Fascists before war seriously threatened. Similarities: Both wars were in many ways conflicts that began in Europe or developed out of European concerns and then spread to or affected other parts of the world..

Visualizing History

Answer to Caption: *The attack brought the United States into World War II on the side of the Allies.*

RETEACH

Review Chart Organize the class into two groups. Have one group prepare a review chart featuring the causes, main events, and consequences of World War I, and the other group do the same for World War II. **L1**

 Reteaching Activities 17, 18, 19, 20

 Chapter Digests Audiocassettes, Chapters 17, 18, 19, 20

ABCNEWS INTERACTIVE™

VIDEODISC
Turning Points in World History

Side Two
Chapter 4

Title: *Assassination Ignites World War I*

Ask: Why did the assassination of the archduke plunge Europe into war? *(A web of European alliances caused most major nations to declare war.)*

0:00 **OUT OF TIME?**

If time does not permit teaching each chapter in Unit 6, you may use the Unit Digest beginning on page 803, in conjunction with the Unit Digest Transparencies and Chapter Digest Audiocassettes with accompanying activities and tests.

Introducing the Unit

Unit 6 focuses on the political trends of the post-World War II era, including the origins and effects of the cold war; decolonization in Asia, Africa, and the Middle East; and the decline of communism and the end of the cold war since 1989.

Unit Objectives

After reading Unit 6, students will be able to:

1. summarize the causes and impact of the cold war.
2. describe conflicts in Asia and the region's emergence as an economic powerhouse.
3. analyze the legacy of colonial rule in Africa and the challenges facing that continent.
4. examine the rival nationalisms of the Middle East and the region's search for peace.
5. identify political and economic trends in Latin America.
6. analyze factors that are leading toward globalization.

Portfolio Project

Have students work together in groups on related topics such as debt, poverty, and urbanization in developing countries. This activity may be an appropriate method of authentic assessment.

Unit 6

1945–Present

The Contemporary World

Then & Now

International tension continued after World War II. Two blocs of nations aligned themselves behind the United States and the Soviet Union to dominate world politics. The two sides fought a cold war using economic powers, diplomacy, espionage, and the threat of nuclear war. When the cold war ended, leaders struggled to address the long-standing problems of nationalism, poverty in the developing nations, distribution of resources, and environmental damage.

The pace of scientific and technological change quickened. Satellite communications and computers linked in a global network offered undreamed of challenges and opportunities. When you turn on your computer, remember that it has been just a few years since this technology was invented. No one can guess the nature or degree of change it will bring to your future.

A Global Chronology

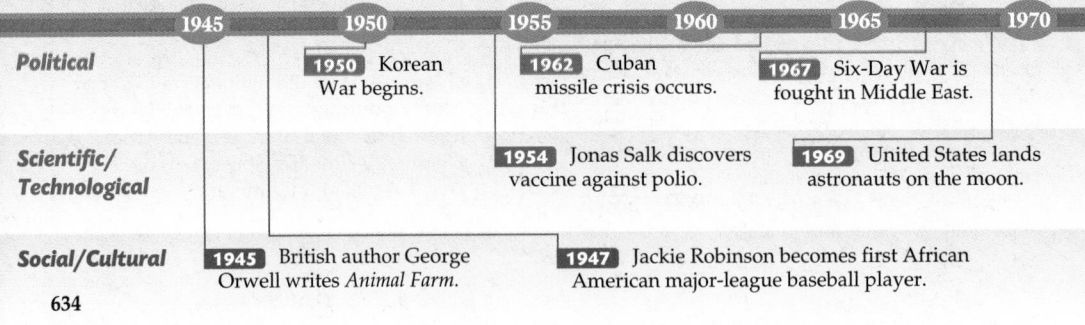

	1945	1950	1955	1960	1965	1970
Political		**1950** Korean War begins.	**1962** Cuban missile crisis occurs.		**1967** Six-Day War is fought in Middle East.	
Scientific/ Technological			**1954** Jonas Salk discovers vaccine against polio.		**1969** United States lands astronauts on the moon.	
Social/Cultural	**1945** British author George Orwell writes *Animal Farm.*	**1947** Jackie Robinson becomes first African American major-league baseball player.				

634

Then & Now

Declaring Independence In this unit, students will learn about the problems faced by the newly independent nations of Africa, the Middle East, and Asia, as well as efforts by Latin American countries to end their economic dependency on the industrialized nations.

Point out to students that the nations that have emerged from colonial rule since World War II won their independence nearly 200 years after the United States became the first colony in modern history to become a sovereign nation. What are the main problems that newly independent nations face in the modern world? *(Answers will vary. Students may say that setting up a representative*

Computer Pentium chip

History *and the* Humanities

📖 Focus on World Art Print
•24, Bridget Riley. *Current*

🗿 World History and Art Transparencies
•43 *The Persistence of Memory*
•44 *Sydney Opera House*
•45 *The Liberated African Woman*
•46 *Bedouin Woman's Headpiece*
•47 *Iranian Mihrab*
•48 *The Twelve Tribes of Israel*
•49 *Figura*
•50 *Diego and I*
•51 *Vietnam Memorial*
•52 *Sky Above Clouds II*

🎵 World Music: Cultural Traditions, Lessons 1, 2, 3, 4, 5, 6, 8

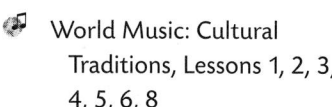

VIDEODISC
Turning Points in World History

Side Two
Chapter 8

Title: *The Moon Landing*
Ask: Competition between what two countries led to the space race? *(the United States and Soviet Union)*

Portfolio Project

Choose an ongoing worldwide problem or situation such as ethnic wars or rivalries, the conflict between Arabs and Israelis, economic difficulties in former Soviet states, population growth in overcrowded cities, oil or other resource shortages, debt in developing nations, the spread of arms, hunger and homelessness, or terrorism. Collect and study news articles about this subject. Write a one-page essay offering suggestions for dealing with the issue.

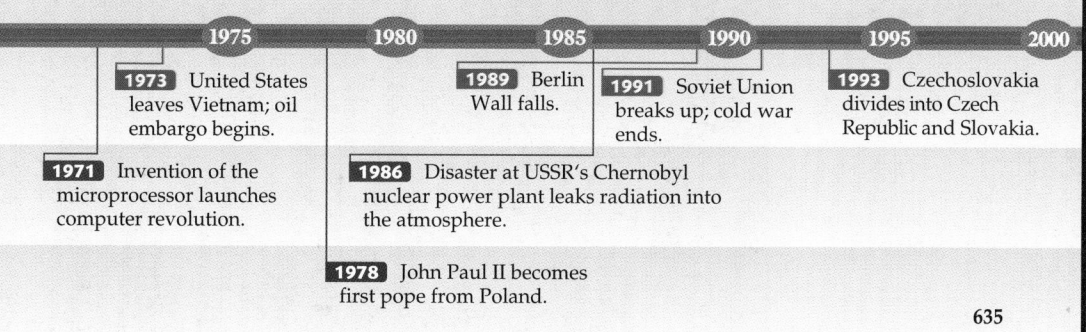

| 1975 | 1980 | 1985 | 1990 | 1995 | 2000 |

1973 United States leaves Vietnam; oil embargo begins.

1971 Invention of the microprocessor launches computer revolution.

1989 Berlin Wall falls.

1986 Disaster at USSR's Chernobyl nuclear power plant leaks radiation into the atmosphere.

1978 John Paul II becomes first pope from Poland.

1991 Soviet Union breaks up; cold war ends.

1993 Czechoslovakia divides into Czech Republic and Slovakia.

635

government and creating a vigorous, independent economy are main challenges.) **How do the challenges facing new nations today differ from those faced by the United States after 1776?** *(Answers will vary. Students may say that the economy was simpler in the 1700s; the United States did not have to worry about the technology gap. On the other hand, as the world's first democracy the United States had to pioneer an untested system of government.)* **How did the cold war affect the transition of many colonies to independence?** *(Answers will vary. Some students may realize that in Vietnam, Algeria, and elsewhere independence movements backed by the Soviet Union were opposed by the United States and its allies, leading to bloody wars.)*

Visualizing History
Since World War II, computers have revolutionized the world economy. A single pentium chip holds more computing capacity than did the earliest mainframe computers.

The Spread of Ideas

TEACH

Introduction

This feature focuses on the political consequences of the development of modern international communications through satellite broadcasting and the Internet.

Background Notes

Linking Past and Present

The early days of the space race that was triggered by the Soviet launching of *Sputnik I* were the subject of Tom Wolfe's recent novel *The Right Stuff* and the popular film by the same title. Students interested in learning more about the period may want to read the book or watch a video of the movie.

Geography

Movement The United States is the leading source of television programs and films for the world market. Many countries have taken steps to limit the consumption of American cultural products in order to support their own film and television industries. Attempts by European nations to limit imports from the United States have led to conflicts under GATT (General Agreement on Tariffs and Trade), which seeks to open markets and reduce trade restrictions.

The Spread of Ideas

Communications

The invention of writing reshaped history. So did Johannes Gutenberg's use of movable type. Today, however, electronics technology is moving communications forward at a startling rate. Two of the biggest changes have been the linking of people around the world via satellite broadcasts and the creation of a vast computer network known as the "information highway."

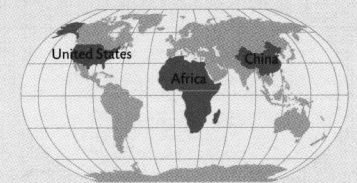

The United States
Satellite Communications

In October 1957, a special announcement interrupted radio broadcasts across the United States. "Listen now … for the sound which forever separates the old from the new," said the broadcaster. Then a voice from outer space—and eerie beep … beep … beep.

The former Soviet Union had taken the lead in space exploration by launching a tiny communications satellite named *Sputnik I*. A crudely simple device by today's standards, the first satellite could do little more than beam back radio signals. In the cold war era, however, it sent shock waves through American society.

Three years later, the United States launched *Echo* and *Courier*. Instead of beeps, these satellites relayed telephone calls between Europe and the United States. In 1962, the United States launched *Telstar*—the first satellite to relay live television programs from one place to another. By the 1980s people around the world with satellite dish antennas could tune in to hundreds of television programs. The effect was revolutionary. Repressive governments in Eastern Europe and elsewhere could not legislate against free speech beamed down from the skies.

Telstar

Scientist and Soviet Sputnik I

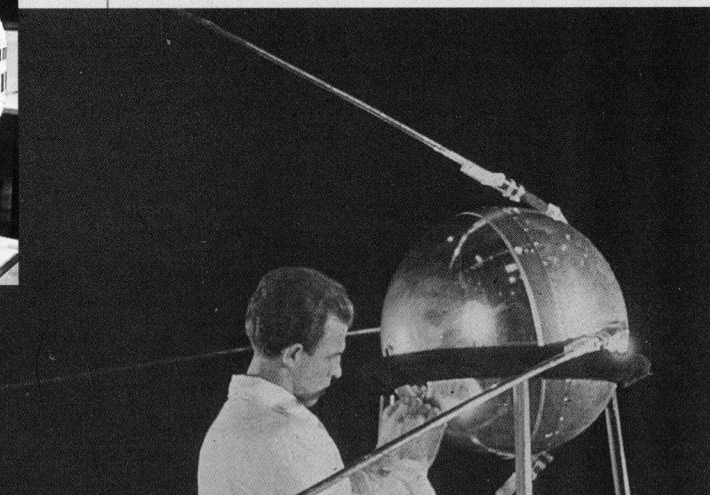

636 Unit 6

COOPERATIVE LEARNING ACTIVITY

Multimedia Presentation Organize students into small groups and have each group select one medium of communication, such as films, television, radio, newspapers, CD-ROM, or the Internet. Then ask each group to choose a current international news story and create a news feature on that topic for the medium they have chosen. Have each group present its report, explaining the features of the presentation that were specially adapted to the medium they chose, and estimating the size and nature of the audience they hoped to reach. L3

China
Satellite Dishes

In the 1990s, satellite dishes sprouted like mushrooms across the People's Republic of China. Star TV, a pan-Asian satellite service, boomed down Mandarin-speaking rappers out of Hong Kong, English broadcasts of CNN News, NFL football games, and movies from Japan. The uncensored broadcasts enraged government officials. However, a 1993 ban against satellite dishes proved nearly impossible to enforce. Even while officials tried to dismantle the thousands of large dishes, kits for smaller dishes were being smuggled into the country.

The example of China was repeated in other repressive nations. Iran, Myanmar (Burma), and other countries tried and failed to ban satellite reception. Even free governments, such as India, expressed concern about the "cultural invasion," but satellite television, a part of the information age, was here to stay.

Communications satellite

Who? What? Where? When?

Sputnik I The launching of *Sputnik I* in 1957 created near-panic in the United States. One senator called the Soviet breakthrough "a devastating blow to the prestige of the United States as the leader in the scientific and technical world," while *The New Republic* said it proved "that the Soviet Union gained a commanding lead in certain vital sectors of the race for world scientific and technological supremacy."

Cultural Diffusion

Hollywood Abroad The internationalization of the film industry has changed the content of Hollywood films. Many American films now earn as much or more money in foreign distribution as they do inside the United States. Since these films are either dubbed or subtitled, those based on action and adventure rather than dialogue tend to be more successful. This phenomenon in part explains the trend toward producing Hollywood blockbuster action thrillers.

Africa
The Internet

High school students on the Internet

A telephone line and a personal computer—that is all someone needs to jump on the information highway. Internet Web sites exist globally, putting individuals in touch with databases and other computer users on every continent.

In Africa, the least electronic continent, UNESCO is helping the Pan-African News Agency to link up with the Internet. The project will help Africans overcome one of the legacies of imperialism—a communications system that linked African nations with European capitals rather than with each other. The driving force behind the project, a Senegalese journalist named Babacar Fall, sees the Internet as one of the keys to unlocking Africa's economic potential. "Without information," explained Fall, "there can be no development."

LINKING THE IDEAS

1. How did the revolution in satellite communications get its start?
2. How has this revolution affected nondemocratic political systems?

Critical Thinking

3. **Drawing Conclusions** How has the revolution in communications made our world more interdependent?

ANSWERS TO LINKING THE IDEAS

1. The Soviet Union launched *Sputnik I* in 1957.
2. They have been unable to stop the flow of information from democratic nations that comes via satellites and the Internet.
3. Sharing of information has been greatly enhanced by satellite technology and the Internet, bringing all parts of the world into closer communication. Development and growth are frequently dependent on this shared information.

A complete, 1-page lesson plan is provided for each section in the *Reproducible Lesson Plans* booklet.

The Cold War

CHAPTER RESOURCES

	Reproducible Resources	Multimedia Resources
Chapter Opener	Chapter Themes: Graphic Organizer 21 Historical Significance Chapter Activity 21	MindJogger Videoquiz
Chapter Enrichment	Vocabulary Activity 21* Time Line Activity 21 Mapping History Activity 21 History Simulation 21 Geography and History Activity 21 Source Reading 21 People in World History Profiles 61, 62 World Art and Music Activity 21 Enrichment Activity 21 Critical Thinking Activity 21 Skill Reinforcement Activity 21 Building Skills in Geography Workbook, Unit 1, Lesson 10 Performance Assessment Activity 21	Focus on World Art Print 24, Bridget Riley. *Current* World History and Art Transparency 43, *The Persistence of Memory* Mapping History Overlay Transparency 22, *The United Nations*; 23, *The Commonwealth of Nations* Chapter Transparency 21 Vocabulary PuzzleMaker Software World Music: Cultural Traditions, Lessons 3, 4 Turning Points in World History Lessons of War Communism and the Cold War
Chapter Review/Reteaching	Reteaching Activity 21 Skill Reinforcement Activity 21 Spanish Chapter Summary 21	Chapter 21 Digest Audiocassette, Activity, Test* Vocabulary PuzzleMaker Software Student Self-Test and Review Software MindJogger Videoquiz
Chapter Evaluation/Testing	Performance Assessment Activity 21 Chapter 21 Test, Forms A and B	Testmaker

* Also available in Spanish

0:00 OUT OF TIME? Assign the Chapter 21 summary in the Unit 6 Digest on pages 803–805, and the Chapter 21 Audiocassettes.

Block Schedule

Block scheduling differs from traditional class scheduling in the amount of time allotted to each period. The extended time frame provided by block scheduling affords you the opportunity to implement a greater number of research-oriented and activity-intense projects to motivate and involve your students. Activities that are particularly suited to use within the block scheduling framework are identified throughout this chapter by the following designation.

KEY TO ABILITY LEVELS

Teaching strategies have been coded for varying learning styles and abilities.

- **L1 BASIC** activities for all students
- **L2 AVERAGE** activities for average to above-average students
- **L3 CHALLENGING** activities for above-average students
- **LEP LIMITED ENGLISH PROFICIENCY** activities

SECTION RESOURCES

Daily Objectives	Reproducible Resources	Multimedia Resources
Section 1 **The East-West Split** Identify the events that caused and heightened the cold war.	Reproducible Lesson Plan 21-1 Guided Reading Activity 21-1* Time Line Activity 21 Geography and History Activity 21 Section Quiz 21-1*	Section Focus Transparency 21-1 Chapter Transparency 21 World History and Art Transparency 43, *The Persistence of Memory* Mapping History Overlay Transparency 22, *The United Nations* Vocabulary PuzzleMaker Software Student Self-Test and Review Software Testmaker World Music: Cultural Traditions, Lesson 4 Communism and the Cold War
Section 2 **The Communist Bloc** Explain how the Soviet Union carried out Communist policies after the death of Stalin.	Reproducible Lesson Plan 21-2 Vocabulary Activity 21* Guided Reading Activity 21-2* Section Quiz 21-2*	Section Focus Transparency 21-2 Student Self-Test and Review Software Testmaker Communism and the Cold War
Section 3 **Western Europe** Describe how Western Europe moved toward greater political and economic unity during the cold war.	Reproducible Lesson Plan 21-3 Vocabulary Activity 21* Guided Reading Activity 21-3* History Simulation 21 Section Quiz 21-3*	Focus on World Art Print 24 Section Focus Transparency 21-3 Mapping History Overlay Transparency 23, *The Commonwealth of Nations* Student Self-Test and Review Software Testmaker
Section 4 **The United States and Canada** Trace the political and social changes that the people of the United States and Canada experienced during the cold war years.	Reproducible Lesson Plan 21-4 Guided Reading Activity 21-4* Reteaching Activity 21 Enrichment Activity 21 Section Quiz 21-4* Performance Assessment Activity 21 Spanish Chapter Summary 21	Section Focus Transparency 21-4 Vocabulary PuzzleMaker Software Student Self-Test and Review Software Testmaker Communism and the Cold War Turning Points in World History Lessons of War

* Also available in Spanish

Chapter Activities

✔ Performance Assessment Activity

Another Berlin Wall Assign students to groups of four to create an expressive version of the Berlin Wall. Give each group a piece of poster board to use for their wall. On one side of the wall, have students use visuals, words, and graffiti to represent sentiments and beliefs held by the Soviet Union. On the other side, have students represent beliefs held by the West. Important events of the era should also be included. Have the students write an individual reflection listing and explaining each item included on their wall.

Possible Rubric Features

Accuracy of content information, concept attainment, originality and creativity of product, collaborative skills, thoroughness of explanation

• *For an additional activity, refer to Activity 21 in the* Performance Assessment Strategies and Activities *booklet.*

ACTIVITY

From the Classroom of...

Robert W. Gardner
New Canaan High
School
New Canaan, CT

Preventing the Cold War

On the chalkboard, list the leaders of the United States and the Soviet Union who played key roles during the cold war era: Harry Truman, Joseph Stalin, Nikita Khrushchev, Leonid Brezhnev, Dwight Eisenhower, John Kennedy, Lyndon Johnson, and Richard Nixon.

Have partners pick an issue, event, or crisis faced by these leaders during the cold war. One student analyzes the problem from the point of view of the American president at the time, the other from the perspective of the Soviet leader. Have students attempt to negotiate a solution to the problem and describe it in a paragraph.

Have pairs present the problem, the world leaders they represent, and the solution they agreed on. Then have the class discuss whether the cold war could have been avoided, or at least ameliorated.

MULTIPLE LEARNING STYLES

Verbal/Linguistic
Have students obtain and read short selections from a collection of *samizdat*—underground literature circulated by Soviet dissidents.

Logical/Mathematical
Have students debate the following proposition: The United States and the Soviet Union were equally to blame for the cold war.

Visual/Spatial
Have students create a poster, based on conditions in the early days of the cold war, warning Americans against the "Communist menace."

Auditory/Musical
Have students listen to a tape or CD of music from the early era of rock and roll, featuring such performers as Chuck Berry and Elvis Presley. Discussion might focus on why this music aroused so much opposition from mainstream America at the time.

Additional Resources

NATIONAL GEOGRAPHIC SOCIETY

Teacher's Corner

INDEX TO
NATIONAL GEOGRAPHIC MAGAZINE

The following articles may be used for research relating to this chapter:

- "Kaliningrad," by Pritt J. Vesilind, March 1997.
- "The New Saigon," by Tracy Dahlby, April 1995.
- "East Europe's Dark Dawn," by Jon Thompson, June 1991.
- "Bikini: A Way of Life Lost," by William S. Ellis, June 1986.

NATIONAL GEOGRAPHIC SOCIETY
PRODUCTS AVAILABLE FROM GLENCOE

To order the following products for use with this chapter, contact your local Glencoe sales representative, or call Glencoe at 1-800-334-7344:

- *GTV: The American People (Videodisc)*
- *GTV: A Geographic Perspective on American History (Videodisc)*

ADDITIONAL NATIONAL GEOGRAPHIC
SOCIETY PRODUCTS

To order the following products for use with this chapter, call National Geographic Society at 1-800-368-2728:

- *1945–1989: The Cold War (Video)*
- *Capitalism, Socialism, Communism Series, "Communism." (Video)*
- *Europe: The Road to Unity (Video)*

BIBLIOGRAPHY

Literature of the Period
Ellison, Ralph. *The Invisible Man.* New York: Random House, 1952. An idealistic young African American man meets disappointment in Harlem.
Solzhenitsyn, Alexander. *One Day in the Life of Ivan Denisovich.* New York: Dutton, 1963. The story of an inmate in one of Stalin's forced-labor camps.
Readings for the Student
le Carré, John. *The Spy Who Came in from the Cold.* New York: Coward-McCann, 1964. Classic espionage fiction set in postwar Europe.
Readings for the Teacher
Patterson, Thomas G. *On Every Front: The Making and Unmaking of the Cold War.* New York: Norton, 1992. Objective explanation of the motives and tactics of both sides.

LOCAL OBJECTIVES

_____
_____
_____
_____
_____
_____
_____
_____
_____
_____
_____
_____
_____
_____
_____
_____
_____
_____
_____
_____
_____
_____
_____

interNET
CONNECTION
Cold War resources on the World Wide Web
Cold War Hot Links:
http://www. stmartin.edu/ ~dprice/cold.war.html

Chapter
21
1945–1979
The Cold War

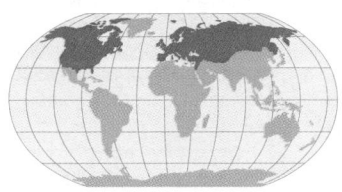

Chapter Themes

▶ **Conflict** A cold war develops between the United States and the Soviet Union, the two superpowers that emerged after World War II. *Section 1*

▶ **Change** The Soviet Union tries to move away from the legacy of Stalin while maintaining its control over Eastern Europe. *Section 2*

▶ **Regionalism** Western European democracies develop closer regional unity. *Section 3*

▶ **Cooperation** The United States and Canada build strong economies and forge closer ties. *Section 4*

The Storyteller

In 1948 the city of West Berlin was an island in the middle of a hostile sea. The Soviets had cut off all land routes into the German city in the hope of driving out the Western Allies. For 11 months the United States airlifted food to 2 million stranded residents in West Berlin.

One day while his plane was on the ground in West Berlin, an American pilot, Lieutenant Gale S. Halvorsen, met a group of German children. Although they had received few sweets to eat during the blockade, they did not beg. He told them to wait for his plane at the end of the airport runway the next day. The children came, and, to their delight, packets of gum and chocolate showered down from Halvorsen's plane.

Soon other pilots joined "Operation Little Vittles," and the crowds of children grew. The children named Halvorsen "the Chocolate Pilot."

Historical Significance

What developments led to a cold war between the Western democracies and the Soviet Union? How did this East-West split affect world affairs during the next 40 years?

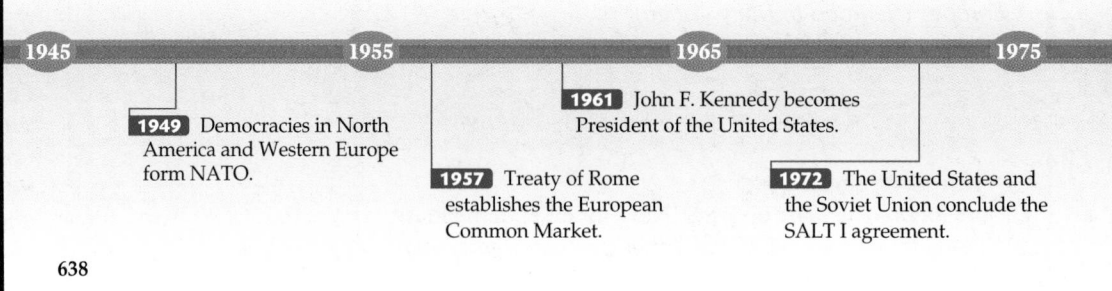

| 1945 | 1955 | 1965 | 1975 |

1949 Democracies in North America and Western Europe form NATO.

1957 Treaty of Rome establishes the European Common Market.

1961 John F. Kennedy becomes President of the United States.

1972 The United States and the Soviet Union conclude the SALT I agreement.

638

GEOGRAPHY CONNECTION

Location Ask students to locate Moscow, Berlin, Bonn, Paris, and London in the Atlas of their textbooks or on a wall map. What were the Eastern European countries that fell behind the iron curtain? *(Albania, Bulgaria, Czechoslovakia, East Germany, Hungary, Poland, Romania, Yugoslavia)* **L1**

Visualizing History During the Soviet era, vast numbers of military vehicles and marchers paraded past Soviet leaders in Moscow's famous Red Square to celebrate May Day (May 1st), the Communist workers' holiday.

Visualizing History

Point out that May Day has been the "labor day" for Socialist and Communist countries since 1889. *What message is conveyed by a parade like this one?* (that the country is prepared militarily; it has the latest weapons; its people are united behind it) Kremlinologists used to study the lineup of leaders at these parades to see, by their positions (or nonappearance), who was in favor and who was not.

✔ Performance Assessment

Refer to the activity on page 638C of the Planning Guide.

📁 For an additional activity, refer to Activity 21 in the *Performance Assessment Strategies and Activities* booklet.

Using Your History Journal

Students may want to make an audiocassette or videotape of their interview. 📼

GLENCOE TECHNOLOGY

VIDEODISC
Use MindJogger to preview chapter content.

MindJogger Videoquiz
 Chapter 21
Disc 3 Side A

 Also available in VHS.

Your History Journal

Interview people who can remember the early period of the cold war. Evaluate the reliability of their accounts by analyzing their background, biases, and closeness to the events.

Chapter 21 *The Cold War* **639**

✚ EXTRA CREDIT PROJECT

Report Almost as soon as the war ended, the Allies began trials of several leading Nazis at Nuremberg, Germany. The men were accused of murder, enslavement, and other crimes against humanity. Have students research and report on the Nuremberg trials and their outcome. They should also deal with the controversy surrounding the trials—the first in which a nation's leaders were tried for war crimes. 📼

640   Chapter 21   *The Cold War*

1945   1955   1965

1947 The United States announces the Truman Doctrine and the Marshall Plan.

1955 West Germany joins NATO.

1961 Soviets and East Germans build the Berlin Wall.

SECTION THEME

▶ **Conflict** A cold war develops between the United States and the Soviet Union, the two superpowers that emerged after World War II.

ind Out

Answer: *the extension of Soviet control over Eastern Europe; the division of Germany; the Berlin blockade; the formation of rival military and economic alliances*

FOCUS

Section Objective

Identify the events that caused and heightened the cold war.

BELLRINGER
Motivational Activity

Before taking roll at the beginning of the class period, project Section Focus Transparency 21-1 and have students answer the activity questions. Discuss students' responses.

This activity is also available as a blackline master.

Vocabulary Pre-check

Use the Vocabulary PuzzleMaker to create a puzzle that reinforces the vocabulary terms in this section. **L1**

Section 1

The East-West Split

Setting the Scene

▶ **Terms to Define**
   superpower, cold war, satellite, iron curtain, containment, arms race, ideology, bloc

▶ **People to Meet**
   Joseph Stalin, Harry S Truman, George C. Marshall

▶ **Places to Locate**
   San Francisco, Greece, West Berlin

 **ind Out** What key events caused and heightened the cold war?

The Storyteller

Nikita Khrushchev recalled the beginning of the arms race: "We are surrounded by American air bases.... For many years after the war, bombers were to represent the major threat in our enemy's arsenal of weapons. It took time and a great deal of work for us to develop a bomber force on our own.... Two of our famous designers ...

developed the MiG-15, which in time was acknowledged as the best jet fighter in the world.... However, our superiority was short-lived. During the Korean War the U.S. started making a jet fighter that was better than the MiG-15, and soon the Americans ruled the air over Korea."

—from *Khrushchev Remembers, The Last Testament*, translated and edited by Strobe Talbott, 1974

Nikita Khrushchev

640   Chapter 21   *The Cold War*

---

he United States and the Soviet Union emerged from World War II as the world's two superpowers. No other countries were equal to them in military power or political influence. Differences in political beliefs and policies soon pulled the two superpowers apart and led to a struggle between them known as the cold war. In the cold war, each superpower sought world influence by means short of total war. This was because the possibility of nuclear war made the costs of a "hot" war too high. The "weapons" used in the cold war included the threat of force, the use of propaganda, and the sending of military and economic aid to weaker nations.

The United Nations

In the closing months of World War II, the Allies started planning for the postwar world. To handle future global problems, they had agreed at Yalta to replace the League of Nations with the United Nations, a new, permanent international organization. The purpose of the United Nations (UN) was to maintain peace by guaranteeing the security of member nations. It would foster good relations among nations based on the principles of equal rights and self-determination. It would also encourage cooperation on economic, cultural, and humanitarian problems.

In April 1945, representatives from 50 nations gathered in **San Francisco** to draft the Charter of the United Nations, which was completed and signed in June. The United Nations, headquartered in New York City, held its first sessions in 1946.

Although the UN Charter provided for six major bodies, it assigned the bulk of power to only two of them—the Security Council and the General Assembly. The Security Council, which decided diplomatic, political, and military disputes, was made up of 11 members. The five permanent members were Great Britain, China, France, the

---

SECTION RESOURCES

Reproducible Masters
- Reproducible Lesson Plan 21-1
- Guided Reading Activity 21-1
- Time Line Activity 21
- Geography and History Activity 21
- Section Quiz 21-1

Transparencies
- Section Focus Transparency 21-1
- Chapter Transparency 21
- World History and Art Transparency 43, *The Persistence of Memory*
- Mapping History Overlay Transparency 22, *The United Nations*

Multimedia
- Vocabulary PuzzleMaker Software
- Student Self-Test and Review Software
- Testmaker
- World Music: Cultural Traditions, Lesson 4
- Communism and the Cold War

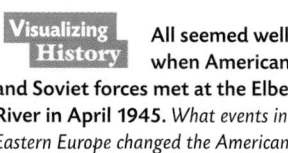 **All seemed well when American and Soviet forces met at the Elbe River in April 1945.** *What events in Eastern Europe changed the American attitude toward the Soviet Union?*

United States, and the Soviet Union. Each was given the right to veto any Security Council decision. The other six members served two-year terms. The General Assembly, the policy-making body, was made up of representatives from all UN member nations. Each nation had one vote.

The third body, the Economic and Social Council, oversaw the fights against poverty, ignorance, and disease. The fourth, the International Court of Justice, handled international legal disputes. The fifth, the Trusteeship Council, promoted the welfare of people in colonial territories and helped them toward self-rule. The sixth, the Secretariat, handled the UN's administrative work.

During the postwar period, the UN effectively resolved many crises. However, the right of veto granted the Security Council's permanent members made the UN powerless to resolve any dispute involving the United States and the Soviet Union. The United Nations became deadlocked. It was criticized as being a "debating society"—far from what the signers of the Charter had hoped it would be.

From Allies to Arch Enemies

After World War II, the Western Allies—the United States, Great Britain, and France—believed the best way to achieve security was to strengthen democracy and to build prosperous economies in Europe. The Soviets, however, had different goals. Historically, they had well-justified fears of invasion and had lost more than 20 million people in

World War II. The Soviet dictator **Joseph Stalin** wanted to establish pro-Soviet governments in Eastern Europe not only to prevent any future attacks but also to expand his empire. He made sure Eastern Europe's Communist parties were loyal to him and worked to strengthen their position throughout the region.

President Franklin D. Roosevelt had believed that postwar cooperation with Stalin was possible, although he was starting to change his mind shortly before his death in April 1945. In the months afterward, Roosevelt's successor, President **Harry S Truman**, and other leaders adopted a much darker view of Stalin. They concluded that the Soviet dictator wanted to control Eastern Europe with the same ruthlessness that he used to govern the Soviet Union.

The Iron Curtain

Eastern Europe thus became the first region where Soviet and Western interests came into conflict. In Albania and Yugoslavia, local Communist parties, which had led the resistance against Axis forces in their countries, took control with little help from the Soviets. In Poland, Romania, and Bulgaria, where Soviet troops were in full command, the Soviet Union made sure that government ministries included Communists. Later, breaking his promise made at Yalta, Stalin refused to allow free elections. Non-Communists were ousted from governments, and Communists took charge. By 1947, most of the nations of the region had become Soviet satellites, controlled by the Soviet Union.

Chapter 21 *The Cold War* **641**

TEACH

Guided Practice

THEME Conflict

Review with students the important differences between the Soviet Union and the United States that predated the end of World War II. *(different political systems: totalitarian versus democratic; different economic systems: planned Communist economy versus market capitalism; also, far different wartime experiences)* **L1 LEP**

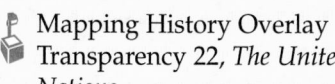 **At this time,** Russian troops were poised to push on to Berlin. American troops did not join them because American generals feared that casualties would be too high, and in fact Soviet casualties may have reached 100,000 in the assault on Berlin.

Answer to Caption: *the extension of Soviet control over Poland and other Eastern European countries*

Politics Review with the class the main agreements made at the Yalta conference in February 1945. *(The Allies agreed to divide Germany and Berlin. Stalin agreed to hold free elections in Soviet-occupied countries and to aid the Allies against Japan; in return, he received eastern Poland and territories in Asia.)* **L2**

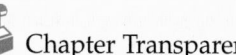 Mapping History Overlay Transparency 22, *The United Nations*

Chapter Transparency 21

World History and Art Transparency 43, *The Persistence of Memory*

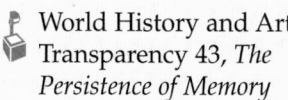 World Music: Cultural Traditions, Lesson 4

COOPERATIVE LEARNING ACTIVITY

Debate After the war, the Russians stripped East Germany of its industrial resources and equipment, while the Allies helped their three zones—what later became West Germany—toward economic recovery. Organize the class into two groups for a debate, one side representing the Soviet Union and the other the Allies. Each side should present its case for acting as it did. Students should try to answer why the differing policies were adopted and what their long-term effects were. **L3**

Map Study

Answer
Austria, Finland, Republic of Ireland, Spain, Sweden, Switzerland

Map Skills Practice

Reading a Map What Communist nation did not join the Warsaw Pact? *(Yugoslavia)*

Regionalism Ask students to explain how the circumstances of Soviet expansion differed in: (1) Albania, Yugoslavia, and Czechoslovakia; (2) Poland, Romania, Bulgaria, and Hungary; and (3) East Germany. *(1: Local Communists took control; 2: Soviet troops occupied during the war; 3: originally agreed on as the Soviet zone.)* **L3**

Who? What? Where? When?

Harry S Truman, a little-known senator from Missouri before he became Franklin Roosevelt's Vice President, had relatively little experience in foreign affairs. When he succeeded to the presidency on Roosevelt's death, he had been Vice President only 82 days and had met with the President just twice.

Independent Practice

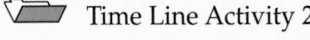 Guided Reading Activity 21-1 **L1**

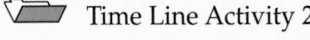 Time Line Activity 21

 Geography and History Activity 21

Literature Have students read George Orwell's *Animal Farm*, the satire of Russian totalitarianism. Some of them may want to read selected portions to the class for discussion. **L2**

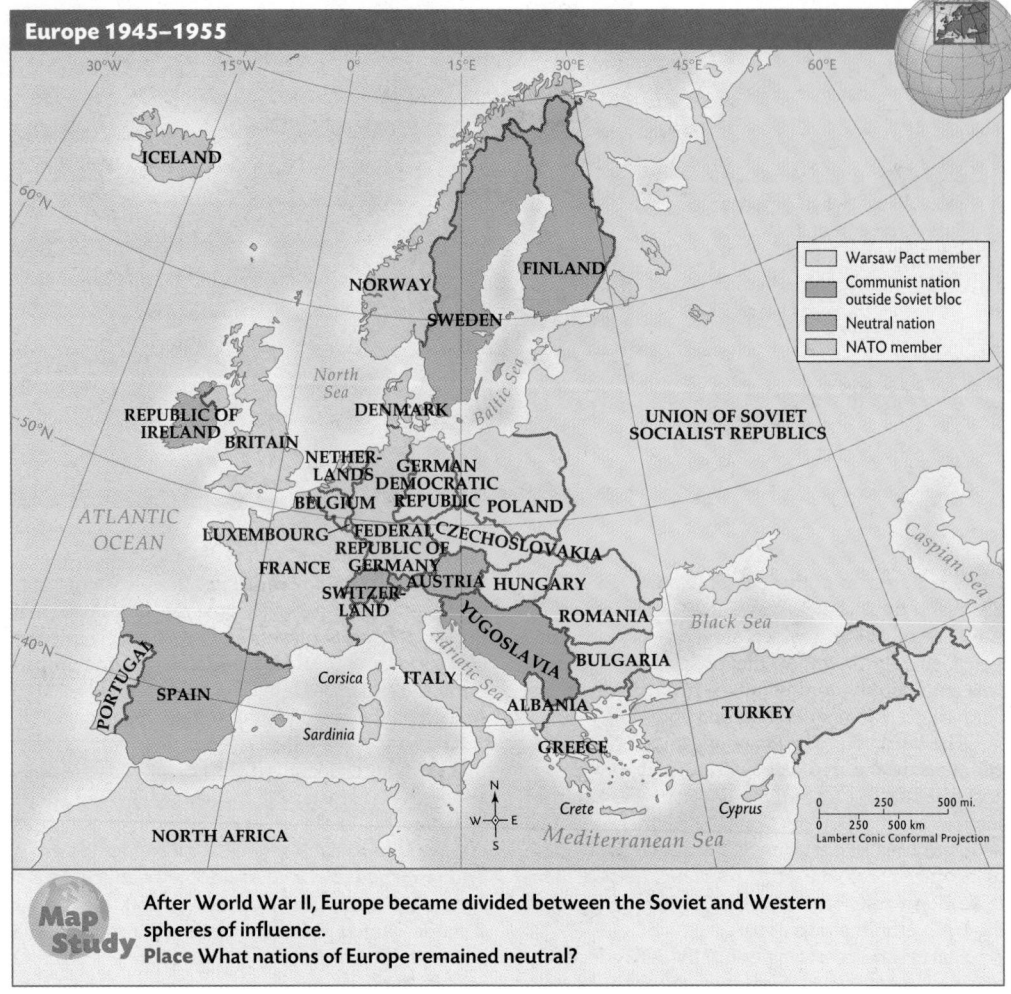

Europe 1945–1955

Map Study After World War II, Europe became divided between the Soviet and Western spheres of influence.
Place What nations of Europe remained neutral?

Stalin's actions in Eastern Europe convinced President Truman that the United States had to resist further Soviet moves. Truman was backed by British statesman Winston Churchill. In March 1946, Churchill had first used the phrase "iron curtain" in a speech in Fulton, Missouri: "From Stettin in the Baltic to Trieste in the Adriatic an iron curtain has descended across the continent of Europe." Thereafter, iron curtain referred to the Soviet-made barrier that split Europe into non-Communist Western Europe and Communist Eastern Europe.

Containing Communism

To counter any expansionist threat from the Soviet Union, the United States developed a new foreign policy in 1947. The idea for the new policy was presented in early 1947 by George Kennan, a State Department expert on the Soviet Union. Believing that the Soviets sought to expand their territory without war, he suggested a policy of containment—holding back the spread of communism. By standing firm, the United States hoped to keep communism inside its existing borders.

The Truman Doctrine

In the spring of 1947, President Truman applied the containment policy for the first time in the eastern Mediterranean. In **Greece**, local Communists were fighting a guerrilla war against the pro-Western monarchy. They were aided by Communists from neighboring Yugoslavia and Albania. The West feared that the fall of Greece to

642 Chapter 21 *The Cold War*

MEETING SPECIAL NEEDS ACTIVITY

Study Strategy Events unfolded rapidly in the early years of the cold war. To understand the events that were happening in many parts of Europe, students can construct a chart. Along the side, suggest that they put the years 1945 to 1947, divided into two- or three-month intervals. Along the top, students should enter the names of the countries most involved in the cold war, either alphabetically or by region. At the appropriate place, they should then indicate important events in the cold war. **L2**

Cornell Capa, Magnum

Cold War

In 1961 Soviet Premier Nikita Khrushchev (left) and United States President John F. Kennedy held a cold war meeting. Khrushchev insisted that troops of the Soviet Union's former World War II Allies—France, Great Britain, and the United States—must leave West Berlin. The Allies' sector of Berlin was entirely inside East Germany, a separate nation from West Germany and an ally of the Soviet Union. Kennedy refused, believing that the Soviets would take control over West Berlin if the Allies departed. Two months later the Soviets shocked the people of both Berlins—and the world—by building the Berlin Wall.

The Berlin Wall became an important symbol of the cold war. For nearly a half century after the end of World War II the world's two superpowers, the United States and the Union of Soviet Socialist Republics, dominated the world and fought a "cold" war. In fact, it was not always cold. The two powers fought a number of regional conflicts either directly or through allies, including the Korean and Vietnam Wars. In 1989 the Berlin Wall was torn down; in 1991, the Soviet Union crumbled and the cold war came to an end. ⊕

Chapter 21 *The Cold War* **643**

TEACH

Tell students that, although the United States could not prevent the building of the Berlin Wall, American leaders never abandoned their goal of reuniting Germany. Two years after this meeting, in June 1963, Kennedy appeared before a huge outdoor rally in West Berlin and delivered an address that included this famous declaration: "All free men, wherever they may live, are citizens of Berlin, and, therefore, as a free man, I take pride in the words 'Ich bin ein Berliner' (I am a Berliner)."

Linking Past and Present

Green Berets One tactic advanced by the West against the East during the cold war was counterinsurgency—organized military action to counteract revolutionary activity. A prime U.S. counterinsurgent force, the Green Berets, received its name because of its distinctive headgear, specifically authorized by President Kennedy.

VIDEODISC
Communism and the Cold War

Side One, Chapter 15
Frames 26867–29413
Title: *Berlin Wall*
Ask: What reason did the Soviets give for blockading East and West Berlin? *(They were attempting to keep agents from the West from coming into the Soviet Union.)*

you don't say...

"Iron curtain" was an expression that Churchill popularized but did not originate. As long ago as the early 1800s, it was used to refer to a fireproof curtain in theaters, installed to prevent the spread of flames between the stage area and the audience.

communism would endanger Western influence in the eastern Mediterranean region.

Great Britain was the traditional defender of the eastern Mediterranean. Economic weaknesses at home, however, prevented the British from continuing their commitment. In February 1947, Great Britain informed President Truman of this fact and asked the United States to assume British responsibilities in the area. A month later, Truman asked Congress for a $400 million aid program for Greece and Turkey. In asking Congress for support, Truman made a new statement of foreign policy that became known as the Truman Doctrine. He stated:

❝ I believe that it must be the policy of the United States to support free peoples who are resisting attempted subjugation by armed minorities or by outside pressures…. [W]e must assist free peoples to work out their own destiny in their own way. ❞

Congress approved Truman's aid request. With the acceptance of the Truman Doctrine, the United States took on international responsibilities as the leader of the Western world. American military aid would now be available to any nation threatened by communism. As a result of American assistance, Greece was able to defeat the Communist guerrillas and the spread of communism in the eastern Mediterranean was blocked.

The Marshall Plan

Conditions in Europe posed immediate and long-term challenges for the United States. World War II had severely weakened European economies. The Truman administration feared that a European economic collapse would open Europe to communism. It believed that the military and economic security of the United States depended on a strong and democratic Europe.

Therefore, the United States government devised a new approach to provide aid to Europe. Speaking at Harvard University on June 5, 1947,

Images *of the* Times

Rebuilding Europe

Fearing the spread of communism, the United States adopted strong economic programs to rebuild Europe after World War II. The Soviets responded with a rival plan in Eastern Europe.

Devastation in the divided city of Berlin challenged the resolve of the West to restore not only the structures but the spirit of the people.

644

Images *of the* Times

Rebuilding Europe

By 1945 and 1946, Europe had begun to recover from the war. But an extremely harsh winter in 1947 caused a setback. For this reason, economic aid such as the Marshall Plan was crucial. By the mid-1960s, European industrial output totaled more than two and a half times what it had been before the war.

Secretary of State **George C. Marshall** proposed a European aid program that became known as the Marshall Plan. Its purpose, he said, was to restore "the confidence of European people in the economic future of their own countries." For the plan to work, Marshall urged a united effort to determine where Europe's economic needs lay and how the United States could help.

Western European countries responded enthusiastically to the Marshall Plan; however, the Soviet Union refused to participate in the plan and forced its Eastern European allies to do the same. Despite their great need for economic aid, the Soviets felt they could not afford to give out information about their economy. They also opposed linking their Communist economy with the largely capitalist ones of Western Europe.

The Marshall Plan was a great success. Western European nations worked together to boost productivity, reduce trade barriers, and use resources efficiently. They received about $13 billion in aid from the United States during the next four years.

By 1951, Western Europe's economies were prospering, and Communist prospects in these countries had declined.

The Marshall Plan extended American influence in Western Europe and helped unite the region into a single economic group to counter the Soviets. In reaction to the Marshall Plan, in 1949 the Soviet Union set up a rival plan known as the Council for Mutual Economic Assistance, or COMECON. Eastern Europe was thus formed into a competing economic group led by the Soviet Union.

Germany Divided

In 1945, Germany had been divided into four zones, controlled by Great Britain, France, the United States, and the Soviet Union. The zones of the Western Allies included the western part of Germany, while the Soviet zone encompassed eastern Germany. The city of Berlin, deep within the Soviet zone, was also divided into four sectors.

Modern Warsaw finally emerged from behind the iron curtain when Poland overthrew its Communist government in 1989.

Threatened by revolt, Greece received economic aid under the Truman Doctrine until the Marshall Plan went into effect.

REFLECTING ON THE TIMES

1. Why was it difficult for the United States to send supplies into Berlin in 1948?
2. What is the purpose of the large sign on the railway car delivering goods in Greece?
3. Why did the Soviet Union prevent its allies from participating in the Marshall Plan?

645

Cooperation The UN, which began with 51 members, now has 184. Have students research the changes in membership and what these changes have meant to the operation of the United Nations. **L3**

Who?What?Where?When?

Denazification After the war the Allies agreed that Nazis should be punished—a process called denazification. One aspect of this process consisted of trials of wartime leaders. But many low-level collaborators were also purged—some tried and executed or imprisoned, many simply fired from their jobs.

ABCNEWS INTERACTIVE™

 VIDEODISC Communism and the Cold War

Side One, Chapter 6
Frames 11768–13455
Title: *The Arms Race*
Subject: Development of the arms race between the United States and the Soviet Union
Ask: What was the arms race? *(It was a competition between the United States and the Soviet Union in the development of high-tech weaponry.)*

ANSWERS TO REFLECTING ON THE TIMES

1. The Soviet Union had cut off access by land.
2. to publicize the role of the United States in bringing about European recovery
3. The Soviets did not want to give out information about their economy, and they did not want to link their economies with the non-Communist West.

Map Study

Answer
the Soviet zone

Map Skills Practice

Reading a Map In what zone was the port city of Bremen? *(U.S. zone)*

Linking Past and Present

NATO Although the Warsaw Pact came to an end in 1991, NATO continues to flourish. Representatives of its 16 member nations form the North Atlantic Council, with headquarters in Brussels, Belgium. Since its beginnings, NATO has been dominated by the United States, and its supreme allied commander in Europe has always been an American.

ASSESS

Check for Understanding

Assign Section 1 Review as homework or as an in-class activity.

🔲 Use Student Self-Test and Review Software to review Section 1.

Evaluate

 Section Quiz 21-1

🔲 Use the Testmaker to create a customized quiz for Section 1.

Occupation of Germany and Austria 1945

Map Study Germany and Austria were divided into zones. In 1955, Austria reunited as a neutral country. **Place** What zone surrounded Berlin?

Zones of Occupation

The Western Allies and the Soviets could not reach agreement on a final peace treaty for Germany. As relations with Stalin soured, the United States, Great Britain, and France decided to include their zones in the Marshall Plan as means to contain communism.

While the Soviets stripped their German zone of its industrial resources and equipment, the three Western powers aided their zones toward economic recovery. Free elections for local governments were held in the Western zones. The United States, Great Britain, and France also agreed to combine their sectors of Berlin to form what became known as the city of **West Berlin**. They also planned to form an independent West German state by joining their zones of occupation.

The Berlin Blockade

In June 1948, the Soviets tried to block this merger plan by cutting all land access from the West into West Berlin. Two million Berliners depended on the Western Allies for all their food, fuel, and other needs. The United States and other Western countries considered and rejected the idea of using force to regain access to Berlin. Instead, they came up with a plan to airlift needed supplies

to the isolated city.

To keep the city alive, at least 4,000 tons of supplies were needed every day. Airplanes surpassed this goal by landing every 3 minutes at West Berlin's 2 airports. At the peak of the airlift, 13,000 tons were landed in one day. The airlift would continue for 11 months. Its success finally forced the Soviets to lift the blockade in May 1949.

That same month, the Western Allies went ahead with their plans to form an independent West German state. A constitution was approved that set up a federal system of 10 states. In the fall of 1949, the Federal Republic of Germany, or West Germany, was proclaimed. Its capital was at Bonn. The Soviets then set up the German Democratic Republic, or East Germany, with its capital at East Berlin. Thus, Germany was divided into 2 separate countries.

New Alliances

Just before the Berlin blockade, another crisis had occurred in Europe. In February 1948, Czechoslovakia was taken over by Communists and incorporated into the Soviet alliance system. The Czechoslovak and Berlin crises heightened Western concerns about military defense. In April 1949, shortly before the end of the Berlin blockade, the North Atlantic Treaty Organization (NATO) was formed by the United States, Great Britain, France, Belgium, the Netherlands, Luxembourg, Italy, Portugal, Denmark, Iceland, Norway, and Canada. NATO expanded to include Greece and Turkey in 1952 and West Germany in 1955. Members of this military alliance agreed that an attack on one would be considered an attack on all. In response to NATO, the Soviet Union and its Eastern European allies signed a military agreement known as the Warsaw Pact in 1955.

Later events showed that the purpose of the Warsaw Pact was as much to strengthen the Soviet

---

MAKING CONNECTIONS ACTIVITIES

Military History The United States has stationed troops in Germany ever since the end of World War II. Have students research and report on the reasons for their presence; the location of the main bases; and troop totals and how they have varied over the years. **L2**

Daily Life At its height the cold war had a strong impact on many nonpolitical aspects of life, including sports. Have students research and report on how the cold war affected the Olympic Games. **L1**

hold on Eastern Europe as to defend it. Soviet troops stationed in Hungary under the terms of the Warsaw Pact were used to suppress a 1956 uprising there. In 1968 the Soviet Union appealed to the treaty to justify its invasion of Czechoslovakia, which had introduced a liberal form of communism.

Worldwide Struggle

The cold war soon turned into a global struggle. In 1949, the Soviets successfully exploded their first atomic bomb. International tensions further increased as the two superpowers engaged in an **arms race**, or a competition to strengthen their armed forces and weapons systems.

Meanwhile, communism made rapid advances in Asia. In the late 1940s, Communist governments came to power in China and North Korea. In 1950, the North Koreans, allied to the Soviet Union and Communist-ruled China, attacked South Korea, a pro-Western republic. Although the North Koreans were forced back to their territory, the Korean conflict fed Western fears that in communism, it faced a single, powerful enemy seeking world conquest.

Beginning in the 1950s, the cold war also came to be not only a test of military strength, but also a test of the superpowers' competing **ideologies**, or political and economic philosophies—democratic capitalism on the part of the United States, and communism on the part of the Soviet Union. Military buildups, space exploration, and local and regional conflicts around the globe became entangled in the cold war as the two superpowers sought to win support and to block gains by the other.

Germany

Germany became a critical flash point in the cold war during the 1950s and 1960s. Nikita Khrushchev (krush•CHAWF), who became Soviet leader in the mid-1950s, set out to test the resolve of the new United States President John F. Kennedy in 1961 by threatening to force the Allies out of West Berlin. Stating that the West would defend West Berlin's freedom, Kennedy bolstered the United States military presence, and Khrushchev did not act on his threats.

Meanwhile, large numbers of East Germans were fleeing to West Berlin, which was easily accessible to them. In an effort to halt the drain of its workforce, the East German government, with Soviet backing, built a concrete wall across the divided city in August 1961. The Berlin Wall stemmed the flow of East Germans fleeing communism and raised East-West tensions. It became a symbol of the cold war and the hostile confrontation between democracy and communism.

The Developing World

After the early 1960s, superpower competition directly affected developing nations in Asia, Africa, and Latin America. In most areas, such as in Africa and the Caribbean area, the superpowers provided aid to their allies in the particular region. Sometimes—as in the case of the Soviet Union in Afghanistan and the United States in Vietnam—they became militarily involved themselves.

By the late 1970s, however, the division of the world into two **blocs**, or groups of nations, each headed by a superpower, was coming to an end. The United States, wary of military involvements, faced growing challenges to its hold on world markets. Western Europe and Japan, less dependent on the United States, were prosperous economic powers in their own right. The Soviet Union, faltering economically, was facing internal pressures for change. Finally, many smaller nations, aligned with neither superpower, were following their own paths of development. All of these events marked the move away from a world dominated by the superpowers to one in which there were many competing groups of countries.

Worldwide Struggle
What made the cold war a unique development?
It was a long struggle between global superpowers that involved all means short of all-out war. The conditions of the cold war were set by the superpowers' possession of nuclear weapons and their fear of mass destruction in the event of these weapons being used.

Reteach

Have students review the events that precipitated the cold war by brainstorming a list on the chalkboard and then putting the events in chronological order.

Enrich

Have students watch a video of a film made during the cold war such as *Fail Safe, Dr. Strangelove,* or *The Russians Are Coming! The Russians Are Coming!* Have them write a brief analysis of the view of U.S.-Soviet relations in the film they see.

CLOSE

Have students list, in order, the American Presidents who held office during the cold war and the major events related to the cold war that took place during their administrations.

SECTION 1 REVIEW

Recall
1. **Define** superpower, cold war, satellite, iron curtain, containment, arms race, ideology, bloc.
2. **Identify** Joseph Stalin, Harry S Truman, George C. Marshall, the Marshall Plan, NATO, Warsaw Pact.
3. **Use** the map on page 642 to name the European nations under Soviet control.

Critical Thinking
4. **Analyzing Information** What geographic factor made it possible for Stalin to impose the Berlin blockade?

Understanding Themes
5. **Conflict** What were some of the political and economic "weapons" of the cold war? What goals did the superpowers hope to accomplish using these varying strategies?

SECTION 1 REVIEW ANSWERS

1. All vocabulary words are defined in the Glossary.
2. Joseph Stalin, 641; Harry S Truman, 641; George C. Marshall, 645; Marshall Plan, 645; NATO, 646; Warsaw Pact, 646
3. East Germany, Poland, Czechoslovakia, Hungary, Romania, Bulgaria, Albania
4. West Berlin was totally surrounded by the Soviet zone.
5. **CONFLICT** Political weapons: transforming governments into Communist or democratic states; active military intervention. Economic weapons: aid and trade links. Goals included extending actual rule or at least influence.

1955

1955 Nikita Khrushchev becomes the dominant leader in the Soviet Union.

1965

1968 The Soviets invade Czechoslovakia.

1972 Soviet and American leaders hold summit meeting in Moscow.

1975

SECTION THEME

▶ **Change** The Soviet Union tries to move away from the legacy of Stalin while maintaining its control over Eastern Europe.

ind Out

Answer: *Along with maintaining its authoritarian system of Communist rule, it continued the arms race and exercised tight control over its Eastern European satellites.*

FOCUS

Section Objective

Explain how the Soviet Union carried out Communist policies after the death of Stalin.

BELLRINGER
Motivational Activity

Before taking roll at the beginning of the class period, project Section Focus Transparency 21-2 and have students answer the activity questions. Discuss students' responses.

🗁 This activity is also available as a blackline master.

Vocabulary Pre-check

🗁 Use Vocabulary Activity 21 to introduce vocabulary terms.
L1 LEP

Section 2

The Communist Bloc

Setting the Scene

▶ **Terms to Define**
peaceful coexistence, intercontinental ballistic missile (ICBM), dissident, detente

▶ **People to Meet**
Nikita Khrushchev, Leonid Brezhnev, Josip Broz Tito, Alexander Dubček

▶ **Places to Locate**
Yugoslavia, East Germany, Poland, Hungary, Czechoslovakia

ind Out How did the Soviet Union carry out Communist policies after the death of Stalin?

ʄtoryteller

Peter Hauptman and Willi Pfeiffer had been best friends since childhood. Although their homes were only two blocks apart, they lived in different sectors of Berlin. Now, literally overnight, their frequent visits ended. The Soviet sector was walled off. Not just a barricade or a lowered gate, it was a wall, protected by barbed wire and concrete blocks. Peter stood on the western side of the wall, strain-

ing to catch a glimpse of Willi. But it was to no avail. Everyone living near the wall's eastern side had been forcibly relocated, and the nearby apartment doors and windows were sealed shut.

—adapted from *People and Politics: The Years 1960–1975,* translated and edited by Strobe Talbott, 1974

Children play near the Berlin Wall

The cold war affected the internal policies of the Soviet Union and its Eastern European satellites. During the late 1940s and early 1950s, Joseph Stalin believed that a full-scale conflict with the West was inevitable. To confront the West, the Soviet leader increased his control over the Soviet Union and Eastern Europe. He purged Communist parties of officials suspected of disloyalty. He also forbade writers and artists to use Western ideas in their works.

The Soviet Union

After World War II, Stalin worked to rebuild the Soviet Union's heavy industry and to boost its military strength. The Soviet Union surpassed its prewar rates of production in several major products, including coal, steel, and oil. It continued a high level of military spending and exploded its first nuclear bomb. In spite of the country's military prestige, life for the average Soviet citizen was difficult. Towns and cities destroyed by the war were rebuilt. Consumer goods, food, and clothing, however, remained in short supply because of high military spending.

Stalin died in March 1953. He was succeeded by a collective leadership of top Communist officials. **Nikita Khrushchev**, who served as Communist party secretary, emerged as the dominant leader in 1955.

De-Stalinization

In the following year, the 20th Congress of the Soviet Communist Party was held in Moscow. At a secret session, Nikita Khrushchev gave a controversial speech about Stalin. He denounced the Soviet dictator for the purges in the 1930s, in which thousands of loyal party members had been tortured

---

SECTION RESOURCES

🗁 **Reproducible Masters**
• Reproducible Lesson Plan 21-2
• Vocabulary Activity 21
• Guided Reading Activity 21-2
• Section Quiz 21-2

Transparencies
• Section Focus Transparency 21-2

Multimedia
• Student Self-Test and Review Software
• Testmaker
• Communism and the Cold War:
  • *Rebellion Behind the Iron Curtain*
  • *Sputnik Launches the Space Race*
  • *Cuban Missile Crisis*

Visualizing History President Eisenhower hosts Premier Nikita Khrushchev in Washington, D.C., in 1959. *What prevented the four-power summit meeting planned for May 1960 from taking place?*

by improving working conditions. He sought to improve housing and to increase the production of consumer goods. The Soviet leader also put new emphasis on technological research. This paid off in 1957 with the launch of *Sputnik I,* the world's first space satellite. *Sputnik* stunned the United States and boosted the prestige of the Soviet Union and its leader.

Despite the cold war "thaw," both superpowers continued a massive military buildup. In the late 1950s, the Americans and Soviets successfully tested long-range rockets known as intercontinental ballistic missiles, or ICBMs, and added them to their arsenals. ICBMs for the first time could target locations in both countries. A nuclear war would result in what was known as mutual assured destruction—that is, the certain destruction of both nations.

Even as they pursued this deadly race, United States and Soviet leaders sought to maintain peace. Summit meetings were the most visible of many contacts between Soviets and the United States. United States President Dwight Eisenhower and Soviet Premier Khrushchev met in Geneva, Switzerland, in 1955 and again in 1959 at Camp David, in Maryland. They recognized the deadly threat of nuclear war and agreed on the need to end the arms race. They planned a four-power summit for Paris in May 1960 and Khrushchev invited Eisenhower to visit the Soviet Union later in the year. But shortly before the Paris summit, the Soviets shot down an American U-2 spy plane over their territory and captured its pilot. Facing criticism from the Soviet military, Khrushchev strongly

and condemned to death or sent to labor camps. He also accused Stalin of creating a "cult of personality," in which he boosted his own image at the expense of the Communist party.

Khrushchev's anti-Stalin speech was part of a broader program of de-Stalinization, which he undertook from 1956 to 1964 to reverse some of the policies that had existed under Stalin. Khrushchev understood that many Soviet citizens wanted a relaxation of government controls and an improved standard of living. While keeping Stalin's Five-Year Plans and collective farms, he promised better wages and more consumer goods. He gave artists and intellectuals more freedom. He also reduced the terror of the secret police and freed many political prisoners from labor camps.

Cold War "Thaw"

By the mid-1950s, both American and Soviet leaders were interested in reducing cold-war tensions. Khrushchev called for a policy of peaceful coexistence in which the Soviets would compete with the West but avoid war. He stated the Soviet Union would surpass the West economically and encouraged other countries to follow the Communist model.

To make the Soviet Union more economically competitive, Khrushchev tried to boost production

Footnotes to History

The Kitchen Debate
In 1959, Vice President Richard M. Nixon, on a tour of the Soviet Union, visited an exhibition of American products with Soviet leader Nikita Khrushchev. The two leaders soon got into a heated argument on the merits of capitalism versus communism. The argument became known as the "kitchen debate" because the two men were standing in front of a model kitchen display.

Chapter 21 *The Cold War* 649

TEACH

Guided Practice

THEME Change
After Stalin's death in 1953, the Soviet leadership instituted some changes to ease living conditions. *What were the most important aspects of de-Stalinization? (promises of higher wages and more consumer goods; more freedom for artists and intellectuals; a lessening of secret police activities; and the release from labor camps of many political prisoners)* **L1 LEP**

Visualizing History On this 1959 trip, Khrushchev dined at the White House, visited a farm in Iowa, and dropped in on a supermarket in San Francisco. In Hollywood he watched a rehearsal of the movie *Can Can,* later criticizing it as immoral.
Answer to Caption: *An American U-2 spy plane was shot down by Soviets.*

 VIDEODISC
Communism and the Cold War

Side One, Chapter 14
Frames 24964–26834
Title: *Sputnik Launches the Space Race*
Subject: The beginning of the space race
Ask: Why did the United States panic when the Soviet Union unveiled *Sputnik*? *(The U.S. feared that the enemy was more technologically prepared.)*

COOPERATIVE LEARNING ACTIVITY

Press Conference Organize the class into two groups, one to represent reporters and the other to play the roles of President Eisenhower and his staff. The teams should research to plan questions and answers for a news conference after the announcement of the shooting down of the U-2 spy plane. Encourage students to address the larger issues of the cold war. The conference should be enacted as if it were actually happening, and you may want to videotape it. **L3**

Politics Ask students when and how the Soviet Union dealt with reactions against its rule in East Germany, Hungary, and Czechoslovakia. *(East Germany: military intervention in 1953, built the Berlin Wall in 1961; Hungary, armed force in 1956; Czechoslovakia, armed force in 1968)* **L3 LEP**

 VIDEODISC
Communism and the Cold War

Side One, Chapter 16
Frames 29427–32782
Title: *Cuban Missile Crisis*
Subject: Summary and different perspectives of the Cuban missile crisis
Ask: Why did the United States panic when the Soviet Union put missiles in Cuba? *(The U.S. felt threatened because Cuba was located so close to the United States.)*

Independent Practice

 Guided Reading Activity
21-2 **L1**

CURRICULUM CONNECTION

SCIENCE
Under Stalin every aspect of intellectual life was scrutinized and controlled. Biology fell under the control of an eccentric scientist named T. D. Lysenko. Among other things, he taught that acquired characteristics could be inherited and that wheat plants could produce rye seeds.

---

denounced the United States and canceled Eisenhower's visit. Relations soon worsened further.

The Cuban Missile Crisis

The Soviet Union and the United States came to the brink of nuclear war in 1962. In 1961, Eisenhower was succeeded as United States President by John F. Kennedy, who adopted a dynamic foreign policy to impress the Soviets with American strength and boost American prestige abroad. Testing Kennedy's resolve, Khrushchev used pressure to try to remove the Allies from Berlin. Then in 1962 he secretly began to install nuclear missiles on Cuba 90 miles (145 km) from Florida. In his gamble, the Soviet leader hoped to offset American missiles based in Turkey that were aimed at the Soviet Union. He also wanted to get from Kennedy a promise not to overthrow Cuba's Communist government. Devising a strong response short of attack, Kennedy blockaded Cuba. Khrushchev then agreed to withdraw the missiles; and in return, Kennedy pledged not to invade Cuba.

The Cuban missile crisis was one of the most significant events in the cold war. Having come so close to nuclear conflict, the superpowers decided to establish a better relationship. In 1963, a telephone "hot line" linked Washington and Moscow to provide instant communication. That same year, the Soviets and the Western Allies also signed a treaty banning nuclear weapons tests in the atmosphere.

Meanwhile, Khrushchev's position within the Soviet Union weakened. In addition to his poor handling of the Cuban missile crisis, relations with China had soured, and Khrushchev's economic policies were in trouble. Heavy spending on technology, defense, and heavy industry had left little for improving agriculture and consumer goods. Far from surpassing the United States, the Soviet Union was forced to import grain from the United States. Sharply rising meat and butter prices provoked angry public demonstrations. In October 1964, Khrushchev was removed from office.

The Brezhnev Era

The Communist party chose a new collective leadership: Aleksei Kosygin (kuh•SEE•guhn) was premier and **Leonid Brezhnev** (BREHZH•NEHF) was general secretary of the party. By the mid-1970s, Brezhnev emerged as the dominant leader. He remained in control until his death in 1982.

Cautious and traditional, Brezhnev reversed Khrushchev's de-Stalinization policies. He clamped down again on intellectuals and dissidents—those who criticized the party or regime. Two prominent

---

dissidents refused to be silenced. Alexander Solzhenitsyn (SOHL•zhuh•NEET•suhn), author of many works including *The Gulag Archipelago*, an account of the horrors of Soviet prison camps, was eventually deported and settled in the United States. Dr. Andrei Sakharov (SAH•kuh•RAWF), scientist and developer of the Soviet hydrogen bomb, later denounced the arms race and was sentenced to internal exile in Gorki.

Brezhnev's military and economic policies were similar to Khrushchev's. Concerned that there was a missile gap with the United States, he greatly increased the Soviet nuclear arsenal and its supplies of conventional weapons. He felt that military power gave the Soviet Union a stronger position in world diplomacy.

Under Brezhnev, economic conditions, however, worsened in the Soviet Union. Heavy military spending stifled growth in other sectors of the economy. Soviet workers had to make do with outdated equipment. Technologically, many industries were at least 20 years behind the times. Consumer goods were shoddy and in short supply. Farmers were only one-sixth as productive as their American counterparts. Poor harvests forced the Soviet Union to again import grain from the West.

Detente

By 1972, Brezhnev was ready to reduce tensions with the West. He hoped to find a way to cut military spending without falling behind the United States militarily. He also needed access to Western technology, grain, and consumer goods.

The United States was ready for Brezhnev's policy of detente. Derived from the French word meaning "relaxation," detente referred to an improvement of American-Soviet relations. A 1972 summit meeting between Brezhnev and United States President Richard Nixon in Moscow began a period of detente that lasted seven years. The Brezhnev-Nixon summit led to the signing of the Strategic Arms Limitation Agreement (SALT) Treaty, under which both sides agreed to limit the number of nuclear warheads and missiles each country could maintain. SALT did not reduce the number of weapons or end the arms race; it did slow it significantly.

Detente did not end the rivalry between the United States and the Soviet Union. The countries continued to compete for influence in various parts of the world. In 1979, the Soviets invaded neighboring Afghanistan to reinforce local Communist control. The move shocked the West and marked the end of detente. It also drew the Soviet Union into a 10-year guerrilla war against tough Afghan

---

MEETING SPECIAL NEEDS ACTIVITY

Attention Deficiency To help students understand the many personalities and events discussed in this section, make out a card for each key person, from Stalin to Dubček. Then organize the class into two teams and have students from each team take turns picking a card, sight unseen. Have that team identify the person, citing his nationality and an event associated with him. Give points based on correct answers. **L1 LEP**

Visualizing History While the Soviets constructed the Berlin Wall in 1961, Russian and American tanks maneuvered within sight of each other.
What was the real purpose of the wall?

nationalists. The occupation of Afghanistan drained the national treasury, brought about the deaths of thousands of young Soviet soldiers, and became extremely unpopular at home.

Soviet Satellites

For most of the cold war, the Soviet Union maintained tight control over its Eastern European satellites. The peoples of these nations resented Soviet domination, but were largely powerless against the secret police and Soviet troops.

Yugoslavia

After World War II, **Yugoslavia** became the only large Communist state in Eastern Europe to resist Soviet control. Its leader, **Josip Broz Tito**, had participated in the resistance against the Nazis. As much a nationalist as a Communist, Tito insisted on developing his own national policies. Angered by Tito's independence, Stalin expelled Yugoslavia from the international Communist movement. Throughout Eastern Europe, Stalin waged a propaganda war against what he called Titoism, or the tendency of some Communists to place their national interests above those of the Soviet Union. With the support of his people, Tito resisted Soviet pressure, developed his own form of communism, held together the different religious and ethnic groups of the country, and won aid from the West. He led Yugoslavia until his death in 1980.

East Germany

Although it recovered from World War II more slowly than West Germany, **East Germany** became the most prosperous of the Soviet satellites. Its people deeply resented Soviet controls, however. In the aftermath of Stalin's death in 1953, East German workers went on strike and rioted when the government tried to lengthen the work day without an increase in wages. Soviet troops and tanks easily put down the revolt.

In the years that followed, nearly 3 million East Germans migrated to West Germany, by way of West Berlin, the only safe access available once the Soviets sealed the East German-West German border. A large percentage of the migrants were well-educated professionals who were attracted by West Germany's higher standard of living and greater

Chapter 21 Section 2

Visualizing History When the Berlin Wall was first erected, it bisected some buildings. Thus people were able to enter the premises in East Berlin and leave—jumping out a window if necessary—in West Berlin. East German authorities acted quickly, however, to brick up escape routes of this sort.
Answer to Caption: *to stop the flow of people from East Berlin to West Berlin*

Report Have students research and report on the pilot of the U-2 mission in 1960, Francis Gary Powers, explaining what happened to him after he was shot down over the Soviet Union. **L2**

A&E HOME VIDEO.

The following videotape program is available from Glencoe:

- **Soviet Space: The Secret Designer**

To find classroom resources to accompany this video, check the following home page:
A&E Television:
http://www.AandE.com/

MAKING CONNECTIONS ACTIVITIES

Music Artistic activity was closely regulated in the Soviet Union. Even composers were expected to glorify the Communist state. Have students research and report on what this meant for such important composers as Sergey Prokofiev, Dmitry Shostakovich, and Aram Khachaturian. **L3**

Religion Although the Soviet Union officially embraced atheism and placed many restrictions on the Russian Orthodox Church, religion survived and even flourished. Have students research and report on religion in the Soviet Union during the cold war and its role in Russian or Eastern European societies today. **L2**

VIDEODISC
Communism and the Cold War

Side One, Chapter 10
Frames 17333–20021
Title: *Rebellion Behind the Iron Curtain*
Subject: Discussion of rebellions in Soviet satellite nations, Soviet reaction, and why the United States did not support the rebellion acts
Ask: Why would the Soviet Union not allow democratic reforms in Czechoslovakia and Hungary? *(due to the fear that the reform movements would spread into the Soviet Union)*

freedoms. This "brain drain" was an embarrassment to the Soviets and an economic blow to the nation.

East Germany's problems contributed to a new cold war crisis in 1959. By then, West Germany had recovered from the war and was fully armed with tanks, bombs, and guns. It also had nuclear weapons on its soil under the control of NATO command. Alarmed at this development, Khrushchev called for negotiations on European security and on a nuclear-free Germany. He also demanded that the Western powers withdraw from Berlin.

Frustrated by the lack of a settlement and the continuing flight of East Germans, Khrushchev ordered the construction of what became the notorious Berlin Wall. In 1961, East German soldiers began work on the wall, a massive concrete structure 26 miles (42 km) long and up to 15 feet (4.6 m) high, topped with electrified wire.

The stated purpose of the wall was to keep Westerners out, but its true purpose was to halt the exodus of East Germans from East Berlin. To escape to West Berlin, people now had to survive mined trenches, guard dogs, and self-activating guns. Then they had to scale the wall itself. Stories reached the West of heroic escapes, but scores of East Germans died trying to run to freedom. Although the Berlin Wall did halt the flow of East German refugees, it became the most visible and powerful physical symbol of the iron curtain.

Poland

Under Communist rule, **Poland** industrialized and, among the satellites, became second in manufacturing only to East Germany. Poles, however, resented Soviet controls. They were angered by the government's efforts to collectivize farms and by its anti-Catholic policies. In June 1956 workers demanding better wages rioted in the city of Poznan. Upheavals in other cities forced Poland's Communist leaders to remove hard-line officials from office.

Poland's new leader was Wladyslaw Gomulka (VLAH•dee•slah goh•MUL•kuh), a popular Communist who had been accused of anti-Soviet activities and jailed during the late 1940s. Gomulka freed political prisoners, ended forced collectivization, and eased relations with the Catholic Church. He retained close ties with the Soviet Union, however. By the mid-1960s many of the Polish freedoms had again been lost.

In the 1970s, there was a new wave of anti-government strikes, with workers demanding better living conditions, and political and economic reforms. Gomulka resigned under the pressure.

Continued economic problems led to food riots in 1976 and the growth of an underground anti-Soviet movement, aided by the Catholic Church.

Hungary

Hungary, a largely agricultural nation, experienced harsh Communist rule after 1947. The Hungarian government required peasants to join collective farms, and nationalized banking, trade and industry. Central planners emphasized heavy industry, at the expense of consumer goods. The Communist leadership silenced or disbanded potential opposition groups, such as trade unions or other political parties. Catholic Church property was seized, and Church schools taken over by the government. Opponents within the Communist party were purged and executed.

After Stalin's death in 1953, Hungary's Communist leaders eased controls for two years and then reimposed them when the economy did not reach its goals. Bitter opposition turned into full revolt in the fall of 1956. As in Poland, worker uprisings brought a liberal Communist government to power. However, Imre Nagy, the new Hungarian prime minister, went further than the Polish leaders. He announced Hungary's neutrality and its withdrawal from the Warsaw Pact. This raised the danger the Soviet Union feared most—the loss of Soviet control over Eastern Europe.

Two days after Nagy's announcement, Soviet tanks and troops poured into Hungary to crush the revolt. Realizing that intervention could cause World War III, the West sympathized with the Hungarians, but did nothing to help. Order in Hungary was restored under a Soviet-controlled government led by János Kádár. More than 200,000 Hungarian refugees fled to the West.

During the 1960s and 1970s, Hungary's Communist government tried to increase production, sometimes tightening controls, while at other times encouraging initiative through small private enterprises. Support of economic reform would eventually spur political reform efforts in the 1980s.

Czechoslovakia

Czechoslovakia, with its developed industry and democratic traditions, was the last Eastern European country to become Communist. After the Communist takeover in 1948, the country was forced to conform to the Soviet model, like Hungary. Purges against officials in Czechoslovakia were the bloodiest outside of the Soviet Union. The Czechoslovak leader, Antonin Novotny, kept the country under such rigid control that

CRITICAL THINKING ACTIVITY

Identifying Cause and Effect The cold war period was one of shifting policies and frequent international crises. Identifying cause-and-effect relationships makes these events easier to understand. For example, the death of Stalin and Khrushchev's desire to lessen discontent were causes that led to the effect of de-Stalinization. Have students write short essays that identify the causes of each of the following: the policies of peaceful coexistence and of détente and Soviet military intervention in East Germany, Hungary, and Czechoslovakia; the building of the Berlin Wall. **L2**

Visualizing History Czech citizens reacted in anger and defiance when Soviet and other Warsaw Pact troops invaded Prague. *How did the Soviets justify the invasion?*

de-Stalinization did not begin in Czechoslovakia until the 1960s.

At this time, public pressure for reform finally gained strength because of Czechoslovakia's economic stagnation. A liberal Communist reformer, **Alexander Dubček** (DOOB•chehk), replaced Novotny as leader in 1968 when Brezhnev signaled his approval. For a brief time, known as "the Prague spring," reform was allowed. Dubček eased press censorship and began to allow some political groups to meet freely.

Although Dubček assured the Soviets that Czechoslovakia was still loyal to the Warsaw Pact and to communism, the Soviets became alarmed at the direction the reform movement was taking. Many Czechoslovak thinkers wanted more freedom, and there were hints that opposition parties might

be allowed to operate. To the Soviets, their hold on Eastern Europe again seemed threatened.

On August 20, 1968, about 500,000 troops from the Soviet Union and its Warsaw Pact allies invaded Czechoslovakia. They took control of Prague and sent Dubček and other Czechoslovak leaders to Moscow. Most of Dubček's reforms were withdrawn and a new constitution put into effect. In April 1969, Dubček was replaced as party leader. In 1970 he was expelled from the party entirely.

The Soviet Union declared its right to intervene in Communist states to counter any opposition that threatened communism or the unity of the Soviet bloc. This principle, called the Brezhnev Doctrine, was the basis for relations between the Soviet Union and its Eastern European satellites for the next 20 years.

SECTION 2 REVIEW

Recall
1. **Define** peaceful coexistence, intercontinental ballistic missile (ICBM), dissident, detente.
2. **Identify** Nikita Khrushchev, Leonid Brezhnev, Josip Broz Tito, Alexander Dubček, the Brezhnev Doctrine.

3. **Explain** why the Soviet Union and East Germany built the Berlin Wall.
Critical Thinking
4. **Analyzing Information** Analyze church-government relations in Eastern Europe during the cold war. How did

Communist rule affect religion in the region?
Understanding Themes
5. **Change** What impact do you think Nikita Khrushchev's 1956 de-Stalinization speech had in the satellites of Eastern Europe?

Check for Understanding
Assign Section 2 Review as homework or as an in-class activity.

 Use Student Self-Test and Review Software to review Section 2.

Evaluate
Section Quiz 21-2

 Use the Testmaker to create a customized quiz for Section 2.

Reteach
Have students use an outline map of the world to locate, date, and label hot spots during the cold war.

Enrich
Have students draw political cartoons criticizing Soviet control over its satellites.

CLOSE

Have students create a time line that includes the major events discussed in this section.

SECTION 2 REVIEW ANSWERS

1. All vocabulary words are defined in the Glossary.
2. Nikita Khrushchev, 648; Leonid Brezhnev, 650; Josip Broz Tito, 651; Alexander Dubček, 653; the Brezhnev Doctrine, 653
3. The Berlin Wall was built to restrict the flow of people from East Berlin to West Berlin.
4. Relations were tense, because communism

opposed religious practices, seized church property, and closed church schools. In Poland, the Catholic Church aided the growth of an underground movement against Soviet controls.

5. **CHANGE** It probably raised hopes for greater freedom and may have encouraged dissident activities.

Timeline

1945

1945 Great Britain elects a Labour party government.

1955

1958 Charles de Gaulle heads France's Fifth Republic.

1965

1963 Konrad Adenauer retires as West German chancellor.

1975

1978 Spain introduces a new democratic constitution.

Find Out

Answer: *by joining NATO and by forming the European Coal and Steel Community and the Common Market*

FOCUS

Section Objective

Describe how Western Europe moved toward greater political and economic unity during the cold war.

BELLRINGER
Motivational Activity

Before taking roll at the beginning of the class period, project Section Focus Transparency 21-3 and have students answer the activity questions. Discuss students' responses.

☞ This activity is also available as a blackline master.

Vocabulary Pre-check

☞ Use Vocabulary Activity 21 to introduce vocabulary terms.
L1 LEP

Section 3

Western Europe

Setting the Scene

▶ **Terms to Define**
welfare state, coalition

▶ **People to Meet**
Clement Attlee, Charles de Gaulle, Valéry Giscard d'Estaing, Konrad Adenauer, Willy Brandt

▶ **Places to Locate**
Rome

 **Find Out** How did Western Europe move toward greater political and economic unity during the period of the cold war?

The Storyteller

Jacques LeMoine nervously held the rifle issued to him just that morning. Like many other citizens of Paris, the 17-year-old had been pressed into service, guarding the city's perimeter. President de Gaulle's announced plans to guide

Paris street disturbance

Algeria to independence had aroused furious opposition. In reaction to the independence policy for Algeria, a threat had been received: Paris would be invaded. Paratroopers under the leadership of four retired French generals had seized key overseas bases and planned to bring citizens like Jacques LeMoine to defend the city.

—adapted from *The 1962 World Year Book*, "France," Fred J. Pannwitt, 1962

---

fter World War II, the non-Communist nations of Western Europe were concerned about two major issues: economic recovery and military security. They came to realize that only through united action would they be able to improve their economies, strengthen the Western Alliance, and contribute to world affairs.

Great Britain

After World War II, Great Britain's position as a world power further declined. The British had bankrupted themselves to win the war. Therefore, they had to sharply reduce their worldwide military, political, and economic role.

A Reduced Role

Even with financial cutbacks, Great Britain's recovery was slow. Many British industries were too inefficient and outdated to compete successfully in world markets that were increasingly dominated by the United States, Japan, and other Western European nations.

Because of economic weakness, the British passed on many of their international obligations to the United States. To maintain its pride and a level of independent security, Great Britain, however, developed its own nuclear force. It also maintained a close relationship with other members of the Western Alliance.

Loss of Empire

The British also could no longer afford to support a vast global empire. During the 1950s and 1960s, many of Great Britain's important Asian and African colonies became independent. Most of these new nations joined as equals with Great Britain in the Commonwealth of Nations, an organization that promoted cooperation among the nations of the former British Empire.

654 Chapter 21 *The Cold War*

The Welfare State

Internally, Great Britain underwent many changes after World War II. In 1945 Churchill and the Conservatives were voted out of office. They were replaced by the Labour party, which appealed to many Britons who wanted greater economic equality. Under Prime Minister **Clement Attlee**, the Labour government continued wartime restrictions to improve the economy. However, it also promised a better standard of living for all British citizens.

Carrying out a moderate Socialist program, the Labour government nationalized the coal, steel, and transportation industries. Greater freedom was given to labor unions to strike and to participate in political activities. Like many other Western European governments, Britain's Labour government created a welfare state, a system in which the national government provides programs for the well-being of its citizens. Social security was expanded to provide lifetime benefits for the needy. Free education was provided to all children up to the age of 16. The government also introduced a national health service that provided free medical care for everyone.

As the economic situation improved in the early 1950s, the Conservatives returned to power and ruled until 1964. Although they ended many government controls over the economy, Conservative prime ministers, such as Winston Churchill, Anthony Eden, and Harold Macmillan did not eliminate the social welfare programs introduced by the Labour party.

The Monarchy

In 1952, the popular wartime monarch, George VI, died and was succeeded by his elder daughter, Elizabeth. As queen, Elizabeth II had little, if any, power. But, for many Britons, she served as a reassuring symbol of traditional British values during a period of rapid, and sometimes discouraging, change. For other Britons, however, the monarchy represented all that they believed was wrong with Great Britain—its preoccupation with past imperial glories and its failure to discard the trappings of an outdated class system.

France

Germany's occupation of France during World War II had ended the Third French Republic created in 1870. After the war, a new constitution established the Fourth French Republic. Like the Third Republic, it, too, had a strong legislature and a weak presidency.

Visualizing History Riots between Hindus and Muslims led to the division of British India in 1947 into two nations: India and Pakistan. Both joined the Commonwealth of Nations. *What was the Commonwealth of Nations?*

The Fourth French Republic

In spite of economic growth, France in the 1950s was plagued with domestic and international problems. The existence of many political parties undermined hopes for a stable government. No single political party was strong enough to obtain a working majority in the National Assembly. Cabinets were formed by coalitions, or temporary alliances, of several parties. When one of the parties disagreed with policy, the cabinet members had to resign and form a new government.

Overseas, France's Asian and African colonies demanded their independence. Unlike Great Britain, France at first clung to its empire. It fought, and lost, expensive and bloody wars in Indochina and North Africa.

The Fifth French Republic

In 1958, the threat of civil war in the North African colony of Algeria resulted in the downfall of France's ineffective Fourth Republic. **Charles de Gaulle**, leader of the French Resistance during World War II, was called from retirement to head an emergency government. De Gaulle asked the

Chapter 21 *The Cold War* **655**

TEACH

Guided Practice

THEME Regionalism

Ask students to discuss what regionalism means to them. They should focus on the concept as it applies to their own area. What region do you live in? How do people in this region cooperate with one another? With other regions? **L1 LEP**

Visualizing History In a 1942 speech, Prime Minister Winston Churchill declared proudly: "I have not become the King's First Minister in order to preside over the liquidation of the British Empire." But the process began under his successor and was almost complete by the mid-1960s.

Answer to Caption: *an organization to promote cooperation among former nations of the British Empire*

Who?What?Where?When?

Vatican II This general council of the Roman Catholic Church, held from 1962 to 1965, had far-reaching consequences for Catholics worldwide. Among the changes it instituted was the substitution, in the Mass, of people's native languages for the Latin that had been used for centuries.

Economics Britain, France, and West Germany all instituted programs to promote citizens' well-being during the cold war period. What programs in the United States provide for our well-being? *(Answers might include Social Security, Medicare, Medicaid, and welfare.)* **L2**

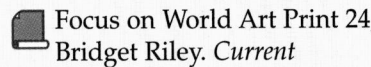
Movement Since World War II, millions of Africans, Asians, and West Indians have resettled in the former colonial powers, especially Britain and France. At the same time, Germany allowed millions of Turks to ease labor shortages. Today the presence of non-Europeans in these countries has led to racist violence. Have students investigate and report on the situation of immigrants in Europe. **L3**

History Simulation 21

Focus on World Art Print 24, Bridget Riley. *Current*

Mapping History Overlay Transparency 23, *The Commonwealth of Nations*

Independent Practice

Guided Reading Activity 21-3 **L1**

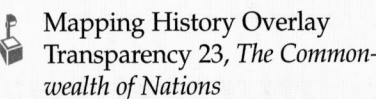

De Gaulle saw himself as the personification of France. "There were many things I would have liked to do but could not," he once said, "for they would not have been fitting for General de Gaulle."
Answer to Caption: *He allowed Algeria to become independent.*

French people to approve a new constitiution providing for a strong presidency. French voters overwhelmingly responded to de Gaulle's appeal. Thus, the Fifth French Republic was born.

De Gaulle became the first president of the Fifth Republic. His political party, the Gaullist Union, formed a working majority in the National Assembly. As president, de Gaulle recognized that France could not stubbornly hold on to its empire against strong nationalist opposition. In the early 1960s, he allowed France's African colonies, including Algeria, to become independent.

With the loss of France's empire, de Gaulle worked to strengthen French cultural and economic influence in Europe and throughout the rest of the world. His strongly nationalistic policies angered France's allies, especially Great Britain and the United States. In 1963, de Gaulle blocked Great Britain's application for membership in the European Common Market. Three years later, the French president decided to withdraw all French troops from NATO's military command and requested that all NATO bases and headquarters be removed from French soil. At the same time, he insisted on maintaining France's political ties to NATO. De Gaulle's ultimate expression of nationalism was the building of an independent French nuclear force.

De Gaulle's successor, Georges Pompidou (PAHM•pih•DOO), by contrast, worked to build

Visualizing History **France gave Charles de Gaulle broad presidential powers and election by direct popular vote.** *How did de Gaulle solve the problem of nationalist opposition in Algeria?*

---

closer relations with Great Britain and the United States. He also focused on economic growth rather than on nationalistic projects. After Pompidou's death in 1974, **Valéry Giscard d'Estaing** (zhihs •KAHR dehs•TAN) was elected president. Giscard continued Pompidou's domestic and international policies. He set out to lessen state economic controls and to encourage the expansion of French private enterprise. Giscard's pro-business policies, however, were crippled by the worldwide economic downturn of the 1970s.

Germany

During the postwar years, West Germany rebuilt its economy and became Western Europe's leading industrial nation. Many experts called West Germany's reconstruction an "economic miracle." New industries used the latest in modern equipment, and industrial production more than tripled in the 1950s. Prosperity enabled West Germany to create a welfare state closely resembling that in Great Britain and France. West Germany also absorbed 10 million refugees from Eastern Europe. Another 1 million people settled in Germany from other parts of the continent.

The Adenauer Years

West Germany's democratic political system was dominated by two parties: the Christian Democrats and the Social Democrats. In 1949, the Christian Democrats, led by **Konrad Adenauer** (A•duhn•OWR), formed the first West German government. They created a capitalist economy with close ties to the West. In 1955 West Germany joined NATO and developed its own armed forces.

As chancellor, Adenauer was known as a strong leader devoted to the Western Alliance, European unity, and the reunification of Germany under a democratic government. During his tenure, West Germany became one of the world's most stable democracies. Adenauer retired in 1963. He was succeeded as chancellor by the economic minister Ludwig Erhard, who served until 1966.

Willy Brandt

During the 1960s, the Christian Democrats lost support to the Social Democrats, a moderate socialist party led by West Berlin's mayor, **Willy Brandt**. The Social Democrats maintained strong support for NATO while seeking improved relations with the Soviet bloc.

Brandt became chancellor of Germany in 1969. During the 1970s, he worked to reduce tensions

---

MEETING SPECIAL NEEDS ACTIVITY

Reading Comprehension Organize the class into four groups, one for each major subsection of Section 3. Then have each group develop a topic sentence for each paragraph in its subsection. After completing the sentences, each group should share its list with other students, then review and comment on their topic sentences. **L2**

between West Germany and the Soviet bloc. This policy, known as *Ostpolitik* (German for "Eastern policy") led West Germany to reach agreements to normalize relations with the Soviet Union and Poland in 1972. Brandt's initiative eventually led to the establishment of diplomatic ties between West Germany and East Germany a year later.

European Unity

Throughout Europe's history, local disputes between two or more nations often drew the entire continent into war. In the twentieth century, developments in technology, such as nuclear weapons, made it clear that future wars could lead to global catastrophe. This possibility prompted leaders to seek regional solutions to European issues.

As World War II ended, European leaders discussed plans for the postwar unification of European countries. These plans included organizations for economic cooperation and the resolution of disputes. Some even raised the idea of a United States of Europe. Others proposed that each nation retain its national identity but hand over control of defense and foreign policy to an all-European government. This arrangement, it was felt, would prevent European nations from waging war on each other.

To coordinate economic policies, six nations— France, Italy, West Germany, Belgium, the Netherlands, and Luxembourg established the European Coal and Steel Community in 1952. The organization's goal was to create a tariff-free market for European coal and steel products. By ending trade barriers and developing uniform standards, the European Coal and Steel Community would further European industrial growth.

The Community was so successful that the same countries decided to bring together the rest of their economies. In 1957, representatives of the six nations meeting in **Rome**, Italy, signed the Treaty of

Edmund Hillary Climbs Mount Everest

Nepal-Tibet, 1953
Located in the Himalayas, on the Nepal-Tibet border, Mount Everest is the world's highest peak. A British expedition set out in 1953 to scale the south slope, which was considered unclimbable. The climbers established a series of camps as they advanced up the mountain. The last camp was set up by Edmund Hillary of New Zealand and Tenzing Norgay of Nepal. On May 29, 1953, they became the first climbers to reach the top of Mount Everest. Queen Elizabeth II knighted Hillary for his achievement.

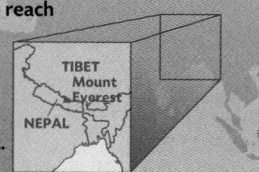

Rome. This agreement created the European Economic Community, also known as the Common Market. The six members of the Common Market planned to abolish all tariffs among themselves and form a single economic market by 1970. During the 1960s and 1970s, Great Britain, attracted by the Common Market's success, ended its traditional aloofness from European affairs and sought membership in the European organization.

The Common Market benefited Western Europe in several ways. By promoting economic cooperation among individual European nations, it reduced the threat of conflict and contributed to European prosperity. It also enabled Western Europe to pursue cooperative technological programs in fields such as space research and nuclear energy. These programs were too expensive for any one nation to pursue on its own. Finally, it enabled Europe to compete on an equal basis with North America and East Asia in world markets.

SECTION 3 REVIEW

Recall
1. **Define** welfare state, coalition.
2. **Identify** Clement Attlee, Charles de Gaulle, Valéry Giscard d'Estaing, Konrad Adenauer, Willy Brandt, *Ostpolitik*, European Economic Community (Common Market).

3. **Explain** why Charles de Gaulle of France was considered an independent leader.

Critical Thinking
4. **Synthesizing Information** Why was a strong European economy vital to world peace after World War II? What fac-

tors contributed to the economic recovery of Western Europe during the postwar years?

Understanding Themes
5. **Regionalism** What do you think would be the advantages and disadvantages of a United States of Europe?

Regionalism Have students research and report on the following European regions in the cold war period: Scandinavia, Italy, Spain. **L3**

ASSESS

Check for Understanding
Assign Section 3 Review as homework or as an in-class activity.

▣ Use Student Self-Test and Review Software to review Section 3.

Evaluate
▱ Section Quiz 21-3

▣ Use the Testmaker to create a customized quiz for Section 3.

Reteach
Have students review the factors that moved Western Europe toward greater cooperation in the postwar period.

Enrich
Have students watch a video of the film *The Mouse That Roared* and then discuss the European attitude toward the United States that is reflected in the film.

CLOSE

Have students summarize the ways Western democracies cooperated during the cold war era.

SECTION 3 REVIEW ANSWERS

1. All vocabulary words are defined in the Glossary.
2. Clement Attlee, 655; Charles de Gaulle, 655; Valéry Giscard d'Estaing, 656; Konrad Adenauer, 656; Willy Brandt, 656; *Ostpolitik*, 657; European Economic Community (Common Market), 657
3. He relinquished France's African

colonies and pursued a nationalistic policy toward the Common Market and NATO.
4. It contributed to political stability and decreased the likelihood of future conflicts. Economic recovery was aided by the Marshall Plan, the European Coal and Steel Community, and the Common

Market.
5. **REGIONALISM** Answers will vary but might include the following ideas. Advantages: lower trade barriers, cooperative research and development in industry, pooling of resources. Disadvantages: loss of sovereignty, weakening of national identity.

1947 U.S. Congress conducts hearings on Communist influence in American life.

1955 Martin Luther King, Jr., begins nonviolent civil rights campaign for African Americans.

1967 Canada celebrates 100th anniversary of nationhood.

1974 Richard M. Nixon becomes the first United States President to resign his office.

SECTION THEME

▶ **Cooperation** The United States and Canada build strong economies and forge closer ties.

ind Out

Answer: *United States: political: anti-Communist crusade, new foreign alliances, arms race, strong presidency, social: domination of automobile, growth of suburbs, civil rights movement. Canada: political: increased independence from Britain, new foreign alliances, social: search for national identity in face of separatism.*

FOCUS

Section Objective

Trace the political and social changes that the people of the United States and Canada experienced during the cold war years.

BELLRINGER
Motivational Activity

Before taking roll at the beginning of the class period, project Section Focus Transparency 21-4. This activity is also available as a blackline master.

Vocabulary Pre-check

Use the Vocabulary PuzzleMaker to create a puzzle that reinforces the vocabulary terms in this section. **L1**

Section 4

The United States and Canada

Setting the Scene

▶ **Terms to Define**
automation, racial segregation, imperial presidency, stagflation, embargo, double-digit inflation, trade deficit, middle power, multicultural, separatism

▶ **People to Meet**
Dwight D. Eisenhower, John F. Kennedy, Lyndon B. Johnson, Richard M. Nixon, Martin Luther King, Jr., Gerald R. Ford, Jimmy Carter, Lester B. Pearson, Pierre Elliott Trudeau

▶ **Places to Locate**
Vietnam, Cambodia, Washington, D.C., St. Lawrence Seaway, Toronto, Montreal, Quebec

 **ind Out** What political and social changes did the people of the United States and Canada experience during the cold war years?

The Storyteller

By the time President Eisenhower began his first term, 33,629 Americans had been killed in the Korean War. Then on March 5, 1953, Joseph Stalin died. Hearing of Stalin's death, Eisenhower asked his associates, "Well, what do you think we can do about this?" He was advised to seek improved relations with Russia. The new Soviet leaders also wanted reduced tensions. As a result, a truce ending the war in Korea was signed on July 28th.

—adapted from *The Glorious Burden*, Stefan Lorant, 1968

President Dwight D. Eisenhower

---

*B*ecause they were spared the destruction of their territory in World War II, the United States and Canada emerged from the war with prosperous economies. During the postwar era, the stunning technological achievements of the United States, its high standard of living, and business success were admired and envied around the globe.

In the 1960s and the 1970s, however, the United States was shaken by domestic political crises, economic difficulties, and its involvement in the Vietnam War. By the 1980s other nations were catching up economically, but the United States retained its role as the leader of the non-Communist world.

During this time, the United States' northern neighbor, Canada, sought to maintain unity between its French-speaking and English-speaking populations. It also attracted immigrants from all parts of the world. Moving away from its traditional British connection, Canada sought a new identity in international affairs and developed closer economic ties with the United States.

American Prosperity

After World War II, the United States entered an era of economic growth that brought material wealth to a larger group of Americans. Demand for American goods was high, and business responded to meet this need. Production soared, and new industries appeared. Higher wages and better benefits gave Americans more money to spend. American shoppers pushed up demand as they eagerly purchased consumer goods that had been scarce during the war. Future prospects were also bright. The postwar "baby boom," or soaring birthrate, added to the potential number of consumers and promised increased economic growth.

SECTION RESOURCES

Reproducible Masters
- Reproducible Lesson Plan 21-4
- Guided Reading Activity 21-4
- Reteaching Activity 21
- Enrichment Activity 21
- Section Quiz 21-4
- Performance Assessment Activity 21
- Spanish Chapter Summary 21

Transparencies
- Section Focus Transparency 21-4

Multimedia
- Vocabulary PuzzleMaker Software
- Student Self-Test and Review Software
- Testmaker
- Communism and the Cold War
- Turning Points in World History
- Lessons of War

Science and Technology

During the postwar years, the United States made spectacular leaps in the field of science and technology. With more money to spend, an increase in the number of university-trained scientists, and a growing commitment to the future, the United States led the world in new technological developments.

During the 1950s and 1960s, American factories and industries began to use automation, the technique of operating a production system using mechanical or electronic devices. With automated methods of production, goods could be produced more efficiently than with human workers.

Beginning in the 1950s, the use of computers began to revolutionize American industry. Businesses used computers for many purposes, including billing and inventory control. Computers were also used for such things as making hotel reservations, sorting bank checks, tracking space satellites, forecasting weather conditions, and setting type for printing. Automation and computers in the workplace caused many workers to lose their jobs. In the long run, however, computers and automation created more jobs than they eliminated. In addition, the new jobs usually demanded a higher level of education.

American technological skills brought the United States into competition with the Soviet Union in space exploration and missile development. The two superpowers experimented with moon probes, weather and communications satellites, and extended flights of humans orbiting the earth. The grand prize of the "space race" was putting a human on the moon. United States astronaut Neil Armstrong won that honor on July 20, 1969.

Social Changes

Many social changes came to the United States during the period from the late 1940s to the late 1970s. In the 1950s the automobile changed the face of America. No longer did people have to live near their places of work. Those who lived and worked in the city could move to less-crowded places. This migration of city residents caused the rapid growth of suburbs.

In the years after World War II, American cities became ringed by seemingly endless housing developments carved out of the less densely settled country land. Shopping centers with vast parking lots were built to serve the new suburban population. Businesses and factories also began relocating from the cities to the suburbs, where their workers now lived. The Highway Act of 1956 contributed to the growth of the suburbs by adding 41,000 miles (66,000 km) to the interstate highway system.

Visualizing History Cold war tensions and fear of nuclear attack led to "duck and cover" drills in public schools. *How did the government react to the fear of the "enemy within"?*

In addition to the automobile, another symbol of American prosperity was the television set. In 1945, fewer than 1 in every 20,000 people had a television. But within a few years, televisions were everywhere, and they were almost as common as telephones. Some critics worried that television would make Americans desire entertainment more than solid information. However, other experts pointed out the positive impact of television in making people directly aware of national and international events.

The Cold War at Home

Despite this time of prosperity, the cold war created deep political divisions in the United States. During the late 1940s and early 1950s, conservatives blamed President Harry S Truman and State Department officials for allowing the Communists to make gains in Eastern Europe and Asia. They also charged that Communists were serving in high government positions. A "red scare" swept the country. The growing fear of the "enemy within"—of subversion within the United States government and society—helped to launch a controversial anti-Communist crusade to discover and expose

Chapter 21 *The Cold War* 659

COOPERATIVE LEARNING ACTIVITY

The Anti-Communist Crusade Organize the class into small groups, one for each year from 1947 through 1954, the years of the post-World War II "red scare." Have each group research and report on relevant anti-Communist activities in its year. Then have groups work together to agree on a format to present their information; suggest either radio or TV reports. **L3**

TEACH

Guided Practice

THEME Cooperation

The United States and Canada have had a cooperative relationship throughout the twentieth century. What factors have served to promote this relationship? *(geographic proximity, a common language, and similar political and social institutions based on British models)* **L1 LEP**

Visualizing History In the late 1950s, some Americans called for the construction of an extensive network of fallout shelters to protect civilians in case of atomic attack. Congress and state legislatures, however, refused to appropriate the massive funds needed.
Answer to Caption: *Congress investigated suspected Communists, and many people lost their jobs.*

Daily Life Fear of Communist influence was very strong in American society during the cold war years. Ask students whether they think attitudes are different today, and if so, why. **L2**

ABCNEWS
INTERACTIVE™

VIDEODISC
Turning Points in World History

Side Two, Chapter 8
Title: *The Moon Landing*
Ask: Who was aboard *Apollo 11* in 1969 when it headed to the moon? *(Neil Armstrong, Edwin "Buzz" Aldrin, and Michael Collins)*

VIDEODISC
Communism and the Cold War

Side One, Chapter 11
Frames 20050–21335
Title: *Communists in Our Midst: McCarthyism*
Ask: How were Americans who believed in Communist ideas treated in the 1940s and 1950s? *(They were investigated, shunned, and considered treasonous.)*

Linking Past and Present

Abstract Painting

European abstract painting of the early 1900s tended to be cool and geometrical. What was new in the 1940s, when American painters set the trend, was a heightened, energetic emotionalism—in other words, abstract *expressionism*. While some artists dripped paint on canvas (Pollock), others experimented with wild colors (Willem de Kooning) or used thin washes that allowed the canvas to show through (Mark Rothko).

ANSWERS
It is a highly emotional form of abstract (nonobjective) painting. Answers will vary but might include dissatisfaction with realism and reaction against European traditions.

---

suspected Communists. The search was concentrated on diplomats, intellectuals, liberals, and other leaders of public opinion whose views could be interpreted as sympathetic toward, or even tolerant of, communism.

Congressional Investigations

Both houses of Congress set up panels to investigate suspected Communists. In 1947, the House Committee on Un-American Activities held hearings on suspected Communist influence in the entertainment industry and in labor unions. As a result, several well-known writers were jailed or found their careers ruined.

The Senate Committee on Investigation was headed by Senator Joseph McCarthy of Wisconsin. In the early 1950s, McCarthy charged there was a vast Communist conspiracy within the State Department and called government employees before the committee to defend themselves. He never proved a single case. But the climate of opinion was such that the accusation alone was enough to label someone a Communist, and many lost their jobs. The term *McCarthyism* came to mean the leveling of public accusations of political subversion without regard to evidence.

Forming Alliances

Between the 1950s and the 1980s, the cold war influenced national political campaigns, and many aspects of domestic policy, as well as most major foreign policy decisions of the United States. In its dealings with Eastern Europe, Africa, the Middle East, Latin America, and Asia, the United States saw its diplomacy as an extension of the struggle against communism.

During the 1950s, the United States expanded the nation's network of alliances in order to contain communism. In Western Europe, the Americans took a leading role in NATO. In Southeast Asia, the United States helped to create the Southeast Asia Treaty Organization (SEATO). In the Middle East, the United States counted on the cooperation of the Central Treaty Organization (CENTO), and in Latin America, the United States promoted the Organization of American States (OAS). These alliances created a formidable counterbalance to the influence of the Soviet Union.

Military Buildup

When necessary, American Presidents also used espionage and military power to fight the cold war. During the 1950s, the effort to contain

---

CONNECTIONS
The Arts

Abstract Painting

Out of the Web *by Jackson Pollock*

Abstract expressionism was a movement in American painting that flourished from the mid-1940s to the mid-1950s. Abstract expressionist artists rejected many of the rules of earlier art. Instead of showing recognizable subject matter in their works, they emphasized the techniques or basic elements of painting, such as color, brushstrokes, lines, and shapes.

One of the important abstract expressionist painters was Jackson Pollock. His usual painting technique involved placing a huge canvas on the floor and then dripping paint from above onto it. The drippings formed sweeping, rhythmic

patterns that seemed to move across the surface. About his highly unusual method of painting, Pollock said, "I feel nearer, more a part of the painting, since this way I can walk around it, work from the four sides, and literally be in the painting."

Although abstract expressionist styles differed, all of the artists in the movement believed that art should express immediate personal feelings and attitudes toward life. Their nontraditional, revolutionary approach to art has influenced painters throughout the world.

Linking Past and Present ACTIVITY

Explain how abstract expressionist painting differs from traditional forms of art. Why do you think abstract expressionist art developed in the United States during the cold war era?

MEETING SPECIAL NEEDS ACTIVITY

Mixed Learners List on the chalkboard some key terms that occur in this section, including all or some of the following: *baby boom, computers, television, Communist subversion, McCarthyism, abstract expressionism, military-industrial complex, teach-ins, Vietnamization, Watergate scandal.* Have students define each term and tell why it is relevant to a discussion of the cold war period. **L2 LEP**

communism, strongly backed by the American public, caused the United States to send troops to fight Communist forces in Korea. It also led President **Dwight D. Eisenhower** in 1954 to agree to shoulder France's efforts to stop Communist military activity in **Vietnam**. The United States engaged in an unprecedented military buildup during this time, even during the cold war "thaw" in the late 1950s.

By the closing months of his presidency, Dwight D. Eisenhower, though a proponent of a strong military, was deeply concerned about the global arms race, or the competition between the superpowers for new and better weapons. On leaving office in 1961, he warned of a growing "military-industrial complex" in the United States. According to Eisenhower, the superpower rivalry, the competition for sophisticated weapons, and the role of arms production in supporting economic growth had created a built-in incentive to increase military spending.

Battle of Ideas

John F. Kennedy, a young senator from Massachusetts, succeeded Eisenhower as President in 1961. During the 1960 presidential race, Kennedy had campaigned on the theme of restoring the strength and prestige the United States had lost after the embarrassments of the U-2 spying incident and *Sputnik*.

Kennedy engaged in cold-war maneuvering on several fronts. He acted quickly to create the Peace Corps, a program that sent young American volunteers overseas to help impoverished countries that were open to Communist influence. Kennedy's cold-war views influenced his actions in several major foreign policy crises, including the building of the Berlin Wall and the Cuban missile crisis.

The Vietnam War

Kennedy's assassination in 1963 brought **Lyndon B. Johnson** to the White House. Johnson supported civil rights laws and reforms in education and social welfare to achieve what he

Nuclear Battlefield

UNION OF SOVIET SOCIALIST REPUBLICS

PACIFIC OCEAN

ARCTIC OCEAN

North Pole

DEW Line radars

CANADA

Cadin Pinetree Line radars

PACIFIC OCEAN

ATLANTIC OCEAN

UNITED STATES

| ABM (antiballistic missile) Sites
| ICBM (intercontinental ballistic missile) Fields
☢ Nuclear Production Sites
ᚠ Radars

0   500   1000 mi.
0   500 1000 km
Stereographic Projection

Map Study By the 1980s the United States and the Soviet Union each had more than 12,000 ICBMs aimed at the other. The Distant Early Warning Line (DEW Line) was a radar system built in 1957 to detect incoming missiles. It was replaced in 1994 with a more sophisticated North Warning System.
Region Why were DEW Line radars placed in northern Canada rather than along the east and west coasts of the United States?

Chapter 21 Section 4

Map Study

Answer
the most direct path of the missiles would be over the North Pole

Map Skills Practice

Reading a Map Why are the Soviet Union's missile sites located mostly on its western borders? *(located near Europe and NATO forces)*

Independent Practice

📁 Guided Reading Activity 21-4

Who?What?Where?When?

Eleanor Roosevelt A moderate voice in the controversial postwar period was that of Eleanor Roosevelt, who continued her public career after the death of her husband, Franklin, in 1945. As a member of the UN Commission on Human Rights, she tried to meet the Russians halfway. "All of us are going to die together or we are going to learn to live together," she said, "and if we are to live together we have to talk."

Report Two notable trials of the cold war era were those of Alger Hiss, accused of Communist ties, and Julius and Ethel Rosenberg, convicted of spying for Russia. Have students research and report on one of these trials. **L3**

MAKING CONNECTIONS ACTIVITIES

Military History One of the most notorious incidents of the Vietnam War was the My Lai massacre of 1968. Have students research and report on the event and on the subsequent trial of William L. Calley, Jr., the American officer accused of responsibility for it. **L2**

Architecture Few war monuments have moved and inspired Americans as much as the Vietnam Veterans Memorial in Washington, D.C. Have students research and report on this structure: who designed it, what it looks like, when it was dedicated, and the controversy about its design. If possible, they should include illustrations to show the class or post on the bulletin board. **L2**

VIDEODISC
Communism and the Cold War

Side Two, Chapter 8
Title: *Vietnam War*
Ask: In what way did the United States view Vietnam as a conflict not between North and South Vietnam but rather between the United States and the Soviet Union? *(The United States believed they were also fighting the Soviet Union because of Soviet military/economic support for North Vietnam.)*

Struggle for Civil Rights
How did the civil rights struggle of the 1960s affect American society?
It brought greater equality to African Americans and other marginalized groups and helped alter American attitudes toward race, discrimination, and poverty.

you don't say...

Hawks and doves are terms that were used widely in the 1960s. Supporters of the Vietnam War were called hawks, while opponents were known as doves. The use of *hawk* to describe a warlike person goes back to the War of 1812. Doves have long been thought of as peaceful; the symbolism was reinforced by a poster by Pablo Picasso that was popular during the 1950s and 1960s.

---

called the Great Society. However, the consuming issue during Johnson's five years in office became the Vietnam War, in which the United States assisted South Vietnam in resisting a Communist takeover.

American involvement in Vietnam, described in Chapter 22, began under Presidents Eisenhower and Kennedy and grew out of their desire to keep communism from spreading throughout Southeast Asia. During the Eisenhower and Kennedy years, American civilian and military advisers had arrived in Vietnam to aid the South Vietnamese. The role of the United States in the Southeast Asian nation was later expanded into full-scale participation by President Johnson. During Johnson's administration, large numbers of American combat soldiers were sent to fight in Vietnam.

Opposition to the War

By 1968, large-scale American intervention had not been able to overcome the Communist Vietnamese forces. As a result, domestic opposition to the war became widespread, and Vietnam became the central issue in the presidential race of that year. President Johnson, condemned for his handling of the lengthy, costly, and indecisive war, decided not to run for reelection. Former Vice President **Richard M. Nixon**, a strong anti-Communist, won the election with his pledge to stop the war and bring the American people together.

President Nixon soon found that ending the war was difficult. As he struggled to find a politically acceptable solution, his administration was besieged by the antiwar forces that had overwhelmed Johnson's presidency.

Although many young Americans believed that it was their duty to serve in the military if they were called, others stated that they would refuse to serve. Some young men eligible for the draft—the mandatory enrollment in the United States armed forces—burned their draft cards, which was an illegal act. Others fled to Canada to avoid the draft, choosing to spend years in exile from their country rather than fight in the war. Demonstrators marched in front of the White House, carrying signs and shouting antiwar slogans. College professors cancelled classes and held antiwar protests called "teach-ins." Most protests across the country were peaceful, but many incidents of violence occurred, including the bombing of military facilities and other institutions that symbolized America's political and military power.

Ending the War

President Nixon's plans for ending the war for the United States was called "Vietnamization"—a

---

gradual withdrawal of American troops while handing over control of war operations to South Vietnam. In a November 1969 speech, the President tried to counter the antiwar protests by appealing to what he called the silent majority of Americans whom he said supported his policies.

Simultaneously with the American withdrawal from Vietnam, Nixon ordered fierce bombing raids on neighboring **Cambodia**. The bombings prompted renewed protests, creating a superheated atmosphere of anger and distrust between supporters and opponents of the war. The situation exploded tragically in May 1970, when National Guard soldiers fired into a crowd of demonstrators at Kent State University in Ohio, killing four students.

In 1973, the last of the active American forces withdrew from Vietnam, and the Paris Accords were signed. Of the 2,700,000 Americans who served in Vietnam, about 58,000 died and more than 300,000 were wounded. The war cost the United States $150 billion. In addition, it made the nation more cautious of foreign involvement.

Struggle for Civil Rights

Despite the general economic prosperity of the United States after World War II, millions of Americans continued to live in poverty. The poor included members of all ethnic groups, but the plight of the nation's poor in the African American community seemed especially critical. Ever since emancipation in the 1860s, African Americans in both the North and the South had faced discrimination in jobs, housing, education, and other areas. After World War II, an increasing number of Americans realized that continuing poverty and racial discrimination were at odds with the basic American values of equality and justice for all. A civil rights movement begun by African Americans in the early 1900s gained momentum and affected many areas of American life.

Changing Social Attitudes

Changing social attitudes helped civil rights advances. The war against Germany played a part. The horrifying racism of the Nazis helped to make some Americans more sensitive to racism in their own country. They began to realize that not only African Americans, but also Asian Americans, Hispanic Americans, and other ethnic groups had been treated unfairly and denied social and educational opportunities.

CRITICAL THINKING ACTIVITY

Making Comparisons Write two headings on the chalkboard, *United States* and *Canada*. Under each, have students enter data given in this section, supplemented by research in reference works. Data should include size, population, major resources, and main ethnic groups. **L2**

Court Decisions

During the 1940s and 1950s, African Americans worked hard to gain civil rights. The war years saw the membership of the National Association for the Advancement of Colored People (NAACP) increase from 100,000 to 351,000. In the late 1940s, the NAACP hired teams of able lawyers to bring a series of lawsuits to the federal courts to end violations of the constitutional rights of African American citizens.

This effort resulted in several United States Supreme Court decisions that attacked discrimination. In the best known case, *Brown* v. *Board of Education of Topeka, Kansas* (1954), the United States Supreme Court ruled that racial segregation, or the separation of the races, in public schools was illegal. President Eisenhower used federal agencies to enforce the Court's decision.

Martin Luther King, Jr.

In the following years, the civil rights movement broadened and changed tactics. **Martin Luther King, Jr.**, a Baptist minister, advocated the use of nonviolent sit-ins and marches to focus attention on discrimination in housing, public facilities, and voting. Media coverage of the segregationist opposition to the movement's efforts helped convince many Americans of the injustice of discrimination.

In 1963, more than 200,000 African Americans, whites, and people of other ethnic groups converged on Washington, D.C., for the largest civil rights demonstration in the nation's history. At the Lincoln Memorial, the marchers heard eloquent speeches, especially from Martin Luther King, Jr., who, in a famous address, described his dream of freedom and equality for all people:

> ❝ I have a dream that one day this nation will rise up and live out the true meaning of its creed: 'We hold these truths to be self-evident; that all men are created equal'…. And when this happens, and when we allow freedom to ring, when we let it ring from every village and hamlet, from every state and every city, we will be able to speed up that day when all God's children … [will] join hands and sing in the words of the old … spiritual: 'Free at last, Free at last, Thank God Almighty, we're free at last.' ❞

The civil rights movement peaked in the 1960s with the passage of major civil rights laws under President Johnson. These measures banned discrimination in public places and education as well as strengthened the right to vote. In addition to helping African Americans, the civil rights legislation also advanced opportunities for other groups, such as Hispanic Americans.

After Martin Luther King, Jr.'s assassination in 1968, the civil rights movement faced the loss or delay of some of its hard-won gains. Beginning in the late 1960s, much of the United States government's social policies shifted to the right, away from earlier liberal policies. However, despite the setback, the movement for civil rights continued. It strongly influenced other groups in the United States—women, Hispanic Americans, and Native Americans—that wanted better opportunities and social equality. It also was an inspiration to civil rights groups in other parts of the world.

Visualizing History Dr. Martin Luther King, Jr., spoke to more than 200,000 people on the 100th anniversary of the Emancipation Proclamation. *What civil rights did legislation in the 1960s address?*

Biography

The following videotape programs are available from Glencoe:

- **Senator Joseph McCarthy: An American Inquisitor**
- **Malcolm X: A Search for Identity**
- **Jackie Robinson**

CURRICULUM CONNECTION

SCIENCE
A great scientific breakthrough of the cold war period was the conquest of polio. This disease had menaced both children and adults all over the world for centuries. (Franklin D. Roosevelt was one of its most prominent victims.) An inoculation, pioneered by Jonas Salk, was pronounced safe in 1955. An oral vaccine, developed by Albert Sabin, was approved in 1961. Today polio has been all but eliminated globally.

Visualizing History King came to prominence in 1955, when African Americans in Montgomery, Alabama, began a boycott against the local bus company, which practiced discrimination in seating and hiring. **Answer to Caption:** *the right to vote, the right to education, and the use of public accommodations without discrimination*

MORE ABOUT...

The Civil Rights Struggle Students and other young people played a key role in the civil rights struggle. In 1960 college students in North Carolina organized the first sit-ins, occupying seats at a segregated lunch counter as a form of protest. The following year many students took part in freedom rides, demonstrating against segregated buses. In 1964 three young men—two white (Michael Schwerner and Andrew Goodman) and one black (James Chaney)—were murdered while organizing voter registration in Mississippi.

Who?What?Where?When?

Accidental Executives When Gerald Ford became President, he named Nelson Rockefeller, former governor of New York, as his Vice President. For the first time in history, the two Chief Executives of the United States occupied their offices by appointment rather than by election.

ABCNEWS INTERACTIVE™

VIDEODISC
Lessons of War

Side Two, Chapter 6
Frames 12636–20751
Title: *Philosophy of Nonviolence*
Subject: The philosophies of Mohandas Gandhi and Martin Luther King, Jr., and how their philosophies were used in protests and demonstrations
Ask: For what cause did Martin Luther King, Jr., peacefully protest? *(civil rights)*

Visualizing History
Long lines formed at gasoline stations because of shortages when OPEC placed an embargo on oil exports. *How did the embargo affect the prices of other goods?*

The Changing Presidency

During the cold war, United States Presidents gradually began to exercise powers beyond those spelled out in the United States Constitution. Claiming a need for a quick military response to counter communism, Presidents began to assume the war-making powers of Congress, committing American military forces to combat without congressional approval. The two largest commitments to undeclared wars were in Korea and Vietnam.

The Imperial Presidency

As the cold war continued into the 1960s and 1970s, many people felt that the increased presidential power was subject to abuses and a violation of the Constitution. The term imperial presidency came into use, reflecting this concern.

The term was most often applied to Presidents Lyndon B. Johnson and Richard M. Nixon, both of whom expanded the conflict in Vietnam without a congressional declaration of war, as called for in the Constitution, and often kept their actions secret from Congress. In 1973 Congress overrode Nixon's veto to pass the War Powers Limitation Act. The measure required the President to consult Congress before committing United States troops to combat.

664 Chapter 21 *The Cold War*

The Watergate Scandal

Political scandals rocked the United States during the 1970s. Investigations revealed many cases of corruption in local and state government, but the country's attention focused primarily on charges of corruption in the federal government. Early in President Nixon's second term, scandal engulfed his administration. Vice President Spiro Agnew was accused of taking bribes when he was governor of Maryland and was forced to resign. Then the President himself came under fire in a scandal that became known as Watergate.

The Watergate scandal began on June 17, 1972, when five men were caught trying to plant electronic listening devices in the offices of the Democratic National Committee, located in the Watergate building in downtown **Washington, D.C.** The break-in was traced to Nixon's reelection committee.

A congressional probe revealed that the White House knew of the burglary and tried to cover it up. The President denied the charges at first, but tape recordings of Oval Office conversations proved that he had participated in the cover-up. Under the threat of impeachment, Nixon resigned on August 9, 1974. He was the first United States President ever to do so.

Gerald R. Ford, the Republican congressman from Michigan who had replaced Spiro Agnew as Vice President, became President when Nixon stepped down. Ford was the first United States President not to have been elected to either of the nation's top two offices. He assumed a presidency that had been weakened and tarnished. Watergate had shaken public confidence in the American political system. In addition, Ford had no personal mandate from the voters, since he had not been elected. As a former congressman, Ford maintained close ties with Congress. That, coupled with his acknowledged personal integrity, enabled him to function effectively. Both Ford and his Democratic successor, **Jimmy Carter**, a former governor of Georgia, worked to restore ethics to the presidency. In addition, as a result of Watergate, the media became far more vigilant in pursuing wrong-doing of public officials.

The Economy

During the late 1960s and 1970s, the United States economy was buffeted by the effects of the cold war and a changing world economy. The country suffered serious inflation in the l970s as a result of the costs of the Vietnam War and increased

TEACHER NOTES

_____

_____

_____

_____

_____

government spending for social programs. Administrations and congressional leaders were reluctant to offset spiraling costs with either cuts in programs or tax increases. Meanwhile, inflation combined with high unemployment to produce an economic trend called stagflation. Low productivity in factories and increased competition from foreign companies also slowed the American economy.

Soaring gas prices were part of an energy crisis that crippled economies around the world during the 1970s. In the United States, rapid economic growth had been dependent on cheap, abundant oil. Wanting to gain from increased world oil prices, OPEC (Organization of Petroleum Exporting Countries) countries in 1973 refused to ship oil to foreign customers. This oil embargo was damaging to American—and world—economic stability because it increased the cost of producing a wide range of goods.

Sharp rises in the price of oil and gasoline contributed to double-digit inflation, or a rise in the general level of prices of 10 percent or more. By 1980 it cost more than $200 to purchase the same goods that $100 would have bought only 10 years earlier. At the same time, the United States government raised interest rates to all-time highs in an effort to discourage borrowing and bring the economy under control. These policies helped reduce inflation but caused a severe recession.

During the 1970s, the United States also experienced a trade deficit, or importing more goods than it was exporting, and the steady loss of American jobs. As other nations in the world became more industrialized, they began to compete with American companies for sales to American consumers. In the late 1970s for example, rising gasoline prices led Americans to buy more fuel efficient Japanese cars rather than larger American cars. The shift of American factories abroad to take advantage of cheaper, talented labor also had a chilling impact on the employment situation in the United States.

Canada

Canada thrived economically after World War II. By 1960, it had changed from a primarily agricultural country to one of the world's most important industrial nations. Like the United States, production in Canada boomed after World War II as consumers demanded household goods and new homes. The exploitation of Canada's rich mineral resources also enabled the Canadian economy to flourish. Foreign investors, mainly from the neighboring United States, financed the development of many new industries.

Improved communications and transportation strengthened Canada's trade links with the United States. One significant joint venture of both countries in the 1950s was the completion of the **St. Lawrence Seaway**, a system of locks and canals that allows ships to travel between the Great Lakes and the Atlantic Ocean.

Canada's World Role

Traditionally linked to Great Britain, Canada's loyalties to the parent country gradually diminished as British global influence plummeted after World War II. Meanwhile, Canada's new and growing economic strength convinced many Canadians that their country needed to play a more active, independent role in world affairs. In 1945, Canada became a founding member of the United Nations and sent troops to Korea as part of the UN forces in 1950. Canada also joined NATO when it was formed in 1949. During the 1950s, cold war tensions brought the United States and Canada into a close defensive partnership.

In pursuing their foreign policy, Canadians were suspicious of a world dominated by superpowers. Over time, Canada advanced a role for itself as a middle power—that is, one that is strong economically, if not militarily. The Canadians used what military strength they had to promote peace. In 1956, Canada helped to bring about peace in the Middle East after Great Britain, France, and Israel had invaded Egypt. **Lester B. Pearson**, Canada's secretary of state for external affairs, won the 1957 Nobel Peace Prize for proposing and organizing a UN peacekeeping force for the troubled area.

A National Identity

In internal affairs, Canada struggled to find its own national identity during the period after World War II. While breaking many of their traditional ties to Europe, Canadians found themselves increasingly influenced by American ideas and practices. Most Canadians favored a continued close relationship to the United States. However, there were growing concerns that the "Americanization" of Canada posed a threat to Canada's newly emerging culture. In 1963, Pearson became Canada's prime minister. His administration expanded the country's social welfare programs and worked to strengthen Canadian national identity. Pearson achieved a personal goal when the Canadian parliament in 1965 adopted a new national flag, one that featured a red maple leaf as a symbol of Canada. The maple leaf soon became very popular

United States An American innovation that has spread around the world is the fast-food restaurant. From humble origins in hot-dog stands in the 1950s, fast-food outlets began to grow into a multibillion-dollar industry. Although their staple fare has been the American hamburger with fries and soft drinks, they now sell everything from minestrone soup to burritos. One of the factors encouraging fast-food growth has been an increase in the number of women who work outside the home.

Who?What?Where?When?

Ice Hockey More than 25 countries now play ice hockey, a game that originated in Canada. The sport began in military garrisons in the 1800s, when soldiers had time—and a lot of winter weather—on their hands.

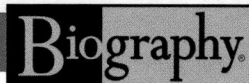

The following videotape programs are available from Glencoe:

- **John F. Kennedy: A Personal Story**
- **Jimmy Carter**

ASSESS

Check for Understanding

Assign Section 4 Review as homework or as an in-class activity.

Use Student Self-Test and Review Software to review Section 4.

TEACHER NOTES

_____

_____

_____

_____

_____

Chapter 21
Section 4

Visualizing History

In a referendum held in Quebec in 1995, citizens narrowly defeated a proposal that would have led to independence for the province.
Answer to Caption: *Sixty-five percent are of British or French descent, and the rest come from many different backgrounds.*

Evaluate

 Section Quiz 21-4

▣ Use the Testmaker to create a customized quiz for Section 4.

Reteach

Have students brainstorm a list of similarities and differences between the experiences of the United States and Canada during the cold war years.

 Reteaching Activity 21

Enrich

Have students view one or more episodes of *Eyes on the Prize,* the public television series about the civil rights movement. Then have them describe their reactions to the video.

📁 Enrichment Activity 21

CLOSE

Have students discuss which they think was the most important event or development in the United States and in Canada during the cold war period.

Visualizing History

The movement for an independent Quebec continued to gain strength through the 1990s. *How ethnically diverse is the population of Canada?*

among Canadians, who for years had honored some form of the Union Jack, or the British flag, as their national flag.

In 1967, Pearson presided over celebrations marking Canada's 100th anniversary of its nationhood. Many Canadians were especially proud of the fact that Canada had become a multicultural country, made up of people from many different ethnic groups. From 1945 to 1956, more than a million people from Germany, Italy, and other wartorn European countries had moved to farms or to **Toronto, Montreal,** and other large Canadian cities. In addition, other Canadians claimed Native American, Asian, African, or Latin American ancestry. Canada's two major ethnic groups,

however, were still people of British descent, who make up about 35 percent of the population, and those of French descent, who make up about 30 percent.

Separatism

While celebrating their nationhood, Canadians also faced a growing challenge to their country's unity. During the 1960s, French Canadians began a movement to defend their rights throughout Canada. They also wanted English-speaking Canadians to recognize and respect their culture in the province of **Quebec,** where 80 percent of the people are French-speaking.

A growing debate arose over the issue of separatism, a movement favoring the establishment of Quebec as an independent country. The issue gave rise to the Parti Quebecois (kay•beh•KWAH), or Quebec party, sometimes known as the Separatist party. Opposing the separatist drive for Quebec independence was Canadian Prime Minister **Pierre Elliott Trudeau,** himself a French Canadian, who had been elected to office in 1968. Trudeau promised to protect French Canadian language and cultural rights while supporting a strong united Canada. In 1969, he had the Canadian parliament pass the Official Languages Act. This law required federal government offices to provide service in both French and English if 10 percent of the people in a particular area spoke either language.

The Official Languages Act brought many changes to Canada's government. However, it had little effect on the growing separatist movement. In 1976, the Parti Quebecois won control of Quebec's government and declared French the province's official language. It also promised to hold an election to decide Quebec's future.

SECTION 4 REVIEW

Recall
1. **Define** automation, racial segregation, imperial presidency, stagflation, embargo, double-digit inflation, trade deficit, middle power, multicultural, separatism.
2. **Identify** Dwight D. Eisenhower, John F. Kennedy, Lyndon B.

Johnson, Richard M. Nixon, Martin Luther King, Jr., Gerald R. Ford, Jimmy Carter, Lester B. Pearson, Pierre Elliott Trudeau.
3. **Describe** the Supreme Court ruling in *Brown* v. *Board of Education of Topeka, Kansas.*

Critical Thinking
4. **Analyzing Information** Why

did President Eisenhower believe that the military-industrial complex was dangerous? Has his warning been borne out by history?
Understanding Themes
5. **Cooperation** Why did the United States and Canada develop close ties after 1945?

SECTION 4 REVIEW ANSWERS

1. All vocabulary words are defined in the Glossary.
2. Dwight D. Eisenhower, 661; John F. Kennedy, 661; Lyndon B. Johnson, 661; Richard M. Nixon, 662; Martin Luther King, Jr., 663; Gerald R. Ford, 664; Lester B. Pearson, 665; Pierre Elliott Trudeau, 666
3. This decision held that racial segregation in

public schools was unconstitutional.
4. He believed that it created an incentive to increase military spending and expand the arms race. Answers will vary.
5. **COOPERATION** As Canada's ties with Europe weakened, its relationship with the United States intensified.

Understanding World Time Zones

Imagine that you work in an office in New Jersey. Your boss asks you to place a telephone call to a client in London. At 2:00 P.M. you place the call, but no one answers. Why? When it is 2:00 P.M. in New Jersey, it is already 7:00 P.M. in London. The times differ because the world is divided into time zones.

Learning the Skill

In 1884 an international conference established standard time zones around the world. The Prime Meridian (0° longitude), which runs through Greenwich, England, became the reference point for measuring time. The conference divided the world into 24 time zones, each 15° of longitude apart. Traveling east from Greenwich, the time is one hour later in each time zone. Traveling west from Greenwich, the time is one hour earlier.

The conference also established the International Date Line at 180° longitude. When crossing this line from west to east, you lose one day; when crossing in the opposite direction, you gain a day.

The map on this page illustrates the world time zones. To use this map, locate a reference point and note its time. Then locate the place for which you wish to know the time. Determine whether this place lies east or west of the reference point. Then count the number of time zones and add or subtract as needed. If the International Date Line lies between two points, add or subtract a day.

Practicing the Skill

Use the map to calculate these times.
1. If it is 3:00 P.M. in Greenwich, what time is it in Moscow?
2. If it is 9:00 A.M. in Cape Town, what time is it in Washington, D.C.?
3. If it is Tuesday, 4:30 P.M. in Japan, what day and time is it in Honolulu?
4. If it is Friday, 8:15 A.M. in Rio de Janeiro, what day and time is it in Beijing?

Applying the Skill

Make up four time zone problems and compute the answers. Exchange your problems with a friend. See who can answer them most quickly.

For More Practice

Turn to the Skill Practice in the Chapter Review on page 669 for more practice in understanding world time zones.

Time Zones of the World

Understanding World Time Zones
Point out that the United States has had standard time zones only since 1883, when they were instituted by America's railroads, which found the 100 different time zones in that era too difficult to cope with. Have students use the hour your class begins and then figure out what the time would be in the following places: Washington, D.C.; Toronto, Ontario; Budapest, Hungary; and Cairo, Egypt.

Additional Practice

📁 Skill Reinforcement Activity 21

📁 Building Skills in Geography Workbook, Unit 1, Lesson 10

ANSWERS TO PRACTICING THE SKILL

1. 5 P.M.
2. 3 A.M.
3. Students will either answer Monday, 9:00 P.M. or Monday, 9:30 P.M. depending on which Japanese island student is using to count.
4. Saturday, 6:15 P.M.

Chapter 21 Review

GLENCOE
TECHNOLOGY

VIDEODISC

Use MindJogger to review students' knowledge of the chapter.

MindJogger Videoquiz

Chapter 21
Disc 3 Side A

Also available in VHS.

Answers

Using Key Terms

1. d   4. g
2. b   5. i
3. f

Using Your History Journal

Headings may include *Politics*, *The Economy*, and *Daily Life*.

Reviewing Facts

1. It provided financial aid to Europe in order to further economic and political stability. It spurred economic recovery.
2. to try to force the Western powers out of Berlin
3. In Albania, Yugoslavia, and Czechoslovakia, local communists took control. In Poland, East Germany, and Bulgaria, it was Soviet troops. Communist governments imposed Soviet government on their countries.
4. He eased censorship and allowed some political groups to meet freely.
5. publicly accusing people of political subversion without regard to evidence
6. King supported nonviolent sit-ins and marches to protest discrimination.

Connections Across Time

Historical Significance The cold war between the United States and the Soviet Union divided Europe and the large areas of the rest of the world into two camps. Long-range nuclear weapons made the superpowers' quarrel dangerous because of the threat of nuclear war that would destroy civilization.

Gradually, this realization compelled the superpowers to seek ways of reducing tensions. Ultimately, the economic strength and democratic principles of the United States and Western Europe undermined communism and stimulated demands for change within the Communist bloc. Meanwhile, nationalism replaced ideology as a source of conflict.

Using Key Terms

Write the key term that completes each sentence. Then write a sentence for each term not chosen.

a. cold war
b. containment
c. ICBMs
d. iron curtain
e. welfare states
f. stagflation
g. dissidents
h. separatism
i. racial segregation
j. imperial presidency
k. peaceful coexistence
l. middle power

1. The term _____ referred to the Soviet-made barrier that divided Europe into non-Communist and Communist areas.
2. To counter any expansionist threat from the Soviet Union, the Truman administration in 1947 developed a policy known as _____.
3. In the 1970s, inflation combined with high unemployment to produce _____.
4. Soviet leader Leonid Brezhnev applied harsh measures to _____ who criticized the Communist party or the Soviet government.
5. In *Brown* v. *Board of Education of Topeka, Kansas*, the United States Supreme Court ruled that _____ in public schools was illegal.

Technology Activity

Using E-mail In the 1950s it would have been hard to imagine the role computers would play in our lives today. One by-product of the computer revolution is the hundreds of new computer-related words we have added to our language, such as *surfing* and *modem*. Using E-mail, compose and send a message requesting a list of words that probably did not exist before computers were invented in the 1950s. Share your responses with the class.

Using Your History Journal

From your notes on the interviews with the people who remember the events of the 1950s or early 1960s, write a newspaper feature piece titled "Living Through the Cold War."

Reviewing Facts

1. **History** Explain the purpose of the Marshall Plan. In what ways was the plan effective?
2. **History** Explain why Joseph Stalin ordered the Berlin blockade.
3. **Government** Describe how Communists came to power in Eastern Europe. How did they govern?
4. **History** Identify the reforms that Dubček introduced in Czechoslovakia.
5. **History** Explain the meaning of *McCarthyism*.
6. **Citizenship** Identify the role of Martin Luther King, Jr., in the civil rights struggle.

Critical Thinking

1. **Apply** What postwar developments launched the cold war?
2. **Analyze** In your view, why did the United States assume global responsibility for containing communism?
3. **Synthesize** Create a time line showing major events in the spread of communism from 1945 to 1979. What effect did Communist expansion have on global affairs during this period?
4. **Evaluate** Was Americans' fear of communism during the 1950s justified? Do you think the actions that Congress took to counter

Critical Thinking

1. the Soviet imposition of communism in Eastern Europe; the division of Germany; the Berlin blockade; the formation of military and economic alliances
2. because it was a democratic superpower, firmly opposed to the spread of communism
3. Time line shows dates for communist takeovers, formation of Warsaw Pact, Korean War, and revolutions in China and Cuba. It

contributed to the cold war competition in arms and diplomatic alliances.

4. Some students may feel communism posed little threat to the United States; others may say the Soviet Union was engaged in aggression. Congressional actions seem inappropriate because they exposed minimal Communist danger while destroying many careers.
5. It heightened fears of Soviet intervention while encouraging moves toward European unity.

communism were appropriate? Explain your reasoning.

5. **Apply** How do you think the cold war affected politics in Western European countries?

6. **Synthesize** Compare the economic systems of the United States, Great Britain, and the Soviet Union during the cold war era.

7. **Apply** Is the United States presidency today an imperial presidency? Why or why not?

8. **Apply** What was the major source of tension that led to French Canadian separatism?

Understanding Themes

1. **Conflict** By the 1950s the superpowers had enough nuclear weapons to eliminate each other. What effect did this power have on super-power relations during the cold war?

2. **Change** What might have happened if the Soviet Union had not used force to keep its Eastern European satellite countries under control?

3. **Regionalism** How did the European Common Market benefit member countries?

4. **Cooperation** How did the foreign policy of Canada compare and contrast with that of the United States during the cold war era?

Linking Past and Present

1. Key cold war issues continued until about 1989, when they reached a dramatic conclusion. Name these issues and explain their link to recent events.

2. Name a previous period in history when Europe was united. When did the continent become fragmented again?

3. Is containment an important or pressing issue in American foreign policy today? Explain your reasoning.

Geography in History

1. **Location** Refer to the map of Berlin on this page. What side of the city of Berlin became the Soviet sector after World War II?

2. **Place** What nations maintained army headquarters in Berlin following the war?

Berlin After World War II

- Berlin Wall
- ○ Control points
- ■ Army HQ 1945–1949
- Main roads
- International railways

3. **Movement** Approximately how long was the wall that the Soviets built to keep East Germans from crossing to the West?

4. **Location** How many control points were located along the Berlin Wall?

Skill Practice

Refer to the map of World Time Zones on page 667 to answer the following questions.

1. Name some areas of the world in which you find non-standard time.

2. You are in New York and you want to call someone in Rome, Italy, at noon Rome time. When would you call?

3. Assume that flying from New York to London requires 6 hours. When would a flight leaving New York on a Wednesday at 6:00 P.M. arrive in London?

4. You are flying from Los Angeles to Moscow. You leave Los Angeles at 10:00 A.M. on Saturday and you arrive in Moscow on Sunday at 9:00 A.M. How many hours did you actually spend flying?

5. You are planning a flight from Mumbai, India, to Washington, D.C., that must connect through several cities. You will leave Mumbai on August 2, at 8:00 A.M., and will continue directly through Beijing and Los Angeles to Washington, D.C. What time is it in Washington, D.C., when you begin your trip? What will be the date when you arrive in Washington, D.C.?

Chapter 21 *The Cold War* **669**

themselves with the West

3. **REGIONALISM** It reduced conflict, lessened trade barriers, and helped raise the standard of living.

4. **COOPERATION** Although Canada, joined the UN and NATO, it saw itself as a middle power and thus a peace-keeper.

Linking Past and Present

1. The iron curtain lifted and the Berlin Wall fell in 1989; Eastern Europe abandoned communism and instituted democratic reforms; the Warsaw Pact was dissolved.

2. Much of it was united under the Roman Empire; after the death of Charlemagne

3. No, because the cold war is over and the threat of Soviet expansion appears to have ended.

Geography in History

1. east

2. France, Britain, United States, Soviet Union

3. approximately 26 miles (42 km)

4. 7

Skill Practice

1. Cook Islands, Newfoundland, Suriname, area north of Iceland, Saudi Arabia, Afghanistan, India and the Bay of Bengal, Cocos Islands, central Australia

2. 6:00 A.M.

3. 5:00 A.M. Wednesday

4. 12 hours

5. 10 P.M. August 1; August 2

---

6. U.S. has a prosperous free enterprise system, with recurring challenges of inflation and balancing budgets; the Soviet Union had a government-run economy based on heavy industry with consumer goods in short supply; Great Britain practiced democratic Socialism with some government economic controls and a welfare state.

7. Some may feel the President has a great deal of power; others may say system of checks

and balances works to limit the presidency.

8. Quebecois fear that their culture would not be recognized and respected

Understanding Themes

1. **CONFLICT** Both sides, realizing that using nuclear weapons was unacceptable, sought ways to limit the arms race.

2. **CHANGE** broken away from its influence and become independent or allied

? Chapter Bonus Test Question

Ask students: Do you think the cold war could have been prevented? *(Yes, the West should have acted quickly after Stalin's first takeovers in Eastern Europe; no, Stalin was willing to risk war to get what he wanted.)*

A complete, 1-page lesson plan is provided for each section in the *Reproducible Lesson Plans* booklet.

Asia and the Pacific

CHAPTER RESOURCES

	Reproducible Resources	Multimedia Resources
Chapter Opener	Chapter Themes: Graphic Organizer 22 Historical Significance Chapter Activity 22	MindJogger Videoquiz
Chapter Enrichment	Vocabulary Activity 22* Time Line Activity 22 Mapping History Activity 22 History Simulation 22 Geography and History Activity 22 Source Reading 22 People in World History Profiles 63, 64 World Art and Music Activity 22 Enrichment Activity 22 Critical Thinking Activity 22 Skill Reinforcement Activity 22 Performance Assessment Activity 22	World History and Art Transparency 44, *Sydney Opera House* Mapping History Overlay Transparency 24 Chapter Transparency 22 Vocabulary PuzzleMaker Software World Music: Cultural Traditions, Lessons 7, 8, 9, 10 Lessons of War: *Philosophy of Nonviolence* Communism and the Cold War: • *Revolution in China* • *Korean War* • *Vietnam War* • *Tiananmen Square*
Chapter Review/Reteaching	Reteaching Activity 22 Skill Reinforcement Activity 22 Spanish Chapter Summary 22	Chapter 22 Digest Audiocassette, Activity, Test* Vocabulary PuzzleMaker Software Student Self-Test and Review Software MindJogger Videoquiz
Chapter Evaluation/Testing	Performance Assessment Activity 22 Chapter 22 Test, Forms A and B	Testmaker

* Also available in Spanish

0:00 OUT OF TIME? Assign the Chapter 22 summary in the Unit 6 Digest on pages 803–805, and the Chapter 22 Audiocassettes.

Block Schedule

Block scheduling differs from traditional class scheduling in the amount of time allotted to each period. The extended time frame provided by block scheduling affords you the opportunity to implement a greater number of research-oriented and activity-intense projects to motivate and involve your students. Activities that are particularly suited to use within the block scheduling framework are identified throughout this chapter by the following designation.

KEY TO ABILITY LEVELS

Teaching strategies have been coded for varying learning styles and abilities.

L1 BASIC activities for all students
L2 AVERAGE activities for average to above-average students
L3 CHALLENGING activities for above-average students
LEP LIMITED ENGLISH PROFICIENCY activities

Use Glencoe's *Presentation Plus!* multimedia teacher tool to easily present dynamic lessons that visually excite your students. Using Microsoft PowerPoint® you can customize the presentations to create your own personalized lessons.

SECTION RESOURCES

Daily Objectives	Reproducible Resources	Multimedia Resources
Section 1 **Japan's Economic Rise** List the factors that have contributed to the economic success of Japan.	Reproducible Lesson Plan 22-1 Vocabulary Activity 22* Guided Reading Activity 22-1* History Simulation 22 Section Quiz 22-1*	Section Focus Transparency 22-1 Mapping History Overlay Transparency 24, *Trade Between the U.S. and Japan* Chapter Transparency 22 Student Self-Test and Review Software World Music: Cultural Traditions, Lesson 8
Section 2 **China in Revolution** Explain how communism has affected the domestic and international affairs of China since the late 1940s.	Reproducible Lesson Plan 22-2 Vocabulary Activity 22* Guided Reading Activity 22-2* Geography and History Activity 22 Section Quiz 22-2*	Section Focus Transparency 22-2 Student Self-Test and Review Software World Music: Cultural Traditions, Lesson 8 Communism and the Cold War
Section 3 **A Divided Korea** Describe how South Korea and North Korea have differed in their political and economic development.	Reproducible Lesson Plan 22-3 Vocabulary Activity 22* Guided Reading Activity 22-3* Section Quiz 22-3*	Section Focus Transparency 22-3 Student Self-Test and Review Software Communism and the Cold War
Section 4 **Southeast Asia** Explain how nationalism, the cold war, and the rise of a global economy have affected Southeast Asia.	Reproducible Lesson Plan 22-4 Vocabulary Activity 22* Guided Reading Activity 22-4* Section Quiz 22-4*	Section Focus Transparency 22-4 Student Self-Test and Review Software World Music: Cultural Traditions, Lesson 9 Communism and the Cold War
Section 5 **South Asia** Identify the challenges that have faced the countries of South Asia since independence.	Reproducible Lesson Plan 22-5 Vocabulary Activity 22* Guided Reading Activity 22-5* Section Quiz 22-5*	Section Focus Transparency 22-5 Student Self-Test and Review Software World Music: Cultural Traditions, Lesson 7 Lessons of War
Section 6 **The Pacific** List the factors that have helped Pacific nations develop prosperous economies and new national identities since World War II.	Reproducible Lesson Plan 22-6 Guided Reading Activity 22-6* Reteaching Activity 22 Enrichment Activity 22 Section Quiz 22-6* Performance Assessment Activity 22 Spanish Chapter Summary 22	Section Focus Transparency 22-6 World History and Art Transparency 44, *Sydney Opera House* Vocabulary PuzzleMaker Software Student Self-Test and Review Software Testmaker World Music: Cultural Traditions, Lesson 10

* *Also available in Spanish*

Chapter Activities

 Performance Assessment Activity

A Page on the Internet Many of the physical and ideological conflicts in Korea, Vietnam, and China, as well as the economic conflicts the United States has had with Japan, still affect Americans today. Many people have lived through these times, and others have strong opinions about them. Have students design a page for the Internet giving information about one of these historical conflicts, their own opinions, information regarding interviews they have had with Americans who have experiences to share, and current laws or reforms that can be traced back to these conflicts.

Possible Rubric Features
Research skills, interviewing techniques, accuracy of content information, appropriateness to audience and purpose, clarity and organization, and use of technology

• *For an additional activity, refer to Activity 22 in the* Performance Assessment Strategies and Activities *booklet.*

ACTIVITY

From the Classroom of...

**Anna Mae Grimm
Homestead High School
Mequon, WI**

Leading a Developing Republic
Students will play the roles of the newly elected president and cabinet of a fictitious developing country, to gain a perspective on the complexities involved in national development. Students should take the roles of president; military leader; ministers of health, industry, finance, trade, agriculture, public works; leaders of two religious groups; farmers; businesspeople; feminists; and the unemployed—all of them with competing interests.

Have students participate in a roundtable discussion and try to create a national structure that keeps everyone happy. Students should keep in mind that their country is poor, with health and literacy problems. It does, however, have abundant untapped natural resources. Remind students that their contribution to the discussion should reflect the interests of their chosen role. Ask students to discuss whether their discussion gave them insight into the complexities involved in industrializing a developing country.

MULTIPLE LEARNING STYLES

Verbal/Linguistic
Ask students to conduct an interview of a veteran of the Korean or Vietnam War, focusing on wartime experiences and postwar reflections. Have students write up the interview for possible classroom presentation.

Visual/Spatial
Have students draw the national flag for each country in this chapter. Ask them to research the meaning of any symbols, colors, and wording on the flags.

Auditory/Musical
Have the class listen to a tape or CD of *Miss Saigon*, the musical about the relationship between a young Vietnamese woman and an American soldier in 1975 at the end of the Vietnam War.

Kinesthetic
Have students investigate the degree to which Western styles of dress have been adopted in the countries discussed in this chapter and the extent to which traditional styles are still worn. Suggest that students make drawings illustrating existing traditional styles.

Additional Resources

NATIONAL GEOGRAPHIC SOCIETY

Teacher's Corner

INDEX TO NATIONAL GEOGRAPHIC MAGAZINE

The following articles may be used for research relating to this chapter:

- "The New Saigon," by Tracy Dahlby, April 1995.
- "Shanghai: Where China's Past and Future Meet," by William S. Ellis, March 1994.
- "Kyushu: Japan's Southern Gateway," by Tracy Dahlby, January 1994.
- "Taiwan: The Other China Changes Course," by Arthur Zich, November 1993.

NATIONAL GEOGRAPHIC SOCIETY PRODUCTS AVAILABLE FROM GLENCOE

To order the following products for use with this chapter, contact your local Glencoe sales representative, or call Glencoe at 1-800-334-7344:

- *Capitalism, Socialism, Communism Series, "Communism."* (Video)
- *Democratic Governments Series, "Japan."* (Video)
- *The Changing Faces of Communism Series, "Vietnam."* (Video)
- *Nations of the World Series, "Japan."* (Video)

BIBLIOGRAPHY

Literature of the Period
Oe, Kenzaburo. *Nip the Buds, Shoot the Kids.* Translated by Paul St. John Mackintosh and Maki Sugiyama. New York: Marion Boyars, 1995. This first novel by the winner of the 1994 Nobel Prize in literature tells the story of a band of teenage delinquents in wartime.

Readings for the Student
Marrin, Albert. *America and Vietnam: The Elephant and the Tiger.* New York: Viking, 1992. The causes and effects of the Vietnam War.

Readings for the Teacher
Paik, Sun Yup. *From Pusan to Panmunjom.* New York: Macmillan, 1992. A South Korean commander describes his involvement in the Korean War.

LOCAL OBJECTIVES

interNET CONNECTION
Southeast Asia resources on the World Wide Web
Links to Southeast Asia: http://www.irdu.nus.sg/ multilingual/sea/

Introducing
Chapter 22

CHAPTER THEMES

Chapter Themes are listed by section on this chapter opening page of the Student Edition. A corresponding theme-based activity is available under "TEACH," and a theme-based question is asked in the Section and Chapter Reviews.

The Storyteller

Historical Setting Although the kimono is universally recognized as a Japanese garment, this familiar ankle-length gown with long, wide sleeves actually derives from a Chinese robe. The transformation of the kimono into a work of art, however, is attributable to Japanese designers of the 1600s and 1700s. Their stylistic prowess turned a simple garment into one of the world's most beautiful articles of clothing. Although Japanese men and women have worn the kimono since the Early Nara period (A.D. 645–724), the broad sash, or obi, that holds the buttonless garment together is of more recent origin, dating from the 1700s.

Historical Significance

Answers: *The countries of Asia play an important role in world politics, economics, and culture.*

Several Asian nations have emerged as economic models; Asian cinema, music, and religion have had a growing influence; and world peace has been affected by Asia since 1945.

Chapter
22

1945–Present

Asia and the Pacific

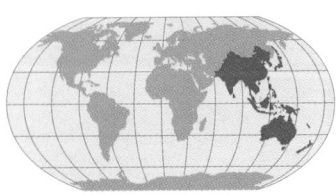

Chapter Themes

▶ **Change** Japan builds a democracy and becomes a global economic power. *Section 1*
▶ **Revolution** Communists in China introduce socialist measures, and then promote a limited free enterprise economy. *Section 2*
▶ **Regionalism** After decades of conflict and cold war tensions, North Korea and South Korea take first steps toward unification. *Section 3*
▶ **Conflict** The rise of nationalism and cold war competition leads to conflict in post-World War II Southeast Asia. *Section 4*
▶ **Diversity** A diversity of religious and ethnic groups challenges the unity in South Asia. *Section 5*
▶ **Cultural Diffusion** Changing political and economic roles open the nations of the Pacific to other parts of the globe. *Section 6*

The Storyteller

"My methods are old, " declares Japanese artist Kako Muriguchi, "but my designs are new." Muriguchi designs innovative patterns for kimonos, the traditional Japanese garment for women. The people of Japan have such respect for his contributions to their heritage that they have declared him a "living national treasure." As a result of this designation, Muriguchi is entitled to lifetime national support for his art. Like Muriguchi, Japan and other countries in Asia have found success by combining old and new. Traditional values that encourage education and hard work, combined with modern developments, such as computer technology, have brought prosperity to many countries in Asia since the end of World War II.

Historical Significance

What role do the countries of Asia and the Pacific play in the contemporary world? How have they contributed to the world's economy, culture, and politics since 1945?

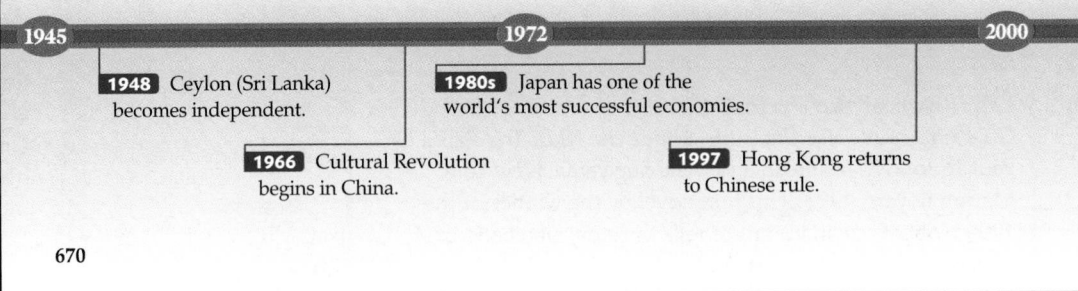

1945

1948 Ceylon (Sri Lanka) becomes independent.

1966 Cultural Revolution begins in China.

1972

1980s Japan has one of the world's most successful economies.

1997 Hong Kong returns to Chinese rule.

2000

670

GEOGRAPHY CONNECTION

Location Have students use a globe to locate the countries discussed in this chapter: Japan, China, Taiwan, North Korea, South Korea, India, Pakistan, Bangladesh, Myanmar, Sri Lanka, Vietnam, Cambodia, Laos, Thailand, Indonesia, Singapore, the Philippines, Australia, and New Zealand. **Which of the countries are large?** *(China, India, Australia)* **Do you think that size is a measure of a country's power or importance?** *(No. India is relatively big, but much of its population is poor. Japan is small but economically advanced.)*

Visualizing History On June 30, 1997, ceremonies were held to commemorate the transfer of Hong Kong from British to Chinese rule. A band of Scots Guards played "God Save the Queen" as Britain's Union Jack flag was lowered. On the other side of the stage, the Chinese flag was raised as a band played the Chinese national anthem. The festivities were televised throughout China.

Visualizing History Hong Kong's skyline is aglow with lights in celebration of the territory's return to Chinese rule on June 30, 1997.

Performance Assessment

Refer to the activity on page 670C of the Planning Guide.

For an additional activity, refer to Activity 22 in the *Performance Assessment Strategies and Activities* booklet.

Your History Journal

Interview someone who migrated to the United States from an Asian or Pacific nation, or research the culture of an Asian or Pacific nation. Write a short report on the cultural adjustments a person from that nation would make to live in the United States.

Using Your History Journal

Advise students to prepare a specific list of questions they want to have answered before they begin their interviews.

GLENCOE TECHNOLOGY

VIDEODISC
Use MindJogger to preview chapter content.

MindJogger Videoquiz
Chapter 22
Disc 3 Side A

Also available in VHS.

Chapter 22 *Asia and the Pacific* **671**

✚ EXTRA CREDIT PROJECT

Oral Report Ask students to research the industrial and economic development of China from the Communist takeover to the present. Advise them to consider the effects of the First Five-Year Plan, the Great Leap Forward, the Cultural Revolution, and the reform measures introduced following Mao's death. Have students summarize their findings in a brief oral report. Suggested resources: J. K. Fairbank, *China: A New History*; Feng Jicai, *Voices from the Whirlwind: An Oral History of the Chinese Cultural Revolution*; W. Overholt, *The Rise of China*; R. Terrill, *China in Our Time*.

SECTION THEME

▶ **Change** Japan builds a democracy and becomes a global economic power.

Find Out

Answer: *MacArthur's postwar reform policies, America's need for supplies in the vicinity during the Korean War, Japanese government-business cooperation, political stability, and normalization of relations with China have contributed to the economic success of Japan.*

FOCUS

Section Objective

List the factors that have contributed to the economic success of Japan.

**BELLRINGER
Motivational Activity**

Before taking roll at the beginning of the class period, project Section Focus Transparency 22-1 and have students answer the activity questions. Discuss students' responses.

📁 This activity is also available as a blackline master.

Vocabulary Pre-check

📁 Use Vocabulary Activity 22 to introduce vocabulary terms.
L1 LEP

1945   1972   2000

1947 Japan adopts democratic constitution.

1980s Japan has one of the world's most successful economies.

1995 Severe earthquake strikes Kobe area.

Section 1

Japan's Economic Rise

Setting the Scene

▶ **Terms to Define**
gross domestic product, pollution, sect, quota

▶ **People to Meet**
Douglas MacArthur, Hirohito

▶ **Places to Locate**
Tokyo, Kobe

Find Out What factors have contributed to the economic success of Japan?

The Storyteller

Kyoichi Tabuchi's plane landed in Bangkok, the city he would now call home. He had accepted a position as manager of an industrial complex. The Thai government eagerly received Tabuchi and his fellow Japanese for establishing economic opportunities. The age of Heisei, or peaceful achievement, had begun. Japan's economy was booming; her industry was welcomed throughout the region she had occupied militarily just 50 years earlier. As Tabuchi drove to the Japanese district, he heard the radio play a song that clearly defined the beneficial situation: "The Samurai Are Here."

Ascendant electronics

—adapted from "Japan's Sun Rises Over the Pacific," *National Geographic,* November, 1995, Arthur Zich

The end of World War II brought dramatic changes to Asia; Japan was stripped of the lands it had conquered. Great Britain, France, and the Netherlands were forced to withdraw from their Asian colonies, and new nations arose. Communists won control in China and North Korea, and the cold war affected the entire region. Out of the turmoil, vigorous industrial powers have emerged. Japan's transformation into a global economic giant has been one of the most important changes of the post-World War II era.

Occupation and Reform

Japan, a proud nation with a long history of self-reliance, ended World War II with its pride crushed, its economy wrecked, and its people demoralized by the humiliating defeat. The victorious countries established an occupation government, the Supreme Command of the Allied Powers (SCAP), to govern Japan after the war. Although planned as a joint venture of the Allies, the occupation government became entirely a United States enterprise, headed by General **Douglas MacArthur**. The general was determined not to plant the seeds of future war by imposing an unjust and unworkable system on the Japanese. MacArthur's reform policies affected Japan's political and economic spheres, and Japan made a remarkable recovery.

A New Constitution

SCAP required Japan to adopt a new constitution in 1947. The constitution stripped the imperial family of its political power and gave it to the Japanese citizens. No longer could Japanese emperors rule by their claim to divine authority. Instead, Emperor **Hirohito** remained in office as a symbol of the state. The constitution also established a cabinet based on the British model. Both houses of the Diet, or legislature, were made elective, and citizens over the age of 20 could vote. A bill of rights guaranteed basic freedoms.

672 Chapter 22 *Asia and the Pacific*

The new constitution included an unusual provision. Article 9 barred Japan from all warfare except for defense—"The Japanese people forever renounce war as a sovereign right of the nation.... Land, sea, and air forces, as well as other war potential, will never be maintained." SCAP hoped that this would prevent Japan from ever threatening its neighbors again. The United States agreed to protect Japan militarily. In the late 1990s, the United States still had troops—47,000 in all—stationed on Japanese territory, most of them on the island of Okinawa. This military arrangement enabled Japan to concentrate more of its resources on consumer goods than on military equipment. It also reassured other nations of the region who feared the revival of a militarily strong Japan.

Economic Reform

SCAP also set out to decentralize Japanese agriculture and industry. Landlords not living on their property could own only 2.5 acres (1.1 ha) of land. The law required them to sell off holdings above this figure at very low prices. Those who actually farmed the soil were permitted to own up to 7.5 acres (3.1 ha). Decentralization changed the face of Japanese agriculture, resulting in the transfer of more than 5 million acres (2 million ha). Although Japanese farmers have prospered, small-scale farming has been costly and inefficient. Today, the Japanese government subsidizes farmers by buying their crops at high prices to cover farmers' costs and then resells the crops to consumers at a loss.

SCAP took steps to decentralize the *zaibatsu*, the giant industrial and banking organizations that controlled Japanese industry. General MacArthur believed that removal of *zaibatsu* control would prevent Japan from rearming. The Korean War, however, led the United States to change this policy and gave renewed life to Japan's large industrial organizations. It was hoped by the United States that a strong Japanese economy would help contain the spread of communism in Asia.

Japan's Dramatic Recovery

Japan's shattered economy recovered quickly in the early 1950s with assistance from the United States. The Korean War created a vast need for all kinds of war supplies, ranging from trucks to uniforms and medical supplies. To have sources of supply close at hand, the United States poured $3.5 billion into Japan—an amount nearly equal to what

Japan's Emperor Hirohito (center) reigned from 1926 until his death in 1989. His son, Akihito, succeeded him. *What changes came to Japan's government during the late 1940s?*

the United States gave Germany under the Marshall Plan. The United States also provided training in management skills so that Japan was able to rebuild its factories to the latest standards. Japanese shipbuilders, car manufacturers, electronics and pharmaceutical industries all benefited from American aid and later became major leaders in the global economy.

As part of its recognition of Japan's support to the United States during the Korean War, a formal peace treaty with Japan was reached in 1951 and the American occupation of Japan ended.

Government-Business Cooperation

The Japanese government and Japan's well-educated workforce took advantage of the boom created by the United States. Although Japan had to import most of its raw materials, the Japanese economy expanded quickly. Japan's engineers, managers, and laborers worked hard to boost the country's prosperity. The Japanese government worked closely with large corporations to plan and promote industrial growth. They brought vision to long-range planning and then followed through on their

---

TEACH

Guided Practice

THEME Change

Have students give examples of political, economic, and cultural reforms instituted by MacArthur in Japan. Ask students if they think making these changes was easy. **L1**

Visualizing History Hirohito was the longest-reigning ruler in Japan's history. From the outset, the period of his rule was named *Showa*, or "Enlightened Peace." Even though World War II took place during Hirohito's reign, he wound up accepting the Allied terms of surrender. A few months later he renounced the tradition of conferring divine status on Japan's emperors.

Answer to Caption: *A new constitution stripped the imperial family of its political power, established a cabinet based on the British model, and barred Japan from all warfare except for defense.*

Japan's Dramatic Recovery
What changes came to Japan's economy after World War II? *American aid and Japanese know-how enabled Japan to rebuild its economy. Japan's government and business leaders invested heavily in electronics and automobiles for export. By the 1970s Japan had become a leader in the world market.*

The Arts Arrange a classroom showing of the Japanese director Akira Kurosawa's *Rhapsody in August*, about the bombing of Nagasaki during World War II. After viewing the film, have the class discuss it. **L2**

COOPERATIVE LEARNING ACTIVITY

TV Interview Organize the class into two groups: one group to prepare interview questions to ask General MacArthur, the other group to prepare questions for Emperor Hirohito. Questions should be based on research of topics such as demilitarization, government, economic reform, and world affairs. Have students from both groups meet to combine their questions into a satisfactory list. Then appoint students to act as MacArthur, Hirohito, and an interviewer, and have them practice role-playing a TV interview. When students are prepared, invite another class or families to attend the mock broadcast. **L3**

Visualizing History

By 1980, Japan had overtaken West Germany, France, Great Britain, and the United States to become the world's leading automotive producer.
Answer to Caption: *Japan increased its share of world automobile production from 3 percent in 1960 to 29 percent in 1980.*

Geography: Location Have students locate Japan, China, Taiwan, Korea, and Indonesia on a map. Point out how proximity would cause these countries to be involved in one another's affairs. Have students note examples of this involvement as study of the chapter proceeds. **L2 LEP**

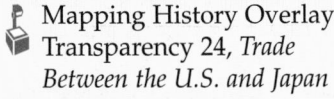 Mapping History Overlay Transparency 24, *Trade Between the U.S. and Japan*

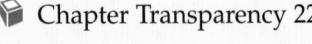 Chapter Transparency 22

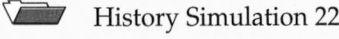 History Simulation 22

World Music: Cultural Traditions, Lesson 8

Biography

The following videotape program is available from Glencoe:
- **Hirohito**

Independent Practice

Guided Reading Activity 22-1 **L1**

decisions. For example, in the late 1950s government and industry agreed to invest heavily in research and development in the home electronics field. By the early 1970s, Japanese radios, televisions, stereos, and other items were challenging American dominance in the world market.

Similarly, the Japanese government and industrial leaders targeted the automobile industry as one they thought could help bring prosperity to Japan. The government helped fund researchers who developed dependable, high-mileage automobiles. Managers and laborers worked together to develop newer and more efficient production techniques. As a result of these innovations, Japan began producing high-quality cars at competitive prices, and sales of Japanese automobiles around the world soared. Japan increased its share of world automobile production from 3 percent in 1960 to a full 29 percent in 1980.

By 1980 Japan had one of the world's most successful economies. Although only as big as California, Japan's gross domestic product (GDP)—the sum value of all goods and services it produced—was about half that of the United States. Its per capita GDP, the amount of production per individual, was among the highest in the industrialized world.

Japan's rapid growth continued through the 1980s. Between 1988 and 1992, the annual growth rate was 5 percent, one of the highest rates in the world. Japanese businesses invested heavily overseas in real estate, banks, and factories.

In 1992, Japan was hit by a recession that lasted into the mid-1990s. The value of many of its foreign investments dropped, and Japanese banks were hard hit. Day laborers were badly hurt by the recession. Even some salaried workers who previously had lifetime employment with large corporations lost their jobs. The long-term prospect for Japan is continued economic growth, but at a slower pace than in the past.

Side Effects of Growth

Like many other industrialized countries, Japan had solid economic growth that raised the standard of living of its citizens. However, the spread of industry also caused environmental damage. Japan's industries clustered along a narrow coastal belt between the city of **Tokyo** and the southernmost Japanese island, Kyushu. Along with industry came a dense concentration of people and automobiles and pollution, or the release of impure or poisonous substances into land, water, and air. In addition, rapid industrial development had created severe housing shortages in urban areas. Government and business leaders began to take steps to balance industrial growth with environmental protection.

Politics and Government

Until recently, Japan's economic growth had been bolstered by an extraordinary level of political stability. From 1955 to 1993, one political party dominated the Japanese government. Despite its name, the Liberal Democratic Party (LDP) is a conservative, pro-business party that has had broad Japanese support. The LDP has traditionally been strong among Japan's farming population, but it also receives heavy financial support from the country's large corporations. Voters liked the party's dependability, especially during the uncertainty of the cold war.

MEETING SPECIAL NEEDS ACTIVITY

Learning Style: Logical/Mathematical Have students create a time line of important events in Japan's history between World War II and the present. Before advising students on the appropriate scale to use (for example, three inches per year), determine how much wall space you have available to display the five time lines that students will generate as they study other sections in this chapter. Tell students to include political, religious, economic, and cultural events, as well as natural disasters such as the 1995 Kobe earthquake. **L1**

In 1993, Japanese voters defeated the scandal-weakened LDP. With the collapse of the Soviet Union, and the end of the cold war, it seemed safe to support the chief opposition party, the Social Democratic Party of Japan (SDPJ). The splintered SDPJ was forced to form a coalition government and to include many LDP leaders in the cabinet.

Because of its political diversity, the new government had difficulty steering Japan through a number of crises. In January 1995, a severe earthquake struck the area around the port city of **Kobe**. It was one of the deadliest natural disasters to hit Japan in the twentieth century. Political opponents criticized the government for not responding rapidly to provide relief to the quake victims. In addition many SDPJ members, unhappy about their party's linkage to the LDP, were leaving the party to form another political party: the New Democratic League.

Japan also encountered the ugly face of terrorism. In March 1995, a Japanese **sect**, or small religious group, carried out a nerve gas attack in Tokyo's subway system, leaving 12 people dead and 5,000 injured. A month later, another gas attack in a railroad station in the city of Yokohama injured more than 300 people. The two attacks stunned most Japanese, who considered their society violence-free, and heightened security concerns among government officials and business leaders.

In early 1996, the LDP regained its influence over Japanese politics. A new prime minister, Ryutaro Hashimoto (ree•you•TAH•roh hah•shee•MOH•toh), promised to rid Japan's government of corruption and promote economic growth.

Japan in World Affairs

As a result of its economic growth since World War II, once self-reliant and isolated Japan became tightly interwoven into the world economy. Economic power has made Japan a world political leader as well, but the Japanese have been unsure how to use their power in world affairs.

Trade Tensions

Japan's economic prosperity has created tensions with other countries in the area of trade. Japan today exports more products than it imports. It therefore has trade surpluses with many countries. By contrast, Japan's major trading partners—the United States, Europe, and neighboring Asian

Religion and Government In 1868 the Japanese government set up an official religion, State Shinto, which emphasized loyalty to the nation and worship of the emperor as a god. When the government abolished State Shinto after World War II in a historic radio broadcast on January 1, 1946, Hirohito claimed that the emperor was not a divine being. Thirteen years later, in 1959, Hirohito's son, Akihito, broke a 1,500-year-old tradition when he married a commoner, Shoda Michiko. Akihito became emperor upon Hirohito's death in 1989.

Japan's Steel Industry

Japan has proved that by industrializing, non-Western nations can become not only the equals of the Western powers but also economically superior to some of the strongest.

ANSWERS

continuous casting, computer-controlled production systems, and speed smelting; Japanese and American steelmakers competed against each other in the 1980s, but in the 1990s they began joint steelmaking ventures

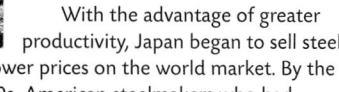

CONNECTIONS — Economics

Japan's Steel Industry

Japan's steel industry was devastated by World War II. Steel, like other Japanese industries, needed a major rebuilding effort.

Beginning in the 1950s Japan poured capital into new steelmaking facilities. An efficient method of continuous casting, computer-controlled production systems, and speed smelting made Japanese plants the most efficient in the world.

With the advantage of greater productivity, Japan began to sell steel at lower prices on the world market. By the 1980s, American steelmakers who had dominated world production were complaining that the Japanese were dumping underpriced steel on the market.

The United States responded with voluntary restraint agreements to hold imported steel to 20 percent of its domestic market. Japanese companies began to buy into United States steel companies, partially owning several by the 1990s.

By the 1990s, however, American steel companies had regained the lead in productivity. Then Japanese and American steelmakers started joint ventures to find even more efficient methods of making steel.

Japanese steel mill

Linking Past and Present — ACTIVITY

Discuss three methods that enabled Japan to become the world's most efficient steel producer. How did competition in the making of steel change from the 1980s to the 1990s?

MAKING CONNECTIONS ACTIVITIES

Science, Technology, and Society The Japanese have a deep reverence for nature and longevity. Both are reflected in the ancient Japanese art of bonsai, in which trees are carefully pruned to be no more than a few feet tall and may live for centuries. Have students research the techniques used in bonsai and do a demonstration for the class. **L3**

Earthquakes Have students use *Readers' Guide to Periodical Literature* to find articles about Japan's reaction to the 1995 Kobe earthquake and the United States's reaction to the 1989 San Francisco earthquake. Ask them to write a comparison and contrast of the national responses to the two events. **L2**

ASSESS

Check for Understanding

Assign Section 1 Review as homework or as an in-class activity.

 Use Student Self-Test and Review Software to review Section 1.

Evaluate

Section Quiz 22-1

Use the Testmaker to create a customized quiz for Section 1.

Reteach

Ask students to explain the relevance of each of the following to the modern history of Japan: SCAP, 1947 constitution, and decentralization. *(The Supreme Command of the Allied Powers, or SCAP, governed postwar Japan; the new constitution provided democratic reforms; business and agricultural monopolies were decentralized right after the war, dramatically changing the face of Japanese agriculture.)*

Enrich

Have students write short biographical sketches of the two recent Japanese winners of the Nobel Prize in literature: Yasunari Kawabata (1968) and Kenzaburo Oe (1994).

CLOSE

Have students write one or two paragraphs assessing whether it was right for MacArthur to impose his political views on an entire nation. *(Answers will vary. Students may point to the great success Japan enjoys today and say that the end justifies the means.)*

---

lands—have trade deficits with Japan. That is, they import more goods from Japan than they export to it. Because of this trade imbalance, other industrialized countries have pressured Japan to change its trade laws to make it easier for their companies to sell their products to Japanese consumers.

Japanese government regulations limit the ability of foreign companies to sell goods in Japan. Japanese retailers have long-standing ties with local producers that they want to maintain. Japanese farmers want to continue trade protection for their crops and livestock rather than face competition with lower-priced imports. Japanese consumers prefer to purchase goods made in Japan because the goods are well made and because they wish to protect the jobs of Japanese citizens.

Overcoming Japanese trade barriers has been difficult and frustrating for foreigners. In 1995 a trade war between the United States and Japan was prevented by a compromise agreement. In the accord, the United States agreed not to impose trade quotas, or specified restrictions, on Japanese goods. In return, Japan agreed to encourage its auto companies to increase purchases of American car parts and to step up production at their plants in the United States. In 1997 the United States urged Japan to make further changes that would open the Japanese home market to foreign goods.

Military Issues

Since the early 1950s, Japan has relied on the United States for its national security. However, the fall of Soviet communism in 1991 greatly reduced Japanese fears of an attack from the Russians. Today most Japanese still expect American help in any emergency, but many of them question the need for large numbers of American troops in their country. Tensions have flared on Okinawa between local residents and American troops. In 1996 Japan and the United States agreed that some of the American military sites on Okinawa would be returned to Japan by 2003. In the meantime, American troop strength would remain the same.

Japan also faces the issue of taking on more responsibility for its own defense and that of other parts of Asia. Some American leaders claim that Japan's low defense budget gives Japan an economic advantage in non-defense industries. They also believe that Japan's economic strength requires that it play a part in maintaining peace in Asia. Many Japanese, however, oppose an expansion of the country's military role. In 1990, when the Middle Eastern country of Iraq invaded its neighbor Kuwait, the United States called upon Japan to help force Iraq out of Kuwait. The Japanese government responded with a financial contribution to the military effort but refused to send troops. Two years later, however, Japan did send troops overseas as part of a United Nations peacekeeping mission in war-torn Cambodia.

In 1997 Japan cautiously took steps to increase its role in the military alliance with the United States. It stated that, in any emergency, the Japanese military would support American forces with sea operations, facilities, equipment, and fuel. In return for changes in the alliance, Japan wants a permanent seat on the U.N. Security Council.

Japan and Its Neighbors

With the most advanced economy in East Asia, Japan since the 1970s has increased its influence in the region. Beginning in 1978, Japan improved relations and forged new trading links with China. Today large amounts of Japanese aid and investment flow to the Chinese. Japan also has developed ties with South Korea, but is more hesitant with Communist North Korea because of concerns that North Korea is intent on pursuing aggressive policies in Asia. Since the late 1970s, the Japanese have greatly expanded trade and investment links with Southeast Asia, one of their fastest growing markets. Still Japan's past continues to trouble relations with its neighbors. Many people in China, Korea, and Southeast Asia recall with bitterness Japan's harsh occupation of their lands during World War II. They fear a renewal of Japanese power in East Asia, whether economic or military.

SECTION 1 REVIEW

Recall
1. **Define** gross domestic product, pollution, sect, quota.
2. **Identify** Douglas MacArthur, Hirohito, Liberal Democratic Party.
3. **Describe** two major reforms instituted during the Allied occupation of Japan after World War II.

Critical Thinking
4. **Synthesizing Information** Imagine how Japan's modern history might have been different if General MacArthur had wanted to punish Japan for its actions in World War II.

Understanding Themes
5. **Change** What economic policies have promoted Japan's prosperity since World War II?

SECTION 1 REVIEW ANSWERS

1. All vocabulary words are defined in the Glossary.
2. MacArthur, 672; Hirohito, 672; LDP, 674
3. Answers might include a new constitution and land redistribution.
4. Answers will vary. Students might suggest that Japan may have resented MacArthur and returned to militarism.
5. **CHANGE** Japan has focused on building a strong economy rather than a strong military, and the government has worked closely with large corporations to plan and promote industrial growth.

1949 Communists proclaim the People's Republic of China.

1972 United States President Richard M. Nixon visits China.

1989 Chinese students in Beijing call for democracy.

Section 2

China in Revolution

Setting the Scene

▶ **Terms to Define**
 communes, pragmatists, special economic zone

▶ **People to Meet**
 Chiang Kai-shek, Mao Zedong, Deng Xiaoping, Jiang Jing, Zhou Enlai, Jiang Zemin, Dalai Lama

▶ **Places to Locate**
 Beijing, Taiwan, Taipei, Shanghai, Tibet, Hong Kong

ind Out How has communism affected the domestic and international affairs of China since the late 1940s?

The Storyteller

Wang Xin had heard his father and grandfather talk about the old days in China. As peasants, they owned no land. If someone was unable to work, he was dismissed by the landlord and had to beg or live off his family. But when Wang was a small boy, things changed. The peasants became masters, receiving shares of farmland. They were no longer starving. Wang's family of 10 people moved from a three-room house to one with seven rooms and a tile roof. For the rest of his life, Wang Xin would remember how happy the peasants were that spring of 1950.

—adapted from "A Peasant Maps His Road to Wealth," *Beijing Review*, reprinted in *Documents in World History*, Peter Stearns, 1988

Chinese peasant's house

After World War II, the Nationalists under **Chiang Kai-shek** and the Communists led by **Mao Zedong** fought a bitter civil war in China. By 1949, Mao's Communist forces had defeated the Nationalists. That year, the Communists proclaimed the People's Republic of China, with **Beijing** as the capital. The defeated Nationalists fled to the offshore island of **Taiwan**, where they set up the new capital of the Republic of China at **Taipei**.

Mao's revolution was one of the major upheavals of the century. It succeeded in part because the Communists' self-proclaimed patriotism and sense of duty appealed to many Chinese citizens disgusted with foreign controls and the corruption of Chiang's officials. Above all, Mao won over China's peasants with his promises of land reform and an end to oppression by landlords.

The Mao Era

After coming to power, the Chinese Communists worked to remake Chinese society along totalitarian Communist lines. Having absolute control of the Chinese government, the Communist party set out to impose its will on the country. Its leaders were determined to uproot both traditional Chinese and Western attitudes in the process.

In theory, the Chinese Communists promoted equality. Women, for example, were made equal with men under the law and benefited from social reforms, such as state-run nurseries that provided child care. They also were expected to enter the workplace alongside men; however, few women were freed from traditional household chores, and even fewer gained top positions in government and industry.

Chapter 22 *Asia and the Pacific* **677**

SECTION THEME

▶ **Revolution** Communists in China introduce socialist measures and then promote a limited free enterprise economy.

ind Out

Answer: *Domestically, Communist rule encourages some privately owned business, but government repression continues; internationally, Communists have increased trade and cultural contact with the West.*

FOCUS

Section Objective
Explain how communism has affected the domestic and international affairs of China since the late 1940s.

BELLRINGER
Motivational Activity

Before taking roll at the beginning of the class period, project Section Focus Transparency 22-2 and have students answer the activity questions.
 This activity is also available as a blackline master.

Vocabulary Pre-check
 Use Vocabulary Activity 22 to introduce vocabulary terms.
L1 LEP

SECTION RESOURCES

Reproducible Masters
• Reproducible Lesson Plan 22-2
• Vocabulary Activity 22
• Guided Reading Activity 22-2
• Geography and History Activity 22
• Section Quiz 22-2

Transparencies
• Section Focus Transparency 22-2

Multimedia
 Student Self-Test and Review Software
 Testmaker
 World Music: Cultural Traditions, Lesson 8
 Communism and the Cold War:
  • *Revolution in China*
  • *Tiananmen Square*

TEACH

Guided Practice

 **Revolution**

Write *Five-Year Plan, Great Leap Forward, Red Guards, Gang of Four, Four Modernizations,* and *Tiananmen Square* on the chalkboard. Ask students to describe the role each played in initiating or preserving revolutionary change in China. **L1**

The Mao Era

How did Mao Zedong's rule affect China and its place in world affairs?

Mao imposed a Communist system on China and tried to uproot traditional ways. Mao's China later became an independent Communist power, and in the 1970s began to normalize relations with the West.

ABCNEWS INTERACTIVE™

VIDEODISC
Communism and the Cold War

Side Two, Chapter 4
Frames 5825–7229
Title: *Revolution in China*
Subject: Transformation of China into a Communist country
Ask: Why was it a shock to the U.S. when China became Communist? *(During World War II, the U.S. backed the Nationalist Chiang Kai-shek and believed that China would be an ally after the war.)*

Building a New Economy

One of the major Communist goals was China's transformation into a modern industrial and agricultural nation. In rural areas, the Communists drove landlords from their property and distributed land to the peasants. Several million people may have died in this often bloody struggle.

Once in power, the Communists worked to improve living conditions and education in the countryside. Health workers and teachers loyal to communism set up clinics and schools in rural villages. Despite limited training, they helped to reduce disease and to increase literacy.

China's Communist government also set out to establish a state-controlled economy that would advance industrial and agricultural development. In 1953 it launched its first Soviet-style Five-Year Plan, which stressed heavy industry and agricultural efficiency. The Plan brought private industries under government control and had peasants merge their individual landholdings into large cooperatives. With Soviet help, the Chinese Communists built roads, railroads, factories, and canals. While industrial output rose significantly under this first Plan, agricultural production improved more slowly.

The Great Leap Forward

In 1958 the Chinese launched an ambitious economic plan known as the Great Leap Forward. Under this plan the cooperatives were merged into larger government-controlled units called communes. In producing goods, the Great Leap Forward stressed human labor over complex technology. Members of communes worked in production brigades on tasks ranging from farming to making steel in small backyard furnaces.

Within two years it was clear that the Great Leap Forward was a disaster. Food shortages, mismanagement, and peasant resistance to communes brought the program to a halt. While it lasted, the Great Leap Forward caused massive suffering—as many as 20 million people died of starvation.

The Cultural Revolution

After the Great Leap Forward, a deep division occurred within the Chinese Communist party. Pragmatists, headed by **Deng Xiaoping** (DUNG SHOW•PIHNG), party general secretary, wanted practical reforms. Radicals, led by Mao and his wife **Jiang Jing**, insisted on strict obedience to revolutionary principles.

To end the influence of the pragmatists, Mao in 1966 launched the Cultural Revolution. In response to Mao's direction, young people formed bands of Red Guards. Waving copies of the "Little Red Book" of Mao's sayings, the Red Guards attacked local politicians, teachers, and other leaders for betraying Mao and the revolution. The accused were denounced, publicly humiliated, and sometimes killed.

The Cultural Revolution was a time of disorder and confusion. Schools closed, factory production dropped, and violence erupted. Finally, in 1968, Mao called on the army to restore order. By the time Mao acted, however, the lives of millions of people had been disrupted, and tens of thousands of people had died.

China's Foreign Policy

After the Communist victory in 1949, Mao Zedong followed the Soviet example and opposed the United States and other capitalist countries. In the early 1950s, China actively supported Communist North Korea in its war against American-backed South Korea. In 1954 Chinese Premier **Zhou Enlai** (joh ehn•LY) took part in talks that ended French rule in Indochina and paved the way for a Communist state in northern Vietnam.

During the late 1950s, Chinese-Soviet relations soured and led to an open split. Mao's version of Marxism, based on Chinese experience, held that peasants, rather than workers, were the leaders of revolutions in largely agricultural societies. The Soviets viewed Mao's ideas as a threat to their leadership of world communism. Mao, for his part, demanded that the Soviets take a firmer line against the West. The two Communist powers soon became rivals for influence in the developing

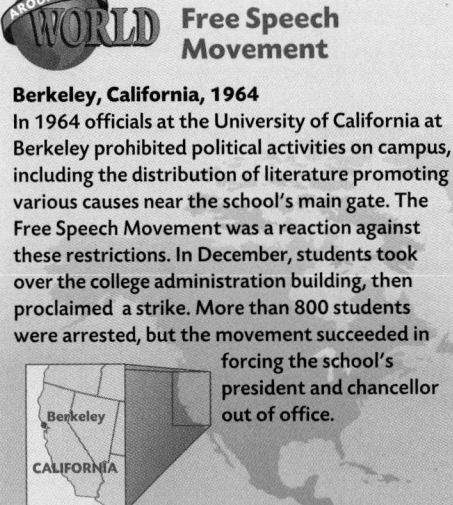

Free Speech Movement

Berkeley, California, 1964
In 1964 officials at the University of California at Berkeley prohibited political activities on campus, including the distribution of literature promoting various causes near the school's main gate. The Free Speech Movement was a reaction against these restrictions. In December, students took over the college administration building, then proclaimed a strike. More than 800 students were arrested, but the movement succeeded in forcing the school's president and chancellor out of office.

Berkeley
CALIFORNIA

COOPERATIVE LEARNING ACTIVITY

Oral-Visual Presentations Have students form five groups to research one of the following topics: the 1949 civil war, the Five-Year Plans of the 1950s, the Cultural Revolution of the 1960s, the pragmatists versus the Gang of Four in the 1970s, and the Tiananmen Square crackdown in 1989.

Tell students to use their texts as well as outside research materials. After they have completed their research, they can make charts and other visuals to present their findings. Each group should then choose one student to present its research orally, using the visual materials. **L2**

world. They also had disputes over their long border, with China wanting back the territory seized from it by the Russians in the late 1600s. In 1960 the Soviets finally withdrew their advisers from China, and the alliance came to an end.

During the 1960s, internal upheavals largely isolated China from the rest of the world. The Chinese, however, were able in 1964 to explode their first atomic bomb. By the 1970s the desire for advanced technology made the Chinese reach out to other countries, especially the United States. Since 1949, the United States had regarded China as an aggressive Communist power and maintained ties with the Nationalist government on Taiwan. But the Chinese-Soviet split gave the United States and China an opportunity to improve relations. In 1972 United States President Richard Nixon made a historic visit to China, and seven years later the United States and China established diplomatic ties.

Visualizing History Students at a commune perform a play supporting Mao Zedong. *What was the role of the Red Guards in the Cultural Revolution?*

The Deng Era

After Mao's death in 1976, the pragmatists under Deng Xiaoping gained power. They arrested the Gang of Four, the name given to Jiang Jing and three of her radical supporters. Deng then began to move China in a new direction. Under Deng, the Communist party remained in firm control of political affairs. In making economic policy, however, Deng was willing to learn from the capitalist West if it could contribute to China's well-being.

The Four Modernizations

Deng backed a plan called the Four Modernizations that stressed the need for improvements in agriculture, industry, science, and defense. To boost food production, the government replaced the communes with the rural "responsibility system," in which families farmed individual plots. The government received some of the produce; the family could keep or sell the rest.

Although the government still controlled major industries, factory managers were encouraged to make plants more efficient. They could now base production on supply and demand rather than by government decree. In addition, economic reforms allowed some privately owned small businesses and private property.

Deng also welcomed foreign businesses and technology to China. European, American, and Japanese investment flowed into the country, and the Chinese set up special economic zones where foreigners could own and operate businesses with little government interference.

The Four Modernizations sparked economic growth and raised standards of living. For the first time, many Chinese were able to buy consumer goods, such as televisions and household appliances. The reforms, however, had created a social gap between a new wealthy class and the rest of the Chinese population. Other problems included increased crime and corruption, more unemployment, and rising prices. By the late 1980s, discontent was stirring in China despite the progress that had been made.

Tiananmen Square Massacre

While Deng encouraged some free enterprise, he refused to grant political freedoms. By the late 1980s, students and intellectuals in Beijing, **Shanghai**, and other Chinese cities had organized movements to demand a more open political system. In May and June 1989, more than 100,000 people rallied for democracy and other reforms in Beijing's Tiananmen Square. Determined to maintain control, government

Footnotes to History **Chinese Students Abroad** In the spirit of improving and expanding relations with Western countries, the Chinese government allowed more students to study in foreign countries. By the early 1900s there were about 40,000 Chinese students studying in American universities.

**Chapter 22
Section 2**

Visualizing History The Red Guards were named for the real army units Mao had organized in 1927. Formed into paramilitary units in 1966, the Red Guard movement subsided by 1969.
Answer to Caption: *They spread the Cultural Revolution throughout the country, using such methods as burning books and destroying treasures of traditional Chinese culture, as well as harassing and arresting their opponents.*

World Music: Cultural Traditions, Lesson 8

POINT

The Deng Era
Why was Deng Xiaoping an important leader of twentieth-century China?
He promoted modernization of China's economy by allowing some free enterprise and extending contacts with the West. However, he maintained the Communist party's hold over political affairs and suppressed a pro-democracy movement.

Independent Practice

Guided Reading Activity 22-2 **L1**

Geography and History Activity 22

Literature Have students read a work by a Chinese American writer, such as Betty Bao Lord, Amy Tan, or Maxine Hong Kingston. Ask them to write a short report that illuminates how the writer incorporates Chinese historical events from this period in her work. **L2**

MEETING SPECIAL NEEDS ACTIVITY

Learning Style: Logical/Mathematical Have students work together to create a time line of important events in China's history between World War II and the present. This time line will be displayed along with the time line they completed for Japanese history of the same period, so students should use the same scale for this project. Tell students to include political, economic, and cultural events. **L1**

ABCNEWS INTERACTIVE™

VIDEODISC
Communism and the Cold War

Side Two, Chapter 19
Frames 46766–49626
Title: *Tiananmen Square*
Ask: What were the protests in Tiananmen Square about? (*students and others protesting for democratic reform in China*)

Linking Past and Present

"Ownership" of Taiwan Taiwan, originally called Formosa, was "discovered" by Portugal, then controlled by the Dutch and later by Spain. Still later it was acquired by China, then Japan, then China again. Taiwanese moves toward independence are strongly resisted by China. In early March 1996, as a threat, China launched 3 unarmed missiles in the water only 20 miles (32 km) from Taiwan's coast.

Visualizing History Demonstrating for more freedoms, students carry a hastily constructed model of the Statue of Liberty through Tiananmen Square. *How was this demonstration broken up?*

leaders sent in troops and tanks when the demonstrators refused to disperse. Thousands of demonstrators were killed or wounded. Throughout the country, those who supported political change were shot, imprisoned, tortured, or silenced.

The Tiananmen Square massacre damaged China's prestige abroad. The United States and other democratic nations condemned Deng's use of force. Fearing political instability, foreign investors backed off from doing business with the Chinese. Later, they resumed dealings when the Chinese government continued with economic reforms.

China After Deng

Following the Tiananmen Square massacre, Deng Xiaoping, elderly and in poor health, named Chinese President **Jiang Zemin** as his successor. Deng, however, retained power from behind the scenes until his death in 1997. Deng at that time was hailed worldwide for his free enterprise reforms, but he was criticized for his use of force against the pro-democracy movement.

The Economy

Since Deng's death, China's economic growth has remained strong, but uneven. A gap has widened between prosperous industrial areas on the coast and less wealthy agricultural regions of the interior. Since the 1980s, millions of peasants have moved to

the cities seeking work. This mass migration has put pressure on housing and various city social services.

Deng's successors have continued his emphasis on capitalist-style economic reforms. In 1997 Jiang Zemin allowed ailing state-run industries to sell stock, although the government would hold the majority of shares. Chinese authorities also moved ahead with the world's largest public works project: the Three Gorges Dam on the Chang Jiang in central China. When completed in 2009, the dam is expected to prevent dangerous flooding and will provide electricity for new commercial ventures. Almost 2 million people will be relocated before the dam's giant reservoir covers up farms, villages, and canyons. Critics charge that the project is destroying one of the world's most scenic areas.

Human Rights

China's leaders continue to affirm Communist party control over government and the military. However, they have also raised the possibility that they might consider some political reforms. One of the challenges faced by Chinese leaders is growing unrest among China's many ethnic groups. Of every 100 people in China, 93 are Chinese; the remainder are from at least 55 other groups, including Kazakhstanis, Mongols, Uyghurs, and Tibetans. Opposition to Chinese Communist rule is particularly strong in **Tibet**, a mountainous region in the southwestern part of the country. Once an independent Buddhist kingdom, Tibet came under direct Chinese

680   Chapter 22   *Asia and the Pacific*

MAKING CONNECTIONS ACTIVITY

International Affairs Have students research to find out about China's behavior as a permanent member of the United Nations Security Council. Ask them to write short reports summarizing their findings. Make sure they include information comparing China's use of the veto with that of the Soviet Union and the United States. **L3**

control in 1950. Since an unsuccessful Tibetan rebellion in 1959, the **Dalai Lama**, the spiritual leader of Tibet, has led a worldwide movement in support of Tibetan rights from his place of exile in India.

International Relations

During most of the 1990s, China's relations with the West have been strained. China wants Western trade and investment but resents Western pressures on human rights issues and continuing American support for the Nationalists on Taiwan. The United States especially opposes Chinese sales of missiles and nuclear technology to countries in the Middle East and South Asia. In spite of differences, China and the West have tried to stress the positive aspects of their relationship.

China also expanded contacts with its neighbors in East Asia. Although some Chinese remain bitter about Japan's harsh occupation policies in World War II, Japan now ranks as one of China's major trade partners. China has ties to both North Korea and South Korea, and has developed friendly relations with Russia since the fall of the Soviet Union. It also has expanded trade with various countries in Southeast Asia.

Hong Kong and Taiwan

Economic growth has increased Chinese national pride. In recent years, China's leaders have set as their goal the return of all separated territories to the Chinese homeland. In 1997, they regained **Hong Kong** from the British; in 1999, they will acquire the port of Macao from the Portuguese. Their most controversial demand, however, is the reuniting of Taiwan with the People's Republic of China.

Hong Kong

In 1997 Hong Kong, one of the world's major ports and financial centers, became part of China after 156 years of British rule. Under a "one country, two systems" plan, Hong Kong keeps its capitalist system and some of its freedoms for 50 years after its return to China. Many Hong Kong residents, however, are concerned about their territory's future under Communist control.

During the early 1990s, Great Britain introduced democratic reforms such as a freely elected legislative council. The Chinese Communists, however, opposed these reforms and developed their own institutions for the territory. On June 30, 1997, the date of transfer, Tung Chee-hwa, a local businessman favored by Beijing, became Hong Kong's leader. A China-backed provisional legislature replaced the democratically-elected legislative council. Although China promises to respect Hong Kong's unique status, many Hong Kong residents resent the limits on their political rights.

Taiwan

The status of Taiwan has been a prominent issue in Chinese affairs since 1949. Both the Chinese Nationalists and the Chinese Communists believe that Taiwan is a province of China. Each government claims to be the legal ruler of all of China.

Under Chiang Kai-shek and his son Chiang Ching-kuo, Taiwan prospered from the export of manufactured goods. In 1988 Lee Teng-hui became president of the country. He moved Taiwan toward democracy by allowing other political parties to challenge the Nationalists. Popular with voters, Lee Teng-hui in 1997 was reelected in Taiwan's first democratic presidential race.

Today, Taiwan's economy remains strong, but its political future is uncertain. In recent years, many Taiwanese have come to accept separation from China as a fact and want to declare Taiwan an independent country. The Chinese government in Beijing, however, opposes such a move and has threatened to use force against Taiwan if the island declares its independence.

Who?What?Where?When?

Dalai Lama For his nonviolent struggle to end China's rule of Tibet, the Dalai Lama was awarded the 1989 Nobel Peace Prize.

ASSESS

Check for Understanding

Assign Section 2 Review as homework or as an in-class activity.

 Use Student Self-Test and Review Software to review Section 2.

Evaluate

Section Quiz 22-2

 Use the Testmaker to create a customized quiz for Section 2.

Reteach

Assign one student to be timekeeper and organize the rest of the class into two teams. Play a game in which you give the teams names or terms such as Mao Zedong, Taipei, and the First Five-Year Plan. Have students explain the importance of each term or name within 10 seconds. Score one point for a correct answer.

Enrich

Have students write and perform skits that dramatize events in this section. Each scene should show how the event affected a segment of society, such as students, peasants, or factory workers.

CLOSE

Have students write a paragraph summarizing China's current position in world affairs.

SECTION 2 REVIEW

Recall
1. **Define** communes, pragmatists, special economic zone.
2. **Identify** Chiang Kai-shek, Mao Zedong, Great Leap Forward, Cultural Revolution, Deng Xiaoping, Jiang Jing, Zhou Enlai, Tiananmen Square, Jiang Zemin, Dalai Lama.

3. **Describe** the changes that occurred in China's relations with the United States and with the Soviet Union between 1949 and 1973.

Critical Thinking
4. **Making Comparisons** How did Mao's policies for the economic development of China

differ with those of MacArthur in Japan?

Understanding Themes
5. **Revolution** Can political struggles within a country always be viewed as a battle between pragmatists and radicals? In your answer use different historical examples.

SECTION 2 REVIEW ANSWERS

1. All vocabulary words are defined in the Glossary.
2. Chiang Kai-shek, 677; Mao Zedong, 677; Great Leap Forward, 678; Cultural Revolution, 678; Deng Xiaoping, 678; Jiang Jing, 678; Zhou Enlai, 678; Tiananmen Square, 679; Jiang Zemin, 680; Dalai Lama, 681
3. Relations with the Soviets worsened, and

those with the United States improved.
4. Each promoted equality and economic reform. Unlike MacArthur's policies, Mao's were harsh and repressive.
5. **REVOLUTION** Answers should include examples from earlier periods, such as the French Revolution or the Russian Revolution.

1945   1972   2000

1945 Soviets and Americans divide Korea at the 38th parallel.   **1950** North Koreans invade South Korea.   **1953** Korean War ends.   **1997** North Korea and South Korea partici in preliminary peace ta

SECTION THEME

▶ **Regionalism** After decades of conflict and cold war tensions, North Korea and South Korea take first steps toward unification.

ind Out

Answer: *North Korea, led by a Communist dictator, has focused on the development of heavy industry and military expenditures; South Korea, which moved from repressive military government to greater democracy, has a more technologically advanced economy and higher standard of living than North Korea.*

FOCUS

Section Objective

Describe how South Korea and North Korea have differed in their political and economic development.

BELLRINGER
Motivational Activity

Before taking roll at the beginning of the class period, project Section Focus Transparency 22-3 and have students answer the activity questions.

This activity is also available as a blackline master.

Vocabulary Pre-check

Use Vocabulary Activity 22 to introduce terms. **L1 LEP**

Section 3

A Divided Korea

Setting the Scene

▶ **Terms to Define**
    stalemate, referendum

▶ **People to Meet**
    Kim Il Sung, Kim Young Sam, Kim Jong Il

▶ **Places to Locate**
    Pyongyang, Seoul

 **ind Out**   How have South Korea and North Korea differed in their political and economic development?

The Storyteller

South Korean government officials watched as teams from 161 nations marched into the stadium. It was a proud day for South Korea, host of the 1988 Olympic games. North Korea had called for a boycott, had even threatened violence, but only 6 national teams had chosen to stay at home. In fact, most communist states had openly supported the Seoul Olympics. Even now, as the torch entered the stadium, American, Japanese, and Soviet ships off the peninsula kept North Korea under surveillance. As South Koreans watched 300 of China's finest athletes in the opening ceremonies, they wondered, was it a sign of a new era dawning?

—adapted from "The Politics of the Olympics," *The World and I*, October 1988

1988 Olympics in Seoul

 orea's modern history has been heavily shaped by international politics. In 1910 the Korean Peninsula was annexed by the Japanese, who ruled it as a colony until the end of World War II, when Japan was stripped of its territorial possessions.

During the war, the Allied powers had agreed that Korea was to be temporarily occupied. In 1945 Soviet troops moved into the northern part of Korea down to the 38th parallel. United States forces occupied the southern area. The occupation was to end as soon as a Korean government could be freely elected. The Soviets and Americans, however, could not agree on procedures for the election.

By 1948, two separate governments had emerged, each claiming to be the legal ruler of all of Korea. North Korea, officially called the Democratic People's Republic of Korea, with its capital at **Pyongyang**, kept close ties with the Soviet Union and China. South Korea, officially the Republic of Korea, established its capital at **Seoul**. It maintained links with the United States. The Soviets withdrew their troops from North Korea in late 1948 and the United States withdrew their troops from South Korea in mid-1949.

TURNING POINT

The Korean War

In June 1950, North Korea, hoping to unify the country under a Communist government, invaded South Korea. The United Nations Security Council immediately voted to condemn the invasion and organized an army to oppose it. At that time the Soviets could not use their veto because of their absence from the Council in protest at the United Nations' refusal to recognize Communist China. While 16 countries contributed troops to the UN force, more than 90 percent of the soldiers came from the United States.

SECTION RESOURCES

Reproducible Masters
- Reproducible Lesson Plan 22-3
- Vocabulary Activity 22
- Guided Reading Activity 22-3
- Section Quiz 22-3

Transparencies
- Section Focus Transparency 22-3

Multimedia
- Student Self-Test and Review Software
- Testmaker
- Communism and the Cold War: *Korean War*

In the first months of the war, the North Koreans swept southward, conquering almost all of South Korea. However, in September 1950, the UN troops led by United States General Douglas MacArthur counterattacked. MacArthur launched a surprise invasion at Inchon, along Korea's west coast and far behind North Korean lines. The daring move gave UN forces the offensive they needed. Within six weeks, the UN forces had pushed the North Koreans out of South Korea and had advanced into North Korea, reaching the Yalu River at the Chinese border.

At this point in the war, Communist China came to the aid of North Korea. Chinese forces crossed into Korea in such large numbers that the UN forces were forced to retreat southward. By mid-1951, each army dug in along a line near the 38th parallel. There the fighting reached a *stalemate*, a situation in which two opponents are unable to move significantly or make further gains. Talks between the two sides began in July 1951 and lasted until July 1953, when a truce was signed. After the deaths of nearly 5 million people and the devastation of much of Korea, the fighting ended with Korea once again divided near the 38th parallel.

Korea Since 1953

The stalemate in the Korean War for a long time was matched by a stalemate in diplomacy. The two Koreas continued to draw economic and military aid from their respective sponsors, the United States and China.

North Korea

From 1948 to 1994, North Korea was led by the Communist dictator, **Kim Il Sung**. A cult of personality developed around Kim, and North Koreans revered him as a god-like figure. Called the "Great Leader," Kim established a repressive and tightly controlled government that largely isolated North Korea from the rest of the world.

Like the Soviet Union and China, North Korea implemented a Communist program of economic development. Under Kim's direction, all of the country's farmland was organized into collective farms between 1953 and 1956. In 1954 the North Korean government announced the first Five-Year Plan for building an industrial economy. North Korea stressed the growth of heavy industry and built up its military power.

Until the early 1990s, North Korea made some progress in developing its economy, but it did not match South Korea's growth. About 20 percent of North Korea's gross domestic product (GDP) was

annually devoted to military expenditures, including the development of nuclear capabilities. Improvements in the standard of living were limited by this heavy military spending.

In the mid-1990s, another factor limiting North Korea's growth was widespread crop failure. This agricultural collapse was due to floods, drought, and government policies that provided few incentives for farmers to produce. The resulting food shortages brought starvation to many of North Korea's people. As catastrophe loomed on the horizon, the Communist government reluctantly admitted its need for foreign aid. In 1997 relief organizations in the United States and other countries began sending food to North Korea.

South Korea

In contrast, South Korea after the mid-1960s enjoyed tremendous economic success. By the mid-1980s, the South Korean economy was growing at the remarkable rate of 10 percent a year. To promote

Chapter 22 *Asia and the Pacific* **683**

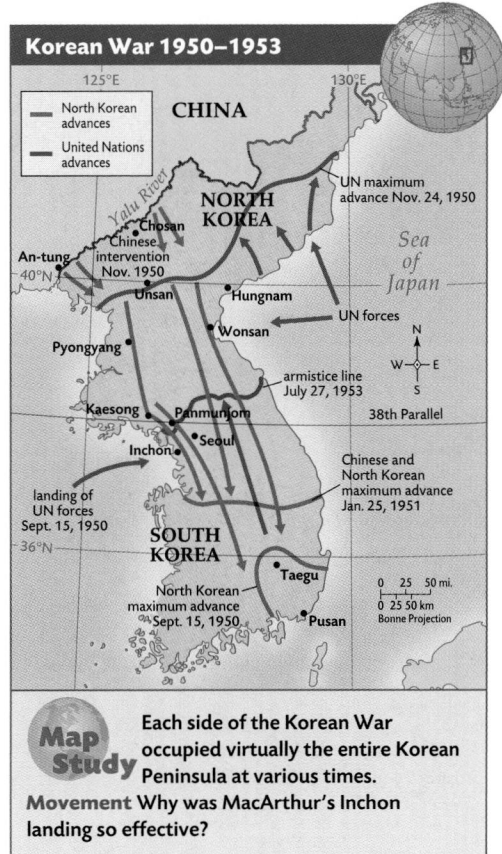

Korean War 1950–1953

CHINA

North Korean advances

United Nations advances

Yalu River

NORTH KOREA

Sea of Japan

An-tung 40°N

Chosan

Chinese intervention Nov. 1950

Unsan

Hungnam

UN maximum advance Nov. 24, 1950

Wonsan

UN forces

Pyongyang

Kaesong

Panmunjom

armistice line July 27, 1953

38th Parallel

Inchon

Seoul

Chinese and North Korean maximum advance Jan. 25, 1951

landing of UN forces Sept. 15, 1950

36°N

SOUTH KOREA

North Korean maximum advance Sept. 15, 1950

Taegu

Pusan

0   25   50 mi.
0 25 50 km
Bonne Projection

 Map Study

Each side of the Korean War occupied virtually the entire Korean Peninsula at various times.
Movement Why was MacArthur's Inchon landing so effective?

Chapter 22 Section 3

TEACH

Guided Practice

THEME **Regionalism**

Discuss ways that life in North Korea and South Korea are different as a result of their different forms of government.

Map Study

Answer
The surprise attack cut off enemy troops behind their front lines.

Independent Practice

Guided Reading Activity 22-3 **L1**

TURNING POINT

The Korean War
Why was the Korean conflict a significant event in the cold war?
It was the first "hot" conflict of the cold war, pitting American-led UN forces against those of Communist North Korea and China. The fighting ended in a stalemate that kept Korea divided at the 38th parallel.

ABCNEWS INTERACTIVE™

VIDEODISC
Communism and the Cold War

Side Two, Chapter 7
Frames 16806–18713
Title: *Korean War*
Ask: What was the policy of containment? (*U.S. policy to stop the spread of communism*)

COOPERATIVE LEARNING ACTIVITY

An Exchange of Letters One of the most controversial episodes of the Korean War was President Truman's firing of General Douglas MacArthur, head of the UN forces in Korea. Organize students into two groups, one to research Truman's role in the war and the other to research MacArthur's role. Direct them to study the two men's personalities, political views, and leadership styles. Then have the groups plan and write mock dispatches between the two men—one exchange following the Inchon landing and another during the dismissal. The letters should contain historical detail and reflect knowledge of war strategy. Choose students to read the letters to the class. **L3**

ASSESS

Check for Understanding

Assign Section 3 Review as homework or as an in-class activity.

 Use Student Self-Test and Review Software to review Section 3.

Evaluate

Section Quiz 22-3

 Use the Testmaker to create a customized quiz for Section 3.

Reteach

Write the following dates on the chalkboard and ask students to identify their significance in Korean history: June 25, 1950 (*North Korea invades South Korea*); September 15, 1950 (*Inchon invasion*); July 27, 1953 (*both sides accept a temporary armistice line*); October 1990 (*unification talks begin*); December 1991 (*a treaty is signed, officially ending the state of war*).

Enrich

Have students research the life and career of Douglas MacArthur in a brief biographical essay.

CLOSE

Have students write a summary of Korea's history from 1945 to the present.

Visualizing History The central area of Seoul, South Korea, reflects the city's economic prosperity in recent years. *What challenges face South Korea as it approaches the year 2000?*

prosperity, the South Korean government strongly encouraged the export of electronics products, textiles, ships, trucks, automobiles, and other industrial goods.

South Korea's economic boom, however, was achieved under repressive governments. Beginning in the early 1960s, the military used the Communist threat to play a strong role in the government. Despite elections, South Korea's president was essentially a military-backed dictator, limiting speech, press, and opposition.

During the 1980s, massive student protests led to greater democracy. In 1987 a new constitution allowing almost complete political freedoms was adopted by referendum, an election in which all voters approve or disapprove a measure. That same year, South Korean voters for the first time elected a new president—Roh Tae Woo—by direct vote instead of indirectly by an electoral college. Six years later, the same method was used to select **Kim Young Sam** as president.

During this period, students and workers also pressed for social reforms, higher wages, and better working conditions. Government efforts to meet these demands caused inflation and slowed economic growth. In 1997 Kim Young Sam tried to roll back some of the reforms, but nationwide labor strikes forced him to back down. Kim lost further credibility when his son and other politicians were linked to corruption scandals. Meanwhile, the country's economy slumped further as unemployment rose and South Korean industries faced stiffer competition in world markets.

North-South Relations

The end of the cold war in the early 1990s raised hopes for uniting the two Koreas. North Korea and South Korea took halting steps toward better relations, but continuing resentments on both sides hampered progress. The death of Kim Il Sung in 1994 and uncertainty about the intentions of his son and successor, **Kim Jong Il**, further delayed any movement toward peace.

By the late 1990s, however, North Korea's food crisis had forced the North Korean government to increase its contacts with the outside world. Hoping to get commitments for food aid, North Korea in 1997 entered into talks with South Korea, the United States, and China. The purpose of the talks was to prepare for further discussions on a peace treaty ending the state of war that still exists between the two Koreas.

SECTION 3 REVIEW

Recall
1. **Define** stalemate, referendum.
2. **Identify** Inchon, Kim Il Sung, Kim Young Sam, Kim Jong Il.
3. **Explain** the political significance of the 38th parallel

in the history of modern Korea.
Critical Thinking
4. **Making Comparisons** How are North Korea and South Korea similar? In what ways are the two Koreas different?

Understanding Themes
5. **Regionalism** How might the two Koreas' futures be influenced by recent global events such as the end of the cold war?

SECTION 3 REVIEW ANSWERS

1. All vocabulary words are defined in the Glossary.
2. Inchon, 683; Kim Il Sung, 683; Roh Tae Woo, 684; Kim Young Sam, 684; Kim Il Jong, 684
3. The UN divided Korea at the end of World War II at the 38th parallel, and the current north-south border is close to this line.

4. Both have had stable, authoritarian governments. South Korea has prospered more than North Korea and has also moved toward democracy.
5. **REGIONALISM** The easing of tensions and weakening of communism might promote reunification.

1949 Indonesia wins its independence from Dutch rule.

1954 Vietminh defeats French forces at Dien Bien Phu.

1965 U.S. President Johnson sends first American ground troops to Vietnam.

1994 Cambodia establishes a democracy.

Section 4

Southeast Asia

Setting the Scene

▶ **Terms to Define**
domino theory, refugee

▶ **People to Meet**
Ho Chi Minh, Norodom Sihanouk, Pol Pot, Aung San Suu Kyi, Achmed Sukarno, Suharto, Lee Kuan Yew

▶ **Places to Locate**
Vietnam, Cambodia, Laos, Thailand, Myanmar, Indonesia, Malaysia, Singapore

 How have nationalism, the cold war, and the rise of a global economy affected Southeast Asia?

The Storyteller

Once again it was Tet. Tran Van Dinh could recall when that most joyous of Vietnamese holidays was the background for twenty-six days of bloody fighting between American and Viet Cong forces. Thousands had died. But throughout Vietnam's history, whether independent or under foreign domination, Tet was an occasion to meditate on the past, enjoy the present, and contemplate the future. Tran, who had made his life in France since 1968, bought flowers from the street vendor to mark the new beginning. It was deeply satisfying to return to his native city of Hue for the celebration.

—adapted from "Hue: My City, Myself," *National Geographic*, November, 1989, Tran Van Dinh.

Celebrating Tet

During the cold war years, Southeast Asia was thrust into the middle of the superpower contest and also suffered because of regional hostilities. The ongoing struggle between Communists and anti-Communists brought instability and war to much of the region of Southeast Asia known as Indochina. Only in recent years have Indochinese countries such as **Vietnam** and **Cambodia** begun to recover from earlier conflicts.

Struggle for Indochina

Before Japan conquered Southeast Asia in World War II, France ruled most of Indochina as a colony. When Japanese forces withdrew following the war, France attempted to reestablish its control. By then, however, nationalist movements demanding independence had gained strength. Vietnamese nationalists in the Indochinese Communist party, later known as the Vietminh, declared the formation of the independent Democratic Republic of Vietnam in 1945. The Vietminh were supported by the Soviet Union and the Communist Chinese.

The Vietminh, under the leadership of **Ho Chi Minh**, and the French could not reach an agreement on how to share power. In 1946 the two sides went to war. The United States, fearing Ho's Communist ties and wanting to support its ally France, provided military and financial aid to France to subdue the Vietminh. Despite American aid, the French could not win a military victory. In May 1954 the Vietminh defeated French forces in the decisive battle at Dien Bien Phu. After their loss, the French agreed to a cease-fire and decided to pull out of Vietnam completely.

A month before the battle, the Vietminh, the French, the United States, and several other countries had agreed to meet in Geneva, Switzerland, to negotiate a settlement to the Vietnam conflict. Negotiators divided Vietnam along the 17th parallel, creating a Communist North Vietnam and a

TEACH

Guided Practice

THEME Conflict

Have students examine the map of Vietnam on page 688. **Describe the physical outline of the country.** *(long and narrow)* **What influence might Vietnam's shape have had on its conflicts?** *(It was difficult to integrate the territory of Vietnam. Few roads or railroads connected the north with the south. Internal divisions within the nation increased.)* **L1**

The Vietnam War

Why was the Vietnam War fought?

Communist Vietnamese forces sought to overthrow the pro-American government of South Vietnam and unify all of Vietnam under Communist rule. In its effort to contain communism, the United States sent troops to support the non-Communist government of South Vietnam.

 VIDEODISC
Communism and the Cold War

Side Two, Chapter 8
Frames 18729–22891
Title: *Vietnam War*
Ask: Why was Vietnam known as a television war? *(For the first time, a war was televised. Showing the reality of war proved detrimental to public support.)*

pro-Western South Vietnam. This arrangement was to last only until elections could be held in 1956. With United States approval, Ngo Dinh Diem, South Vietnam's leader, rejected the proposed elections. He claimed that the Communists would not allow fair elections in North Vietnam. Diem also may have feared that elections would reveal Ho's popularity. Guerrillas in South Vietnam, known as the Viet Cong, fought Diem in hope of uniting Vietnam under Ho. The United States sent financial aid and several hundred advisers to help Diem.

However, Diem was a weak and unpopular leader. In 1963 the South Vietnamese military, despairing of Diem's leadership and fearing that the South would fall to the Communists, staged a coup in which Diem was killed. This was done with the quiet approval of the United States government and President John F. Kennedy.

Reflecting on France's earlier troubles in Vietnam, French President Charles de Gaulle urged Kennedy to withdraw. "I predict you will sink step by step into a bottomless quagmire," he warned.

The Vietnam War

Since the early 1950s, American officials had accepted the domino theory—that if one Southeast Asian land fell to communism, its neighbors would fall as well. To halt communism, the United States moved deeper into the conflict. By late 1963, 16,000 American advisers were in Vietnam.

In 1964 the United States approved secret South Vietnamese naval raids against North Vietnam. On August 2, 1964, United States President Lyndon Johnson announced that North Vietnam had fired on two American destroyers off the coast of Vietnam. Although the incident could not be confirmed, Johnson used it to increase American involvement in the war. He ordered air strikes on North Vietnam. At his request Congress passed the Gulf of Tonkin Resolution, which gave the

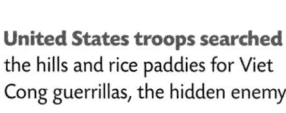

Vietnam War, 1964–1975

Americans, forced to consider the cost of war in terms of human and economic sacrifice, debated for years before withdrawing troops in 1973.

United States troops searched the hills and rice paddies for Viet Cong guerrillas, the hidden enemy.

686

Images *of the* Times Vietnam War, 1964–1975

The human costs of the war included 58,000 Americans killed in action and an additional 305,000 wounded. Vietnamese casualties were much higher (400,000 in North Vietnam; 900,000 in South Vietnam), and many civilians were killed by American bombs. The economic costs of the war were also high. For the United States, the cost of the war has been estimated at $200 billion. The war also had devastating effects on Vietnamese agriculture, business, and industry.

The Vietcong concentrated their efforts on the countryside, where their guerrilla tactics included ambush, terrorism, and sabotage.

President broad war powers. In March 1965 Johnson sent the first ground troops to Vietnam.

By 1968, American forces numbered more than 500,000, and United States planes were bombing Vietnam heavily. The South Vietnamese army was about 800,000; the Vietcong and their North Vietnamese allies about 300,000. The Soviet Union and China sent aid but no troops to help North Vietnam. North Vietnam sent troops and supplies southward over the Ho Chi Minh Trail. Despite greater numbers and advanced technology, the Americans could not defeat the Communists, who relied on surprise and mobility and avoided open battle. As the war intensified, antiwar attitudes spread within the United States and overseas.

The Tet Offensive

The turning point in the war came in early 1968. The Viet Cong launched a major military offensive during the Vietnamese New Year holiday, Tet. Although they failed to capture any major cities, the bitter fighting made more and more Americans real- ize that several years of United States involvement had failed to significantly weaken the Viet Cong. Opposition to Johnson's war policy became so fierce that Johnson decided not to seek reelection in 1968.

Ending the War

Opposition to the war grew rapidly during the Nixon presidency. As a result, the United States began withdrawing its troops. With the war becoming costly to both sides, South Vietnam, the United States, and the Communists in 1973 agreed to a cease-fire, and the last United States troops left Vietnam. The war resumed in 1975, however, when North Vietnamese and Viet Cong forces defeated the South Vietnamese.

After more than 20 years of fighting, Vietnam was reunited under the Communists. However, at least 2 million people, including 58,000 Americans, had died in the conflict. About 10 million South Vietnamese were **refugees**, people who flee to another country for safety from danger or disaster. In addition, large areas of Vietnam lay devastated.

South Vietnamese villagers from Quang Tri Province assemble at a refugee camp. Many hope to leave Vietnam.

Student war protest demonstrations on United States college campuses became common in the early 1970s.

REFLECTING ON THE TIMES

1. Why did college students play a significant role in the antiwar protest movement?
2. Why was the war so difficult for a powerful nation like the United States to win?

687

ANSWERS TO REFLECTING ON THE TIMES

1. Many college students who opposed the war did not want to serve in the army.
2. American soldiers did not know the terrain of Vietnam as well as the Vietcong—a necessity for the guerrilla-style war the Vietcong waged.

Daily Life Have students plan a reenactment of a 30-minute radio broadcast on a particular day in the United States in the late 1960s or early 1970s. Advise them to look through old newspapers to find the events of the day they want to report. In addition to news bulletins reporting that day's significant events, have students include popular music and ads for foods, fashions, and fads. **L2**

World Music: Cultural Traditions, Lesson 9

Independent Practice

Guided Reading Activity 22-4 **L1**

The Arts Have students watch films involving the Vietnam War, such as *Apocalypse Now; Born on the Fourth of July; The Deer Hunter; Good Morning, Vietnam;* and *Platoon*. Then have them write reports that compare and contrast the points of view of the different directors. **L2**

Critical Thinking Have students compare and contrast the Vietnam War with the Korean War. As resources, suggest J. C. Goulden, *Korea: The Untold Story of the War* and S. Karnow, *Vietnam: A History*. Ask students to write a short report summarizing the similarities and differences between the two conflicts. **L3**

Global Gourmet

Indonesia *Nasi goreng* is similar to Chinese fried rice, but instead of the meat and vegetables being cooked together with the rice, the individual ingredients surround a pile of fried rice. In the course of eating, the diner mixes them together.

Map Study

Answer

Cambodia and Laos

Map Skills Practice

Reading a Map What is the name of the trail used by North Vietnam and Vietcong forces for transport and communication among North and South Vietnam, Laos, and Cambodia? *(Ho Chi Minh Trail)*

Linking Past and Present

Cambodia The 1984 film *The Killing Fields* told the story of the relationship between an American reporter covering the invasion of Cambodia and a local translator, Dith Pran, who was caught and tortured by the Khmer Rouge but escaped. Even though Haing S. Ngor, the Cambodian refugee who played the latter role, was a physician with no acting experience, his portrayal was so convincing that he won an Academy Award for best supporting actor. In February 1996, Ngor was shot to death outside his Los Angeles home. He had spent his years in the United States helping survivors of the Khmer Rouge and trying to bring to justice those responsible for the Cambodian massacres.

Who?What?Where?When?

The Year of Living Dangerously (1983) was set in Indonesia in the mid-1960s, when the Sukarno regime was unstable and the war in Vietnam was intensifying. The film stars Mel Gibson as a foreign correspondent from Australia and Sigourney Weaver as a British attaché.

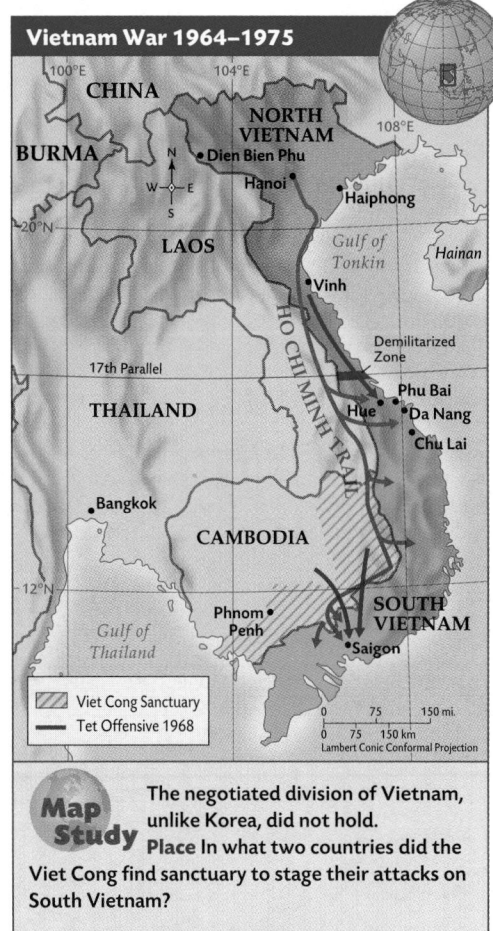

Vietnam War 1964–1975

CHINA
BURMA
NORTH VIETNAM
• Dien Bien Phu
Hanoi •
• Haiphong
LAOS
Gulf of Tonkin
Hainan
• Vinh
HO CHI MINH TRAIL
17th Parallel
Demilitarized Zone
THAILAND
Hue • • Phu Bai
• Da Nang
• Chu Lai
• Bangkok
CAMBODIA
Gulf of Thailand
Phnom • Penh
SOUTH VIETNAM
• Saigon

Viet Cong Sanctuary
Tet Offensive 1968

0   75   150 mi.
0 75 150 km
Lambert Conic Conformal Projection

Map Study
The negotiated division of Vietnam, unlike Korea, did not hold.
Place In what two countries did the Viet Cong find sanctuary to stage their attacks on South Vietnam?

Vietnam's Relations with the West

Since the war, Vietnam has faced economic difficulties. To improve the economy, the government in the late 1980s encouraged limited private enterprise and sought contacts with the West.

In recent years, relations between the United States and Vietnam have begun to improve. The Vietnamese government has helped locate and return many of the bodies of American soldiers killed in Vietnam. Unfortunately, the remains of many United States soldiers have not been found. Some former American soldiers have returned to Vietnam to help disarm land mines they planted during the war.

A major step toward normal relations was made in 1995 when the United States and Vietnam established diplomatic ties. Vietnam also moved to improve its relations and trade with the industrial-ized nations of western Europe as a way to gain funds to rebuild and strengthen its desperately poor economy.

A Legacy of Violence

The Vietnam War affected many areas of Southeast Asia other than Vietnam. Fighting and civil war engulfed Vietnam's neighbors, Laos and Cambodia. Other countries of Southeast Asia, such as Thailand, escaped combat but were flooded by refugees. Since the late 1970s, the region has slowly recovered from the effects of conflict.

Cambodia

In 1953 Cambodia won its independence from France. The country became a constitutional monarchy led by King **Norodom Sihanouk** (noo•roh•DAHM SEE•ah•nuk), a member of Cambodia's historic ruling family. In 1955 Sihanouk abdicated the Cambodian throne in order to become prime minister.

Sihanouk refused to take sides in cold war power struggles. However, as the war intensified in Vietnam, Cambodia became an unwilling participant. In 1969 American planes began to bomb Cambodia in an effort to destroy Viet Cong bases there. The bombings were also intended to stop the flow of supplies and troops moving through Cambodia from North Vietnam to South Vietnam.

The bombing failed to achieve its objectives but did intensify the conflict between Cambodian Communists and Sihanouk's government. In 1970 an American-backed army officer, Lon Nol, ousted Sihanouk. Lon Nol charged that Sihanouk was not battling the Communists aggressively enough.

Civil war broke out after the American bombings and Lon Nol's seizure of power. Cambodian Communists, known as the Khmer Rouge, finally defeated Lon Nol's forces in 1975. Khmer Rouge troops, under the leadership of **Pol Pot**, took control of Cambodia's capital, Phnom Penh.

The Khmer Rouge wanted Cambodia, which they renamed Kampuchea, to become an independent, self-sufficient agricultural country. In the attempt to achieve this goal, the Khmer Rouge devastated the country. They destroyed all money and books. Soldiers forced city residents into the countryside to work on farms. Troops murdered civil servants, teachers, and students who may have supported the old system. Starvation, torture, and executions by the brutal government killed more than 3 million people—nearly one-third of the entire Cambodian population.

COOPERATIVE LEARNING ACTIVITY

Research Organize students into groups. Assign each group one of the countries studied in this chapter. Tell them to research types of arts and crafts produced in these countries. As much as possible, divide each country's art forms and crafts among group members. Make sure that each student has a specific role to play in the research effort. Have each group prepare a short presentation summarizing its findings, using visual examples wherever possible. **L1 LEP**

National Geographic photographer Jodi Cobb

Boat People

Two decades after the Vietnam War, Vietnamese refugees waiting to go elsewhere remained stranded in Hong Kong. In this photograph, Vietnamese refugees in Hong Kong live inside huge concrete-and-metal dormitories where whole families sleep together in shelf-like bunks.

Vietnam suffered decades of war. In the 1800s the area was colonized by the French, who often proved to be brutal masters of rubber plantations and tin works. By the beginning of the 1900s an independence movement had begun in Vietnam. Not until 1975 did Vietnam free itself from foreign interference. But the price was high: economic devastation and domination of South Vietnam by North Vietnam. During the second half of the 1970s—years of poverty and political persecution—hundreds of thousands of Vietnamese left their country, many by boat. Untold numbers died. Some came to the United States; others scattered across Asia. By 1996, international pressure had forced Vietnam to increase its efforts to bring home the boat people. ⊕

Chapter 22 *Asia and the Pacific* **689**

TEACH

Tell students that sometimes the boat people fled political tensions only to find themselves caught up in racial tensions. For example, in 1979, Vietnamese boat people who were mostly ethnic Chinese arrived in Malaysia, already an ethnically diverse country. So intense was the fear that the arrival of the Vietnamese would upset the country's ethnic balance that, instead of welcoming the newcomers, the Malaysian government issued orders to shoot any boat person found landing on Malaysian shores. What current movement in the United States reflects Malaysia's response to the boat people? *(the movement to put an end to immigration)*

Linking Past and Present

Racial tensions between Malays and ethnic Chinese have been a problem in Malaysia since its formation in 1963. In May 1969, racial riots between Malays and Chinese led to a state of emergency that lasted for nearly two years, with the suspension of parliamentary rule. Differences in income between the two groups remain a serious problem, with Malays forming a majority in five of Malaysia's six poorest states.

A&E HOME VIDEO®

The following videotape program is available from Glencoe:

- **Vietnam/Cuban Missile Crisis**

To find classroom resources to accompany this video, check the following home page:

A&E Television:
http://www.AandE.com/

ASSESS

Check for Understanding

Assign Section 4 Review as homework or as an in-class activity.

Use Student Self-Test and Review Software to review Section 4.

Visualizing History Aung San Suu Kyi addresses a pro-democracy rally in Yangon, Myanmar's capital. *What group rules Myanmar?*

In 1978, after a series of border incidents, Vietnam invaded Cambodia and ousted Pol Pot. Cambodian Communists friendly to Vietnam took control of the government, but other Communist groups continued the civil war. In October 1991, representatives of the four major political groups in Cambodia signed an agreement that ended the civil war and called for an election under UN peace-keeping forces.

Cambodian voters in 1993 elected a government under Prince Norodom Ranariddh. However, Hun Sen, a political rival, demanded a role in the government. He gradually forced his way into power, finally removing the prince in July 1997. At that time, Cambodia began still another round of civil war. Continuing political instability has hindered growth of Cambodia's largely agricultural economy.

Laos

Laos became independent of France in 1954. While war raged in neighboring Vietnam, Laos had its own civil war between Laotian Communists and the American-backed government.

After United States forces withdrew from the region, Laos fell under the domination of Vietnam in 1975. A Communist government was formed, and the economy was reorganized along socialist lines. The Lao People's Revolutionary party abandoned those policies 20 years later after the collapse of the Soviet Union. They have reintroduced private land ownership and free markets. With investments from Thailand, Australia, and other foreign countries, the Lao government has built new roads, bridges, and railroads to advance regional trade and to gain access to timber and mineral resources.

Thailand

Thailand's post-World War II history was less violent than that of its neighbors because it had not been a European colony. It did not have to fight a war of national independence or struggle to forge a new national identity. The monarchy continued as a stabilizing force in Thai society, but the real power was often held by top military leaders.

During the Vietnam War, Thailand held to a firm anti-Communist policy, aligning itself decisively with the United States. In recent years, Thailand has adopted a more relaxed policy toward China and its neighbors, while remaining an ally of the United States.

During the 1980s, Thailand had one of Southeast Asia's fast-growing "tiger" economies, with a yearly growth rate of 8 percent. By 1997, high foreign borrowing and slow export growth had cast a dark shadow over the Thai economy. As hardships mounted for the Thai people, the government devalued its currency to make Thai exports cheaper and relied on an international loan. Its economic woes threatened to spill over into neighboring Southeast Asian lands with similar problems.

Myanmar

Myanmar is the northernmost country of Southeast Asia. Once called Burma, it was for many years part of British India but became a separate independent republic in 1948. The new Burmese government faced opposition from Communists and various ethnic groups. To restore order, military leaders took control of the country in 1962.

During the 1960s and 1970s, the military leadership turned Myanmar into a dictatorship. The government took control of the economy and forbade any criticism of its policies. It also limited Myanmar's contacts with the outside world.

During the late 1980s, large numbers of Burmese began to protest the government's policies and call for democracy. Military leaders finally promised free elections in 1990, but before the voting took place they arrested the leader of the main opposition party, **Aung San Suu Kyi** (AWNG SAHN SOO SHE). In spite of her arrest, her party won the elections.

MEETING SPECIAL NEEDS ACTIVITY

Learning Style: Logical/Mathematical Have students work together to create a time line of important events in Vietnam's history from World War II to the present. Advise students to use the same scale for this project, so that their time lines for Japanese, Chinese, and Vietnamese history can be juxtaposed, making simultaneous events easy to see. **L1**

The military leaders refused to accept the election results, but Aung San Suu Kyi won increased international support. While under house arrest, she received the 1991 Nobel Peace Prize. Released in 1995, she has continued efforts to achieve democracy in Myanmar.

Rim of Southeast Asia

Indonesia, Malaysia, Singapore, and the Philippines won their independence following World War II. They went through periods of turmoil and have emerged 50 years later with stable, booming economies. Their people and leaders are optimistic about the future of their countries.

Indonesia

Under Dutch rule for nearly 350 years, **Indonesia** won its freedom in 1949. Largely Muslim in religion, the new nation was very diverse in other ways. It consisted of a string of 14,000 islands stretching 3,000 miles (4,827 km) as well as nearly 80 million people of many cultures and languages. Therefore, forging a national identity was an early goal. Indonesia's first president, **Achmed Sukarno**, did much to unite the country. He ensured the adoption of a national language that put all Indonesians on an equal footing.

In 1965 Indonesia's Communists tried to seize power. In a bloody crackdown, the army killed about 300,000 allegedly pro-Communist ethnic Chinese. The anti-Communist General **Suharto** then replaced Sukarno as ruler.

By the mid-1990s, Suharto's leadership had brought economic growth to Indonesia despite charges of corruption and human rights violations. With oil and other natural resources, Indonesia attracted the attention of Western and Japanese businesses.

Meanwhile, Indonesia acted to crush an independence movement in East Timor. The Indonesians had seized control of the former Portuguese colony in 1975. Since then, the largely Roman Catholic population has resisted Indonesian rule. About 200,000 East Timorans have died as a result of Indonesia's use of force. In 1997 two human rights advocates in East Timor, Jose Ramos Horta and Bishop Carlos Belo, received the Nobel Peace Prize.

Malaysia

Created by the merger of several former British colonies in 1963, **Malaysia** is made up of territory on the Malay Peninsula and on the island of Borneo. Conflict between Malays and Chinese—the country's two largest ethnic groups—has been a frequent source of tension.

Since the early 1970s, however, Malaysia has been relatively stable. Like other nations on the rim of Southeast Asia, Malaysia has enjoyed an economic boom. Its well-educated labor force, good transportation networks, and tax incentives have helped attract foreign investment. Large public-works projects, however, have greatly increased the country's debt.

Singapore

Singapore is a small island republic off the tip of the Malay Peninsula. Independent since 1965, Singapore is a leading international port and commercial center, involved in shipping, banking, insurance, and telecommunications. Today, Singapore's people are well-educated and prosperous. Their standard of living is second only to Japan's in Asia.

Singapore's modern economic growth occurred under the authoritarian leadership of **Lee Kuan Yew** (lee kwahn yoo), who was prime minister from 1965 to 1990. Closely involved with Singapore's economic development, the government focused on encouraging high-technology industries and welcomed foreign business investment. A prosperous economy and the high rate of savings by Singapore citizens helped finance quality housing, health care, and education. In spite of having these benefits, Singapore's people have had limits placed on their freedom of speech and other rights.

Evaluate

 Section Quiz 22-4

🖳 Use the Testmaker to create a customized quiz for Section 4.

Reteach

Organize the class into eight groups and assign each group one of the countries covered in this section: Vietnam, Cambodia, Laos, Thailand, Myanmar, Indonesia, Malaysia, and Singapore. Ask each group to write a succinct paragraph summarizing the information in this section about their country. Reproduce the eight summaries and distribute them as study aids.

Enrich

Ask students to research the role played by Henry Kissinger in the events covered in this section. Have them summarize their findings in brief written reports.

CLOSE

Have students write a paragraph in which they explain whether and why they would have supported or opposed American military involvement in Vietnam if they had been of college age at the time.

SECTION 4 REVIEW

Recall
1. **Define** domino theory, refugee.
2. **Identify** Ho Chi Minh, Norodom Sihanouk, Pol Pot, Aung San Suu Kyi, Achmed Sukarno, Suharto,

Lee Kuan Yew.
3. **Locate** the Ho Chi Minh Trail on the map on page 688. Why was the trail significant in the war?

Critical Thinking
4. **Analyzing Information** How have the economies of

Southeast Asian nations changed since the end of World War II?

Understanding Themes
5. **Conflict** Evaluate whether the domino theory was proven correct by events in Southeast Asia. Explain your reasoning.

SECTION 4 REVIEW ANSWERS

1. All vocabulary words are defined in the Glossary.
2. Ho Chi Minh, 685; Norodom Sihanouk, 688; Pol Pot, 688; Aung San Suu Kyi, 690; Achmed Sukarno, 691; Suharto, 691; Lee Kuan Yew, 691
3. North Vietnam used the route to send troops and supplies to South Vietnam.

4. Vietnam has encouraged limited private enterprise; Cambodia has restored free market policies; Laos has reintroduced private land ownership and free markets; Thailand's economy and standard of living have grown rapidly; Myanmar's military dictatorship has taken control of the economy; Indonesia, Malaysia, and

Singapore have experienced an economic boom.
5. **CONFLICT** Answers will vary. Laos and Cambodia became Communist soon after Vietnam did, but Cambodia might not have if the United States had not bombed it.

1945		1972		2000

1947 India and Pakistan become independent nations.

1971 Civil war in Pakistan leads to independence of Bangladesh.

1984 Sikh unrest leads to assassination of Indira Gandhi.

Section 5

South Asia

Setting the Scene

▶ **Terms to Define**
　nonaligned

▶ **People to Meet**
　Muhammad Ali Jinnah, Jawaharlal Nehru, Indira Gandhi, Benazir Ali Bhutto

▶ **Places to Locate**
　India, Pakistan, Kashmir, Bangladesh, Sri Lanka

ind Out What challenges have the countries of South Asia faced since independence?

The Storyteller

Pradeep Bandhari was deeply shaken. Yet another Indian leader had been assassinated. Confused and distressed, he asked his professor to explain why visionary leaders were repeatedly struck down. "I have no immediate answer to give," replied the professor. "However, you might find some meaning in the eulogy for Mohandas Gandhi written by Jawaharlal Nehru." Pradeep was struck by the timeliness of the message:
　　　"Long ages afterwards history will judge of this period we have passed through. We are too near to be proper judges and to understand what has happened and what has not happened."

　　　　—adapted from Independence and After, "A Glory Has Departed," Jawaharlal Nehru, reprinted in Great Speeches from Pericles to Kennedy, 1965

Nehru and Mohandas Gandhi

ritish rule of South Asia came to an end after World War II. The creation of independent states in the region, however, was marred by religious and ethnic conflicts. The cold war also had an impact. In recent years, dramatic changes in the world have made South Asian nations rethink their policies and relationships.

POINT

Dividing the Subcontinent

After World War II, the British finally agreed to give **India** its freedom. Growing political disunity, however, divided the subcontinent. **Muhammad Ali Jinnah**, leader of the Muslim League, wanted Muslims to have their own state named **Pakistan**. Riots between Hindus and Muslims finally convinced the British to partition, or divide, India. In early 1947, Lord Louis Mountbatten, a World War II military hero, became British India's last viceroy. He and other officials quickly drew borders for two separate states, a difficult task because many Hindus and Muslims lived side by side. Heavily Muslim areas in the far west and far east became Pakistan. The vast area in between, where most of the people were Hindus, became India.

On August 15, 1947, independence came to both countries, but not peace. The division of the subcontinent led to one of the largest single mass movements of people in history. About 12 million Hindus and Muslims crossed the borders of India and Pakistan in both directions. Centuries of mistrust between religious groups led to violence that resulted in the deaths of a million or more people. Tragically, another casualty of the conflict was Mohandas Gandhi, killed in January 1948 by a Hindu extremist who was angered at Gandhi's call for peace and reconciliation.

The migrations and the killings did not end the conflicts between Hindus and Muslims. More than

692 Chapter 22 *Asia and the Pacific*

60 million Muslims remained in India, ensuring future tensions. Bitter hostilities between India and Pakistan would also continue.

India

India's first prime minister was **Jawaharlal Nehru** (jah•wah•HAR•lahl NAY•roo), a British-educated lawyer who had led the fight for freedom along with Gandhi. Nehru headed India's government from 1947 until his death in 1964.

The Nehru "Dynasty"

For forty years after independence, India was ruled by a member of the Nehru family. Jawaharlal Nehru aimed to make India a modern, industrialized state based on secular ideas. His government worked for religious freedom and greater social equality. India's constitution granted universal suffrage, and aimed to ban caste distinctions and improve the status of women.

Nehru favored a mixed economy of privately owned and government-run businesses. Attention was also given to raising food production. Increased food supplies, however, were accompanied by rapid population growth and the increased migration of people from rural areas to the cities.

Under Nehru, India became a leader among the new nations of Asia and Africa. Nehru argued that recently independent countries such as India should not participate in the cold war. By remaining nonaligned—that is, tied to neither superpower—the less powerful countries of the world could forge their own way in global affairs. In the early 1960s, however, tense relations with China helped bring India into a closer relationship with China's new rival, the Soviet Union.

Two years after Nehru's death in 1964, his daughter **Indira Gandhi** became prime minister. An energetic leader, Gandhi continued her father's policies; however, her crackdown on political opponents in 1977 made her unpopular and eventually swept her from office.

When Gandhi returned to power in 1980, India faced growing religious and ethnic unrest. In the Punjab region of northern India, some Sikhs wanted their own state. Sikh separatists occupied the Golden Temple of Amritsar, Sikhism's holiest shrine. When talks failed, Indira Gandhi in 1984 drove out the separatists with troops and tanks. Outraged at the shrine's violation, two of Gandhi's bodyguards, themselves Sikhs, later assassinated her.

Gandhi's son, Rajiv Gandhi, served as prime minister from 1984 to 1989. In 1991 he was assassi-

Visualizing History Indira Gandhi had been a leader in the Congress party and minister of information and broadcasting in India before becoming prime minister. *Why did she lose the 1977 election?*

nated while campaigning to become prime minister again. Rajiv's death seemed to mark the end of the Nehru "dynasty" in politics.

A New Course

In the 1990s India's prime ministers have not had the influence or power of the Nehru "dynasty." However, with workable parliamentary institutions, India's democracy may have been strengthened. Although India still struggles with poverty, disease, and illiteracy, recent reforms have improved its economy by promoting free enterprise, less government regulation, and increased trade.

A major challenge still facing India is religious and ethnic conflict. Uncertainties caused by modernization have led to a revival of traditional Hinduism mixed with modern politics. In the early 1990s, the Hindu nationalist party increased its support. Its desire to promote Hindu principles has disturbed many non-Hindu Indians who view it as a threat to India's secular government. Violence has also erupted between religious groups. In 1992 fierce battles broke out between Hindus and Muslims over the ownership of a religious site at Ayodhya.

Since 1947, India has faced periodic conflicts with Pakistan. A major source of hostility between the two countries has been the disputed northern territory of **Kashmir**. Although most of Kashmir's people are Muslim, two-thirds of the territory is governed by India. Since the 1980s, Muslims in the

Chapter 22 *Asia and the Pacific* **693**

COOPERATIVE LEARNING ACTIVITY

Research Organize the class into four teams, one for each country being studied—India, Pakistan, Bangladesh, and Sri Lanka. Each team should assign individual members to research one of the following topics: religion, economy, language, education, government (type, current leadership, and perceived strengths and weaknesses). Instruct each team to create a chart in poster form that will summarize what they learn about their assigned country. Have students display the completed charts and compare and contrast the four nations. **L1**

TEACH

Guided Practice

THEME Diversity
Ask students to read the section, looking for signs of how diversity contributed to developments in this region. (*Not only did British India break up into India and Pakistan because of religious differences, but Bangladesh later broke off from Pakistan because of language and cultural differences. Religious and ethnic diversity within India, Pakistan, and Sri Lanka continues to create unrest.*) **L1**

Visualizing History One of Indira Gandhi's assassins died soon after the assassination. The second, as well as a third coconspirator, was tried and sentenced to death.
Answer to Caption: *She had moved away from democracy toward authoritarian rule.*

TURNING POINT

Dividing the Subcontinent
How was independence finally achieved in South Asia?
The British withdrew from the subcontinent, but religious differences resulted in the formation of two independent states: India and Pakistan.

World Music: Cultural Traditions, Lesson 7

Independent Practice
Guided Reading Activity 22-5 **L1**

Chapter 22
Section 5

Map Study

Answer

The large number of island nations made regional unity difficult to achieve.

Map Skills Practice

Reading a Map Which country achieved independence most recently? *(Brunei)*

Critical Thinking Have students research and summarize the militant activities of the Sikhs since Indian independence in order to explain the Sikh wish to establish a separate nation.

VIDEODISC
Lessons of War

Side Two, Chapter 6
Frames 12636–20751
Title: *Philosophy of Nonviolence*
Subject: The philosophies of Mohandas Gandhi and Martin Luther King, Jr., and how their philosophies were used in protests and demonstrations
Ask: What form of demonstration did Mohandas Gandhi stress? *(nonviolent protest)*

ASSESS

Check for Understanding

Assign Section 5 Review as homework or as an in-class activity.

Use Student Self-Test and Review Software to review Section 5.

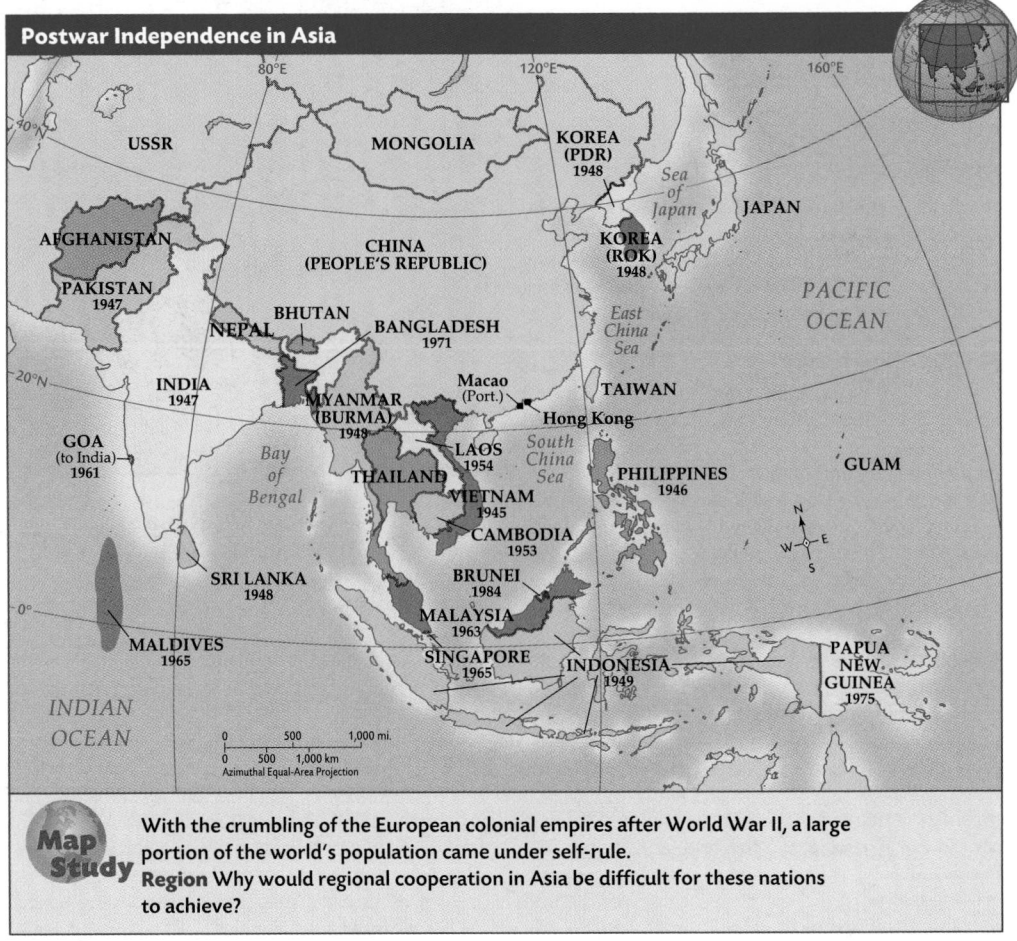

Postwar Independence in Asia

Map Study
With the crumbling of the European colonial empires after World War II, a large portion of the world's population came under self-rule.
Region Why would regional cooperation in Asia be difficult for these nations to achieve?

Indian section of Kashmir have organized to oppose Indian rule.

Observers fear a nuclear arms race between India and Pakistan over Kashmir and other issues. Since the 1970s, India has had its own nuclear weapons. In reaction, Pakistan is working to develop its nuclear capability. International efforts are underway to halt the race before it leads to a nuclear conflict in South Asia.

Pakistan and Bangladesh

After independence in 1947, Pakistan faced difficulties in joining two distinct regions separated by over 1,000 miles (1,609 km) of Indian territory. West Pakistan was a dry, mountainous region in which most people spoke Urdu. East Pakistan was a wet

lowlands region in which most people spoke Bengali. The religion of Islam was their only common bond.

In March 1971, a fierce civil war broke out between the two regions of Pakistan. In December 1971, India joined the war in support of East Pakistan. This military action spread the fighting to West Pakistan and Kashmir. The war ended quickly, and East Pakistan won its independence as the republic of Bangladesh.

Bangladesh

Bangladesh is one of the most densely populated nations of the world. More than 125 million people live in an area about the size of New York State. Most people are located in rural areas where illiteracy and the birthrate are high and the life expectancy is low.

694   Chapter 22   *Asia and the Pacific*

MEETING SPECIAL NEEDS ACTIVITY

Learning Style: Logical/Mathematical Have students work together to create two time lines, one of important events in India's history between World War II and the present, and the second of important events in Pakistan's history over the same period. Tell students to include political, economic, and cultural events. Advise students to use the same scale for this project so that their five time lines can be studied together. **L1**

Achieving stable rule has been difficult in Bangladesh. Since independence, two leaders of the country have been assassinated, and military officials often have controlled the government. Beginning in 1991, free elections have been held, however, and political power has alternated between the female leaders of the two major parties. In 1996 Sheik Hasina Wazid became prime minister.

In spite of economic growth and substantial foreign aid, the future of Bangladesh remains uncertain. The average annual per capita (per person) income of $150 is one of the world's lowest. The country also is subject to intense summer storms and flooding.

Pakistan Since 1971

Pakistan suffered from political instability and military rule after 1971. A move toward a stable democracy seemed likely in 1993 when **Benazir Ali Bhutto** became prime minister. In 1996, however, her government fell as a result of corruption charges. Elections brought to power the opposition party under Nawaz Sharif. Sharif's government promised to reduce government regulations over the economy.

During the 1970s and 1980s, Pakistan allied with the United States in order to counter India's ties with the Soviet Union. The Pakistani government allowed the Americans to channel military arms to anti-Soviet rebels in neighboring Afghanistan. It also permitted Afghani fighters to use Pakistan as a base of operations, and sheltered 3 million Afghani refugees. Despite United States aid, the presence of so many refugees was costly and worsened ethnic tensions within Pakistan.

Military spending has taken a large share of Pakistan's budget because of tensions with India. This has drained resources that could have been used for the economic development of the country. Pakistan's efforts to develop nuclear weapons have raised international concern about a South Asian arms race.

Visualizing History Sheik Hasina Wazid became prime minister of Bangladesh in 1996. Her father, Sheik Mujibar Rahman, is regarded as Bangladesh's founder. *What challenges does Bangladesh face?*

Sri Lanka

In 1948, the year after the partition of India, Great Britain granted independence to Ceylon, known since 1972 as **Sri Lanka**. This beautiful island off the southeast coast of India has been the site of ethnic civil war since the 1980s. The Sinhalese, who make up about about 75 percent of the population, are Buddhists. The Tamils, who make up about 20 percent, are Hindus. In recent years the Tamils, complaining of discrimination against them by the Sinhalese, have demanded their own state within Sri Lanka. Hundreds of people have died in conflicts between government troops and Tamil guerrillas. Efforts to improve the economy have been helped by developing privately owned businesses and by attracting foreign investments.

SECTION 5 REVIEW

Recall
1. **Define** nonaligned.
2. **Identify** Muhammad Ali Jinnah, Jawaharlal Nehru, Indira Gandhi, Benazir Ali Bhutto.
3. **Explain** the consequences of

Great Britain's withdrawal from South Asia.
Critical Thinking
4. **Analyzing Information** What do you think are the underlying causes of continuing

political strife in India?
Understanding Themes
5. **Diversity** Has the division of the Indian subcontinent into separate countries been beneficial? Explain your answer.

Visualizing History Sheik Hasina Wazid graduated from Dhaka University in 1973. Despite a forced exile and the deaths of her family members, she returned to Bangladesh to become its second female Prime Minister.
Answer to Caption: *Bangladesh has a low GDP and a high birthrate. It is vulnerable to drought and floods.*

Evaluate

Section Quiz 22-5

Use the Testmaker to create a customized quiz for Section 5.

Reteach

Have students locate India, Pakistan, Bangladesh, and Sri Lanka on a map. Ask them to identify the year each country achieved independence and to summarize the contemporary challenges each country faces.

Enrich

Have students each choose one of the 22 states of India and write a short report on its ethnic, cultural, and religious aspects. Some students may organize the class findings visually as a poster.

CLOSE

Have students write a short paragraph summarizing modern history and contemporary problems of each of the four countries studied in this section.

SECTION 5 REVIEW ANSWERS

1. All vocabulary words are defined in the Glossary.
2. Muhammad Ali Jinnah, 692; Jawaharlal Nehru, 693; Indira Gandhi, 693; Benazir Ali Bhutto, 695
3. violence between Hindus and Muslims and

the division of the Indian subcontinent
4. Answers will vary but should refer to religious and ethnic conflict.
5. **DIVERSITY** Answers will vary. The division allowed groups more autonomy but left a legacy of conflict.

1945   1972   2000

1946 The Philippines wins independence from the United States.   **1970s** Australia admits non-British European and Asian immigrants for the first time.   **1995** Pacific nations protest French nuclear testing.

SECTION THEME

▶ **Cultural Diffusion** Changing political and economic roles open the nations of the Pacific to other parts of the globe.

Find Out

Answer: *foreign investment, close trading ties to Pacific Rim and other Asian nations, economic diversification; a rethinking of military relationships with the United States, and concern over nuclear proliferation*

FOCUS

Section Objective

List the factors that have helped Pacific nations develop prosperous economies and new national identities since World War II.

BELLRINGER
Motivational Activity

Before taking roll at the beginning of the class period, project Section Focus Transparency 22-6 and have students answer the activity questions.

This activity is also available as a blackline master.

Vocabulary Pre-check

▣ Use the Vocabulary PuzzleMaker to create a puzzle that reinforces the vocabulary terms in this section. **L1**

Section 6

The Pacific

Setting the Scene

▶ **Terms to Define**
archipelago

▶ **People to Meet**
Ferdinand Marcos, Corazon Aquino, Paul Keating, David Lange, Jim Bolger

▶ **Places to Locate**
The Philippines, Australia, New Zealand, Papua New Guinea

Find Out
What factors have helped Pacific nations develop prosperous economies and new national identities since World War II?

The Storyteller

Toby Doust knew what to expect between the Great Sandy Desert and the Gibson Desert in northwestern Australia—and it wasn't water. Earlier explorers had expected water, but Lake Disappointment had water only when a rare inland cyclone brought a spattering shower to the dry bed. Toby, however, was prospecting for more commercial materials—iron, zinc, bauxite—to sell throughout the Pacific Basin. Perhaps there was even gold or uranium. One thing Toby never lacked was nerve. Nearing a remote outcrop, he unstrapped his bag and got out his metal detector, ready to strike it rich.

—adapted from "Journey into the Daytime," *National Geographic*, January 1991

Australia's Uluru (Ayers Rock)

The Pacific region east and south of Asia contains Australia, the world's only island continent, and numerous other islands that spread out across millions of miles of the Pacific Ocean. Until recently, long distances and rugged landscapes kept many parts of the region isolated from each other and the rest of the world. Beginning in the 1700s, Western powers exercised a strong influence in the region. Since World War II, the Pacific countries, now mostly independent, have forged new identities from a mix of European, traditional Pacific, and Asian cultures. Many of them have close trading ties to Japan, Singapore, and other nations of the Pacific Rim, a region of economically prosperous countries bordering the Pacific Ocean.

The Philippines

The Philippines is an archipelago, or group of islands, in the Pacific Ocean east of Vietnam. The Philippines faced severe challenges when it became independent from the United States in 1946. Philippine Communists, known as the Huks, pressed for land reform and tried to take over the government. The Philippine army defeated them in 1954, but the Huks have arisen periodically to challenge later leaders.

Between 1965 and 1986, the Philippines was led by President **Ferdinand Marcos**. Marcos at first was popular because he tried to improve education and transportation. Evidence of corruption later fueled bitter protests against him. Marcos's downfall finally came about as a result of his suspected involvement in the killing of the political opposition leader, Benigno Aquino, Jr.

A massive public outcry over the assassination forced new elections, which Marcos won by fraud. Popular outrage at his deceit forced Marcos to flee the country. **Corazon Aquino**, the widow of the assassinated opposition leader, became the new president.

SECTION RESOURCES

📁 **Reproducible Masters**
• Reproducible Lesson Plan 22-6
• Guided Reading Activity 22-6
• Reteaching Activity 22
• Enrichment Activity 22
• Section Quiz 22-6
• Performance Assessment Activity 22
• Spanish Chapter Summary 22

📗 **Transparencies**
• Section Focus Transparency 22-6
• World History and Art Transparency 44, *Sydney Opera House*

Multimedia
▣ Vocabulary PuzzleMaker Software
▣ Student Self-Test and Review Software
▣ Testmaker
🎵 World Music: Cultural Traditions, Lesson 10

Visualizing History President Corazon Aquino pledged to restore democracy to the Philippines under a new constitution in 1987. *What four groups opposed her rule?*

Optimism that Corazon Aquino would begin a new era of reform and economic growth soon faded. She faced opposition from Marcos supporters, the Huks, the military, and nationalist Filipinos opposed to American military bases in the Philippines. An attempt to overthrow her failed due to American support. In 1992 Fidel Ramos, a former general, succeeded her as president.

That same year, the United States withdrew from its last military base in the Philippines. Although this was the desire of the Philippine government, the loss of revenue to the Philippine economy was substantial. Japan has since become the foreign country with the most economic influence in the Philippines.

Australia

Before World War II, **Australia** was a largely agricultural country dependent on Great Britain. Beef, wool, wheat, and dairy products were the country's main exports. Since 1945, Australia has changed to an industrial economy with close links to the United States and Asian countries. With the help of foreign investment, Australians have developed assembly and manufacturing plants for consumer goods, processed foods, paper, textiles, and transportation equipment.

Since the 1970s, Australia has strengthened ties with Japan and Southeast Asia. Today more than 60 percent of Australia's trade is with Asian countries. Meanwhile, Australia is gradually ending its links to Great Britain and the monarchy. **Paul Keating**, who was prime minister in the early 1990s, pushed for the creation of an Australian republic by the year 2000.

Australia's shift from Great Britain to its Asian and Pacific neighbors has been influenced by the country's changing population. After World War II, large numbers of southern and eastern Europeans—Greeks, Italians, and Slavs—made new homes in Australia. Then, in the 1970s, the Australian government liberalized its immigration laws and allowed Asian immigrants into the country. Today, about 50 percent of immigrants to Australia each year come from neighboring Asian countries. By the 1990s, only about 35 percent of Australians were of British descent; this was down from 75 percent in 1949.

On the World Stage

Since World War II Australia has also sought a greater role in world affairs. It became a founding member of the United Nations in 1945. Five years later, Australian troops joined the UN forces fighting in the Korean War. In 1951 Australia signed the ANZUS treaty, which linked Australia, New Zealand, and the United States in a mutual defense pact. As part of the effort to contain communism, Australia sent forces to fight alongside the United States in the Vietnam War. It later backed the UN effort against Iraq in 1990 by sending Australian warships to the Persian Gulf.

Australians continue to support close military ties with the United States but are concerned about

Chapter 22 *Asia and the Pacific* **697**

TEACH

Guided Practice

THEME Cultural Diffusion

Ask students to list the cultural influences that have affected the development of Australia (*population: Aborigines, British, southern and eastern European; military: United States; trade: Japan, Southeast Asia*), New Zealand (*population: Maori, British, other European; military: United States; trade: Japan, Australia, United States, Europe*), and Papua New Guinea (*population: ethnic groups speaking nearly 700 different languages*). **L1**

Visualizing History Corazon Aquino called for only nonviolent demonstrations, boycotts, and strikes to protest the corrupt Marcos regime.
Answer to Caption: *Marcos supporters, the Huks, the military, and nationalist Filipinos opposed to American military bases in the Philippines*

World History and Art Transparency 44, *Sydney Opera House*

World Music: Cultural Traditions, Lesson 10

Linking Past and Present

Philippine Government In February 1986, Marcos dispatched columns of tanks against a group of rebel soldiers in Manila. They were stopped by the crowds assembled at the corner of Ortigas Avenue and the highway. In February 1996, Filipinos celebrated the tenth anniversary of the "People Power" revolution against Marcos. President Fidel V. Ramos addressed a rally at that corner.

COOPERATIVE LEARNING ACTIVITY

The Arts Organize the class into four groups to research Australian, Melanesian, Polynesian, and Micronesian art. Each group member should have a specific area to research, such as visual art, music, dance, literature, or specific crafts. When the groups have completed their research, ask them to prepare class presentations combining oral commentary with visual and aural examples. After all the groups have made their presentations, hold a class discussion in which students compare and contrast Australian, Melanesian, Polynesian, and Micronesian arts and crafts. **L2**

Independent Practice

 Guided Reading Activity 22-6 **L1**

Literature Have students choose a book by Australian novelist Patrick White, who won the 1973 Nobel Prize in literature. Ask them to write a book report that focuses on life in Australia. **L2**

ASSESS

Check for Understanding

Assign Section 6 Review as homework or as an in-class activity.

⬚ Use Student Self-Test Software to review Section 6.

Evaluate

 Section Quiz 22-6

⬚ Use the Testmaker to create a customized quiz for Section 6.

Reteach

Have students write one-sentence identifications of each of the terms, people, and places listed in "Setting the Scene," on page 696.

 Reteaching Activity 22

Enrich

Have students locate articles about recent antinuclear activities in the Pacific region. Ask them to summarize their findings in a brief written report.

⬚ Enrichment Activity 22

CLOSE

Have students write a short paragraph for each of the countries covered in this section (the Philippines, Australia, New Zealand, and Papua New Guinea) summarizing recent developments.

---

the presence of nuclear weapons in the Pacific region. Australia has been a major sponsor of a South Pacific Nuclear-Free Zone. Even so, it sided with the United States in the United States's dispute with New Zealand about American nuclear-armed vessels entering into New Zealand waters.

New Zealand

Consisting of two major islands and many small ones, **New Zealand** lies about 1,000 miles (1,600 km) to the southeast of Australia. Most of New Zealand's 3.5 million people are of British, other European, or Maori descent. Like Australia, New Zealand traditionally was joined by trade, politics, and culture to Great Britain. After World War II, it began to ally itself more closely with the United States and Asian countries.

New Zealand also added more variety to its economy. While agriculture—mainly sheep and dairy farming—remain important, New Zealand now has many manufacturing and service industries. It trades with Japan, Australia, the United States, and the countries of Western Europe.

Fear of Japanese attack during World War II made New Zealand turn to the United States for defense when the war was over. In 1951, New Zealand welcomed the creation of the ANZUS alliance and participated in the Korean and Vietnam conflicts.

Since the 1980s, however, New Zealand's opposition to nuclear weapons has strained its relationship with the United States and has drawn it closer to other Pacific countries that also oppose nuclear weapons. In 1985, New Zealand Prime Minister **David Lange** announced that ships carrying nuclear weapons, including those from the United States, could no longer enter New Zealand ports. In the early 1990s, Lange's successor as prime minister, **Jim Bolger**, worked to improve relations with the United States on the nuclear issue.

South Pacific Island Countries

Thousands of islands dot the Pacific Ocean. Many are small and uninhabited. Others were first settled thousands of years ago by various Asian and Pacific peoples. Their descendants today belong to three major groups: Melanesians, Micronesians, and Polynesians.

Nations and Colonies

Since World War II, some of the islands—such as Fiji—have become independent of Western rule. Other islands—such as Tahiti—continue to be held by Western powers as colonial territories valued for military reasons. France, for example, in 1995 conducted nuclear tests on an atoll, or ring-shaped coral island, in French Polynesia. French actions aroused antinuclear protests. The international outcry led to an early end of the tests.

Papua New Guinea

Among the larger island countries in the Pacific region is **Papua New Guinea**. Made up of 700 islands, Papua New Guinea has most of its territory on the eastern half of the island of New Guinea. Formerly held by Germany and Great Britain, and later by Australia, Papua New Guinea became independent in 1975.

Papua New Guinea faces many challenges in its efforts to achieve national unity. Its population is made up of many ethnic groups that speak nearly 700 different languages. Because of this ethnic diversity, Papua New Guinea has little sense of nationhood. Tensions and conflict between ethnic groups is common.

In addition, most of Papua New Guinea's people are poor and illiterate. Copper and gold mining has boosted the economy since the 1980s, but other economic sectors remain to be developed. The government of Papua New Guinea is working to interest companies in Japan, the United States, Hong Kong, and Singapore to invest in the country.

SECTION 6 REVIEW

Recall
1. **Define** archipelago.
2. **Identify** Ferdinand Marcos, Corazon Aquino, Paul Keating, ANZUS, David Lange, Jim Bolger.

3. **Explain** what events led to Marcos's downfall in the Philippines.

Critical Thinking
4. **Analyzing Information** How has the economy of Australia changed since World War II?

Understanding Themes
5. **Cultural Diffusion** What cultural influences have affected the development of South Pacific island countries?

SECTION 6 REVIEW ANSWERS

1. All vocabulary words are defined in the Glossary.
2. Ferdinand Marcos, 696; Corazon Aquino, 696; Paul Keating, 697; ANZUS, 697; David Lange, 698; Jim Bolger, 698
3. his suspected involvement in the killing of Benigno Aquino, Jr., and his corrupt government

4. It has changed from a largely agricultural country dependent on Great Britain to an industrial economy with close links to the United States and Asia.
5. **CULTURAL DIFFUSION** Melanesian, Micronesian, and Polynesian influences have affected the development of South Pacific island countries.

Using a Spreadsheet

Electronic spreadsheets can help people manage numbers quickly and easily. You can use a spreadsheet any time a problem involves numbers that can be arranged in rows and columns.

Learning the Skill

A spreadsheet is an electronic worksheet. All spreadsheets follow a basic design of rows and columns. Each *column* (vertical) is assigned a letter or number. Each *row* (horizontal) is assigned a number. Each point where a column and row intersect is called a *cell*. The cell's position on the spreadsheet is labeled according to its corresponding column and row—Column A, Row 1 (A1); Column B, Row 2 (B2), and so on.

Spreadsheets use *standard formulas* to calculate the numbers. You create a simple mathematical equation that uses these standard formulas and the computer does the calculations for you.

Practicing the Skill

Suppose you want to know the population densities (population per square mile) of the countries in South Asia. Use these steps to create a spreadsheet that will provide this information.

1. In cell A1 type *Country*, in cell B1 type *Population*, in cell C1 type *Land Area (square miles)*, and in cell D1 type *Population per square mile.*
2. In cells A2-A5 respectively, type one of the following country's name: *India, Pakistan, Bangladesh,* and *Sri Lanka*. In cell A6, type the words *Total for South Asia.*
3. In cells B2-B5, enter the population area of each country shown in cells A2-A5.
4. In cells C2-C5, enter the land area (square miles) of each country shown in cells A2-A5.
5. In cell D2, create a formula to calculate the population per square mile. The formula for the equation tells what cells (B1 ÷ C1) to divide. Copy this formula into cells D3-D5.

6. Use the process in step 5 to create and copy a formula to calculate the total population of South Asia (B2 + B3 + B4 + B5) for cell B6; to calculate the total Land Area of South Asia (C2 + C3 + C4 + C5) for cell C6.
7. Use the process in step 5 to create and copy a formula to calculate the population per square mile of South Asia (B6 ÷ C6) for cell D6.

Applying the Skill

Use a spreadsheet to enter your test scores and your homework grades. At the end of the grading period, the spreadsheet can calculate your average grade.

For More Practice

Turn to the Skill Practice in the Chapter Review on page 701 for more practice in using a spreadsheet.

Technology

SKILLS

TEACH

Using a Spreadsheet This skill teaches students to work with a spreadsheet program on the computer. Review **Learning the Skill** with students. What types of information could be placed on spreadsheets? (*Budgets, grades, schedules, populations, temperatures, amount of precipitation, and so on.*) Next review **Practicing the Skill** with students. Then allow them computer time to apply the directions. Students can find the information they need to complete **Practicing the Skill** in *The World Almanac, Statesmen's Yearbook,* and *The Population Data Sheet* from the Population Bureau, Inc.

Additional Practice

📁 Skill Reinforcement Activity 22

ANSWERS TO PRACTICING THE SKILL

Students will create a spreadsheet that shows the population density of the countries of South Asia as well as the average population density of all of South Asia. The population densities will vary depending on the population figures (year) used in the calculations.

CHAPTER 22 REVIEW

GLENCOE
TECHNOLOGY

VIDEODISC
Use MindJogger to review students' knowledge of the chapter.

MindJogger Videoquiz

Chapter 22
Disc 3 Side A

 Also available in VHS.

Answers

Using Key Terms
1. i   4. h
2. j   5. a
3. f

Using Your History Journal
Suggest that students reflect on political, cultural, and economic changes they confront as new immigrants.

Reviewing Facts
1. Indira Gandhi (prime minister, India); Benazir Ali Bhutto (prime minister, Pakistan); Sheik Hasina Wazid (prime minister, Bangladesh)
2. He is the spiritual leader of Tibet and has defended Tibetan rights against the Chinese since 1950.
3. Mao Zedong established a totalitarian Communist suppressed state and human rights; he raised living standards, but carried out policies (the Cultural Revolution) that killed millions. Deng introduced market reforms but kept Communist controls.
4. Advances: Aquino's victory in the Philippines; India's maintenance of democratic rule; Violations: the Tiananmen Square massacre in China; the Khmer Rouge atrocities in Cambodia; and suppression of democracy in Myanmar

Connections Across Time

Historical Significance The most dramatic change in Asia since 1945 is the dazzling economic achievements of Japan, South Korea, Hong Kong, Taiwan, and Singapore. In these nations, stable governments have worked with private companies to foster economic growth and high standards of living. Experts from around the world study Japan and other prosperous Asian countries to learn the reasons for their success.

Meanwhile, India and other Asian countries are developing their agriculture and industries. While the gap between rich and poor remains wide in many areas, standards of living are rising.

Using Key Terms

Write the key term that completes each sentence. Then write a sentence for each term not chosen.

a. referendum
b. stalemate
c. archipelago
d. refugee
e. quota
f. pragmatists
g. sect
h. special economic zones
i. domino theory
j. nonaligned
k. pollution
l. gross domestic product

1. In the 1960s the growing American role in Vietnam was justified by those who accepted the _____.
2. Jawaharlal Nehru believed if India and other less powerful countries remained _____ in the cold war, they could provide alternatives to the superpowers.
3. In China, a group known as _____ favored modernizing China through increased trade and contacts with the West.
4. The Chinese government has allowed foreign privately owned businesses to flourish in _____ located in southeastern China.
5. In a _____, voters are asked to accept or reject a measure.

Technology Activity

Using a Word Processor Locate sources about present-day North Korea and South Korea. Organize your findings by creating a fact sheet comparing the two countries. Use a word processor to create a chart. Headings to include are population, type of economy, GDP, type of government, currency, infant mortality rate, literacy rate, and official religion. Provide a map of each country that shows political boundaries, major cities, and natural resources.

Using Your History Journal

Imagine that you and your family have moved to an Asian country. Write a letter back to your friends in the United States about your experiences during the first year in your new country.

Reviewing Facts

1. **Culture** Identify examples of women who have been successful in Asian politics.
2. **Culture** Explain the role of the Dalai Lama.
3. **History** Discuss the policies of Mao Zedong and Deng Xiaoping, and describe their effects on the Chinese people.
4. **Citizenship** Identify examples of how human rights have advanced and how they have been violated in Asia since World War II.
5. **History** Identify the causes and outcome of the Korean War.
6. **History** Describe the impact of the Vietnam War on Southeast Asia and the United States.

Critical Thinking

1. **Apply** Using examples from Asia, explain whether a country's economic progress is related to its form of government.
2. **Analyze** What impact has Japan's recovery since World War II had on global affairs?
3. **Synthesize** Explain how events in Asia since 1945 have influenced the population profile of the people of the United States.
4. **Analyze** How do you think the return of Hong Kong to China will affect China and Hong Kong?

---

5. North Korea's aim to unite Korea under communism; cold war tensions; stalemate with truce talks; Korea remained divided at 38th parallel
6. Vietnam devastated with about 2 million dead and 10 million refugees; all of Vietnam became Communist; conflict spread to other parts of Southeast Asia; discontent with the war at home and an American withdrawal from the conflict

Critical Thinking

1. Countries with relatively stable governments—such as the sometimes authoritarian Singapore and democratic Japan—have had the greatest economic success.
2. Japan's creation of an economy geared for exports has made Japan one of the world's economic giants.
3. Turmoil in Southeast Asia caused a large immigration to the United States.

5. Analyze United States President Richard Nixon visited China in 1972. What historic change in United States policy did this visit signal?

Understanding Themes

1. **Change** What factors account for Japan's economic recovery and prosperity since World War II?
2. **Revolution** What changes did the Communist takeover of 1949 bring to China during the 1950s? How have policies changed since the 1970s?
3. **Regionalism** What basic reason keeps Korea divided into two nations?
4. **Conflict** How did the United States get involved in the war in Vietnam?
5. **Diversity** Why was India partitioned in 1947? Why did Pakistan later split into two separate nations?
6. **Cultural Diffusion** What new national and ethnic groups have come to once predominately British Australia as a result of changes in immigration since World War II?

Linking Past and Present

1. The era from about 1950 to the present and on into the twenty-first century has been called the Asian Century. Explain what name you would give to the 100 years prior to 1950.
2. The involvement by the United States in Vietnam was based on the domino theory and the Truman Doctrine, both of which declared the United States commitment to containing communism. What circumstances, if any, do you think would justify United States involvement overseas today?

Geography in History

1. **Region** Refer to the map on this page. What generalization describes the diverse economies of East Asia and the Pacific?
2. **Place** What nations make up the middle-income economies group?
3. **Region** What do the economies of Japan and Australia have in common according to the map?

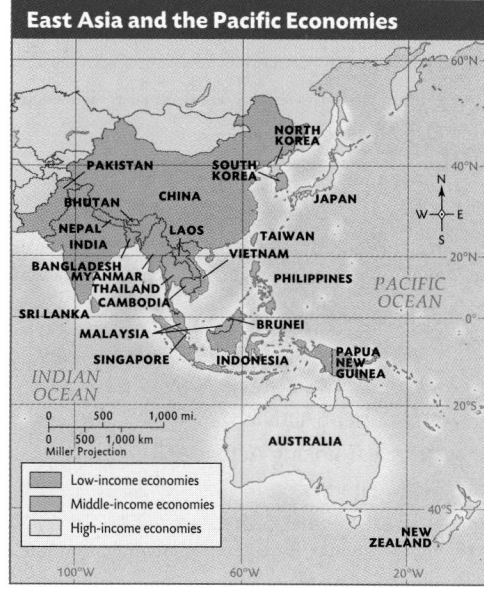

East Asia and the Pacific Economies

- Low-income economies
- Middle-income economies
- High-income economies

Skill Practice

Look at the weather page in a newspaper or on the Internet. Choose a city in Asia or the Pacific that is listed in the weather report for international cities. Using an electronic spreadsheet over a 4-week period, note both the high and low temperature for each day. Insert an equation to calculate the average temperature for the first day. Copy the equation to calculate the average temperature for each day. Using your spreadsheet software, create a line graph showing the daily high, daily low, and the daily average temperature for this 4-week period.

---

between Hindus and Muslims; a civil war between Urdu-speaking West Pakistan and Bengali-speaking East Pakistan

6. **CULTURAL DIFFUSION** southern and eastern Europeans, Asians

Linking Past and Present

1. The American Century or the European Century, because of their economic and political dominance.
2. prevention of genocide and other types of humanitarian aid

Geography in History

1. Most are low-income; only 3 high-income
2. South Korea, Thailand, Malaysia, Philippines, Brunei, Papua New Guinea
3. high-income economies

Skill Practice

Answers will vary depending on the city chosen to track.

? Chapter Bonus Test Question

Ask students: How convincing are arguments by developing nations that democracy should be sacrificed in the name of promoting economic growth and public safety? Support your answer with examples from specific countries studied in this chapter. *(The end justifies the means, and countries such as Singapore are cleaner and safer than the United States, with a higher general standard of living, even if there is political repression; or, the end does not justify the means, and people are better served by democratic countries, even if some citizens do not have an economic safety net.)*

---

4. Hong Kong's economic power may further open China to outside influences; or China may limit Hong Kong's liberties.
5. It led to the establishment of diplomatic relations with the People's Republic of China.

Understanding Themes

1. **CHANGE** MacArthur's policies, Japanese government-business cooperation, political stability
2. **REVOLUTION** the 1950s: state-run economy, close ties to Soviets; since the 1970s: split with Soviets, closer ties to West, market reforms with Communist political controls
3. **REGIONALISM** North Korea remains a Communist dictatorship, and South Korea fears its military threat.
4. **CONFLICT** support of its ally, France in Indochina
5. **DIVERSITY** because of differences

A complete, 1-page lesson plan is provided for each section in the *Reproducible Lesson Plans* booklet.

Africa

CHAPTER RESOURCES

	Reproducible Resources	Multimedia Resources
Chapter Opener	Chapter Themes: Graphic Organizer 23 Historical Significance Chapter Activity 23	MindJogger Videoquiz
Chapter Enrichment	Vocabulary Activity 23* Time Line Activity 23 Mapping History Activity 23 History Simulation 23 Geography and History Activity 23 Source Reading 23 People in World History Profiles 65, 66 World Art and Music Activity 23 Enrichment Activity 23 Critical Thinking Activity 23 Skill Reinforcement Activity 23 Writer's Guidebook, Lesson 12 Performance Assessment Activity 23	World History and Art Transparency 45, *The Liberated African Woman*; 46, *Bedouin Woman's Headpiece* Chapter Transparency 23 NGS PicturePack Transparencies: Physical Geography of the World Vocabulary PuzzleMaker Software Picture Atlas of the World World Music: Cultural Traditions, Lesson 6 Turning Points in World History: *End of Apartheid* STV: World Geography, Vol. 2, *Africa*
Chapter Review/Reteaching	Reteaching Activity 23 Skill Reinforcement Activity 23 Spanish Chapter Summary 23	Chapter 23 Digest Audiocassette, Activity, Test* Vocabulary PuzzleMaker Software Student Self-Test and Review Software MindJogger Videoquiz
Chapter Evaluation/Testing	Performance Assessment Activity 23 Chapter 23 Test, Forms A and B	Testmaker

* Also available in Spanish

0:00 OUT OF TIME? Assign the Chapter 23 summary in the Unit 6 Digest on pages 803–805, and the Chapter 23 Audiocassettes.

Block Schedule

Block scheduling differs from traditional class scheduling in the amount of time allotted to each period. The extended time frame provided by block scheduling affords you the opportunity to implement a greater number of research-oriented and activity-intense projects to motivate and involve your students. Activities that are particularly suited to use within the block scheduling framework are identified throughout this chapter by the following designation.

KEY TO ABILITY LEVELS

Teaching strategies have been coded for varying learning styles and abilities.

L1 **BASIC** activities for all students
L2 **AVERAGE** activities for average to above-average students
L3 **CHALLENGING** activities for above-average students
LEP **LIMITED ENGLISH PROFICIENCY** activities

Use Glencoe's *Presentation Plus!* multimedia teacher tool to easily present dynamic lessons that visually excite your students. Using Microsoft PowerPoint® you can customize the presentations to create your own personalized lessons.

SECTION RESOURCES

Daily Objectives	Reproducible Resources	Multimedia Resources
Section 1 **African Independence** Describe how African nations won their independence after World War II.	Reproducible Lesson Plan 23-1 Vocabulary Activity 23* Guided Reading Activity 23-1* Time Line Activity 23 People in World History Profile 65 Section Quiz 23-1*	Section Focus Transparency 23-1 Chapter Transparency 23 World History and Art Transparency 46, *Bedouin Woman's Headpiece* NGS PicturePack Transparencies: Physical Geography of the World Student Self-Test and Review Software Testmaker Picture Atlas of the World
Section 2 **Africa Today** Explain what kinds of governments ruled in Africa from the 1970s to the 1990s.	Reproducible Lesson Plan 23-2 Vocabulary Activity 23* Guided Reading Activity 23-2* People in World History Profile 66 Section Quiz 23-2*	Section Focus Transparency 23-2 Student Self-Test and Review Software Testmaker World Music: Cultural Traditions, Lesson 6 Picture Atlas of the World Turning Points in World History: *End of Apartheid*
Section 3 **Africa's Challenges** Identify the challenges faced by modern African nations in their quest for political and economic independence.	Reproducible Lesson Plan 23-3 Guided Reading Activity 23-3* Reteaching Activity 23 Enrichment Activity 23 Section Quiz 23-3* Performance Assessment Activity 23 Spanish Chapter Summary 23	Section Focus Transparency 23-3 World History and Art Transparency 45, *The Liberated African Woman* Vocabulary PuzzleMaker Software Student Self-Test and Review Software Testmaker Picture Atlas of the World STV: World Geography, Vol. 2, *Africa*

* Also available in Spanish

Chapter Activities

✔ Performance Assessment Activity

A Letter to a Young African Have students write letters to a high school student in Africa who is living with the challenges addressed in this chapter. Have students organize their letters around the question of why political independence was easier to achieve than economic independence for most African nations. Ask students to suggest reasons why it is sometimes easier to solve political problems than economic problems and have them give examples from their own experiences or from recent United States history.

Possible Rubric Features
Concept attainment, critical thinking, elaboration and organization of letter, analysis of relationships, persuasion

• *For an additional activity, refer to Activity 23 in the* Performance Assessment Strategies and Activities *booklet.*

ACTIVITY

From the Classroom of...

**Anna Mae Grimm
Homestead High School
Mequon, WI**

Experiencing Apartheid
For one class period, designate about half the students in the class to be part of an "underclass" that will not be allowed to participate in activities with the rest of the class. Have the "underclass" sit at the back of the room. Provide an interesting activity for the rest of the class, and assign the separated students routine worksheets. Hold an election during the class period (for example, elect a discussion leader) and exclude the separated students from the voting.

During the next class period, discuss how students felt during the simulation—both those in the "underclass" and those in the mainstream. Use this as a springboard for discussing apartheid in South Africa.

MULTIPLE LEARNING STYLES

Verbal/Linguistic
Have students read and write brief reviews of a short story, play, novel, or poem by a contemporary African author.

Visual/Spatial
Have students create a piece of art based on an African model.

Auditory/Musical
Have students find recordings of modern African music by such popular artists as King Sunny Ade and Babatunde Olanji of Nigeria, Baaba Maal or Youssou N'Dour of Senegal, Ladysmith Black Mambazo of South Africa, or Thomas Mapfumo of Zimbabwe and play selected songs for the class.

Kinesthetic
Have students plan and attend a field trip to a nearby museum that displays African art and artifacts.

Additional Resources

NATIONAL GEOGRAPHIC SOCIETY

Teacher's Corner

INDEX TO NATIONAL GEOGRAPHIC MAGAZINE

The following articles may be used for research relating to this chapter:

- "Down the Zambezi," by Paul Theroux, October 1997.
- "African Gold," by Carol Beckwith and Angela Fisher, October 1996.
- "Ndoki—The Last Place on Earth," by Douglas Chadwick, July 1995.

NATIONAL GEOGRAPHIC SOCIETY PRODUCTS AVAILABLE FROM GLENCOE

To order the following products for use with this chapter, contact your local Glencoe sales representative, or call Glencoe at 1-800-334-7344:

- *STV: World Geography, Vol. 2, Africa (Videodisc)*
- *Picture Atlas of the World (CD-ROM)*
- *Physical Geography of the World (Transparencies)*

ADDITIONAL NATIONAL GEOGRAPHIC SOCIETY PRODUCTS

To order the following products for use with this chapter, call National Geographic Society at 1-800-368-2728:

- *South Africa: After Apartheid (Video)*
- *Baka: People of the Forest (Video)*

LOCAL OBJECTIVES

_____
_____
_____
_____
_____
_____
_____
_____
_____
_____
_____
_____
_____
_____
_____
_____
_____
_____
_____
_____
_____
_____

BIBLIOGRAPHY

Literature of the Period
Achebe, Chinua, and C. L. Innes, eds. **Heinemann Book of Contemporary African Short Stories.** Portsmouth, NH: Heinemann, 1992. Fiction about African social life and customs.
Readings for the Student
Davidson, Basil. **The Black Man's Burden: Africa and the Curse of the Nation-State.** New York: Times Books, 1992. Underlying causes of political conflict and instability in Africa since independence.
Readings for the Teacher
Malan, Rian. **My Traitor's Heart: A South African Exile Returns to Face His Country, His Tribe, and His Conscience.** New York: Atlantic Monthly Press, 1990. Reflections on South Africa by a descendant of one of the builders of apartheid.

*inter***NET**
CONNECTION
African resources on the World Wide Web
afrika.com:
http://www.afrika.com/index2.html

Introducing Chapter 23

CHAPTER THEMES

Chapter Themes are listed by section on this chapter opening page of the Student Edition. A corresponding theme-based activity is available under "TEACH," and a theme-based question is asked in the Section and Chapter Reviews.

The Storyteller

Historical Setting Mandela, born in 1918, spent 28 years (1962–1990) in prison for conspiring to overthrow the white-minority government of South Africa. During those years, his wife, Winnie, helped focus the world's attention on Mandela and make him a symbol of the struggle against apartheid. After his release from prison, his negotiations with white leaders led to the end of apartheid and establishment of a nonracial government system. For their joint efforts to end apartheid, Mandela and F. W. de Klerk, his predecessor as president of South Africa, shared the 1993 Nobel Peace Prize.

Historical Significance

Answers: *The European colonial empires in Africa were replaced by independent nations.*

Africa has become an international force, wielding more than a third of the votes in the United Nations General Assembly.

Using Your History Journal

Advise students, as they begin their clipping or paraphrasing, to concentrate on a single country or region of Africa about which they would like to learn more after concluding the chapter.

Chapter

23

1945–Present

Africa

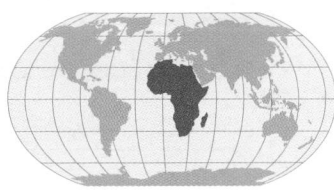

Chapter Themes

▶ **Nationalism** European empires crumble, and independent nations emerge in Africa. *Section 1*
▶ **Change** Some African nations move toward democracy and free enterprise economies. *Section 2*
▶ **Change** Ethnic, cultural, environmental, and economic challenges face newly independent African nations. *Section 3*

The Storyteller

From April 26 to 29, 1994, South Africa held its first election in which all of its citizens, regardless of race, could vote. The outcome was a landslide victory for nationalist leader Nelson Mandela and his African National Congress party.

On May 10, during his inauguration as South Africa's first black president, Mandela declared, "The people of South Africa … want change…. Our plan is to create jobs, promote peace and reconciliation and to guarantee freedom for all South Africans." Mandela's rise to office signaled a joyous dawn of freedom after decades of white-minority rule and racial discrimination in South Africa.

By the 1990s nearly 700 million people in more than 50 African countries had thrown off various forms of colonial rule and were charting new courses as independent nations.

Historical Significance

What sweeping changes came to Africa after World War II? What role does Africa play in world affairs today?

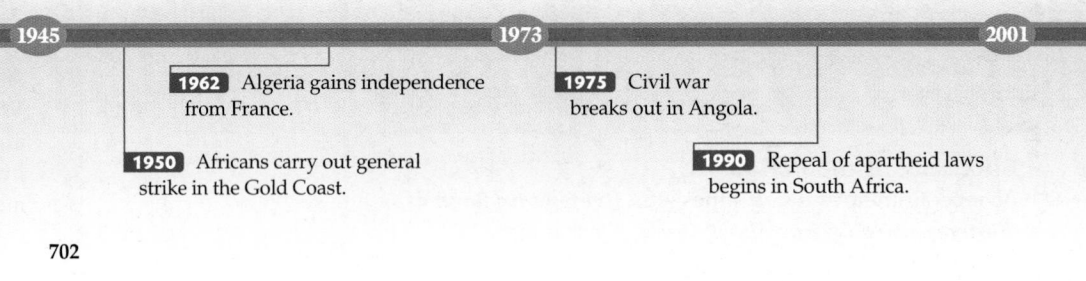

1945   1973   2001

1962 Algeria gains independence from France.

1950 Africans carry out general strike in the Gold Coast.

1975 Civil war breaks out in Angola.

1990 Repeal of apartheid laws begins in South Africa.

702

GEOGRAPHY CONNECTION

Location Have students use a world map to locate Africa. Compare the size of Africa with the size of the United States. *(It is much larger, closer to the size of North America.)* Show students a landform or vegetation map of Africa and ask them to describe the continent. *(About one-third is desert; it has grasslands, rain forests, and hot, dry savannas.)*

Visualizing History Children in Somalia, like this student, were doing their daily schoolwork in the midst of civil war, when United Nations troops arrived in 1992.

Visualizing History In 1991 fighting broke out among rebel groups in Somalia. By late 1992 the fighting had led to the deaths of about 30,000 people and had disrupted food production, threatening millions with starvation. With UN authorization, a coalition of military forces from several countries, led by the United States, went into Somalia to provide security for relief organizations distributing food. U.S. troops were withdrawn in March 1994, and the remaining UN forces left Somalia in March 1995.

✔ *Performance Assessment*

Refer to the activity on page 702C of the Planning Guide.

📁 For an additional activity, refer to Activity 23 in the *Performance Assessment Strategies and Activities* booklet.

Your History Journal

Watch for current articles about African nations in newspapers and magazines. Clip and paste or write headlines and paraphrase short excerpts from these articles in your History Journal.

GLENCOE
TECHNOLOGY

VIDEODISC
Use MindJogger to preview chapter content.

MindJogger Videoquiz

Chapter 23
Disc 3 Side B

Also available in VHS.

Chapter 23 *Africa* **703**

✚ EXTRA CREDIT PROJECT

Oral Report Ask students to choose three African countries, one in western Africa, one on the Mediterranean Sea, and one in eastern or central Africa. Have them research the economic problems each country faces and the policies each country is adopting to solve them. Have students summarize their findings in a brief oral report. Suggested resources: C. Wekesser and C. Pierce, *Africa: Opposing Viewpoints*; S. Baynham, *Africa from 1945*; B. Davidson, *The Black Man's Burden: Africa and the Curse of the Nation-State*; S. J. Ungar, *Africa: The People and Politics of an Emerging Continent.*

1948 South Africa introduces apartheid policies.

1957 Ghana becomes independent.

1970 Biafran conflict ends in Nigeria.

 **ind Out**

Answer: *Relatively small prewar efforts for freedom swelled into powerful mass movements.*

FOCUS

Section Objective

Describe how African nations won their independence after World War II.

**BELLRINGER
Motivational Activity**

Before taking roll at the beginning of the class period, project Section Focus Transparency 23-1 and have students answer the activity questions. Discuss students' responses.

This activity is also available as a blackline master.

Vocabulary Pre-check

Use Vocabulary Activity 23 to introduce vocabulary terms.
L1 LEP

Section 1

African Independence

Setting the Scene

▶ **Terms to Define**
colons, general strike, apartheid

▶ **People to Meet**
Muammar al-Qaddafi, Kwame Nkrumah, Ahmed Sékou Touré, Jomo Kenyatta, Nelson Mandela, Desmond Tutu

▶ **Places to Locate**
Sudan, Algeria, Ghana, Nigeria, Congo (Zaire), Kenya, Angola, Mozambique, Malawi, Zambia, Zimbabwe, South Africa

 **ind Out** How did African nations win their independence after World War II?

Storyteller

Meeting in an open field at Kliptown, South Africa, 3,000 delegates adopted the Freedom Charter in 1955. The Charter held out hope for a democratic nation: "We the people of South Africa, declare for all our country and the world to know: that South Africa belongs to all who live in it, black and white, and that no government can claim authority unless it is based on the will of all the people ... that our country will never be prosperous and free until all people live in brotherhood, enjoying equal rights and opportunities."

—from *South Africa, Challenge and Hope,* American Friends Service Committee, Lyle Tatum, editor, 1987

First free election in South Africa

After World War II, the desire for liberation that found expression in Asia also spread to Africa. On the vast African continent in 1945, only Egypt, Ethiopia, and Liberia were independent states. South Africa, although independent, was governed by a white minority that withheld freedom from most of the country's population. In other areas, Great Britain, France, Portugal, Spain, and Belgium still exercised direct colonial rule.

By the mid-1960s, these European countries had freed most of their African colonies. The southern part of Africa remained the only area of the continent where liberation movements encountered obstacles—in this case, from sizable European settler populations. The path to independence in Africa was often bloody, and once free, the new nations faced the enormous task of building modern societies.

TURNING POINT

A Changing Africa

Since the beginning of the colonial era, nationalist groups in Africa had resisted European rule, often violently. But following World War II, these relatively small efforts for freedom swelled into powerful mass movements.

Opposition to Empire

The democratic ideals for which the Allies fought in the war—self-rule and freedom from tyranny—inspired Africans, many of whom had fought in the Allied armies. "[We] overseas soldiers are coming back home with new ideas," wrote Nigerian Theo Ayoola, stationed with British troops in India. "We have been told what we fought for. That is freedom! We want freedom, nothing but freedom!"

Many people throughout the world were recognizing the hypocrisy and injustice of European

nations continuing to rule African populations while professing democratic values. In addition to the moral argument against colonialism, European nations faced political and economic changes that made it impractical to retain their African possessions. The European continent itself was devastated by World War II, and debt-ridden Europeans could scarcely afford to maintain empires abroad. Even so, the imperial nations of Europe as a matter of pride clung stubbornly to the idea of empire, making the inevitable changes more painful.

African Nationalism

What European imperial nations did not recognize were the changes occurring throughout Africa. In many colonies, nationalism was growing among the European-educated African elite who worked in colonial governments and in businesses. In the late 1940s, leaders emerged among this group, and rallied support for African independence.

Nationalist leaders found a ready audience for their ideas among workers in the fields, mines, and factories owned by overseas investors. World demand for African minerals and crops boomed after World War II, but Africa's European-owned industries appropriated the profits. Africans saw little change in their conditions, and their resentment of foreign rule grew.

North Africa

The movement for independence from European rule saw its first successes in North Africa. Italy ruled Libya, a large country west of Egypt, under a UN trusteeship. France owned colonial possessions—Tunisia, Algeria, and Morocco—in the rest of North Africa. All of the territories of North

Africa were Muslim and shared in a common Arab culture.

The only exception was **Sudan**—ruled jointly by Great Britain and Egypt—which had a large non-Muslim African population in its southern part. Sudan eventually became independent in 1956.

Libya

In 1951, Libya, once an Italian colony, became an independent monarchy. The discovery of oil in Libya in 1959 transformed the country from a poor, desert nation into one of the wealthiest in the world. Widespread discontent against the monarchy and the ruling class owning the oil wealth led to a military takeover in 1969 under Colonel **Muammar al-Qaddafi** (kuh•DAH•fee). Qaddafi established a socialist government to redistribute the national wealth. He also sought to spread his radical brand of nationalism to other parts of Africa and the Arab world.

Chapter 23   *Africa*   705

African Independence

Map showing African nations and independence dates

MOROCCO 1956, TUNISIA 1956, ALGERIA 1962, LIBYA 1951, EGYPT 1922, Western Sahara (Disputed Territory), MAURITANIA 1960, SENEGAL 1960, GAMBIA 1965, MALI 1960, BURKINA FASO 1960, NIGER 1960, GUINEA-BISSAU 1974, GUINEA 1958, BENIN 1960, CHAD 1960, SUDAN 1956, ERITREA 1993, DJIBOUTI 1977, GHANA 1957, TOGO 1960, NIGERIA 1960, CENTRAL AFRICAN REPUBLIC 1960, ETHIOPIA*, SIERRA LEONE 1961, CÔTE D'IVOIRE 1960, CAMEROON 1960, SOMALIA 1960, LIBERIA 1847, EQUATORIAL GUINEA 1968, GABON 1960, CONGO 1960, RWANDA 1962, UGANDA 1962, KENYA 1963, SÃO TOMÉ AND PRÍNCIPE 1975, DEMOCRATIC REPUBLIC OF THE CONGO 1960, Cabinda (Angola), BURUNDI 1962, TANZANIA 1961, SEYCHELLES 1976, MALAWI 1964, COMOROS 1975, ANGOLA 1975, ZAMBIA 1964, MOZAMBIQUE 1975, ZIMBABWE 1980, MADAGASCAR 1960, NAMIBIA 1990, BOTSWANA 1966, MAURITIUS 1968, LESOTHO 1966, SOUTH AFRICA 1931, SWAZILAND 1968, CAPE VERDE 1975

*Ethiopia was conquered by Italy in 1939 but regained independence in 1945.

Map Study
Between 1951 and 1993 more than 50 African colonies achieved independence.
Place What four African nations were independent before 1950?

Chapter 23
Section 1

TEACH

Guided Practice

THEME   Nationalism

Write on the chalkboard the following sentence from the statement of Theo Ayoola quoted on page 928: "[We] overseas soldiers are coming back home with new ideas." Ask students to describe some of the postwar ideas that led to the rise of African nationalism. (*realization that ideals for which the Allies fought the war were not being applied to Africans; realization that Africans were not sharing in wealth resulting from postwar demands for African resources*) **L1**

Map Study

Answer
Liberia, Egypt, Ethiopia, South Africa

Map Skills Practice

Reading a Map What African nations have gained their independence in the 1990s? (*Eritrea, Namibia*)

POINT

A Changing Africa
How did Africa change after World War II?
European empires came to an end, and independent states emerged in Africa after World War II.

 Chapter Transparency 23

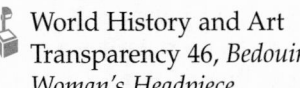 World History and Art Transparency 46, *Bedouin Woman's Headpiece*

COOPERATIVE LEARNING ACTIVITY

Geographical Map Have students separate the countries of Africa into five regions: north, west, central, east, and south. Organize the class into five teams, assigning one region to each team. Have the class create a wall-size map of the African continent, with each group researching its area and coordinating with other groups to produce the final map. Students should research the climate, landforms, and waterways of their region. Have team members illustrate the map and present a short oral presentation about their region. **L2**

TEACH

Tell students that the city of Banjul was formerly called Bathurst, after Henry Bathurst, who was British colonial secretary in 1816. In that year the British established a military post on the Gambia River to stop the slave trade and to serve as a trade center. **Why does the Gambian woman's dress include the portrait of a Senegalese leader?** *(The Gambia is completely surrounded by Senegal, and relations between the two countries have always been close.)*

CURRICULUM CONNECTION

THE ARTS
Tell students that only recently has the influence of African art on modern European art been fully recognized. Have students look at reproductions of traditional African sculptures and masks and then compare these works with the sculpture and painting of European modernists such as Picasso, Matisse, Brancusi, and Braque.

NATIONAL GEOGRAPHIC SOCIETY

PHYSICAL GEOGRAPHY OF THE WORLD TRANSPARENCIES

Display and discuss the physical features shown on the following transparencies:
41. Atlas Mountains, Morocco
42. Sahara in North Africa
44. Nile River, Egypt
51. Namib Desert, Namibia
53. Rain Forest, Zaire
57. Lake Victoria in East Africa

Michael Kirtley

Africa and Independence

This mother in Banjul, capital of The Gambia, combines something old and something new. She wears a traditional West African dress stamped with the colors of Africa: red, black, yellow, and green. Printed on the fabric is a portrait of two of Africa's independence leaders. On the left is Sir Dawda Jawara, who led The Gambia to independence in 1965. He remained president until 1994, when Captain Yahya Ajj Jammeh took power. On the right is President Abdou Diouf, who succeeded Senegal's great independence leader Léopold Sédar Senghor in 1981.

Keeping local traditions and languages—the pride in being African—while discarding the years of colonial rule and white supremacy became the task of the new leaders of West Africa. Where once there were 3 colonial empires, today there are 14 sovereign states in the region.

Independence from France, Great Britain, and Portugal was won peacefully. The task that now remains is to create and to sustain expanding economies. This is the hope of all West Africans, including this young mother and her children on Perseverance Street in The Gambia's capital. ⊕

Algeria

The French colonies of Morocco, Tunisia, and Algeria also wanted independence. France reluctantly granted independence to Morocco and Tunisia in 1956, but refused to do so in the case of Algeria.

Freedom for **Algeria** came only after one of the most costly wars in African colonial history. French settlers, called colons, had been coming to Algeria since the 1830s. By 1940 nearly 1 million colons had taken the best land and jobs in Algeria, ignoring the needs of 9 million Muslim Algerians.

Backed by Egypt, Morocco, and Tunisia, Algerian guerrilla fighters launched a war for independence in 1954. In response to guerrilla raids, French troops destroyed Algerian property, herded people into concentration camps, and used helicopters and heavy artillery to hunt down the rebels.

Despite French firepower, the guerrillas fought on. The controversial war forced the collapse of France's government, the Fourth Republic. After General Charles de Gaulle became president in May 1958, he promised self-determination for Algeria. Despite fierce resistance from the colons, de Gaulle arranged talks with the rebels that led to independence on July 3, 1962. The price of freedom had been eight years of warfare and more than 1 million deaths.

Ghana

In Africa south of the Sahara, mass independence movements pressured the colonial powers to relinquish control. Great Britain's richest colony, the Gold Coast, traveled a relatively easy road to independence, raising the hopes of other African nations for a smooth transition.

Before World War II ended, the British had begun to give the Africans of the Gold Coast more political rights. By then, well-educated African leaders had organized an independence movement. In 1947 the group asked the political activist **Kwame Nkrumah** (kwah•may ehn•KROO•muh) to lead them. Three years later, Nkrumah led a general strike, in which a large number of workers pressured the British for independence.

For his role in the strike, Nkrumah was jailed, but his efforts were effective. He soon moved from his jail cell to head a new government. In 1957 the

Visualizing History Kwame Nkrumah celebrates independence. Ten years of struggle had won freedom for Ghana and inspired other African nations to form national movements. *What led to Nkrumah's loss of power in Ghana?*

Gold Coast, now renamed **Ghana**, became the first African nation south of the Sahara to gain full independence after World War II.

The Nkrumah years came to represent the best and the worst in African leadership after independence. Ghana got off to a strong start, exporting cocoa, gold, and diamonds. It also had a skilled labor force. The Nkrumah government, however, mismanaged the economy. After Nkrumah was ousted by the army in 1966, one regime after another ruled Ghana, forcing the nation into a slow decline.

Guinea

Nationalist movements also took hold in France's African colonies south of the Sahara. Seeking to head off another "Algeria-like" conflict, France's President de Gaulle in 1958 proposed the creation of a French Community. Under this plan, France's African colonies south of the Sahara could choose to remain linked to France, with their foreign and economic policies under French control. The other option was for them to become completely

---

Visualizing History After the army deposed Nkrumah, President Sékou Touré of Guinea not only gave him political asylum but also declared him cohead of state.
Answer to Caption: *He was ousted by the army in 1966.*

Compare Remind students that American colonists had to fight for their independence from Britain and that Latin Americans fought Spain to create independent nations in the early 1800s. By the 1950s, why had European powers not learned that colonized people prefer independence over foreign rule? *(Students may realize that imperialism brought economic and other advantages that Europeans would not easily give up.)* **L2**

Independent Practice

Guided Reading Activity 23-1 **L1**

Time Line Activity 23

People in World History Profile 65

Literature Have students read Wole Soyinka's short drama *Death and the King's Horseman* and write a brief report describing the contrast it develops between Yoruba culture and British power. **L3**

Who?What?Where?When?

Buchi Emecheta was born in 1944 near Lagos, Nigeria, and moved to London in 1962. Her 1976 novel, *The Bride Price*, focuses on an intelligent Nigerian girl who confronts conflicts with her family when she elopes with a low-caste schoolmaster.

MEETING SPECIAL NEEDS ACTIVITY

Learning Style: Visual/Spatial Have students who learn best by producing graphic information create a "home page" for several African nations. Each page should consist of the country's flag, a picture of its ruler, a map and legend showing the major cities and geographic features, and other references appropriate to a web site. Have students share their home pages with the class. **L2**

Apartheid Have students research the policy of apartheid as practiced in South Africa from the 1940s until the 1990s. Ask them to write short reports explaining how the racial laws developed; how they affected the civil, human, and economic rights of black South Africans; and how they were ultimately abolished. **L3**

NATIONAL GEOGRAPHIC SOCIETY

CD-ROM

PICTURE ATLAS OF THE WORLD

Click the "Video" button of Botswana to see the wildlife of the Linyanti River.

Linking Past and Present

Ecological Imperialism The centuries of white settlement in South Africa have affected the region's ecology and worsened its droughts. The native thorn trees and baobabs resist drought, as do traditional crops such as sorghum and tubers. The European settlers, however, planted crops that required more water and put in lawns and swimming pools. They also imported pine and eucalyptus trees, which use great amounts of water.

Visualizing History Crowds in eastern Nigeria celebrate Nigeria's independence in 1960 with a folk-dancing and sports festival. *Why was the path to Nigerian independence easier than that of other African countries?*

independent—with no economic support from France.

Only Guinea (GIH•nee) under its nationalist leader, **Ahmed Sékou Touré** (ah•MEHD SEH•koo TOO•ray), wanted full independence. De Gaulle swiftly ordered all French officials out of Guinea and vowed not to help the new nation. The Soviet Union, however, promised aid to the new nation.

In a world dominated by the cold war, Sékou Touré's link to the Soviets angered de Gaulle, who feared that other African colonies would follow suit. To prevent this, France gave its remaining African colonies independence in 1960, this time with French help.

Nigeria

In the West African country of **Nigeria**, Africa's most populous nation, few Europeans had settled during the period of British colonial rule. The path to independence was therefore easier there than in the colonies that had sizable European minorities. With little resistance, the Nigerians won independence from Great Britain in 1960. Creating

a stable democratic nation was far more difficult, however.

Because Nigeria was contained within old colonial boundaries, the country's population consisted of 250 ethnic groups speaking 395 languages, as well as 3 major religious groups. Muslims dominated the north, followers of traditional African religions the east, and Christians the west. From 1960 to 1965, first one group, then another seized control of the central government.

By the mid-1960s, ethnic conflict drove the Ibo to set up the independent Republic of Biafra in the eastern part of Nigeria. After the creation of Biafra, civil war ravaged Nigeria for three years, killing more than 600,000. About 2 million Biafrans died of hunger as a result of the fighting. Biafra surrendered in January 1970. The Nigerian government then turned to rebuilding the country, developing the nation's rich oil reserves.

Congo

By the late 1950s the vast Belgian Congo in central Africa was ready for change. Belgian authorities, however, responded slowly to the independence movement and imprisoned nationalist leaders who demanded radical changes. Following riots in 1959, however, Belgium hastily granted independence in June 1960. The new country was called **Congo**. In the 1970s, it became known as **Zaire**.

Civil war broke out in Congo following independence between rival political groups and different regions. The rich copper-mining province of Katanga (now the Shaba region) seceded from the new nation in July 1960. UN peacekeeping forces arrived in Congo to prevent the superpowers from becoming involved. After settling differences with the central government, Katanga finally returned to Congolese rule, and UN forces withdrew in 1964. However, conflicts among rival political and ethnic groups continued to divide the country. Not until General Joseph D. Mobutu became dictator in 1965 was order restored.

East Africa

After World War II, nationalism also swept the East African countries of Uganda, Tanzania, and Kenya, all ruled by Great Britain. Uganda, which won independence in 1962, fell prey to ethnic conflicts and brutal military dictatorship.

By contrast, Tanzania, independent in 1961, developed a stable government that followed

MAKING CONNECTIONS ACTIVITY

Flora and Fauna Have students research to find out about the native plants and animals of Africa and how human behavior has affected them. Ask students to summarize their research in a brief written report in which they also consider the effect on the environment of the plants and animals introduced from elsewhere. **L2 LEP**

socialic principles. **Kenya**, however, attracted considerable global attention because of a combination of unique geographic and political characteristics.

Under British colonial rule, Kenya was dominated by European settlers who held control of the fertile highlands of central Kenya. The Kikuyu, the local African ethnic group, regarded this region as their homeland. Moreover, the Europeans banned all Africans from owning land. This discrimination fanned the flames of nationalism in Kenya.

During the postwar period, the nationalist leader **Jomo Kenyatta**, who had been living in Great Britain, brought his battle for independence home to Kenya. By this time, nationalist feelings in Kenya had become intense. A political movement for independence—the Kenya African Union—was formed, and it chose Kenyatta as its president in 1947.

Meanwhile, some Kenyans had formed an underground freedom movement, which the Europeans called the Mau Mau. The movement sought to unite Kenya's many African ethnic groups against British rule. In the early 1950s, it carried out attacks on European settlers, and the British government took military action against the movement. British authorities jailed thousands of nationalists, including Kenyatta, whom they accused of leading the rebellion. By 1956, the uprising had been crushed, but calls for freedom continued. The British finally granted Kenya its independence in 1963.

Kenyatta was elected Kenya's first president in 1964 and held office until 1978. He maintained a free market economy and made Kenya a popular spot for tourists and international businesses.

Angola and Mozambique

Portugal ruled the southern African countries of **Angola** and **Mozambique** with an iron hand. The Portuguese, governed by a dictatorship at home, refused to listen to nationalist demands and created conditions for brutal uprisings.

Starting in 1961 in Angola and 1964 in Mozambique, rebel groups waged guerrilla wars against Portugal. For over a decade, Portuguese troops were able to suppress the guerrillas. In 1974, however, Portugal itself underwent a revolution that overthrew the dictatorship. The new democratic Portuguese government, facing many problems at home, freed Angola and Mozambique in 1975. Both African countries eventually came under Marxist governments that took complete control of their economies.

Malawi, Zambia, and Zimbabwe

Throughout the late 1950s and early 1960s, Great Britain slowly gave up control of its other African colonies. In 1964, Nyasaland became **Malawi** (mah•LAH•wee), and Northern Rhodesia became **Zambia**. The future, however, remained uncertain for Rhodesia, with 4 million Africans and 250,000 Europeans.

As European Rhodesians saw new African nations coming into existence in the 1960s, they formed a party called the Rhodesian Front. Two years later, the Front took control of Rhodesian politics to keep Africans from gaining power.

Great Britain opposed the Front's goals and asked that Africans be given a greater share of political power. White Rhodesians were enraged. In 1965 Rhodesian Prime Minister Ian Smith declared Rhodesia independent. Although most of the world refused to recognize or trade with Rhodesia, the country did get support from South Africa, where a white minority also ruled.

In the 1970s, bands of guerrilla fighters began attacking Rhodesia's Europeans. European settlers began to flee, and the nation's economy was disrupted. In 1979 Smith agreed to negotiate with the African majority, and in 1980, Rhodesia—renamed **Zimbabwe**—won its freedom.

South Africa

After World War II, independent **South Africa** was governed by a white minority—most of British and Afrikaner descent—that denied basic freedoms to other minorities and the majority African population. British and pro-British Afrikaner South Africans controlled the government until elections in 1948 brought to power the nationalist Afrikaners. The nationalist Afrikaner government opposed

Footnotes to History

The Great Zimbabwe
Once winning freedom, many African nations took new names with great meaning for their people. Zimbabwe, for example, refers to the 1,000-year-old city of Great Zimbabwe. Massive, protective stone walls gave the city its name—*zimbabwe*—which means "stone enclosure."

Global Gourmet

South Africa Among the traditional specialties eaten by white South Africans is *boerewors*, an Afrikaner sausage dish. A staple food for black South Africans is *mealies*, a corn porridge.

Who?What?Where?When?

The *lukasa*, or memory board, is a small rectangular wooden panel produced by the Luba people of the Democratic Republic of the Congo (formerly Zaire). Each *lukasa* is used to store the history of the Luba kings, who reigned from the 1600s to the early 1900s.

NATIONAL GEOGRAPHIC SOCIETY

CD-ROM

PICTURE ATLAS OF THE WORLD

You and your students can see and read about the physical features of Africa by clicking the "Photos" and "Essay" buttons of individual countries in the region.

ASSESS

Check for Understanding
Assign Section 1 Review as homework or as an in-class activity.

▣ Use Student Self-Test and Review Software to review Section 1.

Evaluate
▱ Section Quiz 23-1

▣ Use the Testmaker to create a customized quiz for Section 1.

CRITICAL THINKING ACTIVITY

Synthesizing Information Have students reread the section and write two sentences for each of the countries discussed, summarizing how each attained independence. Then ask students to write a paragraph that answers the "Find Out" question on page 928. **L2**

Visualizing History Smoke rises from a burning tanker, set aflame by rioting students in Soweto, outside Johannesburg, South Africa. *What conditions in Soweto led to student protests and riots?*

Visualizing History The Soweto uprising began as a protest against a government order that students in the township's high schools be taught in Afrikaans, which blacks associated with their oppressors. **Answer to Caption:** *The inhabitants of the township, like other black South Africans, were oppressed economically and politically.*

Reteach

Have students state the country associated with the following names or terms: colons (*Algeria*); Nkrumah (*Ghana*); Sékou Touré (*Guinea*); Lumumba, Tshombe, Mobutu (*Democratic Republic of the Congo, fromerly Zaire*); Ibo, Biafra (*Nigeria*); Kenyatta (*Kenya*); Smith, Mugabe (*Zimbabwe*); apartheid, Afrikaners, ANC, Mandela, Botha, de Klerk (*South Africa*).

Enrich

Have students write a report on *Things Fall Apart*, the first novel of Nigerian author Chinua Achebe, or watch the film *The Camp at Thiaroye* by Ousmane Sembene, Africa's premier director.

CLOSE

Have students write one paragraph in which they describe the main differences between pre-World War II Africa and Africa today. (*Answers should include mention of independence and the independent nations' attempts to establish more economic autonomy and diversification, increased political involvement of the population, and accelerated modernization of national infrastructures.*)

South Africa's remaining ties to Great Britain and had a strong belief in its divine right to rule the country. Committed to white supremacy, the nationalist Afrikaners legalized and strengthened a policy of racial separation between blacks and whites called apartheid.

Enforcement of Apartheid

Under apartheid—meaning "apartness"—white, black, and mixed races were strictly segregated. Black South Africans suffered the worst under this legalized segregation. Apartheid laws defined whom blacks could marry and where they could travel, eat, and go to school. Blacks could not vote or own property. To enforce separation of the races, the government moved thousands of blacks to desolate rural areas that it called "homelands," where jobs and food were scarce. Those who were able to get low-paying jobs in the cities were forced to live in wretched, fenced-in townships like Soweto, on the outskirts of Johannesburg. Blacks had to carry identity cards at all times. Under the repressive police state, blacks could be jailed indefinitely without cause.

African Resistance

Black nationalist groups, such as the African National Congress (ANC), peacefully demanded reforms, but the government moved against the resistance. By the 1960s ANC leader **Nelson Mandela** was leading a military operation to press for change. In 1962 he was jailed on charges of treason, becoming a symbol of the struggle for freedom in South Africa.

International criticism of apartheid led to South Africa's increasing political isolation from the 1960s to the 1980s. South Africa, for example, was not welcome in the Commonwealth of Nations, the United Nations, and the Olympics. Many nations eventually imposed sanctions on South Africa, moves designed to hurt South Africa's economy. Within South Africa itself, massive protests developed after police fired on a student march in the black township of Soweto in 1976. During the 1980s, Archbishop **Desmond Tutu**, the head of South Africa's Anglican Church, emerged as a major advocate of nonviolence and interracial reconciliation in the struggle against apartheid. In 1984 he was awarded the Nobel Peace Prize.

SECTION 1 REVIEW

Recall
1. **Define** colon, general strike, apartheid.
2. **Identify** Muammar al-Qaddafi, Kwame Nkrumah, Ahmed Sékou Touré, Jomo Kenyatta, Nelson Mandela, Desmond Tutu.

3. **Explain** How did Ghana serve as a model for nationalists in other African countries?

Critical Thinking
4. **Applying Information** How did the presence of large populations of European descent in Algeria, Kenya, Zimbabwe, and South Africa affect African nationalist movements?

Understanding Themes
5. **Nationalism** What impact did nationalist movements have on Africa after World War II?

SECTION 1 REVIEW ANSWERS

1. The words are defined in the Glossary.
2. Qaddafi, 705; Nkrumah, 707; Sékou Touré, 708; Kenyatta, 709; Mandela, 710; Tutu, 710
3. the first sub-Saharan colony to gain full independence; it did so with relative ease, encouraging other nationalists
4. White colonists resisted efforts to give black majorities political control. In Algeria and Rhodesia, colonists even defied their home countries' demands for political change.
5. **NATIONALISM** Nationalist movements paved the way for independence.

1978 Daniel T. arap Moi becomes president of Kenya.

1994 African National Congress wins South Africa's first open, multiracial elections.

Section 2

Africa Today

Setting the Scene

▶ **Terms to Define**
genocide, clan

▶ **People to Meet**
Muammar al-Qaddafi, Mobutu Sese Seko, Daniel T. arap Moi, F.W. de Klerk, Nelson Mandela

▶ **Places to Locate**
Namibia, Eritrea, Libya, Democratic Republic of the Congo, Rwanda, Burundi, Somalia

 **ind Out** What kinds of governments ruled in Africa from the 1970s to the 1990s?

The Storyteller

Fidele Nshogoza had been monitoring gorillas for 18 years. In the gorilla parks of the Virunga volcano range of east central Africa, he worked to prevent war and poaching from wiping out the animals he loved. "Gorillas are better than us," he explained. "They are peaceful. They have no tribes. When they fight it is for good reason." Fidele knew the horror of warfare. An ethnic Hutu, he fled over the volcanoes after the 1994 Tutsi victory. Two of his children almost died in a refugee camp—one of seven huge camps in Zaire [now the Democratic Republic of the Congo] that sheltered more than 700,000 ethnic Hutus.

Hutu children in a refugee camp

—adapted from "Gorillas and Humans: An Uneasy Truce," by Paul F. Salopek in *National Geographic*, October 1995.

By the late 1990s, Africa had experienced both setbacks and gains. Beginning in the early 1980s, devastating droughts ravaged large areas of the continent. The ups and downs of the world economy as well as political and ethnic conflict also negatively affected African nations.

Still there were reasons for celebration. Since the late 1970s, three new nations had emerged—Zimbabwe and **Namibia** in southern Africa (1980 and 1990), and **Eritrea** in the northeastern part of the continent (1993). Progress also was made in settling some of the civil wars that ravaged the continent. The most remarkable achievement was the dismantling of apartheid in the Republic of South Africa.

North Africa

The 1980s and 1990s saw widespread economic and political unrest in the North African countries of Algeria, Morocco, and Tunisia. A soaring population and increased industrialization led to the growth of the cities. Urban growth rates were further heightened as people from the countryside crowded into urban areas in hope of finding food, shelter, and work. When governments proved unable to provide decent housing and steady jobs, many people turned to a strict practice of Islam or to radical political movements in an effort to solve their problems.

Algeria

The greatest challenge to established government in the region took place in Algeria. In a free election in 1992, the people of Algeria elected to the national legislature a majority of members who favored greater recognition of Islamic laws and values. The more moderate government, however, ignored the election results and dissolved the legislature. Military leaders then took control of Algeria.

Chapter 23 *Africa* **711**

SECTION THEME

▶ **Change** Some African nations move toward democracy and free enterprise economies.

 **ind Out**

Answer: *African governments from the 1970s to the 1990s included one-party dictatorships, military rule, and multiparty systems.*

FOCUS

Section Objective

Explain what kinds of governments ruled in Africa from the 1970s to the 1990s.

BELLRINGER
Motivational Activity

Before taking roll at the beginning of the class period, project Section Focus Transparency 23-2 and have students answer the activity questions. Discuss students' responses.

This activity is also available as a blackline master.

Vocabulary Pre-check

Use Vocabulary Activity 23 to introduce vocabulary terms.
L1 LEP

SECTION RESOURCES

📁 **Reproducible Masters**
• Reproducible Lesson Plan 23-2
• Vocabulary Activity 23
• Guided Reading Activity 23-2
• People in World History Profile 66
• Section Quiz 23-2

📊 **Transparencies**
• Section Focus Transparency 23-2

Multimedia
💿 Student Self-Test and Review Software
💿 Testmaker
💿 World Music: Cultural Traditions, Lesson 6
💿 Picture Atlas of the World
💿 Turning Points in World History: *End of Apartheid*

TEACH

Guided Practice

THEME Change

On the chalkboard copy the section's opening sentence from page 711: "By the late 1990s, Africa had experienced both setbacks and gains." Underneath it, create two columns headed *Setbacks* and *Gains*. As you work through the section with the class, have students enter events in the appropriate columns. **L1**

Government Ask students to discuss the aftermath of the elections of 1992 in Algeria as described on pages 711–712. **Can the military's banning of the Islamic movement be justified in any way?** *(Some students might argue that the end—the suppression of theocratic rule—justifies the means. Others might argue that denying power to the Islamic movement can only further radicalize its supporters, and any subversion of democracy is wrong.)* **L2**

ABCNEWS INTERACTIVE™

VIDEODISC
Turning Points in World History

Side Two
Chapter 10

Title: *End of Apartheid*
Ask: What did the international community do to show disapproval of South African apartheid policies? *(South Africa was banned from the UN and Olympic Games and boycotted.)*

They banned the Islamic movement and arrested many of its members.

Armed conflict soon developed between the government and the Islamic opposition. By 1997, the unrest had claimed more than 60,000 lives. That year, the government claimed victory in a legislative election, but opposition groups questioned the election's fairness. Meanwhile, conflict continued to rage between government forces and the Islamic guerrillas.

Libya

During the 1980s, Colonel **Muammar al-Qaddafi** of **Libya** aroused great resentment among Western countries because of his foreign policy. The United States, accusing Qaddafi of aiding international terrorists, broke economic ties with Libya in 1986. Qaddafi in turn charged the United States with attempting to overthrow his government. Military encounters in the air between aircraft of the two countries were accompanied by United States bombing of Libyan military installations. Since the mid-1980s, declining oil revenue and a worsening Libyan economy have prompted Qaddafi to improve his relations with neighboring countries. Libya's suspected involvement with terrorist bombings of civilian airlines, however, has kept Libya isolated from the international community.

Nigeria

After independence, Nigeria and other nations in West Africa faced political conflicts and economic hardships. Some relied on military leaders or one-party systems to maintain order. By the late 1980s, a trend toward democracy and stability had emerged in the region. However, in the 1990s, some countries, such as Liberia and Sierra Leone, were torn by fierce conflicts between rival political and military groups.

Nigeria, the most populous West African country, continued to remain under military rule. After the Biafran war of the 1960s, Nigeria's military

Images *of the* Times

Toward a New Africa

Beyond independence, African nations work to promote economic growth, while preserving cultural traditions and developing democracy.

An earth satellite station 30 miles (48 km) from Nairobi, Kenya, signals Africa's connection to the telecommunications revolution.

712

Images *of the* Times Toward a New Africa

As in other parts of the developing world, Africans experience sharp contrasts between older ways of life and the latest technological developments. In the continent's rapidly growing cities, newcomers from small villages encounter movies, fax machines, and computers for the first time.

One sign that the telecommunications revolution has not yet saturated the African countryside is the fact that on average, there is only one television set for every 25 Africans. In the United States, by contrast, more than 98 percent of households have at least one television. In most of rural Africa, radios, not televisions or computers, are the lifeline to the rest of the world.

leaders worked to rebuild the country. They relied on oil for the country's economic prosperity. As oil prices rose in the 1970s, Nigeria grew wealthy. Its military leaders set as their goals industrial development, new schools, improved transportation, and development programs to raise the standard of living of all Nigerians.

World oil surpluses in the 1980s, however, dealt crippling blows to the Nigerian economy and weakened the military government. When oil revenues rose during the early 1990s, pressures increased for political reform. Nigeria's military government allowed free elections but prevented the newly elected government from taking power. It also cracked down on critics of its policies. In 1995, ignoring international protests, the military authorities hanged 9 opposition leaders. Two years later, they leveled charges of treason against the exiled writer Wole Soyinka, winner of the 1986 Nobel Prize for Literature. As the Nigerian government increased its crackdown, the international community mobilized an effort to impose economic sanctions on Nigeria.

Democratic Republic of the Congo

From the 1970s to the 1990s Congo continued under the rule of Mobutu, who took the name **Mobutu Sese Seko** and changed the country's name to Zaire. During his rule, copper prices rose and fell, bringing a boom and then a decline to Zaire's economy. Meanwhile, Mobutu ruled as a dictator, stole from the country's resources, and banned rival political groups.

Angered by Mobutu's misrule, guerrilla forces led by Laurent Kabila began a rebellion in late 1996. During the next several months, they took control of most of Zaire with little opposition from demoralized government forces. In May 1997, Mobutu gave up power and fled abroad. Kabila's forces then entered the capital, Kinshasa, where he named himself the new leader and changed the country's name to the **Democratic Republic of the Congo**. Kabila promised eventual elections, but his com-

World Music: Cultural Traditions, Lesson 6

Who?What?Where?When?

The Nobel Prize in literature was awarded to two Africans in recent years, Nigeria's Wole Soyinka (1986) and South Africa's Nadine Gordimer (1991).

Independent Practice

Guided Reading Activity 23-2 **L1**

People in World History Profile 66

Human Rights Have students use *Readers' Guide to Periodical Literature* to find articles about the execution of Ken Saro-Wiwa and the role played by the oil industry in that controversial event. Ask them to summarize their findings in a brief oral report. **L2**

Biography

The following videotape program is available from Glencoe:

- **Nelson Mandela: Journey to Freedom**

NATIONAL GEOGRAPHIC SOCIETY

CD-ROM

PICTURE ATLAS OF THE WORLD

Click the "Video" button of Tanzania to view the Masai people and Serengeti National Park.

Modern office buildings rise above a newly built monument and public garden in Pretoria, South Africa.

Tea pickers toil on a plantation in Kenya. Tea is one of Kenya's chief cash crops and a major export.

REFLECTING ON THE TIMES

1. In what ways could the connection to global telecommunications affect African economies? Cultural traditions?
2. Why are export products key to economic development?

713

ANSWERS TO REFLECTING ON THE TIMES

1. Access to global telecommunications might make Africa a more inviting place for international business and thus might strengthen African economies. The widespread exposure to foreign media might further erode African cultural traditions.
2. Exports bring in foreign capital and strengthen a country's balance of trade, although reliance on a single export makes the economies of some African countries dangerously sensitive to changes in world market prices.

714   Chapter 23   *Africa*

Visualizing History The young Nelson Mandela was groomed to assume high office. Instead, he decided to become a lawyer and also dreamed of contributing to the freedom struggle of his people. Later, working with the then-banned ANC, Mandela became known as the "Black Pimpernel" because of his numerous disguises and successful evasion of the police.
Answer to Caption: *South Africa held its first election open to all races.*

Global Gourmet

Ethiopia A popular Ethiopian food now being served in Ethiopian restaurants in the United States is a thick stew called *wat*. Vegetarian *wats* are made with lentils or chickpeas flavored with spices. Other *wats* contain chicken or meat and are sometimes served with hard-cooked egg. Most *wats* are flavored with a very spicy berbere sauce.

ASSESS

Check for Understanding

Assign Section 2 Review as homework or as an in-class activity.

 Use Student Self-Test and Review Software to review Section 2.

Evaluate

Section Quiz 23-2

 Use the Testmaker to create a customized quiz for Section 2.

Visualizing History South African President Nelson Mandela arrives in Paris, France, on a 1996 state visit with French President Jacques Chirac. *What event in 1994 was a turning point in South Africa's history?*

mitment to democracy was questioned when he banned political parties.

East Africa

In East Africa, ethnic unrest tore apart the inland countries of **Rwanda** and **Burundi**. Some countries in the region, however, enjoyed political stability. Uganda, after a period of harsh rule in the 1970s under dictator Idi Amin, moved toward a one-party system that at the same time encouraged free enterprise. Uganda's southern neighbor, Tanzania, combined a tradition of stable government with socialism. Economic difficulties in the 1990s, however, moved Tanzania toward free enterprise.

Kenya

From the early 1960s to the late 1970s, Kenya enjoyed political stability and economic prosperity under a one-party system. After President Kenyatta's death in 1978, **Daniel T. arap Moi** became the leader. In the 1980s Moi dealt harshly with political opponents wanting a multiparty system. A decade

later, he allowed a multiparty election in which he won endorsement. However, critics charged that the elections were not free or fair. In 1997 a powerful reform movement led by opposition politicians, human rights activists, and Christian and Muslim religious leaders pressured Moi to carry out genuine democratic reforms. At the same time, European governments threatened to cut aid to Kenya if Moi resisted change.

Rwanda and Burundi

During the 1990s, ethnic tensions in Rwanda and Burundi led to violent conflict. Most people in Rwanda and Burundi belong to the Hutu and the Tutsi ethnic groups. The Hutu are the largest group in both countries. Under Belgian colonial rule, the Tutsi were favored over the Hutu. Since the independence of Rwanda and Burundi in 1962, the Hutu have worked to regain power.

In 1994 the Hutu-led Rwandan government battled Tutsi-led guerrillas. In a genocide, or the deliberate killing of a racial or cultural group, Hutu forces killed some 500,000 people, mostly Tutsi, before the Tutsi guerrillas declared victory. Another 2 million people fled Rwanda and settled in camps on the border of Zaire and neighboring countries.

In 1996, conflict broke out in Burundi between the Tutsi-led government and Hutu rebels. Meanwhile, about 1.2 million Rwandan Hutu refugees in eastern Zaire faced mass starvation as ethnic and political conflict erupted in that country. A human catastrophe was avoided when hundreds of thousands of refugees voluntarily returned to Rwanda. In early 1997, tribunals in Tanzania and Rwanda began bringing to justice people accused of participating in the 1994 genocide.

Ethiopia and Somalia

In Ethiopia, military leaders in 1974 ousted the ancient monarchy of Emperor Haile Selassie I and replaced it with a Marxist dictatorship. While implementing land reforms, the new government persecuted and killed many of its opponents. These policies led to civil war. Movements for independence arose in the regions of Tigre and Eritrea.

By the early 1990s, widespread suffering caused by drought and civil war led to the fall of the military dictatorship. In 1991, rebel forces took control of the government and moved Ethiopia onto the path toward democracy. As a result of their victory, Eritrea became independent in 1993.

Drought and civil war also ravaged Ethiopia's neighbor, **Somalia**. There, in the 1980s, rival clans,

---

COOPERATIVE LEARNING ACTIVITY

The Arts Have students form five teams, one for each region of Africa: north, west, central, east, and south. Individual team members should choose different types of African art to research within their region, such as painting, pottery, metal and wood sculpture, textiles, body ornamentation, and music. Have students find examples of each type of art and copy or record them to bring to class. Have the teams work together to create a classroom or hallway exhibit, complete with captions explaining the display. Organize the exhibit by region or by type of art. **L2 LEP**

or groups of people related to one another, fought for control of the government. When a drought struck a few years later, many Somalis starved. Other countries sent food, but the fierce fighting kept much of it from reaching the starving.

In 1992, a UN-sponsored coalition of military forces led by the United States arrived in Somalia to protect relief organizations that were distributing food to needy Somalis. A year later, UN forces replaced most of the coalition troops. Tensions heightened when fighting broke out between the UN soldiers and the forces of one of the Somali clan leaders. By 1995, foreign troops, including United States forces, had withdrawn from Somalia after the worst of the famine had ended, and rival clan leaders had signed a peace settlement. Continued fighting, however, delayed progress toward stability.

South Africa

From the 1970s to the 1990s, South Africa and its neighbors Mozambique, Angola, and Zimbabwe experienced many sweeping changes. After a period of civil wars between Marxist and non-Marxist groups, Mozambique, Angola, and Zimbabwe moved toward peace and gradually abandoned socialism for free enterprise.

In South Africa, mounting pressure from the antiapartheid movement and from foreign countries brought a gradual end to apartheid. During the 1980s, the white-dominated South African government lifted the ban on interracial marriage, and the nation's sizable population of Asian and mixed-race people won voting rights.

In February 1990, South African President **F. W. de Klerk** surprised the world by releasing the black nationalist leader **Nelson Mandela** from prison. During the next few years, the South African government repealed the remaining apartheid laws. Talks began in 1992 between white

Kwanzaa Celebrates African American Culture

United States, 1966
Kwanzaa is a holiday based on a traditional African harvest festival. Developed in the United States in 1966 by Maulana Karenga, an African American cultural leader, Kwanzaa begins on December 26 and lasts for seven days. Each day is dedicated to one of the seven principles of African American culture that Karenga established. African American families celebrate Kwanzaa by lighting candles and exchanging gifts.

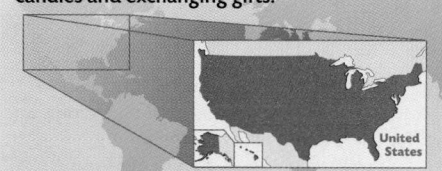

and black political groups that paved the way for a constitution, ending apartheid, and granting political equality to all South Africans regardless of race. A year later, black South Africans won full voting rights.

In April 1994, South Africa held its first election open to all races. The African National Congress won nearly two-thirds of the seats in the national legislature, and the legislature then elected Nelson Mandela president. Mandela recognized the importance of reconciling racial and ethnic groups and bridging the social and economic gap that separated white and nonwhite South Africans. He faced the challenge of raising the standard of living of disadvantaged South Africans while maintaining economic growth.

In 1997 South Africa began to prepare for a transition of power from Mandela to his successor. The likely person to become president of South Africa after the 1999 general election is the current deputy president, Thabo Mbeki.

South Africa
Why was 1994 a significant year for South Africa?
South Africa held its first election open to all races. For the first time, after years of apartheid, the country's black majority had a fair voice in the country's political life.

Reteach

Have students write a sentence to define each term and to identify each individual and each country listed in "Setting the Scene" on page 711.

Enrich

Have students watch the 1992 film *Sarafina!*, based on a popular antiapartheid stage musical, and write a brief review.

CLOSE

Have students list the ten countries discussed in this section (*Algeria, Libya, Nigeria, Democratic Republic of the Congo, Kenya, Rwanda, Burundi, Ethiopia, Somalia, South Africa*) and write a sentence for each that summarizes the changes it has undergone since the 1980s.

SECTION 2 REVIEW

Recall
1. **Define** genocide, clan.
2. **Identify** Muammar al-Qaddafi, Mobutu Sese Seko, Daniel T. arap Moi, F.W. de Klerk, Nelson Mandela.

3. **State** the causes and effects of the civil war in Rwanda.
Critical Thinking
4. **Synthesize** If you were a citizen of South Africa today, how would you describe recent

changes there?
Understanding Themes
5. **Change** What worldwide factors do you think account for the recent trend toward democracy in Africa?

SECTION 2 REVIEW ANSWERS

1. All vocabulary words are defined in the Glossary.
2. Qaddafi, 712; Mobutu Sese Seko, 713; Daniel T. arap Moi, 714; F. W. de Klerk, 715; Nelson Mandela, 715

3. ethnic tensions between the Hutu majority and the Tutsi; widespread fighting, genocide, and homelessness
4. Answers will vary depending on the race of the South African citizen students describe.

5. **CHANGE** Answers will vary. Students might feel that the democratic trend has been encouraged by the end of the cold war.

TEACH

Writing a Research Report Have students review the process of choosing a topic. Practice this process with them by suggesting a number of general topics about Africa that students must narrow down. General topics might include Africa since the cold war, Africa's natural resources, democracy in Africa, or the role of women in Africa. These could be narrowed down to Angola since the cold war, northern Africa's natural resources, democracy in Algeria, and African women in politics.

Additional Practice

📁 Skill Reinforcement Activity 23

📁 Writer's Guidebook, Lesson 12

Writing a Research Report

Writing a research report is similar to most other complex tasks. There are tools to use, skills to master, and steps to follow.

Learning the Skill

Select a topic that interests you. Brainstorming, skimming books and magazines, and talking with classmates can help.

Do preliminary research to determine whether your topic is too broad or too specific. Suppose you've chosen "Problems Facing Africa Today." The library's computers list more than 100 books on this topic. A more manageable topic might be: "Environmental Problems in the Sahara."

As early as possible, write a statement defining what you want to prove, discover, or illustrate in your report. For this topic, your statement might be: "Deforestation is the greatest environmental threat to North Africa."

- **Prepare to do research**. Formulate a list of main idea questions.
- **Research your topic and take notes**. At the library, use the computerized referral service to find suitable research sources. Note cards are a great tool for preparing a research report. They let you record and combine related facts and ideas from several sources. Prepare note cards on each main idea question listing the source information. Keep all the facts for each main idea together.
- **Organize your information**. Build an outline or another kind of organizer. Follow your outline or organizer in writing a rough draft.
- **Write a rough draft**. A research report should have three main parts: the introduction, the body, and the conclusion. The introduction briefly presents the topic and gives your thesis statement. In the body, follow your outline to develop the important ideas in your argument. Connect

these ideas with transitions. The conclusion summarizes and restates your findings.

In writing the rough draft write as quickly as possible without editing. Imagine that you are explaining your findings and ideas to an interested listener.

Revise the draft into a final report. Put it away for a day or so; then reread it with the cold, clear eye of an editor. Does the report have a clear structure—an introduction, a body, and a conclusion? Does the body contain all the main ideas arranged logically? Are there transitions to lead the reader from one thought to the next? If not, revise it and repeat the writing process. Correct spelling, punctuation, and grammar. Finally, make a clean copy.

Practicing the Skill

Suppose you are writing a report on recent changes in South Africa. Answer the following questions about the writing process.
1. How could you narrow this topic?
2. What are three main idea questions to use?
3. Name three possible sources of information.
4. What are the next two steps in the process of writing a research report?

Applying the Skill

Choose a topic and prepare note cards. Continue your research on this topic, organize your information, and write a short report.

For More Practice

Turn to the Skill Practice in the Chapter Review on page 723 for more practice in writing a research report.

ANSWERS TO PRACTICING THE SKILL

1. Answers will vary. Possible answers include: end of apartheid; voting rights for black South Africans; the African National Congress; Nelson Mandela; challenges for future government
2. Answers will vary depending on the topic.
3. Sources include books, magazines, and newspapers.
4. After selecting sources, students should prepare note cards, organize them, and then write a rough draft.

1963 African nations form Organization of African Unity (OAU).

1980s Famine ravages Ethiopia, Somalia, and other areas of Africa.

1990s A trend develops in Africa toward democracy and free enterprise.

Section 3

Africa's Challenge

Setting the Scene

▶ **Terms to Define**
Pan-Africanism, cash crop, subsistence farmer, desertification, literacy rate, negritude

▶ **People to Meet**
Kofi Annan, Léopold Sédar Senghor

▶ **Places to Locate**
the Sahel

 What challenges have modern African nations faced in their quest for political and economic development?

The Storyteller

The Sahara has its own voices. The abrupt changes from darkness to daylight are often accompanied by the shattering of the desert rocks, with a grating sound or a loud noise. Even the sand dunes talk: wind or even the pressure of a human foot will cause shocks and tremblings; then the countless grains of sand, rubbing gently together, will make a strange snoring noise.

Desert oasis

According to legend, these mysterious noises are the bursts of laughter of a genie named Rul—the bad angel of strayed travelers. When the wanderer has lost his way, when fatigue and thirst begin to confuse the mind, then the traveler is tormented by "the laughter of Rul."

—adapted from *Sahara, the Great Desert*, Emile Felix Gautier, 1935

African nations have seen enormous changes in less than half a century. In that short time, a largely rural continent has become increasingly urban, with ties to all parts of the globe. By the mid-1990s, African economies were growing at an average rate of nearly 5 percent, faster than for two decades. Africa also has become an international force, wielding more than a third of the votes in the United Nations General Assembly. In 1997 **Kofi Annan**, a career diplomat from the West African nation of Ghana, became secretary-general of the United Nations. He was the first African from south of the Sahara to serve in the post.

Search for Unity

After the excitement of independence celebrations had passed, Africa's new nations entered a difficult period. Many of them adopted the political borders that had been drawn by the colonial powers. These boundaries divided people with similar customs and faiths. Old ruling families and ethnic groups began to struggle for power, and civil wars often erupted.

National Unity

African politicians and parliaments were unable to stop the violence that sprang from these ethnic divisions. At first, many leaders in Africa governed through political systems inherited from their colonial predecessors—systems that were unfamiliar to many Africans. Often these systems did not work for African countries in the postindependence years. All too often, a nation's most powerful group, the military, stepped in to restore order.

By the 1970s, military leaders or one-party dictatorships ruled about half of Africa's newly freed nations. In some, like Nigeria, dividing strong regional groups into smaller states helped to break down some regional rivalry. By the late 1980s, however, military rule and one-party political systems

Chapter 23 *Africa* **717**

SECTION THEME

▶ **Change** Ethnic, cultural, environmental, and economic challenges face newly independent African nations.

 **Find Out**

Answer: *They have faced ethnic and cultural division, environmental obstacles, and economic development.*

FOCUS

Section Objective

Identify the challenges faced by modern African nations in their quest for political and economic independence.

BELLRINGER
Motivational Activity

Before taking roll at the beginning of the class period, project Section Focus Transparency 23-3 and have students answer the activity questions. Discuss students' responses.

This activity is also available as a blackline master.

Vocabulary Pre-check

Use the Vocabulary PuzzleMaker to create a puzzle that reinforces the vocabulary terms in this section. **L1**

SECTION RESOURCES

Reproducible Masters
- Reproducible Lesson Plan 23-3
- Guided Reading Activity 23-3
- Reteaching Activity 23
- Enrichment Activity 23
- Section Quiz 23-3
- Performance Assessment Activity 23
- Spanish Chapter Summary 23

Transparencies
- Section Focus Transparency 23-3
- World History and Art Transparency 45, *The Liberated African Woman*

Multimedia
- Vocabulary PuzzleMaker Software
- Student Self-Test and Review Software
- Testmaker
- Picture Atlas of the World
- STV: World Geography, Vol. 2

TEACH

Guided Practice

THEME Change

Write on the chalkboard each of the terms listed in "Setting the Scene" on page 717. Ask students to explain the relationship between each term and a change Africa has undergone in recent times. **L1**

History The modern city takes its name from *Enkare Nairobi,* or "cold water," referring to a freshwater spring that used to be located on the site.
Answer to Caption: *the creation of an all-African common market to promote Africa's economic growth and development*

NATIONAL GEOGRAPHIC SOCIETY

VIDEODISC
STV: WORLD GEOGRAPHY, VOLUME 2

Side 1
Frames 00001–49739
Title: *Africa* (in its entirety)
Subject: Describes the geographic contrasts and how people and animals have affected the natural environment of Africa
Ask: What desert in Africa is the world's largest? *(the Sahara)* What kind of technique is used to clear the land for planting? *(slash-and-burn)*

World History and Art Transparency 45, *The Liberated African Woman*

Visualizing History The Kenyatta Conference Center, named after Jomo Kenyatta—Kenya's first president, reflects the rapid growth and modernity of Nairobi, Kenya's capital. Founded in the late 1890s as a small railway settlement, Nairobi today is a busy metropolis of more than 1.5 million people. *What major goal has been set by the Organization of African Unity?*

had failed to fulfill their promises of order and economic progress. They were in decline in certain countries of Africa. Meanwhile, the end of the cold war and the collapse of the Soviet Union discredited the socialist economic model once popular among many African leaders. By the mid-1990s, some African countries had adopted multiparty systems and free enterprise approaches to economic development.

Pan-Africanism

Through a movement called Pan-Africanism, African leaders have sought to promote cooperation among all nations of the continent. In 1963, 32 African nations formed the Organization of African Unity (OAU) in Addis Ababa, Ethiopia. Although the original vision of creating a United States of Africa failed, the OAU did help to build a strong African identity and to coordinate national defense, health, and other policies.

Since its founding, the OAU has increased its influence in African and global affairs. During the 1970s and 1980s, member nations of the OAU pledged to remain neutral in cold war politics. To rid Africa of colonialism, the OAU backed nationalist movements in Angola, Mozambique, and Zimbabwe. As part of this undertaking, OAU members put pressure on white-ruled South Africa to end apartheid. A major achievement of the OAU during this period was the settlement of border disputes among member states.

In addition to working through the OAU, African states have cooperated on a regional level. In 1996, the Economic Community of West African States (ECOWAS) provided a 10,000-strong peacekeeping force to implement a cease-fire between warring groups in the West African nation of Liberia. Their efforts helped end a 7-year civil war that had killed 150,000 of Liberia's 2.4 million people and had left the country in ruins.

As they look to the twenty-first century, the OAU and other African organizations have set as their major goal Africa's economic growth and development. Member states of the OAU eventually plan to create an all-African free trade area.

Economic Development

In addition to creating a united continent, post-independence leaders of Africa worked to build strong economies in their nations. To move Africa's rural economies into the world of mining, manufacturing, and service industries, millions of people

---

COOPERATIVE LEARNING ACTIVITY

Debate Have pairs of students select one African country to represent at a mock session of the UN General Assembly. Before the session, have students brainstorm a list of issues they will discuss; these should include economic development, the environment, foreign aid, free trade, and urbanization. Have students research their country so they can represent its interests at the General Assembly session. **L2**

had to learn to read and write. Workers who made a living with their hands had to learn to operate machines in factories. Governments had to repair aging phone lines, railroads, and highways. Tanzania's President Julius Nyerere in the 1960s stated "while the great powers are trying to get to the moon, we are trying to get to the village."

Legacy of Colonialism

After independence, most African countries suffered from the economies created by colonial rule. As you remember from Chapter 16, Europeans obtained raw materials in Africa for their home industries and developed little industry in Africa. Under colonial rule, some Africans worked on European-owned plantations that produced **cash crops**, or crops grown for profit and exported. Most, however, were **subsistence farmers**, who grew only enough food to meet the needs of a family or village.

After independence, African leaders tried to remedy the imbalance between farming and industry. Many African countries were rich in one or two key resources or crops, but their economies could not provide the basic needs of their populations.

One-product economies, such as Ghana with cocoa and Burundi with coffee, were constantly at the mercy of changing prices for products on world markets. In addition, internal conflicts left some countries with ruined land and heavy war debts.

Economic Challenges

To bring economic advancement, African leaders decided to push the export of cash crops and raw materials while promoting industrialization. A lack of capital, skilled workers, and transportation systems, however, stood in the way of industrial growth. Seeking to overcome these obstacles, African countries turned to foreign governments and banks for loans to build factories, airports, harbors, and roads.

Reliance on foreign aid, however, provoked different reactions among Africans. Some nations followed a capitalist model and developed close ties with the West. Resource-rich nations, such as Nigeria with its oil wealth, tried to fund development from their exports of minerals and other raw materials. To assert their sovereignty, other nations decided to organize various kinds of

CONNECTIONS

Geography

The Moving Sahara

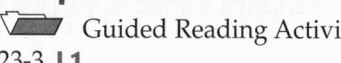

Deep in the Sahara, ancient rock paintings show grazing cattle and grasses where now there is only rock and sand. In recent times, farmers also grazed cattle in areas bordering the Sahara. But now those grasslands too are giving way to desert.

Before Africa was colonized, farmers cultivated fields until the soil was exhausted. When they moved to new plots of land, they let the old ones lie fallow, replenishing the soil. Under colonialism,

The encroaching desert better medical care caused a population boom and a growing demand for food. Europeans pushed Africans to grow big cash crops for export.

Destruction of the land increased. Farmers cut down trees to open up new fields and farmed land year after year without allowing the fields to lie fallow. Droughts in the 1980s brought disaster. People had to use grains for food instead of for seed. Without plants to anchor the soil, tons of topsoil disappeared. The mixture of overfarming, overgrazing, cutting trees, and drought pushed the Sahara south as fast as 90 miles (145 km) a year.

The solution to this problem lies with individual farmers. By planting trees, terracing fields, and fertilizing the soil, they may be able to slow the shifting of the Sahara.

Linking Past and Present — ACTIVITY

Examine what is causing the Sahara to spread south. Why do you think it is difficult to get individual farmers to change their agricultural practices?

Linking Past and Present

The Moving Sahara

Tell students that the name *Sahara* comes from *sahrá*, the Arabic word for "desert." From the late 1800s through the mid-1900s, France, Spain, Italy, and Britain occupied parts of the Sahara. In 1976 Spain became the last European country to give up control of the portion of the Sahara it claimed as its own.

ANSWERS

drought and poor farming practices; students may suggest that individual farmers may not understand the larger problems caused by their methods

Independent Practice

Guided Reading Activity 23-3 **L1**

Economics Have students compare the current economic situations in five African countries. Students should look up such information as per capita income and percentage of the labor force in agriculture and industry in a current almanac or other reference work. Have students display the data they have collected in chart form. **L2**

CD-ROM

PICTURE ATLAS OF THE WORLD

You and your students can see apartheid's legacy by clicking the "Video" button of South Africa.

MEETING SPECIAL NEEDS ACTIVITY

Mixed Learners Have language-delayed students and visual learners identify the different African nations by researching the current flags of several nations from different African regions. On a large sheet of paper or poster board, have students draw and color each nation's flag and describe briefly what the colors and the symbols mean. Encourage students to display their completed work in the classroom. **L1 LEP**

Linking Past and Present

African Music American singer, songwriter, and performer Paul Simon has helped to popularize African pop music around the world. Simon worked with black South African musicians to create his 1986 album, *Graceland*.

ASSESS

Check for Understanding

Assign Section 3 Review as homework or as an in-class activity.

 Use Student Self-Test and Review Software to review Section 3.

Evaluate

Section Quiz 23-3

 Use the Testmaker to create a customized quiz for Section 3.

Visualizing History The education of children like these kindergarten students in Angola is the key to the nation's future. *What is happening with literacy rates in Africa?*

government-controlled economies. This turn to socialism pleased many nationalists, who equated capitalism with colonialism.

No matter how they organized their economies, however, many countries failed to develop agriculture in their push to industrialize. Soon food crops for the domestic markets began to suffer and thousands of unskilled rural people moved to the cities, searching in vain for jobs. With many people out of work and unable to buy the products of new African industries, economies suffered.

Africa's soaring population also caused problems for economic growth. With economies geared for export, not enough food was produced for domestic needs. Governments had to increase borrowing from foreign sources, often to buy food, and their debts grew. As a result, not enough money was available to develop health care, food production, and industry necessary to improve overall standards of living.

Famine

Severe droughts in Africa also hindered economic development, causing food shortages and starvation in various parts of western, central, and eastern Africa. The causes of famine in Africa, as in other parts of the world, are complex and varied.

In the case of Africa in the 1980s, growing populations, a lack of capital, and overdependence on cash crops all contributed to this problem.

Another factor was the expansion of desert into formerly fertile areas. Countries crossed by the Sahara, Africa's largest desert, particularly faced the effects of desertification, or the transformation of fertile land into desert land. The worst occurrence of desertification took place in **the Sahel**, a West African grassland area bordering the Sahara. In addition to the ravages of nature, human activities, such as grazing livestock, planting, and the harvesting of trees, left the land in this environmentally fragile area dangerously exposed to erosion.

Signs of Hope

In the 1980s, Africa was a continent in crisis. A World Bank study showed that 21 of the world's 34 poorest countries were in Africa. More than 60 percent of all Africans received too little food each day, and more than 5 million children died every year. Relying on foreign help to remedy these problems, sub-Saharan African nations by the mid-1980s were $130 billion in debt.

As the year 2000 approaches, the problems of inadequate food, growing populations, and foreign debt still plague Africa, but some hopeful signs exist. More Africans than ever are attending school. Literacy rates, or the percentages of people who can read and write, have risen. Through education, many Africans are developing the skills needed to improve their standard of living.

In various parts of the continent, Africans are cooperating to improve their economies. To break their dependency on foreign countries, some African nations have formed regional associations that promote trade and economic contacts. An example of this type of organization is the Economic Community of West African States (ECOWAS), in which a number of West African nations have agreed to barter among themselves, trading products for oil instead of for scarce cash. In late 1992 Ugandan President Yoweri Museveni expressed a viewpoint that had become increasingly widespread throughout Africa: "We have to go back to the year 1500 [prior to colonialism], where we left off building an African economy, able to produce its own food, its own tools, its own weapons.... In short, we have to rely on ourselves."

MAKING CONNECTIONS ACTIVITIES

Languages More than 800 languages are spoken in Africa. Ask students to research and write a short report on Swahili or other native African languages; Amharic or other Afro-Asian languages; or Afrikaans, which is an Indo-European language. **L2**

Marriage Ask students to research and write a short report on marriage practices in different parts of Africa, including dowries and bride wealth. **L1**

Visualizing History African American children celebrate Kwanzaa, a festival held in late December since 1966. *What is the purpose of such poems as "My Africa"?*

African Identity

❝ I love a world,
This priceless world,
Sweet home of haunting melodies
And roll of tom-toms—
My Africa. ❞

—Michael Dei-Anang,
from the poem "My Africa"

In 1963 the African American poet Langston Hughes gathered nearly 100 African poems into a collection called *Poems from Black Africa*. It includes this one by Dei-Anang, a poet and government official in Ghana.

"Usually," Hughes wrote in the foreword, "poets have their fingers on the emotional pulse of their peoples." The poetry of Dei-Anang, like that of other Africans, had begun to rekindle a deep pride among Africans in their heritage.

During the colonial era, Africans had learned much, both good and bad, from Europeans. There remained the idea, although not accepted by all Africans, that European culture was superior to African culture in art, music, literature, and technology.

As independent nations emerged on the continent, many African leaders stressed the need to take pride in Africa. In Senegal, a former French colony, President **Léopold Sédar Senghor** published poems that expressed his love of Africa. Because Africans had never lost touch with nature, he thought, they could help restore "a world that has died of machines and cannons." Senghor helped found a poetry movement called negritude, an effort to recapture black Africa's past dignity.

During the decades since independence, African artists and writers have built on this foundation of pride. Theater groups, filmmakers, novelists, painters, and others have explored the pain of colonialism as well as the modern problems of corruption and hunger. Music, in particular, developed as a form of social protest in countries such as South Africa.

Open now to influences from around the globe, Africans have also created exciting new art forms. Congolese music, for instance, a mix of African, Latin American, and Caribbean styles, brings pleasure and delight to people in all of Africa and around the world.

Reteach

Ask students to explain (1) the relevance of the Pan-African movement and the OAU to Africa's search for political unity; (2) the causes and significance of drought in Africa; and (3) the role of negritude in the formation of an African identity.

 Reteaching Activity 23

Enrich

Have students read a work by Nobel laureates Wole Soyinka or Nadine Gordimer and write a short report describing the novel's treatment of challenges facing Africa in recent times.

 Enrichment Activity 23

CLOSE

Have students write one paragraph in which they summarize the main challenges facing African countries today. (*Answers should include a search for unity, economic development, and the preservation of an African identity.*)

SECTION 3 REVIEW

Recall
1. **Define** Pan-Africanism, cash crop, subsistence farmer, desertification, literacy rate, negritude.
2. **Identify** Kofi Annan, Organization of African Unity, Economic Community of West African States, Léopold Sédar Senghor.

3. **Discuss** the goal the OAU has for the future development of African economies.
Critical Thinking
4. **Evaluating Information** What might have happened if African nations had spent funds producing more food for their people instead of growing cash crops and industrializing their economies?
Understanding Themes
5. **Change** What trend influenced African political systems by the early 1990s? How do you think this will affect the political future of African nations?

SECTION 3 REVIEW ANSWERS

1. The words are defined in the Glossary.
2. Annan, 717; OAU, 718; Economic Community, 720; Senghor, 721
3. promote Africa's economic growth and development by creating an all-African common market by the year 2000
4. Students may feel that a better balance between food and export crops might have reduced hunger and lessened dependence on foreign governments and banks for loans.
5. **CHANGE** The new trend favored multiparty systems and free enterprise approaches. Students may feel that these changes promise to improve life for Africans.

Chapter 23 Review

GLENCOE
TECHNOLOGY

VIDEODISC
Use MindJogger to review students' knowledge of the chapter.

MindJogger Videoquiz

Chapter 23
Disc 3 Side B

Also available in VHS.

Answers

Using Key Terms
1. e   **4.** i
2. f   **5.** j
3. h

Using Your History Journal

Suggest that students write their essay as if it were the year 2020 and that they are looking back on how their chosen nation has fared over the previous two decades.

Reviewing Facts

1. The democratic ideals for which the Allies fought in the war inspired Africans. African nationalists found support among workers who resented foreign exploitation of Africa.
2. opposition politicians, human rights activists, and Christian and Muslim religious leaders
3. Oil was discovered there in 1959.
4. The Rhodesian Front thwarted Britain's wish to share political power with Africans and in 1965 declared independence; guerrilla warfare caused European settlers to flee and the economy to crumble, driving the Front to negotiate with the African majority and leading to the emergence of a free Zimbabwe.
5. Both led the struggle against

722 Chapter 23 *Africa*

Connections Across Time

Historical Significance The nations of Africa are very old—and very new. They have ancient cultures, but their political systems are still young. Most have been independent for only a generation. Their efforts to forge effective governments are complicated by debt, hunger, and ethnic strife.

Despite difficulties, Africans have made progress. Nations, such as Angola, South Africa, and Zimbabwe, have developed peaceful ways of dealing with their challenges. Also, education and a higher standard of living are being enjoyed by more people now than in the past.

Using Key Terms

Write the key term that completes each sentence. Then write a sentence for each term not chosen.

a. general strike   f. desertification
b. colons   g. cash crops
c. clans   h. apartheid
d. negritude   i. genocide
e. Pan-Africanism   j. literacy rate

1. Through the movement of _____, African nations seek to promote oneness and cooperation throughout the continent.
2. _____, or the transformation of fertile land into desert land, affected countries near the Sahara.
3. In 1948, the South African government began legalizing and strengthening a policy of racial separation known as _____.
4. The deliberate killing of a racial, ethnic, or national group is known as _____.
5. _____, the percentage of people who can read and write, has increased in Africa in recent years.

Technology Activity

Using a Spreadsheet Search the Internet or a library for sources about the independence of three African countries. Use a spreadsheet to organize your information. Include headings such as name of country, highlights of colonial history, year of independence, how independence was attained, current economy, and present form of government. Include a map showing the political borders of the three countries and their capitals.

722   Chapter 23   *Africa*

Using Your History Journal

Review your news clippings on Africa. Write a short essay on the future of an African nation. What are the challenges that your chosen nation faces? What are the prospects for peace and progress?

Reviewing Facts

1. **History** Discuss the reasons for the growth of nationalism in Africa after 1945.
2. **Culture** Identify the groups that pressed for reform in Kenya during the 1990s.
3. **Economics** Explain the reason for Libya's postwar economic prosperity.
4. **History** Discuss the events leading to Zimbabwe's late independence in 1980.
5. **History/Culture** Describe the roles of Nelson Mandela and Desmond Tutu in South Africa from the 1960s to the 1990s. What was the outcome of their efforts?
6. **History** Discuss developments in Somalia during the 1980s and early 1990s.
7. **Culture** Identify the changes that are occurring in African culture.

Critical Thinking

1. **Analyze** What are the benefits and drawbacks of Africa's cultural and ethnic diversity?
2. **Apply** How would you solve the problem of food shortages in various parts of Africa?
3. **Analyze** How did the political boundaries drawn by European colonial powers cause

---

apartheid in South Africa; ANC president Mandela carried out military operations, was jailed, and became a symbol of the struggle; Tutu was Anglican archbishop of Cape Town and urged nonviolent action and interracial reconciliation. Their efforts, with the help of the international community, brought an end to apartheid and the founding of genuine democracy in South Africa.
6. Rival clans fought for control of the govern-

ment, keeping food aid from reaching famine victims. UN forces sent in to protect the distribution of food were withdrawn because they were becoming involved in the fighting.
7. African artists have been developing art expressing pride in their heritage.

Critical Thinking

1. Benefits may include a variety of perspectives with which to approach problems. Draw-

problems for many African nations after they gained independence?

4. **Synthesize** How would you respond if you had lived under the system of apartheid?

5. **Apply** How has migration of people from the countryside to cities affected many African countries?

6. **Analyze** In the photograph below Nigerian farmers irrigate a field. How does this show the transition to a new Africa?

Understanding Themes

1. **Nationalism** What was the purpose of the African National Congress (ANC) in South Africa? How has its role changed since 1994?

2. **Change** What political changes came to Angola and Mozambique between the 1970s and 1990s?

3. **Change** How has the Organization of African Unity (OAU) affected African affairs since its founding in 1963?

Skill Practice

Exchange with another student the research reports you completed in "Applying the Skill" for this chapter. Critique the reports using the following questions. For each question, find examples in the report and present them to the author.

1. Does the report have an introduction, body, and conclusion?

2. Does the introduction define the writer's thesis or main point of the report?

3. Is the body of the report organized in a logical way?

4. Are there clear transitions between ideas? Give an example of a good transition and a weak one.

5. Does the conclusion restate and summarize the thesis of the report?

Geography in History

1. **Region** Refer to the map below. What is the largest uninhabited region of Africa?

2. **Human/Environment Interaction** Why is a narrow strip of land in northeast Africa heavily populated?

3. **Location** Near what city in South Africa is the heaviest population?

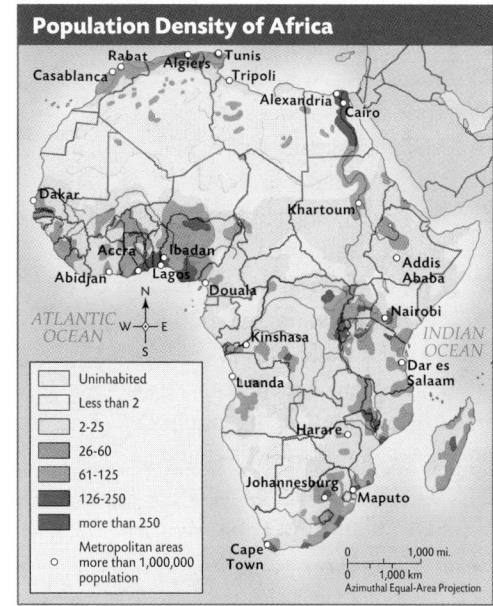

Population Density of Africa

Uninhabited
Less than 2
2-25
26-60
61-125
126-250
more than 250
○ Metropolitan areas more than 1,000,000 population

0   1,000 mi.
0   1,000 km
Azimuthal Equal-Area Projection

Linking Past and Present

1. In the 1980s, droughts brought widespread famine to Africa. What efforts to relieve food shortages continue there today?

2. In 1994, power passed relatively peacefully from the white minority government of South Africa to an all-racial government that includes black South Africans. How might the South African solution serve as a model for solving political problems in other countries that are torn by ethnic unrest?

Chapter 23 *Africa* **723**

peace and gradually abandoned socialism for free enterprise.

3. **CHANGE** Although it failed in creating a United States of Africa, it urged its members to remain neutral during the cold war, put pressure on South Africa to end apartheid, supported pro-independence movements, settled boundary disputes among member nations, and has set as a major goal the creation of an all-African common market by the year 2000.

Skill Practice

Answers will vary but should be based on critical evaluation of the written report and on the elements of the lesson on page 716.

Geography in History

1. North Africa
2. It borders the Nile River.
3. Johannesburg

Linking Past and Present

1. Students might mention international relief programs and attempts to improve agricultural productivity in the Sahel.

2. Students might argue that if blacks and whites can overcome the racial divide, Hutus and Tutsis and different Somali clans should be able to live in peace also.

Chapter Bonus Test Question

Ask students: What situations elsewhere in the world suggest that optimism about Africa's future is warranted? What situations suggest otherwise? *(Answers will vary but may include: Peace developments in the Middle East and the movement toward peace in the Balkans suggest that optimism is warranted; ongoing ethnic conflicts elsewhere suggest otherwise.)*

backs include conflict and a lack of unity.

2. Solutions may include short-term relief efforts or long-term agricultural reform.

3. Old boundaries often divided ethnic and religious groups; divisions created factionalism.

4. Answers should reflect familiarity with South Africa's former racial policies.

5. Unskilled rural people remain unemployed and unable to buy African products, weakening national economies.

6. shows more advanced agricultural techniques

Understanding Themes

1. **NATIONALISM** The ANC's original purpose was to press the white government for reform. Since 1994 it has been the country's ruling party, with many new responsibilities.

2. **CHANGE** After a period of civil war between Marxist and non-Marxist groups, Angola and Mozambique moved toward

A complete, 1-page lesson plan is provided for each section in the *Reproducible Lesson Plans* booklet.

The Middle East

CHAPTER RESOURCES

	Reproducible Resources	Multimedia Resources
Chapter Opener	Chapter Themes: Graphic Organizer 24 Historical Significance Chapter Activity 24	MindJogger Videoquiz
Chapter Enrichment	Vocabulary Activity 24* Time Line Activity 24 Mapping History Activity 24 History Simulation 24 Geography and History Activity 24 Source Reading 24 People in World History Profiles 67, 68 World Literature Selection 8 World Art and Music Activity 24 Enrichment Activity 24 Critical Thinking Activity 24 Skill Reinforcement Activity 24 Writer's Guidebook, Lessons 9, 13 Performance Assessment Activity 24	World History and Art Transparency 47, *Iranian Mihrab*; 48, *The Twelve Tribes of Israel* Chapter Transparency 24 Vocabulary PuzzleMaker Software World Music: Cultural Traditions, Lesson 5 Turning Points in World History: *Middle East Peace Accords* In the Holy Land: • *State of Israel Proclaimed: 1948* • *Six-Day War: Scenes* • *Intifadah (The Uprising)*
Chapter Review/Reteaching	Reteaching Activity 24 Skill Reinforcement Activity 24 Spanish Chapter Summary 24	Chapter 24 Digest Audiocassette, Activity, Test* Vocabulary PuzzleMaker Software Student Self-Test and Review Software MindJogger Videoquiz
Chapter Evaluation/Testing	Performance Assessment Activity 24 Chapter 24 Test, Forms A and B	Testmaker

* Also available in Spanish

0:00 OUT OF TIME? Assign the Chapter 24 summary in the Unit 6 Digest on pages 803–805, and the Chapter 24 Audiocassettes.

Block Schedule

Block scheduling differs from traditional class scheduling in the amount of time allotted to each period. The extended time frame provided by block scheduling affords you the opportunity to implement a greater number of research-oriented and activity-intense projects to motivate and involve your students. Activities that are particularly suited to use within the block scheduling framework are identified throughout this chapter by the following designation.

KEY TO ABILITY LEVELS

Teaching strategies have been coded for varying learning styles and abilities.

L1 **BASIC** activities for all students
L2 **AVERAGE** activities for average to above-average students
L3 **CHALLENGING** activities for above-average students
LEP **LIMITED ENGLISH PROFICIENCY** activities

Use Glencoe's *Presentation Plus!* multimedia teacher tool to easily present dynamic lessons that visually excite your students. Using Microsoft PowerPoint® you can customize the presentations to create your own personalized lessons.

SECTION RESOURCES

Daily Objectives	Reproducible Resources	Multimedia Resources
Section 1 **Nationalism in the Middle East** Explain how nationalism established independent nations and created conflict in the Middle East after World War II.	Reproducible Lesson Plan 24-1 Vocabulary Activity 24* Guided Reading Activity 24-1* Time Line Activity 24 Section Quiz 24-1*	Section Focus Transparency 24-1 Chapter Transparency 24 Student Self-Test and Review Software Testmaker In the Holy Land: *State of Israel Proclaimed: 1948*

Section 2
War and Peace in the Middle East
Summarize how issues of peace and war have been decided in the Middle East since the mid-1960s.
	Reproducible Lesson Plan 24-2
	Vocabulary Activity 24*
	Guided Reading Activity 24-2*
	People in World History Profile 68
	Geography and History Activity 24
	Section Quiz 24-2*
		Section Focus Transparency 24-2
		World History and Art Transparency 47, *Iranian Mihrab;* 48, *The Twelve Tribes of Israel*
		Student Self-Test and Review Software
		Testmaker
		World Music: Cultural Traditions, Lesson 5
		Turning Points in World History: *Middle East Peace Accords*
		In the Holy Land:
		   • *Six-Day War: Scenes*
		   • *Intifadah (The Uprising)*

Section 3 **Challenges Facing the Middle East** Describe how people in the Middle East have handled the conflict between traditional ways and modern values.	Reproducible Lesson Plan 24-3 Guided Reading Activity 24-3* People in World History Profile 67 Reteaching Activity 24 Enrichment Activity 24 Section Quiz 24-3* Performance Assessment Activity 24 Spanish Chapter Summary 24	Section Focus Transparency 24-3 Vocabulary PuzzleMaker Software Student Self-Test and Review Software Testmaker

* Also available in Spanish

Chapter Activities

 Performance Assessment Activity

An Awareness Campaign Events in the Middle East affect the United States in major ways. Have students work through the following steps: (1) list Middle East conflicts and events that have affected the United States in the past; (2) list the areas and issues of continued tensions in the region; (3) for each tension, predict future problems or implications for Americans; and (4) prioritize the list according to the degree of impact on Americans.

Have students work in groups to create an awareness campaign to inform Americans about the severity of the issues. This campaign may include talk-shows, leaflets, newspaper ads, interviews on the evening news, and so on. For each venue chosen, have students explain what would be said or shown, or have them actually create the visual product.

Possible Rubric Features
Concept attainment, accuracy of content information, plausibility of predictions, analysis skills, originality of products, elaboration and detail, persuasion, and collaborative skills

• For an additional activity, refer to Activity 24 in the Performance Assessment Strategies and Activities booklet.

ACTIVITY

From the Classroom of...

Peter Twomey
Brockton High School
Brockton, MA
Israel/Palestine—
A Solution?

Assign each student a Middle Eastern or North African country to research. Then, utilizing the text, library books, and current newspaper articles, each student should write a brief history of his or her country from the end of World War II to the present, including an economic profile. Supply each student with a summary sheet of Arab-Israeli conflicts from 1948 to the present accompanied by maps of the Israeli-Palestinian area in 1948, 1967, and today. When students' research is completed, call a peacekeeping meeting. In round one, each country introduces itself and gives an oral summary of its recent history, including an economic profile. In round two, the countries give their views on the question at hand: What should be the nature of the Israeli and Palestinian states? Why?

To conclude, students should compare their views with current Israeli and Palestinian politicians.

MULTIPLE LEARNING STYLES

Verbal/Linguistic
Have students find examples of different types of literature from modern Middle Eastern writers, including myths, folktales, poetry, drama, novels, and short stories. Have students present to the class oral reports that include brief readings from the literature and that explain how the literature reflects the history and/or current conditions in the Middle East.

Logical/Mathematical
Have students make charts that show the per capita income and the literacy rate of each country in the Middle East. Ask students to compare the charts of several Middle Eastern countries to see if any conclusions can be drawn about the relationship between per capita income and literacy.

Visual/Spatial
Students may research the current flags of each country in the Middle East and then draw or reproduce the flags on poster board. Ask students to include in their posters the meaning of each flag's colors and symbols. Display the posters around the classroom.

Auditory/Musical
Have students collect representative recordings of secular and religious music from the Middle East and play them for the class. Ask students to point out similarities and differences between this music and Western music.

Kinesthetic
Ask students to construct a model that shows the strategies and outcome of the following Middle East conflicts: the Six-Day War, the October War, and the Persian Gulf War.

Additional Resources

NATIONAL GEOGRAPHIC SOCIETY — Teacher's Corner

INDEX TO NATIONAL GEOGRAPHIC MAGAZINE

The following articles may be used for research relating to this chapter:

- "Beirut Rising," by Peter Theroux, September 1997.
- "Syria Behind the Mask," by Peter Theroux, July 1996.
- "Israel's Galilee: Living in the Shadow of Peace," by Don Belt, June 1995.
- "Water: The Middle East's Critical Resource," by Priit J. Vesilind, May 1993.
- "Struggle of the Kurds," by Christopher Hitchens, August 1992.
- "Who Are the Palestinians?" by Tad Szulc, June 1992.

ADDITIONAL NATIONAL GEOGRAPHIC SOCIETY PRODUCTS

To order the following products for use with this chapter, call National Geographic Society at 1-800-368-2728:

- *Nations of the World Series, "Egypt." (Video)*
- *Nations of the World Series, "Israel." (Video)*

LOCAL OBJECTIVES

_____

_____

_____

_____

_____

_____

_____

_____

_____

_____

_____

_____

_____

_____

_____

_____

_____

_____

_____

_____

_____

BIBLIOGRAPHY

Literature of the Period

Yesoshea, A. B. *Mr. Mani.* Translated by Hillel Halkin. New York: Harcourt, 1992. This contemporary Israeli novel gives a great deal of history on the Zionist movement and Israel today.

Readings for the Student

Moore, Molly. *A Woman at War: Storming Kuwait with the U.S. Marines.* New York: Macmillan, 1993. Eyewitness account from the battlefield of the Persian Gulf War by a reporter.

Readings for the Teacher

Decosse, David E., ed. *But Was It Just? Reflections on the Morality of the Persian Gulf War.* New York: Doubleday, 1992. Five essays from differing points of view on the war's justness.

Peres, Shimon. *The New Middle East.* New York: Henry Holt, 1993. An analysis of how the Middle East can achieve a social and economic revival based on peace.

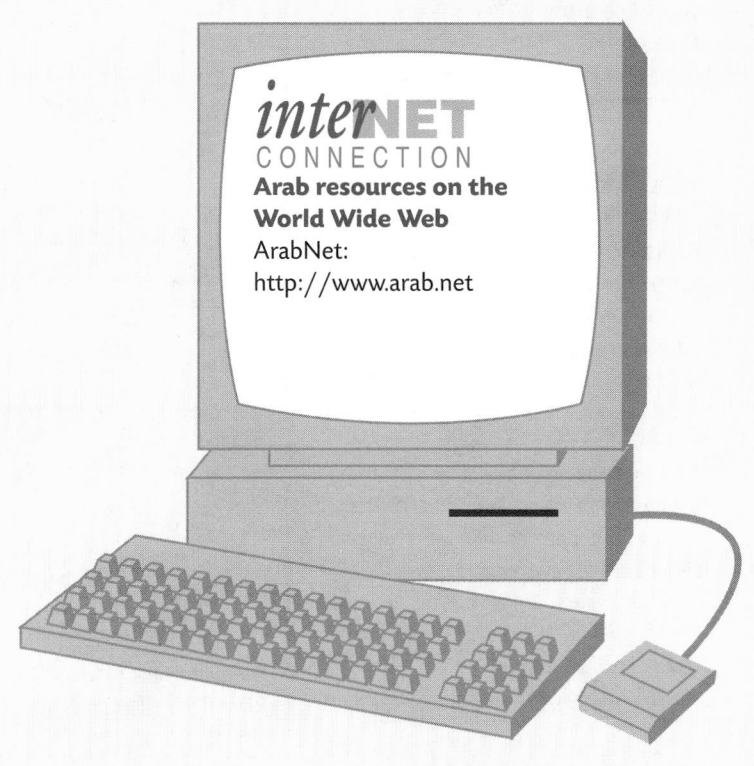

*inter*NET CONNECTION
Arab resources on the World Wide Web
ArabNet:
http://www.arab.net

Chapter Themes are listed by section on this chapter opening page of the Student Edition. A corresponding theme-based activity is available under "TEACH," and a theme-based question is asked in the Section and Chapter Reviews.

The
Storyteller

Historical Setting Both Yitzhak Rabin and Yasir Arafat were born in Jerusalem, Palestine. Rabin fought the British to form an independent Israeli state and led the defense of Jerusalem during Israel's war for independence (1947–1949). Rising through the ranks of the army, Rabin later became a leader of Israel's Labor party and a forceful opponent of the PLO.

Yasir Arafat left Jerusalem in 1948 when Israel became a nation. He led raids into Israel, became a leader of the PLO, and dreamed of establishing a new state of Palestine. In 1993 after secret negotiations, these two old enemies sat down at a special ceremony at the White House, signed a peace accord, and shook hands as the world watched.

Historical Significance

Answers: *Protecting the Middle East's waterways and oil resources caused the Western powers and the Soviet Union to back opposing Middle Eastern countries during the cold war. The United Nations administered the partition of Palestine in 1947 and has sent troops in peace-keeping roles to many places in the Middle East since then. The United States played an important role in the negotiation of peace between Israel and its Arab neighbors.*

Egypt, Jordan, and the Palestinians have signed peace agreements with Israel, and Syria has begun negotiations.

Chapter
24
1945–Present
The Middle East

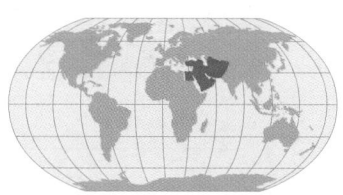

Chapter Themes

▶ **Nationalism** The cold war and rival nationalisms affect the politics of the Middle East. *Section 1*
▶ **Cooperation** Middle Eastern nations take steps toward peace after years of conflict. *Section 2*
▶ **Cultural Diffusion** Middle Eastern countries search for a reconciliation between traditional and modern values. *Section 3*

The
Storyteller

In the fall of 1993, a remarkable event occurred that, to many people, seemed like a miracle. Yitzhak Rabin, the prime minister of Israel, and Yasir Arafat, the chairman of the Palestine Liberation Organization (PLO) signed an agreement to end the decades-long conflict between Israel and the Arabs, known as Palestinians.

In 1995, Rabin's assassination stunned Israel and the world, revealing that the quest for peace is often an uphill struggle marked by tragedy. Since 1945, the Middle East has shown itself to be a complex region where violence has been a constant feature of life but where hopes for peace remain unquenchable.

Historical Significance

How have Middle Eastern developments affected world affairs since 1945? What steps have the nations of the Middle East taken to resolve their differences?

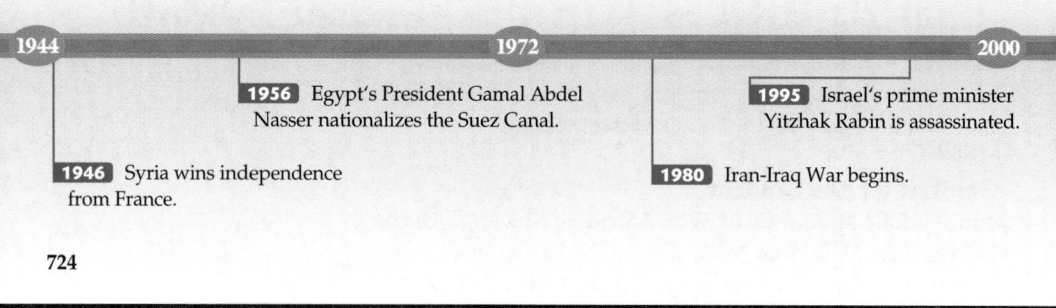

1944		1972		2000
	1956 Egypt's President Gamal Abdel Nasser nationalizes the Suez Canal.		**1995** Israel's prime minister Yitzhak Rabin is assassinated.	
1946 Syria wins independence from France.			**1980** Iran-Iraq War begins.	

724

GEOGRAPHY CONNECTION

Region Point out the locator map of the Middle East on page 724. What has long made the Middle East an important region of the world? *(The Middle East links Europe, Asia, and Africa.)* What makes it an especially important region today? *(its plentiful oil reserves)* Have students turn to the map of the Middle East in the Atlas in their textbook. Ask them to make a list of the 15 countries in the Middle East and their capitals. Also ask them to write down one characteristic of each country. *(For example: The Nile River flows through Egypt; Kuwait borders the Persian Gulf.)*

Istanbul (formerly Constantinople) is Turkey's largest city and one of the busiest ports in the Middle East.

Your History Journal

Create an illustrated time line of conflicts and peace conferences or accords in the Middle East beginning in 1948 and ending at the present. Illustrate your time line with symbols of peace and war.

Chapter 24   *The Middle East*   **725**

Visualizing History

Tell students that Istanbul straddles the Bosporus Strait that divides Europe from Asia. As Constantinople, the city was once the capital of the Byzantine Empire and then the Ottoman Empire. Today the city is a shipbuilding center and a major center for the manufacture of cement, cigarettes, and leather products. Why has Istanbul's location made it an important city throughout history? *(It has been a link between Europe and Asia.)*

✓ Performance Assessment

Refer to the activity on page 724C of the Planning Guide.

 Refer to Activity 24 in the *Performance Assessment Strategies and Activities* **booklet.**

Using Your History Journal

Suggest that students also include on their time lines the names, and if possible, the pictures of people important in the conflicts and peace conferences.

GLENCOE TECHNOLOGY

VIDEODISC
Use MindJogger to preview chapter content.

MindJogger Videoquiz

 Chapter 24
Disc 3 Side B

 Also available in VHS.

✚ EXTRA CREDIT PROJECT

Country Fact Booklet Have students select one of the Middle Eastern countries, conduct in-depth research on it, and compile a fact booklet. Tell students to include the following types of information in their booklets: geography (bordering countries, physical features, plants, animals); government, politics, and army; economy (agriculture, natural resources, industry, trade); society (social classes, religion, education, daily life, literature, the arts, sports and recreation, role of women, role of children and teens); and history.

1945 · 1955 · 1965

1948 Israel and Arab states fight first conflict.

1951 Iran nationalizes foreign-owned oil industries.

1958 Political crisis engulfs Lebanon.

Nationalism in the Middle East

SECTION THEME

▶ **Nationalism** The cold war and rival nationalisms affect the politics of the Middle East.

ind Out

Answer: *led to the establishment of the independent states of Lebanon, Syria, Transjordan (present-day Jordan), and Israel; led to conflicts between Israel and the ousted Palestinians, between Israel and its Arab neighbors; nationalism in Egypt, Lebanon, and Iran led to anti-Western feelings.*

FOCUS

Section Objective

Explain how nationalism established independent nations and created conflict in the Middle East after World War II.

BELLRINGER
Motivational Activity

Before taking roll at the beginning of the class period, project Section Focus Transparency 24-1 and have students answer the activity questions.

This activity is also available as a blackline master.

Vocabulary Pre-check

Use Vocabulary Activity 24 to introduce vocabulary terms.
L1 LEP

Setting the Scene

▶ **Terms to Define**
   Pan-Arabism, kibbutzim, nationalize, pact

▶ **People to Meet**
   David Ben-Gurion, Gamal Abdel Nasser, Hussein I, Mohammad Reza Pahlavi, Mohammad Mossadeg

▶ **Places to Locate**
   Egypt, Iraq, Lebanon, Syria, Jordan, Saudi Arabia, Yemen, Israel, Suez Canal, Turkey, Iran

 **ind Out** How did nationalism establish independent nations and create conflict in the Middle East after World War II?

The Storyteller

In spite of the separate living arrangements, members of a kibbutz family do not become strangers to one another.... Kibbutz parents spend a great deal of their free time with their children.... Parents and children enjoy each other all the more when they meet just for fun and companionship. Kibbutz-niks [residents of a kibbutz] take good care of their elderly parents, too. There is less friction among kibbutz grandparents, parents, and children.... There is less divorce—fewer marriage problems.

—adapted from *Israel Today*, Harry Essrig and Abraham Segal, 1977

Children in a kibbutz

726 Chapter 24 *The Middle East*

In the decades after World War II, nationalist movements took hold in the Middle East. For more than 20 years, Great Britain and France had governed much of the area under the terms of post–World War I agreements. Gradually the presence of foreign officials and troops on Middle Eastern soil revived the desire for independence, as it did in Asia and Africa.

While most Middle Eastern countries shook off European control in the postwar years, foreign influence in the region remained strong. With its valuable waterways and oil reserves, the Middle East became the scene of superpower maneuvering for influence during the cold war.

Arab Independence

Several Arab countries, such as **Egypt** and **Iraq**, had achieved independence before World War II. During the 1940s, other European-ruled Arab territories followed. The Mediterranean coastal lands of **Lebanon** and **Syria** won their freedom from France. In Lebanon, Christian and Muslim leaders agreed to share power under a new constitution, while Syria elected its first parliamentary government. The largely desert kingdom of Transjordan (present-day **Jordan**) gained its independence from Great Britain. In all of these new states, however, Western influences remained strong after independence.

As independent Arab states emerged, Pan-Arabism, a movement aimed at building closer cultural and political ties among Arabs, grew stronger, especially among the educated urban middle class. In 1945, leaders of Egypt, Iraq, Transjordan, Syria, Lebanon, **Saudi Arabia**, and **Yemen** formed the Arab League. Its mission was to unify the Arab world.

SECTION RESOURCES

Reproducible Masters
- Reproducible Lesson Plan 24-1
- Vocabulary Activity 24
- Guided Reading Activity 24-1
- Time Line Activity 24
- Section Quiz 24-1

Transparencies
- Section Focus Transparency 24-1
- Chapter Transparency 24

Multimedia
- Student Self-Test and Review Software
- Testmaker
- In the Holy Land:
   State of Israel Proclaimed: 1948

Formation of Israel

By 1947, Palestine remained the only significant European-ruled territory in the region. Arabs, who had lived in Palestine for centuries, wanted the British to honor their promise of freedom made in the early 1900s. Zionist Jews wanted to build a Jewish state on the same land—land that their ancestors had claimed since Biblical times and that the British had also promised to them.

The Holocaust in Nazi-occupied Europe had boosted support in Western countries for the Zionist movement. Fearing that the British would allow increased Jewish immigration, Arabs in Palestine increased attacks on Jewish settlers. Many of Palestine's Jews lived on kibbutzim, or collective farms, where they struggled to turn swamps and boulder-strewn hillsides into productive farms. To defend themselves, Jewish settlements relied on a military force called the Haganah. Meanwhile, Jewish underground forces carried out attacks on British soldiers and Palestinian Arabs. As hostilities mounted, Great Britain admitted its inability to keep the peace and turned Palestine over to the United Nations in 1947.

For months, world leaders debated the future of Palestine. The United States and much of the West wanted to divide Palestine into a Jewish and an Arab state. Arab nations, along with several European and Pacific nations, rejected the idea and called for a single Palestinian state. At a meeting of the General Assembly on November 29, 1947, the United Nations voted to partition Palestine and to place Jerusalem under UN administration.

Jewish leaders were quick to accept the UN partition plan, while embittered Arab leaders rejected it. Great Britain relinquished control of Palestine on May 14, 1948, as Prime Minister David Ben-Gurion proclaimed the new state of Israel. Within 24 hours, the armies of Syria, Lebanon, Iraq, Egypt, and Transjordan attacked the new Jewish state. With foreign aid and effective civilian and military organization, the Israelis defeated the Arab forces in nine months.

When the fighting ended in early 1949, Israel held more territory. Jerusalem was divided, with the eastern part of the city in Arab hands. Transjordan annexed East Jerusalem and the West Bank of the Jordan River. Egypt held the Gaza Strip. The war was a resounding victory for Israel. To the Arabs, the war spelled disaster. As a result of partition, more than 700,000 Palestinians became homeless. Many fled to neighboring Arab lands, where a large number settled in refugee camps hoping to eventually return home.

Visualizing History Despite British restrictions on immigration, Jews aboard the *Exodus* tried to migrate to Palestine in 1947. *Why did Great Britain turn Palestine over to the United Nations in 1947?*

Arab Unity

The 1948–1949 war had other serious consequences for the Arab world. In Egypt, many people blamed rich, corrupt King Farouk for the Arab defeat and the country's weak economy. In 1952 army officers seized control of the government and proclaimed a republic. Within a year, Colonel Gamal Abdel Nasser, a leader of the coup, took over as president.

Nasser profoundly disliked Western influence in the Middle East, and quickly launched new policies through which he hoped Egypt would lead the Arab world to greatness. In an extremely popular move, Nasser broke up the estates of wealthy Egyptian landowners and gave plots of land to the peasants. Then he negotiated the British withdrawal from the Suez Canal. Finally, he set out to modernize Egypt and build up its military muscle to confront Israel.

The Suez Crisis

Nasser wanted to help Egypt by building a dam at Aswan in the Upper Nile River valley. Known as the Aswan High Dam, the massive structure—36 stories high and more than 2 miles (3 km) wide—would end flooding, increase irrigation, and give farmers two extra harvests a year. Electricity generated by the dam would power new industries.

Seeking political influence in the economic development of Egypt, the United States offered Egypt a $270 million loan to build the dam. However, Nasser's growing Soviet leanings, including a major arms deal with the Soviet Union, caused the United States to angrily withdraw

---

TEACH

Guided Practice

THEME Nationalism
Help students recall the meaning of *nationalism*. *(the desire of a people to achieve independence from foreign control and to govern themselves)* Lead students in a discussion on how Egypt's seizure of the Suez Canal increased the spirit of Arab nationalism in the Middle East. *(Nasser emerged from the Suez crisis as a powerful Arab leader and his brand of nationalism spread throughout the Arab world.)* L1

Visualizing History Tell students that the British did not allow the *Exodus* to disembark its 4,500 Jewish refugee passengers in Palestine. After the ship was badly damaged by British destroyers, its passengers were taken by other ships to France and Germany.
Answer to Caption: *Great Britain was unable to keep the peace between Jewish settlers and Arabs in Palestine.*

Politics Have students make a chart that shows the parties involved, the goals, and the outcomes of the following events in the Middle East: the Arab-Jewish War (1948–1949), the Suez crisis, the civil war in Lebanon (1958), the crisis in Iran (early 1950s). L2

 Chapter Transparency 24

International Relations Have students compare the role the United States played in Turkish affairs with its role in Iranian affairs. L3

Independent Practice

 Guided Reading Activity 24-1 L1

 Time Line Activity 24

Chapter 24 *The Middle East* **727**

Map Study

Answer

It is a crucial waterway linking the Persian Gulf and the Arabian Sea. Through it pass oil tankers and other commercial vessels.

Map Skills Practice

Reading a Map What nations border Israel? *(Egypt, Jordan, Lebanon, Syria)*

Daily Life Have students research life in a Palestinian refugee camp or in an Israeli kibbutz. Ask students to write diary entries for a week from the point of view of a teenager in a camp or on a kibbutz. **L2**

Geography: Movement Have students draw a map that shows the route of a ship from Jiddah, Saudi Arabia, to Marseilles, France, before and after the closing of the Suez Canal. Ask students to estimate the difference in distance between the two routes and research the difference in travel time. **L3 LEP**

VIDEODISC
In the Holy Land

Side One, Chapter 20
Frame: 27441
Title: *State of Israel Proclaimed: 1948*
Ask: What was the significance of the founding of the State of Israel? *(Now there was a Jewish nation.)*

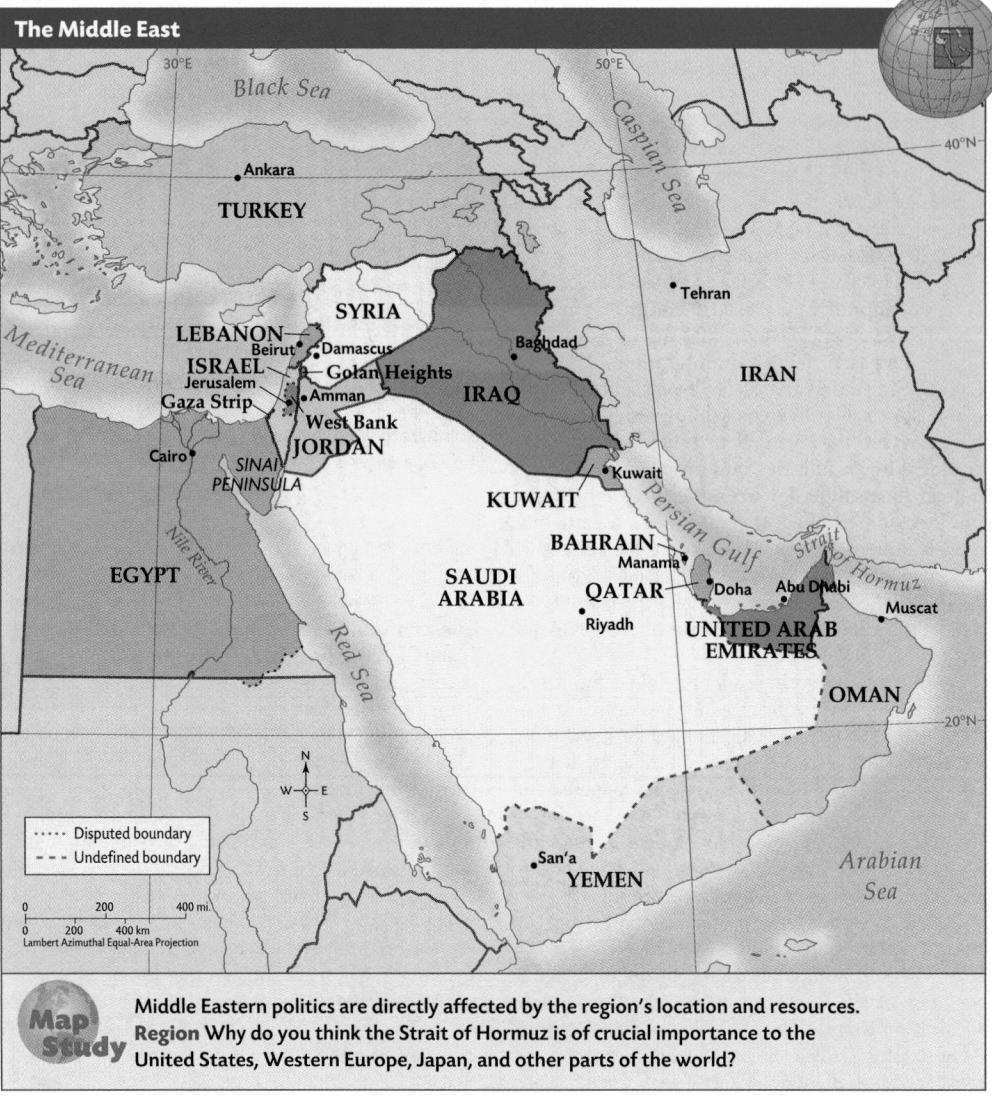

The Middle East

Map Study

Middle Eastern politics are directly affected by the region's location and resources.
Region Why do you think the Strait of Hormuz is of crucial importance to the United States, Western Europe, Japan, and other parts of the world?

its offer. In July 1956 Nasser retaliated against the Western powers by nationalizing, or bringing under government control, the Suez Canal. He vowed to use millions of dollars in canal fees to finance the building of the dam.

President Eisenhower was opposed to Western intervention, and the United States tried to negotiate an end to the crisis. Great Britain and France, however, feared that Nasser might close the canal and cut off shipments of oil between the Middle East and Western Europe. In October, the two European powers joined Israel in invading Egypt. Great Britain and France hoped to overthrow Nasser and seize the canal. Israel wanted to end Egyptian guerrilla attacks on its borders. The United States immediately sponsored a United Nations resolution calling for British and French withdrawal from Egypt. The Russians threatened rocket attacks on British and French cities. Eisenhower, opposed to Soviet interference, put the Strategic Air Command on alert. In face of this pressure, the three nations pulled out of Egypt. United Nations forces were sent to patrol the Egyptian-Israeli border. Nasser then accepted the Soviet offer to build the Aswan High Dam.

MEETING SPECIAL NEEDS ACTIVITY

Study Strategy Have students make a flash card for each of the following countries: Egypt, Iraq, Syria, Lebanon, Jordan, Israel, Turkey, and Iran. Tell students to write the country's name on one side of the card. On the other side, they should write the names of the main leaders from 1948 to 1960; the leaders' positions—pro-Western or pro-Arab, pro-Nasser, and so forth; and main crises or events for the country during those years. **L2**

Middle East Crises

Nasser emerged from the Suez crisis as a powerful Arab leader. He had embarrassed Great Britain and France, won control of the Suez Canal, and had stopped Israel from taking more territory. Pro-Nasser parties began forming throughout the Arab world. It seemed that Nasser might rise to lead a unified Arab world.

In early 1958 Syria and Egypt merged to form a Nasser-led state called the United Arab Republic (UAR). The union lasted about three years. At that point, Syrian leaders had grown resentful of the loss of their power, and Syria withdrew from the UAR.

That same year, Nasser's brand of Arab nationalism seemed to be taking hold in Iraq. There, King Faisal II, Nasser's strongest Arab opponent and a friend of the West, was killed by radical political and military forces in his country. They set up a one-party regime like Nasser's and broke ties with the West.

In the face of pro-Nasser pressure, some Arab leaders turned to the West for support. Jordan's **Hussein I** asked for British and American help when pro-Nasser forces threatened his government. In Lebanon, violence broke out between the Christians, who dominated the nation, and a huge Muslim population that sympathized with Nasser and the UAR. Christian President Camille Chamoun, a supporter of the West, sought election to a new term. Anti-Western elements revolted, and a civil war followed. Chamoun asked for Western help to stop the violence. At first, Eisenhower refused. However, when an unexpected coup overthrew the government of Iraq, Eisenhower decided to uphold political stability in the region. He sent 15,000 Marines to Lebanon in July 1958. When order was restored that fall, the troops pulled out.

By 1960 Arab nationalism had made gains, but the Middle East was in a state of uncertainty. A fragile truce held between Arabs and Israelis; competing Arab groups were at an impasse; and neither superpower had managed to achieve dominance in the region.

Pro-Western Tier

Two other Middle Eastern countries, **Turkey** and **Iran**, experienced the upheaval of nationalism and rapid modernization. Both bordered the Soviet Union, making them pawns in cold war struggles.

Turkey

At the end of World War II, Turkey received American aid to modernize its economy and to ward off Soviet advances. During the 1950s, the Turks joined NATO and the Baghdad Pact, alliances aimed at blocking Soviet expansion. Turkey also made strides toward democracy, encouraged foreign investment, and strengthened its capitalist economy. By the 1960s, however, government corruption, inflation, and a huge international debt discredited Turkey's ruling politicians and increased the political influence of the military.

Iran

By contrast, Western influence in oil-rich Iran was shaken after World War II. The young shah, **Mohammad Reza Pahlavi**, relied on Western help to block Soviet influence. Many Iranian people, however, resented the West. For decades, the British had grown rich on Iranian oil at Iran's expense.

In 1951, a wealthy politician, **Mohammad Mossadeg**, became prime minister. He nationalized the British-owned oil industry and declared that all oil money would be used for social and economic reforms. Great Britain called for a world boycott of Iranian oil. As Iranians began to suffer, their hatred of the West and the shah grew.

In 1953 growing support for Mossadeg forced the shah to flee the country. He returned after a military coup—promoted by the United States—deposed Mossadeg. The shah increased his ties to the United States and signed the Baghdad Pact. A pact is a treaty between two or more nations. He also signed an agreement with Western oil companies. Backed by the army and Western powers, the shah was firmly in control by the 1960s.

SECTION I REVIEW

Recall
1. **Define** Pan-Arabism, kibbutzim, nationalize, pact.
2. **Identify** David Ben-Gurion, Gamal Abdel Nasser, United Arab Republic, Hussein I, Mohammad Reza Pahlavi, Mohammad Mossadeg.
3. **Explain** why the United Nations divided Palestine into an Arab and a Jewish state.

Critical Thinking
4. **Applying Information** How did the Holocaust in Europe contribute to the development of the Jewish state in Palestine?

Understanding Themes
5. **Nationalism** How was Nasser viewed by the Arab world after his nationalization of the Suez Canal?

ASSESS

Check for Understanding

Assign Section 1 Review as homework or as an in-class activity.

◉ Use Student Self-Test and Review Software to review Section 1.

Global Gourmet

Middle East Pita bread, or pocket bread, began with nomads in the Middle East. After pitching their tents at the end of the day, they mixed powdered grain and water to form a dough, patted it into flat rounds, and baked them over an open fire.

Evaluate

 Section Quiz 24-1

◉ Use the Testmaker to create a customized quiz for Section 1.

Reteach

Have students identify the relation of the following people to a Middle Eastern country and to major events in the Middle East: David Ben-Gurion, King Farouk, Gamal Abdel Nasser, Hussein I, Camille Chamoun, Mohammad Reza Pahlavi, and Mohammad Mossadeg.

Enrich

Have students research and write a short report explaining how and why Lebanon's government was divided between Christians and Muslims.

CLOSE

Have students summarize the results of anti-Western feelings in Egypt, Iraq, Lebanon, and Iran.

SECTION I REVIEW ANSWERS

1. The words are defined in the Glossary.
2. Ben-Gurion, 727; Nasser, 727; Arab League, 729; Hussein I, 729; Pahlavi, 729; Mossadeg, 729
3. The United Nations divided Palestine in order to grant freedom and independence to the Palestinian Arabs and to create a Jewish state in Palestine for Zionist Jews.
4. boosted support among Western countries for the Zionist movement
5. **NATIONALISM** Nasser was viewed as a great Arab leader because he had embarrassed Great Britain and France and had stopped Israel from taking more territory.

SECTION THEME

▶ **Cooperation** Middle Eastern nations take steps toward peace after years of conflict.

Find Out

Answer: *Syria's threat led Israel to respond with force in the Six-Day War. Resentment over Israel's occupation of Palestinian lands led Egypt to strike back in the Yom Kippur War. Peaceful resolution to Arab-Israeli conflicts was finally achieved in the Camp David Accords and the 1993 peace treaty. Whether armed members of the PLO should be allowed in Lebanon led to fighting in that country. An Iraqi invasion of Kuwait was resolved by the use of force.*

FOCUS

Section Objective

Summarize how issues of peace and war have been decided in the Middle East since the mid-1960s.

BELLRINGER
Motivational Activity

Before taking roll at the beginning of the class period, project Section Focus Transparency 24-2 and have students answer the activity questions. This activity is also available as a blackline master.

Vocabulary Pre-check

 Vocabulary Activity 24

1965 **1975** **1985** **1995**

1967 Israel and Arab nations fight Six-Day War.

1979 Revolution establishes Islamic republic in Iran.

1990 Iraq invades Kuwait.

1993 Israelis and Palestinians agree to end their conflicts.

Section 2

War and Peace in the Middle East

Setting the Scene

▶ **Terms to Define**
disengagement, cartel, *intifada*, embargo

▶ **People to Meet**
Yasir Arafat, Anwar el-Sadat, Menachem Begin, Hosni Mubarak, Yitzhak Rabin, Shimon Peres, Benjamin Netanyahu, Ayatollah Ruhollah Khomeini, Saddam Hussein

▶ **Places to Locate**
Gaza Strip, Golan Heights, West Bank, Beirut, Strait of Hormuz, Kuwait

Find Out How have issues of peace and war been decided in the Middle East since the mid-1960s?

The Storyteller

When Shah Mohammad Reza Pahlavi was overthrown in 1979, Iran had male tailors fitting women's clothes and male teachers in girls' classrooms. The revolutionaries, however, refused to allow unrelated men and women to work closely together. The result: many more job opportunities for women. In the media, for example, the need for women to cover women's sports opened jobs for directors and reporters.
—adapted from *Nine Parts of Desire, The Hidden World of Islamic Women*, Geraldine Brooks, 1995

Shah Mohammad Reza Pahlavi

From the 1960s to the 1990s, many sweeping changes came to the Middle East. Wars broke out between various nations and groups in the region, but hopes for peace were also high, especially in the early 1990s.

As the 1960s opened, the most prolonged and bitter dispute was between Israel, its Arab neighbors, and the Palestinians. In their struggle for nationhood, the Palestinians in 1964 formed the Palestine Liberation Organization (PLO) to eliminate Israel and to create a Palestinian state. Later, however, many Palestinians and Israelis came to accept a two-state solution: a state for Israelis and a state for Palestinians.

TURNING POINT

Arab-Israeli Conflict

The cease-fire between Israel and its Arab neighbors fell apart during the 1960s. A new radical regime in Syria sought the end of Israel and the creation of an Arab Palestine. Syrian and Israeli troops engaged in border clashes in early 1967. Egypt's President Nasser aided Syria by closing the Gulf of Aqaba to Israel and by having United Nations forces removed from the Israeli-Egyptian border.

Six-Day War

Fearing possible attack, Israel responded with force on June 5, 1967. At 8:45 A.M., Israeli fighter jets bore down on 17 Egyptian airfields, destroying 300 of Egypt's 350 warplanes. Hundreds of miles away, Israeli jets also demolished the air forces of Iraq, Jordan, and Syria.

In the Six-Day War, Israeli forces tripled Israel's land holdings, seizing the Sinai Peninsula and the **Gaza Strip** from Egypt, and the **Golan Heights**

SECTION RESOURCES

 Reproducible Masters
- Reproducible Lesson Plan 24-2
- Vocabulary Activity 24
- Guided Reading Activity 24-2
- People in World History Profile 68
- Geography and History Activity 24
- Section Quiz 24-2

Transparencies
- Section Focus Transparency 24-2
- World History and Art Transparency 47, *Iranian Mihrab*; 48, *The Twelve Tribes of Israel*

Multimedia
- Student Self-Test and Review Software
- Testmaker
- World Music: Cultural Traditions, Lesson 5
- Turning Points in World History
- In the Holy Land

from Syria. When Jordan entered the war, Israeli troops also took East Jerusalem.

In a move that spawned decades of upheaval, Israel occupied the **West Bank** of the Jordan River. The West Bank was land that had been designated as part of Arab Palestine in the United Nations partition plan in 1947. Palestinian Arabs had never achieved self-rule, however; they had been under Jordanian rule ever since 1949, when Jordan annexed the West Bank. Now, as a result of the Six-Day War, the area's more than 1 million Palestinians found themselves under Israeli military occupation.

Thousands more Palestinians fled to neighboring countries such as Lebanon. They turned more than ever to the PLO and its militant leader, **Yasir Arafat**, who vowed to use armed struggle to establish a Palestinian state.

The United Nations asked Israel to pull out of occupied territories and asked Arab nations to recognize Israel's right to exist. Both sides refused. Terrorist attacks and border raids continued for many years.

Oil and Conflict

Nasser died in 1970. His successor, President **Anwar el-Sadat**, led Arab forces in a new war against Israel. On October 6, 1973, Egyptian and Syrian forces launched a surprise attack on Israel on the Jewish holy day of Yom Kippur and during the Muslim holy month of Ramadan. In early battles, many Israeli planes were shot down. Egyptian troops crossed over into the Sinai, and Syria moved into the Golan Heights. With an American airlift of weapons, Israel struck back. Israeli troops crossed the Suez Canal and occupied Egyptian territory. The fighting raged until the UN negotiated a cease-fire. Secretary of State Henry Kissinger negotiated a disengagement, or military withdrawal, agreement in early 1974.

American support of Israel during the 1973 war angered Arab countries. Attempting to halt Western support, Arab oil countries imposed an embargo on oil sales to Israel's allies in 1973. Additional pressure came from the Organization of Petroleum Exporting Countries (OPEC), a cartel, or group of businesses formed to regulate production and prices among its members. OPEC, which included Arab and non-Arab oil producers, quadrupled the price of oil. However, the embargo threatened such dire economic problems for the world, including Arab countries, that it was lifted in 1974.

The Camp David Accords

In 1977, Egypt's President Sadat acted independently to break the deadlock. He accepted an invitation to visit Israel, becoming the first Arab

Visualizing History Yasir Arafat became chairman of the Palestine Liberation Organization (PLO) in 1969. The PLO, formed in 1964, is a confederation of various Palestinian Arab groups. *Why was the PLO formed?*

leader to step in peace on Israeli soil. In a speech before Israel's parliament, Sadat called for Arab acceptance of Israel, a just solution to the Palestinian problem, and an end to hostilities between Israelis and Arabs.

The next year Sadat accepted an invitation from United States President Jimmy Carter to meet with Israeli Prime Minister **Menachem Begin** (BAY•gihn). The 12 days of meetings at Camp David in Maryland resulted in the Camp David Accords, the basis for an Arab-Israeli peace treaty.

Sadat and Begin signed the treaty in March 1979—the first time an Arab nation recognized Israel's right to exist. In return, Israel gave up the Sinai Peninsula. Many nations applauded Sadat's actions, but several Arab states broke ties with Egypt. Sadat's separate peace with Israel, they said, threatened Arab unity.

In 1981 Muslim extremists assassinated Sadat, and **Hosni Mubarak** succeeded him as president. Mubarak supported Egypt's peace with Israel but also worked to improve Egypt's relations with other Arab nations in the region. At home, he faced economic pressures caused by Egypt's soaring population and lack of resources. Another challenge to Mubarak came from a growing opposition movement led by Islamic groups that wanted to end Western influences in Egypt.

Chapter 24 *The Middle East* **731**

COOPERATIVE LEARNING ACTIVITY

Group Presentations Organize the class into five groups. Have each group choose a slip of paper from a box with one of the following types of people on it: Palestinians who took part in the *intifada*; Israelis who participated in the Six-Day War; Lebanese Christian merchants during Lebanon's civil war; American hostages during Iran's revolution; or Kuwaiti civilians during the Persian Gulf War. Have each group research to present its people's view of the cause of violence in the Middle East. Let each team decide the format of its presentation—skit, interview, role playing, or lecture. Suggest that one person from the group record on the chalkboard the main points of the presentation. **L2**

Chapter 24
Section 2

Guided Practice

THEME Cooperation

Have students find examples in Section 2 of countries or political groups cooperating. *Arab countries aiding one another against Israel in the Six-Day and Yom Kippur Wars; OPEC oil embargo; Camp David Accords; peace accords between Israel and PLO; Arab-Western coalition in Persian Gulf War.)* **L1**

Visualizing History Tell students that Yasir Arafat, who once backed the destruction of Israel through terrorist acts, denounced the acts of violence perpetrated by Muslim extremists against Israeli civilians in February and March 1996. **Why do you think he did this?** *(to further the peace process aimed at achieving the establishment of a Palestinian state as outlined in the 1993 peace agreement)* **Answer to Caption:** *to eliminate Israel and establish a Palestinian state*

TURNING POINT

Arab-Israeli Conflict

How did the Arab-Israeli conflict affect Middle Eastern and world events in the 1970s? *War between Arabs and Israelis in 1967 and 1973 resulted in Israeli territorial gains. Many Palestinians came under Israeli rule. The 1973 war sparked an oil embargo that placed pressure on the economies of Israel's allies. In the late 1970s, efforts toward peace were underway, and Egypt became the first Arab state to recognize Israel.*

Time Line Have students make a time line that shows Arab-Israeli relations in the following years: 1967, 1973, 1978, 1987, and 1993. **L2 LEP**

Chapter 24 *The Middle East* **731**

Cultural Perspectives

Religions Ramadan and Yom Kippur are both periods of atonement and fasting. During Ramadan, the ninth month of the Islamic year, Muslims fast from sunrise to sunset. Each evening they recite long passages from the Quran. The most sacred of Jewish holidays, Yom Kippur, falls in late September or early October. Jews spend the day fasting and praying for the forgiveness of sins committed during the year.

ABCNEWS INTERACTIVE™

VIDEODISC
In the Holy Land

Side One, Chapter 26
Frame: 36164
Title: *Six-Day War: Scenes*
Ask: In 1967, which areas were captured by Israeli forces? *(the Sinai Peninsula, West Bank of Jordan River, and Jerusalem)*

Side Two, Chapter 6
Frame: 9840
Title: *Intifadah (The Uprising)*
Subject: Different perspectives
Ask: What were the Palestinians' reasons for the uprising? *(They felt that Israeli policies had been repressive.)* How did the Israeli soldier feel about putting down the Palestinian uprising? *(He said he had been trained to fight military enemies, not civilians, and that it was very difficult.)*

The Palestinian Issue

For 20 years after the 1967 war, Arabs and Israelis could not agree on the future of the West Bank and Gaza Strip. Resenting Israeli rule, Palestinians lived in a smoldering rage. Most could get only low-paying jobs; those who protested could be arrested. During this time, the PLO staged hijackings and bombings in Israel and in foreign countries.

In 1987 the Palestinians carried out an *intifada*, or uprising, against the Israelis. The uprising spread from the Gaza Strip to the West Bank. Workers went on strike, and protesters hurled stones at Israeli soldiers and civilians. The *intifada* focused world attention on the Palestinian issue.

In 1988 the PLO's leader Arafat stated that he would renounce terrorism and accept Israel's right to exist. However, believing that Arafat would not be true to his word, Israel refused to hold talks with the PLO and to halt the growth of Jewish settlements in the West Bank.

The Peace Process

Despite continuing tensions in the Middle East, the United States pressed the Arabs and Israelis to hold peace talks beginning in 1991. The Israeli Prime Minister **Yitzhak Rabin** (YIHT•zahk rah•BEEN), elected in 1992, agreed in principle to exchange some of the occupied land for security guarantees and to accept self-rule by the Palestinians. Many Arab leaders also showed a new flexibility in their positions.

In 1993, Israel and the PLO recognized each other and agreed to eventual self-rule for Palestinians in the West Bank and the Gaza Strip. The Israelis also stated they would gradually withdraw militarily from both areas. By mid-1996, the Palestinians had gained significant self-rule with Yasir Arafat as their first president.

The peace process also reached out to Israel's Arab neighbors: Jordan and Syria. In 1994, Israel and Jordan signed a peace treaty, the first such agreement between Israel and an Arab country since the Israeli-Egyptian peace treaty of 1979. Syria

Images *of the* Times

Living in the Middle East

Daily life in the Middle East today is a blend of modern and traditional ways as well as urban and rural lifestyles.

Beirut, Lebanon, is rebuilding its neighborhoods after a long period of civil war.

Jiddah, Saudi Arabia, is a modern port city on the Red Sea that has prospered from the country's oil wealth.

732

Images *of the* Times — Living in the Middle East

Money from oil provides most of Kuwait's income. These oil revenues pay for medical care, education, and social security for the Kuwaitis. Kuwaitis pay no taxes other than customs duties. Because Kuwaiti families share in the country's oil wealth, they can afford to hire household help. This help and workers in other service industries come from immigrants from Asian and other Arab countries. As a result of immigration, the ethnic Kuwaiti population now makes up a minority of only 45 percent. To keep Kuwait for the Kuwaitis, the government limits voting rights to Kuwaiti males over 21 years of age who can trace their families' residence in the country back to 1921.

and Israel began talks, but a major obstacle between them was the future status of the Golan Heights, occupied by Israel since the 1967 war.

Increased Tensions

Although many Israelis and Palestinians supported the peace process, a large number on both sides opposed it. Some Palestinians feared that peace would lead to a less-than-independent Palestinian state subject to Israeli restrictions. Israeli opponents of the process feared that a self-governing Palestinian state could threaten Israel.

Tragically, in November 1995, Rabin was shot to death by an Israeli student who opposed the peace process. Rabin's successor, **Shimon Peres** (shee•MOHN PEHR•ehs), pledged to continue efforts toward peace, and Yasir Arafat made the same commitment. However, events followed that heightened tensions and hardened positions on both sides.

Opposed to the peace process, the militant Palestinian group Hamas in early 1996 began a series of suicide bombings that killed a number of Israelis. Shocked by the violence, Israeli voters that May narrowly elected **Benjamin Netanyahu** (neh•tahn•YAH•hoo), leader of the conservative Likud party, over Peres and the Labor party. As a candidate and later as prime minister, Netanyahu stressed Israel's security needs over peace with the Palestinians.

After the Israeli elections, Hamas stepped up its bombings and attacks on Israeli citizens. Although Arafat publicly denounced Hamas's actions, Prime Minister Netanyahu and many Israelis believed that Arafat was unable or unwilling to control the militants. To keep would-be bombers out of Israeli cities, Netanyahu closed off Palestinian areas from Israel. These closings kept tens of thousands of Palestinian workers from jobs in Israel and restricted travel between West Bank cities and villages. The Israelis also refused to carry out promises to withdraw military forces from remaining Palestinian areas (except for the town of Hebron) until the bombings stopped.

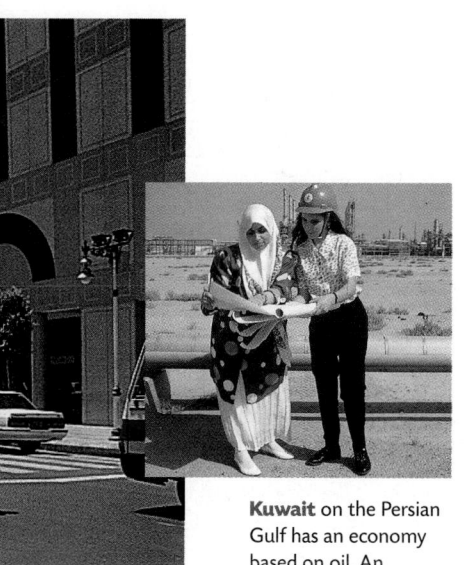

Kuwait on the Persian Gulf has an economy based on oil. An increasing number of women in the Middle East, as in other areas of the world, earn university degrees and work in businesses.

The Galilee region of Israel has areas where swamps and lakes have been drained to create productive farmlands.

REFLECTING ON THE TIMES

1. What impact has oil had on various countries of the Middle East?
2. What country in the Middle East is rebuilding after a long period of civil war?

733

ANSWERS TO REFLECTING ON THE TIMES

1. The economies of countries such as Kuwait and Saudi Arabia are based on oil. Oil production has brought prosperity to these countries.
2. Lebanon

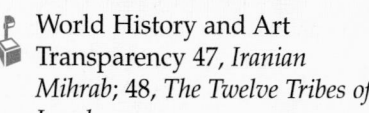

🎵 World Music: Cultural Traditions, Lesson 5

📦 World History and Art Transparency 47, *Iranian Mihrab*; 48, *The Twelve Tribes of Israel*

ABCNEWS INTERACTIVE™

VIDEODISC
 Turning Points in World History

Side Two
Chapter 11

Title: *Middle East Peace Accords*
Ask: Why is it likely that the Middle East peace talks will be ongoing? *(The disputes are centuries old and many difficult issues are involved; thus, negotiations will likely take a long time.)*

you don't say...

Intifada literally translated means "shaking off." The Palestinians in the Israeli-controlled East Jerusalem, the Gaza Strip, and the West Bank tried to "shake off" Israeli control and end the expansion of Jewish settlements in these areas.

Who? What? Where? When?

Nobel Peace Prizes were awarded in 1978 to Anwar el-Sadat and Menachem Begin for signing the Camp David Accords and in 1994 to Yasir Arafat, Yitzhak Rabin, and Shimon Peres for starting the peace process between Israel and the PLO.

Independent Practice

📁 Guided Reading Activity 24-2 **L1**

Multicultural Have students research to make a chart that shows the majority religion, official language, and current leader of Egypt, Israel, Iran, Iraq, Jordan, Lebanon, and Syria. **L2**

Literature Have students write a one-page report on the extent of censorship under the Shiite regime in Iran, using as an example the case of the novelist Salman Rushdie. **L3**

Linking Past and Present

The Hanging Gardens of Babylon, one of the Seven Wonders of the Ancient World, were built about 4,000 years ago by Nebuchadnezzar. In the 1980s, Saddam Hussein had started rebuilding the gardens using 15 million bricks baked in the ancient way. The Persian Gulf War ended this ambitious project.

Visualizing History Educated in the United States, Israeli Prime Minister Benjamin Netanyahu favored strengthening free enterprise in Israel. *What was Netanyahu's position in dealing with the Palestinians?*

While Israelis feared continued attacks, Israeli policies angered Palestinians, who believed that their hopes for an independent Palestinian state were being derailed by Israel's conservative government. The Palestinians opposed Israeli expansion of Jewish settlements in the West Bank and Jerusalem. They expressed their anger in demonstrations that turned into violent clashes between Israeli troops and Palestinian security forces. As turmoil erupted, the United States and other countries engaged in an uphill struggle to get the two sides together and to keep the stalled peace process alive.

Lebanon

The Palestinian issue also affected neighboring Lebanon. In 1975 a civil war broke out between Lebanon's Christian and Muslim groups. As the Muslim population grew to outnumber Christians, unrest had spread. Adding to these tensions was the presence of armed PLO forces in the country. Most Lebanese Muslims supported the PLO; most Lebanese Christians did not.

As fighting erupted, the weakened Lebanese government asked Syria to send in troops to keep order. In 1982 the Israelis invaded southern Lebanon to wipe out PLO bases that had been attacking Israel. A multinational peacekeeping force finally arranged a PLO withdrawal to other Arab countries; however, private armies continued fighting among themselves. After foreign troops became victims of terrorist bombings, the peacekeeping force departed by 1985.

In the early 1990s, some signs of hope appeared. Lebanon agreed to give Muslims an equitable say in the political process, and the various private armies in **Beirut** pulled out of the city, which made rapid strides in rebuilding. By the mid-1990s, Lebanon had made progress toward stability. Tensions remained, however, and both Syria and Israel kept troops in the country.

Iran's Revolution

During the 1960s and 1970s, Iran became a major military power in the Persian Gulf area. Shah Mohammad Reza Pahlavi worked to build a modern industrial economy based on oil. Shiite Muslim religious leaders, however, disliked the influx of Western values into Iran and called for a return to Muslim traditions. The shah silenced all protests and dissent.

In the late 1970s, anti-shah forces rallied around **Ayatollah Ruhollah Khomeini** (ko•MAY•nee), a powerful Shiite Muslim leader, living in exile in France. Khomeini had long preached the overthrow of the shah and the creation of an Islamic republic. By January 1979, widespread unrest forced the shah to flee Iran. Khomeini returned to form a government based on Muslim values.

Iranian hatred for the shah was also directed at the United States. The Americans had long supported the shah, valuing Iran as a major supplier of oil and a reliable buffer against Soviet expansion. Anti-American feelings were so strong that on November 4, 1979, militants stormed the American embassy in Tehran, the capital, and took 52 Americans hostage. United States President Carter's efforts to free the hostages were unsuccessful, thus sealing his defeat in the 1980 presidential election. Only after his successor, Ronald Reagan, was sworn in on January 20, 1981, did Iran release the Americans.

During most of the 1980s, Iran fought a devastating war with neighboring Iraq. The Iraqis first seized a disputed border area and then pushed into Iran. The Iranians, hoping to spread their revolution into Iraq, responded with a fierce counter-

734 Chapter 24 *The Middle East*

Steve McCurry, Magnum

Mohsen Shandiz, SYGMA

Mortal Enemies

This giant portrait of Iraqi President Saddam Hussein (left) overlooks a Baghdad street. An inscription under the portrait in red Arabic characters praises the Arab forces in Iraq's struggle with its Islamic but non-Arab enemy neighbor, Iran. In Iran the stern gaze of the Ayatollah Ruhollah Khomeini peers from a mural behind women attending the departure of soldiers for the battlefront in September 1988. With his zealous view of Islam, Khomeini, who died in 1989, regarded the secular Saddam Hussein as both an enemy and an infidel.

The Middle East has changed profoundly since World War II. What was once an area largely held by the Ottoman Empire and then by European colonial powers is now a region of independent nations. With the end of imperialism came the rise of nationalism. At the same time parts of the Islamic world have witnessed the rise of a fiercely held fundamentalism that views the secular world, even the Muslim secular world, as evil and corrupt. In this context Iran and Iraq fought a long and devastating war that lasted from 1980 to 1988. ⊕

Chapter 24 *The Middle East* **735**

TEACH

Tell students that the dispute between Iran and Iraq was about religious and political issues more than it was a struggle over territory. Before the ayatollah came to power in Iran, he listed his enemies as, "First the Shah; then the American Satan; then Saddam Hussein and his infidel Ba'ath party." Iraq's Ba'ath party was made up of Sunni Muslims and promoted pan-Arabism. It was also the party in charge of expelling Khomeini in 1978 at the request of the shah of Iran. Because Iran is not an Arab country, the fundamentalist Shiite Muslims promote a universal Islam that is indifferent to nationality and aims to unite all Muslim peoples.

Linking Past and Present

Iran and Iraq The present-day countries of Iran and Iraq were sites of ancient empires and kingdoms that are often called "cradles of civilization." Iran was part of the Persian Empire; and Iraq, known as Mesopotamia, is heir to the civilizations of Sumer, Akkad, Babylonia, and Assyria. The two peoples clashed in ancient times also. In 539 B.C., Cyrus the Great, founder of the Persian Empire, captured the present-day Iraqi city of Babylon and conquered the Babylonian Empire.

People in World History
Profile 68

 Geography and History
Activity 24

ASSESS

Check for Understanding

Assign Section 2 Review as home-work or as an in-class activity.

■ Use Student Self-Test and Review Software to review Section 2.

Evaluate

 Section Quiz 24-2

■ Use the Testmaker to create a customized quiz for Section 2.

Reteach

Have students take turns summa-rizing major events in Israel, Egypt, Lebanon, Iran, and Iraq from 1967 to 1996.

Enrich

Have students research and give a short oral report on how the 1973 oil embargo affected daily life in the United States.

CLOSE

Have students create a time line on the chalkboard that shows major events in the Middle East from 1967 to 1996.

Footnotes to History

War and the Environment

During the Persian Gulf War, Iraqi troops spilled an estimated 250 million gallons (947 million l) of Kuwait's oil into the Persian Gulf. Thousands of birds, fish, and other marine life perished when the oil spill spread for 350 miles (563 km) along the Persian Gulf coastline.

attack. The Iraqis had superior weapons and used poison gas; the Iranians, however, relied on larger numbers of troops. When both sides targeted com-mercial vessels in the Persian Gulf, the United States sent naval forces to protect the vital shipping lanes running through the **Strait of Hormuz**. In 1988 Iran and Iraq, both exhausted, agreed to end the fighting.

After Khomeini's death a year later, his succes-sors worked to rebuild Iran's crippled economy. In 1997 a moderate religious leader, Mohammad Khatami, became president. Khatami supported a reduction in press censorship and closer economic ties with the West. Observers, however, did not expect a significant improvement in Iran's relations with the West. The United States, for example, still was concerned about Iran's use of nuclear technol-ogy and linked Iran to terrorist attacks in other countries.

Iraq's Bid for Power

The war with Iran left Iraq near collapse and in debt to its small, but oil-rich, neighbor, **Kuwait**. In August 1990, Iraq's President **Saddam Hussein** sent Iraqi forces into Kuwait, claiming that the country was a historic part of Iraq. In occupying Kuwait, Hussein also wanted to expand Iraq's influence in the Persian Gulf region.

The Persian Gulf War

Fearing an Iraqi attack, oil-rich Saudi Arabia asked the United States for protection. United States President George Bush responded by send-ing troops to the Saudi desert. Eight Arab nations also sent forces to Saudi Arabia. At the urging of the UN, Western nations, the Soviet Union, and Japan imposed a trade embargo, or a ban on the export of goods, against Iraq.

In January 1991, after a UN deadline for an Iraqi withdrawal expired, the United States rained medium-range missiles on the Iraqi capital of Baghdad. During the next month, coalition forces from the United States, Great Britain, France, Syria, Saudi Arabia, Egypt, and Kuwait conducted a mas-sive air war against Iraq. Iraq responded by launch-ing missiles against Saudi Arabia and Israel. Iraqi forces in Kuwait also set fire to oil fields. When Iraq still refused to withdraw, coalition land forces moved into Iraq and Kuwait, defeating the Iraqis after 100 hours of fighting. With Kuwait freed, a cease-fire went into effect. Allied war deaths totaled just over 100, with tens of thousands of Iraqi sol-diers believed killed.

Iraq After the War

After their victory, coalition forces withdrew from Iraq. Saddam Hussein, however, remained in power. He brutally crushed Kurdish and Shiite groups in Iraq that used the war to rebel against his authority. World public opinion condemned Hussein's attacks on his civilian population.

Meanwhile, the UN trade embargo continued in an effort to force Iraq to end its chemical and nuclear weapons program. The embargo caused much hardship to Iraqis. In December 1996, the UN allowed Iraq to resume oil exports on a limited basis to pay for badly needed food and medical supplies. Iraq, however, refused to allow UN teams that included Americans to inspect its weapons plants for chemical and biological weapons. In a show of military strength, a large United States naval force went to the Persian Gulf in November 1997.

SECTION 2 REVIEW

Recall
1. **Define** disengagement, cartel, *intifada*, embargo.
2. **Identify** PLO, Yasir Arafat, Anwar el-Sadat, OPEC, Menachem Begin, Camp David Accords, Hosni Mubarak, Yitzhak Rabin, Shimon Peres, Benjamin Netanyahu, Ayatollah Ruhollah Khomeini, Saddam Hussein.
3. **Explain** the outcome of the Six-Day War.

Critical Thinking
4. **Analyzing Information** How has the Persian Gulf War affected the Middle East?

Understanding Themes
5. **Cooperation** What were the major points of the 1993 agree-ment between Israel and the Palestinians?

SECTION 2 REVIEW ANSWERS

1. All vocabulary words are defined in the Glossary.
2. PLO, 730; Arafat, 731; Sadat, 731; OPEC, 731; Begin, 731; Camp David Accords, 731; Mubarak, 731; Rabin, 732; Peres, 733; Netanyahu, 733; Khomeini, 734; Hussein, 736
3. Israel seized the Sinai Peninsula and the Gaza Strip from Egypt, the Golan Heights from Syria, and East Jerusalem and the West Bank from Jordan. Arab nations refused to recognize Israel's right to exist. Terrorist attacks continued.
4. A coalition of Middle Eastern countries worked with Western forces to stop a common enemy; Israel, by accepting protection from the United States instead of responding to Iraqi attacks, helped hold the coalition together.
5. **COOPERATION** Israel and the PLO recognized each other and agreed to eventual self-government for Palestini-ans in the West Bank and the Gaza Strip and a gradual withdrawal of Israeli forces.

Preparing a Bibliography

In the last chapter, you wrote a research report on some topic of interest. To complete your report, you have one more step—preparing a bibliography.

Learning the Skill

A bibliography is a list of sources used in a research report. These sources include: books; articles from newspapers, magazines, and journals; interviews; films, videotapes, audiotapes, and compact discs. Why do you need a bibliography? What purpose does it serve?

There are two main reasons to write a bibliography. First, those who read your report may want to learn more about the topic. Second, a bibliography supports the reliability of your report.

A bibliography should follow a definite format. The entry for each source must contain all the information needed to find that source: author, title, publisher information, and publication date. You should have this information already on note cards. If you neglected this step earlier, you must return to the library to find the sources again.

In a bibliography, arrange entries alphabetically by the author's last name. The following are accepted formats for bibliography entries, followed by sample entries. Note the form of punctuation used between parts of the entry.

Books
Author's last name, first name. Full Title. Place of
   publication: publisher, copyright date.
Hay, Peter. Ordinary Heroes: The Life and Death
   of Chana Szenes, Israel's National Heroine.
   New York: Paragon House, 1986.

Articles
Author's last name, first name. "Title of Article."
   Name of Periodical in which article appears,
   Volume number (date of issue): page
   numbers.
Watson, Bruce. "The New Peace Corps in the

New Kazakhstan." Smithsonian, Vol. 25
(August 1994): pp. 26–35.

Other Sources
For other kinds of sources, adapt the format for book entries.

Practicing the Skill

Review the sample bibliography below for a report on Mexico. Then answer the questions that follow.

Caste–eda, Jorge G. The Mexican Shock: Its
   Meaning for the United States. New York:
   The New Press, 1995.
Marquez, Viviane Brachet de. The Dynamics of
   Domination: State, Class and Social Reform
   in Mexico, 1910–1990. Pittsburgh, Penn.,
   University of Pittsburgh Press, 1994.
Cockburn, A., "The Fire This Time." Cond—Nast
   Traveler, Vol. 30 (June 1995): pp. 104–113.
Smith, G. "The Brave New World of Mexican
   Politics." Business Week (August 28, 1995)
   pp. 42–44.

1. Are the bibliography entries in the correct order? Why or why not?
2. What is missing from the second book listing?
3. What is missing from the second article listing?

Applying the Skill

Compile a bibliography for your research report. Include at least five sources, preferably a mix of books and articles. Exchange bibliographies with another student and check each other for proper format and arrangement.

For More Practice

Turn to the Skill Practice in the Chapter Review on page 747 for more practice in preparing a bibliography.

TEACH

Preparing a Bibliography Write the following list on the chalkboard: *Author's name, Title, Place of publication, Publisher, Date of publication*. Ask students to find this information for their textbook. If necessary, guide students to the title and copyright pages. Have volunteers write the correct information from their text opposite the five categories on the chalkboard. Then tell students that this information is required for books in a bibliography. Direct students to read the skill and complete the practice questions to learn more about the purposes and formats of a bibliography.

Additional Practice

📁 Skill Reinforcement Activity 24

📁 Writer's Guidebook, Lessons 9, 13

ANSWERS TO PRACTICING THE SKILL

1. No; the entries should be in alphabetical order by author's last name.
2. The title of the book should be underlined.
3. The volume number is missing, and the title of the periodical should be underlined.

1945 Arab nations form the Arab League.

1979 Israel and Egypt sign peace treaty.

1994 Jordan and Israel end their state of war.

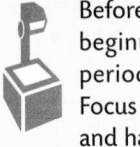
Section 3

Challenges Facing the Middle East

Setting the Scene

▶ **Terms to Define**
  sovereignty, desalination, fundamentalism

▶ **People to Meet**
  Shimon Peres, Hafez al-Assad, Benjamin Netanyahu, Golda Meir, Tansu Çiller

▶ **Places to Locate**
  West Bank, Gaza Strip, Jerusalem, Golan Heights, Saudi Arabia, Cairo, Turkey, Euphrates River

ind Out   How have people in the Middle East handled the conflict between traditional ways and modern values?

The Storyteller

An Israeli observer records the expulsion of Arabs from Israeli-held territory: "Masses of people marched on behind the next. Women bore bundles and sacks on their heads; mothers dragged children after them. From close up it was sad to watch this trek of thousands going into exile. As soon as they left the city, they began to divest themselves of things … and the roads were cluttered with the belongings that people had abandoned to make their walk easier."

Palestinian Arabs in exile

—from *The People of Nowhere,* Danny Rubenstein, 1991

The tragic cycle of violence, wars between nations, and civil wars within nations have brought much suffering to the people of the Middle East since the end of World War II. Besides the lost lives, billions of dollars of precious resources are spent each year on weapons. If you speak to Middle Easterners about their hopes for the future, they consistently include peace and stability. But peace and stability have been hard to achieve.

War and Peace

Since Egypt and Israel agreed to peace in 1979, major steps have been taken in ending the state of war between Israel and the rest of the Arab world. In 1993, the Israelis and the Palestinians came to an agreement, and a year later, Jordan and Israel finally ended their conflict. Contacts also began between Israel and Syria for the settlement of issues stemming from the Six-Day War of 1967.

West Bank and Gaza Strip

After successful efforts toward peace in the early 1990s, Israeli-Palestinian relations worsened by 1997. Hamas bombings and the tougher position of Israel's conservative government both threatened to derail the peace process. Increasing tensions delayed indefinitely any resolution of the major issues dividing Israelis and Palestinians. These issues include the timing of Israeli military withdrawals from Palestinian areas in the **West Bank** and **Gaza Strip**, the ownership of **Jerusalem**, and the status and security of Israeli Jewish settlers on the West Bank.

Still another major issue is the resettlement of Palestinians who fled their homes beginning in the 1948 Arab-Israeli conflict. Today, more than 6

---

million Palestinian Arabs live in the Middle East, North Africa, Europe, and the Americas. About 2 million Palestinians live in the West Bank and Gaza Strip. In addition, about 850,000 Israeli Arabs live inside Israel itself and try to combine Israeli citizenship with their Arab heritage.

Golan Heights and Lebanon

Relations between Israel and its northern neighbor, Syria, also need to improve before a general peace can be achieved. The **Golan Heights**, which has been in Israeli hands since 1967, is a major area of dispute. Israeli Prime Minister **Shimon Peres** and Syrian President **Hafez al-Assad** committed themselves to settling this issue, but talks between Israel and Syria have been deadlocked since the election of Israeli Prime Minister **Benjamin Netanyahu** in 1996.

In neighboring Lebanon, the civil war has ended, but Israeli and Syrian troops remain. Some Israelis would like their troops to withdraw, but the Netanyahu government believes an Israeli military presence in Lebanon is vital for Israel's security. In Lebanon, Israeli forces are opposed by Shiite Muslim guerrillas. Attacks repeatedly occur between the two sides. In 1997 Netanyahu called on Syria, the major power in Lebanon, to restrain the guerrillas.

The Elusive Dream

Unity among Arab people has long been a powerful desire. For many centuries, millions of people throughout the Arab world have shared strong cultural ties, such as the Arabic language, traditions, religious beliefs, and a common history. British and French imperialism in the 1800s and 1900s increased division among the Arabs and created numerous states with artificial boundaries. Many Arabs thought that with independence from foreign powers they would be able to achieve unity. They began to take steps to strengthen the common links among them.

In 1945 political unity seemed within reach when Egypt, Transjordan (present-day Jordan), Syria, Lebanon, Iraq, **Saudi Arabia**, and Yemen formed the Arab League, a step toward unity. By 1995 membership in the Arab League had grown to 22 participants (including the PLO) covering an area larger than the United States, with a population of about 200 million. But disagreements among governments and the unwillingness of some Arab nations to give up their sovereignty, or independent decision-making powers, frustrated any move toward further unity.

Visualizing History Banking and financial services are important to the economies of many Middle Eastern countries. *In what other ways have Middle Eastern economies changed in the past 40 years?*

Some political leaders and government officials have advocated a cautious move toward unity. They formed cooperative councils among their countries to coordinate trade, economic development, and travel. Peoples' aspirations and political realities, in time, may lead to some type of loose union in which each state would retain independence and contribute to stability in the region.

Economic Developments

In the past 40 years the Middle East has seen greatly changed economic and social conditions. Light and heavy industry has been developed in most countries of the region. Irrigation for agriculture spread as hydroelectric projects were constructed on major rivers, such as the Nile and the Euphrates. At the same time as production rose and jobs became available, the region's population grew rapidly. If the current rate of increase continues, the population will double in the next 25 years. The increase has been most apparent in major urban centers. By the mid-1990s, more than 6 cities had populations exceeding 3 million each. The largest is **Cairo**, Egypt's capital, with 12 million people. It is also the largest in the whole African continent. The needs and the challenges of rapidly growing populations are on the minds of every major leader in the Middle East.

Chapter 24 *The Middle East* **739**

TEACH

Guided Practice

THEME **Cultural Diffusion**
Remind students that cultural diffusion is the spread of ideas or ways of living from one culture to another. Help students find examples of cultural diffusion in this section. *(Palestinians in Israel combining Israeli citizenship with Arabic heritage; goods and ideas from the West changing Islamic society)* **L1 LEP**

Visualizing History Have students differentiate between the modern and traditional styles of clothing shown in the picture. Tell students that the long, loose robe, called a *thwab*, and the head covering, a *keffiyah*, are suited to the climate of the Middle East.
Answer to Caption: *Industry has developed in most Middle Eastern countries. Agricultural production has increased because of irrigation.*

Economics Have students make a flowchart that shows how economic development (industrialization, improved agriculture) in the Middle East has led to challenges (increase in population, gap between oil-producing and non-oil-producing countries, water shortages). **L2**

COOPERATIVE LEARNING ACTIVITY

Panel Discussions Organize the class into five groups. Have each group choose one of the following topics: role of women in Muslim nations; dam building on the Nile and Euphrates Rivers; Middle Eastern desalination projects; dispersal of oil wealth among citizens in oil-producing countries; or the debate about moving toward more democratic government in Kuwait and Saudi Arabia. Tell students to research their topic using recent newspaper, magazine, and journal indexes. Suggest that each group break its topic into subtopics so that each group member has a specific topic to research. Before each group presents its panel discussion, have students choose a moderator for their panel. **L3**

Independent Practice

 Guided Reading Activity
24-3 **L1**

 People in World History
Profile 67

Linking Past and Present

Water from the Euphrates

Because Turkey had not worked out an agreement with Syria and Iraq for sharing water from the Euphrates, the World Bank refused to extend Turkey a loan to build Ataturk Dam. Turkey obtained independent financing to build the dam.

ANSWERS

Answers will vary but should mention shadoofs and other early technology compared to modern dams and reservoirs; ancient peoples, include Sumerians, Babylonians, and Persians; modern lands: Turkey, Syria, Iraq. Turkey needs water to irrigate farmland to supply food for its people, but its dams should not hurt the people of Iraq and Syria.

CURRICULUM CONNECTION

GOVERNMENT

The royal family of Saudi Arabia holds daily *majlis*, audiences with ordinary citizens who come to petition for help in settling a dispute or to receive special aid from the government. The royal princes receive up to 300 people a day; the king, far fewer and on a less regular basis.

Oil and Water

Oil-producing countries of the Middle East have built wealthy and highly developed societies in recent years. The region's highest per capita incomes, or the total national incomes divided by the number of people in each nation, are found in the Persian Gulf countries. Their prosperity, however, contrasts sharply with the poverty of some other countries in the region. Hoping to lessen the gap between rich and poor nations, oil-producing countries have invested in and loaned large sums of money to the non-oil producing countries.

Another valuable, but scarce, resource in the Middle East is water. The region has long had critical water shortages caused by an unequal distribution of water. However, as Middle Eastern countries develop industrially and face population increases, they are working to meet their water needs. For example, **Turkey** has built dams and other water facilities on the **Euphrates River** to irrigate fertile, but dry, areas.

Other countries with water shortages include Israel, Syria, and Jordan. If all three countries settle their political differences, they will be able to coordinate their water resources and build plants for **desalination**, the removal of salt from sea water to make it usable for drinking and farming. In 1997 Israel and Jordan settled a dispute about the sharing of water. At present, both countries are constructing dams on the Yarmuk River, which serves as part of the Jordanian-Israeli border.

Social Change

Throughout the Middle East, modernization has turned traditional societies upside down. With the discovery of oil, desert cities bloomed and new industrial areas were created. Urban areas now contain high-rise offices, shopping centers, and freeways. Foreign investment has created new jobs and raised living standards. New wealth has led to better education and health care. In addition, women in the region have made a growing impact on business and politics. In politics, for example, **Golda Meir** (meh•IHR), who served as Israeli prime min-

---

CONNECTIONS: Science and Technology

Water From the Euphrates

Like their ancient ancestors, people in the Middle East today rely on the Euphrates River for water. The technology used to obtain the water, however, has changed considerably over the centuries. To ensure their water supply, the people of Turkey today rely on a series of huge dams on the Euphrates. The dams' reservoirs provide water for Turkey's expanding industries and urban centers.

Turkey's solution for its water problem, however, deprives Syria and Iraq of water from the same river. Iraq would be especially worse off because it is the last country that is situated along the river.

The Turks claim they need the river to better their economy. They hope to turn more of the Anatolian Peninsula into farmland. Crops grown there are needed to feed Turkey's growing population, they say.

Syria and Iraq claim that Turkey does not own the entire Euphrates River. They point out that not only will they lose water from the reduced flow, but that more will be lost through evaporation from the Turkish reservoirs.

Experts state that this crisis can be eased by all three countries repairing existing equipment, improving irrigation and water conservation methods, and expanding water recycling. The countries also need to grow some crops that do not require so much water. Above all, experts state that the countries need to better manage their population growth.

Turkish dam on the Euphrates River

Linking Past and Present ACTIVITY

Compare water technology today with that used in the past. What peoples relied on the Euphrates in ancient times? What lands depend on the Euphrates today? Does Turkey have a right to build dams on the river?

MEETING SPECIAL NEEDS ACTIVITY

Learning Style: Visual/Spatial Have students create a bulletin-board display of various aspects of traditional Islamic life. They might include drawings of traditional dress for both men and women and photographs of Islamic religious rituals or such rituals of daily life as eating, entertaining, and shopping. Be sure all images are clearly labeled with explanatory captions. **L1 LEP**

ister from 1969 to 1974, was the modern Middle East's first female head of government. In early 1990s **Tansu Çiller** (TAHN•soo see•LAHR) of Turkey became the first female prime minister to govern a Middle Eastern Muslim country.

Challenges

As in other parts of the world, the rapid pace of change in the Middle East also had its negative side. Cities experienced rising crime, and there was a growing gap between the rich and the poor. The greater independence of family members led to a loosening of traditional family ties. The availability of cars, TVs, VCRs, and personal computers brought a new materialism to daily life. Many people in the Middle East blamed the West for the new social trends.

Saudi Arabia

In Saudi Arabia, the birthplace of Islam, most people have fiercely resisted undesirable Western cultural influences. For hundreds of years, the land that is now Saudi Arabia was divided among many tribes. During the early 1900s, these groups joined together under the Saud family to form the kingdom of Saudi Arabia. Beginning in the mid-1900s, the Saudi royal family used income from the oil industry to support modernization programs. As a result, many Saudis have developed skills for management and technical jobs. However, the Saudi royal family, which still maintains a close hold on the country's affairs, has used tight censorship to shield Saudis from exposure to many Western ideas and practices. By contrast, more liberal lifestyles are permitted in Iraq, Lebanon, Syria, Jordan, Egypt, and Israel.

A Return to Religion

In recent years many Middle Easterners have sought solutions to their problems in fundamentalism, or adherence to traditional religious values. This development has also occurred, although in different ways, in other parts of the world. For example, in the United States, conservative Protestantism has flourished and has expressed itself politically; in India, Hindu nationalists have won widespread support.

Some observers view support for fundamentalism as a natural reaction by people who are overwhelmed by massive change and desire to seek security in long-valued traditions. Other experts, however, point out that the continued growth of religious fundamentalism deepens mistrust and hardens divisions at a time when the world's peoples need to develop greater understanding and cooperation.

In the Middle East, the revival of traditional religion has increased the political influence of Islam in many countries. Since 1979, Shiite Muslim religious leaders have ruled Iran. In Turkey, Egypt, and Jordan, the political power of Islam poses a serious challenge to secular forms of government. Israel's Jewish right-wing religious parties, although small in size, have contributed to the rising strength of political conservatism and nationalism there.

The most direct confrontation in the Middle East between traditional religion and secularism has occurred in Turkey. In 1996 Necmettin Erbakan became Turkey's first prime minister from an Islamic party. Military leaders, however, saw Erbakan's pro-Islamic policies as a threat to Turkey's secular political traditions. They forced Erbakan from power in 1997, and secular politicians then formed a new government. Many of the new leaders believe that the country's Islamic schools promote militancy among students. They have proposed a plan that would force the closing of many Islamic schools. Devout Muslims have protested this plan as a violation of their religious freedom.

Egypt also has seen religious conflict. Since 1992, Muslims in southern Egypt have sought to oust President Hosni Mubarak's secular government and establish a government based on Islamic principles. By late 1997, more than 1,150 people had been killed in battles between Muslim supporters and the police.

SECTION 3 REVIEW

Recall
1. **Define** sovereignty, desalination, fundamentalism.
2. **Identify** Shimon Peres, Hafez al-Assad, Benjamin Netanyahu, Arab League, Golda Meir, Tansu

Çiller.
3. **Explain** three challenges to stability in the Middle East today.

Critical Thinking
4. **Applying Information** What impact has religious fundamen-

talism had on the Middle East?

Understanding Themes
5. **Cultural Diffusion** In what ways have foreign influences affected modern Middle Eastern society?

ASSESS

Check for Understanding
Assign Section 3 Review as homework or as an in-class activity.

 Use Student Self-Test and Review Software to review Section 3.

Evaluate
Section Quiz 24-3

 Use the Testmaker to create a customized quiz for Section 3.

Reteach
Have students make charts that describe the positive and the negative aspects of the political, economic, and social changes that have taken place since the 1970s in the Middle East.

Reteaching Activity 24

Enrich
Have students write a short report on the effect of the Islamic militant groups Hamas and Jihad on the Israel-PLO peace process since 1994.

 Enrichment Activity 24

CLOSE

Have students hold a mock UN meeting in which they offer possible solutions to Middle East problems.

SECTION 3 REVIEW ANSWERS

1. All vocabulary words are defined in the Glossary.
2. Peres, 739; Assad, 739; Netanyahu, 739; Arab League, 739; Meir, 740; Ciller, 741
3. disagreements between Israel and the PLO; Muslim and Israeli religious fundamentalism; the gap between the oil-rich

and non-oil countries; the increasing population; water shortages
4. Muslim fundamentalists have taken control of the government in Iran and pose a challenge to secular governments in other nations. Fundamentalist Jewish parties have contributed to the rise of political conservatism in Israel.

5. **CULTURAL DIFFUSION** Foreign investment and material goods have affected Middle Eastern society. Many Middle Easterners blame the West for materialistic values that threaten cherished traditions.

Block Schedule

Team Teaching This selection of modern poems may be presented in a team-teaching context, in conjunction with English or Language Arts.

Modern Poems

Historical Connection

The three poems in this feature were written by poets from developing countries: Mexico, Turkey, and Nigeria. The increasing prominence in the West of literature from developing nations suggests that people in Europe and the United States are more aware of the achievements of people in other parts of the world.

Background Information

Setting The setting for each poem appears to be the homeland of the poet. Students may wish to discuss, however, whether these poems could be set in another country just as well.

Literary Elements Personification means giving human characteristics to an inanimate object. For example, in "The Window," Torres Bodet talks about the world issuing a "great, rough, hoarse cry." Giving the world the power of speech is personification.

A stanza is a collection of lines in a poem, separated from other lines or stanzas. In "Once Upon a Time," most stanzas are six lines long. In modern poetry, stanza length varies.

Metaphor is a comparison of two objects. For example, Nazim Hikmet compares the earth to "a mere toy next to the sun."

from

Modern Poems

by

Jaime Torres Bodet, Nazim Hikmet, and Gabriel Okara

Modern poets have continued to explore both universal themes, such as friendship and loneliness, as well as individual preferences for a particular place or group of people.

The following poem was written by one of Mexico's greatest writers, Jaime Torres Bodet, who was born in 1902 and was active in politics. Bodet served the government as an administrator and diplomat. In this poem, Bodet urges people to take risks in their lives. Bodet died in 1974.

The Window

Translated from Spanish by George Kearns

You closed the window, And it was the world,
the world that wanted to enter, all at once,
the world that gave that great shout,
that great, deep, rough cry
you did not want to hear—and now
will never call to you again as it called today,
asking your mercy!

The whole of life was in that cry:
the wind, the sea, the land
with its poles and its tropics,
the unreachable skies,
the ripened grain in the resounding wheat field,
the thick heat above the wine presses,
dawn on the mountains, shadowy woods,
parched lips stuck together longing for
cool water condensed in pools,
and all pleasures, all sufferings,
all loves, all hates,
were in this day, anxiously
asking your mercy …

But you were afraid of life,
And you remained alone,
behind the closed and silent window,
not understanding that the world calls to a man
only once that way, and with that kind of cry,
with that great, rough, hoarse cry!

ABOUT THE AUTHORS

Jaime Torres Bodet was supervisor of Mexico's libraries in the 1920s. Later he served as director-general of the United Nations Educational, Scientific, and Cultural Organization (UNESCO).

Nazim Hikmet's outspoken views on behalf of the poor and oppressed in Turkey led to his imprisonment by the government. When he was released in 1951, he left the country. Many of his works were not published in Turkey during his lifetime, yet he became a popular hero there.

Gabriel Okara received little formal schooling in Nigeria. He learned enough on his own, however, to become a widely respected writer. He usually writes in his native language, Ijaw.

N azim Hikmet, who lived from 1902 to 1963, often criticized the government of his native Turkey for serving only the wealthy. In 1951 he left Turkey, never to return, and settled in Europe. His sympathy for the peasants of his country, his love of nature, and his hope for humanity are all suggested in the following poem.

The World, My Friends, My Enemies, You, and the Earth

Translated from Turkish by
Randy Blasing and Mutlu Konuk

I'm wonderfully happy I came into the world,
I love its earth, its light, its struggle, and its bread.
Even though I know its dimensions from pole to pole to the
  centimeter,
and while I'm not unaware that it's a mere toy next to the sun,
the world for me is unbelievably big.
I would have liked to go around the world
and see the fish, the fruits, and the stars that I haven't seen.
However,
I made my European trip only in books and pictures.
In all my life I never got one letter
          with its blue stamp canceled in Asia.
Me and our corner grocer,
we're both mightily unknown in America.
Nevertheless,
from China to Spain, from the Cape of Good Hope to Alaska,
in every nautical mile, in every kilometer, I have friends and
      enemies.
Such friends that we haven't met even once—
we can die for the same bread, the same freedom, the same dream.
And such enemies that they're thirsty for my blood,
          I am thirsty for their blood.
My strength
is that I'm not alone in this big world.
The world and its people are no secret in my heart,
          no mystery in my science.
Calmly and openly
      I took my place
          in the great struggle.
And without it,
      you and the earth
          are not enough for me.
And yet you are astonishingly beautiful,
          the earth is warm and beautiful.

Nazim Hikmet

FOCUS

Before students read the poems, have them speculate about what writers from such different countries as Mexico, Turkey, and Nigeria might have in common. Have them read the biographical statement about each poet and then ask them to consider what the poets' attitudes might be toward European culture, political change, economic development, and nationalism. After they have read the poems, ask them if the works have anything in common. *(Students may say that, in distinct ways, each poet deals with his attitude toward the wider world.)*

CURRICULUM CONNECTION

POLITICS

Many writers from developing countries are actively involved in their countries' politics. Other politically active Latin American, Middle Eastern, and African writers include Mario Vargas Llosa, Carlos Fuentes, Naguib Mahfouz, Chinua Achebe, and Wole Soyinka.

Chapter 24 *The Middle East* **743**

OTHER WORKS BY THE AUTHORS

Other Works by Jaime Torres Bodet
Karser, Sonja, trans. *Selected Poems.* Bloomington: Indiana University Press, 1964.
Other Works by Nazim Hikmet
The Moscow Symphony and Other Poems. Chicago: Swallow Press, 1971.

Blasing, Randy, and Mutlu Konuk, trans. *Things I Didn't Know I Loved.* New York: Persea Books, 1975.
Other Works by Gabriel Okara
The Voice. New York: Africana Publishing Corp., 1970.

Chapter 24 *The Middle East* **743**

TEACH

Interpretation

Ask students to decide for which age group Torres Bodet wrote this poem. (*Possible answer: Young people trying to choose a direction in life might benefit from the challenge he presents, but the message can apply to people of any age.*)

Definition

Hikmet's claim to know the dimensions of the world "to the centimeter" is an example of hyperbole. Discuss with students how Hikmet uses overstatement as a way of suggesting his love of the world.

Literary Analysis

Okara effectively uses the technique of repetition when he lists the many faces that one must learn to wear as one grows older. Ask students to cite other examples of repetition in the poem. Have volunteers read the verses aloud and guide them to see how repetition gives the verses a certain rhythm.

Evaluation

Ask students to choose their favorite poem of the three and to write a paragraph on why they like it. Tell them to support their view with specific details.

 World Literature Selection 8

Gabriel Okara, born in 1921, is one of many Nigerian writers to achieve international acclaim since the 1960s. Others include Chinua Achebe, Christopher Okigbo, and Wole Soyinka. Some of Okara's poems deal with the problems of living in a country that is influenced by European culture. Others deal with family, friends, and daily life.

Once Upon a Time

Once upon a time, son,
they used to laugh with their hearts
and laugh with their eyes;
but now they only laugh with their teeth,
while their ice-block-cold eyes
search behind my shadow.

There was a time indeed
they used to shake hands with their hearts;
but that's gone, son.
Now they shake hands without hearts
while their left hands search
my empty pockets.

"Feel at home," "Come again,"
they say, and when I come
again and feel
at home, once, twice,
there will be no thrice—
for then I find doors shut on me.

So I have learned many things, son.
I have learned to wear many faces
like dresses—homeface,
officeface, streetface, hostface, cock-
tailface, with all their conforming smiles
like a fixed portrait smile.

And I have learned, too,
to laugh with only my teeth
and shake hands without my heart.
I have also learned to say, "Goodbye,"
when I mean, "Good-riddance";
to say "Glad to meet you,"
without being glad; and to say "It's been
nice talking to you," after being bored.

ADDITIONAL LITERARY WORKS OF THE PERIOD

García Márquez, Gabriel. ***One Hundred Years of Solitude.*** A mystical novel by a prominent Colombian writer about life in a Latin American village.

Head, Bessy. ***A Question of Power.*** A powerful and disturbing novel by one of South Africa's leading women writers.

Mahfouz, Naguib. ***The Beginning and the End.*** A novel by one of Egypt's greatest writers, winner of the 1988 Nobel Prize in literature.

Senghor, Léopold Sédar. ***Poems.*** Poetry about African culture by a West African.

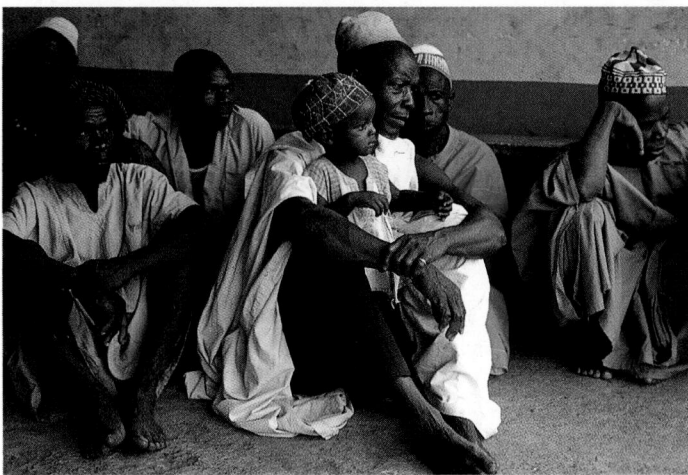

Visualizing History National unity has been difficult for Nigeria to achieve because of its diverse ethnic groups. *How does the author remember his childhood years before strife divided the country?*

But believe me, son.
I want to be what I used to be
when I was like you. I want
to unlearn all these muting things.
Most of all, I want to relearn
how to laugh, for my laugh in the mirror
shows only my teeth like a snake's bare fangs!

So show me, son,
how to laugh; show me how
I used to laugh and smile
once upon a time when I was like you.

RESPONDING TO LITERATURE

1. In your own words, define "the great struggle" that Hikmet refers to near the end of his poem.
2. Explain whether you think the poem by Bodet is written just to the people of Mexico or whether it applies to people throughout the world.
3. What is the main point of the poem by Okara?
4. **Demonstrating Reasoned Judgment** How does each poet view individuals who are willing to act boldly?

ANSWERS TO RESPONDING TO LITERATURE

1. Answers will vary. Some students may feel Hikmet means that life itself is a struggle, while others may feel he refers to class struggle between the rich and poor.
2. Torres Bodet's challenge seems directed to people everywhere but may have special significance for people in Mexico and other developing countries.
3. Students may feel the poet is reflecting on the insincerity that comes with success in the world.
4. Each poet seems to value boldness: Torres Bodet criticizes one who is "afraid of life"; Hikmet praises those who dared to struggle; Okara is nostalgic for the honesty of his early years.

Visualizing History Nigeria's people belong to more than 250 ethnic groups.
Answer to Caption: *as happy times*

ASSESS

Assign **Responding to Literature** questions.

CLOSE

After students have read the poems, ask them if they think that writers and artists in the developing world have special responsibilities to their people.

Contemporary Connection

Students interested in learning more about the culture of Nigeria can listen to the music of such world-famous "Afropop" musicians as King Sunny Ade, Fela Anikulapo Kuti, Babatunde Olatunji, or Shina Peters.

Portfolio Project

Have students read a poem on one of the themes touched on in these selections but written by a Western poet. Walt Whitman and T.S. Eliot are two possible choices. Then have students write an essay comparing the two poems. Have them answer these questions: Do you think any of the differences between the two poems can be traced to the differences in the poets' backgrounds? Is poetry a universal language?

GLENCOE
TECHNOLOGY

VIDEODISC
Use MindJogger to review students' knowledge of the chapter.

MindJogger Videoquiz

Chapter 24
Disc 3 Side B

 Also available in VHS.

Answers

Using Key Terms
1. a   4. c
2. g   5. d
3. e

Using Your History Journal

Have students use their time lines on conflicts, peace conferences, and accords as a basis for essays.

Reviewing Facts
1. As a strategic crossroads and with its valuable waterways, the Middle East was affected by superpower rivalries.
2. After U.S. refusal to help build the Aswan Dam, Nasser took over the Suez Canal.
3. He invited Egyptian and Israeli leaders to Camp David, where they worked out accords.
4. These places, still held by Israel, were taken in the 1967 war. Peace depends on agreement about their status.
5. to ward off Soviet influence
6. He claimed that Kuwait was part of Iraq.
7. They resented his emphasis on Western values.
8. anger at Israeli rule and poor jobs

Critical Thinking
1. Acts of terrorism occurred in the struggle for American

Connections Across Time

Historical Significance The nations of the Middle East have ancient cultures, but their political systems are still being developed. This undertaking has often been complicated by conflicts among themselves and by the great difficulties of reconciling traditional and modern ways of life.

Solutions for the challenges facing the Middle East often seem elusive, and progress has to be measured in gradual steps. An example is the complicated peace process among Israel and its Arab neighbors. In spite of setbacks, some factors weigh on the side of progress and peace. The end of the cold war has made cooperation among Middle Eastern nations a greater possibility.

Using Key Terms

Write the key term that completes each sentence. Then write a sentence for each term not chosen.

a. disengagement   g. sovereignty
b. nationalized   h. Pan-Arabism
c. fundamentalism   i. pact
d. *intifada*   j. desalination
e. kibbutzim   k. cartel
f. embargo

1. In 1974 United States Secretary of State Henry Kissinger negotiated a _____, or military withdrawal, agreement between Egypt and Israel.
2. In the quest for regional unity, some Arab nations refuse to yield their _____ to an international body.
3. Some Jewish immigrants to Palestine settled on _____, or collective farms.
4. In recent years, some Middle Easterners have supported religious _____ in their efforts to defend traditional values and to oppose governments they dislike.
5. In 1987, Palestinians in the West Bank and Gaza Strip carried out an _____ to oppose Israeli rule of their areas.

Technology Activity

Using the Internet Use the Internet to search for an online newspaper with current articles about the Middle East. Find a recent article pertaining to any news from the Middle East. Evaluate your findings by writing a report that contains the source of information, title, date, and summary of the article. Include an opinion of whether or not this particular current event impacts your life.

Using Your History Journal

Write an essay about an unresolved Middle Eastern issue shown on your time line. Gather information about the issue, consider ways of solving the problems it poses, and evaluate which resolution you believe is most effective.

Reviewing Facts

1. **Geography** Discuss how geography helped make the Middle East a scene of cold war rivalry.
2. **History** Explain the link between the Aswan High Dam and the Suez crisis of 1956.
3. **History** Describe United States President Jimmy Carter's role in improving relations between Israel and Egypt.
4. **Geography** Explain the importance of the West Bank, the Gaza Strip, and the Golan Heights.
5. **History** Explain why the United States gave support to Turkey and to Iran.
6. **History** State the reasons for Saddam Hussein's invasion of Kuwait in 1990.
7. **Citizenship** Discuss why Iran's Muslim leaders opposed the rule of the shah.
8. **Citizenship** Describe the factors that sparked the outbreak of the Palestinian *intifada*.

Critical Thinking

1. **Evaluate** Do you think that terrorism can be justified as a means of attaining political goals? Why or why not?

---

independence.
2. Women have more opportunities for education and jobs. Some women have made advances in business and politics. Students should note general progress in women's rights worldwide, although some areas have progressed faster than others.
3. Answers should point out the varieties of government and differing attitudes toward human rights; Israel is a democracy, although

Palestinians point out violation of their rights; Turkey and Lebanon are democratic, but the military has influence; Iran and Iraq have authoritarian regimes.
4. No country or people should be forced to become part of another country.

Geography in History
1. Saudia Arabia
2. Persian Gulf

2. **Apply** How have women's roles changed in the Middle East in recent years? Compare the position of women in the Middle East today with those of women in other parts of the world.
3. **Evaluate** To what degree do you think human rights and democratic government have made advances in the Middle East since 1945?
4. **Evaluate** Saddam Hussein justified Iraq's invasion of Kuwait, in part, on the grounds of nationalism and Arab unity. Analyze this reasoning. Do you think it is justified?

Geography in History

1. **Place** Refer to the map below. What country of the Middle East produced the most oil in 1990?
2. **Location** The four main producers of oil in the Middle East all border what body of water?
3. **Region** What correlation is there between the size, in area, and the amount of oil produced in the countries shown?

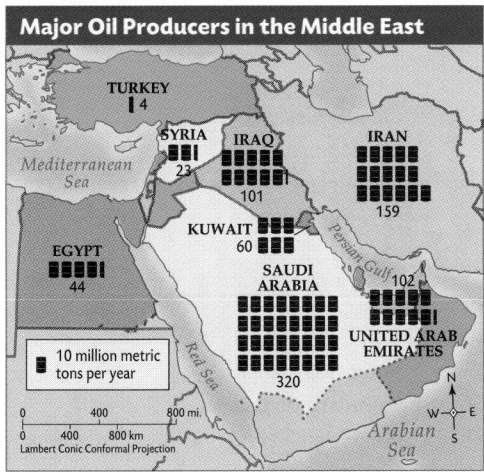

Major Oil Producers in the Middle East

TURKEY 4
SYRIA
IRAQ 23
101
IRAN 159
Mediterranean Sea
EGYPT 44
KUWAIT 60
SAUDI ARABIA 320
102
UNITED ARAB EMIRATES
Persian Gulf
Red Sea
Arabian Sea

10 million metric tons per year

0   400   800 mi.
0   400   800 km
Lambert Conic Conformal Projection

Understanding Themes

1. **Nationalism** How did the cold war contribute to the development of the Suez crisis in 1956?
2. **Cooperation** Why can the Camp David Accords be considered a turning point in the history of the modern Middle East?
3. **Cultural Diffusion** Do you think Saudi Arabia

will succeed in resisting unwanted foreign influences while developing its economy and society? Explain.

Linking Past and Present

1. When the state of Israel was founded in 1948, Israelis and Palestinians were bitter enemies. What was the basic issue that divided them in 1948? By 1995, how had their relationship changed? What issues continue to divide them?
2. Religion continues to influence life in the Middle East. What recent developments reflect this influence? How have religious ideas and movements shaped events in other parts of the world since World War II? What impact will they have in the future?

Skill Practice

Review the sample bibliography below for a report on the South American country of Brazil. Then answer the questions that follow.

Page, Joseph A. The Brazilians. Addison-Wesley Publishing Company, 1995.
Kirch, John. Why is This Country Dancing: One-Man Samba to the Beat of Brazil. New York: Simon & Schuster, 1993.
Rambali, Paul. In the cities and the Jungles of Brazil. New York, 1994.
J. F. Hage, "Fulfilling Brazil's Promise: a Conversation with President Cardoso." Foreign Affairs, Vol. 74, July–August 1995: pp. 62–75.
Levine, J. "The Dance Drink: Brazil's Samba Soft Drink to be Marketed in the U.S." Vol. 154: p. 232.

1. The entries presented above are not listed in the correct order. What author do you think should be listed first?
2. What is missing from the Joseph A. Page book listing?
3. What is wrong or missing in the Paul Rambali book listing?
4. Rewrite the J.F. Hage article listing correctly.
5. What do you think is missing from the J. Levine listing?

Linking Past and Present

1. partition into Jewish and Arab states; by 1995, both sides working toward a settlement; Palestinian fear of Israeli restrictions; Israeli fear of threat by independent Palestine
2. Islam's influence in Iran and Turkey, conservative Judaism's fostering of Israeli links to West Bank, Catholic opposition to communism in Eastern Europe. Regarding the future, religion's role in promoting human rights; feuding caused by religious intolerance.

Skill Practice

1. J. F. Hage
2. The title should be underlined, and the place of publication is missing.
3. The author's name should not be underlined, the word *cities* should be capitalized, and the publisher is missing.
4. Hage, J. F. "Fulfilling Brazil's Promise: A Conversation with President Cardoso." Foreign Affairs, Vol. 74 (July–August 1995): pp. 62–75.
5. the title of the periodical and the date

? **Chapter Bonus Test Question**

Ask students: What role did the end of the cold war play in the formation of the coalition of nations that opposed Iraq in the Persian Gulf War? *(If the cold war had not ended, the Soviet Union might have backed Iraq against the United States, Saudi Arabia, and Kuwait.)*

---

3. The larger the country, the more oil it produces.

Understanding Themes

1. **NATIONALISM** superpower desire for influence, Soviet grant of weapons led to U.S. refusal to help build Aswan High Dam; Nasser sized Suez Canal to obtain its fees
2. **COOPERATION** They represented the first break in the cycle of war between Israel

and its Arab neighbors and led to the first peace treaty between an Arab state (Egypt) and Israel. They laid the foundation for later agreements.

3. **CULTURAL DIFFUSION** Students might point out the difficulties involved in promoting changes in some areas of life while trying to block related changes in other areas.

A complete, 1-page lesson plan is provided for each section in the *Reproducible Lesson Plans* booklet.

Latin America

CHAPTER RESOURCES

	Reproducible Resources	Multimedia Resources
Chapter Opener	Chapter Themes: Graphic Organizer 25 Historical Significance Chapter Activity 25	MindJogger Videoquiz
Chapter Enrichment	Vocabulary Activity 25* Time Line Activity 25 Mapping History Activity 25 History Simulation 25 Geography and History Activity 25 Source Reading 25 People in World History Profiles 69, 70 World Art and Music Activity 25 Enrichment Activity 25 Critical Thinking Activity 25 Skill Reinforcement Activity 25 Performance Assessment Activity 25	World History and Art Transparency 49, *Figura*; 50, *Diego and I* Chapter Transparency 25 Vocabulary PuzzleMaker Software Communism and the Cold War: • *Perspectives on Communism* • *Bay of Pigs* • *Cuban Missile Crisis* • *Revolution in Cuba* • *Nicaragua* • *El Salvador* • *Chile*
Chapter Review/Reteaching	Reteaching Activity 25 Skill Reinforcement Activity 25 Spanish Chapter Summary 25	Chapter 25 Digest Audiocassette, Activity, Test* Vocabulary PuzzleMaker Software Student Self-Test and Review Software MindJogger Videoquiz
Chapter Evaluation/Testing	Performance Assessment Activity 25 Chapter 25 Test, Forms A and B	Testmaker

* *Also available in Spanish*

0:00 OUT OF TIME? Assign the Chapter 25 summary in the Unit 6 Digest on pages 803–805, and the Chapter 25 Audiocassettes.

Block Schedule

Block scheduling differs from traditional class scheduling in the amount of time allotted to each period. The extended time frame provided by block scheduling affords you the opportunity to implement a greater number of research-oriented and activity-intense projects to motivate and involve your students. Activities that are particularly suited to use within the block scheduling framework are identified throughout this chapter by the following designation.

KEY TO ABILITY LEVELS

Teaching strategies have been coded for varying learning styles and abilities.

L1 **BASIC** activities for all students
L2 **AVERAGE** activities for average to above-average students
L3 **CHALLENGING** activities for above-average students
LEP **LIMITED ENGLISH PROFICIENCY** activities

Use Glencoe's *Presentation Plus!* multimedia teacher tool to easily present dynamic lessons that visually excite your students. Using Microsoft PowerPoint® you can customize the presentations to create your own personalized lessons.

SECTION RESOURCES

Daily Objectives	Reproducible Resources	Multimedia Resources
Section 1 **Latin American Challenges** List the social and political challenges facing Latin America after World War II.	Reproducible Lesson Plan 25-1 Vocabulary Activity 25* Guided Reading Activity 25-1* Time Line Activity 25 Section Quiz 25-1*	Section Focus Transparency 25-1 Chapter Transparency 25 Student Self-Test and Review Software Testmaker Communism and the Cold War: *Perspectives on Communism*
Section 2 **Mexico and the Caribbean** Describe the political and economic crises faced by Mexico and the Caribbean after World War II.	Reproducible Lesson Plan 25-2 Vocabulary Activity 25* Guided Reading Activity 25-2* History Simulation 25 People in World History Profile 70 Section Quiz 25-2*	Section Focus Transparency 25-2 World History and Art Transparency 49, *Figura;* 50, *Diego and I* Student Self-Test and Review Software Testmaker Communism and the Cold War: • *Bay of Pigs* • *Cuban Missile Crisis* • *Revolution in Cuba*
Section 3 **Central America** Summarize the factors that led to conflicts in Central America from the 1970s to the 1990s.	Reproducible Lesson Plan 25-3 Vocabulary Activity 25* Guided Reading Activity 25-3* Mapping History Activity 25 Section Quiz 25-3*	Section Focus Transparency 25-3 Student Self-Test and Review Software Testmaker Communism and the Cold War: • *Nicaragua* • *El Salvador*
Section 4 **South America** Explain how democracy has advanced in South America since the late 1980s.	Reproducible Lesson Plan 25-4 Vocabulary Activity 25* Guided Reading Activity 25-4* People in World History Profile 69 Reteaching Activity 25 Enrichment Activity 25 Section Quiz 25-4* Performance Assessment Activity 25 Spanish Chapter Summary 25	Section Focus Transparency 25-4 Student Self-Test and Review Software Testmaker Communism and the Cold War: *Chile*

* Also available in Spanish

Chapter Activities

 Performance Assessment Activity

A Conversation Among Immigrants Have students list situations and locations from the postwar era that produced refugees or immigrants. In each instance have them identify reasons people would want to immigrate to the United States. Students should then role-play a conversation among a group of refugees representing several of the countries from their list. In the conversation students should use information from their lists, from the chapter, and from their own research. The conversation should include opinion statements about standing policies or potential laws that could affect them.

Possible Rubric Features
Accuracy of content information, concept attainment, elaboration and detail, research skills, analytical skills, and persuasion

• *For an additional activity, refer to Activity 25 in the* Performance Assessment Strategies and Activities *booklet.*

ACTIVITY

From the Classroom of...

Mark Manning
Egg Harbor Township
High School
Egg Harbor Township, NJ

Value of the Amazon Rain Forest

After students have read about the Amazon region, organize the class into two groups. Have one group research the economic potential of the rain forest, while the other investigates the region's unique ecology. Then have the class generate two lists comparing the economic and ecological worth of the Amazon region.

Have the full class discuss both sides of the issue of developing the Amazon rain forest. Given the struggling economies of the nations of the region, should economic development be a priority? Can economic development and ecological preservation be balanced?

MULTIPLE LEARNING STYLES

Verbal/Linguistic
Have students locate Latin American literature, including folktales, poetry, drama, nonfiction, novels, and short stories. Direct them to create an annotated bibliography.

Visual/Spatial
Have students draw or reproduce the flag of each nation studied. Ask them to find out what the flag symbols mean and to provide a key to them. They should then display the flags to the class.

Auditory/Musical
Play recordings of the music of several of the countries studied and ask students to compare musical styles. Possible examples include reggae from Jamaica, merengue from the Dominican Republic, tango from Argentina, and samba from Brazil.

Kinesthetic
Show the class examples of murals by such Latin American artists as Diego Rivera and José Orozco. Have students choose aspects of life in Latin America and illustrate them. Create a colorful classroom mural, using all of the illustrations.

Additional Resources

NATIONAL GEOGRAPHIC SOCIETY

Teacher's Corner

INDEX TO NATIONAL GEOGRAPHIC MAGAZINE

The following articles may be used for research relating to this chapter:

- "Peru Begins Again," by John McCarry, May 1996.
- "El Salvador," by Mike Edwards, September 1995.
- "Buenos Aires: Making Up for Lost Time," by John J. Putman, December 1994.

ADDITIONAL NATIONAL GEOGRAPHIC SOCIETY PRODUCTS

To order the following products for use with this chapter, call National Geographic Society at 1-800-368-2728:

- *Capitalism, Socialism, Communism Series, "Communism."* (Video)
- *Nations of the World Series, "Mexico."* (Video)
- *Nations of the World Series, "Central America."* (Video)
- *Physical Geography of the Continents Series: South America* (Video)
- *The Mexicans: Through Their Eyes* (Video)

LOCAL OBJECTIVES

_____
_____
_____
_____
_____
_____
_____
_____
_____
_____
_____
_____
_____
_____
_____
_____
_____
_____
_____
_____
_____
_____
_____
_____
_____
_____
_____
_____
_____

BIBLIOGRAPHY

Literature of the Period
García Márquez, Gabriel. *One Hundred Years of Solitude.* New York: Harper, 1970. The rise and fall of the fictional town of Macondo is an allegory of Colombian history.
Vargas Llosa, Mario. *The Time of the Hero.* New York: Grove Press, 1966. Adolescents struggle for survival in a military school.
Readings for the Student
Guillermoprieto, Alma. *The Heart That Bleeds: Latin America Now.* New York: Knopf, 1994. Personal encounters in major cities.
Readings for the Teacher
Winn, Peter. *Americas: The Changing Face of Latin America and the Caribbean.* New York: Pantheon, 1992. Past and present, with an emphasis on human interest.

*inter*NET
CONNECTION
Latin American resources on the World Wide Web
Latin World:
http://www.latinworld.com/

Chapter Themes are listed by section on this chapter opening page of the Student Edition. A corresponding theme-based activity is available under "TEACH," and a theme-based question is asked in the Section and Chapter Reviews.

The Storyteller

Historical Setting Fidel Castro came from a family of well-to-do landowners. But he claimed that his "vocation" was "being a revolutionary." As a young man, he took part in an unsuccessful invasion of the neighboring Dominican Republic to try to overthrow that nation's dictator, and he organized riots that disrupted the 1948 Pan-American Conference at Bogotá, Colombia.

Historical Significance

Answers: *They have tried to institute democratic reforms and industrialize their countries, as well as joining economic and political alliances.*

Countries have become more democratic, and their economies have grown. Their populations have also skyrocketed.

Chapter
25
1945–Present
Latin America

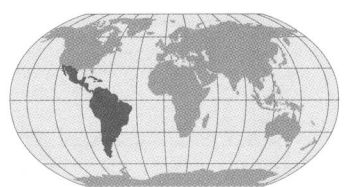

Chapter Themes

▶ **Cooperation** New organizations promote economic ties in Latin America. *Section 1*
▶ **Revolution** The overthrow of dictatorial government in Cuba opens the door to communism in the Western Hemisphere. *Section 2*
▶ **Conflict** Calls for land reform and political freedom lead to civil wars in Latin America. *Section 3*
▶ **Change** Latin American countries work to develop their struggling economies and to establish democracies. *Section 4*

The Storyteller

On New Year's Day, 1959, the island of Cuba went mad with joy. Tall, bearded Fidel Castro, a lawyer turned soldier, and his band of guerrillas had overthrown dictator Fulgencio Batista.

Along the road to Santiago, crowds of people waved and cheered as Castro's ragtag troops passed by in battered jeeps and trucks. "Viva, Fidel! Viva la revolución!" they cried. So delirious were the throngs, so swept away by the power of the moment, that a friend of Castro's later recalled, "It was like a messiah arriving. We were walking on a cloud."

Castro's revolution was not the first in Latin America, nor the last. Over the next few decades, tensions between rich and poor would erupt in violence repeatedly as the nations of Latin America struggled toward economic and political development.

Historical Significance

How have Latin American countries worked toward political reform and economic growth? What changes have come to Latin America since the end of the cold war?

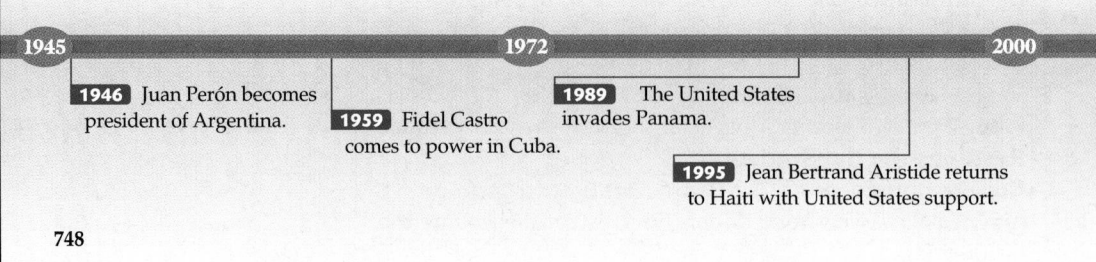

1945	1972	2000

1946 Juan Perón becomes president of Argentina.

1959 Fidel Castro comes to power in Cuba.

1989 The United States invades Panama.

1995 Jean Bertrand Aristide returns to Haiti with United States support.

748

GEOGRAPHY CONNECTION

Location Have students locate Latin America on a map. Ask them to point out the following: Mexico; the Caribbean region; Central America; South America; the Isthmus of Panama. **What major American cities are closest to the Caribbean, Mexico, and Central America?** *(Answers include Miami, New Orleans, Houston, San Antonio, and Los Angeles.)* **Why is this region called Latin America?** *(Except for indigenous people, most of the inhabitants of this region speak Spanish, Portuguese, or French—languages based on Latin.)*

Visualizing History

Portuguese sailors named Rio de Janeiro; the words mean "river of January." Arriving on January 1, 1502, they thought that Guanabara Bay was the mouth of a river. What is special about the culture of Brazil? *(Brazil is the only South American country where Portuguese, not Spanish or French, is spoken.)*

Visualizing History Amid the glow of night lights, Sugarloaf Mountain overlooks the city of Rio de Janeiro, Brazil.

Performance Assessment

Refer to the activity on page 748C of the Planning Guide.

For an additional activity, refer to Activity 25 in the *Performance Assessment Strategies and Activities* booklet.

Your History Journal

Research population statistics of either Central or South American nations. Draw a cartogram that shows the relative population sizes of these nations today.

Using Your History Journal

Suggest that students use a current almanac or recent encyclopedia for up-to-date statistics.

GLENCOE TECHNOLOGY

VIDEODISC
Use MindJogger to preview chapter content.

MindJogger Videoquiz
Chapter 25
Disc 3 Side B

  Also available in VHS.

Chapter 25 *Latin America* **749**

✚ EXTRA CREDIT PROJECT

Native Americans In pre-Columbian times, Latin America had the most advanced Native American cultures in the Western Hemisphere and the largest population of Native Americans. Ask students what has happened to the descendants of the Maya, Aztec, Inca, and other indigenous peoples. Have them research and report on the Native Americans of Latin America today—where most of them are concentrated and how they live.

1945   1972   2000

1948 The United States and Latin American nations form the Organization of American States (OAS).

1968 Catholic clergy in Latin America support social reform efforts.

1990s Civilian democratic governments begin to replace military rule throughout Latin America.

SECTION THEME

▶ **Cooperation** New organizations promote economic ties in Latin America.

ind Out

Answer: *social: population growth, urbanization, gap between elites and rest of population; economic: large foreign debt, industrialization; political: conflicts between conservatives and liberals, guerrilla movements*

FOCUS

Section Objective

List the social and political challenges facing Latin America after World War II.

BELLRINGER
Motivational Activity

Before taking roll at the beginning of the class period, project Section Focus Transparency 25-1 and have students answer the activity questions. Discuss students' responses.

🗁   This activity is also available as a blackline master.

Vocabulary Pre-check

🗁   Use Vocabulary Activity 25 to introduce vocabulary terms.
L1 LEP

Section 1

Latin American Challenges

Setting the Scene

▶ **Terms to Define**
   campesino, elite, liberation theology, free trade

▶ **People to Meet**
   Luis Echeverría, Javier Pérez de Cuéllar, Jacobo Arbenz Guzmán

▶ **Places to Locate**
   Mexico City, Brazil, Rio de Janeiro

 **ind Out**   What social and political challenges did Latin America face after World War II?

The Storyteller

The university student volunteers reached the Guatemalan Indian village after nightfall. Eating tortillas and drinking fresh milk around the fire came first; then the cursillo *began—city and mountain people coming together to talk about liberation. The program included talks about the common good, the right of people to organize, and how to organize for greater strength. Standing before the gathering, Juan took a stick and snapped it. "Alone we are like this," he said. Then he picked up a bundle of sticks that he could not break. "Together we are like this. You and I and your children."*

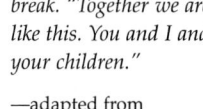

—adapted from *Guerrillas of Peace, Liberation Theology and the Central America Revolution*, Blase Bonpane, 1985

Guatemalan village

In the years after World War II, powerful changes began to reshape Latin America. Between 1940 and 1970, many Latin American nations industrialized as rapidly as did the United States in the late 1800s. Social changes followed this economic transformation. For example, schools and health-care facilities spread, and women won the right to vote.

Yet a dark cloud hung over these bright and hopeful achievements. Much of the region's newfound wealth flowed into the hands of the well-to-do, leaving millions of farmers and workers in the grip of desperate poverty. As the gap between rich and poor widened, the huge peasant class grew hungry and angry. Communism, with its appeal to the oppressed and its promise of social and economic equality, won many converts. As the peasants' demands increased, strong military dictators emerged to quell political upheaval through repression and terror.

These military leaders, in turn, were unable to solve mounting political and economic problems during the 1970s, and their failures inspired calls for democratic reform. By the early 1990s, new civilian democratic governments had replaced many of the old, harsh regimes in a number of Latin American countries.

Population Growth

Since World War II, Latin America's population has skyrocketed. In 1940 Latin America's population was 126 million. With a growth rate of about 2.3 percent a year—about three times the rate of the United States and other industrialized countries—the region's population may expand to nearly 600 million by the year 2000.

Rapid growth has resulted from a combination

🗁 **Reproducible Masters**
- Reproducible Lesson Plan 25-1
- Vocabulary Activity 25
- Guided Reading Activity 25-1
- Time Line Activity 25
- Section Quiz 25-1

Transparencies
- Section Focus Transparency 25-1
- Chapter Transparency 25

Multimedia
- Student Self-Test and Review Software
- Testmaker
- Communism and the Cold War: *Perspectives on Communism*

Visualizing History Deforestation by slash-and-burn methods and by excessive logging threatens the rainforests of Latin America. Despite increased agricultural acreage, there are not enough jobs in rural areas. *Where do people from these areas go to find work?*

of tradition and progress. Traditionally, families had many children. But because so many died in infancy, the population grew slowly. Latin American women still have many children. The average number of births per 1,000 Latin American women is twice the number in the United States, but improved health care has sharply lowered the infant mortality rate.

The rate of infant deaths, though five times that in the United States, is lower than in the past. Thus, more babies live to adulthood, and Latin America's population is increasing.

The population growth of Latin America has strained its economic and political systems. The expanding population requires increased supplies of food, clean drinking water, housing, schools, health care, jobs, and transportation.

Urbanization

As the population of rural areas expanded, the poor farmers—known as campesinos—headed to cities in search of work in factories or stores and of better living conditions. With more schools, medical facilities, and other social services than rural areas have, larger cities continue to attract many rural people. In the 1950s about 10 percent of Latin Americans lived in a city of at least 1 million people. Today, over 25 percent do; another 45 percent live in smaller cities.

Cities, however, could not absorb easily the heavy flow of campesinos. The new residents clustered in sprawling, dilapidated shantytowns, many with no electricity, running water, or sanitary facilities. In his 1969 book *A Death in the Sanchez Family*, Oscar Lewis captured the bleakness of life in one such **Mexico City** slum:

> ❝ The [place] where she [Guadalupe] lived consisted of a row of 14 one-room adobe huts about 10 feet by 15 feet, built along the left side and across the back of a 30-foot-wide bare lot.... Five of the dwellings had makeshift sheds, constructed by setting up two poles and extending the kitchen roofs of tarpaper, tin, and corrugated metal over the low front doorways.... Toward the rear of the yard, two large cement water troughs, each with a faucet, were the sole sources of water for the 84 inhabitants. ❞

Such miserable surroundings offered little comfort or hope for the future. Even so, thousands of campesinos kept coming. The president of Venezuela observed, "The poor country peasant would rather come to the city and try to make a living selling lottery tickets than remain in the [countryside] where he has absolutely nothing."

Social Inequalities

Latin America's social structure—masses of poor people dominated by a small but wealthy class of elite—was established during the colonial period. Today the elite includes large landowners, industrialists, top church officials, and military leaders. Many of the elite in Latin America today

Chapter 25 *Latin America* **751**

TEACH

Guided Practice

THEME Cooperation

Have students list ways the United States and Latin America can cooperate and the benefits that would result for each region. (*The United States can help Latin American nations become economically stable, enabling them to improve living conditions, prevent environmental degradation, and repay their debts to U.S. banks. Cooperating to curb the drug trade would reduce crime in both regions.*) **L1 LEP**

Visualizing History In some cases, deforestation is aimed at clearing land on which to graze cattle (often for export to the Northern Hemisphere). Elsewhere, it is done to create more farmland; unfortunately, much of the cleared soil lacks fertility. **Answer to Caption:** *to cities*

Population A major challenge to development in Latin America has been its growing population. **How does population growth in Latin America compare with that in the United States?** (*It is about three times as great in Latin America.*) **L2**

 Chapter Transparency 25

Independent Practice

 Guided Reading Activity 25-1 **L1**

Time Line Activity 25

COOPERATIVE LEARNING ACTIVITY

Posters Have students form five teams, each one to make a poster graphically representing one of the challenges faced by Latin America: population growth, urbanization, economic development, the growth of democracy, and foreign relations. Students should focus on these aspects: background of the challenge, a clear statement of the issue, key individuals or countries involved with the issue, and possible solutions. **L2**

Cooperation The Organization of American States (OAS), formed in 1948, has worked to encourage political and economic ties among its members. Have students research and report on how this organization is set up and how it operates. **L2**

Economics Land reform has been a controversial issue in many Latin American countries for many years. Have students research and report on land-reform efforts since World War II. They may wish to choose a specific country. **L3**

Who?What?Where?When?

Woman Suffrage For decades, left-wing politicians in Latin America opposed woman suffrage because they thought that women would vote for right-wing candidates. In Ecuador, the first Latin American country to give women the vote, voting was mandatory for men but optional for women.

Linking Past and Present

Booming Buenos Aires

Visitors to the city enjoy shopping—especially for fine woolens and leather goods—eating steak dinners at reasonable prices (Argentina remains a major beef producer); and dancing the tango, the Argentine national dance.

ANSWERS

its pleasant climate and its prosperity as a commercial and industrial center; students may suggest that growth will likely increase pollution and strain city services

are the descendants of the Europeans who colonized the region centuries ago. The increase in wealth brought by industrialization in this century simply made these families richer. By the late 1980s, 50 percent of the newly generated wealth in **Brazil** flowed into the hands of the wealthiest 10 percent of the people. As of 1992, 33 million Brazilians, about 21 percent of the population, lived in extreme poverty.

The majority of Latin America's population consists of poor people: peasants, landless farm workers, and factory workers. Many countries in recent decades have a small but growing middle class consisting of professionals, managers, clerks, and government workers.

A more important change has been in the development of the role of women in Latin America. Traditionally women had important but restricted roles in society. They were expected to work at home and raise children. In the late 1800s, women established their right to get an education and to enter a variety of careers. However, not until the mid-1960s did all Latin American women win the right to vote.

Economic Development

In recent decades many Latin American leaders pushed for increased industrialization. They hoped that their countries could manufacture their own products instead of importing them, thereby reducing their trade deficits. In just a few decades, Latin American steel production grew by 20 percent, while the production of metals, machines, and energy rose by 10 percent. Manufacturers flooded the markets with consumer products aimed at the upper and middle classes—fashions, sports cars, toys, and appliances. Since industrialization did little to increase the buying power of the poor, the market for consumer goods was limited to the small elite. Latin American firms quickly produced more than they could sell at home, so they turned to exporting goods to stay in business.

The efforts at industrialization brought results. Between 1950 and 1995, Latin America achieved a remarkable economic growth rate. Much of the money to finance industrial growth, however, came from large multinational corporations and banks. For every dollar they invested in Latin America,

CONNECTIONS

Geography

Booming Buenos Aires

Downtown Buenos Aires

Latin America is one of the world's most rapidly urbanizing continents. For example, today more than 12 million people—well over one-third of all Argentinians—live in the port city and capital of Buenos Aires. One attractive feature of the city is the pleasant, temperate climate. The people of Buenos Aires, called *porteños*, or port dwellers, are descendants of immigrants from all over the world—Spain, Italy, England, France, Poland, and the Middle East.

In the mid-1800s, British and Argentinian investors built a network of rail lines spreading outward from Buenos Aires. On these rail lines, wheat, corn, cattle, and

sheep are now sent to Buenos Aires for export. Building on its foundation of trade in agricultural products, Buenos Aires grew into a prosperous industrial center. Among the major industries are food processing and textiles.

Buenos Aires' rapid growth typifies the recent expansion of cities throughout the region. In 1909 Buenos Aires topped the 1 million mark. Immigration from overseas and from rural areas in Argentina added to the population in the succeeding decades. During the 1940s, Buenos Aires had 4.5 million people, and in forty years the population had nearly tripled, reaching over 12 million.

Linking Past and Present ACTIVITY

Discuss the features of Buenos Aires that have attracted immigrants. What effects do you think continued growth will have on Buenos Aires' future?

MEETING SPECIAL NEEDS ACTIVITY

Mixed Learners Students with learning disabilities and those with limited English proficiency will benefit from organizing the chapter information in a visual way. Have students create wall maps of Latin America to reinforce the location of each country. Have students find, copy, or create images of important aspects of life in the various countries: people, places, farming, industry, and so on. Gifted students may write captions explaining the meaning and importance of the images for each country. **L1 LEP**

these business and banking enterprises took out more than three dollars in profits and dividends.

Agricultural growth did not match industrial growth. More land was allocated for growing cash crops for export, such as coffee, bananas, and coca, which is used to make cocaine. But as farmers converted more land to growing cash crops, they grew less food for the local population. Although the landowners prospered from selling their crops abroad, local people had to pay more to buy food from farther away. Most campesinos remained poor.

Hoping to stimulate economic growth, many Latin American leaders borrowed heavily from large banks in the United States and other countries. Between 1975 and 1985, Latin American debt to other parts of the world rose 318 percent. By the 1980s, a worldwide recession made matters worse—cutting global demand for Latin American products and further raising interest rates and Latin American debts. By 1984, the region's debt totaled $350 billion; by 1993, it had climbed to over $465 billion.

In spite of economic improvements in the 1990s, Latin American debt remains a major problem for the region. If debts are not paid, banks may fail, threatening the stability of the global economy. In the mid-1990s, a political and economic crisis in Mexico nearly led to Mexico's failure to meet its international debt payments. The United States came to Mexico's rescue with an aid package to bolster the Mexican economy. The United States government has also worked with Latin American countries to reschedule international loan payments to avoid potential crises.

Another economic area in which the United States and Latin America work together is the war on drugs. Powerful dealers profit from international trading in illegal drugs made from certain crops grown in Latin America. The United States and Latin American governments both aim to end the illegal drug trade, but difficulties often hamper cooperation. The United States often expresses concern about the corrupt influence drug dealers have on Latin American governments, while Latin American countries claim the United States needs to take stronger measures at home to lessen the demand for drugs.

Growth of Democracy

The economic problems of Latin America made the growth of democracy almost impossible. In most countries, the elite controlled the government as well as the economy. The elite did not trust the masses enough to allow any form of majority rule to take hold. The majority of people, long dominated by a few powerful leaders, had little experience in making decisions or choosing leaders.

Political conflicts in most of Latin America were between liberals and conservatives. Liberals tried to help the masses through land and tax reforms. Conservatives wanted to maintain the traditional social structure and opposed any redistribution of wealth. Clashes between liberals and conservatives have often been bloody.

The failure of democracy and social reform prompted calls for more radical change. Armed guerrilla movements, that sought to change society by force, emerged in many countries. These groups often relied on the support and protection of campesinos. Many guerrilla organizations included at least some Communists. In countries such as Cuba and Nicaragua, guerrilla movements successfully overthrew governments and took power themselves.

Fear of communism combined with outrage at the poverty of so many people caused changes in the Catholic Church. Since colonial times, the Church had generally supported rule by elites in most Latin American countries. Individual priests sometimes called for reforms to help the poor, but they were exceptions. After a meeting of Latin American bishops in Colombia in 1968, however, an increasing number of Catholic clergy began supporting land reform, democracy, and other changes that campesinos and workers had long demanded. They began emphasizing the role of Christianity in

Visualizing History Workers load bananas for shipment in Ecuador, where petroleum and agricultural products are the main exports. *How did the emphasis on production of cash crops affect the campesinos?*

Visualizing History Agriculture continues to be the leading occupation in most of Latin America. Have students use an almanac or encyclopedia to identify which nations in Latin America have economies based on agriculture and what crops they export.
Answer to Caption: *They grew less food for their own use and thus had to buy it, increasing their need for income.*

ABCNEWS INTERACTIVE™

VIDEODISC
Communism and the Cold War

Side One, Chapter 8
Frames 14264–14893
Title: *Perspectives on Communism*
Subject: Discussion of the ideals of communism
Ask: In Communist philosophy, what was the ideal society? *(The ideal society was one in which everyone was happy; in which all were "master and owner of everything" with no competition.)*

Chapter 25 *Latin America* 753

MAKING CONNECTIONS ACTIVITIES

Literature Latin American literature has gained worldwide fame in recent decades. The first writer from this region to win the Nobel Prize was the Chilean poet Gabriela Mistral, in 1945. Have students research her work or the poetry of such writers as Pablo Neruda, Octavio Paz, or Derek Walcott and then present selections to the class, reading in both Spanish (where relevant) and English if possible. **L3**

History Several Nazi leaders fled to South America after the defeat of Germany in World War II. One of the best known was Adolf Eichmann, who was arrested in Argentina in 1960. Have students research and report on how he was found and captured and his subsequent fate. **L3**

ASSESS

Check for Understanding

Assign Section 1 Review as home-work or as an in-class activity.

 Use Student Self-Test and Review Software to review Section 1.

Evaluate

📁 Section Quiz 25-1

📷 Use the Testmaker to create a customized quiz for Section 1.

Reteach

Have students brainstorm a list of the main challenges facing Latin America in the post-World War II period and then rank them by importance.

Enrich

Have students watch the 1983 movie *El Norte*, a moving depiction of illegal immigrants who make a dangerous journey from Guatemala to California, and write a short essay on why immigrants are willing to take great risks to reach the United States.

CLOSE

Have students list all the organizations through which Latin American nations cooperate for economic, social, and political progress.

---

liberating people from oppression. Their beliefs became known as liberation theology. One Latin American religious worker explained the new movement this way:

> **❝** For example, if, as the book of Genesis teaches, human beings have been created in God's image, they have a great dignity; hence, to torture another human being is to disfigure God's image. If the Lord gave the Earth to Adam and Eve, he meant it for all—not just a few plantation owners. **❞**
> —Philip Berryman, *Inside Central America*, 1985

The combined pressure of guerrillas, liberal Catholic clergy, and organized citizens began to bring changes in the 1980s. Argentina, Brazil, Chile, and other countries threw off their dictators and adopted democratic governments. However, these young democracies inherited international debts, widespread poverty, and social unrest. The most controversial issue in many countries has been land reform, which is still opposed by the military and wealthy landowners.

International Relations

Since the end of World War II, Latin America has become involved with the rest of the world. Latin American nations have forged new trading relationships with Western Europe, Asia, Africa, and Japan. In addition, many Latin American leaders have taken leadership positions in world diplomacy. For example, in the 1970s, Mexico's president, **Luis Echeverría** (AY•chuh•vuh•REE•uh) was a leader in the nonaligned movement. Peruvian diplomat **Javier Pérez de Cuéllar** (kway•YAHR) served as the secretary general of the United Nations from 1982 to 1991.

The most important relations of Latin American nations, however, have been with each other and with the United States. In **Rio de Janeiro**,

Brazil, in 1947, representatives of the United States and most of the Latin American nations signed the Rio Treaty. This defense pact provided that any attack on one member would be considered an attack on all members.

A year later, the Organization of American States (OAS) was set up to develop political and economic ties among the nations of the Western Hemisphere. One of its most important successes was in 1995, when OAS members Brazil, the United States, Argentina, and Chile intervened to stop a war between Peru and Ecuador.

Relations between Latin America and the United States were shaped by the cold war. The United States often provided military aid to conservative regimes while undermining left-wing governments. In 1954 the U.S. CIA helped overthrow a left-wing government in Guatemala led by **Jacobo Arbenz Guzmán**. Guzmán's efforts to redistribute land to the peasants was viewed as a threat to American business interests.

Another way to fight communism was through financial assistance. In 1961 President John F. Kennedy launched the Alliance for Progress. It provided $10 billion for Latin American industry, housing, medical care, and military development. However, much of the money sent to Latin America was used to buy American-made goods.

As the cold war ended in the 1980s nations in the Americas began working toward free trade, or the elimination of trade barriers among countries. Throughout the Western Hemisphere, groups of countries formed regional economic pacts, such as the North American Free Trade Agreement (NAFTA), the Andean Pact, the Southern Common Market (Mercosur), the Caribbean Community and Common Market (Caricom), and the Central American Common Market.

Western Hemisphere governments also took steps to bring together all of the region's free trade organizations. In 1994 leaders from 34 Western Hemisphere nations planned for a free trade area by the year 2005.

| **SECTION 1 REVIEW** |

Recall
1. **Define** campesino, elite, liberation theology, free trade.
2. **Identify** Luis Echeverría, Javier Pérez de Cuéllar, Jacobo Arbenz Guzmán, Alliance for Progress, NAFTA.

3. **State** how the role of the Roman Catholic Church in Latin America has changed since World War II.

Critical Thinking
4. **Evaluating Information** Has the cause of human rights

advanced in Latin America since the 1980s? Explain.

Understanding Themes
5. **Cooperation** How might increased United States–Latin American trade affect the campesinos of Latin America?

| **SECTION 1 REVIEW ANSWERS** |

1. All vocabulary words are defined in the Glossary.
2. Luis Echeverría, 754; Javier Pérez de Cuéllar, 754; Jacobo Arbenz Guzmán, 754; Alliance for Progress, 754; NAFTA, 754
3. Once a pillar of the establishment, it has been influenced by liberation theology

to advocate reform, especially advancement of the poor.
4. Students might discuss the return of democratic rule in Chile, Argentina, and various Central American nations that had poor civil rights records in the 1970s.
5. **COOPERATION** It might benefit

them if the increased income is distributed more widely than in the past; if only the rich profit, campesinos will make no progress.

1945   1972   2000

1961 U.S.-trained exiles stage Bay of Pigs invasion in Cuba.

1971 The first Duvalier presidency ends in Haiti.

1993 United States, Mexico, and Canada enact NAFTA.

Section 2
Mexico and the Caribbean

Setting the Scene

▶ **Terms to Define**
standard of living, privatization

▶ **People to Meet**
Carlos Salinas de Gortari, Zapatistas, Ernesto Zedillo Ponce de León, Fidel Castro, Jean Bertrand Aristide

▶ **Places to Locate**
Mexico, Cuba, Dominican Republic, Haiti

 **ind Out** How did Mexico and the Caribbean face political and economic crises after World War II?

The Storyteller

The revolutionary leader Fidel Castro spoke of revolutionaries: "Whoever stops to wait for ideas to triumph among the majority of the masses before initiating revolutionary action will never be a revolutionary.... It is obvious that in Latin America there are already in many places a number of men who … have started revolutionary action. And what distinguished the true revolutionary from the false revolutionary is precisely this: one acts to move the masses, the other waits for the masses to have a conscience already before starting to act."

—*Fidel Castro Speaks*, edited by Martin Kenner and James Petras, 1969

Castro as a young rebel fighter

After World War II, Mexico and the Caribbean nations of Cuba, the Dominican Republic, and Haiti were ruled frequently by either a single political party or by dictators. Mexico's single-party government controlled much of its economy, while American businesses played an important role in the Caribbean economies. In Cuba, a Communist government took power in 1959, bringing the cold war to the Western Hemisphere. In recent decades, Mexico and the Caribbean countries have tried to reform their political systems and develop their economies. Growing populations and political turmoil, however, have made these goals difficult to reach.

Mexico

Of all the countries in Latin America, **Mexico** was among the most stable after World War II. Since 1929, it had been dominated by one political party, the Institutional Revolutionary Party (PRI). Restricted by the constitution to single, six-year terms, strong PRI presidents, using their appointment powers, kept tight control over national and local governments. State-controlled businesses produced rapid industrialization and a growing middle class.

From the late 1940s to the 1960s, Mexico's standard of living—the overall wealth of its people—increased. Industrial growth was concentrated in the central region of the country around Mexico City. There, more goods and services were available to a growing number of people. Rural areas, especially in the south, lagged far behind, and millions of peasants remained desperately poor. Today 40 percent of Mexico's population lives in poverty.

Chapter 25 *Latin America* **755**

TEACH

Guided Practice

THEME Revolution

Cuba's government was over-thrown in 1959. What dissatisfactions led to this uprising? *(foreign domination of the economy, together with Batista's repressive and corrupt rule)* **L1 LEP**

Linking Past and Present

Three Cultures Mexico City boasts a dramatic example of how the present builds on the past. The Plaza of the Three Cultures contains the ruins of Aztec temples, the remains of a Spanish colonial church, and a modern housing complex.

Politics In spite of economic progress under Mexico's President Salinas, his regime faced opposition. What were three causes of this opposition? *(Economic benefits were slow to reach the poor; many resented the political domination of the PRI; many opposed NAFTA, fearing the loss of their lands.)* **L2**

 History Simulation 25

World History and Art Transparency 49, *Figura*; 50, *Diego and I*

Who?What?Where?When?

Zapata The name of Emiliano Zapata is written in gold in Mexico's chamber of deputies. An uneducated, landless Native American, Zapata became a powerful spokesperson for others like himself. In 1919, during the violence of the Mexican Revolution, he was assassinated by political foes.

Economic Problems

In the 1970s, oil seemed to offer Mexico a way to prosperity. New oil discoveries and rising world oil prices brought profits to the state-owned Mexican oil industry and boosted the Mexican economy. The government borrowed money from foreign sources to finance economic development, assuming that oil revenues would make repaying the loans easy.

Global recession in the early 1980s and increased oil supplies caused world oil prices to drop. The Mexican government was forced to cut back jobs and services to save money. To boost exports, the value of the peso, the Mexican unit of currency, was cut by nearly half. Some wealthy Mexicans responded by fleeing the country with their money.

Mexico soon faced an economic crisis, owing foreign investors $100 billion, one of the highest national debts in the developing world. The gap between rich and poor widened, as the population continued to grow rapidly. The growing demand for jobs, goods, and services could not be met. Then in 1985, a devastating earthquake hit Mexico City, the capital, killing thousands of people and causing billions of dollars in damages.

Relations worsened with the United States during this period, too, as a result of differences over drug smuggling and illegal immigration. The United States wanted the Mexican government to do more to stop the flow of illegal drugs into United States territory. In addition, growing numbers of Mexicans and Central Americans were crossing the United States-Mexico border without visas in hopes of finding work.

The Salinas Era

In 1988 Mexican president **Carlos Salinas de Gortari** promised broad reforms. To improve relations with the United States, he pledged to crack down on drug smuggling and illegal immigration. He also rolled back the policy of government ownership of major industries. With privatization, or a shift to private ownership of businesses, Salinas

Images *of the* Times

Mexico Today

Mexico faces economic, social, and political change as the nation attempts to provide a better living for its growing population.

Native Mexican crafts delight shoppers in the Sunday craft market in Oaxaca.

Petroleum and petroleum products play an important role in Mexico's trade. World oil prices affect the nation's economy.

756

Images *of the* Times Mexico Today

Every year some 800,000 people move to Mexico City. This migration has made the city the largest metropolitan area in the world. Almost one-fourth of the Mexican people live in the *distrito federal*—on less than one-half of one percent of the country's land.

hoped that Mexican industries would be run more efficiently.

Salinas also sought to create jobs for Mexicans by attracting more foreign investment. The centerpiece of his effort was NAFTA, the North American Free Trade Agreement. Begun in 1993, NAFTA committed Mexico, Canada, and the United States to removing trade barriers among all three countries over a 15-year period.

While Salinas's reforms were expected to succeed in the long run, Mexico at first faced setbacks. Economic benefits were slow to reach the poorest Mexicans. In addition, there was growing opposition to the PRI's hold on political power. In 1994 a guerrilla army of Native American peasants in the southern Mexican state of Chiapas rebelled against the government. Calling themselves the **Zapatistas**, after the revolutionary leader Emiliano Zapata, they demanded that the government aid the poor and advance democracy. They also vehemently opposed NAFTA, which they feared would hand their lands over to large corporations.

Zedillo and Reform

Also in 1994, the PRI candidate for president was assassinated during the campaign. **Ernesto Zedillo Ponce de Léon**, the new PRI candidate, won easily, but there was widespread dissatisfaction about the extent of government corruption, which allegedly reached even to the Salinas family.

As president, Zedillo continued free enterprise reforms, while promising to improve the lot of the poor. In late 1994, however, he faced a trade deficit that forced him to devalue the peso, a move that shook international business confidence in Mexico. American financial aid helped support Mexico's economy, but Mexican government cutbacks in jobs and services imposed hardships on many Mexicans.

To counter growing public discontent, Zedillo held talks with the Zapatistas and opened up the political system to other political parties. In 1997 elections, the PRI, for the first time since 1929, lost its majority in the lower house of the Mexican legislature. The two major opposition parties—the

Independent Practice

📁 Guided Reading Activity 25-2 **L1**

📁 People in World History Profile 70

The following videotape program is available from Glencoe:

- **Fidel Castro: El Commandante**

you don't say...

Buckaroos—and more Mexicans were the first cowboys, so many of the words we associate with the American West are of Spanish origin. They include *buckaroo* (vaquero, cowboy), *bronco* (rough, unruly), *chaps* (chaparejos), *corral* (enclosed yard), *lariat* (la reata), and *ranch* (rancho).

Mexico City, home to more than 20 million people and one of the world's most rapidly growing cities, faces pollution, crime, and inadequate housing.

Ballet Folklórico enhances the cultural life of Mexico City, the nation's leading business, industrial, and cultural center.

REFLECTING ON THE TIMES

1. How do world oil prices affect Mexico's economy?
2. What challenges does Mexico City face because of its rapidly growing population?

757

Who? What? Where? When?

Ernesto "Che" Guevara, an Argentinian, was one of Castro's ablest guerrilla fighters. After Castro came to power, Guevara occupied several important posts until 1965, when he dropped out of public life in Cuba. Apparently Guevara went to South America to preach revolution. He was captured and shot in Bolivia in 1967. His eloquent writings made him a hero to revolutionaries everywhere.

ANSWERS TO REFLECTING ON THE TIMES

1. Since Mexico is a prime oil producer, high world prices help its economy and low ones harm it.
2. dealing with pollution, crime, and inadequate services

Map Study

Answer
about 2,300 miles (3,700 kilometers)

Cuba and the Cold War
Why did Cuba become an important "flash point" in the cold war?
The United States saw Fidel Castro's Communist revolution in Cuba as a threat to the rest of Latin America. The Soviet Union sought to protect Cuba from the Americans by installing missiles in the island republic. To defuse the Cuban missile crisis, the United States promised not to invade Cuba in return for Soviet withdrawal of the missiles.

ABCNEWS INTERACTIVE™

VIDEODISC
Communism and the Cold War

Side Two, Chapter 13
Frames 30190–31200
Title: *Bay of Pigs*
Ask: What does this footage portray? *(American forces in Cuba as a result of the threat of communism.)*

Side One, Chapter 16
Frames 29427–32782
Title: *Cuban Missile Crisis*
Ask: What part of the United States was in the most danger from the missiles? *(the southeastern United States)*

Cuban Missile Crisis 1962

The Cuban missile crisis of 1962 brought the United States and the Soviet Union to the brink of a nuclear conflict.
Region From east to west, how large was the area covered by the United States blockade of Cuba?

---

conservative National Action Party (PAN) and the leftist Democratic Revolutionary Party (PRD) gained a significant influence in national politics.

Meanwhile, United States-Mexican relations remained strained over the drug trade and illegal immigration. Mexican nationalists were angered by American doubts about Mexico's commitment to the war against drugs. They also opposed a new United States law that sought to crack down on illegal immigration.

Cuba

From 1952 to 1959, the Caribbean island nation of **Cuba** was ruled by the dictator Fulgencio Batista. Batista's government—often accused of employing corrupt practices—allowed American corporations to dominate the Cuban economy. By the early 1950s, United States companies, taking full advantage of this policy, owned or controlled many of Cuba's mines and ranches as well as much of the oil and sugar industries.

In 1956 a young lawyer named **Fidel Castro** began a guerrilla movement against Batista. Castro opposed Batista's repressive and corrupt practices and called for political reforms. For three years, he

---

and his soldiers carried out attacks on Batista's forces. On January 1, 1959, Batista fled the country, and Castro took control. Many former political officials and army officers were tried and executed. Independent newspapers were closed. Many Cubans who opposed Castro left the country and settled in the United States.

Castro's Domestic Policies

Castro promised democratic reforms and a better standard of living for the Cuban people. Instead of establishing a democracy, however, Castro suspended elections. He did push through reforms to improve wages, health care, and basic education. He took control of the land and nationalized plantations and major industries. Castro's seizure of American-owned property and his disregard of Cuban civil liberties angered the United States.

In retaliation, the United States cut off all sugar imports from Cuba in 1960. Castro meanwhile allied Cuba with the Soviet Union. Soviet Premier Nikita Khrushchev agreed to buy Cuban sugar and to sell arms to Cuba. Castro's dictatorship was openly Communist two years after the revolution.

Cuba and the Cold War

Castro's friendship with the Soviet Union made Cuba the focal point of the cold war in the Western Hemisphere. Castro supported revolutions in Latin America and Africa by supplying military aid and troops and by urging people to join the cause:

> ❝ The revolution will triumph in America and throughout the world, but it is not for revolutionaries to sit in the doorways of their houses waiting for the corpse of imperialism to pass by. ❞
> —From a 1962 speech by Fidel Castro

Castro's defiance of the United States put him in danger. During this period the Central Intelligence Agency (CIA), the intelligence-gathering agency of the United States government, made many attempts to assassinate Castro.

In April 1961 the United States tried and failed to overthrow Castro in a secretly planned invasion. About 1,500 anti-Castro exiles trained by the CIA landed in Cuba at the Bay of Pigs, hoping to rally the Cubans to revolt and topple Castro. At the last moment, United States President John F. Kennedy barred open American military support for the

---

COOPERATIVE LEARNING ACTIVITY

Debate Have students hold a debate about the Cuban missile crisis of 1962. Organize the students into two groups, one taking the position that Soviet missiles had to be removed from Cuba at any cost, the other defending a negotiated settlement or even allowing the missiles to remain. Refer students to Samuel Dinerstein, *The Making of a Missile Crisis*, October 1962; Robert A. Divine, *The Cuban Missile Crisis*; and Robert F. Kennedy, *Thirteen Days: A Memoir of the Cuban Missile Crisis.*

L2

James L. Stanfield

Rich Heritage

Havana, the capital city of Cuba, dates to the 1500s. The Old City has endured, essentially unchanged for four centuries. Today more than 900 buildings—including palaces, churches, mansions, and humble dwellings—remain so uniquely preserved that the United Nations has classified Old Havana as a world heritage site. This palace, being restored from the ground up, reveals the faded grandeur and splendor of the colonial era. Once home to a Spanish conquistador's widow and later to orphans, the building now houses one of the few restaurants in Old Havana.

In 1959 Fidel Castro led a successful Cuban Revolution. After the United States rejected Castro, he turned to the Soviet Union, and for the next 30 years Cuba was a critical stronghold of communism in the Western Hemisphere. Castro's revolution kept out modern developers—along with tourist dollars. But it is partly as a result of Cuba's poverty and relative isolation that the island has preserved its heritage of architectural wonders like the building above. ⊕

Chapter 25 *Latin America* **759**

TEACH

Tell students that Havana is also famous for fortresses originally built by Spain to defend the port city. One of them, Morro Castle, has become the symbol of Havana. Another, the Castillo de la Fuerza, was begun in 1538 and is the oldest colonial military building in the Americas. What historic sites are preserved in or near your community? (*Examples might include birthplaces or residences of famous people; forts or other military installations; and buildings of architectural interest.*)

Linking Past and Present

Cuban Exiles More than half a million Cubans fled to the United States after the Cuban Revolution. The vast majority settled in south Florida, where they transformed Miami into "Little Havana." The annual Calle Ocho (formerly Eighth Street) Festival draws as many as a million visitors.

ABCNEWS INTERACTIVE™

VIDEODISC
Communism and the Cold War

Side Two, Chapter 12
Frames 28259–30174
Title: *Revolution in Cuba*
Ask: According to Gennadi Gerasimov, how did the United States push Fidel Castro toward communism? (*by trying to stop the revolution instead of supporting it*)

ASSESS

Check for Understanding

Assign Section 2 Review as homework or as an in-class activity.

 Use Student Self-Test and Review Software to review Section 2.

Evaluate

Section Quiz 25-2

 Use the Testmaker to create a customized quiz for Section 2.

Reteach

Review with the class key events in relations between the United States and Cuba since the 1950s.

Enrich

Have students draw a cartoon from the point of view of another Latin American country that reacts to the Cuban missile crisis.

CLOSE

Have students discuss whether the United States should lift the economic embargo it placed on Cuba in 1962.

---

effort. The Cuban people failed to revolt, and Castro's forces captured or killed most of the invaders within a few days. Kennedy's new presidency and the global image of the United States were badly damaged by the disaster.

A year later, the Cuban missile crisis brought the world to the brink of nuclear war. Soviet leader Khrushchev's installation of nuclear missiles on Cuba met with stiff American opposition. President Kennedy ordered nearly 200 American warships to blockade Cuba and stop military shipments from the Soviet Union. American B-52 bombers with nuclear warheads took to the skies, and American forces worldwide went on full alert. As Soviet ships steamed toward Cuba, a tense world waited.

Four days later, after tense negotiations, the crisis ended. Khrushchev agreed to dismantle the bases and withdraw the missiles, if the United States promised never to attack Cuba again. Separately the United States agreed to remove American missiles in Turkey aimed at the Soviet Union. The most dangerous confrontation of the cold war left the world shaken but relieved. Castro, however, was outraged at Khrushchev's yielding to American pressure.

United States-Cuban relations also continued to be icy. In 1962, the United States imposed an economic embargo on Cuba. Travel between the two countries was tightly restricted. Due to its ties with the Communist world, Cuba was isolated by other countries in the Western Hemisphere.

For brief periods, in 1980 and 1994, Castro allowed thousands of Cubans to sail to the United States. Most of these people were opponents of Castro's authoritarian rule. Others were criminals, mentally ill, or impoverished peasants. ◼

Cuba After the Cold War

In the 1970s, Cuba sent troops to Africa to aid Marxists in Angola. With the fall of Soviet communism two decades later, the Cubans could no longer export revolution. Due to loss of Soviet aid, poor sugar harvests, and the American embargo, they had to devote primary attention to their devastated economy.

Despite strong American pressures, Castro resisted abandoning his Communist system. However, he allowed limited private enterprise in mining and tourism to obtain needed foreign investment. Castro also improved ties with Canada and other capitalist countries. The United States, however, refused to end the embargo. As a result, Cuba remained as the last remnant of the cold war.

Haiti

East of Cuba is the large, mountainous island of Hispaniola, which is divided into two nations. The eastern two-thirds of the island is the **Dominican Republic**, a Spanish-speaking country. The western third is French-speaking **Haiti**. The two countries are among the poorest in the Western Hemisphere. Relations between the two countries have often been tense because of their cultural differences.

Economically poorer than the Dominican Republic, Haiti has been ruled by dictatorships during much of its recent history. The dictator François Duvalier (du•VAL•YAY) ruled Haiti from 1957 to 1971. His son, Jean-Claude Duvalier, then became Haiti's leader but was overthrown in 1986. After four years of strife, **Jean Bertrand Aristide** (ah•reh•STEED), a popular reform-minded priest, was elected president. A military coup forced Aristide to flee the country in 1991. With broad international support, and the intervention of American military forces, Aristide returned to power in 1994. A United Nations peacekeeping mission helped in the country's transition from military rule to democracy. Mistrust and violence among rival political groups, however, slowed progress toward stable government and economic recovery. In December 1995, however, a peacefully conducted election brought René Preval to power as Aristide's successor to the presidency.

SECTION 2 REVIEW

Recall
1. **Define** standard of living, privatization.
2. **Identify** Carlos Salinas de Gortari, Zapatistas, Ernesto Zedillo Ponce de León, Fidel Castro, Jean Bertrand Aristide.

3. **Locate** Cuba on the map on page 758. Why might Americans have felt threatened by a Soviet military presence there?

Critical Thinking
4. **Analyzing Information** How was citizens' participation in

government advanced in Mexico during the 1990s?

Understanding Themes
5. **Revolution** Explain why revolutions have been so common in the Caribbean and in other parts of Latin America since 1945.

SECTION 2 REVIEW ANSWERS

1. All vocabulary words are defined in the Glossary.
2. Carlos Salinas de Gortari, 756; Zapatistas, 757; Ernesto Zedillo Ponce de León, 757; Fidel Castro, 758; Jean Bertrand Aristide, 760

3. Cuba lies within 90 miles of the United States mainland; Soviet missiles in Cuba posed a close threat to American cities.
4. President Zedillo opened up the one-party political system to other political parties. In 1997, the opposition parties

together won a majority of seats in the lower house of the national legislature.
5. **REVOLUTION** The region has been dominated, politically and economically, by elites or dictators; it has also been subject to foreign intervention.

1970   1980   1990   2000

1979 The Sandinistas overthrow Somoza rule in Nicaragua.

1981 United States begins aid to the contras in Nicaragua.

1999 U.S.-owned Panama Canal to come under Panamanian control.

Section 3

Central America

Setting the Scene

▶ **Terms to Define**
covert, death squad

▶ **People to Meet**
Anastasio Somoza Debayle, Sandinistas, contras, Oscar Arias, Violeta Chamorro, Oscar Romero, Manuel Noriega

▶ **Places to Locate**
Nicaragua, El Salvador, Panama

ind Out What factors led to conflicts in Central America from the 1970s to the 1990s?

The Storyteller

An American journalist interviewed a Nicaraguan mother whose daughter, a schoolteacher, had been killed. The teacher, who had volunteered to help young children in a small remote village in the war zone, was ambushed by the contras. "My daughter gave her life fighting for freedom, like my son who died in the insurrection. Losing a child is like losing your life." She stopped for a moment to wipe her cheeks, and then looked up again. "My children were my whole life," she said. "My daughter never hurt anyone. All she was doing was teaching poor children in the mountains how to read."

—adapted from *Blood of Brothers, Life and War in Nicaragua*, Stephen Kinzer, 1991

Contra soldiers

lthough independent since the 1800s, the nations of Central America have suffered from wars, civil unrest, and interference by foreign powers. Ruled by wealthy elites, several nations were gripped by revolution and civil war from the late 1970s. Only in the early 1990s was some stability restored to the region. This achievement gave hope that the desperate needs of the people could finally be addressed.

Nicaragua

Nowhere was the hold of the wealthy elite tighter than it was in **Nicaragua**. There the Somoza family took power in 1937, and, with the exception of one four-year period, remained in control, backed by the American-trained army known as the National Guard until 1979. By 1967, when **Anastasio Somoza Debayle** took over the presidency, the Somoza family owned one-quarter of the land in Nicaragua and most of the country's industries, banks, and businesses.

The Somozas' rule of Nicaragua caused increasing resentment; and by the late 1970s, the United States had ended its support. In 1978 peasants, Catholic priests, business people, and Marxists united to challenge Somoza. Leading the anti-Somoza alliance was the Sandinista National Liberation Front (FSLN). The **Sandinistas** took their name from Augustino Sandino, the popular hero who had waged guerrilla attacks on American occupation forces in Nicaragua in the 1920s. Sandino had been killed by the father of Anastasio Somoza in 1934.

After the Revolution

The rebel alliance succeeded in overthrowing Somoza in 1979. Although the majority of Nicaraguans cheered the revolution, they differed on how the new government should operate. Some Nicaraguans believed in capitalism and wanted to

Chapter 25 *Latin America* **761**

SECTION THEME

▶ **Conflict** Calls for land reform and political freedom lead to civil wars in Latin America.

ind Out

Answer: *domination by elites; political control by Communists or Socialists; foreign intervention; drug trafficking*

FOCUS

Section Objective

Summarize the factors that led to conflicts in Central America from the 1970s to the 1990s.

BELLRINGER
Motivational Activity

Before taking roll at the beginning of the class period, project Section Focus Transparency 25-3 and have students answer the activity questions. Discuss students' responses.

This activity is also available as a blackline master.

Vocabulary Pre-check

Use Vocabulary Activity 25 to introduce vocabulary terms.
L1 LEP

SECTION RESOURCES

📁 **Reproducible Masters**
• Reproducible Lesson Plan 25-3
• Vocabulary Activity 25
• Guided Reading Activity 25-3
• Mapping History Activity 25
• Section Quiz 25-3

📊 **Transparencies**
• Section Focus Transparency 25-3

Multimedia
💻 Student Self-Test and Review Software
💻 Testmaker
💿 Communism and the Cold War:
  • *Nicaragua*
  • *El Salvador*

TEACH

Guided Practice

THEME Conflict

The United States played a key part in the conflicts in both Nicaragua and El Salvador. Which side did the United States aid in Nicaragua? (*the* contras) Which side did the United States help in El Salvador? (*the government*) What was its motive in both cases? (*fear of communism*) **L1 LEP**

Map Study

Answer

Guatemala, Nicaragua, and El Salvador

Map Skills Practice

Reading a Map Besides the three countries that experienced civil wars in the 1980s, what nations are located in Central America? (*Panama, Honduras, Costa Rica, Belize, Mexico*)

Independent Practice

 Guided Reading Activity 25-3 **L1**

Critical Thinking One of the slogans of FMLN supporters was "no justice, no peace." Ask students what the slogan meant in the context of El Salvador's civil war and whether it might be relevant in other parts of Latin America. **L2**

Mapping History Activity 25

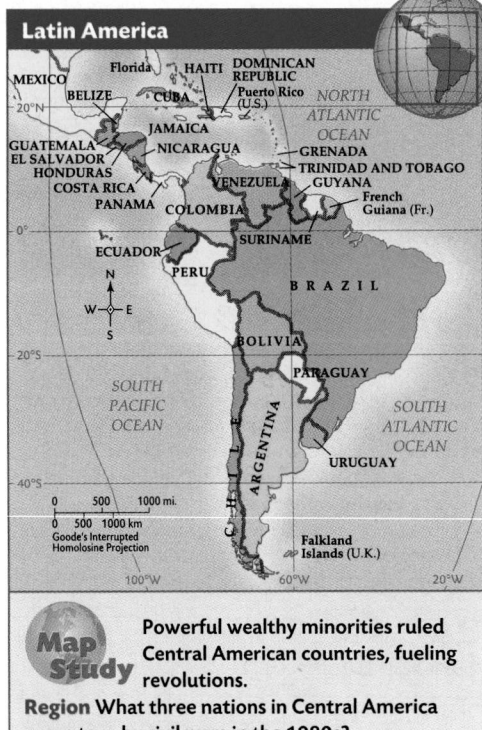

Latin America

Map Study

Powerful wealthy minorities ruled Central American countries, fueling revolutions.

Region What three nations in Central America were torn by civil wars in the 1980s?

maintain close ties with the United States. Others called for socialism and a lessening of dependence on the United States.

The Sandinistas, many of whom were Socialists or Communists, held control and began a series of popular reforms. They seized land that belonged to Somoza supporters and turned it over to peasant groups. With Castro's help, they taught people to read and write and improved rural health care.

Within a year after taking power, however, the new Nicaraguan government faced growing opposition. Upper- and middle-class Nicaraguans who had lost property to the Sandinistas opposed the creation of what they saw as a socialist dictatorship. Many of them fled to the United States. Meanwhile, disgruntled former allies of the Sandinistas joined forces with former Somoza supporters to try to overthrow the government. These opponents were called the **contras**, from the Spanish word meaning "against."

Civil War

The Nicaraguan government received financial and military aid from Cuba, the Soviet Union, and

many western European countries. However, the United States, fearing the influence of the Soviets and the Cubans, decided to support the contras. In 1981 the United States government sent $19.5 million to the contras, the first official aid to the rebels. By 1985 contra forces numbered approximately 12,000 soldiers. From bases in Honduras and Costa Rica, they attacked Nicaraguan military bases and businesses.

By 1985 the American public began to fear that the United States would be drawn into another conflict like that in Vietnam. The United States Congress banned military aid to the contras. Despite the ban, members of President Ronald Reagan's staff continued to send covert, or secret, funds to the contras. This illegal use of funds was part of the so-called Iran-Contra scandal that became public in 1987, embarrassing the Reagan administration and leading to indictments of some of the President's staff. Critics charged that an undercover foreign policy was being carried out against the express will of Congress.

Through negotiations, which were led by Costa Rican president **Oscar Arias**, the contras and the Nicaraguan government agreed to a cease-fire and to hold presidential elections in 1990. With American financial and political backing, **Violeta Chamorro**, the widow of a popular newspaper editor killed by Somoza in 1978, won the election. Chamorro led a wide-ranging coalition of parties. After her victory, she faced immense challenges. Her inclusion of key Sandinistas in her government cost her support among the conservative opposition. Despite efforts to introduce reforms, Nicaragua by the mid-1990s had a staggering foreign debt, high inflation, and massive unemployment. In 1996 Arnoldo Aleman, a conservative, was elected president over his Sandinista challenger Daniel Ortega. After a campaign marked by bitter political rivalry, the new president called for national unity to solve Nicaragua's problems.

Footnotes to History

Nicaragua's Literacy Campaign

In 1980 over one-half of adult Nicaraguans were unable to read or write. The Nicaraguan government decided that those who were literate must help those who were not literate. Over the next 5 months, almost 100,000 students helped teach 500,000 people, most of whom were peasants. At the end of the period, Nicaragua's illiteracy rate was less than 15 percent.

COOPERATIVE LEARNING ACTIVITY

News Coverage Organize students into three teams, one each for Nicaragua, El Salvador, and Guatemala. Have each team investigate news coverage about its country. Students should listen to radio news broadcasts, watch TV news broadcasts, and read newspapers and newsmagazines. They may use *Readers' Guide to Periodical Literature* to find stories that have appeared recently. Students should summarize the information they gather and share it with the class. As a wrap-up, have the class discuss how well and how fairly these countries are covered by the media. **L2**

El Salvador

By the early 1970s, **El Salvador** was one of the most industrialized countries in Central America, boasting modern highways, railroads, airports, and office buildings. However, nearly 90 percent of the country's wealth was held by a small group of landowning families. About 40 percent of the population consisted of landless peasants.

The unequal distribution of wealth led to demands for change. Fearing a revolution, wealthy landowners hired death squads—bands of killers who murdered their political opponents. As many as 1,000 people were being killed a month. One of the leading critics of the murder of innocent civilians was Roman Catholic archbishop **Oscar Romero**. When a death squad killed him as he celebrated Mass on March 24, 1980, the country erupted into a civil war. In her poem, "Because I Want," Claribel Alegría described the feelings of many Salvadorans:

> **❝** Because there are clandestine
> cemeteries
> and Squadrons of Death
> drug-crazed killers
> who torture
> who maim
> who assassinate
> I want to keep on fighting....
> Because there are liberated
> territories
> where people
> learn how to read
> and the sick are cured
> and the fruits of the soil
> belong to all
> I have to keep on fighting.
> Because I want peace
> and not war. **❞**

Moderates in the El Salvadoran government supported land reform but were powerless to stop the death squads. As the killing continued, the Farabundo Martí National Liberation Front (FMLN),—a coalition of leftist guerrilla groups—won greater popular support. The United States, fearing Communist influence within the FMLN, gave military aid to the El Salvadoran government. In 1992 the government and the FMLN finally agreed to a peace settlement. Over 70,000 people had died in the 12-year civil war. Another 1.5 million became refugees. Since the end of fighting, the government has made progress toward economic recovery and cooperation with its Central American neighbors.

Visualizing History Civil war in El Salvador claimed more than 70,000 lives before the 12-year war ended in 1992. *What was the FMLN?*

Guatemala

In recent decades Guatemala, the northernmost Central American country, has been torn by conflict arising from deep-rooted ethnic and social divisions. Most Guatemalans are rural Native Americans, but political and economic power has long been held by Spanish-speaking urban dwellers. Beginning in the 1960s, the wide social gap between rich and poor contributed to tensions between these two groups. A small number of Europeanized families owned most of the nation's wealth, while the majority of the Native American population were landless and faced discrimination.

In the early 1960s, leftist guerrillas supporting land reform took up arms against the Guatemalan government. The conflict heightened in the 1970s

Visualizing History During this period, the United States gave El Salvador more than $5 billion in aid; these funds allowed the government's armed forces to quadruple in size and modernize their tactics and weaponry.
Answer to Caption: *a coalition of guerrilla groups*

ABCNEWS INTERACTIVE™

VIDEODISC
Communism and the Cold War

Side Two, Chapter 15
Frames 33016–35726
Title: *Nicaragua*
Ask: Why did Nicaragua *contra* rebels fight? *(because they believed the Communist regime was taking over Nicaragua)*

Side Two, Chapter 16
Frames 35749–38013
Title: *El Salvador*
Ask: What threat did San Salvador represent to the United States, according to President Reagan? *(Communist influence in close proximity to the United States)*

Visualizing History Rigoberta Menchú received the 1992 Nobel Peace Prize for her work on behalf of Native American rights in Guatemala. *Why was Guatemala engulfed in civil war from about 1960 to 1996?*

Visualizing History Death squads killed thousands in Guatemala—especially among the Maya—in the 1970s and 1980s. Rigoberta Menchú, whose father, mother, and brother were killed by security forces, organized resistance among her people and was finally forced to flee for her life.

Answer to Caption: *Ethnic and social conflict between the small Europeanized elite that controlled the government and the Native American majority that faced widespread discrimination.*

ASSESS

Check for Understanding

Assign Section 3 Review as homework or as an in-class activity.

 Use Student Self-Test and Review Software to review Section 3.

Evaluate

◢◣ Section Quiz 25-3

 Use the Testmaker to create a customized quiz for Section 3.

Reteach

Review with the class the various motives behind U.S. intervention in Central America.

Enrich

Have students watch the 1989 film *Romero*, starring Raul Julia, which tells the story of the Salvadoran archbishop murdered in 1980, and write a short essay on the role of the Catholic Church in El Salvador's civil war.

CLOSE

Have students debate whether they think U.S. intervention helped or harmed the three Central American countries discussed in this section.

and 1980s as the guerrillas strengthened their hold on the countryside. In response, the military harshly treated rural villagers, whom it suspected of aiding the guerrillas.

In the late 1980s, the government and the guerrillas agreed to talks. The 36-year civil war finally ended with a peace agreement in 1996. Although making no promises about land reform, the government agreed to reduce the military's size and to end discrimination against Native Americans. The guerrillas in turn agreed to disarm and return to their homes. As a result of the conflict, more than 100,000 people had died, 46,000 others were missing, and about 1 million civilians were refugees.

Panama

Despite periods of dictatorship, **Panama** was relatively prosperous and peaceful after World War II. Much of this prosperity came from the American-owned Panama Canal. Many Panamanians, however, resented what they saw as foreign domination. In 1977 United States President Jimmy Carter and Panamanian President Omar Torrijos (toh•REE•hohs) signed the Panama Canal Treaties. According to the agreements, Panama would take control of the canal by December 31, 1999, the canal would remain open to the ships of all nations, and the United States would have the right to protect the canal's neutrality.

In 1988 General **Manuel Noriega** took power as president. Despite Noriega's former position as a CIA agent, his role in drug smuggling increased tensions with the United States. When Noriega arrested Americans in Panama, United States President George Bush sent American troops into the country in December 1989. Noriega was seized a month later and taken to Florida, where in 1992 he was tried and convicted of drug smuggling. Panama's new President Ernesto Pérez Balladares worked to attract foreign investors and to end the legacy of the drug trade.

SECTION 3 REVIEW

Recall
1. **Define** covert, death squad.
2. **Identify** Anastasio Somoza Debayle, Sandinistas, contras, Oscar Arias, Violeta Chamorro, Oscar Romero, Manuel Noriega.
3. **List** the terms of the 1977 Panama Canal Treaty.

Critical Thinking
4. **Applying Information** President Kennedy once said of Central America: "Those who make peaceful change impossible make violent change inevitable." Show how events in El Salvador supported this observation.

Understanding Themes
5. **Conflict** What role do you think the United States should play in Central America? What role do you think other countries should play?

SECTION 3 REVIEW ANSWERS

1. All vocabulary words are defined in the Glossary.
2. Anastasio Somoza Debayle, 761; Sandinistas, 761; *contras*, 762; Oscar Arias, 762; Violeta Chamorro, 762; Oscar Romero, 763; Manuel Noriega, 764
3. Panama would take control of the canal by the end of 1999, and the canal would remain open to the ships of all nations.
4. The elite resisted demands for change and used death squads to silence opposition; the result was a violent revolution.
5. **CONFLICT** Answers should consider the security of other Western Hemisphere nations, fears of elites, and poverty of the masses.

Developing a Database

Do you have a collection of sports cards or CDs? Have you ever kept a list of the names, addresses, and phone numbers of friends and relatives? If you have collected information and kept some sort of list or file, then you have created a database.

Learning the Skill

An electronic database is a collection of facts that are stored in a file on the computer. The information is organized in fields.

A database can be organized and reorganized in any way that is useful to you. By using a database management system (DBMS)—special software developed for record keeping—you can easily add, delete, change, or update information. You give commands to the computer telling it what to do with the information, and it follows your commands. When you want to retrieve information, the computer searches through the file, finds the information, and displays it on the screen.

Practicing the Skill

Fidel Castro is one of the Latin American leaders discussed in this chapter. Follow these steps to build a database of the political events that have taken place during his years as Cuba's leader.

1. Determine what facts you want to include in your database.
2. Follow instructions in the DBMS that you are using to set up fields. Then enter each item of data in its assigned field.
3. Determine how you want to organize the facts in the database—chronologically by the date of the event, or alphabetically by the name of the event.
4. Follow the instructions in your computer program to place the information in order of importance.

5. Check that the information in your database is all correct. If necessary, add, delete, or change information or fields.

Applying the Skill

Bring to class current newspapers. Using the steps just described, build a database of current political events in Latin American countries. Explain to a partner why the database is organized the way it is and how it might be used in this class.

For More Practice

Turn to the Skill Practice in the Chapter Review on page 771 for more practice in developing a database.

TEACH

Developing a Database Students who know how to use and construct a database will have a valuable skill that can save them time in locating specific facts and figuring out relationships among facts. Begin a discussion of this page by taking a class survey to find out if any students have done computer database searches. (Students who have used a computerized card catalog at the library have used a database.)

When discussing the information in **Learning the Skill,** give students some examples of *fields*—for example, the year that an event takes place, the name of the event, or the main people connected with the event. Then explain that all of the data fields related to the same subject make up a record, and that a collection of records is a data file. If possible, show students examples of data files, records, and fields on a computer as well as the use of a database management system.

You might have students work in pairs to complete **Applying the Skill.** Have students share information about the organization and use of their databases. Point out notable similarities and differences.

Additional Practice

📁 Skill Reinforcement Activity 25

ind Out

Answer: *In several countries—notably Argentina, Chile, and Brazil—authoritarian governments have been replaced by more democratic regimes.*

FOCUS

Section Objective

Explain how democracy has advanced in South America since the late 1980s.

BELLRINGER
Motivational Activity

Before taking roll at the beginning of the class period, project Section Focus Transparency 25-4 and have students answer the activity questions. Discuss students' responses.

This activity is also available as a blackline master.

Vocabulary Pre-check

Use Vocabulary Activity 25 to introduce vocabulary terms.
L1 LEP

1945 — 1972 — 2000

1973 Military forces overthrow Allende presidency in Chile.

1982 Argentina and Great Britain fight the Falkland Islands War.

Section 4

South America

Setting the Scene

▶ **Terms to Define**
hyperinflation, cartel

▶ **People to Meet**
Juan Perón, Eva Perón, Carlos Menem, Salvador Allende, Augusto Pinochet, Alberto Fujimori

▶ **Places to Locate**
Argentina, Falkland Islands, Chile, Colombia, Peru, Brazil

ind Out How has democracy advanced in South America since the late 1980s?

The Storyteller

Eva Perón expressed herself about many topics, including feminismo, *the women's movement in Argentina: "I felt that the women's movement in my country and all over the world had a*

Eva Perón

sublime mission to fulfill … and everything I knew about feminism seemed to me ridiculous. For, not led by women but by those who aspired to be men, it ceased to be womanly and was nothing: feminism had taken the step from the sublime to the ridiculous. And that is the step I always try to avoid taking."

—from *Feminismo!* by Marifran Carlson, 1988

ince the end of World War II, South America has become a region of sharp contrasts. Rapidly growing cities have sprawling slum areas as well as suburbs for the well-to-do and glamorous tourist resorts. While new industries have developed in the coastal urban areas, traditional forms of agriculture still dominate much of the interior of the continent. Despite areas of modernization and prosperity, widespread poverty continues to shape the politics and social structures of South American nations.

Argentina

Before a world depression and the rise of fascism in **Argentina** in the 1930s, the country was one of the 10 wealthiest in the world. Since then, the country has often been under military rule, and its prosperity has declined.

The Perón Era

The dominant political figure in Argentina from the 1940s to the 1970s was Colonel **Juan Perón** (pay•ROHN). When he was first elected president in 1946, Perón enjoyed great popularity, even though he was an authoritarian ruler. Perón and his glamorous wife, **Eva Perón**, a former film and radio star, became the heroes of the downtrodden. By increasing the military budget and supporting pay raises for union members, Perón won the loyalty of soldiers and workers. By nationalizing foreign-owned industries, he appealed to Argentinian pride over controlling its own resources. Eva supported construction of hospitals, schools, clinics, and nursing homes and distributed millions of shoes, sewing machines, and other household goods to the poor.

However, Perón's popularity began to wane in the 1950s. The much-loved Eva died in 1952. Perón's policy of taxing agriculture to fuel industrial growth led to a decline in food production. As the economy declined, anti-Perón protests increased.

766 Chapter 25 *Latin America*

Visualizing History More than 100,000 people rally in Buenos Aires, Argentina, in support of democratic government in 1987. The nation has had long periods of military rule interrupted by brief intervals of constitutional government. *Why has the military often seized power?*

In 1973, after almost 20 years of military rule, Perón returned briefly to power. When he died in 1974, his new wife Isabel took over, becoming the first woman president in the Americas. Economic problems led the military to oust her in 1976.

Argentina's military leaders sparked an economic recovery but ruled brutally. Death squads roamed the country, torturing and killing those who dissented. About 20,000 people simply disappeared. Mothers of missing children brought these human rights abuses to the world's attention through their weekly silent protest in Buenos Aires.

Toward Democracy

In 1982, in an effort to unite Argentina and to end one of the last outposts of colonialism, the military leadership sent Argentinian troops to seize the **Falkland Islands**, also known as the Malvinas. These islands off the coast of Argentina had been controlled by the British since 1833. Seventy-four days later, the Argentinians returned home defeated by the British forces.

After the Falklands humiliation, the military was discredited, and democracy was gradually restored. Economically, Argentina came dangerously close to collapse. In 1989 inflation reached 5,000 percent. This **hyperinflation**—extremely sharp and rapid price increases—caused a severe depression, and much of the middle class fell into poverty.

In 1989 Argentinians elected **Carlos Menem** as president and in 1995 reelected him. Menem has brought inflation under control, attracted foreign investment, and sold off inefficient state-owned industries. Despite a growing economy, many Argentinians worry about high unemployment, deteriorating public education, and government corruption. Regionally, Argentina has joined with Brazil, Paraguay, and Uruguay to form Mercosur, a free trade area. Internationally, its role has been enhanced by joining in UN peacekeeping missions.

Chile

The long coastal country of **Chile** has one of the strongest traditions of democracy in Latin America. In 1970 the voters elected socialist **Salvador Allende** (ah•YEHN•day) to the presidency. He was the first Marxist in the Western Hemisphere to come to power through peaceful means.

Chapter 25 *Latin America* 767

Biography

The following videotape program is available from Glencoe:

- **Evita: The Woman Behind the Myth**

Independent Practice

Guided Reading Activity 25-4 **L1**

People in World History Profile 69

ABCNEWS INTERACTIVE™

VIDEODISC
Communism and the Cold War

Side Two, Chapter 14
Frames 31217–32996
Title: *Chile*
Subject: Inauguration of President Salvador Allende
Ask: To what does President Nixon refer by saying that Latin America will be all "red" eventually due to the election of a Marxist leader in Chile? *(He believes Chile will spread communism across Latin America.)*

Visualizing History From 1965, when Cuba sponsored guerrilla fighters against the government, to the 1990s, Bolivia has had an unstable political system. *What neighboring country also faced struggles between the military and Socialists in this period?*

To stimulate the faltering economy, Allende nationalized businesses, including American copper-mining companies, and distributed land to the poor. He also boosted wages and put a ceiling on prices. In two years, the economy grew 13.5 percent and unemployment was cut in half.

Not all of Allende's policies were successful, however. For example, the breakup of big farms resulted in a decline in food production, which in turn caused food shortages. And the increased wages led to inflation.

More important, though, Allende's policies made him powerful enemies. Wealthy Chileans, frightened by Allende's ties to Castro's Cuba, took their money out of Chile and invested it in other countries. In addition, the United States decided to undermine the Allende government by funding opposition candidates, promoting strikes and protests, and convincing the World Bank to halt loans to Chile. By 1972 Chile's economy was near collapse.

In 1973 Chilean military leaders who had worked closely with the CIA led a coup against Allende. After the successful uprising, Allende was found dead in his office. The military leaders claimed Allende had killed himself with a machine gun that Castro had given him as a gift. It was reported that thousands of people died during and after the coup.

The new government was led by a ruthless and powerful dictator, General **Augusto Pinochet** (PEE•noh•CHEHT). Immediately, Pinochet put an end to Chile's long-standing democracy. He dissolved the congress, censored the press, canceled civil liberties, and issued a new constitution. He killed or imprisoned as many as 1 in every 100 Chileans.

To improve the Chilean economy, Pinochet imposed higher taxes and encouraged foreign investment. Inflation, which had reached 600 percent in 1973, fell to 10 percent by 1981. Soon, store shelves were filled with consumer goods.

Popular opposition to Pinochet, however, remained strong. Many Catholic leaders continued to risk arrest, torture, and death by protesting against Pinochet's cruelty. In 1988, at long last Pinochet gave in to mounting pressure and allowed the people to have elections, which brought Patricio Aylwin to power. With the threat of another military coup still strong, Aylwin tried to revive Chile's democratic tradition.

In 1993, Eduardo Frei Ruiz-Tagle succeeded Aylwin as Chile's president. He has continued many of Aylwin's policies: decreasing the number of people in poverty by increased spending on education, health, and housing; and achieving steady economic growth. By 1997, Chile had one of the strongest economies in Latin America and prepared to join NAFTA.

Colombia

Since World War II, **Colombia** has had long periods of instability. Between the late 1940s and the mid-1960s, battles between liberals and conservatives caused the deaths of about 200,000 people. Colombians refer to this period as *La Violencia*, or the Violence.

During the 1970s and 1980s, the ever-growing power of drug dealers infected Colombian politics. Drugs, including marijuana and cocaine, became Colombia's largest export. Drug dealers in the city of Medellín amassed tremendous fortunes. They murdered more than 350 judges and prosecutors who tried to stop the drug business. By the

mid-1990s, some progress was made in curtailing the power of the Colombian drug cartels, associations formed to establish an international monopoly by price fixing and regulating production. Yet, the illegal trade continued to flourish. In 1996, President Ernest Samper and other government officials faced charges that they had accepted campaign contributions from drug dealers.

Peru

Since World War II, **Peru** has experienced both military and civilian rule. In the early 1970s, military leaders distributed land to peasants, nationalized foreign-owned industries, and aided the urban poor. However, inflation and unemployment remained high. By the early 1980s, democracy had been restored under a new constitution.

In 1990, and again in 1995, Peruvians elected **Alberto Fujimori**, the son of Japanese immigrants, as president. Although criticized for his dictatorial ways, Fujimori worked to improve government effiency and increase free enterprise. During Fujimori's term, Peru has increased economic links with other Pacific countries, especially Japan.

In 1995 Fujimori succeeded in ending a 15-year civil war with a Marxist guerrilla group known as the Shining Path. A year later, militant leftists seized the Japanese ambassador's residence in Lima, the capital, and took a number of hostages. Four months later, Fujimori had Peruvian troops storm the residence to rescue the hostages. The successful outcome of the crisis boosted Fujimori's popularity and increased business confidence in Peru's stability.

Brazil

From the late 1940s to the early 1960s, **Brazil** was generally a democracy. During this period, Brazil's economy expanded as foreign investors opened steel plants and auto factories. In the early 1960s, labor unions helped elect leaders

Live Aid Concert

Philadelphia and London, 1985
A rock concert, organized by Irish singer Bob Geldof, raised money to help feed starving people in Africa. The day-long event was held simultaneously in Philadelphia and London on July 13, 1985. Performers included Paul McCartney, Bob Dylan, Mick Jagger, Madonna, and Joan Baez. Live Aid drew crowds in excess of 160,000. It was televised worldwide to an audience estimated at 1.5 billion people.

who promoted social reforms as well. However, military leaders, fearing that the reforms would lead to communism, took control of the government in 1964.

In the late 1960s, Brazil's military rulers pressed for greater industrial growth. They reduced social programs, increased foreign investment, and weakened labor unions. Although the economy prospered, workers' wages remained low, and poverty remained widespread.

By the late 1980s, increasing opposition at home and abroad forced the military to gradually return Brazil to democracy. Hopes for both economic growth and social reforms were raised with the election of Fernando Collor de Mello as president in 1990. Collor's concern for the environment, including efforts to slow the destruction of the Amazon rain forest, won him international support. However, in 1992 Collor faced charges of corruption and resigned. The new president, Fernando Henrique Cardoso, faced many economic challenges, among them reducing inflation and government waste.

SECTION 4 REVIEW

Recall
1. **Define** hyperinflation, cartel.
2. **Identify** Juan Perón, Eva Perón, Carlos Menem, Salvador Allende, Augusto Pinochet, Alberto Fujimori.

3. **Describe** major developments in Peru under the presidency of Alberto Fujimori.

Critical Thinking
4. **Making Comparisons** How do the economies of Chile and

Cuba differ?

Understanding Themes
5. **Change** How did military governments both improve and damage various South American nations?

ASSESS

Check for Understanding
Assign Section 4 Review as homework or as an in-class activity.

■ Use Student Self-Test and Review Software to review Section 4.

Evaluate
📁 Section Quiz 25-4

■ Use the Testmaker to create a customized quiz for Section 4.

Reteach
Have students review the changes in government in Argentina, Chile, and Brazil since the 1980s.

📁 Reteaching Activity 25

Enrich
Have students watch the 1982 film *Missing*, starring Jack Lemmon and Sissy Spacek, based on the true story of an American who disappeared in Chile after Allende's overthrow in 1973.

📁 Enrichment Activity 25

CLOSE

Have students list the challenges facing the countries of South America today.

SECTION 4 REVIEW ANSWERS

1. All vocabulary words are defined in the Glossary.
2. Juan Perón, 766; Eva Perón, 766; Carlos Menem, 767; Salvador Allende, 767; Augusto Pinochet, 768; Alberto Fujimori, 769
3. Peru has moved toward stronger government, increased free enterprise, successfully concluded civil war with leftist guerrillas, and ended hostage crisis.
4. Chile has a prosperous free enterprise economy and is preparing to join NAFTA; Cuba has a declining socialist economy with only limited free enterprise; it has improved contacts with a number of capitalist countries but remains under an American-imposed embargo.
5. **CHANGE** They improved them by making economic reforms and encouraging development; they damaged them by discarding democratic institutions and carrying out reigns of terror.

CHAPTER 25 REVIEW

GLENCOE
TECHNOLOGY

VIDEODISC
Use MindJogger to review students' knowledge of the chapter.
MindJogger Videoquiz

Chapter 25
Disc 3 Side B

 Also available in VHS.

Answers

Using Key Terms

1. c   4. i
2. e   5. d
3. g

Using Your History Journal

Point out that gross domestic product (GDP) is the total goods and services produced by an economy in a year, while gross national product (GNP) is GDP plus the income from foreign investments.

Reviewing Facts

1. population growth, urbanization, domination by elites, foreign intervention and debt
2. Politically, PRI control has somewhat relaxed; economically, it has privatized some industries and joined NAFTA.
3. Nicaragua: Somoza family owned one-quarter of the land and most industry, banks, and businesses. El Salvador: A small group of families controlled 90 percent of the country's wealth.
4. After four years of turmoil, Aristide was elected president but was forced to flee; reinstated in 1994, he served until 1995,

---

Connections Across Time

Historical Significance The history of Latin America since World War II shows the challenge of establishing democracy in societies traditionally ruled by a small elite. In most countries, the bitter conflict between the rich and the poor has limited the development of stable democracies.

A second significant challenge in Latin America is economic development. Increasing agricultural exports and building industry have brought increases in total national wealth. However, the majority of the population has not always benefited from these changes.

Using Key Terms

Write the key term that completes each sentence. Then write a sentence for each term not chosen.

a. campesinos   f. free trade
b. death squads   g. liberation theology
c. elite   h. covert
d. privatization   i. cartels
e. standard of living j. hyperinflation

1. Since colonial times, Latin American society has consisted of masses of poor people dominated by a small but wealthy _____.
2. From 1945 to the 1960s, Mexico's _____— the overall wealth of its people—increased.
3. Beginning in the 1960s, many Catholics in Latin America supported social change and promoted the ideas of _____.
4. Since the 1970s, Colombia has been affected by the drug _____, who control the illegal drug trade by fixing prices and regulating production.
5. By the mid-1980s, Mexico and other Latin American countries were supporting programs of _____, shifting control of industry from governments to private owners.

Technology Activity

Creating a Multimedia Presentation Locate information about the history of colonialism in Central America. Create a multimedia presentation about an individual country from that region. Include information about the history of colonialism, cultural influences of colonial powers and how that country achieved its independence. Before you begin, plan the type of multimedia presentation you would like to develop and the steps you will need to take. Cite all electronic resources used.

Using Your History Journal

Research statistics about the gross national (or gross domestic) product of Central American or South American nations. Draw a cartogram that shows the relative economic strength of these nations.

Reviewing Facts

1. **Government/Economics** List various political and economic challenges that confront Latin American countries.
2. **Government** Describe Mexico's political and economic system since the 1980s.
3. **History** List the causes of the civil wars in Nicaragua and El Salvador.
4. **History** Discuss political developments in Haiti since the fall of the Duvaliers.
5. **History** Explain how the Soviet collapse affected Cuba.
6. **History** Explain the purpose of the Organization of American States (OAS).
7. **Culture** Discuss the role of women in the struggle for human rights in Argentina.
8. **History** State why Juan and Eva Perón were popular in Argentina.

Critical Thinking

1. **Evaluate** How did the policies of the United States and Canada differ in the mid–1990s regarding Cuba? Which country do you think had the better approach in dealing with Castro?
2. **Apply** How would you solve the problem of the illegal drug trade between Colombia and criminals in the United States?

---

when a successor was elected.
5. Cuba lost Soviet aid and saw its economy devastated.
6. to develop political and economic ties among nations of Western Hemisphere
7. Mothers of missing persons staged a weekly silent vigil in Buenos Aires, winning world attention for the plight of Argentine citizens.
8. They increased funds for the military and unionized workers, built public facilities,

aided the poor, and stimulated national pride.

Critical Thinking

1. The U.S. believed in isolating Castro with an embargo; Canada traded with Castro, hoping that contact would move Cuba toward reforms; answers will vary.
2. Suggestions may include education, interdiction, eradication, or legalization.
3. The Somozas dictatorially ruled Nicaragua

3. Synthesize Imagine that you were a citizen of Nicaragua in the 1970s and 1980s. How would you feel about the Somoza government? The Sandinistas? The contras?

4. Synthesize Describe the goal of NAFTA. What are the advantages and disadvantages of NAFTA to Mexico and the United States?

Geography in History

1. Region Refer to the map below. What large area of South America has an economy largely based on hunting, fishing, and gathering?

2. Movement Why are most manufacturing and commercial areas located along the seacoast?

3. Place Judging from the type of economic activity, where are South America's largest plains?

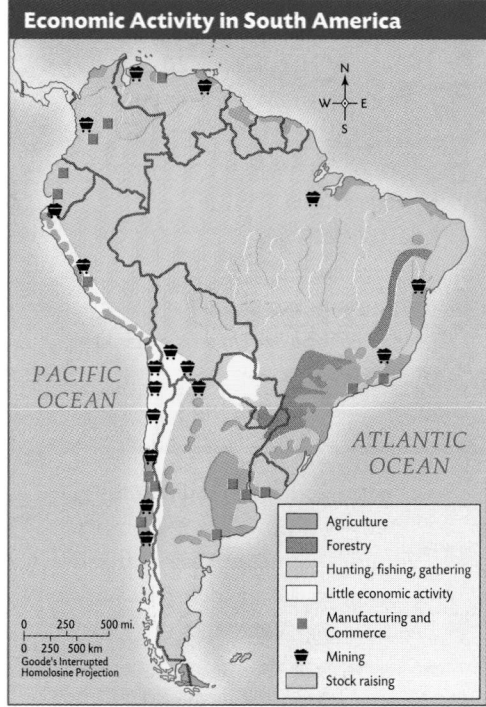

Economic Activity in South America

PACIFIC OCEAN

ATLANTIC OCEAN

N W E S

0   250   500 mi.
0   250   500 km
Goode's Interrupted Homolosine Projection

- Agriculture
- Forestry
- Hunting, fishing, gathering
- Little economic activity
- Manufacturing and Commerce
- Mining
- Stock raising

Understanding Themes

1. Cooperation How has Latin America's interdependence with global and hemispheric

markets affected its ability to develop economically?

2. Revolution How did Cuba's revolution affect the United States and the Soviet Union?

3. Conflict How did the cold war affect revolutions and civil wars in Central America?

4. Change How have South American countries changed politically and economically since the late 1980s and early 1990s?

Linking Past and Present

1. How have American responses to Latin American crises today differed from American responses a century ago? How do you think the United States might respond in years to come?

2. In both the Monroe Doctrine and the Rio Treaty of 1947, the United States pledged to protect Latin American nations from outside powers. In the Falkland Islands War, however, the United States supported Great Britain. How do you think Latin Americans responded to this?

Skill Practice

Prepare a database of the major political events in South America from the 1970s to the 1990s. Include the following information in your database.

- Year
- Country
- Event

Be sure to follow these steps to build your database.

1. Determine what facts to include.
2. Follow instructions in the DBMS that you are using. Then enter each item in its assigned field.
3. Determine how you want to organize the facts in the database.
4. Place the information in order of importance.
5. Check the accuracy of the information. Make necessary changes.

---

2. REVOLUTION The Cuban Revolution brought the cold war to Latin America. The U.S. worked to rid Cuba of Castro and to halt the spread of revolutionary ideas in Latin America through the Alliance for Progress and the Peace Corps; the Soviet Union gained a foothold in the Americas and used Cuba to further its foreign policy interests.

3. CONFLICT U.S. fear of communism led it to intervene in the affairs of many countries.

4. CHANGE Several countries have become democratic. Some rely heavily on foreign investors.

Linking Past and Present

1. U.S. military intervention during era of imperialism; the relationship was unequal. Today, U.S. deals with Latin America on a more equal basis, but intervention has occurred in some cases; importance of economic cooperation and free trade.

2. Some saw it as a violation of U.S. pledges, but others did not object since they had not supported Argentina's move in the first place.

Skill Practice
Databases will vary depending on events.

Chapter Bonus Test Question

Ask students: Which of the three regional groupings in this chapter—Mexico and the Caribbean, Central America, or South America—do you think has the best prospects for the future? *(When predicting, students should keep in mind the region's history, government, economic resources, and social structure.)*

---

for decades, the Sandinistas were a left-wing alliance that overthrew the Somozas, and the contras were U.S.-backed right-wing groups organized to oppose the new leftist regime.

4. NAFTA will remove trade barriers among the U.S., Mexico, and Canada. Mexico: economic growth; expansion of agro-businesses; loss of traditions; environmental and labor concerns; U.S.: more trade and markets; job losses and gains; environmental and labor concerns.

Geography in History
1. the north
2. for access to the sea for easy transport of raw materials and finished goods
3. east and southeast

Understanding Themes
1. **COOPERATION** It has brought industry and more exports but has not boosted living standards.

A complete, 1-page lesson plan is provided for each section in the *Reproducible Lesson Plans* booklet.

The World in Transition

CHAPTER RESOURCES

Chapter Opener	**Reproducible Resources**	**Multimedia Resources**
Chapter Opener	Chapter Themes: Graphic Organizer 26 Historical Significance Chapter Activity 26	MindJogger Videoquiz
Chapter Enrichment	Vocabulary Activity 26* Time Line Activity 26 Mapping History Activity 26 History Simulation 26 Geography and History Activity 26 Source Reading 26 People in World History Profiles 71, 72 World Art and Music Activity 26 Enrichment Activity 26 Critical Thinking Activity 26 Skill Reinforcement Activity 26 Building Skills in Geography Workbook, Unit 2, Lesson 11 Performance Assessment Activity 26	World History and Art Transparencies 51, 52 Mapping History Overlay Transparency 25 Chapter Transparency 26 Vocabulary PuzzleMaker Software Picture Atlas of the World Turning Points in World History: *Fall of the Berlin Wall* Lessons of War: *The Nature of Violence* Communism and the Cold War: • *A New Soviet Union: Communist Rule Ends* • *Challenge of Reform*
Chapter Review/Reteaching	Reteaching Activity 26 Skill Reinforcement Activity 26 Spanish Chapter Summary 26	Chapter 26 Digest Audiocassette, Activity, Test* Vocabulary PuzzleMaker Software Student Self-Test and Review Software MindJogger Videoquiz
Chapter Evaluation/Testing	Performance Assessment Activity 26 Chapter 26 Test, Forms A and B	Testmaker

* Also available in Spanish

0:00 OUT OF TIME? Assign the Chapter 26 summary in the Unit 6 Digest on pages 803–805, and the Chapter 26 Audiocassettes.

Block Schedule

Block scheduling differs from traditional class scheduling in the amount of time allotted to each period. The extended time frame provided by block scheduling affords you the opportunity to implement a greater number of research-oriented and activity-intense projects to motivate and involve your students. Activities that are particularly suited to use within the block scheduling framework are identified throughout this chapter by the following designation.

KEY TO ABILITY LEVELS

Teaching strategies have been coded for varying learning styles and abilities.

L1 BASIC activities for all students
L2 AVERAGE activities for average to above-average students
L3 CHALLENGING activities for above-average students
LEP LIMITED ENGLISH PROFICIENCY activities

Use Glencoe's *Presentation Plus!* multimedia teacher tool to easily present dynamic lessons that visually excite your students. Using Microsoft PowerPoint® you can customize the presentations to create your own personalized lessons.

SECTION RESOURCES

Daily Objectives	Reproducible Resources	Multimedia Resources
Section 1 **The End of the Cold War** Identify the developments that changed the relationship of the superpowers by the mid-1990s.	Reproducible Lesson Plan 26-1 Guided Reading Activity 26-1* Section Quiz 26-1*	Section Focus Transparency 26-1 Chapter Transparency 26 World History and Art Transparency 51, *Vietnam Memorial* Vocabulary PuzzleMaker Software Student Self-Test and Review Software Communism and the Cold War: *A New Soviet Union: Communist Rule Ends*
Section 2 **The Crumbling Wall** Describe how Soviet Communist controls came to an end in Eastern Europe.	Reproducible Lesson Plan 26-2 Vocabulary Activity 26* Guided Reading Activity 26-2* People in World History Profile 71 Section Quiz 26-2*	Section Focus Transparency 26-2 Student Self-Test and Review Software Turning Points in World History: *Fall of the Berlin Wall* Communism and the Cold War: *Challenge of Reform*
Section 3 **Toward a European Union** Identify the steps Western European nations have taken to unify their governments and economies.	Reproducible Lesson Plan 26-3 Vocabulary Activity 26* Guided Reading Activity 26-3* Section Quiz 26-3*	Section Focus Transparency 26-3 Student Self-Test and Review Software Testmaker Picture Atlas of the World
Section 4 **National and Ethnic Conflicts** Recognize the areas of the world that have been in ethnic discord since the end of the cold war.	Reproducible Lesson Plan 26-4 Vocabulary Activity 26* Guided Reading Activity 26-4* People in World History Profile 72 Section Quiz 26-4*	Section Focus Transparency 26-4 Student Self-Test and Review Software Testmaker Lessons of War: *The Nature of Violence*
Section 5 **Global Interdependence** Explain how recent advances in technology have affected the world's cultures.	Reproducible Lesson Plan 26-5 Guided Reading Activity 26-5* Geography and History Activity 26 History Simulation 26 Reteaching Activity 26 Enrichment Activity 26 Section Quiz 26-5* Performance Assessment Activity 26 Spanish Chapter Summary 26	Section Focus Transparency 26-5 World History and Art Transparency 52, *Sky Above Clouds II* Mapping History Overlay Transparency 25, *World Population Growth* Vocabulary PuzzleMaker Software Student Self-Test and Review Software Testmaker

* Also available in Spanish

Chapter Activities

Performance Assessment Activity

An Awards Ceremony Have the students take the roles of producers and judges of a competition of persons and developments of the last 20 years. Have students create a name for the awards ceremony and identify the different types of awards that might be given, the nominees for each award (based on accomplishments found in the chapter or researched), and the winners (as determined by greatest impact). As a final product, students should create one of the following: (1) a newspaper article summarizing the awards ceremony, giving the categories, nominees and winners; (2) a videotape of the actual awards program; or (3) a set of radio interviews with the winners.

Possible Rubric Features

Accuracy of content information, decision-making skills, originality, ability to analyze relationships and classify information, oral presentation skills (if applicable), clarity of writing (if applicable)

• For an additional activity, refer to Activity 26 in the Performance Assessment Strategies and Activities booklet.

ACTIVITY

From the Classroom of...

Trent Steele
Kearney High School
Kearney, NE

[Name]'s Excellent Adventure!

Organize the class into five teams and give each team a current physical/political map of Europe with roads and train routes. Each team must plan a trip across modern-day Europe; for example, from London to Athens. Each group must plot the route on a map, following major roadways, trains, and water routes. Then, on poster paper, each group should list all countries, major cities, and major physical geographic features they will encounter on their journey, as well as at least ten major points of interest. Finally, each group should provide an approximate mileage [kilometer] figure for the entire trip. Have each group present the details of their journey to the class. After comparing current maps of Europe with some older ones, have the class draw conclusions about European geography. How has Europe changed? What features have stayed the same?

MULTIPLE LEARNING STYLES

Verbal/Linguistic
Have students choose one of the global concerns covered in this chapter (political, economic, social, or environmental), research the problem, and prepare a report to share with the class.

Logical/Mathematical
Have students who are computer buffs create a "bibliography" of interesting and useful web sites from around the world.

Visual/Spatial
Have students create a series of cartoons focusing on global environmental problems.

Kinesthetic
Ask students to make a time line banner for the bulletin board or wall that covers the years 1980 to 2000. They should fill in events and places from this chapter and leave spaces for filling in current events and predictions.

Additional Resources

NATIONAL GEOGRAPHIC SOCIETY

Teacher's Corner

INDEX TO
NATIONAL GEOGRAPHIC MAGAZINE

The following articles may be used for research
relating to this chapter:

- "A Dream Called Nunavut," by Michael Parfit, September 1997.
- "Sri Lanka," by Priit J. Vesilind, January 1997.
- "Information Revolution," by Joel L. Swerdlow, October 1995.

NATIONAL GEOGRAPHIC SOCIETY
PRODUCTS AVAILABLE FROM GLENCOE

To order the following products for use with this chapter, contact your
local Glencoe sales representative, or call Glencoe at 1-800-334-7344:

- *GTV: The American People (Videodisc)*
- *GTV: A Geographic Perspective on American History (Videodisc)*
- *Picture Atlas of the World (CD-ROM)*

ADDITIONAL NATIONAL GEOGRAPHIC
SOCIETY PRODUCTS

To order the following products for use with this chapter, call National
Geographic Society at 1-800-368-2728:

- *Voices of Leningrad (Video)*
- *The Rise and Fall of the Soviet Union (Video)*
- *Europe: The Road to Unity (Video)*
- *Technology's Price (Video)*
- *For All Mankind (Video)*

BIBLIOGRAPHY

Literature of the Period
Shields, Carol. *The Stone Diaries.* New York: Penguin Books,
1993. A novel of a woman's journey through life in the changing twentieth century.
Readings for the Student
Weiner, Jonathan. *The Next One Hundred Years.* New York:
Bantam Books, 1990. Prospects for life on this planet in light
of the accelerated changes of the twentieth century.
Readings for the Teacher
Walker, Martin. *The Cold War.* New York: Henry Holt, 1993.
An overview of the origins and course of the cold war and
related foreign policy challenges of the future.

LOCAL OBJECTIVES

*inter*NET
CONNECTION
**Global resources on the
World Wide Web**
The United Nations:
http://www.un.org/

Chapter Themes are listed by section on this chapter opening page of the Student Edition. A corresponding theme-based activity is available under "TEACH," and a theme-based question is asked in the Section and Chapter Reviews.

Historical Setting More than a year had passed since a group of Soviet economists had prepared a 500-day plan for transition to a semifree market that was based on Western economic support and cuts in Soviet defense spending. Opposition to this plan came from the senior ranks of the Soviet military and from directors of the defense industries. Gorbachev also failed to get the Western financial support he counted on, and by August 1991, a coup could not be held off. When Gorbachev spoke over television, the Soviet Union had ended.

Historical Significance

Answers: *Gorbachev's policies of glasnost, perestroika, and military concessions to the West, together with the growing world influence of blocs of nations other than the United States and the Soviet Union, helped bring about the end of the cold war.*

The Soviet Union broke up, and in its place the former Soviet republics formed a commonwealth. Communist systems collapsed in most Eastern European nations. Nationalist sentiments grew, leading to war in the Balkans and ethnic conflicts in CIS republics and elsewhere. The movement for European unity took on increased momentum, resulting in the formation of the European Union.

Nations became more interdependent economically. European and Pacific Rim nations are now economic giants.

Chapter
26

1980–Present

The World in Transition

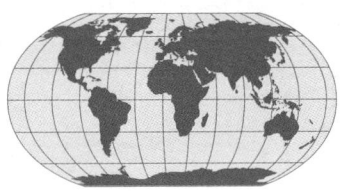

Chapter Themes

▶ **Change** The end of the cold war and the collapse of communism transform the relationship of the United States and the Soviet Union. *Section 1*

▶ **Change** The weakening of the Soviet Union and the rise of reform movements bring an end to Soviet control in Eastern Europe. *Section 2*

▶ **Cooperation** The European Union works to create a united Europe that will be a major economic power. *Section 3*

▶ **Conflict** National and ethnic conflicts intensify worldwide after the end of the cold war. *Section 4*

▶ **Cultural Diffusion** New technology and an integrated world communications system speed the transfer of ideas and practices throughout the world. *Section 5*

Storyteller

On December 25, 1991, Soviet President Mikhail Gorbachev resigned his office in a speech on national television:

"We live in a new world. The Cold War has ended, the arms race has stopped, as has the insane militarization that mutilated our economy, public psyche and morals. The threat of world war has been removed....

We opened ourselves to the rest of the world, abandoned the practices of interfering in others' internal affairs ..., and we were reciprocated with trust, solidarity, and respect.... "

With these words, Gorbachev pronounced the end of the cold war. The road that had led to the end of this war was long and dangerous. The last ten years were no exception. Now, amid the jubilation and hope, the question was raised: "Where do we go from here?"

Historical Significance

What developments brought about the end of the cold war? How has the world changed politically and economically since the beginning of the 1980s?

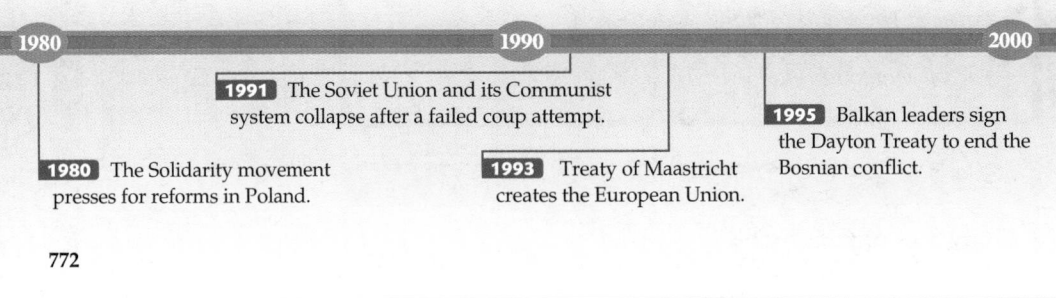

| 1980 | 1990 | 2000 |

1991 The Soviet Union and its Communist system collapse after a failed coup attempt.

1980 The Solidarity movement presses for reforms in Poland.

1993 Treaty of Maastricht creates the European Union.

1995 Balkan leaders sign the Dayton Treaty to end the Bosnian conflict.

772

GEOGRAPHY CONNECTION

Location Display a world map. Before studying each section of the chapter, ask students to find the region covered on the map. Have students put markers on the map for the areas of ongoing conflict as they study them. How does the location of European countries present a special problem not encountered by the United States? *(They are so close together that they are in the midst of each other's conflicts; uprisings can easily spread beyond national boundaries. The United States, by contrast, is physically removed.)*

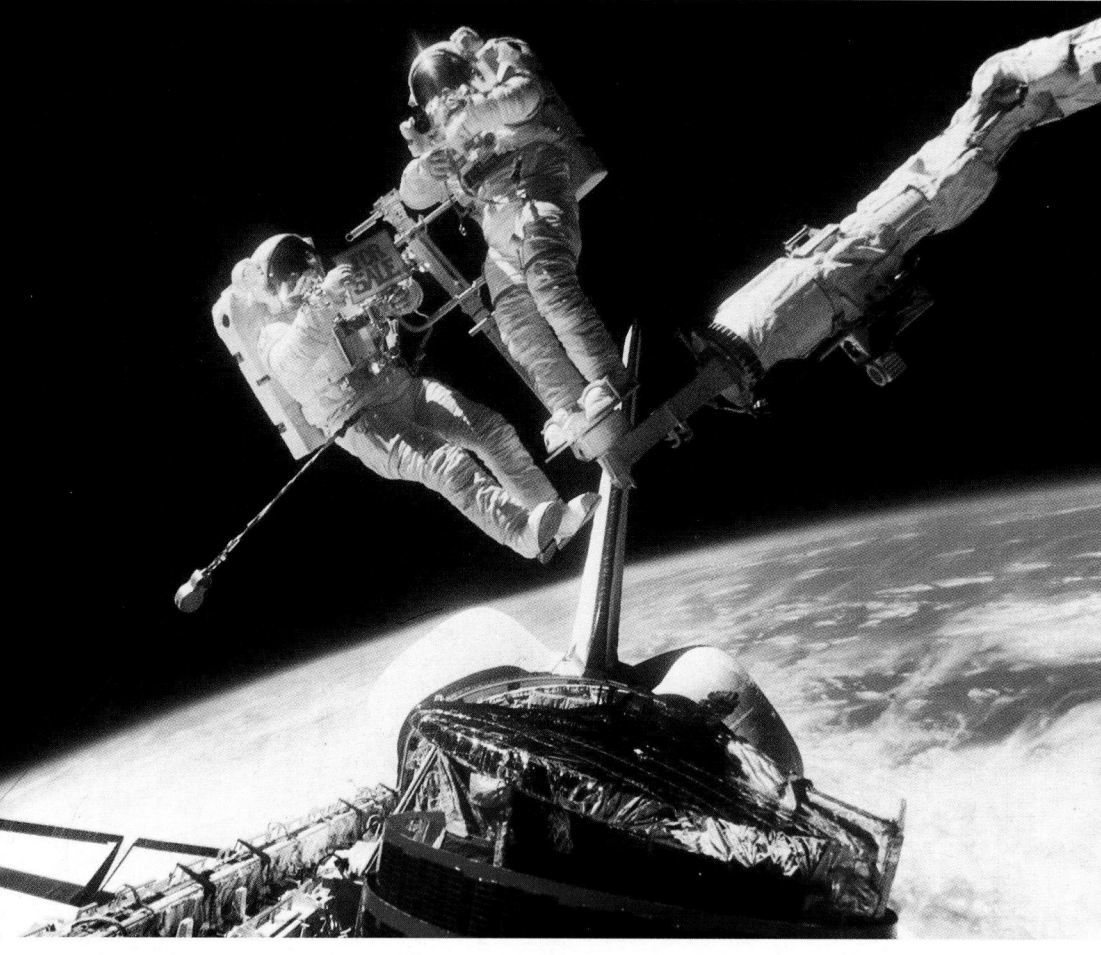

**Visualizing
History** New technology has helped advance space exploration. The earth's people now can view the earth as a single unit with a shared environment.

Your History Journal

Choose a region of the world that is having difficulty keeping peace. Imagine that you are part of a delegation of diplomats from the United Nations who have been sent to the region to talk with leaders. Write your opening statement.

Chapter 26 *The World in Transition* **773**

**Visualizing
History** Space has become a laboratory in which scientists can assess what is happening to our planet. Spacecraft can orbit the earth and photograph areas of the planet to monitor changes. Scientists hope to be able to "watch the planet breathe" and study global change with the aim of preventing more damage to the earth.

 **Performance
Assessment**

Refer to the activity on page 772C of the Planning Guide.

For an additional activity, refer to Activity 26 in the *Performance Assessment Strategies and Activities* booklet.

Using Your History Journal

Remind students to think first about how the people native to the region they are visiting differ from them culturally. Remind them of the need to be sensitive to and respect their values and needs.

**GLENCOE
TECHNOLOGY**

 VIDEODISC
Use MindJogger to preview chapter content.

MindJogger Videoquiz

 Chapter 26
Disc 3 Side B

 Also available in VHS.

+ EXTRA CREDIT PROJECT

Global Issues Daily newspapers, television broadcasts, and newsmagazines cover and update most of the topics in this chapter. Have students gather up-to-the-minute information on the issues, people, and places they study and compile articles to put into a "Global Issues" newspaper. They can work in groups or individually; one or two students might volunteer to be the editors and oversee the articles coming in. By the end of the chapter, they should have current information on most of the topics to print in the newspaper for class distribution.

1980   1990   2000

1980 Ronald Reagan is elected President of the United States.

1985 Mikhail Gorbachev becomes leader of the Soviet Union.

1991 Former Soviet republics form the CIS.

1995 Russian and American soldiers take part in NATO-led Bosnian peacekeeping mission.

SECTION THEME

▶ **Change** The end of the cold war and the collapse of communism transform the relationship of the United States and the Soviet Union.

Find Out

Answer: *Domestic problems and the growing influence of other blocs of nations changed superpower relations.*

FOCUS

Section Objective

Identify the developments that changed superpower relations by the mid-1990s.

BELLRINGER
Motivational Activity

Before taking roll at the beginning of the class period, project Section Focus Transparency 26-1 and have students answer the activity questions. Discuss students' responses.
This activity is also available as a blackline master.

Vocabulary Pre-check

Use the Vocabulary PuzzleMaker to create a puzzle that reinforces the vocabulary terms in this section. **L1**

Section 1

The End of the Cold War

Setting the Scene

▶ **Terms to Define**
trade deficit, budget deficit, glasnost, perestroika, privatization

▶ **People to Meet**
Ronald Reagan, George Bush, Bill Clinton, Madeleine Albright, Mikhail Gorbachev, Boris Yeltsin

▶ **Places to Locate**
Moscow, Latvia, Lithuania, Estonia, Russia, Ukraine, Belarus, Kazakhstan, Georgia, Armenia, Azerbaijan, Uzbekistan, Tajikistan, Turkmenistan

Find Out
What developments changed superpower relations by the mid-1990s?

The Storyteller

As the U.S. government's deficit soared out of control, the budget became the focus of debate. Aaron Wildavsky explained what may be the heart of the problem: "There are times when an agency wishes to cut its budget…. If the agency [has] effective clientele groups (special interests), however, it may not only fail in this purpose but may actually see the appropriation increased as this threat mobilizes the affected interests."

—from "Political Implications of Budgetary Reform," Aaron Wildavsky in *Classic Readings in American Politics*, 1986

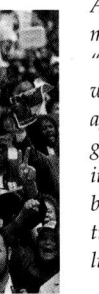

U.S. group protesting budget cuts

---

*I*n the early 1980s, cold war tensions between the United States and the Soviet Union increased dramatically. However, the world had changed since the 1950s when the superpowers competed alone in the arena of world affairs. Now other blocs of nations, with their own separate concerns, were influencing global developments. In addition, the two superpowers faced growing political and economic problems at home. Together, domestic and international changes would lead to the end of the cold war.

The United States

By the early 1980s, the United States was losing its dominance of the global market. It had changed from a lending nation to a borrowing nation. America also experienced trade deficits, buying more from foreign nations than it sold in foreign markets. As other industrialized lands developed powerful economies, their industries competed with American industries in sales to American consumers.

Reinventing Government

Meanwhile, the United States government found it difficult to live within its means. In 1980 Republican **Ronald Reagan** won the presidency partly on his promise to reduce the budget deficit, or the difference between the amount of money the government earns in revenues and what it spends. As President, Reagan cut spending on social programs and lowered taxes to stimulate economic growth. During his two terms, inflation slowed and the economy improved. However, increased military spending by Reagan and his Republican successor, **George Bush**, pushed the budget deficit to new heights.

SECTION RESOURCES

Reproducible Masters
- Reproducible Lesson Plan 26-1
- Guided Reading Activity 26-1
- Section Quiz 26-1

Transparencies
- Section Focus Transparency 26-1
- Chapter Transparency 26
- World History and Art Transparency 51, *Vietnam Memorial*

Multimedia
- Vocabulary PuzzleMaker Software
- Student Self-Test and Review Software
- Testmaker
- Communism and the Cold War: *A New Soviet Union: Communist Rule Ends*

By 1992, American voters wanted a change and elected Democrat **Bill Clinton** as President. Clinton favored both moderate deficit reduction and increased spending. He pushed—unsuccessfully—for guaranteed health benefits for all Americans. Attacking the President for favoring big, costly government, the Republicans in 1994 won control of both houses of Congress for the first time in 40 years. After strong disagreements, Clinton and the Republican-led Congress in 1996 accepted a compromise plan to balance the budget by the year 2002. They also introduced reforms to move people from welfare rolls to jobs. By 1997, government cutbacks had helped reduce the annual federal budget deficit.

This turnaround was part of a general improvement in the American economy since the early 1990s. Despite an overall trade deficit, the United States had strengthened its global economic position by streamlining industries, using new technology, and opening new markets. The economic good news helped Clinton win reelection in 1996 over his Republican opponent, Robert Dole, and Reform party candidate Ross Perot. However, campaign fund-raising controversies and accusations against his personal morals and financial ethics posed challenges for Clinton well into his second term.

American Foreign Policy

During the 1980s and 1990s, sweeping changes in the world affected American foreign policy. In the early 1980s, tensions heightened between the United States and the Soviet Union. Both superpowers engaged in military buildups, and the Soviet army continued to occupy Afghanistan. By mid-decade, however, relations had improved as the Soviets undertook reforms. With the collapse of the Soviet Union in 1991, George Bush, and later Bill Clinton, supported the growth of democracy in Russia and other former Communist nations.

In the 1990s, the United States sought to develop a new foreign policy for the postwar world. Cuts were made in defense spending, and both Bush and Clinton generally conducted foreign policy through diplomacy or by using economic pressures. However, as the world's only superpower, the United States also joined in multinational military operations in such trouble spots as the Persian Gulf, Somalia, Haiti, and the Balkans. One of the architects of the new foreign policy was **Madeleine Albright**, who in 1997 became the first woman to serve as Secretary of State. Previously the American ambassador to the UN, Albright supported United States efforts to strengthen democracy in Europe, advance peace in the Middle East, and establish effective partnerships with Latin American and Asian countries.

American Society

As the twentieth century draws to a close, opportunities and challenges face the United States. The technological revolution has created opportunities for workers trained in new skills. However, workers without such training have not always benefited. In 1996, the income gap between rich and poor was wider than at any time since the 1930s. As a result, Americans now recognize the need for more effective ways to improve education and provide people with relevant job skills.

Crime and violence is another challenge. In 1995 the bombing of a federal office building in Oklahoma City claimed the lives of 168 people and focused national attention on the violent anti-government feelings of private American militia groups. To combat terrorism, the government has sought new powers, such as increased wiretapping, but this raises the question of whether Americans would accept limits on their civil liberties.

In the 1990s there were increased risks to the health of Americans. Diseases such as AIDS (acquired immunodeficiency syndrome) have killed thousands in the United States. Drug addiction continues to be a concern, which causes many to demand more government involvement to halt the problem.

Immigration became a pressing issue in the 1990s, when economic and political ills around the world brought a new tide of immigrants to the United States. Some newcomers were illegal aliens, people who enter a country without a permit. Many Americans blamed increased immigration for loss of jobs and higher taxes. In 1996 Congress passed legislation that imposed new restrictions on both legal and illegal immigrants. The new rules, however, were opposed by civil rights groups.

Related to immigration is the question of diversity. Some Americans believe that the different peoples who make up the United States should retain their individual cultural heritages. Others believe that the United States should be a melting-pot society in which immigrants from around the world blend into one unique people.

Gorbachev's USSR

In the mid-1980s, **Mikhail Gorbachev**, a reform-minded leader, came to power in the Soviet Union. To transform the inefficient, state-run economy and halt the decay of Soviet society, Gorbachev was willing to make drastic changes. Under his policy of glasnost, meaning "openness," Gorbachev allowed freedom of expression for Soviet citizens and eased harsh measures against critics of the Soviet system.

TEACH

Guided Practice

THEME Change

Put the heads *U.S.* and *USSR* on the chalkboard and ask students to list the economic problems these countries faced in the 1980s and the changes leaders sought. **L1 LEP**

Critical Thinking With the freedom to leave the Soviet Union, Soviet Jews poured into Israel in the early 1990s. Ask students to suggest what problems Israel faced as a result of this influx. *(shortage of jobs, newcomers don't understand the language or such basic things as the banking system; inadequate housing)* **L3**

Biography

The following videotape programs are available from Glencoe:

- **Ronald Regan: The Role of a Lifetime**
- **George Bush: A Sense of Duty**

ABCNEWS
INTERACTIVE™

 VIDEODISC
Communism and the Cold War

Side One, Chapter 21
Frames 38662–44504
Title: *A New Soviet Union: Communist Rule Ends*
Ask: What changes were made by Gorbachev's reforms? *(The people were allowed to vote, political prisoners were set free, and the ruling party was no longer required to be Communist.)*

COOPERATIVE LEARNING ACTIVITY

Geography: Place Organize the class into small groups. Assign each group one of the republics of the Soviet Union to research and prepare an oral report. Students should find out about the geographic features, the people, the resources, the cities, and daily life. Suggest that each group divide the tasks and prepare information, including a map or copies of photographs, about one aspect of their republic. When the research is complete, ask each group to give a class presentation on its assigned republic. **L2**

Chapter Transparency 26

 World History and Art Transparency 51, *Vietnam Memorial*

Independent Practice

Guided Reading Activity 26-1 **L1**

Visualizing History By speaking directly with citizens and listening to their complaints and hopes, Gorbachev sought to soften the government's image and encourage greater citizen participation.
Answer to Caption: *He wanted to publicly acknowledge the nation's problems and rebuild the Soviet economy, moving toward greater reliance on free enterprise.*

POINT

The Soviet Breakup
How did communism in the Soviet Union come to an end? *Gorbachev's efforts to reform the Communist system led only to the Soviet Union's further decay. Attempts by hard-liners to regain power led to public resistance and the complete collapse of Soviet communism.*

Critical Thinking Gorbachev has written that the end of the cold war "… has also brought to the fore tensions that were latent, frozen as it were, during the confrontation between global alliances. Many of these tensions have exploded into bloody conflicts." Have students comment on this statement in view of material in this section. **L3**

Visualizing History Soviet leader Mikhail Gorbachev (right) and his wife Raisa (center) greet Soviet citizens at a public meeting. *What changes did Gorbachev want to make in 1985?*

Departing from rigid state controls, Gorbachev also pushed for a rebuilding of the Soviet economy, a policy the Soviets called perestroika (PEHR•uh•STROY•kuh). Gorbachev encouraged limited moves toward free enterprise. He began to dismantle the national bureaucracy that controlled industrial production, allowing more decision making at local levels.

Gorbachev's Foreign Policy

Facing the enormous American military buildup under President Reagan, Gorbachev needed to negotiate new arms-reduction agreements with the United States. Since Soviet economic progress depended on military cutbacks, Gorbachev made large concessions to settle long-stalled treaty negotiations. His offers to cancel nuclear tests and to withdraw Soviet missiles from Eastern Europe was so sweeping that they took Western leaders by surprise. To further ease global tensions, Gorbachev withdrew Soviet troops from Afghanistan.

Gorbachev also encouraged Eastern European Communist leaders to carry out reforms. His policies inspired discontented majorities in these repressed countries. Scattered demands for democracy grew into a wave of anti-Communist protest that eventually brought down the Iron Curtain.

New Challenges

Gorbachev's fresh outlook and friendly personality made him popular in the Western countries he visited. At home, however, Gorbachev was increas-

ingly criticized. Economic problems continued, and even worsened, while reforms stalled. At the same time, the conservative bureaucracy and military resisted change, fearing the loss of jobs and the weakening of Soviet might. To maintain control, Gorbachev zigzagged between reformist and hard-line positions, creating uncertainty throughout government and business.

By 1990, perestroika's slow pace had brought forward rivals to Gorbachev's leadership. The most powerful of these challengers was **Boris Yeltsin**, a former Gorbachev ally. Wanting to increase the pace of reforms, Yeltsin took his case to the people, winning election to the presidency of the Russian Republic, the largest of the Soviet republics. As an elected leader, Yeltsin had a stronger base of support than did Gorbachev.

POINT

The Soviet Breakup

While Gorbachev faced mounting opposition from political rivals, nationalist and ethnic unrest began to sweep the Soviet Union. As its name reflected, the Union of Soviet Socialist Republics (USSR) was a union of 15 separate republics, or states. The largest was Russia, which included the Soviet capital, **Moscow**. The non-Russian republics resented the dominance of the Russians over their affairs. A strong Soviet secret police and army had long kept opposition and nationalist groups under control. But in the relaxed atmosphere of glasnost, old hatreds resurfaced. Throughout the republics there were strong demands for self-rule, if not outright secession. In 1990 **Latvia**, **Lithuania**, and **Estonia** became the first republics to declare their independence from the Soviet Union.

A Dangerous Course

To appease the conservatives who feared a breakup of the Soviet Union, Gorbachev began a rollback of glasnost in the early 1990s and adopted new hard-line positions. Among them were the tightening of controls on the Soviet press to curb dissent and the restoration of powers to the secret police. Some of Gorbachev's reform-minded political aides resigned in protest, and Soviet citizens, led by Yeltsin, called for Gorbachev to step down.

The Coup Attempt

In August 1991 events in the Soviet Union finally reached a climax. Hard-liners in the military and secret police staged a coup to remove Gorbachev

---

MEETING SPECIAL NEEDS ACTIVITY

Physical Disability Students with a hearing loss are usually stronger visual learners. To help them study this section, encourage them to write down the main ideas under each of the section headings and to copy any charts or words put on the chalkboard. Have students who give oral reports provide copies for these students so they can highlight important facts and learn visually. **L1**

from power and to restore the old order. In three tense days the coup unraveled. Early support for the coup evaporated in the face of the heroic leadership of Boris Yeltsin in Moscow. Resistance spread to other parts of the country. Military units refused to carry out the orders of the coup leaders.

The coup turned out to be the turning point for the Soviet Union. Gorbachev was seen as unable to solve the country's problems and unable to shake off his Communist roots. Yeltsin became the real leader of the Soviet Union. Popular anger at the Communist party and the secret police swept the land, and the party dissolved. Statues of party leaders were torn down; many cities chose to return to their pre-1917 names. One such city was Leningrad, which had given birth to the 1917 Bolshevik Revolution. It took back its historic name —St. Petersburg.

Independent Republics

By late September all the Soviet republics had announced their independence from the Soviet Union. Gorbachev failed to win their support for a Union Treaty guaranteeing the republics greater self-rule within the old Soviet framework. Yeltsin, however, chose another plan to maintain some form of unity among the republics. In December 1991, the three Slavic republics—**Russia**, **Ukraine**, and **Belarus**—announced the formation of the Commonwealth of Independent States (CIS), a loose association of republics to take the place of the Soviet Union. Other republics quickly joined. Mikhail Gorbachev, now a man without a country to govern, resigned the Soviet presidency.

Foreign Policy

After the Soviet breakup, Russian president Yeltsin moved to ensure the security of the Soviet nuclear arsenal. He and the leaders of the other republics holding nuclear weapons—Ukraine, Belarus, and **Kazakhstan**—agreed that Russia would assume command of the weapons. Ukraine later declared itself a nuclear-free zone and dismantled its arsenal of nuclear warheads. A further agreement between Russia and the United States was reached. The two nations agreed on a mutual reduction in the number of nuclear weapons that each had. By 1997, Russia and the United States no

Russia and the Independent Republics

Map Study By December 1991 all the republics had declared independence from the Soviet Union. From 1994 to 1996, Russia fought a war against the breakaway republic of Chechnya.
Place What independent republic has the best access to warm water ports?

Chapter 26 *The World in Transition* **777**

Map Study

Answer
Russia

Map Skills Practice

Reading a Map What bodies of water does Russia border? (*Baltic Sea, Barents Sea, Black Sea, Caspian Sea, Sea of Japan, Sea of Okhotsk, Bering Sea, Arctic Ocean*)

Who?What?Where?When?

Soviet Exodus With glasnost came the freedom for Soviet Jews to emigrate. Half a million Jews moved to Israel between 1989 and 1992.

Linking Past and Present

Alexander Pushkin, perhaps Russia's greatest poet, was born in 1799 and lived only 26 years, but he is an enduring part of Russian culture. He was a champion of liberty and wrote drama and some prose as well as poetry. His masterpiece, *Eugene Onegin*, inspired an opera by Tchaikovsky and was translated into English by Vladimir Nabokov. Russian poet Yevgeny Yevtushenko, a modern-day champion of freedom, says, "Pushkin stands out as that rare Russian, an independent man."

ASSESS

Check for Understanding

Assign Section 1 Review as homework or as an in-class activity.

Use Student Self-Test and Review Software to review Section 1.

NATIONAL GEOGRAPHIC PICTURING HISTORY

Explain that the new freedom of expression allowed under Gorbachev opened a floodgate after years of repression. Ask students to try to imagine the courage it took, after such ingrained habits of watching one's words, to openly confront a Russian colonel as the man in this photograph is doing. What other forms of protest could people make under glasnost? *(open display of banners of protest, telegrams of criticism to politicians, publicly airing grievances through demonstrations, publishing books critical of the government, even jokes about the system)*

Who?What?Where?When?

Mikhail Gorbachev, who is now chairman of the International Institute for Social, Economic, and Political Studies in Moscow, has written a book called *The Search for a New Beginning: Developing a New Civilization*. The views expressed in the book reflect a man who has taken a careful look at the past, has learned from it, and has changed. About the early years of glasnost and perestroika, he says: "... we formulated the principle 'Start perestroika with yourself.' In fact, however, we rushed to change society while leaving the change of ourselves for later ... the root cause of many of our ... failures."

Steve Raymer

Seeing Red

Traitor! A flag-waving Russian colonel shouts at a demonstrator who wants to end the 70-year-long rule of communism in the Soviet Union. Opposing visions divided the Russian people as they faced their uncertain future in the spring of 1990. Would their children live in the Union of Soviet Socialist Republics where they had grown up? Would communism prevail, after all the sacrifices made in the name of Lenin or Stalin? Would the state plan a national economy, or would the forces of the market prevail? Who would win and who would lose?

Communism first began to crumble in the satellite nations of Eastern Europe. As early as 1956 the Hungarians revolted, and in 1968 the Czechs rebelled. In these early years of the cold war the Communist regime was strong enough to withstand those assaults. In 1989 Germany's Berlin Wall crumbled. In 1990 the Soviet Union itself began to fall apart, first in the Baltic States and then throughout the country as the various republics proclaimed their independence. No wonder anger and fear line the faces of the two men pictured above, as they confront the end of the world they know. ⊕

longer targeted nuclear warheads at each other; however, mounting disorder in Russia increased Western concerns about foreign dictators and terrorists buying or stealing Soviet-era nuclear technology.

During the 1990s, Russia at first opposed the West's effort to turn NATO into a collective security alliance embracing much of Europe, including Eastern European countries formerly under Soviet control. To allay Russian security fears, the West pledged not to place nuclear weapons in Eastern Europe. Russia then agreed to the plan, while promising to continue its partnership with NATO in peacekeeping ventures. It also strengthened economic and political ties with the West by joining the leading free enterprise democracies in periodic discussions that became known as the Group of Eight.

Economic and Social Changes

At home, Yeltsin introduced reforms to move Russia's economy from government control to free enterprise. These measures included removing price controls, closing inefficient factories, and promoting **privatization**, the setting up of privately owned businesses. The immediate result, however, was an increase in both prices and unemployment, causing much discontent. Many of the other CIS countries—for example, Ukraine, **Georgia**, **Armenia**, **Azerbaijan**, **Uzbekistan**, **Tajikistan**, and **Turkmenistan**—pushed similar economic reforms while facing unrest among their populations.

By the mid-1990s, some progress had been made in stabilizing prices, and new businesses and a new middle class were growing in the former Soviet republics. Yet many reforms were stalled or had little immediate impact. In Russia, production fell sharply, and the government lacked funds to meets its obligations, mainly due to mismanagement, corruption, and difficulty in collecting taxes. To receive badly needed financial aid from abroad, Yeltsin had to cut spending for the military .

Russia also faced mounting social problems. Workers, the elderly, and the poor suffered economic hardships. Street violence, organized crime, and ethnic unrest increased public fears about the collapse of law and order. Pollution caused by Soviet-era industrialization presented a major health risk.

Taking advantage of widespread dissatisfaction, nationalists and Communists in Russia tried to block Yeltsin's reforms. Despite this opposition and his poor health, Yeltsin in 1996 defeated his Communist rival in presidential elections. To win nationalist voters, he had brought a popular general, Alexander Lebed, into his government; but after several months, Yeltsin fired Lebed when the general criticized his policies. During his second term, Yeltsin pressed ahead with reforms, naming a cabinet made up of free enterprise supporters.

Visualizing History Soviet President Boris Yeltsin tried to promote free enterprise reforms but faced powerful opposition. *What two groups opposed Yeltsin's reforms?*

SECTION 1 REVIEW

Recall
1. **Define** trade deficit, budget deficit, glasnost, perestroika, privatization.
2. **Identify** Ronald Reagan, George Bush, Bill Clinton, Madeleine Albright, Mikhail Gorbachev, Boris Yeltsin.

3. **State** the major issues facing the United States during the 1980s and 1990s.
Critical Thinking
4. **Applying Information** Why do you think the transition from communism to free enterprise has been difficult in the former Soviet republics?
Understanding Themes
5. **Change** How did Gorbachev's policy of glasnost contribute to ethnic unrest in the former Soviet republics and open the way for independence movements there?

SECTION 1 REVIEW ANSWERS

1. All vocabulary words are defined in the Glossary.
2. Ronald Reagan, 774; George Bush, 775; Bill Clinton, 775; Madeleine Albright, 775; Mikhail Gorbachev, 775; Boris Yeltsin, 775
3. sluggish economy in 1980s, with improvement in the 1990s; federal government budget deficits; welfare reform; crime and violence; health issues; technological revolution and workers' retraining; campaign funding; foreign policy adjustment to post-cold war world; immigration controls; cultural diversity
4. Answers will vary. Possible answer: Not all people favor the change and some have wanted to block the transition.
5. **CHANGE** It allowed people to express discontent and admit problems; rigid controls were dropped and old resentments resurfaced.

SECTION THEME

▶ **Change** The weakening of the Soviet Union and the rise of reform movements bring an end to Soviet control in Eastern Europe.

Find Out

Answer: *When the Soviet Union began to change under Gorbachev and signaled that it would not object to changes in Eastern Europe, the Communist systems there collapsed.*

FOCUS

Section Objective

Describe how Soviet Communist controls came to an end in Eastern Europe.

BELLRINGER
Motivational Activity

Before taking roll at the beginning of the class period, project Section Focus Transparency 26-2 and have students answer the activity questions. Discuss students' responses.

This activity is also available as a blackline master.

Vocabulary Pre-check

Use Vocabulary Activity 26 to introduce vocabulary terms.
L1 LEP

Section 2

The Crumbling Wall

Setting the Scene

▶ **Terms to Define**
autonomy

▶ **People to Meet**
Pope John Paul II, Lech Walesa, Nicolae Ceaușescu, Václav Havel, Aleksander Kwasniewski, Slobodan Milosevic

▶ **Places to Locate**
Poland, Gdansk, East Germany, Hungary, Romania, Bulgaria, Berlin, the Czech Republic, Slovakia, Albania, Bosnia-Herzegovina, Croatia, Macedonia, Slovenia, Serbia, Montenegro, Dayton

Find Out
How did Soviet Communist controls come to an end in Eastern Europe?

The Storyteller

The wall was coming down. West Berliners chipped away at it with hammers and chisels, while impatient East Berliners used heavy equipment. Finally a gap opened and a crowd of people surged through. Young people who had never visited the West sampled the goods of a market economy. Older people looked for friends whom they had not seen for nearly three decades. "It's been so long, it's a wonder we recognized each other!" With joyful exclamations, two old friends met by the ruins of the wall that had separated them as teenagers.

—adapted from "Berlin's Ode to Joy," Prit J. Vesilind in *National Geographic*, April 1990

Fall of the Berlin Wall

During the 1980s, the Communist nations of Eastern Europe, like the Soviet Union, faced massive problems. Their government-controlled economies failed to produce high-quality consumer goods and had fallen far behind the economies of the West. Reform had to be tried, but the Communist system was too flawed. When the Soviet Union began to change and signaled that it would not object to changes in Eastern Europe, the Communist systems collapsed.

The Rise of Solidarity

The final round of unrest in Eastern Europe began in the 1970s and continued into the 1980s. In **Poland**, the antigovernment movement had received a strong boost in 1978, when the Roman Catholic Church selected a Polish church leader, Karol Wojtyla (voy•TEE•wah), as its pope. The elevation of **Pope John Paul II**, a staunch anti-Communist, inspired confidence among the largely Catholic Poles and enabled them to take further steps toward liberation from Communist control.

In 1980 Polish workers in the Baltic port of **Gdansk** organized a trade union called Solidarity. **Lech Walesa** (lehk vah•LEHN•suh), an electrical worker at the Lenin Shipyard in Gdansk, was a founder and leader of Solidarity.

Solidarity backed up its demands for better living and working conditions with strikes, including one led by Walesa at the Gdansk shipyards. In a remarkable victory, the strikers forced the Polish government to recognize Solidarity in October 1980. Until this time, self-governing trade unions independent of Communist control had not been allowed to exist in Communist countries.

Under Walesa's leadership, Solidarity demanded free elections and a voice for workers in forming government policy. The Polish government responded by demanding that strikes and other "antistate" activities be ended. Under pressure

---

Visualizing History Lech Walesa began his career as an electrician and eventually became Poland's first democratically elected president of the post-Communist era. *What role did Walesa have in Polish affairs during the early 1980s?*

from the Soviet Union, Polish authorities outlawed the union 16 months later and jailed many of its leaders. Despite this, Walesa and others continued their activities underground.

Although Solidarity's activities were not immediately successful, the courage of its members inspired people in other Eastern European countries. Walesa became a symbol of freedom and an international hero. He was awarded the Nobel Peace Prize in 1983. By the end of the decade, the Soviet Union itself was changing under Gorbachev, and unrest had spread across Eastern Europe.

TURNING POINT

1989: A Year of Miracles

By the late 1980s, reduced production, decreases in labor productivity, high inflation, and trade deficits had virtually paralyzed the economies of Eastern Europe. This meant fewer goods at ever-increasing prices. The highly centralized economies, out of touch with consumer needs, caused widespread food shortages. Dissent against communism reached its peak in 1989.

Soviet Policies

As democratic movements gathered force across Eastern Europe during the late 1980s, many people wondered: Would Mikhail Gorbachev exer-

cise the terms of the Brezhnev Doctrine and put down rebellions? In a speech in January 1989, Gorbachev announced that he had ordered a cutback of 500,000 troops in the Soviet army—about half of that number to come from troops stationed in Eastern Europe. The troops had been put there to keep the Soviet satellites in line.

In March he pledged not to interfere with democratic reforms in Hungary. Referring to the 1956 and 1968 invasions of Hungary and Czechoslovakia, Gorbachev declared that "all possible safeguards should be provided so that no external force can interfere in the domestic affairs of socialist countries."

Gorbachev decided that most Eastern-bloc governments—which lacked popular support—would continue to provoke opposition. The Soviet Union would be forced to intervene militarily at great cost. Soviet interests would be better served if he simply let these governments fall. Gorbachev would then establish friendly relations with new governments.

Collapse of Communism

In 1989 Communist governments in Eastern Europe crumbled under the weight of staggering problems. All the satellite countries had ruined economies. Many had terrible environmental damage that had been ignored in the push to industrialize. Other countries, such as Yugoslavia, were being shaken by internal ethnic conflicts.

As economic and political instability increased, Communist regimes either resigned or were overturned in **East Germany**, Czechoslovakia, **Hungary**, Poland, **Romania**, and **Bulgaria**. Throughout this remarkable year of 1989, Gorbachev astounded the world by not only refusing to intervene in democratic uprisings, but actually encouraging reform in the region.

In mid-1989 Hungary, which had been quietly moving toward democratic reform for more than a decade, opened its sealed borders. A flood of East German refugees poured through this new "hole" in the Iron Curtain, seeking sanctuary in the West. The exodus called attention to the failed government of East Germany's leader, Erich Honecker.

The Wall's Fall

Amid mass demonstrations and calls for democratic reform, Honecker's government was toppled in October and replaced by a more moderate Communist administration. The move did not satisfy the reform movement but made its supporters bolder and more demanding. The next month, in an attempt to defuse the situation, the government lifted all travel restrictions between East and West. It

---

Guided Practice

THEME Change

Write *1989: A Year of Miracles* on the chalkboard and ask students to list the events and changes from this section that made 1989 a year of "miracles." **L1 LEP**

Visualizing History  Walesa was jailed for his involvement with Solidarity, and after his release suffered harassment from the government. Influenced by its economic problems, however, in 1988 the government agreed to recognize Solidarity and to allow the union to have seats in the legislature.
Answer to Caption: *He led the drive for free elections and became a symbol of freedom.*

TURNING POINT

1989: A Year of Miracles
Why was 1989 a significant year in the history of Eastern Europe?
Economic decline and popular unrest, aided by Gorbachev's disinclination to intervene, led to the collapse of Communist governments in Eastern Europe.

Television Broadcast Organize the class into news teams and assign one team to cover West Germany, one to cover East Germany, and one to represent the team in the news studio in the United States. Each team will need to research the November 1989 reuniting of Berlin as the wall came down. Students are to conduct interviews to get firsthand reactions and accounts of reunited families and friends. (Teams should decide what parts each member will play.) The studio team should research details about the people in the West and the East and alert news teams about the questions they might ask when they air the show. If possible, have a video camera available to tape the broadcast. **L2**

Government Guide students in naming the different countries mentioned in this section whose Communist regimes ended. *(Poland, East Germany, Hungary, Romania, Bulgaria, Czechoslovakia, Albania, Yugoslavia)* Have students create a chart on the chalkboard that lists the names of the rulers involved in each country and that tells whether the change in each country was peaceful or violent. **L2 LEP**

Critical Thinking Ask students to discuss the issues of freedom and control. Point out how difficult it has been for the newly freed countries to build democracies and stability without new outbreaks of fighting and chaos. Ask students to give examples from this section of the results of too much control and of the results of sudden freedom. **L3**

ABCNEWS INTERACTIVE™

VIDEODISC
Turning Points in World History

Side Two
Chapter 9

Title: *Fall of the Berlin Wall*
Subject: The building of the Berlin Wall, its symbolic and literal 28-year division between East and West Germany, the fall of the wall as a symbol of the failure of communism
Ask: What was desirable about the West for East Germany's people? *("Good wages, affordable homes, and most of all freedom.")* What did the fall of the wall represent to Germany? *(that East and West Germany were unified once again)*

hoped the refugees would remain in East Germany under a reformed but still Communist government.

On the evening of November 9, 1989, the famous Brandenburg Gate at the **Berlin** Wall was opened. All through the night East Germans and West Germans, hearing the wall had been opened, rushed there to see for themselves, overwhelming the guards and passing through the gate in both directions. Others swarmed over the wall, dancing and singing atop it.

In the following days, people on both sides of the wall attacked it with picks and shovels, opening huge holes—even selling chunks as souvenirs. More gates were opened, and the flow of people increased. Families and friends who had not seen each other in decades were reunited. The government, helpless before this popular uprising, ordered the rest of the wall torn down.

Violence in Romania

The overthrow of Communist governments in Eastern Europe was, for the most part, nonviolent. The one grim chapter in the story took place in Romania, where dictator **Nicolae Ceauşescu** (NEE•koh•lay chow•SHEHS•koo) had ruled for 24 years. Ceauşescu's methods had become increasingly brutal over the years, and his reaction to freedom protests in his country was violent. Hundreds of people were killed before the Romanians revolted and ousted the dictator in December 1989. Ceauşescu and his wife, Elena, were tried and shot.

Throughout Europe and the West, crowds celebrated the fall of Ceauşescu. They were also celebrating the end of Soviet control in Eastern Europe and, in a larger sense, the end of the cold war.

New Leaders in a New Age

Following the downfall of Communist governments, reformers looked for new leaders to bring democracy and stability to their countries. They wanted leaders who had not been tainted by collaboration or membership in the Communist

Images *of the* Times

A New Era

A wave of unrest swept Eastern Europe in the late 1980s, leading to the fall of hard-line Communist governments. By the mid-1990s, some countries in the region had become sound democracies; others, plagued by economic uncertainties, turned to nationalist or former Communist leaders.

Solidarity led the movement for democracy in Poland. The labor union began in the shipyards of the Baltic port of Gdansk and soon spread to other parts of the country.

782

Images *of the* Times

A New Era

With the fall of communism and rise of nationalism came ethnic conflicts that have resulted in a major international problem: refugees. The UN founded an agency known as the United Nations High Commission for Refugees (UNHCR) after World War II. Its mission is to assist people who are refugees, including those living like refugees in their own country. The UNHCR staff attempts to get food and medicine to refugees. The Yugoslavian breakup had created nearly 4 million refugees by 1994, 600,000 of them children. The UNHCR has airlifted supplies to Kurds, Rwandans, residents of Sarajevo, and to the people in Bosnia-Herzegovina.

party—a particularly difficult task in East Germany and Romania.

In East Germany, the fall of the Berlin Wall quickly led to calls for the reunification of Germany. On December 2, 1990, Helmut Kohl, riding a wave of pro-unification sentiment, was elected in a landslide as the first chancellor of a reunited Germany. Other countries looked to their national heroes to lead their new regimes. Czechoslovakia elected a dissident playwright, **Václav Havel** (VAHT•SLAHF HAH•vehl), who had been in jail only months before. Then, in 1992, Czech and Slovak leaders agreed to split Czechoslovakia into two separate nations. **The Czech Republic** and the Republic of **Slovakia** became separate sovereign nations in January 1993. The countries maintain close economic and political ties. In Poland, voters made a choice that surprised no one: Lech Walesa was elected president in 1990.

Even staunchly Communist **Albania**, the lone holdout against the reforms of 1989, was finally swept up in the wave of protests. It opened its sealed borders, allowed opposition parties to form, and held elections in 1991. Other nations, such as Romania, organized coalition governments from a multitude of political parties.

Facing Challenges

After coming to power, new Eastern European governments faced the awesome task of shifting from communism to democracy and free enterprise. State-run economies were in shambles, and new governments inherited a host of problems. These included inefficient or outdated industries, huge national debts, workforces paid regardless of the quality of their work, artificially low prices for basic goods, and currencies considered worthless by the rest of the world. In addition, little investment was available in Eastern Europe to modernize old industries or fund new ones. To attract foreign investment and financial aid, new governments had to reform their economies by cutting spending,

Refugees push across the border from Hungary into Austria after Hungary in 1989 became the first Communist state to open its sealed borders.

A reunited Germany was celebrated by throngs of people near Berlin's Brandenburg Gate on October 3, 1990.

REFLECTING ON THE TIMES

1. How did the fall of communism in Eastern Europe affect Germany?
2. What movement rallied public support for democracy in Poland?

783

ANSWERS TO REFLECTING ON THE TIMES

1. It led to the reunification of Germany.
2. Solidarity movement

Chapter 26 Section 2

Independent Practice

📁 Guided Reading Activity 26-2 **L1**

📁 People in World History Profile 71

Daily Life Have students research and depict in a letter to a newspaper what everyday life is like in one of the Eastern European countries studied in this section. **L2**

Linking Past and Present

Nazi War Crimes Germans have decided to remember the victims of Nazi war crimes by establishing January 27, the anniversary of the liberation of Auschwitz by Red Army troops, as a national day of commemoration. In establishing this day, the German president expressed the desire that young people who did not experience the Nazi regime maintain awareness of racism and totalitarianism in order to resist them.

ABCNEWS INTERACTIVE™

 VIDEODISC
Communism and the Cold War

Side Two, Chapter 17
Frames 38033–42654
Title: *Challenge of Reform*
Subject: Challenges facing Eastern European countries
Ask: What happened as Poland tried to establish a free market system? *(Prices and unemployment rose.)*

Critical Thinking Have students research Yugoslavia and its collapse. Ask them to study resources other than newspapers and to analyze the factors that led to its collapse. **L3**

Who?What?Where?When?

Women from East Germany have lost benefits with reunification. They were used to working with a year's paid maternity leave and free day-care centers. The unemployment after unity has left many jobless.

ASSESS

Check for Understanding

Assign Section 2 Review as homework or as an in-class activity.

🖥 Use Student Self-Test and Review Software to review Section 2.

Evaluate

 Section Quiz 26-2

🖥 Use the Testmaker to create a customized quiz for Section 2.

---

balancing budgets, closing or selling off inefficient state-run firms, and training workers in new skills.

Reforms and Stability

With their strong industrial bases, the Czech Republic, Hungary, and Poland seemed the most likely to succeed in the transition from communism to capitalism. However, even in these lands, economic reforms imposed hardships on citizens, with many workers facing unemployment and reductions in social benefits. In Hungary and Poland, dissatisfied voters in the mid-1990s returned ex-Communists to power. For example, a 41-year-old former Communist, **Aleksander Kwasniewski** (kvash•NYEHF•skee) defeated Lech Walesa for Poland's presidency. Eastern Europe's reformed communists, however, supported democracy and favored their countries joining NATO, although they wanted a slower pace to privatization and opposed radical cuts in social welfare programs. Yet by decade's end, voters seemed to be moving back toward the political center. In 1997 Solidarity and other non-Communist candidates triumphed over their ex-Communist opponents in Poland's parliamentary elections. Encouraging this trend was the decision of NATO to admit Poland, Hungary, and the Czech Republic in 1999.

Upheavals

The post-Communist era not only brought economic hardships but political instability and widespread violence to countries in the southern part of Eastern Europe. There, democratic traditions were not as strong, and economies had only recently been industrialized. In Bulgaria, ex-Communist leaders poorly managed the state-run economy and rejected any reforms until the country was hit by a grain shortage and severe inflation. In 1997 citizen protests finally forced the government to call elections, which brought anti-Communists to power. Bulgaria's new leaders promised to introduce free enterprise and won international financial help.

In Albania, Eastern Europe's poorest country, democracy and free enterprise were nearly engulfed in chaos. During the early 1990s, almost every Albanian family had put money in investment schemes, which abruptly collapsed in 1997. With their life savings wiped out, Albanians rioted throughout the country, blaming the government for the collapse and demanding payment. Rebel groups took control of southern Albania, and many Albanians in other areas fought each other with weapons looted from the country's arsenals. A UN-sponsored peacekeeping force finally restored order, and new elections were held. The new gov-

ernment stated that it could not pay back investors but that it would work to revive the economy.

War in the Balkans

After communism's fall, Eastern Europe experienced a rebirth of nationalist feeling. The most serious outbreak of nationalist conflict occurred in Yugoslavia. For centuries, tensions had existed among Yugoslavia's many ethnic groups. However, these hatreds were muted under the Communist leadership of Josip Broz Tito. After Tito's death in 1980, Communist controls gradually weakened, and in 1990, opposition political parties were allowed to form.

Multiparty elections in Yugoslavia were held later that year. Non-Communist parties won most seats in the parliaments of **Bosnia-Herzegovina**, **Croatia**, **Macedonia**, and **Slovenia**. In **Serbia** and **Montenegro**, the former Communist parties, renamed as Socialist parties, won majorities. The leader of Serbia, **Slobodan Milosevic** (swoh •boh•dahn mee•LAH•soh•veech), renounced communism but was intent on expanding his power. After the elections, the most industrialized republics—Croatia and Slovenia—charged that Serbia sought to dominate the rest of the country. In 1991, when Serbia opposed any restructuring of Yugoslavia that would give the other republics more autonomy, or self-rule, Slovenia and Croatia declared their independence.

Fighting in Croatia

Fighting then broke out in Croatia between the Croat army and ethnic Serbs who refused to be under Croat rule. Serbia and Montenegro, which together became known as Yugoslavia, backed the ethnic Serbs of Croatia. With this aid, ethnic Serb forces gained control of one-third of Croatia's territory.

A cease-fire in 1992 finally ended much of the fighting in Croatia, and UN peacekeeping forces patrolled the borders between Serb-held and Croat-held areas. A Croat offensive in 1995 finally brought the Serb-held territory back into Croatia. Since then, international human rights groups have accused the Croat government of abuses in its treatment of the ethnic Serbs in Croatia.

Bosnia-Herzegovina

In the fall of 1991, another republic, Macedonia, declared its independence. The following year, most of the Muslim population and the ethnic Croats in still another republic—Bosnia-Herzegovina—voted for independence from Serb-controlled

784 **Chapter 26** *The World in Transition*

Visualizing
History On November 21, 1995, the leaders of Serbia, Bosnia-Herzegovina, and Croatia joined U.S. Secretary of State Warren Christopher in initialing an accord. *What decision was reached at the Dayton peace talks?*

Visualizing History After this accord, Bosnian Muslims began returning to the ruins of their homes in Sarajevo. The Dayton agreement brought change, but it does not prevent countries from seeking assistance in military training. In 1996 the Bosnian government sent soldiers to Iran for more training.

Answer to Caption: *A Bosnian state divided into a Croatian-Muslim and a Serb region was established.*

Yugoslavia. Ethnic Serbs living in Bosnia-Herzegovina opposed the election and its outcome.

Fighting then broke out between the ethnic Serbs in Bosnia-Herzegovina and the rest of the population—the Bosnian Muslims and the Croats. Yugoslavia, Serbia and Montenegro provided aid to the Bosnian Serbs, who soon controlled most of Bosnia-Herzegovina.

In 1994 the exhausted Bosnian Muslims and Croats formed a federation, and the United States asked the Bosnian Serbs to end the fighting and join as well. After military pressure from Croatia's land forces and NATO air strikes, the Bosnian Serbs accepted a cease-fire and American-sponsored peace talks. In 1995 the leaders of Bosnia-Herzegovina, Yugoslavia (Serbia and Montenegro), and Croatia met at **Dayton**, Ohio, and agreed to set up a Bosnian state divided into separate Croat-Muslim and Serb regions.

Milosevic's Serbia

Dissatisfaction with Slobodan Milosevic led to discord in Serbia. In 1996, Milosevic's government refused to accept the victory of opposition parties in local elections. Numerous protests were staged in Belgrade, the Serbian capital, and other towns to protest the government's action. In 1997 Milosevic finally yielded and acknowledged the opposition's victories. However, he also worked to strengthen his hold on the country.

Reteach

Have the class make a flowchart documenting what happened to Eastern Europe after the collapse of the Soviet Union.

Enrich

Ask students to collect information from the library or a travel agency about the historic sights and the natural beauties of the Eastern European countries before civil wars changed some of them.

CLOSE

Ask students to summarize the recent changes in the Balkans and predict what might change in Eastern Europe in the next decade.

SECTION 2 REVIEW

Recall
1. **Define** autonomy.
2. **Identify** Pope John Paul II, Solidarity, Lech Walesa, Nicolae Ceauşescu, Václav Havel, Aleksander Kwasniewski, Slobodan Milosevic.

3. **Explain** Why were some of the revolutions in Eastern Europe more violent than others?

Critical Thinking
4. **Applying Information** What kinds of changes have occurred rapidly in Eastern European

countries? Which changes are occurring slowly?

Understanding Themes
5. **Change** What changes came to the Yugoslav area with the fall of communism in the late 1980s and early 1990s?

SECTION 2 REVIEW ANSWERS

1. All vocabulary words are defined in the Glossary.
2. Pope John Paul II, 780; Solidarity, 780; Lech Walesa, 780; Nicolae Ceauşescu, 782; Václav Havel, 783; Aleksander Kwasniewski, 783; Slobodan Milosevic, 784
3. The Romanian dictator resisted the

freedom protests and had hundreds of people killed, whereas most other Communist regimes responded to protests peacefully.

4. The collapse of Communist systems and establishment of new governments has been rapid; privatization and the establishment of a free market has been

a slower process.

5. **CHANGE** Individual republics declared independence, fighting broke out in Croatia and Bosnia-Herzegovina, and a Bosnian state with two separate regions was established.

1980   1990   2000

1981 France elects its first Socialist president.

1986 Spain and Portugal join the European Community.

1990 East Germany and West Germany reunite.

1995 The British and Irish governments announce talks to resolve Northern Ireland's future.

Find Out

Answer: *The Common Market was transformed into the European Community. Members signed the Maastricht Treaty establishing the European Union. The Single Europe Act ended most obstacles to trade and movement among European Union members.*

FOCUS

Section Objective

Identify the steps Western European nations have taken to unify their governments and economies.

Vocabulary Pre-check

Use Vocabulary Activity 26 to introduce vocabulary terms.
L1 LEP

Section 3

Toward a European Union

Setting the Scene

▶ **Terms to Define**
referendum, collective security

▶ **People to Meet**
Margaret Thatcher, John Major, Tony Blair, François Mitterrand, Jacques Chirac, Helmut Kohl, Juan Carlos I, Felipe González, Andreas Papandreou

▶ **Places to Locate**
Northern Ireland, Cyprus

 **Find Out** What steps have Western European nations taken to unify their governments and economies?

The Storyteller

Paddy Ashdown believed in the European Union. As a businessman and a member of Parliament, he saw the benefits of Britain's participation. Already he had seen imports and exports move more freely, unhampered by restrictive tariffs. The last remaining hurdle was that of a common currency. Ashdown took the floor of Parliament to argue for the proposition. "We face the prospect of either joining an imperfect monetary union at a later date, or staying out altogether. This is exactly what happened over the EU itself. We must not make the same mistake twice."

European Union Currency

—adapted from "The Case for a Single Currency," Paddy Ashdown, in *The Economist Newspaper, Ltd.*, March 4, 1995

786 Chapter 26 *The World in Transition*

*S*ince the 1970s, Western European nations have faced economic recession, budget deficits, and high unemployment. However, they also have worked to modernize their societies and to balance economic growth with the social needs of their peoples. By 1995, Western Europe as a whole had made great strides toward full economic and political unity. Yet it faced a number of economic and political challenges resulting from economic restructuring, increasing immigration, the reunification of Germany, the collapse of the Soviet bloc, and the outbreak of fierce ethnic conflict in the Balkans.

Great Britain

During the 1970s, Great Britain's economic woes continued under Labour governments. In 1979 voters, dissatisfied with a weak economy, high taxes, and trade union strikes, brought the Conservative party into a long period of power.

Thatcher and Major

As Great Britain's first woman prime minister, Conservative party leader **Margaret Thatcher** aggressively introduced free market measures. She privatized state-owned industries, scaled back welfare programs, and limited trade union powers. Although Thatcher's policies aided business growth, they created high unemployment. Declining popularity and the loss of Conservative support led to her resignation in 1990.

Thatcher's successor, **John Major**, led a Conservative party increasingly divided over Great Britain's ties to Europe. Some Conservatives wanted British participation in a united Europe, while others feared a future European union would mean a loss of British independence.

Visualizing History Political murals cover buildings in both Protestant and Catholic Northern Ireland neighborhoods. *What issue has led to conflict in Northern Ireland?*

During the 1990s, the British economy continued to grow, with falling unemployment and relatively low inflation. However, after nearly 18 years of Conservative rule, voters wanted a change and in 1997 brought the Labour party to power. Known for his youthful, energetic style, the new prime minister, **Tony Blair**, moved away from Labour's traditional socialism and favored low taxes, tightly controlled social spending, and closer ties to Europe.

The most innovative of Blair's plans was the reform of British government. In response to growing nationalism in Scotland and Wales, Blair favored home rule for these parts of Great Britain.

In 1997 Scottish voters approved creation of their own parliament to tax and legislate on local issues, and Welsh voters backed plans for a less powerful assembly that would spend funds provided by the British Parliament. Blair also pressured the long-established but scandal-plagued monarchy to be more in touch with the people.

Ireland

A major European issue from the 1970s to the 1990s was the status of **Northern Ireland**, the British-ruled province torn by divisions between Protestants and Catholics. The Protestant majority wanted to remain British, while the Catholic minority wanted to be part of the Republic of Ireland. Long-standing Protestant discrimination of Roman Catholics in the province had led to civil rights protests during the 1960s. As clashes between the two communities increased, the British government sent troops to Northern Ireland and imposed direct rule during the early 1970s. Meanwhile, the outlawed Irish Republican Army (IRA) fought British rule by attacking British military forces and civilians in the province and in Great Britain.

In the 1980s, Margaret Thatcher took stern measures by suspending the civil liberties of suspected IRA terrorists. However, John Major contacted the IRA to end the violence in Northern Ireland. In 1995 a cease-fire paved the way for peace talks among all sides, but the IRA's resort to arms hampered any progress. Two years later, the IRA agreed to another cease-fire, and Sinn Fein, the IRA's political wing, entered talks with British and Irish officials.

France

France enjoyed political stability from the 1970s to the 1990s. In 1981 French voters elected **François Mitterand** as France's first Socialist president. Mitterand nationalized major industries and funded new social programs. His measures, however, increased inflation, and he eventually was forced to make cutbacks. By the mid-1990s, Mitterand also had to work with a largely conservative legislature. Meanwhile, voter concerns about government corruption, unemployment, high taxes, and increasing immigration from northern Africa and Asia remained high.

In 1995 **Jacques Chirac**, the conservative mayor of Paris, was elected president of France. Chirac promised a referendum, or popular vote, on France's future relationship with a united Europe. He also tried to balance the budget by further cuts in government spending. To protest Chirac's economic policies, workers and students staged nationwide strikes and demonstrations. In 1997 a majority of voters rebuffed Chirac and elected Socialists and other leftists to France's legislature. A period of difficult relations began between the conservative president and the leftist legislature. Chirac pushed for less spending and more business growth, while his Socialist opponents stressed jobs for unemployed workers and the protection of social benefits.

Germany

During the 1970s West Germany, under Chancellor Willy Brandt and his successor, Helmut Schmidt, enjoyed prosperity. But the early 1980s

---

TEACH

Guided Practice

THEME **Cooperation**
Have students list the ways members of the European Union cooperate now or hope to cooperate in the future. *(cooperation in areas of defense policy, crime, immigration; ending most obstacles to trade and movement among member nations; establishing a common currency and a central bank)* **L1**

Visualizing History Point out the open hostility the murals on the buildings portray. Militaristic murals and street decorations can be seen in the cities of Northern Ireland, but by contrast, the countryside is a place of peace and natural beauty.
Answer to Caption: *The Protestant majority in Northern Ireland favors continued union with Great Britain, while the Catholic minority there wants to join the Republic of Ireland.*

Critical Thinking Explain that *xenophobia* means "fear of foreigners." Tell students that German reunification caused an upsurge of xenophobia in the early 1990s. Neo-Nazi sects preached German superiority and targeted foreigners. Ask students to comment on why this might have occurred. *(new problems of housing shortages and public deficit blamed on refugees from Eastern Europe)* **L3**

COOPERATIVE LEARNING ACTIVITY

Panel Presentations Organize students into small groups. Have each group choose one of the countries studied in this section to research in depth. Have individual students in each group look at the people and culture, the music and literature, places of interest to visit, the politics, economics, and social conditions. They should try to collect any visual materials they feel will help the presentation. Have them present these reports as panels of experts. **L2**

Cultural Perspectives
London There is a mix of cultures in this city that is unparalleled in Europe. Each of 34 countries ranging from Ireland and the United States to Mauritius and Malaysia are represented in London communities.

Independent Practice

 Guided Reading Activity 26-3 **L1**

Politics Have students draw cartoons about one of the political situations discussed in this section. Each cartoon should express a specific point of view. **L2 LEP**

Linking Past and Present

Madrid's Plaza Mayor This Spanish city square was built in the seventeenth century and served as the site for public tortures during the Spanish Inquisition. Today it is a place of pleasure; where people enjoy refreshments and conversation at its courtyard cafés.

Civil Strife Ask students to look at a map showing Turkey and Greece in relation to Cyprus. Ask volunteers to research and report to the class about the conflicts in Cyprus between the Greek and Turkish communities. **L2**

 NATIONAL GEOGRAPHIC SOCIETY

CD-ROM

PICTURE ATLAS OF THE WORLD

You and your students can view the streets of London, the moors of the United Kingdom, the vineyards of Germany, and the hillsides of Greece by clicking the "Video" button of selected countries.

---

saw a growth of inflation and unemployment. Promising better times, a conservative chancellor, **Helmut Kohl**, came to power. In 1990 Kohl presided over the reunification of Germany following the collapse of communism in Eastern Europe. He made preparations for the transfer of the German capital from Bonn to Berlin by the year 2000.

When the excitement of reunification wore off, Germans realized that the economic costs of reunification were far higher than anyone had foreseen. Eastern Germany's economic rebuilding after years of Communist rule required vast expenditures, and Germans in the western part had to pay higher taxes to support this restructuring. In eastern Germany, the closing of inefficient industries caused unemployment to soar, although economic rebuilding in the long term would provide eastern Germany with the most modern technology in Europe.

By 1997, unemployment was at its highest level throughout Germany since the 1930s. Meanwhile, the government faced the dilemma of trying to maintain generous welfare programs while controlling its budget deficit. Further progress toward greater European economic unity required Germany to keep its deficit under control, but workers opposed any government effort to roll back price supports for certain goods.

Social and political unrest accompanied economic difficulties throughout Germany. Neo-Nazis and other right-wing Germans protested against immigration from southern Europe and the Middle East. Some of them attacked foreigners, resulting in a number of deaths. Large numbers of Germans protested the attacks, but the German parliament in 1993 amended the constitution to reduce the flow of immigrants into Germany.

That same year, Germany's highest court ruled that German troops could take part in international peacekeeping missions. Until then, the constitution

---

ᖴootnotes to ᕼistory

The Chunnel
In 1994 Great Britain and France, separated for thousands of years by the English Channel, were once again joined. The Channel Tunnel, nicknamed the Chunnel, linked the island country to mainland Europe. By the year 2003 the Chunnel is expected to carry more than 120,000 people between Great Britain and France each day. At night, tons of freight will now move through the Chunnel.

---

had banned all military activities except those related to collective security, or joint agreement by nations to protect themselves from attack.

Mediterranean Europe

Mediterranean Europe made great strides in political and economic development from the 1970s to the 1990s. Dictatorships fell and democracies arose in Spain and Portugal. Economic recession, however, hurt the Mediterranean countries.

Italy

From the 1970s to the 1990s, a variety of economic, social, and political problems plagued Italy. Among these were the uneven distribution of wealth, especially between north and south, an inefficient government bureaucracy, and constantly changing governments.

During the 1970s, Italy had the largest Communist party in western Europe. The party was popular in part because it promoted a less authoritarian view of communism. It sought to share power with the ruling conservative Christian Democrats. Many conservative Italians, however, were alarmed at this prospect. Adding to the political uncertainty was a wave of murders, kidnappings, and bombings by leftist groups.

Christian Democrats, later renamed the Populists, controlled the government during the late 1980s and early 1990s. During this time, the leftist parties—Communists and Socialists—suffered from policy disputes and political scandals. By the late 1990s, government power shifted back and forth between conservative and leftist coalitions. The leaders of these governments faced the challenge of shrinking Italy's enormous budget deficit.

Spain and Portugal

After nearly 35 years of dictatorship under Francisco Franco, Spain in the late 1970s entered a new era of democracy guided by its new king, **Juan Carlos I**. For most of the 1980s and 1990s, Spain's democratic government was in the hands of the Socialists and their leader, **Felipe González**. In 1996 Spanish voters replaced the Socialists with a conservative government under José Maria Aznar.

Since the restoration of democracy, the Spanish government has granted the Basque Provinces and other regions of Spain increased self-rule after years of repression under Franco. Nevertheless, it has been unable to stop terrorist attacks by Basques wanting full independence for their region. In foreign affairs, Spain has strengthened its links to the

---

MEETING SPECIAL NEEDS ACTIVITY

Language Delayed Have students trace an outline map of Europe. Ask them to label the countries studied in this section and then color-code each country. Have them make a color-code key for the map and in the key give specific information about each country, such as political leaders, important dates and events, and any other details they want to include. **L1 LEP**

---

rest of Europe after joining NATO and the European Community in the 1980s.

A turn toward democracy also occurred in Portugal. There, dictatorship ended with a military coup in 1974, and two years later the nation held its first free elections in 50 years. During this time, Portugal freed most of its African and Asian colonies and in 1986 joined the European Community.

Greece

From the mid-1960s to the early 1970s, Greece was ruled by a repressive military government. In 1974 democracy was restored, and for the next two decades the country was ruled by either conservatives or Socialists. In 1981 the Socialists under Premier **Andreas Papandreou** (pah•pahn•DRAY •yoo) brought Greece into the European Community.

In recent years, Greece has had differences with neighboring Turkey over **Cyprus**, a Mediterranean island republic divided between feuding Greek and Turkish communities. Since 1974, Turkish forces have occupied northern Cyprus, while the southern part of the island remains under an internationally recognized government led by Greek Cypriots.

 **POINT**

A United Europe

During the 1980s and 1990s, the Common Market broadened its activities to include political and financial affairs and became known as the European Community. In 1992 European Community members met in Maastricht, the Netherlands, and signed the Treaty of Maastricht, setting up the European Union (EU). This new body aimed to extend cooperation among members.

In 1993 another measure—the Single Europe Act—ended most obstacles to trade among EU members. Two years later, seven EU nations allowed their citizens to freely travel from one member country to another without a passport. The year 1995 also saw the admission of Austria, Finland, and Sweden to the EU.

The EU looks ahead to even closer unity among its members. Plans are underway to include Eastern European countries and to create an Economic and Monetary Union (EMU) by the year 1999. The principal features of the EMU will be a common currency known as the euro and a central bank.

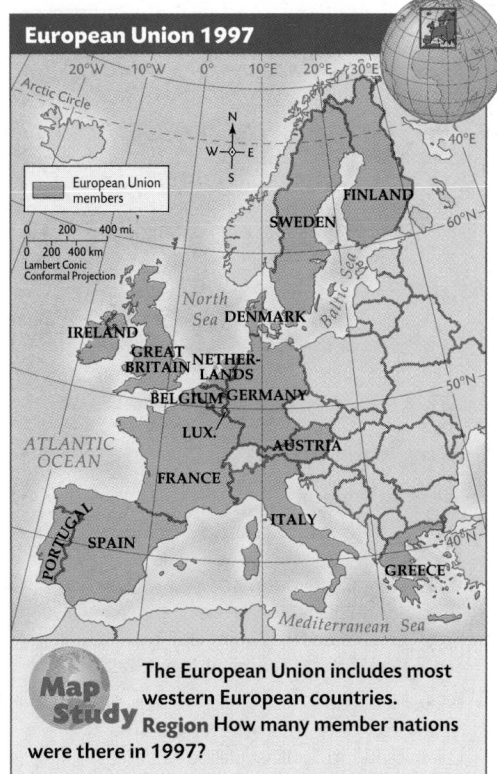

European Union 1997

The European Union includes most western European countries. **Region** How many member nations were there in 1997?

Map Study

Answer
15

 **POINT**

A United Europe
Why was the signing of the Treaty of Maastricht an important event for Europeans?
It created the European Union (EU), which furthered the economic and political union of member nations.

ASSESS

Check for Understanding
Assign Section 3 Review as homework or as an in-class activity.

Use Student Self-Test and Review Software to review Section 3.

Evaluate
Section Quiz 26-3

Reteach
Create a diagram or chart with the students identifying the countries and the leading political groups discussed in this section and the problems they faced in the 1980s and 1990s.

Enrich
Have students research the European Union and create a chart of its current members. Summarize any goals it has for further unity.

CLOSE

Ask students to write a brief summary of the evidence of growing cooperation among European countries since 1990.

SECTION 3 REVIEW

Recall
1. **Define** referendum, collective security.
2. **Identify** Margaret Thatcher, John Major, Tony Blair, the Irish Republican Army, François Mitterrand, Jacques Chirac, Helmut Kohl, Juan Carlos I,

Felipe González, Andreas Papandreou, Treaty of Maastricht.
3. **Explain** the purpose of the European Union.

Critical Thinking
4. **Applying Information** Explain why Great Britain has shown reluctance to fully

participate in plans for full European unity.

Understanding Themes
5. **Cooperation** How do relationships among countries in the European Union compare with those among states in the United States?

SECTION 3 REVIEW ANSWERS

1. The words are defined in the Glossary.
2. Thatcher, 786; Major, 787; Blair, 787; IRA, 787; Mitterrand, 787; Chirac, 787; Kohl, 788; Juan Carlos I, 788; González, 788; Papandreou, 789; Maastricht, 789
3. to increase the cooperation among members of the European Community
4. Great Britain fears a loss of independence.

5. **COOPERATION** Countries in European Union do not share a common government, legal system, or currency as the states in the United States do. Free trade and movement among member nations resemble the same freedoms among the states of the United States.

1980　　　　　　　　1990　　　　　　　　2000

1982 Canada enacts new constitution.　　**1992** Civil war begins in Bosnia.　　**1994** Russian troops enter Chechnya.

SECTION THEME

▶ **Conflict** National and ethnic conflicts intensify worldwide after the end of the cold war.

ind Out

Answer: *The Balkans, southern Russia and the Caucasus, the Middle East, Sri Lanka, and Canada have suffered ethnic discord in the 1990s.*

FOCUS

Section Objective

Recognize the areas of the world that have been in ethnic discord since the end of the cold war.

BELLRINGER
Motivational Activity

Before taking roll at the beginning of the class period, project Section Focus Transparency 26-4 and have students answer the activity questions. Discuss students' responses.

📁　This activity is also available as a blackline master.

Vocabulary Pre-check

📁 Use Vocabulary Activity 26 to introduce vocabulary terms.
L1 LEP

Section 4
....

National and Ethnic Conflicts

Setting the Scene

▶ **Terms to Define**
ethnic cleansing, atrocity, embargo, enclave

▶ **People to Meet**
Slobodan Milosevic, Alija Izetbegovic, Franjo Tudjman, the Chechens, the Ossetians, the Abkhazians, the Kurds, the Sinhalese, the Tamils, Brian Mulroney, Jean Chretien

▶ **Places to Locate**
Sarajevo, Dayton, Chechnya, Nagorno-Karabakh, Sri Lanka, Quebec

ind Out 　What areas of the world have been in ethnic discord since the end of the cold war?

The Storyteller

Zahid Olorcic remembered how things had been just a few years ago. People in Sarajevo had gotten along with their neighbors. Even though coming from diverse backgrounds, the city's multiethnic population lived in harmony. Then the situation changed as radical groups stirred up ethnic hatred. Zahid recalled earlier times:

War damage in Sarajevo

"Funerals, weddings, birthdays, we never counted how many Muslims were there, how many Serbs, how many Croats. The only important thing was to be together.... "

—adapted from "Bosnians Recall Karadzic, a Neighbor Turned Enemy," Tracy Wilkinson, in *The Los Angeles Times*, July 23, 1995

he end of the cold war brought about communism's fall and the triumph of democracy. A new world was at hand—or so it seemed. The aftermath has proven to be more complex. During the cold war, even regional conflicts were often linked to the East-West struggle. Now that the superpower rivalry was over, each issue stood on its own terms, and predictability and stability had given way to uncertainty and confusion.

During the 1990s, long-hidden national and ethnic rivalries flared into violence in various parts of the world. The threats to peace included not only fighting, but also human tragedies such as starvation and the flow of refugees. Often, the global community, through the United Nations and other organizations, seemed helpless in dealing with these crises. However, there were bright spots—for example, South Africa, the Balkans, and the Middle East. In all three places, the 1990s saw efforts, either fulfilled or in progress, to peacefully resolve disputes or deeply rooted injustices.

Fighting in Bosnia

The most serious ethnic fighting in Europe took place in Bosnia-Herzegovina, where the creation of an independent state led to conflict among Croats, Muslims, and Serbs in the early 1990s. With the support of neighboring Serbia and Montenegro, the Bosnian Serbs conquered most of Bosnia-Herzegovina. In April 1992, they began a siege of **Sarajevo**, the Bosnian capital, which was largely controlled by Muslims. Following a policy called **ethnic cleansing**, the Serbs ruthlessly expelled rival ethnic groups from the areas taken by their army. The Croats and Muslims also carried out **atrocities**, or cruel actions, against the Serbs.

SECTION RESOURCES

📁 **Reproducible Masters**
• Reproducible Lesson Plan 26-4
• Vocabulary Activity 26
• Guided Reading Activity 26-4
• People in World History Profile 72
• Section Quiz 26-4

📑 **Transparencies**
• Section Focus Transparency 26-4

Multimedia
💿 Student Self-Test and Review Software
💿 Testmaker
💿 Lessons of War:
　The Nature of Violence

The UN imposed an embargo, a ban on trade, against Serbia in 1992, hoping to get the Serbs to stop supplying the ethnic Serbs in Bosnia. UN peacekeeping forces also arrived in the war-torn republic to protect food and medicine sent to the Bosnian people. Since the war began, thousands of Bosnians had been killed, and hundreds of thousands left homeless.

The United States and other UN members also reported human rights abuses in Bosnia. The reports indicated that Bosnian Serbs had tortured and killed Bosnian Muslims and Croats in detention camps. In 1995 an international court charged Bosnian Serb leaders with genocide for operating thousands of Nazi-style concentration camps and ruthlessly attacking civilian populations.

Steps Toward Peace

In 1994 Serbia, hurting from the effects of the UN embargo, called on Bosnian Serbs to cease fighting. Later that year, the United States offered a peace plan that proposed dividing Bosnia between the Serbs and a new Muslim-Croat federation. Hostilities, however, continued into 1995. When Bosnian Serbs stepped up their attacks on Sarajevo, NATO responded with air attacks on Serb positions around the city. Meanwhile, Croatia completed a land offensive to regain land held by its own Serb minority. With a possible defeat looming, the Bosnian Serbs finally decided to negotiate.

In November 1995, three presidents—**Slobodan Milosevic** (swoh•boh•dahn mee•LAH•soh•veech) of Serbia, **Alija Izetbegovic** (ah•LEE•hah ee•zeht•BEH•goh•veech) of Bosnia-Herzegovina, and **Franjo Tudjman** (FRAHN•hoh TOOZH•mahn) of Croatia—met in **Dayton**, Ohio, and agreed to the partition of Bosnia into distinct Serb and Muslim-Croat areas. In December the Dayton Treaty was signed in Paris, ending the Bosnian conflict. In response to the agreement, the UN Security Council voted to lift the embargo on Serbia. By the time of the Dayton agreement, the Bosnian conflict had resulted in the deaths of 200,000 people and the forced removal of 3 million people from their homes.

Keeping the Peace

To safeguard the peace, a 60,000-strong NATO-led force arrived in Bosnia to replace the exhausted UN troops. American and Russian troops served as part of the peacekeeping force. In 1996 Bosnian voters elected Muslim, Serb, and Croat leaders to serve on a three-person panel that would govern the country. Despite these steps toward peace, the three Bosnian communities disputed territory and blocked refugees from returning to their homes. Another problem was the difficulty in bringing indicted war criminals to justice. However, in 1997 as conflicts erupted between moderate and extremist Bosnian Serbs, NATO forces began attacks against positions held by the war criminals and their supporters.

Unrest in the CIS

With the collapse of communism, fierce ethnic hatreds boiled to the surface in Russia and the other CIS republics. During the Soviet era, the Russian-dominated government in Moscow had repressed the nationalism of non-Russian ethnic groups. This policy increased resentment among many peoples.

Russia and the CIS

Even after the Soviet collapse, relations among the Commonwealth republics were strained. Russia was clearly the most powerful nation, and European republics, such as Ukraine, were reluctant to concede their hard-won independence to a Russian-dominated federation. During the late 1990s, however, Russia worked to improve relations with these countries in order to offset NATO's eastward expansion. In 1997 Russia and Ukraine signed a treaty that recognized Ukrainian rule over the Crimea and divided the disputed Black Sea naval fleet between them. Also that year, Russia and Belarus forged a close union, allowing Russian and Belarussian citizens to move freely between the two countries, own property in either country, and vote in each other's local elections.

Wary of Russia, the Central Asian republics and those in the Caucasus region balanced ties to Russia with new links to Middle Eastern and Western countries. Largely Muslim in religious background, the Caucasus republic of Azerbaijan and the Central Asian republics rediscovered the spiritual and cultural traditions they shared with the Middle East. Rich in oil deposits awaiting development, these lands also were eager to attract Western businesses.

Although Commonwealth ties were often weak, the CIS remained intact as member nations worked together to resolve conflicts between them and within their territories. For example, the CIS backed peacekeeping forces in the Central Asian republic of Tajikistan, which until 1997 had been torn apart by a civil war between its ex-Communist leadership and Muslim opposition forces. Since the Soviet collapse, ethnic unrest had also arisen within some of the individual CIS republics. Each republic had dominant ethnic groups and many smaller ones. Many of

---

TEACH

Guided Practice

THEME Conflict

Trace the steps of the Bosnian conflict with the class, making a time line on the chalkboard as students list events from this section. Start the time line with Bosnian independence in 1992. **L1 LEP**

Summarize Ask students to summarize the pressures applied by the UN against Serbia and the peace plan that was finally agreed on. **L2**

Critical Thinking Have students discuss the stand Boris Yeltsin took against Chechnya. Have them suggest how they think Yeltsin should have responded to the Chechens. **L3**

 **VIDEODISC**
Lessons of War

Side Two, Chapter 10
Title: *The Nature of Violence*
Subject: Various perspectives concerning the nature of violence
Ask: Is violence inherent in human nature? *(Answers will vary, but one theory is that if provoked, all humans are capable of violence.)* How can violence be stopped? *(perhaps through peaceful negotiations)*

COOPERATIVE LEARNING ACTIVITY

Global Peace Union Organize students into small groups to plan and organize a cooperative international effort to educate people in techniques for peaceful resolution of conflicts. First students should brainstorm ideas in their small groups, then have a joint meeting of all the groups and write guidelines for the organization and a plan of action for use in future conflicts. **L2**

Independent Practice

📁 Guided Reading Activity 26-4 **L1**

📁 People in World History Profile 72

Visualizing History The Russian military took over Grozny and expanded into the countryside. According to some reports, the Russians' "total-war strategy" in Chechnya made it a terrifying war zone. **Answer to Caption:** *He wanted to prevent the breakup of Russia that might occur if other ethnic groups followed the example of the Chechens.*

Culture Have students research Sri Lanka and prepare a bulletin-board display of the land, its people, and its culture. **L2**

Who?What?Where?When?

Village Divided On the border between the United States and Canada, a village is divided. On the United States side, in Escourt Station, Maine, live five French-speaking families and an American wildlife warden. On the Canadian side is Escourt, Quebec. One of the households in the village is bisected by the border line.

ASSESS
Check for Understanding

Assign Section 4 Review as homework or as an in-class activity.

💿 Use Student Self-Test and Review Software to review Section 4.

Visualizing History In December 1994, Russian soldiers with tanks (above) attacked Chechen fighters (left), some of whom were dressed in traditional Chechen clothing. *Why did Yeltsin send troops to Chechnya?*

these groups were concentrated in a particular area and had their own local governments. With the collapse of Soviet power, they asserted pride in their traditions and demanded greater self-rule.

The Chechens

The **Chechens** are among the ethnic groups of Russia. Their territory, **Chechnya** (chehch•NYA), lies in southern Russia near the Caspian Sea. In 1994 the Chechens declared their independence from Russia. Fearing Russia's breakup if other groups did the same, Russian leader Boris Yeltsin sent Russian troops into Chechnya. He was widely criticized at home and abroad for the invasion, in which hundreds of civilians were killed in bombing attacks.

The Chechens fought extremely well against poorly trained and disheartened Russian forces. At the same time, the conflict divided Russian public opinion and further strained the economy. In 1996, when Chechen forces took back their capital from the Russians, Yeltsin sent his aide General Alexander Lebed to Chechnya to work out an agreement to end the conflict. Russia and Chechnya soon signed a peace treaty in which both pledged to renounce force in any future disputes. Although the treaty avoided mention of independence, the Chechens claimed victory and proceeded to build an independent state.

The Caucasus Republics

Ethnic conflicts troubled other republics in the CIS. In the Caucasus region, Armenia and Azerbaijan both claimed ownership of the enclave of **Nagorno-Karabakh**. An *enclave* is a small territory entirely surrounded by another territory.

Nagorno-Karabakh lies entirely within Azerbaijan, but its majority population of Armenians wanted it to separate from Azerbaijan and join Armenia. In 1993 Armenia and Azerbaijan went to war over Nagorno-Karabakh. Armenian forces made significant advances and took control of much of the disputed territory.

Neighboring Georgia has faced separatist uprisings by minority ethnic groups, such as **the Ossetians** and **the Abkhazians**. In 1994 the Abkhazians declared their region an independent republic. Meanwhile, Georgia has received support from Russia in the effort to preserve its national unity. The Russians hold three military bases in Georgia and train and equip the Georgian army.

Africa and Asia

During the 1990s, ethnic conflicts erupted in various parts of Africa and Asia. In Africa, full-scale fighting broke out between Hutu and Tutsi peoples in the East African republics of Rwanda and Burundi. The unleashed hatreds led to genocides within these nations, and the violence spilled over into neighboring Zaire, later called the Democratic Republic of the Congo. Other ethnic divisions contributed to civil wars in West Africa, especially in the nations of Sierra Leone and Liberia.

The Kurds

In the Middle East, one of the most divisive ethnic disputes was between **the Kurds** and the governments of Iraq and Turkey. The 20 million Kurds are Sunni Muslims and live mostly in Armenia, Iran, Iraq, Syria, and Turkey. They have never had their

792 **Chapter 26** *The World in Transition*

MEETING SPECIAL NEEDS ACTIVITY

Attention Deficiency Suggest that students who find it easier to break up study into short sessions concentrate on the information under one subhead for a short time, then go to the resource center and find additional information about that subject. This physical activity will help them to focus again when they return to studying. These students could be responsible for gathering current information about conflicts for the newspaper project suggested for this chapter. **L1**

own nation but have long sought their freedom. This goal has been thwarted by divisions among themselves and by the scheming of the governments that rule them. In the 1980s and 1990s, the Kurds of Turkey and Iraq carried out separate revolts against their respective governments. Before and after the Persian Gulf War, Iraqi forces used bombings and poison gas to put down Kurdish uprisings, which left over 1 million Kurds as refugees. Turkish forces have staged offensives against Turkish Kurdish bases in remote mountain areas along the border of Turkey and Iran.

Sri Lanka

Another place torn by ethnic discord was the Indian Ocean island republic of **Sri Lanka**. Sri Lanka's 18 million people largely belong to two ethnic groups, **the Sinhalese** and **the Tamils**. The Sinhalese, who make up about 75 percent of the population, are Buddhist. The Tamils, most of whom are Hindus, form about 18 percent of the population and live in northern and eastern areas of Sri Lanka.

For decades, the Tamils had resented discrimination by the Sinhalese-controlled government. In 1983 fighting broke out between Tamil guerrillas and Sinhalese government troops. Despite peace efforts, the fighting continued into the 1990s. Nearly 40,000 were killed, and hundreds of thousands of Tamil refugees fled to India.

Canada's Fragile Unity

During the 1980s and 1990s, Canada faced growing uncertainty about its future. Many French-speaking people in the province of **Quebec** wanted independence from English-speaking Canada. When Quebec voters in 1980 narrowly defeated an independence proposal, the Canadian federal government worked to strengthen national unity while respecting regional differences. In 1982 a new Canadian constitution was enacted that granted more power to the provinces and guaranteed the language and cultural rights of all Canadians.

Quebec, however, rejected the constitution because it did not allow individual provinces to veto future amendments. Prime Minister **Brian Mulroney**, whose Conservative party came to power in 1984, tried in vain to get English-speaking Canada to accept a special status for Quebec. Ten years later, the Liberal party won parliamentary elections, and **Jean Chretien** (cray•TYEHN) became prime minister. Although a French-speaking Quebecer, Chretien was a firm believer in national unity and opposed Quebec separatism.

In 1995 Quebec voters again turned down independence for the province, but only by a margin of a little over 1 percent. In addition, nearly 60 percent of French-speaking Quebecers had voted for the proposal. Canada in theory remained united, but the Quebec referendum left Canada's people deeply divided.

In June 1997 Canadian voters elected a new parliament, splitting their vote along regional lines. Running on its record of reducing government spending, Prime Minister Jean Chretien's Liberal party captured a majority of seats—19 less than it held in parliament before the vote. Most Liberals were elected in Ontario, Canada's most populous province, and in the Atlantic provinces of Prince Edward Island and Newfoundland.

In second place was the Reform party, a conservative group that had strong support in the western Canadian provinces. There, opposition to a special status for Quebec was strongest in Canada. The Bloc Quebeçois, the Quebec separatist party, was third. Because of divisions within its ranks, however, the Bloc's total number of party seats went down from 50 before the vote.

SECTION 4 REVIEW

Recall
1. **Define** ethnic cleansing, atrocity, embargo, enclave.
2. **Identify** Slobodan Milosevic, Alija Izetbegovic, Franjo Tudjman, the Chechens, the Ossetians, the Abkhazians, the Kurds, the Sinhalese, the Tamils, Brian Mulroney, Jean Chretien.

3. **List** the nations involved in the Nagorno-Karabakh dispute. What geographic factor makes any settlement difficult to achieve?

Critical Thinking
4. **Making Comparisons** How was Quebec's expression of dissatisfaction with Canada different from that of the Tamils with Sri Lanka? What do you think accounts for the differences between the two disputes?

Understanding Themes
5. **Conflict** Why did the Bosnian Serbs in 1992 oppose the creation of an independent Bosnia? Why did they agree to peace talks in 1995?

Linking Past and Present

United Nations Fiftieth Anniversary On June 26, 1945, fifty nations joined to sign the UN Charter. Fifty years later there were 185 members planning a celebration in New York City at the UN headquarters. This organization has received the Nobel Peace Prize numerous times. Although it has not succeeded in resolving some major conflicts, most members believe that the problems countries face are too great for any one nation to solve alone.

Evaluate

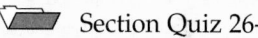 Section Quiz 26-4

⚙ Use the Testmaker to create a customized quiz for Section 4.

Reteach

Ask students to write five opening statements for a national TV news broadcast covering issues in this section.

Enrich

Have students scan newspapers and magazines for articles related to the regions or issues mentioned in this section. Then have them share the articles with the class.

CLOSE

Ask students to discuss which conflicts that they have studied in this section cause them the greatest concern and why.

SECTION 4 REVIEW ANSWERS

1. All vocabulary words are defined in the Glossary.
2. Milosevic, 791; Izetbegovic, 791; Tudjman, 791; Chechens, 792; Ossetians, 792; Abkhazians, 792; Kurds, 792; Sinhalese, 793; Tamils, 793; Mulroney, 793; Chretien, 793
3. Armenia, Azerbaijan; Nagorno-Karabakh is inhabited largely by Armenians, but is an enclave, lying entirely within Azerbaijan
4. Quebec sought separation from Canada through the election process; the Tamils' discord was expressed through violent fighting. Answers will vary. Possible answer: responding to an unjust blocking of basic opportunities for education and employment; people in Quebec were not having rights withheld.
5. **CONFLICT** Bosnian Serbs feared domination by the Croatians and Muslims if Bosnia became independent. Bosnian Serbs agreed to peace talks because it looked like they would be defeated and would lose territory.

1980 1990 2000

1987 The Montreal Protocol calls for global reduction of chemical pollutants.

1992 The first Earth Summit is held in Rio de Janeiro, Brazil.

1995 The United States space shuttle *Atlantis* docks with the Russian space station *Mir*.

Section 5

Global Interdependence

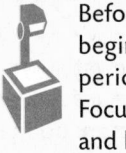
Setting the Scene

▶ **Terms to Define**
interdependent, developing nations, developed nations, deforestation, Internet, genetic engineering

▶ **People to Meet**
Neil Armstrong, Jean Paul Sartre, Mother Teresa

▶ **Places to Locate**
Montreal, Rio de Janeiro

ind Out How have recent advances in technology affected the world's cultures?

The Storyteller

Robert "Hoot" Gibson, the American astronaut, carefully maneuvered Atlantis *closer to* Mir, *the Russian space station. Finally, just after 9:00 A.M. eastern standard time, June 29, 1995, Gibson gently docked the 100-ton shuttle with the* Mir's *central docking port. On Earth, at the Russian mission control, NASA chief Dan Goldin leaped from his seat to hug his Russian counterpart, Yuri Koptev. When the hatch was opened, Gibson floated along the pathway into the Russian ship. After decades of competition, American and Russian space programs had launched a promising partnership.*

—adapted from "Mir Reflections," Frank Sietzen, in *Final Frontier*, November/December 1995

Partnership in space

n 1900 most of the world's people knew little about other people in distant places on the planet. As the year 2000 approaches, however, people communicate instantly with others thousands of miles away and access vast amounts of information with their fingertips. Today, we share in a technological and communications revolution that has made people increasingly interdependent, or reliant on each other.

The Global Community

Today's nations have become economically interdependent through world trade, which now exceeds $8 trillion per year. Since World War II, technological advances and the removal of tariff and other barriers to free trade have led to a tremendous increase in the global exchange of goods and services. The forging of new trade links among different regions has ensured that an economic boom or bust in one region will impact economies in other parts of the world.

The world's economic superpowers include the United States, the European Union, and Japan. These areas, along with South Korea, Taiwan, and other countries of Asia's Pacific Rim, are the leading competitors in international markets and will probably remain so into the next century.

Developing and Developed Nations

With the rise of the global economy, some observers claim that the nation-state is no longer the key economic and political institution it was a hundred years ago. They point out that large multinational organizations and corporations now have greater control over international flows of people, goods, funds, and technology. Others, while recognizing the growing importance of international bodies such as the EU, believe that nation-states are still crucial in making and carrying out basic economic policies.

One of the major global issues involving nations is the gap between rich and poor countries. Developing nations in Asia, Africa, and Latin America are newly industrializing countries, and many of their people still follow traditional ways of life. These developing nations are dependent on developed nations, such as the United States, that have long been industrialized and have the technology to produce a great quantity and variety of goods.

Building Strong Economies

To raise standards of living, developing nations often try to diversify, or increase the variety of, the goods they supply to the world. This enables them to avoid relying on a single crop or product. The transition to a diversified economy, however, can be difficult because of lack of funds and skilled workers. Developing countries often rely on outside lending sources for funding. The World Bank and the International Monetary Fund (IMF) were set up after World War II to assist global economic development. Private banks and international corporations also invest in developing nations.

Borrowing funds for economic growth has placed many countries in monumental debt. When loans cannot be paid, banks suffer huge losses that hurt businesses. Many strategies have been tried to solve international debt problems. In some cases, the banks involved have issued new loans to enable developing countries to pay off old debts. While such practices have helped to offset immediate concerns, the debt question remains a threat to the world's economic health.

Population Growth

The number of people on our planet affects both human well-being and the environment. Developed nations point to the rapid growth of population in developing countries as a major cause in straining world resources. As much as 97 percent of the world's population growth occurs in the developing world. Families are large in very poor countries because many children are needed to help earn money and to assist parents in their old age. At the present rate of growth, the world's population is expected to increase from the present 5.8 billion to more than 6 billion by 2000 and about 12 billion by 2050.

People in developing countries consume far less per person than do people in developed countries. However, the large populations in the developing world are exhausting the resources of many areas. In Africa and Asia, for example, population pressures have forced farmers to make a living on

Visualizing History Hong Kong is one of the busiest ports of Asia's Pacific Rim. *In addition to Asia's Pacific Rim, what other prosperous area of the world trades extensively with the United States?*

fragile, poorly productive lands. In some places erosion and landslides have caused irreversible environmental damage. Throughout the developing world, millions of people leave the countryside each year and crowd into cities in the hope of improving their lives. Urban growth has been so rapid that cities cannot keep up with the needs for shelter, food, and jobs. To remedy these problems, developing countries are working to link population, development, and environmental needs in their planning.

The Environment

Protecting the environment is another challenge facing the planet. For much of human history, the abundance of the earth's resources was taken for granted. Today, however, human use and abuse of resources—especially the high consumption of resources in the developed world—has reached such levels that the planet may no longer be able to

Chapter 26 The World in Transition **795**

TEACH

Guided Practice

THEME Cultural Diffusion

Have students discuss how increasing economic interdependence can hasten the spread of different cultures. (*Answers may include that an increase in international trade encourages foreign travel by the businesspeople of many nations and brings people into contact with the goods from other countries.*) **L1**

Visualizing History Hong Kong is a 400-square-mile (1,036-sq.-km) area with a population of 6 million. It is one of the world's largest financial centers. Life expectancy there is higher than in the United States. **Answer to Caption:** *Western Europe*

Economics Explain that the World Bank is a specialized agency of the United Nations which was founded to provide loans to developing countries to finance investments that will help their economic growth. Discuss the issues this bank would have to consider in making such loans. (*environmental concerns, human rights, political upheavals*) **L2**

Critical Thinking Ask students to consider the problem and effects of overpopulation at the individual and family level. Have some students participate in an impromptu panel discussion about how overcrowding can affect people's daily lives. **L3**

 History Simulation 26

COOPERATIVE LEARNING ACTIVITY

Environmental Responsibilities Display Have students choose an environmental concern (for example, energy conservation, deforestation, species extinction) and make one poster graphically dramatizing the problem and another poster displaying a possible solution. Have students gather visual materials to go with the posters and make a wall display to promote environmental awareness. They should include global as well as local examples. **L1 LEP**

- World History and Art Transparency 52, *Sky Above Clouds II*

- Mapping History Overlay Transparency 25, *World Population Growth*

Independent Practice

📁 Guided Reading Activity 26-5 **L1**

📁 Geography and History Activity 26

Economics Have students do a survey of where the foods they eat and other things they purchase or consume are produced. Have them bring labels to class and use these as a basis for making a rough assessment of how the world is catching up to the United States in trade. **L2**

Linking Past and Present

Global Economy

China is another Asian nation on its way to becoming an economic giant. Its economy is expected to boom in the next century. It has been growing rapidly and is expected to expand to $6 trillion over the next 25 years, a nearly tenfold growth since 1994. With this explosion of growth, however, has come increased pollution; in 1991, industries there created more polluted water than in the entire Western world.

ANSWERS

to increase trade and coordinate economic growth among members; possible answer: They help the global economy since they help member nations achieve economic health and stability.

---

heal itself. Damage to the atmosphere, land, water, and air, has an impact on all living things.

Land and Water

Vast areas of the earth's land have been destroyed by overgrazing, pesticides, and deforestation, the widespread clearing of forests for logging or farming. Particularly at risk are semi-arid areas near the edge of deserts. Between 1970 and 1990, developing countries lost 40 percent of their farmland. This loss will make it increasingly difficult for poorer countries to raise enough food for their growing populations.

The oceans and freshwater supplies of the planet also are showing signs of overuse and abuse. Coastal waters are heavily polluted with chemicals and litter. The bulk of contamination comes from poisonous industrial wastes, municipal sewage, and runoffs of fertilizers, pesticides, and salts. Instead of being swept out to sea, most of this contamination settles into the coastal soil. Environmental damage is reflected in epidemics spread by contaminated fish, in increasing numbers of diseased wildlife, and in the decay of coral reefs.

Meanwhile, demand for fresh water has grown. Conflicts over the distribution of limited water supplies have already developed in the southwestern United States, the Middle East, and North Africa. Efforts are underway to achieve some fair distribution of scarce water supplies among countries, as well as between rural and urban areas.

Environmental Awareness

Since the 1970s, the world's people have become increasingly aware of environmental issues, and a number of international gatherings have stressed the urgency of dealing with the environmental crisis. In 1987 delegates from 46 countries met in **Montreal**, Canada, and signed the Montreal Protocol, which called for reductions in the use of chemicals damaging to the earth's atmosphere. Other important gatherings were the 1992 Earth Summit in **Rio de Janeiro**, Brazil and the follow-up 1997 Earth Summit+5 in New York City. These UN-sponsored conferences called on nations to plan economic growth to meet present global needs without sacrificing the environmental needs of future generations.

CONNECTIONS
Economics

Global Economy

Since 1945, many of the world's nations have joined together to create large regional economic markets. The goal of each of these markets is to increase trade and to coordinate economic growth among member nations.

In North America the United States, Canada, and Mexico have implemented the North American Free Trade Agreement (NAFTA). In southern South America several nations participate in the Southern Common Market (Mercosur), while in the Caribbean region a number of countries form the Association of Caribbean States (ACS).

Western European nations have not only promoted economic interdependence among themselves. In the 1993 Treaty of Maastricht, they also took steps toward political unity by creating the European Union.

The creation of large economic blocs in the Americas and in Europe in part stems from the increasing competition these two regions have faced from the growing economic might of the countries of Asia's Pacific Rim. During the past few decades Japan, South Korea, Taiwan, and Hong Kong have become economic giants and are very active in world trade. In the near future, China, (now including Hong Kong) and the Association of Southeast Asian Nations (ASEAN) will powerfully impact the global economy.

Japanese cars for export

Linking Past and Present ACTIVITY

Explain why individual countries have joined in forming large regional economic markets. Do you think regional economic blocs benefit or hinder the global economy?

796 Chapter 26 *The World in Transition*

MEETING SPECIAL NEEDS ACTIVITY

Language Delayed Students with a need for help with language would benefit by making a set of flash cards for the names of places and the special vocabulary in this section. They might want to go on to compile a set of cards for the entire chapter and use them in studying the material. **L1 LEP**

TURNING POINT

The Technological Revolution

Since 1945, the world has undergone a technological revolution as significant as the Industrial Revolution of the early 1800s. Computers are at the heart of this transformation. They process information that can analyze a nation's economy, forecast the weather, interpret public opinion polls, or calculate the flight path of a rocket. Nations that can afford the latest computer technology gain a distinct advantage—whether through increased productivity or ultimately a higher standard of living—over those still struggling with outdated equipment.

The applications of computer technology are varied. The "brain" driving the computer is the microchip, a mesh of circuits etched on a silicon wafer. In medicine, doctors use these chips to power artificial limbs worn by people who need them. Industrial robots programmed to assemble machines and perform tasks such as welding and painting represent another application of microchip technology.

The Internet

Computers are playing an important role in the expansion of global communications. The most dramatic leap in communications in recent years has been the development of the Internet, a massive number of computers linked together through a worldwide, high-speed, telecommunications network. Using a computer and a modem, a device linking two compatible computers together by a direct connection to the telephone line, a user can research and share information with millions of other participants around the globe. One can create a World Wide Web page to present research results or send a message through E-mail, or electronic mail, to any place in the world in seconds.

Space Exploration

Computer and other new technologies have made space exploration possible. Since the Soviet launching of *Sputnik*, the first satellite into orbit, in 1957, the Americans and Russians have sent hundreds of satellites and human-operated spacecraft into outer space. In July 1969 American astronaut **Neil Armstrong** became the first human to step on the moon's surface. In the early 1980s, American scientists developed the space shuttle, a reusable spacecraft that takes off like a rocket and lands like an airplane. From the shuttle, astronauts can launch, retrieve, and repair satellites. In the mid-

Visualizing History Air pollution from factories is a problem in industrialized countries. In this scene, clouds containing industrial pollutants cover an area in Germany. *How has pollution affected the planet's water?*

1990s the American space shuttle *Atlantis* docked with the Russian space station *Mir*. Symbolizing a new era of space cooperation, this linkage prepared the way for the building of an internationally operated space station.

Medical Advances

Medical science also has benefited from technological progress. Lasers, or devices that emit narrow, powerful beams of light, allow doctors to perform delicate surgery with minimal discomfort to patients. Current medicines can even correct chemical imbalances in the brain, thereby treating the severe depression that can cripple some people's lives. Organ transplants, have become possible with new technologies. Kidneys and livers are among the most commonly transplanted organs, and many people now live for years with transplanted hearts as well.

Recent DNA (deoxyribonucleic acid) technology has led to the new field of genetic engineering, a process that involves the alteration of cells to

Chapter 26 *The World in Transition* **797**

Visualizing History

One of the problems facing a unified Germany was that of serious air and water pollution in former East Germany. The cleaning of the air is a costly and important task for all industrialized countries.
Answer to Caption: *It has contaminated much freshwater.*

Linking Past and Present

Forests The North American continent was once covered with great forests. With the movement west, rising populations, and decades of logging, these temperate rain forests that are home to many plants, fish, and wildlife are shrinking.

TURNING POINT

The Technological Revolution
In what ways has the technological revolution been a turning point?
Computers and the Internet enable millions of people throughout the world to communicate with one another; new technologies have furthered space exploration, and new medical technologies have improved quality of life and research possibilities.

MAKING CONNECTIONS ACTIVITY

Science, Technology, and Society Every day new and more advanced forms of technology are produced, such as computers, diagnostic equipment for medical problems, and video and audio equipment. Have students interview people who grew up in the 1950s or earlier to find out how daily life then, without this technology, differed from life today. For example, students can find out whether their subjects have learned to use a computer. Then ask students to write the interview as a magazine article and include an assessment of how their own lives would be different without the technology they use every day. **L1**

ASSESS

Check for Understanding

Assign Section 5 Review as homework or as an in-class activity.

 Use Student Self-Test and Review Software to review Section 5.

Evaluate

 Section Quiz 26-5

Reteach

Lead a class discussion on developments of the last decade in communications technology, medicine, environment, and cultural global interdependence.

 Reteaching Activity 26

Enrich

Have students prepare written reports on an international environmental issue. Allow an opportunity for them to share these studies.

 Enrichment Activity 26

CLOSE

Have students create a wall chart showing the major technological changes in communication and transportation that have occurred in the twentieth century.

---

produce new life-forms. Further molecular research may yield insights into the origins and cure of diseases such as cancer and AIDS that affect millions of people worldwide.

The Global Culture

Technological advances have hastened the growth of a global culture. Jet travel, television, and communications satellites have spread ideas and practices from one part of the globe to another. Today the cultures of various regions meet and blend. American rock music now echoes in clubs around the world. Asian folk dancers perform their artistry on tour in Europe, while Latin American poets recite their works before audiences in Japan.

The Search for Life's Meaning

Today's rapid and often complex changes have sent many people on a search for life's meaning. After World War II, the French thinker **Jean Paul Sartre** stated a viewpoint known as existentialism that became popular among intellectuals in the West. According to Sartre, each person is essentially alone, but free to choose his or her path in life.

Individual freedom has become a key goal during the last half of the twentieth century. Civil rights movements have advanced racial equality in the United States and South Africa; and in many countries, the women's movement has altered traditional female roles and opened new career opportunities for women.

While secular viewpoints have spread, religious individuals and groups have sought to meet society's needs. For example, the Vatican Council II (1962–1965) related Roman Catholic teaching to modern life and simplified many church practices. The Roman Catholic nun **Mother Teresa** inspired many people with her care of the needy in the slums of Calcutta, India. Also, the Dalai Lama, Tibet's Buddhist leader, and Desmond Tutu, South

African Anglican archbishop, spoke out for human rights. Within Islam and Protestant Christianity, powerful conservative movements have attracted many followers. Although religious hostilities persist in areas such as the Balkans and South Asia, efforts have increased to promote understanding among global religions.

Human Rights

In recent decades, the issue of human rights has captured world attention. According to human rights groups, despite democratic advances since the 1980s, many governments still imprison and abuse people for speaking their minds. Among the countries accused of human rights violations are China, Indonesia, Nigeria, Saudi Arabia, Afghanistan, and Myanmar. Others, such as Iran, Iraq, Cuba, Libya, North Korea, Sudan, and Syria have also been charged with sponsoring terrorist acts outside of their borders.

The good news is that human rights abuses are more carefully monitored than they were. In South Africa, Haiti, and El Salvador, for example, national truth commissions have investigated abuses of past governments, and international tribunals for Bosnia and Rwanda have called individuals to account for their war crimes. The increased visibility of each government's actions and the accompanying accountability that many nations and groups feel is showing results.

In 1948 the United Nations adopted what has become the most important human-rights document of the postwar years—the Universal Declaration of Human Rights. Addressing social and economic as well as political rights, the Declaration is a statement not of the way things are, but of the way they should be. As new technologies develop, more will have to be done to provide the basic needs and a decent quality of life for the planet's inhabitants. As the year 2000 approaches, the Universal Declaration of Human Rights gives the world's people a common goal and ideal for the twenty-first century.

SECTION 5 REVIEW

Recall
1. **Define** interdependent, developing nations, developed nations, deforestation, Internet, genetic engineering.
2. **Identify** NAFTA, ASEAN, Montreal Protocol, Neil Armstrong, Jean Paul Sartre, Mother Teresa
3. **Explain** how population changes have affected lifestyles in developing countries.

Critical Thinking
4. **Analyze** Why do environmental dangers to the planet require global solutions?

Understanding Themes
5. **Cultural Diffusion** What is the most powerful source of cultural diffusion today? Explain the reasoning behind your answer.

SECTION 5 REVIEW ANSWERS

1. All vocabulary words are defined in the Glossary.
2. NAFTA, 796; ASEAN, 796; Montreal Protocol, 797; Neil Armstrong, 798; Jean Paul Sartre, 798; Mother Teresa, 798
3. Large populations in developing nations are consuming natural resources, including land; the movement of people from countryside to cities has exhausted urban resources.
4. Possible answer: Damage to one part of the planet affects other parts of the planet, as all environments are interconnected.
5. **CULTURAL DIFFUSION** Answers will vary. Possible answer: Computer technology has made instant global communication possible, which has allowed the sharing of art, language, and science within seconds.

Interpreting Statistics

Statistics seem to support a claim or an opinion with a ring of authority. We have heard that statistics can be misleading, but do we really understand how to interpret statistics?

Learning the Skill

Statistics are sets of tabulated information that may be gathered through surveys and other sources. When studying statistics, consider each of the following:

Biased sample A sample, or group of the total population surveyed, may affect the results. A sample that does not represent the entire population is called a biased sample. An unbiased sample is called a representative sample.

Correlation Two sets of data may be related or unrelated. If they are related, we say that there is a correlation between them. For example, there is a positive correlation between academic achievement and wages. There is a negative correlation, however, between smoking and life expectancy. Statistics may seem to show a correlation when none exists. For example, a report that "people who go fishing are less likely to get cancer" may be statistically true but lack any correlation.

Statistical Significance Using statistics, researchers determine whether the data support a generalization or whether the results are due to chance. If the probability that the results were due to chance is less than 5 percent, researchers say that the result is statistically significant.

Practicing the Skill

Study the table below (the amount of economic freedom is shown on a scale from 0–8, with 8 being most free). Then answer the questions that follow.

1. Is there a correlation between wage rates and the percentage of government employees? Explain.
2. What statistics deny a correlation between the percentage of government employees and the index of economic freedom?

Applying the Skill

Create a survey with two questions for which you believe the answers may show a correlation. For example, "How many hours of television do you watch per day?" and "How many hours of sleep do you average per night?" Gather a representative sample of responses. Tabulate and evaluate your statistics.

For More Practice

Turn to the Skill Practice in the Chapter Review on page 801 for more practice in interpreting statistics.

Wages, Government Employment, and Economic Freedom			
Nation	**Hourly Wage Rate (1994)**	**Government employees as percent of total**	**Index of Economic Freedom 1993–1995***
Germany	$27	16.2	6.5
Japan	$21	8.4	7.0
Sweden	$19	33.2	5.5
United States	$17	15.4	7.5
Great Britain	$14	18.1	7.0
New Zealand	$10	15.3	8.0
South Korea	$6	na	7.0
Mexico	$5	31.8	5.5

* Index compiled by survey of economists for "Economic Freedom of the World: 1975–1995," James Gwartney, Robert Lawson, and Walter Block.

TEACH

Interpreting Statistics Explain to students that finding a correlation does not mean you have found its cause. When two things are correlated, you cannot tell whether one factor causes the other. For example, if students who did particularly well on an exam were found to have consumed more caffeine the night before, it would not mean that this was the reason for the better performance. The real reason might have been that these students spent more time studying. Remind students to be on guard against inferring a causative relationship where none exists when analyzing statistical data.

Additional Practice

☞ Skill Reinforcement Activity 26

☞ Building Skills in Geography Workbook, Unit 2, Lesson 11

ANSWERS TO PRACTICING THE SKILL

1. No; wages are highest in Germany, but percentage of government employees is highest in Sweden.
2. They all do. For example, Sweden has the highest percentage of government employees but its index is 5.5; Japan has the lowest percentage of government employees and its index is high, 7.0.

Chapter 26 Review

GLENCOE TECHNOLOGY

VIDEODISC

Use MindJogger to review students' knowledge of the chapter.

MindJogger Videoquiz

Chapter 26
Disc 3 Side B

 Also available in VHS.

Answers

Using Key Terms

1. a
2. f
3. d
4. e
5. k

Using Your History Journal

Students should include several specific issues with their effects.

Reviewing Facts

1. U.S. free enterprise economy had trade deficits and high inflation and unemployment, but was basically sound; the Soviet Union had a state-run economy, inefficient and in decay.
2. He worked for reform and agreements with the West.
3. **1980:** Solidarity strikes in Poland; **1985:** Gorbachev comes to power; **1989:** Communist governments fall in Eastern Europe; **Aug. 1991:** failed coup in Moscow; **Dec. 1991**: End of Soviet Union and formation of CIS
4. Yeltsin removed price controls, closed inefficient factories, and pushed toward privatization; this increased prices and caused job losses at first, then led to gradual new business and middle-class growth.
5. The Soviet collapse led to new

Connections Across Time

Historical Significance Since World War II, the world has undergone tremendous changes. The cold war between the United States and the Soviet Union was resolved peacefully, and the global supremacy of the superpowers has given way to a world of regional blocs. Capitalist economies have triumphed over Communist ones, and efforts toward democracy are yielding results in many parts of the world. New technology also has linked world regions more closely together, creating a global economy and culture. The planet, however, faces complex political, economic, and environmental challenges. The world's nations must learn to cooperate to find solutions and to meet the needs of all people.

Using Key Terms

Write the key term that completes each sentence. Then write a sentence for each term not chosen.

a. interdependent
b. glasnost
c. privatization
d. genetic engineering
e. developing nations
f. ethnic cleansing
g. Internet
h. referendum
i. perestroika
j. trade deficit
k. enclave
l. deforestation

1. The growth of technology, communications, and transportation since 1945 has made the regions of the world increasingly _____.
2. In the war in Bosnia, ethnic Serb forces carried out _____, a policy of forcibly removing rival ethnic groups.
3. Through _____, scientists can now alter cells to produce new life-forms.
4. _____ have established new industries, but many of their people still follow traditional ways of earning a living.
5. The territory of Nagorno-Karabakh is an _____ completely surrounded by Azerbaijan.

Technology Activity

Using the Internet Search the Internet for information about the latest technological innovations that are influencing our global culture. Use a search engine to focus your search by using phrases such as *information technology innovations*, *global communications* and *technology revolution*. Create a bulletin board using the information retrieved on the Internet. Include illustrations or pictures of the latest technological innovations.

Using Your History Journal

How will world events affect your future? Write an essay entitled "The World's Future and My Own" identifying important international issues and explaining how events could affect your life.

Reviewing Facts

1. **Economics** Describe the economic challenges faced by Americans and Soviets during the 1980s.
2. **History** Explain how Mikhail Gorbachev differed from earlier Soviet leaders.
3. **History** List in chronological order, the significant events that led to the fall of communism.
4. **Economics** Discuss Boris Yeltsin's economic policy and its effects on Russia.
5. **History** Describe how the Soviet collapse and the fall of communism affected global affairs.
6. **Culture** Explain the role of religion in the anti-Communist movements of Eastern Europe during the late 1970s and early 1980s.
7. **Geography** Explain how developed and developing nations affect the environment.
8. **History** Describe the roles of Pope John Paul II, the Dalai Lama, and Mother Teresa.
9. **Citizenship** Discuss the advances made in human rights since World War II. How has the UN dealt with this issue?
10. **Science/Technology** Explain how the cold war affected space exploration.

republics; the end of the cold war, and expansion of free enterprise.

6. John Paul II inspired Catholic Poles and other Europeans to resist communism
7. developed nations consume resources; developing nations are overpopulated
8. major religious leaders; John Paul II inspired activities in Eastern Europe; the Dalai Lama spoke for Tibet; Mother Teresa, cared for poor

9. Despite violations, greater global awareness, monitoring of government actions, and use of tribunals to punish violators. U.N. has defined human rights and supported peacekeeping missions

Critical Thinking

1. Answers may vary. Students may say yes, because the new freedom caused many uprisings and ethnic conflicts.

Critical Thinking

1. **Analyze** Is Europe less stable now than it was during the cold war? Why or why not?
2. **Analyze** How would you identify the era after 1989? What are its major features?
3. **Evaluate** How does a global economy affect developing nations?
4. **Analyze** How have recent developments in medical technology affected humans?

Geography in History

1. **Region** Refer to the map below. What continent has the largest population?
2. **Place** Why do economists believe that the Pacific Rim is likely to become the world's fastest-growing market in the next decades?
3. **Human/Environment Interaction** How does this map help to identify regions of extreme climate and unsuitable living conditions?

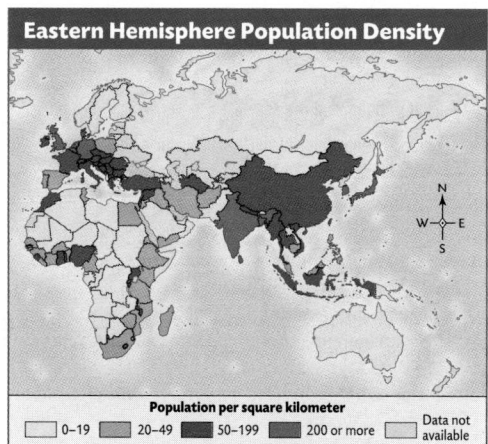

Eastern Hemisphere Population Density

Population per square kilometer
0–19 20–49 50–199 200 or more Data not available

Understanding Themes

1. **Change** What factors do you think led both superpowers to seek an end to the cold war?
2. **Change** Evaluate Mikhail Gorbachev's response to the uprisings in Eastern Europe. What might have happened if he had tried to stop the changes? How were changes in the Soviet Union and its satellites linked?

3. **Cooperation** What are two future goals of the European Union that was created by the 1993 Treaty of Maastricht?
4. **Conflict** How did the Dayton peace settlement attempt to bring peace to Bosnia?
5. **Cultural Diffusion** What factors have led to the emergence of a global culture?

Linking Past and Present

1. How have many people's attitudes toward natural resources and their use changed over the past fifty years?
2. Placing a person on the moon was the primary goal of the space race between the United States and the Soviet Union. Has a new goal for the space programs of the United States and Russia emerged? Explain.

Skill Practice

Study the statistics in the chart below and answer the questions that follow.

1. Is there a correlation between energy consumed and per capita GDP?
2. What factors may explain the correlation between energy consumption and GDP?
3. Is the sample of countries used in the chart statistically significant? Explain.

Energy Use and Per Capita GDP

Country	Energy Consumed* per capita (kilograms)	GDP** per capita
Bahrain	15,608	$12,000
United States	10,798	$24,000
Netherlands	7,248	$9,700
New Zealand	5,838	$15,700
Poland	3,167	$4,400
Argentina	1,977	$5,500
Thailand	833	$5,500
India	336	$1,300
Sudan	62	$750

* figures for 1991
** Gross Domestic Product: the sum of all goods and services produced within the country (1993).

Understanding Themes

1.  **CHANGE** political and economic problems at home; other nations were influencing world affairs
2. **CHANGE** Uprisings may have occurred anyway but would have been violent if Gorbachev had opposed them.
3. **COOPERATION** inclusion of Eastern Europe and to form an economic union with a common currency and bank
4. **CONFLICT** by dividing Bosnia into Serb and Muslim–Croat areas
5. **CULTURAL DIFFUSION** jet travel, TV, computers

Linking Past and Present

1. People have become concerned about using up world resources.
2. Advancing scientific knowledge or developing space stations.

Skill Practice

1. Yes; in most cases, the higher GDP, the more energy consumed
2. The higher the GDP, the better off people are likely to be, thus the use of more energy-consuming devices
3. It looks like a fairly good cross section from all over the world.

Chapter Bonus Test Question

Ask students: What do you think is the future of communism as an international political ideology? *(Answers should reflect an understanding of the overthrowing of Communist regimes in the former Soviet Union and Eastern Europe and of more recent events in these countries, such as the election of former Communists in Hungary and Poland.)*

2. Answers should relate to end of cold war; cessation of superpower rivalry, rise of noncommunist governments, expansion of democracy and free enterprise; global economy; communications revolution
3. Developing nations supply raw materials to developed nations in exchange for manufactured goods.
4. Lasers allow doctors to perform delicate surgery with minimal discomfort; drugs can help relieve depression; organs can be transplanted; genetic engineering may lead to cures for diseases such as cancer and AIDS.

Geography in History

1. Asia
2. because it has such a large population
3. Those are the regions where population is least dense.

ABCNEWS INTERACTIVE™

VIDEODISC
Turning Points in World History

Side Two
Chapter 9

Title: *Fall of the Berlin Wall*

 If you do not have access to a videodisc player, **Turning Points in World History** is also available in VHS.

Internet Sites

The following are possible sites for completing the "Net" activities:

The United Nations
http://www.un.org/

Not on the "Net"...

If students have limited or no access to the Internet, have them complete the "Human Rights" activity by using resources in the school or public library to find information on human rights. Encourage students to use the following subjects to help them locate sources in the library's computerized or traditional card catalog: United Nations, human rights document, peace.

Students may use the information they locate to help them design a poster.

 **ABCNEWS INTERACTIVE™** **Turning Points in World History**

Fall of the Berlin Wall

Setting up the Video

Work with a group of your classmates to view "Fall of the Berlin Wall" on the videodisc Turning Points in World History. On New Year's Eve, 1990, the two Germanys celebrated reunification. Afterward, Germany was faced with many economic problems to address—such as high unemployment and the arrival of refugees from Eastern Europe that placed a strain on social services.

Hands-On Activity

Create an economic fact sheet about Germany's present economic status. Include information such as GDP, unemployment rate, imports, exports, rate of currency, and other related information.

Side Two, Chapter 9

View the video by scanning the bar code or by entering the chapter number on your keypad and pressing Search. (Also available in VHS format.)

Surfing the "Net"

Human Rights

The protection of human rights has been a major priority for the United Nations since its creation in 1945. In 1948, the United Nations adopted an important human-rights document known as the Universal Declaration of Human Rights. This document addresses economic, social, and political rights. To find out about the content of the United Nations Universal Declaration of Human Rights document, look on the Internet.

Getting There

Follow these steps to gather in-depth information about the content of the Universal Declaration of Human Rights.
1. Go to a search engine. Type in *united nations.*

2. After typing in the phrase, enter terms such as the following to focus your search.
 • *human rights document* • *peace*
3. The search engine should provide you with a number of links to follow. Links are "pointers" to different sites on the Internet and commonly appear as blue underlined words.

What to Do When You Are There

Click on the links to navigate through the pages of information and gather your findings. Design a poster illustrating the different articles of the United Nations Declaration of Human Rights. Hang posters around your classroom.

INTERNET ADDRESS BOOK

Use this space to record frequently used addresses.

*F*rom 1945 to the present, major political shifts have occurred throughout the world. During most of this period, the United States—promoting democracy—and the Soviet Union—promoting communism—were locked in the cold war, a struggle for global dominance short of total war. Meanwhile, Europe's imperial powers, weakened by World War II and facing nationalist upheavals, withdrew from Asia and Africa. New nations emerged from the remains of the European empires to establish their roles in the global community.

By the 1980s, the United States and Soviet Union no longer dominated the world scene. New groups of nations—especially those located on Asia's Pacific Rim—began to influence world trade and economics. The United States began to adjust to this challenge, but the Soviet Union and the Eastern European nations under its sway faced severe economic difficulties. Communism proved incapable of reform; and as Soviet controls loos-ened, popular uprisings toppled Communist governments in Eastern Europe. The collapse of the Soviet Union itself and the emergence of new republics in 1991 signaled both the end of communism and the cold war. Hope for a new era of global cooperation faded, however, as ethnic rivalries led to bloody conflicts in various parts of the world.

Chapter 21
The Cold War

After World War II, Europe was divided into the Eastern bloc, dominated by the Soviet Union, and the Western bloc, tied to the United States. To maintain control of Eastern Europe, the Soviets in 1955 created the Warsaw Pact and later used force against uprisings in Hungary and Czechoslovakia. The United States, as the leader of the non-Communist world, developed the Truman Doctrine to aid countries threatened by Communist takeover. Under the American-sponsored Marshall Plan, Western Europe's democratic nations rebuilt their economies and soon enjoyed economic prosperity. With the United States and Canada, they formed the NATO alliance in 1949 for mutual defense against Soviet attack.

The United States and Canada developed strong, closely-linked economies after World War II. The cold war affected American politics during the 1950s, when concern arose about Communist influences in American government and society. During the 1960s women, African Americans, Hispanic Americans, and Native Americans began to make advances in civil rights. The Vietnam War divided American society and led to a questioning of the United States's military role in world trouble spots.

Chapter 22
Asia and the Pacific

The era after World War II brought profound changes to Asian and Pacific nations. Japan went from defeat to become a major world economic power. A Communist victory in 1949 established the People's Republic of China on the Chinese

Visualizing History The cold war led to an arms race between the United States and the Soviet Union. This Soviet rocket launcher was based in Ukraine. *What major step did the Western allies take in 1949 to contain communism?*

The Unit Digest offers a chapter-by-chapter summary that can be used for any of the following:
- **Preview** one chapter or an entire unit,
- **Review** some or all of the chapters,
- **Condense** when specific chapters or units have not been taught, or
- **Reteach** chapters that students have studied in the unit.

PREVIEW

Use the Unit 6 Digest Transparencies to preview the highlights of the unit.

Visualizing History

Answer to Caption: *They formed the NATO alliance.*

Time Capsule Have students create a time capsule representing the state of the world at the end of its second millennium. Have students work together in small groups based on their interests: technology, politics, economics, human rights, the environment, the arts, sports, and so on. If actual articles cannot be obtained, students may list items to be included in the capsule. **L2**

REVIEW

Use Student Self-Test and Review Software to review any chapters that students have studied in Unit 6.

CLASSROOM RESOURCES FOR UNIT 8 DIGEST

Preview
- Unit 6 Digest Transparencies

Review
- Time Line Activities 21, 22, 23, 24, 25, 26
- Student Self-Test and Review Software, Chapters 21, 22, 23, 24, 25, 26
- MindJogger Videoquiz, Chapters 21, 22, 23, 24, 25, 26

Condense
- Chapter Digests Audiocassettes, Chapters 21, 22, 23, 24, 25, 26

Reteach
- Reteaching Activities 21, 22, 23, 24, 25, 26
- Chapter Digests Audiocassettes, Chapters 21, 22, 23, 24, 25, 26

CONDENSE

 Use Chapter Digests Audiocassettes to introduce chapters that students have not studied in Unit 6. Spanish Chapter Digests Audiocassettes are also available.

Discuss Have students read the **Unit Digest** and discuss the **Surveying the Unit** questions. **L1**

GLENCOE TECHNOLOGY

VIDEODISC
Use MindJogger to review any chapter in Unit 6.

MindJogger Videoquiz

 Chapter 21
Disc 3 Side A

 Chapter 22
Disc 3 Side A

 Chapter 23
Disc 3 Side B

 Chapter 24
Disc 3 Side B

Chapter 25
Disc 3 Side B

 Chapter 26
Disc 3 Side B

 Also available in VHS.

mainland, with the Nationalist government based on the island of Taiwan. Beginning in the 1970s, China combined its Communist system with free enterprise and contacts with the West. In South Asia, nationalist movements created four new nations: India, Pakistan, Sri Lanka, and later, Bangladesh. In spite of economic progress, ethnic and religious rivalries hampered unity within and among these countries.

Korea and Vietnam, both divided into Communist and non-Communist parts, became cold war hot spots. During the Korean War, fought from 1950 to 1953, American-led United Nations forces fought back a Communist advance, but the conflict ended in a stalemate, with Korea returning to its divided status. In Vietnam, however, Communist forces defeated American and anti-Communist Vietnamese forces and united the entire country under Communist rule. The Vietnam conflict lasted from the 1950s to the mid-1970s, with direct American military involvement beginning in the mid-1960s.

Since the Korean and Vietnam conflicts, economic prosperity has come to the nations along Asia's Pacific Rim, stretching from South Korea through Japan and Taiwan to Southeast Asia. Australia, New Zealand, and other South Pacific nations are increasingly involved in trade with their Asian neighbors.

Visualizing History Since the 1960s, Taiwan has developed a booming economy that exports goods to other parts of the world. *How was Taiwan affected by events in China during the late 1940s?*

Chapter 23
Africa

The collapse of European colonialism from the mid-1950s to the mid-1990s led to the rise of new nations throughout Africa. Newly independent African nations worked to build stable governments, resolve ethnic conflicts, and create modern economies. The colonial legacy, however, often interfered with these efforts. Some African countries, forced by European colonial rulers to rely on a single product, had difficulty protecting their economies from sharp declines in world commodity prices. Others, based on boundaries set up by the European powers without regard to ethnic loyalties, faced internal unrest.

In other ways, Africa's future seemed full of promise. Many Africans were reestablishing their cultural identities by throwing off reminders of the colonial past. A movement for African unity created new political and economic links among the nations on the continent. Meanwhile, after years of struggle against racial separation, South Africa in the mid-1990s became a full democracy open to all its races, especially the black majority.

Chapter 24
The Middle East

After 1945, fully independent nations arose in the Middle East as European influence declined. Huge oil reserves brought economic growth to some Middle Eastern nations; but they also drew the Middle East into the cold war struggle between the superpowers the United States and the Soviet Union.

Arabs united in opposing the formation of the Jewish state of Israel in 1948. During the years of the Arab-Israeli conflict, the Israelis were able to preserve their independence and even extend their territory. A major issue related to the fighting was the status of the Palestinian Arabs, who claimed the land that Israel occupied.

After years of struggle, Israel and its Arab neighbors began to make peace in the 1970s and 1980s. With the end of the cold war, this task became less complicated. By the early 1990s, Israel had agreed to give back some of the territory it had taken in the 1967 war in return for guarantees of peace and security from the Arabs. The peace process, however, moved slowly. It was often marred by violence from opponents of peace on both sides.

ANSWERS TO SURVEYING THE UNIT

CHAPTER 21 The cold war divided Europe into an Eastern bloc, dominated by the Soviet Union, and a Western bloc, linked to the United States. With the end of the cold war, Soviet controls ended in Eastern Europe, and the nations of the region set up new governments. In Western Europe, nations moved closer toward political and economic unity in the European Union (EU).

CHAPTER 22 The Pacific Rim of Asia. The Asian Pacific Rim's economic growth has made it an important center of global trade and has posed a challenge to the United States and other industrialized nations.

CHAPTER 23 Colonialism locked Africans into one-product economies that are at the mercy

Chapter 25
Latin America

Latin American nations faced many challenges during the postwar era. Rapid industrialization brought new wealth to the region, but the sharp divide between rich and poor often led to political unrest. In the late 1950s, Fidel Castro's revolution in Cuba brought communism to the Western Hemisphere. To contain communism's spread, the United States often supported military dictatorships in various Latin American countries.

During the 1980s and 1990s, pro-democracy movements overturned dictatorships in several Latin American countries. A new generation of political leaders began to encourage free enterprise, free trade, and a limited role for government. In spite of economic advances, the region still faced rapid population growth, heavy foreign debt, and deep divisions between rich and poor.

Chapter 26
The World in Transition

During the 1980s and 1990s, superpower relations warmed considerably, signaling the end of the cold war. Under Republican Presidents Ronald Reagan and George Bush and Democratic President Bill Clinton, the United States carried out a military role in world trouble spots while reducing government spending on social programs at home. In the Soviet Union, leader Mikhail Gorbachev introduced sweeping economic and social changes that led to the collapse of the Soviet Union and its Communist system. Russia's leader Boris Yeltsin and the other leaders of the now independent republics moved toward free enterprise, but the transition from communism to capitalism brought hardships to many citizens accustomed to government controls.

The reform movement spread to Eastern European countries, which broke free of the Soviet grip and launched new governments. Meanwhile, the nations of Western Europe moved forward toward economic and political unity as members of the European Union (EU).

During the mid-1990s, ethnic and national divisions affected peoples and governments in various parts of the world. In places such as Yugoslavia, Czechoslovakia, and Canada, disputes split or nearly split countries in two. The bloodiest encounters took place along the southern borders of the former Soviet Union and in the Balkans.

As the world heads into the twenty-first century, the interdependence and common purpose of nations and peoples are being recognized. Advances in technology have enabled instantaneous communication around the globe, creating an electronic neighborhood of the world's peoples. Such advances, however, are offset by rapid increases in world population and industrial growth. These trends have created critical environmental problems that affect the entire world. It is apparent that global cooperation is essential to protecting the future of the planet.

SURVEYING UNIT 6

1. **Chapter 21** How did the cold war affect the continent of Europe? How has Europe changed since the end of the cold war?
2. **Chapter 22** What area of Asia is entering a new era of economic prosperity? How has its economic growth affected global affairs?
3. **Chapter 23** How has the colonial legacy affected Africa? In what ways have Africans overcome this legacy?
4. **Chapter 24** How has the relationship between Israelis and Arabs evolved since 1948?
5. **Chapter 25** What changes have come to Latin America since the 1980s?
6. **Chapter 26** How have global environmental problems changed people's thinking about political relationships among nations?

Unit 6 *The Contemporary World* **805**

ANSWERS TO SURVEYING THE UNIT

of world prices. It also ignored ethnic interests when dividing Africa into political units. Africans, however, have thrown off colonialism and reasserted their own identities.

CHAPTER 24 After a long period of hostility, Israel and some of its Arab neighbors are working to resolve their differences. The status of the Palestinians, however, remains a divisive issue.

CHAPTER 25 Democracy has replaced dictatorship in many Latin American lands. Major concerns in the region are economic growth, free trade, and political reform. Latin America still faces rapid population growth, foreign debt, and deep divisions between rich and poor.

Chapter 26 Common challenges are making people think "globally," realizing that international cooperation is necessary if these problems are to be solved.

APPENDIX

GLOSSARY

absolutism – capital

absolutism political system in which a monarch (or group) holds supreme, unlimited power or theory that supports such a system (p. 258)

acupuncture traditional technique of Chinese medicine using thin needles at vital body points (p. 87)

age set in traditional Africa, a group of males or females of similar age who learn skills and go through life stages together (p. 81)

alchemist person who practiced alchemy, an early form of chemistry emphasizing changes in substances, such as lead into gold (p. 296)

alliance system series of defense agreements involving two or more nations (p. 516)

alphabet system of symbols or characters that represent the sounds of a language (p. 36)

anarchy absence of political authority (p. 468)

animism belief that spirits are found in both living and nonliving things (pp. 130, 252)

apartheid official policy of strict racial separation and discrimination practiced in South Africa from 1948 to the early 1990s (p. 710)

appeasement policy of granting concessions to a potential enemy in order to maintain peace (p. 605)

apportion to divide into assigned shares (p. 424)

aqueduct a channel built to carry water (p. 73)

"Arabic numerals" counting symbols (1-9) devised by mathematicians in Gupta India (p. 84)

arbitration process of settling a dispute by submitting it to an impartial third party (p. 498)

archipelago a group or chain of islands (p. 696)

armada (ahr•MAH•duh) a fleet of warships (p. 259)

armistice an agreement to stop fighting (p. 537)

arms race the cold war competition between the U.S. and Soviet Union to build up their respective armed forces and weapons (p. 647)

atomic theory scientific idea that all matter is made up of tiny particles called atoms (p. 404)

atrocity a cruel and evil action, such as torture (p. 791)

autocracy government ruled by one person with unlimited authority (p. 466)

automation process in which electronic devices or machines do work once done by humans (p. 659)

autonomy self-government (p. 784)

balance of power the distribution of power among rival nations so that no one is dominant (p. 265)

balance of trade difference in value between what a nation imports and what it exports over a period of time (p. 224)

baroque (buh•ROHK) ornate, dramatic artistic style developed in Europe in the 1550s (p. 200)

bazaar marketplace in an Islamic city (p. 110)

belligerent engaged in fighting or war (p. 522)

blitz a series of intensive air raids (p. 610)

blitzkrieg (German, "lightning war") a swift, sudden Nazi offensive (p. 607)

bloc a group of political factions or nations acting together (p. 647)

bourgeoisie (boorzh•wah•ZEE) the middle class, between aristocrats and workers (pp. 337, 401)

boyar a landowning noble of early Russia (p. 275)

boycott a refusal to buy or use certain goods as a protest against an action (p. 324)

budget deficit the amount by which government spending exceeds government income (p. 774)

buffer state neutral territory between rival powers, intended to prevent conflict (p. 358)

bullion gold or silver in the form of bars or plate (p. 224)

bureaucracy a group of government officials headed by an administrator (p. 30)

C

cabinet group of advisers to a ruler or head of state (p. 320)

calculus system of mathematics developed by Newton to analyze changing quantities (p. 295)

caliph (KAY•lihf) supreme leader of Islam, chosen as the "successor" of Muhammad (p. 106)

calligraphy the art of beautiful handwriting (p. 111)

campesino (kahm•puh•SEE•noh) a poor Latin American farm worker (p. 751)

capital money available to invest in business (p. 380)

cartel (kahr•TELL) an association of businesses supplying the same product that regulates its members' prices and production (pp. 731, 769)

cartographer person who makes maps (p. 212)

cash-and-carry policy World War II program allowing Great Britain to pay cash and transport needed supplies from the U.S. (p. 611)

cash crop farm product grown to be sold or traded, not used by the farmer (p. 719)

cell theory scientific theory that small units called cells make up all living things (p. 402)

chancellor title of the chief minister of some European countries (p. 461)

charter formal document granting the right of self-rule (p. 148)

châteaux (sing., chateau [Fr.]) castles (p. 189)

chivalry code of conduct for medieval knights, based on ideals of honor and courtesy (p. 116)

choreographer person who creates dances (p. 551)

circumnavigation sailing completely around something, such as the world (p. 215)

city-state an independent state consisting of a city and the surrounding land and villages (p. 35)

civil disobedience nonviolent refusal to obey a law or practice thought unjust (p. 578)

civil service system by which government offices are given on the basis of examinations (p. 85)

civilization highly organized society marked by advanced knowledge of trade, government, arts, science, and often written language (p. 24)

clan group based on family ties (pp. 127, 715)

classical describing the artistic style of ancient Greece and Rome, characterized by balance, elegance, and simplicity (p. 61)

classicism style and attitudes derived from the ideals of ancient Greece and Rome (p. 304)

coalition a temporary alliance of differing political factions (pp. 556, 655)

cold war era of political tension in which the United States and the Soviet Union competed for world influence without actual armed conflict (p. 640)

collective bargaining negotiations between union representatives and employers (p. 392)

collective security the common defense interests of several nations against an enemy (pp. 602, 788)

collectivization under Stalin, a system to combine land into large farms owned by the government and worked by peasants (p. 566)

colon (koh•LOHN) a French settler in the colony of Algeria (p. 707)

colony a settlement of people outside their homeland, linked with the parent country by trade and direct government control (pp. 251, 482)

comedy story or play intended to entertain and amuse, usually with a happy ending (p. 62)

common law body of English law based on tradition and court decisions, not specific laws (p. 121)

commonwealth a nation or state governed by the people or their representatives (p. 315)

commune people who live communally, with collective ownership and use of property (p. 678)

communism in the theories of Marx and Engels, a society without class distinctions or private property (pp. 401, 534)

concentration camp prison camp where political prisoners or refugees are held (p. 562)

confederation a loose alliance or union of several states or groups (pp. 164, 330)

conquistador (kon•KEES•tuh•dohr) a Spanish "conqueror" or soldier in the Americas (p. 217)

conscription compulsory call to military service; the draft (pp. 345, 516)

constitution plan of government (p. 60)

constitutional monarchy state in which a monarch's power is limited by a constitution (p. 317)

containment U.S. policy designed to prevent the spread of communism (p. 642)

contraband goods that may not legally be transported, particularly during wartime (p. 527)

convoy group of merchant ships traveling together with warships for safety (p. 536)

cooperative a farm organization owned and managed by members, who share profits (p. 588)

cordon sanitaire (kawr•dahn sah•nee•TEHR) a line of "quarantine" or buffer states (p. 539)

corporate state Mussolini's concept of a government with representation by industrial corporations, not political parties (p. 559)

corporation business organization that is owned by stockholders who buy shares, and is run by professional managers (p. 385)

coup d'état (koo day•TAH) sudden overthrow of government leaders by a small group (pp. 349, 433)

covert (KOH•vert) secret (p. 762)

Creole a person of European ancestry born in colonial Latin America (p. 443)

Crusades military expeditions by European Christians in the 11th–13th centuries to regain the Holy Land from the Muslims (p. 144)

cubism 20th-century art style that abstracts natural forms into geometric shapes (p. 549)

cultural diffusion the exchange of goods, ideas, and customs among different cultures (p. 25)

culture the way of life of a given people at a given time, including language, behavior, and beliefs (p. 21)

culture system in Dutch colonies in Asia, a system of forced labor to get raw materials (p. 494)

czar (from "caesar") title taken by rulers of Russia beginning in the late 1400s (p. 152)

D

D-Day the day of the Allied invasion of Normandy, France (June 6, 1944)(p. 622)

daimyo (DY•mee•oh) a powerful local noble in feudal Japan (p. 129)

datus local rulers in the Philippines (p. 251)

death squad in Central America, a band of killers hired by landowners to murder political opponents (p. 763)

deforestation process of cutting trees and clearing forests on large areas of land (p. 796)

deism religious philosophy of the 1700s based on reason and the idea of natural law (p. 299)

democracy form of government in which the citizens hold power (p. 60)

depression economic situation characterized by a business slump and unemployment (p. 385)

desalination process of removing salt from seawater to produce drinkable water (p. 740)

desertification process of fertile land becoming desert (p. 720)

détente (day•TAHNT) the relaxing of tensions between the United States and the Soviet Union in the 1970s (p. 650)

developed nation an industrialized nation with advanced technology (p. 795)

developing nation a country in the process of industrializing, where people often follow traditional lifestyles (p. 795)

dharma duties and rights of members of each class in traditional Hindu society (p. 45)

dictatorship government headed by a ruler with absolute authority (p. 350)

dictatorship of the proletariat in the former Soviet Union, theoretical control of the state by the working class (p. 565)

direct tax a tax paid directly to the government (p. 324)

disarmament limiting or reducing military forces and weapons (p. 554)

disciple an active follower of a teacher (p. 76)

disenfranchised denied the right to vote (p. 425)

disengagement act of freeing oneself or withdrawing from a situation (p. 731)

dissident a person who openly criticizes the policies of his or her government (p. 650)

divine right political theory that a ruler derives his or her power directly from God and is accountable only to God (pp. 258, 312)

division of labor production technique in which each worker does one specialized task (p. 385)

doge (DOHJ) the elected leader of the republic in the city-states of Venice and Genoa (p. 184)

domestic system early industrial labor system in which workers produced goods at home (p. 378)

dominion a self-governing nation within the British Empire, later the Commonwealth (p. 429)

domino theory cold war belief that if one nation became Communist, its neighbors would follow (p. 686)

double-digit inflation a quick rise in prices of 10 percent or more (p. 665)

dual monarchy two states with one monarch (p. 472)

duma the Russian national legislature (p. 470)

duty a tax on imports (p. 322)

dvorianie (dvoh•ree•YAH•nee•yuh) new class of Russian landed nobility established by Peter the Great (p. 277)

dynasty a line of rulers who belong to the same family (p. 30)

E

elite a select group of people (p. 751)

ellipse an oval (not round) closed curve (p. 293)

emancipation legally granting freedom (p. 467)

embargo an order restricting trade (pp. 665, 736, 791)

emigration leaving one's home country or region to settle elsewhere (p. 406)

émigré (EH•mih•GRAY) person who fled France during the Revolution (p. 342)

empire group of territories or nations ruled by a single ruler or government (p. 31)

enclave (EHN•klayv) a small territory entirely surrounded by the territory of another country or group (p. 792)

enclosure movement the trend for large landowners gradually to fence and include public and private common lands in their own estates (p. 379)

enlightened despot a monarch who began social changes based on Enlightenment ideas (p. 303)

entente (ahn•TAHNT) an agreement, but not a formal alliance, between nations (p. 516)

entrepreneur person who undertakes risks to establish a business (pp. 224, 380)

estate one of three distinct social classes in France during the 1700s: clergy, nobility, and commoners (the Third Estate) (p. 336)

ethnic cleansing term used in the Bosnian conflict for a policy of forcibly removing or killing members of another ethnic group (pp. 790–91)

evolution theory that species of living things change over long periods of time (p. 402)

F

factory system method of production in which goods are made by workers and machines in one location (a factory) outside their homes (p. 382)

fascism (FASH•ihz•uhm) political philosophy based on nationalism and an all-powerful state (p. 558)

federal system form of government in which power is divided between a central authority and its political subdivisions (p. 310)

feudalism medieval political system in which monarchs and lesser nobles made alliances based on exchanging land grants for loyalty (p. 115)

fez traditional hat worn by Turkish men (p. 573)

free trade the elimination of trade barriers between nations (p. 754)

friar member of a Catholic order who preached in towns and practiced poverty (p. 120)

fundamentalism movement emphasizing adherence to traditional religious laws and practices (p. 741)

G

geisha Japanese woman trained as a professional entertainer (p. 248)

general strike a strike involving workers from many parts of a nation's economy (pp. 555, 707)

genetic engineering scientific field in which cell structures can be altered to produce new or different organisms (p. 798)

genetics the study of biological heredity (p. 403)

genocide deliberate attempt to kill all members of a racial, cultural, or ethnic group (pp. 616, 714)

gentry in Elizabethan England, the social group including minor nobility and landowners (p. 264)

ghana title of the ruler of a region in ancient Africa, later applied to the kingdom (p. 155)

glasnost Russian term for the policy of "openness" and free expression introduced by Mikhail Gorbachev (p. 775)

grand vizier (vih•ZEER) prime minister to the sultan of a Muslim country (p. 233)

gross domestic product (GDP) total value of goods and services produced within a country in a year (p. 674)

guerrilla warfare method of fighting in which small groups strike unexpectedly (p. 455)

guild medieval business association of merchants or craftsworkers (p. 148)

H

habeas corpus legal principle that requires authorities to show reasons why a person should be held in custody and to provide a speedy trial (p. 318)

haiku (HY•koo) Japanese poetry form with 17 syllables, usually in three lines (p. 248)

hajj pilgrimage to Makkah that every able-bodied Muslim is expected to make at least once (p. 106)

heavy industry the manufacture of machines and equipment for factories and mines (p. 584)

heresy disagreement with or denial of the basic teachings of a religion (p. 120)

hierarchy group of people organized according to levels of rank or importance (p. 164)

Holocaust name given to the Nazis' mass murder of European Jews in World War II (p. 615)

home rule self-government, especially when granted to a dependent country (p. 427)

hominid (HAH•muh•nihd) member of the group that includes human beings and earlier humanlike creatures (p. 20)

humanism Renaissance movement based on the literature and ideas of ancient Greece and Rome, such as the worth of each individual (p. 180)

hyperinflation an extreme form of inflation, with sharp, rapid price increases (p. 767)

hypothesis solution proposed to explain a set of facts, which can be tested (p. 293)

I

icon a Christian religious image or picture (p. 102)

ideology the system of beliefs and attitudes that guides the actions of a group or nation (p. 647)

immigration entering a new country or region to settle permanently there (p. 406)

imperialism policy of building an empire (p. 480)

imperial presidency term for a President and executive branch who assume powers beyond those defined in the Constitution (p. 664)

impressionism artistic style of the late 1800s in which painters tried to capture quick impressions and the effects of light (p. 414)

individualism emphasis on the dignity and worth of the individual person (pp. 180–81)

indulgence pardon sold by the Catholic Church to reduce one's punishment for sins (p. 192)

industrial capitalism economic system in which individuals continually reinvest profits and expand their businesses (p. 384)

inflation situation in which prices rise quickly while the value of money decreases (p. 260)

intendant an agent representing the king of France in local government (p. 267)

interchangeable parts production method using identical, easy-to-assemble parts (p. 385)

intercontinental ballistic missile (ICBM) a long-range rocket carrying a warhead (p. 649)

interdependent relying on one another (p. 794)

Internet popular term for the advanced communications network linking people and computers around the world (p. 797)

intifada the 1987 uprising by Palestinians against Israeli occupation (p. 732)

iron curtain term coined by Winston Churchill for the political barrier isolating Soviet-dominated Eastern Europe from Western Europe (p. 642)

J

janissary member of an elite corps of soldiers in the Ottoman Empire (p. 233)

jati groups based on occupation formed within larger social classes (varna) in ancient India, each with its own rules and customs (p. 45)

jazz American musical style incorporating African rhythms with American and European sounds (p. 549)

jingoism attitude of extreme patriotism, usually directed toward a foreign power (p. 474)

joint-stock company trading venture that sold shares to divide costs and profits (p. 223)

junk a Chinese sailing ship (p. 240)

justification by faith Martin Luther's concept that faith alone is enough to bring salvation (p. 191)

K

kaiser title of the German emperor (p. 461)

kamikaze in World War II, the Japanese pilots who crashed bomb-filled planes in suicide attacks on Allied targets (p. 621)

karma in Hinduism, the idea that one's actions in life determine one's destiny and future (p. 47)

khan an absolute ruler of the Mongols (p. 139)

kibbutz (pl. kibbutzim) a collective farm community in Israel (p. 727)

Kristallnacht ("night of broken glass") Nazi terrorist attacks, November 9-10, 1938, on Jewish property in Germany and Austria (p. 562)

kulak a well-to-do peasant in the USSR (p. 566)

L

labor-intensive farming agriculture that relies on human labor, not animals or machines (p. 242)

labor union organization of workers formed to pressure business owners to improve wages and working conditions (p. 392)

laissez-faire (leh•say•FAYR) economic principle that government should not regulate businesses (p. 398)

lay investiture medieval practice in which secular rulers appointed and inaugurated church officials such as bishops (p. 120)

lend-lease World War II policy allowing the loan of equipment to friendly countries (p. 612)

liberalism political philosophy that promotes social change and individual freedoms (p. 358)

liberation theology movement led by Catholic clergy in Latin America emphasizing the Church's role in improving people's lives (p. 754)

line of demarcation imaginary line in the Atlantic Ocean, drawn by the pope in 1493 to divide the world's lands between Spain and Portugal (p. 215)

literacy rate the percentage of a country's adult population who can read and write (p. 720)

M

mandarin member of the elite class of civil servants in Chinese government (p. 85)

mandate (1) in ancient China, authority granted by heaven to deserving rulers, called the Mandate of Heaven (p. 71); (2) a territory administered by another nation before independence (p. 539)

manorialism medieval economic system linking nobles and the peasants on their land (p. 116)

martial law temporary military rule, limiting rights such as free speech (p. 313)

matrilineal tracing family descent through the mother and her ancestors (p. 81)

mercantilism economic policy of European nations in the 1600s, equating wealth and power (p. 224)

meritocracy system in which people gain success on the basis of ability and performance (p. 124)

messiah in Judaism, a savior promised by the Hebrew prophets, who would bring peace (p. 75)

mestizo (meh•STEE•zoh) in Latin America, a person of Native American and European ancestry (p. 443)

metaphysics aspects of philosophy dealing with basic questions of existence and reality (p. 306)

metsuke group of officials who gathered information for the Tokugawa shoguns (p. 245)

Middle Passage middle section of the triangular trade, in which enslaved Africans were brought by ship to the Americas (p. 221)

middle power a nation that is economically strong but not a military power (p. 665)

militarism national policy based on military strength and glorification of war (pp. 465, 516)

millet community of non-Muslims within the Ottoman Empire (p. 234)

mobilization act of assembling and preparing troops and equipment for war (p. 519)

monarchy rule by a king or a queen (p. 30)

monastery a community of men who have taken religious vows (p. 102)

money economy economic system in which money (not barter) is used to buy and sell (p. 148)

monopoly control of all (or almost all) trade or production of a given good (p. 159)

monotheism belief in one God (p. 36)

mosaic picture made up of tiny pieces of colored glass, tile, or stone set in mortar (p. 102)

mosque a Muslim house of worship (p. 110)

multicultural representing several different cultural and ethnic groups (pp. 159, 666)

N

nationalism pride in one's own nation; desire for independence (pp. 352, 452)

nationalization placing a privately owned business under government ownership (pp. 513, 589)

nationalize to bring a private industry under government control (p. 728)

nation-state a political state whose people also share the same language and culture (p. 453)

natural law a universal truth or principle that 17th-century thinkers believed could be found through reason (p. 297)

natural rights rights belonging to all persons from birth (p. 299)

negritude a literary movement that emphasizes and takes pride in Africa's cultural heritage (p. 721)

nihilist member of a Russian political movement of the late 1800s that rejected all authority and advocated terrorism (p. 468)

nirvana in Buddhism, a state of oneness with the universe, the end of the cycle of rebirth (p. 49)

nonaligned not taking sides with either of the superpowers in the cold war (p. 693)

O

obsidian black volcanic glass (p. 91)

oligarchy form of government in which a small group holds political power (p. 60)

oral tradition the legends and history of a culture preserved by word of mouth (p. 78)

P

pacifism opposition to war or violence as a way to settle disputes (p. 299)

pacifist a believer in pacifism (p. 578)

pact a treaty between several nations (p. 729)

Pan-Africanism movement encouraging unity and cooperation among African nations (p. 718)

Pan-Arabism movement intended to build cultural and political ties among Arabs (p. 726)

papal infallibility Roman Catholic doctrine that the pope cannot make an error in speaking about faith and morals (p. 462)

partisan World War II term for an underground resistance fighter, especially in Italy and Yugoslavia (p. 624)

partition to divide a region (p. 483)

partnership business owned by two or more entrepreneurs who share management, profits, and losses (p. 385)

patrician a member of the wealthy aristocratic class of ancient Rome (p. 70)

peaceful coexistence Soviet policy of competing with the United States while avoiding war (p. 649)

peninsulares officials born in Spain or Portugal who led society in colonial Latin America (p. 443)

perestroika (pehr•uh•STROY•kuh) Russian term for "restructuring," the changes in the Soviet economy begun by Mikhail Gorbachev (p. 776)

philosophe (fee•luh•ZAWF) a social or political thinker of the Enlightenment (p. 300)

plebeian (plih•BEE•uhn) a citizen of ancient Rome who was not an aristocrat (p. 70)

plebiscite (PLEB•uh•syt) a direct popular vote on a program or issue (pp. 351, 433)

pogrom organized persecution of a minority group, usually Jews, in czarist Russia (p. 469)

polis city-state of ancient Greece (p. 59)

pollution putting toxic or impure substances into the air, land, or water (p. 674)

polytheism worship of many gods (p. 32)

pope the bishop of Rome, later the head of the Roman Catholic Church (p. 77)

population explosion a large, sudden increase in the human population (p. 584)

Postimpressionism artistic movement whose members experimented with form and color (p. 415)

potlatch feast held by Native Americans of the Pacific Northwest to display their wealth (p. 162)

pragmatic sanction decree issued by a ruler on an important question (p. 271)

pragmatist in China, a moderate who advocated economic reform and trade with the West (p. 678)

predestination doctrine of John Calvin that each person's fate is predetermined by God (p. 195)

prehistory time before written history (p. 20)

prime minister the chief executive of a parliamentary government (p. 320)

principality territory ruled by a prince (p. 104)

privatization the return of government-owned industries to private owners (pp. 756–57)

proletariat in Marxist theory, the working class (p. 401)

propaganda news and information intended to influence people's feelings about a cause (p. 522)

prophet a person who preaches or interprets what are thought to be messages from God (p. 36)

protectorate a country whose policies are guided by a foreign nation (p. 482)

provisional government a temporary government set up while waiting for elections (p. 533)

psychology study of behavior and its causes (p. 404)

purge an official effort to remove people that a government considers undesirable (p. 567)

Q

queue (KYOO) single braid of hair at the back of the head (p. 242)

quota a specified number or amount (p. 676)

R

racial segregation the social separation of people according to their race (p. 663)

ratify to give formal approval (p. 441)

reactionary one who opposes progress or change and wants to return to earlier ways (p. 358)

realism artistic and literary style of the mid-1800s that pictured the realities of everyday life (p. 412)

realpolitik political theory that national success justifies the use of any means (p. 458)

referendum a direct popular vote on a measure or proposed law (pp. 684, 787)

refugee person who must leave his or her home and flee elsewhere for safety (p. 687)

reincarnation the rebirth of the soul or spirit in different bodies over time (p. 47)

reparation compensation for war damage (p. 539)

republic a government in which citizens elect the leaders (p. 70)

revolution a sudden, radical change; change of government by force (p. 330)

romanticism artistic movement of the early 1800s emphasizing individuality and emotion (pp. 306, 411)

royalist person who supports a monarchy (p. 315)

Russification policy of imposing Russian language and customs on other peoples (p. 468)

S

sacrament one of the established formal rituals of the Roman Catholic Church, such as baptism, holy communion, or matrimony (p. 118)

salon in France, a gathering where Enlightenment intellectuals met for conversation (p. 301)

samurai class of landowning warriors in feudal Japan, who pledged loyalty to a daimyo (p. 129)

sanctions penalties and restrictions imposed on a nation for breaking international law (p. 603)

sankin-kotai ("alternate attendance") in feudal Japan, system in which a daimyo had to spend every other year at the shogun's court (p. 245)

satellite a country politically dominated by a nearby power (p. 641)

satyagraha ("truth force") term for nonviolent protests led by Gandhi (p. 578)

savanna a flat grassland, with few trees, in tropical or subtropical regions (p. 78)

schism (SIH•zuhm) the division of the Christian Church in 1054 that separated the Roman Catholic Church and the Eastern Orthodox Church (p. 101)

scholasticism medieval school of thought that tried to bring together Aristotle's philosophy and the teachings of Church scholars (p. 149)

scientific method steps to find scientific truth through observation and experiments (p. 294)

scorched-earth policy Stalin's order for the Soviet people to destroy buildings, land, and anything that Nazi invaders could use (p. 614)

secede to withdraw formally from membership in a political organization (p. 439)

sect a subgroup with distinct beliefs within a larger religious group (p. 675)

sectionalism overemphasis on the political and economic interests of one's own region (p. 439)

secular worldly, not overtly or specifically religious (p. 180)

self-determination the right of a people to decide their own political status or government (p. 572)

seminary school for educating priests, as ordered by the Council of Trent (p. 199)

separatism in Canada, a political movement favoring the independence of Quebec (p. 666)

sepoy an Indian soldier in the British army (p. 489)

serf a peasant laborer legally bound to the lands of a noble (pp. 118, 277)

shah the ruler of a Middle Eastern country (p. 573)

shamanism belief that spirits inhabit living and nonliving things, communicating with humans through priests called shamans (p. 126)

shogun military ruler of feudal Japan (p. 129)

shogunate government established by a shogun's family and followers in feudal Japan (p. 129)

slash-and-burn farming farming method in which land for crops is cleared by cutting and burning trees to fertilize the soil (p. 52)

socialism political theory that society as a whole should control the means of production, such as factories and land (p. 400)

Socialist realism under Stalin, an artistic style that glorified the Soviet way of life (p. 567)

sociology study of human group behavior (p. 404)

sonnet poetry form with 14 lines and a fixed pattern of rhyme and meter (p. 181)

sovereignty the independent decision-making power of a group or nation (p. 739)

soviet a workers' council formed early in the Russian Revolution; later, a unit of government in the Soviet Union (p. 470)

special economic zone areas of China where foreign businesses and a free market were allowed to operate in the 1990s (p. 679)

sphere of influence area in a country where a foreign power has exclusive rights to trade or invest (pp. 482, 491)

stagflation slow growth with high inflation and unemployment (p. 665)

stalemate a deadlock, or situation in which neither of two opponents can move further (p. 683)

standard of living a general measure of people's overall wealth and quality of life (p. 755)

steppe wide, grassy, semiarid plains of Eurasia, from the Black Sea to the Altai Mountains (p. 138)

subsistence farmer farmer who grows only enough to supply a family or village (p. 719)

suffragette woman who actively worked to win voting rights for women (p. 427)

sultan political leader with absolute authority over a Muslim country (p. 233)

superpower a powerful, influential nation with a bloc of allies; specifically, the United States and the Soviet Union during the cold war (p. 640)

surrealism 20th-century art movement using distorted, surprising images (p. 549)

symbolism antirealism artistic movement that focused on dreamlike images and symbols (p. 414)

syndicate under fascism, an organization of workers and employers in an industry (p. 559)

T

technology the skills and knowledge used by people to make tools and do work (p. 21)

theocracy government headed by religious leaders or a leader regarded as a god (p. 194)

theology study of religious questions (p. 101)

tithe a 10 percent tax on income, paid to the clergy (p. 337)

totalitarianism idea that a dictatorial government should control all aspects of citizens' lives (p. 557)

trade deficit the economic imbalance when a country's imports exceeds its exports (pp. 665, 774)

tragedy story or play in which the central character struggles against destiny but meets an unhappy end (p. 62)

trench a ditch dug to protect soldiers (p. 523)

triangular trade three-directional trade route between Europe, Africa, and America in the 1600s (p. 220)

tribune in ancient Rome, an official who represented the plebeians (p. 71)

tyrant in ancient Greece, a person who seized power and established one-man rule (p. 60)

U V

ultimatum a final demand or statement of terms, implying a threat of serious penalties (p. 578)

ultraroyalist an extremely conservative aristocrat in France in the 1820s (p. 431)

unicameral legislature assembly or lawmaking body with one house (p. 341)

urbanization the spread of cities and city living (p. 407)

utilitarianism economic philosophy, developed by Jeremy Bentham, that social and political actions should be useful and helpful to humanity (p. 400)

varna one of four main social classes in Aryan society of ancient India (p. 45)

vernacular the language of everyday speech, not of scholars, in a country or region (p. 149)

viceroy governor representing a monarch (p. 490)

vocation a calling from God to take up certain work (p. 193)

W X Y Z

war of attrition conflict in which each side tries to win by wearing down the other (p. 523)

warlord local military leader in China (p. 580)

welfare state government system in which the state provides programs to protect people's social and economic well-being (p. 655)

westernization the spread of European culture (p. 494)

yeoman (YOH•mun) in English society, a farmer who owned land (p. 264)

yin and yang in Chinese thinking, the opposing principles present in all nature (p. 51)

zaibatsu (zy•BAHT•soo) large Japanese industrial firms owned by a few families (p. 584)

zemstvo local assembly in czarist Russia (p. 468)

A

absolutism/absolutismo sistema político en el cual un monarca (o grupo) tiene poder supremo e ilimitado, o teoría que sustenta tal sistema (pág. 258)

acupuncture/acupuntura técnica tradicional de la medicina china que utiliza agujas finas en puntos vitales del cuerpo (pág. 87)

age set/grupo etario en el África tradicional, un grupo de varones o hembras de edad semejante que adquieren destrezas y siguen juntos a través de las distintas etapas de la vida (pág. 81)

alchemist/alquimista persona que practica la alquimia, forma primitiva de la química, que enfatizaba cambios en las sustancias, como la conversión del plomo en oro (pág. 296)

alliance system/sistema de alianzas serie de acuerdos sobre la defensa en que participan dos o más naciones (pág. 516)

alphabet/alfabeto sistema de símbolos o caracteres que representan los sonidos de un lenguaje (pág. 36)

anarchy/anarquía ausencia de autoridad política (pág. 468)

animism/animismo creencia de que los espíritus residen tanto en los seres vivos como en las cosas inanimadas (págs. 130, 252)

apartheid/apartheid política oficial de estricta segregación y discriminación racial practicada en África del Sur desde 1948 hasta principios de la década de 1990 (pág. 710)

appeasement/apaciguamiento la política de hacer concesiones a un enemigo en potencia a fin de mantener la paz (pág. 605)

apportion/prorratear dividir en partes proporcionales (pág. 424)

aqueduct/acueducto canal construido para conducir las aguas (pág. 73)

"Arabic numerals"/números arábigos símbolos de numeración diseñados por matemáticos en Gupta, India (pág. 84)

arbitration/arbitraje proceso de poner fin a una disputa sometiéndola a una tercera parte imparcial (pág. 498)

archipelago/archipiélago grupo o cadena de islas (pág. 696)

armada/armada escuadra de buques de guerra (pág. 259)

armistice/armisticio acuerdo para dar fin a una guerra (pág. 537)

arms race/carrera armamentista la competencia durante la Guerra Fría entre Estados Unidos y la Unión Soviética para fortalecer sus respectivas fuerzas militares y armamentos (pág. 647)

atomic theory/teoría atómica idea científica de que la materia está hecha de partículas pequeñas llamadas átomos (pág. 404)

atrocity/atrocidad acción cruel y maligna, tal como la tortura (pág. 791)

autocracy/autocracia gobierno regido por una persona con poder ilimitado (pág. 466)

automation/automatización proceso por el cual dispositivos electrónicos o máquinas hacen el trabajo antes realizado por humanos (pág. 659)

autonomy/autonomía gobierno propio (pág. 784)

B

balance of power/equilibrio de poder la distribución del poder entra naciones rivales de modo que ninguna predomine (pág. 265)

balance of trade/equilibrio comercial diferencia en valor entre lo que una nación importa y lo que exporta durante un período de tiempo (pág. 224)

baroque/barroco estilo artístico recargado y dramático, desarrollado en Europa a mediados del siglo XVI (pág. 200)

bazaar/bazar mercado público en una ciudad islámica (pág. 110)

belligerent/beligerante enfrascado en una guerra (pág. 522)

blitz/ataque relámpago serie de ataques aéreos intensos (pág. 610)

blitzkrieg/guerra relámpago ofensiva nazi rápida e inesperada (pág. 607)

bloc/bloque grupo de facciones políticas o agrupación de naciones que actúan conjuntamente (pág. 647)

bourgeoisie/burguesía la clase media, entre los aristócratas y los trabajadores (págs. 337, 401)

boyar/boyardo un noble propietario de tierras en la Rusia primitiva (pág. 275)

boycott/boicot rechazo a comprar ciertos productos como protesta por alguna acción (pág. 324)

budget deficit/déficit presupuestario la cantidad por la cual los gastos del gobierno exceden a sus ingresos (pág. 774)

buffer state/estado parachoques territorio neutral entre potencias rivales, destinado a prevenir un conflicto (pág. 358)

bullion/lingote oro o plata en forma de barras o planchas (pág. 224)

bureaucracy/burocracia un grupo de funcionarios del gobierno encabezado por un administrador (pág. 30)

C

cabinet/gabinete grupo de consejeros de un gobernante o jefe de estado (pág. 320)

calculus/cálculo sistema de matemáticas desarrollado por Newton para analizar cantidades variables (pág. 295)

caliph/califa líder supremo de Islam, escogido como sucesor de Mahoma (pág. 106)

calligraphy/caligrafía el arte de escribir con letra hermosa (pág. 111)

campesino/campesino agricultor pobre de Latinoamérica que trabaja en una finca (pág. 751)

capital/capital dinero disponible para invertir en negocios (pág. 380)

cartel/cartel convenio entre empresas que ofrecen el mismo producto, que regula los precios de sus miembros y su producción (págs. 731, 769)

cartographer/cartógrafo persona que dibuja mapas (pág. 212)

cash-and-carry policy/política de compra al contado programa de la Segunda Guerra Mundial que permitía a Gran Bretaña pagar en efectivo y transportar desde los Estados Unidos las mercancías que necesitara (pág. 611)

cash crop/cosecha comercial producto agrícola cultivado para la venta o el intercambio, no usado por el agricultor (pág. 719)

cell theory/teoría celular teoría científica que sostiene que las pequeñas unidades llamadas células constituyen todas las cosas vivas (pág. 402)

chancellor/canciller título del primer ministro en algunos países europeos (pág. 461)

charter/carta constitucional documento formal que concede el derecho al gobierno propio (pág. 148)

chateaux/castillos un tipo de fortaleza (pág. 189)

chivalry/caballería código de conducta de los caballeros medievales basado en ideales de honor y cortesía (pág. 116)

choreographer/coreógrafo persona que crea bailes (pág. 551)

circumnavigation/circunnavegación viaje marítimo completamente alrededor de algo, como por ejemplo, el mundo (pág. 215)

city-state/ciudad-estado un estado independiente que consistía en una ciudad y las tierras y aldeas que la rodeaban (pág. 35)

civil disobedience/desobediencia civil rechazo sin violencia a obedecer una ley o práctica considerada injusta (pág. 578)

civil service/servicio civil sistema mediante el cual puestos del gobierno son concedidos mediante exámenes (pág. 85)

civilization/civilización sociedad altamente organizada caracterizada por el conocimiento avanzado del comercio, gobierno, artes, ciencia y a menudo, lenguaje escrito (pág. 24)

clan/clan grupo unido por lazos familiares (págs. 127, 715)

classical/clásico que describe el estilo artístico de las antiguas Gracia y Roma, caracterizado por el equilibrio, la elegancia y la simpleza (pág. 61)

classicism/clasicismo estilo y actitudes derivadas de los ideales de las antiguas Gracia y Roma (pág. 304)

coalition/coalición alianza temporal de facciones políticas en desacuerdo (págs. 556, 655)

cold war/Guerra Fría período de tensión política en el que Estados Unidos y la Unión Soviética rivalizaron por obtener el dominio mundial sin llegar a un conflicto armado real (pág. 640)

collective bargaining/convenios colectivos negociaciones entre los delegados sindicales y los patronos acerca de asuntos (pág. 392)

collective security/seguridad colectiva los intereses de defensa comunes a varias naciones frente a un enemigo (págs. 602, 788)

collectivization/colectivización bajo Stalin, sistema de unificar tierras en grandes fincas que pertenecían al gobierno y las trabajaban los campesinos (pág. 566)

colon/colon colonizador francés en la colonia de Algeria (pág. 707)

colony/colonia establecimiento de personas que están fuera de su país, enlazado a la madre patria por el comercio y el control directo del gobierno (págs. 251, 482)

comedy/comedia historia o representación que se propone entretener y divertir usualmente con un desenlace feliz (pág. 62)

common law/derecho consuetudinario sistema de leyes inglesas basadas en la tradición y decisiones de la corte, no en leyes específicas (pág. 121)

commonwealth/mancomunidad nación o estado gobernado por el pueblo o representantes del mismo (pág. 315)

commune/comuna Un grupo de personas que viven en comuna, con posesión y uso colectivo de la sociedad (pág. 678)

communism/comunismo según las teorías de Marx y Engels, una sociedad sin distinciones de clases ni propiedad privada (págs. 401, 534)

concentration camp/campo de concentración recinto donde se encierra a prisioneros políticos o a refugiados (pág. 562)

confederation/confederación alianza flexible o unión de varios estados o grupos (págs. 164, 330)

conquistador/conquistador aventurero o soldado español en las Américas (pág. 217)

conscription/reclutamiento llamado obligatorio al servicio militar (págs. 345, 516)

constitution/constitución plan de gobierno (pág. 60)

constitutional monarchy/monarquía constitucional estado en el cual el poder del monarca está limitado por una constitución (pág. 317)

containment/contención política de Estados Unidos proyectada para prevenir la propagación del comunismo (pág. 642)

contraband/contrabando mercancías que no pueden ser transportadas legalmente, particularmente en tiempo de guerra (pág. 527)

convoy/convoy grupo de naves mercantes que viajan junto a buques de guerra para su seguridad (pág. 536)

cooperative/cooperativa sociedad de fincas que pertenece y es administrada por sus miembros, los cuales comparten sus ganancias (pág. 588)

cordon sanitaire/cordón sanitario línea de cuarentena o estados "parachoques" (pág. 539)

corporate state/estado corporativo concepto de Mussolini de un gobierno con representación de corporaciones, y no de partidos políticos (pág. 559)

corporation/corporación organización de empresas que es propiedad de socios que compran acciones y que es dirigida por administradores profesionales (pág. 385)

coup d'état/golpe de estado derrocamiento repentino de líderes del gobierno por un pequeño grupo (págs. 349, 433)

covert/encubierto secreto (pág. 762)

Creole/criollo persona de ascendencia europea nacida en la América Latina colonial (pág. 443)

Crusades/Cruzadas expediciones militares por cristianos europeos en los siglos XI al XIII para conquistar la Tierra Santa de manos de los musulmanes (pág. 144)

cubism/cubismo estilo artístico del siglo XX que representa las formas naturales por medio de formas geométricas (pág. 549)

cultural diffusion/difusión cultural intercambio de bienes, ideas y costumbres entre diferentes culturas (pág. 25)

culture/cultura modo de vida de un pueblo en un tiempo determinado, que incluye su lenguaje, conducta y creencias (pág. 21)

culture system/sistema de cultivo en las colonias holandesas en Asia, sistema de trabajos forzados para obtener materias primas (pág. 494)

czar/zar (de "caesar") título adoptado por los gobernantes de Rusia desde finales del siglo XV (pág. 152)

D-Day/Día D día de la invasión de Normandía, Francia por los Aliados (junio 6 de 1944) (pág. 622)

daimyo/daimyo poderoso noble local en el Japón feudal (pág. 129)

datus/datus gobernantes locales en las Filipinas (pág. 251)

death squad/escuadrón de la muerte en la América Central, una banda de asesinos contratados por terratenientes para asesinar a sus contrincantes políticos (pág. 763)

deforastation/deforestación proceso de talar los árboles y desmontar los bosques en grandes extensiones de tierra (pág. 796)

deism/deísmo filosofía religiosa del siglo XVIII basada en la razón y en la idea de leyes naturales (pág. 299)

democracy/democracia forma de gobierno en la cual los ciudadanos ejercen el poder (pág. 60)

depression/depresión situación económica caracterizada por la quiebra de los negocios y el desempleo (pág. 385)

desalination/desalinización proceso de extraer la sal del agua de mar para producir agua potable (pág. 740)

desertification/desertización proceso por el cual una tierra fértil se convierte en un desierto (pág. 720)

détente/detente la relajación de las tensiones entre los Estados Unidos y la Unión Soviética en la década de 1970 (pág. 650)

developed country/país desarrollado nación industrializada, con una tecnología avanzada (pág. 795)

developing country/país en desarrollo país en proceso de industrialización, donde el pueblo mantiene frecuentemente los estilos de vida tradicionales (pág. 795)

dharma/dharma deberes y derechos de los miembros de cada clase en la sociedad hindú tradicional (pág. 45)

dictatorship/dictadura gobierno encabezado por un gobernante con poder absoluto (pág. 35)

dictatorship of the proletariat/dictadura del proletariado en la antigua Unión Soviética, control teórico del estado por la clase trabajadora (pág. 565)

direct tax/impuesto directo impuesto pagado directamente al gobierno (pág. 324)

disarmament/desarme limitación o reducción de las fuerzas militares y de las armas (pág. 554)

disciple/discípulo activo seguidor de un maestro (pág. 76)

disenfranchised/privado del derecho al sufragio negado el derecho al voto (pág. 425)

disengagement/desembarazo acto de liberarse o retirarse uno mismo de una situación (pág. 731)

dissident/disidente persona que critica abiertamente las maneras de actuar de su gobierno (pág. 650)

divine right/derecho divino teoría política que mantiene que un gobernante deriva su autoridad directamente de Dios y es responsable de sus actos sólo ante Dios (págs. 258, 312)

division of labor/división del trabajo técnica de producción en la cual cada obrero realiza un trabajo especializado (pág. 385)

doge/dux líder electo de la república en las ciudades-estados de Venecia y Génova (pág. 184)

domestic system/sistema doméstico sistema primitivo de trabajo industrial en el cual los obreros producían los bienes en sus hogares (pág. 378)

dominion/dominio nación de gobierno propio dentro del Imperio Británico; más tarde, mancomunidad (pág. 429)

domino theory/teoría del dominó creencia de la época de la Guerra Fría por la que si una nación se hacía comunista, sus vecinos seguirían el ejemplo (pág. 686)

double-digit inflation/inflación de dos dígitos rápida elevación de los precios en un diez por ciento o más (pag. 665)

dual monarchy/monarquía dual dos estados con un solo monarca (pág. 472)

duma/duma legislatura nacional rusa (pág. 470)

duty/arancel de aduana impuesto sobre productos importados (pág. 322)

dvorianie/dvorianie nueva clase de nobleza rusa dueña de tierras, establecida por Pedro I el Grande (pág. 277)

dynasty/dinastía sucesión de gobernantes que pertenecen a la misma familia (pág. 30)

elite/elite un grupo de personas selecto (pág. 751)

ellipse/elipse curva cerrada ovalada (no redonda) (pág. 293)

emancipation/emancipación acción de conceder la libertad legalmente (pág. 467)

embargo/embargo orden restringiendo el tráfico comercial (págs. 665, 736, 791)

emigration/emigración abandono del país o región natal para establecerse en otro lugar (pág. 406)

émigré/émigré emigrado o persona que huyó de Francia durante la Revolución (pág. 342)

empire/imperio grupo de territorios o naciones regidos por un solo emperador o gobierno (pág. 31)

enclave/enclave pequeño territorio completamente rodeado por el territorio de otro país o grupo (pag. 792)

enclosure movement/expansión por apropiación tendencia de los grandes terratenientes a cercar e incluir tierras comunes públicas y privadas en sus propios terrenos (pág. 379)

enlightened despot/déspota iluminista monarca que comenzaba cambios sociales basados en las ideas del iluminismo (pág. 303)

entente/entente acuerdo, pero no alianza formal, entre naciones (pág. 516)

entrepreneur/empresario persona que corre riesgos para fundar un negocio (págs. 224, 380)

estate/estado una de las tres clases sociales distintas en Francia durante el Siglo XVIII: el clero, la nobleza y los plebeyos (el Tercer Estado) (pág. 336)

ethnic cleansing/limpieza étnica término usado en el conflicto de Bosnia, para referirse a una política de traslado forzoso o de dar muerte a los miembros de otro grupo étnico (págs. 790–91)

evolution/evolución teoría de que las especies de seres vivos se transforman a través de largos períodos de tiempo (pág. 402)

factory system/sistema de fábrica método de producción en el cual los bienes son producidos por obreros y máquinas en un local (una fábrica) fuera de sus hogares (pág. 382)

fascism/fascismo filosofía política basada en el nacionalismo y en un estado todopoderoso (pág. 558)

federal system/sistema federal forma de gobierno en la cual el poder se halla dividido entre la autoridad central y sus subdivisiones políticas (pág. 310)

feudalism/feudalismo sistema político medieval en el cual los monarcas y los nobles menores hacían alianzas basadas en el intercambio de concesiones de tierras por lealtad (pág. 115)

fez/fez sombrero tradicional usado por los hombres turcos (pág. 573)

free trade/comercio libre la eliminación de barreras comerciales entre naciones (pág. 754)

friar/fraile miembro de una orden religiosa católica que predicaba en los pueblos y practicaba la pobreza (pág. 120)

fundamentalism/fundamentalismo movimiento que enfatiza el cumplimiento de las leyes y prácticas religiosas tradicionales (pág. 741)

G

geisha/geisha mujer japonesa adiestrada profesionalmente para entretener (pág. 248)

general strike/huelga general huelga en que participan obreros de muchas áreas de la economía de la nación (págs. 555, 707)

genetic engineering/ingeniería genética campo científico en el cual la estructura de las células puede ser alterada para producir organismos nuevos o distintos (pág. 798)

genetics/genética el estudio de la herencia biológica (pág. 403)

genocide/genocidio intento deliberado de matar a todos los miembros de un grupo racial, cultural o étnico (págs. 616, 714)

gentry/gentry en la Inglaterra isabelina, el grupo social que incluía a la nobleza menor y a los terratenientes (pág. 264)

ghana/ghana título del gobernante de una región en el África antigua, que más tarde fue aplicado al reinado (pág. 155)

glasnost/glasnost palabra rusa aplicada a la política de "apertura" o "transparencia" y de libre expresión, introducida por Mijail Gorbachov (pág. 775)

grand vizier/gran visir primer ministro del sultán de un país musulmán (pág. 233)

gross domestic product/producto territorial bruto valor total de las mercancías y los servicios producidos en un país en un año (pág. 674)

guerrilla warfare/guerra de guerrillas método de lucha en el cual pequeños grupos atacan de modo inesperado (pág. 455)

guild/gremio asociación comercial medieval de mercaderes o artesanos (pág. 148)

H

habeas corpus/hábeas corpus principio legal que requiere que las autoridades muestren las razones por las cuales una persona debe ser detenida y garanticen un juicio rápido (pág. 318)

haiku/hai kai forma de poesía japonesa generalmente con tres versos de 17 sílabas (pág. 248)

hajj/hajj peregrinación a La Meca que todo musulmán en buenas condiciones físicas se supone realice por lo menos una vez en su vida (pág. 106)

heavy industry/industria pesada la manufactura de máquinas y equipo para fábricas y minas (pág. 584)

heresy/herejía desacuerdo con la enseñanzas básicas de una religión o negación de las mismas (pág. 120)

hierarchy/jerarquía grupo de personas organizadas de acuerdo con niveles de rango o importancia (pág. 164)

Holocaust/Holocausto nombre dado al asesinato en masa de judíos europeos por los nazis en la Segunda Guerra Mundial (pág. 615)

home rule/autonomía local gobierno propio, especialmente cuando se concede a un país dependiente (pág. 427)

hominid/homínido miembro del grupo que incluye a los seres humanos y a las criaturas primates primitivas (pág. 20)

humanism/Humanismo movimiento renacentista basado en la literatura e ideas de las antiguas Grecia y Roma, tales como el valor de cada individuo (pág. 180)

hyperinflation/hiperinflación forma extrema de inflación, con aumentos violentos y rápidos de los precios (pág. 767)

hypothesis/hipótesis solución propuesta para explicar una serie de hechos, que puede ser probada (pág. 293)

I

icon/ícono imagen religiosa cristiana o cuadro que representa a un santo u otra persona sagrada (pág. 249)

ideology/ideología sistema de creencias y actitudes que guían las acciones de un grupo o nación (pág. 647)

immigration/inmigración entrada a un nuevo país o región para asentarse allí permanentemente (pág. 406)

imperialism/imperialismo política de erigir un imperio para extender el poderío y el territorio de una nación (pág. 480)

imperial presidency/presidencia imperial término aplicado a un presidente y al poder ejecutivo que asumen poderes que van más allá de los estipulados en la Constitución (pág. 664)

impressionism/impresionismo estilo artístico del Siglo XIX en el cual los pintores trataban de captar impresiones rápidas y los efectos de la luz (pág. 414)

individualism/individualismo énfasis en la aignidad de la persona (págs. 180–81)

indulgence/indulgencia perdón vendido por la Iglesia Católica para reducir el castigo de pecados (pág. 192)

industrial capitalism/capitalismo industrial sistema económico en en cual individuos continuamente reinvierten sus ganancias y expanden sus negocios (pág. 384)

inflation/inflación situación en la cual los precios suben rápidamente mientras que el valor del dinero disminuye (pág. 260)

intendant/intendente agente que representaba al rey de Francia en el gobierno local (pág. 267)

interchangeable parts/piezas intercambiables método de producción que utiliza piezas idénticas, fáciles de ensamblar (pág. 385)

intercontinental ballistic missile (ICBM)/misil balístico intercontinental un cohete de combate de largo alcance que lleva una carga explosiva en la punta (pág. 649)

interdependent/interdependiente confianza mutua (pág. 794)

Internet/Internet término popular para la red avanzada de comunicación que vincula a personas y computadoras a nivel mundial (pág. 797)

intifada/intifada el levantamiento de los palestinos contra la ocupación israelita (pág. 732)

iron curtain/Cortina de Hierro término acuñado por Winston Churchill para referirse a la barrera política que aislaba a la Europa Oriental dominada por los soviéticos de la Europa Occidental (pág. 642)

janissary/jenízaro miembro del cuerpo más selecto de soldados del Imperio Otomano (pág. 233)

jati/jati grupos formados dentro de las mayores clases sociales *(varna)* en la antigua India según las ocupaciones de sus miembros y con sus propias reglas y costumbres (pág. 45)

jazz/jazz estilo de música de Estados Unidos que incorpora ritmos africanos a sonidos estadounidenses y europeos (pág. 549)

jingoism/jingoísmo actitud de patriotismo extremo, usualmente dirigida hacia un poder extranjero (pág. 474)

joint-stock company/compañía por acciones empresa comercial que vende acciones para dividir entre los participantes los costos y las ganancias (pág. 223)

junk/junco embarcación china (pág. 240)

justification by faith/justificación por la fe concepto de Martín Lutero de que la fe por sí sola es suficiente para alcanzar la salvación (pág. 191)

kaiser/káiser título del emperador de Alemania (pág. 461)

kamikaze/kamikaze en la Segunda Guerra Mundial, pilotos japoneses que hacían estallar aviones llenos de bombas en ataques suicidas contra objetivos Aliados (pág. 621)

karma/karma en el hinduismo, la idea de que las acciones de los hombres en la vida determinaban sus destinos y sus futuros (pág. 47)

khan/kan gobernante absoluto de los mongoles (pág. 139)

kibbutz/kibbutz comunidad de granjas colectivas en Israel (pág. 727)

Kristallnacht/la noche de las vidrieras rotas ataques terroristas nazis en noviembre 9 y 10 de 1938, contra propiedades judías en Alemania y Austria (pág. 562)

kulak/kulak labriego en la Unión Soviética que vivía holgadamente (pág. 566)

L

labor-intensive farming/agricultura manual intensiva agricultura que confía en el trabajo humano, no en animales o máquinas (pág. 242)

labor union/sindicato obrero organización de obreros formada para presionar a los dueños de los negocios a que mejoren los salarios y las condiciones en el trabajo (pág. 392)

laissez-faire/laissez-faire doctrina económica según la cual el gobierno no debe regular los negocios (pág. 398)

lay investiture/investidura seglar práctica medieval en la cual las autoridades seglares designaban e investían a funcionarios de la iglesia tales como los obispos (pág. 120)

lend-lease/préstamo-arriendo política de la Segunda Guerra Mundial de permitir el préstamo de equipo a países amigos (pág. 612)

liberalism/liberalismo filosofía política que promueve el cambio social y las libertades individuales (pág. 358)

liberation theology/teología de la liberación movimiento dirigido por el clero católico en la América Latina que enfatizaba el papel de la Iglesia en el mejoramiento de las vidas humanas (pág. 754)

line of demarcation/línea de demarcación línea imaginaria en el Océano Atlántico, trazada por el papa en 1493 para dividir las tierras del mundo entre España y Portugal (pág. 215)

literacy rate/tasa de alfabetización el porcentaje de población adulta de un país que sabe leer y escribir (pág. 720)

mandarin/mandarín miembro de la clase más selecta de funcionarios en el gobierno chino (pág. 85)

mandate/mandato (1) en la antigua China, la autoridad concedida por el cielo a gobernantes merecedores de ello, llamada el Mandato del Cielo (pág. 71); (2) territorio administrado por otra nación antes de su independencia (pág. 539)

manorialism/economía feudal sistema económico medieval que ataba a los nobles y a los campesinos a su tierra (pág. 116)

martial law/ley marcial ley militar temporal, que limita derechos tales como la libertad de expresión (pág. 313)

matrilineal/línea materna que traza el origen de una familia a través de la madre y los ancestros de ésta (pág. 81)

mercantilism/mercantilismo política económica de las naciones europeas en el Siglo XVII, que igualaba la riqueza al poder (pág. 224)

meritocracy/sistema de ascenso por méritos sistema en el cual las personas obtienen éxito a base de su habilidad y actuación (pág. 124)

messiah/mesías en el judaísmo, el salvador prometido por los profetas hebreos, quien traería la paz (pág. 75)

mestizo/mestizo en América Latina, persona de ancestro indígena americano y europeo (pág. 443)

metaphysics/metafísica aspectos de la filosofía relativos a los problemas básicos de la existencia y la realidad (pág. 306)

metsuke/metsuke grupo de funcionarios que recolectaban información para los shogúnes de Tokugawa (pag. 245)

Middle Passage/Paso Central sección intermedia del comercio triangular, en el cual los africanos esclavizados eran traídos a la América por barco (pág. 221)

middle power/potencia mediana nación que es fuerte económicamente pero que no es una potencia militar (pág. 665)

militarism/militarismo política nacional basada en la fuerza militar y la glorificación de la guerra (págs. 456, 516)

millet/millet comunidad de los no-musulmanes dentro del imperio otomano (pág. 234)

mobilization/movilización acción de reunir y preparar tropas y equipo para la guerra (pág. 519)

monarchy/monarquía gobierno de un rey o una reina (pág. 30)

monastery/monasterio comunidad de hombres que han tomado votos religiosos (pág. 102)

money economy/economía monetaria sistema económico en el cual se usa el dinero y no el trueque para comprar y vender (pág. 148)

monopoly/monopolio control de todo (o casi todo) el comercio o la producción de un producto determinado (pág. 159)

monotheism/monoteísmo creencia en un solo dios (pág. 36)

mosaic/mosaico cuadro hecho de pedazos de vidrio de colores, barro cocido o piedra unidos con mortero (pág. 102)

mosque/mezquita templo mahometano (pág. 110)

multicultural/multicultural que representa varios grupos culturales y étnicos diferentes (págs. 159, 666)

nationalism/nacionalismo orgullo en la nación o grupo propios y sus tradiciones; deseo de independencia de un gobierno extranjero (págs. 352, 452)

nationalization/nacionalización traspaso de un negocio de propiedad privada al gobierno (págs. 513, 589)

nationalize/nacionalizar traspasar una industria privada al control del gobierno (pág. 728)

nation-state/estado-nación un estado político cuyos habitantes comparten también el mismo idioma y la misma cultura (pág. 453)

natural law/ley natural verdad o principio universal que los pensadores del Siglo XVII creían podía ser hallado mediante la razón (pág. 297)

natural rights/dereches naturales derechas que poseen todas las personas al nacer (pág. 299)

negritude/negritud movimiento literario que enfatiza y se enorgullece de la herencia cultural del África (pág. 721)

nihilist/nihilista miembro de un movimiento político ruso de finales del Siglo XIX que rechazaba toda autoridad y abogaba a favor del terrorismo (pág. 468)

nirvana/nirvana en el budismo, estado de unidad con el universo; el final del ciclo de renacimiento (pág. 49)

nonaligned/no alineado que no toma partido con ninguna de las superpotencias en una guerra fría (pág. 693)

O

obsidian/obsidiana cristal volcánico negro (pág. 91)

oligarchy/oligarquía forma de gobierno en la cual un grupo pequeño ejerce el poder político (pág. 60)

oral tradition/tradición oral las leyendas e historia de una cultura preservada de viva voz (pág. 78)

P

pacifism/pacifismo oposición a la guerra o a la violencia como medio de resolver disputas (pág. 299)

pacifist/pacifista creyente en el pacifismo (pág. 578)

pact/pacto tratado entre varias naciones (pág. 729)

Pan-Africanism/Panafricanismo movimiento que aboga por la unidad y la cooperación entre las naciones africanas (pág. 718)

Pan-Arabism/Panarabismo movimiento de mediados del siglo XX que pretendía construir lazos culturales y políticos entre los árabes (pág. 726)

papal infallibility/infalibilidad papal doctrina católica romana que sostiene que el papa no puede cometer un error al hablar acerca de la fe y la moral (pág. 462)

partisan/partisano en la Segunda Guerra Mundial, término aplicado a un guerrillero de la resistencia clandestina, especialmente en Italia y Yugoeslavia (pág. 624)

partition/partición división de una región (pág. 483)

partnership/sociedad negocio que es propiedad de dos o más empresarios que comparten el manejo, las ganancias y las pérdidas (pág. 385)

patrician/patricio miembro de una clase aristocrática acaudalada en la antigua Roma (pág. 70)

peaceful coexistence/coexistencia pacífica política soviética de competir con los Estados unidos para evitar la guerra (pág. 649)

peninsulares/peninsulares funcionarios nacidos en España o Portugal que dirigían la sociedad en la América Latina colonial (pág. 443)

perestroika/perestroika término ruso que significa "reestructuración"; los cambios en la economía soviética iniciados por Mikhail Gorbachev (pág. 776)

philosophe/filósofo pensador social o político del Siglo de las Luces (pág. 300)

plebeian/plebeyo ciudadano de la antigua Roma que no era un aristócrata (pág. 70)

plebiscite/plebiscito voto popular directo sobre un programa o asunto (págs. 351, 433)

pogrom/pogrom persecución organizada de un grupo minoritario, usualmente judíos, en la Rusia de los zares (pág. 469)

polis/polis ciudad-estado de la antigua Grecia (pág. 59)

pollution/contaminación incorporación de sustancias tóxicas o impuras en el aire, tierra o agua (pág. 674)

polytheism/politeísmo adoración de varios dioses (pág. 32)

pope/papa el obispo de Roma, más tarde el jefe de la Iglesia Católica Romana (pág. 77)

population explosion/explosión demográfica aumento grande y repentino de la población humana (pág. 584)

Postimpressionism/Posimpresionismo movimiento artístico cuyos miembros experimentaban con la forma y el color (pág. 415)

potlatch festín celebrado por los americanos nativos del Noroeste del Pacífico (pág. 162)

pragmatic sanction/sanción pragmática decreto emitido por un gobernante sobre un asunto importante (pág. 271)

pragmatist/pragmatista en China, una persona moderada que abogaba por reformas económicas y por el comercio con Occidente (pág. 678)

predestination/predestinación doctrina de John Calvin (fundador del calvinismo) que predicaba que el destino de una persona estaba predeterminado por Dios (pág. 195)

prehistory/prehistoria tiempo anterior a la historia escrita (pág. 20)

prime minister/primer ministro jefe ejecutivo de un gobierno parlamentario (pág. 320)

principality/principado territorio gobernado por un príncipe (pág. 104)

privatization/privatización la devolución de industrias que eran propiedad del gobierno, a dueños privados (págs. 756–57)

proletariat/proletariado según la teoría marxista, la clase trabajadora (pág. 401)

propaganda/propaganda noticias e información destinadas a influir en los sentimientos de las personas hacia una causa (pág. 522)

prophet/profeta persona que predica o interpreta lo que se cree son mensajes de Dios (pág. 36)

protectorate/protectorado país cuya política es dirigida por una nación extranjera (pág. 482)

provisional government/gobierno provisional gobierno temporal establecido mientras se espera por un proceso electoral (pág. 533)

psychology/psicología estudio del comportamiento y sus causas (pág. 404)

purge/purga esfuerzo oficial para eliminar a las personas que un gobierno considera indeseables (pág. 567)

Q

queue/coleta trenza de pelo única en la parte posterior de la cabeza (pág. 242)

quota/cuota número o cantidad específica (pág. 676)

R

racial segregation/segregación racial separación social de las personas de acuerdo a su raza (pág. 663)

ratify/ratificar dar aprobación oficial (pág. 441)

reactionary/reaccionario el individuo que se opone al progreso o al cambio y desea retornar a costumbres antiguas (pág. 358)

realism/realismo estilo y literatura de mediados del Siglo XIX, que reflejaba las realidades de la vida cotidiana (pág. 412)

realpolitik/realpolitik teoría política según la cual el éxito nacional justifica el uso de cualquier medio (pág. 458)

referendum/referéndum voto popular directo para ratificar una disposición o una ley propuesta (págs. 684, 787)

refugee/refugiado persona que tiene que abandonar su patria y escapar a otro lugar buscando seguridad (pág. 687)

reincarnation/reencarnación el renacimiento del alma o el espíritu en diferentes cuerpos a través del tiempo (pág. 47)

reparation/indemnización de guerra compensación por daños producidos durante una guerra (pág. 539)

republic/república gobierno en el cual los ciudadanos eligen a sus dirigentes (pág. 70)

revolution/revolución cambio de gobierno mediante la fuerza (pág. 330)

romanticism/romanticismo movimiento artístico de principios del siglo XIX, que enfatizaba la individualidad y la emoción (págs. 306, 411)

royalist/realista persona que apoya una monarquía (pág. 315)

Russification/rusificación política de imponer la lengua y costumbres rusas a otros pueblos (pág. 468)

S

sacrament/sacramento uno de los rituales formales establecidos por la Iglesia Católica Romana, tales como el bautismo, la sagrada comunión o el matrimonio (pág. 118)

salon/salón en Francia, tertulia donde los intelectuales del Siglo de las Luces se reunían para conversar (pág. 303)

samurai/samurai clase de guerreros terratenientes en el Japón feudal que juraban lealtad a un *daimyo* (pág. 129)

sanctions/sanciones penalidades y restricciones impuestas a una nación por haber infringido la ley internacional (pág. 603)

sankin-kotai/sankin-kotai ("presencia alterna") en el Japón feudal, el sistema en el cual un *daimyo* tenía que residir en años alternos en la corte de un shogún (pág. 245)

satellite/satélite país dominado políticamente por un poder vecino (pág. 641)

satyagraha/satyagraha ("fuerza de la verdad") término para referirse a las protestas no violentas guiadas por Ghandi (pág. 578)

savanna/sabana llanura cubierta de vegetación, con pocos árboles, en las regiones tropicales o subtropicales (pág. 78)

schism/Cisma de Oriente la división de la Iglesia cristiana en 1054, que separó a la Iglesia Católica Romana de la Iglesia Ortodoxa Oriental (pág. 101)

scholasticism/escolasticismo enseñanza medieval que trataba de combinar la filosofía de Aristóteles con las enseñanzas de los sabios de la Iglesia (pág. 149)

scientific method/método científico pasos para descubrir la verdad científica por medio de la observación y la experimentación (pág. 294)

scorched-earth policy/política de tierra arrasada orden dada por Stalin para que el pueblo soviético destruyera edificios, tierras y cualquier cosa que pudiera ser usada por los invasores nazis (pág. 614)

secede/separarse retirarse formalmente de la membresía de una organización política (pág. 439)

sect/secta subgrupo con sus propias creencias dentro de un grupo religioso mayor (pág. 675)

sectionalism/regionalismo énfasis exagerado en los intereses políticos y económicos de la región propia (pág. 439)

secular/seglar mundano, que no es abierta o específicamente religioso (pág. 180)

self-determination/autodeterminación el derecho de un pueblo de decidir su propio gobierno o estado político (pág. 572)

seminary/seminario escuela destinada para la enseñanza de los sacerdotes, según ordenó el Concilio de Trento (pág. 199)

separatism/separatismo en el Canadá, movimiento político que favorecía la independencia de Quebec (pág. 666)

sepoy/cipayo soldado natural de la India en el ejército británico (pág. 489)

serf/siervo campesino labrador que dependía de las tierras de un noble (págs. 118, 277)

shah/sha el soberano de un país del Oriente Medio (pág. 573)

shamanism/chamanismo creencia de que los espíritus habitan en cosas vivas y muertas, y que se comunican con los humanos a través de unos sacerdotes llamados chamanes (pág. 126)

shogun/shogún gobernador militar en el Japón feudal (pág. 129)

shogunate/shogunado gobierno fundado por la familia de un shogún y sus seguidores en el Japón feudal (pág. 129)

slash-and-burn farming/sistema de quema y siembra método de labranza en el cual la tierra cosechable se limpia talando y quemando los árboles para fertilizar el terreno (pág. 52)

socialism/socialismo teoría política que propugna que la sociedad como un todo debe tener el control de los medios de producción, tales como las fábricas y la tierra (pág. 400)

Socialist realism/realismo socialista bajo Stalin, un estilo artístico que glorificaba el modo de vida soviético (pág. 567)

sociology/sociología el estudio del comportamiento de grupos humanos (pág. 404)

sonnet/soneto composición poética de 14 versos y con un patrón de rima y métrica (pág. 181)

sovereignty/soberanía el poder independiente de un grupo o nación de tomar sus propias decisiones (pág. 739)

soviet/soviet un consejo de trabajadores formado al principio de la Revolución Rusa; más tarde, una unidad del gobierno en la Unión Soviética (pág. 470)

special economic zone/zona económica especial áreas de China donde se han permitido que negocios extranjeros y un mercado libre desarrollaran sus actividades en la década de 1990 (pág. 679)

sphere of influence/esfera de influencia área de un país donde una potencia extranjera tiene derechos exclusivos para comerciar o hacer inversiones (págs. 482, 491)

stagflation/estanflación tendencia económica que combina el estancamiento con la elevada inflación y el desempleo (pág. 665)

stalemate/estancamiento una detención o una situación en la que ninguna de las dos partes opuestas pueden avanzar (pág. 683)

standard of living/nivel de vida la medida general de la riqueza global de las personas y su calidad de vida (pág. 755)

steppe/estepa llanuras de Eurasia, extensas, herbáceas, semiáridas, que se extienden desde el Mar Negro hasta los montes Altai (pág. 138)

subsistence farmer/agricultor de subsistencia campesino que cultiva sólo lo suficiente para mantener a su familia o a una aldea (pág. 719)

suffragette/sufragista mujer que trabajaba activamente para obtener el derecho al voto femenino (pág. 427)

sultan/sultán líder político con autoridad absoluta sobre un país mahometano (pág. 233)

superpower/superpotencia nación poderosa e influyente, con un bloque de aliados, específicamente, los Estados Unidos y la Unión Soviética durante la Guerra Fría (pág. 640)

surrealism/surrealismo movimiento artístico que utilizaba sorpresivas imágenes distorsionadas (pág. 549)

symbolism/simbolismo movimiento artístico antirrealista que se centraba alrededor de imágenes y símbolos fantásticos (pág. 414)

syndicate/sindicato bajo el fascismo, agrupación de obreros y patronos en una industria (pág. 559)

technology/tecnología las habilidades y conocimientos empleados por las personas para fabricar herramientas y trabajar (pág. 21)

theocracy/teocracia gobierno encabezado por líderes religiosos o por un líder considerado como un dios (pág. 194)

theology/teología el estudio de temas religiosos (pág. 101)

tithe/diezmo contribución de un 10 por ciento de los ingresos que se pagaba al clero (pág. 337)

totalitarianism/totalitarismo idea en que un gobierno dictatorial debe controlar todos los aspectos de la vida de los ciudadanos (pág. 557)

trade deficit/déficit comercial el desequilibrio económico que ocurre cuando el valor de las importaciones excede el valor de las exportaciones (págs. 665, 774)

tragedy/tragedia historia o representación teatral en la que el personaje central lucha contra el destino pero que desemboca en un final trágico (pág. 62)

trench/trinchera zanja cavada para dar protección a los soldados (pág. 523)

triangular trade/comercio triangular ruta de tres direcciones entre Europa, África y América en el Siglo XVII (pág. 220)

tribune/tribuna en la antigua Roma, magistrado que representaba a los plebeyos (pág. 71)

tyrant/tirano en la antigua Grecia, persona que usurpaba el poder y establecía un gobierno unipersonal (pág. 60)

ultimatum/ultimátum última disposición o declaración de condiciones, que implica una amenaza de penalidades severas (pág. 578)

ultraroyalist/ultrarrealista aristócrata extremadamente conservador en la Francia de principios del Siglo XIX (pág. 431)

unicameral legislature/legislatura unicameral asamblea o cuerpo legislativo de una sola cámara (pág. 341)

urbanization/urbanización la expansión de las ciudades y la vida citadina (pág. 407)

utilitarianism/utilitarismo filosofía económica desarrollada por Jeremy Bentham que considera que las acciones sociales y políticas deben ser de utilidad y ayuda a la humanidad (pág. 400)

varna/varna una de las cuatro clases sociales principales en la sociedad aria de la antigua India (pág. 45)

vernacular/vernáculo el lenguaje del habla diaria, no de los eruditos, en un país o región (pág. 149)

viceroy/virrey gobernante que representa a un monarca (pág. 490)

vocation/vocación llamado de Dios para asumir cierto trabajo (pág. 193)

war of attrition/guerra de desgaste conflicto en el cual cada bando trata de ganar agotando al contrario (pág. 523)

warlord/señor de la guerra líder militar local en China (pág. 580)

welfare state/estado de proteccionismo social sistema de gobierno en el cual el estado provee programas para proteger el bienestar económico y social del pueblo (pág. 655)

westernization/occidentalización la expansión de la cultura europea (pág. 494)

yeoman/campesino propietario en la sociedad inglesa, un campesino que poseía tierras (pág. 264)

yin and yang/yin y yan en el pensamiento chino, los principios opuestos presentes en toda naturaleza (pág. 51)

zaibatsu/zaibatsu grandes firmas industriales japonesas que pertenecían a varias familias (pág. 584)

zemstvo/zemstvo asamblea local en la Rusia zarista (pág. 468)

ACKNOWLEDGMENTS

Text

Grateful acknowledgment is given authors and publishers for permission to reprint the following copyrighted material.
66 From "Antigone" in *Sophocles, the Oedipus Cycle: An English Version* by Dudley Fitts and Robert Fitzgerald, copyright 1939 by Harcourt Brace & Company and renewed 1967 by Dudley Fitts and Robert Fitzgerald, reprinted by permission of Harcourt Brace & Company. CAUTION: All rights, including professional, amateur, motion picture, recitation, lecturing, performance, public reading, radio broadcasting, and television are strictly reserved. Inquiries on all rights should be addressed to Harcourt Brace & Company, Permissions Dept., Orlando, FL 32887; **202** Niccolò Machiavelli, The Prince, translated and edited by Thomas G. Bergin. Copyright © 1947 by F. S. Crofts & Co. Inc. Reprinted by permission of Viking-Dutton, Inc.; **360** From *Les Misérables* by Victor Hugo, translated by Lee Fahnestock and Norman MacAfee. Translation copyright © 1987 by Lee Fahnestock and Norman MacAfee. Used by permission of Dutton Signet, a division of Penguin Books USA Inc.; **416** "The Beggar" from *The Short Stories of Anton Chekhov* by Anton Chekhov, edited with introduction by Robert Linscott. Copyright © 1932 and renewed 1960 by The Modern Library, Inc. Reprinted by permission of Random House, Inc.; **523** "Dulce et Decorum Est" by Wilfred Owen, from *The Collected Poems of Wilfred Owen.* Copyright © 1963 by Chatto & Windus. Reprinted by permission of New Directions Publishing Corp.; **594** From "By Any Other Name" from *Gifts of Passage* by Santha Rama Rau. Copyright © 1951 by Vasanthi Rama Rau Bowers. Copyright renewed. Reprinted by permission of HarperCollins Publishers, Inc. "By Any Other Name" originally appeared in The New Yorker; **613** From *Central Zionist Archives, Jerusalem 1939–1945,* edited by Francis R. Nicosia, Volume 4 of the *Archives of the Holocaust,* Garland Publishing, 1990; **721** Michael Dei-Anang, "My Africa" from Poems from Black Africa, edited by Langston Hughes. Copyright © 1963 by Langston Hughes. Reprinted by permission of Indiana University Press; **742** Jaime Torres Bodet, "The Window," translated by George Kearns. Translation copyright © 1974, 1963 by the McGraw-Hill Book Company, Inc.; **743** "The World, My Friends, My Enemies, You, and the Earth" from *Things I Didn't Know I Loved* by Nazim Hikmet, translated by Randy Blasing and Mutlu Konuk, copyright © 1975 by Randy Blasing and Mutlu Konuk. Reprinted by permission of Persea Books, Inc.; **744** Gabriel Okara, "Once Upon a Time," from African Voices, edited by Howard Sergeant. Copyright © 1973 by Howard Sergeant. Used by permission of Evans Brothers Ltd, London; **763** "Because I Want Peace" by Claribel Alegría, from *El Salvador: Testament of Terror,* edited by Joe Fish and Cristina Sganga. Copyright © 1988. Reprinted by permission of Interlink Publishing Group, Inc.

Maps

Cartographic Services provided by Ortelius Design, and GeoSystems Global Corp.

Photographs

Cover (shuttle) NASA, (other) Biblioteca Ambrosiana, Milan, Italy/Art Resource, NY; **15** Jacksonville Museum of Contemporary Art, FL/SuperStock; **16–17** Anthony Howard/Woodfin Camp & Associates; **16** Heraklion Museum, Crete/Kurt Scholz/SuperStock; **17** (t)David David Gallery, Philadelphia/SuperStock, (b)National Museum, Lagos, Nigeria/Kurt Scholz/SuperStock; **19** The British Museum, London/Bridgeman Art Library/SuperStock; **20** Boltin Picture Library; **21** John Reader/Science Photo Library/Photo Researchers; **24** Borromeo/Art Resource, NY; **30** Giraudon/Art Resource, NY; **34** Egyptian Expedition of the Metropolitan Museum of Art, The Rogers Fund, 1930 (30.4.21); **36** David Forbest/SuperStock; **37** SuperStock; **44** Christies, London/Bridgeman Art Library/SuperStock; **46–47** B. Kapbor/SuperStock; **46** Robert Harding Picture Library; **47** Art Resource, NY; **48** Victoria & Albert Museum, London/Art Resource, NY; **48–49** Bridgeman/Art Resource, NY; **51** Giraudon/Art Resource, NY; **52** Museum of Mankind/E.T. Archives, London SuperStock; **57** Scala/Art Resource, NY; **58** William Katz/Photo Researchers; **60** Giraudon/Art Resource, NY; **62** Museo Delle Terme, Rome/E.T. Archives, London/SuperStock; **63** Erich Lessing/Art Resource, NY; **64** Musee du Louvre, Paris/E.T. Archives, London/SuperStock; **66 67 68** Art Resource, NY; **70** Robert Emmett Bright/Photo Researchers; **71** Prenestino Museum, Rome/E.T. Archives, London/SuperStock; **74–75** Scala/Art Resource, NY; **76** Scala/Art Resource, NY; **78** Roger K. Burnard; **79** file photo; **83** Ancient Art & Architecture Collection; **88** Bettmann Archive; **89** S. Vidler/SuperStock; **90** Jacksonville Museum of Contemporary Art, FL/SuperStock; **99** Bibliotheque Nationale, Paris/AKG Berlin/SuperStock; **100** Scala/Art Resource, NY; **102** Ancient Art & Architecture Collection; **103** Bettmann Archive; **106** Ancient Art & Architecture Collection; **105** Bibliotheque Nationale, Paris/The Bridgeman Art Library International Ltd; **108–109** Lerner Fine Art Collection/SuperStock; **111** Michael Holford; **112** SuperStock; **113** Robert Smith/Ancient Art & Architecture Collection; **116** The Metropolitan Museum of Art, Munsey Fund, 1932(32.130.6); **118** Ancient Art & Architecture Collection; **119** Ronald Sheridan/Ancient Art & Architecture Collection; **123** Naomi Duguid/Asia Access; **124** Laurie Platt Winfrey, Inc.; **126** Rick Browne/Photo Researchers; **127** Masao Hayashi/Dunq/Photo Researchers; **128** Private Collection/Bridgeman Art Library/SuperStock; **129** Bettmann Archive; **132** A. Hubrich/H. Armstrong Roberts; **137** Scala/Art Resource, NY; **138** Laurie Platt Winfrey, Inc.; **139** J. Bertrand/Photo Researchers; **143** SEF/Art Resource, NY; **144** Ancient Art & Architecture Collection; **145** Giraudon/Art Resource, NY; **147** Giraudon/Art Resource, NY; **150** Erich Lessing/Art Resource, NY; **153** The British Library, London/Bridgeman Art Library/SuperStock; **154** The Metropolitan Museum of Art, The Michael C. Rockefeller Collection, Gift of Nelson A. Rockefeller, 1972 (1978.412.310); **156–157** The Elliott Elisofon Archives, Museum of African Art, The Smithsonian Institution; **160** H. von Meiss/Photo Researchers; **161** Steve Smith/Westlight; **162** J. Warden/SuperStock; **173** Giraudon/Art Resource, NY; **175** Scala/Art Resource, NY; **177** Wolfgang Kaehler; **179** Palazzo Ducale, Mantua, Italy/M. Magliari/SuperStock; **182–183** Vatican Museums & Galleries, Rome/Fratelli Alinari/SuperStock; **182** Galleria Dell'Academia, Florence/Scala/SuperStock; **183** Erich Lessing/Art Resource, NY; **184** Scala/Art Resource, NY; **186** Victor R. Boswell, Jr.; **187** Vatican Museums & Galleries, Rome/Canali PhotoBank, Milan/SuperStock; **188** AKG, Berlin/SuperStock; **189** Scala/Art Resource, NY; **190** Erich Lessing/Art Resource, NY; **191** SuperStock; **192** Erich Lessing/Art Resource, NY; **193** (l)Erich Lessing/Art Resource, NY, (r)National Museum, Copenhagen/E.T. Archives, London/SuperStock; **194** Mary Evans Picture Library/Photo Researchers; **196** Scala/Art Resource, NY; **197** Erich Lessing/Art Resource, NY; **198** Michael Holford; **199** Giraudon/Art Resource, NY; **201** Werner Forman Archive/Art Institute of Chicago/Art Resource, NY; **202 through 205** Scala/Art Resource, NY; **207** Erich Lessing/Art Resource, NY; **209** National Maritime Museum; **210** Karen Kasmauski/Woodfin Camp & Associates; **212** (l)SuperStock, (r)Michael Holford; **214** National Museum of American Art, Washington DC/Art Resource, NY; **215 216** AKG, Berlin/SuperStock; **218–219** Alinari/Art Resource, NY; **218** Erich Lessing/Art Resource, NY; **219** (t)Scala/Art Resource, NY, (b)Brent Turner/BLT Productions; **221** Bettmann Archive; **222 223** SuperStock; **224** Bridgeman/Art Resource, NY; **225** Michael Holford; **226** Bridgeman/Art Resource, NY; **231 232** Giraudon/Art Resource, NY; **234** Art Resource, NY; **235** Adam Woolfitt/Woodfin Camp & Associates; **237** by courtesy of the Board of Trustees of the Victoria & Albert Museum, London/Bridgeman Art Library/SuperStock; **238** Bibliotheque Nationale, Paris; **239** Dallas & John Heaton/Westlight; **240–241** Philadelphia Free Library/AKG, Berlin/SuperStock; **240** G. Hunter/SuperStock; **241** (l)Art Trade, Bonhams, London/Bridgeman Art Library/SuperStock, (r)SEF/Art Resource, NY; **242** D.E. Cox/Tony Stone Images; **244** Werner Forman Archive/Art Resource, NY; **245** Culver Pictures Inc./SuperStock; **246** Kita-In Saitumi/Werner Foreman Archive/Art Resource, NY; **247** Michael Holford; **249** Doug Martin; **250** George Holton/Photo Researchers; **251** SuperStock; **252** Scala/Art Resource, NY; **253** Bettmann Archive; **257** Giraudon/Art Resource, NY; **258** Bridgeman Art Library, London/SuperStock; **259** Bettmann Archive; **261** Victoria & Albert Museum/Art Resource, NY; **262** Michael Holford; **263** (l)Bridgeman/Art Resource, NY, (r)National Portrait Gallery, London; **264 265** National Portrait Gallery, London/SuperStock; **266** Giraudon/Art Resource, NY; **267** Lauros-Giraudon/Art Resource, NY; **268** A&F Pears Ltd., London/SuperStock; **270** Museum of Art History, Vienna/AKG, Berlin/SuperStock; **272** AKG, Berlin/SuperStock; **274** Novosti from Sovfoto; **275** Michael Holford; **278** Giraudon/Art Resource, NY; **281** Bridgeman/Art Resource, NY; **283** National Gallery, London/SuperStock; **284** Bridgeman/Art Resource, NY; **285** Giraudon/Art Resource, NY; **287** Scala/Art Resource, NY; **288** Architect of the Capitol, Washington D.C.; **289** Bettmann Archive; **291** Giraudon/Art Resource, NY; **292** Royal Society of London **293** Private Collection/Bridgeman Art Library/SuperStock; **295** Bettmann Archive; **297** (detail)Erich Lessing/Art Resource, NY; **300** Giraudon/Art Resource, NY; **301** Derby Museum and Art Gallery,

England/Bridgeman Art Library/SuperStock; **302–303** Erich Lessing/Art Resource, NY; **302** Christies, London/SuperStock; **303** Bettmann Archive; **304 305** Ronald Sheridan/Ancient Art & Architecture Collection; **306 307** Archive Photos; **311** Bridgeman/Art Resource, NY; **312** Ronald Sheridan/Ancient Art & Architecture Collection; **313** Bettmann Archive; **314** courtesy The Pilgrim Society; **316** National Portrait Gallery, London/SuperStock; **317 319** Ronald Sheridan/Ancient Art & Architecture Collection; **320** Bettmann Archive; **321** Scala/Art Resource, NY; **322–323** Bettmann Archive; **322** Historic Deerfield Inc.: photo by Amanda Merullo; **323** (l)John Carter Brown Library, Brown University, (r)Massachusetts Historical Society; **324** Bettmann Archive; **326** Archive Photos; **327** Ronald Sheridan/Ancient Art & Architecture Collection; **328** Chicago Historical Society; **329** Yale University Art Gallery; **335** AKG, Berlin/SuperStock; **336** Bettmann Archive; **337** Scala/Art Resource, NY; **339** Mary Evans Picture Library/Photo Researchers; **340** Bettmann Archive; **341** Giraudon/Art Resource, NY; **343** Photo Researchers; **344** AKG, Berlin/SuperStock; **346–347** Stock Montage; **346** Photo Researchers; **347** Archiv/Photo Researchers; **349** Erich Lessing/Art Resource, NY; **350** Bettmann Archive; **351 354** Giraudon/Art Resource, NY; **356** Photo Researchers; **358 359** Bettmann Archive; **360** Giraudon/Art Resource, NY; **361** The Metropolitan Museum of Art, Gift of Mrs. Herbert N. Straus, 1942(42.203.1) Photo by Derry Moore; **362** Mary Evans Picture Library/Photo Researchers; **367** (l)Stock Montage, (r)Scala/Art Resource, NY; **367** (t)Bettmann Archive, (b)Original painting hangs in the Selectmen's Meeting Room, Abbot Hall, Marblehead MA; **369** Scala/Art Resource, NY; **371** L. Berger/SuperStock; **372** Stock Montage; **373** (t)Library of Congress, (b)Laurie Platt Winfrey, Inc.; **375** The Science Museum, London; **376** Waterhouse and Dodd, London/Bridgeman Art Library/SuperStock; **377** Christies, London/SuperStock; **379** Archive Photos; **380** Ronald Sheridan/Ancient Art & Architecture Collection; **381** file photo; **382 383** The Smithsonian Institution; **384** Royal Museum of Fine Arts, Copenhagen/Bridgeman Art Library/SuperStock; **388** International Museum of Photography/George Eastman House; **389 390** Collection of Picture Research Consultants; **390–391** Snark/Art Resource, NY; **391** Library of Congress; **392** Courtesy Labor Archives and Research Center, San Francisco State University; **397 398** Giraudon/Art Resource, NY; **399** Library of Congress; **400** file photo; **402** Bettmann Archive; **403** Erich Lessing/Art Resource, NY; **405** National Portrait Gallery, London/SuperStock; **406–407** Christies, London/SuperStock; **406** Library of Congress; **407** Missouri Historical Society; **409** Tate Gallery, London/Art Resource, NY; **411** Gemaldegalerie, Dresden, Germany/A.K.G., Berlin/SuperStock; **412** Christies, London/SuperStock; **415** Erich Lessing/Art Resource, NY; **416** Archive Photos; **417** Scala/Art Resource, NY; **418** Russian Sate Museum, St. Petersburg/Bourka-touskey/SuperStock; **421** National Portrait Gallery, London/SuperStock; **423** Giraudon/Art Resource, NY; **424** Library of Congress; **425** Snark/Art Resource, NY; **427 428** Bettmann Archive; **429** Archive Photos; **431** Erich Lessing/Art Resource, NY; **432** Stock Montage; **433** Giraudon/Art Resource, NY; **434 436 438** Bettmann Archive; **438–439** Scala/Art Resource, NY; **439** Mark Burnett; **441** Library of Congress; **442** Bettmann Archive; **444** Schalkwijk/Art Resource, NY; **451 452** Scala/Art Resource, NY; **454–455** Giraudon/Art Resource, NY; **455** (l)Scala/Art Resource, NY, (r)Vince Streano/Tony Stone Images; **456** Bettmann Archive; **457** Archive for Art & History, Berlin/AKG, Berlin/SuperStock; **459** Bryan F. Peterson/The Stock Market; **471** Erich Lessing/Art Resource, NY; **472** FPG International; **463** SuperStock; **465** Bettmann Archive; **466** FPG International; **469** Bettmann Archive; **471** Corbis-Bettmann; **472** SEF/Art Resource, NY; **478** Mark Burnett; **479** Bridgeman/Art Resource, NY; **480** Laurie Platt Winfrey, Inc.; **481** Bettmann Archive; **483** Archive Photos/Popperfoto; **484** Bettmann Archive; **485** Werner Forman Archive/Art Resource, NY; **487** Bettmann Archive; **488** Thierry Prat/Sygma; **489** Stock Concepts; **492–493** Bridgeman/Art Resource, NY; **493** (l)Bettmann Archive, (r)Bridgeman Art Library/Art Resource, NY; **495** Bettmann Archive; **496** file photo; **497 498** Bettmann Archive; **503** Historical Picture Service; **505** Musee de Petit Palais, Paris/Bridgeman Art Library/SuperStock; **507** Stock Montage; **509** Aaron Haupt; **510** UPI/Bettmann Archive; **511** (t)AP/Wide World Photos, (b)Lena Kara/SIPA; **513** West Point Museum/Joshua Nefsky; **514** SuperStock; **517** Bettmann Archive; **520** Archive Photos; **522–523** Bridgeman/Art Resource, NY; **522** Collection of Colonel Stuart S. Corning. Photo: Rob Huntley: Lightstream; **523** UPI/Bettmann Archive; **524** Erich Lessing/Art Resource, NY; **525** Bettmann Archive; **532** Snark/Art Resource, NY; **533** AP/Wide World Photos; **536** Collection of Colonel Stuart S. Corning. Photo: Rob Huntley:Lightstream; **537** Bettmann Archive; **545** Des Moines Art Center Permanent Collection, 1958.2. Photo: Craig Anderson; **546** Archive Photos; **548** The Metropolitan Museum of Art, bequest of Gertrude Stein, 1946(47.106); **549** Centro de Arte Reina Sofia, Madrid, Spain/Giraudon, Paris/SuperStock; **552** Archive Photos; **553** National Museum of American Art/Art Resource, NY; **554** Bettmann Archive; **555** UPI/Bettmann; **557** AKG, Berlin/SuperStock; **558** L'Illustration/Sygma; **559 560** Bettmann Archive; **560–561** AP/Wide World Photos; **561** Bettmann Archive; **562** Hugo Jaeger/LIFE Magazine, Time Inc.; **563** David Low/London Evening Standard/Solo Syndication Limited; **564** Sovfoto; **565 567** Bettmann Archive; **569** (l) Museum of Modern Art, New York/Bridegeman Art Library/SuperStock, Demart Pro Arte, Geneva/Artists' Rights Society, NY; (r) Stock Montage, Inc.; **571** Schalkwijk/Art Resource, NY; **571** Archive Photos; **574** UPI/Bettmann; **575** Eliot Elisofon National Museum of African Art, Eliot Elisofon Archives, Smithsonian Institution; **576** John Moss/Black Star; **577** Bridgeman/Art Resource, NY; **578** file photo; **579** Keystone, Paris/Sygma; **581** AP/Wide World Photos; **582** SIPA Press; **583 584** Bettmann Archive; **586** John Moss/Black Star; **587** SuperStock; **588 589** Schalkwijk/Art Resource, NY; **590 594** UPI/Bettmann; **595** Laurie Platt Winfrey, Inc.; **597** Rudi Von Briel; **601** U.S. Naval Photographic Center; **602** UPI/Bettmann; **603** AP/Wide World Photos; **605** Sygma; **607** Archive Photos; **610–611** UPI/Bettmann; **610** AP/Wide World Photos; **611** (l)Bettmann Archive, (r)Archive Photos; **612** Popperfoto/Archive Photos; **614 615 618** UPI/Bettmann; **622** Archive Photos; **624** RIA-Novosti/Sovphoto; **625** UPI/Bettmann; **626** Archive Photos; **627** UPI/Bettmann; **632** B. Swersey/Gamma-Liaison; **633** AP/Wide World Photos; **635** Chuck O'Rear/Westlight; **636** (l)UPI/Corbis-Bettmann, (r)Sovfoto/Eastfoto; **637** (l)T. Rosenthal/SuperStock, (r)NASA; **639** Sovfoto/Eastfoto; **640** Archive Photos; **641** SuperStock; **644–645** AP/Wide World Photos; **644** UPI/Bettmann; **645** S. Vidler/SuperStock; **648** Archive Photos; **649** UPI/Bettmann; **651** Black Star; **653** UPI/Bettmann; **654** Roger-Viollet; **655** AP/Wide World Photos; **656** UPI/Bettmann; **658** Bettmann Archive; **659** UPI/Bettmann; **660** SIPA Press; **663** AP/Wide World Photos; **664** UPI/Corbis-Bettmann; **666** Reuters/Bettmann; **671** M. Setboun/Sygma; **672** P. Amranand/SuperStock; **673** T. Matsumoto/Sygma; **674** Tom Wagner/SABA; **675** Michael Yamashita/Westlight; **677** George Matchneer; **679** Bettmann Archive; **680** Langevin/Sygma; **682** Duclos/Guichard/Gouver/Gamma-Liaison; **684** R. Ian Lloyd/The Stock Market; **685** UPI/Bettmann; **686–687** file photo; **687** UPI/Bettmann; **690** Howard/Spooner/Gamma; **692** Sygma; **693** UPI/Bettmann; **695** V. Miladinovic/Sygma; **696** G.R. Robert; **697 701** Sygma; **703** Klaus Reisinger/Black Star; **704** Louis Gubb/JB Pictures; **707** UPI/Bettmann; **708** Archive Photos/Express News/D.E.1; **710** David Keith Jones/Images of Africa Photobank; **711** Haviv/SABA; **712 713** (l)David Keith Jones/Images of Africa Photobank; **714** Alain Buu/Gamma Liaison Network; **716** Mark Burnett; **717** J.M. Bertrand/SuperStock; **718** David Travers/The Stock Market; **719** Doug Menuez/SABA; **720** P. Schmidt/SuperStock; **721** Lawrence Migdale/Tony Stone Images; **723** Betty Press/Woodfin Camp & Associates; **725** Robert Frerck/Woodfin Camp & Associates; **726** Jesse Nemerofsky/Photoreporters; **727** Sygma; **730** L. de Raemy/Sygma; **731** UPPA/Photoreporters; **732 733** Barry Iverson/Woodfin Camp & Associates; **733** (l)Penny Tweedie/Woodfin Camp & Associates, (r)Esaias Baitel/Gamma-Liaison; **734** Terry Ashe/The Gamma Liaison Network; **738** Reuters/Bettmann; **739** Tony Stone Images; **740** Ed Kashi; **743** AP/Wide World Photos; **745** Dennis Stock/Magnum; **749** Ary Diesendruck/Tony Stone Images; **750** Alain Keler/Sygma; **751** David L. Perry; **752** Neil Beer/Tony Stone Images; **753** Carrion/Sygma; **755** Bettmann Archive; **756–757** Sergio Dorantes/Sygma; **756** Robert Frerck/Tony Stone Images; **757** (l)Robert Frerck/Woodfin Camp & Associates, (r)Russell Cheyne/Tony Stone Images; **761** Javier Bauluz/SABA; **763** Sygma; **764** Sergio Dorantes/Sygma; **765** Gary Payne/Gamma Liaison; **766** UPI/Bettmann; **767** Reuters/Bettmann; **768** David L. Perry; **773** NASA; **774** Les Stone/Sygma; **776** Novosti/Gamma-Liaison; **779 780** Reuters/Bettmann; **781** AP/Wide World Photos; **782 783** Reuters/Bettmann; **785** AFP/Bettmann; **786** AP/Wide World Photos; **787** Peter Turnley/Black Star; **790** AP/Wide World Photos; **792** (l)AP/Wide World Photos, (r)Reuters/Bettmann; **794** NASA/Gamma-Liaison; **795** SuperStock; **796** J.L. Atlan/Sygma; **797** Hans Peter Merten/Tony Stone Images; **802** Epix/Sygma; **803** Adrian Bradshaw/SABA; **804** David L. Perry.